McGRAW-HILL ENCYCLOPEDIA OF
Science &
Technology

3

BOR-CLE

McGRAW-HILL ENCYCLOPEDIA OF
Science &
Technology

3

BOR-CLE

8th Edition
An international reference work in twenty volumes including an index

McGraw-Hill

New York   San Francisco   Washington, D.C.   Auckland   Bogotá   Caracas   Lisbon   London   Madrid
Mexico City   Milan   Montreal   New Delhi   San Juan   Singapore   Sydney   Tokyo   Toronto

Library of Congress Cataloging in Publication data

McGraw-Hill encyclopedia of science & technology. — 8th ed.
    p.   cm.
    Includes bibliographical references and index.
    ISBN 0-07-911504-7 (alk. paper)
    1. Science—Encyclopedias.   2. Technology—Encyclopedias.
Q121.M3   1997
503—dc21   96-52375

ISBN 0-07-911504-7 (set)

McGraw-Hill

A Division of The **McGraw·Hill** *Companies*

This book set was printed on acid-free paper.

*It was set in Neue Helvetica Black Condensed and Garamond Light
by ATLIS Graphics & Design, Inc., Mechanicsburg, Pennsylvania. It was
printed and bound by R. R. Donnelley & Sons Company, The Lakeside Press.*

Organization of the Encyclopedia

This Encyclopedia presents pertinent information in every field of modern science and technology. The 7100 article titles are alphabetically sequenced, so that often the reader can quickly find information by choosing from the 19 text volumes that one bearing the appropriate letter for the subject.

As for the organization of the material throughout the volumes, broad survey articles for each of the disciplines or large subject areas give even the uninitiated reader the basic concepts or rudiments. From the lead article the reader may proceed to other articles that are more restricted in scope by utilizing the cross-referencing system. These cross references are set in small capitals for emphasis and are inserted at the relevant points in the text. In all, some 60,000 cross references are given. In a survey article such as **Petroleum engineering** the reader is directed to other articles such as **Oil and gas well drilling, Petroleum reservoir models,** and **Well logging.** The references may lead to subjects that have not occurred to the reader. For example, the article **Chlorine** has such diverse cross references as **Antimicrobial agents, Halogen elements, Industrial health and safety,** and **Oxidizing agent.**

The pattern of proceeding from the general to the specific has been employed not only in the plan of the Encyclopedia but within the body of the articles. Each article begins with a definition of the subject, followed by sufficient background material to give a frame of reference and permit the reader to move into the detailed text of the article. Within the text are centered heads and two levels of side-heads which outline the article; they are intended to enhance understanding, and can guide the user who prefers to read selectively the sections of a long article.

Alphabetization of article titles is by word, not by letter, with a comma providing a stop in occasional inverted article titles (so that subject matter can be grouped). Two examples of sequence are:

Air	**Earth, age of**
Air-cushion vehicle	**Earth, heat flow in**
Air mass	**Earth crust**
Air-traffic control	**Earth tides**
Aircraft fuel	**Earthquake**

Copious illustrations, both line drawings and half-tones, contribute to the utility, clarity, and interest of the text. Each illustration (as well as each table) is called out in boldface at its first mention in the text. This emphasis enables the browsing reader to move from an illustration to the specific point in the text where the illustration is often discussed in detail.

Measurements are given in dual systems of units. The U.S. Customary System, continuing in wide application, is used throughout the text. To meet the needs of the Encyclopedia's broad readership, equivalent measurements are given in the International System of Units. In particular cases, such as references to measurements in some illustrations or tables, conversion factors may be given for simplicity.

The contributor's full name appears at the end of an article section or an entire article. Each author is identified in an alphabetical Contributors list in volume 20, which cites the university, laboratory, business, or other organization with which the author is affiliated and the titles of the articles written.

Most of the articles contain bibliographies citing useful sources. The bibliographies are placed at the ends of articles or occasionally at the ends of major sections in long articles. To utilize additional bibliographies, the reader should refer to related articles which are indicated by cross references.

Thus, the alphabetical arrangement of article titles, the text headings, the cross references, and the bibliographies permit the reader to pursue a particular interest by simply taking a volume from the shelf. However, the reader can also find information in the Encyclopedia by using the Analytical Index and the Topical Index in volume 20. The Analytical Index contains each important term, concept, and person—170,000 in all—mentioned throughout the 19 text volumes. It guides the reader to the volume numbers and page numbers concerned with a specific point. The reader wishing to consult everything in the Encyclopedia on a particular aspect of a subject will find that the Analytical Index is the best approach. A broader survey may be made through the Topical Index, which groups all article titles of the Encyclopedia under 78 general headings. For example, under "Geophysics" 59 articles are listed, and under "Organic chemistry," 190. The Topical Index thus enables the reader quickly to identify all articles in the Encyclopedia in a particular subject area.

The Study Guides in volume 20 provide highly structured outlines of six major scientific disciplines (Biology, Chemistry, and so on), and relate groups of Encyclopedia articles to each outline heading. By following a guide, the reader is led through pertinent Encyclopedia articles in a sequence that provides an overall grasp of the discipline.

A useful feature is the section "Scientific Notation" in volume 20. It clarifies usage of symbols, abbreviations, and nomenclature, and is especially valuable in making conversions between International System, U.S. Customary, and metric measurements.

McGRAW-HILL ENCYCLOPEDIA OF
Science &
Technology

3

BOR-CLE

Boracite

A borate mineral with chemical composition $Mg_3B_7O_{13}Cl$. It occurs in Germany, England, and the United States, usually in bedded sedimentary deposits of anhydrite ($CaSO_4$), gypsum ($CaSO_4 \cdot 2H_2O$), and halite ($NaCl$), and in potash deposits of oceanic type. The chemical composition of natural boracites varies, with Fe^{2+} or Mn^{2+} replacing part of the Mg^{2+} to yield ferroan boracite or manganoan boracite.

Boracite occurs in crystals which appear to be isometric in external form, despite the fact that the arrangement of the atoms in the crystal structure has only orthorhombic symmetry (see **illus.**). When this natural low-temperature form is heated to 510°F (265°C), a slight readjustment of the atoms takes place internally without change in external form. The atomic symmetry of this resulting high-temperature form, which does not occur naturally, is then consistent with the external habit.

The hardness is $7-7^1/_2$ on Mohs scale, and specific gravity is 2.91–2.97 for colorless crystals and 2.97–3.10 for green and ferroan types. Luster is vitreous, inclining toward adamantine. Boracite is colorless to white, inclining to gray, yellow, and green, and rarely pink (manganoan); its streak is white; and it is transparent to translucent. It is strongly piezoelectric and pyroelectric and does not cleave. *See* BORATE MINERALS.　　Charles L. Christ

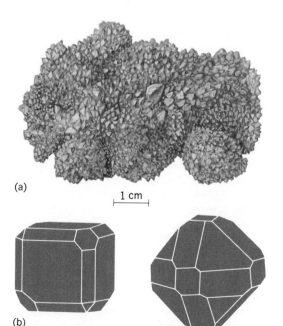

(a)

1 cm

(b)

Boracite. (a) Specimen from Segeberg, Germany (*specimen from Department of Geology, Bryn Mawr College*). (b) Crystal habits (*after C. S. Hurlbut, Jr., Dana's Manual of Mineralogy, 17th ed., John Wiley and Sons, 1959*).

Borane

One of a class of binary compounds of boron and hydrogen, often referred to as boron hydrides. The term borane is sometimes used to denote substances which may be considered to be derivatives of the boron-hydrogen compounds, such as BCl_3 and $B_{10}H_{12}I_2$.

The simplest borane is B_2H_6; other boranes of increasingly higher molecular weight are known, one of the least volatile of which is an apparently polymeric solid of composition $(BH)_x$. Certain boranes, such as BH_3 and B_3H_7, are not known as such, but can be prepared in the form of adducts with electron-donor molecules. The formulas, names, melting points, and boiling points of some of the commoner boranes are listed in the **table**.

The most spectacular projected large-scale use of the boranes and their derivatives is in the field of high-energy fuels for jet planes and rockets. The heats of combustion of the boranes per unit weight

Properties of boranes		
Name* and formula	Melting point, °C (°F)	Boiling point, °C (°F)
Diborane (6) B_2H_6	−165 (−265)	−92.5 (−134)
Tetraborane (10) B_4H_{10}	−120 (−184)	16 (61)
Pentaborane (9) B_5H_9	−47 (−53)	58.4 (137)
Pentaborane (11) B_5B_{11}	−123 (−189)	65† (150)
Decaborane (14) $B_{10}H_{14}$	99.5 (211)	213 (415)

*The nomenclature used is that of G. W. Schaeffer and T. Wartik, as presented at the March 1954 meetings of the American Chemical Society in Kansas City. The prefix designates the number of boron atoms in the molecule, and the numeral suffix indicates the number of hydrogen atoms.
†Extrapolated boiling point.

are such as to permit specific impulses approaching 300 s, a distinct improvement over hydrocarbon fuels. The thermal decomposition of B_2H_6 has been used to produce coatings of pure elementary boron for neutron-detecting devices and for applications requiring hard, corrosion-resistant surfaces. Boranes can be used as vulcanizing agents for natural and synthetic rubbers, and are especially effective in the preparation of silicone rubbers.

Structure. The molecular structures possessed by the boranes are exhibited by no other class of substances. Because of the lack of sufficient electrons for the formation of the requisite number of covalent bonds, normal covalently bonded structures of the hydrocarbon type are not possible. The boranes are sometimes referred to as electron-deficient substances. The hydrogen bridge bonding in B_2H_6 is shown below; here only four electrons

are utilized to link the two central hydrogen atoms to the two boron atoms. This is illustrative of the type of bonding which prevails in the boranes. In no case are the simple chain and ring configurations of carbon chemistry encountered in the more complex boranes. Instead, the boron atoms are situated at the corners of polyhedrons. An example of such a structure is that of pentaborane (9), which is shown below.

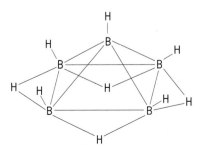

Preparation. The first important work on the boranes was that of Alfred Stock and coworkers, whose investigations in this field began about 1912. Their method of preparation, which utilized the decomposition of metallic borides (mainly magnesium boride) by mineral acids as a first step, yielded exceedingly small amounts of the boranes. The discouragingly small yields reported by Stock were significantly improved upon by H. I. Schlesinger and A. Burg, who developed an electrical discharge method based on the overall reaction shown by reaction (1). Later a number

$$6H_2 + 2BBr_3 \rightarrow B_2H_6 + 6HBr \qquad (1)$$

of chemical methods involving the metathetical exchange of hydride ion for halide or alkoxy groups were evolved by Schlesinger, H. C. Brown, and coworkers. One example of the latter is reaction (2),

$$6LiH + 2BF_3 \xrightarrow{Et_2O} 6LiF + B_2H_6 \qquad (2)$$

where $Et = C_2H_5$. Reactions of this type have been utilized to prepare B_2H_6 on a commercial scale. *See* HYDROBORATION.

No practical direct routes to the higher-molecular-weight boranes are known. Instead, substances such as B_4H_{10}, B_5H_9, and $B_{10}H_{14}$ are generally prepared by the thermal decomposition of B_2H_6, a process in some ways analogous to the cracking of hydrocarbons.

Reactions. As a class, the boranes are quite reactive substances and are generally decomposed, at times explosively, on contact with air. Their reactivities with air and water decrease with increasing molecular weight; B_2H_6 reacts instantaneously, whereas $B_{10}H_{14}$ must be heated with air or water to obtain an appreciable reaction rate. Because boranes react readily with air, laboratory investigations are almost invariably carried out in all-glass vacuum apparatus or in inert-atmosphere dry boxes. Prolonged exposure to hydrocarbon greases, in which the boranes dissolve and with which they slowly react, must be avoided. Animal tests have indicated that the boranes are quite toxic, and severe physical discomfort can result from the inhalation of their vapors. However the characteristic odor of boranes, which has been compared with that of chocolate but which is distinctly disagreeable, is so intense that it provides adequate warning before a dangerous level of exposure is reached.

With the possible exception of $B_{10}H_{14}$, the known boranes are not indefinitely stable at room temperature. They decompose more or less rapidly to yield elementary hydrogen and boranes richer in boron. When stored as a gas at approximately one atmosphere pressure, a sample of B_2H_6 at room temperature will normally decompose to the extent of several percent per month. The order of stability for the well-characterized boranes is $B_{10}H_9 > B_5H_9 > B_2H_6 > B_5H_{11} > B_4H_{10}$. B_2H_6 can be complete decomposed to its elements of 500–600°C (930–1110°F), whereas temperatures several hundred degrees higher are required for the quantitative conversion of $B_{10}H_{14}$ to its elements.

Because of its ready availability, the chemistry of B_2H_6 has been studied much more extensively than that of the other boranes. The previously mentioned reaction of B_2H_6 with oxygen proceeds according to reaction (3), and that with water yields hydrogen and boric acid, as shown by reaction (4). Both of these reactions, particularly the former,

$$B_2H_6 + 3O_2 \rightarrow B_2O_3 + 3H_2O \rightleftharpoons 3B(OH)_3 \qquad (3)$$

$$B_2H_6 + 6H_2O \rightarrow 6H_2 + 2B(OH)_3 \qquad (4)$$

are highly exothermic. Stable partial hydrolysis or partial oxidation products have not been isolated. Alcoholysis yields alkoxyboranes and hydrogen.

With electron-donor molecules, B_2H_6 often forms simple addition compounds of BH_3, as shown by reaction (5). More complex boranes can sometimes

$$B_2H_6 + 2NMe_3 \rightarrow 2Me_3NBH_3 \qquad (5)$$

be split into more complex component boranes; reaction (6) represents the splitting.

$$B_4H_{10} + OR_2 \rightarrow {}^1\!/_2B_2H_6 + B_3H_7 \cdot OR_2 \qquad (6)$$

With ammonia at low temperatures, B_2H_6 forms a solid product commonly called the diammoniate or diborane; this is shown by reaction (7).

$$B_2H_6 + 2NH_3 \rightarrow B_2H_6 \cdot 2NH_3 \qquad (7)$$

The structure of this solid has been extensively investigated, and the evidence is strongly in favor of the formulation $[BH_2(NH_3)_2]^+[BH_4]^-$. When the diammoniate of diborane is heated at elevated temperatures, hydrogen elimination occurs, as in reaction (8). The reaction product, borazine, has

$$3B_2H_6 + 6NH_3 \rightarrow 2B_3N_3H_6 + 12H_2 \qquad (8)$$

physical (but not chemical) properties closely resembling those of benzene, and its molecular structure, shown below, is formally similar to that

of the carbon compound.

An important class of compounds, the borohydrides, results from the reaction of B_2H_6 with metal hydrides. With lithium hydride, for instance, lithium borohydride is formed, as in reaction (9). A simi-

$$2LiH + B_2H_6 \xrightarrow{Et_2O} 2LiBH_4 \qquad (9)$$

lar reaction, which gives rise to a triborohydride, is indicated by reaction (10).

$$NaH + B_4H_{10} \xrightarrow{Et_2O} {}^1\!/_2B_2H_6 + NaB_3H_8 \qquad (10)$$

Treatment of B_2H_6 with ethylenic compounds produces alkyl boranes, as shown by reaction (11).

$$B_2H_6 + C_2H_4 \rightarrow B_2H_5C_2H_5 \qquad (11)$$

A large excess of ethylene leads to the formation of triethylborane. *See* CARBORANE.

The known derivatives of the boranes (other than BH_3) are relatively few in number. Several halo, alkyl, and amino boranes have been reported but, in general, these have not been extensively characterized. *See* BORON; METAL HYDRIDES.

Thomas Wartik

Bibliography. H. C. Brown, *Boranes in Organic Chemistry,* 1972; J. F. Liebman, A. Greenberg, and R. E. Williams (eds.), *Advances in Boron and the Boranes,* 1988; P. A. Mellor, *A Comprehensive Treatise on Inorganic and Theoretical Chemistry,* pt. 5: *Boron,* 1981; A. Pelter, *Borane Reagents,* 1988.

Borate minerals

A large and complex group of naturally occurring crystalline solids in which boron occurs in chemical combination with oxygen; hence the term borate. With the exception of avogadrite, $(K,Cs)BF_4$, and ferrucite, $NaBF_4$, all known boron minerals are borates. Boron, having an oxidation number (valence) of $+3$, does not act as a cation; for example, compounds of the type $B(NO_3)_3$ are not known to exist. Rather, boron combines with oxygen to form anions of varying degrees of complexity. Borate minerals may contain silicon, phosphorus, or arsenic. These, specifically, are the borosilicates, the borophosphates, and the boroarsenates. Of these three groups, the first is by far the largest. *See* BORON.

Occurrence. The average amount of boron in the Earth's crust is estimated as 3 ppm. Fortunately, large quantities are concentrated in deposits of hydrated borate minerals that are easily worked, and boron is not, like some minor elements, so completely dispersed that it is hard to find and use. Deposits are found in the United States (Mojave Desert), Turkey, Russia (Inder district), Tibet, Italy, Germany, Argentina, Bolivia, Canada, China, India, Iran, New Zealand, New Guinea, and Syria. The minerals of chief commercial importance are borax, $Na_2B_4O_7 \cdot 10H_2O$, and kernite, $Na_2B_4O_7 \cdot 4H_2O$. Large quantities of these minerals are mined at the Kramper deposit, Boron, California. Borax is extracted in large amounts from brine at Searles Lake, California. *See* KERNITE.

Structural classification. Any rational classification of the borate minerals must rest directly on a knowledge of their crystal structures. Not all of the structures are known, but a large number have been worked out so that a satisfactory classification can be made. The crystal chemistry of the borates is similar to that of the silicates, with the additional complication that boron can occur in either triangular or tetrahedral coordination. Boron will combine with three oxygen atoms

Borate minerals		
Mineral name	Empirical formula	Structural formula
Anhydrous borates		
Suanite	$Mg_2B_2O_5$	$Mg_2(B_2O_5)$
Kotoite	$Mg_3B_2O_6$	$Mg_3(BO_3)_2$
Nordenskiöldine	$CaSnB_2O_6$	$CaSn(BO_3)_2$
Ludwigite	$(Mg,Fe^{2+})_2Fe^{3+}BO_5$	$(Mg,Fe^{3+})_2Fe^{3+}BO_3O_2$
Boracite	$Mg_3B_7O_{13}Cl$	Complex three-dimensional network
Hydrated borates		
Sassolite	H_3BO_3	$B(OH)_3$
Pinnoite	$Mg(BO_2)_2 \cdot 3H_2O$	$Mg[B_2O(OH)_6]$
Teepleite	$Na_2BO_2Cl \cdot 2H_2O$	$Na_2[B(OH)_4]Cl$
Fluoborite	$Mg_3(BO_3)(OH,F)_3$	Same
Colemanite	$Ca_2B_6O_{11} \cdot 5H_2O$	$Ca[B_3O_4(OH)_3] \cdot H_2O$
Meyerhofferite	$Ca_2B_6O_{11} \cdot 7H_2O$	$Ca[B_3O_3(OH)_5] \cdot H_2O$
Inyoite	$Ca_2B_6O_{11} \cdot 13H_2O$	$Ca[B_3O_3(OH)_5] \cdot 4H_2O$
Inderite	$Mg_2B_6O_{11} \cdot 15H_2O$	$Mg[B_3O_3(OH)_5] \cdot 5H_2O$
Borax	$Na_2B_4O_7 \cdot 10H_2O$	$Na_2[B_4O_5(OH)_4] \cdot 8H_2O$
Tincalconite	$Na_2B_4O_7 \cdot 5H_2O$	$Na_2[B_4O_5(OH)_4] \cdot 3H_2O$
Kernite	$Na_2B_4O_7 \cdot 4H_2O$	$Na_2[B_4O_6(OH)_2] \cdot 3H_2O$
Veatchite	$Sr_4B_{22}O_{37} \cdot 7H_2O$	$Sr_2[B_5O_8(OH)]_2 \cdot B(OH)_3 \cdot H_2O$
Probertite	$NaCaB_5O_9 \cdot 5H_2O$	$NaCa[B_5O_7(OH)_4] \cdot 3H_2O$
Ulexite	$NaCaB_5O_9 \cdot 8H_2O$	$NaCa[B_5O_6(OH)_6] \cdot 5H_2O$
Borosilicates		
Datolite	$CaBSiO_5 \cdot H_2O$	$Ca_4[BSiO_4(OH)]_4$
Reedmergnerite	$NaBSi_3O_8$	Feldspar structure
Danburite	$CaB_2Si_2O_8$	Feldspar structure
Tourmaline	$(Na,Ca)(Li,Al)_3Al_6(OH)_4(BO_3)_3Si_6O_{18}$	Same
Borophosphates and boroarsenates		
Lunebergite	$Mg_3B_2(OH)_6(PO_4)_2 \cdot 6H_2O$	
Seamanite	$Mn_3(PO_4)(BO_3) \cdot 3H_2O$	
Cahnite	$Ca_2B(OH)_4(AsO_4)$	

to form a planar triangular group BO_3, or with four oxygen atoms to form a tetrahedral group BO_4. These groups of threefold and fourfold coordination result in isolated ions such as BO_3^{3-}, or $B(OH)_4^-$, or the molecule $B(OH)_3$, contained in sassolite. Alternatively, the groups may share corners in various ways to form polyanions of varying complexity. These polyanions may be relatively simple, as in the pyro ion $O_2B-O-BO_2$, or more complicated. For example, the mineral meyerhofferite, $Ca_2B_6O_{11} \cdot 7H_2O$, contains insular polyions of composition $[B_3O_3(OH)_5]^{2-}$, formed by corner sharing of two $BO_2(OH)_2$ tetrahedra with a $BO_2(OH)$ triangle, as shown in the **illustration**. Other examples shown are the insular polyion $[B_4O_5(OH)_4]^{2-}$ that is found in borax, $Na_2B_4O_7 \cdot 10H_2O$, and the infinite chains of composition $[B_3O_4(OH)_3]_n^{2-}$ that is found in colemanite,

$Ca_2B_6O_{11} \cdot 5H_2O$. Three rules have emerged for predicting the nature of the polyanions in borates (in the absence of Si, P, or As): (1) Polyanions are formed by the corner sharing only of triangles and tetrahedra in such manner that a compact insular group of low negative charge results; (2) these insular groups may polymerize to form infinite chains; an example is the equation below; (3) in hydrated

$$n[B_3O_3(OH)_5]^{2n-} = [B_3O_4(OH)_3]_n^{2n-} + nH_2O$$
Meyerhofferite   Colemanite

borates those oxygens not shared between two borons or more always attach a hydrogen atom and become hydroxyl groups.

In the borosilicates there is much evidence for the linking of boron-oxygen polyanions with silicon-oxygen tetrahedra, but the details for most minerals are unknown. In borophosphates and boroarsenates there does not appear to be sharing between phosphate or arsenate tetrahedra and borate polyanions. In the **table** is a list of some of the commoner borate minerals. Structural formulas are given where it is possible to do so. The table also includes several minerals that serve as examples of structural types, even though they actually may be comparatively rare in occurrence. *See* BORACITE; DATOLITE; TOURMALINE.

Charles L. Christ

Bibliography. D. Dana et al., *The System of Mineralogy*, vol. 2, 7th ed.; D. L. Martin (ed.), *Borax to Boranes*, 1961; C. T. Walker, *Geochemistry of Boron*, 1975.

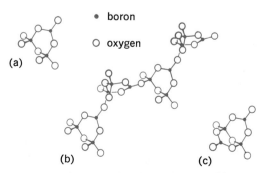

Some structural elements of borate minerals. (*a*) Meyerhofferite. (*b*) Colemanite. (*c*) Borax.

Bordetella

A bacterial genus named for Jules Bordet, who together with O. Gengou discovered in 1905 the organisms causing whooping cough (pertussis). The organisms are minute (0.2–0.3 by 0.5–1.0 micrometer), nonsporulating, gram-negative coccobacilli. They grow within 2–5 days at 95°F (35°C) in the presence of oxygen on potato-glycerol-blood agar (Bordet-Gengou agar) or in chemically defined media. Litmus milk is made alkaline. Carbohydrates are not fermented. Indole and gelatinase reactions are negative. Three species are mammalian parasites and one is an avian parasite; they may cause respiratory diseases. A variety of antigenic or toxic factors are secreted or contained in the cell walls. Genetic investigations have shown that the genus *Bordetella* is most closely related to the *Alcaligenes denitrificans/Achromobacter xylosoxidans* and *Alcaligenes faecalis* group. The genome deoxyribonucleic acid (DNA) of the mammalian bordetellas contains 67–70 mol%, that of the avian species 61–63 mol% guanine plus cytosine. *See* WHOOPING COUGH.

Bordetella pertussis, the most fastidious species, causes whooping cough and subacute bronchitis in humans, with high mortality in the young baby. It is hemolytic, oxidase- and mostly catalase-positive, and urease-negative, and does not brown peptone agar media. The specific heat-labile antigen known as factor 1 is always present. The genome DNA exhibits high degrees of base sequence relatedness to the genome DNAs of *B. parapertussis* and *B. bronchiseptica*.

Bordetella parapertussis may cause similar but less severe respiratory infections in humans. It differs from *B. pertussis* by a weaker or lacking oxidase reaction, by urease and tyrosinase (browning) activities, faster growth, and the presence of the specific heat-labile antigen factor 14.

Bordetella bronchiseptica is only rarely found affecting humans, but is a common respiratory parasite in many domestic and wild mammals, including horses, swine, dogs, and rodents, and may cause a variety of respiratory diseases in them. The organism is motile by peritrichous flagella, grows more rapidly than the former species, and reduces nitrates to nitrites. It contains the specific antigen factor 12.

Bordetella avium is a newly described species of the genus that causes respiratory infections in birds.

Several antibacterial chemotherapeutics, such as tetracyclines, chloramphenicol, and specific antisera, are clinically effective against *B. pertussis* and *B. bronchiseptica* in early stages of the infection, but less effective in eliminating the bacteria. Drug resistance in *Bordetella* species has been frequently observed. Erythromycin is used for chemoprophylaxis. Vaccines consisting of killed *B. pertussis* organisms are protective in the young baby, but so far nontoxic vaccines are not available. *See* ANTIBIOTIC; DRUG RESISTANCE; MEDICAL BACTERIOLOGY; VACCINATION.

Walter Mannheim

Bibliography. N. R. Krieg and J. G. Holt (eds.), *Bergey's Manual of Systematic Bacteriology*, vol. 1, 4th ed., 1984.

Boring and drilling, geotechnical

The drilling of holes for exploration, extractive development, extraction of mineral deposits, and site evaluation. Exploration holes are drilled to locate mineral deposits, define their extent, determine their ore dressing characteristics, determine mining or quarrying conditions to be met in their development or extraction, and otherwise to establish the commercial value of the deposit. Holes for extractive development are drilled for blasting, mine dewatering, access for utility lines, grouting for water control, pilot holes for shaft sinking, and as small shafts for backfilling, ventilation, portals, and escapeways. Drilling employed in site evaluation is used to determine whether specific locations are suitable for the construction of structures or roads. Environmental drilling is done to determine the extent of contamination left by industrial or other activity. Samples of soils, rock, and ground water are analyzed for chemical, biological, or radiological contamination to enable the remediation designers to determine the best method of improvement of the site. *See* MINING; OIL AND GAS WELL DRILLING.

Elements of drilling. The two essentials are a process to detach particles of soil or rock from the floor of the hole, and a way to remove the loosened particles from the hole. The principles that can be applied to these processes are limited by the confines of the drill hole, but they can be combined into an innumerable variety of drilling methods, applicable to mineral work.

Drills and equipment. Energy and action required for the two processes of drilling are furnished in various ways. Drills are designed to create rotary or linear motion or a combination of both. Auxiliary drill-rig equipment (pumps, compressors, generators) may introduce additional energy into the hole in the form of hydraulic, pneumatic, or electric power. Another source of energy may be created at the bit by conversion of gases into heat.

The energy of motion created by the drill may be transmitted to the drill bit by a shaft (drill rods) or by a flexible cable (wire-line, rope). Drill rods are tubular so that they may be used for the injection of fluids, compressed air, or gases.

Principal drilling methods. Five commonly used drilling techniques are (1) rotary drilling, penetration by the abrasive action of a drill bit in rotary motion; (2) core drilling, rotary drilling an annular groove leaving a central core; (3) percussion drilling, penetration by the chipping or crushing action produced by a drill bit in linear motion; (4) rotary-percussion drilling, a combination of rotary and linear motions to produce penetration; and (5) fusion piercing, penetration by flaking or melting caused by the application of heat. Many drills may be adapted to a variety of drilling methods, particularly those drills that are designed to produce penetration by rotary motion and that also incorporate dual linear motion mechanisms, one for control and one for hoisting. Some drills are specifically designed for a combination of drilling methods (see **illus.**).

Drilling methods have terminology generally indicative of the outstanding feature of the method, but the same term may be used for a method that is also used for a type of drilling, as in the use of the term rotary drilling.

Rotary drilling. In this type of drilling, a rotary motion is induced in the drill rods and transmitted to the drill bit. The cutting action is accomplished by the use of either a roller bit, which has rolling cutters with hard projecting teeth, or drag bits, which have fixed hardened cutting edges. The roller bit penetrates the rock by the crushing action of the teeth. Weight is placed on the bit either by using heavy drill pipe or collars or by pushing on the tools with the drill rig while rotating the tools. The drag bit cuts with a scraping action at the bottom of the hole, lifting the rock particles away from the rock. The removal of the cuttings from the hole is by injection of air, fluid, or foam into the rock through a swivel that stays stationary as the rods are rotated. The air or fluid is transmitted down the rods under pressure to the bit, where it cools the cutting surfaces and flushes the rock particles from the hole between the rod surface and the hole wall. The most common use of rotary drilling is gas and oil drilling, where the fluid used is drilling mud. The mud actually serves three functions in the deep gas and oil work: it stabilizes the walls of the hole, cools

the cutting edges, and flushes the cuttings from the hole.

Auger drilling. Rotary-type auger methods penetrate by the cutting or gouging action of chisel-type cutting edges forced into the formation by down pressure and rotation of the bit. Cuttings are removed by mechanical action. Auger flights are made with a continuous helical projecting surface so that they act as screw conveyors to remove the cuttings. Auger drills are of various sizes, and usually incorporate a hydraulic cylinder to increase bit pressure and to withdraw the tools. The method is used for drilling blast holes and for reconnaissance prospecting. A special type is used as a mining tool.

Diamond core drilling. Another rotary type, this drilling utilizes the extreme hardness of the diamond to penetrate rock by abrasive action. Core drills rotate an annular bit to cut a narrow kerf around a central core and thus obtain unaltered samples of the formation drilled. Diamond drills are the principal tools for exploration of mineral deposits.

The diamond drill furnishes rotary motion for penetration, and generally also has dual linear motion mechanisms, a hydraulic cylinder to control the feed of the bit against the rock, and a wire-line hoist for tool withdrawal. The drill head on some drills swivels for drilling at any angle. Tubular drill rods transmit rotary motion to the core barrel, which has a core-retaining device just above the diamond bit. The ring-shaped diamond bit is set with industrial-grade diamonds, those with imperfections that prohibit their use as gems. Water or mud circulation cools the bit and removes the cuttings. Double-tube core barrels are used to keep water circulation from washing the core (see **table**).

A few variations are developed. Surface-set bits contain a single layer of diamonds. Impregnated bits have diamond fragments distributed through the crown so that fresh cutting points are exposed as the bit wears. Noncoring diamond bits may be used where a core is not desired, as in diamond blast-hole drilling. *See* DIAMOND.

Raise drilling. This method, a variation on the rotary drilling technique, is mainly used for the drilling of large air shafts and access ways in mining operations. The hole is actually drilled from the bottom up. First, a hole usually less than 15 in. (380 mm) in diameter is drilled from the surface to an open entry in the mine. The raise drill rods are then placed in the hole to its bottom by the raise boring machine. The raise drill bit is transported into the mine through the system of mine entries, assembled, and attached to the drill rods. The bit is then rotated and pulled toward the surface. Cuttings from the drilling fall to the mine floor and are collected and hauled out of the mine by the conventional material-handling methods. Because of the tremendous forces that can be applied in the drilling by the raise boring equipment, holes of over 20 ft (6 m) in diameter can be drilled.

Combined auger-core drill. (*Mobile Drilling Co.*)

Standard diamond core bit sizes	
Hole diameter, in. (mm)	Core diameter, in. (mm)
1.160 (29.4)	0.735 (18.6)
1.470 (37.3)	0.905 (22.9)
1.875 (47.6)	1.281 (32.5)
2.345 (59.5)	1.750 (44.4)
2.965 (75.3)	2.313 (58.7)
3.890 (98.8)	3.187 (80.9)
5.435 (138.0)	3.970 (100.8)
7.655 (194.4)	5.970 (151.6)

Air percussion drilling. Penetration of this drilling is by crushing action under pneumatically powered impact. The drill bit is chisel type, commonly with four cutting edges in the form of a cross. The drill produces linear impact motion by means of a reciprocating pneumatically powered piston to strike a rapid series of blows against a tubular drill steel, which transmits the energy to the bit. The drills also provide pneumatically powered rotary motion constantly to change the position of the bit against the floor of the hole. Cuttings are usually blown out of the hole by compressed air injected through the hollow drill steel and bit, although water may be substituted with drills designed for hazardous dust conditions. Dust collectors may be used to reduce hazard and also to collect samples.

Air percussion drills are primarily used for blasthole drilling, in various sizes and mountings, for both surface and underground work. The method is limited in hole size and depth by two considerations—constant loss of bit gage and absorption of dynamic energy by the drill steel. Tungsten carbide cutting inserts help retain gage, and special down-the-hole drills are of aid in the latter problem. Detachable drill bits are commonly used in pneumatic drilling operations.

Cable tool (churn) drilling. A different percussion-type method, this penetrates by crushing impact of a falling heavy chisel bit. The drill creates an oscillating vertical linear motion, which is transmitted to the drilling tools by wire-line cable, so that they are alternately lifted and dropped. The cuttings are suspended in water by the churning action of the tools, and then periodically removed by bailing. Churn drills are usually used for drilling water wells and for drilling access holes for utility lines into mines.

Fusion piercing methods. For these, an oxygen-acetylene blow pipe applies intense heat to the floor of the hole and penetrates by flaking or melting. Drills must produce both linear and rotary motion to handle the blow pipe and break up slag formed in the process. The cuttings and slag are blown from the hole. Fusion piercing methods have been used successfully for drilling blast holes in hard rocks, such as taconite and granite.

Other drilling methods. Innumerable combinations of the basic drilling methods described above provide a wide range of variations in drilling methods.

Auger mining utilizes the conveyor action of continuous-flight augers for actual mining operations in large-diameter horizontal holes, such as for mining coal in the high wall beyond the economical limits of strip mining. The science of electronics has been applied to guide such an auger and keep it within the bed.

Auger stem drilling uses a short helix, run on a solid or telescoping stem, as a bit for gouging out and collecting cuttings. With a derrick higher than the hole is deep, or high enough to withdraw the entire string of tools in telescoped position, the auger can be withdrawn quickly and spun rapidly to throw off the cuttings by centrifugal force. The method is suitable for holes 12–72-in. (310–1800-mm) or larger diameter. When a bit incorporating a steel cylinder to confine the cuttings is substituted, the technique is termed bucket drilling.

Reverse-circulation drilling usually refers to a variation of the rotary drilling method in which the cuttings are pumped up and out of the drill pipe. This is advantageous in certain large-diameter holes. The term is also applied to diamond core drilling when the water is injected through a stuffing box into the annular space around the drill rods and thus forced up special large drill rods. Here the water forces the core up through the drill rods like a piston through a cylinder.

Rotary blast-hole drilling is a term commonly applied to two types of drilling. In quarrying and open-pit mining, it implies rotary drilling with roller-type bits, using compressed air for cuttings removal, either a conventional rotary table drive or a hydraulic motor to produce rotation, and hydraulic or wire-line mechanisms to add part of the weight of the drill to the weight of the tools and thereby increase bit pressure. In underground mining, and sometimes above-ground, rotary blast-hole drilling implies the drilling of small-diameter blast holes with a diamond drill, using either coring or noncoring diamond bits.

Rotary-percussion drilling increases the penetration speed of a roller bit by adding pneumatic impact in linear motion to the normal abrading action of the bit in rotary motion.

Shaft drilling is shaft sinking by drilling a hole the size of the shaft, as contrasted with conventional shaft-sinking methods of drilling small holes and blasting. The perfect arch action of the smooth-cut circular wall of a drilled shaft makes shaft lining unnecessary in hard massive rocks, and much safer and more economical in others, because a blasted wall is shattered and requires more concrete for lining due to overbreak. Both shot core drilling and rotary drilling methods are used in shaft drilling, with variations such as the use of carbide or rolling cutters on the core barrel, rotary reaming a pilot hole in successively larger stages, use of reverse circulation, and down-the-hole-type rotary drills.

Down-the-hole drilling is air percussion type (for large-diameter blast holes) with the reciprocating pneumatic piston placed in the drill tools close to the bit for minimizing energy losses.

Sonic drilling methods are percussion or rotary-percussion type, utilizing for impact the energy of a drill stem vibrating at sonic frequency. One method of producing sonic vibration is by use of eccentric weights driven by a mud turbine.

Turbodrilling is rotary drilling with rotary motion created in the hole close to the bit by a turbine driven by the circulating mud.

Wash boring or jet drilling utilizes a chopping bit with a water jet run on a string of hollow drill rods to chop through soils and wash the cuttings to the surface.

Wire-line coring is a method of removing core by pulling the inner tube of the core barrel, with the bit, core barrel, and drill rods remaining in the hole. The inner tube is dropped or pumped down through the drill rods, and recovered by running a retriever on a wire line, so the periodic removal of core can be done in deep drill holes in less time than required for removal and replacement of drill pipe or drill rods. Most of the deep diamond drill holes are drilled with wire-line diamond core drilling equipment.

Site evaluation. Drilling is done in a variety of ways to investigate sites for buildings, roads, bridges, and other structures. The supporting characteristics of the underlying soil and rock are determined by the drilling of test borings. Most common in site investigations is the use of the American Society for Testing and Materials Standard Penetration Test for soil properties. In this test a standard sampler is driven into the soil with a specific weight falling a set distance. Many other tests are available both in place and in the soils laboratory to measure moisture content, plasticity, grain size, shear strength, permeability, axial strength, deformation over time, and other properties. Some of these tests are performed on disturbed samples obtained with the Standard Penetration Test, and some are performed on larger samples obtained with test pits or undisturbed sampling with Shelby tubes. In Shelby-tube sampling, a thin-walled metal tube with a formed, sharpened edge is pressed into the soil with the hydraulic feed apparatus on the drill rig.

Rock core drilling provides rock samples for visual examination and laboratory testing. The cores are tested in the laboratory for strength, permeability, freeze-thaw cycle deterioration, weathering characteristics, deformation under load over time, and other characteristics.

In-place borehole testing for engineering properties also includes pressure testing, falling-head and constant-head permeability, pressure meter testing, pump testing for aquifer information, and cross-hole seismic tests.

Site evaluation for chemical properties of the underlying soil and rock has become the standard for property transfer because of the prevalence of subsurface contamination. Drilling and sampling is done, and monitoring wells of appropriate materials are installed to determine the extent, if any, of contamination generated by prior illegal dumping or substandard manufacturing processes. Purchasers of contaminated real estate can incur tremendous cleanup costs if proper investigations are not conducted. *See* BOREHOLE LOGGING.

Frank C. Sturges; Thomas B. Sturges III

Boring bivalves

A variety of marine bivalve mollusks which penetrate solid substrata. They represent seven families and vary in the extent to which they are specialized, in the type of substrata they utilize, and in their method of boring. It is difficult to differentiate borers, burrowers, and nestlers because some species, such as *Hiatella arctica*, not only bore into hard limestones, calcareous sandstones, and chalks, but also burrow in peat or sand-filled crevices in hard rocks, or nestle in holdfasts of *Laminaria*. Undoubtedly the true borers evolved from burrowers via forms that were living in increasingly harder substrata.

Unlike other bivalves which use their shells as abrasive "tools," date mussels (*Lithophaga*, Mytilidae) penetrate calcareous rocks, corals, and shells by chemical means, possibly a weak carbonic acid. These borers are byssally attached and move back and forth in their burrows by alternate contractions of the anterior and posterior byssal retractor muscles. This action presses the thickened, fused, anterior mantle lobes against the end of the burrow, and when they are withdrawn they are covered with fine particles of rock which are ejected through the incurrent siphon along with the pseudofeces. Larvae of *Botula* (another small, elongate mytilid), which settle in crevices of soft rock, corals, or wood, abrade their way into the substrate by continued movement of their shells and siphons.

Rupellaria and *Petricola* (Petricolidae) are non-specialized borers in peat, firm mud, and soft rock. *Petricola* are usually found in peat, but *Rupellaria* larvae settling in crevices of limestone and coral gradually enlarge their burrows as they grow. *Platyodon* (Myidae), closely related to the soft-shelled clam, press their valves against the walls of the burrow by engorging the mantle and then abrade the soft rock by continued movement of their unspecialized valves.

Gastrochaena and *Spengleria* (Gastrochaenidae) are specialized for boring by having a closed mantle cavity, a large pedal gape, and a truncate foot, allowing them to press the foot and shell against the burrow wall. Despite their thin, fragile shells, they drill into limestone and coral blocks by mechanical means, making flask-shaped burrows which they line posteriorly with calcareous material to ensure a snug fit around the siphons.

The Pholadacea (Pholadidae and Teredinidae)

are worldwide in distribution and are highly specialized for boring into hard substrata. The family Pholodidae (common name: piddocks) is composed of 17 genera, of which 5 are restricted to wood. All species of Teredinidae are obligate wood, nut, or plant-stem borers. The major difference between these two families is the presence of accessory plates in the pholads and pallets in the teredinids. For a discussion of the latter group *see* SHIPWORM.

Most pholads are marine, living at depths ranging from intertidal to about 1000 ft (300 m), with some of the deep-sea wood borers (Xylophagainae) extending to 16,500 ft (5000 m). Specializations for boring include filelike sculpture on the shell, a large pedal gape, a truncate foot, a closed mantle cavity, the reduction of the hinge and ligament, the insertion of the anterior adductor muscle on the outside of the valves anterior to the umbos so that it works in opposition to the posterior adductor muscle, and the pivoting of the valves on a dorsoventral axis passing through the umbos and ventral condyle (**Fig. 1**). The contraction of the anterior adductor muscle brings the valves

Fig. 2. Typical boring bivalves: (*a*) *Diplothyra smithii* boring in *Crassostrea virginica*; (*b*) *Penitella penita* boring in shale; (*c*) *Zirfaea crispata* removed from burrow, showing foot, anterior adductor muscle, and siphons (*from R. D. Turner, The family Pholadidae in the western Atlantic and eastern Pacific, Johnsonia, 3(33–34):1–160, 1954–1955*); (*d*) *Petricola pholadiformis* removed from burrow, showing extended siphons.

together anteriorly; the attachment of the foot anteriorly and the contraction of the pedal muscles pull the shell forward against the anterior end of the burrow; and then the forceful contraction of the posterior adductor muscle spreads the valves anteriorly and scrapes the filelike ridges against the wall of the burrow. Water jetted anteriorly from the mantle cavity flushes the burrow, and the debris is ejected from the incurrent siphon as pseudofeces. Accessory plates, developed to protect the exposed anterior adductor muscle, are unique to the Pholadidae. Additional dorsal, ventral, and siphonal plates are produced, and the pedal gape is closed with a callum when adult Martesiinae cease boring (Figs. 1 and **Fig. 2***a*, *b*).

Species in the genera *Zirfaea* (Fig. 2*c*) and *Barnea* hasten the recycling of submerged peat beds, and the activity of rock borers such as *Penitella* (Fig. 2*b*), *Parapholas*, *Pholas*, and *Chaceia* contribute to the breakdown of intertidal and submerged cliffs and even cement bulkheading. *Pholas dactylus* of Europe, known to penetrate schistose rock, is also famous for its luminescent properties. *Diplothyra smithii* (Fig. 2*a*) and *Penitella parva*, both shell borers, are pests of oysters and abalones respectively. The wood-boring *Martesia* are important pests of waterfront structures and may even bore into polyvinyl chloride pipes in tropical and warm temperate areas. The Xylophagainae are the most important organisms involved in recycling wood in the deep sea. This subfamily includes three genera and about 30 species. *See* MOLLUSCA.

Ruth D. Turner

Bibliography. G. L. Kennedy, *West American*

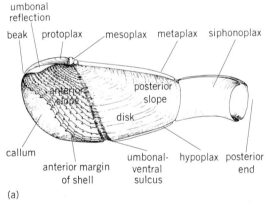

umbonal reflection
beak | protoplax | mesoplax | metaplax | siphonoplax
anterior slope
posterior slope
disk
callum
anterior margin of shell
umbonal-ventral sulcus
hypoplax | posterior end

(a)

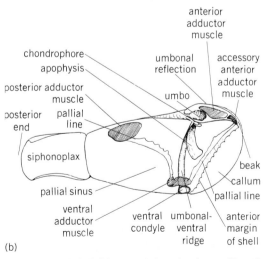

anterior adductor muscle
chondrophore
apophysis
umbonal reflection
accessory anterior adductor muscle
posterior adductor muscle
umbo
posterior end | pallial line
pallial line
posterior | pallial line
siphonoplax
beak
callum
pallial line
pallial sinus
ventral adductor muscle
ventral condyle | umbonal-ventral ridge
anterior margin of shell

(b)

Fig. 1. A pholad shell: (*a*) external view, showing position of accessory plates and parts of the valve; (*b*) internal view, showing position of muscle and parts of the valves. (*After R. D. Turner, The family Pholadidae in the western Atlantic and eastern Pacific, Johnsonia, 3(33–34):1–160, 1954–1955*)

Cenozoic Pholadidae (Mollusca: Bivalvia), San Diego Soc. Nat. Hist. Mem. 8, pp. 1–128, 1974; R. C. Moore (ed.), *Treatise on Invertebrate Paleontology*, pt. N, vol. 2, 1969; R. D. Purchon, The structure and function of British Pholadidae, *Proc. Zool. Soc. London*, 124:859–911, 1955; R. D. Turner, The family Pholadidae in the western Atlantic and eastern Pacific, *Johnsonia*, 3(33–34):1–160, 1954–1955.

Boring sponges

Sponges that excavate galleries in mollusk shells, corals, limestone, and other calcareous matter. Boring sponges are known in three families of the class Demospongiae; they are also called burrowing sponges. All species of the family Clionidae, order Hadromerida, excavate burrows in calcium carbonate substrata, as do some species of the genera *Anthosigmella* and *Spheciospongia* (family Spirastrellidae, order Hadromerida) and all species of *Siphonodictyon* (family Adociidae, order Haplosclerida). Water currents are maintained through the tissues of these boring sponges exactly as in other Demospongiae. They do not obtain food from their hosts when the calcareous matter into which they burrow happens to be the shell or skeleton of a living organism. Instead, boring sponges feed on bacteria, flagellates, and other kinds of particulate organic matter drawn in from the surrounding seawater by way of ostia. In *Cliona*, ostia and oscula are localized on contractile tubules that protrude through holes in the calcareous substratum continuous with the extensive galleries within (**Fig. 1**). In

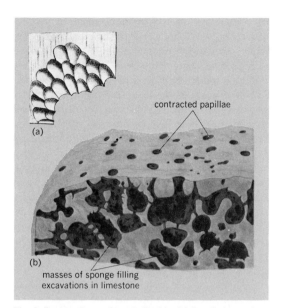

Fig. 2. Destructive action of clionids. (a) Small piece of calcite showing how a clionid has excavated uniform chips from it. (b) Section through a piece of limestone (enlarged) to show the excavations made by a clionid. Contracted papillae can be seen on the upper surface.

Siphonodictyon, minute to conspicuous chimneys protrude from the host, usually a coral in this genus.

The most widespread genus, *Cliona*, has a skeleton of monactinal siliceous megascleres provided with terminal knobs. Microscleres may be present in the form of spined diactinal spicules or spirasters or both. *Anthosigmella* and *Spheciospongia* have tylostyles as megascleres and spirasters of distinctive shapes as microscleres. *Siphonidictyon* has only diactinal spicules.

The burrowing process is similar in all genera and involves the excavation of numerous minute particles of calcium carbonate (20–70 micrometers in diameter) that pass out by way of the exhalant canals and oscula. Piles of such calcareous chips often accumulate around the bases of the oscular tubules. In *Cliona*, special etching cells bear filopodia that extend into etched crevices of the substratum. The filopodia branch and fuse to form a meshwork like a basket, the size of which will correspond to that of the chip excavated. A localized acidic secretion presumably accounts for the etching capacity of the filopodia; an enzymic component of the secretion probably accounts for the ability of the cells to remove bits of the organic matrix of skeletal materials (such as the conchiolin of mollusk shells). Only 2–3% of the calcium carbonate removed by the etching cells is in solution; most of it is freed as particles that are added to the bottom sediments of the sea as silt. In coral reef environments, up to 30–40% of fine sediment particles may be derived from the activities of burrowing sponges in low-energy environments; lesser proportions (5–22%) characterize sediments in high-energy environments.

Clionids are regarded as a nuisance in oyster beds because their excavations weaken the shells

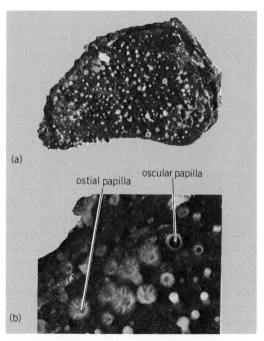

ostial papilla   oscular papilla

Fig. 1. *Cliona celata*, a common boring sponge. (a) Sponge living in oyster shell. (b) Enlarged portion of a showing several expanded ostial and oscular papillae.

of these mollusks and thus hinder processing in the canning factories. Boring sponges also become economically important when they attack limestone breakwaters (**Fig. 2**).

Clionid boring sponges are found in all seas, chiefly in tidal and shallow waters. A few species reach a depth of at most 3300 ft (1000 m). Their excavations are known in fossil mollusk shells at least as far back as the Devonian Period. Burrowing species of the genera *Anthosigmella, Spheciospongia,* and *Siphonodictyon* are found on coral reefs at depths of more than 200 ft (60 m). *See* DEMOSPONGIAE.   Willard D. Hartman

Bibliography. K. Rützler and C. Rieger, Sponge burrowing: Fine structure of *Cliona lampa* penetrating calcareous substrata, *Mar. Biol.*, 21:144–162, 1973.

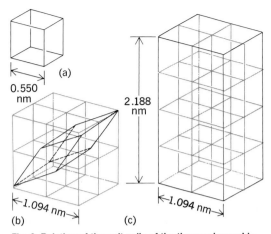

Fig. 2. Relation of the unit cells of the three polymorphic modifications of bornite to a face-centered cubic array of sulfur atoms. (*a*) High-temperature cubic form (one sulfur subcell). (*b*) Metastable rhombohedral form. (*c*) Low-temperature tetragonal form.

Bornite

A sulfide of composition Cu_5FeS_4, specific gravity 5.07, and hardness 3 (Mohs scale), commonly occurring as a primary mineral in many copper ore deposits. Crystals are rare; bornite is usually massive or granular (**Fig. 1**). The metallic and brassy color of a fresh surface rapidly tarnishes upon exposure to air to a characteristic iridescent purple, giving rise to the name "peacock ore." Bornite exhibits considerable solid solution at elevated temperatures. Upon cooling, other copper sulfides, such as chalcopyrite, chalcocite, and digenite, may be exsolved. Association or intergrowths of bornite with these minerals is common. Though of lesser importance as an ore than chalcocite or chalcopyrite, masses of bornite have been mined in Chile, Peru, Bolivia, and Mexico and in the United States in Arizona and Montana. *See* CHALCOCITE; CHALCOPYRITE.

Three polymorphic modifications of bornite are known. A cubic form, stable above 442°F (228°C), cannot be quenched, and transforms into a metastable rhombohedral structure upon rapid cooling. This intermediate form slowly transforms into a tetragonal modification stable at room temperature. The atomic arrangement in all three phases is based upon a face-centered

cubic arrangement of sulfur atoms (**Fig. 2**). The metal atoms are statistically distributed among the tetrahedral interstices available in this array: $3/4$ atom is disordered among 24 equivalent sites within every available tetrahedron in the high-temperature phase; and 1 atom is distributed over 4 positions within 3 of the 4 tetrahedral sites available in the rhombohedral modification. The rhombohedral and tetragonal phases both mimic cubic symmetry because of fine-scale twinning. *See* COPPER.

Bernhardt J. Wuensch

Fig. 1. Example of bornite from Messina, Transvaal, South Africa. (*Specimen from Department of Geology, Bryn Mawr College*)

Boron

A chemical element, symbol B, atomic number 5, atomic weight 10.811, in group III of the periodic table. It has three valence electrons and is nonmetallic in behavior. It is classified as a metalloid and is the only nonmetallic element which has fewer than four electrons in its outer shell. *See* METALLOID.

The free element is prepared in crystalline or amorphous form. The crystalline form is an extremely hard, brittle solid. It is of jet-black to silvery-gray color with a metallic luster. One form of crystalline boron is bright red. The amorphous form is less dense than the crystalline and is a dark-brown to black powder.

In the naturally occurring compounds, boron exists as a mixture of two stable isotopes with atomic weights of 10 and 11. The ^{10}B isotope, which normally makes up 18.8% of the total boron, is an effective absorber for thermal neutrons. The large relative difference between the atomic masses of the isotopes ^{10}B and ^{11}B permits their separation and concentration by fractional distillation and diffusion processes. Such processes have been operated on a large scale using boron trifluoride etherate as the reaction medium.

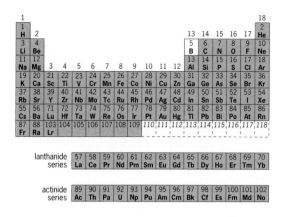

Humphry Davy and Joseph Gay-Lussac with Louis Jacques Thénard obtained the element from boric acid almost concurrently in 1807 and 1808, respectively. Davy used electrolysis, whereas Gay-Lussac and Thénard used potassium to reduce the boric acid.

Very little in the way of analyses accompanied the work of these original investigators. The first serious investigation pertaining to boron was carried out at the end of the nineteenth century by Henri Moissan, who in 1892 first obtained boron of better than 98% purity. He also repeated the work of earlier investigators and reported for the first time analyses which showed large amounts of impurities, usually oxygen and the reducing metal.

Properties. Many properties of boron have not been sufficiently established experimentally. The literature shows considerable inconsistency in physical properties; this is the result of the questionable purity of some sources of boron, as well as of the variations in the methods and temperatures of preparation. A summary of the physical properties is shown in **Table 1**. Samples of boron having the highest purity, whether crystalline or amorphous, are black in color. The samples of so-called Moissan (amorphous) boron exhibit various shades of brown, which are associated with the presence of various amounts of boron suboxide impurities. Crystalline boron, although relatively brittle compared to diamond, is second only to diamond in hardness. Facets on the minute single crystals are clearly visible when viewed through a microscope of at least 30 power.

Three crystalline modifications of boron have been established. A tetragonal form contains 50 boron atoms in its unit cell. Its density is 2.31 g/cm^3. Two rhombohedral modifications (α and β) have densities of 2.46 and 2.35 g/cm^3, respectively. The α-rhombohedral modification is said to form in the 800–1100°C (1500–2000°F) temperature range. The tetragonal modification is prepared in the 1100–1300°C (2000–2400°F) range, while the β-rhombohedral form may be obtained above 1300°C (2400°F). Boron possesses a large, negative temperature coefficient of resistivity, which means that its electrical conductivity rises rapidly with increase in temperature. E. Weintraub's data show an increase by a factor of almost 2×10^6 over the 100–1000°C (212–1800°F) temperature range. W. C. Shaw found that the resistivity of boron decreases by a factor of almost 10^{10} between the temperatures of -70 and 700°C (-90 and 1300°F).

The chemical properties of boron depend largely on the physical form as well as on the purity of samples. Amorphous boron oxidizes slowly in the air even at room temperature, and is spontaneously flammable at about 800°C (1500°F). A special reactive form of amorphous boron may be prepared by the magnesiothermic reduction of anhydrous alkali borates. This form may catch fire in air at temperatures below 100°C (212°F), and is generally characterized by an extremely small particle size (smaller than 1 micrometer) and high alkali-metal impurity (5–10%) content.

Boron is not affected by either hydrochloric or hydrofluoric acids, even on prolonged boiling. Crystalline boron is quite stable to heat and oxidation even at relatively high temperatures. It is slowly attacked and oxidized by hot concentrated nitric acid and by mixtures of sodium dichromate and sulfuric acid. Hydrogen peroxide and ammonium persulfate also slowly oxidize crystalline boron. These reagents are found to act violently on samples of amorphous boron. All varieties of boron are completely oxidized by molten mixtures of alkali carbonates and hydroxides. Chlorine, bromine, and fluorine act easily on boron with formation of the corresponding boron halides [bromine acts at 700°C (1300°F), chlorine at 410°C (770°F), and fluorine at room temperature]. Boron reacts vigorously with sulfur at about 600°C (1100°F) to form a mixture of boron sulfides. Boron nitride is formed when boron is heated in a nitrogen or ammonia atmosphere above 1000°C (1800°F). At high temperatures, boron combines with phosphorus and with arsenic to form a phosphide, BP, and an arsenide, BAs. On further heating, these materials lose phos-

TABLE 1. Physical properties of boron		
Property	Temp., °C	Value
Density		
Crystalline	25–27	2.31 g/cm^3
Amorphous	25–27	2.3 g/cm^3
Mohs hardness		
Crystalline		9.3
Melting point		2100°C (3800°F)
Boiling point		2500°C (4500°F)
Resistivity	25	1.7×10^6 ohm-cm
Coefficient of thermal expansion	20–750	8.3×10^{-6} cm/°C
Heat of combustion	25	302.0 ± 3.4 kcal/mole
Entropy		
Crystalline	25	1.403 cal/(mole)(deg)
Amorphous	25	1.564 cal/(mole)(deg)
Heat capacity		
Gas	25	4.97 cal/(mole)(deg)
Crystalline	25	2.65 cal/(mole)(deg)
Amorphous	25	2.86 cal/(mole)(deg)

phorus and arsenic, respectively, and form more stable phosphorus and arsenic hexaborides, B_6P and $B_{5-7}As$. Boron is not reactive with hydrogen until temperatures of 1800–2000°C (3300–3600°F) are reached. It reacts with silicon to form silicon borides at temperatures above 2000°C (3600°F).

Boron reacts with a majority of metals and metallic oxides at high temperatures to form metallic borides. Boron does not conform to the usual rules of valence in forming these compounds. The borides, along with the carbides and the nitrides, are called interstitial compounds. These compounds have crystal structures and properties very similar to those of the original metal; hence, it is suggested that the boron is located in the cavities of the metallic lattice. *See* SOLID-STATE CHEMISTRY.

Borates are salts related to boric oxide, B_2O_3, and are commonly the salts of orthoboric acid, H_3BO_3. Only orthoboric acid is important in its free state. Some of the other boric acids are known only in the form of salts (**Table 2**).

The naming of borate compounds is additionally complicated by the fact that other polyborates are known and several systems for naming the salts are used. For example, borax is also known as pyroborate, diborate, or sodium (1:2) borate, this last name being based on the formula $Na_2O \cdot 2B_2O_3$. A dilute solution of any sodium borate contains mainly $(H_2BO_3)^-$ and $(BO_2)^-$ ions.

Inorganic compounds. Refined boric acid, H_3BO_3, is used as a raw material to make other boron compounds. It is used in leather manufacturing, electroplating, antiseptics, cosmetics, electrolytic condensers, and hydrogen-ion control.

Sodium perborate, $NaBO_3 \cdot 4H_2O$, usually prepared electrolytically from borax and caustic, is used as a bleach and disinfectant, in toothpastes and mouthwashes, and in electroplating.

Anhydrous sodium tetraborate, $Na_2B_4O_7$, prepared by high-temperature dehydration of borax, is used extensively as a replacement for the parent material.

Boric oxide or boric anhydride, B_2O_3, is produced by the dehydration of boric acid. In addition to its wide use as an intermediate in the production of boron halides and metallic borides, it is used in the atomic energy industry as a thermal neutron absorber (boraxal). It is used in glass manufacture, welding fluxes, and ore processing.

Boron carbide, B_4C, is produced by the high-temperature (about 2500°C or 4500°F) interaction of boric oxide, B_2O_3, and carbon in an electrical resistance–type furnace. It is a black, lustrous solid. It is used extensively as an abrasive, because its hardness approaches that of the diamond. It is also used as an alloying agent, particularly in molybdenum steels.

The use of boron carbide in nuclear engineering, both as a construction material and as a neutron absorber, is believed to be potentially of considerable magnitude.

Metallic borides are usually prepared by hot sintering of the elements. They may also be prepared by carbothermic and aluminothermic reduction of metal oxide–boron oxide mixtures. A number of metallic borides of high purity have been prepared on a semicommercial scale by vapor-deposition methods, in which the volatile halides of the elements are deposited on a hot substrate, such as tungsten or tantalum wire, in an atmosphere of hydrogen. Borides have much in common with true metals. They have a high electrical conductivity, high melting points, and extreme hardness. Many metal borides are used as components of cermet compositions in the ever-growing technology of high-temperature refractory materials. *See* CERMET.

Boron combines with hydrogen to form a series of compounds known as boranes, alternatively known as boron hydrides. *See* BORANE; HYDRIDE.

Nitrogen compounds. Boron forms a large number of compounds with nitrogen. At low temperatures, diborane, B_2H_6, reacts with ammonia, NH_3, or amines, RNH_2, to form ammoniates or the amine boranes. When diborane and ammonia are heated above 200°C (390°F), hydrogen is eliminated and a six-membered boron-nitrogen ring compound, borazine, is formed [reaction (1)]. By analogous

$$3B_2H_6 + 6NH_3 \longrightarrow 2 \underset{\substack{\displaystyle HN \diagdown \underset{\textstyle B}{} \diagup NH \\ \displaystyle H}}{\overset{\substack{\displaystyle H \\ \displaystyle N \\ \displaystyle HB \diagup \diagdown BH}}{}} + 12H_2 \quad (1)$$

methods, substituted borazines may be obtained from amines and diborane. The reaction of boron trichloride with ammonium chloride at elevated temperatures produces a substituted borazene, in which a chlorine atom is attached to each boron atom [reaction (2)]. Borazines are of interest

$$3NH_4Cl + 3BCl_3 \longrightarrow \underset{\substack{\displaystyle HN \diagdown \underset{\textstyle B}{} \diagup NH \\ \displaystyle Cl}}{\overset{\substack{\displaystyle H \\ \displaystyle N \\ \displaystyle ClB \diagup \diagdown BCl}}{}} + 9HCl \quad (2)$$

because of their similarity in physical properties to aromatic organic compounds. Borazine is structurally very similar to benzene, and has been

---

TABLE 2. Boric acids and their salts

Formula	Name
H_3BO_3 or $B_2O_3 \cdot 3H_2O$	Boric or orthoboric acid; salt Na_3BO_3 (sodium borate, sodium orthoborate)
HBO_2 or $B_2O_3 \cdot H_2O$	Metaboric acid; salt $Na_2BO_2 \cdot 4H_2O$ (sodium metaborate)
$H_4B_4O_7$ or $2B_2O_3 \cdot H_2O$	Tetra- or pyroboric acid; salt $Na_2B_4O_7 \cdot 10H_2O$ (borax, sodium tetraborate)

referred to as inorganic benzene.

In addition to the ring compounds of borazine type, boron halides, boron hydrides, and borate esters form a number of addition compounds with ammonia and amines, in which boron acts as a Lewis acid. Some of these compounds, particularly the amine-boranes, are useful as reducing agents in organic synthesis and have been suggested as polymerization catalysts and petroleum additives. *See* ACID AND BASE.

Because of the unusual stability of the boron-nitrogen chemical bond, the compounds containing this bond are converted to boron nitride on heating to high temperatures. These and similar compounds that boron forms with phosphorus and arsenic have been extensively investigated as possible building blocks in the field of polymer chemistry.

Boron nitride, BN, has many potential commercial applications. It is a white, fluffy powder with a greasy feel. It has an x-ray diffraction pattern almost identical with that of graphite, indicating a close similarity in structure, but it does not conduct electricity. Boron nitride may be prepared in a variety of ways, for example, by the reaction of boric oxide with ammonia, alkali cyanides, and ammonium chloride, or of boron halides and ammonia. The unusually high chemical and thermal stability, combined with the high electrical resistance of boron nitride, suggests numerous uses for this compound in the field of high-temperature technology. Boron nitride can be hot-pressed into molds and worked into desired shapes. A cubic form of boron nitride, called borazon, has been prepared at pressures near 65,000 atm (6500 megapascals) and temperatures near 1500°C (2700°F). It is comparable to diamond in hardness and apparently has properties superior to those of diamond with regard to oxidation, electrical resistance, and thermal stability. This material will probably take its place with diamond for industrial grinding.

A tough, coherent, hard abrasive compact, consisting of a cubic form of boron nitride bonded with boron carbide, has been developed.

Halides. Boron trihalides are colorless, volatile compounds that are extremely susceptible to moisture. Boron trifluoride is a gas (boiling point −101°C or −150°F) and has been an article of commerce for a considerable period. Boron trichloride (bp 12.4°C or 54.3°F) and boron tribromide (bp 90.4°C or 195°F) have also become available on a commercial scale. Boron triiodide is a white crystalline solid (melting point 49.6°C or 121°F). Boron halides, with the exception of the iodide, can be made by heating elemental boron or borides with halogens. The iodide can be prepared only indirectly, for example, from boron trichloride and hydriodic acid or from iodine and sodium borohydride. Boron trifluoride is most readily obtained from the reaction of boric acid, hydrogen (or a metallic) fluoride, and sulfuric acid.

Boron halides, and in particular the trifluoride and trichloride, are valuable catalysts and are used extensively in the chemical industry. They are valuable intermediates in the production of metal borohydrides and various boron-hydrogen compounds. Boron trichloride is used in the refining of aluminum, magnesium, zinc, and copper, and as a fire-extinguishing agent for magnesium and other metal fires.

Boron trifluoride combines with fluoride ions to form fluoroborate (borofluoride) ions, $(BF_4)^-$. Several of the metallic fluoroborates and fluoroboric acid have important uses in the electroplating industry. *See* HALOGEN ELEMENTS.

Subhalides. A number of boron subhalides, in which the halogen−boron ratio is less than three, have been prepared and studied. They are relatively unstable substances and include the diboron tetrahalides B_2Cl_4, B_2F_4, B_2Br_4, and B_2I_4.

Organic compounds. Organic compounds of boron are numerous and varied. They may be broadly subdivided into two classes: alkyl and aryl derivatives of boron, in which boron is directly bonded to carbon; and boron-oxygen-carbon compounds, such as borate esters and boroxines. These latter substances may be regarded as derivatives of boric acid or boric oxide.

Boron alkyls, such as trimethyl boron (a gas, bp −21.8°C or −7.24°F) and triethyl boron (liquid, bp 95°C or 203°F), are extremely reactive materials. Most of the boron alkyls are spontaneously inflammable in air. Controlled oxidation yields alkyl boron oxides, R · BO, which dissolve in water to form alkyl boric acids, R · $B(OH)_2$. Boron alkyls are usually prepared from boron halides and metal alkyls, such as zinc, or Grignard reagents, RMgX, or by the reaction of diborane with unsaturated hydrocarbons. *See* GRIGNARD REACTION.

Boron aryls, such as triphenyl boron (mp 142°C or 288°F), are usually solids. The aryl compounds are also prepared by the Grignard method from boron halides. The boron aryls are somewhat less sensitive to oxygen than their alkyl analogs.

The aryl and the alkyl compounds of boron are potentially useful intermediates for the synthesis of other boron compounds. Sodium tetraphenyl borohydride, an analytical reagent, is used for the estimation of potassium, rubidium, and cesium.

Borate esters are derivatives of boric acid (or oxide) and alcohols or phenols. They may be prepared either directly from parent materials or indirectly from the reaction of boron halides with alcohols or phenols, or by ester interchange reactions. In general borate esters are extremely sensitive to hydrolysis, but if the alcohol is sufficiently hindered sterically, this hydrolytic tendency can be appreciably reduced. The simplest borate ester, trimethyl borate, is a valuable intermediate for the preparation of metal borohydrides. In addition to synthetic possibilities for borate esters, a number of miscellaneous uses have been described, principally in the patent literature. Some of these include the use of borate esters in cosmetic preparations, as antioxidants for rubber and alcohols, as curing agents for epoxy resins, as petroleum additives, in pharmaceutical preparations, in plasticizers, and as surface-action agents.

Boric oxide dissolves readily in borate esters to form materials known as boroxines. Although most of these boroxines will burn in the air, their combustion product is glassy boric oxide, and for these reasons they are being employed as extinguishing agents for metal fires. Boroxines can also be used as polymerization catalysts. *See* ORGANOMETALLIC COMPOUND.

Analysis. The detection of boron is generally based upon the green coloration which is imparted by its volatile compounds to an alcohol flame or a nonluminous gas flame. Minerals are tested for boric acid by mixing them with calcium fluoride and sulfuric acid and introducing them close to the lower margin of a flame. If boric acid is present, volatile boron trifluoride is formed; this gives a green coloration to the flame.

With yellow turmeric paper, free boric acid or acidified solutions of borates give a red-brown coloration, which appears only after the paper is dried. If the paper is then moistened with ammonia, it is temporarily colored blue-black.

Boric acid can be determined quantitatively by conversion to methyl borate and subsequent saponification with calcium hydroxide. If a weighed amount of calcium oxide is used, the increase in weight after ignition represents directly the amount of boric oxide taken up.

Boric acid (or soluble borates) are conveniently determined volumetrically. For this purpose, the alkali content is first determined by titration with standard acid (usually hydrochloric); methyl orange serves as indicator. Then, by addition of glycerol, or better, mannitol or invert sugar (fructose), the weak boric acid is converted into a stronger monobasic acid; this can then be titrated directly with standard sodium hydroxide, using phenolphthalein as indicator. *See* TITRATION.

For the estimation of boron in metallic borides, boron carbide, boron nitride, and elemental boron, the sample is first digested to a soluble sodium borate by fusion in a mixture of sodium carbonate and sodium nitrate. The boron in the resultant melt is converted to boric acid by treatment with hydrochloric acid, and the resulting solution is titrated with standard sodium hydroxide in the presence of mannitol.

Preparation. The literature describes a variety of methods for the preparation of elemental boron from boron oxide, halides, hydrides, and other boron-containing compounds. These methods involve electrothermic, electrochemical, and direct pyrolysis procedures, and may be classified as follows: thermoreduction of boron-oxygen compounds with an active metal, reaction (3); alkali

$$B_2O_3 + 3Mg \rightarrow 2B + 3MgO \qquad (3)$$

reduction of boron halides, reaction (4); hydrogen

$$BCl_3 + 3Na \rightarrow B + 3NaCl \qquad (4)$$

reduction of the halides, reaction (5); carbother-

$$2BCl_3 + 3H_2 \rightarrow 2B + 6HCl \qquad (5)$$

mic reduction of borates, reaction (6); electrolysis

$$Na_2B_4O_7 + 7C \rightarrow 2Na + 7CO + 4B \qquad (6)$$

of fused borates or other boron-containing compounds, reaction (7); and thermal decomposition

$$2KBF_4 + 6KCl \rightarrow 2B + 8KF + 3Cl_2 \qquad (7)$$

of boron hydrides, reaction (8). Of these methods,

$$B_2H_6 \rightarrow 2B + 3H_2 \qquad (8)$$

reactions (3), (5), and (7) are used for the commercial production of boron.

In general, production of high-purity (above 99%) boron involves secondary treatment (such as vacuum degassing, or controlled halogenation) of the crude products as obtained by any of the above methods.

Natural occurrence. Boron makes up 0.001% of the Earth's crust. It is never found in the uncombined or elementary state in nature. Beside being present to the extent of a few parts per million in seawater, it occurs as a trace element in most soils and is an essential constituent of several rock-forming silicate minerals, such as tourmaline and datolite. The presence of boron in extremely small amounts seems to be necessary in nearly all forms of plant life, but in larger concentrations, it becomes quite toxic to vegetation. Only in a very limited number of localities are high concentrations of boron or large deposits of boron minerals to be found in nature; the more important of these seem to be primarily of volcanic origin.

As a result, the world's important deposits of borates are to be found only in such localities as the barren wastes of south-central and southwestern Asia, portions of Asia Minor, the pampas of South America, and the desert areas of California and Nevada, all of which are immediately adjacent to regions characterized by evidence of former intensive volcanic activity.

The United States accounts for about 95% of the world's reported output of borax. Argentina, Italy, and Turkey are also producers of borates. It is believed that there are considerable deposits of borate ores in the Russia, but the extent of present exploitation is unknown. *See* BORATE MINERALS.

Extraction and refining. Borax is produced from bedded deposits and from natural brines found in the United States. The entire output comes from California.

The deposit of kernite (rasorite) and borax (tincal) in the Kramer district of California is the world's principal source of boron compounds. The deposit consists of two beds of borate minerals approximately 200–250 ft (60–75 m) thick interspersed with shale and covered by 150–750 ft (45–230 m) of overburden. After the overburden is stripped off, open-pit mining operations are carried out. The crude ore is crushed and concentrated by magnetic separators, calciners, and various air-classifying units to yield a borate concentrate of the desired composition and density. The ore concentrates are then further refined at the mine site by specially adapted crystallization techniques.

A variety of refined borate products, such as sodium metaborate, potassium pentaborate, and ammonium borate, and several grades of boric acid, obtained from acidification of borax with sulfuric acid, are routinely produced.

Another important source of borate minerals is a dry lake containing an alkaline brine permeating the mineral bed that carries, in addition to borax, various other alkaline and miscellaneous mineral salts. This dry lake, known as Searles Lake, is located in northwestern San Bernardino County, California.

In the Trona process, brine is obtained from wells drilled in the salt body, approximately 60–70 ft (18–21 m) below the surface of the lake. This brine is transported to the plant, where it is stirred and blended with various end liquors resulting from previous operations of the process. It is then evaporated to a desired concentration. During this evaporation, carbonate, sulfate, and chloride of sodium are removed by means of salt traps and filters. At the end of the evaporation process, the brine is essentially saturated with potassium chloride. It is then cooled rapidly under conditions that cause potassium chloride to crystallize, whereas borax and other salts remain in solution. The crude borax of the supersaturated solution is crystallized upon further cooling and is further refined by recrystallization techniques. Various grades of sodium tetraborate and of boric acid are manufactured by this process.

In another process, boron values are directly recovered from the Searles Lake brine with the aid of an aliphatic polyol dissolved in kerosine. Sodium, potassium, and borate ions form a chelate complex with the polyol. The kerosine solution is then contacted with dilute sulfuric acid, giving a solution containing boric acid and sodium and potassium sulfates. After a combined evaporation and crystallization operation, high-purity boric acid and mixed sodium-potassium sulfates are recovered as separate products.

Another process for the recovery of borax consists of carbonating the alkaline brine with carbon dioxide (CO_2) gas. Sodium bicarbonate is precipitated, and this procedure serves to recover sodium carbonate. The resulting reduction in alkalinity increases the borax solubility by permitting the formation of the more soluble acid borates. After filtering off the bicarbonate crop, a portion of fresh raw brine is added to adjust the alkalinity back to that of the tetraborate. The mixture is then cooled to crystallize a substantial crop of borax.

In the Tuscan region of Italy, boric acid, together with ammonium salts and carbon dioxide, is recovered from hot springs and fumaroles. In addition to supplying considerable amounts of borates, sufficient to satisfy most of Italy's domestic needs, these hot springs generate appreciable quantities of electrical power at low cost.

Uses. Boron and boron compounds have numerous uses in many fields, although elemental boron is employed chiefly in the metal industry. Its extreme reactivity at high temperatures, particularly with oxygen and nitrogen, makes it a suitable metallurgical degasifying agent. It is used to refine the grain of aluminum castings and to facilitate the heat treatment of malleable iron. Boron considerably increases the high-temperature strength characteristics of alloy steels. Elemental boron is used in the atomic reactor and in high-temperature technologies.

In combination with plastics or aluminum, boron provides an effective lightweight neutron-shielding material. Boron-containing shields are valuable because of their satisfactory mechanical properties and because boron absorbs neutrons without producing high-energy gamma rays. Rods and strips of boron steel have been used extensively as control rods in atomic reactors.

The physical properties that make boron attractive as a construction material in missile and rocket technology are its low density (15% lighter than aluminum), extreme hardness, high melting point, and remarkable tensile strength in filament form. Production of boron fibers by vapor deposition methods has been developed on a commercial scale. These fibers are being used in an epoxy (or other plastic) carrier material or matrix. The resulting composite is stronger and stiffer than steel and 25% lighter than aluminum. The composite's balance of strength and stiffness makes it ideal for aircraft applications, where high performance is of primary importance. Another development in this area is the incorporation of boron filaments in metal matrices. *See* COMPOSITE MATERIAL; METAL MATRIX COMPOSITE.

Boron can be produced in various shapes by conventional hot-pressing methods. Temperatures of the order of 2000°C (3600°F) are required and the operation must be carried out in an inert atmosphere. The use of boron has been patented for such diversified applications as in motor-starting devices, phonograph needles, lightning arresters, thermal cutouts for transformers, igniters in rectifier and control tubes, alloys resistant to high-temperature abrasion and scaling, constant-potential controllers, thermoelectric couples, and resistance thermometers.

Certain compounds of boron, such as borax and boric acid, have been known and used for a long time in glass, enamel, ceramic, and mining industries. Refined borax, $Na_2B_4O_7 \cdot 10H_2O$, is an important ingredient of a variety of detergents, soaps, water-softening compounds, laundry starches, adhesives, toilet preparations, cosmetics, talcum powder, and glazed paper. It is also used in fireproofing, disinfecting of fruit and lumber, weed control, and insecticides, as well as in the manufacture of leather, paper, and plastics.

F. H. May; V. V. Levasheff

Bibliography. F. A. Cotton and G. Wilkinson, *Advanced Inorganic Chemistry*, 5th ed., 1988; *Kirk-Othmer Encyclopedia of Chemical Technology*, vol. 4, 4th ed., 1992; J. J. Pouch and S. A. Alterovitz, *Synthesis and Properties of Boron Nitride*, 1990; K. Smith, *Organometallic Compounds of Boron*, 1985; S. E. Thomas, *Organic Synthesis: The Role of Boron and Silicon*, 1992.

Borrelia

A genus of spirochetes. They are motile, helical organisms with 4–30 uneven, irregular coils, and are 5–25 micrometers long and 0.2–0.5 μm wide. Their locomotory apparatus consists of 15–22 fibrils coiled around the cell body and situated between the elastic envelope and a cytoplasmic membrane. Motion is forward and backward, laterally by bending and looping, and corkscrewlike. *See* BACTERIA.

All borreliae are arthropod-borne. Of the 19 recognized species, 17 cause relapsing fevers and similar diseases in human and rodents; of the remaining 2, one is responsible for infections in ruminants and horses, the other for borreliosis in birds.

The borreliae of human relapsing fevers are transmitted by the body louse, *Pediculus humanus humanus*, or by a large variety of soft-shelled ticks of the genus *Ornithodoros*. The species *B. burgdorferi*, the etiologic agent of Lyme disease and related disorders, is transmitted by ticks of the genus *Ixodes (I. dammini, I. pacificus, I. ricinus)*. *Borrelia anserina*, which causes borreliosis in geese, ducks, turkeys, pheasants, chickens, and other birds, is propagated by ticks of the genus *Argas*. Various species of ixodid ticks are responsible for transmitting *B. theileri* among cattle, horses, and sheep. *See* RELAPSING FEVER.

Borreliae stain well with nearly all aniline dyes and can be demonstrated in tissue sections by silver impregnation techniques. Dark-field microscopy is used for rapid examination and detection of spirochetes in peripheral blood or in tissues of vectors.

Strictly anaerobic, borreliae can readily be cultivated in their tick vectors or animal hosts. Kelly's medium and modifications thereof are suitable for culturing several species of relapsing fever spirochetes and the agent of Lyme disease. Penicillin and tetracyclines are the most effective antibiotics for treatment. *See* ANTIBIOTIC; MEDICAL BACTERIOLOGY.

Willy Burgdorfer

Bibliography. A. G. Barbour et al., Isolation of a cultivable spirochete from *Ixodes ricinus* ticks of Switzerland, *Curr. Microbiol.*, 8:123–126, 1983; R. E. Buchanan and N. E. Gibbons (eds.), *Bergey's Manual of Determinative Bacteriology*, 1974; W. Burgdorfer et al., Lyme disease: A tick-borne spirochetosis?, *Science*, 216:1317–1319, 1982; R. C. Johnson (ed.), *Biology of Parasitic Spirochetes*, 1976; R. Kelly, Cultivation of *Borrelia hermsi*, *Science*, 172:443–444, 1971.

Bose-Einstein statistics

The statistical description of quantum-mechanical systems in which there is no restriction on the way in which particles can be distributed over the individual energy levels. This description applies when the system has a symmetric wave function. This in turn has to be the case when the particles described are of integer spin.

Distribution probability. Suppose one describes a system by giving the number of particles n_i in an energy state ϵ_i, where the n_i are called occupation numbers and the index i labels the various states. The energy level ϵ_i is of finite width, being really a range of energies comprising, say, g_i individual (nondegenerate) quantum levels. If any arrangement of particles over individual energy levels is allowed, one obtains for the probability of a specific distribution, Eq. (1a). In Boltzmann statistics, this same probability would be written as Eq. (1b).

$$W = \prod_i \frac{(n_i + g_i - 1)!}{n_i!(g_i - 1)!} \qquad (1a)$$

$$W = \prod_i \frac{g_i^{\,n_i}}{n_i!} \qquad (1b)$$

See BOLTZMANN STATISTICS.

The equilibrium state is defined as the most probable state of the system. To obtain it, one must maximize Eq. (1a) under the conditions given by Eqs. (2a) and (2b), which express the fact

$$\sum n_i = N \qquad (2a)$$

$$\sum \epsilon_i n_i = E \qquad (2b)$$

that the total number of particles N and the total energy E are fixed. One finds for the most probable distribution that Eq. (3) holds. Here, A and β are

$$n_i = \frac{g_i}{\dfrac{1}{A} e^{\beta \epsilon i} - 1} \qquad (3)$$

parameters to be determined from Eqs. (2a) and (2b); actually, $\beta = 1/kT$ where k is the Boltzmann constant and T is the absolute temperature.

In the classical case, that is, when Boltzmann statistics is employed, the equilibrium distribution may be obtained from a specific assumption about the number of collisions of a certain kind. One assumes that the number of collisions per second in which molecules with velocities in cells i and j in phase space produce molecules with velocities in cells k and l is given by Eq. (4), where a_{ij}^{kl} is a

$$A_{ij}^{kl} = n_i n_j a_{ij}^{kl} \qquad (4)$$

geometrical factor. In the Bose case, Eq. (3) may be obtained in a similar way from a collision number assumption, which is written as Eq. (5).

$$A_{ij}^{kl} = a_{ij}^{kl} n_i n_j \left(\frac{g_k + n_k}{g_k} \right) \left(\frac{g_l + n_l}{g_l} \right) \qquad (5)$$

One observes the interesting fact that the number of collisions depends on the number of particles in the state to which the colliding particles are going. The more heavily populated these states are, the more likely a collision is. Quite often one defines f_i, the distribution function, by Eq. (6).

$$n_i = f_i g_i \qquad (6)$$

Applications. An interesting and important result emerges when one applies Eq. (3) to a gas of photons, that is, a large number of photons in an enclosure. (Since photons have integer spin, this is legitimate.) For photons one has Eqs. (7a) and (7b), where h is the Planck constant, v the

$$\epsilon = hv \qquad (7a)$$

$$p = \frac{hv}{c} \qquad (7b)$$

frequency of the photon, c the velocity of light, ϵ the energy of the photon, and p the momentum of the photon. The number of photons in a given energy or frequency range is given by Eq. (8),

$$g = \frac{8\pi}{c^3} V v^2 \, dv \qquad (8)$$

where V is the volume of the enclosure containing the photons. Actually, for a gas of photons, Eq. (2a) is not necessary (the number of photons is not fixed), and thus the distribution function depends on just one parameter, β; A can be shown to be unity. If one also uses the fact that $\beta = 1/kT$, one obtains from Eq. (3), for the number of photons in the frequency range dv, Eq. (9). The energy density

$$n(v) \, dv = \frac{8\pi}{c^3} V \frac{v^2 \, dv}{e^{hv/kT} - 1} \qquad (9)$$

(energy per unit volume) in the frequency range dv is, by Eqs. (9) and (7a), Eq. (10). Equation (10) is the

$$\rho(v) \, dv = \frac{8\pi h}{c^3} \frac{v^3 \, dv}{e^{hv/kT} - 1} \qquad (10)$$

Planck radiation formula for blackbody radiation. Thus, blackbody radiation must be considered as a photon gas, with the photons satisfying Bose-Einstein statistics. *See* HEAT RADIATION.

For material particles of mass m contained in a volume V, one may write Eq. (3) as (11), where

$$f(v_x v_y v_z) \, dv_x \, dv_y \, dv_z$$
$$= \left(\frac{m}{h} \right)^3 V \frac{dv_x \, dv_y \, dv_z}{\frac{1}{A} e^{mv^2/2kT} - 1} \qquad (11)$$

$v = \sqrt{v_x^2 + v_y^2 + v_z^2}$ is the total velocity. Equations (2a) and (2b) may now be written as integrals. If the so-called virial theorem, written as Eq. (12), is

$$PV = {}^2/_3 E \qquad (12)$$

used where P is the pressure, V the volume, and E the energy, Eqs. (2a) and (2b) yield a pair of implicit equations, which give the equation of state of an ideal Bose gas, Eqs. (13a) and (13b). Here λ^3

$$\frac{N}{V} \lambda^3 = B_{1/2}(A) \qquad (13a)$$

$$\lambda^3 \frac{P}{kT} = B_{3/2}(A) \qquad (13b)$$

is defined as in Eq. (14) while Eq. (15) holds. In Eq.

$$\lambda^3 = \frac{h^2}{2\pi mkT} \qquad (14)$$

$$B_\rho(A) = \frac{1}{\Gamma(\rho + 1)} \int_0^\infty \frac{u^\rho \, du}{\frac{1}{A} e^u - 1} \qquad (15)$$

(15) Γ is the usual Γ function and $u = mv^2/2kT$. From Eqs. (13a) and (13b), one obtains the relation between P, V, and T by eliminating A.

Now if one develops the numerator of the integral in Eq. (15) in an infinite series, one obtains the so-called Einstein equations, Eqs. (16a) and (16b).

$$\frac{N}{V} = \frac{1}{\lambda^3} \sum_{l=1}^\infty \frac{A^l}{l_{3/2}} \qquad (16a)$$

$$P = \frac{kT}{\lambda^3} \sum_{l=1}^\infty \frac{A^l}{l^{5/2}} \qquad (16b)$$

It is easy to verify that the sums of Eqs. (16a) and (16b) diverge for $A > 1$; however, they still converge for $A = 1$. For $A = 1$, $N/V = 2.61/\lambda^3$ and $P = 1.34kT/\lambda^3$. Einstein interpreted $N/V = 2.61/\lambda^3$ as a maximum possible density. If the gas is compressed beyond this point, the superfluous particles will condense in a zero state, where they do not contribute to the density or the pressure. If the volume is decreased, this curious Bose-Einstein condensation phenomenon results, yielding the zero state which has the paradoxical properties of not contributing to the pressure, volume, or density. The particles in the zero state are coherently matched with each other, analogous to the photons in a laser beam sharing a common quantum-mechanical wave function and losing their individual identities. Many of the superfluid properties exhibited by liquid helium are believed to be manifestations of such a condensation. In 1995, Bose-Einstein condensation was first observed directly in a cloud of rubidium atoms that had been cooled to 1.7×10^{-7} K through laser cooling followed by evaporative cooling in a magnetic trap. *See* COHERENCE; FERMI-DIRAC STATISTICS; LASER COOLING; LIQUID HELIUM; NONRELATIVISTIC QUANTUM THEORY; PARTICLE TRAP; QUANTUM STATISTICS; STATISTICAL MECHANICS.

Max Dresden

Botanical gardens

A garden for the culture of plants collected chiefly for scientific and educational purposes. Such a garden is more properly called a botanical institution, in which the outdoor garden is but one portion of an organization including the greenhouse, the herbarium, the library, and the research laboratory. *See* HERBARIUM.

Famous botanical gardens. It was only in modern Europe, after the foundation of the great medieval universities, that botanical gardens for educational purposes began to be established in connection with the schools. The oldest gardens are those in Padua (established 1533) and at Pisa (1543). The botanical garden of the University of Leiden was begun in 1587 and the first greenhouse is said to have been constructed there in 1599. Louis XIII authorized the establishment of a royal garden in Paris "for the instruction of students"; it was opened to the public in 1640 under the name Jardin du Roy. Later the name was changed to the Museé National d'Histoire Naturelle. The Oxford University Botanic Garden, the first in Great Britain, was established in 1621. In Berlin the Botanischer Garten was established in 1646. In 1655 a garden was founded at Uppsala, Sweden, of which Carolus Linnaeus, the father of modern plant taxonomy, was director from 1742 to 1777. In Russia Peter the Great's Druggist's Garden was founded at St. Petersburg in 1713. In 1817 the Conservatoire et Jardin Botanique were established at Geneva and became one of the leading botanical centers of the world. The Royal Botanical Gardens at Kew, England, were officially opened in 1841. This institution came to be known as the botanical capital of the world.

The first of the great tropical gardens was founded at Calcutta in 1787. The original name, Royal Botanic Garden, was changed in 1947 to Indian Botanic Garden. Another great tropical garden, the Jardin Botanico of Rio de Janeiro, was founded in 1808. The great tropical botanical graden of Buitenzorg (Bogor), Java, which originated in 1817, has an area of 205 acres with an additional 150 acres in the Mountain Garden.

Gardens in North America. The first great garden of the United States was founded by Henry Shaw at St. Louis in 1859, and in now known as the Missouri Botanical Garden. The New York Botanical Garden was chartered in 1891 and the Brooklyn Botanic Garden in 1910. The Jardin Botanique of Montreal, the leading garden of Canada, was opened in 1936. *See* ARBORETUM.   Earl L. Core

Botany

That branch of biological science which embraces the study of plants and plant life. According to the specific objectives of the investigators, botanical studies may range from microscopic observations of the smallest and obscurest plants to the study of the trees of the forest. One botanist may be interested mainly in the relationships among plants and in their geographic distribution, whereas another may be primarily concerned with structure or with the study of the life processes taking place in plants.

Botany may be divided by subject matter into several specialties, such as plant anatomy, plant chemistry, plant cytology, plant ecology (including autecology and synecology), plant embryology, plant genetics, plant morphology, plant physiology, plant taxonomy, ethnobotany, and paleobotany. It may also be divided according to the group of plants being studied; for example, agrostology, the study of grasses; algology (phycology), the study of algae; bryology, the study of mosses; mycology, the study of fungi; and pteridology, the study of ferns. Bacteriology and virology are also parts of botany in a broad sense. Furthermore, a number of agricultural subjects have botany as their foundation. Among these are agronomy, floriculture, forestry, horticulture, landscape architecture, and plant breeding. *See* AGRICULTURE; AGRONOMY; BACTERIOLOGY; BREEDING (PLANT); CELL BIOLOGY; ECOLOGY; EMBRYOLOGY; FLORICULTURE; FOREST AND FORESTRY; GENETICS; LANDSCAPE ARCHITECTURE; PALEOBOTANY; PLANT ANATOMY; PLANT GROWTH; PLANT MORPHOGENESIS; PLANT PATHOLOGY; PLANT PHYSIOLOGY; PLANT TAXONOMY.   Arthur Cronquist

Bothriocidaroida

An order of Perischoechinoidea in which the ambulacra comprise two columns of plates, the interambulacra comprise two column, and the madreporite is placed radially. *Bothriocidaris* (see **illus.**), the only known genus, occurs in the Upper Ordovician of Estonia, and is the oldest recognized echinoid.

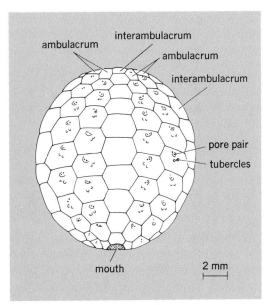

Bothriocidaris, **reconstruction of test.**

See ECHINODERMATA; ECHINOIDEA; PERISCHOECHINOIDEA.
Howard B. Fell

Botulism

An illness produced by the exotoxin of *Clostridium botulinum* and occasionally other clostridia and characterized primarily by paralysis and other neurological abnormalities. There are seven (A–G) principal toxin types involved, but only types A, B, E, and F have been implicated in human disease; types C and D produce illness in birds and mammals. Strains of *C. barati* and *C. butyricum* have been found to produce toxins E and F and have been implicated in infant botulism. There is serologic cross-reactivity between *C. botulinum* and *C. sporogenes* and *C. novyi*. Botulinal toxin is among the most potent poisons known; it has a heavy chain (molecular weight about 100,000) and a light chain (about 50,000) joined by a disulfide bond. The toxin attaches to neuromuscular junctions and prevents release of acetylcholine, resulting in paralysis. *See* ACETYLCHOLINE; ANAEROBIC INFECTION; CLOSTRIDIUM; VIRULENCE.

Forms. There are three clinical forms of botulism: classic botulism is typically due to ingestion of preformed toxin; infant botulism involves ingestion of *C. botulinum* spores with subsequent germination and toxin production in the gastrointestinal tract; and wound botulism involves production of toxin by the organism infecting or colonizing a wound. The incubation period ranges from a few hours to more than a week, but is usually 1–2 days, depending primarily on the amount of toxin ingested or absorbed.

Symptoms and diagnosis. There is an acute onset of bilateral cranial nerve impairment and subsequent symmetrical descending paralysis or weakness. Nausea and vomiting, fatigue, difficulty in swallowing, dry mouth, double vision, difficulty in articulating, and blurred vision are common symptoms. Bowel irregularities and constipation are much more typical than diarrhea, and there may also be urinary retention and dry mucous membranes. Central nervous system function and sensation remain intact, and fever is absent if no complications develop. Fever may be absent even in wound botulism.

The diagnosis can be made clinically, and can be confirmed by demonstrating the toxin in serum, stool, or epidemiologically implicated foods or by recovering the organism from the stools or wound of the patient. Toxin is identified by mouse toxicity and neutralization tests with type-specific antitoxin. *See* TOXIN.

Epidemiology. In food-borne botulism, home-canned or home-processed foods (particularly vegetables) are commonly implicated, with commercially canned foods involved infrequently. In infant botulism, honey and corn syrups have been implicated as vehicles. Therapy involves measures to rid the body of unabsorbed toxin, neutralization of unfixed toxin by antitoxin, and adequate intensive care support. *See* FOOD POISONING; MEDICAL BACTERIOLOGY; POISON.
Sydney M. Finegold

Boundary-layer flow

That portion of a fluid flow, near a solid surface, where shear stresses are significant and the inviscid-flow assumption may not be used. All solid surfaces interact with a viscous fluid flow because of the no-slip condition, a physical requirement that the fluid and solid have equal velocities at their interface. Thus a fluid flow is retarded by a fixed solid surface, and a finite, slow-moving boundary layer is formed.

A requirement for the boundary layer to be thin is that the Reynolds number, $Re = \rho UL/\mu$, of the body be large, 10^3 or more, where ρ and μ are the fluid density and viscosity, respectively, U is the stream velocity, and L is the body length. Under these conditions, as first pointed out by L. Prandtl in 1904, the flow outside the boundary layer is essentially inviscid and plays the role of a driving mechanism for the layer. *See* REYNOLDS NUMBER.

A typical low-speed or laminar boundary layer is shown in **Fig. 1**. Such a display of the streamwise flow vector variation near the wall is called a velocity profile. The no-slip condition requires that $u(x,0) = 0$, as shown. The velocity rises monotonically with distance y from the wall, finally merging smoothly with the outer (inviscid) stream velocity $U(x)$. At any point in the boundary layer, the fluid shear stress τ is related to the local velocity gradient by Eq. (1), assuming a newtonian fluid.

$$\tau = \mu(\partial u/\partial y) \tag{1}$$

The value of the shear stress at the wall, τ_w, is most important, since it relates not only to the drag of the body but often also to its heat transfer. At the edge of the boundary layer, τ approaches zero asymptotically. There is no exact spot where $\tau = 0$; therefore the thickness δ of a boundary layer is

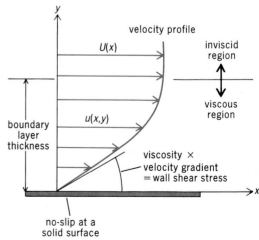

Fig. 1. Typical laminar boundary-layer velocity profile.

usually defined arbitrarily as the point where $u = 0.99U$. *See* LAMINAR FLOW.

Boundary-layer approximations. A boundary layer is mathematically different from a general viscous flow. In a steady, two-dimensional, incompressible flow (Fig. 1), the three unknowns would be pressure $p(x,y)$, streamwise velocity $u(x,y)$, and velocity normal to the wall, $v(x, y)$. These would be solved for simultaneously from the conservation of mass and the x- and y-momentum or Navier-Stokes equations. The solution would apply throughout the entire flow field.

If, however, the viscous region is thin, the boundary-layer approximations apply in the form of Eqs. (2). Many terms may then be dropped from

$$v \ll u \qquad \partial u/\partial x \ll \partial u/\partial y$$
$$\partial v/\partial x \ll \partial v/\partial y \qquad \partial p/\partial y \cong 0 \qquad (2)$$

the basic Navier-Stokes equations, and the resulting boundary-layer equations eliminate pressure as a variable and solve merely for u and v by extending downstream between the wall, where no-slip obtains, and the inviscid outer stream, where $U(x)$ is assumed directly related to the pressure $P(x)$ by the Bernoulli relation (3).

$$P(x) + 0.5\rho U^2(x) = \text{constant} \qquad (3)$$

This is a profound mathematical simplification which permits designers to compute boundary-layer velocity, shear, temperature, and heat transfer without recourse to massive digital computer codes. *See* BERNOULLI'S THEOREM; NAVIER-STOKES EQUATIONS.

Boundary layers in duct flow. When a flow enters a duct or confined region, boundary layers immediately begin to grow on the duct walls (**Fig. 2**). An inviscid core accelerates down the duct center, but soon vanishes as the boundary layers meet and fill the duct with viscous flow. Constrained by the duct walls into a no-growth condition, the velocity profile settles into a fully developed shape which is independent of the streamwise coordinate. The pressure drops linearly downstream, balanced by the mean wall-shear stress. This is a classic and simple case of boundary-layer flow which is well documented by both theory and experiment.

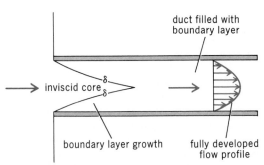

Fig. 2. Boundary-layer development in the entrance of a duct.

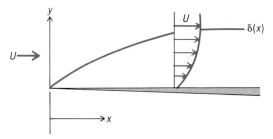

Fig. 3. Laminar boundary-layer flow past a sharp flat plate.

Flat-plate flow. A classic incompressible boundary-layer flow is a uniform stream at velocity U, moving past a sharp flat plate parallel to the stream (**Fig. 3**). In the Reynolds number range $\rho UL/\mu = 1 \times 10^3$ to 5×10^5, the flow is laminar and orderly, with no superimposed fluctuations. The boundary-layer thickness δ grows monotonically with x, and the shape of the velocity profile is independent of x when normalized, that is, u/U is a function of y/δ. The profiles are said to be similar, and they are now called Blasius profiles, after the engineer who first analyzed them in 1908.

The Blasius flat-plate flow results in closed-form algebraic formulas for such parameters as wall-shear stress and boundary-layer thickness, given by Eqs. (4). Similar expressions can be formulated

$$\delta \approx 5.0(\mu x/\rho U)^{1/2}$$
$$\qquad (4)$$
$$\tau_W \approx 0.332(\rho\mu U^3/x)^{1/2}$$

for temperature and heat-transfer parameters. These results are useful in estimating viscous effects in flow past thin bodies such as airfoils, turbine blades, and heat-exchanger plates.

Momentum and displacement thickness. As mentioned above, δ is defined arbitrarily as the point where $u = 0.99U$. This position is difficult to define experimentally. More definitive thickness measures are the two integral scales which arise from the conservation of mass and streamwise momentum. These are the displacement thickness δ^* and the momentum thickness θ, as defined in Eqs. (5).

$$\delta^* = \int_0^\infty (1 - u/U)\,dy$$
$$\qquad (5)$$
$$\theta = \int_0^\infty (u/U)(1 - u/U)\,dy$$

These two terms are unambiguous and are often used to correlate data on local friction and heat transfer and on transition to turbulence of boundary layers. The displacement thickness represents the local deflection of the outer inviscid streamlines, whereas the momentum thickness is a measure of local wall-friction effects.

For flat-plate flow, if δ is given by Eq. (4), the Blasius theory predicts that $\delta^*/\delta = 0.344$ and $\theta/\delta = 0.133$.

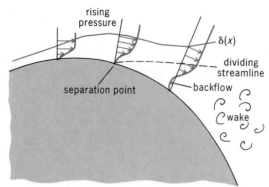

Fig. 4. Boundary-layer separation in a region of persistent rising pressure velocity.

Boundary-layer separation. The flat plate is very distinctive in that it causes no change in outer-stream velocity U. Most body shapes immersed in a stream flow, such as cylinders, airfoils, or ships, induce a variable outer stream $U(x)$ near the surface. If U increases with x, which means from Eq. (3) that pressure decreases with x, the boundary layer is said to be in a favorable gradient and remains thin and attached to the surface. If, however, velocity falls and pressure rises with x, the pressure gradient is unfavorable or adverse (**Fig. 4**). The low-velocity fluid near the wall is strongly decelerated by the rising pressure, and the wall-shear stress drops off to zero. Downstream of this zero-shear or separation point, there is backflow and the wall shear is upstream. The boundary layer thickens markedly to conserve mass, and the outer stream separates from the body, leaving a broad, low-pressure wake downstream. Flow separation may be predicted by boundary-layer theory, but the theory is not able to estimate the wake properties accurately. *See* WAKE FLOW.

In most immersed-body flows, the separation and wake occur on the rear or lee side of the body, with higher pressure and no separation on the front. The body thus experiences a large downstream pressure force called pressure drag. This happens to all blunt bodies such as spheres and cylinders and also to airfoils and turbomachinery blades if their angle of attack with respect to the oncoming stream is too large. The airfoil or blade is said to be stalled, and its performance suffers.

Instability and transition. All laminar boundary layers, if they grow thick enough and have sufficient velocity, become unstable. Slight disturbances, whether naturally occurring or imposed artificially, tend to grow in amplitude, at least in a certain frequency and wavelength range. The growth begins as a selective group of two-dimensional periodic disturbances, called Tollmien-Schlichting waves, which become three-dimensional and nonlinear downstream and eventually burst into the strong random fluctuations called turbulence. The critical parameter is the Reynolds number, usually based on boundary-layer displacement thickness, $\mathrm{Re}_{\delta*} = \rho U \delta^*/\mu$. The process of change from laminar to turbulent flow is called transition. *See* TURBULENT FLOW.

In **Fig. 5**, the classic flat-plate flow is shown as an example. The leading-edge flow is the laminar, Blasius profile from Fig. 3. The point of first instability is at $\mathrm{Re}_{\delta*} \approx 520$ or $\mathrm{Re}_x \equiv \rho U x/\mu \approx 10^5$. Tollmien-Schlichting waves are formed with wavelengths of about six boundary-layer thicknesses and frequencies of approximately $0.1 U/\delta$. These waves grow, are joined by other frequencies and wavelengths, become three-dimensional, and burst into turbulence further downstream, typically at $\mathrm{Re}_{x,\mathrm{tr}} \approx 5 \times 10^5$. The flow downstream of this transition point is fully turbulent and remains so in almost all cases. For very smooth flows, $\mathrm{Re}_{x,\mathrm{tr}}$ can be as high as 5×10^6.

The transition process is affected by many parameters. The transition is delayed by favorable pressure gradients, smooth walls, and a quiet outer stream. It is hastened by adverse pressure gradients, rough walls, and a noisy freestream. The transition can be triggered abruptly by inserting an unsteady, wake-producing tripping device, such as a wire or large particle, into the boundary layer near the instability point.

The prediction of the point of first instability for various boundary-layer flows is well developed and experimentally verified. The prediction of final transition, however, is quantitatively less successful because of the many important competing parameters affecting the process.

In rare cases, a fully turbulent flow can be made to relaminarize by subjecting the boundary layer to extreme deceleration.

Turbulent boundary layers. The turbulent flow regime is characterized by random, three-dimensional fluctuations superimposed upon time-mean fluid properties, including velocity, pressure, and temperature. The fluctuations are typically 3–6% of the mean values and range in size over three orders of magnitude, from microscale movements to large eddies of size comparable to the boundary-layer thickness. They are readily measured by modern instruments such as hot wires and laser-Doppler velocimeters.

The effect of superimposing a wide spectrum of eddies on a viscous flow is to greatly increase mixing and transport of mass, momentum, and heat across the flow. Turbulent boundary layers are thicker than laminar layers and have higher heat transfer and friction. The turbulent mean-velocity profile is rather flat, with a steep gradient at the wall (Fig. 5). The edge of the boundary layer is a ragged, fluctuating interface, as shown in Fig. 5, which separates the nonturbulent outer flow from large turbulent eddies in the layer. The thickness of such a layer is defined only in the time mean, and a probe placed in the outer half of the layer would show intermittently turbulent and nonturbulent flow.

No theory for turbulent flow is based on first principles, but many successful empirical models have been proposed. A turbulent boundary layer may be broken into three regions: a narrow sublayer near the wall, of approximate thickness $5\mu/(\rho\tau_w)^{1/2}$, too small to be seen in Fig. 5, where eddies are damped out and molecular viscosity dominates; an intermediate layer, approximately logarithmic in shape, extending to about one-fourth of the layer thickness; and an outer wake layer, dependent on stream parameters, which rises from the log layer to merge smoothly with the stream velocity U.

The intermediate or logarithmic layer is dependent entirely on wall-related parameters and is approximated by Eq. (6). In flows with constant or

$$u/v^* \approx 2.44\log(\rho v^* y/\mu) + 5.0 \qquad (6)$$
$$v^* = (\tau_w/\rho)^{1/2}$$

falling stream pressure, the wake layer is small, and Eq. (6) can be employed to develop useful formulas for predicting turbulent boundary-layer friction and heat transfer. For example, formulas (7) result for flat-plate turbulent boundary-layer thickness

$$\delta \approx 0.16(\mu x^6/\rho U)^{1/7} \qquad (7)$$
$$\tau_W \approx 0.0135(\mu\rho^6 U^{13}/x)^{1/7}$$

and wall friction. They may be compared with their laminar-flow counterparts in Eqs. (4). For a given x, the turbulent layer is thicker and has a wall-shear stress several times larger; the wall-heat transfer is also higher.

The reason the turbulent-velocity profile in Fig. 5 is so flat is that its effective viscosity is very large. By analogy with the laminar shear-stress formula (1), an equivalent turbulent eddy viscosity may be defined to compute shear stress in a turbulent layer, Eq. (8). The eddy viscosity is much larger than the

$$\tau_{\text{turb}} \approx \mu_{\text{turb}}(\partial u/\partial y) \qquad (8)$$

molecular viscosity μ and is not a physical property, but depends upon flow parameters such as stream velocity and wall-shear stress. For example, the

logarithmic layer of Eq. (6) may be used to infer the eddy viscosity formula of Eq. (9). Many digital

$$\mu_{\text{turb}} \approx 0.41\rho v^* y \qquad (9)$$

computer codes for predicting turbulent boundary layers use eddy-viscosity correlations to complete the equations of motion. Similarly, in turbulent heat-transfer analysis, an eddy thermal conductivity is often used.

Compressible boundary layers. As the stream velocity U becomes larger, its kinetic energy, $U^2/2$, becomes comparable to stream enthalpy, c_pT, where c_p is the specific heat at constant pressure and T is the absolute temperature. Changes in temperature and density begin to be important, and the flow can no longer be considered incompressible. An equivalent statement is that the stream Mach number Ma_∞, defined by Eq. (10), where a is

$$\text{Ma}_\infty = U/a \qquad (10)$$

the speed of sound of the stream, becomes significant when Ma_∞ is greater than 0.5. Liquids flow at very small Mach numbers, and compressible flows are primarily gas flows. For an ideal gas of absolute temperature T, the speed of sound is given by Eq. (11), where R is the gas constant and γ, defined

$$a = \gamma R T^{1/2} \qquad (11)$$

by Eq. (12) where c_p is the specific heat at con-

$$\gamma = c_p/c_v \qquad (12)$$

stant pressure, is approximately 1.4 for air. If Ma_∞ is greater than 1, the flow is said to be supersonic. *See* GAS; GAS DYNAMICS; MACH NUMBER.

In a flow with supersonic stream velocity, the noslip condition is still valid, and much of the boundary-layer flow near the wall is at low speed or subsonic. The fluid enters the boundary layer and loses much of its kinetic energy, of which a small part is conducted away although most is converted into thermal energy. Thus the near-wall region of a highly compressible boundary layer is very hot, even if the wall is cold and is drawing heat away.

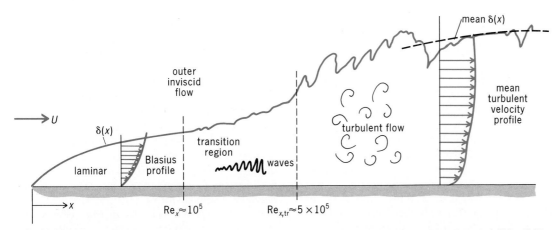

Fig. 5. Transition process in viscous flow past a sharp flat plate. The boundary-layer thickness is exaggerated. (*After F. M. White, Heat and Mass Transfer, Addison-Wesley, 1988*).

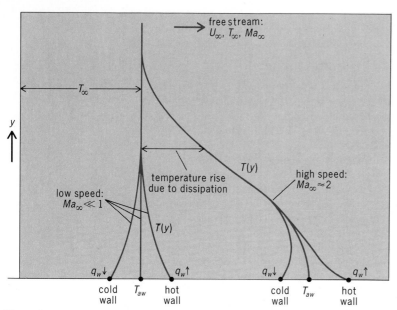

Fig. 6. Boundary-layer temperature profiles for incompressible and compressible (supersonic) stream velocities. (*After F. M. White, Heat and Mass Transfer, Addison-Wesley, 1988*).

This situation is illustrated in **Fig. 6**, comparing an incompressible and a compressible ($Ma_\infty = 2$) thermal boundary layer. The basic difference between low and high speed is the conversion of kinetic energy into higher temperatures across the entire boundary layer.

In a low-speed (incompressible) boundary layer, a cold wall simply means that the wall temperature T_w is less than the free-stream temperature T_∞. The heat flow q_w is from high toward lower temperature, that is, into the wall (Fig. 6). For a low-speed insulated wall, the boundary-layer temperature is uniform. For a high-speed flow, however, an insulated wall has a high surface temperature because of the viscous dissipation energy exchange in the layer. This adiabatic wall temperature T_{aw} may be estimated from Eq. (13).

$$T_{aw} \approx T_\infty \left[1 + 0.5r\,(\gamma - 1)\,Ma_\infty^2\right] \qquad (13)$$

The parameter r is the recovery factor, indicating the efficiency of energy exchange; it varies from 0.85 to 0.89 for compressible air flows. For example, if $Ma_\infty = 2.0$, as in Fig. 6, then $T_{aw} \approx 1.7T_\infty$. Equation (13) requires that temperatures be in absolute units. In such a flow, a cold wall means only that $T_w < T_{aw}$; the wall temperature itself may be considerably higher than the stream temperature, yet the fluid temperature drops off at the wall, into which heat flows.

Except for the added complexity of having to consider fluid pressure, temperature, and density as coupled variables, compressible boundary layers have similar characteristics to their low-speed counterparts. They undergo transition from laminar to turbulent flow (Fig. 5) but typically at somewhat higher Reynolds numbers. Compressible layers tend to be somewhat thicker than incompressible boundary layers, with proportionally smaller wall-

shear stresses. They tend to resist flow separation (Fig. 4) slightly better than incompressible flows.

In a supersonic outer stream, shock waves can always occur. Shocks may form in the boundary layer because of obstacles in the layer or downstream, or they may be formed elsewhere and impinge upon a boundary. In either case, the pressure rises sharply behind the shock, an adverse gradient, and this tends to cause early transition to turbulence and early flow separation. Special care must be taken to design aerodynamic surfaces to accommodate or avoid shockwave formation in transonic and supersonic flows. *See* COMPRESSIBLE FLOW; SHOCK WAVE.

Boundary-layer control. As boundary layers move downstream, they tend to grow naturally and undergo transition to turbulence. Boundary layers encountering rising pressure undergo flow separation. Both phenomena can be controlled at least partially. Airfoils and hydrofoils can be shaped to delay adverse pressure gradients and thus move separation downstream. Proper shaping can also delay transition. Wall suction removes the low-momentum fluid and delays both transition and separation. Wall blowing into the boundary layer, from downward-facing slots, delays separation but not transition. Changing the wall temperature to hotter for liquids and colder for gases delays transition. Practical systems have been designed for boundary-layer control, but they are often expensive and mechanically complex. *See* AIRFOIL; FLUID FLOW; FLUID-FLOW PRINCIPLES; STREAMLINING; VISCOSITY.

Frank M. White

Bibliography. *Illustrated Experiments in Fluid Mechanics*, NCFMF Book of Film Notes, 1972; J. A. Schetz, *Boundary Layer Analysis*, 1992; H. Schlichting, *Boundary-Layer Theory*, 7th ed., 1979; F. S. Sherman, *Viscous Flow*, 1990; M. Van Dyke, *An Album of Fluid Motion*, 1982; F. M. White, *Viscous Fluid Flow*, 2d ed., 1991.

Bovine virus diarrhea

A disease of cattle induced by bovine viral diarrhea virus. The virus is common worldwide, infects cattle of all ages, and causes a variety of disease processes.

The virus. The mature virion is approximately 50 nanometers in diameter. The viral genome consists of a single strand of positive-sense ribonucleic acid (RNA) that contains approximately 12,500 nucleotides. In the mature virion, viral RNA is packaged in an icosahedral nucleocapsid that is surrounded by a membranous envelope. The virus is sensitive to lipid solvents. All bovine viral diarrhea viruses are serologically related. There are, however, antigenic, genetic, and biologic differences among viruses.

Two biotypes of bovine viral diarrhea virus exist. The noncytopathic biotype, which is predominant in nature, grows in cell cultures without inducing harmful effects. The cytopathic biotype induces formation of characteristic cytoplasmic vacuoles in cultured cells and causes cell death. Viral biotype in cell culture, however, does not correlate with virulence in the host. Cattle are the natural hosts for bovine viral diarrhea virus, but the virus infects most even-toed ungulates, including sheep, swine, goats, deer, and antelope. *See* ANIMAL VIRUS.

Clinical disease. Cattle infected with the bovine viral diarrhea virus usually develop an acute disease that is inapparent or clinically mild. The acute form is characterized by fever, low white blood cell counts, mild depression, and a brief loss of appetite. Occasionally, acute bovine viral diarrhea is clinically severe, and then cattle may have diarrhea, develop ulcers in the mouth and intestine, show respiratory distress, hemorrhage internally, and die. Acute bovine viral diarrhea seldom lasts longer than a few days.

The virus replicates in lymphoid cells and induces a transient suppression that affects function of lymphocytes and neutrophils, potentially lowering the host's resistance to other infectious agents. Adverse effects on the fetus are common following infection of pregnant cattle. Embryonic resorption, abortion, stillbirth, and congenital anomalies result from fetal infections with the virus.

Fetal infection with noncytopathic bovine viral diarrhea virus during the first 4 months of pregnancy may lead to persistent viral infection. During this period of development, the bovine fetus does not produce an immune response against the virus, and a lifelong persistent infection may be established. Many persistently infected cattle are clinically normal and live several years, but they are uniquely susceptible to a fatal condition termed mucosal disease. The characteristic signs of mucosal disease are fever, low white blood cell counts, diarrhea, dehydration, depression, and ulcerations on the mucosal surfaces of the alimentary tract. Mucosal disease often causes death within a few days, but a chronic disease may develop that leads to death after several weeks. Mucosal disease occurs when persistently infected cattle become superinfected with a complementary cytopathic bovine viral disease virus. A mutation of the noncytopathic virus that persistently infects the animal may produce the complementary cytopathic virus, but the complementary virus also may come from other animals or vaccines.

Pathology. Postmortem examination of cattle that have acute bovine viral disease or mucosal disease often reveals lesions in the lymphoid centers and mucosa of the alimentary tract. Erosions and ulcerations in the mouth and esophagus are classic lesions of the disease. Other frequently observed lesions include mucosal ulcerations in the abomasum and over lymphoid follicles in the small intestine. Similar lesions occur at the ileocecal junction, in the proximal large intestine, and in the rectum. In hemorrhagic syndrome, a clinically severe form of acute bovine viral diarrhea, platelet counts are reduced and hemorrhages occur in the mouth and on serosal surfaces of internal organs. The primary microscopic lesion for all forms of bovine viral diarrhea consists of a depletion of lymphoid cells in the lymphoid follicles of the intestine. Viral antigen is found in lymphoid, neuronal, and endocrine cells.

Mode of transmission. Persistently infected cattle are instrumental in the spread of bovine viral disease. These cattle shed the virus in saliva, nasal secretions, urine, milk, and semen. Susceptible cattle become infected within 1 h of direct contact with a persistently infected animal. Because bovine viral diarrhea virus infects several species, wildlife or other farm animals may spread infection. Biting insects, contaminated hypodermic needles, and contaminated farm equipment also spread the virus.

Diagnosis, treatment, and control. Ulcerations of the mouth, diarrhea, and fever support a diagnosis of bovine viral diarrhea. Postmortem examination and isolation of the virus from tissues, white blood cells, or nasal swab specimens are used to confirm the diagnosis. Also, an increase in specific antibody titer in serum samples obtained 2 weeks apart from convalescent cattle indicates recent infection. Persistently infected cattle are identified by isolation of the virus from blood samples obtained 3 weeks apart.

Treatment of bovine viral disease is based on supportive care. Administration of antiserum during the early stages of acute bovine viral disease may be beneficial, but controlling the disease is accomplished by vaccination, and by identification and elimination of persistently infected cattle.

Steven R. Bolin

Bibliography. D. C. Blood and O. M. Radostits, *Veterinary Medicine*, 1989; R. I. B. Francki et al. (eds.), Classification and nomenclature of viruses, *Arch. Virol.*, suppl. 2, 1991; M. C. Horzinek, *Non-arthropod-borne Togaviruses*, 1981; J. L. Howard (ed.), *Current Veterinary Therapy 3: Food Animal Practice*, 1993.

Boyle's law

A law of gases which states that at constant temperature the volume of a gas varies inversely with its pressure. This law, formulated by Robert Boyle (1627–1691), can also be stated thus: The product of the volume of a gas times the pressure exerted on it is a constant at a fixed temperature. The relation is approximately true for most gases, but is not followed at high pressures. The phenomenon was discovered independently by Edme Mariotte about 1650 and is known in Europe as Mariotte's law. *See* GAS; KINETIC THEORY OF MATTER.   Frank H. Rockett

Brachiopoda

A phylum of solitary, exclusively marine, coelomate, bivalved animals, with both valves symmetrical about a median longitudinal plane. They are typically attached to the substrate by a posteriorly located fleshy stalk or pedicle. Anteriorly, a relatively large mantle cavity is always developed between the valves, and the filamentous feeding organ, or lophophore, is suspended in it, projecting forward from the anterior body wall (**Fig. 1**).

Although this brief description serves to differentiate a brachiopod from any other animal, it conceals a division into two clearly defined groups within the phylum, a division that is particularly marked if only Recent animals are considered. These two groups are regarded as classes; several names have been given to them, but Inarticulata and Articulata are the most widely used and are based on one of the most readily observed differences between them, the presence or absence of articulation between the two valves of the shell. Among the Articulata the valves are typically hinged together by a pair of teeth with complementary sockets in the opposing valve; these hinge teeth are lacking in the Inarticulata, whose valves are held together only by the soft tissue of the living animal.

Classification. The zoological affinities of the phylum with the remainder of the animal kingdom are not well understood. In spite of gross morphological differences in the adult forms, similarities in embryological development, coupled with the presence of a lophophore, suggest that the brachiopods may be more closely related to the Bryozoa and the Phoronida than to any other group. It is at least conceivable that these lophophorates may have been derived independently from a protozoan ancestry. *See* BRYOZOA; PHORONIDA.

The phylum may be classified as follows:

Class Inarticulata
  Order: Lingulida
          Acrotretida
          Obolellida
          Paterinida
Class Incertae Sedis
  Order Kutorginida
Class Articulata
  Order: Orthida
          Strophomenida
          Pentamerida
          Rhynchonellida
          Spiriferida
          Terebratulida

Orientation. The pedicle either protrudes between the valves or more commonly emerges from a variably modified opening in one valve. Whatever the form of the pedicle opening, it is always at the posterior end of the animal and its enclosing shell, the opposite end being regarded as anterior. The two valves are best known as pedicle valve and brachial valve, although ventral valve and dorsal valve are frequently employed alternatives. In the majority of forms the pedicle opening is confined to the pedicle valve, and among articulate brachiopods it is this valve which bears the teeth. Both valves have a characteristic distribution of muscles, and any skeletal support for the lophophore is invariably developed from the brachial valve (**Fig. 2**).

Morphology. The pedicle is the only organ protruding outside the valves, for the remainder

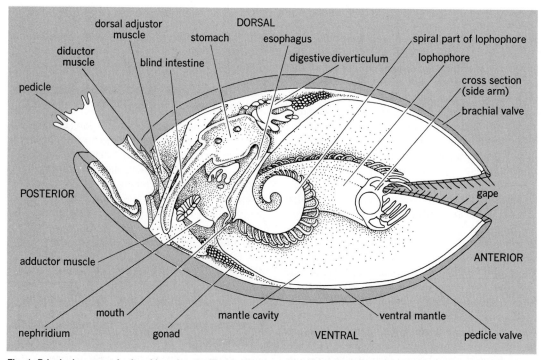

Fig. 1. Principal organs of a brachiopod as typified by *Terebratulina*. (*After R. C. Moore, ed., Treatise on Invertebrate Paleontology, pt. H, Geological Society of America, Inc., and University of Kansas Press, 1965*)

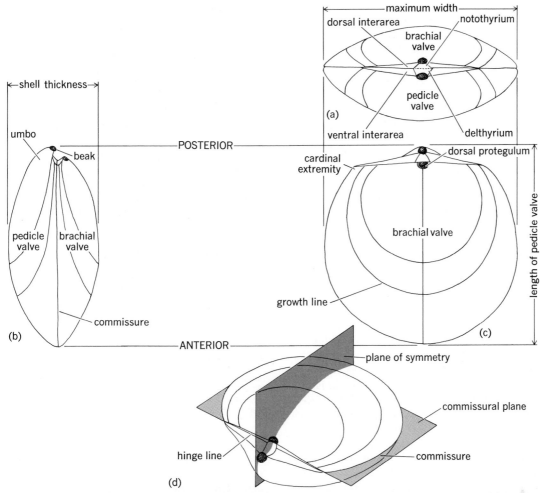

Fig. 2. Diagrammatic representation of the external features of generalized brachiopod seen in (a) the posterior, (b) the left lateral, (c) the dorsal, and (d) the dorsolateral views. (After R. C. Moore, ed., Treatise on Invertebrate Paleontology, pt. H, Geological Society of America, Inc., and University of Kansas Press, 1965)

of the animal is enclosed in the space between them. This space is divided into two unequal parts, a smaller posteriorly located body cavity and an anterior mantle cavity. The ectoderm underlying the shell bounding the body cavity is in a single layer; but anteriorly, laterally, and even posteriorly in the inarticulate brachiopods, it is prolonged as a pair of folds forming the ventral and dorsal mantles. The two mantles approach each other and ultimately fuse along the posterior margin of articulate brachiopods; in contrast, the mantles are invariably discrete in the inarticulates and are separated by a strip of body wall (**Fig. 3**).

The body cavity contains the musculature; the alimentary canal; the nephridia, which are paired excretory organs also functioning as gonoducts; the reproductive organs; and primitive circulatory and nervous systems. Except for the openings through the nephridia, the body cavity is enclosed, but the mantle cavity communicates freely with the sea when the valves are opened. The lophophore is suspended from the anterior body wall within the mantle cavity and is always symmetrically disposed about the median plane. The lophophore consists

of a variably disposed, ciliated, filament-bearing tube, with the ciliary beat producing an ordered flow of water within the cavity, flowing across the filaments. The latter trap food particles which are carried along a groove in the lophophore to the medially situated mouth.

The alimentary canal of all brachiopods is broadly similar; the mouth opens into a muscular tube, the esophagus, which continues to a stomach and intestine. In addition, there are a variable number of digestive diverticula which communicate with the stomach through narrow ducts. In all articulate brachiopods the intestine ends blindly; in the inarticulates, however, the intestine terminates in an anus which discharges on the right-hand side of the body.

The muscles which control the opening and closing of the valves are contained within the body cavity, but their distribution varies considerably between the articulate and inarticulate brachiopods. In the former class they are disposed to effect a rotation of the valves about a hinge axis, but no such constraint is imposed on the majority of the Inarticulata, whose valves are free to rotate or even slide longitudinally relative to each other. Because of a differential rate of secretion of shell material by the epithelium at the bases of the muscles, the site of muscle attachment is commonly impressed in the valves, producing muscle scars. More rarely, the muscle scars are elevated above the adjacent shell.

Although hermaphroditic species are known, the sexes are separate in the majority of brachiopods. The gonads, or reproductive organs, are located either within the body cavity (as in the inarticulate lingulids and discinids), or more typically, in slender tubelike extensions of the body cavity which project into the mantle, the mantle canals. The mantle canal pattern may be retained on the inner surface of the valves by processes of differential secretion comparable with those which produce the muscle scars.

Ontogeny. The anatomical differences between Recent inarticulate and articulate brachiopods are emphasized in a comparison of the early stages of development of typical representatives of the two classes. In all brachiopods fertilization is external and usually on the sea floor, although a few species are known to brood their eggs. The larval existence of the articulate brachiopods is relatively brief, usually less than a week. Early in the life history of the animal the pedicle develops posteriorly as a primary larval segment, while the two mantle rudiments also grow posteriorly as folds of epithelium partially covering the pedicle. After settling, when the distal tip of the pedicle becomes attached to the substratum, the animal undergoes metamorphosis. The mantles are reversed so that they are oriented anteriorly, partially covering

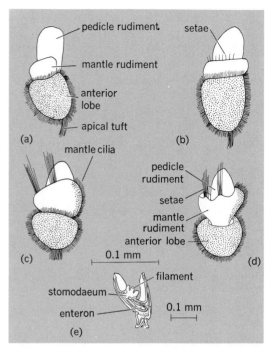

Fig. 4. Larval development of the articulate brachiopod *Notosaria*. (*a–d*) Stages in the differentiation of the anterior lobe, mantle, and pedicle rudiments; and (*e*) longitudinal section after mantle reversal and attachment. (*After R. C. Moore, ed., Treatise on Invertebrate Paleontology, pt. H, Geological Society of America, Inc., and University of Kansas Press, 1965*)

what was the apical lobe of the larva, and with the original inner surface of the mantle forming the outer surface. They subsequently secrete the earliest, first-formed shell, the protegulum. It is not until after settling that the rudimentary lophophore, alimentary canal, and adult musculature make their appearance (**Fig. 4**).

The development of Recent inarticulate brachiopods differs in a number of respects. The period of free-swimming existence is longer, in *Lingula* about a month. Possibly associated with this longer larval life, the alimentary canal, lophophore, shell, and many or even all of the adult muscles make their appearance before the animal settles. The larvae do not undergo metamorphosis or suffer mantle reversal, and the two mantle rudiments are separated from each other early in larval life, not being fused along the posterior margin in the manner characteristic of the articulate brachiopods.

The origin of the pedicle is also completely different, for it arises relatively late and is not protruded between the valves until immediately prior to settlement. It does not develop from a primary segment of the larva, but is formed as an evagination of part of the larval posterior ventral mantle lobe, immediately behind the posterior body wall. Unlike the pedicle of the articulate brachiopods, it is hollow and the lumen is in communication with the body cavity (**Fig. 5**).

Shell morphology. Because of the wide variation within the phylum, only outlines are presented

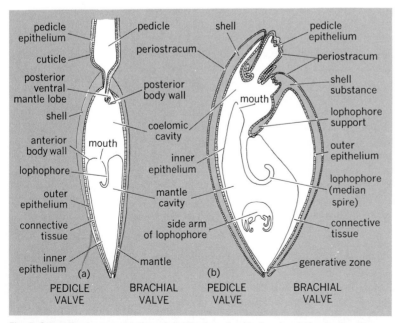

Fig. 3. Generalized representation of distribution of epithelium in relation to the other tissues and organs in (*a*) inarticulates (lingulids) and (*b*) articulates (terebratulids). (*After R. C. Moore, ed., Treatise on Invertebrate Paleontology, pt. H, Geological Society of America, Inc., and University of Kansas Press, 1965*)

here. For additional information consult articles under class and order titles listed earlier.

The two valves are of unequal size, with the pedicle valve typically larger. Because the shell increases in size by increments laid down at the mantle margin, ontogenetic changes in shape are faithfully recorded by growth lines. The valves may be further ornamented by concentric folds (rugae), growth lamellae, or radially disposed ribs of various amplitude and wavelength. Numerous genera are characterized by extravagant development of spines. The posterior region of one or both valves is commonly differentiated from the remainder of the valve as a somewhat flattened cardinal area. The ventral area is typically further modified by the pedicle opening; among articulate brachiopods this consists of a triangular delthyrium which may be partially closed by a pseudodeltidium or a pair of deltidial plates. A corresponding triangular opening, the notothyrium, may be developed on the dorsal cardinal area. Internally, muscle scars and mantle canal impressions may be apparent, together with structures of varying complexity associated with articulation and support of the lophophore.

Beneath the thin outer layer of organic periostracum, the shell of the Articulata is invariably calcite and typically secreted in two clearly defined layers. This layered structure is absent in the few inarticulates which possess calcareous shells, and the majority of this class have a shell of calcium phosphate containing a considerable quantity of organic chitin.

Ecology and distribution. All modern brachiopods are marine, and there is little doubt from the fossil record that brachiopods have always been confined to the sea. A few genera, however, notably the closely related inarticulates *Lingula* and *Glottidia*, can tolerate reduced salinities and may survive in environments that would be lethal to the majority of forms. Recent brachiopods occur most commonly beneath the relatively shallow waters of the continental shelves, which seems to have been the most favored environment, but the bathymetric range of the phylum is large. A few modern species live intertidally and, at the other extreme, a limited number have been dredged from depths of over 16,500 ft (5000 m).

The majority of brachiopods form part of the sessile benthos and are attached by their pedicle during postlarval life. *Glottidia* and *Lingula* are exceptional in being infaunal and making burrows. A commoner modification involves loss of the pedicle, either complete suppression or atrophy early in the life history of the individual. Such forms either lie free on the sea floor, are attached by cementation of part or all of the pedicle valve, or are anchored by spines. The geographic distribution and geological setting of some fossil species suggest that they may have been epiplanktonic, attached to floating weed, but such a mode of life is unknown in modern faunas.

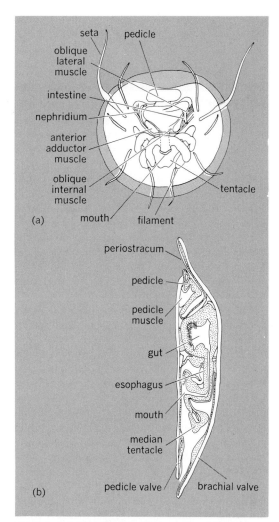

Fig. 5. Larval *Palagodiscus* with four pairs of filaments. (*a*) Ventral view. (*b*) Median longitudinal section. (*After R. C. Moore, ed., Treatise on Invertebrate Paleontology, pt. H, Geological Society of America, Inc., and University of Kansas Press, 1965*)

Chronological distribution. The oldest undoubted brachiopods occur in the Early Cambrian, when representatives of 6 of the 11 known orders were present. Throughout the Cambrian, inarticulates were more abundant than articulates, but during the Early Ordovician this situation was reversed and remains so the present day. The Ordovician was a period of considerable increase in diversity and abundance of the phylum, which formed an important part of the marine faunas throughout the Paleozoic. Toward the close of the Paleozoic Era and during the early part of the Mesozoic many of the older stocks became extinct, although the phylum was still strongly represented numerically. It dwindled in importance on a worldwide basis during the late Mesozoic Era and has remained at approximately that level up to the present. In the present-day oceans, approximately 95 genera are recognized. *See* ARTICULATA (BRACHIOPODA); INARTICULATA.   A. J. Rowell

Bibliography. R. C. Moore (ed.), *Treatise on Invertebrate Paleontology*, pt. H, 1965; S. P.

Parker (ed.), *Synopsis and Classification of Living Organisms*, 2 vols., 1982; M. J. S. Rudwick, *Living and Fossil Brachiopods*, 1970.

Bradyodonti

An order, perhaps composite in nature, of Paleozoic cartilaginous fishes (Chondrichthyes), presumably derived from primitive sharks. They are mainly represented by dentitions, which appear to have been adapted to the eating of mollusks and other shelled invertebrates; the body (seldom preserved) appears to have been broad and flattened, with large pectoral fins, as in the later skates and rays of similar habits. The first bradyodonts appear at the end of the Devonian; they flourished during the Carboniferous, but declined and vanished by the end of the Permian, concomitantly with a reduction in the invertebrate fauna at that time.

There are four families. In the Cochliodontidae the main tooth structures consist of a large spirally twisted tooth plate in each jaw half, each plate formed by the fusion of a row of successional teeth. In the Petalodontidae teeth with deep roots and flattened diamond-shaped crowns were numerous and formed crushing pavements. In the Psammodontidae upper and lower dentitions consisted of a few large quadrilateral plates arranged in two rows meeting in the midline. In the obscurely known Copodontidae, there was but a single subquadrate tooth medially placed at the front end of the upper and lower jaws. *See* CHIMAERIFORMES; CHONDRICHTHYES; ELASMOBRANCHII.   Alfred S. Romer

Brain

A collection of specialized cells (neurons) in the head that regulates behavior as well as sensory and motor functions. Neurons grow long threadlike structures—an axon and a dendritic tree—from their cell bodies, which provide them with a rapid communication network throughout the body. The axon transmits pulses as it signals to thousands of other neurons or to muscle cells or gland cells. The dendrites integrate the pulses from thousands of other neurons. Groups of neurons form ganglia in chains along both sides of the body axis from "head to tail." The largest of these paired groups, the brain, is in the head, where the distance receptors (nose, eyes, and ears) are located. These receptors respond to smells, sights, and sounds coming so far from the collective that the collective has time to receive the inputs, interpret them as signals, plan an action before being overtaken by circumstance, and act while monitoring and correcting its action. These are the minimal functions of a brain. The power of a brain lies not in its size but in the complexity of the connections among its functional parts. *See* NEURON.

Parts. The three main parts of the brain in vertebrates are the cerebrum, the cerebellum, and the brainstem that connects them with each other and with the spinal cord (**Fig. 1**). The two cerebral hemispheres are separated by a midline fissure that is bridged by a massive bundle of axons running in both directions, the corpus callosum. Each hemisphere has a core of groups of neurons (the basal ganglia); an outer shell of neurons in layers (the cerebral cortex); and massive bundles of axons for communication within the cerebrum and with the rest of the brain. These bundles are called white matter because of the waxy myelin sheaths surrounding the axons.

Basal ganglia. This component of the brain comprises three main groups. (1) The thalamus receives axons from all sensory systems and transmits information to the cortex. It also receives feedback from cortical neurons during sensory processing. (2) The corpus, comprising striatum bundles of axons cutting through the groups of neurons, also has two-way communication with the cortex and assists in the organization of body movement. (3) The hypothalamus receives orders from the cortex and organizes the chemical systems that support body movement. One output channel is hormonal, and controls the pituitary gland (hypophysis) which in turn controls the endocrine system. The other channel is neural, comprising axons coursing through the brainstem and spinal cord to the motor neurons of the autonomic nervous system, which regulates the heart, blood vessels, lungs, gastrointestinal tract, sex organs, and skin. The autonomic and endocrine systems are largely self regulating, but they are subject to control by the cortex through the hypothalamus. *See* AUTONOMIC NERVOUS SYSTEM; ENDOCRINE SYSTEM (VERTEBRATE); NEUROBIOLOGY.

Cortex. This section of the brain is also called gray matter because it contains the axons, cell bodies, and dendrites of neurons but there is very little myelin. An index of the capacity of a brain is cortical surface area. In higher mammals, the cortical surface increases more rapidly than the volume during fetal development, and as a result the surface folds, taking the form of wrinkles, that is, convexities (gyri) and fissures (sulci) that vary in their details from one brain to another. However, they are sufficiently reliable to serve as landmarks on the cerebral hemisphere that it can be subdivided into lobes.

Lobes. Four lobes make up the shell of each hemisphere (**Fig. 2**), namely the frontal, parietal, temporal, and occipital lobes. Each lobe contains a motor or sensory map, which is an orderly arrangement of cortical neurons associated with muscles and sensory receptors on the body surface. The central sulcus delimits the frontal and parietal lobes. The precentral gyrus contains the motor cortex whose neurons transmit signals to motor neurons in the brainstem and spinal cord which control the muscles in the feet, legs, trunk, arms, face, and tongue of the opposite side of the body, in that order from medial to lateral position in the motor cortex. The number of neurons for each section is determined by the fineness of control, not the size of the muscle; for example, the lips and tongue have larger areas than the trunk. Within the postcentral gyrus is the primary somatosensory cortex. Sensory receptors in the skin, muscles, and joints send messages to the somatosensory cortical cells through relays in the spinal cord and the thalamus to a map of the opposite side of the body in parallel to the map in the motor cortex. The lateral fissure separates the temporal lobe from the parietal and frontal lobes. The cortex on the inferior border of the fissure receives input relayed through the thalamus from the ears to the primary auditory cortex. The occipital lobe receives thalamic input from the eyes and functions as the primary visual cortex.

In humans, the association cortex surrounds the primary sensory and motor areas that make up a small fraction of each lobe. The occipital lobe has many specialized areas for recognizing visual patterns of color, motion, and texture. The parietal cortex has areas that support perception of the body and its surrounding personal space. Its operation is manifested by the phenomenon of phantom limb, in which the perception of a missing limb persists for an amputee. Conversely, individuals with damage to these areas suffer from sensory neglect, because parts of the body may no longer exist for them. The temporal cortex contains areas that provide recognition of faces and of rhythmic patterns, including those of speech, dance, and music. The frontal cortex provides the neural capabilities for constructing patterns of motor behavior and social behavior. It was the rapid enlargement of the frontal and temporal lobes in human evolution over the past half million years that supported the transcendence of humans over other species. This is where the capacity to create works of art, and also to anticipate pain and death is located. Insight and foresight are both lost with bilateral frontal lobe damage, leading to reduced experience of anxiety, asocial behavior, and a disregard of consequences of actions.

Motor systems. A small part of frontal lobe output goes directly to motor neurons in the brainstem and spinal cord for fine control of motor activities, such as search movements by the eyes, head, and fingers, but most goes either to the striatum from which it is relayed to the thalamus and then back to the cortex, or to the brainstem from which it is sent to the cerebellum and then through the thalamus back to the cortex. In the cerebellum, the cortical messages are integrated with sensory input predominantly from the muscles, tendons, and joints, but also from the eyes and inner ears (for balance) to provide split-second timing for rapid and complex movements. The cerebellum also has a cortex and a core of nuclei to relay input and output. Their connections, along with those in the cerebral cortex, are subject to modification with learning in the formation of a working memory (the basis for learned skills). *See* MEMORY; MOTOR SYSTEMS.

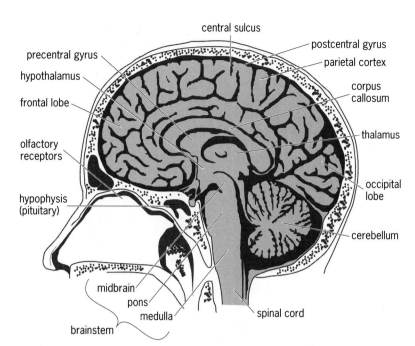

Fig. 1. Midsagittal (midline, medial) section through the human brain. (*After C. R. Noback, The Human Nervous System, 4th ed., McGraw-Hill, 1991*)

Limbic system. The cerebellum and striatum do not set goals, initiate movements, store temporal sequences of sensory input, or provide orientation to the spatial environment. These functions are performed by parts of the cortex and striatum deep in the brain that constitute another loop, the limbic system. Its main site of entry is the entorhinal cortex, which receives input from all of the sensory cortexes, including the olfactory system. The input from all the sensory cortexes is combined and sent to the hippocampus, where it is integrated

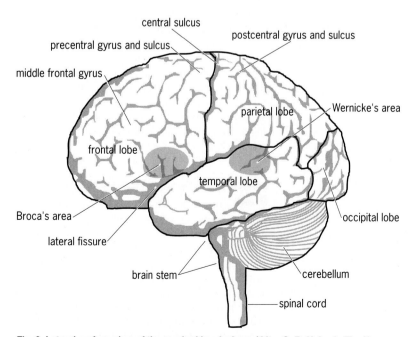

Fig. 2. Lateral surface view of the cerebral hemisphere. (*After C. R. Noback, The Human Nervous System, 4th ed., McGraw-Hill, 1991*)

over time. Hippocampal output returns to the entorhinal cortex, which distributes the integrated sensory information to all of the sensory cortexes, updates them, and prepares them to receive new sensory input. This new information also reaches the hypothalamus and part of the striatum (the amygdaloid nucleus) for regulating emotional behavior. Bilateral damage to the temporal lobe including the hippocampus results in loss of short-term memory. Damage to the amygdaloid nucleus can cause serious emotional impairment. The Papez circuit is formed by transmission from the hippocampus to the hypothalamus by the fornix, then to the thalamus, parietal lobe, and entorhinal cortex. The limbic system generates and issues goal-directed motor commands, with corollary discharge to the sensory systems that prepares them for the changes in sensory input caused by motor activity (for example, when one speaks and hears oneself, as distinct from another).

Split brain. Each hemisphere has its own limbic, Papez, cortico-thalamic, cortico-striatal, and cortico-cerebellar loops, together with sensory and motor connections. When isolated by surgically severing the callosum, each hemisphere functions independently, as though two conscious persons occupied the same skull, but with differing levels of skills in abstract reasoning and language. The right brain (spatial)–left brain (linguistic) cognitive differences are largely due to preeminent development of the speech areas in the left hemisphere in most right- and left-handed persons. Injury to Broca's area (located in the frontal lobe) and Wernicke's area (located in the temporal lobe) [Fig. 2] leads to loss of the ability, respectively, to speak (motor aphasia) or to understand speech (sensory aphasia), appearing as a loss of declarative memory for facts and words. Studies of blood flow show that brain activity during intellectual pursuits is scattered broadly over the four lobes in both hemispheres. *See* CENTRAL NERVOUS SYSTEM; HEMISPHERIC LATERALITY.

Walter J. Freeman

Bibliography. F. E. Bloom and A. Lazerson, *Brain, Mind and Behavior*, 1988; E. R. Kandel, J. H. Schwartz, and T. M. Jessel, *Principles of Neural Science*, 1993; C. R. Noback, *The Human Nervous System*, 4th ed., 1991; H. K. Yusef, *Understanding the Brain and Its Development: A Chemical Approach*, 1992.

Brake

A machine element for applying a force to a moving surface to slow it down or bring it to rest in a controlled manner. In doing so, it converts the kinetic energy of motion into heat which is dissipated into the atmosphere. Brakes are used in motor vehicles, trains, airplanes, elevators, and other machines. Most brakes are of a friction type in which a fixed surface is brought into contact with a moving part that is to be slowed or stopped. Brakes in general connect a moving and

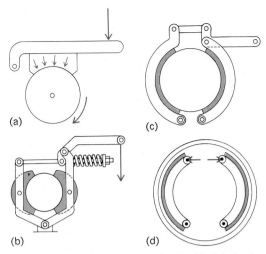

Fig. 1. Brakes. (*a*) Single-block brake. The block is fixed to the operating lever; force in the direction of the arrow applies the brake. (*b*) Double-block brake. The blocks are pivoted on their levers; force in the direction of the arrow releases the brake. (*c*) External shoe brake. Shoes are lined with friction material. (*d*) Internal shoe brake with lining.

a stationary body, whereas clutches and couplings usually connect two moving bodies. *See* AILERON; CLUTCH; COUPLING.

The limitations on the applications of brakes are similar to those of clutches, except that the service conditions are more severe because the entire energy is absorbed by slippage which is converted to heat that must be dissipated. The important thing is the rate at which energy is absorbed and heat dissipated. With friction brakes, if the temperature of the brake becomes too high, the result is a lowering of the friction force, called fading.

There are also electrical and hydrodynamic brakes. The electrical type may be electromagnetic, eddy-current, hysteresis, or magnetic-particle. The hydrodynamic type works somewhat like a fluid coupling with one element stationary. Another type, used on electric trains, is the regenerative brake. This electrical machine can be used as a motor or a generator. As a generator, it brakes the train and stores the generated electricity in an accumulator. Another type of brake is the air brake (flaps) on an airplane.

Friction types. Friction brakes are classified according to the kind of friction element employed and the means of applying the friction forces. *See* FRICTION.

Single-block. The simplest form of brake consists of a short block fitted to the contour of a wheel or drum and pressed against its surface by means of a lever on a fulcrum, as widely used on railroad cars. The block may have the contour lined with friction-brake material, which gives long wear and a high coefficient of friction. The fulcrum may be located with respect to the lever in a manner to aid or retard the braking torque of the block. The lever may be operated manually or by a remotely controlled force (**Fig. 1***a*).

Double-block. Two single-block brakes in symmetrical opposition, where the operating force on the end of one lever is the reaction of the other, make up a double-block brake (Fig. 1*b*). External thrust loads are balanced on the rim of the rotating wheel.

External-shoe. An external-shoe brake operates in the same manner as the block brake, and the designation indicates the application of externally contracting elements. In this brake the shoes are appreciably longer, extending over a greater portion of the drum (Fig. 1*c*). This construction allows more combinations for special applications than the simple shoe, although assumptions of uniform pressure and concentrated forces are no longer possible. In particular, it is used on elevator installations for locking the hoisting sheave by means of a heavy spring when the electric current is off and the elevator is at rest. Self-energization is possible, as with block brakes, depending upon the arrangement of the supporting mechanism. *See* ELEVATOR.

Internal-shoe. An internal shoe has several advantages over an external shoe. Because the internal shoe works on the inner surface of the drum, it is protected from water and grit (Fig. 1*d*). It may be designed in a more compact package, is easily activated, and is effective for drives with rotations in both directions. The internal shoe is used in the automotive drum brake, with hydraulic piston actuation. *See* AUTOMOTIVE BRAKE.

Band. Hoists, excavating machinery, and hydraulic clutch-controlled transmissions have band brakes. They operate on the same principle as flat belts on pulleys. In the simplest band brake, one end of the belt is fastened near the drum surface, and the other end is then pulled over the drum in the direction of rotation so that a lever on a fulcrum may apply tension to the belt.

The belt may be a thin metallic strip with a friction lining. The method of applying the lever on the fulcrum and attaching the belt determines the structural operation of the brake. These variations make possible a sensitive differential brake, self-energizing brakes, and brakes operating with equal effectiveness in both directions. The radial force of the brake is proportional to the tension in the band. In automotive automatic transmissions, the bands are almost completely circular (**Fig. 2**). They are applied by hydraulic pressure and released by spring force, usually aided by redirecting the hydraulic pressure.

Disk. Structurally similar to disk clutches, disk brakes have long been used on hoisting and similar apparatus. Because more energy is absorbed in prolonged braking than in clutch startup, additional heat dissipation must be provided in equivalent disk brakes. Disk brakes are used for the wheels of aircraft, where segmented rotary elements are pressed against stationary plates by hydraulic pistons. Flexibility, self-alignment, and rapid cooling are inherent in this design. Another application is the bicycle coaster brake.

The caliper disk brake (**Fig. 3**) is widely used on automotive vehicles. It consists of a rotating disk which can be gripped between two friction pads. The caliper disk brake is hydraulically operated,

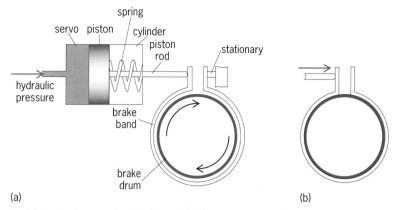

Fig. 2. Band brake around a brake drum. (*a*) Brake band released; the drum is free to rotate. (*b*) Brake applied; tightening the band stops rotation of the drum and holds it stationary. (*Automotive & Technical Writing, Charlottesville, Virginia*)

and the pads cover between one-sixth and one-ninth of the swept area of the disk. *See* AUTOMOTIVE BRAKE.

Actuators. A brake can be arranged so that it is normally either released or applied, a spring usually forcing it into the normal condition. A controllable external force then applies or releases the brake. This force can be, for example, mechanical through a linkage or cable to a lever, pneumatic or hydraulic through a cylinder to a piston, or electric through a solenoid to a plunger.

Air brake. Railway brakes are normally applied air brakes; if the air coupling to a car is broken, the brakes are applied automatically. To apply the brakes, the brake operator releases the compressed air that is restraining the brakes by means of a diaphragm and linkage. Over-the-road trucks and buses use air brakes. Another form of air brake consists of an annular air tube surrounding a jointed brake lining that extends completely around the outside of a brake drum. Air pressure expands the tube, pressing the lining against the drum. *See* AIR BRAKE.

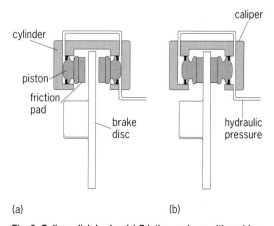

(a)   (b)

Fig. 3. Caliper disk brake. (*a*) Friction pads on either side of a disk that is free to rotate. (*b*) Brake applied, hydraulic pressure forces the pistons toward the disk to stop its rotation and hold it stationary. (*Automotive & Technical Writing, Charlottesville, Virginia*)

Electromagnetic brake. In commonly encountered electromagnetic brakes, the actuating force is applied by an electric current through a solenoid. Direct current (dc) gives greater braking force than alternating current (ac), and is therefore used almost exclusively; ac is rectified if used. Usually the electromagnetic force releases the brake against a compression spring, which provides braking action if the power fails, and overspeed protection when the brake is used with dc series motors.

In a towed highway vehicle, such as a boat trailer, the trailer brakes are applied by electromagnets at each wheel. When the driver operates a controller, the electromagnets are attracted to disks on the rotating wheels. This causes the electromagnets to shift through a limited arc which forces the brake shoes into contact with the drum. Further movement of the controller allows more current to flow in the electromagnets, producing stronger magnetic fields and greater braking action.

Donald L. Anglin

Bibliography. E. A. Avallone and T. Baumeister III, *Marks' Standard Handbook for Mechanical Engineers*, 10th ed., 1996; J. E. Shigley and C. R. Mischke, *Machine Design Fundamentals*, 1989.

Branch circuit

The portion of an electrical wiring system that extends beyond the final, automatic overcurrent protective device (circuit breaker or fuse), which is recognized by the National Electrical Code for use as a branch-circuit overcurrent protector, and that terminates at the utilization device (such as a lighting fixture, motor, or heater). Thermal cutouts, motor overload devices, and fuses in luminaires or plug connections are not approved for branch-circuit protection and do not establish the point of origin of a branch circuit (see **illus.**).

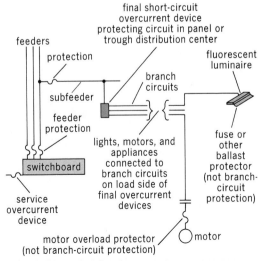

Typical electrical wiring system. Branch circuits are those portions of system beyond the final overcurrent device approved for branch-circuit protection.

Motor branch circuits must have conductors with current-carrying capacity at least 125% of the motor full-load current rating. Overcurrent protection must be capable of carrying the starting current of the motor. Maximum values are tabulated for various currents in the National Electrical Code. *See* ELECTRICAL CODES.

Branch circuits, other than motor branch circuits, are classified by the maximum rating of the overcurrent device. Thus a branch circuit with a 20-A circuit breaker is designated a 20-A branch circuit, even though the conductors may be capable of carrying higher current.

Individual branch circuits serving a single fixed appliance, such as a clothes dryer or a water heater, may be of any size if the overcurrent protection (fuse or circuit breaker) does not exceed 150% of the rated current of the appliance (where it is 10 A or more). For continuous loads of 3 h or longer duration, the branch circuit rating must be at least 125% of the continuous current.

Branch circuits serving more than one outlet or load are limited by the National Electrical Code to three types:

1. Circuits of 15 or 20 A may serve lights and appliances; the rating of one portable appliance may not exceed 80% of the circuit capacity; the total rating of fixed appliances may not exceed 50% of circuit capacity if lights or portable appliances are also supplied.

2. Circuits of 30 A may serve fixed lighting units with heavy-duty lampholders in other than dwellings or appliances in any occupancy.

3. Circuits of 40 or 50 A may serve fixed lighting with heavy-duty lampholders in other than dwellings, fixed cooking appliances, or infrared heating units.

Multiwire branch circuits consist of two or more ungrounded conductors having a potential difference (voltage) between them and a (neutral) grounded conductor having equal potential difference between it and each ungrounded conductor.

Conventionally the current-carrying capacity of conductors may be the same as the branch-circuit rating (for example, no. 12 conductors in a 20-A branch circuit); however, larger conductors may be required to avoid excessive voltage drop. *See* WIRING. Brian J. McPartland; J. F. McPartland

Bibliography. J. F. McPartland, *The Handbook of Practical Electrical Design*, 1982; J. F. McPartland and B. J. McPartland, *National Electrical Code Handbook*, 21st ed., 1993; *National Electrical Code*, NFPA 70-1987 (ANSI), 1987; H. P. Richter and W. C. Schwan, *Practical Electrical Wiring*, 16th ed., 1993.

Branched polymer

A polymer chain having branch points that connect three or more chain segments. Examples of branched polymers include long chains having occasional and usually short branches comprising the same repeat units as the main chain (nominally termed a branched polymer); long chains having occasional branches comprising repeat units different from those of the main chain (termed graft copolymers); main chains having one long branch per repeat unit (referred to as comb polymers); and small core molecules with branches radiating from the core (star polymers). So-called starburst or dendritic polymers are a special class of star polymer in which the branches are multifunctional, leading to further branching with polymer growth. Star, comb, and starburst polymers, (**Fig. 1**), especially the last, represent interesting molecular structures that may lead to unusual supramolecular structures (for example, micelles and liposomes) that mimic the functions of complex biomolecules.

Classic type. A classic example of a branched polymer where the branches have the same chemical composition as the backbone is low-density polyethylene (LDPE). When ethylene is polymerized by using free-radical initiators, short branches, typically ethyl and *n*-butyl along with lesser amounts of a few other types including very long branches, are generated by a process known as chain transfer to polymer. A propagating radical at the end of a growing polyethylene chain, which is a primary alkyl radical, is capable of abstracting a backbone hydrogen atom from the polymer backbone, leading to a more stable secondary radical. The preponderance of ethyl and *n*-butyl groups is thought to be the result of intramolecular chain transfer proceeding via conformations involving six-membered ring transition states, as in the reaction below.

The short branches interfere to some degree with crystallization of the backbone and, since the chains cannot pack as efficiently, the density is lower than that of high-density polyethylene (HDPE). However, LDPE is somewhat tougher because of its greater amorphous content. The amorphous regions are above their glass transition temperature at room temperature, and the liquidlike nature of these regions provides for energy dissipation and hence toughness. Much LDPE is prepared by copolymerization of ethylene with α-olefins such as 1-hexene using organometallic initiators, a route that offers more control over branch type and concentration, and hence properties. This type is known as linear low-density polyethylene (LLDPE).

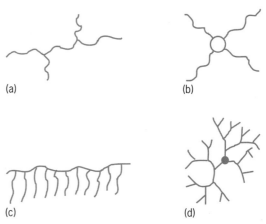

Fig. 1. Examples of branched polymers. (*a*) Branched polymer (if arms are of composition similar to backbone) or graft polymer (if compositions are different). (*b*) Star polymer. (*c*) Comb polymer. (*d*) Dendritic polymer.

Branching can occur to some extent in the polymerization of other monomers, including vinyl acetate (radical polymerization), the base-initiated ring-opening polymerization of caprolactam, and the cationic ring-opening polymerization of ethyleneimine. Step-growth polymerizations using monomers with an average functionality greater than two can also lead to branching and, in many cases, crosslinking. An example of branching in biopolymers is the structure of amylopectin, a component of starch [monomer, structure (**1**)]; in amy-

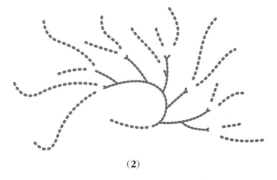

lopectin, the branches on the main backbone are themselves branched [structure (**2**)]. Glycogen, the

storage polymer of glucose in animals, is even more heavily branched than amylopectin. *See* BIOPOLYMER; GLYCOGEN; POLYOLEFIN RESINS; STARCH.

Graft and comb. There are many examples of graft copolymers. They can be prepared by generation of a radical on a polymer backbone via ultraviolet or ionizing radiation in the presence of a monomer, or by polymerization of a monomer in the presence of a polymer with a polymerizable linkage such as a carbon-carbon double bond. An important example of the latter type is a graft copolymer of polystyrene and polybutadiene [structure (**3**)]. The resulting material is far tougher

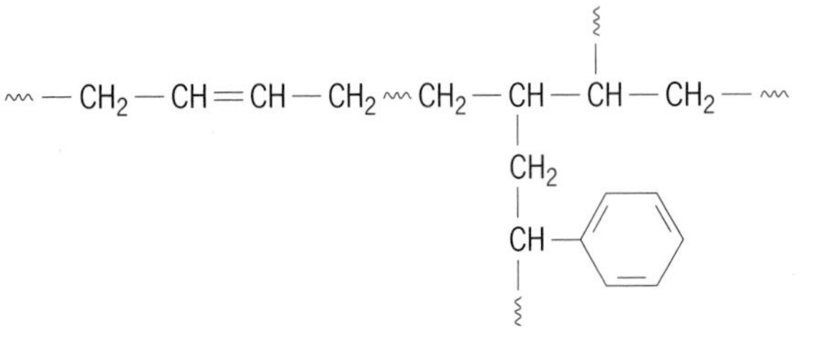

$$\text{∿} - CH_2 - CH = CH - CH_2 \text{∿} CH_2 - CH - CH - CH_2 - \text{∿}$$

(**3**)

than polystyrene itself because of the presence of small domains of rubbery polybutadiene. Graft copolymers can also be prepared by coupling polymers having reactive groups at one chain end with different polymers having functional groups on their backbones. Preformed polymers with a polymerizable end (referred to as macromonomers) can be homopolymerized to form comb polymers or can be copolymerized with a variety of monomers to yield graft copolymers. Finally, graft copolymers can be prepared by mechanically blending different polymers. Homolytic bond cleavage resulting from shearing leads to the formation of free radicals on the polymer chains, and the coupling of these onto different polymer chains results in grafting. *See* COPOLYMER; FREE RADICAL.

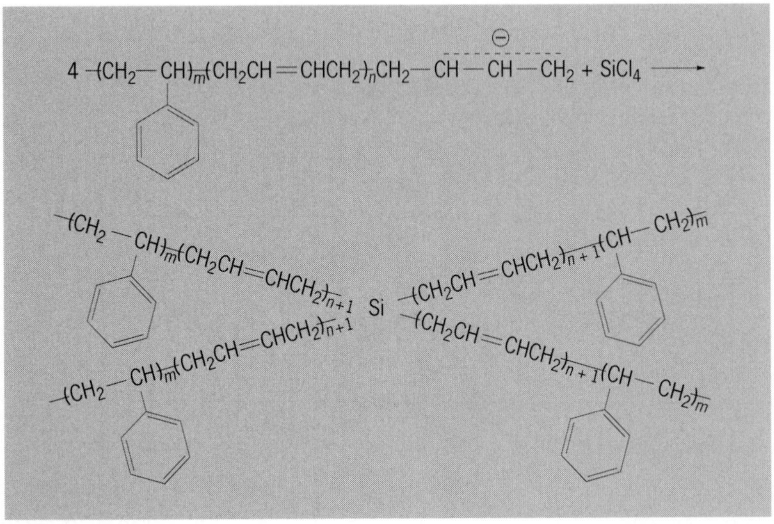

Star and comb. Star polymers can be prepared by a core-first or arm-first approach. In the former, initiation of polymerization occurs from a multifunctional core molecule. In the latter, polymer chains are synthesized and then coupled to a core molecule via reactive end groups. Steric considerations dictate the efficiency of the coupling process. For example, reaction of polystyryl anions with tetrachlorosilane yields a mixture of three- and four-arm star polymers along with a coupled polymer and a homopolymer. A similar reaction with the less sterically demanding polybutadienyl anion gives an almost quantitative yield of four-arm star polymer. The arms need not be homopolymers. For example, star polymers with styrene-butadiene block copolymer arms have been prepared by reaction of polybutadienyl anionic ends with reactive core molecules such as tetrachlorosilane (**Fig. 2**). Star polymers are of interest because they are smaller in size than a linear polymer of comparable molecular weight and therefore will usually have lower softening points and solution viscosities, which can facilitate processing. Comb polymers can also be prepared by using the ideas employed for the synthesis of star polymers, as well as via polymerization of macromonomers, which are polymers terminated with polymerizable groups such as vinyl and epoxy.

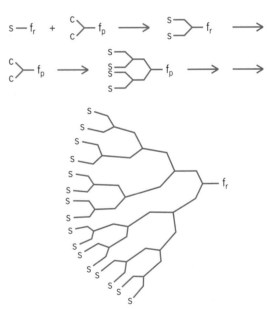

Fig. 3. Steps in the synthesis of a starburst polymer. s = surface. c = interior. f_r = reactive group. f_p = protected group.

Starburst and dendritic. The field of branched polymers also includes starburst, or dendritic, polymers (also referred to as arborols and cascade molecules). These unique materials are characterized by a highly branched, three-dimensional structure emanating from a central, multifunctional molecule. The difference between dendritic polymers and other so-called hyperbranched polymers

Fig. 2. Reaction for preparation of a star polymer with styrene-butadiene block copolymer arms.

such as amylopectin is that in the former each monomer unit has at least one branch point, and therefore the extent of branching is extraordinarily high. The pronounced branching allows the attainment of spherical molecules that resemble micelles.

Numerous syntheses of starburst polymers have been developed. An initial example involved the addition of ammonia to methyl acrylate. The resulting triester was then reacted with a diamine such as ethylenediamine, resulting in a new triamine that was effectively the core molecule. Repetition of these steps led to the production of a starburst polymer (**Fig. 3**). This approach, in which the synthesis is begun at the center of the polymer, is termed the divergent method, and the repetitions of the reactions are referred to as generations. The number of reactions that need to be performed increases geometrically with the number of generations. The molecule will tend toward a spherical shape as the number of generations increases. The size of the molecule can be predicted from the number of generations, and indeed experimentally determined diameters (via electron microscopy and size exclusion chromatography) are in excellent agreement with predictions. Also, the surface of the molecule will have a high concentration of functional groups (amines in this case).

An alternative approach to dendrimer synthesis is the convergent method, where the synthesis is begun at the outside of the dendrimer. Here portions of what will ultimately be a dendrimer, referred to as dendrons, are synthesized and then coupled to yield the dendrimer. Use is made of series of protection or deprotection steps. One advantage of this approach is that it does not limit the type and concentration of a particular functional group at the surface of the dendrimer. It has been successfully employed to prepare a wide variety of dendrimers, including polyesters and poly(aryl ethers), as well as novel block copolymers.

Dendrimers can be viewed as nanostructural compounds that can be used as building blocks for novel supramolecular assemblies. For example, it is possible to react dendrimers bearing nucleophilic surface groups (for example, amines) with others bearing electrophilic groups to form dendrimer clusters. Dendrimers can also be reacted with functionally terminal polymers to obtain networks having junction points of very high functionality. The high concentration of surface functionality and the ability to manipulate the functionality through simple organic reactions has spurred interest in their potential use as targeted drug carriers. Indeed, it may be that applications of dendrimers will be particularly significant in biological science in view of the ability to control functionality and supramolecular structure. *See* ORGANIC SYNTHESIS; POLYMER; POLYMERIZATION.

Gary E. Wnek

Bibliography. G. Odian, *Principles of Polymerization*, 3d ed., 1991.

Branchiopoda

A class of crustaceans. Formerly, four extant orders were recognized: Anostraca, Notostraca, Conchostraca, and Cladocera, the first two of which are well defined. The Conchostraca consist of two groups which, although superficially similar, differ in so many fundamental features that they have been placed in separate orders, Laevicaudata and Spinicaudata. The Cladocera are in fact a heterogeneous assemblage of organisms that have now been split into four orders: Anomopoda, Ctenopoda, Onychopoda, and Haplopoda. Although the name Cladocera has to be abandoned as a taxonomic unit, it will doubtless continue to be used as a convenient descriptive term for members of these four orders. There are also two extinct orders, Lipostraca and Kazacharthra. Branchiopods have a long history. Both the Lipostraca and Spinicaudata were differentiated by Devonian times, and their ancestors doubtless originated even earlier. *See* ANOMOPODA; ANOSTRACA; CTENOPODA; HAPLOPODA; LAEVICAUDATA; NOTOSTRACA; ONYCHOPODA; SPINICAUDATA.

Living members of the Branchiopoda range from less than 0.5 mm (0.02 in.) to (exceptionally) 100 mm (4 in.) in length. Form is exceedingly diverse. The trunk may be abbreviated and of probably as few as 5 segments (although segmentation is sometimes obscure) or elongate and of more than 40 segments. Trunk limbs range from 5 to about 70 pairs. A carapace is often present, either as a dorsal shield or as a bivalved structure; anostracans lack a carapace. The eyes were primitively paired and are sometimes stalked and sometimes sessile; in several orders they have fused to give a single median sessile eye. Members of several orders use their antennae as organs of locomotion—a retention of the similar mechanism used by the nauplius larva. Others swim by means of trunk limbs. The mandibles are usually of the crushing, rolling type; only in a few cases have biting or piercing mandibles been acquired. Other mouthparts are usually small, but important. Trunk limb structure is extremely diverse. Many-limbed orders tend to have limbs that differ from each other only in degree; the Anomopoda have limbs that differ greatly from each other in form and from species to species in relation to habits.

Most species are microphagous. Microphagous forms collect their food either by direct scraping from surfaces, which may or may not be followed by filtration, or by abstracting suspended particles by the use of complicated filtering devices. A few species are omnivores or carnivores.

Reproductive habits are diverse. Parthenogenesis

is widespread, and the production of highly resistant resting eggs that can withstand freezing and drying and retain their viability for several years is highly characteristic. Almost all species live in fresh water, but a few are marine and some frequent highly saline situations. Branchiopods have a worldwide distribution. *See* CRUSTACEA.

Geoffrey Fryer

Branchiura

A subclass of the Crustacea known as the fish lice. They are ectoparasites of fresh-water and marine fish on such areas as the base of fins and the gill chamber walls. *Argulus* (see **illus.**) is a common genus. They are a small homogeneous group, less than 100 species, with worldwide distribution, and very much alike in appearance. The disklike head and thorax (cephalothorax) is strongly flattened and bears a small unsegmented abdomen bilobed at its distal end. Larger species may exceed 1 in. (25 mm) in length.

Taxonomy. The Branchiura have often been included within the Copepoda either as the subclass Branchiura, opposed to the remainder grouped under Eucopepoda, or as the order Arguloida equivalent in rank to the Calanoida, Cyclopoida, and Harpacticoida. Though widespread acknowledgment is not yet apparent, critical appraisal of branchiuran morphology, ontogeny, and ethology has revealed several basic characteristics which have no homologs in the eucopepods. On the basis of these fundamental differences, linkage to the Copepoda is no more justified than placement within the Branchiopoda, Ostracoda, or even Cirripedia. *See* COPEPODA.

Some of the morphological characteristics distinguishing Branchiura from Copepoda include the presence of compound eyes, totally different segmentation of the swimming legs, location of the genital orifice on the thorax, absence of a spermatophore, and use of the second, third, and fourth pairs of legs in copulation. The absence of larval stages, either suppressed in the embryonic period or as a free-swimming nauplius followed by metamorphosis into the immature adult form, is noteworthy. Behavioral differences occur in the method of spawning; branchiurans attach small masses of eggs enveloped in gelatinous sheaths to stones and other firm objects on the bottom.

Morphology. The appendages, all on the cephalothorax, consist of two pairs of antennae, the mouthparts which are one pair of mandibles and two pairs of maxillae, and four pairs of swimming legs. They originate on the underside of the body near the midline and extend laterally, perpendicular to the longitudinal axis. The wafer-thin cephalothorax with its appendages appressed to the underside permits fish lice to flatten themselves against a fish's skin. The resulting highly streamlined contour serves to minimize the considerable force of frictional drag found in a dense medium like water.

Other adaptations for holding fast to a mucus-covered swimming fish include numerous spinules and strategically placed hooks on the underside of the body and utilization of specialized portions of the body as suction cups. Despite these elaborate specializations, fish lice never lose the ability to abandon a host and swim. At least some of this activity is associated with mating and spawning.

Reproduction. Breeding males seek the female which remains passively on the host. Use is made of the second to fourth pairs of swimming legs in copulation, these appendages bearing pegs and corresponding sockets arranged in a manner unique to each species. Spawning females swim from the host to find firm objects, such as stones, on which to fix the mass of eggs encased in a gelatinous sheath. Following direct embryonic development the hatching juvenile resembles the parent although the appendages do not assume an adult form until later. Sexual maturity, occurring about a month after hatching, requires at least seven molt stages and does not seem to stop growth.

Nutrition. Branchiurans feed on tissue fluids, especially blood. The mouth, located at the end of a movable proboscis, is applied to the host's skin and the rasping mandibles make the necessary wound. Fish lice usually are no threat to fish populations. In restricted areas such as hatchery ponds, however, an infestation can increase to levels that bring about high fish mortality. Treatment may require such drastic measures as drainage and cleaning before restocking can be successful. *See* CRUSTACEA.

Abraham Fleminger

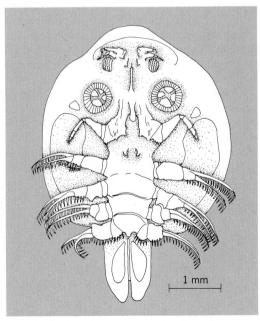

Argulus japonicus, male fish louse of the Branchiura.

1 mm

Bibliography. M. F. Martin, On the morphology and classification of *Argulus* (Crustacea), *Proc. Zool. Soc. London*, 1932:771–806, 1932; O. L. Meehean, A review of the parasitic Crustacea of the genus *Argulus* in the collections of the United States National Museum, *Proc. U.S. Nat. Mus.*, 88:459–522, 1940; S. P. Parker (ed.), *Synopsis and Classification of Living Organisms*, 2 vols., 1982; C. B. Wilson, Parasitic copepods in the United States National Museum, *Proc. U.S. Nat. Mus.*, 94:529–582, 1944.

Brass

An alloy of copper and zinc. In manufacture, lump zinc is added to molten copper, and the mixture is poured either into castings ready for use or into billets for further working by rolling, extruding, forging, or a similar process. Brasses containing 75–85% copper are red-gold and malleable; those containing 60–70% are yellow and also malleable; and those containing 50% or less copper are white, brittle, and not malleable. Alpha brass contains up to 36% zinc; beta brass contains nearly equal proportions of copper and zinc. Specific brasses are designated as follows: gilding (95% copper: 5% zinc), red (85:15), low (80:20), and admiralty (70:29, with balance of tin). Naval brass is 59–62% copper with about 1% tin, less than that of lead and iron, and the remainder zinc. The nickel silvers contain 55–70% copper and the balance nickel. With small amounts of other metals, other names are used. Leaded brass is used for castings.

Addition of zinc to copper produces a material that is harder and stronger than copper, as shown in the **illustration**, yet retains the malleability, ductility, and corrosion resistance of copper. Mechanical and heat treatment greatly vary the properties of the finished product. Because brass with 64% or more copper (α-brass) forms a single solid solution, it combines high strength, ductility, and corrosion resistance. The β solid solution is harder and more brittle. With 61% zinc the compound Cu_2Zn_3 forms; it is brittle, having the lowest tensile strength of the brasses. Higher percents of zinc produce other brittle constituents.

Brass stains in moist air; however, the oxide so formed is sufficiently continuous and adherent to retard further oxidation. When brass is required to remain bright, it is either washed in nitric acid and then coated with clear lacquer, or it is regularly polished and waxed. For brightwork or other corrosion-resistant applications, α-brass is usually used. In atmospheres containing traces of ammonia, cold-worked brass or annealed brass highly stressed in tension may fail by cracking. This is called season cracking or stress corrosion cracking. Susceptibility of cold-worked brass to failure of this kind is reduced by proper annealing.

Brass is widely used in cartridge cases, plumbing fixtures, valves and pipes, screws, clocks, and

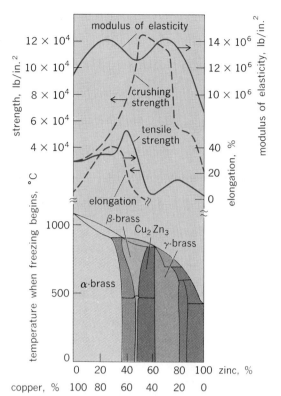

Approximate mechanical properties of cast brass in relation to alloy composition in simplified phase diagram.

musical instruments. *See* ALLOY; BRONZE; COPPER; COPPER ALLOYS; CORROSION; ZINC; ZINC ALLOYS.

Frank H. Rockett

Bibliography. R. M. Brick et al., *Structure and Properties of Engineering Materials*, 4th ed., 1977; K. G. Budinski, *Engineering Materials: Properties and Selection*, 4th ed., 1992.

Brayton cycle

A thermodynamic cycle (also variously called the Joule or complete expansion diesel cycle) consisting of two constant-pressure (isobaric) processes interspersed with two reversible adiabatic (isentropic) processes (**Fig. 1**). The ideal cycle performance, predicated on the use of perfect gases, is given by relationships (1) and (2). Thermal

$$V_3/V_2 = V_4/V_1 = T_3/T_2 = T_4/T_1 \qquad (1)$$

$$\frac{T_2}{T_1} = \frac{T_3}{T_4} = \left(\frac{V_1}{V_2}\right)^{k-1} = \left(\frac{V_4}{V_3}\right)^{k-1} = \left(\frac{p_2}{p_1}\right)^{\frac{k-1}{k}} \qquad (2)$$

efficiency η_T, the work done per unit of heat added, is given by Eq. (3). In these relationships V is the

$$\eta_T = [1 - (T_1/T_2)] = \left[1 - \left(\frac{1}{r^{k-1}}\right)\right] \qquad (3)$$

volume in cubic feet, p is the pressure in pounds per square foot, T is the absolute temperature in degrees Rankine, k is the c_p/c_v, or ratio of specific heats at constant pressure and constant volume, and

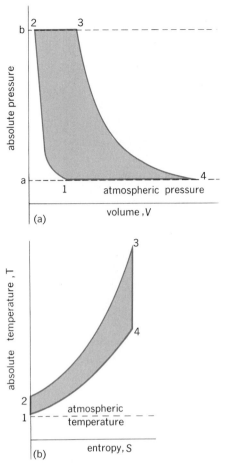

Fig. 1. Brayton cycle, air-card standard. (*a*) *p-V* cycle diagram. (*b*) *p-S* diagram. Phases: 1–2, compression; 2–3, heat addition; 3–4, expansion; and 4–1, heat abstraction.

r is the compression ratio, V_1/V_2.

The thermal efficiency for a given gas, air, is solely a function of the ratio of compression. This is also the case with the Otto cycle. For the diesel cycle with incomplete expansion, the thermal efficiency is lower. The overriding importance of high compression ratio for intrinsic high efficiency is clearly demonstrated by these data.

A reciprocating engine, operating on the cycle of Fig. 1, was patented in 1872 by G. B. Brayton and was the first successful gas engine built in the United States. The Brayton cycle, with its high inherent thermal efficiency, requires the maximum volume of gas flow for a given power output. The Otto and diesel cycles require much lower gas flow rates, but have the disadvantage of higher peak pressures and temperatures. These conflicting elements led to many designs, all attempting to achieve practical compromises. With a piston and cylinder mechanism the Brayton cycle, calling for the maximum displacement per horsepower, led to proposals such as compound engines and variable-stroke mechanisms. They suffered overall disadvantages because of the low mean effective pressures. The positive displacement engine consequently preempted the field for the Otto and diesel cycles.

With the subsequent development of fluid acceleration devices for the compression and expansion of gases, the Brayton cycle found mechanisms which could economically handle the large volumes of working fluid. This is perfected today in the gas turbine power plant. The mechanism (**Fig. 2**) basically is a steady-flow device with a centrifugal or axial compressor, a combustion chamber where heat is added, and an expander-turbine element. Each of the phases of the cycle is accomplished with steady flow in its own mechanism rather than intermittently, as with the piston and cylinder mechanism of the usual Otto and diesel cycle engines. Practical gas-turbine engines have various recognized advantages and disadvantages which are evaluated by comparison with alternative engines available in the competitive marketplace. *See* AUTOMOBILE; GAS TURBINE; INTERNAL COMBUSTION ENGINE.

The net power output P_{net}, or salable power, of the gas-turbine plant (Fig. 2) can be expressed as shown by Eq. (4), where W_e is the ideal power

$$P_{net} = W_e \times \text{eff}_e - \frac{W_c}{\text{eff}_c} \qquad (4)$$

output of the expander (area b34a, Fig. 1), W_c the ideal power input to the compressor (area a12b, Fig. 1), eff_e the efficiency of expander, and eff_c the efficiency of compressor. This net power output for the ideal case, where both efficiencies are 1.0, is represented by net area (shaded) of the p-V cycle diagram of Fig. 1a. The larger the volume increase from point 2 to point 3, the greater will be the net power output for a given size of compressor. This volume increase is accomplished by utilizing the maximum possible temperature at point 3 of the cycle.

The difference in the two terms on the right-hand side of Eq. (4) is thus basically increased by the use of maximum temperatures at the inlet to the expander. These high temperatures introduce metallurgical and heat-transfer problems which must be properly solved.

The efficiency terms of Eq. (4) are of vital practical significance. If the efficiencies of the real compressor and of the real expander are low, it is entirely possible to vitiate the difference in the ideal powers W_e and W_c, so that there will be no useful output of the plant. In present practice this means that for adaptations of the Brayton cycle to acceptable and reliable gas-turbine

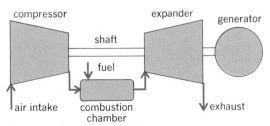

Fig. 2. Simple, open-cycle gas-turbine plant.

plants, the engineering design must provide for high temperatures at the expander inlet and utilize high built-in efficiencies of the compressor and expander elements. No amount of cycle alteration, regeneration, or reheat can offset this intrinsic requirement for mechanisms which will safely operate at temperatures of about 1500°F (816°C). *See* CARNOT CYCLE; DIESEL CYCLE; OTTO CYCLE; THERMODYNAMIC CYCLE.   Theodore Baumeister

Bibliography. E. A. Avallone and T. Baumeister III (eds.), *Marks' Standard Handbook for Mechanical Engineers*, 9th ed., 1987; J. B. Jones and G. A. Hawkins, *Engineering Thermodynamics*, 1960; H. Cohen et al., *Gas Turbine Theory*, 2d ed., 1975; R. T. Harman, *Gas Turbine Engineering: Applications, Cycles, and Characteristics*, 1981; G. N. Hatsopoulos and J. H. Keenan, *Principles of General Thermodynamics*, 1965, reprint 1981; M. J. Zucrow and J. D. Hoffman, *Gas Dynamics*, vol. 1, 1976, vol. 2, 1977.

Brazil nut

A large broad-leafed evergreen tree, *Bertholettia excelsa*, that grows wild in the forests of the Amazon valley of Brazil and Bolivia. The fruit is a spherical capsule, 3–6 in. (7.5–15 cm) in diameter and weighing 2–4 lb (0.9–1.8 kg) which, when mature, consists of an outer hard indehiscent husk about $1/2$ in. (1.2 cm) thick enclosing an inner hard-shelled container or pod filled with about 20 rather triangular seeds or nuts. *See* LECYTHIDALES.

Although there are a few plantations in Brazil, almost the entire production is gathered from wild trees. The quantity that gets into commercial channels varies with the price paid on the world market. The nuts are gathered either by local people who live in the forest or migrants who come into the area for the harvest season. The ripened capsules fall to the ground, and because of their weight and the height of the trees are a hazard to the harvesters. The fruits are carried to the stream bank and transported in small boats to local huts, where the capsules are split open to free the nuts. These are sold to traders who ship them downstream to brokers. They are mostly exported to Europe, Canada, and the United States. About one-fourth of the crop is shelled in Brazil before export.

Brazil nuts have a high oil and protein content and require careful handling and refrigeration to prevent spoilage. The nuts are used in confectionery, baked goods, and nut mixtures. *See* NUT CROP CULTURE.   Laurence H. MacDaniels

Brazing

A group of welding processes in which coalescence is produced by heating to suitable temperatures above 450°C and by using a filler metal that must have a liquidus temperature above 450°C and below the solidus temperature of the base metal. The filler metal is distributed between the closely fitted surfaces of the joint by capillary attraction. Brazing is distinguished from soldering in that the latter employs a filler metal having a liquidus below 450°C. *See* SOLDERING.

Brazing provides advantages over other welding processes, especially because it permits joining of dissimilar metals that, because of metallurgical incompatibilities, cannot be joined by traditional fusion processes. Since base metals do not have to be melted to be joined, it does not matter that they have widely different melting points. Therefore, steel can be brazed to copper as easily as steel to steel.

Brazing also generally produces less thermally induced distortion (warping) than fusion welding does, because an entire part can be brought up to the same brazing temperature, thereby preventing the kind of localized heating that can cause distortion in welding.

Finally, and perhaps most important to the manufacturing specialist, brazing readily lends itself to mass-production techniques.

Brazing process. The important elements of the brazing process are filler-metal flow, base-metal and filler-metal characteristics, surface preparation, joint design and clearance, temperature and time, and rate and source of heating.

A brazed joint is a heterogeneous assembly that is composed of different materials with different physical and chemical properties. In the simplest case, it consists of the base-metal parts to be joined and the added brazing filler metal. Diffusion processes, however, can change the composition and therefore the chemical and physical properties of the boundary zone formed at the interface between base metal and filler metal.

Small clearances should be used because the smaller the clearance, the easier it will be for capillarity to distribute the brazing filler metal throughout the joint area, and there will be less likelihood that voids or shrinkage cavities will form as the brazing filler metal solidifies. Small clearances and correspondingly thin filler-metal films make sound joints. The soundest joints are at least as high in tensile strength as the filler metal itself, and often higher. Clearances ranging from 0.03 to 0.08 mm are designed for the best capillary action and greatest joint strength.

Joint design. A number of factors must be considered in designing joints. First is composition and strength of the brazing filler metal. Generally, the bulk strength of the brazing filler metal is lower than that of the base metals, and so a correctly designed joint is required to obtain adequate mechanical strength. Second is capillary attraction. Because brazing depends on the principle of capillary attraction for distribution of molten brazing filler metal, joint clearance is a critical factor. Third is flux and air displacement. Not only must the filler metal be drawn into the joint, but flux and air must be displaced from it. Fourth is type of stress. In general, it is preferred that any load on a brazed joint be transmitted as shear stress rather than as tensile stress. Fifth is composition and strength of the base metals. In a joint made according to recommendations between high-strength members, the filler-metal film in the joint may actually be stronger than the base metal itself.

There are basically only two types of brazed joints, butt and lap, with all other joints being only modifications.

Butt and lap joints. The butt joint (**Fig. 1***a*) has the advantage of a single thickness at the joint. Preparation is relatively simple; however, the strength of any joint depends in part on the bonding area available. The thinnest member, therefore, dictates the maximum strength of the joint.

Strength is only one reason for the use of the lap design. Lap joints (Fig. 1*b*) can be readily designed to be self-jigging or, as in the case of tubing, self-aligning. Also, preplaced filler metal can be held in position better with such joints.

Butt-lap and scarf joints. The butt-lap joint (Fig. 1*c*) is an attempt to combine the advantage of a single thickness with maximum bonding area and strength. The scarf joint (Fig. 1*d*) represents another attempt to increase the cross-sectional area of the joint without increasing its thickness. Because the scarf joint is at an angle to the axis of tensile loading, its load-carrying capacity is similar to that of the lap joint and greater than that of the butt joint.

Joint clearance. The single most important design consideration in achieving good brazements is joint clearance—the distance between the faying surfaces to be joined. The ideal clearance for production work is frequently cited as 0.05–0.13 mm. However, some metals actually require interference fits, whereas others require clearances as great as 0.25 mm.

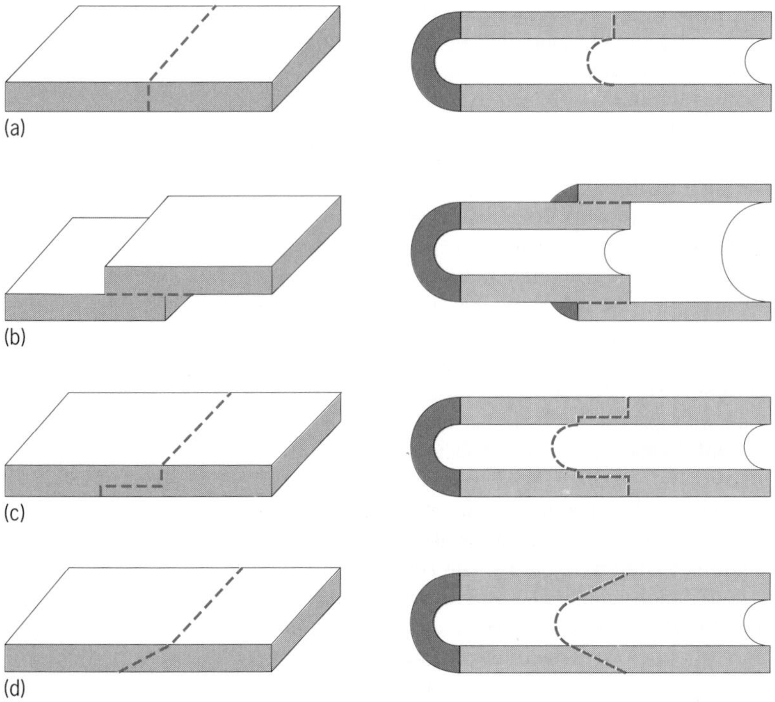

Selection of materials. Selection involves consideration of both the base metal and the filler metal.

Base metals. The base metal has a prime effect on joint strength. A high-strength base metal produces joints of greater strength than those made with softer base metals. In addition to the base-metal effects and the normal mechanical requirements of the base metal in the brazement, the effect of the brazing cycle on the base metal and the final joint strength must be considered. The brazing cycle by its very nature will usually anneal the cold-worked base metal, unless the brazing temperature is very low and the time at heat is very short. When it is essential to design a brazement having strength above the annealed strength of the base metals after the brazing operation, it will be necessary to specify a heat-treatable base metal.

Braze filler metals. The brazing filler metal is also known as the brazing alloy. A specific brazing filler metal cannot be chosen to produce a specific joint strength. Actually, strong joints can be brazed with almost any commercial brazing filler metal if brazing methods and joint design are done correctly.

The degree to which brazing filler metal penetrates and alloys with the base metal during brazing is referred to as diffusion. In applications requiring strong joints for high-temperature, high-stress service conditions (such as turbine rotor assemblies and jet components), it is generally good practice to specify a brazing filler metal that has high diffusion and solution properties with the base metal. When the assembly is constructed of extremely thin base metals (as in honeycomb structures and some heat exchangers), good practice generally calls for a brazing filler metal with a low-diffusion characteristic relative to the base metal.

In choosing a brazing filler metal, the first criterion is the working temperature. Very few brazing filler metals possess distinct melting points. A brazing filler metal may have to melt below the temperature at which members of the joint lose strength or above the temperature at which oxides are reduced or dissociated. Joining may have to be carried out above the solution treatment temperature of the base metal, at a structure refining temperature, or below the remelt temperature of a brazing filler metal used previously in producing a brazed subassembly.

Methods of heating. There are a variety of heating methods available for brazing. Effective capillary joining requires efficient transfer of heat from the heat source into the joint. The seven commonly used methods are torch, furnace, induction, dip, resistance, infrared, and diffusion brazing.

Fig. 1. Types of brazed joints, showing flat (left) and tubular (right) configurations. (*a*) Butt. (*b*) Lap. (*c*) Butt-lap. (*d*) Scarf.

Torch brazing. Manual torch brazing is most frequently used for repairs, one-of-a-kind brazing jobs, and short production runs as an alternative to fusion welding. Any joint that can be reached by a torch and brought to brazing temperature can be readily brazed by this technique. The adjustment of the torch flame is important. Generally, a slightly reducing flame is desirable.

In manual torch brazing, the brazing filler metal is usually face fed in the form of wire or rod, or preplaced. To ensure uniform heating throughout the joint, an important consideration, it may be advisable to use a multiple-tip torch or more than one torch.

Torch brazing can be automated relatively easily. Usually, such systems involve multiple-station rotary indexing tables. The part is fed into a holding fixture at the first station, then indexed to one or more preheating stations, depending on the heating time required. A brazing station is next, followed by a cooling station and an ejection station (**Fig. 2**).

Furnace brazing. Furnace brazing is used extensively where the parts to be brazed can be assembled with the brazing filler metal preplaced or in the joint. There are two basic types of furnaces used for brazing: the batch and the continuous. Furnace brazing is particularly applicable for high-production brazing in which continuous-conveyor-type furnaces are used. For medium-production work, batch-type furnaces are best. When continuous-type furnaces are used, several different temperature zones may be used to provide the proper preheating, brazing, and cooling temperatures. Heating is usually produced by electrical resistance.

The parts should be self-jigging or fixtured and assembled with brazing filler metal preplaced near or in the joint. The preplaced filler metal may be in the form of wire, foil, powder, paste, slugs, or preformed shapes. Fluxing is used except when a reducing atmosphere, such as hydrogen gas, can be introduced into the furnace. Pure, dry, inert gases, such as argon and helium, are used to obtain special atmospheric properties.

A large volume of furnace brazing is performed in vacuum, which prevents oxidation and often eliminates the need for flux. Vacuum brazing has found wide application in the aerospace and nuclear fields, where reactive metals are joined or where entrapped fluxes would be intolerable.

Induction brazing. The high-frequency induction heating method for brazing is clean and rapid, lends itself to close control of temperature and location, and requires little operator skill. The heat for induction brazing is created by a rapidly alternating electric current that is induced into the workpiece by an adjacent coil. The workpiece is placed in or near a coil carrying alternating current, which induces the heating current in the desired area. Brazing filler metal is normally preplaced in the joint, and the brazing can be done in air, in an inert atmosphere, or in a vacuum. Induction brazing is

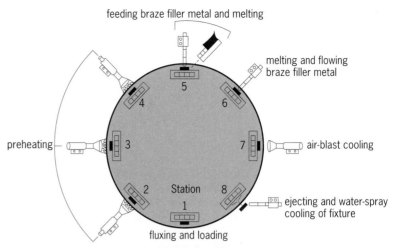

Fig. 2. Automatic eight-station torch brazing machine.

well suited for mass production, and mechanized systems for moving the assemblies to and from the coils are very common.

Dip brazing. This process involves immersion of assembled parts into a suitable molten bath to effect brazing. The bath can be either molten brazing filler metal or molten chemical flux. The molten-flux method is used extensively for brazing aluminum and its alloys. The brazing filler metal is preplaced and the assembly immersed in the flux bath, which has been raised to brazing temperature. The flux bath provides excellent protection against reoxidation of the metal, which can occur quite easily with aluminum.

Resistance brazing. The process is most applicable to relatively simple joints in metals that have high electrical conductivity. The workpieces are heated locally, and brazing filler metal that is preplaced between the workpieces is melted by the heat obtained from resistance to the flow of electric current through the electrodes and the work. In the usual application of resistance brazing, the heating current, which is normally alternating current, is passed through the joint itself. Equipment is the same as that used for resistance welding.

Infrared brazing. The development of high-intensity quartz lamps and the availability of suitable reflectors have made infrared heat a commercially important generator for brazing. Lamps are often arranged in a toasterlike configuration, with parts traveling between two banks of lamps.

Diffusion brazing. This process is defined not by the method of heating but by the degree of mutual filler-metal solution and diffusion with the base metal resulting from the temperature used, and the time interval at heat. Temperature, time, in some cases pressure, and selection of base and filler materials are so controlled that the filler metal is partially or totally diffused into the base metal. For example, a nickel filler metal with a solidus temperature of 960°C, when partially diffused at a temperature of 1095–1150°C, will have a remelt temperature in excess of 1370°C.

Brazing environment. Fluxes, gas atmospheres, and vacuum conditions promote formation of brazed joints. They may be used to surround the work, exclude reactants, and provide active or inert protective atmospheres, thus preventing undesirable reactions during brazing.

Fluxes. The primary purpose of brazing fluxes is to promote wetting of the base metal by the brazing filler metal. The efficiency of flux activity, which is commonly referred to as wetting, can be expressed as a function of brazeability. The flux must be capable of dissolving any oxide remaining on the base metal after it has been cleaned, and also any oxide films on the liquid filler metal. To effectively protect the surfaces to be brazed, the flux must completely cover and protect them until the brazing temperature is reached. It must remain active throughout the brazing cycle.

Many chemical compounds are used in the preparation of fluxes. When a flux is heated, reactions take place between the various chemical ingredients, forming new compounds at brazing temperatures that are quite different chemically and physically from the unreacted constituents. Composition of the flux must be carefully tailored to suit all the factors of the brazing cycle.

Controlled atmospheres. The second way to control the formation of oxides during brazing and also reduce oxides present after precleaning is to surround the braze area with an appropriate controlled atmosphere. Like fluxes, controlled atmospheres are not intended to perform primary cleaning for removal of oxides, coatings, grease, oil, dirt, or other foreign materials.

In controlled-atmosphere applications postbraze cleaning is generally not necessary. Controlled atmospheres for brazing fall into three broad categories: reducing atmospheres, inert atmospheres, and vacuum conditions. They are used extensively for high-temperature brazing.

Cleaning. Cleaning of all surfaces that are involved in the formation of the desired brazed joint is necessary to achieve successful and repeatable braze joining. The presence of contaminants on one or both surfaces may result in formation of voids, restriction or misdirection of filler-metal flow, and inclusion of contaminants within the solidified braze area.

Inspection techniques. Inspection of the completed assembly or subassembly is the last step in the brazing process and is essential for ensuring satisfactory and uniform quality of the brazed unit. This operation also provides a means of evaluating the adequacy with which the prior steps in the process have been carried out with regard to ultimate integrity of the brazed joint.

The inspection methods chosen to evaluate the brazing procedure and the serviceability of the product will be largely dependent on the service requirements of the brazed assembly.

Applications. A myriad of applications of brazing occur in many fields, including automotive and aircraft designs; engines and engine compo-nents; electron tubes, vacuum equipment, and nuclear components, such as production of reliable ceramic-to-metal joints; and miscellaneous applications such as fabrication of food-service dispensers (scoops) used for ice cream and corrosion-resistant and leakproof joints in stainless steel blood-cell washers. *See* WELDING AND CUTTING OF METALS.

Mel M. Schwartz

Bibliography. American Society for Metals, *Welding, Brazing, and Soldering*, vol. 6, 9th ed., 1993; American Welding Society, *Brazing Manual*, 4th ed., 1992; M. Schwartz, *Brazing for the Engineering Technologist*, 1995; M. Schwartz, *Joining Composite Materials*, 1994.

Breadboarding

Assembling an electronic circuit in the most convenient manner on a board or other flat surface, without regard for final locations of components, to prove the feasibility of the circuit and to facilitate changes when necessary. Standard breadboards for experimental work are made with mounting holes and terminals closely spaced at regular intervals, so that parts can be mounted and connected without drilling additional holes.

Printed-circuit boards having similar patterns of punched holes, with various combinations of holes connected together by printed wiring on each side, are often used for breadboarding when the final version is to be a printed circuit. *See* CIRCUIT (ELECTRONICS); PRINTED CIRCUIT. John Markus

Breadfruit

The multiple fruit of an Indo-Malaysian tree, *Artocarpus altilis*, of the mulberry family (Moraceae), now cultivated in tropical lowlands around the

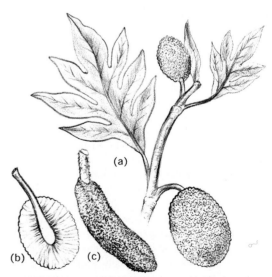

Breadfruit (*Artocarpus altilis*). (*a*) End of branch with multiple fruits. (*b*) Longitudinal section of multiple fruit. (*c*) Staminate flower cluster.

world (see **illus.**). Captain William Bligh was bringing plants from Tahiti to America when the mutiny on the *Bounty* occurred. The perianth, pericarp, and receptacle are all joined in a multiple fruit having a high carbohydrate content. The fruits vary considerably in size and are often borne in small clusters. Breadfruit is a wholesome food for both humans and animals. It is eaten fresh or baked, boiled, roasted, fried, or ground up and made into bread. There are many varieties, both with and without seeds. *See* URTICALES.   Earl L. Core

Breakdown potential

The potential difference at which an electrically stressed gas is tranformed from an insulator to a conductor. In an electrically stressed gas, as the voltage is increased, the free electrons present in the gas gain energy from the electric field. When the applied voltage is increased to such a level that an appreciable number of these electrons are energetically capable of ionizing the gas, the gas makes the transition from an insulator to a conductor; that is, it breaks down. The potential difference at which this transition occurs is known as the breakdown potential for the particular gaseous medium.

The breakdown potential depends on the nature, number density, and temperature of the gas; on the material, state, and geometry of the electrodes; on the type of voltage applied (steady, alternating, impulsive); and on the degree of preexisting ionization. Areas of surface roughness at the electrodes (especially the cathode) or the presence of conducting particles in the gas greatly reduces the breakdown potential because at such points the electric field is significantly enhanced, increasing the electron energies and thus gas ionization. The breakdown voltage varies considerably from one gaseous medium to another; it is very low for the rare gases, such as neon, for which a 0.394-in. (1-cm) uniform-field gap at 1 atm (101.3 kilopascals) breaks down at 0.53 kV; and very high for polyatomic, especially electronegative, gases such as sulfur hexafluoride (SF_6), for which a 0.394-in. (1-cm) uniform-field gap at 1 atm (101.3 kPa) breaks down at 88.9 kV.

The transition of a gas from an insulator to a conductor under an imposed electrical potential occurs in times ranging from milliseconds to nanoseconds, depending on the form of the applied field and the gas density. This transition depends on the behavior of electrons, ions, and photons in the gas, especially the processes which produce or deplete free electrons. Knowledge of these processes often allows prediction of the breakdown voltage of gases and the tailoring of gas mixtures which can withstand high electrical potentials for practical uses. *See* ELECTRICAL BREAKDOWN; ELECTRICAL CONDUCTION IN GASES.

Increasing the breakdown potential. Fundamental research on the microscopic physical processes which take place in an electrically stressed gas—especially those involving the interaction of slow (less than about 20 eV) electrons with atoms and molecules—has led to a better understanding of the electrical "breakdown" of gases. It has also led to the realization that an effective way of increasing the breakdown potential is to prevent the free electrons in the gas from initiating the breakdown by attaching them to gas molecules forming negative ions, which—being much heavier than the electrons—do not ionize the gas. (In such cases the breakdown potential can be defined as that value of the applied potential for which the rate of electron production by ionization is equal to the rate of electron depletion by attachment.) The ability of molecules to capture free electrons is large in the extreme low-energy range (less than about 1 eV) and decreases as the electron energy increases. For this reason, the gas itself—or an additive to it, as in a gas mixture—must be capable of reducing the energies of the free electrons and effectively scattering them into the low-energy region, where they can be captured most efficiently. Knowledge of the electron-scattering properties of gases permits selection of suitable gases for the slowing down of free electrons in dielectric gas mixtures. Combinations of two or more electron-attaching and electron-slowing-down gases have been developed in this manner which effectively control the energies and number densities of free electrons in electrically stressed gases. This approach allows the systematic identification of unitary gases (for example, sulfur hexafluoride and perfluorocarbons) and the systematic development of multicomponent gaseous dielectrics (for example, sulfur hexafluoride–nitrogen; perfluorocarbon–nitrogen; and sulfur exafluoride–perfluorocarbon–nitrogen) which are able to withstand very high potentials before breaking down and are suitable for many applications.

Applications. The systematic development of gaseous dielectrics with high dielectric strength (that is, high breakdown potential) is most significant for high-voltage technology, which has a multiplicity of gas insulation needs. Dielectric gases are widely used as insulating media in high-voltage transmission lines, circuit breakers, transformers, substations, high-voltage research apparatus, and other electrical equipment (such as Van de Graaff accelerators). In transmission lines the high-voltage conductor is held in place by solid insulators and is enclosed in a vacuum-tight pipe, the earthed electrode (often buried underground), which is filled with the insulating gas at pressures usually ranging from 1 to 10 atm (100 to 1000 kPa) depending on the voltage. The voltages in such systems can be higher than 1,000,000 V, resulting in considerable reduction of resistive losses and hence substantial energy savings. The use of compressed-gas–insulated transmission lines and other gas-insulated high-voltage electrical equipment is expected to continue increasing. *See* CIRCUIT BREAKER; DIELECTRIC MATERIAL; TRANSMISSION LINES.   L. G. Christophorou

Bibliography. L. G. Christophorou (ed.), *Gaseous Dielectrics VI*, 1991; L. G. Christophorou, D. R. James, and R. Y. Pai, Gas breakdown and high voltage insulating gases, in *Applied Atomic Collisions*, vol. 5, pp. 87–167, 1982; E. E. Kunhardt and L. H. Luessen (eds.), *Electrical Breakdown and Discharges in Gases*, vols. 89a and 89b, NATO Advanced Science Institutes Series, 1983; J. M. Meek and J. D. Craggs (eds.), *Electrical Breakdown in Gases*, 1978.

Breast

The human mammary gland, usually well developed in the adult female but rudimentary in the male. Each adult female breast contains 15–20 separate, branching glands that radiate from the nipple. During lactation their secretions are discharged through separate openings at the base of the nipple.

In both sexes paired ridges (milk lines) develop in the 6-week-old fetus and extend from the axilla downward, converging toward the abdomen. Most portions of the milk lines regress, leaving only slight prominences in the region destined to become the breasts. During the middle part of fetal life clusters of epidermal cells grow inwardly in these areas, forming cords which develop into hollow ducts. After birth slow increase in size and branching of each primary duct occurs. Development in the male usually ends at this stage. Supernumerary nipples or breasts along the milk lines are not rare. They are of minor clinical significance because they are usually rudimentary, but may constitute a severe cosmetic or psychic problem, which is readily amenable to surgery.

In the female, hormonal changes in adolescence cause enlargement of breast tissue, but much of this is connective tissue although some glandular buds form. With the advent of full menstruation ovarian estrogenic hormones influence breast development. If pregnancy ensues, the glandular tissue reaches full development and full lactation begins shortly after birth. After cessation of lactation the breasts regress considerably and once again reflect cyclic regulation. *See* MENSTRUATION; PREGNANCY.

Occasionally the male breasts will be stimulated by estrogens, possibly of adrenal origin. Liver disease may prevent normal destruction of estrogen so that gynecomastia (enlargement of breasts in the male) results.

The breasts of infants may respond to maternal hormones during the first few days or weeks of life, but regression usually occurs spontaneously. *See* LACTATION.   Walter Bock

Breast disorders

Benign and malignant lesions of the human mammary glands. Benign breast disorders are often symptomatic and bothersome but do not have malignant potential. Malignant disorders have the potential to grow locally in the breast and spread through the bloodstream to other parts of the body.

Physiologic changes. The breast is an organ that changes in response to fluctuations in hormone levels. Physiologic changes in the breast are often confused with disease. Fibrocystic disease, chronic cystic mastitis, and mammary dysplasia are terms that have been used to describe cyclical pain, tenderness, and lumpiness in the breast. These terms are imprecise and represent the normal physiologic responses to hormonal changes in the body rather than distinct clinical entities. Cyclic breast pain can occur in response to estrogens endogenous in premenopausal women or supplemental in postmenopausal women. Diffuse, palpable irregularities or lumps in the breast are also associated with this cyclical pain. Unlike malignant masses, however, these irregularities fluctuate in size and tenderness with the menstrual cycle, and are better described as physiologic nodularity of the breast. *See* MENOPAUSE.

Benign disorders. Common benign disorders include breast masses, cysts, gynecomastia, nipple discharge, and breast infections. Breast masses or dominant lumps are different from lumpiness; they are persistent over time and are palpably distinct from the surrounding breast tissue. They can develop in any age group and should be carefully evaluated. Mammography and ultrasound can help to determine the character of the mass, depending on the age of the patient.

Dominant lumps include fibroadenomas, gross cysts, pseudolumps, and cancer. Fibroadenomas may occur in any age group but are most commonly seen in young women. They are benign tumors consisting of smooth, rounded masses that are easily palpable in the breast. The cause is unknown; however, there is evidence to support the presence of an imbalance in circulating hormone levels that might be responsible for tumor growth. Breast cysts may be difficult to identify by physical examination or mammography, but can be distinguished from solid masses by using ultrasound imaging. Treatment of a cyst involves draining it with a small needle and syringe. If the cyst completely disappears, no further treatments are required. However, if the cyst remains or recurs or the cyst fluid is bloody, further examinations are required to rule out an underlying carcinoma. *See* MAMMOGRAPHY.

Gynecomastia, a benign enlargement of the male breast which can occur at any age and in one or both breasts, is a physiologic response to hormones, drugs, or an underlying medical condition. Nipple discharge does not always indicate a pathologic process; the character of the discharge is significant. A watery bilateral discharge from multiple ducts is usually normal. A milky discharge (galactorrhea) is often physiologic but sometimes can be associated with a tumor of the pituitary gland, which secretes prolactin. Unilateral, and especially spontaneous, nipple discharge generally signifies underlying pathology. Bloody nipple discharge is of most concern. About 80% of the time, however, the underlying cause is a benign papilloma within a duct. Breast infections are a common problem seen in both lactating and nonlactating individuals. *See* LACTATION.

Proliferative breast disorders include ductal and lobular hyperplasias. It is thought that some of these disorders might represent precancerous changes since they signal an increased risk for the development of breast cancer. Women who have hyperplasia without atypical cell changes have a mildly elevated risk for the subsequent development of breast cancer when they are compared with the general population. Women with atypical hyperplasia have a risk of developing breast cancer 4.4 times that of women without identifiable risk factors. This lesion is seen in only about 4–10% of breast biopsies. It does not characteristically form lumps or show up on mammography. Other benign neoplasms of the breast include adenomas, intraductal papillomas, adenosis, and radial sclerosing lesions.

Precancer. Ductal carcinoma is a precancer. It does not have the ability to disseminate throughout the body but can progress to an invasive carcinoma if left untreated. Once discovered, this lesion can be treated with breast conservation surgery, that is, excision of the tumor with a margin of normal tissue, with or without radiation, or with total mastectomy. Lobular carcinoma, however, is a misnomer since it is not a premalignant lesion but a marker for subsequent cancer. Women with lobular carcinoma who subsequently develop cancer do so in either breast with a relative risk 5.7 times that of the general population. Treatment options include close observation with physical examination and mammography, or bilateral mastectomies.

Cancer. Breast cancer is the most common cancer in women and is the second leading cause of cancer deaths among all American women, particularly in the fifth and sixth decades of life. Almost 80% of invasive carcinomas of the breast are of ductal origin; the remainder are lobular carcinomas or other special histologic types. Invasive ductal carcinomas can be subtyped if they have one or more characteristics of a specific histologic type, including tubular, medullary, papillary, or mucinous differentiation. When a large part of the tumor is differentiated into one of these subtypes, they generally carry a more favorable prognosis.

There are no significant differences in the rates of local recurrence and survival when breast conservation surgery is combined with radiation therapy to the breast as compared with total mastectomy. Removal of axillary lymph nodes continues to be an important tool in the staging and prognosis of invasive carcinomas of the breast. If axillary lymph node metastases are detected, systemic therapy is indicated to decrease the incidence of distant metastses, and will usually decrease the risk of mortality by one-third. Combination chemotherapy is generally recommended for premenopausal women, and its use has been extended to healthy postmenopausal women. Hormonal therapy is used to treat postmenopausal women with axillary lymph node metastases and hormone receptor positive tumors. Tamoxifen (an antiestrogen) is a hormonal agent which has been shown to decrease the risk of recurrence and the development of second primary tumors in postmenopausal women. *See* CANCER (MEDICINE); CHEMOTHERAPY.

Thirty percent of all women with negative lymph nodes will have developed micrometastases at the time of diagnosis and will eventually die of breast cancer. Chemotherapy or hormone therapy is therefore often recommended even for women with negative nodes. The use of chemotherapy or hormone therapy in women without axillary lymph node metastases is determined by multiple factors. The most important determinant is tumor size. Women with tumors greater than 2 cm (0.8 in.) in diameter, with negative axillary nodes, should receive systemic therapy. For individuals without axillary lymph node metastases and tumors less than 1 cm (0.4 in.) in diameter, the probability of relapse 10 years after diagnosis is less than 10%. Therefore, systemic chemotherapy is generally not recommended in this group.

Screening. Breast cancer screening is the most effective way of detecting breast cancer in its early stages. Screenings involve self-examination of the breast, physical examination, and mammography. The guidelines for when these examinations should be administered depend on the individual's age. A mammogram is the most reliable screening test for the early detection of breast cancer; mammograms are recommended every 2–3 years from age 40 to 50 and annually after age 50. As the density of the breast parenchyma changes with increasing age, mammography is better able to detect abnormalities within the breast.   Kelly K. Hunt; Susan M. Love

Bibliography. I. M. Ariel and A. C. Cahan, *Treatment of Precancerous Lesions and Early Breast Cancer: Diagnosis and Management*, 1993; J. R. Harris et al., *Breast Diseases*, 1991; D. F. Hayes (ed.), *Atlas of Breast Cancer*, 1993; P. A. Tavassoli, *Pathology of the Breast*, 1992; A. K. Tucker (ed.), *Textbook of Mammography*, 1993.

Breccia

A clastic rock composed of angular gravel-size fragments; the consolidated equivalent of rubble. The designation gravel-size refers to a mean particle diameter greater than 0.08 in. (2 mm), which means that 50% or more of the particles (by volume) are this size or larger. Various classifications specify different values for the degree of angularity. One system specifies angular or subangular fragments (roundness ≤ 0.25), whereas another restricts the term breccia to aggregates with angular fragments (roundness ≤ 0.10). *See* GRAVEL.

Most classifications recognize three major types of breccia: sedimentary, igneous, and cataclastic. Sedimentary breccias are characterized as exogenic, that is, formed by processes at the surface of the Earth, while igneous and cataclastic breccias are characterized as endogenic, that is, formed within the Earth. A minor exogenic type is impact breccia, which is formed by the impact of extraterrestrial bodies, such as meteorites and comets. This type is rare on Earth, but it is abundant on the Moon, Mercury, and other heavily cratered planetary bodies.

Sedimentary breccia. These breccias, referred to as sharpstone conglomerates according to one classification, are significant because the angularity of their fragments indicates either proximity to the source or transportation by a mechanism that does not cause significant rounding of the fragments. Examples of the first condition are talus breccia formed at the base of a scarp, and reef breccia deposited adjacent to a reef margin. Transport mechanisms that can preserve the angularity of clasts over significant distances include debris flows, slumps, and glacial transport, although rounded fragments may also be carried. All of these mechanisms incorporate a large proportion of fine sediment in the transporting medium, which effectively cushions interparticle collisions and inhibits rounding. *See* CONGLOMERATE; REEF; SEDIMENTOLOGY; TALUS.

Intraformational or intraclastic breccias are an important class of sedimentary breccias. They are formed by the breakup and incorporation of sediment aggregates from within the same formation, which requires either early cementation (for example, the formation of nodules or duricrusts) or uncemented aggregates sufficiently cohesive to be transported a short distance without disaggregation. Thus, uncemented aggregates are basically limited to sediments that are rich in clay or clay-size carbonates (calcilutites). The mechanisms for formation of intraformational breccias include bank slumping or desiccation fracturing of mud in river or tidal channels, and erosion and incorporation of mud blocks in mass flows such as slumps or turbidity currents. *See* SEDIMENTARY ROCKS.

Igneous breccia. These breccias are mainly of pyroclastic origin but may also form as intrusive breccias by forceful intrusion of magma. In the latter case the operative agent is fluid pressure; in the former it is the explosive escape of gas from solidifying viscous lava. These rocks, termed pyroclastic or volcanic breccias, are distinct from agglomerates, which accumulate mainly as lava bombs solidified during flight and which are commonly rounded. *See* PYROCLASTIC ROCKS.

Cataclastic breccia. These breccias result from the fracture of rocks by tectonic or gravitational stresses. However, since many tectonic processes are at least partly gravitational, the two processes can be considered together. Tectonic breccias in-

clude fault and fold breccias, the latter formed by fracturing of brittle layers within incompetent plastic strata during folding. In one classification, landslide and slump breccias are included in the gravitational category, but here they are considered to be sedimentary, commonly intraformational. Solution or collapse breccias are a type of nontectonic gravitational breccia. They result from the creation by ground-water solution of unsupported rock masses which collapse under their own weight to form breccia   Brain Rust

Bibliography. H. Blatt, *Sedimentary Petrology*, 2d ed., 1991; W. C. Krumbein and F. J. Pettijohn, *Manual of Sedimentary Petrography*, 1938, reprint 1988; D. W. Lewis and D. M. McConchie, *Practical Sedimentology*, 2d ed., 1993.

Breeding (animal)

The application of genetic principles to improving heredity for economically important traits in domestic animals. Examples are improvement of milk production in dairy cattle, meatiness in pigs, feed requirements or growth rate in beef cattle, and egg production in chickens. Even after thousands of years of domestication, domestic animals respond readily to selection. Selection permits the best parents to leave more offspring in the next generation than poor parents. Many specialized breeds and strains have been developed that are adapted to different environmental and economic conditions for the production of meat, fiber, milk, and draft.

The science of animal breeding is based on genetic principles; however, the current application of these principles relies heavily on statistical knowledge. Measurement of performance of individuals, such as growth rate or milk production, is essential. Use of computers has become an integral part of both animal breeding research and application. Modern computers allow the application of complicated statistical procedures to large volumes of performance data to choose the best individuals as parents of the next generation. Selection thus can be efficient.

Methods of selection. Selection is the primary tool for generating directed hereditary changes in animals. Selection may be concentrated on one characteristic, may be directed independently on several traits, or may be conducted on an index or total score which includes information on several important traits. The first method is most effective in generating improvement in the one chosen trait, but generates only correlated response in other traits. The second method, independent culling levels, generates greater overall improvement in total merit than the first, but is less effective for the chosen trait. The third method, index selection, generates maximum improvement by weighing each trait by its relative economic importance and by the observed or phenotypic and genetic relations among the traits. In some species, index selection has the disadvantage of delaying selection decisions until measurements are completed on all traits, taken at different times in the life of the animals.

In general, the second and third methods are preferable to the first when several important and heritable traits need attention. In practice, selection is likely to be a mixture of the second and third methods.

Accuracy of selection. Heritability, the fraction of the total variation in a trait that is due to additive genetic differences, is a key parameter in making decisions in selection. Traits for which environmental effects cause most of the variation are lowly heritable. Most traits are strongly to moderately influenced by environmental or managemental differences. So, managing animals to equalize environmental influences on them, or statistically adjusting for environmental differences between animals, is necessary to accurately choose those with the best inheritance for various traits.

The improvement achieved by selection is directly related to the accuracy with which the breeding values of the subjects can be recognized. Accuracy, in turn, depends upon the heritabilities of the traits and upon whether they can be measured directly upon the subjects for selection (mass selection), upon their parents (pedigree selection), upon their brothers and sisters (family selection), or upon their progeny (progeny testing). Mass selection is effective for traits with high heritability which are expressed before breeding age. Pedigree selection is most useful for traits which are expressed relatively late in life and for traits which are limited in expression to only one sex. Pedigree selection can never be highly accurate as compared with other kinds of selection, because a subject can have only two parents, a maximum of four different grandparents, and so on, whereas the number of siblings or progeny can be large. For traits of medium heritability, the following sources of information are approximately equally accurate for predicting breeding values of subjects: (1) one record measured on the subject; (2) one record on each ancestor for three previous generations; (3) one record each on five brothers or sisters where there is no environmental correlation between family members; and (4) one record each on five progeny having no environmental correlations, each from a different mate.

Artificial insemination is an effective tool for increasing the intensity of selection, especially in males. Artificial insemination allows one male to breed many more females than with natural mating. It has been most widely applied in dairy cattle, where carefully planned young sire sampling programs are being combined with thoroughly conducted progeny testing schemes to identify genetically superior sires. Superior dairy sires produce thousands of progeny. The use of artificial insemination with sheep and pigs has been limited to date but is increasing in beef cattle. Performance testing and family selection have played more important roles in the notable improvement in meatiness in pigs than has progeny testing.

Purebred breeds. Propagation of improved animal seed stocks is achieved primarily with purebred strains descended from imported or locally developed groups of animals which have been selected and interbred for a long enough period to be reasonably uniform for certain trademark characteristics, such as coat color. Each breed is promoted and sponsored by its farmer breeders organized as a purebred society. Because the number of breeding animals is finite and because breeders tend to prefer certain bloodlines and sires, some inbreeding occurs within the pure breeds, but this has not limited productivity in most of these breeds.

As a rule, each breed is characterized by certain easily identifiable characteristics, such as coat color, size and shape of ear, and horns or polledness. The genes controlling such traits are almost homozygous in breeds that have been subjected to intense selection for many generations. The frequency of genes influencing functional traits of economic importance is likely to be much lower for several reasons. First, functional characteristics, such as growth rate or milk production, are influenced by many genes, including those concerned with appetite, ability to obtain and digest food, temperament, disease resistance, and energy metabolism. Second, the effects of individual genes upon functional characteristics are likely to be small relative to the total variation. Hence, selection for improved performance changes the frequency of any one desired gene only slightly, although the cumulative improvement over many generations may be large. Third, selection has not always been consistently for the same goal, frequently changing intensity or direction as a consequence of changing styles or economic conditions.

Crossbreeding. The reason for crossbreeding is to make use of the genetic phenomenon of heterosis. Heterosis is noted when the performance of crossbred progeny exceeds the average performance of their parents. Most commercial pigs, sheep, and beef cattle are produced by crossbreeding. In rotational crossbreeding, females are mated to males of a different breed, and crossbred females are mated to males of a second breed, and so on until males of three or four breeds are used. The cycle is then repeated. Males are marketed, and enough females are retained for replacement stock. Terminal crossing is another type of crossbreeding. An example is the mating of females from breeds with superior mothering ability but average meatiness to males from breeds with superior meatiness and average mothering ability. This breeding technique results in more animals for market with a higher proportion of lean meat. *See* GENETICS.

New developments. New discoveries that have application or potential application for improving domestic animals are in four areas: statistical methodology, molecular genetics, immunogenetics, and reproductive physiology.

Statistical methods provide the data that enable choices of the superior animals to be parents for the next generation. A procedure called best linear unbiased prediction is widely used to accurately rank animals for their breeding value. In addition, it is possible to use information about all relatives of an individual to more accurately predict the breeding value of that individual. These statistical procedures allow unbiased ranking of animals, even if they are in different herds or flocks, provided they have relatives in common. These procedures are being used to evaluate all dairy cattle in the United States. A supercomputer is required to solve the 25 million equations that result from evaluating the cattle. These same procedures are also being used, but less extensively, to evaluate all domestic food-producing animals that have major economic importance.

Knowledge is available that has the potential to increase efficiency of food production. The use of bovine somatotropin (a naturally occurring hormone) can increase milk production by 10–20% and efficiency of converting feed to milk by 5–15%. Superovulation and embryo transfer is now commonly used in cattle. A superior cow can be made to produce several ova, which when fertilized can be transplanted to recipient cows to be carried to birth. This technique allows increasing the number of offspring from superior cows but is, as yet, too expensive for routine use.

Developments in the fields of immunobiology and molecular biology have great potential use. Vaccines are being developed that are more effective, and genetic lines and sires whose progeny have a greater resistance to disease are being sought. Transgenic animals, which have had cloned deoxyribonucleic acid (DNA) transplanted from one animal to another of the same species or to another of a different species, have potential usefulness. Injecting multiple copies of genes, from either the same or other species, could result in increased growth rates or increased protein content of milk. Hereditary defects could be alleviated. There are many ways in which application of such technology could eventually result in more efficient food production. There has not yet been much commercial impact from discoveries at the cellular and molecular level. Examples of knowledge that is available and has the potential to increase food production are use of bovine somatotropin, and superovulation combined with embryo transfer. Bovine somatotrophin is a naturally occuring hormone from cattle that can increase milk production by 10–20% and increase feed efficiency by 5–10%. Superior cows can be made to produce several ova, which can be fertilized and then transplanted to recipient cows. This practice is becoming more common for cows of superior merit. The use of genetically altered animals, plants, or microorganisms must be carefully screened for any potential harmful effects on humans or on the environment. Ultimately, new discoveries must be integrated with statistical procedures to develop the most useful breeding programs.

Developments in reproductive physiology could allow additional genetic gain. Breeders are interested in gain per unit of time. Thus, speeding up the time between generations allows less time between selecting offspring from superior parents. By mating one superior sire to several superior females, sets of full sisters (all born from a single mother and father) can be produced. The sets of full sisters are produced by superovulation and embryo transplantation. Half-sisters are also produced from a common sire but have different mothers. Pedigree selection using records from these full and half-sisters allows selecting parents of the next generation earlier compared with waiting for records on the new parents. Accuracy of selection may be reduced slightly, compared to direct selection on the new parents, but generation interval is decreased enough to more than compensate for the loss in accuracy, so the result is more genetic gain per unit of time. *See* AGRICULTURAL SCIENCE (ANIMAL); GENETIC ENGINEERING; REPRODUCTIVE SYSTEM.

A. E. Freeman

Bibliography. D. S. Falconer, *Introduction to Quantitative Genetics*, 2d ed., 1981; L. D. Van Vleck, E. J. Pollack, and E. A. B. Oltenacu, *Genetics for the Animal Sciences*, 1987.

Breeding (plant)

The application of genetic principles to the improvement of cultivated plants, with heavy dependence upon the related sciences of statistics, pathology, physiology, and biochemistry. The aim of plant breeding is to produce new and improved types of farm crops or decorative plants, to better serve the needs of the farmer, the processor, and the ultimate consumer. New varieties of cultivated plants can result only from genetic reorganization that gives rise to improvements over the existing varieties in particular characteristics or in combinations of characteristics. In consequence, plant breeding can be regarded as a branch of applied genetics, but it also makes use of the knowledge and techniques of many aspects of plant science, especially physiology and pathology. Related disciplines, like biochemistry and entomology, are also important, and the application of mathematical statistics in the design and analysis of experiments is essential. *See* GENETICS.

Scientific Method

The cornerstone of all plant breeding is selection. By selection the plant breeder means the picking out of plants with the best combinations of agricultural and quality characteristics from populations of plants with a variety of genetic constitutions. Seeds from the selected plants are used to produce the next generation, from which a further cycle of selection may be carried out if there are still differences. Much of the early development of the oldest crop plants from their wild relatives resulted from unconscious selection by the first farmers. Subsequent conscious acts of selection slowly molded crops into the forms of today. Finally, since the early years of the century, plant breeders have been able to rationalize their activities in the light of a rapidly expanding understanding of genetics and of the detailed biology of the species studies.

Conventional breeding is divided into three categories on the basis of ways in which the species are propagated. Species that reproduce sexually and that are normally propagated by seeds occupy two of these categories. First come the species that set seeds by self-pollination, that is, fertilization usually follows the germination of pollen on the stigmas of the same plant on which it was produced. The second category of species sets seeds by cross-pollination, that is, fertilization usually follows the germination of pollen on the stigmas of different plants from those on which it was produced. The third category comprises the species that are asexually propagated, that is, the commerical crop results from planting vegetative parts or by grafting. Consequently, vast areas can be occupied by genetically identical plants of a single clone that have, so to speak, been budded off from one superior individual. The procedures used in breeding differ according to the pattern of propagation of the species. While conventional methods involving crossbreeding have been used very successfully for several decades, several innovative techniques have been explored to enhance the scope, speed, and efficiency of producing new, superior cultivars. Advances have been made in extending conventional sexual crossing procedures by laboratory culture of plant organs and tissues and by somatic hybridization through protoplast fusion.

Self-pollinating species. The essential attribute of self-pollinating crop species, such as wheat, barley, oats, and many edible legumes, is that, once they are genetically pure, varieties can be maintained without change for many generations. When improvement of an existing variety is desired, it is necessary to produce genetic variation among which selection can be practiced. This is achieved by artificially hybridizing between parental varieties that may contrast with each other in possessing different desirable attributes. All members of the first hybrid (F_1) generation will be genetically identical, but plants in the second (F_2) generation and in subsequent generations will differ from each other because of the rearrangement and reassortment of the different genetic attributes of the parents. During this segregation period the breeder can exercise selection, favoring for further propagation those plants that most nearly match the breeder's ideal and discarding the remainder.

In this way the genetic structure is remolded so that some generations later, given skill and good fortune, when genetic segregation ceases and the products of the cross are again true-breeding, a new and superior variety of the crop will have been produced.

This system is known as pedigree breeding, and while it is the method most commonly employed, it can be varied in several ways. For example, instead of selecting from the F_2 generation onward, a bulk population of derivatives of the F_2 may be maintained for several generations. Subsequently, when all the derivatives are essentially true-breeding, the population will consist of a mixture of forms. Selection can then be practiced, and it is assumed, given a large scale of operation, that no useful segregant will have been overlooked. By whatever method they are selected, the new potential varieties must be subjected to replicated field trials at a number of locations and over several years before they can be accepted as suitable for commercial use.

Another form of breeding that is often employed with self-pollinating species involves a procedure known as backcrossing. This is used when an existing variety is broadly satisfactory but lacks one useful and simply inherited trait that is to be found in some other variety. Hybrids are made between the two varieties, and the F_1 is crossed, or backcrossed, with the broadly satisfactory variety which is known as the recurrent parent. Among the members of the resulting first backcross (B_1) generation, selection is practiced in favor of those showing the useful trait of the nonrecurrent parent and these are again crossed with the recurrent parent. A series of six or more backcrosses will be necessary to restore the structure of the recurrent parent, which ideally should be modified only by the incorporation of the single useful attribute sought from the nonrecurrent parent. Backcrossing has been exceedingly useful in practice and has been extensively employed in adding resistance to disease, such as rust, smut, or mildew, to established and acceptable varieties of oats, wheat, and barley. *See* PLANT PATHOLOGY.

Cross-pollinating species. Natural populations of cross-pollinating species are characterized by extreme genetic diversity. No seed parent is true-breeding, first because it was itself derived from a fertilization in which genetically different parents participated, and second because of the genetic diversity of the pollen it will have received. In dealing with cultivated plants with this breeding structure, the essential concern in seed production is to employ systems in which hybrid vigor is exploited, the range of variation in the crop is diminished, and only parents likely to give rise to superior offspring are retained.

Inbred lines. Here plant breeders have made use either of inbreeding followed by hybridization (see **illus.**) or of some form of selection. During inbreeding programs normally cross-pollinated species,

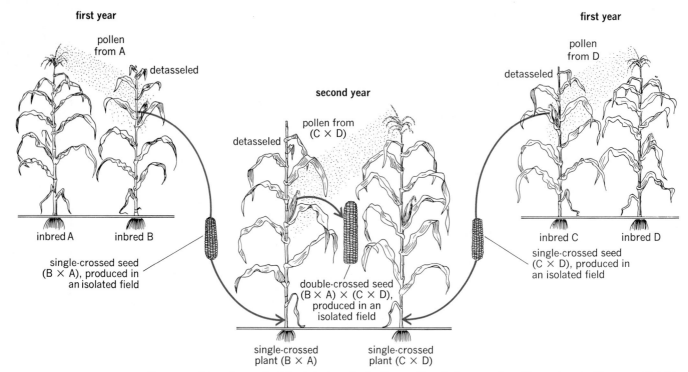

first year

pollen from A

detasseled

inbred A   inbred B

single-crossed seed (B × A), produced in an isolated field

second year

detasseled

pollen from (C × D)

double-crossed seed (B × A) × (C × D), produced in an isolated field

single-crossed plant (B × A)   single-crossed plant (C × D)

first year

pollen from D

detasseled

inbred C   inbred D

single-crossed seed (C × D), produced in an isolated field

Sequence of steps in crossing inbred plants and using the resulting single-crossed seed to produce double-crossed hybrid seed. (*Crops Research Division, Agricultural Research Service, USDA*)

such as corn, are compelled to self-pollinate by artificial means. Inbreeding is continued for a number of generations until genetically pure, truebreeding, and uniform inbred lines are produced. During the production of the inbred lines rigorous selection is practiced for general vigor and yield and disease resistance, as well as for other important characteristics. In this way desirable attributes can be maintained in the inbred lines, which are nevertheless usually of poor vigor and somewhat infertile. Their usefulness lies in the vigor, high yield, uniformity, and agronomic merit of the hybrids produced by crossing different inbreds. Unfortunately, it is not possible from a mere inspection of inbred lines to predict the usefulness of the hybrids to which they can give rise. To estimate their values as the parents of hybrids, it is necessary to make tests of their combining ability. The test that is used depends upon the crop and on the ease with which controlled cross-pollination can be effected.

Tests may involve top crosses (inbred × variety), single crosses (inbred × inbred), or three-way crosses (inbred × single cross). Seeds produced from crosses of this kind must then be grown in carefully controlled field experiments designed to permit the statistical evaluation of the yields of a range of combinations in a range of agronomic environments like those normally encountered by the crop in agricultural use. From these tests it is possible to recognize which inbred lines are likely to be successful as parents in the development of seed stocks for commercial growing. The principal advantages from the exploitation of hybrids in crop production derive from the high yields produced by hybrid vigor, or heterosis, in certain species when particular parents are combined.

Economic considerations. The way in which inbred lines are used in seed production is dictated by the costs involved. Where the cost of producing F_1 hybrid seeds is high, as with many forage crops or with sugarbeet, superior inbreds are combined into a synthetic strain which is propagated under conditions of open pollination. The commercial crop then contains a high frequency of superior hybrids in a population that has a similar level of variability to that of an open-pollinated variety. However, because of the selection practiced in the isolation and testing of the inbreds, the level of yield is higher because of the elimination of the less productive variants.

When the cost of seed is not of major significance relative to the value of the crop produced, and where uniformity is important, F_1 hybrids from a single cross between two inbred lines are grown. Cucumbers and sweet corn are handled in this way. By contrast, when the cost of the seeds is of greater significance relative to the value of the crop, the use of single-cross hybrids is too expensive and then double-cross hybrids (single cross A × single cross B) are used, as in field corn. As an alternative to this, triple-cross hybrids can be grown, as in marrow stem kale, in the production of which six different inbred lines are used. The commerical crop is grown from seeds resulting from hybridization between two different three-way crosses.

Recurrent selection. Breeding procedures designated as recurrent selection are coming into limited use with open-pollinated species. In theory, this method visualizes a controlled approach to homozygosity, with selection and evaluation in each cycle to permit the desired stepwise changes in gene frequency. Experimental evaluation of the procedure indicates that it has real possibilities. Four types of recurrent selection have been suggested: on the basis of phenotype, for general combining ability, for specific combining ability, and reciprocal selection. The methods are similar in the procedures involved, but vary in the type of tester parent chosen, and therefore in the efficiency with which different types of gene action (additive and nonadditive) are measured. A brief description is given for the reciprocal recurrent selection.

Two open-pollinated varieties or synthetics are chosen as source material, for example, A and B. Individual selected plants in source A are self-pollinated and at the same time outcrossed to a sample of B plants. The same procedure is repeated in source B, using A as the tester parent. The two series of testcrosses are evaluated in yield trials. The following year inbred seed of those A plants demonstrated to be superior on the basis of testcross performance are intercrossed to form a new composite, which might be designated A_1. Then B_1 population would be formed in a similar manner. The intercrossing of selected strains to produce A_1 approximately restores the original level of variability or heterozygosity, but permits the fixation of certain desirable gene combinations. The process, in theory, may be continued as long as genetic variability exists. In practice, the hybrid $A_n \times B_n$ may be used commercially at any stage of the process if it is equal to, or superior to, existing commercial hybrids.

Asexually propagated crops. A very few asexually propagated crop species are sexually sterile, like the banana, but the majority have some sexual fertility. The cultivated forms of such species are usually of widely mixed parentage, and when propagated by seed, following sexual reproduction, the offspring are very variable and rarely retain the beneficial combination of characters that contributes to the success of their parents. This applies to such species as the potato, to fruit trees like apples and pears that are propagated by grafting, and to raspberries, grapes, and pineapples.

Varieties of asexually propagated crops consist of large assemblages of genetically identical plants, and there are only two ways of introducing new and improved varieties. The first is by sexual reproduction and the second is by the isolation of sports or somatic mutations. The latter method has often been used successfully with decorative plants, such as chrysanthemum, and new forms of potato have occasionally arisen in this way. When sexual reproduction is used, hybrids are produced on a large scale between existing varieties with different desirable attributes in the hope of obtaining a derivative possessing the valuable characters of both parents. In some potato-breeding programs many thousands of hybrid seedlings are examined each year. The small number that have useful arrays of characters are propagated vegetatively until sufficient numbers can be planted to allow the agronomic evaluation of the potential new variety.

Ralph Riley

Special Techniques

Breeding for new, improved varieties of crop plants is generally based on cross-pollination and hybrid production. Such breeding is limited to compatible plants, that is, plants that permit cross-pollination, fertilization of the egg cell, and development of an embryo and seedling. Compatibility lessens with increasing distance in the relationship between plants. Breeding would benefit from access to traits inherent in sexually noncompatible plants. For instance, it is desirable to breed disease resistance from mustard (*Brassica nigra*) or oil quality of Meadow foam (*Limnanthes douglasii*) into rapeseed (*B. napus*). Special techniques, collectively referred to as biotechnology, are employed to overcome incompatibility barriers. Cell biology, molecular genetics, and biological chemistry are the scientific disciplines which nurture the development of special breeding techniques.

True-to-type reproduction of plant stock is another goal of plant breeding. Traditionally it is accomplished by cuttings, tubers, and bulbs, that is, asexually. Such technique applies, for example, to propagation of sugarcane, banana, potato, or lilies. Cell technologies have been used to extend the range and efficiency of asexual plant propagation. The process is often referred to as micropropagation. *See* PLANT PROPAGATION.

Cell technologies. The regeneration of entire, fertile or mature plants from single cells excised from a source plant and cultured in a nutrient medium in an incubator constitutes the primary goal of plant cell culture. Cell development leads either to shoot and root formation or to embryo (as in seeds) and plantlet formation. Cell technologies underlie all of the following special techniques. *See* TISSUE CULTURE.

Micropropagation and cloning. Cell technologies have been applied to mass propagation of a great number of species and varieties; particularly in the realm of horticulture. Conventionally, tissues rather than single cells are excised from root, stem, petiole, or seedling and induced to regenerate plantlets. All regenerants from tissues of one source plant constitute a clone. Nutrient formulas and growth conditions are specific for cells and tissues of each plant variety. Once sufficient growth has been achieved, plantlets are acclimatized to greenhouse and field conditions on location, or via air freight close to market. The Boston fern was one of the first plants to leave micropropagation labs and arrive in stores. High-priced ornamentals (for example, orchids) have been prime targets of micropropagation. Mass propagation of nursery stock has been aided by devices for automated processing (robotics).

Micropropagation has been used to eliminate virus from contaminated stock and is being practiced in quarantine stations. This technology has also been implemented in the restoration of natural habitats (propagation of *Cypripedium*) and of species on the brink of extinction. It complements other techniques whenever seed production of prototype plants is doubtful and asexual means of propagation are called for.

Microspore or anther culture. A technique of propagation particularly useful for plant breeders is the generation of plants from cells with but one set of chromosomes, haploid cells, as occurs in the development of pollen, referred to as microspore culture. Microspores are isolated from anthers and cultured on nutrient media, or entire anthers are cultured in this manner. Given properly conditioned source plants, a high-sugar nutrient medium, and growth conditions with specific temperature regimes, embryos may form directly or subsequent to callus formation. Doubling of chromosomes that may occur spontaneously or can be induced by treatment of callus, embryos, or plantlets with colchicine leads to the formation of homozygous di-haploid plants. Such material instantly stabilizes a (new) genotype, F-1plants, due to hybridization. *Brassica napus* (rapeseed), which responds to these techniques particularly well, enables several hundred microspores per macerated bud to develop into embryos. Anthers of certain barley varieties can yield up to 20 plantlets. Microspore culture relieves the plant breeder of several cycles of inbreeding to obtain pure lines. *See* POLLEN.

Cryopreservation. Regeneration of plants from cells and tissues opens new ways of preserving stock or germplasm. Treating pieces of tissue with cryoprotectants like sorbitol or dimethylsulfoxide followed by controlled freezing permits storage of such material in vials under low temperature ($-280°$F or $-196°$C) for years. Thereafter the tissues may be quickly thawed in a waterbath and, upon return to nutrient media, grown to plants. Shoot tips of a variety of horticultural species and of experimental plants are being preserved in this manner. Gene resources centers around the world have adopted cryopreservation as a standard practice. *See* CRYOBIOLOGY.

In vitro fertilization. Sexual incompatibility between plants can be caused by inadequate pollen tube growth and sperm cell development. Such problems could be overcome by in vitro fertilization. Compared to animal systems, in vitro fertilization in plants is compounded by the participation of the embryo sac, accessibility of the egg cell, and complementary function of auxiliary cells. Advances have led to the isolation of viable sperm cells from pollen tubes, the regeneration of plants from embryo sacs 1 day after fertilization, the electrofusion of sperm cells with isolated egg cells, and the injection of sperm cells into the embryo sac.

Embryo rescue. The excision and culture of embryos on nutrient media under in vitro conditions has become an important technique to overcome postfertilization problems, for example, deficiencies in the development of endosperm, the tissue that stores nutrients and surrounds the embryo. The younger the embryo, the more development depends on employing ovules rather than isolated embryos. The technique is used also to overcome natural seed dormancy or to accelerate seed germination. *See* SEED.

Somaclonal variation. Cells and tissues cultured on nutrient media may undergo spontaneous changes. Frequently these changes result in declining capacity for plant regeneration over time. Also, plants regenerated from cells cultured over several months may show increasing variation in phenotype. As a result, regenerated plants may become a pool for selection of plants with desirable traits. Introduction of such plants into a breeding program requires prior demonstration of the heritability of the variant trait by analysis of the progeny of the selected regenerant. A pool of di-haploid, homozygous plants with stable regenerants obtained by culturing microspores as in the case of rapeseed is preferred by breeders.

Somatic hybridization. Enzymatic removal of walls from cells of leaves and seedlings furnishes individual naked cells, that is, protoplasts. Naked cells permit the process of cell fusion. Exposure of protoplasts to electric current or to high concentrations of polyethylene glycol induces adhesion followed by fusion of cell membranes. Similarity of membrane structure throughout the plant kingdom permits the fusion of distantly related protoplasts. Fusion may lead to nuclear fusion prior to and during nuclear division, resulting in amphi-diploid somatic hybrid cells. Such fusion products may divide. Fusion products of closely related, yet sexually incompatible plants have been grown to flowering plants; the most famous example is the potato + tomato hybrid = pomato (*Solanum tuberosum* + *Lycopersicon esculentum*). These plants did not set seeds. Rapeseed (*Brassica napus*) obtained by conventional breeding has been recreated by somatic hybridization using protoplasts from *B. campestris* and *B. oleracea* Furthermore, intergeneric fertile hybrids have been obtained via protoplast fusion of various rapeseed (*Brassica*) plants with *Eruca, Sinapis,* and *Diplotaxis* species. The difference between artificial cross-pollination and fertilization is the fusion not only of nuclei but also of the cytoplasm with mitochondria and plastids of both parents. *See* PLANT CELL; SOMATIC CELL GENETICS.

DNA technologies. The development of technologies that enable the isolation of desirable genes from bacteria, plants, and animals (genes that confer herbicide resistance or tolerance to environmental stress, or encode enzymes and proteins of value to the processing industry) and the insertion of such genes into cells and tissues of target plants by direct or indirect uptake has led to the genetic transformation of plant cells. Desirable genes often are constructed to include regulatory deoxyribonucleic acid (DNA) sequences and genes which enable targeted expression, selection, and visualization of transformed cells and tissues.

Transformation technology began with the observation that nature practices this very process when crown-gall bacteria, which live in the soil, adhere to wounded tissue and release DNA with genes for hormone synthesis into neighboring nonwounded cells. The hormones subsequently drive the growth of the crown gall. In laboratories, this process is mimicked when the genes for hormones are excised from the extrachromosomal DNA of *Agrobacterium* and are replaced by desirable genes. Transformation of plant cells with this indirect method is widely used with plants which naturally respond to *Agrobacterium*, including dicotyledonous herbs and perennials, and trees like poplar. Cells and tissues of monocotyledonous plants (wheat, barley, corn, and rice) but also of conifers and a host of dicots are successfully transformed by an array of direct uptake and transformation processes, the most important of which is based on ballistic technology. Here, recombinant DNA is coated on microscopic particles of gold or tungsten, and these are introduced into cells under high velocity mediated either by gunpowder discharge or helium gas pressure. Initially, transformation success is measured by a response to products of selectable marker gene activity (such as resistance to antibiotics or pigmentation due to β-glucuronidase activity). *See* CROWN GALL; MOLECULAR BIOLOGY.

Assays for the expression of foreign genes in cells and tissues of target plants vary in technology: Southern blot analysis demonstrates the presence of the gene in a host genome; the Northern dot blot analysis, its transcription to ribonucleic acid (RNA); and the Western dot blot analysis, its translation into a gene product (protein or enzyme). The overall expression of a gene is regulated by associated genes that promote, enhance, or silence gene activity.

Transgenic plants. The regeneration of transformed plant cells and tissues results in new and novel genotypes to be assessed for transgenic phenotype. Contrary to hybrids obtained by cross-pollination, such plants are different from their parent by only one or two single, defined traits. Since the production of the first herbicide-resistant tobacco plant in 1985, transgenics of numerous species have successfully been grown and planted in field plots. Herbicide-resistant and insect pest–tolerant crops, both single-gene transgenics, have been entered into breeding programs and are close to commercialization.

Limitations to fast application of DNA technologies include the identification and isolation of useful genes, optimum combination with regulatory genes (promoters, enhancer sequences), the position of the transgene in the host genome, translation and fi-nal structure of the gene product, as well as survival of select transformed cells and refinement of nutrient and culture conditions for plant development and growth from these cells, avoiding of chimeric products. While DNA techniques generally add to or reinforce plant traits, suppression can also be valuable.

Trait changes based on the recombination of single genes represent state-of-the art biotechnology. Multigene traits such as yield or nitrogen fixation are too complex to manipulate and transfer. Still, genes can be introduced one at a time. Rapeseed plants with genes for male sterility and fertility restoration responding to different cues have been produced, and are being assessed for hybrid seed production.

DNA-based genetic diagnostics. Traditional plant breeding is based on selection of superior plants among segregating progeny of a cross. The selection is usually based on a visible or measurable phenotype (vigor, seed color, yield and disease resistance). Using DNA markers, which cosegregate with the genes of interest, allows for greater precision in breeding assessment. Analysis of DNA restriction fragment length polymorphisms (RFLPs) has become the method of choice. It is based on a variation in length of DNA fragments obtained after treatment of a given strand of DNA with restriction enzymes and visualized by electrophoresis. Molecular markers such as RFLPs have been tagged to specific agronomic traits such as disease resistance or male sterility. Generally, they are employed to map phenotypic traits, select superior plants, reduce the transfer of unwanted traits to hybrids (linkage drag), and fingerprint cultivars prior to patent application. The RFLP assay, however, is a laborious procedure, undesirable for breeding projects with high sample throughput. The random amplification of polymorphic DNA (RAPD) assay, however, is based on the use of short sequences of nucleotides as primers for the amplification through polymerase chain reaction of randomly selected segments of the target genome. RAPD markers have assisted in mapping a variety of traits with higher cost efficiency. The polymerase chain reaction is a technique for the enzymatic amplification of specific nucleotide sequences and results in an exponential increase in copies of such sequences. Apart from facilitating RAPDs, this technology promises to assist in reconstituting the genes of extinct species such as ancestors of present-day crop plants. *See* GENETIC ENGINEERING.

Friedrich Constabel

Bibliography. A. M. R. Ferrie, C. E. Palmer, and W. A. Keller, *In vitro Embryogenesis in Plants*, 1994; K. K. Kartha (ed.), *Cryopreservation of Plant Cells and Organs*, 1985; H. T. Stalker and J. P. Murphy, *Plant Breeding in the 1990s*, 1992; T. A. Steeves and I. M. Sussex, *Patterns in Plant Development*, 1989; I. K. Vasil (ed.), *Scale-up and Automation in Plant Propagation*, 1991; I. K. Vasil and T. A. Thorpe (eds.), *Plant Cell and Tissue Culture*, 1994.

Bremsstrahlung

In a narrow sense, the electromagnetic radiation emitted by electrons when they pass through matter. Charged particles radiate when accelerated, and in this case the electric fields of the atomic nuclei provide the force which accelerates the electrons. The continuous spectrum of x-rays from an x-ray tube is that of the bremsstrahlung; in addition, there is a characteristic x-ray spectrum due to excitation of the target atoms by the incident electron beam. The major energy loss of high-energy (relativistic) electrons (energy greater than about 10 MeV, depending somewhat upon material) occurs from the emission of bremsstrahlung, and this is the major source of gamma rays in a high-energy cosmic-ray shower. *See* COSMIC RAYS; ELECTROMAGNETIC RADIATION.

Properties. The spectrum of bremsstrahlung resulting from the collision of an electron with an atom is continuous and is roughly constant between $v = 0$ and $v = v_{max}$; v_{max} is the maximum frequency of a photon which can be emitted; that is, $h v_{max} = T$, where T is the initial kinetic energy of the electron and h is Planck's constant. The angular distribution of bremsstrahlung is roughly isotropic at low (nonrelativistic) electron energies, but is largely restricted to the forward direction at high energies. Very little bremsstrahlung is emitted at an angle much larger than $\theta_c = m_e c^2 / T$ radians, where m_e is the electron mass and c is the velocity of light. Bremsstrahlung emitted at the angle θ_c is polarized with the electric vector perpendicular to the plane containing the direction of radiation and the incident electron velocity. It is difficult to observe the polarization, because it is small except near the angle θ_c. A longitudinally polarized electron (that is, one with its spin parallel to its velocity) emits circularly polarized bremsstrahlung; this effect is not sensitive to angle, and has proved useful in analysis of the longitudinal polarization of electrons emitted in beta decay.

Synchrotron radiation. In a broader sense, bremsstrahlung is the radiation emitted when any charged particle is accelerated by any force. To a great extent, as a source of photons in the ultraviolet and soft x-ray region for the investigation of atomic structure (particularly in solids), bremsstrahlung from x-ray tubes has been replaced by synchrotron radiation. Synchrotron radiation is an analog to bremsstrahlung, differing in that the force which accelerates the electron is a macroscopic (large-scale) magnetic field. Like bremsstrahlung, the synchrotron radiation spectrum is continuous and slowly varying. The main advantage of synchrotron radiation light sources is that the spectrum is accurately calculable and is uncontaminated by spectral lines from atomic transitions. In addition, they have a much higher efficiency, that is, a larger ratio of brightness to power input. This is partly because the electrons' only loss of energy is the emission of the synchrotron radiation, but mainly because the nuclear electric fields which accelerate the electrons to produce bremsstrahlung also scatter the electrons, thus broadening the angular distribution of subsequently emitted photons. *See* SYNCHROTRON RADIATION.

Nonelectronic bremsstrahlung. Because all other charged particles are much heavier than the electron, their accelerations are generally much smaller and so their bremsstrahlung is generally much weaker. But although nonelectronic bremsstrahlung is not a useful source of photons, its observation can be a useful indicator of the accelerations undergone in a particular process. An example is proton–proton scattering; the rate of the process $p + p \rightarrow p + p + \gamma$ yields information on the p-p nuclear force. *See* PLASMA (PHYSICS).   Charles Goebel

Bibliography. A. Bienenstock and H. Winnick, Synchrotron-radiation research: An overview, *Phys. Today*, 36(6):48–58, 1983; W. Heitler, *The Quantum Theory of Radiation*, 3d ed., 1954; J. D. Jackson, *Classical Electrodynamics*, 2d ed., 1975; E. M. Rowe and J. H. Weaver, The uses of synchrotron radiation, *Sci. Amer.*, 236(6):32–41, 1977; Special issue on synchrotron radiation, *Phys. Today*, 34(5):27–71, 1983.

Brick

A construction material usually made of clay and extruded or molded as a rectangular block. Three types of clay are used in the manufacture of bricks: surface clay, fire clay, and shale. Adobe brick is a sun-dried molded mix of clay, straw, and water, manufactured mainly in Mexico and some southern regions of the United States. *See* CLAY; CLAY, COMMERCIAL.

The first step in manufacture is crushing the clay. The clay is then ground, mixed with water, and shaped. Then the bricks are fired in a kiln at approximately 2000°F (1093°C). A modern brick manufacturing plant includes a tunnel kiln that permits a nonstop firing process. Some older plants operate beehive kilns, which require periodic firing. After manufacture, the bricks are normally packaged into a steel-strapped cube with openings for handling by a forklift; this module generally contains 500 bricks. *See* REFRACTORY.

Substances in the clay such as ferrous, magnesium, and calcium oxides impart color to the bricks during the firing process. The color may be uniform throughout the bricks, or the bricks may be manufactured with a coated face. The latter are classified as glazed, claycoat, or engobe. Engobes are coatings, also called slurries, which are applied to plastic or dry body brick units to develop the desired color and texture. Claycoat is a type of engobe that is sprayed on as a coating of liquid clay and pigments.

Clay bricks are manufactured for various applications. In the United States the specifications are determined by the American Society for

Testing and Materials (ASTM).

The most commonly used brick product is known as facing brick. In the United States the standard dimensions (modular brick size) are $3^5/_8$ in. × $2^1/_4$ in. × $7^5/_8$ in. (90 mm × 57 mm × 190 mm). However, 11 other brick sizes are used for specific applications.

In addition to standard bricks, decorative bricks molded in special shapes are available in both standard and custom sizes. They are used to form certain architectural details such as water tables, arches, copings, and corners. Bricks are also used to create sculptures and murals.   Michael Gurevich

Bridge

A structure built to provide ready passage over natural or artificial obstacles, or under another passageway. Bridges serve highways, railways, canals, aqueducts, utility pipelines, and pedestrian walkways. In many jurisdictions, bridges are defined as those structures spanning an arbitrary minimum distance, generally about 10–20 ft (3–6 m); shorter structures are classified as culverts or tunnels. In addition, natural formations eroded into bridgelike form are often called bridges. This article covers only bridges providing conventional transportation passageways.

The longest single span provided by a bridge—the Humber suspension bridge in England—is 4626 ft (1410 m); the longest multiple-span bridge—the Lake Pontchartrain Causeway at New Orleans, Louisiana—126,055 ft (38,422 m).

History. Bridges undoubtedly have been built since the origin of humankind, perhaps first as trees felled over waterways and later as structures of timber or stone. The art of constructing stone bridges reached a high degree of development during the Roman era, and for a thousand years or so thereafter, it continued as an empirical art rather than a science. During the nineteenth century the theories of physics and mathematics were first applied to bridges in efforts to produce structures which would be rationally and economically proportioned to take the intended loads. During the midnineteenth century, with application of wrought iron as a material for construction (in the Brittania railway bridge in England), model testing and materials testing were initiated in a scientific manner. At this time, too, and continuing nearly until the end of the century, many firms in the United States developed proprietary bridges which were competitively peddled to railroads and governmental divisions. Eventually the failures of bridges, particularly railroad bridges, because of either faulty design or skimpy construction intended to lower cost, led in the 1880s to the establishment of consulting bridge engineering as a specialized discipline of civil engineering.

Parts. Bridges generally are considered to be composed of three separate parts: substructure, superstructure, and deck. The substructure or foundation of a bridge consists of the piers and abutments which carry the superimposed load of the superstructure to the underlying soil or rock. The superstructure is that portion of a bridge lying above the piers and abutments. The deck or flooring is supported on the bridge superstructure; it carries and is in direct contact with the traffic for which passage is provided.

Types. Bridges are classified in several ways. Thus, according to the use they serve, they may be termed railway, highway, canal, aqueduct, utility pipeline, or pedestrian bridges. If they are classified by the materials of which they are constructed (principally the superstructure), they are called steel, concrete, timber, stone, or aluminum bridges. Deck bridges carry the deck on the very top of the superstructure. Through bridges carry the deck within the superstructure. The type of structural action is denoted by the application of terms such as truss, arch, suspension, stringer or girder, stayed-girder, composite construction, hybrid girder, continuous, cantilever, or orthotropic (steel deck plate), prestressed, or segmental (concrete).

The main load-carrying member or members of a bridge are almost invariably parallel to the alignment of the bridge. When the alignment of the bridge and the obstacle being bridged are not square with one another, the main structural members may not be opposite one another, and the deck may be a parallelogram in plan; in this case the bridge is said to be a skewed bridge. Otherwise, it is known as square.

Many bridges are also designed on horizontally curved alignments to conform with curved approach roadways.

The two most general classifications are the fixed and the movable. In the former, the horizontal and vertical alignments of the bridge are permanent; in the latter, either the horizontal or vertical alignment is such that it can be readily changed to permit the passage beneath the bridge of traffic, generally waterbound, which otherwise could not pass because of restricted vertical clearance. Movable bridges are sometimes called drawbridges in reference to an obsolete type of movable bridge spanning the moats of castles.

A singular type of bridge is the floating or pontoon bridge, which can be a movable bridge if it is designed so that a portion of it can be moved to permit the passage of water traffic.

The term trestle is used to describe a series of stringer or girder spans supported by braced towers or bents, and the term viaduct is used to describe a structure of many spans, often of arch construction.

Fixed Bridges

Fixed-bridge construction is selected when the vertical clearance provided beneath the bridge exceeds the clearance required by the traffic it spans. For very short spans, construction may be a solid slab or a number of beams; for longer spans, the choice may be girders or trusses. Still longer spans may dictate the use of arch construction, and if the spans are even longer, stayed-girder bridges are used. Suspension bridges are used for the longest spans.

Each of the above types of bridge is generally designed so that the substructure, superstructure, and deck are each considered to carry only the loads directly imposed upon them. In certain types of construction, the deck and the main load-carrying superstructure members are made to participate in carrying the load in order to make the bridge more economical than ordinary stringer or girder bridges with a concrete deck. This is known as composite or hybrid construction, depending upon the type of stringers. If there is stringer or girder-type construction, with a deck partly of steel topped by an asphalt surfacing material, the bridge is known as an orthotropic bridge. When the substructure and superstructure act together, the bridge is described as being of rigid frame construction.

The longer the span of a bridge, the greater is the relative cost per unit of deck area.

The choice of type of bridge superstructure may depend not only on the obstacle to be spanned but also on the substructure. Thus, if an expensive substructure is required because of water depth or unsatisfactory foundation conditions, the selection of a longer-span superstructure may be indicated even though it may not in itself be the economical choice.

Beam bridge. Beam stringer bridges consist of a series of beams, usually of rolled steel, supporting the roadway directly on their top flanges. The beams are placed parallel to traffic and extend from abutment to abutment. When foundation conditions permit the economical construction of piers or intermediate bents, a low-cost multiple-span structure can be built. Spans of 50 ft (15 m) for railroad beam bridges and 100 ft (30 m) for highway beam bridges may be economical.

Composite I-beam bridges are beam bridges in which the concrete roadway is mechanically bonded to the I beams by means of shear connectors, which develop horizontal shear between the concrete slab and the beam. Such a connection forces a portion of the slab to act with the beam, resulting in a composite T beam. This construction yields a saving in the weight of the beams. Rolled shapes such as the channel, angle, and I, bars in serpentine form or in the form of a longitudinal helix, and steel studs are used as shear connectors. These connectors are usually welded to the flange of the steel beam and should extend at least halfway into the slab. *See* COMPOSITE BEAM.

Plate-girder bridge. Plate-girder bridges are used for longer spans than can be practically traversed with a beam bridge. In its simplest form, the plate girder consists of two flange plates welded to a web plate, the whole having the shape of an I.

The railroad deck plate-girder bridge consists of two girders which support the floor system for a single track directly on their top flanges. A double-track bridge usually consists of two single-track bridges placed side by side on common abutments or piers. Through plate-girder bridges are used when clearance below the structure is limited. For railroad traffic, the floor system consists of a number of transverse floor beams which are supported by the girders just above their lower flanges. *See* PLATE GIRDER.

Box-girder bridge. Steel girders fabricated by welding four plates into a box section have been used for spans from 100 to more than 850 ft (30 to 259 m). The Rhine River crossing at Cologne, Germany, is an example of an 850-ft (259-m) span. In the United States, a 750-ft (229-m) box-girder span is used in the San Mateo–Hayward Bridge in California. Conventional floor beams and stringers can be used on box-girder bridges, but the more economical arrangement is to widen the top flange plate of the box so that it serves as the deck. When this is done, the plate is stiffened to desired rigidity by closely spaced bar stiffeners or by corrugated or honeycomb-type plates. These stiffened decks, which double as the top flange of the box girders, are termed orthotropic. The wearing surface on such bridges is usually a relatively thin layer of asphalt. Single lines of box girders with orthotropic decks can be used for two-lane bridges, but when wider decks are required, two or more box-girder bridges can be placed parallel to each other.

Curved-girder bridge. Bridges on curved roadways present special problems. Such bridges must be deck bridges. For lightly curved roadways, or when the spans are short, straight stringers or girders usually are used and are positioned under the roadway parallel to a chord of the circular arc of the roadway. When the spans are long or when the curved roadway is of short radius, girders that are curved horizontally are used. These girders parallel the curved edges of the roadway. Sometimes curved girders are chosen for esthetic considerations even when straight girders might be practical, because straight girders on curved bridges are sometimes considered unattractive.

Prior to 1961 there were only a few curved-girder bridges. Both their design and fabrication are difficult, and their erection can be troublesome. Their design involves not only the usual vertical bending forces but also torsional forces caused by the unbalanced loading of a span whose supports are offset from its center of gravity. Early in their use, design was somewhat empirical and overly conservative. However, development of reliable computer programs for curved-girder design has made the use of curved girders more practical.

In addition to individual curved girders, curved steel box girders and curved concrete box girders are used.

Truss bridge. Truss bridges, consisting of members vertically arranged in a triangular pattern, can be used when the crossing is too long to be spanned economically by simple plate girders. Where there is sufficient clearance underneath the bridge, the deck bridge is more economical than the through bridge because the trusses can be placed closer together, reducing the span of the floor beams. For multiple spans, a saving is also effected in the height of piers. *See* TRUSS.

Through-truss. A through-truss bridge is illustrated in **Fig. 1**. The top and bottom series of truss members parallel to the roadway are called top chords and bottom chords, respectively. The diagonals and verticals form the web system and connect the top and bottom chords. The point at which web members and a chord intersect is called a panel point. Gusset plates connect the members intersecting at a panel point.

Lateral bracing of a bridge ties the two trusses together and assures a stable and rigid structure. The top lateral bracing consists of cross struts connecting the top chords at opposite panel points and the diagonals joining the diagonally opposite ends of adjacent cross struts. It decreases the unsupported length of the top chord members, reducing the cross-sectional area they require. The floor beams and the diagonals connecting the opposite ends of adjacent floor beams constitute the bottom lateral system. Although the floor system of a highway bridge can take over the function of a lateral truss, the lateral bracing must be provided to stiffen the structure during erection and to furnish wind resistance until the steel or concrete floor slab is in place.

The stringers of an open-floor railroad bridge must be braced to relieve them of bending due to lateral forces from the train. In addition, the floor beams should be provided with bracing to relieve the bending due to tractional forces.

Portal and sway bracing are systems of bracing in transverse vertical planes of a bridge. Intermediate sway frames in the plane of opposite verticals give added rigidity.

The end posts of the through-truss bridge are tied together to form a rigid frame or portal capable of transferring the end reaction of the top lateral system to the abutments. To keep the bending stresses in the end posts as small as possible and to provide a rigid portal, portal bracing should be as deep as headroom allows. Also, the end post should be braced by brackets or diagonal members.

Simple-span trusses. Common types of simple-span bridge trusses are shown in **Fig. 2**. The Pratt truss, with its various modifications (Fig. 2a and b), has tension diagonals and compression verticals. The diagonal in every other panel of a Warren truss (Fig. 2c–e) is in compression. The depth of short-span trusses is usually determined by the depth necessary for clearance at the portal. For long spans, it is usually economical to make the depth of the truss greater at the center than at the ends. If the depth is increased in proportion to the increase in the forces tending to bend the bridge, the force in the chord members can be more nearly equalized. Figure 2b shows a curved-chord Pratt truss.

Trusses of economical proportions usually result if the ratio of depth of truss to length of span is approximately 1:5 to 1:8 and if the diagonals make angles of 45–60° with the horizontal. The panel length produced in long-span trusses when both of these factors are considered results in an uneconomical floor system. Subdivided trusses (Fig. 2f–h) are used to get reasonable length panels.

Arch bridge. In an arch bridge the main structural system supporting the deck is a curved member (or members), higher vertically at its center than its ends, acting almost entirely in compression, with this compressive load being maintained by thrust against immovable abutments. Arch bridges have been constructed of stone, brick, timber, cast iron, steel, and reinforced concrete, all of which can adequately take compressive loads. Sophistication of construction of stone masonry arch bridges reached a peak during the nineteenth century, spurred by road improvements, and the construction first of canals and then of railroads. Cast iron as a construction material was introduced at this time. *See* ARCH.

Stone masonry arch bridges are rarely constructed anymore. Almost all modern arch bridges are constructed of steel or reinforced concrete, and occasionally of timber. Also, the main structural load-carrying arch system in a modern bridge consists of a number of ribs, generally two, supporting a deck by columns, termed spandrel columns, or by suspenders, in place of the single barrel of stone masonry construction supporting the deck by walls and earth fill, termed spandrel fill. Thus the road carried by the arch no longer must be above the arch ribs, as in the stone masonry construction, but can pass between the ribs similar to through-truss spans. The choice of arch construction depends largely on foundation conditions at the site,

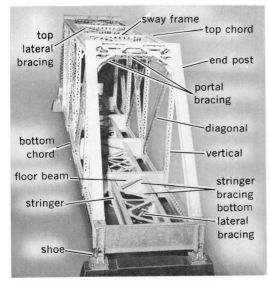

Fig. 1. Model of a through-truss railroad bridge.

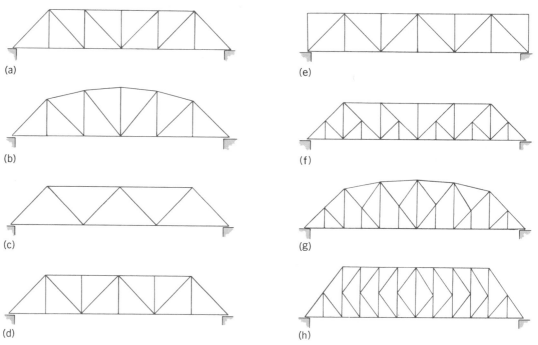

Fig. 2. Examples of simple-span trusses. (*a*, *b*) Pratt trusses. (*c–e*) Warren trusses. (*f–h*) Subdivided trusses.

as they must be suitable to economically take the tremendous thrust of the arch ribs. A deck-type arch generally would be used only if the ground level was high at the site, such as at a gorge, in order to obviate long approaches. *See* REINFORCED CONCRETE; STRUCTURAL STEEL.

Arches of steel have reached a maximum span of 1700 ft (518 m) in a bridge over the New River in West Virginia, and arches of concrete a span of 1000 ft (305 m) in the Gladesville Bridge over the Parramatta River at Sydney, Australia. Spans of less than about 150 ft (46 m) generally are not economical because the cost of construction of the

Fig. 3. Lewiston-Queenston Bridge over Niagara River. (*Niagara Falls Bridge Commission and Hardesty & Hanover*)

curved arch ribs far exceeds any advantage of an arch over other types of bridges for such short spans.

Ribs. The ribs of an arch bridge terminate at inclined faces, termed skewbacks, of the bridge abutments. While arch ribs are essentially compression members, they are also subjected to bending due to partial live loadings, expansion or contraction due to temperature changes, contraction due to shrinkage in the case of concrete ribs, and the transfer of the deck load to the rib at discrete locations. However, the geometrical shape of the vertical curve of the arch ribs is selected to fit the conditions of the site and the loadings so that ribs act mainly as compression members, and then, for the bending, to make sure that no stress exceeds the allowable. The arch ribs of concrete arch bridges are of reinforced concrete, rectangular in section, varying in depth or width from crown to abutment. The ribs of steel arch bridges may be box-shaped in section, of constant width and depth, but varying in thicknesses of steel material from crown to abutment; or, like a truss bridge with bottom and top chord sections with web members, the ribs may be of constant depth, but varying in chord section from crown to abutment. In all cases, since the ribs are compression members, they generally are braced one to the other.

Hinges. If the arch rib extends continuously from skewback to skewback, and is fixed at the skewbacks so no rotation can occur, the bridge is called a fixed arch. An example is shown in **Fig. 3**. If devices known as hinges are introduced in the arch ribs, the bridge is called a two- or three-hinged arch. The three-hinge arch has hinges at the center (or crown of the rib) and at the skewbacks, and the two-hinged arch has hinges only at the skewbacks. These hinges permit the transfer of axial compressive loads from one section of arch rib to another or to the abutments without transfer of bending moments.

The choice of the number of hinges depends on several considerations. Hinges at the skewbacks simplify the abutment design; and hinges at crown and skewbacks simplify the design of the arch rib as well as the abutment, eliminate stresses due to change in temperature, and allow the arch to tolerate minor movements of the abutments. The fixed arch is more rigid, but much more difficult to analyze, and requires the abutment to take bending loads. Arch bridges have been built in all three types, and also with a single hinge at the crown.

Fig. 4. Some major United States bridges. (a) Greater New Orleans cantilever bridge, across the Mississippi River (*Bethlehem Steel Co.*). (b) Looking from south tower during construction of Mackinac Bridge, connecting upper and lower peninsulas of Michigan (*Mackinac Bridge Authority*). (c) Verrazano-Narrows Bridge, New York City (*Triborough Bridge and Tunnel Authority*). (d) Vertical-lift span and swing bridge across Arthur Kill, between Staten Island and New Jersey. The vertical-lift bridge replaced the swing bridge, in use since 1888 (*Baltimore and Ohio Railroad Co.*).

Tied arches. While most arch bridges have abutments to take the thrust of the arch action, there are a number in which one end of the arch rib is tied to the other with a structural tension member to take the thrust of the rib. These are called tied arches. Usually these are through-arches; the tie is at about deck level and the deck is suspended from the arch rib. These spans may also be a part of another type of construction, a bridge with cantilever and anchor spans, and the tied arch suspended from the cantilever spans, known as a tied arch cantilever.

Continuous bridge. The continuous bridge is a structure supported at three or more points and capable of resisting bending and shearing forces at all sections throughout its length. The bending forces in the center of the span are reduced by the bending forces acting oppositely at the piers. Trusses, plate girders, and box girders can be made continuous. The advantages of a continuous bridge over a simple-span bridge (that is, one that does not extend beyond its two supports) are economy of material, convenience of erection (without need for falsework), and increased rigidity under traffic. Its relative economy increases with the length of span. No increase in rigidity is obtained by making more than three spans continuous. The disadvantages are its sensitivity to relative change in the levels of supporting piers, the difficulty of constructing the bridge to make it function as it is supposed to, and the occurrence of large movements at one location due to thermal changes.

Cantilever bridge. The cantilever bridge consists of two spans projecting toward each other and joined at their ends by a suspended simple span. The projecting spans are known as cantilever arms, and these, plus the suspended span, constitute the main span. The cantilever arms also extend back to shore, and the section from shore to the piers offshore is termed the anchor span (**Fig. 4**a). Trusses, plate girders, and box girders can be built as cantilever bridges.

The chief advantages of the cantilever design are the saving in material and ease of erection of the main span, both of which are due to the fact that no falsework is needed. By adding continuity of members after erection, the cantilever bridge is made to act as a continuous structure under live load. *See* CANTILEVER.

Cable-stayed bridge. A modification of the cantilever lever bridge which has come into modern use resembles a suspension bridge, and it is termed a cable-stayed bridge. It consists of girders or trusses cantilevering both ways from a central tower and supported by inclined cables attached to the tower at the top or sometimes at several levels (**Fig. 5**). Usually two such assemblies are placed end to end to provide a bridge with a long center span.

Suspension bridge. The suspension bridge is a structure consisting of either a roadway or a truss suspended from two or more cables which pass over two towers and are anchored by backstays to a firm foundation (Fig. 4b and c). If the roadway is attached directly to the cables by suspenders, the structure lacks rigidity, with the result that wind loads and moving live loads distort the cables and produce a wave motion on the roadway. When the roadway is supported by a truss which is hung from the cable, the structure is called a stiffened suspension bridge. The stiffening truss distributes the concentrated live loads over a considerable length of the cable.

Cables of the larger sizes, such as those up to 36 in. (91 cm) in diameter used for the George Washington Bridge in New York City, are assembled (or spun) in the field by using pencil-thick wires laid parallel. For smaller cables, strands of wire wound spirally in the factory are assembled into cables. Factory-made strands of parallel wires were used for the first time in 1968 for the 15-in.-diameter (38-cm) cables of the Newport Bridge in Rhode Island.

The longest bridge spans in the world are all of the suspension type. The longest main spans occur in the Humber Bridge of England (4626 ft or 1410 m), the Verrazano-Narrows Bridge in New York City (4260 ft or 1298 m; Fig. 4c), the Golden Gate Bridge in San Francisco (4200 ft or 1280 m), and the Mackinac Bridge in northern Michigan (3800 ft or 1158 m). The Akashi Strait Bridge in Japan, scheduled for completion in 1998, with a 6633-ft (2022-m) center span, will be the world's longest suspension bridge.

Pontoon bridge. The pontoon bridge is a floating bridge supported by pontoons. The structure may be a temporary one, as for military usage, or a permanent one, if the level of the water can be carefully controlled. A pontoon bridge may be advantageous where deep water and adverse bottom conditions make piers expensive. Seattle's Lake Washington is crossed by three floating concrete bridges. Typically, the pontoons are 360 ft (110 m) long, 60 ft (18 m) wide, and 14.5 ft (4.4 m) deep. A 378-ft (115-m) pontoon is used as a floating draw span to give a clear channel opening 200 ft (61 m) wide. Adjacent pontoons are bolted together, and each is secured by a pair of anchors, one on each side. Cast-in-place reinforced concrete was used for the pontoons of the first bridge, but the later bridges are of prestressed concrete.

Concrete bridge. The bridges that have been discussed above are usually made of steel, although they may carry a concrete roadway. Increasingly, however, since the development of the prestressing method, bridges of almost every type are being constructed of concrete. Prior to the advent of prestressing, these bridges were of three types: (1) arch bridges, which were built in either short or long spans, even up to 1000 ft (305 m) for the Gladesville Bridge in Sydney, Australia; (2) slab bridges of quite short spans, which were simply reinforced concrete slabs extending from abutment to abutment; and (3) deck girder bridges, consisting of concrete slabs built integrally with a series of concrete girders placed parallel to traffic. The

Fig. 5. Sunshine Skyway Bridge in Tampa, Florida. (*Florida Department of Transportation and Figg and Muller Engineers, Inc.*)

advent of prestressed concrete greatly extended the utility and economy of concrete for bridges, particularly by making the hollow box-girder type practicable. One of the longest such spans, 682 ft (208 m), is in a bridge over the Rhine River near Koblenz, Germany. *See* PRESTRESSED CONCRETE.

The objective in prestressing concrete is to reduce or eliminate tensile stresses in the concrete by applying a force that greatly increases internal compressive stress in the concrete member. The force is applied by stretching the reinforcing tendons, which may be either wires or bars, by means of hydraulic jacks that react against the ends of the concrete member. Prestressing may be done to precast members, or it may be done as the concrete is being placed in the field. It may be done by either pretensioning or posttensioning. In pretensioning, the reinforcing tendons are stretched prior to the placing of the concrete. In posttensioning, the reinforcing tendons are installed in tubes so that they are isolated from the concrete while it is being placed. When the concrete hardens, the tendons are stretched by jacks reacting against and compressing the concrete member.

Bridge bearings. Almost all bridges have devices known as bearings or shoes where the superstructure transfers its vertical and horizontal loads to the substructure. Exceptions can be arch bridges, rigid frame bridges, and suspension or cable-stayed bridges, where other devices or actions obviate the need of bearings. These bearings are either fixed, expansion, or sliding. All the main structural members of a single-span bridge—the stringers, girders, and trusses—have a fixed bearing at one end of the support and an expansion bearing at the other. Multiple-span bridges have a single fixed bearing and one or two expansion bearings and sliding bearings between fixed and expansion bearings on each main structural member.

The fixed bearing transfers not only vertical loads

to the substructure but also the longitudinal horizontal wind or traffic tractive forces. The expansion bearing takes vertical loads but allows longitudinal movements of the end of the member it supports. These movements are caused by temperature changes and changes in the length of the span caused by loadings. Sliding bearings function similarly. All bearings accommodate rotation of the ends of the span when the span or spans deflect under loading. Also, all bearings transfer transverse wind forces from the superstructure to the substructure of the bridge.

Depending on the span of the bridge, bearings can vary from simple steel plates curved on their undersides, one of which slides, to large cast-steel devices with a rocker, or nest of cylindrical rollers at the expansion bearing.

Expansion bearings are one of the most troublesome parts of the bridge as they are exposed to deterioration from moisture and debris sifting down from expansion openings in the bridge deck. In fact, a few single- and multiple-stringer bridges have been built experimentally without bearings, depending upon the restraint of the bridge abutments and the reversed stress induced in the superstructure to substitute for allowed expansion.

Also, since the mid-1960s bearings known as elastomeric bearings have been used for spans up to about 100 ft (30 m). These are blocks of resilient synthetic rubber which deform to accommodate the expansion and rotational forces.

Movable Bridges

Modern movable bridges are either bascule, vertical lift, or swing; with few exceptions, they span waterways. They are said to be closed when they are set for the traffic they carry, and open when set to permit marine traffic to pass through the waterway they cross.

Both bascule and vertical-lift bridges operate well and reliably. Sometimes the bascule is chosen

Fig. 6. Stanley Stroffolino Bridge in Norwalk, Connecticut. (*Connecticut Department of Transportation and Hardesty & Hanover*)

because its appearance may be pleasing and creates less of a visual impact than do the towers and ropes of vertical-lift bridges.

Swing bridges are now considered almost obsolete because the center pier, on which the span rotates, occupies the portion of the waterway that is most desirable from the standpoint of mariners. However, one feature of a swing bridge, which dictates its use near airports, is that it does not encroach on flight paths as would the towers of lift bridges or the raised leaves of bascule bridges.

Bascule, swing, and lift bridges may be of either stringer, girder, or truss construction, depending

upon the length of their span.

Other types of movable spans, such as the retractable, are generally obsolete.

Bascule and swing bridges provide unlimited vertical clearance in the open position, whereas the vertical clearance of a lift bridge is limited by its design.

Bascule bridge. The bascule bridge consists primarily of a cantilever span, which may be either a truss or a plate girder, extending across the channel (**Fig. 6**). This type is generally chosen for spans up to about 175 ft (53 m) for highway use. Because of the large deflection of the cantilevered leaves of the double-leaf bascule, which is excessive under railway loadings and intolerable to railroad operation, bascule spans for railway usage are exclusively single-leaf bridges with maximum spans of about 250 ft (76 m).

Bascule bridges rotate about a horizontal axis parallel with the waterway. The portion of the bridge on the land side of the axis, carrying a counterweight to ease the mechanical effort of moving the bridge, drops downward, while the forward part of the leaf opens up over the channel much like the action of a playground seesaw. Bascule bridges may be either single-leaf, where the entire leaf rotates over the waterway about a single axis on one side of the waterway, or double-leaf, where two leaves over the waterway rotate about two different axes on opposite sides of the waterway. The two leaves of double-leaf bascule bridges are locked together where they meet when the bridge is closed. If the bridge actually rotates about an axis, it is called a trunnion-type bascule. If it rolls back on a track, it is called a rolling lift span.

Vertical-lift bridge. The vertical-lift bridge has a span similar to that of a fixed bridge, and is lifted by steel ropes running over large sheaves at the tops of its towers to the counterweights, which fall as the lift span rises and rise as it falls. If the bridge is operated by machinery on each tower, it is known as a tower drive. If it is driven by machinery located on the lift span, it is known as a span drive. The 585-ft (178-m) span of the lift bridge over the Arthur Kill, an arm of New York harbor, is the longest of this type in the world (Fig. 4*d*). Another example of a vertical-lift bridge is shown in **Fig. 7**.

Swing bridge. Swing bridges rotate about a vertical axis on a pier, called the pivot pier, in the waterway (Fig. 4*d*). There are three general classes of swing bridges: the rim-bearing, the center-bearing, and the combined rim-bearing and center-bearing. A rim-bearing bridge is carried on a cylindrical girder on rollers, and a center-bearing on a single large bearing at the center of rotation. Swing bridges have been classified also as to the character of their main girders—that is, plate girder swing spans or truss swing spans.

Machinery. Almost all modern movable bridges are driven by electric motors which operate gear trains that convert the high-speed low-torque

Fig. 7. Stratford Avenue Bridge in Bridgeport, Connecticut. (*Connecticut Department of Transportation and Hardesty & Hanover*)

output of the motor to a low-speed high-torque output of the gear train at a pinion, acting on a rack.

Originally, movable bridges were operated by steam engines, and until recently, many still were. At least one former steam-operated bridge was operated for many years by compressed air driving the old steam engine. A very few bridges have been operated hydraulically. Some small bridges are operated by hand power. Provisions are still made on most movable bridges to operate by hand power in the event of power failure or malfunction of the bridge's electrical controls.

Machinery for early movable bridges consisted of simple custom-made components produced by the numerous small foundries, forge shops, and machine shops. Such components consisted of cast and roughcut gears of various tooth profiles, babbitt and bronze bushed bearings, custom-designed mounts for individual bearings, and common frames for the mounting of multiple bearings for open sets of reduction gears and various combination drive assemblies (**Fig. 8**). After World War II, a wide variety of standardized gear reducers, shaft bearings, and other machinery components suitable for use on bridge drives became available (**Fig. 9**). These components have generally replaced the custom-made components previously used.

Welded components have replaced cast components. Speed-reducer housings are essentially all welded. Even the huge sheaves for vertical-lift bridges are commonly manufactured as weldments instead of castings.

Electrical equipment. Except on the simplest small movable bridges, the electrical control of a movable bridge is so interlocked that the bridge cannot be moved until a series of prior operations have been made in correct order. Thus, on a highway bridge, first the traffic lights must be turned to red, then a set of traffic gates lowered, next the barrier gates set, and finally the locks or wedges pulled before the bridge can be moved.

The movable span generally can be completely opened or closed in from 1 to 2 min. However, the prior operations, particularly closing the bridge to

Fig. 9. Enclosed gear reducers on a later bascule bridge. (*Earle Gear and Machine Co.*)

traffic and making sure that the bridge is cleared of all vehicles between traffic gates, may run the cycle of operation up to 15 min or longer, depending upon the speed of passage through the span of the vessel for which the bridge has opened.

The drive systems on movable bridges have progressed from the early simpler forms of technology to the solid-state control devices permitting pushbutton operation.

Design

Bridges are designed according to the laws of physics pertaining to statics. The primary members of bridges act in tension, compression, shear, or bending, or in combinations of these. Secondary members act in the same fashion, sometimes participating in carrying the principal loads, especially if failure of any primary members should occur. Redundancy, so that failure of a single member or part of a member will not cause immediate collapse of the bridge, is now recognized as a desirable feature of design, particularly since collapse of the eyebar suspension bridge across the Ohio River at Point Pleasant, West Virginia, in 1967.

Modern design of bridges follows standards established by their principal users, the state highway or transportation departments and the railroads. In the United States, these standards are those of the American Association of State Highway and Transportation Officials and the American Railway Engineering Association, respectively. These specifications are developments of those for bridge design formulated by the early bridge engineers. While they are advisory, they are generally followed, albeit at times with modifications. Other countries

Fig. 8. Exposed gear reductions on an early bascule bridge.

have similar specifications.

The traffic load, called live load, is given in these specifications. It depends on the service to which the bridge will be subjected. The highway loadings are in terms of a simulated conventional truck or, for long spans, a uniform load with a roving concentrated load representing a line of average traffic. Railroad loadings are a simulated conventional locomotive load followed by a uniform load representing loaded freight cars. In both cases, in design, the live loads are positioned to give maximum load in the member being designed. In addition, dead load, the structure's own weight, and loads from impact, wind, temperature changes, ice, traction or braking of traffic, earthquake, and, in the case of highway bridges, pedestrians are specified. Allowable stresses and limiting deflections, too, are specified.

Other specifications followed in the design and construction of bridges include those of the American Society for Testing and Materials, the American Welding Society, and the American Institute of Steel Construction, and the construction specifications of the individual owners, and special specifications, when no other covers the situation. *See* STRUCTURAL DESIGN.

Vibration

Bridges are generally considered to be statically loaded structures under their own dead load, with dynamic loadings from the live load and from the wind.

Vibrations of bridges or individual components of a bridge occur when a resonant frequency of the bridge or a component is excited by one or more of the applied dynamic loadings. Excitation from live loads is more apt to happen on bridges carrying rail traffic than on those carrying highway traffic because of the uniform spacing of railroad cars. Excitation from wind is caused by the repeated formation of eddies or vortices as the wind travels past nonstreamlined members. Such aerodynamically induced vibrations caused the failure of the Tacoma Narrows Bridge in the state of Washington in 1941. A similar failure is recorded for a suspension bridge over the Ohio River at Wheeling, West Virginia, in 1854. In both cases, the formation of vortices built up as the torsional movements of the deck increased, ultimately leading to failure. Long, thin, H-shaped truss members have failed from similar wind-induced torsional vibrations. Wind velocities necessary to excite such vibrations need not be excessively high. The Tacoma Narrows Bridge failed under a 40 mi/h (18 m/s) wind, less than half the equivalent static wind load for which it was designed, and less than 20% of the load which would have caused structural distress.

Light lateral bracing on many spans will vibrate under the passage of live load.

Sufficient data exist on aerodynamically induced vibration to predict the possibility of its occurrence and thus modify the design when necessary to prevent serious problems.

Substructure

Bridge substructure consists of those elements that support the trusses, girders, stringers, floorbeams, and decks of the bridge superstructure. Piers and abutments are the primary bridge substructure elements. Other types of substructure, such as skewbacks for arch bridges, pile bents for trestles, and various forms of support wall, are also commonly used for specific applications.

The type of substructure provided for a bridge is greatly affected by the conditions of the site. Studies must be made on topography, stream currents, floating drift and ice, seismic potential, wind, and soil conditions. Forces and loads encountered in the design of substructure elements include dead load, live load, impact loads, braking forces, earth pressure, buoyancy, wind forces, centrifugal forces, earthquake loads, stream flow, and ice pressure.

Both piers and abutments are generally supported on either spread footings or pile footings. A spread footing is usually a concrete pad large enough in area to transmit all superimposed loads

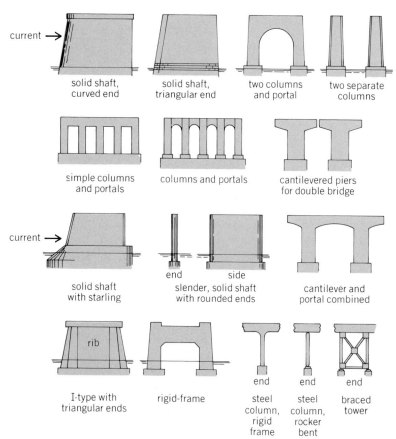

current →

solid shaft, curved end

solid shaft, triangular end

two columns and portal

two separate columns

simple columns and portals

columns and portals

cantilevered piers for double bridge

current →

solid shaft with starling

end   side
slender, solid shaft with rounded ends

cantilever and portal combined

rib

I-type with triangular ends

rigid-frame

end
steel column, rigid frame

end
steel column, rocker bent

end
braced tower

Fig. 10. General shapes of some piers for small bridges. (*After C. W. Dunham, Foundations of Structures, McGraw-Hill, 2d ed., 1962*)

and forces directly to the soil on which it is founded. The size of the spread footing is related to the bearing capacity of the soil on which it rests and the external forces on the substructure which will be transmitted to the spread footing.

A pile footing is usually a large concrete block supported on piles, so that the superimposed substructure loads and forces are transmitted to the support piles through the footing. The footing piles are used primarily to transmit loads through soil formations having poor supporting properties into or onto formations that are capable of supporting the loads. Piles may be point-bearing or friction types or the two in combination, and they may be timber, steel, precast concrete, cast-in-place concrete, or prestressed concrete. They may be driven by the use of a pile driver equipped with a hammer; they may be augered, jetted or prebored, or predrilled and cast-in-place. *See* FOUNDATIONS.

Bridge piers. Bridge piers are the intermediate support systems of bridges and viaducts. They may be located in water or on dry land. When located in water, piers may be subjected to scour by current and collision by vessels. Bridge piers support the superstructure and must carry dead loads and live loads, and withstand braking forces and other induced forces peculiar to the location of the pier, such as wind, ice, earthquake, and stream flow. A major consideration in pier design is stability and the ability to support all loads without appreciable settlement.

The shape, type, and location of piers are based on many factors; the major ones are horizontal and vertical clearance requirements, subsurface conditions, architectural and esthetic considerations, political and urban planning factors, traffic, and cost.

The most common pier shapes are solid shafts, multiple columns and portal, two columns and portal, separate columns, T or hammerhead, and cantilever. There are many variations of these pier shapes, which are constructed using concrete, steel, or wood (**Fig. 10**). A pier should have sufficient horizontal area at its top to receive the superstructure bearings. Architecturally, it should give the appearance of strength; it should not look weak and flimsy, although calculations may have shown the design to be adequate.

Piers in water are sometimes faced with stone, steel, or other protective devices below the high-water line to protect the pier from scour, ice, and other floating matter. At spans over navigable waterways, the piers of the channel span are provided with resilient timber fenders and clusters of timber piles for the protection of the piers and vessels.

Abutments. The abutments of a bridge are the substructure elements that support the ends of a bridge (**Fig. 11**). Bridge abutments are generally constructed of concrete or masonry and are designed to be pleasing esthetically as well as

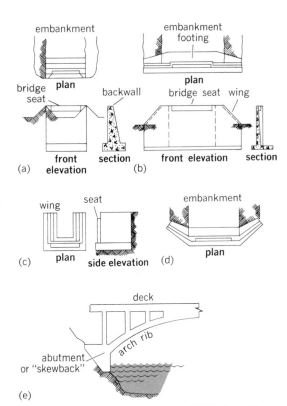

Fig. 11. Abutment designs for bridges. (*a*) Wingless. (*b*) Straight wing. (*c*) U-shaped. (*d*) Beveled wing. (*e*) Abutment for arch bridge.

architecturally and functionally sound. Major loads to which abutments are subjected are dead loads, live loads, braking forces, ice, wind, earthquake, stream flow, and earth pressure. The last is applied at the rear of the abutment wall.

An abutment is generally composed of a footing, a wall with a bridge seat supporting the superstructure bearings, and a backwall to retain the earth. Abutments may have wingwalls to retain the earth of the approach fill to the bridge. Proper drainage behind abutment walls is essential to avoid increasing the lateral pressure forces.

Skewbacks. A skewback is a common expression for an abutment for an arch; it is practically nothing more than an inclined footing that receives the thrust from the arch superstructure (Fig. 11).

A skewback differs from common abutments in the type and direction of forces that are applied to it. The horizontal component of an arch reaction is usually very large and exceeds the vertical component.

The large thrusts which are supported by skewbacks require good foundations. The ideal foundations are rock gorges which have strong, sound, and suitably sloping rock.

In general, a skewback for a fixed arch must provide practically no yielding. Some hinged arches, which are statically determinate structures, can sustain slight yield of the foundation. Skewbacks for these may be supported on piles or on spread footings on earth.

Caissons. A caisson is a boxlike structure, round or rectangular, which is sunk from the surface of either land or water to the desired depth as excavation proceeds inside or under it. It is an aid in making excavations for bridge piers or abutments and remains in place as part of the permanent structure.

The most common types are open caissons, which, as the name implies, have no top or bottom. Pneumatic caissons have permanent or temporary tops and are so arranged that people can work in the compressed air trapped under the structure.

An innovation in caissons was used for the Tappan Zee Bridge, which carries the New York State Thruway across the Hudson River 13 mi (22 km) north of New York City. Here eight buoyant precast concrete box caissons reduce the structure's dead load on supporting piles by 70%. The buoyant effect is maintained by keeping the boxes dewatered. Each of the two 15,000-ton (13,600-metric-ton) caissons supporting the main piers measures 100 ft (30 m) by 190 ft (58 m) and 40 ft (12 m) high.

Generally, the ultimate purpose of caisson construction is to reach a bearing stratum which will carry the load of supporting piers and abutments. *See* CAISSON FOUNDATION.

Cofferdam. A cofferdam, generally, is an enclosed temporary structure used to protect an excavation against lateral earth pressure or water pressure during construction. The material within the confines of the cofferdam is removed to allow the construction of piers and abutments below ground or water level.

In constructing cofferdams to counterbalance the upward pressure which may exist at the bottom of the caissons or cofferdams, a concrete seal, also known as tremie seal, is placed prior to dewatering. Concrete is placed in water using vertical pipes known as tremies. These pipes are continually filled with concrete. The bottom of the pipe is submerged in the plastic concrete while the concrete is poured through a funnellike top. During the pour, the tremie pipe is pounded, vibrated, and raised and lowered to increase the hydraulic head of the concrete in the tube and to cause the concrete to flow. The depth of the tremie concrete pour is a function of the upward pressure encountered after dewatering. *See* COFFERDAM.

Inspection and maintenance. It is imperative that bridges are structurally able to carry the traffic for which they are intended. Consequently, they must be inspected regularly for any defects which may have developed and must be appropiately repaired.

A bridge inspection and maintenance program resulted from the 1967 collapse of the U.S. Route 35 highway bridge over the Ohio River between Ohio and West Virginia. Subsequently, a policy for the inspection of highway bridges was developed by the Federal Highway Administration. Initially the program required interim inspections of bridges every 2 years, giving priority to those built before

1935, and in-depth inspections not to exceed 5-year intervals. The first round of inspections of approximately 600,000 highway bridges found that almost 40% of the nation's bridges were structurally deficient or functionally obsolete.

Bridge inspection entails a close-up examination of all parts of the structure, sometimes called a tactile examination, by a team of structural engineers supervised by a licensed professional engineer. At one time inspection was made by climbing and rigging or scaffolding for access. While the early methods are still used to some extent, special automotive equipment, such as snoopers and cherry pickers, are now employed for quick and easy access below the decks.

After inspection, the condition of a bridge is rated on a sliding scale. If a bridge is rated at the low end of the scale, the bridge may be closed or a load limit established until repairs can be made. If deterioration of primary structual members is found, the bridge is rated as to its load-carrying capacity related to the load-carrying cross-sectional area, known as loss of section, found in those members.

Maintenance of bridges, much of which is developed from the ongoing inspection program, is a priority function. The most common maintenance problems are deterioration of reinforced concrete decks; corrosion of steel caused by salt usage for snow and ice removal; nonfunctioning bridge bearings and drainage; deterioration of substructure elements such as piers, abutments, and walls; damage to bridges by natural causes such as floods and earthquakes; and damage by fire and allision (striking of the bridge by a vessel).

Another common maintenance issue, metal fatigue, results from unforeseen high stresses that eventually cause failure. It occurs particularly in details that are unduly restrained or that have defects. Likewise, when a crack emanating from a defect in a member or a weld (existing, accidentally induced, or developing) reaches a critical length, it will propagate through the member and may cause failure.

Steel construction requires a protective coating of the material to prevent corrosion. The most common coating found on bridges is lead-based paint. The condition of the paint is a subject of inspection. Painting of bridges involves cleaning of the existing paint work, including removal of loose or deteriorated paint. For many bridges, dependable red lead primer followed by two coats of a lead-based colored finish paint were customarily used. However, the materials were hazardous to those who applied them, and lead poisoning was a common sickness of bridge painters. There is a major problem involving the preparation of the surface of an existing lead-based paint for repainting. Normally the paint is blasted with grit to make the surface clean and acceptable for receiving new paint. Federal regulations require that enclosures be used for areas of bridges from which paint is removed, and the paint debris must be collected and discarded in approved hazardous waste disposal sites. In the past, the paint debris, which was practically all lead based, was allowed to fall to the ground or waterway. That which fell to the ground could present a hazard to those who worked under the bridge or used the area as a playground. Depending upon the current of the waterway, the debris has been carried over distances and lies in the loose soil of the river bottom. *See* CORROSION; HAZARDOUS WASTE; METAL COATINGS.

E. R. Hardesty; H. W. Fischer; R. W. Christie; B. Haber

Bibliography. E. DeLong, *Landmark American Bridges*, 1993; G. A. Hool and W. S. Kinne, *Movable and Long Span Steel Bridges*, 1943; D. Plowden, *Bridges: The Spans of North America*, 1974; S. M. Shaker and R. D. Wakefield, *Modular Steel Bridges*, 1995; J. Toneas, *Bridge Engineering*, 1995 ; J. A. L. Waddell, *Bridge Engineering,* 1916; C. S. Whitney, *Bridges, A Study in Their Art, Science and Evolution*, 1929.

Bridge circuit

A circuit composed of a source and four impedances that is used in the measurement of a wide range of physical quantities. The bridge circuit is useful in measuring impedances (resistors, capacitors, and inductors) and in converting signals from transducers to related voltage or current signals. *See* CAPACITOR; ELECTRICAL IMPEDANCE; INDUCTOR; RESISTOR; TRANSDUCER.

The bridge impedances Z_1, Z_2, Z_3, Z_4, shown in the **illustration**, may be single impedances (resistor, capacitor, or inductor), combinations of impedances, or a transducer with varying impedance. For example, strain gages are resistive transducers whose resistance changes when they are deformed. *See* STRAIN GAGE.

Bridge circuits are often used with transducers to convert physical quantities (temperature, displacement, pressure) to electrical quantities (voltage and current). High-accuracy voltmeters and ammeters are relatively inexpensive, and the voltage form of a signal is usually most convenient for information display, control decisions, and data storage.

Another important advantage of the bridge circuit is that it provides greater measurement sensitivity than the transducer. When a strain gage resistance increases from 120 to 120.10 ohms, the percentage

change is small (less than 0.1%). If the same strain gage is placed in a bridge with 120-ohm resistors and a 10-V source, the output read by the meter changes from 0 to 4.167 mV. The circuit has two advantages: the percentage change may be very large (if the initial output was close to zero), and the small output voltage is more easily read. Much more precision is required of a meter to resolve small differences in larger voltages than to resolve small signals near zero.

The bridge circuit is balanced when the output read by the meter is zero. In this condition the voltages on both sides of the meter are identical, as shown in Eqs. (1) and (2), and the equality

$$V_{12} = \frac{V_s Z_2}{Z_1 + Z_2} \qquad (1)$$

$$V_{34} = \frac{V_s Z_4}{Z_3 + Z_4} \qquad (2)$$

$V_{12} = V_{34}$ implies that the output is zero and that Eq. (3), which is known as the balance condition,

$$Z_1 Z_4 = Z_2 Z_3 \qquad (3)$$

is satisfied. The measurement sensitivity is highest when the bridge circuit is nearly balanced, because the values read on the meter are near zero.

The bridge is used in two forms. The null adjustment method requires adjustment of a calibrated impedance to balance it. In this case the meter is usually a highly sensitive current-measuring galvanometer. The null adjustment method is often used to measure impedances, with the output read from a dial attached to the adjustable impedance. The deflection method requires on accurate meter in the bridge to measure the deviation from the balance condition. The deviation (change in $V_{12} - V_{34}$) is proportional to the quantity being measured.

There are many special forms of the bridge circuit. When all of the impedances are resistive, it is commonly called a Wheatstone bridge. Other common forms use a current source in place of the voltage source, a sinusoidal source in place of a constant (dc) source, or branch impedances which are specific combinations of single passive impedances, for example, the Hayes bridge and the Owen bridge. The bridge circuit is also used in a variety of electrical applications varying from oscillators (Wien bridge oscillator) to instrumentation amplifier circuits for extremely accurate measurements. *See* INSTRUMENTATION AMPLIFIER; OSCILLATOR; RESISTANCE MEASUREMENT; WHEATSTONE BRIDGE. Kirk D. Peterson

Bibliography. T. G. Beckwith, J. H. Lienhard, and R. D. Marangoni, *Mechanical Measurements*, 5th ed., 1993; E. O. Doebelin, *Measurement Systems: Application and Design*, 4th ed., 1990; J. P. Holman, *Experimental Methods for Engineers*, 6th ed., 1993; E. J. Kennedy, *Operational Amplifier Circuits: Theory and Applications*, 1988.

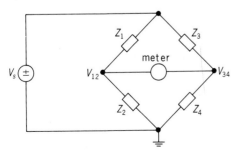

Bridge circuit with source and impedances.

Brillouin zone

In the propagation of any type of wave motion through a crystal lattice, the frequency is a periodic function of wave vector **k**. This function may be complicated by being multivalued; that is, it may have more than one branch. Discontinuities may also occur. In order to simplify the treatment of wave motion in a crystal, a zone in **k**-space is defined which forms the fundamental periodic region, such that the frequency or energy for a **k** outside this region may be determined from one of those in it. This region is known as the Brillouin zone (sometimes called the first or the central Brillouin zone). It is usually possible to restrict attention to **k** values inside the zone. Discontinuities occur only on the boundaries. If the zone is repeated indefinitely, all **k**-space will be filled. Sometimes it is also convenient to define larger figures with similar properties which are combinations of the first zone and portions of those formed by replication. These are referred to as higher Brillouin zones.

The central Brillouin zone for a particular solid type is a solid which has the same volume as the primitive unit cell in reciprocal space, that is, the space of the reciprocal lattice vectors, and is of such a shape as to be invariant under the symmetry operations of the crystal. *See* CRYSTAL STRUCTURE; CRYSTALLOGRAPHY.

Zone construction. Let $\mathbf{a}_1$, $\mathbf{a}_2$, $\mathbf{a}_3$ be the primitive translation vectors for some crystal lattice. New vectors $\mathbf{b}_i$ with $i = 1, 2, 3$, are defined by Eq. (1),

$$\mathbf{a}_i \cdot \mathbf{b}_j = 2\pi \delta_{ij} \tag{1}$$

where δ_{ij} is unity when $i = j$, and zero for other values of i. The vectors $\mathbf{b}_i$ are then given by Eqs. (2).

$$\mathbf{b}_1 = \frac{2\pi \mathbf{a}_2 \times \mathbf{a}_3}{\mathbf{a}_1 \cdot \mathbf{a}_2 \times \mathbf{a}_3} \quad \mathbf{b}_2 = \frac{2\pi \mathbf{a}_3 \times \mathbf{a}_1}{\mathbf{a}_1 \cdot \mathbf{a}_2 \times \mathbf{a}_3}$$
$$\mathbf{b}_3 = \frac{2\pi \mathbf{a}_1 \times \mathbf{a}_2}{\mathbf{a}_1 \cdot \mathbf{a}_2 \times \mathbf{a}_3} \tag{2}$$

Now vectors $\mathbf{K}_i$ are defined by Eq. (3), where

$$\mathbf{K}_i = h_1 \mathbf{b}_1 + h_2 \mathbf{b}_2 + h_3 \mathbf{b}_3 \tag{3}$$

the h_i's are arbitrary integers. The subscript i stands for some particular combination of the h. The end points of the vectors $\mathbf{K}_i$ form a lattice of points in reciprocal space. The vectors $\mathbf{K}_i$ have the property that plane waves of the form $e^{i\mathbf{K}_i \cdot \mathbf{r}}$ are periodic in the crystal lattice, since if some $\mathbf{r}' = \mathbf{r} + \mathbf{R}_n$ is considered, where $\mathbf{R}_n$ is a translation vector of the crystal, Eq. (4) holds.

$$e^{i\mathbf{K}_i \cdot \mathbf{r}'} = e^{i\mathbf{K}_i \cdot \mathbf{r}} e^{i\mathbf{K}_i \cdot \mathbf{R}_n} = e^{i\mathbf{K}_i \cdot \mathbf{r}} \tag{4}$$

The last step follows since $\mathbf{K}_i \cdot \mathbf{R}_n$ is an integer times 2π. Consequently, the plane waves $e^{i\mathbf{K} \cdot \mathbf{r}}$ are suitable functions for the Fourier expansion of any function which is periodic in the lattice.

Unit cells can be constructed in the reciprocal space of the lattice of the ends of the vectors $\mathbf{K}_i$, just as is done in the real crystal space. The lines connecting one point with the other lattice sites are drawn, and the planes which are the perpendicular bisectors of these lines are constructed. The smallest enclosed solid figure is the first Brillouin zone. It is the smallest unit cell in the reciprocal lattice which has the symmetry of the entire lattice. Higher Brillouin zones are also formed.

Brillouin zones for the body-centered cubic, face-centered cubic, and hexagonal close-packed lattices are shown in **illus.** *a–c*.

Application to band theory. Each electron wave function in the crystal can be classified according to some **k** inside the first Brillouin zone. For if **k'** is a vector in reciprocal space whose end point lies outside the zone, then it can be written as Eq. (5),

$$\mathbf{k}' = \mathbf{k} + \mathbf{K}_n \tag{5}$$

where **k** lies inside the zone and $\mathbf{K}_n$ is a reciprocal lattice vector. According to the Bloch theorem, Eq. (6a) holds. But since $\mathbf{K}_n \cdot \mathbf{R}_j$ is an integer times 2π, Eq. (6b) is valid. Thus **k'** and **k** are equivalent

$$\psi(\mathbf{k}', \mathbf{r} + \mathbf{R}_j) = e^{i\mathbf{k}' \cdot \mathbf{R}_j} \psi(\mathbf{k}', \mathbf{r}) \tag{6a}$$
$$e^{i\mathbf{k}' \cdot \mathbf{R}_j} = e^{i\mathbf{k} \cdot \mathbf{R}_j} e^{i\mathbf{K}_n \cdot \mathbf{R}_j} = e^{i\mathbf{k} \cdot \mathbf{R}_j} \tag{6b}$$

in a certain sense. For this reason, it is possible to consider only the first zone in discussing the properties of solids.

A fundamental point in the application of Brillouin zone theory to the study of the properties of solids is that the energy $E(\mathbf{k})$ of the states ψ_k must be a continuous function of **k** inside the zone (although it will be multivalued if the reduced zone scheme is employed). Discontinuities can occur only across the faces of the zone. The number of allowed states inside each Brillouin zone can be determined as follows: The number of allowed states per unit volume in the space of the vector **k** is $1/(2\pi)^3$ for each spin per unit volume of the crystal, or $2/(2\pi)^3$ altogether. Thus, the number of states in the zone for each atom in the crystal is $2V/(2\pi)^3N$, where N is the number of atoms of the crystal and V is the volume. A substance which has just enough electrons per atom to fill some zone

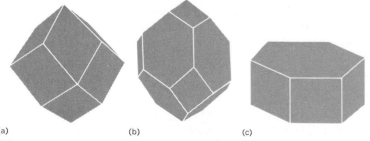

(a)   (b)   (c)

Brillouin zone for (a) body-centered cubic lattice, (b) face-centered cubic lattice, (c) hexagonal close-packed lattice.

may be an insulator or semiconductor. If there are not enough electrons to fill a zone, it must be a metallic conductor.

Alkali metals. These metals are body-centered cubic at high temperatures. (Sodium and lithium undergo phase transitions at low temperatures.) The volume of the zone is $2(2\pi/a)^3$, where a is the lattice constant. The number of atoms per unit volume is $2/a^3$ so that the first zone can contain two electrons per atom. However, the atoms possess only one valence electron, so that these metals are good conductors.

Noble metals. Copper, silver, and gold are face-centered cubic metals with one valence electron per atom, and again the zone can hold two electrons per atom. Thus, these also are good conductors. If noble metals were adequately described by a free electron model, the Fermi surface (the surface bounding the occupied volume of reciprocal space) would be a sphere which would approach close to the surface of the zone. It is known, however, that the free electron model is not adequate for electrons near the Fermi surface, and that the Fermi surface touches the Brillouin zone boundary near the extremities of the (111) axes.

Divalent metals. Except for barium and mercury, the divalent metals have either hexagonal close-packed or face-centered cubic structures. The zones hold two valence electrons per atom, and on the basis of simple arguments, it would be expected that these materials should be insulators. However, some of the electrons go over into the next Brillouin zone, leaving pockets of holes behind in the first zone.

Semiconductors and insulators. In diamond, silicon, and germanium, all of which have the diamond structure of two interpenetrating face-centered cubic (fcc) lattices, the Brillouin zone has the same form as for the fcc. It can hold four electrons per atom. Occupied states are separated from higher states by an energy gap, since these materials are semiconductors or insulators. Graphite, which has a hexagonal layer structure, can be regarded as a semiconductor with a vanishing energy gap. The Brillouin zone in a simple model is full at a temperature of 0 K, but there is no gap along the edges of the zone. In bismuth there is a higher Brillouin zone which holds five electrons per atom. There is a very small overlap of electrons across the faces of the zone, leading to the presence of a small number (about 10^{-5} per atom) of both electrons and holes at 0 K. *See* SEMICONDUCTOR.

Binary alloys. Many of the properties of binary alloys which form substitutional solid solutions can be explained on the hypothesis that the solute contributes its valence electrons to form a composite system whose fundamental parameter is the electron per atom ratio. The electronic structure is assumed to be essentially unaltered. Many changes of the properties, such as the lattice parameter, the concentration at which the various phases appear, and the Hall coefficient, can be explained in terms of overlap or contact of the Fermi surface with the Brillouin zone. *See* ALLOY STRUCTURES; BAND THEORY OF SOLIDS.

Joseph Callaway

Bibliography. N. W. Ashcroft and N. D. Mermin, *Solid State Physics*, 1976; W. Hume-Rothery and R. E. Smallman, *The Structure of Metals and Alloys*, 1988; C. Kittel, *Introduction to Solid State Physics*, 6th ed., 1986 ; M. N. Rudden and J. Wilson, *Elements of Solid State Physics*, 2d ed., 1993.

Brittleness

That characteristic of a material that is manifested by sudden or abrupt failure without appreciable prior ductile or plastic deformation. A brittle fracture occurs on a cleavage plane which has a crystalline appearance at failure because each crystal tends to fracture on a single plane. On the other hand, a shear fracture has a fibrous appearance because of the sliding of the fracture surfaces over each other. Brittle failures are caused by high tensile stresses, high carbon content, rapid rate of loading, and the presence of notches. Materials such as glass, cast iron, and concrete are examples of brittle materials.

John B. Scalzi

Broccoli

A cool-season biennial crucifer, *Brassica oleracea* var. *italica*, of Mediterranean origin, belonging to the plant order Papaverales. Broccoli is grown for its thick branching flower stalks which terminate in clusters of loose green flower buds (see **illus.**). Stalks and buds are cooked as a vegetable or may be processed in either canned or frozen form. Cultural practices for broccoli are similar to those used for cabbage. *See* CABBAGE; PAPAVERALES.

New varieties (cultivars) with greater disease resistance and higher quality are continually being developed. Broccoli is slightly tolerant of acid

Flower buds of broccoli. (*Asgrow Seed Co., Subsidiary of the Upjohn Co.*)

soils and has high requirements for boron and molybdenum. Terminal and axillary clusters are cut 80–140 days after planting. California and Texas are important broccoli-producing states.   H. John Carew

Bromegrass

A common name designating a number of grasses found in the North Temperate Zone that produce highly palatable and nutritious forage. Of these, smooth bromegrass (*Bromus inermis*) is the most important (see **illus.**). This species was introduced to the United States during the 1880s from central Europe and Russia, where it is native. It proved to be well adapted to regions of cold winters and limited rainfall. Although first widely used in the eastern Great Plains and western Corn Belt regions, improved strains are now grown extensively for hay and rotation pastures north of the Mason-Dixon line, from the Plains to the Atlantic. Smooth bromegrass is a long-lived perennial, spreads by underground creeping stems, and is fairly deep rooted and drought-tolerant. Top growth is 2–4 ft (0.6–1.2 m) tall and is used for hay or pasture. Regional strains are available for Canada and the northern two-thirds of the United States. Bromegrass tolerates a wide range of soil conditions, but responds well to higher levels of

Smooth bromegrass (*Bromus inermis*). (*a*) Entire plant. (*b*) Fruit. (*c*) Inflorescence.

fertility. Where the moisture supply is adequate, smooth bromegrass grows well in mixtures with alfalfa and red clover. The seeds of bromegrass are large, light, and chaffy, and successful planting requires special seeders. *See* CYPERALES; GRASS CROPS.   Howard B. Sprague

Bromeliales

An order of flowering plants, division Magnoliophyta (Angiospermae) in the subclass Zingiberidae of the class Liliopsida (monocotyledons). It consists of the single family Bromeliaceae, with about 45 genera and 2000 species, occurring chiefly in tropical and subtropical America. They are firm-leaved, terrestrial xerophytes (adapted structurally to live and grow with a limited water supply), or very often epiphytes (living on other plants nonparasitically), with six stamens and regular or somewhat irregular flowers that usually have septal nectaries and an inferior ovary. The order has often been associated with several related ones in a larger order, Farinosae, marked by its starchy endosperm. Spanish moss (*Tillandsia*) and the cultivated pineapple (*Ananas*) are familiar members of the Bromeliales, and many others attract attention as houseplants. *See* FLOWER; LILIOPSIDA; MAGNOLIOPHYTA; PINA; PINEAPPLE; PLANT KINGDOM; SECRETORY STRUCTURES (PLANT).

Arthur Cronquist; T. M. Barkley

Bromine

A chemical element, Br, atomic number 35, atomic weight 79.909, which normally exists as Br_2, a dark-red, low-boiling but high-density liquid of intensely irritating odor. The name is derived from the Greek *bromos*, meaning stench. This is the only nonmetallic element that is liquid at normal temperature and pressure. Bromine is very reactive chemically; one of the halogen group of elements, it has properties which are intermediate between those of chlorine and iodine.

The most stable valence states of bromine in its salts are 1− and 5+, although 1+, 3+, and 7+ are known. Within wide limits of temperature and pressure, molecules of the liquid and vapor are diatomic, Br_2, with a formula weight of 159.818. There are two stable isotopes (^{79}Br and ^{81}Br) that occur naturally in nearly equal proportion, so that the atomic weight is 79.909. A number of radioisotopes are also known. A. J. Balard is recognized as the discoverer of this element in 1826, even though it appears that other workers made the discovery simultaneously. The most notable of these was J. von Liebig, who appropriately called it "chloro-iodide."

Physical properties. The solubility of bromine in water at 20°C is 3.38 g/100 g solution, but its solubility is increased tremendously in the

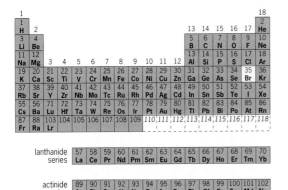

lanthanide series: 57 La, 58 Ce, 59 Pr, 60 Nd, 61 Pm, 62 Sm, 63 Eu, 64 Gd, 65 Tb, 66 Dy, 67 Ho, 68 Er, 69 Tm, 70 Yb

actinide series: 89 Ac, 90 Th, 91 Pa, 92 U, 93 Np, 94 Pu, 95 Am, 96 Cm, 97 Bk, 98 Cf, 99 Es, 100 Fm, 101 Md, 102 No

presence of its salts and in hydrobromic acid. Thus, in a solution of 359 g/liter of sodium bromide, the solubility of bromine is 641.6 g/liter. Bromine is completely miscible with 48% hydrobromic acid and with common solvents, such as carbon disulfide, carbon tetrachloride, chloroform, ether, and glacial acetic acid. The ability of this inorganic element to dissolve in organic solvents is of considerable importance in its reactions. **Table 1** summarizes the physical properties of bromine.

Inorganic bromides and bromates. Major intermediates in the manufacture of bromides, second only to bromine as a means of introducing bromine into a molecule, are gaseous hydrogen bromide, HBr, and aqueous hydrobromic acid, usually as the constant-boiling solution containing approximately 48% HBr. The reaction of hydrogen and bromine at high temperature in the absence of air is the principal method of manufacture; HBr as the by-product of an organic substitution reaction may also be utilized. Liquefied hydrogen bromide is available commercially in cylinders, and vari-

ous strengths of aqueous hydrobromic acid, usually 48%, are available in carboys, drums, or tank cars. The physical properties of anhydrous hydrogen bromide are listed in **Table 2**. With water at 760 mmHg (101 kPa) pressure, the constant-boiling solution contains 47.63% HBr and boils at 124.3°C (255.7°F).

Other valuable inorganic brominating agents include phosphorus tribromide, bromine chloride, aluminum bromide, barium bromide, thionyl bromide, and sulfur bromide.

The alkali bromides can be manufactured by several processes. Thus, ammonia, bromine, and an alkali hydroxide or carbonate will react according to type reaction (1). Also, the reaction

$$2NH_3 + 6NaOH + 3Br_2 \rightarrow 6NaBr + N_2 + 6H_2O \qquad (1)$$

of HBr with an alkali hydroxide or carbonate gives the desired product, shown in reaction (2).

$$2HBr + Na_2CO_3 \rightarrow 2NaBr + CO_2 + H_2O \qquad (2)$$

As shown previously, absorption of bromine by alkali carbonates or hydroxides in the blowing-out process of manufacture produces alkali bromide and alkali bromate in a 5:1 mole ratio. If bromate $[(BrO_3)^-]$ is the desired product, it may be formed from the bromide electrolytically, or by the oxidative action of chlorine in reaction (3). The bromides of calcium, strontium, barium,

$$NaBr + 6NaOH + 3Cl_3 \rightarrow NaBrO_3 + 6NaCl + 3H_2O \qquad (3)$$

magnesium, cesium, and lithium are of commercial importance.

Ammonium bromide (NH_4Br) is most easily formed by the reaction of ammonia and bromine in water solution with the liberation of nitrogen, as in reaction (4). Aluminum bromide made by direct

$$3Br_2 + 8NH_4OH \rightarrow 6NH_4Br + N_2 + 8H_2O \qquad (4)$$

reaction of aluminum and bromine is a valuable catalyst in alkylation and isomerization reactions. It is preferable to aluminum chloride in some cases because it can be liquefied easily (mp 97.5°C or 208°F), and it is more soluble and more reactive in organic liquids.

Organic bromides. As numerous as are the inorganic bromides that have found industrial use, the organic bromides have even wider application. Because of the ease of reaction of bromine with organic compounds and the ease of its subsequent removal or replacement, organic bromides have been much studied and used as chemical intermediates. In addition, many of the bromine reactions are so clean-cut that they can be used for the study of reaction mechanisms without complication of side reactions. The ability of bromine to add into unusual places on organic molecules has added to its value as a research tool.

There are several reactions by which bromine and its bromides may be added to an organic molecule. Many of these reactions will give essentially 100% yield of the desired product.

TABLE 1. Physical properties of bromine			
Property			Value
Flash point			None
Fire point			None
Freezing point			−7.27°C
			(18.9°F)
Density, 20°C			3.1226
Pounds per gallon, 25°C			25.8
Boiling point, 760 mmHg, °C			58.8
Refractive index, 20°C			1.6083
Latent heat of fusion, cal/g			15.8
Latent heat of vaporization, cal/g, bp			44.9
Vapor density, g/liter, standard conditions			
(0°C, 1 atm)			7.139
Viscosity, centistokes, 20°C			0.314
Surface tension, dynes/cm, 20°C			49.5
30°C			47.3
40°C			45.2
Dielectric constant, 10^5 freq, 25°C			3.33
Compressibility, vapors, 25°C			0.998
Thermodynamic data, cal/(mole K)			
	T, K	Entropy	Heat capacity
Solid	265.9	24.786	14.732
Liquid	265.9	34.290	18.579

TABLE 2. Physical properties of hydrogen bromide

Property	Value
Formula weight	80.9
Melting point	$-86.8°C$ ($-124°F$)
Boiling point	$-66.7°C$ ($-88.1°F$)
Specific heat, liquid, cal/g	0.176
Specific heat, vapor, 27°C, cal/g	0.085
Heat of fusion at mp, cal/g	71.1
Heat of vaporization at 66.7°C, cal/g	52.0
Critical temperature, °C	89.8
Critical pressure, atm	84

The ability of bromine to dissolve both in many common organic solvents and in inorganic bromide solutions permits easy control of the reactions.

The addition of bromine to a double or triple bond to saturate the molecule is usually done very easily, as shown in reaction (5). One exception

$$
\begin{array}{c}
\text{H} \quad \text{H} \qquad\qquad \text{H} \quad \text{H}\\
| \quad\; | \qquad\qquad\quad | \quad\; |\\
\text{RC} - \text{CR} + \text{Br}_2 \longrightarrow \text{C} - \text{CR} \qquad (5)\\
| \quad\; |\\
\text{Br} \quad \text{Br}
\end{array}
$$

is perchloroethylene (1,1,2,2-tetrachloroethylene), which resists bromination and requires a catalyst to speed the reaction.

Substitution reactions of bromine on the ring in aromatic molecules take place readily with the aid of a catalyst, such as iron, iron bromide, or aluminum bromide. Direct bromination of saturated aliphatic hydrocarbons requires higher temperatures, with the result that a multitude of products is formed. In the presence of catalysts, the substitution of bromine to the α position of aliphatic acids, aldehydes, and ketones takes place readily. Hydrogen bromide is a mole-for-mole by-product of substitution reactions, as in reaction (6).

$$ RCH_2CO_2H + Br_2 \rightarrow RCHBrCO_2H + HBr \qquad (6) $$

Bromine compounds such as phosphorus tribromide, N-bromosuccinimide, 1,3-dibromo-5,5-dimethylhydantoin, and 1,2-dibromotetrachloroethane will react with olefins under the influence of peroxides or ultraviolet light (uv) to yield the corresponding allylic bromide. The reaction proceeds with cyclohexene, as in reaction (7). Phosphorus

tribromide is a mild brominating agent that can be used when bromine itself acts too vigorously on a molecule.

A commercially useful reaction for the replacement of hydroxyl groups on organic molecules utilizes sulfur bromide, as shown in reaction (8). Alkyl

$$ S + 3Br_2 + 6ROH \rightarrow 6RBr + H_2SO_4 + 2H_2O \qquad (8) $$

bromides may also be prepared by the action of hydrogen bromide or hydrobromic acid on alcohols. Sulfuric acid may be added to take up water and drive the reaction to completion.

Another method for the manufacture of alkyl bromides illustrates a reaction unique to hydrogen bromide. In this method, the addition of hydrogen bromide to an olefin, such as allyl chloride, gives the 1,2-chlorobromo compound, as expected from Markownikoff's rule. However, if the reaction is carried out in the presence of free-radical-type catalysts, such as peroxides, or in ultraviolet light, the addition is reversed and the 1,3 compound formed, as shown in reactions (9) and (10). This

$$ CH_2\!=\!CHCH_2Cl + HBr \rightarrow CH_3CHBrCH_2Cl \qquad (9) $$

$$ CH_2\!=\!CHCH_2Cl + HBr \xrightarrow[\text{catalyst}]{\text{free-radical}} $$
$$ CH_2BrCH_2CH_2Cl \qquad (10) $$

reverse reaction does not occur with hydrochloric acid, HCl. The reaction is of particular value in placing a reactive bromine on a terminal carbon of a compound for use as an intermediate. Thus, the 1,3 product above finds use in the production of cyclopropane, an anesthetic.

The preparation of alkyl bromides by replacement of chlorine with $AlBr_3$ has been used commercially, particularly for the methane family. However, this preparation is more easily and economically accomplished by the action of hydrogen bromide in the presence of only catalytic amounts of aluminum bromide or aluminum chloride, as shown in reaction (11). Replacement of the hydrogen in

$$ CHCl_3 + 3HBr \xrightarrow{AlCl_3} CHBr_3 + 3HCl \qquad (11) $$

such a molecule can be accomplished by high-temperature, vapor-phase bromination.

Both chlorine and bromine are ortho-para directing in their influence on aromatic molecules. Thus, the second bromine that will substitute in benzene will be found predominantly in the para position with some o-dibromobenzene, but little or no m-dibromobenzene. Each subsequent bromine atom becomes more difficult to add, but with more reactive compounds, such as phenol or aniline, it is difficult to stop short of the symmetrical 2,4,6-tribromo compound. In the case of phenol or aniline, the hydroxyl (OH) and amine (NH$_2$) groups are stronger ortho-para directors than halogen is, so these groups will determine the position of substitution. With aromatic compounds having saturated side chains, the presence of heat and light and the absence of metals such as iron favor side-chain substitution, whereas lower temperatures, darkness, and iron favor ring brominations.

The usefulness of organic bromine compounds as chemical intermediates is illustrated by their reactions with alkalies to form either the corresponding alcohols or olefins, with ammonia to form amines, and with phenols to form the corresponding ethers. The carbon-to-carbon chain lengths of organic molecules may be increased by the action of alkyl bromides, utilizing the Grignard or Friedel-Crafts actions. An interesting alkylating agent is bromotrichloromethane, which adds to olefins as shown in reaction (12). Many other methods for

$$CBrCl_3 + CH_2 = CH_2 \rightarrow CCl_3CH_2CH_2Br \qquad (12)$$

using bromine compounds as building blocks for more complex molecules are available. *See* CHEMICAL DYNAMICS; HALOGENATED HYDROCARBON.

Bromine compounds have a number of properties that make them useful. High specific gravity is a general characteristic, and some bromine compounds are among the most dense organic liquids known. The compound 1,1,2,2-tetrabromoethane has a specific gravity of 2.96, for example. Many of the compounds possess bacteriological and fungicidal activity, and the ability of some, such as aluminum bromide, to act as catalysts has been utilized. The ease of the addition of bromine to a molecule and its subsequent replacement by a more complex molecule makes bromine a useful tool in organic synthesis.

Natural occurrence. Although it is estimated that from 10^{15} to 10^{16} tons (9×10^{14} to 9×10^{15} metric tons) of bromine are contained in the Earth's crust, the element is widely distributed and found only in low concentrations in the form of its salts. The bulk of the recoverable bromine, however, is found in the hydrosphere. Seawater contains an average of 65 parts per million (ppm) of bromine, which means that 308,000 tons (277,000 metric tons) of bromine are held in a cubic mile of ocean. Though 15,000 tons (14,000 metric tons) of seawater must be processed to obtain 1 ton (0.9 metric ton) of bromine, seawater is a major commercial source of bromine. *See* SEAWATER.

The other major sources of bromine in the United States are underground brines and salt lakes, with commercial production in Michigan, Arkansas, and California. Brines from wells contain 1000–6000 ppm of bromine, but they must be obtained by drilling to depths as great as a mile and more. Chlorine is 300 times more abundant in both brines and seawater. This same ratio is maintained generally in the Earth's crust, which contains an average of 1.6 ppm bromine.

Manufacture. The discovery of potash in the salt deposits at Strassfurt in 1856 opened the way for the initial recovery of bromine as a by-product in Germany in 1858. Bromine was first produced in the United States in 1845 by D. Altes from salt brine.

Commercial recovery of bromine from brines and from seawater involves the oxidation of the bromide ions in solution to free elemental bromine, which is then vaporized from the solution either by air or by steam. Although oxidation was accomplished at one time by electrolysis, all modern processes utilize chlorine, according to reaction (13). Vaporization by steam results in the

$$Cl_2 + 2Br^- \rightarrow 2Cl^- + Br_2 \qquad (13)$$

recovery of free bromine directly.

With seawater, bromine must first be concentrated before the steaming-out process becomes economically practical. Consequently, air is used to vaporize the bromine from chlorinated seawater, and then sulfur dioxide (SO_2) is introduced into the dilute bromine-laden air. Subsequent absorption of the hydrogen bromide in a controlled amount of water produces a much more concentrated bromide solution, as shown in reaction (14). Elemental

$$SO_2 + Br_2 + 2H_2O \rightarrow 2HBr + H_2SO_4 \qquad (14)$$

bromine must then be released again by chlorine and steamed from the solution. The by-product hydrochloric and sulfuric acids are recycled to acidify the incoming seawater to the pH necessary for efficient chlorination. The steps in the process are shown in the **illustration**.

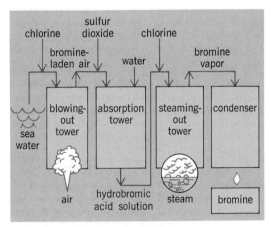

Steps in the extraction process for bromine.

The air-blowing process can also be used when an alkali bromide is the desired end product. Absorption of the bromine from the airstream by sodium carbonate ($NaCO_3$), for instance, produces sodium bromide and sodium bromate, as in reaction (15). The sodium bromate may then be

$$3Br_2 + 3Na_2CO_3 \rightarrow 5NaBr + NaBrO_3 + 3CO_2 \qquad (15)$$

crystallized from solution, or can be reduced with iron, if NaBr is the only desired product. One process utilizes NaBr solution as the absorbing medium for bromine from bromine-laden air.

Uses. At one time a substantial part of bromine production in the United States was used to form ethylene dibromide, an ingredient in leaded gasoline. The ethylene dibromide was used as a scavenger to remove residual lead in internal combustion engines by combining with the lead to form volatile lead bromide which was expelled from the engine via the exhaust gases. However, there has been a severe reduction of the use of leaded gasolines because of the air-pollution problems caused by this application. *See* SPARK KNOCK.

Other chemicals containing bromine have been produced in increased volumes. A major and fast-growing use for bromine is in completion fluids for oil and gas wells, specifically calcium bromide and zinc bromide. These products are useful because of the high specific gravity which can be reached by aqueous solutions of these salts: as high as 1.8 g/cm^3 for calcium bromide and upward of 2.4 g/cm^3 for zinc bromide. Where abnormally high bottom hole pressures are expected, the high density of these fluids controls the oil or gas formation pressure because of the hydrostatic head of the fluid in the well bore. These fluids, being solid-free in nature, are less damaging to the oil-producing formation than fluids that obtain their density by the use of suspended weighting materials, such as barium sulfate. Such solid-weight materials tend to reduce the permeability of the oil-producing formation, and thus restrict production. *See* OIL AND GAS WELL COMPLETION.

Of prime importance for many years has been the use of bromine in the production of sodium and potassium bromides that are used in the photographic industry. Also, several organic bromides have found utility as chemical intermediates in the production of complex chemicals used as herbicides and insecticides. Alkali bromates are also used as oxidizing agents in the production of hair-waving preparations and also in the oxidation of sulfur dyes in the textile industry. Methyl bromide and ethylene dibromide have also found wide use in agriculture as soil and space fumigants. *See* HERBICIDE; INSECTICIDE; PHOTOGRAPHIC MATERIALS.

Another use for bromine compounds is in the area of flame retardants. Compounds that are high in halogen content, for example, chlorine or bromine, are resistant to ignition and burning. Incorporation of these halogen-containing flame retardants into flammable material often reduces the ease of ignition. The addition of these compounds to the base material can be accomplished in two ways. The easier is to blend or disperse the compound physically into the flammable material. Such compounds are called additive-type flame retardants. The second approach is to react the bromine compound chemically into the substrate. Such compounds are known as reactive-type flame retardants. The reactive type are usually more durable than the additive type. *See* FLAMEPROOFING.

Bromine and its compounds have found acceptance as disinfection and sanitizing agents in swimming pools and potable water. Certain bromine-containing compounds are safer to use than the analogous chlorine compounds due to certain persistent residuals found in the chlorine-containing materials. Other bromine chemicals are used as working fluid in gages, as hydraulic fluids, as chemical intermediates in the manufacture of organic dyes, in storage batteries, and in explosion-suppressant and fire-extinguishing systems. Bromine compounds, because of their density, also find use in the gradation of coal and other minerals where separations are effected by density gradients. Their versatility is illustrated by the commercial use of over 100 compounds containing bromine.

Handling and safety. Bromine is almost instantaneously injurious to the skin, and it is difficult to remove quickly enough to prevent a painful burn that heals slowly. Extreme precaution, including protective clothing, must be used when handling bromine. Bromine vapor is extremely toxic, but its odor gives good warning; it is difficult to remain in an area of sufficient concentration to be permanently damaging. Bromine can be handled safely, but the recommendations of the manufacturers should be respected.

Bromine is available in 6.5-lb (3-kg) bottles, in 225-lb (102-kg) Monel alloy drums, and in nickel- and lead-lined tank cars and trucks. Wet bromine is corrosive to most metals except tantalum, but dry bromine (containing 20 ppm or less water) can be handled at room temperatures with essentially no corrosion in Monel, nickel, and lead. Steel and stainless steel are not usually satisfactory, even for dry bromine. This is because dry bromine can absorb moisture rapidly, and bromine containing more than 50 ppm water is usually very corrosive to steel and stainless steel. *See* HALOGEN ELEMENTS.

Randy C. Stauffer

Bibliography. F. A. Cotton (ed.), *Inorganic Syntheses*, vol. 13, 1972; F. A. Cotton and G. Wilkinson, *Advanced Inorganic Chemistry*, 5th ed., 1988; A. J. Downs and C. J. Adams, *The Chemistry of Chlorine, Bromine, Iodine, and Astatine*, vol. 7, 1975; D. Price, B. Iddon, and B. J. Wakefield (eds.), *Bromine Compounds: Chemistry and Applications*, 1988.

Bronze

Usually an alloy of copper and tin. Bronze is used in bearings, bushings, gears, valves, and other fittings both for water and steam. Lead, zinc, silver, and other metals are added for special-purpose bronzes. Tin bronze, including statuary bronze, contains 2–20% tin; bell metal 15–25%; and speculum metal up to 33%. Gun metal contains 8–10% tin plus 2–4% zinc.

The properties of bronze depend on its composition and working. Phosphor bronze is tin bronze hardened and strengthened with traces of phosphorus; it is used for fine tubing, wire springs, and machine parts. Lead bronze may contain up to 30% lead; it is used for cast parts such as low-pressure valves and fittings. Manganese bronze with 0.5–5% manganese plus other metals, but often no tin, has high strength. Aluminum bronze also contains no tin; its mechanical properties are superior to those of tin bronze, but it is difficult to cast. Silicon bronze, with up to 3% silicon, casts well and can be worked hot or cold by rolling, forging, and similar methods. Beryllium bronze (also called beryllium copper) has about 2% beryllium and no tin. The alloy is hard and strong and can be further hardened and strengthened by precipitation hardening; it is one of the few copper alloys that responds to heat treatment, approaching three times the strength of structural steel.

Tin bronze is harder, stronger in compression, and more resistant to corrosion than the brasses. Bronze that will not be exposed to extremes of weather can be protected from corrosion by warming it to slightly over 212°F (100°C) in an oxygen atmosphere. A thin layer of oxide or patina forms to prevent further oxidation. A patina may be formed on art objects by exposure first to acid fumes and then drying as above. While still warm, the object can be further protected by a spray of wax in a solvent.

For bearings, sintered bronze is compacted from 10% tin, up to 2% graphite, and the balance by weight of copper. The aggregate is formed under pressure at a temperature below the melting point of its constituents but high enough to reduce their oxides. After forming, a bearing is repressed or sized and impregnated with oil, the pores retaining the lubricant until needed. In place of copper, alpha-bronze powder may be used; zinc may replace some of the tin. At forming temperatures below 1290°F (700°C), properties depend primarily on compacting pressure. At higher temperatures, properties depend first on temperature, although heat treatment beyond 30 min has minor influence. *See* ALLOY; ANTIFRICTION BEARING; BELL; COPPER; COPPER ALLOYS; TIN; TIN ALLOYS. Frank H. Rockett

Brown dwarf

One of the least massive self-gravitating objects that are formed in the fragmentation of an interstellar cloud. Brown dwarfs are less massive than the least massive true stars, the red dwarf stars, and are comparable to or heavier than the most massive planets, that is, the gas-giant planets such as Jupiter.

Brown dwarfs are distinguished from stars in that they are insufficiently massive to sustain long-term nuclear burning of hydrogen, although they undergo a brief period of deuterium (heavy-hydrogen) burning. Accordingly, brown dwarfs cool and fade away over periods of time that are short compared to the age of the Sun (5×10^9 years), while red dwarf stars burn hydrogen continuously at a relatively low rate and should continue to shine over times longer than the present age of the universe (about 10–20×10^9 years). The current search for brown dwarfs is important because studying them may elucidate the processes by which interstellar clouds break up and condense, and should demonstrate how to distinguish brown dwarfs from extrasolar planets (the planets of stars other than the Sun).

Mass range. Because the origin of a given object in space is rarely observed and the nature of the nuclear burning within an object is also not observed, astronomers use the working definition that objects in the mass range from 10 to 80 jupiters are brown dwarfs. One jupiter, the mass of the planet Jupiter, is equal to about one-thousandth the mass of the Sun. However, the definition of a planet, namely an object that does not sustain nuclear energy generation and that is formed by accretion in a viscous disk surrounding a star or protostar, does not necessarily exclude objects that may be as massive as 20 jupiters. Further, the theory of the internal constitution and nuclear-energy generation of red dwarf stars and brown dwarfs is sufficiently imprecise that the possibility exists that objects as light as 80 jupiters are red dwarf stars or that objects as heavy as 90 jupiters are brown dwarfs. These definitions can be improved only when brown dwarfs are identified with certainty and are subjected to detailed study.

Search for brown dwarfs. Several brown-dwarf candidates have been discovered, and one case is considered proven. Methods used to search for brown dwarfs that may be associated with known stars are astrometry, infrared photometry, infrared speckle interferometry, radial-velocity monitoring, and cluster population analysis. Astrometry seeks to detect brown dwarfs that are companions of known stars through the slight wobbling that the presence of a brown dwarf must induce in the motion of its accompanying star. Infrared photometry seeks to detect the infrared radiation of a brown dwarf that is the companion of a small hot star such as a white dwarf star. Infrared speckle interferometry is used to attempt to obtain images of infrared radiation sources, such as brown dwarfs, that are close companions of known stars. Radial-velocity monitoring is conducted to detect the orbital motion of a known star around the center of mass of the binary system that it forms with a brown dwarf. In cluster population analysis, the brightnesses and temperatures of stars in a galactic or open star cluster are compared to see if some stars are so much fainter and cooler than the others that they must be brown dwarfs. *See* ASTROMETRY; ASTRONOMICAL SPECTROSCOPY; SPECKLE; STAR CLUSTERS.

It appears from radial-velocity monitoring that sunlike stars are not likely to have brown dwarf companions. A striking result from infrared speckle interferometry is that red dwarf stars generally lack brown dwarf companions. Astrometry and infrared speckle interferometry have detected a few objects which may be brown dwarf companions of low-mass stars but which could well be very light red dwarf stars. Population analyses of the Hyades and Pleiades star clusters have identified several possible brown dwarfs. However, none of these cases has been proven. The detection of unseen, gravitating objects (MACHOs) in the galactic halo and galactic bulge has prompted speculation that they may be brown dwarfs. *See* HYADES; PLEIADES.

Positive but not certain evidence for brown dwarfs comes from infrared photometry, which has revealed the existence of faint companions, glowing in infrared light, to the white dwarf stars Giclas 29-38 and GD165. The object GD165B (the companion of GD165) is clearly seen on infrared images, but may be an extremely low-mass red dwarf. However, a faint companion of the nearby star Gliese 229 has been detected and definitely identified as a brown dwarf. The near-infrared spectrum of this object, Gl 229B, establishes the presence of methane and water vapor in its atmosphere, implying a temperature less than 1000 K (1350°F), much cooler than any known star. The object's mass is about 20–50 jupiters and its luminosity about $1/250{,}000$ that of the Sun. *See* BINARY STAR; INFRARED ASTRONOMY; MACHOS; PLANET; RED DWARF STAR; STAR; STELLAR EVOLUTION.   Stephen P. Maran

Bibliography. M. C. Kafatos, R. S. Harrington, and S. P. Maran (eds.), *Astrophysics of Brown Dwarfs*, 1986; S. P. Maran, Very-low-mass companions—extrasolar planets?, *Physics News in 1987*, p. S-14, 1988, and *Phys. Today*, 40(1):S-14, January 1988.

Brownian movement

The irregular motion of a body arising from the thermal motion of the molecules of the material in which the body is immersed. Such a body will of course suffer many collisions with the molecules, which will impart energy and momentum to it. Because, however, there will be fluctuations in the magnitude and direction of the average momentum transferred, the motion of the body will appear irregular and erratic, as shown in the **illustration**.

In principle, this motion exists for any foreign body suspended in gases, liquids, or solids. To observe it, one needs first of all a macroscopically visible body; however, the mass of the body cannot be too large. If its mass is M, one can estimate the root-mean-square velocity $\bar{v}$ by the equipartition law, written as Eq. (1). Here, k is the Boltzmann

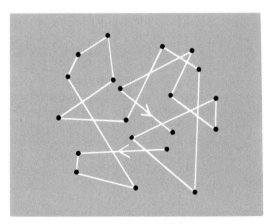

Random brownian movement of a particle.

$$\tfrac{1}{2}M\overline{v^2} = \tfrac{3}{2}kT$$

$$\sqrt{\overline{v^2}} = \sqrt{\frac{3kT}{M}} \tag{1}$$

constant and T is the absolute temperature. Hence, for a large mass, the velocity becomes small. For example, a 0.01-g mass has at 300 K a root-mean-square velocity of 3.5×10^{-6} cm/s. *See* KINETIC THEORY OF MATTER.

Mirror in a gas. A simple observable example of brownian motion is the motion of a mirror in a gas. If a mirror of moment of inertia I is suspended by a fine fiber, this mirror will execute a simple harmonic motion of natural frequency ω_0. Its mechanical equation of motion is written as Eq. (2), where θ

$$\frac{d^2\theta}{dt^2} + \omega_0^2\theta = 0 \tag{2}$$

is the angular displacement and $\omega = d\theta/dt$ the angular velocity. If this mirror is placed in the gas, the unequal forces on the two sides of it, which are due to the fluctuations in the momentum transferred by the molecules, will cause fluctuations around the harmonic oscillations. After a time, one will have equipartition of energy. For the rotational kinetic energy, one has Eq. (3a). For the rotational potential energy, one has Eq. (3b).

$$\tfrac{1}{2}I\overline{\omega^2} = \tfrac{1}{2}kT \tag{3a}$$

$$\tfrac{1}{2}I\omega_0^2\overline{\theta^2} = \tfrac{1}{2}kT \tag{3b}$$

By careful measurement, relations such as Eqs. (3a) and (3b) may be checked. Brownian motion also yields a limit for the accuracy which may be obtained in a given experiment. *See* HARMONIC MOTION.

Langevin equation. If a small particle is suspended in a liquid, its displacement x in the course of time can be observed. The displacement will of course be erratic, but one can still calculate the average displacements, or root-mean-square displacements, at any time t. It is possible to compare these experimental results with theoretical calculations. If a small body moves through a liquid, it will the usual viscous drag, $-\beta Mv$, where M is the mass, v is the velocity, and β is a numerical coefficient depending on the viscosity. For a sphere of radius R, $M\beta$ has the value given by Stokes' law: $M\beta = 6\pi R\eta$, where η is the coefficient of viscosity. In addition, a fluctuating force $MA(t)$, varying rapidly in the course of time, but of average value zero, acts on the particle. One may therefore write an equation of motion as Eq. (4).

$$\frac{dv}{dt} = -\beta v + A(t) \tag{4}$$

See VISCOSITY.

If one now multiplies Eq. (4), the Langevin equation, by x, averages over time, and applies the equipartition law, one obtains for a Stokes case Eq. (5). This result was originally derived by

$$\overline{x^2} = \frac{kTt}{3\pi R\eta} \qquad (5)$$

Albert Einstein; it expresses the root-mean-square displacement explicitly in terms of observable parameters. Equation (5) has been verified with an accuracy of about 0.5%. *See* COLLOID.   **Max Dresden**

Bibliography. R. Durrett and H. Kesten (eds.), *Random Walks, Brownian Motion and Interacting Particle Systems.*, 15(1), 2d ed., 1991; A. Einstein, *Investigations on the Theory of Brownian Movement*, 1926; D. Freedman, *Brownian Motion and Diffusion*, 1971, reprint 1983; T. Hida, *Brownian Motion*, 1980; I. Karatzas and S. E. Shreve, *Brownian Motion and Stochastic Calculus*, 2d ed., 1991; F. B. Knight (ed.), *Essentials of Brownian Motion and Diffusion*, 1981, reprint 1989; S. C. Port and C. J. Stone, *Brownian Motion and Classical Potential Theory*, 1978.

Brucellosis

An infectious disease of animals and humans caused by bacteria of the genus *Brucella*. The organisms are *B. melitensis*, found in sheep and goats, *B. abortus* in cattle, and *B. suis* in swine. Humans become infected through direct contact with infected animals or by ingesting their unpasteurized milk. The principal animal reservoirs of the disease are cattle, swine, goats, and sheep. *Brucella ovis* infects goats, but not humans; *B. canis* infects dogs, and rarely humans. Brucellosis occurs throughout the world and is one of the most important of the nearly 100 diseases of animals transmissible to human beings.

The brucellae are small, nonmotile, nonsporing, gram-negative coccobacilli. *Brucella militensis* and *B. suis* will grow aerobically in trypticase soy broth, but *B. abortus* requires 10% carbon dioxide. Differentiation of all the species is made by biochemical reactions, growth requirements, and serological tests.

Animals. The brucellae localize in the reproductive organs and mammary glands of animals. This makes the disease of serious economic concern to livestock producers and dairy producers because it causes abortions and reduces the production of milk. The disease in cattle is known as Bang's disease, or contagious abortion.

Humans. Brucellosis in humans, also known as undulant fever or Malta fever, is primarily an occupational disease in which infection through the skin is acquired by contact with the tissues of freshly killed animals, or with the contaminated environment of the animals. The disease is also contracted by drinking unpasteurized milk and by eating fresh cheese prepared from unpasteurized milk.

The acute illness is characterized by chills, fever, sweats, and weakness. Chronic disease results in weakness and mental depression. The usual course of the disease is less than 3 months, but antibiotic therapy (chlortetracycline) reduces the length of the illness. It may also prevent both recurrence and complications, such as osteomyelitis, orchitis, subacute endocarditis, and diseases of the kidney and liver.

Diagnosis. In animals the diagnosis is made by detecting brucella antibodies in the milk (whey test or ring test) or in the blood. The diagnosis in humans is established by the presence of brucella agglutinins in the blood and by isolating brucellae from blood cultures. A standardized brucella antigen is used in tests for brucella agglutinins. The brucella skin test is of doubtful diagnostic value.

Prevention. Human brucellosis can be eliminated only by eradicating the disease in animals. The disease is controlled in cattle by eliminating infected animals. Successful vaccination of cattle against the disease has been achieved with a live brucella culture having stable, attenuated virulence. An effective vaccine has been developed for the protection of sheep and goats, but not for swine.

The incidence of human brucellosis can be reduced by using only pasteurized animal milk for human consumption. *See* EPIDEMIOLOGY; MEDICAL BACTERIOLOGY.   **Wesley W. Spink**

Bibliography. K. Nielsen and R. J. Duncan (eds.), *Animal Brucellosis*, 1990; M. M. Rementsova, *Brucellosis in Wild Animals*, 1987.

Brucite

A magnesium hydroxide mineral, $Mg(OH)_2$, crystallizing in the trigonal system with space group $P\bar{3}m$. It is a member of $Cd(OH)_2$ structure type, consisting

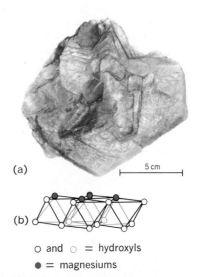

(a)   5 cm

(b)

○ and ◌ = hydroxyls

● = magnesiums

Brucite. (*a*) Specimen found in Texas, Pennsylvania (*American Museum of Natural History specimens*). (*b*) Trioctahedral brucite structure (*after R. E. Grim, Clay Mineralogy, McGraw-Hill, 1953*).

of hexagonal close-packed oxygen atoms with alternate octahedral layers occupied by Mg. The "brucite layer" is an important structural component in the clay, mica, and chlorite mineral groups.

Brucite occurs as tabular crystals and as elongated fibers (as the variety nemalite), cleavage on {0001} perfect, hardness 2.5 (Mohs scale), color white to greenish, and specific gravity 2.4. Fe^{2+} and Mn^{2+} commonly substitute for Mg^{2+}. The structural unit consists of two sheets of closely packed hydroxyl ions in which magnesium atoms are octahedrally considered (see **illus**.).

Brucite often occurs in a low-temperature vein paragenesis, usually with serpentine and accessory magnesite. It is also derived by the action of water on periclase, MgO, which results from the thermal metamorphism of dolomites and limestones. Carbonate rocks rich in periclase and brucite are called predazzites. *See* DOLOMITE; MAGNESITE; SERPENTINE.   Paul B. Moore

Brussels sprouts

A cool-season biennial crucifer (*Brassica oleracea* var. *gemmifera*), which is of northern European origin and belongs to the plant order Capparales. The plant is grown for its small headlike buds formed in the axils of the leaves along the plant stem (see **illus.**). These buds are eaten as a cooked vegetable. Cultural practices are similar to those used for cabbage; however, monthly mean temperatures below 70°F (21°C) are necessary for firm sprouts. Brussels sprouts are moderately tolerant of acid soils and have a high requirement for boron. Popular varieties (cultivars) are Half Dwarf and Catskill; however, hybrid varieties are increasingly planted. Harvesting begins when the lower sprouts are firm and 1–2 in. (2.5–5 cm) in diameter, usually 3 months after planting. California and New York are important producing states. *See* CABBAGE; CAPPARALES.   H. John Carew

Brussels sprouts (*Brassica oleracea var. gemmifera*), Jade Cross. (*Joseph Harris Co., Rochester, New York*)

Bryales

An order of the subclass Bryidae. With 11 families and perhaps 44 genera, it is defined in terms of terminal inflorescences, with rare exceptions, and perfect, double peristomes which are papillose on the outer surface. The capsules are generally inclined and more or less pear-shaped. Erect capsules are associated with reduced peristomes.

These mosses often grow in disturbed places. They are perennial and grow in tufts, with stems erect and simple or forked and often densely covered with rhizoids. The leaves are generally bordered by elongate cells and often toothed. The midrib often ends in a hairpoint. The cells, usually smooth, are not differentiated at the basal angles. The sporophytes are nearly always terminal. The setae are generally elongate, and the operculate capsules are usually symmetric but generally inclined to pendulous and commonly pyriform owing to the development of a sizable neck. The peristome is normally double, with a well-developed endostome. The 16 lanceolate teeth of the exostome are evenly tapered and papillose on the outer surface. Keeled and perforate endostome segments alternate with the teeth and arise from a generally high basal membrane. Alternating with the segments are usually one to four cilia. The calyptrae are cucullate and naked. Chromosome numbers are 5, 6, 10, 11, 12, often in polyploid series. *See* BRYIDAE; BRYOPHYTA; BRYOPSIDA.
          Howard Crum

Bryidae

A subclass of the class Bryopsida. Most genera of true mosses (Bryopsida) belong in the 16 orders of the Bryidae. The most characteristic feature is the peristome consisting of one or two series of teeth, derived from parts of cells rather than whole cells, as in the Tetraphididae, Dawsoniidae, and Polytrichidae. (The Buxbaumiidae have some resemblance in peristome structure to Bryidae.) The stems may be erect and merely forked, or prostrate and freely branched, with sporophytes produced terminally or laterally, respectively. The leaves are inserted in many rows, though sometimes flattened together and appearing two-ranked, but only rarely actually in two rows. The costa may be single or double, sometimes very short, and rarely lacking. The cells are short or elongate, thin- or thick-walled, and often papillose-roughened. The basal and especially the basal angular cells are often differentiated. The setae are generally present and elongate. The capsules dehisce by means of an operculum except in a few genera that show extreme reduction. The number of peristome teeth and segments of the inner peristome are usually 16. The spores are produced by two layers of spore mother cells; they are generally small. The calyptra may be cucullate or mitrate. *See* ARCHIDIIDAE; BRYALES; BRYOPHYTA; BRYOPSIDA; BRYOXIPHIALES; DAWSONIIDAE; DICRANALES; ENCALYPTALES; FISSIDENTALES; FUNARIALES; GRIMMIALES; HOOKERIALES; HYPNALES; ISOBRYALES; MITTENIALES; ORTHOTRICHALES; POLYTRICHIDAE; POTTIALES; SELIGERIALES; SPLACHNALES; TETRAPHIDIDAE.   Howard Crum

Bibliography. G. C. S. Clarke and J. G. Duckett, *Modern Approaches in Bryophyte Systematics*, 1979; S. P. Parker (ed.), *Synopsis and Classification of Living Organisms*, 2 vols., 1982; H. Robinson, A revised classification for the orders and families of mosses, *Phytologia*, 21:289–293, 1971; R. J. Taylor and A. E. Leviton (eds.), *The Mosses of North America*, 1980.

Bryophyta

A division that consists of some 23,000 species of small and relatively simple plants commonly known as mosses, granite mosses, peat mosses, liverworts, and hornworts (see **illus.**). The bryophytes display a distinct alternation of sexual and asexual generations; the sexual gametophyte, with a haploid chromosome number, is the more diversified. The sporebearing, diploid sporophyte is reduced in size and structure, attached to the gametophyte, and partially or almost completely dependent on it.

Structure. The gametophytes may consist of leafy stems or flat thalli. They have no roots but are anchored to the substrate by hairlike rhizoids. Vascular tissue is at best poorly differentiated, with no lignification of cells. Growth results from the divisions of single cells (rather than meristematic tissues) located at stem tips or in notches at the margins of thalli. The sex organs are multicellular and have a jacket of sterile cells surrounding either the single egg produced in flask-shaped archegonia or the vast number of sperms produced in globose to cylindric, stalked antheridia. The sperms swim by means of two flagella. The sporophyte develops, at least during the early stages, inside a calyptra of gametophytic tissue. The sporophyte commonly consists of a capsule that produces a large number of spores, a stalklike seta, and a swollen foot anchored in the gametophyte. The seta is sometimes lacking and, in a very few thallose liverworts, the foot as well. The spores, nearly always single-celled,

are dispersed in the air, except in the case of a small number of aquatics. They germinate directly or produce a juvenile stage called a protonema. *See* REPRODUCTION (PLANT).

Diversity and phylogeny. The division can be divided into five classes: Sphagnopsida (peat mosses), Andreaeopsida (granite mosses), Bryopsida (true mosses), Hepaticopsida (liverworts), and Anthocerotopsida (hornworts). The mosses have radially organized leafy gametophytes that develop from a protonema and have multicellular rhizoids with slanted crosswalls. The liverworts and hornworts are mostly flat and dorsiventrally organized and have no protonematal stage; the rhizoids are unicellular. Though obviously related, as evidenced by

Brophytes. (*a*) Moss plant, *Polytrichum juniperinum* (*General Biological Supply House*). (*b*) Male and female plants of liverwort, *Marchantia*. (*c*) Hornwort, *Anthoceros* (*Carolina Biological Supply Co.*).

similar sex organs and attachment of a simplified sporophyte to a more complex and independent gametophyte, the classes differ greatly in structural detail. Swimming sperms and relative simplicity suggest an origin among the aquatic green algae, but the attachment of sporophyte to gametophyte and the frequent occurrence of trilete spores, stomata in the capsule wall, rudiments of vascular tissue of some similarity to xylem and phloem (especially in the gametophyte), protection of sex organs, and development of a sporangium that produces countless airborne spores are strong evidence for an origin on land, perhaps from a stock ancestral to the earliest vascular plants, or psilophytes. A significant difference from that group is that bryophytes never have branched sporophytes.

An outline of the Bryophyta is shown below. See separate articles on each group listed.

Class Hepaticopsida (liverworts)
Subclass Jungermanniidae
Order: Takakiales
Calobryales
Jungermanniales
Metzgeriales
Subclass Marchantiidae
Order: Sphaerocarpales
Monocleales
Marchantiales
Class Anthocerotopsida (hornworts)
Class Sphagnopsida (peat mosses)
Class Andreaeopsida (granite mosses)
Class Bryopsida (true mosses)
Subclass: Archidiidae
Subclass: Bryidae
Order: Fissidentales
Bryoxiphiales
Schistostegales
Dicranales
Pottiales
Grimmiales
Seligeriales
Encalyptales
Funariales
Splachnales
Bryales
Mitteniales
Orthotrichales
Isobryales
Hookeriales
Hypnales
Subclass: Buxbaumiidae
Tetraphididae
Dawsoniidae
Polytrichidae

See PLANT EVOLUTION; PLANT KINGDOM.

Howard Crum

Bibliography. N. S. Parihar, *An Introduction to Embryophyta,* vol. 1, 1961; P. Puri, *Bryophytes: A Broad Perspective,* 1973; D. H. S. Richardson, *The Biology of Mosses,* 1981; F. Verdoorn, *Manual of Bryology,* 1932; E. V. Watson, *The Structure and Life of Bryophytes,* 3d ed., 1971.

Bryopsida

The largest class of the division Bryophyta, the true mosses. Members of the class are best characterized by operculate capsules and a peristome that aids in the dispersal of spores, and are generally perennial. The class consists of about 14,000 species distributed in six subclasses based primarily on the structure and developmental history of the sporophyte and especially the peristome. The orders and families are likewise based primarily on stable sporophytic details, whereas genera and species are most often differentiated in terms of gametophytic features.

Gametophyte. The filamentous, freely branched protonema of Bryopsida gametophytes produces an abundance of leafy plants which may be erect, simple or sparsely forked, and growing in tufts and producing archegonia at the stem tips (**Fig. 1**); or, alternatively, plants may be prostrate, freely branched, growing in intertangled mats, and producing archegonia laterally. If the apical cell is used up by the formation of archegonia, growth usually continues by the formation of a new subapical branch, called an innovation. But if the terminal cell is not used up and the archegonia are produced laterally, the stems are indeterminate in growth and form numerous branches. Growth results from the activity of a single apical cell with three cutting faces, or in a few genera with two-

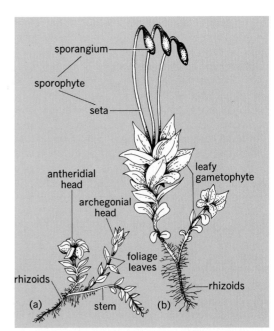

Fig. 1. True moss (*Mnium*). (a) Location of sex organs (male antheridia and female archegonia). (b) Gametophyte with attached sporophytes. (*After W. W. Robbins et al., Botany, 3d ed., 1964*)

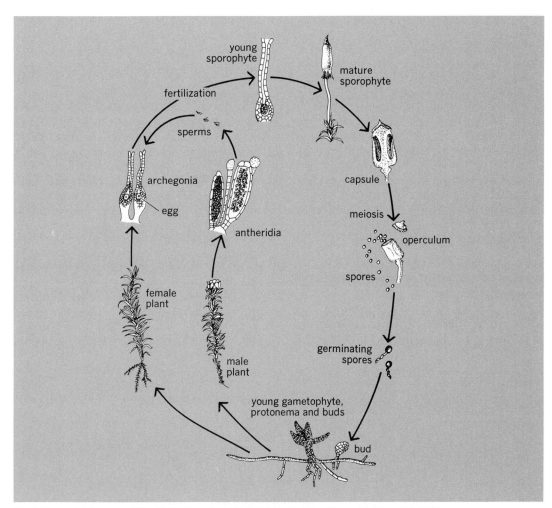

Fig. 2. Life cycle of a moss. (*After E. W. Sinnott and K. S. Wilson, Botany, 6th ed., McGraw-Hill, 1963*)

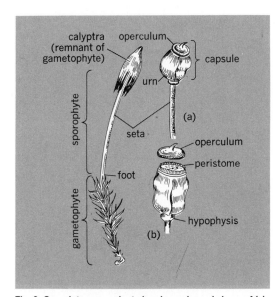

Fig. 3. Complete moss plant showing enlarged views of (*a*) tip of sporophyte with calyptra removed and (*b*) capsule (sporangium), with operculum and peristome and, beneath the capsule, the hypophysis. (*After F. W. Emerson, Basic Botany, 2d ed., Blakiston, 1954*)

ranked leaves the apical cell becomes, secondarily, two-faced. In large, erect-growing plants, the stems may have a central strand of vascular tissues similar to xylem and phloem but without lignification. In smaller plants, the vascular tissue is reduced or lacking. The rhizoids are multicellular, with slanted crosswalls. The inflorescences are usually enveloped in differentiated leaves, and the sex organs, of superficial origin, are often mingled with paraphyses, especially in the male inflorescence. The archegonia are flask-shaped; the antheridia are banana-shaped and stalked (**Fig. 2**). *See* PHLOEM; XYLEM.

Sporophyte. The long-lived sporophytes are abundantly green until maturity and largely self-supporting. They consist of foot and capsule, usually also a seta (**Fig. 3**). The capsules dehisce by means of a lidlike operculum, or rarely irregularly by rupture. Operculate capsules are provided with a single or double fringe of peristome teeth in multiples of four at the mouth. The peristome is generally derived from the amphithecium (the outer tissue of the embryonic capsule). The capsule wall is usually spongy, especially in the neck portion below the spore sac. Stomata are usually present, especially in the neck or at the junction of capsule and seta; the stomata usually have two guard cells. The spore sac is derived from the endothecium; it surrounds but does not overarch the slender columella. The calyptra may be mitrate (conic and lobed) or cucullate (slit up one side and hoodlike). The chromosome numbers are exceedingly diverse; polyploidy is common, both within species and among related ones. *See* ARCHIDIIDAE; BRYIDAE; BRYOPHYTA; BUXBAUMIIDAE; DAWSONIIDAE; POLYTRICHIDAE; TETRAPHIDIDAE.

Howard Crum

Bibliography. F. Cavers, The inter-relationships of the Bryophyta, *New Phytol.*, 9:81–112, 157–186, 196–234, 269–304, 341–353, 1910, and 10:1–46, 84–86, 1911; E. V. Watson, *The Structure and Life of Bryophytes*, 3d ed., 1971.

Bryopsidales

An order of the green algae (Chlorophyceae), also called Caulerpales, Codiales, or Siphonales, in which the plant body (thallus) is a coenocytic filament (tube or siphon). The filaments may be discrete with free or laterally coherent branches, or organized into a dense plexus exhibiting distinctive morphological features. Septa, which are generally infrequent and incomplete, are formed by centripetal deposition of wall material. A large, continuous central vacuole restricts the cytoplasm to a thin layer just beneath the wall. The cytoplasm contains innumerable nuclei, discoid plastids, and other organelles. Pigments are similar to those in higher plants but include two distinctive xanthophylls, siphonein and siphonaxanthin. Some genera have distinct plastids for the storage of starch. The chief constituent of the wall is frequently xylan or mannan, polysaccharides in which the monomer is xylose and mannose, respectively. Vegetative reproduction is common, usually by rhizomes or fragments. The life history, known for only a few genera, comprises either one somatic phase, with meiosis occurring in the production of gametes, or an alternation of strikingly dissimilar somatic phases, with meiosis occurring in the production of zoospores. Motile gametes are

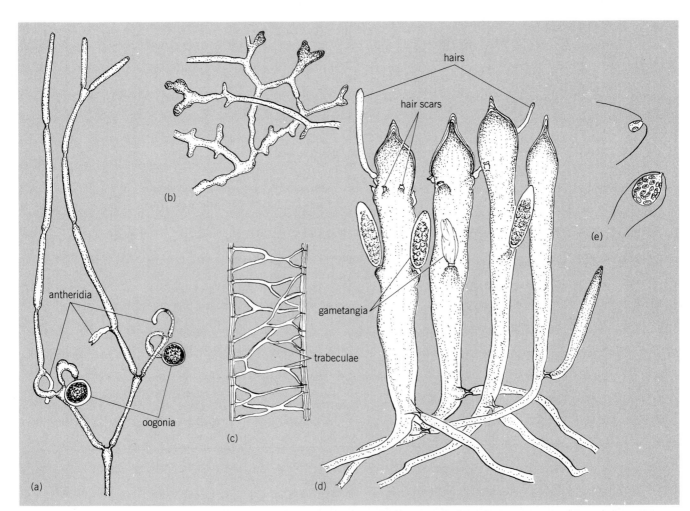

Fig. 1. Anatomical structures of selected members of Bryopsidales. (*a*) *Dichotomosiphon,* filament with oogonia and antheridia. (*b*) *Ostreobium,* filaments. (*c*) *Caulerpa,* section of filament showing trabeculae. (*d*) *Codium,* group of utricles with gametangia and hairs (or hair scars). (*e*) *Codium* gametes, male above and female below.

biflagellate, while zoospores have a subapical crown of flagella. Reproductive cells may be formed in unmodified or slightly modified portions of the filament or in special organs.

The order Bryopsidales comprises six families with about 24 genera. The Dichotomosiphonaceae, represented by a single species, *Dichotomosiphon tuberosus* (**Fig. 1***a*), occurs in fresh water, growing at the surface of pools and at depths of at least 50 ft (15 m) in lakes, where it becomes entangled in fish nets. The remaining families are marine and are most abundant and diverse in tropical and subtropical waters. *Bryopsis* (**Fig. 2***a*), an inhabitant of exposed rocky shores as well as wooden pilings in harbors, is the most commonly encountered member of the family Bryopsidaceae. The gametophyte of *Bryopsis* forms a dense tuft of profusely branched filaments, and is mosslike. The Ostreobiaceae includes a single, poorly defined genus (*Ostreobium;* Fig. 1*b*) with six species, all growing in calcareous substrates (old mollusk shells, corals, calcified red algae). *Caulerpa* (Fig. 2*b*), the only genus of the Caulerpaceae, has large filaments reinforced by strands of wall material (trabeculae; Fig. 1*c*) extending into and across the interior. The filaments may be threadlike, but usually they are coarsely cylindrical or flattened. The erect fronds may be very similar in general appearance to other plants, such as club moss and cypress. *Caulerpa* is extremely abundant and diverse in tropical and subtropical waters and (as an exception) in temperate southern Australia. Certain species prefer a rocky substrate, while others spread over large expanses of mud or fine calcareous sand by means of rhizoids. Some species produce a toxin, caulerpicin, which may enter the food chain of the tropical Pacific.

In Udoteaceae, the basic structural unit is a dichotomously or trichotomously branched threadlike filament that is often constricted in a regular pattern. The filaments often form a dense tuft borne on a stem (or stipe), as in *Penicillus* (Neptune's shaving brush; Fig. 2*c*). The most distinctive and ecologically important genus is *Halimeda* (Fig. 2*d*), in which the thallus is an articulate series of flattened or cylindrical segments that are heavily impregnated with aragonite, a form of calcium carbonate. *Halimeda* is nearly ubiquitous in tropical and subtropical seas, and its calcified remains have contributed to the buildup of coral reefs and the infilling of atoll lagoons since the Late Cretaceous. In *Codium* (Fig. 2*e*), the only genus of the Codiaceae, the basic structural unit is similar to that in the Udoteaceae, but the filaments are intertwined to form a spongy thallus that may be crustose, spheroidal, bladelike, or dichotomously branched and up to 33 ft (10 m) long. The chloroplasts are localized in swollen segments called utricles (Fig. 1*d*), which form a palisadelike surface layer. The genus is represented in all parts of the world except the Arctic and Antarctic, but is most diverse in tem-

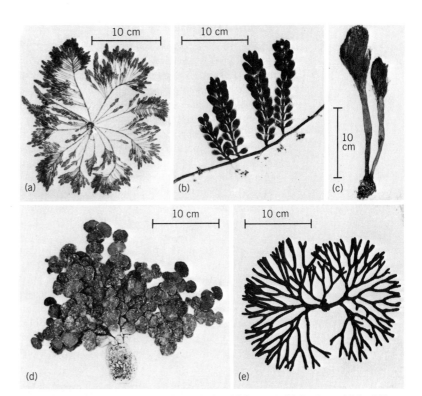

Fig. 2. Representative members of Bryopsidales. (a) *Bryopsis*; **(b)** *Caulerpa*; **(c)** *Penicillus*; **(d)** *Halimeda*; **(e)** *Codium*.

perate regions. *Codium fragile* ssp. *tomentosoides* is a notorious weed, spreading rapidly in the Atlantic and Pacific by fragmentation and parthenogenesis, and damaging shellfish plantings. *See* ALGAE; CHLOROPHYCEAE.   Paul C. Silva; Richard L. Moe

Bibliography. L. Hillis-Colinvaux, Ecology and taxonomy of *Halimeda*: Primary producer of coral reefs, *Adv. Mar. Biol.,* 17:1–327, 1980; J. Ramus, *Codium*: The invader, *Discovery* (Yale Univ.), 6(2):59–68, 1971.

Bryoxiphiales

An order of the class Bryopsida in the subclass Bryidae. The order consists of a single genus and species, *Bryoxiphium norvegicum,* the sword moss. This order is characterized by a swordlike appearance owing to leaves overlapping in two rows. The shiny, rigid leaves are keeled and conduplicate-folded. The apex is long-awned at the stem tip and progressively shorter-pointed downward. The midrib bears at back a low ridge of one to four rows of cells. The leaf cells are smooth and subquadrate within, longer and narrower toward the margins. The plants are dioecious with terminal archegonia. The capsules are immersed and have an operculum but no peristome. The calyptra is cucullate, and the haploid chromosome number 14. *See* BRYIDAE; BRYOPHYTA; BRYOPSIDA.

Howard Crum

Bibliography. A. Löve and D. Löve, Studies on *Bryoxiphium, Bryologist,* 56:73–94, 183–203, 1953.

Bryozoa

A phylum of sessile aquatic invertebrates (also called Polyzoa) which form colonies of zooids. Each zooid, in its basic form, has a lophophore of ciliated tentacles situated distally on an introvert, a looped gut with the mouth inside the lophophore and the anus outside, a coelomic body cavity, and (commonly) a protective exoskeleton (**Fig. 1**). The colonies are variable in size and habit (**Figs. 2**, **3**, and **5**). Some are known as lace corals and others as sea mats, but the only general name is bryozoans (sea mosses).

General Characteristics

Byrozoans form colonies by asexual budding from a primary zooid, or ancestrula, formed by metamorphosis of a sexually produced larva or from some kind of resting bud. Structurally the zooids are metazoan, triploblastic, unsegmented, and bilaterally symmetrical, with a regionated fluid-filled body cavity that is considered to be a coelom.

The body wall comprises epidermis underlain by a feebly developed peritoneum, between which muscle may be present. The epidermis secretes a chitinlike cuticle or gelatinous layer, and the cuticle may become calcified as a rigid exoskeleton.

Much of the zooid consists of the lophophore, alimentary canal, and associated musculature, together known as the polypide. The lophophore comprises a circle or crescent of slender, ciliated tentacles plus their supporting ridge. When spread for feeding, the tentacles form a funnel with the mouth at its vertex. During withdrawal the tentacles close, and are pulled downward from their base through the simultaneously in-rolling introvert. They then lie within the introvert, called the tentacle sheath. The open distal end of the in-rolled tentacle sheath is termed the orifice, and it may be closed simply by a sphincter muscle or by more elaborate structures.

The alimentary canal is deeply looped, and regionated into pharynx, stomach, and rectum. The limb descending from the mouth consists basically of the pharynx and stomach cardia; the central stomach and its dilatation, the cecum, form the base of the loop; and the stomach pylorus and the rectum constitute the ascending limb. The anus opens outside the lophophore. The nerve ganglion, center of a system that may be complex, lies between the mouth and the anus. There are no special excretory or respiratory organs, and no circulatory system. Colonies, but not all zooids, are hermaphroditic. Zooids are generally not more than 0.04 in. (1 mm) long.

The colony may be minute, of not more than a single feeding zooid and its immediate buds, or substantial, forming masses 3 ft (1 m) in circumference, festoons 1.5 ft (0.5 m) in length, or patches 0.67 ft^2 (0.25 m^2) in area. Commonly the colonies form incrustations not more than a few square centimeters in area, small twiggy bushes up to about 1.2 in. (3 cm) in height, or soft masses up to about 4 in. (10 cm) in the largest dimension. In many colonies much of the bulk consists of the zooid exoskeletons, termed zooecia, which may persist long after the death of the organism and account for the abundance of fossilized bryozoan remains.

Many bryozoans display polymorphism, having certain zooids adapted in particular ways to perform specialized functions, such as protection, cleaning the surface, anchoring the colony, or sheltering the embryo. The evolution of nonfeeding polymorphs is dependent upon some form of intercommunication between zooids.

All bryozoans are epibenthic, and are generally attached to firm substrata, less often anchored in or resting on sand. Most are marine, but one complete class (Phylactolaemata) is confined to fresh water. In the latter habitat, statoblasts and hibernacula, resting bodies resistant to cold and desiccation, are produced. Sexual reproduction leads either to a distinctive, planktotrophic larva,

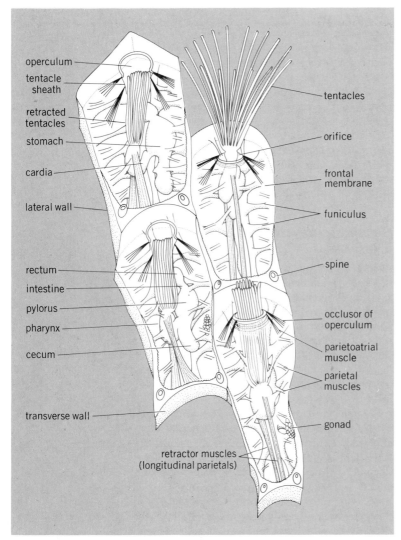

labels: operculum, tentacle sheath, retracted tentacles, stomach, cardia, lateral wall, rectum, intestine, pylorus, pharynx, cecum, transverse wall, retractor muscles (longitudinal parietals), tentacles, orifice, frontal membrane, funiculus, spine, occlusor of operculum, parietoatrial muscle, parietal muscles, gonad

Fig. 1. Morphological features of autozooids, in frontal view.

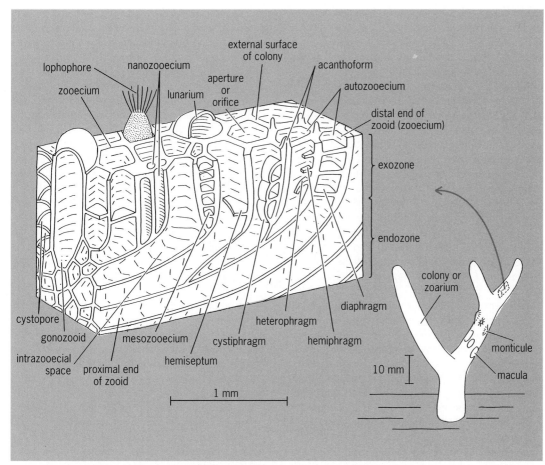

Fig. 2. Stenolaemate morphologic features, some of which are found only in living colonies and others only in fossil colonies. The enlarged oblique view is from the colony at the lower right.

called the cyphonautes, or more usually to a subspherical, nonfeeding, short-lived type that has had no particular name until recently distinguished as "coronate," because of its extensive ciliary corona.

Taxonomy and classification. Bryozoa is the name of a phylum for which Ectoprocta is generally regarded as a synonym, these names being used by zoologists according to personal preference. Entoprocta (synonym Calyssozoa) is likewise regarded as an independent phylum. A minority regard Ectoprocta and Entoprocta as subphyla within the Bryozoa, while others maintain Ectoprocta and Entoprocta as phyla but link them under Bryozoa as a name of convenience. *See* ENTOPROCTA.

The phylum contains some 20,000 described species, one-fifth of them living. These are distributed among three classes and a somewhat variable number of orders.

Class Phylactolaemata
    Order Plumatellida
Class Gymnolaemata
    Order: Ctenostomata
           Cheilostomata
Class Stenolaemata

    Order: Cyclostomata
           Cystoporata
           Trepostomata
           Cryptostomata
           Hederellida

See GYMNOLAEMATA; PHYLACTOLAEMATA; STENOLAEMATA.

Until somewhat over 200 years ago bryozoans went unrecognized. When discovered they were thought, with coelenterates, to be plants—a confusion that led Linnaeus to invent the term zoophyte. In 1830 J. Vaughan Thompson characterized bryozoans, separating them from other zoophytes, but at the same time ambiguously introducing a class Polyzoa. G. C. Ehrenberg's name Bryozoa followed in 1831. *See* CHEILOSTOMATA; CRYPTOSTOMATA; CTENOSTOMATA; CYCLOSTOMATA (BRYOZOA); CYSTOPORATA; HEDERELLIDA; TREPOSTOMATA.

Comparative morphologists link the Bryozoa with the Phoronida and the Brachiopoda, characterized especially by possession of a lophophore, which L. H. Hyman defined as "a tentaculated extension of the mesosome that embraces the mouth but not the anus, and has a coelomic lumen." The tentacle circlet of the Entoprocta is postanal and noncoelomic. The designation of the bryozoan lophophore as mesosomal, and its body cavity as mesocoelic, rests entirely on the interpretation of a supraoral flap of tissue, the epistome, present in phylactolaemates, as the protosome or first region of a tripartite body. In addition to the lophophore and presumed tripartite body, all three phyla have a U-shaped alimentary tract. The lophophore is crescentic in some members of all three groups. Even if the relationship is correct, however, it sheds little light on bryozoan origins. The soft-bodied Phylactolaemata have left no fossil record, but comparative anatomy suggests that they, the Stenolaemata, and the Gymnolaemata must already have been distinct by the Ordovician. The view that Bryozoa arose from entoprocts, perhaps by internal budding from the larva, seems tenuous, and implies at most no more than a similarity between larvae such as that which links Mollusca to Annelida. Certainly the immediate ancestor must have been vermiform and sedentary, for cylindrical zooids, terminal lophophores, and deeply recurved digestive tracts with the anus rather close to the mouth represent the primitive state in all classes.

Functional morphology of zooid. Zooids in all three byrozoan classes display the same ground plan: eversible lophophore, U-shaped gut, fluid-filled coelom, and deformable body wall. The lophophore is everted by increase in hydrostatic pressure caused by inflexion of the body wall; withdrawal is achieved by the direct pull of retractor muscles anchored to the wall. The flexible phylactolaemate wall incorporates circular and longitudinal muscle, and its contraction everts the lophophore. Recent work indicates that stenolaemates, as evidenced by the extant Cyclostomata, have a remarkably modified system. Throughout this class the zooid is cylindrical (often inaccurately described as tubular; only the exoskeleton is tubular). Except in the immediate vicinity of the orifice, the cuticle is calcified and totally rigid. The peritoneum, with a hypertrophied basal membrane and associated bands of circular muscle, has detached from the epidermis and lies freely as a bag, the membranous sac, anchored at some points to the body wall. The endosaccal cavity is coelomic, but the exosaccal cavity, external to the mesoderm, is not. The sac contracts to evert the lophophore; exosaccal fluid must be displaced proximally as the polypide is eased toward the orifice.

The simplest gymnolaemates (Ctenostomata) have cylindrical zooids and deformable walls, although the musculature is extrinsic. The circular (now renamed transverse parietal) muscles lie inside the peritoneum, and the longitudinal muscles are reduced and specialized. Mechanically the system works as in Phylactolaemata. An early trend of zooidal evolution in the Gymnolaemata was toward a flat, membranous, coffinlike shape, adherent to the substratum. It seems probable that the cheilostomes arose from ctenostomes like that by calcification of the lateral walls and the differentiation of a cuticular lid, the operculum, to close the orifice. Cheilostomes of this plan, classified as the suborder Anasca, preserve a wholly or partially flexible front wall. Transverse parietal muscles, relocated to span the coelom from the rigid lateral walls to the frontal membrane, bring about its inflexion.

Natural selection in cheilostomes has favored modifications which better protect the polypide while preserving the function of the frontal membrane. Thus the frontal membrane can be underlain by a shelf, at a distance sufficient to permit inflexion; or it can be overarched by flattened spines or by a meshwork of partially fused spines. In the subclass Ascophora the membrane may be overgrown or replaced by a calcified frontal wall, but the flexible membrane either remains or is replaced more deeply by a functional equivalent. A saclike cavity or ascus, opening just behind the orifice, is created either by overgrowth of the wall or by involution from the orifice underneath the wall. Transverse parietal muscles insert on the lower face of the ascus, which is pulled down to evert the lophophore, while water to compensate for the volume change enters the ascus through its opening.

Feeding. The expanded lophophore of marine bryozoans forms an almost radially symmetrical funnel of 8–30 tentacles, although fixed or transient bilateral symmetry may occur. In gymnolaemates the base of this funnel stands free above the surface of the zooid, but in stenolaemates it lies concealed within the orificial region of the exoskeleton. The top diameter is in the range of 0.01 to 0.05 in. (0.25 to 1.25 mm). In primitive phylactolaemates 20–30 tentacles form a funnel, but in most members of this class the large lophophore comprises 100 or more tentacles disposed in a horseshoe, the lobes

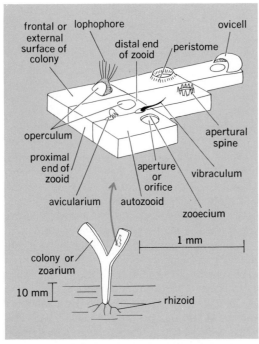

Fig. 3. Morphological features of gymnolaemate colony, and enlarged oblique view of block from it.

of which project from the adanal side.

The base of the lophophore is the most complex part of the polypide. Essentially it is a hollow epidermal annulus, with thickened basement membrane. The lumen (mesocoel) opens into the main body cavity (metacoel) by an adanal pore. The cerebral ganglion partly occludes this pore, and a nerve tract parallels the mesocoel. Radial and circular muscles open and close the mouth. The tentacles rise from the annulus as slender hollow cylinders. Their central coelom is surrounded by a thick, flanged collagenous tube, the hypertrophied basement membrane of the epidermal cells. The lumen, which opens terminally through a minute pore, is lined by peritoneum and contains frontal (that is, facing into the funnel) and abfrontal longitudinal muscles. The lateral epidermal cells bear long cilia (about 25 micrometers) and the frontal cells shorter cilia (about 15 μm). Laterofrontally is a line of static sensory cilia. The tentacles contain motor and sensory nerves.

The lateral cilia generate a water current that enters the top of the funnel and flows downward and outward between the tentacles. Particles such as bacteria and phytoplankton are separated from the water and directed at the mouth by the frontal cilia without the use of mucus. The mechanism of separation is uncertain, but a likely explanation is that particles passing out between the tentacles, perhaps sensed by the rigid laterofrontal cilia, are flicked back into the funnel by localized reversal of ciliary beat. Small particles accumulate just above the mouth; heavier particles may be projected down the funnel and directly into the partly open mouth.

Unwanted particles are rejected by closing the mouth, flicking the tentacles, closure or concerted movements of the funnel, and ejection from the pharynx (see below). A few bryozoans with large lophophores have rejection tracts leading centrifugally between the ventromedial (abanal) tentacles. Bryozoans are vigorous feeders, and it has been calculated that the lophophore of even a small zooid filters about 0.3 ml/h (and a colony may contain thousands of zooids).

Bryozoan colonies may have exhalant chimneys or set points of water outflow. The reason is clear: if the colony is large, solid, flat, and uniformly covered by tentacular funnels pumping toward its surface, the filtered water requires a means to get away. Small colonies may have a single, central chimney; large colonies may have a mamillate surface, the summit of each mamilla marking a chimney; and wholly flat colonies produce chimneys by an apparently coordinated bending away of lophophores from predetermined points. Filtered water flows toward the chimneys, through which it is expelled. Lophophores surrounding a chimney display strong bilateral symmetry, with the bordering tentacles standing tall and upright instead of curving into the chimney. A consequence of the posture is that the beat of the current-generating lateral cilia becomes centripetal to the chimney rather than being unhelpfully directed toward its base.

The pharynx is a remarkable organ. It is short, thick-walled, and situated immediately below the mouth. Its exterior is circular in section, its interior deeply furrowed. The frontal ciliation from the lophophore continues through the mouth and may cover the distal part of the pharynx: the midventral groove is ciliated, even when the rest of the pharynx is not, and its cilia beat upward, whether there is a ventromedial rejection tract or not. Between the grooves, the inwardly bulging walls are made up of vacuolated cells which incorporate intracellular myofibrils. The simultaneous contraction of all the myofibrils, acting against the fluid-filled vacuole, causes a brief convulsive dilation of the pharynx, engulfing the particles accumulated outside the mouth.

A sphincter and valve separate the pharynx from the cardia (descending arm of the stomach). In some ctenostomes, and a few other bryozoans, part of the cardia is differentiated as a gizzard, armed internally with teeth or keratinized plates, presumably for crushing the frustules of diatoms. The unmodified wall of the cardia contains secretory cells. The floor of the central stomach is ciliated, evidently to carry particles into the cecum, which is the main locus of extra- and intracellular digestion and absorption. The epithelium of the pylorus is ciliated and serves to compact the undigested remains into a revolving cord. A sphincter separates the pylorus from the rectum, which has an absorptive function and modifies the cord of reject material into fecal pellets. The pellet is moved through and expelled from the rectum by peristalsis. At summer temperatures (72°F or 22°C) the gut transit time is less than 1 h but at 43°F (6°C) it is 2 h.

Metabolic integration and colony evolution. The simplest bryozoan colonies presumably consisted of loosely interconnected, monomorphic feeding zooids. In the most ancient fossil stenolaemates, confluence of coeloms had been achieved either by means of internal pores or by the so-called double wall, in which a superficial (or hypostegal) coelom unites the colony outside the calcification. The hypostegal coelom must have been reasonably effective as a means of distributing metabolites, since the colonies of trepostomes were large by bryozoan standards, and the fenestrates evolved colony forms of considerable complexity. However, rapid growth and the proliferation of nonfeeding zooid polymorphs requires a transport system more efficient than aqueous diffusion. The funiculus provides such a system.

In living single-walled stenolaemates (cyclostomes) zooids communicate via small, open interzooidal pores. The funiculus is a small muscular strand linking the proximal end of the cecum with the base of the membranous sac at its attachment to the zooid wall. The testis is positioned where the funiculus joins the cecum. The phylactolaemate funiculus similarly is muscular, supports the testis, and links the cecum to the proximal end of the ventral body wall. More importantly, it contains a core of blastogenic tissue from which the statoblasts arise. These are the future resting buds and become richly supplied with yolk. The obvious inference is that the products of digestion are transported, perhaps to the testis but certainly to the developing statoblasts, along the funiculus. Communication between zooids in phylactolaemates is by open pores; indeed in many of them the dividing walls have almost completely broken down, so that the polypides are suspended in a communal coelom.

The adaptive radiation of zooid form has been very slight in both Cyclostomata and Phylactolaemata. Cyclostome zooids have remained as slender cylinders, while the colonies have evolved mainly in terms of the way in which the zooids are disposed. Thus regular, alternating placement of zooid orifices is replaced by a pattern of separated short rows or fascicles, presumably to improve feeding efficiency; and erect or partially erect colonies have evolved from creeping ones. The reproductive zooids, at first clearly in series with the rest, become larger, more central, and often truly colonial by incorporating neighboring structures. Phylactolaemates have evolved larger, deeply crescentic lophophores, but the zooids have not diversified. Evolution of the colony has been toward unity by confluence of coeloms.

Primitive gymnolaemates have an organization very like that of the simpler phylactolaemates: elongate zooids connected by simple open pores, with the funiculus confined within each zooid. The radiation of stolonate ctenostomes has been facilitated by the development of a colonial, essentially nonmuscular funiculus which passes through the internal pores between zooids and along the stolons. A flux of lipid from feeding zooids into the stolonal funiculus occurs and spreads toward the growth and budding zones. The funiculus has become a colony-wide metabolic expressway.

When cheilostomes evolved from ctenostomes, they inherited the funicular system. They added mural calcification and developed complex communicating pores in the lateral walls, while retaining simple pores in the end walls. The main funicular trunks are longitudinal, passing from the proximal pores to the distal pores via the cecum, with branches to the lateral pores. The success of the Cheilostomata, in terms of species numbers, adaptive radiation, and polymorphism, is evidently the result of a high-potential module, plus the distributive efficiency of the funiculus in nourishing large numbers of specialized, nonfeeding zooids.

Nervous system. The cerebral ganglion is dorsally (adanally) situated in the lophophore base and has a diameter of 30–60 μm. It is extended circumorally as a ring or deep crescent. Apart from the fibrillar component, the anascan ganglion contains distal, central, and proximal groupings of cell bodies. The principal nerves are the following. (1) Sensory and motor lophophoral nerves. (2) Paired direct tentacle sheath nerves which unite with the first branch of the trifid nerve to form (3) the compound tentacle sheath nerves: these extend up the tentacle sheath to the superficial part of the zooid, including the sensitive region near the orifice. (4) The trifid motor nerve; of its three branches, the first, 4a, is visceral, meeting its opposite number at a small suprapharyngeal visceral ganglion; the second, 4b, innervates the paired retractor muscles of the polypide; and the third, 4c, joins the compound tentacle sheath nerve and innervates the tentacle sheath muscles, the orificial sphincter, occlusors of the operculum, and the transverse parietal muscles that deflect the frontal membrane. It will be noted that 4b and 4c innervate the antagonistic effectors in polypide withdrawal and eversion. (5) Paired parietal nerves parallel the direct tentacle sheath nerves, but pass deep to join a peripheral encircling ring which enters in turn each of the interzooidal pores. Here the parietal nerves of neighboring zooids make contact. (6) Paired visceral nerves originate in the suprapharyngeal ganglion.

Electrophysiological research has confirmed the existence of a functional colony-wide nervous system in anascans. Stimulation near the orifice results in the immediate withdrawal of all nearby expanded lophophores (while stimulation of a lophophore results only in its withdrawal).

Polymorphism. Phylactolaemates have achieved integration at the expense of zooid individuality, so that polymorphs have not evolved (unless the statoblasts are so regarded). Stenolaemates have metabolic integration dependent on diffusion gradients, and display weakly developed polymorphism. In living cyclostomes, four morphs are commonly encountered: (1) normal-feeding or autozooids; (2) empty or kenozooids of various kinds, which support colonies, make up attachment rhizoids and stolons, in-fill spaces, and project as spines; (3) female or gynozooids, also called brooding or gonozooids, that do not feed but produce ova and shelter the developing embryos; and (4) dwarf or nanozooids, containing a reduced unitentaculate polypide which sweeps and cleans the surface of the colony. All zooids which are not autozooids may be termed heterozooids.

Among gymnolaemates, which have metabolic integration via the funiculus, the ctenostomes have limited polymorphism. Apart from the autozooids, only kenozooids are commonly present, either as stolon segments or as spines attached to autozooids. The cylindrical type of zooid, whether calcified or cuticularized, has not provided the potential for extensive polymorphism. In cheilostomes, on the contrary, one sees a wide range of heterozooids, high numbers of heteromorphs per colony, and the grouping of polymorphs into functional units or cormidia (colonies within colonies). Of importance in contributing to such impressive adaptive radiation seem to be the funicular system, the retention of individualistic zooids, and the calcified, boxlike zooid with its partly membranous front and hinged, lidlike operculum closing the orifice.

Cheilostome zooid types merge with one another, but the following may usefully be recognized: (1) sterile or fertile autozooids, which may also brood embryos but do feed, at least for most of the time; (2) androzooids or nonfeeding males with reduced polypides; (3) gynozooids (gonozooids), nonfeeding females which produce ova and sometimes brood the embryo; (4) avicularia, in which the operculum is enlarged; (5) vibracula, in which the operculum is lengthened to whiplike proportions; (6) kenozooids for in-filling, or associated with attachment rootlets and stolons; (7) kenozooids in the form of spines; and (8) ooecia or brood chambers.

Avicularia appear to be zooids modified for grasping. They vary in form from something close to an autozooid, differing only in having an enlarged operculum, or mandible, to diminutive and highly modified structures. The large ones often obviously replace autozooids in the colony, and are termed vicarious; the smaller ones are attached to autozooids, and are termed adventitious. Often a zooid may bear several adventitious avicularia of different kinds and in a variety of positions. Abductor muscles open the mandible by pulling down the small frontal membrane just behind the hingeline, whereas larger adductors snap it shut. In its most evolved form, the bird's-head avicularium, the zooid is pedunculate and mobile. The avicularian polypide is much reduced, and is believed to fulfill a sensory role.

Some avicularia have a long slender mandible, and may be precursors of vibracula, in which the operculum has become a whiplike seta. The vibracular seta, however, is mounted on asymmetrical condyles and can be swiveled by gyrator muscles, as well as being moved through a regular arc. In some species the vibracula remove sediment from the colony surface, and in nonattached sand-living forms they also act as struts or legs.

Spines are small kenozooids of varied form. They are normally adventitious and presumably have a protective role. The arguments for regarding cheilostome spines as zooids are basically three: they are separated from their bearing autozooid by a communication pore of standard morphology; they terminate with a flat membrane, seen as homologous to a frontal membrane; and they may replace an undoubted polymorph, for example, an autozooid or avicularium. The fundamental arrangement of spines in anascans is as a marginal ring around the frontal membrane. One worker sees this as the vestige of an ancient type of budding, each spine representing what was once a free-rising series of zooids. Even when this annular pattern is modified, as in certain erect, branching anascans and in ascophorans, the basic arrangement frequently persists in the founding zooid or ancestrula. In later zooids the spines are confined to the immediate region of the orifice.

Marginal spines may be modified, as when one or a series overarches the frontal membrane. One major fossil group (with a few extant species) has a porous, protective frontal shield formed by the fusion of such spines.

Most cheilostomes brood their embryos in special external chambers of standard plan: a hoodlike upfolding from the distal/proximal boundary of two zooids, which may become partly or wholly immersed in or between these zooids. It is called an ooecium and is double-walled, with outer ectooecium and inner entooecium separated by a coelomic lumen. In some species at least, the lumen is confluent with the coelom of the bearing zooid, and the ooecium appears to be a spinous polymorph. However, its development is inconsistent, for example, commencing with paired outgrowths from the proximal zooid or with a single outgrowth from the distal zooid. It is easy to interpret the former as representing the distal pair of marginal spines, especially since these are usually otherwise lacking in ooeciferous zooids. Development from the distal zooid is more difficult to explain, although it should be noted that proximally situated spinelike zooids are not unknown in cheilostomes.

The bryozoan colony is made up from replicated zooids. The simpler polymorphs are vicarious and dispersed through the colony in an ordered or apparently random manner. With the development of adventitious polymorphs, however, a second-order unit, the cormidium, becomes recognizable. Cormidia are groupings of dissimilar polymorphs. Siphonophora (Cnidaria) provide the standard example of colonies with cormidia and it seems generally unappreciated that cheilostomes have cormidia that are at least as complex and probably better integrated. Thus an autozooid may bear spines, an ooecium, adventitious avicularia, and perhaps a vibraculum. Little is known about behavioral coordination in cormidia; much more is known about the metabolic relationships between a female zooid and its ooecium.

Reproduction and growth. Propagation by statoblasts is important in Phylactolaemata. They develop in large numbers on the funiculi, and are liberated when the colony breaks up. Statoblasts have a protective coat, often a float, and sometimes hooked spines. They are resistant to cold and desiccation and give rise to a new colony under favorable conditions. Nonphylactolaemates in fresh and brackish water may produce resting zooids or hibernacula, and many marine species overwinter as nutrient-filled stolons. Asexual reproduction by fragmentation occurs in a few marine bryozoans, and is said to be important to the free-living sand forms. Lobulation of colonies is characteristic of the more evolved phylactolaemates.

Gonads in bryozoans are associated with the peritoneum: testes on the funiculus, ovaries more often on the zooid wall. Cyclostome spermatozoa develop in tetrads, but in phylactolaemates and gymnolaemates large numbers develop around a common mass, the cytophore. In marine bryozoans (at least) they escape from the body via the mesocoel and the terminal pore in two (the dorsomedial pair) or all of the tentacles. Special male zooids with nonfeeding polypides may be localized in chimneys, thereby taking advantage of the exhalant current to disperse the spermatozoa.

The fertilized egg in phylactolaemates develops in an invagination of the body wall. When released, it is already essentially a motile zooid ready to settle and found a colony. The cyclostome gynozooid is inflated and may occupy much of the colony. Its embryo, having reached the blastula stage, lobulates a series of secondary blastulae, which may repeat the process, until the brood chamber contains 100 or more embryos. Each develops into a simple, ovoid, coronate larva which swims for a short time and then metamorphoses into a proancestrula or incomplete primary zooid. This lengthens and becomes functional.

Sexual reproduction in gymnolaemates follows one of three general patterns. (1) Small eggs are discharged into the sea via the intertentacular organ, an inflated tube situated between the dorsomedial tentacles. Fertilization takes place there. The zygote develops into a planktonic, feeding, triangular, flattened, bivalved larva or cyphonautes. This probably lives for several weeks before it settles. (2) A large, fully yolked egg is produced in the coelom, and extruded through the supraneural coelomopore (replacing the intertentacular organ) into an external brood chamber. If this is an ovicell, the embryo receives no nourishment, for its size is unchanged during development. A nonfeeding coronate larva is liberated. (3) Smallish yolky eggs are transferred to the lumen of an ovicell via the supraneural pore. The ovicell comprises the ooecium, previously described, and an internal membranous extension of the mother zooid, the inner vesicle. The fertilized egg lies between the ooecium and the inner vesicle. The vesicular epithelium, well supplied with funicular strands, hypertrophies where it is in contact with the embryo and becomes a pseudoplacenta. That food is supplied to the embryo is evidenced by its growth during development. A nonfeeding coronate larva is liberated.

The larva responds to light and other stimuli. It achieves limited dispersal and selects a settlement site. Prior to metamorphosis the larva explores a surface with special long cilia; at the moment of attachment a hollow organ, the adhesive sac, is everted, spreads as a disk, and flattens onto the surface. Metamorphosis is total and its details are complex, but the larval organization disappears and a reversed polarity emerges. (Phylactolaemate development does not include this reversal.) The ancestrular polypide differentiates from the upper wall, and colonial budding commences.

The method of budding differs between the three classes. In phylactolaemates new polypide rudiments appear, abanally to the parent, in an ordered manner which determines the branching pattern of the colony. Differentiation of cystids (the zooid walls), insofar as they are present, follows the polypides.

In stenolaemates polypide rudiments also appear first, but are adanal to the parent zooid. Since the cystids are essentially tubular, they grow around the polypide rudiments following division of the longitudinal walls. However, it is important whether these calcified walls meet or remain slightly distant from the terminal epithelium. In the latter case, coelomic confluence remains around their distal end (the double-walled structure), whereas in the former, cystids are separate once formed and communicate only through interzooidal pores.

Gymnolaemate budding is different again, and dependent from the outset on the connecting pores and funiculus. The cystid is produced first, adanally to the mother zooid, and the polypide develops within it.

The pattern of colony formation is termed astogeny. Early on, it is often characterized by sequential change in the size and morphology of the zooids; later astogeny is repetitive, with the production of virtually identical zooids, groupings of zooids, cormidia, or groups of cormidia. The continuous colony in cheilostomes arises from the apposition of repeatedly dividing lines of zooids. The walls between contiguous lines are therefore morphologically double, and the communication pores in them have differentiated from potential zooid buds, which is one reason why they are more complex than the pores in end walls. Frontal budding, of a layer of zooids above the existing layer or layers, may also occur.

Initial formation does not complete the zooid's development. Wall thickening may continue, phases of reproductive activity come and go, while a cycle of polypide aging and renewal continues until senescence. This cycle, in which the whole polypide regresses, and is histolyzed until only a compacted, fibrous "brown body" remains, is peculiar to bryozoans. Old zooids may consist only of an accumulation of brown bodies.

Ecology. Fresh-water bryozoans are present on submerged tree roots and aquatic plants in most lakes, ponds, and rivers, especially in clear water of alkaline pH. Their presence is best confirmed by dip-netting for statoblasts at the water's edge. Most other bryozoans are marine, although some gymnolaemates inhabit brackish water. They are common in the sea, ranging from the middle shore to a depth of over 26,000 ft (8000 m), and are maximally abundant in waters of the continental shelf. Most attach to firm substrata, so that their distribution is primarily determined by the availability of support. Mud is unfavorable and so is sand unless well provided with stone, dead shells, hydroids, or large foraminiferans, as in regions of strong current, where colony densities may reach 470/ft² (5000/m²) of hard substrate.

Intertidal bryozoans shun the light, and are found under boulders, below overhangs, and on algae, particularly under conditions of high flow; they avoid turbid water and accumulating sediment. The seaweed dwellers are mainly fleshy ctenostomes and specially flexible cheilostomes, or are very small. Experiments with larvae have demonstrated high selectivity with regard to substrate, for example, algal species or shell surface. Settlement is influenced by texture and contour, with larvae often preferring concavities.

Colony form in bryozoans is to some extent related to habitat. Encrusting and bushy flexible species are adapted to wave exposure; brittle twiglike and foliaceous species are found deeper; some erect branching species tolerate sediment deposition. One group of tiny discoid species lives on sand in warm seas, and in one genus the colonies are so small that they live actually among the sand grains; a few species live anchored by long kenozooidal stems in mud. A number of stolonate ctenostomes bore into the substance of mollusk shells; other species are associated only with hermit crabs, and a few are commensal with shrimps or polychaete worms.

Primarily, however, bryozoans are inhabitants of shaded rock surfaces, where they compete with each other, sponges, and compound ascidians for space. They have no set size or shape, and reproductive capacity is simply a function of size. Some display adaptations, such as raised margins, long spines, or frontal budding, to resist being overgrown. When colonies meet, there is often a mutual cessation of growth, but with different species the one with larger zooids may overgrow its

rival or impair its feeding efficiency. Closely related species sometimes display slightly different habitat preferences, thereby avoiding direct competition. Pendent and outgrowing colonies escape the surface competition and become better placed for feeding; they include elegant lace corals and robust fans rising 6–12 in. (15–30 cm) in height.

Bryozoans have few serious predators. Nudibranch mollusks and pycnogonids (sea spiders) specialize in feeding on zooids but are rarely destructive of entire colonies. Loxosomatids (Entoprocta) and a hydroid (*Zanclea*) are common commensals.

Life spans vary. Small algal dwellers complete their life cycle in a few months. Many species survive a year but have two overlapping generations; others are perennial, with one known to survive for 12 years.

Bryozoans may be a nuisance in colonizing ship hulls and the insides of water pipes, and one species has caused severe dermatitis in fishers. Recently some delicate kinds have been used in costume jewelry, and green-dyed clumps of dried *Bugula* are often sold as "everlasting plants."

John S. Ryland

Fossils

Fossil Bryozoa, also called fossil ectoprocts, have a long geological history from early in the Ordovician Period [500 million years ago (m.y.a.)] to the Recent (**Fig. 4**). Individual colonies range in size

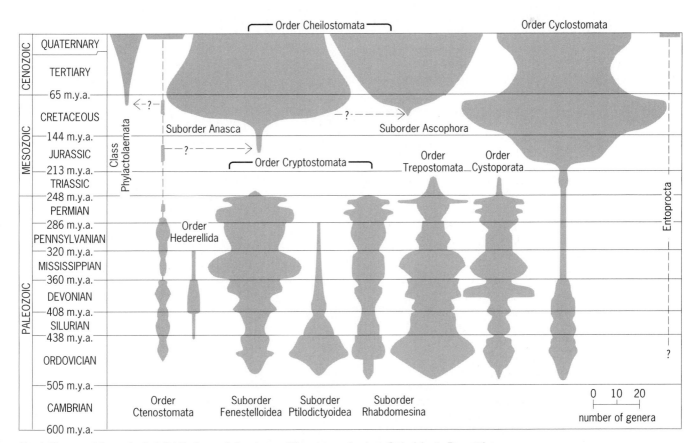

Fig. 4. Diagram of the geological distribution and abundance of Bryozoa ranging from Ordovician to Recent time.

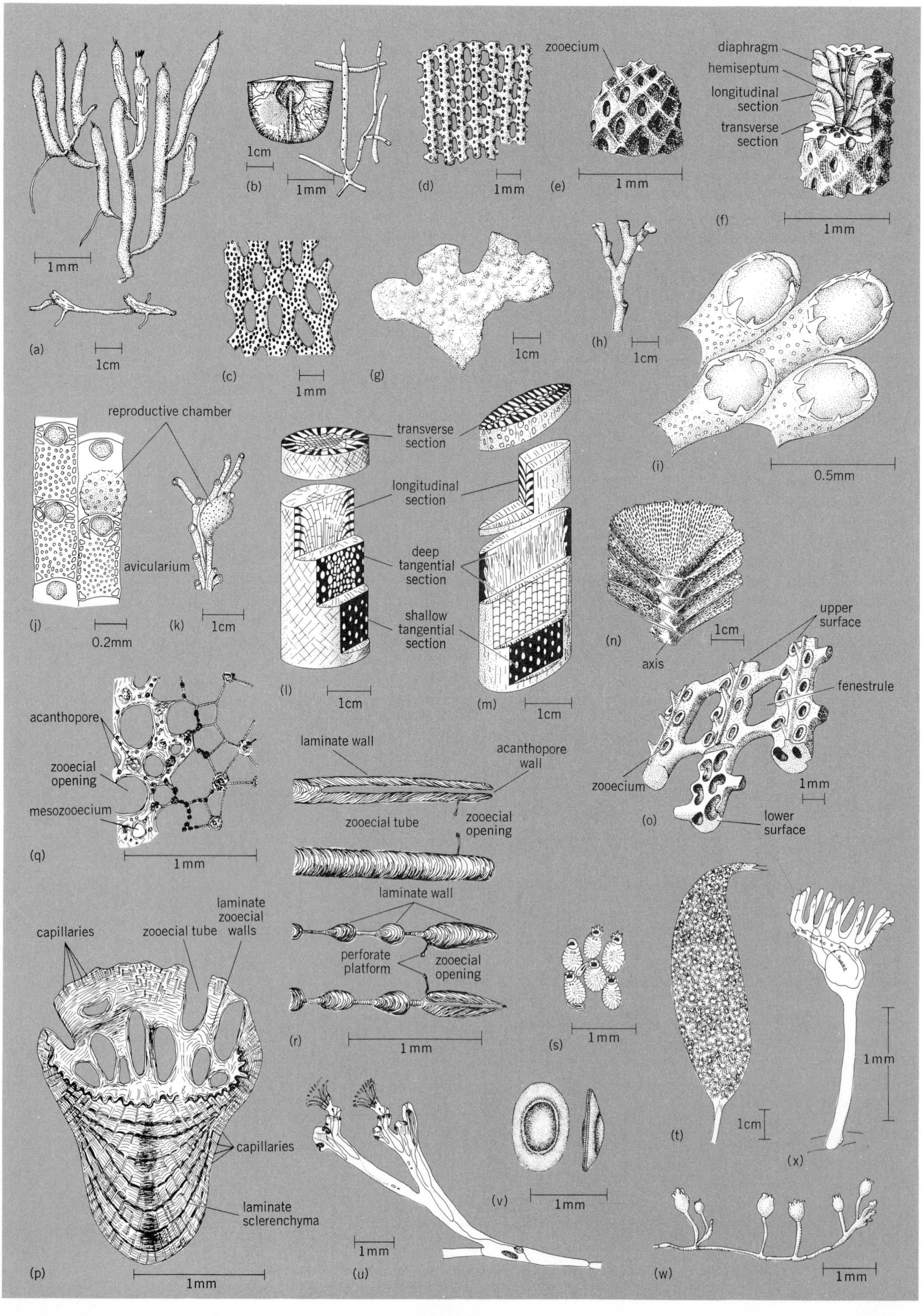

(a)

(b) 1cm / 1mm

(c) 1mm

(d) 1mm

(e) zooecium / 1mm

(f) diaphragm / hemiseptum / longitudinal section / transverse section / 1mm

(g) 1cm

(h) 1cm

(i) 0.5mm

(j) reproductive chamber / avicularium / 0.2mm

(k) 1cm

(l) transverse section / longitudinal section / deep tangential section / shallow tangential section / 1cm

(m) 1cm

(n) axis / 1cm

(o) upper surface / fenestrule / zooecium / lower surface / 1mm

(q) acanthopore / zooecial opening / mesozooecium / 1mm

(r) laminate wall / acanthopore wall / zooecial tube / zooecial opening / laminate wall / perforate platform / zooecial opening / 1mm

(s) 1mm

(p) capillaries / zooecial tube / laminate zooecial walls / capillaries / laminate sclerenchyma / 1mm

(t) 1cm

(u) 1mm

(v) 1mm

(w) 1mm

(x) 1mm

from a few millimeters to several meters in height. A vast array of diverse colony forms record the heterogeneity of this phylum (**Fig. 5**a–n). There are about 1100 known fossil genera and about 15,000 known fossil species. Representatives of the marine orders that secreted calcareous skeletons (Cryptostomata, Cyclostomata, Cystoporata, Trepostomata, and Cheilostomata) commonly are abundant in sedimentary rocks deposited in various environments of marine basins where sessile benthic animals flourished. The calcareous skeletons are generally calcite, but some are aragonite or a mixture of calcite and aragonite. The Ctenostomata with only soft membranous or gelatinous colonies are preserved as impressions, excavations, or borings generally in marine shells. The fresh-water Phylactolaemata with soft gelatinous colonies are mostly not preserved except for statoblasts (dormant reproductive bodies) [Fig. 5v] that are reported from Quaternary (2 m.y.a.) rocks.

Bryozoan-bearing rocks. Fossil Bryozoa are most abundant in impure calcareous rocks, such as limestone, calcareous shale and siltstone, and shelly marl. Accumulations of fragments of bryozoan colonies are readily collected from weathered thin-bedded limestones alternating with shales. Fossil Bryozoa are uncommon in quartzose clastic rocks and fissile black shales; they are poorly preserved in dolomites. Bryozoa were common contributors to fossil reefs and carbonate banks and formed extensive reef-flanking deposits from the Ordovician Period onward. They also were part of the fauna of bioherms and biostromes (reefal mound accumulations of organisms on the shallow continental shelves in the epeiric seas). *See* BIOHERM; BIOSTROME.

Paleoecology. Fossil groups associated with bryozoans are mainly sessile benthic organisms, such as articulate brachiopods, algae, corals, and echinoderms in Paleozoic rocks (500–250 m.y.a.) and mollusks in post-Paleozoic rocks (225 m.y.a. to present). In the early Paleozoic such nonsessile groups as trilobites and cephalopods formed a consistent part of the faunal association. A firm or rocky substrate or shells of other marine organisms were necessary for the settlement and attachment of bryozoans. Bryozoans flourished best on stable bottoms in the shallow waters (less than 330 ft or 100 m depth) of continental shelves where current action was marked but wave action was not extensive.

Methods and techniques. In the study of bryozoans, preparation of material for examination with a microscope is necessary. Although colonies of many species are large in size, the individual skeletons of each animal composing a colony range from 0.002 to 0.008 in. (0.05 to 0.20 mm) in diameter. Identification is based on numerous external and internal features that require study with a microscope using magnifications ranging from 10 to 500 times. Thin sections are generally essential to classify most species unless the species of a particular fauna are well known to the investigator. Commonly a minimum of three differently oriented thin sections (transverse, longitudinal, and tangential) of a colony is necessary to identify the species (Fig. 5l, m). Sections made in different parts of a colony show growth changes, including various stages of calcification of the older parts of the colony. Thin sections may be made of free specimens which weathered from rock and also from

Fig. 5. (*Opposite*) Representative bryozoans; sketches of parts of colonies. (*a*) Ctenostome, general view of colony and enlargement of stolons, *Victorella*, Recent. (*b*) Tubular stolons of fossil ctenostome on brachiopod shell and an enlargement of stolons, *Vinella*, Ordovician–Cretaceous. (*c*) Reticulate colony of phylloporinid fenestrate, *Phylloporina*, Ordovician–Silurian. (*d*) Upper surface of fenestellid fenestrate colony, *Fenestella*, Ordovician–Permian. (*e*) Growing tip at upper end of branch of rhabdomesid colony, *Rhombopora*, Devonian–Permian. (*f*) Transverse and longitudinal views of a branch of rhabdomesid colony, *Rhombopora*, Devonian–Permian. (*g*) Branching explanate colony of fistuliporid cystoporate, *Fistulipora* Ordovician?–Permian. (*h*) Branching colony of trepostome, *Monotrypella*, Ordovician–Triassic? (*i*) Parallel series of zooecia of anascan cheilostome, *Electra*, Early Tertiary–Recent. (*j*) Zooecia with accessory structures in encrusting explanate colony of ascophoran cheilostome, *Schizoporella*, Early Tertiary–Recent. (*k*) Part of cyclostome colony with reproductive chamber, *Crisia*, Early Tertiary–Recent. (*l*) Orientations of different sections cut from part of a trepostome colony, *Rhombotrypa*, Ordovician–Silurian. (*m*) Orientation of different sections cut from part of bifoliate cryptostome colony, *Stictopora*, Ordovician–Silurian. (*n*) Colony with spiraling fenestellid fronds, *Archimedes*, Carboniferous–Permian. (*o*) Longitudinal, transverse, and tangential sections across a fenestellid fenestrate colony, *Fenestella*, Ordovician–Permian. (*p*) Longitudinal section through a single branch of a fenestellid fenestrate to show laminate patterns of calcareous matrix, *Polypora*, Ordovician–Triassic. (*q*) Tangential section deep into surface of a trepostome, *Tabulipora*, Devonian–Permian. (*r*) Longitudinal sections through zooecial tubes of a trepostome, *Tabulipora*, Devonian–Permian, and a trepostome, *Rhombotrypella*, Carboniferous–Permian. (*s*) Zooecia in encrusting colony of cribrimorph cheilostome, *Cribrilaria*, Early Tertiary–Recent. (*t*) Gelatinous phylactoaemate, general view of colony on twig, *Pectinatella*, Recent. (*u*) Chitinous phylactolaemate, enlargement of zooecia adhering to substrate, *Fredericella*, Recent. (*v*) Ventral and side views of statoblast of phylactolaemate, *Hyalinella*, Recent. (*w*) Colonial entoproct, view of colony, *Pedicellina*, Recent. (*x*) Zooid of solitary entoproct, *Loxosoma*, Recent. (*Parts a, i after J. S. Ryland, Catalogue of main marine fouling organisms, vol. 2: Polyzoa, Organization for Economic Cooperation and Development, Paris, 1965; b after R. S. Bassler, The Early Paleozoic Bryozoa of the Baltic Provinces, U.S. Nat. Mus. Bull. 77, pp. 1–382, 1911; c–f, n, o after R. C. Moore, C. G. Lalicker, and A. G. Fischer, Invertebrate Fossils, McGraw-Hill, 1952; g, h after E. O. Ulrich, Paleozoic Bryozoa, Illinois Geological Survey, Geology and Paleontology, vol. 8, pp. 283–688, plates 29–78, 1890; j after K. W. McCain and J. R. P. Ross, Annotated Faunal List of Cheilostome Ectoprocta of Washington State, Northwest Science, vol. 48, no. 1, pp. 9–16, 1974; k after J. R. P. Ross, Keys to the Recent Cyclostome Ectoprocta of Marine Waters of Northwest Washington State, Northwest Science, vol. 44, no. 3, pp. 154–169, 1970; l, m after J. R. P. Ross and C. A. Ross, Bryozoans, in B. Kummel and D. Raup, eds., Handbook of Paleontological Techniques, pp. 40–44, W. H. Freeman, 1965; p–r after J. R. P. Ross and C. A. Ross, Faunas and Correlation of the Late Paleozoic Rocks of Northeast Greenland, pt. 4: Bryozoa, Meddelelser om Gronland, bd. 167, no. 7, pp. 1–65, 1962; s after R. S. Bassler, Treatise on Invertebrate Paleontology, pt. G: Bryozoa, Geological Society of America and University of Kansas Press, 1953; t–v after L. H. Hyman, The Invertebrates, vol. 5: Smaller Coelomate Groups, McGraw-Hill, 1959; w, x after L. H. Hyman, The Invertebrates, vol. 3: Acanthocephala, Aschelminthes, and Entoprocta, McGraw-Hill, 1951*) large bulk samples of rock containing bryozoans. The rock is cut into thin slabs, and the surface of the slab is scanned for bryozoans with a microscope. Selected slabs having bryozoans of the desired orientation are trimmed and polished using fine carborundum powder. These polished and trimmed specimens are mounted on glass slides, and then the mounted specimen is ground from the other unpolished surface using carborundum powder until the rock specimen is thin enough to transmit light as a thin section. A great variety of embedding and mounting materials may be used in the preparations of thin sections.

Silicified limestones, in which the calcareous skeletons of bryozoans have been replaced by silica, can be etched with acetic acid to release the bryozoans from the rock. Surface features of such colonies may be excellently preserved, but internal features generally are incompletely preserved and the ultrastructure of the walls has been obliterated in the silica replacement process. Scanning and transmission electron microscopy may be used in determining ultrastructural features and patterns.

Classification. Features of the colony as well as the morphology of the individual calcareous chambers (that is, zooecia) and accessory structures (for example, avicularia in Cheilostomata, and mesozooecia in Trepostomata) are used to classify bryozoans. Many of the accessory structures are the result of polymorphism, which is a phenomenon found in all groups of ectoprocts. The typical zooecium contained a fully developed animal, but other kinds of zooecia, such as avicularia and mesozooecia, were formed by reduction of other animals in the same colony which had no nutritive or reproductive functions. A bryozoan colony, therefore, shows various polymorphic tubes that are modified for specific types of individuals which performed specialized functions.

Wall structure (Fig. 5o–r) and morphology of reproductive chambers (Fig. 5j, k) are important characters in many groups. The wall structure of several groups of Paleozoic bryozoans shows fine calcareous laminae that arch convexly and interweave so that the resulting zooecial walls between two zooecial tubes appear continuous. In other Paleozoic bryozoans the arching laminae of adjacent walls abut and form an irregular boundary that appears as a jagged line. Wall structure in Mesozoic and Tertiary bryozoans has received relatively little study.

The exquisite and delicate character and the great variety in shape, size, and anatomy in bryozoan colonies (that is, zoaria) are astounding. Encrusting, lamellate, reticulate, and dendroid colonies are found in most orders that have calcareous colonies. Commonly the type of colony is the only feature that is determinable without the use of a microscope. The type of colony form is generally constant in most species, some genera, and a few families. Under different environmental conditions, colony form of a species may be modified; for example, an encrusting fan-shaped colony may become erect and grow as a free, explanate colony, or an erect, dendroid colony may become a narrow, encrusting colony.

The class Stenolaemata includes the orders Cryptostomata, Cyclostomata, Cystoporata, Hederellida, and Trepostomata (Fig. 5c–h, k, n–r. The Cryptostomata commonly are bifoliate colonies (Fig. 5m). The Cyclostomata have numerous genera with long, minutely porous zooecial tubes and distinctive reproductive chambers (Fig. 5k). The Cystoporata have a recrystallized wall structure suggesting the original calcareous skeleton was aragonite (Fig. 5g). The kind of zooecial opening is useful in differentiating members of this order. In the suborder Fenestelloidea, colonies are commonly reticulate (Fig. 5c, d, o, p). The suborder Rhabdomesina, comprising small twiglike dendroid colonies, have tubular zooecia arranged in various distinctive geometric patterns (Fig. 5e, f). The Trepostomata also have long zooecial tubes, and these may be crossed by curved or flat platforms (Fig. 5h, l, r).

The class Gymnolaemata includes the orders Ctenostomata and Cheilostomata; the cheilostomes have an extensive fossil record. In many cheilostome genera the zooecial tubes have evolved into calcified cylindrical or boxlike structures. Extrusion of the individual animal, particularly in the cheilostomes, from its tube or box is accomplished by adjustments in its internal fluid pressure, and this resulted in distinctive modes of construction of the zooecium. Some groups (anascan and cribrimorph cheilostomes; Fig. 5i, s) maintained the internal fluid pressure by means of a noncalcified flexible frontal layer across the zooecium that would be depressed or elevated. Others (ascophorans and gymnocystids; Fig. 5j) evolved a calcified frontal wall and controlled the internal fluid pressure with a sac directly beneath it; the sac had only one opening which led to the exterior of the zooecium, and filled and emptied of seawater to compensate for changes in the internal volume of the bryozoan animal.

Geologic history. The earliest bryozoans (representatives of the Ctenostomata, Cryptostomata, Trepostomata, Cyclostomata, and Cystoporata) are recorded from Lower Ordovician rocks (a few fossils from the Cambrian have been assigned erroneously to the Bryozoa). At the beginning of Middle Ordovician time, diverse groups of these various bryozoan orders, including the suborder of Ptilodictyoidea of the order Cryptostomata, had a broad geographic distribution (Fig. 4). The phylum continued to evolve rapidly, and toward the end of the Ordovician Period the Cryptostomata and Trepostomata were dominant. During the Ordovician Period some bryozoans had a high rate of speciation; for example, one species evolved into another species within an interval of 4 m.y. The Cystoporata, Cyclostomata, Hederellida, and Ctenostomata were less important faunal elements of the time period.

In the Silurian, the Trepostomata and Cryptostomata were still dominant. New groups evolved in other orders, including the family Fenestellidae (Cryptostomata), which occurred sparsely in the Late Ordovician. The cystoporates also became a more distinctive part of the bryozoan faunas. Less is known about the Silurian bryozoans of many regions because the principal sedimentary rocks are dolomites and evaporites and the bryozoans are either poorly preserved or they did not inhabit these environments.

Diversity of genera and species further increased in the Devonian Period. Fenestelliod and rhabdomesine cryptostomes were very abundant, and the number of fistuliporid cystoporates increased. The trepostomes continued to be well represented by new species and genera. The Cyclostomata and Hederellida were far more prominent than in earlier periods.

The Carboniferous and Permian bryozoans were dominated by various kinds of fenestelloids, rhabdomesines, and cystoporates. The trepostomes and cyclostomes were far less numerous. Toward the end of the Permian Period, almost all trepostomes, cryptostomes, cystoporates, and hederellids became extinct. This drastic reduction in bryozoan groups was a gradual process throughout much of the Permian and parallels similar patterns in other Paleozoic fossil groups.

Bryozoans are sparse in the Triassic Period. A few trepostomes, rhabdomesines, fenestelloids, and cyclostomes are reported from Triassic rocks, but some of these occurrences, particularly the trepostomes, rhabdomesines, and fenestelloids, appear to be reworked late Paleozoic pebbles that have been redeposited in Triassic sediments. In the Triassic Period, the Trepostomata, Cystoporata, and Cryptostomata became extinct. A new and highly successful group of cyclostomes, the cerioporids, appeared in the Late Triassic.

The Jurassic Period witnessed a great expansion of the Cyclostomata. This order dominated bryozoan faunas until the Late Cretaceous. The Cheilostomata, initially represented by anascans, which first appeared late in the Jurassic, rapidly became the dominant bryozoan group undergoing explosive diversification. Many of the major cheilostome groups had evolved by the Late Cretaceous. The cyclostomes continued to evolve new groups, but by the end of the Cretaceous less than half of the Cretaceous cyclostome genera survived into and through the Tertiary (65–2 m.y.a.). The Bryozoa of the Tertiary Period, like the present-day fauna, were principally cheilostomes. Some of the groups, such as the cribrimorphs, which flourished in the Late Cretaceous, declined in numbers in the Tertiary, many becoming extinct in the Early Tertiary. The anascans, a dominant group in the Cretaceous, continued to maintain their importance in the Tertiary bryozoan faunas and onward to the present day. The ascophorans and gymnocystids diversified rapidly, evolving new groups until the Early Tertiary, and they maintained good representation through the Tertiary to the present.

Evolutionary relationships. The evolutionary relationships within the phylum Bryozoa based on the fossil record leads back to the problem of the process of calcification and how organisms evolved methods to calcify tissue. Calcification of tissues permitted soft-bodied organisms, such as bryozoans, to use the mineralized material in the construction of colonies. Such a process opened up vast avenues of structural possibilities which otherwise would not have been available to them. They developed a more rigid framework which permitted better leverage for muscle action and a permanent supporting structure for connective tissue.

During the Cambrian Period, some phyla, such as the Arthropoda (for example, trilobites), evolved the ability to secrete hard, mineralized tissue composed of calcium phosphate and calcium carbonate. In the succeeding Ordovician Period, many additional phyla, such as Bryozoa and Brachiopoda, evolved methods to calcify tissue using calcium carbonate as the principal chemical material. In the fossil record, borings of the soft-bodied ctenostomes and the calcified colonies of all orders of the stenolaemates represent the oldest known bryozoans. These two Early Ordovician groups provide no morphological evidence to hypothesize a close evolutionary relationship. They all appear as a sudden evolutionary burst showing great diversification, but no well-defined evolutionary relations have been established between the different orders. It is presumed that all these Ordovician fossil groups evolved as independent lineages from an earlier ancestral group.

The origin of the cheilostomes which evolved in the Late Jurassic is uncertain. Ctenostomes and cheilostomes are commonly assumed to have arisen from a common ancestor. So far no definite evidence provides a link of the primitive anascan cheilostomes with the ctenostomes. Presently one hypothesis regarded with much favor is that the cheilostomes were derived from a ctenostome ancestor in Late Jurassic time. The discovery of a few cheilostomes in the Late Jurassic that are an encrusting, uniserial chain of pear-shaped zooecia is considered to support this interpretation because such a colony arrangement is similar to that of some ctenostomes. The evolution of the cheilostomes proceeded from primitive anascan cheilostomes having a noncalcified frontal layer with the progressive calcification of this frontal layer in different ways to lead to the great diversity of cheilostome groups (ascophorans, gymnocystids, spinocystids, and cribrimorphs) in the Cretaceous, Tertiary, and the present.   June R. P. Ross

Bibliography. F. P. Bigey (ed.), *Bryozoa: Living and Fossil*, 1991; S. P. Parker (ed.), *Synopsis and Classification of Living Organisms*, 2 vols.,

1982; R. A. Robison, *Treatise on Invertebrate Paleontology*, rev, 1983; J. P. Ross (ed.), *Bryozoa: Present and Past*, 1987; R. M. Woolacott and R. L. Zimmer, *Biology of the Bryozoans*, 1977.

Buckeye

A genus, *Aesculus*, of deciduous trees or shrubs belonging to the plant order Sapindales. Buckeyes grow in North America, southeast Europe, and eastern Asia to India. The distinctive features are opposite, palmately compound leaves and a large fruit having a firm outer coat and containing usually one large seed with a conspicuous hilum. The Ohio buckeye (*A. glabra*), a small tree which may grow to a height of 30 ft (9 m), is found mainly in the Ohio valley and in the southern Appalachians. It can be recognized by the glabrous winter buds, prickly fruits 1–2 in. (2.5–5 cm) long, and compound leaves having five leaflets. *See* SAPINDALES.

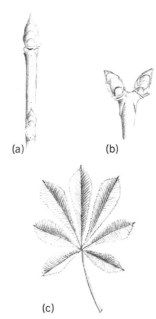

Horse chestnut (*Aesculus hippocastanum*): (*a*) twig, (*b*) buds, (*c*) leaf.

Another important species, the yellow buckeye (*A. octandra*), which may reach to 90 ft (27 m), is native in the Central states, has five leaflets and smooth buds, but differs in its smooth, larger fruit, which may be 2–2½ in. (5–6 cm) long. The horse chestnut (*A. hippocastanum*), which usually has seven leaflets and resinous buds (see **illus.**), is a native of the Balkan Peninsula. It is planted throughout the United States and is a beautiful ornamental tree bearing cone-shaped flower clusters in early summer. The seeds of all species contain a bitter and narcotic principle. The wood of the native tree species is used for furniture, boxes, crates, baskets, and artificial legs. *See* FOREST AND FORESTRY; TREE.

Arthur H. Graves / Kenneth P. Davis

Buckwheat

A herbaceous, erect annual, the dry seed or grain of which is used as a source of food and feed. It is not a true cereal and is one of the very few plants, other than those of the Gramineae family, used for their starchy seed, which is processed as a meal or flour.

Buckwheat belongs to the Polygonaceae family, which also includes the common weeds dock, sorrel, knotweed, bindweed, smartweed, and climbing false buckwheat. Species of buckwheat that have been commercially grown are *Fagopyrum sagittatum* (*F. esculentum*), *F. emarginatum*, and *F. tataricum*. *See* POLYGONALES.

The plant grows to a height of 2–5 ft (0.6–1.5 m), with many broad heart-shaped leaves. It produces a single main stem which usually bears several branches, and is grooved, succulent, and smooth except for nodes (see **illus.**). Buckwheat is an indeterminate species in response to photoperiod, and produces flowers and fruits (so-called seeds) until the beginning of frost. *See* PHOTOPERIODISM.

Species differentiation. *Fagopyrum sagittatum* and *F. emarginatum* produce flowers that are densely clustered in racemes at ends of branches or on short pedicels that arise from the axils of the leaves. Individual flowers have no petals, but the calyx is composed of five petallike sepals which may be light green, white, pink, or red. Populations

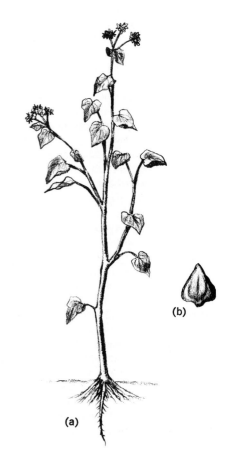

Buckwheat. (*a*) Mature plant. (*b*) Seed.

include plants typically of two floral types: the pin type which has flowers with long pistils and short stamens and the thrum type which has flowers with short pistils and long stamens. The pistil consists of a one-celled ovary, three-parted style with knoblike stigmas, and eight stamens. Glands (usually eight) which secrete nectar are located at the base of the ovary. Generally, self-fertilization is prevented by a heteromorphic incompatibility system, and seeds are produced only when cross-pollination occurs between the pin and thrum stylar types. The so-called seed of buckwheat (actually a fruit which is an achene) usually has three angles and varies in shape, size, and color. *See* FLOWER; FRUIT; SECRETORY STRUCTURES (PLANT).

Fagopyrum tataricum (commonly known as tartary buckwheat, rye buckwheat, duck wheat, or hulless) differs from the two previously described species. The leaves are narrower and arrow-shaped, and the flowers are smaller with inconspicuous greenish-white sepals. Plants are only of one flower type and are self-fertile.

Cultivation and use. Buckwheat is of minor importance as a grain crop in the United States, and is principally grown in areas of the Northeast where the weather is likely to be moist and cool. It is usually grown on land too rough or poor for other grain crops or, since it matures within 10–12 weeks, as an emergency crop where previous crops have failed. The crop is also used to smother weeds, as green manure, and as food and cover for various game birds and wildlife. Buckwheat is often used as bee pasture, and is the source of a dark, strong-flavored honey. H. G. Marshall

Processing. The production of buckwheat flour requires cleaning, grinding, and fractionation in a manner similar to that used for wheat flour. The distinctive polygonal shape of the grain kernel enables the use of sieving screens with triangular openings to facilitate separation of weed seeds and other foreign material. Sieving by size and the use of air aspiration enables separation of good-quality grain. Poor-quality, low-density seed and trash are removed by air aspiration. Successive cleaning of the grain is essential for premium quality. *See* WHEAT.

Hot-water steeping or steam pretreatment of the grain may be used to improve the nutritional properties, yield, and market value of buckwheat products. Dry heating or steaming of the grain prior to drying with temperatures less than 158°F (70°C) improves the efficiency of hull removal and reduces cooking time of selected products. Hulling is accomplished by using roller mills adjusted to crack the husk with minimum damage to the kernel. This operation must be precisely controlled to avoid excessive kernel fracture. Hulls, constituting about one-fifth of the grain by weight, are separated by sieving. Buckwheat hulls provide little food value and are utilized as animal litter.

The products of dehulled buckwheat include whole groats, split kernels, middlings or farina, and flour. Whole groats, splits, and farina are obtained by selective sieving and may be utilized as breakfast cereals and porridges or as thickening agents. Dry roasting of whole groats may be employed to increase color and flavor while decreasing their preparation time. When milled as flour, buckwheat will yield 60–75% extraction. The flour is typically more coarse and more highly colored than wheat flour. Buckwheat middlings, which include the layer immediately below the hull and the germ, provide valuable animal feed stock. In the United States, buckwheat flour is used primarily in pancake mix formulations, blended with wheat, corn, rice, or oat flour. Japanese soba, a dried noodle product, is prepared from blends of buckwheat and wheat flours. *See* CEREAL; FOOD MANUFACTURING; GRAIN CROPS. Mark A. Uebersax

Bibliography. H. G. Marshall and Y. Pomeranz, Buckwheat: Description, breeding, production, and utilization, in *Advances in Cereal Science and Technology*, vol. 5, American Association of Cereal Chemists, 1982; H. K. Wilson, *Grain Crops*, 2d ed., 1955.

Bud

An embryonic shoot containing the growing stem tip surrounded by young leaves or flowers or both, and the whole frequently enclosed by special protective leaves, the bud scales.

Position. The bud at the apex of the stem is called a terminal bud (**Fig. 1***a*). Any bud that develops on the side of a stem is a lateral bud. The lateral bud borne in the axil (angle between base of leaf and stem) of a leaf is the axillary bud (Fig. 1*a* and *d*). It develops concurrently with the leaf which subtends it, but usually such buds do not unfold and grow rapidly until the next season. Because of the inhibitory influence of the apical or other buds, many axillary buds never develop actively or may not do so for many years. These are known as latent or dormant buds. Above or beside the axil-

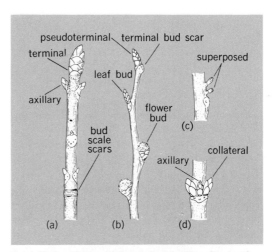

Fig. 1. Bud positions. (*a*) **Terminal and axillary (buckeye).** (*b*) **Pseudoterminal (elm).** (*c*) **Superposed (butternut).** (*d*) **Collateral (red maple).**

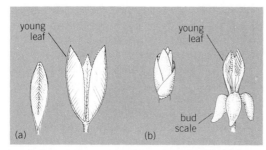

Fig. 2. Bud coverings. (*a*) Closed and open naked buds (hobblebush). (*b*) Closed and open scaly bud (hickory).

lary buds, some plants regularly produce additional buds called accessory, or supernumerary, buds. Accessory buds which occur above the axillary bud are called superposed buds (Fig. 1*c*), and those beside it collateral buds (Fig. 1 *d*). Under certain conditions, such as removal of terminal and auxillary buds, other buds may arise at almost any point on the stem, or even on roots or leaves. Such buds are known as adventitious buds. *See* PLANT GROWTH.

Composition. Buds that give rise to flowers only are termed flower buds (Fig. 1*b*), or in some cases, fruit buds. If a bud grows into a leafy shoot, it is called a leaf bud (Fig. 1*b*), or more accurately, a branch bud. A bud which contains both young leaves and flowers is called a mixed bud.

Covering. Buds of herbaceous plants and of some woody plants are covered by rudimentary foliage leaves only. Such buds are called naked buds (**Fig. 2*a***). In most woody plants, however, the buds are covered with modified protective leaves in the form of scales. These buds are called scaly buds or winter buds (Fig. 2*b*). In the different species of plants, the bud scales differ markedly. They may be covered with hairs or with water-repellent secretions of resin, gum, or wax. Ordinarily when a bud opens, the scales fall off, leaving characteristic markings on the stem (bud scale scars).

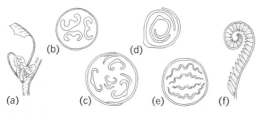

Fig. 3. Some types of vernation (prefoliation). (*a*) Conduplicate (tulip tree). (*b*) Revolute (dock). (*c*) Involute (poplar). (*d*) Convolute (cherry). (*e*) Plicate (sycamore). (*f*) Circinate (fern).

Vernation. The characteristic arrangement of young leaves within the bud is known as vernation or prefoliation (**Fig. 3**). Within the buds, the leaves may be folded on the midrib, plaited, rolled, coiled, or twisted in exact order and precision, each kind of plant having its distinctive inner bud pattern. Many ferns have a coiled leaf arrangement which is known as circinate vernation. *See* LEAF; PLANT ORGANS; PLANT TAXONOMY.   Neele Ammons

Buffalo

The name for members of the family Bovidae in the mammalian order Artiodactyla. The buffalo is an Old World species and resembles the oxen in general appearance. The North American bison is often called a buffalo, but is not related to the true buffalo. The Asiatic buffalo (*Bubalus bubalis*), known as the Indian or water buffalo and also as the carabao, is found as a domestic animal in the Balkans, Asia Minor, and Egypt. These buffalo exist in the wild state in southern Asia and Borneo, where they are considered to be ferocious and dangerous. Water buffalo are stocky, heavy-built animals that are not quite 6 ft (2 m) at shoulder height. They have very short hair and the shortest, most splayed horns of any variety (see **illus.**). Like all buffalo, they have a liking for marshes, where they wallow and become caked with mud that affords protection against insects. Their wide, flattened hooves allow them to stand firmly on the soft, marshy soil. They are hardy animals, being able to resist the infections and insect-borne diseases of the country, and they can withstand cold so well that they do not need shelters. Their diet consists entirely of reeds, rushes, and other aquatic plants. Domestic herds of 200–300 animals may provide 300 pints (1400 liters) of milk a year. This milk is rich in cream and is used to make butter and yogurt. *See* MILK.

Two other Asiatic species related to, but smaller than, the water buffalo are the tamarau (*Anoa mindorensis*), which is indigenous to the Philippines, and the still smaller (40 in. or 1 m high) anoa (*A. depressicornis*), or wild dwarf buffalo, found in the Celebes.

The African buffalo, classed in the genus *Syncerus*, was very numerous until the turn of the century, when the infectious disease rinderpest caused many deaths. They are still abundant though widely hunted by the natives. There are several varieties of African buffalo, and it is thought that all may be subspecies of *S. caffer*, the Cape buffalo, which attains a height of about 5 ft (1.5 m) at the

Herd of Indian or water buffalo (*Bubalus bubalis*).

shoulder and weighs more than 1500 lb (675 kg). They live in the open country of central, eastern, and southern Africa. Mating occurs early in the year, and a single calf is born after a gestation period of 11 months. Except for its size, this animal is difficult to distinguish from the rare dwarf or forest buffalo (*S. caffer nanus*), which is less than 4 ft (1.2 m) high at the shoulder and weighs a little more than 400 lb (180 kg). It lives in marshy, forested areas of western Africa, where it is known as the bush cow. This species has not been domesticated and occurs in herds of up to 1000. *See* ARTIODACTYLA; BISON; MAMMALIA; MUSK-OX; YAK.   Charles B. Curtin

Buffers (chemistry)

Solutions selected or prepared to minimize changes in hydrogen ion concentration which would otherwise tend to occur as a result of a chemical reaction. In general, chemical buffers are systems which, once constituted, tend to resist further change due to external influences. Thus it is possible, for example, to make buffers resistant to changes in temperature, pressure, volume, redox potential, or acidity. The commonest buffer in chemical solution systems is the acid-base buffer.

Chemical reactions known or suspected to be dependent on the acidity of the solution, as well as on other variables, are frequently studied by measurements in comixture with an appropriate buffer. For example, it may be desirable to investigate how the rate of a chemical reaction depends upon the hydrogen ion activity (pH). This is accomplished by measurements in several buffer systems, each of which provides a nearly constant, different pH. Alternatively, it may be desirable to measure the effects of other variables on a pH-sensitive system, by stabilizing the pH at a convenient value with a particular buffer.

Effectiveness. Buffer action depends upon the fact that, if two or more reactions coexist in a solution, then the chemical potential of any species is common to all reactions in which it takes part, and may be defined by specification of the chemical potentials of all other species in any one of the reactions. To be effective, a buffer must be able to respond to an increase as well as a decrease of the species to be buffered. In order to do so, it is necessary that the proton transfer step of the buffer be reversible with respect to the species involved, in the reaction to be buffered. In aqueous solution the proton transfer between most acids, their conjugate bases and water, is so rapid and reversible that the dominant <u>direct</u> source of protons for a chemical reaction is H_3O^+, the hydronium ion.

An acid-base buffer reaction in water is defined by reversible reaction (1), and the equilibrium

$$BH^+ + H_2O \rightleftharpoons B + H_3O^+ \qquad (1)$$

constant K_a shown by Eq. (2).

$$K_a = \frac{[H_3O^+][B]}{[BH^+][H_2O]} \qquad (2)$$

In Eq. (2) the square brackets designate the activity of the species involved. In normal concentrations of buffer (0.1 mole/liter) the activity of the solvent water is essentially constant and approximately that of pure water (55.5 M). Thus the position of the equilibrium may be defined by specifying the activity of any two of the three variable species in reaction (1). Normally this is by means of the equilibrium expression shown as Eq. (3) which, upon converting to a logarithmic form, can be reduced to Eq. (4). Here f is the fraction of the total buffer

$$[H_3O^+] = K_a \frac{[BH^+]}{[B]} \qquad (3)$$

$$pH = pK_a - \log \frac{(1-f)}{f} - \log \frac{\gamma_{BH+}}{\gamma_B} \qquad (4)$$

concentration, $(BH^+) + (B)$ existing as B, and γ is the activity coefficient relating activity a to concentration X. This relation is shown by Eq. (5). Thus a

$$a_x = \gamma_x(X) \qquad (5)$$

buffer pH is approximately defined by the dissociation constant K_a of the weak acid system and the ratio of acid to conjugate base concentrations. However, the third term in Eq. (4) indicates that the pH is dependent on the change in activity coefficients with concentration. Effects of this dependency may be eliminated in practice by providing a high and essentially invariant ionic environment in the form of an added pH-neutral strong electrolyte such as KNO_3 or NaCl.

Buffer capacity π is defined as the change in added H_3O^+ necessary to produce a given change in pH, $d[H_3O^+]/d$pH. Since the buffer comes to equilibrium with added H_3O^+, $1/\pi$ may also be defined as dpH/df. Inspection of Eq. (4) shows $1/\pi$ to be a minimum when $f = 1 - f$; hence a given buffer system has its highest capacity in a solution composed of equal parts BH^+ and B, and the capacity is directly proportional to the concentrations of BH^+ and B. For these reasons buffers are normally used at concentrations 10–100 times higher than the system to be controlled and, if possible, are selected so that the desired pH is approximately equal to pK_a for the buffer system. As a general rule, weak acid systems are not used to stabilize solutions whose pH is more than 2 pH units removed from pK_a, to ensure that the ratio of BH^+ to B will fall in the range 100–0.01.

Water as solvent. Buffers are particularly effective in water, because of the unusual properties of water as a solvent. Its high dielectic constant (80) tends to promote the existence of formally charged ions (ionization). Because it has both an acidic (H) and a basic (O) group, it may form bonds with ionic species leading to an organized sheath of solvent surrounding an ion (solvation). Water also tends to self-ionize to form its own conjugate acid-base system as shown by Eq. (6*b*), in which K_{ap} is the

$$2H_2O \rightleftharpoons H_3O^+ + OH^- \qquad (6a)$$

$$K_{ap} = [H_3O^+][OH^-] = 10^{-14} \qquad (6b)$$

autoprotolysis constant. The strength of an acid (or base) in solvent water cannot be separated from reaction (6a) and the familiar acid (or base) dissociation equilibrium reaction (1). Strong acids are those for which the K_a of Eq. (2) is very large; weak acids do not completely transfer the proton to water. The strongest acid which may exist in water is H_3O^+; the strongest base is OH^-. Thus, the maximum range of acid level which a solvent can support is governed by its own acid-base properties. In water this range is 14 pH units, or 14 orders of magnitude change in activity of H_3O^+. *See* SUPERACID.

The mechanism of buffer action may be regarded as a sequence of the proton transfer steps implied in reaction (1) coupled with reaction (6a). For example, the result of the chemical production or deliberate addition of an acid, HA, is to cause the water autoprotolysis reaction and the buffer acid reaction to respond to the change shown by reactions (7) and (8). Addition of a base would be accommodated by the reverse of (7) and (8).

$$HA + H_2O \rightleftharpoons H_3O^+ + A^- \qquad (7)$$

$$H_3O^+ + B \longrightarrow BH^+ + H_2O \qquad (8)$$

The effect of adding HA depends on the position of the equilibrium shown in reaction (7); buffer capacity π is usually defined in terms of H_3O^+ added because H_3O^+ is the strongest possible acid in aqueous solution, and would tend to create the maximum possible change in solution pH per mole of added acid. If HA is relatively weak so its degree of dissociation, in reaction (1), is small, its effective H_3O^+ addition may be calculated through Eq. (9),

$$[H_3O^+] \cong \sqrt{K_a C_a} \qquad (9)$$

where C_a is the concentration of added HA. A simple calculation using Eq. (9) shows that a given buffer solution will undergo the same change in pH for the addition of 0.1 mole/liter of a weak acid such as acetic acid ($K_a = 10^{-5}$) as for the addition of 0.01 mole/liter of strong acids such as HCl, $HClO_4$, or HNO_3.

In studies of rates of chemical reactions at constant pH, it is necessary that the proton transfer processes of the buffer acid and base and the solvent be rapid with respect to the primary reaction. The phosphate ($HPO_4^{2-}-PO_4^{3-}$) and carbonate ($HCO_3^--CO_3^{2-}$) systems, among others, sometimes give anomalous effects because this condition may not be obtained. Buffer rate effects are manifested in different reaction rates for a chemical system in two different buffers or otherwise identical ionic strength and nominal (equilibrium) pH. Later evidence seems to suggest that buffers of low-change type, for example, $NH_3-NH_4^+$, react more rapidly than high-charge

types such as $HPO_4^{2-}-PO_4^{3-}$. *See* ACID AND BASE; ACID-BASE INDICATOR; IONIC EQUILIBRIUM.

A. M. Hartley

Bibliography. J. J. Cohen and J. P. Kassirer, *Acid-Base*, 1982; H. A. Laitinen, *Chemical Analysis*, 2d ed., 1975; D. D. Perrin and B. Dempsey, *Buffers for pH and Metal Ion Control*, 1979; D. A. Skoog, D. M. West, and F. J. Holler, *Fundamentals of Analytical Chemistry*, 6th ed., 1992.

Buffers (electronics)

Electronic circuits whose primary function is to connect a high-impedance source to a low-impedance load without significant attenuation or distortion of the signal. Thus, the output voltage of a buffer replicates the input voltage without loading the source. An ideal voltage buffer is an amplifier with the following properties: unity gain, $A_B = 1$; zero output impedance, $Z_{out} = 0$; and infinite input impedance, $Z_{in} = \infty$. For example, if the voltage from a high-impedance source, say a strain-gage sensor with 100 kΩ output resistance, must be processed by further circuitry with an input impedance of, say, 500 Ω, the signal will be attenuated to only $500/100,500 \approx 0.5\%$ of the sensor voltage if the two circuits are directly connected, whereas the full strain-gage voltage will be available if a buffer is used.

Operation. Buffers are generally applied in analog systems to minimize loss of signal strength due to excessive loading of output nodes (**Fig. 1**a). Two kinds of circuits are frequently used: the operational-amplifier-based buffer and the transistor follower.

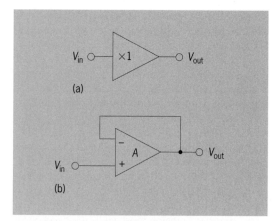

Fig. 1. Buffer circuit. (a) Circuit schematic symbol. (b) Operational-amplifier-based circuit.

Operational-amplifier-based buffer. This circuit (Fig. 1b) is based on an operational amplifier (op amp) with unity-gain feedback. The open-loop gain, $A(s)$, of the operational amplifier should be very high. To form the buffer, the amplifier is placed in a feedback loop. The buffer gain, $A_B(s)$, is then given by Eq. (1). Here, $s = j\omega$ is the Laplace transform

$$A_B(s) = \frac{V_{\text{out}}}{V_{\text{in}}} = \frac{A(s)}{1 + A(s)} \qquad (1)$$

variable, $j = \sqrt{-1}$; $\omega = 2\pi f$ is the radian frequency in radians per second (rad/s); and f is the frequency in hertz (Hz). The magnitude of A_B is approximately equal to unity, that is, $|A_B|$ approaches 1, if $|A|$ becomes very large. A common representation of the frequency dependence of the operational-amplifier gain is given by Eq. (2), where ω_t is

$$A(s) = \frac{\omega_t}{s} \qquad (2)$$

the operational amplifier's unity-gain frequency. By using this notation, Eq. (1) becomes Eq. (3), which

$$A_B = \frac{\omega_t}{s + \omega_t} \qquad (3)$$

shows that the buffer's bandwidth is approximately equal to the unity-gain frequency of the operational amplifier, typically 1 MHz or higher.

Under the assumption that the frequency of interest is much less than ω_t, it follows from Eq. (2) that the magnitude of the operational-amplifier gain, $A(s)$, is much greater than 1. In that case, it can be shown that, because of the feedback action, the buffer's input impedance is much larger than that of the operational amplifier itself [by a factor of $A(s)$]. Similarly, the buffer's output impedance is much smaller than that of the operational amplifier [again, by a factor of $A(s)$].

The very low output impedance of operational-amplifier-based buffers assures that a load impedance, $Z_L(s)$, does not affect the buffer's gain, A_B. Also, operational-amplifier-based buffers have no systematic offset. The high-impedance input node of a buffer may in practice have to be shielded to prevent random noise from coupling into the circuit. This shielding can be accomplished with a coaxial cable. To eliminate the capacitive loading of the source by the effective input capacitance of the cable, the shield can be driven with the output voltage of the buffer so that no voltage difference exists between the signal line and the shield. The driven shield is referred to as the guard. *See* AMPLIFIER; ELECTRICAL SHIELDING; ELECTROMAGNETIC COMPATIBILITY; OPERATIONAL AMPLIFIER.

Transistor followers. The bipolar junction transistor (BJT) emitter follower (**Fig. 2**a) and the field-effect transistor (FET) source follower (Fig. 2b) are very simple but effective buffer circuits. Both consist of a single transistor and a bias-current source; they are used in applications where power consumption and circuit area must be reduced to a minimum or where specifications are not too demanding.

An important parameter for BJT operation is the current gain, β, a number of the order of 100. For large values of β, the small-signal voltage gain of the common-collector circuit or emitter follower is close to but smaller than 1. The other two parameters that are important for the buffer's operation are the input and output impedances. The input impedance is obtained approximately by multiplying the load

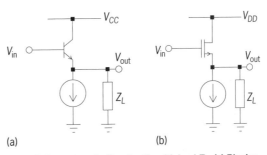

Fig. 2. Follower-type buffer circuits with load Z_L. (a) Bipolar emitter follower. An *npn* follower circuit is shown. V_{CC} = collector supply voltage. (b) Field-effect-transistor (FET) source follower. An *n*-type metal oxide semiconductor FET (MOSFET) follower circuit is shown. V_{DD} = drain supply voltage.

impedance by the current gain, and the output impedance is approximately equal to the resistance at the base divided by the current gain.

The FET source follower also has an ac voltage gain that is less than 1. The output impedance is approximately the reciprocal of the transconductance of the FET transistor, g_m. The input impedance of the FET buffer is infinite, apart from a small gate capacitance.

The performance of a transistor follower circuit depends strongly on the source and load impedances, that is, on the surrounding circuitry. In fact, the transistors are so fast that the frequency response is usually determined by loading. In general, follower circuits exhibit a systematic direct-current (dc) offset equal to the base-to-emitter voltage, V_{BE}, in BJTs and equal to the gate-to-source voltage, V_{GS}, for FET. Only followers made with depletion-mode field-effect transistors can be biased with zero V_{GS} to avoid this offset. *See* EMITTER FOLLOWER; TRANSISTOR.

Other specifications. Specifications that apply to buffer circuits comprise dc and large-signal parameters on the one hand and ac and small-signal parameters on the other.

DC and large-signal parameters. Buffer circuits should have small dc offset voltages (dc outputs when no input is applied), small bias currents (to minimize the effect of high-impedance sources), large linear signal swing (to minimize distortion), and high slew rate (to handle fast transitions of the applied signals).

AC and small-signal parameters. Buffers should have a low-frequency gain of unity and wide bandwidth (to reproduce the applied signals faithfully), low phase margins (to prevent peaking and overshoots), and low equivalent input-referred noise (to have wide dynamic range). Field-effect-transistor input buffers exhibit the lowest noise for high-impedance signal sources. *See* ELECTRICAL NOISE; GAIN.

Rolf Schaumann

Bibliography. P. R. Gray and R. G. Meyer, *Analysis and Design of Analog Integrated Circuits*, 3d ed., 1993; R. Gregorian and G. C. Temes, *Analog MOS Integrated Circuits for Signal Processing*, 1986; A. S. Sedra and K. C. Smith, *Microelectronic Circuits*, 3d ed., 1991.

Buhrstone mill

A mill for grinding or pulverizing, in which a flat siliceous rock, generally of cellular quartz, rotates against a stationary stone of the same material. The Buhrstone mill is one of the oldest types of mill and, with either horizontal or vertical stones, has long been used to grind grains and hard materials. Grooves in the stones facilitate the movement of the material. Fineness of the product is controlled by the pressure between the stones and by the grinding speed. A finely ground product is achieved by slowly rotating the stone at a high pressure against the materials and its mate (see **illus.**). The

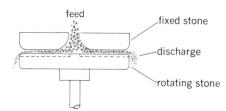

Buhrstone mill. Material moves toward outer edge of the stones where finely ground product is discharged.

capacity, or output, of a Buhrstone mill is low and its power requirements are high. The stones require frequent maintenance, even when grinding only slightly abrasive materials. *See* CRUSHING AND PULVERIZING; GRINDING MILL.   George W. Kessler

Buildings

Fixed permanent structures, more or less enclosed and designed to use as housing or shelter or to serve the needs of commerce and industry. The history of buildings is almost as old as human history. Most contemporary building techniques are possible because of materials and methods of construction that have been introduced since about 1800.

Iron and steel. With the use of cast and wrought iron early in the nineteenth century and the growth of the steel industry at the end of that century, large-scale buildings became common, and many were constructed. Notable were the Crystal Palace (London, 1851) where mass production and a demountable building were first demonstrated, the great London train sheds (Paddington Station, Victoria Station), the Eiffel Tower (Paris, 1889), and the first skyscrapers (Chicago, 1890s).

Iron and steel building components are noncombustible, and their basic strength is excellent compared to both masonry and timber of similar dimension. The strength-to-weight ratio of steel is also good. Steel is equally strong in tension and compression and possesses excellent ductility, a highly desirable quality in building design.

Contemporary applications of structural steel in building construction generally utilize rolled shapes in the form of wide flange and I beams, pipes and tubes, channels, angles, and plates. These are fabricated and erected into frameworks of beams, girders, and columns. Floors are usually concrete slabs cast on corrugated metal deck or on removable wood forms. *See* FLOOR CONSTRUCTION; STRUCTURAL STEEL.

Concrete. Another important building material, concrete, was known to builders in Roman times. Concrete is a mixture of cement, coarse and fine aggregate (usually stone and sand), and water, with other chemical admixtures sometimes introduced to impart special qualities. The material is inherently weak in tension and must be reinforced by means of steel bars embedded in and bonded to the concrete matrix. This combination of nonhomogeneous materials, called reinforced concrete, is utilized in many areas of building construction, including foundations, walls, columns, beams, floors, and roofs. *See* COLUMN; FOUNDATIONS; ROOF CONSTRUCTION; WALL CONSTRUCTION.

In its early applications in the late nineteenth century, reinforced concrete was primarily used in industrial buildings. However, because of its ability to be molded into any shape, its inherent resistance to fire and weather, and its relatively low cost, reinforced concrete has become a desirable material for all types of buildings. Construction of reinforced concrete structures is more labor intensive than steel structures because of the need to construct elaborate formwork, place the reinforcement accurately where it is required, convey the concrete materials from the mixer to the final destination, and finish and cure any exposed surfaces. Reinforced concrete structures of 40 stories and more are not uncommon. While beam and column frames are often used, reinforced concrete construction frequently involves the flat plate, a system in which the floor slab is of uniform depth with no beams projecting beneath it and with the plate supported only by columns, which may be randomly spaced rather than on a regular grid. *See* REINFORCED CONCRETE.

Concrete is subject to plastic flow (sometimes called creep) when subjected to compressive forces over a period of time. Therefore collateral building materials such as exterior walls, interior partitions, and vertical pipes and ducts must be detailed to accommodate this movement. *See* CONCRETE.

Timber. Two inventions made the use of timber extremely viable in small-scale structures: the machine-powered sawmill and the automatic nail-making machine. Previously, timbers were either hand hewed or sawed and nails were hand forged.

In North America, where large softwood forests were plentiful, the milling of small-dimension lumber [2–3 in. (5–7.5 cm) wide by 4–12 in. (10–30 cm) deep] gave rise to the balloon frame house in the latter part of the nineteenth century. In this technique, closely space studs, joists, and rafters [no more than 24 in. (60 cm) on center] are fastened together with simple square cuts and nails. The balloon frame allowed relatively unskilled persons to erect simple frame houses. In the twentieth century, the balloon frame gave way to the platform frame, in which the studs were capped at each floor rather than running continuously for two stories (**Fig. 1**). The platform technique further simplified the framing system and compensated more uniformly for the drying shrinkage of newly milled wood with high moisture content that was often employed in construction.

Masonry. Masonry is a widely used construction technique, and perhaps the oldest building material. The three most common masonry materials are stone (quarried from natural geologic formations), brick (manufactured from clay that is exposed to high temperature in kilns), and concrete masonry units (solid or hollow blocks manufactured from carefully controlled concrete mixes). These materials are used alone or in combination, with each unit separated from the adjacent one by a bed of mortar. *See* BRICK; MORTAR; STONE AND STONE PRODUCTS.

The strength of a masonry wall depends greatly on the quality of construction. Since quality varies widely, it is desirable to introduce a relatively large factor of safety into the design. Masonry has been used in structural supporting walls built as high as 20 stories, although commonly the limit is 8–12 stories. Reinforcement can be introduced in the form of steel wires in horizontal bed joints as well as vertically in the form of rods set into grouted hollow cells of concrete masonry or in the grouted space between wythes of a brick wall. Reinforcement greatly enhances the strength of a masonry wall. *See* MASONRY.

Other materials. As new materials were developed, the technology of constructing buildings advanced, and it is anticipated that progress will continue. Newer metals include high-strength alloys of steel as well as products developed for space programs that have very high strength-to-weight ratios. Other desirable properties involve increased strength as well as resistance to corrosion, high temperature from fires, and fatigue.

Reinforced concrete with compressive strength increased from the older common range of 3000–5000 lb/in.^{2} (21–35 megapascals) up to 15,000–18,000 lb/in.^{2} (103–124 MPa) has been developed. This is of particular value in the design of columns in very tall buildings. Plastics are used in many building applications. However, these materials require improvements in strength and stiffness, long-term dimensional stability, resistance to high temperature and the degrading effects of ultraviolet radiation, and ease in being fastened and connected. Composite materials have been developed for application in buildings, and include sandwich panels in which the surfaces are bonded to a core. Combinations of steel and concrete, (**Fig. 2**), masonry and steel reinforcement or prestress, timber and concrete, and timber and steel are in use. Other novel materials include high-performance fabric for roof coverings, structural adhesives, carbon fiber, and glass-fiber products.

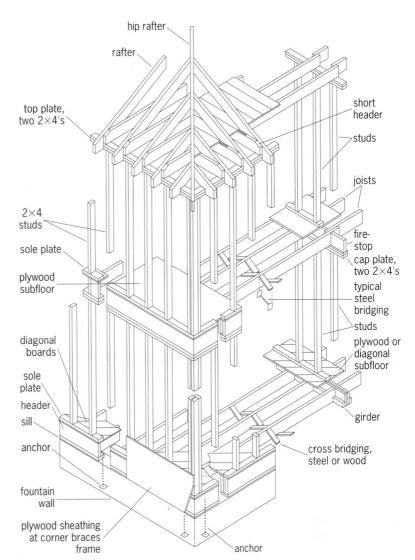

Fig. 1. Configuration of the platform frame construction. (*After C. Ramsey, Architectural Graphic Standards, 7th ed., John Wiley and Sons, 1989*)

These modern materials are often lighter in weight than conventional products, facilitating long-span roofs that are made of steel or alloy cables and struts, coated fabric membranes, and reinforced plastic panels. An additional benefit of lightweight structures is their ability to be prefabricated in a factory and shipped to the job site, either as panels or as completed three-dimensional modules. Materials of high strength allow the construction of taller buildings, using columns of smaller dimensions. In addition, durability can be substantially improved in basic materials that will resist corrosion and deterioration due to atmospheric conditions including pollution and acid rain, as well as in secondary materials such as sealants (at building joints and junctures of dissimilar materials), adhesives, and connections (including bolts, screws, and nails).

Many building components are subassembled in factories prior to delivery to the job site. Wood structural members are made into glue-laminated beams using strip lumber, veneer lumber, particle board, or parallel strand lumber. Steel components

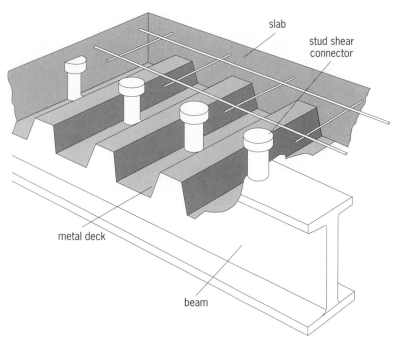

Fig. 2. Metal deck of composite design, providing a permanent form for concrete as well as a work platform. (*Nelson Studs Welding Systems*)

on parcels of land in urban environments. Earlier heavy-masonry-bearing-wall buildings had walls up to 6 ft (2 m) thick at their base to support as much as 16 stories of load. These walls occupied valuable space that could otherwise be rented to tenants. This drawback provided stimulus to the development of the skeleton steel frame, in which the thin exterior cladding does not participate in the support of the building but functions as a weather enclosure and a visual expression. These external skins (curtain walls) are often constructed of light aluminum or steel supports infilled with glass or metal panels. Curtain walls may also be fabricated of masonry veneer or precast concrete panels. They are designed to resist water and wind pressure and infiltration, and they are attached to the building frame for their primary support. Curtain walls may be built up of mullions and muntins, with the glass and metal in place on the building (the so-called stick system), or may be installed as a unit, with the framing members and glazing preassembled offsite.

The major structural problem that must be considered in the design of skyscrapers is the ability of the frame to resist lateral wind loads. The building must be both strong enough to resist the applied forces and stiff enough to limit the lateral displacement or drift to amounts that are tolerable to human comfort levels and to the performance of the collateral materials such as glass, interior partitions, and ceilings. In order to meet these criteria, methods have evolved since the skeleton frame was introduced. The simplest method of providing lateral rigidity is to ensure that the joints between girders and columns remain rigid, that is, their geometry remains unchanged. Thus if two members meet at a 90° angle, the design must ensure that this angle will not be changed when

include prefabricated open-web trusses and joists as well as three-dimensional space frames. Concrete components are factory precast to form hollow core planks and tee-shaped sections, often using a techniques for reinforcing called prestressing, in which steel wires or strands are stretched taut in the forms prior to concrete being cast around them.

Skyscrapers. Following the invention of the high-speed safety elevator, skyscrapers were developed at the end of the nineteenth and early in the twentieth century to maximize the economic return

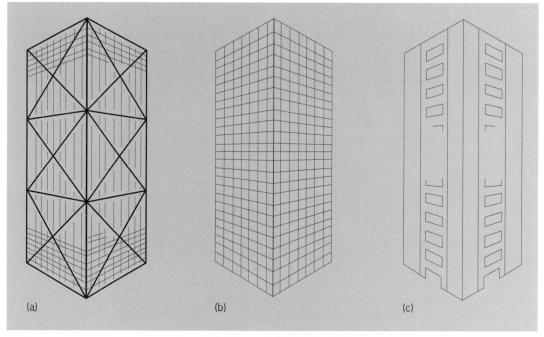

Fig. 3. Tube structural systems: (*a*) braced, (*b*) framed, and (*c*) shear wall.

a load is applied. In steel frames, this requirement is accomplished by connecting the two members with adequately sized and spaced bolts, rivets, or welds. In reinforced concrete construction, the design must provide for adequately sized members and reinforcing steel that act together by virtue of the monolithic nature of the material. Rigid frame design is still the most economical method of framing buildings up to 20 stories tall. *See* STRUCTURAL ANALYSIS.

As buildings became taller than 20 stories, it was recognized that diagonal braces could be introduced between the top of one column and the bottom of an adjacent one to form a truss type of framework. The diagonals could form X's, V's, or K's and were found to be very efficient for buildings up to about 60 stories. The principle of a truss is that a series of triangles is interconnected, and these are found to be immutable shapes; that is, their geometry cannot be changed except by changing the lengths of the members. In reinforced concrete buildings, solid shear walls are used rather than diagonals. *See* TRUSS.

Special systems have been developed for constructing very tall buildings. One of the most effective is the tube system (used in the World Trade Center, New York), in which the perimeter framework of the building is composed of closely spaced columns (with small windows) and very rigid spandrel beams connected to form almost a solid tube with small penetrations. This is an efficient system because it maximizes the use of the framing material by locating it as far as possible from the center of the building, that is, at the perimeter (**Fig. 3**). Variations on the tube system include large-scale external X-bracing (as in the John Hancock Building, Chicago; **Fig. 4**) and the bundled tube (such as the Sears Tower, Chicago). In addition to these so-called passive framing systems, buildings can resist wind forces by means of tuned mass dampers. These are large weights, as much as 300–400 tons (270–360 metric tons), mounted on guided rollers or pendulums and located at the top of a skyscraper; they move counter to the direction of the wind, minimizing the deflection. The dampers are activated by the actual movement of the building, and they alter its dynamic response to wind.

Special-purpose types. Modern technology has created the need for different types of structures. Examples include aircraft maintenance hangars (the largest building in the world is the vertical assembly building at Cape Canaveral, Florida), communications and entertainment production centers, large stadiums (many of which were formerly outdoors but are now covered and climate controlled), transportation terminals, convention centers, specialized medical facilities and scientific laboratories, and high-technology manufacturing buildings. Some require long spans, others extremely stringent climate or vibration controls, and still others superclean environments.

Building services. In order for buildings to be fully functional, they must be able to provide

Fig. 4. Large-scale external X-bracing as used in the John Hancock Building, Chicago. (*ESTO*).

adequate levels of comfort and service. There are many methods used to supply the services of heating and cooling. Heating may be provided by radiation, conduction, or convection. Commonly, pipes containing steam or hot water from a central boiler are installed throughout a structure and connected to radiators or convectors in each room. Alternatively, air heated in a furnace may be delivered by means of fans blowing through sheet metal or fiber-glass ducts. Fuels commonly used in boilers are oil or gas. Cooling requires that warm air inside the building pass over coils containing cold water or refrigerant that exchange the heat, so that the cooled air is delivered to the interior while the heat is conveyed to the outside. *See* AIR CONDITIONING; COMFORT HEATING.

Electrical systems are installed throughout buildings to provide lighting as well as power to operate appliances and machinery. In large buildings, high-voltage power is reduced by means of transformers to usable voltage. Elaborate distribution systems of conduits and cables, wired to circuit-breaker panels for overload protection, are installed. Signal systems for telephones, computers, and alarms are also commonly specified and built. Finally, there is plumbing service, which delivers hot and cold water and carries away wastewater as well as storm water into disposal systems such as sewers or septic systems.

Loads. Buildings are designed to resist loads due to their own weight, to environmental phenomena, and from the occupants' usage. The self-weight of a building, called dead load, is relatively easy to calculate if the composition and thickness of all of the materials are known. Included in the dead load are the building frame, walls, floors, roof, ceilings, partitions, finishes, and service equipment—that is, everything that is fixed and immovable.

Environmentally applied loads include rain, which may cause ponding, and snow and ice. Snow loads are calculated based on the weather history of the area in which the building is located. All of the loads mentioned thus far are vertical loads, but the effect of wind on a building is usually experienced as a lateral, horizontal force. Wind velocity records are kept by local weather bureaus; loads are then calculated and based on statistical probability of occurrence (usually a 50- or a 100-year return period) of peak wind speeds. These wind velocities are converted to force units, with gust loads as well as allowances for the shape of the building, its height, and exposure factored in.

Another significant load to which buildings are subjected is the force of earthquakes. The understanding of seismic activity is an emerging science. So too is the understanding of how buildings respond to seismic forces. Calculation of the probability of an earthquake occurring in any given area is based on past seismic experience as well as determination of the locations of fault lines and tectonic plates. However, it has not been possible to predict timing, location, or specific intensity of earthquakes. In fact, earthquake record-keeping, like that of snow and wind, has been effective for slightly more than 100 years, a very short period of time in the history of the Earth. Thus the models of statistical probability of the occurrence or the magnitude of an event or a storm are based on incomplete information. In many locations, building structures have been inadequately designed to meet unexpectedly large forces due to these environmental loads. *See* EARTHQUAKE.

Seismic loads, unlike most other loads except for wind, are dynamic in character rather than static. Furthermore, each seismic event produces a unique spectrum of vibrations to which a building may be subjected. The shaking of the ground causes both horizontal and vertical acceleration in a building, whose response may go through a number of vibration modes.

Engineers have devised a number of methods by which buildings can resist significant seismic loads. One is to design a maximum of energy absorption into the building by providing ductility in the frame and its connections. A second method involves an attempt to separate the superstructure of the building from ground-induced vibration—a method called base isolation. In this system, shock-absorbent material is inserted between the foundation and the superstructure to prevent vibrations from traveling up into the building. Other principles of seismic resistance require that all parts of the building be connected, that ornamental and other nonstructural features be securely attached to the building frame, and that mechanical and electrical systems be designed to accommodate anticipated movement. *See* SEISMIC RISK.

Fire protection. The danger of fire in buildings has several aspects. Of primary importance is the assurance that all occupants can exit safely and that firefighters can perform their work with minimal danger. The second consideration involves the protection of property, the building, and its contents. In the initial planning of a building, the location, number, and size of exits must be carefully considered in relation to the anticipated occupancy and the material of construction. Where it is not possible to provide sufficient access to exit doors at ground level, fire escapes (generally steel-bar platforms and stairs) are affixed to the sides of buildings.

Sophisticated fire detection systems are available that can sense both smoke and heat. These sound audible alarms and directly contact municipal fire departments and building safety officers. In addition, the alarm may automatically shut down ventilation systems to prevent smoke from spreading, may cause elevators to return to the ground floor where they remain until the danger is passed, and may close fire doors and dampers to compartmentalize the spread of smoke or flames. Supplementing this passive detection are automatic sprinkler systems, in which water is delivered to spray heads spaced to provide complete coverage of the area to be protected. The sprinklers are activated by heat or by the alarm system. *See* ALARM SYSTEMS; AUTOMATIC SPRINKLER SYSTEM; FIRE DETECTOR; FIRE TECHNOLOGY.

Building framing system are rated for their ability to withstand fires. Actual assemblages of building materials are tested in simulated fire conditions where they are exposed to flames of a certain temperature and a water-hose stream of a specified pressure. They are then rated based on how long (generally between 1 and 4 h) they can remain intact when exposed to the design fire conditions. Structural steel rapidly loses its ability to safely support loads when its temperature exceeds 800°F (427°C). Thus steel is protected by encasing the structural members with sprayed-on mineral fibers (formerly asbestos was used), concrete, masonry, plaster, or gypsum dry wall. In one technology a thin sprayed or troweled intumescent coating turns into foam when exposed to heat; the foam then serves as an insulator for a given period of time. Wood members can be impregnated with salts (zinc chloride, ammonium sulfate, borax, or boric acid) that render the wood resistant to combustion. Reinforced concrete and masonry are naturally resistant to fire for a minimum of several hours.

Certain building materials release toxic substances when exposed to high temperature. Thus while a building structure may be safe, the occupants can be injured or killed by toxic emissions (smoke and fumes) before they have an opportunity to exit. Such materials are no longer allowed in many buildings.

In high-rise buildings the problems of fire safety are exacerbated by the inherent difficulties in avoiding a chimney stack effect for smoke and flames in elevator shafts, stairwells, ventilation shafts, and heating/cooling air ducts. Efforts are directed at compartmentalizing flames and smoke. This is often difficult to achieve, since doorways to exit stairs are frequently opened by persons fleeing the danger. These exit passages can be positively pressurized with air to deter the intrusion of smoke. Planning for evacuation of occupants without panic includes providing emergency lighting, smoke-free access routes, frequent fire drills, and positive communications during an emergency.

Building codes. The process of building is often regulated by governmental authorities through the use of building codes that have the force of law. In the United States there is no national code; rather there are regional, state, or even city building codes. Some of the more widely accepted codes are the Building Officials Conference of American (BOCA), used widely in the eastern United States; the Uniform Building Code (UBC), used in the western United States; and the Southern Building Code, used in the south. In Europe there are national codes and codes that transcend national boundaries (Eurocodes).

Codes establish classifications of buildings according to the proposed occupancy or use. Then, for any given type of construction (for example, wood, steel, or concrete), they establish minimum standards for exit and egress requirements, for height and area, and for fire resistance ratings. In addition, minimum loads are designated as well as requirements for natural light, ventilation, plumbing, and electrical services. Local codes are written to regulate zoning, stipulating items such as building type, occupancy, size, height, setbacks from property lines, and historic considerations.

Environmental concerns. The process of building raises large numbers of environmental issues. In many cases the owner must prepare an official environmental impact statement that considers the potential effect of the proposed building on traffic, air quality, sun and shadow, wind patterns, archeology, wildlife, and wetlands, as well as demands on existing utilities and services. Many building projects have had their original schemes severely altered or have been abandoned to avoid adverse effects on the environment.

One of the primary environmental concerns is energy conservation. In the initial design of a building, all systems are studied to obtain maximum efficiency. Heating and cooling are two of the largest consumers of energy, and a great deal of effort is directed toward minimizing energy consumption by techniques such as building orientation, sun shading, insulation, use of natural ventilation and outside air, recapture of waste heat, cogeneration (using waste heat to generate electricity), use of solar energy both actively and passively, and limiting heat generation from lighting. Efforts at reducing electric power consumption by designing more efficient lighting, power distribution, and machinery are also of high priority. Consumption of water and disposal of liquid and solid waste are additional concerns. Yet another aspect of energy conservation deals with the study of the quantity of embodied energy required to construct the original building. Considerations involve energy required to produce the material, transport it, and install it. *See* COGENERATION; HEAT INSULATION; SOLARHEATING AND COOLING; VENTILATION.

Planners are concerned with sustainable design and development. Included within this broad topic are not only considerations of energy conservation but also issues such as use of renewable resources, human scale, bioregionalism, and awareness of the need to nurture the planet for future inhabitants.

Robert Silman

Bibliography. E. Allen, *Fundamentals of Building Construction*, 2d ed., 1990; L. S. Beedle (ed.), *Second Century of the Skyscraper*, Council on Tall Buildings and Urban Habitat, 1988; C. W. Condit, *American Building*, 2d ed., 1992; M. Salvadori, *Why Buildings Stand Up*, 1992.

Bulk-handling machines

A diversified group of materials-handling machines specialized in design and construction for handling unpackaged, divided materials.

Bulk material. Solid, free-flowing materials are said to be in bulk. The handling of these unpackaged, divided materials requires that the machinery both support their weight and confine them either to a desired path of travel for continuous conveyance or within a container for handling in discrete loads. Wet or sticky materials may also be handled successfully by some of the same machines used for bulk materials. Characteristics of materials that affect the selection of equipment for bulk handling include (1) the size of component particles, (2) flowability, (3) abrasiveness, (4) corrosiveness, (5) sensitivity to contamination, and (6) general conditions such as dampness, structure, or the presence of dust or noxious fumes.

Particles range in size from those that would pass through a fine mesh screen to those that would be encountered in earth-moving and mining processes. Fine granular materials are usually designated by their mesh size, which is an indication of the smallest mesh screen through which all or a specified percent of the particles will pass. As an example, a 100-mesh screen is one in which there are 100 openings per linear inch. Where the size of the bulk material varies, it is customary to indicate the percentage of each size in each mixture.

Flowability, corrosiveness, abrasiveness, and similar terms are relative and are usually modified by adjectives to indicate the degree of the characteristic, such as "mildly" corrosive or "highly" abrasive.

Many products are sensitive to contamination; this characteristic may be a determining factor in selecting bulk-handling equipment and its material of construction. For example, an enclosed conveyor is used to protect the material from exterior contamination; and construction from noncorrosive material, such as stainless steel, may be required to protect the handled material from interior contamination.

Consideration also must be given to the angle of repose and the angle of slide of the material (**Fig. 1**). The angle of repose is the maximum slope, expressed in degrees, which piled material will stand without sliding on itself. The angle of slide, also expressed in degrees, is the angle at which material flows freely on an inclined surface such as a chute.

Corrosiveness and other handling characteristics of materials are compiled and updated in literature provided by manufacturers of bulk-handling machines. Trade associations also publish technical bulletins on the relations of machines to jobs, applications, and operating costs. Related data are published by various governmental departments, especially the U.S. Department of Commerce.

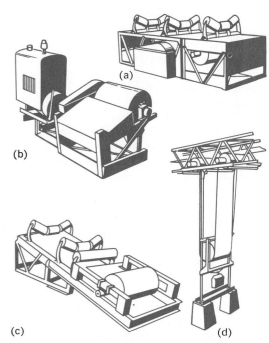

Fig. 2. Typical components of belt conveyor. (a) Electric motor wrap drive. (b) Gasoline engine head-end drive. (c) Screw type take-up. (d) Vertical gravity take-up.

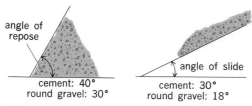

Fig. 1. Critical angles for bulk materials.

angle of repose

cement: 40°
round gravel: 30°

angle of slide

cement: 30°
round gravel: 18°

Continuous bulk conveyor. Equipment that transports material continuously in a horizontal, inclined, or vertical direction in a predetermined path is a form of conveyor. The many different means used to convey bulk materials include gravity, belt, apron, bucket, skip hoist, flight or screw, dragline, vibrating or oscillating, and pneumatic conveyors. Wheel or roller conveyors cannot handle bulk materials.

Gravity chutes are the only unpowered conveyors used for bulk material. They permit only a downward movement of material. Variations such as chutes with steps or cleats are employed as a means of slowing product movement.

Belt conveyors of many varieties move bulk materials. Fabric belt conveyors have essentially the same operating components as those used for package service; however, these components are constructed more ruggedly to stand up under the more rigorous conditions imposed by carrying coal, gravel, chemicals, and other similar heavy bulk materials (**Fig. 2**). In the latter type, the belt runs on a bed of closely spaced rollers positioned to form a flat or troughed conveyor bed. Belts may also be made of such materials as rubber, metal, or open wire. Belt conveyors are only used within angles of 28° from horizontal. Materials feed onto belt

conveyors from hoppers or from storage facilities overhead and may discharge over the end (**Fig. 3a**) or, if the belt is flat, by being diverted off one side. Belt conveyors can handle most materials over long distances and up and down slopes. Their advantages include low power requirements, high capacities, simplicity, and dependable operation.

An apron conveyor is a form of belt conveyor, but differs in that the carrying surface is constructed of a series of metal aprons or pans pivotally linked together to make a continuous loop. The pans, which may overlap one another, are usually attached at each end to two strands of roller chain. The chain runs on steel tracks, movement being provided by suitable chain sprockets. Turned-up edges or side wings provide a troughed carrying surface (Fig. 3b). As in the case of the belt conveyor, the top strand of the apron is the carrying surface. This type of conveyor is suitable for handling large quantities of bulk material under severe service conditions and can operate at speeds up to approximately 100 ft (30 m) per minute, handling up to approximately 300 tons (270 metric tons) per hour; with the addition of cleats, an apron

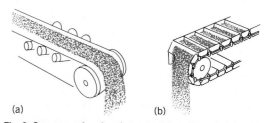

Fig. 3. Conveyors for abrasive materials, with material and conveying surface moving together. (a) Belt conveyor. (b) Apron conveyor.

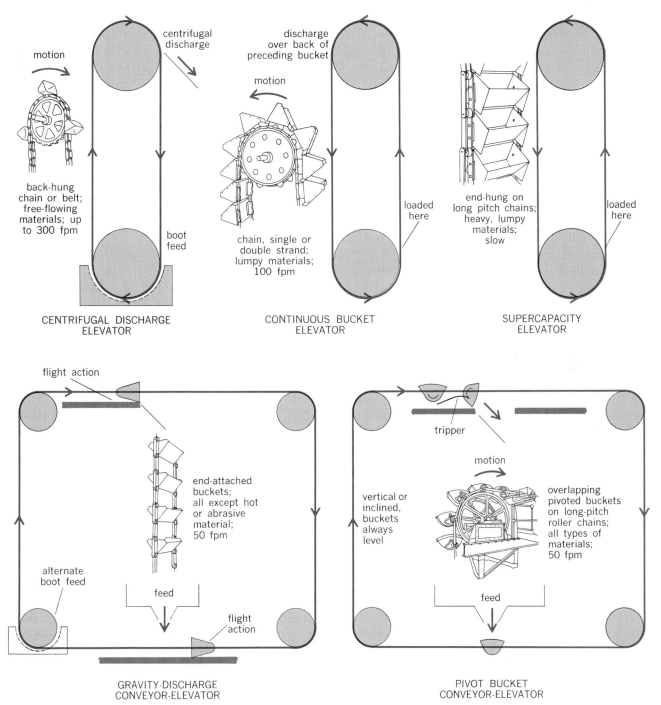

Fig. 4. Components of bucket conveyor-elevators and typical paths of travel for which they are used.

can convey up inclines to as steep as 60°. Apron conveyors are most suitable for heavy, abrasive, or lumpy materials.

Bucket conveyors, as the name implies, are constructed of a series of buckets attached to one or two strands of chain or in some instances to a belt. These conveyors are most suitable for operating on a steep incline or vertical path, sometimes being referred to as elevating conveyors (**Fig. 4**). Bucket construction makes this type of conveyor most ideal for bulk materials such as sand or coal. Buckets are provided in a variety of shapes and are usually constructed of steel.

Flight conveyors employ flights, or bars attached to single or double strands of chain. The bars drag or push the material within an enclosed duct or trough. These are frequently referred to as drag conveyors. Although modifications of this type of conveyor are employed in a number of ways, its commonest usage is in a horizontal trough in which the lower strand of the flights actually moves the material. This type of conveyor is commonly used for moving bulk material such as coal or metal chips from machine tools (**Fig. 5**). Constant dragging action along the trough makes this type of conveyor unsuitable for materials which are

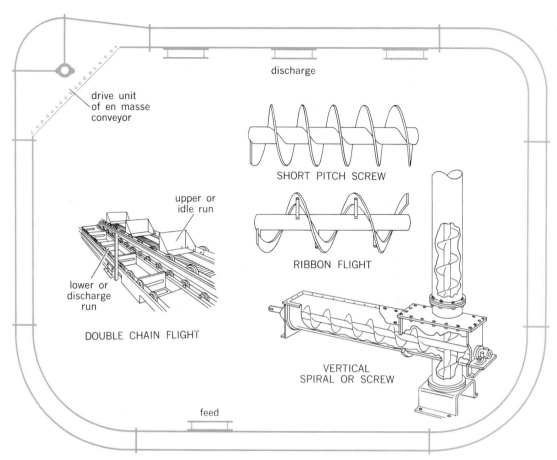

Fig. 5. Diagram of an en masse conveyor trough. The insets show some of the flight conveyors used to move bulk materials: double chain flight, and horizontal and vertical screw or spiral conveyors.

extremely abrasive. Materials can be fed to the conveyor from any desired intermediate point and, by the use of gating, can be discharged at any desired point.

Dragline conveyors operate on basically the same principle as flight conveyors, as previously described. The chain, ruggedly made for this service, drags the material, such as clinkers and slag, along the bottom of a concrete trough. The dragging is done entirely by the links of the chain.

Spiral or screw conveyors rotate upon a single shaft to which are attached flights in the form of a helical screw. When the screw turns within a stationary trough or casing, the material advances (**Fig. 6***b*). These conveyors are used primarily for bulk materials of fine and moderate sizes, and can move material on horizontal, inclined, or vertical planes (Fig. 5). The addition of bars or paddles to the flight conveyor shaft also makes it ideal for mixing or blending the materials while they are being handled. In addition, enclosed troughs may be water- or steam-jacketed for cooling, heating, drying, and so forth.

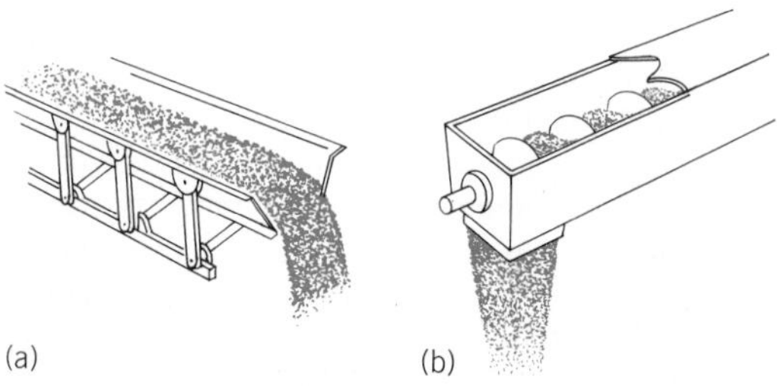

Vibrating or oscillating conveyors employ the use of a pan or trough bed, attached to a vibrator or oscillating mechanism, designed to move forward slowly and draw back quickly (Fig. 6*a*). The inertia of the material keeps the load from being carried back so that it is automatically placed in a more advanced position on the carrying surface. Adaptations of this principle are also used for moving material up spiral paths vertically. Mechanical (spring), pneumatic (vibrator), and electrical (vibrator) devices provide the oscillating motion. These conveyors can handle hot, abrasive, stringy, or irregularly shaped materials. The trough can be made leakproof or, by enclosing it, dustproof.

Pneumatic, or air, conveyors employ air as the propelling media to move materials. One implementation of this principle is the movement within an air duct of cylindrical carriers, into which are placed currency, mail, and small parts for movement from one point to discharge at one of

Fig. 6. Open and closed troughs. (*a***) Oscillating conveyor, with whole trough oscillating. (***b***) Screw conveyor, with helix driving material along trough.**

several points by use of diverters. Pneumatic pipe conveyors are widely used in industry, where they move granular materials, fine to moderate size, in original bulk form without need of internal carriers. An air compressor provides the air to move the material either by pressure or vacuum. Materials are introduced to the system by means of air locks, which are of the rotary or slide type. These locks are designed to permit the entry of the material with negligible loss of air. By means of diverted valves in the pneumatic pipe, a discharge can be effected at any one of a number of predetermined points. The small number of moving parts, the ability to move material in any direction, and the need for minimal prime plant floor space are among the advantages of this type of bulk-handling machine.

A pneumatic conveyor may form part of a conveyor system. The system comprises a network of machines, each handling the same product through its various processing stages; a single system may well employ numerous varieties of conveyors, such as pneumatic, screw, and vibrating conveyors. **Figure 7** shows a system for handling pebble lime in a water-treatment plant. The lime is received in railroad cars or trucks, unloaded and conveyed by a pneumatic vacuum system to a receiver filter, and discharged to a screw conveyor, from which it is selectively delivered to any desired storage bin. From the bins, the lime can be delivered on demand to the slakers below.

Another adaptation of the pneumatic conveyor is to activate a gravity conveyor. Such a conveyor handles dry pulverized materials through slightly inclined chutes. Air flows through the bottom of the chute, which is usually constructed of a porous medium, fluidizing the material and causing it to flow in the manner of a liquid. An advantage of this conveyor is that there are no moving parts.

Aerial tramways and cableways employ the use of a cab or carrier suspended by a grooved wheel on an overhead cable to transport materials over long distances, particularly where the terrain is such that truck or rail transportation is impractical. They are used primarily to meet the needs of such activities as dam construction, loading ships, bringing coal to and from power houses, and stock piling in open country.

Discontinuous bulk handlers. Power cranes and shovels perform many operations moving bulk materials in discrete loads. When functioning as

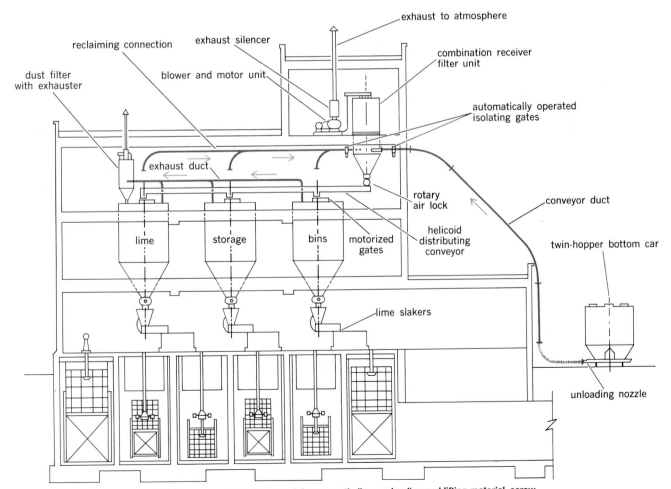

Fig. 7. Typical conveyor system, with hopper car delivering material, pneumatic lines unloading and lifting material, screw flight transferring it to bins, and gravity chutes discharging it. (*National Conveyors Co.*)

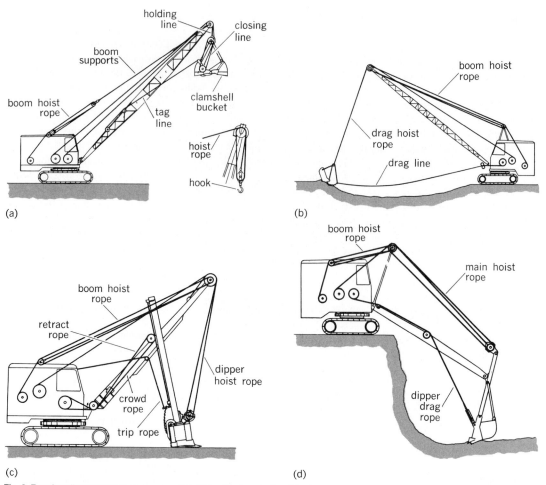

Fig. 8. Reeving diagrams for power crane fitted (*a*) with clamshell or (*b*) with scoop and for shovel fitted (*c*) with forward dipper or (*d*) with back hoe (backdigger or drag-shovel). (*United States Steel Corp.*)

cranes and fitted with the many below-the-hook devices available, they are used on construction jobs and in and around industrial plants. Such fittings as magnets, buckets, grabs, skullcrackers, and pile drivers enable cranes to handle many products.

The machines of the convertible, full-revolving type are mounted on crawlers, trucks, or wheels. Specialized front-end operating equipment is required for clamshell, dragline, lifting-crane, pile-driver, shovel, and hoe operations. Commercial sizes of these machines are nominally from $1/4$ to $2^1/2$ yd^3 (0.19 to 1.9 m^3) as shovels and from $2^1/2$ to 60 tons (2.25 to 54 metric tons).

The revolving superstructure consists of the rotating frame and the operating machinery thereon. It may be carried on a crawler mount, consisting of two continuous parallel crawler belts. A truck mount is a heavy-framed, rubber-tired carrier supported by two or more axles and having the general characteristics of a heavy-duty truck. The carrier may be controlled for road travel from a cab mounted on the carrier or located on the revolving superstructure. Machines of this type can also be secured on railroad mountings.

Six types of front-end operating equipment are standard: crane, clamshell, dragline, pile driver, shovel, and hoe. Common crane-boom equipment is used with crane, clamshell, dragline, and pile driver. The boom usually consists of two sections, between which additional sections may be inserted. Shovel and hoe equipment have their distinctive mechanisms for operation (**Fig. 8**).

Scoops and shovels are used for handling bulk materials in plants and yards. Lighter models are

Fig. 9. Tractor fitted with shovel for up-and-over operation. (*Service Supply Corp.*)

usually wheel-mounted, while those for heavier duty are apt to be carried on tractors. Two basic types are recognized: those that load and dump only at the front or at the rear, and those with an up-and-over action which permits loading at the front end and discharging at the rear (**Fig. 9**). This last arrangement is frequently a time-saver in that it eliminates the need for maneuvering when loading wagons.

Specialized equipment for mechanized pit mining has been developed. Power cranes, shovels, and scoops are actively engaged in strip mines, quarries, and other earth-moving operations.

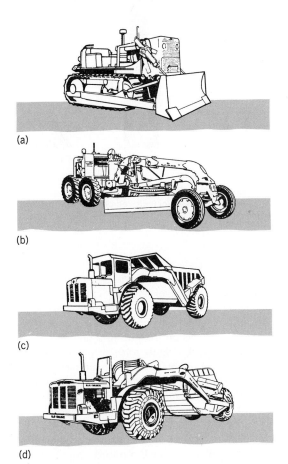

Fig. 10. Road-making machines. (*a*) Front-end shovel. (*b*) Motor grader. (*c*) Motor wagon. (*d*) Motor scraper.

The rapid expansion of highway systems has led to the widespread use of road-making machines (**Fig. 10**). Some of these are modifications of equipment standard to this kind of work; others are highly specialized. Among the former are machines that have evolved by the addition of attachments to wheel and crawler tractors. Machines such as bulldozers and graders do not function as true handling equipment in that they do not pick up and transport materials but push them. On the other hand, self-loading scrapers do transport materials and are usually constructed so that they are either side- or end-dumping. Other general-purpose machines used in highway construction are trench diggers, hole diggers for utility poles, and cable-laying machines. Highly specialized equipment is used for surfacing the road with concrete or other material. *See* CONVEYOR; ELEVATING MACHINES; HOISTING MACHINES; INDUSTRIAL TRUCKS; MATERIALS-HANDLING EQUIPMENT; MONORAIL.   Arthur M. Perrin

Bibliography. S. C. Cowin (ed.), *Mechanics Applied to the Transport of Bulk Materials*, 1979; M. N. Kraus, *Pneumatic Conveying Systems for Bulk Materials*, 3d ed., 1991; F. J. Loeffler and C. R. Proctor (eds.), *Unit and Bulk Materials Handling*, 1980; J. S. Mason and A. S. Goldberg, *Bulk Solids Handling: An Introduction to the Practice and Technology*, 1986.

Buoy

An anchored or moored floating object, other than a lightship, intended as an aid to navigation. Buoys are the most numerous of all engineered aids to navigation, with some 20,000 in United States waters alone.

A great variety of buoys are in use. All are intended to serve as daymarks. Some buoys, particularly those at turning points in channels, are provided with lights of distinctive characteristics for location and identification at night. Some buoys are equipped with apparatus for providing distinctive sounds at intervals so they can be used as aids to navigation in fog and darkness. Some buoys are equipped with radio beacons, and some have reflectors to make them more conspicuous to radar.

Over the years, a number of different buoyage systems have been developed in various parts of the world. In an effort to reduce the differences, the International Association of Lighthouse Authorities (IALA) conducted an extensive study culminating in a recommended uniform system that has been adopted by most European, African, and Asian nations.

This system, identified as IALA system A, has one feature that has not been acceptable to most nations in the Western Hemisphere and some Asian countries. The objectionable feature is the use of red buoys to port while entering a channel from seaward. The United States and other nations were unwilling to give up their traditional "red right returning." To accommodate these nations, IALA proposed an optional system B, similar to system A but with the red buoys on the opposite side of the channel. The United States started installation of system B in 1983; with completion in 1989, the 6-year period coincides with the normal overhaul period of the buoys.

The principal features of IALA system B are shown in the **illustration**. All of these buoys are red and green. In addition, yellow buoys (with yellow lights if such are used) are employed for ocean data acquisition systems, traffic separation schemes, dredging operations, fishnet areas, spoil grounds, military exercise zones, and anchorage

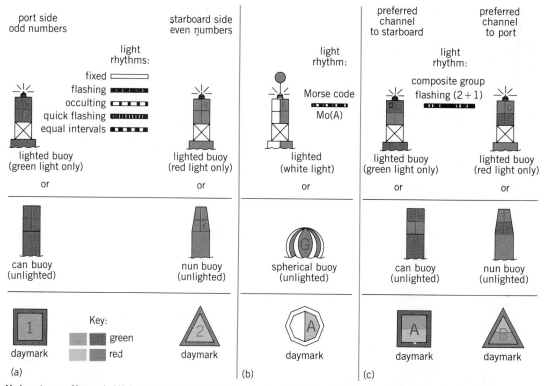

Various types of buoys in IALA system B. (*a*) Lateral aids, marking the sides of channels as seen when entering from seaward. These are marked with numbers. (*b*) Safe-water aids, marking midchannels and fairways. (*c*) Preferred-channel aids, marking bifurcations. Both safe-water and preferred-channel aids have no numbers but may be lettered. (*After U.S. Coast Guard, Modifications for a New Look in U.S. Aids to Navigation, ANSC 5N 3022, 1983*)

areas. Orange and white buoys are used for regulatory and information markers. *See* PILOTING.

Alton B Moody

Bibliography. N. Bowditch, *American Practical Navigator*, U.S. Defense Map. Agency Hydrogr./Topogr. Publ. 9, vol. 1, 1984, vol. 2, 1981; B. Clearman, *International Marine Aids to Navigation*, 2d ed., 1988; U.S. Coast Guard, *Aids to Navigation Manual*, CG-222, 1982.

Buoyancy

The resultant vertical force exerted on a body by a static fluid in which it is submerged or floating. The buoyant force F_B acts vertically upward, in opposition to the gravitational force that causes it. Its magnitude is equal to the weight of fluid displaced, and its line of action is through the centroid of the displaced volume, which is known as the center of buoyancy. With V the displaced volume of fluid and γ the specific weight of fluid (weight per unit volume), the buoyant force equation becomes $F_B = \gamma V$. The magnitude of the buoyant force must also be given by the difference of vertical components of fluid force on the lower and upper sides of the body. *See* AEROSTATICS; FLUID STATICS; HYDROSTATICS.

By weighing an object when it is suspended in two different fluids of known specific weight, the volume and weight of the solid may be determined.

See ARCHIMEDES' PRINCIPLE.

Horizontal buoyancy. Another form of buoyancy, called horizontal buoyancy, is experienced by models tested in wind or water tunnels. Horizontal buoyancy results from variations in static pressure along the test section, producing a drag in closed test sections and a thrust force in open sections. These extraneous forces must be subtracted from data as a boundary correction. Wind tunnel test sections usually diverge slightly in a downstream direction to provide some correction for horizontal buoyancy. *See* WATER TUNNEL; WIND TUNNEL.

Stability. A body floating on a static fluid has vertical stability. A small upward displacement decreases the volume of fluid displaced, hence decreasing the buoyant force and leaving an unbalanced force tending to return the body to its original position. Similarly, a small downward displacement results in a greater buoyant force, which causes an unbalanced upward force.

A body has rotational stability when a small angular displacement sets up a restoring couple that tends to return the body to its orignal position. When the center of gravity of the floating body is lower than its center of buoyancy, it will always have rotational stability. Many a floating body, such as a ship, has its center of gravity above its center of buoyancy. Whether such an object is rotationally stable depends upon the shape of the body. When it floats in equilibrium, its center of buoyancy and center of gravity are in the same vertical line. When the body is tipped, its center of buoyancy shifts to the new centroid of the displaced fluid and exerts its force vertically upward, intersecting the original line through the center of gravity and center of buoyancy at a point called the metacenter. A floating body is rotationally stable if the metacenter lies above the center of gravity. The distance of the metacenter above the center of gravity is the metacentric height and is a direct measure of the stability of the object. *See* SHIP DESIGN.

Victor L. Streeter

Buret

An instrument used to deliver variable volumes of a liquid. Burets are usually made from uniform-bore glass tubing in capacities of 5–100 ml, the commonest being 50 ml. The uniform portion is graduated in small divisions, so that volumes of liquid accurate to a small fraction of a milliliter may be measured by reading the volumes in the buret before and after a sample has been withdrawn. For the most accurate use of burets, the graduations should be calibrated by the user, and liquid levels in the buret should be estimated to one-tenth of the smallest interval between graduations. Most burets are equipped with a stopcock to control the flow of liquid (see **illus.**). Various modifications of the

A common buret, with stopcock.

basic design of a buret have been introduced to simplify its use or to increase its accuracy. For example, with a weight buret, the quantity of liquid delivered is determined from the change in weight. Special modifications have been employed in microanalysis, where a capacity of 0.1 ml is frequently employed. *See* TITRATION; VOLUMETRIC ANALYSIS.

Clark E. Bricker

Burgess Shale

Part of a clay and silt sequence that accumulated at the foot of a colossal "reef" during the Cambrian explosion, a dramatic evolutionary radiation of animals beginning about 545 million years ago. Although this explosion is most obvious from the geologically abrupt appearance of skeletons, the bulk of the radiation consisted of soft-bodied animals. The Burgess Shale fauna, located near Field in southern British Columbia, is the finest of the soft-bodied assemblages. It is Middle Cambrian—approximately 520 million years old. Of the more than 30 other Burgess Shale–type faunas that have been recognized in various parts of the world, Lower Cambrian examples from Chengiang (southern China) and Sirius Passet (northern Greenland) are especially significant.

Diversity of fauna. The Burgess Shale fauna remains the most diverse, however, with about 120 genera. Its approximate composition is arthropods 37%, sponges 15%, brachiopods 4%, priapulids 5%, annelids 5%, chordates and hemichordates 5%, echinoderms 5%, coelenterates 2%, mollusks 3%, and other fauna 19%. Although arthropods are the most important group, the trilobites, normally dominant among Cambrian arthropods, are entirely overshadowed both in number of species and in absolute number of specimens by a remarkable variety of other arthropods with delicate exoskeletons. Primitive crustaceans and chelicerates are complemented by the lobopods *Aysheaia* and *Hallucigenia*, presumed to be distantly related to the onychophorans and uniramians. Many other arthropods show puzzling combinations of anatomy that make precise placement in major groups difficult. Phylogenies based on cladistics, however, are placing them in an ordered evolutionary context.

Cambrian evolution. The Burgess Shale has revealed many other aspects of the Cambrian explosion. First, a census of the collections reveals marine ecology that is fundamentally unchanged to the present day. Predators, long thought to be insignificant in the Cambrian, are an important component. Second, although many of the species are a product of the Cambrian explosion, rare species are clear holdovers from the primitive Ediacaran faunas of late Precambrian age. Third, some species are of particular evolutionary importance. Most significant is the worm *Pikaia*, which is interpreted as the earliest chordate, and as a predecessor of fish it lies near the beginning of the evolutionary path that ultimately leads to humans. A number of species appear so bizarre that earlier they were interpreted as new phyla, representing extinct body plans. This view is a simplification, because as new information accumulates from both the Burgess Shale and comparable faunas, it transpires that such taxa are giving unique insights into the very early stages of diversification and the interrelationships between known phyla. *See* EDIACARAN FAUNA.

Much remains to be understood about Cambrian

life in the context of Burgess Shale–type faunas. Some taxa are still enigmatic, and reasons for the prevalence of soft-bodied preservation are obscure. In the Burgess Shale itself, rapid burial in silts and muds at the foot of an enormous carbonate escarpment and in anoxic conditions were certainly contributory factors, but they are unlikely to be the entire explanation. *See* CAMBRIAN; FOSSIL; PALEONTOLOGY.   Simon Conway Morris

Bibliography. S. J. Gould, *Wonderful Life: The Burgess Shale and the Nature of History*, 1990; H. B. Whittington, *The Burgess Shale*, 1985.

Burn

The reaction that occurs when tissue (usually skin) receives more energy (heat, chemical energy, electrical energy, or radiation) than it can absorb without injury. Factors such as the duration of contact, temperature, volume of chemical, and voltage influence the severity of the injury. The notable pathologic changes are denaturation of protein and coagulation of blood vessels. Local destruction of tissue leads to bacterial invasion and infection; loss of fluid, electrolytes, and protein; loss of temperature control; and pain. Systemic reactions include altered blood flow and temperature regulation, fluid and electrolyte imbalances, shock, infections, and catabolism. Associated problems—other illnesses (particularly cardiopulmonary), trauma, and injuries caused by inhaling carbon monoxide, smoke, and occasionally heat—may be lethal or contribute significantly to mortality and morbidity from burn injuries. *See* SKIN.

Classification. Burns are classified according to location, percentage of total body surface involved, and depth of injury (see **illus.**).

First-degree burns, for example, sunburn, are superficial burns that result in some redness, pain, and swelling. Blister formation and necrosis (tissue death) do not extend beyond the epidermis (outer layer of skin). Healing is completed in a few days, and there is no scarring.

Second-degree burns, for example, scalds, are burns that show destruction of the entire epidermis

and variable portions of the dermis (inner layer of skin); blistering and swelling occur and pain is severe. The degree of scarring depends on the depth of injury to the dermis. Skin grafting may be necessary if burns are deep or if trauma or secondary infection ensues and deepens the necrosis. *See* TRANSPLANTATION BIOLOGY.

Third-degree burns, for example, flame burns, are characterized by necrosis of the epidermis and dermis, including the dermal appendages (hair follicles and sweat glands). A pearly white, tan, or brownish-black eschar ("scab") with coagulated dermal blood vessels results. After 14 to 21 days, the eschar sloughs, leaving a raw surface. Skin grafting is usually necessary.

Fourth-degree burns, for example, severe electrical injuries, involve all layers of skin, as well as the underlying fat, muscle, nerves, or bone. These injuries may require both amputation and skin grafting to heal.

Treatment. The initial step in management for a burn is to remove the injuring source from the burned patient. Attention should be directed to assessing the airway and breathing, particularly in individuals with inhalation or associated injuries. Patients with severe, extensive burns must be given large amounts of fluids and electrolytes intravenously, during the first 24 h and lesser amounts, with the addition of protein and other electrolytes, thereafter. Wound care involves removing dead tissue, preventing infection by applying antibiotics, and replacing the skin if indicated; the skin may be temporarily replaced by allografts (skin from other humans—for example, that obtained from cadavers), xenografts (skin from other species), or synthetic membranes or permanently replaced by autografts (skin from elsewhere on the patient's body). Nutritional support involves giving calories, protein, fat, and minerals by mouth and intravenously; requirements can be up to twice normal levels. Psychological support must overcome anxiety, denial, disbelief, guilt, depression, as well as fear of death, disfigurement, and disability, in order to provide coping mechanisms and enable planning for the future.

The more severe the burn or the more vulnerable the injured person (patients who are very young or very old, have other systemic diseases, or have other associated injuries are especially vulnerable), the more likely are complications. The most significant of these are systemic infections and the consequences of treating them. In addition, there may be specific or nonspecific injury to certain organs, such as Curling's ulcer (superficial ulceration of the stomach), renal damage related to inadequate fluid support, red cell or myoglobin destruction, adrenal changes, focal liver necrosis, or multiple organ failure.

Electrical burns. Electrical burns result from the amount of heat incident to the flow of a certain amount of electricity through the resistance offered by the tissues. The initial resistance is from dry skin. Large nerves and blood vessels carry electricity

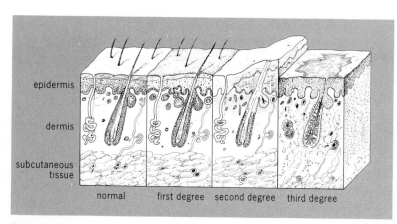

epidermis

dermis

subcutaneous tissue

normal   first degree   second degree   third degree

Anatomic diagram of normal and burned skin.

efficiently, but smaller blood vessels, muscle, and especially bone have higher resistance. Therefore, most electrothermal injuries consist of damage to the skin and immediately subjacent tissues, along with muscle necrosis due to the heat from bones and destruction of nutrient vessels. Deep penetration of the burn may follow large voltages. Small pitlike entrance and exit wounds may occur from arcing across adjacent flexed surfaces (for example, elbow, armpit, groin, and knee). Often the injury below a small entrance or exit wound is significantly larger and resembles tissue injured by crushing. Effects on the heart and brain are well documented and are evidenced in electric chair executions.

Chemical burns. Chemical burns result from corrosive agents that destroy tissues at the point of contact. Injury to the skin, eyes, and gastrointestinal tract are most common. The corrosives may be either acid or alkali; alkalis cause damage longer than acids. Extremes of pH above 11.5 or below 2.5 almost always result in irreversible damage. Protein coagulation, precipitation, and actual dissolution of tissue constituents may occur. The initial treatment is to dilute and thus remove the chemical by irrigating the area copiously with water; in addition, a few chemicals, for example, hydrogen fluoride, require specific neutralization. In general, chemicals should not be neutralized on the skin. In addition to causing burns, some chemicals injure specific organs; for example, phenol and carbon tetrachloride damage the liver.

Epidemiology and prevention. Annually, 1% of the United States population is burned significantly enough to prevent participation in activities of daily living. Most burns occur in the kitchen, with scalds being the most frequent mechanism of injury; the next most frequent site of injury is the bathroom. Fire and flames cause most of the burn or inhalation injuries leading to hospital admissions and deaths. Most deaths from burns due to fire occur in the bedroom at night.

Burn prevention requires changes in behavior (conducting exit drills in the home and school, and not smoking in bed), in manufacturing (producing fire-retardant garments, fire-safe cigarettes, and lower-temperature thermostats on water heaters), in codes (requiring fire and smoke detectors, and sprinkling systems), and in laws.   Thomas L. Wachtel

Bibliography. J. A. Boswick, *The Art and Science of Burn Care*, 1987; T. L. Wachtel, Burns, *Critical Care Clinics*, vol. 1, no. 1, 1985; T. L. Wachtel, V. Kahn, and H. A. Frank, *Current Topics in Burn Care*, 1983.

Burning velocity measurement

The velocity at which the combustible gases move through a flame in the direction perpendicular to the flame surface defines the burning velocity. The term flame as used here refers to the burning of combustible gases. The process of combustion, or burning, is described as a chemical reaction of two

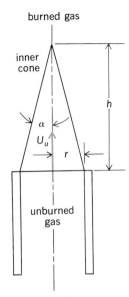

Fig. 1. Geometry of Bunsen flame.

or more substances in which a large quantity of heat is evolved. This heat is self-absorbed and goes into heating the products of combustion. Part of the light that is emitted is due to the heat of the flame, and part is due to the chemical reaction within the flame zones or thickness. It is the combustion of gases that forms the basis of a flame; and the zone in which chemical reactions occur, together with the concomitant temperature gradient, determines the location of the flame. An expression of the laminar flame speed for premixed homogeneous combustible gases has been obtained analytically, and indicates that the flame speed is proportional to the square root of the diffusivity and the reaction rate. The diffusion of heat and mass cause the flame to propagate. The reaction rate determines the temperature gradient by its effect on the thickness of the reaction zone: the slower the reaction, the thicker the zone.

A general definition of burning velocity consonant with measurement techniques cannot be formulated free from all possible objections. Ideally, if an infinite plane flame surface, considered stationary in a one-dimensional flow field, is cut perpendicularly by a stream tube, the area of the flame surface enclosed in the stream tube does not depend on how the flame is structured. The area of all parallel surfaces is the same no matter what property is chosen to define the surface, and this area is equal to the luminous surface of the flame. Where the flame surface is curved, the determination of the reference area within the flame, that is, the reaction zone, is much more difficult. For example, consider a combustible gas mixture which is supplied at a point at a steady rate and which flows radially outward in a laminar manner to a radially spherical flame. In this case the area of the surface of the combustion wave will depend on where the surface is located. Since the mass flow of the gases through the surface is constant, the flame speed will depend on the selected surface. In addition, since source flow with spherical symmetry exists, there is no constant asymptotic value for the velocity of the unburned gases. In this case, if it is assumed that the flame curvature is large compared with the flame thickness, then the burning velocity is the minimum value of the gas velocity upstream of the flame front.

Other difficulties are experimental and can arise because of the apparatus used to measure the flame speed. For example, probes cause the flow field to distort and can serve as heat sinks or catalytic surfaces for the reacting gases. In addition, where optical means are employed to measure temperature gradients in a flame, nonequilibrium effects can introduce errors in locating the reference surface for the determination of flame speed. Thus, measurement techniques that do not distort or interact with the chemistry of the flow field are preferred.

Idealized and actual flames. Experimental measurements of burning velocities have been made on both stationary and moving flames. Bunsen burners furnish a familiar example of stationary flames (**Fig. 1**). If the inner cone of a bunsen flame were a geometric cone whose base coincided with the port, the burning velocity S_u would be simply the volume of unburned gas entering per unit time per unit area of flame cone, as shown by Eq. (1). Expressed in terms of the port radius r, cone height h,

$$S_u = \frac{\text{area of port } \times \text{ average gas velocity}}{\text{area of flame cone}} \quad (1)$$

pressed in terms of the port radius r, cone height h, angle α which one side of the cone makes with its axis, and average gas velocity U_u, burning velocity is given by Eq. (2).

$$S_u = \frac{r U_u}{\sqrt{r^2 + h^2}} = U_u \sin \alpha \quad (2)$$

In this idealized flame, all unburned gas must have the same velocity and must flow parallel to the axis of the burner; there must be no heating of the unburned gases; and the reaction zone must be infinitely thin. Actual flames deviate appreciably from this ideal. For example, consider the following methods of observation: shadowgraph, schlieren, and interferometry. Shadowgraph measures the derivative of the gas density gradient, and it is not well defined spatially. Schlieren measures the gas density gradient which corresponds more closely to the ignition temperature and is more readily defined and preferable. Interferometry measures the density, is very sensitive, and yields complicated graphical results which are difficult to define quantitatively. The flame cone defining the front of the combustion wave is not infinitely thin, yielding different locations for the flame surface and therefore different burning velocities. *See* FLAME.

Measurement techniques. The various methods used to measure flame speeds can be grouped under the following headings: conical stationary flames; flames in tubes; soap bubble methods; constant-volume explosions in spherical vessels; flat-flame burner methods; and laser diagnostic techniques. These are briefly described below.

Bunsen burner method. Premixed gases flow up a cylindrical tube long enough to ensure fully developed laminar flow. The gas burns at the mouth of the tube, and the shape of the flame cone is recorded by photography or an equivalent method. The flame area is determined by various means of geometrical methods and the flame speed thus determined, as in Eq. (3). It is agreed that

$$S_u = \frac{\text{volume of gas flow}}{\text{surface area of flame cone}} \quad (3)$$

the schlieren cone is the most suitable for the determination of flame speed. The cone angle is measured at the central portion of the cone in about 30% of the internal portion of the cone. Wall effects which produce flame cooling, lower reaction rates, and lower flame speeds cannot be completely eliminated.

Cylindrical tube method. In this case, a premixed gas is placed in a horizontal or vertical tube. The gas is ignited at one end, and the rate of flame propagation into the unburned gases is measured. Provided that the tube is not too short, and the energy released by the spark used for ignition is not much larger than the minimum ignition energy, the combustion wave is observed to be nearly plane and to travel at almost constant speed between 2 and 10 tube diameters from the spark. This constant speed is the empirical burning velocity. This method is approximate and suffers from errors due to wall effects, buoyancy, combustion-wave distortion, and friction.

Soap bubble method. In an effort to eliminate wall effects, two spherical methods were developed. Soap bubbles blown with homogeneous combustible gas mixtures have been used as a containing medium. Spark ignition at the center of the bubble will propagate a combustion wave at constant pressure through the mixture. The flame speed is amplified by expansion of the burned gases behind the flame front.

Measurements on such a flame are made photographically by observing the growth of the flame radius through a slit as the film moves past

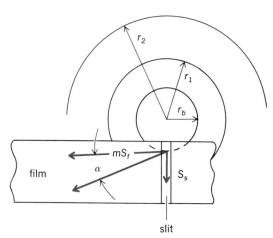

Fig. 2. Film moving past slit to record growth of flame by measurement of its radius.

the slit (**Fig. 2**). If an initial volume of gas of radius r_1 burns to a final volume of radius r_2 and is measured on a film moving with a velocity S_f and a magnification factor m, the flame speed S_s in space is given by Eq. (4), where α is the angle made

$$S_s = m S_f \tan \alpha \qquad (4)$$

with the film axis due to growth of the flame. The expansion ratio E is also a function of the burned gas density ρ_b and unburned gas density ρ_u, as expressed in Eq. (5). The mass of gas entering

$$E = \left(\frac{r_2}{r_1}\right)^3 = \frac{\rho_u}{\rho_b} \qquad (5)$$

and leaving a unit area of combustion wave per unit time is derived from Eqs. (5) and (6) and shown in Eq. (7). Afterburning, which affects the

$$S_u \rho_u = S_s \rho_b \qquad (6)$$

$$S_u = \frac{S_s \rho_b}{\rho_u} = \frac{S_s}{E} \qquad (7)$$

precision of measurement of the final radius, can be eliminated by surrounding the bubble with inert gas. The method can be used at various pressures by placing the entire apparatus inside a pressure-controlled chamber.

Closed spherical bomb method. Another technique for measuring burning velocity in which adequate control of gas composition is maintained is combustion in spherical bombs with central ignition. Since reaction occurs under constant-volume conditions in this apparatus, the calculations to find the burning velocity are much more complex.

Flat-flame burner method. The flat-flame burner method is probably the most accurate because it offers the simplest flame front and one in which the area of the shadow schlieren and visible parts are the same. A combustible gas mixture flows up a tube in which a porous plug or grid is placed at the end. The grid stabilizes the flame. If the combustion gas speed is too great, a flame cone occurs; if too slow, flashback and quenching occur. Finally the tube is shrouded by inert gas to better define the flame. This method applies to mixtures having low burning velocities and can be applied as well to low pressures.

Laser diagnostic techniques. Through the combined use of laser Raman scattering and laser Doppler velocimetry, simultaneous nonintrusive, instantaneous, and pointwise measurements of temperature, specie concentration, and velocity can be obtained in flames. The nature of this diagnostic technique is also rather complicated. *See* LASER.

Maximum burning velocity in air mixtures of most hydrocarbons under atmospheric conditions varies from 10 to 40 in./s (25 to 100 cm/s). Typical gasoline hydrocarbons have burning velocities in the range of 12–16 in./s (30–40 cm/s). *See* COMBUSTION.   Vito Agosta

Bibliography. I. Glassman, *Combination*, 1977; S. Lederman, The use of laser Raman diagnostics in flow fields and combustion, *Progress of Energy and Combustion Sciences*, vol. 3, pp. 1–34, 1977; S. Lederman, A. Celentano, and J. Glaser, Temperature, concentration and velocity in jets, flames and shock tubes, *Phys. Fluids*, 22(6):1065–1072, 1979; H. Taylor (ed.), *Physical Measurement in Gas Dynamics*, vol. 9, 1954; L. A. Vulis, *Thermal Regimes of Combustion*, 1961; F. A. Williams, *Combustion Theory*, 1965.

Burrowing animals

Some terrestrial and aquatic animals are capable of excavating holes in the ground for protection from adverse environmental conditions, as well as for storing food. Burrows vary from temporary structures of simple design (for example, the nesting burrows of some birds) to more permanent underground networks that may be inhabited for several generations (for example, rabbit warrens, badger sets, fox earths, and prairie dog burrows). They vary in structure from blind burrows with a single opening to extensive systems with several openings. Some animals (for example, some species of moles) live permanently underground, and their burrows have no obvious large openings to the surface. Burrows may be shared by a number of species, and abandoned burrows may be used by other species. Animals with limbs usually excavate their burrows by using their legs, but many burrowing animals are limbless and the mechanism of progression is not always obvious.

Terrestrial burrowers. Worms, slugs, many insects, and many vertebrates live in burrows. Earthworms are important soil organisms because their burrows improve drainage and aeration, their feeding habits enhance leaf decomposition, and their droppings increase soil fertility. Earthworms burrow by contracting circular muscles in their body wall to push forward, and contracting the longitudinal muscles to widen the burrow. Termites (Isoptera) and ants (Hymenoptera) are social insects, most of which live underground. Termites are major consumers of vegetation in warm climates, and many construct extensive underground galleries extending from the mound located on the surface. The conditions in the mound are carefully regulated by the termites. Most ants are predators or scavengers, but leaf-cutter ants feed on a fungus that grows on the harvested pieces of leaf in carefully tended underground galleries. Male mole crickets (*Gryllotalpa viniae*) attract mates by singing (they rub their wings together to generate sound) in their burrows; the burrow has a double, trumpet-shaped opening which acoustically focuses the sound, thereby increasing efficiency.

Some animals bury themselves to avoid adverse conditions, abandoning the burrow when conditions improve. Lungfish, for example, inhabit seasonal rivers in Australia, Africa, and South America. They bury themselves in the mud of drying rivers, breathe with the aid of an organ resembling a lung, and become active again when the next rainy season fills the river.

Several groups of burrowing vertebrates have small limbs or, in some cases, are limbless. For example, caecilians are amphibians that resemble earthworms. Burrowing skinks show varying limb reduction. Slow worms and snakes are burrowing, limbless reptiles, though many snakes live in other habitats.

Moles are highly adapted for a permanent life underground. European moles are solitary, feed mainly on earthworms, and have shovellike front limbs and well-developed tactile and olfactory senses, but their vision is reduced. Some moles are blind. The golden mole of Namibia effectively "swims," surprisingly quickly, through the desert sand by using its front feet and its head.

Most small and medium-sized mammals (for example, shrews, mice, voles, rabbits, prairie dogs, foxes, and badgers) live in burrows, though they have few anatomical adaptations to burrowing. Small animals are more susceptible to adverse environmental conditions than large ones. Very large mammals do not burrow.

Naked mole rats (*Heterocephalus glaber*) live in East Africa in underground colonies of up to 100 individuals; a colony may have 2.5 mi (4 km) of burrows. They feed on roots and tubers. They use their large incisor teeth to excavate the burrow and scrape away the soil to widen the opening. Uniquely among mammals, mole rats show a social order similar to that of social insects: each colony has only a single breeding female and several breeding males; all others are infertile and are called helpers. Foraging and burrowing are carried out mainly by small helpers, while defensive duties are performed by large helpers.

One problem all burrow dwellers face is ventilation. Diffusion alone is insufficient for extensive burrows. In order to overcome this difficulty, prairie dogs (*Cynomys ludovicianus*) construct burrows up to 98 ft (30 m) long with two or three entrances and mounds of different shapes for each entrance. The force produced by wind creates a pressure differential between the entrances which causes air to flow through the burrow.

Aquatic burrowers. Many marine animals, including flatfish, crabs, and shrimps, take temporary refuge or live more permanently in sand or mud by burying themselves just below the surface. Aquatic sand and mud pose several problems for burrowing animals. First, the particles are usually tightly packed together, restricting movement and requiring these organisms to expend 10–1000 times as much energy to move a given distance compared to other forms of locomotion. Second, burrows readily collapse unless reinforced or consolidated. The wall of burrows may simply be consolidated with mucus, but some animals make a more permanent, substantial tube of particles stuck together with mucus. Finally, all burrowing animals must be able to create a current of water through the burrow so that

they can breathe. Many animals also feed partly or wholly on particles carried in such currents.

Animals with limbs or similar appendages use them to burrow or move through sand. Crabs and shrimps use their legs. The burrowing crab (*Corystes cassivellaunus*) uses its unusually long antennae to breathe when it is buried. Interlocking setae hold the antennae together and form a tube, rather like a snorkel. The burrowing sea urchin uses spatulate spines to burrow. Many burrowing worms and mollusks have no such appendages.

Saturated sediments have two properties that such animals exploit. When an intermittent force is applied to sediments, they become liquefied (thixotropic), and when a steady force is applied they become solid (dilatant). Many burrowing animals utilize these properties to burrow in a two-stage process that is clearly demonstrated in burrowing bivalved mollusks such as clams. The shell valves open against the sediment, forming a penetration anchor. Meanwhile, the foot repeatedly extends into the sediment. The siphons (breathing tubes) then close to prevent water leakage, and adductor muscles partly close the shell. These actions have several consequences: the penetration anchor is released; water is ejected from the shell margin, excavating a cavity in the sand; blood is forced from the body into the foot, which swells to form a terminal anchor; and the elastic hinge ligament of the shell is compressed. The muscles then pull the shell downward into the cavity. Finally, stored energy in the ligament is released so that the shell reopens. This cycle is repeated several times. *See* MOLLUSCA.

The alternation of penetration and terminal anchors can be recognized in many different kinds of burrowing animals. Burrowing worms and sea anemones use circular and longitudinal muscles in the body wall to elongate or thicken the body. The liquid contents of the body cavity act as a hydrostatic skeleton, allowing the two sets of muscle to antagonize.

Lugworms (*Arenicola*) are commonly found on sandy beaches, where each inhabits a U-shaped burrow. Coiled worm casts accumulate at the rear end of the burrow, and a small depression marks the front end. The worms pump water from back to front through the burrow to produce a current that provides for respiration and feeding. The sand in front of the head acts as a filter and is enriched with planktonic food before it is swallowed and digested. The indigestible sand is then deposited as casts on the surface at regular intervals.

Nereis diversicolor is a worm found in abundance in the mud of estuaries. It also inhabits a U-shaped burrow. It has a pair of jaws and can feed either as a predator or a scavenger or by filtering. It secretes a conical net of fine mucus strands in the front part of the burrow and pumps water through the net by undulating the body within the burrow. After about 7 min of pumping, the worm moves forward in the burrow, eating the net and the trapped food particles. It then secretes another net (the whole cycle takes about 10 min). A single worm may pump over half a quart of water in an hour.

Fiddler crabs (*Uca*) are common on many tropical and subtropical muddy shores such as mangrove swamps. They are air breathing and feed when the tide is out by sieving through surface mud for food. When the tide comes in, each crab retreats to its burrow and blocks the entrance with a plug of sand.   Hugh D. Jones

Bibliography. J. Bailey, *The Life Cycle of a Crab*, 1990; M. L. Gorman and R. D. Stone, *The Natural History of Moles*, 1990; P. W. Sherman, J. U. M. Jarvis, and R. D. Alexander (eds.), *The Biology of the Naked Mole-Rat*, 1991.

Bursa

A simple sac or cavity with smooth walls and containing a clear, slightly sticky fluid interposed between two moving surfaces of the body to reduce friction. Subcutaneous bursae are found where the skin stretches around the greater curvature of a joint, as in the elbow or knee, and considerable chafing may occur; they may be single or multiple sacs. These bursae may enlarge as a result of continuous excessive irritation, as in housemaid's knee or miner's elbow. *See* BURSITIS; JOINT DISORDERS.

Synovial bursae are small closed sacs of fibrous tissue continuous with the joint cavity of a diarthrosis. They are lined with a complex membrane that secretes a clear lubricating fluid, serving to reduce friction between the opposing surfaces of the articulation.

Bursae may exist in the form of elongated sheaths surrounding tendons or ligaments, where these moving bands are in contact with another structure, such as a bone, muscle, or another tendon or ligament. Tendon sheaths are especially common where tendons bend around the ends of two bones at an articulation. *See* JOINT (ANATOMY); MUSCULAR SYSTEM; SKELETAL SYSTEM.   Walter Bock

Bursitis

Any inflammation of a bursa. Bursae are synovial pouches, positioned to minimize friction between moving parts of the body. They are cystic in appearance and are filled with fluid. More than 80 bursae have been identified on each side of the body around joints and between tendons, muscles, and ligaments. In many cases, they are continuous with or near a regular joint cavity. It is generally thought that bursae exist as normal but irregularly apparent structures, but there is some evidence that they are pathologic alterations of connective tissue produced by irritation and friction. In any case, they rarely produce symptoms unless inflammation occurs. Bursitis most often occurs near the shoulder,

hip, elbow, or knee. *See* BURSA; JOINT (ANATOMY).

Inflammatory changes in bursae produce acute or chronic swelling, an increase in the fluid content, and variable degrees of pain and tenderness. Acute bursitis may be septic (caused by microorganisms) or nonseptic. Nonseptic bursitis can be further subdivided into idiopathic (of unknown cause), traumatic, and crystal-induced bursitis. Septic bursitis may result from direct penetration by microorganisms through medical instrumentation or trauma; rarely, microorganisms may reach bursae through the blood. Most cases of bursitis are nonseptic; they may result from trauma or physical stress. The fluid aspirated from an inflamed nonseptic bursa does not contain microorganisms.

In chronic bursitis, the wall of the bursa becomes thickened, shaggy, and irregular, with calcium deposits commonly being present. The fluid, which is normally clear, changes to a reddish-brown or black gritty mass as a result of repeated hemorrhages and precipitation of calcium. The treatment depends on whether the bursitis is septic or nonseptic. Septic bursitis is most commonly due to *Staphylococcus aureus* and requires prompt administration of appropriate antibiotics and repeated drainage of fluid containing pus. Nonseptic bursitis can be treated conservatively by withdrawal of fluid and administration of nonsteroidal, anti-inflammatory drugs. In nonseptic bursitis, withdrawal of the fluid can also be followed by injection of a steroid, but side effects, including chronic pain, may occur. Surgical incision and drainage are rarely necessary. Crystal-induced nonseptic bursitis is most frequently due to gout and usually responds well to drug therapy. Avoidance of trauma can help to prevent occupation-related cases of bursitis. Most cases of bursitis have a favorable prognosis. *See* CONNECTIVE TISSUE; GOUT.   Robert P. Searles

Bus

A motor vehicle for mass transit, built in various capacities and sizes, designed for carrying from 10 to 60 passengers or more on school, local, intercity, or interstate routes. A commercial bus usually operates on a regular schedule and travels a fixed route, and each passenger pays a fare. In general, a bus has a long body with the passengers sitting on benches or seats. A double-deck bus has two separate passenger compartments, one above the other. The articulated bus has two connected passenger compartments that bend at their connecting point as the bus turns.

Most commercial buses have diesel engines, air conditioning, air suspension, and automatic transmission. Restroom facilities are usually included in buses for long-distance service. Basic bus design retains many passenger car and truck components. Gross weight is kept at a minimum for economic operation and for maximum utilization of space for entry, aisle, and exit areas. Seating and safety devices must comply with federal regulations. Heavy frames perform the same functions as those in other commercial vehicles for load-bearing capacity, rigidity, and resistance to impact. *See* AUTOMOBILE.

The chassis assembly includes all the components and systems essential to operation, usually the fundamental package upon which bus bodies built by other manufacturers are mounted. Body styles, seating, passenger capacity, power plant, and other equipment and passenger conveniences are available in great variety.

Gasoline and diesel engines are the principal sources of motive power. Engine installation may be at the front, under the floor, at the rear (either laterally or transversely), or on the frame, according to capacity or operating specifications for the operator's unobstructed view of front entry and rear exit areas. *See* DIESEL ENGINE; INTERNAL COMBUSTION ENGINE.

Power trains resemble those used in other large commercial vehicles, and transmissions may be manual, semiautomatic, or automatic, depending upon cost and operating requirements. Brake, steering, and suspension systems are available on the same basis. *See* MOTOR VEHICLE.   Donald L. Anglin

Bus-bar

An aluminum or copper conductor supported by insulators that interconnects the loads and the sources of electric power in an electric power system. A typical application is the interconnection of the incoming and outgoing transmission lines and transformers at an electrical substation. Bus-bars also interconnect the generator and the main transformers in a power plant. In an industrial plant such as an aluminum smelter, large bus-bars supply several tens of thousands of amperes to the electrolytic process. A line diagram of a typical substation bus-bar system is shown in **Fig. 1**. The bus-bar distributes the current of the two incoming lines between the outgoing line and the transformer. In this example, bus-bar failure interrupts the load connected to the transformer and the outgoing line. In a large station, the bus-bar failure may affect thousands of customers. The reliability of a system including bus-bars can be improved by using double bus-bars, where the loads automatically switch to the operating bus-bar in case of a fault. The ring bus-bar provides two supply routes for each load, which increases the system fault tolerance. A three-phase system has three bus-bars, which collectively are called a bus. *See* ELECTRIC POWER SUBSTATION.

Types. The major types are (1) rigid bus-bars, used at low, medium, and high voltage; (2) strain bus-bars, used mainly for high voltage; (3) insulated-phase bus-bars, used at medium voltage; and (4) sulfur hexafluoride (SF_6)–insulated bus-

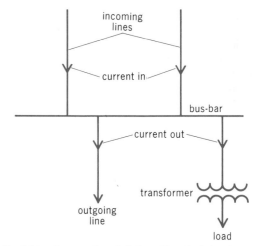

Fig. 1. Line diagram of a substation with a single bus-bar for distribution of current.

bars, used in medium- and high-voltage systems.

The rigid bus-bar is an aluminum or copper bar supported by porcelain insulators. The most frequently used bar types are rectangular, U-shape, and tube. In some cases, the bus-bars are protected by a metal duct, which surrounds all three phases.

The strain bus-bar is a flexible, stranded conductor which is strung between substation metal structures and held by suspension-type insulators. Its construction is similar to that of a common transmission line.

The insulated-phase bus-bar is a rigid bar supported by insulators and covered by a grounded metal shield (**Fig. 2**). The duct is often ventilated to assure better cooling of the conductor. The main advantage of this system is the elimination of short circuits between adjacent phases.

The sulfur hexafluoride–insulated bus-bar is a rigid aluminum tube, supported by insulators and installed in a larger metal tube, which is filled with high-pressure sulfur hexafluoride gas. The high-pressure sulfur hexafluoride has very high electric flashover strength, which permits the reduction of the bus-bar size at high voltage by a factor of 10 to 20. *See* ELECTRICAL INSULATION.

Design. Bus-bars are major components of electrical systems because they distribute large amounts of energy. A bus-bar failure is a major system dis-

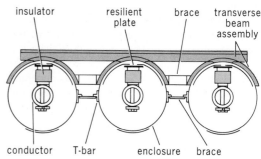

Fig. 2. Cross section of insulated-phase bus-bar.

turbance which should be avoided, and bus-bars are therefore designed with extreme care. The major design considerations are that the bus-bar must carry the maximum load current continuously without overheating, and the mechanical forces generated by short circuits should not cause any damage. *See* CONDUCTOR (ELECTRICITY); WIRING.

George G. Karady

Bushing

A removable metal lining, usually in the form of a bearing to carry a shaft. Generally a bushing is a small bearing in the form of a cylinder and is made of soft metal or graphite-filled sintered material. Bushings are also used as cylindrical liners for holes to preserve the dimensional requirements, such as in the guide bearings in jigs and fixtures for drilling holes in machine parts. *See* CYLINDER.

James J. Ryan

Butter

A food product made by churning cream. In the United States, butter is not defined by Standard of Identity in the Food, Drug and Cosmetic Act as are most foods, but instead it was defined in 1923 by an act of Congress. Butter must contain at least 80% milk fat and may contain added salt or color. In antiquity, butter and cheese were made as a means of preserving the surplus milk for later use. *See* MILK.

Butter is a water-in-fat emulsion. Cream is a fat-in-water emulsion. Cream consists of discrete fat globules, 6–16 micrometers in size, suspended in skim milk. Fat globules have a membrane or coating consisting of natural emulsifiers, lipoproteins, fat-soluble vitamins, cholesterol, and some other materials in lesser concentrations. The membrane provides stability for the globule and protects it from attack by lipase enzymes. *See* EMULSION.

Manufacturing. In the United States and Europe, negligible amounts of farm-separated cream are produced, and little butter is made by batch churning. Thus, the handling of cream and butter has advanced technologically to improve markedly the sanitary conditions under which it is produced and the quality of the finished food that reaches the consumer.

Cream that is to be used for making butter arrives at the manufacturer's processing plant from many sources, but the major source is those dairies where whole milk is separated into skim milk and cream by centrifugal force in a separator. Skim milk in these processing plants is converted to nonfat dry milk, and the cream is sold to other users. Another source of cream is fluid milk plants, where whole milk is partially or totally separated to produce standardized whole milk, 3.25% milk fat; low-fat milks, 1 and 2% milk fat; and skim milk, no more than 0.5% milk fat. The third source of cream is the cheese industry, where incoming milk supplies may be partially separated. Also, all cheese whey is separated to recover the milk fat that was lost in making the cheese. This is known as whey cream and is somewhat inferior to the sweet cream made directly from whole milk. These two sources of cream may be combined or stored separately. *See* CHEESE.

All cream is perishable and must be handled with care to retain high quality. After separation, cream is held in stainless steel tanks and refrigerated at 39–45°F (4–7°C). The fat content of creams ranges 35–45%.

Butter manufacturers buy and transport cream from many dairy plants. In the United States, some manufacturers buy cream in 20 or more states. Cream in large tankers is delivered to a butter manufacturer and is examined on arrival for flavor and odor, followed by taking of a sample for analysis. If the cream passes the flavor and odor test, it is pumped into the butter plant and is stored in another large tank. The next step is to pasteurize the cream. This heat treatment destroys bacteria, inactivates enzymes, and gives the cream a cooked or heated flavor. Pasteurization can either be a batch process where cream is heated to a minimum of 165°F (74°C) and held at the temperature for 30 min, or continuous at 185°F (85°C) where the hold is only 15 s. *See* PASTEURIZATION.

Following pasteurization, rapid cooling promotes fat crystals on the exterior and liquid fat on the interior of the fat globules. If the cream were churned after this step, the loss of fat to the buttermilk would be high. Thus, a tempering step is used in which the cream is held at about 50°F (10°C) to allow rearrangement of the fat crystals. Then, liquid fat is on the outside of the globules to allow rapid aggregation during churning.

In the summer season, consumption of green feed by dairy cattle elevates the oleic acid content of the milk fat. This phenomenon alters the melting point so that cream during tempering must be held 3.6°F (2°C) lower in summer to minimize fat loss to buttermilk and also to allow for suitable plasticity at wrapping and packaging.

Continuous churns produce as much as 15,000 lb (6800 kg) of butter per hour. They convert cream to butter in a few minutes; with the batch churn, about 45 min is needed to produce butter, and then at least 30 min to standardize the composition and get water dispersed in tiny droplets.

Churning. In the continuous churn the entering pasteurized and tempered cream is agitated vigorously by beater bars. This causes stripping of the fat globule membrane and aggregation of the fat globules into chunks 0.2–0.4 in. (0.5–1 cm) in diameter. At this point the emulsion has been inverted. The slope of the continuous churn allows the buttermilk to drain out the rear of the churn and the butter granules to continue through the churn barrel. The next flow-through position continues the kneading process to produce butter with finely dispersed droplets of moisture. If composition or color adjustment is required, it is done in this step; also, a salt solution is added to give the finished butter 1.2–1.5% salt. As the butter continues through the last step, more kneading is done with finer bars to complete the blending process and provide for fat crystallization that will yield optimum spreadability in the finished butter. A continuous ribbon of yellow butter streams from the end of the continuous churn. Butter drops into a hopper, where it is pumped to packaging machinery.

Packaging. Butter is delivered by stainless steel pipeline to a variety of packaging machinery. A paper parchment overwrap is used on $1/4$- and 1-lb prints (molded portions), then a waxed cardboard overwrap. Some product is delivered to machinery that makes individual patties and wrapped pieces. For a whipped product, nitrogen gas is injected into the butter; this product is sold in tubs of many sizes both retail and wholesale. In many plants, boxes fitted with plastic bags having a capacity of 68 lb (31 kg) are filled with butter either for government purchase from approved plants or for frozen storage.

Buttermilk. This by-product of butter manufacture has many uses. The composition of buttermilk is similar to that of skim milk except that it is higher in materials found in the fat globule membrane. Buttermilk sold in supermarkets and labeled "cultured buttermilk" has been cultured with acid and flavor-producing bacteria and may be different in composition. Buttermilk from the churn is condensed and spray-dried; in this form it is in great demand by the ice cream and bakery industries.

Composition and grading. Butter in the package has a composition close to 80.0% milk fat, 1.2–1.5% salt, 17.5–17.8% water, and 1% milk solids. If butter is salt-free, the moisture and fat contents are adjusted to a slightly higher value to compensate. Salted butter has a shelf life of 3–6 months refrigerated; salt is a preservative and is about 7–8% of the water phase. Salt-free butter must be frozen to hold it for table use; otherwise, its shelf life is only 30 days. *See* COLD STORAGE.

In the United States, all butter in commercial channels is graded by licensed inspectors from the Department of Agriculture. This evaluation is organoleptic, using the senses of sight, taste, and odor, and requires highly trained technicians working in facilities that provide adequate room and excellent control of product temperature. Top-quality butter is graded as USDA-AA. If it is slightly off in texture or flavor, it receives USDA-A grade. Unacceptable product receives no grade or is rated below grade.   **Robert Bradley**

Butter oil. This product is made by heating butter to break the emulsion and settling or centrifuging to separate the milk serum from the fat. It may also be prepared by deemulsifying cream. Moisture is reduced to a low level by drying, the butterfat content being over 99%. Although little butter oil is produced in the United States, it is of importance in Australia and New Zealand. It is usually canned, is much more stable than butter, and does not require refrigeration. Because it is practically anhydrous, spoilage by hydrolysis and microbiological action is eliminated. Butterfat consists principally of mixed glycerides of saturated and unsaturated fatty acids in approximately the following percentages: butyric, 3.5; caproic, 1.4; caprylic, 1.7; capric, 2.6; lauric, 4.5; myristic, 14.6; palmitic, 30.2; stearic, 10.5; longer-chain saturated, 1.6; decenoic, 0.3; dodecenoic, 0.2; tetradecenoic, 1.5; hexadecenoic, 5.7; octadecenoic (oleic), 18.7; octadecadienoic (linoleic), 2.1; and longer-chain unsaturated, 0.9.

Ghee. A common food fat in India, ghee is produced from boiled buffalo milk. Its manufacture is similar to that of butter oil. It can be kept for months, or years, without refrigeration, and has a more intense flavor than butter or butter oil.

Frank G. Dollear

Microbiology. Seven major groups of microorganisms may be found in dairy products: bacteria, molds, yeasts, rickettsiae, viruses, algae, and protozoa. Only the first four are significant for butter.

Public health. The almost complete conversion from farm to factory manufacture of butter has all but eliminated public health hazards. All commercial butter is produced from pasteurized cream. When properly performed, pasteurization destroys all pathogens. Postpasteurization carelessness is, therefore, the only avenue for infection.

Pathogenic organisms which could, under some circumstances, enter and exist in butter include *Staphylococcus aureus* (which produces a toxin that survives pasteurization), some genera of Enterobacteriaceae (*Proteus* and *Salmonella*), *Clostridium*, *Corynebacterium diphtheriae*, *Brucella abortus* (undulant fever), *Mycobacterium tuberculosis*, and *Coxiella burneti* (Q fever).

Defects. Proper pasteurization destroys upward of 99.9% of all ordinary organisms present in milk or cream. Microbiologically induced flavors, developed prior to pasteurization, may carry over into butter. Attempts to minimize this carryover include the use of soluble food additives (illegal in the United States on the basis of the definition of butter by an Act of Congress in 1923) which are largely removed in the buttermilk, or by vacuum treatment following pasteurization. Neither method is completely effective.

Organisms responsible for flavor defects originate from dirty utensils, water, and air (indirectly from soil or plants). The name of an organism is often indicative of the flavor it produces. Among the organisms most responsible for flavor and other defects in butter are *Pseudomonas putrifaciens*; *P. nigrifaciens*; *P. fragi* and *P. fluorescens* (hydrolytic rancidity); acid-producing types; *Streptococcus lactis* var. *maltigenes*; such yeasts as *Saccharomyces*, *Candida mycoderma*, and *Torulopsis holmii*; and the molds *Geotrichum candidum*, *Penicillium*, *Alternaria*, and *Cladosporium*. Molds are responsible for musty flavors, but they, as well as some yeasts and *Pseudomonas nigrifaciens*, may also cause color defects.

All of the *Pseudomonas* groups found in butter are psychrotrophs; that is, they grow well at refrigerator temperatures of about 42°F (5.5°C). They may cause putrid or lipolytic flavors in 5–10 days.

Factors responsible for inhibiting the development of microbiological flavor defects in butter include common salt, pH, butter structure, and storage temperatures.

Butter with 1.5% salt and 17.5% water has an overall brine concentration of 8.6%, which is inhibitory to some organisms. The growth of psychrotrophs is inhibited by a lower pH. In properly worked (mixed) butter, fat is the continuous phase and surrounds the tiny moisture droplets. Unless the water used in the manufacture of butter is contaminated, the waterdroplets are overwhelmingly sterile. Also, their size is such that growth of bacteria is impossible. Only molds whose mycelia can penetrate the fat phase can reproduce. Where the interval between manufacture and sale is less than 4–6 weeks, the butter is maintained at 35–55°F (1.7–12.8°C); hence some growth of organisms may be expected to continue, but where storage is from a month to a year or more, temperatures range from 0 to −15°F (−17.8 to −26.1°C) and growth ceases. The number of living organisms may actually decrease.

Palatability development. Not all nationalities prefer butter of the same flavor intensity. Butter made from sweet pasteurized cream is bland but may have a slight nutty or scalded-milk flavor. In general, Americans, Australians, and New Zealanders prefer this flavor. Europeans, Latin Americans, and some Asiatics prefer a more intense flavor. The desired flavor can be developed by the use of milk cultures of certain organisms. These cultures are referred to as starters. They may be added to the pasteurized and cooled cream at temperatures of 72°F (22.2°C) or less, or to the butter at about the time of salting. The latter practice is more economical and facilitates flavor control. The presence of citrates or citric acid is necessary for the development of diacetyl, $CH_3COCOCH_3$, recognized as the chief compound responsible for butter aroma (see **illus**.). Most unsalted butter is made by the use of starters, because they tend to inhibit the growth of psychrotrophs.

The organisms present in the starter determine how the flavor compounds develop, and their quantity and intensity. For use in buttermaking, a mixture of two or more of the following organisms is desirable: *Streptococcus lactis*, *Leuconostoc cremoris*, and *S. diacetilactis*; in recent years the last has been used alone or in combination with *S. lactis*. In some areas of Europe, *Candida krusii* (a yeast) has been tried in mixed cultures.

Starter distillates, made by steam distillation of starter cultures, are commercially available.

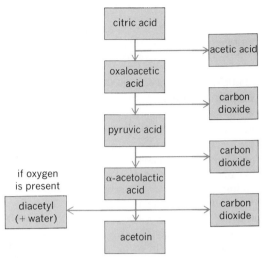

Decomposition of citric acid to diacetyl, chief component responsible for cultured butter aroma.

Their advantages are economy, convenience, and uniformity. Their disadvantages are lack of delicate flavor and aroma and failure to inhibit the growth of some undesirable bacteria. Addition of lactic or other food-grade acids or of synthetic flavoring compounds could compensate for the latter disadvantage; however, such additions may not comply with the legal definition of butter.

Control. Standards and procedures for controlling the quality of butter have been developed collectively by the butter industry, dairy schools and experiment stations, the U.S. Department of Agriculture, and state regulatory agencies. By education, inspection, and the use of various tests standardized by the American Public Health Association for the maintenance of quality, butter has been greatly improved since the early 1940s.

Procedures for ascertaining the numbers of psychrotrophs (as represented by *Pseudomonas putrifaciens*) and for yeasts and molds are especially important because they are, to a great extent, an indication of postpasteurization handling practices.

The introduction of stainless steel churns and the use of metal in all other equipment have eliminated many flavor problems—especially those due to yeasts and molds. The practice of all-welded pipelines and cleaning in place, when combined with the proper use of cleaners and sanitizers, likewise has been an important factor in the production of high-quality butter. *See* FOOD MANUFACTURING; FOOD MICROBIOLOGY; INDUSTRIAL MICROBIOLOGY; MICROBIOLOGY.

L. C. Thomsen

Bibliography. F. W. Bodyfelt, J. Tobias, and G. M. Trout, *The Sensory Evaluation of Dairy Products*, 1988; E. M. Foster et al., *Dairy Microbiology*, 1983; Y. H. Hui (ed.), *Dairy Science and Technology Handbook*, 3 vols., 1993; G. R. Richardson, *Standard Methods for the Examination of Dairy Products*, American Public Health Association, 16th ed., 1992; D. Swern (ed.), *Bailey's Industrial Oil and Fat Products*, vol. 1, 4th ed., 1986; N. P. Wong, *Fundamentals of Dairy Chemistry*, 3d ed., 1988.

Buxbaumiidae

A subclass of the class Bryopsida, the true mosses. It consists of a single family with four genera. The peristome shows some similarities to the double-peristome members of the subclass Bryidae, but the numerous series of teeth external to the endostomial cone are distinctive. *See* BRYIDAE.

The Buxbaumiidae is very distinctive in every way and most significantly in the structure of the peristome. The plants are small and occur especially on soil. The gametophyte is greatly reduced (*Buxbaumia*), with no stem and with leaves few and readily disappearing, or is better developed with well-formed leaves having a single costa and short cells. The sporophytes are terminal; the perichaetial leaves, if present, are conspicuous and exceed the capsules (see **illus.**). The capsules are disproportionately large and immersed or elevated on a seta (*Buxbaumia*). They are strongly inclined and asymmetric, tapered to a small mouth from a broad base. The operculum is small and conic. The exostome teeth of the peristome are greatly reduced in one to four series (representing several concentric series of amphithecial cells and con-

sisting of thickenings deposited on the adjoining tangential walls between the series); the endostome consists of a tall, white, plicate cone. The calyptrae are small, conic, and naked. Chromosome numbers are 8 and 9. *See* BRYOPHYTA; BRYOPSIDA.

Howard Crum

Bibliography. M. R. Crosby, *Florschuetzia*, a new genus of Buxbaumiaceae (Musci) from southern Chile, *Bryologist*, 80:149–152, 1977; A. Engler and K. Prantl, *Die natürlichen Pflanzenfamilien,* 2d ed., vol. 2, 1925.

Bytownite

A member of the plagioclase feldspar solid-solution series with a composition ranging from $Ab_{30}An_{70}$ to $Ab_{10}An_{90}$ (Ab = $NaAlSi_3O_8$ and An = $CaAl_2Si_2O_8$) [see **illus.**]. In the high-temperature form, bytownite

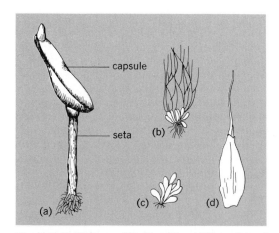

Morphological features of Buxbaumiidae. (*a*) Sporophyte of *Buxbaumia aphylla* (*after W. H. Welch, Mosses of Indiana, Indiana Department of Conservation, 1957*). *Diphyscium foliosum* (*b*) habit sketch, (*c*) leaves, and (*d*) perichaetial leaf (*after H. S. Conard, How to Know the Mosses and Liverworts, William C. Brown, 1956*).

Bytownite, from Crystal Bay, Minnesota. (*Specimen from Department of Geology, Bryn Mawr College*)

has the high-albite structure type in which Al and Si atoms are completely disordered; that is, neither element shows a preference for any of the four distinct tetrahedral sites. During cooling, natural material changes its Al/Si distribution, tending toward an ordered state in which Al and Si concentrate in different sites which alternate with one another in all directions. Bytownite is very abundant in basic igneous rocks, where it is the first plagioclase to crystallize under plutonic conditions; it forms the cores of zoned plagioclase phenocrysts in basaltic volcanics; and it sometimes occurs in anorthosites. *See* ANORTHITE; FELDSPAR; IGNEOUS ROCKS.

Lawrence Grossman

Cabbage

A hardy, cool-season crucifer (*Brassica oleracea* var. *capitata*) of Mediterranean origin and belonging to the plant order Capparales. Cabbage is grown for its head of overlapping leaves (see **illus.**), which are generally eaten raw in salads, cooked fresh, or processed into sauerkraut. Because it normally produces seed the second year, cabbage is considered to be a biennial by most authorities. Others regard it as a perennial because it will remain vegetative unless subjected to cold weather. *See* CAPPARALES.

Chinese cabbage is a related annual of Asiatic origin. Two species are grown in the United States, petsai (*B. pekinensis*) and pakchoi (*B. chinensis*).

Propagation of cabbage is by seed planted in the field, or in greenhouses and outdoor beds for the production of transplants. Field spacing varies; plants are usually 8–18 in. (20–46 cm) apart in 30–36 in. (76–91 cm) rows.

Cool, moist climate favors maximum yields of firm heads. However, exposure of young plants to prolonged low temperatures favors seed-stalk formation without production of normal heads.

Varieties. Cabbage varieties (cultivars) are generally classified according to season of maturity, leaf surface (smooth, savoyed, or wrinkled), head shape (flattened, round, or pointed), and color (green or red). Round, smooth-leaved, green heads are commonest. Popular varieties are Golden Acre and strains of Danish Ballhead; hybrid varieties are increasingly planted. Principal varieties of other types are Chieftain (savoy), Jersey Wakefield (pointed), Red Danish (red), and Wong Bok (Chinese cabbage). Strains of Danish Ballhead are also used for sauerkraut manufacture and for late storing. Varieties differ in their resistance to disease and in the tendency for heads to crack or split in the field.

Harvesting. Harvesting of fresh market varieties begins when the heads are hard enough to be accepted on the market, generally 60–90 days after field planting. Buyer preference for heads weighing no more than 2–3 lb (0.9–1.4 kg) has encouraged close spacing and early harvesting. In the northern states production of cabbage for winter storage has declined as the Texas and Florida winter areas have expanded production, providing green cabbage as competition on the market for the white stored heads.

Texas and Florida are important winter crop producing states; Georgia, Mississippi, and North Carolina produce large acreages in the spring; and New York, North Carolina, and Wisconsin are important for the summer and fall crops. New York and Wisconsin are the important kraut cabbage states.

H. John Carew

Cabbage (*Brassica oleracea* var. *capitata*). (*Joseph Harris Co., Inc., Rochester, New York*)

Diseases. About 40 diseases of cabbage and other cole crops share the worldwide distribution of these important vegetables. The most important diseases are clubroot (caused by *Plasmodiophora brassicae*), blackleg (*Phoma lingam*), yellows (*Fusarium oxysporum* f. sp. *conglutinans*), black rot (*Xanthomonas campestris*), downy mildew (*Peronospora parasitica*), and Alternaria spot (*Alternaria* sp.).

Clubroot. The clubroot organism persists in infested soils for several years. When infected, young roots are enlarged and produce masses of abnormal root tissues instead of a normal root system. Proper absorption of water and minerals from the soil is prevented, and infected plants are stunted and often wilt during the day. Moist, acid soils favor the disease. Amendments such as lime to raise the soil pH can reduce disease damage. In some countries, fungicides can control the disease. Some cultivars that are resistant to clubroot are available.

Yellows. The fungus that causes yellows can also persist in the soil for many years. The fungus infects young roots and invades the entire vascular system, causing the leaves to wilt and drop off. Xylem vessels turn brown, and the plants are severely stunted or killed. Good heads are seldom produced. Cabbage cultivars resistant to yellows are available. The letters "YR" following the cultivar name signify that it is resistant to yellows. Yellows is seldom a problem in cole crops other than cabbage.

Blackleg and black rot. Blackleg and black rot are serious diseases in seedbeds and in the field. Both pathogens may be seed-borne and can spread rapidly from plant to plant by spattering or windblown rain. Thus, a very small amount of disease may soon develop throughout the entire crop. Neither organism persists in the soil more than a few years. Control is achieved by crop rotation and by using pathogen-free seed. Chemical and hot water treatments can eliminate these pathogens from infested seed.

Blackleg produces grayish-brown dead areas on leaves and stems and often extends to the roots. Plants may be killed or stunted. Black rot bacteria enter leaves through hydathodes at the leaf margin and invade the plant systemically. Yellow, triangular spots appear at the leaf margin, and the vascular system turns black. Leaves are killed, and affected heads are rotted.

Downy mildew. Downy mildew is destructive on young plants and mature heads. Small, dark flecks are produced in abundance on the undersides of cotyledons and leaves and on the outer head leaves. Young seedlings are frequently killed. Fungal structures and spores may be seen as downy-white masses on the undersides of affected leaves early in the day while dew is present.

Alternaria. Alternaria leaf spot is most destructive on cabbage approaching maturity. Dark spots up to 1 in. (2.5 cm) in diameter, with concentric rings, are formed on leaves and heads. Alternaria and downy mildew can be controlled with fungicides.

Other diseases. Virus diseases sometimes affect cabbage. Symptoms include mottling, ringlike dead spots, black flecking, and stunting. Many cultivars are resistant to common viruses. Black speck, a physiological disorder, produces abundant black specks throughout the head leaves, especially after a period of storage at low temperature. *See* CAULIFLOWER; PLANT PATHOLOGY; PLANT VIRUSES AND VIROIDS. J. O. Strandberg

Bibliography. L. V. Boone et al., *Producing Farm Crops*, 4th ed., 1991; R. E. Nyvall, *Field Crop Diseases Handbook*, 1989.

Cable television system

A system that receives and processes television signals from various sources and retransmits these signals through coaxial or optical-fiber cables to subscribers' homes. The sources of the signals include broadcast transmissions, satellite-delivered programming, and local television studio productions. The facility that receives, processes, and retransmits the signals is called a headend.

Types of service. Cable television service is provided to subscribers by cable system operators that are awarded contracts or franchises by local or state governments to provide cable service to local communities. Cable television systems typically offer the customers in their franchise area four types of service options: basic service, expanded basic service, premium networks, and pay-per-view service. In exchange for being allowed to develop franchises, cable systems pay franchise fees and often set aside channels for public, educational, and governmental use, as well as providing studio and production facilities that enable community members, schools, and governments to produce and televise programs over these channels.

Frequency spectrum. Compared to almost any other communications need, video requires extensive bandwidth. While telephone-quality voice transmissions require only 3 kHz of spectrum and high-fidelity sound requires about 20 kHz (double for stereo), the current United States video standard requires a bandwidth of 4.2 MHz. Uncompressed high-definition television requires about 30 MHz for each of the components of the color picture. In order to carry numerous channels of programming, a separate enclosed spectrum is needed because the terrestrial broadcast frequency spectrum is too limited in bandwidth. *See* BANDWIDTH REQUIREMENTS (COMMUNICATIONS).

Unlike broadcast television signals, which travel through free space, cable signals travel through coaxial cable or optical fiber, with different programs or channels traveling at different frequencies (much the same as frequency-division multiplex). In effect, the coaxial cable or optical fiber acts as a self-contained, closed, noninterfering frequency spectrum, created inside the cable by the reuse of the spectrum already in use for other purposes. *See*

MULTIPLEXING AND MULTIPLE ACCESS.

Transmission technology. Cable television is made possible by the technology of coaxial and optical-fiber cable and is subject to the principles of transmission-line theory. The primary disadvantage of coaxial-cable distribution systems is their relatively high loss or attenuation to television signals at the frequencies normally used in cable television systems (50–550 MHz, extending up to 1 GHz in newer systems). Amplifiers are required to overcome this signal loss, and the farther the subscriber is from the cable headend the more amplifiers are needed (**illus.** *a*). Noise and intermodulation distortions created by many cascaded amplifiers limit the practical length of any coaxial cable network. *See* COAXIAL CABLE.

Optical fiber does not have the same high attenuation or loss characteristics as coaxial cable, and optical-fiber networks can therefore be built without amplifiers (illus. *b*). Most cable systems that use optical fibers do so in a hybrid fashion. Optical fiber is connected from the headend to some localized node or terminating location. The subscriber is then connected to the optical-fiber

node by short distances of coaxial cable. The short coaxial cable subscriber connection in most cases eliminates the need for amplification, except in rare instances where one or at most two amplifiers are required. *See* COMMUNICATIONS CABLE; OPTICAL COMMUNICATIONS; OPTICAL FIBERS.

System architecture. The system design or architecture is known as a tree-and-branch design. The tree-and-branch architecture is the most efficient way to transmit a package of multiple channels of programming from a headend to all subscribers.

There is one major difference between a switched telephone network and a cable television system. Cable systems are usually built on a nonswitched basis, meaning that every subscriber receives the same channels unless physically restricted by the cable television operator. Since cable television systems are not a general-purpose communications mechanism but a specialized system for transmitting numerous television channels in a sealed spectrum, the topology can be customized for maximum efficiency. A cable television system comprises five major parts: the headend, the trunk cable, the distribution (or feeder) cable in the neighborhood,

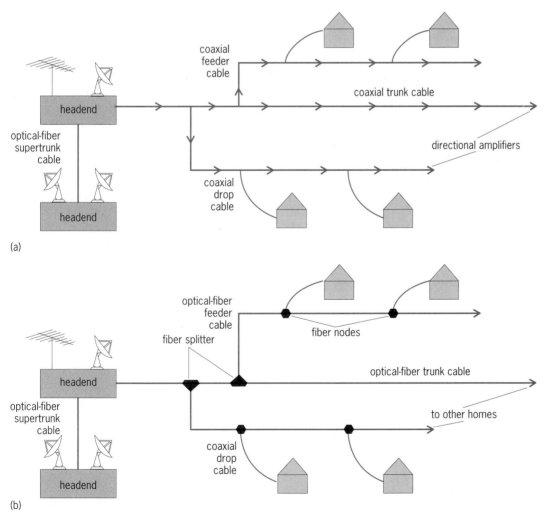

Cable television systems with (*a*) coaxial feeder cables and (*b*) optical-fiber feeder cables.

the drop cable to the home, and the in-home wiring and terminal equipment (that is, the set-top converter-descrambler). Generally, multiple-trunk cables carry the television signals from the headend to feeder or neighborhood distribution cables, and subscribers are connected through drop cables.

Headend. The headend is the origination point or location where all of the cable television channels are received and assembled. Generally, the headend is centrally located in the cable television system for maximum efficiency. One or more trunk cables emanate from the headend.

Trunk cable. The primary goal of the trunk cable is to cover maximum distance while preserving signal quality in a cost-effective manner. Broadband amplifiers are required about every 2000 ft (600 m), depending upon coaxial-cable type and diameter, and frequency spectrum bandwidth of the system. As mentioned above, noise and other distortions limit the number of amplifiers that may be cascaded or connected in series to extend the trunk cable's reach. The accepted number of cascaded amplifiers is about 20.

Distribution cable. The distribution cable interfaces with the trunk cable through a bridger amplifier, which increases the signal level for delivery to multiple subscribers. This distribution cable runs past the homes and is tapped with passive directional couplers so that multiple subscribers may be connected. One or two specialized amplifiers may be included in this cable. *See* DIRECTIONAL COUPLER.

Drop cable. A small, flexible cable is used to connect an individual subscriber to the distribution cable through a tap or directional coupler. In the subscriber's home, this flexible drop cable delivers the signal to the terminal device, cable-ready television receiver, or video cassette recorder.

Terminal device. Commonly called a set-top converter, the terminal device may perform several functions. A converter allows noncable-ready consumer devices to tune the multiple channels delivered by the cable television system to the subscriber. A descrambler, however, may also perform the function of a converter, but its primary purpose is to allow subscribers who have paid for premium programming channels to receive them. Addressability is another function of the terminal device, which allows the cable operator to authorize or deauthorize subscriber access levels without requiring a technician to visit the subscriber premise.

Advanced technology. In the past, most cable television systems were designed to maximize delivery of analog video signals in only one direction. However, the minimum transmission quality criteria are well above the demands of digital transmissions. Optical fiber also improves the quality of the cable television signal, primarily because few or no amplifiers are needed. In order for cable television systems to provide full-duplex data communications, the system must be built for two-way transmissions, by utilizing part of the spectrum for forward or downstream transmissions

and another part for the reverse. Alternatively, a second and separate cable can be used to provide the duplex transmission path.

Most cable systems are now constructed to provide full-duplex communications capability. Because of the great amounts of bandwidth provided by optical fiber and coaxial cable as compared with other communications media, cable systems are in a unique position to provide expanded television programming and data services, and to support advanced technologies such as high-definition television, digital communications, and video-on-demand. *See* CLOSED-CIRCUIT TELEVISION; DATA COMMUNICATIONS; DATA COMPRESSION; TELE-VISION.   Roger D. Pierce

Bibliography. D. P. Dulchinos, *Twenty First Century Television: Cable Television in the Information Age*, 1993; B. Harrell, *The Cable Television Technical Handbook*, 1985; B. E. Keiser, *Broadband Coding, Modulation, and Transmission Engineering*, 1989.

Cacao

Theobroma cacao, a small tropical tree 13–19 ft (4–6 m) in height that is cultivated for the almond-shaped seeds, 0.8–1.2 in. (2–3 cm) long, which are used to make chocolate. It is a member of the tea family (Thealeae) in the order Theales. The species is native to the rainforest of the Amazon basin, and two regions of distribution in pre-Columbian times are recognized. The crop was first cultivated in Central America and northern South America, the varieties found there being known as Criollos. The second region comprises the Amazon and Orinoco basins, where the cacao populations are known as Amazonian Forastero. The second type is more commonly cultivated, particularly in Brazil, Ivory Coast, Ghana, and Nigeria, which produce 75% of the world annual output. *See* THEALES.

As a typical crop of the humid tropics, cacao is grown commercially between 15°N and 15°S, where mean annual temperatures vary from 73 to 79°F (23 to 26°C). It is generally accepted that the lower limits for successful growth are a mean monthly minimum temperature of 59°F (15°C) and an absolute minimum of 50°F (10°C). Annual rainfall in growing areas varies from 56 to 80 in. (1400 to 2000 mm).

Cultivation. Cacao can be grown in many different soils, provided they have good moisture retention and are well drained and aerated. Loose, crumbly, soft, and plastic soils facilitating root penetration are preferred. Cacao appears to have high soil fertility requirements, but can be cultivated in relatively poor soils if suitable management practices such as liming and fertilization are used.

In its natural forest habitat, cacao grows under taller trees. Traditional cultivation practices simulate such conditions by using thinned forest stands or planted shade trees. The main role of shade is to counteract unfavorable ecological factors, such as low soil fertility, wind damage, high transpiration

Fig. 1. Cacao (*Theobroma cacao*). (*USDA*)

Marketing. The produce is generally exported in the form of dry beans. The farmers' production is purchased by dealers and exported by registered exporters or government marketing boards. Sales are effected through contracts or futures markets, principally in New York and London. Growers' prices may be fixed at predetermined levels or may fluctuate according to market trends. International standards have been adopted to bring about uniformity. Accordingly, exported produce is subject to grading and treatment to avoid spoilage. The market distinguishes between bulk and fine cocoas. The latter have preferred flavor or other characteristics and receive a premium price. *See* COCOA POWDER AND CHOCOLATE.   **Paulo de T. Alvim**

Diseases. The most serious disease of cacao is black pod (**Fig. 2**), caused by the fungus *Phytophthora palmivora*, now recognized as having three morphological forms; two of these may be distinct species. This fungus causes great economic loss following wet weather favorable for disease development. The fungus can also attack leaves, branches, and trunks. Some control can be achieved with copper fungicides, and there is genetic material with some resistance. Another pod rot, associated with the fungus *Botryodiplodia theobromae*, is occasionally a problem following wounding of pods by various vertebrates.

Witches'-broom, caused by the fungus *Crinipellis perniciosa* (formerly *Marasmius perniciosus*), occurs in tropical South America and in the West In-

leading to moisture stress, and increased insect attack. If all such factors can be controlled by other methods, the highest production is obtained without shade.

Cacao can be propagated by seeds or by vegetative methods (rooted cuttings or budding). The former is practically the only method used for commercial planting, with cultivars produced by hybridization. Seedlings are usually grown in shaded nurseries for 4–6 months and then transplanted to the field under temporary shade, such as that provided by banana plants. The recommended planting distance is 9 × 9 ft (3 × 3 m). The permanent shade trees are spaced at 77 ft (24 m).

Fruit and seeds. The first commercial crops are obtained in 4–5 years. In areas with even rainfall distribution, flowering may occur almost throughout the year. The flowers are borne directly on the trunk and larger branches. The fruit, an indehiscent drupe with a usually woody shell (**Fig. 1**), is red or green when unripe, and varies between 6 and 12 in. (15 and 30 cm) in length. The fruits ripen in 5–6 months and change in color to yellow or orange.

The seeds, which may number up to 65 per fruit (average is 35–40), are surrounded by a mucilaginous pulp. The dry weight of the beans constitutes about one-third of the total dry weight of the pod. In most producing areas the mean annual yield varies from 660 to 1100 lb (300 to 500 kg) of dry beans per hectare, but yields of 4400–6600 lb (2000–3000 kg) may be obtained with superior cultivars and improved cultural practices. Harvesting consists of cutting the pods from the tree and opening them with a machete to remove the seeds. Following a period of 4–6 days of fermentation in heaps or "sweatboxes," the seeds (cocoa) are dried on sun-platforms or artificially until the final moisture content is about 7%.

Fig. 2. The most widespread and most severe disease of cacao, caused by *Phytophthora palmivora*. (*Inter-American Institute of Agricultural Sciences*)

dies. The fungus causes distorted growth of aerial plant parts, resulting in witches'-broom, and forms fruiting bodies ("mushrooms") on dead tissue. Some control is possible with sanitation and use of resistant varieties. Another New World (northwest South America, Panama, Costa Rica) disease is Monilia pod rot (watery pod rot), caused by the fungus *Monilia roreri*. Damage to pods can be severe. Control measures include removal of affected pods and use of resistant varieties. Swollen shoot, a virus disease transmitted by mealybugs, occurs only in western Africa and causes deformation of the tree and considerable economic loss. Eradication programs have been attempted. Some tolerance to the disease has been found. Other occasional problems include wilt, caused by the fungus *Ceratocystis fimbriata* and commonly spread by *Xyleborus* borers; and cushion galls, caused by a species of *Calonectria*. *See* PLANT PATHOLOGY; PLANT VIRUSES AND VIROIDS.   George A. Zentmyer

Bibliography. P. H. Gregory (ed.), *Phytophthora Disease of Cocoa*, 1974; C. A. Thorold, *Diseases of Cocoa*, 1975.

Cachexia

The severe wasting syndrome that accompanies such diseases as cancer, infection, or parasitic infestation. Occasionally, it is also observed in noninvasive conditions, such as severe cardiac failure. The causes of cachexia are only partially understood. However, it is clear that most cachexia is caused by diminished consumption of nutrients rather than by a hypermetabolic state.

Anorexia, the proximal cause of this problem, is thought to be related to the expression of endogenous factors collectively termed cytokines, some of which have now been identified. For example, tumor necrosis factor, a protein (also known as cachectin), when administered to animals for a long period of time, causes a syndrome of cachexia indistinguishable from that produced by chronic disease. Inhibitors of tumor necrosis factor activity may partially alleviate cachexia caused by experimental tumors. It is likely that other cytokines are also involved, and that together these agents cause wasting of such severity that it may lead to death in a wide variety of diseases. *See* ANOREXIA NERVOSA; CYTOKINE.

It is unclear whether cytokines suppress appetite through a direct action on satiety centers in the hypothalamus or through peripheral effects (such as effects on the bowel or other enteric structures), which then project to the central nervous system. Another clinical feature related to cachexia appears to be caused by a direct effect of cytokines (notably tumor necrosis factor and interleukin-1) on stem cells and stromal cells of the bone marrow. Tumor necrosis factor and interleukin-1 also appear to mobilize lipid through direct effects on adipocytes.

The cytokines that cause cachexia are produced mainly by cells of the immune system, especially macrophages. Synthesis is triggered by contact with molecules produced by microbial pathogens or tumor cells. Induction of synthesis depends upon both transcriptional and translational activation pathways. Rational strategies for alleviation of cachexia include eradicating the underlying infection or tumor, blocking cytokine synthesis with agents that specifically interrupt the requisite signaling pathways, or inhibiting cytokine activity with specific antibodies or other antagonists. Oral or intravenous administration of nutrients is likely to be effective if the process has not advanced to a point at which utilization of nutrients is impaired. *See* ONCOLOGY.   Bruce Beutler

Cactus

The common name for any member of the cactus family (Cactaceae). There are 120 genera with perhaps 1700 species, nearly all indigenous to America.

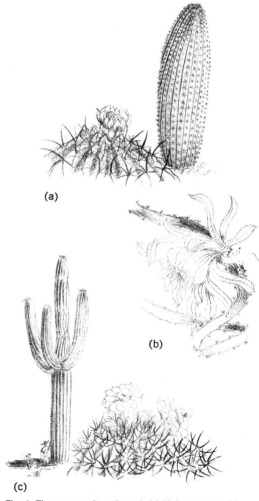

Fig. 1. Three examples of cacti. (*a*) Mule cactus, with closeup of flower, maximum height of 6 ft (2 m). (*b*) Flower of night-blooming *Cereus*, maximum height of 40 ft (12 m). (*c*) Saguaro, maximum height of 70 ft (21 m), with closeup of flower.

The cacti are among the most extremely drought-resistant plants, and consequently they thrive in very arid regions. The group is characterized by a fleshy habit, presence of spines and bristles and large, brightly colored, solitary flowers. There is a great variety of body shapes and patterns, and many of the species are grown as ornamentals or oddities (**Fig. 1**). A few have edible fruits. The cochineal insect, which produces a valuable red dye, is cultivated chiefly on the cochineal cactus (*Nopalea coccinellifera*). The saguaro (*Cereus giganteus*) of Arizona and Sonora is the largest of the cacti, attaining a height of 70 ft (21m). *See* CARYOPHYLLALES.

Perry D. Strausbaugh/Earl L. Core

Several diseases of wild cacti are known. The most conspicuous of these is probably bacterial soft rot of saguaro cacti, which is usually seen in older plants. Affected tissues appear as dark, soft lesions that usually develop a light-green border; these lesions frequently leak a dark, odorous fluid. Infected branches may fall, and the fleshy tissue of diseased plants may be destroyed in several weeks to a few months, leaving bare the woody supportive ribs (xylem elements) of the plant. Control by chemical sprays or soil drenches is not feasible. Therefore, when symptoms are first noted, rotting tissues should be removed. If the rot is limited, $1/2$ in. (13 mm) of surrounding healthy tissue should also be discarded. Immediately the cavity should be washed thoroughly with a solution of one part household bleach and nine parts water with the washing repeated in 18 to 24 h; the wound should be left open. Infections so treated frequently do not spread. Plants with numerous or large lesions should be removed and the debris thoroughly treated with the diluted bleach, or burned, or deeply buried.

The same controls apply to similarly infected organ-pipe cacti. Infected prickly-pear cacti initially have similar symptoms, but internal tissues can become so liquefied that pads bulge. The infected pad should be promptly destroyed, and the former point of attachment treated with bleach.

Recent studies in the United States have established that the soft-rot disease is caused by bacteria in the genus *Erwinia*, particularly *E. cacticida*. This species has also been isolated from rotting cacti in Australia and Mexico.

Saguaro cacti may be toppled by heavy winds following soil-soaking rains. Roots of these plants usually have been previously weakened by the root- and wood-rotting fungus *Poria carnegieana*. Wind-thrown plants tend to be mature specimens; no control is known.

Prickly pears can be infected by other pathogens. Certain viruses cause whitish rings or irregularly shaped patterns to develop on pads (**Fig. 2**), Severely affected plants also are stunted. The light-colored lines usually are narrow. By contrast, rings caused by the feeding of sap-sucking insects have small, central green areas with broad, light-colored margins (Fig. 2). Presumably, sap-sucking

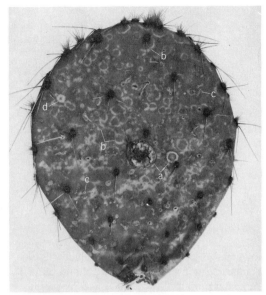

Fig. 2. Disease symptoms on prickly-pear pad: (*a*) lesions caused by *Phyllosticta concava*; (*b*) virus-induced symptoms; (*c*) injuries from penetrating cactus spines; (*d*) ring pattern caused by feeding insects. (*From S. M. Alcorn, R. L. Gilbertson, and M. R. Nelson, Some diseases of cacti in Arizona, Prog. Agr. Ariz., 27(3):3–5, 1975*)

insects carry the viruses between plants, but "new," infected plants will develop if diseased pads root after their detachment from the parent plant. The fungus *Phyllosticta concava* causes the formation of generally circular, whitish to tan, depressed, dry lesions on pads; these areas usually become covered with black, slightly raised "dots" (Fig. 2). An infection may penetrate to the opposite side, where a similar lesion forms. Infected tissue can disintegrate, leaving a hole through the pad. Fungicidal sprays will minimize infections, which start in cool, rainy periods. *See* PLANT PATHOLOGY.

Stanley M. Alcorn

Bibliography. S. M. Alcorn, R. L. Gilbertson, and M. R. Nelson, Some diseases of cacti in Arizona, *Prog. Agr. Ariz.*, 27(3):3–5, 1975; S. M. Alcorn et al., Taxonomy and pathogenicity of *Erwinia cacticida* sp. nov., *Int. J. Sys. Bacteriol.*, 41 (2): 197–212, 1991; L. Benson, *The Cacti of the United States and Canada*, 1982; G. M. Milbrath, M. R. Nelson, and R. E. Wheeler, The distribution and electron microscopy of viruses of cacti in southern Arizona, *Phytopathology*, 63:1133–1139, 1973.

Cadmium

A relatively rare chemical element, symbol Cd, atomic number 48, closely related to zinc, with which it is usually associated in nature. Cadmium was discovered by F. Stromeyer in Germany in 1817 in a sample of zinc carbonate. It does not occur uncombined in nature, and the one true cadmium

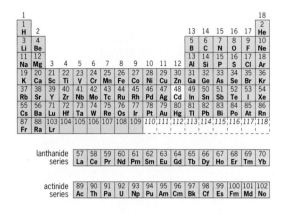

1																	18
1 H	2											13	14	15	16	17	2 He
3 Li	4 Be											5 B	6 C	7 N	8 O	9 F	10 Ne
11 Na	12 Mg	3	4	5	6	7	8	9	10	11	12	13 Al	14 Si	15 P	16 S	17 Cl	18 Ar
19 K	20 Ca	21 Sc	22 Ti	23 V	24 Cr	25 Mn	26 Fe	27 Co	28 Ni	29 Cu	30 Zn	31 Ga	32 Ge	33 As	34 Se	35 Br	36 Kr
37 Rb	38 Sr	39 Y	40 Zr	41 Nb	42 Mo	43 Tc	44 Ru	45 Rh	46 Pd	47 Ag	48 Cd	49 In	50 Sn	51 Sb	52 Te	53 I	54 Xe
55 Cs	56 Ba	71 Lu	72 Hf	73 Ta	74 W	75 Re	76 Os	77 Ir	78 Pt	79 Au	80 Hg	81 Tl	82 Pb	83 Bi	84 Po	85 At	86 Rn
87 Fr	88 Ra	103 Lr	104	105	106	107	108	109	110	111	112	113	114	115	116	117	118

lanthanide series	57 La	58 Ce	59 Pr	60 Nd	61 Pm	62 Sm	63 Eu	64 Gd	65 Tb	66 Dy	67 Ho	68 Er	69 Tm	70 Yb

actinide series	89 Ac	90 Th	91 Pa	92 U	93 Np	94 Pu	95 Am	96 Cm	97 Bk	98 Cf	99 Es	100 Fm	101 Md	102 No

mineral, greenockite (cadmium sulfide), is not a commercial source of the metal. Almost all of the cadmium produced is obtained as a by-product of the smelting and refining of zinc ores, which usually contain 0.2–0.4% cadmium.

The United States, Canada, Mexico, Australia, Belgium-Luxembourg, and the Republic of Korea are principal sources, although not all are producers.

Physical properties. Cadmium is a silvery-white ductile metal with a faint bluish tinge. It is softer and more malleable than zinc, but slightly harder than tin. It has an atomic weight of 112.40, a specific gravity (sp gr) of 8.65 at 20°C (68°F), and its metallic radius is 0.154 nanometer. Its melting point of 321°C (610°F) and boiling point of 765°C (1409°F) are lower than those of zinc. There are eight naturally occurring stable isotopes, and eleven artificial unstable radio isotopes have been reported. *See* TIN; ZINC.

Chemical properties. Cadmium is the middle member of group II (zinc, cadmium, and mercury) in the periodic table, and its chemical properties generally are intermediate between zinc and mercury. Like zinc, cadmium loses its luster in moist air and is rapidly corroded by moist ammonia and moist sulfur dioxide. Most acids will dissolve cadmium, but not as rapidly as zinc. Cadmium is very soluble in concentrated ammonium nitrate solution, and such solutions are used by electroplaters to strip cadmium from plated steel or iron objects. Cadmium oxide and hydroxide, unlike those of zinc, are insoluble in excess sodium hydroxide. The cadmium ion is displaced by zinc metal in acidic sulfate solutions. Cadmium is bivalent in all its stable compounds, and its ion is colorless. It forms the complex ions $Cd(NH_3)_4^{2+}$, $Cd(CN)_4^{2-}$, and CdI_4^{2-}. *See* MERCURY (ELEMENT).

Cadmium oxide, CdO, is a brown powder (sp gr 6.95 at 20°C or 78°F) used mainly to prepare cadmium electroplating baths, and can be made by heating the hydroxide or burning the metal. It is more easily reduced to a metal by heating with carbon than zinc oxide. This property, as well as the fact that cadmium is more volatile than zinc,

is important in the recovery of cadmium in zinc ore smelting operations and from lead and copper smelting where zinc and cadmium are present.

Cadmium sulfide, CdS, is obtained as a bright yellow precipitate by passing hydrogen sulfide through a solution containing cadmium ions. The precipitate is insoluble in cold dilute acid, and use is made of this property in the detection of the presence of cadmium by qualitative analysis procedures. CdS (cadmium yellow) and cadmium sulfoselenide (cadmium red) are permanent useful pigments. These compounds exhibit a strong photovoltaic response to visible light, and are becoming of interest in solar energy applications.

The Weston standard cell, which gives a nearly constant potential (1.0186 V), uses cadmium sulfate, $3CdSO_4 \cdot 8H_2O$, as an electrolyte.

Cadmium halide compounds are generally similar to the corresponding zinc halide compounds, except that the cadmium halides are less ionized and do not hydrolyze in water as much as the corresponding zinc compounds. Except for the fluoride, cadmium halides are considerably less soluble in water than the zinc compounds. Cadmium iodide is the least ionized of the cadmium and zinc halides and, like cadmium fluoride, does not form hydrates.

Toxicity. The fumes of cadmium, its compounds, and solutions of its compounds are very toxic, and cadmium-plated articles should not be used in food, nor should cadmium-coated articles be welded or used in ovens.

Analytical methods. Cadmium can be determined gravimetrically by the sulfate method, by precipitation as the beta-napthoquinoline complex, or by electrodeposition from faintly alkaline cyanide solution. Volumetrically, the cadmium ion can be titrated with the chelating agent ethylenediaminetetraacetate (EDTA), using Eriochrome Black T indicator. It is also easily determined polarographically, a method particularly suitable when zinc is present, and also by emission spectroscopy, by atomic absorption spectroscopy, and by electron microprobe analysis.

Uses. The main use of cadmium is in the plating of iron and steel, and to a much less extent of other alloys, such as copper and brass, to protect them from corrosion. Although cadmium can be deposited from acidic baths such as the sulfate (used in the electrowinning of cadmium) and the fluoborate, nearly all commercial plating for protective coatings is done in cyanide baths (composed of 20–25 g/liter cadmium oxide dissolved in 100–125 g/liter concentration sodium cyanide solution) because of its ease of operation and its good throwing power (good distribution of deposit over a complex shape). Cadmium anodes of 99.95% purity are used to replenish the metal as it is deposited on the cathode. The plating process is usually done at temperatures of 20–30°C (70–90°F), voltages of 2–12 V, and current densities of about 1–6 A/dm² (10–60 A/ft²), depending mainly on metal concentration, stirring, and temperature.

Certain organic compounds (glue, cellulose compounds, wetting agents) are used in the baths to improve deposit brightness and covering power, and to decrease grain size. To further brighten and to improve tarnish resistance, or to form visible passive films which help improve corrosion protection, plated coatings are often given brief dips in chromic acid solutions. Thin (0.0002 in. or 0.005 mm) cadmium deposits offer good protection to iron and steel, especially in marine or rural exposure.

Cadmium solders easily and, unlike zinc, is resistant to alkali. It does not form voluminous corrosion products like zinc does, and therefore is preferred for plating bolts, nuts, and fasteners. It plates much more readily on malleable cast iron than zinc. For all these various reasons it is used extensively. Within the past few years proprietary noncyanide cadmium plating baths have been introduced, but their use is very small. *See* ELECTROPLATING OF METALS.

The commercial use of cadmium as an electrodeposited coating on iron and steel for corrosion protection started in 1919 and by 1941 had become by far the largest application of cadmium. Due to its cost and the waste disposal problems associated with its toxicity, however, the use of cadmium in electroplating has decreased to less than half of the present total consumption. Zinc electrodeposited coatings have replaced much of the cadmium. Nickel-cadmium batteries are the second-largest application, with pigment and chemical uses third. Sizable amounts are used in low-melting-point alloys, similar to Wood's metal, and in automatic fire sprinklers, and relatively smaller uses are in brazing alloys, solders, and bearings. Cadmium compounds are used as stabilizers in plastics and the production of cadmium phosphors. Because of its great neutron-absorbing capacity, especially the isotope 113, cadmium is used in control rods and shielding for nuclear reactors. *See* ALLOY; CADMIUM METALLURGY.   Wilbur Hague

Bibliography. J. C. Bailar et al. (eds.), *Comprehensive Inorganic Chemistry*, vol. 3, 1973; F. A. Cotton and G. Wilkinson, *Advanced Inorganic Chemistry*, 5th ed., 1988; C. A. Hampel (ed.), *Rare Metals Handbook*, 2d ed., 1971; D. R. Lide, *Handbook of Chemistry and Physics*, 72d ed., 1993; F. A. Lowenheim (ed.), *Modern Electroplating*, 3d ed., 1974.

Cadmium metallurgy

Cadmium resembles zinc in its chemical properties, and its occurrence for commercial purposes is with zinc ores. A relatively rare element in the Earth's crust, cadmium ranks in abundance between mercury and silver. Most cadmium occurs in solid solution in the zinc sulfide mineral called sphalerite. Although cadmium may be recovered from some lead and copper ores, it is associated with the zinc which is also found in these ores. Although a few zinc concentrates contain as much as 1–2% cadmium, typical content ranges from 0.06 to 0.5%. Since cadmium is entirely a by-product metal, the supply available is closely aligned with zinc production, averaging about 0.4% of zinc production. *See* SPHALERITE.

Recovery methods. All cadmium recovery processes involve the dissolution of cadmium-bearing feed material (sinter fume from the sintering of zinc ores or calcines, residue from the electrolyte purification of electrolytic zinc plants or from the purification of zinc sulfate solutions in the manufacture of zinc salts and pigments, and so on) followed by various purification and cadmium displacement steps. Methods of processing can be grouped conveniently into two basic categories, electrolytic and electromotive. In the former case, cadmium is recovered by electrolyzing purified solutions; in the latter case, cadmium in the form of a metallic sponge is displaced from purified solutions by a less noble metal, zinc being used in every known commercial application, and the sponge is melted or distilled, or both.

Electrolytic recovery. In electrolytic cadmium recovery, the feed material is dissolved in spent electrolyte either from the cadmium cells or from an electrolytic zinc circuit. The leach solution is neutralized to a pH of 5.0 or above, and troublesome impurities, such as copper, are removed by adding a small amount of zinc dust. Thallium can be removed from solution by precipitating with potassium permanganate or sodium chromate. Cadmium is electrolyzed from purified solutions at cell voltages of 2.4–2.8 V. Most electrolytic cadmium plants employ a current density of 3–8 A/ft^2 (32–86 A/m^2). Extensive refining of cathode cadmium is not required to produce metal that meets market specifications. In the usual case, the cathode metal is melted under a layer of caustic at a temperature of 716–950°F (380–510°C) for 3–18 h before it is cast into commercial shapes.

Electromotive recovery. Electromotive cadmium producers recover the metal from fume produced in the sintering of zinc calcines or zinc concentrates. Most fume contains appreciable concentrations of troublesome impurities, such as arsenic. Prior to leaching, fume may be oxidized by roasting or sulfated by baking with sulfuric acid. Roasted fume is leached in sulfuric acid solution; sulfated fume is leached with water. Leach solutions are purified to remove arsenic, iron, copper, thallium, and lead. For example, a small amount of zinc dust may be added to remove copper, and the filtered solution treated with potassium permanganate to oxidize iron (which is precipitated with caustic) and remove arsenic, following which a small amount of sodium chromate may be added to precipitate lead and thallium. Cadmium sponge is precipitated from purified solutions with zinc dust (zinc is higher in the electromotive series than cadmium is, and it displaces cadmium from solutions). Most electromotive producers densify the cadmium sponge by briquetting it in a press at pressures of 3000–12,000 $lb/in.^2$

(20–80 megapascals). If the cadmium sponge is sufficiently pure, metal meeting ASTM specifications may be produced by melting the compacted sponge under caustic. Less pure sponge may require retorting (distilling) to meet product cadmium specifications.

Product specifications and applications. Product specifications are set forth in the **table**. Major end uses for cadmium are in corrosion-resistant plating and in cadmium compounds for use as pigments in paints, ceramics, and plastics. These two uses account for about 45% and 15%, respectively, of total cadmium production. The remainder is used in alloys, plastic stabilizers, batteries, and television picture tube phosphors. Other uses for cadmium include solar energy cells and energy storage systems.

Cadmium chemical requirements*	
Element	Composition, %[†]
Cadmium	99.90
Zinc	0.035
Copper	0.015
Lead	0.025
Tin	0.01
Silver	0.01
Antimony	0.001
Arsenic	0.003
Thallium	0.003

*ASTM designation: B 440–69.
[†]The minimum percentage is indicated for cadmium, the maximum percentage for the other elements.

Cadmium is a toxic element. Care must be exercised to avoid breathing or ingesting it or its compounds. *See* CADMIUM; ZINC.   Robert E. Lund

Bibliography. American Society for Testing and Materials, *Annual Book of ASTM Standards*, 02.0, *Nonferrous Metals*, 1992; R. A. Burkin, *Topics in Non-Ferrous Extractive Metallurgy*, 1980; C. H. Cotterill (ed.), *AIME World Symposium on Mining and Metallurgy of Lead-Zinc*, vol. 2, 1970; C. B. Gill, *Nonferrous Extractive Metallurgy*, 1988.

Caffeine

An alkaloid, formerly synthesized by methylation of theobromine isolated from cacao, but now recovered from the solvents used in the manufacture of decaffeinated coffee. Chemically, caffeine is 1,3,7-trimethylxanthine, and has the formula below. It

is widely used in medicine as a stimulant for the central nervous system and as a diuretic. It occurs naturally in tea, coffee, and yerba maté, and small amounts are found in cola nuts and cacao. Caffeine crystallizes into long, white needlelike crystals that slowly lose their water of hydration to give a white solid that melts at 235–237.2°C (455–459.0°F). It sublimes without decomposition at lower temperatures. Caffeine has an intensely bitter taste, though it is neutral to litmus. *See* ALKALOID.   Frank Wagner

Cage hydrocarbon

A compound that is composed of only carbon and hydrogen atoms and contains three or more rings arranged topologically so as to enclose a volume of space. In general, the "hole" within a cage hydrocarbon is too small to accommodate even a proton. The carbon frameworks of many cage hydrocarbons are quite rigid. Consequently, the geometric relationships between substituents on the cage are well defined. This quality makes these compounds exceptionally valuable for testing concepts concerning bonding, reactivity, structure-activity relationships, and structure-property relationships. *See* CHEMICAL BONDING.

Platonic solids. The carbocyclic analogs of the platonic solids that are tenable are tetrahedrane (**1**, where X = —H), cubane (**2**), and dodecahedrane (**3**). According to theory, tetrahedrane is

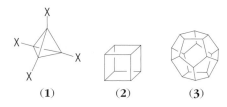

so highly strained that it should dissociate spontaneously to two molecules of acetylene. Nevertheless, G. Maier was able to synthesize tetra-*t*-butyl tetrahedrane [**1**, X = —C(CH₃)₃] in 1978. The symmetry of the carbon skeleton of the tetrahedron permits the distances among all the bulky *t*-butyl groups [—C(CH₃)₃] to be maximized, and so their intramolecular repulsions are minimized. Cubane also requires the bond angles and bond lengths of its skeletal carbon atoms to be substantially distorted. Cubane was first prepared in 1964 by P. Eaton. Calculations suggest that octanitrocubane may be a high-density, high-energy material. Although the synthesis of dodecahedrane is difficult, independent preparations of this nearly globular cage hydrocarbon were reported in 1982 and 1987. *See* ALICYCLIC HYDROCARBON; BOND ANGLE AND DISTANCE.

Prismanes. An unsubstituted prismane has the general formula of $(CH)_n$, and the carbon atoms are located at the corners of a regular prism. Prismane (**4**), cubane, pentaprismane (**5**), and hexaprismane (**6**, unknown) are the simplest members of this

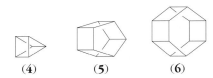

(**4**) (**5**) (**6**)

family of cage hydrocarbons. Despite their high strain energies(which in most ring structures would facilitate ring opening), the prismanes have unusual kinetic stabilities due to the symmetry-imposed barriers that exist toward any ring opening. *See* MOLECULAR ORBITAL THEORY.

Adamantane. The monomer of the diamond carbon skeleton is adamantane (**7**, where X = —H). Although this compound has been isolated from petroleum, its availability is a result of a chance observation in 1957 that tetrahydrodicyclopentadiene (**8**), an inexpensive compound, isomerizes to

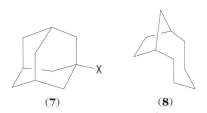

(**7**) (**8**)

adamantane in the presence of aluminum halide catalysts. Eventually, it was recognized that drugs containing adamantyl groups are fat soluble and not readily degraded in the human body. Thus, such drugs are more persistent and longer acting than formulations based on long-chain hydrocarbons. Amantadine (**7**, where X = —NH$_2$) was developed commercially as the first orally active antiviral drug for the prevention of respiratory illness due to influenza A2-Asian viruses. Amantadine also has been found to be clinically effective for treating the symptoms of Parkinson's disease. *See* VIRUS CHEMOPROPHYLAXIS.

The other simple diamondoid hydrocarbons, diamantane (**9**) and triamantane (**10**), can be synthe-

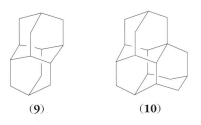

(**9**) (**10**)

sized by the Lewis acid–catalyzed rearrangement of isomeric hydrocarbons that possess a moderate degree of strain energy. Thus, treatment of (**11**) and (**12**) with appropriate catalysts give (**9**) and (**10**), respectively.

(**11**) (**12**)

Other structures. Organic chemists have prepared a wide variety of cage hydrocarbons that do not occur in nature. Among these compounds are triasterane (**13**), iceane or wurtzitane (**14**), and pagodane (**15**). Each of these compounds is

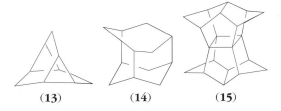

(**13**) (**14**) (**15**)

prepared by a complex multistep organic synthesis. *See* ORGANIC CHEMISTRY; ORGANIC SYNTHESIS.

Roger K. Murray, Jr.

Bibliography. G. A. Olah (ed.), *Cage Hydrocarbons*, 1990; E. Osawa and O. Yonemitsu (eds.), *Carbocyclic Cage Compounds: Chemistry and Applications*, 1992.

Caisson foundation

A permanent substructure that, while being sunk into position, permits excavation to proceed inside and also provides protection for the workers against water pressure and collapse of soil. The term caisson covers a wide range of foundation structures. Caissons may be open, pneumatic, or floating type; deep or shallow; large or small; and of circular, square, or rectangular cross section. The walls may consist of timber, temporary or permanent steel shells, or thin or massive concrete. Large caissons are used as foundations for bridge piers, deep-water wharves, and other structures. Small caissons are used singly or in groups to carry such loads as building columns. Caissons are used where they provide the most feasible method of passing obstructions, where soil cannot otherwise be kept out of the bottom or where cofferdams cannot be used. *See* BRIDGE; PILE FOUNDATION.

The bottom rim of the caisson is called the cutting edge. The edge is sharp or narrow and is made of, or faced with, structural steel. The narrowness of the edge facilitates removal of ground under the shell and reduces the resistance of the soil to descent of the caisson.

Open caisson. An open caisson is a shaft open at both ends. It is used in dry ground or in moderate amounts of water. A bottom section, having a cutting edge (**Fig. 1**), is set on the ground and soil is removed from inside while the caisson sinks by its own weight. Sections are added as excavation and sinking proceed. After excavation is completed, the hollow interior of the shaft is filled with concrete.

Open caissons are usually constructed of reinforced concrete, but if steel shells are used, concrete may also be required to provide weight. When an open caisson is to be towed into place, hollow walls

Fig. 1. Underside of open caisson for Greater New Orleans bridge over Mississippi River. (*Dravo Corp.*)

Figure 2 shows the major types of caissons in use. Chicago caissons (open well) are formed by excavating a few feet of soil, installing short vertical pieces of wood or concrete lagging beveled to form a circle, bracing with segmental hoops, and repeating. Such caissons are used in clay that is not strong enough to carry the permanent load alone but will permit excavation for the lagging without flowing in at the bottom. The clay is hoisted out in buckets or elevators. The bottom may be belled out. Lagging and bracing are generally left in place.

Sheeted caissons are similar to Chicago caissons, except that vertical sheeting is continuous and is driven by hand or pile-driving hammers either in advance of excavation or as it proceeds. Bracing rings are placed every few feet. Sheeting may be wood, concrete plank, or steel, and is left in place. Sheeted caissons may be round or square.

Small cylindrical caissons, 2–12 ft (0.6–3.6 m) in diameter, consist of a concrete shell or steel pipe sunk into the ground by its own or by a temporarily superimposed weight. Excavation is done by hand or mechanically, and the caisson is finally filled with concrete.

Drilled caissons are drilled holes that are filled with concrete. Rock socketing may be used at the bottom, or the bottom may be belled up to 30 ft (9 m) in diameter. The caisson may be as long as 150 ft (46 m). Cohesive soils are drilled with augers or bucket-type drills. Granular soils are drilled in the same manner with the aid of a binding agent or by rotary drills using drilling mud

or false bottoms are provided to give it buoyancy; they are removed after the caisson is in position. Open caissons can be sunk in water to practically any depth.

In deep water an open caisson is sometimes sunk by the sand-island method. A cofferdam is constructed and filled with sand to form an artificial island. The island serves as a working platform and guide for sinking the caisson. This method also avoids the necessity of transporting a fabricated shell and holding it in position.

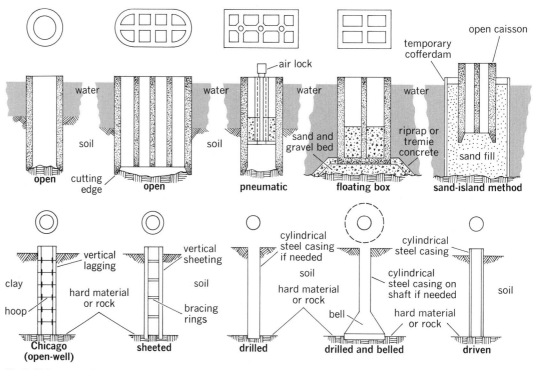

Fig. 2. Major types of caissons as they appear from top and in cross section from side.

or water to keep the hole from caving in. Steel-shaft casings are used where needed to shut off water or keep soil out of the hole. Casings are removed before concreting, or during concreting in unstable ground.

Driven caissons are formed by driving a cylindrical steel shell with one or more pile-driving hammers. After excavation by grabs, buckets, or jetting, concrete is placed inside. The shells usually are withdrawn as the concrete rises, unless the soil is so soft or water conditions are such that they must be left in place.

Pneumatic caisson. A pneumatic caisson is like a box or cylinder in shape; but the top is closed and thus compressed air can be forced inside to keep water and soil from entering the bottom of the shaft. A pneumatic caisson is used where the soil cannot be excavated through open shafts (for instance, where there are concrete, timbers, boulders, or masonry lying underwater) or where soil conditions are such that the upward pressure must be balanced. The air pressure must balance or slightly exceed the hydrostatic head and is increased as the caisson descends. The maximum depth is about 120 ft (37 m), corresponding to an air pressure of 52 lb/in.^{2} (360 kilopascals), which is about the limit of human endurance. Workers and materials must pass through air locks. Too rapid decompression may result in caisson disease or "bends," resulting from the expansion of bubbles of air trapped in joints, muscles, or blood. The length of time that workers can perform under pressure and the speed of decompression are regulated by law. Pneumatic caissons may be started as open caissons, then closed and air applied. They are made of reinforced concrete, which may be faced on one or both sides with steel plates. *See* DIVING.

Floating caisson. A floating or box caisson consists of an open box with sides and closed bottom, but no top. It is usually built on shore and floated to the site where it is weighted and lowered onto a bed previously prepared by divers. The caisson is then filled with sand, gravel, or concrete. This type is most suitable where there is no danger of scour. Floating caissons may be built of reinforced concrete, steel, or wood.

Small box caissons usually consist of a single cell. Large caissons are usually divided into compartments; this braces the side walls and permits more accurate control during loading and sinking. *See* FOUNDATIONS.   Robert D. Chellis

Calamine

A term that may refer to either a zinc mineral, $Zn_4Si_2O_7(OH)_2 \cdot H_2O$, which is also known as hemimorphite, or to zinc oxide, ZnO, which is used in medicinal or pharmaceutical products and in cosmetics. *See* HEMIMORPHITE; ZINC.

E. Eugene Weaver

Calanoida

An order of Copepoda that includes the larger and more abundant of the pelagic species. Some authorities consider the Calanoida an order of the subclass Copepoda. In the food cycles of the sea these copepods are the most important group of marine animals because of their overwhelming numbers, ubiquitous distribution, and position at the base of the animal food chain. *See* COPEPODA.

The anterior part of the body is cylindrical with five or six segments, and much broader than the posterior part, usually with two, three, or four segments in the female and five segments in the male. A pair of caudal rami bear short setae, often of nearly equal length. The first antennae have 20 to 25 segments and usually extend to the ends of the caudal rami or beyond. They are not for locomotion, but are stabilizers and sinking retarders, and also have an olfactory function. In the male the right first antenna is often geniculate for grasping the female. The second antennae and mandibular palps are biramous and create water currents for feeding and slow movement. These and the first and second maxillae and maxillipedes have long setae and create feeding-current eddies and strain small food organisms from the water. The five pairs of swimming legs are biramous, but the last pair is sometimes reduced or absent in the female, and the male's right fifth leg may be modified for grasping the female (see **illus.**). There is a small oval, dorsal thoracic heart with an anterior aortic opening, two posterior venous openings, and one ventral venous opening. A pair of excretory glands are in the second maxillae, and an oil storage sac is usually found dorsal to the digestive tract in the thorax.

In this order there are 120 or more recognized genera, some with numerous species. In the freshwater genus *Diaptomus* about 100 species are known. However, except in surveys over very wide geographic areas, the number of species to be found in any one genus is usually less than 10 or 15.

Calanus is the most outstanding genus in boreal and arctic seas. *Calanus. finmarchicus* (Gunnerus) was the first copepod to be described. It is a cold-water species, 0.12–0.24 in. (3–6 mm) long, which ranks first among North Atlantic copepods, and several researchers have claimed that, feeding at the second trophic level, it may be the world's most numerous animal species.

In biomass, the calanoids exceed all other copepod groups. In the Gulf of Maine alone the total standing crop of calanoids has been calculated at 4,000,000 tons.

Nearly all calanoids are planktonic and, as a group, occur in all parts of the oceans from the surface to abyssal depths. The geographic and bathymetric ranges of many species are, however, restricted by the nature of water currents and the chemical and physical conditions of the water. In their southernmost range the northern species are found at greater depths.

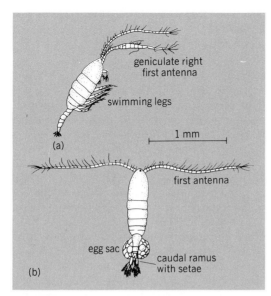

Diaptomus. (*a*) Lateral view of male. (*b*) Dorsal view of female.

Many species live at depths of 650–1000 ft (200–300 m) during the day, but migrate upward at night and return to usual levels again at dawn. These diurnal migrations are doubtless in response to conditions of light, but are modified by the temperature tolerances of the species and by other factors.

In keeping with their planktonic habit, many calanoids are provided with long plumose setae and long antennae to aid in flotation. Often the body or plumes are brightly pigmented. Common colors are pink, red, green, blue, and violet. Some are mostly black or entirely hyaline. A number of species, especially of the genera *Metridia* and *Pleuromomma*, are bioluminescent, emitting flashes of phosphorescent light. *See* BIOLUMINESCENCE; ZOOPLANKTON.   Harry C. Yeatman

Bibliography. J. Green, *Biology of Crustacea*, 1961; S. M. Marshall and A. P. Orr, *The Biology of a Marine Copepod, Calanus finmarchicus (Gunnerus)*, 1955; S. P. Parker (ed.), *Synopsis and Classification of Living Organisms*, 2 vols., 1982; G. O. Sars, *Crustacea of Norway*, vol. 4, 1903; T. H. Waterman (ed.), *The Physiology of Crustacea*, 2 vols., 1960, 1961.

Calcarea

A class of the phylum Porifera, including sponges with a skeleton composed of spicules of calcium carbonate. Calcarea vary from radially symmetrical vase-shaped species to colonies made up of a reticulum of thin tubes to irregular massive forms. Calcareous sponges are mostly of small size and inhabit the shallow waters of all seas, from tidal areas to depths of 660 ft (200 m), with a few species extending down to at least 13,120 ft (4000 m).

Morphology. Primitive calcareous sponges with an ascon grade of construction consist of colonies of upright tubes with unfolded walls made up of an outer epidermis of pinacocytes and an inner lining of choanocytes (**Fig. 1**). Between these layers of cells is a stratum of mesoglea containing amebocytes and spicules. Cells called porocytes, each perforated by a tubular canal, pierce the walls at intervals and allow water to enter the central cavity or spongocoel (**Fig. 2***a*). Water leaves by way of a terminal osculum.

A somewhat more complicated structure is seen in calcareous sponges of the sycon grade of construction (Fig. 2*b*). Syconoid sponges are usually individual vase-shaped forms with a thick wall enclosing a large central spongocoel opening out through a terminal osculum. In the simplest forms the wall is pushed out at intervals into fingerlike projections, called radial canals, in which the choanocytes are localized. Water enters the radial canals directly through pores without the intervention of special inhalant canals. In most syconoid species, however, a dermal membrane made up of pinacocytes and mesenchyme forms a cortex of greater or less thickness which joins the outer ends of the radial canals. Pores or ostia pierce the dermis and open into inhalant canals which are simply the spaces between the radial canals in some cases. In forms with a thick cortex (Fig. 2*c*), the inhalant canals run a course through the cortical mesenchyme before reaching the outer ends of the radial canals (flagellated chambers).

The leuconoid grade of construction has probably evolved independently among the several lines of calcareous sponges. In those with a syconoid ancestry, the radial canals subdivide into many small flagellated chambers which arise as outpocketings of the radial canal wall. A common intermediate stage is seen in genera in which each radial canal is subdivided into elongate flagellated chambers

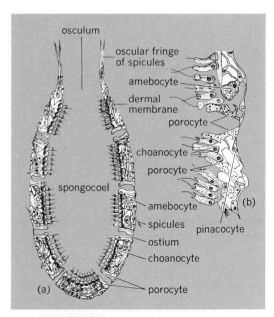

Fig. 1. Morphology of asconoid calcareous sponge. (*a*) Shown in longitudinal section. (*b*) Cross section through *Clathrina* showing cell types.

grouped around a common exhalant canal (Fig. 2d). Several lines of calcareous sponges have apparently reached the leuconoid grade of construction during the course of evolution through the anastomosis of ascon tubes, rather than by the branching of the radial canals of a syconoid sponge (Fig. 2e).

Spicules. Calcareous sponge spicules are monaxonid, triradiate, or quadriradiate in form. Monaxons, where present, tend to occur in the cortex from which they may project to form a bristly surface. In some species monaxons project around the osculum. Either triradiates or quadriradiates or both, depending on the species, are distributed in the mesenchyme, often arranged in definite patterns with relation to the cortex and internal structures. It has been found in *Leucosolenia,* an asconoid sponge, that the mesoglea alone is capable of supporting this tubular sponge after the spicules have been dissolved. The spicules provide increased rigidity for the tube and serve as protective elements. They may also buffer the mesoglea against a fall in pH which would lead to hardening of this substance.

Monaxonid calcareous spicules are secreted by binucleate scleroblasts. The calcium carbonate is laid down around an organic axial thread. As the spicule grows in length, the cell divides. One cell establishes the length and shape of the spicule, while the other lays down additional layers of calcium carbonate. In the case of triradiate and quadriradiate spicules each ray is laid down separately as described above (**Fig. 3**). The groups of scleroblasts are so oriented that the individual rays fuse basally to form a triradiate or quadriradiate pattern.

Phylogeny. As in the Demospongiae, the Calcarea may be divided into two evolutionary lines based on differences in development. In the subclass Calcaronea, including the asconoid genus *Leucosolenia* and its syconoid and leuconoid relatives, the free-swimming larvae are amphiblastulae (**Fig. 4a**). These are hollow larvae, each with an anterior hemisphere of flagellated cells and a posterior mass of nonflagellated cells. The fate of these two categories of cells is determined at an early stage of cleavage. The egg cells always lie just beneath the maternal choanocyte layer. After fertilization three successive meridional cleavages are followed by an equatorial cleavage to produce a 16-celled embryo. The eight cells which lie next to the maternal choanocyte layer are future external and mesenchymal cells; the other eight cells are future choanocytes. After a short free-swimming period the amphiblastula larva settles down on its anterior end and gastrulation occurs by invagination of the flagellated hemisphere or by downgrowth of the nonflagellated cells. A small tubular asconoid sponge called an olynthus results and this may retain the asconoid structure or differentiate later into a syconoid or leuconoid structure according to species. Flagellated cells become choanocytes, while nonflagellated cells are totipotent and give rise to all other cell types of the

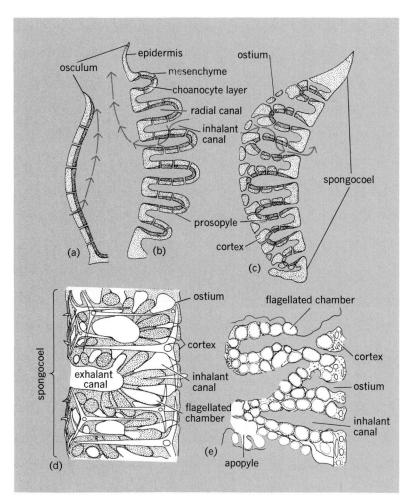

Fig. 2. Grades of construction of water-current system in Calcarea. (a) Asconoid type. (b) Syconoid type without cortex. (c) Syconoid type with cortex. (d) Intermediate or transitional stage between syconoid and leuconoid type. (e) Leuconoid type.

adult sponge. *See* DEMOSPONGIAE.

In the subclass Calcinea, including asconoid genus *Clathrina* and its leuconoid relatives, *Leucetta,* and others, the free-swimming larva is a blastula (Fig. 4b). In this case cleavage results in a hollow blastula made up of a single layer of

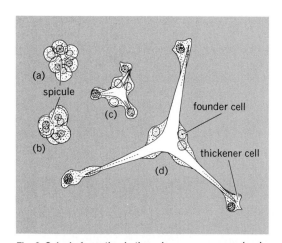

Fig. 3. Spicule formation in the calcareous sponges. (a–c) Early stages in secretion of triradiate spicule, with founder and thickener cells. (d) Late stage of spicule formation.

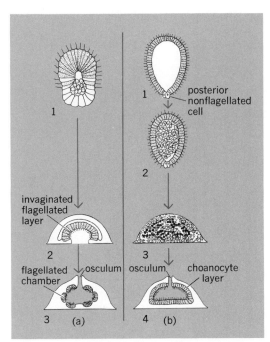

Fig. 4. Larval structure and metamorphosis in calcareous sponges. (a) Developmental stages characteristic of the Calcaronea: 1, amphiblastula larva; 2, newly settled larva showing metamorphosis; 3, young syconoid stage. (b) Developmental stages characteristic of the Calcinea: 1, coeloblastula larva; 2, solid larva; 3, newly settled larva; 4, young sponge of asconoid grade.

flagellated cells. One to several cells at the posterior pole may be nonflagellated. Cells now wander into the interior of the embryo from all points except the anterior pole or from the posterior pole only. The larva so produced leads a short free-swimming life and then settles to the bottom where it attaches by the anterior pole and flattens out. The cells of the larva differentiate according to their position in the metamorphosing sponge. Cells of the outer layer become pinacocytes; those of the interior become choanocytes that line the spongocoel. A young asconoid sponge or olynthus is thus formed that will develop into the adult condition. *See* CALCARONEA; CALCINEA.   Willard D. Hartman

Fossils. Fossil Calcarea are of two kinds. One kind, which are known as pharetrones, has a massive calcareous skeleton, often spherulitic, in which calcite triradiates, typical of the Calcarea, may be embedded. This skeleton may be in the form of fibers outlining interconnecting tubular spaces, or it may be in the form of an external wall pierced by pores, or more frequently the skeleton is a combination of these forms. The other kind, which are known as lithonines, has a rigid skeleton of interlocking, or cemented, four-rayed spicules arranged so that three curving rays point downward or inward and one straight ray points upward or outward. Living representatives of the first kind (such as *Murrayona*) belong to the subclass Calcinea, and living representatives of the second kind (such as *Minchinella*) belong to the subclass Calcaronea. Both kinds sometimes have a peculiar three-rayed spicule called a tuning fork in which

two rays are subparallel. Tuning-fork spicules also occur in a living calcaronean group, exemplified by *Lelapia*, in which the spicules are organized in bundles but are not cemented together.

There are, however, large groups of fossils of considerable abundance, often forming reefs (as do the pharetrones), which have a massive calcareous skeleton but whose living representatives appear to be demosponges. These groups include the sclerosponges, the stromatoporoids, the chaetetids (and possibly all the tabulate corals), and some sphinctozoans. Because many of them lack spicules (when spicules are present they are siliceous monaxons), they are sometimes difficult to distinguish from pharetrones. *See* COELENTERATA; STROMATOPOROIDEA.

Another group, the Heteractinida, which is confined to the Paleozoic Era, probably belongs to the class Calcarea. Their typical spicule has six rays in one plane, sometimes with two more at right angles to the six. This type of spicule can be thought of as a double triradiate (or tetraradiate), and the interpretation is strengthened by the simultaneous occurrence of triradiates and tetraradiates (typical of Calcarea), together with the six-rayed forms, in late Paleozoic representatives of the group such as *Wewokella*.

Another possibly related group is the Archaeocyatha. This exclusively Cambrian group has a pharetronelike skeleton, but the double-walled conical growth form is not a typical pharetrone shape. *See* ARCHAEOCYATHA.

Although pharetrones have existed from the Cambrian to the present day, they were most abundant and diversified in the late Paleozoic and Mesozoic. The lithonines are not known before the Jurassic. *See* ECHINODERMATA.   Robert M. Finks

Bibliography. W. D. Hartman, A re-examination of Bidder's classification of the Calcarea, *Syst. Zool.,* 7(3):97–110, 1958.

Calcarenite

A mechanically deposited (clastic) limestone in which the constituent particles of carbonate are sand-grain size. If the grains are larger than 0.08 in. (2 mm), the rock is a calcirudite. If the grains are smaller than 0.0025 in. (0.06 mm), it is a calcilutite. The calcarenites are normally cemented by clear calcite. The detrital carbonate grains are fossil fragments, broken fragments of calcilutite, oolites, and fecal pellets. The detritus is fairly well sorted as to size, and many grains show slightly abraded edges, indicating a normal, current-deposited sediment. Where oolites are dominant, the rock is called an oolite or oolitic limestone. Calcarenites are often found with orthoquartzites, either interbedded or grading laterally into them. They have the same sedimentary structures as the orthoquartzites, dominantly cross-bedding.

The fine-grained equivalent of calcarenite, calcilutite, is called lithographic limestone if it is homogeneous, dense, and very fine-grained and breaks with conchoidal or subconchoidal fracture; the name is derived from the use of the rock for lithography. The very fine-grained particles may be the product of inorganic precipitation or of finely comminuted algal debris. *See* COQUINA; LIMESTONE; SEDIMENTARY ROCKS.   Raymond Siever

Calcaronea

A subclass of sponges of the class Calcarea, in which the larvae are amphiblastulae. This subclass may be divided into the orders Leucosoleniida and Sycettida. The nucleus of the choanocytes is apical in position, and the flagellum arises directly from the nucleus (see **illus.**). The triradiate spicules in species of this subclass characteristically have one ray longer than the other two. Monaxonid spicules are usually present. The canal system is asconoid, syconoid, or leuconoid. Species with a leuconoid structure give evidence of having had a syconoid ancestry.

Species of the family Lelapiidae have a rigid skeleton composed of tracts or bundles of modified triradiates. They bear a superficial resemblance to pharetronid sponges, with which they are often erroneously classified. The fossil history of the Lelapiidae extends back to the Permian Period. *See* CALCAREA; CALCINEA; LEUCOSOLENIIDA; SYCETTIDA.
Willard D. Hartman

Most of the fossil representatives of this group are similar to the living species *Minchinella lamellosa*. They are sometimes referred to as lithonines. Their principal skeleton consists of four-rayed spicules, often spinose, which interlock or are cemented together to form a rigid skeleton. Three of the rays curve downward and the fourth projects upward, so that the entire skeleton tends to consist of layers of somewhat uniformly oriented spicules. In addition, there are separate spicules of more typical calcaronean type, often organized around an exhalant opening. Members of this group first appear in the Jurassic and are moderately common in the Cretaceous and Tertiary periods, particularly in chalky facies.

In addition, there is a Jurassic species, *Leucandra walfordi*, which is built of loose spicules organized as in the living calcaronean *Leucandra*, and there are isolated equiangular triradiate spicules which occur as far back as the Early Carboniferous Period and may belong to the Calcaronea (based on the predominance of equiangular triradiates among living calcaroneans).   Robert M. Finks

Calcichordates

Primitive fossil members of the phylum Chordata with a calcite skeleton of echinoderm type. They occur in marine rocks of Cambrian to Pennsylvanian age (530–300 million years old) and, because of their skeletons, have traditionally been placed in the phylum Echinodermata. They are shown to be chordates, however, by many chordate anatomical features. Their calcite skeletons merely confirm an old view—that echinoderms and chordates are closely related. *See* CHORDATA; ECHINODERMATA.

There are three main groups of calcichordates—the Soluta, the Cornuta, and the Mitrata. **Figure 1** shows the relationships of these groups to each other, to the extant echinoderms and chordates, and to the recent hemichordate *Cephalodiscus*. The last is a small marine animal (**Fig. 2**) with a head shield, several pairs of arms, a trunk region with a pair of gill slits, and a locomotory stalk. *See* HEMICHORDATA.

In the common ancestry of echinoderms and chordates, a *Cephalodiscus*-like animal probably lay down on its right side (dexiothetism) on the sea floor (Fig. 2). The right arms and right gill slit were lost as a result. Primitive right became ventral while primitive left became dorsal. The resulting animal, called the dexiothetic ancestor, acquired a calcite skeleton and gave rise both to the echinoderms and to the chordates.

The Soluta (**Fig. 3***a*) had an echinodermlike feeding arm and a tail homologous with the stalk of *Cephalodiscus* and with the tail of chordates. There was a gill slit at posterior left in the head, equivalent to the left gill slit of *Cephalodiscus*. The

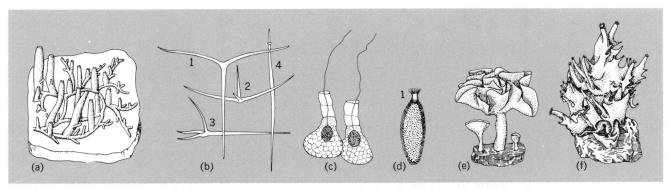

Representative calcaronean sponges. (*a***)** *Leucosolenia botryoides.* **(***b***)** Spicules of *L. complicata*: 1, triradiate with one long ray; 2 and 3, quadriradiates; and 4, monaxon. **(***c***)** Choanocytes of *L. complicata*, showing apical nuclei from which flagella arise. **(***d***)** *Sycon.* **(***e***)** *Teichonopsis labyrinthica.* **(***f***)** *Leucandra aspera.*

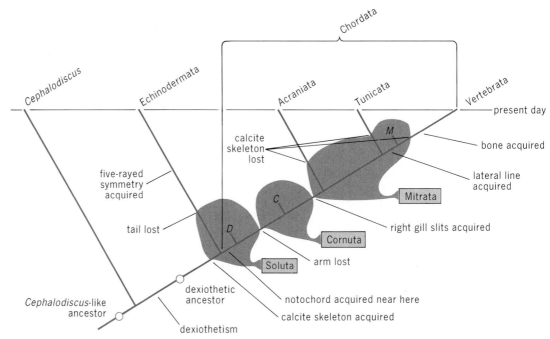

Fig. 1. Evolutionary relationships of calcichordates (Soluta, Cornuta, and Mitrata). The oldest events are at the bottom and the most recent are at the top. *D* = *Dendrocystoides*; *C* = *Cothurnocystis*; *M* = *Mitrocystites*.

tail probably contained a notochord and would have pulled the head rearward across the sea floor, as it probably did in cornutes and mitrates also. By loss of the tail, solutes gave rise to echinoderms.

The Cornuta (Fig. 3b) arose from Soluta by loss of the feeding arm. Cornutes had many gill slits at left posterior in the roof of the head.

The Mitrata (Fig. 3c) arose from Cornuta by acquiring right gill slits. They had a complicated fishlike brain and nervous system. Right and left gill slits were inside the head. The lateral line of *Mitrocystites* is a special resemblance to vertebrates.

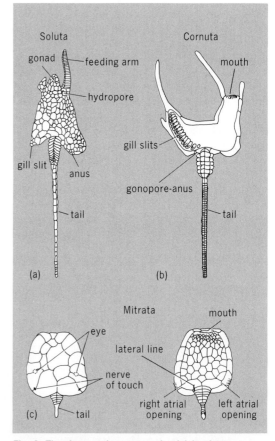

Fig. 3. The three main groups of calcichordates. (*a*) Soluta; dorsal view of *Dendrocystoides* (Ordovician, Scotland, about 440 million years old). (*b*) Cornuta; dorsal view of *Cothurnocystis* (Ordovician, Scotland, about 440 million years old). (*c*) Mitrata; dorsal and ventral views of *Mitrocystites* (Ordovician, Czechoslovakia, about 460 million years old). The atrial openings are external outlets for groups of gill slits inside the head. The lateral line is a sense organ found also in fishes.

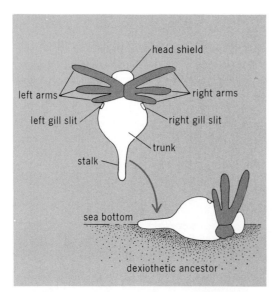

Fig. 2. The *Cephalodiscus*-like ancestor, by falling over on its right side, became the dexiothetic ancestor. This form acquired a calcite skeleton and gave rise both to the echinoderms and to the chordates.

By losing their calcite skeleton three times, mitrates gave rise to the extant groups of chordates. The phosphatic skeleton of vertebrates arose after the calcite skeleton had disappeared. *See* ANIMAL EVOLUTION.
R. P. S. Jefferies

Bibliography. A. P. Cripps, A new species of stem-group chordate from the Upper Ordovician of Northern Ireland, *Palaeontology*, 31:1053–1077, 1988; R. P. S. Jefferies, *The Ancestry of the Vertebrates*, British Museum (Natural History), 1986; R. P. S. Jefferies, The solute *Dendrocystoides scoticus* from the Upper Ordovician of Scotland and the shared ancestry of chordates and echinoderms, *Palaeontology*, 1990; R. L. Parsley, Feeding and respiratory strategies in Stylophora, in C. R. C. Paul and A. B. Smith (eds.), *Echinoderm Phylogeny and Evolutionary Biology*, Liverpool Geological Society, 1989; G. M. Philip, Carpoids: Echinoderms or chordates?, *Biol. Rev.*, 54:439–471, 1979; G. Ubaghs, Réflexions sur la nature et la fonction de l'appendice articulé des carpoides Stylophora (Echinodermata), *Ann. Paléontol. (Invert.)*, 67:33–48, 1981.

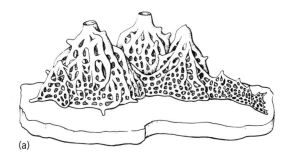
(a)

(b)

Calcinea

A subclass of sponges of the class Calcarea, in which the larvae are blastulae (see **illus.**). The flagellum in the choanocytes arises independently of the nucleus, which occupies a basal position in the cells. Most species possess at least some triradiate spicules which have equal rays and equal angles between the rays. Monaxonid spicules are present or absent. The leuconoid grade of construction shows no trace of syconoid ancestry in this group but has apparently been derived from reticulate asconoid species.

Included in this subclass are two orders: the Clathrinida and Leucettida. *See* CALCAREA; CALCARONEA; CLATHRINIDA; LEUCETTIDA.
Willard D. Hartman

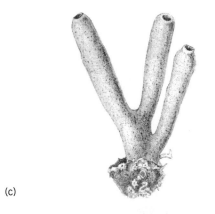
(c)

Representative calcinean sponges. (a) *Clathrina clathrus*. (b) *Leucaltis clathria*. (c) *Leucettusa tabulosa*.

The majority of fossils of the class Calcarea may belong to this subclass. They are often called pharetrones. These sponges have a massive calcareous skeleton which is usually divided into an internal trabecular skeleton that outlines interpenetrating tubular spaces, and an external cortical skeleton that forms a solid layer pierced by pores. Both types of massive skeleton are built of spherulites (round or flake-shaped masses of radiating needles of aragonite or calcite) in which the calcite spicules typical of the class Calcarea may be embedded. A living species, *Murrayona phanolepis*, has such a skeleton, and its soft parts are those of a calcinean. In *Murrayona* the spherulites are fused together in the internal trabecular skeleton but are separate flakes in the external cortical skeleton.

In the fossils the trabecular skeleton is often dominant, and such forms are referred to the suborder Inozoa. In other fossils there is a dominantly cortical skeleton, with sometimes a reduced trabeculate skeleton also present. These forms appear to grow by forming a new unit of the body in the soft parts and then secreting a layer of cortex to cover it. The resulting skeleton is a series of hollow, or partly hollow, chambers. The chambered forms are referred to the suborder Sphinctozoa. The only living sponge with a sphinctozoan type of skeleton, *Vaceletia crypta*, has the soft parts characteristic of a member of the class Demospongea and has no spicules; its calcareous skeleton is not spherulitic. Some fossil sphinctozoans have spicules typical of the class Calcarea embedded in the calcareous skeleton, which is also not spherulitic. Still other fossil Sphinctozoa have spherulitic skeletons and no spicules. It is thus possible that there are several distinct lineages among the sphinctozoans, some to be assigned to the class Demospongea and others to the class Calcarea.

Fossil Sphinctozoa are known from as early

as the Cambrian Period and Inozoa from the Ordovician, both groups extending to the present day. They were important reef builders, particularly the Sphinctozoa, during the Permian and Triassic periods. This was a time during which corals were in a decline, the rugose corals becoming extinct at the end of the Permian, and their successors, the Scleractinia, just getting started in the Triassic. The reefs were confined to the low latitudes of those times just as coral reefs are today. The inozoans remained abundant during the Jurassic and Cretaceous periods, but after that both Inozoa and Sphinctozoa form a minor element in the fossil record.   Robert M. Finks

Calcite

A mineral composed of calcium carbonate ($CaCO_3$); one of the most common and widespread minerals in the Earth's crust. Calcite may be found in a great variety of sedimentary, metamorphic, and igneous rocks. It is also an important rock-forming mineral and is the sole major constituent in limestones, marbles, and many carbonatites. Calcite in such rocks is the main source of the world's quicklime and hydrated, or slaked, lime. It is also widely used as a metallurgical flux to scavenge siliceous impurities by forming a slag in smelting furnaces. It provides the essential calcium oxide component in common glasses and cement. Limestones and marbles of lower purity may find uses as dimension stone, soil conditioners, industrial acid neutralizers, and aggregate in concrete and road building. Calcite in transparent well-formed crystals is used in certain optical instruments. *See* CARBONATITE; CRYSTAL OPTICS; LIME (INDUSTRY); LIMESTONE; STONE AND STONE PRODUCTS.

Calcite is the most stable polymorph of $CaCO_3$ under the pressure-temperature conditions existing in most of the Earth's crust. It is by far the most common polymorph to form as a result of carbon dioxide (CO_2) in the atmosphere, hydrosphere, and lithosphere, and in the upper mantle reacting with the calcium oxide (CaO) component in magmas, crustal rocks, and the oceans. Although it is commonly of high purity, calcite itself may contain other cations such as manganese, iron, magnesium, cobalt, barium, and strontium, substituting for the calcium in variable amounts. Well-developed crystals of calcite are common in cavities in limestones and basic igneous rocks. Of special interest are the large crystals of optical quality obtained from near the Eskefiord, Iceland. This material is known as Iceland spar, and single crystals several feet across have been reported. In the United States very large crystals have been mined in Taos County, New Mexico.

Crystallography. Calcite crystals may exhibit a wide variety of external forms in addition to the most common rhombohedra. Tabular, prismatic, and scalenohedral varieties are not unusual, and twinned crystals are often found (**Fig. 1**). Some

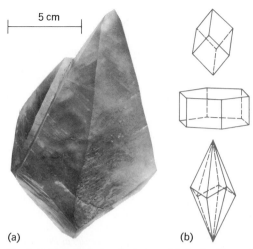

Fig. 1. Calcite. (*a*) Scalenohedral crystal, Joplin, Missouri (*American Museum of Natural History specimens*). (*b*) Common crystal forms (*after C. S. Hurlbut, Jr., Dana's Manual of Mineralogy, 17th ed., John Wiley and Sons, 1959*).

fibrous varieties of calcite known as satin spar yield specimens of gem quality. Deposits in streams in calcareous regions and forming stalactites and stalagmites in limestone caves occur as masses with overall rounded forms made up of very small crystals. Travertine and onyx often consist of such material. *See* ONYX; STALACTITES AND STALAGMITES; TRAVERTINE.

Calcite has hexagonal (rhombohedral) symmetry and a structure built up of alternate layers of calcium ions (Ca^{2+}) and carbonate groups (CO_3^{2-}) stacked so that the layers lie perpendicular to the main axis of symmetry (**Fig. 2**). The structure may be compared with the much simpler sodium chloride structure by aligning the main symmetry axis of calcite with any of the four threefold axes in halite. If the sodium ions (Na^+) and the chloride ions (Cl^-) in the halite model are replaced by Ca^{2+} ions and CO_3^{2-} groups respectively, the selected threefold axis of halite becomes shortened to accommodate the planar CO_3^{2-} groups aligned perpendicular to it. The original halite cube is thus pulled into an obtuse rhomb to give a model of the calcite structure (Fig. 2). *See* CRYSTAL STRUCTURE.

Properties. Pure calcite is either colorless or white, but impurities can introduce a wide variety of colors; blues, pinks, yellow-browns, greens, and grays have all been reported. Hardness is 3 on Mohs

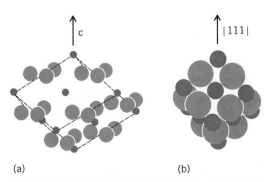

Fig. 2. Structures of (*a*) calcite and (*b*) halite. (*After K. Frye, Modern Mineralogy, Prentice-Hall, 1974*)

scale. The specific gravity of pure calcite is 2.7102 ± 0.0002 at 68°F (20°C).

Calcite has a very low solubility in pure water (less than 0.001% at 77°F or 25°C), but the solubility increases considerably with CO_2 added, as in natural systems from the atmosphere, when more bicarbonate ions and carbonic acid are formed. The solubility is also increased by falling temperature and rising total pressure. Shallow warm seas are supersaturated with calcite, while enormous quantities of calcite are dissolved in the unsaturated deep oceans.

The equilibrium amounts of certain cations that replace calcium in the calcite structure have been determined experimentally for magnesium, iron, and manganese. The amounts of each have been found to increase with temperature. At a fixed temperature the equilibrium amounts increase in the order Mg—Fe—Mn as the size of the substituting cation approaches that of calcium.

The temperature at which calcite dissociates to calcium oxide and carbon dioxide at atmospheric pressure depends on the heating rate, grain size, presence of moisture, and partial pressure of carbon dioxide. Dissociation temperatures range from 1290°F (700°C) to at least 2000°F (1100°C) [at 34 atm or 3.4 megapascals CO_2]. The equilibrium thermal dissociation temperatures have been determined experimentally, and nearly pure calcite has been melted at approximately 2440°F (1340°C) and 1000 atm (100 MPa) of carbon dioxide. Attempts to grow large single crystals of calcite of optical quality by high-temperature and high-pressure techniques have been encouraging, although the dimensions of synthetic crystals do not yet compete with those of natural crystals. *See* HIGH-PRESSURE MINERAL SYNTHESIS.

Partly because it is available in pure, clear, well-developed crystals, calcite has played an important role in the formation of certain fundamental concepts in crystallography and mineralogy. The phenomenon of double refraction was first observed in calcite, and the discovery of the polarization of light resulted from studies of this mineral. Detailed work has shown anisotropism in most of its physical properties. *See* BIREFRINGENCE; POLARIZED LIGHT. Robert I. Harker

Calcium carbonate relations. Calcium carbonate has a variety of polymorphs, but only calcite, aragonite, and vaterite occur in nature. Vaterite is a rare mineral and occurs as tissues of fractured shells of some gastropods, as gallstones, and as an alteration product after larnite. It probably forms under metastable conditions. The synthetic phase of vaterite has been encountered as high-temperature precipitates of calcium carbonate.

As many as five additional polymorphs not known in nature either have been encountered experimentally or have been presumed to exist. All are apparently closely related to calcite in structure and are not stable at room temperature. **Figure 3** shows the range of pressures and temperatures for which most of these phases occur; the polymorphs

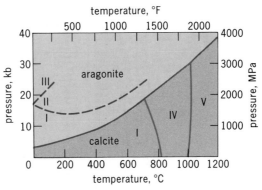

Fig. 3. Phase relations in the unary system $CaCO_3$. Broken lines represent metastable equilibria. Calcite polymorphs are identified as I–V. (*After R. J. Reeder, ed., Reviews in Mineralogy, vol. 11: Carbonates: Mineralogy and Chemistry, Mineralogical Society of America, 1983*)

$CaCO_3$(II) and $CaCO_3$(III) do not possess pressure-temperature stability fields and are metastable with respect to aragonite. Two additional $CaCO_3$ polymorphs, designated as $CaCO_3$(IV) and $CaCO_3$(V), exist at temperatures above 1470°F (800°C). Phase transformations among these polymorphs appear to be rapid, and the $CaCO_3$(V) decomposes to CaO + CO_2 at temperatures above 1800°F (1000°C).

The aragonite–calcite transition has long been of interest to chemists and geologists. The determination of the aragonite stability field at high pressures and temperatures and the positive identification of aragonite in blueschist facies rocks in California have led petrologists to consider the utility of metamorphic aragonite as a geobarometer for blueschist facies metamorphism, and much effort has been directed to both phase relations and kinetics for the transition. The pressure-temperature slope of the equilibrium boundary for the aragonite–calcite transition changes between 660 and 930°F (350 and 500°C), as shown in Fig. 3. This change has been attributed to either a phase transition between $CaCO_3$(I) and $CaCO_3$(II) or a gradual disordering of the carbonate (CO_3) groups with increasing temperature. The presence of small amounts of strontium (Sr) in aragonite extends its stability field toward lower pressures; the opposite effect was observed for the presence of magnesium (Mg) in calcite.

Aragonite has been recognized in high-pressure metamorphic rocks such as blueschists. Its rare occurrence is attributed to rapid inversion of aragonite to calcite under shallow crustal conditions. Aragonite cannot survive in rocks in the presence of a fluid phase or in dry rocks subjected to temperatures greater than 570°F (300°C). Partial preservation of aragonite within the calcite stability field requires fast uplift rates (0.004–0.4 in./year or 0.1–10 mm/year) and temperatures of less than 250–370°F (120–190°C) along the uplift pressure-temperature-time path. The occurrence of aragonite may have been overlooked in many blueschist terranes; it does imply depths of 9–19 mi (15–30 km) for its formation. However, because the aragonite can be completely converted to calcite, the absence of aragonite does not limit the rocks to less than these depths. The common aragonite occurrence in Franciscan blueschists in California and its rarity in other blueschist terranes suggests that Franciscan metamorphism reached a lower maximum temperature (for example, 720°F or 380°C), remained dry upon uplifting, or was uplifted much more rapidly than other blueschist terranes. *See* ARAGONITE; BLUESCHIST METAMORPHISM; CARBONATE MINERALS.   J. G. Liou

Bibliography. C. Klein and C. S. Hurlbut, Jr., *Manual of Mineralogy*, 21st ed., 1993; R. J. Reeder (ed.), *Reviews in Mineralogy*, vol. 11: *Carbonates: Mineralogy and Chemistry*, 1983.

Calcium

A chemical-element, symbol Ca, of atomic number 20, fifth among elements and third among metals in abundance in the Earth's crust. Calcium compounds make up 3.64% of the Earth's crust. Occurrence of

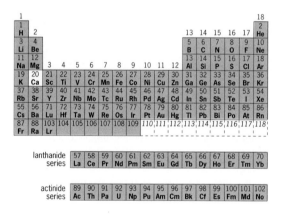

calcium is very widespread; it is found in every major land area of the world. This element is essential to plant and animal life, and is present in bones, teeth, eggshell, coral, and many soils. Calcium chloride is present in seawater to the extent of 0.15%. In **Table 1** are listed the major calcium minerals and their formulas.

Lime, calcium oxide, was known and used by the ancient Greeks and Egyptians in the manufacture of mortar.

Principal compounds. In general, sodium compounds are preferable to calcium compounds, if they may be substituted for a particular application, because the cost of sodium is approximately one-fifth or one-sixth that of calcium. However, lime, CaO, is a cheaper alkali than is sodium hydroxide. Calcium metal reacts directly with hydrogen at 400°C (750°F) to form calcium hydride, CaH_2. The product is stable in dry oxygen to 400–500°C (750–930°F), and at elevated temperatures it becomes an excellent reducing agent. It will reduce many inorganic oxides, such as rutile and baddeleyite, ZrO_2, to their metals (Hydrimet process). Sodium chloride may be reduced to sodium, and carbon monoxide to formaldehyde. The hydride also acts as a condensing agent in converting acetone to mesitylene oxide and as a hydrogenation catalyst in converting ethylene to ethane. It has also served as a portable source of hydrogen for cooking and meteorological balloons; the trade names are Hydrolith and Hydrogenate. In this capacity the reaction of 1 lb of the hydride with water gives 16 ft³ (STP) of hydrogen at pressures as high as 1800 lb/in.² (12 megapascals) at rates as high as 1.5 ft³/lb [0.094 m³/(min)(kg)].

Oxide and hydroxide. Calcium oxide is made by the thermal decomposition of carbonate minerals in tall kilns using a continuous-feed process. Care must be taken during the heating to decompose the limestone at a low enough temperature so that the oxide will slake freely with water. If too high a temperature is used, the so-called dead-burnt lime is formed. The oxide is used in high-intensity arc lights (limelights) because of its unusual spectral features and as an industrial dehydrating agent. At high temperatures, lime combines with sand and other siliceous material to form fusible slags; hence the metallurgical industry makes wide use of it during the reduction of ferrous alloys.

The slaking or hydrolysis process for lime produces the slightly soluble [0.219 g $Ca(OH)_2$/100 g H_2O] calcium hydroxide, whose basicity is limited only by its insolubility. Because of the low cost of calcium hydroxide, it is used in many applications where hydroxide ion is needed. During the slaking process, the volume of the slaked lime produced expands to twice that of quicklime, and because of this, it can be used for the splitting of rock or wood. Slaked lime is an excellent absorbent for carbon dioxide to produce the carbonate. Because of the great insolubility of the carbonate, gases are easily tested qualitatively for carbon dioxide by passing them through a saturated lime-water solution and watching for a carbonate cloudiness. The hydroxide is also used in the formation of mortar, which is composed of slaked lime (1 volume), sand (3–4 volumes), and enough water to make a thick paste. The mortar gradually hardens because of the evaporation of the water and the cementing action of the deposition of calcium hydroxide, and because of the absorption of carbon dioxide. *See* LIME (INDUSTRY).

Silicide and carbide. Calcium silicide, CaSi, is an electric-furnace product made from lime, silica, and a carbonaceous reducing agent. This material is

TABLE 1. Major calcium minerals	
Mineral	Formula
Marble*	$CaCO_3$
Limestone*	$CaCO_3$
Iceland spar	$CaCO_3$
Calcite*	$CaCO_3$
Dolomite*	$MgCO_3 \cdot CaCO_3$
Fluorite*	CaF_2
Anhydrite*	$CaSO_4$
Gypsum*	$CaSO_4 \cdot 2H_2O$
Apatite*	$Ca_5(PO_4)_3F$
Asbestos*	$CaMg_3(SiO_3)_4$

*See separate article.

useful as a steel deoxidizer because of its ability to form calcium silicate, which has a low melting point. Calcium carbide is produced in enormous quantities each year by heating a mixture of lime and carbon to 3000°C (5430°F) in an electric furnace. The compound, CaC_2, is an acetylide which contains the ionic structure $[C\equiv C]^{2-}$, and it yields acetylene upon hydrolysis. Acetylene is the starting material for a great number of chemicals important in the organic chemicals industry. The carbide absorbs atmospheric nitrogen at red heat to form calcium cyanamide, and this reaction is the basis for the cyanamide process for the fixation of atmospheric nitrogen. *See* CYANAMIDE.

Carbonate. Pure calcium carbonate exists in two crystalline forms: calcite, the hexagonal form, which possesses the property of birefringence, and aragonite, the rhombohedral form. Naturally occurring carbonates are the most abundant of the calcium minerals, as is indicated in Table 1. Iceland spar and calcite are essentially pure carbonate forms, whereas marble is a somewhat impure and much more compact variety which, because it may be given a high polish, is much in demand as a construction stone. Although calcium carbonate is quite insoluble in water, it has considerable solubility in water containing dissolved carbon dioxide, because in these solutions it dissolves to form the bicarbonate. This fact accounts for cave formation in which limestone deposits have been leached away by the acidic ground waters. *See* CAVE; KARST TOPOGRAPHY.

Halides. The halides of calcium include the phosphorescent fluoride, which is the most widely distributed calcium compound and which, because of its transparency to ultraviolet and infrared radiation, has important applications in spectroscopy. Calcium chloride, obtained as a waste product in the Solvay process, has in the anhydrous form important deliquescent properties which make it useful as an industrial drying agent and a dust quieter on roads. The equilibrium vapor pressure of water vapor in contact with the system shown in reaction (1) is 0.34 mm at 25°C (72°F).

$$CaCl_2 + 2H_2O \rightleftharpoons CaCl_2 \cdot 2H_2O \qquad (1)$$

Also, this halide finds use in refrigeration plants because of its high solubility in water at low temperatures. The calcium chloride hexahydrate and water system has a eutectic point at −54.9°C (−66.8°F). Calcium chloride hypochlorite (bleaching powder) is produced industrially by passing chlorine into slaked lime, and has been used as a bleaching agent and a water purifier. *See* BLEACHING; CHLORINE.

Sulfate. Calcium sulfate dihydrate is called gypsum; this mineral is mined in New York, Michigan, Texas, Iowa, and Ohio. It constitutes the major portion of portland cement, and has been used to help reduce soil alkalinity. A hemihydrate of calcium sulfate, produced by heating gypsum at elevated temperatures, is sold under the commercial name plaster of paris. When mixed with water, the hemihydrate reforms the dihydrate, evolving con-

siderable heat and expanding in the process, so that a very sharp imprint of the mold is formed. Thus, plaster of paris finds use in the casting of small art objects and mold testing. *See* PLASTER OF PARIS.

Miscellaneous compounds. Calcium sulfide is formed industrially by the reduction of the sulfate with carbon and, because it dissolves hair, has found some use as a depilatory. Calcium forms a mixed alkyl with diethyl zinc, $CaZn(CH_2CH_3)_4$, which is exceedingly reactive. The reaction of calcium metal with phenyl iodide, reaction (2), shows the

formation of a calcium Grignard reagent.

Calcium boride, CaB_6, has a metallic lattice with interstitial boron atoms. It has been shown to have metallic conductivity. *See* GRIGNARD REACTION.

Extraction of the metal. Calcium metal is prepared industrially by the electrolysis of molten calcium chloride, although the reduction of lime with aluminum metal in vacuum followed by distillation of the calcium metal has been used in times of short supply. Calcium chloride, the raw material, is obtained either by treatment of a carbonate ore with hydrochloric acid or as a waste product from the Solvay carbonate process. *See* ELECTROMETALLURGY.

The physical properties of calcium metal are given in **Table 2**. The metal is trimorphous and is harder than sodium, but softer than aluminum. Like beryllium and aluminum, but unlike the alkali metals, it will not cause burns on the skin. It is less reactive chemically than the alkali metals and the other alkaline-earth metals. The pure metal may be machined in a lathe, threaded, sawed, extruded, drawn into wire, pressed, and hammered into plates. The wire may be extruded at temperatures as low as 420–460°C (790–860°F). Calcium has a tensile strength of 8700 lb/in.² (60 MPa), and may be cast if one of the suitable protective fluxes is employed.

In air, calcium forms a thin film of oxide and nitride, which protects it from further attack. At

TABLE 2. Properties of calcium metal

Property	Value
Atomic number	20
Atomic weight	40.08
Isotopes (stable)	40, 42, 43, 44, 46, 48
Atomic volume, cm³/g-atom	25.9
Crystal form	Face-centered cubic
Valence	2+
Ionic radius, nm	0.099
Electron configuration	2 8 8 2
Boiling point	(?) 1487°C (2709°F)
Melting point	(?) 810°C (1490°F)
Density, g/cm³ at 20°C (68°F)	1.55
Latent heat of vaporization at boiling point, kJ/g-atom	399

elevated temperatures, it burns in air to form largely the nitride. The commercially produced metal reacts easily with water and acids, yielding hydrogen that contains noticeable amounts of ammonia and hydrocarbons as impurities.

The metal is employed as an alloying agent for aluminum-bearing metal, as an aid in removing bismuth from lead, and as a controller for graphitic carbon in cast iron. It is also used as a deoxidizer in the manufacture of many steels, as a reducing agent in preparation of such metals as chromium, thorium, zirconium, and uranium, and as a separating material for gaseous mixtures of nitrogen and argon. When added to magnesium alloys (0.25%), it refines the grain structure, reduces their tendency to take fire, and modifies the strengthening heat treatment. It finds use also in the precipitation-hardening lead-calcium alloys. Alloys of lead, calcium, and barium are produced by the electrolysis of fused salts in which the fused chlorides of barium and calcium are electrolyzed over a bath of molten lead as a cathode. The ability of calcium to fix the residual gases nitrogen and oxygen in vacuum tubes makes it important as a getter. The phase diagrams of the systems composed of calcium with aluminum, copper, hydrogen, gold, lead, magnesium, nickel, silicon, silver, tin, and zinc have been investigated.

Analytical methods. The presence of calcium may be detected qualitatively either by forming its insoluble carbonate or by igniting the unknown in a burner flame, to which the calcium imparts a brilliant crimson color. Quantitatively, calcium is determined by precipitation as the oxalate after separation of the strontium and barium. The oxalate is then either ignited to the oxide or oxidized with a standardized solution of potassium permanganate.

Calcium in the biosphere. Calcium is an invariable constituent of all plants because it is essential for their growth. It is contained both as a structural constituent and as a physiological ion. The calcium ion is able to counteract the toxic effects of potassium, sodium, and magnesium ions. Calcium may also affect the growth of plants because its presence in soil affects the alkalinity of the latter.

Calcium is found in all animals in the soft tissues, in tissue fluid, and in the skeletal structures. The bones of vertebrates contain calcium as calcium fluoride, calcium carbonate, and calcium phosphate. In some lower animals, magnesium replaces either totally or partially the skeletal calcium. The importance of calcium in animals as a structural constituent is based on its abundance and on the low solubility of the three calcium salts just listed. Calcium is also essential in many biological functions of the vertebrates. *See* CALCIUM METABOLISM; CARBONATE MINERALS; METAL HYDRIDES.   Reed F. Riley

Bibliography. F. A. Cotton and G. Wilkinson, *Advanced Inorganic Chemistry: A Comprehensive Text*, 5th ed., 1988; D. Pletcher and F. C. Walsh, *Industrial Electrochemistry*, 2d ed., 1993; B. E. Nordin (ed.), *Calcium in Human Biology*, 1988; R. P. Rubin, G. B. Weiss, and J. W. Putney, Jr., *Calcium in Biological Systems*, 1985.

Calcium metabolism

The calcium ion is essential to the normal function of all living cells. In the human, some 99% of total body calcium resides in the skeleton, and 1% is distributed in the soft tissues and extracellular fluids. The concentration of free calcium ions in the cytoplasm of resting cells and in the extracellular fluids is rigidly maintained, in keeping with the critical physiological importance of calcium to a wide variety of biological processes.

The calcium salts in bone provide structural integrity to the skeleton. In bone, calcium exists largely in the form of hydroxylapatite, a crystalline structure composed of calcium, phosphate, and hydroxyl ions. As a tissue, bone is metabolically active and is continuously being destroyed (by a process known as resorption) and renewed (by the processes of formation and subsequent mineralization). These processes are controlled by a number of hormonal and local factors. Normally, the rates of bone destruction and renewal are tightly coupled, so that no net change in bone mineral content occurs. The two most important diseases of bone are osteoporosis and osteomalacia. Osteoporosis is characterized by a reduced volume of normally mineralized bone. Osteomalacia is characterized by bone that has not been reduced in volume but has become soft through a deficiency of vitamin D. *See* BONE; OSTEOPOROSIS; RICKETS.

The total concentration of calcium in serum is approximately 10 milligrams per deciliter (2.5 millimoles per liter). Only about one-half of this concentration is represented by free calcium ions, the biologically important fraction, the remainder being bound to proteins and complexed to other ionic species. The concentration of free calcium ions in the extracellular fluids is involved in the maintenance of plasma membrane integrity and permeability, functions as a cofactor for certain clotting factors, and is of crucial importance to normal skeletal mineralization. *See* BLOOD; CELL MEMBRANES; CELL PERMEABILITY.

The concentration of calcium ions in the cytoplasm of resting cells is approximately 10^{-6} molar, only about one-thousandth that present in the extracellular fluids. The cytosolic calcium concentration is tightly regulated by calcium transport mechanisms in the plasma membrane, mitochondria, and microsomes. Calcium ions play various roles in cellular physiology, including coupling of excitation and contraction in skeletal and heart muscle, participation in nerve excitation, regulation of cellular secretion and ion transport, and regulation of the activities of cytosolic enzymes. *See* BIOPOTENTIALS AND IONIC CURRENTS.

At a systemic level, the metabolism of calcium and phosphate ions is intimately related. The two most important hormones that are responsible for regulating the extracellular concentration of these ions are parathyroid hormone and 1,25-dihydroxyvitamin D [1,25-$(OH)_2D$]; there is little evidence that calcitonin has an important physiological role in humans. The secretion of parathyroid hormone is rigidly controlled by the extracellular concentration of calcium ions, and parathyroid hormone is responsible for the fine regulation of the serum calcium concentration on a minute-to-minute basis, by virtue of its effects on calcium mobilization from bone and the rate of calcium (and phosphate) excretion into the urine. 1,25-Dihydroxyvitamin D is primarily responsible for regulating the quantity of calcium absorbed in the small intestine, and it also participates with parathyroid hormone in the regulation of mineral mobilization from bone. The demonstration of prominent 1,25-$(OH)_2D$ effects requires hours rather than minutes, so that it may be viewed as more important to the long-term maintenance of systemic calcium balance than to the minute-to-minute regulation of the serum concentration of calcium ions. There are a large number of human disorders affecting the parathyroid glands and vitamin D metabolism. *See* PARATHYROID HORMONE; PHOSPHATE METABOLISM; VITAMIN D.

Arthur E. Broadus

Bibliography. L. J. DeGroot (ed.), *Endocrinology*, vol. 2, 1988; P. Felig et al. (eds.), *Endocrinology and Metabolism*, 1987; H. Rasmussen, *Calcium and Cyclic AMP as Synarchic Messengers*, 1981; J. D. Wilson and D. W. Foster (eds.), *Textbook of Endocrinology*, 1985.

Calculators

Portable or desktop devices, primarily electronic, that are used to perform arithmetic and other numerical processing operations at the direction of an operator or a stored program.

Mechanical calculators. Early calculators were exclusively mechanical. An older mechanical calculator provided identical columns of numeral selection keys, one column for each digit of the operand range, with the units selection keys as the rightmost column. A numerical value was selected by depressing one or more keys, one in each column for which a nonzero value was desired. The selected operand was added to the accumulated sum or subtracted from the remaining difference either as the selection of value was made or as the operator took some further action. The result was displayed in a mechanical accumulator register.

Mechanical calculators performed only additions. Multiplication was accomplished by repeated addition of the multiplicand to form a series of partial sums. Additions for the units digit of the multiplier were made into the rightmost accumulator locations. A shift of one position to the left preceded the additions for each subsequent multiplier digit. Subtraction involved addition of the tens complement of the subtrahend. Division consisted of repeated subtractions, beginning in the leftmost accumulator

locations and shifting right by one location for each quotient digit to be determined.

Improvement in mechanical calculators consisted of incorporating motors to effect additions upon key command and adding mechanisms to automatically control execution of the repeated additions needed in multiplication and division. Mechanical calculators have been almost completely replaced by quieter, more efficient, and more capable electronic units.

In addition to mechanical digital calculators, the slide rule, a mechanical analog computing aid, was used for multiplication and division and, to a lesser degree, for looking up functions. In its most common form, a slide rule consisted of a body formed from two parallel members rigidly fastened together, a slide which could be moved left or right between the body members, and a transparent indicator which carried a hairline and could be moved left or right over the face of the body and slide. Slide rules have been almost completely replaced by electronic digital calculators.

Electronic calculators. Calculators changed radically in the mid-1960s when transistorized models were developed to replace the mechanical units. The early electronic units were faster and quieter, but merely emulated their mechanical predecessors—only arithmetic operations were executed. As development continued, the capabilities of the electronic calculators increased and sizes decreased. By 1975, inexpensive hand-held calculators employing large-scale integrated circuits as processing elements were in wide use. *See* ELECTRONICS.

The rapid evolution of the electronic calculator has been made possible by technological improvements in integrated circuits. An integrated circuit can hold all the circuit elements needed to implement the algorithms and the control and timing functions of a calculator. Multiplication, for example, is still accomplished by multiple additions and shifts, but every step in the operation is under the direction of the integrated circuit. Forty or more algorithms may be held in memory, to be retrieved and used when requested by depression of a function key. A hand-held calculator may use a single integrated circuit to interpret key-switch closures, carry out the requested operation, and multiplex the individual digits of the result to the display. *See* INTEGRATED CIRCUITS.

Although most electronic calculators are similar with regard to basic operation, wide differences in functional capabilities exist between models. The user must evaluate the application and select a unit providing the needed features. Some of the differences in calculator capabilities are discussed below.

Display. Several display formats are prevalent. The simple fixed-point display, in which the decimal point remains in a fixed position and answers are automatically aligned on the decimal point by the calculating unit, appeared in early electronic models but was seldom used in subsequent designs. The floating-point format, in which the decimal point can appear in any display location, is more flexible. The processor carries information on decimal-point location along with each operand, aligns decimal points of operands involved in additions and subtractions, and calculates decimal-point locations for results of all other arithmetic processes, passing this information to the display.

More elaborate calculators generally employ scientific notation. In scientific notation, any displayed result consists of a mantissa and a characteristic, the characteristic being the power of 10 associated with the number. The characteristic may be positive or negative. The mantissa always has one digit, which may be a zero, to the left of the decimal point. For example, the displayed value 4.86750 07 corresponds to the floating-point number 4.86750×10^7, or 48,675,000. A display of 2.13447-02 represents 2.13447×10^{-2}, or 0.0213447. Some units capable of scientific notation routinely display results in floating-point form and automatically shift to scientific notation when the results are too large or too small to be accurately represented in floating-point form. The calculator definition of floating-point format does not conform to the same expression in computer terminology, where scientific notation is considered floating-point.

The numbers of display digit locations vary with the calculator model and the mode of display. A floating-point display might have 8 digit positions and a sign location. Scientific and engineering formats usually occupy 12 or 14 display positions, with 8 or 10 digit locations for the mantissa, 2 for the characteristic, and 1 each for the sign of the mantissa and the sign of the characteristic. The operator can select the number of mantissa digits displayed and the display mode on some models.

Early electronic calculators used high-voltage gas discharge tubes for display. Later units utilized the more reliable and power-saving light-emitting diode (LED) displays, which are energized at a low voltage level and which can be readily multiplexed from the calculator integrated circuit. Since the display can account for most of the power consumed in a calculator, and therefore for battery drain, many units automatically remove power from the displays after a predetermined interval of inactivity, retaining the displayed value in semiconductor memory for recall. *See* LIGHT-EMITTING DIODE.

Some designs now make use of liquid-crystal display (LCD) elements which avoid the current drain of LED displays. An LCD assembly provides a significant saving in power consumption over an LED display, but is less easily viewed by the operator, particularly in a bright light environment. *See* LIQUID CRYSTALS.

A display usually provides an overflow or underflow indication when answers exceed the range of the calculator, or an error indication, such as a blinking display, if an illegal operation is requested or unacceptable results are generated. Most displays also indicate impending battery discharge.

Some LCDs on the more capable units have been given alphanumeric capability, to display letters as well as numbers. Specific error and diagnostic messages can be provided to the operator on such a unit as an aid to locating and rectifying mistakes in a program or calculation sequence. *See* ELECTRONIC DISPLAY.

Operand range. The range of operands that can be accepted, processed, and displayed by a calculator is a function of the display and the processing capabilities of the unit. An eight-digit floating-point display can exhibit numbers between .00000001 and 99,999,999, a 16-decade dynamic range. A 12-location scientific display can represent numbers from 1.0×10^{-99} to 9.9999999×10^{99}, a range of about 200 decades. If the available range is exceeded, the operator must reformulate or rescale the problem.

Entry notation. The user of a calculator must enter a sequence of operands and commands to direct the unit through the required processing. For entry, most calculators use either algebraic notation or reverse polish notation (RPN). With algebraic notation, the calculator accepts and processes data and commands in the order in which they would be written in an equation. If, for example, the operator wishes to add 21 and 38 and divide the result by 14, the operator would enter, in sequence, the number 21, an add command (+), the number 38, a divide command (÷), the number 14, and a command to complete the calculation (=). Some calculators using algebraic notation must perform special operations or impose restrictions on the operator in order to handle the nesting of parentheses that occurs in more complex equations.

The RPN entry mode is more convenient for evaluation of complex expressions. This is also known as postfix notation because an operational command always follows the operand to which it applies. For the example provided previously, the operator would enter 21, an ENTER command, 38, an add command (+), 14, and a divide command (÷).

Storage registers. Availability of registers in which operands and intermediate results can be stored is of importance in many applications. If storage is inadequate, the operator may be forced to record intermediate results by hand and reenter them as they are needed for the calculation. Most calculators supply at least one memory register, to be exercised by store and recall keys. Some units contain stacks of three or four registers each; selection of one register in a stack is made by shifting the contents of the registers through the visual display until the desired location reaches the display. Any of a number of scientific calculators provides 10 or more storage locations. Storage and retrieval (into the displayed register) are done by activation of the store or recall key and a location-designating key, in sequence.

Speed. Calculators are designed to carry out computations previously performed by hand, the automation yielding speed and accuracy advantages. By computer standards, calculators are slow. A scientific calculator may require a second or more to execute one of its more complex operations. Execution time may also be dependent upon operand value since some operations involve iterative computations. The relatively slow speed of the calculator is seldom perceived as a handicap by the user.

Power. The power requirements of hand-held calculators have been reduced by the application of LCDs, as noted above. Further reductions have been made by the use of complementary metal-oxide semiconductor (CMOS) circuitry, which exhibits very low power consumption in its quiescent modes, for the processing elements within the units. Desktop calculators include internal power converters and are energized from normal household power lines. Many hand-held units operate from small batteries housed within the cases. Solar cells have been incorporated into a number of designs that make use of LCDs and CMOS circuitry. These cells are placed on an exposed upper surface of the calculator case and convert even normal levels of room light into power sufficient to run the calculator, making batteries or connection to power lines unnecessary. *See* SOLAR CELL.

Programmable calculators. Any calculator can be considered a computer in that it contains in nonvolatile memory a fixed set of algorithms for execution of the processing operations in its repertoire. These algorithms are available whenever power is applied to the unit. Programmable calculators are able to accept and act upon a higher level of programming that directs the units through sequences of processing steps without operator intervention other than operand entry. Programming may be done by the operator or, in advance, by the manufacturer, and storage of the program may be volatile or nonvolatile. Programming relieves the drudgery of repeated keystroke entry when a repetitive calculation must be made. *See* ALGORITHM.

Programming by the operator on the unit to be used for the calculation is known as keystroke programming. The desired sequence of operations is entered into calculator memory by depression of keys as though a calculation were being made, but with the unit in program mode. Each keystroke enters an instruction into the semiconductor memory of the unit. When the unit is returned to the normal run mode, the program sequence can be initiated by the operator through depression of a special function key on the keyboard. Three or more special function keys may be provided; a number of programs can simultaneously reside in memory.

The semiconductor storage in a calculator is usually volatile—program information is lost when power is removed. Some units can accept magnetic tape cartridges or miniaturized magnetic cards, from which the volatile memory can be loaded and to which the memory contents can be written. The magnetic medium provides a means of saving and reentering a program written by the keystroke method. Manufacturers also offer preprogrammed tapes and cards for specialized calculations in a wide range of fields, such as surveying, statistics, financial decisions, mathematics, and circuit analysis. A tape or card can customize a general-purpose calculator to a particular application. Since the miniaturized cards are easily carried with a calculator, the nonvolatile storage capacity greatly improves the computational capacity, and hence the value of a hand-held calculator, especially for use in the field.

Memory of the CMOS type, which consumes little power when storage or retrieval is not under way, has been incorporated into many models. These units prevent program loss by continuously maintaining power on the memory section even when the main unit is powered down. The combination of a CMOS memory and an LCD readout can provide long battery life and protection against program loss in a self-sufficient calculator unit.

Hand-held units that provide the user with the capability to enter a program in the popular BASIC language or to use a set of programming commands more specialized to a scientific, statistical, or financial application have been offered commercially as calculators. A unit of this type incorporates a full alpha-numeric keyboard, although miniaturized, for entry of program commands and names of variables. Programming may be of the type employed for desktop personal computers as well as of the keystroke type. Programmer assistance may be provided in the form of prompting or error messages written on a two-dimensional dot-matrix LCD. Some calculators accept plug-in peripheral elements, such as memory extender modules, read-only memory modules that store programs for specialized computations, magnetic card readers, and printers or plotters. Given that personal computers typically provide calculation commands, the expansion of the range of capabilities of hand-held units called calculators and the variety of peripheral devices that can be attached to them has made a clear distinction between calculators and personal computers impossible. *See* COMPUTER; COMPUTER PROGRAMMING; DIGITAL COMPUTER; MICROCOMPUTER; PROGRAMMING LANGUAGES.

Special-purpose calculators. Although any programmable calculator with sufficient capability can be specialized to a task by insertion of a program, some units are designed for particular applications. Calculators performing all the basic engineering, scientific, or statistical calculations are numerous. A financial calculator can carry out determinations of yields, compound interest, loan and mortgage amortization, depreciation, and many related items. Some calculators perform arithmetic in, and conversions between, the several number systems used in computer programming. A checkbook calculator maintains current balance in its memory. Several models serve as teaching aids by posing arithmetic problems to elementary students and evaluating answers. Calculatorlike units provide synonyms; remember phone numbers, addresses and appointments; serve as teaching aids for spelling; assist in translation between languages; and offer a variety of electronic games. W. W. Moyer

Calculus

The branch of mathematics dealing with two fundamental operations, differentiation and integration, which are carried out on functions. The subject, as traditionally developed in college textbooks, is partly an elementary development of the purely theoretical aspects of these operations and their interrelation, partly a development of rules and formulas for applying calculus to the standard functions which arise in algebra and trigonometry (with exponentials and logarithms included), and partly a collection of applications to problems of geometry, physics, chemistry, engineering, economics, and perhaps a few other subjects.

Derivative. The fundamental concept of differential calculus is that of the derivative of a function of one variable. The classical physical prototype of this concept is that of instantaneous velocity, which is the derivative of distance as a function of time. The derivative also has a highly significant geometrical realization which depends upon the graphical representation of a function in rectangular coordinates (x,y). If y is a differentiable function of x, perhaps as x increases from x_1 to x_2, the graph of the function is a continuous curve with exactly one y for each x, and at each point the curve has a tangent line which is not parallel to the y axis. If ϕ is the angle, measured counterclockwise, from the positive x direction to the tangent (**Fig. 1**), then $\tan \phi$ is equal to the derivative of y with respect to x. (This is on the supposition that the same unit of length is used along the two axes.) This $\tan \phi$ is also called the slope of the curve.

The standard notation for the derivative of y with respect to x is dy/dx. If the functional notation $y = f(x)$ is used, the derivative is often denoted by $f'(x)$. Modern practice is to use f for the function as an abstract entity, while $f(x)$ denotes the value of f at c. Then f' denotes the derivative as a function, and $f'(x)$ is the value of f' at x. For a precise definition of the derivative *see* DIFFERENTIATION.

Functions. To say that y is a function of x means that, as a consequence of some rule or definite agreement, there is a designated collection of permissible values of x (called the domain of the function) and an associated set of corresponding values of y (called the range of the function), of such a character that with each permissible value of x is paired a unique well-determined value of y. The function itself is the collection of all the pairs (x, y) which arise in this way. This collection exemplifies the rule or agreement. If f denotes the function, it is customary to write $y = f(x)$ to represent the dependence of y on x.

In calculus the domain of the function is usually composed of one or more intervals of the x axis.

Definite integral. If f is a function defined on the finite interval from x_1 to x_2 inclusive, the definite integral of f from x_1 to x_2, denoted by

$$\int_{x_1}^{x_2} f(x)\,dx$$

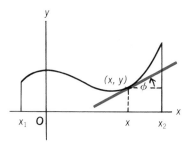

Fig. 1. Graphical representation of the derivative of *f(x)*.

is defined by applying to f a rather intricate process which entails the consideration of what are called approximating sums. When the function f is subjected to certain restrictions, this process culminates in the determination of a number as the limit of the approximating sums, and this number is called the definite integral of f from x_1 to x_2. The integral is not defined unless the approximating sums do converge to a well-defined limit. A sufficient condition that this be so is that the function f be continuous.

There is a geometrical representation of the process of defining the definite integral, and it furnishes a plausible argument for the convergence of the approximating sums to a limit. Divide the interval from x_1 to x_2 into a finite number N of not necessarily equal parts. Let the lengths of these parts be $h_1, h_2, \ldots, h_N$, and let t_k be a value of x in the kth part (**Fig. 2**). Then the expression

$$f(t_1)h_1 + f(t_2)h_2 + \cdots + f(t_N)h_N$$

is called an approximating sum. In Fig. 2, where the function is continuous and the function values are all positive, each term $f(t_k)h_k$ in the approximating sum is equal to the area of a certain shaded rectangle, and the whole sum is an approximation of the area between the graph of the function and the x axis, from x_1 to x_2 inclusive. The limiting process is carried on by increasing N and making the largest of the h_k's approach 0. It is then intuitively clear that the definite integral is the number which represents the exact area between the x axis and the graph. This geometrical interpretation of the integral is the basis of an important application of integral calculus, to the calculation of areas.

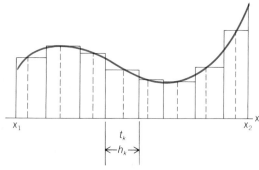

Fig. 2. The definite integral.

It would be tedious and difficult in practice to compute definite integrals by actually working out the limits of approximating sums. It is therefore fortunate that by purely mathematical reasoning it is possible to demonstrate a theorem which links derivatives and integrals and makes it possible, in many important instances, to compute definite integrals by an easier procedure. *See* INTEGRATION.

In the next paragraph are stated the two fundamental theorems of calculus. In these statements the adjective "continuous" appears. For a function $y = f(x)$ to be continuous means, roughly, that as x changes gradually, y must either change gradually, or not at all. Absolutely abrupt jumps are forbidden, and so are many more bizarre modes of irregular behavior. For a precise definition of continuity *see* DIFFERENTIATION.

Fundamental theorems. For the calculation of

$$\int_{x_1}^{x_2} f(x)dx$$

find, if possible, a function F with continuous derivative F' such that $F'(x) = f(x)$ when $x_1 \leq x \leq x_2$. Then Eq. (1) can be written. This is one

$$\int_{x_1}^{x_2} f(x)dx = F(x_2) - F(x_1) \qquad (1)$$

of the two central theorems. The other is stated as follows: Suppose f is continuous, and consider the function F defined by Eq. (2). Then F has a derivative given by $F'(x) = f(x)$.

$$F(x) = \int_{x_1}^{x} f(t)\,dt \qquad (2)$$

Law of the mean. The most important theorem about derivatives, exclusive of those which involve integrals, is variously called "the law of the mean" and "the mean-value theorem of differential calculus." It is stated in this form: Suppose f is continuous for x from x_1 to x_2 inclusive, and suppose f has a derivative for each x between x_1 and x_2. Then there is some x of this kind for which Eq. (3) holds true. This theorem enables one to prove

$$f'(x) = \frac{f(x_2) - f(x_1)}{x_2 - x_1} \qquad (3)$$

that, if $f'(x)$ is always positive, then $f(x)$ is always zero, then $f(x)$ remains constant as x changes. The first of these results is important for applications to the investigations of graphs. The second is virtually indispensable in the proof of the fundamental theorems of calculus stated above, and in establishing the uniqueness of the solutions for certain problems which involve antidifferentiation (the process of surmising what a function is from a knowledge of its derivative). Such problems abound in application of calculus to problems of motion.

Applications of derivatives. If y is a function of x, the derivative dy/dx is interpretable as the rate of change of y with respect to x. If y is distance and x is time, dy/dx is velocity. If y is work done by a force and x is time, dy/dx is power. Many motion problems, such as those

arising in mechanics and formulated by Newton's second law, are expressible by posing an equation which a function and its derivative or derivatives must satisfy. These are called differential equations. The study of such equations is an extension and ramification of calculus. Differential equations are important in all branches of physics. They also arise in many problems of engineering and chemistry, for example, in the deformation of columns and beams, in the study of chemical reactions, and in radioactive decay. *See* DIFFERENTIAL EQUATION.

Problems of maximizing or minimizing a function usually involve derivatives. If a differentiable function f reaches a relative maximum or minimum at a point in the interior of an interval of its domain, then $f'(x)$ must be zero there. This helps in finding extreme values of f.

Applications of integrals. Integrals are used to compute areas bounded by curves in a plane. They are also used to compute other geometrical quantities, such as lengths of curves, areas of surfaces, and volumes of solids. For computing volumes and surface areas the natural tools are multiple integrals. Integrals are also used to compute quantities which occur in physics, such as center of mass, moment of inertia, work done by a variable force, and attraction due to gravitation. The concepts of first, second, and higher moments of a function, as used in statistics, are stated in terms of integrals.

Functions of several variables. To each pair (x_1, x_2) in a specified collection of number pairs, let there correspond a certain definite number y. This defines $y = f(x_1, x_2)$ as a function of two variables. Functions of three or more variables may also be considered. Differential calculus is extended to such functions through the study of partial derivatives with respect to the separate variables $x_1, x_2, \ldots$. A concept of total differential is also relevant. For details *see* PARTIAL DIFFERENTIATION.

Integral calculus for functions of several variables is developed through the concept of a multiple integral. For instance, in the case of functions of two variables there is a concept of double integral. The theory of the subject deals with how the double integral is expressible in terms of two successive definite integrals of the sort occurring in calculus of functions of one variable. There is also a concept of a line integral, which is a kind of integral along a curve. There are relations between this concept, the concept of total differential, and the concept of double integral.

New developments. Calculus belongs to the branch of mathematics called analysis. One characteristic of analysis is its concern with infinite limiting processes. Current research in analysis is mostly on a level of development far beyond the elements of calculus. However, the ideas of calculus persist, though in much more generalized and abstract form, in the theory of functions and in functional analysis.

Angus E. Taylor

Bibliography. R. Courant and F. John, *Introduction to Calculus and Analysis*, vols. 1 and 2, 1965, 1974, reprint 1993; W. Kaplan, *Advanced Calculus*, 4th ed., 1991; S. Lang, *A First Course in Calculus*, 5th ed., 1986, reprint 1993; S. L. Salas and E. Hille, *Calculus: Single Variable*, 6th ed., 1990; S. K. Stein and A. Barcellos, *Calculus and Analytical Geometry*, 3d ed., 1982; E. W. Swokowski et al., *Calculus*, 6th ed., 1994; A. E. Taylor and R. W. Mann, *Advanced Calculus*, 5th ed., 1992.

Calculus of variations

An extension of the part of differential calculus which deals with maxima and minima of functions of a single variable. The functions of the calculus of variations depend in an essential way upon infinitely many independent variables. Classically these functions are usually integrals whose integrand depends on a function whose specification by any finite number of parameters is impossible. For example, let C be a smooth bounded region of a space of m variables, $x_1, x_2, \ldots, x_m$, let y be any function of some smooth class on C and its boundary into real numbers or into n-tuples of real numbers and taking specified values on the boundary, and let $f(x,y,p)$ be a smooth function of $2m + 1$ variables $x_1, x_2, \ldots, x_m, y, p_1, p_2, \ldots, p_m$. Then the integral, Eq. (1), is a function on the space

$$J = \int \cdots \int_C f(x, y, y_x) \qquad (1)$$

of functions y to the real numbers, and this space of functions is infinite dimensional unless excessive restrictions are placed on it. Here y_x denotes the derivatives $\partial y/\partial x$, and throughout this article subscripts will be used to denote derivatives and occasionally where the context is clear to denote particular values.

The calculus of variations studies such functions and their maxima and minima. The limitation of the competing functions is made realistically, and with sufficient restrictions it is possible to arrive at a rewarding theory; these restrictions do not always include the fixed boundary conditions stated above.

Principal applications may be to physical systems involving flexible components or time-dependent orbits; equilibrium positions or orbits may be determined by minimizing energy or action integrals. The problems are of mathematical interest because of intrinsic difficulties (largely related to lack of topological compactness of bounded regions in spaces of infinitely many dimensions) and possibly because more progress with difficult nonlinear problems has been made here than elsewhere. *See* HAMILTON'S PRINCIPLE; LEAST-ACTION PRINCIPLE.

Theoretical basis. The classical theorems of differential calculus which are used and generalized are the following.

1. Necessary conditions for a function f of a single variable x to attain a local minimum at $x = x_0$ are $f'(x_0) = 0$ if the derivative exists at x_0 and if there are neighboring points of definition of f for arguments on each side of x_0; $f'(x_0) \geqq 0$ if the

derivative exists at x_0 and if there are neighboring points of definition of f arguments larger than x_0.

2. If $f'(x_0) = 0$, if f is defined at some points neighboring x_0, and if $f'(x_0)$ exists, then a necessary condition for f to attain a local minimum at $x = x_0$ is $f''(x_0) \geqq 0$; conversely the conditions $f'(x_0) = 0$ and $f''(x_0) > 0$ guarantee a local minimum at x_0. *See* DIFFERENTIATION.

One standard technique of the calculus of variations is to derive necessary conditions for minima by restricting variations to a set of admissible variations depending smoothly on a single parameter and then to apply these theorems 1 and 2 from differential calculus.

For example, in the integral above, suppose that the function $f(x,y,p)$ is defined for all (x,y) in some region of $(m + 1)$-space and for all p, and that f and all its first and second partial derivatives are continuous in this region. Suppose that the admissible functions y are restricted to functions which have continuous second derivatives in C and which take on the required boundary values. Let $g(x)$ be such an admissible function lying in the interior of the region over which $f(x,y,p)$ is defined, and let $z(x)$ be any function with continuous second derivatives on C and taking the value 0 at all points on the boundary of C. Then for e neighboring zero, the function $y = g(x) + ez(x)$ is admissible in the problem (it has continuous second derivatives and takes the prescribed values on the boundary). Then $z(x)$ is an admissible variation. If g does indeed afford a local minimum to J and if it is specified that the functions $y = g(x) + ez(x)$ are close to g for e neighboring zero, then propositions 1 and 2 above may be applied to the function $J(e)$ of the single variable e, where $J(e)$ is the value taken by J for y defined in terms of g and z as above. Under the conditions stated, the derivative $J'(0)$ does exist, and it may be computed by differentiating under the integral sign. The result is shown in Eq. (2).

$$J'(0) = \int \cdots \int_C \left[z(x) f_y(x, g, g_x) + \sum_j z_{x,j} f_{p,j}(x, g, g_x) \right] \qquad (2)$$

This expression must be zero for any admissible $z(x)$ according to proposition 1. Under the restrictions set here each term of the expression to be summed may be integrated by parts, the integration of the term with factor $z_{x,j}$ being with respect to the single variable x_j; for the formula

$$\int u \, dv = uv - \int v \, du$$

(with boundary values assigned to the term uv) one sets $dv = z_{x,j} dx_j$ and takes the remainder of the term as u. This yields, after due account is taken of the vanishing of z on the boundary, Eq. (3). A fundamental technique of the calculus of variations lies in exploiting the necessity of this last integral

$$J'(0) = \int \cdots \int_C z(x)$$

$$\times \left[f_y(x, g, g_x) - \sum_j \frac{\partial}{\partial x_j} f_{p,j}(x, g, g_x) \right] \quad (3)$$

being zero independent of the admissible variation $z(x)$. The integral divided by the measure of C is the average over C of z times the expression in brackets, and the requirement that any function of a sufficiently wide class times a given function averages to zero is met only if the given function is itself zero. Care must be taken to assure that this fundamental condition is met—that is, that the admissible variations are sufficiently general to permit invoking this lemma. In this case the bracketed expression must be zero, and the necessary condition becomes a differential equation, the Euler equation. For the function in Eq. (4), so that Eq. (5) holds, the Euler equation is just the Laplace equation (6).

$$f(x, y, p) = p_1^2 + p_2^2 \quad (4)$$

$$J = \int \int \left[\left(\frac{\partial y}{\partial x_1} \right)^2 + \left(\frac{\partial y}{\partial x_2} \right)^2 \right] \quad (5)$$

$$\frac{\partial^2 y}{\partial x_1^2} + \frac{\partial^2 y}{\partial x_2^2} = 0 \quad (6)$$

See DIFFERENTIAL EQUATION; INTEGRATION; LAPLACE'S DIFFERENTIAL EQUATION.

Second variations are studied in a similar way, applying proposition 2 above to $J''(0)$. These give rise to conditions of Jacobi for a minimum. Generally, there are a set of conditions including Euler's condition above, a condition of Weierstrass, a condition of Legendre which may be derived from the Weierstrass condition, and the Jacobi condition, all known as necessary conditions for a minimum. These are generally set in terms of inequalities, and when the conditions are strengthened to demand strong inequalities (excluding equality) the conditions become sufficient for many interesting problems.

Multidimensional derivatives. Much of the work on the calculus of variations is devoted to meticulous detail with regard to the number of derivatives assumed to be available for various functions, particularly the competitive admissible functions $y(x)$. If too many derivatives are assumed, minima may not exist; if too few are assumed, the solution might not be sufficiently smooth to be acceptable in the light of the original statement of the problem. In an attempt to use fewer derivatives, different approaches are used depending on the number of independent variables x. For the multidimensional case, an approach by A. Haar leads to extended complications which are not amenable to description here. Haar introduced an additional function which has the effect of replacing the Laplace equation in the simple Dirichlet problem stated above by the Cauchy-Riemann equations. *See* COMPLEX NUMBERS AND COMPLEX VARIABLES.

Single-integral problems. For the case of single integrals, however, a lemma of du Bois–Reymond is applicable. This lemma states that a function must be a constant if the average of its product with every function of a sufficiently broad class is zero, where the class may be restricted to have average value zero. The proof takes the given function to be $u(x)$ and its average over the interval to be some constant c, and requires that $u(x) - c$ be one of the admissible functions for comparison. This leads to a requirement that $[u(x) - c]^2$ average zero, and this means that $u(x)$ is essentially c.

Additional illustrative material of general results obtainable will now be presented in terms of single integral problems. Here take Eq. (7) and enlarge the

$$J = \int_a^b f(x, y, y') \, dx \quad (7)$$

class of admissible curves somewhat. The precise nature of this enlargement will not be important for the moment, but assume that among the admissible curves $y = g(x)$, $a(0) \leq x \leq b(0)$ affords a minimum to J. Assume also that a family of curves $y = z(x, e)$, $a(e) \leq x \leq b(e)$ is admissible and that the value of $z(x,e)$ as e tends to zero is $g(x)$. Most particularly, however, it is desired to avoid the restriction that $z_x(x,e) \to g'(x)$, which was implied above by the variation $y = g(x) + ez(x)$. This allows variations more general than the ones above with regard to the variations of the end points of the curve, the limits of integration, and the behavior of the derivatives.

Curves of the type of $z(x,e)$ introduced here may be admitted as neighboring $y(x)$ for e neighboring zero either by using $\max_x |z(x,e) - y(x)|$ (possibly modified by some measure of disparity between the intervals of definition) or $\int [z(x,e) - y(x)]^2$ as a measure of distance between two points in the function space. In either case, $J(e)$ may be defined as the value of the integral J with f evaluated for x, $z(x, e)$, and $z_x(x,e)$, and it is again possible to study $J'(0)$ if it exists. However, it should be noted that there is no reason for expecting $J'(0)$ to exist in this case, for the integrand involves derivatives z_x which may not vary continuously. Actually a simple example of length shows what may happen; if J is a length integral, the z curves may be taken as zigzagging broken lines approaching a straight line segment but always making an angle of perhaps $45°$ with it. Then $J(e)$ for any e not zero is $\sqrt{2}$ times $J(0)$. There is illustrated here an important property known as lower semicontinuity. Although $J(e)$ is not continuous, its limit as the argument varies is never less than its value for the limiting value of the argument. This property, along with some compactness properties, suffices for all purposes of the calculus of variations, but it must be noted that it is reasonable to expect semicontinuity but not continuity in problems of the calculus of variations.

The method used before may be used to derive a

formula for $J'(0)$; it is Eq. (8), where Eq. (9) holds.

$$J'(0) = f[b_0, g(b_0), z_x(b_0, 0)]b'(0)$$
$$- f[a_0, g(a_0), z_x(a_0, 0)]a'(0) + \overline{J} \quad (8)$$

$$\overline{J} = \int_{a_0}^{b_0} \{z_e f_y[x, g, z_x(x, 0)]$$
$$+ z_{xe} f_p[x, g, z_x(x, 0)]\} \quad (9)$$

This may be integrated by parts to give either Eq. (10) or Eq. (11), where H is a function of x such that Eq. (12) holds. In all these formulas $z_x(x,0)$ has

$$\overline{J} = \left\{z_e f_p[x, g, z_x]\right\}_{a_0}^{b_0} + \int_{a_0}^{b_0} z_e \left\{f_y - \frac{d}{dx} f_p\right\} \quad (10)$$

$$\overline{J} = \left\{z_e H\right\}_{a_0}^{b_0} + \int_{a_0}^{b_0} z_{xe} \left\{f_p - H\right\} \quad (11)$$

$$H' = f_y[x, g(x), g'(x)] \quad (12)$$

been retained instead of $g'(x)$ to indicate ambiguity in case of discontinuous derivatives.

End-point problems. If variations with fixed end points are admissible near g, it is possible to choose z with $z_e = 0$ at the end points, and so that a' and b' are zero for $e = 0$ and only $\overline{J}$ is left, so that $J'(0) = 0$ implies $\overline{J} = 0$. In the expression above for $\overline{J}$, Eq. (11), the first term is zero since $z_e = 0$ at the end points, the average of z_{xe} over the interval is zero, since $z_e = 0$ at both end points, and the lemma of du Bois–Reymond mentioned above may be applied. This means that the expression in curly brackets in the integrand is constant whether $f_p(x,g')$ is known to be differentiable or not. Since H is obviously differentiable if g and z have first derivatives which are continuous on each of a finite set of closed intervals covering $[a,b]$, then the whole expression is differentiable, and the Euler equation follows under these weakened conditions. Furthermore, under some conditions of regularity, it is demonstrable that the solutions of this Euler equation have two continuous derivatives, so that minimizing functions in a wide class of functions are comfortably smooth.

The same formula may be used to get conditions which must exist in a corner. It is also applicable to problems with variable end conditions. It may be applied to a special variation to get the Weierstrass condition (**Fig. 1**). These are curves with no

general properties except that they vary slowly, approaching straightness at the top and conforming with the continuing curve at the bottom.

Here the lower curve $y = g(x)$ is assumed to be the extremal, and at a point $x = x_1$ on this curve a line with slope q is erected. The variations corresponding to e are taken by proceeding along g to x_1, then up the line to a point with abscissa $x_1 + e$, then along a curve of a smooth family rejoining g at a fixed point x_2, and then along g to b. The family between the line and the point of rejoining g is assumed to be smooth and to approach g with the $z_x,(x,e)$ approaching g'. Thus the difficulty about limits of $z_x(x,0)$ is avoided except at the point $x = x_1$. Note that the variation is defined only for nonnegative values of e, and hence the value $J'(0)$ must be nonnegative if g is a minimum, but not necessarily zero. Intelligent straightforward application of the formulas developed just above yields this condition in the form shown in Eq. (13).

$$E(x, g, g', q) = f(x, g, q) - f(x, g, q')$$
$$- (q - g')f_p(x, q, g')] \geq 0 \quad (13)$$

In problems with variable end points (which end points may, for example, be constrained to lie on prescribed curves) the end-point conditions which appear in these formulas must be taken into account. Here it is often possible to assume that $\overline{J}$ in the formula is zero, because of admissibility of sufficiently large classes of variations with fixed end points. The remaining conditions are called transversality conditions.

Alternative methods. In classical single-integral problems it is frequently possible to integrate the Euler equations into a family of curves depending on a finite set of parameters (the initial conditions, for example). However, in other cases it is not possible to do this, and a solution must be arrived at or proved to exist in more direct ways. Frequently a minimizing sequence of functions is used; that is, a set of functions y_n is chosen so that the values of J corresponding to y_n approach their greatest lower bound. If there is a convergent subsequence of these y_n and if J itself is lower semicontinuous, then a limit y to the sequence must afford a minimum to J.

Other methods of solution and of proving the existence of solutions depend on general studies of Hilbert spaces. In these studies the integrals appear as operators in Hilbert space, and they are frequently reduced to quadratic forms by some majorizing process.

Problem of Bolza. Here the admissible class of functions is restricted by differential conditions. Problems of Bolza include the classical isoperimetric problems, in which the length of the admissible curves is specified. The problem of Bolza gives rise to multiplier rules which are based on the implicit function theorem. The theorem is applied by noting that if the rank of a matrix which can be caused to arise is maximal, then the restrictions imposed on

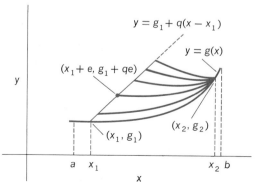

Fig. 1. Weierstrass condition. Symbols explained in text.

admissible curves may be retained unchanged (in particular, or more generally they may be changed arbitrarily) and the function J may still be changed arbitrarily, hence reduced. A submaximal rank for this matrix is a necessary condition for a minimum; using this result the problem of Bolza may be transformed to an ordinary problem whose integral is a linear combination of the integrand of J and functions describing the original restrictions. The coefficients of this linear combination are initially undetermined; they are called Lagrange multipliers.

Critical points. Finally, studies in the spirit of differential calculus but not restricted to local minima should be noted. Here the interest includes not only minima but all critical points (that is, all functions satisfying the Euler condition), and also other studies. It is true that classical problems in mechanics may have stable solutions corresponding to nonminimizing critical points. For sufficiently restricted problems it can be shown that the homology group of the space for which $J \leq c$ for any c does not change as c varies until a critical level is reached; this is a level of J at which a critical point exists. The change in homology groups at critical points is related closely to the nature of the critical point. For example, in a finite-dimensional space, on a sphere the number of pits minus the number of simple passes plus the number of peaks is two; on a torus the corresponding number is zero; a pass with three grooves running down and three ridges running up from it is to be counted as two simple passes for topological reasons. This is the Morse theory. *See* TOPOLOGY.   Charles B. Tompkins

Multivariable problems. This section deals primarily with the case where the function y is vector-valued. Thus the associated Euler equation is a vector equation, or equivalently a system of real-valued equations.

There are two main cases, one where the approach through the Euler partial differential equation (PDE) has been fruitful, and one where it has been more useful to treat the problem in its original, integral form by rewriting the integral as an integral over the image set rather than the parameter domain. Most of the results discussed are for elliptic problems, but reference is made to some of the work on nonelliptic problems in the calculus of variations.

PDE approach. It will be assumed that the domain C is a bounded open subset of R^m (where R is the real numbers) with a smooth boundary and that the real-valued function f of Eq. (14) is continuous in all its

$$f(x, y, p) : C \times R^n \times R^{mn} \to R^1 \qquad (14)$$

variables (though somewhat weaker assumptions are possible); as before, $J[y]$ is given by Eq. (15).

$$J[y] = \int_C f(x, y, y_x) dx \qquad (15)$$

The key ingredients for the existence of a minimum of J within an admissible class of functions are as follows:

1. The integral J has the property that if a sequence of admissible functions y_i converges to an admissible function y, then $\lim \inf J[y_i]$ is no larger than $J[y]$ (this property is called sequential lower semicontinuity).

2. There exists a minimizing sequence of admissible functions which converges to an admissible function. (Typically this is arranged by requiring the set of admissible functions to have the property that any sequence has some convergent subsequence with limit in the set, which is the property of compactness.)

When these two conditions hold, the direct method can be used to find a minimizer: take any sequence y_i such that $J[y_i]$ converges toward the infimum of the possible values of J, and extract a convergent subsequence.

To have these conditions hold, it is sufficient that f be convex in the last set of variables (so that the Euler equations form a so-called strongly elliptic system of partial differential equations), that either f increases with $|y_x|$ at least as fast as $|y_x|^\alpha$ for some $\alpha > 1$ or there be some known bound given in advance on the slopes $|y_x|$ of a minimizer, and that the class of admissible functions be an appropriate Sobolev space. In particular, the class of admissible functions must allow some kinds of discontinuities, and the first derivatives of y need exist only in a "weak" sense (analogous to Schwartz's generalized functions or distributions).

This leads to the regularity problem: Are the functions obtained by this procedure indeed classical functions with enough derivatives that they are classical solutions to the Euler system of equations?

When $n = 1$ (and under the above assumption of convexity), the answer is yes. But for $n \geq 2$, the answer is, in general, no. For example, there are integrands f satisfying all the above hypotheses such that the function $y = x/|x|$ (which is discontinuous at the origin) is the unique minimizer among functions with its boundary values.

The problem thus shifts to characterizing the set of points x such that y is not a continuously differentiable function in a neighborhood of x (that is, to characterizing the singular set of y). It has been shown that the singular set has Hausdorff dimension less than $m - 2$; it is an open question in general whether the dimension of the singular set is always less than or equal to $m - 3$. (Fractal sets can have dimensions which are not whole numbers, and the possibility of fractal singular sets has not been ruled out.) *See* FRACTALS.

One particular such case where $y = x/|x|$ is the unique minimizer is with $m = n = 3$, C the unit ball in R^3, $f(x, y, y_x) = y|_x|^2$ (for this f, $J[y]$ is often called the elastic energy of the mapping y), and boundary values $y(x) = x$ for x on the boundary of the unit ball, provided the additional requirement is imposed that the image of y lies on the boundary of the unit ball. Such energy-minimizing mappings where the image is constrained to lie on a unit sphere are typical of the director fields of liquid crystals. The subject of looking for energy-

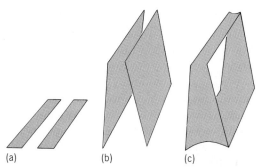

Fig. 2. Example of an area-minimizing surface that cannot be written as the graph of a single function. (a) Nonconvex domain C. (b) Minimal graph over C that is not area-minimizing. (c) Second surface over C that has less area. (After F. Morgan, Geometric Measure Theory: A Beginner's Guide, Academic Press, 1988)

minimizing mappings, or at least for mappings which are critical points of this J (called harmonic maps), is an active field of mathematics research. An example where there is no energy-minimizing mapping arises in the attempt to map a torus (an inner tube) so as to cover a sphere (a beach ball): in the limit of an energy-minimizing sequence, the torus tears apart. *See* LIQUID CRYSTALS.

The major problem with this PDE approach is that many variational problems, when formulated in this way, do not result in a strongly elliptic system of partial differential equations. For example, when a two-dimensional surface in R^3 is written as the graph of a single real-valued function y over a domain C in the plane, its area is given by Eq. (16), and if C is convex the above theory can be

$$J[y] = \int (1 + |y_x|^2)^{1/2} dx \qquad (16)$$

applied. But if the same surface is written parametrically, as a mapping from a parameter domain in R^2 into three-dimensional space, the area is given by integrating a different integrand, and this integrand is no longer convex in the derivatives. (For mappings of two-dimensional disks, it is possible to chose a particular parametrization so that minimizing area is equivalent to minimizing the elastic energy of the mapping, but for higher-dimensional

surfaces, for example, three-dimensional surfaces in R^4, there is no such choice of parametrization or equivalence.) Furthermore, in any dimension a typical area-minimizing surface usually cannot be written as the graph of a single function (**Fig. 2**), and thus (except for special parametrizations of some two-dimensional surfaces) the above theory simply cannot be applied. *See* PARAMETRIC EQUATION.

Geometric variational problems. For functions J such that the value of J depends only on the image surface and not on the particular parametrization chosen (as is the case for area), there is an alternative approach. Integrands F with this property are commonly (and perversely) known as parametric integrands. Since the solution to a variational problem with a parametric integrand is really a surface and not a particular parametrization of it, it has proven fruitful to translate the problem to one of integrating over the image set and not over the parameter domain. This is the point of view adopted in geometric measure theory, a subject whose modern history dates to 1960. Written in this form, the integral has the form given in Eq. (17). Here $\vec{S}(x)$ denotes the

$$J = \int_{x \in S} F[x, \vec{S}(x)]\, d\sigma \qquad (17)$$

tangent plane to the surface S at the point x on the surface, and $d\sigma$ denotes integration over the surface (specifically, with respect to Hausdorff m-dimensional measure). For example, F is just constantly 1 for all points and all tangent plane directions when J is the area functional. The integrand F is defined to be elliptic if a piece of a plane always has uniquely (and uniformly, in a certain sense) the least integral, compared to any other surface having the same boundary. If F is elliptic, then when a minimizing surface can be written as the graph of a function, the corresponding system of Euler partial differential equations is strongly elliptic.

If integration over the image set is considered, then it makes sense to speak about minimizing integrals over possible changing surface geometries. For example, surfaces with different numbers of handles or connected components can be compared. A handle is defined topologically by the operation of cutting out two disks from a surface and gluing in a cylinder. The surface in **Fig. 3a** has no handles and more area than the surface in Fig. 3b with one handle, which in turn has more area than the surface in Fig. 3c with two handles. In Fig. 3d, e, and f, these three surfaces are deformed to show that they do have zero, one, and two handles, respectively; the cylinders (tubes) are evident in Fig. 3e and f, compared to Fig. 3d. An infinite sequence of handle additions results in a surface with infinitely many handles that is area-minimizing.

In this context, previously intractable problems, such as that of seeking area-minimizing surfaces with prescribed boundaries which are not graphs of functions, become elliptic and amenable to analysis. Some nonelliptic problems can also be handled. More elaborate problems can also be considered, such as that of finding the shape of the interface

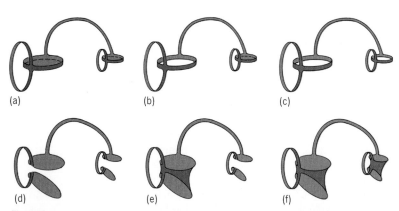

Fig. 3. Comparison of surfaces. (a) Surface with no handles. (b) Surface with one handle and less area. (c) Surface with two handles and still less area. (d, e, f) These three surfaces are deformed to show that they do have zero, one, and two handles, respectively.

between two substances of prescribed volume filling a given knobby container with tubes running through it. The three types of surface energy per unit area—that between the two fluids as well as that between each fluid and the wall of the container—must be specified, as well as the direction and magnitude of any gravitational attractions. The object here is to minimize the sum of the gravitational energy of the bulk and the integrals of the surface energies over the relevant surfaces.

Many general results on existence, regularity, singularity structure, and computation for geometric variational problems have been developed in this context. The former questions become here questions of the existence of a minimizing surface, the existence of tangent planes to the surface and their smooth variation from point to point, and the possible structures of the surface around points where tangent planes do not exist.

There are four basic classes of surfaces considered in geometric measure theory (playing the role of admissible functions above). These four classes were created in order to solve different types of problems in the calculus of variations.

1. Integral currents are most analogous to mappings; the orientation and multiplicity (number of times a point is hit in the mapping) are included in the definition, and the boundary is defined by Stokes' theorem. An appropriately bounded set of integral currents is compact, and elliptic integrands on integral currents have the lower-semicontinuity property; thus the direct method in the calculus of variations is applicable. The singular set of an m-dimensional area-minimizing integral current is known to have dimension at most $m - 2$ [dimension $m - 7$ if the area-minimizing surface happens to lie in an $(m + 1)$-dimensional space], and there are examples which have singular sets this large. Much less is known about the possible singularities in integral currents minimizing the integral of a general elliptic integrand, except that they can be much larger. See STOKES' THEOREM.

2. Flat chains modulo 2 are used for unorientable surfaces like the Möbius band; in other ways, they are similar to integral currents. See MANIFOLD (MATHEMATICS).

3. (F,ϵ,δ)-minimal sets are useful in modeling a large variety of complicated physical surfaces, such as soap bubble clusters and soap films or the total grain-boundary structure of polycrystalline materials. Neither orientation nor multiplicity is counted for these surfaces; the defining idea is that of being close to minimizing in small balls. When F is elliptic, singularities can have dimension at most $m - 1$. (The liquid edges in soap bubble clusters form singularities of dimension 1.)

4. Varifolds are quite general (all integrands are continuous on this class of surfaces) and are useful, in particular, in the consideration of infinitesimally corrugated surfaces such as the limit of the sawtooth curves discussed above or certain boundaries of crystalline grains in materials, where the surface energy is so highly anisotropic that the integrand

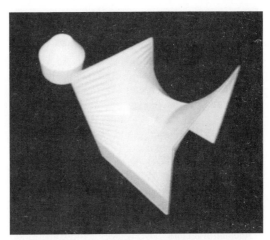

Fig. 4. Examples of surfaces minimizing the integral of a nonelliptic integrand among all bodies having the same volume (the surface at upper left) and among all surfaces having the same boundary (the saddle-shaped surface). Surfaces were computed as part of the Geometry Supercomputer Project sponsored by the National Science Foundation and the University of Minnesota.

is not elliptic. (When varifoldlike solutions arise in the context of partial differential equations, they are often referred to as Young measures.) See MINIMAL SURFACES.

Computation. Research in geometric measure theory includes developing and implementing algorithms for the computation and display of surface-energy-minimizing surfaces with a variety of constraints. The integrands (surface energies) that are considered range from the constant 1 (for area-minimizing surfaces) through other elliptic integrands to integrands that are so nonelliptic that the analog of a soap bubble is a polyhedron (**Fig. 4**).

Additional directions. When the system of Euler equations is not strongly elliptic, and the problem is one where it is not reasonable to switch to integration over the image set, some additional techniques such as compensated compactness and homogenization have been developed; they are somewhat analogous to the use of varifolds in geometric variational problems.

There is at least one variational formulation for all partial differential equations, although some variational formulations are more useful than others. In the past, it has been most useful to pass from calculus of variations problems to partial differential equations, but now it is sometimes better to travel the opposite way.   Jean E. Taylor

Bibliography. N. I. Akhiezer, *Calculus of Variations*, 1988; U. Brechtken-Menderscheid, *An Introduction to the Calculus of Variations*, 1991; F. Morgan, *Geometric Measure Theory: A Beginner's Guide*, 1988; M. Morse, *Calculus of Variations in the Large*, 8th ed., 1986, reprint 1993; B. Nicolaenko, D. D. Holm, and J. M. Hyman (eds.), *Nonlinear Systems of Partial Differential Equations in Applied Mathematics*, Lectures in Applied Mathematics, vol. 23, 1986; E. R. Pinch, *Optimal Control and the Calculus of Variations*, 1993; F. Y. Wan, *Introduction to the Calculus of Variations and Its Applications*, 1991.

Calculus of vectors

In its simplest form, a vector is a directed line segment. Physical quantities, such as velocity, acceleration, force, and displacement, are vector quantities, or simply vectors, because they can be represented by directed line segments. The algebra of vectors was initiated principally through the works of W. R. Hamilton and H. G. Grassmann in the middle of the nineteenth century, and brought to the form presented here by the efforts of O. Heaviside and J. W. Gibbs in the late nineteenth century. Vector analysis is a tool of the mathematical physicist, because many physical laws can be expressed in vector form.

Addition of vectors. Two vectors **a** and **b** are added according to the parallelogram law (**Fig. 1**). An equivalent definition is as follows: From the end point of **a**, a vector is constructed parallel to **b**, of the same magnitude and direction as **b**. The vector from the origin of **a** to the end point of **b** yields the vector sum **s** = **a** + **b** (**Fig. 2**). Any number of vectors can be added by this rule.

Given a vector **a**, a class of vectors can be formed which are parallel to **a** but of different magnitudes. If x is a real number, the vector x**a** is defined to be parallel to **a** of magnitude $|x|$ times that of **a**. For $x > 0$, the two vectors **a** and x**a** have the same sense of direction, whereas for $x < 0$ the vector x**a** is in a reverse direction from that of **a**. The vector $-$**a** is the negative of the vector **a**, such that **a** + ($-$**a**) = **0**, with **0** designated as the zero vector (a vector with zero magnitude). Subtraction of two vectors is defined by

$$\mathbf{a} - \mathbf{b} = \mathbf{a} + (-\mathbf{b})$$

The rules shown in notation (1), which conform

$$
\begin{aligned}
\mathbf{a} + \mathbf{b} &= \mathbf{b} + \mathbf{a} \\
(\mathbf{a} + \mathbf{b}) + \mathbf{c} &= \mathbf{a} + (\mathbf{b} + \mathbf{c}) \\
x(\mathbf{a} + \mathbf{b}) &= x\mathbf{a} + x\mathbf{b} \\
x(y\mathbf{a}) &= (xy)\mathbf{a} \\
(x + y)\mathbf{a} &= x\mathbf{a} + y\mathbf{a} \\
0 \cdot \mathbf{a} &= 0 \\
\mathbf{a} + 0 &= \mathbf{a} \\
\mathbf{a} + \mathbf{b} &= \mathbf{a} + \mathbf{c} \text{ implies } \mathbf{b} = \mathbf{c} \\
\mathbf{a} = \mathbf{c}, \mathbf{b} &= \mathbf{d} \text{ implies } \mathbf{a} + \mathbf{b} = \mathbf{c} + \mathbf{d}
\end{aligned}
\tag{1}
$$

$|\mathbf{a} + \mathbf{b}| \leq |\mathbf{a}| + |\mathbf{b}|$, with $|\mathbf{a}|$ = magnitude of **a**, etc.

to the rules of elementary arithmetic, can be readily deduced.

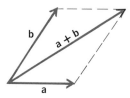

Fig. 1. Addition of two vectors.

Coordinate systems. The cartesian coordinate frame of analytic geometry is very useful for yielding a description of a vector (**Fig. 3**). The unit vectors **i**, **j**, **k** lie parallel to the positive x, y, and z axes, respectively. Any vector can be written as a linear combination of **i**, **j**, **k**. From Fig. 3, it is noted that Eq. (2) holds. Furthermore, the scalars a_x, a_y,

$$\mathbf{a} = a_x\mathbf{i} + a_y\mathbf{j} + a_z\mathbf{k} \tag{2}$$

a_z are simply the projections of **a** on the x, y, and z axes, respectively, and are designated as the components of **a**. Thus, a_x is the x component of **a**, and so on. If the vector **b** is described by $\mathbf{b} = b_x\mathbf{i} + b_y\mathbf{j} + b_z\mathbf{k}$, then Eq. (3) holds.

$$
\alpha\mathbf{a} + \beta\mathbf{b} = (\alpha a_x + \beta b_x)\mathbf{i} \\
+ (\alpha a_y + \beta y_y)\mathbf{j} + (\alpha a_z + \beta b_z)\mathbf{k} \tag{3}
$$

In general, the components of a vector will be functions of the space coordinates and the time. To be more specific, consider a fluid in motion. At any time t the particle which is located at the point $P(x,y,z)$ will have velocity components which depend on the coordinates x,y,z, as well as the time t. Thus, the velocity field **v** of the fluid is represented by Eq. (4). A steady-state vector field

$$
\mathbf{v} = v_x(x, y, z, t)\mathbf{i} + v_y(x, y, z, t)\mathbf{j} \\
+ v_z(x, y, z, t)\mathbf{k} \tag{4}
$$

exists if the components are time-independent. The force field of a fixed gravitating particle is of this type.

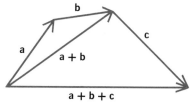

Fig. 2. Addition of three vectors.

It is not necessary to describe a vector in terms of rectangular coordinates (**Fig. 4**). Let **a** be a vector in the xy plane with origin at the point $P(x,y)$. The point P can also be described in terms of polar coordinates (r, ϕ). Let $\mathbf{u}_r$, $\mathbf{u}_\phi$ be unit vectors in the directions of increasing r and θ, respectively. From Fig. 4 it follows that Eq. (5) holds

$$\mathbf{a} = a_x\mathbf{i} + a_y\mathbf{j} = a_r\mathbf{u}_r + a_\theta\mathbf{u}_\theta \tag{5}$$

with
$$
a_r = a_x \cos\theta + a_y \sin\theta \\
a_\theta = -a_x \sin\theta + a_y \cos\theta
$$

The components a_r, a_θ yield a description of the same vector **a**. Thus coordinate systems are simply a means of describing a vector. The vector is independent of the description.

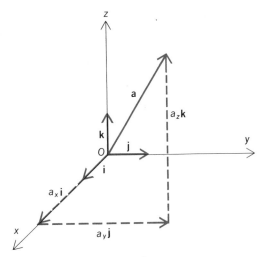

Fig. 3. Vectors in cartesian coordinate system.

Scalar or dot product of two vectors. From two vectors **a** and **b**, a scalar quantity is formed from the definition in Eq. (6), where θ is the angle between

$$\mathbf{a} \cdot \mathbf{b} = |\mathbf{a}| \cdot |\mathbf{b}| \cos \theta \qquad (6)$$

the two vectors when drawn from a common origin (**Fig. 5**). It is quickly verified that Eqs. (7) hold. Here

$$\mathbf{a} \cdot \mathbf{b} = \mathbf{b} \cdot \mathbf{a}$$
$$\mathbf{a} \cdot \mathbf{a} = |\mathbf{a}|^2$$
$$(\mathbf{a}+\mathbf{b}) \cdot (\mathbf{c}+\mathbf{d}) = \mathbf{a} \cdot \mathbf{c} + \mathbf{a} \cdot \mathbf{d} + \mathbf{b} \cdot \mathbf{c} + \mathbf{b} \cdot \mathbf{d} \qquad (7)$$
$$\mathbf{i} \cdot \mathbf{i} = \mathbf{j} \cdot \mathbf{j} = \mathbf{k} \cdot \mathbf{k} = 1$$
$$\mathbf{i} \cdot \mathbf{j} = \mathbf{j} \cdot \mathbf{k} = \mathbf{k} \cdot \mathbf{i} = 0$$

$\mathbf{a} \perp \mathbf{b}$ implies $\mathbf{a} \cdot \mathbf{b} = 0$, and conversely, provided $|\mathbf{a}| \cdot |\mathbf{b}| \neq 0$.

For $\mathbf{a} = a_x \mathbf{i} + a_y \mathbf{j} + a_z \mathbf{k}$, $\mathbf{b} = b_x \mathbf{i} + b_y \mathbf{j} + b_z \mathbf{k}$, it follows from Eqs. (7) that Eq. (8) can be written. If

$$\mathbf{a} \cdot \mathbf{b} = a_x b_x + a_y b_y + a_z b_z \qquad (8)$$

a is a force field displaced along the vector **b**, then $\mathbf{a} \cdot \mathbf{b}$ represents the work performed by this force field.

Referring to Eq. (5), let $\mathbf{b} = b_x \mathbf{i} + b_y \mathbf{j} = b_r \mathbf{u}_r + b_\theta \mathbf{u}_\theta$. Then

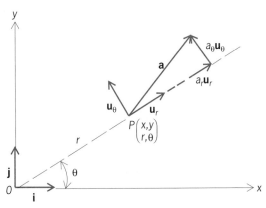

Fig. 4. Vectors in polar coordinate system.

$$\mathbf{a} \cdot \mathbf{b} = a_x b_x + a_y b_y = a_r b_r + a_\theta b_\theta$$
$$\equiv (a_x \cos\theta + a_y \sin\theta)(b_x \cos\theta + b_y \sin\theta)$$
$$+ (-a_x \sin\theta + a_y \cos\theta)$$
$$\times (-b_x \sin\theta + b_y \cos\theta)$$

Thus the scalar product of two vectors is independent of the descriptive coordinate system as is evident from the definition of the scalar product given by Eq. (6).

Vector or cross product of two vectors. In three-dimensional space, a vector can be formed from two vectors **a** and **b** in the following manner if they are nonparallel. Let **a** and **b** have a common origin defining a plane, and let **c** be that vector perpendicular to this plane of magnitude $|\mathbf{c}| = |\mathbf{a}| \, |\mathbf{b}| \sin\theta$. If **a** is rotated into **b** through the angle θ, a right-hand screw will advance in the direction of **c** (**Fig. 6**). Thus Eq. (9) can be written.

$$\mathbf{c} = \mathbf{a} \times \mathbf{b} = |\mathbf{a}| \, |\mathbf{b}| \sin\theta \, \mathbf{n} \qquad (9)$$

It follows that $\mathbf{a} \times \mathbf{b} = -(\mathbf{b} \times \mathbf{a})$, and that if **a** is parallel to **b**, $\mathbf{a} \times \mathbf{b} = \mathbf{0}$. Conversely, if $\mathbf{a} \times \mathbf{b} = \mathbf{0}$, then **a** is parallel to **b** provided $|\mathbf{a}| \, |\mathbf{b}| \neq 0$.

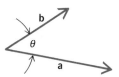

Fig. 5. Scalar product of two vectors.

The distributive law can be shown to hold for the vector product so that Eq. (10) holds.

$$(\mathbf{a}+\mathbf{b}) \times (\mathbf{c}+\mathbf{d})$$
$$= \mathbf{a} \times \mathbf{c} + \mathbf{a} \times \mathbf{d} + \mathbf{b} \times \mathbf{c} + \mathbf{b} \times \mathbf{d} \qquad (10)$$

It follows from

$$\mathbf{i} \times \mathbf{i} = \mathbf{j} \times \mathbf{j} = \mathbf{k} \times \mathbf{k} = 0$$
$$\mathbf{i} \times \mathbf{j} = \mathbf{k}, \mathbf{j} \times \mathbf{k} = \mathbf{i}, \mathbf{k} \times \mathbf{i} = \mathbf{j}$$

that for

$$\mathbf{a} = a_x \mathbf{i} + a_z \mathbf{j} + a_z \mathbf{k} \qquad \mathbf{b} = b_x \mathbf{i} + b_y \mathbf{j} + b_z \mathbf{k}$$

Eq. (11) holds. The expression in Eq. (11) is

$$\mathbf{a} \times \mathbf{b} = \begin{vmatrix} \mathbf{i} & \mathbf{j} & \mathbf{k} \\ a_x & a_y & a_z \\ b_x & b_y & b_z \end{vmatrix} \qquad (11)$$

to be expanded by the ordinary rules governing determinants.

Multiple products involving vector and scalar products can be generated. The triple scalar product $\mathbf{a} \cdot (\mathbf{b} \times \mathbf{c})$ is given by Eq. (12). It can be shown

$$\mathbf{a} \cdot (\mathbf{b} \times \mathbf{c}) = \begin{vmatrix} a_x & a_y & a_z \\ b_x & b_y & b_z \\ c_x & c_y & c_z \end{vmatrix} \qquad (12)$$

that Eq. (13) is true. Geometrically, the scalar triple

$$\mathbf{a} \cdot (\mathbf{b} \times \mathbf{c}) = (\mathbf{a} \times \mathbf{b}) \cdot \mathbf{c} \equiv (\mathbf{abc}) \qquad (13)$$

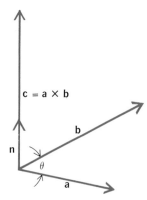

Fig. 6. Vector product of two vectors.

product represents the volume of a parallelepiped formed with **a**, **b**, **c** as coterminous sides,

$$\mathbf{V} = |\mathbf{a} \cdot (\mathbf{b} \times \mathbf{c})|$$

Of importance in the study of rigid-body motions is the triple vector product shown in Eq. (14). From Eqs. (13) and (14) follow Eqs. (15) and (16).

$$\mathbf{a} \times (\mathbf{b} \times \mathbf{c}) = (\mathbf{a} \cdot \mathbf{c})\mathbf{b} - (\mathbf{a} \cdot \mathbf{b})\mathbf{c}$$
$$(\mathbf{a} \times \mathbf{b}) \times \mathbf{c} = (\mathbf{a} \cdot \mathbf{c})\mathbf{b} - (\mathbf{b} \cdot \mathbf{c})\mathbf{a} \qquad (14)$$

$$(\mathbf{a} \times \mathbf{b}) \cdot (\mathbf{c} \times \mathbf{d}) = (\mathbf{a} \cdot [\mathbf{b} \times (\mathbf{c} \times \mathbf{d})])$$
$$= (\mathbf{a} \cdot \mathbf{c})(\mathbf{b} \cdot \mathbf{d}) - (\mathbf{a} \cdot \mathbf{d})(\mathbf{b} \cdot \mathbf{c}) \qquad (15)$$

$$(\mathbf{a} \times \mathbf{b}) \times (\mathbf{c} \times \mathbf{d}) = (\mathbf{acd})\mathbf{b} - (\mathbf{bcd})\mathbf{a}$$
$$= (\mathbf{abd})\mathbf{c} - (\mathbf{abc})\mathbf{d} \qquad (16)$$

Pseudovectors. It is easy to verify that a reflection of the space coordinates given by $x' = -x$, $y' = -y$, $z' = -z$, reverses the sign of the components of a vector. Under a space reflection, however, the components of the vector $\mathbf{a} \times \mathbf{b}$ do not change sign. This is seen from Eq. (11), for if a_x, a_y, a_z are replaced by $-a_x$, $-a_y$, $-a_z$, and if $-b_x$, $-b_y$, $-b_z$ are replaced by $-b_x$, $-b_y$, $-b_z$, the components of $\mathbf{a} \times \mathbf{b}$ remain invariant. Hence, $\mathbf{a} \times \mathbf{b}$ is not a true vector and therefore is given the title pseudovector. In electricity theory the magnetic field vector $\mathbf{B}$ is a pseudovector, whereas the electric field vector is a true vector provided the electric charge is a true scalar under a reflection of axes. Pseudovectors belong properly to the domain of the tensor calculus. In general, vectors associated with rotations belong to the category of pseudovectors. In particular, the angular velocity vector associated with the motion of a rigid body is a pseudovector. *See* TENSOR ANALYSIS.

Differentiation. There are three differentiation processes that are of conceptual value in the study of vectors; the gradient of a scalar, the divergence of a vector, and the curl of a vector.

Gradient of a scalar. The vector field **v** given by Eq. (17) has the property that the components of **v**

$$\mathbf{v} = v_1(x, y, z)\mathbf{i} + v_2(x, y, z)\mathbf{j} + v_3(x, y, z)\mathbf{k} \qquad (17)$$

differ at individual points $P(x,y,z)$. The differential change in the individual components of **v** in moving

from $P(x,y,z)$ to $Q(x + dx, y + dy, z + dz)$ is given by Eq. (18). It is suggestive to define the differential

$$dv_i = \frac{\partial v_i}{\partial x}dx + \frac{\partial v_i}{\partial y}dy + \frac{\partial v_i}{\partial z}dz \qquad (18)$$
$$i = 1, \ 2, \ 3$$

of **v** by Eq. (19), because **i**, **j**, **k** are constant vectors

$$d\mathbf{v} = dv_1\mathbf{i} + dv_2\mathbf{j} + dv_3\mathbf{k} \qquad (19)$$

(both in magnitude and direction).

If the components of a vector **v** are functions of a single parameter λ, the derivative of v with respect to λ is defined by Eq. (20).

$$\frac{d\mathbf{v}}{d\lambda} = \frac{dv_1}{d\lambda}\mathbf{i} + \frac{dv_2}{d\lambda}\mathbf{j} + \frac{dv_3}{d\lambda}\mathbf{k} \qquad (20)$$

The position vector of a particle is designated by $\mathbf{r} = x\mathbf{i} + y\mathbf{j} + z\mathbf{k}$. If the particle moves along a trajectory, the velocity and acceleration vectors associated with the motion of the particle are described by Eqs. (21).

$$\mathbf{v} = \frac{d\mathbf{r}}{dt} = \frac{dx}{dt}\mathbf{i} + \frac{dy}{dt}\mathbf{j} + \frac{dz}{dt}\mathbf{k}$$
$$\mathbf{a} = \frac{d\mathbf{v}}{dt} = \frac{d^2\mathbf{r}}{dt^2} = \frac{d^2x}{dt^2}\mathbf{i} + \frac{d^2y}{dt^2}\mathbf{j} + \frac{d^2z}{dt^2}\mathbf{k} \qquad (21)$$

The expression for the derivative of a vector described in curvilinear coordinates becomes more involved simply because the unit vectors in the curvilinear coordinate system need not remain fixed in space. Referring to Eq. (5),

$$\frac{d\mathbf{a}}{dt} = \frac{da_x}{dt}\mathbf{i} + \frac{da_y}{dt}\mathbf{j}$$
$$= \frac{da_r}{dt}\mathbf{u}_r + \frac{da_\theta}{dt}\mathbf{u}_\theta + a_r\frac{d\mathbf{u}_r}{dt} + a_\theta\frac{d\mathbf{u}_\theta}{dt}$$

From $\mathbf{u}_r = \mathbf{i}\cos\theta + \mathbf{j}\sin\theta$ and $\mathbf{u}_\theta = -\mathbf{i}\sin\theta + \mathbf{j}\cos\theta$, it follows that

$$\frac{d\mathbf{a}}{dt} = \left(\frac{da_r}{dt} - a_\theta\frac{d\theta}{dt}\right)\mathbf{u}_r + \left(\frac{da_\theta}{dt} + a_r\frac{d\theta}{dt}\right)\mathbf{u}_\theta$$

The differentiation rules shown in Eq. (22) exist.

$$\frac{d}{d\lambda}(\mathbf{u} \cdot \mathbf{u}) \cdot \frac{d\mathbf{v}}{d\lambda} + \frac{d\mathbf{u}}{d\lambda} \cdot \mathbf{v}$$
$$\frac{d}{d\lambda}(\mathbf{u} \times \mathbf{v}) = \mathbf{u} \times \frac{d\mathbf{v}}{d\lambda} + \frac{d\mathbf{u}}{d\lambda} \times \mathbf{v} \qquad (22)$$
$$\frac{d}{d\lambda}(f\mathbf{v}) = f\frac{d\mathbf{v}}{d\lambda} + \frac{df}{d\lambda}\mathbf{v}$$

From the scalar $\phi(x,y,z)$, one can form the three partial derivatives $\partial\phi/\partial x$, $\partial\phi/\partial y$, $\partial\phi/\partial z$, from which the vector in Eq. (23) can be formed. The vector,

$$\left.\begin{array}{c} \text{gradient of } \phi \\ \text{grad } \phi \\ \text{del } \phi \equiv \nabla\phi \end{array}\right\} = \frac{\partial\phi}{\partial x}\mathbf{i} + \frac{\partial\phi}{\partial y}\mathbf{j} + \frac{\partial\phi}{\partial z}\mathbf{k} \qquad (23)$$

grad ϕ, has two important properties. Grad ϕ is a vector field normal to the surface $\phi(x,y,z) =$ constant at every point of the surface. Moreover, grad ϕ yields that unique direction such that ϕ increases at its greatest rate. If $T(x,y,z)$ is the temperature at any point in space, then ∇T at any point yields that direction for which the temperature increases most rapidly. If $\phi(x,y,z)$ represents the electrostatic potential, then $\mathbf{E} = -\nabla\phi$ yields the electric field vector.

Divergence and curl of a vector. The del operator defined by Eq. (24) plays an important role in the

$$\nabla = \mathbf{i}\frac{\partial}{\partial x} + \mathbf{j}\frac{\partial}{\partial y} + \mathbf{k}\frac{\partial}{\partial z} \qquad (24)$$

development of the differential vector calculus. For the vector field of Eq. (17), the divergence of v is defined by Eq. (25). The divergence of a vector is a scalar.

$$\text{div } \mathbf{v} = \nabla \cdot \mathbf{v} = \frac{\partial v_1}{\partial x} + \frac{\partial v_2}{\partial y} + \frac{\partial v_3}{\partial z} \qquad (25)$$

If ρ is the density of a fluid and $\mathbf{v}$ the velocity field of the fluid, then div $(\rho\mathbf{v})$ represents the rate of loss of mass of fluid per unit time per unit volume. The total loss of mass of fluid per unit time for a fixed volume V is given by the volume integral of notation (26).

$$\iiint_v \text{div } (\rho\mathbf{v}) \, dz \, dy \, dx \qquad (26)$$

In electricity theory, the divergence of the displacement vector $\mathbf{D}$ is a measure of the charge density, $\nabla \cdot \mathbf{D} = \rho$.

By use of the del operator one obtains quite formally Eq. (27). The vector $\nabla \times \mathbf{v}$ is called the

$$\nabla \times \mathbf{v} = \begin{vmatrix} \mathbf{i} & \mathbf{j} & \mathbf{k} \\ \dfrac{\partial}{\partial x} & \dfrac{\partial}{\partial y} & \dfrac{\partial}{\partial z} \\ v_1 & v_2 & v_3 \end{vmatrix}$$

$$= \left(\frac{\partial v_3}{\partial y} - \frac{\partial v_2}{\partial z}\right)\mathbf{i} + \left(\frac{\partial v_1}{\partial z} - \frac{\partial v_3}{\partial x}\right)\mathbf{j}$$

$$+ \left(\frac{\partial v_2}{\partial x} - \frac{\partial v_1}{\partial y}\right)\mathbf{k} \quad (27)$$

curl of $\mathbf{v}$ (curl $\mathbf{v}$). Under a reflection of space coordinates, $\partial v_3/\partial y \to \partial(-v_3)/\partial(-y) = \partial v_3/y$ the curl of $\mathbf{v}$ is a pseudovector. As has been noted previously, the class of pseudovectors is associated with rotations in space; thus, it is not strange that the curl of a velocity field is closely associated with an angular velocity vector field. The velocity of a fluid at a point $Q(x + dx, y + dy, z + dz)$ near $P(x,y,z)$ can be characterized as shown in Eq. (28), where $\mathbf{r}$ is the vector from P to Q and Eq. (29)

$$\mathbf{v}_Q = \mathbf{v}_P + \frac{1}{2}(\nabla \times \mathbf{v})_P \times \mathbf{r} + \frac{1}{2}\nabla(\mathbf{r} \cdot \mathbf{w}) \quad (28)$$

$$\mathbf{w} = [(\mathbf{r} \cdot \nabla)\mathbf{v}]_P = \left(x\frac{\partial \mathbf{v}}{\partial x} + y\frac{\partial \mathbf{v}}{\partial y} + z\frac{\partial \mathbf{v}}{\partial z}\right)_P \quad (29)$$

holds. Now in general, $\boldsymbol{\omega} \times \mathbf{r}$ is the velocity of a point due to the angular velocity $\boldsymbol{\omega}$; thus, $\nabla \times \mathbf{v} = 2\boldsymbol{\omega}$. The velocity at Q is simply the sum of a translatory velocity $\mathbf{v}_P$ plus a rigid-body rotational

velocity $\boldsymbol{\omega} \times \mathbf{r}$, plus a nonrigid-body deformation, $\frac{1}{2}\nabla(\mathbf{r} \cdot \mathbf{w})$.

Formulas involving gradient, divergence, curl.

1. $\nabla(uv) = u\nabla v + v\nabla u$
2. $\nabla \cdot (\phi\mathbf{v}) = \phi\nabla \cdot \mathbf{v} + (\nabla\phi) \cdot \mathbf{v}$
3. $\nabla \times (\nabla\phi) = \mathbf{0}$
4. $\nabla \cdot (\nabla \times \mathbf{v}) = 0$
5. $\nabla \times (\phi\mathbf{v}) = \phi\nabla \times \mathbf{v} + (\nabla\phi) \times \mathbf{v}$
6. $\nabla \cdot (\mathbf{u} \times \mathbf{v}) = (\nabla \times \mathbf{u}) \cdot \mathbf{v} - (\nabla \times \mathbf{v}) \cdot \mathbf{u}$
7. $\nabla \times (\mathbf{u} \times \mathbf{v}) = (\mathbf{v} \cdot \nabla)\mathbf{u} - \mathbf{v}(\nabla \cdot \mathbf{u})$
   $\qquad\qquad + \mathbf{u}(\nabla \cdot \mathbf{v}) - (\mathbf{u} \cdot \nabla)\mathbf{v}$
8. $\nabla(\mathbf{u} \cdot \mathbf{v}) = \mathbf{u} \times (\nabla \times \mathbf{v}) + \mathbf{v} \times (\nabla \times \mathbf{u})$
   $\qquad\qquad + (\mathbf{u} \cdot \nabla)\mathbf{v} + (\mathbf{v} \cdot \nabla)\mathbf{u}$
9. $\nabla \times (\nabla \times \mathbf{v}) = \nabla(\nabla \cdot \mathbf{v}) - \nabla^2\mathbf{v}$
10. $d\phi = d\mathbf{r} \cdot \nabla\phi + \partial\phi/\partial t \, dt$ for $\phi = \phi(x,y,z,t,)$
11. $\nabla \cdot (\nabla\phi) \equiv \nabla^2\phi = \partial^2\phi/\partial x^2 + \partial^2\phi/\partial y^2$
12. If $\nabla \cdot \mathbf{f} = 0$, then $\mathbf{f} = \nabla \times \mathbf{A}$ ($\mathbf{A}$ is called the vector potential)
13. If $\nabla \times \mathbf{f} = \mathbf{0}$, then $\mathbf{f} = \nabla\phi$ (ϕ is called the scalar potential)

Integration. If a closed surface is decomposed into a large number of small surfaces, a vector field normal to the surface can be constructed, each normal element being represented by $d\boldsymbol{\sigma}$. The magnitude of $d\boldsymbol{\sigma}$ is the area of the surface element dS, $d\boldsymbol{\sigma} = \mathbf{N}\, dS$.

If $\mathbf{f}$ is a vector field defined at every point of the surface, then notation (30) represents the total flux

$$\iint_S \mathbf{f} \cdot d\boldsymbol{\sigma} \qquad (30)$$

of $\mathbf{f}$ through the surface S. The elements $d\sigma$ point outward from the interior of S.

The divergence theorem of Gauss states that Eq. (31) is true, where R is the region enclosed by S, $d\tau$

$$\iint_S \mathbf{f} \cdot d\sigma = \iiint_R (\nabla \cdot \mathbf{f}) \, d\tau \qquad (31)$$

a volume element of R. For $\mathbf{f} = \rho\mathbf{v}$, the divergence theorem states that the net loss of fluid per unit time can be accounted for by measuring the total outward flux of the vector $\rho\mathbf{v}$ through the closed surface S bounding R. See GAUSS' THEOREM.

The line integral of a vector field is described as follows: Let Γ be a space curve, and let $\mathbf{t}$ be the unit vector field tangent to Γ at every point of Γ in progressing from A to B, the initial and end points of the trajectory Γ.

The scalar integral in notation (32) is called the

$$\int_A^B (\mathbf{f} \cdot \mathbf{t}) \, ds \qquad (32)$$

line integral of $\mathbf{f}$ along Γ, with arc length s measured along Γ. If $\mathbf{f}$ is a force field, notation (32) represents the work performed by the force field if a unit test particle is taken from A to B along Γ.

The value of the integral of notation (32) will generally depend on the path from A to B. However, if $\mathbf{f} = \nabla\phi$, then

$$\int_A^B (\mathbf{f} \cdot \mathbf{t})\, ds = \int_A^B \nabla \phi \cdot d\mathbf{r}$$

$$= \int_A^B d\phi = \phi(B) - \phi(A)$$

and the line integral is independent of the path of integration.

The theorem of Stokes states that Eq. (33) holds,

$$\oint_\Gamma \mathbf{f} \cdot d\mathbf{r} = \int\!\!\int_S (\nabla \times \mathbf{f}) \cdot d\boldsymbol{\sigma} \qquad (33)$$

where Γ is the boundary of the open surface S. If S is a closed surface, then

$$\oiint_S (\nabla \times \mathbf{f}) \cdot d\boldsymbol{\sigma} = 0$$

In electricity theory, a time-changing magnetic flux through an open surface induces a voltage in the boundary of the surface, so that

$$-\frac{\partial}{\partial t} \int\!\!\int_S \mathbf{B} \cdot d\boldsymbol{\sigma} = \oint_\Gamma \mathbf{E} \cdot d\mathbf{r}$$

Applying Stokes' theorem yields one of Maxwell's equations,

$$\nabla \times \mathbf{E} = -\frac{\partial \mathbf{B}}{\partial t}$$

See OPERATOR THEORY; POTENTIALS.   Harry Lass

Bibliography. P. Baxandall and H. Liebeck, *Vector Calculus*, 1987; D. Bourne and P. C. Kendall, *Vector Analysis and Cartesian Tensors*, 3d ed., 1992; B. Davis, H. Porta, and J. J. Uhl, *Vector Calculus: Measuring in Two and Three Dimensions*, 1994; H. F. Davis and A. D. Snider, *Introduction to Vector Analysis*, 6th ed., 1991; P. C. DuChateau, *Vector Analysis*, 1993; J. E. Marsden and A. J. Tromba, *Vector Calculus*, 3d ed., 1988; E. C. Young, *Vector and Tensor Analysis*, 1992.

Caldera

A large volcanic collapse depression, typically circular to slightly elongate in shape, the dimensions of which are many times greater than any included vent (**Figs. 1** and **2**). Calderas range from a few miles to 37 mi (60 km) in diameter. A caldera may resemble a volcanic crater in form, but differs genetically in that it is a collapse rather than a constructional feature. The topographic depression resulting from collapse is commonly widened by slumping of the sides along concentric faults, so that the topographic crater wall lies outside the caldera wall. A caldera may include vents formed by postcollapse volcanism. The term caldera comes from the Portuguese *caldeira* or Spanish *caldera*, meaning caldron or kettle. As originally defined, the term caldron referred to volcanic subsidence structures, and caldera referred only to the topographic depression formed at the surface by collapse. However, the term caldera is now common as a synonym for caldron, denoting all features of collapse, both topographic and structural. Caldera may also refer to a depression resulting from explosive removal of the upper part of a volcanic cone (explosion calderas) or from erosion of a volcanic cone (erosion caldera), but these usages are no longer favored. *See* PETROLOGY.

Occurrence. Calderas occur primarily in three different volcanic settings, each of which affects their shape and evolution: basaltic shield cones, stratovolcanoes, and volcanic centers consisting of preexisting clusters of volcanoes. These last calderas, associated with broad, large-volume andesitic to rhyolitic ignimbrite sheets, are generally the largest and most impressive, and are those generally denoted by the term. Calderas have been formed throughout much of the Earth's history, ranging in age from Precambrian (greater than 1.4 billion years old) to Holocene (for example, Krakatau in Indonesia, which erupted in 1883). *See* RHYOLITE; VOLCANO.

In regions of recurrent, shallow magmatic activity giving rise to large volcanic fields, numerous calderas may be partially or entirely superimposed upon each other. In the San Juan volcanic field of Colorado, an area which has been of seminal importance in understanding the features and significance of calderas, 17 of them occur, many of which partially overlap each other (**Fig. 3**). Valles caldera in the Jemez volcanic field of New Mexico (Figs. 1 and 2) is almost perfectly confocal with the Toledo caldera, which formed 330,000 years earlier. The Toledo caldera is recognized only by its ignimbrite sheet and by several postcollapse rhyolite domes lying slightly outside the ring fracture associated with the Valles caldera. These two calderas represent multiple collapses of a single caldera.

In addition to Earth, large calderas occur on Mars, Venus, and Jupiter's moon Io. The presence of calderas on four solar system bodies indicates that the underlying mechanisms of shallow intrusion and caldera collapse are basic processes in planetary geology. *See* MAGMA.

Collapse. Collapse occurs because of withdrawal of magma from an underlying chamber some 2.4–3.6 mi (4–6 km) beneath the surface, resulting in foundering of the roof into the chamber. Withdrawal of magma may occur either by relatively passive eruption of lavas, as in the case of calderas formed on basaltic shield cones, or by catastrophic eruption of pyroclastic material, as accompanies formation of the largest calderas. Eruption of small volumes (no more than 0.24 mi^3 or 1 km^3) of pyroclastic rock, such as was observed in historical times, does not necessarily involve caldera collapse. Formation of calderas typically begins with pyroclastic eruptions of 6–12 mi^3 (25–50 km^3) volume. In this range, collapse may result in incomplete, hinged caldera subsidence or structural sags, or may even occur piecemeal. Some small calderas collapse late during the associated pyroclastic eruptions. Larger systems are bounded by complete ring faults; subsidence may be pistonlike or asymmetric (trapdoor). Subsidence begins after partial evacuation of the magma chamber, occurring during, not after, eruption. Eruption of larger volumes of pyroclastic material appears always to be associated with caldera collapse, since roofs of such large chambers cannot support themselves. Collapse occurs along vertical or steeply inward-dipping ring faults or zones of ring faults. The area of caldera collapse is roughly proportional to the volume of erupted material. Following collapse, the caldera may be a closed sedimentary basin. With appropriate meteorological conditions, a lake will form (for example, Crater Lake in Oregon, a caldera formed on the site of a former volcanic area, Mount Mazama).

Pyroclastic eruption. Caldera-forming eruptions probably last only a few hours or days. Eruption of pyroclastic material begins as gases (predominantly water) that are dissolved in the magma come out of solution at shallow depths. Magma is explosively fragmented into particles ranging in size from micrometers to meters. An eruption column develops, rising several miles into the atmosphere. This first and most explosive phase of the eruption, known as the Plinian phase, covers the area around the vent with pumice. The Plinian phase erupts from a single conduit or from a group of closely spaced conduits. Caldera subsidence occurs during eruption, as shown by the thick wedge of ignimbrite (up to 3 mi or 5 km; **Fig. 4**) within calderas, and probably begins after about 20% of the total volume of associated pyroclastic material has been erupted. The thickness of intracaldera tuff typically is much greater than that of the corresponding outflow sheets. Evidence for intermittent collapse is provided by landslide deposits, formed by the caving inward of the steep, unstable walls, that interfinger with pyroclastic rocks within the caldera, and by the presence of individual cooling units in the tuffs.

As caldera subsidence proceeds and eruption becomes less explosive, the Plinian eruption column collapses. This collapse produces pyroclastic flows made of volcanic particles buoyed up and fluidized by hot gases (**Fig. 5**). These hot, ground-hugging pyroclastic flows can travel as far as 93 mi (150 km) outward from the vent at speeds of 330 ft/s (100 m/s). Successive collapses of the column produce multiple flow units with an aggregate thickness that may be several hundreds of feet thick near the caldera. Ignimbrites may be erupted from multiple vents distributed around the ring fracture, but there may be a complex shift in vent geometry during caldera collapse. The ash and pumice of these ignimbrites are compacted, and individual particles are welded together by the intense heat (932–1112°F or 500–600°C) of the trapped gases.

Postcollapse volcanism. Volcanism may resume following caldera collapse and cessation of the

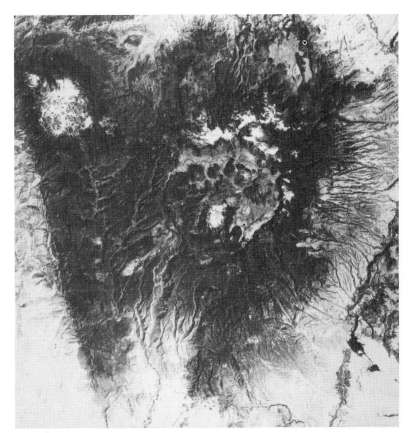

Fig. 1. Landsat Thematic Mapper image (bands 1, 3, and 4) of Valles caldera in the Jemez volcanic field of New Mexico. Note resurgent dome (Redondo Peak) with an axial graben near the center of the caldera, and a concentric pattern of ring domes surrounding the resurgent dome. Diameter of the topographic depression is about 13 mi (21 km). (*H. Foote, Battelle–Pacific Northwest Laboratories*)

massive pyroclastic eruptions. This phase of activity is predominantly passive because the remaining magma is depleted in volatile components. Eruptive activity may begin shortly after caldera collapse and continue intermittently for millions of years. Eruptions may occur from vents within the caldera. Most prominent, however, are the eruptions of lava domes and flows from a series of vents along the ring fractures. These probably mark the intrusion of a ring dike, a feature exposed in eroded

Fig. 2. Computer-generated image of Valles caldera, as viewed obliquely toward the southwest. (*Produced from digital elevation data by H. Foote, Battelle–Pacific Northwest Laboratories*)

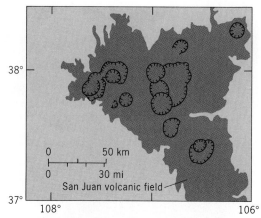

Fig. 3. Oligocene San Juan volcanic field, showing overlapping calderas. (*After P. W. Lipman, The roots of ash flow calderas in western North America: Windows into the tops of granitic batholiths, J. Geophys. Res. 89:8801–8841, 1984*)

calderas or in subvolcanic igneous centers such as the Mesozoic White Mountains (New Hampshire) and the Permian Oslo graben (Norway). In Valles caldera (Figs. 1 and 2), eight domes (up to 2300 ft or 700 m thick) and an obsidian flow were erupted in an approximately counterclockwise sequence along the main ring fracture from 1,000,000 to about 300,000 years ago. *See* GRABEN; OBSIDIAN.

Resurgence. The floors of many of the largest calderas (typically those with diameters exceeding 6 mi or 10 km) have been domed upward, resulting in a central massif or resurgent dome. Uplift, which probably occurs intermittently over a period of thousands of years, may exceed 0.6 mi (1 km). Resurgence is not a simple, pistonlike rise of the caldera floor along the ring faults. Rather, the caldera floor may be forced upward so that geological units constituting the caldera

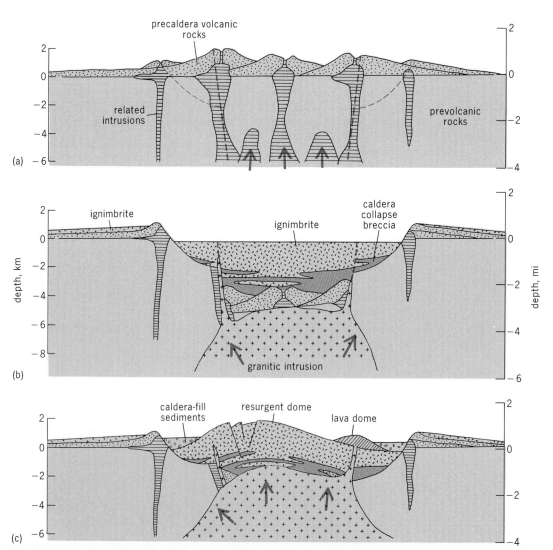

Fig. 4. Generalized evolution of a caldera associated with a pyroclastic eruption. (*a*) Precollapse volcanism. Isolated, small plutons move upward to accumulate into a single large magma chamber. Incipient ring faults are indicated by heavy broken lines, site of subsequent caldera collapse by light broken lines. (*b*) Caldera geometry just after pyroclastic eruptions and concurrent caldera collapse. Collapse along the ring faults is followed by slumping of the oversteepened walls. (*c*) Resurgence and postcaldera deposition. Magma body has risen and intrudes intracaldera ignimbrite and breccia. Sediments and lava domes partly fill the caldera. (*After P. W. Lipman, The roots of ash flow calderas in western North America: Windows into the tops of granitic batholiths, J. Geophys. Res., 89:8801–8841, 1984*)

Fig. 5. Pyroclastic flows from the eruption that accompanied collapse of the Crater Lake caldera in Oregon.

example of resurgence (Fig. 2). During uplift of the resurgent dome (Redondo Peak) of Valles caldera, somewhat elongated in shape, the upper portion of the dome was subjected to extension, resulting in formation of an axial graben. However, resurgence is not always so symmetrical, and it may instead cause broad uplift of adjacent areas of the volcanic field. The intrusions responsible for resurgence are exposed in the centers of deeply eroded calderas.

Geothermal systems. Calderas typically contain or are associated with extensive hydrothermal systems, because of two factors: (1) the shallow magma chambers that underlie them provide a readily available source of heat; and (2) the floors of calderas may be extensively fractured, which, along with the main ring faults, allows meteoric water to penetrate deeply into the crust beneath calderas. Hydrothermal activity related to a caldera system can occur any time after magmas rise to shallow crustal levels, but it is dominant late in caldera evolution. In young calderas, such as those of the Yellowstone Plateau and the Valles caldera, hydrothermal systems are still active and may be a source of commercial power. The spectacular geysers, hot springs, and boiling mud pots of Yellowstone National Park are part of the hydrothermal system associated with a series of three overlapping, young calderas.

Much of the high heat flow in calderas is conductive; convective heat transfer occurs mostly along fault zones. Magma bodies beneath large calderas cool slowly and may be important heat sources for as long as 2,000,000 years following collapse. The hydrothermal system within Valles caldera (**Fig. 6**) is one of the best-studied systems

fill—typically ignimbrites and possibly lake beds—have steep dips, often exceeding 45°, away from a central point or axis. Resurgence results from the continued or renewed buoyant rise of magma after collapse. Valles caldera, where the details of uplift and doming have been well studied, is a typical

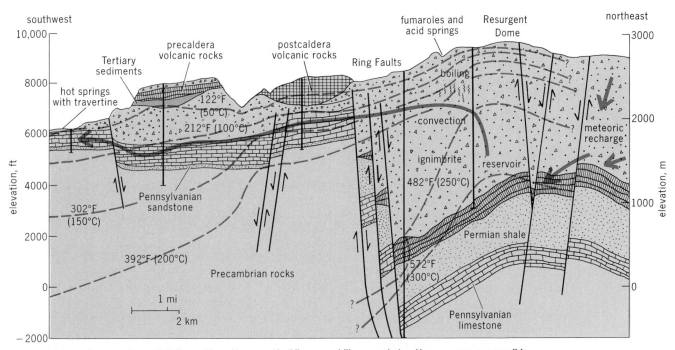

Fig. 6. Hydrothermal system beneath Valles caldera. Heavy vertical lines are drill or core holes. Heavy arrows are possible paths of thermal fluid flow. (*After F. Goff et al., The hydrothermal outflow plume of Valles caldera, New Mexico, and a comparison with other outflow plumes, J. Geophys. Res., 93:6041–6058, 1988*)

in the world, largely because of extensive drilling to explore for potentially commercial quantities of geothermal energy. In this system, meteoric water percolates to a depth of 1.2–1.9 mi (2–3 km) in caldera-fill ignimbrites and precaldera volcanic rocks, where it is heated to temperatures of about 572°F (300°C). The heated water then rises convectively to depths of approximately 1640–1968 ft (500–600 m) before flowing laterally southwestward toward the caldera wall. A boiling interface at about 392°F (200°C) marks the upper surface of a convecting liquid-dominated system. Above this interface is a vapor-dominated zone containing steam, carbon dioxide (CO_2), hydrogen sulfide (H_2S), and other volatile components. Acid springs, mud pots, and fumaroles occur in a surface condensation zone a few feet thick. The present (post–Valles caldera) hydrothermal system was probably initiated about 1,000,000 years ago, immediately after caldera collapse.

Mineralization. Many metals, including such base and precious metals as molybdenum, copper, lead, zinc, silver, gold, mercury, uranium, tungsten, and antimony, are mobile in hydrothermal circulation systems driven by the shallow intrusions which underlie and give rise to large calderas. Many economically important ore deposits in the western United States lie within calderas. The relationship of caldera collapse to mineralization is, however, complex. Many mineral deposits are related to precaldera volcanism, and others to activity which significantly postdates collapse (in some places by millions of years) that is simply localized by caldera structures. Deep core holes within Valles caldera indicate that mineralization is presently occurring there. *See* ORE AND MINERAL DEPOSITS.

Consequences of eruption. Large pyroclastic eruptions associated with such giant (6 mi or 10 km or more in diameter), young calderas as Yellowstone, Long Valley (California), and Valles, are, with the exception of impacts of large meteorites or asteroids, the most violent geological phenomena on Earth. In human terms, eruptions of this magnitude are rare. No giant calderas have occurred in historical times, and probably no more than 10 have occurred worldwide in the last 1,000,000 years. However, formation of smaller calderas, such as Tambora (Indonesia) in 1815 and Krakatau 1883, affirms that such an eruption would have catastrophic effect on human life, both regionally and globally, with enormous economic and political consequences. A large area of land would collapse; additional huge areas, the exact amount depending on the details of topography, size of the eruption, and prevailing wind, would be covered by pyroclastic flows and ash. Large volumes of dust and aerosols would be injected into the stratosphere. The resulting cooling could disrupt agriculture worldwide, possibly for years.   W. Scott Baldridge

Bibliography. P. Francis, Giant volcanic calderas, *Sci. Amer.*, 248(6):60–70, 1983; P. W. Lipman, S. Self, and G. Heiken (eds.), Calderas and associated igneous rocks, *J. Geophys. Res.*, 89:8219–8841, 1984; K. Wohletz and G. Heiken, *Volcanology and Geothermal Energy*, 1992.

Calendar

A list, usually in the form of a table, showing the correspondence between days of the week and days of the month; also, a list of special observances with their dates, especially those that fall on different dates in different years, as a church calendar; also, a set of rules that serves to attach to any day a specific number or name or combination of number and name. The calendars used at various times and places are numerous and diverse. Most represent attempts to divide the synodic month or the tropical year into numbered days. According to whether the emphasis is on month or year, calendars are called lunar or solar.

Gregorian calendar. The calendar used for civil purposes throughout the world, known in Western countries as the Gregorian calendar, was established by Pope Gregory XIII, who decreed that the day following Thursday, October 4, 1582, should be Friday, October 15, 1582, and that thereafter centennial years (1600, 1700, and so on) should be leap years only when divisible by 400 (1600, 2000, and so on), other years being leap years when divisible by four, as previously. The effect of the reform was to restore the vernal equinox (beginning of spring, which governs the observance of Easter) to March 21, and to reduce the number of days in 400 calendar years by 3, making the average number of days in the calendar year 365.2425, instead of 365.24220 days. The new calendar was adopted by Great Britain in 1752, but did not become universal until well into the twentieth century.

Although the Gregorian calendar is a solar calendar, lunar vestiges remain in it, as is shown by the division of the year into months. The week is independent of any astronomical phenomenon; it was established before the beginning of the Christian Era, and the cyclical succession of the days of the week has not since been disturbed. The connection between the week and the ancient Jewish cycle of seven days has not been established; for example, it is not known whether the modern Saturday is identical with the ancient seventh day.

The calendar generally used before the adoption of the Gregorian calendar is called the Julian calendar; their relationship is shown in the **table**. Dates recorded for civil and commercial purposes before October 4, 1582, may be assumed to be in the Julian calendar, but dates recorded since then may require considerable care in interpretation.

Calendar reform. The Gregorian calendar is not perfectly adjusted to the tropical year, the error accumulating to 1 day after about 3300 years. Numerous proposals for calendar reform have been made with the object of reducing the error, and there have also been many proposals for altering

Perpetual calendar*

Day of the week for any known date from the beginning of the Christian Era to the year 2400

		Julian calendar								Gregorian calendar			
Century:	0†	0‡ 700 1400	100 800 1500¶	200 900	300 1000	400 1100	500 1200	600 1300	1600 2000	1700 2100	1800 2200	1500§ 1900 2300
Year												
0	...	DC	ED	FE	GF	AG	BA	CB	BA	C	E	G
1 29 57 85	A	B	C	D	E	F	G	A	G	B	D	F
2 30 58 86	G	A	B	C	D	E	F	G	F	A	C	E
3 31 59 87	F	G	A	B	C	D	E	F	E	G	B	D
4 32 60 88	E	FE	GF	AG	BA	CB	DC	ED	DC	FE	AG	CB
5 33 61 89	...	D	E	F	G	A	B	C	B	D	F	A
6 34 62 90	...	C	D	E	F	G	A	B	A	C	E	G
7 35 63 91	...	B	C	D	E	F	G	A	G	B	D	F
8 36 64 92	...	AG	BA	CB	DC	ED	FE	GF	FE	AG	CB	ED
9 37 65 93	...	F	G	A	B	C	D	E	D	F	A	C
10 38 66 94	...	E	F	G	A	B	C	D	C	E	G	B
11 39 67 95	...	D	E	F	G	A	B	C	B	D	F	A
12 40 68 96	...	CB	DC	ED	FE	GF	AG	BA	AG	CB	ED	GF
13 41 69 97	...	A	B	C	D	E	F	G	F	A	C	E
14 42 70 98	...	G	A	B	C	D	E	F	E	G	B	D
15 43 71 99	...	F	G	A	B	C	D	E	D	F	A	C
16 44 72	...	ED	FE	GF	AG	BA	CB	DC	CB	ED	GF	BA
17 45 73	...	C	D	E	F	G	A	B	A	C	E	G
18 46 74	...	B	C	D	E	F	G	A	G	B	D	F
19 47 75	...	A	B	C	D	E	F	G	F	A	C	E
20 48 76	...	GF	AG	BA	CB	DC	ED	FE	ED	GF	BA	DC
21 49 77	...	E	F	G	A	B	C	D	C	E	G	B
22 50 78	...	D	E	F	G	A	B	C	B	D	F	A
23 51 79	...	C	D	E	F	G	A	B	A	C	E	G
24 52 80	...	BA	CB	DC	ED	FE	GF	AG	GF	BA	DC	FE
25 53 81	...	G	A	B	C	D	E	F	E	G	B	D
26 54 82	...	F	G	A	B	C	D	E	D	F	A	C
27 55 83	...	E	F	G	A	B	C	D	C	E	G	B
28 56 84	...	DC	ED	FE	GF	AG	BA	CB	BA	DC	FE	AG

Month	Dominical letter						
Jan., Oct.	A	B	C	D	E	F	G
Feb., Mar., Nov.	D	E	F	G	A	B	C
Apr., July	G	A	B	C	D	E	F
May	B	C	D	E	F	G	A
June	E	F	G.	A	B	C	D
Aug.	C	D	E	F	G	A	B
Sept., Dec.	F	G	A	B	C	D	E

1	8	15	22	29	Sun.	Sat.	Fri.	Thurs.	Wed.	Tues.	Mon.
2	9	16	23	30	Mon.	Sun.	Sat.	Fri.	Thurs.	Wed.	Tues.
3	10	17	24	31	Tues.	Mon.	Sun.	Sat.	Fri.	Thurs.	Wed.
4	11	18	25		Wed.	Tues.	Mon.	Sun.	Sat.	Fri.	Thurs.
5	12	19	26		Thurs.	Wed.	Tues.	Mon.	Sun.	Sat.	Fri.
6	13	20	27		Fri.	Thurs.	Wed.	Tues.	Mon.	Sun.	Sat.
7	14	21	28		Sat.	Fri.	Thurs.	Wed.	Tues.	Mon.	Sun.
											Mon.

To find the calendar for any year of the Christian Era, first find the Dominical letter for the year in the upper section of the table. Two letters are given for leap years; the first is to be used with January and February, the second for the other months. In the lower section of the table, find the column in which the Dominical letter for the same line with the month for which the calendar is desired; this column gives the days of the week that are to be used with the month. For example, in the table of Dominical letters the letter for 1962 is G; in the line with July, this letter occurs in the first column; hence July 4, 1962, is Wednesday.

*After *Smithsonian Physical Tables*, 9th ed., Washington, D.C., 1954.
†A.D. 1 through A.D. 4 only.
‡A.D. 5 through A.D. 99 only.
§On and after 1582, October 15 only.
¶On and before 1582, October 4 only.

the succession of days for the purpose of bringing greater regularity into the calendar. For example, one proposal would divide the year into 13 months of 4 weeks each, which would make 364 days. The 365th day, and the 366th in leap years, would have a special name and would not belong to any month or to any week. Thus, every month of every year would begin on Sunday and end with Saturday, and annual calendars would become unnecessary. The 13-month calendar has the disadvantage, serious from the standpoint of business, of not being divisible into quarters. Another proposal, which overcomes this difficulty, retains 12 months but would give them successively 31, 30, 30, 31, 30,

30, 31, 30, 30, 31, 30, 30 days, the extra day or days again being outside the system. No attempt to regularize the calendar can succeed if the succession of week days and the average length of the calendar year are both preserved. *See* DAY; MONTH; TIME; YEAR.   Gerald M. Clemence

Bibliography. E. Achelis, *The Calendar for Everybody*, 1943, reprint 1990; H. J. Cowan, *Time and Its Measurement: From the Stone Age to the Nuclear Age*, 1958; W. M. O'Neil, *Time and the Calendars*, rev. ed., 1978.

Calibration

The process of determining the performance parameters of an artifact, instrument, or system by comparing it with measurement standards. Adjustment may be a part of a calibration, but not necessarily.

All calibrations involve one or more measurement processes, which may be simple or complex. A calibration assures that a device or system will produce results which meet or exceed some defined criteria with a specified degree of confidence. The measurement standards, the process, and the device or system being calibrated must all be capable of satisfying these defined criteria.

Two important measurement concepts related to calibration are precision and accuracy. Precision refers to the minimum discernible change in the parameter being measured, while accuracy refers to the actual amount of error that exists in a calibration.

All measurement processes used for calibration are subject to various sources of error. It is common practice to classify them as random or systematic errors. When a measurement is repeated many times, the results will exhibit random statistical fluctuations which may or may not be significant. Indeed, under some conditions, they may not even be noticeable. Systematic errors are offsets from the true value of a parameter and, if they are known, corrections are generally applied, eliminating their effect on the calibration. If they are not known, they can have an adverse effect on the accuracy of the calibration. High-accuracy calibrations are usually accompanied by an analysis of the sources of error and a statement of the uncertainty of the calibration. Uncertainty indicates how much the accuracy of a calibration could be degraded as a result of the combined errors. Experts in metrology, the science of measurement, are not always in agreement as to how to combine the errors due to various sources in order to arrive at an overall uncertainty. *See* ANALYSIS OF VARIANCE; DISTRIBUTION (PROBABILITY); INSTRUMENT SCIENCE; PHYSICAL MEASUREMENT; PROBABILITY; PROBABILITY (PHYSICS); STATISTICS.   Bill Bruce

Bibliography. C. Eisenhart, Realistic evaluation of the precision and accuracy of instrument calibration systems, *J. Res. Nat. Bur. Stand.*, 67C(2):161–187, April-June 1963; J. M. Juran, F. M. Gryna, Jr., and R. S. Bingham, Jr., *Juran's Quality Control Handbook*, 4th ed., 1988.

Caliche

A soil that is mineralogically an impure limestone. Such soils are also known as duricrust, kunkar, nari, kafkalla, Omdurman lime, croute, and race. Many soil profiles in semiarid climates (that is, those characterized by a rainfall of 4–20 in. or 10–50 cm per year) contain concentrations of calcium carbonate ($CaCO_3$). This calcium carbonate is not an original feature of the soils but has been added to the C horizon during soil formation either by direct precipitation in soil pores or by replacement of preexisting material. Fossil analogs of caliche, which are widely reported in ancient sedimentary sequences, are referred to as calcrete or cornstone. *See* LIMESTONE.

Formation. The principal control on the formation of caliche is a hydrologic regime in which there is sufficient moisture to introduce calcium carbonate in solution to the soil but not enough to leach it through the system. As a result, calcium carbonate precipitates in the soil during periods of evaporation, and it will slowly increase in amount as long as the hydrologic setting remains stable. The source of the carbonate may be from the dissolution of adjacent limestones, from the hydrolysis of plagioclase and other silicates, or from carbonate loess.

Within the climatic constraints noted above, most caliche forms in river floodplains and near the surface of alluvial fans. In addition, caliche deposits may form within exposed marine and lacustrine limestones during periods of sea-level fall or lake desiccation. Caliche may also form at inert pediment (eroded rock) surfaces; in the geological record such surfaces will be seen as unconformities. In this context it is interesting that the first unconformity ever recognized as such, by James Hutton in 1787 on the Isle of Arran, western Scotland, is characterized by a development of caliche. *See* UNCONFORMITY.

The mineralogy of the host soil or rock in which a caliche develops may vary considerably; it is not essential for there to be any preexisting carbonate grains within the regolith. The most favorable medium is a clay-rich soil of limited permeability. Low permeability provides the residence time in the soil pores necessary for calcite to precipitate. *See* CALCITE; REGOLITH.

Textures. A variety of textures records the growth of the calcrete. Initially, small nodules of limestone nucleate within the soil; these nodules are usually roughly spherical but may form as elongate tubules and filaments. The latter probably form as casts around roots in the soil. Subsequently, nodules coalesce to form an increasingly solid mass of carbonate, and as a result the soil becomes

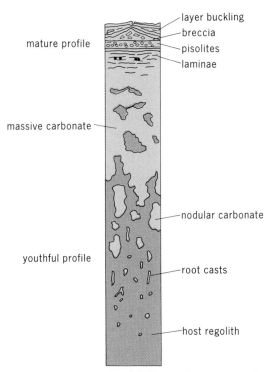

mature profile
— layer buckling
— breccia
— pisolites
— laminae

massive carbonate

nodular carbonate

youthful profile

root casts

host regolith

Typical profie through a mature caliche. The lower part of the profile is essentially a mimic of a juvenile caliche.

increasingly rocklike. Eventually the soil profile may become plugged by a massive impermeable limestone. Above the plugged horizon a perched aquifer develops; further calcite precipitation above such a horizon may produce laminated and pisolitic deposits. Continued addition of calcite may result in the buckling and brecciation of laminae. Deoxygenated conditions may develop below the plugged zone; in the reducing environment so formed, elements held in solution in oxygenated waters may precipitate (for example, uranium). *See* OOLITE.

Microscopic fabrics in caliche are initially very fine-grained mosaics of nonferroan low-magnesian calcite crystals. However, more complicated fabrics develop as the paleosol matures. Repeated wetting and drying of the soil results in expansion and contraction of the soil; as a result nodules frequently show signs of multiple cracking. Typically these cracks have been healed because of the precipitation of coarse drusy calcite. This later calcite may be ferroan, that is, may contain some iron. Non-carbonate grains in the caliche usually show signs of intense chemical corrosion and may show signs of physical displacement by precipitating calcite crystals. During the mature stage of development, highly alkaline conditions may develop in caliches. In such conditions quartz in the soil profile may temporarily pass into solution and subsequently re-precipitate as chert, forming a silcrete. *See* CHERT; PALEOSOL.

Mature profile. When the full range of textures referred to above is developed, the caliche is regarded as a mature profile. The vertical profile

of such a caliche (see **illus.**) shows a characteristic sequence passing downward from a laminated carbonate into a massive limestone, which in turn passes into increasingly more disconnected nodules. Thus the vertical profile recapitulates the growth of the caliche.

Fully mature caliche profiles may be up to 40 ft (12 m) thick, although 10–20 ft (3–6 m) is more typical. Various workers have tried to estimate the length of time required for the development of a mature caliche. Values of the order of 10,000 years are typical of such estimates. Such lengths of time imply the existence of an environment of great geomorphic stability as continued growth of the caliche requires a constant hydrologic regime. Major fluctuations of climate, variations in base level, and major pulses of tectonic activity are precluded. Environmental stability during caliche formation means that such horizons function as "time lines" in the geological record. In other words, they are important chronostratigraphic markers that permit correlation between adjacent sequences, and thus they help unravel geological history in a more rigorous fashion than would otherwise be the case. *See* SOIL.   Nowell Donovan

Bibliography. V. P. Wright (ed.), *Paleosols: Their Recognition and Interpretation*, 1986.

Caliciales

An order of the Ascolichenes. This order is characterized by an unusual apothecium. The hymenial layer originates normally, but by the time the spores are mature, the asci and paraphyses have partially disintegrated into a mass of spores and hymenial tissues known as a mazaedium. In the family Caliciaceae the disk is borne on a short stalk 0.04–0.32 in. (1–8 mm) high, a peculiar structure that is also known in the nonlichenized Roesleriaceae. These two families are so close that some species in either one may or may not lichenize symbiotic algae. The primary thallus of the Caliciaceae is a powdery grayish or lemon-yellow crust on soil or rotten wood. There are six genera separated by spore septation and color. The family Cypheliaceae with seven genera is more typically crustose, with sessile apothecia and a more fully developed thallus. The Sphaerophoraceae are fruticose, much like *Cladonia* sp., but the thallus is solid. The apothecia are open or enclosed in a spherical chamber at the tips of branches. The largest genus, *Sphaerophorus*, is widespread in boreal zones and mountains of both hemispheres.   Mason E. Hale

Californium

A chemical element, symbol Cf, atomic number 98, the ninth member of the actinide series of elements. Its discovery and production have been based upon artificial nuclear transmutation of radioactive isotopes of lighter elements. All isotopes of californium are radioactive, with half-lives ranging from a minute to about 1000 years. Because of its nuclear instability, californium does not exist in the Earth's crust. *See* ACTINIDE ELEMENTS; BERKELIUM; RADIOACTIVITY.

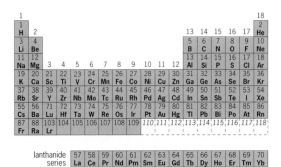

Californium was discovered in 1950 by S. G. Thompson, K. Street, A. Ghiorso, and G. T. Seaborg. The experiments were carried out at the University of California Radiation Laboratory, and the new element was named in honor of the university and the state. The discoverers bombarded a target, consisting of a few millionths of a gram of ^{242}Cm (curium-242), with helium ions accelerated in a cyclotron. Combination of helium nuclei with nuclei of ^{242}Cm, followed by loss of a neutron, gave the mass-245 isotope of element 98. Californium-245 was found to decay partly by capture of an orbital electron and partly by emission of an alpha particle, with a half-life of 45 min.

Several other isotopes of californium (mass numbers 239–256) have been discovered by using a variety of combinations of target isotopes and bombarding particles. The production of ^{246}Cf by bombardment of ^{238}U with carbon ions is an example of the possibility of using comparatively heavy bombarding particles and more abundant target isotopes for synthesis of new elements. For production of amounts of californium isotopes ranging up to a few grams, kilogram amounts of ^{239}Pu have been irradiated with neutrons in nuclear reactors. Successive capture of neutrons by newly formed isotopes and subsequent beta decay to next heavier elements lead eventually to formation of the californium isotopes. Mixtures of californium isotopes with considerably different isotopic composition have been produced by multiple neutron capture in the high, instantaneous neutron flux from thermonuclear explosions (fast time scale). In this latter case compositions especially rich in ^{254}Cf are obtained.

An interesting property of the californium isotopes is that spontaneous fission becomes a very important mode of decay. The isotope ^{254}Cf decays predominantly (99%) by spontaneous fission and

has a half-life of about 60 days. This property has resulted in speculation that this isotope might be responsible for the decay of the light intensity of supernovae, which have a similar half-life, but this is not generally accepted. It is also in the region of californium isotopes that a nuclear subshell at neutron number 152 has an important influence on the stabilities of nuclei and in their alpha decay and spontaneous fission half-lives.

The most easily produced isotope for many purposes is ^{252}Cf, which is obtained in gram quantities in nuclear reactors and has a half-life of 2.6 years. It decays partially by spontaneous fission, and has been very useful for the study of fission. It has also had an important influence on the development of counters and electronic systems with applications not only in nuclear physics but in medical research as well. There are also important potential applications of ^{252}Cf for high-intensity neutron sources. The most useful isotope for chemical investigations is ^{249}Cf, which has a half-life of 350 years and is obtained from the beta decay of ^{249}Bk. This californium isotope was first used to measure the magnetic susceptibility of Cf(III) adsorbed on a single resin bead. The susceptibility is similar to that of its lanthanide analog, Dy(III). There is no evidence for an oxidation state of californium other than 3+ in aqueous solution, but +4 and +2 solid compounds exist. Solid compounds include Cf_2O_3, CfO_2 (and intermediate oxides), CfF_3, CfF_4, $CfCl_3$, $CfBr_2$, $CfBr_3$, CfI_2, and CfI_3. Solutions of the tripositive ions are green in color. The color arises from distinct absorption bands in the visible region of the spectrum, the strongest of which appear at 489–493, 590–618, 670–680, and 720–760 nanometers.

The chemical properties are similar to those observed for other 3+ actinide elements: a water-soluble nitrate, sulfate, chloride, and perchlorate. Californium is precipitated as the fluoride, oxalate, or hydroxide. Ion-exchange chromatography can be used for the isolation and identification of californium in the presence of other actinide elements. A solution of a complexing agent (α-hydroxyisobutyric acid, for example) desorbs actinides from a cation-exchange resin at different rates; the elements leave the column of resin in distinct fractions and can be identified by their characteristic radioactivities. Solvent extraction with hydrogen di(2-ethylhexyl)phosphoric acid (HDEHP) or quaternary ammonium salts is also used.

Californium metal is quite volatile and can be distilled at temperatures of the order of 1100–1200°C (2000–2200°F). It is chemically reactive and appears to exist in two different crystalline modifications between room temperature and its melting point, 900°C (1700°F). *See* TRANSURANIUM ELEMENTS.   Glenn T. Seaborg

Bibliography. S. Ahrland et al., *The Chemistry of the Actinides*, 1975 ; B. B. Cunningham, Berkelium and californium, *J. Chem. Educ.*, 36:32–37, 1959;

E. K. Hyde, I. Perlman, and G. T. Seaborg, *The Nuclear Properties of the Heavy Elements*, vols. 1 and 2, 1964; J. J. Katz et al., *The Chemistry of the Actinide Elements*, 2 vols., 2d ed., 1986; F. L. Oetting et al., *The Chemical Thermodynamics of Actinide Elements and Compounds*, 2 vols., 1977; G. T. Seaborg, History of the synthetic actinide elements, *Actinides Rev.*, 1:3–38, 1967; G. T. Seaborg, *The Transuranium Elements*, 1958.

Caliper

An instrument with two legs used for measuring linear dimensions. Calipers may be fixed, adjustable, or movable. Fixed calipers are used in routine inspection of standard products; adjustable calipers are used similarly but can be reset to slightly different dimensions if necessary. Movable calipers can be set to match the distance being measured. The legs may pivot about a rivet or screw in a firm-joint pair of calipers; they may pivot about a pin, being held against the pin by a spring and set in position by a knurled nut on a threaded rod; or the legs may slide either directly (caliper rule) or along a screw (micrometer caliper) relative to each other. *See* MICROMETER.

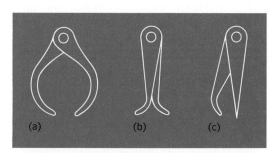

Some typical machinist's calipers. (*a*) Outside. (*b*) Inside. (*c*) Hermaphrodite. (*After R. J. Sweeney, Measurement Techniques in Mechanical Engineering, Wiley, 1953*)

The legs may be shaped to facilitate measuring outside dimensions, inside dimensions, surface dimensions as between points on a plate, or from a surface into a hole as in a keyway (see **illus.**). Other forms are adapted to special needs. *See* GAGES.

Frank H. Rockett

Callitrichales

An order of flowering plants, division Magnoliophyta (Angiospermae), in the subclass Asteridae of the class Magnoliopsida (dicotyledons). The order consists of three small families with about 50 species, most of which are aquatics or small herbs of wet places, and have much reduced vascular systems. The flowers are small and solitary in the axils of leaves or bracts. The perianth is nearly or completely absent. The pistil consists of two carpels united to form a compound, unilocular or four-chambered ovary, or sometimes the pistil appears to be of a single carpel. The Callitrichales are placed in the Asteridae largely on the basis of their embryology and phytochemistry. The ovules are anatropous and tenuinucellar and have a single integument, and the plants generally produce iridoid substances. *See* ASTERIDAE; MAGNOLIOPHYTA; MAGNOLIOPSIDA; PLANT KINGDOM.   T. M. Barkley

Calobryales

An order of liverworts. They are characterized by prostrate, simple or branched, leafless stems and erect, leafy branches of a radial organization. The order consists of a single genus, *Calobryum*, and 12 species, most of them occupying restricted ranges in apparently relic areas indicative of an ancient origin and dispersal. The order is considered primitive in comparison with the Jungermanniales, in which the leafy axis tends to be prostrate and the underleaves reduced.

The stems are thick and fleshy, with no differentiated outer layers. Rhizoids are lacking. The leaves may be small or lacking below, larger and more crowded above. They are three-ranked, with those of one rank sometimes more or less reduced. They are broad, unlobed, and entire. The cells, large and thin-walled, are often two- or three-layered at the leaf base. Slime papillae at the base of leaves secrete mucilage. The antheridia occur in axils of upper leaves or in terminal clusters subtended by three leaves; the stalk is long, four-seriate, and enlarged above. The archegonia are clustered in a terminal disk but in the absence of fertilization become lateral; the neck is long and four-seriate. The sporophyte is protected by a cylindric upgrowth of gametophytic tissue. The seta consists of numerous rows of cells, and the long-ellipsoid capsule dehisces by four valves remaining attached at the tip. The wall is unistratose below and bistratose at the apex; its cells have one or two longitudinally oriented bands. The haploid chromosome number is 9. *See* BRYOPHYTA; HEPATICOPSIDA; JUNGERMANNIALES; JUNGERMANNIIDAE.   Howard Crum

Bibliography. E. O. Campbell, The structure and development of *Calobryum gibbsiae* Steph., *Trans. Roy. Soc. N. Z.* 47:243–254; R. M. Schuster, Studies on Hepaticae, XV: Calobryales, *Nova Hedwigia*, 13:1–63, 1966.

Calomel

Mercury(I) chloride, Hg_2Cl_2, a covalent compound which is insoluble in water. The substance sublimes when heated. The formula weight is 472.086 and the specific gravity is 7.16 at 20°C (68°F). The material is a white, impalpable powder consisting of fine tetragonal crystals. Calomel is manufactured by precipitation when sodium chloride is added to a solution of mercury(I) nitrate or by direct combination of the elements.

Calomel is used in preparing insecticides and medicines. It is well known in the laboratory as the constituent of the calomel reference electrodes which are commonly used in conjunction with a glass electrode to measure pH. *See* MERCURY (ELEMENT); REFERENCE ELECTRODE.

E. Eugene Weaver

Calorimetry

The measurement of the quantity of heat energy involved in processes such as chemical reactions, changes of state, and mixing of substances, or in the determination of heat capacities of substances.

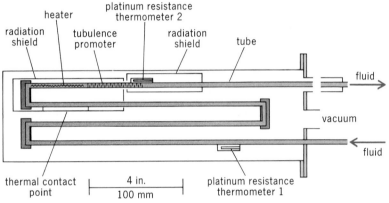

Fig. 1. Schematic diagram of a high-pressure flow calorimeter for measurement of heat capacity. (*After G. Ernst, G. Maurer, and E. Wiederoh, Flow calorimeter for the accurate determination of the isobaric heat capacity at high pressures: Results for carbon dioxide, J. Chem. Thermodyn., 21:53–65, 1989*)

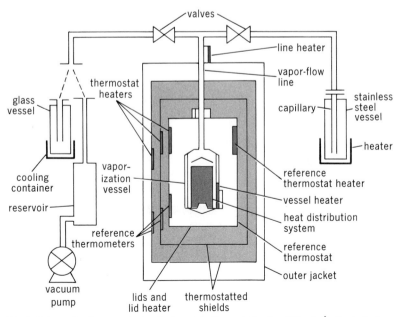

Fig. 2. Schematic diagram of a heat-of-vaporization calorimeter. (*After L. Šváb et al., A calorimeter for the determination of enthalpies of vaporization at high temperatures and pressures, J. Chem. Thermodyn., 20:545–550, 1988*)

The unit of energy in the International System of Units is the joule. Another unit still being used is the calorie, defined as 4.184 joules.

Types of calorimeters. A calorimeter is an apparatus for measuring the quantity of heat energy released or absorbed during a process. Since there are many processes that can be studied over a wide range of temperature and pressure, a large variety of calorimeters have been developed.

Nonisothermal calorimeters. These instruments measure the temperature change that occurs during the process. An aneroid-type nonisothermal calorimeter is normally constructed of a material having a high thermal conductivity, such as copper, so that there is rapid temperature equilibration. It is isolated from its surroundings by a high vacuum to reduce heat leaks. This type of calorimeter can be used for determining the heat capacity of materials when measurements involve low temperatures. Aneroid-type nonisothermal calorimeters have also been developed for measuring the energy of combustion for small samples of rare materials.

Another type of nonisothermal calorimeter uses a liquid as a heat sink, so that even if there is a large amount of energy released in the process, the temperature rise is not excessive. The liquid is kept at a uniform temperature by stirring, and the change in temperature can be measured accurately. In general, the size of the liquid heat sink is designed so that the temperature change is of the order of 5°C (9°F). For measurements near room temperature, water is commonly used as the working fluid; measurements at higher temperatures use less volatile organic liquids.

With most nonisothermal calorimeters, it is necessary to relate the temperature rise to the quantity of energy released in the process. This is done by determining the calorimeter constant, which is the amount of energy required to increase the temperature of the calorimeter itself by 1°. This value can be determined by electrical calibration or by measurement on a well-defined test system. For example, in bomb calorimetry the calorimeter constant is often determined from the temperature rise which occurs when a known mass of a very pure standard sample of benzoic acid is burned.

Isothermal calorimeters. These instruments make the measurements at constant temperature. The simplest example is a calorimeter containing an outer annular space filled with a liquid in equilibrium with a crystalline solid at its melting point, arranged so that any volume change will displace mercury along a capillary tube. The Bunsen ice calorimeter operates at 0°C (32°F) with a mixture of ice and water. Changes as a result of the process being studied cause the ice to melt or the water to freeze, and the consequent volume change is determined by measurement of the movement of the mercury meniscus in the capillary tube. While these calorimeters can yield accurate results, they are limited to operation at the equilibrium temperature of the two-phase system. Other types of isothermal calorimeters use the addition of electrical energy to achieve exact balance of the heat absorption that occurs during an endothermic process.

Calorimeter components. All calorimeters consist of the calorimeter proper and a jacket or a bath, which is used to control the temperature of the calorimeter and the rate of heat leak to the environment. For temperatures not too far removed from room temperature, the jacket or bath contains liquid at a controlled temperature. For measurements at extreme temperatures, the jacket usually consists of a metal block containing a heater to control the temperature. With nonisothermal calorimeters, where the jacket is kept at a constant temperature, there will be some heat leak to the jacket when the temperature of the calorimeter changes. It is necessary to correct the temperature change observed to the value it would have been if there were no leak. This is achieved by measuring the temperature of the calorimeter for a time period both before and after the process and applying Newton's law of cooling. This correction can be avoided by using the technique of adiabatic calorimetry, where the temperature of the jacket is kept equal to the temperature of the calorimeter as a change occurs. This technique requires more elaborate temperature control, and its primary use is for accurate heat capacity measurements at low temperatures.

Thermometry. In calorimetric experiments it is necessary to measure temperature differences accurately; in some cases the temperature itself must be accurately known. Modern calorimeters use resistance thermometers to measure both temperatures and temperature differences, while thermocouples or thermistors are used to measure smaller temperature differences. A calibrated standard platinum resistance thermometer can measure temperature differences to $0.00001°C$ $(0.000018°F)$ and temperatures ranging from -260 to $630°C$ $(-436$ to $1166°F)$ to an accuracy of $\pm0.001°C$ $(0.0018°F)$ Multiple-junction thermocouples and thermistors can measure smaller temperature differences, allowing precise measurements of very small heat effects. *See* TEMPERATURE MEASUREMENT; THERMISTOR; THERMOCOUPLE; THERMOMETER.

Calorimetric measurements. Heat capacities of materials and heats of combustion are processes that are routinely measured with calorimeters. Calorimeters are also used to measure the heat involved in phase changes, for example, the change from a liquid to a solid (fusion) or from a liquid to a gas (vaporization). Calorimetry has also been applied to the measurement of heats of hydrogenation of unsaturated organic compounds, the heat of dissolution of a solid in a liquid, or the heat change on mixing two liquids.

Heat-capacity calorimeter. Heat capacities of gases or liquid can be determined in a flow calorimeter. Some essential features are shown in **Fig. 1**. A known mass of fluid flowing at a constant rate is pumped through the calorimeter. The inlet temperature is measured with platinum resistance

thermometer 1. The fluid is heated with a known amount of electrical energy, and the change in temperature is observed at thermometer 2. The radiation shields reduce heat losses to the surroundings.

Heat-of-vaporization calorimeter. A modern heat-of-vaporization calorimeter is shown in **Fig. 2**. The material in the vaporization vessel is heated with a known amount of electrical energy, and the mass of material vaporized is determined from the change in weight of the glass collection vessel. The thermostated shields, which are maintained at the same temperature as the vaporization vessel, ensure that all the electrical energy goes to vaporize the sample and none is lost to the surroundings. *See* CHEMICAL THERMODYNAMICS; HEAT CAPACITY; HEAT TRANSFER; THERMOCHEMISTRY.

Kenneth M. Marsh

Bibliography. J. P. McCullough and D. W. Scott (eds.), *Experimental Thermodynamics*, vol. 1: *Calorimetry of Non-Reacting Systems*, 1968; M. L. McGlashan, *Chemical Thermodynamics*, 1979; R. S. Porter and J. F. Johnson (eds.), *Analytical Chemistry*, vols. 2–4, 1970–1977; W. R. Parrish, Recent advances in calorimetry, *Fluid Phase Equilibria*, 29:172–192, 1986.

Calycerales

An order of flowering plants, division Magnoliophyta (Angiospermae), in the subclass Asteridae of the class Magnoliopsida (dicotyledons). The order consists of a single family with about 60 species native to tropical America. The plants are herbs with alternate, simple leaves that do not have stipules. The flowers are borne in involucrate heads with centripetal flowering sequence. The calyx is reduced to small lobes or teeth, and the corolla consists of (4)5(6) fused lobes and is regular or somewhat irregular. The stamens are attached near the summit of the corolla tube, and the filaments are more or less connate. The pistil consists of two united carpels, which form a compound, inferior ovary wth a single, pendulous ovule. The order Calycerales is sometimes included within the Dipsacales, and the order has attracted attention because of the overall resemblance of the inflorescence to that of the Asteraceae. *See* ASTERALES; ASTERIDAE; DIPSACALES; MAGNOLIOPHYTA; MAGNOLIOPSIDA; PLANT KINGDOM.   T. M. Barkley

Cam mechanism

A mechanical linkage whose purpose is to produce, by means of a contoured cam surface, a prescribed motion of the output link of the linkage, called the follower. Cam and follower are a higher pair. *See* LINKAGE (MECHANISM).

A familiar application of a cam mechanism is in the opening and closing of valves in an automotive engine (**Fig. 1**). The cam rotates with the cam

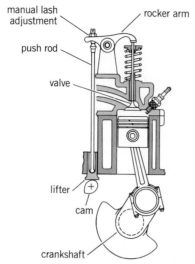

Fig. 1. Cam mechanism for opening and closing valves in automotive engine. (*Texaco, Inc*.)

shaft, usually at constant angular velocity, while the follower moves up and down as controlled by the cam surface. A cam is sometimes made in the form of a translating cam (**Fig. 2***a*). Other cam mechanisms, employed in elementary mechanical analog computers, are simple memory devices, in which the position of the cam (input) determines the position of the follower (output or readout).

Although many requisite motions in machinery are accomplished by use of pin-joined mechanisms, such as four-bar linkages, a cam mechanism frequently is the only practical solution to the problem of converting the available input, usually rotating or reciprocating, to a desired output, which may be an exceedingly complex motion. No other mechanism is as versatile and as straightforward in design. However, a cam may be difficult and costly to manufacture, and it is often noisy and susceptible to wear, fatigue, and vibration.

Cams are used in many machines. They are numerous in automatic packaging, shoemaking, typesetting machines, and the like, but are often found as well in machine tools, reciprocating engines, and compressors. They are occasionally used in rotating machinery.

Cams are classified as translating, disk, plate, cylindrical, or drum (Fig. 2). The link having the contoured surface that prescribes the motion of the follower is called the cam. Cams are usually made of steel, often hardened to resist wear and, for high-speed application, precisely ground.

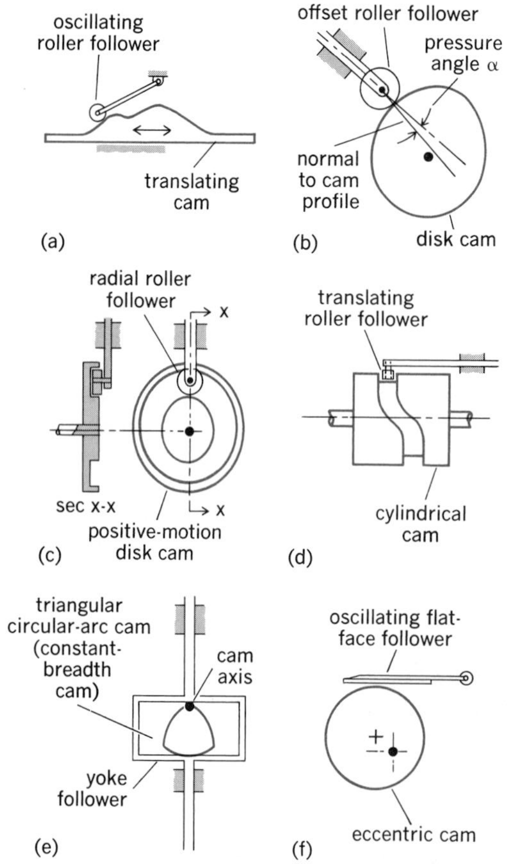

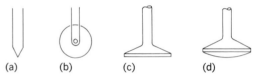

Fig. 3. Cam followers. (*a*) Knife edge. (*b*) Roller. (*c*) Flat face. (*d*) Spherical face.

The output link, which is maintained in contact with the cam surface, is the follower. Followers are classified by their shape as roller, flat face, and spherical face (**Fig. 3**). The point or knife-edge follower is of academic interest in developing cam profile relationships. Followers are also described by the nature of their constraints, for example, radial, in which motion is reciprocating along a radius from the cam's axis of rotation (Fig. 1); offset, in which motion is reciprocating along a line that does not intersect the axis of rotation (Fig. 2*b*); and oscillating, or pivoted (Fig. 2*a*. Three-dimensional cam-and-follower systems are coming into more frequent use, where the follower may travel over a lumpy surface.

Motion of cam follower. The first step in the design of a cam mechanism is the determination of the motion of the cam follower. In a packaging machine, for example, the ends of a carton may be folded by cam-operated fingers that advance at the proper times, retract as soon as the fold has been made, and then rest or dwell until the next carton is in position. The motion of the cam follower, which in turn moves the folder fingers, can be represented by a displacement-time diagram (**Fig. 4**). The time axis is usually laid off in degrees of cam rotation. The conventional meanings of follower dwell, rise, and return are indicated in the figure.

Fig. 2. Classification of cams. (*a*) Translating. (*b*) Disk. (*c*) Positive motion. (*d*) Cylindrical. (*e*) With yoke follower. (*f*) With flat-face follower.

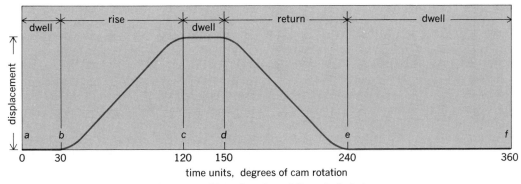

Fig. 4. Displacement-time diagram for a cam, with motion of cam follower indicated.

The maximum displacement of the follower and the periods of dwell are determined, more or less arbitrarily, by the designer, who has the choice of any curve to connect the dwell portions of the complete displacement-time diagram. The practical form for this curve is determined largely by the maximum acceleration that can be tolerated by the follower linkage. In addition, the pressure angle (α in Fig. 2b) must be kept fairly small, usually less than 30°, to avoid undue friction and possible jamming of the reciprocating follower in its guides. The space that is available for the cam will affect the maximum pressure angle. Usually, a small cam is preferred; yet the larger the cam can be made (which in effect physically increases the length of the time axis for the same time interval), the smaller the maximum pressure angle will be. The final form may further represent a compromise to make possible economical manufacture of the cam.

If the diagram of Fig. 4 were laid out on and cut out of steel and a knife-edge follower were constrained to move vertically, the translating cam mechanism of **Fig. 5a** would result. The process of wrapping this translating cam around a disk (Fig. 5b), thus producing a disk cam whose follower action would be similar to that of Fig. 5a, can be visualized readily. The introduction of a roller or flat-face follower complicates the determination of the actual cam contour that will produce a desired follower displacement-time relationship; but recognition of the similarity between the displacement-time diagram and the final cam contour makes it easier to visualize the conditions that must be met to design a cam

that will operate satisfactorily.

Consider the dwell-rise-dwell portion of the curve of Fig. 4. Displacement of the follower might be plotted arbitrarily as a straight line (**Fig. 6a**).

The slope $\Delta s/\Delta t$ of a displacement-time ($s - t$) curve is equal to velocity ($s/t = v$) so that velocity of the follower from A to B (dwell) will be zero, from B to C it will be constant and finite, and from C to D velocity will be zero again (Fig. 6b).

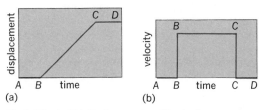

Fig. 6. Effect of (a) displacement on (b) velocity.

The slope $\Delta v//\Delta t = a$ of the velocity-time curve is correspondingly equal to acceleration. Thus, the acceleration of the follower necessary to increase velocity from zero to a finite value in zero time (B to B in Fig. 6b) is infinite. Likewise, the deceleration that occurs at C must also be infinite. The acceleration along the constant velocity line, from B to C, would be zero. Thus the curve chosen in Fig. 6a for displacement is unrealistic because of the high inertial forces that would result from abrupt changes of velocity.

Choice of acceleration curve. Therefore, a curve having a gradual transition from dwell to maximum velocity is necessary. Three such curves are plotted in **Fig. 7** and are superimposed in **Fig. 8** for comparison. The derived curves for velocity and acceleration are also plotted so comparisons may be made.

The constant acceleration–constant deceleration curve, in which displacement s is proportional to t^2, is desirable except for the instantaneous reversal of acceleration at the point of maximum velocity; such a reversal would cause high stresses in the mechanism. If the follower were spring-loaded, a heavy spring would be required to prevent the follower's leaving the cam face momentarily, with

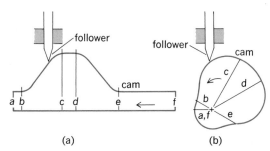

(a)   **(b)**

Fig. 5. Converting (a) translating to (b) disk cam.

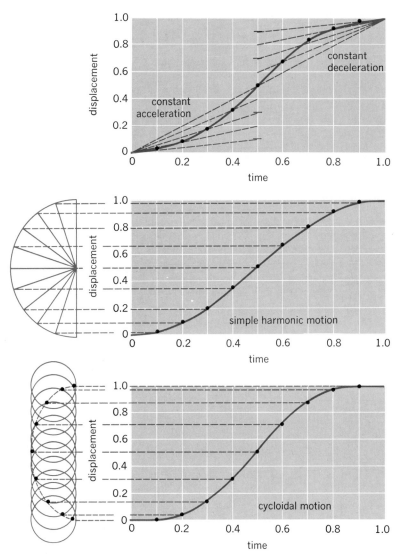

Fig. 7. Displacement-time diagrams for cam contours.

Comparison of the three curves is shown in Fig. 8. The cycloidal curve exhibits a higher pressure angle α for a radial translating follower than the other curves, but its acceleration characteristics are much superior.

Today's extensive use of cams and the extreme demands upon them under increasing speeds of modern manufacturing have yielded still another form of cam profile, which might be called catenoidal because of its association with the catenary [the curve in which a rope or chain (catena) hangs freely]. This curve has an equation expressed primarily in terms of exponential functions ϵ^x, whose slope variation is a curve with the remarkable property that it partakes of the same general form as the original function. Hence the velocity and acceleration curves show patterns similar to that of displacement rather than being so different, as was markedly so with the constant acceleration-deceleration profile, and less so with others. This curve (catenoidal) also is shown in the figures; it is alleged to give even smoother performance and less vibration than the cycloidal type. Its slope (jerk)

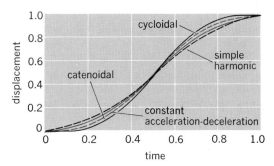

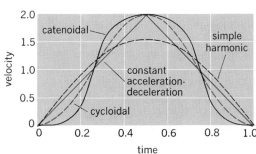

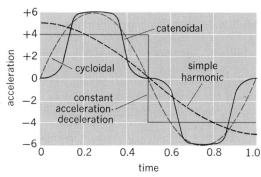

Fig. 8. Comparison of motions for three shapes of rise-return regions. Fourth motion, for catenoidal shape, also superposed. (*After G. L. Guillet and A. H. Church, Kinematics of Machines, 5th ed., Wiley, 1950*)

resulting shock to the linkage as it returned.

The simple harmonic displacement curve is plotted by projecting onto the diameter (equal to follower displacement) of a circle a point moving with constant velocity around the circle's circumference. Although maximum acceleration is higher than in the preceding curve, the abrupt changes of acceleration occur only at the beginning and end of the rise. Both of these curves have been used in cam design; both are satisfactory if speeds are low to moderate and follower mass is not large. However, serious difficulties are encountered when high speeds or heavy followers accentuate the stresses resulting from acceleration.

The cycloidal curve is plotted by projecting points from a cycloid whose generating circle has a diameter equal to follower displacement divided by π, as in Fig. 7. This curve has desirable acceleration characteristics, but requires that the cam face be accurately machined at the beginning and end of rise to accomplish in fact the theoretical performance.

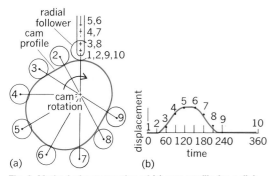

Fig. 9. Method of construction of (a) cam profile for a disk cam having a radial translating roller follower from (b) displacement curve.

will be zero four times in each cycle.

The manufacture of cam and follower from a master model is dwindling in favor of manufacture using a computer tape, which accurately directs the cutting of the surface. This procedure avoids the expensive manufacture of master cams.

In certain high-speed cam mechanisms, for example, an automotive engine valve gear, the elasticity and vibration characteristics of the follower linkage must be taken into account if faulty operation is to be avoided. The polydyne method derives its name from use of a polynomial displacement curve that suits the dynamic characteristics of the follower linkage.

Construction of cam profile. Empirically, a cam profile can be plotted to as large a scale as desired if the displacement curve and the configuration of the follower linkage are known. The method consists essentially in inverting the mechanism by fixing the cam and rotating the follower linkage about it, plotting only enough of the follower linkage to establish the successive positions of the follower face that will bear on the cam. **Figure 9** shows the method of constructing the profile for a disk cam having a radial translating roller follower whose displacement curve is given. The cam profile is faired in, being at every point tangent to the follower roller. (Accuracy is improved by using a larger scale and by plotting additional positions.)

The method of constructing a cam profile for a flat face, offset, or oscillating follower is similar to that shown in the figure. It is important, however, that the location of the point in the follower linkage whose displacement is described by the displacement-time curve be kept constantly in view while the follower linkage is plotted in various successive positions.

Analytically, a profile can be calculated to any desired accuracy and the cam profile may be shown in tabular form, giving, for example, displacement of the follower for each degree of cam rotation. If a milling cutter or grinding wheel of the same size and shape as the follower is then used to cut the cam contour, the resulting contour will be true except for the small ridges that remain between given positions. These ridges can be removed by hand, using a file or a stone.   Douglas P. Adams

Bibliography. J. Chakraborty and S. G. Dhande, *Kinematics and Geometry of Planer and Spatial Cam Mechanisms*, 1977; F. J. Ogozalek, *Theory of Catenoidal-Pulse Motion and Its Application to High-Speed Cams*, ASME Publ. 66-Mech-45, 1966; J. E. Shigley and J. J. Uiker, *Theory of Machines and Mechanisms*, 1980.

Cambrian

An interval of time in Earth history (Cambrian Period) and its rock record (Cambrian System). The Cambrian Period spanned about 35,000,000 years and began with the first appearance of marine animals with mineralized (calcium carbonate, calcium phosphate) shells. The Cambrian System includes many different kinds of marine sandstones, shales, limestones, dolomites, and volcanics. There is very little provable record of nonmarine Cambrian environments.

CENOZOIC	QUATERNARY	
	TERTIARY	
MESOZOIC	CRETACEOUS	
	JURASSIC	
	TRIASSIC	
PALEOZOIC	PERMIAN	
	CARBONIFEROUS	PENNSYLVANIAN
		MISSISSIPPIAN
	DEVONIAN	
	SILURIAN	
	ORDOVICIAN	
	CAMBRIAN	
PRECAMBRIAN		

The concept that great systems of rocks recorded successive periods of Earth history was developed in England in the early nineteenth century. The Cambrian, which was one of the first systems to be formally named, was proposed by the Reverend Adam Sedgwick in 1835 for a series

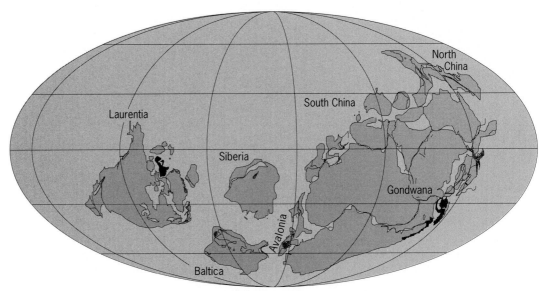

Fig. 1. Reconstruction of the Lower Cambrian world. (*After W. S. McKerrow, C. R. Scotese, and M. D. Brasier, Early Cambrian continental reconstructions. J. Geol. Soc., 149:599–606, 1992*)

of sedimentary rocks in Wales that seemed to constitute the oldest sediments in the British Isles. At that time, there was no real idea of the antiquity of Cambrian rocks. They were recognized by distinctive fossils and by their geologic relations to other systems. In the early part of the twentieth century, radiometric techniques for obtaining the ages of igneous and metamorphic rocks evolved. Because of the difficulty of finding rocks that can be dated radiometrically in association with rocks that can be dated empirically by fossils, the age in years of most Cambrian deposits is only approximate. The best present estimates suggest that Cambrian time began about 540 million years ago and ended about 505 million years ago. It is one of the longest Phanerozoic periods.

Geography. Knowledge of Cambrian geography and of the dynamic aspects of evolution and history in Cambrian time is derived from rocks of this age that have been exposed by present-day erosion or penetrated by borings into the Earth's surface. Despite the antiquity of Cambrian time, a surprisingly good record of marine rocks of Cambrian age has been preserved at many localities throughout the world. Each of the different rock types contains clues about its environment of deposition that have been derived from analogy with modern marine environments. From this information, together with knowledge gained from fossils of about the same age within the Cambrian and information about the present geographic distribution of each Cambrian locality, a general picture of world geography and its changes through Cambrian time is available.

Plate tectonics. The theory of plate tectonics has provided criteria whereby ancient continental margins can be identified. By using these criteria and the spatial information about marine environments

derived from study of the rocks, the Cambrian world can be resolved into at least four major continents that were quite different from those of today (**Fig. 1**). These were (1) Laurentia, which is essentially North America, minus a narrow belt along the eastern coast from eastern Newfoundland to southern New England that belonged to a separate microcontinent, Avalonia. This microcontinent, which also included present-day England, and another microcontinent now incorporated in South Carolina were originally marginal to Gondwana; (2) Baltica, consisting of present-day northern Europe north of France and west of the Ural Mountains but excluding most of Scotland and northern Ireland, which are fragments of Laurentia; (3) Gondwana, a giant continent whose present-day fragments are Africa, South America, India, Australia, Antarctica, parts of southern Europe, the Middle East, and Southeast Asia; and (4) Siberia, including much of the northeastern quarter of Asia. Unfortunately, there is not enough reliable information to accurately locate these continents relative to one another on the Cambrian globe. *See* CONTINENTAL MARGIN; CONTINENTS, EVOLUTION OF; PLATE TECTONICS.

Time divisions. For most practical purposes, rocks of Cambrian age are recognized by their content of distinctive fossils. On the basis of the successive changes in the evolutionary record of Cambrian life that have been worked out during the past century, the Cambrian System has been divided globally into Lower, Middle, and Upper series, each of which has been further divided on each continent into stages, each stage consisting of several zones (**Fig. 2**). Despite the amount of work already done, precise intercontinental correlation of series and stage boundaries, and of zones, is still difficult, and refinement of intercontinental correlation of these ancient rocks is a topic of research.

Life. The record preserved in rocks indicates that essentially all Cambrian plants and animals lived in the sea. The few places where terrestrial sediments have been preserved suggest that the land was barren of major plant life, and there are no known records of Cambrian insects or of terrestrial vertebrate animals of any kind.

Plants. The plant record consists entirely of algae, preserved either as carbonized impressions in marine black shales or as filamentous or blotchy microstructures within marine buildups of calcium carbonate, called stromatolites, produced by the actions of these organisms. Cambrian algal stromatolites were generally low domal structures, rarely more than a few meters high or wide, which were built up by the trapping or precipitation of calcium carbonate by one or more species of algae. Such structures, often composed of upwardly arched laminae, were common in regions of carbonate sedimentation in the shallow Cambrian seas. *See* STROMATOLITE.

Animals. The animal record is composed almost entirely of invertebrates that had either calcareous or phosphatic shells (**Fig. 3**). The fossils of shell-bearing organisms include representatives of several different classes of arthropods, mollusks, echinoderms, brachiopods, and poriferans. Coelenterates and radiolarians are extremely rare, and bryozoans, radiolarians, and foraminiferans are unknown from Cambrian rocks. A few rare occurrences of impressions or of carbonized remains of a variety of soft-bodied organisms indicate that the fossil record, particularly of arthropods, is incomplete and biased in favor of shell-bearing organisms. Some widespread fossil groups, such as Archaeocyatha, are known only from Cambrian rocks, and several extinct groups of Paleozoic organisms such as hyolithids and conodonts have their first appearance in Cambrian rocks. *See* ARTHROPODA; CONODONT; PORIFERA.

Diversity. Although the record of marine life in the Cambrian seems rich, one of the dramatic differences between Cambrian marine rocks and those of younger periods is the low phyletic diversity of most fossiliferous localities. The most diverse faunas of Cambrian age have been found along the ocean-facing margins of the shallow seas that covered large areas of the Cambrian continents. Because these margins were often involved in later geologic upheavals, their rich record of Cambrian life has been largely destroyed. Only a few localities in the world remain to provide a more accurate picture of the diversity of organisms living in Cambrian time. In Laurentia, the richest localities are in the Kinzers Formation of southeastern Pennsylvania, the Spence Shale of northern Utah, the Wheeler Shale and Marjum Formation of western Utah, the Buen Formation of northern Greenland, and the Burgess Shale of British Columbia.

Trilobites. The most abundant remains of organ-

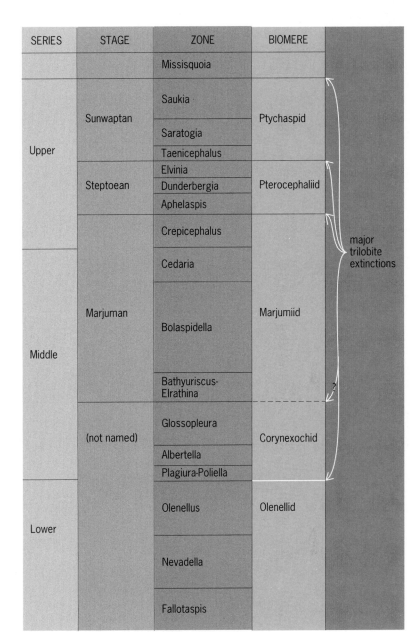

SERIES	STAGE	ZONE	BIOMERE	
		Missisquoia		
Upper	Sunwaptan	Saukia	Ptychaspid	major trilobite extinctions
		Saratogia		
		Taenicephalus		
	Steptoean	Elvinia	Pterocephaliid	
		Dunderbergia		
		Aphelaspis		
Middle	Marjuman	Crepicephalus	Marjumiid	
		Cedaria		
		Bolaspidella		
		Bathyuriscus-Elrathina	?	
	(not named)	Glossopleura	Corynexochid	
		Albertella		
		Plagiura-Poliella		
Lower		Olenellus	Olenellid	
		Nevadella		
		Fallotaspis		

Fig. 2. North American divisions of the Cambrian System.

isms in Cambrian rocks are of trilobites (Fig. 3*a–c*). They are present in almost every fossiliferous Cambrian deposit and are the principal tools used to describe divisions of Cambrian time and to correlate Cambrian rocks. These marine arthropods ranged from a few millimeters to 20 in. (50 cm) in length, but most were less than 4 in. (10 cm) long. Although some groups of trilobites such as the Agnostida (Fig. 3*a*) were predominantly pelagic in habitat, most trilobites seem to have been benthic or nektobenthic and show a reasonably close correlation with bottom environments. For this reason, there are distinct regional differences in the Cambrian trilobite faunas of the shallow seas of different parts of the Cambrian world. *See* TRILOBITA.

Brachiopods. The next most abundant Cambrian

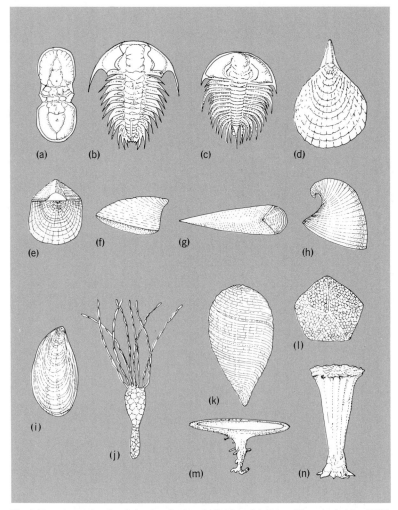

Fig. 3. Representative Cambrian fossils: (*a–c*) trilobites; (*d–f*) brachiopods; (*g*) hyolithid; (*h–i*) mollusks; (*j–l*) echinoderms; and (*m, n*) archaeocyathids.

for only short periods of time and left no clear descendants. Representatives of these phyla, such as cephalopods, clams, and true crinoids, which are abundant in younger rocks, are rare in Cambrian rocks. Snails, however, are found throughout the Cambrian. Discoveries of primitive clams have been made in Early Cambrian beds, but they are apparently absent from the later record of life for tens of millions of years until post-Cambrian time. *See* ECHINODERMATA; MOLLUSCA.

Corals. Except for rare jellyfish impressions, the Coelenterata were thought to be unrepresented in Cambrian rocks. Corals have now been discovered in early Middle Cambrian rocks in Australia. However, like clams, they are not seen again as fossils until Middle Ordovician time, many tens of millions of years later. *See* COELENTERATA.

Extinction. The stratigraphic record of Cambrian life in Laurentia (North America) shows perhaps five major extinctions of most of the organisms living in the shallow seas. These extinction events form the boundaries of evolutionary units called biomeres (Fig. 2). Their cause, and their presence in the Cambrian records of other continents, is under investigation. However, perhaps it was these periodic disasters that prevented clear continuity in the evolutionary records of many groups and which led, particularly, to the discontinuous records of the echinoderms, corals, and mollusks. *See* ANIMAL EVOLUTION; EXTINCTION (BIOLOGY).

Faunal origin. One major unsolved problem is the origin of the entire Cambrian fauna. Animal life was already quite diverse before Cambrian time. The earliest Cambrian beds contain representatives of more than 20 distinctly different invertebrate groups. All of these have calcified shells, but none of the Precambrian organisms have any evidence of shells. There is still no clear evidence to determine whether shells evolved in response to predation or to environmental stress, or as the result of some change in oceanic or atmospheric chemistry. *See* PRECAMBRIAN.

History. At the beginning of Cambrian time, the continents were largely exposed, much as they are now. Following some still-unexplained event, the seas were suddenly populated by a rich fauna of shell-bearing invertebrates after 3 billion years of supporting only simple plants and perhaps 100 million years with shell-less invertebrates. *See* PRECAMBRIAN.

Belts of volcanic islands comparable to those of the western Pacific Ocean today fringed eastern Laurentia, the Australian and western Antarctic margins of Gondwana, and southern Siberia. These belts suggest that crustal plates analogous to those of the present day were in motion at that time. Thick evaporites in Siberia and the Middle Eastern and Indian parts of Gondwana suggest regions of warm temperature and high evaporation rate. Absence of significant development of limestones around Baltica suggest that it was a cool region, probably at high latitudes. Near the con-

fossils are brachiopods (Fig. 3*d–f*). These bivalved animals were often gregarious and lived on the sediment surface or on the surfaces of other organisms. Brachiopods with phosphatic shells, referred to the Acrotretida (Fig. 3*f*), are particularly abundant in many limestones and can be recovered in nearly perfect condition by dissolving these limestones in acetic or formic acids. Upper Cambrian limestones from Texas, Oklahoma, and the Rocky Mountains yield excellent silicified shells of formerly calcareous brachiopods when they are dissolved in dilute hydrochloric acid. *See* BRACHIOPODA.

Archaeocyathids. Limestones of Early Cambrian age may contain large reeflike structures formed by an association of algae and an extinct phylum of invertebrates called Archaeocyatha (Fig. 3*m* and *n*). Typical archeocyathids grew conical or cylindrical shells with two walls separated by elaborate radial partitions. The walls often have characteristic patterns of perforations. *See* ARCHAEOCYATHA.

Mollusks and echinoderms. The Cambrian record of mollusks and echinoderms is characterized by many strange-looking forms (Fig. 3*g–l*). Some lived tinental margins of eastern and western Laurentia, on and around Siberia, and on the western Antarctic, eastern Australian, northwestern African, and southern European margins of Gondwana, archaeocyathid bioherms developed and flourished. By the end of Early Cambrian time, archaeocyathids had become extinct, and shell-bearing organisms capable of building bioherms did not reappear until Middle Ordovician time, at least 40,000,000 years later.

Volcanism and evaporitic conditions continued into the Middle Cambrian in Siberia and parts of Gondwana, and evaporites of this age are also known from northern Canada. However, a dramatic change took place in the southern European and northwestern African parts of Gondwana. Carbonate sedimentation virtually ceased throughout that region as those parts of Gondwana reached areas of cooler water and probably higher latitudes. Sea level was rising over much of the world throughout Middle Cambrian time, flooding the interiors of most continents.

In the Late Cambrian, parts of western Baltica and eastern Laurentia began to show signs of crustal deformation suggesting that Iapetus, the ocean between Laurentia, Gondwana, and Baltica, was beginning to close. Crustal deformation was also taking place in southern Siberia, eastern Australia, and western Antarctica. In the broad, shallow seas over all of the continents except Baltica and the southern European and northwestern African parts of Gondwana, extensive areas of carbonate sediments developed. At least five times in the shallow seas covering Laurentia, large parts of the animal populations became extinct and had to be replenished from the oceanic regions. The last of these extinction events marks the end of Cambrian time in Laurentia.

Throughout Cambrian time, terrestrial landscapes were stark and barren. Life in the sea was primitive and struggling for existence. Only in post-Cambrian time did the shallow marine environment stabilize and marine life really flourish. Only then did vertebrates evolve and plants and animals invade the land.

Allison R. Palmer

Bibliography. C. H. Holland (ed.), *Cambrian of the British Isles, Norden and Spitzbergen*, 1974; C. H. Holland (ed.), *Cambrian of the New World*, 1971; C. H. Holland (ed.), *Lower Paleozoic of the Middle East, Eastern and Southern Africa, and Antarctica*, 1981; W. S. McKerrow, C. R. Scotese, and M. D. Brasier, Early continental reconstructions, *J. Geol. Soc.*, 149:559–606, 1992; M. A. McMenamin and D. L. McMenamin, *The Emergence of Animals: The Cambrian Breakthrough*, 1990; A. R. Palmer, Search for the Cambrian world, *Amer. Sci.*, 62:216–224, 1974; R. A. Robinson and C. Tiechert (eds.), *Treatise on Invertebrate Paleontology*, pt. A: *Biogeography*, 1979; J. A. Secord, *Controversy in Victorian Geology: The Cambrian-Silurian Dispute*, 1986; H. B. Whittington, *The Burgess Shale*, 1985.

Camel

The name given to two species of mammals which are members of the family Camelidae in the order Artiodactyla. These are the bactrian camel (*Camelus bactrianus*) and the Arabian or dromedary camel (*C. dromedarius*). Both species are domesticated, but a few wild herds of bactrian camels are still in existence in the Gobi desert.

The legs of these animals are long and slender and terminate in two toes. The neck and head are elongate, and there is a cleft upper lip. The upper jaw has both canines and incisors, and the dental formula is I 1/3 C 1/1 Pm 3/3 M 3/3 for a total of 36 teeth. These animals do not have a gall bladder and the stomach has three divisions. The period of gestation is about 1 year and the female breeds every second year, producing one young (colt).

Bactrian camel. The bactrian camel (see **illus.**) is stronger and more heavily built than the dromedary and is more suitable as a pack animal. The long, shaggy hair allows it to withstand the cold climate of its range in central Asia. There are two humps of fatty tissue, one over the shoulders and the other atop the hindquarters. The shoulder height, excluding the hump, is about 6 ft (2 m). This animal is economically important to the region as it provides milk, meat, and leather for the nomads.

Arabian camel. The Arabian camel is taller than the bactrian and has a single hump of fatty tissue, which can be used as a food reserve. There are two varieties of this species found in the desert. One is the baggage camel, used as a beast of burden, which can average 40 mi (65 km) a day carrying a load of about 400 lb (180 kg). The other type is the more slightly built racing camel, which can travel up to 100 mi (160 km) a day, but with a very light load. This species is well suited to desert life with its broad feet, adapted to walking on sand, its ability to close its nostrils completely, and its double row of interlocking eyelashes.

Adaptations. These two species are able to interbreed. They have a most important physiological adapation in their ability to conserve water. Camels

Bactrian camel (*Camelus bactrianus*).

do not store water but conserve it, since the body is well insulated by fur and has a temperature range of over 12°F (7°C) before it perspires sufficiently to prevent a further rise. The body temperature is about 93°F (34°C) in the morning and may rise to 106°F (41°C) during daytime activity before water is expended in any appreciable quantity. The camel can lose over 40% of its body water without fear of dehydration. However, although able to survive for long periods without water, it may drink as much as 15 gal (57 liters) when water is available. *See* ARTIODACTYLA.
                                    Charles B. Curtin

Camel's hair

A fine hair known to the American consumer chiefly in the form of high-quality coat fabrics. This textile fiber is obtained from the two-humped bactrian camel, which is native to all parts of Asia. The protective hair covering of the camel is a nonconductor of both heat and cold, also water repellent. In the spring the year's growth of hair, which hangs from the camel in matted strands and tufts, falls off in clumps. This growth, plus the masses of hair shed throughout the year, is the chief source of supply. The camel is sometimes plucked to obtain the down or underhair.

Camel's-hair fabrics are ideal for comfort, particularly when used for overcoating, as they are especially warm and light in weight. Camel's hair is characterized by strength, luster, and smoothness. The best quality is expensive. It is often mixed with wool to improve the quality of the wool fabric. The price of such a mixed cloth is much less than that of a 100% camel's-hair fabric.

In the textile industry camel's hair is divided into three grades. Grade 1 is the soft and silky light-tan underhair. This is short staple or noil of 1–5 in. (2.5–12.5 cm) but is the choicest quality. This was once the only true camel's hair used in the manufacture of apparel. Grade 2 is the intermediate growth, consisting partly of short hairs and partly of coarse outer hairs. Grade 3 consists entirely of coarse outer hairs measuring up to 15 in. (27.5 cm) in length and varying in color from brownish-black to reddish brown. This grade has no value for apparel manufacture; it is suitable only for cordage and for low-quality rugs. *See* ALPACA; CAMEL; CASHMERE; LLAMA; MOHAIR; NATURAL FIBER; VICUNA; WOOL.
                                    M. David Potter

Cameo

A type of carved gemstone in which the background is cut away to leave the subject in relief. Often cameos are cut from stones in which the coloring is layered, resulting in a figure of one color and a background of another. The term cameo, when used without qualification, is usually reserved for those cut from a gem mineral, although they are known also as stone cameos. The commonly encountered cameo cut from shell is properly called a shell cameo.

Most cameos are cut from onyx or agate, but many other varieties of quartz, such as tiger's-eye, bloodstone, sard, carnelian, and amethyst, are used; other materials used include beryl, malachite, hematite, labrodorite, and moonstone. *See* GEM; INTAGLIO (GEMOLOGY).   Richard T. Liddicoat, Jr.

Camera

A device for forming and recording images; the basic tool of photography. In its simplest form, a camera is a light-tight box in which an image is formed by a pinhole or lens at one end on a light-sensitive material at the opposite end. Most cameras contain an aperture and shutter for controlling the amount of light reaching the light-sensitive material (exposure). The receiving material, the film, is usually a plastic sheet or flexible strip coated with a photosensitive silver halide emulsion. It can also be an electronic device such as a Newvicon tube or charge-coupled device, or a photosensitive material for a specific purpose.

Types. The camera was originally a light-tight chamber in which observers saw and sometimes traced the image projected by a pinhole and later by a simple biconvex lens (camera obscura); the first portable model using a lens (camera lucida) was introduced in the mid-1600s. Since the first photographic camera was built by Nicephore Niepce in 1826, many different types have been devised. They can be distinguished by function, application, film size, or format. Distinctions are also based on type of viewfinder and body construction.

Cameras for still photography include box, point-and-shoot, view-and-press, roll film, 35-mm, instant-picture, stereo, underwater, and panoramic. Some categories overlap. Still video and digital cameras use electronic sensors instead of film, and store the image in solid-state memory or on magnetic media or optical disks. Motion picture or cine cameras record movement at regular intervals in a series of frames, which are projected on a screen to create an illusion of movement. Television and video cameras record movement electronically for broadcast and storage on magnetic media or optical disks. Camcorders are video cameras which contain both the image sensor and recording media in a single unit.

Box and simple cameras. These cameras have no (or very few) adjustments and are generally easy to use. They do not require focusing; called focus-free, universal, or fixed-focus, they have a lens with a small aperture. This design maximizes the range of distances from the subject over which sharp images can be formed. This range is called the depth of field. The focus is preset to produce the greatest depth of field, known as the hyperfocal distance.

See GEOMETRICAL OPTICS; LENS (OPTICS).

Simple cameras rely on the wide latitude, that is, the range of exposure which yields acceptable negatives, of modern photographic films and in particular that of color-negative emulsions. Most have a single shutter speed of $\frac{1}{30}$ to $\frac{1}{125}$ s and a single aperture, although a limited selection of settings such as indoors, outdoors, or sunny and cloudy may be provided. A film advance mechanism that prevents double exposure and a basic aiming device are usually present. Many cameras can trigger a flash device (**Fig. 1**).

Disposable cameras (also known as recyclable or single-use) are simple cameras that come loaded with film, which is not replaced after use. The basic disk camera is a modern derivative of the box camera, with automatic film advance and built-in electronic flash.

Many cameras have few controls and are as simple to operate as the box cameras, but they have automatic electronic adjustment of the lens opening and shutter speed to produce the correct exposure. These cameras may have a switch to set the film speed, according to the International Standard Organization (ISO), and are often limited to two settings, ISO 100 and ISO 400.

Simple cameras rely on compromises for focus and exposure control. Although they can produce good photographs under average conditions, much better results can be obtained over a wider range of conditions with adjustable focus and exposure.

Zone focusing cameras are similar to the simple cameras described above, except that the focus can be set within limits. Focus settings may exist for close-up, portrait, group portrait, and landscape.

Point-and-shoot cameras. Some cameras operate as box or simple cameras but with automatic electronic adjustments for producing good pictures. These cameras set exposure control automatically. The focus may be fixed or subject to automatic electronic adjustment. They often feature drop-in or automatic film loading and built-in flash. Some have user overrides, which enable the photographer to choose manual settings in extreme situations, such as strong spot or back lighting.

Although the lens is fixed, many models have dual (switchable) focal length or continuously variable focal length (zoom lenses).

Folding cameras. Except for instant-picture cameras, few folding cameras are now being made; a collapsible bellows between the back and the lens permits compact folding for carrying. They have been made for most film sizes, especially the larger. Some modern cameras use a collapsible or retractable lens which is stored in the camera body when not in use.

View cameras. These large cameras were originally designed for landscapes or views, but are equally useful in commercial studio photography. A flexible bellows is attached to front and rear panels that swing on a rigid base. The front panel holds the lens mounted on a board. The rear panel usually

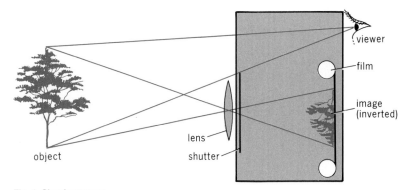

Fig. 1. Simple camera.

contains a ground-glass plate that can be replaced by a film holder. View cameras can be folded for transport; the bellows is primarily functional, connecting the lens board to the film holder, while allowing great freedom of movement between them. These cameras offer a wide range of positions for correcting perspective and controlling the image distortion that results when the subject and film plane are not parallel. Studio or stand cameras used for portraiture are similar in construction, but they may have more limited movements.

Instant-picture cameras. Introduced in 1948, these cameras directly produce a print. The development chemicals are contained within the film package in a pod, which is broken by rollers upon ejection of the print from the camera. Instant-picture cameras must be comparatively large, since the full-size image is used. Instant-picture-type backs are made for other cameras, particularly medium- and large-format view cameras, to produce fast proofs to check lighting and composition before making an exposure on conventional film.

Motion picture cameras. Commonly called movie or cine cameras, they photograph moving objects in a series of images for sequential playback to create an illusion of movement. They differ from still cameras principally in the need to advance the film rapidly during the brief time that the shutter closes between frames. Rates of 18 to 24 frames per second are common, with other rates for special purposes such as time-lapse or high-speed photography. The format is usually specified by the width of the film: 8-mm and super-8-mm (slightly larger image with different sprocketing) cameras are amateur formats, popular for home movies; 16-mm cameras are used for news, scientific, and some theatrical films; and 35- and 70-mm cameras are used primarily for theatrical films. *See* CINEMATOGRAPHY.

Electronic cameras. In these cameras, an electronic detector is used in place of film. The image formed on the detector is changed into an electronic signal which is transmitted or recorded. Since the image is not recorded directly on the sensor, the recording medium does not have to be located in the camera and can be a separate unit connected by wire or by a wireless system.

Electronic cameras that can store images in

analog form on a 2-in. magnetic disk are called still video cameras. Digital cameras capture images electronically and hold the images in encoded form in solid-state memory, usually for transfer to a magnetic or optical medium for more permanent storage and for later retrieval.

Video and television cameras are electronic cameras that capture frame sequences similar to those recorded by motion picture cameras at 30 frames per second. Video cameras that also contain the electronics and medium for recording the images are called camcorders. *See* TELEVISION CAMERA.

Reflex cameras. Reflex cameras use mirrors to reflect the object scene onto a viewing (and often focusing) screen. The mirror erects the inverted image, making viewing easier, although motion left and right is still reversed in the finder. A camera that uses this mirror with a pair of matched lenses (one for viewing and focusing, the other for picture taking) is called a twin-lens reflex. In such a camera the two lenses are coupled, and the mirror and focusing screen are so placed that a sharp image on the focusing screen corresponds to a sharp image on the film plane (**Fig. 2**).

To eliminate parallax, various methods of viewing through the lens have been used. A beam splitter may be placed behind the lens, channeling part of the image to the viewfinder and part to the film. This arrangement reduces the efficiency of both the focusing and picture taking. A mirror placed directly behind the lens can reflect the image from it directly to the viewing screen. By removing the mirror from the light path during the exposure, the film receives the full intensity of the image.

The single-lens reflex camera uses the same lens with the aid of a mirror for viewing and photographing (**Fig. 3**). Since picture taking and viewing use the same lens, the single-lens reflex has the advantage that the viewfinder always shows the precise scene to be recorded by the film. In some single-lens reflexes, particulary larger ones, the mirror must be reset manually after exposure, usually by using the film advance lever. Most single-lens reflexes employ an instant-return mirror,

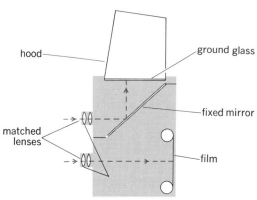

Fig. 2. Twin-lens reflex camera.

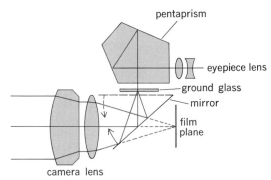

Fig. 3. Single-lens reflex camera.

which is virtually always in the viewing position but flips out of the way immediately before and during the exposure. A pentaprism (or a group of mirrors called a Poro prism) may be used between the focusing screen and viewfinder eyepiece to restore proper left-right motion while viewing an image oriented like the subject. This makes it easy to aim the camera and follow moving subjects. Various focusing aids may be present on the built-in focusing screen, including a central split image which is brought into alignment at the point of focus. Some single-lens reflex cameras allow for a change of focusing screen for various purposes.

Autofocusing single-lens reflexes. The semisilvered mirror found in some metering cameras can be used to channel the light to a charge-coupled-device array sensor for detecting focus. The camera electronics can then be used to focus the lens. This type of autofocusing single-lens reflex is widely used by amateurs and some professional photographers and is a leading feature of current 35-mm camera design. *See* CHARGE-COUPLED DEVICES.

Like the focusing screen, the sensor array must be at the same distance from the mirror as the film plane. The array may detect the intensity maximum or compare two beams to check focus. The result of the measurement may be relayed to the operator via a display in the viewfinder indicating "focus" or "out of focus" or the direction to turn the lens to achieve focus.

The camera itself may focus the lens by using a motor and connecting shaft or by controlling a motor built into the lens.

Other types. Many cameras have been devised for specific purposes. Wide-field or panoramic cameras take extreme wide-angle views, some up to a full 360°. This can be useful in photographing landscapes or for photographing large groups of people. In extreme wide-angle photography, some cameras swing the lens during exposure in synchronization with the shutter.

Underwater cameras must be watertight up to a pressure of several atmospheres. Some are specialized in design, although many are conventional cameras placed in a watertight container with linkages to the exterior for control of focus and exposure. *See* UNDERWATER PHOTOGRAPHY.

Aerial cameras may use special mounts to

counteract vibration. They may also move the film during exposure to compensate for aircraft motion relative to the ground. These cameras can be used for reconnaissance, mapping, or scientific surveys. *See* AERIAL PHOTOGRAPH.

Stereo cameras have multiple lenses for taking pictures in pairs. When these pictures are viewed simultaneously, each with a different eye, the original three-dimensional depth is created.

Many cameras have been devised for scientific studies. Medical cameras can photograph inside the human body. Streak and slit cameras record images for time-motion studies. Holographic cameras record diffraction patterns instead of real images for reconstruction of three-dimensional subjects. Lenses adapted to ultraviolet or infrared rather than visible light are used with film of corresponding sensitivity. Cameras aboard space satellites gave the first view of the Earth from space and of the dark side of the Moon. *See* APPLICATIONS SATELLITES; HOLOGRAPHY; REMOTE SENSING.

Films. Camera images were originally recorded full size, and cameras were built accordingly. When the recorded images are enlarged and printed, or transparencies projected to the same size, the best results are obtained from the largest recorded image. Advances in film technology, however, have produced better images of smaller format compared to older film. Cameras can accommodate a variety of film types, sizes, shapes, and aspect ratios (ratio of image height to width). Cameras may accommodate film in sheets, cartridges, or roll with or without backing. For instant photography, photostatting, and some special purposes, the recorded image is often used full size, and consequently determines the shape and size of the camera.

The most popular format for still photography is the 24×36 mm ($1 \times 1\frac{1}{2}$ in.) image produced by the 35-mm camera on a roll of edge-perforated 35-mm film. Considered as miniature devices when introduced, 35-mm cameras typically take film containing 24 or 36 exposures and are used for amateur, professional, and some studio photography. Smaller formats are widely used for security and some leisure photography. The extremely compact disk and 110, 126, and half-frame 35-mm cameras are employed in amateur and snapshot photography. A variety of image formats may be produced on a single film size. A paper-backed roll $2\frac{1}{2} \times 32\frac{1}{2}$ in. (6×81 cm), so-called 120-size film, is used in cameras that create images of various sizes. Some cameras can produce images in more than one size by changing the film holder or masking the film plane and adjusting the film advancement. View cameras use sheets of film ranging from 4×5 in. (10×13 cm) to 8×10 in. (20×25 cm) and larger. *See* PHOTOGRAPHIC MATERIALS.

Viewfinders and focusing aids. The image is viewed most accurately on the film plane. The operator places a ground-glass plate at the film plane and adjusts the camera position and lens focus until the desired image appears sharp (and inverted) on the glass, which is replaced by the film in a holder for exposure. This time-consuming process is impractical for many applications, particularly if the subject is moving.

The photographer looks through the viewfinder to see exactly what the camera will photograph and to determine the focus. Viewfinders range from simple frames to screens with focusing aids surrounded by information displays.

Viewfinders of simple cameras may consist only of a plastic or metal frame that is held up to the eye to approximate the angle of view of the lens. Many cameras have a lens or group of lenses that compensates for the magnification or reduction of the picture-taking lens. Since viewfinder and photographic lenses are often separate, they do not see precisely the same images; their difference is called parallax. Although this is not usually a problem, subjects near the edge of a picture may not appear on the film. This error increases as the focusing distance decreases, and can be especially troublesome for close-up photography.

Cameras are focused either by changing the distance between lens and film or by moving specific elements within a complex lens, often by turning the outer lens barrel. Some cameras are focused by turning the lens barrel until a pointer is aligned with a point on a scale that represents the distance from the camera to the subject. A rangefinder may be placed on the camera which uses a split image to determine the object distance. When a lever or dial on the rangefinder is adjusted until the two images coincide, the distance can be read from a scale on the rangefinder. Some cameras connect the rangefinder to the lens via a cam, so that turning the lens adjusts the rangefinder to bring both to a focus at the same point. These are called rangefinder-coupled cameras. *See* RANGEFINDER (OPTICS).

Electronic rangefinding devices built into the camera may be used instead of the optical type. These may measure object distance by timing the reflection of a sound wave emanating from the camera (sonar), or by projecting an infrared beam from a small window on the camera and locating the beam by rotating a mirror behind a second window. By knowing the angle of the mirror and the distance between the mirror and the infrared emitter, the subject distance is electronically calculated by trigonometry. The lens is automatically set to the proper focus or focus zone.

Viewfinders of electronic and video cameras may be simple optical finders like those found in point-and-shoot cameras, but most use electronic viewfinders. Since the electronic sensor at the film plane relays the image information to an electronic recording device, this image can be relayed simultaneously to a small television monitor. This is usually a miniature cathode-ray tube viewed through a magnifying eyepiece. Because power requirements and cost are high, black and white monitors are often used, although color liquid-crystal displays are becoming more popular.

Exposure control. To produce a photograph or electronic image, the camera must match the image brightness to the sensitivity of the receiving medium or device. When that medium is photographic film, sensitivity is reported as ISO film speed, with each doubling of speed indicating an increase of one photographic stop of sensitivity; that is, one smaller aperture, half the shutter speed, or half the subject illumination would be required to expose the image properly. Electronic sensors may be rated with an equivalent ISO. Image intensity is usually controlled by an iris diaphragm serving as the lens aperture. The ratio of the lens focal length to this aperture is called the f/stop. Although technically a function of the lens, in some designs the aperture is located inside the camera. Many cameras can control the aperture in the lens, keeping it at the widest possible setting for bright viewing and focusing of single-lens reflexes and closing the aperture to the proper setting during exposure.

Shutters. The shutter controls exactly when and for how long the light is admitted to the image-forming material. This can be simply a cap that is removed and then replaced over a pinhole; or a metal flap, or a group of such blades (leaf shutter), that swings aside behind the lens to create the exposure; or a slit that moves across the film plane during the exposure (focal-plane shutter). Shutters can provide exposures ranging from several seconds to small fractions of a second. Speeds up to $^1/_{500}$ s are common for leaf shutters, with focal-plane shutters routinely producing exposures as short as $^1/_{1000}$ s, and some reaching $^1/_{12,000}$ s.

Exposure meters. To determine the optimal shutter speed and aperture combination for the film or image sensor, it is necessary to determine the brightness of the scene being recorded. A photosensitive device such as a cadmium sulfide cell or silicon photodiode is often employed to measure illumination. Originally a separate device, the light meter was used to determine f/stop and shutter speed combinations for proper exposures. Today this device is often built into the camera, although it can only measure the light reflected from the subject. In some cameras, particularly 35-mm point-and-shoot cameras, the cell is placed on the front behind a small lens element designed to approximate the angle of view of the photographic lens. On the most basic cameras, this shows when light is sufficient to take a picture with the recording medium of given sensitivity and the available range of shutter speeds and apertures. Some cameras automatically adjust aperture and shutter speed to obtain the proper exposure as shown by the cell. Other cameras, particularly single-lens reflexes, have an indicator in the viewfinder to show when the shutter speed–aperture combination will give

proper exposure. *See* PHOTOCONDUCTIVE CELL; PHOTOELECTRIC DEVICES.

Like viewing, metering through the photographic lens has proved effective and is widely used. Some single-lens reflex cameras have photocells in the mirror box which look forward through the lens and are aimed at the subject. Others use similar cells to measure the intensity of the image (or parts thereof) formed on the focusing screen. Since the image changes with the angle of view provided by the lens, the angle of the metering is proportional to lens coverage and changes with changes of focal length.

Sometimes a semisilvered mirror is used as the instant return mirror. This mirror acts as a beam splitter, allowing a small portion of the light to pass through it to the metering device while reflecting most of the light to the focusing screen. Some cameras have cells facing toward the film plane to monitor the exposure directly from the film. Some cells are intended to measure electronic flash exposures, which are so short in duration that they can be measured only during the actual exposure.

Metering cells may not measure the entire subject evenly. Those that do so, even approximately, are called averaging meters. Meters that concentrate their sensitivity on the center of the frame (where the main subject is often placed) are called center-weighted systems. Some systems measure only a small central portion, in so-called spot metering. Some cameras use more than one metering system. *See* EXPOSURE METER.

Automatic modes. Still cameras control the combination of shutter speed and f/stop used for each exposure. (Motion picture and video cameras usually offer less control of shutter speed, which must be higher than the frame rates.) Many combinations of shutter speed and aperture yield the same exposure at the image plane. Different selections produce different photographic results: higher shutter speeds freeze action or reduce blurring caused by camera motion during exposure; smaller apertures yield greater depth of field. The photographer may want the camera to select either or both settings automatically.

A camera selecting both shutter speed and aperture is said to be in a programmed autoexposure mode. Some cameras offer a choice of exposure programs, either automatically selected by the camera according to lens focal length, or operator-selected with a preference for greater depth of field or higher shutter speeds.

Some cameras allow the photographer to choose shutter speed or f/stop and automatically make the corresponding setting. When the operator sets only the shutter speed, the camera is set to shutter-priority autoexposure. Multimode cameras allow the photographer to select among autoexposure options, often including full manual control, in which the operator sets both f/stop and shutter speed.

So-called multimode cameras offer a choice

of automated exposure modes. This versatility
is especially prominent in 35-mm single-lens
reflexes. Some cameras offer variations of the basic
autoexposure options. Some have autoexposure
modes in which the photographer, instead of
selecting the actual shutter speed, selects the
minimum shutter speed acceptable, and the camera
acts as if it were in a special program mode if there
is enough light for a higher shutter speed.

Automatic multipattern metering. By dividing the scene
into sections, the camera can often automatically
set the best exposure in situations where a
conventional, single photocell might err, as with a
subject lit in silhouette or a strong spotlight. Several
variations exist, but they all measure the light in the
center of the subject and in one or more adjoining
areas. By comparing combinations of specific
values and checking illumination differences in
adjoining sections (and sometimes considering
the subject's position and distance from the
autofocusing system), the best estimate for proper
exposure setting is made electronically.

Auxiliary equipment. Many cameras accommodate
a variety of lenses. Those with focal lengths
close to the diagonal of the camera format
are considered normal and produce an image
magnification roughly equivalent to human vision.
Lenses with shorter focal lengths are wide-angle
and may give coverage up to 240°. Telephoto
lenses have focal lengths longer than the format
diagonal. The narrow angle of view increases
the image magnification, allowing photography of
small details at greater distances.

A flash unit produces a brief burst of bright
light to allow photography under dim illumination.
The camera must open the shutter fully during
the brightest portion of the flash. An electronic
flash can have various durations. Some cameras,
particularly single-lens reflexes, can measure the
subject through the lens and then control the
flash via a special contact. *See* STROBOSCOPIC
PHOTOGRAPHY.

Tripod stands hold cameras steady, giving sharp
pictures at longer shutter speeds than are possible
with hand-held cameras. Winders and motor drives
allow still cameras to take short sequences at rates
from one to almost six frames per second.

Special backs used on some cameras imprint
digital information on or between the negatives.
Accessories can fire the cameras automatically at
specified intervals (intervalometers) or for specific
events (remote triggers). Some backs can even
change the film in midroll. *See* PHOTOGRAPHY.

Lawrence R. White

Camerata

An extinct subclass of stalked Crinoidea comprising
about 210 Paleozoic genera ranging from the Lower
Ordovician to the upper Permian. The calyx was
composed of a rigid, boxlike structure of many

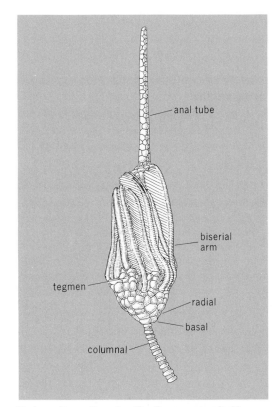

Thylacocrinus, a Devonian dicyclic camerate crinoid.

small, polygonal plates. The lower arm plates
(brachials) were solidly incorporated into the upper
part of the calyx, and were separated by small
interbrachial and interradial plates (see **illus.**). The
tegmen was rigid and roofed over the mouth and
proximal food grooves. Advanced forms had a long,
slender, solid anal tube with the anal opening at the
tip. All but a few primitive Ordovician forms had
biserial arms, and the arms bore pinnules.

Both dicyclic forms with infrabasal plates (order
Diplobathrida; 50 genera) and monocyclic forms
without infrabasals (order Monobathrida; 160 genera) are known. The former became extinct during middle Mississippian time, the latter persisted to
the close of the Paleozoic Era and flourished during Mississippian time. Silurian camerates were important reef dwellers. Pennsylvanian and Permian
monobathrids had a much simplified calyx, with
the arms free above the radials, and were homeo-
morphs of the more diversified inadunate crinoids
of the time. The youngest known camerate crinoids
are from Permian rocks on the island of Timor in
Indonesia. *See* MISSISSIPPIAN.

The origin of the Camerata is obscure but
presumably occurred during Cambrian or earliest
Ordovician time. Camerates are not closely related
to the other two large subclasses of Paleozoic
crinoids, the flexibles and the inadunates. *See*
CRINOIDEA; ECHINODERMATA.   N. Gary Lane

Bibliography. R. C. Moore and C. Teichert (eds.),
Treatise on Invertebrate Paleontology, part T:
Echinodermata 2, vols. 1 and 2, 1978; G. D.

Webster, *Bibliography and Index of Paleozoic Crinoids, 1974–1980,* Geol. Soc. Amer. Microform Publ. 16, 1986.

Campanulales

An order of flowering plants, division Magnoliophyta in the subclass Asteridae of the class Magnoliopsida (dicotyledons). It consists of 7 families and about 2500 species. The order is distinguished in this subclass by its chiefly herbaceous habit, alternate leaves, inferior ovary, and stamens which are free from the corolla or attached at the base of the tube. About 2000 of the species belong to the single family Campanulaceae. This family and two others in the order have a specialized pollen presentation mechanism. The anthers converge or unite around the young style, which grows up through the anther tube and pushes out the pollen. Several familiar ornamentals, including the Canterbury bell (*Campanula medium*) and the cardinal flower (*Lobelia cardinalis*), belong to the Campanulaceae. *See* ASTERIDAE; MAGNOLIOPHYTA; MAGNOLIOPSIDA; ORNAMENTAL PLANTS; PLANT KINGDOM.

Arthur Cronquist; T. M. Barkley

Camphor

A bicyclic, saturated terpene ketone. It exists in the optically active dextro and levo forms, and as the racemic mixture of the two forms. All of these melt within a degree of 178°C (352°F). The principal form is *dextro*-camphor, which occurs in the wood and leaves of the camphor tree (*Cinnamomum camphora*). Taiwan is the chief source of natural camphor which is distilled from the wood of this tree. Camphor is also synthesized commercially on a large scale from pinene which yields mainly the racemic variety. The structural formula of the molecule is shown below.

Camphor has a characteristic odor; it crystallizes in thin plates and sublimes readily at ordinary temperatures.

Camphor has use in liniments and as a mild rubefacient, analgesic, and antipruritic. It has a local action on the gastrointestinal tract, producing a feeling of warmth and comfort in the stomach. It is also used in photographic film and as a plasticizer in the manufacture of plastics. *See* KETONE; PINE TERPENE; TERPENE.

Everett L. Saul

Bibliography. T. W. Solomons, *Organic Chemistry,* 5th ed., 1991.

Camphor tree

The plant *Cinnamomum camphora*, a member of the laurel family (Lauraceae) and a native of China, Japan, and Taiwan (see **illus.**). The tree grows to a height of 40 ft (12 m), is dense-topped, and has shiny, dark, evergreen leaves. It is widely planted

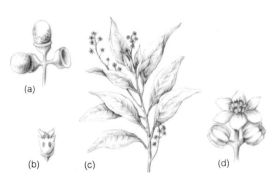

Camphor tree (*Cinnamomum camphora*). (*a*) Fruits. (*b*) Stamen. (*c*) Branch. (*d*) Flower.

as an ornamental tree. All parts of the tree contain camphor, as essential oil which is obtained from the finely ground wood and leaves by distillation with steam. The crude camphor crystallizes on the surface of the still. After it is removed and refined, it is the commercial gum camphor, which is used medicinally, in perfumes and in the manufacture of celluloid and nitrocellulose compounds. *See* CAMPHOR; MAGNOLIALES.

Perry D. Strausbaugh / Earl L. Core

Camptostromatoidea

A small class of primitive echinoderms (subphylum Echinozoa) known from the single species *Camptostroma roddyi* based on about 200 specimens from the Early Cambrian (*Bonnia-Olenellus* Zone) in southeastern Pennsylvania. *Camptostroma* was originally described as a hydrozoan or jellyfish, but it was recognized as an echinoderm and the new class Camptostromatoidea was set up for it. *Camptostroma* has been reinterpreted as an early edrioasteroid, and as a "stem echinoderm" ancestral to several other groups including edrioasteroids. Because of *Camptostroma*'s puzzling morphology, different reconstructions of it have been made (see **illus.**). It has a conical or domal theca or body with a nearly circular outline, divided into a pleated lower theca with larger and smaller overlapping plates, and a domed upper theca made up of large plates with pores on their margins surrounded by numerous smaller plates. The upper theca bears five straight to curved ambulacra protected by numerous cover plates and radiating from the central mouth, and a small anal pyramid at one edge. *Camptostroma* probably had the lower theca either embedded in the soft sediment or attached to objects lying on the sea floor, making it a stationary or attached,

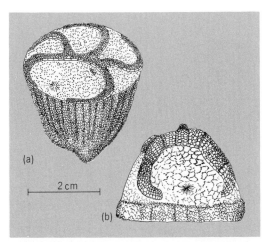

Camptostroma roddyi from the Early Cambrian of Pennsylvania. (*a*) Reconstructed oblique side view showing theca with conical lower part inferred to have been partly buried in the sea floor (*after C. R. C. Paul and A. B. Smith, Biol. Rev., 59:451, 1984*). (*b*) Reconstructed side view showing domed theca with flat lower surface inferred to have been attached to the sea floor or to objects on it (*after K. Derstler, Ph.D. dissertation, University of California, Davis, p. 120, 1985*).

low-level suspension feeder using tube feet in the ambulacra to capture small food particles drifting by the theca. The unusual thecal plating is the main feature separating *Camptostroma* from later Edrioasteroidea, which it otherwise resembles, but this genus may also have been ancestral to other classes such as the Eocrinoidea. *See* ECHINODERMATA; ECHINOZOA; EDRIOASTEROIDEA.

James Sprinkle

Bibliography. K. Derstler, Ph.D. dissertation, University of California, Davis, 1985; J. W. Durham, *J. Paleontol.*, 40:1216–1220, 1966; C. R. C. Paul and A. B. Smith, *Biol. Rev.*, 59:443–481, 1984.

Canal

An artificial open channel usually used to convey water or vessels from one point to another. Canals are generally classified according to use as irrigation, power, flood-control, drainage, or navigation canals or channels. All but the last type are regarded as water conveyance canals.

Canals may be lined or unlined. Linings may consist of plain or reinforced concrete, cement mortar, asphalt, brick, stone, buried synthetic membranes, or compacted earth materials. Linings serve to reduce water losses by seepage or percolation through pervious foundations or embankments and to lessen the cost of weed control. Concrete and other hard-surface linings also permit higher water velocities and, therefore, steeper gradients and smaller cross sections, which may reduce costs and the amount of right-of-way required.

Water conveyance canals. The character of material along the bottom and sides of a canal must be considered in determining whether lining is re-

quired. The velocity in an irrigation canal must be sufficiently low to avoid erosion of the canal banks and bottom, and it must be high enough to prevent deposition of silt: Velocities of 1.5–3.5 ft/s (0.46–1.1 m/s) are normally used for earth canals, and about 7 ft/s (2 m/s) is the usual maximum for concrete-lined irrigation canals. The velocity depends on canal slope, boundary roughness, and proportions of the cross-sectional area. Canal capacity Q in ft^3/s may be expressed by the formula $Q = AV$, where A is the cross-sectional area in square feet, and V is the average velocity in ft/s.

Most irrigation canals are trapezoidal in cross section. Their side slopes are generally either 1.5:1 or 2:1 (horizontal to vertical) depending on the type of soil, but flatter slopes are used in unstable materials. Side slopes of concrete-lined irrigation canals are generally 1.25:1 or 1.5:1. They occasionally may be as high as 2:1, as for example in the San Luis Canal (**Fig. 1**). Freeboard, or the vertical distance between maximum water surface and top of canal bank, generally ranges from 1 ft (0.3 m) for small earth laterals to 4 ft (1.2 m) for earth canals. Freeboard for concrete-lined canals ranges from 0.5 to 3.5 ft (0.15 to 1.1 m) to the top of the lining, depending on capacity.

Irrigation canal intakes usually consist of a headworks and a river control structure with some form of intake gates to regulate the quantity of water admitted or stop the flow into the canal. Frequently, when the canal diverts from a stream that transports considerable sediment, the intake may be designed to keep out as much sediment as possible. This is accomplished by (1) locating the canal intake on the stream where the bed load is the smallest; (2) using weirs that divert water from the less silty upper layers of the flowing stream called skimming weirs; or (3) interposing basins in which much of the sand and silt are deposited before the water enters the canal. The deposited material is removed from these settling or desilting basins by occasional sluicing or dredging.

Irrigation canals usually require check structures in them to regulate the elevation of the water on the upstream side and wasteways as a safety device to carry off surplus water. The checks hold back the water in case of a break in the canal banks and retard the flow when the canal is being emptied to prevent a sudden evacuation and resulting uplift in the lining or sloughing of saturated banks. Hard-surfaced linings are frequently protected from uplift by automatic relief valves placed in the bottom and sides of the canal. *See* IRRIGATION (AGRICULTURE).

Although generally similar to irrigation canals in design, power, flood-control, and drainage canals or channels have special requirements. Power canals are placed on minimum grade to conserve head for power development; hence velocities are usually low. Rectangular wooden, concrete, or steel flumes with high ratio of depth to width are often used for this purpose. Because power canals are subject to sudden changes in flow, overflow wasteways are usually provided

Fig. 1. Segment of the San Luis irrigation canal in California. A major waterway in the western United States, it is 103 mi (165 km) long, 200 ft (60 m) wide, and 36 ft (11 m) deep. (*U.S. Bureau of Reclamation and State of California*)

as well as ample freeboard.

Banks of flood-control channels constructed in earth are lined with grass or rock riprap for protection against erosion by flood flows. Grass protection is used for velocities from about 3 to 8 ft/s (0.9 to 2.4 m/s), and riprap for velocities

Fig. 2. Walter F. George Lock, Dam and Powerhouse on the Chattahoochee River, Alabama-Georgia boundary. The lock chamber can be seen at right center of the photograph. (*U.S. Army Corps of Engineers*)

of 8 to 18 ft/s (2.4 to 5.5 m/s). Either rectangular or trapezoidal concrete-lined channels are used for velocities exceeding 18 ft/s (5.5 m/s), although in some cases concrete lining is used for lower velocities to reduce the size of channel.

Drainage canals are deeply excavated to facilitate the drainage of surrounding land. They usually have a minimum grade and small depths of water flow.

Navigation canals and canalized rivers. Navigation canals are artificial inland waterways for boats, barges, or ships. A canalized river is one that has been made navigable by construction of one or more weirs or overflow dams (**Fig. 2**) to impound river flow, thereby providing navigable depths. Locks may be built in navigation canals and canalized rivers to enable vessels to move to higher or lower water levels.

Navigation canals are often built along portions of canalized rivers or located so as to connect two such rivers. They are adapted to the topography by a series of level reaches connected by locks. Sea-level navigation canals, connecting two tidal bodies of water, are excavated sufficiently deep to preclude the need for locks, if the tidal flow permits.

The dimensions of a navigation canal are determined primarily by the size, and to some extent by the speed, of the vessels that are to use it. Depth must be sufficient to assure bottom clearance under all operating conditions, and ordinarily the width allows vessels to pass each other safely. The canal cross section is usually trapezoidal, with side slopes ranging from 1.5:1 to 3:1 or flatter, depending on the stability of the bank material. Sections cut in rock may have vertical or near-vertical sides. Earth banks of some navigation canals are protected against erosion from wave action by placing rock riprap or similar protection near the water surface. *See* INLAND WATERWAYS TRANSPORTATION.

Locks. A lock (Fig. 2) is a chamber equipped with gates at both upstream and downstream ends. Water impounded in the chamber is used to raise or lower a vessel from one elevation to another. The lock chamber is filled and emptied by means of filling and emptying valves and a culvert system usually located in the walls and bottom of the lock.

After a vessel enters the lock chamber, the afterward gates are closed and the water level is lowered (if the vessel is headed downstream) by operation of the emptying valve, or raised (if the vessel is headed upstream) by operation of the filling valve. When the water level in the chamber reaches the water level forward of the vessel, the forward set of gates is opened and the vessel leaves the lock.

Maximum lift of a lock is the vertical distance from the normal pool upstream of the lock to the low-water surface downstream of the lock. Low lifts simplify design problems, but generally in developing a major waterway it will be more economical to use fewer higher-lift locks. Lock lifts vary from a few feet in tidal canals to over 100 ft (30 m) in major rivers, such as the Columbia and Snake. Lock widths vary from 56 to 110 ft (17 to 33 m) and usable lengths vary from 400 to 1200 ft (120 to 370 m), except that smaller locks are used when all the traffic consists of small craft.

On some canalized rivers having low-lift locks, dams contain movable sections which are lowered during periods of moderate or high flow to permit the unobstructed passage of vessels and barges over the dam. The locks are used in these rivers only during periods of low flow when the movable sections of the dams are closed to create sufficient depth of water for navigation. *See* OPEN CHANNEL.

Corps of Engineers; Bureau of Reclamation

Bibliography. A. J. Chadwick and J. C. Morfett, *Hydraulics in Civil and Environmental Engineering*, 2d ed., 1993; H. W. King and E. F. Brater, *Handbook of Hydraulics*, 6th ed., 1976; J. K. Vennard and R. L. Street, *Elementary Fluid Mechanics*, 6th ed., 1983.

Cancer (constellation)

The Crab, in astronomy, a winter constellation and the faintest of the zodiacal groups. Cancer, the fourth sign of the zodiac, is important because during early times it marked the northernmost limit of the ecliptic, when the zodiacal system was adopted. The Tropic of Cancer takes its name from

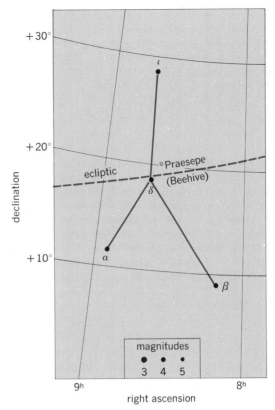

Line pattern of constellation Cancer. Grid lines represent the coordinates of the sky. Apparent brightness, or magnitudes, of stars are shown by sizes of dots, which are graded by appropriate numbers as indicated.

this constellation. The four faint stars, α, β, δ, and ι, form a rough Y outline, which is suggestive of a crab (see **illus.**). In the center of Cancer is a hazy object. This is a magnificent cluster of faint stars called Praesepe (the Beehive) or the Manger. *See* CONSTELLATION; ZODIAC.

Ching-Sung Yu

Cancer (medicine)

The common name for a malignant neoplasm or tumor. Neoplasms are new growths and can be divided into benign and malignant types, although in some instances the distinction is unclear. The most important differentiating feature is that a malignant tumor will invade surrounding structures and metastasize (spread) to distant sites whereas a benign tumor will not. Other distinctions between benign and malignant growth include the following: malignancies but not benign types are composed of highly atypical cells; malignancies tend to show more rapid growth than benign neoplasms, and are composed, in part, of cells showing frequent mitotic activity; and malignant tumors tend to grow progressively without self-limitation. *See* MITOSIS; TUMOR.

Malignant neoplasms that arise from cells of mesenchymal origin (for example, bone muscle, connective tissue) are called sarcomas. Those that develop from epithelial cells and tissues (for example, skin, mucosal membranes, and glandular tissues) are termed carcinomas. Carcinomas usually metastasize initially by way of lymphatic channels, whereas sarcomas spread to distant organs through the bloodstream.

Etiology. The cause of most types of human cancers is unknown. However, a number of factors are thought to be operative in the development of some malignant neoplasms. Genetic factors are thought to be causally related to some human malignancies such as lung cancer in that the incidence of cancer among persons with a positive family history of cancer may be three times as high as in those who do not have a family history. A number of different neoplasms are known to be genetically related and may be due to damage or changes in chromosome structure. These include such neoplasms as retinoblastoma (an eye tumor), pheochromocytoma and medullary thyroid carcinoma (adrenal and thyroid neoplasms), and several types of neoplasms that occur in people who have genetically caused immune deficiency syndromes; in these individuals there is a marked increase in lymphoma (cancer of the lymph glands). *See* IMMUNOLOGICAL DEFICIENCY; LYMPHOMA.

Radiation in various forms is thought to be responsible for up to 3% of all cancers. Persons who receive radiation therapy for some other type of malignant neoplasm, or who are exposed to ionizing radiation from atomic blasts or accidents, have an increase in leukemia. Also, people who receive radiation to the neck have a higher incidence of thyroid carcinoma. Electromagnetic radiation from the Sun (solar radiation) is associated with a higher incidence of many types of skin cancer, including malignant melanoma. There has been a distinct and growing concern about naturally occurring radon gas, from the decay of radioactive rocks in the Earth's crust, concentrated in certain areas of the world such as the Redding Prong in the northeastern United States. Radon gas has been stated to cause up to 10% of all lung cancers, a finding that would be consistent with studies showing that certain types of lung cancer are increased in uranium miners. *See* LEUKEMIA; RADIATION BIOLOGY.

In the United States the carcinogens in tobacco account for up to one-third of all cancer deaths in men and 5–10% in women. The increasing incidence and death rate from cancer of the lung in women is alarming, and is directly related to the increasing prevalence of cigarette smoking by women. There is absolutely no doubt that the single most important action that could be taken to reduce the incidence of cancer in the United States would be to markedly reduce or to eliminate cigarette smoking. Cigarette smoking and the heavy consumption of ethyl alcohol appear to act synergistically in the development of oral, esophageal, and gastric cancers.

There are several carcinogens to which people are exposed occupationally that result in the development of cancer, although the mechanisms by which they cause neoplasms are sometimes poorly understood. For example, arsenic is associated with lung, skin, and liver cancer; asbestos causes mesotheliomas (cancer of the pleural, peritoneal, and pericardial cavities); benzene causes leukemia; and vinyl chloride causes angiosarcomas (tumors of blood vessels) of the liver. *See* MUTAGENS AND CARCINOGENS.

Certain drugs and hormones have been found to cause certain types of neoplasms. Postmenopausal women taking estrogen hormones have a much higher incidence of endometrial cancer (cancer of the lining of the uterine cavity). Alkylating agents that are used in the treatment of a variety of cancers have been shown to cause acute leukemia. Persons who receive organ transplants and are treated with immunosuppressive drugs, such as azathioprine, have an increased incidence of cancer of the lymphoid cells (lymphomas). *See* IMMUNOSUPPRESSION.

The role of diet and nutrition in the development of malignant tumors is controversial and still under investigation. Some epidemiologic studies have shown that certain diets, such as those high in saturated fats, are associated with an increased incidence of certain types of neoplasm, such as colon cancer. Vitamin A–containing compounds have also been shown epidemiologically to prevent some cancers, including lung cancers. In addition, some substances, such as nitrites, used to cure such foods as bacon, are causally associated with gastrointestinal cancers.

The role of viruses in the development of human cancers is being studied. A type of lymphoma that occurs primarily in southern Japan is known to be caused by a retrovirus referred to as human T-cell lymphoma and leukemia virus type I (HTLV-I). Epstein-Barr virus, a deoxyribonucleic acid (DNA) virus of the herpes family, is closely associated with African Burkitt's lymphoma and a tumor of the nasopharynx (nasopharyngeal carcinoma). There is an increased incidence of cancer of liver cells in people who are infected with hepatitis B virus. Whether hepatitis B virus directly causes the tumor or is one of many factors in the development of this type of tumor is uncertain. Certain strains of human papilloma virus (HPV) are thought to cause some cases of uterine cervical carcinoma. *See* EPSTEIN-BARR VIRUS; HERPES; RETROVIRUS; TUMOR VIRUSES.

It is generally accepted that the neoplastic condition is caused by alterations in genetic mechanisms involved in cellular differentiation. In malignant cells, normal cellular processes are bypassed due to the actions of a select group of genes called oncogenes which regulate cellular activities. A group of these highly conserved genes exist in normal cells and are called proto-oncogenes. These genes appear to be important in regulating cellular growth during embryonic development. Although these genes were originally identified in oncogenic retroviruses, proto-oncogenes have been found in normal tissue and also have been identified in a variety of human cancers. Increased amounts of these proto-oncogenes have been seen in small-cell undifferentiated cancer of the lung, colon cancer, breast cancer, and lymphomas. Since proto-oncogenes seem to be important in embryonic growth, it is not surprising that in the process of carcinogenesis these genes can be expressed and can lead to the proliferation of malignant cells. It is thought that in carcinogenesis these proto-oncogenes become unmasked or changed during the breakage or translocation of chromosomes. These genes that were previously suppressed in the cell then become functional, and in some instances lead to the excessive production of growth factors which could be important in the neoplastic state. *See* ONCOGENES.

Incidence. The incidence of malignancies varies with regard to race, geographical location, sex, age, hereditary factors, and socioeconomic status. In certain parts of Africa, for example, liver cancer is the most common malignant neoplasm, whereas in the United States lung cancer in men and breast cancer in women are the most common neoplasms. There has been a marked rise in the incidence of lung cancer in both men and women due to cigarette smoking, whereas most other common tumors, such as cancer of the colon and stomach, have remained stable or even decreased.

Signs, symptoms, and staging. The physical changes that cancer produces in the body vary considerably, depending on the type of tumor, location, rate of growth, and whether it has metastasized. The American Cancer Society has widely publicized cancer's seven warning signals: (1) a change in bowel or bladder habits; (2) a sore that does not heal; (3) unusual bleeding or discharge; (4) a thickening or lump in the breast or elsewhere; (5) indigestion or difficulty in swallowing; (6) an obvious change in a wart or mole; and (7) a nagging cough or hoarseness.

In current medical practice, most cancers are staged according to tumor size, metastases to lymph nodes, and distant metastases. This type of staging is useful in determining the most effective therapy and the prognosis.

Treatment. The progression, or lack thereof, of a given cancer is highly variable and depends on the type of neoplasm and the response to treatment. Treatment modalities include surgery, chemotherapy, radiation therapy, hormonal manipulation, and immunotherapy. In general, each type of cancer is treated very specifically, and often a combination of the various modalities is used, for example, surgery preceded or followed by radiation therapy. The response to treatment depends on the type of tumor, its size, and whether it has spread. *See* CHEMOTHERAPY; IMMUNOTHERAPY; ONCOLOGY; RADIOGRAPHY.

Samuel P. Hammar

Bibliography. V. T. DeVita, Jr., et al., *Cancer: Principles and Practices of Oncology*, 1985; V. T. DeVita, Jr., et al. (eds.), *Important Advances in Oncology*, 1985; J. F. Holland and E. Frei, *Cancer Medicine*, 1982.

Cancrinite

A family of minerals, related to the scapolite family, characteristically occurring in basic rocks such as nepheline syenites and sodalite syenites. A typical specimen is shown in the **illustration**. Cancrinite is hexagonal, $a = 1.28$, $c = 0.52$ nanometers respectively, space group $P6_3$, and is based on a three-dimensional linkage of $[AlO_4]$ and $[SiO_4]$ tetrahedra. Four-, six-, and twelve-membered aluminosilicate rings can be discerned in the structure. Large anions such as $[SO_4]^{2-}$ and $[CO_3]^{2-}$ occur in the hexagonal channels of the structure. The cancrinite member is white, yellow, greenish, or reddish. It has perfect prismatic cleavage, hardness is 5–6 on Mohs scale, and the specific gravity is 2.45.

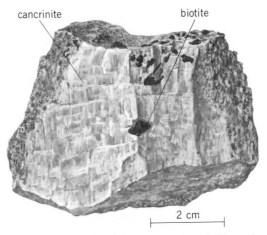

cancrinite   biotite

2 cm

Cancrinite with biotite in nepheline syenite rock, Bigwood Township, Ontario, Canada. (*Specimen from Department of Geology, Bryn Mawr College*)

Compositionally, four members of the cancrinite family are:

Cancrinite	$Na_6Ca_2[AlSiO_4]_6$	(CO_3)	$(OH)_2$
Vishnevite	$Na_6Ca_2[AlSiO_4]_6$	(SO_4)	$(OH)_2$
Haüyne	$K_2Na_4Ca_2[AlSiO_4]_6$	(SO_4)	$(OH)_2$
Afghanite	$Na_4Ca_2[AlSiO_4]_4$	(SO_4)	$(OH)Cl$

The cancrinite structure has been proposed as a possible crystalline storage site for nuclear wastes, in particular the gases. Cancrinite can be derived from reaction of far more common nepheline with calcite.

Localities include the Fen area, southern Norway; the Kola Peninsula, Russia; Bancroft, Ontario, Canada; and Litchfield, Maine. *See* FELDSPATHOID; NEPHELINE SYENITE; SILICATE MINERALS.

Paul B. Moore

Candlepower

Luminous intensity expressed in candelas. The term refers only to the intensity in a particular direction and by itself does not give an indication of the total light emitted. The candlepower in a given direction from a light source is equal to the illumination in footcandles falling on a surface normal to that direction, multiplied by the square of the distance from the light source in feet. The candlepower is also equal to the illumination of metercandles (lux) multiplied by the square of the distance in meters.

The apparent candlepower is the candlepower of a point source which will produce the same illumination at a given distance as produced by a given light source.

The mean horizontal candlepower is the average candlepower of a light source in the horizontal plane passing through the luminous center of the light source.

The mean spherical candlepower is the average candlepower in all directions from a light source as a center. Since there is a total solid angle of 4π (steradians) emanating from a point, the mean spherical candlepower is equal to the total luminous flux (in lumens) of a light source divided by 4π (steradians). *See* LUMINOUS INTENSITY; PHOTOMETRY.   Russell C. Putnam

Canine distemper

A fatal viral disease of dogs and other carnivores, with a worldwide distribution. Canine distemper virus has a wide host range; most terrestrial carnivores are susceptible to natural canine distemper virus infection. All animals in the families Canidae (for example, dog, dingo, fox, coyote, wolf, jackal), Mustelidae (for example, weasel, ferret, mink, skunk, badger, stoat, marten, otter), and Procyonidae (for example, kinkajou, coati, bassariscus, raccoon, panda) may succumb to canine distemper virus infection. Members of other Carnivora families, including domestic cats and swine, may become subclinically infected. The virus has also been isolated from large cats (lions, tigers, leopards) that have died in zoological parks in North America, from wild lions in the Serengeti National Park (Tanzania), and from wild javelinas (collared peccaries). *See* CARNIVORA.

Etiologic agent. Canine distemper virus is classified as a morbillivirus within the Paramyxoviridae family, closely related to measles virus and rinderpest virus of cattle and the phocine (seal) and dolphin distemper virus. The virus is enveloped with a negative-sense ribonucleic acid and consists of six structural proteins: the nucleoprotein and two enzymes in the nucleocapsid, the membrane protein on the inside, and the hemagglutinating and fusion proteins on the outside of the lipoprotein envelope. *See* ANIMAL VIRUS; PARAMYXOVIRUS.

Transmission. Canine distemper is enzootic worldwide. Aerosol transmission in respiratory secretions is the main route of transmission. Virus shedding begins approximately 7 days after the initial infection. Acutely infected dogs and other carnivores shed virus in all body excretions, regardless of whether they show clinical signs or not.

Canine distemper virus affects susceptible dogs of all ages, but puppies are most vulnerable when their maternal antibodies are lost. Dogs that completely recover from canine distemper virus infection are immune for years and probably for life. They do not shed the virus and they are not persistently infected. Outside the host, canine distemper virus becomes inactivated rapidly, and all of the available common disinfectants are effective against it.

Disease signs. Great variations occur in the duration and severity of canine distemper, which may range from no visible signs to severe disease, often with central nervous system involvement, with approximately 50% mortality in dogs.

The first fever 3–6 days after infection may pass unnoticed; the second peak (several days later and intermittent thereafter) is usually associated with nasal and ocular discharge, depression, and anorexia. A low lymphocyte count is always present during the early stages of infection. Gastrointestinal and respiratory signs may follow, often enhanced by secondary infection.

Many infected dogs develop central nervous system disorders following systemic disease. Depending on the virus strain, the signs may be more related to acute gray matter disease or subacute white matter disease. Seizures and muscle spasms accompanied by depression predominate in gray matter disease; lack of muscle coordination, partial paralysis, and muscle tremors occur in white matter disease. Brain and spinal inflammation and cervical rigidity may be seen in both. Inflammation of the optic nerve and retinal lesions in dogs with canine distemper virus are not uncommon. Hardening of the foot pads (hyperkeratosis) and nose is produced by some virus strains. In growing dogs, loss of enamel from the teeth after canine distemper virus infection is common. Old dog encephalitis, a rare disease of middle-aged or older dogs caused by canine distemper virus, is characterized by progressive deterioration and is ultimately fatal. Postvaccinal encephalitis may develop 1–2 weeks after vaccination and usually causes behavioral changes, seizures, and blindness; but this condition is rare.

Pathology. Atrophy of the thymus gland and hardening of lung tissue are the main lesions. Discharges of mucus and pus from the nose and eyes, diarrhea, hardening of nose and foot pads, and skin pustules may be present. Depletion of lymphocytes in lymphoid tissues, interstitial pneumonia, and intracytoplasmic inclusion bodies in epithelium of the respiratory, alimentary, and urinary tracts are characteristic. In the central nervous system, the degeneration of neurons is typical, but not always present. Intracytoplasmic and intranuclear bodies can be found, predominantly in astrocytes and neurons.

Dogs with old dog encephalitis have extensive

infiltration of the surrounding vessels by lymphocytes in the central nervous system, degeneration of neurons, and minimal depletion of myelin. Postvaccinal encephalitis causes lesions predominantly in the brainstem.

Treatment. A specific antiviral drug having an effect on canine distemper virus in dogs is not presently available. Treatment of canine distemper, therefore, is nonspecific and supportive. Antibiotic therapy is recommended because of the common occurrence of secondary bacterial infections of the respiratory and alimentary tracts. Administration of fluids and electrolytes may be the most important therapy for canine distemper because diseased dogs with diarrhea are often dehydrated.

Treatment of neurologic forms of canine distemper is usually not very successful. Sedatives and anticonvulsants may temporarily relieve clinical signs, but they do not have a healing effect. When central nervous system disorders are progressive and dogs become recumbent, euthanasia is usually prescribed. Some dogs with central nervous system disorders, however, recover quite well, and residual signs such as muscle spasms or inflammation of the optic nerve can improve with time.

Vaccination and control. Immunization by controlled vaccination is the only effective approach to canine distemper prophylaxis. Active immunization with modified-live virus vaccines induces long-lasting immunity and keeps the disease in dogs under control. With a few exceptions, modified-live canine distemper virus vaccines are derived from either egg and avian cell or canine cell culture adaptations. Both methods of adaptation produce vaccines that are very effective in inducing an immunity that lasts for at least 1 year and probably for several years in most dogs. Any modified-live canine distemper virus vaccine may be fatal for certain wildlife and zoo animals (such as red pandas or black-footed ferrets). Inactivated virus vaccines must be used in some species, but they are not commercially available in the United States.

Heterotypic (measles) virus vaccination has been the best approach to overcome maternal antibody interference with immunization. As with inactivated canine distemper virus vaccines, measles virus induces a limited immunity that can protect dogs against canine distemper virus disease but not against canine distemper virus infection. A combination of attenuated measles virus and canine distemper virus is still commonly used in 6–10-week-old pups. It offers the advantage of complete protection in the absence of, and partial protection in the presence of, maternal antibody. In addition, measles virus antibody titers induced by vaccination usually are below a level that would interfere with measles virus vaccination in the next generation when used in 6–10-week-old pups.

A vaccination schedule for pups against canine distemper should include a combined modified-live measle virus–canine distemper virus vaccination at 6–8 weeks of age. Two additional canine distemper virus vaccinations at 3–4-week intervals should be given. Annual booster inoculations are recommended because some dogs lose antibody titers in that time period. Pups deprived of colostrum (the first milk from the mammary gland) should not be vaccinated with modified-live canine distemper virus before they are 3–4 weeks of age. Modified-live canine distemper virus can be fatal in unprotected younger pups, as it can be in some wild or zoo animals.

Besides immunization, strict isolation of dogs with canine distemper appears to be the most important step in controlling the disease. The virus is shed in all body excretions during the acute systemic disease, and direct dog-to-dog contact appears to be the main route of viral spread. Dogs with subacute canine distemper encephalitis still may infect susceptible contact dogs. Disinfection of the environment can be accomplished with commonly used products because the enveloped virus is rapidly destroyed outside the host.

M. J. G. Appel; B. A. Summers

Bibliography. C. E. Green (ed.), *Canine Distemper in Infectious Diseases of the Dog and Cat*, 1990; M. Horzinek (ed.), *Virus Infections of Vertebrates*, 1987.

Canine parvovirus infection

Severe enteritis caused by a small nonenveloped single-stranded deoxyribonucleic acid (DNA) virus that is resistant to inactivation and remains infectious in the environment for 5–7 months. First observed in dogs in 1976, canine parvovirus may have originated by mutation of a closely related parvovirus of cats or wildlife. The original virus was designated as canine parvovirus, type 2 (CPV-2); however, since its discovery the virus has undergone two minor genetic alterations, designated CPV-2a and CPV-2b. These alterations may have enabled the virus to adapt to its new host, replicate, and spread more effectively.

Epidemiology. Canine parvovirus is transmitted between dogs by the fecal-oral route. The incubation period is 3–7 days. Virus is first shed in the feces on day 3, and shedding continues for an additional 10 days. Chronically infected dogs that shed virus intermittently are rare. Most naturally occurring infections in dogs are subclinical or result in mild signs of the disease. Dogs with subclinical infections play an important role in the spread of the disease by shedding large amounts of virus into the environment. This shedding, along with the ability of the virus to persist in the environment, contributes to the endemicity of the disease. The development of disease following infection ranges from 20 to 90%, and mortality between 0 to 50%.

Pathogenesis. Only mitotically active cells, such as those of the intestine, lymphoid system, bone marrow, and fetal tissues, support replication of the canine parvovirus. After ingestion, the virus replicates in the regional lymphoid tissues of the oropharynx, spreading to other lymphoid tissues, bone marrow, and intestinal epithelial cells by way of the blood. Viral replication in the lymphoid tissue and bone marrow leads to necrosis of the lymphoid cells and a decrease in circulating white blood cells. Viral replication in the germinal epithelium of the intestinal glands of the jejunum and ileum leads to blunting and fusing of the intestinal villi. Diarrhea results from disruption of the normal absorptive and digestive processes. In severe cases, hemorrhaging into the intestine occurs. Secondary bacterial infections occur in severely affected animals.

Diagnosis and treatment. Severe enteritis is commonly observed in dogs 6–20 weeks of age. Initial signs include depression, anorexia, and lethargy, followed by fever, abdominal pain, vomiting, and diarrhea. Blood may be found in both the vomitus and stool. Dehydration, hypothermia, and weakness develop if the vomiting and diarrhea are severe. Signs are more severe in pups that are undernourished, stressed, or concurrently infected with other organisms. Diagnosis is based on history, clinical signs, vaccination status, physical exam, and laboratory tests. The white blood cell count is usually low. Detection of virus in the feces provides a definitive diagnosis. The bowel lumen is often empty, but on occasion there may be watery or hemorrhagic intestinal matter.

The goal of treatment is to support the animal until the infection runs its course. There are no specific antiviral therapies available. The intensity of treatment depends on the severity of signs. Dehydrated pups require intensive intravenous fluid therapy. Antimicrobial drugs are useful because of the risk of secondary bacterial infections, and antiemetic drugs help control vomiting and nausea. Good nursing care is essential. All food and water should be withheld until the pup is no longer vomiting, and the pup should be kept warm, clean, and dry. Because of the infectious nature of the disease, pups should be isolated from other dogs.

Prevention. Canine parvovirus infection in pups is prevented by minimizing exposure and by vaccination. Keeping pups isolated from other dogs until completion of the vaccination series is optimal. If strict isolation is not possible, limiting the exposure of pups to areas where large numbers of dogs congregate is useful. Immunity to canine parvovirus infection can be either passive or active. Passive immunity results from absorption of maternal antibodies following ingestion of colostrum; active immunity develops following natural infection or vaccination. The maternal antibodies protect the pup from natural infection, with the duration of protection dependent on the quantity of immunoglobulins absorbed. Inactivated and modified-live forms of the canine parvovirus vaccine are available. Vaccines that include a modified-live attenuated canine parvovirus strain are preferred because immunity develops more rapidly and is of longer duration. Pups are vaccinated at 2–3-week intervals starting at 6–8 weeks of age and continuing to 16–20 weeks of age. The immune response following vaccination depends on the amount of maternal antibodies present. High levels of antibodies block the immune response to vaccination. This period of nonresponsiveness may extend up to 16–20 weeks of age. *See* ANIMAL VIRUS; IMMUNITY; VACCINATION.

Michael J. Coyne

Bibliography. M. S. Leib (ed.), *Gasteroenterology: The 1990's*, 1993; P. Tijssen (ed.), *Handbook of Parvoviruses*, 1989; C. Vella and S. W. Ketteridge, *Canine Parvovirus: A New Pathogen*, 1991.

Canonical transformations

Transformations of the variables describing a dynamical system which preserve the canonical form of Hamilton's canonical equations of motion for that system. One advantage of the advanced methods of analytical mechanics over the original formulation of Newton's laws of motion is that with the advanced methods the equations of motion can easily be derived in terms of any convenient system of coordinates, within specified limitations. The ability to transform from coordinates in which the system is easily specified to ones which are particularly suited to discuss its motion, while preserving the form of the equations, provides a powerful tool for discussing this motion. For example, in the lagrangian formulation the spatial coordinates can be freely chosen. This flexibility is greatly extended in the hamiltonian formulation of mechanics. In this formulation, the equations of motion make it possible not only to use any convenient system of coordinates but even to use variables which are mixtures of spatial coordinates and momenta.

However, this greater flexibility exacts a price: In the lagrangian formulation, any set of independent generalized coordinates are suitable variables; whereas in the hamiltonian formulation, an arbitrary transformation of the generalized coordinates and momenta will not necessarily lead to variables that satisfy Hamilton's equations of motion. The derivation of the canonical transformations, that is, the transformations that do preserve the form of Hamilton's equations, will now be discussed. *See* HAMILTON'S EQUATIONS OF MOTION; LAGRANGE'S EQUATIONS; LAGRANGIAN FUNCTION.

General principles. The equations of motion for a nondissipative system are derivable from Hamilton's principle, which states that the time integral of the lagrangian function L specifying the system between two fixed configurations of the system at two fixed times is an extremum for the actual trajectory of the system as compared with any nearby paths. Hamilton's principle can be used as a basis for deriving the canonical transformations, since a set of transformed variables that preserves Hamilton's principle will obey Hamilton's equations of motion. However, in order to apply it, Hamilton's principle must be restated in terms of the variables that appear in Hamilton's equations. This restatement can be done by using Eq. (1), which relates

$$L(q, \dot{q}, t) + H(q, p, t) = \sum_{j=1}^{f} p_j \dot{q}_j \qquad (1)$$

the lagrangian function L and the hamiltonian function H of a system. Here, f is the number of degrees of freedom of the system, and q represents the f generalized coordinates of the system, $\dot{q}$ the time derivatives of these coordinates (the generalized velocities), p the corresponding generalized momenta, and t the time. (In the lagrangian formulation, the generalized momenta are specified in terms of the generalized coordinates and velocities; whereas in the hamiltonian formulation, the generalized momenta are among the independent variables.) By using Eq. (1), Hamilton's principle can be written as Eq. (2), where Δ is the variation

$$\Delta \int_{t_1}^{t_2} \left[\sum_{j=1}^{f} p_j \dot{q}_j - H(q, p, t) \right] dt = 0 \qquad (2)$$

in the integral produced by a variation in the dependence of the variables on time without varying the end points. *See* HAMILTON'S PRINCIPLE.

Now, the content of Hamilton's principle is not changed by subtracting the total time derivative of any function from the integrand, because the time integral of a total time derivative depends only on the value of that function at the end points, which are not varied. This feature provides a means of introducing canonical transformations of the coordinates and momenta.

The function ϕ whose total time derivative will be subtracted from the integrand of Eq. (2) is chosen as a function of the f coordinates q_j, of f other variables q'_j (which will emerge below as the transformed coordinates), and perhaps the time t. Its total time derivative is given by Eq. (3). The

$$\frac{d\phi}{dt} = \sum_{j=1}^{f} \frac{\partial \phi}{\partial q_j} \frac{dq_j}{dt} + \sum_{j=1}^{f} \frac{\partial \phi}{\partial q'_j} \frac{dq'_j}{dt} + \frac{\partial \phi}{\partial t} \qquad (3)$$

partial derivatives $\partial \phi / \partial q_j$ are then identified with the momenta p_j, and the quantities $-\partial \phi / \partial q'_j$ are called p'_j (which will emerge as the transformed momenta). The resulting set of $2f$ equations, Eqs. (4), may be solved for the $2f$ primed variables

$$p_j = \frac{\partial \phi}{\partial q_j} \qquad p'_j = -\frac{\partial \phi}{\partial q'_j} \qquad (4)$$

q'_j p'_j in terms of the corresponding unprimed variables and the time. A new function $H'(q'_j, p'_j)$ [which will be the transformed hamiltonian] is defined by Eq. (5). In this equation the variables

$$H'(q', p', t) = H(q, p, t) + \frac{\partial \phi}{\partial t} \qquad (5)$$

q, p appearing on the right side must be expressed

in terms of the primed variables by using the transformation equations. The total derivative $d\phi / dt$ as given by Eq. (3) is then subtracted from the integrand in the statement, Eq. (2), of Hamilton's principle, and Eq. (5) is used to obtain Eq. (6).

$$\Delta \int_{t_1}^{t_2} \left[\sum_{j=1}^{f} p'_j \dot{q}'_j - H'(\dot{q}', p', t) \right] dt = 0 \qquad (6)$$

This is a statement of Hamilton's principle in the new, primed variables, and so these variables satisfy Hamilton's equations of motion and constitute a set of canonical variables. The transformation between the variables q, p and q', p' is therefore a canonical transformation.

The function $\phi(q, q', t)$ is called a generator of the canonical transformation. In the above discussion, the generator was a function of the old and new coordinates, but canonical transformations can be generated by functions of any combination of f unprimed and f new variables (either coordinates or momenta) with distinct indices.

Canonical transformations constitute a group. The generator of two successive transformations is the sum of the generators of the separate transformations, the arguments of the generators undergoing the corresponding transformations in the appropriate order. *See* GROUP THEORY.

Applications. Canonical transformations have a number of important applications, a few of which will be briefly described.

Phase space. The value of the $2f$ coordinates and momenta of a dynamical system at any time specify the state of motion of the system completely. It is useful to introduce a $2f$-dimensional phase space for the system. This is an abstract space with a cartesian coordinate system whose axes are labeled by the canonical coordinates and momenta. The state of the dynamical system is completely described by the location of its phase point in this phase space, and its motion is described by the motion of this phase point through the phase space. In statistical physics an ensemble of systems is represented by a cloud of phase points in a common phase space. The density of this cloud is of great importance. An essential feature of canonical transformations is that they preserve volume elements in phase space so that carrying one out does not affect this density.

Hamilton-Jacobi equation. A time-dependent canonical transformation changes the value of the hamiltonian according to Eq. (5). The transformation can be chosen to make the new hamiltonian vanish, and according to Hamilton's equations the new canonical variables are then constant in time. A transformation which accomplishes this is generated by a solution of the Hamilton-Jacobi equation (7), con-

$$H\left(q, \frac{\partial \phi}{\partial q}, t \right) + \frac{\partial \phi}{\partial t} = 0 \qquad (7)$$

taining f nonadditive constants. Such a solution of Eq. (7) is called a complete integral of the equation.

See HAMILTON-JACOBI THEORY.

Infinitesimal canonical transformations. The generating function given by Eq. (8), where ϵ is a small

$$\psi'(q, p', t) = \sum_{j=1}^{f} q_j p'_j + \epsilon X(q, p', t) \qquad (8)$$

parameter whose square is negligible, generates an infinitesimal canonical transformation, that is, a canonical transformation in which the changes in the coordinates and momenta, given by Eqs. (9), are

$$\begin{aligned} \delta q_j &= q'_j - q_j = \epsilon \frac{\partial X}{\partial p'_j} \\ \delta p_j &= p'_j - p_j = -\epsilon \frac{\partial X}{\partial q_j} \end{aligned} \qquad (9)$$

very small. Such transformations are important in deriving relations between the symmetry properties of a system and its constants of motion.

Since X appears with the infinitesimal coefficient ϵ, within X the arguments p' can be replaced by p, because these differ only by order ϵ. Thus, X can be written as a function of q, p, and t, and is therefore a dynamical variable of the system. Infinitesimal canonical transformations are thus generated by dynamical variables.

For example, if X is the z component of linear momentum of a particle, it generates an infinitesimal displacement in the z direction. A component of angular momentum generates an infinitesimal rotation. The hamiltonian generates the changes corresponding to a time displacement, ϵ.

Poisson brackets. The symmetry properties of a system under an infinitesimal canonical transformation are often of interest, and, in particular, whether another dynamical variable, $Y(q, p, t)$, distinct from X, is invariant under the transformation generated by X. In order that the value of Y not be altered by carrying out the infinitesimal canonical transformation generated by X, the functional form of Y must change, the change in the functional form compensating for the change in the value of the arguments. The change in functional form may be defined by Eq. (10), where the variables q', p' on the right are

$$\delta Y = Y(q', p', t) - Y(q, p, t) \qquad (10)$$

to be expressed in terms of the unprimed variables by using Eq. (9). Then the change in functional form is given by Eq. (11). Here (Y, X) is known

$$\begin{aligned} \delta Y &= \sum_{j=1}^{f} \left(\frac{\partial Y}{\partial q_j} \delta q_j + \frac{\partial Y}{\partial p_j} \delta p_j \right) \\ &= \sum_{j=1}^{f} \epsilon \left(\frac{\partial Y}{\partial q_j} \frac{\partial X}{\partial p_j} - \frac{\partial X}{\partial q_j} \frac{\partial Y}{\partial p_j} \right)_0 \\ &= \epsilon (Y, X) \end{aligned} \qquad (11)$$

as the Poisson bracket of the two dynamical variables Y and X. Clearly $(Y, X) = -(X, Y)$; that is, the Poisson bracket is antisymmetric.

If Y is the hamiltonian H, then the Poisson bracket of X with H is given by Eq. (12). This

$$\begin{aligned} (X, H) &= \sum_{j=1}^{f} \left(\frac{\partial X}{\partial q_j} \frac{\partial H}{\partial p_j} - \frac{\partial H}{\partial q_j} \frac{\partial X}{\partial p_j} \right) \\ &= \frac{dX}{dt} - \frac{\partial X}{\partial t} \end{aligned} \qquad (12)$$

equation shows that when a dynamical variable does not depend explicitly on the time, that is, when $\partial X / \partial t = 0$, its Poisson bracket with the hamiltonian gives its time derivative.

If the Poisson bracket of a dynamical variable X with the hamiltonian vanishes, then it follows from Eq. (12) that X is a constant of the motion, and it follows from Eq. (11) that the hamiltonian is invariant under the infinitesimal canonical transformation generated by X. This relation connects the symmetry of a system directly with constants of motion. *See* CONSERVATION LAWS (PHYSICS); SYMMETRY LAWS (PHYSICS).

Transition to quantum theory. Quantum mechanics is related to classical mechanics through the identification of the quantum commutator of two dynamical variables with $ih/(2\pi)$ times the Poisson bracket of the classically analogous dynamical variables, if they exist, where h is Planck's constant. This is one reason for the great importance of Poisson brackets. Thus, for example, classically the angular momentum components j_x and so forth satisfy the Poisson bracket relations of Eq. (13). The corresponding op-

$$(j_x, j_y) = j_z \qquad (13)$$

erators in quantum mechanics obey the commutation relations of Eq. (14).

$$j_x j_y - j_y j_x = \frac{ih}{2\pi} j_z \qquad (14)$$

See ANGULAR MOMENTUM; NONRELATIVISTIC QUANTUM THEORY.

Perturbation theory. The Hamilton-Jacobi equation is useful for problems in perturbation theory in classical mechanics. Here, the hamiltonian H of a classical dynamical system is given by Eq. (15), where

$$H = H_0 + V \qquad (15)$$

the hamiltonian H_0 yields a soluble Hamilton-Jacobi equation with a complete integral ϕ_0, and V is a small perturbation. The solution ϕ of the exact Hamilton-Jacobi equation may be approximated by Eq. (16), where ϕ_1 is of order V and only terms

$$\phi = \phi_0 + \phi_1 \qquad (16)$$

linear in V and ϕ_1 are retained. The solution of the approximate equation is given by Eq. (17),

$$\phi_1 = \int_{C_0} V \left(q, \frac{\partial \phi_0}{\partial q}, t \right) dt \qquad (17)$$

where the integral is evaluated along the unperturbed trajectory C_0. The function $\phi_0 + \phi_1$ generates the canonical transformation from the initial state to the later state, correct to first order in the perturbation V. *See* PERTURBATION (ASTRONOMY); PERTURBATION (MATHEMATICS); PERTURBATION; (QUANTUM MECHANICS).   Philip Stehle

Bibliography. M. Born, *Problems of Atomic Dynamics*, 1970; H. C. Corben and P. Stehle, *Classical Mechanics*, 2d ed., 1994; H. Goldstein, *Classical Mechanics*, 2d ed., 1980.

Cantaloupe

In the United States the name applied to muskmelon cultivars belonging to *Cucumis melo* var. *reticulatus* of the family Cucurbitaceae. *See* VIOLALES.

Description. The fruits weigh 2.4 lb (1.1 kg) and are round to oval; the surface is netted and has shallow vein tracts (see **illus.**). At maturity the skin color changes from dark green or gray to light gray or yellow. The flesh is usually salmon-colored, but it may vary from green to deep salmon-orange. When mature the melon is sweet, averages 6–8% sugar, and has a distinct aroma and flavor. The flesh is high in potassium and vitamin C, and when deep orange, rich in vitamin A. The vines usually bear andromonoecious flowers which are pollinated by bees, and the fruit generally separates from the stem when mature. Melons harvested at less than full-slip maturity do not achieve their full potential for sugar content, flavor, texture, and aroma. *See* ASCORBIC ACID; VITAMIN A.

The use of the name cantaloupe to indicate these medium-sized, netted melons with green and yellow-green rinds has become firmly established in the United States. However, this is a misnomer, and the name cantaloupe should be restricted to cultivars of *C. melo* var. *cantalupensis*. The fruits of this group are rough and scaly, with deep vein tracts and a hard rind. Cultivars of the variety *cantalupensis* are grown in Europe and Asia, but seldom in the United States.

Cantaloupe culture in the United States began with the introduction of the Netted Gem cultivar by the Burpee Seed Company in 1881.

Cultivation and production. Cantaloupes require a frost-free season of about 95 days to mature.

Cantaloupes (*Cucumis melo*).

Average temperatures of 70°F (21°C) are favorable for the production of high-quality melons. Most of the United States production is on irrigated land in the arid and semiarid Southwest because of favorable temperatures and lack of rain during the growing season. California grows approximately 51% of the United States acreage, followed by Texas with 22% and Arizona with 13%. Most of the California production is in the summer in the Sacramento and San Joaquin valleys, while Texas produces in the spring. High harvest and transportation costs tend to make cantaloupes a luxury product on the eastern markets. *See* MUSKMELON.   Oscar A. Lorenz

Diseases. Cantaloupe plants can be infected with bacterial wilt, angular leaf spot, downy mildew, scab, and cucumber mosaic. In addition, there are other fungal and viral diseases which can greatly reduce plant vigor and fruit quantity or quality.

Fungal diseases. Anthracnose may be the most destructive of all diseases affecting cantaloupe. All plant parts, excluding the roots, are susceptible to the pathogen *Colletotrichum lagenarium*. Lesions may coalesce to kill entire leaves, stems and runners. Depressed spots are formed on the fruits and, when wet conditions persist, are covered with a mass of pink spores. Spores easily spread to uninfected plants by splashing rain or are carried by cucumber beetles. The fungus has as many as seven races which are capable of infecting different cultivars. The disease can be controlled by using resistant varieties, although breeding for disease resistance in cantaloupes has lagged behind that in cucumbers and watermelons. Control can be achieved by crop rotation, proper drainage, and fungicides such as the dithiocarbamates.

Powdery mildew is a destructive disease caused by either *Spaerotheca fulginea* or *Erysiphe cichoracearum*. These fungi form a fuzzy white growth on the fruit, stem, or leaf. Tissue covered by the fungus for extended periods of time may be killed. Overwintering structures are tiny black fruiting bodies. Infection is most likely to occur when humidity is high and temperatures are moderately high. Powdery mildew is controlled by dusting plants with Karathane or sulfur. Resistant cultivars derived from P.M.R. 45, Georgia 47, Honey Ball 306, and Homegarden can also be planted.

Fusarium wilt, caused by *Fusarium oxysporum* f. *melonis*, is a particular problem in the northern states from Maine to Minnesota. The fungus either causes damping-off in young seedlings or a root rot and stem blight in older plants. Badly affected plant stems crack open, and the plants desiccate. The pathogen lives in old plant debris and as propagules in the soil. Hence crop rotation is not an effective control measure. The only worthwhile means of control is to plant resistant varieties, such as Honey Dew, Golden Gopher, Iroquois, Delicious 51, and Harvest Queen.

Viral diseases. Muskmelon mosaic and squash mosaic cause serious crop losses from time to time. Muskmelon mosaic virus is seed- and aphid-transmitted. Leaves develop a mottling and may be distorted in shape. Fruit production is greatly decreased. Squash mosaic virus is seed-transmitted and causes symptoms similar to those caused by muskmelon mosaic virus. Both virus diseases can be controlled by using certified disease-free seed and by eliminating wild cucurbit weeds from nearby locations. *See* PLANT VIRUSES AND VIROIDS.

Frank L. Caruso

Bibliography. R. A. Seelig, *Cantaloupes*, United Fresh Fruit and Vegetable Association, 1973; T. W. Whitaker and G. N. Davis, *Cucurbits*, 1961.

Cantilever

A linear structural member supported both transversely and rotationally at one end only; the other end of the member is free to deflect and rotate. Cantilevers are common throughout nature and engineered structures; examples are a bird's wing, an airplane wing, a roof overhang, and a balcony. *See* WING.

Horizontal axis. If the main axis of the member is horizontal and the member is loaded with a downward gravity load, the member will support the load by forming a structural couple, with the upper portion of the member being in tension and the lower portion being in compression. This is the principle on which the design of a horizontal cantilever truss is based. When a horizontal cantilever truss is under a gravity load, the top member is in tension and the bottom member is in compression. If there are no external horizontal forces, the internal forces in the top and bottom members must be equal. Because these internal forces are separated by a distance, they can resist moments and rotation. The resisting moment is defined as a couple, that is, two equal and opposite forces separated by a distance. The translation force of the cantilever (defined as the shear) is resisted by the diagonals in a truss or the web of a wide flange beam. *See* TRUSS.

For a cantilever to function, it must be counterbalanced at its one support against rotation. This requirement is simply achieved in the design of a playground seesaw, with its double-balanced cantilever, or of a chemical balance. This principle of counterbalancing the cantilever is part of the basic design of a crane, such as a tower crane (see **illus.**). More commonly, horizontal cantilevers are resisted by being continuous with a backup span that is supported at both ends. This design is common for cantilever bridges; the largest of the cantilever bridges is an 1800-ft (540-m) railroad bridge in Quebec, Canada. Cantilever bridges are simpler to erect since they can be built out from their supports. All swing bridges or drawbridges are cantilevers. *See* BRIDGE.

Vertical axis. Cantilevers also occur with the member's main axis being vertical. Vertical can-

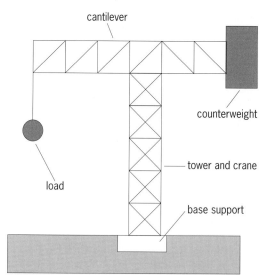

Cantilever configuration in the form of a tower support crane.

tilevers primarily resist lateral wind loads and horizontal loads created by earthquakes. Common vertical cantilevers are chimneys, stacks, masts, flagpoles, lampposts, and railings or fences. Trees are the largest vertical cantilevers found in nature.

All skyscrapers are vertical cantilevers. One common system to provide the strength to resist lateral loads acting on the skyscraper is the use of a truss (known as bracing), which cantilevers out from the foundation in the walls of the core of the building that encloses the elevators and the stairs. In apartment buildings and hotels, vertical walls that separate different living units (demising walls or shear walls) cantilever out of the foundation to resist lateral loads. *See* BUILDINGS; SHEAR.

Applications. Some of the largest cantilevers are used in the roofs of airplane hangars. The reason is that typically at one edge of an airplane hangar there is a sliding door that can be removed; thus it cannot provide support to the roof's edge. Cantilevers of up to 300 ft (90 m) have been used to enclose 747 airplanes. It has become common practice to include cantilevers in the design of theaters and stadiums, where an unobstructed view is desired, balconies and tiers are supported in the back and cantilevered out toward the stage or playing field so that the audience has column-free viewing. *See* BEAM; ROOF CONSTRUCTION.

I. Paul Lew

Bibliography. M. Salvadori, *Structure in Architecture*, 1986; M. Salvadori, *Why Buidlings Stand Up*, 1990.

Capacitance

The ratio of the charge q on one of the plates of a capacitor (there being an equal and opposite charge on the other plate) to the potential difference v between the plates; that is, capacitance (formerly called capacity) is $C = q/v$.

In general, a capacitor, often called a condenser, consists of two metal plates insulated from each other by a dielectric. The capacitance of a capacitor depends on the geometry of the plates and the kind of dielectric used since these factors determine the charge which can be put on the plates by a unit potential difference existing between the plates. *See* DIELECTRIC MATERIALS.

For a capacitor of fixed geometry and with constant properties of the dielectric between its plates, C is a constant independent of q or v, since as v changes, q changes with it in the same proportion. This statement assumes that the dielectric strength is not exceeded and thus that dielectric breakdown does not occur. (If it does occur, the device is no longer a capacitor.) If either the geometry or dielectric properties, or both, of a capacitor change with time, C will change with time.

In an ideal capacitor, no conduction current flows between the plates. A real capacitor of good quality is the circuit equivalent of an ideal capacitor with a very high resistance in parallel or, in alternating-current (ac) circuits, of an ideal capacitor with a low resistance in series.

Properties of capacitors. One classification system for capacitors follows from the physical state of their dielectrics. For a discussion based on this classification *see* CAPACITOR..

Charging and discharging. These processes can occur for capacitors while the potential difference across the capacitor is changing if C is fixed; that is, q increases if v increases and q decreases if v decreases. If C and v both change with time, the rate of change of q with time is given by Eq. (1).

$$\frac{dq}{dt} = C\frac{dv}{dt} + v\frac{dC}{dt} \tag{1}$$

Since the current i flowing in the wires leading to the capacitor plates is equal to dq/dt, Eq. (1) gives i in the wires. In many cases, C is constant so $i = C\,dv/dt$.

Energy of charged capacitor. This energy W_c is given by the formula $W_c = vq/2$, and is equal to the work the source must do in placing the charge on the capacitor. It is, in turn, the work the capacitor will do when it discharges.

Geometrical types. The geometry of a capacitor may take any one of several forms. The most common type is the parallel-plate capacitor whose capacitance C in farads is given in the ideal case by Eq. (2), where A is the area in square meters of one

$$C = \frac{A\epsilon_r\epsilon_0}{d} \tag{2}$$

of the plates, d is the distance in meters between the plates, ϵ_0 is the permittivity of empty space with the numerical value 8.85×10^{-12} farad/m, and ϵ_r is the relative permittivity of the dielectric material between the plates. The value of ϵ_r is unity for empty space and almost unity for gases. For other

dielectric materials, ϵ_r ranges in value from one to several hundred. In order for Eq. (2) to give a good value of C for an actual capacitor, d must be very small compared to the linear dimensions of either plate. *See* DIELECTRICS; PERMITTIVITY.

Each plate of a parallel-plate capacitor may be made up of many thin sheets of metal connected electrically with a corresponding number of thin sheets of metal making up the other plate. The sheets of metal and their intervening layers of dielectric are chosen and stacked in such a way that A will be large and d small without making the whole capacitor too bulky. The result is appreciable capacitance in a reasonable volume.

The spherical capacitor is made of two concentric metal spheres with a dielectric of relative dielectric constant ϵ_r filling the space between the spheres. The capacitance in farads of such a capacitor is given by Eq. (3), where r_2 is the radius in meters

$$C = 4\pi\epsilon_r\epsilon_0 \frac{r_1 r_2}{r_2 - r_1} \tag{3}$$

of the outer sphere and r_1 that of the inner sphere.

The cylindrical capacitor, as the name implies, is made of two concentric metal cylinders, each of length l in meters, with a dielectric filling the space between the cylinders. If r_2 and r_1 are the radii in meters of the outer and inner cylinders, respectively, and l is very large compared to $r_2 - r_1$, the capacitance C in farads is given by

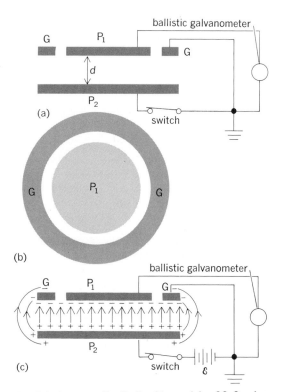

Parallel-plate capacitor P_1, P_2 with guard ring GG. Spacing between guard ring and plate is exaggerated. (*a*) Cross section with all parts of capacitor at ground potential. (*b*) Top view showing plate P_1 surrounded by guard ring. (*c*) Cross section of capacitor charged from battery whose electromotive force is $\mathscr{E}$.

Eq. (4), where ϵ_r is the relative dielectric constant

$$C = \frac{2\pi \epsilon_r \epsilon_0 l}{\ln (r_2/r_1)} \qquad (4)$$

of the dielectric and $\ln (r_2/r_1)$ indicates the natural logarithm of the ratio r_2/r_1.

Guard ring. This is often used with a standard parallel-plate capacitor, as shown in the **illustration**, in order that Eq. (2) shall more accurately represent its capacitance. It is the fringing of the electric lines of force which makes Eq. (2) inaccurate for an actual capacitor and, as shown in illus. c, the fringing is nearly all at the outside edge of the guard ring, and thus is not associated with the charge Q which is put onto plate P_1 while the capacitor is being charged. It is the charge Q that determines the deflection of the ballistic galvanometer during the charging process. Then Eq. (2) gives the correct value of C that is needed to relate Q to the potential difference $\mathscr{E}$ across the plates by the equation $Q = C\mathscr{E}$. Thus, with C known from Eq. (2) and $\mathscr{E}$, known from a potentiometer measurement, Q may be computed and the ballistic galvanometer calibrated. This illustrates one use of a standard capacitor with a guard ring.

Body capacitance. When a part of the human body, say the hand, is brought near a high-impedance network, the body serves as one plate of a capacitor and the adjacent part of the network as the other plate. This situation is the equivalent of a capacitor of very low capacitance, in parallel between that part of the network and ground, since the human body can usually be considered as being a grounded conductor. This capacitance is known as body capacitance and enters as a part of the distributed capacitance of the network. A high-impedance network must be well shielded in order to eliminate the variable and undesirable effects of body capacitance. *See* CAPACITOR. **Ralph P. Winch**

Bibliography. W. J. Duffin, *Electricity and Magnetism*, 4th ed., 1990; D. Halliday, R. Resnick, and K. Krane, *Physics*, 4th ed., 1992; E. M. Purcell, *Electricity and Magnetism*, 2d ed., 1985; F. W. Sears, M. W. Zemansky, and H. D. Young, *University Physics*, 7th ed., 1987.

Capacitance measurement

The measurement of the ratio of the charge induced on a conductor to the change in potential of a neighboring conductor which induces the charge. In a multiconductor system there are capacitances between each of the conductors. In general, these capacitances are functions of the total geometry, that is, the location of each and every conducting and dielectric body. When, as is usually true, only the capacitance between two conductors is of interest, the presence of other conductors is an undesirable complication. It is then customary to distinguish between two-terminal and three-terminal capacitors and capacitance measurements.

In the case of a two-terminal capacitor, either one of the conductors of primary interest surrounds the other, in which case the capacitance between them is independent of the location of other bodies except in the vicinity of the terminals; or the somewhat indefinite contributions of the other conductors to the capacitance of interest are accepted.

A three-terminal capacitor consists of two active electrodes surrounded by a third, or shield, conductor. The direct capacitance between the two active electrodes is the capacitance of interest, and, when shielded leads are used, it is independent of the location of all other conductors except the shield. Only certain of the methods described are suitable for the measurement of three-terminal capacitors.

Every physically realizable capacitor has associated loss in the dielectric and in the metal electrodes. At a single frequency these are indistinguishable, and the capacitor may be represented by either a parallel or series combination of pure capacitance and pure resistance. The measurement of capacitance, then, in general involves the simultaneous measurement of, or allowance for, an associated resistive element. *See* PERMITTIVITY.

Most capacitance measurements involve simply a comparison of the capacitor to be measured with a capacitor of known value. Methods which permit comparison of essentially equal capacitors by simple substitution of one for the other at the same point in a circuit are frequently possible and almost always preferable.

Properties of standard capacitors. The most stable capacitor is one with fused quartz dielectric having a value of 10 picofarads. The dielectric is a quartz disk about 2.8 in. (70 mm) in diameter and 0.4 in. (10 mm) thick. Electrodes are fired onto the two faces of the disk, and a guard electrode is fired onto the circumferential surface. Because fused quartz has a temperature coefficient of permittivity of about 5 parts per million per degree Fahrenheit (10 parts per million per kelvin) it is essential to measure the temperature accurately, and a resistance thermometer is placed around the disk. The unit is in a hermetically sealed container and can be put in an oil-bath or other constant-temperature enclosure.

Other good capacitors with values up to 1 nanofarad have parallel plates or cylindrical electrodes; they are hermetically sealed and evacuated or filled with dry gas. Capacitors of larger value have a solid dielectric, such as mica or polystyrene or other plastic film, and are less constant in value. When they are used as standards, a three-terminal arrangement is normal, and there is a screening case with a separate connection. A three-terminal capacitor can be measured satisfactorily if the screen can be maintained at the potential of one of the capacitor terminals, but at high frequencies—above about 100 kHz—it becomes increasingly difficult to satisfy this condition, and a two-terminal capacitor may be advantageous. The disadvantage of a two-terminal capacitor is the uncertainty arising from the fringing field of its terminals, which may be a few tenths of a picofarad; however, a change in capacitance will be precise if the fringing field is unaltered. For example, the difference in the value of two capacitors with identical terminal arrangements can be measured accurately even if their total capacitance cannot be determined with high accuracy. This applies even to capacitors with precision coaxial connectors for use up to a few gigahertz; with one type of such capacitor, when it is unmated, the inner conductor length can differ slightly from one connector to another, thereby giving a corresponding different capacitance for an unmated connector. Such capacitors have a series inductance of only a few nanohenries, and they and transmission lines of accurately known dimensions provide the standards for high-frequency measurements. *See* INDUCTANCE; TRANSMISSION LINES.

At the other end of the frequency range, measurements are required on capacitors up to 1 farad in value at frequencies around 100 Hz. The stability of these capacitors is such that the standards used in their measurement need have an accuracy of no better than 0.01% and are often considerably worse. For this range, the standards comprise a capacitor combined with transformers for the input and output connections. A single capacitor, which may be a 1-microfarad mica dielectric capacitor, and multitapped input and output transformers can be used to provide values between 1 μF and 1 F. However, a better performance is obtained if a transformer designed to give the optimum properties is used to provide each value of the capacitance, and plastic-film capacitors of value larger than 1 μF are used.

Frequency-dependence of capacitors. The effective value of a capacitor C_e (the value that is measured at its terminals) may be affected by three factors. First, series inductance l apparently increases the actual capacitance C, according to Eq. (1), where ω is the

$$C_e = \frac{C}{1 - \omega^2 l C} \qquad (1)$$

angular frequency. Second, dielectric absorption in a capacitor with a solid dielectric normally causes a reduction in capacitance as the frequency is raised. Third, mechanical displacement of the electrodes due to the electric forces between them may alter the capacitance in a voltage- or frequency-dependent manner; this effect should be detectable only in air or gas dielectric capacitors, and it can be quite appreciable in high-voltage capacitors.

The series inductance can be obtained from a measurement of the self-resonant frequency f of the capacitor with its terminals connected together by a link of low and calculable inductance. The total inductance is $1/[(2\pi f)^2 C]$.

The effect of dielectric absorption is measured

by ultimate reference to an air or gas dielectric capacitor whose plates have clean metal surfaces.

The electric forces between the electrodes of standard capacitors produce capacitance changes that are usually too small to be significant, except when the highest accuracy is required at more than a single applied voltage or at a frequency near that of a mechanical resonance.

Distributed capacitance. An inductor is a particularly impure circuit component. In addition to the series resistance of the winding, distributed capacitance is always present from turn to turn and layer to layer, making the effective inductance a function of frequency. It is customary to assume that the effect of the distributed capacitance in an inductance coil may be represented by a single capacitor connected between the coil terminals. In some cases the value of this equivalent capacitor may be obtained by a determination of the self-resonant frequency of the coil; however, as a result of the distributed nature of both the inductance and the capacitance, the coil may exhibit several resonance modes, and a self-resonance determination is then ambiguous.

A procedure that usually surmounts this difficulty is that of determining the resonant frequency for several settings of a variable capacitor connected in parallel with the coil. A plot of the capacitance of the observed auxiliary capacitor against the reciprocal of the square of the corresponding resonant frequency and extrapolated to infinite frequency then gives a value for the lumped equivalent of the distributed capacitance.

Bridge comparison methods. When capacitors must be compared with high accuracy, bridge methods must be adopted. *See* BRIDGE CIRCUIT; WHEATSTONE BRIDGE.

Resistance-ratio bridges. These are Wheatstone-bridge configurations in which the potential division and either a parallel combination of a loss-free capacitor C_s and a conductance G_s (**Fig. 1**a) or a series combination of C_s and a resistor R_s (Fig. 1b) is equated, when the detector is nulled, to the ratio of potentials across resistors R_1 and R_2. More commonly now, the reference potential division is that of a variable-ratio autotransformer known as an inductive voltage divider (IVD). *See* INDUCTIVE VOLTAGE DIVIDER.

For the parallel arrangement, equality of potential division leads to Eqs. (2) and (3) for the unknown

$$C_x = C_s \frac{R_1}{R_2} \qquad (2)$$

$$G_x = G_s \frac{R_1}{R_2} \qquad (3)$$

capacitance C_x and conductance G_x; while, for the series arrangement, this equality leads to Eqs. (4) and (5) for C_x and the unknown resistance R_x.

$$C_x = C_s \frac{R_1}{R_2} \qquad (4)$$

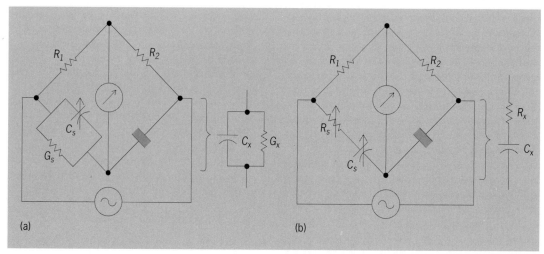

Fig. 1. Resistance-ratio bridges, in which two adjacent arms are resistors. (*a*) Parallel arrangement. (*b*) Series arrangements.

$$R_x = R_s \frac{R_2}{R_1} \qquad (5)$$

Schering bridge. This bridge yields a measurement of the equivalent series-circuit representation of a capacitor (**Fig. 2**). The equations of balance are written as Eqs. (6) and (7).

$$C_x = C_s \frac{R_1}{R_2} \qquad (6)$$

$$R_x = R_2 \frac{C_1}{C_s} \qquad (7)$$

As with any balanced bridge network, the positions of source and detector may be interchanged without affecting the balance condition. This change may be done to gain an advantage in, for example, sensitivity to the balance condition or the voltage rating of some component.

Wagner branch. The resistance-ratio and Schering bridges are useful for two-terminal capacitance measurements. Their use may be extended to three-terminal measurements and extended in accuracy and range by the introduction of shielding and the addition of the Wagner branch (**Fig. 3**).

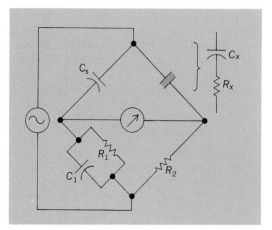

Fig. 2. Schering bridge for measurement of the equivalent series-circuit representation of a capacitor.

Balance is effected alternately by adjustment of the main bridge arms with the switch open, and by adjustment of the Wagner branch elements with the switch closed. The final balance is obtained with the switch open. Capacitances to the shield at two opposite corners of the bridge then shunt the Wagner arms and do not affect the balance of the main bridge. Capacitances to the shield at the other two corners carry no current at balance and therefore cannot introduce error.

Bridged-T and parallel-T networks. These complex bridges possess a significant advantage over four-arm bridges for medium-accuracy radio-frequency measurements of capacitance because the source and detector have a common point of connection. (**Fig. 4**). Use of the Y-delta network transformation permits reduction of either the bridged-T (Fig. 4*a*) or the parallel-T (Fig. 4*b*) to an equivalent circuit (Fig. 4*c*). Balance, or null indication of the detector, is achieved by variation of the network components until the equivalent impedance linking the source and the detector is infinite. *See* Y-DELTA TRANSFORMATIONS.

Time-constant methods. If a direct voltage is suddenly applied to the series combination of a resistor and an initially discharged capacitor, the charge and the voltage on the capacitor increase exponentially toward their full magnitudes with a time constant equal in seconds to the product of the resistance in ohms and the capacitance in farads. Similarly, when a charged capacitor is discharged through a resistor, the charge and the voltage decay with the same time constant. Various methods are available for the measurement of capacitance by measurement of the time constant of charge or discharge through a known resistor. *See* TIME CONSTANT.

In one such method the time required for the output voltage of an operational amplifier to increase to a value equal to the step-function input voltage is determined by an electronic voltage-comparison circuit and timer. With the assumption of ideal characteristics for the amplifier, such as infinite gain without feedback, infinite

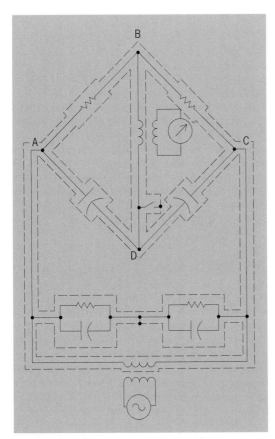

Fig. 3. Shielded resistance ratio-arm bridge with a Wagner branch for three-terminal measurements. With the switch open, capacitances to the shield at A and C shunt the Wagner arms. At balance, capacitances to the shield at B and D carry no current.

input impedance, and zero output impedance, the measured time interval is equal to the product of the values of the known resistance and the capacitance being measured. *See* OPERATIONAL AMPLIFIER.

Thompson-Lampard capacitor. The value of a capacitor of a fixed shape is proportional to its size; that is, a single dimension might be used to establish its value. A. M. Thompson and D. G. Lampard showed how this principle could be applied to a precise and practical capacitor. The value of such a capacitor requires only a single length to be measured accurately, and this is readily accomplished by interferometry. Because of its high

accuracy, this capacitor provides the standard for the unit of capacitance defined in the International System of Units (SI).

Thompson and Lampard's theorem relates to a capacitor which, in its simple form, comprises four equal electrodes of parallel round bars arranged with their axes at the corners of a square and with small gaps between adjacent bars (**Fig. 5**). In vacuum, the cross-capacitance between diagonally opposite electrodes per unit length is given by notation (8). If the two cross-capacitances are not

$$C_0 = 1.95354902 \text{ pF/m} \qquad (8)$$

quite equal and differ by ΔC, the mean capacitance is given approximately by Eq. (9).

$$C = C_0[1 + 0.0866(\Delta C/C)^2] \qquad (9)$$

Grounded electric shields around the assembly and at the ends of the capacitor eliminate from a measurement all capacitances except the required internal ones. The capacitor is in an evacuated enclosure to avoid uncertainties arising from the relative permittivity and the refractive index.

If a grounded bar or tube is inserted into the central space between the electrodes, with a small gap between the bar and the electrodes, it forms an electric shield and the cross-capacitance is zero. A short, fixed tube is inserted at one end, and at the other there is a long tube that can be moved axially to alter the active length of the capacitor. The change of length is measured interferometrically; for this, interferometer plates are mounted at the inner ends of the fixed and movable tubes. There is a minimum separation of the tubes—about three times the space between opposing electrodes— below which the capacitance change with length becomes significantly nonlinear.

A practical cross-capacitor departs slightly from the ideal geometry in a number of ways, so that the accuracy is limited to about 1×10^{-8} pF; if the working range of the capacitor is 0.5 pF (equivalent to a change of length of 10 in. or 25 cm), the overall accuracy on this account is 2 parts in 10^8. The repeatability is appreciably better.

Calibration of standard capacitors. The Thompson-Lampard capacitor provides the starting point for the calibration of standard capacitors, which are compared in 1:10 steps by using an accurately

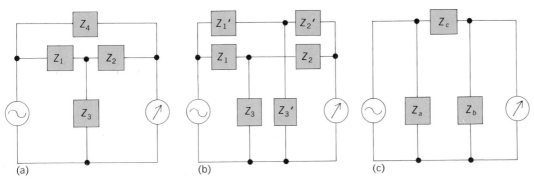

(a)   (b)   (c)

Fig. 4. T networks. (*a*) Bridged-T. (*b*) Parallel-T. (*c*) Equivalent circuit. Balance is achieved by varying network components until the equivalent impedance Z_c is infinite.

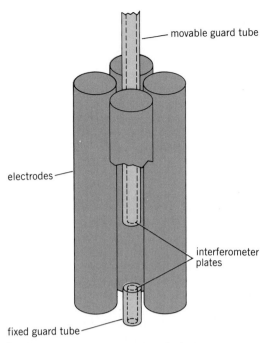

Fig. 5. Essential arrangement of a calculable capacitor with an interferometer for length measurement. Grounded electric shields are omitted.

calibrated transformer in a coaxial alternating-current bridge. When the highest accuracy of comparison is required, the capacitors must be four-terminal-pair components and used in an appropriate bridge (**Fig. 6**). A four-terminal-pair impedance has two coaxial connections at the input and two at the output terminations. The source is connected to one input connection, and the defining voltage appears at the other input connection; similarly, the current through the impedance passes through one output connector, while the potential difference and current at the other output connection are kept at zero. The defining conditions can be departed from, provided that the bridge balance is not thereby altered. The coaxial connections have screens and outer conductors. Every mesh has a current equalizer which ensures that equal currents of opposite sign flow in the inner and the outer conductors of every coaxial connection. The transformer is of the two-stage type; thus there is an energizing winding on the first core followed by a winding which supplies the current to the impedances to be compared, and finally, a second core and the overall winding, which provides a precise potential ratio for comparing the two four-terminal-pair impedances. *See* INSTRUMENT TRANSFORMER.

The bridge is balanced by injecting a small known voltage into the potential circuit of one of the impedances. Adjustment of the combining network for the detector is also required. For this, the switch in the conductor joining the output current connections of the two impedances is opened, the detector is rebalanced by adjusting the combining network, and the switch is closed. *See* CAPACITANCE; CAPACITOR; ELECTRICAL MEASUREMENTS.

Bryan P. Kibble; F. Ralph Kotter; G. H. Rayner

Bibliography. B. P. Kibble and G. H. Rayner, *Coaxial A. C. Bridges*, 1984; L. Schnell, *Technology of Electrical Measurements*, 1993.

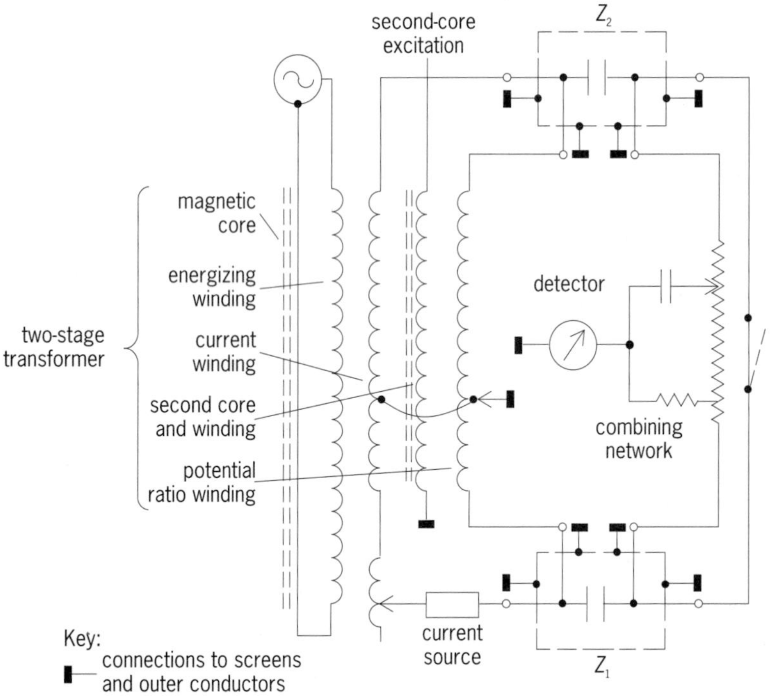

Capacitance multiplication

The generation of a capacitance which is some multiple of that of an actual capacitor. Capacitance multiplication circuits have an input impedance which is capacitive and which is proportional to that of an actual capacitor appearing somewhere in the circuit. In most applications, capacitance multiplication circuits are used to generate an equivalent input capacitance which is much larger than that of the actual capacitor. One scenario where capacitance multiplication might prove useful is where a physical capacitor of a required capacitance may be too large, too expensive, or unavailable. A second is where the capacitor must be reasonably large and capable of handling bidirectional signals, thus precluding the direct use of widely available electrolytic capacitors and hence making practical the utilization of a much smaller nonelectrolytic capacitor in a capacitance multiplication circuit. *See* CAPACITANCE; CAPACITOR.

Capacitance multiplication circuits are often made from operational amplifiers and resistors along with the capacitor that is to be scaled, although transistors and other active devices can also be used. Capacitance multiplication circuits are closely related to classes of circuits termed generalized immittance converters and negative impedance

Fig. 6. Transformer bridge for the precise comparison of two similar impedances Z_1 and Z_2. Screens and outer conductors of the coaxial connections have been omitted for clarity, but connections to them are shown.

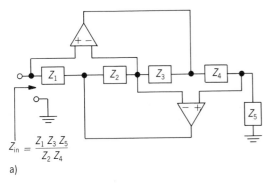

$$Z_{in} = \frac{Z_1 Z_3 Z_5}{Z_2 Z_4}$$

a)

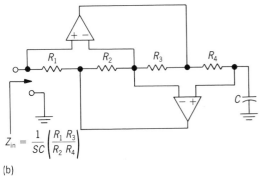

$$Z_{in} = \frac{1}{SC}\left(\frac{R_1 R_3}{R_2 R_4}\right)$$

(b)

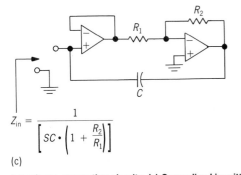

$$Z_{in} = \frac{1}{\left[SC \cdot \left(1 + \frac{R_2}{R_1}\right)\right]}$$

(c)

Impedance-generation circuits. (a) Generalized immittance converter. (b) Capacitance multiplier based on generalized immittance converter. (c) Miller capacitance multiplier. Input impedance Z_{in} is given in Laplace transform notation; S is the Laplace transform variable.

converters. Generalized immittance converters are used to generate an equivalent input impedance that is proportional to products or quotients of specific impedances that appear in the circuit. Generalized immittance converters are often used for capacitance multiplication. Related applications of generalized immittance converters are synthetic inductance simulation and negative-resistance generation. Negative-impedance converters are also used for the generation of negative impedances. *See* ELECTRICAL IMPEDANCE; IMMITTANCE; INDUCTANCE; NEGATIVE-RESISTANCE CIRCUITS; OPERATIONAL AMPLIFIER.

A generalized immittance converter circuit is shown in **illus.** *a*. The input impedance Z_{in} of this circuit is given by Eq. (1). I f the impedances

$$Z_{in} = \frac{Z_1 Z_3 Z_5}{Z_2 Z_4} \tag{1}$$

$Z_1 - Z_4$ are resistors and Z_5 is a capacitor, the capacitance multiplication circuit of illus. *b* is

obtained. The equivalent impedance of this circuit is that of a capacitor of value C_{eq} given by Eq. (2). The resistor ratio $(R_2 R_4)/(R_1 R_3)$ determines

$$C_{eq} = \frac{C R_2 R_4}{R_1 R_3} \tag{2}$$

the capacitance multiplication factor. A second capacitance multiplication circuit based upon the Miller effect is shown in illus. *c*. The equivalent capacitance of this circuit is given by Eq. (3).

$$C_{eq} = C\left(1 + \frac{R_2}{R_1}\right) \tag{3}$$

Capacitance multiplication circuits have some practical limitations. For example, the input impedance of the circuits of illus. *b* and *c* will remain capacitive only provided the operational amplifiers are operating linearly. This requirement places some restrictions on how capacitance multiplication circuits can be used. For example, the output voltage swing, the output current, and the slew rate of the operational amplifier all have hard limits imposed by the design of the operational amplifier itself, and these limits must not be violated at either internal or external nodes of the capacitance multiplication circuits. The bandwidth of the operational amplifier is also limited. These limits on the operational amplifier restrict the magnitude and frequency of signals that can be placed on capacitance multiplication circuits, as well as how fast these capacitors can be discharged. Although violation of these limits is usually nondestructive (provided the input voltage does not exceed the maximum allowed for the operational amplifier), violations will result in significant signal distortion. These limitations become increasingly problematic when realizing very large capacitors or when using large capacitance multiplication factors. Other capacitance multiplication circuits beyond those shown in the illustration are available which offer varying trade-offs between capacitance multiplication, signal swing, frequency response, and complexity.

Randall L. Geiger

Bibliography. L. T. Bruton, *RC-Active Circuits, Theory and Design*, 1980; A. Sedra and K. Smith, *Microelectronic Circuits*, 3d ed., 1992; F. W. Stephenson (ed.), *RC Active Filter Design Handbook*, 1985.

Capacitor

An electrical device capable of storing electrical energy. In general, a capacitor consists of two metal plates insulated from each other by a dielectric. The capacitance of a capacitor depends primarily upon its shape and size and upon the relative permittivity ϵ_r of the medium between the plates. In vacuum, in air, and in most gases, ϵ_r ranges from one to several hundred. *See* CAPACITANCE; PERMITTIVITY.

Classification. One classification of capacitors comes from the physical state of their dielectrics, which may be gas (or vacuum), liquid, solid, or a combination of these. Each of these classifications

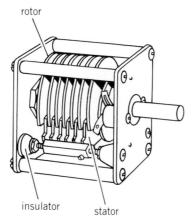

Fig. 1. **Variable air capacitor.**

may be subdivided according to the specific dielectric used. Capacitors may be further classified by their ability to be used in alternating-current (ac) or direct-current (dc) circuits with various current levels.

Capacitors are also classified as fixed, adjustable, or variable. The capacitance of fixed capacitors remains unchanged, except for small variations caused by temperature fluctuations. The capacitance of adjustable capacitors may be set at any one of several discrete values. The capacitance of variable capacitors may be adjusted continuously and set at any value between minimum and maximum limits fixed by construction. Trimmer capacitors are relatively small variable capacitors used in parallel with larger variable or fixed capacitors to permit exact adjustment of the capacitance of the parallel combination.

Air, gas, and vacuum types. Made in both fixed and variable types, these capacitors are constructed with flat parallel metallic plates (or cylindrical concentric metallic plates) with air, gas, or vacuum as the dielectric between plates. Alternate plates are connected, with one or both sets supported by means of a solid insulating material such as glass, quartz, ceramic, or plastic. **Figure 1** shows a variable air capacitor. Gas capacitors are similarly built but are enclosed in a leakproof case. If the gas capacitor is variable, the shaft supporting the movable plates, or rotor, is brought out through

a pressure-tight insulated seal. Vacuum capacitors are of concentric-cylindrical construction and are enclosed in highly evacuated glass envelopes.

The purpose of a high vacuum, or a gas under pressure, is to increase the voltage breakdown value for a given plate spacing. For high-voltage applications, when increasing the spacing between plates is undesirable, the breakdown voltage of air capacitors may be increased by rounding the edges of the plates. Air, gas, and vacuum capacitors are used in high-frequency circuits. Fixed and variable air capacitors incorporating special design are used as standards in electrical measurements. *See* CAPACITANCE MEASUREMENT; ELECTRICAL UNITS AND STANDARDS.

Solid-dielectric types. These capacitors use one of several dieletrics such as a ceramic, mica, glass, or plastic film. Alternate plates of metal, or metallic foil, are stacked with the dielectric, or the dielectric may be metal-plated on both sides. Some of the more popular dielectric materials are listed in **Table 1**, along with their relative permittivities and power factors. *See* DIELECTRIC MATERIALS; POWER FACTOR.

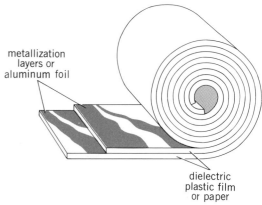

Fig. 2. **Wound-roll construction of plastic film and paper capacitors.**

Plastic-film types. These capacitors use dielectrics such as polypropylene, polyester, polycarbonate, or polysulfone with a relative permittivity ranging from 2.2 to 3.2. This plastic film may be used alone or in combination with Kraft paper. The dielectric thicknesses range from 0.06 to over 0.8 mil (1.5 to over 20 micrometers). The most common electrodes are aluminum or zinc vacuum-deposited on the film, although aluminum foil is also used. These types generally utilize wound-roll construction (**Fig. 2**). *See* POLYESTER RESINS; POLYOLEFIN RESINS; POLYSULFONE RESINS.

Plastic-film capacitors may be constructed in a dry roll for dc and low-voltage ac applications. For ac applications above about 250 V, the capacitor winding is usually impregnated with a dielectric fluid to avoid degradation of the dielectric due to partial discharges.

Mica types. These capacitors use thin rectangular sheets of mica as the dielectric. The relative

TABLE 1. Dielectric materials used in capacitors

Dielectric material	Relative permittivity (ϵ_r)	Power factor, %
Vacuum or air	1	0
Kraft paper	4.0–6.5	3
Polyester	3.0	0.5
Polypropylene	2.2	0.01
Polystyrene	2.5	0.05
Glass	6.7	0.06
Mica	6–8	0.02
Aluminum oxide	10.0	5–10
Tantalum oxide	11.0	5–10
Barium titanate	10.60	0.2–2.5

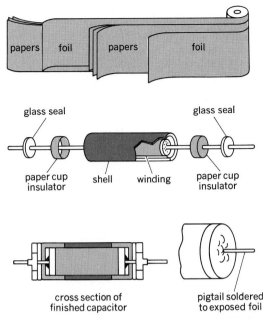

Fig. 3. Ceramic capacitor constructed in chip form, showing cutaway of finished chip.

permittivity of mica is in the range of 6–8. The electrodes are either thin sheets of metal foil stacked alternately with the mica sheets, or thin deposits of silver applied directly to the surface of the mica sheets. Mica capacitors are used chiefly in radio-frequency applications. They have a low dielectric loss at very high frequencies, good temperature, frequency, and aging characteristics, and low power factor, but have a low ratio of capacitance to volume or to mass. They are made with dc voltage ratings

from a few hundred to many thousands of volts and with radio-frequency current ratings up to about 50 A. *See* MICA.

Paper types. A dielectric of Kraft paper usually impregnated with mineral oil, or ester, is used in paper capacitors. Paper and plastic-film capacitors (Fig. 2) are constructed by stacking, or forming into a roll, alternate layers of foil and dielectric. Paper capacitors are gradually being replaced by metallized polypropylene and polyester films with lower cost, smaller size, and lower power factor. *See* PAPER.

Ceramic types. The monolithic ceramic capacitor consists of dielectric layers interleaved with electrode layers; the assembly is then compressed and sintered to form a solid monolithic block (**Fig. 3**). The dielectric layer may be as thin as 0.8 mil (20 μm), and as many as 40–50 layers may be interleaved. The most common dielectric material is barium titanate. The electrodes are composed of materials such as a silver-palladium mixture. The end termination is usually composed of several layers of silver-palladium, nickel, and tin. These capacitors may be constructed in radial, axial, or chip form. The chip construction is especially popular for surface mounting on electronic circuits. The chips have a typical size of $1/8$ in. × $1/6$ in. × $1/40$ in. (3.2 mm × 1.6 mm × 0.65 mm). These capacitors have the ability to withstand the 450°F (230°C) reflow solder and 540°F (280°C) wave solder mounting temperatures. *See* CERAMICS.

Electrolytic types. A large capacitance-to-volume ratio and a low cost per microfarad of capacitance are chief advantages of electrolytic capacitors. These use aluminum or tantalum plates (**Fig. 4**).

TABLE 2. Major types of capacitors*

Type	Capacitance	Voltage (working voltage, dc), V	Applications
Monolithic ceramics	1 pF–2.2 μF	50–200	Ultrahigh frequency, rf coupling, computers
Disk and tube ceramics	1 pF–1 μF	50–1000	General, very high frequency
Paper	0.001–1 μF	200–1600	Motors, power supplies
Film			
Polypropylene	0.0001–0.47 μF	400–1600	Television vertical circuits, rf circuits
Polyester	0.001–4.7 μF	50–600	Entertainment electronics
Polystyrene	0.001–1 μF	100–200	General, high stability
Polycarbonate	0.01–18 μF	50–200	General
Metallized polypropylene	4–60 μF	400†	Alternating-current motors
Metallized polyester	0.001–22 μF	100–1000	Coupling, rf filtering
Electrolytic			
Aluminum	1 100,00 μF	5–500	Power supplies, filters
Tantalum	0.1–2200 μF	3–150	Small space requirement, low leakage
Gold	0.022–10 F	2.5–5.5	Memory backup
Nonpolarized (either aluminum or tantalum)	0.47–1000 μF	10–200	Loudspeaker crossovers
Mica	330 pF–0.05 μF	50–1000	High frequency
Silver-mica	5–820 pF	50–500	High frequency
Variable			
Ceramic	1–5 to 16–100 pF	200	Radio, television, communications
Film	0.8–5 to 1.2–30 pF	50	Oscillators, antenna, rf circuits
Air	10–365 pF	50	Broadcast receiver
Poly(tetrafluoroethylene)	0.25–1.5 pF	2000	Very high frequency, ultrahigh frequency

*After A. Mottershead, *Electricity and Electronics*, Prentice Hall, 1990.
†Alternating-current voltage at 60 Hz.

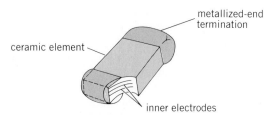

Fig. 4. Tantalum electrolytic capacitor showing cross section. (*General Electric Co.*)

A paste electrolyte is placed between the plates, and a dc forming voltage is applied. A current flows and by a process of electrolysis builds up a molecule-thin layer of oxide bubbles on the positive plate. This serves as the dieletric. The rest of the electrolyte and the other plate make up the negative electrode (**Fig. 5***a*). Such a device is said to be polarized and must be connected in a circuit with the proper polarity. To ensure proper connection, the polarization of the capacitor is clearly marked by polarity signs for the axial type (Fig. 5*b*) or by a longer lead for the positive side in the radial type (Fig. 5*c*). Polarized capacitors can be used only in circuits in which the dc component of voltage across the capacitors exceeds the crest value of the ac ripple.

Another type of electrolytic capacitor utilizes compressed tantalum powder and the baking of manganese oxide (MnO_2) as an electrolyte. These capacitors may be constructed with either radial, axial, or chip configurations.

Nonpolarized electrolytic capacitors can be constructed for use in ac circuits. In effect, they are two polarized capacitors placed in series with their polarities reversed.

Table 2 provides a summary of the major types of

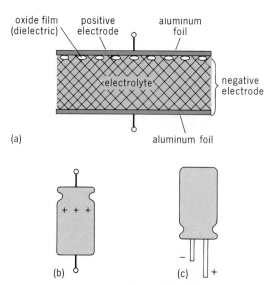

(a)

(b)   **(c)**

Fig. 5. Construction and polarity markings of aluminum electrolytic capacitor. (*a*) Cross section. (*b* Polarization markings for tabular capacitor with axial leads. (*c*) Polarization markings for capacitor with radial leads. (*After A. Mottershead, Electricity and Electronics, Prentice Hall, 1990*)

discrete capacitors and some of their applications.

Thick-film types. These capacitors are made by means of successive screen-printing and firing processes in the fabrication of certain types of microcircuits used in electronic computers and other electronic systems. They are formed, together with their connecting conductors and associated thick-film resistors, upon a ceramic substrate. Their characteristics and the materials are similar to those of ceramic capacitors. *See* PRINTED CIRCUIT.

Thin-film types. Thin-film dielectrics are deposited on ceramic and integrated-circuit substrates and then metallized with aluminum to form capacitive components. These are usually single-layer capacitors. The most common dielectrics are silicon nitride and silicon dioxide. Thin-film dieletrics may be deposited by plasma deposition or sputtering. *See* INTEGRATED CIRCUITS; SPUTTERING.

Allen Mottershead

Bibliography. C. J. Kaiser, *The Capacitor Handbook*, 1990, reprint 1993; A. Mottershead, *Electricity and Electronics*, 1990.

Capparales

An order of flowering plants, division Magnoliophyta (Angiospermae), in the subclass Dilleniidae of the class Magnoliopsida (dicotyledons). It consists of 5 families and nearly 4000 species.

The families Brassicaceae (Cruciferae), with about 3000 species, and Capparaceae (often spelled Capparidaceae), with about 800 species, form the core of the order. These two families have alternate, usually compound or dissected leaves, and hypogynous flowers with mostly four sepals, four petals, centrifugal stamens, and (at least apparently) two carpels which form a compound ovary with more or less distinctly parietal placentation. Nearly all the Brassicaceae and many of the Capparaceae have specialized myrosin cells, which are chiefly but not entirely restricted to this order. Myrosin is an enzyme involved in the formation of mustard oil. The Brassicaceae are further marked by a distinctive ovary, which is bilocular, with the ovules attached to the margins of the partition; and by the mostly tetradynamous stamens, the two outer stamens being shorter than the four inner ones. Several common vegetables, including cabbage, radish, rutabaga, turnip, water cress, and the various kinds of mustards, belong to the Brassicaceae. A number of familiar ornamentals, including candytuft (*Iberis*), stock (*Matthiola*), and sweet alyssum (*Lobularia maritima*) in the Brassicaceae, spider flower (*Cleome spinosa*) in the Capparaceae, and mignonette (*Reseda*) in the Resedaceae belong to the Capparales. *See* BROCCOLI; BRUSSELS SPROUTS; CABBAGE; CAULIFLOWER; COLLARD; CRESS; HORSERADISH; KALE; KOHLRABI; MUSTARD; ORNAMENTAL PLANTS; RADISH; RAPE; RUTABAGA; TURNIP.

In the past the Capparales have often been united with the Papaverales in the order Rhoeadales, but it is now generally believed that the two groups are not closely related. *See* MAGNOLIOPHYTA; MAGNOLIOPSIDA; PAPAVERALES; PLANT KINGDOM.

Arthur Cronquist; T. M. Barkley

Caprellidea

A common crustacean suborder in marine and estuarine environments, belonging to the superorder Peracarida, order Amphipoda. As peracarids, female Caprellidea have a ventral brood pouch and eggs develop directly (that is, there are no planktonic larvae); as amphipods, Caprellidea have the second and third thoracic appendages formed into enlarged subchelate claws (gnathopods). Many amphipods use their abdominal appendages for swimming, but the abdomen and abdominal appendages of caprellideans are reduced. Thus caprellideans are restricted to a clinging and crawling life-style. Almost all caprellideans use other organisms as substrata. Family distinctions within the Caprellidea are being reevaluated, but the classical divisions are the families Caprellidae and Cyamidae. The ecology of both families is poorly understood.

Caprellidae. Caprellids are slender organisms 0.4–1.2 in. (1–3 cm) in length which resemble praying mantises. They are commonly found clinging to algae, bryozoans, and hydroids (easily found on boat docks and pilings) and crawl through the habitats in an inchworm fashion. Caprellids assume an upright stance (see **illus.**) when not moving. Most caprellids are color-camouflaged with their biotic habitats, and therefore difficult to distinguish. Some species have poisonous spines on their second gnathopods which are used in aggressive encounters and to capture prey. Caprellids occur globally to depths of 10,000 ft (3000 m); their distribution is surprising considering their direct life cycle and limited dispersal mechanisms. Two ecological groups are separable by second antennae setation; the filter-feeding genera have long, paired setae that arise in a V pattern from the ventral margin, whereas the predatory genera lack these specialized setae.

Cyamidae. Cyamids are the whale lice; they are so named for their occurrence on the skin of baleen and toothed whales and their resemblance to terrestrial lice (Insecta). Cyamid bodies are dorsoventrally flattened, so that water drag is reduced on the cyamid as the whale swims. The thoracic appendages are robust, an adaptation that enables the cyamid to firmly grasp the whale. Whale lice have piercing mouthparts and feed on the exposed tissues of the whales. Thus cyamids are true ectoparasites. *See* AMPHIPODA; CRUSTACEA.

Edsel A. Caine

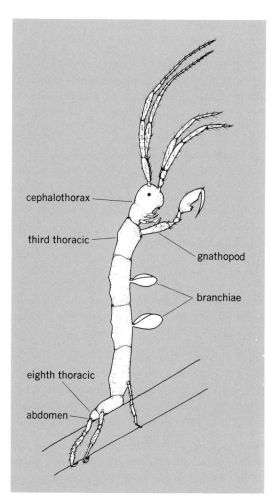

Generalized predatory caprellid in an upright stance.

Capricornus

The Sea Goat, in astronomy, an inconspicuous zodiacal constellation in the southern sky lying between Aquarius and Sagittarius. Capricornus is the tenth sign of the zodiac. It has two third-magnitude stars, β and δ, the remainder being of fourth magnitude or fainter. The constellation has been described from the earliest times as a goat, or

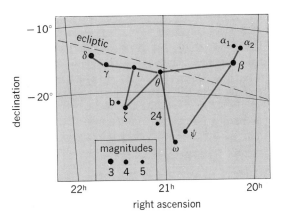

Line pattern of constellation Capricornus. Grid lines represent coordinates of the sky. Apparent brightness, or magnitudes, of stars are shown by size of dots, which are graded by appropriate numbers as indicated.

as a figure that is part goat with the tail of a fish (see **illus.**). Together with the neighboring zodiacal constellations Aquarius and Pisces, Capricornus forms the great heavenly sea; all the names are related to water. The Tropic of Capricorn originates from this constellation, which marked the southern limit of the ecliptic in ancient times. *See* AQUARIUS; CONSTELLATION; PISCES (CONSTELLATION); ZODIAC.

Ching-Sung Yu

Caprimulgiformes

An order of crepuscular or mainly nocturnal birds collectively known as the goatsuckers. The group is apparently most closely related to the owls (Strigiformes) and is found worldwide, mainly in the tropics and warm temperate regions. Species breeding in the Arctic and cooler temperate regions are migratory. *See* STRIGIFORMES.

Classification. The order Caprimulgiformes is divided into the suborder Steatornithes, containing the single family Steatornithidae (oilbirds; 1 species), and the suborder Caprimulgi, including the families Podargidae (frogmouths; 13 species), Aegothelidae (owlet-frogmouths; 8 species), Nyctibiidae (potoos; 6 species), and Caprimulgidae (nightjars or goatsuckers; 77 species). The largest family, Caprimulgidae, is found worldwide and is usually divided into two subfamilies, the Caprimulginae (nightjars) and the Chordeilinae (nighthawks). The Steatornithidae are restricted to northern South America. The Podargidae live in the Old World tropics from India to Australia, while the smaller related Aegothelidae are restricted to Australia and surrounding islands. The Nyctibiidae are found in the New World tropics.

Fossil record. The goatsuckers have a poor fossil record, but with some interesting forms known from the early Tertiary well outside the current range of the different families. Specimens assigned to the oilbirds, the frogmouths, and the owlet-frogmouths have been reported from the Eocene of France.

Characteristics. The goatsuckers are primarily insectivorous, although the large frogmouths also feed on small vertebrates; the oilbird is unique in feeding on fruits, especially of palms. Goatsuckers have a huge, generally weak mouth with long, stout bristles surrounding it to make an effective trap for insects caught in flight. The wings are well developed, but the feet are weak and serve mainly for perching. The plumage is soft and fluffy, and is mottled and barred brown and gray, serving as a cryptic protective coloration. White patches may exist on the wings, tail, and throat, which are visible only in flight. Some species have greatly elongated tail feathers, and a few have very elongated primary feathers forming pennants from their wings. Goatsuckers are solitary but may migrate in loose flocks (nighthawks). Most species are highly vocal, using the calls to attract mates and

defend territories. The English names of a number of species, such as the whippoorwill and chuck-will's-widow, are based on their calls. Goatsuckers nest on the ground or in trees, laying one to five eggs. Young are downy and remain in the nest until they are able to fly. A few species are known to hibernate. Poorwills in the deserts of the southwestern United States hibernate in rock holes for several months at a time, often returning to the same hole in successive winters. Their body temperature falls from a normal 104–105°F (40–41°C) to 64–66°F (18–19°C).

The oilbirds are colonial nesters, placing their nest of seeds and droppings on ledges deep in caves. Paired adults remain together throughout the year, roosting on their breeding ledge. The young become very fat, reaching twice the weight of the adults; they were once harvested in large numbers and boiled down for cooking oil. Oilbirds have excellent night vision, but inside their often totally dark caves they find their way by using echolocation based on pulses of sound of about 7000 Hz which are audible to the human ear. *See* AVES; ECHOLOCATION.

Walter J. Bock

Captorhinida

A moderately coherent group of primitive reptiles constituting an order of the subclass Anapsida. Most members are characterized by a closed cheek (temporal) region. The order is divided into four suborders: Captorhinomorpha, Millerosauria, Procolophonia, and Pareiasauria. Except for the Procolophonia, which continue into the Late Triassic, Captorhinida are confined to the Permo-Carboniferous. They lived in lowlands, where they were associated with amphibians and synapsid reptiles. Some of the smaller animals of the Captorhinomorpha and the Millerosauria fed primarily on insects and small vertebrates, but the larger genera were exclusively herbivorous. Along with the caseid pelycosaurs, they were the dominant consumers of vegetation in the middle Permian ecosystems.

At one time the Captorhinida were joined with the Diadectamorpha and Seymouriamorpha to form the order Cotylosauria (stem reptiles). This assemblage, now known to include both reptiles and amphibians, has been dropped because it is polyphyletic and also because it has carried many different meanings.

The Captorhinomorpha are the most diversified of the Captorhinida; the best-known genus is *Captorhinus* of the early Permian (**illus.** *a*). It was preceded, however, by more primitive genera from the upper Carboniferous and very early Permian and succeeded by specialized genera during the later portions of the Permian. *Captorhinus* and its successors were notable in the possession of multiple rows of teeth on the jaws and palates, related to increasingly herbivorous diets. The captorhinomorph evolutionary radiation culminated in a large, mas-

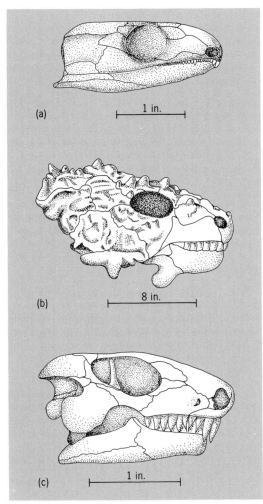

Captorhinid skulls. (*a*) *Captorhinus.* (*b*) *Pareiasaurus.* (*c*) *Procolophon.*

sive genus, *Moradisaurus,* from the upper Permian of Niger, Africa; it measured about 6 ft (2 m) in length.

Millerosasaurs are poorly known small reptiles from the middle Permian of South Africa. Unlike most Captorhinida, they developed partially to fully open cheek regions. They have been considered to be close relatives of the lizards, but currently are thought to be merely a somewhat specialized branch of the Captorhinida.

Procolophonia were small to medium-sized animals with generalized skeletons and specialized skulls. Skulls of some of the Late Triassic procolophons such as *Hypsognathus* were set with sharp, bony projections somewhat reminiscent of those in living horned lizards. The teeth of procolophons were arrayed in single rows and were rather blunt, suggesting a herbivorous diet.

Pareiasaurs were the giants of the Captorhinida, rivaled only by *Moradisaurus.* They ranged up to about 6 ft (2 m) in length and were characterized by broad vertebrae, heavy limbs, and massive feet. Pareiasaurs were prominent herbivores during the middle and late Permian of Eurasia and Africa, where their skeletons occasionally occur in profusion in deposits formed in ancient waterholes. During the late Permian their role as primary consumers was gradually taken over by evolving herbivorous therapsids. *See* ANAPSIDA; REPTILIA; SYNAPSIDA; THERAPSIDA.   Everett C. Olson

Bibliography. C. L. Carroll, *Vertebrate Paleontology and Evolution,* 1987; A. S. Romer, *Osteology of the Reptiles,* 1956.

Carat

The unit of weight now used for all gemstones except pearls. It is also called the metric carat (m.c.). By international agreement, the carat weight is set at 200 milligrams (0.00704 oz). Pearls are weighed in grains, a unit of weight equal to 50 mg (0.0018 oz), or $^1/_4$ carat.

Despite the great value of many of the gemstones weighed against a unit called the carat, the weight differed from country to country until early in the twentieth century. Although most of the weights to which the name was applied were near 205 mg (0.00722 oz), the range was from less than 190 to over 210 mg (less than 0.00669 to over 0.00739 oz). The 200-mg (0.00704-oz) carat was proposed in 1907 in Paris. This weight slowly gained acceptance, and by 1914 most of the important nations in the gem trade had accepted the metric carat as the legal standard for gemstones.

The word carat comes from the Greek word for the locust tree that is common in the Mediterranean area. This tree produces seeds that are fairly uniform in weight, averaging about 205 mg (0.00722 oz) each. As a result, locust seeds came to be used for gem weight comparisons.

The application of the term carat as a unit of weight must not be confused with the term karat used to indicate fineness or purity of the gold in which gems are mounted. *See* GEM.

Richard T. Liddicoat, Jr.

Caraway

An important spice from the fruits of the perennial herb *Carum carvi,* of the family Apiaceae. A native of Europe and western Asia, it is now cultivated in many temperate areas of both hemispheres. The small, brown, slightly curved fruits are used in perfumery, cookery, confectionery, in medicine, and for flavoring beverages. *See* APIALES; SPICE AND FLAVORING.   Perry D. Strausbaugh/Earl L. Core

Carbohydrate

A term applied to a group of substances which include the sugars, starches, and cellulose, along with many other related substances. This group of compounds is vital in the lives of plants and animals, both as structural elements and in the maintenance of functional activity. Plants are unique in that they have the power to synthesize carbohydrates from carbon dioxide and water in the presence of the green pigment chlorophyll through the energy derived from sunlight, by the process of photosynthesis. This process is responsible not only for the existence of plants but for the maintenance of animal life as well, since animals obtain their entire food supply directly or indirectly from the carbohydrates of plants. *See* PHOTOSYNTHESIS.

The carbohydrates as a group are comparable in importance with the proteins and fats. Cane or beet sugar, D-glucose, D-fructose, starch, and cellulose may be cited as typical representatives. A number of members of this group are of great industrial importance. Among undertakings dependent on carbohydrate materials are the cotton industry, explosives manufacture, brewing, and manufacture of alcohol.

The term carbohydrate originated in the belief that naturally occurring compounds of this class, for example, D-glucose ($C_6H_{12}O_6$), sucrose ($C_{12}H_{22}O_{11}$), and cellulose ($C_6H_{10}O_5)_n$, could be represented formally as hydrates of carbon, that is, $C_x(H_2O)_y$. Later it became evident that this definition for carbohydrates was not a satisfactory one. New substances were discovered whose properties clearly indicated that they had the characteristics of sugars and belonged in the carbohydrate class, but which nevertheless showed a deviation from the required hydrogen-to-oxygen ratio. Examples of these are the important deoxy sugars, D-deoxyribose, L-fucose, and L-rhamnose, the uronic acids, and such compounds as ascorbic acid (vitamin C). The retention of the term carbohydrate is therefore a matter of convenience rather than of exact definition. A carbohydrate is usually defined as either a polyhydroxy aldehyde (aldose) or ketone (ketose), or as a substance which yields one of these compounds on hydrolysis. However, included within this class of compounds are substances also containing nitrogen and sulfur. *See* DEOXYRIBOSE; L-FUCOSE; L-RHAMNOSE.

The properties of many carbohydrates differ enormously from one substance to another. The sugars, such as D-glucose or sucrose, are easily soluble, sweet-tasting and crystalline; the starches are colloidal and paste-forming; and cellulose is completely insoluble. Yet chemical analysis shows that they have a common basis; the starches and cellulose may be degraded by different methods to the same crystalline sugar, D-glucose.

Classification. The carbohydrates usually are classified into three main groups according to complexity: monosaccharides, oligosaccharides, and polysaccharides.

Monosaccharides. These simple sugars consist of a single carbohydrate unit which cannot be hydrolyzed into simpler substances. These are characterized, according to their length of carbon chain, as trioses ($C_3H_6O_3$), tetroses ($C_4H_8O_4$), pentoses ($C_5H_{10}O_5$), hexoses ($C_6H_{12}O_6$), heptoses ($C_7H_{14}O_7$), and so on. A monosaccharide may be an aldose or a ketose, depending on the type of carbonyl group ($C{=}O$) present. This system gives rise to such names as aldotriose, aldotetrose, aldopentose, and aldohexose for the aldose forms and by such names as ketopentoses and ketohexoses when the ketone group is present. More recently the tendency is to indicate the presence of a ketone group by the ending "ulose" in names such as pentuloses and heptuloses. *See* MONOSACCHARIDE.

Oligosaccharides. These compound sugars are condensation products of two to five molecules of simple sugars and are subclassified into disaccharides, trisaccharides, tetrasaccharides, and pentasaccharides, according to the number of monosaccharide molecules yielded upon hydrolysis.

The sugars which include the monosaccharides and oligosaccharides are mostly crystalline compounds. The monosaccharides and disaccharides have a sweet taste. Products obtained from hydrolysis of higher molecular weight polysaccharides and consisting of compound sugars that contain as many as nine monosaccharide units are also termed oligosaccharides. However, these higher members are not crystalline compounds. The disaccharides and other groups of oligosaccharides are subclassified into reducing and nonreducing sugars, depending on whether or not the sugar has a functional carbonyl group. In a nonreducing oligosaccharide, the carbonyl groups of the constituent monosaccharide units are involved in glycosidic linkage. The compound sugars are in reality sugarlike polysaccharides, but the prefix "poly" is reserved for carbohydrates which consist of large aggregates of monosaccharide units. *See* OLIGOSACCHARIDE.

Polysaccharides. These comprise a heterogeneous group of compounds which represent large aggregates of monosaccharide units, joined through glycosidic bonds. They are tasteless, nonreducing, amorphous substances that yield a large and indefinite number of monosaccharide units on hydrolysis. Their molecular weight is usually very high, and many of them, like starch or glycogen, have molecular weights of several million. They form colloidal solutions, but some polysaccharides, of which cellulose is an example, are completely insoluble in water. On account of their heterogeneity they are difficult to classify. One common system of classification is based primarily upon the class of monosaccharide yielded on hydrolysis. Thus a polysaccharide that yields hexose monosaccharides on hydrolysis is called hexoglycan, ($C_6H_{10}O_5)_n$, where n represents the number of monosaccharide units present. A polysaccharide yielding a pentose sugar is called pentoglycan, ($C_5H_8O_4)_n$. Each major class is further subdivided according to the particular hexose or pentose produced. Thus, a polysaccharide composed of the hexose sugar D-glucose is called glucan; those composed of the pentose sugars D-xylose and L-arabinose are called xylan and araban, respectively.

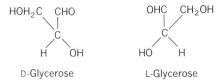

Fig. 1. Spatial arrangement of the groups around the asymmetric carbons of the two isomers of glycerose.

Some polysaccharides, however, yield both hexose and pentose sugars on hydrolysis and are classified as mixed hexosans and pentosans; others, in addition to hexoses and pentoses, frequently on acid hydrolysis yield the uronic acids, D-glucuronic, D-galacturonic, or D-mannuronic acid. Such polysaccharides are often called polyuronides. *See* POLYSACCHARIDE.

Reducing and nonreducing sugars. The sugars are also classified into two general groups, the reducing and nonreducing. The reducing sugars are distinguished by the fact that because of their free, or potentially free, aldehyde or ketone groups they possess the property of readily reducing alkaline solutions of many metallic salts, such as those of copper, silver, bismuth, mercury, and iron. The most widely used reagent for this purpose is Fehling's solution, in which the oxidizing agent is the cupric tartrate ion, formed in a strongly alkaline solution of copper sulfate and a salt of tartaric acid. The nonreducing sugars do not exhibit this property. The reducing sugars constitute by far the larger group. The monosaccharides and many of their derivatives reduce Fehling's solution. Most of the disaccharides, including maltose, lactose, and the rarer sugars cellobiose, gentiobiose, melibiose, and turanose, are also reducing sugars. The best-known nonreducing sugar is the disaccharide sucrose. Among other nonreducing sugars are the disaccharide trehalose, the trisaccharides raffinose and melezitose, the tetrasaccharide stachyose, and the pentasaccharide verbascose.

The alkali in the Fehling solution, or other such reagents used for the determination of reducing sugars, causes considerable decomposition of the sugar molecule into reactive fragments which may also reduce the metal ions. Thus, while the total reduction for a given sugar may be constant under carefully controlled conditions and can therefore be used for quantitative purposes, it is impossible to write a balanced equation for the reaction in terms of the simple oxidation of the sugar and reduction of the metal ion.

Analysis. This involves separation of the carbohydrate mixtures, identification of the individual carbohydrates, and estimation of their quantities.

Separation and identification. Sugars, in most cases, occur in living tissues as mixtures. Before a sugar can be identified, it must be isolated in pure form, preferably as a crystalline substance. The pure crystalline compound is readily identified by its melting point, optical rotation, and x-ray diffraction pattern. Preparation of certain crystalline derivatives

facilitates isolation and identification of reducing sugars. The phenylhydrazone and phenylosazone derivatives of these sugars are especially useful, chiefly because of their ease of preparation. The phenylosatriazoles, benzimidazoles, and diothioacetal acetates are more advantageous for the purpose of identification.

Application of chromatographic technique provides a useful and rapid method for the separation and identification of sugars. The great advantage of this process lies in the fact that it can be applied to minute amounts as well as to relatively large quantities. For micro amounts chromatography on filter paper is used. The mixed sugar solution is applied as a spot on the narrow edge of a strip of filter paper. The sugars are then separated by using a mixture of water and a partially immiscible organic solvent, such as *n*-butanol or phenol. The paper is then dried and sprayed with coloring reagents, such as *p*-anisidine hydrochloride or aniline hydrogen phthalate, which show the location of the individual sugars. For separation of larger quantities of material, column chromatography is used. In this method the proper choice of solvents and absorbents is important. The solvent is passed through a column containing powdered cellulose, silicic acid, alumina, clay, carbon, or other adsorbent by gravity, suction, or pressure. After sufficient development to form the different zones, the products may be eluted from the column in successive batches. *See* CHROMATOGRAPHY.

Color tests. There are a number of color tests which are helpful in the identification of carbohydrates. These tests are based on the condensation of various aromatic amines or phenolic substances with the degradation products of sugars. The Molisch test is used for the general detection of carbohydrates. In this test a purple color is produced when the solution containing carbohydrate is treated with strong sulfuric acid in the presence of α-naphthol.

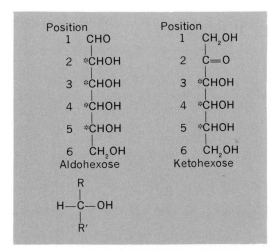

Fig. 2. Structural formulas showing asymmetric carbons (asterisk) for an aldohexose and a ketohexose. Detail of carbon at position 2 in aldohexose is shown where R = CHO and R′ = everything below carbon atom 2.

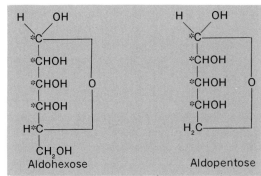

Fig. 3. Structural formulas for ring forms of an aldohexose and an aldopentose. Asymmetric carbons are marked by an asterisk.

In the Tauber test pentose sugars produce a cherry-red color when heated with a solution of benzidine in glacial acetic acid. Another test for pentoses and uronic acids is based on the fact that a violet-red color develops when these sugars are treated with hydrochloric acid and phloroglucinol. Seliwanoff's test is used for ketoses, which give a red color with resorcinol in hydrochloric acid. The Tollens naphthoresorcinol and the Dische carbazole tests are used for the detection of the uronic acids, D-glucuronic acid, D-galacturonic acid, and D-mannuronic acid. The polysaccharide, starch, produces a blue color when treated with a dilute solution of iodine in potassium iodide, while glycogen gives a reddish-brown color with this reagent.

Paper chromatography and color tests only indicate the probable presence of a particular carbohydrate. For unequivocal proof it is necessary to resort to isolation procedures.

Estimation. The reducing properties of aldoses and ketoses are most frequently utilized for the quantitative analysis of these sugars. A nonreducing sugar such as sucrose or raffinose, or a polysaccharide such as starch, must be first hydrolyzed with acid or with an appropriate enzyme to its constituent reducing monosaccharide units before it is analyzed. Upon heating the reducing sugars with Fehling's solution, containing copper sulfate, tartrate ion, and sodium hydroxide, a brick-red color develops, a result of the formation and precipitation of cuprous oxide.

The quantity of the cuprous oxide precipitate is a measure of the amount of reducing sugar present. Several modifications of this reaction have been used for the quantitative determination of reducing sugars. The estimation of sugar by the Benedict method involves the determination of the reduced

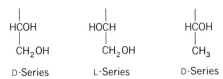

Fig. 4. Spatial configurations of D and L series showing reference carbon attached to the terminal group.

cuprous ions colorimetrically after treatment with phosphomolybdic acid. In the Somogyi-Shaffer-Hartmann method, the sugar is estimated by iodometric titration of reduced copper. Several other quantitative methods for the determination of sugars are based on the reduction of ferricyanide ions in an alkaline solution. These reactions can be applied to micro quantities of sugars. There are also spectrophotometric methods, devised by Dische, which are based on light absorption by the reaction products resulting from treatment of sugars with carbazole or cysteine-carbazole in sulfuric acid. Sugars can be accurately identified and determined by their specific optical rotations, provided they are available in sufficient quantities and no other interfering optically active material is present. *See* ALDEHYDE; SPECTROPHOTOMETRIC ANALYSIS; TITRATION.

Stereoisomerism. The sugars consist of chains of carbon atoms which are united to one another at a tetrahedral angle of 109°28′. A carbon atom to which are attached four different groups is called asymmetric. A sugar, or any other compound containing one or more asymmetric carbon atoms, possesses optical activity; that is, it rotates the plane of polarized light to the right or left. The specific rotation of a substance possessing optical activity is the rotation expressed in angular degrees which is afforded by 1 gram of substance dissolved in 1 milliliter of water in a tube 1 decimeter in length. It is usually given for the sodium D line at a definite temperature, for example, 20°C (68°F), and is designated by $[\alpha]_D^{20}$. *See* OPTICAL ACTIVITY.

The triose glycerose, or glyceraldehyde, has one asymmetric carbon atom and therefore exists in two optically active forms, one dextrorotatory and the other levorotatory (**Fig. 1**).

The D and L forms of glycerose are related to each other as the right hand is to the left hand, being similar, but not identical. One may not be superposed upon the other. If one model is held before a mirror, the image in the mirror corresponds to the arrangement of the other model. The two compounds whose molecules are mirror images of each other are called optical antipodes or enantiomorphs.

It is difficult to represent stereochemically the more complex sugars having several asymmetric carbon atoms. An examination of the formula for an aldohexose (**Fig. 2**) reveals that it contains four different asymmetric carbon atoms; that is, each of the atoms marked with an asterisk, at positions 2, 3, 4, and 5, carries four different groups or atoms. The ketohexose contains three asymmetric carbon atoms, at 3, 4, and 5 (Fig. 2).

As the number of asymmetric carbon atoms in the sugar molecule increases, from the trioses to the higher monosaccharides, the number of stereoisomers increases in accordance with the van't Hoff formula 2^n where n represents the number of asymmetric carbon atoms.

Thus the possible number of stereoisomers of

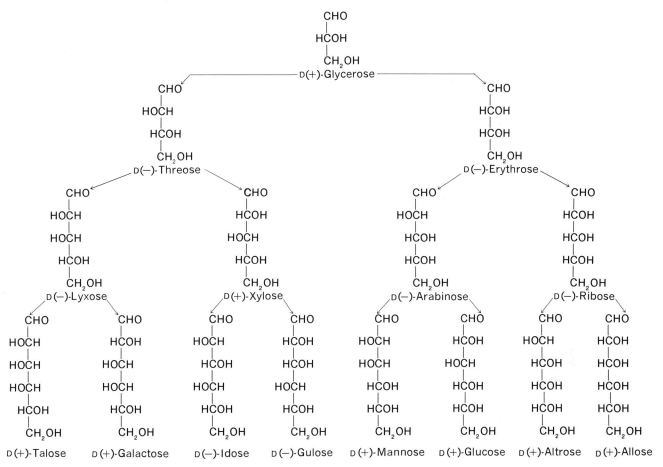

Fig. 5. The D-series of aldose sugars as related to D-glycerose.

an aldohexose, such as glucose or galactose, when written in open-chain form, is 2^4 or 16 (eight enantiomorphous pairs). In the ketose sugars, there is one less asymmetric center than in the aldoses of equal chain length; therefore the number of isomers is reduced by a factor of 2. The possible number of stereoisomers of a ketohexose, exemplified by fructose or sorbose, is 2^3 or 8 (four enantiomorphous pairs). Eight stereoisomers, consisting of four pairs of enantiomorphs, are possible for an aldopentose like xylose or arabinose. If, as seen in **Fig. 3**, the formulas of these sugars are represented in ring form, the first carbon atom in the monosaccharide chain becomes asymmetric because of formation of a cyclic hemiacetal with a new OH group and

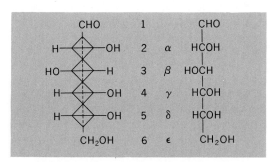

Fig. 6. Projection formula for the aldohexose D-glucose.

another center of asymmetry at carbon atom 1. The possible isomers for a cyclic aldohexose therefore become 2^5 or 32, and for an aldopentose 2^4 or 16.

The spatial arrangement of the groups around the asymmetric carbon atom of the dextrorotatory form of glyceraldehyde (glycerose) is arbitrarily called the D configuration, while that of the levorotatory form is called the L configuration. This connotation of the D and L refers to spatial configuration only and is not an indication of the direction of rotation of the plane of polarized light by the sugar. The reference carbon atom regarding D or L configuration is, for sugars containing more than one asymmetric carbon atom, the asymmetric carbon atom farthest removed from the active (that is, the aldehyde or ketone) end of the molecule and adjacent to the terminal group (**Fig. 4**).

Rosanoff, who introduced this criterion for designating the D and L form of sugars, regarded all sugars of the D series as built up, in theory, from D-glycerose, and those of the L series from L-glycerose. Although not accomplished in practice throughout the series, such a process is rendered possible without interfering with the original asymmetric carbon atom by the stepwise addition of the repeating unit CHOH through the Kiliani cyanohydrin synthesis. It must be emphasized that Rosanoff's representation of the D and L forms of sugar is merely a convention and has no relation to their direction of rotation. If it is desired to indicate the direction of rotation of the compound, the symbols (+), meaning dextrorotatory, and (−), meaning levorotatory, are used. Thus a dextrorotatory sugar with the D configuration is indicated by the symbol D(+), while a levorotatory sugar of the same configuration is represented by D(−). **Figure 5** shows the relationship of D-glycerose to the D-trioses, D-tetroses, D-pentoses, and D-hexoses.

Formulation. Thus far the monosaccharides have been considered as open-chain compounds, designated by projection formulas. The projection formula, introduced by Emil Fischer, is based on the convention that tetrahedrons, representing individual asymmetric carbons of a sugar, viewed as though supported by their carbon to carbon bonds with the hydrogen and hydroxyl groups extending outward, are projected upon the depicting plane. This formula is quite convenient, because the relationship between various sugars is easily demonstrated. Its numbering begins at the terminal position associated with the carbonyl group; in ketoses the carbonyl group is in carbon atom 2 position. When Greek letters are used, as in the older literature, the carbon next to the CHO group is called the α-carbon atom.

Although an aldohexose such as D-glucose or an aldopentose such as D-xylose exhibits many of the properties of common aldehydes, its reactivity, when compared with acyclic hydroxyaldehydes such as glycolic aldehyde or glyceraldehyde, is not as great as would be expected if the sugar possessed the simple aldehydic projection formula (**Fig. 6**). Furthermore, the cyanohydrin reaction proceeds with difficulty, and sugars fail to give the Schiff test for aldehydes. Thus, the straight-chain aldehydic projection formula does not represent the essential features of the sugar molecules, particularly their tendency to form five- and six-membered rings. In reality, because of the tetrahedral angles between bonds of the carbon atoms, the chain tends to form a ring. Thus, the ends of a six-carbon chain approach each other as shown in **Fig. 7**, permitting a reaction between the carbonyl group and a hydroxyl on the fourth or fifth carbon atom and forming a hemiacetal.

The reaction is analogous to the formation of hemiacetals from simple aldehydes and alcohols. Admixture of an aldehyde and an alcohol produces first a hemiacetal. Long standing in an excess of

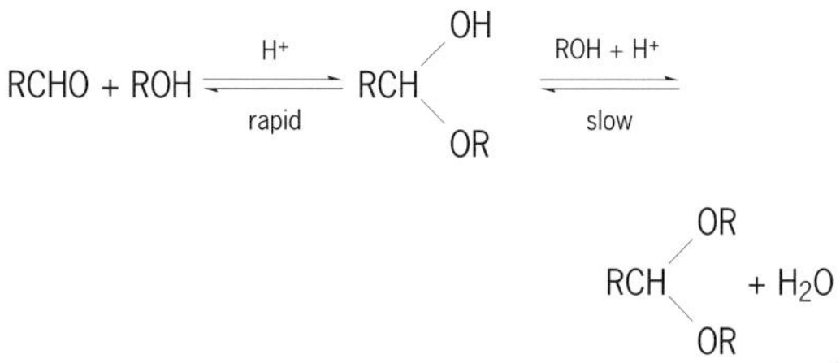

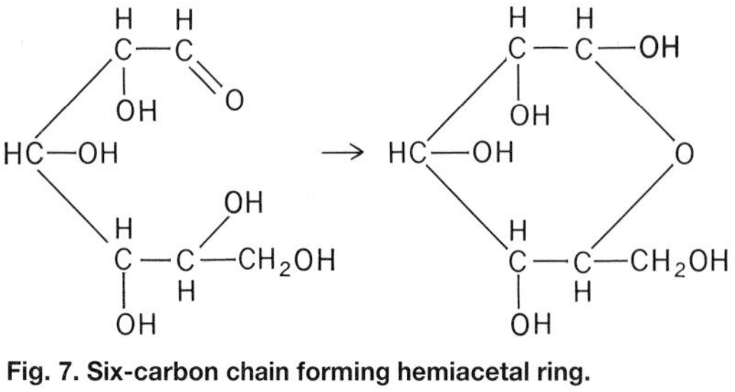

Fig. 7. Six-carbon chain forming hemiacetal ring.

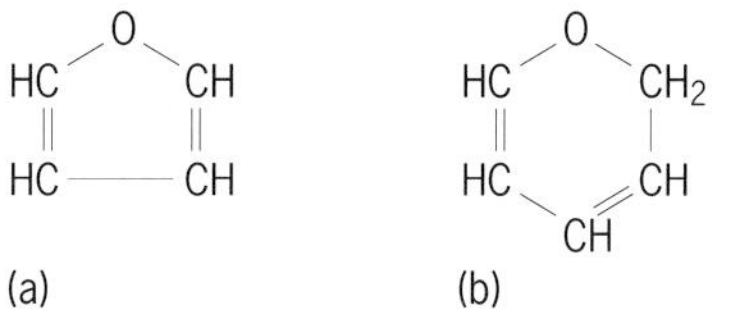

Fig. 8. Structural formulas for (a) furan and (b) pyran.

alcohol in the presence of an acid catalyst converts the hemiacetal into a complete acetal, as shown below.

Such a reaction occurs not only with aldose but also with ketose sugars. Formation of a hemiacetal in a hexose monosaccharide from a reaction between carbon atom 1 and the OH group of carbon atom 6 is not likely, because this would produce a strained seven-membered ring. Six- and five-membered rings are more easily formed because there is very little distortion of the bond angles. Rings of four carbon atoms or less do not form easily.

There is abundant evidence that sugars actually exist as cyclic compounds. Most decisive proof is furnished by the phenomenon of mutarotation, by the existence of two isomeric methylglycosides, and by Haworth's methylation experiments, in which he was unable to demonstrate open-chain structure.

In the older literature the six-membered ring structure of the aldohexoses in which the first carbon atom is linked to the fifth carbon atom through an oxygen atom had been named amylene oxide or δ-oxide configuration. The five-membered rings in which carbon atom 1 is linked to carbon atom 4 had been termed butylene oxide or γ-oxide configuration. In 1927 W. N. Haworth suggested that the five-atom ring sugars should be regarded as derived from furan and the six-atom ring configuration from pyran (**Fig. 8**).

Thus a sugar containing a γ-oxide or 1,4-oxide ring is called a furanose sugar, and if it is present as a glycoside, it is described as a furanoside. It must be noted, however, that unsubstituted furanose sugars have never been isolated, although they do exist in small proportion in solution. Although the 1,4 ring is stable and the 1,5 ring is relatively unstable in the sugar lactones, the reverse is true for the sugars and glycosides. Furanose structures are therefore found either in substituted sugars such as 2,3,5,6-O-methyl-D-glucose, where there is no free hydroxyl on carbon atom 5, or more commonly, when the monosaccharide (D-fructose or L-arabinose) is a constituent of complex sugars, the oligosaccharides or polysaccharides. Similarly

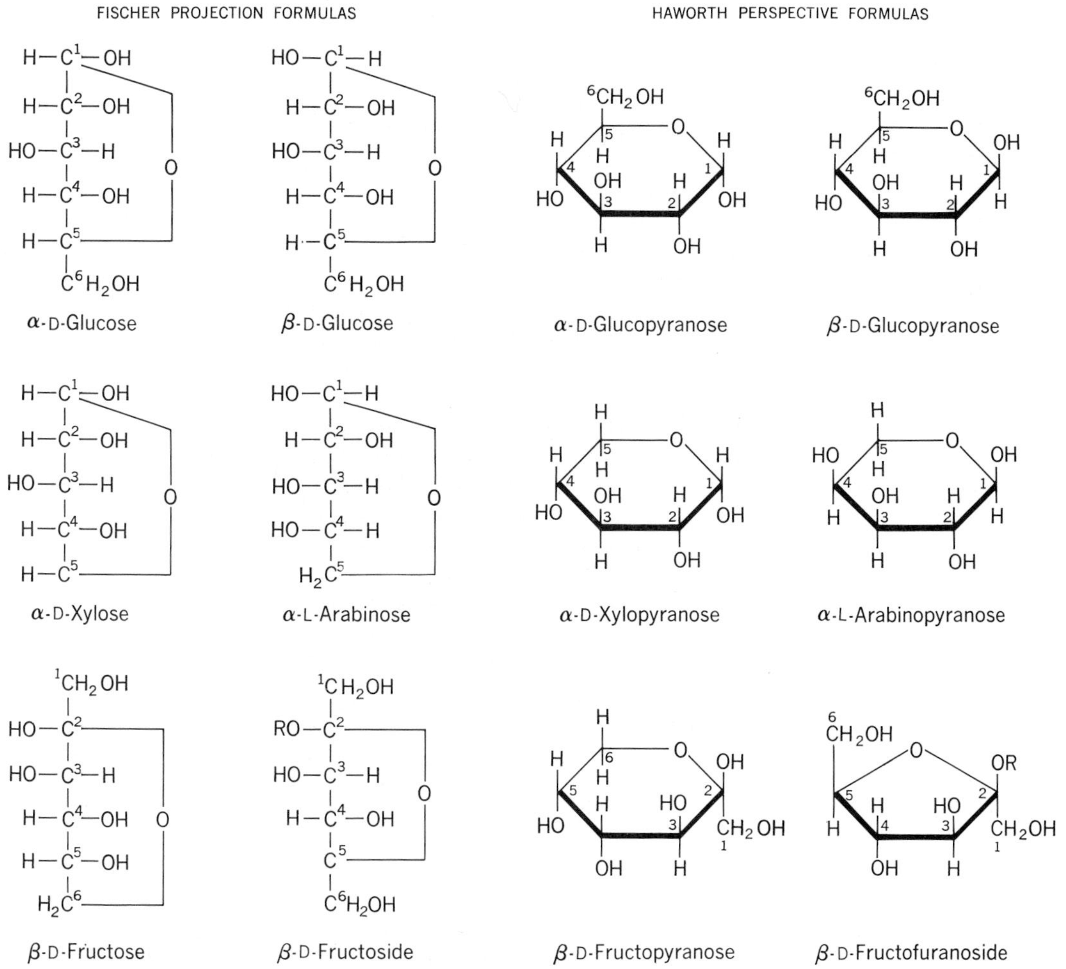

FISCHER PROJECTION FORMULAS   HAWORTH PERSPECTIVE FORMULAS

α-D-Glucose   β-D-Glucose   α-D-Glucopyranose   β-D-Glucopyranose

α-D-Xylose   α-L-Arabinose   α-D-Xylopyranose   α-L-Arabinopyranose

β-D-Fructose   β-D-Fructoside   β-D-Fructopyranose   β-D-Fructofuranoside

Fig. 9. Fischer projection formulas and Haworth perspective formulas.

the names pyranose and pyranoside are applied to the sugars and sugar derivatives having the six-membered, δ-oxide, or 1,5 rings. *See* GLYCOSIDE.

In the Haworth perspective formulas, carbon atoms 1–5 and the ring oxygen are represented in a single plane projecting from the plane of the paper on which it is written. The valences of the carbon atoms not involved in ring formation are situated above or below the plane of the ring. The thickened lines at the bottom of the ring formulas represent the sides of the hexagon nearest to the observer.

When the carbon atoms in the ring are numbered clockwise, as in α-D-glycopyranose, the groups that are written on the right-hand side in the projection formula are represented as projecting below the plane of the ring, and the corresponding groups on the left-hand side are projecting above. However, there is a discrepancy in the relative positions of the substituent groups on carbon atom 5 in that the H atom appears in the perspective formula below instead of above the plane of the ring. This apparent anomaly is the result of torsion required to effect ring closure. In forming a ring from the straight-chain aldehydic form, the fifth carbon atom must be rotated so that the oxygen atom in the OH group on this carbon atom is brought into the plane of the first five carbon atoms. Consequently, the H atom

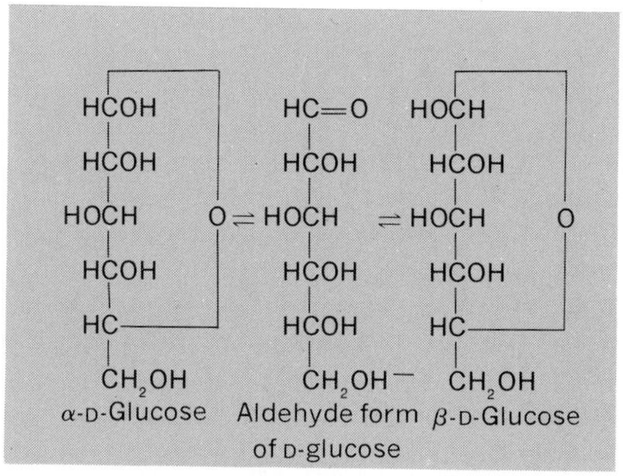

α-D-Glucose   Aldehyde form   β-D-Glucose
of D-glucose

Fig. 10. Possibilities during mutarotation of D-glucose.

chair   boat

Fig. 11. Conformations of a cyclohexane.

Fig. 12. Geometrical arrangements of carbon-hydrogen bonds on the chair form of a cyclohexane.

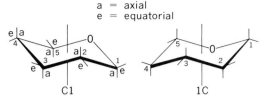

Fig. 14. Interchangeable conformations of a pyranose sugar, designated as C1 and 1C.

attached to carbon atom 5 is now shifted to the other side of the chain, because this carbon atom has been rotated through more than a 90° angle.

The projection and perspective formulas for the α- and β-isomers of D-glucose and for α-D-xylose, α-L-arabinose, and β-D-fructose are shown in **Fig. 9**.

Since free D-fructose primarily exists in the pyranose configuration, the furanose ring structure of this sugar is shown with the active hydrogen of the potential reducing group substituted. The substituent R may be a D-glucopyranosyl unit as in the disaccharide, sucrose, or a chain of other fructofuranosyl units as in the polysaccharide, inulin.

Mutarotation. Two forms of glucose are known. The α-form is obtained by dissolving the sugar, D-glucose, in water and allowing it to crystallize through evaporation of the solvent. The β form is obtained by crystallizing D-glucose from pyridine or acetic acid. The products are not merely different crystallographic forms of the same substance, because they have different properties when dissolved. At 20°C (68°F) a freshly prepared solution of α-D-glucose has a specific rotation, $[\alpha]_D^{20}$, of +113°, and a freshly prepared aqueous solution of β-D-glucose at the same temperature has a specific rotation of +19°. Upon standing, both solutions gradually change in rotatory power. The optical rotation of the α-D form decreases and that of the β-D form increases until they reach the same equilibrium value of $[\alpha]_D$ + 52.5°, which corresponds to a mixture of 37% α and 63% β. This phenomenon of change in its optical property is called mutarotation. It is displayed not only with glucose but with all crystalline sugars that have a free or potentially free aldehyde or ketone group in the molecule. To account for the existence of two structures, it is assumed that the monosaccharides exist in the form of cyclic hemiacetals rather than in open-chain form (**Fig. 10**).

The process of mutarotation is due to the labile nature of the hemiacetal linkage and the interconversion of the α and β forms through the acyclic aldehyde form which exists in solution to a very small extent (about 0.1%). Mutarotation is catalyzed by both acid and base, with the base being by far more effective.

The α- and β-sugars are stereoisomeric, but they are not mirror images. They are known as anomers, differing from each other only in the positions of the atoms or groups attached to the terminal asymmetric carbon atom.

To avoid confusion in the matter of new isomers or anomers, a convention was proposed by C. Hudson which is generally accepted. This states that for pairs of α and β isomers of the D series, the one with the higher rotation in the positive sense shall be called the α form, whereas the isomer with the lower rotation is designated as β. The reverse holds good for the L series, the enantiomorph of α-D-glucose being α-L-glucose with a lower specific rotation of $[\alpha]_D - 113°$ than β-L-glucose, $[\alpha]_D - 19°$. In the α-anomer of D-glucose the OH group that is attached to the aldehydic carbon atom and the OH group that is on the adjacent carbon atom are on the same side of the ring (cis position). In the β form these hydroxyl groups are on opposite sides of the hemiacetal ring (trans position).

Sugar conformations. Although the Haworth formulas are an improvement over the Fischer formulas, they still represent an oversimplification of the true configuration of the monosaccharides in space. While the five-membered furanose ring of a sugar is almost planar, a strainless six-membered pyranose ring is not. A nonplanar arrangement of the molecule must be adopted to maintain the normal valency angles in the pyranose ring. The term "conformations" was coined for the various arrangements of atoms in space that can arise by rotation about single bonds.

Since the only difference between a pyranose ring of a monosaccharide and that of a cyclohexane is the presence of an oxygen in the ring of the former compound, there is a close similarity between the molecular geometries of the two types of rings. The concepts developed for the cyclohexane ring can, therefore, be applied to the sugars containing the pyranose rings.

Results obtained by several investigators show that arrangements of cyclohexane which are free from angle strain are either of the "chair" conformation or the "boat" conformation (**Fig. 11**).

Examination of the chair form of cyclohexane shows that its carbon-hydrogen bonds can be divided into two geometrically different types. Six of them are perpendicular to the plane of the ring and are termed axial (a) bonds, while the other six radiate out from the ring and are termed equatorial (e) bonds (**Fig. 12**). Because of the

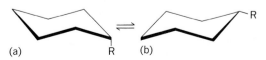

Fig. 13. Interconversion of (a) axial and (b) equatorial positions for R group of a cyclohexane derivative.

staggered arrangements of the hydrogen atoms, the chair conformation (which minimizes repulsions between them) has a lower energy content and is thus more stable than the boat form. Consequently, cyclohexane and most of its derivatives tend to assume the chair conformation.

In cyclohexane derivatives, the group R is axial in one conformation but is readily convertible into the equatorial position (**Fig. 13**).

Similarly, pyranose sugars can exist in two interchangeable conformations, designated by R. E. Reeves as C1 and 1C (**Fig. 14**).

The greatest nonbonded interactions in a sugar are due to the hydroxyl groups. In considering preferred conformational stability for any sugar, conformations with large axial substituents should be avoided. In the absence of large polar interactions in the pyranose series, that chair conformation in which the largest number of the bulky groups are in equatorial position is the most stable one. In this connection it should be noted that the CH₂OH group is bulkier than the hydroxyl.

The relationship between the Haworth formulas and the two chair forms for the pyranose sugars is shown in **Fig. 15**. In each of the pyranose sugars in the illustration there are fewer axial hydroxyl groups and fewer repulsive interactions in the C1 conformation, which is the preferred form.

In conformational formulas, direction of bonds is determined by the tetrahedral valencies of the carbon atoms (**Fig. 16**).

The application of conformational analysis in carbohydrate chemistry is useful in many cases in predicting relative rates of reactions and the extent to which some reactions will proceed. As an example, the greater proportion of β-D-glucose (in which all hydroxyls are equatorial) in the equilibrium mixture compared with α-D-glucose (in which all hydroxyls are equatorial) in the equilibrium mixture compared with α-D-glucose (which has an axial hydroxyl at carbon atom 1) can be explained. Similarly, the equilibrium between α-D-galactose 1-phosphate (axial hydroxyl at carbon atom 4 in C1 conformation) and α-D-glucose 1-phosphate, which has an equatorial hydroxyl at C = 4, resulting in smaller nonbonded interactions, favors the glucose derivative.

Methyl glucosides. When a solution of glucose in cold methanol is treated with dry hydrogen chloride as catalyst, an acetal is formed. Such a compound formed from glucose is called a glucoside (**Fig. 17**); if the sugar galactose were used, the acetal would be called a galactoside. Methyl glucoside is perhaps the simplest example of a large group of substances in which the hydroxyl of the hemiacetal group at carbon atom 1 of an aldose monosaccharide has been condensed with the hydroxyl group of an alcohol.

In aqueous solution D-glucose exists chiefly as D-glucopyranose. However, a small proportion of this sugar exists in the furanose as well as in the open-chain aldehyde forms, the last in a minute amount.

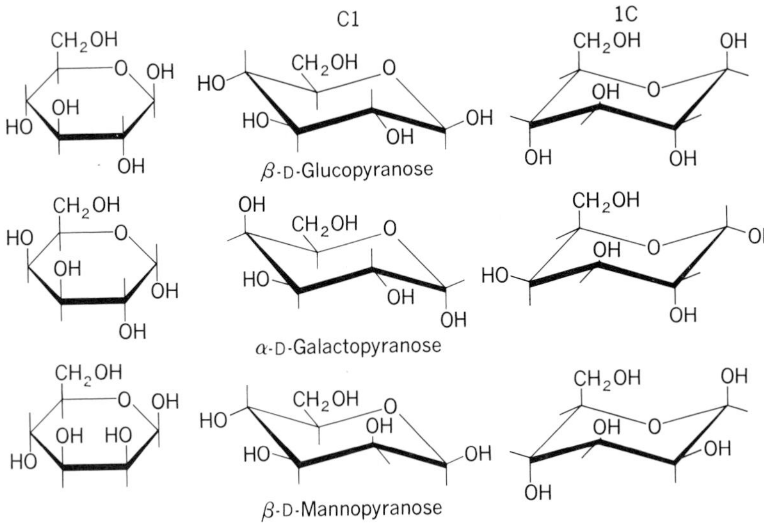

Fig. 15. Relationship between Haworth formula and chair forms for pyranose sugars.

Since the furanose structure reacts more rapidly to form the glucoside than does the pyranose configuration of the sugar, a considerable amount of labile methylglucofuranoside is formed in the first few hours. On prolonged standing or heating, the more stable methyl α-D-glucopyranoside and methyl β-D-glucopyranoside appear. Thus it is evident that when glucose is treated with methanolic hydrochloric acid, the yield of methylglucoside of a particular configuration has little bearing on the structure of the original sugar; that is, the structure of the glucoside may or may not correspond to the structure of the crystalline sugar. However, a relationship in this case can be established through hydrolysis of a methylglucoside. When pure methyl α-D-glucoside is hydrolyzed, the subsequent mutarotation of the hydrolysis product is found to be in the same direction as that of pure α-D-glucopyranose. It is therefore concluded that α-D-glucose and α-D-glucoside have the same configuration about the first carbon atom.

Fig. 16. Glycosidic carbon links in the C1 conformation must be as in (a) not (b).

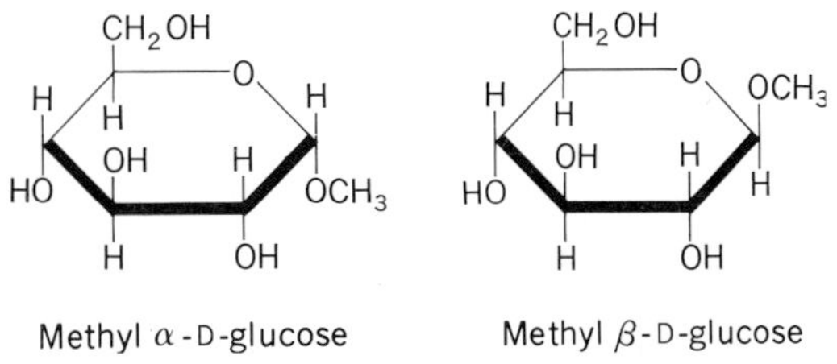

Methyl α-D-glucose   Methyl β-D-glucose

Fig. 17. Formulas for α and β forms of methyl D-glucose.

The α- and β-methylglucosides are crystalline compounds. They may be separated by fractional crystallization or through the agency of enzymes. The enzymes maltase and emulsin act selectively upon the two glucosides, the former hydrolyzing the α form only and the latter acting upon the anomeric β compound. The specific rotation of methyl α-D-glucopyranoside is $+159°$, while that of methyl β-D-glucopyranoside is $-33°$. *See* BIOCHEMISTRY. William Z. Hassid

Bibliography. G. D. Aspinall, *Carbohydrate Chemistry*, 1976; V. Ginsburg, *Biology of Carbohydrates*, 1981; W. W. Pigman, *The Carbohydrates: Chemistry and Biochemistry*, 2d ed., 1981; J. Staněk et al., *The Monosaccharides*, 1964; J. Staněk, M. Černý, and J. Pacák, *The Oligosaccharides*, 1965.

Carbohydrate metabolism

The fields of biochemistry and physiology deal with the breakdown and synthesis of simple sugars, oligosaccharides, and polysaccharides, and with the transport of sugars across cell membranes and tissues. The breakdown or dissimilation of simple sugars, particularly glucose, is one of the principal sources of energy for living organisms. The dissimilation may be anaerobic, as in fermentations, or aerobic, that is, respiratory. In both types of metabolism, the breakdown is accompanied by the formation of energy-rich bonds, chiefly the pyrophosphate bond of the coenzyme adenosinetriphosphate (ATP), which serves as a coupling agent between different metabolic processes. In higher animals, glucose is the carbohydrate constituent of blood, which carries it to the tissues of the body. In higher plants, the disaccharide sucrose is often stored and transported by the tissues. Certain polysaccharides, especially starch and glycogen, are stored as endogenous food reserves in the cells of plants, animals, and microorganisms. Others, such as cellulose, chitin, and bacterial polysaccharides, serve as structural components of cell walls. As constituents of plant and animal tissues, various carbohydrates become available to those organisms which depend on other living or dead organisms for their source of nutrients. Hence, all naturally occurring carbohydrates can be dissimilated by some animals or microorganisms. *See* ADENOSINETRIPHOSPHATE (ATP); CARBOHYDRATE; CELLULOSE; CHITIN; GLYCOGEN; STARCH.

Dietary carbohydrates. Certain carbohydrates cannot be used as nutrients by humans. For example, the polysaccharide cellulose, which is one of the main constituents of plants, cannot be digested by humans or other mammals and is a useful food only for those, such as the ruminants, that harbor cellulose-decomposing microorganisms in their digestive tracts. The principal dietary carbohydrates available to humans are the simple sugars glucose and fructose, the disaccharides sucrose and lactose, and the polysaccharides glycogen and starch. Lactose is the carbohydrate constituent of milk and hence one of the main sources of food during infancy. The disaccharides and polysaccharides that cannot be absorbed directly from the intestine are first digested and hydrolyzed by enzymes secreted into the alimentary canal. The nature of these enzymes, which are known as glycosidases, will be discussed later. *See* FRUCTOSE; LACTOSE.

Intestinal absorption and transport. The simple sugars, of which glucose is the major component, reach the intestine or are produced there through the digestion of oligosaccharides. They are absorbed by the intestinal mucosa and transported across the tissue into the bloodstream. This process involves the accumulation of sugar against a concentration gradient and requires active metabolism of the mucosal tissue as a source of energy. The sugars are absorbed from the blood by the liver and are stored there as glycogen. The liver glycogen serves as a constant source of glucose in the bloodstream. The mechanisms of transport of sugars across cell membranes and tissues are not yet understood, but they appear to be highly specific for different sugars and to depend on enzymelike components of the cells.

Dissimilation of simple sugars. The degradation of monosaccharides may follow one of several types of metabolic pathways. In the phosphorylative pathways, the sugar is first converted to a phosphate ester (phosphorylated) in a reaction with ATP. The phosphorylated sugar is then split into smaller units, either before or after oxidation. In the nonphosphorylative pathways, the sugar is usually oxidized to the corresponding aldonic acid. This may subsequently be broken down either with or without phosphorylation of the intermediate products. Among the principal intermediates in carbohydrate metabolism are glyceraldehyde-3-phosphate and pyruvic acid. The end products of metabolism depend on the organism and, to some extent, on the environmental conditions. Besides cell material that is formed through various biosynthetic reactions, the products may include carbon dioxide (CO_2), alcohols, organic acids, and hydrogen gas. In the so-called complete oxidations, CO_2 is the only excreted end product. In incomplete oxidations, characteristic of the vinegar bacteria and of certain fungi, oxidized end products such as gluconic, ketogluconic, citric, or fumaric acids may accumulate. Organic end products are invariably found in fermentations, since fermentative metabolism requires the reduction as well as the oxidation of some of the products of intermediary metabolism. The energy available from the complete oxidation of 1 mole of glucose with molecular oxygen is approximately 688,000 cal (2.98 megajoules), while that which can be derived from fermentation is very much less; for example, alcoholic fermentation yields about 58,000 cal (243,000 joules). In aerobic metabolism, a great deal of the available energy is harnessed for the needs of the organism as energy-rich bonds primarily in ATP through the process known as oxidative phosphorylation. In fermentation, a much smaller amount of ATP is produced. Hence, the amount of biosynthesis and mechanical work that an organism can do at the expense of a given amount of sugar is many times greater in respiration than in fermentation. *See* FERMENTATION.

Glycolysis. The principal phosphorylative pathway involved in fermentations is known as the glycolytic, hexose diphosphate, or Embden-Meyerhof pathway (see **illus.**). This sequence of reactions is the basis of the lactic acid fermentation of mammalian muscle and of the alcoholic fermentation of yeast. Its main features may be summarized as follows:

1. Glucose is phosphorylated to yield glucose-6-phosphate by the enzyme hexokinase with the conversion of a molecule of ATP to adenosinediphosphate (ADP).

2. Glucose-6-phosphate is epimerized to fructose-6-phosphate by phosphoglucoisomerase.

3. Fructose-6-phosphate is phosphorylated with ATP to yield fructose-1,6-diphosphate. This reaction is catalyzed by phosphofructokinase.

4. Fructose-1,6-diphosphate is split to two molecules of triose phosphate (dihydroxyacetone phosphate and glyceraldehyde phosphate) by aldolase.

5. Both molecules of triose phosphate, which are interconverted by triose phosphate isomerase, are oxidized to 1,3-diphosphoglyceric acid by triose phosphate dehydrogenase. Inorganic phosphate is esterified in this reaction, and the coenzyme nicotinamide adenine dinucleotide NAD becomes reduced to NADH.

6. 1,3-Diphosphoglyceric acid reacts with ADP to yield ATP and 3-phosphoglyceric acid in the presence of phosphoglycerate kinase.

7. 3-Phosphoglyceric acid is converted to 2-phosphoglyceric acid by phosphoglyceric acid mutase, and the product is dehydrated to phosphoenolpyruvic acid by enolase.

8. In a reaction catalyzed by pyruvic kinase, phosphoenolpyruvic acid reacts with ADP to give pyruvic acid and ATP.

9. Pyruvic acid is converted to the various end products of metabolism. In the lactic acid fermentation, it is reduced to lactic acid with the simultaneous reoxidation of NADH, which had been formed in step 5, to NAD. In alcoholic fermentation, pyruvic acid is decarboxylated to yield CO_2 and acetaldehyde, and the latter compound is reduced to alcohol with NADH.

For every molecule of glucose fermented through the glycolytic sequence, two molecules of ATP are used for phosphorylation (steps 1 and 3), while four are produced (steps 6 and 8). Thus, fermentation results in the net gain of two energy-rich phosphate bonds as ATP at the expense of inorganic phosphate esterified in step 5. The excess ATP is converted back to ADP and inorganic phosphate through coupled reactions useful to the organism, such as the mechanical work done by the contraction of muscle or biosynthetic reactions associated with growth. *See* ADENOSINEDIPHOSPHATE (ADP); NICOTINAMIDE ADENINE DINUCLEOTIDE (NAD).

Oxidative mechanisms. The oxidative or respiratory metabolism of sugars differs in several respects from fermentative dissimilation. First, the oxidative steps, that is, the reoxidation of NADH, are linked to the reduction of molecular oxygen. Second, the pyruvic acid produced through glycolytic or other mechanisms is further oxidized, usually to CO_2 and H_2O. Third, in most aerobic organisms, alternative pathways either supplement or completely replace the glycolytic sequence of reactions for the oxidation of sugars. Where pyruvic acid appears as a metabolic intermediate, it is generally oxidatively decarboxylated to yield CO_2 and the two-carbon acetyl fragment which combines with coenzyme A. The acetyl group is then further oxidized via the Krebs cycle. *See* CITRIC ACID CYCLE.

The principal alternative pathways by which sugars are dissimilated involve the oxidation of glucose-6-phosphate to the lactone of 6-phosphogluconic acid and are known as the hexose monophosphate pathways. In the best-known hexose monophosphate pathway, 6-phosphogluconic acid is formed from its lactone by hydrolysis and is oxidatively decarboxylated to yield CO_2 and the five-carbon sugar, ribulose-5-phosphate. Ribulose-5-phosphate is then converted to glucose-6-phosphate through a series of reactions in which phosphorylated sugars containing three, four, five, six, and seven carbon atoms are formed as intermediates. The principal enzymes involved in these transformations are transaldolase, transketolase, and epimerases. Since the glucose-6-phosphate that is produced from ribulose-5-phosphate is oxidized

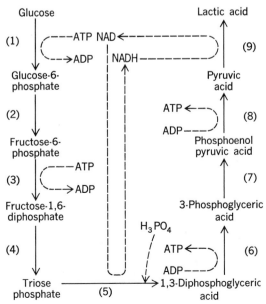

Glycolysis in lactic acid fermentation.

by the same sequence of reactions, the cyclic operation of this mechanism results in complete oxidation of glucose. Some of the enzymatic steps involved in this pathway provide the pentoses necessary for the synthesis of nucleotides and participate in the photosynthesis of green plants.

Simple sugars other than glucose. The metabolism of simple sugars other than glucose usually involves the conversion of the sugar to one of the intermediates of the phosphorylative pathways described for glucose metabolism. For example, fructose may be phosphorylated to fructose-6-phosphate, which can then be degraded via the glycolytic pathway or converted to glucose-6-phosphate and oxidized through the hexose monophosphate pathway. Similarly, mannose may be phosphorylated to mannose-6-phosphate, which is then transformed to fructose-6-phosphate by phosphomannose isomerase. Alternatively, in some bacteria, mannose is epimerized to fructose before phosphorylation. The principal mechanism for galactose metabolism requires the phosphorylation of the sugar to galactose-1-phosphate and the conversion of this ester to glucose-1-phosphate through the mediation of uridine diphosphoglucose. Glucose-1-phosphate is then converted to glucose-6-phosphate by phosphoglucomutase. The pentoses may be metabolized via their phosphate esters, which are converted to glucose-6-phosphate as described in the discussion of the hexose monophosphate pathway. *See* URIDINE DIPHOSPHOGLUCOSE (UDPG).

Disaccharides and polysaccharides. The dissimilation and biosynthesis of the oligosaccharides are effected through the enzymatic cleavage or formation of glycosidic bonds between simple monosaccharide constituents of the complex carbohydrates. The principal types of enzyme which split or synthesize glycosidic bonds are the hydrolases or glycosidases, phosphorylases, and transglycosylases. The enzymes are generally highly specific with respect to the glycosidic portion, or moiety, and the type of linkage of the substrates which they attack. For example, the glycosidic moiety may be glucosidic or galactosidic and the linkage may be α or β. The essential function of all three types of enzymes is the transfer of the glycosyl moiety of the substrate, which may be designated as the glycosyl donor, to an appropriate glycosyl acceptor, with the liberation of the aglycone. The different types of enzymes generally require different types of acceptors for the transfer reactions, but some enzymes can use a variety of acceptors and can act in more than one capacity. For example, an enzyme can act as a phosphorylase, transglycosylase, or hydrolase for the same substrate.

Hydrolytic cleavage is an essentially irreversible process and hence is used mostly in dissimilative metabolism. Phosphorylases and transglycosylases, on the other hand, may function in biosynthesis as well as the degradation of oligosaccharides.

The glycosidases or hydrolytic enzymes use preferentially the hydroxyl ion of water as the glycosyl acceptor. The aglycone is liberated after combining with the remaining hydrogen ion.

Lactases, for example, are β-galactosidases, and they combine the β-galactosyl portion of the disaccharide lactose with hydroxyl ion of water to yield galactose, liberating glucose. These enzymes can also hydrolyze methyl- or phenyl-β-galactosides with the formation of galactose and methanol or phenol, respectively.

Maltases are α-glucosidases which can hydrolyze maltose to two molecules of glucose.

Sucrases or invertases are enzymes which hydrolyze sucrose to yield glucose and fructose. The typical yeast invertase is a β-fructosidase, specific for the β-fructosyl portion of sucrose. The sucrase found in the human intestinal mucosa, on the other hand, is an α-glucosidase.

Amylases or diastases are enzymes which hydrolyze (digest) starch. The α-amylases, such as the human salivary and pancreatic amylases, split starch to smaller polysaccharide units, known as dextrins, and the disaccharide maltose. The β-amylase of malt, on the other hand, produces maltose as the main product of hydrolysis. *See* DEXTRIN.

The phosphorylases catalyze the reversible phosphorolysis of certain disaccharides, polysaccharides, and nucleosides by transferring the glycosyl moieties to inorganic phosphate. The breakdown of glycogen and starch by the enzymes known as amylophophorylases is an example of biologically important phosphorolytic reactions. α-D-Glucose-1-phosphate, which is the product of this process, can be metabolized after conversion to glucose-6-phosphate. Starch and glycogen can be synthesized from glucose-1-phosphate by the reverse reaction. The polysaccharide chain acts as either donor or acceptor for glucosyl groups, inorganic phosphate being the alternative acceptor. The reversible synthesis of sucrose, sucrose phosphate, and cellulose from uridine diphosphoglucose is similar to the phosphorolytic reactions, with the uridine compound serving as glucosyl donor.

The transglycosylases interconvert various disaccharides and polysaccharides by the transfer of glycosyl groups. For instance, dextrins can be synthesized from maltose in a reversible reaction catalyzed by the bacterial enzyme, amylomaltase:

$$nC_{12}H_{22}O_{11} \rightleftharpoons (C_6H_{10}O_5)_{11} + nC_6H_{12}O_6$$

| Maltose | Detrin | Glucose |

Many glucosidases have marked transglycosylase activity. *See* BIOCHEMISTRY.   Michael Doudoroff

Carbon

A chemical element, symbolized C, with an atomic number of 6 and an atomic weight of 12.01115. Carbon is unique in chemistry because it forms a vast number of compounds, larger than the sum total of all other elements combined. By far the largest group of these compounds are those composed of carbon and hydrogen. It has been estimated that there are at least 1 million known organic compounds, and this number is increasing rapidly each year. Although the classification is not rigorous, carbon forms another series of compounds, classified as inorganic, comprising a much smaller number than the organic compounds. *See* ORGANIC CHEMISTRY.

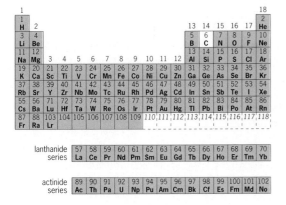

Physical and chemical properties. Elemental carbon exists in two well-defined crystalline allotropic forms, diamond and graphite. Other forms, which are poorly developed in crystallinity, are charcoal, coke, and carbon black.

Charcoal is prepared by the ignition of wood, sugar, blood, and other carbon-containing compounds in the absence of air. X-ray diffraction studies reveal that it has a graphite structure but is not very well developed in crystallinity. The lack of crystallinity is the result of defects in the crystal structure and the high surface area. In the activated state, charcoal adsorbs gases, liquids, and solids. Activation of the charcoal is accomplished by treatment of the substance with steam; this tends to remove the adsorbed hydrocarbons from the surface. The adsorbing property of charcoal is related to the large surface area present. It is stated that 1 cm^3 of charcoal has a surface area of 1000 m^2, or 1 in.^{3} has a surface area of 200,000 ft^2. *See* ADSORPTION.

Coke, another form of amorphous carbon, is prepared by heating coal in the absence of air. It is used primarily for the reduction of metal oxides to the free metals. *See* COKE.

Chemically pure carbon is prepared by the thermal decomposition of sugar (sucrose) in the absence of air. Impurities in the carbon are removed by treatment with chlorine gas at red heat. The substance is then washed with water and the residual chlorine is removed by heating in an atmosphere of hydrogen gas.

The physical and chemical properties of carbon are dependent on the crystal structure of the element. The density varies from 2.25 g/cm^3 for graphite to 3.51 g/cm^3 for diamond. For graphite, the melting point is 3500°C (6330°F) and the extrapolated boiling point is 4830°C (8726°F). This is abnormally high because a large amount of energy is required to break the three-dimensional covalent bonding in the crystal.

Elemental carbon is a fairly inert substance. It is insoluble in water, dilute acids and bases, and organic solvents. At elevated temperatures, it combines with oxygen to form carbon monoxide or carbon dioxide. With hot oxidizing agents, such as nitric acid and potassium nitrate, mellitic acid, $C_6(CO_2H)_6$, is obtained. Of the halogens, only fluorine reacts with elemental carbon. A number of metals combine with the element at elevated temperatures to form carbides.

Principal compounds. Carbon forms three compounds with oxygen: carbon monoxide, CO; carbon dioxide, CO_2; and carbon suboxide, C_3O_2. The first two oxides are the more important from an industrial standpoint.

Oxides of carbon. Carbon monoxide is prepared in the laboratory, as in reaction (1), by the

$$HCOOH + H_2SO_4 \longrightarrow CO + H_2SO_4 \cdot H_2O \qquad (1)$$

dehydration of formic acid with concentrated sulfuric acid. Similarly, other organic acids can be used, for example, oxalic acid, $H_2C_2O_4$. However, in this case, carbon dioxide is obtained along with the carbon monoxide. The highest-purity carbon monoxide is prepared by the thermal decomposition of nickel carbonyl at 200°C (390°F), as in reaction (2).

$$Ni(CO)_4 \longrightarrow Ni + 4CO \qquad (2)$$

The industrial preparation of carbon monoxide is by the water gas reaction. Water, in the form of steam, is passed over hot coke or coal at 600–1000°C (1100–1800°F), as represented by reaction (3). The temperature of the reaction must

$$C + H_2O(g) \rightleftharpoons CO + H_2 \qquad (3)$$

be carefully controlled because at 500°C (930°F) carbon dioxide is obtained instead of carbon monoxide. Also, as the reaction is endothermic, air must be passed over the heated coke or coal at regular intervals to maintain the minimum 600°C (1100°F) temperature. *See* FUEL GAS.

Carbon monoxide is a highly poisonous, colorless, odorless, tasteless gas having a melting point of −205.1°C (−337.2°F) and a boiling point of −190°C (−310°F). The gas is stable at room temperature but at elevated temperatures it disproportionates into carbon and carbon dioxide, as shown by reaction (4). This reaction is accelerated by the presence

$$2CO \rightleftharpoons C + CO_2 \qquad (4)$$

of certain metal catalysts. At elevated temperatures, the gas is an excellent reducing agent. With metal oxides, such as copper(II) oxide, it gives copper metal and carbon dioxide, as shown by reaction (5). Many other applications of this reducing prop-

$$CuO + CO \longrightarrow Cu + CO_2 \qquad (5)$$

erty are known, and perhaps the most important is

the blast furnace reduction of iron(III) oxide to pig iron. *See* IRON METALLURGY.

Carbon monoxide combines with many metals and nonmetals. With chlorine, in the presence of sunlight, it forms highly poisonous phosgene, $COCl_2$; with sulfur, carbonyl sulfide, COS, is obtained. A number of other carbonyl compounds are known, such as carbonyl fluoride, COF_2; carbonyl bromide, $COBr_2$; and carbonyl selenide, COSe.

With metals, a class of compounds known as metal carbonyls are formed. These metals are from groups I, II, VI, VII, and VIII of the periodic table. The metal carbonyls can be prepared by the direct combination of the metal with carbon monoxide, although several of the compounds require fairly high pressures. With finely divided nickel, the compound $Ni(CO)_4$ is formed at 50°C (122°F) and normal atmospheric pressure, as shown by reaction (6). With others such as iron, cobalt,

$$Ni + 4CO \longrightarrow Ni(CO)_4 \qquad (6)$$

molybdenum, and tungsten, pressures of 200–450 atm (20–45 megapascals) and temperatures above 200°C (390°F) are necessary to prepare $Fe(CO)_5$, $CO_2(CO)_8$, $Mo(CO)_5$, and $W(CO)_6$, respectively.

The metal carbonyls react with the halogens to produce metal carbonyl halides. With hydrogen, a similar reaction takes place to form metal carbonyl hydrides.

Nickel carbonyl finds application in the purification and separation of nickel from other metals. Iron carbonyl has been used in antiknock gasoline preparations and to prepare high-purity iron metal. *See* METAL CARBONYL; NICKEL.

Carbon monoxide may be considered to be the anhydride of formic acid. It does not react with water, however, to form an acid solution. It reacts with a sodium hydroxide solution, at 140°C (284°F) and under pressure, to give sodium formate, $NaCO_2H$. This solution, on acidification, gives formic acid.

Carbon monoxide is very important in the field of synthetic organic chemistry. By use of pressures of 100–200 atm (10–20 MPa), temperatures of 300–600°C (570–1100°F), and various mixed metal oxide catalysts, direct combination reactions with hydrogen can be carried out to produce methyl alcohol and benzene, as seen by reactions (7) and (8). Many other similar reactions utilize carbon monoxide.

$$CO + 2H_2 \longrightarrow CH_3OH \qquad (7)$$

$$12CO + 3H_2 \longrightarrow C_6H_6 + 6CO_2 \qquad (8)$$

As stated previously, carbon monoxide is extremely poisonous. As little as 9 parts of the gas in 10,000 parts of air will cause nausea and headache, and slightly larger amounts will cause death. The physiological action of carbon monoxide poisoning is based upon the formation of a stable compound with the hemoglobin of the blood. This compound is more stable than oxyhemoglobin; thus, body tissues are prevented from receiving the necessary oxygen. Caution should be exercised in handling carbon monoxide at all times. Automobile exhaust gas is a common source of carbon monoxide poisoning.

Carbon monoxide can be detected by the green color produced with a mixture of iodine pentoxide and fuming sulfuric acid adsorbed on pumice. Another test is the black color of finely divided palladium metal produced by bubbling the gas through a palladium(II) chloride solution. The gas can be absorbed in an aqueous solution of copper(I) chloride containing hydrochloric acid.

Carbon dioxide is prepared by the combustion of carbon in air or by the decomposition of a metal carbonate with an acid or by heat. *See* CARBON DIOXIDE.

Carbon suboxide, C_3O_2, is a less known oxide of carbon. It is prepared by the dehydration of malonic acid, $HOOCCH_2COOH$, with phosphorus(V) oxide in a vacuum at 140–150°C (280–300°F), as represented by reaction (9). Carbon suboxide is a gas

$$HOOCCH_2COOH \xrightarrow{P_4O_{10}} C_3O_2 + 2H_2O \qquad (9)$$

with an obnoxious odor and a boiling point of −6.8°C (−19.8°F). It combines readily with water to form malonic acid, thus reversing the above reaction.

Carbonates. Carbon forms carbonate (CO_3^{2-}), an ion derived from carbonic acid, H_2CO_3, which is a solution of carbon dioxide, CO_2, in water. Because there are two replaceable hydrogen ions in carbonic acid, the salts obtained by neutralizing only one hydrogen are called bicarbonates, for example, sodium bicarbonate, $NaHCO_3$.

Carbonates can be converted into bicarbonates by adding excess carbon dioxide [reaction (10)].

$$Na_2CO_3 + CO_2 + H_2O \rightleftharpoons 2NaHCO_3 \qquad (10)$$

The reaction can be reversed by heating: at even higher temperatures a second reaction takes place; for example, limestone is converted to lime [reaction (11)]. This reaction is commercially

$$CaCO_3 \xrightarrow{\Delta} CaO + CO_2 \qquad (11)$$

important in the production of lime and portland cement.

Reaction (10) is the mechanism whereby the ground water in limestone areas dissolves calcium carbonate (Ca_2CO_3) to give hard water. Bicarbonates in general are more soluble than carbonates. All the carbonates except those of the alkali metals are insoluble.

Sodium carbonate is produced by the Solvay process from the raw materials ammonia, carbon dioxide, and sodium chloride. Sodium carbonate is used in the manufacture of glass, paper, and textiles. *See* LIMESTONE.

Carbon tetrahalides. Carbon forms compounds with the halogens which have the general formula CX_4, where X is fluorine, chlorine, bromine, or iodine.

At room temperature, carbon tetrafluoride is a gas, carbon tetrachloride is a liquid, and the other two compounds are solids. All are covalent compounds with the usual tetrahedral structure.

By far the most important carbon halide is carbon tetrachloride, CCl_4. It is prepared, as shown by reaction (12), by passing chlorine gas into

$$CS_2 + 3Cl_2 \longrightarrow CCl_4 + S_2Cl_2 \qquad (12)$$

carbon disulfide, CS_2, containing a small amount of iodine or antimony(III) chloride. The carbon tetrachloride is separated from the reaction mixture by fractional distillation. Carbon tetrachloride is a colorless, pleasant-smelling, nonflammable liquid with a melting point of $-22.9°C$ ($-9.2°F$), a boiling point of $76.4°C$ ($170°F$), and a density of 1.595 g/ml at $20°C$ ($68°F$). The compound is an excellent solvent and finds much use as a solvent for fats, greases, waxes, and many other organic compounds. It is commonly used as a dry-cleaning fluid and also as a spot remover for clothing.

The heavy, nonflammable vapor finds use in fire extinguishers. The dense vapors exclude air and oxygen from the combustion area. It should not be used to extinguish fires where hot metal surfaces are present. In the presence of hot metals as catalysts, water vapor reacts with carbon tetrachloride to produce, among other products, poisonous phosgene.

Carbon tetrabromide and tetraiodide are prepared from the tetrachloride by reaction with aluminum bromide and aluminum iodide, respectively. Both of these substances are thermally unstable at elevated temperatures.

Mixed carbon tetrahalides are also known. Perhaps the most important of them is dichlorodifluoromethane, CCl_2F_2, commonly called Freon. It is prepared by the reaction of hydrogen fluoride with carbon tetrachloride in the presence of antimony(III) chloride. *See* HALOGENATED HYDROCARBON.

Carbide. Carbon forms binary compounds known as carbides with elements less electronegative than carbon (carbon-hydrogen compounds are excluded). Effectively then, carbides are composed of metal-carbon compounds if boron (B) and silicon (Si) are included among the normal metals. Essentially no volatile compounds [except aluminum carbide (AlC) or its dimer] are known, because decomposition sets in at higher temperatures before volatilization of the carbide as such can occur.

Most carbides can be prepared by heating a mixture of the powdered metal and carbon, usually to high temperatures, but not necessarily as high as the melting point. Generally, the same result is possible by heating a mixture of the oxide of the metal with carbon [reaction (13)]. Some may be prepared

$$CaO + 3C \longrightarrow CaC_2 + CO \qquad (13)$$

by passing a hydrocarbon vapor over the hot metal in the form of an electrically heated filament. The

alkali metal carbides (Li_2C_2, Na_2C_2, K_2C_2, Rb_2C_2, and Cs_2C_2) are best prepared by passing acetylene (C_2H_2) into solutions of the metals in liquid ammonia [reaction (14)], followed by heating [reaction (15)]. The very unstable carbides (Cu_2C_2, Ag_2C_2,

$$2Na + 2C_2H_2 \longrightarrow 2NaHC_2 + H_2 \qquad (14)$$

$$2NaHC_2 \longrightarrow Na_2C_2 + C_2H_2 \qquad (15)$$

Au_2C_2, ZnC_2, CdC_2, and HgC_2) are prepared by passing acetylene into solutions of the metal salts [reaction (16)]. The carbides of these two series of

$$2CuCl + C_2H_2 \longrightarrow Cu_2C_2 + 2HCl \qquad (16)$$

elements are often regarded as acetylides partly in view of the preparative method, but primarily because they react with water to give off acetylene gas [reaction (17)].

$$Na_2C_2 + 2H_2O \longrightarrow C_2H_2 + 2NaOH \qquad (17)$$

See ACETYLENE.

It is useful to classify carbides as ionic (saltlike), metallic (interstitial), and covalent. The more electropositive elements (groups I, II, and III, and to some extent, members of the lanthanide and actinide series of the periodic system) form ionic carbides with transparent (or saltlike) crystals. Belonging to this class are the acetylides listed above and BeC_2, MgC_2, CaC_2, SrC_2, BaC_2, Al_2C_6, and Ce_2C_6. Others yielding predominantly acetylene on reaction with water but also producing additional hydrocarbons are YC_2, LaC_2, CeC_2, PrC_2, NdC_2, SmC_2, ThC_2, UC_2, and NpC_2. The acetylides contain pairs of carbon atoms in ion units, C_2^{2-}. Other ionic carbides (methanides) which with water yield primarily methane but also other hydrocarbons and hydrogen [an example is given in reaction (18)] are

$$Al_4C_3 + 12H_2O \longrightarrow 4Al(OH)_3 + 3CH_4 \qquad (18)$$

Be_2C and Al_4C_3, and probably also Sc_4C_3.

Highly refactory covalent carbides are formed with silicon and boron. In the electric-arc furnace, SiC (diamond structure) is formed from a mixture of SiO_2 and coke. The very hard B_4C can be made similarly from its oxide; it is unusual both structurally and in having a fairly high electrical conductivity.

The carbides of Cr, Mn, Fe, Co, and Ni are intermediate between the interstitial and covalent types, but are much nearer the former in properties. The presence of Fe_3C in iron is an important factor in the properties of steel. *See* ABRASIVE; CERMET; HYDRIDE.

Analytical methods. Carbon is usually determined as carbon dioxide. The free element can be burned in air; metal carbonates can be decomposed by acids or heat; carbon monoxide can be burned in air; and organic compounds containing carbon can be oxidized to give carbon dioxide. The evolved carbon dioxide is weighed directly by adsorption in a mixture of sodium hydroxide and calcium hydroxide contained in a glass tube. A qualitative test for carbon dioxide is to pass the gas through limewater, a solution of calcium hydroxide [$Ca(OH)_2$], and observe the presence of a white precipitate of calcium carbonate, $CaCO_3$.

Occurrence. Carbon and its compounds are found widely distributed in nature. It is estimated that carbon makes up 0.032% of the Earth's crust. Free carbon is found in large deposits as coal, an amorphous form of the element which contains additional complex carbon-hydrogen-nitrogen compounds. Pure crystalline carbon is found as graphite and in small amounts as diamonds.

Extensive amounts of carbon are found in the form of its compounds. In the atmosphere, carbon is present in amounts up to 0.03% by volume as carbon dioxide. Various minerals such as limestone, dolomite, marble, and chalk all contain carbon in the form of carbonate. All plant and animal life is composed of complex organic compounds containing carbon combined with hydrogen, oxygen, nitrogen, and other elements. The remains of past plant and animal life are found as deposits of petroleum, asphalt, and bitumen. Deposits of natural gas contain compounds that are composed of carbon and hydrogen. *See* CARBONATE MINERALS; COAL; ELEMENTS, GEOCHEMICAL DISTRIBUTION OF; RADIOCARBON DATING.

Uses. The free element has many uses, ranging from ornamental applications of the diamond in jewelry to the black-colored pigment of carbon black in automobile tires and printing inks. Another form of carbon, graphite, is used for high-temperature crucibles, arc-light and dry-cell electrodes, lead pencils, and as a lubricant. Charcoal, an amorphous form of carbon, is used as an absorbent for gases and as a decolorizing agent. *See* CARBON BLACK; CHARCOAL; DIAMOND; GRAPHITE.

The compounds of carbon find many uses. Carbon dioxide is used for the carbonation of beverages, for fire extinguishers, and in the solid state as a refrigerant. Another oxide of carbon, carbon monoxide, finds use as a reducing agent for many metallurgical processes. Carbon tetrachloride and carbon disulfide are important solvents for industrial uses. Gaseous dichlorodifluoromethane, commonly known as Freon, is used in refrigeration devices. Calcium carbide is used to prepare acetylene, which is used for the welding and cutting of metals as well as for the preparation of other organic compounds. Other metal carbides find important uses as refractories and metal cutters. *See* ACTIVATED CARBON; GERMANIUM; SILICON.

E. Eugene Weaver

Bibliography. F. Albert Cotton and G. Wilkinson, *Advanced Inorganic Chemistry*, 5th ed., 1988; G. S. Hammond and V. J. Kuck (eds.), *Fullerenes: Synthesis, Properties, and Chemistry of Large Carbon Clusters*, 1992; *Kirk-Othmer Encyclopedia of Chemical Technology*, vol. 4, 4th ed., 1992; P. A. Thrower, *Chemistry and Physics of Carbon*, 1993.

Carbon black

An amorphous form of carbon produced commercially by thermal or oxidative decomposition of hydrocarbons, It is used principally in rubber goods, pigments, and printer's ink.

Because of the irregular arrangement of its carbon atoms, the physical properties of carbon black differ from the graphite and diamond forms of carbon. The surface area of blacks used for rubber reinforcement ranges 3100–46000 ft²/oz (10–150 m²/g) when determined by nitrogen adsorption, and the ultimate black particle has an average diameter of 20 to 300 nanometers. Pigment-grade blacks have surface areas of 150,000 ft²/oz (300–500 m²/g). Loose carbon black has a density of 2–3 lb/ft³ (0.032–0.048 g/cm³), but it is usually compressed for bag shipment or pelleted for bulk shipment in hopper cars.

Principal noncarbon components of carbon black are oxygen, hydrogen, and sulfur. Oxygen and hydrogen are combined chemically with carbon on the surface of the particle. The ratio of hydrogen to oxygen varies with the manufacturing process. In contact (channel) blacks, oxygen content is 2–5% while hydrogen amounts to about 0.5%; in furnace blacks the oxygen content of the black depends on that of the hydrocarbon feed.

Manufacturing processes may be classed as contact, furnace, or thermal. In the channel (contact) process, natural gas is burned with insufficient air for complete combustion. The smoky flame from individual burners impinges on a cool channel iron, and carbon black deposited on the channel is removed by a scraper blade. The yield of channel black is dependent upon the composition of the gas and the grade of black produced. Yield of black decreases as the heating value of the natural gas decreases. Of the three grades of black produced—easy (EPC), medium (MPC), or hard (HPC) processing channel—the yield of EPC is lowest and averages about 1.3 lb/1000 ft³ (21 kg/1000 m³) of natural gas.

In the furnace process, the hydrocarbon and air are fed into a reactor. Combustion of part of the hydrocarbon raises the temperature to 2000–3000°F (1100–1700°C), causing decomposition of the unburned hydrocarbon to carbon black. A water spray quickly cools the hot reaction products, and the finely divided black is recovered by cyclones and bag filters. Natural gas was the principal feed to the furnace process until 1943, when a furnace process utilizing heavy petroleum oils was introduced. The oil black produced was superior for reinforcing synthetic rubber, and oil furnace blacks now constitute the major type of carbon black produced. Yield of carbon black from the furnace process depends on feed stock used and type of black produced, ranging from 2 to 16 lb per 1000 ft³ (32–260 kg/1000 m³) of natural gas and 2.5 to 6 lb per gallon (0.3–0.7 kg/liter) of oil.

The oil furnace process can produce a variety of blacks specifically designed for use with various types of rubbers. For many years particle size was used as an approximate guide for black quality, the finer-particle blacks generally showing better abrasion resistance in performance tests. However, the physicochemical nature of the black surface, or "structure," became increasingly important. Structure affects the ease of compounding and modulus, stiffness, and extrusion properties of the rubber black mixture. Another development was the production of channel black substitutes from oil furnace blacks.

In the thermal process, natural gas is decomposed to carbon and hydrogen by heated refractories. Because this decomposition cools the refractories rapidly, it must be periodically interrupted to reheat the refractories. In one variant of this process employing acetylene as the feed, heat is liberated during the decomposition of acetylene. Acetylene black is distinguished by unusually high electric conductivity, and it is used in the manufacture of dry cells.

Over 90% of the production of carbon black in the United States is used by the rubber industry; hence, carbon black and rubber technology are interrelated. It is not an inert filler but enhances and reinforces various properties of rubber. Carbon black may be dispersed in rubber latex (masterbatch process) to produce, after coagulation, an intimate solid mixture of black and rubber, ready for fabrication of rubber goods.

Prior to 1940, channel black accounted for nearly 90% of domestic carbon black production; the last plant producing channel black closed in September 1976. This dramatic shift from contact to oil furnace processes was the result of the rapid price increase of natural gas along with the superior performance of oil blacks in tire manufacture. *See* DIAMOND; GRAPHITE; RUBBER; TIRE.   Carl J. Helmers

Carbon dioxide

A colorless, odorless, tasteless gas, formula CO_2, about 1.5 times as heavy as air. The specific volume at atmospheric pressure (100 kilopascals) and 70°F (21°C) is 8.74 ft^3/lb (0.546 m^3/kg). Under normal conditions, it is stable, inert, and nontoxic.

The decay (slow oxidation) of all organic materials produces CO_2. The burning of hydrocarbon fuels also produces CO_2. Fresh air contains approximately 0.033% CO_2 by volume. In the respiratory action (breathing) of all animals and humans, CO_2 is exhaled. *See* RESPIRATORY SYSTEM.

Carbon dioxide gas may be liquefied or solidified. For example, if the gas is compressed to 300 pounds per square inch gage (psig; 2 megapascals) and cooled to 0°F (-18°C) it becomes a liquid; or it may be liquefied at 70°F (21°C) by being compressed to 838 psig (5.78 MPa). Above the critical temperature of 87.9°F (31.1°C), CO_2 exists only as a gas, regardless of the pressure applied.

If liquid CO_2 is cooled to -69.9°F (-56.6°C) the

pressure drops to 60.4 psig (417 kPa), and dry ice snow is formed. This condition of pressure and temperature is known as the triple point of CO_2, at which all three phases, solid, liquid, and gas, may exist in equilibrium with one another. Carbon dioxide cannot exist as a liquid below the triple-point temperature and pressure. If the pressure on dry-ice snow is reduced to atmospheric, its temperature drops to -109.3°F (-78.5°C). As solid CO_2 absorbs heat from its surroundings, it transforms directly to a gas (sublimes), hence the name dry ice. In still air, a film of gaseous CO_2 surrounds the dry ice, and the sublimation temperature is -109.3°F (-78.5°C); but in a vacuum or in rapidly moving air in which the CO_2 gas film is stripped away, the sublimation temperature drops to -130°F (-90°C) or lower.

Carbon dioxide is obtained commercially from four sources: gas wells, fermentation, combustion of carbonaceous fuels, and as a by-product of chemical processing.

Applications. Carbon dioxide may be used as a refrigerant, inerting medium, chemical reactant, neutralizing agent for alkalies, and pressurizing agent.

Refrigeration. Solid CO_2 has a greater refrigeration effect than water ice; the latent heat of sublimation of dry ice is 253.8 Btu/lb (595.0 kilojoules/kg), whereas the latent heat of fusion of water ice is 143.4 Btu/lb (336.2 kilojoules/kg). Furthermore, it is much colder than water ice and sublimes to a gas as it absorbs heat. Solid CO_2 may be furnished to the user in pressed blocks weighting 50–60 lb (23–27 kg) each, or as extruded pellets. It may also be made as snow at the point of use by expanding liquid CO_2 to atmospheric pressure; upon release to the atmosphere, liquid CO_2 at a pressure of 285 psig (1.97 MPa) produces about 47% dry ice snow and 53% gas by weight. However, of the total refrigerating effect originally available in the liquid, 85% remains in the ice and 15% in the vapor when the liquid CO_2 is warmed to 0°F (-18°C).

Dry ice blocks and pellets are used to chill, firm, and freeze meats, vegetables, and other perishable foods for preservation during transport. Dry ice snow produced from the expansion of liquid CO_2 may be applied directly to the surface of foods in a freezing chamber or tunnel, or it may be deposited on the contents of a container. Refrigeration may be achieved in trucks and other transport modes by vaporization of either solid or liquid CO_2. *See* DRY ICE.

Liquid CO_2 is injected into pneumatic conveyor systems to cool the contents during transport. Such items as flour, sugar, plastics, and core sand are quickly chilled by the dry ice snow and cold gas produced in the pneumatic line as liquid CO_2 is introduced through a thermostatically controlled orifice.

In low-temperature testing of aircraft and electronic parts to meet military or manufacturing specifications at -65°F (-54°C) and below, liquid CO_2 is expanded through an orifice to form dry-ice snow, which is either blown directly on the part or circulated in a test chamber; solid CO_2 is used in certain kinds of testing.

Carbon dioxide liquid injected into a hollow plastic shape while it is still in the mold reduces the temperature of the internal surface and, in turn, decreases the time required for the plastic to become sufficiently hardened to be self-supporting, allowing the part to be removed from the mold more quickly. Thus blow-molding equipment can operate on a shorter cycle time, and production can be speeded up.

Carbon dioxide liquid or ice may be used to advantage for removing the flash (mold marks) from molded rubber parts. This is done in an insulated tumbling barrel in which the mechanical action easily removes the flash that has been embrittled by contact with solid CO_2.

Carbon dioxide snow is added directly to choppers and mixers used in the preparation of hamburger, sausage, and prepared meat products such as bologna. The quick chilling reduces meat temperature rapidly, retarding bacterial growth.

Carbon dioxide is used to stiffen shortening for homogeneous blending with the dry ingredients used in piecrust mixes; to chill spices, chemicals, sugar, and rubber during high-speed grinding; and to prevent softening of thermoplastic materials during pulverizing.

Inerting. Carbon dioxide does not react with oxygen, nor does it normally function as an oxidizing agent. At high temperatures, it dissociates into carbon monoxide and oxygen (about 1% at 2800°F or 1538°C).

Liquid CO_2 is an effective fire-extinguishing agent because it rapidly reduces the temperature of burning materials below the ignition point, and the gas, being heavy and inert, displaces air, usually the source of oxygen, and blankets the flames. It is particularly effective in extinguishing fires when water cannot be used, for example, in oil and electrical fires. *See* FIRE EXTINGUISHER.

Oil tankers, barges, storage vessels, and pipelines are quickly and safely inerted with CO_2 to allow welding and other repairs. In the automatic electric–tungsten–inert gas welding of steel using a filler wire, CO_2 is used to blanket the arc, thus preventing oxidation of the molten metal. *See* WELDING AND CUTTING OF METALS.

Carbon dioxide is useful in many other applications in which an inert gas is required to prevent oxidation, as in packaging foodstuffs, spray-drying eggs and other solids, blanketing paint ingredients during manufacture to prevent the formation of "skin," and protecting grain and other bulk foods stored in silos.

Chemical applications. The largest single market for CO_2 for chemical purposes is in the preparation of carbonated beverages, in which the weak carbonic acid formed by the CO_2 acts as a taste enhancer and preservative. Other uses include the hardening of foundry cores in the core box by the reaction of CO_2 with the sand binder, the neutralization of excess alkalinity in water or industrial wastes, the manufacture of salicylic acid for aspirin, the production of pure carbonates and bicarbonates, as an intermediate in the preparation of titanium dioxide, and the stimulation of oil and gas wells.

Pressure medium. Life rafts and life preservers are packaged to include small CO_2 cartridges which permit rapid inflation upon operation of a quick-opening valve. Carbon dioxide in a cartridge is used as the propellent in certain pistols. It is also used as a propellent in pressure packaging, for example, in aerosol cans, and in many instances can replace fluorinated hydrocarbons at a fraction of the cost.

Manufacture. Most CO_2 is obtained as a by-product from steam-hydrocarbon reformers used in the production of ammonia, gasoline, and other chemicals; other sources include fermentation, deep gas wells, and direct production from carbonaceous fuels. Whatever the source, the crude CO_2 (containing at least 90% CO_2) is compressed in either two or three stages, cooled, purified, condensed to the liquid phase, and placed in insulated storage vessels. Commercial liquid CO_2 is usually stored at a pressure of 225–325 psig (1.55–2.2 MPa) and is maintained in this range by refrigeration. When the liquid is placed into high-pressure cylinders and stored at ambient temperature, however, the pressure in the liquid rises to 1071 psig (7.385 MPa) when the temperature is 87.8°F (31.0°C) [the initial point], or higher, if the cylinder is completely filled with liquid.

Distribution. Carbon dioxide is distributed in three ways: in high-pressure uninsulated steel cylinders; as a low-pressure liquid in insulated truck trailers or rail tank cars; and as dry ice in insulated boxes, trucks, or boxcars.

The size of the high-pressure cylinders is limited because of the weight involved. Most commercial cylinders contain either 20 or 50 lb (9 or 23 kg) of CO_2 and are designed to deliver CO_2 gas, which can be reduced to the pressure required by the user through the action of a pressure regulator. However, some cylinders are equipped with a tube that reaches to the bottom of the cylinder and siphons liquid CO_2 to the outlet, provided the temperature of the contents is below the critical temperature (87.9°F or 31.1°C).

Truck trailer capacity is restricted by laws which govern the gross vehicle weight. Up to 20 tons (18 metric tons) of liquid CO_2 may be shipped in an insulated trailer. Suppliers of CO_2 provide their customers with storage vessels varying in capacity from 4 to 150 tons (3.6 to 135 metric tons).

When CO_2 is manufactured and transported as dry ice, losses occur because of sublimation. By storing the dry ice in a well-insulated container, losses may be kept within economical limits.

Solid CO_2 can be converted to the liquid form by placing it in a heavy-walled steel vessel known as a converter. After the vessel is sealed, it is allowed to warm to room temperature. As the temperature of the CO_2 rises past the triple point, it is converted to liquid.   J. S. Lindsey

Bibliography. American Society of Heating, Refrigerating, and Air-Conditioning Engineers, *ASHRAE Handbook of Fundamentals*, 1993; W. C. Clark, *Carbon Dioxide Review*, 1982; J. Wisniewski and R. N. Sampson (eds.), *Terrestrial Carbon Fluxes: Quantification of Sinks and Sources of CO₂*, 1993; A. S. Young, *Carbon Dioxide*, 1993.

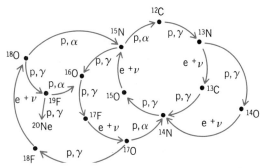

Carbon-nitrogen-oxygen cycles. (*After J. Audouze, ed., CNO Isotopes in Astrophysics, D. Reidel, 1977*)

Carbon-nitrogen-oxygen cycles

A group of nuclear reactions that involve the interaction of protons (nuclei of hydrogen atoms, designated by ^{1}H) with carbon, nitrogen, and oxygen nuclei. The cycle involving only isotopes of carbon and nitrogen is well known as the carbon-nitrogen (CN) cycle. These cycles are thought to be the main source of energy in main-sequence stars with mass 20% or more in excess of that of the Sun. Completion of any one of the cycles results in consumption of four protons (4 ^{1}H) and the production of a helium (^{4}He) nucleus plus two positrons (e^+) and two neutrinos (ν). The two positrons are annihilated with two electrons (e^-), and the total energy release is 26.73 MeV. Approximately 1.7 MeV is released as neutrino energy and is not available as thermal energy in the star. The energy $E = 26.73$ MeV arises from the mass difference between four hydrogen atoms and the helium atom, and is calculated from the Einstein mass-energy equation $E = \Delta mc^2$, where Δm is the mass difference and c^2 is the square of the velocity of light. Completion of a chain can be thought of as conversion of four hydrogen atoms into a helium atom. Because the nuclear fuel that is consumed in these processes is hydrogen, they are referred to as hydrogen-burning processes by means of the carbon-nitrogen-oxygen (CNO) cycles. *See* SOLAR NEUTRINOS.

Carbon-nitrogen cycle. The original carbon-nitrogen cycle was suggested independently by H. A. Bethe and C. F. von Weiszäcker in 1938 as the source of energy in stars. In the first reaction of the carbon-nitrogen cycle, a carbon nucleus of mass 12 captures a proton, forming a nitrogen nucleus of mass 13 and releasing a photon of energy, 1.943 MeV. This may be written: ^{12}C + ^{1}H → ^{13}N + γ, or ^{12}C$(p,\gamma)^{13}$N. The nucleus ^{13}N is unstable and decays by emitting a positron (e^+) and a neutrino (ν). In reaction form, ^{13}N → ^{13}C + e^+ + ν or ^{13}N$(e^+\nu)$-^{13}C. The cycle continues through ^{14}N, ^{15}O, and ^{15}N by the reactions and decays shown in ^{12}C$(p,\gamma)^{13}$N$(e^+\nu)^{13}$C$(p,\gamma)^{14}$N$(p,\gamma)^{15}$O$(e^+\nu)^{15}$N$(p, \alpha)^{12}$C. These reactions form the second cycle from the right in the **illustration**. The reaction ^{15}N$(p,\alpha)^{12}$C represents emission of an alpha particle (^{4}He nucleus) when ^{15}N captures a proton and this cycle returns to ^{12}C. Because of the cycling, the total number of carbon, nitrogen, and oxygen nuclei remains constant, so these nuclei act as catalysts in the production of a helium nucleus plus two positrons and two neutrinos with the release of en-

ergy. The positrons that are created annihilate with free electrons rapidly after creation, so the energy used in their creation is returned to the energy fund. Synthesis of some of the rare carbon, nitrogen, and oxygen isotopes is accomplished through hydrogen burning by means of the carbon-nitrogen-oxygen cycles.

Table 1 shows the energy release, Q, and the average release of thermal energy, Q (thermal), in each reaction of the cycle, as well as the maximum neutrino energy E_ν^{max} in the two reactions in which a neutrino is produced.

A standard model for the Sun has been developed by J. N. Bahcall and colleagues to determine the flux of solar neutrinos that should be coming to the Earth. In this model, the site of maximum hydrogen burning is just outside the central core of the Sun. At a distance of 0.0511 solar radius from the center, chosen to lie in the most active part of that site for hydrogen burning in the proton-proton chains, the temperature is 14×10^6 K (25×10^6 °F), the density is $\rho = 112$ g/cm³ (112 times the density of water), and the mass fraction of hydrogen is $X(^1$H$) = 0.483$. The reaction rates, R, calculated for the carbon-nitrogen cycle reactions at that temperature, are shown in **Table 2**. Small corrections for screening of the Coulomb field between nuclei by electrons have been neglected. Taking into account the mass fraction of hydrogen and the density at the site, the number of reactions per nucleus per second is given by $\lambda = \rho R X(^1$H$)/1.0078$. By inverting λ, the mean lifetimes, τ, of the carbon, nitrogen, and oxygen nuclei are obtained; these are shown in the last column of Table 2 in years. The fraction of energy from CNO cycles in the Sun is calculated to be only 1.5%; the remaining 98.5% of the energy is from hydrogen burning in the proton-proton chains.

TABLE 1. Energies involved in the carbon-nitrogen cycle, in MeV

Reaction	Q	Q (thermal)	E_ν^{max}
^{12}C + ^{1}H → ^{13}N + γ	1.943	1.943	
^{13}N → ^{13}C + e^+ + ν	2.221	1.51	1.199
^{13}C + ^{1}H → ^{14}N + γ	7.551	7.551	
^{14}N + ^{1}H → ^{15}O + γ	7.297	7.297	
^{15}O → ^{15}N + e^+ + ν	2.753	1.75	1.731
^{15}N + ^{1}H → ^{12}C + ^{4}He	4.966	4.966	

TABLE 2. Reaction rates and mean lifetimes for carbon-nitrogen cycle in the Sun

Reaction	R, s^{-1}/(mole)(cm^3)*	λ, s^{-1}	τ, years
$^{12}C + {}^{1}H \rightarrow {}^{13}N + \gamma$	8.19×10^{-17}	4.40×10^{-15}	7.20×10^{6}
$^{13}N \rightarrow {}^{13}C + e^+ + \nu$		1.16×10^{-3}	2.73×10^{-5}
$^{13}C + {}^{1}H \rightarrow {}^{14}N + \gamma$	2.83×10^{-16}	1.52×10^{-14}	2.08×10^{6}
$^{14}N + {}^{1}H \rightarrow {}^{15}O + \gamma$	2.94×10^{-19}	1.58×10^{-17}	2.01×10^{9}
$^{15}O \rightarrow {}^{15}N + e^+ + \nu$		5.68×10^{-3}	5.58×10^{-6}
$^{15}N + {}^{1}H \rightarrow {}^{12}C + {}^{4}He$	7.27×10^{-15}	3.91×10^{-13}	8.11×10^{4}

*From G. R. Caughlan and W. A. Fowler, Thermonuclear reaction rates, V, *Atom. Nucl. Data Tables*, vol. 40, 1988.

CNO bicycle. Nuclear research in the 1950s led to the addition of a second cycle to the processes of hydrogen burning by the CNO cycles. Laboratory research has shown that in a very small number of proton captures by ^{15}N a photon is emitted with the formation of an oxygen nucleus of mass 16, leading to reactions which may cycle back to ^{14}N by $^{15}N(p,\gamma)^{16}O(p,\gamma)^{17}F(e^+\nu)^{17}O(p,\alpha)^{14}N$. The pair of cycles consisting of this cycle and the carbon-nitrogen cycle, that forms the main cycle and the first cycle to the left of it in the illustration, is called the carbon-nitrogen-oxygen bicycle. The rate of the $^{12}N(p,\alpha)^{12}C$ reaction is of the order of 10^3 times that of the $^{15}N(p,\gamma)^{16}O$ reaction at most temperatures expected in stellar interiors.

Other CNO cycles. In research since 1960, it has become apparent that many possible branches among the nuclei must be included in any analysis of hydrogen burning by carbon, nitrogen, and oxygen nuclei. For example, if the unstable nucleus ^{13}N to capture a proton before it decays in its mean lifetime of 862 s, a third cycle can occur through $^{13}N(p,\gamma)^{14}O(e^+\nu)^{14}N$. This cycle is displayed in the illustration by the branch on the right-hand side of the main carbon-nitrogen cycle and is known as the fast or the hot carbon-nitrogen cycle. The other possible branches leading to additional cycles shown in the diagram are due to competition between (p,γ) and (p,α) reactions. The added reactions are $^{17}O(p,\alpha)^{18}F(e^+\nu)^{18}O(p,\alpha)^{15}N$ and $^{18}O(p,\alpha)^{19}F(p,\alpha)^{16}O$. The reaction $^{19}F(p,\gamma)^{20}Ne$ shown in the illustration leads out of the carbon, nitrogen, and oxygen nuclei and hence away from CNO cycles.

There are two additional branches that may occur if the unstable fluorine nuclei (^{17}F and ^{18}F) capture protons before they can decay. *See* NUCLEAR FUSION; NUCLEAR REACTION; NUCLEOSYNTHESIS; PROTON-PROTON CHAIN; STELLAR EVOLUTION.

Georgeanne R. Caughlan

Bibliography. J. Audouze (ed.), *CNO Isotopes in Astrophysics*, 1977; J. N. Bahcall et al., Standard solar models and the uncertainties in predicted capture rates of solar neutrinos, *Rev. Mod. Phys.*, 54:767–799, 1982; G. R. Caughlan and W. A. Fowler, Thermonuclear reaction rates, V, *Atom. Nucl. Data Tables*, vol. 40, 1988; W. A. Fowler, *Nuclear Astrophysics*, 1967; M. J. Harris et al., Thermonuclear reaction rates, III, *Annu. Rev. Astron. Astrophys.*, 21:165–176, 1983.

Carbon star

Any of a class of stars with an apparently high abundance ratio of carbon to hydrogen. In normal stars, oxygen is more abundant than carbon, and carbon and nitrogen are about equal. In carbon stars, however, carbon is more abundant than oxygen. The majority of the carbon-rich stars are low-temperature red giants of the C class, showing bands of C_2, CN, and CH (the older designation of this is R or N). A few hot carbon-rich stars are also known. An excess abundance of carbon is also found in the S (zirconium oxide) stars and the barium (heavy-element) stars. The C-class stars have surface temperatures in the range 5500–2500 K (9500–4000°F). Heavy absorption produced by bands ascribed to C_3 and SiC_2 exists in cooler objects. An unexpected peculiarity is the strength of the resonance lines of neutral lithium; this element is easily destroyed by nuclear reactions with hydrogen. Its synthesis by helium burning may occur in late stages of red giant evolution.

The degree of enhancement of carbon varies from star to star. In a related phenomenon found in global clusters, variations in the C/N/O ratios are found. An outstanding peculiarity is the presence of the isotope ^{13}C in some of these stars, as shown by the presence of $^{12}C^{13}C$ and $^{13}C^{13}C$ isotope bands, with an abnormally high $^{13}C/^{12}C$ ratio. between 1 to 4 and 1 to 10. In some other C-class stars the $^{12}C^{13}C$ bands are absent, indicating a low $^{13}C/^{12}C$ ratio, possibly near the terrestrial value of 1 to 90. An important discovery was that nearly all red giants, not only carbon stars, have systematically higher values of the $^{13}C/^{12}C$ ratio than the Sun.

The difference between normal red giant spectra and those of the carbon-rich group arises apparently because of the strong binding of the compound CO. In stars for which there is more oxygen than carbon, at temperatures below 5000 K (8500°F), almost all the carbon is bound in the form of CO and therefore unavailable to form further carbon compounds. In the carbon-rich stars the CO consumes all the oxygen, but leaves some carbon in free atomic form, available for carbon compounds. The importance of the C/O ratio lies in the theory of the origin of chemical elements, in which it is shown that carbon is easily synthesized at temperatures found in cores of evolving red giants. *See* NUCLEOSYNTHESIS; STAR.

Jesse L. Greenstein

Carbonate minerals

Mineral species containing CO_3^- ion as the fundamental anionic unit. The carbonate minerals can be classified as (1) anhydrous normal carbonates, (2) hydrated normal carbonates, (3) acid carbonates (bicarbonates), and (4) compound carbonates containing hydroxide, halide, or other anions in addition to the carbonate.

Most of the common carbonate minerals belong to group (1), and can be further classified according to their structures. The rhombohedral carbonates are typified by calcite, $CaCO_3$, and by dolomite, $CaMg(CO_3)_2$. Minerals with the calcite structure include magnesite, $MgCO_3$; siderite, $FeCO_3$; rhodochrosite, $MnCO_3$; smithsonite, $ZnCO_3$; cobaltocalcite, $CoCO_3$; otavite, $CdCO_3$; and gaspeite, $NiCO_3$. Ankerite, $Ca(Fe,Mg)(CO_3)_2$, and kutnahorite, $CaMn(CO_3)_2$, have the dolomite structure. The other structural type within this group is that of aragonite, a metastable high-pressure polymorph of $CaCO_3$, which has orthorhombic symmetry. Minerals with the aragonite structure are strontianite, $SrCO_3$; witherite, $BaCO_3$; and cerussite, $PbCO_3$. Less common group (1) minerals which do not fall into these three structural types include vaterite, another metastable polymorph of $CaCO_3$; huntite, $Mg_3Ca(CO_3)_4$; and other multication minerals. *See* ANKERITE; ARAGONITE; CALCITE; CERUSSITE; DOLOMITE; MAGNESITE; RHODOCHROSITE; SIDERITE; SMITHSONITE; STRONTIANITE; WITHERITE.

The minerals in groups (2) and (3) all decompose at relatively low temperatures and therefore occur only in sedimentary deposits (typically evaporites) and as low-temperature hydrothermal alteration products. The only common mineral in these groups is trona, $Na_3H(CO_3)_2 \cdot 2H_2O$. *See* SALINE EVAPORITE.

Similarly, the group (4) minerals are relatively rare and are characteristically low-temperature hydrothermal alteration products. The commonest members of this group are malachite, $Cu_2CO_3(OH)_2$, and azurite, $Cu_3(CO_3)_2(OH)_2$, which are often found in copper ore deposits. *See* AZURITE; MALACHITE.

Important occurrences of carbonates include ultrabasic igneous rocks such as carbonatites and serpentinites, and metamorphosed carbonate sediments, which may recrystallize to form marble. The major occurrences of carbonates, however, are in sedimentary deposits as limestone and dolomite rock. *See* DOLOMITE ROCK; LIMESTONE; MARBLE; ROCK; SEDIMENTARY ROCKS.   Alan M. Gaines

Bibliography. R. G. Bathurst, *Carbonate Sediments and Their Diagenesis*, 2d ed., 1975; W. A. Deer, R. A. Howie, and J. Zussman, *An Introduction to the Rock-Forming Minerals*, 2d ed., 1992; W. A. Deer, R. A. Howie, and J. Zussman, *Rock Forming Minerals*, vol. 5: *Non-silicates*, 2d ed., 1986; E. T. Degens, *Geochemistry of Sediments*, 1965; C. Klein and C. S. Hurlbut, Jr., *Manual of Mineralogy*, 21th ed., 1993.

Carbonatite

An igneous rock in which carbonate minerals make up at least half the volume. Individual occurrences of carbonatite are not numerous (about 330 have been recognized) and generally are small, but they are widely distributed. Carbonatites are scientifically important because they reveal clues concerning the composition and thermal history of the Earth's mantle. Economically, carbonatites provide important mines for some mineral commodities and are virtually the only sources of a few. *See* CARBONATE MINERALS.

Mineralogy. The carbonate minerals that dominate the carbonatites are, in order of decreasing abundance, calcite, dolomite, ankerite, and rarely siderite and magnesite. Sodium- and potassium-rich carbonate minerals have been confirmed in igneous rocks at only one locality, the active volcano Oldoinyo Lengai in Tanzania. Noncarbonate minerals that typify carbonatites are apatite, magnetite, phlogopite or biotite, clinopyroxene, amphibole, monticellite, perovskite, and rarely olivine or melilite. Secondary minerals, produced by alteration of primary magmatic minerals, include barite, alkali feldspar, quartz, fluorite, hematite, rutile, pyrite, and chlorite. Minerals that are important in some carbonatites because they carry niobium, rare-earth elements, and other metals in concentrations high enough for profitable extraction are pyrochlore, bastnaesite, monazite, baddeleyite, and bornite.

Styles of occurrence. Carbonatites occur in a variety of forms, both intrusive and volcanic. Lava flows are small and rare, but pyroclastic carbonatites are numerous as thick near-vent accumulations (tuff cones) and thin but widespread airfall and surge deposits. Some pyroclastic carbonatites are especially important, because they preserve the forms of quenched droplets of carbonate-rich liquid and also record the mineral assemblages that are nearly always erased in intrusive rocks by low-temperature alteration. Carbonatite airfall tuffs are paleontologically important, because they tend to be fine grained and rapidly become lithified, preserving delicate organic structures. The hominid footprints at Laetolil, Tanzania, and remarkably detailed molds of plants and caterpillars are examples. *See* TUFF.

Most intrusive carbonatites form arrays of dikes that may be parallel, radiating, or concentric and arcuate. More irregular intrusive bodies are also known, but all are small compared to those of silicate-rich igneous rocks; the largest known carbonatite body, at Sokli in Finland, has a surface area of only 20 km^2 (8 mi^2). Carbonate-rich magmas appear in many examples to have had low viscosities, but some were emplaced with explosive violence because of their high gas content. A few carbonatites extend for several kilometers along fault surfaces; they may have been older igneous bodies that were caught up in the fault displacement and acted as cold but weak ductile lubricant between the rock masses; or they may have been injected as magma. Except for the absence of large homogeneous plutons, carbonatites form the full array of igneous rock styles that are shown by silicate-rich igneous rocks. *See* MAGMA; PLUTON.

Associated rocks. Carbonatites usually have been found with low-silica, high-alkali igneous rocks, typically melilitites, nephelinites, tephrites, and phonolites. The silicate and carbonate rocks are intimately mixed in many intrusive complexes, and the carbonatites are among the youngest and generally least abundant of rock types in any complex. Carbonatites that are unaccompanied by other igneous rocks have been recognized. Examples are at Fort Portal, Uganda; Kaluwe, Zaire; and Sarfartoq, Greenland.

Geographic distribution. Carbonatites are widely scattered. The only occurrences known on oceanic crust are in the Canary and Cape Verde islands; however, carbonatite associated with deep-water marine sediments occurs under the Semail ophiolite in the United Arab Emirates. These occurrences suggest that carbonatites might actually be common on and within oceanic crust but are usually buried or destroyed by subduction. *See* OPHIOLITE.

In North America, localities include Magnet Cove, Arkansas; Mountain Pass, California; Iron Hill, Colorado; and Oka, Quebec, Canada. In South America, carbonatites include those at Cerro Manomo, Bolivia; Araxa, Jacupiranga, and several others in southern Brazil and Paraguay; and at least four in the northern Amazon Basin.

About half of all carbonatite occurrences so far recognized are in Africa. Many of these occur in a south-trending belt from southern Sudan through Kenya, Uganda, Tanzania, Zambia, and Malawi to South Africa; they are of diverse ages, from 2047 million years to less than 10,000 years. Another belt runs south from Zaire through Angola to Namibia. A third belt, with fewer carbonatites, trends eastward from Mauritania and Morocco through Mali and Libya to Egypt.

European localities include Fen, Norway; Alno, Sweden; Sokli and Siilinjarvi, Finland; many in the Kola Peninsula of Russia; the Ukraine; and Kaiserstuhl and Hegau, Germany. In Asia, large numbers of carbonatites have been found in Siberia, the Aldan and Sayan-Tuva regions, Mongolia, Afghanistan, Pakistan, southern and western India, and at Bayan Obo, China. A few carbonatites have been recognized in Australia and the South Island, New Zealand.

Chemical compositions. Carbonatites, compared to the inferred composition of the Earth's mantle and to other igneous rocks, are greatly enriched in niobium, rare-earth elements, barium, strontium, phosphorus, and fluorine, and they are relatively depleted in silicon, aluminum, iron, magnesium, nickel, titanium, sodium, potassium, and chlorine. These extreme differences are attributed to strong fractionation between carbonate liquid on the one

hand and silicate and oxide solid phases on the other during separation of the carbonate liquid from its source. Strontium and neodymium isotope ratios indicate that the sources of carbonatites are geologically old, inhomogeneous, and variably depleted in the radioactive parent elements rubidium and samarium.

Genesis of carbonate-rich magma. For more than two centuries, it has been known that calcite decomposes to lime (calcium oxide; CaO) and carbon dioxide (CO_2) when exposed to high temperature at atmospheric pressure. Furthermore, at high pressure calcium carbonate ($CaCO_3$) liquid is stable only at temperatures far higher than are reasonably expected in the Earth's crust. It was therefore difficult for geologists to imagine liquid carbonate being stable at or near the Earth's surface. In 1960 it was demonstrated experimentally that the addition of water (H_2O) to the system $CaO-CO_2$ at high pressure will stabilize a carbonate liquid at temperatures expectable in the Earth's crust. Also in 1960, the volcano Oldoinyo Lengai in Tanzania erupted carbonate-rich ash and subsequently carbonatite lava. Geologic mapping has confirmed that most carbonatites occur in small volumes associated with mantle-derived, high-alkali, low-silica igneous rocks. *See* CALCITE.

There are three possible origins (not mutually exclusive) for carbonatite magmas: (1) they are "primary" liquids, arriving directly from their mantle sources without change during ascent; (2) they are products of fractional crystallization from carbonate-bearing silicate magmas (as silicate minerals crystallize from the magma, carbonate concentration builds up in the remaining liquid); or (3) they are products of immiscible separation of carbonate-rich and silicate-rich liquids (the properties of highly ionic carbonate liquid are so different from those of silicate liquid that, during cooling, carbonate-bearing silicate magma separates into two liquids, one containing nearly all the carbonate, the other nearly all the silicate).

The first origin is favored by evidence from altered mantle xenoliths (rock fragments enclosed by an unrelated igneous rock) carried to the surface by basalts, nephelinites, and kimberlites; these altered fragments demonstrate that carbonatite liquid has percolated through the mantle. A primary liquid origin is also supported by the presence in carbonatites, rarely, of magnesium- and chromium-rich spinels typical of mantle rocks, and by the absence, in some carbonatite occurrences, of associated silicate rocks that could represent parents or siblings of the carbonatites. The lack of mantle xenoliths in carbonatites is evidence against the primary liquid status, but the low density and low viscosity of carbonatite liquid may permit such dense fragments to settle out quickly. *See* SPINEL; XENOLITH.

The second and third origins are favored by the small volume of carbonatite relative to silicate rocks in most occurrences, and by the lateness of carbonatites in intrusive and eruptive sequences;

but they are opposed by differences in isotopic ratios between carbonatite and silicate rocks in some occurrences (neither fractional crystallization nor immiscible liquid separation should change the isotopic ratios). The third origin is further supported by experiments demonstrating that a carbonate-bearing silicate liquid can split into carbonate-rich and silicate-rich liquids, and by the natural occurrence of "rock emulsions" consisting of blobs of one composition enclosed in the other. On balance, the evidence is still inconclusive, and probably any of the three mechanisms of origin can operate at different times and places.

Criteria for recognition. It is not easy to discriminate carbonatites from thoroughly recrystallized and metamorphosed marbles or from vein fillings deposited by dilute, low-temperature aqueous solutions. Because calcite has very low strength and easily deforms by plastic flow, carbonate-rich rocks can intrude their more brittle surroundings and thus imitate magmatic rocks. Furthermore, because marbles and recrystallized carbonatites converge toward the same textures and mineral assemblages, carbonatites can be misidentified as metamorphosed sedimentary rocks. The strongest indications of igneous origin for a carbonate-rich rock are considered to be quenched carbonate-rich liquid in the form of droplets or bubble walls, association with nepheline- or melilite-bearing rocks, presence of strontium-rich calcite, presence of pyrochlore and other minerals that are rich in niobium or rare-earth elements, and presence of apatite that has higher concentrations of rare-earth elements and silicon than apatite from other rock types. *See* APATITE; NIOBIUM; RARE-EARTH ELEMENTS.

Economic significance. Carbonatites yield a variety of mineral commodities, including phosphate, lime, niobium, rare-earth elements, anatase, fluorite, and copper. Agricultural phosphate for fertilizer is the most valuable single product from carbonatites; most is obtained from apatite in lateritic soils that have developed by tropical weathering of carbonatites, dissolving the carbonates and thereby concentrating the less soluble apatite. Lime for agriculture and for cement manufacture is obtained from carbonatites in regions where limestones are lacking.

Tectonic significance. Ultramafic xenoliths from lithospheric mantle commonly show textures and mineral assemblages that indicate modification of the original rock. This alteration typically results in strong enrichment in light rare-earth elements, uranium, thorium, and lead, but much less enrichment in titanium, zirconium, niobium, and strontium. These changes are commonly attributed to interaction of lithospheric mantle with an invading carbonate-rich magma. The wide geographic dispersal of these altered xenoliths suggests that carbonate-rich liquid has been more common in the upper mantle than the sparse distribution of carbonatites in the upper crust would suggest. According to the testimony of these samples, carbonatite magma, ascending through lithospheric mantle, commonly is trapped before it can invade the crust. In addition to the factors that can stop the rise of any magma (heat loss, increase of solidus temperature with decrease in pressure, decrease in density and increase in strength of wall rock), carbonatite magma can be halted by reaction with wall rock to form calcium and magnesium silicates plus CO_2, and by less oxidizing conditions to reduce carbonate to elemental carbon (graphite or diamond) or to methane. Both of these changes subtract dissolved CO_2 from the magma, causing crystallization. *See* DIAMOND; GRAPHITE.

In some regions carbonatite magmatism has recurred after intervals of 100 million years, suggesting that carbonate-rich liquids can be regenerated by a small degree of partial fusion of locally and repeatedly carbonated mantle. This possibility, in turn, suggests that carbonate in the mantle is replenished by recycling of sedimentary carbonate at subduction zones. *See* SUBDUCTION ZONES.

Carbonatites are not restricted to a single tectonic regime. They occur in oceanic and continental crust and have formed in compressional fold belts and stable cratons as well as regions of crustal extension. Rather than indicating the stress field in the shallow crust in which they were emplaced, carbonatites are useful in modeling the long-term thermal and chemical development of the mantle. *See* IGNEOUS ROCKS.   Daniel S. Barker

Bibliography. K. Bell (ed.), *Carbonatites: Genesis and Evolution*, 1989; A. R. Woolley, *Alkaline Rocks and Carbonatites of the World*, pt. 1: *North and South America*, 1987; P. J. Wyllie and O. F. Tuttle, The system $CaO-CO_2-H_2O$ and the origin of carbonatites, *J. Petrology*, 1:1–46, 1960.

Carboniferous

The fifth period of the Paleozoic Era. The Carboniferous Period spanned from about 355 million years to about 285 million years ago. The rocks that formed during this time interval are known as the Carboniferous System; they include a wide variety of sedimentary, igneous, and metamorphic rocks. Sedimentary rocks in the lower portion of the Carboniferous are typically carbonates, such as limestones and dolostones, and locally some evaporites. The upper portions of the system are usually composed of cyclically repeated successions of sandstones, coals, shales, and thin limestones. *See* SEDIMENTARY ROCKS.

The economic importance of the Carboniferous is evident in its name, which refers to coal, the important energy source that fueled the industrialization of northwestern Europe in the early 1800s and led to the Carboniferous being one of the first geologic systems to be studied in detail. Carboniferous coal formed in coastal and fluvial environments and is found in much of the world. In addition, petroleum, another important energy resource, accumulated in many Carboniferous marine carbonate

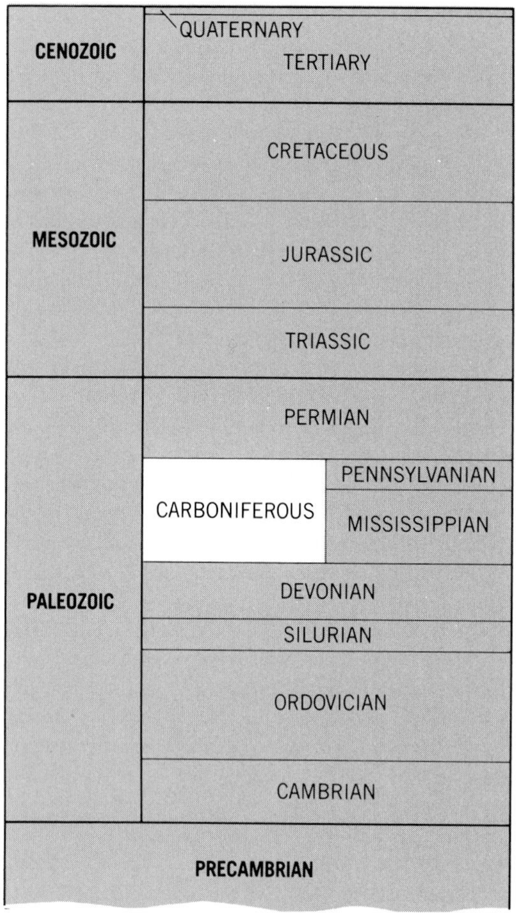

CENOZOIC	QUATERNARY	
	TERTIARY	
MESOZOIC	CRETACEOUS	
	JURASSIC	
	TRIASSIC	
PALEOZOIC	PERMIAN	
	CARBONIFEROUS	PENNSYLVANIAN
		MISSISSIPPIAN
	DEVONIAN	
	SILURIAN	
	ORDOVICIAN	
	CAMBRIAN	
PRECAMBRIAN		

sediments, particularly near shelf margins adjacent to basinal black shale source rocks. In many regions the cyclical history of deposition and exposure has enhanced the permeability and porosity of these rocks to make them excellent petroleum reservoirs.

The limestones of the Lower Carboniferous are extensively quarried and used for building stone, especially in northwestern Europe and the central and eastern United States. *See* COAL; PETROLEUM.

The base of the Carboniferous is placed at the first appearance of the conodont *Siphonodella sulcata*, a fossil that marks a widely recognized biozone in most marine sedimentary rocks. The reference locality for this base is an outcrop in Belgium. The top of the Carboniferous is placed below the first appearance of the Permian fusulinacean foraminiferal zone of *Sphaeroschwagerina fusiformis*, and the reference locality is in an outcrop in the southern Ural region of Kazakhstan. The equivalent biozone is at the base of *Pseudoschwagerina beedei* in North America. *See* CONODONT; FUSULINACEA.

Subdivisions. The term Carboniferous Order was originally applied by W. D. Conybeare and J. Phillips in 1822 to rocks in the British Isles that included the Old Red Sandstone, Mountain Limestone, Millstone Grit, and Coal Measures (**Fig. 1**). Later, after the Old Red Sandstone was recognized as being a continental facies of the Devonian System, the Mountain Limestone became the Lower Carboniferous and the Millstone Grit and Coal Measures were combined to be the Upper Carboniferous. In North America, the Coal Measures were readily recognized (as Upper Carboniferous), and the underlying, mainly noncoaly beds were initially called Subcarboniferous. *See* DEVONIAN.

In 1891, the U.S. Geological Survey introduced the terms Pennsylvanian Series for the Coal Measures and Mississippian Series for the Subcarboniferous. In 1906 T. C. Chamberlain and R. D. Salisbury raised the Mississippian and Pennsylvanian to the rank of Systems (Fig. 1), noting that they were separated by a major unconformity and were quite

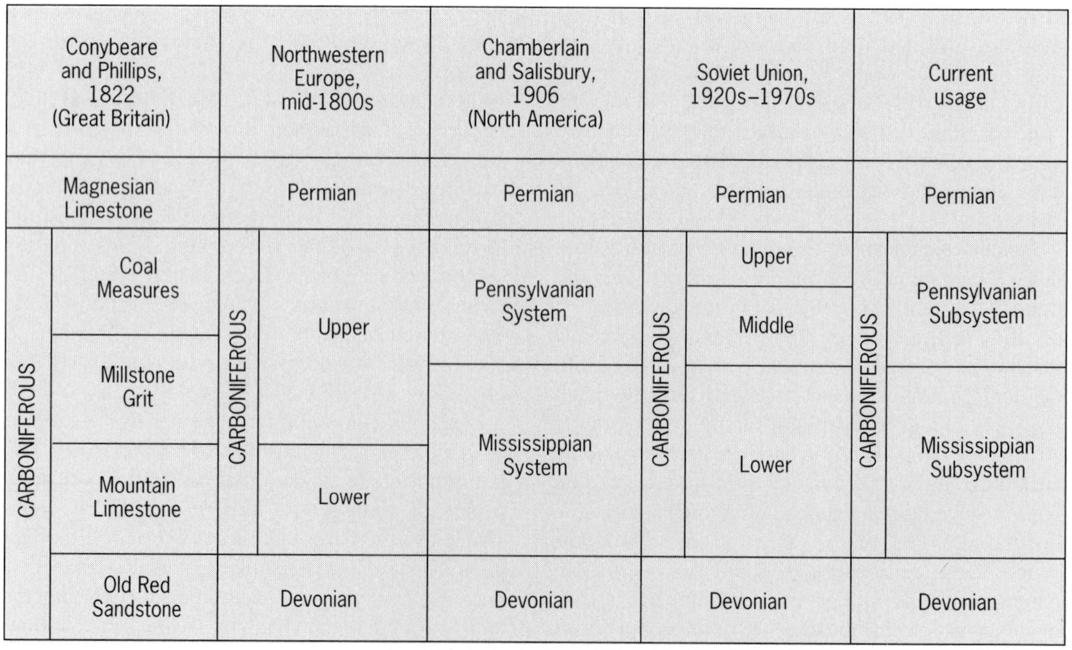

Conybeare and Phillips, 1822 (Great Britain)		Northwestern Europe, mid-1800s		Chamberlain and Salisbury, 1906 (North America)	Soviet Union, 1920s–1970s		Current usage	
Magnesian Limestone		Permian		Permian	Permian		Permian	
CARBONIFEROUS	Coal Measures	**CARBONIFEROUS**	Upper	Pennsylvanian System	**CARBONIFEROUS**	Upper	**CARBONIFEROUS**	Pennsylvanian Subsystem
	Millstone Grit					Middle		
	Mountain Limestone		Lower	Mississippian System		Lower		Mississippian Subsystem
	Old Red Sandstone		Devonian	Devonian	Devonian		Devonian	

Fig. 1. Development of stratigraphic nomenclature for the Carboniferous. Placement of the Lower-Upper Carboniferous boundary varies depending upon which sequence boundary was selected as locally most significant.

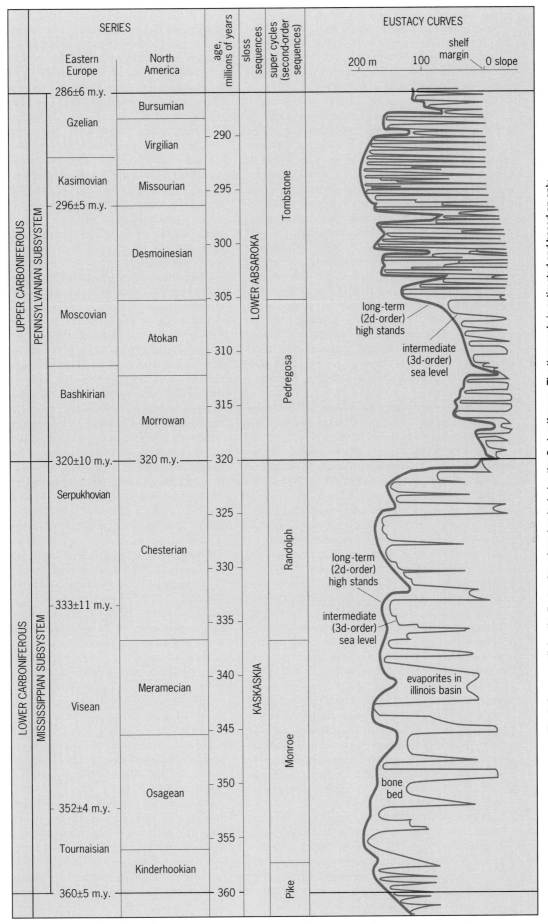

Fig. 2 Curves outlining the fluctuation of sea levels during the Carboniferous. The time scale is estimated and based on only a few reliable radiometric ages for the interval. 1 m = 3.3 ft. (*After C. A. Ross and J. R. P. Ross, Late Paleozoic Sea Levels and Depositional Sequences and Biostratigraphic Zonation of Late Paleozoic Depositional Sequences, Cushman Found. Foraminiferal Res. Spec. Publ. 24, 1987*)

different lithologically in North American and in Europe. This nomenclature was extensively adopted in North America but not in other parts of the world. *See* MISSISSIPPIAN; PENNSYLVANIAN.

A third means of subdividing the Carboniferous was developed during the 1920s and 1930s on the Russian Platform, the western slopes of the Urals, and the greater Donetz Basin areas of Ukrainia. There, the limestone succession of the Lower Carboniferous could be widely recognized. On the platform, this succession was separated by a major unconformity and a hiatus from the overlying Upper Carboniferous. However, on the platform margins and slopes and toward the center of the Donetz Basin, sediments progressively filled the hiatus, so that a complete sedimentary record could be studied in marine facies. Within the upper portion of the Carboniferous, a second regional unconformity of considerable duration is documented on the Russian Platform; and as a result, the Soviet Carboniferous was subdivided into a Lower, Middle, and Upper (Fig. 1). The boundary between the Middle and Upper Carboniferous on the Russian Platform is correlated with the boundary between the Middle and Upper Pennsylvanian in the North American midcontinent region.

After many meetings, discussions, and field trips to outcrops, the International Subcommission on Carboniferous Stratigraphy reached general agreement in the 1980s that the Carboniferous would be divided into a Lower Carboniferous Mississippian Subsystem and an Upper Carboniferous Pennsylvanian Subsystem.

The two Carboniferous subsystems are subdivided into a number of series and stages (**Fig. 2**) that are variously identified in different parts of the world based on biostratigraphic evidence using evolutionary successions in fossils or overlapping assemblage zones. Many fossil groups have been studied in order to establish consistent worldwide zonations; they have included foraminifers, corals, ammonoid cephalopods, brachiopods, bryozoans, sponges, bivalves, crinoids, radiolarians, conodonts, and plants. To a large extent the distribution of each of these fossil groups was determined by climate, temperature, and other environmental and ecological conditions, evolutionary adaptations, and paleobiogeographic opportunities. As the Carboniferous progressed, changes in each of these factors caused biotic redistributions and dispersals and, at other times, strongly provincial biotic associations. These changes have made detailed correlations between some regions more difficult. *See* INDEX FOSSIL; STRATIGRAPHY.

Paleogeography and lithology. Perhaps the strongest of the many ecological factors that controlled biotic distributions were the paleogeographic changes within the Carboniferous that were brought about by the initial assembling of the supercontinent Pangaea and the associated mountain-building activities, which greatly modified climate, ocean currents, and seaways. During Tournaisian and Visean

time in the Early Carboniferous (**Fig. 3***a*), a nearly continuous equatorial seaway encouraged extensive tropical and subtropical carbonate sedimentation on the shelves and platforms in North America, northern and southern Europe, Kazakhstan, North and South China, and the northern shores of the protocontinent Gondwana (such as northern Africa).

Beginning near the end of the Visean, the gradual collision of northern Gondwana against northern Europe–North America (also called Euramerica or Laurussia) started the formation of Pangaea, and by the Late Carboniferous had divided the tropical equatorial seaway into two segments (Fig. 3*b*). One, which represented the beginning of the Paleotethys faunal region, lay to the east of Pangaea as a large arcuate ocean with a number of small island arcs and oceanic plateaus. This warm-water ocean with vast west-flowing equatorial currents resulted in warm-water currents being directed to both the north and south of their normal latitudes.

The other segment of the former equatorial seaway lay to the west of Pangaea and faced a relatively large, deep Panthalassa Ocean basin, which had considerably fewer island arcs and ocean plateaus. This edge of Pangaea was not bathed by warm-water currents; it was the site of cold-water upwelling and cool-water currents from both the Northern and Southern hemispheres. When these reached equatorial areas they began to warm, and they formed the beginnings of the westward-flowing equatorial currents. As a consequence, the paleolatitudinal extent of carbonate platforms on the western margin of Pangaea was less than in the Paleotethys region. *See* CONTINENTAL DRIFT; CONTINENTS, EVOLUTION OF; PALEOGEOGRAPHY; PLATE TECTONICS.

Orogeny. The collision of Gondwana with North America–northern Europe, in addition to changing the patterns of equatorial ocean currents, created the long chain of mountains that made up the Ouachita-Appalachian-Hercynian orogenic belt. This complex set of mountains also is evident in the sedimentary patterns of clastic rocks, such as conglomerates, river and shoreline sandstones, and coals and other nonmarine clastic deposits, as well as in thick turbidite successions in several foredeep marine basins that formed along the front of the advancing orogenic thrust belts. Although this chain of mountains was mainly within the tropics and subtropics, it became very elevated, perhaps similar to the present-day Himalaya ranges; it disrupted terrestrial climates to a similar degree. *See* OROGENY.

Glaciation. An additional ramification of the formation of Pangaea was the beginning of very extensive glaciation in the polar and high-latitude regions of the supercontinent. Glacial deposits are also known from smaller continental fragments that were at high paleolatitudes in the Northern Hemisphere. The cause for this great increase in ice accumulation is not entirely known. It may be that the diversion of warm-water currents into more southerly (and northerly) latitudes increased precipitation (as snow). Perhaps the mountain heights of the newly formed orogenic belts disrupted general atmospheric circulation from the tropics into high latitudes. Solar radiation possibly was reduced a few percent to initiate these more extensive glacial conditions. Or other, still unknown factors may be the primary causes. In any case, the Earth's climate cooled, tropical carbonate-producing areas became restricted toward the

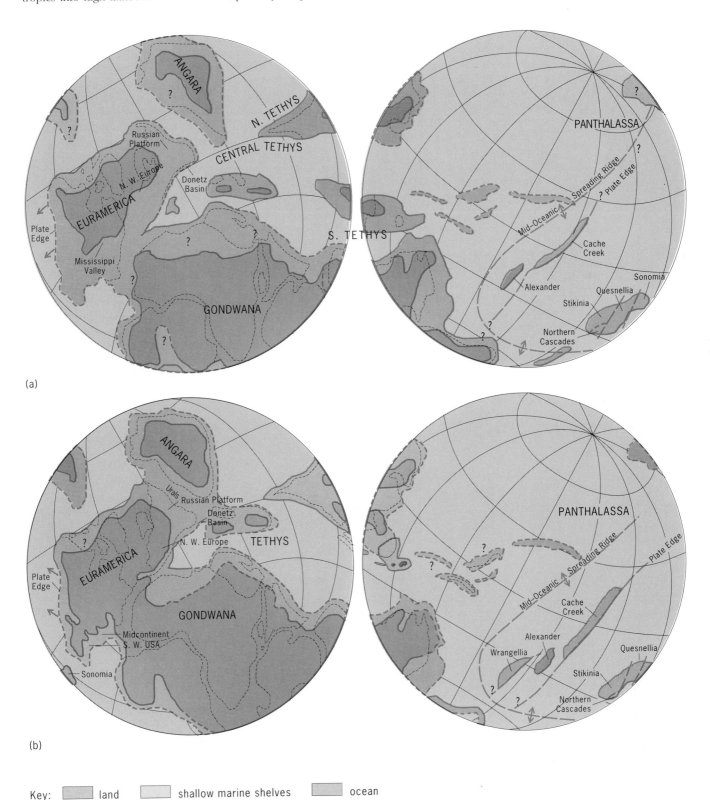

(a)

(b)

Key: ▢ land ▢ shallow marine shelves ▢ ocean

Fig. 3. Paleogeography of the Carboniferous. (*a*) Early Carboniferous (Mississippian) Tournaisian and Visean epochs, with a major east-west equatorial seaway between Euramerica and Gondwana. (*b*) Late Carboniferous (Pennsylvanian) Moscovian (or Desmoinesian) epochs with the seaway closed by the Ouachita-Appalachian-Hercynian orogeny and the land separation of a Tethys equatorial region from an eastern Panthalassa equatorial region.

Equator, and eustatic sea-level fluctuations became prominent in the sedimentary record. *See* GLACIAL EPOCH.

Sea-level changes. The sedimentary record of sea-level changes is well documented from the beginning of the latest Mississippian through the Pennsylvanian and into the Permian. These are cyclical sediments in which the succession of depositional facies is regularly repeated by each sea-level fluctuation. As a result, these depositional sequences have great lateral extent and continuity. Because local depositional conditions depended on many other, often unique circumstances, the sedimentary patterns have considerable lateral variation (**Fig. 4**). For example, the cyclical sediments near the Appalachian orogenic belt contain vast amounts of clastic debris, such as sands, silts, and gravels, which were transported and deposited in rivers, lakes, deltas, and coastal features. Many of these cycles are nonmarine or only marginally marine, and many are viewed as being more strongly influenced by changes in tectonic activity and climate. The suggestion is that the amount of clastic material was supplied mainly by erosion, and sedimentation responded only indirectly to sea-level fluctuations. In marine-dominated sequences, supratidal carbonates commonly passed upward into thin, fluvial and eolian beds that were usually reworked as debris into the succeeding basal marine transgressive beds. *See* DEPOSITIONAL SYSTEMS AND ENVIRONMENTS; FLUVIAL EROSION CYCLE.

Farther west (Fig. 4) at greater distances from the Appalachian orogenic belt, as in Ohio, many of these clastic-rich cyclic sediments intertongue with marine sediments, and the influence of sea-level fluctuations becomes increasingly evident. The Illinois-Kentucky basin has about equal representation of marine deposits and fluvial channels and delta deposits. Western Missouri and eastern Kansas were far enough away from the large influx of clastic materials to have predominantly marine sediments and minor amounts of nonmarine, mostly silt and fine sand clastics. Carbonate sedimentation dominated farther from sources of clastic sediments. Oceanic plateaus in the Paleotethys and Panthalassa ocean basins, which lacked influxes of clastic materials, have cyclical sediments that are entirely in various carbonate facies that reflect differences in water depth.

The fluctuations in sea level during the Carboniferous reflect different rates of sea-level change, different durations, and different magnitudes. Minor sea-level fluctuations of a meter or two (3–6 ft) with cyclicities of 20,000–40,000 years and intermediate fluctuations of 4–6 m (13–20 ft) with cyclicities of about 100,000 years may be preserved. More easily recognized are fluctuations of about 1–3 million years, which have amplitudes of 60–200 m (200–660 ft) [Fig. 2]. Late in the Mississippian and early in the Pennsylvanian, for an interval of approximately 15–20 million years, sea-level high-stands were consistently low and infrequently reached

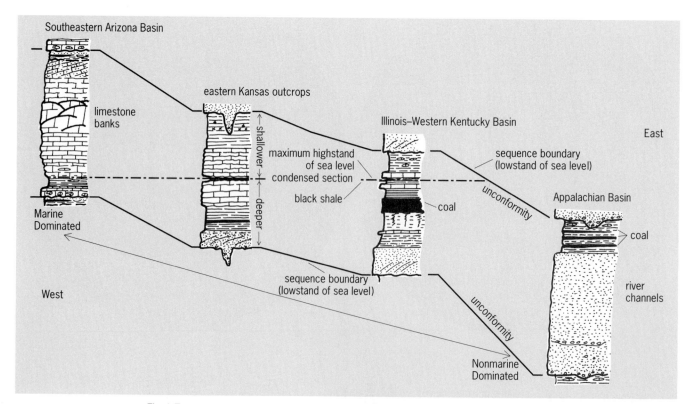

Fig. 4. Typical sedimentary patterns in Carboniferous depositional sequences. The broken line shows the condensed section that is present in three of the four types of depositional sequences and represents a maximum high stand of sea level. The prominent unconformity at the base of the nonmarine parts of the sequences in areas having well-developed fluvial beds becomes less pronounced in marine dominated sequences.

higher than the continental shelf margins (Fig. 4), a condition that was not repeated until quite late in the Permian Period. *See* CONTINENTAL MARGIN.

The sea-level fluctuations resulted in large areas of the cratonic shelves being frequently exposed to long intervals of weathering, erosion, and diagenesis. The effects of these exposure-related events suggest that within the Carboniferous climates were not uniform and that the events reflect changes in world climate as well as the continued northward motion of continents across latitudinal climatic belts as a result of plate tectonics and sea-floor spreading. *See* PALEOCLIMATOLOGY; SEDIMENTOLOGY; WEATHERING PROCESSES.

Life. During the Carboniferous, life evolved to exploit fully the numerous marine and nonmarine aquatic environments and terrestrial and aerial habitats. Single-cell protozoan foraminifers evolved new abilities to construct layered, calcareous walls and internally complex tests. These single-celled organisms diversified into nearly all shallow-water, carbonate-producing environments from the intertidal, lagoon, shelf, shelf margin, and upper parts (within the photic zone) of the shelf slope. Ammonoid cephalopods, from their first appearance in the later part of the Devonian, diversified rapidly during the Early Carboniferous, and their occurrences were used to establish one of the earliest biostratigraphic zonation schemes for the Lower Carboniferous. Brachiopods, bryozoans, and corals were also widespread and locally important parts of the marine faunas. The Tournaisian and Visean shallow tropical seas abounded in blastoid echinoderms; however, these creatures became nearly extinct and were geographically restricted to a small area in the eastern Panthalassa Ocean after the end of the Early Pennsylvanian (Morrowan). Conodonts were widespread in deeper-water deposits, where they have been used to establish a zonation for parts of the Lower and lower Upper Carboniferous.

Insects have one of the most remarkable evolutionary histories of the Carboniferous, during which they adapted to flight and dispersed into many habitats. Carboniferous insects include many unusual orders, such as one with three pairs of wings (although it is not clear that the foremost pair functioned directly in propulsion). By the Late Pennsylvanian, many large cockroachlike orders were present and also several huge dragonflylike groups, some of which reached wingspans of 90 cm (3 ft). Carboniferous insects included representatives of five Paleoptera orders (mayflies and dragonflylike orders) and at least six orthopterid (cockroachlike) orders. Insects are commonly preserved in coal swamp deposits and display the amazing diversity of life within these swamps. *See* INSECTA.

Vertebrates also evolved rapidly. Although acanthodian fish declined from their Devonian peak, sharklike fishes and primitive bony fishes adapted well to the expanded environments and the new ecological food chains of the Carboniferous. Some sharklike groups invaded fresh-water habitats, where they were associated with coal swamp deposits. For the bony fish (ray-finned fish and air-breathing choanate fishes with lobed fins), the Late Devonian and Carboniferous was a time of considerable evolutionary diversity and ecological expansion, with many lineages independently adapting to both fresh-water and marine conditions. One of the fresh-water choanate lineages was the rhipidistians, some of which evolved adaptations for survival in temporarily dry lakes and rivers. Near the Devonian-Carboniferous boundary, a lineage from these fish had evolved into the first amphibians. *See* VERTEBRATA.

Carboniferous amphibians evolved rapidly in several directions. The earliest were the labyrinthodont embolomeres, which had labyrinthodont teeth and were mainly aquatic. Another significant labyrinthodont group was the rhachitomes, which originated in the Early Carboniferous and became abundant, commonly reaching about 1 m (3 ft) or more; they were widespread in terrestrial habitats during the Late Carboniferous and Permian. Some of the Carboniferous amphibians reverted to totally aquatic habitats, such as the lepospondyls, which lost their bony vertebrae and limbs, had large flattened broad heads, and were snakelike in appearance. Ancestors of the present-day anurans (frogs), urodeles (salamanders), and caecilians (apodans) probably date from the later part of the Carboniferous, but their record as fossils is meager. *See* AMPHIBIA.

Primitive reptiles evolved from one of the embolomere amphibian lineages during the Late Carboniferous. They formed the basal stock from which all other reptiles have evolved. Although their Late Carboniferous history is incompletely recorded, they coexisted with several advanced amphibian groups which shared at least some, but probably not all, of their reptilelike characters. *See* REPTILIA.

Terrestrial plants also showed major diversification of habitats and the evolution of important new lineages during the Carboniferous. Initially, Early Carboniferous plants were predominantly a continuation of latest Devonian groups; however, they were distinguished in part by their large sizes with many arborescent lycopods and large articulates, and pteridosperms (seed ferns) and ferns became increasingly abundant and varied. By the Late Carboniferous, extensive swamps formed along the broad, nearly flat coastal areas; and these coal-forming environments tended to move laterally across the coastal plain areas as the sea level repeatedly rose. Other coal-forming marshes were common in the floodplains and channel fills of the broad rivers of upper delta distributary systems. During the Late Carboniferous primitive conifers appeared and included araucarias, which became common in some, probably drier ecological habitats. One of the features of Late Carboniferous plant paleogeographic distributions is the recognition of a southern, high-latitude Gondwanan floral province, the *Glossopteris* province, and a northern high-latitude Anagaran floral province, which were cool adapted. These provinces contrasted with an extensive equatorial belt of much greater plant diversity. *See* PALEOBOTANY; PALEOZOIC.   C. A. Ross

Bibliography. R. H. Dott, Jr., and D. R. Prothero, *Evolution of the Earth*, 5th ed., 1994; H. L. Levin, *The Earth Through Time*, 4th ed., 1994; A. L. Palmer (general ed.), Decade of North American Geology (DNAG) Project, *The Geology of North America*, Geological Society of America, 1986–1994; R. C. Moore et al., *The Kansas Rock Column*, State Geol. Surv. Kans. Bull. 89, 1951; C. A. Ross and J. R. P. Ross, *Late Paleozoic Sea Levels and Depositional Sequences and Biostratigraphic Zonation of Late Paleozoic Depositional Sequences*, Cushman Found. Foraminiferal Res. Spec. Publ. 24, 1987; H. R. Wanless and C. R. Wright, *Paleoenvironmental Maps of Pennsylvanian Rocks, Illinois Basin and Northern Midcontinent Region*, Geol. Soc. Amer. MC-23, 1978.

Carbonyl

A functional group found in organic compounds in which a carbon atom is doubly bonded to an oxygen atom:

$$\begin{matrix} X \\ \diagdown \\ C=O \\ \diagup \\ Y \end{matrix}$$

Depending upon the nature of the other groups attached to carbon, the most common compounds containing the carbonyl group are aldehydes (X and Y = H; X = H, Y = alkyl or aryl), ketones (X and Y = alkyl or aryl), carboxylic acids (X = OH, Y = H, alkyl, or aryl), esters (X = O-alkyl or aryl; Y = H, alkyl, or aryl), and amides (X = N—H, N-alkyl, or N-aryl; Y = H, alkyl, or aryl). Other compounds that contain the carbonyl group are acid halides, acid anhydrides, lactones, and lactams. *See* ACID ANHYDRIDE; ACID HALIDE; ALDEHYDE; AMIDE; ESTER; KETONE; LACTONE.

The direct introduction of the carbonyl group (carbonylation) has been accomplished by the reaction of alkenes with a mixture of carbon monoxide and hydrogen (synthesis gas) in the presence of metal carbonyls, of which the cobalt derivatives are the most important. This industrially important process, known as the oxo process, is shown in the reaction below. It is a principal

$$RCH=CH_2 + CO + H_2 \xrightarrow{CO_2(CO)_8} RH_2C-CH_2CH\overset{\displaystyle O}{\overset{\|}{}}$$

commercial source of straight-chain aldehydes.

Another mode of direct introduction is by the action of Grignard reagents with carbon dioxide, which produces carboxylic acids. Formally, this reaction is analogous to the fixation of carbon dioxide in plants to produce glucose and fructose and ultimately starch and cellulose. *See* CARBOXYLIC ACID; GRIGNARD REACTION.

Indirectly, the carbonyl group can be introduced by the oxidation of primary and secondary alcohols, the former a source of aldehydes and carboxylic acids, and the latter of ketones. The hydrolysis of organic cyanides is another source of carboxylic acids.

The presence of a carbonyl group in a molecule often leads to highly desirable properties of taste and odor. Thus a large number of flavoring and perfume components are carbonyl compounds. Familiar examples are oil of spearmint, oil of peppermint, oil of cloves, oil of vanilla, and camphor. *See* ESSENTIAL OILS.

Most of the important materials of nature, including fats and oils, steroids, proteins, many carbohydrates, and other such familiar compounds as caffeine, aspirin, and pencillin, contain the carbonyl group. *See* ASPIRIN; CAFFEINE; CARBOHYDRATE; FAT AND OIL; PROTEIN; STEROID.

Synthetic fibers such as nylon and Dacron, acrylic plastics and latexes, and many adhesives and paper finishes are polymeric materials containing carbonyl groups, principally of the amide and ester type. *See* MANUFACTURED FIBER; POLYMER.

All the compounds containing this functional group are referred to in a general way as carbonyl compounds. It is important, however, to distinguish these compounds from a large group formed from metals and carbon monoxide, which are known as metal carbonyls. In these latter compounds, there is only one group attached to the carbon in addition to the oxygen, and the carbon atom is viewed as triply bonded to the oxygen. *See* METAL CARBONYL.

Jeremiah P. Freeman

Bibliography. R. Fessenden and J. Fessenden, *Organic Chemistry*, 4th ed., 1990; R. T. Morrison and R. N. Boyd, *Organic Chemistry*, 6th ed., 1992; S. E. Patai and Z. Rappoport, *Chemistry of Enones and Related Compounds*, 1989.

Carborane

A cluster compound containing both carbon (C) and boron (B) atoms as well as hydrogen (H) atoms external to the framework of the cluster. A cluster compound is one with insufficient electrons to allow for classical two-center two-electron bonds between all adjacent atoms. Sometimes the term carborane is used as a synonym for *closo*-1,2-$C_2B_{10}H_{12}$, commonly referred to as *ortho*-carborane. Carboranes are of interest because of their nonclassical bonding, their relatively high thermal stability, and their ability, when containing the ^{10}B isotope, to capture neutrons efficiently. *See* BORANE.

Structure. The structures of carboranes are based upon a series of three-dimensional, cagelike geometric shapes possessing triangulated faces; such shapes are termed delta polyhedra. The structure for any given carborane may be predicted by determining the framework electrons, by determining the number of electrons involved in bonding the boron and carbon atoms of the cluster framework together, and by using Wade's rule. Wade's rule states that a cluster containing n framework electrons will be derived from a delta polyhedron containing $(n - 2)/2$ vertices, the parent cluster. Once this parent cluster has been determined, the geometry of the cluster framework may be predicted by clipping off vertices from the parent cluster until a polyhedron whose number of vertices is equivalent to the sum of boron and carbon atoms in the cluster framework is obtained.

Carboranes are placed, according to their structure, into several classifications. The most common classifications are closo (closed), nido (nestlike), and arachno (cobweb). If a carborane's framework structure is that of a closed delta polyhedron, the carborane is said to be a *closo*-carborane. If a carborane's framework structure is that of a closed delta polyhedron minus one or two vertices, the carborane is said to be a *nido*- or *arachno*-carborane, respectively.

The carborane *nido*-$C_2B_4H_8$ can be used as an example for predicting the structure of a carborane. The first step is to sum all the electrons for the compound: the eight valence electrons of the two carbon atoms (four each), the twelve valence electrons of the four boron atoms (three each), and the eight valence electrons of the eight hydrogen atoms (one each). There is then a total of twenty-eight valence electrons contained in *nido*-$C_2B_4H_8$. In the second step, the number of framework electrons is calculated, assuming that each carbon atom and each boron atom contains one bond to a hydrogen atom that is directed away from the center of the cluster, that is, a terminal hydrogen atom. For *nido*-$C_2B_4H_8$, six terminal hydrogen atoms are assumed. Then, since terminal hydrogen atoms are not involved in holding the cluster framework together, for each terminal hydrogen two electrons (the number of electrons involved in the bond between carbon or boron and the terminal hydrogen) are subtracted from the total number of valence electrons to obtain the number of cluster framework electrons—sixteen framework electrons for *nido*-$C_2B_4H_8$. Third, the number of vertices in the parent cluster can then be calculated by using Wade's formula, where $n = 16$, and the number of vertices = $(16 - 2)/2 = 7$. Therefore, the structure of *nido*-$C_2B_4H_8$ is derived from a seven-vertex delta polyhedron (see **Fig. 1**: seven vertices, closo column). However, since the sum of carbon and boron atoms in the cluster framework is only six, one of the vertices of the seven-vertex delta polyhedron must be removed. The result is a framework structure containing a plane of five atoms capped by one atom, a pentagonal pyramid (see Fig. 1: six vertices, nido column). The nonterminal hydrogen atoms are then distributed as bridging hydrogen atoms between boron atoms about the open face that resulted from the removal of the vertex from the parent

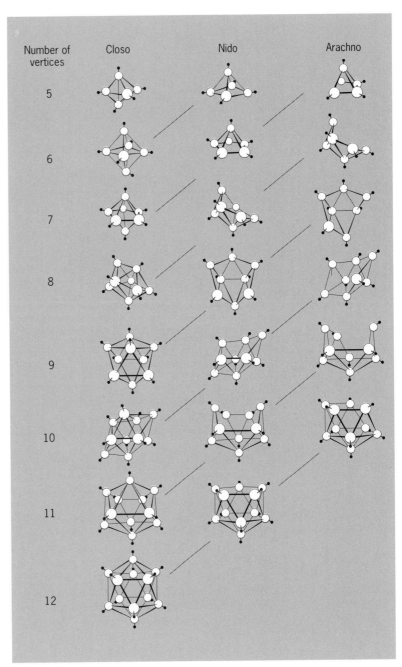

Fig. 1. Parent clusters from which carborane structures are determined. The diagonal lines define series of related closo, nido, and arachno structures.

cluster. The structures of other carboranes may be predicted in a similar manner.

Isomers. Since the framework structures of carboranes are based upon multivertex polyhedra, it might be expected that isomers exist in which the arrangement of the carbon and boron atoms within the cluster framework varies. Indeed, this type of isomerism is commonly observed. For carboranes containing two carbon atoms in the framework structure, dicarbon carboranes, the isomer with adjacent carbon atoms is frequently the one initially synthesized, although it is rarely, if ever, the thermodynamically preferred isomer. Typically, the thermodynamically preferred isomer in dicarbon carboranes is the one in which the

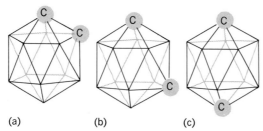

Fig. 2. Skeletal structures of the (a) 1,2-, (b) 1,7-, and (c) 1,12-isomers of C₂B₁₀H₁₂.

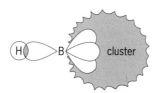

Fig. 3. Vertex boron atom with the three *sp³* orbitals that it employs in cluster bonding. The BH unit contributes three orbitals and only two electrons to the bonding that holds the cluster together (framework bonding).

carbon atoms have moved as far apart within the cluster as possible. Three isomers of *closo*-C₂B₁₀H₁₂ result from moving the carbons farther apart from one another (**Fig. 2**). *See* MOLECULAR ISOMERISM.

Numbering. The rules for numbering carboranes can be quite complicated; however, following is a brief explanation of the numbering employed here. The numbers directly preceding the carbon atoms in a formula indicate the numbers assigned to those carbon atoms. For example, in the formula *closo*-1,2-C₂B₁₀H₁₂ the 1 and 2 indicate that the carbon atoms have been assigned as atoms 1 and 2. A functional group immediately following a number in a formula indicates that the functional group is bound to the atom assigned that number. For example, in the formula *closo*-1-R-2-R′-1,2-C₂B₁₀H₁₀ the 1 preceding the functional group R indicates that it is bound to carbon 1, while the 2 preceding the functional group R′ indicates that it is bound to carbon 2. *See* STRUCTURAL CHEMISTRY.

Bonding. The bonding within a carborane can be thought of in terms of localized atomic orbitals forming both classical two-center two-electron bonds and nonclassical three-center two-electron bonds. Each vertex boron and carbon atom can be thought of as being *sp³* hybridized, with three of these hybrid orbitals of each vertex atom employed in framework bonding (**Fig. 3**). Employing this simple approach, the bonding within carboranes can be represented by employing resonance structures. For example, *nido*-C₂B₄H₈ exhibits three resonance structures (**Fig. 4**). The existence of resonance structures implies a delocalization of electron density throughout the cluster framework. Indeed, carboranes exhibit a high degree of electron density delocalization, and their bonding can be described more accurately by employing molecular orbital theory. *See* CHEMICAL BONDING; DELOCALIZATION; MOLECULAR ORBITAL THEORY; RESONANCE (MOLECULAR STRUCTURE).

Preparation. The typical synthesis of a carborane involves the reaction of a boron hydride cluster, containing only boron and hydrogen, with an alkyne. The resulting carborane contains two carbon atoms in its skeletal structure, a dicarbon carborane. The dicarbon carboranes, because of their relative ease of preparation, have been the most widely studied group of carboranes. In particular, *closo*-1,2-C₂B₁₀H₁₂, the most readily available carborane, has been extensively studied. Other common groups of carboranes include the monocarbon and tetracarbon carboranes. In order to illustrate the general synthetic routes to carboranes, the synthesis of several common mono-, di-, and tetracarbon carboranes are described below. *See* ALKYNE.

Monocarbon carboranes. There are two common routes to the monocarbon carboranes. One involves the incorporation of the carbon atom of [B₁₀H₁₃CN]²⁻ into the skeletal structure [reaction (1)], and the other involves the degradation of [*nido*-7,9-C₂B₁₀H₁₃]⁻ [reactions (2) and (3)].

$$B_{10}H_{14} + 2NaCN \xrightarrow{-HCN} Na_2B_{10}H_{13}CN \xrightarrow{H^+}$$

$$B_{10}C(NH_3)H_{12} \xrightarrow{(CH_3)_2SO_4} \xrightarrow[2.\ H_2O]{1.\ Na} [CB_{10}H_{13}]^- \quad (1)$$

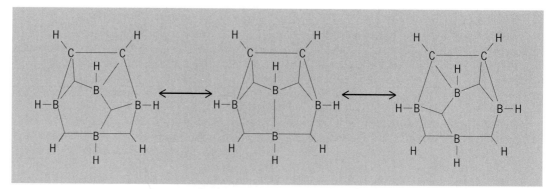

Fig. 4. Three resonance structures of *nido*-C₂B₄H₈.

$$[C_2B_{10}H_{13}]^- \xrightarrow[N(CH_3)_3]{C_4H_8O_{(aq)}}$$

$$9\text{-}CH_3\text{-}8\text{-}(CH_3)_3N\text{-}arachno\text{-}6\text{-}CB_9H_{12} \xrightarrow[K_2CO_3]{(CH_3)_2CO}$$

$$9\text{-}CH_3\text{-}8\text{-}(CH_3)_3N\text{-}nido\text{-}6\text{-}CB_9H_{10} \quad (2)$$

$$[C_2B_{10}H_{13}]^- \xrightarrow[(CH_3)_2S]{H_3O^+} \xrightarrow{[BH_4]^-} [CB_9H_{12}]^- \quad (3)$$

Dicarbon carboranes. The most common carboranes are the twelve-vertex carboranes, *closo*-1,2-$C_2B_{10}H_{12}$ and its carbon-substituted derivatives. They are readily prepared by the reaction of acteylene or substituted alkynes with compounds of the form $B_{10}H_{12}L_2$ [where L = CH_3CN or $(CH_3CH_2)_2S$]. Such adducts are readily obtained by the reaction of the appropriate Lewis base with decaborane (14), $B_{10}H_{14}$ [reaction (4)]. Yields of the *closo*-twelve-

$$B_{10}H_{14} + 2L \xrightarrow{-H_2}$$

$$B_{10}H_{12}L_2 \xrightarrow{RC{\equiv}CR'} 1\text{-}R\text{-}2\text{-}R'\text{-}1,2\text{-}C_2B_{10}H_{10} \quad (4)$$

vertex carboranes depend upon the substituents R and R′ of the alkyne. With R = R′ = H, the yield is typically about 60%. The substituents R and R′ can be any number of functional groups, including acetoxy, alkoxy, alkyl, aryl, carboranyl, dimethylaminomethyl, halomethyl, and olefin. In all these syntheses, the 1,2-isomers of the corresponding carboranes are obtained.

Another readily prepared class of dicarbon carboranes are the ten-vertex carboranes, *nido*-$C_2B_8H_{12}$ and *closo*-$C_2B_8H_{10}$ and their carbon-substituted derivatives. A convenient method for the preparation of carbon-substituted derivatives, *nido*-5,6-R,R′-5,6-$C_2B_8H_{10}$, is the reaction of the appropriately substituted alkyne with $B_9H_{13}\cdot O(C_2H_5)_2$ as in reaction (5). The reaction proceeds with the

$$B_9H_{13} \cdot O(C_2H_5)_2 \xrightarrow[-B(CR{=}CR'H)_3]{4RC{\equiv}CR'}$$

$$nido\text{-}5,6\text{-}R,R'\text{-}5,6\text{-}C_2B_8H_{10} \quad (5)$$

displacement of the $(C_2H_5)_2O$ and the abstraction (removal) of a BH_3 unit, by excess alkyne, from $B_9H_{13}\cdot O(C_2H_5)_2$. The unsubstituted *nido*-5,6-$C_2B_8H_{12}$ is most readily prepared by the aqueous iron(III) chloride oxidation of [*nido*-7,8-$C_2B_9H_{12}$]⁻. The *nido*-5,6-$C_2B_8H_{12}$ obtained by this procedure can then, if desired, be converted to *closo*-1,10-$C_2B_8H_{10}$ by vacuum pyrolysis at 525°C (977°F).

The *nido*-six-vertex carboranes, *nido*-2,3-R_2-2,3-$C_2B_4H_6$, further serve to exemplify the preparation

of dicarbon carboranes. This class of carboranes is readily prepared by the reaction of pentaborane with triethylamine and the appropriate alkyne. Carboranes with the functional groups CH_3, C_2H_5, C_3H_7, or $Si(CH_3)_3$ are readily prepared via this method.

Tetracarbon carboranes. The tetracarbon carboranes are unusual in that their structures are not that of a regular delta polyhedron. Instead they are twelve-vertex clusters that possess two square and sixteen triangular faces (**Fig. 5**). The carboranes 2,3,7,8-R_4-2,3,7,8-$C_4B_8H_8$ are prepared by the oxidative fusion of two 2,3-R_2-2,3-$C_2B_4H_4$ fragments from the metallacarboranes $[R_2C_2B_4H_4]_2FeH_2$, where R = CH_3, C_2H_5, C_3H_7. These tetracarbon carboranes have cluster framework structures (Fig. 5).

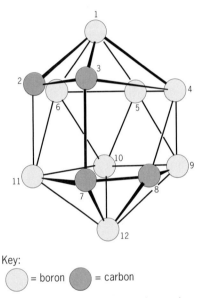

Key:

= boron   = carbon

Fig. 5. Skeletal structures of the tetracarbon carboranes, $R_4C_4B_8H_8$.

Chemistry. The chemistry of *closo*-1,2-$C_2B_{10}H_{12}$ and carboranes derived from it provides a reasonable representation of the entire class of carboranes. The most commonly exploited reaction of *closo*-1,2-$C_2B_{10}H_{12}$ is the deprotonation (removal of hydrogen) of its carbon atoms by a lithium alkyl group. Depending on the stoichiometry of the lithium alkyl employed, either one or both of the carbon atoms may be deprotonated [reactions (6) and (7), where BuLi is the lithium alkyl].The result-

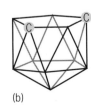
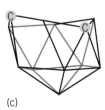

(a)   (b)   (c)   (d)

Fig. 6. Skeletal structures. (a) [*nido*-7,8-$C_2B_9H_{12}$]⁻. (b) [*nido*-7,9-$C_2B_9H_{12}$]⁻. (c) [*nido*-$C_2B_{10}H_{12}$]²⁻ anions. (d) $(C_2B_9H_{11})_2M^{N-4}$ complexes, where N = oxidation state of the metal.

$$1,2\text{-}C_2B_{10}H_{12} + BuLi \longrightarrow 1\text{-}Li\text{-}1,2\text{-}C_2B_{10}H_{11} + butane \qquad (6)$$

$$1,2\text{-}C_2B_{10}H_{12} + BuLi \longrightarrow$$
$$1,2\text{-}Li_2\text{-}1,2\text{-}C_2B_{10}H_{10} + 2\,butane \qquad (7)$$

ing lithiated carboranes can then be employed as nucleophiles in a variety of organic reactions.

Closo-1,2-$C_2B_{10}H_{12}$ is thermally robust, that is, not easily degraded by heat, and is isomerized to *closo*-1,7-$C_2B_{10}H_{12}$ upon heating to $450°C$ ($842°F$) under an atmosphere of nitrogen or argon. Even upon heating to $500°C$ ($932°F$) under an atmosphere of nitrogen or argon, no decomposition is observed. However, upon heating to $600°C$ ($1112°F$), significant decomposition occurs and rearrangement to *closo*-1,12-$C_2B_{10}H_{12}$ is observed, the *closo*-1,12-$C_2B_{10}H_{12}$ being obtained in low yield. These twelve-vertex carboranes are very resistant to degradation by acid. However, both *closo*-1,2-$C_2B_{10}H_{12}$ and *closo*-1,7-$C_2B_{10}H_{12}$ are degraded by strong bases such as methoxide, resulting in the removal of a BH vertex that is adjacent to both carbon atoms. This base degradation results in the formation of the isomeric [*nido*-7,8-$C_2B_9H_{12}$]$^-$ and [*nido*-7,9-$C_2B_9H_{12}$]$^-$ anions from the 1,2- and 1,7-isomers, respectively (**Fig. 6***a–b*).

The two-electron reduction of a *closo*-carborane results in an opening of the cluster framework and the formation of a *nido*-carborane. This type of reductive opening of a cluster is observed when *closo*-1,2-$C_2B_{10}H_{12}$ reacts with sodium metal in solution to form [*nido*-$C_2B_{10}H_{12}$]$^{2-}$ [Fig. 6*c*].

One unique feature of carboranes is the ability of those with open faces to incorporate a wide variety of atomic groups into vertex positions. Anions of such carboranes are readily capped by a variety of atomic groups representing many of the elements of the periodic table. Additionally, an atom may be sandwiched between two *nido*-carborane anions; such structures are known as sandwich compounds (Fig. 6*d*).　　　　　Thomas D. Getman

Bibliography. R. N. Grimes, *Carboranes*, 1970; J. Plesek, Potential applications of the boron cluster compounds, *Chem. Rev.*, 92:269–278, 1992; B. Stibr, Carboranes other than $C_2B_{10}H_{12}$, *Chem. Rev.*, 92:225–250, 1992; R. E. Williams, The polyborane, carborane, carbocation continuum: Architectural patterns, *Chem. Rev.*, 92:177–207, 1992.

Carboxylic acid

One of a large family of organic substances widely distributed in nature, and characterized by the presence of one or more carboxyl groups (—COOH). These groups typically yield protons in aqueous solution. *See* ACID AND BASE.

In the type formula, R(CXY)$_n$COOH, symbols R, X, and Y can be hydrogen, saturated, or unsaturated groups, carboxyl, alicyclic, or aromatic groups, halogens, or other substituents, and *n* may vary from zero (formic acid, HCOOH) to more than 100, provided that the normal carbon

covalence of four is maintained.

Nomenclature and general properties. According to the International Union of Pure and Applied Chemistry, an acid is named by its relation to the parent hydrocarbon, but in common practice trivial names are used often to indicate the origin of the substance. Thus HCOOH, formic acid (from Latin *formica*, ant), is properly methanoic acid, and $CH_3(CH_2)_7COOH$, pelargonic acid, from the leaves of *Pelargonium roseum*, is nonanoic acid. Substituents are located numerically on the carbon chain, counting the carboxylic carbon as 1, but an older, common method uses Greek letters, beginning with the carbon adjacent to the carboxyl. The following exemplifies both systems:

$$\overset{\epsilon}{\underset{6}{CH_2OH}}\overset{\delta}{\underset{5}{CH_2}}\overset{\gamma}{\underset{4}{CHBr}}\overset{\beta}{\underset{3}{CHBr}}\overset{\alpha}{\underset{2}{CH_2}}\underset{1}{COOH}$$

is 3,4-dibromo-6-hydroxyhexanoic acid, or β,γ-dibromo-ϵ-hydroxycaproic acid. *See* ORGANIC CHEMISTRY.

Physical and chemical properties of carboxylic acids are represented, grossly, by the resultant of the various chemical groupings present in the molecule. A short-chain aliphatic acid, wherein the carboxyl is dominant, is a pungent, corrosive, water-soluble liquid of abnormally high boiling point (because of molecular association), with specific gravity close to 1 (higher for formic and acetic acids). With increasing molecular weight, the hydrocarbon grouping overbalances the carboxyl; sharpness of odor diminishes, boiling and melting points rise, the specific gravity falls toward that of the parent hydrocarbon, and the water-solubility decreases. Thus the typical high-molecular-weight saturated acid is a bland, waxlike solid.

Ionization and acidity. Ionization occurs on exposure to a proton acceptor (base, in the Brønsted-Lowry sense); in water the opposing equations shown in reaction (1) describe the fundamental

$$R(CXY)_nCOOH + H_2O \rightleftharpoons R(CXY)_nCOO^- + H_3O^+ \qquad (1)$$

equilibrium encountered with any feebly ionized, or weak, acid. Hydration of the proton to form H_3O^+ is virtually complete; thus, the process of ionization is analogous to that of neutralization, the degree to which ionization proceeds varying directly with the basicity of the solvent (proton acceptor), and inversely with the O-H bond strength of the carboxylic hydroxyl group.

The above equilibrium leads to the dissociation constant K_a defined as reaction (2), wherein the

$$K_a = \frac{[H_3O^+][R(CXY)_nCOO^-]}{[R(CXY)_nCOOH]} \qquad (2)$$

square brackets signify concentration, measured in moles per liter of solution. With simple, saturated acids, wherein X and Y are hydrogen, the value of K_a is always small (acetic acid, 1.75×10^{-5}), which means that simple organic acids are only slightly ionized in aqueous solution. However, the degree of dissociation is sensitive to electronegative (electron-attracting) substituents, particularly when located on the α- or 2-carbon (for example, K_a for trichloroacetic acid, 1.3×10^{-1}). *See* IONIC EQUILIBRIUM.

Table 1 presents a list of 30 saturated, monocarboxylic acids, together with their important constants and main sources.

Structure and properties. The un-ionized carboxyl group has been shown via many classical studies to have the structure

$$R - \underset{1}{C} - \underset{2}{C} \overset{\displaystyle \overset{O}{\underset{1}{\|}}}{\underset{\underset{2}{O} - H}{}}$$

in which carbon 2 is doubly bonded to oxygen 1 and singly bonded to oxygen 2. Geometrical considerations lead to the conclusions that distance

$$\underset{2}{C} = \underset{1}{O}$$

should be shorter than

$$\underset{2}{C} - \underset{2}{O}$$

and the angle

$$\underset{1}{C} - \underset{2}{C} = \underset{1}{O}$$

should be greater than angle

$$\underset{1}{C} - \underset{2}{C} - \underset{2}{O}$$

This is confirmed by measurements on crystalline acids, although the fact that the single bond

$$\underset{2}{C} - \underset{2}{O}$$

never reaches the normal length (about 0.144 nm) means that some resonance is involved between the two forms

$$R - C \overset{\displaystyle O}{\underset{\displaystyle O - H}{}} \qquad R - C \overset{\displaystyle O^{-}}{\underset{\displaystyle \underset{+}{O - H}}{}}$$

In the ionized state, however, the two resonating forms of the anion are electronically equivalent,

$$R - C \overset{\displaystyle O}{\underset{\displaystyle O^{-}}{}} \qquad R - C \overset{\displaystyle O^{-}}{\underset{\displaystyle O}{}}$$

TABLE 1. Saturated monocarboxylic acids

Name	Formula	Main source*	Melting point, °C (°F)	Boiling point, °C (°F)
Formic	HCOOH	S	8.4 (47.1)	100.5 (212.9)
Acetic	CH_3COOH	S and fermentation	16.7 (62.1)	118.1 (244.6)
Propionic	CH_3CH_2COOH	S	−22.0 (−7.6)	141.0 (285.8)
Butyric	$CH_3(CH_2)_2COOH$	F, S, and ferm.	−4.7 (23.5)	164.1 (327.4)
Valeric	$CH_3(CH_2)_3COOH$	S and *Valeriana officinalls*	−34.5 (−30.1)	186.4 (367.5)
Isovaleric	$(CH_3)_2CHCH_2COOH$	F and S	−29.3 (−20.7)	176.5 (349.7)
Caproic	$CH_3(CH_2)_4COOH$	F and S and by-product in butyric fermentation	−1.5 (29.3)	205.8 (442.4)
Heptanoic	$CH_3(CH_2)_5COOH$	S from heptaldehyde	−7.5 (18.5)	223.0 (433.4)
Caprylic	$CH_3(CH_2)_6COOH$	F and S; goat's butter	16.3 (61.3)	239.7 (463.5)
Pelargonic	$CH_3(CH_2)_7COOH$	S; oxidation of oleic and *Pelargonium roseum*	12.5 (54.5)	255.6 (492.1)
Capric	$CH_3(CH_2)_8COOH$	F; coconut; palm kernel oils	31.5 (88.7)	268.7 (515.7)
Undecylic	$CH_3(CH_2)_9COOH$	S; reduction of undecenoic acid	29.3 (84.7)	228 (442)/21 kPa
Lauric	$CH_3(CH_2)_{10}COOH$	F; coconut and laurel oils	44.1 (111.4)	225 (437)/13 kPa
Tridecylic	$CH_3(CH_2)_{11}COOH$	S	41.0 (105.8)	236 (457)/13 kPa
Myristic	$CH_3(CH_2)_{12}COOH$	F; nutmeg oil	58.0 (136.4)	250 (482)/13 kPa
Pentadecylic	$CH_3(CH_2)_{13}COOH$	S	54.0 (129.2)	257 (495)/13 kPa
Palmitic	$CH_3(CH_2)_{14}COOH$	F; palm and olive oils	62.8 (145.0)	271.5 (520.7)/13 kPa
Margaric	$CH_3(CH_2)_{15}COOH$	S	59.9 (139.8)	227 (441)/13 kPa
Stearic	$CH_3(CH_2)_{16}COOH$	F; tallow and reduction of oleic acid	69.9 (157.8)	291 (556)/15 kPa
Nonadecylic	$CH_3(CH_2)_{17}COOH$	S	66.5 (151.7)	298 (568)/13 kPa
Arachidic	$CH_3(CH_2)_{18}COOH$	F; peanut oil	77.0 (170.6)	205 (401)/130 Pa
Heneicosanoic	$CH_3(CH_2)_{19}COOH$	S	75.2 (167.4)	
Behenic	$CH_3(CH_2)_{20}COOH$	F; reduction of erucic acid	80.2 (176.3)	306 (583)/8 kPa
Tricosanoic	$CH_3(CH_2)_{21}COOH$	S	79.1 (174.4)	
Lignoceric	$CH_3(CH_2)_{22}COOH$	F; *Adenanthera pavonina* seed; beechwood tar; rotten oak	84.2 (183.6)	
Pentacosanoic	$CH_3(CH_2)_{23}COOH$	S	83.0 (181.4)	
Cerotic	$CH_3(CH_2)_{24}COOH$	Beeswax; carnauba wax	87.7 (189.9)	
Heptacosanoic	$CH_3(CH_2)_{25}COOH$	S	87.6 (189.7)	
Montanic	$CH_3(CH_2)_{26}COOH$	Montan wax from lignite	90.9 (195.6)	
Nonacosanoic	$CH_3(CH_2)_{27}COOH$	S	90.3 (194.5)	
Melissic	$CH_3(CH_2)_{28}COOH$	Beeswax	93.6 (200.5)	

*S stands for synthetic, meaning that the acid is manufactured commercially by one or more methods. F stands for fats; the fatty acids comprise a group of carboxylic acids, both saturated and unsaturated, which may be obtained by hydrolysis of animal or vegetable fats and oils.

TABLE 2. Dicarboxylic, aromatic, and unsaturated acids

Name	Formula	Melting point, °C (°F)*	Boiling point, °C (°F)*
Dicarboxylic acids			
Oxalic	HOOC—COOH	189.5 (373.1) (dec)	
Malonic	$CH_2(COOH)_2$	135 (275) (dec)	
Succinic	$(CH_2)_2(COOH)_2$	185–187 (365–369)	235 (455)
Glutaric	$(CH_2)_3(COOH)_2$	98.0 (208)	302–304 (576–579)
Adipic	$(CH_2)_4(COOH)_2$	152 (306)	337.5 (639.5)
Pimelic	$(CH_2)_5(COOH)_2$	105–107 (221–225) (subl)	272 (522) at 13 kPa
Suberic	$(CH_2)_6(COOH)_2$	142 (288)	279 (534) at 13 kPa
Azelaic	$(CH_2)_7(COOH)_2$	106.5 (223.7)	286 (547) at 13 kPa
Sebacic	$(CH_2)_8(COOH)_2$	134 (273)	295 (563) at 13 kPa
Aromatic acids			
Benzoic	C_6H_5COOH	121.7 (251.1)	249 (480)
o-Toluic	$o\text{-}CH_3C_6H_4COOH$	104 (219)	259 (498) at 100 kPa
m-Toluic	$m\text{-}CH_3C_6H_4COOH$	111 (232)	263 (505)
p-Toluic	$p\text{-}CH_3C_6H_4COOH$	180 (356)	275 (527)
o-Ethylbenzoic	$o\text{-}C_2H_5C_6H_4COOH$	68 (154)	259 (498) at 100 kPa
m-Ethylbenzoic	$m\text{-}C_2H_5C_6H_4COOH$	47 (117)	
p-Ethylbenzoic	$p\text{-}C_2H_5C_6H_4COOH$	113 (235)	
o-Fluorobenzoic	$o\text{-}FC_6H_4COOH$	122 (252)	
m-Fluorobenzoic	$m\text{-}FC_6H_4COOH$	124 (255)	
p-Fluorobenzoic	$p\text{-}FC_6H_4COOH$	182–184 (360–363)	
o-Chlorobenzoic	$o\text{-}ClC_6H_4COOH$	140.2 (284.4)	
m-Chlorobenzoic	$m\text{-}ClC_6H_4COOH$	154.3 (309.7)	
p-Chlorobenzoic	$p\text{-}ClC_6H_4COOH$	239.7 (463.5)	Subl
o-Bromobenzoic	$o\text{-}BrC_6H_4COOH$	148–150 (298–302)	Subl
m-Bromobenzoic	$m\text{-}BrC_6H_4COOH$	154–155 (309–311)	
p-Bromobenzoic	$p\text{-}BrC_6H_4COOH$	251–253 (484–487)	
o-Iodobenzoic	$o\text{-}IC_6H_4COOH$	162 (324)	
o-Iodobenzoic	$o\text{-}IC_6H_4COOH$	162 (324)	
m-Iodobenzoic	$m\text{-}IC_6H_4COOH$	187 (367)	Subl
p-Iodobenzoic	$p\text{-}IC_6H_4COOH$	270 (518)	Subl
Salicylic	$o\text{-}HOC_6H_4COOH$	158.3 (316.9)	211 (412) at 2.7 kPa
m-Hydroxybenzoic	$m\text{-}HOC_6H_4COOH$	201 (394)	
p-Hydroxybenzoic	$p\text{-}HOC_6H_4COOH$	215 (419)	
Gallic	$3,4,5\text{-}(HO)_3C_6H_4COOH$	235 (455) (dec)	
Anthranilic	$o\text{-}H_2NC_6H_4COOH$	144–145 (291–293)	Subl
m-Anthranilic	$m\text{-}H_2NC_6H_4COOH$	173–174 (343–345)	
p-Anthranilic	$p\text{-}H_2NC_6H_4COOH$	187–188 (369–370)	
α-Naphthoic	$\alpha\text{-}C_{10}H_7COOH$	160–161 (320–322)	300 (572)
β-Naphthoic	$\beta\text{-}C_{10}H_7COOH$	184 (363)	>300 (572)
Unsaturated acids			
Acrylic	$CH_2{=}CH{-}COOH$	14 (57)	141
Crotonic (trans)	$CH_3CH{=}CHCOOH$	71.6 (161)	
i-Crotonic (cis)		15.5 (59.9)	185
Mesaconic (trans)	$HOOCC{=}CHCOOH$, with CH_3	202 (396)	
Citraconic (cis)		91 (196)	250 (482) (dec)
Tiglic (trans)	$CH_3CH{=}CCOOH$, with CH_3	64 (147)	198 (388)
Angelic (cis)		45 (133)	185 (365)
Cinnamic (trans)	$C_6H_5CH{=}CHCOOH$	133 (271)	300 (572)
Allocinnamic (cis)		68 (154)	125 (257) at 2.4 kPa
Fumaric (trans)	$HOOCCH{=}CHCOOH$	287 (549)	
Maleic (cis)		130 (266)	
Elaidic (trans)	$CH_3(CH_2)_7CH{=}$ $HOOC(CH_2)_7CH$	44 (111)	288 (550) at 13 kPa
Oleic (cis)		13 (55)	288 (550) at 13 kPa

*dec = decomposes, subl = sublimes.

and the actual structure of the carboxylate ion is a stable hybrid of these. *See* RESONANCE (MOLECULAR STRUCTURE).

In the free state (solid, liquid, or gas), the lower acids tend to exist as dimers, in which two molecules are associated through relatively weak hydrogen bonds (the energy is about 5 kcal/mole):

$$R-C\underset{O-H\cdots O}{\overset{O\cdots H-O}{<}}\underset{}{>}C-R$$

The hydrogen bonds (indicated by dotted valences) account for the abnormally high boiling points of the smaller acids. With longer-chain acids (from C_8) there is a tendency toward polymorphism, ascribable to hydrogen bonding of the following type:

$$R-C\overset{O}{\underset{O-H\cdots O=C}{<}}\overset{R}{\underset{O-H}{>}}$$

As determined by x-ray diffraction studies, the carboxyl and terminal methyl groups of acids containing an odd number of carbons are on the same side of the molecule; with acids containing an even number of carbons, these groups are on opposite sides, permitting closer packing in the crystal lattice and consequent increased van der Waals forces. Thus, the melting point of any even-numbered acid lies above that of the preceding and following odd-numbered acid.

Structural variations. These are of two types: those not involving the carboxyl group, and those involving the carboxyl, leading to the acid derivatives.

In the first type are such distinctive classes as branched-chain acids, for example, pivalic acid, $(CH_3)_3CCOOH$; alicyclic acids, for example, cyclopropane carboxylic acid,

$$H_2C\overset{\overset{H_2}{C}}{-}\underset{H}{\overset{}{C}}-COOH$$

halogenated acids, fluoro, chloro, or bromo, rarely, iodo; hydroxy acids (*see* LACTONE; TARTARIC ACID); dicarboxylic and polycarboxylic acids; aromatic acids .(*see* BENZOIC ACID); β-keto acids or amino acids (*see* AMINO ACIDS; LACTAM; PROTEIN).

An important class of acids contains unsaturated groups, for example, acrylic acid ($CH_2{=}CHCOOH$). Acids of this type are unstable and polymerize readily; hence they and their esters are much studied. *See* POLYACRYLATE RESIN.

Among the variations involving the carboxyl group are found many important classes of substances, derived from acids by suitable substitution within the carboxylic group. Thus, replacement of the hydroxyl group with alkoxyl gives esters (*see* ESTER; FAT AND OIL; WAX, ANIMAL AND VEGETABLE); replacement of OH by halogen forms acid halides (*see* ACID HALIDE; ACYLATION); substitution of OH by amino (NH_2) group gives amides (*see* AMIDE; UREA); intermolecular dehydration of two acids generates the anhydride structure

$$\underset{}{R}-\overset{O}{\overset{\|}{C}}-O-\overset{O}{\overset{\|}{C}}-R$$

(*see* ACID ANHYDRIDE); the hydrolysis of long-chain esters by alkali hydroxides forms soaps. *See also* DETERGENT; SOAP.

Table 2 lists some important dicarboxylic acids, aromatic acids, and unsaturated acids, together with their important physical constants.

Reactions and uses. Acids are used in large quantities in the production of esters, acid halides, acid amides, and acid anhydrides. Decarboxylation of acids to form hydrocarbons containing one less carbon is accomplished by pyrolyzing the sodium or barium salt with soda lime. If the potassium salt is electrolyzed at a platinum anode (Kolbe electrolysis), the hydrocarbon RCH_2CH_2R is produced by the acid $RCH_2COO^-K^+$. Ethylenic and acetylenic acids containing unsaturation α,β to the carboxyl are easily decarboxylated by heat. Aromatic acids, such as benzoic and toluic, are frequently used as sources of hydrocarbons; the decarboxylation is effected by treating the acid in boiling quinoline with a copper powder catalyst.

Many acids obtained by acid hydrolysis of fats or waxes are reduced to the corresponding alcohols, for example, lauric acid to lauryl alcohol. The reaction is carried out in the laboratory by means of lithium aluminum hydride; the industrial procedure utilizes hydrogen at elevated temperatures, over a mixed catalyst of the oxides of copper and chromium.

Acids find use in the manufacture of soaps and detergents, in thickening lubricating greases (stearate soaps), in modifying rigidity in plastics, in compounding buffing bricks and abrasives, and in the manufacture of crayons, dictaphone cylinders, and phonograph records. The solvent action of acids finds use in manufacture of carbon paper, inks, and in the compounding of synthetic and natural rubber. Because of the stability of saturated fatty acids toward oxidation, these are often used as solvents for carrying out oxidation reactions upon the sensitive compounds.   Evans B. Reid

Carburetor

The device that controls the power output and fuel feed of internal combustion spark-ignition engines generally used for automotive, aircraft, and auxiliary services. Its duties include control of the engine power by the air throttle; metering, delivery, and mixing of fuel in the airstream; and graduating the fuel-air ratio according to engine requirements in starting, idling, and load and altitude changes. The fuel is usually gasoline or similar liquid hydrocarbon compounds, although some engines with a carburetor may also operate on a gaseous fuel such as propane or compressed natural gas. A carburetor may be classified as having either a fixed venturi, in which the diameter of the air opening ahead of the throttle valve remains constant, or a variable venturi, which changes area to meet the changing demand. *See* AUTOMOBILE; ENGINE; FUEL SYSTEM; VENTURI TUBE.

Engine air charge. A simple updraft carburetor with a fixed venturi illustrates basic carburetor action (**Fig. 1**). Intake air charge, at full or reduced atmospheric pressure as controlled by the throttle, is drawn into the cylinder by the downward motion of the piston to mix with the unscavenged exhaust remaining in the cylinder from the previous combustion. The total air-charge weight per unit time is approximately proportional to the square root of its pressure drop in the carburetor venturi (with a square-root correction, direct for change in air pressure, and inverse for change in air absolute temperature). Also, each individual cylinder air-charge volume follows the intake pressure minus about one-sixth the exhaust pressure, so that the intake manifold pressure and temperature are often taken as an approximate indication of the engine torque; this factor multiplied by the engine speed is similarly taken as a measure of the engine power output. Any given fixed part-throttle opening gives higher intake manifold pressure, increased individual-cylinder air charge, and greater engine torque, as the engine speed is decreased. *See* TORQUE.

A cylinder is most completely filled with the fuel-air mixture when no other cylinder is drawing in through the same intake passage at the same time. For high speed, best power is usually obtained with multiple carburetor and intake passages. However, on an engine so equipped, it is often difficult to throttle all the cylinders equally. *See* VOLUMETRIC EFFICIENCY.

Fuel charge. The fuel is usually metered through a calibrated orifice, or jet, at a differential pressure derived from the pressure drop in a venturi in the intake air passage. Since this fuel flow also follows the square root of its differential pressure, the fuel and air rates tend to be accurately parallel, particularly if a small bleed of air is fed into the fuel

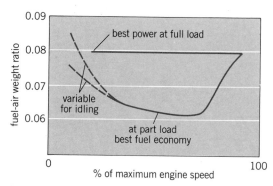

Fig. 2. Fuel-air ratios required for engine operation.

delivery or spray nozzle to overcome the retarding effect of surface tension.

Fuel-air requirements. For normal steady speed, the limits of consistent ignition lie between 0.055 and 0.09 fuel-air by weight (**Fig. 2**). Richer mixtures (more fuel) give higher power, apparently cooler combustion, and less detonation. Leaner mixtures (less fuel) give better fuel economy. *See* COMBUSTION; COMBUSTION CHAMBER.

A narrowly controlled rich mixture is required for idling because low charge densities and relatively high contamination with residual exhaust gas make combustion conditions unfavorable. Individual adjustments may be provided both for the idling fuel feed and for the throttle closure stop to keep the engine running at minimum speed. Slight intake or exhaust valve leaks can make smooth idling impossible.

Cold-engine operation. Engine fuels are a mixture of components varying in volatility, usually selected so that they evaporate completely in the intake manifold at ordinary operating temperatures at the reduced pressures of part throttle, but not at full throttle. For starting at low temperatures and for the first few ignitions with cylinder walls cold, a great increase in fuel feed is momentarily required since only the most volatile part of the fuel can vaporize and burn. *See* GASOLINE.

The higher metering suction necessary to give the excess fuel feed required for cold starting may be created by a manually or automatically operated choke valve. Partial closure of this valve also yields the moderate enrichment needed during warmup. An additional linkage is generally supplied on automotive carburetors so that pressing the accelerator pedal all the way down will open the choke valve and permit return to normal fuel feed.

Automotive carburetion. An automotive engine performs through a wider range of loads and speeds than most prime movers. Furthermore, its transient response to changes of load is highly important. For these reasons, the functions of an automotive carburetor are complex. The multiple main and boost venturi structure is used to increase the fuel metering force for a given air delivery; also, it yields better metering regulation at the higher air velocities.

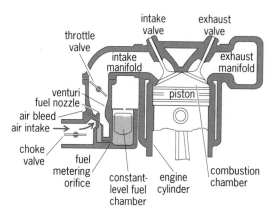

Fig. 1. Elements that basically determine air and fuel charges received by the engine through the carburetor.

Idling system. To obtain adequate metering forces at low air speeds and small throttle openings, the fuel passes through the main metering jet and is bypassed to an idle metering jet. Then the fuel mixes with air bled in through the idle air bleed, and this fuel and air are delivered to an idle port in the high suction at the edge of the throttle valve. Some graduation of fuel feed from low to high idling speed is obtained as the throttle valve edge passes across the idle port, which may include multiple delivery holes.

Because of increased piston and other friction with a cold engine, a greater throttle opening as well as more fuel is required for idle at that time. The choke valve is usually interconnected so that, in its partly closed or cold-engine position, the minimum-throttle area is increased.

Power enrichment. The richer fuel feeds necessary for best power are customarily obtained by varying the area of the main metering jet, using a valve responsive to intake manifold pressure beyond the throttle. At light loads the lowered manifold pressure draws the enrichment valve down. A rise in manifold pressure resulting either from a drop in engine speed or added throttle opening will allow the plunger spring to open the metering jet further. An approximation of this function is obtained in some carburetors by mechanical linkage between the enrichment valve and the throttle valve. On most carbureted automotive engines with a catalytic converter, the enrichment valve is computer controlled to help maintain stoichiometry.

Transitional requirements. Proper regulation under change of throttle is a major problem in obtaining good carburetor action. Any lag in evaporation of the fuel when the throttle is opened tends to give a momentary delay in power response, which is usually compensated by an accelerator pump. The pump gives a quick squirt of fuel as the throttle is opened. The apparent willingness of the engine to respond to the accelerator pedal is largely determined by how accurately the accelerator pump discharge is proportioned to the existing engine temperature and to the volatility of the fuel.

A converse transitional problem is associated with sudden closing of the throttle, when wet fuel is present on the intake manifold walls. The sudden drop in pressure causes the liquid to flash into vapor, resulting in a temporarily overrich condition in the cylinder, with subsequent misfiring and incompletely burned combustion products in the exhaust. Better manifold heating helps, as does injection of fuel at cylinder intake ports. *See* FUEL INJECTION.

Aircraft carburetion. Early aviation carburetors followed automobile carburetor practice, but in the 1940s the pressure or injection type came into use. These incorporated the following advantages: (1) The whole metering system is kept under pressure, to prevent formation of bubbles and disturbances to the metering under the reduced pressures at higher altitudes. (2) The fuel spray can be delivered into a heated part of the intake system so that ice formation resulting from fuel evaporation becomes impossible. (3) Correction of the metering function under changes of altitude and temperature is automatically provided. (4) The closed system avoids disturbance of the fuel metering, or leakage from vents, during vigorous maneuvers of the airplane.

In the most commonly used form, the metering function of the automobile carburetor is retained. The fuel metering differential (**Fig. 3**) is derived from the multiple venturi air differential by the system of opposed synthetic-rubber diaphragms. The idling spring adds a small positive increment to provide the required rich idle fuel flow.

The fuel pressure in the carburetor is held to a desired value above the surrounding atmosphere by the fuel-pressure valve and its regulating diaphragm and spring. Beyond the pressure valve the fuel may be led to a spinner ring which has multiple discharge orifices. The ring is mounted on, and rotates with, the supercharger shaft. On other installations, the fuel, after metering, is taken to an injection pump which divides the charge equally and delivers a portion at much higher pressure to the interior of each engine cylinder on its intake stroke.

Pressure from the engine-driven fuel pump, as regulated by its bypass valve, must be adequate to maintain flow through the system at the highest powers, but beyond this it does not affect the fuel metering. Fuel-air ratio, as desired for light or full

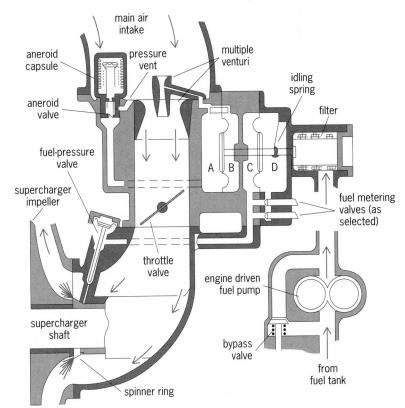

Fig. 3. Schematic diagram of an aircraft injection-type or pressure-type carburetor.

load or as selected by the pilot, is controlled by one or more metering valves which collectively determine the flow area between the two fuel-metering chambers. A variety of combinations have been used, but all are directed toward the regulation illustrated in Fig. 2.

Correction of the fuel-air ratio at increased altitude or temperature is accomplished by differentials. A small fixed-size depression vent is provided between the innermost multiple venturi chamber and the venturi communication channel, while a large pressure vent between the main air intake and the chamber is varied by the aneroid valve. This valve is connected to the aneroid capsule, a metallic bellows filled with inert gas and extended by a spring. As the airplane gains altitude, or as the temperature of the entering air rises, the capsule extends to reduce the area of the entering air vent to the innermost chamber. This action reduces the differential between the multiple venturi chambers at a rate determined by the profile and adjustment of the aneroid valve.

Deviations from the form that provides power enrichment by varying the main metering orifice have been used on smaller aircraft engines. Similar construction has also been used to regulate fuel feed by the parameters of engine speed and intake manifold pressure. This operation is commonly called speed-density metering.

Carburetor icing. There are two reasons for condensation of atmospheric moisture and formation of ice in the intake system. First, at partly closed throttle, the adiabatic pressure drop across the throttle orifice generates a temperature drop. When atmospheric humidity is high, ice sometimes partly clogs the throttle orifice, requiring further throttle opening to keep the engine running for a short period after starting and before the engine heat has had time to build up. With carburetors having a fuel discharge at the throttle edge, the addition of water-soluble antifreeze to the fuel may reduce such icing tendency.

The other source of temperature drop in the intake system is the evaporation of fuel. Ice tends to form wherever fuel spray impinges upon an unheated surface. Such icing was formerly encountered frequently in aircraft operation and was dealt with by heating the intake air, which reduced the engine power and sometimes caused detonation. The problem was largely eliminated by use of the injection carburetor or a fuel-injection system.   Donald L. Anglin

Bibliography. W. H. Crouse and D. L. Anglin, *Automotive Engines*, 1995; J. B. Heywood, *Internal Combustion Engine Fundamentals*, 1988.

Cardamon

A spice from the plant *Elettaria cardamomum* (Zingiberaceae), a perennial herb 6–12 ft (1.8–3.6 m) tall and native to India. The small, light-colored seeds, borne in capsules, have a delicate flavor.

An important spice in the Orient for centuries, they are used in curries, cakes, pickles, and in general cooking, as well as in medicine. In India the seeds are a favorite masticatory. *See* SPICE AND FLAVORING; ZINGIBERALES.

Perry D. Strausbaugh/Earl L. Core

Cardiac electrophysiology

The science of the electrical activity of the heart. The heartbeat results from the development and organized control of cardiac excitability, including ionic current flow across the cardiac membrane, within and between cells, and throughout the body, which in turn allows the orderly contraction of heart muscle and the efficient pumping of blood. Cellular electrophysiologic events lead to the establishment of extracellular potentials on the surface of the body. Electrocardiographic, vectorcardiographic, and other recording systems are used to determine the orientation and magnitude of that extracellular potential. The normal heart produces characteristic sequences of extracellular potentials that may be altered by disease.

Cellular electrophysiology. Cardiac excitability depends on the interaction among the determinants of the resting potential and both the active and passive cellular properties, which can be considered elements in an electrophysiologic matrix. The inside and outside of a cardiac cell are connected by channels that run through a membrane consisting of a lipid bilayer. Electrochemical gradients are established across the membrane in which the ionic activities differ inside and outside the cell. The extracellular activity of sodium ions (Na^+) and calcium ions (Ca^{2+}) exceeds the intracellular activity, which causes an inward leak; the reverse is true for potassium ion (K^+) activity. Energy-requiring pumps and other exchange mechanisms maintain the distribution of the ionic activities across the membrane. The unequal distribution of each ion species charge across the semipermeable membrane is well described by the Nernst equation, which determines the potential required to oppose the activity gradient and is termed the equilibrium potential (E_{ion}). *See* BIOPOTENTIALS AND IONIC CURRENTS; CELL PERMEABILITY.

Active cellular properties relate to the opening and closing of channels that carry the currents responsible for the ionic currents, which in turn are responsible for rapid depolarization and repolarization of the action potential. The channels are selectively permeable to different ionic species and are controlled by gates that open and close as a function of voltage, time, or, sometimes, binding by a hormone, drug, or other ligand. The current flow of an ionic species (i_{ion}) depends on the driving force (the difference between the transmembrane voltage, V_m, and the ion's equilibrium potential, E_{ion}) and the membrane conductance (g_{ion}), that is, the ease with which ions pass through the channels. In other words, $i_{ion} = g_{ion}(E_{ion} - V_m)$. Conductance

(g) is the reciprocal of resistance (R).

Some tissues, such as those in the atria, the Purkinje fibers of the specialized infranodal conduction system, and ventricles, depend on the inrush of sodium ion current (i_{Na^+}) to produce the phase of rapid depolarization, phase 0. The kinetics of the channel, the inrush of sodium ion current, and the maximum rate of rise of voltage (V_{max}) during phase 0 are rapid. Because of that characteristic, these tissues are

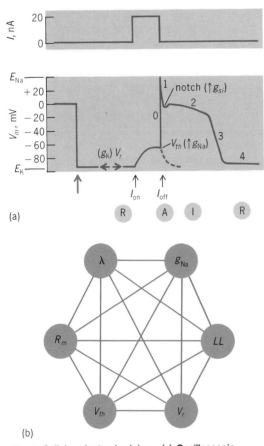

(a)

(b)

Fig. 1. Cellular electrophysiology. (*a*) Oscilloscopic representations of current (*I*) and V_m. When the microelectrode is in the extracellular space, V_m is Φ. With impalement of the tissue, V_m falls from 0 to −95 mV (colored vertical arrow) which is the resting potential (V_r). With physiologic extracellular K$^+$ activities, V_r approximates the potassium equilibrium potential (E_K). Depolarizing current (I_{on}) causes V_m to become more positive and to approach V_{th} for regenerative phase Φ depolarization. If the liminal length requirements are not met, V_m decays exponentially (broken line following I_{off}) because of passive membrane resistive-capacitive properties. Membrane conductance for both resting membrane and subthreshold voltage range are determined primarily by membrane potassium conductance (g_K). If liminal length requirements are met, an action potential results, and the overshoot approaches the equilibrium potential for sodium (E_{Na}). States of the sodium channel are indicated by R (resting), A (open or activated), and I (inactivated). The phases of the action potential are shown, as are the conductances of particular importance to each phase (g_K, g_{Na}, g_{si}). **(*b*)** Simple matrix of selected active and passive cellular properties that determine cardiac excitability. The determinants depicted include the resting potential (V_r), threshold voltage (V_{th}), sodium conductance (g_{Na}), membrane resistance (R_m), the length constant (λ), and, as a measure of overall excitability, the liminal length (*LL*). Note that each has its own determinants, but other determinants are also important, so that the scheme is multidimensional and more complex than illustrated.

often called fast-response tissues. Much of what is known about cardiac electrophysiology has been determined by using microelectrodes that are inserted through the cell membrane into the interior of the cell, thus allowing the recording and perturbation of transmembrane voltages (**Fig. 1**). The resting potential (V_r) and subthreshold conductance (before excitation) in fast-response tissues are determined primarily by potassium conductance (g_K). As the cell is depolarized from a resting potential of about −90 millivolts to about −60 mV, a point often termed the threshold voltage (V_{th}), the response becomes regenerative and out of proportion to the stimulus. This regenerative response is called the action potential.

The membrane potential in fast-response tissues depends on a strictly controlled balance between depolarizing inward currents, which help maintain the action potential plateau, and repolarizing outward currents, which favor a return to the resting potential. Phase 1 depends on the interactivation of sodium conductance and, in Purkinje fibers, perhaps on the activation of the positive dynamic current, which may be a calcium-activated potassium ion current. Events during phase 2, the plateau phase, are complex. The reduced transmembrane current opens the channel for the mixed calcium ion–sodium ion, or "slow inward," current (i_{si}), which helps maintain the plateau. An inward sodium current, the "window" current, is distinct from that active during phase 0 and helps maintain the plateau. At the transmembrane voltage of the plateau, potassium ion conductance decreases in the outward direction but increases in the inward direction, thus repolarization is more difficult—a process called inward rectification. That mechanism helps maintain the plateau.

Phase 3 repolarization has also been termed the rapid repolarization phase. During phase 3, a rapid return to resting potential results from inactivation of the slow inward current, reversal of the process of inward rectification, and activation of repolarizing outward potassium currents. During phase 3, enough of the sodium system is normally reactivated so that another action potential can be electrically induced. Sodium channels may exist in several states: the resting state (R) predominates in normally polarized tissues; the activated state (A) occurs transiently with opening of the sodium channel; and the inactivated state (I) dominates at more positive transmembrane conductance, such as during the plateau or in tissues that have been depolarized because of injury.

Other tissues, such as the sinoatrial (SA) and atrioventricular (AV) nodes, depend on a slow inward current of mixed calcium and sodium ions for phase 0 depolarization. They have been termed slow-response tissues because the current flows through a kinetically slow channel distinct from the channel that controls sodium. Because the channel preferentially carries calcium ions, it is often called the calcium current. Phase 0 in the sinoatrial and atrioventricular nodes normally depends on a slow inward current, and depolarized fast-response tissues may switch over to action potentials dependent on slow inward current. Fast-response tissues have a resting potential of about −60 mV, a transmembrane voltage at which the sodium system is virtually inactivated. The slow channel is voltage-dependent and has resting, active, and inactivated phases. The phase of inactivation depends on both voltage and time and extends into electrical diastole, a characteristic that limits the number of impulses that can transverse the atrioventricular node in atrial fibrillation and flutter.

The cardiac cell has a low-resistance myoplasm surrounded by a membrane that has both capacitative elements and a high resistance; it is analogous to a telegraph cable with a low-resistance core and high-resistance insulation. Cells are connected and communicate with each other through gap junctions, which normally have a low resistance to ionic flow. With injury, gap junction resistance may increase and cells may uncouple—actions mediated by changes in pH and intracellular calcium activity. Membrane insulation is imperfect, and so current leaks out, resulting in a drop in available current for the longitudinal flow of ions through the myoplasm and the gap junctions.

Liminal length. Liminal length is the amount of tissue that must be raised above threshold so that the inward depolarizing current from one region is sufficiently greater than the repolarizing influences of the adjacent tissues to permit regenerative depolarization of neighboring tissues. The liminal length is directly proportional to the charge developed by the active cellular properties and inversely proportional to the membrane capacitance and the length constant. If the liminal length requirements of an element are fulfilled, that element will influence its neighboring element. If the electrotonic influence from the first membrane element is sufficient to bring its adjacent membrane element up to threshold (or, more properly, to fulfill its liminal length requirements), regenerative depolarization and an action potential are produced in the second element. If the electrotonic influence is insufficient, the current continues to decay exponentially. Clearly, cardiac excitability depends both on the current strength created by active cellular properties and on the "sink" of the tissue's cable properties. Each membrane element that fulfills its liminal length requirement will bring about regenerative depolarization, and an action potential will propagate one unit further. Impulse propagation, then, depends on both active and passive cellular properties. Conduction velocity is much more rapid in fast-response, as compared to slow-response, tissues.

Excitation-contraction coupling. Excitation-contraction coupling in heart tissue is complex. A rise in intracellular calcium ions is required to activate the proteins responsible for myocardial contraction. The slow inward current seems to trigger and modulate the release of calcium ions from the sarcoplasmic reticulum and other intracellular storage sites and

to be involved in replenishing calcium ions in those stores. Sodium current, resultant changes in intracellular sodium activity, and sodium ion–calcium ion exchange, which influences the intracellular milieu, also affect contractility.

Automaticity. True spontaneous or automatic activity arises in the absence of direct external causes. Such automaticity may be physiological, as in the sinoatrial node and the lower escape pacemakers, or pathological, as in states of accelerated, depressed, or abnormal pacemaker function. Yet another type is triggered automaticity. In triggered automaticity, nondriven action potentials are initiated by one or more driven action potentials. Normally, the sinoatrial node is the predominant cardiac pacemaker and controls the overall heart rhythm. Pacemaker activity is the product of a changing balance between positive inward currents, which favor depolarization, and positive outward currents, which favor repolarization. The depolarization current of importance is slow inward current, although a second inward current may also play a role. A slowly decaying outward potassium current may also be involved in causing pacemaker activity. *See* HEART (VERTEBRATE); MUSCLE.

Recording extracellular potentials. A dipole consists of two separated, equal but opposite charges. Positive charges flow along force lines from the positive pole to the negative pole, creating current and, perpendicular to the current flow, an electrical field. The separation of charge across the cell membrane discussed above can be considered to be a dipole layer. The changes in transmembrane voltages during depolarization, repolarization, and impulse propagation alters the polarity of the dipole layer in the activated region. The separation of charge between activated and quiescent tissues results in a boundary between surface dipoles. The dipoles are the source of extracellular current flow across the boundary and throughout the surrounding volume conductor of the human thorax; the distribution of the potential in the electrical field is at right angles to the current flow and is detected electrocardiographically.

The magnitude of the recorded extracellular potential is determined by the size and relationship of the boundary to the recording electrode, by the transmembrane voltage gradient across the boundary, and by a conductivity term. The conductivity term incorporates intercellular conductivity, which is determined largely by gap junctions, and extracellular conductivity, which incorporates the characteristics of the volume conductor of the thorax, skin, fat, muscle, mediastinal structures, electrode paste, and the electrode itself. Dipoles have magnitude and direction and, therefore, can be represented by spatial vectors. Multiple vectors may be summed and expressed as a single equivalent vector, which may be translated to a common origin. In classic physiology, the heart has been considered a single dipole current source, represented by a single equivalent spatial vector that is fixed in position but is allowed to vary in magnitude and direction

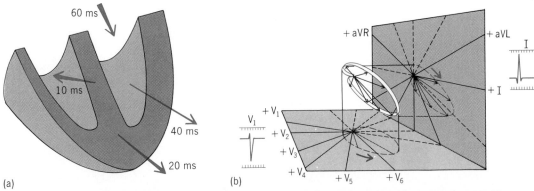

Fig. 2. Spatial vectors after onset of ventricular depolarization. (*a*) Ventricular activation at 10, 20, and 40 ms. At 10 ms the subendocardial Purkinje system is depolarized, and ventricular vectorial forces are balanced except for left septal depolarization; the resultant spatial vector normally has a rightward, anterior, and superior orientation. The 20-ms vector results from activation of the septum and apex and has a leftward, anterior, and inferior orientation. The 40-ms vector arises from depolarization of the inferior and lateral walls of the left ventricle, with lesser contributions from the septum and right ventricle, and has a leftward, posterior and inferior orientation. At 60 ms the inferior posterolateral and basal walls of the left ventricle are activated, and the spatial vector has a leftward, inferior and even more posterior orientation. (*b*) The spatial vectors of ventricular depolarization translated in space with a common origin. The spatial QRS loop depicted is projected onto the frontal plane of the hexaxial reference system consisting of Einthoven and Goldberger leads and onto the horizontal plane created by unipolar Wilson leads. The projected loop is interrupted every 2.5 ms. The scalar recordings are shown in leads I and V_1. By convention, when the spatial vector approaches the positive terminal of the lead, the scalar recording is positive, and when directed away from the positive terminal of the lead, negative. (*After M. F. Arnsdorf, Electrocardiography, American Physiological Society, 1978*)

during the cardiac cycle. More complex multidipole models have also been proposed.

An equivalent spatial vector may be projected onto a plane or, as with the electrocardiograph onto a lead axis system. Leads detect potential differences between two or more sites. The Einthoven reference system uses bipolar leads that compare left arm and right arm, with the left arm being positive (lead I), as well as the right arm and left leg (lead II) and the left arm and left leg (lead III), with the left leg being positive. Unipolar leads compare an exploring electrode against two or three standard limb leads (Goldberger augmented limb leads and Wilson precordial leads, respectively). The spatial vector, then, can be projected onto a hexaxial lead system (Einthoven and Goldberger leads) that defines the frontal plane (superior, inferior, left, and right) and a precordial lead system (Wilson leads) that approximates a horizontal plane (anterior, posterior, left, and right). Other lead systems provide a more orthogonal, that is, less distorted, three-dimensional axis system. The Frank vectorcardiographic system, for example, uses an X lead (left, right) similar to standard lead I, a Y lead (inferior, superior) similar to the augmented left foot lead, and a Z lead (posterior, anterior) similar to an inverted second unipolar chest lead (V_2).

In electrocardiography the potential in a given lead system is displayed against time, usually with 12 separate leads: I, II, III, augmented right arm (aVR), augmented left arm (aVL), augmented left foot (aVF), and six unipolar chest leads, designated V_1 through V_6. In vectorcardiography the spatial orientation of successive vectors is displayed for the frontal, horizontal, or sagittal plane. The vectorcardiographic loop is formed by the instantaneous plot of one orthogonal lead against another, with the time frame indicated by an interruption in the inscribed loop every 2.0 or 2.5 milliseconds.

Body surface mapping based on recordings made at many sites has been used because each recording has both redundant and unique information, and computer analysis can extract the unique information. Signal averaging in the time domain and with Fourier analysis yields data that are not available with the standard electrocardiographic and vectorcardiographic approaches.

Extracellular potential measurements. The sinoatrial node is the normal pacemaker of the heart. Its mass is small, and therefore it does not appear on surface electrocardiograms. The sinoatrial nodal potential, however, initiates the activation of the atria. Atrial depolarization appears as the P wave on the electrocardiogram. Conduction from the atria to the ventricles normally takes place through the atrioventricular node and is quite slow. The impulse emerges from the atrioventricular node, penetrates the bundle of His and bundle branches, and enters the terminal Purkinje network. Because the tissue mass of the atrioventricular node, His bundle, bundle branches, and terminal Purkinje network is too small to produce a signal strong enough to be recorded at the body surface, the P wave is followed by an isoelectric interval.

The wavefront enters the ventricular muscle from the Purkinje network. (The QRS complex demonstrates the phase of depolarization of the large mass of ventricular muscle.) It is followed by the T wave, the rapid phase of ventricular repolarization. U waves, which sometimes are recorded, may reflect repolarization of the terminal Purkinje system. The interval from atrial activation to the beginning of ventricular depolarization is shown as the PR interval, and the isoelectric segment is the PR segment. The ST segment is inscribed during the plateau phase of ventricular action potential repolarization, which follows QRS

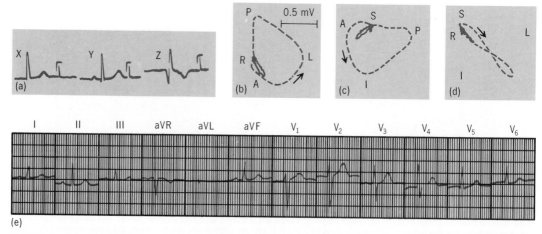

Fig. 3. Normal electrocardiograms and vectorcardiograms. (*a*) Normal orthogonal X, Y, and Z leads that are used to construct the vectorcardiogram (VCG). The X lead defines a left-right lead with the positive terminal on the left; the Y lead defines a superior-inferior lead with the positive terminal inferiority; and the Z lead defines an anterior-posterior lead with the positive terminal posteriorly. (*b–d*) Normal P, QRS, and T vectorcardiographic loops. The beam is interrupted every 2.5 ms, and the direction of inscription is indicated. Orientation in the vectorcardiograph is as follows: A, anterior; P, posterior; L, left, R, right; S, superior; I, inferior. (*b*) The horizontal plane has a left-hand (X lead) and anterior-posterior (Z lead) orientation; (*c*) the sagittal plane has a superior-inferior (Y lead) and anterior-posterior (Z lead) orientation; and (*d*) the frontal plane has a left-right (X lead) and superior-inferior (Y lead) orientation. The P loop is very small, the QRS loop is the large dominant inscription, and the T loop is the intermediate-size inscription. The P and T loops are magnified for analysis. (*e*) Normal 12-lead electrocardiogram. Note the similarity between the electrocardiographic and the orthogonal vectorcardiographic recordings: left-right (I, X), inferior-superior (aVF, Y), and the mirror image of V₁ with anterior positivity and Z with posterior positivity.

depolarization, and it may be abnormal in disease states. The QT interval represents the entire depolarization and repolarization process of the ventricle. Vectorcardiography records P, QRS, and T loops in a frontal, sagittal, and transverse or horizontal plane. Time intervals are represented by interruptions in the recording. The spatial vectors in **Fig. 2** point in the direction of the net potential.

The electrocardiograph and vectorcardiograph are sensitive to abnormal sequences of depolarization such as bundle branch block and preexcitation. They often are useful in detecting increase in myocardial mass, such as atrial and ventricular enlargement. They can detect ischemia and myocardial infarction and often suggest myocardial or pericardial disease, electrolyte disturbance, and drug effects.

Pacemakers. The heartbeat is controlled primarily by the sinoatrial node, which is normally the fastest pacemaker. A marked slowing or failure of the sinus node or a conduction defect that prevents an impulse initiated by the sinus node from reaching all of the heart usually leads to the appearance of a lower escape pacemaker to assume control of the heart. Such escape pacemakers, which have intrinsic rates slower than that found in the normal sinoatrial node, may arise in the atrium, the junction (the His bundle and the region of the atrioventricular node adjacent to it), the subjunction (fascicles and bundle branches), and the terminal Purkinje fibers. The so-called idioventricular escape rhythm probably originates in the terminal Purkinje fibers rather than in the ventricle, although pathological pacemakers may arise in the ventricular tissue. Time-dependent inward and outward currents are involved in lower pacemaker function. Abnormalities in automaticity

and in impulse propagation may lead to cardiac rhythm disturbances, but electrocardiography is very useful in evaluating the rhythm and conduction of the heart. Normal electrocardiograms and vectorcardiograms are shown in **Fig. 3**.

At times, pacemaker catheters are inserted into the cavities of the heart to stimulate the myocardium, provoking cardiac arrhythmias, and to record extracellular potentials. Intracavitary

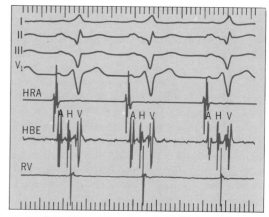

Fig. 4. Body surface and intracavitary electrocardiographic recordings. The electrocardiogram body surface leads I, II, III, and V₁ are shown in the four traces at the top. A catheter with recording electrodes was advanced through the femoral vein, the inferior vena cava, the right atrium, and right ventricle. Recordings were made in the high right atrium (HRA), in the area of the tricuspid valve (HBE, His bundle electrogram), and the right ventricle (RV). Note that the HBE records the atrial (A), His bundle (H), and ventricular (V) depolarization. The ventricular electrogram in the HBE is primarily due to left ventricular depolarization, is delayed because of a conduction block in the left bundle branch, and occurs after the right ventricular depolarization. (*Dr. Thomas Bump, University of Chicago*)

recordings can record small potentials from the sinoatrial node, His bundle, bundle branches, and terminal Purkinje fibers. Multiple intracavitary recording catheters permit the identification and mechanisms of reentrant arrhythmias and the localization of anomalous connections between the atria and ventricles, such as those that occur in preexcitation. An example of an intracavitary recording is shown in **Fig. 4**.

Body surface mapping and signal averaging techniques show promise for detecting abnormal potentials that indicate myocardial disease. Some studies suggest that the presence of such abnormal potentials may allow identification of the individual at risk for serious rhythm disturbances and sudden death. *See* BIOPHYSICS; CARDIOVASCULAR SYSTEM; VASCULAR DISORDERS.   Morton Arnsdorf

Bibliography. M. F. Arnsdorf, *Electrocardiography: I. Fundamental Theory*, and *II. Applied Theory*, 1978; H. A. Fozzard et al. (eds.), *The Heart and Cardiovascular System*, 2 vols., 1986; O. Garfein (ed.), *Cardiovascular Physiology*, 1989; R. Holland and M. F. Arnsdorf, Solid angle theory and the electrocardiogram, *Prog. Cardiovasc. Dis.*, 19:431–457, 1977; P. W. Macfarlane and T. D. V. Lawrie (eds.), *Comprehensive Electrocardiography*, 3 vols. 1989; N. Sperelakis (ed.), *Physiology and Pathophysiology of the Heart*, 2d ed., 1989.

Cardinal points

The four intersections of the horizon with the meridian and with the prime vertical circle, or simply prime vertical, the intersections with the meridian being designated north and south, and the intersections with the prime vertical being designated east and west (see **illus.**). The cardinal

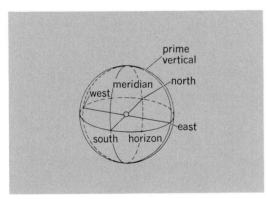

Cardinal points around horizon.

points are 90° apart; they lie in a plane with each other and correspond to the cardinal regions of the heavens. The four intermediate points, northeast, southeast, northwest, and southwest, are the collateral points. *See* ASTRONOMICAL COORDINATE SYSTEMS.   Frank H. Rockett

Cardioid

A heart-shaped curve generated by a point of a circle that rolls (without slipping) on a fixed circle of the same diameter. In point-wise construction of the curve, let O be a fixed point of a circle C of diameter a, and Q a variable point of C. Lay off distance a along the secant OQ, in both directions from Q. The locus of the two points thus obtained is a cardioid (see **illus.**). If a rectangular coordinate

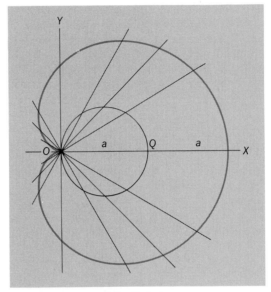

Cardioid. Symbols explained in text.

system is chosen with O for origin initially and y axis tangent to C at O, the cardioid has the equation $(x^2 + y^2 - ax)^2 = a^2(x^2 + y^2)$. The equation expressed in polar coordinates is $\rho = a(1 + \cos\theta)$. The cardioid's area is $3/2\pi a^2$, or six times the area of C, and its length is $8a$. *See* ANALYTIC GEOMETRY.   Leonard M. Blumenthal

Cardiovascular system

Those structures, such as the heart, or pumping mechanism, and the arteries, veins, and capillaries, which provide channels for the flow of blood. The cardiovascular system is sometimes called the blood-vascular system. The circulatory system includes both the cardiovascular and lymphatic systems; the latter consists of lymph channels (lymphatics), nodes, and fluid lymph which finally empties into the bloodstream. This article discusses the cardiovascular system under the following major headings: comparative anatomy, comparative embryology, functional development of the heart, human fetal circulation at term, postnatal circulation, and comparative physiology. *See* BLOOD; LYMPHATIC SYSTEM.

Comparative Anatomy

All vertebrates feature a closed system of branched vessels, a ventral heart, and a basic pattern of organization that ranges from the single system in most fishes to the double system in land forms.

Heart. The hearts of vertebrates differ from those of animals in the lower phyla in their ventral rather than dorsal location. Blood is pumped anteriorly through arteries and forced to the dorsal side. The greater part then courses posteriorly through arteries which terminate in capillaries in various parts of the body. The blood returns to the heart through veins. *See* HEART (VERTEBRATE).

Phylogeny. In lower vertebrates the heart is located far forward in the body, but there is a gradual backward shifting as the vertebrate scale is ascended. The heart lies in a pericardial cavity which is surrounded by an investing membrane, the pericardium. The pericardial cavity is a portion of the coelom which has been separated from the remainder of the body cavity. In elasmobranchs, the separation is incomplete and the two portions of the coelom are connected by a pericardioperitoneal canal. A thin serous membrane, the epicardium, covers the surface of the heart. It is continuous with the lining of the pericardial cavity.

The heart is primarily a pulsating tube, the lining (endocardium) of which is derived from fusion of two vitelline veins. Its muscular wall (myocardium) and the epicardium originate from surrounding splanchnic mesoderm. It becomes divided into chambers called atria and ventricles. In addition, two accessory chambers, called the sinus venosus and conus arteriosus, respectively, may be present. Cyclostomes and most fishes have two-chambered hearts with one atrium and one ventricle. A sinus venosus connects with the atrium and a conus arteriosus leads from the ventricle. Dipnoans and amphibians have three-chambered hearts with two atria and one ventricle. The three-chambered heart of most reptiles is similar to that of amphibians, but an incomplete partition appears in the ventricle. In crocodiles and alligators this becomes complete, forming a four-chambered heart with two atria and two ventricles. Birds and mammals have four-chambered hearts. Valves are present to regulate the direction of blood flow.

Circulation in the heart. Vertebrates with two-chambered hearts have the single type of circulation (**Fig. 1**) in which only unoxygenated blood passes through the heart, which pumps it to the gills for aeration. The double type of circulation (**Fig. 2**) exists in three- and four-chambered hearts through which pass two streams of blood, one oxygenated and the other unoxygenated or partly oxygenated. Even in three-chambered hearts these streams do not mix to any appreciable extent. Partitioning of the heart has been associated in evolution with development of pulmonary circulation accompanying the appearance of lungs.

The conus arteriosus no longer exists as such in adults of higher forms; it is split into trunks leading

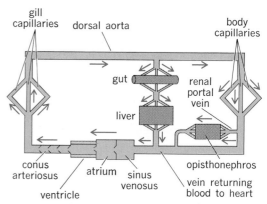

Fig. 1. Single type of circulatory system. *(After C. K. Weichert, Anatomy of the Chordates, 3d ed., McGraw-Hill, 1965)*

to the aorta and lungs, respectively.

In those forms having two-chambered hearts unoxygenated blood from all parts of the body is collected by the sinus venosus which joins the atrium. In the three-chambered hearts of dipnoans and amphibians the sinus venosus has shifted its position and joins the right atrium. A large sinus venosus is present in certain reptiles, but in most it is very small or is lacking. Birds and mammals possess a sinus venosus only during early embryonic development. In vertebrates having three- or four-chambered hearts, unoxygenated blood is returned to the heart through the sinus venosus or directly to the right atrium, as the case may be.

Arterial system. Although the arterial systems of various adult vertebrates appear to be very different in arrangement, a study of development reveals that all systems are built upon the same fundamental plan.

Ventral and dorsal aortas. In lower vertebrates the conus arteriosus leads forward to a ventral aorta. During early development this vessel divides anteriorly into two aortic arches which course dorsally in the mandibular region. These continue posteriorly as the paired dorsal aortas. Additional pairs of aortic arches then appear, forming

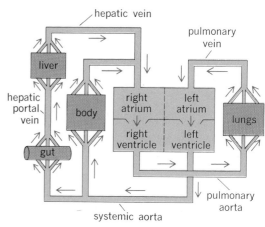

Fig. 2. Double type of circulatory system in a vertebrate having a four-chambered heart (ventral view). *(After C. K. Weichert, Anatomy of the Chordates, 3d ed., McGraw-Hill, 1965)*

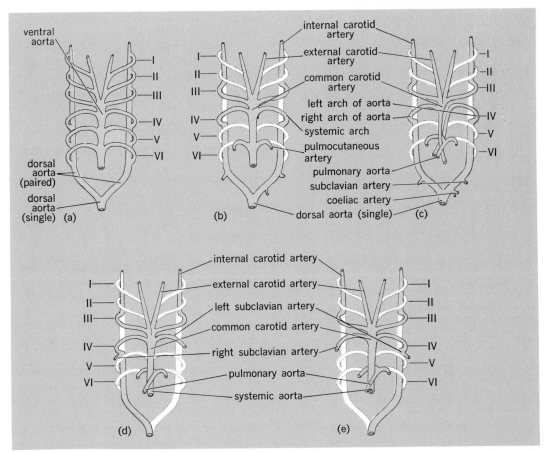

Fig. 3. Modifications of aortic arches in vertebrates, ventral views. (a) Typical condition in vertebrate embryos. Six pairs of arches connect dorsal and ventral aortas. (b) In anuran amphibians. (c) In reptiles. Ventral aorta has split into three vessels, right and left systemic trunks and a pulmonary trunk or aorta. (d) In birds. (e) In mammals. *(After C. K. Weichert, Anatomy of the Chordates, 3d ed., McGraw-Hill, 1965)*

connections between ventral and dorsal aortas on each side. They appear in sequence in an anteroposterior direction, each coursing through the tissues between adjacent pharyngeal pouches. The typical number of aortic arches to form in vertebrates is six pairs (**Fig. 3***a*), although there are certain discrepancies among lower forms. The paired dorsal aortas unite posterior to the pharyngeal region to form a single vessel. This single dorsal aorta continues posteriorly into the tail as the caudal artery.

Various paired and unpaired arteries arise along the length of the dorsal aorta to supply all structures of the body posterior to the pharyngeal region. Anterior continuations of the ventral aorta and the anterior remnants of the paired dorsal aortas supply the head and anterior branchial regions. Although the vessels arising from the dorsal aorta are fairly uniform throughout the vertebrate series, the aortic arches undergo profound modifications. The changes are similar in members of a given class.

Blood, pumped anteriorly by the heart, passes to the aortic arches. These vessels then carry the blood to the dorsal aorta or aortas from which it goes either anteriorly to the head or posteriorly to the remainder of the body.

Aortic arches. Changes in the aortic arch region constitute the chief differences in the arterial systems of the separate vertebrate classes. A progressive reduction in the number of aortic arches occurs as the evolutionary scale is ascended. In cyclostomes and in most fishes, in which gills are used in respiration, the aortic arches break up into afferent and efferent portions connected by numerous gill capillaries in which blood is oxygenated.

The changes in this region involve primarily a routing of the blood through certain preferred aortic arches with a consequent atrophy or disappearance of those which are no longer used, and a splitting of the conus arteriosus and ventral aorta, particularly in reptiles, birds, and mammals, in such a manner that systemic and pulmonary trunks are established (Fig. 3*b–e*). The systemic trunk, coming from the left ventricle (or left side of the ventricle), distributes oxygenated (or partially oxygenated) blood to the body in general. The pulmonary trunk, coming from the right ventricle (or right side of the ventricle), carries blood to the lungs. Oxygenated blood returns through veins from the lungs to the left atrium. Vessels which carry blood from the heart to the lungs and back constitute the pulmonary circulation. Branches of the sixth pair of aortic arches give rise to the pulmonary arteries.

Coronary arteries, supplying the tissues of the heart itself, arise as branches of certain aortic arches

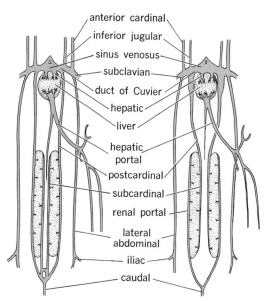

anterior cardinal
inferior jugular
sinus venosus
subclavian
duct of Cuvier
hepatic
liver
hepatic portal
postcardinal
subcardinal
renal portal
lateral abdominal
iliac
caudal

Fig. 4. Changes over the primitive condition which occur in the venous system of lower fishes, ventral view. *(After C. K. Weichert, Anatomy of the Chordates, 3d ed., McGraw-Hill, 1965)*

or of the systemic trunk near the point where it emerges from the heart.

Somatic arteries. The arteries supplying the body proper are usually paired structures which clearly show evidences of segmental arrangement (metamerism). They spring from the dorsolateral regions of the dorsal aorta. Fusion of two or more segmental arteries may take place, obscuring the fundamental metameric arrangement. *See* METAMERES.

Visceral arteries. Arteries supplying the viscera are of two kinds, paired and unpaired. The paired arteries, usually restricted to certain regions, are segmentally arranged. They supply structures derived from the part of the embryo from which the urogenital organs and their ducts arise.

Unpaired visceral arteries supply the spleen and digestive tract. There are usually three such vessels in vertebrates. The celiac artery supplies the stomach, spleen, pancreas, liver, and duodenum; the superior mesenteric artery supplies most of the intestine and a portion of the pancreas; and the inferior mesenteric artery goes to the posterior part of the large intestine and rectum. Variations from this condition are accounted for by fusions or separations.

Venous system. A comparison of veins in the various vertebrate groups shows that they too are arranged according to the same fundamental plan and that the variations encountered form a logical sequence as the vertebrate scale is ascended. In its development the venous system of higher forms passes through certain stages common to the embryos of lower forms.

Sinus venosus. The accessory chamber present in the hearts of lower vertebrates through which blood from all over the body is returned to the heart is the sinus venosus.

In cyclostomes and fishes the sinus venosus

typically receives a pair of common cardinal veins, or ducts of Cuvier, formed by the union of anterior and posterior cardinals, a pair of small inferior jugular veins from the ventrolateral part of the head, and a pair of hepatic veins coming from the liver. In lower fishes a lateral abdominal vein also joins each duct of Cuvier. Each lateral abdominal vein receives a subclavian vein from the pectoral fin and an iliac vein from the pelvic appendage (**Fig. 4**). In some fishes the inferior jugular veins are lacking; in others they have fused. Teleost fishes lack lateral abdominal veins; rather, the subclavians enter the common cardinals. In the dipnoan *Epiceratodus*, the lateral abdominal veins fuse to form a single anterior abdominal vein which joins the sinus venosus directly.

The sinus venosus in amphibians is conspicuous. The ducts of Cuvier have consolidated to form two precaval veins, each of which, in addition to the usual vessels, receives a large musculocutaneous vein from the skin and body wall before joining the sinus venosus. A postcava, derived partly from the sinus venosus and partly from the vitelline veins, joins the sinus venosus posteriorly.

A large sinus venosus is present in turtles; in most reptiles, however, it has been greatly reduced and much of it may be incorporated within the wall of the right atrium. In such reptiles and in adult birds and mammals which lack a sinus venosus, precaval and postcaval veins enter the right atrium directly. Valves that are present where veins enter the right atrium represent vestiges of the sinus venosus.

Cardinal veins. Anterior cardinal, or jugular, veins are prominent in cyclostomes and fishes. In amphibians, reptiles, birds, and mammals they receive internal and external tributaries before joining the precaval veins. In some mammals a single precava is present, an anastomosis having developed between the two original vessels.

Postcardinal veins, which originally course along the lateral borders of the kidneys, at first carry blood away from the kidneys. In fishes they separate into anterior and posterior portions. The posterior sections terminate in the kidneys to become the renal portal veins. The anterior sections connect with a new pair of vessels, the subcardinals, which appear along the medial borders of the kidneys. These now carry blood from the kidneys to the heart. In caudate amphibians and a few salientians the condition is similar to that of fishes, but in most salientians the anterior portions of the postcardinals disappear, and the blood from the kidneys reaches the sinus venosus by way of the postcava. In reptiles and birds the renal portal veins have lost most of their significance, and in mammals they disappear entirely. A remnant of the anterior end of the right postcardinal of mammals becomes the azygos vein, a branch of the right precava which drains the intercostal muscles.

Abdominal veins. The lateral abdominal veins of amphibians and reptiles, like those of the lungfish *Epiceratodus*, have fused to form a single anterior abdominal vein. Instead of entering the sinus venosus, however, it joins the hepatic portal vein. In reptiles, birds, and mammals the lateral abdominal veins are represented during embryonic life by allantoic or umbilical veins which lose their direct connections with the sinus venosus when the liver develops. In adult birds the anterior abdominal vein may possibly be represented by the coccygeomesenteric vein or the epigastric vein. It disappears entirely in all mammals, with the exception of the echidnas.

Portal systems. A portal system is a system of veins that breaks up into a capillary network before the blood which courses through it is returned to the heart. All vertebrates have a hepatic portal system in which blood collected from the digestive tract and spleen passes through capillaries (sinusoids) in the liver before reaching the heart. The embryonic vitelline (subintestinal) vessels are represented in adults by the hepatic portal vein and its tributaries. The renal portal system of lower vertebrates has already been mentioned. Another small but important portal system is found associated with the blood vessels draining the pituitary gland. *See* LIVER.

Miscellaneous. Coronary veins draining the tissues of the heart enter the sinus venosus in lower forms or the right atrium in higher vertebrates. Pulmonary veins, found in amphibians, reptiles, birds, and mammals, first appear in the dipnoan fishes, where their function is to drain the swim bladder. They enter the left atrium. *See* RESPIRATORY SYSTEM; SWIM BLADDER.
                                    Charles K. Weichert

Comparative Embryology

The cardiovascular system in vertebrates arises from the splanchnic mesoderm, with the first blood and vessels formed in the wall of the yolk sac.

Heart. The heart of each species attains its characteristic morphology through an orderly series of changes which begin in early embryonic life. Although the details of development differ for different animals, there are a number of basic principles which apply to all species. Emphasis will be placed on the general principles first, and

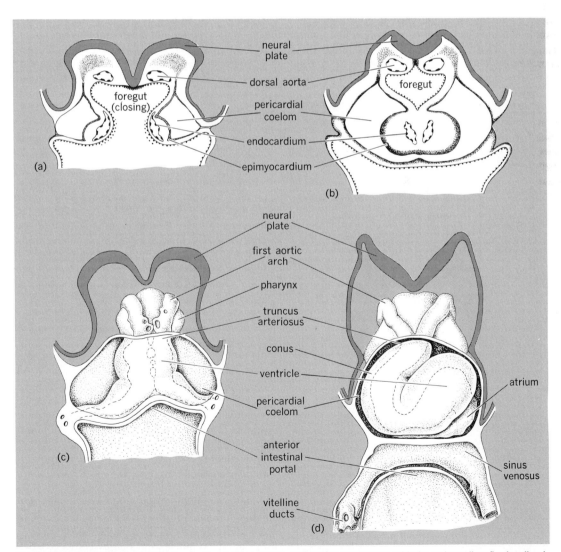

Fig. 5. Stages in development of the human heart. The organ is depicted as translucent, with the endocardium (broken lines) visible through the myocardium. (*a***) Cross section from a four-somite embryo. (***b***) Cross section at seven somites. (***c***) Ventral view at four somites. (***d***) Ventral view at thirteen somites.**

species characteristics will be noted subsequently.

The prospective heart rudiment, that is, the tissue which eventually differentiates into the heart, can be located by experimental procedures (exploration, transplantation, vital dyes, and autoradiographs) before morphological differentiation is observable. The rudiment consists of bilateral areas of splanchnic mesoderm located near the blastopore in the early amphibian gastrulae and near the pharyngeal arches just prior to initial morphological differentiation. *See* AUTORADIOGRAPHY.

The heart field, the mesoderm with potency for heart development, is more extensive than the prospective rudiment which normally forms the organ. For example, a normal heart can develop in amphibians after complete removal of a visibly differentiated primordium. This results from migration of mesoderm from the periphery of the field to the region of extirpation.

The heart field, like the prospective rudiment, is bilateral. The potency for cardiac development is greatest at the center of the field and least at the periphery. The limits of the fields have been determined precisely in chick embryos by studies on the fates of small areas transplanted to the chorioallantoic membrane. *See* FATE MAPS (EMBRYOLOGY).

Induction. The prospective rudiment in amphibian embryos becomes destined (determined) for heart development at the time of gastrulation through an inductive effect exerted by tissue adjacent to the blastopore. Endoderm has a further inductive role on the heart-forming mesoderm at the neurula stage, as evidenced by lack of heart development following extirpation of the endoderm. *See* EMBRYONIC INDUCTION.

Determination and self-differentiation. The prospective rudiment is determined early, as outlined above. This is tested by transplantation to abnormal positions and by explantation as in tissue culture. The rudiment is described as self-differentiating when it attains the ability to develop in a foreign environment.

Polarity. Polarity or axial determination occurs at different times for the different axes. For example, when the anteroposterior axis is changed by 180° in neurula-stage amphibians, the heart develops with reversed morphology and beat. When the early rudiment is rotated around the long axis, altering only the dorsoventral and ventrolateral axes, the heart develops normally.

Totipotency. The ability of part of an organ rudiment to develop the whole organ is called totipotency. Experiments on amphibians, birds, and mammals show that either of the bilateral rudiments is capable of developing a complete organ. Furthermore, a whole organ may form from less than one-half; that is, several hearts can form from one rudiment.

Tubular heart formation. The heart is usually described as tubular during its early morphological differentiation, although it is saccular in shape in most species.

Mesenchymal cells arising from the splanchnic mesoderm of the heart rudiment differentiate into endocardium continuous with the subintestinal blood capillaries. The endocardial channels are bilateral at first; they eventually fuse into a single median tubular endocardium (**Fig. 5**a and b).

The ventral portion of the splanchnic mesoderm of each bilateral heart rudiment thickens and differentiates into epimyocardium around the endocardium (Fig. 5). A space between endocardium and myocardium during early development is filled with homogeneous material known as cardiac jelly. It is eventually replaced by connective tissue uniting the endocardium and myocardium.

The space between the splanchnic and somatic mesoderm of the heart rudiment becomes the pericardial cavity, and a part of the somatic mesoderm differentiates into parietal pericardium.

The bilateral portions of the tubular heart approach the midline and unite to form a single tubular or saccular heart (Fig. 5). Fusion progresses in a cephalocaudal direction. Likewise, structural and functional differentiation of the chambers progresses cephalocaudally. These chambers, beginning with the most caudal one, are the sinus venosus, atrium, ventricle, and bulbus cordis (conus). The sinus venosus receives the blood from the veins; the bulbus empties into the truncus arteriosus

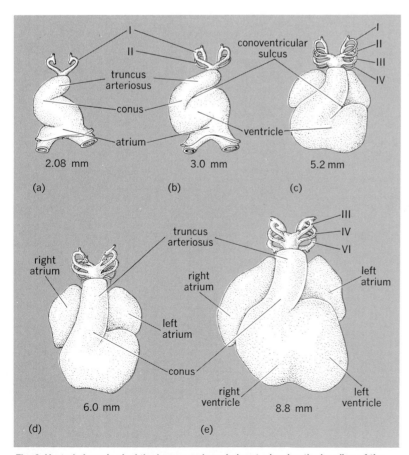

Fig. 6. Ventral views (*a-e*) of the human embryonic heart, showing the bending of the cardiac tube and the establishment of its regional divisions. The roman numerals I to VI indicate the aortic arches of corresponding numbers. (*After T. C. Kramer, Amer. J. Anat., 71(3):343–370, 1942*)

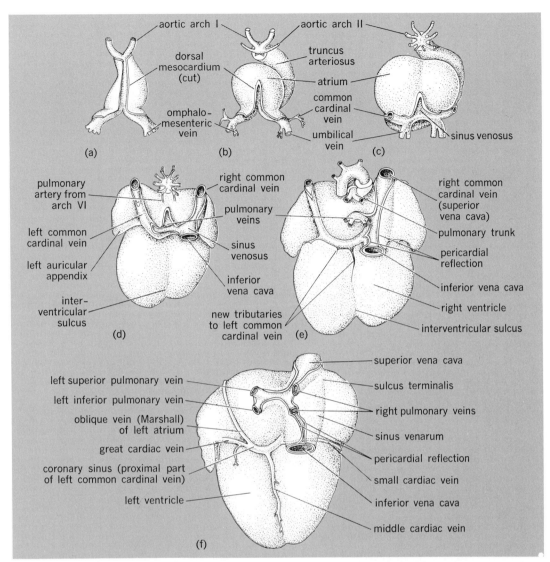

Fig. 7. Six stages in development of the heart, in dorsal aspect to show changing relations of the sinus venosus and great veins entering the heart. (*a*) 2½ weeks (8–10 somites). (*b*) 3 weeks (12–14 somites). (*c*) 3½ weeks (17–19 somites). (*d*) 5 weeks (6–8 mm or 0.24–0.31 in., crown-rump). (*e*) 8 weeks (about 25 mm or 1 in.). (*f*) 11 weeks (about 60 mm or 2 in.). (*After B. M. Patten, Human Embryology, 3d ed., Blakiston–McGraw-Hill, 1968*)

and thence into the aortic arches.

The amount of morphological differentiation seen in the bilateral heart rudiments when they reach the midventral region of the body differs for different species. For example, the bilateral rudiments of the amphibian heart are only slightly differentiated at this time, whereas those of birds and mammals show considerable differentiation prior to union in the midline (Fig. 5a and c). This is because the heart of birds and mammals develops relatively early, while the mesoderm is spread out over the yolk sac. The two sides cannot come together until the head end of the body grows and folds off from the yolk sac. An early development of the circulatory system is particularly important in mammalian embryos since they have very little yolk and come to depend very early upon metabolic exchange with the mother through a placental circulation. It is significant that the heart is the first organ to function.

Cardiac loop and regional development. The tubular heart is attached by its vascular trunks and by a continuity of visceral pericardium with the serous portion of the parietal pericardium at its venous and arterial ends. It is attached by a dorsal pericardium for only a brief period.

The heart becomes curved primarily due to its rapid growth. The heart increases in length so much faster than the cavity in which it lies that it first makes a U-shaped bend to the right and is then twisted into a loop. This moves the venous end cephalically and the arterial end caudally until the entering and exiting vessels approximate the same level in mammals (**Figs. 6***e* and **7***f*).

With the formation of the cardiac loop during the fifth week of human gestation, the primary regional divisions become clearly recognizable (Fig. 6). This is a result of the curvature and of different intrinsic growth rates in different regions. Blood flow also plays a part in the regional differentiation.

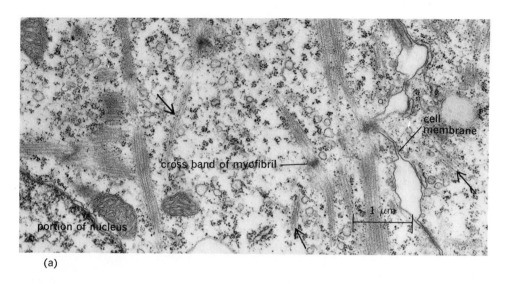

(a)

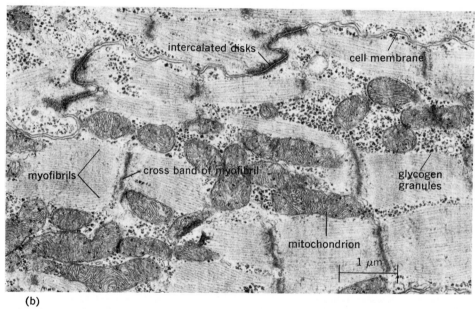

(b)

Fig. 8. Electron micrographs of cardiac muscle at different stages of development. (*a*) Section of sinus venosus from the heart of a tadpole just before the feeding stage. (*b*) Section of ventricle of adult frog. Note that the tadpole sinus has irregularly arranged myofilaments (at arrows) and poor alignment of filaments into myofibrils with only a few cross bands.

The sinus venosus is the thin-walled most caudal chamber into which the great veins enter (Fig. 7*c*). The atrial region is established by transverse dilation of the heart just cephalic to the sinus venosus, and the ventricle is formed by the bent midportion of the original cardiac tube (Figs. 5, 6, and 7). Between the atrium and ventricle, the heart remains relatively undilated to form the atrioventricular canal. The conus is distinguishable as a separate region prior to its later incorporation into the right ventricle. The most cephalic part of the cardiac tube undergoes the least change in appearance, persisting as the truncus arteriosus connecting the conoventricular region to the aortic arches (Figs. 5 and 6).

Studies on amphibians, birds, and mammals show that initial cardiac contractions begin in the ventricular region. The heart at this time is just slightly less developed than that illustrated in Fig. 6 for a human embryo 0.08 in. (2 mm) long (beginning of fourth week of development). With further cardiac differentiation in a cephalocaudal direction, the atrium and sinus venosus acquire the ability to contract, each with a successively higher intrinsic rate which dominates its predecessor.

Innervation of the heart occurs subsequent to the time when the sinus differentiates and takes over the pacemaker function. The fact that the embryonic heart pulsates rhythmically and carries on circulation prior to innervation indicates the beat is myogenic rather than neurogenic in origin.

The myocardium shows cytological differentiation relatively early. Electron micrographs of developing heart muscle cells show randomly oriented myofilaments (actin and myosin) prior to the time when striations appear due to the alignment of the filaments in register in myofibrils. A compact, well-oriented arrangement of myofibrils, each composed of many myofilaments, occurs earlier in the ventricle than in the atrium. The sinus venosus (shown in **Fig. 8** for the tadpole heart just prior to the time of innervation) retains an irregular arrangement in adult amphibians. In mammals, where the sinus venosus becomes incorporated into the right atrium, the sinoatrial node is composed of cells which have sparse randomly oriented myofibrils, like those which are found in the amphibian sinus venosus. The irregular arrangement is one of the characteristics of pacemaker cells. *See* HEART (INVERTEBRATE); MUSCLE.

Formation of definitive heart. The morphological changes which occur in the heart while it differentiates from a tubular structure to its definitive adult form vary for different classes and species of vertebrates in correlation with different functional requirements. The changes in elasmobranch fishes are few and simple. The heart retains all its primitive chambers in sequence (sinus, atrium, ventricle, and conus) and each chamber remains unpartitioned.

In adult amphibians the heart attains an external form and curvature beyond that illustrated in Fig. 5 for a mammalian embryo, but it retains the chambers in sequence. In urodele amphibians there is a partial division of the atrium into right and left sides; in anuran amphibians the atrial division is complete, but other parts remain undivided.

The heart of reptiles has the atrium divided completely into right and left chambers while the ventricle is divided only partially.

In birds and mammals the sinus venosus is incorporated into the right atrium, which is divided completely from the left atrium; the primitive ventricle is completely divided into right and left chambers; the conus is incorporated into the right ventricle; and the truncus arteriosus is divided into right and left sides to form the roots and proximal portions of the pulmonary artery and aorta.

The fusion of the sinus venosus with the right atrium is somewhat more complete in most mammals than in birds. In mammals specialized tissues develop in certain areas of the original sinus region to form the sinoatrial and atrioventricular nodes. The sinoatrial node, located near the entrance of the superior vena cava, serves as the cardiac pacemaker.

Complete division of the heart into right and left sides, that is, a complete separation of respiratory and systemic circulations, is achieved only in birds and mammals. This supplies a higher arterial pressure on the systemic side and distributes oxygenated blood to the tissues more rapidly than in animals with partial separation (reptiles and amphibians) or those with no separation (fishes).

Partitioning of mammalian heart. The division of the heart into right and left sides has been studied in detail in humans and in a number of other mammals. The following account applies

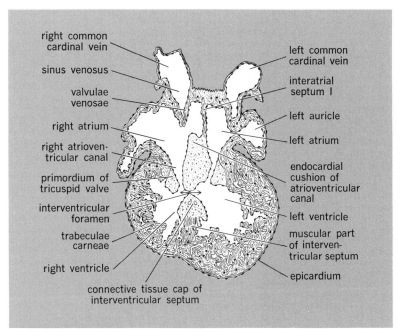

Fig. 9. Section through heart of a 9.4-mm (0.37-in.) pig embryo. Stage of development corresponds to that in a human embryo of the sixth week. (*After B. M. Patten, Foundations of Embryology, 2d ed., McGraw-Hill, 1965*)

primarily to the human heart, but the general plan of partitioning is similar in other mammals. It should be noted that the partitioning of the embryonic heart involves more than its structural division into parts. The process is beset by striking functional exigencies. Cardiac partitioning in the human embryo does not begin until about the fifth week of development, 0.2 in. (6 mm) long, when the heart (Fig. 6d) is already maintaining a circulation essential for embryonic life. All of the complex changes in partitioning must be made without interruption of the blood supply to any part of the growing embryo. Starting with a stage when the blood is flowing through it in an undivided stream, the heart, by the time of birth, must become converted into an elaborately valved, four-chambered organ, pumping from its right side a pulmonary stream which is returned to its left side to be pumped out again over the aorta as the systemic bloodstream. Moreover, at the end of gestation, the vascular mechanism must be prepared for air breathing. At the moment of birth the lungs, their blood vessels, and the right ventricle (which pumps the pulmonary circuit) must be ready to take over from the placenta the entire responsibility of oxygenating the blood.

The systemic part of the circulation must also be prepared. During intrauterine life the left side of the heart receives less blood from the pulmonary veins than the right side receives from the vena cavae. Immediately after birth the left ventricle is called on to do more work than the right ventricle. It must pump sufficient blood through the myriad peripheral vessels of the systemic circulation to care for the metabolism and continued growth of all parts of the body. These are just some of the striking functional situations which the growing heart must encounter before it can attain its adult condition.

Division of atrium and ventricles. Almost from their earliest appearance, the atrium and ventricle show external indication of their impending division into right and left sides. A distinct median furrow appears at the apex of the ventricle (Figs. 7*d* and *e* and 6*c–e*). The atrium meanwhile bulges out on either side of the midline (Fig. 7). Its bilobed configuration is emphasized by the manner in which the truncus arteriosus compresses it midventrally (Fig. 6*c–e*). These superficial features suggest the more important internal changes.

As the wall of the ventricle increases in thickness, it develops internally a meshwork of interlacing muscular bands, the trabeculae carneae. Opposite the external furrow these muscular bands become consolidated as a partition which projects from the apex of the ventricle toward the atrium. This is the interventricular septum (**Fig. 9**).

Meanwhile, two conspicuous masses of the loosely organized mesenchyme called endocardial cushion tissue develop in the walls of the narrowed portion of the heart between the atrium and ventricle. One of these endocardial cushions of the atrioventricular canal is formed in its dorsal wall

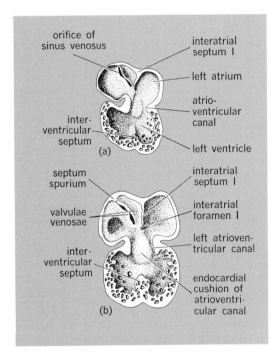

Fig. 10. Interior of heart showing initial steps in its partitioning. (a) Cardiac septa in human embryos early in fifth week, showing primary relations of interatrial septum primum. Based on original reconstruction of heart of a 3.7-mm (0.15-in.) pig embryo and on Tandler's reconstructions of corresponding stages of the human heart. **(b)** Cardiac septa in human embryos of sixth week. Note restriction of interatrial foramen primum by growth of interatrial septum primum. Based on original reconstructions of the heart of 6-mm (0.24-in.) pig embryo, on Born's reconstructions of rabbit heart, and Tandler's reconstructions of corresponding stages of the human heart. (*After B. M. Patten, Human Embryology, 3d ed., Blakiston–McGraw-Hill, 1968*)

(**Fig. 10***b*). A similar one is formed opposite it on the ventral wall. When these two masses meet, they divide the atrioventricular canal into right and left channels (**Fig. 11**).

Septum primum. Concurrently, a median partition appears in the cephalic wall of the atrium. Because another closely related partition will form adjacent to it later, this is called the first interatrial septum or septum primum. It is composed of a thin layer of young cardiac muscle covered by endothelium. It is crescent-shaped, with its concavity directed toward the ventricle. The apices of the crescent extend to the atrioventricular canal where they merge, respectively, with its dorsal and ventral endocardial cushions (Fig. 10). This leaves the atria separated from each other except for a diminishing opening called the interatrial foramen primum (Fig. 10*b*).

While these changes have been occurring, the sinus venosus has been shifted out of the midline so that it opens into the atrium to the right of the interatrial septum (Fig. 7). The heart is now in a critical stage of development. Its original simple tubular form has been altered so that the four chambers characteristic of the adult heart are clearly suggested. Partitioning of the heart into right and left sides is well under way, but there are still open communications from the right to the left side in both atrium and ventricle. If partitioning were completed now, the left side of the heart would be left almost literally dry, because the sinus venosus, into which systemic, portal, and placental currents all enter, opens on the right of the interatrial septum. Not until much later do the lungs and their vessels develop sufficiently to return any considerable volume of blood to the left atrium. The partitions in the ventricle and in the atrioventricular canal do progress rapidly to completion (Figs. 10, 11, and **Fig. 12**), but an interesting series of events takes place in the interatrial septal complex which assures that an adequate supply of blood will reach the left atrium and thence the left ventricle.

In the sixth week, just when the septum primum is about to fuse with the endocardial cushions of the atrioventricular canal, thus closing the interatrial foramen primum, a new opening is established. The more cephalic part of the septum primum becomes perforated, at first by multiple small holes. These soon coalesce to form the interatrial foramen secundum, thus keeping a route open from the right to the left atrium (Fig. 11).

Septum secundum. During the seventh week the second interatrial partition makes its appearance just to the right of the first. Like the septum primum, the septum secundum is crescent-shaped. The concavity of its crescent is, however, differently oriented. Whereas the open part of the septum primum is directed toward the atrioventricular canal, the open part of the septum secundum is directed toward the lower part of the sinus entrance which later becomes the opening of the inferior vena cava into the right atrium (Figs. 11 and 12). This difference in the direction of growth in the two interatrial septa is of vital functional significance because it means that as the septum secundum grows, the opening remaining in it is carried out of line with the interatrial foramen secundum in the septum primum (Fig. 12). The opening in the septum secundum, although it becomes relatively smaller as development progresses, will not be completely closed but will remain as the foramen ovale.

The flaplike persisting portion of the septum primum overlying the foramen ovale constitutes an efficient valvular mechanism between the two atria. When the atria are filling, some of the blood returning by way of the great veins can pass freely through the foramen ovale merely by pushing aside the flap of the septum primum. When the atria start to contract, pressure of the blood within the left atrium forces the septum primum against the septum secundum, effectively closing the foramen ovale against return flow into the right atrium. Without some such mechanism to afford a fair share of blood to the left atrium, the fetal left ventricle would receive a low blood volume, and as a result its muscular wall would not develop adequately to carry its postnatal pumping load. The strength of cardiac muscle and other muscles in the body depends on the work the muscle is called upon to do.

Division of the truncus. While these changes are going on in the main part of the heart, the truncus arteriosus is being divided into two separate channels. This process starts where the truncus joins the ventral roots of the aortic arches. Continuing toward the ventricle, the division is effected by the formation of longitudinal ridges of plastic young connective tissue of the same type as that making up the endocardial cushions of the atrioventricular canal. These ridges, called truncus ridges, bulge progressively further into the lumen of the truncus arteriosus and finally meet to separate it into aortic and pulmonary channels (**Figs. 13** and **14**). The semilunar valves of the aorta and the pulmonary trunk develop as local specializations of these truncus ridges. Toward the ventricles from the site of formation of the semilunar valves, the ridges are continued into the conus of the ventricles (**Fig. 15**). The truncoconal ridges follow a spiral course through the truncus and extend down into the ventricles, where they meet and become continuous with the margins of the interventricular septum. This reduces the relative size of the interventricular foramen but does not close it completely. Its final closure is brought about by a mass of endocardial cushion tissue from three sources. Bordering the interventricular foramen ventrocaudally is the interventricular septum, the crest of which, above its main muscular portion, is made up of endocardial cushion tissue (Fig. 9).

Toward the atrioventricular canal lie the masses of endocardial cushion tissue which were responsible for its partitioning (Fig. 15). In the conus outlet are the ridges that were just considered. From all three of these adjacent areas, endocardial cush-

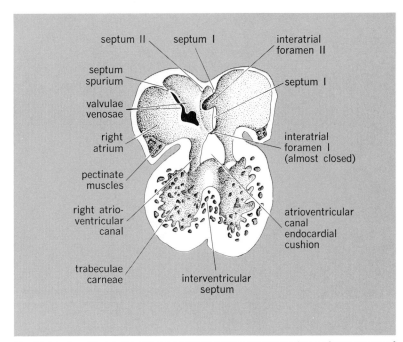

Fig. 11. Interior of heart showing start of interatrial septum secundum and appearance of interatrial foramen secundum in septum primum. Based on original reconstructions of the hearts of pig embryos and on Tandler's reconstructions of the heart of human embryos of the seventh week. (*After B. M. Patten, Human Embryology, 3d ed., Blakiston–McGraw-Hill, 1968*)

ion tissue encroaches on the opening. About the end of the seventh week, the interventricular foramen is completely plugged with a loose mass of this young, readily molded connective tissue. Later this mass differentiates into the membranous portion of the interventricular septum and the septal cusps of the atrioventricular valves. When the interventricular septum has thus been completed, the right ventricle leads into the pulmonary trunk and

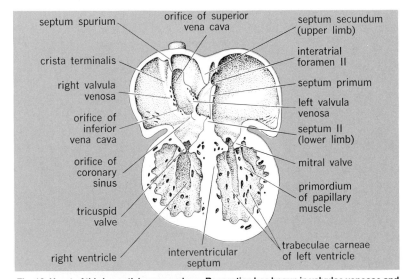

Fig. 12. Heart of third-month human embryo. Resorption has begun in valvulae venosae and septum spurium as indicated by many small perforations in their margins. Left venous valve is coming to lie against and fuse with septum secundum; it usually leaves no recognizable traces in the adult, but occasionally delicate lacelike remains can be seen adhering to septum secundum, and more rarely, extending a short distance onto the valvula foraminis ovalis. (*After B. M. Patten, Foundations of Embryology, 2d ed., McGraw-Hill, 1964*)

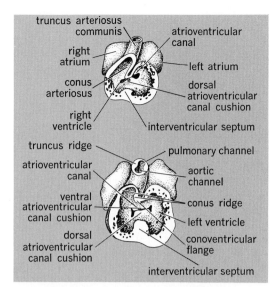

Fig. 13. Dissections of developing hearts in frontal aspect to show relations of importance in establishing aortic and pulmonary outlets. (*After T. C. Kramer, Amer. J. Anat., 71(3):343–370, 1942*)

the left leads into the ascending aorta. With this condition established, the heart is completely divided into right and left sides except for the interatrial valve at the foramen ovale which must remain open throughout fetal life until after birth, when the lungs attain their full functional capacity and the entire volume of the pulmonary stream passes through them to be returned to the left atrium.

Ductus arteriosus. This leaves only one of the functional exigencies of heart development still to be accounted for. If, during early fetal life and before the lungs are well developed, the vessels to the lungs were the only exit from the right side of the heart, the right ventricle would not have an outlet adequate to develop its pumping power. It

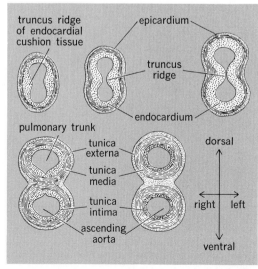

Fig. 14. Partitioning of the truncus arteriosus to form the ascending aorta and the pulmonary trunk. (*After S. E. Gould, Pathology of the Heart, Charles C. Thomas, 1953*)

is only late in fetal life that the lungs and their vessels develop to a degree which prepares them for assuming their postnatal activity, and the power of the heart muscle can be built up only gradually by continued functional activity. This situation is met by the ductus arteriosus, leading from the pulmonary trunk to the aorta. Throughout fetal life any blood from the right ventricle that cannot be accepted within the pulmonary circuit is shunted by way of the ductus into the descending aorta. Thus the right ventricle is able to develop its muscular walls by pumping throughout prenatal life its full share of the cardiac load.

The foregoing account of cardiac partitioning applies particularly to the human. There are some notable exceptions in cardiac development in the opossum, a mammal in which the young are born in a primitive stage and continue their development for several weeks in the mother's pouch. This species does not have a secondary interatrial septum or a fossa ovalis. The primary septum has multiple perforations, a few of which persist until birth. The sinus venosus remains in a more primitive stage, clearly defined from the right atrium. The left superior vena cava also persists, opening into the sinus portion of the atrium by way of the coronary sinus.

The rabbit also maintains a more primitive arrangement of the vessels and a more evident sinus region much like the opossum.

Embryogenesis of blood vessels. The endothelial lining of the earliest embryonic vessels arises from mesenchyme, with differentiation occurring first in the wall of the trophoblast and only slightly later in the body stalk and yolk sac. The mesenchymal cells with potency to form endothelium are designated as angioblasts.

According to one view (angioblastic theory), the vessels within the body of the embryo arise by migration of angioblasts from the body stalk and yolk sac. According to the local origin theory, the main intraembryonic vessels, such as the aorta, arise by in situ differentiation from vasoformative mesenchymal cells. Most experimental evidence favors the latter view.

After main embryonic vessels have arisen, new vessels arise by vascular sprouts from preexisting vessels. Regeneration of endothelium of new vessels following injury in adult life is likewise dependent upon outgrowth from preexisting endothelium.

Angiogenesis. The earliest observable differentiation of endothelium occurs in blood islands of the trophoblast, body stalk, and yolk sac. Each island consists of mesenchymal cell clusters in which the central cells differentiate into blood corpuscles and the peripheral cells elongate and transform into endothelium. Growth and union of the isolated vascular spaces give a plexus of primitive vascular channels. Endothelium of the main vessels of the body of the embryo differentiates also but without relationship to blood islands.

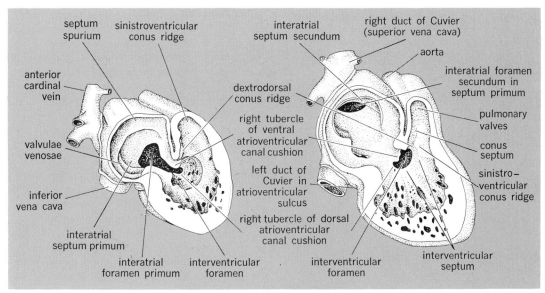

Fig. 15. Lateral dissections showing the relations of the various septa in the developing heart. (*After B. M. Patten, Human Embryology, 3d ed., Blakiston–McGraw-Hill, 1968*)

Circulatory system morphogenesis. The earliest vessels are anastomosing, thin-walled tubes (capillaries) lined only by endothelium. In the course of differentiation, some of the capillaries enlarge to form arteries and veins, some remain as capillaries, and some fall into disuse and atrophy. It seems well established that the amount rather than the rate of blood flow through any given portion of a capillary plexus determines whether a vessel merely persists as a capillary or enlarges to form an artery or vein. In a similar manner, alterations in vascular pathways occur after the capillary plexus stage of differentiation. For example, arteries atrophy when their blood flow is diverted to newly formed vessels.

Formation of ventral aorta. The aorta arises from bilateral primordia continuous with the bilateral cardiac primordia. The bilateral rudiments quickly fuse to form a common truncus arteriosus continuous with the bulbus cordis. By formation and fusion of two longitudinal ridges along the inner surface of the distal portion of the bulbus, the primitive aortic bulb is split into a pulmonary trunk and an ascending aorta. The latter is relatively short in mammals. It connects with the dorsal aorta by means of aortic arches which vary at different embryonic stages, and the final pattern differs in different species.

Formation of aortic arches. In mammalian embryos there are usually six pairs of arches, but these do not all function simultaneously. Furthermore, the fifth pair is very rudimentary. The arch which follows the questionable fifth one is usually called the pulmonary arch because it becomes a part of the pulmonary arterial system.

The first pair of aortic arches forms in human embryos at the beginning of the fourth week, and the remaining pairs develop in sequence during the fourth week. Transformations (**Fig. 16**) occupy the fifth to seventh weeks.

The first and second pairs become dysfunctional and atrophy as the third and fourth pairs enlarge, and form more direct pathways from the ventral to the dorsal aortas. Following atrophy of portions of the dorsal aortas between levels of the third and fourth arches, the third arches and cephalic portions of the dorsal aortas remain as paired primitive internal carotid arteries. After the external carotid grows out from the third arch, the proximal portion is known as the common carotid.

The fate of the fourth arches differs for different classes of vertebrates. In mammals the left fourth arch persists as the arch of the aorta, whereas the right fourth arch forms a portion of the innominate artery and the proximal portion of the subclavian artery (Fig. 16). In birds the condition is the reverse, with the arch of the aorta forming on the left. In reptiles and amphibians both fourth arches retain their connection with the dorsal aorta.

Formation of dorsal aorta. The dorsal aorta arises from bilateral primordia which persist as the paired internal carotids cephalically (Fig. 16) and fuse caudally to form the descending aorta.

The aorta has dorsal, lateral, and ventral branches which are arranged serially. There are about 30 pairs of dorsal branches, which are also known as intersegmental arteries because they occur between successive body segments. Each of the intersegmental arteries divides into dorsal and ventral rami; the dorsal rami give rise to the spinal and vertebral arteries and the ventral rami form the intercostals and lumbars. The lateral aortic branches are not segmentally arranged. They form the renal, suprarenal, inferior phrenic, and internal spermatic or ovarian arteries. The ventral aortic branches develop as paired vitelline arteries to the yolk sac. They fuse when the paired aortas fuse. Later, they are reduced until they occur only at three levels, forming the celiac, superior mesenteric, and inferior mesenteric arteries.

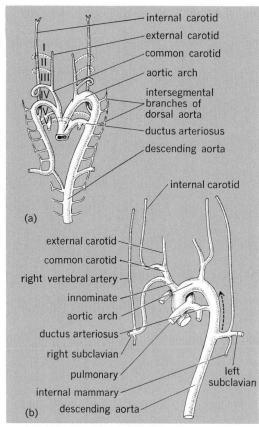

internal carotid
external carotid
common carotid
aortic arch
intersegmental branches of dorsal aorta
ductus arteriosus
descending aorta

(a)

internal carotid

external carotid
common carotid
right vertebral artery
innominate
aortic arch
ductus arteriosus
right subclavian
pulmonary
internal mammary
descending aorta

left subclavian

(b)

Fig. 16. Transformations of human aortic arches, ventral view. (a) Diagram of early stage of transformation when first, second, and fifth pairs of vessels (broken lines) have degenerated. (b) Adult derivatives. Diagram, from fetus, shows left subclavian arising from caudal part of arch, but shifts to a higher position at a later stage, indicated by arrow. Ductus arteriosus normally atrophies after birth.

Arteries of the extremities. Vascularization of the extremities illustrates the growth of given pathways within a plexus of vessels. At first, each extremity has a blood supply from several lateral aortic branches. Then, one lateral branch enlarges and the others fall into disuse. In the arm the main stem is the brachial artery which is a continuation from the subclavian. The extension of the brachial into the arm progresses by differential growth of pathways of a capillary plexus. At one stage, the brachial continues by the interosseous to the vessels of the hand. Later, when the median artery arises as a brachial branch and annexes the vessels of the hand, the interosseous becomes less prominent. At a still later stage, the ulnar and radial arteries develop as brachial branches and become the main vessels of the forearm.

The first axial vessel of the leg is known as the sciatic artery. Later, it is superseded by the femoral artery which is a continuation of the external iliac, a branch of the common iliac. After the femoral joins and annexes portions of the sciatic, the proximal portion of the sciatic persists merely as the inferior gluteal, whereas the distal part of the sciatic becomes the popliteal artery in continuity with the femoral.

Primitive venous system. In the early embryo there are three sets of paired veins of particular significance: vitellines carrying blood from the yolk sac to the heart, umbilicals from the placenta, and cardinals from the head and body.

Changes in vitelline veins. Changes in these vessels are correlated with the developing liver in the sense that there is a mutual intergrowth between cords of hepatic cells and endothelial sprouts from the vitelline veins. Thus the vitelline veins are interrupted by liver sinusoids. By enlargement of some of the sinusoids, a direct channel is formed between the left umbilical vein and the proximal portion of the right vitelline (the future hepatic); the channel is known as the ductus venosus.

Caudal to the liver, the right and left vitelline veins become united by three cross anastomoses. By growth of some parts and atrophy of other parts of this system, the S-shaped portal vein arises.

The segment of the right vitelline between the liver and the heart becomes the hepatic vein; the left vitelline of this level disappears.

Changes in umbilical veins. During its growth, the liver encroaches on the umbilical veins until all the umbilical blood enters the liver. Then the entire right umbilical vein atrophies, leaving the left vein which empties into the ductus venosus. The left umbilical vein and the ductus venosus persist as important vessels until birth; then they atrophy and become the ligamentum teres and the ligamentum venosum, respectively.

Plan of the cardinal veins. Paired precardinal veins from the head join paired postcardinals from the body at the level of the heart to form the common cardinals (ducts of Cuvier). During development, parts of the postcardinals are replaced and superseded by subcardinals and supracardinals. The major veins of the body arise through transformation of the cardinal system.

Changes in precardinals, common cardinals. The precardinal of each side is composed of a primary head vein and the precardinal proper extending from the head to the common cardinal. The head vein drains anterior, median, and lateral plexuses over the brain. The rostral portion of the head vein becomes the cavernous sinus; portions of the anterior plexus enlarge to become the superior sagittal sinus; and a dorsal connection between the middle and posterior plexuses becomes the transverse sinus. The main precardinal stem of each side becomes the internal jugular vein as far caudal as the level of a shunt from the left to the right precardinal (**Fig. 17**). The shunt itself becomes the left brachiocephalic (left innominate), and the left precardinal caudal to the shunt remains as the relatively small first intercostal.

The right common cardinal with the right precardinal up to the point of intercardinal anastomosis forms the superior vena cava. The left common cardinal of humans persists as the small oblique vein of the left atrium. As a congenital anomaly, it may remain as a left superior vena cava.

In some mammals and in the lower vertebrates, two superior venae cavae (left and right) occur normally.

Postcardinal system transformations. Postcardinals develop primarily as vessels of the mesonephroi and their fate in different species varies with that of the mesonephroi. In *Petromyzon* the postcardinal of each side remains, as in the embryo; in elasmobranchs the plan is modified by a renal portal system; and in humans and some other mammals the postcardinals become altered, as shown in Fig. 17. This transformation is related to the development of subcardinal veins ventral to the mesonephroi, and supracardinals dorsomedial to the postcardinals. Parts of each of these systems contribute to the formation of the inferior vena cava (Fig. 17).

Veins of the extremities. These develop by channels within capillary plexuses, as already described for the arteries. Each extremity of an early embryo develops a peripheral or border vein. In the upper extremity the border vein persists on the ulnar side

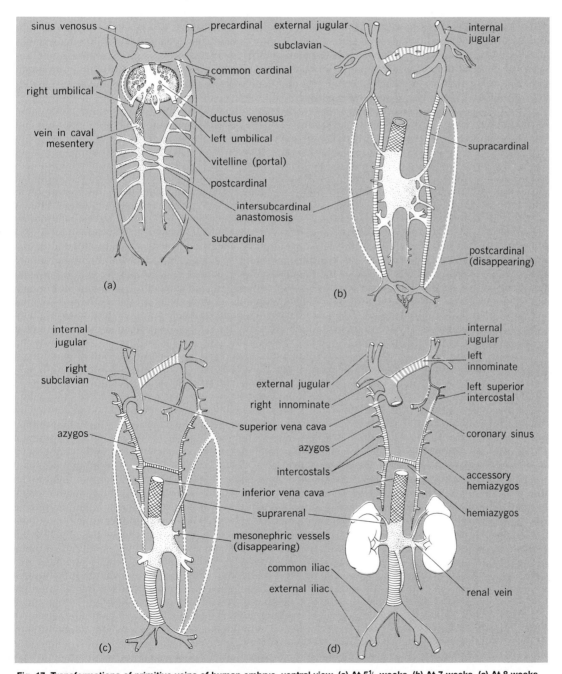

Fig. 17. Transformations of primitive veins of human embryo, ventral view. (*a*) At 5½ weeks. (*b*) At 7 weeks. (*c*) At 8 weeks. (*d*) At term. In *a*, proximal portions of umbilicals (broken lines) have atrophied. Remainder of the right umbilical atrophies later. Vitellines (omphalomesenterics) have been interrupted by liver sinusoids. Right proximal vitelline has enlarged and will become the hepatic. Caudal portions of vitellines are transforming into the portal vein. A connection from hepatic to subcardinals via ventral mesentery will form hepatic segment of inferior vena cava. Vessels associated with liver are omitted from *b*, *c*, and *d*.

as the subclavian, axillary, and basilic veins; in the lower extremity the border vein persists on the fibular side.

Pulmonary veins. These develop from pulmonary plexuses. At one stage of development, all branches combine to open by a single stem into the left atrium. By growth of the atrium, more of the pulmonary vessel is drawn into the atrial wall until there are four pulmonary vein openings into the atrium, two from each lung.   W. M. Copenhaver

Functional Development of Heart

The heart begins to beat before all its parts have been formed. The character of the heartbeat changes with the sequential formation of the regions of the heart. The heart arises by the fusion of bilateral primordia which converge from positions on opposite sides of the embryo. In the human embryo virtually the entire development of the heart and major blood vessels occurs between the third and eighth weeks of embryonic life. In the chick embryo, one of the principal objects of experimental analysis, the bilateral primordia begin to fuse in the seven-somite stage. The first beats can be recorded in the embryo of nine somites, where the first cross striations also occur.

Contractions of the heart. The first contractions occur along the right side of the developing ventricle, the first part of the heart to form. The beat is at first slow but rhythmical and gradually involves the whole wall of the ventricle. The first contractions may be described as rhythmic but intermittent, that is, rhythmic contractions interrupted by rest periods. Next is added the atrium, which begins to contract at a higher rate than that of the ventricle, stepping up the rate of the entire heart, because the part of the tube with the highest rate of contraction sets the pace for the heart as a whole. At this time the blood is set in motion. The sinus venosus begins to contract somewhat later; again, its inclusion steps up the heartbeat. Contractions begin before any of the nerve fibers (which in their development grow out from the central nervous system), reach the heart and before the specialized system for conducting impulses in the heart is established. The nervous system secondarily assumes the regulation of the rate of the pulsations originating in the myocardium, retarding and accelerating functions being by the vagus and cervical sympathetic fibers, respectively.

Heart-forming areas. The first pulsations of the heart are foreshadowed by the localization of the heart-forming cells to well-demarcated regions of the embryo in the head-process stage, about 10 h earlier. **Figure 18** shows the position of the heart-forming areas as demonstrated by experimental tests of the histogenetic capacity of isolated fragments of the early embryo. Although cardiac muscle arises from the mesoderm, it is impossible to state whether it develops independently in the chick or whether interactions between the mesoderm and endoderm are required. Such an inductive interaction appears to be required for normal development of the heart in the salamander embryo.

Contractile proteins. The question has been raised as to what extent the early localization of heart-forming cells reflects the early differentiation of specificity in chemical composition or metabolism. It has also been questioned whether the heart-forming areas differ chemically from adjacent regions of the embryo. Immunochemical techniques employing as tools specific antiheart sera reveal that the early embryo contains macromolecules identical with or closely related to those of the adult heart, a conclusion that is supported by the additional finding that when early embryos are cultured in a medium containing antiheart serum the development of the heart is differentially suppressed. Similar techniques show time of origin and pattern of localization of the cardiac contractile proteins, myosin and actin.

Synthesis of contractile proteins. The synthesis of cardiac myosin is initiated during the formation of the mesoderm, the protein being detected first during the movement of prospective mesodermal cells through the primitive streak. As these formative movements are terminated, myosin is distributed widely in the ectoderm and mesoderm, but cannot be detected in the endoderm. At the head-process stage, cardiac myosin is restricted to the heart-forming regions of the embryo where, at the same time, the synthesis of cardiac actin is initiated. It is impossible at the present time to say whether the myosin first detected is adult myosin, or a complete myosin molecule closely related to but not identical with the adult protein, a situation that exists in the sequential formation of fetal and adult hemoglobin molecules. It is postulated that, in the formation of cardiac muscle, the contractile proteins

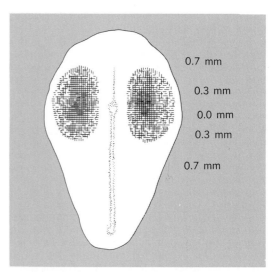

Fig. 18. Heart-forming areas in a head-process stage chick blastoderm. Numerals show distances from level of primitive pit. (*After M. E. Rawles, The heart-forming areas of the early chick blastoderm, Physiol. Zool., 16:22–42, University of Chicago Press, 1943*)

are synthesized and subsequently aggregated to form fibrils. Although this hypothesis of stepwise organization agrees with the limited information available on the development of the fine structure of heart muscle, a note of caution must be expressed, because in skeletal muscle myosin has been detected simultaneously with the formation of the first simple muscle fibrils, and not before. *See* HEMATOPOIESIS.

Action of inhibitors. In further studies of the biochemical differentiation of the heart-forming areas, it has been found that the metabolic pathways operating in the development of the brain and heart differ markedly. When early chick embryos are cultured in vitro on a medium containing traces of the metabolic inhibitor antimycin A, the development of the regions destined to form muscle is inhibited almost completely, whereas the developing brain and spinal cord remain intact. The heart is more sensitive than other mesodermal tissues. Another compound, sodium fluoride, also inhibits development of the heart. The inhibition of the embryo produced by sodium fluoride follows a clear-cut, reproducible pattern, in which the initial sites of inhibition are the heart-forming regions. At succeeding stages in the establishment of the heart, the locations of the cells destroyed by sodium fluoride reflect the sites of highest ability to form pulsatile heart and the area of greatest capacity for the synthesis of actin and myosin. Thus the primary forces operating in the formation of the heart must be sought at the very outset of development.

James D. Ebert

Human Fetal Circulation at Term

The circulation in the mammalian fetus at term must be thoroughly understood as a basis for the consideration of postnatal circulatory changes, because the very mechanisms which ensure intracardiac balance during prenatal life maintain a balanced cardiac load during the changes to the postnatal basis. In this discussion of the fetal circulation at term, the basic conditions presented are essentially applicable to all the higher mammals. Reference to ages and to other specific details are, however, based on the conditions in humans.

By the last trimester of pregnancy all the major blood vessels have been developed in essentially their adult pattern, and all the steps in the partitioning of the embryonic heart are leading progressively closer to the final adult condition, in which the heart is a four-chambered organ completely divided into right and left sides. However, from the nature of its living conditions it is not possible for the fetus in utero to attain fully the adult type of circulation. The plan of the divided circulation of postnatal life is predicated on lung breathing. After birth the right side of the heart receives the blood returning from a circuit of the body and pumps it to the lungs, where it is relieved of carbon dioxide and acquires a fresh supply of oxygen. The left side of the heart then receives the blood that has just been aerated in the lungs and pumps it through ramifying channels to all the tissues of the body. In the last part of intrauterine life the lungs and their blood vessels are fully formed and ready to function, but they cannot actually try out their functional competence until after birth. Nevertheless, in the first minutes of its postnatal life a fetus must successfully change from an existence submerged in the amniotic fluid to air breathing with its hitherto untested lungs. Moreover, this abrupt change must be accomplished without the sudden overloading of any part of the cardiac pump.

It is in the light of these functional exigencies that the fetal circulation at term must be considered. Of primary importance is the fact that at no time during the prenatal life are the atria completely separated from each other. This permits the left atrium to receive a contribution of blood from the inferior vena cava by a transseptal flow which compensates for the relatively small amount of blood entering the left atrium directly by way of the pulmonary circuit. The routes and the relative amounts of this interatrial shunt are different at different ages. Very early in development, before the lungs have grown to any great extent, the pulmonary return is negligible and the flow from the right atrium through the interatrial ostium primum constitutes practically the entire intake of the left atrium (**Fig. 19***b*). After the ostium primum has been closed and while the lungs are but little developed, flow through the interatrial ostium secundum must provide for the major part of the blood entering the left atrium (Fig. 19*d*). During the latter part of fetal life the foramen ovale in the septum secundum becomes the transseptal route for blood (Fig. 19*e* and *f*).

Intracardiac circulatory balance. The precise manner in which this balancing transseptal flow occurs in a fetus at term and where and to what extent the various bloodstreams are mixed has long been a controversial subject. By a synthesis of the most significant of the anatomical evidence with the newer experimental evidence, the course followed by the blood in passing through the heart may be summarized as follows. The inferior caval entrance is so directed with reference to the foramen ovale that a considerable portion of its stream passes directly into the left atrium (**Figs. 20** and **21**). Careful measurements have shown, however, that the interatrial communication through the foramen ovale is considerably smaller than the inferior caval inlet. This implies that the portion of the inferior caval stream which could not pass through this opening into the left atrium must eddy back and mix with the rest of the blood entering the right atrium. Angiocardiographic studies confirm this inference.

Prenatal pulmonary circulation. As the lungs grow and the pulmonary circulation increases in volume relatively less of the left atrial intake comes by way of the foramen ovale and relatively more from the vessels of the growing lungs.

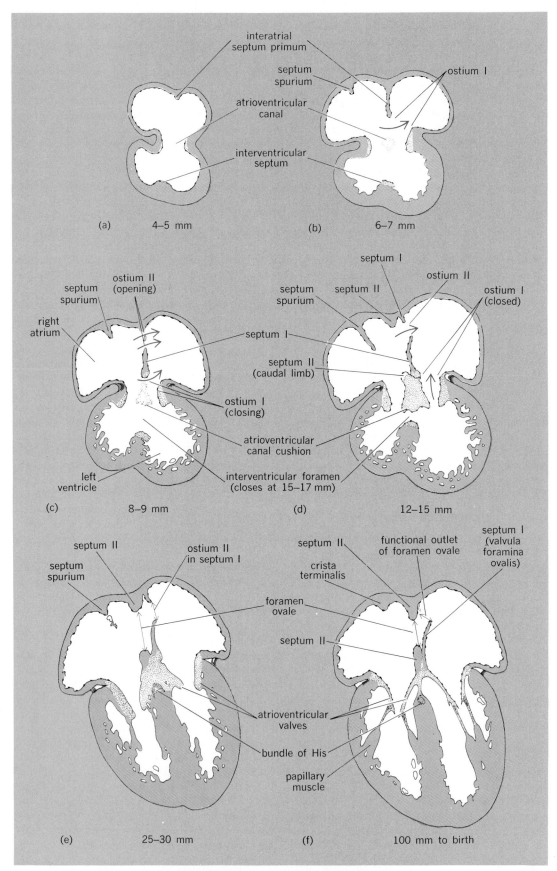

Fig. 19. Sectional plan (*a–f*) of the embryonic heart in frontal plane, showing progress of partitioning in the human embryo. The endocardial cushion tissue is indicated by stippled areas, the muscle by gray areas, and the epicardium by solid black outline. Parts *b* and *c* show the location of endocardial cushions of the atrioventricular canal before they have grown sufficiently to fuse in the plane of the diagram. (*After B. M. Patten, Developmental defects at the foramen ovale, Amer. J. Pathol., 14(2)135–161, 1938*)

However, the circulation of the lungs, although increased as compared with earlier stages, has been shown by angiocardiographic studies to be much less in volume than the caliber of the pulmonary vessels would lead one to expect. Until the lungs are inflated, there are evidently factors, either vasomotor or mechanical or both, which restrict flow through the smaller pulmonary vessels. Therefore, even in the terminal months of pregnancy, a considerable right-left flow must still be maintained through the foramen ovale to keep the left atrial intake equal to that of the right.

Balancing ventricular output. The balanced atrial intake thus maintained implies a balanced ventricular intake, and this in turn implies the necessity of a balanced ventricular output. Although not in the heart itself, there is, in the closely associated great vessels, a mechanism which affords an adequate outlet from the right ventricle during the period when the pulmonary circuit is developing. When the pulmonary arteries are formed as downgrowths from the sixth pair of aortic arches, the right sixth arch soon loses its original connection with the dorsal aorta. On the left, however, a portion of the sixth arch persists as the ductus arteriosus connecting the pulmonary artery with the dorsal aorta (Fig. 21). This vessel remains open throughout fetal life and acts as a shunt, carrying over to the aorta whatever blood the pulmonary vessels at any particular phase of their development are not prepared to receive from the right ventricle. The ductus arteriosus can therefore be called the exercising channel of the right ventricle because it allows the right ventricle to do its full share of work throughout development and thus be prepared to pump its full quota of blood through the lungs at birth.

Thus by means of intake and output shunts there is maintained, throughout prenatal development, an effective right-left balance in the pumping load of the heart. The importance of this for the attainment of normal cardiac structure is forcefully shown by the abnormalities that appear when the balancing mechanisms are in any way disturbed. The importance of these same mechanisms in accomplishing postnatal circulatory changes is discussed in the following section.

Human Postnatal Circulation

The changes in circulation following birth involve some of the most dramatic and fascinating biological processes. One of the most impressive phenomena in embryology is the perfect preparedness for these changes which has been built into the very architecture of the circulatory system during its development. The shunt at the ductus arteriosus, which has been one of the factors in balancing ventricular output throughout intrauterine development, and the valvular mechanism at the foramen ovale, which has been balancing atrial intakes, are perfectly adapted to prevent any abrupt unbalancing of cardiac load as a result of postnatal changes in circulatory routes.

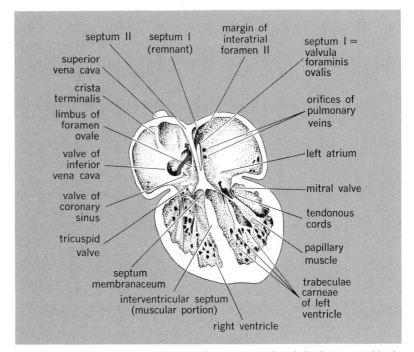

Fig. 20. Interrelations of septum primum and septum secundum during latter part of fetal life. Lower part of septum primum is situated to act as a one-way valve at the foramen ovale in septum secundum. Split arrow indicates the way a considerable part of blood from inferior vena cava passes through foramen ovale to the left atrium while remainder eddies back into the right atrium to mingle with the blood being returned by way of the superior vena cava. (_After B. M. Patten, Foundations of Embryology, 2d ed., McGraw-Hill, 1964_)

Pulmonary circuit and ductus. In much of the older literature, great emphasis was placed on what happened at the foramen ovale. It is now known that these changes are secondary and that the events of primary significance occur in connection with the pulmonary circuit and the ductus arteriosus. In the section on fetal circulation at term, the importance of the ductus arteriosus as an exercising channel for the right ventricle was emphasized. From the standpoint of postnatal circulatory changes, the reciprocal relation between flow through the ductus and flow through the lungs becomes the center of interest. As the lungs increase in size, relatively more of the blood leaving the right ventricle by way of the pulmonary trunk goes to the lungs, and relatively less goes through the ductus arteriosus to the dorsal aorta.

By the end of gestation the pulmonary vessels must be large enough to handle a blood volume adequate to care for oxygenating the blood. Injection preparations of fetuses clearly show that the vascular channels in the lungs are of generous size for this function well before birth. However, such postmortem material does not show that before birth these large vessels are not carrying the blood volume their size would suggest.

Prenatal pulmonary blood flow. The brilliant work of C. Wegelius and J. Lind, utilizing angiocardiographic methods on living fetuses, has shown that the flow of blood through the pulmonary circuit is actually restricted to a volume much below the potential capacity of the vessels. How much of this is the result of mechanical factors, such as the unexpanded condition of the lungs, and how much it depends upon differential vasoconstriction of the smaller vessels within the lungs remains to be determined. It is clear, however, that pulmonary channels of the requisite size have been formed and are ready to increase their blood flow radically and promptly with the beginning of respiration. Within a short time after birth, under the stimulus of functional activity, the lungs are able to take all the blood from the right side of the heart.

Abandonment and closure of ductus. When the lungs accept all the blood entering the pulmonary trunk, blood flow through the ductus arteriosus ceases. Following its functional abandonment, the ductus arteriosus is gradually occluded by an overgrowth of its intimal tissue. This process in the wall of the ductus is as characteristic and regular a feature of the development of the circulatory system as the formation of the cardiac septa. Its earliest phases

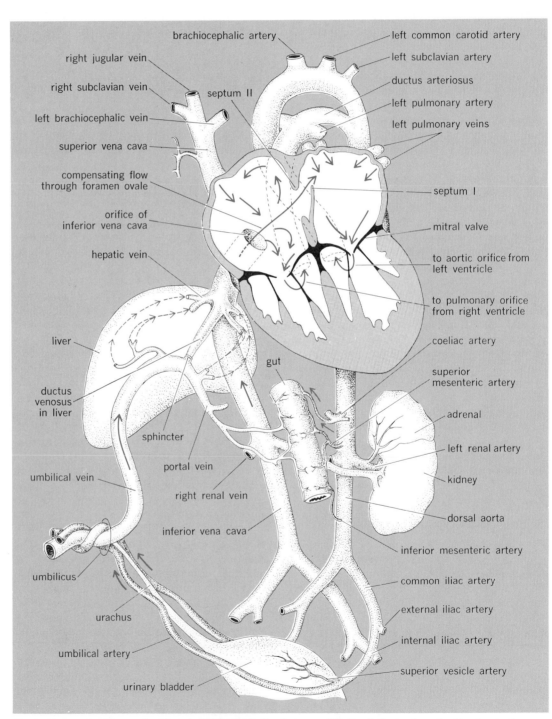

Fig. 21. Heart and major vessels of fetus just before birth. Small arrows within liver indicate alternative blood routes by way of hepatic sinusoids. (*After B. M. Patten, Human Embryology, 3d ed., McGraw-Hill, 1968*)

begin to be recognizable in the fetus as the time of birth approaches, and postnatally the process continues at an accelerated rate, to terminate in complete anatomical occlusion of the lumen of the ductus some 6–8 weeks after birth.

Postnatal readjustment of the circulation cannot, however, wait on this protracted structural closure. Following birth there appears to be an immediate reduction in the bore of the ductus as a result of its muscular contraction. This is accompanied by a reduced flow of blood through it. This reduction in the shunt from the pulmonary circuit to the aorta, acting together with the lowering of resistance in the vascular bed of the lungs which accompanies their newly assumed respiratory activity, aids in raising the pulmonary circulation promptly to full functional level. At the same time, the functional closure of the ductus arteriosus paves the way for the ultimate anatomical obliteration of its lumen by the active growth of its intimal connective tissue.

Closure of foramen ovale. The results of increased pulmonary circulation with the concomitant increase in the direct intake of the left atrium are manifested secondarily at the foramen ovale. Following birth, as the pulmonary return increases, compensatory blood flow from the right atrium to the left decreases correspondingly, and shortly ceases altogether. In other words, when equalization of atrial intakes has occurred, the compensating one-way valve at the foramen ovale falls into disuse and the foramen may be regarded as functionally closed. The abandonment of the shunt at the foramen ovale is indicated anatomically by a progressive reduction in the looseness of the valvula foraminis ovalis and the consequent diminution of the interatrial communication to a progressively narrower slit between the valvula and the septum.

Anatomical obliteration of the foramen ovale slowly follows its functional abandonment (**Fig. 22**). There is a highly variable interval of 3–9 months following birth before the septum primum fuses with the septum secundum to seal the foramen ovale. This delay is, however, of no functional import because as long as the pulmonary circuit is normal and pressure in the left atrium equals or exceeds that in the right, the orifice between them is functionally inoperative. It is not uncommon to find the fusion of these two septa incomplete in the hearts of individuals who have, as far as circulatory disturbances are concerned, lived uneventfully to maturity. Such a condition can be characterized as probe patency of the foramen ovale. When, in such hearts, a probe is inserted under the margin of the fossa ovalis and pushed toward the left atrium, the probe is prying behind the no longer used, but still unfastened, interatrial door.

Physiological aspects of transition. Much yet remains to be learned concerning the more precise physiology of the fetal circulation and concerning the interaction of various factors during the transition from intrauterine to postnatal conditions. Nevertheless, it is quite apparent that the changes in

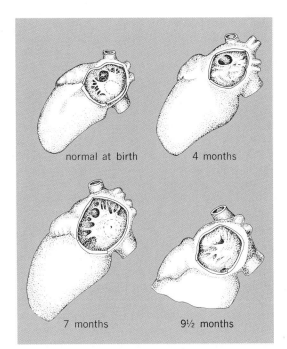

Fig. 22. Hearts with left atrium opened to show gross changes in relations of valvula during period in which foramen ovale closes anatomically. (*After B. M. Patten, The closure of the foramen ovale, Amer. J. Anat., 48:19–44, 1931*)

the circulation which occur following birth involve no revolutionary disturbances of the load carried by different parts of the heart. The fact that the pulmonary vessels are already so well developed before birth means that the changes which must occur following birth have been thoroughly prepared for, and the compensatory mechanisms at the foramen ovale and the ductus arteriosus which have been functioning throughout fetal life are entirely competent to effect the final postnatal reroutings of the circulation with a minimum of functional disturbance. The change from living in water to living in air is crowded into a few crucial moments that in phylogeny must have been spread over eons of transitional amphibious existence.   Bradley M. Patten

Comparative Physiology

Comparative physiology describes the structure and operation of the circulation in animals, and inquires as to how or why the circulatory system may have evolved. Comparing the circulatory system in different animal groups leads to an understanding of general principles and also to various applications of them, adapting animals to a wide range of habitats. The circulatory system in all vertebrates has multiple functions, but all functions are involved in regulating the internal environment of the animal (promoting homeostasis).

General physiology of circulation. In all vertebrates the circulatory system consists of a central pump, the heart, which drives a liquid transport medium, the blood, continuously around a closed system of tubes, the vascular system. The arterial portion of this system is divided into larger elastic and smaller resistance vessels (arterioles) which distribute blood to specialized regions or organs (such as muscles, gut, and lungs) where transfer of nutrients, oxygen, or waste products takes place across the walls of a fine network of microscopic capillaries. Blood from the capillaries passes through the venules (small venous vessels) into the main veins and returns to the heart (**Fig. 23**). The arterioles, venules, and capillaries make up the microcirculation, which is arguably the most important role of the vertebrate circulatory system from a functional point of view.

Blood flow in the circulation occurs from regions of high to regions of low fluid energy (or down an energy gradient). The total fluid energy consists of "pressure" energy (created by the heart) and energy contained in the blood due to its motion (kinetic energy). The latter component is small (1 to 2% of the pressure energy in main arteries) and is usually ignored. Hence, the term "pressure" has become synonymous with the total fluid energy. However, this is not always the case as pressures usually recorded in the circulation are transmural pressures; that is, pressure across the wall of the vessel.

The transmural pressure can be very misleading if it is taken as representing the energy for flow. For example, in a recumbent person, transmural pressure in the foot arteries is 1.7 lb in.$^{-2}$ or 12 kilopascals, but in an erect person, the column of fluid between the heart and foot is subjected to the gravitational force, which means the column bears down on the foot arteries with a pressure equivalent to its height (4 ft or 1.2 m), and adds to the pressure created by the pump. Due to this hydrostatic effect, transmural pressure in the foot may be 2.4 lb in.$^{-2}$ or 24 kPa. However, this hydrostatic effect is also added to the veins so the energy gradient for flow through the vascular beds remains unchanged. In other words, in a closed circulation, flow cannot be maintained by differences in fluid level (hydrostatic pressure). Flow occurs as a result of difference in total fluid energy between two points in the circulation; if these points are at the same fluid level (central arteries and veins), then the energy difference can be measured in terms of pressure.

Energy is dissipated unevenly around the circulation, the major portion being expended to force blood through the arterial resistance vessels (Fig. 23, energy shown as pressure). Even so, loss of energy is not altogether due to friction between the vessel wall and blood but rather to overcoming the internal friction (or viscosity) of the blood. In the circulation, blood flow is usually streamlined or laminar. If blood, flowing in a vessel, is imagined as made up of a series of thin concentric tubes (or laminae), the layer of fluid next to the wall is stationary while that in the center flows fastest. Therefore, successive layers of blood slide past one another, and friction between these layers of fluid dissipates mechanical energy as heat.

The relation between mean pressures (energy) and flows in the body circulation (equally appli-

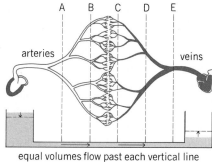

(a)

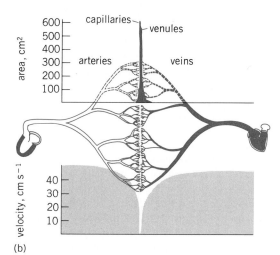

(b)

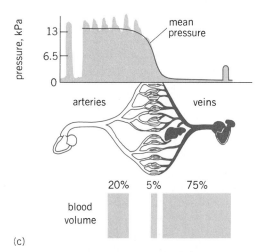

(c)

Fig. 23. Systemic circulatory system in a dog (13 kg or 28.7 lb). (a) Representation of the aborization of the system. All vessels of the same caliber are arranged vertically (at A, B, C, and so on). (b) Increase in cross-sectional area of the various segments. The velocity of blood flow (cm · s⁻¹) is inversely proportional to the cross-sectional area of the tubes through which it flows. (c) Pulsatile and mean pressures in the various vascular segments. At the extreme left is a representation of left ventricular pressure, while right ventricular pressure is shown at the extreme right. The boxes show the proportion of blood volume (approximately 85% of total blood volume) in the systemic arteries (including the heart), capillaries, and veins (the pulmonary circulation has about 10–15% of the total blood volume). (After R. F. Rushmer, Cardiovascular Dynamics, W. B. Saunders, 1961)

cable in general principle to the pulmonary circulation) is shown in Fig. 23. At every division of a blood vessel the cross-sectional area of the branches always exceeds that of the parent vessel (with two branches by a factor of 1.2 to 1.3), so there is a tremendous increase in area as the capillaries are approached (Fig. 23b). In a closed circulation what goes in at one end must come out the other, so the total blood flow through each region must be the same, but the rate of flow will be inversely proportional to the cross-sectional area of any given region (Fig. 23a and b). Since the cross-sectional area of the veins is not much greater than that of the arteries, venous flow rates are high (Fig. 23b). On the other hand, mean pressure in the circulation falls from the arteries to the veins. The major pressure drop in the circulation occurs across the arterial resistance vessels which lead to the capillaries (Fig. 23c). Consequently, venous pressure is low, despite high blood flow rates, and this explains why blood does not spurt out when one severs a vein. The majority of the total blood volume is stored in the venous vessels (Fig. 23c).

Microcirculation. The microcirculation consists of arterial (arterioles) and venous (venules) resistance vessels on either side of the capillaries. The arterioles and venules constitute the pre- and postcapillary resistances respectively. A capillary is a single layer of endothelial cells enclosed by a basement membrane. Blood flow through the capillary is low (at rest, less than 1 mm $\cdot$ s^{-1}) and is controlled by the opening and closing activity of a short muscular region of blood vessel at the capillary entrance (precapillary sphincter). The total number of capillaries, and therefore their surface area for exchange of materials with the cells, is enormous. The systemic (or body) circulation of humans has 40 billion capillaries with a surface area of 10,800 ft^2 (1000 m^2). In the pulmonary (or lung) circuit there are 8 billion capillaries with a combined surface area of 650 ft^2 (60 m^2). Lipid-soluble substances, including oxygen and carbon dioxide, and some water cross the capillary cell walls, whereas most water and all water-soluble substances are exchanged through pores either within or between the cells.

The structure of capillaries is dictated by their function in the organ supplied and falls into three main types which are basically similar in all vertebrates. Fenestrated capillaries have holes through the cells permitting large and rapid exchange of solvent and solutes; the pores may be closed by a delicate membrane. This type of capillary is found in kidney, intestine, and glands. Discontinuous capillaries have large gaps between the cells of the wall, and are found where macromolecules or even red blood cells are exchanged, as in bone marrow, liver, and spleen. Continuous capillaries have an apparently continuous layer of cells and occur in muscle, lungs, and central nervous system. However, there are small-diameter pores between the cells in all tissues except the brain. The brain capillaries of all vertebrates, except those of lampreys and hagfishes, appear to present an extremely effective barrier to the transport of materials across their walls. In conjunction with the astrocytes, modified nonnervous brain cells which invest the brain capillaries, they form an effective blood-brain barrier. Metabolites must cross the blood-brain barrier by specialized carrier systems or active transport, and this explains the abundance of mitochondria in the brain capillaries. Neurons are more sensitive than most cells to an imbalance in their environment, and homeostasis of the neuronal environment is the function of the blood-brain barrier.

Capillaries are generally about the diameter of the red blood cells (RBCs) which flow through them. Hence, in some amphibians (RBC diameter, 80 micrometers) the capillaries are far larger than, for example, in the mouse deer (RBC diameter, 1.5 micrometers). This relation between size of the RBC and capillary means that blood cells move through capillaries one at a time acting as a moving plug, sweeping unstirred fluid layers away from the capillary wall and facilitating exchange across the wall by diffusion, by reducing the diffusion distance. This is referred to as bolus flow.

Pressure and flow. The pulsatility of pressure and flow allied to the anomalous viscosity of blood greatly complicates any attempt to describe mathematically the relationship between pressure and flow in large arteries. However, in arterial resistance vessels both pressure and flow pulsations are dissipated so that a condition of steady pressure and flow is approached in the microcirculation. In large vessels, blood viscosity is high (some four times that of water) and, due to the presence of RBCs, appears to change with flow velocity (anomalous properties). In small vessels (less than 200 μm diameter) the apparent viscosity falls and, in capillaries, appears constant and similar to that of water (Fähraeus-Lindqvist effect).

Given conditions of steady pressure, flow, and viscosity, the relation between pressure and flow in the microcirculation can be described by the Hagen-Poiseuille law, Eq. (1), where $\dot{Q}$ = flow

$$\dot{Q} = \frac{\pi r^4 \cdot [P_1 - P_2]}{8 \eta L} \qquad (1)$$

per unit time, r = radius of the vessel, $P_1 - P_2$ = pressure difference between the upstream and downstream ends of a pipe of length L, and η = blood viscosity. An important relationship emerging from the Hagen-Poiseuille law is that flow varies with the radius of the vessel raised to the fourth power. Thus, if r is halved (by constriction of a blood vessel), then flow through that vessel will be reduced to one-sixteenth [$(^1/_2)^4 = {}^1/_{16}$] of that existing formerly for the same pressure difference.

Hagen-Poiseuille's law is often rewritten in a simplified form, Eq. (2) [where R = resistance

$$\dot{Q} = \frac{P_1 - P_2}{R} \tag{2}$$

$= 8\eta L/\pi r^4$], as a direct analog of Ohm's law describing the relation between electric current, voltage and resistance. This "Ohmic" relation is frequently applied to the whole circulation (not just the microcirculation) to determine total peripheral resistance (TPR) when Q = cardiac output (volume per unit time), P_1 = mean arterial pressure (kPa), and P_2 = mean venous pressure (kPa). TPR is generally expressed in peripheral resistance units (PRU; $kPa \cdot ml^{-1} \cdot unit\ time^{-1}$). To simplify comparisons between animals of vastly different sizes (or even between individual vascular beds in the same animal), cardiac output is usually expressed on a unit weight basis yielding PRU per unit weight (see **table**).

Since flow per unit time ($ml \cdot min^{-1}$) through the vascular system is the same at any two points, capillary pressure (P_c) may be calculated from arterial (P_a) and venous (P_v) pressure by application of the Hagen-Poiseuille law, yielding Eq. (3), where R_a and R_v are the pre- and

$$P_c = \frac{P_a \cdot (R_v/R_a) + P_v}{1 + (R_v/R_a)} \tag{3}$$

postcapillary resistances. Since it is the ratio of these resistances which determines capillary pressure, capillary pressure is largely independent of arterial blood pressure over a wide range. For instance, an R_a/R_v ratio of 5:1 gives $P_c = 1.875$ kPa when $P_a = 10$ kPa and $P_v = 0.25$ kPa. Now if P_a rose to 15 kPa, an adjustment of the ratio to 8:1 would leave P_c unchanged.

Measured capillary pressures are in the range of 1.33 to 4 kPa. This raises the question of why the single layer of cells in the capillary is not disrupted by these high internal pressures. The answer is contained in Laplace's law. This law describes how the wall tension (T) which opposes the distending force of the blood pressure (P) is critically dependent on the radius of the vessel, for Eq. (4). Hence, wall tension in a capillary in

$$P = \frac{T}{r} \tag{4}$$

a human is 1/10,000 of that in the aorta, even though the pressure within is one-fifth of that in the aorta. Not surprisingly the aortic wall is 10,000 times thicker than the capillary wall.

Fluid exchange across capillaries. Water is exchanged

Some cardiovascular variables in selected vertebrates*

Species name (common name)	Conditions	Body mass and temp.	Heart rate, beats · min⁻¹	Cardiac output, ml · min⁻¹ · 100 g⁻¹	Mean arterial pressure, kPa	Mean pulmonary pressure, kPa	Peripheral resistance of body (PRU₁₀₀), kPa · ml⁻¹ · min⁻¹ · 100 g⁻¹	Peripheral resistance of gas exchanger (PRU₁₀₀), kPa · ml⁻¹ · min⁻¹ · 100 g⁻¹
Salmo gairdneri (rainbow trout)	Unrestrained, rest	1.25 kg, 10°C	38	1.76	4[†]	5.06[‡]	2.26	0.6
	Unrestrained, exercise		51	5.26	4.8[†]	8[‡]	0.9	0.6
Xenopus laevis (clawed toad)	Restrained, rest, breathing	0.1 kg, 20°C	45	11	3.74	2.8	0.57	0.43[§]
	Restrained, rest, not breathing		40	6.4	4	3.7	0.56	3.2[§]
Pseudemys scripta (red-eared turtle)	Unrestrained, rest, breathing	1.25 kg, 21°C	23	5.7	3.74	2.4	1.73	0.65
	Unrestrained, rest, not breathing		11	2.65	2.8	2.0	1.94	1.73
Anas platyrhynchos (white pekin duck)	Restrained, anesthetized	2.5 kg, 41°C	219	22	19	2.0	0.87	0.1
	Diving, unanesthetized		30	2	18	1.67	8.33	0.17
Homo sapiens (human)	Unrestrained, rest	70 kg, 37°C	72	8	12	1.75	1.5	0.2
	Maximum exercise		193	33	14.5	2.4	0.44	0.07

*In fish the gills are in series with the body circulation, so the resistances were calculated by using the pressure difference between the ventral and dorsal aorta and the dorsal aorta and veins, respectively. In fish, amphibians, and reptiles the heart is undivided and cardiac output is the total amount of blood pumped per unit time, whereas in birds and mammals cardiac output is the output of only one ventricle or half the output of the whole heart. In all cases, central venous pressures were assumed to be insignificant, except during diving in ducks when both pulmonary and central venous pressure rise to 1.3 kPa.
[†] Dorsal aorta.
[‡] Ventral aorta.
[§] Includes skin.

both across the wall of the capillary and through pores. It is driven out by the blood pressure in the vessel, which is much higher than the pressure in the fluid between cells. In fact, the extracellular fluid pressure is frequently subatmospheric (negative). The venules (small veins), as well as capillaries, are apparently involved in this exchange because the venules are also highly permeable to water. The pressure which filters water out of the capillary (filtration pressure) is opposed by the colloid osmotic pressure (COP) of the blood; COP tends to pull water back into the blood vessel. The COP difference between the blood and the fluid between the cells (interstitial fluid) is almost entirely due to a higher concentration of relatively impermeable proteins in blood plasma; it is equivalent to a pressure of 1.3 to 4 kPa depending on the animal.

At the arterial end of the capillary there is usually a net loss of water because the blood pressure is higher than COP. As water leaves, the blood is concentrated, and its COP increases. This increase in COP, coupled with the fall in blood pressure along the capillary, causes fluid absorption at the venous end. In a human perhaps 21 quarts (20 liters) of fluid is filtered from the body capillaries each day, excluding kidney filtration. Of this filtrate, 17–19 quarts (16–18 liters) are reabsorbed, and the remainder returns to the blood by the lymphatic system. When filtration and absorption are more or less in balance, a Starling equilibrium is said to exist (named after E. H. Starling). However, the degree of equilibrium in individual tissues may vary; some may be exclusively involved in filtration, and others in absorption due to the independent regulation of capillary blood pressure in different tissues.

Obviously, capillary fluid exchange must be regulated if the volume of the blood is to be controlled. The vital importance of this control is seen when animals, such as humans, assume an erect posture. A column of fluid stretching from the heart to the feet applies an additional pressure of 12 kPa to the capillary pressure. This results in a pressure across the capillary wall (transmural pressure) of perhaps 16 kPa. This pressure is added to both arterial and venous sides of the circulation so the pressure gradient for flow across the vascular bed remains unchanged (except that flow resistance may drop because the vessels expand a bit due to the high transmural pressures). However, capillary pressure now greatly exceeds COP, and fluid should be filtered throughout the microcirculation. In fact, this is prevented by a marked reduction in the permeability of the microcirculation due, it is thought, to precapillary sphincters closing off capillaries and thereby reducing the surface area for capillary exchange.

In the brain of erect animals, the hydrostatic effect due to standing is reversed. The blood column must be lifted against gravity from the heart. Thus, in the head of an erect human, there is a negative hydrostatic pressure of 5 kPa, whereas in the giraffe it is 20 kPa. Consequently, a positive capillary pressure, even at the arterial end of the microvasculature, can only be achieved by a high arterial blood pressure. This is the explanation for the extremely high arterial blood pressure in the giraffe. However, at the venous end of the microcirculation, pressures could still be negative, causing veins to collapse. Even though the brain is enclosed within a rigid box, which would tend to prevent blood vessel collapse, many veins are tethered to surrounding skeletal structures to ensure that they remain open.

Control. Microvascular activity is coupled to local tissue function through intrinsic mechanisms which are independent of control by the nervous or hormonal systems. The arterioles, metarterioles, and precapillary sphincters are muscular vessels in which muscle fibers contract spontaneously (myogenic activity), keeping these vessels in a state of partial constriction (basal vascular tone). Increases in blood pressure stretch the vessels, causing an increase in myogenic activity in the vascular smooth muscle and a return toward their original diameter. Any tendency for vessels to close completely is prevented by the accumulation of vasodilator metabolites in the tissues as flow is reduced. Decreases in oxygen and increases in carbon dioxide, both in the blood and tissues, cause muscle relaxation and an increase in vessel diameter (vasodilation). However, in the lung circuit, low oxygen causes blood vessel diameter to decrease (vasoconstriction). This reversal of blood vessel response is related to the lung's role as a supplier, rather than user, of oxygen and has important consequences for distributing blood to areas of the lung where oxygen is available.

The arterioles and metarterioles are also subject to remote control by the nervous system. They are innervated by vasodilator and vasoconstrictor nerve fibers which modulate and sometimes dominate local control systems. In contrast, the precapillary sphincters lack innervation and can only be affected by local or blood-borne excitatory or inhibitory influences.

The endothelial (inner) layer of cells of the blood vessels makes an important contribution to regulation of resistance to flow. Physical stimuli such as stretch, flow, and pressure as well as hormonal influences cause the release of contracting and relaxing factors from the endothelial cells, which affect adjacent smooth muscle. These endothelium-dependent regulatory mechanisms integrate blood vessel responses, and may explain regional differences in responses of vascular beds to the same hormone. The most well-known relaxing factor is nitric oxide (NO), produced from L-arginine, which very rapidly loses its potency in the circulation. Contracting factors include peptides, such as endothelin and prostaglandin which remain active for a considerably longer period of time.

The efficacy of the local control system as an

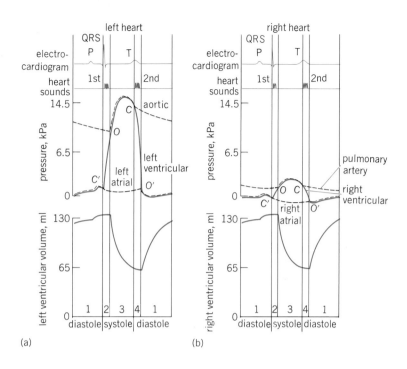

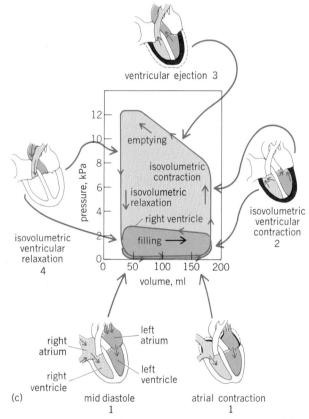

Fig. 24. Mammalian heart. Events in the (a) left heart and aorta and (b) right heart and pulmonary arteries during a cardiac cycle. In a: At C' the atrioventricular valve closes; at O' it opens. At O the aortic valve opens; at C it closes. In b: At C' the atrioventricular valve closes; at O' it opens. At O the pulmonary valve opens; at C it closes (after A. J. Vander et al., Human Physiology, McGraw-Hill, 1975). (c) Pressure-volume loops for the right and left ventricles. The area enclosed by the loop is a measure of the work done by the heart in ejecting blood. Diagrammatic representations of the heart during one cardiac cycle surround the loops and are linked by arrows with their appropriate position (in time) on the loop. The contracting portions of the heart are shown in black. The numbers (1 to 4) under each heart diagram refer to the phases of the cardiac cycle in a and b (after R. Eckert and D. J. Randall, Animal Physiology, W. H. Freeman, 1978)

unaided regulator of blood supply to the tissues is remarkable. For example, blood flow to the brain can be maintained constant despite induced arterial blood pressure changes from 8 to 18 kPa. Such control, in the absence of nerves or blood-borne factors, is referred to as autoregulation.

Heart. The heart is a pump imparting propulsive energy to the blood. Primitively, the heart is a tubular structure equipped with valves to prevent backflow. In more advanced animals it is differentiated into receiving and storage chambers (sinus venosus and atrium) and pumping chambers (ventricle and conus arteriosus). During evolution, these chambers have become folded upon one another; some were incorporated into others, and some subdivided. Sharks and rays have all four chambers, whereas in birds and mammals, the sinus venosus is incorporated into the right atrium and the conus arteriosus into the outflow tract of the ventricle. In birds and mammals the two remaining chambers (atrium and ventricle) are subdivided to form two parallel circulations, one supplying the body and the other the lungs.

In all vertebrates the heart is enclosed in a double-layered membranous pericardium; a liquid-filled space separates the layers. The inner layer of the pericardium is applied to the ventricular surface. In elasmobranchs, the outer layer of the pericardium is extremely thick and is attached to surrounding skeletal structures. As a result, ventricular contraction creates a subatmospheric pressure within the pericardium which tends to stretch the thin-walled atrium so that it fills with blood by aspiration.

Cardiac cycle. In all vertebrates the period of one heartbeat, or cardiac cycle, can be divided into four phases (**Fig. 24**a and b).

1. Filling phase: the inflow valves are open and the outflow valves shut. Ventricular pressure at the start of this phase is low and falling; when it falls below that in the atrium, the atrioventricular valves open and blood flows rapidly into the ventricle. Flow into the ventricle is driven by the energy contained in venous blood. As ventricular pressure rises, flow slows, and atrial contraction "tops up" the ventricle. The end of the ventricular relaxation phase (diastole) is marked by the start of ventricular contraction (systole) which increases ventricular pressure and shuts the atrioventricular valves.

2. Isovolumetric contraction (contraction without a change in volume): both inlet and outlet valves are shut. The ventricular muscle contracts, developing tension, and the pressure of the contained blood increases. In hearts with large and rapid pressure generation the free edges of the atrioventricular valves have guy ropes (chordae tendineae), attached to papillary muscles of the ventricular wall; these prevent the valves being turned inside out.

3. Ejection phase: the rising ventricular pressure exceeds that in the arteries and the outlet valves open; the inlet valves remain closed. Blood is

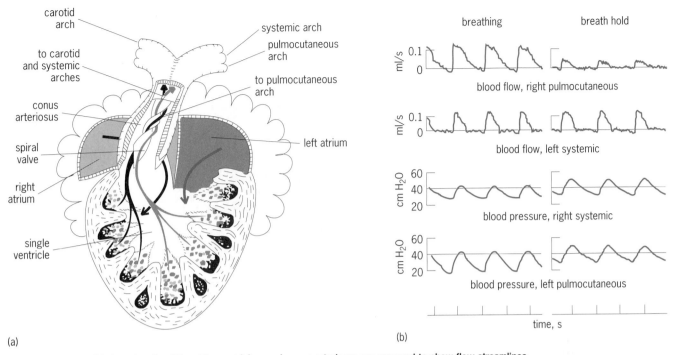

(a)

(b)

Fig. 25. Frog heart. (a) Ventral walls of the atria, ventricles, and conus arteriosus are removed to show flow streamlines that account for selective distribution of oxygenated blood to the head and body via the carotid and systemic arteries, and deoxygenated blood to the lungs via the pulmocutaneous arteries. (b) Blood pressures and flows in the blood vessels supplying the lungs (pulmocutaneous) and body (systemic) during a period of breathing and during a breath hold in the anuran amphibian *Xenopus laevis*. (*After P. S. Davies, Perspectives in Experimental Biology, vol. 1, Pergamon Press, 1976*)

ejected rapidly, but pressure continues to rise in both ventricle and outflow tract until peak systolic pressure is reached. About two-thirds through this phase, ventricular contraction stops and pressure falls; when it falls below arterial pressure, the outflow valves shut, causing a disturbance in the arterial pressure pulse (incisura or dichrotic notch). The amount of blood pumped in this phase, by a single ventricle, is the stroke volume (ml), while cardiac output (ml · min^{-1}) is the product of stroke volume and heart rate (beats · min^{-1}). Backflow of blood is not necessary to shut the outflow valves. When the valve opens during blood ejection, vortices are created between the valve cusp (free edges of the valve) and the aortic wall, and the pressure distribution associated with these vortices deflects the cusps toward apposition (closure) as outflow from the ventricle decelerates. Leonardo da Vinci is credited with first describing the role of vortices in valve closure more than 100 years before W. Harvey's discovery of the circulation. Some lower vertebrates have an extra contractile chamber (conus arteriosus) on the ventricular outflow tract; the conus shuts the outflow valves when it contracts.

4. Isovolumetric relaxation: inflow and outflow valves shut and pressure falls rapidly as the ventricular muscle relaxes. Subatmospheric pressure can occur in this phase due to "elastic recoil" of the walls of the ventricle.

The plot of ventricular pressure against volume describes a closed loop circling counterclockwise with respect to time (Fig. 24c). The area enclosed by the loop is a measure of the work done by the ventricle in ejecting blood. Since pressures in the lung circuit of birds and mammals (see table) are lower than those in the body circulation, the work required to circulate the blood to the lungs is much less.

The ventricles are not divided in amphibians and noncrocodilian reptiles. Since both the lung and body circulations are connected to the same pressure source, flow in each circuit is inversely proportional to the resistance of that circuit. In amphibians such as frogs and toads, during periods of breath holding (apnea) blood can be circulated away from the lung circuit and sent to the body by increasing pulmonary flow resistance (**Fig. 25**). Hence, unlike the situation in avian and mammalian hearts, flows in lung and body circuits can be independent of one another. However, in incompletely divided hearts peak pressures during cardiac contraction have to be the same in both lung and body circuits because they are connected to the same pressure source. The peak pressure must be low; otherwise plasma will filter out of the lung capillaries into the lung and the animal will drown. Only when the heart is completely divided can pressures in lung and body circuits be independent of one another (high pressure in the body, low pressure in the lung), but the price to be paid is that flows in each circuit must now be exquisitely balanced.

Varanid reptiles (for example, monitor lizards),

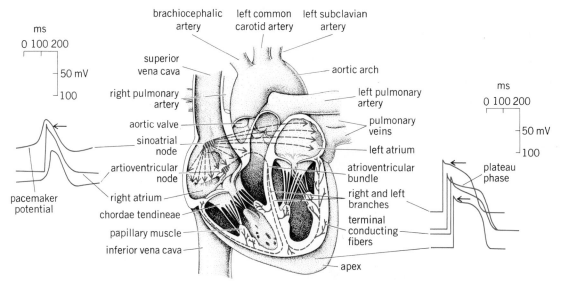

Fig. 26. Anterior view of the opened human heart, showing the pacemaker in the sinus node, the atrioventricular node, and the specialized conduction pathways of the ventricle. Intracellular action potential shapes were recorded at identified sites of the heart during one cardiac cycle. The arrows link the action potentials to the site. Time and voltage calibrations are shown at the left and right. Zero transmembrane voltage is indicated on some of the action potentials by the arrowhead. (*After J. E. Crouch, Functional Human Anatomy, Lea and Febinger, 1978*)

however, show clear pressure separation between lung (low pressure) and body circuits (high pressure), yet the varanid ventricle is morphologically undivided. This extraordinary triumph of physiology over morphology is achieved by partitioning the ventricular cavity during the contraction and relaxation phases. An interventricular partition formed by the atrioventricular valves divides the ventricle during diastole, whereas a musclar ridge within the ventricle divides it at a different site during systole. Crocodilians also have a high-pressure body and low-pressure lung circulation. The heart is completely divided by an interventricular septum, but the left aorta, supplying the body, arises along with the pulmonary artery from the right ventricle. Furthermore, the left and right aortas are joined just outside the heart by a hole in their common wall (foramen of Panizza) and again by a connection behind the heart. Hence, in the crocodilians a unique situation exists, because it is possible for venous blood to be transferred away from the lung circulation and sent back to the body through the left aorta so that both flows and pressures are independent of one another.

In birds and mammals the heart is completely divided, and the flows in both lung and body circuits must be matched. This matching of flows is largely achieved by nervous control although an automatic mechanism, referred to as Starling's law of the heart, could play a role. Starling's law (which also applies to the hearts of lower vertebrates) states that the energy of contraction of ventricular muscle is a function of the length of the muscle fiber. Thus, if in a particular beat a ventricle is filled to a greater extent than the previous one, the next contraction would be more vigorous and a greater volume of blood (stroke volume) would be ejected.

So, if there is an increase in pumping by the right heart, a few beats later more blood will return to the left heart and increase its filling, so its output will rise, maintaining a balance between flows in the two circuits without intervention of any nervous or humoral (blood-borne) control mechanisms.

Pacemaker. The cardiac rhythm is myogenic in all vertebrates, the heartbeat being initiated in a specialized group of muscle cells which form the pacemaker. From the pacemaker, a wave of electrical excitation passes across the heart, activating the contractile process in cardiac muscle. This wave of excitation may pass across the muscle tissue itself or along specialized conducting pathways (Purkinje fibers, which are modified muscle cells; **Fig. 26**). Pacemaker cells are different from other cardiac cells in that the electrical charge across their cell membranes spontaneously and repetitively declines (depolarization). These repeated depolarizations are called pacemaker potentials. They reach a threshold, after a depolarization of some 15 mV, and an action potential is generated (a sudden reversal of the membrane electrical charge). The action potential is propagated from cell to cell, initiating muscle contraction (Fig. 26). The cycle then repeats. An unusual feature of the cardiac action potential is its long duration, compared, for instance, with the action potential in skeletal muscle. If a muscle action potential is short, then further action potentials and contractions can be generated before the muscle relaxes. Consequently, in skeletal muscle a sequence of contractions may sum. However, in the heart the shortest possible interval between two action potentials is still longer than the relaxation time of cardiac muscle. Thus, the sustained contractions (tetanus) characteristic of skeletal muscle, and due to the fusion of individual waves of contraction, cannot occur in cardiac muscle. Tetanus in cardiac muscle would, of course, be maladaptive.

The sum of the electrical events occurring during the synchronous activity of all the cardiac cells can be detected as a series of small voltage changes at points all over the body (Fig. 24a and b). The record of small voltage changes is the electrocardiogram; it exhibits waves associated with atrial depolarization (P-wave), ventricular depolarization (QRS complex), and repolarization (T-wave) [Fig. 24a and b].

In all vertebrate hearts there is a hierarchy of pacemakers. This is reflected in embryonic development where the ventricle is formed and begins beating before the other parts of the heart have differentiated. The ventricular pacemaker sets a slow rate and is superseded by pacemakers, first in the atrium, and ultimately in the sinus venosus. In fish and frogs heart rate is set by the pacemaker in the sinus venosus because it beats fastest and drives the other pacemakers. In birds and mammals the sinus venous is incorporated into the right atrium, and the pacemaker zone is called the sinoatrial node (Fig. 26). The wave of excitation crosses the atrium (in some mammals specialized conducting pathways have been described) at a rate of up to 1 $m \cdot s^{-1}$, but it can only cross to the ventricle through the atrioventricular node. In the atrioventricular node, the rate of conduction slows to 0.05–0.1 $m \cdot s^{-1}$, allowing time for the atrium to complete its contraction before the ventricle is activated. From the atrioventricular node the wave of excitation is propagated rapidly (0.05–2.5 $m \cdot s^{-1}$). In birds and mammals propagation takes place via specialized conducting fibers called in mammals the right and left bundles of His. Lower vertebrates lack specialized conducting fibers and even a discrete atrioventricular node; in noncrocodilian reptiles there is an almost complete ring of junctional tissue between the atria and ventricle.

In all except the lowest vertebrates the pacemaker region receives innervation both from excitatory (sympathetic) and depressor (parasympathetic) nerves. The sympathetic nerves liberate catecholamines which increase the rate of spontaneous depolarization, and therefore heart rate. The parasympathetic nerves liberate acetylcholine which stabilizes the membrane potential and decreases the rate of spontaneous depolarization, so heart rate falls. The extent to which these nerves innervate cardiac muscle or other structures, such as the atrioventricular node, is variable. However, when muscle innervation is dense, catecholamines increase the force of contraction (positive inotropic effect) while acetylcholine decreases it (negative inotropic effect).

The effects of chemicals released by nerves are due to the activation of receptors on the cardiac cell which are specific for that particular chemical. For noradrenaline and adrenaline the receptors are called α and β receptors, respectively. Adrenaline and noradrenaline increase in the circulation in response to stress and stimulate the heart. In many vertebrates, however, the effects are different from those caused by nerves. For instance, circulating adrenaline is unable to reach the same receptors which are activated neurally because the nerve ending is so closely attached to the cardiac cell. Receptors stimulated by nerves have different effects on pacemaker potentials from those accessed from the circulation.

Arteries. The arteries are the connecting tubes between the heart and the microcirculatory vessels. They are largest and most distensible just outside the heart. They decrease in diameter and flexibility at every bifurcation, so the arterial tree is said to display both geometric and elastic taper. The vessels within the thorax are extremely distensible due to a much higher proportion of rubbery (elastin) to stiff (collagen) fibers in their walls. In nonthoracic arteries collagen dominates the wall composition, but its proportion remains constant as the vessels get stiffer with their approach to the periphery.

During the ejection phase of the cardiac cycle much of the blood is temporarily stored in the central arteries as these become distended by the pressure rise. This blood is fed into the peripheral circulation, by the rebound of the stretched elastic walls, throughout diastole. Consequently, a highly pulsatile input is transformed into a more even outflow (**Fig. 27**a). However, in a large number of animals (such as humans, dogs, and ducks) this is not the case with the pressure pulse. The pressure pulse is amplified in the peripheral vessels (peaking), and both the size and rate of rise of the pulse wave is greater than in the more central vessels (Fig. 27a). On the other hand, small high-frequency components such as the incisura disappear from the peripheral pulse as they are damped out (Fig. 27a).

The pressure pulse wave travels through the arteries at a velocity which depends on the viscosity of the fluid and distensibility of the vessel. In humans it picks up speed, from 3 $m \cdot s^{-1}$ centrally, to 5–10 $m \cdot s^{-1}$ in peripheral arteries. At every discontinuity in the arterial tree (regions of geometric and elastic taper and, more importantly, the terminal vascular beds) the incident wave will be reflected toward the heart. At any major reflecting sites, such as the terminal vascular beds, the incident wave and the reflected wave will be almost in phase and will sum so that the pressure pulse increases in size (Fig. 27a). If the heart is positioned one-quarter of a wavelength back from the major reflecting sites (wavelength is the pulse velocity divided by the cycle length), the incident wave will have passed here one-quarter wavelength before (with respect to the reflecting sites) and the reflected wave will arrive here one-quarter wavelength later (with respect to the reflecting sites) so the two waves will be out of phase, by half a wavelength, and will cancel one another out. Hence, the pressure pulsations in central arteries will be reduced by wave reflection

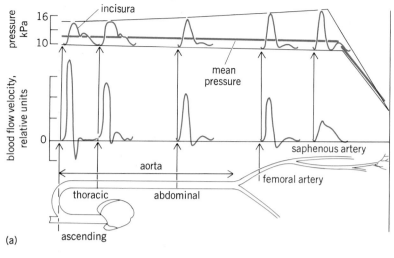

(a)

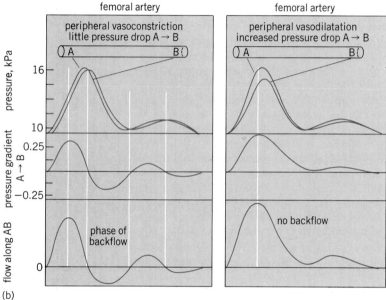

(b)

Fig. 27. Arterial circulation. (*a*) Comparison of the behavior of the pressure and flow velocity pulses from the ascending aorta until the saphenous artery. (*b*) The propagation of the pulse wave along an artery, with deduction of the pressure gradient and the phasic flow. (*After B. Folkow and E. Neil, Circulation, Oxford University Press, 1971*)

(Fig. 27*a*). In mammals about 30% of cardiac power is invested in pulsatile pressure and subsequent flow, so by reducing the pressure pulsations just outside the heart, energy can be saved. Peaking occurs only if the transit time is a significant proportion of the cardiac cycle. In humans mean pulse wave velocity is around 5–6 m · s⁻¹ at a cardiac interval of 1 s, so the transit time is about a quarter of the cardiac cycle (quarter wavelength) and, as described above, pulse amplification occurs. However, arteriosclerotic individuals (be they ducks, dogs, or humans) do not show peaking of the pressure pulse since the pulse wave velocity in the "hardened" arteries is extremely fast and transit time through the circulation is greatly reduced. This lack of pulse wave amplification may contribute to the deleterious effects of this condition on the heart. In frogs mean pulse wave velocity is around 3 m · s⁻¹ at a cardiac interval of 1 s, so

the transit time is about 50 ms, and the shape of the peripheral pulse in frogs is, except for damping of fast components (incisura), identical in shape to that in central arteries.

As blood is pumped through the circulation, energy is dissipated and mean pressure drops (Fig. 27*a*). Mean pressure is a steady pressure obtained by integrating the pressure pulse over one or several cardiac cycles and is somewhat lower than the arithmetic mean of systolic and diastolic pressures. When peaking occurs, the pressure pulse gets bigger but much narrower (Fig. 27*a*), and mean pressure is still lower in the peripheral arteries compared with the central arteries. Therefore, the flow occurs down the mean pressure gradient.

Unfortunately, an analysis in terms of steady pressures and flows tells little about the shapes of the pressure and flow pulses. Why does flow reverse at certain portions of the cardiac cycle? The reason is that the pulsatile pressure gradient reverses in those phases (Fig. 27*b*). The pressure pulse travels through the arterial tree with a velocity from 3 to 10 m · s⁻¹. If pressure is recorded at two sites in a vessel that are a small distance apart, then as the wave passes the upstream point, pressure will exceed that downstream and forward flow will occur (Fig. 27*b*). When the wave moves on and passes the downstream point, pressure there will exceed the pressure upstream and the flow will reverse (Fig. 27*b*). In fact, it is the pressure difference between the upstream and downstream points (the pressure gradient) which oscillates about a mean and is closely linked to the flow velocity (Fig. 27*b*).

Arterial blood pressure is controlled, at least in the short term, through the agency of arterial baroreceptors. Baroreceptors are specialized nerve endings located in the walls of major vessels; they are stimulated when the wall is expanded by the blood pressure. They have been found in the aortic arch and carotid sinus of mammals, the aortic arch of birds, and the carotid labyrinth of amphibians. Claims have been made for their existence in fishes. Blood pressure is controlled using the negative feedback principle. A rise in blood pressure stimulates baroreceptors which send electrical messages (action potentials) to the brain where they are directed to regions involved in control and adjustment of heart rate, stroke volume, and resistance in the peripheral blood vessels. In response to a rise in blood pressure, heart rate, stroke volume, and peripheral resistance are reduced. Input from mechanically stimulated receptors in the heart and lungs, and from chemoreceptors (measuring blood oxygen and carbon dioxide) in the vascular system and brain, are also involved in regulating the circulatory system.

Venous system. From the capillaries the blood passes through venules to successively larger veins and returns to the heart. Aside from being conduits for returning blood to the heart, the major function of the venous system is as a storage site for blood (Fig. 23). Veins are thin-walled, although the larger ones have a muscular coat, and are distended by small changes in pressure across their walls (transmural pressure). A pressure rise causes the veins to change from an elliptical cross-sectional profile to one that is nearly circular, greatly increasing blood storage while reducing flow resistance. Contraction of the muscles in the walls of the larger veins (venomotor activity) reverses the effects of increases in transmural pressure. Venoconstriction is under the control of the sympathetic nervous system.

In larger veins, valves appear as intimal folds and ensure that flow moves only in one direction. In humans some veins such as the vena cava, hepatic, pulmonary, and cerebral veins lack valves, a feature shared with the major veins running the length of the body in fishes. In elasmobranchs, these long veins have a unique structure; they are invested with such a thick connective tissue sheath that they are virtually incompressible tubes. Elasmobranch fishes and some seals also have a muscular venous sphincter located between the liver and heart which regulates venous return when venous pressure rises during exercise (elasmobranch) or diving (seal).

In most animals the majority of the venous reservoir is placed level with or above the heart (even in giraffes). However, in erect animals (primarily humans) the majority of the venous reservoir is below the heart. Consequently, due to the hydrostatic effect (as described above), transmural pressure will increase in veins below the heart and will decrease in those above. Hence, when the animal is upright, leg veins distend and head veins may collapse. This hydrostatic effect has no "direct" effect on flow (aside from the fact that flow resistance will fall as vessels distend or increase if they collapse) since it is added to both arterial and venous sides of the circulation.

Venous return is caused by the forward push of the blood generated by the heart and transmitted in the form of a positive pressure across the capillaries (*vis à tergo*). In the pulmonary circulation and, on the body side in some lower vertebrates, the arterial pressure pulse may be transmitted across the capillaries. Even when these pulsations are damped out, venous pressure pulsations occur in central veins as heart movements are transmitted "backward" to these veins. In some animals venous return is promoted by a suction force (*vis à fronte*) due to subatomospheric pressures in the cardiac cavities caused either by a negative intrapericardial pressure stretching the atrium, as in elasmobranchs, or, in animals lacking a rigid pericardium, to "elastic recoil" of the ventricles, or atrial volume changes associated with ventricular relaxation. When veins with valves run through blocks of skeletal muscle, contraction of these muscles squeezes blood toward the heart (muscle pump).

The muscle pump works in all vertebrates; in some fishes, even the arteries within the muscle mass have valves to ensure unidirectional flow of blood. In animals that have a diaphragm, inspiration aids venous return; since pressure within the thorax is at subatmospheric level, the transmural pressure of intrathoracic veins increases, and they expand. At the same time, abdominal pressure rises, so the transmural pressure in extrathoracic veins will decrease and they will be compressed, thus forcing blood toward the heart. Hence, at the diaphragm a sharp drop in venous pressure occurs which is referred to as a vascular waterfall.   David R. Jones

Bibliography. C. R. Austin and R. V. Short, *Embryonic and Fetal Development*, 1983; H. S. Badeer, *Cardiovascular Physiology*, 1983; R. W. Blake (ed.), *Efficiency and Economy in Animal Physiology*, 1991; W. W. Nichols and M. F. Rourke, *McDonald's Blood Flow in Arteries*, 1990; C. L. Prosser, *Comparative Animal Physiology*, 4th ed., 1991; A. S. Romer and T. S. Parsons, *The Vertebrate Body*, 6th ed., 1986.

Carnauba wax

Product exuded from the leaves of the wax palm, *Copernicia cerifera* (Palmae), a native of Brazil and other regions in tropical South America. The wax accumulates on the surface of the leaves; these are cut from the trees and dried, whereupon the layer of wax becomes loose and is easily removed by flailing. It is the hardest, highest-melting natural wax and is used in making candles, shoe polish, high-luster wax, varnishes, phonograph records, and surface coating of automobiles. *See* ARECALES; WAX, ANIMAL AND VEGETABLE.   Earl L. Core

Carnivora

One of the larger orders of placental mammals, including fossil and living dogs, raccoons, pandas, bears, weasels, skunks, badgers, otters, mongooses, civets, cats, hyenas, seals, walruses, and many extinct groups organized into 12 families, with about 112 living genera and more than twice as many extinct genera. The primary adaptation in this order was for predation on other vertebrates and invertebrates. A few carnivorans (for example, bear and panda) have secondarily become largely or entirely herbivorous, but even then the ancestral adaptations for predation are still clearly evident in the structure of the teeth and jaws. The Carnivora have been highly successful animals since their first appearance in the early Paleocene. During the early Tertiary they shared the predatory mode of life with carnivorous members of some other placental orders, particularly the Deltatheridia, to the extent that few other mammals succeeded in invading this adaptive zone. *See* DELTATHERIDIA.

Structural adaptations. Meat-eating adaptations involving the teeth and jaws appeared early in the history of Carnivora. The dentition is sharply

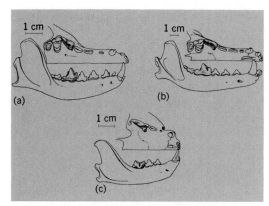

Fig. 1. Upper and lower dentition of the right side representing the superfamilies of Carnivora, carnassials shaded. (a) Miacoidea, *Miacis*, Eocene. (b) Canoidea, *Canis*, Recent. (c) Feloidea, *Felis*, Recent.

divided into three functional units. The incisors act as a tool for nipping and delicate prehension, and the large interlocking upper and lower canines for heavy piercing and tearing during the killing of prey. The cheek teeth are divided into premolars (for heavy prehension) and molars (for slicing and grinding), which may be variously modified depending on the specific adaptation. A diagnostic feature of the Carnivora is the enlargement of the last (fourth) upper premolar and the first lower molar to form longitudinally aligned opposed shearing blades. This important pair of teeth are termed the carnassials. Primitively, the dental formula was that common to all early placentals, but in most carnivores there is often loss of anterior premolars and posterior molars, with the strictly carnivorous forms, such as cats, reducing the number of cheek teeth the most (**Fig. 1**). *See* DENTITION.

In all carnivorans the jaw articulation is arranged in such a manner that movement is limited to vertical hinge motions and transverse sliding. The temporal muscle dominates the jaw musculature, forming at least one-half of the total mass of the jaw muscles. Cursorial adaptations of the limbs appeared early in carnivore history and have always been characteristic of the order. In all modern carnivorans the brain is large and the cerebral hemispheres are highly developed; evolution of the brain seems to have proceeded at an accelerated pace during the latter half of the Cenozoic.

Phylogeny. The history of the Carnivora is relatively well documented despite the fact that fossils are rarely abundant. The earliest records are early Paleocene, but the earliest well-represented material comes from the middle Paleocene of North America. During the Paleocene and Eocene the stem-carnivorans, or miacoids, underwent considerable diversification in both the Old and New worlds. These animals were small- to medium-sized, usually with the full eutherian dental formula, and the fourth upper premolars and first lower molars were developed as carnassials. The feet were plantigrade or subdigitigrade with separate scaphoid and lunar bones in the wrist. The middle-

ear region lacked a completely ossified cover or bulla, although the bony tympanic ring was present. The internal carotid artery was primitively three-branched (median, promontory, and stapedial branches).

At the end of Eocene and beginning of Oligocene time throughout the Northern Hemisphere, a dramatic change took place within the Carnivora— the appearance of primitive representatives of modern carnivoran families (**Fig. 2**). These animals had more cursorial limbs than their miacoid predecessors, with fused scaphoid and lunar bones, and completely ossified bullae, and the internal carotid was reduced to a two-branched (median and promontory) or single (median) vessel. Commonly the dentition showed reduction or loss of anterior premolars and posterior molars. There is little doubt that the miacoids are the progenitors of the earliest members of the modern carnivoran families, but analysis of available fossil evidence has allowed only limited determination of the exact lineages.

A second adaptive radiation of the Carnivora was initiated by these primitive members of the living families. Eventually this radiation brought about the extinction of contemporary carnivores, the Creodonta (family Hyaenodontidae did persist into late Miocene in the Old World tropics). During this second adaptive radiation of the Carnivora, a wider variety of ecologic niches was exploited than is shown by the fossil record of the early Cenozoic radiation. Striking among these are the development of crushing dentitions for omnivorous diets, loss of teeth for ant and termite feeding, hypertrophy of both premolars and molars for bone crushing, and most spectacularly the total modifications of skeleton and soft parts for aquatic existence in the open ocean.

Taxonomy. Historically, the order Carnivora has been divided into suborders Creodonta, Fissipeda, and Pinnipedia. Research on early Cenozoic fossils casts serious doubt on the affinity of the creodonts with the remainder of the Carnivora; they appear to be a convergent group of eutherians, some of which occupied the same adaptive zone as the Fissipeda. They are now placed in their own order, Creodonta. Furthermore, the Fissipeda and Pinnipedia do not denote a primary subdivision of the Carnivora as historically conceived. Although the living pelagic carnivorans and fossil allies (Pinnipedia) do seem to form a natural (that is, monophyletic) group, they originate from carnivorans embedded within the fissiped group. Such a twofold subdivision of the order Carnivora no longer expresses knowledge of the group's phylogeny. A threefold subdivision of the order has long been practiced, and the following superfamilies seem a better expression of the phylogenetic relationships: Miacoidea, Canoidea, and Feloidea. *See* CONDYLARTHRA; EUTHERIA.

Miacoidea. The basic features of these ancestral carnivorans are mentioned above. Two families, the Miacidae and the Viverravidae, are often recognized. These animals occur in early Paleocene through late Eocene deposits in North America. In Europe they are known only from the Eocene. They have not been recognized in Africa. Members of the Viverravidae occur earliest in the fossil record. They have reduced dentitions that suggest special affinity with the Feloidea. The miacids include forms that resemble the Canoidea, and some may eventually be recognized as members of canoid families.

Canoidea. This group of doglike carnivorans first appears in the late Eocene of North America and Eurasia. They possess an auditory bulla, formed from both the entotympanic and ectotympanic (tympanic ring), that primitively lacks an internal septum. The Canoidea consists of seven living families: Canidae (dogs and their allies), Procyonidae (raccoons and their allies), Ursidae (bears and their allies), Mustelidae (weasels and their allies), and the pinniped families, Otariidae (sea lions), Odobenidae (walruses), and Phocidae (seals). All the terrestrial families appear in the fossil record during the Oligocene, and there seems little doubt that they are a closely related group. The pinniped families appear to be related to an extinct group that lies within the Ursidae. The fossil record reveals an eighth canoid family, the Amphicyonidae, that lies near the base of the canoid phyletic tree. This group, which included giant predators in the

Miocene, persisted into the late Miocene of Eurasia. *See* BADGER; BEAR; COATI; DOG; FERRET; FISHER; MARTEN; MINK; OTTER; PANDA; PINNIPEDS; RACCOON; SEALS AND ALLIES; SKUNK; WEASEL; WOLVERINE.

Feloidea. The catlike carnivorans also first appear in the late Eocene or early Oligocene in both the Old and New worlds. Four living families are currently recognized: Viverridae (civets) Herpestidae (mongooses), Hyaenidae (hyenas and aardwolf), and Felidae (cats and saber-toothed cats). Nearly all the fossil and living members of these families possess an auditory bulla divided by a septum formed at the junction of the entotympanic and ectotympanic bones. An exception is the living African palm civet (*Nandinia*) in which only the ectotympanic is fully ossified and the entotympanic is cartilaginous or poorly ossified. In addition, *Nandinia* appears to represent the primitive condition of the bulla in feloids. The herpestids and hyaenids appear in early to medial Miocene time and may be the youngest terrestrial carnivoran families to arise. Members of extinct family of feloids, the Nimravidae, often assigned to the Felidae, retained their primitive cranial features although possessing felid teeth and skeletons. Representatives of this group appeared first in the late Eocene of North America, and by the Oligocene the nimravids were dis-

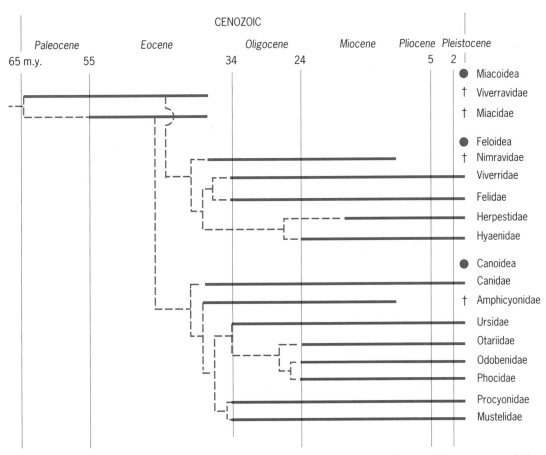

Fig. 2. Phylogenetic relationships and geologic ranges of the carnivoran families. The heavy lines indicate known geologic ranges, and the broken lines indicate predicted ranges inferred from phylogenetic relationships. Daggers indicate extinct families.

tributed across the continents of the Northern Hemisphere. All nimravid species have bladelike upper canine teeth, and in some, such as the late Cenozoic saber-toothed felids, the canines are greatly lengthened. Saberlike upper canines also evolved in other orders of carnivorous mammals such as the Credonta (family Hyaenodontidae) and the Marsupialia (family Borhyaenidae), and at least twice within the Carnivora (families Nimravidae and Felidae), providing a striking case of convergence in a specialized feeding mechanism. *See* CAT; CIVET; HYAENA; MAMMALIA; MONGOOSE.   **Richard H. Tedford**

Carnot cycle

A hypothetical thermodynamic cycle originated by Sadi Carnot and used as a standard of comparison for actual cycles. The Carnot cycle shows that, even under ideal conditions, a heat engine cannot convert all the heat energy supplied to it into mechanical energy; some of the heat energy must be rejected. In a Carnot cycle, an engine accepts heat energy from a high-temperature source, or hot body, converts part of the received energy into mechanical (or electrical) work, and rejects the remainder to a low-temperature sink, or cold body. The greater the temperature difference between the source and sink, the greater the efficiency of the heat engine.

The Carnot cycle (**Fig. 1**) consists first of an isentropic compression, then an isothermal heat addition, followed by an isothermal expansion, and concludes with an isentropic heat rejection process. In short, the processes are compression, addition of heat, expansion, and rejection of heat, all in a qualified and definite manner.

Processes. The air-standard engine, in which air alone constitutes the working medium, illustrates the Carnot cycle. A cylinder of air has perfectly insulated walls and a frictionless piston. The top of the cylinder, called the cylinder head, can either be covered with a thermal insulator, or, if the insulation is removed, can serve as a heat transfer surface for heating or cooling the cylinder contents.

Initially, the piston is somewhere between the top and the bottom of the engine's stroke, and the air is at some corresponding intermediate pressure but at low temperature. Insulation covers the cylinder head. By employing mechanical work from the surroundings, the system undergoes a reversible adiabatic, or an isentropic, compression. With no heat transfer, this compression process raises both the pressure and the temperature of the air, and is shown as the path *a-b* on Fig. 1.

After the isentropic compression carries the piston to the top of its stroke, the piston is ready to reverse its direction and start down. The second process is one of constant-temperature heat addition. The insulation is removed from the cylinder head, and a heat source, or hot body, applied that is so large that any heat flow from it will not affect its temperature. The hot body is at

a temperature just barely higher than that of the gas it is to heat. The temperature gradient is so small it is considered reversible; that is, if the temperature changed slightly the heat might flow in the other direction, from the gas into the hot body. In the heat addition process, enough heat flows from the hot body into the gas to maintain the temperature of the gas while it slowly expands and does useful work on the surroundings. All the heat is added to the working substance at this constant top temperature of the cycle. This second process is shown as *b-c* on Fig. 1.

Part way down the cylinder, the piston is stopped; the hot body is removed from the cylinder head, and an insulating cover is put in its place. Then the third process of the cycle begins; it is a frictionless expansion, devoid of heat transfer, and carries the piston to the bottom of its travel. This isentropic expansion reduces both the pressure and the temperature to the bottom values of the cycle. For comparable piston motion, this isentropic expansion drops the pressure to a greater extent than the isothermal process would do. The path *c-d* on Fig. 1 represents this third process, and is steeper on the *P-v* plane than process *b-c*.

The last process is the return of the piston to

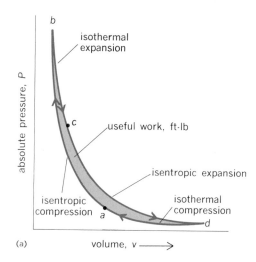

(a)

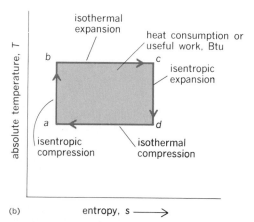

(b)

Fig. 1. Carnot cycle for air. (a) Pressure-volume diagram. (b) Temperature-entropy diagram.

the same position in the cylinder as at the start. This last process is an isothermal compression and simultaneous rejection of heat to a cold body which has replaced the insulation on the cylinder head. Again, the cold body is so large that heat flow to it does not change its temperature, and its temperature is only infinitesimally lower than that of the gas in the system. Thus, the heat rejected during the cycle flows from the system at a constant low-temperature level. The path *d-a* on Fig. 1 shows this last process.

The net effect of the cycle is that heat is added at a constant high temperature, somewhat less heat is rejected at a constant low temperature, and the algebraic sum of these heat quantities is equal to the work done by the cycle.

Figure 1 shows a Carnot cycle when air is used as the working substance. The *P-υ* diagram for this cycle changes somewhat when a vapor or a liquid is used, or when a phase change occurs during the cycle, but the *T-s* diagram always remains a rectangle regardless of phase changes or of working substances employed.

It is significant that this cycle is always a rectangle on the *T-s* plane, independent of substances used, for Carnot was thus able to show that neither pressure, volume, nor any other factor except temperature could affect the thermal efficiency of his cycle. Raising the hot-body temperature raises the upper boundary of the rectangular figure, increases the area, and thereby increases the work done and the efficiency, because this area represents the net work output of the cycle. Similarly, lowering the cold-body temperature increases the area, the work done, and the efficiency. In practice, nature establishes the temperature of the coldest body available, such as the temperature of ambient air or river water, and the bottom line of the rectangle cannot circumvent this natural limit.

The thermal efficiency of the Carnot cycle is solely a function of the temperature at which heat is added (phase *b-c*) and the temperature at which heat is rejected (phase *d-a*) [Fig. 1]. The rectangular area of the *T-s* diagram represents the work done in the cycle so that thermal efficiency, which is the ratio of work done to the heat added, equals $(T_{hot} - T_{cold})T_{hot}$. For the case of atmospheric temperature for the heat sink ($T_{cold} = 500°R$), the thermal efficiency, as a function of the temperature of the heat source, T_{hot}, is shown in **Fig. 2**.

Carnot cycle with steam. If steam is used in a Carnot cycle, it can be handled by the following flow arrangement. Let saturated dry steam at 500°F (260°C) flow to the throttle of a perfect turbine where it expands isentropically down to a pressure corresponding to a saturation temperature of the cold body. The exhausted steam from the turbine, which is no longer dry, but contains several percent moisture, is led to a heat exchanger called a condenser. In this device there is a constant-pressure, constant-temperature, heat-rejection process during which more of the steam with a particular pre-

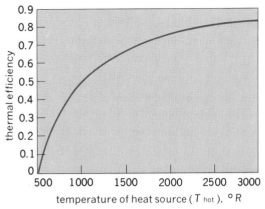

Fig. 2. Thermal efficiency of the Carnot cycle with heat-rejection temperature T_{cold} equal to 500°R (278 K).

termined amount of condensed liquid is then handled by an ideal compression device. The isentropically compressed mixture may emerge from the compressor as completely saturated liquid at the saturation pressure corresponding to the hot-body temperature. The cycle is closed by the hot body's evaporating the liquid to dry saturated vapor ready to flow to the turbine.

The cycle is depicted in **Fig. 3** by *c-d* as the isentropic expansion in the turbine; *d-a* is the constant-temperature condensation and heat rejection to the cold body; *a-b* is the isentropic compression; and *b-c* is the constant-temperature boiling by heat transferred from the hot body. *See* STEAM ENGINE.

Carnot cycle with radiant energy. Because a Carnot cycle can be carried out with any arbitrary system, it has been analyzed when the working substance was considered to be a batch of radiant energy in an evacuated cylinder. If the system boundaries are perfectly reflecting thermal insulators, the enclosed radiant energy will be reflected and re-reflected with no loss of radiant energy and no change of wavelength.

The electromagnetic theory of radiation asserts that the radiant energy applies pressure P to the cylinder walls. This radiation pressure is equal to $u/3$, where u represents the radiant energy density, or the amount of radiant energy per unit volume.

The piston moves so that the cylinder boundaries expand, and additional radiant energy is supplied

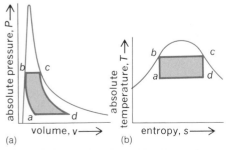

Fig. 3. Carnot cycle with steam. (*a*) Pressure-volume diagram. (*b*) Temperature-entropy diagram.

to the system so that the temperature remains constant. Then, cutting off any further supply of radiant energy, the system undergoes a further infinitesimal expansion with its associated pressure drop and temperature drop. The third process is an isothermal compression at the low-temperature level, accompanied by some rejection of radiant energy. One last process closes the cycle with a reversible compression that raises the temperature to the original level. The assumption is made throughout this analysis that energy density is a function of temperature alone. Thus, because this last compression process increases the energy density, it raises the temperature.

A record of all energy quantities in this radiant-energy Carnot cycle indicates that energy density u is proportional to the fourth power of the absolute temperature. Consequently the total rate of emission of radiant energy from the surface of a blackbody is also proportional to the fourth power of its absolute temperature, thereby using a Carnot cycle to provide a relationship by theoretical analysis, the same relationship which had previously been determined experimentally and labeled as Stefan's law.

Conversion of heat to electricity. Several physical phenomena convert heat energy directly into electrical energy. The extent of this direct conversion of heat to electricity is limited by the temperature levels between which the process operates. The ideal efficiency of such direct-conversion thermoelectric cycles equals the efficiency of a Carnot cycle that operates between the same temperature limits of heat source and heat sink. However, the conversion efficiency obtained in practice is only a small fraction of the ideal efficiency at the present stage of development.

The most widely known physical arrangement for direct thermoelectric generation is the thermocouple, which produces an electromotive force, or voltage, when one junction of two dissimilar conductors is heated while the other junction is kept cool. Thermocouples made of metals are inefficient converters of heat energy to electric energy, because metals that have good electrical conductivity unfortunately have equally good thermal conductivity, which permits heat loss by conduction from the hot to the cold junction. In contrast, thermocouples made of semiconductors offer the prospect of operation at high temperatures and with high temperature gradients, because semiconductors are good electrical conductors but poor heat conductors. Semiconductor thermocouples may have as large a junction potential as the metal couples do. *See* THERMOCOUPLE.

Thermionic emission is another phenomenon that permits the partial conversion of heat energy directly into electrical energy. Externally applied heat imparts kinetic energy to electrons, liberating them from a surface. The density of the emission current is a function of the absolute temperature and work function of the emitter material.

For many years thermionic emission received little attention as a source of power because of its very low conversion efficiency. However, interest was stimulated by development of a contact potential thermionic emission cell. In this device, current flows between the surfaces of two materials which have different work functions. These materials are held at different temperatures, and the gap between the electrode surfaces is filled with gas at low pressure. *See* THERMIONIC EMISSION.

Such direct-conversion techniques show promise of becoming small-scale, if unconventional, power sources. Although these techniques ideally can convert heat to electrical energy with the efficiency of a Carnot cycle operating between the same temperature levels, laboratory devices do not surpass about 8% efficiency, which is just a fraction of the ideal performance.

Reversed Carnot cycle. A Carnot cycle consists entirely of reversible processes; thus it can theoretically operate to withdraw heat from a cold body and to discharge that heat to a hot body. To do so, the cycle requires work input from its surroundings. The heat equivalent of this work input is also discharged to the hot body.

Just as the Carnot cycle provides the highest efficiency for a power cycle operating between two fixed temperatures, so does the reversed Carnot cycle provide the best coefficient of performance for a device pumping heat from a low temperature to a higher one. This coefficient of performance is defined as the ratio of the quantity of heat pumped to the amount of work required, or it equals $T_{hot}(T_{hot} - T_{cold})$ for a warming machine, and $T_{cold}(T_{hot} - T_{cold})$ for a cooling machine, where all temperatures are in degrees absolute. This is one of the few engineering indices with numerical values greater than unity. *See* HEAT PUMP; REFRIGERATION CYCLE.

Practical limitations. Good as the ideal Carnot cycle may be, there are serious difficulties that emerge when one wishes to make an actual Carnot engine. The method of heat transfer through the cylinder head either limits the operation of the engine to very low speeds, or requires an engine with a huge bore and small stroke. Moreover, the material of the cylinder head is subjected to the full top temperature of the cycle, imposing a metallurgical upper limit on the cycle's temperature. *See* HEAT TRANSFER.

A practical solution to the heat transfer difficulties which beset the Carnot cycle is to burn a fuel in the air inside the engine cylinder. The result is an internal combustion engine that consumes and replaces its working substance while undergoing a periodic sequence of processes.

The working substance in such an internal combustion engine can attain very high temperatures, far above the melting point of the metal of the cylinder walls, because succeeding lower-temperature processes will keep the metal parts adequately cool.

Thus, as the contents change temperature rapidly between wide extremes, the metal walls hover near a median temperature. The fuel-air mixture can be ignited by a spark, or by the rise in temperature from the compression stroke. *See* DIESEL CYCLE; DIESEL ENGINE; INTERNAL COMBUSTION ENGINE; OTTO CYCLE.

Even so, the necessarily high peak pressures and temperatures limit the practical thermal efficiency that an actual engine can achieve. The same theoretical efficiency can be obtained from a cycle consisting of two isobaric processes interspersed by two isentropic processes. The isobaric process requires that the cycle handle large volumes of low-pressure gas, which can best be done in a rotating turbine. *See* BRAYTON CYCLE; GAS TURBINE.

Although the Carnot cycle is independent of the working substance, and hence is applicable to a vapor cycle, the difficulty of efficiently compressing a vapor-liquid mixture renders the cycle impractical. In a steam power plant the sequence of states assumed by the working substance is (1) condensate and feedwater are compressed and pumped into the boiler, (2) heat is added to the water first at constantly increasing temperature and then at constant pressure and temperature, (3) the steam expands in the engine, and (4) the cycle is completed by a constant-temperature heat-rejection process which condenses the exhausted steam. *See* VAPOR CYCLE.

By comparison to the Carnot cycle, in which heat is added only at the highest temperature, this steam cycle with heat added over a range of temperatures is necessarily less efficient than is theoretically possible. An analysis of engine operations in terms of thermodynamic cycles indicates what efficiencies can be expected and how the operations should be modified to increase engine performance, such as high compression ratios for reciprocating internal combustion engines and high steam temperatures for steam engines. *See* POWER PLANT; THERMODYNAMIC CYCLE; THERMODYNAMIC PRINCIPLES.

Theodore Baumeister

Bibliography. E. A. Avallone and T. Baumeister III (eds.), *Marks' Standard Handbook for Mechanical Engineers*, 9th ed, 1987; K. E. Bett et al., *Thermodynamic's for Chemical Engineers*, 1975; T. D. Eastop and A. McConkey, *Applied Thermodynamics for Engineering Technologists*, 5th ed., 1993; D. P. Tassios, *Applied Chemical Engineering Thermodynamics*, 1993; M. W. Zemansky and R. Dittman, *Heat and Thermodynamics*, 6th ed., 1981.

Carnotite

A mineral that is a hydrous vanadate of potassium and hexavalent uranium with the formula $K_2(UO_2)_2V_2O_8 \cdot n\,H_2O$. Its water content varies with the humidity at ordinary temperatures. The fully hydrated mineral contains $3H_2O$, and n ranges down to about 1 for only partly hydrated material. Carnotite transforms easily into tyuyamunite, $Ca(UO_2)_2V_2O_8 \cdot n\,H_2O$, by exchange of $2K^+$ by one Ca^{2+}.

Carnotite is one of 12 known uranyl vanadates with similar structures; of these, carnotite and tyuyamunite are the most common. These uranyl vanadates all contain a polyanionic complex of composition $(V_2O_8)^{6-}$ as part of their structures. This anionic complex is the result of two VO_5 groups sharing an edge. The form of the VO_5 group is that of a square pyramid with V located at its center. Carnotite, as well as the other 11 uranyl vanadates, contains sheetlike linkages of pentagonal dipyramids of UO_2 and the V_2O_8 groups; the cations such as K^+ and Ca^{2+} are interleaved between these sheets. The sheets are oriented parallel to the (001) in the carnotite structure, giving rise to excellent cleavage parallel to {001}.

Carnotite is monoclinic with space group $P\,2_1/a$. Its unit cell dimensions are $a = 1.047$ nanometers, $b = 0.841$ nm, $c = 0.659$ nm, A and $\beta = 103°50'$. Its color ranges from bright yellow, to lemon yellow, to greenish yellow. The mineral most commonly occurs as a powder or as loosely coherent, very fine grained aggregates and also as tiny platy crystals with a rhombic outline or as very small terminated prisms.

Carnotite is a secondary mineral that occurs in the alteration zone of many uranium deposits. It results from the action of ground water on preexisting uranium and vanadium minerals such as uraninite (UO_2), and montroseite, $[(V^{3+},Fe^{3+})O(OH)]$. It forms in close associations with tyuyamunite and metatyuyamunite. *See* CRYSTAL STRUCTURE; CRYSTALLOGRAPHY.

Carnotite is an important source of uranium and also a source of vanadium in the United States. In the United States, the principal region of carnotite mineralization is the Colorado Plateau and adjacent districts of Utah, New Mexico, and Arizona, where it occurs chiefly as disseminated grains in cross-bedded sandstone of Triassic and Jurassic age, but also in relatively pure masses near fossilized trunks, leaves, and other organic matter. Deposits are also found in the Powder River Basin, Wyoming; in Duval County, Texas; and in Carbon County, Pennsylvania. Carnotite is found at Radium Hill near Olary, Australia; at El Boroui, Louis Gentil, and Assaikidji, Morocco; at Franceville, Gabon, together with francevillite; at Kambove and West Mashamba in southern Shaba, Zaire (at West Mashamba, carnotite occurs as well-developed platy crystals). Other deposits are in northern Ferghana, Republic of Kirghizistan; Lussagues, Aveyron, France; and Schellkopf near Brenk in the volcanic area of Eifel, Germany (at Schellkopf carnotite is characterized by a larger cell with $c = 0.766$ nm). *See* RADIOACTIVE MINERALS; RADIUM; URANIUM; VANADIUM.

Michael Deliens; Cornelis Klein

Bibliography. C. Frondel, *Systematic Mineralogy of Uranium*, USGS Bull. 1064, 1958; Institution of Mining and Metallurgy, London, *Uranium Geochemistry, Mineralogy, Geology, Exploration and Resources*, 1984.

Carotenoid

Any of a class of yellow, orange, red, and purple pigments that are widely distributed in nature, including vegetables, fruits, insects, fishes, and birds. Most of these pigments are carotenoids, which are generally fat-soluble unless they are complexed with proteins. In plants, carotenoids are usually located in quantity in the grana of chloroplasts in the form of carotenoprotein complexes. Carotenoprotein complexes give blue, green, purple, red, or other colors to the outer surfaces or eggs of crustaceans, such as the lobster and crab. Echinoderms, nudibranch mollusks, and other invertebrate animals also contain carotenoproteins. Some coral coelenterates exhibit purple, pink, orange, or other colors due to carotenoids in the calcareous skeletal material. Cooked or denatured lobster, crab, and shrimp show the modified colors of their carotenoproteins.

Colors exhibited by carotenoid pigments are due to the absorption of quanta of visible wavelength light by the conjugated double-bond network of carotenoids. The absorption of a light quantum by the carotenoid molecule promotes an electron (π electron) of the double-bond system to a higher-energy orbital.

Astaxanthin is the carotenoid component of crustacyanin, a carotenoprotein that determines the color of the lobster shells. The native α-crustacyanin of fresh lobster maximally absorbs light of 632-nanometer wavelength whereas the denatured pigment protein of boiled lobster shows an absorption maximum at 540 nanometers, exhibiting dark green and orange-pink colors, respectively. These color changes are apparently due to an alteration of the interactions among the carotenoid molecules or between the carotenoid and protein moieties upon heat denaturation of the crustacyanin.

The total carotenoid production in nature is estimated at about 110,000,000 tons (100,000,000 metric tons) a year. The widespread occurrence of carotenoids in nature suggests that the distribution pattern of carotenoid pigments may be valuable in chemotaxonomic analyses. Patterns of evolution of algal groups have indeed been proposed on the basis of carotenoid pigmentation patterns. *See* PIGMENTATION.

Chemical structure and classification. The general structure of carotenoids is that of aliphatic and aliphatic-alicyclic polyenes, with a few aromatic-type polyenes (**Fig. 1**). Most carotenoid pigments are tetraterpenes with a 40-carbon (C_{40}) skeleton, traditionally regarded as results from the conjugation of eight isoprene units. C_{30}, C_{45}, and C_{50} carotenoids are also known in nature. Carotenes such as α-, β-, γ-, and δ-carotene are C_{40} carotenoids containing 11 or fewer conjugated carbon-carbon double bonds. Oxygenated carotenoids with hydroxyl, epoxy, ether, aldehyde, ketone, or acid groups are generally called xanthophylls. Carotenoids may exist in either cis or trans isomeric forms, with the latter being more stable than the former. The cis-trans isomerization may be catalyzed by iodine, and blue light of 450-nm wavelength may also induce the isomerization (photoisomerization). *See* PHOTOCHEMISTRY.

More than 400 carotenoids of known structure are recognized, and the number is still on the rise.

Isolation and characterization. A rough separation of carotenes and xanthophylls (oxygen-containing carotenoids) can be achieved by partitioning a crude extract of pigment mixture between two immiscible solvents, petroleum ether or *n*-hexane and aqueous methanol (90%). Petroleum ether or *n*-hexane dissolves carotenes preferentially (epiphasic fraction), whereas aqueous methanol dissolves

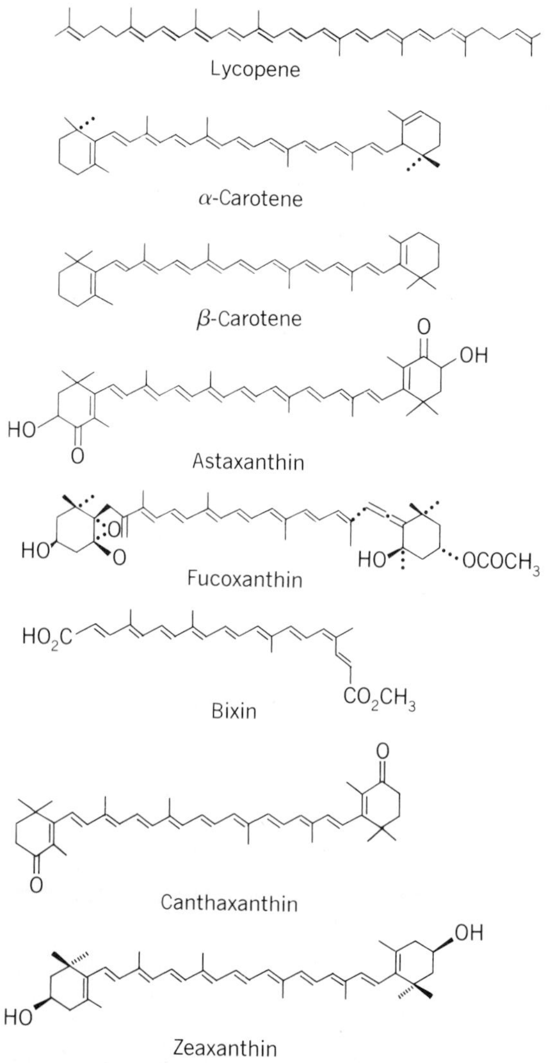

Fig. 1. Chemical structures of typical carotenoids.

xanthophylls with two or more hydroxyl groups (hypophasic fraction). Monohydroxy carotenoids tend to be distributed equally between both phases.

Chromatographic methods are most effective and popular for isolation and purification of carotenoids. These include column chromatography, thin-layer chromatography, and high-pressure liquid chromatography, among others. Both column and thin-layer chromatography are based on the differential adsorption of various carotenoids to adsorbents. Adsorbents chosen for the column method depend on the polarity of the carotenoids to be separated. For example, sucrose powder and magnesium silicate are used for separating strongly polar carotenoids, whereas carotenes are readily separated on an activated alumina column, by eluting them from the column stepwise, with a solvent mixture of increasing polarity. Thin-layer chromatography utilizes adsorbents such as silica gel, alumina, or sucrose, developed with mixtures of organic solvents. Thin-layer chromatography on cellulose layers as the stationary phase can also be used for separating different carotenoids on the basis of their partitioning between the stationary phase and the mobile phase (for example, acetone-methanol-water). Thin-layer chromatographic separation is usually more satisfactory for carotenoids than is column chromatography. **Figure 2** shows an example of the thin-layer chromatographic separation of five representative carotenoids. High-pressure liquid chromatography yields the highest resolution in separating carotenoids for identification and

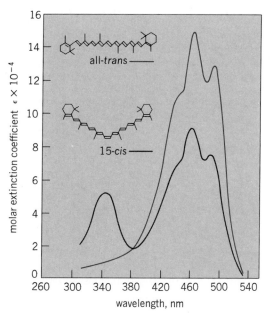

Fig. 3. Absorption spectra of all-trans carotene and 15,15′-mono-*cis*-β-carotene.

preparative purposes. Stereochemical isomers including cis-trans and enantiomeric isomers can be separated by high-pressure liquid chromatography. For characterization of carotenoids, various chemical and modern physical techniques such as spectroscopic and x-ray crystallographic determinations have been widely used. *See* CHROMATOGRAPHY.

Since carotenoids are blue light–absorbing pigments, absorption spectroscopy is routinely employed for the characterization of carotenoids with regard to the degree of conjugation and geometric isomerism. **Figure 3** illustrates spectral changes of β-carotene upon isomerization of the central carbon-carbon double bond. The near-ultraviolet peak gains its absorptivity, as the electronic system of β-carotene changes from a fully linear all-trans to a bent cis form. In contrast to linear polyenes, cyclic polyenes such as porphyrins exhibit a much stronger near-ultraviolet absorption band (Soret band) than a visible light band. Thus isomerization of fucoxanthin to isofucoxanthin by alkali can be followed spectrophotometrically at the near-ultraviolet band. Alkali also facilitates oxidation of certain carotenoids; for example, astaxanthin is oxidized to astacene. Acids also cause chemical changes in carotenoids; certain acids also form Lewis acid–carotenoid complexes.

Biosynthesis. The carbon skeletons of carotenoids are derived from the starting material, acetic acid, via a biosynthetic route similar to those of rubber and steroid syntheses. The biosynthetic pathway involves enzymatic reactions, such as hydrogenation, condensation, and dehydrogenation, followed finally by conjugation of the carbon-carbon double bonds forming the carotenoid π-electron system. Some xanthophylls are derived from β-carotene. **Figure 4** shows a simplified scheme for the biosynthesis of carotenoids.

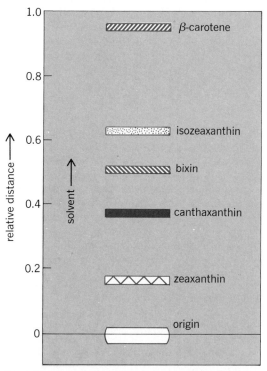

Fig. 2. Thin-layer chromatogram showing the separation of carotenoids. The adsorbent is silica gel, and the developing solvent consists of three parts *n*-hexane and seven parts ether.

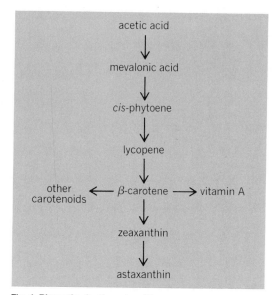

Fig. 4. Biosynthesis of carotenoids.

The biosynthesis of carotenoids can be regulated by a number of exogenously added compounds. Some amines and compounds containing ammonium groups inhibit carotenoid biosynthesis in fungi and higher plants. On the other hand, many others stimulate carotenoid biosynthesis. A classic example of a compound that stimulates carotenoid biosynthesis is β-ionone, which is the ring structure occurring in β-carotene (Fig. 1). It is known that β-ionone itself is not incorporated into the carotenoid structure during the biosynthesis of β-ionone-containing carotenoids. It is known too that the regulation of the carotenoid biosynthesis is rather specific with respect to different geometric carotenoid isomers; thus, compounds such as diethyl alkylamines stimulate the formation of all-trans carotenes. Specifically, diethyl octylamine and diethyl nonylamine greatly enhance the biosynthesis of the cyclic carotenes, α-, β-, and δ-carotenes, along with the noncyclic pigment lycopene (Fig. 1).

The substituted benzylamines, such as N-benzylphenylamines and N-benzyl 2-naphthalene methylamine, induce the accumulation of cis-carotenoids in certain plant fruits, for example, grapefruit.

There are two major regulatory modes of action for these bioregulators in trans-carotenoid biosynthesis. One mode of action includes the inhibition of the enzyme cyclase in the formation of the monocyclic δ-carotene and the bicyclic β-carotene (Fig. 4), as shown in the scheme where X indicates a blocked pathway. The other includes activation or transcriptional induction of a gene regulating the synthesis of specific enzymes required for the biosynthetic pathway of carotenoid pigments.

The mode of action of the bioregulators for the biosynthesis of cis-carotenoids is less clear. The cyclases are not inhibited by the cis-regulators. Thus, the most likely mode of action of these regulators appears to be gene activation that results in biosynthesis of cis-carotenoids at the expense of all-trans carotenoid biosynthesis.

β-Carotene serves as a major precursor to various oxygen-containing carotenoids called xanthophylls. For example, in lobster and crab the biosynthetic pathway from β-carotene to astaxanthin (Fig. 1 and 4) involves several intermediates, as outlined in **Fig. 5**. Zeaxanthin has also been proposed as a precursor to astaxanthin in lobster.

Biosynthesis of carotenoids can be enhanced by light. For example, blue light stimulates the formation of carotenoids in the fungi *Fusarium*, *Phycomyces*, and *Neurospora*. *Fusarium* synthesizes very little quantity of carotenoids in the dark, but blue light markedly stimulates the biosynthesis of carotenoids, including β-carotene and neurosporaxanthin. Blue light does so by regulating the expression of genes for the enzymes or regulatory proteins involved in the biosynthesis of carotenoids, and by photoinducing the production of certain factors used for the biosynthetic pathway of carotenoids. In addition, blue light stimulates the biosynthesis of carotenoids in algae, bacteria, and possibly in certain crustaceans and higher plants, such as angiosperms.

Red light also enhances the biosynthesis of carotenoids in higher plants; the pigment protein phytochrome acts as the red-light receptor. The red-light effect may be coupled to the blue-light effect in enhancing the biosynthetic formation of carotenoids in higher plants.

Function. The biochemical function of carotenoids is still largely unknown, although there are several biochemical functions in which the role of carotenoids is well understood. These include carotenoids in the photosynthetic apparatus of green plants, algae, and photosynthetic bacteria, where carotenoids function as a blue-light–harvesting pigment (antenna or accessory pigment) for photosynthesis. Thus carotenoids make it possible for photosynthetic organisms more fully to utilize the solar energy in the visible spectral region. Although the mechanism for the transfer of absorbed solar energy from carotenoid to chlorophyll is yet to be elucidated, it appears that carotenoid structures involving interactions of carotenoid-carotenoid as well as carotenoid-chlorophyll ag-

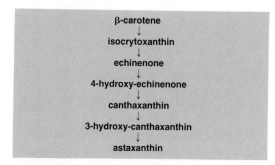

Fig. 5. Biosynthesis of astaxanthin from β-carotene in lobster and crab.

gregate pairs are essential for the efficient energy transfer. This feature has been elucidated for the blue-light–harvesting carotenoid-chlorophyll protein complexes of marine dinoflagellates. **Figure 6** shows two sets of peridinin pairs (dimer) which stabilize the excited state of peridinin produced by light absorption, thus enhancing the probability of energy transfer from the carotenoid to chlorophyll. Without such interactions through exciton coupling between the two excited states of the peridinin dimer, each individual peridinin molecule does not possess a long enough lifetime for the energy transfer to chlorophyll to take place. *See* CHLOROPHYLL; PHOTOSYNTHESIS.

In addition to the light-harvesting function of carotenoids for photosynthesis, it is possible that carotenoid acts as an electron donor to the reactive chlorophyll (so-called P680), resulting in the formation of a carotenoid cation radical which may participate as an intermediate in the oxygen-evolving reaction of photosynthesis. However, this possibility remains to be studied.

Many algae, including dinoflagellates, utilize similar carotenoprotein pigments as the photoreceptor for phototaxis (swimming toward or away from blue light) and photophobic response (light-avoiding behavior). Apparently carotenoproteins in these systems serve as the antenna pigment and transfer the absorbed energy to the primary photoreceptor, probably chlorophyll, of the photosyn-

thetic machinery which may control flagellum motion of algae in response to blue light by providing the necessary source of energy for the transduction network.

Another function of carotenoids is to protect biological systems such as the photosynthetic apparatus from photodynamic damage. Thus, plants lacking carotenoids are readily damaged by light. Certain herbicides kill weeds by blocking the biosynthesis of carotenoids so that the weed's photosynthetic apparatus is unprotected from photodynamic damage. Protection from photodynamic damage is achieved by quenching the powerful photodynamic oxidizing agent, singlet oxygen, produced as an undesirable by-product of the exposure of pigmented organisms to light. Carotenoids also protect plants from photodynamic damage by quenching the so-called triplet-state chlorophyll (where two of the π electrons in chlorophyll have their magnetic moments in parallel) in the photosynthetic apparatus.

Carotenoids are synthesized concomitantly with other photosynthetic membrane constituents for photosynthesis in the alga *Euglena*. This simultaneous synthesis appears to ensure that the membrane being assembled for the photosynthetic apparatus is stabilized by carotenoids and protected from photodynamic damage. However, this is not the case in higher plants where assembling of the photosynthetic apparatus takes place before the biosynthesis of carotenoids.

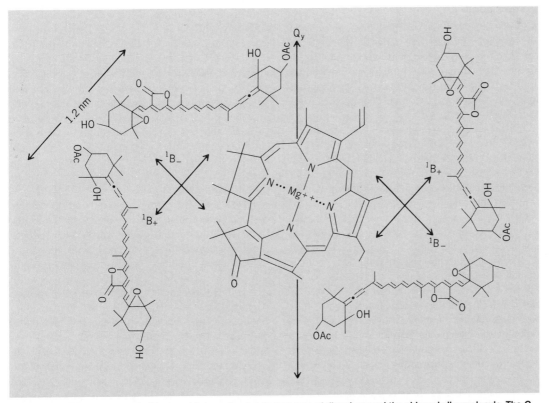

Fig. 6. A possible arrangement of four peridinin molecules (in two sets of dimer) around the chlorophyll *a* molecule. The Q_y axis of chlorophyll *a* represents the direction of fluorescence emission. B₊ and B₋ represent two exciton states resulting from dimeric interactions between the peridinin molecules. Energy transfer takes place from the B₊ state to the chlorophyll molecule.

There may be many other functions of carotenoids as yet unknown. For example, it is possible that carotenoids, as important flower-petal pigments, may function in attracting insect pollinators.

Usage. Certain carotenoids are metabolized in biological systems, and some of them possess nutritional value. In particular, β-carotene is widely used as the vitamin A precursor, since it is metabolically oxidized to retinol (vitamin A) in animals, except cats. It is also used as an effective sunscreen agent in erythropoietic protoporphyria. Carotenoids, as well as a derivative, vitamin A, exhibit antitumor activity, for example, against ultraviolet-radiation–induced skin tumors. *See* VITAMIN A.

Perhaps the most important industrial application of carotenoids, including β-carotene and lycopene, which are rich in carrot and tomato, respectively, is in safe coloration of foods, as exemplified in the coloring and fortification of margarine and poultry feedstuff. *See* FOOD MANUFACTURING.

Pill-Soon Song

Bibliography. G. Britton and T. W. Goodwin (eds.), *Carotenoid Chemistry and Biochemistry*, 1982; O. Isler (ed.), *Carotenoids*, 1971; H. Senger (ed.), *Blue Light Responses: Phenomena and Occurrence in Plants and Microorganisms*, 1987; P. S. Song, *Trends Biochem. Sci.*, pp. 25–27, February 1978.

Carotid body

A special sensory organ (glomus caroticum) located in the angle of the branching of the common carotid artery into the external and internal carotid arteries (see **illus.**). The human carotid body is an ovoid organ approximately 0.2 in. (5 mm) long, embedded in the outer connective tissue (adventitia) of the blood vessel. The carotid body is called a chemoreceptor because it is sensitive to oxygen and carbon dioxide in the blood. There is evidence that suggests that the carotid body is also sensitive to changes in blood pressure, blood flow, and blood osmolarity (salt content). *See* CHEMORECEPTION.

Histology. The carotid bodies are highly vascular structures composed of cords or lobules of epithelioid cells. The glomus cells, which constitute the principal cell type in the carotid body, contain numerous cytoplasmic vesicles or granules that are known to contain special transmitter substances called catecholamines. Stored together with these catecholamines are putative transmitter substances called neuropeptides that may modulate the action of the catecholamine neurotransmitter. The carotid body also contains supporting cells, which are less abundant than glomus cells, do not contain vesicles, and partially envelop glomus cells and adjacent nerve fibers in their attenuated processes.

The glomus cells are richly innervated by sensory nerve fibers derived from the ninth cranial

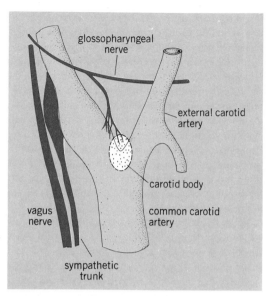

Location of the carotid body in relation to the carotid arteries.

(glossopharyngeal) nerve, and to a lesser extent by the ganglioglomerular nerve from the superior cervical ganglion. The nerve fibers enter the carotid body and travel between and around the lobules of glomus cells, forming an interstitial plexus. Small unmyelinated nerve fibers from this plexus ultimately end on the glomus cells in a variety of synaptic configurations.

The embryology of the carotid body is controversial; experiments in birds, however, suggest that all of the cells are derived from a specialized portion of the neuroectoderm (neural crest), and there is little reason to suspect a different origin for the mammalian carotid body. The neural crest also gives rise to the adrenal medulla, whose cells closely resemble those of the carotid body. The adrenal medullary cells, however, secrete the hormones epinephrine (adrenaline) and norepinephrine (noradrenaline), whereas glomus cells release primarily dopamine and norepinephrine as neurotransmitters. *See* ADRENAL GLAND; EPINEPHRINE.

Physiology. The 1930s marked an epoch in carotid body research. It was demonstrated at that time that the carotid body and similar glomus tissue accumulations associated with the aortic arch (aortic bodies) possessed chemoreceptor properties. It was found that blood low in oxygen (hypoxemia) or high in carbon dioxide (hypercapnia) stimulated an increase in respiration and a secondary increase in heart rate and blood pressure. The increase in respiration observed after carotid body stimulation provides for an increase in the oxygenation of the red blood cells (erythrocytes). Likewise, secondary reflexes originating from the lungs cause an increase in heart rate that results in a greater blood flow from the heart to the lungs and, ultimately, the whole body. These important reflexes protect the organism from conditions of hypoxia (low tissue oxygen) such as may be experienced at high altitudes, during exercise, or during various cardiopulmonary disease states. *See* AORTIC BODY.

Although much is known about reflexes initiated by the carotid body, it is still not known how the chemical information derived from the blood is converted into electrical signals that are then transmitted to the cardiopulmonary brain centers. Current hypotheses center on the glomus cell as the immediate chemosensor which responds to stimuli by triggering nerve impulses in the sensory nerve endings. Alternatively, some studies suggest that both glomus cells and sensory nerve endings have chemosensory properties and that these elements coparticipate in the chemoresponse. Experiments to differentiate between these two possibilities are difficult to design. Moreover, different cellular elements within the carotid body may respond to different stimuli, thereby complicating the transduction mechanisms that normally are operative. Regardless of how chemoreception occurs, the carotid body is uniquely suited for the task of "sampling" the arterial blood. Because of its high vascularity and small size, the carotid body has one of the highest blood flow rates of any tissue in the body.

Pathological and physiological changes. Tumors of the carotid body are termed chemodectomas and are similar histologically to tumors of the adrenal medulla (pheochromocytomas) that secrete catecholamines. Carotid body tumors usually are benign, asymptomatic, and slow-growing. Individuals living at high altitudes have larger carotid bodies, and a higher incidence of carotid body tumors, although compared to all neoplasms the incidence is low. Finally, there is some evidence that the carotid body may be involved in sudden infant death syndrome (SIDS) or "crib death." It is still not known, however, whether SIDS arises from a peripheral (such as the carotid body) or from a central (such as brainstem) defect in respiratory integration. *See* CARDIOVASCULAR SYSTEM; SUDDEN INFANT DEATH SYNDROME (SIDS).   John T. Hansen

Bibliography. *Handbook of Physiology*, sec. 3: *The Respiratory System*, vol. 3: *Control of Breathing*, ed. by A. P. Fishman, 1986.

Carp

The common name for a number of cypriniform fishes of the family Cyprinidae. The carp originated in China, where for centuries it was raised for food. It was imported into the United States from Europe, where it also has been raised for years as a source of food.

Two varieties or forms of carp occur in nature (see **illus.**), but are commoner in captivity in breeding ponds. These are the mirror carp, which has a few large scales, and the leather carp,

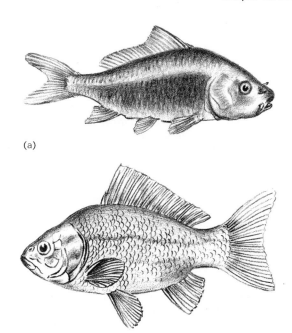

(a)

(b)

Two varieties of carp: (*a*) the carp (*Cyprinus carpio*) and (*b*) the goldfish (*Crassius auratus*).

which has no scales. In America the carp has invaded many natural bodies of water, where it has destroyed the weeds which are part of the natural breeding places of native fishes.

The carp (*Cyprinus carpio*) is a member of the Cyprinidae and is closely related to the goldfish (*Crassius auratus*). The silver carp (*Hypopthalmichthys*) is an Asiatic species in which the fourth gill arch is modified to form the helical organ, which is an accessory feeding structure. Fine, particulate food that escapes the gill rakers is entrapped in the mucus of the helical organ and passed into the stomach. The carp has pharyngeal teeth and a suckerlike mouth. A very long dorsal fin is preceded by a strong spine. The swim bladder of the carp is associated with a group of small bones at the anterior end, the Weberian ossicles. This structural modification enables the carp to perceive sound quite well. *See* ACTINOPTERYGII; CYPRINIFORMES; SWIM BLADDER.   Charles B. Curtin

Carpal tunnel syndrome

A condition caused by the thickening of ligaments and tendon sheaths at the wrist, with consequent compression of the median nerve at the palm. Affected individuals report numbness, tingling, and pain in the hand; the discomfort often becomes worse at night or after use of the hand. A physical examination of the injured hand during the early stages of the syndrome often reveals no abnormality. With more severe nerve compression, the individual experiences sensory loss over some or all of the digits innervated by the median nerve (thumb, index finger, middle finger, and ring finger) and weakness of thumb movement.

Assessment. Electrodiagnostic testing is important for an accurate diagnosis. The electromyographer uses sensory fibers to measure the nerve conduction velocity from the finger or the palm to the wrist and the motor conduction velocity from the wrist to the thumb muscles. Approximately half the individuals with carpal tunnel syndrome have abnormalities of the opposite median nerve. Electrodiagnostic values of these individuals therefore need to be compared with reference values obtained from normal subjects and with ulnar or radial nerve values. No other test has a higher diagnostic accuracy for individuals who have a final diagnosis of carpal tunnel syndrome, but to make a final diagnosis clinical data, including the individual's response to treatment, must be obtained.

False positive and false negative results are illustrated by the high rate of abnormalities in the opposite, nonsymptomatic hands of individuals with carpal tunnel syndrome. As testing becomes more complex and sophisticated, it becomes increasingly likely that results beyond the normal range (false positive) will be generated. The number of individuals with false negative results should be below 8%.

Thermography shows clear abnormalities in carpal tunnel syndrome, but an abnormal thermogram is found in many other conditions in which the pattern of blood flow to the hand is altered. Computed tomography and magnetic resonance imaging have not been widely used for carpal tunnel syndrome and have no role in management at this time. *See* THERMOGRAPHY.

Prevalence. Carpal tunnel syndrome is common. One study reported that 125 individuals per 100,000 were affected from 1976 to 1980. Another study estimated that 515 of every 100,000 patients sought medical attention for carpal tunnel syndrome in 1988; the syndrome in half of these patients was thought to be occupational in origin.

The incidence of carpal tunnel syndrome is greater among electronic-parts assemblers, frozen-food processors, musicians, and dental hygienists. Highly repetitive wrist movements, use of vibrating tools, awkward wrist positions, and movements involving great force seem to be correlated with the disorder. Awkward and repetitive wrist motions occur in many office tasks, such as typing and word processing. In some occupations, such as shellfish packing, the incidence is more than 200 times higher than in the baseline data. The highest reported incidence in an industrial setting, based on the numbers of carpal tunnel syndrome–based releases, was 15% among a group of meatpackers.

Carpal tunnel syndrome probably accounts for a minority of the cases of overuse syndrome (cumulative trauma syndrome), which is a common problem in occupational settings. Overuse syndrome symptoms include muscle pain, tendinitis, fibrositis (inflammation of connective tissue in a joint region), and epicondylitis (inflammation of the eminence on the condyle of a bone). Although the causative relationship between the two disorders has not been conclusively proven, the incidence of both carpal tunnel syndrome and overuse syndrome appears to increase in tandem in individuals who are at risk.

Pathophysiology. Under normal circumstances, the pressure within the tissues of a limb is 7–8 mmHg. In carpal tunnel syndrome, the pressure is often 30 mmHg, approaching the level at which nerve dysfunction occurs. With wrist flexion or extension, pressures may increase to 90 mmHg or more.

The increase in pressure within the carpal canal is usually caused by nonspecific inflammation of flexor tendon sheaths. Diabetes, pregnancy, rheumatoid arthritis, and hypothyroidism are the most common medical conditions associated with carpal tunnel syndrome. Amyloidosis, acromegaly, and mycobacterial infections are rare causes. A reduction in the flow of blood to the nerve can account for the intermittent tingling that occurs at night or with wrist flexion. *See* AMYLOIDOSIS; ARTHRITIS; DIABETES; THYROID GLAND DISORDERS.

Treatment. Nonsurgical treatment includes avoidance of the use of the wrist, use of a splint to keep the wrist in a neutral position, and anti-inflammatory medications. These treatments are especially useful in individuals with an acute flare-up and in those with minimal and intermittent symptoms. Conservative nonsurgical treatment will not succeed for individuals over the age of 50, for those who have had the syndrome for more than 10 months, and for those with constant tingling.

Surgical treatment may be used if conservative approaches fail. The procedure is usually done on an outpatient basis with prognoses of good to excellent in 80% of the cases. Although 40% of the individuals regain normal function, the condition of 5% may worsen. Most individuals return to an office job within a week of surgery, but it may be 4–6 months before carpenters, construction workers, or athletes are able to return to work. Many individuals with work-related carpal tunnel syndrome should consider changing jobs.

Surprisingly little information is available regarding the redesign of workstations and its effect on the reversal of symptoms or the prevention of carpal tunnel syndrome. Ergonomic redesign is widely practiced, but rarely described in medical terms.

David M. Dawson

Bibliography. D. M. Dawson, M. Hallett, and L. H. Millender, *Entrapment Neuropathies*, 2d ed., 1990; R. B. Rosenbaum and J. L. Ochoa, *Carpal Tunnel Syndrome and Other Disorders of the Median Nerve*, 1993.

Carpoids

The common name for four extinct classes of primitive echinoderms that have a flattened theca or body lacking radial symmetry. These enigmatic fossils were originally classified together in the class Carpoidea, but more recent echinoderm researchers

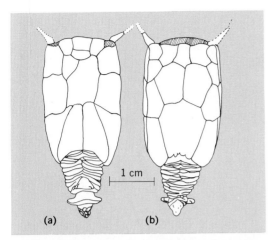

Enoploura popei, a stylophoran carpoid from the Late Ordovician of Ohio. (*a*) Concave lower side and (*b*) convex upper side of the plated theca showing part of the attached, tapering appendage used for locomotion and feeding at the bottom.

have assigned them to four separate classes in the subphylum Homalozoa: the Stylophora (or Calcichordates), Homoiostelea, Homostelea, and Ctenocystoidea. These four classes include about 50 genera that range from the Early or Middle Cambrian to the Late Carboniferous.

Carpoids have a flattened theca that varies from asymmetrical to nearly bilaterally symmetrical (see **illus.**) and is made up of sutured, multiporous, single-crystal, calcite plates like those found in other echinoderms. Three of the classes have a long plated appendage attached to the theca that was used for locomotion and, in the Stylophora, also for feeding. The mouth was either on the anterior margin of the theca with ambulacral grooves leading to it or at the base of the feeding appendage; the anal pyramid was usually on the opposite thecal margin or nearby at a thecal corner. Carpoids were apparently mobile, bottom-living or shallow-burrowing, detritus or suspension feeders, sifting out small food particles from the top layer of soft sediment or from the surrounding seawater. Because of the distinctive skeletons, most researchers consider carpoids as true echinoderms, although they seem only distantly related to other fossil and living echinoderms that have well-developed pentameral symmetry. *See* ECHINODERMATA; HOMALOZOA.   James Sprinkle

Bibliography. R. C. Moore (ed.), *Treatise on Invertebrate Paleontology*, pt. S, 1968.

Carrageenan

A polysaccharide that is a major constituent of the cell walls of certain red algae (Rhodophyceae), especially members of the families Gigartinaceae, Hypneaceae, Phyllophoraceae, and Solieriaceae. Extracted for its suspending, emulsifying, stabilizing, and gelling properties, it is one of three algal polysaccharides of major economic importance, the others being agar and alginate. *See* AGAR; ALGINATE.

Carrageenans form a family of linear (unbranched) sulfated polysaccharides in which the basic repeating units are exclusively D-galactose, or D-galactose and 3,6-anhydro-D-galactose, linked alternately α-1,3- and β-1,4-. Different types of carrageenans, which are designated by Greek letters, are found in different species and sometimes in different somatic phases of the same species or in different regions of the same plant. The κ- and ι-carrageenans are soluble in hot water but not cold, and gel upon cooling in the presence of potassium ion. The λ-, ϵ-, and π-carrageenans are soluble in hot water or cold, forming a viscous solution but not a gel.

Carrageenan is prepared by boiling the dried algae in slightly alkaline water. The hot solution is filtered and poured into isopropyl alcohol, which causes the carrageenan to precipitate. The product is purified, dried, ground, and packaged as a powder.

The main sources of carrageenan are *Chondrus crispus* (Gigartinaceae) from the Maritime Provinces of Canada and various species of *Eucheuma* (Solieriaceae) from the Philippines. *Chondrus*, popularly called Irish moss, is harvested from naturally occurring intertidal stands, while *Eucheuma* is successfully grown in mariculture on nets and lines.

About 80% of the refined carrageenan is used in food processing, with the dairy industry being the chief consumer. The remainder is used in the cosmetic, pharmaceutical, printing, and textile industries. *See* RHODOPHYCEAE.

Paul C. Silva; Richard L. Moe

Carrier

A periodic waveform upon which an information-bearing signal is impressed. This process is known as modulation and comprises a variety of forms such as amplitude, phase, and frequency modulation. The most common type of carrier is the sinusoidal carrier (**illus.** *a*), but in reality, any periodic waveform followed by a band-pass filter can serve as a carrier.

The validity of the last statement can be verified by considering a periodic function $c(t)$, and

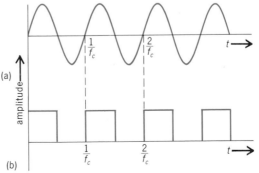

Carriers. (*a*) Sinusoidal carrier. (*b*) Square-wave carrier.

assuming that it is desired to have a message $m(t)$ double-sideband (DSB)-modulate a carrier. Since the function $c(t)$ is periodic, it can be expanded in a Fourier series of the form given by Eq. (1),

$$c(t) = \sum_{n=-\infty}^{\infty} c_n e^{j2\pi n f_c t} \qquad (1)$$

where the $\{c_n\}$ are the coefficients of the Fourier series, and f_c is the carrier frequency, chosen so that it exceeds W, the bandwidth of the message $m(t)$. This results in the waveform given by Eq. (2).

$$m(t)c(t) = \sum_{n=-\infty}^{\infty} c_n m(t) e^{j2\pi n f_c t} \qquad (2)$$

The Fourier transform of this waveform is given by Eq. (3), where $M(\omega)$ is the Fourier transform

$$F(\omega) = \sum_{n=-\infty}^{\infty} c_n M(\omega - n\omega_c) \qquad (3)$$

of $m(t)$, and $\omega_c = 2\pi f_c$. If this signal is now put through a band-pass filter with center frequency f_c and bandwidth $2W$, a waveform proportional to $m(t) \cos \omega_c t$ results (that is, a double-sideband signal has been generated). *See* FOURIER SERIES AND TRANSFORMS.

A periodic waveform that is very simple to generate is a square wave composed of ones and zeros of equal duration. This allows the multiplication function inherent in the modulation process represented by the function $m(t)c(t)$ to be replaced by an on-off switch. Indeed, such a modulator is commonly known as a switching modulator, and results in a periodic square wave (illus. *b*).

At times, it is convenient to use subcarriers in addition to the main carrier. Such a situation arises when frequency-division multiplexing (FDM) is used. A set of, say, N information-bearing waveforms individually modulate their own subcarrier, whereby the spacing of the subcarriers is chosen so that it results in (virtually) no spectral overlap of the resulting N spectra. This composite baseband waveform then modulates the main carrier in preparation for transmission over the channel. For voice communications, the modulation on the subcarriers is often single-sideband (SSB), whereas typically the modulation on the carrier itself is frequency-modulation. *See* AMPLITUDE MODULATION; FREQUENCY MODULATION; MODULATION; MULTIPLEXING AND MULTIPLE ACCESS; SINGLE SIDEBAND.   Laurence B. Milstein

Carrot

A biennial umbellifer (*Daucus carota*) of Asiatic and Mediterranean origin belonging to the plant order Umbellales. The carrot is grown for its edible roots which are eaten raw or cooked (**Fig. 1**). *See* APIALES.

Fig. 1. Carrots. (*Asgrow Co., Subsidiary of the Upjohn Co.*)

Cultivation and harvesting. Propagation is by seed planted directly in the field. Spacing varies; plants are usually planted $1/2$–2 in. (1.2–5 cm) apart in rows of 18–24 in. (45–60 cm). Temperature and soil moisture affect root color and shape; 60–70°F (15–21°C) is optimum for high yields of long, deep-colored roots.

Exposure of the young carrot plants to prolonged cold weather (40–50°F, or 4–10°C, for 15 or more days) favors seed-stalk formation. Misshapen roots commonly result from nematodes, aster yellows disease, or compacted soils. Most commercial plantings are weeded chemically.

Varieties (cultivars) are classified according to length of root (long or short or stump-rooted) and use (fresh market or processing). Popular varieties for fresh market are Imperator and Gold Pak; for processing, Red Cored Chantenay and Royal Chantenay are often chosen.

Harvesting of carrots for fresh market begins when the roots are $3/4$–2 in. (1.8–5 cm) in diameter, usually 60 to 90 days after planting. Harvesting by machine is common. Marketing in bunches is declining; most carrots are sold in plastic bags with the foliage removed. Carrots for canning generally have shorter roots and are grown to a larger diameter.

Texas, California, and Arizona are three important carrot-producing states. *See* NEMATA.   H. John Carew

Diseases. Carrots are affected in the field by two important leaf spot diseases and by aster yellows. In storage and transit, the roots are attacked by several kinds of rot-inducing organisms.

Carrot leaf spots are caused by the fungi *Cercospora carotae* and *Alternaria dauci*. Cercospora blight occurs on young leaves and Alternaria blight on older leaves. These fungi overwinter in debris of the previous crop. During the growing season, repeated disease cycles are caused by airborne spores. In humid weather, both diseases increase rapidly, and severe defoliation results. Control of these leaf spots is achieved by repeated application of a suitable fungicide.

Aster yellows is caused by a mycoplasmalike organism that can infect many weed and crop hosts. Leafhoppers, principally *Macrosteles fascifrons*, are the insect vectors. Aster yellows causes the development of many adventitious chlorotic shoots to give a witches'-broom condition. These malformed and bushy tops eventually turn bronze or reddish. Roots are also malformed and produce numerous woolly secondary roots (**Fig. 2**) and tough woody tissue in the carrot. Control of aster yellows is by control of the leafhopper vectors. Spraying with an approved insecticide should begin early in the season as vectors begin to migrate from nearby diseased weeds into carrot fields.

Fig. 2. Carrot yellows. (*Courtesy of Arden Sherf, College of Agriculture, Cornell University*)

Rots of carrots in storage or transit are caused by several different bacteria or fungi. The classic rot is bacterial soft rot caused by *Erwinia carotovora*. This bacterium is a wound parasite and enters the carrot through openings at the crown, insect wounds, or harvest bruises. At temperatures about 40°F (4°C), the rot advances rapidly. Diseased tissues become soft and slimy and have a putrid odor. Control of soft rot requires careful handling during harvest and packing in order to reduce bruising. Storage temperature should be just above freezing, and relative humidity below 90%. *See* PLANT PATHOLOGY.   Thomas H. Barksdale

Bibliography. L. V. Boone et al., *Producing Farm Crops*, 3d ed., 1981; T. W. Whitaker et al., *Carrot Production in the United States*, U.S. Department of Agriculture, Agr. Handb. 375, 1970.

Cartilage

A firm, resilient connective tissue of vertebrates and some invertebrates. Isolated pieces act as a skeleton to provide support and anchor muscles, or cartilage is with bone to contribute its resilience and interstitial growth to bony skeletal functions. Cartilage comprises a firm extracellular matrix synthesized by large, ovoid cells (chondrocytes) located in holes called lacunae. The matrix elements are water bound by the high negative charge of extended proteoglycan (protein-polysaccharide) molecules, and a network of fine collagen fibrils. The elements furnish mechanical stability, give, and tensile strength, but allow the diffusion of nutrients and waste to keep the cells alive. Generally, blood vessels reach only to the perichondrium of fibrous connective tissue, wrapping around the cartilage and attaching it to other tissues. *See* BONE; COLLAGEN.

Cartilage is modified in several ways. In elastic cartilage, the chondrocytes add elastic fibers to the matrix to increase resilience, as in cartilages supporting the Eustachian tube, mammalian external ear, and parts of the larynx. Where cartilage joins bones tightly at certain joints with limited mobility, for example, at the pubic symphysis and between vertebrae, the matrix of fibrocartilage contains prominent collagen fibers and has less proteoglycan than the typical hyaline variety. Hyaline cartilage, named for its glassy translucence, is the major support in the airway; and throughout the embryo, pieces of it develop as a cartilaginous precursor to the bony skeleton, except in the face and upper skull.

The primitive cartilaginous skeleton undergoes another modification, by locally calcifying its matrix. At sites of calcification, invading cells destroy the cartilage and mostly replace it by bone, leaving permanent hyaline cartilage only at the joint or articular surfaces, in some ribs, and, until maturity, at growth plates set back from the joints and perpendicular to the long axis of limb bones. The precarious physiological balance between chondrocytes and matrix materials in the heavily loaded articular cartilage breaks down in old age or in inflamed joints. *See* ARTHRITIS; CONNECTIVE TISSUE; JOINT (ANATOMY); SKELETAL SYSTEM.   William A. Beresford

Bibliography. B. K. Hall (ed.), *Cartilage*, 3 vols., 1983.

Cartography

The techniques concerned with constructing maps from geographic information. Maps are spatial representations of the environment. Typically, maps take graphic form, appearing on computer screens or printed on paper, but they may also take tactile or auditory forms for the visually impaired. Other representations such as digital files of locational coordinates or even mental images of the environment are also sometimes considered to be maps, or virtual maps.

Maps and uses. Because the environment is complex and everchanging, the variety of maps and map uses is unlimited. For instance, maps are indispensable tools for navigating over land, sea, or air. Maps are effective both in exploiting natural resources and in protecting them. They are used to investigate geographic phenomena, including environmental pollution, climate change, even the spread of diseases and the distribution of social phenomena such as poverty and illiteracy. In addition, maps can be used to communicate insights derived from geographic research through publication in periodicals and books and through distribution over computer networks and broadcast media. Every private business, government agency, and academic discipline whose products, services, or objects of study are geographically dispersed benefits from detailed, up-to-date maps. Unfortunately, appropriate maps often are unavailable.

Map scale and geographic detail. Maps often include insufficient or excessive detail for the task at hand. The amount of usable detail on a map varies with its scale, because human visual acuity and the resolution of printing and imaging devices are limited. Maps that depict extensive areas in relatively small spaces are called small-scale maps. For example, on a 1-ft-wide (30-cm) map of the world, on which the ratio of map distance to ground distance is approximately 1:125,000,000, very little perceptible detail can be preserved. As the scale of a map increases, so may the level of geographic detail it represents. Geographic features selected to appear on small-scale maps must be exaggerated in size and simplified in shape so as to be recognizable by the map user. These map generalization operations constitute an intriguing field of research by cartographers attempting to formalize, and ultimately to automate, the map creation process.

Reference maps. Topographic maps record the positions and elevations of physical characteristics of the landscape. They serve as locational dictionaries for many endeavors, including environmental planning, resource management, and recreation. The 1:24,000 scale United States Geological Survey (USGS) series covers the continental United States with approximately 57,000 map sheets and depicts 17 categories of physiographic and cultural features with more than 130 distinct graphic symbols. The enormous costs involved in compiling, producing, and revising a topographic map series account for the fact that only about 15% of Earth's surface is topographically mapped at a scale of 1:25,000 or larger (**Fig. 1**). *See* TOPOGRAPHIC SURVEYING AND MAPPING.

Thematic maps. Another problem with available maps is that they often fail to include a feature of particular interest. Maps that emphasize one or a few related geographic phenomena in the service of a specific purpose are called thematic maps. An example is a thematic map that reveals the uneven distribution of topographic map coverage around the world (Fig. 1). Thematic maps are powerful alternatives to text, tables, and graphs for visualizing potentially meaningful patterns in

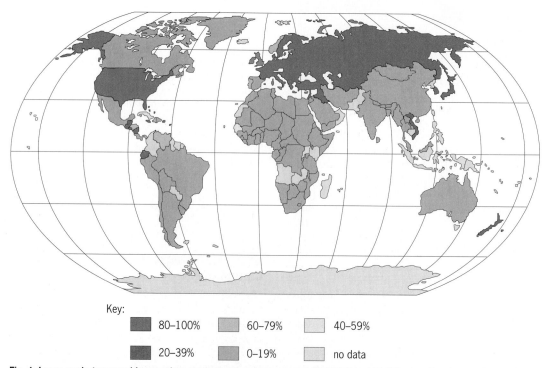

Key:

■ 80–100%   ■ 60–79%   ■ 40–59%

■ 20–39%   ■ 0–19%   □ no data

Fig. 1. Large-scale topographic mapping, percent area coverage area at 1:1000 to 1:36,680, showing the uneven spatial distribution of map coverage. (*After United Nations, World Cartography, vol. 20, 1990*)

geographic information. Although the production of large-scale topographic map series requires the resources of large private or government agencies, individuals and small organizations with access to relatively inexpensive personal computers, mapping software, and databases can afford to produce thematic maps in support of business, scientific, political, and creative endeavors.

Constructing geographic information. Maps are composed of two kinds of geographic information: attribute data and locational data. Attribute data are quantitative or qualitative measures of characteristics of the landscape, such as terrain elevation, land use, or population density. Locations of features on the Earth's surface are specified by use of coordinate systems; among these, the most common is the geographical coordinate system of latitudes and longitudes.

Geographical coordinates describe positions on the spherical Earth. These must be transformed to positions on a two-dimensional plane before they can be depicted on a printed sheet or a computer screen. Hundreds of map projections—mathematical transformations between spherical and planar coordinates—have been devised, but no map projection can represent the spherical Earth in two dimensions without distorting spatial relationships among features on Earth's surface in some way. One specialized body of knowledge that cartographers bring to science is the ability to specify map projections that preserve the subset of geometric characteristics that are most important for particular mapping applications.

Prior to World War II, locational data were compiled mainly by field surveys. Aerial surveillance techniques developed for the war effort were then adapted for use in civilian mapmaking. The scale distortions inherent in aerial photographs can be corrected by photogrammetric methods, yielding planimetrically correct projections on which all locations appear to be viewed simultaneously from directly above. Rectified aerial photographs (orthophotos) can be used either as bases for topographic mapping or directly as base maps. *See* AERIAL PHOTOGRAPH; LATITUDE AND LONGITUDE; PHOTOGRAMMETRY.

Influence of computing technology. Periodically, cartographic practice has been transformed by new technologies. Few have had such a profound effect as the development of computer-based mapping techniques. While printed paper maps still constitute the richest store of geographic information, cartography has become as much a digital as a paper-based enterprise. With more and more geographic data available in digital form, the computer has changed the very idea of a map from a static caricature of the environment to a dynamic interface for generating and testing hypotheses about complex environmental and social processes.

Digital geographic data. There are two major approaches to encoding geographic data for computer processing. One, commonly called raster encoding, involves sampling attribute values at some regular interval across the landscape. Imagery scanned from Earth-observing satellites works this way, recording surface reflectance values for grid cells (pixels) from 80 to 30 m (250 to 100 ft) or less in resolution. Digital elevation models are matrices of terrain elevations derived from satellite imagery or sampled from topographic maps (**Fig. 2**).

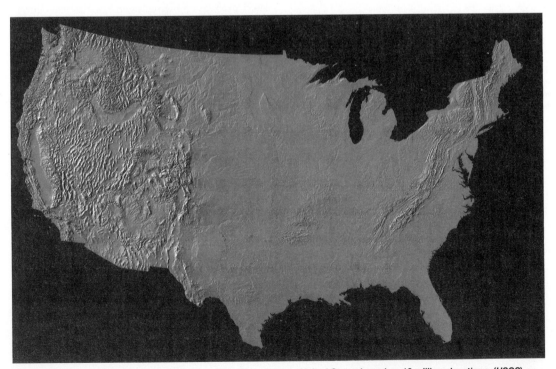

Fig. 2. Computer rendering of the topography of the 48 contiguous United States based on 12 million elevations. (*USGS*)

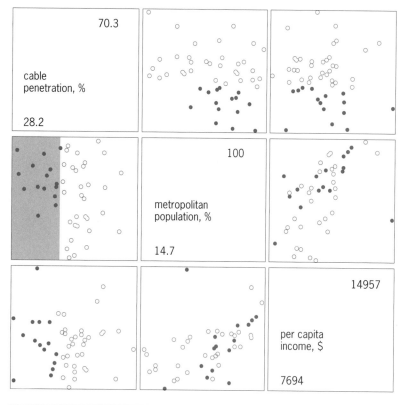

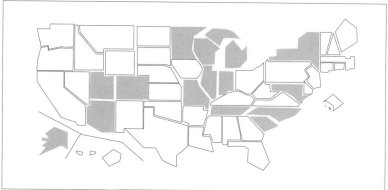

Fig. 3. Three geographic data variables related in a scatterplot matrix and linked to a map. Locations of observations selected in a scatterplot are automatically highlighted on the map. (*From M. Monmonier, Geographic brushing: Enhancing exploratory analysis of the scatterplot matrix, Geog. Anal., 21(1):81–84, 1989*)

plemented in dozens of idiosyncratic data formats designed to suit individual mapping agencies and computer vendors. Incompatible formats have impeded data sharing and have resulted in expensive redundancies in database construction. A committee of United States academic and government cartographers specified a Spatial Data Transfer Standard to improve cooperation and data sharing among federal government agencies. The development of international data standards is needed. *See* COMPUTER GRAPHICS.

Constructing geographic understanding. Geographic illiteracy is thought to put afflicted societies at a disadvantage in an increasingly integrated international economy. Access to geographic information is a necessary but insufficient condition for constructing geographic understanding. Access to analytical expertise is required to learn from the available information.

Geographic information systems. Guiding much of the research and development efforts of academic cartographers is the concept of automated geography—an amalgam of computer databases and procedures by which analysts might model, simulate, and ideally predict the behavior of physical and social systems on the landscape. Concurrently, increasing social concern for environmental protection stimulates a market for computerized geographic information systems (GIS) that combine mapping capabilities with techniques in quantitative spatial analysis. Many of the analytical procedures in these systems—such as calculations of distances, areas, and volumes; of terrain surface slope and aspect; defining buffer regions surrounding landscape features; and generating maps of new features formed by the intersection of several related map layers—have been codified by cartographers. Some cartographers have investigated the potential of computerized expert systems that may be used to assist nonspecialists in performing quantitative geographic analyses. *See* EXPERT SYSTEMS; GEOGRAPHIC INFORMATION SYSTEMS.

Cartographic communication. With few exceptions, the outcomes of analyses performed with geographic information systems are maps. Just as careless or biased quantitative analyses result in erroneous conclusions, so can unskilled map designs mislead users, and even the analysts themselves. Concern for the integrity of thematic maps motivated cartography's largest research project—the search for objective guidelines, based on psychological research, to optimize map communication. Map design issues that have garnered the most attention include classification techniques for grouping attribute data into discernible map categories and logical systems for choosing appropriate graphic symbols for representing different types of attribute data.

Interactive cartography. Although many broadly applicable map design principles have been established, the goal of specifying an optimal map for a particular task is less compelling than it once

A second method, known as vector encoding, involves digitizing outlines of landscape features that are homogeneous with regard to some attribute, such as a river, a watershed, a road, or a state boundary. Vector encoding is more expensive than raster encoding, but it is more flexible for many applications. One U.S. government database, for example, includes street descriptions and address ranges for 345 metropolitan areas by which U.S. census statistics can be matched and precisely mapped. The U.S. government's Digital Chart of the World vector database includes 16 distinct feature layers, including coastlines, rivers, roads, political boundaries, and 1000-ft (300-m) terrain elevation contours for the entire world at 1:1,000,000 scale.

Although the raster and vector approaches for digital encoding predominate, these have been imwas. Instead, there is interest in the potential of providing map users with multiple, modifiable representations via dynamic media such as CD-ROM, computer networks, and interactive television. Even as computer graphics technologies and numerical models provide ever more realistic environmental simulations, innovative, highly abstract display methods are being developed and tested to help analysts discover meaningful patterns in multivariate geographic data sets (**Fig. 3**). Maps, graphs, diagrams, movies, text, and sound can be incorporated in multimedia software applications that enable users to navigate through vast electronic archives of geographic information. Interactive computer graphics are eliminating the distinction between the mapmaker and the map user. Modern cartography's challenge is to provide access to geographic information and to cartographic expertise through well-designed user interfaces. *See* LAND-USE PLANNING; MAP DESIGN; MAP PROJECTIONS; MAP REPRODUCTION.   David DiBiase

Bibliography. L. Gaile and C. J. Wilmott (eds.), *Geography in America*, 1989; J. Makower (ed.), *The Map Catalog*, 1986; C. Muerhcke and J. O. Muerhcke, *Map Use*, 3d ed., 1992; R. J. Pike and G. P. Thelin, Mapping the nation's physiography by computer, *Cartog. Perspect.*, no. 8, pp. 15–24, Winter 1990–1991; D. Wood, *The Power of Maps*, 1992.

Caryophyllales

An order of flowering plants, division Magnoliophyta (Angiospermae), in subclass Caryophyllidae, class Magnoliopsida (dicotyledons). It consists of 12 families and about 10,000 species. The names Centrospermae and Centrospermales have often been applied to this order, in reference to the free-central or basal placentation. The order is further marked by its curved, peripheral embryo and a series of other embryological features; by the frequent occurrence of anomalous secondary thickening; by the substitution of betalains (unique to this order) for anthocyanins in most families; and by the frequently succulent habit.

The four largest families of the Caryophyllales are the Aizoaceae (about 2500 species), Cactaceae (about 2000 species), Caryophyllaceae (about 2000 species), and Chenopodiaceae (about 1500 species). The Aizoaceae are unarmed leaf-succulents, chiefly of Africa, with numerous tepals and stamens and often with an inferior ovary. The Cactaceae are American stem-succulents, mostly spiny and with much reduced leaves, with numerous tepals and stamens and an inferior ovary; in the past they have often been treated as the separate order Opuntiales, but their relationship to the other betalain-containing families is now generally acknowledged. The Caryophyllaceae lack betalains but are otherwise typical of the order. The Chenopodiaceae have reduced, mostly greenish flowers and usually a single ovule.

Familiar garden plants belonging to the Caryophyllales include beet (*Beta vulgaris*) and spinach (*Spinacia oleracea*), both of the Chenopodiaceae; sweet william (*Dianthus barbatus*) and carnation (*D. caryophyllus*), of the Caryophyllaceae; rose moss (*Portulaca grandiflora*), of the Portulacaceae; and the four-o'clock (*Mirabilis jalapa*), of the Nyctaginaceae. *See* BEET; MAGNOLIOPHYTA; MAGNOLIOPSIDA; PLANT KINGDOM; SPINACH; SUGARBEET.
                    Arthur Cronquist

Caryophyllidae

A relatively small subclass of the class Magnoliopsida (dicotyledons) of the division Magnoliophyta (Angiospermae), the flowering plants, consisting of 3 orders, 14 families, and about 11,000 species. They have mostly trinucleate pollen and ovules with two integuments (bitegmic) and a nucellus that is more than one cell thick (crassinucellate). Also, the ovules are often distorted by unequal growth so that the micropyle is brought near the funiculus and the chalazal end (campylotropous), or half inverted so the funiculus is attached near the middle (amphitropous) and these are usually borne on a free-central or basal placenta.

Most of these plants contain betalain pigments instead of anthocyanins, and the seeds very often have a perisperm. Most of the families and species of the subclass belong to the order Caryophyllales. The other orders (Plumbaginales and Polygonales) have only a single family each. *See* CARYOPHYLLALES; MAGNOLIOPHYTA; MAGNOLIOPSIDA; PLANT KINGDOM; PLUMBAGINALES; POLYGONALES.
                    Arthur Cronquist; T. M. Barkley

Cascode amplifier

An amplifier stage consisting of a common-emitter transistor cascaded with a common-base transistor (see **illus.**). The common-emitter–common-base (CE-CB) transistor pair constitutes a multiple active device which essentially corresponds to a common-emitter stage with improved high-frequency performance. In monolithic integrated-circuit design the use of such active compound devices is much more economical than in discrete designs. A similar compound device is the common-collector–common-emitter connection (CC-CE), also known as the Darlington pair. *See* INTEGRATED CIRCUITS.

The cascode connection is especially useful in wideband amplifier design as well as the design of high-frequency tuned amplifier stages. The improvement in high-frequency performance is due to the impedance mismatch between the output of the common-emitter stage and the input of the common-base stage. Thus the influence of the Miller effect on the first (common-emitter) transistor is minimal even when the load resistance of the amplifier, R_L, is large, because the load

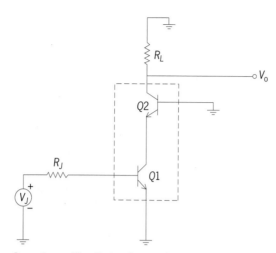

Cascode amplifier. Broken lines enclose a transistor pair consisting of a common-emitter transistor Q1 and a common-base transistor Q2.

resistance of the first transistor is no longer R_L but the much lower input resistance of the second transistor. Furthermore, since the second transistor is in the common-base configuration, it does not suffer from the Miller effect. This effect limits the frequency response of a common-emitter stage by essentially multiplying the base-to-collector junction capacitance by the voltage gain and making it appear much larger at the input of the stage between base and emitter.

Another important characteristic of the cascode connection is the higher isolation between its input and output than for a single common-emitter stage, because the reverse transmission across the compound device stage is much smaller than for the common-emitter stage. In effect, the second (common-base) transistor acts as an impedance transformer. This isolation effect makes the cascode configuration particularly attractive for the design of high-frequency tuned amplifier stages where the parasitic cross-coupling between the input and the output circuits can make the amplifier alignment very difficult. *See* AMPLIFIER; TRANSISTOR.

Christos C. Halkias

Bibliography. A. S. Sedra and K. C. Smith, *Microelectronic Circuits*, 1991.

Casein

The principal protein fraction of cows' milk. It accounts for about 80% of the protein content and is present in concentrations of 2.5–3.2%. The term casein, derived from the Latin word for cheese, *caseus*, was introduced into the scientific literature early in the nineteenth century to describe the primary protein of milk. Casein is a mixed complex of phosphoproteins existing in milk as colloidally dispersed micelles 50 to 600 nanometers in diameter. The variable-sized micelles are assembled from spherical subunits of nearly uniform diameter (10 to 20 nm), containing 25–30 casein molecules,

and from small amounts of calcium phosphate which, together with serum ionic calcium, plays a significant role in micellar structure. Critical to the stability and size distribution of the micellar state is a calcium-insensitive phosphoprotein component which functions as a so-called protective colloid to the system. When hydrolyzed by rennin (chymosin) as in the cheese-making process, it loses its hydrophilic, carboxy-terminal segment, predisposing the altered micellar system to the aggregation activity of calcium ions and subsequent clot formation. *See* COLLOID; MICELLE.

Caseins can be separated from the whey proteins of cows' milk by gel filtration, high-speed centrifugation, salting-out with appropriate concentrations of neutral salts, acid precipitation at pH 4.3–4.6, and coagulation with rennet (or other proteolytic enzymes), and as a coprecipitate with whey proteins. The first three methods yield preparations in essentially their native micellar state, but are impractical for commercial exploitation. Thus, commercial ca-

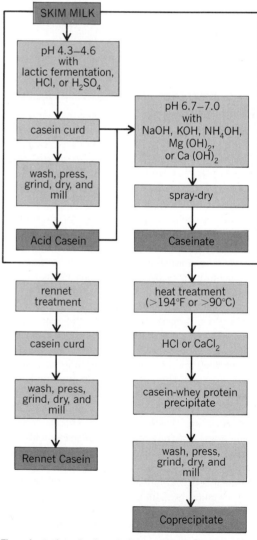

Flow chart of production of commercial casein products from skim milk.

Approximate composition of commercial casein products, in percent					
Component	Sodium caseinate	Calcium caseinate	Acid casein	Rennet casein	Coprecipitate
Protein	94	93.5	95	89	89–94
Ash (max.)	4.0	4.5	2.2	7.5	4.5
Sodium	1.3	0.05	0.1	0.02	—
Calcium	0.1	1.5	0.08	3.0	—
Phosphorus	0.8	0.8	0.9	1.5	—
Lactose (max.)	0.2	0.2	0.2	—	1.5
Fat (max.)	1.5	1.5	1.5	1.5	1.5
Moisture (max.)	4.0	4.0	10.0	12.0	5.0
pH	6.6	6.8	—	7.0	6.8

seins are produced by methods more amenable to industrial practices (see **illus**).

Acid casein. Fat-free, separated milk (skim milk) is cultured with lactic acid–producing organisms, namely *Streptococcus lactic* or *S. cremoris*, until it clots at pH 4.3–4.6 (isoelectric pH of the casein complex). The clot is broken and heated to about 122°F (50°C) to expel whey, thoroughly washed, pressed, ground, dried, and milled. Alternatively, food-grade HCl or H_2SO_4 is added slowly to agitated skim milk at 86–95°F (30–35°C). The temperature is raised to 111–115°F (44–46°C) to enhance precipitation of the casein, which is collected and processed. Acid caseins are designated according to the acid utilized in their production, such as lactic casein, HCl casein, or H_2SO_4 casein. Acid caseins are insoluble and possess low ash content (see **table**).

Rennet casein. When rennet is added to skim milk, colloidal casein is destabilized and forms a gel. Sufficient rennet and $CaCl_2$ is added to skim milk at about 86°F (30°C) to yield a coagulum in 20 to 30 min. Agitation is initiated following the onset of coagulation to reduce the particle size to optimize processing. After raising the temperature to 131–149°F (55–65°C) to expel whey, the curd is collected and processed. Rennet casein is frequently referred to as *para*-calcium caseinate. It is insoluble and contains a relatively high ash content consisting largely of calcium phosphate (see table). *See* RENNIN.

Coprecipitates. In the production of casein isolates, only 80% of the milk protein is recovered, since undenatured whey proteins are soluble at pH 4.6 and are unaffected by rennet. Efforts to increase protein recovery and improve the nutritional quality and functionality of isolates led to the development of coprecipitates. Skim milk is heated to more than 194°F (90°C) to denature the whey proteins and induce protein-protein interactions. Either HCl or $CaCl_2$ is added to induce precipitation of the protein complex, which varies in ash content according to the amount of $CaCl_2$ and HCl employed (see table). $CaCl_2$-induced coprecipitates are usually dispersed with polyphosphate salts prior to drying.

Caseinates. Many applications for casein isolates require that they be water-soluble or dispersable. This is achieved by the slow addition of a suitable alkali to the wet curd of an acid casein, being careful not to exceed a pH of 6.7–7.0. Protein concentrations of about 20% are spray-dried. Although sodium caseinate is most commonly used in the food industry, caseinates containing cations of K, NH_4, Mg, and Ca are produced.

The early production of casein isolates was stimulated by their application in industrial products such as paper, glue, paint, and plastics. These applications have been replaced by petroleum-based polymers. Thus the emphasis has shifted to their utilization in food systems, where they add enhanced nutritional and functional characteristics. They are widely used in the formulation of comminuted meat products, coffee whitener, processed cereal products, bakery products, and cheese analogs. *See* CHEESE; FOOD MANUFACTURING; MILK.

J. Robert Brunner

Bibliography. P. F. Fox (ed.), *Developments in Dairy Chemistry*, vol. 1: *Proteins*, 1982; N. P. Wong, *Fundamentals of Dairy Chemistry*, 3d ed., 1988.

Cashew

A medium-sized (20–30 ft or 6–9 m high), spreading evergreen tree (*Anacardium occidentale*) native to Brazil, but now grown widely in the tropics for its edible nuts and the resinous oil contained in the shells. Cashews belong to the family Anacardiaceae in the order Sapindales. The fruit consists of a fleshy, red or yellow, pear-shaped receptacle, termed the apple, 2–3$^1/_2$ in. (5–8.7 cm) long, at the distal end of which is borne a hard-shelled, kidney-shaped ovary or nut about 1$^1/_2$ in. (3.7 cm) long. The shell of this nut is about $^1/_8$-in. (3-mm) thick and consists of a smooth, relatively thin outer layer (exocarp) and an inner hard layer (endocarp). Between these layers is a porous layer (mesocarp), which is filled with a caustic black liquid that blisters the skin and makes the processing of the nut difficult. *See* SAPINDALES.

Although cashew trees are spread throughout the tropics, commercial production is centered in India, which handles 90% of the world trade. The trees, mostly seedlings, grow on wastelands with a minimum of care, reach full bearing at 8 years of age, and may continue for 25 years or more. Usually the fruits fall from the trees when mature and are gathered by local labor; the nuts are separated from the apples by hand. Some of the apples are marketed locally but most are wasted.

Processing the nuts is a difficult operation because of the caustic liquid in the shells. The nuts are dried in the sun, cleaned, moistened, and kept for 12 h in heaps or silos to soften the shells. They are then roasted at 350–400°F (176–204°C). In the roasting process the cashew shell liquid is released and collected as a by-product. The kernels are extracted from the shells, heated to remove the enclosing membrane (testa), graded, and packed in tin cans for export.

Shelled cashew nuts, plus cashew shell liquid, are second only to jute in India's exports. More than half of these go to the United States; Europe and Russia are heavy importers also. *See* JUTE.

Cashew nut kernels are eaten as nuts and used extensively in the confectionery and baking trade. The cashew shell liquid is a valuable by-product, containing 90% anacardic acid and 10% cardol, and is used in the varnish and plastic industries.

The cashew apples are too astringent for eating without being processed, but when processed may be used for jams, chutney, pickles, and wine. In India much attention is being given to extending and improving the cashew industry. *See* NUT CROP CULTURE.

Laurence H. MacDaniels

Cashmere

The natural fiber obtained from the Cashmere goat, native to the Himalayan region of China and India. The fleece of this goat has long, straight, coarse outer hair of little value; but the small quantity of underhair, or down, is made into luxuriously soft woollike yarns with a characteristic highly napped finish. This fine cashmere fiber is obtained by frequent combings during the shedding season. A microscopic examination reveals that cashmere is a much finer fiber than mohair or wool fiber obtained from sheep. The scales being less distinct and farther apart, the fiber appears to be made of telescoped sections.

Cashmere first became familiar in the beautiful soft, light cashmere shawls for which India has been famous. Today, it is used for such garments as sweaters, sports jackets, and overcoats. Cashmere is soft, lighter in weight than wool, and quite warm; but because of its soft, delicate texture, cashmere is not as durable as wool. *See* ALPACA; CAMEL'S HAIR; LLAMA; MOHAIR; NATURAL FIBER; VICUÑA; WOOL.

M. David Potter

Cassava

The plant *Manihot esculenta* (family Euphorbiaceae), also called manioc. It is one of the 10 most important food plants, and the most important

Tuberous roots from a single cassava plant.

starchy root or tuber of the tropics. It originated in Central or South America, possibly Brazil, and was domesticated and widely distributed well before the time of Columbus. Subsequent distribution has established cassava as a major crop in eastern and western Africa, in India, and in Indonesia. Brazil continues to be the largest producer. *See* GERANIALES.

Description and cultivation. The cassava plant is a slightly woody, perennial shrub reaching 10 ft (3 m) in height. The leaves are deeply palmately lobed; the flowers are inconspicuous, and the prominent capsules are three-seeded and explosive at maturity. The roots (see **illus.**) are enlarged by the deposition of starch and constitute the principal source of food from the plant. Normal yields are about 10 lb (4.5 kg) per plant. The leaves are also eaten (after cooking), and are noteworthy for their high protein content. The plant is propagated from mature stems which are planted without special treatment. Tuberization occurs gradually; about 10 or 12 months from planting to harvest is normal. Cassava can be grown for 2 or more years, however, and thus is a food that can be used at any season. Once it is harvested, however, the roots deteriorate within a few days.

Use and food value. The chief use of cassava is as a boiled vegetable. It is also a source of flour, called farinha in Brazil and gari in western Africa, and of toasted starch granules, the familiar tapioca. It can be processed into macaroni and a ricelike food. In the form of dried chips, cassava root is an important animal feed in the international market and is used extensively in Europe. In spite of its popularity, however, cassava root is a poor food. Its protein content is extremely low, and its consumption as a staple food is associated with the protein deficiency disease kwashiorkor. In addition, all parts of the plant contain glucosides of hydrocyanic acid, substances which on decomposition yield the poisonous hydrocyanic acid (HCN, prussic acid). Chronic diseases including goiter are common in regions where cassava is a staple food.

Franklin W. Martin

Diseases. Much of the older literature implies that cassava diseases are of minor importance, but this is not the case. Numerous diseases caused by fungi, bacteria, viruses, and nematodes affect cassava. The most important cassava disease in Africa is African common cassava mosaic, which possibly also occurs in Asia. The causal agent is a virus transmitted by whiteflies. Most plants in Africa are infected, and losses of 30–80% are reported. Some lines with resistance are available, but losses can also be minimized where disease-free planting material can be produced.

Cassava bacterial blight, caused by *Xanthomonas manihotis*, is distributed worldwide and is perhaps the most devastating disease on a worldwide basis. Disease-free planting material and resistant varieties are control measures. The four species of *Cercospora* that induce leaf spots are widespread and cause significant losses. Some varieties resistant to Cercospora leaf spots occur, and wider spacing to reduce humidity can also reduce disease severity. Other important foliar diseases are superelongation (caused by *Sphaceloma manihoticola*), Phoma leaf spot, cassava rust (caused by *Uromyces* spp.), anthracnose (caused by *Colletotrichum* spp.), and cassava ash (caused by *Oidium manihotis*). Stem pathogens (*Glomerella* spp. and *Botryodiplodia* spp.) and root rot pathogens (*Phytophthora* spp. and *Pythium* spp.) may be destructive in some areas. *See* PLANT PATHOLOGY.

H. David Thurston

Bibliography. T. Brekelbaum, A. Bellotti, and J. C. Lozano (eds.), *Proceedings of the Cassava Protection Workshop*, CIAT, Cali, Colombia, 1977; J. H. Cock, *Cassava*, 1984; J. H. Cock, *Cassava: New Potential for a Neglected Crop*, 1985; W. O. Jones, *Manioc in Africa*, 1959; J. C. Lozano and R. H. Booth, Diseases of cassava (*Manihot esculenta* Crantz), *Pest Articles and New Summaries*, 20:30–54, 1974; H. D. Thurston, *Tropical Plant Disease, American Phytopathological Society*, 1984.

Cassiduloida

An order of exocyclic Euechinoidea in the superorder Neognathostomata which possess five similar ambulacra which form petal-shaped areas, phyllodes, around the mouth. The innermost interambulacral plate between each pair of adjoining phyllodes is swollen and is termed a bourrelet. The five bourrelets and five phyllodes thus form a flower-shaped pattern around the mouth, collectively termed the floscelle. The apical system is monobasal; that is, the genital plates fuse together (see **illus.**). The adult stages lack teeth and fascioles. All extant forms live in shallow or moderately deep tropical seas, partly buried in sand. The oldest-known cassiduloids occur in Jurassic strata. The order was most abundant during the Eocene Epoch, after which a gradual decline occurred. Of 500

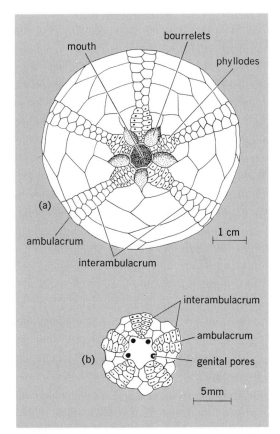

Diagnostic features of Cassiduloida. (*a*) Adoral aspect of test with the mouth at the center, surrounded by the floscelle. (*b*) Monobasal apical system.

species reported from Tertiary horizons, no more than 16 survivors are known from existing seas. The group seems to have been essentially tropical and subtropical in distribution, and the extinction of most members may in part be due to the deterioration of sea temperatures toward the end of the Tertiary. In the latest revision of the Cassiduloida, 10 families are recognized. *See* ECHINODERMATA; ECHINOIDEA; EUECHINOIDEA; NEOGNATHOSTOMATA.

Howard B. Fell

Bibliography. R. C. Moore (ed.), *Treatise on Invertebrate Paleontology*, vol. U, pt. 3, 1966; A. Smith, *Echinoid Palaeobiology*, 1984.

Cassiopeia

In astronomy, a prominent northern circumpolar constellation as seen from the middle latitudes. The five main bright second- and third-magnitude stars of Cassiopeia form the rather distorted W or M by which the constellation is usually identified (see **illus.**). The W is also called Cassiopeia's Chair, because on its side the W suggests the shape of a chair. Most old sky maps show Cassiopeia as a queen seated upon a throne. Lying as it does in the Milky Way, the entire region of Cassiopeia is rich in star fields containing several beautiful star clusters. Cassiopeia and the Big

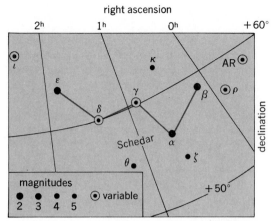

Line pattern of the constellation Cassiopeia. The grid lines represent the coordinates of the sky. Magnitudes of the stars are shown by the sizes of the "dots."

Dipper lie across the opposite sides of the North Celestial Pole. *See* CONSTELLATION; URSA MAJOR.

Ching-Sung Yu

Cassiterite

A mineral having the composition SnO_2. Cassiterite is the principal ore of tin. Its crystals are of the tetragonal rutile structure type, usually in prisms terminated by dipyramids. Twins with a characteristic notch called visor tin are common. Cassiterite is usually massive granular, but may be in radiating fibrous aggregates with reniform shapes (wood tin). The hardness is 6–7 (Mohs scale), and the specific gravity is 6.8–7.1 (unusually high for a nonmetallic mineral). The luster is adamantine to submetallic. Pure tin oxide is white, but cassiterite is usually yellow, brown, or black because of the presence of iron.

Cassiterite is genetically associated with granitic rocks and pegmatites and may be present as a primary constituent. More commonly it is found in quartz veins in or near such rocks associated with tourmaline, topaz, and wolframite. Cassiterite is most abundantly found as stream tin (rolled pebbles in placer deposits). Early production of tin came from cassiterite mined at Cornwall, England, but at present, the world's supply comes mostly from placer or residual deposits in the Malay States, Indonesia, Zaire, and Nigeria. It is also mined in Bolivia. *See* RUTILE; TIN.   Cornelius S. Hurlbut, Jr.

Cast iron

A generic term describing a family of iron alloys containing 1.8–4.5% carbon. Cast iron usually is made into specified shapes, called castings, for direct use or for processing by machining, heat treating, or assembly. In special cases it may be forged or rolled moderately. Generally, it is unsuitable for drawing into rods or wire, although to a limited extent it has been continuously cast into rods and shapes from a liquid bath or swaged from bars into smaller-dimensional units. Silicon usually is present in amounts up to 3%, but special compositions are made containing up to 6% (Silal) and up to 12% (Duriron).

Cast iron of the above composition range is often made into blocks or rough shapes and called pig iron. It is an intermediate form of cast iron used for remelting into iron castings. Pig iron usually is produced from iron ore and coke smelted into liquid iron in the blast furnace. This liquid iron may be poured into sand molds of specific design which, when cleaned and trimmed, become ingot molds for steel manufacture. In these instances the cast iron may be referred to as direct metal, indicating its production in the blast furnace without the intermediate remelting in the cupola furnace of the foundry, which is common practice in the manufacture of iron castings.

Classification. Cast iron may be purchased in several commercial grades called gray iron, chilled iron, mottled iron, white iron, malleable iron, ductile iron, spheroidal graphite iron, nodular iron, and austenitic cast iron.

Originally, cast iron was graded by examination of fracture characteristics of the surfaces produced when a sample was broken; its true composition was unknown. This method of grading first was applied to pig iron, which was classified similarly as white, mottled, or gray. The color of the fracture governed the classification of the product until about 1888, when extensive work by W. J. Keep revealed that the silicon content in a large measure determined the character of the fracture. Further work clarified the relationships between composition, microstructure, and fracture characteristics, and gradually the importance of the examination of fractures receded until the present time, when it is used only to classify the products generally. The chemistry of cast iron today is quite well known, and gray, white, and mottled iron can be selected on the basis of composition charts which mark the areas of their occurrence.

Further developments in cast irons have adapted heat-treatment processes to produce special properties that permit classification of special grades of gray, malleable, and white cast irons. Also, metals such as cerium and magnesium have been used to produce the spheroidal graphite structures which are characteristic of ductile irons.

Properties and uses. Gray iron is an iron-base material within the broad composition limits mentioned above. Of its total carbon content, more than one-half is in the form of graphite flakes. It is the presence of the graphite flakes which produce a gray color in a fresh fracture. The remaining carbon is dissolved in the metal and is called combined carbon. It may be present in amounts ranging from 0.05 to 1.20%. Gray iron is the mainstay of iron foundry production. Its application covers practically all engineering fields involving construction, machinery, engines, power, transport, mining, and many daily uses, such as stove parts, pots and pans, and hardware.

Mottled iron solidifies as a mixture of white and gray irons. The fracture is a mottled mixture of white and gray areas. The fracture may contain as few as 10% white areas in a gray background or the reverse, namely, 10% gray areas in a white background. Mottled irons are useful for abrasion- or erosion-resisting services, where their composite structure provides a hard surface with some ability to deform. The high frictional resistance of its surface is occasionally utilized.

Chilled iron has all but disappeared as a descriptive term. It was applied to cast iron which was poured into a metal mold or chill. Frequently, a gray iron would be processed in this manner, and if the cooling rate was rapid enough, a white-iron casting or a surface zone of white iron on the casting would develop, backed by the less rapidly cooled gray iron inside. Since glass molds, for example, are often made by casting one of their surfaces against a chill, such castings would be called chilled iron. Unfortunately, the term spread to the part-white, part-gray types of cast iron and more inaccurately to a solid white iron which had been cast in a chill.

White iron is an iron-base material within the broad composition limits mentioned above whose total carbon content is in the combined form. It therefore contains little or no graphite. A fresh fracture is white (ground-glass white). Its characteristic structure usually is obtained by lowering the carbon content or the silicon content or both, so that the graphitizing power of the composition is subdued.

Malleable cast iron is made as a white-iron casting within the narrower composition range that the term implies. Annealing produces a tough, bendable, and machinable cast iron. During the anneal, all or most of the carbon is precipitated in ragged nodules of graphite. The end product is available in a number of grades that vary in strength, hardness, and toughness. Malleable iron is used widely in the transportation, valve, fitting, and hardware industries for innumerable small parts.

Ductile iron (also called spheroidal graphite iron or nodular iron) is a product of high carbon and high silicon content in which most of the carbon has been coagulated into spheres during processing in the liquid state. During processing, an ingredient such as magnesium or cerium is added, followed by another substance such as silicon, calcium, or combinations of these ingredients. The resulting product acquires the structure of steel peppered with spheres of graphite. Its strength closely approaches that of steel, and it may be heat-treated to develop a ductility exceeding that of malleable cast iron. Its properties make it useful for a great many engineering applications requiring strength and toughness levels which previously were beyond the reach of iron foundry products.

Austenitic cast irons are available in the gray-iron and ductile-iron classifications. When gray or ductile iron is alloyed with substantial amounts of nickel, manganese, silicon, or other elements to alter the basic crystalline structure from magnetic alpha iron to nonmagnetic gamma iron, the resulting product becomes austenitic cast iron. These irons generally offer better corrosion- and heat-resistance than the low-alloy irons. *See* ALLOY; HEAT TREATMENT (METALLURGY); IRON; IRON ALLOYS; METAL CASTING; STEEL; WROUGHT IRON.

James S. Vanick

Bibliography. H. T. Angus, *Cast Iron: Physical and Engineering Properties*, 2d ed., 1978; E. Dorazil, *High Strength Austempered Ductile Cast Iron*, 1991; H. Fredriksson and M. Milert (eds.), *Physical Metallurgy of Cast Iron: Materials Research Society Symposia Proceedings*, 1985; Metallurgical Society of the American Institute of Mining, Metallurgical and Petroleum Engineers, *History of Iron and Steelmaking in the United States*, 1961; L. H. Van Vlack, *Elements of Materials Science and Engineering*, 6th ed., 1989.

Castor plant

A plant, *Ricinus communis*, belonging to the spurge family (Euphorbiaceae). Castor varies greatly in height and in color of foliage, stems, and seeds and also in size and oil content of the seeds. The palmately lobed leaves are borne more or less alternately. The main stem is terminated by a raceme (primary). After appearance of the primary raceme, branches on the main stem are each in turn terminated by a raceme. Growth continues sequentially as long as the plant lives, with branches arising from recently terminated branches. Thus a plant can have racemes in all stages of development from mature to prebloom. Mature racemes mostly have 10 to 70 capsules, each capsule containing three seeds. In frost-free areas castor can attain heights of 9 to 11 m (30 to 36 ft). Castor seeds are poisonous and also contain allergens.

Distribution is in the warmer regions of the world, the plant often growing in waste places. The castor oil plant has been of utilitarian value since antiquity. Oil from the seeds is among the world's oldest nonfood products in commerce. Castor oil contains about 85% ricinoleic acid, used in making industrial products such as alkyde resins for surface coatings, blown oil used in plasticizers, cracked oil for production of synthetic perfumes, nylon, sebacic acid, synthetic detergents, drying oils, and special lubricating oils.

Farmers usually grow castors on less productive land. Culture usually is not mechanized. However, plant breeders in the United States developed types (nonshattering capsules, dwarfs, and F_1 hybrids similar to hybrid corn) suitable for completely mechanized production; concurrently, engineers developed harvesting machinery. Production in the

United States, mostly in west Texas, peaked in 1968 but declined to nil because of larger economic return from food and fiber crops. Brazil is the world's largest producer and exporter of castor seed and oil.
Leroy H. Zimmerman

Bibliography. E. A. Weiss, *Castor, Sesame and Safflower*, 1971.

Casuarinales

An order of flowering plants, division Magnoliophyta (Angiospermae), in the subclass Hamamelidae of the class Magnoliopsida (dicotyledons). The order consists of a single family (Casuarinaceae) and genus (*Casuarina*), with about 50 species. Native to the southwestern Pacific region, especially Australia, they are sometimes called Australian pine. They are trees with much reduced flowers and green twigs that bear whorls of scalelike, much reduced leaves. Some species are grown as street trees in tropical and subtropical regions. *See* HAMAMELIDAE; MAGNOLIOPHYTA; MAGNOLIOPSIDA; PLANT KINGDOM.
Arthur Cronquist

Cat

The term used to describe any member of the mammalian family Felidae. Commonly, the term is restricted to the domestic cat and those felids that resemble it in size, shape, and habits. Those that are larger in size are referred to as the big cats.

All members of the cat family have a round head, are digitigrade (walk on their toes), have retractile claws (with the exception of the cheetah), and have 30 teeth with the dental formula I 3/3 C 1/1 Pm 3/3 M 1/1. All species are carnivorous.

Domestic cats. The origin of domestic cats is unknown, but it is established that they have been associated with humans for many centuries. Remains of the cat have been found with artifacts and remains of cave people, but it is generally conceded that these were not domesticated species. It has been suggested that domestic cats are descended from Old World wildcats such as the caffer cat (*Felis lybica*), an African species. However, there is no evidence for this belief, although it is known that wild and domestic species interbreed. Domestic cats are generally characterized by long, thin tails, straight ears, and short hair of a variety of colorations. These are the so-called alley cats and are mixed breeds. The pure breeds, however, are notable exceptions to this general description. There is a long-haired race, apparently developed in Persia, which is represented by the Persian and the Angora. The Abyssinian breed, in contrast to the common domestic cat, is characterized by being ruddy brown in color and having a longer face and ears. Each short hair is ticked or grizzled in appearance because of its alternate dark and light banding. This is known as an agouti condition.

There are at least two tailless breeds, of which the best known is the Manx from the Isle of Man. It has a boneless tuft of hair instead of a tail. The other tailless variety is found in Japan, and there is a question as to whether the Manx was a mutation or was imported. One of the most popular breeds is the Siamese cat, an animal with great independence and individuality. Its eyes are deep blue, it has a long, kinky tail, and its fur is short and cream to buff in color.

Most cats have two periods of heat each year. After a gestation period of about 8 weeks, a litter of about five kittens is born in April and August. They are helpless, blind, and entirely dependent upon the mother after birth. The kittens are protected by the female since the male will sometimes attack them. Scientific breeding of cats is difficult, since the cat is a vagabond by nature and interbreeding usually occurs in time, making it difficult to keep races pure.

Wildcats. In addition to cats such as the lynx, bobcat, serval, ocelot, puma, leopard, lion, tiger, jaguar, and cheetah, there are a few lesser known forms that are of interest to the biologist and naturalist. Among these are the Scottish wildcat and the caracal. The Scottish wildcat resembles the domestic species but is more heavily built. It has become virtually extinct, except for the small numbers in the Scottish Highlands. It is a nocturnal animal and is both ferocious and untamable. This cat is regarded as a separate subspecies of the European wildcat (*F. sylvestris*). The long-legged caracal (*Caracal caracal*) is built better for running than are other cats. It is found in the deserts of North Africa and western Asia, where it hunts and kills many types of animals. It resembles a lynx in having ear tufts but is more closely related to the serval.

Lynx. There are a number of species of cats known by this name. The Canadian lynx (*Lynx canadensis*) is the largest North American lynx. It is found in pine-forested areas of Canada and the northern United States, where it feeds upon rabbits, mice, and birds, and during the winter on the remains of animals left by other scavengers. This animal has become relatively rare as a result of land settlement. It is a stout-bodied cat about the size of a cocker spaniel. It is trapped for its fur, and the flesh is reputed to be edible. Usually two cubs are born each year, and the gestation period is about 10 weeks. The maximum weight of the adult is about 30 lb (13 kg), and the life-span is about 10 years.

The European lynx (*L. lynx*) ranges throughout the large forested areas of northern and central Europe. Unlike the Canadian lynx, it will leave the forest to attack sheep and goats when food is scarce. *Lynx pardellus* is known as the Spanish lynx and is the smallest of the species. It is found in the Pyrenees, on the French side of the ranges. *Lynx rufus*, known as the bobcat, bay lynx, or wildcat, is very similar to the Canadian lynx but is smaller, and its ears are not conspicuously tufted. It ranges over the eastern United States from Maine to Georgia and has been divided into a number of subspecies. It is fierce and feeds on mammals and birds.

Lynx differ from other felids in having 28 instead of 30 teeth; an upper premolar is absent.

Serval. Found in the scrub grass regions south of the Sahara desert, this cat (*Leptailurus serval*) usually feeds on birds and small mammals. Being fawn colored with black spots, it blends with the landscape. It is one of the fastest-running felids and can leap up to 6 ft (2 m) to catch a flying bird.

Ocelot. This species (*F. pardalis*) is arboreal and feeds on monkeys and birds in the forested regions of South America, its native habitat. Smaller and more ornamental than the jaguar, it is known as the painted leopard. The head and back are golden and the flanks are silvery, and there are rows of somewhat metallic spots on the body with stripes on the head and neck. Near habitations this cat will feed on domestic and farmyard animals. The adult, which is almost 3 ft (0.9 m) long, can be easily trained when captured young and is apparently harmless to humans.

Puma. This member of the cat family, also known as the cougar or mountain lion, is found in various habitats in the Americas and nowhere else. The puma (*F. concolor*) has been described as resembling a small, short-legged lioness because of its uniform color. It is a good climber and is nocturnally active in its hunting. It has been theorized that the puma aided the extinction of the horse in the Americas before the discovery of these continents. The male may weigh as much as 200 lb (90 kg) and have a length of about 7 ft (2 m), and the female is nearly as large. The male is not adverse to eating the young.

Jaguar. This cat (*F. onca*) is indigenous to Central and South America, where it is found along the banks of forested rivers and in marshy areas. Remaining hidden during the day, it is a nocturnal hunter, a strong swimmer, the largest cat, and a fierce carnivore. The jaguar has been called the leopard of the New World, and its pelts are commercially important.

Cheetah. This is a peculiar animal in that it has some doglike characteristics although it is included in the cat family. Its claws are nonretractile, its legs are long, and it does not climb. A single species, *Acinonyx jubatus*, occurs from northern Africa to Asia as far south as India. This animal is doubtless the fastest animal in running over short distances. It hunts in small groups and attacks such animals as gazelles and antelopes.

Leopard. This species ranges throughout Africa and Asia and is regarded as the most athletic member of the cat family, being equally adept at climbing, swimming, jumping, and running. *Felis pardus* is the only species of true leopard; however, *Uncia uncia*, the snow leopard or ounce, also is called a leopard. This latter species occurs in the Himalayas of central Asia at high altitudes. The leopard has a more extensive distribution than any other species of Felidae. These animals hunt ceaselessly and have been known to eat humans.

Tiger (*Felis tigris*).

They can be tamed in captivity when young, but few are tamed since they cannot be trusted.

Lion. *Felis leo* was a common animal in the Near East, and its range extended into Europe during prehistoric times. In historical times it was recorded as continuing to inhabit the Balkan Peninsula. It has come to be restricted in its distribution as a result of the advances of humans. It is still abundant in the savanna areas between Senegal and East Africa, where there is much herbivorous fauna to prey upon. It is not found in deserts or thickly forested regions. The lion may weigh as much as 550 lb (248 kg) and reach a height of 3 ft (0.9 m) and a length of $6\frac{1}{2}$ ft (1.9 m). It is the largest African carnivore. There is one litter of 2–4 young per year after a gestation period of about 15 weeks. The life-span may be as long as 40 years. The lion hunts at night and is silent while approaching its prey in order to surprise it. Various races of this species have been described, such as Cape, Masai, Somali, and Indian lions, but they show few differences in color and size.

Tiger. The tiger is represented by a single species, *F. tigris* (see **illus.**). It inhabits the forests of Asia, Sumatra, Java, and southern Siberia. As a consequence of the wide climatic and geographical distribution of tigers, they show a wide range of coloration and size, and a number of varieties are recognized. After a gestation period of 3 months, two or three cubs are born helpless and blind. There is one litter every second year, and usually only one cub of each litter survives. Tigers breed in captivity, and crosses between the lion and tigress (the liger) and between the tiger and lioness (the tigron) have been obtained. The tiger takes any food available and, like many members of the cat family, returns to the kill until it is consumed. *See* CARNIVORA.

Charles B. Curtin

Cat scratch disease

A benign, mild localized illness transmitted principally by cats and characterized in humans by an enlargement of the lymph nodes (lymphadenopathy), resulting from dermal inoculation of *Bartonella* (formerly *Rochalimaea*) *henselae*. This bacterium was first isolated from immunocompromised individuals with bacillary angiomatosis, a distinctive and potentially deadly vascular proliferative host response in skin, bone, or other organs associated with the presence of clumps of bacteria. The cat seems to be the major reservoir of *B. henselae*, and the cat flea, *Ctenocephalides felis*, could be involved in the transmission of *B. henselae* from cat to cat.

Epidemiology. Cat scratch disease occurs in immunocompetent individuals of all ages; however, a higher proportion of cases is reported among children and teenagers than adults (45–50% of the cases are of individuals younger than 15 years). The disease is considered the most common cause of chronic benign adenopathy in children and young adults, but can easily be confused with neoplastic conditions. More than 90% of the individuals have a history of some type of contact with cats, and 57–83% have received a cat scratch in the past. Incidence varies by season, and most of the cases are reported in fall and winter. More cases are observed in males than females.

Clinical signs. One to three weeks elapse between the scratch (or bite) and the appearance of clinical signs. In 50% of the cases, a small skin lesion, often resembling an insect bite, appears at the inoculation site (usually on the hand or forearm) and evolves from a papule to a vesicle and partially healed ulcers. These lesions resolve within a few days to a few weeks. Inflammation of a lymph node develops approximately three weeks after exposure, and is generally unilateral, commonly appearing in the epitrochlear, axillary, or cervical lymph nodes. Swelling of the lymph node is usually painful and persists for several weeks to several months. In 25% of the cases, a discharge of pus occurs. A large majority of cases shows signs of systemic infection such as fever, chills, malaise, anorexia, and headaches. In general, the disease is benign and heals spontaneously without aftereffects. Atypical manifestations of cat scratch disease occur in 5–9% of the cases. Most common is Parinaud's oculoglandular syndrome (periauricular lymphadenopathy and conjunctivitis), but encephalitis, degenerative bone lesions, and thrombocytopenic purpura (a bleeding disorder due to decreased platelet levels) may occur. Usually, complete recovery occurs with few aftereffects.

No clinical signs of cat scratch disease have ever been reported in cats. Whether members of the genus *Bartonella* are pathogenic for cats or contribute to persistent lymphadenopathy in cats remains to be determined.

Diagnosis. For years, diagnosis was based on clinical criteria, exposure to a cat, failure to isolate other bacteria, and histologic examination of biopsies of lymph nodes. A skin test was also developed and used. However, the antigen, prepared from pasteurized pus from lymph nodes of patients with cat scratch disease, was not standardized, and concerns about the safety of the product were raised. Since discovery of the causative agent, a serological test and techniques to isolate the organism from human specimens have been developed, and the polymerase chain reaction is used to confirm *Bartonella* infection. Diagnosis is mainly based on a serological titer $\geq 1{:}64$ (or a fourfold titer increase between early and late serum samples) and a history of a cat scratch or bite.

Treatment. Most individuals with cat scratch disease experience mild illness and require minimal treatment. Usually antimicrobial therapy is not necessary since spontaneous resolution is common. In severe forms, especially in immunocompromised patients, antibiotics such as ciprofloxacin, rifampin, or gentamicin have been recommended. Erythromycin and doxyxycline are effective antibiotics in the treatment of bacillary angiomatosis and may be recommended in immunodeficient persons suffering from cat scratch disease.   Bruno B. Chomel

Cataclysmic variable

A member of a wide class of short-period binary stars, one of whose components is a white dwarf (degenerate) star, capable of irregularly timed but recurrent outbursts of brightness by factors of 2 to 10,000. The other component can be a main-sequence (core-hydrogen-burning) star like the Sun, a red giant (evolved, low-mass) star like that which the Sun will become, or another white dwarf. Classical novae make up the most spectacular, but not the commonest, category of cataclysmic variables. The systems are also called cataclysmic binaries.

Origin. Stars with initial masses between 0.8 and 8 solar masses complete hydrogen and helium burning within the present age of the universe, shed their outer layers, which are seen as planetary nebulae, and settle down as white dwarfs with radii of about 10,000 km (6000 mi) and no further sources of nuclear or gravitational energy. If the star was originally part of a binary system, as about half are, the pair remains bound through this process, leaving the white dwarf in orbit with a normal star. The second star, after an additional time span of about $10^{10} \, (M/M_\odot)^{-2}$ years (where M is the mass of the second star and $M_\odot$ is the solar mass), in turn evolves first into a red giant and then into another white dwarf. Such a pair, at any stage, constitutes a minimal cataclysmic variable. *See* PLANETARY NEBULA.

The more interesting manifestations occur when gas flows from the normal star down into the deep gravitational potential well of the compact white dwarf, releasing energy as it goes. Such a transfer can happen in two ways. First, if the stars are close enough together, the normal one fills a critical surface called its Roche lobe, and gas from its surface streams through a neck (called the inner lagrangian point, L_1) between the two stars and feeds a disk around the white dwarf (see **illus.**). The stream, the disk, and the

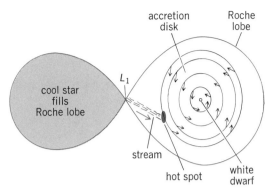

accretion disk

Roche lobe

L_1

cool star fills Roche lobe

stream

hot spot

white dwarf

Idealization of a typical cataclysmic binary system. Light curves and spectra, especially those of dwarf novae, provide evidence for all the components shown. The Roche lobe is an equipotential surface, that is, gas can flow along it without gaining or losing energy. *(After V. Trimble, How to survive the cataclysmic binaries, Mercury, 9(1): 8, 1980)*

spot where one hits the other are all hot and radiate with variable brightness, depending on the instantaneous gas flow rate. This accretion-powered luminosity normally exceeds that intrinsic to the stars themselves. Second, material will be transferred when the companion star becomes a red giant with a strong stellar wind blowing off its surface. Part of the wind hits the white dwarf, heats up, and radiates; but no disk is formed.

Variations in the mass-transfer rate give rise to variable brightness and outbursts. In addition, the transferred hydrogen eventually builds up a layer so thick that its bottom becomes hot and dense enough for nuclear reactions to occur. The hydrogen is degenerate, so that its pressure depends only on density, not on temperature. Thus, when burning starts, the gas heats up but does not expand and cool again, in the way a normal gas would. Instead, the higher temperature drives more rapid hydrogen burning, and so forth, leading to an explosion called a nova. *See* NOVA.

Types of behavior. Several types of cataclysmic variables are known (see **table**). Classical novae display the greatest outburst amplitudes, increasing luminosity by 9–14 magnitudes during outbursts.

They are followed by recurrent novae and dwarf novae with outburst amplitudes of 7–9 and 2–6 magnitudes, respectively. The interval between outbursts can range from as little as 10 days to 30 years for dwarf novae and from 10 to 100 years for recurrent novae, while classical novae also recur but only after 10^4–10^5 years or more. The nova-like variables, V471 Tauri stars, and symbiotic stars display irregular variability but no outbursts, while brightness changes in AM CV stars are due entirely to eclipses, which sometimes occur in V471 Tauri stars as well.

The number of binary systems belonging to each type is more a reflection of the observational difficulties in identifying a type than of its real frequency in the Galaxy. For instance, V471 Tauri stars (where neither component fills its Roche lobe) must be quite common, but are very inconspicuous since the only light comes from the two faint stars. In addition to the strong outbursts in the various types of novae, most cataclysmic variables also display irregular brightness variations on time scales from seconds to years. These variations are caused by the pulsation and rotation of the white dwarfs, changes in disk structure, and so forth. Many cataclysmic variables are seen as radio and x-ray sources, the emission coming from the hot spot and other regions of diffuse gas. *See* RADIO ASTRONOMY; X-RAY ASTRONOMY.

The magnetic fields of the white dwarfs in polars are 2000–5000 tesla (20–50 megagauss) and strong enough to keep the rotation of the stars synchronized with their orbit periods. Accretion occurs only at the magnetic poles, so that brightness varies with a period equal to that of the white dwarf's rotation. Intermediate polar fields of 500–1000 tesla (5–10 megagauss) do not synchronize the rotation, and accretion occurs partly at the poles and partly from a disk. Both polars and intermediate polars can have outbursts like those of classical novae, dwarf novae, and novalike variables. The two classes may constitute an evolutionary sequence.

All cataclysmic variables with white dwarfs

Subtypes of cataclysmic variables						
System type	Outburst factor	Number known	Recurrence time	Component stars*	Features seen in light curves and spectra	Cause of mass transfer
Classical novae (CN)	≥1000	~200	≥10^5 years	WD + MS	Disk, stream	Roche lobe overflow
Recurrent novae (RN)	~100–1000	5–6	Decades	WD + RG	Disk	Roche lobe overflow or wind
Dwarf novae (DN)	≲10	~300	Months	WD + MS	Disk, stream, hot spot	Roche lobe overflow
Novalike (NL) variables		~100		WD + MS	Disk and/or stream, hot spot	Roche lobe overflow
Polars		20		WD + MS	Strong magnetic field, no disk	Roche lobe overflow
Intermediate polars		20		WD + MS	Moderate magnetic field, some disk	Roche lobe overflow
V471 Tau stars		12 in planetary nebulae		pre-WD + MS	Surrounding gas of planetary nebula	—
		20 others		WD + MS	Possible old planetary nebula	—
Symbiotic stars		Dozens		WD + RG	Hot gas of wind	Wind
AM CVn stars		4		WD + WD	Stars both fill Roche lobes	Contact

*WD = white dwarf, MS = main sequence, RG = red giant.

made of carbon and oxygen or of oxygen, neon, and magnesium that accrete hydrogen from their companions will eventually explode as novae, when the hydrogen layer becomes sufficiently thick. Thus the dwarf novae (with slow mass transfer) and the novalike variables (with larger transfer rates) are really just novae that have not been seen yet. The V471 Tauri stars evolve into more conspicuous types of systems when their normal stars expand as they age enough to fill their Roche lobes, initiating mass transfer by Roche-lobe overflow.

Controversy long surrounded the mechanisms responsible for outbursts in dwarf novae. The rapid changes in their transfer rates could be connected with changes in the structure of the donor star or with an instability in the accretion disk, having to do with the viscosity of the gas as a function of density and temperature. Simultaneous observation at ultraviolet, visible, and infrared wavelengths finally established that disk instabilities are responsible.

True nova explosions, powered by nuclear reactions, always blow off material that can be observed in spectra of the events. The amount expelled generally exceeds the amount of hydrogen accreted between explosions, and the ejected gas has been enriched in carbon and oxygen dredged up from the white dwarf. Thus, although the white dwarf survives any one explosion, it is gradually eroded away, rather than increasing in mass as a result of the accretion.

Ultimate fate. The erosion process just described leads to a pair of low-mass white dwarfs in orbit that will eventually merge to a single white dwarf, less massive than the Chandrasekhar mass of 1.4 solar masses, and therefore stable. If the white dwarf in a cataclysmic variable is initially more massive than about 1 solar mass and accretion occurs either very rapidly (as in the recurrent novae) or very slowly (as in some symbiotic stars), then explosions may not blow off all the accreted material that has burned. Retained helium can then gradually increase the mass of the white dwarf to the Chandrasekhar limit. If the stellar core is still very hot when this event happens, the entire body of the star burns and blows apart in an explosion that is perhaps responsible for one kind of supernova. If the center has cooled, the overmassive white dwarf undergoes accretion-induced collapse to a neutron star. Continued mass transfer onto the neutron star gives rise to emission of x-rays in what is called a low-mass x-ray binary. If the accretion stops, the neutron star can radiate as a pulsar with a close companion. Both sorts of systems occur in the centers of globular clusters and elsewhere. *See* BINARY STAR; NEUTRON STAR; PULSAR; STAR CLUSTERS; STELLAR EVOLUTION; SUPERNOVA; SYMBIOTIC STAR; VARIABLE STAR; WHITE DWARF STAR.   Virginia Trimble

Bibliography. S. Kenyon, *The Symbiotic Stars*, 1989; O. Regev and G. Shaviv (eds.), *Cataclysmic Variables and Related Physics*, 1993; N. Vogt (ed.), *Cataclysmic Variable Stars*, 1992.

Catalysis

The phenomenon in which a relatively small amount of foreign material, called a catalyst, augments the rate of a chemical reaction (positive catalysis), or decreases it (negative catalysis) without itself being consumed. A catalyst is material, and not light or heat. It changes a reaction rate. *See* ANTIOXIDANT; INHIBITOR (CHEMISTRY).

If the reaction $A + B \rightarrow D$ occurs very slowly but is catalyzed by some catalyst (Cat), the addition of Cat must open new channels for the reaction. In a very simple case [reactions (1)], the two

$$
\left.
\begin{array}{rcl}
A + Cat & \rightarrow & ACat \\
ACat + B & \rightarrow & D + Cat
\end{array}
\right\} \text{Chain propagation}
$$
$$
A + B \rightarrow D \qquad \text{Overall reaction} \tag{1}
$$

propagation processes, which are fast compared to the uncatalyzed reactions, $A + B \rightarrow D$, provide the new channel for the reaction. The catalyst reacts in the first step, but is regenerated in the second step to commence a new cycle. A catalytic reaction is thus a kind of chain reaction. *See* CHAIN REACTION (CHEMISTRY).

If a reaction is in chemical equilibrium under some fixed conditions, the addition of a catalyst cannot change the position of equilibrium without violating the second law of thermodynamics. Therefore, if a catalyst augments the rate of $A + B \rightarrow D$, it must also augment the reverse rate, $D \rightarrow A + B$. *See* CHEMICAL THERMODYNAMICS.

Categories. Catalysis is conventionally divided into three categories: homogeneous, heterogeneous, and enzyme. Heterogeneous catalysis plays a dominant role in chemical processes in the petroleum, petrochemical, and chemical industries. Homogeneous catalysis is important in the petrochemical and chemical industries. Enzyme catalysis plays a key role in all metabolic processes and in some industries, such as the fermentation industry. The mechanisms of these categories involve chemical interaction between the catalyst and one or more reactants. In phase-transfer catalysis the interaction is physical. Electrocatalysis and photocatalysis are more specialized forms of catalysis.

Homogeneous. In homogeneous catalysis, reactants, products, and catalyst are all present molecularly in one phase, usually liquid. Examples are the hydrogenation of 1-hexene in a hydrocarbon solvent catalyzed by dissolved $[(C_6H_5)_3P]_3RhH$ [reaction (2)] and the hydrolysis of an ester catalyzed by acid [reaction (3)].

$$H_2C=CHCH_2CH_2CH_2CH_3 + H_2 \longrightarrow$$

$$CH_3CH_2CH_2CH_2CH_2CH_3 \quad (2)$$

$$CH_3COOC_2H_5 + H_2O \xrightarrow{H^+} CH_3COOH + HOC_2H_5 \quad (3)$$

See HOMOGENEOUS CATALYSIS.

Heterogeneous. In heterogeneous catalysis, the catalyst is in a separate phase. Usually the reactants and products are in gaseous or liquid phases and the catalyst is a solid. The catalytic reaction occurs on the surface of the solid. Examples are the dehydration and the dehydrogenation of isopropyl alcohol [reactions (4) and (5)]. Reaction (4) can be

$$CH_3CHOHCH_3 \longrightarrow$$

$$CH_3HC=CH_2 + H_2O \quad \text{Dehydration} \quad (4)$$

$$CH_3CHOHCH_3 \longrightarrow$$

$$CH_3COCH_3 + H_2 \quad \text{Dehydrogenation} \quad (5)$$

affected by passing the vapors of the alcohol over alumina at about 300°C (570°F), and reaction (5) over copper at 200°C (390°F). *See* HETEROGENEOUS CATALYSIS.

Enzyme. Transformations of matter in living organisms occur by an elaborate sequence of reactions, most of which are catalyzed by biocatalysts called enzymes. Enzymes are proteins and therefore of colloidal dimensions. Although studies of interrelations between homogeneous catalysis and heterogeneous catalysis have been developing, enzyme catalysis remains a rather separate area in the nature of the catalyst and in the type of reactions catalyzed. *See* ENZYME.

Phase transfer. In phase-transfer catalysis the two reactants start in separate phases: a salt as a solid or dissolved in water, and a water-insoluble organic compound as a liquid or dissolved in a nonpolar solvent such as benzene. Mere agitation of the two phases will usually lead to little reaction. However, addition of a suitable phase-transfer catalyst such as an onium salt or a crown ether will considerably augment the rate, ordinarily by carrying the anion into the organic phase, where it is relatively unsolvated and therefore reactive. Such catalytic reactions are run in batch reactors with catalyst at the 1–3% level. Thus, the turnover number (a value related to the number of sets of molecules that react) is about 50 in typical phase-transfer catalysis. For example, an alkyl halide (RX) dissolved in benzene agitated with aqueous potassium cyanide (KCN) forms RCN + KX in the presence of tetrabutyl ammonium chloride as a catalyst. *See* PHASE-TRANSFER CATALYSIS.

Electrocatalysis. Electrochemical processes ordinarily involve an overpotential (overvoltage). Electrocatalysis aims at reducing the overpotential with consequent increase in rate and often of selectivity. The catalytic action may be innate to the electrode

(for example, platinum electrodes in a hydrocarbon reaction where dissociative adsorption is involved); it may result from derivatization of the electrode (for example, by a porphyrin); or it may be indirect [for example, the electrochemical hydrogenolysis of halobenzene (RX) with added anthracene (Ar); reactions (6)].

$$Ar + e \rightleftharpoons AR^- \cdot \xrightarrow{RX} R \cdot + X^- + Ar$$

$$R \cdot + e \rightleftharpoons R^- \xrightarrow{H_2O} RH + OH^- \quad (6)$$

See OVERVOLTAGE.

Photocatalysis. Photocatalysis is a rather vague term, and in some cases it represents a nonstandard usage of catalysis. Clearly a photogenerated catalyst could exist. A more common usage is given in the following example. Water is irradiated with light of $\nu = 320$ nanometers. No light is adsorbed so nothing happens. Fine particles of titanium dioxide are now suspended in the water. Light is adsorbed and hydrogen and oxygen are evolved. This sequence has been called photocatalysis, but not all chemists would agree that it really represents catalysis. It is a complex issue.

Selectivity. In most cases, a given set of reactants could react in two or more ways, as exemplified by reactions (4) and (5). The degree to which just one of the possible reactions is favored over the other is called selectivity. The fraction of reactants that react by a specific path, for example, reaction (4), is called the selectivity by that path, and it will vary from catalyst to catalyst. Selectivity is a key property of a catalyst in any practical application of the catalyst.

Turnover. The number of sets of molecules that react consequent to the presence of a catalytic site (heterogeneous or enzyme catalysis) or molecule of catalyst (homogeneous catalysis), the turnover number is substantially greater than unity and may be very large. The turnover frequency is the number of sets of molecules that react per site or catalyst molecule per second.

Catalyst life. In practical applications, catalyst life, that is, the time or number of turnovers before the reaction rate becomes uselessly low, is important. It will be reduced by the presence of molecules that adsorb at (react with) and block the active site (poisons). *See* ADSORPTION.   Robert L. Burwell, Jr.

Bibliography. D. K. Kyriacou and D. A. Jannakoudakis, *Electrocatalysis for Organic Synthesis*, 1986; N. Schiavello (ed.), *Photoelectrochemistry, Photocatalysis, and Photoreactors: Fundamentals and Developments*, 1985.

Catalytic antibody

An antibody that can cause useful chemical reactions. Catalytic antibodies are produced through immunization with a hapten molecule that is usually designed to resemble the transition state or intermediate of a desired reaction. Catalytic antibodies combine programmable selectivity with catalytic activity because a molecule must first bind inside the binding pocket of a catalytic antibody before any reaction takes place. The net result is a high level of control over the catalyzed reaction, control that is reminiscent of enzymes. It is possible that catalytic antibodies may be utilized in the synthesis of complex, valuable molecules, such as pharmaceuticals, or perhaps in some specialized therapeutic applications.

Selectivity. Generally, chemists must rely on collisions between molecules in solution to cause chemical reactions. Often, a reaction will produce a distribution of unwanted side-products along with the desired molecule. This lack of selectivity is a result of the different possible trajectories of the molecules just before a collision, and the different atoms on each molecule that can make contact during a collision.

In nature, enzymes serve as catalysts for chemical reactions, and have evolved to produce only a single desired product by requiring a precise binding event prior to reaction. A substrate or substrates (the molecule or molecules that will undergo the reaction) must fit exactly into an enzyme's binding pocket (active site) prior to any chemical reaction. Such fitting is often referred to as being analogous to a key fitting into a lock. This prerequisite and precise binding event allows enzymes to exert several levels of control over chemical reactions of bound substrates, levels of control that are not possible for reactions that occur free in solution. See ENZYME.

For example, as a first level of control, only the desired substrate molecules fit in the active site of an enzyme. Thus, the enzymes are provided with the necessary substrate discrimination required to operate effectively in the complex molecular mixtures inside living cells. That is, although many different molecules in a cell could potentially take part in a given reaction, only the desired substrate can bind properly in the enzyme and thus actually undergo the transformation.

As a next level of control, only the desired portions of even complex molecules react inside enzymes. The binding event precisely positions the substrate molecule within the enzyme active site, so that only the correct group of the substrate is in the proper location to react. Control over the location of reaction in a complex molecule is referred to as regioselectivity. Because of substrate binding, enzymes are capable of remarkable regioselectivity with even complex substrates that would give many products if they were left to react via random collisions free in solution.

The final level of control that enzymes can exert over chemical reactions can be described as molecular handedness. In certain cases, two molecules with the same molecular formula can be identical in all of their normal properties, but they are still different because one is "left-handed" and the other is "right-handed." This is analogous to a pair of hands being mirror images of each other but not superposable, even though they each have four fingers and a thumb. For molecules, handedness is a consequence of the tetrahedral geometry around carbon atoms with four different groups attached, since the four groups can be placed in a tetrahedral array in two different ways (a left-handed way and a right-handed way) around a central carbon atom. Molecular handedness is of critical importance because within living organisms usually only one version of a molecule is active in a particular organism, either the left-handed or right-handed version. Often, the wrong version is inactive, or in extreme cases even hazardous. The term stereochemistry is used to describe the handedness properties of molecular structures.

Stereoselectivity refers to how much of one handed version of the molecule is produced in a reaction relative to the other version. Typically, reactions in solution exhibit no stereoselectivity. That is, both handed versions of a product are created in equal amounts. Enzymes, however, can produce a single-handed version of a product as a consequence of the precise fashion in which the substrate is bound prior to the reaction and the handedness properties of the enzymes themselves.

Thus, as opposed to reactions in solution that take place through random collisions, substrates must first bind inside enzyme active sites. This binding provides for discrimination between different substrates, as well as regioselectivity and stereoselectivity in the catalyzed reaction. See STEREOCHEMISTRY.

Reaction requirements. Chemical reactions have energy barriers that must be overcome before a reaction can take place and the products created; the higher the energy barrier, the slower the reaction. A catalyst such as an enzyme accelerates a chemical reaction by somehow lowering the energy barrier. An enzyme, like any true catalyst, is itself not permanently modified during a reaction, so each enzyme molecule can cause the reaction of many substrate molecules, a process referred to as catalytic turnover. See CATALYSIS.

As starting materials are transformed into products, they must adopt, for a fleeting instant, very unstable structures corresponding to the highest points of the energy barrier for the process, and these highest-energy structures are called transition states. The higher the energy of a structure, the less stable it is. Often, there are also other high-energy species called intermediates that occur at a saddle point, near the top of energy barriers. The key to accelerating a chemical reaction is to lower the energy of the transition state(s) and intermediate(s), thus lowering the overall energy barrier. See CHEMICAL DYNAMICS; REACTIVE INTERMEDIATES.

Antibody production. Antibodies are the recognition arm of the immune system. They are elicited, for example, when an animal is infected with a bacterium or virus. The animal produces antibodies with binding sites that are exactly complementary to some molecular feature of the invader. The antibodies can thus recognize and bind only to the invader, even in the presence of the animal's complex internal molecular landscape. The antibody binding identifies the invader as foreign, leading to its destruction by the rest of the immune system.

Antibodies are also elicited in large quantity when an animal is injected with molecules, a process known as immunization. A small molecule used for immunization is called a hapten. Ordinarily, only large molecules effectively elicit antibodies via immunization, so small-molecule haptens must be attached to a large protein molecule, called a carrier protein, prior to the actual immunization. Antibodies that are produced after immunization with the hapten-carrier protein conjugate are complementary to, and thus specifically bind, the hapten. This situation is analogous to a molecular key (the hapten) fitting into a highly complementary molecular lock (the elicited antibody binding pocket). *See* ANTIBODY; ANTIGEN-ANTIBODY REACTION; IMMUNITY.

Transition states. Ordinarily, antibody molecules simply bind; they do not catalyze reactions. However, catalytic antibodies are produced when animals are immunized with hapten molecules that are specially designed to elicit antibodies that have binding pockets capable of catalyzing chemical reactions. For example, in the simplest cases, binding forces within the antibody binding pocket are enlisted to stabilize transition states and intermediates, thereby lowering a reaction's energy barrier and increasing its rate. This can occur when the antibodies have a binding site that is complementary to a transition state or intermediate structure in terms of both three-dimensional geometry and charge distribution. This complementarity leads to catalysis by encouraging the substrate to adopt a transition state–like geometry and charge distribution. Not only is the energy barrier lowered for the desired reaction,

but other geometries and charge distributions that would lead to unwanted products can be prevented, increasing reaction selectivity.

Making antibodies with binding pockets complementary to transition states is complicated by the fact that true transition states and most reaction intermediates are absolutely unstable. They exist for only a fleeting moment during the course of a reaction. Thus, true transition states or intermediates cannot be isolated or used as haptens for immunization. Instead, so-called transition-state analog molecules are used for the immunizations that produce catalytic antibodies. Transition-state analog molecules are not real transition states or intermediates; rather they are stable molecules that simply resemble a transition state (or intermediate) for a reaction of interest in terms of geometry and charge distribution. To the extent that the transition-state analog molecule resembles a true reaction transition state or intermediate, the elicited antibodies will also be complementary to that transition state or intermediate. This complementarity to the transition state can lower a reaction's energy barrier and thus lead to the catalytic acceleration of that reaction.

For example, phosphonate molecules have been used extensively as transition-state analog haptens for ester hydrolysis reactions, as shown in the reaction below. The tetrahedral geometry around the phosphorus atom and negative charge on oxygen of the phosphonate are good mimics for these features in the tetrahedral intermediate that occurs during the ester hydrolysis reaction. Thus, antibodies elicited by the phosphonate hapten have binding pockets that are complementary not only to the phosphonate but also to the tetrahedral intermediate for ester hydrolysis. This complementarity to the reaction intermediate results in its stabilization, and thus a lowering of the reaction barrier leading to acceleration of the reaction. In the catalyzed reaction, an ester molecule is hydrolyzed to give one carboxylate molecule and one alcohol molecule. Following reaction, the products depart, another substrate binds, and the catalytic cycle is repeated.

Characterization. The antibodies elicited by a transition-state analog hapten are isolated, usually

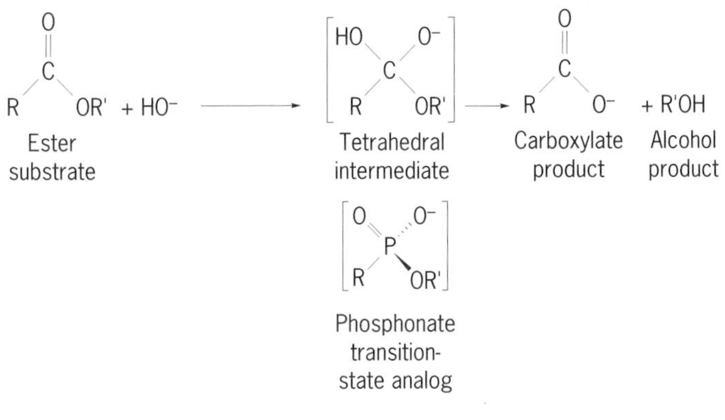

Ester substrate · Tetrahedral intermediate · Carboxylate product · Alcohol product · Phosphonate transition-state analog

as monoclonal antibodies using hybridoma technology, and then analyzed for catalytic activity. Catalytic antibodies, like enzymes, require a substrate to bind before reacting. For this reason, antibody-catalyzed reactions display the same type of general reaction parameters as enzymes, namely Michaelis-Menten, or so-called saturation, kinetics. Thus the standard types of analyses used to characterize enzymes are also used with catalytic antibodies.

In addition to the similar reaction parameters, some catalytic antibodies display detailed mechanistic features in common with analogous enzymes. Furthermore, some important structural features of an enzyme active site are also found in the binding pockets of catalytic antibodies.

Catalytic antibodies bind very tightly to the transition-state analog haptens that were used to produce them during the immunization process. The transition-state analog haptens, such as the phosphonate haptens, only bind and do not react with catalytic antibodies. It is the substrates, for example, the analogous ester molecules, that react. For this reason, transition-state analog haptens can interfere with the catalytic reaction by binding in the antibody binding pocket, thereby preventing any substrate molecules from binding and reacting. This inhibition by the transition-state analog hapten is always observed with catalytic antibodies, and is used as a first level of proof that catalytic antibodies are responsible for any observed catalytic reaction.

Importance of antibody catalysis. The important feature of catalysis by antibodies is that, like enzymes, the substrate must fit precisely inside the antibody binding pocket before any reaction occurs. Thus, precise enzymelike control over the catalyzed reaction is possible with catalytic antibodies. However, unlike enzymes, a desired reaction selectivity can be programmed into the antibody by using an appropriately designed hapten.

Catalytic antibodies almost always demonstrate a high degree of substrate selectivity. That is, only substrates that closely resemble the hapten take part in the antibody-catalyzed reaction. In addition, catalytic antibodies have been produced that have regioselectivity sufficient to produce a single product for a reaction in which other products are normally observed in the absence of the antibody. Antibodies can be programmed with such a high degree of regioselectivity that some have the ability to generate products that cannot even be produced by random collisions when free in solution. The antibody not only accelerates formation of the desired product but also prevents the unwanted reactions that completely predominate in solution.

Finally, catalytic antibodies have been produced by immunization with a single-handed version of a hapten, and only substrates with the same handedness can act as substrates for the resulting catalytic antibodies. The net result is that a high degree of stereoselectivity is observed in the antibody-catalyzed reaction.

Scope of reactions. By using transition-state analogs and other more complex strategies, catalytic antibodies have been programmed to carry out many different types of reactions. In particular, antibodies have been elicited that have the ability to catalyze reactions involving the breaking of bonds, including the breaking of carbon-oxygen bonds (ester, carbonate, glycoside, and ether hydrolysis), carbon-nitrogen bonds (amide and imide hydrolysis), carbon-fluorine and carbon-hydrogen bonds (elimination reaction), carbon-carbon bonds (Claisen rearrangement, decarboxylation), and phosphorus-oxygen bonds (phosphate ester hydrolysis). In addition, antibodies have been produced that catalyze the making of new bonds, including the formation of carbon-carbon bonds (Diels-Alder reaction, Claisen rearrangement), carbon-hydrogen bonds (reduction), carbon-oxygen bonds (lactonization, ester formation, ether formation), and carbon-nitrogen bonds (amide formation). Included within these categories are many examples of substrate specificity, regioselectivity, and stereoselectivity.   Brent Iverson

Bibliography. R. Lerner et al., At the crossroads of chemistry and immunology: Catalytic antibodies, *Science*, 252:659–667, 1991; K. Janda et al., Antibody catalysis of a disfavored chemical transformation, *Science*, 259:490–493, 1993; M. R. Haynes et al., Routes to catalysis: Structure of a catalytic antibody and comparison with its natural counterpart, *Science*, 263:646–652, 1994; D. W. Landry et al., Antibody-catalyzed degradation of cocaine, *Science*, 259:1899–1901, 1993.

Catalytic converter

An aftertreatment device used for pollutant removal from automotive exhaust. Since the 1975 model year, increasingly stringent government regulations for the allowable emission levels of carbon monoxide (CO), hydrocarbons (HC), and oxides of nitrogen (NO_x) have resulted in the use of catalytic converters on most passenger vehicles sold in the United States. The task of the catalytic converter is to promote chemical reactions for the conversion of these pollutants to carbon dioxide, water, and nitrogen.

By definition a catalyst is an agent which promotes the rates at which chemical reactions occur, without affecting the final equilibrium as dictated by thermodynamics, but which itself remains unchanged. For automotive exhaust applications, the pollutant removal reactions are the oxidation of carbon monoxide and hydrocarbons and the reduction of nitrogen oxides. Metals, base and noble, are the catalytic agents most often employed for this task. Small quantities of these metals, when present in a highly dispersed form (often as individual atoms), provide sites upon which the reactant molecules may interact and the reaction proceed.

In addition to the active metal, the converter contains a support component whose functions include yielding structural integrity to the device, providing a large surface area for metal dispersion, and promoting intimate contact between the exhaust gas and the catalyst. Two types of supports are used: pellets and monoliths. The pelleted converter consists of a packed bed of small, porous, ceramic spheres whose outer shell is impregnated with the active metal. The monolith is a honeycomb structure consisting of a large number of channels parallel to the direction of exhaust gas flow. The active metals reside in a thin layer of high-surface-area ceramic (usually γ-alumina) placed on the walls of the honeycomb. In either system the support is contained in a stainless steel can installed in the exhaust system ahead of the muffler.

Two types of catalyst systems, oxidation and three-way, are found in automotive applications. Oxidation catalysts remove only CO and HC, leaving NO_x unchanged. An air pump is often used to add air to the engine exhaust upstream of the catalyst, thus ensuring an oxidizing atmosphere. Platinum and palladium are generally used as the active metals in oxidation catalysts. Three-way catalysts are capable of removing all three pollutants simultaneously, provided that the catalyst is maintained in a "chemically correct" environment that is neither overly oxidizing or reducing. To achieve this requires that the engine air-fuel ratio always be at, or very near, stoichiometry under all vehicle operating conditions. Feedback air-fuel ratio control systems are often used to satisfy this requirement. Platinum, palladium, and rhodium are the metals most often used in three-way catalysts. In addition, base metals are frequently added to improve the ability of the catalyst to withstand small, transient perturbations in air-fuel ratio. In both oxidation and three-way catalyst systems, the production of undesirable reaction products, such as sulfates and ammonia, must be avoided.

Maintaining effective catalytic function over long periods of vehicle operation is often a major problem. Catalytic activity will deteriorate due to two causes, poisoning of the active sites by contaminants, such as lead and phosphorus, and exposure to excessively high temperatures. Catalyst overtemperature is often associated with engine malfunctions such as excessively rich operation or a large amount of cylinder misfire. To achieve efficient emission control, it is thus paramount that catalyst-equipped vehicles be operated only with lead-free fuel and that proper engine maintenance procedures be followed. In such cases catalytic converters have proved to be a very effective means for reducing emissions without sacrificing fuel economy. *See* AUTOMOTIVE ENGINE; CATALYSIS.

Norman Otto

Cataract

Any clouding or opacity of the crystalline lens of the eye. Cataracts vary markedly in degree of density and may be due to many causes, but the majority are associated with aging. Cataracts are the single leading cause of blindness in the world.

The lens consists of fibers arranged in regular layers, similar to the structure of an onion. It is composed of three distinct parts: an elastic capsule, the epithelium from which the lens fibers originate, and the lens substance which is plastic and capable (below the age of 40) of altering shape according to the condition of the capsule. The average diameter of the lens is 0.36 in. (9 mm), and it has a greater radius of convexity on its posterior surface. This lens is supported by the suspensory ligament and lies between the back of the iris and the anterior base of the vitreous, which is the jelly that fills the space behind the lens and in front of the retina. The lens has no blood supply, so it cannot be inflamed, but it is easily affected by metabolic changes. The essential biochemical change in a cataractous lens is the coagulation of its protein.

Senile cataract occurs with aging and is by far the most common type. Progressively blurred vision is the only symptom. There are a number of other varieties (congenital, metabolic, secondary, or traumatic; see **illus.**) and causes (such as a reaction to certain drugs or irradiation). Cataracts may also be associated with systemic diseases such as hypoparathyroidism, myotonic dystrophy, atopic dermatitis, galactosemia, and Lowe's, Werner's, and Down syndromes.

At present the treatment for cataracts, when they are sufficiently advanced to impair the vision, is surgical removal. When a cataract is surgically removed, the crystalline lens of the eye is removed much as a lens would be removed from a camera. Cataract surgery may be performed in one of three ways: (1) Intracapsular extraction: the lens, enclosed in its complete capsule, is entirely removed through a large 0.48–0.56-in. (12–14-mm) incision in the eye; this remains the most successful and common method of cataract removal in the United States. (2) Extracapsular cataract extraction: the capsule is opened, and the lens contents are removed; the posterior capsule is left intact, while the anterior capsule is partially or totally removed. (3) Ultrasound cataract surgery or phacoemulsification: an ultrasonic needle is introduced into the lens, and the lens is emulsified, fragmented, or broken up and sucked out through

(a) (b) (c)

Types of cataracts: (*a*) traumatic "star-shaped," (*b*) senile "cuneiform," and (*c*) senile "morgagnian."

a small (0.12-in. or 3-mm) opening in the eye; this is a form of extracapsular cataract extraction since the anterior capsule is opened and removed along with the contents, leaving the posterior capsule intact.

In order to restore normal vision after surgery, any of a number of methods may be followed. Cataract glasses may be prescribed. Contact lenses may be fitted, but these have not been too successful in elderly cataract patients because of their inability to handle lenses. However, since soft contact lenses have been approved for extended wear, they can be left in the eye for weeks or even months, thus obviating the need for handling. Intraocular lenses made of the plastic polymethylmethacrylate can be inserted into the eye to replace the cataractous lens. There are numerous types of intraocular lenses. Their theoretical advantages include permanent placement and less distortion and magnification. Some of the disadvantages include the increased difficulty of the cataract operation, an increased incidence of operative and postoperative complications, and the inability to easily remove a lens of incorrect power. *See* EYE (VERTEBRATE).

Jack Hartstein

Bibliography. O. R. Caldwell (ed.), *Cataracts*, 1988; E. L. Greve (ed.), *Surgical Management of Coexisting Glaucoma and Cataract*, 1987; J. Schulman (ed.), *Cataracts*, 1993; R. W. Young, *Age-Related Cataract*, 1990.

Catastrophe theory

A theory of mathematical structure in which smooth continuous inputs lead to discontinuous responses. Water suddenly boils, ice melts, a building crashes to the ground, or the earth unexpectedly buckles and quakes. The French mathematician René Thom conceived and developed an eclectic collection of ideas into catastrophe theory. His idea was to establish a new basis for a more mathematical approach to biology. Connotations of disaster are misleading, since Thom's intention was to emphasize sudden, abrupt changes.

Advanced areas of modern mathematics, including algebraic geometry, differential topology, and dynamical system theory, contributed to the creation of catastrophe theory. A complete mathematical theory exists for the elementary catastrophes, which can be written as the gradient of an energylike function. The physical, chemical, and engineering applications are less developed, although many are known in optics, laser theory, thermodynamics, elasticity, and chemical reaction theory. The Thom classification theorem gives exactly seven elementary catastrophes. Although a theory of generalized catastrophes exists, which extends the theory beyond gradient systems, it is not nearly as well developed mathematically or physically as that of elementary catastrophes. It does include remarkable examples of chaos (or stochastic behavior) in the solutions to nonlinear deterministic equations. These solutions include strange attractors and omega explosions among the examples of nonelementary catastrophes. *See* GEOMETRY; PERIOD DOUBLING; TOPOLOGY.

Two important aspects of catastrophe theory are frequently overlooked or misconstrued. First, as it is a rigorous mathematical theory, the characteristic catastrophe features can be proved. These features include jumps in the response; hysteresis or a path dependence in the response, representing a storage of energy for some paths; divergence, where a small path change produces a large response change (as if a source or sink were crossed); and type changes in the response, where a smooth response occurs on one path that becomes discontinuous along a nearby path.

Second, all of these features are topological, so that they are independent of the coordinates used to describe the potential. They are, therefore, qualitative features of the solutions. Some critics have concluded that because these aspects were qualitative, they could not be quantitative. This is contradicted by the solid and growing body of quantitative studies in catastrophe theory. (Problems in quantum optics, thermodynamics, and scattering theory have all been clarified by catastrophe theory.)

Definitions. The object V whose possible behavior is to be classified is a smooth, real function, having the general form given by Eq. (1), the set of real numbers, or, equivalently, Eq. (2). The r real

$$V : R^r \times R^n \mapsto R \qquad (1)$$

$$V_{a_1,a_2,\ldots,a_r}(x_1,\ldots,x_n) = V a_1,\ldots,a_r(x_1,\ldots,x_n) \qquad (2)$$

variables $a_1, a_2, \ldots, a_r$ are called the control parameters; the n variables $x_1, \ldots, x_n$ are the variables; and V is the response function. In mechanics, V represents a potential energy surface, and the control parameters are coupling constants, that is, the strengths of various terms in the expression for the potential energy. For a two-dimensional potential function, $V_{abc}(x_1,x_2)$, the response is the height of hills and valleys in a perpendicular x_3 direction. If a ball (with negligible inertia) is rolled onto this surface, it will roll into the lowest possible position. This lowers its potential energy to a local minimum. This is a simple example of a critical point. *See* ENERGY; PARAMETER; POTENTIALS.

In general, the critical points of $V_{a_1}, \ldots, _{ar}(x_1, \ldots, x_n)$ are the set of all points $P_i = (x_{1i}, x_{2i}, \ldots, x_{ni})$ for which Eq. (3) is satisfied, and may be

$$\left(\frac{\partial V_{a_1,\ldots,a_r}}{\partial x_j}\right)\bigg|_{P_i} = 0 \qquad (3)$$

maxima, minima, or inflection points. The hessian matrix **H** of the function $V_{a_2,\ldots,a_r}$ is the $n \times n$ matrix with ijth element given by Eq. (4). A point x_0 is called structurally stable if it is a critical point and satisfies inequality (5).

$$h_{ij} = \frac{\partial^2 V_{a_1,\dots,a_r}}{\partial x_i \partial x_j} \qquad (4)$$

$$\det (H)_{x_0} \neq 0 \qquad (5)$$

If S is a space of points with boundary ∂S, its codimension is dimension (S) − dimension (∂S). Two subspaces V_1, V_2 of S are transverse if dimension (V_1) + dimension (V_2) = dimension (S). The Morse lemma and splitting lemma allow the number of variables considered to be reduced. The codimension is the number of variables which must be studied.

Thom classification theorem. Consider an r-parameter family of smooth real functions $V : R^r \times R^n \to R$, for any value of n and any value of $r \leq 5$. The Thom classification theorem states that either the family is structurally stable, and is equivalent about any point to noncritical or a nondegenerate critical point (these are not catastrophes); or it is structurally unstable and is equivalent to one of the seven elementary catastrophes: (1) the fold; (2) the cusp; (3) the swallowtail; (4) the butterfly; (5) the elliptic umbecile; (6) the hyperbolic umbecile; or (7) the parabolic umbecile. If the number of parameters is finite and greater than five, complicated combinations of these seven catastrophes can occur. If r is made very large, the elementary class of catastrophes is not complete. Catastrophe geometry becomes increasingly complicated both as n increases and as the numbers of possible catastrophes increase.

One-variable cusp catastrophe. A simple example of a catastrophe is the one-variable cusp catastrophe. The response function for this catastrophe, $V_{ab}(x)$, is given by Eq. (6). A sketch of Eq. (6) for

$$V_{ab}(x) = {}^1\!/_4 x^4 + {}^1\!/_2 a x^2 + bx \qquad (6)$$

$x = x_0$, a critical point, is given in **Fig. 1**. Since the value of the critical point x_0 depends on the control parameters, a and b, in a complicated fashion, it follows that V_{ab}, evaluated at $x = x_0$, is a complicated nonlinear function of a and b. This is plotted in Fig. 1. Assuming that V_{ab} is a potential energy surface, a ball placed on the surface in Fig. 1 will roll downhill toward the right. The curves A, B, and C indicate three possible paths and, in **Fig. 2**, points 1 to 10 are labeled on these curves. Suppose further that points (1,3,5) and points (2,4,10) all have the same potential energy. This example will be used to illustrate each of the characteristic features of elementary catastrophes. It is the dependence of the response upon control parameters which is under study.

The curves A, B, and C of Fig. 1 are redrawn in Fig. 2. To see the jumps in response, consider a ball set in motion from point 5 on curve C. It will roll past point 6, and at point 7 it will fall to point 9 (**Fig. 3***a*). In addition, it is impossible to go from point 10 to point 5 along curve C.

To exhibit the hysteresis effect (Fig. 3*b*), first roll

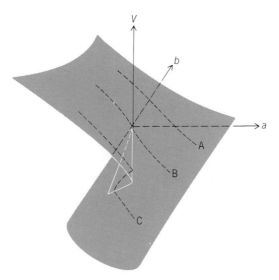

Fig. 1. Cusp catastrophe surface for the response function V_{ab} as a function of (a,b) at a critical point. Paths A, B, and C are labeled.

a ball from point 2 to point 1 on curve A; from there to point 3 on curve B. Then roll it from point 3 to point 4 and back to the starting point 2. The area enclosed in the figure is a hysteresis effect and is quite similar to hysteresis in magnetism. *See* HYSTERESIS; MAGNETIC HYSTERESIS.

The divergence effect can be understood by considering a small counterclockwise circular path about the (a, b) origin. A ball which rolls in this path will see the hill at negative b as a source of energy. The ball will act as if it had received a divergence of

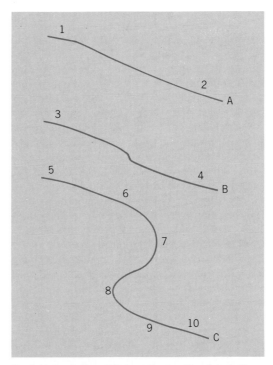

Fig. 2. Paths A, B, and C from Fig. 1, with points 1–10 marked. The response function V_{ab} has the same values at (1,3,5) and at (2,4,10).

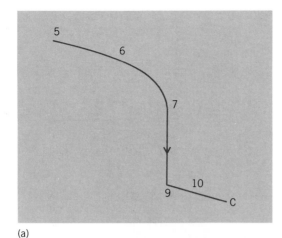

(a)

(b)

Fig. 3. Paths that exhibit features of catastrophe theory. (a) Path on curve C showing a jump in the response function. (b) Path using curves A and B which shows hysteresis. No change in potential energy V_{ab} is required to go from 1 to 3 or from 2 to 4. The area enclosed between curves is proportional to an energy stored from the overall process.

potential (that is, a nonconservative force) on each trip.

To see the change in type of path, simply consider the difference in paths A and C. If the scale of the b control parameter is such that these paths are very "near" one another, then a small change in the bx term can dramatically change the path from a smooth and continuous path A to a discontinuous path C.

Applications. Many physical problems involve some or all of the four nonlinear effects just described. Phase transitions include many aspects which are surprisingly similar to these four. The jump in the latent heat at a liquid-vapor phase transition is very similar to the jump shown in Fig. 3a. However, the cusp catastrophe given in Eq. (6) is quite definite. It contains no cx^3 term, as such effects are transformed away by coordinate transformations in obtaining the generic form. Unfortunately, careful experiments and their analysis show that the liquid-vapor phase transition is not any of the elementary catastrophes. On the other hand, the hysteresis of ferroelectrics is accurately described by the butterfly catastrophe. The conclusion is that catastrophe theory has an important role to play in phase transition physics even if it is not the whole story. *See* FERROELECTRICS; PHASE TRANSITIONS.

In ecology, sharp boundaries are often important. A predator may eliminate some competing species from an area; a parasite may eliminate the food supply of another. An explanation can be obtained from curve C in Fig. 2. Along the segment 5 to 6, the conditions assure the dominance of species A. Point 7 is a catastrophe point. The segment 8-9-10 is a region where another species, species B, dominates. This simple model is, of course, nonunique. Any other model whose solution is approximately such a polynomial is an equally good candidate. Thus, some collaboration from ecology is required to determine the correct response function, but the model can help in finding this. After several successful iterations of this kind, the surviving models have a sound basis. *See* ECOLOGY.

Status. There have been vigorous controversies, as some scientists have argued that catastrophe theory is unmathematical and scientifically empty, and that some applications are foolish. The first two claims are simply false. The first objection was based on the articles which were explicitly written to popularize the subject, while conveniently ignoring the scholarly articles which contained the mathematical proofs and examples. The second objection was based upon a very careless search of the literature; articles by many mathematicians meet the highest scientific standards. The third criticism is partially correct. Attempts to use simple models on drunkenness, prison disorders, and social problems are questionable. Even in these cases, however, the criticism seems harsh.

Catastrophe theory is an important tool for the physical sciences. If Thom's vision is correct, it may be even more important for biology and the social sciences.   Brian DeFacio

Bibliography. M. V. Berry, *Adv. Phys.*, 25:1–26, 1976; R. Gilmore, *Catastrophe Theory for Engineers and Scientists*, 1982; T. Poston and I. Stewart, *Catastrophe Theory and Its Applications*, 1978; H. T. Sussmann, *Synthesis*, 31:229–270, 1975; R. Thom, *Structural Stability and Morphogenesis*, 1975; E. C. Zeeman, Catastrophe theory, *Sci. Amer.*, 234(4):65–83, April 1976; E. C. Zeeman, *Catastrophe Theory: Selected Papers (1972–1977)*, 1977.

Catenary

The curve formed by an ideal heavy uniform string hanging freely from two points of support. The lowest point A (**Fig. 1**) is the vertex. The portion AP is an equilibrium under the horizontal tension H at A, the tension F directed along the tangent at P, and the weight W of AP. If the weight of the string is w per unit length and s is the arc AP, $W = ws$; and from the force triangle, $\tan \psi = ws/H = s/c$, where $c = H/w$, is called the parameter of the catenary. Thus the catenary has the differential equation (1).

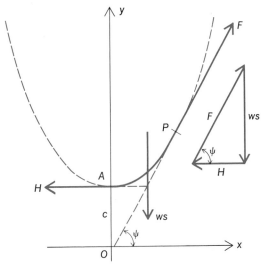

Fig. 1. Catenary and force triangle which keeps a portion of the string in equilibrium.

$$dy/dx = s/c \qquad (1)$$

The horizontal line at a distance c below the vertex A is the directrix of the catenary. With the x axis as directrix and the y axis through the vertex, the integration of Eq. (1) yields

$$y = c \, \cosh \frac{x}{c} \qquad s = c \, \sinh \frac{x}{c}$$

for the ordinate and arc of the catenary. All catenaries are geometrically similar to the hyperbolic cosine curve, $y = \cosh x$. These equations show that $g^2 = s^2 + c^2$, and from Eq. (1), Eqs. (2) are written.

$$s = c \, \tan \psi \qquad y = c \, \sec \psi \qquad (2)$$

The radius of curvature of the catenary at P is the length of the normal cut off by the x axis:

$$\rho = ds/d\psi = c \sec^2 \psi = y \sec \psi = PN$$

The tension at P,

$$F = H \sec \psi = wc \sec \psi = wy$$

varies as the height above the directrix.

In **Fig. 2** the tangent PT is tangent to a circle of radius c about Q, the foot of the ordinate; and

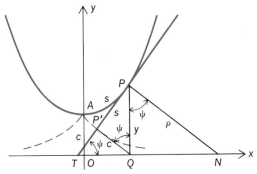

Fig. 2. Relation of catenary to the tractrix which is its involute.

since $\tan \psi = s/c$, $P'P = s =$ arc AP. Thus arc AP unwraps on the segment $P'P$. The locus of P' is a curve whose tangent $P'Q$ has the constant length c, namely a tractrix; hence the tractrix is an involute of the catenary. *See* TRACTRIX.

The surface generated by revolving a catenary about its directrix is a minimal surface, the catenoid. The catenary is an extremal for the problem of finding a curve joining two given points so that the surface generated by revolving it about a given line has minimum area. *See* HYPERBOLIC FUNCTION.

Louis Brand

Bibliography. P. A. Laurent, A. LeMehaute, and L. L. Schumaker (eds.), *Curves and Surfaces*, 1991; D. H. von Seggern (ed.), *Handbook of Mathematical Curves and Surfaces*, 2d ed. 1992.

Cathode-ray tube

An electron tube in which a beam of electrons can be focused to a small cross section and varied in position and intensity on a display surface. In common usage, the term cathode-ray tube (CRT) is usually reserved for devices in which the display surface is cathodoluminescent under electron bombardment, and the output information is presented in the form of a pattern of light. The character of this pattern is related to, and controlled by, one or more electrical signals applied to the cathode-ray tube as input information. *See* CATHODOLUMINESCENCE; ELECTRON TUBE.

Development. The technology of the cathode-ray tube was both a product of certain late-nineteenth-century experiments which led to modern physics and an indispensable element in the conduct of such experiments. In particular, the discovery of x-rays in 1895 by William Roentgen and the discovery of the electron in 1897 by J. J. Thompson both resulted from experiments in which early cathode-ray devices were involved. *See* ELECTRON; X-RAYS.

While experiments with cathode rays within partial vacuum devices had been conducted by various scientists for at least the previous 200 years, Ferdinand Braun is credited with inventing in 1897 a "cathode-ray indicator tube" from which all modern cathode-ray tubes are derived. Braun's interest in the cathode-ray tube was primarily as a device for the study of phenomena related to electricity. The cathode-ray tube was well suited to this use because of its ability to provide a visual indication of alternating electric currents at low frequencies. Oscillography was thus a natural first application for the new device. To this day, the cathode-ray oscilloscope continues to be an indispensable tool in nearly all fields of electronics.

Early experimenters in television who were attempting to develop electronic scanning realized the potential usefulness of the cathode-ray tube as a television display device. In the 1920s V. K. Zworykin developed a cathode-ray tube which was improved in ways which made it particularly suitable for the display of television images. This tube, the kinescope, first demonstrated in 1929, was the forerunner of the monochrome television picture tubes which were produced commercially in the late 1940s and the 1950s. Modifications to the kinescope, including the addition of a shadow mask, led to the commercial introduction of the color picture tube in 1953. *See* PICTURE TUBE; TELEVISION.

During the 1930s, it had become apparent that the cathode-ray tube would make an excellent display device for use with the new radar technology. Many of the early television pioneers were recruited into the effort to complete the development of radar for use in World War II. *See* RADAR.

In the 1960s and 1970s the cathode-ray tube became established as a widely used device for the display of computer output information. Modifications have been made to television picture tubes, both monochrome and color, to improve characteristics which are of importance to observers of computer output information. Cathode-ray tubes specialized for this use are called data display tubes. Their use has grown rapidly, particularly because of the popularity of personal computers. *See* COMPUTER; MICROCOMPUTER.

Basic elements. In the following description of a typical cathode-ray tube, emphasis is given to those features which are common to most of the tubes now produced. Some variations in construction and function from this basic cathode-ray-tube configuration are described later in the article.

The three elements of the basic cathode-ray tube are the envelope, the electron gun, and the phosphor screen (**Fig. 1**).

Envelope. The envelope is usually made of glass, although ceramic envelopes and metal envelopes have been used. The envelope is typically funnel-shaped. The small opening is terminated by the stem, a disk of glass through which pass metal leads that apply voltages to the several elements of the electron gun. A tubulation that passes through the stem is used to evacuate the air from the

tube during manufacture, and is then sealed off. The electron gun is mounted within the neck portion of the envelope and is connected to the leads coming through the stem. The neck is often made sufficiently narrow to allow positioning of deflection and focusing components outside of it.

The large end of the funnel is closed by a faceplate, on the inside of which the phosphor screen is deposited. The faceplate is made of high-quality clear glass in order to provide an undistorted view of the display on the phosphor screen.

Electron gun. The electron gun consists of an electrical element called a heater, a thermionic cathode, and an assemblage of cylinders, caps, and apertures which are all held in the proper orientation by devices such as glass beads, ceramic rods and spacers.

The cathode is a source of electrons when maintained at about 1750°F (1100 K) by thermal radiation from the heater. The heater requires from 0.5 to 5 W of input power, depending on its design. Electrons emitted by the cathode are formed into a beam, and controlled in intensity by other elements of the electron gun. Depending on the design and application of the cathode-ray tube, the current of the electron beam will have an instantaneous peak value from 0.5 to 5000 microamperes. Means are provided, either within the electron gun itself or externally, to focus the electron beam to a small cross section at its intersection with the phosphor screen and to deflect it to various locations on the screen. *See* CHARGED PARTICLE OPTICS; ELECTRON EMISSION.

A monochrome cathode-ray tube is designed to display information in a single color, usually white, although green, orange, and other colors are used. A color cathode-ray tube, such as a color picture tube, is designed to display information in a full range of colors. In most cases, monochrome cathode-ray tubes employ a single electron gun. Nearly all color picture tubes employ the shadow-mask principle and use three electron guns.

The deflection path of the electron beam on the phosphor screen depends on the intended use of the cathode-ray tube. In oscillography, a horizontal trace is swept across the phosphor screen, with vertical excursions of the beam which coincide with variations in the strength of some electrical signal. In television, a raster of closely spaced horizontal lines is scanned on the phosphor screen by the electron beam, which is intensity-modulated to produce a visible picture. Radar makes use of a variety of specialized electron-beam scanning patterns to present information to an observer. It is also a common practice to apply scan-conversion techniques to the radar signals so that they may be displayed by using a television raster scan.

In the display of computer output information, two general approaches to beam deflection are used: The raster-scan technique may be identical in format to that used for television or may utilize a greater number of scanning lines for increased

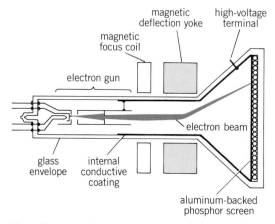

Fig. 1. Elements of a cathode-ray tube.

magnetic deflection yoke

high-voltage terminal

magnetic focus coil

electron gun

electron beam

glass envelope

internal conductive coating

aluminum-backed phosphor screen

definition. The random-scan technique involves computer control to direct the electron beam to locations which may be anywhere on the tube face.

Phosphor screen. The phosphor screen consists of a layer of luminescent material coated on the inner surface of the glass faceplate. Typically, the luminescent material is in the form of particles whose size is from 1 to 100 micrometers, depending upon the design and intended use of the cathode-ray tube. Monochrome cathode-ray tubes generally use a single layer of a homogeneous luminescent material. Color cathode-ray tubes typically utilize a composite screen made up of separate red-, green-, and blue-emitting luminous materials. *See* LUMINESCENCE; PHOSPHORESCENCE.

Design considerations. There are certain concerns which must be dealt with in the design of all types of cathode-ray tubes.

Safety. Foremost is the matter of safety. While cathode-ray tubes now in use generally can be considered safe, when employed as intended by their manufacturer, there are potential health hazards which must be considered in the design both of the cathode-ray tubes and of the equipment incorporating them. For example, as discussed below, it is frequently desirable to operate cathode-ray tubes at high voltages and currents, for example, tens of kilovolts and hundreds to thousands of microamperes. Consequently, there are possible hazards of electrical shock, x-radiation, and high temperatures. Designers of cathode-ray tubes and equipment using the tubes are generally quite aware of these possible hazards and are able to effectively utilize designs without undue risk to health and safety.

Vacuum maintenance. Another general concern is the absolute necessity of maintaining a high vacuum within the envelope of the cathode-ray tube so that the electron beam can travel unimpeded from the electron gun to the phosphor screen. Also, it is frequently not possible for the various electrodes within the cathode-ray tube to withstand electrical breakdown except under high vacuum. Cathode-ray tubes are exhausted by vacuum pumps for periods of up to several hours before being tipped off (permanently sealed at the exhaust tubulation). Cathode-ray tubes are typically raised to temperatures of a few hundred degrees Celsius during exhaust in order to outgas the internal parts. Internal pressure in a cathode-ray tube at tip-off is typically in the range of 10^{-4} to 10^{-8} torr (10^{-2} to 10^{-6} pascal), the desired value being determined by the design and intended use of the cathode-ray tube.

With very few exceptions, commercial cathode-ray tubes are never again vacuum-pumped after tip-off, and are expected to maintain an acceptable high level of vacuum. Leaks through the vacuum envelope are extremely rare; those problems which do arise are generally from the outgassing of internal parts. In order to assist in maintaining a high internal vacuum throughout many years of storage and use, it is now a universal practice to include within the cathode-ray tube one or more small devices called getters. Getters, through chemical action, absorb residual gas molecules within an envelope, and will continue to do so usually for several years.

Voltage control. Another general concern is the need to have several different voltages applied to structures within the cathode-ray-tube envelope. These voltages must be individually passed through the vacuum envelope, either through the stem leads or through metal buttons or pins sealed into the envelope. Frequently, an electrical cable carrying voltages as high as 50 kV will be encapsulated to a button terminal on the outside of the cathode-ray tube. Inside the cathode-ray tube, it is important that all envelope surfaces, as well as all electrode structures, be set at definite, known electric potentials. For this reason, conductive coatings which include materials such as graphite, iron oxide, stannous chloride, or evaporated aluminum are applied to nearly all interior envelope surfaces. This is one of the functions of the aluminum coating on the back of the phosphor screen. By these means, the path of the electron beam is fully established and controlled.

Performance. Two major considerations in cathode-ray-tube design are the choice of the overall operating voltage, that is, the potential difference between the cathode and the phosphor screen, and the electron-beam current to the phosphor screen. The product of the overall operating voltage (called the screen voltage) and the average value of the screen current gives the power input to the phosphor screen. For example, a cathode-ray tube operating at a screen voltage of 20 kV and screen current of 500 μA has 10 W of input power. A small fraction of this power, typically 10 to 20%, is converted into visible light by the phosphor. Less than 1% of the input power is converted into x-radiation, nearly all of which is absorbed within the glass walls of the envelope. The remainder of the input power is dissipated in the faceplate as heat. Most cathode-ray tubes operate at power levels such that this heat is allowed to radiate away or otherwise be removed by conduction and convection. Tubes which operate at very high voltages and currents, such as projection tubes, sometimes require special means, such as cooling fans, to remove heat from the faceplate.

The choice of operating screen voltage and current can have considerable effect on the design and construction of the cathode-ray-tube envelope, electron gun, and phosphor screen. It is important to consider the tradeoffs involved in making these choices. The higher the screen voltage, the greater the level of performance which can be obtained from the cathode-ray tube. The performance characteristics most directly affected by choice of screen voltage and current are screen brightness and resolution. While higher values of screen voltage will improve both brightness and resolution, higher values of screen current will improve brightness but degrade resolution performance. For any particular cathode-ray-tube design, the upper level of screen current which can be utilized is set by the allowable level of resolution degradation. On the other hand, the upper limit of screen voltage that can be utilized is set by (1) the capability of the internal tube elements, as well as the glass wall of the envelope, to withstand high potential gradients without electrical breakdown; (2) the practical problems involved in generating a very high voltage and delivering it to the cathode-ray-tube high-voltage terminal; (3) added power requirements for the deflection drive circuits; and (4) additional precautions necessary to ensure safe operation at high voltages as far as electrical and x-radiation safety are concerned.

A great deal of the design effort for any cathode-ray tube goes into obtaining the maximum attainable brightness and resolution at a selected screen voltage and current. The required brightness and resolution vary greatly, depending on the intended use of the cathode-ray tube (**Table 1**).

Envelopes. Cathode-ray-tube envelopes have been made from metal, ceramic, and glass materials. Glass is now used more than any other material, because it has the most desirable combination of mechanical, electrical, and optical properties. A variety of specialized glasses have been developed for use in cathode-ray tubes. *See* GLASS.

Electrical resistance. An important characteristic of glass for cathode-ray tubes is its electrical resistance. Early oscilloscope cathode-ray tubes, operating at voltages from 500 to 2000 V, were made by using a soda-lime-silica combination similar to that used in windows and bottles. This glass was found to be useless at higher voltages because of low electrical resistance. *See* ELECTRICAL RESISTANCE.

X-ray absorption. A second important characteristic is produced any time that electrons traveling at high speed strike a stationary target. The amount of x-radiation produced is proportional to the square of the energy of the electron and to the first power of the atomic number of the constituents of the target material. The target material is that of the phosphor screen, the faceplate, and shadow mask, if one is present. The amount of x-radiation generated within the cathode-ray tube can be substantial at higher voltages. Manufacturers and users of cathode-ray tubes depend on the material of the envelope to absorb nearly all of this radiation. Absorption of x-radiation within the envelope depends on the thickness of the envelope and its composition, and is given by Eq. (1), where I is

$$I = I_0 e^{-\mu t} \tag{1}$$

the intensity of x-radiation at the outside surface of the cathode-ray tube; I_0 is the intensity of x-radiation at the inside surface of the cathode-ray tube; μ is the linear x-ray absorption coefficient of the particular type of glass used (usually expressed in units of 1/cm); and t is the thickness of glass (usually expressed in centimeters). *See* X-RAYS.

Optical properties. A third important characteristic for glass used in cathode-ray tubes is the optical properties of the faceplate glass. These properties vary widely, depending on the design and intended use of the cathode-ray tube. The best cathode-ray-tube faceplates have optical characteristics and quality equivalent to those of the finest photographic lenses. Cathode-ray-tube faceplates may be clear or may may have intentionally reduced optical transmission in order to improve the contrast of the display. Special-purpose cathode-ray tubes have been built with fiber-optic faceplates which make possible direct-contact exposure of photosensitive film and paper.

Shapes and sizes. **Figure 2** shows a variety of cathode-ray tubes having different shapes and sizes. Cathode-ray-tube envelopes are generally round or are rectangular with a 3 × 4 product aspect ratio, although numerous other shapes have been built. Extremes in sizes of cathode-ray tubes are exhibited by 1-in.-diameter (2.5-cm) and 36-in.-diameter (91-cm) round cathode-ray tubes.

Another parameter characterizing the shape of a cathode-ray tube envelope is its deflection angle. The deflection angle is related roughly to the angular dimension of the opening of the funnel. Cathode-ray tubes with deflection angles of from 15 to 110° have been built.

Electron gun. The electron gun and its associated neck components generate the electron beam and direct it toward the phosphor screen. This assembly may conveniently be broken down into three separate systems: the electron emission system, the

TABLE 1. Characteristics of cathode-ray tubes

Type of cathode-ray tube	Screen voltage, kV	Screen current, μA	Brightness, footlamberts (candelas/m²)	Resolution expressed as spot size, in. (mm)	Typical application
Oscilloscope	5	100	40 (137)	0.050 (1.3)	Oscilloscope
Photorecording	15	5	3 (10)	0.001 (0.025)	Phototypesetter
Picture tube (monochrome)	20	300	100 (340)	0.015 (0.4)	Television or data display
Picture tube (color; 3 guns)	30	400	100 (340)	0.020 (0.5)	Television or data display
Projection	45	2000	10,000 (34,000)	0.004 (0.1)	Data display

Fig. 2. Typical cathode-ray tubes.

focusing system, and the deflection system.

Emission systems. An emission system may consist of the cathode with its associated heater, a control grid, also called grid #1, and an accelerating grid (**Fig. 3**).

The voltage applied to the accelerating grid sets up a field which penetrates the opening in the control grid and determines the magnitude of the space-charge–limited current drawn from the cathode. As the control grid is made more negative in potential, the penetration of the accelerating field and, consequently, the beam current are reduced.

The electrostatic field in the emission system of an electron gun is so shaped by the geometry of the several elements that electrons perpendicularly leaving the cathode enter trajectories which carry them across the axis of the system in the vicinity of the control-grid–accelerator-grid space. The

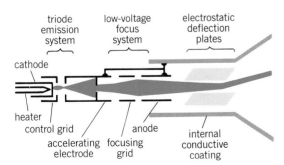

Fig. 3. Simplified electron gun with triode emission system, electrostatic focus, and electrostatic deflection.

location at which the electrons cross the axis is called the crossover point and represents the minimum beam cross section in the vicinity of the cathode surface. Beyond this point, beam electrons enter the field-free drift space within the cylindrical electrode attached to the accelerating grid and travel along straight diverging trajectories toward the focusing system. *See* ELECTRON MOTION IN VACUUM.

A key parameter for the emission system of an electron gun is the cutoff voltage, that voltage between the control grid and the cathode which is just necessary to extinguish the flow of electrons from the cathode. Depending on a particular design, this value may lie between −15 and −150 V, the grid being at a negative voltage with respect to the cathode.

The control grid can be modulated by a video signal, or otherwise varied in voltage between cutoff and zero volts, in order to produce a desired level of beam current. The total current from the cathode (known as the Child-Langmuir current) is given by Eq. (2), where I is the actual cathode

$$I = K V_d^3 V_c^{-3/2} \qquad (2)$$

current in microamperes, K is a constant whose value typically is in the range of 3 to 5, V_d is the grid drive which is equal to the difference between the actual voltage on the control grid and the cutoff voltage, and V_c is the cutoff voltage. Absolute values are used for both V_d and V_c.

Emission-system operation, as described above,

in which the cathode is grounded and the control grid is modulated, is termed grid drive. Another mode of operation is cathode drive, in which grid #1 is grounded and the cathode is modulated. The formula for cathode current in the cathode-drive mode is more complicated than that given above for the grid-drive mode.

Often, a circular baffle termed a limiting aperture is introduced in the path of the electron beam. The limiting aperture intercepts the outer portions of the beam and prevents their reaching the phosphor screen, thus improving the resolution of the display. The portion of the beam intercepted may be from 0 to 98%, depending on the design and intended use of the cathode-ray tube. For this reason, the electron-beam current reaching the phosphor screen may be a small fraction of the current emitted by the cathode.

An emission system consisting of a cathode, a control grid, and an accelerating grid is termed a triode emission system. A tetrode emission system (**Fig. 4**) has an additional electrode, called grid #2, inserted between the control grid and the accelerating grid. A primary purpose of grid #2 is to electrically isolate the emission system from the focusing system and the high-voltage portion of the envelope, so that changes in focusing or anode voltage will not affect cutoff and drive voltages. Grid #2 is typically operated within a range of 150 to 1500 V positive with respect to the cathode, depending on the design of the electron gun. Grid #2 may be adjusted in voltage to select a desired cutoff voltage. Increasing the grid #2 voltage will raise the magnitude of the cutoff voltage, and vice versa.

The element within the cathode-ray tube set at the highest voltage to which the electron beam is subjected prior to its deflection is termed the anode, or sometimes the ultor. Except in the special case of cathode-ray tubes which utilize postdeflection acceleration, the anode is the element at the highest positive direct-current voltage in the cathode-ray tube and is the element to which the aluminum backing of the phosphor screen is connected. In many cathode-ray tubes, the anode will function as the emission-system accelerating electrode.

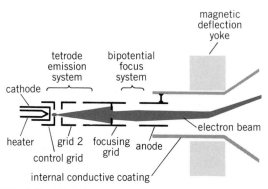

Fig. 4. Simplified electron gun with tetrode emission system, electrostatic focus, and magnetic deflection.

Focusing systems. The two basic types of focusing used in cathode-ray tubes, magnetic and electrostatic, have been extensively used in many different cathode-ray-tube designs with fully acceptable performance. Electrostatic focus has the advantage of being generally less costly and easier to implement for most applications. In certain applications where resolution at high beam current is required, there is usually a performance advantage in using magnetic focus.

1. Magnetic focusing. In magnetic focusing systems, a short focus coil is fitted externally to the neck of the envelope of the cathode-ray tube. The coil is arranged so that magnetic flux lines flow within the neck parallel to the direction of travel of the electron beam. The focus coil is positioned toward the phosphor screen from the anode portion of the electron gun, so that focusing will take place in a region free from electrostatic potential gradients. Current through the focus coil is adjusted to bring the electron beam to a sharp focus on the phosphor screen. Many designs will require dynamic changes in the focus current to maintain sharp focus as the electron beam is deflected to various positions on the tube face. *See* MAGNETIC LENS.

2. Electrostatic focusing. In electrostatic focusing systems, an electrostatic lens is formed between two or more electrodes within the neck of the tube. Many different electrode arrangements which will give satisfactory focus are in use. Two frequently encountered arrangements are the bipotential lens (Fig. 4) and the low-voltage focus lens (Fig. 3). These lenses are often used with tetrode emission systems, where the presence of grid #2 serves to prevent variations in focus voltage from altering the emission-system cutoff voltage. The bipotential lens requires an additional electrode, the focus electrode, inserted between grid #2 and the anode. The focus electrode operates at an intermediate voltage between that of grid #2 and the anode. Typically, this voltage is in the range of 20 to 40% of the anode voltage, depending on lens design, and is adjusted in value for optimum focus. In the bipotential lens, the main focusing action takes place in the region between the focus electrode and the anode.

In the low-voltage lens, the anode is split into two separate cylinders and an additional electrode, the focus electrode, is inserted into the gap between them. This focus electrode operates at a potential which is only a few tens of volts above cathode voltage, compared to a few thousand volts for the bipotential focus electrode. The bipotential lens generally will provide superior focus quality.

Some newer designs for electrostatic focusing lens involve the introduction of several focusing electrodes stacked together, each operating at a slightly different voltage. *See* ELECTRON LENS; ELECTROSTATIC LENS.

Deflection systems. Two basic types of deflection are electrostatic deflection and magnetic deflection. In principle, either types of deflection can be used for any application, although each has advantages which have led to its being favored for certain classes of use.

1. *Electrostatic deflection.* With electrostatic deflection, it is possible to very quickly deflect the beam from one location to any other location on the screen. Electrostatic deflection is usually preferred over magnetic deflection for cathode-ray tubes intended for oscillography and other instrumentation applications, because operation is possible over a wider frequency range. The band pass of an electrostatic deflection system is limited in a practical sense by the amount of power the equipment designer can justifiably expend in achieving adequate display brightness and size. Laboratory oscilloscopes designed around conventional cathode-ray tubes and having useful band pass to the order of 50 MHz are readily obtained.

Deflection systems, particularly of the electrostatic type, invariably distort to some degree the circular cross section of an electron beam which undergoes deflection. This distortion increases with angle of deflection. Taking all factors into consideration, the designer of practical cathode-ray tubes with electrostatic deflection rarely attempts to design for angles of deflection much greater than 15° with respect to the gun axis.

In the electrostatic-deflection electron gun shown in Fig. 3, the deflecting system consists of a single pair of parallel electrodes mounted symmetrically about the axis of the gun. The electron beam entering and traversing the space between the electrodes does so at a constant axial velocity corresponding to the average potential of the electrodes. This potential is usually adjusted to be essentially that of the anode. Signals to be applied to the deflecting electrodes are first passed through a paraphrase amplifier in which two components equal in voltage but opposite in polarity are generated. These two components can be applied to the opposing deflecting electrodes without affecting the average potential in the space between them. Under the influence of the applied deflection signals, an electric field is set up between the electrodes. This field imparts an acceleration to the electron beam which is perpendicular to the direction of the constant beam velocity. In the space between the electrodes, therefore, the beam travels in a parabolic path. After leaving this transverse field, the beam continues to the phosphor screen on a straight path tangent to the parabola. The assumption is made that no postdeflection acceleration is present. If the signals applied to the electrodes vary linearly with time, a straight line is traced out upon the phosphor screen. In a practical tube, a second pair of deflecting electrodes is mounted farther along the gun axis at right angles to the first. These electrodes provide a second independent axis of deflection, orthogonal to the first.

The deflection produced by a pair of parallel electrodes is given by Eq. (3), where y is the

$$y = \frac{LbV_d}{2aV} \qquad (3)$$

deflection observed at the phosphor screen in any linear units, L is the distance from the axial midpoint of the electrodes to the phosphor screen in the same linear units, b is the deflecting-electrode length in the same linear units, a is the deflecting-electrode spacing in the same linear units, V_d is the potential difference between electrodes in volts, and V is the beam acceleration potential in volts.

The effectiveness of a pair of deflecting electrodes is often described in terms of its deflection factor: the number of volts necessary to deflect the beam a unit distance (usually in inches) at the phosphor screen for a given accelerating potential (usually 1 kV).

Plane-parallel electrodes are rarely found in modern cathode-ray tubes. Overall improvements in performance are obtained by forming the electrodes so that the spacing between plates increases with distance in the direction of beam travel.

2. *Magnetic deflection.* Magnetic deflection systems generally require more time, perhaps tens of microseconds, to deflect the electron beam from one location on the screen to another. This is because a change in position requires a change in the value of the current through an inductive coil. Magnetic deflection systems do have an important advantage in that they can deflect the beam through a much wider deflection angle with less distortion in the shape of the cross section of the beam than is possible with electrostatic deflection. Also, with high anode voltages of 20–30 kV, the current required for magnetic deflection yokes can readily be provided; whereas the high dynamic voltages which would be required for electrostatic deflection plates, on the order of 3–4 kV peak to peak, cannot easily and economically be achieved. For these reasons, cathode-ray tubes employing magnetic deflection are widely used, particularly in television, radar, and data display.

An elementary magnetic deflection system takes the form of a pair of coils, each wound on a rectangular form, positioned externally to the cathode-ray tube with major planes parallel to beam direction on opposite sides of the neck. The magnetic field lines are thus perpendicular to the axis of the electron gun mounted therein. On entering this field, the beam electrons encounter forces which impart to them acceleration perpendicular to their velocity. If the flux density is uniform, the path followed by the electrons is circular and lies in a plane perpendicular to the lines of flux. On leaving the deflection field, the beam travels in a straight-line path tangent to the circle just described. The deflection given an electron beam which traverses a field of uniform flux density limited to the space between two planes perpendicular to the initial direction of the beam motion (that is, the tube axis) is given approximately by Eq. (4), where y is the deflec-

$$y \approx \frac{LbB}{3.37\sqrt{V}} \qquad (4)$$

tion observed at the phosphor screen in centimeters (1 in. = 2.54 cm), L is the distance from the axial midpoint of the magnetic field to the phosphor screen in centimeters, b is the axial extent of the magnetic field in centimeters, B is the flux density in gauss (1 tesla = 10^4 gauss), and V is the beam acceleration potential in volts. By an appropriate arrangement of the windings of a magnetic-deflection coil pair, more commonly called a deflecting yoke, it is possible to obtain useful total deflection angles up to 110°.

3. *Postdeflection acceleration.* As discussed above, brighter and sharper cathode-ray-tube displays can be obtained at higher anode voltages. It is apparent from Eqs. (3) and (4), however, that high anode voltages require either high levels of magnetic deflection flux or high peak-to-peak electrostatic deflection voltages. A variety of schemes have been employed in cathode-ray tubes to arrange for acceleration of the electron beam to a higher voltage after deflection, thus avoiding the need for very high deflection voltages or magnetic flux. While postdeflection acceleration, as it is called, can be used with either magnetic or electrostatic deflection, it is far more important in the case of electrostatic deflection. From Eqs. (3) and (4) it follows that while electrostatic deflection varies inversely with anode voltage, magnetic deflection varies inversely only with the square root of the anode voltage.

The most successful scheme for providing postdeflection acceleration involves the addition of a shaped open-mesh electrode to the interior of the cathode-ray tube at some point between the electron gun and the phosphor screen, usually within the neck of the envelope. The mesh serves to separate the high- and low-voltage sections of the interior of the envelope. By suitable selection of voltages and appropriately shaping the mesh, scan magnification or enhancement can be attained in addition to postdeflection acceleration.

Phosphor screen. This element converts electrical energy to visible radiation. Materials known as phosphors are said to be luminescent; that is, they are able to emit light at temperatures substantially below those which produce incandescence. A phosphor which is excited to luminescence by electron bombardment is described as cathodoluminescent. In the case of phosphors for cathode-ray tubes, luminescence invariably persists after cessation of excitation. Luminescence which continues for more than 10^{-8} s after excitation is removed is called phosphorescence. Luminescence which is coincident in time with excitation is known as fluorescence.

A wide variety of materials display the property of cathodoluminescence. Phosphors used in commercially fabricated cathode-ray tubes are generally inorganic, nonmetallic, crystalline materials. Many phosphors now make use of materials which incorporate transition elements, such as yttrium, and the lanthanoid metals: lanthanum, cerium, europium, gadolinium, and terbium. Phosphors made from materials using these elements are known for their high luminous output, purity of color, and stability.

Some of these materials will emit radiation in the pure state. Most, however, display practical luminescence only when activated by an impurity (**Table 2**). These impurities, deliberately introduced in amounts ranging from 1 part in 100,000 to 1 part in 100, play a profound role in determining the efficiency, color, and persistence of the emission obtained from a given phosphor. **Figure 5** shows the spectral emission density curves which plot relative radiant energy versus wavelength for certain of these phosphor screens.

One of the criteria by which a phosphor material is judged is its ability to convert electrical energy to useful radiation. In many cases, cathode-ray-tube screens are intended to be viewed by human observers. It is appropriate, therefore, to speak in terms of visible flux output. The luminous efficiencies of practically all commercially significant phosphors are within the range 5–50 lumens per watt of exciting power. Light output increases with increasing bombarding-current density, eventually exhibiting evidence of saturation at current-density levels which are characteristic of particular phosphors. For some phosphors, saturation effects are quite evident at the 10 μA/cm^2 level. Others display relatively undiminished luminous efficiencies at levels of several hundred microamperes per square centimeter.

The color of the emission from a phosphor is governed both by the base material and by the activator. The spectral-energy distributions of most phosphors are fairly broad, although colors of high saturation are readily obtained. Phosphors made from materials incorporating rare-earth and

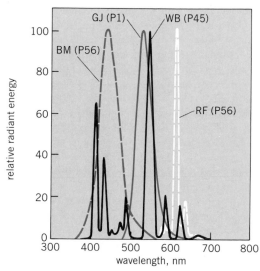

Fig. 5. Spectral emission density curves for phosphor screens.

TABLE 2. Characteristics of some phosphor screens used in cathode-ray tubes

WTDS* designation	Previous EIA† designation	Base material (activator)	Color of luminous emission‡	Persistence classification§	Typical application
BE	P11	Zinc sulfide (silver)	Blue	Medium short	Photorecording
BH	P47	Yttrium silicate (cerium)	Purplish blue	Very short	Flying-spot scanner
BM	P55	Zinc sulfide (silver)	Blue	Medium short	Projection, large screen
GH	P31	Zinc sulfide (copper)	Green	Medium short	Data display, oscillography
GJ	P1	Zinc orthosilicate (manganese)	Yellowish green	Medium	Projection, oscillography
GM	P7	Zinc sulfide (silver) on top of zinc cadmium sulfide (copper)	Yellowish green	Long	Radar
GY	P43	Gadolinium oxysulfide (terbium)	Yellowish green	Medium	Data display
KA	P20	Zinc cadmium sulfide (silver)	Yellow green	Medium	Storage tubes
KG	P46	Yttrium aluminate (cerium)	Yellow green	Very short	Flying-spot scanner
KH	P48	Yttrium aluminate (cerium) and yttrium silicate (cerium)	Yellow green	Very short	Flying-spot scanner
KJ	P53	Yttrium aluminum garnet (terbium)	Yellowish green	Medium	Data display
RF	P56	Yttrium oxide (europium)	Red	Medium	Projection, large screen
WB	P45	Yttrium oxysulfide (terbium)	White	Medium	Projection, large screen
WW	P4	Zinc sulfide (silver) and zinc cadmium sulfide (silver)	White	Medium short	Monochrome television, data display
		Zinc sulfide (silver)	Blue	Medium short	Color television, data display
X	P22¶	Zinc cadmium sulfide (silver)	Green	Medium short	
		Yttrium oxysulfide (europium)	Red	Medium short	

*World Wide Type Designation System. Designation administered by the Electronic Industries Association.
†Electronic Industries Association.
‡Color shown is that of phosphorescence, that is, the color after cessation of phosphor excitation.
§Persistence categories are based upon time for radiant output to drop to 10% of initial level following interruption of excitation: very long, 1 s or more; long, 100 ms to 1 s; medium, 1 ms to 100 ms; medium short, 10 μs to 1 ms; short, 1 μs to 10 μs; very short, less than 1 μs.
¶Composite structured screen used in conjunction with shadow mask for full color display. The materials shown are one example of several sets of materials used for this screen.

related elements are noted for having spectral-energy distributions in which the radiant energy is concentrated into very narrow emission bands at just a few wavelengths.

As is evident from Table 2, a wide range of colors is available; the tube designer is restricted in this matter only insofar as particular efficiencies and persistences must be achieved simultaneously with a given color.

A great majority of cathode-ray-tube screens now being produced are aluminized. The side of the phosphor screen facing the electron gun is coated with a thin electron-transparent film of aluminum by vacuum-deposition techniques. This process not only stabilizes the phosphor potential at the applied acceleration voltage, but also provides an increased light output because of the mirror effect of the highly reflective layer, which redirects radiation that could otherwise be lost in the interior of the envelope.

The fineness of detail in an image presented on a phosphor screen is limited to some extent by the granular nature of the screen. Both particle size and layer thickness affect performance. Phosphor screens intended for very high-resolution cathode-ray tubes employ thin layers of phosphor with particles as fine as 1 μm in size.

Varieties of tubes. A wide variety of available envelopes, electron guns, and phosphor screens are combined in different ways to fashion cathode-ray tubes which are specialized to meet the needs of a host of different applications. A few of these tubes are described here.

Oscillography. Equipments to be used as oscilloscopes, spectrum analyzers, computer waveform analyzers, and related applications require cathode-ray tubes with fast deflection, high writing speed, and highly visible displays. Also important are small size, low weight, and ruggedness to fit a variety of working environments. Generally, less importance is given to resolution. Such tubes will usually employ electrostatic focus and deflection with small deflection angles of 10 to 15°, round or rectangular envelopes with a largest display dimension of 3 to 8 in. (7.5 to 20 cm), and a highly visible phosphor screen such as GH(P31) or GJ(P1) [Table 2]. If there is a need for longer persistence due to a low refresh rate, a long-persistence phosphor such as GM(P7) may be used. These cathode-ray tubes generally use operating anode voltages of from 0.5 to 10 kV. Some envelopes for these tubes are made from ceramic materials. *See* OSCILLOSCOPE.

Radar. The most widely used display mode for radar, the plan position indicator (PPI) mode, is readily adapted to electrostatic-focus, magnetic-deflection electron guns of moderate current capability and resolution, operating at 5 to 15 kV. Typically, round envelopes will be employed which are 1 to 36 in. (2.5 to 91 cm) in diameter, although the most common sizes are 5 to 10 in. (12.5 to 25 cm).

The most important requirement for cathode-ray tubes for use as radar-display indicators has been a long-persistent image. This is important because the refresh period of most radar antennas has been several seconds. The phosphor screen GM(P7), which has persistence at a low light level of several seconds, was developed during World War II to meet this need. After World War II, a special class of tubes called cathode-ray charge-storage tubes was developed to meet the need of providing a persistent radar display image. Such tubes have been in use in radar display indicators in both commercial and military aircraft for many years.

In the 1970s, the availability of solid-state memory devices at acceptable cost levels obviated the need for special cathode-ray tubes with built-in capability of providing long-persistent images. Many radar displays since the early 1970s use cathode-ray tubes more closely related to those used for television and data display. The storage necessary for long-persistent radar images is provided by solid-state memory circuits external to the tube. The cathode-ray tube is fed an appropriate video signal at or near television scan rates.

Pictorial. A large class of applications for cathode-ray tubes involves either the presentation on the cathode-ray-tube screen of an actual picture with a full black and white halftone range or with full color, such as is required for television, or the presentation of a computer-generated display which may consist of alphanumerics, graphics, or a variety of pictorial subjects. Tubes for the direct viewing of such presentations are required to have large display sizes, high brightness, high resolution, and in many cases a full halftone range and full color capability.

Cathode-ray tubes for these presentations have always employed magnetic deflection and generally electrostatic-focus electron guns operating at high voltages from 15 to 35 kV. Envelopes for television cathode-ray tubes have traditionally been rectangular, of 3 × 4 aspect ratio. Popular usable screen diagonals have been 10 to 27 in. (25 to 70 cm). Deflection angles have ranged from 10 to 110°.

Cathode-ray tubes for computer-generated data-display applications are very similar to television picture tubes but may use other rectangular or square display formats. The need for uniformity of resolution in the display, particularly from the center of the picture to the edge, is even more acute for tubes intended for data display than it is for tubes intended for television only. Particular attention is paid to this need in the design of cathode-ray tubes for data-display applications.

One special class of pictorial applications comprises displays for use in automobiles, airplanes, boats, and military vehicles of all types. While cathode-ray tubes for such applications are similar to those described above, they tend to be smaller and brighter, and they must be quite rugged.

Another special class is projection tubes, but these are not intended to be directly viewed. The display on the phosphor screen is projected by using an optical system, such as a lens, onto large screens. Screen sizes vary widely, the largest being those in theaters and sports arenas that are equipped for projection television.

Cathode-ray tubes for projection applications are usually of the general type described above but optimized for extremely high brightness and resolution capability. Projection cathode-ray tubes generally have a largest phosphor screen dimension of 3 to 8 in. (7.5 to 20 cm). This smaller size is compatible with available high-efficiency optical systems. Projection cathode-ray tubes generally operate at higher voltages than direct-view tubes. Tubes which can be operated at voltages as high as 80 kV have been built.

Photorecording. Another class of cathode-ray tubes which are not intended for direct viewing by human observers comprises photorecording tubes. The applications for these tubes require that the phosphor screen display be projected by an optical system, such as a lens, onto a photosensitive medium, such as photographic film. Applications include electronic phototypesetting and the storage of computer output information on microfilm. Photorecording cathode-ray tubes are required to have extremely high resolution capability, to be extremely stable over long periods of time, and to have accurate and precise display geometry. A photorecording display may have 50 times the information content of a typical broadcast television picture. *See* PRINTING.

Photorecording tubes usually employ magnetic deflection and may utilize either magnetic or electrostatic focus. They operate at anode voltages in the range 10 to 20 kV. Many photorecording cathode-ray tubes use envelopes with 3- or 5-in. (7.5- or 12.5-cm) round faceplates of optical quality. Displays on these faceplates are projected through a lens onto the photosensitive medium. Other photorecording tubes have faceplates made from fiber-optic plates which, in use, are in direct contact with the photosensitive medium. *See* OPTICAL FIBERS.

A special cathode-ray tube which is closely related to the photorecording tube is the flying-spot scanner. The flying-spot-scanner display consists of a spot of light moving across the phosphor screen to scan a raster such as that used in television. This raster is blank and includes no video modulation other than retrace blanking. In a typical application, the raster will be projected through a lens onto a slide transparency. The light passing through the transparency is picked up by one or more photomultiplier tubes. The pictorial content of the transparency in this way is made available as a video signal, provided by the photomultiplier, which can then be displayed on a television monitor.

A special group of phosphor screens having extremely short persistence, on the order of 150 nanoseconds, has been developed for use with flying-spot scanners. These are identified in Table 2. Short persistence is necessary to avoid severe distortion of the video signal.

Competing technologies. Considering the length of time that the cathode-ray tube has been in use, and the number of uses to which it has been put, it must be considered one of the most successful electronic devices ever conceived. There are, nonetheless, certain drawbacks inherent in the use of the cathode-ray tube: (1) it must have a certain size and weight to provide a vacuum-tight enclosure and sufficient room internally for generation and deflection of the electron beam; (2) it has a long but finite lifetime, limited by degradation processes associated with the high temperatures at which the heater and cathode are operated; and (3) it is essentially an analog device which must be interfaced with other electronic devices, an increasing proportion of which are exclusively digital.

Display technologies not involving the use of cathode-ray tubes have been under development for many years. The more promising make use of plasma or gas discharge, electroluminescent, and liquid-crystal devices. Some of these devices have gained a degree of acceptance in data display applications which have also made use of cathode-ray tubes. *See* ELECTRONIC DISPLAY.

In spite of certain drawbacks and the advent of other display technologies, there are advantages to the use of cathode-ray tubes which ensure their continuing presence: (1) the ease with which the electron beam can be deflected to address any desired display location; (2) the ease and efficiency with which electrical energy can be converted into radiant energy at visible wavelengths in the phosphor screen; and (3) the flexibility of cathode-ray-tube technology, which has allowed a high degree of customization to meet the special requirements of diverse applications. The cathode-ray tube is still the most widely used display device in those equipments which originally use the tube at the time of their introduction. These include the oscilloscope, the radar display, the television set, and the personal computer.   Norman W. Patrick

Bibliography. P. A. Keller, *The Cathode-Ray Tube*: *Technology, History, and Applications*, 1992; S. Sherr, *Electronic Displays*, 2d ed., 1993; J. Whitaker, *Electronic Displays*: *Technology, Design, and Applications*, 1994.

Cathode rays

The name given to the electrons originating at the cathodes of gaseous discharge devices. The term has now been extended to include low-pressure devices such as cathode-ray tubes. Furthermore, cathode rays are now used to designate electron beams originating from thermionic cathodes, whereas the term was formerly applied only to cold-cathode devices. *See* CATHODE-RAY TUBE.

The basis for the nomenclature is purely historical. The first outward evidence was flourescence from the glass walls of cold-cathode discharge tubes. This fluorescence appeared as the pressure was reduced to the region where the mean free path became greater than the tube dimensions. At these pressures, the gas in the tube no longer emitted an appreciable amount of light. It was as-

certained that the wall fluorescence had its origin in rays of particles coming from the cathode. Furthermore, it was demonstrated that these particles traveled in approximately straight lines. If an object was interposed between the cathode and the wall, the fluorescence disappeared in the optically shadowed region of the wall. In 1897 J. J. Thomson was able to show, using electric and magnetic fields, that the particles were negatively charged. In his experimental arrangement, he eliminated all but a very narrow beam of these rays. By producing an electrostatic deflection of the beam and then counteracting this with a magnetic deflection, he was able to determine the charge-mass ratio e/m. This was found to be the same as that of the electron, and resulted in the identification of these particles. *See* ELECTRON.

Thomson's measurements also form the basis for modern beta-particle spectroscopy. In this case e/m is known, so that either an electric or magnetic field may be used to determine the energy of the electrons which emanate from various radioactive materials, such as beta particles. *See* BETA PARTICLES; ELECTRICAL CONDUCTION IN GASES; ELECTRON EMISSION; PARTICLE ACCELERATOR; X-RAYS.   Glenn H. Miller

Bibliography. J. W. Rohlf, *Modern Physics from Alpha to the Z^0*, 1994; T. R. Sandin, *Essentials of Modern Physics*, 1989; J. Taylor and C. Zafaritos, *Modern Physics for Scientists and Engineers*, 1991.

Cathodoluminescence

A luminescence resulting from the bombardment of a substance with an electron (cathode-ray) beam. The principal applications of cathodoluminescence are in television, computer, radar, and oscilloscope displays. In these a thin layer of luminescent powder (phosphor) is evenly deposited on the transparent glass faceplate of a cathode-ray tube. After undergoing acceleration, focusing, and deflection by various electrodes in the tube, the electron beam originating in the cathode impinges on the phosphor. The resulting emission of light is observed through the glass faceplate, that is, from the unbombarded side of the phosphor coating. *See* CATHODE-RAY TUBE.

The luminescence of most phosphors comes from a few sites (activator centers) occupied by selected chemical impurities which have been incorporated into the matrix or host solid. The interaction of cathode rays with the phosphor involves a collective excitation of all the atoms of the host rather than a selective excitation of the luminescent centers, a condition that allows the dissipation of beam energy by competing nonluminescent processes. An appreciable energy loss occurs as soon as the primary cathode-ray beam strikes the phosphor; 25–35% of the electrons are immediately reflected (backscattered) due to coulombic repulsion. The electrons that actually penetrate the phosphor give rise to a combination of several processes that can be described only qualitatively. Some x-rays are produced, but in the main the high-energy electron beam ionizes the solid, producing a plasma of many lower-energy (secondary) electrons. These electrons are multiply scattered, successively losing more and more energy to the solid by various nonradiative paths. Although the bombarded phosphor is in the complex excited condition described above, a small part of the excitation energy is transferred by various mechanisms to the activator centers, causing them to luminesce. Because of the complex mode of interaction of cathode rays with phosphors, the energy efficiency of light production by cathodoluminescence is lower than the best efficiencies obtainable with photoluminescence. Conversion efficiencies of currently used display phosphors are between 2 and 23%.

The brightness B of a phosphor under cathode-ray excitation depends on the accelerating voltage V and the current density j. Many phosphors exhibit a dead voltage V_0 below which they show diminished output, presumably due to radiationless dissipation of the energy by poison centers, which are present only at the surface where this low voltage excitation occurs. Above V_0, the brightness is proportional to $(V - V_0)^q$, where q is between 1 and 3. At a given voltage, the brightness initially varies linearly with the current density, and then may increase more slowly with increasing j (saturation). The blue-emitting zinc sulfide (ZnS) and green-emitting zinc-cadmium sulfide [(Zn,Cd)S] phosphors used in color television exhibit this saturation effect, as well as a color shift and shorter afterglow at high current density, but the red-emitting europium-activated phosphor and other rare earth–activated phosphors do not. Linearity at high current density is an important requirement for phosphors to be used in projection television or aircraft pilot displays.

The blue and green phosphors for television are broadband emitters with dominant wavelengths of 464 and 556 nanometers, respectively; the red europium-activated yttrium oxysulfide phosphor is a line emitter at 605 nm. Their luminous efficiencies are 7.5, 65, and 17 lumens per input watt, respectively, and all have persistences of less than 10^{-4} s to reduce the smearing of fast-moving objects in television pictures. For easy viewing of slowly scanned radar screens, however, phosphors with persistences of up to 0.5 s are used.

The activators in zinc sulfide and zinc-cadmium sulfide are parts-per-million traces of donor-acceptor pairs of impurities, chlorine and silver in the former and aluminum and copper in the latter. Luminescence in these phosphors is produced when electrons trapped at donors recombine with holes trapped at acceptors. The broad emission band is a complex of emissions of slightly different wavelengths from pairs having a variety of separations in the host lattice. This mechanism can also explain phosphor saturation, shortened

persistence, and color shifts in the sulfides at high current density. In the rare earth–activated phosphor, the emitting center Eu^{3+} is present at a concentration of 4 mole %. The deep-lying atomic orbits of Eu^{3+} are not appreciably affected by interaction with the other constituent atoms of the phosphor, and the red light therefore appears in a very narrow range of wavelengths. *See* HOLE STATES IN SOLIDS; SEMICONDUCTOR.

An important requirement for a good cathodoluminescent phosphor is the possession of good secondary electron emission properties; otherwise, it charges up negatively and reduces the effective potential of the bombarding beam. In most cases the secondary electron emission coefficient R is less than 1, and the screen must be coated with a film of aluminum to provide conductance to the power supply in order to prevent charge buildup. The film provides two additional benefits. Its action as an optical mirror nearly doubles the display brightness, and it shields the phosphor from bombardment by residual gas ions that remain or are generated in the tube (ion burn). The phosphor host crystal structure can be disrupted by ion bombardment, and to a lesser extent by prolonged electron bombardment, creating absorbing centers (discoloration), poison centers, and other lattice defects which can reduce the efficiency of the luminescence. *See* LUMINESCENCE; SECONDARY EMISSION.

Herbert N. Hersh; James H. Schulman

Cauliflower

A cool-season biennial crucifer (*Brassica oleracea* var. *botrytis*) of Mediterranean origin. Cauliflower belongs to the plant order Capparales. It is grown for its white head or curd, a tight mass of flower stalks, which terminates the main stem (see **illus.**). Cauliflower is commonly cooked fresh as a vegetable; to a lesser extent, it is frozen or pickled and consumed as a relish. Cultural practices are similar to those used for cabbage; however, cauliflower is more sensitive

Head of cauliflower. (*Burpee Seeds*)

to unfavorable environment. Strains of the variety (cultivar) Snowball are most popular; purple-headed varieties are less common. Cauliflower is slightly tolerant of acid soils and has high requirements for boron and molybdenum. A cool, moist climate favors high quality. Harvest is generally 3–4 months after planting. California and New York are important cauliflower-producing states. *See* CABBAGE; CAPPARALES.   H. John Carew

Causality

In physics, the requirement that interactions in any space-time region can influence the evolution of the system only at subsequent times; that is, past events are causes of future events, and future events can never be the causes of events in the past. Causality thus depends on time orientability, the possibility of distinguishing past from future. Not all spacetimes are orientable.

Causality and determinism. The laws of a deterministic theory (for example, classical mechanics) are such that the state of a closed system (for example, the positions and momenta of particles in the system) at one instant determines the state of that system at any future time. Deterministic causality does not necessarily imply practical predictability. It was long implicitly assumed that slight differences in initial conditions would not lead to rapid divergence of later behavior, so that predictability was a consequence of determinism. Behavior in which two particles starting at slightly different positions and velocities diverge rapidly is called chaotic. Such behavior is ubiquitous in nature, and can lead to the practical impossibility of prediction of future states despite the deterministic character of the physical laws. *See* CHAOS.

Quantum mechanics is deterministic in the sense that, given the state of a system at one instant, it is possible to calculate later states. However, the situation differs from that in classical mechanics in two fundamental respects. First, conjugate variables, for example, position x and momentum p, cannot be simultaneously determined with complete precision, the relation between their indeterminacies being $\Delta x\ \Delta p \geq \hbar$, where $\hbar$ is Planck's constant divided by 2π. Second, the state variable ψ gives only probabilities that a given eigenstate will be found after the performance of a measurement, and such probabilities are also all that is calculable about a later state ψ' by the deterministic prediction. Despite its probabilistic character, the quantum state still evolves deterministically. However, which eigenvalue (say, of position) will actually be found in a measurement is unpredictable. *See* DETERMINISM; EIGENVALUE (QUANTUM MECHANICS); NONRELATIVISTIC QUANTUM THEORY; QUANTUM MECHANICS; QUANTUM THEORY OF MEASUREMENT; UNCERTAINTY PRINCIPLE.

Causal structure of spacetimes. Nonrelativistic mechanics assumes that causal action can be prop-

agated instantaneously, and thus that an absolute simultaneity is definable. This is not true in special relativity. While the state of a system can still be understood in terms of the positions and momenta of its particles, time order, as well as temporal and spatial length, becomes relative to the observer's frame, and there is no possible choice of simultaneous events in the universe that is the same in all reference frames. Only space-time intervals in a fused "spacetime" are invariant with respect to choice of reference frame. The theory of special relativity thus rejects the possibility of instantaneous causal action. Instead, the existence of a maximum velocity of signal transmission determines which events can causally influence others and which cannot. *See* SPACE-TIME.

The investigation of a spacetime with regard to which events can causally influence (signal) other regions and which cannot is known as the study of the causal structure of the spacetime. Thus, in the Minkowski spacetime of special relativity, an event E can causally affect another E' if and only if there is a timelike curve which joins E and E', and E' lies in the future of E. Such a curve is contained within the future light cone of E and connects E and E'. The light-cone surface is generated by null geodesics representing the velocity of light. One of the two halves of the light cone intersecting at the "present" is specified as the future, the other as the past. Paths lying within the light cone are timelike, those in the past region (or the present) being capable of influencing later events. Curves joining E with events outside the light cone are called spacelike. Their traversal requires velocities greater than that of light, and thus events which are spacelike-related cannot causally influence one another.

Closed causal curves. Different spacetimes, for example, those allowed by general relativity, are distinguished by their different causal structures. Because general relativity admits distinct spacetime metrics at adjacent points, the future directions of light cones can vary over short distances. (Light cones at adjacent points tilt with respect to one another.) Under these circumstances, it is possible for a continuous sequence of tilted cones to result in a timelike curve intersecting itself, producing a closed curve. An event on such a curve, however, both precedes and succeeds itself, and can be both its own cause and effect. Some solutions of the general relativistic field equations, for example, Gödel and Taub-Nut spacetimes, contain such closed causal curves.

However, many physicists hold that the existence of such curves is unphysical, and seek criteria to exclude them. Among the many such conditions that have been extensively discussed are the following. The causality condition excludes closed nonspacelike (that is, null or timelike) curves. Strong causality further excludes "almost closed" causal curves, wherein a nonspacelike curve returns more than once to the same infinitesimal neighborhood. Need for yet a further condition arises from the possibility that, in a quantum theory of gravity, the uncertainty principle would prevent the metric from having an exact value at every point, leading to the possibility that small variations in the metric would generate closed timelike curves. The condition of causal stability prevents such occurrences by defining a neighborhood of a point in which there are no closed timelike curves. Causal stability is the strongest condition excluding causal anomalies: violations of weaker conditions necessarily violate causal stability. If a spacetime is causally stable, the topology of its manifold follows from the causal structure, as do the differentiable and the conformal structures. Clearly a study of the causal structure gives deep insight into the characteristics of a spacetime.

In contrast, there are also many physicists who do not consider solutions of the equations of general relativity which contain closed causal curves to be unphysical, pointing out that, in the past, possibilities treated as unphysical have frequently turned out to be physically significant. For this reason (among others), they hold that solutions with closed causal curves should be taken seriously, and should be included among, for example, the possible histories of the universe in path-integral calculations in quantum theories of gravity.

Other causality violations. Violations of conventional causality could (hypothetically) arise in ways other than through closed causal curves. For example, the possibility has been considered that tachyons, faster-than-light particles, might exist. This is tantamount to the speculation that the past (or present) could be influenced by future events through the transmission of tachyons. Existence of such particles is generally rejected on both experimental and theoretical grounds. Causality violation would also result if there were more than one dimension of time, as there are of space. Such assignments are therefore usually excluded in theories of quantum gravity. *See* QUANTUM GRAVITATION; RELATIVITY; TACHYON.

Dudley Shapere

Bibliography. R. Geroch and G. Horowitz, Global structure of spacetimes, in S. Hawking and W. Israel, *General Relativity,* 1979; S. Hawking and G. Ellis, *The Large-Scale Structure of Space-Time,* 1973; P. S. Joshi, *Global Aspects in Gravitation and Cosmology,* 1993; R. Torretti, *Relativity and Geometry,* 1983; R. Wald, *General Relativity,* 1984.

Cave

A natural cavity located underground or in the side of a hill or cliff, generally of a size to admit a human. Caves occur in all types of rocks and topographic situations. They may be formed by many different erosion processes. The most important are created by ground waters that dissolve the common soluble rocks—limestone, dolomite, gypsum, and salt. Limestone caves are the most frequent, longest, and deepest. Lava-tube caves, sea caves created by wave action, and caves caused by piping in unconsolidated rocks are the other important types. The science of caves is known as speleology. *See* DOLOMITE; GYPSUM; HALITE; LIMESTONE.

Dissolution caves. The principal processes of aqueous dissolution are simple molecular dissociation for salt (NaCl, and other water-soluble salts) and gypsum ($CaSO_4 \cdot 2H_2O$), and bicarbonate solution for limestone ($CaCO_3 + H_2O + CO_2 = Ca^{2+} + 2HCO_3$) and dolomite ($CaMg \cdot 2HCO_3$). Dissociation of salt proceeds until an equilibrium concentration of 360 g/liter is achieved in standard conditions; that is, there is very rapid creation and destruction, with the consequence that salt caves survive only in arid regions and are rarely longer than 1 km (0.6 mi). Gypsum solutions equilibrate at about 2.4 g/liter, allowing enterable caves to develop in tens to hundreds of years where there is abundant water and ground-water hydraulic gradients are steep. Limestone (calcite) and dolomite solutions normally equilibrate at 0.1–0.3 g/liter; such caves require 10^3–10^6 years to be initiated and then enlarged for human entry, but then may also survive for many millions of years. *See* CALCITE; GROUND-WATER HYDROLOGY.

Limestone and dolomite dissolution is augmented or accelerated at certain locations by addition of carbon dioxide (CO_2) or hydrogen sulfide (H_2S) [oxidizing to sulfuric acid (H_2SO_4)] from deep crustal sources, and along sea coasts where mixing of fresh and salt water enhances the solubility. Microbiological processes (nanobacteria producing CO_2) may also be important. Condensation corrosion by carbonic acid (H_2CO_3) or H_2SO_4 can be significant where periodic high humidity combines with excess release of CO_2 or H_2S in some coastal or arid-zone caves.

Types. Dissolution caves have been classified by their plan morphology (see **table**). In most regions the caves are formed by meteoric water recharging through karst depressions, creating systems that are combinations of the fracture and bedding plane types. Significant karst caves from intergranular dissolution are uncommon, as are caves created by diffusion beneath porous but insoluble sandstones. Spongeworks and rudimentary networks are associated mostly with coastal mixing-zone dissolution in young (late Tertiary–Quaternary) limestones. Hypogene (ascending, deeper crustal) waters sometimes create a single-stem, treelike cave in their rise to the surface. More often they ramify into networks of fissures and rooms; the greatest known examples have invaded filled paleokarst cavities of different kinds. *See* KARST TOPOGRAPHY.

There are four principal varieties of common meteoric water caves (see **illus.**). Where densities of penetrable fissures are low or stratal dips are steep, the cave system may consist largely of a single deep (phreatic zone) loop beneath a water table that was lowered, then stabilized, by expansion of the cave (illus. *a*). Where fissure frequency is high or there is significant intergranular

Limestone cave patterns and their relationship to types of recharge and porosity*

		Type of Recharge				
		Via karst depressions		Diffuse		Hypogenic
		sinkholes (limited discharge fluctuation)	sinking streams (great discharge fluctuation)	through sandstone	into porous soluble rock	dissolution by acids of deep-seated source or by cooling of thermal water
		branchworks (usually several levels) and single passages	single passages and crude branchworks, usually with the following features superimposed:	most caves enlarged further by recharge from other sources	most caves formed by mixing at depth	
Type of Presolutional Porosity	Fractures	angular passages	fissures, irregular networks	fissures, networks	isolated fissures and rudimentary networks	networks, single passages, fissures
	Bedding partings	curvilinear passages	anastomoses, anastomotic mazes	profile: sandstone — shaft and canyon complexes, interstratal solution	spongework	ramiform caves, rare single-passage and anastomotic caves
	Intergranular	rudimentary branchworks	spongework	profile: sandstone — rudimentary spongework	spongework	ramiform and spongework caves

*After A. N. Palmer, Origin and morphology of limestone caves, *Geol. Soc. Amer. Bull.*, 103:1–21, 1991.

porosity, or where strata are nearly flat lying, a subhorizontal, water-table passage may collect waters from higher (vadose zone) feeder galleries that were drained by the early enlargement of the cave (illus. *b*). There are two intermediate types (illus. *c*, *d*). Most of the larger cave systems that are known also display multiple phases (levels) in their development.

In the United States, Mammoth Cave National Park, Kentucky, provides excellent examples of meteoric water caves. Jewel Cave and Wind Cave, South Dakota, are superb examples of thermal water caves. Carlsbad Caverns, New Mexico, are outstanding for sulfur corrosion and magnificent speleothems.

Passages. In cross section (as they are seen by visitors), meteoric water passages display three basic shapes, alone or in combination. Phreatic passages are created below a water table, where pressure flow applies. Their ideal shape is circular (that is, minimum-friction cross section, as in a domestic pipe), but more often there is an ellipse extended along the host fissure. Vadose passages develop in the aerated zone where gravity flow prevails; shapes are varieties of entrenched canyons interspersed with fluted shafts, and there may be widening at the base to undercut the walls. In breakdown passages, parts or all of the walls or ceilings are collapsed into blocks or rubble. Breakdown is caused by loss of buoyant support upon draining, by vadose stream undercutting, by tributary waters descending through roofs, as well as other processes. Most large underground rooms are developed by progressive breakdown.

Shapes in hypogene and mixing-zone caves are phreatic, but with a greater frequency of deep, rounded dissolution alcoves (pockets) than is common in meteoric water caves. Fissure passages taper rapidly in some hydrogen sulfide caves. A swiss-cheese texture is often reported in the walls of mixing-zone caves.

Large systems. The longest known cave system is Mammoth Cave, Kentucky, a meteoric water cave in near-horizontal strata; more than 500 km (300 mi) of interconnected passages have been mapped. Phreatic tubes, vadose, and breakdown

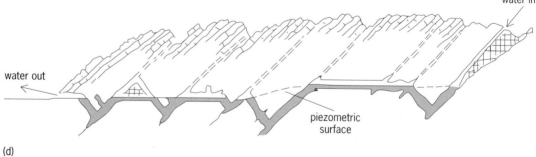

Principal types of meteoric water caves, longitudinal cross sections. The piezometric surface is an imaginary surface that represents the static head of ground water and is defined by the level to which the water will rise. (*a*) Bathyphreatic cave. (*b*) Ideal water-table cave. (*c*) Phreatic cave with multiple loops. (*d*) Cave with mixture of phreatic and water-table-leveled components. The letters represent the distribution (density) of major penetrable fissures in which the cave will develop. As fissure density increases, the vertical amplitude of looping in the cave diminishes. (*From D. C. Ford and P. W. Williams, Karst Geomorphology and Hydrology, Routledge, Chapman and Hall, 1989*)

rooms are all common in this system, which has evolved through at least four phases at successively lower spring levels. Other caves exceeding 100 km (60 mi) include hypogene mazes such as Jewel Cave and Wind Cave, South Dakota, which are in limestone and dolomite, and Optimists' and Ozernaya, Ukraine, which are contained in a thin gypsum formation. Exploration in the Americas, western Europe, China, and southeastern Asia is revealing many more meteoric caves around or approaching the 100-km (60-mi) mark. Flooded (still phreatic) caves have been explored to lengths of 8 km (5 mi) in Australia, Europe, and Florida. The deepest known caves occur in high mountain areas such as the Alps, Pyrenees, Caucasus, and southern Mexico: Reseau Bernard (France) is 1590 m (5170 ft) deep, and there are at least 20 others exceeding 1000 m (3300 ft). Underwater, great springs at Mante (Mexico) and Vaucluse (France) have been explored by divers to depths of 250 m (825 ft) and 315 m (1040 ft) respectively; the latter was investigated with a remotely controlled submersible. The greatest room is in Lubang Nasib Bagus Cave, Sarawak: it measures 720 m (2400 ft), long, 400 m (1300 ft) wide, and 70 m (230 ft) high and has a volume of approximately 20,000,000 m³ (700,000,000 ft³). It is far larger than any space built by humans.

Cave deposits. Caves are important sediment traps, preserving evidences of past erosional, botanic, and other phases that may be obliterated aboveground. Clastic sediments include breakdown, weathering earths, water-laid gravels, sands, silts and clays, windborne dust, colluvium, beach deposits, and even tills injected from glaciers. Organic materials of every kind can be trapped in them. The finer-grained deposits may also contain good paleomagnetic records. *See* EROSION; PALEOMAGNETISM; WEATHERING PROCESSES.

Chemical deposits are very important. More than 100 different minerals are known to precipitate in caves. Most abundant and significant are stalactites, stalagmites, and flowstones of calcite. These may be dated with uranium series methods, thus establishing minimum ages for the host caves. They contain paleomagnetic records. Their oxygen and carbon isotope ratios and trapped organic materials may record long-term changes of climate and vegetation aboveground that can be dated with great precision. As a consequence, cave deposits are proving to be among the most valuable paleoenvironmental records preserved on the continents. *See* STALACTITES AND STALAGMITES.

All kinds of faunal remains are found in cave deposits, including human artifacts and bones. Most known sites of early *Homo sapiens, H. neanderthalensis,* and *H. erectus* are caves. Cave fauna specially adapted to the permanent darkness of underground are termed troglodytes. They include many species of fishes, insects, and crustaceans. Eyeless animals are common. *See* FOSSIL HUMAN.   Derek C. Ford

Bibliography. W. Dreybrodt, *Processes in Karst Systems: Physics, Chemistry and Geology,* 1988; D. C. Ford et al., Uranium series dating of the draining of an aquifer: The example of Wind Cave, Black Hills, S.D., *Bull. Geol. Soc. Amer.,* 105:241–250, 1993; D. C. Ford and P. W. Williams, *Karst Geomorphology and Hydrology,* 1989; C. A. Hill and P. Forti, *Cave Minerals of the World,* 1986; A. N. Palmer, Origin and morphology of limestone caves, *Bull. Geol. Soc. Amer.,* 103:1–21, 1991; W. B. White, *Geomorphology and Hydrology of Karst Terrains,* 1988; I. J. Winograd et al., Continuous 500,000 year climate record from vein calcite in Devils Hole, Nevada, *Science,* 258:255–260, 1992.

Cavies

Rodents comprising the family Caviidae, which includes the guinea pig, rock cavies, mountain cavies, capybara, salt-desert cavy, and mara. All members of the group are indigenous to South America and comprise 15 species in six genera. Cavies have either rounded bodies with large heads and short ears and limbs, or rabbitlike bodies with long limbs and moderately long ears. They have 20 teeth with short incisors and a dental formula of I 1/1 C 0/0 Pm 1/1 M 3/3.

The guinea pig (*Cavia aperea*) originated in Peru, where there is still a wild stock. The domestic form (*C. porcellus*) [see **illus.**] has been produced by selective breeding and is a valuable laboratory animal with a life-span of 3–5 years. They are stocky animals; adults measure 8–12 in. (20–30 cm) in length and weigh less than 2 lb (0.9 kg). There are two or three litters each year with two to six young born after a gestation period of 2 months. The young cavies can see at birth and are fairly independent of the mother. These animals are docile, are easily reared in captivity, and make excellent pets.

The guinea pig has been used as an experimental animal in numerous studies. Geneticists have studied coat color and hair length and type, and have carried out numerous studies on the effects of inbreeding. Mating behavior in the guinea pig has been thoroughly studied by ethologists; in fact, it is probably the best-known insofar as mating

The guinea pig (*Cavia aperea*).

behavior is concerned. Immunological studies using this animal are continually conducted.

A large cavy which is closely related to the guinea pig is the mara or Patagonian cavy (*Dolichotis patagonum*). It resembles a large hare, being 1 ft (0.3 m) high and having a length of 2–3 ft (0.6–0.9 m). It is a burrowing, herbivorous animal that lives in small colonies in drier areas of Argentina and Patagonia. The mara is active during the day, and is quite swift as it runs and leaps. Two litters of usually three offspring each are born in the burrows each year. The salt-desert cavy (*Pediolagus salinicola*) is a smaller species found in the salt deserts of southern Argentina.

The largest of all rodents is the capybara or carpincho (*Hydrochoerus hydrochaeris*). It grows to the size of a small pig, about 4 ft (1.2 m) long and 120 lb (54 kg). It is essentially an aquatic animal which lives in small groups along the banks of lakes and streams in tropical South America. It is a vegetarian, is easily tamed, and breeds well in captivity. The female produces one litter each year after a gestation period of 4 months with from three to eight self-sufficient young; domestication increases fertility. The life-span of the animal is about 10 years. *See* RODENTIA.   Charles B. Curtin

Cavitation

The formation of vapor- or gas-filled cavities in liquids. If understood in this broad sense, cavitation includes the familiar phenomenon of bubble formation when water is brought to a boil under constant pressure and the effervescence of champagne wines and carbonated soft drinks due to the diffusion of dissolved gases. In engineering terminology, the term cavitation is used in a narrower sense, namely, to describe the formation of vapor-filled cavities in the interior or on the solid boundaries created by a localized pressure reduction produced by the dynamic action of a liquid system without change in ambient temperature. Cavitation in the engineering sense is characterized by an explosive growth and occurs at suitable combinations of low pressure and high speed in pipelines; in hydraulic machines such as turbines, pumps, and propellers; on submerged hydrofoils; behind blunt submerged bodies; and in the cores of vortical structures. This type of cavitation has great practical significance because it restricts the speed at which hydraulic machines may be operated and, when severe, lowers efficiency, produces noise and vibrations, and causes rapid erosion of the boundary surfaces, even though these surfaces consist of concrete, cast iron, bronze, or other hard and normally durable material.

Acoustic cavitation occurs whenever a liquid is subjected to sufficiently intense sound or ultrasound (that is, sound with frequencies of roughly 20 kHz to 10 MHz). When sound passes through a liquid, it consists of expansion (negative-pressure)

waves and compression (positive-pressure) waves. If the intensity of the sound field is high enough, it can cause the formation, growth, and rapid recompression of vapor bubbles in the liquid. The implosive bubble collapse generates localized heating, a pressure pulse, and associated high-energy chemistry. *See* SOUND; ULTRASONICS.

Bernoulli's principle. As mentioned, cavitation occurs when the pressure in a liquid is reduced to a critical value. For the present, it will be assumed that this critical value is the vapor pressure p_v of the liquid. For clean, fresh water at 70°F (21°C), p_v has a value of about 52 lb/ft² (2.5 kilopascals); hence, when a liquid is moving with velocity V over a body at ordinary temperature and the pressure on the body surface is reduced to or near 52 lb/ft² (2.5 kPa), cavitation may be expected to occur. The condition for the onset of cavitation is therefore given by relation (1), where p_m is the minimum

$$p_m \leq p_v \tag{1}$$

pressure at any point on the surface of a moving body and p_v is the vapor pressure of the liquid at the prevailing temperature. Inversely, the condition for avoidance of cavitation is given by relation (2).

$$p_m > p_v \tag{2}$$

See VAPOR PRESSURE.

A more practical relation than (2) is obtained when the pressure p_m is expressed in terms of easily measurable reference values. This can be done by use of Bernoulli's principle. According to this principle, the sum of pressure head and velocity head in a frictionless incompressible medium remains constant along a streamline. This may be understood by considering a hydrofoil in a stream

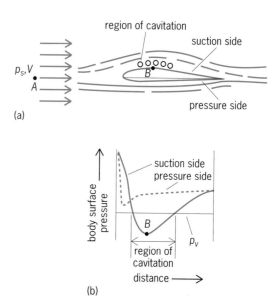

Fig. 1. Flow around a hydrofoil in a frictionless, incompressible fluid. (a) Cross section of flow. At point A, p_s = absolute static pressure, V = velocity of undisturbed flow. (b) Variation of body surface pressure along the two sides of the hydrofoil. p_v = vapor pressure of fluid.

flowing from left to right with constant velocity V (**Fig. 1**). Writing Bernoulli's equation for two points A and B lying on the same streamline, where the local pressure is minimum at point B, yields Eq. (3),

$$p_m = p_s - \frac{\rho}{2}V^2\left[\left(\frac{v}{V}\right)^2 - 1\right] \qquad (3)$$

where p_m = absolute local pressure at point B, v = velocity at point B, V = velocity of undisturbed flow at point A, p_s = absolute static pressure at point A, and ρ = density of liquid. The term in the square brackets is independent of the absolute speed V, because v changes proportionally to V. It follows that for a constant value of p_s the pressure p_m may be reduced to the vapor pressure p_v, to zero, or even to negative values by increasing the speed V. Negative values for p_m have been obtained in carefully conducted laboratory tests, proving that a pure liquid, such as clean air-free water, may sustain tension. However, in most practical cases, negative values are not obtained; instead, the flow is disrupted when cavities are formed. Combining (2) and (3), the condition for avoidance of cavitation becomes relation (4).

$$\frac{p_s - p_v}{(\rho/2)V^2} > \left[\left(\frac{v}{V}\right)^2 - 1\right] \qquad (4)$$

See BERNOULLI'S THEOREM.

Cavitation number. The term on the left of inequality (4) contains easily measurable values and is usually denoted by σ, which is called the cavitation number. The magnitude of the term on the right can be calculated for simple bodies, but for more complex configurations it cannot be calculated and must be obtained by experiment. Denoting this value by σ_c, the condition for avoidance of cavitation has the form of relation (5).

$$\sigma = \frac{p_s - p_v}{(\rho/2)V^2} > \sigma_c \qquad (5)$$

The cavitation number σ is used for flow through pipes, flow around submerged bodies, and in the design of marine propellers. In pump and hydraulic turbine work, slightly different expressions are used. The simplest one is the expression first introduced by D. Thoma which has form of relation (6), where H_{sv} is the net positive suction head at

$$\sigma_T = \frac{H_{sv}}{H} > (\sigma_T)_c \qquad (6)$$

the pump inlet, or just below the turbine runner, and H is the total head under which the turbine or pump operates. The value of $(\sigma_T)_c$, like the value of σ_c, is a fixed number for a given design of pump or turbine which in general must be found by experiment.

Experiments to determine σ_c and $(\sigma_T)_c$ are usually made on models geometrically similar to, but smaller than, the prototype installations. This has the advantage of less cost and more precise

Fig. 2. Examples of cavitation on screw propellers in water tunnels. (*a*) Bubble or traveling cavitation (*U.S. Navy*). (*b*) Sheet and tip vortex cavitation (*Applied Research Laboratory, Pennsylvania State University*)

control of the experiments and permits correction of undesirable characteristics of a design before the prototype machine is actually constructed. For instance, should it be found in a model test that a given propeller design cavitates heavily at the design operating value, different combinations of diameter and pitch, revolutions, blade width and outline, or section shape may be tried to eliminate or alleviate the observed cavitation. The same procedure is followed in the case of pumps and turbines.

The term scale effect is given to any deviations from the elementary similarity relations linking cavitation number to geometric and kinematic conditions. The many factors producing scale effects can be divided into two types: those which affect the minimum pressure in the liquid flow, and those which cause the cavitation pressure to be different from the equilibrium vapor pressure. *See* DYNAMIC SIMILARITY.

Types. It has been found convenient to differentiate between a type of cavitation in which small bubbles suddenly appear on the solid boundary, grow in extent, and disappear, and another type in which cavities form on the boundary and remain attached as long as the conditions that led to their formation remain unaltered. The former type is known as bubble or traveling cavitation (**Fig. 2**a) and the latter as sheet or attached cavitation (Fig. 2b). Tip vortex cavitation (Fig. 2b). occurs in the low-pressure center of a vortex formed at the tip of a lifting blade.

Physical causes. Both experiments and calculations show that with ordinary flowing water cavitation commences as the pressure approaches or reaches the vapor pressure, because of impurities in the water. These impurities, called cavitation nuclei, cause weak spots in the liquid and thus prevent it from supporting higher tensions. The various forms of cavitation nuclei are classified in two general groups, stream nuclei and surface nuclei. Stream nuclei exist in the liquid in such forms as inorganic or organic particulates or microbubbles. Surface nuclei originate at the surface of the fluid boundary by means of cracks and crevices in the boundary. Several techniques to measure stream nuclei have been standardized, and two significantly different approaches have developed. One is to measure the particulate or microbubble distribution by utilizing acoustical (wave-velocity, tone-attenuation), electrical (Coulter counter), or optical (photography, holography, laser light-scattering) techniques. The other approach measures a cavitation event rate for a liquid under various tensions (measured by a head-form venturi tube) and establishes a cavitation susceptibility. See VENTURI TUBE.

The exact mechanism of bubble growth is generally described by mathematical relationships which depend upon the cavitation nuclei. Cavitation commences when these nuclei enter a low-pressure region where the equilibrium between the various forces acting on the nuclei surface cannot be established. As a result, bubbles appear at discrete spots in low-pressure regions, grow quickly to relatively large size, and suddenly collapse as they are swept into regions of higher pressure.

Effects. It was mentioned initially that cavitation produces noise, and, when severe, lowers the efficiency of a machine, and causes rapid erosion of boundary surfaces. The destructive effect of cavitation on solid surfaces may be explained as follows. When cavitation bubbles form in a low-pressure region, the growth is explosive, with high bubble wall velocity. The growth time interval is too short for much air or gas to come out of solution, so that the bubbles are filled primarily with vapor. On subsequent collapse in the high-pressure region, the liquid particles rush toward the center of the bubble virtually unimpeded and form a very high velocity jet. Impingement of this jet and the resulting pressure wave on a solid boundary cause very high impulsive forces. It is estimated that the surface stress caused by the impingement is of the order of 1000 atm (100 megapascals), sufficiently high to cause fatigue failure of the material in a relatively short time. Some investigators hold that the explosive formation of the bubbles, intercrystalline electrolytic action, and the collapse of the bubbles all are factors contributing to the observed destruction.   Michael L. Billet

Supercavitating propellers. The limitation on ship speed caused by loss of thrust when cavitation is severe has been overcome by a radical departure from conventional propeller designs. In this new design (**Fig. 3**), cavitation on the backs of the blades (forward side) is induced by special blade sections at relatively low forward speed so that, when revolutions and engine power are increased, the whole back of each blade becomes enveloped by a sheet of cavitation. When this is completed, further increase in thrust at still higher engine power and revolutions per minute is obtained by the increase in positive pressure on the blade face (rear side); erosion is avoided because the collapse of the cavitation bubbles occurs some distance behind the trailing edges of the blades. The blade sections are usually wedge-shaped with a sharp leading edge to initiate cavitation at this point, a blunt trailing edge, and a concave face. The supercavitating propeller is no replacement for the conventional propeller, being suitable only for very high ship and engine speeds.

Fig. 3. Supercavitating propeller in water tunnel. (*U.S. Navy*)

In 1968 the supercavitating propeller was applied in two experimental hydrofoil boats: the *Denison* constructed for the U.S. Maritime Administration and another constructed for the Royal Canadian Navy. Probably it has also been used on patrol boats of various navies, but no performance data have been published. In the known installations the propellers functioned as anticipated, but some difficulties have been encountered in finding materials for these propellers strong enough to withstand the very high blade stresses. *See* PROPELLER (MARINE CRAFT).   Jacques B. Hadler

Sonochemistry. The chemical and biological effects of ultrasound were first reported by A. L. Loomis in the 1930s. With the advent of inexpensive and reliable sources of ultrasound, there has been a resurgence of interest in the chemical applications of ultrasound. Ultrasound has been found to enhance a very wide range of chemical reactions, and there has been special interest in organometallic reactions. It has been used to increase rates and yields for both stoichiometric and catalytic reactions, both in homogeneous liquids and in liquid–solid heterogeneous systems.

Since ultrasound has acoustic wavelengths of roughly 0.15–75 mm, clearly no direct coupling of the acoustic field with chemical species on a molecular level can account for sonochemistry. Instead, the chemical effects of ultrasound derive from several different physical mechanisms, depending on the nature of the system. The most important of these is cavitation. The dynamics of cavity growth and collapse are strikingly dependent on local environment, and cavitation in a homogeneous liquid should be considered separately from cavitation near a solid interface.

In homogeneous media, the generally accepted sonochemical mechanism involves pyrolysis by a localized hot spot due to the adiabatic heating which is produced by the implosive collapse of a bubble during cavitation. A measurement of the temperature generated during this implosive collapse established that the effective temperature in the gas-phase reaction zone is about 8900°F (5200 K) with pressures of hundreds of atmospheres (tens of megapascals).

When a liquid–solid interface is subjected to ultrasound, cavitation still occurs, but with major changes in the nature of the bubble collapse. No longer do cavities implode spherically. Instead, a markedly asymmetric collapse occurs, which generates a jet of liquid directed at the surface, just as in propeller-induced cavitation. The jet velocities are greater than 300 ft/s (100 m/s). The origin of this jet formation is essentially a shaped-charge effect. The impingement of this jet creates a localized erosion responsible for surface pitting and ultrasonic cleaning. Enhanced chemical reactivity of solid surfaces is associated with these processes. The cavitational erosion generates unpassivated, highly reactive surfaces; causes short-lived high temperatures and pressures at the surface; produces surface defects and deformations; creates high-velocity interparticle collisions; increases the surface area of friable solid supports; and ejects material in unknown form into solution. Finally, the local turbulent flow associated with acoustic streaming improves mass transport between the liquid phase and the surface, thus increasing observed reaction rates. In general, all of these effects are likely to occur simultaneously. *See* SEMICONDUCTOR.   Kenneth S. Suslick

Bibliography. C. E. Brennen, *Cavitation and Bubble Dynamics*, 1995; F. G. Hammitt, *Cavitation and Multiphase Flow Phenomena*, 1980; K. S. Suslick (ed.), *Ultrasound: Its Chemical, Physical and Biological Effects*, 1988; J. P. Tullis, *Hydraulics of Pipelines: Pumps, Valves, Cavitation and Transients*, 1989; F. R. Young, *Cavitation*, 1989.

Cavity resonator

An enclosure capable of resounding or resonating and thereby intensifying sound tones or electromagnetic waves. Resonance is the phenomenon which results when the frequency of the impressed

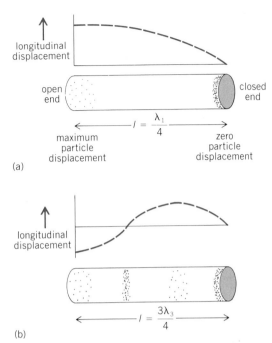

Fig. 1. Closed-end sound pipe resonating (*a*) at the fundamental frequency f_1 (the first harmonic) with wavelength λ_1, and (*b*) at an overtone, $f_3 \approx 3f_1$ (the third harmonic), with wavelength λ_3.

driving force is the same as the natural vibration of the cavity. Vibrating rods, the tuning fork, musical instrument strings, radio and television channel tuners, and so forth, constitute resonating systems as well. The cavity resonator enclosure has a volume which stores energy oscillating between one form and another. In the case of sound, the oscillation is between displacement and velocity of particles. In the case of electromagnetic waves, the energy oscillates between the magnetic and the electric fields. *See* MUSICAL INSTRUMENTS; TUNING FORK; VIBRATION.

Sound-resonant pipes. Cavity pipes are used as resonators in musical instruments such as pipe organs and flutes to increase their sonority. The frequency of resonance is determined (to a degree of approximation) by the length of the pipe, by the velocity of sound at the ambient temperature and pressure, by the intensity of the driving force, and by the condition at the ends of the pipe: closed or open. The resulting frequency is related to multiples of quarter-wavelengths or half-wavelengths (depending on the end conditions) contained in the length of pipe. The driving force, if sufficiently strong, can force oscillations to occur at overtone frequencies which are higher multiples of the lowest or fundamental frequency, as well as at the fundamental. **Figure 1** illustrates simple cavity resonators for sound for a pipe open at one end and closed at the other. Other resonators have both ends open or both ends closed, with a small hole through which the driving force is introduced. For the case of both ends open as well as for the case of both ends closed, the resonant frequencies are those frequencies for which the pipe length is a whole number of half-wavelengths. *See* ACOUSTIC RESONATOR; SOUND.

Microwave-resonant cavities. At very high radio frequencies, losses due to radiation can be eliminated and resistive losses can be minimized by using closed resonant cavities instead of lumped-circuit resonators. A cavity resonator stores both magnetic and electric fields, the energy oscillating between the two, losing energy only to the conducting walls if a perfect dielectric fills the space. The resonant frequency of the cavity is determined by the shape of the cavity and the mode, or allowable field distribution, of the electromagnetic energy that the cavity contains. The usual cavities consist of closed sections of cylindrical or rectangular waveguides, or of hollow spheres or other symmetrical shapes. The choice of the shape is determined by the ease of fabrication or by the cavity's application. In the case of the cylindrical cavity resonator, the resonant frequency f_0 is computed from Eq. (1),

$$f_0 = \frac{c}{2L}\left[1 + \left(\frac{2L}{K_{nl}a}\right)^2\right]^{1/2} \quad (1)$$

where a = radius

L = cavity length

c = velocity of light

K_{nl} = lth root of $J_n'(K) = 0$ for tranverse electric (TE) modes

K_{nl} = lth root of $J_n(K) = 0$ for tranverse magnetic (TM) modes (J_n is the nth order Bessel function and J_n' is its derivative)

If one of the end walls of the cavity is adjustable, the cavity can act as a wavemeter; that is, the resonance frequency can change as L is adjusted. **Figure 2** illustrates how this can be done. *See* WAVELENGTH MEASUREMENT; WAVEMETER.

For the case of a rectangular cavity, the resonance frequency is determined by Eq. (2), where a, b, and

$$f_0 = \frac{c}{2}\left[\left(\frac{m}{a}\right)^2 + \left(\frac{n}{b}\right)^2 + \left(\frac{p}{d}\right)^2\right]^{1/2} \quad (2)$$

d are dimensions of the cavity and m, n, and p are integers (or zero in certain cases) as determined by the mode of the enclosed fields. *See* MICROWAVE; WAVEGUIDE.

Coupling. Coupling to cavities may be accomplished by (1) introduction of a conducting probe or antenna oriented so it coincides with the direction of the electron field; (2) introduction of a conducting loop with plane normal to the magnetic field; (3) placement of a hole or iris between the cavity and a driving waveguide, the iris being placed so that a field component in the cavity mode has a common direction with one in the waveguide or other cavity; and (4) introduction of a pulsating electron beam

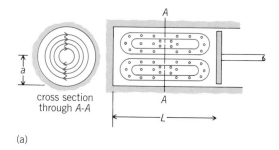

cross section through A-A

(a)

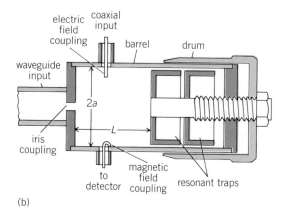

(b)

Fig. 2. Wavemeters. (a) Wavemeter consisting of cylindrical cavity with an adjustable end-wall, resonating in the TE$_{011}$ mode. The free-space wavelength λ_0 corresponding to the resonant frequency f_0 is given by $\lambda_0 = 2L[1 + (2L/1.64a)]^{-1/2}$ **(b)** Practical wavemeter for the TE$_{111}$ mode.

passing through a small gap into the cavity and in the direction of the electric field of the cavity. The first three coupling methods are illustrated in Fig. 2b.

Quality factor. A good measure of the quality of a typical cavity resonator is expressed by the amount of stored energy as compared with the energy lost to the imperfectly conducting walls (and if present, to the imperfect dielectric of the cavity region).

More precisely defined, the quality factor is represented by Eq. (3). The formula for any

$$Q = \frac{2\pi f_0 \times \text{(energy stored)}}{\text{average power loss}}$$
$$= \frac{\pi \text{(energy stored)}}{\text{energy loss per half cycle}} \quad (3)$$

particular cavity configuration operating in a particular mode is derived by calculating the energy stored (either in the magnetic field or in the electric field), determining the losses due to the currents flowing on the imperfect conducting walls, and substituting in Eq. (3) for Q. The formula then contains the dimensions of the cavity relevant to the mode of the field configuration and an expression for the surface resistance of the conducting walls.

If a resonant cavity which has a quality factor Q is coupled to an external load which has a factor denoted by Q_e, the combination of the two leads to a loaded quality factor Q_L, which is related to the others by Eq. (4).

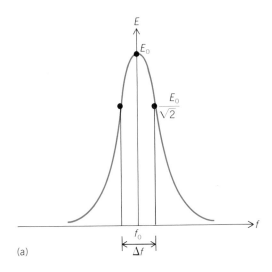

(a)

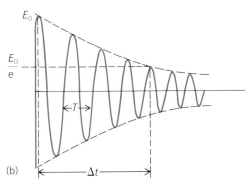

(b)

Fig. 3. Determination of the Q of a cavity resonator by (*a*) measuring the bandwidth and (*b*) measuring the damping rate of the oscillations.

$$1/Q_L = 1/Q_e + 1/Q \qquad (4)$$

The Q can be measured by using two basic techniques. The first is to monitor the field intensity E as the frequency of the driving force is increased and decreased off the resonance of the cavity. **Figure 3***a* shows the response of such a detuning. The two points representing a drop in field intensity to 0.707 or $1/\sqrt{2}$ of its peak value (half-power points) also represent the bandwidth, or Δf. Under this condition, it can be shown that Q is given by Eq. (5).

$$Q = \frac{f_0}{\Delta f} \qquad (5)$$

Another approach is to make use of the damping properties which indicate the rate at which oscillations would decay if the driving source were removed. For this method the fields E decay as given in Eq. (6), where E_0 is the initial field and

$$E = E_0 e^{-(\pi f_0/Q)t} \qquad (6)$$

$e = 2.718 \ldots$. Consequently, if, as shown in Fig. 3*b*, a measure of the time taken for the field to drop to $(1/e)$th of its initial value is denoted as Δt, then Q is given by Eq. (7), and, since $1/f_0$ is the period of the oscillation T_0, then Eq. (8) is valid.

$$Q = \pi f_0 \Delta t \qquad (7)$$

$$Q = \pi \Delta t / T_0 = \pi \times (\text{number of cycles in } \Delta t) \qquad (8)$$

See Q (ELECTRICITY); RESONANCE (ALTERNATING-CURRENT CIRCUITS).

Optical cavity resonators. As the frequency of oscillation of the electromagnetic waves gets higher and well beyond the microwave range, the microwave cavity resonators described above become impractical. For lasers, with operation in the visible range, the infrared, or ultraviolet, the corresponding wavelengths are of the order of micrometers. The resonant cavity would have to be extremely small. If one was constructed with dimensions of millimeters, then the resonances of the possible modes of operation would be extremely close together and it would be impractical to separate them. Removing the sides of a closed cavity eliminates a large number of modes which in the absence of walls would radiate and thus be damped out. It has been shown that proper shaping and placing of the ends does support low-loss modes. Parallel plane mirrors is one system. Another consists of curved mirrors facing each other. Combinations of curved-planar mirrors, confocal mirrors, concentric mirrors, and spherical mirror configurations also constitute optical resonators. The objective in each design is to stabilize (contain) low-loss modes. *See* LASER.

The system of parallel plane reflectors has been used in interferometry and is referred to as a Fabry-Pérot resonator or etalon. *See* INTERFEROMETRY.

Optical resonators have also been made using loops of low-loss optical fibers, and in integrated optical circuits. *See* INTEGRATED OPTICS; OPTICAL FIBERS; RESONANCE (ACOUSTICS AND MECHANICS).

Diogenes J. Angelakos

Bibliography. R. E. Collin, *Foundations for Microwave Engineering*, 2d ed., 1992; J. D. Krause and K. R. Carver, *Electromagnetics*, 4th ed., 1992; M. I. Skolnik, *Radar Handbook*, 2d ed., 1990.

Cayley-Klein parameters

A set of four numbers used to specify the orientation of a body, or equivalently, the rotation R which produces that orientation, starting from some reference orientation. They can be expressed in terms of the Euler angles ψ, θ, and ϕ, as in Eqs. (1).

$$\alpha = \cos\frac{\theta}{2}e^{-i(\psi-\phi)/2} \qquad \beta = -i\sin\frac{\theta}{2}e^{i(\psi-\phi)/2}$$
$$\gamma = -i\sin\frac{\theta}{2}e^{-i(\psi-\phi)/2} \qquad \delta = \cos\frac{\theta}{2}e^{i(\psi-\phi)/2} \qquad (1)$$

Often the set δ, $-\beta$, $-\gamma$, α is used with slightly different properties from those given here. The four complex numbers contain eight real numbers and satisfy relations in Eqs. (2), where the

$$\delta = \overline{\alpha} \qquad \gamma = -\beta$$
$$\alpha\delta - \beta\gamma = \alpha\overline{\alpha} + \beta\overline{\beta} = 1 \qquad (2)$$

bar denotes complex conjugate. These constitute

five real conditions, leaving three independent parameters as required. *See* EULER ANGLES.

The Cayley-Klein parameters combine in a simple way under compound rotations when they are arranged in the square matrix array shown in (3).

$$\begin{pmatrix} \alpha & \beta \\ \gamma & \delta \end{pmatrix} \qquad (3)$$

If α, β, γ, δ correspond to the rotation R_1 and α', β', γ', δ' to R_2, then the paramters α'', β'', γ'', δ'' of the rotation $R_2 R_1$ (R_1 first, then R_2) are found by matrix multiplication. Thus Eq. (4) holds.

$$\begin{pmatrix} \alpha'' & \beta'' \\ \gamma'' & \delta'' \end{pmatrix} = \begin{pmatrix} \alpha' & \beta' \\ \gamma' & \delta' \end{pmatrix} \begin{pmatrix} \alpha & \beta \\ \gamma & \delta \end{pmatrix} \qquad (4)$$

A rotation $R(\psi, \theta, \phi)$ can be produced by three successive rotations. The corresponding decomposition of the parameter matrix is given by Eq. (5).

$$\begin{pmatrix} \alpha & \beta \\ \gamma & \delta \end{pmatrix} =$$

$$\begin{pmatrix} e^{-i\phi/2} & 0 \\ 0 & e^{i\phi/2} \end{pmatrix} \begin{pmatrix} \cos\dfrac{\theta}{2} & -i\sin\dfrac{\theta}{2} \\ -i\sin\dfrac{\theta}{2} & \cos\dfrac{\theta}{2} \end{pmatrix} \begin{pmatrix} e^{-i\psi/2} & 0 \\ 0 & e^{i\psi/2} \end{pmatrix}$$

$$(5)$$

Although these parameters have been used to simplify somewhat the mathematic of spinning top motion, their main use is in quantum mechanics. There they are related to the Pauli spin matrices and represent the change in the spin state of an electron or other particle of half-integer spin under the space rotation $R(\psi, \theta, \phi)$. *See* MATRIX THEORY; SPIN (QUANTUM MECHANICS).   Bernard Goodman

Bibliography. H. Goldstein, *Classical Mechanics*, 2d ed., 1980; L. Shepley and R. Matzner, *Classical Mechanics*, 1991.

Caytoniales

A group of Mesozoic plants first recognized in 1925. The remains consist of palmately compound leaves with 3–6 lanceolate leaflets previously known as *Sagenopteris phillipsi*, pinnately branched microsporophylls (named *Caytonanthus arberi*) that bore winged pollen in four-chambered microsporangia, and fruit-bearing inflorescences, *Caytonia* (with two species), which bore a dozen or more globular, short-stalked fruits in subopposite rows. Each fruit was 0.2 in. (5 mm) or less in diameter. Near the attachment stalk at the lower part of the fruit was a small transverse lip beneath which was a minute depression marking the place where a small opening formed at pollination time. This opening admitted the pollen into the interior, where small orthotropous ovules were attached to the surface. The inflorescence thus resembled a simply pinnate frond, of which the individual pinnules were curved

so as to enclose the seeds. When first discovered, it was believed that the flap served as a stigmatic surface to receive the pollen in a manner similar to the stigma of a modern flower. Later it was found that the pollen actually entered the young fruit through the small opening and germinated on the nucellus of the ovule after the manner in gymnosperms (Pinopsida). The Caytoniales appear related to the pteridosperms. They range from the Triassic to the Cretaceous. *See* PALEOBOTANY.   Chester A. Arnold

Cedar

Any of a large number of evergreen trees having fragrant wood of great durability. Arborvitae is sometimes called northern white cedar. *Chamaecyparis thyoides* is the botanical name of the southern white cedar, which may grow to 75 ft (22 m). It is characterized by small, spherical cones with peltate, seed-bearing scales fitted together to form a little ball, and by small scalelike evergreen leaves (**illus.** *a*). It grows only in swamps near the eastern coast of North America, where it is also known as Atlantic white cedar. The wood is soft, fragrant, and durable in the soil and is used for boxes, crates, small boats, tanks, woodenware, poles, and shingles. *See* ARBORVITAE; PINALES.

The Port Orford cedar (*C. lawsoniana*), also known as Lawson cypress, grows to 180 ft (54 m), has spherical cones larger than those of the eastern species, and is native to southwestern Oregon and northwestern California. It is the principal wood for storage battery separators, but is also used for venetian blinds and construction purposes. It is an ornamental tree which is sometimes used in shelter belts.

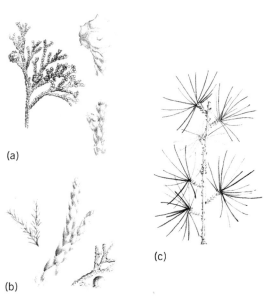

(a)

(b)

(c)

Characteristic leaf arrangements for three cedar species: (*a*) Southern white cedar (*Chamaecyparis thyoides*), (*b*) eastern red cedar (*Juniperus virginiana*), and (*c*) Atlas cedar (*Cedrus atlantica*).

Alaska cedar (*C. nootkatensis*), found from Oregon to Alaska, grows to 120 ft (36 m), and has larger spherical cones which are nearly ¹/₂ in. (0.6 cm) in diameter. The wood is used for interior finish, cabinetwork, small boats, and furniture. It is also grown as an ornamental tree.

Incense cedar (*Libocedrus decurrens*), a beautifully formed tree which grows to 135 ft (41 m), is found from Oregon to western Nevada and Lower California. The cones, ³/₄–1 in. (1.8–2.5 cm) long, resemble those of arborvitae. Incense cedar is one of the chief woods for pencils, and is also used for venetian blinds, rough construction, and fence posts and as an ornamental and shade tree.

Eastern red cedar (*Juniperus virginiana*), which may reach a height of 90 ft (27 m), is distributed over the eastern United States and adjacent Canada. Its leaves, evergreen and scalelike, occur in four rows lengthwise on the branchlets, giving a four-sided appearance (illus. *b*). On young trees or on vigorous shoots the leaves are needlelike, sometimes in threes. The fruit is spherical, berrylike, about ¹/₂ in. (0.6 cm) in diameter, and borne on the female tree. Male trees bear only stamens. The very fragrant wood is durable in the soil and is used for fence posts, chests, wardrobes, flooring, and pencils. Cedarwood oil is used in medicine and perfumes.

Cedar of Lebanon (*Cedrus libani*) and Atlas cedar (*C. atlantica*) resemble the larch, but the leaves are evergreen and the cones are much larger and erect on the branches. The cedar of Lebanon, a native of Asia Minor, has cones 3–4 in. (7.5–10 cm) long and 1¹/₂–2¹/₂ (4.3–6.8 cm) in diameter, and is sometimes cultivated in the United States. The Atlas cedar is hardier, and the variety *glauca* is popular as an ornamental (illus. *c*). *See* LARCH.

The deodar cedar (*Cedrus deodara*), a beautiful tree with large leaves and drooping branches, is a native of India, and although not hardy in the northern United States, it is widely cultivated in the Southeast and in California.

The cigarbox cedar (*Cedrela odorata*), also known as the West Indian cedar, belongs to the mahogany family, is a broad-leaved tree with pinnate, deciduous leaves and is related to the *Ailanthus* and sumac. The wood is very durable and fragrant and is valued in the West Indies for the manufacture of cabinets, furniture, and canoes. It seldom grows well in the northern United States. *See* FOREST AND FORESTRY; TREE.

Arthur H. Graves/Kenneth P. Davis

Celastrales

An order of flowering plants, division Magnoliophyta (Angiospermae), in the subclass Rosidae of the class Magnoliopsida (dicotyledons). The order consists of 11 families and more than 2000 species, with the families Celastraceae (about 800 species), Aquifoliaceae (about 400 species), Icaci-

American holly (*Ilex opaca*), a characteristic member of the family Aquifoliaceae in the order Celastrales. The spiny leaves are typical of several species of holly, but not of the whole family or order. (*Photograph by Eric J. Hosking, from National Audubon Society*)

naceae (about 400 species), and Hippocrateaceae (about 300 species) forming the core of the group. The order is marked by its simple leaves and regular flowers, varying from hypogynous (those with the perianth and stamens attached directly to the receptacle, beneath the ovary) to perigynous (those with the perianth and stamens united at the base into a hyphanthium distinct from the ovary) and with a single set of stamens which alternate with the petals. Nearly all of the species are woody plants. Various species of holly (*Ilex*, family Aquifoliaceae; see **illus.**) and *Euonymus* (Celastraceae) are often cultivated. *See* HOLLY; MAGNOLIOPHYTA; MAGNOLIOPSIDA; PLANT KINGDOM; ROSIDAE.

Arthur Cronquist; T. M. Barkley

Celery

A biennial umbellifer (*Apium graveolens* var. *dulce*) of Mediterranean origin and belonging to the plant order Apiales. Celery is grown for its petioles or leafstalks, which are most commonly eaten as a salad but occasionally cooked as a vegetable (see **illus.**). Celeriac or knob celery (*A. graveolens* var. *rapaceum*) is grown for its enlarged rootlike stem and is commonly eaten as a cooked vegetable in Europe.

Propagation of celery is by seed planted in the field or sown in greenhouses or outdoor beds for the production of transplants. Field spacing varies; plants are generally grown 6–10 in. (15–25 cm) apart in 18–36-in. (0.4–0.9-m) rows. Celery requires a long growing season, cool weather, and unusually abundant soil moisture. It has a high requirement for boron; a deficiency results in "cracked stem." Exposure to prolonged cold weather (39–48°F or 4–9°C for 10–30 days) favors "bolting" or seed-stalk formation.

Varieties (cultivars) are classified primarily ac-

Celery (*Apium graveolens* var. *dulce*). (*Joseph Harris Co., Inc., Rochester, New York*)

cording to their color, green or yellow (self-blanching). The most popular green variety is Utah, of which a large number of strains are grown, such as Summer Pascal and Utah 52–70H. The acreage of yellow celery has been declining. Pink and red varieties are grown in England.

Harvesting begins generally when the plants are fully grown but before the petioles become pithy, usually 3–4 months after field planting. In periods of high prices, earlier harvesting is often practiced.

California, Florida, and Michigan are important producing states. *See* APIALES.　　　　H. John Carew

Celery seedlings are often severely damaged by a variety of soil-inhabiting fungi that cause "damping-off" diseases in seedbeds. Extensive chemical fumigation treatments are commonly used to reduce seedbed losses. Some diseases caused by fungi such as *Fusarium oxysporum* f. sp. *apii* and *Septoria apii* can lead to early plant losses in the seedbed, but they usually damage plants after transplanting in the field. The crown, roots, and petioles are rotted and killed. Basal stalk rot and pink rot are other important fungal diseases in this group.

Foliar diseases caused by both fungi and bacteria reduce quality and affect the appearance of the harvested product. In most celery production areas, pesticides are routinely applied to protect the foliage from infection and damage. Common foliar diseases are caused by the fungi *Cercospora apii* and *Septoria apii*, leading to the early and late blight diseases, respectively. Bacterial leaf blight commonly damages celery foliage in seedbeds and in the field. Virus diseases cause sporadic losses. Cucumber mosaic and western celery mosaic viruses are commonly encountered.

Celery exhibits several physiological disorders traceable to mineral deficiencies or imbalances. Among the most common and important disorders are blackheart, due to calcium deficiency, and cracked stem due to boron deficiency. *See* PLANT PATHOLOGY; PLANT VIRUSES AND VIROIDS.

　　　　　　　　　　　　　　　　　J. O. Strandberg

Bibliography. G. N. Agrios, *Plant Pathology*, 1988; A. F. Sherf and A. A. MacNab, *Vegetable Diseases and Their Control*, 2d ed., 1986.

Celestial mechanics

The field of dynamics as applied to celestial bodies moving under their mutual gravitational influence in systems with few bodies. It usually describes and predicts motions in the solar system, both of natural bodies such as planets, satellites, asteroids, and comets, and of artificial bodies such as space probes. It can also be applied to small stellar systems.

Newton's laws. Isaac Newton's law of universal gravitation is the foundation of most of the field. It states that the force produced by one particle upon another is attractive along the line connecting the bodies, is proportional to the product of the masses of the bodies, and is inversely proportional to the square of the distance between the bodies. The constant of proportionality is G, the universal constant of gravitation. Newton's second law of motion then says that the acceleration experienced by a body is equal to the force on that body divided by its mass. *See* FORCE; KINETICS (CLASSICAL MECHANICS); NEWTON'S LAWS OF MOTION.

Two-body problem. The simplest and only exactly solvable problem in celestial mechanics is that of one particle moving about another. Since any body with spherical symmetry looks gravitationally like a point mass from the outside, the results from this problem may be used to describe approximately the relative motion of two finite bodies, such as a planet around the Sun or a satellite around a planet. The principal results from this problem had already been recognized empirically by Johannes Kepler and are embodied in his three laws of planetary motion. Usually the motion of the smaller body (the secondary) is described relative to the larger one (the primary). This relative motion is confined to a plane, and the path traced is a conic section such that the primary occupies one focus. If the bodies are gravitationally bound, the conic is an ellipse. The longest segment connecting opposite points on the ellipse is called the major axis, and half this length is called the semimajor axis a (see **illus.**). The departure of the ellipse from a circle is called the eccentricity e, which is usually quite small for planetary orbits. The tilt of the plane from some reference plane is called the inclination, and for the solar system that reference plane is the plane of the Earth's orbit, known as the ecliptic plane. Planetary inclinations are also usually quite small. The line of intersection of the plane of motion with the reference plane is called the line of nodes. The point on the orbit closest to the primary, which is at one end of the major axis, is called the pericenter (specifically for planetary orbits, the perihelion), and its angular distance from the node is called the argument of pericenter. The time at which the secondary passes through the pericenter is called the epoch of pericenter. A seventh parameter is the period of revolution, and the cube of the semimajor axis divided by the square of the period is proportional to the sum of the two masses. Since a planetary mass is small compared to that of the Sun, this ratio is essentially constant for the planets; this is Kepler's third law, also known as the harmonic law. *See* ELLIPSE.

A second result applies whenever the forces are directed along the line connecting the two bodies. Angular momentum is conserved, which causes the line connecting the two bodies to sweep out equal areas in equal times, a result stated in Kepler's second law. This results in the relative velocity in the orbit being inversely proportional to the square root of the separation. Ellipses are not the only type of relative motion permitted, and the type of conic depends on the total energy in the orbit. If there is just enough energy for the bodies to escape from each other, the relative orbit is a parabola. If there is more than enough energy for escape, such that some relative velocity would still remain, the orbit is a hyperbola. A hyperbola would also describe the relative motion of two independent bodies encountering each other, as in the case of two stars within the galaxy. *See* CONIC SECTION; ESCAPE VELOCITY; ORBITAL MOTION; PLANET.

Orbit determination. One of the major operational problems of celestial mechanics is that of determining the orbit of a body in the solar system from observations of its position, or distance plus line-of-sight velocity, at various times. The objective is to determine the numerical values of the parameters characterizing the orbit, known as orbital elements. It is usually first assumed that the motion is that of a two-body system and that the mass of the body is negligible. Thus, six elements must be determined. Each observation consists of two values at each time. Since six numbers are needed to solve for six other ones, a minimum of three observations is required. Usually there are more than three observations, which means a unique solution is not possible, but best values must be estimated in some statistical sense.

The problem is made difficult because observations are being made from the surface of the Earth, and hence parameters easily described by the two-body problem are not observed. The location of the point of observation with respect to the Sun must be accurately known, and this is often the limiting factor in orbit determination. In many cases, it is the improvement in knowledge of the orbit of the Earth that is the most useful result of a set of observations. *See* EARTH ROTATION AND ORBITAL MOTION.

Ephemeris generation. Once the orbit is known, the future locations of the object can be predicted. A table of predicted positions is called an ephemeris, and the generation of such a table is relatively straightforward. Usually, further observations are then obtained and checked for discrepancies, which in turn leads to improved values for the elements in a continually repeated cycle. *See* EPHEMERIS.

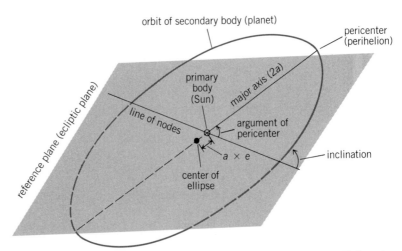

Relative motion of one body about another when the bodies are gravitationally bound. Parameters used to describe the motion are shown. (Terms used to describe the motion of a planet about the Sun are given in parentheses.) e = eccentricity.

Space flight and ballistics. Another important problem is determining the proper orbit to get from one point at one time to another point at another time. This may involve getting from one body to another (space flight) or from one point to another on the same body (ballistics). For space flight, the approach is to consider several two-body problems and then patch them together. For instance, for interplanetary flight, there is an initial hyperbolic orbit with respect to one planet, an elliptic orbit with respect to the Sun for the most part, and a final hyperbolic orbit with respect to the other planet. For economy, an orbit with as little energy change as possible is desired. This dictates an elliptic heliocentric orbit that is just tangent to one planetary orbit at one extreme and just tangent to the other orbit at the other extreme. Such an orbit is known as a Hohmann transfer orbit, and it is unique for each pair of planets. The period of the orbit is known, and the tangent points are at opposite ends of the major axis. Therefore, the launch time is dictated by the relative locations of the planets. Since in practice there is a little room for adjustment, there usually is a period of time, known as the launch window, during which a launch is possible. *See* SPACE NAVIGATION AND GUIDANCE; SPACE PROBE.

The ballistic problem requires determining an Earth-centered elliptic orbit that will connect launch and target points. The actual path will be that part of the ellipse above the Earth's surface. Usually the two points are at least approximately at the same distance from the center of the Earth, but the Earth rotates. This requires a cyclic procedure of estimating travel time, allowing for the shift in target location during that time, improving the orbit, and so on. *See* BALLISTICS.

Binary stars. An astronomical application of the two-body problem is the relative motion of components of a binary star. It was realized in the eighteenth century that this motion obeys the same laws as the solar system, which established the case for the universality of the law of gravitation. In this application, there is the advantage of being on the outside looking in, but there is no information on separation in the line of sight. The same techniques of orbit determination can be applied in usually simplified form, but since the masses are not known, period must be treated as a seventh independent parameter. This leads to the primary astronomical interest in these objects, because if the orbit is known, the masses can be determined, and this is the only presently known way to determine directly these important stellar data. *See* BINARY STAR.

Restricted three-body problem. Only slightly increased in complexity is this problem of the motion of a massless particle moving in the gravitational field of two bodies moving around each other in two-body motion. The simplest version of this problem is called planar circular, which means the particle moves in the plane of revolution of the two bodies which are themselves in circular orbits. This can be applied to objects like a spacecraft going from the Earth to the Moon or asteroids under the influence of the Sun and Jupiter. This problem has no general solution; the analytic and numerical study of the problem is concerned with stability, periodic orbits, and topology of solutions. There are five specific solutions—the fixed points or libration points. If the massless particle is placed at any of these points with zero velocity in the coordinate system rotating with the primaries, it will remain at that point in the rotating system. Three of these points are located along the line connecting the primaries, one between them and one outside of each; these are known as the linear points. Their exact distances from the primaries depend on the ratio of the masses of the primaries.

The other two points form equilateral triangles with the primaries, one ahead and one behind as they revolve. Unlike the linear points, these triangular points can be stable, in that a slight displacement of the massless particle away from the point will not produce unbounded motion but rather an oscillation (called a libration) about the point. The requirement for this is that the primaries' mass ratio must be below about 0.04. This is indeed true for the Sun-Jupiter system, and there are asteroids, known as the Trojans, librating about both triangular points in this system. It is also true for the Earth-Moon systems but the presence of the Sun makes matters more complicated. However, it is possible to keep the particle reasonably close to one of these lagrangian or L points for extended periods of time if initial conditions are chosen properly. *See* TROJAN ASTEROIDS.

Perturbations. If there are three or more bodies, all of which have mass and therefore all of which influence each other, the problem becomes almost hopeless. The degree of complexity is essentially independent of the number of bodies, so the problem is called the n-body problem. This is usually studied by purely numerical means, but in two extreme cases some analytical progress can be made. One is when the number of bodies, n, becomes so large that statistical approaches are possible; this leads into the dynamics of star clusters and galaxies and out of the field of celestial mechanics. The other is when relative geometries or masses are such that the situation becomes a series of two-body problems with small coupling influences, or perturbations. These perturbations can be treated in some approximate way, such as series expansions or iterative solutions. *See* GALAXY, EXTERNAL; MILKY WAY GALAXY; STAR CLUSTERS.

The major efforts in these perturbation studies have been the development of general theories of motion. These are elaborate mathematical approximate solutions which almost invariably involve series expansions in some small parameter of the problem. These can be solutions for slow variations of the elements that are fixed in the two-body problem, or they can be for slow divergence from the coordinates that would result from the two-body problem, or a mixture of the two. The numerical parameters are carried as literal expressions as far as possible, but before application, actual numerical values must be estimated. This usually involves a first estimate from two-body results, then similar ephemeris generation, comparison with observations, improved estimates of the parameters, and so on.

There are two classical areas of general perturbation theory. One is the development of lunar theory, the representation of the motion of the Moon about the Earth, under the influence of rather strong perturbations from the Sun. The small parameter is the period of the Moon (a month) compared to the period of the Earth (a year), and the motion of the Earth-Moon system about the Sun is considered known. This parameter is not really very small, producing slow rates of convergence and thus expressions with thousands of terms. *See* MOON.

The other major development has been planetary theory, the description of the motion of planets (either major or minor) about the Sun, under the influence of (other) major planets. The small parameter is the mass of the perturbing planet or planets compared with the Sun, but series expansions involving powers of ratios of mutual distances are also required. These ratios can become quite large (for Neptune and Pluto, it can become unity), again producing slow convergence. Furthermore, there are many planets, which add more terms to the resulting expressions. However, the biggest complication is resonances, a situation realized when the revolution periods of two planets are related by small integers. (The most famous of these is the great inequality of Jupiter-Saturn, produced by five of Jupiter's almost-12-year periods being almost exactly the same as two of Saturn's almost-30-year periods). Fortunately, these perturbations are long-period, large-amplitude, and sensitive to the perturbing mass, making them useful for planetary mass determinations.

The use of the general theory is now giving way to that of the special or numerical theory. The full equations of motion are solved on computers in approximated numerical form to simulate the motions of the bodies and produce tables of coordinates as functions of time. Again, ephemerides must be generated and compared to observations to establish the best numerical values of the starting conditions. In addition, the extrapolatory value of these theories is more uncertain than that of analytic ones, because of the approximations inherent in the numerical solutions. *See* PERTURBATION (ASTRONOMY).

Oblateness and tides. Another set of perturbations from two-body theory arises from the finite sizes of the actual bodies. Because of rotation during the time of formation, no body is completely spherically symmetric, but rather possesses at least a small bulge around its equator. This bulge will cause slow changes in the orientation of the orbit of any object circling the oblate body. It will also cause the orbiter to pull asymmetrically on the oblate body and change its orientation in space. These slow changes in orientation are collectively referred to as precession. *See* PRECESSION OF EQUINOXES.

If a body of finite size is under the influence of another one, the parts closer to the perturber will feel a stronger pull and the parts farther away will feel a weaker pull. If the body is not infinitely rigid, this will result in a deformation known as tides. If it has a liquid or gaseous surface and is rotating, the tidal bulges will be carried at least part way around the body, but will reach a point at which the horizontal tidal forces compensate frictional drag and an equilibrium is reached. This drag will change the rotation rate of the body, at the same time releasing energy from the system, and the asymmetric bulge will perturb the orbit of the circling body to change its period and distance. The end result in one extreme is that the system will evolve until rotation and revolution rates are equal. Many planetary satellites are thus locked into synchronous rotation with their planets, and the Earth-Moon system is evolving to a time when both the day and the month will be equal to about 47 of our present days. However, solar tides will carry Earth rotation past the synchronous state, and the lunar distance will start to decrease again. Eventually the opposite extreme situation will arise, when the tidal forces on the Moon will exceed the cohesive ones and the Moon will break up. The limit on how closely a body can approach another one without breaking up is known as Roche's limit. Its exact value depends on the nature of the bodies involved, but it is usually around $2^{1}/_{2}$ times the radius of the larger body. *See* ROCHE LIMIT; SATURN; TIDE.

Unseen companions. The most complex situation is where there is a perturbation but no visible perturber. Unexplained variations can exist in observed orbits that can be due only to bodies not yet seen and therefore not yet modeled. Such was the case for Uranus after its discovery, and ultimately Neptune was discovered. Such is the case for both Uranus and Neptune, and while Pluto has been discovered, its mass is much too low to be responsible for the observed perturbations. A comparable situation can arise for a star, in which a wobble is seen in its motion across the sky, due to an unseen companion. Such detections have led to the discovery of many faint, substellar objects and may even result in the location of extrasolar planets. *See* ASTROMETRY; NEPTUNE.

Post-newtonian theories. The newtonian law of universal gravitation has been remarkably successful in explaining most astronomical dynamical phenomena. However, there have been some discrepancies, the most glaring being a small unexplainable motion in the perihelion of Mercury. For a time, a planet interior to Mercury ("Vulcan") was suspected, but the problem was resolved by Einstein's theory of general relativity. Philosophically, gravitation is quite different in the two theories, but the mathematical description of motion in general relativity shows that Newton's simple relationship is "almost" correct. The errors depend on such quantities as the square of the object's velocity compared to the square of the speed of light, which make them virtually undetectable for astronomical bodies (with the exception of Mercury). These effects are, however, easily detectable in spacecraft trajectories, and thus now have to be routinely considered. Post-Einstein theories of gravitation have also been proposed, but there is no observational support for them and thus no observational need to adopt a more complex theory. *See* GRAVITATION; RELATIVITY.   Robert S. Harrington

Bibliography. R. R. Bates, D. D. Mueller, and J. E. White, *Fundamentals of Astrodynamics*, 1971; J. M. Danby, *Fundamentals of Celestial Mechanics*, 1988; W. G. Hoyt, *Planets X and Pluto*, 1980; G. Marchal, *The Three-Body Problem*, 1990; V. Szebehely, *Adventures in Celestial Mechanics: A First Course in the Theory of Orbits*, 1989.

Celestial navigation

Navigation with the aid of celestial bodies, primarily for determination of position when landmarks are not available. In celestial navigation, position is not determined relative to the objects observed, as in navigation by piloting, but in relation to the points on the Earth having certain celestial bodies directly overhead.

Celestial bodies are also used for determination of horizontal direction on the Earth, and for regulating time, which is of primary importance in celestial navigation because of the changing positions of celestial bodies in the sky as the Earth rotates daily on its axis.

The navigator is concerned less with the actual motions of celestial bodies than with their apparent motions as viewed from the Earth. The heavens are pictured as a hollow celestial sphere of infinite radius, with the Earth as its center and the various celestial bodies on its inner surface. The navigator visualizes this sphere as rotating on its axis once in about 23 h 56 min—one sidereal day. The stars are then back where they were when the period started.

Bodies closer to the Earth appear to change position at a different rate than do those at a distance. The Sun appears to make a complete revolution among the stars once a year, as the Earth makes one revolution in its orbit. The apparent motion is along a great circle called the ecliptic, which is inclined nearly 23.5° to the plane of the Equator of the Earth. All of the planets stay within 8° of the ecliptic, in a band called the zodiac. Within this band they appear to move among the stars. The Moon, too, stays within the zodiac as it revolves around the Earth—or more properly as the Earth and Moon revolve around their common center of mass—once each lunar month. *See* EARTH ROTATION AND ORBITAL MOTION.

Body selection and identification. The navigator uses a limited number of celestial bodies—the Sun, Moon, 4 planets, and perhaps 20–30 stars. Although 173 stars are listed in the *Nautical Almanac*, and 57 of these are listed in the *Air Almanac* and on the daily pages of the *Nautical Almanac*, the majority of them are normally not used unless the navigator's favorite ones are unavailable. Some of the navigational stars are not seen at the latitudes traveled by many navigators. *See* ALMANAC.

With relatively few bodies in use and little change in star positions from one evening to the next, identification is seldom a problem. A tentative selection is often made in advance by means of some form of star finder. When set for the latitude of the observer and the time and date of observation, this device provides a graphical indication of the approximate altitude and azimuth of each star shown. The relative positions of other bodies can be plotted by the user. Star finders, tables, and star charts may be used to identify bodies observed before identification.

Celestial equator coordinate system. Several systems of coordinates are available to identify points on the celestial sphere. The celestial equator system of coordinates is an extension of the equatorial system commonly used on the Earth. The intersection of the plane of the terrestrial Equator, extended, with the celestial sphere is a great circle called the celestial equator. The Earth's axis, extended, intersects the celestial sphere at the north and south celestial poles. Small circles parallel to the celestial equator, similar to parallels of latitude on the Earth, are called parallels of declination. Each of these connects points of equal declination, the celestial coordinate similar to latitude on the Earth.

Great circles through the celestial poles, similar to meridians on the Earth, are called celestial meridians if they are considered to remain fixed in relation to terrestrial meridians, and hour circles if

considered to remain fixed on the rotating celestial sphere.

Several different quantities on the celestial sphere are analogous to those of longitude on the Earth. Greenwich hour angle is measured westward from the Greenwich celestial meridian, through 360°. Local hour angle is similarly measured from the celestial meridian of the observer. Meridian angle is measured eastward and westward from the local meridian, through 180°. Sidereal hour angle is measured westward from the hour circle of the veneral equinox, the point at which the Sun crosses the celestial equator on its northward travel in spring, through 360°. Right ascension is measured eastward from the hour circle of the vernal equinox, usually in hours, minutes, and seconds, from 0 through 24 h. The various relationships of the celestial equator system are shown in **Fig. 1**.

With the exception of right ascension, all of these quantities are customarily stated to a precision of one minute of arc by the air navigator, and to one-tenth of a minute of arc by the marine navigator. The celestial equator system is used in the almanacs for indicating positions of celestial bodies at various times. *See* ASTRONOMICAL COORDINATE SYSTEMS.

Horizon system of coordinates. The navigator also uses the horizon system of coordinates, which is similar to the celestial equator system. The primary great circle is the horizon of the observer. The pole vertically overhead is the zenith, and the opposite pole is the nadir. Small circles parallel to the horizon are called parallels of altitude, each connecting all points having the same altitude. Angular distance downward from the zenith is called zenith distance. Great circles through the zenith and nadir are vertical circles. The prime vertical circle passes through the east and west points of the horizon. Azimuth is measured clockwise around the horizon, from 000° (it is generally expressed in three figures)

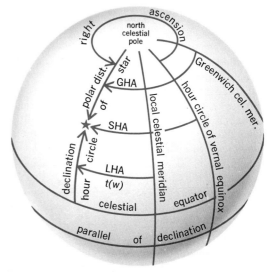

Fig. 1. Celestial equator system of coordinates. GHA is Greenwich hour angle, SHA is sidereal hour angle, LHA is local hour angle, and *t* is meridian angle (shown here as westerly).

at the north point, to 360°. Azimuth angle is measured eastward and westward to 180°, starting from north in the Northern Hemisphere, and from south in the Southern Hemisphere. Thus, it starts directly below the elevated pole, the celestial pole above the horizon. The relationships of the horizon system are shown in **Fig. 2**. The navigator uses the horizon system because it offers the most practical references for the origin of his or her measurements.

Altitude and zenith distance are customarily stated by the air navigator to a precision of one minute of arc, and azimuth and azimuth angle to a precision of one degree; the marine navigator states them to one-tenth of a minute and one-tenth of a degree, respectively.

Two similar systems based upon the ecliptic and the galactic equator are used by astronomers, but not by navigators.

Position determination. Position determination in celestial navigation is primarily a matter of converting one set of coordinates to the other. This is done by solution of a spherical triangle called the navigational triangle.

The concept of the spherical navigational triangle is graphically shown in **Fig. 3**, a diagram on the plane of the celestial meridian. The celestial meridian passes through the zenith of the observer, and is therefore a vertical circle of the horizon system. Elements of both systems are shown in Fig. 3, indicating that an approximate solution can be made graphically.

The vertices of the navigational triangle are the elevated pole (P_n), the zenith (Z), and the celestial body (M). The angles at the vertices are, respectively, the meridian angle (t), the azimuth angle (Z), and the parallactic angle (X). The sides of the triangle are the codeclination of the zenith or the colatitude (colat) of the observer, the coaltitude or zenith distance (z) of the body, and the codeclination or polar distance (p) of the body.

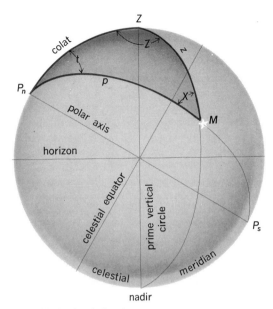

Fig. 3. Navigational triangle.

A navigational triangle is solved, usually by computation, and compared with an observed altitude to obtain a line of position by a procedure known as sight reduction.

Observed altitude. To establish a celestial line of position, the navigator observes the altitude of a celestial body, noting the time of observation. Observation is made by a sextant, so named because early instruments had an arc of one-sixth of a circle. By means of the double reflecting principle, the altitude of the body is double the amount of arc used. Similar instruments were called octants, quintants, and quadrants, depending upon the length of the arc. Today, all such instruments, regardless of length of the arc, are generally called sextants.

The marine sextant uses the visible horizon as the horizontal reference. An air sextant has an artificial, built-in horizontal reference based upon a bubble or occasionally a pendulum or gyroscope. The sextant altitude, however measured, is subject to certain errors, for which corrections are applied. *See* SEXTANT.

When a marine sextant is used, observations can be made only when both the horizon and one or more celestial bodies are visible. This requirement generally eliminates the period between the end of evening twilight and the beginning of morning twilight. The navigational stars and planets are therefore usually observable only during twilight. Air navigation is not subject to this limitation, star and planet observations being available all night.

In selecting bodies for observation, the navigator considers difference in azimuth, magnitude (brightness of the body), altitude (avoiding both extremes), and sometimes other factors. If speed is of particular concern, the navigator selects a body nearly ahead or astern to provide a speed line. A body near the ship's beam provides a course line.

Fig. 2. Horizon system of coordinates.

One north or south provides a latitude line, while one east or west provides a longitude line. One perpendicular to a shoreline provides an indication of distance offshore.

Many navigators prefer to observe three bodies differing in azimuth by about 120°, or four bodies differing by 90°, and preferably at about the same altitude. In this way any constant error in the altitudes is eliminated.

Sight reduction. The process of deriving from an observation the information needed for establishing a line of position is called sight reduction. A great variety of methods have been devised. That now in general use is called the Marcq St.-Hilaire method, after the French naval officer who proposed it in 1875, and is described as follows.

Having obtained the body's corrected sextant altitude, called the observed altitude, the navigator uses the almanac to obtain the Greenwich hour angle and declination of the body. The navigator converts the former to local hour angle or meridian angle for an assumed position in the vicinity of actual position. With these two quantities and the latitude of the assumed position, the navigator solves the navigational triangle for altitude and azimuth.

Each altitude of a given celestial body at any one instant defines a circle having the geographical position of the body (the point on the Earth at which the body is momentarily vertically overhead) as the center, and the zenith distance as the radius. The difference between the computed altitude for the assumed position and the observed altitude at the actual position of the observer, called the altitude difference or altitude intercept, is the difference in radii of the circles of equal altitude through the two positions.

This difference is measured along an azimuth line through the assumed position, each minute of altitude difference being considered one nautical mile. A perpendicular through the point so located is considered a part of the circle of equal altitude through the position of the observer. This is the line of position sought. The intersection of two or more nonparallel lines of position adjusted to a common time defines a fix (or running fix if the elapsed time between observations is more than a few minutes) locating the position of the observer at the time of observation. Although two lines of position are sufficient for a fix, most navigators prefer to observe three or more to provide a check and to decrease somewhat the probable error of the fix.

Sometimes, however, the navigational triangle is solved in reverse, starting with altitude, assumed latitude, and declination, and solving for meridian angle. This is then compared with Greenwich hour angle at the time of observation to determine the longitude at which the line of position crosses the assumed latitude. An American, Capt. Charles H. Sumner, used this method in his discovery in 1837 of the celestial line of position. Others used one point, found by this so-called time sight method, and the azimuth of the celestial body to establish a line of position.

Special short-cut methods have been used for a body observed on or near the celestial meridian and for Polaris. Since simple methods of sight reduction have become widely used, the popularity of such special methods has decreased.

A large number of methods have been devised for solution of the navigational triangle. The most widely accepted have been mathematical, but a great many graphical and mechanical solutions have been proposed. Many of these methods are discussed in U.S. Defense Mapping Agency Hydrographic Topographic Center Publication 9, *American Practical Navigator*, originally by N. Bowditch. Most American navigators and many of other nationalities now use one of two methods, both published by the U.S. Defense Mapping Agency Hydrographic Topographic Center. Publication 229, *Sight Reduction Tables for Marine and Air Navigation*, is intended for use with the *Nautical Almanac* for marine navigation and with the *Air Almanac* for air navigation. Editions of both of these sets of tables are also published in certain other countries.

With the emergence of electronic computers and hand-held calculators, sight reduction has been performed increasingly with limited use or elimination of tables. The extent to which a computer replaces tables depends upon the capability of the available computer and the preference of the navigator. The principal use of a nonprogrammable hand-held calculator is to perform simple arithmetical calculations such as addition, subtraction, and interpolation, with respect to both the almanac and slight reduction tables. If a programmable calculator with stored programs is available, the complete sight reduction process can be performed without the aid of tables, and if suitable data are available, even the ephemerides of celestial bodies can be computed, eliminating the need for an almanac in the usual form. An *Almanac for Computers*, providing the essential data, is published by the U.S. Naval Observatory. In the most sophisticated systems, a central computer combines sight reduction data with outputs of electronic positioning systems, perhaps including those associated with navigational satellites, and dead-reckoning data to provide continuous readout of the current most probable position. *See* CALCULATORS.

Time relationships. Time is repeatedly mentioned as an important element of a celestial observation because the Earth rotates at the approximate rate of 1 minute of arc each 4 s of time. An error of 1 s in the timing of an observation might introduce an error in the line of position of as much as one-quarter of a mile. Time directly affects longitude determination, but not latitude. The long search for a method of ascertaining longitude at sea was finally solved two centuries ago by the invention of the marine chronometer, a timepiece with a nearly steady rate.

Several different kinds of time are used by the navigator. A timepiece, which keeps watch time, usually has a small watch error. When this is applied to watch time, the result is usually zone time. This is familiar to most people as standard time (such as Pacific Standard Time) or, when clocks are set an hour ahead, as daylight saving time (such as Central Daylight Saving Time). At sea the zones may be set by each vessel or aircraft, but they are generally 15° wide, centered on the meridians exactly divisible by 15°.

When zone time is increased or decreased by 1 h per 15° longitude (the amount of the zone description, for example, +7 for Mountain Standard Time), Greenwich mean time is obtained. This is the time used in the almanacs.

Local mean time differs from zone time by the difference in longitude between the meridian of the observer and the zone meridian, at the rate of 4 min of time for each degree of longitude, the meridian to the eastward having the later time. Local mean time is used in tables indicating time of sunrise, sunset, moonrise, moonset, and beginning and ending of twilight.

All forms of mean time are based upon apparent motions of a fictitious mean sun which provides an essentially uniform time. Apparent time, based upon the apparent (visible) Sun, may differ from mean time by a maximum of nearly $16\frac{1}{2}$ min. Apparent time, plus or minus 12 h, indicates the actual position of the Sun with respect to the celestial meridian. At local apparent noon the Sun is on the celestial meridian, and the local apparent time is 1200. (Navigators customarily state time in four digits without punctuation, from 0000 at the start of a day to 2400 at the end of a day.)

Sidereal time, based upon motion of the stars, is used (indirectly in many cases) with a star finder or a star chart.

The custom of setting navigational timepieces to Greenwich mean time is growing, particularly among air navigators. This time is used almost invariably in polar regions.

Time signals are broadcast from a number of stations throughout the world to permit checking of standard timepieces. Marine chronometers are not reset by the user, an accurate record being kept of chronometer time, chronometer error, and chronometer rate. *See* TIME.

Day's work. A typical day's work of a marine navigator at sea, when using celestial navigation, is as follows:

1. Plot of dead reckoning.
2. Morning twilight observations for a fix.
3. Report of 0800 position to the commanding officer.
4. Morning sun line and compass check.
5. Winding of chronometers and determination of error and rate.
6. Noon sun line, advance of morning sun line for running fix, and report of 1200 position to the commanding officer.
7. Afternoon sun line and compass check.
8. Determination of time of sunset and preparation of a list of bodies available for observation during evening twilight.

9. Evening twilight observations for a fix.
10. Report of 2000 position to the commanding officer.
11. Determination of time of beginning of morning twilight, time of sunrise, and preparation of a list of bodies available for observation during morning twilight.
12. Time of moonrise and moonset.

Electronic applications, however, have gradually changed the pattern of celestial navigation in at least three important respects: (1) by providing noncelestial position information at sea, (2) by providing devices for automatic observation and sight reduction, and (3) by extending use of celestial navigation to all weather conditions at all times of day or night, by the use of electronic star trackers and of radio astronomy. *See* DEAD RECKONING; NAVIGATION; PILOTING; POLAR NAVIGATION; RADIO ASTRONOMY. Alton B Moody

Bibliography. E. S. Maloney, *Dutton's Navigation and Piloting*, 14th ed., 1985; W. B. Paulk, *Basic and Intermediate Celestial Navigation*, 1989; H. Schlereth, *Progressive Celestial Navigation*, 1994; U.S. Defense Mapping Agency Hydrographic Topographic Center, *American Practical Navigator*, (2 vols., Publ. 9), *Sight Reduction Tables for Marine and Air Navigation* (6 vols., Publ. 229), published periodically; U.S. Naval Observatory, *Air Almanac, Almanac for Computers*, and *Nautical Almanac*.

Celestial sphere

The imaginary sphere, on the inside surface of which the astronomical objects appear to be located. Its center is the center of the Earth. The sphere is so large in proportion to the size of the Earth that its center can be considered as the same point as the observer, wherever he or she may be on the Earth.

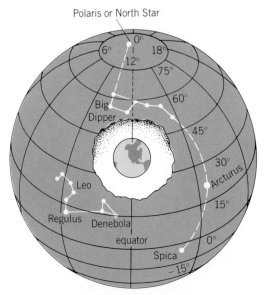

The celestial sphere and the Earth. (*After C. H. Cleminshaw, The Beginner's Guide to the Skies, T. Y. Crowell, 1977*)

A small section of the celestial sphere has been removed in the **illustration** to show the Earth at the center. The Earth's axis has been extended from the North Pole to intersect the celestial sphere in a point called the north celestial pole, which is only about 1° from Polaris, the North Star. Since the northern part of the Earth is tilted outward from the page in the illustration, the south poles of the Earth and the celestial sphere are not shown. *See* POLARIS.

Halfway between the north and south celestial poles is the celestial equator. Parallel to it are circles of declination. Declination is the angular distance north or south of the celestial equator, corresponding to latitude on the Earth.

Corresponding to the Earth's meridians, which run from pole to pole, are the hour circles on the celestial sphere. Similar to the way in which longitude is measured on Earth, right ascension is measured along the celestial equator in hours of time. *See* LATITUDE AND LONGITUDE.

The celestial sphere is always viewed from the inside, but the illustration and a celestial globe represent it as it would appear from the outside. Hence the constellations of the Big Dipper and Leo, which are shown in the illustration, appear backward from the way in which they look to an observer on the Earth. *See* ASTRONOMICAL COORDINATE SYSTEMS.   Clarence H. Cleminshaw

Celestite

A mineral with the chemical composition $SrSO_4$. Celestite occurs commonly in colorless to sky-blue, orthorhombic, tabular crystals. Fracture is

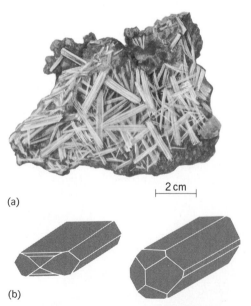

(a)

2 cm

(b)

Celestite. (*a*) Bladed crystals in limestone from Clay Center, Ohio (*specimen from Department of Geology, Bryn Mawr College*). (*b*) Crystal habits (*after C. S. Hurlbut, Jr., Dana's Manual of Mineralogy, 17th ed., John Wiley and Sons, Inc., 1959*).

uneven and luster is vitreous. Hardness is 3–3.5 on Mohs scale and specific gravity is 3.97. It fuses readily to a white pearl. It is only slowly soluble in hot concentrated acids or alkali carbonate solutions. The strontium present in celestite imparts a characteristic crimson color to the flame.

Celestite occurs in association with gypsum, anhydrite, salt beds, limestone, and dolomite. Large crystals are found in vugs or cavities of limestone (see **illus.**). It is deposited directly from seawater, by groundwater, or from hydrothermal solutions. Celestite is the major source of strontium. The principal use of strontium is in tracer bullets and in various red flares used by the armed forces. Minor applications of strontium compounds are in ceramics, depilatories, and medicine. Although celestite deposits occur in Arizona and California, domestic production of celestite has been small and sporadic. Much of the strontium demand is satisfied by imported ores from England and Mexico. *See* STRONTIUM.   Edward C. T. Chao

Cell (biology)

All organisms from the simplest bacterium to the most complex plant or animal are composed of cells. Bacteria, protozoa, some fungi, and some algae consist of a single cell and are called unicellular organisms. Some species of fungi and algae, and all plants and animals, are multicellular, containing from a few hundred to many trillions of cells. Groups of cells in a multicellular organism form tissues that are specialized for performance of various tasks, as in the case of skin, nerve, muscle, liver, and blood cells.

All cells are classified into two groups, prokaryotes and eukaryotes, on the basis of several characteristics. Prokaryotes are the bacteria; all other organisms (protozoa, fungi, algae, plants, and animals) consist of eukaryotic cells.

Prokaryotes. Tens of thousands of different species of bacteria occur in virtually every environment on Earth, ranging from soils to the oceans, to all bodies of fresh water, to the intestinal lumen of animals and the roots of plants. Some species of marine, soil, and fresh-water bacteria are photosynthetic, producing a large fraction of the atmospheric oxygen. Among these, the blue-green bacteria, or cyanobacteria, form a major group. *See* BACTERIA.

Prokaryotes are small cells, usually measuring a few micrometers in their longest dimension. Bacteria called mycoplasmas are the smallest cells known; some are only a few tenths of a micrometer in diameter. Most bacteria are enclosed by a tough cell wall (**Fig. 1**) that protects the cell from mechanical injury and from osmotic pressure. The wall is made of protein and polysaccharide molecules secreted by the bacterial cell. The bacteria of the mycoplasma group lack a cell wall. *See* MYCOPLASMAS.

Like eukaryotic cells, prokaryotic cells are

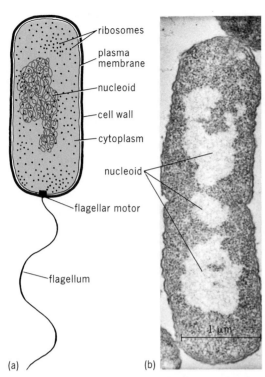

Fig. 1. Bacterial cell. (*a*) Diagram showing the structures that can be seen by electron microscopy. (*b*) Electron micrograph of a section cut through a bacterial cell. The lighter area is the irregularly shaped nucleoid. The rest of the cell is filled with ribosomes. This cell was about to divide, as indicated by the slight crimping in the surface at the middle of the cell. (*Courtesy of N. Nanninga*)

enclosed by a plasma membrane made of a double layer of lipid molecules and various proteins. The plasma membrane governs the movement of ions and molecules into and out of the cell. Some of the proteins in the plasma membrane work as transport systems that pump useful molecules, such as sugars and amino acids, into the cell. Other proteins in the plasma membrane are enzymes that break down sugars and other organic molecules to obtain energy to drive all the processes of the cell. Two structural compartments, the cytoplasm and the nucleoid, are clearly recognizable inside the plasma membrane. The cytoplasm consists of a solution of many kinds of ions, enzymes, and other oganic molecules that carry out most cell metabolism. Within this solution are thousands of ribonucleic acid (RNA)–protein particles, called ribosomes, each of which is a factory for the synthesis of proteins. The nucleoid consists of the single chromosome of deoxyribonucleic acid (DNA) in the bacterial cell. By contrast, eukaryotic cells usually contain many chromosomes, and these are separated from the cytoplasm by a membranous envelope, giving rise to a well-defined nucleus. The absence of a nuclear envelope in bacteria is the origin of the name prokaryote (before a nucleus). *See* CELL MEMBRANES; CELL PERMEABILITY.

The single chromosome in a prokaryotic cell, containing a single, long DNA molecule, encodes all the genes needed for the metabolism, self-maintenance, growth, cell division, and other activities of the cell. The DNA molecule is a closed loop that is extensively folded and compacted into a nucleoid by proteins that attach to it. In the reproduction of a bacterial cell the DNA in the nucleoid replicates, producing two identical DNA molecules. The DNA molecules form two daughter nucleoids that move to different sides or ends of the cell; then division of the cell into two daughter cells occurs by formation of a septum across the cell between the two daughter nucleoids. *See* CELL DIVISION; CHROMOSOME; DEOXYRIBONUCLEIC ACID (DNA); GENE.

Prokaryotes lack the many membranous organelles that are present in the cytoplasm of all eukaryotic cell species. Although prokaryotes are structurally simple, they are biochemically complex. Many species possess the anabolic pathways for synthesis of all 20 of the biologically important amino acids, as well as nucleotides, vitamins, fatty acids, and other biomolecules needed for cell metabolism and growth. Prokaryotic cells can reproduce much faster than eukaryotic cells. The bacterium *Escherichia coli*, which inhabits the large intestine of mammals, doubles its size and divides into two daughter cells every 20 min in a rich, nutrient culture medium. At this rate a single bacterial cell can give rise to over 1.7×10^{10} cells in 12 h. *See* BACTERIAL GROWTH; BACTERIAL PHYSIOLOGY AND METABOLISM.

Some species of bacteria possess one or more flagella by which they can swim rapidly. A flagellum (Fig. 1) consists of a long string of protein molecules arranged to produce a thread with a permanent helical twist. The flagellum is rotated on its long axis by a molecular motor just inside the cell surface; because of its helical twist the flagellum acts as a corkscrew-shaped propeller. By means of sensory receptors that influence operation of the flagellum, bacterial cells can move toward higher concentrations of certain useful nutrients and away from toxic chemicals in their microenvironment. *See* CILIA AND FLAGELLA; PROKARYOTAE.

Eukaryotes. Eukaryotic organisms form a much larger group of species than prokaryotes; some eukaryotes are unicellular (protozoa, some algae, and some fungi) and some are multicellular (some algae, some fungi, plants, and animals). Eukaryotic cells are larger than prokaryotic cells, usually measuring several to many micrometers in diameter. Among the smallest are yeast cells, and among the largest are giant algal cells that reach lengths of several centimeters. Most cells in an animal such as a human measure 10–20 micrometers in diameter. In addition to a nucleus, eukaryotic cells possess numerous organelles and structures that are not present in prokaryotic cells (**Fig. 2**). *See* EUKARYOTAE.

Nucleus. In contrast to prokaryotes, eukaryotic cells possess an envelope that surrounds the chromosomes, separating them from the cytoplasm and forming a well-defined nucleus (Fig. 2). Eukaryotic

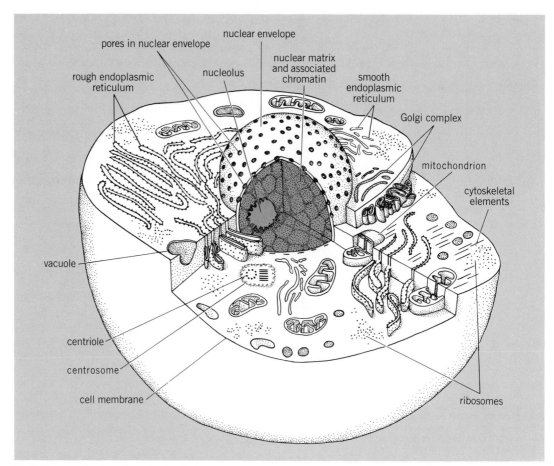

Fig. 2. Cutaway drawing of an animal cell showing the major structures and organelles as seen with an electron microscope. (*After G. Karp, Cell Biology, 2d ed., McGraw-Hill, 1984*)

cells possess several chromosomes, usually many; the DNA molecule in each chromosome carries a large group of genes. The nuclear envelope is composed of two closely apposed membranes. At many places the two membranes fuse to form tiny circular openings, called nuclear pores, through which molecules and ions can pass between the nucleus and cytoplasm. For example, almost all RNA is synthesized in the nucleus, from which it passes into the cytoplasm to function in protein synthesis. Except during cell division, the chromosomes do not appear as distinct individual structures, but rather as a dense network of fibers called chromatin that fills the nucleus. Parts of chromosomes and occasionally whole chromosomes are more tightly packed, forming darkly staining material in the nucleus called heterochromatin. The more loosely organized chromosomes stain less densely and are known as euchromatin. The nucleus typically contains one to several nucleoli, which are distinct, roughly spherical bodies. Nucleoli are sites of synthesis of ribosomal RNA and assembly of ribosomal RNA and proteins. The ribosomes migrate from the nucleolus through nuclear pores into the cytoplasm. *See* CELL NUCLEUS.

Cytoplasm. Eukaryotic cells, like prokaryotic cells, possess a plasma membrane, which envelopes the cell. Similarly, the cytoplasm of eukaryotic cells is a solution of ions and biomolecules called the cytosol, containing a large number of ribosomes, on which protein synthesis takes place. In contrast to prokaryotes, the cytoplasm of a eukaryotic cell also has a variety of structures and membranous organelles not found in prokaryotes. Among these are mitochondria, chloroplasts (in algal and plant cells), lysosomes, Golgi membranes, an endoplasmic reticulum, peroxisomes, a centrosome, and a cytoskeleton. *See* CENTROSOME; CYTOPLASM.

Mitochondria. Because of their role in generating a useful form of chemical energy, mitochondria are called the powerhouses of the cell. Mitochondria are oval or elongated vesicles, usually measuring a few micrometers in diameter and a few to many micrometers in length. Usually, many mitochondria are present in a cell, sometimes several thousand, as in a cell of the liver or an ameba. A mitochondrion is enclosed by a double membrane. The inner membrane has many folds, called cristae, that extend into the mitochondrion. Enzymes in the space enclosed by the inner membrane, the matrix space, work cooperatively with other enzymes anchored in the cristae of the inner membrane to transfer electrons from carbohydrates and fats to oxygen, yielding in the process carbon dioxide and water. In the transfer of electrons, chemical energy is obtained in the form of adenosinetriphosphate (ATP), which is used to fuel all of the energy-requiring activities in the cell. *See* ADENOSINETRIPHOSPHATE (ATP).

Mitochondria also contain several copies of a small, circular DNA molecule, which encodes several of the proteins and RNA molecules needed for mitochondrial function. Most mitochondrial proteins are encoded by nuclear genes and are synthesized by ribosomes in the cytoplasm, from where they are imported into mitochondria. Mitochondria grow and divide by simple binary fission coordinately with the growth of the cell. *See* MITOCHONDRIA.

Chloroplasts. Chloroplasts, found in the cytoplasm of algal and plant cells, carry out photosynthesis. A chloroplast usually has an ovoid shape and is a few micrometers in diameter, although some algal cells have a single giant chloroplast. Like a mitochondrion, a chloroplast is enclosed by a double membrane but without cristae on the inner membrane. The internal compartment enclosed by the double membrane, the stromal space, contains several identical circular DNA molecules. They encode many of the proteins needed for chloroplast structure and function, although many more are encoded by nuclear genes. The stromal compartment also contains an internal set of membranes called thylakoids. Chlorophyll and other pigments embedded in the thylakoid membranes absorb energy of light (photons), which is used by enzymes also embedded in the thylakoids, working together with enzymes in the inner space of the chloroplast, to produce sugar molecules. Chloroplasts produce oxygen as a by-product of photosynthesis. *See* CELL PLASTIDS; PHOTOSYNTHESIS.

Endoplasmic reticulum. The endoplasmic reticulum is an extensive set of membranes found in the cytoplasm of all eukaryotic cell species. Usually the membranes of the endoplasmic reticulum occur as flattened sacs enclosing a narrow space called the cisterna, although in some unicellular organisms the endoplasmic reticulum consists of roughly spherical, membrane-bound vesicles. Membranes of the endoplasmic reticulum occasionally connect with the outer membrane of the nuclear envelope, which is considered to be part of the endoplasmic reticulum. Some parts of the endoplasmic reticulum have large numbers of ribosomes attached to the cytoplasmic faces of its membranes. An endoplasmic reticulum studded with ribosomes is called a rough endoplasmic reticulum, distinguishing it from a smooth endoplasmic reticulum, without ribosomes. The smooth endoplasmic reticulum has several functions. It contains enzymes that catalyze the synthesis of lipids, and possesses other enzymes called oxidases that break down drugs and toxic substances that may enter cells. This is particularly a major function of the smooth endoplasmic reticulum in liver cells. Ribosomes of the rough endoplasmic reticulum synthesize proteins that are destined for delivery to certain other organelles in the cell or for secretion from the cell. These proteins are transferred into the cisternae of the rough endoplasmic reticulum. In the cisternae, sugars are added to the protein molecules, a process called glycosylation. Within the rough endoplasmic reticulum the glycosylated proteins collect into membrane-bound vesicles that bud off from it and travel to and fuse with the Golgi complex. *See* ENDOPLASMIC RETICULUM.

Golgi complex. The Golgi complex consists of a discrete stack of flattened membrane sacs, distinct from the endoplasmic reticulum. Protein-laden vesicles arriving from the rough endoplasmic reticulum fuse with membranes of the Golgi complex, releasing the proteins into the spaces enclosed by the membranes. In the Golgi complex, some sugars are removed from the proteins, new ones are added, and phosphate groups are added to some of the proteins. Finally, the proteins are sorted, concentrated, and packaged in vesicles for transport to lysosomes in the cytoplasm or to the cell surface. At the cell surface the membrane of the vesicle fuses with the plasma membrane, resulting in the opening of the vesicle to the outer surface of the cell and the releasing of its cargo of protein molecules. The latter activity is very prominent in pancreas cells, which produce and release digestive enzymes (which are proteins) that are carried by a duct to the small intestine, where they have a major role in digestion of food. *See* GOLGI APPARATUS.

Lysosomes. Lysosomes are spherical vesicles, usually measuring about a micrometer in diameter, that contain a large variety of digestive enzymes in an inactive state. Lysosomes fuse with vesicles formed by a cell when it ingests particles such as bacteria, or food organisms in the case of protozoa, a process called phagocytosis. Fusion activates and releases the digestive enzymes into the phagocytosis vesicle, forming a secondary lysosome. Ingested bacteria or food organisms are digested by the lysosomal enzymes. Lysosomes also serve as so-called suicide bags, releasing activated enzymes into a cell that has died and digesting the cell's contents, a process called autolysis. *See* LYSOSOME; PHAGOCYTOSIS.

Peroxisomes. Peroxisomes are small, inconspicuous cytoplasmic vesicles that contain enzymes that catalyze oxidation of certain kinds of organic molecules. During oxidation, peroxisomes produce hydrogen peroxide, hence the name peroxisomes. Peroxisomes contain the enzyme catalase, which catalyzes the conversion of hydrogen peroxide, which is toxic, into water and molecular oxygen. In plants, peroxisomes have additional functions and are called glyoxysomes.

Cytoskeleton. Within the membranous structures just described, the cytoplasm of eukaryotic cells contains a cytoskeleton made up of two and sometimes three kinds of filamentous elements. One of these elements is the microtubules, which are present in all eukaryotic cells and absent in all prokaryotes. Microtubules are hollow cylinders measuring 30 nanometers in outside diameter and ranging up to many micrometers in length. They are formed by aggregation of many thousands of identical protein subunits called tubulin. Microtubules form and disassemble continuously during the constant remodeling of the cytoskeleton in cells that change shape. The assembly of a microtubule begins in the centrosome, an ill-defined, spherical structure that usually occupies a position next to the nuclear envelope. Growth of a microtubule occurs by addition of tubulin subunits to the microtubule end projecting from the centrosome. During mitosis the microtubules are disassembled and then reassembled by centrosomes into the spindle-shaped mitotic apparatus, which functions in the distribution of chromosomes to daughter cells. In the interphase cell, microtubules serve as tracks along which cytoplasmic vesicles and particles rapidly migrate. Microtubules also form the structural core of cilia and flagella, where they do not undergo disassembly.

Microfilaments are the second filamentous element of the cytoskeleton. These are rodlike structures about 9 nm in diameter and of variable length. Microfilaments are composed of the protin actin; like microtubules, they continuously assemble and disassemble. They grow by addition of actin molecules to one or both ends. Usually they occur in bundles or networks. Bundles can be seen by light microscopy using special staining methods, and are called stress fibers. In networks, microfilaments are arranged in three-dimensional orthogonal arrays. A variety of proteins interact with microfilaments to regulate their assembly and disassembly and to cross-link them into bundles and networks. Microfilaments interact with yet other proteins to bring about the contraction that underlies ameboid cell movement. Actin-based movement is present in eukaryotic cells generally, but is particularly prominent in muscle cells. In protozoa and animal cells that are undergoing cell division, actin forms a ring around the equator of the cell just inside the plasma membrane that contracts to pinch the cell into two daughter cells. See CELL MOTILITY; MUSCLE PROTEINS.

The third filamentous element of the cytoskeleton comprises intermediate filaments. There are five classes of intermediate filaments, which are distinguished by their diameters (7–12 nm) and by their different protein compositions. They occur in animal cells especially. Unlike microtubules and microfilaments, they do not undergo turnover but remain as stable rods. Intermediate filaments provide great mechanical strength to various epithelial cell layers. In skin cells they are composed of keratin and give the skin its toughness. See CYTOSKELETON.

Cell maintenance and function. The maintenance and function of a cell depend on interactions with the environment. Cells gain nutrients, energy, and raw materials from their surroundings and release by-products, waste products, and other secreted materials. The plasma membrane mediates uptake and excretion from a cell by using several mechanisms. A few materials, such as water, oxygen, and carbon dioxide, diffuse across the plasma membrane at rates sufficient to meet cell needs. The uptake of molecules and ions by cells is called endocytosis. Endocytosis of many molecules, for example, sugars, amino acids, and several kinds of inorganic ions, is mediated by proteins that span the lipid bilayer of the membrane. In some cases the uptake of materials driven by a concentration difference is simply facilitated by membrane proteins. Other membrane proteins work as pumps to take in or excrete molecules and ions. These are energy-requiring processes known collectively as active transport. High-molecular-weight substances, for example, proteins, may be taken up by pinocytosis. Pinocytosis is a drinking process in which the cell encloses tiny amounts of fluid by an infolding of the plasma membrane to form a vesicle that is internalized in the cell. A special form of pinocytosis called receptor-mediated endocytosis is induced by binding of viruses and particles to specific receptors on the cell surface. Low-density lipoprotein particles, each of which carries thousands of cholesterol molecules, and the acquired immune deficiency syndrome (AIDS) virus gain entry into cells by receptor-mediated endocytosis. Many kinds of cells ingest larger particulate materials by phagocytosis, such as many kinds of protozoa which ingest food organisms, and specialized lymphocytes which ingest bacteria. See ENDOCYTOSIS.

The release of substances from a cell is called exocytosis. Certain types of viruses are released from cells by budding from the cell surface. Many cells release proteins into their surroundings by fusion of protein-containing vesicles with the plasma membrane. A prominent form of this is the release of massive amounts of digestive enzymes (proteins) from cells of the pancreas for delivery by a duct to the intestinal lumen, where the enzymes are required for food digestion.

Many kinds of cells, particularly in animal tissues, possess receptors on their surfaces that are specific binding sites for various hormone molecules. Binding of hormone molecules by membrane proteins creates a signal that is transmitted across the membrane into the cell, where it may profoundly affect cell activities. Finally, glycoproteins at the cell surface serve to guide the migration of cells and to bind cells into specific groups to form tissues.

Nutrients, energy, and raw materials obtained from the environment are used by cells to maintain their structural and functional capacities. Proteins, nucleic acids, and other molecules are continuously damaged by the intense thermal motions of ions and molecules in the cell. Much cellular synthetic activity is devoted to replacing damaged components in the cell.

Cell reproduction. In general, the most important function of prokaryotic and eukaryotic cells is reproduction. Ultimately, the survival and success of every species depends on the ability of its cells to reproduce. Cell reproduction consists of cell growth, chromosome replication, and physical division of the cell into two daughters.

The events of cell reproduction occur as a cycle, the cell cycle, that repeats itself each time a cell divides. A new daughter cell grows by doubling all of its structures, components, and functional capacities during interphase, the period between cell divisions. Also, in interphase the chromosomes replicate so that each daughter cell can receive a copy of every chromosome at the subsequent cell division. See CELL CYCLE.

The central event of chromosome replication is the replication of the genetic material, the DNA. With the completion of cell growth and DNA replication, the cell initiates prophase of cell division, the condensation of its chromosomes into compact bodies, each of which is composed of two identical, thick rods (chromatids). As the chromosomes condense, the nuclear envelope disintegrates. Next, the fully condensed chromosomes align in the central plane of the cell in a stage called metaphase. The two identical chromatids in each chromosome separate to become two daughter chromosomes, which migrate during the ensuing anaphase to opposite sides of the cell. The two groups of daughter chromosomes begin to decondense in telophase, losing their distinct rod-shaped form. A nuclear envelope forms around each group, creating two daughter nuclei. The cytoplasm divides by pinching in two between the new daughter nuclei (protozoan and animal cells) or by formation of a septum (fungal, algal, and plant cells) to create two new daughter cells, each of which then repeats the cell cycle. Typically, animal cells complete the entire process of cell division in an hour or less. The period between division lasts many hours.

Among unicellular organisms, each cell cycle increases the population of organisms. In multicellular organisms, cell reproduction provides the cells for formation of the organism. Multicellular organisms begin as a single cell, the fertilized ovum (egg cell), that repeats the cell cycle to create first a multicellular embryo and subsequently an adult organism. In humans, cell reproduction, starting with the fertilized ovum, ultimately produces an adult composed of more than 100 trillion cells. The cells in a developing organism differentiate into various types (skin, liver, kidney, muscle, and so forth) specialized to carry out different kinds of work. In the various tissues of an adult human, a total of more than 10 million cells dies each second and is replaced by completion of 10 million cell divisions per second. Reproduction of cells in a multicellular organism is precisely regulated. Cancer begins as a mutation in a single cell that causes the loss of regulation, resulting in overproduction of cells. A single cancer cell that reproduces every 24 h can produce a cancer mass of 5 kg (11 lb) in 6 weeks; few kinds of cancer cells reproduce that rapidly. See CELL DIFFERENTIATION; MEIOSIS; MITOSIS.

Cell culture. Cells taken from various tissues of multicellular plants and animals and maintained in cultures are commonly used to analyze cell reproduction, cell differentiation, and other functions under easily controlled conditions. Cell culture is now one of the main tools in the study not only of normal cell behavior but also of cell behavior in many human diseases, particularly cancer. It is possible to create cancer cells from normal cells in culture by using radiation, chemicals, or viruses as cancer-causing agents. See CANCER (MEDICINE); CELL BIOLOGY; CELL ORGANIZATION; PLANT CELL; TISSUE CULTURE.
David M. Prescott

Bibliography. W. M. Becker, *The World of the Cell*, 2d ed., 1991; G. Karp, *Cell Biology,* 2d ed., 1984; L. J. Kleinsmith and V. M. Kish, *Principles of Cell and Molecular Biology*, 2d ed., 1994; D. M. Prescott, *Cells: Principles of Molecular Structure and Function*, 1988.

Cell, spectral analysis of

Living cells contain various substances, the concentrations and biological activity of which can be investigated by observing the spectrum of light passed through the cells. Such investigations take advantage of the fact that many substances absorb light in an individually characteristic manner. Thus, the spectrum of light passed through a green leaf has two black bands where red and blue light should appear. The absorption of red and blue light is characteristic of the chlorophylls, the photosynthetic pigments. Today, investigations of cells by optical methods go far beyond the routine analysis of brightly colored pigments that are found widespread and in high concentration, for example, hemoglobin and chlorophyll. Such methods allow the investigation of light-absorbing molecules within the cell whose concentration is 1000 times smaller that that of hemoglobin or of chlorophyll. See CHLOROPHYLL; HEMOGLOBIN.

Because the color of biological molecules changes when they undergo chemical reactions, such reactions in the cell can be monitored by spectral analyses. These analyses can be used to monitor reactions occurring in times ranging from 10^{-15} s to minutes. In some cases, the spectral properties can also indicate the environment of the biological molecules in the cell, that is, whether they are rigidly held or free to move and how they react with one another within the cell.

Useful kinds of spectra. Different parts of the spectrum provide different information about molecules in cells.

Infrared spectra (700–5000 nanometers) give information about the structure of molecules; all molecules absorb in the infrared in a characteristic manner.

Visible light spectra (400–700 nm) give information concerning those relatively few biological molecules that absorb light in this region. These molecules thus can be specifically studied in a cell that may contain tens of thousands of other types of molecules.

Ultraviolet spectra (200–400 nm) give information on those molecules that absorb light in this region. Such spectra are not very useful when working with living cells or other light-scattering samples.

Fluorescence and phosphorescence spectra are produced by light emission. When some molecules absorb light in the ultraviolet and visible spectral regions, they can be energized into various electronic excited states. In many instances, the energy of the excited states is dissipated rapidly as heat, and the molecule returns to its original ground state. However, the appropriate excited state can also be dissipated relatively slowly by emitting light at wavelengths slightly longer than that of the excitation light. The emitted light can take one of two forms: fluorescence, which occurs rapidly after excitation and lasts 10^{-9} to 10^{-6} s; and phosphorescence, which has a longer decay time and wavelength range than fluorescence and lasts on the order of 10^{-6} to 10^{2} s. Relatively few molecules emit light after absorption.

Light scattering is of two types. When light is scattered without changing wavelength (elastic scattering), the scattering reveals the size and shape of molecules. Another type of scattering is called Raman scattering. In this case, molecules alter the light by slightly shifting the wavelength in a manner that is very specific for the particular molecule. *See* RAMAN EFFECT; SCATTERING OF ELECTROMAGNETIC RADIATION.

Magnetic resonance spectroscopy techniques frequently can resolve components of cells that cannot be visualized by optical methods. *See* ELECTROMAGNETIC RADIATION; MAGNETIC RESONANCE.

Intracellular substances. Spectral analysis by optical methods is limited to those substances which show characteristic peaks, or maxima, of absorption when light absorption is plotted as a function of light wavelength. Whether or not a given substance can be detected depends on the intensity of absorption relative to other substances present at a given absorption maximum. The molecular extinction coefficient quantitatively describes the light absorption of a given substance at a given wavelength. The dependence of absorption A on extinction coefficient ϵ, concentration c, and optical path l is expressed as Beer's law, $A = 10 \exp(-\epsilon \cdot C \cdot l)$. This dependence imposes limitations on the application of optical methods to the study of living cells; only those substances with a high extinction coefficient can be investigated successfully.

Hemoproteins. There are a variety of substances present within living cells, but the number of those of biological interest which also possess a useful extinction coefficient is limited; often these substances are pigments. A large group of biologically interesting pigments belongs to the class known as hemoproteins. Included in this group are the hemoglobins, myoglobins, catalase, peroxidase, and the cytochromes, a large family of hemoproteins that are universally present in all cells. Reduced hemoproteins are characterized by well-defined absorption maxima in the visible spectrum, while the spectra of oxidized hemoproteins are quite different. The absorption spectrum of each hemoprotein is characteristic and individual to that hemoprotein only, a property that gives a considerable degree of specificity to the optical study of these components in cells. Among the hemoproteins, the cytochromes are of particular interest because of the intimate role they play in various processes, for example, in cellular respiration and in photosynthesis. From the cytochrome spectra obtained from an investigation of cells, the ratio of oxidized to reduced forms (the oxidation state) can be determined. The oxidation state of the cytochromes, in turn, depends on the conditions under which the cell is placed. Given any steady-state condition, the oxidation state of each cytochrome component in the cell will reach a definite value, a value which can be determined by spectral analysis. *See* CYTOCHROME.

Flavoproteins and pyridine nucleotides. Other substances of biological interest that are found in cells and that can be studied optically include flavoproteins, a family of proteins that occur abundantly in nature, and the pyridine nucleotides. As in the hemoproteins, the spectral properties of flavoproteins and pyridine nucleotides depend on their oxidation state. Flavoproteins in their oxidized state absorb light in the yellow portion of the visible spectrum and fluoresce strongly in the green; light absorption and fluorescence is quenched when these proteins are reduced. Reduced pyridine nucleotides, NADH and NADPH, show strong light absorption in the blue portion of the spectrum and also fluoresce strongly at longer wavelengths, also in the blue. In the oxidized forms NAD^+ and $NADP^+$, the molecules do not absorb light or fluoresce. Because of the strong fluorescence, it is often most convenient to study these components by fluorescent techniques.

Iron-sulfur clusters. There is a large group of proteins, the iron-sulfur proteins, which are of considerable biological importance. These substances, referred to individually as iron-sulfur clusters, do not have the properties that can be characterized by optical spectroscopy. However, they can be studied in considerable detail by magnetic resonance spectroscopy, a technique where the spectrum involves magnetic fields and light in the microwave spectral region. This technique is also used to study the position of protein complexes relative to one another in biological membranes.

Subcellular structures. The living cell is a highly organized biological unit. Within the cell there are a variety of structures, each one of which carries out specific functions. The necessary interactions between the subcellular structures that must provide for the normal processes of cell functions and metabolism are not yet well understood. Examples of the well-organized subcellular structures are the mitochondria, where the respiratory processes of the cell are localized, microsomes, peroxisomes, and chloroplasts. In many instances, the study of suspensions of cells, for example, yeast and algal cells, has been reasonably fruitful. However, because of light-scattering problems and the limited numbers of single cells available, it is extraordinarily difficult to study specific processes within a single cell. Rather, it has proven much more profitable to investigate suspensions of subcellular organelles which can be isolated in a reasonably undamaged state, for example, mitochondria and chloroplasts. Such suspensions, prepared by destroying the cell structure, contain a variety of substances suitable for optical, fluorescent, and magnetic resonance analysis and in sufficient concentration to allow precise and quantitative study. Suspensions of mitochondria and chloroplasts have been used extensively in the development of the understanding of cellular respiration and of photosynthesis. *See* CELL (BIOLOGY); CELL PLASTIDS; MITOCHONDRIA.

It is characteristic of biological processes that various proteins, enzymes, and coenzymes react with one another in cycles or sequences. In the processes of cellular respiration, there is a sequence of reactions which involve pyridine nucleotides, flavoproteins, iron-sulfur clusters, and cytochromes in processes involving energy transfer and oxygen consumption. Similarly, photosynthesis involves chlorophylls and accessory pigments, cytochromes, pyridine-nucleotides, and iron-sulfur clusters. It is particularly important to discover which components are included in various biological processes and the order in which they react with one another; spectral analysis provides the methods for such investigations.

Methods. Any spectral analysis, regardless of its application, utilizes the components in **Fig. 1.** These components consist of a light source from which the light is focused by means of a lens on a narrow slit. The narrow beam of light is then resolved into its component wavelengths by means of a prism or a grating. Lasers have been used as a source of monochromatic light. A narrow band of such light is isolated by means of a second narrow slit and passes through the sample onto an appropriate detector. The signal produced on activation of the detector may be amplified and displayed or recorded on a suitable device. Instruments for measuring light absorption at varying wavelengths utilize the above basic components and are suitable for the study of clear solutions—solutions that do not impose any restrictions, other than those of Beer's law, on the amount of light passing through them. *See* SPECTROPHOTOMETRIC ANALYSIS.

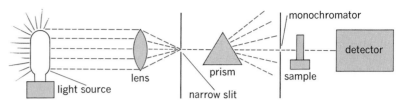

Fig. 1. Basic components used for spectral analysis.

The spectral analysis of living cells and of subcellular organelles is complicated because some suspensions of particulate matter scatter light and thus limit the amount of light that can pass through them. Suspensions of biological material scatter light by refraction and reflection, and the problem is intensified by changes in the state of the particulate matter in the suspension—such as changes of size with time: swelling and shrinking. Problems of light scattering are magnified by monochromatic light, where high light intensities are difficult to obtain. The most important problem is the

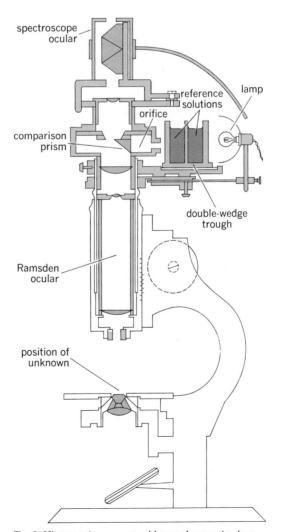

Fig. 2. Microspectroscope used by an observer to view the spectra of the specimen and reference solution simultaneously. (*After D. Keilin and Y. L. Wang, Haemoglobin of Gastrophilus larvae, Biochem. J. 40(5,6):855–866, 1946*)

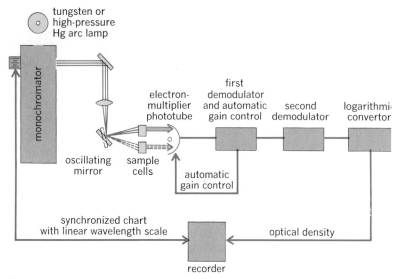

Fig. 3. Split-beam recording spectrophotometer.

impossibility of observing spectra of specific light-absorbing species. Problems of light scattering can be avoided in various ways, for example, by using a low-dispersion spectroscope or a dual-wavelength spectrophotometer.

Microspectroscope. Much of early understanding of blood and muscle pigments and of cellular respiration was obtained through the use of the microspectroscope (**Fig. 2**). Basically, this instrument is a hand spectroscope that uses the human eye as the detector. Within a narrow but biologically interesting spectral region, the human eye is capable of sharp delineation between light and dark; hence, absorption bands can be observed with a considerable degree of accuracy. This

instrument is now regarded as a museum piece, but many investigators still find that it is useful for quick observations.

Spectrophotometers. Special photoelectric devices have almost completely replaced visual spectroscopy for examination of light-scattering samples.

The split-beam spectrophotometer measures the difference in absorption between two nearly identical biological suspensions. Monochromatic light is passed alternately through the two samples by means of a vibrating mirror and onto a light detector. If the suspensions under study are identical except for their oxidation state, light scattering will be the same in both, and the light detector will measure only the difference in light adsorption between the two samples. The result is an oxidized-minus-reduced difference spectrum and will give the absorption maxima between the reduced and oxidized redox components present in the sample. Such a spectrophotometer is capable of scanning difference spectra in the visible and near-ultraviolet regions (**Fig. 3**).

The dual-wavelength spectrophotometer uses two sources of monochromatic light that are passed through a single light-scattering sample, again by means of a vibrating mirror. If one light beam is set at a known absorption maximum and the other at wavelength where there is no absorption change between the oxidized and reduced species, the photoelectric circuit will measure the true absorption difference between these two wavelengths and will reject almost completely changes of light transmission that are independent of wavelength. With such a device, one can measure rates of oxidation or reduction of redox components. As with the split-beam spectrophotometer, difference spectra of redox components of biological samples can be scanned.

Temperature studies. The light-absorbing properties of many pigments important to the economy of living cells are altered at low temperatures. Not only is there a marked sharpening of the absorption bands at low temperature, but also a considerably increased absorbancy because of increased path length due to reflections from interfaces on the ice surfaces. Thus, the use of low temperatures, 77 K and below, increases the sensitivity and specificity of detection. The effects of low temperature are illustrated in **Fig. 4** in a suspension of yeast cells, measured at 77°F (25°C) and at 77 K (−196°C). Different path lengths were used at each temperature; hence, the increased absorbancy at low temperature is not shown. The 77 K spectrum clearly shows the sharp delineation of absorbing components that can be realized at that temperature. Note that there is a shift of absorption maxima toward shorter wavelengths at 77 K.

Microspectrophotometer. Spectrophotometers, utilizing the principles discussed above but including a microscope for the localization of the object under

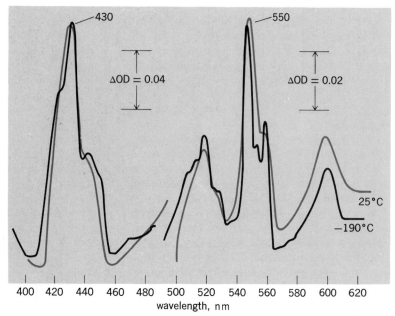

Fig. 4. Spectra, by difference, of the pigments present in suspensions of yeast cells. These spectra show the changes in absorbency plotted as a function of wavelength. △OD is optical density increment.

study, have also been developed. Such microspectrophotometers are capable of carrying out spectral analyses within the dimensions of a single cell.

Ultraviolet studies. Such studies are difficult to carry out with intact cells and tissues, light-scattering problems increase with decreasing wavelengths, and there are too many substances with low extinction coefficients and overlapping absorbancies in this spectral region. Pertinent information is most easily obtained by using clear extracts of cells and tissues. Extracts can be prepared that contain nucleic acids, amino acids, various metabolites, and quinones, for example, the ubiquinones.

Infrared studies and Raman spectra. Both of these reflect the vibrational structure of the molecule. Water absorbs in the infrared region, so most infrared studies are done on concentrated solutions in order to increase the signal over that of water. Infrared studies are particularly useful for monitoring protein conformation and the structure of lipids in membranes. Raman spectra are relatively weak, but very useful for studying the heme proteins, where they can help determine the structure of the heme.

Fluorescence and phosphorescence. Fluorescence is widely used as an analytical tool for the investigation of cells. Similar to the spectrophotometer, a spectrofluorimeter consists of a light source from which the light is made monochromatic by a prism or grating. Instead of measuring how much light is absorbed, however, the light that is emitted from the sample is measured. The light is emitted at higher wavelengths than those of the absorbed light, and it is measured at right angles relative to the exciting light by passing it through a second monochromator. In the absorption instrument the difference in intensity between two light beams is measured. In the fluorescence spectrofluorimeter the absolute value of light intensity is measured. Because single photons of light can be measured with modern equipment, fluorescence can measure very low concentrations of molecules. However, the technique is limited to only those molecules which fluoresce.

Fluorescence measurements are especially adaptable for investigating the environment of molecules. The rotational motion of a molecule depends upon its size and viscosity. These can be measured by fluorescence polarization. In this technique the molecule is excited with polarized light. If the molecule moves in the time scale of the fluorescent excited state (1–100 nanoseconds), the emitted light will be partially depolarized, the amount of depolarization depending upon the molecular rotation. This technique has been used to determine molecular size and the viscosity of the environment around cells.

Phosphorescence can be used in much the same way as fluorescence, but molecular oxygen interferes with the phosphorescence light intensity. By measuring phosphorescence intensity or lifetime, the concentration of oxygen within the cells can be determined. *See* FLUORESCENCE; PHOSPHORESCENCE.

Measurement of cell component interaction. The reactions of the cell occur very specifically, for example, if A→B→C, the scheme A→C→B will never occur. Spectral analysis is very useful for finding the order and rate of reactions of cell components. A common method for carrying out such experiments is to initiate the reactions with a strong light signal, usually from a laser, and then to follow the reactions by measuring the absorption of the components with a weaker light. This method has been used to study photosynthesis, where reactions occur in as fast as 1 picosecond (10^{-12} s).

Walter D. Bonner, Jr.; Jane M. Vanderkooi

Bibliography. C. R. Cantor and P. R. Schimmel, *Biophysical Chemistry II: Techniques for the Study of Biological Structure and Function*, 1980; S. P. Colowick and N. O. Kaplan (eds.), *Special Techniques for the Enzymologist*, vol. 4 of *Methods in Enzymology*, 1957; D. C. Youvan and B. L. Marrs, Molecular mechanisms of photosynthesis, *Sci. Amer.*, 256(6):42–49, 1987.

Cell biology

The study of the activities, functions, properties, and structures of cells. Cells were discovered in the middle of the seventeenth century after the microscope was invented. In the following two centuries, with steadily improved microscopes, cells were studied in a wide variety of plants, animals, and microorganisms, leading to the discovery of the cell nucleus and several other major cell parts. By the 1830s biologists recognized that all organisms are composed of cells, a realization that is now known as the Cell Doctrine. The Cell Doctrine constitutes the first major tenet upon which the contemporary science of cell biology is founded. By the late 1800s biologists had established that cells do not arise de novo, but come only by cell division, that is, division of a preexisting cell into two daughter cells. This is the second major tenet upon which the modern study of cells is based. *See* CELL DIVISION; MICROSCOPE.

By the end of the nineteenth century chromosomes had been discovered, and biologists had described mitosis—the distribution at cell division of chromosomes to daughter cells. Subsequent studies showed that the chromosomes contain genes and that mitosis distributes a copy of every chromosome and hence every gene to each daughter cell during cell division. This established the basis of cell heredity and ultimately the basis of heredity in multicellular organisms. *See* CHROMOSOME; MITOSIS.

Microscope studies established that some kinds of organisms are composed of a single cell and some, such as plants and animals, are made up of many cells—usually many billions. Unicellular organisms are the bacteria, protozoa, some fungi, and some algae. All other organisms are multicellular. An adult human, for example, consists of about 200 cell types that collectively amount to more than 10^{14} cells. Microscope studies revealed that all organisms fall into two major groups, the prokaryotes and the eukaryotes. In prokaryotes, the genetic material is not segregated by a membranous envelope into a distinct nucleus. Prokaryotes are the bacteria, of which there are many thousands of species. Eukaryotes are organisms whose cells possess a nucleus that is clearly defined by an enveloping double membrane. Eukaryotes are the protozoa, fungi, algae, plants, and animals; some are unicellular and some are multicellular. The number of species is unknown, but exceeds 10 million. *See* EUKARYOTAE; PROKARYOTAE.

All modern research recognizes that in both unicellular and multicellular organisms the cell is the fundamental unit, housing the genetic material and the biochemical organization that account for the existence of life. Many millions of different species of cells, showing tremendous diversity in structure and metabolic capabilities, exist on Earth. Cells as different as a bacterium, an ameba, a plant leaf cell, and a human liver cell appear to be so unrelated in structure and life-style that they might seem to have little in common; however, the study of cells has shown that the similarities among these diverse cell types are more profound than the differences. These studies have established a modern set of tenets that bring unity to the study of many diverse cell types. These tenets are: (1) All cells store information in genes made of deoxyribonucleic acid (DNA). (2) The genetic code used in the genes is the same in all species of cells. (3) All cells decode the genes in their DNA by a ribonucleic acid (RNA) system that translates genetic information into proteins. (4) All cells synthesize proteins by using a structure called the ribosome. (5) Proteins govern the activities, functions, and structures in all cells. (6) All cells need energy to operate; they all use the molecule adenosinetriphosphate (ATP) as the currency for transfer of energy from energy sources to energy needs. (7) All cells are enclosed by a plasma membrane composed of lipid and protein molecules. *See* CELL MEMBRANES; GENETICS; RIBOSOMES.

In the twentieth century the study of cells, which had been dominated for more than 200 years by microscopy, has been enormously expanded with many other experimental methods. The breaking open of a large mass of cells and the separation of released cell parts into pure fractions led to the discovery of functions contributed by different structures and organelles. For example, mitochondria were shown to be organelles that carry out energy metabolism and supply the entire cell with the energy-rich molecule adenosinetriphosphate, and the thousands of small RNA-protein particles in the cell cytoplasm, called ribosomes, were discovered to be factories that carry out protein synthesis. This work was greatly accelerated after World War II by the availability of radioactive isotopes, which were used to identify and trace biochemical activities of various cell parts. *See* MITOCHONDRIA.

Beginning in the 1950s, the application of the electron microscope, with its great power of magnification, led to discoveries about cell structures, especially the endoplasmic reticulum, mitochrondria and chloroplasts, the nuclear envelope, chromosomes, nucleoli, lysosomes, the Golgi complex of membranes, peroxisomes, centrioles, cilia, flagella, the cell membrane, the cytoskeleton, and cell walls. *See* CELL ORGANIZATION; ELECTRON MICROSCOPE.

Contemporary research in cell biology is concerned with many problems of cell operation and behavior. Cell reproduction is of special concern because it is essential for the survival of all unicellular and multicellular forms of life. Cell reproduction is the means by which a single cell, the fertilized egg, can give rise to the trillions of cells in an adult multicellular organism. Disrupted control of cell reproduction, resulting in accumulation of disorganized masses of functionally useless cells, is the essence of cancer. Indeed, all diseases ultimately result from the death or misfunctioning of one or another group of cells in a plant or animal. The study of cells pervades all areas of medical research and medical treatment. Great advances were made during the 1980s in learning how cells of the immune system combat infection, and the nature of their failure to resist the acquired immune deficiency syndrome (AIDS) virus. *See* ACQUIRED IMMUNE DEFICIENCY SYNDROME (AIDS); CANCER (MEDICINE); CELL SENESCENCE AND DEATH.

The development of methods to grow plant and animal cells in culture has provided new ways to study cells free of the experimental complications encountered with intact plants and animals. Cell culture has greatly facilitated analysis of abnormal cells, including transformation of normal cells into cancer cells. Cultured cells are also used extensively to study cell differentiation, cell aging, cell movement, and many other cell functions. *See* TISSUE CULTURE.

In parallel with cell biology, the fields of genetics, biochemistry, and molecular biology have likewise greatly expanded. As knowledge and understanding have increased, these fields have overlapped and fused more and more with one another, resulting in a unified multidisciplinary approach to the study of life. This confluence will increasingly facilitate research on the cellular basis of life and provide expanded opportunities for the study of many areas in medicine, genetic engineering, agriculture, evolution, and higher functions of the vertebrate brain. *See* BIOCHEMISTRY; CELL (BIOLOGY); GENETIC ENGINEERING; MOLECULAR BIOLOGY.   **David M. Prescott**

Bibliography. B. Alberts et al., *Molecular Biology of the Cell*, 1983; W. M. Becker, *The World of the*

Cell, 1986; J. Darnell et al., *Molecular Cell Biology*, 1986; D. Fawcett, *The Cell*, 2d ed., 1981; L. J. Kleinsmith and V. M. Kish, *Principles of Cell Biology*, 1988; D. M. Prescott, *Cells: Principles of Molecular Structure and Function*, 1988.

Cell constancy

The condition in which the entire body of an adult animal or plant consists of a fixed number of cells that is the same in all members of the species. This phenomenon is also called eutely. The largest group of animals exhibiting eutely are the nematode worms, one of the largest of all animal phyla, and of great medical and agricultural importance as parasites of plants, animals, and humans. A plant that exhibits eutely is usually called a coenobium. Many species of semimicroscopic aquatic green algae exist as coenobia, such as the common *Volvox* and *Pandorina*.

Numerical limitation occurs in certain organs and organ systems, notably the brain and muscles of annelid worms, mollusks, and vertebrates. This is essentially a localized eutely. A related but different phenomenon, observed for many animal cells when cultured, is that normal cells divide some specific number of times and then stop dividing. Thus the life-span, as measured by number of cell cycles, is limited; for many human cell types this is about 50 cell generations.

Investigations on cell constancy and limitation center on three areas. One is the investigation of the factors that limit cell proliferation; this is related to the general problems of growth and differentiation as well as to cancer. A second active area of interest is the use of animals such as mollusks and nematodes in neurophysiological research because they possess nerve centers with a fixed and very small number of cells. Analysis of these simple nervous systems, it is anticipated, will permit better understanding of the organization and functioning of nervous systems, even those of much greater complexity. The third area is muscle development in meat animals such as chickens, beef cattle, and swine. The work on muscle in cattle was stimulated by the discovery of "double-muscled" cattle in which many but not all of the muscles are abnormally enlarged. The muscle hypertrophy in these cattle is due to a single, semidominant gene which has several additional effects, including reduced head size and amount of fatty tissue.

Limiting factors. The factors that sharply limit cell proliferation are unknown. It is clear, however, that in both plants and animals a fundamental distinction exists between growth by cell proliferation and growth by cell enlargement. It is significant in this connection that heavy metals, which will form mercaptides with the sulfhydryl groups of the cell, will block cell division but not cell enlargement. It is also true that the formation of a coenobium in a plant bears a certain resemblance to the cleavage of an egg in an animal. In both cases, a single large cell undergoes a rapid series of mitoses, resulting in a group of many small cells. It is conceivable that in both cases the final slowdown of cell division is due to an exhaustion of the readily available supply of nucleic acids and other constituents required for the rapid formation of new chromosomes.

Although plausible, such a theory gives little insight into why in one case the cells can continue to divide at a slow pace while in the other they must wait until the initial large size is again reached. The work of G. Fankhauser on salamanders has shown that unknown factors correlated with overall size of the animal are somehow important. If these animals are made polyploid so that they have an extra set of chromosomes in every cell, the individual cells are much larger than normal. Nevertheless, the size of the adults remains close to normal. This is because in every tissue, from the brain to the mucous glands of the skin, there has occurred a reduction in cells to compensate exactly for their large size.

The cause or causes of the limit on the number of possible cell divisions in culture for vertebrate cells are unknown. One current theory is that the cumulative effects of thermal, chemical, and background radiation on the cell's deoxyribonucleic acid (DNA) result in a cell which cannot divide. However, why this always occurs after some specific number of cell divisions is hard to explain by this random damage theory. An alternative hypothesis is that cell senescence and the inability to divide are genetically programmed developmental events.

Animals. In rotifers, where cell constancy was first intensively investigated, the number of nuclei in every organ and tissue can be counted exactly. In the common species *Epiphanes* (*Hydatina*) *senta*, which has been studied by several workers, there are 958 nuclei in every individual. The skin and associated structures have 301, the pharynx 167, and the digestive tract 76, of which 15 constitute the esophagus, 35 the stomach, 12 the gastric glands, and 14 the intestine. The urogenital system consists of 43 cells, the general musculature 120, and the nervous system 247, of which 183 are in the brain and 4 in the retrocerebral organ. A. F. Shull, in an investigation of a large number of individuals of this species, found almost no deviations. The presence of 6 nuclei in each gastric gland and of 8 in the vitellarium is common to many species of rotifers.

"An outstanding anatomical feature of nematodes," according to L. H. Hyman, "is their cell constancy." This fact has been confirmed by several workers on various species, including the well-known *Ascaris*, *Turbatrix aceti* (vinegar eel), and *Rhabditis*. In *Turbatrix* there are 251 nerve cells, 1 excretory cell, 18 cells in the midgut, 64 in the body-wall musculature, 59 in the pharynx, 5 in the esophagus, and so on. Since cell division comes to an end before the birth of the worm, all subsequent growth is by cell enlargement. The gonads are exceptions because they produce new eggs or sperms continuously throughout the reproductive life of the individual.

In annelids and vertebrates, cell proliferation is more or less continuous throughout life only in those tissues that are subject to wear. Thus, in adults, cell division may be found in the germinative zones of the skin, hair, finger and toe nails, the lining of the alimentary canal, and especially in the blood cell–forming tissues. The muscles and nervous system, however, appear to undergo no cell division after early embryonic or fetal stages. In both earthworms and mammals, including humans, it has been demonstrated that the number of muscle nuclei and muscle fibers, but not fibrils, is fixed early and does not increase with subsequent growth. An earthworm hatches from its egg cocoon with the adult number of muscle fibers and nuclei. A human fetus, about 5 in. (13 cm) from crown to rump, has as many muscle fibers and nuclei as an adult. It has been shown that the number of glomeruli in each kidney of a rat or human, and therefore presumably of any mammal, is fixed before birth, and that the subsequent growth of the glomeruli, either normally or resulting from compensatory hypertrophy after unilateral nephrectomy, is due entirely to the enlargement of cells already present. The same holds true for the cells of the ciliated nephrostomes of earthworms.

Plants. Coenobia, that is, adult individuals composed of a fixed and predictable number of cells, are characteristic of the species of green algae belonging to the species of *Volvox* in the order Volvocales, and to the species of *Hydrodictyon* and *Scenedesmus* in the order Chlorococcales. In these forms the number of cells in an adult ranges from 4 to 8 in certain species of *Gonium*, 32 to 64 in *Pandorina*, and from 500 (probably 512) to 60,000 (probably 65,536) in *Volvox*. During asexual reproduction in these species, either every cell or, in the larger forms, certain cells undergo a rapid series of cell divisions. This results in the formation of a miniature replica of the adult, as far as cell number is concerned, within every single cell which has so divided. Thus a very small, young volvox has as many cells as a large, mature one. The minute, new individuals are released from the parent cell by the breakdown of the old cell wall. It will be noted that the number of cell generations is always small. Thirty-two is 2^5, which means only 5 cell generations, 512 is 2^9, and even 65,536 is only 2^{16}, which means only 16 cell generations to make the largest volvox. Gairdner B. Moment

Bibliography. B. C. Edgar, Nematodes, *"Elegans Workshops" Worm Breeder's Gazette*, vols. 1 and 2, University of California, Santa Cruz, 1977; D. F. Goldspink, *Development and Specialization of Skeletal Muscle*, 1981; L. Hayflick, Cell biology of human aging, *Sci. Amer.*, 242(1):58–66, 1980; L. H. Hyman, *The Invertebrates*, vol. 3, 1951; T. L. Lawrence (ed.), *Growth in Animals*, 1980.

Cell cycle

The succession of events that culminates in the asexual reproduction of a cell; also known as cell division cycle. In a typical cell cycle, the parent cell doubles its volume, mass, and complement of chromosomes, then sorts its doubled contents to opposite sides of the cell, and finally divides in half to yield two genetically identical offspring. Implicit in the term cycle is the idea that division brings the double-sized parent cell back to its original size and chromosome number, and ready to begin another cell cycle. This idea fits well with the behavior of many unicellular organisms, but for multicellular organisms a cell may be very different in size, shape, and differentiation state at the start of one cell cycle than it was at the start of the previous one.

The time required for completion of a eukaryotic cell cycle varies enormously from cell to cell. Embryonic cells that do not need to grow between divisions can complete a cell cycle in as little as 8 min while cycling times of 10–24 h are typical of the most rapidly dividing somatic cells. Many somatic cells divide much less frequently; liver cells divide about once a year, and mature neurons never divide. Such cells may be thought of as temporarily or permanently withdrawing from the cell cycle.

Phases for eukaryotic cells. The cell cycle is divided into two main parts: interphase and mitosis (**Fig. 1**). During interphase, the cell grows and replicates its chromosomes. Interphase accounts for all but an hour or two of a 24-h cell cycle, and is subdivided into three phases: gap phase 1 (G1), synthesis (S), and gap phase 2 (G2). Interphase is followed by mitosis (nuclear division), and cytokinesis (cell division). This relatively brief part of the cell cycle includes some of the most dramatic events in cell biology. *See* CYTOKINESIS; MITOSIS.

G1 phase. Gap phase 1 begins at the completion of mitosis and cytokinesis and lasts until the beginning of S phase. This phase is generally the longest of the four cell cycle phases and is quite variable in length. During this phase, the cell chooses either to replicate its deoxyribonucleic acid (DNA) or to exit the cell cycle and enter a quiescent state (the G0 phase). A variety of physical and chemical signals influence this decision. Some of the signals are intrinsic; for example, the cell determines whether it has grown sufficiently to warrant cell cycle progression. Other signals, such as peptide growth factors, are provided by neighboring cells. Damaged DNA may be repaired during the G1 phase. Late in this phase, the cell becomes committed to replicating its DNA. In mammalian cells, the time at which this commitment occurs is called the restriction point.

S phase. Replication of the chromosomes is restricted to one specific portion of interphase, called S phase (DNA synthesis phase), which typically lasts about 6 h. In mammalian cells, the start of S phase—the actual initiation of DNA synthesis—takes place several hours after the cell has committed to carrying out DNA

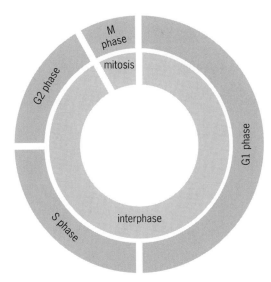

Fig. 1. Phases of the eukaryotic cell cycle.

synthesis. During S phase, each chromosome replicates exactly once to form a pair of physically linked sister chromatids. In animal cells, a pair of centrioles is also duplicated during S phase. *See* CHROMOSOME; GENETICS.

G2 phase. The portion of interphase that follows S phase is called gap phase 2. Some cells can exit the cell cycle from G2 phase, just as they can from G1 phase.

M phase. M phase includes the overlapping processes of mitosis and cytokinesis. Mitosis is divided into five stages: prophase, prometaphase, metaphase, anaphase, and telophase. During prophase, the chromosomes condense and the football-shaped mitotic spindle begins to form. Prometaphase begins when the nuclear envelope abruptly disappears and the chromosomes begin to migrate toward the spindle's midline. When the chromosomes reach the midline, the cell is said to be in metaphase. Metaphase ends and anaphase begins when the sister chromatids abruptly separate from each other and move toward the spindle poles. During telophase, the nuclear envelope reforms around each set of chromosomes, the chromosomes decondense, and mitosis is completed. Cytokinesis usually begins during anaphase and ends at a point after the completion of mitosis. At the end of cytokinesis, the parent cell has formed its two G1 phase progeny and the cell is ready to repeat the cycle.

Mitotic control. The best-understood aspect of eukaryotic cell cycle control is the transition from G2 phase to M phase. Biochemical studies of oocytes from the South African clawed frog (*Xenopus laevis*) indicate that activation of a protein factor brings about the G2-M transition. When a small amount of M-phase cytoplasm is injected into a G2-phase oocyte, the recipient cell enters meiotic M phase. The factor responsible, maturation promoting factor (MPF), is present and active during both meiotic M phase and mitotic M phase, and can be found in M-phase cells from

evolutionarily distant organisms. This suggests that MPF is the universal M-phase trigger.

Other crucial insights into M-phase control came from studies of growth regulation in the yeast *Schizosaccharomyces pombe*. Mutations in genes that regulate M-phase onset of *S. pombe* give rise to organisms that are too long or too short. Once such a mutant strain is isolated, the gene responsible for its altered size can be identified by molecular genetic methods. Two genes identified through this approach were $cdc2^+$ and $cdc13^+$. Genes related to $cdc2^+$ and $cdc13^+$ were found in a variety of other eukaryotes, suggesting that they encoded universal regulators of M-phase onset. *See* GENE ACTION; MOLECULAR BIOLOGY; MUTATION.

Ultimately it was realized that the biochemical studies of M-phase regulation in frog oocytes and the genetic studies of M-phase regulation in *S. pombe* had succeeded in identifying the same M-phase regulators. MPF proved to be a complex of the *Xenopus* homologs of *S. pombe* $cdc2^+$ and $cdc13^+$ (the Cdc13 protein is more usually called a B-type cyclin, because it rises and falls in abundance during the cell cycle). The fact that two very different approaches and two evolutionarily distant organisms had converged upon the same M-phase regulators underscored the importance and universality of the regulators.

The Cdc2/cyclin B complex is essential for initiation of all M phases in all organisms. The complex functions as a protein kinase—an enzyme that adds a phosphate group to specific amino acid residues in target proteins. The catalytic subunit of the complex is Cdc2; cyclin B is necessary for the activation of Cdc2 and is responsible for localizing the complex to the nucleus at the onset of M phase. The nuclear lamin proteins are Cdc2 target proteins, which form a scaffolding that supports the nuclear envelope. The Cdc2/cyclin B complex can phosphorylate lamins, causing the lamin network to disassemble. This disassembly allows the nuclear envelope to break down into small vesicles, which will coalesce and reassemble during telophase after cyclin B has been degraded and the lamins have been dephosphorylated. Other likely targets of Cdc2/cyclin B complex include histone proteins, whose phosphorylation may contribute to chromosome condensation, and a number of regulatory proteins.

At the onset of anaphase, there is a transient increase in intracellular calcium, which is thought to trigger the activation of a protease, an enzyme that degrades specific target proteins. One target of this protease is cyclin B, and destruction of cyclin B (and the consequent deactivation of Cdc2/cyclin B) is thought to allow cytokinesis to proceed. The protease is also thought to cause the separation of the sister chromatids at anaphase, but the target responsible for sister chromatid separation has not yet been identified.

G1 and S-phase control. The other cell cycle transitions, for example, the commitment to DNA synthesis that occurs in G1 phase, and the initiation

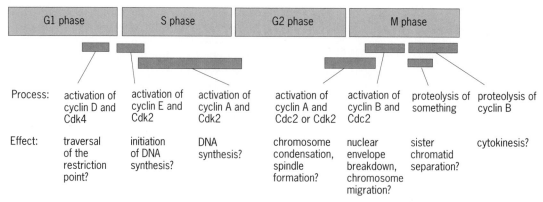

| | G1 phase | | S phase | | G2 phase | | M phase | | |

Fig. 2. Behavior of various Cdk/cyclin complexes and their cellular events.

Process:	activation of cyclin D and Cdk4	activation of cyclin E and Cdk2	activation of cyclin A and Cdk2	activation of cyclin A and Cdc2 or Cdk2	activation of cyclin B and Cdc2	proteolysis of something	proteolysis of cyclin B
Effect:	traversal of the restriction point?	initiation of DNA synthesis?	DNA synthesis?	chromosome condensation, spindle formation?	nuclear envelope breakdown, chromosome migration?	sister chromatid separation?	cytokinesis?

of DNA synthesis at the start of S phase, may be triggered by activation of heterodimeric protein kinases consisting of Cdc2-like catalytic subunits (termed Cdks, for cyclin-dependent kinases) and cyclin-like regulatory subunits. Remarkably, it appears that the entire cell cycle may be driven by sequential activation and inactivation of Cdk/cyclin complexes. At least seven different Cdc2-like catalytic subunits (Cdc2 and Cdks 2–7) are thought to be involved in cell cycle regulation, and they can be paired with cyclins from at least eight classes (cyclins A through H). Sequential activation of various Cdk/cyclin pairs is thought to initiate various cell cycle transitions, and also to regulate entry of quiescent cells into the cell cycle (**Fig. 2**).

Cancer. Cancer cells can differ from normal cells in a great many ways. Foremost among them is that they enter the cell cycle, or fail to exit the cell cycle, at times when they should be quiescent. It is believed that cyclins and Cdks, particularly those that operate in G1 phase, might be deranged in these cells. *See* CANCER (MEDICINE); CELL DIVISION; DEOXYRIBONUCLEIC ACID (DNA).   James E. Ferrell

Bibliography. A. Murray and T. Hunt, *The Cell Cycle: An Introduction*, 1993; A. W. Murray and M. W. Kirschner, What controls the cell cycle?, *Sci. Amer.*, 264:56–63, 1991.

Cell differentiation

The mechanism by which cells in a multicellular organism become specialized to perform specific functions in a variety of tissues and organs. The life cycle of a higher organism begins with a unicellular stage, the fertilized egg, and becomes more complex as the individual grows and takes on its characteristic form. The life cycle of a unicellular organism permits temporary change in shape and chemical composition. Only a multicellular organism can afford irreversibly differentiated cells.

Differentiated cells. The stable differentiated state is a consequence of multicellularity. A complex organism maintains its characteristic form and identity because populations of specialized cell types remain assembled in a certain pattern. Thus several kinds of cells make up a tissue, and different

tissues build organs. The variable assortment of about 200 cell types allows for an almost infinite variety of distinct organisms.

Epithelia, sheets of cells of specific structure and function, cover the outer surface of the vertebrate body and line the lungs, gut, and vascular system. The stable form of a vertebrate is due to its rigid skeleton built from bone and cartilage, forming cells to which the skeletal muscles adhere. All other organs, such as liver and pancreas, are embedded in connective tissue that is derived from fibroblast cells which secrete large amounts of soft matrix material. *See* CONNECTIVE TISSUE; EPITHELIUM.

Some cells, like nerve cells, are so specialized that they need divide no longer in order to maintain a complex network. Their finite number decreases even during embryonic development. Other cell types are constantly worn out and must be replaced; for example, fibroblasts and pancreas cells simply divide as needed, proving that the differentiated state of cells is heritable, as the daughter cells remember and carry out the same special functions. The renewal of terminally differentiated cells that are unable to divide anymore, such as skin and blood cells, is carried out by stem cells. They are immortal and choose, as they double, whether to remain a stem cell or to embark on a path of terminal differentiation. Most stem cells are unipotent because they give rise to a single differentiated cell type. However, all cell types of the blood are derived from a single blood-forming stem cell, a pluripotent stem cell. A fertilized egg is a totipotent stem cell giving rise to all other cell types that make up an individual organism. *See* BLOOD.

Process of differentiation. Specialized cells are the product of differentiation. The process can be understood only from a historical perspective, and the best place to start is the fertilized egg. Different kinds of cell behavior can be observed during embryogenesis: cells double, change in shape, and attach at and migrate to various sites within the embryo without any obvious signs of differentiation. Cleavage is a rapid series of cell cycles during which the large egg cell is divided into a ball of small cells that line the primitive body cavity as a single layer of embryonic cells.

This blastula stage is followed by gastrulation, a complex coordinated cellular migration which not only shapes the embryo but segregates the single-cell layer of the blastula into the three germ layers: endoderm, mesoderm, ectoderm. They give rise to specific cell types; for example, skin and nerves from the ectoderm, the digestive tract from the endoderm, and muscle and connective tissue from the mesoderm. *See* BLASTULATION; CLEAVAGE (EMBRYOLOGY); EMBRYOGENESIS; GASTRULATION.

Descriptive embryology has contributed elaborate body plans, but cannot explain the development of various organisms. Experimental embryologists originally concluded that all organisms can be placed in two categories. They found that either the developmental system represented by an egg acts as a fixed mosaic, or it can regulate and, for example, give rise to four complete mice from the cells produced after the first cleavage divisions. In a philosophical context, the terms preformation and epigenesis describe the two opposite kinds of development, the former claiming that an organism is physically preformed inside the egg, the latter proposing that the organism is newly created in each generation. *See* DEVELOPMENTAL BIOLOGY; EMBRYOLOGY.

Cell determination. An explanation of the two egg types by the timing of a single developmental change came from another experiment. A piece from a salamander blastula, which would have become an eye according to the body plan, was transplanted into the region destined to develop into the gut of another blastula. The implant adapted to the new environment and became part of the gut rather than an eye. A short time later, after gastrulation, the transplant resulted in the development of an eye inside the gut. This experiment holds a key to the cell differentiation process. It reveals a critical event, cell determination, which leads to the fixation of a particular developmental pathway. Before that time the embryo regulates; thereafter it has become a mosaic. Once a cell is committed to function in a specific capacity, it will not forget it, irrespective of environment. Thus, the change brought about by determination affects the internal character of a cell and results in a self-propagating change. The egg cell combines all capacities to build organisms as complex as humans, but it can do so only if its potential is first segregated and divided into groups of stem cells with lesser developmental capacities. Two counteracting tendencies describe the developmental process: as embryonic cells lose their developmental potential, they gain specific characteristics which permit sophisticated division of labor in multicellular organisms. *See* EMBRYONIC DIFFERENTIATION.

Cell differentiation is the realization of the determined state, and since different cell types share the same genes, the central concept, if not dogma, of developmental biology is the theory of differential gene expression. This means that a myoblast becomes a muscle cell because genes responsible for muscle-specific structures, such as the contractile apparatus, are selectively activated. Conversely, muscle-specific genes remain inactive in other cell types. Molecular biologists have accumulated good evidence for selective gene expression in differentiated cells. Specific gene products, such as hemoglobin in red blood cells, have been labeled luxury molecules, because they are not essential for the lives of a cell but are required for the diversification of multicellular organisms. However, the processes of cell determination and differentiation are not accompanied by an overall increase in the number of genes that are expressed during embryonic development. To the contrary, many genes that are active in early embryos become inactivated by the time a cell becomes differentiated. It seems that the loss of developmental capacity is accompanied, or may be the consequence of, massive inactivation of genes of unknown functions. *See* GENE.

The determined state is very stable and inherited over many cell generations, but it is not irreversible. Transdetermination occurs occasionally and alters the developmental course of cells. There are some mutations that cause a similar shift of the developmental pathway. Perhaps the respective genes are "master genes" which control a whole set of cell-type-specific genes that evoke the production of the "luxury" molecules in differentiated cells. About 200 of such regulatory genes would be required to determine all existing cell types. If, however, embryonic cells could be determined by a set of regulatory genes in either "on" or "of" position, eight genes would suffice to program all different cell types ($2^8 = 256$). It can be concluded that these control genes are active in determined cells, which makes them different from those that are not determined. Consequently, committed cells must possess some less obvious luxury molecules yet to be discovered. They are distinct from undetermined cells, although not so grossly altered as the differentiated cells that are their progeny. Cell divisions occur during the transition from cell determination to differentiation. Frequently, a special kind of cell cycle, called the quantal cell cycle, is required, following which the differentiated state becomes obvious by the massive production of the cell-type-specific luxury molecules. *See* CELL CYCLE.

Embryonic induction. Another experiment has shed some light on the determination process. Implantation of that piece from the blastula, which would normally come to lie under the prospective neural tissue after gastrulation, into another blastula turns the host embryo into a monster with two complete nervous systems. This experiment defines embryonic induction. Induction works even with killed inducing cells. This result opened the search for the still elusive inducer substance. Furthermore, the capacity of induction can be traced back through earlier stages into the egg. These observations are consistent with the concept of cytoplasmic localization. It is assumed that cytoplasmic determinants are produced during the process of oogenesis and become deposited in certain areas in the egg. This concept is a modern version of the classical prefor-

mation theory. See OOGENESIS.

There are two ways to explain embryonic induction: either the inducer instructs the reacting tissue to become determined and, later on, differentiated, or the reacting tissue is multipotential and selects one developmental pathway over one of several others. In the first case, instruction can be viewed as a transfer of information in the form of specific protein or nucleic acid molecules. In the second case, the inducer plays a more permissive role, allowing the reacting tissue to decide what to do next. Consequently, the inducer need not confer information and may just provide a cue, like a change in ion concentration. There is evidence for unspecific cueing in the early embryogenesis of the most complex organisms, the mammals. After a few cleavage divisions, the young embryo forms the blastocyst, which consists of an outer layer of cells with a few cells inside. Any cell that happens to be inside the blastocyst takes part in building the embryo, while outside cells do not. This is germane to the inside-out concept, indicating that the cellular environment can provide cues as to the course of cell determination in the absence of localized cytoplasmic determinants. *See* EMBRYONIC INDUCTION.

Cellular nonequivalence. The shaping of an embryo is an essential routine of the developmental program. While embryonic induction leads to cell determination and differentiation, it is a complex patterning process that eventually puts different cell types into their proper territory. For example, a leg and an arm are quite distinct, although they are built from the very same cell types; but they are arranged in different patterns. More than one cell must collaborate to construct body parts, such as a segment or a wing of an insect. This process is initiated among a few founder cells in response to unknown cytoplasmic controls for which terms such as morphogenetic field, gradient, and centers have been applied.

According to the unifying position information hypothesis, embryonic cells secrete substances, perhaps an activator and an inhibitor, that generate a stable dynamic gradient of either diffusible molecules or a macromolecular extracellular network. These cells not only receive information with respect to their position, but are able to interpret that information. Interpretation is the crucial component of this hypothesis. One can assume that receptor molecules at the cell surface measure the size of the supracellular position information signal, and can postulate that they interpret different increments of that signal according to a preset behavior pattern. In the famous "French flag model," a sheet of cells with the potential to become blue, white, or red turn red at a low value, blue at a high value, and white at a medium value of the position signal. An important implication of the position information concept is that cells remember their position value. Consequently, cells of the same differentiated state can be different: they are nonequivalent. As with determination and differentiation, cellular nonequivalence is a self-perpetuating change in character. It may distinguish each cell from all other cells and allow it to home-in during the animated puzzle of embryogenesis and to stay put in a precise location. There is a class of developmental mutants, in which cells of a certain territory, called a compartment, collectively change their course of development and, for example, form a leg instead of an antenna at the head of the fruit fly *Drosophila melanogaster*. A combinational activity pattern of a few selector genes could provide for a mechanism to interpret different positive values.

It is conceivable that a single position information mechanism operates in all organisms during embryogenesis and later permits determined cells to display overt differentiation at the correct place. Together with genetic information that generates biological materials, position information could arrange these materials inside a cell to maintain a specific subcellular organization, or could operate between cells to create multicellular organisms of distinct forms.

Cellular change. In order to accurately describe a specific organism, one must know which cell types are arranged in what pattern. From a developmental perspective three different components describe the system from which a body plan emerges: cellular determination, differentiation, and nonequivalence. The developmental process proceeds according to the timing and interactions of these three kinds of cellular self-perpetuating change. Therefore, it is impossible to project a body plan into an egg cell and thus reveal the blueprint of a particular organism. The remarkable biological change initiated upon fertilization of an egg is perhaps better described as the product of the developmental program.

Molecular biology has unraveled in almost complete detail how genetic information in nucleic acids programs the linear array of amino acids in proteins. Some model systems (for example, bacteriophages and subcellular particles, such as ribosomes) need little if any additional information to assemble predictably into highly complex and functional structures by self-organization. These particles are almost exclusively programmed in the genome, but they are not alive. Even dissociated specialized cells of an adult organism can self-organize to some extent by the processes of sorting-out and differential adhesion. However, a cell is never reformed from its parts; each cell comes from a cell. Over 90% of its genome does not code for any known product. Even most known genes are made up of a mosaic of coding stretches of deoxyribonucleic acid (DNA), exons, and introns that are seemingly devoid of genetic sense. The genome is less stable than originally thought. Subtle rearrangements (by transposons) or differential ribonucleic acid (RNA) splicing may be the source for unprogrammed but essential biological change during embryonic development. In addition, the biomembrane, which is never the result of self-assembly, could store information in a two-dimensional network at its inner face to communicate with the cytoplasm, and at its outer face to respond to signals from the environment. To date, the developmental program, if it exists, has remained elusive. *See* BACTERIOPHAGE; DEOXYRIBONUCLEIC ACID (DNA); EXON; INTRON; MOLECULAR BIOLOGY; NUCLEIC ACID; PROTEIN; RIBONUCLEIC ACID (RNA); RIBOSOMES; TRANSPOSONS.

By comparing the differentiation process of cells to evolution, interesting new insights may be gained. The mechanism of cell differentiation and the establishment of nonequivalence are formally equal to speciation. Although it is hard to imagine how random change in embryonic cells will lead to complex organisms, such as humans, the developmental options of the germ cell are limited. The limitations are the linear patterns of genes, which hold the memory for their successful propagation over evolutionary time, and the constraints posed by the protoplasmic environment and its system of chemical interactions. Extinctions are common in the fossil record and, by analogy, also occur during embryogenesis. For example, the big egg cell, the totipotent stem cell, disappears after a few cleavage divisions and must be reorganized during oogenesis in the adult organism; and all neuroblasts, the precursors of terminally differentiated nerve cells, become extinct before birth. Cell death even becomes a formative tool as the human fingers are carved out from a paddlelike appendage, and the tail of a tadpole is destroyed in building the frog. Eventually the whole organism is survived only by its germ cells and the genes contained in them.

Origins. A living unit must reproduce faster than it is destroyed or taken over by other replicators. It seems that one kind of replicator made of nucleic acid and protein survived all other attempts at forming life, because all life on Earth uses the same genetic code. The most primitive cell was formed when a membrane kept the necessary building blocks close to the replicator. Prokaryotic organisms, such as bacteria and blue-green algae, may be descendants of the first cell. The eukaryotic cell achieved a higher degree of division of labor by segregating and enlarging the genome in the nuclear envelope, and by acquiring organelles, perhaps through ingestion and maintaining other primitive cells in a state of symbiosis. Flagellates may resemble that state which permitted a thousandfold increase in size. All unicellular organisms compete with each other for resources. The third step, following replicator and cell formation, is characterized by specialization of all functions assembled in the eukaryotic cell through cellular differentiation and positioning. Thus multicellularity and cell differentiation, and the switch from competitive to altruistic cellular behavior, are closely related. *See* GENETIC CODE; PREBIOTIC ORGANIC SYNTHESIS.

Some specialized functions in extant organisms may provide information as to how cell differentiation originated. Even the simplest bacterium segregates genetic material into one gene set which controls the routine processes of life, and a small additional genome, a plasmid, that permits shuttling of genetic material within and between cells, a prerequisite for sexuality. *See* BACTERIAL GENETICS.

The ciliates are the most advanced single-celled organisms. They have two nuclei, a micronucleus and a macronucleus. The micronucleus functions in gene replication and sexual recombination; its genes cannot be copied into RNA. Growth and division are controlled by the macronucleus, in which a portion of the genome is segregated, amplified, and transcribed. Ciliates display a highly organized cell surface as the result of intracellular patterning. The positioning of arrays of cilia is to some degree self-perpetuating and independent of the genome. *See* CILIOPHORA.

The switch from competitive to altruistic cell behavior happens in the life cycle of cellular slime molds. They live as individual cells while they have sufficient food. Following starvation, about 10,000 individuals aggregate into a tissuelike structure which forms a fruiting body. In this process many individuals die and allow the survival of others to propagate the genes. Formation of these fruiting bodies is a model case of cellular positioning, reversible differentiation, and altruistic cellular behavior. *See* CELLULAR ADHESION.

A stable association of identical cells has occurred in some algae, which form a sphere from identical individuals that resemble a blastula. Plants may have arisen from algal colonies, and the high degree of regeneration in plants could indicate that cells of a plant tissue have never given up the pluripotent state. *See* ALGAE.

The plasmodial slime molds provide a model of developmental organization beyond unicellularity. These organisms can live as minute competing amebas. Under proper conditions a single cell turns into a large mass of protoplasm. Its new developmental feature is the uncoupling of nuclear divisions from cell divisions. A plasmodium is born, a giant cell which can grow to over a foot in diameter and contains billions of nuclei. In some plasmodial slime molds, cellular transformation into a multinucleated system is coupled to sexual cell differentiation and cell fusion. The life cycle continues with a patterning process in which the giant cell is divided into smaller units of about a million nuclei. Each unit undergoes morphogenesis which results in a fruiting body. During this process most nuclei become eliminated. The surviving nuclei end up in the head of the fruiting body, where each is surrounded by a portion of cytoplasm and a proper cell membrane. Thus, this organism demonstrates major events of embryogenesis, which turn a fertilized egg into a complex organism: growth, patterning, determination, cell differentiation, and morphogenesis. It is a simple model system for two reasons: the transition from the unicellular to the multicellular state occurs in the absence of the still elusive maternal programming during oogenesis, and the giant cell and the building of the fruiting body display, in mutually exclusive fashion, either growth or differentiation. One cannot distinguish whether the plasmodial slime mold represents an evolutionary dead end or whether the animals are its descendants. Once multicellularity is established, all kinds of fungi, plants, and animals can evolve by utilizing the opportunities of specialization to optimize division of labor by differentiated cells, and the constraints posed by the history of their ancestors. *See* CELL (BIOLOGY); CELL SENESCENCE AND DEATH.

Helmut Sauer

Bibliography. B. Alberts et al., *Molecular Biology of the Cell*, 1983; J. T. Bonner (ed.), *Evolution and Development* 1982; F. Jacob, *The Logic of Life*, reissued 1982; G. Karp and N. J. Berrill, *Development*, 2d ed. 1981; N. Maclean, *The Differentiation of Cells: Genetics—Principles and Perspectives* (a series of texts), 1977; R. A. Raff and T. C. Kaufman, *Embryos, Genes, and Evolution*, 1983.

Cell division

The division of a cell into daughter cells that receive identical copies of its genetic material. The cell cycle comprises the period between the formation of a cell as a progeny of division and its own subsequent division into two daughter cells. The cell cycle falls into two parts. A relatively long interphase represents the time during which the cell engages in synthetic activities and reproduces its components, even though there is no visible change. The relatively short period of mitosis provides an interlude during which the actual process of visible division into two daughter cells is accomplished.

Cell cycle. Prokaryotic and eukaryotic cells differ markedly in the coordination of deoxyribonucleic acid (DNA) synthesis and in the subsequent equal partitioning of DNA during cell division. In prokaryotes the cell cycle consists of successive periods of DNA replication and of cell division where a cell wall forms and divides the cell in two, with no visible condensation and decondensation of DNA. Eukaryotes from yeast to humans have similar cell division phases, termed G1, S, G2, and M phases. After each division there is a time gap (G1 phase) before the synthesis of DNA begins. The cell is metabolically active during this part of the cycle in which proteins and DNA precursors are made. The period of DNA synthesis (S phase) involves the replication of chromosomal DNA, and it is followed by another time gap (G2 phase), after which mitosis (M phase) occurs. Interphase is the time that elapses between one M phase and the next. It is composed of successive G1,

S, and G2 phases and normally comprises 90% or more of the total cell cycle time. The cell cycle varies from tissue to tissue and during development. Sea urchin blastomeres, for instance, replicate their DNA at the end of mitosis in telophase of the preceding division, thus eliminating the G1 phase completely.

The products of the series of mitotic divisions that generate the entire organism are called somatic cells. During embryonic development, most of the somatic cells are proceeding through the cell cycle. In the adult organism, however, many cells are terminally differentiated or no longer divide; they remain in a perpetual interphase. These cells are sometimes said to be quiescent or in G0 phase. *See* CELL CYCLE; DEOXYRIBONUCLEIC ACID (DNA).

Mitotic stages. The mitotic or M phase of the cell cycle involves the separation of replicated nuclei into two identical daughter nuclei. Mitosis is divided into six distinct stages: prophase, prometaphase (or late prophase), metaphase, anaphase, telophase, and cytokinesis (see **illus.**). The length of time that a cell takes to complete mitosis varies in different organisms. In rapidly proliferating cells of higher eukaryotes, M phases generally occur only once every 16–24 h, and each M phase itself lasts only 1–2 h.

Prophase. Prior to mitosis, in the S phase of the cell cycle chromosomal DNA replicates, and each chromosome divides into two sister chromatids. At the onset of prophase, these sister chromatids condense while remaining attached at a specific sequence of DNA necessary for chromosome separation called the centromere. At this point, the condensed chromosomes become visible by light microscopy. In interphase, the centrosome also divides, giving rise to two sets of centrioles. The centrioles, which are made from microtubules, also duplicate during interphase and begin to move to opposite sides of the nucleus to form separate poles. As these centrioles move apart, the microtubules disassemble. The new microtubules or asters, which will become intimately involved in the movement of the chromosomes during mitosis, begin to radiate from the centriole pairs in all directions to form the mitotic spindle. The number of microtubules making up the mitotic spindle varies depending on the organism. The microtubules that connect at the center of the chromatid pairs are called kinetochore microtubules; others, called polar microtubules, will extend to the opposite pole. Astral microtubules radiate from the centriole pair outside the mitotic spindle. *See* CENTRIOLE; CENTROSOME.

Prometaphase. Prometaphase, or late prophase, begins with the breakdown of the nuclear membrane. At this point, the kinetochore microtubules interact with the chromosomes to form protein complexes at their centromeres. This association between the microtubules and proteins of the chromatids makes up the structure of the mitotic spindle. The microtubules that extend past the sister chromatids to each pole are stabilized through cross-linking of

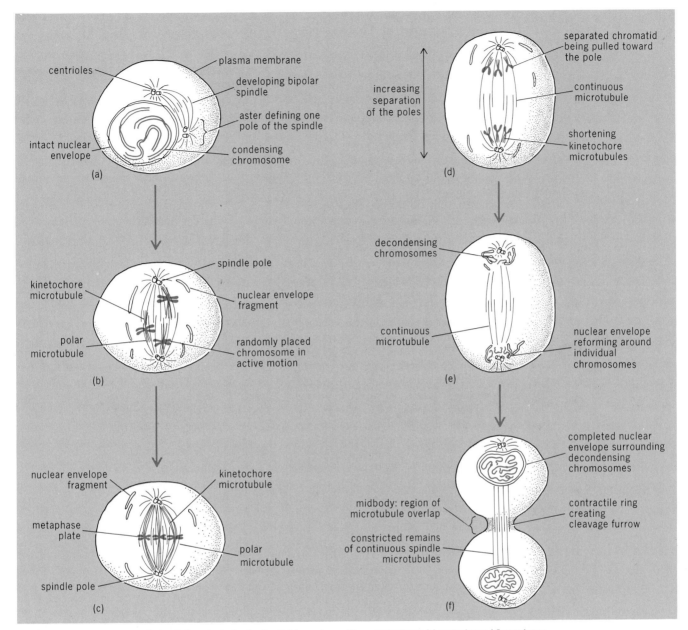

Representation of the stages of mitosis for a typical animal cell: (*a*) prophase; (*b*) prometaphase; (*c*) metaphase; (*d*) anaphase; (*e*) early telophase; (*f*) late telophase.

microtubule binding proteins. These microtubules are also protected from disassembly by the constant formation of new microtubules from tubulin molecules in the fluid portion of the cytoplasm (cytosol). The stabilization of these microtubules is necessary for mitosis, as shown by the effect of the drug colchicine which blocks the assembly of microtubules and makes cells unable to complete mitosis.

Metaphase. At metaphase, the kinetochore microtubules align their chromosomes in one plane called the metaphase plate, half way between the spindle poles, with one kinetochore facing each pole. Each sister chromatid is now perpendicular to the opposite poles. The metaphase stage of mitosis is the longest, lasting up to 30 min in mammalian cells. The kinetochore·microtubules align the sister

chromatids by holding them in tension with the two opposite poles. This tension seems to be necessary for the correct movement of the chromatids in the next stage.

Anaphase. The sister chromatids are triggered to separate and migrate to opposite spindle poles, and assemble there to form the nucleus of a new cell. Anaphase is separated into two stages. During anaphase A, a sister chromatid pair separates at the kinetochore and is guided to an opposite pole as the kinetochore microtubules begin to shorten at a rate of 1 micrometer per minute. This separation occurs simultaneously for all the chromatids. As the chromatids reach the poles, the microtubules begin to disassemble. During anaphase B, the disassembling polar microtubules begin to elongate so that the two poles of the spindle move farther apart.

Telophase. The end stage of mitosis, termed telophase, begins with the arrival of the sister chromatids at each separate pole. As the kinetochore microtubules disappear, the polar microtubules continue to elongate. A new nuclear envelope begins to form around each group of sister chromatids. The chromatin which has been condensed throughout mitosis expands, and nucleoli appear. After this stage, the cell enters cytokinesis. *See* CELL NUCLEUS.

Cytokinesis. Cytokinesis begins during anaphase and ends the mitotic process. The cytoplasm divides by a process known as cleavage to give rise to two separate daughter cells. The forces required for cleavage are generated through actin-myosin interactions, which pull the plasma membrane down a furrow, a puckering of the plasma membrane. The cleavage furrow forms around the equator of the parent cell so that the two daughter cells produced are of approximately equal size and have similar properties.

Induction of mitosis. The alternation between interphase and M phase is controlled by periodic changes in the activity of maturation promoting factor. This factor in amphibian eggs is present only in M-phase cytoplasm, and its activity is regulated by phosphorylations. Activity of maturation promoting factor depends on two protein species associated in equimolar amounts in purified preparations. The first component is the protein kinase catalytic subunit $p34^{cdc2}$. The second component is a 62-kilodalton protein which must be synthesized at each metaphase-anaphase transition in mitosis. Because of this cyclical behavior, this protein was identified as cyclin B; it is the maturation promoting factor activator protein. There is a delay in an organism between the time after which protein synthesis is no longer required and the time when $p34^{cdc2}$ kinase activation occurs. The suggestion is that cyclin B accumulation required for maturation promoting factor activation is not the only factor involved in the activation process.

Disruption. The order of the cell cycle is ensured by dependent relationships, the initiation of late events depending upon the completion of preceding ones. Such dependence can be circumvented by pharmacological intervention, such as the induction of premature chromosome condensation by caffeine, blockade of mitosis, and inhibition of microtubule formation by colcemid, or inhibition of cytokinesis by cytochalasin B. Mutations, which are more specific than inhibitions, can also detect molecules involved in cell division. Mutants and inhibitors aid in the identification of control mechanism in cell division, named checkpoints, that govern mitotic entry and exit. *See* MITOSIS; MUTATION.

Khandan Keyomarsi; Nuala O'Leary; Arthur B. Pardee
Bibliography. N. Akkas (ed.), *Biomechanics of Cell Division*, 1987; B. Alberts et al., *Molecular Biology of the Cell*, 1994; R. Baserga, *The Biology of Cell Reproduction*, 1985; J. S. Hyams and B. R. Brinkley (eds.), *Mitosis*, 1989; J. D. Watson et al., *Recombinant DNA*, 1992.

Cell lineage

A type of embryological study in which the history of individual blastomeres (cells formed during division of the zygote) or meristem cells is traced to their ultimate differentiation into tissues and organs.

Animals. The question of how the animal genome can be regulated to produce the various cell types found in the larval and adult organism is a central concern in developmental biology. A possible approach to this problem would involve tracing the structural fates of the descendants of each of a population of progenitor cells, and then trying to determine which gene products are required for particular steps in the process of cell differentiation. The cleaving embryos of a limited number of invertebrates, such as some flatworms, annelids, mollusks, and ascidians, are suitable for such studies because they show stereotyped cleavage patterns and asymmetries in size and arrangement of the blastomeres. Studies of this sort have been of limited interest because the large number of cells produced make it impossible to follow clones beyond the establishment of the germ layers. *See* CLEAVAGE (EMBRYOLOGY).

Cell lineages are also studied by marking cells in developing tissues and then observing the pattern of marked descendants in the adult structure. X-ray-induced alteration of cellular phenotype is the most powerful method of studying cell lineages in the imaginal development of insects. The x-rays cause a calculable number of chromosome crossing-over events which mark the affected cells by altered phenotype, such as different color or bristle configuration. The spatial pattern of cells with altered phenotype is then observed in the adult and, in ideal cases, represents the progeny of one founder cell. *See* FATE MAPS (EMBRYOLOGY).

Some of the most promising cell lineage studies are conducted on a nematode worm, *Caenorhabditis elegans*, which is a small (1 mm or 0.04 in. in length), nearly transparent worm that lives in soil. Adults are either males or hermaphrodites; the hermaphrodites contain 959 somatic nuclei. The origin of each somatic cell can be traced back to a single blastomere, and the clonal history of each cell has been determined (see **illus.**). A detailed genetic map for the 80,000 kilobase genome has been worked out. The short (3 days) generation time makes it possible to follow the effects of defined mutations upon the differentiation of specific cells. The relative roles of genetic programs as opposed to extrinsic signals can be assessed, for example, by destroying a particular cell during a defined stage of development and observing the effect on the differentiation of surrounding cells. The techniques of molecular genetics, particularly insertion and

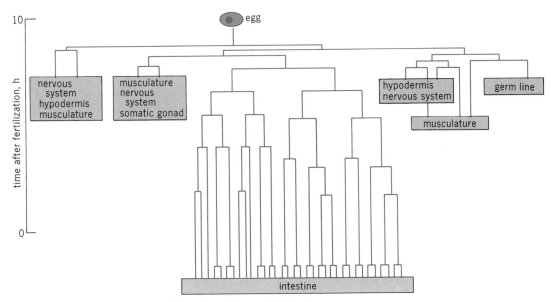

Lineage tree for the cells that form the intestine of *Caenorhabditis elegans*.

deletion of specified stretches of deoxyribonucleic acid (DNA) at specific chromosomal sites in *C. elegans*, should be particularly useful in determining the role of regulatory genes whose product may not be a structural or enzymatic protein. Because each stage of the differentiation of a particular cell can be described, the effects of alteration of the activity of any gene on the differentiation or interaction with surrounding cells can be precisely delineated. *See* DEVELOPMENTAL GENETICS; INVERTEBRATE EMBRYOLOGY; OVUM.

Spencer J. Berry

Plants. Cell lineage analysis in plants, as in animals, involves tracing the origin of particular cells in the adult body back to their progenitor cells. The adult body of a typical plant consists primarily of leaves, stems, and roots. Cells arise continuously during plant life from specialized dividing cell populations called meristems. A shoot apical meristem produces the leaves and stem, and a root apical meristem produces root tissue. The shoot apical meristem will also produce specialized structures, such as cones, flowers, thorns, tendrils, and so on. Because plant cells do not move during development, and in many cases the plane of cell division is constant, lines of cells, called cell files, all derive from a single meristem cell at the base of the file. Cell files are particularly obvious in root tissue of ferns and higher plants. Although the organization of cells in plants follows regular patterns, the fate of individual cells is not as rigidly determined as cell fates are in animals. In plants, anatomical position determines a cell's typical fate, but if the pattern is disrupted by injury, for example, cells can differentiate into a variety of cell types. *See* APICAL MERISTEM.

Study of chimeras. Cell lineage can be examined in a more sophisticated manner by examining individual organs, such as leaves, to determine how many cells form a leaf and how these cells are oriented to one another as the organ forms. Exact cell lineages are most readily followed by using a color marker, such as chlorophyll-deficient cells which are white. Plant developmental biologists have used naturally occurring green-white chimeric plants, such as variegated ivy, or chimeras have been created by mutation. A common practice is to x-irradiate seeds that are heterozygous for one or more color loci (+ for color, − for albino) to create some meristem cells in which the chromosome arm carrying the (+) allele is lost from the cell, leaving only the (−) allele. This (−) cell and all of its progeny will be albino. *See* CHIMERA.

By using such mutated stocks, the contribution of the albino cell lineage to individual organs can be determined. Two types of observations are made. The first is the apparent cell number. If a leaf is 90% green and 10% albino, the simplest explanation is that the leaf was originally composed of 10 cells: 9 normal green ones and 1 mutant albino one. Thus the apparent cell number of the leaf is 10, indicating that 10 cells in the shoot apical meristem contributed to the leaf's formation. The second observation is the extent of the defect. If the albino sector is found in only a single leaf, this suggests that the meristem is very large and that the albino cell, and by inference all other cells in the meristem, typically contributes to only a single leaf on the plant. More often, albino sectors will be found on a number of leaves, indicating that meristem cells contribute to many different leaves. In some cases in which the plant has opposite leaves, all of the leaves on one side may be completely green while those on the opposite side all have an albino sector. Such an observation suggests that there are two groups of cells in the meristem, each producing leaves exclusively on one side of the stem.

Lineage in growing leaves. To gain further information

about the pattern of cell division within an organ such as a leaf, experimentalists have x-irradiated leaves as they are growing. The earlier the mutations are induced, the larger the resulting sectors, because early in development the leaf is composed of few cells, each of which will give rise to a substantial fraction of the final leaf. Mutations induced late in development, when the leaf has thousands of cells, result in sectors that are tiny dots or streaks on the leaf. Such tiny sectors are used to determine where cell divisions are occurring in the leaf late in its development; areas lacking any dots or streaks have their final cell number, so no mutant cell lineages are visible.

Cell lineage analysis is a powerful tool for the study of plant development. By simple rules of observation and analysis, a great deal can be learned about the structure and activity of the meristems and about the timing and pattern of cell division in the developing organs. *See* PLANT GROWTH; PLANT MORPHOGENESIS.   Virginia Walbot

Bibliography. B. Alberts et al., *The Molecular Biology of the Cell*, 1983; E. H. Davidson, *Gene Activity in Early Development*, 2d ed., 1976; A. Garcia-Bellido, P. A. Lawrence, and G. Morata, Compartments in animal development, *Sci. Amer.*, 1979; P. Grant, *Biology of Developing Systems*, 1978; M. M. Johri and E. H. Coe, Jr., Clonal analysis of corn plant development, *Develop. Biol.*, 97:154–172, 1983; C. Kenyon, The nematode *Caenorhabditis elegans, Science*, 240:1448–1453, 1988; N. Le Douarin (ed.), *Cell Lineage, Stem Cells and Cell Differentiation*, 1979; W. F. Loomis, *Development Biology*, 1986; S. Subtelny and I. M. Sussex (eds.), *The Clonal Basis of Development*, 1978; K. M. Wilbur (ed.), *The Mollusca*, vol. 3, 1983.

Cell membranes

The membrane that surrounds the cytoplasm of a cell; it is also called the plasma membrane or, in a more general sense, a unit membrane. This is a very thin, semifluid, sheetlike structure made of four continuous monolayers of molecules. Cells usually contain internal structures called organelles that are made of membranes. The plasma membrane and the membranes making up all the membranous organelles display a common molecular architectural pattern of organization, the unit membrane pattern, even though the particular molecular species making up the various unit membranes differ considerably from membrane to membrane. All unit membranes consist of a bilayer of lipid molecules, the polar surfaces of which are directed outward and covered by at least one monolayer of nonlipid molecules on each side, most of which are protein, packed on the lipid bilayer surfaces and held there by various intermolecular forces. Some of these proteins, called intrinsic proteins, traverse the bilayer and are represented on both sides. These usually can

be removed from the membrane only by disruption of the lipid bilayer with chaotropic agents such as detergents. The segments of the polypeptide chains of these transverse proteins within the core of the lipid bilayer may form channels that provide low-resistance pathways for ions and small molecules to get across the membrane in a controlled fashion. Sugar moieties are found in both the proteins and lipids of the outer half of the unit membrane, but not on the inside next to the cytoplasm. The molecular composition of each lipid monolayer making up the lipid bilayer is different. The unit membrane is thus chemically asymmetric. *See* CELL ORGANIZATION.

Unit membrane. The unit membrane of a cell is a continuous structure having one surface bordered by cytoplasm and the other by the outside world. It appears in thin sections with the electron microscope as a triple-layered structure about 7.5–10 nanometers thick consisting of two parallel dense strata each about 2.5 nm thick separated by a light interzone of about the same thickness (**Fig. 1**). The plasma membrane may become tucked into the cytoplasm and pinch off to make an isolated vesicle containing extracellular material by a process called endocytosis. Cells take in water or external foodstuff materials by this process, and here the special terms pinocytosis and phagocytosis are used. During all these processes the membrane still maintains its orientation, with its cytoplasmic surface remaining next to cytoplasm. In this sense the contents of intracellular organelles, such as the endoplasmic reticulum, Golgi apparatus sacs, nuclear membrane, lysosomes, peroxisomes, and secretion granules, are material of the outside world, since at some time the space occupied by this material may become continuous directly or indirectly with the outside world. Hence the surface of the membrane bordering such material and lying between it and cytoplasm is topographically an external membrane surface even though it may be contained completely within the cell. *See* ENDOCYTOSIS.

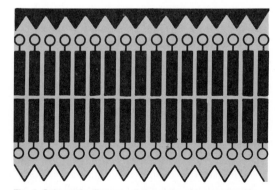

Fig. 1. Schematic diagram of the molecular organization of a unit membrane. Lipid molecules are represented as a solid bar for the hydrophobic carbon chains and by a circle for the polar head groups. Nonlipid is represented by zigzag lines, which are filled in for the outer layer. The nonlipid is protein, but in the outer surface there is also carbohydrate.

Eukaryotic cells are characterized by the triple-layered nature of the unit membrane. The genetic material is segregated into a central region bounded by the nuclear membrane that is penetrated by many pores containing special proteins. It can be thought of as a group of flattened sacs of the endoplasmic reticulum arranged so as to place a pair of unit membranes between the nucleoplasm and the rest of the cytoplasm. Bacteria (prokaryotes) do not contain such elaborate systems of internal membranes, but some have an external unit membrane separated from the plasma membrane by a special material called periplasm. The membrane does not normally flip over, so that the surface that borders the outside world, either at the cell surface or inside the cell, comes to border cytoplasm. This principle is maintained in all membranous organelles.

Mitochondria are a special case because the inner mitochondrial membrane is believed to be the membrane of a primitive one-celled organism that is symbiotically related to the cell and lies inside a cavity containing material of the outside world as defined above. The outer mitochondrial membrane is in this sense a membrane of the cell analogous to a smooth endoplasmic reticulum membrane, and the inner membrane of the mitochondrion is the plasma membrane of the included organism, which normally does not become continuous with the membrane of the cell. Thus it has its own unit membrane, and again the orientation of this unit membrane is always maintained, with one side directed toward the cytoplasm, in this case the cytoplasm of the mitochondrion. *See* MITOCHONDRIA.

Function and origin. The cell membrane functions as a barrier that makes it possible for the cytoplasm to maintain a different composition from the material surrounding the cell. The unit membrane is freely permeable to water molecules but very impermeable to ions and charged molecules. It is permeable to small molecules in inverse proportion to their size but in direct proportion to their lipid solubility. It contains various pumps and channels made of specific transverse membrane proteins that allow concentration gradients to be maintained between the inside and outside of the cell. For example, there is a cation pump that actively extrudes sodium ions (Na^+) from the cytoplasm and builds up a concentration of potassium ions (K^+) within it. The major anions inside the cell are chlorine ions (Cl^-) and negatively charged protein molecules, the latter of which cannot penetrate the membrane. The presence of the charged protein molecules leads to a buildup of a Donnan electroosmotic potential across the membrane with the outside positive. The sodium pump actively extrudes Na^+ to the outside and K^+ to the inside, adding to the Donnan potential. The membrane potential may be as high as 100 mV in nerve and muscle cells capable of conducting an action potential. Action potentials result from the sequential spreading transient opening of Na^+ or calcium ion (Ca^{2+}) channels depolarizing the membrane, followed by an opening of K^+ channels leading to repolarization. This occurs along an excitable membrane such as that of a nerve or muscle fiber, and this is one of the most important functions of membranes, since it makes it possible for the brain to work by sending or receiving signals sent over nerve fibers for great distances, as well as many other things. *See* BIOPOTENTIALS AND IONIC CURRENTS.

The plasma membrane contains numerous receptor molecules that are involved in communication with other cells and the outside world in general. These respond to antigens, hormones, and neurotransmitters in various ways. Thymus lymphocytes (T cells) are activated by attachment of antigens to specific proteins in the external surfaces of the T cells as an important part of the immune responses of an organism. The binding of antigens or other molecules to receptors in the external surfaces of membranes may result in lateral movements of the receptor molecule complexes to sites where they aggregate and become tucked into the cytoplasm by endocytosis. This is mediated by a special cytoplasmic cytoskeletal protein called clathrin which participates with other cytoskeletal proteins in moving the endocytotic vesicles to specific sites in the cell where they may fuse with some organelle such as a lysosome. The lysosome contains many acidic proteolytic enzymes which break down the internalized molecules to small fragments that may then enter the cytoplasm. *See* CELLULAR IMMUNOLOGY; LYSOSOME.

Hormones such as epinephrine and glucagon attach to a receptor protein in the surfaces of cells and cause the activation of adenylate cyclase, which in turn causes the formation of cyclic adenosinemonophosphate, called a second messenger (the hormone is the first messenger). Cyclic adenosinemonophosphate may do various things such as activate specific enzymes like protein kinases, which may phosphorylate channel proteins and affect the flow of ions through the cell membrane with profound effects on cell function. Neurotransmitters attach to the postsynaptic membrane in synapses in the nervous system and mediate the transfer of information between neurons. There is a class of membrane proteins called cell adhesion molecules that are components of the outer surfaces of the membranes of cells in the developing nervous system that is thought to be involved intimately in guiding development during embryonic life.

It is known that under the conditions prevailing in the primitive oceans at the time that life originated, various biological molecules could have been formed. Lipid molecules are generally simpler than the more complex protein and nucleic acid molecules necessary for life, and it seems very likely that lipid molecules were formed first and that lipid bilayer–limited vesicles were available

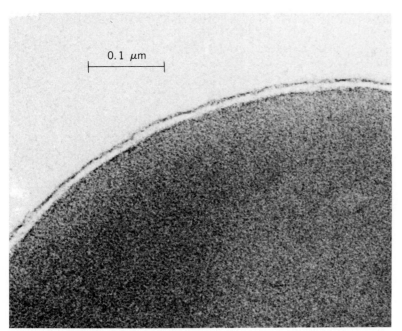

Fig. 2. Thin section of a part of a human red blood cell. Note the triple-layered pattern. The light central zone is somewhat variable in thickness and generally somewhat broadened after this preparation technique.

the definitive conclusion that the Schwann cell membrane consists of a single lipid bilayer core with the polar surfaces of the bilayer directed outward and covered by monolayers of non-lipid as indicated highly schematically in the molecular diagram in Fig. 1. It was further concluded that the Schwann cell membrane was chemically asymmetric and that the asymmetry was likely due to carbohydrate in the external surface of the membrane. It is now accepted that this is generally true of all unit membranes and the asymmetry includes the lipids. Membranes appeared by electron microscopic examination in thin transverse sections of heavy metal–stained cells as two parallel dense lines separated by a light interzone measuring about 7.5–10 nm in overall thickness (**Fig. 2**). This triple-layered structure was demonstrated to be present in all membranes and membranous organelles of animal cells. It was also demonstrated in plant cells, in bacteria, and in those viruses having a membrane. Since this was found to be the fundamental repeating unit of all biological membrane structures, it was called the unit membrane. This general concept is now accepted to be true of all membranes.

In the early 1970s it was postulated that some membrane proteins might traverse the lipid bilayer and be represented by polypeptide moieties on both the cytoplasmic and external surfaces. H. M. Whiteley and H. C. Berg provided the first proof of this in 1974, and the hypothetical fluid mosaic model proposed earlier (**Fig. 3**) by S. J. Singer and G. L. Nicholson became generally accepted. It was realized, however, that the lipid bilayer is not likely to be as naked as this model proposed, because the surface tension of membranes does not fit the model and because the phospholipids of the bilayer are not as accessible to the action of phospholipases as would be the case if this model were correct. Furthermore, membranes, although fluid, are not always as fluid as this model requires them to be. For these and other reasons the model presented in **Fig. 4** and called the hydrophobic barrier model has been proposed as the modern form of the unit

when the first proteins and nucleic acid molecules were produced. The presence of the bilayer would have made it possible for these molecules to be segregated together in an environment that could become specialized, allowing life processes to begin. The unit membrane thus may be considered to be the essential first structure for the origin of life. Certainly its presence has always been necessary for the maintenance of life, since its removal invariably results in rapid death of any cell. *See* PREBIOTIC ORGANIC SYNTHESIS.

Origin of unit membrane concept. In the late nineteenth century, several individuals suggested that cells might be surrounded by a thin membrane that acted as a barrier to the free passage of ions, and since it was noted that lipid soluble molecules crossed the barrier more easily than water-soluble ones of the same size, it was believed that lipid might be involved. Work in the early part of the twentieth century on monomolecular films of lipid molecules led to the idea that monolayers of lipid might be involved, and it was postulated that they might exist in a bilayer. However, there was no proof that the structure was simply a bilayer since there was evidence suggesting that more than two monolayers of lipid might be present in some membranes.

The application of the electron microscope to the problem in the 1950s provided the first definitive evidence that all biological membranes contain as a core structure one and only one lipid bilayer. This concept originated from studies of the myelin sheath of nerve fibers by thin-section electron microscopy with the demonstration that it was made of a single, closely packed, spirally wound Schwann cell membrane. Studies allowed

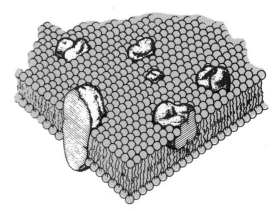

Fig. 3. Diagram of the fluid-mosaic cell membrane model. The lipid bilayer is shown as almost completely naked and with iceberglike dense islands of protein floating in it.

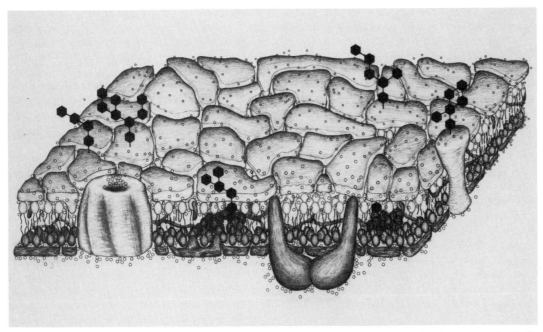

Fig. 4. Diagram of cross section of a unit membrane (hydrophobic barrier model) showing the lipid bilayer covered on both sides by monolayers of protein. The lipid molecules are shown with the head groups filled in on the cytoplasmic (lower) half of the bilayer to indicate the asymmetry of the lipids of the bilayer. The small circles represent water molecules. The shapes of the protein molecules are arbitrary. Three of these have groups of hexagons (sugar residues) attached to their outer surface; some are shown as head groups of glycolipids.

membrane model. It is not meant to imply that this model is not fluid, only that the bilayer is almost completely covered. Some cracks are doubtless present, but they are scarce. Both lipid and protein molecules may move around extensively, but there may be some hindrance due to interactions of the proteins with one another and some of the lipids and proteins may move together as mosaics.

Hydrophilicity, hydrophobicity, and amphiphiles. Molecules that are themselves electrically polarized like water readily dissolve in it and are said to be hydrophilic. The reason these molecules enter water readily is that they have a polar structure like water and hence cause less disruption of the hydrogen-bonded groups of water molecules that characterize liquid water. It thus takes relatively little energy to get these molecules into solution in water. Molecules that are relatively electrically nonpolarized do not so readily enter water and are said to be hydrophobic.

There is a class of molecules, called amphiphiles, that are both hydrophilic and hydrophobic. Typically, such molecules are hydrophilic at one end and hydrophobic at the other. Double bonds may cause kinks to develop in the carbon chain that affect membrane fluidity. There are two kinds of kinks, cis and trans: the former makes a bend like the one in oleic acid (**Fig. 5**), but the latter leaves the chain fairly straight. More than one double bond introduces more complicated kinks, as in linoleic acid (Fig. 5). Different membranes have different fatty acids with varying degrees of unsaturation, and this has important effects on their function and degrees of fluidity. In diagrams like that in Figs. 1 and

2, it is customary to represent such molecules by a circle for the polar head and a line or bar for the hydrophobic tail.

When a small amount of a fatty acid is placed on a water surface, the molecules do not fully penetrate the surface. The head groups enter the water, but the tails do not. If a barrier is moved along the water surface so as to press the molecules together, the head groups come into contact in the water and the tails stick up in the air and associate laterally with one another, picket-fence-like, by very weak London–van der Waals attractive forces, making a

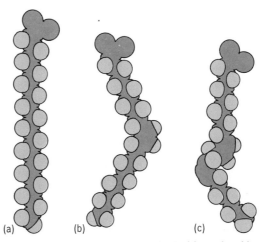

(a)   (b)   (c)

Fig. 5. Space-filling models of three lipids: (a) stearic acid, which is saturated; (b) oleic acid, which has one double bond shown in the cis conformation here; and (c) linoleic acid, which has two double bonds, one in the trans and one in the cis conformation.

lipid monolayer. If the solvent with fatty acid is injected under the water surface, a spherical droplet of solvent forms, and at the boundary between the solvent and the water a similar thing may happen. The hydrophilic head groups enter the water, and the tails come together to make a lipid monolayer. If the solvent is then removed, the two monolayers of lipid may come together with the tails associating to make a lipid bilayer. If there is enough amphiphile present, the edges of such a bilayer may spontaneously zip together to fuse into a spherical vesicle that is a form of micelle. The core structure of all unit membranes is a lipid bilayer such as this, except that the lipid molecules are more complex. Several bilayers may come together to make a larger micelle containing many bilayers. *See* MICELLE.

The hydrophobic bond is very important in the maintenance of membrane structure. The London–van der Waals forces between the carbon chains of lipid molecules in the bilayer are relatively weak and are not the hydrophobic bonds that are usually meant by this term. The term is best defined thermodynamically in terms of free energy. Free-energy change (ΔF) is the sum of heat content or enthalpy (ΔH) minus the product of absolute temperature and entropy ($T\Delta S$): $\Delta F = \Delta H - T\Delta S$. Entropy can be regarded as disorder. A chain of $—CH_2—$ groups in water induces formation of ordered cages of hydrogen-bonded water molecules around it analogous to the clathrate cages that form about noble gases in water. If the $—CH_2—$ group is removed these cages become disordered; that is, there is an increase in entropy. This is of greater magnitude than the decrease in entropy that results from association of the $—CH_2—$ groups, which occurs as they are removed from water. At constant temperature the term $T\Delta S$ thus becomes larger. The enthalpy change is relatively small so that the free energy decreases by about 1000 kcal (4.2 × 10^6 J)/mole for each $—CH_2—$ group transferred from water to a nonaqueous medium. Thus carbon chains tend to be driven out of water. This is the nature of the hydrophobic bond that is the major factor that stabilizes the lipid bilayer of the unit membrane.

Membrane lipids. The fatty acids of membranes are of various chain lengths usually with 15–20 carbon atoms in straight chains, and they are parts of more complex lipid molecules. The major lipids of membranes are phospholipids with a glycerol backbone including phosphophatidyl ethanolamine, phosphatidyl choline, phosphatidyl serine, phosphatidyl inositol, and cardiolipin. Cardiolipin is more complex because it contains two glycerols and four fatty acids. It is important in bacterial membranes and is also found, interestingly, in the mitochondrial inner membrane.

The sphingolipids are another class of membrane lipids having the compound sphingosine as their backbone structure instead of glycerol. Ce-ramide is a fatty acid derivative of sphingosine that is the parent substance of many important membrane lipids. Sphingomyelin is ceramide with phosphatidyl choline added. This is the only phospholipid of membranes not based on glycerol. This molecule, like phosphatidyl choline and phosphatidyl ethanolamine, is a zwitterion at pH 7; that is, it is uncharged. Phosphatidyl serine is negatively charged.

The glycolipids are an important class of lipid not containing phosphorus and based on ceramide. These include the uncharged cerebrosides that have only one sugar group, either glucose or galactose, and the gangliosides that may contain branched chains of as many as seven sugar residues including sialic acid, which is charged.

Cholesterol is a very important membrane lipid. It is present only in eukaryotes and is a prominent constituent of red blood cells, liver cells, and nerve myelin. *See* CHOLESTEROL.

The different lipid molecules are not equally distributed on both sides of the bilayer. The amino lipids, glycolipids, and cholesterol are located primarily in the outer monolayer, and the choline and sphingolipids are located mainly in the internal monolayer. The fatty acids of the outer half of the bilayer tend to have longer, more saturated carbon chains than those of the inner half.

The lipid bilayer has a considerable degree of fluidity, with the lipid molecules tending to rotate and translate easily, but they do not ordinarily flipflop from one side of the bilayer to the other. Furthermore, some lipids are firmly attached to membrane proteins and translate laterally only as the proteins do so. Some membrane proteins form extended two-dimensional crystals, and their lateral movement is thus restricted. Nevertheless, there is a considerable degree of fluidity in membranes overall. *See* LIPID.

Membrane proteins. Most proteins are hydrophilic. They are made of polypeptide chains of polar and nonpolar amino acids. Usually the chain is folded into a globular structure with hydrophilic amino acid side chains to the outside and hydrophobic ones tucked inside. For this reason the common globular protein is hydrophilic. Sometimes stretches of hydrophobic amino acids occur in the chain and may divide it into two hydrophilic domains. If there is a stretch of hydrophobic amino acids long enough (about 20) to stretch across the hydrophobic interior of the bilayer, the extrusion of the protein across the bilayer during protein synthesis may stop, leaving a hydrophilic part of the protein on the cytoplasmic side and another hydrophilic part on the outside. This protein then becomes an intrinsic amphiphilic transmembrane protein. Such proteins are clearly intrinsic, and they can be removed only with chaotropic agents that destroy the bilayer.

The ratio of protein to lipids in membranes is often about 1:1 as is the case with the erythrocyte, but in some cases, such as nerve myelin, there is only about 20% protein. However, even in this case, if certain assumptions are made about the state of the protein, there is enough to cover the lipid polar surfaces on both sides. Furthermore, protein is easily lost during the isolation procedures, and so it is not unreasonable to suppose that the lipid bilayer is generally completely covered by proteins. In addition, there is a good theoretical reason to suppose that the bilayer is covered completely. It is well known that any hydrophilic surface in contact with water containing dissolved protein always becomes completely covered by a monolayer of protein. It seems unlikely, though perhaps not impossible, that the inside of cells contains no dissolved protein in contact with the membrane, but the external surfaces certainly are continually exposed to dissolved protein. The exposed surfaces should be completely covered even if only with denatured protein. Still, some authorities believe there may be extensive areas of naked lipid bilayer even on the external side of unit membranes.

Some proteins clearly become attached to either the inside or outside of the bilayer by more specific interactions with the polar heads of the lipid molecules, and sometimes it is not clear whether such proteins should be called extrinsic or intrinsic. They are extrinsic in that they can be removed without using detergents to disrupt the lipid bilayer completely, but they are intrinsic in that they are permanent parts of the membrane and retain some tightly bound lipids when removed. Spectrin and anchorin in the erythrocyte membrane are firmly bound to the cytoplasmic surfaces presumably by polar head group interactions and can thus be regarded as intrinsic. Another example of such a protein is ligatin, a small (about 10,000 daltons), highly charged membrane protein confined to the outer half of the bilayer in the membranes of the endocytic complex of the cells of the sucking mammalian ileum, where the molecule binds the enzyme *n*-acetyl glucosaminidase to the external surface of the membrane. Ligatin can be removed with high calcium concentrations and takes with it a complement of firmly bound lipid that is mainly triphosphoinositol. Ligatin certainly is an intrinsic protein, but there is no evidence that it is a transmembrane protein. Thus the classification of membrane proteins as intrinsic and extrinsic is not always easy. *See* CELL (BIOLOGY); PLANT CELL; PROTEIN.　　　　　　　　J. David Robertson

Bibliography. R. M. Bailian et al. (eds.), *Membranes and Intercellular Communication*, 1981; E. L. Becker (ed.), *Membrane Activation in Immunologically Relevant Cells*, 1988; G. Benga and J. M. Tager (eds.), *Biomembranes*, 1988; D. C. Chang et al. (eds.), *Structure and Function of Excitable Cells*, 1983; M. P. Chech and C. R. Kahn, *Membrane Receptors and Cellular Regulation*, 1985; J. B. Finean et al., *Membranes and Their Cellular Functions*, 2d ed., 1984; L. Pauling, *The Nature of the Chemical Bond*, 3d ed., 1960; C. Tanford, *The Hydrophobic Effect: Formation of Micelles and Biological Membranes*, 2d ed., 1980; G. Weissmann and R. Claiborne (eds.), *Cell Membranes: Biochemistry, Cell Biology and Pathology*, 1975; P. Yeagle, *The Membranes of Cells*, 1987.

Cell metabolism

The sum of chemical reactions which transpire within cells. The cell is a self-contained chemical factory which interacts with its environment. This factory is unique in that it is a structure which moves, manufactures products for its own use and for the use of other factories, takes in from the outside that which it needs and discards that which it does not, and has the property of producing factories identical to itself from its own substance. The cell performs chemical, osmotic, mechanical, and electrical work, for which it needs energy. Plant cells obtain energy from sunlight; using light energy, they convert simple compounds such as carbon dioxide and various nitrogen, phosphate, and sulfur compounds into more complex materials. The energy in light is thus "stored" as chemical substances, mostly carbohydrates, within plant cells. Animal cells cannot use sunlight directly, and they obtain their energy by breaking down the stored chemical compounds of plant cells. Bacterial cells obtain their energy in various ways, but again mostly by the degradation of some of the simple compounds in their environment. *See* BACTERIAL PHYSIOLOGY AND METABOLISM; PHOTOSYNTHESIS; PLANT METABOLISM.

Dynamic state. The chemical atoms of the biological world are relatively few in number, being mostly carbon, hydrogen, oxygen, nitrogen, phosphorus, sulfur, iron, magnesium, and minute amounts of others. These atoms are grouped together into biological molecules, the most prevalent being proteins, carbohydrates, fats, and nucleic acids. These latter differ greatly among themselves in their chemistry and their functions. Their characteristics are given elsewhere, but they all have one thing in common: They are being continually broken down or degraded and being resynthesized by the cell. Thus, a feature of the cell is continuous metabolism of its chemical constituents.

Furthermore, cells have definite structures, and even the chemical constituents of these structures are being constantly renewed. This continuing turnover has been called the dynamic state of cellular constituents. For example, an animal cell takes in carbohydrate molecules, breaks down some of them to obtain the energy which is necessary to replace the chemical molecules that are being turned over, while another fraction of these molecules is integrated into the substance of the cell or its extracellular coverings. The energy obtained is, of course, also used for all the purposes mentioned above. Another way of stating it is that the cell is constantly striving to maintain an organized structure, a structure which has many functions, not the least of which is to duplicate itself, in the face of an environment which is continuously striving to degrade that structure into a random mixture of chemical molecules.

Chemical specificity. All the large molecules of the cell have rather specific functions: Carbohydrates, fats, and proteins constitute the structures of the cells; these, particularly the former two, are also used for food, or energy, depots; the nucleic acids are the structures involved in the continuity of cell types from generation to generation. All these large molecules are really variegated polymers of smaller molecules. These smaller molecules interact with one another in chemical reactions which are catalyzed at cellular temperature by biological protein catalysts called enzymes. These chemical reactions involve the breakdown of molecules, the condensing of one molecule to another to form a larger one, and the reforming of a third compound from parts of two constituents.

All these reactions are very specific, being catalyzed by specific enzymes, each enzyme being a specific protein, having a singular structure and performing a singular function, only reacting with its own specified substrate or substrates. At present, about a thousand chemical reactions are known which occur within cells; thus, about a thousand specific enzymes are known, some having been purified to crystalline form. *See* CARBOHYDRATE METABOLISM; ENZYME; LIPID METABOLISM; NUCLEIC ACID; PROTEIN METABOLISM.

Metabolic pathways. By studying how these enzymes operate and what substrates they attack, the biochemist has learned in general, and in many cases in specific, how fats, carbohydrates, proteins, and nucleic acids are synthesized and degraded in cells. Mainly through the use of radioactive tracer atoms, the pathways of many chemical compounds within the cell have been realized. For example, it is known what part of the carbohydrate molecule is used for energy production, what part is used in fat storage, and what parts end up in proteins and nucleic acids. Via the vast array of enzymatic reactions which go on inside cells, the substances which a cell "eats" or brings in are completely changed, becoming transformed into cell substance. This changeover, these syntheses of specific cell substances, need energy for accomplishment.

Energy source. As mentioned, this energy comes from the breakdown of various foodstuffs a burning up of substrate, an oxidation; but unlike mechanical machines in which energy is given off as heat, the cell has evolved an energy coin. This coin is a chemical compound called adenosinetriphosphate (ATP); it is synthesized enzymatically by the cell in a number of reactions in which various compounds coming from foodstuffs are oxidized, and thus the energy gained as a result of this oxidation is not lost as heat but stored in ATP. Subsequently, all cellular reactions which require synthesis of cell-specific substances use this ATP as a source of energy for

these syntheses. For example, fats are composed mainly of carbon, oxygen, and hydrogen; when fats are used as foodstuff by the cell, the compounds are degraded, oxygen and hydrogen end up in the form of water and carbon in the form of carbon dioxide, and overall energy is gained in the form of ATP. When fats have to be synthesized by the cell, this ATP is used as an energy source to recombine small chemical molecules containing these atoms into certain kinds of fats. But since the cell needs to synthesize other molecules as well, these same carbon atoms, for example, are also found (via synthetic reactions) in carbohydrates, proteins, and nucleic acids. In this way the molecules, of which these atoms are a part, are being constantly replaced. *See* ADENOSINETRIPHOSPHATE (ATP).

Control and continuity. Remarkably, even with these constant replacements going on, the cell never loses its own distinctive structure and function. The reason is that the ordering of the cell resides in a code of nucleic acids, which directs the syntheses of specific enzymes designed to do specific tasks; when these enzymes, being proteins and being also replaced like the other molecules of the cell, are degraded and have to be resynthesized, they are made again in exactly the same way as before. In this way continuity is ensured. *See* DEOXYRIBONUCLEIC ACID (DNA); GENETICS; RIBONUCLEIC ACID (RNA).

Metabolic differentiation in cells. To accomplish the many tasks outlined above, the cell is comparmentalized into distinctive functioning structures. The production of usable energy in the form of ATP takes place in plant and animal cells in membranous structures called mitochondria. Even in bacteria, which are about the size of mitochondria, these events occur on the membrane surrounding the bacterium. In plants the capture of light energy and the production of ATP therefrom take place in structures called chloroplasts. Proteins, including enzyme proteins, are sythesized by tiny particles called ribosomes. The synthesis of carbohydrates in plants occurs within chloroplasts, while the synthesis of fatty acids in animal cells occurs in mitochondria. The structures involved in the continuity of cell structure and function, in the heredity of the cell, are the nucleic acid–containing chromosomes of the nucleus. In addition, cells have a variety of other structures, not as important as those above, but which nevertheless have distinctive functional tasks, such as storage granules, secretory granules, and lytic granules. *See* CELL PLASTIDS; CHROMOSOME; MITOCHONDRIA; RIBOSOMES.

Control mechanisms. Finally, although a great deal is known of the metabolism of a large variety of compounds, their degradation and syntheses, and the interaction between chemical substances, little is known of how these multitudinous reactions are regulated within the cell to effect growth, particular size, and division into daughter cells having the same structure and functioning characteristics as those of the parent cells. It is known that enzymatic reaction activities within cells are strictly governed so that in quite a few cases knowledge has been gained of how a cell shuts off the synthesis of a compound of which it has enough, or speeds up the syntheses of those in short supply. It is all done by an enzyme so constructed that the compound which it synthesizes, say, can interact with this enzyme to inhibit further activity of the enzyme; thus not too much of the compound is formed at any one time. In the cells of a multicellular organism, cells interact with cells, their metabolism being geared among themselves, and this gearing, or regulation, probably occurs via the action of intercellular messengers or hormones. *See* HORMONE.

In summary, almost the sole justification for cell metabolism is the functioning of a vehicle whose major task is to reproduce as precise a replica of itself as possible. The efficiency of this metabolism has been maximized with this goal in view. *See* CELL (BIOLOGY).   Philip Siekevitz

Bibliography. T. A. Subramanian (ed.), *Cell Metabolism: Growth and Environment*, 2 vols., 1986; G. R. Welch and J. S. Clegg (eds.), *The Organization of Cell Metabolism*, 1987.

Cell motility

The movement of cells, changes in cell shape including cell division, and the movement of materials within cells. Many free-living protozoa are capable of movement, as are sperm and ameboid cells of higher organisms. Coordinated movement of cells occurs during embryogenesis, wound healing, and muscle contraction in higher organisms. Cell division is observed in all organisms and is a requirement for reproduction, growth, and development. Many cells also undergo structural changes as they differentiate, such as the outgrowth of axonal and dendritic processes during nerve cell differentiation. A more subtle form of cell motility involves active transport of membranous organelles within the cytoplasm. This form of movement is required for proper organization of cytoplasmic contents, and the redistribution of metabolites, hormones, and other materials within the cell.

Molecules responsible for movement. There are two basic molecular systems responsible for producing a variety of forms of movement in a wide range of cell types: one system involves filamentous polymers of the globular protein actin; the other involves hollow, tube-shaped polymers of the globular protein tubulin, known as microtubules (see **illus.**). Associated with both actin filaments and microtubules are accessory enzymes that convert the chemical energy stored in adenosinetriphosphate (ATP) into mechanical energy. Other proteins are responsible for regulating the arrangement, assembly, and organization of actin filaments and microtubules within the cell.

Actin and myosin. Muscle contraction represents one of the most extensively studied forms of cell movement, and it is from muscle that much basic knowledge of actin-based movement has been derived. Striated muscle cells found in skeletal muscle and heart muscle contain highly organized arrays of actin filaments interdigitating with filaments of the protein myosin. Myosin has an enzymatic activity that catalyzes the breakdown of ATP to adenosinediphosphate (ADP) and phosphate. The released energy is used to produce force against the actin filaments, which results in sliding between the actin and myosin filaments. *See* MUSCLE PROTEINS.

These proteins have by now been found in virtually all cell types. The actin and myosin filaments are less highly organized in smooth muscle and nonmuscle cells than in striated muscle; however, they act by the same force-producing mechanism.

Microtubules, dynein, and kinesin. Microtubules were initially described as components of eukaryotic cilia and flagella. Like actin filaments, microtubules have by now been found within the cytoplasm of almost all eukaryotic cells.

Two different molecules, dynein and kinesin, have been identified as enzymes that break down ATP to ADP and phosphate to produce force along microtubules. Dynein is a large enzyme complex that was initially identified in cilia and flagella. It has also been found associated with cytoplasmic microtubules. Kinesin is a force-producing enzyme that was initially found in microtubules prepared

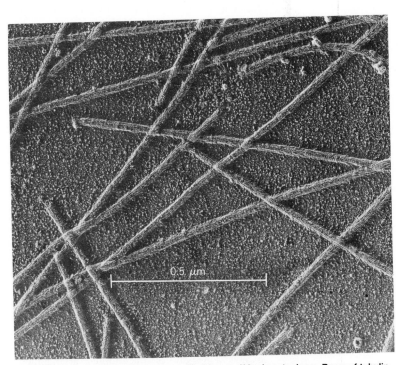

Electron micrograph of microtubules purified from calf brain cytoplasm. Rows of tubulin subunits along the microtubule axis can be discerned by close inspection. (*Courtesy of John Aghajanian*)

from neuronal cells. It is now also known to be widespread.

Despite the basic similarity in how the three force-producing enzymes (myosin, dynein, and kinesin) work, they differ from each other in structure and enzymatic properties and there is no evidence that they are evolutionarily related. Kinesin and dynein differ from each other in another important way: they produce force in opposite directions along microtubules. This suggests that they play complementary roles in the cell. As yet, no enzyme has been identified that produces force along actin filaments in the direction opposite to myosin.

Molecular and genetic analysis of a variety of organisms has revealed a remarkable diversity of kinesin- and myosin-related proteins in cells. The parts of these molecules responsible for producing force are closely related to the corresponding parts of kinesin and myosin. However, the remainder of the kinesin- and myosin-related molecules are structurally diverse. This pattern suggests that the kinesin- and myosin-related proteins attach to different structures within the cell, each individual protein being responsible for a specific type of movement. Multiple forms of dynein have also been identified. The members of the dynein family of proteins are much more closely interrelated than are the members of the myosin and kinesin families. The dyneins fall into two classes: a cytoplasmic dynein and several ciliary and flagellar dyneins. Novel tubulin- and actin-related proteins have been identified. With the exception of γ-tubulin, the functions of these proteins are as yet poorly understood.

Actin and microtubule assembly and organization. Another factor involved in cellular and intracellular movement is the assembly and rearrangement of actin and tubulin polymers. Actin filaments in muscle and microtubules in cilia and flagella are relatively stable structures. However, in other situations, both polymers are in equilibrium with their subunits. Thus the cell can make rapid and reversible changes in the number and organization of polymers.

Actin and microtubule assembly is often initiated at specific sites by specialized structures in the cell. In typical cultured eukaryotic cells, microtubules assemble outward from a centrosome. The centrosome is a complex structure that contains one or two centrioles (composed of a complex array of short microtubules) surrounded by diffusely organized proteinaceous material containing the novel protein γ-tubulin, which may serve to initiate microtubule growth. During the interphase portion of the cell cycle, the microtubules are seen to emanate radially from a single centrosome. During cell division the centrosome splits, and two overlapping radial arrays of microtubules appear. These arrays are subsequently remodeled to form the mitotic spindle. Differentiated cells exhibit a variety of microtubule arrangements consistent with the specific functional requirements of these cells. For example, neuronal cells are filled with parallel microtubules that are required for process formation and also serve as tracks along which materials are transported. Microtubules span epithelial cells and are involved in transport between the two surfaces of the epithelial cell layer. Microtubules form a circular band around blood platelets and are required for maintaining the discoid shapes of these cells. *See* CELL CYCLE; CENTROSOME.

Actin often assembles from sites associated with membranes. These sites may be diffuse or well defined, such as the cytoplasmic face of intercellular junctions. A variety of proteins that may be involved in organizing the actin filaments are localized at these sites, but the precise arrangement of these proteins and their role in initiating the assembly of actin are not fully understood.

Other factors affect the assembly of actin filaments and microtubules. Energy is required for polymerization. In the case of actin filaments, energy is supplied by the breakdown of ATP to ADP and phosphate as actin subunits add to the end of the growing filament. In the case of microtubules, energy is supplied by the breakdown of guanosine triphosphate (GTP) to guanosine diphosphate (GDP) and phosphate. Microtubule assembly is inhibited by calcium, but it is not certain whether this mechanism is actually used to regulate assembly in the cell.

Microtubules contain a variety of associated proteins (microtubule associated proteins, or MAPs) that have the general property of enhancing the rate and extent of polymerization. Several of these proteins appear as elongated fibrous projections on the microtubule surface, and may be involved in organizing the microtubules into parallel arrays in the cytoplasm.

A functionally diverse group of proteins affects actin assembly and organization. Profilin and thymosin $\beta 4$ regulate assembly by binding to free actin subunits and controlling their availability for polymerization. Gelsolin and severin are examples of proteins responsible for breaking actin filaments. Other proteins cross-link actin filaments; some, such as filamin and alpha actinin, produce random gels; and others, such as fascin, produce regularly packed bundles.

The organization of myosin may also be controlled in smooth muscle and nonmuscle cells by the activity of a protein kinase, an enzyme that adds a phosphate group to myosin. In the test tube, this reaction switches on the enzymatic activity of the myosin and causes it to form filaments. The protein kinase is under the control of calcium, which also turns on the severing activity of gelsolin and, in nonmuscle cells, inhibits the cross-linking activity of alpha actinin. These combined effects may be important in the solation and mobilization of gelled cytoplasm.

Actin-based cell movement. Actin is involved in a wide variety of movements in many cell types.

Ameboid movement. Ameboid movement occurs in

a number of free-living amebas, in slime molds, which are colonial amebas, and in a variety of cells of higher organisms, such as white blood cells. Many of these cells are chemotactic, that is, they move toward or away from food, hormonal stimuli, and other factors. This indicates that, despite the lack of a distinct shape, these cells are capable of coordinated movement. In ameboid cells, the actin and myosin filaments are much less organized than in muscle, and may act as a contractile gel. The actin filaments are randomly arranged, and force production occurs in all directions, unlike muscle where it occurs only along the axis of the muscle fiber. The cytoplasm of the ameboid cell contains relatively rigid as well as fluid regions, which respectively reflect the cross-linked and free states of the actin filaments. Movement of the cell occurs by the extension of pseudopodia (false feet), which appears as the oozing of fluid cytoplasm through the zone of gelled cytoplasm surrounding the cell.

Other forms of locomotion. Other forms of movement also use actin and myosin to provide the motive force. The best characterized of these movements is that shown by mammalian cells, commonly fibroblasts and epithelial cells, grown in culture in plastic petri dishes. Unlike ameboid cells, these cells become very flat, and their cytoplasm shows some evidence of organized actin-containing structures. Most prominent are stress fibers, which are long cables of parallel actin filaments spanning the cells. The stress fibers also contain myosin and other proteins known to interact with actin. This suggests that they may act like myofibrils, the organized arrays of actin and myosin filaments in muscle cells, serving to produce force across the entire cell. However, experiments designed to test this possibility have generally shown that stress fibers do not really serve in force production. They may, instead, act as structural struts or simply represent by-products of the constant reshuffling of actin filaments during movement.

Cultured fibroblasts and epithelial cells, like ameboid cells, show evidence of fluid regions of cytoplasm involved in the forward migration of the cell. At the leading edge of the cell, a lamellipodium of clearer, fluid cytoplasm is usually seen, which extends at relatively rapid rates much like an ameboid pseudopodium. New sites of adhesion to the substratum are produced as the leading edge of the cell moves forward. In time, the trailing portion of the cell is released from the substratum, and contracts to join the leading portion of the cell, resulting in net movement.

Similar lamellipodial extension is observed in other forms of cell movement and may be a very general phenomenon. For example, the migration of sheets of epithelial cells that occurs in wound healing and during embryonic development may occur by a concerted extension of the leading edge of a row of cells. Neuronal cells, which produce extremely elongated axonal and dendritic processes, have a growth cone at their leading edge. The growth cone has the appearance and the actin organization of a leading lamellipodium, and seems to extend by a similar mechanism.

Actin filaments may have a relatively simple organization within lamellipodia. The filaments appear to be attached to the leading edge of the lamellipodium and extend in parallel array into the cytoplasm. These filaments may assemble by intercalation of actin subunits at the membrane. In this case, actin assembly alone, without the need for myosin, could be responsible for movement. Clear evidence that actin assembly can be responsible for movement has come from work with sperm of the sea cucumber. When the sperm contacts an egg, a long acrosomal process composed of actin filaments emerges from the head of the sperm within a few seconds and penetrates the vitelline membrane. There is no myosin in the process. Instead, it is the rapid assembly of actin that acts as the motive force for elongation of the process.

Another form of actin-based intracellular movement is cyclosis or cytoplasmic streaming. It occurs in varying patterns in a variety of plant and algal cells, as well as in the cells of a number of protozoa and the acellular slime molds. In some cases, as in the acellular slime molds, the bulk back-and-forth movement of cytoplasm appears to result from the contraction of gelled actin in the cell cortex. In walled cells, like those of plants and algae, arrays of parallel actin filaments near the cell surface are thought to be involved in propelling the cytoplasm in a continuous, circulating stream. Myosin may be involved in force production, but it is not known how force is exerted on the fluid cytoplasm to induce bulk flow.

Cytokinesis. Cell division consists of two processes: mitosis, which is responsible for chromosome separation, and cytokinesis, which divides the other contents of the cell. Mitosis is a microtubule-based process. Cytokinesis in animal cells involves the formation of a contractile ring of actin filaments. During cell division the ring constricts, as a result of the force-producing action of myosin. Ultimately, the cell is completely separated into two progeny cells. Plant cells contain a rigid cell wall, and cytokinesis occurs by a different mechanism. *See* CYTOKINESIS; MITOSIS.

Microtubule-based movement. Microtubules are also involved in a variety of forms of movement.

Ciliary and flagellar movement. Many eukaryotic cells bear cilia or flagella. Unlike the flagella of bacteria, eukaryotic cilia and flagella consist of a bundle of microtubules. The arrangement of microtubules is the same in cilia and flagella, and consists of nine laterally fused pairs of microtubules surrounding a central pair of unfused microtubules. This complex structure, known as the axoneme, whiplashes back and forth at very rapid rates. In the case of free-living cells, including a variety of ciliated and flagellated protozoa and most eukaryotic sperm cells, this movement propels the cell through the surrounding medium. Cilia also coat the surface of many types of epithelial cell layer in eukaryotic organisms (for example, the lining of the lung) and serve to transport the surrounding medium across the cell layer.

The basic mechanism underlying ciliary and flagellar movement is well understood. The enzyme dynein, using ATP as fuel, causes the microtubules to slide against each other. Because other proteins in the cilium or flagellum bind the microtubules together, little net movement of the microtubules relative to each other is possible. Instead, the microtubule bundle bends, much as a bimetallic strip bends in response to changes in temperature. How the elaborate bending movements of the entire structure are coordinated is not yet well understood. *See* CILIA AND FLAGELLA.

Organelle traffic. Many, perhaps all, membrane-bound organelles move about within the cell. This movement occurs in two directions, outward toward the cell membrane and inward toward the nucleus. The outward movement is part of the process of secretion, the export of materials manufactured within the cell. The inward movement represents the processing of materials that have been taken up by endocytosis and pinocytosis, such as peptide hormones that have acted on the cell surface and serum proteins destined for degradation. These movements occur in virtually all cells. In neurons, they are referred to as anterograde (outward) and retrograde (inward) axonal transport, and are responsible for supplying new materials and removing used components from the axon, which has a very limited biosynthetic capability. *See* ENDOCYTOSIS.

The oppositely directed movements of the membrane-bound organelles are thought to be due to the activities of kinesin and dynein, which produce force in opposite directions along microtubules. The tubulin subunits within a microtubule are arranged in a head-to-tail manner, and the microtubule, therefore, has a built-in polarity. The two ends of the microtubule are designated as plus (+) and minus (−). In typical cultured mammalian cells, the plus ends of the microtubules are anchored in the centrosome located on the surface of the nucleus. The plus ends of the microtubules are disposed toward the cell surface. In axons, most of the microtubules are oriented with their minus ends near the nucleus and the plus ends toward the axon terminus where the synapse is located.

Evidence suggests that kinesin and cytoplasmic dynein are attached to the surface of organelles and are responsible for transporting the organelles along microtubules. Based on what is known about the orientation of the microtubules, a simple model for the mechanism of bidirectional organelle traffic is that kinesin is responsible for organelle transport from the nucleus toward the cell surface, or toward the end of the axon, while cytoplasmic dynein is responsible for movement in the opposite, inbound, direction.

Mitosis. All eukaryotic cells reproduce by replication of their deoxyribonucleic acid (DNA) and subsequent separation of the duplicated chromosomes. The process of dividing the genetic material is referred to as karyokinesis or mitosis.

Cell division begins by the condensation of chromatin in the nucleus, followed by the breakdown of the nuclear envelope. The centrosome, the organizing center for microtubules in the interphase cell, duplicates, resulting in two radial arrays of microtubules. The overlapping microtubules interact to form a barrel- or spindle-shaped structure termed the mitotic spindle, also known as the mitotic apparatus. The chromosomes gather at the middle of the spindle, at which time they are found attached to the ends of microtubules. The chromosomal attachment site for microtubules is known as the kinetochore, which is located along a constricted region of the chromosome known as the centromere. *See* CELL DIVISION.

Chromosome movement generally occurs in two stages referred to as anaphase A and B. During anaphase A, the chromosomes move toward the poles of the spindle. During anaphase B, the entire spindle elongates, causing further separation of the chromosomes. During both processes, different classes of microtubules within the spindle shorten or lengthen. It is not known whether this behavior is a cause or a consequence of chromosome movement. Kinesin-related proteins and cytoplasmic dynein are involved in chromosome movement. CHO-1, a kinesin-related protein, has been found associated with microtubules in the middle of the mitotic spindle. It is believed to produce spindle elongation by causing microtubules to slide against one another. Other kinesin-related proteins have been found at the kinetochore, as has cytoplasmic dynein, and may pull on the ends of microtubules at their point of attachment to the kinetochore and draw the chromosome toward the spindle pole. *See* CHROMOSOME.

Other motile proteins. It appears that many forms of movement can be explained by actin and myosin or by microtubules and their associated proteins dynein and kinesin. However, other motile mechanisms certainly exist.

Many bacteria possess flagella. These are very fine helical hairs, unlike the more substantial flagella and cilia of eukaryotic cells. Another important difference is that the bacterial flagella rotate about their axis and propel the bacterium by a corkscrewlike mechanism, unlike the bending and whiplashing movements of eukaryotic cilia and flagella. Bacterial flagella are hollow filamentous polymers, like microtubules, but are composed of the protein flagellin, which has no apparent relationship to tubulin. The flagella are attached at their base to a rotary motor structure in the bacterial cell membrane. *See* BACTERIA.

Other forms of bacteria glide over solid substrata by using an excreted slime for propulsion; the mechanism of gliding is not understood. Gliding motility is also seen in a number of algae and blue-green algae.

The sperm cells of roundworms differ from other types of sperm cells in that they lack flagella and exhibit a form of ameboid movement. These cells, however, contain neither actin, which is involved in ameboid movement in other ameboid cells, nor tubulin. Movement may be produced by insertion of lipid in the forward region of the plasma membrane and rearward flow of the membrane.

A contractile protein, spasmin, has been identified in *Vorticella* and related ciliated protozoa. Spasmin is organized into a long, thick fiber within the stalk portion of the organism. In response to calcium, the fiber undergoes a rapid, drastic contraction. It is not known whether spasmin exists in other organisms. *See* CELL (BIOLOGY).

Relationship to disease. Understanding how cells move increases the ability to control abnormal cell behavior, such as the increased level of cell division responsible for cancer and the migration of cancer cells from their site of origin in the body. Errors in chromosome segregation are also known to be responsible for Down syndrome, and are prevalent during the progression of neoplastic tumors.

Because the normal functioning of cells is so dependent on proteins that compose and regulate microtubules and actin filaments, defects in these proteins are expected to have severe effects on cell viability. An example of a microtubule defect has been identified in Alzheimer's disease: a microtubule-associated protein (termed tau) is found to be a prominent component of abnormal neurofibrillary tangles seen in affected nerve cells. However, it remains unknown whether the defect involving tau is part of the cause of the disease or represents one of its effects. *See* ALZHEIMER'S DISEASE; CANCER (MEDICINE); DOWN SYNDROME.

Richard Vallee

Bibliography. M. De Brabander and J. G. De Mey (eds.), *Microtubules and Microtubule Inhibitors: Nineteen Eighty–Five*, 1987; J. A. De Grado, *Microtubule Proteins*, 1989; P. Dustin, *Microtubules*, 1984.

Cell nucleus

The largest of the membrane-bounded organelles which characterize eukaryotic cells; it is thought of as the control center since it contains the bulk of the cell's genetic information in the form of deoxyribonucleic acid (DNA). The nucleus has two major functions: (1) It is the site of synthesis of ribonucleic acid (RNA), which in turn directs the formation of the protein molecules on which all life depends; and (2) in any cell preparing for division, the nucleus precisely duplicates its DNA for later distribution to cell progeny. The discovery of the nucleus dates back to 1710, when the Dutch microscopist Antonie van Leeuwenhoek noted a centrally located "clear" area in living blood cells

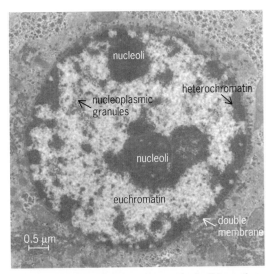

Fig. 1. Transmission electron micrograph of a thin section of a rat liver cell nucleus.

of birds and amphibians. However, it was not until 1831 that the British botanist Robert Brown first used the term nucleus and provided a precise morphological description. *See* DEOXYRIBONUCLEIC ACID (DNA); EUKARYOTAE; PROKARYOTAE.

Structure. The diameter of the nuclei ranges from 1 micrometer in intracellular parasites and yeast cells to several millimeters in some insect sperm. Spherical or ellipsoidal nuclei are found in most cell types, although occasionally spindle-shaped, lobulated, disc-shaped, or cup-shaped nuclei may be observed. Although nuclear size and shape are somewhat consistent features of a particular cell type, these features are more variable in cancer cells. In addition, tumor cell nuclei are characterized by indentation, furrowing, elongation, and budding.

The nucleus is bounded by a double membrane and contains several major components: chromatin, which is composed of DNA and chromosomal proteins; the nucleolus, which is the site of ribosomal RNA (rRNA) synthesis; and nucleoplasmic fibrils and granules, some of which are involved in the processing and transport of messenger RNA out of the nucleus (**Fig. 1**). The constituents of the nucleus are contained within a framework referred to as the nuclear matrix.

Nuclear envelope. The contents of the nucleus are spatially separated from the cytoplasm by a double-membrane-bounded structure called the nuclear envelope. The two membranes are both approximately 10 nanometers thick, and they are separated by a gap of 20–40 nm, known as the perinuclear space. The outer nuclear membrane is continuous with the endoplasmic reticulum and is often studded with ribosomes involved in protein synthesis.

At periodic intervals, the inner and outer membranes appear to be fused together, forming nuclear pores, averaging 120 nm in diameter. A typical mammalian cell contains 3000–4000 pores in its nuclear envelope. Each pore is composed of a nuclear pore complex measuring approximately 80 nm (inside diameter) with an estimated 9-nm open channel. The pores allow for the passage of molecules into and out of the nucleus. The central channel of the nuclear pore complex is thought to be involved in active transport, and eight peripheral channels, each approximately 10 nm in diameter, are proposed to function in passive exchange of small molecules as well as perhaps serving as an anchoring site for interphase chromatin. The transport of molecules into and out of the nucleus may be regulated by the protein components of the nuclear pore complex, which could function as receptors for the translocation of proteins and nucleoprotein complexes across the pore. See RIBOSOME.

Internal and adjacent to the inner membrane of the nuclear envelope is an electron opaque layer termed the nuclear lamina. In most mammalian cells, the lamina is about 10 nm thick and is composed of three major polypeptides, lamins A (70 kilodaltons), B (68 kDa), and C (60 kDa), which are present in equal amounts in the interphase nucleus. Lamins possess all the major structural properties that have been described for intermediate filament polypeptides at the levels both of protomers and of assembled filaments. The lamins are thought to function in regulating nuclear envelope structure and anchoring interphase chromatin at the nuclear periphery. It has also been suggested that the lamins act as a substrate for the formation of DNA replication complexes, or regulate DNA condensation or formation of nuclear matrix elements which are required for efficient replication to occur. See CELL MEMBRANES.

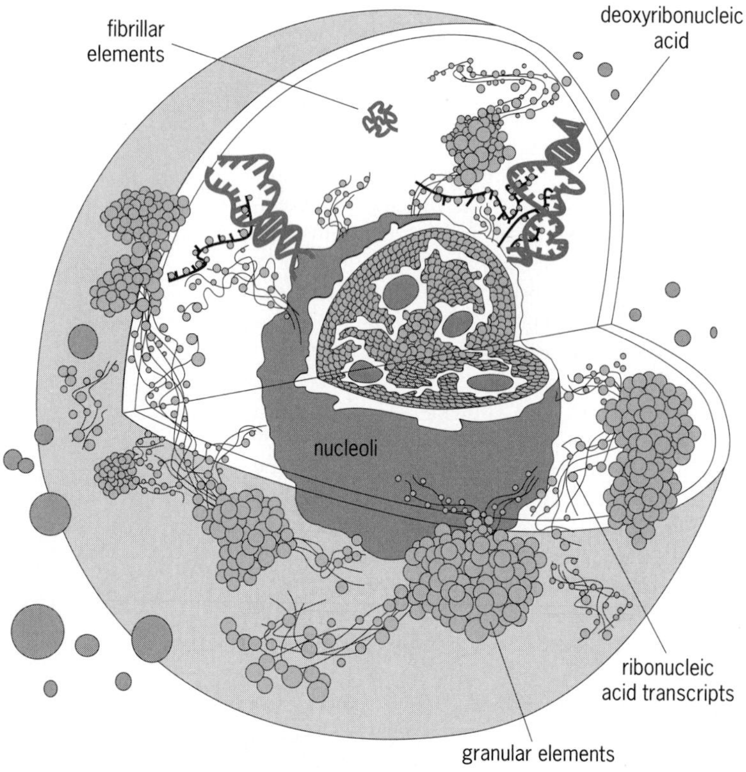

Chromatin and chromosomes. Deoxyribonucleic acid is present in the nucleus as a DNA-protein complex referred to as chromatin. The DNA that is present in a typical human cell is composed of 3 billion base pairs of nucleotide sequence. The DNA is highly compacted, approximately 200,000-fold. If it were stretched out in a linear manner, it would extend for 6.6 ft (2 m). This DNA encodes for the estimated 50–100,000 genes which are present in each human cell. However, a significant portion of the genome does not contain any protein coding information, and it is unclear what role this DNA plays in cellular function.

Classes of chromatin. Eukaryotic chromatin has been divided into two classes, heterochromatin and euchromatin, based on its state of condensation during interphase. Heterochromatin is condensed during interphase and is therefore generally considered to be transcriptionally inactive. It is commonly located in an irregular band around the nuclear periphery (Fig. 1) and around the nucleolus as well as in patches throughout the nucleoplasm. The amount of heterochromatin present in the nucleus varies with transcriptional activity; little heterochromatin is present in transcriptionally active cancer cells whereas the nuclei of orthochromatic erythroblasts and mature spermatozoa, both transcriptionally inactive, are practically filled with condensed chromatin. In an average eukaryotic cell, approximately 90% of the chromatin is transcriptionally inactive at any given time, but all of the inactive chromatin may not be in a condensed state. However, the 10% of the chromatin that is transcriptionally active is always in the form of decondensed euchromatin.

Transcription. The process by which a segment of cellular DNA makes a copy of itself in the form of RNA is referred to as transcription. Transcription can be divided into three systems, each using a different set of enzymes and some similar as well as different factors which function to produce different classes of RNA molecules. The three systems are referred to as RNA polymerase I, II, and III. RNA polymerase I is specifically involved in transcribing ribosomal RNAs, which are components of ribosomes and are involved in the process of protein synthesis. RNA polymerase II is primarily involved in transcribing messenger RNAs which act as the template for the production of specific cellular proteins. A majority of the RNAs that are made by RNA polymerase II must be edited prior to their transport from the nucleus into the cytoplasm. This editing process, referred to as splicing, involves the removal of noncoding regions (introns) which interrupt the protein coding sequence (exons) present in the transcribed RNA molecule. RNA polymerase III is primarily involved in the production of transfer

Fig. 2. Three-dimensional organization of the mammalian cell nucleus.

RNAs, which are involved in directing specific amino acids, the building blocks of proteins, to the ribosomes, where the amino acids become incorporated in a sequence dependent manner into the newly synthesized protein. The production of RNA molecules may be thought of as the major function of the nucleus, and the process is highly regulated, with some RNAs being transcribed at specific times during the cell cycle. *See* EXON; INTRON; RIBONUCLEIC ACID (RNA).

Replication. A second nuclear function equally important to transcription is the process of DNA replication. Because many cells in the human body are continuously dividing, it is essential to their function for each of the daughter cells to obtain a complete copy of the cell's DNA. Replication of DNA takes place only once during the cell cycle in a period referred to as the synthesis phase or S phase. As is the case for transcription, a specific series of enzymes and factors are responsible for the accurate replication of cellular DNA. *See* CELL CYCLE; CHROMOSOME.

Nucleolus. The nucleolus is a subnuclear organelle within which ribosomal genes and their products are naturally sequestered from the rest of the genome and nucleoplasm. Ribosomal gene transcription, ribosomal RNA processing, and pre-ribosomal particle formation all occur within this highly specialized region of the nucleus. Nuclei may contain one or more nucleoli, and generally cancer cells have multiple nucleoli. Although the nucleolus is not bounded by a membrane, specific proteins have been localized to discrete functional regions within this structure and a nucleolar localization signal has been identified. Ultrastructurally, the nucleolus may be regarded as being composed of four organizational areas: a dense fibrillar region, fibrillar center or centers, a granular region, and nucleolar vacuoles. The nucleolus is usually surrounded by a shell of perinucleolar chromatin which is connected with regions of intranucleolar chromatin and is continuous with the fibrillar centers.

The cellular DNA that encodes for ribosomal RNA of higher eukaryotes occurs in multiple copies and is organized in tandem repeats which are separated from each other by nontranscribed spacer regions of DNA. Human cells contain approximately 250 copies of rDNA, and the length of a single rDNA repeat unit is 44,000 base pairs. The nucleolar fibrillar centers or the periphery of the fibrillar centers are the sites that most likely represent the nucleolar regions where rDNA transcription occurs. The dense fibrillar component probably represents elongating RNA transcripts and precursor molecules. Finally, the granular region represents the site of assembling and processing mature ribosomal subunits.

Nuclear matrix. The nuclear components are present within specific macromolecular nuclear domains (**Fig. 2**). The large number of molecules present within the nucleoplasm and the high degree of efficiency with which vital nuclear functions take place suggest a high degree of nuclear organization. The concept of a nuclear matrix or nuclear scaffold seems to satisfy this role. By definition, the nuclear matrix is the residual structure left after DNA, nuclear proteins, and nuclear phospholipid are extracted from the nucleus. Numerous nuclear functions, including transcription, RNA processing, and DNA replication, are thought to take place in association with the nuclear matrix. *See* CELL (BIOLOGY); MOLECULAR BIOLOGY.　David L. Spector

Bibliography. P. S. Agutter, *Between Nucleus and Cytoplasm*, 1990; B. Alberts et al. (eds.), *Molecular Biology of the Cell*, 3d ed., 1994; H. Hillman, *The Living Cell*, 1991; E. Wang et al. (eds.), *Biochemical and Structural Dynamics of the Cell Nucleus*, 1990.

Cell organization

Cells are divided into several compartments, each with a characteristic structure, biochemical composition, and function (**Fig. 1**). These compartments are called organelles. They are delimited by membranes composed of phospholipid bilayers and a number of proteins specialized for each type of organelle. All eukaryotic cells have a nucleus surrounded by a nuclear envelope, and a plasma membrane that borders the whole cell. Most eukaryotic cells also have endoplasmic reticulum, a Golgi apparatus, lysosomes, mitochondria, and peroxisomes. Plant cells have chloroplasts for photosyn-

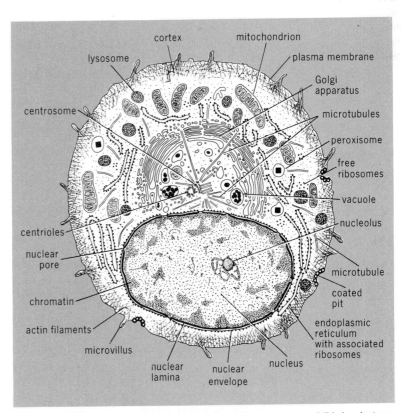

Fig. 1. Section through an animal cell showing the major components visible by electron microscopy. To simplify, a few important components, including intermediate filaments, have been omitted.

thesis in addition to the organelles that both they and animal cells possess. These organelles are suspended in a gellike cytoplasmic matrix composed of three types of protein polymers called actin filaments, microtubules, and intermediate filaments. In addition to holding the cell together, the actin filaments and microtubules act as tracks for several different types of motor proteins that are responsible for cell motility and organelle movements within the cytoplasm.

A major challenge in the field of cell biology is to learn how each organelle and the cytoplasmic matrix are assembled and distributed in the cytoplasm. This is a very complex process since cells consist of more than 2000 different protein molecules together with a large number of lipids, polysaccharides, and nucleic acids, including both deoxyribonucleic acid (DNA) and many different types of ribonucleic acid (RNA). *See* NUCLEIC ACID.

The cell must possess enough information to specify which molecules are to be associated in a specific compartment, to route the appropriate groups of molecules to their compartments, and then to position each type of component appropriately in the cell. As a result of intense research on each of these topics during the 1970s and 1980s, a number of specific chemical reactions that contribute to organizing cells are now recognized, but even more important, a small number of general principles that explain these complex processes of life can be appreciated.

Principles of assembly. The following principles account for many of the processes that result in the assembly and organization of cells.

Normal cells regulate the production and degradation of all of their constituent molecules so that the right balance of molecules is present at any given time. The genes stored in nuclear DNA are duplicated precisely once per cell cycle. The supply of each of thousands of proteins is usually regulated at the level of the genes at the time of biosynthesis and by the rate of degradation. These proteins serve as enzymes that determine the rate of synthesis of themselves as well as of other cellular components such as nucleic acids, carbohydrates, and lipids. Each of these processes is regulated by molecular feedback loops to assure the proper levels of each cellular constituent. *See* CELL CYCLE; CELL METABOLISM.

A large majority of cellular components are generated by the self-assembly of their constituent molecules. Self-assembly means that the information required for molecules to bind together in the proper orientation is contained in the molecules themselves. In other words, no outside information is required. Some examples include the binding of histones to DNA, the formation of bilayers from phospholipids, and the polymerization of actin molecules into filaments. The molecules are usually brought together by diffusion. The energy required to hold them together derives from the exclusion of water from their complementary surfaces as well

as from the formation of ionic bonds and hydrogen bonds. The variety of molecular structures found in proteins allows each type to self-assemble specifically, only with their correct partner molecules.

After biosynthesis, proteins and nucleic acids are routed to their proper cellular compartment by specific recognition signals consisting of parts of the molecule or, in the case of some proteins, by sugar side chains. These signals are recognized by compartment-specific receptors that guide the molecules to the correct compartment. For example, proteins destined for lysosomes have a specific sugar side chain added in the Golgi apparatus that guides them to lysosomes. Similarly, proteins destined for the nucleus all contain short sequences of amino acids that target the proteins for uptake by the nucleus. These so-called nuclear recognition sequences most likely bind to specific receptors associated with the nuclear pores, the channels through the nuclear envelope that connect the nucleus with the cytoplasm.

Most molecules move to their correct compartment by the process of diffusion down concentration gradients, but organelles generally require transport systems composed of microtubules or actin filaments together with specific motor proteins to position them correctly in the cytoplasm. For example, a protein molecule destined to be part of a mitochondrion will diffuse from the site of biosynthesis through the cytoplasm to a mitochondrion, where it will bind to a receptor that guides its incorporation into the mitochondrion. On the other hand, the mitochondrion itself is too large to diffuse through the network of protein fibers in the cytoplasmic matrix, and so it must be pulled through the matrix by a motor protein that moves along microtubules to the correct place in the cell.

Some cellular components, such as ribosomes and the filaments in the cytoplasmic matrix, assemble afresh from their constituent molecules, but all organelles composed of membranes form only by the growth and division of preexisting organelles. The reason that these organelles require precursors is that biological membranes composed of phospholipids can grow only by expansion of preexisting bilayers. As a consequence, organelles such as mitochondria and the endoplasmic reticulum are inherited maternally starting from the egg and expanding into every cell in the body by continued growth and partition into both daughter cells at every cell division. Other membrane-bound organelles, such as lysosomes, form by budding off the Golgi apparatus.

Many of the individual self-assembly reactions required for normal cell growth can be reproduced in the test tube, but the cell is the only place known where the entire range of reactions, including biosynthesis, targeting, and assembly, can go to completion. Thus, cells are such a special environment that the chain of life has required an unbroken lineage of cells stretching from all living cells back through their ancestors to the earliest forms of life. This requirement for cellular continuity explains why extinction is an irreversible process.

Assembly of organelles. All cellular organelles arise by the assembly of their components, either from constituent molecules or from preexisting structures.

Nucleus. The nucleus is a protected environment within the cell where the genes are stored in the form of specific DNA sequences. The genes are organized into units called chromosomes. Each type of chromosome has characteristic genes lined up end-to-end, an organization that results from the fact that each chromosome consists of a single, huge DNA molecule with a specific array of genes. These long DNA molecules are coiled up by interaction with proteins called histones, so that they can fit inside the nucleus. The DNA is replicated once during each cell cycle and supplied with sufficient histones and other accessory proteins to duplicate each chromosome. Between mitotic events the chromosomes are not distinct from each other and are called chromatin (Fig. 1) *See* CELL NUCLEUS; CHROMOSOME; GENE.

The nucleus is separated from the cytoplasm by the nuclear envelope, an extension of the endoplasmic reticulum consisting of two membranes and penetrated by tiny diaphragms called nuclear pores. All of the traffic into and out of the nucleus passes through the nuclear pores. The traffic moving into the nucleus includes all of the proteins found in the nucleus and the proteins required to form ribosomes. The traffic moving out includes messenger RNA and ribosomal subunits assembled in the nucleolus. The integrity of the nuclear envelope is maintained by a network of intermediate filaments composed of protein subunits called lamins (Fig. 1) that are associated with the inner surface of the envelope. They appear to form links between the nuclear pores and between the membrane and the chromatin.

During mitosis the chromosomes must partition equally between the two daughter cells, a process that requires the dissassembly and reassembly of the nuclear envelope. At the outset of mitosis, phosphate groups are added to the nuclear lamins by an enzyme called a mitotic kinase. This causes the lamin intermediate filaments to break up into their protein subunits. The nuclear envelope membranes then break up into small vesicles, releasing the chromosomes into the cytoplasm, where they are divided between the daughter cells by the mitotic apparatus. At the end of mitosis, the chromosomes cluster so close to each other that they exclude soluble macromolecules. The lamins lose their extra phosphates, and together with associated vesicles of nuclear envelope membranes, they repolymerize on the surface of the condensed chromosomes. When these vesicles fuse to form a continuous nuclear envelope, virtually no cytoplasmic macromolecules are included in the nucleus. Remarkably, the entire cycle of chromosome conden-

sation, nuclear envelope breakdown, and nuclear envelope reformation can now be carried out in the test tube. A single process, the phosphorylation and dephosphorylation of the lamins, provides the biochemical cue for this complex process. *See* MITOSIS.

Endoplasmic reticulum. The endoplasmic reticulum forms by expansion of preexisting endoplasmic reticulum. The phospholipids that constitute the lipid bilayer are synthesized by proteins inserted into the lipid bilayer itself. As with all other proteins, the proteins of the endoplasmic reticulum membrane are synthesized by small RNA-protein assemblies called ribosomes. The ribosomes are themselves assembled in the nucleolus by a process that has been reconstituted in the test tube from purified components including more than 20 different proteins and two RNA molecules. Proteins destined for insertion into membranes, or for lysosomes, or for secretion carry signal sequences of amino acids that interact with ribosomal and endoplasmic reticulum receptors. These receptors cause the ribosomes making these proteins to bind to the endoplasmic reticulum and to guide these proteins into or through the lipid bilayer of the membrane. Particular proteins are retained in the lipid bilayer, in the lumen, or in the endoplasmic reticulum; others move on to various parts of the cell. Microtubules seem to play an important role in distributing the endoplasmic reticulum within the cell. Motor proteins bind to the membrane and by moving along microtubules can pull the endoplasmic reticulum into a branching network that spreads throughout the cytoplasm. *See* ENDOPLASMIC RETICULUM; PROTEIN; RIBOSOMES.

Golgi apparatus. These stacks of flattened membrane-bounded sacks (Fig. 1) are responsible for adding sugars to proteins and for sorting membranes and secretory proteins. Membranes with specific proteins and specific proteins in the lumen of the endoplasmic reticulum pinch off from the endoplasmic reticulum and fuse with the Golgi apparatus. These components pass through the Golgi apparatus, most likely by a process of selective budding of membrane components from one Golgi stack and the subsequent fusion of these vesicles with later stacks in the Golgi apparatus. The Golgi apparatus is characteristically located in the middle of the cell near the centrosome. The mechanism of this association is not yet known. *See* GOLGI APPARATUS.

Plasma membrane. The components of the cell membrane (Fig. 1) are originally formed in the endoplasmic reticulum, where both the phospholipids and proteins are synthesized. The proteins are inserted into the bilayer and then transported from the endoplasmic reticulum through the Golgi apparatus via small vesicles to the plasma membrane. It is remarkable that the signals and receptors along this pathway are selective enough to guide the particular plasma membrane proteins to their target, with the total exclusion of proteins that belong in the other membrane compartments. Furthermore, many of the components of the plasma membrane are not permanent residents there; instead, proteins that serve as receptors for extracellular molecules, including nutrients and some hormones, are taken into the cell by specializations called coated pits (Fig. 1) and can recycle in small vesicles from the plasma membrane to internal compartments called endosomes and back to the cell surface from one to hundreds of times before they are degraded. Much larger particles, such as bacteria, are taken in by the related process of phagocytosis and also delivered to lysosomes for degradation. *See* CELL MEMBRANES; ENDOCYTOSIS; PHAGOCYTOSIS.

Lysosomes. The degradative enzymes found in lysosomes are synthesized by ribosomes attached to the endoplasmic reticulum, so that they pass into the lumen of the endoplasmic reticulum. From there they pass to the Golgi apparatus, where some yet to be identified signal on these proteins targets them for the addition of a special sugar called phosphomannose. This then acts as the signal to guide the lysosomal proteins from the Golgi apparatus to the lumen of lysosomes, most likely by budding of small vesicles containing these proteins and their subsequent fusion with forming lysosomes. *See* LYSOSOME.

Mitochondria. Although mitochondria are membrane-bound organelles (Fig. 1), they form in a fundamentally different way from the other organelles since the constituent proteins do not come through the endoplasmic reticulum–Golgi pathway. Most of the proteins are synthesized on free ribosomes, so that they are released into the cytoplasm. From there they diffuse to the mitochondria. They have an identifying sequence of amino acids that react with receptors on the surface of mitochondria. Subsequently they are actively transported across the mitochrondrial membranes into the lumen or are inserted into the membranes. A minority of the mitochondrial proteins are synthesized inside the mitochondria themselves. Remarkably, these organelles have their own genomes, ribosomes, and messenger RNAs that produce these special types of proteins. This process may be an anachronism from a stage of evolution when mitochondria arose from symbiotic bacteria. Most of the mitochondrial components are coded for by nuclear genes. *See* MITOCHONDRIA.

Peroxisomes. As with mitochondria, the constituent proteins are synthesized on free ribosomes and then incorporated into the membranes and lumen of the peroxisome.

Chloroplasts. Plant cells have chloroplasts for photosynthesis. As with mitochondria, they have their own genomes and make a number of their own proteins. Most of the proteins are made in the cytoplasm and imported as in mitochondria and peroxisomes. *See* CELL PLASTIDS; PHOTOSYNTHESIS.

Cytoskeleton. Assembly of the cytoskeleton represents a somewhat different problem for the cell than any of the examples considered above, since the three types of protein polymers making up the cytoskeleton change their form relatively rapidly during the life of the cell. The cytoskeleton is much more dynamic than chromatin, the nuclear envelope, lysosomes, or mitochondria. Consequently, information is required not only to guide assembly but also to remodel these systems on a time scale of seconds to minutes. Since the actin filaments, intermediate filaments, and microtubules are composed of different proteins and each has distinctive functions and dynamics, they will be considered separately. *See* CYTOSKELETON.

1. Actin filaments. Actin filaments (**Fig. 2***a*) occur in all eukaryotic cells, being a fundamental structural component as well as the linear tracks for the movement of myosin molecules. In muscle, actin filaments and myosin filaments form a highly specialized contractile system designed for forceful, rapid, one-dimensional contractions. In other cells, these proteins are responsible for pinching daughter cells in two during cytokinesis and for other less directed movements. *See* CYTOKINESIS; MUSCLE PROTEINS.

Actin is a globular protein that polymerizes into long filaments composed of a double-helical array of actin subunits. Formation of these filaments is a classical example of self-assembly, but the process is tightly controlled in cells by more than a dozen regulatory proteins. Some of these actin-binding proteins bind to actin monomers and influence the number available for polymerization. Others bind to an end of actin filaments. These can help initiate polymerization but allow growth in only one direction. Some can cut actin filaments into two fragments. Others cross-link actin filaments into random networks or parallel bundles. These networks form relatively rigid gels in the cortical cytoplasm of cells (Fig. 1). Since many of these filaments are also anchored to the plasma membrane, they can reinforce the surface of the cell. Tightly packed bundles of actin filaments with closely applied plasma membrane (like fingers in

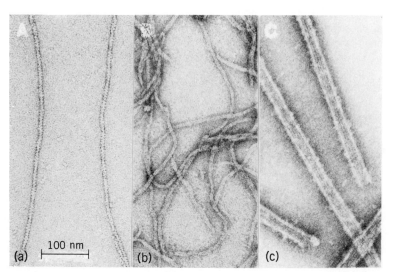

Fig. 2. Electron micrographs of the three cytoskeletal polymers: (*a*) actin filaments, (*b*) intermediate filaments, and (*c*) microtubules.

100 nm

(a)   (b)   (c)

a glove) project from the surface of many cells. These filopodia or microvilli (Fig. 1) increase the surface area of the plasma membrane. Some cells have bundles of actin filaments attached at their ends to the inside of the plasma membrane. These "stress fibers" appear to contribute to reinforce cells that are under mechanical stress such as the cells that line large arteries.

This actin filament system is dynamic, as shown by the way that a cell can change shape as it moves. Such movements require the reorganization of both the cortical network and actin filament bundles. Some of these changes are caused by myosin-mediated contractions such as the contraction of the cleavage furrow during cytokinesis. Other changes such as the extension of the cortical cytoplasm to form a new pseudopod are likely to require the assembly of new actin filaments. External signals such as chemotactic molecules can influence both actin filament organization and the direction of motility. *See* CELL MOTILITY.

Two types of myosin molecules are responsible for actin-based movements. Myosin II, the type originally found in muscle, forms filaments that can pull two actin filaments past each other. Myosin I does not form filaments, but has some affinity for membranes. It may be responsible for the movement of membranes relative to actin filaments. In both cases, the energy for the movements is provided by the hydrolysis of adenosinetriphosphate (ATP). Several types of regulation are known, including phosphorylation of the myosin and calcium-sensitive regulatory proteins bound to the actin filaments. *See* MUSCLE.

2. Intermediate filaments. Somewhat more restricted in their distribution than actin, the intermediate filaments (Fig. 2*b*) appear to be essential as intracellular tendons in higher eukaryotic cells that are subjected to substantial physical stresses such as muscle cells and epithelial cells like skin. The various types of intermediate filaments are composed of a family of protein subunits all related to the keratin molecules found in hair. Intermediate filaments characteristically form bundles that are attached to the plasma membrane (sometimes at specializations called desmosomes) and surround the nucleus. The nuclear lamina is also composed of intermediate filaments. Since intermediate filaments are inextensible (try stretching a hair), they help the cell from being overstretched. The intermediate filaments rearrange during mitosis and cell movements, but the mechanisms involved are not yet known.

3. Microtubules. Microtubules (Fig. 2*c*) are ubiquitous, rigid polymers that form a number of structures, including the mitotic apparatus, an interphase cytoplasmic array radiating from the centrosome (Fig. 1), and the supporting axoneme of cilia and flagella. Microtubules get their name from the cylindrical arrangement of tubulin subunits in the polymer. This architecture accounts for their rigidity, making them the only cytoskeletal polymer that can resist compressive forces. Microtubules are known to provide the internal support for asymmetrical cell processes (such as cilia) and to maintain asymmetrical cell shapes. A simplifying feature of microtubule organization in cells is that virtually all microtubules have the same polarity relative to the centrosome; the rapidly growing end is peripheral. As with actin filament polymerization, microtubule polymerization is a self-assembly process that is modulated by other proteins called microtubule-associated proteins. Some of these proteins can cross-link microtubules to intermediate filaments and actin filaments, unifying the cytoskeleton into a single mechanical structure. *See* CILIA AND FLAGELLA.

Microtubules are also the tracks for rapid movements of membrane-bound vesicles and larger organelles, including mitochondria and the endoplasmic reticulum. In this way the microtubule system is an important determinant of cellular organization. These movements are powered by motor proteins that hydrolyze ATP to provide the energy for the motion. Kinesin moves particles toward the peripheral end of the microtubules, while dynein moves particles toward the cell center. Together they form a two-way transport system in the cell that is particularly well developed in the axons and dendrites of nerve cells, where vesicles can move more than 3 ft (1 m) in a few days' time.

The site and direction of microtubule assembly is determined by the centrosome (or by basal bodies in the case of cilia and flagella). Remarkably, the microtubules radiating into the cytoplasm are not particularly stable, but individually undergo spontaneous fluctuations in length that can involve the alternate loss and reassembly of thousands of tubulin subunits at their peripheral ends. These fluctuations in length seem to be important in the formation of the mitotic spindle and may even be used in the process of chromosome movement. Such microtubule dynamics are modulated by chemical modification of the tubulin subunits and by microtubule-associated proteins. *See* CELL (BIOLOGY); CYTOPLASM.

Thomas Pollard

Bibliography. B. Alberts et al., *Molecular Biology of the Cell*, 2d ed., 1991; J. Darnell and H. Lodish, *Molecular Cell Biology*, 2d ed., 1990.

Cell permeability

The permitting or activating of the passage of substances into, out of, or through cells, or from one cell to another. These materials traverse either the cell surface that demarcates the living cytoplasm from the extracellular space or the boundaries between adjacent cells. In many cases the materials also traverse the cell wall. *See* CELL WALLS (PLANT).

Cell Surface

Living cells are surrounded by specialized surface structures which isolate the cytoplasm, or interior portion of the cells, from the extracellular environment. The cell surface characteristically consists of two components: the glycocalyx and the cell membrane.

Glycocalyx. The outer component of the cell surface is the glycocalyx. Glycocalyces vary from cell to cell in more obvious ways than do the cell membranes or inner components. However, they always contain sugars, usually in polymer form and often attached to strongly acidic groups. These sugars are always associated with other substances, which may be proteins, lipids, lignins, or phosphates. The term glycocalyx, from the Greek for "sweet husk," refers to this sugar coating of cells.

In some cells, such as the human red blood cell, the glycocalyx is very thin and tenuous and cannot be seen easily, even with a powerful electron microscope. The red cell glycocalyx includes an interesting acidic sugar, sialic acid, and amino sugars in polymer form. The latter are responsible for the specificity of the several blood types, which must be properly matched between donor and recipient for safe blood transfusions. At another extreme, thick, robust, relatively rigid glycocalyces are found around woody plant cells. The cell wall in this instance may be regarded as the glycocalyx. The desirable properties of wood as a construction material depend on the cellulose and lignin in the cell walls of constituent plant cells. Many other variants of glycocalyces are known. *See* AMINO SUGAR; BLOOD GROUPS.

Since many glycocalyces contain strongly acidic sugars, they carry negative electric charges. Such a glycocalyx is bound in a layer in close association with the cell membrane, which has a different charge distribution. The combination of two such differently charged layers close together endows the surface of many cells with the properties of electrical rectifiers, permitting electric currents to flow with less resistance in one direction than in the other.

Cell membrane. The inner component, which is immediately adjacent to the cytoplasm, surrounds the cell completely and is known as the cell membrane or plasma membrane. The cell membrane serves to confine the delicate internal chemical components of the cell and to defend them from the effects of substances outside. In general, the cell cytoplasm differs considerably from the surrounding extracellular fluid with respect to the composition of ions, proteins, sugars, fats, and other materials. The intact cell membrane provides excellent protection, but if it is damaged the results are often disastrous for the cell.

Structure. The cell membrane is a thin, flat, flexible, sheetlike structure about 8 nanometers thick. It is composed basically of rather regularly arranged molecules of lipid (fatty substances) in which are embedded protein molecules, many of which project somewhat beyond the curved surfaces defined by the limits of the lipid molecules. The lipid molecules in these membranes are arranged much as they are in soap bubbles. In both, the lipids stand side by side in palisadelike fashion in two closely packed layers, composing a lipid bilayer. Protein molecules embedded in the lipid bilayers are called integral membrane proteins. In addition, there are usually other protein molecules not embedded in the membrane but associated closely with the inner (cytoplasmic) or outer (extracellular) surface of the lipid layer. These are usually called extrinsic or peripheral membrane proteins. Carbohydrate (sugar) residues are attached to the external aspects of many proteins and lipids. These sugar residues are part of the glycocalyx of the cell. Sugar residues are rare in, or absent from, membrane proteins and from lipids presenting toward the inner membrane face.

Control of properties. The cell can control many properties of its membranes, including those related to permeability. Control can be exerted in the following ways: (1) by varying the number and variety; (2) by varying the specific nature of the lipid components in the membrane; (3) by varying the glycocalyx proteins or lipid-associated sugar molecules on the outside of the cell, or the membrane-associated proteins on the inside; (4) by causing large areas of membrane to flow from one place to another, or to fold, indent, evert, or pinch off, carrying with these movements substances bound to one or the other surface of the membrane, or embedded in it; (5) by selectively moving integral membrane proteins in the plane of the membrane, allowing these proteins to carry with them substances, particles, molecules, or other materials bound to them; (6) by varying the properties of a single integral membrane protein or of a closely associated group of them so as to allow or prevent the passage across the membrane of substances such as ions or proteins of a specific character. Each of these six mechanisms can be used by the cell to activate or to control some aspect of permeability of the cell surface. *See* CELL MEMBRANES.

Properties of the lipid bilayer. The lipid bilayer forms an extensive fraction of the membrane of many cells. It is responsible for some of the mechanical, electrical, and selective permeability properties of cell membrane. The lipid bilayer endows the cell membrane with flexibility and plasticity and a capacity to flow like a thin layer of oil on a pond surface. Since the lipid molecules in the bilayer are arranged much as are the molecules in a soap bubble, they give the membrane some of the properties of a soap bubble. Just as two soap bubbles can be fused into one, and just as one soap bubble can be manipulated to pinch off and form two separate bubbles, so can two membrane areas fuse or pinch off with analogous topological consequences. Fusions and pinchings-off of cell membrane areas are normally under the control of the cell and can be activated by appropriate stimuli to move substances into or out of the cell, and hence to mediate permeability phenomena.

The hydrocarbon stratum of the lipid bilayer resists strongly the passage of water and of water-soluble ions and molecules. The lipid bilayer is the principal membrane component endowing the membrane with the properties of a remarkable electrical insulator. The differing ionic concentrations inside and outside the cell, with their resulting electrical potential (voltage) differences, are separated from each other by this nearly water-free hydrocarbon stratum. The hydrocarbon stratum is about 5 nm thick and intervenes between two aqueous fluid compartments (the inside and the outside of the cell), which differ from each other by an electrical potential of 40 to 80 or even 100 millivolts, depending on the type and the physiological state of the cell. It is not uncommon for such a thin hydrocarbon stratum in a cell membrane to withstand comfortably a voltage gradient of well over 10^5 V/cm, thus performing as well as high-quality electrical insulating layers used in industry. *See* BIOPOTENTIALS AND IONIC CURRENTS.

Selective Permeability

The cell membrane (including the lipid bilayer and the integral membrane proteins) and the glycocalyx together endow the cell surface with a remarkable selectivity in allowing or activating passages of materials and substances into or out of the cell.

Selectivity of the lipid bilayer. The lipid bilayer resists strongly the passage of water and water-soluble components, but allows the passage of substances which are soluble in oils, and hence in the hydrocarbon portion of the lipid bilayer. The watery phases on each side of the hydrocarbon stratum resist the passage of water-insoluble substances such as oils, but molecules soluble both in water and in hydrocarbons can move in either medium. Dissolved gases, particularly oxygen, carbon dioxide, and nitrogen, are examples of substances sufficiently soluble in water and in hydrocarbons to enable them to traverse the lipid bilayer as well as the aqueous phases on both sides of the cell membrane. Thus the lipid bilayer, together with the aqueous phases, forms a highly selective system in allowing the passage of substances soluble in both oils and water, but retarding greatly the passage of molecules soluble in only one of these media.

Selectivity of integral membrane proteins. The integral membrane proteins endow the cell membrane with a great variety of rather different capabilities for selective permeability, particularly with respect to allowing or energizing the passage of materials soluble in water but not in oils. The number of species of integral membrane proteins in a single cell is large—certainly in the hundreds and probably in the thousands. Moreover, each species can be represented many times in the membrane of a single cell, and the numbers representing each of the species may vary over a very wide range from cell type to cell type.

Ion channels. In some cases, individual integral membrane proteins are embedded in the lipid bilayer as independent units. However, in many other cases several protein molecules assemble to form a coherent body which is embedded as a well-defined complex of two to five or six (or more) of very closely associated protein molecules. A considerable variety of these proteins are so arranged as to create passages or channels across the membrane. In general, such channels can be opened or closed by molecular mechanisms under the control of the cell or by external influences such as hormones, drugs, poisons, light quanta, mechanical distortion, or electrical potentials; or by the influence of specific substances which may gain access to the proximity of the channel, such as specific peptides or protein configurations, or specific, small, organic molecules such as acetylcholine, or specific inorganic ions. Each channel allows passage of water-soluble materials from one side of the membrane to the other. The nature of the materials allowed to pass depends on the detailed molecular configurations of bonds, atoms, and charges lining the channel and determining its size and other properties. Many of these channel-forming integral membrane protein complexes are analogous to tiny, molecular bushings or grommets inserted into the nearly impermeable (to water) lipid bilayer of the membrane—the channels through these bushings being specific with respect to the materials allowed to pass through them, and with respect to the molecular control mechanisms which open or close them. Because of the great variety of protein molecules made by the cell and inserted into the cell membrane to make up such passages, the channels are present in many different versions, each with its own specific properties. Thus there are potassium channels which specifically allow passage of potassium ions (K^+); there are specific channels for sodium ions (Na^+); calcium ions (Ca^{2+}), and chloride ions (Cl^-), as well as for hydrogen ions or protons (H^+). There are also protein complexes which serve as electrical conductors for electrons (e^-) across a membrane.

Some poisons interfere with the proper functioning of one or another type of ion permeability channel. One example is tetrodotoxin, present in certain organs of the puffer fish but not in its muscles. If tetrodotoxin enters the bloodstream of a person, it can emerge from the capillaries and bind specifically to the integral membrane proteins constituting sodium channels. Tetrodotoxin interferes with their proper functioning, and if enough of these channels become encumbered the results can be fatal. The Japanese refer to this fish as the fugu and esteem its flesh as a delicacy. However, Japanese restaurants are required by law to have specially trained, licensed persons to prepare it to avoid poisoning. *See* TOXIN.

Protein channels. In addition to the ion channels, there are also special channels for proteins. These channels are not indiscriminately permeable to all proteins, but occur in a number of specific types. Each type is made up of specific integral membrane proteins capable of recognizing a specific part of another protein molecule. This specific part has been called a signal sequence. When a given protein sequence comes into contact with a channel-forming integral membrane protein complex which recognizes the specific features of that particular signal sequence, the complex may respond by engaging the molecule bearing the signal sequence and thereafter allowing the whole signal-bearing protein molecule to traverse the channel. Bacterial cells characteristically allow passage of proteins by the signal mechanism from the inside of the cell to the outside. Animal and plant cells, however, though frequently using the signal mechanism to mediate passage of specific protein molecules across the internal membranes of the cell, seem to use this mechanism sparingly, if at all, in their cell or plasma membranes which surround the cell as a whole. Nevertheless, proteins gaining access by means of the signal sequence mechanism to compartments bounded by internal membranes may later find their way to the outside of the cell by mechanisms which will be treated later in this article, and which utilize processes known as exocytosis (or eccytosis), membrane fusions (synhymenosis), membrane flow, and vesicular transport.

Selectivity of the glycocalyx. The glycocalyx can also exercise important influences on permeability, particularly with respect to imparting highly selective and specific features to processes involving entry into a cell; this entry is often called uptake. Some glycocalyces can act as filters, allowing only particles or molecules below a certain size to reach the cell membrane for uptake. Frequently, however, the glycocalyx exercises its selective role on a more subtle and specific basis, utilizing an exceedingly versatile array of specific binding configurations to initiate uptake mechanisms.

In the case of many cells, the glycocalyx, including portions of membrane lipid and protein molecules, presents to the fluids immediately outside the cell a forest of complex and intricate chemical groupings, many of them sugar residues, which endow the external surfaces of cells with a large number of varied binding sites. Here it must be repeated that protein molecules also contribute significantly to the binding sites on the external surfaces of cells, as do lipids to a lesser extent.

Some of these binding sites have a high specificity, such as antigen receptor sites on the surfaces of lymphocytes, or acetylcholine or adrenaline receptor sites on the surfaces of certain portions of muscle cells. There are also many known examples of binding sites of lower specificity, such as the phosphate groups attached to glycocalyx sugar residues on some amebas. These phosphates are versatile binding groups for the ameba, and can entrap simple positive ions such as Ca^{2+} or K^+, or many kinds of protein molecules, such as serum albumin, or even whole

organisms, such as the protozoans *Paramecium* or *Tetrahymena*.

Endocytosis: phagocytosis, pinocytosis. When such specific or nonspecific binding takes place, the chemical configurations on the surface of the cell change; the cell is usually able to perceive this as information and to react to it. There are many types of reactions to such binding situations, and a great number are characterized by permeability changes. To illustrate, one can examine in more detail some of the consequences when the binding sites on the glycocalyx of an ameba engage suitable ions, molecules, or organisms. The response of the ameba to this binding often leads to the uptake of the material. During this uptake process, the material is handled by the cell so as to cause it to move from the outside of the cell to the inside without actually traversing any pore or channel in the membrane. This mechanism of uptake involves active, gross movements of the membrane and membrane components, and corresponds to the membrane activities which characterize phagocytosis, pinocytosis, and receptor-mediated endocytosis. These are all fundamentally the same process and are represented in a large variety of cell types.

Prey organisms, or proteins, or even simple ions captured from the environmental waters by the binding sites on the ameba's glycocalyx are concentrated in relatively small membrane areas by membrane flow and are led down long, slender membrane invaginations which form in response to the earlier binding processes. The invagination reaches a certain distance toward the interior of the cell. When sufficient material has accumulated at the inner extremity of the invagination, its membrane lining pinches off near the bottom, forming an intracellular vesicle lined by membrane and glycocalyx molecules carrying the materials or organisms which bound to them earlier. The vesicle, carrying its load of ingested material, is moved further into the interior of the cell, where the material is digested or otherwise handled in accordance with the physiological and biochemical capabilities of the cell. This example of endocytosis in the ameba is typical of the process in many respects. It is receptor-mediated, the receptors in this case being the phosphate groups fastened to sugar residues of the ameba's glycocalyx.

In the human, uptake by endocytosis has long been recognized as a capability of the phagocytic cells of the blood, bone marrow, and connective tissue. Generally, in endocytosis the molecules or ions are moved from one side of the membrane to the other, not one by one but many thousands or millions of molecules at a time, often in a highly organized array, as in a living protozoon, bacterium, or virus. This process is now recognized in lymphocytes, in liver cells, in endothelial cells lining blood vessels and lymphatics, and even in nerve-cell terminals and in epithelial cells of the mammary gland. Red blood cells can be induced by malaria organisms to take up the parasite by this process. After gaining entry, the malarial parasite proceeds to eat and destroy the contents of the red cell. Many viruses, bacteria, and rickettsia gain entry into cells by this process and subsequently harm them. Endocytosis, then, involves a permeability mechanism which first selects and then permits molecules, particles, or even whole organisms to enter cells without passing through any pores or channels in the membrane, but nevertheless invoking selective and specific binding processes. *See* ENDOCYTOSIS; PHAGOCYTOSIS.

Exocytosis; secretion. A reverse process, exocytosis, is also used by a large variety of cells. Exocytosis constitutes one type of secretion mechanism and can be contrasted with others, such as secretion by the signal mechanism or through other types of transmembrane channels which can permit the passage of simple organic ions a few at a time or of single protein molecules one by one. Like endocytosis, exocytosis provides a means for transferring material in bulk, many millions of molecules at a time, from the inside of a cell to the outside. Proteins, peptides, neurotransmitter substances, and even highly organized bodies such as viruses, the trichocysts of *Paramecium*, the nematocysts of *Hydra*, and the cell-wall scales of certain algae are expelled from the cell by exocytosis. Again, no pore or channel is used for the passage. The pancreas secretes its enzymes into the pancreatic ducts by this process, and liver cells secrete serum albumin and other proteins directly into the blood plasma by exocytosis.

Generally, the exocytosis process is preceded by the utilization of internal membranes of the cell. The cell, using the signal mechanism, may insert proteins into a vesicle surrounded by an internal membrane, or it may cause a membrane to surround certain selected bodies or molecules inside the cell, such as may be recognized by the cell as harmful, foreign, useless, worn out, or disadvantageous. In either case, a vesicle is formed carrying molecules destined for expulsion or secretion. This vesicle, enveloped in membrane compatible with the cell's surface membrane, is transported to a region of cytoplasm very close to the cell membrane; there, upon signal, its membrane can be caused to fuse with the cell membrane so as to discharge the entire contents of the vesicle all at once to the outside.

As a variant, the mammary gland cell, as in the cow, liberates its fat into the milk by transporting fat droplets to positions near the tips of slender cell processes called microvilli. The cell membrane near the tip then pinches off to form an extracellular vesicle containing the fat droplet. The fat, while inside the cell, is not surrounded by an internal cell membrane, but when secreted into the milk it is surrounded by an envelope derived from the membrane area earlier at the tip of the microvillus. This membrane envelopment of each fat droplet prevents the many droplets from coalescing before consumption of the milk by the calf. However, if the cream is churned, these membrane envelopments are broken by the mechanical agitation. The insoluble lipid droplets are then liberated as a separate phase and allowed to coalesce to form butter.

Thus there are permeability mechanisms which allow water-insoluble molecules, like fat, to move from the interior of the cell to the extracellular space in bulk, without traversing any pore or channel piercing the membrane, but utilizing membrane movements and fusions according to a topological scheme somewhat different from the schemes involved in secretion of water-soluble proteins by exocytosis.

Some viruses gain egress from cells by invoking permeability mechanisms similar to those involved in the secretion of fat by the mammary gland. For example, herpes viruses and mammary tumor viruses of mice, after replication in a cell, move to the cytoplasm just under the cell membrane, where each provokes the formation of a fingerlike process or microvillus, near the tip of which the virion takes its place. The virion proceeds further to control the behavior of the membrane areas nearby and prompts the tip of the process to pinch off; the ion is liberated into the extracellular space while completely enveloped in a vesicle of membrane which was once the area of host-cell membrane at the microvillus tip. Many such ions can survive in an external environment for some time, protected by their borrowed surrounding membrane. Virions can use the surrounding membrane to help them gain entry into an uninfected cell. If the virion can approach closely to a potential host cell, the membrane surrounding the virion, derived as it was from the cell membrane of a former host cell, is so constructed as to favor fusion with the newly encountered cell membrane. With this fusion, the virion itself is delivered into the cytoplasm of the new host, there to work its damage. Thus permeability mechanisms normally working to benefit the cell can be turned against it by the molecular machinery of a virus.

In all these mechanisms, whether mediating entrance into or egress from a cell, the processes are selective and take place only in response to specific molecular signals to which the transported molecules contribute.

Loss of selective permeability. While considering selective mechanisms controlling permeability, it is worth mentioning the so-called complement reaction. Complement reaction is highly selective in initiation but, when complete, severely compromises selective features of permeability, though increasing membrane permeability considerably. This is accomplished by creating large defects in the cell membrane which allow a general, nonselective leakage across it, usually so serious as to lead to cell death. This is one mechanism the human body uses to kill off invading organisms such as bacteria, parasites, or foreign cells of many kinds.

Usually the mechanism functions to benefit the individual by combating infection, but it sometimes comes into effect in autoimmune disease or in organ transplant rejection reactions. *See* AUTOIMMUNITY; COMPLEMENT; TRANSPLANTATION BIOLOGY.

As stated above, the selectivity of the reaction is based on the mechanism of its initiation and the consequences are based on the nonselective nature of the result. How is this permeability disaster brought to pass?

The surface coatings of all cells are rich in sugar residues which, together with proteins and other chemical groupings, make up the glycocalyx. The specificities of some of these cell-surface chemicals are determined by a group of genes which, in vertebrates and other organisms with well-developed immune systems, are called histocompatibility genes. Generally, these genes differ in detail from individual to individual. Thus in each individual animal with these genes the cells carry surface-marker molecules which, as a complete set, differ from those of every other individual. Among humans, identical twins constitute the most important exception, as they may possess histocompatibility genes identical in every detail.

Species with well-developed immune systems, such as vertebrates, generate cells called immunocytes which police the body and are specially equipped with molecular feeler molecules on their surfaces. Some of these feeler molecules can read the molecular codes embodied in the specific chemical configurations on the surfaces of cells they encounter. As they read the codes of cell-surface molecules presenting to the outside, they can recognize the molecular configurations which are derived from their own histocompatibility genes; that is, they can recognize cells which belong genetically to that individual organism. These cells they pass by. The immunocytes can also recognize strange or foreign cell-surface coatings, reflecting cells which possess histocompatibility genes differing from those of the host cells. Examples include invading bacteria, parasites, some viruses, or cells from another individual of the same species, such as the cells of a transplanted organ or of unmatched transfused blood. When immunocytes encounter such foreign cells, the latter's surface-coat molecules are recognized as alien. Immunocytes then react in several ways, one of which is to synthesize antibodies directed against the alien molecules. Antibodies are protein molecules, synthesized in many varieties, each of which can recognize and bind to an alien molecule of a very specific configuration. Antibodies synthesized by immunocytes, therefore, are capable of reacting specifically with and binding to surface-molecular components of alien cells with surface-molecular configuration of the kind which earlier triggered the synthesis of the antibody variety. Some of these specific antibodies are liberated by the synthesizing immunocytes, after which these antibodies circulate through the blood, lymph, and other body fluids. Wherever they circulate, they are available to bind only to the specific molecular configurations which they recognize.

What, then, are the consequences of these specific binding reactions? In the examples under consideration here, cells with molecular coatings of foreign types quickly become encumbered with antibody molecules of the correct specificity. This can restrict the activities of the alien cell in several ways, but here only one of several types of consequences will be discussed. Among the many proteins circulating in the blood and other body fluids are a group which are members of the so-called complement system. Complement proteins are of several types which can cooperate when they encounter a cell which has been recognized as alien and which has become encumbered by specific antibody molecules.

One member of the complement group recognizes the bound antibody (though it ignores unbound ones) and binds to the antibody, whereupon the antibody is activated to interact with other molecular members of the complement system; these reactions take place very close to the bound antibody molecule, and hence close to the cell membrane itself. During these reactions, certain molecular members of the reacting complement system are modified in very special ways so that a number of the complement molecules, probably five, are changed: they are no longer stably soluble in the surrounding body fluids, but instead acquire properties which introduce them into the adjacent membrane lipid bilayer of the cell to which the antibody is bound. There the newly inserted molecules associate to form a new complex of integral membrane proteins, creating a large molecular grommet surrounding a channel so wide and uncontrolled as to constitute a serious defect which compromises the selective nature of the cell membrane. As a result, aqueous fluids can move readily through this grommet, leading to leakages and cell death. Thus, by using exquisitely sensitive selection mechanisms which can detect molecules of alien origin, an organism can defend itself with considerable success against harmful invaders by destroying the selective permeability features of the membrane of the foreign cells.

Some parasitic worms which gain entry into the blood vessels of humans protect themselves by appropriating glycocalyx molecules from host cells to cover their own surfaces which are exposed to the host's body fluids. When immunocytes encounter these worms, they interpret the surface molecules as possessing compatible configuration and so pass them by. Such worms usually avoid the complement reaction and seem to be able to live for years in the blood vessels or lymphatics of their hosts.

Driving Forces

The forces which drive the ions, molecules, particles, or organisms as they make their passages will now be considered. Generally, physiologists classify these driving forces into two types: diffusion and active transport. Active transport can be thought of as a molecular pumping process in which energy from chemical reactions in the cell is coupled directly to mechanisms which can move substances or materials from outside the cell into its interior, or in the reverse direction, or from one place to another within the same cell.

Diffusion is a type of movement which depends on thermal motion, that is, on the random agitation which characterizes all matter at temperatures above absolute zero. Diffusion processes can be recognized in gases, liquids, and solids, but those of greatest importance in cell permeability occur in liquids—either in the solutions inside or outside a cell or in the hydrocarbon phase of a lipid bilayer, which is often thought of as a two-dimensional liquid. Diffusion forces are closely related to the generation of osmotic pressures.

Diffusion and osmosis. Diffusion forces depend on random, thermally driven molecular collisions such as activated brownian movement. Water, ions, sugars, and other molecules are bombarded by similar collisions and can move about readily in aqueous media, being impelled by diffusion forces. Diffusion also takes place in water-insoluble liquids such as the hydrocarbon portions of membranes. Though diffusion energy can be transmitted between aqueous and hydrocarbon phases, substances themselves can move by diffusion in a liquid medium only if dissolved or suspended in that medium. Gas molecules of physiological importance, such as nitrogen, oxygen, or carbon dioxide, are sufficiently soluble in both water and hydrocarbons to permit them to diffuse readily through extracellular fluids, hydrocarbon layers of membranes, and intracellular aqueous phases. Water and materials soluble in it but not soluble in oil, however, can diffuse or otherwise move readily through membranes only if the lipid bilayer is pierced by aqueous channels such as can be formed by suitably placed and constituted integral membrane proteins. Many of these transmembrane aqueous channels are selective in allowing some substances to pass while denying passage to others, and are under the control of the cell or of extracellular perturbations so that they can be opened or closed, or their resistance to passage can be increased or decreased over narrow or wide ranges.

The selective permeability of membranes to water and to water-soluble substances requires further elaboration. Cell membranes, though resisting the passage of water molecules, do not form impervious barriers to water. Membranes of different kinds of cells vary considerably in their resistance to water. Thus the membrane of an ameba in distilled water is almost watertight. In the presence of ions in the surrounding water, however, the ameba's cell membrane acts to permit or to activate exchanges of water at more than 50 times the rate in pure water. In either case, excess water taken up is excreted by the ameba, which makes urine and discharges it from a membranous bladder called a contractile vacuole. The ameba, then, is a cell that can regulate the permeability of its membrane and its internal cytoplasmic hydration by using molecular physiological mechanisms.

Another situation occurs in the red cell of vertebrate blood. Although the membrane of this simple cell resists the passage of water, it is far from watertight; it appears to be unable to regulate adequately its permeability to water unless it is in an aqueous medium of closely regulated ionic strength, such as the blood plasma in which the red blood cell normally circulates. However, even in physiologically compatible fluids, the red cell membrane is rather permeable to water and to simple ions. As a consequence, water molecules can diffuse across the red cell membrane sparingly in either direction. Varying concentrations of solutes dissolved in water exert osmotic forces capable of driving water from regions of higher water concentration to regions of lower. If an osmotic force is present, a net movement of water across the membrane is actuated in the direction of the force. Variations in concentrations of dissolved materials in the blood plasma, or in some other aqueous medium in which red cells are suspended, affect the net flow of water across the red cell membrane.

If solutes in the external fluid are more concentrated than inside the cell, osmotic forces cause a net flow of water out of the cytoplasm into the surrounding fluid and the red cell's contents become more concentrated, its volume diminishes, and its membrane crinkles. This continues until the concentration of materials inside the cell produces an osmotic pressure equal to that outside, whereupon water intake and egress become equal, the concentration remains at the new equilibrium condition, and the cell remains intact though distorted. On the other hand, if the external fluid is more dilute than that of the cytoplasm of the red cell, osmotic pressure drives water into the cell faster than it escapes, the cell gains in volume, its contents become more dilute, and the slack portions of the membrane are taken up. If the external solution is dilute enough, such as distilled water or a dilute solution of salt or sugar, the hydrostatic pressure inside the cell soon reaches a level which the membrane cannot withstand. The membrane ruptures and permits much internal substance of the cell to escape. Such destruction of red cells is called hemolysis.

Red cells in the circulating blood of animals are normally well protected from osmotic changes sufficient to bring about hemolysis, as the concentrations of dissolved substances in the blood plasma are regulated by physiological mechanisms. However, hemolysis of red cells can occur, usually not from osmotic rupture but from damage to red cell membranes owing to drugs, malaria, burns, or defective immune mechanisms. When hemolysis occurs, hemoglobin is liberated from red cells into the surrounding blood plasma. If only small amounts of hemoglobin appear in the blood plasma, phagocytic cells can clean it up, but if the hemoglobin is released in quantities sufficient to overwhelm the phagocytic cells, the excess is excreted in the urine. In some severe forms of malaria, large amounts of hemoglobin are released from damaged red cells. Most of this hemoglobin appears in the urine, creating a hemoglobinuria so severe as to give the urine a very dark color. This condition is known as blackwater fever. From these examples, one can see a close relation between permeability of the cell membranes and the state of an individual's health. *See* BILIRUBIN; BLOOD; OSMOSIS.

Active transport. Since there is a slow but appreciable leakage of ions across the cell surface, in time such leakages can impair seriously the internal ionic medium of the cell and compromise the cell's effectiveness. One way that cells meet this problem is by inserting into their membranes very specialized types of integral membrane protein complexes which can act as ion pumps. These pumps are highly selective and function to restore the ionic imbalances created by the leakages. In many cells the concentration of potassium (K^+) is several times higher than in the extracellular fluid, whereas the internal concentration of sodium (Na^+) is much lower than that outside. Significant differences of concentrations of calcium (Ca^{2+}) and magnesium (Mg^{2+}) are also maintained. In such circumstances, the ionic leakages tend to be characterized by a predominant exit of potassium and a lesser ingress of sodium across the cell membrane. The ion pumps can distinguish between these two similar ions and work to pump excess sodium out of the cell and replace potassium losses by selectively pumping potassium into the cell from the extracellular fluid. These ionic pumps can move their respective ions against a chemical potential, that is, from a lower concentration to a higher one. This performance constitutes work in a physical sense. The energy required is derived from chemical reactions, usually from the hydrolysis of adenosinetriphosphate (ATP).

Thus there is a two-way traffic of several sorts of ions across cell membranes. First, a passive leakage of one or more ionic species, predominantly in one direction, is driven by electrical and diffusion forces. Second, an active, selective, energy-utilizing pumping of corresponding ions of the same species takes place in the opposite direction across the same membrane. At equilibrium the movement of each ion in each direction is equal and there is no net change of ionic concentration in the cell, though there is a constant exchange of individual ions.

Physiologists use the term active transport when they speak of the process of pumping ions or other substances up a concentration gradient. However, cells are able also to transport actively many substances that are not simple ions. For example, sugars and proteins can be expelled from a cell or taken in under circumstances that meet the criteria of active transport. Indeed, in phagocytosis or other forms of endocytosis, ions, molecules, bacteria, or particulate matter can be taken selectively into a cell by an energy-utilizing process that displays all the formal features of active transport.

The selective binding to a component of the cell surface appears to underlie the selective nature of active transport, whatever the nature of the material transported. The active transport of sugars, phosphate, amino acids, proteins, and inorganic cations depends on the cell surface. In some cases the acidic sugars present in some glycocalyces can participate in these specific binding reactions. In the ameba, for example, material to be taken up by endocytosis is first bound to binding sites on the glycocalyx and then taken up into the cell by a sequence of processes involving membrane movements, membrane flow, and pinching-off of membrane areas to form vesicles containing the bound extraneous material. Thus, binding sites on the cell surface can do more than merely select the material to be transported; they can also accumulate and concentrate it so that the transport process can convey the material in packaged, bulk quantities. In this way a reduction is achieved in the energy expended per unit of material transported.

In some cells the regulation of active transport mechanisms may be quite complex. For example, in mammals some of the hormones secreted by the adrenal cortex can influence the sodium and potassium pumps of cells so as to affect the ionic levels at which the pumps will respond. As another example, the active uptake of sugars by the ameba can be initiated by the presence of ions in the surrounding fluid. *See* OSMOREGULATORY MECHANISMS.

Excitable Membranes

Dramatic variations in permeability are found in the membranes of nerve and muscle cells and in the cells of electric organs of electric fishes. These variations in permeability are rapid and engender sudden surges of ions that produce substantial electrical transient disturbances, some of which are of great physiological importance. *See* ELECTRIC ORGAN (BIOLOGY).

Impulse conduction. As explained above, the concentration imbalances between the ions inside and those outside the cell and the imbalance of ionic leakage currents lead to a difference in electrical potential between the inside and the outside of the cell. In many cells, differences in concentration rates and diffusion rates of sodium and potassium respectively make large contributions to this electrical potential difference. A membrane separating two fluid compartments at different electrical potentials is said to be polarized. In the case of nerve, muscle, and electric organ cells, the electrical potential difference across the membrane ranges from 0.05 to about 0.1 V. This voltage is called the resting potential of the cell.

Nerve, muscle, and electric organ cells have membranes which are said to be excitable, meaning that some kind of a disturbance can produce a localized and very sudden but temporary change in permeability in a part of the cell surface. The membrane behaves as if it developed a sudden leak or a breakdown in resistance at a certain small point, the leak being sufficient to permit a considerable flow of ions. These leaks probably take place mainly through ion-permeable channels made up of integral membrane proteins. These surges of ions constitute movements of electrically charged particles and hence are electric currents. The leak can develop very rapidly and may reach a peak in a fraction of a millisecond. While the current is flowing, the membrane behaves as if it had a low electrical resistance, and the difference in electrical potential between the inside and the outside of the cell diminishes and may even reverse in sign. A membrane in this state is said to be depolarized. In some nerve and sensory cells, such as the photoreceptor cells of the retina of the eye, the changes in permeability taking place upon activation create a change in potential in the opposite direction, leading to a condition known as hyperpolarization. The electrical transients occurring as a result of such ionic movements are called action potentials or graded potentials, and are characterized by corresponding ionic currents. Such currents and potential changes can be recorded electrically and displayed upon an oscilloscope screen.

The leaky areas or points of diminished resistance quickly heal, restoring the original state locally within a few milliseconds to several seconds. However, such a considerable, localized molecular disturbance in the membrane perturbs neighboring regions as well, so that the permeability of the membrane of adjacent areas becomes altered and permits ionic leaks. In many nerve and muscle cells and in the electric organ cell, an initial depolarizing disturbance occurring in a localized part of the cell membrane propagates in this manner. A wave of depolarization sweeps in rapid sequence over the entire cell surface, with each area permitting a surge of ions resembling in magnitude the initial one, and then "healing," as did the original site.

Propagated disturbances of permeability can sweep along surfaces of nerve or muscle cells at speeds of several tens of meters per second. Such disturbances constitute the impulses of nerve, which hence conduct at velocities much slower than the rate of conduction of electrical transients in wires.

Of course, any transient surge of ions such as occurs in an action current across an excitable membrane reduces the ionic concentration differences between the inside and the outside of the membrane. Normally the transient losses in permeability are so brief that very little effect is felt on ionic concentrations inside the cell. However, the ionic pumps are sensitive to small ionic changes and move quickly to restore any imbalances resulting from the ionic leakages. Thus, under physiological conditions, excitable cells such as nerve, muscle, or electric organ are capable of engendering many repeated depolarizing impulses, and ionic pumps can keep pace.

Impulse initiation. Excitable membrane impulses can be initiated in many ways, some of which are highly specialized. In visual receptor cells such as vertebrate eye rod and cone cells, the absorption of light quanta leads to changes in the shapes of molecules in the membranes of the photoreceptor cells. These changes in shape cause changes in the permeability of the membranes at those sites, initiating a hyperpolarization. In some cases, chemicals or ions coming into contact with an area of membrane equipped with suitable receptors can initiate a permeability change. One example is the effect of acetylcholine on receptor protein complexes on the surface of a muscle cell just under a motor nerve ending. Some sensory cells of the lateral line organ of fishes are sensitive to changes in ionic concentrations in the water in which the fish swims. Some species of sharks and teleost fish have sensory cells which undergo a polarization change when the cells sense a weak electrical signal from the breathing muscles of a fish in the vicinity, perhaps one hidden in the sand on the bottom. Such cells are called electroreceptors. The cells of the human's acoustic system and of the balance-sensing cells in the semicircular canals, and the cells of the lateral line organs of fishes and amphibia are sensitive to leverlike bending or tilting of long, slender processes called cilia or microvilli, which extend from the apical surfaces of the cells into surrounding fluids. Thus, hearing is effected by means of permeability changes induced in these acoustic "hair cells" by mechanical displacement of the angles assumed by slender cell processes. At synapses, action potential can be induced in nerve cells by contact with specific peptides, amino acids, catechol amines, indol amines, acetylchlorine, or other so-called transmitter substances liberated from a nearby portion of another nerve cell and allowed to engage specific binding sites localized in the small area of synaptic membrane of the receptor cell. The venom of a south Asian snake, the krait, contains bungarotoxin. The toxin is distributed in the victim's blood and other body fluids, binds to acetylcholine receptor areas in muscle and nerve cells, and prevents them from responding properly to their normal agonist, acetylcholine, when it is liberated from a nearby nerve cell. As a result, the proper permeability changes do not take place in the receptor cells; their normal function is paralyzed, and death of the victim is a common result. *See* SYNAPTIC TRANSMISSION.

Drugs of abuse, such as the opiates, cocaine, and cannabis, as well as certain prescription drugs such as tranquilizers, also interfere with the proper functioning of one or another of these transmitter substances, and thus produce their effects by confusing the normal mechanisms whereby the permeability of a nerve cell is regulated. Changes in permeability at sensitive areas of nerve cells, especially synapses, can induce depolarizing or hyperpolarizing ionic currents which can sweep over the cell surface and inform distant portions of the cell that an important event has taken place at the site of initiation. *See* CHEMORECEPTION; PHONORECEPTION; SENSE ORGAN.

Transcellular Permeability

In addition to considering permeability across a cell membrane, biologists and physicians must consider the permeability characteristics of more complex membranes, such as those composed of a whole layer of cells or of a layer of cells and a layer of connective tissue. Selective permeation of a barrier composed of cells is called transcellular permeability. For example, the circulating blood is separated from intercellular tissue spaces by the walls of large numbers of blood capillary vessels about 5–10 micrometers in diameter. These vessels have walls composed of many flattened cells (endothelial cells), which join with each other at their edges to form tubular structures. Closely enveloping most endothelial tubes is a sleeve of extracellular, fibrous, matted glycocalyx material that is termed the basement membrane or basal lamina of the capillary. These two structures together—one cellular and one extracellular— stand as barriers between the circulating blood and the cells of the body. However, across the capillary wall, selective exchanges go on constantly between the blood plasma and the cells outside.

Oxygen, carbon dioxide, and nitrogen dissolve readily in the blood plasma; and oxygen and carbon dioxide, the latter in the form of carbonic acid, are carried in concentrated form in red cells. Since these molecular gases are also soluble in lipids, they diffuse readily across the cell membranes of the endothelial cells and the intervening aqueous layers. As does the cell membrane, the capillary barrier permits ready transcellular passage of these lipid-soluble gases.

Fenestrations and other channels. However, movements of water and water-soluble, lipid-insoluble products are greatly hindered by lipid bilayers. Since these water-soluble substances must exchange briskly across blood capillary walls in order to meet the physiological needs of the tissues and organs, capillaries are constituted to allow pathways which bypass all lipid bilayers. These pathways are under physiological control and vary from one capillary bed to another in accordance with the physiological needs of the organ or tissue served. In many tissues, for example, in the liver, kidney, parts of the intestine, and endocrine glands, the endothelial cells lining the capillary blood vessels are provided with numerous holes or fenestrations which allow ready aqueous exchanges between blood and tissue spaces. These fenestrations are lined by the endothelial cell membrane and are so large that they do not prevent exchanges of molecules across the blood vessel wall, yet are small enough to prevent losses of blood cells or platelets.

In the case of liver capillaries, the numerous large windows are unobstructed by any appreciable barriers, so that proteins, such as serum albumin and fibrinogen, synthesized by liver cells and destined for physiological service in the blood plasma, have direct and unencumbered access to the blood plasma. Conversely, circulating blood proteins have direct access to liver cells through these apertures.

In other organs, such as intestine and endocrine glands, the apertures through the endothelial cells are as large and numerous as those through the liver, but instead of being unencumbered are bridged by delicate extracellular diaphragms derived from glycocalyx elements of endothelial cells. Such diaphragms act as filters which allow free passage of water, simple ions, and small molecules but retard the passage of protein molecules, hindering large protein molecules more than small. In the abundantly fenestrated capillaries of the glomeruli of mammalian kidneys there are at least three filters in series. The first is the fenestrated endothelial cell itself, which holds back cells and platelets. The second is a glycocalyx component called the glomerular basement membrane, which intervenes between the capillary endothelium and the glomerular epithelial cells. The third is an extracellular glycocalyx component called the filtration slit membrane, which bridges narrow spaces between elongated, branching foot processes of glomerular epithelial cells. This series of filters does retard the passage of proteins, but allows smaller, positively charged protein molecules to filter through more readily than large ones, or ones with negative charges. Normally, proteins are removed from the filtrate by kidney tubule cells, so that normal urine is almost devoid of protein. *See* ABSORPTION (BIOLOGY).

Many blood capillaries lack abundant fenestrations. Such capillaries dominate the vascular beds of brain, nerve, muscle, tendon, and connective tissue. The pathways taken by aqueous fluids across the walls of these capillaries are less clear. However, one possibility is that some of the water may exchange through interstices between endothelial cells or through relatively small-caliber fenestrations or channels which may form only transiently and which may be spanned by filtering diaphragms derived from glycocalyx material.

Capillary selectivity. In all types of capillaries, aqueous substances use only a small portion of the total capillary surface area as pathways of exchange, whereas gas molecules can diffuse across at any point. Moreover, in all types of capillaries except those of the liver, the aqueous components are hindered according to size, with small units, such as water molecules, inorganic ions, and simple sugars, traversing the barrier most rapidly. The smaller protein molecules move across with greater difficulty, and protein molecules of larger size go through even more sparingly. Even in the case of the liver capillaries, blood cells and platelets are confined to the lumens of the capillaries. Thus the capillary wall acts as a selective permeability barrier.

Mechanisms. There is no evidence that capillary endothelial cells utilize active transport mechanisms to mediate exchanges between blood plasma and extracellular tissue fluids. The driving forces for exchange seem to reside in diffusion and in hydrostatic and osmotic pressure differences between the two fluid compartments. The hydrostatic pressure in the capillaries is derived from the blood pressure generated by heart action.

Very different situations are encountered in some other cellular barriers. The cells making up the walls of vertebrate kidney tubules, the lining of the urinary bladder of a toad, and the skin of a frog are examples of continuous laminar structures composed of cells which separate two fluid compartments, one of which is intercellular fluid in exchange with blood plasma. Transcellular diffusion of gases across these cellular barriers occurs, but movements of water, salts, proteins, and sugars are highly regulated and selective and are actuated by active transport processes. Frog-skin and toad-bladder epithelial cells selectively and actively transport sodium into the tissue fluids and blood plasma, from the pond water in the case of the frog, and from the urine in the case of the toad. The transported sodium ions carry with them chloride ions and some water.

The transcellular permeability of kidney tubule cells is far more complex. These cells also utilize active transport mechanisms. They can move sugars and simple ions from the urinary fluid compartment into the blood and can move other substances in the reverse direction. These active transport processes are highly selective and regulated and display an impressive versatility and sophistication in transcellular permeability. *See* KIDNEY.

Cell-to-Cell Permeability

Cells making up an organized structure such as an organ of the body or an early embryo or the vascular system of a plant can often benefit themselves, the organ, and the organism if the individual constituent cells can communicate effectively with their near or distant neighbors. Two methods of cell-to-cell communication have been described above. One is based on specificity of surface molecular configurations on the glycocalyx of a cell. These configurations can be explored by surface feeler molecules of another cell and recognized as matching or nonmatching. The response to such interactions is often a change in permeability. A second method of cell-to-cell communication has been exemplified in the discussion of some features of synapses. According to this mechanism, one cell liberates a specific substance, for example, a hormone or a neurotransmitter substance or a pheromone. Another cell, nearby or far away, recognizes the substance liberated and responds to it, as do

receptor cells at chemical synapses. Here again, the liberation of the substance by one cell and the response of the second often involve permeability phenomena. This type of cell-to-cell signaling has been introduced herein by citing examples of nerve cells and neurotransmitters, but the method is also of great importance in numerous other cell systems. Many plants use hormones such as auxins or gibberellins to signal from one cell to another. Embryo cells signal to neighboring cells at certain specific times in development, calling on close or distant cells to take this or that timely path in differentiation or growth. In such communication, mammalian embryonic cells secrete specific signaling chemicals, several of which are the same as ones used between nerve cells in transmitting a signal. *See* CELL DIFFERENTIATION; EMBRYONIC INDUCTION.

A third method of cell-to-cell communication functions only between one cell and an immediately adjacent neighbor. It involves establishing direct, permeable channels between the two adjacent cells, in two different ways. One is by providing continuity of the membranes of two adjacent cells so as to enclose the cytoplasms of both cells in one continuous membrane. In this situation, no membrane intervenes between the cells, and free permeability is established through the communicating passage surrounded by the membrane common to the two cells. In the second way, each cell is enclosed completely by its own separate membrane, but where a region of one cell membrane is closely adjacent to that of a next neighbor, the membranes of both cells accommodate integral membrane proteins which form channels. The coupling of two similar channel-forming complexes resembles the end-to-end coupling of two short lengths of pipe. In both cases, the lumens of the channels or passages connecting the two cells are well insulated from the surrounding extracellular space, so that the delicate cytoplasms of both cells are well protected. Rather free permeability is established between the cytoplasm of one cell and that of its neighbor, but not with the extracellular fluids. Details of these two types of intercellular communicating channels are described below.

Synapses and junctions. During the late 1950s, physiologists learned that the electrical resistance between adjacent heart-muscle cells is very low—much lower than the resistance across a cell membrane. Others learned that in some instances the electrical resistance between two adjacent nerve-cell cytoplasms is similarly low, though in most cases where measurements have been made, the resistance between two nerve cells is high, reflecting the two intact cell membranes. It was quickly recognized that where the intercellular resistance is low, intact continuous lipoprotein barriers cannot be separating the two cells and that the two cells must be coupled by continuous aqueous channels large enough to allow rather free flow of ions between them. In other words, there exists no effective permeability barrier to ions between two cells so coupled.

It was also learned that wherever two adjacent nerve cells are connected by such low-resistance channels, if one cell is excited and gives rise to a propagated action potential, this disturbance is transmitted to the second cell without appreciable delay. Thus one cell can communicate with its neighbor very quickly, as ions can flow through the low-resistance channels with great rapidity. In contrast, at a chemical synapse, there is a measurable delay which can be accounted for by the time required for the discharge of neurotransmitter from synaptic vesicles, for the diffusion of the substances so released across the synaptic interspace, for the recognition of the transmitter substances by receptor molecules associated with the receptor-cell synaptic membrane, and for the initiation of the permeability changes in response to the binding of transmitter substance by receptor molecules. Thus it became apparent that low-resistance channels between adjacent excitable cells allow for direct electrical coupling and for very rapid transmission of an excitation impulse from one cell to another. This type of direct coupling between nerve cells came to be known as an electrical synapse, in order to distinguish it from a chemical synapse, where a specific transmitter chemical carries the signal from one cell to another.

In nervous tissue, chemical synapses are more commonly encountered than are electrical synapses. Chemical synapses, though slower, lend themselves better to control, modulation, and regulation. But electrical synapses are not rare, and several have been found, particularly in invertebrate nerve chains where very rapid responses are advantageous. For example, in the nerve cord of an earthworm there are chains of giant nerve fibers connected to each other by electrical synapses. If an earthworm extends its head end above the soil within the range of a predator, a slight disturbance or touch occasioned by the predator can be appreciated by sense organs at the worm's head end and the signal transmitted with great speed to the body muscles. The electrical synapses in the nerve cord allow the worm to withdraw more rapidly than would be possible with chemical synapses. Similarly, in shrimp, prawns, and lobsters, the chain of nerve cells controlling the powerful tail muscles is fitted with electrical synapses, thus speeding up the flick of the tail on which these animals depend when retreating from danger. Electrical synapses are also present in the human brain and spinal cord, though their abundance and roles are not well understood. It appears that chemical synapses are favored in vertebrate nervous systems. In the case of the heart, which like the brain is made up of excitable cells, the constituent muscle cells are connected to their neighbors by low-resistance permeability channels which function in a manner identical to the workings of electrical synapses connecting two nerve cells. Though the term synapse was introduced to refer to specialized regions where one nerve cell could transmit an excitatory or inhibitory signal to an adjacent nerve cell, the term has been extended to apply to specialized regions of communication between nerve and muscle, and can just as aptly be applied to the communicating junctions between heart-muscle cells. Thus one can say that heart-muscle cells are connected to each other by electrical synapses.

During the 1960s, physiologists found that similar, low-resistance channels connect many cells which are not excitable in the sense that nerve and muscle cells are. It became evident that in the early developing embryo, many, or even all, of the cells at certain stages are so connected. Moreover, cells in the liver, kidney, intestinal epithelium, smooth muscle investments, salivary and pancreatic glands, connective tissue, and in many other organized groups are similarly connected to each other by low-resistance aqueous channels.

When the morphological basis for these channels was explored, it was found that the basic units providing for communication are channel-forming integral membrane protein complexes with the essential features already described. Each of these channel-forming unit complexes is typically made up of six protein molecules arranged around a passage about 1.5–2 mm in diameter. Such a channel is selective in accordance with size, allowing free passage of water, inorganic ions, simple sugars, amino acids, and most metabolites, but restricting passage of large proteins and other large polymers. Many channels close down if exposed to high concentrations of intracellular calcium (Ca^{2+}). Each unit is embedded in the membrane of its cell, forming a passage which pierces the membrane, but which connects directly with its aligned identical partner embedded in the membrane of the adjacent cell. The connection is such as to prevent leakage from either cell into the extracellular fluids. The electrical resistance of each channel is that of a cylinder of cytoplasm or of physiological salt solution 2 nm in diameter and 20 nm long. Typically, in a system of cells using these channels, one cell is connected to its neighbor by 10^2 to 10^5 channels in each.

These communicating channels frequently occur in groups or patches of several hundred or several thousand paired units. Such groups can be recognized with the electron microscope as specialized complexes linking two adjacent cells. These patches are called communicating junctions. The term gap junctions is also used but seems less appropriate. Thus the terms electrical synapses, communicating junctions, and gap junctions all refer to the same type of structure: patches or groups of essentially similar channels which permit almost unimpeded ionic communication between adjacent cells through aqueous permeability passages piercing the cell membrane. Each channel is formed by paired, aligned molecular bushings or grommets, each composed of six integral membrane proteins. When such channels connect nerve cells, the term electrical synapse is most appropriate.

Plasmodesmata; syncytia. Another means of communication through permeability pathways is by direct cytoplasmic channels confined by typical lipid bilayer membrane between a cell and its adjacent communicant. In this case, one continuous lipid bilayer membrane with its complement of integral membrane proteins and glycocalyx surrounds the connected cells.

Cell-to-cell permeability channels bounded by cell membrane can be formed in two ways. One is by incomplete cell division. In this case, nuclei divide in the normal manner and separate from each other, but the cytoplasmic division is incomplete and the membrane investment of the original dividing cell does not divide into two separate, complete daughter cells, each bounded by its own membrane. Instead a single, continuous membrane is left to surround both separated daughter nuclei, each of which, however, comes to lie in and to control its own cytoplasmic domain while remaining in direct cytoplasmic contact with its neighboring sister nucleus. A second way to form communicating pathways of this type is by fusion of membranes of two once-separate cells. After the fusion, the two cytoplasmic domains are in direct continuity without any separating membrane.

Formation of cell-to-cell permeability channels by incomplete cell division is common in plants. Plant cells characteristically tend to surround themselves with a hard, woody, rather rigid glycocalyx component rich in cellulose and aptly called the cell wall. After nuclear division, the two nuclei migrate to opposite ends of the plant cell. Between them, usually near the midpoint of the dividing cell, a group of flattened, membrane-bound vesicles align in the plane destined to separate the two daughter cells. This flat accumulation of vesicles is called the cell plate. These vesicles characteristically proceed to fuse with each other. As they fuse, they separate more and more the cytoplasmic domains around the two daughter nuclei. If the fusion process goes to completion, the cytoplasms of the two cells are separated completely. Each cell is then surrounded by its own cell membrane, and no special communicating channels remain to connect the two cells. In plants, however, the fusion of the vesicles of the cell plate is often incomplete, so that membrane-lined channels remain connecting the cytoplasm of two daughter cells. A single membrane can then be traced surrounding both cells without discontinuity. In plants, several such channels can persist, connecting adjacent cells for indefinite periods of time, probably often for the duration of the life of the plant.

After cell division, plant cells often rearrange or restructure their cell walls, removing cellulose in some places and building it up in others. In doing so, they lay down cell-wall cellulose barriers between the two daughter cells. When the separation of the cytoplasm of the two daughter cells is incomplete, the intervening cell wall does not form a solid partition, but has openings or pores which accommodate the residual membrane-bound channels connecting the two cells on either side of the new partition. This cell-wall partition, when viewed face-on with a microscope, clearly shows the pores or fenestrations around which the cellulose fibers of the cell wall were laid. Regions of cell wall showing groups of such pores are called sieve plates, and the cytoplasmic connections which pass through the sieve pores to connect one cell to another are called sieve tubes or plasmodesmata (singular, plasmodesma or plasmodesm). Sieve tubes are so named because of the tubelike sleeve of cell membrane which surrounds each cytoplasmic connection; the membranous sleeve is continuous with the membrane surrounding the two cells connected by it. The term plasmodesma reflects the concept of connecting cytoplasm. The electrical resistance between two cells so connected is low, and water, ions, sugars, metabolites, and even proteins can pass through the channels. The diameters of these tubes may range from 100 to 1000 nm or more. The lengths may range from a few micrometers to a few tens of micrometers. The electrical resistance between the extracellular fluid and the cytoplasms of cells thus connected is high.

After the cells here described have matured and reach a stable structure, the nuclei of some of them disappear and the cells take a simplified form. Such simplified cells are nevertheless able to participate in permeability functions, along with their nucleated fellows, as their connections through the sieve plates persist and perform effectively.

In many plants, very extensive systems of cells are connected to each other through sieve plates and plasmodesmata. Typically in these systems, one cell is connected to several of its neighbors, not only to cells at each end but to cells to the side as well. Thus aqueous fluids can move for long distances in plants, traversing cell after cell, and permeating from one cell to the next through plasmodesmata.

There is a brisk and active two-way traffic in plants. For example, in a redwood tree, water, phosphates, nitrogen, potassium, and other minerals and nutrients are taken up by the roots, which may be as long as 328 ft (100 m). The nutrients are then carried up the trunk and into the crown, the topmost leaves of which may be 328 ft (100 m) above the ground. Conversely, in the leaves sugars are made from carbon dioxide, water, and sunlight. These sugars include the raw material for synthesizing cellulose, some of which is made in the most distant root tips, which may be 656 ft (200 m) from the topmost leaves. Thus sugars must make as long a journey as the phosphates, but in the opposite direction. In most plants, the corresponding journeys are over lesser distances, but the permeability phenomena are similar, and the traffic takes place through series of cells connected by plasmodesmata, without a single membrane offering resistance to the aqueous traffic. In many plant tissues, a single membrane can be traced continuously over very many cells, each cell connected to its immediate neighbors in the same system by plasmodesmata. Thousands of plant cells can thus be connected into a single system with cytoplasmic continuity, and hence low electrical resistance as well as low resistance to aqueous flow can be provided throughout the entire system. In such a system, the cytoplasms of all the participating cells and the plasmodesmata alike are protected by one continuous cell membrane of substantial area but intricate geometric design. Within this membrane, free permeability is allowed to aqueous components through the thousands of participating cells and their numerous tubelike cytoplasmic connections. *See* PLANT TRANSPORT OF SOLUTES.

In animals, transport of nutrients over long distances is achieved in a different fashion, by pumping body fluids such as blood or lymph through specialized channels, the motive power being supplied in most cases by specialized muscular organs such as hearts. Thus animals neither need nor use huge systems of interconnected cells, as do plants.

Nevertheless, there are many circumstances where animal cells can benefit by establishing communicating pathways between cells which allow for intercellular permeability more free even than that provided by electrical synapses or communicating junctions. Such cell-to-cell permeability channels in animal cells can be made either by incomplete cell division or by fusion of cells.

Male germ cells provide striking examples of cell-to-cell permeability channels created by incomplete cell division, or perhaps more accurately, by delayed cytoplasmic division. As male germ cells develop in the testis, they go through a series of maturing stages called spermatogonia, spermatocytes, and spermatids. In a series of accurately timed cell divisions, the nuclei of the germ cells double in number at each division, but cytoplasmic division is incomplete at first and rather wide (5–10 μm) cytoplasmic passages are left connecting the divided cells. Starting with a spermatogonium and continuing through the spermatocyte stages, a clone of 64, 128, or 256 interconnected germ cells forms through a series of six to eight nuclear divisions. One continuous cell membrane surrounds all members of the clone. The cytoplasmic channels through the intercellular connections are so wide as to offer little selectivity, but instead permit very free communication between all members of the clone. These wide permeability channels persist into the spermatid stage, but pinch off as spermatids mature into spermatozoa. With these pinchings-off, cytoplasmic division is completed for all members of the clone, and each resulting spermatozoon has its own intact membrane.

The functional significance of these cytoplasmic

bridges between members of a male germ cell clone is not well understood. It is known, however, that all members of a clone go through the stages of each cell division synchronously. It is supposed that the wide, intercellular, permeable passages may have a role in synchronizing these events.

Examples of cells establishing freely permeable connections with other cells by fusion can be noted in the cases of mammalian striated muscle and of phagocytic giant cells. In both cases, single cells with single nuclei fuse with similar cells to form multinucleate cytoplasmic domains surrounded by a single continuous membrane. The cytoplasms of the fusing cells join so completely that no narrow neck persists after completion of the fusion process. Instead the cytoplasmic mass resulting from many fusions retains no traces of the original boundaries of the participating cells. From the point of view of permeability physiology, the resulting multinucleated cytoplasmic unit can usually be regarded as a very large single cell, as it is surrounded by a single membrane. Such multinucleate cells are commonly called syncytia (singular, syncytium), reflecting the concept that they form by the joining of many cells. However, the term is also used to refer to cells remaining joined to each other after incomplete or delayed cytoplasmic division, as illustrated by developing male germ cells. *See* CELL (BIOLOGY).

H. Stanley Bennett

Bibliography. K. S. Cole, *Membranes, Ions and Impulses: A Chapter of Classical Biophysics*, 1971; G. C. Karp, *Cell Biology*, 2d ed., 1984; G. R. Kepner (ed.), *Cell Membrane Permeability and Transport*, 1982; H.-C. Luttgau, *Membrane Control of Cellular Activity*, 1987; C. Nombela (ed.), *Microbial Cell Wall Synthesis and Autolysis*, 1985.

Cell plastids

Specialized structures found in plant cells, diverse in distribution, size, shape, composition, structure, function, and mode of development.

Types. A number of different types is recognized. Chloroplasts occur in the green parts of plants and

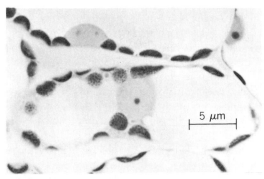

Fig. 1. Light microscope view of part of *Hypochaeris radicata* leaf, showing chloroplasts sectioned in a variety of planes and displaying internal grana.

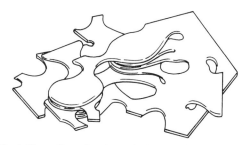

Fig. 2. Three-dimensional model of grana with intergranal connections. (*After W. Wehrmeyer, Planta, 63:13–30, 1964*)

are responsible for the green coloration, for they contain the chlorophyll pigments. These pigments, along with certain others, absorb the light energy that drives the processes of photosynthesis, by which sugars, starch, and other organic materials are synthesized. Amyloplasts, nearly or entirely colorless, are packed with starch grains and occur in cells of storage tissue. Proteoplasts are less common and contain crystalline, fibrillar, or amorphous masses of protein, sometimes along with starch grains. In chromoplasts the green pigment is masked or replaced by others, notably carotenoids, as in the cells of carrot roots and many flowers and fruits. *See* CAROTENOID; CHLOROPHYLL; STARCH.

Occurrence. Plastids lie in the cytoplasm of the cell (**Fig. 1**), normally unattached to other structures but surrounded by a special extension of the nuclear envelope in some algae. There may be from a single plastid to many thousand plastids per cell. A mesophyll cell in a leaf contains up to about 50 chloroplasts. Some specialized cells lose their plastids at maturity. Plastids do not occur in fungi.

Size and shape. The greatest diversity of chloroplast size and shape is found among genera and species of algae, as exemplified by branched and unbranched ribbons 100 micrometers or more in length, flat plates, and cup-shaped or stellate bodies. In some algae and in most other plants, chloroplasts are spherical or lens- or disk-shaped, with the major axis measuring 4–7 μm. *See* ALGAE.

Composition. A chloroplast in a spinach leaf has a dry weight of about 2×10^{-11} g, of which some 70% is protein (about half of this is soluble and half is membrane-bound), slightly more than 20% is lipid, and up to 7% is nucleic acid. Inorganic constituents include calcium, magnesium (largely in chlorophyll molecules), iron (partly in the proteins ferredoxin and cytochrome), manganese, and copper. Of the lipid approximately 21% is chlorophyll (100), 3% is carotenoid (22), 3% is plastoquinone and other quinonoid compounds (22), 9% is phospholipid (50), 44% is glycolipid (mainly mono- and digalactosyl glycerides) (23), 2% is sterol (25), 0.5% is prenol (3), and 17% is as yet unidentified. Figures in parentheses are estimates of the numbers of molecules relative to 100 molecules of chlorophyll.

Structure. All types of plastids have one structural feature in common, a double envelope consisting of two concentric sheets of membrane. The outer of these is in contact with the cytoplasmic ground substance; the inner with the plastid matrix, or stroma. They are separated by a narrow space of about 10 nanometers.

Another system of membranes generally occupies the main body of the plastid. This internal membrane system is especially well developed in chloroplasts, where the unit of construction is known as a thylakoid. In its simplest form this is a sac such as would be obtained if a balloon-shaped, membrane-limited sphere were to be flattened until the internal space was not much thicker than the membrane itself. It is usual, however, for thylakoids to be lobed, branched, or fenestrated. **Figures 2** and **3** show how disk-shaped lobes stack on top of one another to form grana. A granum may have 2–100 layers in it, and there may be more than 50 grana in a chloroplast. It is thought that all the grana are interconnected (**Fig. 4**) and that junctions with the inner layer of the chloroplast envelope are also present. As with their shape and pigmentation, algal chloroplasts are very diverse as regards the architecture of the thylakoids, and often do not possess grana. *See* CELL MEMBRANES.

Functions. The surface area of thylakoids is very large in relation to the volume of the chloro-

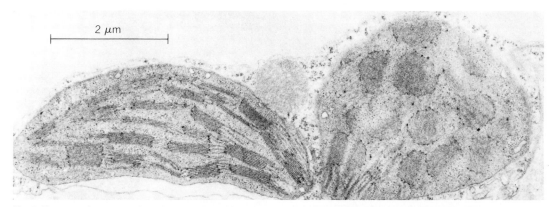

Fig. 3. Electron microscope view of two oat leaf chloroplasts, one showing successive layers of grana in side view, and the other showing grana in face view (disk shape of constituent thylakoid lobes are seen).

2 μm

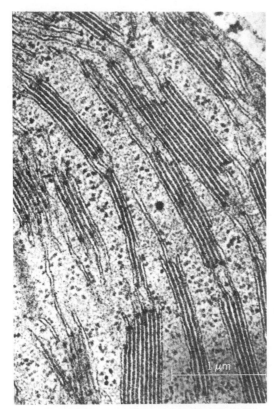

Fig. 4. Part of oat leaf chloroplast at higher magnification. Grana are seen in side view, revealing profiles of membranes. Thylakoids that interconnect grana are shown, with components of stroma, or ground substance, in which thylakoids lie. The dense granules are chloroplast ribosomes.

plast. This is functionally significant, for chlorophyll molecules and other components of the light-reaction systems of photosynthesis are associated with these membranes. Techniques such as shadow casting, negative staining, freeze etching, and small-angle x-ray scattering have revealed subunits within and on the surface of the thylakoid membrane itself. One such unit has been identified as a photophosphorylase enzyme involved in the final stages of the production of adenosinetriphosphate by photosynthetic phosphorylation. Others have not yet had specific functions assigned to them, but since the membranes can be fractionated to yield particles that carry out one or the other of the two light reactions, it may well be that photosynthetic units of function are being visualized. Such units might be based on lipoprotein particles, with chlorophyll and other molecules associated with them.

Utilization of the products of light reactions in the actual fixation of carbon dioxide occurs not in the membranes but in the stroma, or ground substance, of the chloroplast. Here reside the enzymes of the Calvin carbon-reduction cycle, including as a major protein component of green tissues the enzyme ribulose diphosphate carboxylase (carboxydismutase). This large molecule, more than 10 nm in diameter, catalyzes the formation of phosphoglyceric acid from ribulose diphosphate

(the acceptor molecule) and carbon dioxide. It is, like many other molecular species in the cell, restricted to chloroplasts.

A chloroplast is much more than a device for carrying out photosynthesis. It can use light energy for uptake and exchange of ions and to drive conformational changes. The stroma contains the elements of a protein-synthesizing system—as much deoxyribonucleic acid (DNA) as a small bacterium, various types of ribonucleic acid (RNA), distinctive ribosomes, and polyribosomes. There is evidence to indicate that much of the protein synthesis of a leaf takes place within the chloroplasts. *See* DEOXYRIBONUCLEIC ACID (DNA); PHOTOSYNTHESIS; PROTEIN; RIBONUCLEIC ACID (RNA); RIBOSOMES.

Mode of development. In algae, mosses, and ferns mature chloroplasts can divide. In cells of flowering plants divisions occur at a much earlier stage of development. Young, undifferentiated cells near the growing points of the plant, the meristems, contain precursor bodies called proplastids (**Fig. 5**), which apparently can divide and multiply. The proplastids only start to develop into one or other of the categories of plastid when the cell that contains them itself starts to differentiate. The ability of amyloplasts to give rise to chloroplasts (for example, when a potato tuber turns green), of chloroplasts to senesce into chromoplasts, and of chromoplasts to "re-green" to give chloroplasts, demonstrates that, although the different types normally develop from proplastids, interconvertibility is not completely lost.

A complex morphogenetic pathway leads from the proplastid to the chloroplast. Precursor molecules are synthesized; some are incorporated into the thylakoids, and the extending thylakoid surface gradually gives rise to interconnected grana.

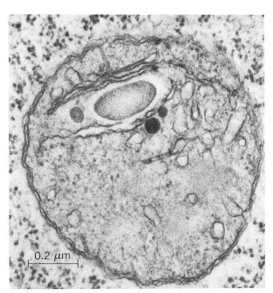

Fig. 5. Proplastid in cell of broad bean root tip. Double membranous envelope is shown and rudimentary nature of internal membrane system is obvious.

In general, light is required for this process. In darkness a precursor of chlorophyll, protochlorophyll, accumulates and the membranes assume a surprisingly different form, the unit of which is a branched tubule some 20–25 nm in diameter. These tubes interconnect to form semicrystalline lattices based on tetrahedral or cubic arrangements. The lattices, or prolamellar bodies, are up to 3 μm across and contain a relatively large surface area of membrane. When the plant is illuminated, the tubular membranes rearrange and the normal arrangement of interconnected grana develops. Since prolamellar bodies occur in etiolated plants, the plastids that contain them are known as etioplasts.

Morphogenetic autonomy. One of the most challenging problems in cell biology concerns the autonomy of organelles, such as the plastids. Chloroplasts, for instance, have their own DNA, DNA-polymerase, and RNA-polymerase; can make proteins; and, significantly, can mutate. All this suggests a measure of independence. It is known, however, that some nuclear genes can influence the production of molecules that are normally found only in chloroplasts, so their autonomy cannot be complete. It remains to be seen whether they control and regulate their own morphogenetic processes.

Brian E. S. Gunning

Bibliography. C. J. Avers, *Molecular Cell Biology*, 2d ed., 1986; R. J. Ellis (ed.), *Chloroplast Biogenesis*, 1985; L. Goldstein and D. M. Prescott (eds.), *Cell Biology: A Comprehensive Treatise*, vol. 4, 1980; L. J. Kliensmith and V. M. Kish, *Principles of Cell Biology*, 1987; J. J. Lee and J. F. Fredrick (eds.), *Endocytobiology III*, 1987; W. Waymouth (ed.), *Modern Cell Biology*, vol. 5: *Molecular Mechanisms in the Regulation of Cell Behavior*, 1987.

Cell polarity (biology)

The highly organized condition in most cells that is characterized by a distinct apical-basal axis with an asymmetric distribution of cytoplasmic organelles. This phenomenon of polarization is critical for living organisms to function. For example, cells in secretory organs such as the gall bladder generally secrete only at one end where secretory vesicles are localized. Another example would be a cell in the intestinal wall that must collect nutrients on the side near the lumen and transport them through the cell to the opposite end, where they can be delivered to the blood supply for transport to the rest of the body. Clearly, this cell must exhibit a polarized distribution of membrane proteins so that those necessary for sugar uptake are concentrated in the membrane facing the lumen and those needed to move the sugar out of the cell are located at the opposite side.

Most organisms begin life as a rather symmetrical, spherical, single cell called an egg. During early development this egg divides many times and forms

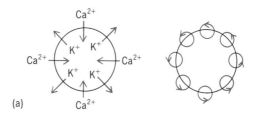

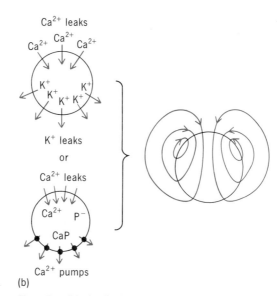

Fig. 1. Possible distribution of ion channels and pumps in a cell's plasma membrane with the resulting current pattern. (a) A uniform distribution of calcium Ca($^{2+}$) and potassium (K$^+$) channels will result in many highly localized current loops. (b) Separation of the Ca^{2+} and K$^+$ channels (above) or Ca^{2+} channels and pumps (below) will result in the transcellular ion current pattern shown on the right.

an embryo, which exhibits much more intricate patterns (such as the polarized intestine) than were initially expressed by the egg. Determining how the embryo controls the development of such patterns has been an area of active research, and there is evidence that the plasma (outer) membrane can influence the development of cell polarity by driving ionic currents through the cell which, in turn, can influence the polarization process by generating ion concentration gradients within the cell or voltage gradients between cells. *See* DEVELOPMENTAL BIOLOGY.

Plant eggs. By far the strongest cases for a direct role of membrane-generated ion currents and concentration gradients in cell polarization are found in plant eggs which exhibit no preformed growth axis. Among the most useful have been the eggs of the brown algae *Fucus* and *Pelvetia*, common seaweeds found in the intertidal zone on both the Atlantic and Pacific coasts. The eggs develop by first secreting wall-softening and wall-building enzymes at one end. They then pump in potassium and chloride ions, and water follows these ions into the eggs to generate a large turgor pressure of about 5 atm (500 kilopascals). The eggs bulge (germinate) in the region where the wall has been softened by the secreted enzymes, thereby producing a structure that will develop into the rhizoid or holdfast. This is the first morphologically obvious axis of polarity. The establishment of the axis of secretion, and thus the morphological polarity, can be influenced by a variety of environmental factors, including unilateral light or unilateral chemical influences from nearby eggs or plants. The response to unilateral light is to germinate on the dark side; this is useful since the rhizoid outgrowth will form the holdfast for the plant and should form opposite the Sun so the plant can be anchored to a rock. Since the light receptors are located in the plasma membrane, it is not surprising that this membrane plays a key role in the signal transduction.

Transcellular ionic currents. The earliest indicator of the polarization process is the movement of ions through the egg via pores in the plasma membrane. These ionic currents crossing the plasma membrane can be detected by using a technique called the vibrating probe which measures small voltage gradients in the fluid just outside the egg. As early as 30 min after fertilization, these currents can be found entering the dark hemisphere of a unilaterally illuminated egg. The early spatial current pattern is unstable and shifts position, often with more than one inward current region. However, the current enters mainly on the side where germination will occur, and is usually largest at the prospective cortical clearing region where the rhizoid forms. The current pattern observed during the 2-h period prior to germination is more stable and looks like the pattern on the right side in **Fig. 1**. The site of inward current always predicts the germination site, even when the axis is reversed by light-direction reversal. The most likely hypothesis is that light receptors in the cell's plasma membrane control the distribution of open ion channels so that current

enters the dark end.

In order to understand how such a transcellular current might be influencing the polarization process, it is important to determine which ions are carrying the current. By varying the composition of the artificial seawaters in which these measurements were made, it was determined that calcium ion (Ca^{2+}) influx was responsible for a small fraction of the current with chloride ion (Cl^-) efflux as the most likely carrier of the bulk of it. This calcium ion component was directly measured by following the movement of radioactive calcium ion through the egg. Therefore, one consequence of the transcellular ionic current in this egg is the generation of a calcium ion flux through the cell, which has been shown to generate a gradient in the intracellular concentration of calcium ion, $[Ca^{2+}]_i$. This gradient appears to play the primary role in polarizing the egg.

Calcium ion gradients. It is known that a central component of the polarization mechanism in the egg of a brown alga involves a cytoplasmic gradient in $[Ca^{2+}]_i$. This hypothesis is supported by the three criteria required for physiological significance: (1) An endogenous $[Ca^{2+}]_i$ gradient exists in the egg (although measured long after polarization); (2) modifying the direction of this gradient during polarization changes the orientation of the axis of polarization; and (3) inhibiting the gradient prevents polarization. The gradient was detected in germinated zygotes by using calcium ion–sensitive microelectrodes, and a 10-fold higher $[Ca^{2+}]_i$ was detected in the tip region than in the subtip region of the rhizoid. A calcium ion gradient was imposed on unpolarized eggs by placing them near a fixed source of calcium ion ionophore in the dark. A majority of the eggs then germinated on the hemisphere facing the ionophore, where the influx of calcium ion is expected to be the

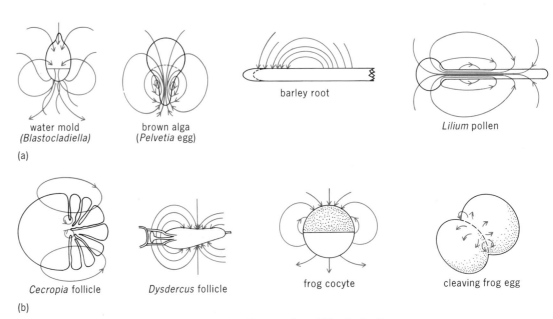

water mold
(*Blastocladiella*)

brown alga
(*Pelvetia* egg)

barley root

Lilium pollen

(a)

Cecropia follicle

Dysdercus follicle

frog cocyte

cleaving frog egg

(b)

Fig. 2. Transcellular ion current patterns measured in (*a*) plant cells and (*b*) animal cells.

greatest. Finally, the magnitude of the gradient can be greatly reduced by injecting the cell with a molecule that can rapidly shuttle calcium ions from regions of high concentration to regions of low concentration. Such a molecule was used to show that polarization could be blocked for weeks while the cell remained viable and even divided. This is the strongest evidence yet that a gradient in $[Ca^{2+}]_i$ is required for cell polarization.

Ionic currents and intracellular ion concentration gradients are not a unique property of brown algae, but have been detected in many other cell types as well. In fact, ionic currents have been detected in nearly every plant and animal cell and tissue investigated with the vibrating probe technique (**Fig. 2**). The transcellular current pattern is usually closely correlated with the axis of polarity. It would therefore appear that most cells do not have a uniform distribution of ion channels and pumps (Fig. 1a) but segregate channel types to varying degrees (Fig. 1b). See BIOPOTENTIALS AND IONIC CURRENTS.

Animal cells. A wide variety of animal systems have been investigated with the vibrating probe, and the best example of the use of ionic currents in maintaining the polarized state comes from the developing egg of the moth *Hyalophora cecropia*. This egg is connected to seven other cells called nurse cells which produce important molecules that are transported into the egg. This transport is polarized since most proteins will move from the nurse cells into the egg but will not move from the egg back to the nurse cells. It was demonstrated that a voltage difference of about 5 millivolts exists between the nurse cells and oocyte in the follicle of the silk moth. The only way that such a voltage gradient can be maintained in the conductive cytoplasm is by a steady current flow. Thus, the plasma membranes of these cells must be driving a steady current along the cytoplasmic bridge between the cells to generate the observed voltage gradient. Moreover, there is strong evidence from the behavior of microinjected proteins that intercellular electrophoresis is involved as a protein segregation mechanism here. The polarity of protein transport across the bridge connecting these two cell types can be reversed by reversing the endogenous electrical field with this bridge.

While it is not too surprising that proteins could be electrophoresed along an intercellular bridge by an imposed field, even more compelling evidence that electrophoresis is involved in this transport has been found. The polarity of movement of given protein across the bridge is dependent only on its net electric charge. Most cellular proteins are negatively charged and so would be driven from the nurse cells into the oocyte by the voltage gradient along the cytoplasmic bridge. Lysozyme is a basic protein with a net positive charge, and when it is injected into either the nurse cells or the oocyte, it is found to move only in the opposite direction, from the oocyte to the nurse cells. However, when the net charge on this protein is reversed by methylcarboxylation, its transport direction was reversed, and it was observed only to move from nurse cells to oocyte. In further support for the electrophoresis mechanism, neutral proteins with no net electric charge move in both directions across the bridge. Thus, in the cecropia follicle, the polarity of protein transport, which is a critical component of the oocyte's polarity, is determined by the electrical field across the intercellular bridge. The cecropia follicle is the best example in which transcellular currents play an active, causal role in polarized transport. See CELL (BIOLOGY).

Richard Nuccitelli

Bibliography. C. Brownlee and J. W. Wood, A gradient of cytoplasmic free calcium in growing rhizoid cells of *Fucus serratus, Nature*, 320:624–626, 1986; L. F. Jaffe and R. Nuccitelli, An ultrasensitive vibrating probe for measuring steady extracellular currents, *J. Cell Biol.*, 63:614–628, 1974; J. R. McIntosh (ed.), *Modern Cell Biology*, vol. 2, 1983; R. Nuccitelli, Ooplasmic segregation and secretion in the *Pelvetia* egg is accompanied by a membrane-generated electrical current, *Dev. Biol.*, 62:13–33, 1978; R. I. Woodruff and W. H. Telfer, Electrophoresis of proteins in intercellular bridges, *Nature*, 286:84–86, 1980.

Cell senescence and death

The limited capacity of all normal human and other animal cells to reproduce and function. The gradual decline in normal physiological function of the cells is referred to as aging or senescence. The aging process ends with the death of individual cells and then, generally, the whole animal. Aging occurs in all animals, except those that do not reach a fixed body size such as some tortoises and sharks, sturgeon, and several other kinds of fishes. These animals die as the result of accidents or disease, but losses in normal physiological function do not seem to occur. Examples of cells that do not age are those composing the germ plasm (sex cells) and many kinds of cancer cells. These cells are presumed to be immortal.

Normal cells. In the mid-1960s it was found that, contrary to the prevailing belief, normal human cells cultured in the laboratory do have a limited capacity to function and to divide. This phenomenon was interpreted as aging at the cellular level. These observations have been extended to include the cells of all other animals tested. See TISSUE CULTURE.

Prior to this finding, it was believed that all cultured cells were potentially immortal. If that were true, aging in animals would be the result of events that occur at organizational levels higher than individual cells. That is, age changes would be attributed to nongenetic events occurring outside cells, such as changes in the substances that bind cells into tissues, externally caused injuries to cells, hormone effects, and other interactions between tissues and organs. Now that it is known that normal human and other animals cells have a limited capacity to divide and function, there is a general belief that cell senescence must be attributed to intracellular events. These events, which would play a major role in senescence or aging, are thought to occur in the deoxyribonucleic acid (DNA) and other information-containing molecules.

Studies have shown that when normal human fibroblasts, derived from human embryos, are

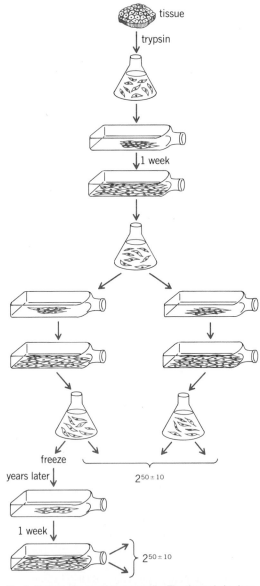

Fig. 1. Culture of normal human cells. The tissue is broken down into individual cells with the digestive enzyme trypsin. The cells are then separated from the trypsin and placed into a flat bottle, where they multiply until they cover the floor of the culture vessel. When they stop multiplying, the cells are divided into equal numbers and placed into two culture vessels. The process is repeated every few days after the cells have covered the available surface area. Each subcultivation results in one population doubling. (*After L. Hayflick, The cell biology of human aging, Sci. Amer., 242(1):58–66, 1980*)

grown in laboratory culture, they can undergo only about 50 population doublings (**Fig. 1**). Fibroblasts are found in virtually all tissues, and besides lending structural support, they produce collagen and other proteins that bind cells into tissues. The maximum number of doublings attainable was inversely proportional to donor age: fibroblasts from older people were found to undergo fewer doublings than those derived from younger donors.

Cultured fibroblasts derived from different animal species seem to undergo a number of population doublings that are directly proportional to the species lifespan (**Fig. 2**).

Nondividing cells. Fibroblasts have a greater capacity to divide in laboratory cultures than any other normal cell type. Nevertheless, since all normal human and other animal cells have a finite capacity to divide or to function, nondividing cells, such as neurons or muscle cells, also age. The loss of function in brain neurons may indeed play a greater role in age changes than do changes in any other cell type.

When normal human embryonic cells are frozen at a particular population doubling, they "remember" at what doubling level they were frozen and, when thawed, continue to divide until the total of 50 is reached. It has been shown that the frozen cells' memory is accurate over a period of at least 22 years.

Normal human and other animal cells are mortal not only when they are grown in laboratory cultures but even when normal tissues are grafted into laboratory animals. When the laboratory animal grows old, the graft can be removed and placed on a younger host animal. This serial animal-to-animal transfer, which is analogous to cell transfers in laboratory cultures, also reveals the finitude in division capacity and function of normal cells.

Changes in senescent cells. Prior to the death of cultured normal human cells, they incur well over 100 changes that herald their approaching demise. These changes occur in lipid content and synthesis; carbohydrate utilization; protein content, synthesis, and breakdown; ribonucleic acid (RNA) and DNA content, synthesis, and turnover; enzyme activity and synthesis; cell-cycle kinetics; morphology; ultrastructure; cell architecture; and incorporation and stimulation. Of great importance is that many of these age changes seen in cultures at the cell level are also observed in humans as they age.

Immortality. Although cultured normal human and other animal cells are mortal, they can be converted to a state of immortality. The conversion can be produced in human cells by the SV40 virus and in other animal cells by other viruses, chemicals, and irradiation. This conversion from mortality to immortality is called transformation, and is characterized by the acquisition of many profound abnormal cell properties, including changes in chromosome number and form, ability of the cells to grow unattached to a solid surface, and the prop-

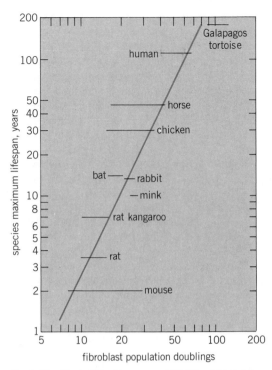

Fig. 2. Fibroblasts from the young of 10 different species multiply in culture roughly proportionate to the maximum lifespan for that species.

erty of immortality. These changes, and many more, are characteristic of most cancer cells. *See* CANCER (MEDICINE); CELL (BIOLOGY); MUTATION; ONCOLOGY; TUMOR VIRUSES.   Leonard Hayflick

Bibliography. A. Comfort, *The Biology of Senescence,* 1979; C. Finch and L. Hayflick (eds.), *Handbook of the Biology of Aging,* 1977; L. Hayflick, The cell biology of aging, *Bioscience,* 25:629–636, 1975; L. Hayflick, The cell biology of human aging, *Sci. Amer.,* 242(1):58–66, 1980; L. Hayflick and P. S. Moorhead, The serial cultivation of human diploid cell strains, *Exp. Cell Res.,* 25:585–621, 1961; A. Rosenfeld, *Prolongevity,* 1976.

Cell-surface ionization

All living cells suspended in aqueous salt solutions at neutral pH values possess a negative charge. The charge is due to the dissociation of ionogenic, or charged, groups (carboxyl, amino, and others) in the cell surface. Studies of the charge carried by bacteria give information regarding the nature of the components in their surfaces; these studies have been used to measure the frequency distribution of bacterial variants in a mixed population and can assist in the selection of material for vaccine production. The occurrence and nature of tumor cells and the selection of yeasts for brewing have been studied electrophoretically. *See* BIOLOGICALS.

Electrophoretic mobility. When an electric field is applied between electrodes placed in a cell suspension, the cells migrate, generally toward the positive electrode. This migration can be observed under a microscope in a microelectrophoresis apparatus (see **illus.**). The electrophoretic mobility $\bar{v}$ (velocity per unit field strength) is measured by timing cells across a fixed distance in the observation chamber under a known field strength. In this method the mobility of individual cells of varying shape and size can be measured with minimal cellular disorganization. Migration occurs because charged groups and ions adsorbed on the surface produce a nonuniform distribution of ions in solution at the cell-liquid interface. This distribution is generally expressed in terms of the ζ potential (volts), which may be calculated from the mobility, $\zeta = 4\pi\eta\bar{v}/D$, where η and D are the viscosity and dielectric constants, respectively, of the medium. The surface charge density in electrostatic units per square centimeter can be calculated from ζ.

Variation of charge. Factors which may affect the charge of cell surfaces are of three types: (1) biological factors—in bacterial and yeast cells, such things as sex, strain, age, growth conditions, presence of capsules or fimbriae, antibiotic resistance, virulence, and toxicity; in mammalian cells, such things as species, type of tissue, normal or pathological conditions, and the like; (2) nature of suspension medium, that is, ionic strength, pH, presence of dyes, drugs, or surface-active agents in the medium; and (3) chemical or enzymatic treatment of the surface. It is often possible to correlate alteration of charge with changes in the nature or number of ionogenic groups in the surface and hence with a particular biological property. Such a correlation is justified only if the variation of charge is measured in media of constant physical properties. An absolute value of the charge under standard conditions of test is without value; the charge carried by particles

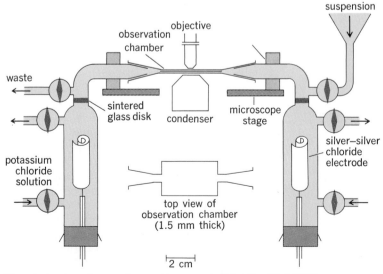

Microelectrophoresis apparatus used to measure electrophoretic mobility.

with ionogenic and nonionogenic surfaces under the same conditions may be identical. However, variations of charge with changes in the nature of the medium are completely different. With living cells, lowering the pH of the medium at constant ionic strength in general produces a lowering of the negative value of the ζ potential; at low pH value, charge reversal may occur. This change results from the decreased dissociation of acidic groups which may be characterized from the dissociation constant pK of the surface. Simultaneously there is an increased ionization of basic groups. At extreme pH values surface and possibly cellular disorganization must be investigated. When the salt concentration of the suspension medium is increased, biological and nonionogenic surfaces behave similarly. The charge-density concentration curve is a typical Langmuir adsorption isotherm, indicating adsorption of anions from solution. *See* ADSORPTION.

Ionogenic groups can be characterized by the binding properties of a series of cations. Their order of effectiveness in reversing the charge of the particles is known as a charge-reversal spectrum. The spectra for various cells can be compared with spectra of model systems with known ionogenic surface groups. Alteration of charge in the presence of anionic surface-active agents can reveal the presence of lipid in the surface. Mild chemical treatment to inactivate specific groups, for example, diazomethane for carboryl, results in marked changes of charge. Enzymatic treatments, for example, using the enzyme trypsin, may produce changes in the charge. *See* ENZYME; LIPID; PROTEIN.

Bacteria. Most strains show slight, if any, variation of charge density during growth. Any drastic alteration of charge always occurs during the period of active cell division, returning to the normal value during the stationary phase, as in hemolytic streptococci. Little alteration of charge generally results from changes in nutrition. Growth in the presence of some drugs, for example, *Aerobacter aerogenes* in crystal violet, results in the formation of a resistant strain with different charge characteristics. The pK values of the surfaces of *Escherichia coli* (2.9) and *A. aerogenes* (3.0), obtained from ζ-pH studies, are the same as those for a large number of polysaccharides, strongly suggesting that carboxyl and not phosphatidic groups (pK = 1.8) are present on the cell surface. Charge-reversal spectra lead to the same general conclusions. Treatment of *E. coli* K12 in aqueous suspension at pH 4.5 with gaseous diazomethane results in an 80% decrease of charge when measured at pH 7.0. Assuming that all the surface carboxyl groups have been esterified, the number of such groups is about 8×10^5 per cell. Spores of *Bacillus subtilis* treated with *p*-toluene sulfonyl chloride in aqueous suspension show a 25% increase in negative charge; this is attributed to the blocking of amino groups.

Teichoic acid, on the surface of cells of *Staphylococcus aureus* in the pH range 4–5, undergoes a change of configuration resulting in a pH-mobility curve which passes through a maximum at pH 4.5. Strains which are resistant to Methicill give a normal curve with no maximum. Cells of *Streptococcus pyogenes* which are resistant to Tetracycline possess larger amounts of surface lipid, as detected by changes of mobility in the presence of surface-active agents, than do sensitive strains.

Yeasts. In suspensions of pH greater than 2.3, yeast cells carry a negative charge. Various strains of *Saccharomyces cerevisiae* and *S. carlsbergensis* have such low charges that ion binding is small, the composition of the wall determining the charge. In some strains the charge is due to combined phosphate in the cell wall and in others to protein. The nature of the growth medium has a pronounced effect on the charge.

Blood cells. The major components on the erythrocyte surface are phospholipid in nature; protein and cholesterol may also be present near the surface. Of sheep blood cells, lymphocytes exhibit an isoelectric point at pH 2.5 (that pH at which there is a zero charge) in contrast to erythrocytes and polymorphonuclear leukocytes, which are damaged at low pH values. Charge-reversal spectra and chemical treatments of aldehyde-treated blood cells indicate that the predominant groups are carboxyl from sialic acid on erythrocytes, carboxyl on polymorphonuclear leukocytes, and both phosphate and amine on lymphocytes and platelets. *See* BACTERIA; BIOPHYSICS; BLOOD; COLLOID; ELECTROKINETIC PHENOMENA; STREAMING POTENTIAL; YEAST.

Arthur M. James

Bibliography. M. Blank, *Surface Chemistry of Biological Systems*, 1970; W. Hoppe, *Biophysics*, 1983.

Cell walls (plant)

The cell wall is the layer of material secreted by the plant cell outside its plasma membrane. All plants have cell walls that are generally very similar in chemical composition, organization, and development. The walls of the Chlorophyta (green algae) show characteristics virtually identical to those of flowering plants, another indication that flowering plants are derived evolutionarily from this division of algae. The wall serves as the first point of entry of materials into cells, functions in the movement of water throughout the plant, and is one of the major mechanical strengthening factors. In addition, the wall must be sufficiently flexible and plastic to withstand mechanical stresses while still permitting the growth of the cell. *See* CELL MEMBRANES.

Cell plate and middle lamella. The plant primary wall is initiated during the process of cell division. After chromosomes line up along the metaphase plate and begin to be pulled apart toward the

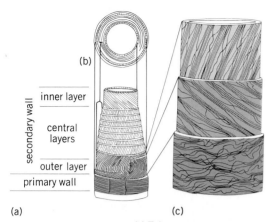

(a)   (c)

Fig. 1. Wall in a cotton fiber. (*a*) Telescoped segment and (*b*) transverse section showing spatial relation of layers and orientation of microfibrils. (*c*) Primary wall has reticulate microfibrillar structure; the outer layer of the secondary wall combines reticulate and parallel orientation of microfibrils, and the first central layer of the secondary wall has a predominantly parallel microfibrillar structure. (*After K. Esau, Plant Anatomy, 2d ed., John Wiley and Sons, 1965*)

poles of the cells by the spindle fibers (the anaphase portion of mitosis), a cell plate or phragmoplast can be observed at the equator of the dividing cell. Vesicles apparently derived from the dictyosomes line up on both sides of the equator to form the proteinaceous cell plate. Elements of the endoplasmic reticulum fuse with the cell plate, marking the location of plasmodesmatal pores and pits which will eventually provide the intercellular connections between adjacent cells. The cell plate forms the matrix within which the middle lamella and primary walls are formed. The middle lamella is composed of pectic substances which are polymers of neutral (arabinogalactans) and acidic (galacturonorhamnans) pectins plus smaller amounts of other sugars, including L-fucose, D-xylose, and D-galactose. The bulk of pectic substances are long chains of α-D-galacturonic acid, with side chains composed of other sugars; the exact chemical composition and organization of pectins are still unclear. Pectins can form reversible gels or viscid solutions in water. As the middle lamella, pectic substances are usually in the water-insoluble gel state, possibly because they are esterified with calcium or magnesium ions. Such gels can be solubilized and extracted from plants. Some tissues, notably those of mature apple and citrus fruits which have high concentrations of pectins, have been extracted and purified, and their pectins have been used as gelling agents in jams, jellies, and some industrial products. The middle lamella provides some of the observed plasticity and extensibility of cell walls during cell growth, and it has also been suggested that pectins are capable of hydrogen-bonding to the cellulose that forms the plant cell primary wall.

Primary wall. Simultaneously with the middle lamella, the primary cell wall begins to form, usually before the end of telophase. During the early stages in cell wall formation, the cellulose wall is isotropic

without any ordered orientation, but as cell walls continue to develop in area and in thickness and the cell grows to mature size, the walls become anisotropic or highly ordered (**Fig. 1**).

Biosynthesis and chemistry of cellulose. Cellulose, like starch, is basically a polymer of glucose, a six-carbon monosaccharide, although the biosynthetic route for cellulose synthesis differs from that of starch. The polyglucose chain of starch is derived by enzymatically regulated condensation of uridine diphosphate glucose (UDPG) or adenine diphosphate glucose (ADPG). However, the monomers that form cellulose are guanosine diphosphate glucose (GDPG) with the resulting polymer being a β-(1–4) glucoside rather than the α-(1–4) polymer characteristic of amylose. In both polymers, the terminal glucose residue can unfold into its open-chain configuration, exposing the aldehyde group that has reducing power.

Each chain of cellulose may be as long as 8000 to 12,000 glucose monomers, or up to 4 micrometers long. These are arranged linearly, with no side branching. Cellulose chains are aggregated into bundles of approximately 40 chains each,

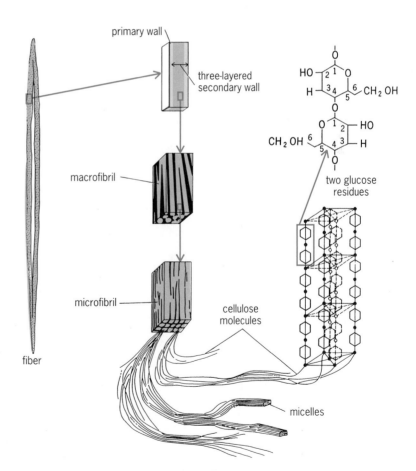

Fig. 2. Interpretation of wall structure. Fiber has a three-layered secondary wall. The macrofibrils consist of numerous microfibrils of cellulose interspersed by microporosities containing noncellulosic wall materials. Microfibrils consist of bundles of cellulose molecules, partly arranged into micelles. Micelles are crystalline because of regular spacing of glucose residues which are connected by β-1,4-glucosidic bonds. (*After K. Esau, Plant Anatomy, 2d ed., John Wiley and Sons, 1965*)

the cellulose micelles, which are held together by hydrogen bonds between the hydrogen atom of a hydroxyl group of one glucose residue and an oxygen atom of another glucose residue which is adjacent to the first glucose. Although the strength of individual hydrogen bonds is rather weak, there may be so many of them joining adjacent chains that total bonding in a micelle is quite high. There is good, albeit incomplete, evidence that all of the chains in the same micelle bundle are directionally oriented, with the reducing groups at the same end of the micelle; and there is some fairly conclusive evidence from the x-ray diffraction patterns of cellulose that the glucose units of one chain are displaced by one-half the length of a glucose monomer, so that there are two hydrogen bonds connecting adjacent monomers. The micelle thus is a very regular, quasicrystalline structure (**Fig. 2**).

Whether isotropic or anisotropic, the micelles themselves are embedded in a matrix of other polysaccharides, the hemicelluloses. Insofar as is known, hemicelluloses are produced by the dictyosomes and associated vesicles and are moved through the cytoplasm and the plasmalemma to enter into the structure of the primary wall. In addition to glucose, seven monosaccharides are involved in hemicellulose composition. About a quarter of this monosaccharide complex is arabinose, with 10–15% each of galactose, galacturonic acid, and xylose plus smaller percentages of rhamnose,

fucose, and mannose. These monosaccharides may form unspecific polymers composed of a single monomer or may be complexes containing two or more monomers. In the primary plant cell wall, these polysaccharides are covalently bonded. One model (**Fig. 3**) suggests that each of the cellulose micelles is completely coated with a monomolecular layer of xyloglucan, with the glucose units of the xyloglucan lying parallel to the long axis of the micelle and hydrogen-bonded to glucose residues in the cellulose. Radiating at right angles from the coated micelle are arabinogalactan polymers, which are then covalently linked to rhamnogalactan polymers which run parallel to the cellulose micelle. Thus, hemicellulose serves to bind the micelle into a fairly rigid unit which retains a good deal of flexibility.

Micelles, in bundles of variable number, are bound together into the cellulose microfibril, a unit sufficiently large to be seen under the electron microscope; these, in turn, are bound together into macrofibrils which are observable under the light microscope. *See* CELLULOSE.

Organization of primary wall. During the formation of the primary wall, at locations predetermined by attachments of endoplasmic reticulum to the middle lamella, cellulose microfibrillar deposition is minimal, leaving a thin place in the primary wall which forms the plasmodesmatal connections. Running through these pores are fine strands of protoplasm, the plasmodesmata proper, which contain a tube of endoplasmic reticulum–like material. The plasmodesmata provide a cytoplasmic connection between adjacent cells. Such connections are found among all the living cells of a plant, a fact which has led to the concept that all plant cells are so interconnected that the entire plant is a cytosymplast or single unit.

In the formation of the primary cell wall, there may be several discrete depositions of cellulose, with changes in the orientation of the micro- and macrofibrils with successive depositions. There has been some equivocation as to whether the added cellulosic fibrils are inserted among those already part of the wall (intussusception) or whether the new fibrils are laid down inside the older portions of the primary wall as a discrete layer or lamella (apposition). Most of the available evidence suggests that apposition is the only method of increasing the thickness of the wall. This can be readily seen in the formation of both primary and secondary walls in the cotton fiber, the hairs attached to the seed coat which are the starting material for cotton thread (Fig. 1).

Secondary wall. Although there are differences in nomenclature and terminology, secondary walls of plant cells are defined as those laid down after the primary wall has stopped increasing in surface area, essentially at that time when the plant cell has reached mature size. This is particularly true of those cells that, at maturity, have irreversibly differentiated into specialized cells, some of which are destined to lose their cytoplasm and become

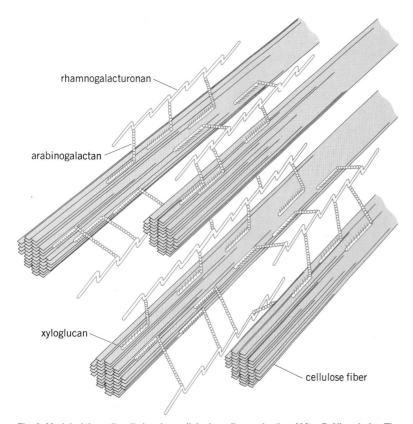

rhamnogalacturonan

arabinogalactan

xyloglucan

cellulose fiber

Fig. 3. Model of the cell wall showing cellulosic wall organization. (*After P. Albersheim, The wall growing plant cells, Sci. Amer., 232(4):80–95, April 1975*)

functional only as dead cells. These include xylem vessels and tracheids, and sclereids (the stone or grit cells of pear fruits). In those xylem cells differentiated from parenchyma cells to form the primary vascular xylem, secondary wall thickenings may not occur uniformly over the surface of the wall but may be in the form of bands, spirals, or reticulate thickenings.

The secondary wall of most plants seems to have the same chemical structure and physical orientation of fibrils and hemicelluloses as do primary walls. While there may be little orientation of fibrils in young primary walls, the secondary walls are composed of fibrils that are highly ordered. In general, there are three layers or lamellae of fibrils. Two of these, usually the inner and outer layers, tend to be thin and birefringent, and the middle layer tends to be thicker and less birefringent. One of the differences between the larger xylem vessels and tracheids of spring wood and the smaller xylem cells of summer wood is the thickness of the middle layer of cellulose fibrils. Part of the difference in birefringence, on the other hand, seems to be due to the reduced anisotropy of the middle secondary wall layer.

Since successive layers of cellulose fibrils are laid down inside one another, with the youngest layer closest to the plasmalemma, the lumen of the cell which contains the protoplast becomes reduced in size and, in some cells, may virtually disappear.

In most secondary walls, and particularly those of the xylem, the fibrillar structure of the primary as well as the secondary walls may become impregnated with more substances, the most prominent of these being lignin. The chemical nature and biological role of lignin is of considerable interest because of the use of wood in the lumber and pulpwood-paper industries. Lignins are polymers of complex phenolic substances (phenylpropanoid C_6-C_3 compounds), and exact composition of the polymer may be species-specific. Certainly the lignins of the softwoods (conifers) and those of hardwoods (broad-leaved trees) are chemically distinguishable based on both chemical and physical properties and on the ratios of the various phenolic monomers composing the polymer. As the secondary walls develop, lignins may be deposited either from the inside layer toward the outermost or the reverse. The primary roles of the lignins include their ability to render walls mechanically strong, rigid, and—at least to some extent—water-impermeable. It has been suggested that lignins may also serve to make wood less subject to microbially caused decay.

Depending on the species, other compounds may form part of the secondary walls of plant cells. In some of the algae, notably the diatoms and phylogenetically related classes in the division Chrysophyta, mature cell walls may consist almost entirely of silica compounds. Although silica is usually not a major component in the walls of vascular plants, grasses and sedges have walls with significant amounts of silica, and the use of the scouring rush (*Equisetum* spp.) was based in part of the silica content of the walls of stem cells. In some algae and in a few flowering plants (including *Ficus*), deposition of calcium carbonate into both primary and secondary walls has been found. In many plants, an ill-characterized compound called callose is found; it is particularly prominent in the end or sieve plates of phloem cells, where it surrounds the sieve pores. Callose may vary in amount with the developmental stage of the plant, with the seasons, and as a result of trauma.

Although frequently not considered to be a structural component of plant cell walls, water is an important constituent. A good deal of the movement of water through a tissue system occurs not by the movement of water into and out of successive and adjacent cells, but through the intercellular spaces between cells and through the primary and secondary walls. Many plant physiologists consider the walls and intercellular spaces to be the apparent free space that permits the movement of water and dissolved substances at rates considerably in excess of that possible were all water to move from cell to cell.

Other components of cell walls have received relatively little attention from chemists and developmental physiologists, although they play important roles in the economy of the plant and may, in some instances, be of commercial value. Walls of red and brown algae contain polymers such as algin, agar, and carrageenan, which form rigid gels used as substrates for growing microorganisms and as thickening and stabilizing agents in ice cream and industrial products. Cutins, waxes, and suberins are lipoidal materials that serve to waterproof cells in whose walls they are deposited. Cutin, found as the outermost layer of the outside wall of epidermal cells, is the primary barrier of the plant, serving to prevent the leaching of cell constituents and functioning as a protective layer to prevent invasion of the plant by microorganisms. Cutins also serve to lessen water loss from leaves and stems. Suberins are prominent components of the walls of cork and bark cells and of the casparian strip of root endodermal cells. Both are polymers of fatty acids. Waxes may also be found on epidermal layers of leaves and fruit. They are usually small polymers and are responsible for the "bloom" which, in apples, allows the fruit to be polished. Waxes can be removed from plants and used in shoe polish and other applications. *See* WAX, ANIMAL AND VEGETABLE.

Pits. As the primary wall develops, areas of the wall surrounding the plasmodesmatal intercellular connections tend to be thinner than the rest of the wall and are called primary pit fields. In some cells, primary pit fields may be deeply depressed as cellulose microfibrillar layers accumulate and the rest of the primary wall becomes thicker. Pit fields are almost always paired, with the pit field of one cell oriented exactly opposite to that of the adjacent cell. Many cells have large numbers of primary pit fields.

In plant secondary walls, pits are readily distinguishable from the rest of the wall because the layers of secondary wall materials are completely interrupted at the pit with only thin coverings, if any, of primary wall. In mature cells with well-developed secondary walls, the pits may be simple or, as seen in the bordered pits common in xylem vessels, tracheids, and fibers, they may be structurally very complex. *See* XYLEM.

In bordered pits, the developing secondary wall arches over the pit to form a thickened rim (the border), enclosing a pit chamber which may be open and continuous with the cell lumen (**Fig. 4**). In conifers, the primary walls in the center become thickened (the torus), while on the edges (the margo) they become thinner as hemicelluloses are digested away. It has been suggested, primarily but not exclusively on anatomical grounds, that bordered pits in xylem may serve as valves to control the rate of water flow between the adjacent cells bearing the pair of pits. Depending on the species, bordered pits may be very complex.

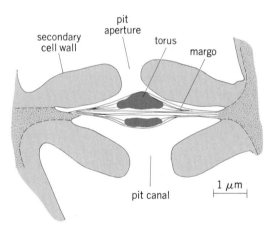

Fig. 4. Cross section through a bordered pit of a transfusion tracheid from a needle of *Pinus sylvestris*, showing the pit membrane. (*After E. G. Cutter, Plant Anatomy: Experiment and Interpretation, pt. 1, Addison-Wesley, 1969*)

Cell elongation and enlargement. In vascular plants, cells grow in length, thickness, or both, primarily by the uptake of water into their vacuoles. The initiation and maintenance of growth is dependent not only upon the availability of water and the concentrations of auxins and other growth-regulating compounds that control cell enlargements, but on characteristics of the cell wall. Even in primary walls the cellulosic components and the matrix in which the fibrils are embedded form a fairly rigid structure, and for growth to occur there must be loosening of the fibrillar matrix. Furthermore, the effects of indoleacetic acid (IAA) on cell elongation are expressed within a minute or even less following presentation of auxin, indicating that the necessary loosening must occur quite rapidly. Any comprehensive theory must also account for the fact that, as a cell elongates, its wall does not become thinner, nor is new wall material

deposited only at the ends of the cell. The new wall fibrils are deposited fairly uniformly over the entire surface of the cell. *See* AUXIN.

On the manifold questions relating to cell elongation and enlargement, the question of the deposition of new cellulose fibrils appears to be the most amenable to answer. Most, if not all, of the fibrillar material is deposited by apposition on the inner portion of the walls adjacent in the middle lamella. Intussusception, if it occurs at all, is a minor factor in new wall deposition during growth. Little attention has been directed toward understanding the possible changes in the middle lamella. Clearly, if the cell is to continue to grow, with increases in surface area of the wall, the middle lamella must either increase proportionally or be drastically thinned; no unequivocal data are available on this point.

Since cell wall area is accompanied by appositional deposition of fibrils, the fibrils existing prior to the period of growth must slide past one another. It has been suggested that this occurs by the enzymatic breaking of bonds that occur between the cross-linked fibrils with almost immediate reformation of these bonds at new sites, but no information has been provided on the chemical nature of the bonds affected or the polymers involved. Other investigators have postulated that the bond breaking and reforming may be due to changes in the proton concentration caused by application of auxin. This "acid growth theory" suggests that IAA stimulates an adenosinetriphosphatase/adenosinetriphosphate (ATPase/ATP) reaction, providing the energy for the mutual exchange of potassium ions and protons across the plasmalemma, and that this may be the mechanism for breaking the bonds linking fibrils together. *See* PLANT CELL; PLANT GROWTH.   Richard M. Klein

Bibliography. J. D. Mauseth, *Plant Anatomy*, 1988; R. D. Preston, *The Physical Biology of Plant Cell Walls*, 1974.

Cellophane

A clear, flexible film made from cellulose. It first appeared commercially in the United States in 1924, and it revolutionized the packaging industry, which had been using opaque waxed paper or glassine as wrapping materials. Cellophane was also the first transparent mending tape. By 1960, petrochemical-based polymers (polyolefins) such as polyethylene had surpassed cellophane for use as a packaging film. Nevertheless, 50,000 tons (45,000 metric tons) of cellophane are used in the United States each year for packaging because cellophane gives a material that is stiffer and more easily imprinted than are polyolefin films. *See* CELLULOSE.

Manufacture. Cellophane is manufactured in a process that is very similar to that for rayon. Special wood pulp, known as dissolving pulp, which is white like cotton and contains 92–98% cellulose, is treated with strong alkali in a process known as mercerization, a treatment used in processing cotton for textiles. The mercerized pulp is aged for several days. *See* TEXTILE CHEMISTRY.

The aged, shredded pulp is then treated with carbon disulfide, which reacts with the cellulose and dissolves it to form a viscous, orange solution of cellulose xanthate known as viscose. Rayon fibers are formed by forcing the viscose through a small hole into an acid bath that regenerates the original cellulose while carbon disulfide is given off. To make cellophane, the viscose passes through a long slot into a bath of ammonium sulfate which causes it to coagulate. The coagulated viscose is then put into an acidic bath that returns the cellulose to its original, insoluble form. The cellophane is now clear. *See* MANUFACTURED FIBERS.

The cellophane is then treated in a glycerol bath and dried. The glycerol acts like a plasticizer, making the dry cellophane less brittle. The cellophane may be coated with nitrocellulose or wax to make it impermeable to water vapor; it is coated with polyethylene or other materials to make it heat sealable for automated wrapping machines. Cellophane is typically 0.03 mm (0.001 in.) thick, is available in widths to 132 cm (52 in.), and can be made to be heat sealable from 82 to 177°C (180 to 350°F). *See* POLYMER.

Uses. Cellophane is used for packaging snacks, cookies, baked goods, candy, and tobacco products. Cellophane can be cast into a ring-shaped structure to be used as sausage casings (wiener), but paper with hemp fiber is used in large sausages. Cellophane enjoys many specialized uses based on its ability to let small molecules pass through it while retaining larger molecules, although some materials are replacing cellophane for these uses. It has been used in kidney dialysis machines, battery separators for silver-zinc cells, and semipermeable membranes. It is also used in denture compression molding. *See* WOOD CHEMICALS; WOOD PRODUCTS.

Christopher J. Biermann

Bibliography. C. J. Biermann, *Essentials of Pulping and Papermaking*, 1993; *Kirk-Othmer Encyclopedia of Chemical Technology*, 4th ed., vol. 5, 1992; A. P. Peck, Cellophane is born, Sci. Amer., 158: 274–275, May 1938; E. Sjöström, *Wood Chemistry: Fundamentals and Applications*, 2d ed., 1993.

Cellular adhesion

The process whereby cells interact and attach to other cells or to inanimate surfaces. Adhesion is mediated by interactions between the molecules on the surface of the cell. This process has been studied extensively in embryonic cells of higher organisms, where species and tissue specificity of adhesion has been shown. However, adhesion is a common feature in the life of most organisms. Prokaryotic microorganisms do not frequently exhibit cell-to-cell interactions, but adhere to surfaces forming biofilms. In these interactions with a surface, some microorganisms cause corrosion of metal by adhering and producing corrosive acid by-products as a result of their metabolism. Adhesion of microorganisms to the cells of higher plants and animals is often a prerequisite for causing disease. Eukaryotic microorganisms often exhibit specific cell-to-cell interactions, allowing complex colonial forms and multicellular organisms to be constructed from individual or free-living cells. Plant cells are rigidly maintained in position by an extracellular matrix that limits their movement. Specific adhesion between different plant cells is apparent in several cases, as in the interaction between a pollen grain and the stigma during fertilization. These interactions between two cell surfaces may be quite specific, involving certain types of cell-surface protein molecules. Also, they may be general, involving production of a sticky extracellular matrix that surrounds the cell, as frequently occurs in bacterial adhesion. As a general process, cellular adhesion is important in cellular recognition, in the generation of form or pattern, and possibly in regulation of cellular differentiation. *See* CELL (BIOLOGY); CELL DIFFERENTIATION; CELL WALLS (PLANT); CORROSION; REPRODUCTION (PLANT).

Cell-surface molecules. All adhesion is mediated by the cell surface, either directly involving integral components of the plasma membrane, or indirectly through material excreted and deposited on the outside of the cell. The plasma membrane is composed of lipids, proteins, and carbohydrates. The basic structure is a lipid bilayer arranged so that the hydrophobic portion of the phospholipids is internal in the bilayer and the hydrophilic portion of the lipid molecules is oriented toward the outside or the inside of the cell. Proteins are arranged in the membrane interacting with the hydrophobic portion of the membrane, interacting with the hydrophilic portion, or spanning both regions. The lipid bilayer is fluid, allowing the proteins to move within the membrane as icebergs would move in an ocean. Some proteins have decreased mobility because they are anchored in position by interactions with cytoskeletal elements inside the cell. The carbohydrate is found associated with either the lipid (glycolipid) or the protein (glycoprotein). Almost all membrane proteins are glycoproteins having the carbohydrate attached to the portion of the protein on the outer surface of the cell. A limited number of different carbohydrates are found in glycoproteins. The diversity of the carbohydrate side chains present in glycoproteins is due to the sequence and branching patterns of the monosaccharides making up the oligosaccharide side chains. The protein and carbohydrate exposed on the outside of the cell is referred to as the cell coat or glycocalyx. The carbohydrate portion of the glycoprotein is believed to be responsible for many cell-surface interactions. *See* CELL MEMBRANES.

Most theories of cellular adhesion suggest that cell-surface glycoproteins serve as ligands

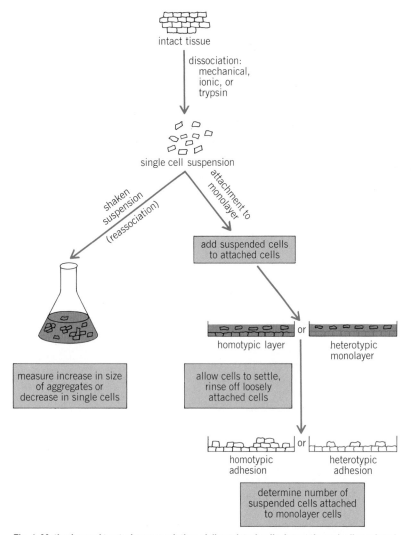

Fig. 1. Methods used to study reassociation of dissociated cells. Intact tissue is dissociated and reassociation is followed either in shaken suspensions or in monolayer culture.

requires the presence of calcium (Ca^{2+}) ions. Ionic requirements, particularly for Ca^{2+} ions, are common in many adhesion mechanisms. The kinds of proteins found in the membrane may differ between cell types and, even within a cell type, may be altered at different stages during the life cycle. Thus proteins are added, removed, and chemically altered, allowing cells to make and break specific adhesive contacts during their life cycle. Due to the fluidity of the membrane, the location or local concentration of specific cell-surface ligands can be changed, allowing for the arrangement or pattern of cell structures to change. *See* LECTINS.

Study methods. There are several methods used in studying cellular adhesion; most involve studying the reassociation of dissociated cells (**Fig. 1**). Several different techniques are used to dissociate cells, including mechanical shear, alteration of the ionic environment, or treatment of cells with proteolytic enzymes, like trypsin, that cleave extracellular proteins from the surface of the cells. One problem with studying the reassociation of dissociated cells is that the rate and extent of reassociation may depend on the method used for dissociation. Also, it is assumed that studying the reassociation of the dissociated cells is equivalent to studying the initial adhesion between these cells. One of the most common methods for the study of adhesion is to shake a suspension of dissociated cells and follow the increase in size of the agglutinated cells or the disappearance of single cells from the population (Fig. 1*a*). The suspension of cells is shaken at a rate sufficient to break nonspecific contacts between cells and allow specific adhesion to take place. This method is useful for studies involving the strength of the adhesive interactions (specific adhesion is stronger than nonspecific) and for cell-cell recognition. A second technique involves two populations of cells, one attached as a cell monolayer to a surface, as in a plastic tissue-culture dish, and a second population of cells in suspension. When the cells in suspension are added to the monolayer cells, adhesion can occur as the suspended cells settle out. Specific interactions between the two groups of cells are determined by washing any loosely associated cells away from the attached monolayer and determining the number of cells remaining attached to the monolayer cells (Fig. 1*b*). This method is useful for studying the rate of attachment of cells and for cell-cell recognition.

One of the most effective means of studying cellular adhesion involves the use of antibodies directed against plasma membrane preparations or individual cell membrane proteins. When an antibody binds to a specific cell-surface ligand involved in cellular adhesion, it is presumed to block the participation of that protein in adhesion. Modified antibodies are used to block adhesion. These modified antibodies are fragments (Fab fragments) of an antibody molecule that are monovalent, having only one antigen recognition site instead of two

involved in attaching cell surfaces together. When a specific cell interacts with an identical cell, the attachment is said to be homotypic. Heterotypic adhesion involves interactions between different cell types. If the ligand-specific attachment involves interaction between identical cell-surface ligands, it is homophilic, and between two different ligands, heterophilic. The interaction between a pollen grain and the stigma cells described previously is an example of a heterotypic, heterophilic interaction. A specific glycoprotein on the surface of the stigma cells interacts with another protein on the surface of the pollen grain. The protein on the surface of the pollen grain is a carbohydrate-binding protein or lectin. The lectin-glycoprotein interaction provides for specific adhesion, due to the structure of the carbohydrate portion of the glycoprotein of the stigma cells and the binding specificity of the lectin on the pollen grain for a single carbohydrate or sequence of carbohydrates. The interaction between sponge cells (described later in this article) is an example of homophilic adhesion. The homophilic ligand interaction in sponge cells present in the untreated bivalent antibodies. The monovalent Fab fragment will bind to its specific antigen (in this case a cell-surface ligand) and block it from forming adhesive contacts. If a bifunctional antibody were used, the cells would be artificially agglutinated because the antibody could bind to one antigen on two separate cells.

Fab fragments have been used extensively to study reassociation of embryonic chick neural retina cells and to study adhesion of the eukaryotic microorganisms *Dictyostelium discoideum* (cellular slime mold). *Dictyostelium discoideum* are ameboid cells that, during the starvation phase of their life cycle, form a multicellular organism based on specific cell-to-cell adhesion and collection of amebas into groups by means of a chemotactic process. One of the ligands responsible for adhesion of the amebas is called the contact site A (CsA) protein. This protein is an 80,000-molecular-weight glycoprotein present in the cell membrane only after the onset of starvation. It is localized at the ends of the cells. If anti-CsA Fab is prepared, it will block adhesion of the amebas and specifically block the end-to-end contacts. Fab fractions can be made more specific and, with the use of monoclonal antibodies, very specific probes for individual cell-surface molecules can be obtained. The importance of the antibody experiments is that they can be used to interfere with normal adhesion and frequently are used to assist in purification of cellular adhesion ligands. *See* MONOCLONAL ANTIBODIES.

Cell sorting and species specificity. One of the earliest studies showing species specificity of cellular adhesion was with sponges. These marine organisms have only five or six different cell types. They are easily dissociated mechanically by forcing them through a fine mesh cloth or screen. When the dissociated cells were allowed to reassociate in a gyrated suspension, initial reaggregation was rapid. The reaggregated cells sorted out slowly, leading to the formation of a normal sponge. Species specificity is shown in most cases of sponge-cell reaggregation. For example, when two different-colored species of sponge cells were dissociated and mixed, the initial aggregates contained both species. With time, sorting out occurred, yielding two distinctly colored individuals. A glycoprotein responsible for the species-specific sorting has been isolated. It functions as a homophilic ligand that depends on Ca^{2+} ions to form adhesive contacts (**Fig. 2**). The glycoprotein binds to the baseplate of the sponge cells, and additional glycoprotein molecules are linked together through Ca^{2+} ions, causing the cells to adhere. *See* PORIFERA.

Adhesion in the cellular slime molds (*D. discoideum*) is also species-specific in that species that will aggregate together because of similarities in their chemotactic systems will sort out into species-specific multicellular organisms prior to continuing their development. In addition, antibodies that block adhesion of one species of slime

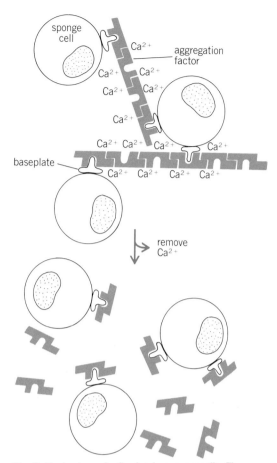

Fig. 2. Mechanism of adhesion in sponge cells. The homophilic adhesion ligand binds to a baseplate on the surface of the sponge cells. In the presence of Ca^{2+} ions, the aggregation factors are linked together forming a network joining the sponge cells into a multicellular organism. Removal of Ca^{2+} ions causes the sponge cells to dissociate. (*After B. Alberts et al.*, Molecular Biology of the Cell, *Garland Publishing, 1983*)

mold will not block adhesion of a different species of slime mold.

In higher organisms, many studies of species and tissue specificity have been done with embryonic chick and mouse systems. In general, it would seem that homotypic adhesion is stronger that heterotypic adhesion. Also, tissue and species-specific adhesion can be shown, but tissue specificity seems to be more frequent. For example, when dissociated embryonic neural retina of mouse and chick are mixed and allowed to aggregate, there is very little sorting, and mosaic tissue is formed. This is not true in all tissues, as heart and liver tissue show much greater species specificity than neural retina. It is generally found that mixtures of different tissue types will aggregate together initially. Sorting out occurs within the aggregate, so that one tissue type will be internal and the other will form a surrounding layer around the first type. For example, mixtures of cartilage and liver cells will sort out to yield aggregates, with the cartilage cells internal and the liver cells surrounding the cartilage cells. When studying reassociation in mixtures of

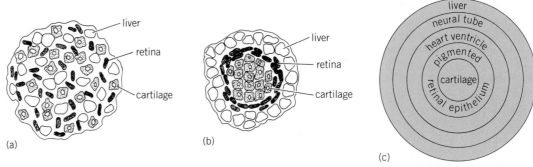

Fig. 3. Hierarchy of positions of disaggregated cells from chick embryos. (*a*) A mixed aggregate of liver, retina, and cartilage cells. (*b*) Sorting out of the cells in *a*. (*c*) Relative position of five different cell types in mixed aggregates. (*After R. G. Ham and M. J. Veomett, Mechanisms of Development, C. V. Mosby, 1980*)

tissues, a hierarchy of locations can be established, as shown in **Fig. 3**. It has been suggested that the internal cells form stronger adhesive contacts than the surrounding cell type, and that the circular internal structure provides for maximum contact for these strongly adhesive cell types. As illustrated in Fig. 3*c*, any cell type farther away from the center will surround any cell type closer to the center in mixtures of two cell types. The cells farthest away from the center are thought to make the weakest adhesive contacts, leading to a hypothesis for cell sorting based on the strength of adhesion (the differential adhesion hypothesis).

Development of form. Throughout development, it is necessary for specific adhesion among cells to establish and maintain form. It is also important during development that cells change position, as occurs during gastrulation, or migrate, as with neural crest cells that move from the neural tube to various positions, forming ganglia. In these cases, it would seem to be necessary for certain cells to dissociate or alter their adhesive properties in response to the proper developmental cues. Throughout development, there are a series of primary and secondary inductions that affect cellular differentiation and pattern formation. These inductions depend on interactions between cell types having different histories, either due to being in different embryonic layers or due to interaction between cells derived from the same layer but previously differentiated.

These changes in form are related to specific changes in cell-adhesion molecules (CAMs). Using Fab against embryonic chick brain and retina cell membranes, a neural-specific glycoprotein (N-CAM) was isolated. N-CAM-specific adhesion occurs using a homophilic mechanism. A liver-specific CAM (L-CAM) has been isolated with techniques similar to those used to isolate N-CAM. Adhesion mediated by L-CAM requires Ca^{2+} ions. It is not known whether L-CAM is homophilic or heterophilic. Both of these CAMs were isolated as tissue-specific glycoproteins. However, during the earliest stages of chick embryogenesis, both N-CAM and L-CAM were distributed uniformly on the cell surface. The first change in distribution was observed when migrating cells were forming the mid-dle layer of the primitive streak. During this particular cellular differentiation, both CAMs disappeared from the cell surface. After this stage, cells that develop into the neural plate acquired N-CAM and surrounding cell types acquired L-CAM. This is an example of appearance, disappearance, and segregation of CAMs that occurs due to an inductive event in development. It is suggested that whenever inductions are occurring, there are dynamic changes in CAMs. A kinetic model for cellular adhesion is used to describe how a pattern is established and changed during development. This kinetic model suggests that the strength of binding, amount and type of CAM, distribution, or chemistry of CAMs can be altered to cause different forms.

CAMs may not be the only component involved in alteration of form, but they are thought to provide constraints on the shape. A large number of different CAMs is not required to allow for the complex interactions in early embryogenesis. Additional CAMs or chemically altered CAMs may be required within tissues to get proper arrangements. Some support for this is obtained from the finding of a later-developing CAM, called Ng-CAM, that is specific for a heterotypic adhesion between neurons and glial cells. *See* DEVELOPMENTAL BIOLOGY; EMBRYOGENESIS; EMBRYONIC INDUCTION.

Adhesion and gene expression. One very active and controversial area of research involves the role of adhesion in controlling differentiation by affecting gene expression. The major controversy seems to center on whether adhesion plays an active or passive role in controlling gene expression. Obviously, development is blocked under conditions where cells are disaggregated, but this does not prove that adhesion plays an active role in determining the biochemical differentiation of the cells after adhesive contacts are made. There are two lines of evidence that begin to address this problem. First, the enzyme glutamine synthetase becomes inducible by hydrocortisone at a specific stage during the development of embryonic chick neural retina. If cells that are inducible are dissociated and kept as single cells, they lose their inducibility, even though the hydrocortisone receptors are present on the cells and the hormone is taken up. However, if the dissociated cells are allowed to reaggregate and begin to sort establishing normal cellular interactions, glutamine synthetase becomes inducible. It has not been fully established where the block of induction occurs. Second, in *D. discoideum*, approximately 2500 new messenger RNA (mRNA) molecules are induced after the amebas have formed a multicellular organism. The induction of gene expression correlates with the establishment of strong cellular adhesive interactions. In defective cells, or mutants, that do not form these adhesive interactions none of the mRNAs is expressed. One possible explanation of these data is that the tight interactions trigger a response leading to the induction of these new mRNAs. Both of these studies point toward a more active role for adhesion in controlling gene expression during development. *See* DEVELOPMENTAL GENETICS.   Michael Hanna

Bibliography. B. Alberts et al., *Molecular Biology of the Cell*, 1994; G. M. Edelman, Cell-adhesion molecules: A molecular basis for animal form, *Sci. Amer.*, 250:118–129, April 1984.

Cellular immunology

The mechanisms and pathways that permit the cells of the lymphoid organs to recognize molecules from invading pathogens and to distinguish them from the body's own molecules. Two main immune systems are involved, the innate and the adaptive. The innate immune system is capable of destroying certain pathogens on first encounter. However, the growth of many pathogens is so rapid that they are able to evade this primitive system. The adaptive immune system, present in all vertebrates, allows for recognition of an invading pathogen, even if the invader has never been previously identified. Upon exposure to a previously encountered pathogen, immune cells that were retained after the first infection are reactivated and respond more efficiently to this subsequent invasion, preventing a recurrence of the disease. In contrast, the innate immune system has no such memory, and it is unable to discriminate one pathogen from another.

The adaptive immune system occasionally may react against the body's own cells, resulting in an autoimmune disease. This attack on self, however, is usually avoided through tolerance, a process in which the cells of the immune system that recognize self-proteins are inactivated while cells that recognize foreign molecules are retained. *See* AUTOIMMUNITY.

Cells involved. The innate immune system operates mainly through the action of large phagocytic cells called macrophages and granulocytes. Another important component of the innate response is the complement system. Some complement components act directly on bacteria, killing them by breaking down their lipid membrane, while others simply coat the bacteria in a process known as opsonization, making it easier for macrophages to ingest and destroy the bacterial cells. *See* COMPLEMENT; PHAGOCYTOSIS.

Types of lymphocytes. The functional cells of the adaptive system are known as lymphocytes. Different types of lymphocytes contribute to two major types of immune responses. The first of these responses is humoral immunity, which occurs through the action of antibodies produced by the class of lymphocytes known as B cells which are formed in the bone marrow. The second type of response is cell-mediated immunity, involving T cells, which are lymphocytes that mature in the thymus. Together, these two classes of lymphocytes are able to respond to antigens in the blood or in virus-infected cells. Activated T cells secrete chemical factors known as lymphokines that can either promote or suppress B-cell production of antibodies. Conversely, when B cells process antigens into a form that is recognized by T cells, the T cells are stimulated to an active state but, under certain conditions, the T-cell response is inhibited. In addition, both T and B cells communicate with other cells by producing lymphokines that activate macrophages, granulocytes, or other white blood cells, which are important elements of the innate immune system. *See* THYMUS GLAND.

Stem cells. The T and B cells originate from parental stem cells that differentiate under separate influences in distinct environments. In embryos, the stem cells that enter the B-cell differentiation pathway undergo early migration to the liver and later to the bone marrow. The signals that cause a stem cell to enter the B-cell pathway secrete the lymphokine interleukin-7 that binds to receptors on B cells in different stages of maturation, signaling them to divide and differentiate.

B-cell development. Each B cell in the mature organism bears a unique antibody receptor complex on its surface which it uses to recognize a specific antigen. Each B cell selects one combination out of millions of possibilities. A process of negative selection begins during development when newly formed B cells first encounter their environment. If the binding to self components is strong, the antibody receptor on the B cells signals the cells to become inactive or die. Only immature B cells that do not react strongly to self antigens survive. These cells migrate to the peripheral lymphoid tissues and take up residence in the spleen, lymph nodes, and Peyer's patches (lymph nodules) of the intestine. After specific stimulation by antigens in these organs, a small portion of the B cells proliferate and interact with T cells to produce terminally differentiated B cells, called plasma cells, that secrete antibodies. Other B cells, called memory cells, increase in number and retain the ability to respond to the same antigen. These cells strongly participate in future responses and enhance the body's defense against previously encountered infections. *See* ANTIBODY; ANTIGEN.

T-cell development. The T-cell developmental pathway is more complex. Early in fetal life, stem cells migrate to the thymus. Once in the thymus, they divide and differentiate through stages that can be distinguished by surface proteins. The T cells whose receptors bind to molecules of the major histocompatibility complex (MHC) survive; the others die. The next step involves the destruction of T cells that react strongly to the body's own antigens. T cells with receptors that recognize both foreign peptides and self-MHC leave the thymus and circulate to the lymphoid organs.

Helper cells and killer cells. There are two classes, I and II, of MHC molecules. Most of the T cells binding to class I MHC molecules become killer cells; those binding to class II become helper cells. The two types of T cells are also distinguished by the expression of different markers on the cell surface. Killer T cells generally express the transmembrane protein CD8, whereas helper cells bear the CD4 protein. Both of these molecules facilitate T-cell activation by stabilizing a low-affinity interaction between the T-cell receptor and the MHC peptide complex. The T-helper cells are further designated as subtypes (T_H1 and T_H2), and are identifiable by the cytokines they express. The T_H1 subtype primarily secretes interleukin-2 and γ-interferon; the T_H2 subtype secretes interleukin-4 and -5. The products of the T_H1 cells primarily trigger cell-mediated responses, while those of T_H2 cells activate B cells and thereby promote the production of antibodies. It is noteworthy that a strong T_H1 response inhibits a strong T_H2 response and vice versa. *See* CYTOKINE; HISTOCOMPATABILITY.

Lymph nodes. Both T and B cells become localized in the peripheral lymphoid tissues. Once the developmental and maturation processes are complete, the immune response can take place in lymph nodes, where T and B cells congregate with antigen-presenting cells. The antigen-presenting cells—macrophages and dendritic cells—present the foreign antigen to T and B cells. A number of other molecules, known as adhesion molecules, participate in the interaction between lymphocytes, endothelial cells, and stromal cells.

Genes and molecules. The B lymphocytes synthesize antibody molecules called immunoglobulins. These molecules initially serve as receptors, with each B cell making a different antibody that recognizes its respective foreign molecule. The genes for immunoglobulins exist as independent deoxyribonucleic acid (DNA) fragments that are recombined to form a complete gene during the differentiation process. Each antibody molecule consists of two types of domains, variable and constant. The variable domains are subdivided into a variable segment, a joining segment, and a diversity segment. There are many gene copies for each segment, allowing for the formation of approximately 2 million different antibody genes. Finally, after the B-lymphocyte receptor binds to its antigen, B cells differentiate and secrete antibodies of

the same specificity as the receptor molecule. *See* IMMUNOGENETICS; IMMUNOGLOBULIN.

T-cell antigen receptor. The T-cell antigen receptor is encoded by two genes that undergo rearrangement during T-cell differentiation. Each T-cell clone expresses a single gene combination at its surface. T-cell receptors are associated with a complex of transmembrane proteins. This complex, CD3, is required for assembly and cell surface expression of the T-cell receptors and also provides signaling functions. Other accessory molecules, CD4 and CD8, are also an integral part of the receptor complex. Identified originally as cell markers which helped to distinguish between helper T cells and cytotoxic T cells, these accessory molecules are of critical importance in positive and negative selection of T cells. *See* IMMUNOCYTOTOXICITY.

Target-cell molecules. There is a set of molecules on target cells which are capable of signaling to the T cells that an infection is present. Viral proteins in an infected cell are cleaved to peptides, which are then carried by transporter molecules to the endoplasmic reticulum where the class I MHC molecules are synthesized. After binding the peptides, the class I MHC molecules migrate to the cell surface as a complex that is detected by the cytotoxic T cell. When a T-cell receptor binds to its specific foreign peptide–MHC complex, the T cell secretes substances that kill the infected cell.

MHC molecules and genes. Both class I and class II MHC molecules bind peptides that arise in different portions of the cell. The T cells that are involved in the recognition of class I–peptide complexes have CD8 proteins on their surface. The class II MHC molecules bind peptides derived from extracellular pathogens. The peptide-MHC complex can then move to the cell surface to interact with CD4 T cells. Unlike CD8 T cells, CD4 T cells do not kill the cells that display the peptide. The CD4 T cells may stimulate a macrophage to kill bacteria inside its own vesicles, or they may instruct nearby B cells to start producing specific antibodies.

The genes that encode MHC molecules are the most polymorphic genes found in humans. These MHC genes are identical in all of an individual's cells but differ from one individual to another. As a consequence, the domains that comprise the MHC molecules differ in their amino acid sequences from person to person. In turn, the differences in the domains of the MHC molecules are responsible for the differences in the peptides that become bound. Each MHC molecule has a groove into which peptides of a specific length bind within pockets formed by the various amino acid sequences. Most of these peptides come from the individual's own proteins; however, it is the presence of foreign peptides that evokes an immune reaction.

Immunological self-tolerance. If an immune cell reacts to a self-product during the developmental stage in the thymus or bone marrow, it is inactivated or killed. A mature T cell whose receptor binds to a self-product is made unresponsive or killed if it fails to receive a second message. Unfortunately, the immune system still makes mistakes. T cells can sometimes respond to self-antigens and cause autoimmune diseases, such as rheumatoid arthritis, multiple sclerosis, and lupus erythematosus. *See* ARTHRITIS; IMMUNOLOGY; MULTIPLE SCLEROSIS; RHEUMATISM.   Ettore Appella

Bibliography. R. M. Coleman, *Fundamental Immunology*, 2d ed., 1992; J. Kuby, *Immunology*, 1992; P. Marrack and W. Kappler, How the immune system recognizes the body, *Sci. Amer.*, 269:81–89, 1993; W. E. Paul (ed.), *Fundamental Immunology*, 3d ed., 1993; A. Weiss, T-cell antigen receptor signal transduction, *Cell*, 73:209–212, 1993.

Cellulose

A linear polymer of (1→4)-linked β-D-glucopyranosyl units, and the most abundant of all naturally occurring substances. Cellulose constitutes approximately a third of all vegetable matter and thus it exists in far greater quantity than any other polysaccharide. It occurs as a principal structural component of the cell walls of mosses and seaweeds (25–30%), annual plants (25–35%), and trees (40–50%); cotton fiber contains 98% cellulose along with 1% protein, 0.65% pectic substance, and 0.15% mineral matter. Cellulose also is produced by some microorganisms, in a few cases reaching amounts of 20–30%. *See* CELL WALLS (PLANT).

Source. Cellulose for chemical modification, particularly for derivatization, is often obtained from cotton linters by boiling them with 1% sodium hydroxide solution. High-quality cellulose may be obtained from bast fibers such as flax (80–90% cellulose), hemp (65–75%), jute (60–70%), and ramie (85%). Cellulose fibers used for paper, for cardboard, or for conversion to film and synthetic fiber are obtained from wood pulp.

Structure. While cellulose is a uniform, linear polymer of a β-D-glucopyranosyl units linked (1→4), the β-D-glucosidic bond causes alternate units to be positioned as shown in the structure here, so that the molecule is essentially a polymer of the disaccharide, cellobiose, actually the cellobiosyl unit. The molecule has a nonreducing end and an aldehyde end, although at times the latter may be oxidized to a carboxyl group. Chain length varies with previous treatment, but native cellulose molecules have 7000 to 15,000 units, which are termed degrees of polymerization. *See* POLYMER.

Cellulose is the principal structural component of plants. The structural strength and integrity of plant cell walls that support even giant trees is due to the ease with which cellulose molecules fit together and bond intermolecularly, with secondary forces, over long lengths. This crystallization is due, for the most part, to hydrogen bonds such as that between the C3 hydroxyl of one chain and the C6 hydroxyl of a neighboring chain. Crystallinity may account for 60–70% of the cellulose in wood pulp and 70–80% in cotton. Rayon regenerated from pulp may redevelop 45% crystallinity. Cellulose in the cell wall is mainly in threadlike fibers, composed of smaller fibrils. These provide the reinforcing material with noncrystalline molecules running from one crystallite to another, providing elasticity in conjunction with that of hemicellulose and other filler material of the cell wall. *See* HEMICELLULOSE; HYDROGEN BOND.

Various crystalline forms of cellulose exist with the native form known as cellulose I. The unit cell is monoclinic with three unequal sides and one non-90° angle. Chains are skewed 180° along the chain axis. Strong alkali alters the polymorph to cellulose II, providing greater hydrogen bonding and a more stable, lower-energy, structure. Some covalent bonding occurs between cellulose and with the lignin of the cell wall and of the middle lamella, but mainly these molecules are free and can be extracted with reagents such as a strong alkaline solution.

Pulp. Commercial cellulose is obtained from woods by pulping procedures designed to remove lignin, hemicelluloses, gums, waxes, and other natural noncellulose constituents. Most commercial wood pulp is consumed in paper manufacture, but pulps of high α-cellulose content (90% or greater for rayon and at least 98% for cellulose ester, mainly acetate, manufacture) are considered good chemical cellulose, or dissolving-grade cellulose. α-Cellulose is that which is not soluble in 17.5% sodium hydroxide solution. Though cellulose is resistant to degradation during the pulping operation, it is partially degraded to lower molecular weights. Pulping is accomplished by mechanical or chemical means, or a combination of the two. Mechanical pulps contain the same constituents as the original wood, but fewer water-soluble substances. These pulps have shorter fibers than do chemical pulps and produce weaker paper. If steam is used to produce a thermomechanical pulp, the fibers are less degraded.

Nonreducing end   Cellobiose repeating unit   Reducing end

The kraft (sulfate) method is the most common chemical pulping method used in the United States, accounting for 70% of pulp production; pulp yield is 40–45%. In this process, wood chips, $^5/_8$–1 in. (1.5–2.5 cm) long by $^1/_4$ in. (0.6 cm) thick, are cooked to a maximum temperature of 334–347°F (168–175°C) for 2–6 h with a solution of sodium hydroxide and sodium sulfide, present in a ratio of 3:1. Other processes used are the sulfite and alkaline. Less than 10% of the pulp made in the United States is produced by the sulfite process. Chemical methods have become focused on improved yield, reduced environmental problems associated with sulfur chemicals, and production of high-strength fibers. Modern processes add anthraquinone to a soda (alkaline) cook, introduce soda-oxygen cooking, or use organic solvent extraction. Combinations of mechanical and chemical pulping tend to produce higher yields of high-strength fibers. *See* PAPER; WOOD CHEMICALS.

Dissolving pulp of 95–98% α-cellulose is used for viscous rayon, cellulose nonwoven materials, and cellulose derivatives. These pulps are made by alkaline washing of sulfite or sulfate pulps or by mild acid hydrolysis of chips followed by kraft pulping and bleaching to give low pulp yields of 29–35%. *See* TEXTILE CHEMISTRY.

Derivatives. Commercial derivatives are ethers that, among other properties, provide water solubility and esters which, in high degrees of substitution, provide organic solubility needed for spinning cellulose into fibers or molding it into shaped objects. One inorganic ester, the nitrate, made by reacting cellulose in a mixture of nitric and sulfuric acids, is used at high derivation as cellulose trinitrate gunpowder. Cellulose trinitrate has a degree of substitution (DS; the average number of hydroxyls substituted per glucose residue) of three. Formerly, it was used at a lower degree of substitution as a lacquer and film former. *See* ESTER; ETHER; MANUFACTURED FIBER.

Commercial ethers are carboxymethyl, methyl, hydroxyethyl, or hydroxypropyl. Mixed ethers are also made that contain methyl and hydroxyethyl or hydroxypropyl groups. All are soluble in water or mild alkaline solution. Solubility is conferred on the linear cellulose molecule by the substituent groups, which provide frequent bumps on the regular cellulose chains. This restricts them from associating when sections of chains meet in solution, thus preventing close association of chains that would lead to partial crystallization and insolubilization. Since these rather inflexible chains are still quite long with degrees of polymerization of 150–250, they sweep out large spherical volumes as they gyrate, and they collide frequently to absorb energy, producing highly viscous solutions. Such derivatives have degrees of substitution of 0.1–2.5. They are used to thicken solutions and to act as suspending agents and sometimes as mild emulsifiers.

Carboxymethylcellulose has a negative charge due to ionization of the carboxyl group, giving the molecule some emulsifying character. This derivative is used in washing powders; the molecules bind slightly to cotton fabrics, giving the cloth a negative charge that prevents negative soil particles from redepositing on the cloth.

Cellulose acetate is the principal commercial ester. Reaction is usually conducted in a mixture of acetic anhydride, acetic acid, and sulfuric acid as the catalyst to produce a degree of substitution of about 2.4, resulting in a product soluble in acetone. This has applications as a quick-drying adhesive, for film formation, or for use in cigarette filters. If proprionic acid or its anhydride is used in the esterification reaction, a mixed ester is produced that forms a shock-resistant plastic useful for football helmets, telephones, and other objects that need to withstand shock. A fully acetylated cellulose (degree of substitution = 3) is used for making high-strength products, acetate rayon, and textile tow. This acetate can be made by acetylation of cellulose in dichloromethane with acetic anhydride and perchloric acid catalyst.

Degradation. Because cellulose molecules bind together so strongly, they are quite resistant to hydrolysis by acids and even cellulytic enzymes, although the free molecules or amorphous regions are hydrolyzed as easily as other polysaccharides. The end product is D-glucose; if it could be produced cheaply from cellulose, it would allow wood to be used as a source of fermentation alcohol. Hot 12% hydrochloric acid converts hemicelluloses mainly to furfural and cellulose to hydroxmethyl-furfural. Unless cellulose molecules are oxidized, they are resistant to alkaline solutions, because like other polysaccharides the aldehyde functions of the D-glucopyranosyl units are tied up as acetal linkages that are resistant to alkaline cleavage.

Cellulose undergoes oxidation by numerous oxidants such as peroxides and hypochlorite. Dinitrogen tetraoxide specifically converts the hydroxymethyl group at C6 of each D-glucopyranosyl unit to a carboxyl or uronic acid. Most oxidations are catalyzed by metal ions. Therefore, iron salts allow oxidation of cotton textiles, causing yellow spots and eventually holes.

Cellulose is hydrolyzed slowly by cellulase enzymes produced by bacteria and fungi. *See* POLYSACCHARIDE.   David G. Barkalow; Roy L. Whistler

Bibliography. J. P. Casey (ed.), *Pulp and Paper Chemistry and Chemical Technology*, vol. 1, 3d ed., 1980; J. F. Kennedy et al. (eds.), *Cellulose and Its Derivatives*: *Chemistry, Biochemistry and Applications*, 1985; T. P. Nevell and S. H. Zeronian (eds.), *Cellulose Chemistry and Its Applications*, 1985; C. E. Shuerch (ed.), *Cellulose and Wood*: *Chemistry and Technology*, 1989; E. Sjostrom, *Wood Chemistry*: *Fundamentals and Applications*, 1993; R. A. Young and R. M. Rowell (eds.), *Cellulose Structure, Modification and Hydrolysis*, 1986.

Cement

A material, usually finely divided, that when mixed with water forms a paste, and when molded sets into a solid mass. The term cement is sometimes used to refer to organic compounds used for adhering or for fastening materials, but these are more correctly known as adhesives. *See* ADHESIVE; ADHESIVE BONDING.

In the fields of architecture, engineering, and construction, the term portland cement is applied to most of the hydraulic cements used for concrete, mortars, and grouts. This article discusses portland cement and other special construction cements.

Portland cement sets and hardens by reacting chemically with water. In concrete, it combines with water and aggregates (sand and gravel, crushed stone, or other granular material) to form a stonelike mass. In grouts and mortars, cement is mixed with water and fine aggregates (sand) or fine granular materials. *See* CLAY, COMMERCIAL; CONCRETE; MORTAR.

Production. Portland cement is ground from nodules, which can vary in dimension from dust to fist-sized chunks, known as clinker. Cement clinker is the product of a high-temperature process. Manufacturing entails introduction of finely ground raw materials—mineral sources of calcium oxide, silica, alumina, and iron oxide—into a horizontally sloping rotary kiln. Raw materials are ground to a fineness to pass a 75-micrometer (200-mesh) screen in order to react within the kiln's residence time.

Materials are introduced either in powdered form, known as the dry process, or in slurry form, known as the wet process. Less energy is required to produce cement in the dry process; energy conservation efforts have led to the phasing-out of wet-process systems. Kiln systems differ, but generally materials are funneled through three major zones: drying and preheating, 70–1650°F (20–900°C), in which water is evaporated and calcination occurs; calcining, 1100–1650°F (600–900°C), where carbon dioxide is driven off but lime needed for subsequent reactions remains; and sintering or burning, 2200–2700°F (1200–1480°C), in which calcium oxide reacts with silica to form calcium silicates.

The intense heat yields clinker, whose principal chemical compounds are tricalcium silicate, dicalcium silicate, tricalcium aluminate, and tetracalcium aluminoferrite. Raw-material sources can vary according to local availability, but generally bear lime, iron, silica, alumina, and magnesia. Sources of these materials include limestone, clay, shale, and slag. Cement clinker is ground to extreme fineness in rotary steel-ball mills. Approximately 85–95% of cement particles are smaller than 45 micrometers. Small amounts of gypsum are interground with clinker to control set time.

Calcium silicates constitute about 75% of the weight of cement. When mixed with water, they form calcium hydroxide and calcium silicate hydrate or tobermorite gel. Hydrated cement contains about 25% calcium hydroxide and 50% tobermorite gel. The latter is primarily responsible for the strength and other properties of hydrated cement.

Standards. Under its C 150 classification, the American Society for Testing and Materials (ASTM) designates five basic types of portland cement. Type I is a general-purpose cement suitable for all uses where special properties are not required. Type II is used for resistance to moderate sulfate exposures. Type III is high-early-strength cement. Type IV is used where the rate and amount of heat generated from hydration must be minimized. Type V is used for resistance to severe sulfate exposure.

Types I, II, and III are also produced in air-entraining varieties. Air entrainment (incorporation of tiny air bubbles) is employed to maintain workability and cohesiveness in the fresh concrete mix and provide durability in the hardened product in climates where the material is subject to cycles of freezing and thawing. The microscopic air bubbles in the mix act as pressure-relief valves during freeze cycles. Air entrainment in a concrete mix can be acheived by using the three air-entraining portland cements (types IA, IIA, IIIA) or admixtures, which impart special properties to fresh or hardened concrete.

Adjustments in the physical and chemical compositions allow for tailoring portland cements and other hydraulic cements to special applications. Blended hydraulic cements are produced with portland cements and materials that by themselves might not possess binding characteristics.

Special varieties. Special cements are produced for mortars and architectural or engineering applications: white portland cement, masonry cement, and oil-well cement, expansive cement, and plastic cement.

In addition to acting as the key ingredient in concrete, mortars, and grouts, portland cements are specified for soil-cement and roller-compacted concrete, used in pavements and in dams, and other water resource structures, and as reagents for stabilization and solidification of organic and inorganic wastes.   Don Marsh

Bibliography. S. H. Kosmatka and W. C. Panarese, *Design and Control of Concrete Mixtures*, 13th ed., 1988; Portland Cement Association, *A New Stone Age: The Making of Portland Cement and Concrete*, 1992.

Cenozoic

The youngest and the shortest of the three Phanerozoic geological eras. The Cenozoic (also known as Cainozoic) includes the Tertiary and Quaternary periods and represents geological time (and rocks deposited during that time) extending

CENOZOIC	QUATERNARY		HOLOCENE
			PLEISTOCENE
	TERTIARY	NEOGENE	PLIOCENE
			MIOCENE
		PALEOGENE	OLIGOCENE
			EOCENE
			PALEOCENE
MESOZOIC	CRETACEOUS		MAASTRICHTIAN

from the close of the Mesozoic Era to the present day.

The concept of the Cenozoic as the youngest era of the Phanerozoic was introduced by J. Phillips in 1941. The Cenozoic was considered to be a unit equivalent to the Tertiary, a term still in use from the old classification of Primary, Secondary, and Tertiary rocks, introduced by G. Arduino in Italy in 1759. Arduino based his classification on physical attributes, such as older magmatic and metamorphic rocks as Primary; limestone, marl, and clay with fossils as Secondary; and youngest fossil-rich rocks as Tertiary. This classification is now largely obsolete, with the exception of the term Tertiary, which is still in use but in a considerably modified form. A. Brogninart first modified the concept of "tertiaire" in 1810, applying it to strata deposited above the Cretaceous chalk in the Paris Basin. The term Quaternary (the second and younger period of the Cenozoic) was introduced by Morlot in 1854. *See* QUATERNARY; TERTIARY.

Modern time scales include all of the past 66 million years (approximately) of geological history in the Cenozoic Era. The distinction of Cenozoic from older eras has been traditionally based on the occurrence of fossils showing affinities to modern organisms, and not on any particular lithostratigraphic criteria. *See* INDEX FOSSIL; PALEONTOLOGY.

Subdivisions. Traditional classifications subdivide the Cenozoic Era into the Tertiary and Quaternary periods and seven epochs (from oldest to youngest): Paleocene, Eocene, Oligocene, Miocene, Pliocene, Pleistocene, and Holocene. The older five epochs that constitute the Tertiary Period span the time interval from around 66 to 1.6 million years before present (B.P.). The Tertiary is often separated into two subperiods, the Paleogene (Paleocene through Oligocene epochs, also sometimes collectively called the Nummulitic in Europe) and the Neogene (Miocene and Pliocene epochs). These subperiods were introduced by Hornes in 1853. The Quaternary Period, which encompasses only

approximately 1.6 million years B.P., includes the two youngest epochs (Pleistocene and Holocene). Holocene is also often referred to as the Recent, a term still in use from the old Lyellian classification. More recent stratigraphic opinions are leaning toward abandoning the use of Tertiary and Quaternary (which are seen as the unnecessary holdovers from obsolete classifications) and in favor of retaining Paleogene and Neogene as the prime subdivisions of the Cenozoic. *See* EOCENE; HOLOCENE; MIOCENE; OLIGOCENE; PALEOCENE; PLEISTOCENE; PLIOCENE.

Tectonics. Many of the tectonic events (mountain-building episodes or orogenies, changes in the rates of sea-floor spreading, plate convergences) that began in the Mesozoic continued into the Cenozoic. The Laramide orogeny, which uplifted the Rocky Mountains in North America, perhaps began as early as late Jurassic and continued into the Cretaceous and early Cenozoic time. In its post-Cretaceous phase the orogeny comprised a series of diastrophic movements that deformed the crust until some 50 million years ago (m.y.a.), when it ended abruptly. The Alpine orogeny, which created much of the Alps, also began in the Mesozoic, but it was most intense in the Cenozoic, when the European and African plates converged at an increased pace. *See* CRETACEOUS; JURASSIC; MESOZOIC; OROGENY.

In the Pacific Ocean the most significant tectonic event in the Cenozoic may have been the progressive consumption of the East Pacific Rise at the Cordilleran Subduction Zone and the concomitant development of the San Andreas Fault System some 30 m.y.a. *See* CORDILLERAN BELT; FAULT AND FAULT STRUCTURES; SUBDUCTION ZONES.

In the intracontinental region of the Tethys between Europe and Africa, the Cenozoic tectonic history is one of successive fragmentation and collision of minor plates and eventual convergence of the African and European plates. Africa's motion was counterclockwise relative to Europe, and began sometime in the early Mesozoic. By mid-Cenozoic, however, the motion between the two plates was largely convergent. The convergence caused a complex series of events that closed the Tethys Seaway between the two continents. In the late Cenozoic (Pliocene) the final collision of the Arabian plate with the Asian plate along Iran produced the Zagros Mountains and partially or completely isolated the Caspian and Black seas. *See* CONTINENTAL DRIFT.

In the Indian Ocean, perhaps the most significant event during the Cenozoic was rapid movement of the Indian plate northward and its collision with Asia. India had already broken loose from eastern Gondwana in the late Cretaceous, but around 80 m.y.a. its motion accelerated, and then increased further in the early Cenozoic. This movement, however, slowed down considerably around 50 m.y.a., when the Indian plate plowed into the Asian mainland. The first encounter of the two plates caused the initial uplift of the Himalayas. The major phase of the Himalayan orogeny, however, extends from the Miocene to the Pleistocene, when much of the high Himalayas were raised and the Tibetan Plateau was created. The encounter also caused major reorganization of the crust both north and south of the collision zone. In the Indian Ocean the plates were reorganized, and spreading was initiated on the Central Indian Ridge system. The collision had important repercussions for the Asian mainland as well. Over 900 mi (1500 km) of crustal shortening has occurred since the collision began. The effects of diastrophism associated with this event extend some 1800 mi (3000 km) northeast of the Himalayas. Included are major strike-slip faults in China and Mongolia, which may account for a major portion of the crustal shortening that continues to the present day. The present convergence between the Indian and Asian plates is at the rate of around 0.2 in. (0.5 cm) per year.

The convergences between India and Asia and between Africa and Europe in the mid-Cenozoic destroyed the ancestral Tethys, leaving behind remnants that include the Mediterranean, Black, and Caspian seas. *See* PLATE TECTONICS.

Oceans and climate. The modern circulation and vertical structure of the oceans and the predominantly glacial mode that the Earth is in at present were initiated in mid-Cenozoic time. The early Cenozoic was a period of transition between the predominantly thermospheric circulation of the Mesozoic and the thermohaline circulation that developed in the mid-Cenozoic. By the mid-Cenozoic the higher latitudes had begun to cool down, especially in the Southern Hemisphere because of the geographic isolation of Antarctica, leading to steeper latitudinal thermal gradients and accentuation of seasonality. The refrigeration of the polar regions gave rise to the cold high-latitude water that sank to form cold bottom water. The development of the psychrosphere (cold deeper layer of the ocean) and the onset of thermohaline circulation are considered to be the most significant events of Cenozoic ocean history, ushering the Earth into its modern glacial-interglacial cyclic mode.

The overall history of the Cenozoic oceans is marked by a long-term withdrawal of the seas from epicontinental and coastal oceans and the accretion of ice on the polar regions. The ice buildup may have been partly favored by the more poleward position of the landmasses and the eventual thermal isolation of the Antarctic continent.

In the early Paleogene, for the first time a deep connection between the North and South Atlantic was developed that allowed deeper water penetration into the southern basin, which intermittently led to extensive erosion on the ocean floor. However, the most likely source area for deep waters in the early Cenozoic was still in the temperate and low-latitude shelves. Farther north, in the Norwegian Sea area there is magnetic evidence of initiation of sea-floor spreading in the late Paleocene. By the middle Eocene, this area may have become a site for the formation of cold bottom waters. Erosional events on the sea floor indicate that North Atlantic Deep Water may have begun to flow southward at approximately the same time as the initial subsidence of the Greenland-Faeroe Ridge below sea level in the late Eocene. Later on, in the Miocene, the ridge subsided more actively, resulting in greater outflow of higher-salinity water to intermediate and abyssal depths of the Central Atlantic. Evidence also points to vigorous bottom waters in the late Eocene, which increased in intensity through Oligocene and Miocene time.

The most prominent feature of the surface circulation in the early Cenozoic was the westward-flowing circumglobal Tethys Current that dominated the oceanic scene in the tropical latitudes. As the Indian plate approached the Asian mainland in the early Cenozoic, it progressively restricted the flow of the Tethys Current to its north. In the middle Eocene, when the general drop in global sea level and the first encounter of the Indian plate with Asia reduced the northern passage, the main flow moved to the west of the Indian plate. By the Oligocene time the westward flow in the Tethys had become intermittent and severely restricted to a narrow western passage. The Tethyan passage had essentially closed by the dawn of the Neogene.

A major paleogeographic event for the overall Cenozoic oceanic patterns was the breaching of the straits between Antarctica and South America at the Drake Passage in the Oligocene. This event led to the eventual thermal isolation of Antarctica, the development of the circum-Antarctic Current, and further enhancement of the ice cap on the continent by the mid-Oligocene. The ice accumulation on the Arctic, which lacks a continent in the polar position, may have also begun by the Oligocene. The increased sequestration of water on ice caps may be responsible for a major global sea-level drop in the mid-Oligocene, as is evidenced along most of the world's continental margins. By late Oligocene time the global surface circulation patterns had essentially evolved the major features of the modern oceans. *See* PALEOCEANOGRAPHY; PALEOGEOGRAPHY.

All climatic indicators point to a general warming trend through the Paleocene, culminating in a period of peak global temperatures in the early Eocene. The latitudinal and vertical thermal gradients in the early Eocene were low, and mean surface temperature was around 50°F (10°C) in the higher latitudes and 70°F (20°C) in the tropics. Terrestrial flora and fauna also corroborate the peak warming of this interval. For example, the Arctic island of Ellesmere has yielded a rich warm-blooded vertebrate fauna that indicates a range of temperature between 50 and 70°F (10 and 20°C). The Eocene time is also characterized by higher global sea levels and increased oceanic productivity and carbonate deposition on the shelves and banks. The climate became more extreme in the late Eocene and through the Oligocene, when the latitudinal contrast increased because of development of ice in the polar regions. Vertical thermal gradients also steepened once the outflow of cold bottom waters began from the higher latitudes.

The late Cenozoic is characterized by further accentuation of the oceanographic and climatic patterns that were initiated in the early Cenozoic. By Miocene time the Tethyan connection between the Indian Ocean and the Mediterranean Sea had been broken. This event modified the circulation patterns in the North Atlantic and the Mediterranean, which for the first time began to resemble their modern analogs. Neogene climatic proxies (such as stable isotopes in cores and glacial records on land) show evidence of considerable climatic fluctuations. Six major climatic deterioration events have been identified in the Mio-Pliocene record. These events were also associated with enhanced surface circulation, bottom erosion, and aridity on land over North Africa. The cooler early Miocene climates were followed by a climatic optimum in mid-Miocene, followed in turn by a significant deterioration in climate which has been ascribed to a major enlargement of the ice sheets on Antarctica. *See* GLACIAL EPOCH.

In the late Miocene the Mediterranean suffered a salinity crisis following a sea-level fall and the isolation of the basin. The growth of ice caps in the Miocene eventually led to the fall of sea level below the depth of Gibraltar Sill, isolating the Mediterranean Basin. The lack of connection to the open Atlantic and excess evaporation led to high salinities and deposition of voluminous quantities of evaporites in a relatively short time. The Mediterranean was reconnected to the Atlantic in the early Pliocene, allowing cold deep waters to suddenly spill over the subsided Gibralter Sill. The Black Sea was also converted into an alkaline lake during the salinity crisis when the Mediterranean inflow was cut off. The early Pliocene reconnection with the Mediterranean was once again followed by isolation of the Black Sea, this time as a fresh-water lake. These conditions lasted into the Quaternary, when the reconnection to the Mediterranean was established through the Bosporus Straits, ushering in the present-day conditions. *See* SALINE EVAPORITE.

Another important threshold event of the late Cenozoic was the closing of the connection between the Central Atlantic and Pacific oceans at the Isthmus of Panama. The connection was operative until the mid-Pliocene, when tectonic events led to its closure some 3 m.y.a. The closure most likely led to more vigorous Gulf Stream flow due to deflected energy, displacing the Stream northward to its present-day position. The modern circulation patterns in the Caribbean also date back

to this event. Another major climatic-oceanographic event of the Cenozoic was the development of an extensive ice cap on the Arctic. Although there is some evidence of ice cover in the Arctic since the Oligocene, evidence of a significant amount of ice accumulation is only as old as mid-Pliocene, some 3 m.y.a., coincident with the closing of the Panama Isthmus. The deflection of the Gulf Stream northward due to the latter event may have provided the excess moisture needed for this accumulation.

The Quaternary climatic history is one of repeated alternations between glacial and interglacial periods. At least five major glacial cycles have been identified in the Quaternary of northwestern Europe. The most recent glacial event occurred some 18,000 years ago, when much of North America and northern Europe were covered with extensive ice sheets. The late Pliocene and Pleistocene glacial cyclicity led to repeated falls in global sea level as a result of sequestration of water as ice sheets in higher latitudes during the glacial intervals. For example, the sea level is estimated to have risen some 360 ft (110 m) since the end of the last glacial maximum some 17,000 years ago. As a by-product of these repeated drops in sea level and movement of the shorelines toward the basins, large deltas developed at the mouths of the world's major drainage systems during the Quaternary. These bodies of sand and silt constitute ideal reservoirs for hydrocarbon accumulation. *See* DELTA; PALEOCLIMATOLOGY.

Life. At the end of the Cretaceous a major extinction event took place that killed off nearly 75% of all biota on Earth. This event also decimated marine biota, and only a few species survived into the Cenozoic. The recovery, however, was relatively rapid. During the interval of the Paleocene through middle Eocene, the overall global sea-level rise enlarged the ecospace for marine organisms, and the associated optimal climatic conditions led to increased speciation through the Paleocene, culminating in a great diversity of marine life during the early and middle Eocene. Limestone-building coral reefs were also widespread in the tropical-temperate climatic belt of the early Cenozoic, and the tropical Tethyan margins were typified by expansive distribution of the larger foraminifera known as *Nummulites* (giving the Paleogene its informal name of the Nummulitic Period). *See* NUMMULITES.

The late Eocene saw a rapid decline in the diversity of marine phyto- and zooplankton due to a global withdrawal of the seas from the continental margins and the ensuing deterioration in climate. Marine diversities reached a new low in the mid-Oligocene, when the sea level was at its lowest, having gone through a major withdrawal of seas from the continental margins. The climates associated with low seas were extreme and much less conducive to biotic diversification. The late Oligocene and Neogene as a whole constitute an interval characterized by increasing partitioning of ecological niches into tropical, temperate, and higher-latitude climatic belts, and greater differentiation of marine fauna and flora.

The terminal Cretaceous event had also decimated the terrestrial biota. Dinosaurs, which had dominated the Mesozoic scene, became extinct. Only a few small shrewlike mammalian species survived into the Paleocene. In the absence of dinosaurian competition, mammals evolved and spread rapidly to become dominant in the Cenozoic. The evolution of grasses in the early Eocene and the wide distribution of grasslands thereafter may have been catalytic in the diversification of browsing mammals. Marsupials and insectivores as well as rodents (which first appeared in the Eocene) diversified rapidly, as did primates, carnivores, and ungulates. The ancestral horse first appeared in the early Eocene in North America, where its lineage evolved into the modern genus *Equus*, only to disappear from the continent in the late Pleistocene. It was brought back to North America from the Old World by the first Europeans. Hominoid evolution began during the Miocene in Africa. Modern hominids are known to have branched off from the hominoids some 5 m.y.a. Over the next 4.5 million years the hominids went through several evolutionary stages to finally evolve into archaic *Homo sapiens* some half million years ago. *See* DINOSAUR; FOSSIL HUMAN; MAMMALIA; ORGANIC EVOLUTION.

Bilal U. Haq

Bibliography. A. Hallam, *Phanerozoic Sea-Level Changes*, 1992; K. J. Hsu (ed.), *Mesozoic and Cenozoic Oceans*, 1986; C. Pomerol, *The Cenozoic Era: Tertiary and Quaternary*, 1982; D. Raup and S. M. Stanley, *Principles of Paleontology*, 2d ed., 1978.

Centaurus

The Centaur, in astronomy, one of the most magnificent of the southern constellations. Two first-magnitude navigational stars, Alpha and Beta Centauri, mark the right and left front feet, respectively, of the centaur. The former is Rigil Kentaurus, or simply Rigil Kent, and the latter Hadar. Rigil Kent is the third brightest star in the whole sky, ranking after Sirius and Canopus. The line joining Rigil Kent and Hadar points to the constellation Crux (Southern Cross). Thus they are also called the Southern Pointers, in contradistinction to the northern pointers of the Big Dipper. *See* CONSTELLATION; CRUX; URSA MAJOR.

Ching-Sung Yu

Center of gravity

A fixed point in a material body through which the resultant force of gravitational attraction acts. The resultant of all forces or attractions produced by the Earth's gravity on a body constitutes its weight.

This weight is considered to be concentrated at the center of gravity in mechanical studies of a rigid body. The location of the center of gravity for a body remains fixed in relation to the body regardless of the orientation of the body. If supported at the center of gravity, a body would remain balanced in its initial position. Coordinates, as for an aircraft, are conveniently chosen with origin at the center of gravity. *See* GRAVITY; RESULTANT OF FORCES.

Nelson S. Fisk

Center of mass

That point of a material body or system of bodies which moves as though the system's total mass existed at the point and all external forces were applied at the point. The Earth-Moon system moves in the Sun's gravitational field as though both masses were located at a center of mass some 3000 mi (4700 km) from the Earth's geometric center. The function of the center-of-mass concept is to permit analysis of the motion of an entire system as distinguished from that of its individual parts.

Consider a system of mass M composed of n bodies with masses m_1, m_2, ... , m_n and radius vectors r_1, r_2, ... , r_n measured from some common reference point. Separate the force on each body into internal and external components $^i f$ and $^e f$. The motion of the jth body is given by Eq. (1). The sum of the motions of all bodies is given by Eq. (2).

$$m_j \frac{d^2 r_j}{dt^2} = {}^e f_j + {}^i f_j \qquad (1)$$

$$\sum_j m_j \frac{d^2 r_j}{dt_2} = \sum_j {}^e f_j + \sum_j {}^i f_j \qquad (2)$$

By Newton's third law, $j^i f_j$ is zero, and sum of the external forces acts as a single resultant force as in Eq. (3).

$$\sum_j {}^e f_j = F \qquad (3)$$

Define a point with radius vector R, such that Eq. (4) holds. Then Eq. (5) can be written, and by substitution from Eq. (2), Eqs. (6) and (7) are obtained.

$$M R = \sum_j m_j r_j \qquad (4)$$

$$\frac{d^2}{dt^2}(MR) = \frac{d^2}{dt^2} \sum_j m_j r_j = \sum_j m_j \frac{d^2 r_j}{dt^2} \qquad (5)$$

$$\frac{d^2}{dt^2}(MR) = F \qquad (6)$$

$$\frac{d^2 R}{dt^2} = \frac{F}{M} \qquad (7)$$

Equation (7), an expression of Newton's second law, states that the center of mass at R moves as though it possessed the total mass of the system and were acted upon by the total external force.

A simplification of the description of collisions can be had by using a coordinate system which moves with the velocity of the center of mass before collision. *See* COLLISION (PHYSICS); RIGID-BODY DYNAMICS. John P. Hagen

Center of pressure

A point on a plane surface through which the resultant force due to pressure passes. Such a surface can be supported by a single mounting fixture at its center of pressure if no other forces act. For example, a water gate in a dam can be supported by a single shaft at its center of pressure. For a nonvertical plane surface submerged in a motionless liquid, the center of pressure is vertically below the centroid of the volume of liquid above the surface. For a vertical submerged surface, the distance from the surface of the liquid to the center of pressure is y_p given by $y_p = I/y_c A$, where A is the area of submerged surface, y_c is the distance below liquid surface to the centroid of area, and I is the moment of inertia of area A about the intersection line of the vertical surface with the liquid surface. *See* CENTROIDS (MATHEMATICS); MOMENT OF INERTIA; RESULTANT OF FORCES. Nelson S. Fisk

Central force

A force whose line of action is always directed toward a fixed point. The central force may attract or repel. The point toward or from which the force acts is called the center of force. If the central force attracts a material particle, the path of the particle is a curve concave toward the center of force; if the central force repels the particle, its orbit is convex to the center of force. Undisturbed orbital motion under the influence of a central force satisfies Kepler's law of areas. *See* CELESTIAL MECHANICS. Raynor L. Duncombe

Central heating and cooling

The use of a single heating or cooling plant to serve a group of buildings, facilities, or even a complete community through a system of distribution pipework that feeds each structure or facility. Central heating plants are basically of two types: steam or hot-water. The latter type uses high-temperature hot water under pressure and has become the more usual because of its considerable advantages. Steam systems are only used today where there is a specific requirement for high-pressure steam. Central cooling plants utilize a central refrigeration plant with a chilled water distribution system serving the air-conditioning systems in each building or facility.

Benefits. Advantages of a central heating or cooling plant over individual ones for each building or facility in a group include reduced labor cost, lower energy cost, less space requirement, and simpler maintenance. Though a central plant may require a 24-h shift of operators, the total number of employees can be substantially less than that required to operate and maintain a number of individual plants.

Firing efficiencies of 85–93%, dependent upon such factors as fuel, boiler, and plant design, are usual with large central heating plants. Corresponding efficiencies for small individual heating boiler plants average 50–70%. Fuel in bulk quantity has a lower unit cost, and single handling for one large plant as distinct from multiple handling for many small plants saves appreciably in labor and transportation. Maintenance costs on a single central plant are considerably lower than for the aggregate of small plants of equal total capacity.

The disadvantages of a central heating plant concern mainly the maintenance of the distribution system where steam is used. Corrosion of the condensate water return lines shortens their life, and the steam drainage traps need particular attention. These disadvantages do not occur with high-temperature hot-water installations.

Central cooling plants, using conventional, electrically driven refrigeration compressors, have the advantage of utilizing bulk electric supply, at voltages as high as 13.5 kV, at wholesale rates. Additionally, their flexible load factor, resulting from load divergency in the various buildings served, results in major operating economies.

Design. Winter heat-load requirements are calculated by the addition of the following for each individual building or facility: winter heat losses; domestic water-heating requirements; and industrial or other special heat requirements. To the sum of these for all buildings or facilities must be added the system distribution heat losses.

The summer load on the central cooling plant is calculated by the addition for each individual building or facility of the summer air-conditioning requirements. To the sum of these for all buildings or facilities must be added the system summer distribution heat losses.

To the individual winter and summer totals a diversity factor of 60–80% is applied because not all loads peak simultaneously. Winter heat loss due to weather conditions must be taken at its maximum. Water-heating and industrial requirements vary throughout the daily cycle. The summer air conditioning load must also be taken at its maximum. System distribution losses must be calculated both for the winter and the summer loads. The individual characteristics of the system must be considered in the diversity factor used.

Individual boiler sizing should allow the best arrangement to meet load variations, such as between individual 24-h peaks for winter loads. Standby capacity is essential. Fuel selection, usually oil, coal, or gas, depends on local conditions and costs, taking into account labor and firing efficiencies to be expected with each fuel. Individual refrigeration machine sizing must allow for cooling load variation over the 24-h cycle and the turn-down range of the machine itself. Considerable flexibility in machine choice thus results.

Distribution pipework sizing follows normal practice using suitable pressure drops with allowance for load variations and diversity factors as indicated.

Economics. The economics of each system must be individually computed because of the many factors involved. There is no average cost unitary basis applicable. The following major factors affect each plant's economics study: (1) system type, that is, steam, low pressure or high pressure; medium- or high-temperature hot water; chilled water temperature used; and so forth; (2) cost and type of energy used, that is, coal, gas, oil, or electricity, (3) type and occupancy of facilities served; (4) labor costs and conditions; (5) terrain; (6) climatic conditions; (7) plant first cost; (8) system life and maintenance costs. *See* DISTRICT HEATING.

Boiler plant. Both high-pressure (125 lb/in.^{2} or 860 kilopascals saturated) and low-pressure (15 lb/in.^{2} or 103 kilopascals saturated) steam plants are used, although the former is the more common. Both types follow conventional design. Feedwater and firing auxiliaries are of conventional type. Chemical treatment of feedwater is necessary. *See* BOILER FEEDWATER.

Either conventional hot-water heating boilers or high-temperature hot-water boilers, depending on size, are used. Design and components for high-temperature hot-water plants are more complex and include nitrogen pressurization and gland-cooled circulating pumps. However, standard manufactured equipment is available for both conventional and high-temperature plants. Hot-water circulation, due to losses in the distribution pipework, should be at maximum temperature-pressure limitation. Circulation through the distribution system is by centrifugal pump with standby equipment being furnished. High-temperature hot-water installations may operate in the 400–500°F (200–260°C) range. *See* BOILER.

Fuel handling, firing, and control arrangements also follow conventional design. Capacity of fuel storage should be on a minimal 3–4 week basis.

Central refrigeration plant. The central refrigeration plant may be electrically driven, or it may be of the steam-turbine-driven centrifugal type or steam absorption type. Steam as the prime energy source can be used where the plant is installed adjacent to a central boiler plant. Otherwise, medium-tension electricity, bought at bulk rates, forms an economical energy source. Gas turbines may also power centrifugal refrigeration compressors.

All equipment, including cooling towers and pumps, is of conventional design. *See* REFRIGERATION.

Distribution systems. Both overhead and underground pipework are used for distribution, although the latter is more usual except for industrial plants. Overhead mains must be strongly supported, insulated, and weatherproofed. Underground heating mains must be insulated and carefully waterproofed, particularly in damp areas. They must be structurally adequate. Steam distribution requires proper drainage of mains and often pumped return of condensate when gravity flow is not practical. In municipal distribution systems in larger cities where steam is used, it is frequently considered uneconomical to return the condensate to the central boiler plant due to pumping costs.

Hot-water distribution systems have the advantage that they are not affected by grade variations, that is, they can be run both uphill and downhill. The circulating pump pressures must be calculated accordingly.

A number of prefabricated insulated piping systems are commercially available. Each requires special handling for its installation and jointing. Hydrocarbon fill may also be used for heating mains insulation. Proper depth of burial must be arranged to give adequate protection against surface loads. Arrangements for expansion by loops or sliding fittings in access manholes are essential, and frequently cathodic protection is necessary. Where high-temperature hot water is used, it may be necessary to provide heat exchangers at each building or facility to furnish secondary heat at more moderate temperatures for uses such as heating systems and hot water. Where low-pressure steam is required, such exchangers may furnish this on the secondary side, if the primary hot water is at sufficiently high temperature.

For chilled water distribution systems, asbestos-cement plastic-lined piping can be used. The plastic lining has a low flow friction coefficient. If the piping is buried 4 ft (1.2 m) or deeper, no insulation is required, provided soil is not waterlogged.

Heat sales. Various methods of heat sale are in use where central plants service public communities or facilities. With steam distribution steam meters to each individual building or facility served are usual, and a utility type of sliding scale rate per pound of steam sold is charged.

For high-temperature and chilled water distribution a combination meter measuring both water flow and temperature differential between supply and return mains may be used. This measures directly Btu per hour furnished. If a constant temperature differential is maintained between supply and return water mains, metering may be by flow only, although this is not very accurate. *See* AIR CONDITIONING; COMFORT HEATING; DEGREE-DAY; STEAM; STEAM HEATING; WARM-AIR HEATING SYSTEM.

John K. M. Pryke

Bibliography. *ASHRAE Systems Handbook*, 1992; R. Havrella, *Heating, Ventilating, and Air Conditioning Fundamentals*, 1981.

Central nervous system

That portion of the nervous system composed of the brain and spinal cord. The brain is enclosed in the skull, and the spinal cord within the spinal canal of the vertebral column. The brain and spinal cord are intimately covered by membranes called meninges and bathed in an extracellular fluid called cerebrospinal fluid. Approximately 90% of the cells of the central nervous sytem are glial cells which support, both physically and metabolically, the other 10% of the cells, which are the nerve cells or neurons. Although the glial cells are much more numerous than neurons, the glial cells are also much smaller and do not directly participate in the propagation and integration of information. *See* MENINGES; NEURON.

Functionally similar groups of neurons are clustered together in so-called nuclei of the central nervous system. When groups of neurons are organized in layers (called laminae) on the outer surface of the brain, the group is called a cortex, such as the cerebral cortex and cerebellar cortex. The long processes (axons) of neurons course in the central nervous sytem in functional groups called tracts. Since many of the axons have a layer of shiny fat (myelin) surrounding them, they appear white and are called the white matter of the central nervous system. The nuclei and cortex of the central nervous system have little myelin in them, appear gray, and are called the gray matter of the central nervous system. The complex of gray and white matter forms the organizational pattern of the central nervous systems of all vertebrates. *See* BRAIN; NERVOUS SYSTEM (VERTEBRATE); SPINAL CORD.   Douglas B. Webster

Centrifugal force

A fictitious or pseudo outward force on a particle rotating about an axis which by Newton's third law is equal and opposite to the centripetal force. Like all such action-reaction pairs of forces, they are equal and opposite but do not act on the same body and so do not cancel each other. Consider a mass M tied by a string of length R to a pin at the center of a smooth horizontal table and whirling around the pin with an angular velocity of ω radians per second. The mass rotates in a circular path because of the centripetal force, $F_c = M\omega^2 R$, exerted on it by the string. The reaction force exerted by the rotating mass M, the so-called centrifugal force, is $M\omega^2 R$ in a direction away from the center of rotation. *See* CENTRIPETAL FORCE.

From another point of view, consider an experimenter in a windowless, circular laboratory that is rotating smoothly about a centrally located vertical axis. No object remains at rest on a smooth surface; all such objects move outward toward the wall of the laboratory as though an outward, centrifugal force were acting. To the experimenter partaking in the rotation, in a rotating frame of reference, the centrifugal force is real. An outside observer would realize that the inward force is real. An outside observer would realize that the inward force which the experimenter in the rotating laboratory must exert to keep the object at rest does not keep it at rest, but furnishes the centripetal force required to keep the object moving in a circular path. The concept of an outward, centrifugal force explains the action of a centrifuge. *See* CENTRIFUGATION.   C. E. Howe/R. J. Stephenson

Centrifugal pump

A machine for moving fluid by accelerating it radially outward. More fluid is moved by centrifugal pumps than by all other types combined. The smooth, essentially pulsationless flow from centrifugal pumps, their adaptability to large capacities, easy control, and low cost make them preferable for most purposes. Exceptions are those in which a relatively high pressure is required at a small capacity, or in which the viscosity of the fluid is too great for reasonable efficiency. *See* CENTRIFUGAL FORCE.

Centrifugal pumps consist basically of one or more rotating impellers in a stationary casing which guides the fluid to and from the impeller or from one impeller to the next in the case of multistage pumps. Impellers may be single suction or double suction (**Fig. 1**). Additional essential parts of all centrifugal pumps are (1) wearing surfaces or rings, which make a close-clearance running joint between the impeller and the casing to minimize the backflow of fluid from the discharge to the suction; (2) the shaft, which supports and drives the impeller; and (3) the stuffing box or seal, which prevents leakage between shaft and casing.

Characteristics. The rotating impeller imparts pressure and kinetic energy to the fluid pumped. A collection chamber in the casing converts much of the kinetic energy into head or pressure energy before the fluid leaves the pump. A free passage exists at all times through the impeller between the discharge and inlet side of the pump. Rotation of the impeller is required to prevent backflow or draining of fluid from the pump. Because of this, only special forms of centrifugal pumps are self-priming. Most types must be filled with liquid or primed, before they are started.

Every centrifugal pump has its characteristic curve, which is the relation between capacity or rate of flow and pressure or head against which it will pump (**Fig. 2**). At zero pressure difference, maximum capacity is obtained, but without useful work. As resistance to flow external to the pump

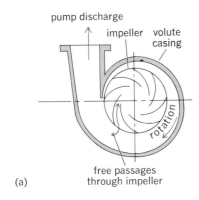

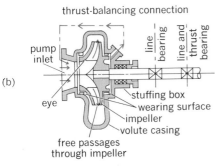

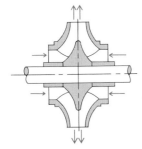

Fig. 1. Views of centrifugal pumps. (*a*) Section across the axis of a single-suction volute pump. (*b*) Section along the axis of a single-suction volute pump. (*c*) Double-suction impeller.

increases, capacity decreases until, at a high pressure, flow ceases entirely. This is called shut-off head and again no useful work is done. Between these extremes, capacity and head vary in a fixed relationship at constant rpm. Input power generally increases from a minimum at shut-off to a maximum at a capacity considerably greater than that at which

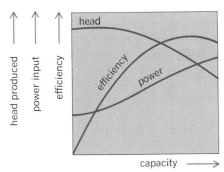

Fig. 2. Some of the typical characteristics of centrifugal pump at constant speed of rotation.

best efficiency is realized. The operating design point is set as close as practical to the point of best efficiency. Operation at higher or lower speed results in a change in the characteristic curves, with capacity varying directly with the speed, and head varying as the square of speed. Since the power required is proportional to the product of the head and capacity, it varies as the cube of the speed. These relations are essentially constant as long as viscosity of the fluid is low enough to be negligible.

Centrifugal impeller (and casing) forms vary with the relation of desired head and capacity at a practical rotating speed. Impellers and pumps are commonly classified as centrifugal, mixed-flow, and axial-flow or propeller (**Fig. 3**). There is a continuous change from the centrifugal impeller to the axial-flow impeller. For maximum practical head at small capacity, the impeller has a large diameter and a narrow waterway with vanes curved only in the plane of rotation. As the desired capacity is increased relative to the head, the diameter of the impeller is reduced, the width of the waterway is increased, and the vanes are given a compound curvature. For higher capacities and less head, the mixed-flow impeller is used. It discharges at an angle approximately midway between radial and axial. For maximum capacity and minimum head, the axial-flow or propeller-type impeller is used.

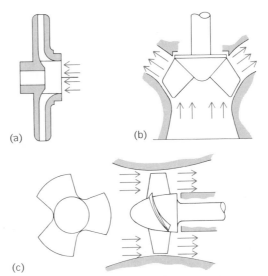

Fig. 3. Common classification of impellers. (*a*) Centrifugal for low speed. (*b*) Mixed-flow for intermediate speed. (*c*) Axial-flow or propeller for high speed.

Capacity. Specific speed is used to identify the place occupied by an impeller in this range of form or type. The narrow, purely radial discharge impeller is at the low end of the specific speed scale while the axial-flow impeller is at the high end. The highest pump efficiency is obtainable at a specific speed of approximately 2000 when the capacity is expressed in gallons per minute (gpm), or 94 when the capacity is expressed in cubic feet per second (cfs). Specific speed $N_s = NQ^{1/2}H^{-3/4}$ where N is

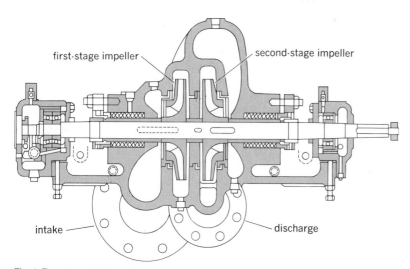

Fig. 4. Two-stage horizontally split casing pump.

rpm, H is head in feet, and Q is capacity in gpm or cfs.

Since the highest efficiency is obtained at a medium specific speed, theoretically an optimum speed of rotation may be calculated for any head and capacity. Such a selection must be adjusted for practical considerations. Because most pumps are driven directly by electric motors, available motor speeds govern operating speeds to a large extent. For small capacities, a lower specific speed is usually necessary. The low limit is set by casting limitations for long vanes and extremely narrow impellers, by the hydraulic losses from flow through the small passages, and by the friction of a large disk rotating in the fluid. At the other end of the scale, for large capacities and low heads, high specific speed

is necessary to keep the driver speed as high as practical. In large pumps the head per stage may be limited by mechanical considerations. At common motor speeds, single-stage pumps are limited to heads of about 600 ft (180 m) per stage. However, at higher speeds heads up to about 2000 ft (600 m) per stage have been attained in multistage boiler feed pumps.

Cavitation limits also play a major part in limiting the operating speed and head per stage for any specified condition. High speeds of rotation require high velocities at the entrance to the impeller. Since the static pressure in a closed stream of fluid drops as velocity is increased, there is a limiting velocity at which the absolute pressure approaches the vapor pressure of the fluid. Beyond this, partial vaporization occurs and the subsequent collapse of these pockets of vapor causes noise, vibration, and ultimately destruction of the surrounding walls. This form of vaporization in a moving stream of fluid is called cavitation. Higher operating speeds require higher suction pressure over the vapor pressure, spoken of as a net positive suction head. *See* CAVITATION.

Multistage pumps. When the required head exceeds that practical for a single-stage pump, several stages are employed. **Figure 4** shows a typical two-stage pump with single-suction impellers mounted back to back to obtain an approximate balance of the hydraulic thrust developed by pressure acting on the greater area of the back side of the impeller. A modern high-pressure multistage centrifugal pump enclosed in a forged steel barrel with all the single-suction impellers facing in the same direction is shown in **Fig. 5**. In this design axial thrust is balanced by a rotating disk mounted

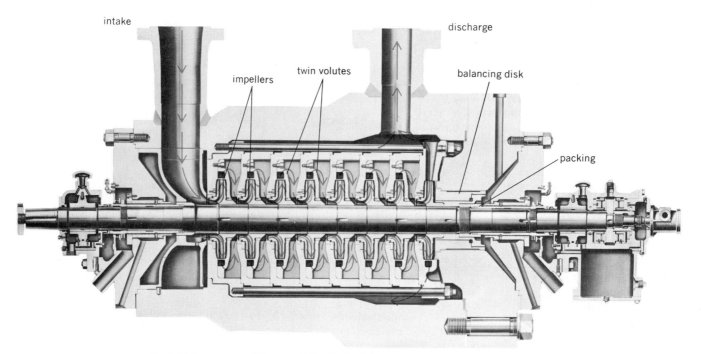

Fig. 5. High-pressure multistage centrifugal boiler-feed pump.

at the high-pressure end of the pump. Leak-off from this balancing device, which is piped back to suction pressure, serves also to reduce, practically to suction pressure, the load on the stuffing box packing or seal at this end of the pump. Pumps of this type are built with 4 to 10 or more stages, depending on the speed, pressure, and capacity desired.

Another type of multistage pump is the vertical turbine or deep-well pump. The details of design and the choice of an impeller of relatively high specific speed are the result of a drastic limitation of the outside diameter required to fit inside drilled-well casings. Pumps of this type are built with as many as 20 or 30 stages for high lifts from relatively small-diameter wells. Pumps with this same arrangement are built with a closed-bottom cylindrical housing with the inlet connected near the top of the housing, for applications at moderate head and limited net positive suction head. The cylindrical housing, or can, is then located in a pit or dry well with suction and discharge connections near ground or floor level. *See* PUMP; PUMPING MACHINERY. Elliott F. Wright

Bibliography. J. W. Dufour and W. Nelson (eds.), *Centrifugal Pump Sourcebook*, 1992; I. J. Karassik and W. C. Krutzch, *Pump Handbook*, 2d ed., 1986; V. S. Lobanoff and R. R. Ross, *Centrifugal Pumps*, 1992; A. J. Stepanoff, *Centrifugal and Axial Flow Pumps: Theory, Design and Application*, 2d ed., 1957, reprint 1993.

Centrifugation

A mechanical method of separating immiscible liquids or solids from liquids by the application of centrifugal force. This force can be very great, and separations which proceed slowly by gravity can be speeded up enormously in centrifugal equipment.

When an object is made to move in a circular path, its direction must constantly be changed. To accomplish this, a force must be applied acting inward toward the center of rotation; otherwise the object would continue on a straight path. An equal and opposite force, the centrifugal force, acts in an outward direction on the rotating elements.

The magnitude of the centrifugal force exerted on an element depends on its angular velocity and its distance from the center of rotation. Centrifugal acceleration is usually compared with the gravitational acceleration at the Earth's surface, and centrifugal force is expressed as a relative force F_R, expressed in multiples of the force of gravity, or G's. Relative centrifugal force is given by Eq. (1), where D is the diameter of the circular path,

$$F_R = 5.59 \times 10^{-4} n^2 D = 0.204 V^2/D \qquad (1)$$

in meters; n is the rotational speed, in rpm; and V is the peripheral speed of an element around the circle of rotation, in meters per second. In a centrifugal machine, the force varies radially from zero at the rotational axis to a maximum where D equals the inside diameter of the bowl or chamber. *See* CENTRIFUGAL FORCE.

Laboratory centrifuges are used for testing, control, and research. Industrial centrifuges find application in such diverse areas as sugar refining, chemical manufacture, dewatering diesel and jet fuel, and municipal waste treatment; they handle large amounts of material, yet require little space.

Stationary equipment: cyclones and nozzles. Centrifugal force is generated inside stationary equipment by introducing a high-velocity fluid stream tangentially into a cylindrical-conical chamber, forming a vortex of considerable intensity. Cyclone separators based on this principle remove liquid drops or solid particles from gases, down to 1 or 2 micrometers in diameter. Smaller units, called liquid cyclones, separate solid particles from liquids. The high velocity required at the inlet of a liquid cyclone is obtained with standard pumps. Units 4 to 12 in. (100 to 300 mm) in diameter make crude separations of large, heavy solid particles from liquids with a pressure drop across the cyclone of about 30–60 lb/in.^{2} (200–400 kilonewtons/m^2). More difficult separations may be done in banks of smaller units called hydroclones, each 0.4 in. (10 mm) in diameter, which can concentrate or remove 2–5-μm particles with a pressure drop of some 100 lb/in.^{2} (700 kN/m^2).

In the separation nozzle process for uranium enrichment, a dilute mixture of gaseous uranium hexafluoride (UF$_6$) and hydrogen is caused to flow at high velocity in a curved path of very small radius of curvature (about 0.004 in. or 0.1 mm). The high centrifugal force tends to concentrate the heavier ^{238}U near the outer wall. The issuing stream is divided in two and sent through a long series of similar nozzles to achieve the desired degree of separation.

Rotating equipment: centrifuges. Much higher centrifugal forces than in stationary equipment are generated in a mechanically driven bowl or basket, usually of metal, turning inside a stationary casing. Rotating a cylinder at high speed induces a considerable tensile stress in the cylinder wall; for a thin-walled cylinder, this self-stress is given by Eq. (2), where S_s is the stress, in N/m^2, and ρ_m is the

$$S_s = 2.74 \times 10^{-3} n^2 D^2 \rho_m \qquad (2)$$

density of the material of the wall, in kg/m^3. This limits the centrifugal force which can be generated in a unit of a given size and material of construction. Dividing Eq. (1) by Eq. (2) and rearranging gives Eq. (3). Thus if S_s is fixed at the maximum

$$F_R = 0.20 S_s/D\rho_m \qquad (3)$$

stress allowable in the material, the maximum relative centrifugal force varies inversely with cylinder diameter. Very high forces, therefore, can be developed only in very small centrifuges. The **table** shows forces generated in various types and sizes

Comparison of bowl diameter and centrifugal force			
Type of centrifuge	Bowl or basket diameter, in. (mm)	Rotational speed, rpm	Centrifugal force, multiples of gravity
Ultracentrifuge	0.2 (6)	230,000	177,000
Laboratory tubular	1.8 (45)	32,000	25,800
Industrial tubular	4 (100)	14,300	11,400
Disk	12 (300)	4,800	3,800
	18 (450)	3,200	2,600
Batch	30 (750)	1,900	1,500
	47 (1200)	1,200	970

of centrifuges at a typical peripheral speed of 246 ft/s (75 m/s).

Centrifuges

There are two major types of centrifuges: sedimenters and filters. Either type may be operated batchwise, with intermittent removal of the separated phase; semibatchwise, with essentially continuous removal of the liquid and intermittent removal of the solids; or continuously, with steady uninterrupted removal of both liquid and solids. Special sedimenting gas centrifuges find application in uranium enrichment.

Sedimenting centrifuges. A sedimenting centrifuge contains a solid-wall cylinder or cone rotating about a horizontal or vertical axis. An annular layer of liquid, of fixed thickness, is held against the wall by centrifugal force; because this force is so large compared with that of gravity, the liquid surface is essentially parallel with the axis of rotation regardless of the orientation of the unit. Heavy phases "sink" outwardly from the center, and less dense phases "rise" inwardly. Heavy solid particles collect on the wall and must be periodically or continuously removed.

The sedimentation velocity of fine particles in a centrifuge is given by the form of Stokes' law shown in Eq. (4), where u is the setting velocity,

$$u = \frac{2\pi^2 n^2 D_p^2 \rho r}{9\mu} \qquad (4)$$

n the rotational speed, D_p the particle diameter, ρ the particle density, r the radial distance from the axis of rotation, and μ the fluid viscosity. The setting velocity of small low-density particles, to which Stokes' law applies, increases directly with the relative centrifugal force. That of large heavy particles, to which Stokes' law does not apply, increases less rapidly with an increase in centrifugal force.

Sedimenting centrifuges are divided into small, high-speed machines, which generate very high centrifugal forces, and large, comparatively slow-speed machines, which handle large amounts of material. Each group is further subdivided into liquid-liquid separators or decanters, clarifiers,

sludge separators, and classifiers. Special machines partially separate gas mixtures for isotope enrichment.

Separators. Bottle centrifuges are batch laboratory centrifuges for research, analysis, or very small-scale production. The mixture to be separated is poured into bottles or test tubes which are placed in a rotor head and spun for a known length of time. An ultracentrifuge is a research unit which generates extremely high centrifugal forces inside a rotor around 0.2 in. (6 mm) in diameter (see table); sedimentation of extremely fine particles or macromolecules may be observed through a microscope and a transparent window in the rotor. *See* ULTRACENTRIFUGE.

Bowls in high-speed centrifuges for industrial use rotate about a vertical axis; liquid feed enters at or near the bottom of the bowl and escapes from the top. Stability considerations dictate one of two preferred bowl shapes: tall narrow cylinders or squat cylinders with a conical top. Tubular centrifuges typify the first design. Industrial models are 4 in. (100 mm) in diameter and 30 in. (750 mm) long and process 1.5 to 10 gal/min (0.3 to 2.5 m³/h) of liquid. They serve as centrifugal decanters and as clarifiers to remove very small amounts of solids from liquids. A maximum of about 11 lb (5 kg) settled solids may accumulate in the bowl before the machine must be stopped and cleaned.

The bowl in a disk centrifuge (**Fig. 1**) is typically 8 to 16 in. (200 to 400 mm) in diameter and contains a large number of closely spaced "disks" which are actually truncated cones stacked one above the other and perforated to form passages for the liquid. The disks shorten the distance that a particle or drop must travel before being separated, compared with the distance in a tubular unit. Despite the somewhat lower centrifugal force, therefore, disk centrifuges are effective separators, especially for emulsion concentration. As shown in Fig. 1, feed enters the top of the machine and flows outward into the bowl near the bottom; separated liquids are removed through outlets at the top, while solids collect in the bowl. Large units can process 660 gal/min (150 m³/h) or more and retain 110 to 130 lb (50 to 60 kg) of settled solids before cleaning becomes necessary.

Clarifiers. In a self-discharging separator, the settled solids are removed in more or less concentrated form through openings in the bowl wall. The bowl in a nozzle-discharge centrifuge is usually conical at the bottom as well as at the top. Where the bowl diameter is a maximum, 2 to 12 nozzles, lined with abrasive-resistant material, allow a slurry to issue continuously from the periphery of the bowl. Part of the slurry may be recycled to the bottom of the bowl to build up the solids concentration. Some nozzle machines are three-way separators, discharging two clarified liquids and a solids suspension. In a valve-discharge centrifuge, the peripheral openings are circumferential slits, covered most of the time by

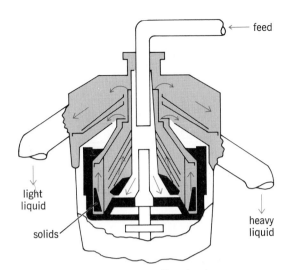

Fig. 1. Cutaway view of disk centrifuge bowl.

a piston. Periodically the piston is lowered by hydraulic or mechanical action, and concentrated solids are forcefully ejected, with some liquid, into the casing.

Sludge separators. In a sludge separator the continuous removal of solids as concentrated sludge requires that settled solids be moved mechanically out of the liquid and allowed to drain while subjected to centrifugal force. This is done in a scroll-conveyor centrifuge (**Fig. 2**), in which a cylindrical bowl with a conical end section rotates about a horizontal axis. Feed enters through a stationary central pipe and sprays outward into a pond or annular layer of liquid inside the bowl. Clarified liquid escapes through overflow ports in the cover plate on the large end of the bowl; the position of these ports fixes the depth of the pond. Solids settle under centrifugal force to the inner wall of the bowl, where a helical or scroll conveyor, turning slightly slower than the bowl, moves the solids out of the pond and up the slanting beach to discharge openings in the small end of the cone. Wash liquid may be sprayed on the solids as they travel up the beach. In some designs, feed enters near the large end of the bowl

and liquid and solids travel in the same direction, with clarified liquid removed by skimmer pipes; this is effective in concentrating fine low-density solid particles encountered in sewage sludge treatment. Industrial sludge separators range in diameter from 16 to 55 in. (400 to 1400 mm), and separate from 1.1 to 2.2 tons/h (1 to 2 metric tons/h) of solids in a small machine to as much as 110 tons/h (100 metric tons/h) in a large one.

Classifiers. Classification is the sorting of solid particles in a fluid stream into two or more fractions according to particle size. Centrifugal classifiers are used when particles are too fine for separations by gravity. Scroll-conveyor centrifuges find application in large-scale wet grinding operations using ball mills, for example, separating acceptably fine particles from the oversize ones which are returned to the mill for regrinding. High-speed tubular centrifuges remove particles of grit from ultrafine cosmetics, dyes, and pigments.

Gas centrifuges. High-speed centrifuges are extensively used for uranium enrichment, partially separating ^{235}U from ^{238}U. They operate on gaseous uranium hexafluoride at moderate temperatures. The centrifugal force tends to compress the gas into a region near the bowl wall, while thermal motion tends to distribute the molecules uniformly throughout the available volume. Since thermal motion has a greater effect on light molecules than on heavy ones, a concentration gradient is established, with a higher concentration of the heavier molecules near the wall. The theoretical separation factor α is given by Eq. (5), where M_A and M_B are

$$\alpha = \exp \frac{(M_A - M_B)V^2}{2RTg_c} \qquad (5)$$

the molecular weights of the heavy and light components, respectively; V is the peripheral velocity; R is the gas constant; T is the absolute temperature; and g_c is the Newton's-law conversion factor. Since α depends on the difference between the molecular weights of the isotopes and not on their ratio,

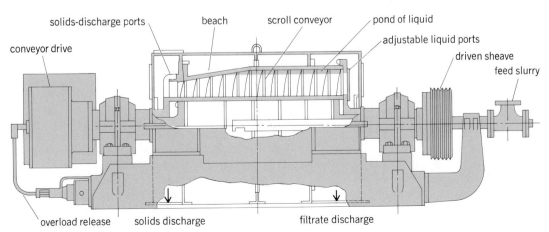

Fig. 2. Cylindrical-conical helical-conveyor centrifuge. (*Bird Machine Co.*)

gas centrifuges have much higher separation factors than do gas diffusion units.

Gas centrifuges operate at very high speeds, for the separative capacity of a given unit depends on the fourth power of the peripheral velocity. In the typical machine shown in **Fig. 3**, a tubular rotor perhaps 8 in. (200 mm) in diameter rotates in an evacuated casing with a peripheral velocity of more than 660 ft/s (200 m/s), about three times that in conventional industrial centrifuges. The centrifugal force at the bowl wall is more than 40,000 G. Feed gas enters the top near the axis of rotation; enriched gas is collected by a gas scoop near the bottom of the bowl, and depleted gas by a scoop near the bottom. Because of the high separation factor, relatively few centrifuges need be connected in series to achieve a substantial change in the concentration of ^{235}U. Productive capacities are low, however, and thousands of machines operating in parallel are needed for practical rates of throughput.

Filtering centrifugals. Centrifuges which separate by filtration are known as centrifugals or centrifugal filters. Solids and liquid are introduced into a rotating basket; after the liquid has been removed through the basket wall, the retained cake of solids is washed, spun dry, and removed. Centrifugals operate batchwise or continuously; various types differ primarily in the length of the cycle times and in the way in which solids are removed from the basket.

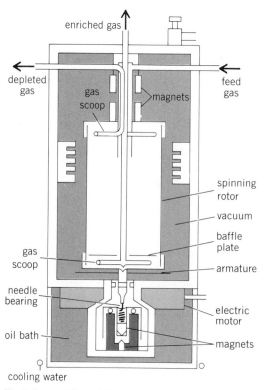

Fig. 3. Gas centrifuge. (*After V. V. Abajian and A. M. Fishman, Supplying enriched uranium, Phys. Today, 26(8):23–29, 1973*)

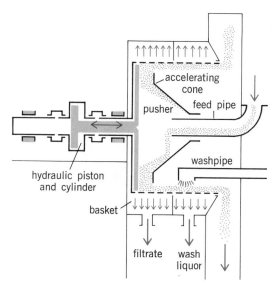

Fig. 4. Pusher-type centrifugal.

In large batch centrifugals, up to 47 in. (1200 mm) in basket diameter, the basket turns about a vertical axis. A solid cake 2–6 in. (50–150 mm) thick is formed, washed, spun (often at a higher speed), and then cut out of the basket, now turning very slowly, with a traveling knife. Discharged solids fall through openings in the basket floor; discharged liquid, or centrate, is removed from the casing. In some machines the cycle steps are fully automated. Free-draining crystals are separated quasicontinuously in short-cycle automatic horizontal-axis machines with baskets 20–40 in. (500–1000 mm) in diameter; solids are cut out every 45–150 s at full basket speed by a heavy-duty knife. Truly continuous filtering units for the large crystals are typified by the pusher centrifugal (**Fig. 4**), in which the solid cake, 1 to 3 in. (25 to 75 mm) thick, is moved over the inner surface of the perforated basket by a reciprocating piston. Each forward piston stroke moves the crystals an inch or so toward the basket lip; on the return stroke, a space is opened on the filtering surface on which more solids can be deposited. When crystals reach the basket lip, they fly outward into the casing. Filtrate and any wash liquid sprayed on the crystals during their travel leave the casing through separate outlets. Multistage pusher centrifugals are used when the solids cannot be pushed the fairly long distances required in the single-stage unit shown in Fig. 4.

A filtering centrifuge operates on the same principle as the spinner in a household washing machine. The basket wall is perforated and lined with a filter medium such as a cloth or a fine screen; liquid passes through the wall, impelled by centrifugal force, leaving behind a cake of solids on the filter medium. The filtration rate increases with the centrifugal force and with the permeability of the solid cake. Some compressible solids do not filter well in a centrifugal because the particles deform under centrifugal force and the permeability of the cake is greatly reduced. The amount of liquid adhering to the solids after they have been spun also depends on the centrifugal force applied; in general, it is substantially less than in the cake from other types of filtration devices. *See* MECHANICAL SEPARATION TECHNIQUES.   Julian C. Smith

Biological Applications

Biologists have long been interested in the effects of high centrifugal forces on cells, developing embryos, and protozoa. These studies have yielded valuable information on the properties of cells, such as surface tension, relative viscosity of the cytoplasm, and the spatial and functional interrelationship of cell organelles when redistributed in intact cells. The last finding led to the discovery that in a variety of invertebrate egg cells any disturbance of the intracellular organization of the cytoplasm will severely affect future development. *See* CELL, PRESSURE-TEMPERATURE EFFECTS IN; DEVELOPMENTAL BIOLOGY.

Another interest, partly in relation to the space program, has been the physiological effects of centrifugal forces on intact organisms, including humans. These forces are identical with the high gravitational forces astronauts must face on leaving and reentering the Earth's atmosphere. Such studies have been useful to determine the maximum forces that a person can tolerate and to develop equipment to offset the drastic effects. *See* AEROSPACE MEDICINE.

Thus the centrifuge has been applied to the whole gamut of biological systems, from humans to cells to subcellular organelles to biological molecules. It is routinely used in hospitals and clinics to collect blood cells, bacteria, and viruses, but its prime importance in biology is to isolate and determine the biological properties and functions of subcellular organelles and large molecules.

Cellular studies. During the first half of the twentieth century those interested in cell biology were generally segregated into two separate disciplines, cell biology and biochemistry. Cell biologists studied sections of tissues that had been subjected to various fixatives and then stained. From these studies evolved the identification of cell structures, but since these organelles had been rendered inactive by fixation, their function could only be guessed. The biochemists viewed living systems as an enzymatic and metabolite "soup." They thoroughly ground up tissues and by primarily chemical procedures isolated enzymes and substrates. Again, however, no attempts were made to correlate the discovered metabolic-enzyme pathways with their location in intact cells. *See* CELL BIOLOGY; CELL METABOLISM; CYTOCHEMISTRY.

The modern technique for the isolation of cell parts was first introduced by R. Bensley and N. L. Hoerr in 1934, when they disrupted guinea pig liver cells and isolated mitochondria. A. Claude soon saw the importance of this technique, and from 1938 to 1946 extended the findings of Bensley and Hoerr by isolating two fractions, a "large granule" fraction, which was mitochondria, and a fraction of submicroscopic granules, which he called microsomes. From these beginnings additional pioneering investigators developed the centrifugal techniques of cell fractionation now commonly used.

Differential centrifugation. A tissue, such as the liver or a population of cells, is broken up in one of several ways. Most common is mechanical disruption, by grinding the tissue in a test tube with a glass or poly(tetrafluoroethylene) pestle or with a high-speed mixer such as a Waring blender. To be certain that the cellular particles retain their structure and function, much care is taken not to destroy them by overvigorous cell disruption, and to place the disrupted cell material, or homogenate, into a sucrose and salt solution that is isotonic and as close as possible to the natural conditions inside the intact cell.

The homogenate is then centrifuged in a medium at various centrifugal forces to separate the cellular organelles from each other. Organelles that differ in density, size, or shape sediment at different rates in a field of centrifugal force. Centrifugation simply magnifies the force of gravitational acceleration, which is normally constant, 392 in./s^2 (980 cm/s^2), and accounts for the weight of objects on Earth. Spinning a particle at high speeds produces a force on it proportional to the mass of the particle, the rotational speed or angular velocity in going in circles, and the distance from the axis or point of rotation to the particle. This is stated in Eq. (6), where G is the gravitational acceleration, ω

$$G = \omega^2 r \qquad (6)$$

is the angular velocity, and r is the distance from the point of rotation to the particle. The angular velocity can be determined by knowing the rotor speed according to Eq. (7). It is thus possible to

$$\omega = \frac{2\pi(\text{rpm})}{60} \qquad (7)$$

calculate the relative centrifugal force G, knowing the revolution per minute (rpm) and the radius r of the centrifuge, using Eq. (8).

$$G = \frac{4\pi^2(\text{rpm})^2 r}{3600} = 1.11 \times 10^{-5}(\text{rpm})^2 r \qquad (8)$$

The rate at which a particle sediments in a centrifugal field is proportional to the centrifugal force, but also is dependent on the density and viscosity of the medium through which it is passing. This relationship is shown by Eq. (9), which states

$$t = \frac{9}{2} \frac{\eta}{\omega^2 r^2 (d_p - d_m)} \cdot 2.3 \log \frac{R_{\max}}{R_{\min}} \qquad (9)$$

that t is the time in which a fairly spherical particle of radius r and density d_p travels from the top of the centrifuge tube, $R_{\min}$, to the bottom of the tube, $R_{\max}$, in a medium having a known viscosity η and density d_m. This makes it possible to determine the time needed to centrifuge to the base of a tube a population of relatively homogenous particles from a larger population of particles of widely varying size and density, such as occurs in a cell homogenate.

This was the basis for the first techniques developed for cell fractionation, and is called differential centrifugation. These procedures have now been standardized. Tissue, such as liver, is homogenized at 32°F (0°C) in a sucrose solution (0.22–45 M) containing both a buffer to stabilize the pH and a salt, usually magnesium chloride. The homogenate is then centrifuged at 600 G for 10 min, also at 32°F (0°C). The sediment, which is forced to the bottom of the centrifuge tube, forms a solid pellet, and the overlying solution, or supernatant, is now removed and placed in another centrifuge tube. Called the nuclear fraction, the sedimented pellet consists mainly of nuclei which are the largest and densest organelles present in cells. The supernatant is centrifuged at a higher speed to attain a higher centrifugal force, 10,000 G, for 15 min. Another group of particles, the mitochondria, now sediment. This process can then be repeated, using higher centrifugal forces, to obtain the lysosome and microsome fractions from each succeeding supernatant medium. Finally, the supernatant, following centrifugation at forces of 100,000 G for one hour or longer, is essentially nonparticulate and is called the soluble fraction, containing enzymes and other small-molecular-weight substances that are not associated with any cell organelles. *See* CELL (BIOLOGY).

Density gradient method. Since there was a great deal of cross-contamination of particles among the various fractions, modifications soon developed to improve the separation of the cell organelles into purer fractions. The chief improvement involved the formation of a density gradient in the medium through which the particles migrate by altering the concentration of the sucrose or the salt. The gradient is so formed that the density is least at the top of the tube and is greatest at the bottom. A tissue homogenate is placed on top of a density gradient, and in the presence of centrifugal force each particle sediments to a specific zone of the gradient with an equivalent density to that of the particle. In this way zones, or bands, of the various cell organelles are formed with a minimum of contamination of other particles of differing size and density. A number of variations of the density gradient centrifugation method have been developed to further refine the quality of separation of particles of similar size and shape but of slightly different density.

Another technique has enabled large volumes of material to undergo separation by a continuous flow system, in which homogenate is continually being added to a centrifugal field while the displaced material, which is essentially nonparticulate supernatant, is being discarded. Large quantities of particulate material may thus be accumulated.

Although biochemists had used centrifuges previously, with the advent of these methods cell biologists began to look at both the chemical nature and the morphology or structures of the isolated particles. In this way function could be correlated with structure and various metabolic processes could be localized in intact cells. It was established that the mitochondria were the centers for oxidative phosphorylation involved in the synthesis of adenosinetriphosphate (ATP). The crude "microsome" fraction was found to consist of membranes and associated particles called ribosomes. Biochemical procedures had shown that nearly all protein synthesis occurred in the microsome fraction. By separating the membranes from the ribosomes by mild detergent treatment, the ribosome fraction retained protein synthetic activity. Several years later, ultracareful homogenization of developing red blood cells (reticulocytes) showed the ribosomes usually were aggregated and held together by a strand of ribonucleic acid (RNA). This has led to the polysome concept, in which the strand of RNA is messenger RNA (mRNA), which contains the genetic information that is obtained from the nucleus to make specific proteins. *See* RIBONUCLEIC ACID (RNA); RIBOSOMES.

A new particle was also discovered by centrifugation procedures, the lysosomes. These particles sediment very close to the mitochondria, but by careful manipulation they were separated. Lysosomes perform many of the digestive functions of the cell and contain many hydrolytic enzymes. *See* LYSOSOME; MITOCHONDRIA.

By these centrifugal procedures, then, it has been possible to isolate cell components, determine their composition and their metabolic activity, and examine the components to discover what they look like in order to find the most comparable structures in intact cells.

Molecular studies. Another valuable avenue of research and discovery opened by density gradient centrifugation techniques has been to find and isolate the large macromolecules that are involved in the various metabolic events of the cell, particularly for the nucleic acids. A complete description is not possible, but key examples may be given. There are slight but definite differences in the density of deoxyribonucleic acid (DNA) of various species isolated and centrifuged in cesium chloride gradients. This centrifugation depends of the base composition of DNA (ratio of adenine and thymine to cytosine and guanine). *See* NUCLEIC ACID.

Isotopic labeling combined with density gradient centrifugation has proved extremely useful to define the nature and role of the various RNAs in protein synthesis. A sedimentation "profile" is illustrated in **Fig. 5**, showing the presence of the two species of RNA found in ribosomes (rRNA-I and rRNA-II) and transfer RNA (tRNA). It is known

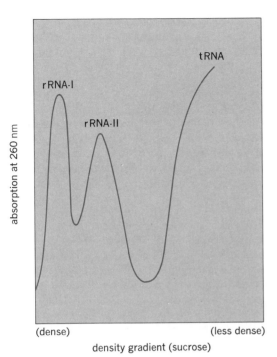

Fig. 5. Sedimentation profile showing ribosomal and transfer ribonucleic acid.

that there is a third type of RNA, messenger mRNA, that is involved with protein synthesis. It is rapidly synthesized and is rather unstable. This synthesis characteristic can be used to advantage by rapidly exposing cells or a tissue to a precursor molecule of RNA labeled with an isotope such as ^{32}P or ^{14}C. After this brief exposure the cells are homogenized and the RNA extracted and centrifuged in a density gradient centrifuge. Fractions are removed drop by drop and analyzed for the presence of RNA by ultraviolet light, which is absorbed at 260 nanometer wavelength, and for radioactivity. **Figure 6** illustrates that most of the radioactivity is localized between the tRNA and rRNA-II peaks, and composes a small portion of the total RNA of the

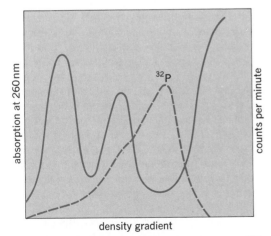

Fig. 6. Localization of radioactivity for RNA labeled with ^{32}P. Sedimentation profile of Fig. 5 is shown.

cell. *See* PROTEIN.

A final distinction in centrifugation methodology may be made. If the contents of the centrifuge are to be analyzed after the centrifuge stops, as shown in Figs. 5 and 6, the procedure is called preparative; if the sample is examined optically during centrifugation, the procedure is called analytical. This last method is particularly important to determine the sedimentation coefficient and the molecular weight of the molecules under investigation. *See* MOLECULAR BIOLOGY.   W. Auclair

Bibliography. D. Green (ed.), *Perry's Chemical Engineer's Handbook*, 6th ed., 1984; W. L. McCabe, J. C. Smith, and P. Harriott, *Unit Operations of Chemical Engineering*, 5th ed., 1993; D. Rickwood (ed.), *Centrifugation*, 2d ed., 1984; D. Rickwood (ed.), *Preparative Centrifugation: A Practical Approach*, 1993; R. W. Rousseau, *Handbook of Separation Process Technology*, 1987.

Centriole

A morphologically complex cellular organelle found at the focus of centrosomes in animal cells and some lower plant cells. Prokaryotes, higher plant cells, and a few animal cells do not have centrioles. Centrioles have a close structural similarity to basal bodies, which organize the axoneme of cilia and flagella. A centriole can act as a basal body during the interphase portion of the cell cycle. Although centrioles and basal bodies are often regarded as equivalent organelles, basal bodies of lower forms are not located in the spindle poles during mitosis and do not seem to have the centriole's ability to organize a spindle pole when the basal bodies are microinjected into dividing cells. *See* CENTROSOME; CILIA AND FLAGELLA.

Structure and composition. Centrioles are typically 300–700 nanometers in length and 250 nm in diameter. Although they can be detected by the light microscope, an electron microscope is required to resolve their substructure. At the electron microscopic level, a centriole consists of a hollow cylinder of nine triplet microtubules in a pinwheel arrangement (see **illus.**). Within each triplet, one microtubule (the A tubule) is a complete microtubule, while the others (the B and C tubules) share a portion of their wall with the adjacent tubule. In some cells these nine triplet microtubules are embedded in a densely straining cylindrical matrix that is spatially distinct from the pericentriolar material of the centrosome. Structures found in the lumen or core of the centriole include linkers between the triplets, granules, fibers, a cartwheel structure at one end of the centriole, and sometimes a small vesicle. Tapered projections, called basal feet, are sometimes observed on the external surface of the centriole. Astral microtubules emanate from the globular tips of the basal feet.

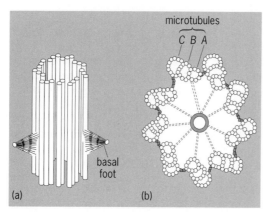

Diagrams of centriole showing (*a*) arrangement of microtubules and (*b*) cross section of proximal end, with nine triplet microtubules (A, B, and C) and central cartwheel structure.

The centriole is a polar organelle, having a proximal and a distal end relative to the cell center. When a centriole acts as a basal body, the ciliary or flagellar axoneme is nucleated from the distal end of the centriole. Daughter centrioles are formed perpendicular to the proximal end of the parent centriole. Within the centriole, the cartwheel structure is located at the proximal end.

The molecular composition of the centriole is poorly understood because it has not been possible to isolate enough centrioles in a sufficiently pure form to conduct biochemical analyses. The microtubule protein, tubulin, is a major constituent of centrioles; however, the identities of the proteins that make up the rest of the centriole are not known. Centrioles probably contain ribonucleic acid (RNA), but it is not known if this RNA is specific to the centriole or only represents general cytoplasmic RNAs that happen to reside there. A centriole-specific role for this RNA, if any, has yet to be clearly demonstrated.

Microtubules. The terms centriole and centrosome are sometimes erroneously used interchangeably; centrioles are not the centrosome itself but rather a part of it. The centrosome of higher animal cells has at its center a pair of centrioles, arranged at right angles to each other and separated by 250 nanometers or less. Spindle microtubules are nucleated by the pericentriolar material, an amorphous cloud of densely staining material surrounding the centriole pair. In some cell types, the older (mother) centriole has basal feet; the globular tips of these basal feet also nucleate some of the spindle microtubules. Centrioles without basal feet do not nucleate spindle microtubules. Gamma tubulin, a molecule involved in the nucleation of microtubules, is found in trace amounts in the pericentriolar material. In some cells the pericentriolar material surrounds primarily the older of the two centrioles; the younger (daughter) centriole acquires pericentriolar material only later in the cell cycle when it separates from its mother and assembles its own daughter centriole.

Distribution and replication. During interphase the centriole pair and associated pericentriolar material lie closely apposed to the nuclear envelope or sometimes lie within a small indentation in the nuclear envelope.

Late in the G1 (first gap) phase of the cell cycle, the two centrioles separate slightly from each other and lose their orthogonal arrangement. When the cell initiates deoxyribonucleic acid (DNA) synthesis, short daughter centrioles (called procentrioles) are assembled at right angles to and separated slightly from the proximal ends of both mature centrioles. It is not known how daughter centrioles are formed in this way. The finding that cells from which centrioles are microsurgically removed cannot reassemble centrioles suggests that daughter centriole formation normally requires a specific organizing activity provided by the mother centriole. The procentrioles later elongate during the S (DNA synthesis) and G2 (second gap) phases of the cell cycle, reaching their mature length during mitosis or the following G1 phase. At a variable time in the G2 phase of the cell cycle, the centrosome as a whole splits, with a mother-daughter pair of centrioles in each daughter centrosome. During mitosis, a pair of centrioles is found at the focus of both spindle poles. *See* CELL CYCLE; MITOSIS.

Functions. The only clearly demonstrated role of the centriole is to organize the axoneme of the primary cilium in cells having this structure, and the flagellar axoneme in sperm cells. Other possible functions for centrioles are a matter of debate. Some authorities assert that when present in the centrosome, centrioles contain activities that serve to organize the centrosome, determine the number of centrosomes in a cell, and control the doubling of the centrosome as a whole before mitosis. Evidence comes from observations that the introduction of extra centrioles into a cell leads to the formation of extra centrosomes. Also, the ability of a centrosome to double between divisions is correlated with the number of centrioles that it contains.

Others believe that centrioles have no role in the formation and doubling of the centrosomes but are associated with the centrosomes only to ensure the equal distribution of basal bodies during cell division. This view is supported by the observation that all higher plant cells, most protozoa, algae, and fungi, and a few animal cells form functional centrosomes without recognizable centrioles. At a minimum, the nine-triplet-microtubule aspect of the centriole is probably not required for centrosome formation or doubling. In principle, the nonmicrotubule components of the centriole might play important roles in centrosome doubling, but this has not yet been proved directly. *See* CELL (BIOLOGY); CELL DIVISION.   Greenfield Sluder

Bibliography. M. Carroll, *Organelles*, 1989; H. Hermann, *Cell Biology*, 1990; J. L. Hiatt et al., *Cell Biology-Histology*, 1993; K. Miller (ed.), *Advances in Cell Biology*, 1989; C. Widnell, *Essentials of Cell Biology*, 1990.

Centripetal force

The inward force required to keep a particle or an object moving in a circular path. It can be shown that a particle moving in a circular path has an acceleration toward the center of the circle along a radius. *See* ACCELERATION.

This radial acceleration, called the centripetal acceleration, is such that, if a particle has a linear or tangential velocity v when moving in a circular path of radius R, the centripetal acceleration is v^2/R. If the particle undergoing the centripetal acceleration has a mass M, then by Newton's second law of motion the centripetal force F_C is in the direction of the acceleration. This is expressed by Eq. (1), where

$$F_C = Mv^2/R = MR\omega^2 \qquad (1)$$

ω is the constant angular velocity and is equal to v/R. From the laws of motion given by Isaac Newton in his treatise *The Principia*, it follows that the natural motion of an object is one with constant speed in a straight line, and that a force is necessary if the object is to depart from this type of motion. Whenever an object moves in a curve, a centripetal force is necessary. In circular motion the tangential speed is constant but is changing direction at the constant rate of ω, so the centripetal force along the radius is the only force involved.

For example, a small heavy object tied by a cord of length R, with the other end of the cord held in the hand, can be whirled in a horizontal circular path. The person holding the cord has to exert an inward pull, the centripetal force, to maintain this circular motion (**Fig. 1**). When turning a corner in a car, the centripetal force necessary for the turn is provided by the frictional force between the road and the wheels. If the road is banked, then a component of the weight of the car can supply the necessary centripetal force. For a given angle of banking and radius of turn it is necessary to maintain a certain speed, if the component of weight is to exactly provide the necessary centripetal force. *See* CENTRIFUGAL FORCE.

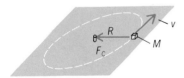

Fig. 1. Diagram of centripetal force in circular motion.

As another example (**Fig. 2**), consider the motion of the Earth or other planet about the Sun. The planets move in elliptical paths about the Sun. This motion is maintained by the gravitational attraction of the planet and Sun. In this case the radial distance between planet and Sun changes during the motion, so that the gravitational force is not in general equal to the centripetal force. If F_G is the gravitational force of attraction between the planet and Sun and R the distance between them, then Eq. (2) holds,

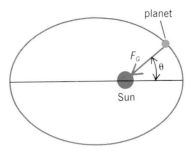

Fig. 2. Planet moving in an ellipse about the Sun.

$$\begin{aligned} F_G &= M(a_R - R\omega^2) \\ &= M[d^2R/dt^2 - R(d\theta/dt)^2] \end{aligned} \qquad (2)$$

where M is the mass of the planet, $a_R = d^2R/dt^2$ is the acceleration along the radial distance R, and $d\theta/dt$ is the instantaneous angular velocity. Since the path of a planet about the Sun is elliptical rather than circular, another force, beside the centripetal one, is required. *See* ORBITAL MOTION.

R. J. Stephenson

Bibliography. F. Bueche, *Principles of Physics*, 5th ed., 1988; D. Halliday, R. Resnick, and K. Krane, *Physics*, 4th ed., 1992; F. Miller, Jr., D. Schroeer, and R. W. Stanley, *College Physics*, 6th ed., 1989; F. W. Sears, M. W. Zemansky, and H. D. Young, *University Physics*, 7th ed., 1987.

Centrode

The path traced by the instantaneous center of a plane figure when it undergoes plane motion. If a plane rigid body is constrained to move in its own plane but is otherwise free to undergo an arbitrary translational and rotational motion, it is found that at any instant there exists a point, called the instantaneous center, about which the body is rotating. The path that this instantaneous center traces out in space as the motion unfolds is called the space centrode. The path that it would trace out in a coordinate system which is rigidly attached to the body is called the body centrode. The motion may therefore be specified, when the two centrodes are given, by allowing one curve to roll without slipping along the other. *See* FOUR-BAR LINKAGE; RIGID-BODY DYNAMICS.

Herbert C. Corben; Bernard Goodman

Centrohelida

An order of the Heliozoia. There is a central cell mass from which thin stiff arms radiate. The arms are supported internally by arrays of microtubules which terminate internally on a central granule, the centroplast, and the nucleus has an eccentric position. In the majority of species, the body is

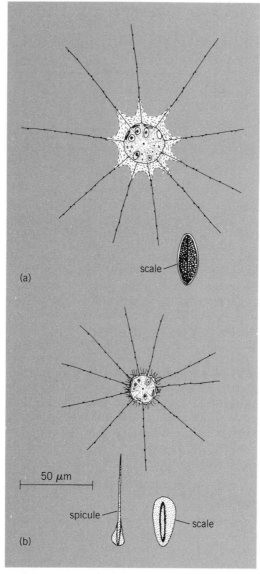

Centrohelida. (a) *Raphidiophrys ambigua*. (b) *Acanthocystis erinaceoides*.

coated with a layer of siliceous spines or spicules and measures from 20 to 50 micrometers. These organisms are found in fresh-water and marine habitats, feeding on other protozoa, which adhere to the arms after colliding with them. In addition to about five genera which certainly are closely related (of which *Acanthocystis* and *Raphidiophrys* are among the most widely represented; see **illus.**), the group contains a variety of other Heliozoia of uncertain affinities. *See* ACTINOPODEA; HELIOZOIA; PROTOZOA; SARCODINA.   David J. Patterson

Bibliography. J. J. Lee, S. H. Hutner, and E. C. Bovee, *Illustrated Guide to the Protozoa*, Society of Protozoologists, 1984.

Centroids (mathematics)

Points positioned identically with the centers of gravity of corresponding homogenous thin plates or thin wires. Centroids are involved in the analysis of certain problems of mechanics, for example, the phenomenon of bending.

Centroids by integration. The centroid of plane area A is point C (**Fig. 1**). Coordinates $\bar{x}$ and $\bar{y}$ of C as referred to the indicated X and Y coordinate axes are given by Eqs. (1). Similarly, the

$$\bar{x} = \frac{\int x \, dA}{\int dA} \qquad \bar{y} = \frac{\int y \, dA}{\int dA} \qquad (1)$$

centroidal coordinates of plane curve L are given by Eqs. (2). In these equations x and y are the

$$\bar{x} = \frac{\int x \, dL}{\int dL} \qquad \bar{y} = \frac{\int y \, dL}{\int dL} \qquad (2)$$

coordinate locations of infinitesimal area element dA and infinitesimal line element dL, respectively.

Centroids by summation. Whether or not the above integrals can be evaluated, approximate values of $\bar{x}$ and $\bar{y}$ may be determined by summation (**Fig. 2**). To this end, area A is divided as shown into n finite elements whose areas $\Delta A_1, \ldots, \Delta A_n$ contain center points $P_1, \ldots, P_n$. Coordinates $\bar{x}, \bar{y}$ of the centroid of area A are then approximately given by Eqs. (3).

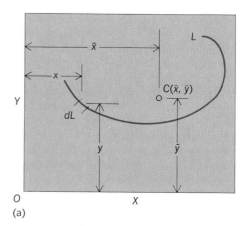

(a)

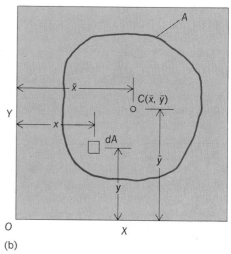

(b)

Fig. 1. Notation of integral equations for centroids. (a) centroid of line. (b) Centroid of area.

$$\bar{x} = \frac{x_1 \Delta A_1 + \cdots + x_n \Delta A_n}{\Delta A_1 + \cdots + \Delta A_n}$$
$$\bar{y} = \frac{y_1 \Delta A_1 + \cdots + y_n \Delta A_n}{\Delta A_1 + \cdots + \Delta A_n} \qquad (3)$$

In analogous fashion, equations for the centroid coordinates of a planar line L are, in summation, given as Eqs. (4). Accuracy of the method increases

$$\bar{x} = \frac{\sum_{i=1}^{n} x_i \Delta L_i}{\sum_{i=1}^{n} \Delta L_i} \qquad \bar{y} = \frac{\sum_{i=1}^{n} y_i \Delta L_i}{\sum_{i=1}^{n} \Delta L_i} \qquad (4)$$

as the number of elements increases.

Principle of symmetry. The centroid of a geometrical figure (line, area, or volume) is at a point on a line or in a plane of symmetry of the figure.

A plane figure is symmetrical about a straight line if the figure may be decomposed into pairs of equal elements so that each pair is in reflected position about a point on the line. If every such pair is reflected in the same point, it is the point of symmetry of the figure.

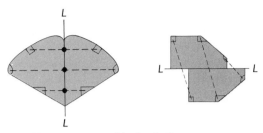

Fig. 3. Plane areas symmetric about a line.

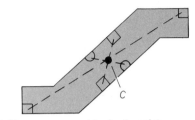

Fig. 4. Plane area symmetric about a point.

Lines LL are lines of symmetry (and contain the centroids) of both the perimeter and area of the outlined shapes (**Fig. 3**). Point C is the point of symmetry (and the centroid) of the figure (**Fig. 4**).

Surface and volume of revolution. By the following theorems stated by Pappus of Alexandria (Greek mathematician, third century) a knowledge of the centroids of plane curves and plane areas may be employed to determine, respectively, surface areas of revolution and volumes of revolution.

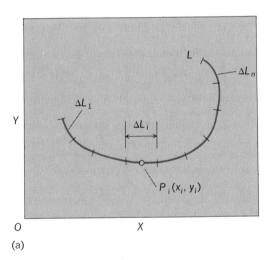

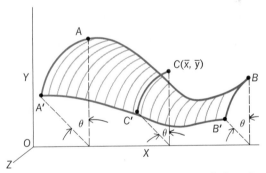

Fig. 5. Use of the centroid of a line to find area of a face of revolution, according to Pappus' theorem.

Pappus' theorem of surface area is that the area of a surface generated by rotating a plane curve about a nonintersecting line in its plane is the product of the length of the curve and the arc length traveled by its centroid. Area S of the surface (indicated by shaded lines in **Fig. 5**) generated by rotating plane curve AB of length L an amount θ radians about the X axis from position AB in OXY to position $A'B'$ is $S = \bar{y}\theta L$, where $\bar{y}$ is the centroidal coordinate of curve AB referred to the OXY coordinate plane, and $\bar{y}\theta = CC'$ is the arc length traveled by its centroid.

Pappus' theorem of volume is that the volume of a solid generated by rotating a plane area about a nonintersecting line in its plane is the product of the area and the arc length traveled by its centroid. *See*

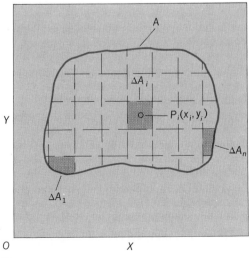

Fig. 2. Determination of centroids by summation. (a) Centroid of line. (b) Centroid of area.

CENTER OF GRAVITY; MOMENT OF INERTIA; SURFACE AND SOLID OF REVOLUTION. Nelson S. Fisk

Centrosome

An organelle located in the cytoplasm of all animal cells and many plants, fungi, and protozoa, that controls the polymerization, position, and polar orientation of many of the cell's microtubules throughout the cell cycle. There is usually one centrosome per cell, located near the cell's center; it doubles during interphase, so there are two when the cell divides. At the onset of mitosis, each centrosome increases the number of microtubules it initiates. These mitotic microtubules are more labile and generally shorter than their interphase counterparts, and as they rapidly grow and shrink they probe the space around the centrosome that initiated them. When the nuclear envelope disperses, the microtubules extend from the centrosome into the former nucleoplasm where the chromosomes have already condensed. Some of these microtubules attach to the chromosomes, while others interact with microtubules produced by the sister centrosome, forming a mitotic spindle that organizes and segregates the chromosomes. During anaphase, sister centrosomes are forced apart as the spindle elongates, allowing each daughter cell to receive one centrosome to organize its microtubules in the next cell generation. *See* CELL CYCLE; CELL MOTILITY.

Morphology and organization. There is no simple morphological description of a centrosome because its shape differs widely between organisms. The centrosomes of animal cells usually contain a pair of perpendicular centrioles (**Fig. 1**), including a parent

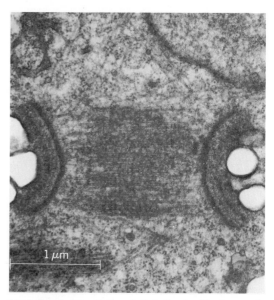

Fig. 2. Developing mitotic spindle in the alga *Stephanopyxis turris*. The microtubules are asymmetrically distributed around each centrosome (spindle pole). (*Courtesy of Kent McDonald*)

centriole formed in an earlier cell generation and a daughter centriole formed during the most recent interphase. Centrioles can serve as basal bodies for the initiation of a cilium or flagellum in the cells that make them. They appear to be essential for the formation of these motile appendages, so centriole inheritance by both daughters at cell division is analogous to the transmission of a gene. *See* CILIA AND FLAGELLA.

The organization of a centrosome is partly dependent on centrioles when they are present. The microtubule initiation that defines the centrosome is accomplished by a matrix that surrounds and is attached to the parent centriole; this matrix is often called pericentriolar material. In many cases, the pericentriolar material forms an almost spherical halo around the parent centriole, and the array of microtubules that forms is radially symmetric. In other cases, the pericentriolar material is highly structured and includes cone-shaped projections from the parent centriole (basal feet) or cross-striated fibers that extend from one end of the centriole (striated rootlets). Many of these appendages can initiate microtubules and should be regarded as a part of the centrosome. *See* CENTRIOLE; CYTOSKELETON.

In many lower eukaryotes there are no centrioles, but centrosomes still serve as both the principal organizer of interphase microtubules and as poles for the mitotic spindle (**Fig. 2**). In these centrosomes, the microtubule-initiating material is usually asymmetrically disposed, leading to the initiation of microtubule arrays without radial symmetry. Cells of higher plants lack visible centrosomes, yet they contain microtubules in both interphase and mitosis. During interphase, microtubule initiation is accomplished by cytoplasmic specializations that lie just beneath the plasma membrane at the

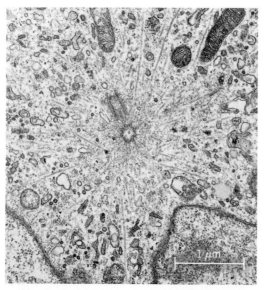

Fig. 1. Centrosome of a mammalian cell. Many microtubules radiate from the cloud of pericentriolar material which surrounds one of the two centrioles. (*Courtesy of Kent McDonald*)

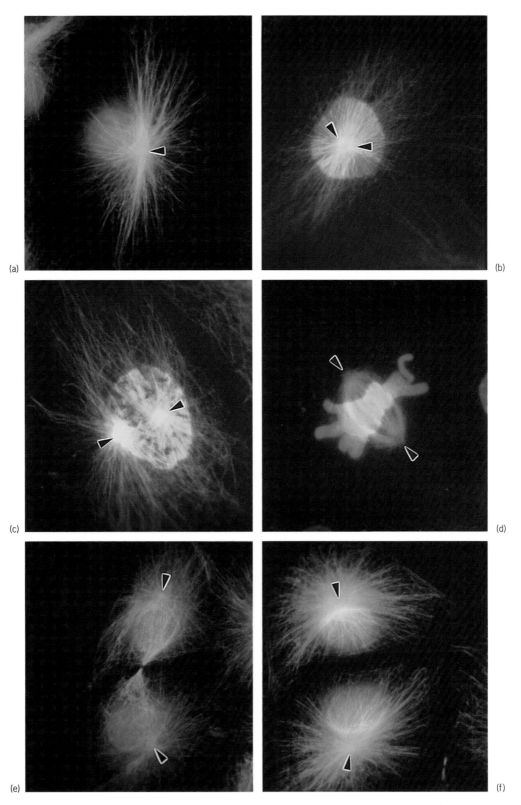

Microtubules (yellow-green) and DNA (red) stained in a cultured mammalian cell and visualized by fluorescence microscopy. The cell-cycle-dependent changes in microtubule morphology and in the position of the centrosome(s) that initiates them (arrowheads) are evident. (a) Interphase. (b) Late interphase with two centrosomes still acting as one. (c) Prophase with centrosomes separate and chromosomes condensing. (d) Metaphase with one centrosome at each spindle pole. (e) Telophase with centrosomes becoming active beside each of the two daughter nuclei whose DNA is largely decondensed, even though the cells are still connected with a microtubule-containing bridge. (f) A pair of interphase cells with microtubule arrays fully reestablished by their centrosomes. (*Courtesy of Mark Ladinsky*)

corners and edges of the cells. During mitosis, microtubules form from two juxtanuclear regions that function similarly to centrosomes but lack a structurally defined microtubule organizing center. The cells of plants that form flagellated sperm also lack organized centrosomes, except in the sperm mother cells. The latter cells contain a more structured organelle associated with the spindle microtubules. The daughters of these cells produce even more structured centrosomes that eventually form many centrioles, each of which serves as a basal body for the formation of a sperm flagellum.

Chemistry. Centrosomes have been isolated from several lower eukaryotes, from embryos of *Drosophila*, and from mammalian cells. Biochemical descriptions of these fractions have now identified numerous centrosome components, but most of these components are unique to the cells from which they were isolated. Legitimate generalizations about the functions of centrosome components are still rare. One essentially universal centrosome component is γ-tubulin, a trace isoform of tubulin that is almost entirely confined to the centrosome. This protein may play a key role in initiating the polymerization of α- and β-tubulin. Mutations of or neutralizing antibodies to γ-tubulin and some other centrosome components prevent microtubule initiation or block cell cycle progression, implicating them in centrosome function. There are many candidates for proteins that might help to organize the centrosome and hold γ-tubulin in place, because several antigens have been localized to the pericentriolar material by using either antibodies raised against centrosome components or sera from humans with autoimmune disorders. *See* ANTIBODY; ANTIGEN.

Centrosome action is regulated as a function of time in the cell cycle. The increase in microtubule number that occurs prior to mitosis is correlated with a significant increase in the extent of phosphorylation of several centrosomal proteins. The protein kinase p34^{cdc2}, which helps to regulate the cell cycle, is concentrated at the centrosome, together with cyclin-B, a positive regulator of this kinase. Indirect evidence suggests that the changes in centrosome phosphorylation do not result simply from p34^{cdc2}, but from other kinases, some of which are regulated by p34^{cdc2}. Moreover, one of the regulatory subunits of cyclic adenosinemonophosphate (cAMP)–dependent protein kinase is bound to a high-molecular-weight centrosome component, suggesting that additional kinases may also contribute to the regulation of centrosome activity. Phosphatases too have been localized to the centrosome.

Structural regulation. Biological reasons for centrosome regulation can be found not only in the importance of microtubules for interphase cell shape and for mitosis but also in the ways that centrosome behavior is modified in differentiative divisions during the development of metazoa. Developmental distinctions between daughter cells are often made at cell divisions that produce daughters of different size. Such divisions result from the asymmetric position of the cleavage furrow, which correlates with asymmetry in the mitotic asters, which in turn correlates with different activities at the two mitotic centrosomes. For example, when blastomeres cleave asymmetrically, the spindle's asters are of different size and shape. When oocytes go through meiosis and throw off polar bodies, one centrosome is usually attached to the cell cortex, while the other is not. *See* CELL (BIOLOGY); MITOSIS.　J. Richard McIntosh

Bibliography. D. M. Glover and J. W. Raff, The centrosome, *Sci. Amer.*, 268:62–68, 1993; V. I. Kalnins (ed.), *The Centrosome*, 1992.

Cephalaspidomorpha

The subclass of Agnatha that includes the jawless vertebrates with a single median nostril, as opposed to the subclass Pteraspidomorpha, in which there are paired nostrils. The Cephalaspidomorpha includes the orders Osteostraci, Galeaspida, Petromyzontida, and Anaspida. *See* AGNATHA; ANASPIDA; CYCLOSTOMATA (CHORDATA); OSTEOSTRACI; PETROMYZONTIDA; PTERASPIDOMORPHA.

Robert H. Denison

Cephalobaenida

One of two orders in the class Pentastomida of the phylum Arthropoda. This order includes primitive pentastomids with six-legged larvae. The hooks are simple, lacking a fulcrum, and disposed in trapeziform pattern, with the anterior pair internal to the posterior pair. The mouth is anterior to the hooks. In both sexes the genital pores are located anteriorly on the abdomen. There is no cirrus sac; the cirrus is short and united with the gubernaculum. In the female the uterus is straight or saccate.

There are two families, Raillietiellidae and Reighardiidae. The Raillietiellidae contains two genera: *Raillietiella*, with 19 species arranged in five groups; and *Cephalobaena*, with a single species. *Cephalobaena* has equal hooks at the ends of retractile, fingerlike appendages, the parapodia. The posterior end of the body is bifid. In *Raillietiella* the body is elongate with rounded ends, and there are lobes at the bases of the hooks. The anterior pair of hooks is the smaller. These animals are parasitic: adult stages occur in the lungs of lizards and snakes, and larval stages are encysted in reptiles, toads, and possibly insects. The life cycle is not well known and may be direct. The family Reighardiidae contains the single genus *Reighardia*, with one species, which infests the air passages of gulls and terns. The posterior end of this species is rounded, without lobes. The cuticula is covered with minute spines, and the hooks are small and equal. Proboscis and parapodia are lacking. *See* PENTASTOMIDA.　Horace W. Stunkard

Cephalocarida

A group of minute marine crustaceans, discovered in 1954, of great interest to students of arthropod evolution because its members have been postulated to possess many primitive characters and to show relationships not only to various other groups of Crustacea but perhaps also to the trilobites. Nine species are recognized, placed in four genera. They have been found in flocculent surface deposits of mud or silty sand, from the intertidal zone down to depths of 5000 ft (1500 m), on the shores of all continents except Europe. Population densities up to an average of 16 individuals/ft^2

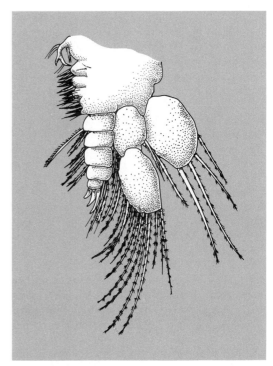

Fig. 2. *Lightiella* **fourth thoracopod. (***After P. A. McLaughlin, A new species of Lightiella (Crustacea: Cephalocarida) from the west coast of Florida, Bull. Mar. Sci., 26:593–599, 1976)*

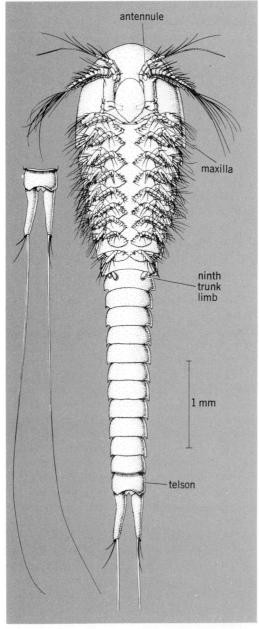

Fig. 1. **Ventral view of** *Hutchinsoniella macracantha*. **(***After H. L. Sanders, The Cephalocarida: Functional morphology: Larval development, comparative external anatomy, Mem. Conn. Acad. Arts Sci., 15:1–80, 1963)*

(177/m^2) have been recorded.

The best-known species is *Hutchinsoniella macracantha*, from the east coast of North and South America, about 0.12–0.16 in. (3–4 mm) long, with a shovel-shaped head and a slender, very flexible body which is not covered by a carapace (**Fig. 1**). Other species are similar. Among the features that appear to be primitive, most notable is the pronounced serial homology seen in the trunk limbs, the trunk musculature, the ventral nerve cord, and the heart. Of the nine pairs of trunk limbs, all but the last two are alike; all are flexible but stiffened by internal turgor; each has a flattened basal protopod bearing several medial endites, a distal leglike endopod, and a distal paddle-shaped exopod; and an epipodite (or pseudepipodite) projects from the base of the exopod (**Fig. 2**). In the ventral nerve cord there is a partial coalescence of the ganglia in the head, but in the trunk a separate pair of ganglia is present in each somite. The heart extends through the limb-bearing trunk somites, in each of which it has one pair of ostia.

Other features in the anatomy of *Hutchinsoniella* that seem likely to be primitive are the uniramous, multisegmented antennules, the biramous antennae with both rami multisegmented, the large, flattened pleura on all the limb-bearing somites, and the telson freely articulated with the trunk and bearing a caudal furca. In the larval development, there is a primitive "nauplius" stage (**Fig. 3**), followed by stages showing an unusually regular addition of new somites and limbs. A relatively slight metamorphosis occurs at the thirteenth molt, when

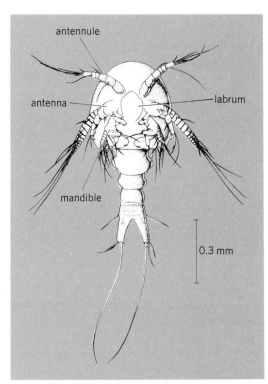

Fig. 3. Stage 1 nauplius larva of *Hutchinsoniella*. (*After H. L. Sanders, The Cephalocarida: Functional morphology, larval development, comparative external anatomy, Mem. Conn. Acad. Arts Sci., 15:1–80, 1963*)

the antennae, mandibles, and maxillules suddenly acquire their adult form.

Hutchinsoniella is a nonselective deposit feeder, subsisting on the organic matter present in its habitat. Cephalocarids are nonswimming, bottom-creeping, nonselective deposit feeders. Distal claws on the endopods of the thoracopods scratch up particles that are passed into the median ventral food groove and moved forward to the mouth by metachronal beating of the thoracopods. *See* FEEDING MECHANISMS (INVERTEBRATE).

Cephalocarids are hermaphroditic, with eggs and sperm that seem to ripen at the same time. The sperm are nonmotile but less simplified than in Branchiopoda. Whether fertilization is by sperm from the same organism or whether cross-fertilization occurs is not yet known. Unusual characteristics are the location of the ovaries beside the maxillary glands in the head and the presence of a pair of common genital ducts, opening on the sixth trunk limbs. The large, yolky eggs become attached, after laying, to the rudimentary ninth trunk limbs, both limbs (or sometimes only one limb) bearing a single egg. There appear to be only three such broods in a season.

The discovery of this presumably primitive class gave rise to speculation that cephalocarids stood close to the ancestral stem of the Crustacea. However, with the more recent discovery of another, and perhaps even more primitive, class, the Remipedia, this hypothesis has been challenged. Some characters of the Cephalocarida are unquestionably advanced. There are no limbs on the last 11 trunk somites. The heart does not extend through these limbless somites. The mandibles of the adult have lost all parts distal to the coxa, and the adult maxillules are also somewhat reduced. The eighth trunk limbs are reduced or absent, and the ninth trunk limbs are greatly reduced. The reproductive system seems to be unique and unlike those of other Crustacea.

There is dispute as to the primitive or specialized nature of certain other characters, such as the lack of a carapace covering the limb-bearing part of the trunk, the attachment of the epipodites to the exopods rather than to the protopods, and the very even width of the long, flexible trunk. The dorsal covering of the head, with its ventrolateral pleural folds, has been variously regarded as a primitive cephalic shield, an incipient carapace, or a carapace that is much reduced from some ancestral condition. These aspects of cephalocarid morphology have caused some carcinologists to suggest that these animals simply are highly specialized progenetic paedomorphs. *See* CRUSTACEA.   John H. Lochhead; Patsy McLaughlin

Bibliography. A. Y. Hessler, R. R. Hessler, and H. L. Sanders, Reproductive system of *Hutchinsoniella macracantha, Science*, 168:1464, 1970 ; R. R. Hessler, Cephalocarida, in R. C. Moore (ed.), *Treatise on Invertebrate Paleontology*, pt. R, Arthropoda 4, vol. 1, pp. R120–R128, 1969 ; S. P. Parker (ed.), *Synopsis and Classification of Living Organisms*, 2 vols., 1982; F. R. Schram (ed.), *Crustacean Issues*, vol. 1: *Crustacean Phylogeny*, 1983.

Cephalochordata

A subphylum of the phylum Chordata comprising the lancelets, including *Branchiostoma* (amphioxus). They are also known as the Leptocardii. Lancelets are small fishlike animals, not exceeding 3.2 in. (80 mm) in length. They burrow in sand on the ocean bed or in estuaries in tropical and temperate regions throughout the world. Only two genera are recognized, *Branchiostoma* with 23 species and *Asymmetron* with 6 species.

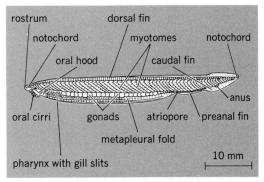

European lancelet (*Branchiostoma lanceolatum*). (*After J. E. Webb, Proc. Zool. Soc. London, 127:131, 1956*)

Morphology. The structure of the lancelet is based on the same fundamental plan as all other chordates, but there is neither head nor paired fins (see **illus.**). The skeletal rod of the back, or notochord, extends the entire length of the body. The animal is thus pointed at both ends, a feature to which the name amphioxus refers, and lanceolate in form, hence the name lancelet. The mouth lies at the base of an oral hood fringed with sensory projections or cirri and opens into a capacious pharynx occupying over half the length of the body. The body wall in the pharyngeal region is perforated on each side by a large number of elongated gill slits. This delicate branchial basket is protected by two folds of tissues, the metapleural folds, which grow down on either side of the body and, joining midventrally, form a sac into which the gill slits open. The cavity of this sac is called the atrium and opens to the exterior through a posterior atriopore. The circulatory system resembles that of a fish, but there is no heart and the blood is colorless. The excretory system is quite unlike that of higher chordates and consists of nephridia situated above the pharynx with ciliated cells similar to those of the Platyhelminthes and the annelid worms. Lancelets are either male or female. The gonads are segmentally arranged pouches arising from the metapleural folds and discharging into the atrium.

Nutrition. Feeding in lancelets is by a ciliary or filter-feeding mechanism. Water is taken in through the mouth, passed through the gill slits into the atrium, and thence out through the atriopore. The water current is maintained by the beating of cilia on the gill bars. Microorganisms and organic debris on which the animal feeds are strained off by the gill bars onto a mucous string, the endostyle, and transported by cilia back to the intestine for digestion.

Life history. The adults burrow in rather coarse sand or shell gravel and usually lie with the mouth open at the surface of the sand. They select by trial and error sands of high permeability with rounded grains coated with microorganisms and free from organic decay. The selection of the optimum sand deposit available results in the congregation of large numbers of lancelets in small areas for spawning. The egg develops into a larvae not unlike the adult except that it is asymmetrical with a long elliptical mouth on the left side of the body and a single series of gills on the right. At first the larva is bottom-living, but later becomes planktonic. Metamorphosis to the symmetrical adult form takes place after about 11–12 weeks of life. The young adult sinks to the bottom and swims actively until a suitable sand in which it can burrow and remain undisturbed is found. Some species complete the life cycle in a year and death evidently occurs after spawning, but others may live 3 or 4 years and spawn annually. In some species metamorphosis occurs late and comparatively large larvae with 20–30 gills are formed. At one time specimens of this type were placed in a separate genus, *Amphioxides*, but these are now generally regarded as larvae of either *Branchiostoma* or *Asymmetron*.

Importance. The importance of lancelets lies chiefly in their being one of the most primitive chordates. However, lancelets are eaten by the Chinese and there are lancelet fisheries at Amoy. Lancelets are also being used as indicator organisms to assist in tracing the pattern of ocean currents on which their distribution appears to depend. *See* CHORDATA..   J. E. Webb

Bibliography. S. P. Parker (ed.), *Synopsis and Classification of Living Organisms*, 2 vols., 1982; J. E. Webb and M. B. Hill, The ecology of Lagos Lagoon, pts. 3 and 4, *Phil. Trans. Roy. Soc. London B*, 241(683):334–391, 1958; C. K. Weichert, *Anatomy of the Chordates*, 4th ed., 1970; J. Z. Young, *The Life of Vertebrates*, 3d ed., 1981.

Cephalopoda

The most highly evolved class of the phylum Mollusca. It consists of squids, cuttlefishes, octopuses, and the chambered nautiluses. The earliest known cephalopods are small, shelled fossils from the Upper Cambrian rocks of northeast China that are 500 million years old. Cephalopods always have been marine, never fresh-water or land animals. Most fossil cephalopods, among them the subclasses Nautiloidea and Ammonoidea, had external shells and generally were shallow-living, slow-moving animals. Of the thousands of species of such shelled cephalopods that evolved, all are extinct except for four species of the only surviving genus, *Nautilus*. All other recent cephalopods belong to four orders of the subclass Coleoidea, which also contains five extinct orders (see **illus.**).

General Characteristics

Living cephalopods are bilaterally symmetrical mollusks with a conspicuously developed head that has a crown of 8–10 appendages (8 arms and 2 tentacles) around the mouth. These appendages are lined with one to several rows of suckers or hooks. *Nautilus* is exceptional in having many simple arms. The mouth contains a pair of hard chitinous jaws that resemble a parrot's beak and a tonguelike, toothed radula (a uniquely molluscan organ). Eyes are lateral on the head; they are large and well developed. The "cranium" contains the highly developed brain, the center of the extensive, proliferated nervous system. The shell of ancestral cephalopods has become, in living forms, internal, highly modified, reduced, or absent; and is contained in the sac- or tubelike, soft muscular body, the mantle. (Only *Nautilus* has an external shell.) A pair of fins may occur on the mantle as an aid to locomotion, but primary movement is achieved through jet propulsion in which water is drawn into the mantle cavity and then forcibly expelled through the nozzlelike funnel. Fewer than

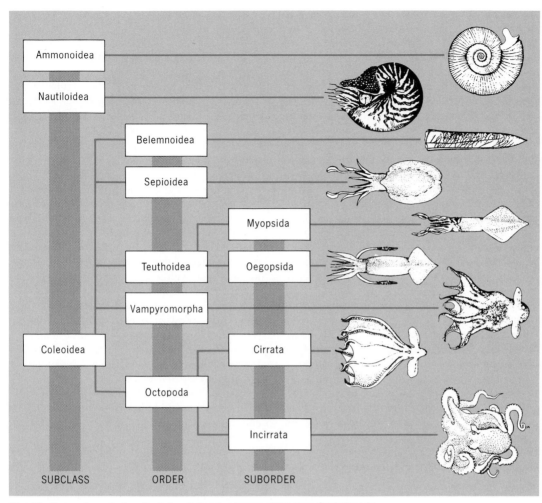

Classification and morphology (body form) of major groups of the class Cephalopoda.

1000 species of living cephalopods inhabit all oceans and seas from intertidal pools to depths of over 16,000 ft (5000 m) in the deep sea.

Classification. The classification given here concentrates on the living groups and lists only the major fossil groups; see separate articles on each subclass and order.

> Class Cephalopoda
> Subclass: Nautiloidea
> Ammonoidea
> Coleoidea
> Order: Belemnoidea
> Sepioidea
> Teuthoidea
> Suborder: Myopsida
> Oegopsida
> Order: Vampyromorpha
> Octopoda
> Suborder: Cirrata
> Incirrata

Habitat. Species of cephalopods inhabit most marine habitats. Chambered nautiluses occur in tropical and subtropical waters of the Indo-West Pacific, where they live in association with reefs

from near-surface to 1600 ft (500 m) deep. The myopsid squid *Lolliguncula brevis* inhabits shallow coastal waters and estuarine bays, where it tolerates salinities of 8.5 parts per thousand; normal ocean salinity is 35 parts per thousand. Some octopuses (for example, *Octopus bimaculatus*) live in water so shallow that only their burrows retain water in the mud flats exposed at low tide. Cephalopods inhabit tide pools, rocky patches, sandy bottoms, coral reefs, grass beds, mangrove swamps, coastal waters, and the open ocean from the surface through the water column to depths on the abyssal bottom at over 16,000 ft (5000 m). Some species are cryptic, spending their lives secluded in holes and crannies; others live in middepths of the open ocean where they undergo vertical migrations from the safety of dimly lit daytime depths of 1600–3200 ft (500–1000 m) to the upper 640 ft (200 m) at night to feed. The only species in the order Vampyromorpha is the bathypelagic (deep midwaters, not associated with bottom) *Vampyroteuthis infernalis*, and it occurs worldwide in tropical and temperate waters at depths of 1600–3800 ft (500–1200 m). Young usually are found deeper than 2900 ft (900 m), then with growth move to shallower depths. Cirrate octopods are worldwide, deep-sea forms with species that live in pelagic (midwater), epibenthic (just above the bottom), or benthic (on the bottom) habitats to depths in excess of 16,000 ft (5000 m).

Brain and nervous system. Cephalopods are, above all, characterized by their capacity to learn, great maneuverability, ability to change color and texture and to produce light, and the extraordinary development of the eye and the central nervous system. The ratio of brain to body weight exceeds that of most fishes and reptiles. Diffuse ganglionated nerve cords found in the arms of octopuses and mantles of squids further indicate the advanced state of the nervous system of cephalopods that approaches that of some birds and mammals. Short- and long-term changes in learned behavior demonstrate the capacity for memory. The lifestyle of living cephalopods, as direct competitors with marine fishes since fishes invaded the sea from ancient fresh waters, has driven the evolution of these unique, advanced animals. *See* NERVOUS SYSTEM (INVERTEBRATE).

Food, feeding, and digestion. Cephalopods are high-level, active predators that feed on a variety of invertebrates, fishes, and even other cephalopods. The relatively sluggish nautiluses feed primarily on slow-moving prey such as reed shrimps, and even are scavengers of the cast-off shells of molted spiny lobsters. Cuttlefishes prey on shrimps, crabs, and small fishes, while squids eat fishes, pelagic crustaceans, and other cephalopods. Benthic octopuses prey mostly on clams, snails, and crabs.

Prey capture in sepioids and teuthoids is accomplished by the two tentacles that shoot out and catch the prey with the expanded sucker-bearing tips, called clubs. The prey is drawn into the crown of arms and held to the mouth by suckers. Some oceanic squids have hooks like cats' claws that ensure capture of prey. Octopuses search for food in crevices and holes with their highly chemotactile arm tips, then secure the discovered prey with several arms covered with scores or hundreds of suckers. Octopuses also may stalk crabs and suddenly pounce on them, enveloping them in the broad web between their arms.

Salivary glands secrete toxins that subdue the prey and, in octopuses, begin digestion. The digestive tract consists of hard, beaklike jaws that bit off chunks of prey that are then rammed into the esophagus with the horny, toothed radula. Because the esophagus passes through the brain, the bites cannot be too big. Digestion and absorption take place in the stomach and cecum with the aid of secretions from the digestive gland ("liver") and pancreas. Waste material passes through the intestine and is excreted from the anus into the mantle cavity, then flushed out through the funnel when water is expelled from the cavity during respiratory or jetting contractions of the mantle (body).

Size, age, and growth. Cephalopods convert their food to tissue very rapidly. Many species of small cuttlefishes, bobtail squids, and octopuses reach reproductive maturity within 8–10 months of hatching, while larger forms hatch in the summer, overwinter, and spawn at 12–14 months of age. Therefore, life cycles of most cephalopods are completed in less than a year. The life span of giant species of octopuses and squids is not known but is estimated to be 5 years or less. The smallest adult cephalopods are the Indian Ocean sepioid *Idiosepius pygamaea* at 0.2–0.8 in. (6–22 mm) body length, the Caribbean myopsid *Pickfordiateuthis pulchella* at 0.8 in. (22 mm), and the octopuses *Octopus micropyrsus* from California at 0.4–1.4 in. (10–35 mm) and *O. nanus* from the Red Sea at 0.5–1 in. (12–26 mm). The true giant squids of the family Architeuthidae are the largest invertebrates in the world, with a total length (tip of tail to tip of outstretched tentacles) of nearly 64 ft (20 m), a body length of 13–16 ft (4–5 m), and a weight of up to 1 ton. Most *Architeuthis* specimens are 32–38 ft (10–12 m) total length, 6–10 ft (2–3 m) body length, and about 450–660 lb (200–300 kg). The largest octopus, *O. dofleini*, can reach 32 ft (10 m) across the outstretched arms.

Defense. To protect themselves from predators cephalopods would rather hide than fight. To this end they have become masters of camouflage and escape. Benthic forms especially (for example, *Sepia* and *Octopus*) have evolved an intricate, complex system of rapid changes in color and patterns via thousands of individually innervated chromatophores (pigment cells) that allow precise matching to the color and pattern of the background. In addition, they regulate the texture of their skins by erecting papillae, flaps, and knobs that simulate the texture of the background. Many midwater oceanic squids camouflage against predation from below by turning on photophores (light organs) that match the light intensity from the surface and eliminate their silhouettes. Most cephalopods have the ability to eject a blob of dark, mucoidal fluid, commonly known as ink, that resembles the form of their body (pseudomorph) and captures the attention of an attacker while the squid or octopus changes to a transparent hue and jets away. The ink is therefore not a "smokescreen." Jet propulsion makes speed an important defense mechanism as well. *See* CHROMATOPHORE; PHOTOPHORE GLAND; PROTECTIVE COLORATION.

Locomotion. Cephalopods have perfected jet propulsion for many modes of locomotion, from hovering motionless, to normal cruising, to extremely rapid escape swimming. Water enters the mantle cavity through an opening around the neck when the muscular mantle (body) expands. The mantle opening seals shut as the mantle contracts and jets the water out through the hoselike funnel, driving the cephalopod tail-first through the water. The functioning of this system is coordinated through a complex of nerves, including the giant axon that enables simultaneous contraction of the mantle along its entire length. The giant axon of cephalopods is the largest single nerve fiber in the animal kingdom. Streamlined body shape and other drag-reducing mechanisms add efficiency to the system, especially in the squids. The fins on the bodies of sepioids, teuthoids, and cirrate octopods serve as rudders and stabilizers, as well as providing locomotory power. Benthic octopuses frequently move about by walking or scuttling on their arms, especially when hunting. To save energy, many cephalopods have buoyancy mechanisms that permit them to maintain their desired depth without constantly swimming; these include gas chambers in the shells (*Nautilus, Sepia, Spirula*), concentrating lightweight ammonium ions in reservoirs (Cranchiidae, Enoploteuthidae) or body tissues (Histioteuthidae, Architeuthidae), and large amounts of oils in the liver (Bathyteuthidae).

Reproduction. The sexes are separate in cephalopods, and many species display complex courtship, mating, spawning, and parental care behavior. In females, eggs are produced in the ovary and when ripe they accumulate in the oviduct (single or double) where they are fertilized by sperm from the male. As they are extruded from the oviduct, the eggs are encased in individual capsules (sepioids, some oceanic squids), or enveloped in a gelatinous matrix formed into fingerlike clusters and attached to the bottom (myopsids, octopuses) or formed into sausage- or ball-shaped masses that drift in the open ocean (some oegopsids). The fragile shell of the epipelagic argonauts (*Argonauta*) is actually a case held by the female into which strands of eggs are attached and incubated until hatching. In males, sperm is produced in the testis and moved through the spermatophoric apparatus where it is encased in long, cylindrical packets (spermatophores) that are then stored in a sac. At mating, the male of most species transfers the spermatophores to the female with a specially modified arm, the hectocotylus. The spermatophores are implanted into the female's mantle cavity, around the neck, under the eyes, or around the mouth, depending on the species. Incubation takes a few weeks to a few months depending on the species. Hatchlings either look like miniature adults and assume the adult habitat, or have a modified "larval" stage, usually planktonic, before assuming the adult habitat.

Ecology. Cephalopods are extremely important in the diets of toothed whales (sperm whales, dolphins), pinnipeds (seals, sea lions), pelagic birds (petrels, albatrosses), and predatory fishes (tunas, billfishes, groupers). For example, pilot whales in the North Atlantic feed almost exclusively on one species of squid, *Illex illecebrosus*, that aggregates for spawning in the summer.

Cephalopods may occur singly, in small groups, or in huge schools that attract natural predators as well as fishing crews. Squids, cuttlefishes, and octopuses support major fisheries for human food throughout the world. Annual catches fluctuate around 1 million metric tons, and scientists believe that cephalopods represent a major underutilized resource that could be developed as a source of nutritious, high-protein, low-fat food. *See* DEEP-SEA FAUNA.
Clyde F. E. Roper

Fossils

Modern representatives of the Cephalopoda are dominated in numbers by forms without a calcareous skeleton (such as *Octopus*) or by those taxa with only a reduced or rudimentary internal skeleton (most squids). Only a small minority of forms, such as the externally shelled *Nautilus* and Argonauta, the internally shelled cuttlefish (*Sepia*), and the squid *Spirula*, possess significant skeletal hard parts.

Fossil record. The fossil record, however, suggests that the typical morphologies of the world's cephalopodan fauna were quite different in the past. During the Paleozoic and Mesozoic eras (from about 560 to 65 million years ago), the majority of cephalopod fossils came from species with external shells, similar to that produced today by *Nautilus*. Although fossils of the subclass Coleoidea (to which squids and octopus are today assigned) are known, and in some deposits can even be extremely common, it appears that they represented only a small fraction of Paleozoic and Mesozoic diversity. Even accounting for their lesser chance of incorporation into the fossil record because of their reduced internal skeletons, it appears that the coleoids were never as abundant as the groups bearing external shells during the Paleozoic and Mesozoic eras. Over 15,000 Paleozoic- and Mesozoic-aged species belonging to the subclasses Nautiloidea and Ammonoidea are now known to science. In contrast, the modern-day cephalopod fauna, dominated by the squids and octopuses, has only several hundred species described to date, and appears to be very different from the typical cephalopod faunas characteristic of the Paleozoic and Mesozoic oceans. Most evidence suggests that the modern fauna is composed of taxa which have evolved only after the end-Mesozoic extinction of most externally shelled forms. *See* MESOZOIC; PALEOZOIC.

Chambered shell. Much of what is known and inferred about the habits of the ancient cephalopods comes from study of the small number of extant forms still possessing the external shells characteristic of the Paleozoic and Mesozoic cephalopod faunas. For this reason the modern-day *Nautilus* has been the subject of much research, for it represents the last living, externally shelled cephalopod. (Although *Argonaut*, a very specialized pelagic octopus, also has an external shell, this shell is produced by females only and serves as a specialized brooding organ for developing eggs.) The *Nautilus* shell has the dual purpose of lending protection to the vulnerable soft parts and serving as a buoyancy device. The rear of the shell contains numerous compartments partitioned by calcareous walls or septa; each chamber contains a central tube within which is a strand of living flesh communicating with the rear of the soft parts. This strand, called the siphuncle, is instrumental in achieving overall neutral buoyancy of the entire animal by removing a seawaterlike liquid from each chamber. Although the modern *Nautilus* shows soft-part specializations which may be adaptations to its typical deepwater existence in front of coral reefs (and hence atypical of most extinct species, which appear to have lived in water depths and environments different from those typical of *Nautilus*), the nautilus shell shows close similarity with the shells of all fossil nautiloids and their closely allied descendants, the ammonoids.

In both nautiloids and ammonoids, the soft parts rest in a large space at the front of the shell. The shell enlarges through new calcification along its aperture. New chambers are produced at the back of the soft parts and are originally filled with the seawaterlike liquid. This liquid is removed via the siphuncle by an osmotic process at a rate that balances the density increases brought about by the production of new shell and tissue growth. After completion of a new chamber, the soft parts of the nautiloid or ammonoid move forward in the shell, creating a space behind the body for another chamber. All fossil cephalopods reached a final mature size and hence ceased shell growth.

With this cessation of shell growth, new chamber formation no longer became necessary. The buoyancy function of the chambered shell portion changed from one primarily dedicated to offsetting density increase due to shell and tissue growth to one concerned with making small buoyancy compensations in response to slight, nongrowth weight changes, such as weight increases brought about by windfall feeding, or concerned with producing weight reduction, which could occur if shell material was broken off during predatory attacks on the nautiloid or ammonoid. There is reason to believe that buoyancy change was not used to power any sort of movement vertically through the water column. At least in the modern *Nautilus* (and by inference in the fossil nautiloids and ammonoids), the process of buoyancy change appears too slow to aid in any type of active locomotion brought about by rapid weight gain or loss.

Origins. The evolution of the chambered cephalopod shell, with its neutral buoyancy capability, dates back to the Cambrian Period; the shell was the central adaptation leading to the origin of the cephalopods from their snaillike molluscan ancestors. The earliest cephalopods are assigned to the subclass Nautiloidea. The first of these, known from Late Cambrian rocks in China, were small (less than 1 ft or 0.3 m long) and bore straight to slightly curved shells. By Ordovician time, however, adaptive radiations among the ancestral nautiloid stocks gave rise to a wide variety of shell shapes and sizes,

including giants at least 10 ft (3 m) long. The subclass Ammonoidea arose from nautiloid ancestors in the Devonian Period, and can be differentiated from the nautiloids in details of shell morphology, especially relating to the complexity and position of the septa and siphuncle. It was also during the Devonian Period that the earliest internally shelled forms assignable to the Coleoidea appeared. *See* CAMBRIAN; DEVONIAN; ORDOVICIAN.

Evolutionary radiations and extinctions. The early Paleozoic nautiloids predated the first-known fishes and hence may have been among the earliest large predators in the sea. The subsequent evolutionary history of the nautiloids and their ammonoid descendants was one of successive waves of rapid evolutionary radiations. These externally shelled forms, however, were also very susceptible to extinction, especially during the rare intervals of mass extinction which occasionally occurred during the Paleozoic and Mesozoic eras. Following a period of extinction, a new fauna of nautiloids and ammonoids would rapidly evolve. This characteristic pattern of rapid speciation rates and high extinction rates tends to make most species chronologically short-ranging and hence useful in subdividing strata through biostratigraphy. Ammonoids are among the most useful known fossils for subdividing the stratigraphic record into small, chronological units.

The modern-day cephalopod fauna originated only after one of the most spectacular of the mass extinctions, occurring at the end of the Cretaceous Period. At this time, about 65 million years ago, a still-flourishing ammonoid fauna was totally destroyed; most nautiloids also died out as well. Although the record of Cenozoic cephalopod fossils is spotty, it appears that much of the cephalopod fauna as it is known today evolved only after the demise of the externally shelled forms. Thus, much as in the case of mammals and dinosaurs, the so-called modern fauna (the coleoid cephalopods) inherited the seas not because they were inherently superior to the ancient shelled nautiloids and ammonoids, but because they found themselves in an ocean emptied by mass extinction. *See* CENOZOIC; EXTINCTION (BIOLOGY); MOLLUSCA.

Peter D. Ward

Bibliography. W. Arkell et al., *Treatise on Invertebrate Paleontology,* pt. L, 1957; M. R. Clarke and E. R. Trueman (eds.), *The Mollusca,* vol. 12: *Paleontology and Neontology of Cephalopods,* 1988; U. Lehmann, *The Ammonites: Their Life and Their World,* 1981; E. R. Trueman and M. R. Clarke (eds.), *The Mollusca,* vol. 11: *Form and Function,* 1988; P. Ward, *The Natural History of Nautilus,* 1987.

Cephalosporins

A group of antibiotics that are effective in eradicating streptococcal, pneumococcal, staphylococcal, *Klebsiella, Neisseria,* enteric gram-negative rod bacteria that produce pulmonary, skin and soft tissue, bone and joint, endocardial, surgical, urinary, and bacteremic infections. They have been used most often in a preventive or prophylactic fashion at the time of various surgical procedures. The pharmacology of the early cephalosporins was such that the agents had to be administered by vein in frequent intervals in serious infections. This problem was overcome since most of the newer agents have much longer half-lives. All the third-generation cephalosporins penetrate well into tissues, and antibacterially active levels in various body fluids (pleural, peritoneal, synovial, biliary) and tissues such as bone are excellent. Toxic potential of the agents, considering their broad antibacterial spectrum, has been minor. Toxicities which are seen are those of bleeding due to vitamin K depletion.

There are many areas in which cephalosporins have been used, particularly respiratory, oral, abdominal, urinary tract, bone, gynecological, and neurological infections, and in septicemia. Roles in skin and soft tissue infections have been advocated for the drugs, but the agents still are a second choice and the investigational agents offer most for the uncommon multiresistant bacterial infection. *See* ANTIBIOTIC.   Harold Neu

Bibliography. H. C. Neu, *J. Antimicrob. Chemother.*, 6(Suppl.A):1–11, 1980.

Cepheids

A class of brightness-variable stars whose prototype is the star Delta Cephei in the constellation Cepheus. Hundreds are known in the Milky Way Galaxy and other nearby galaxies. While both bluer and redder stars also vary in their intrinsic light, the properties of these β Cephei, ZZ Ceti, RV Tauri, and Mira variables are much less understood than the yellow-color Cepheids. These yellow stars are known to be pulsating in radius by as much as 10% or more. Their light variations are due to their changing surface area and, more importantly, changing surface temperature. Larger yellow stars are intrinsically brighter because they have more surface area, and they have larger pulsation periods because they have a larger radius.

The interest in these stars is twofold. If their intrinsic brightnesses can be inferred from their pulsation period, the brightnesses can be used as indicators of their distance from the Earth. The observed period and a calibrated period-luminosity relation is used to give an intrinsic brightness. The observed distance-dependent apparent brightness then gives the actual distance. The second, and more current, interest in Cepheids is that their pulsation properties reveal their masses and internal structure, which help in understanding how stars age. Thus, Cepheids and the related classes of yellow pulsating stars have been extremely useful in mapping the scale of the universe and in probing the details of stellar interiors.

Types of Cepheids. Classical Cepheids are high-luminosity variables with masses 3–18 times that of the Sun. Their pulsation periods range from 2 to over 100 days. They are nearing the end of their thermonuclear energy production lives, having exhausted most of their hydrogen fuel by converting it to helium in their central regions. In most of these variable stars, helium at the very center is being further converted to carbon and oxygen by even higher-temperature thermonuclear burning.

The luminosity of more slowly evolving stars with lower mass, radius, and pulsation period is still due to hydrogen converting to helium. Those stars with masses between 1 and 3 solar masses and periods between about 0.1 and 1 day are in the related class of stars called Delta Scuti variables. Both the Cepheids and the Delta Scuti variables have original hydrogen, helium, and heavier-element compositions similar to that of the Sun, and all are called population I stars.

As stars of about 1 solar mass age, they become Delta Scuti variables and later evolve again to pulsation conditions after some loss of mass. They then are called RR Lyrae variables and are seen mostly in the very old globular star clusters, with their most massive stars already evolved to their death as white dwarfs or other compact objects. These RR Lyrae variables are also seen in the general galactic field. The name population II has been given to these very old stars which have masses like the Sun but ages two or more times longer. Since they were born before some of the elements such as carbon, nitrogen, oxygen, and iron were made in earlier generations of stars, they are very deficient in these elements. As these RR Lyrae variables age and grow even larger in radius, converting their central helium to carbon and oxygen, they become population II Cepheids with periods about the same as the classical, massive, and younger population I Cepheids. *See* NUCLEOSYNTHESIS.

Thus the population I stars become variables when their surface temperatures are 7000–8000 K (12,100–13,940°F) as Delta Scuti variables, and, for more massive and luminous stars, when their surface temperatures are 5000–7000 K (8540–12,100°F) as Cepheids. The population II variable-star history with mass much like that of the Sun is as a Delta Scuti variable (7000–8000 K or 12,140–13,940°F), an RR Lyrae variable (6500–7500 K or 11,240–13,040°F), and finally as a population II Cepheid (5000–7000 K or 8500–12,100°F). The radii of both population types range from just over the solar radius for the shortest-period Delta Scuti variable to over 100 times that value for the longest-period Cepheids. The mean luminosity of these variables is from less than 10 to over 100,000 times that of the Sun.

Observation of pulsations. The pulsations of the Cepheids and the related classes can be detected not only by their varying luminosity but also by their outward and inward motions as detected by the periodic Doppler shifts of their spectral lines. The light range of the Cepheid variation is about one magnitude, and the peak-to-peak velocity range is between 6 and 40 mi/s (10 and 70 km/s). These variations, which are mirror images of one another with maximum light at minimum radial velocity, are frequently smooth. The interpretation of this relative variation is that the surface temperature is largest when the star is passing through its mean position in its outward expansion. However, for the Cepheids between 5- and 15-day periods, bumps occur at a phase that is late in declining light for a period of 5 days, at the peak of the luminosity for a period of 10 days, and at the very start of rising light at a period of 15 days. All these variable stars pulsate in radial modes, that is, they retain their spherical shapes even as they pulsate.

Period-luminosity-color relation. The use of the Cepheids as distance indicators requires calibration of the period-luminosity-color relation. Observations in 1912 of the Cepheids in the Small Magellanic Cloud showed that, for these stars all at the same distance from the Earth, the mean luminosity increased with period. This period-luminosity relationship can also be derived now from stellar evolution and pulsation theories. A further small effect is also known from observation and theory, that is, the period depends also on color or, physically, on the surface temperature. Two stars with the same mean luminosity can have two different mean radii, that is, different temperatures and colors, and therefore have two different periods. This period-luminosity-color relation is calibrated from stars in nearby star clusters or associations with distances known by other considerations. Then the intrinsic mean luminosity and color are directly related to an observed period. Care must be taken that the color is properly corrected for the absorption of light by interstellar matter. Since Cepheids are seen in several other nearby galaxies, they serve to measure these galaxy distances with fair accuracy.

The 1969 period-luminosity-color relation developed by A. Sandage and G. Tammann has been replaced by one based on the infrared colors J, H, and K for bands, respectively, at 1.25, 1.65, and 2.2 micrometers. This new relation is not very dependent on the pulsation phase and temperature, that is, on the color, making it unnecessary to observe the distance-indicating Cepheid around its entire pulsation cycle. It also is very insensitive to the abundance of metals in the atmosphere, the position in the instability strip (discussed below), or the reddening of the light due to interstellar absorption (see **illus.**).

Structure and evolution. Cepheids have also given insight into stellar evolution theory. These yellow variables pulsate because of an instability in the near-surface layers which periodically inhibits the flow of radiation to the surface. The detailed properties of hydrogen and helium as these elements become ionized give the instability, which grows until internal radiative damping

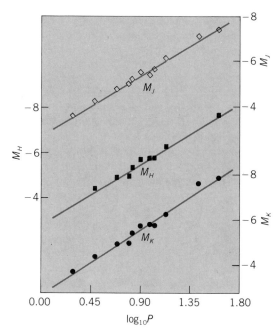

Cepheid period-luminosity relations. The absolute magnitudes M_J, M_H, and M_K, based on infrared colors J, H, and K for bands respectively at 1.25, 1.65, and 2.2 micrometers, are plotted as a function of the logarithm of the period P, in days. Data points indicate measured values; lines indicate best fits to data. (*After R. McGonegal et al., The near infrared Cepheid distance scale. I. Preliminary galactic calibration, Astrophys. J., 269:641–644, 1983*)

exactly balances the ionization driving. Many linear (assuming an infinitesimal amplitude) and nonlinear (allowing for an observable amplitude) calculations have clarified the pulsation details in the several longest-period modes with only a few internal nodes.

There is a definite surface temperature, which is only slightly hotter or cooler for lesser or greater luminosity, above which the Cepheids are not observed to pulsate. The theoretical explanation for this cutoff is that when the ionization mechanisms get too shallow they do not involve much mass and do not give enough driving to overcome the deep damping. This observed blue edge of the pulsation instability strip in the $\log L - \log T_e$ (where L is the luminosity and T_e is the surface effective temperature), or Hertzsprung-Russell, diagram can be used to determine a minimum helium content, because the ionization of the element helium causes most of the driving. *See* HERTZSPRUNG-RUSSELL DIAGRAM.

An observed red edge of the instability strip seems to be caused by the occurrence of convection in the surface layers. While the detailed pulsation damping mechanisms of convection are not so well understood, it is clear that there is a red (or cool) limit to the ionization instability mechanism, even though redder, often irregular variables exist.

The yellow pulsating stars of all classes mentioned here can reveal their mean radii, which can be compared to those predicted from stellar evolution theory. At two different phases of the pulsation cycle, when the surface temperatures are equal, the differing luminosity of the stars is due only to the differing surface areas. Use of simultaneous observations of the light and radial velocity variations can give the actual motion of the stellar surface during this time between equal-temperature phases. Analysis then gives the mean (or Wesselink) radius, which agrees with evolution theory. Further, the use of the theoretical relation between the period and the mean density of the star gives a mass consistent with evolution theory. *See* STAR; STELLAR EVOLUTION; VARIABLE STAR.   Arthur N. Cox

Bibliography. S. A. Becker, L. Iben, and R. S. Tuggle, On the frequency-period distribution of Cepheid variables in galaxies in the Local Group, *Astrophys. J.*, 218:633–653, 1977; M. Breger, Delta Scuti and related stars, *Publ. Astron. Soc. Pacific*, 91:5–26, 1979; A. N. Cox, Cepheid masses from observations and pulsation theory, *Astrophys. J.*, 229:212–222, 1979; B. F. Madore and W. L. Freedman, The Cepheid distance scale, *Publ. Astron. Soc. Pacific*, 103:933–957, 1991; K. A. Strand (ed.), *Stars and Stellar Systems*, vol. 3, 1963.

Ceramics

Inorganic, nonmetallic materials processed or consolidated at high temperature. This definition includes a wide range of materials known as advanced ceramics and is much broader than the common dictionary definition, which includes only pottery, tile, porcelain, and so forth. The classes of materials generally considered to be ceramics are oxides, nitrides, borides, carbides, silicides, and sulfides. Intermetallic compounds such as aluminides and beryllides are also considered ceramics, as are phosphides, antimonides, and arsenides. *See* INTERMETALLIC COMPOUNDS.

Ceramic materials can be subdivided into traditional and advanced ceramics. Traditional ceramics include clay-base materials such as brick, tile, sanitary ware, dinnerware, clay pipe, and electrical porcelain. Common-usage glass, cement, abrasives, and refractories are also important classes of traditional ceramics.

Advanced materials technology is often cited as an enabling technology, enabling engineers to design and build advanced systems for applications in fields such as aerospace, automotive, and electronics. Advanced ceramics are tailored to have premium properties through application of advanced materials science and technology to control composition and internal structure. Examples of advanced ceramic materials are silicon nitride, silicon carbide, toughened zirconia, zirconia-toughened alumina, aluminum nitride, lead magnesium niobate, lead lanthanum zirconate titanate, silicon-carbide-whisker–reinforced alumina, carbon-fiber–reinforced glass ceramic, silicon-carbide-fiber–reinforced silicon carbide, and high-temperature superconductors. Advanced ceramics can be viewed as a class of the broader field of advanced materials, which can be divided into ceramics, metals, polymers, composites, and electronic materials. There is considerable overlap among these classes of materials. *See* CERMET; COMPOSITE MATERIAL; GLASS; POLYMER.

Advanced ceramics can be subdivided into structural and electronic ceramics based on primary function or application. Optical and magnetic materials are usually included in the electronic classification. Structural applications include engine components, cutting tools, bearings, valves, wear- and corrosion-resistant parts, heat exchangers, fibers and whiskers, and biological implants. The electronic-magnetic-optic functions include electronic substrates, electronic packages, capacitors, transducers, magnets, waveguides, lamp envelopes, displays, sensors, and ceramic superconductors. Thermal insulation, membranes, and filters are important advanced ceramic product areas that do not fit well into either the structural or the electronic class of advanced ceramics.

Fabrication Processes

A wide variety of processes are used to fabricate ceramics. The process chosen for a particular product is based on the material, shape complexity, property requirements, and cost. Ceramic fabrication processes can be divided into four generic categories: powder, vapor, chemical, and melt processes.

Powder processes. Traditional clay-base ceramics and most refractories are fabricated by powder processes, as are the majority of advanced ceramics. Powder processing involves a number of sequential steps. These are preparation of the starting powders, forming the desired shape (green forming), removal of water and organics, heating with or without application of pressure to densify the powder, and finishing.

Powder preparation. The starting powders for traditional ceramics are predominantly clays and other natural minerals which have been processed to achieve the purity and particle size desired. The methods of mining, crushing, and milling are similar to those operations in other industries. The starting powders for advanced ceramics are high-purity specialty chemicals. These powders have many similarities to high-quality inorganic pigments. Powder preparation is a critical step in the fabrication of advanced ceramics, since high-quality advanced ceramics require high-purity, submicrometer powders with controlled physical characteristics such as particle size. The availability of high-quality, low-cost powders with reproducible characteristics is a critical requirement for use of advanced ceramic materials in many emerging applications. *See* CRUSHING AND PULVERIZING; GRINDING MILL.

Advanced ceramic powders are produced by a number of processes, including precipitation, calcination, and vapor-phase processes. The primary process is chemical precipitation, followed by calcination (heating) to remove water and other volatiles and to achieve the desired crystallinity and physical characteristics. After calcination, powders are ground, usually in ball mills, to break the bonds between individual crystallites formed by diffusion during calcination, thus producing a powder with a submicrometer particle size. In addition to conventional precipitation, a number of other precipitation processes can be used, including precipitation under pressure (hydrothermal) and simultaneous precipitation of more than one cation (coprecipitation). Hydrothermal precipitation can produce mixed cation precipitates and can precipitate oxides directly, whereas conventional precipitation usually produces hydroxides or salts which must be calcined to form oxides. Coprecipitation is used for many advanced multication powders to obtain more intimate mixing of the cations than can be achieved by mixing oxides or salts of the individual cations, as discussed below under calcination. Because of the intimate mixing produced by coprecipitation, the calcination temperature required to produce the desired crystalline phase in the powder is usually lower than for calcination of mixtures of individual oxides. *See* PRECIPITATION (CHEMISTRY).

Calcination is involved in the production of most advanced ceramic powders. For precipitated powders, a subsequent calcination step is usually required, as described above. Many multi-cation powders, such as an oxide which contains nickel, zinc, and iron [$(Ni,Zn)Fe_2O_4$], are formed by calcining mixtures of the individual oxides or salts of the cations. Many nonoxide powders can also be produced by some form of calcination. Most silicon carbide (SiC) is produced by high-temperature reaction of a mixture of sand (silicon dioxide; SiO_2) and carbon powders. Silicon nitride (Si_3N_4) powder can be produced by reacting a mixture of SiO_2 and carbon at high temperature in a nitrogen atmosphere or by reacting silicon metal powder with nitrogen at high temperatures.

Powders for most advanced ceramics can also be produced by vapor-phase reaction. In this process, reactant gases are mixed and heated to nucleate and grow particles from the gas phase. A number of different heat sources for the reaction can be used, such as a direct-current or induction-coupled plasma, a laser, or a furnace.

Green forming. The ceramic fabrication step in which powders are formed into useful shapes is called green forming. A wide variety of processes are used for green forming. The process chosen is based on the material being fabricated, the shape desired, the property requirements, and the production cost. Green-forming processes include casting, extrusion, jiggering, die pressing, isostatic pressing, tape casting, and injection molding. Some form of treatment of the starting powders is usually required for green forming, and the treatment depends on the green-forming process and the material. Green-forming processes for clay-base ceramics usually take advantage of the plastic behavior of clay–water mixtures. Organic plasticizers are often added to achieve the desired plasticity if clay is not one of the starting powders.

Slip casting is a green-forming process in which the starting powders are suspended in water to form a slip. Green shapes are formed by pouring the slip into porous molds made of plaster of paris or another suitable material. The capillary action of the porous mold draws water from the slip and forms a solid layer on the inside of the mold. When the desired part thickness has been obtained, the excess slip is poured out of the mold (**Fig. 1**). The part is partially dried in the mold to cause it to shrink away from the mold and develop adequate rigidity for handling. This process is an economical way to form complex shapes and is used for hollow objects such as artware and sanitary ware. Slip preparation is critical to slip casting and requires optimization among a number of factors, including viscosity, solids contents, slip stability, casting rate, drying rate, and drying shrinkage. One of the critical factors in developing a slip is controlling the degree of deflocculation. This involves an understanding of the surface chemistry of the particles in the slip. *See* PORCELAIN; POTTERY.

Pressure casting has begun to replace conventional slip casting. In pressure casting, a pressure is applied to the slip to supplement or replace the capillary action of the porous mold. The advantages of pressure casting over conventional slip casting are higher casting rate, ability to automate the process, and extension of the useful application of slip casting to colloidal nonclay powders.

Extrusion is a process in which a stiff plastic mass is forced through a die that has the desired

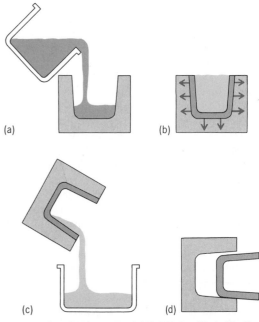

Fig. 1. Drain-casting process. (*a*) Mold being filled with slip. (*b*) Mold extracting liquid, forming compact along mold walls. (*c*) Excess slip being drained. (*d*) Casting removed after partial drying. (*After D. W. Richerson, Modern Ceramic Engineering, Marcel Dekker, 1982*)

cross section of the object to be formed. The extruded column is then cut to the desired length. Secondary shaping processes are often used to further shape the extruded object. Extrusion is the primary process used to fabricate structural clay products such as building brick and clay sewer pipe. The starting materials for these products are primarily clays that have been ground into a powder and blended with 10–15% water to form a stiff mud, which is extruded. Other products which are formed by extrusion include thermocouple insulation tubes and catalyst supports for automotive emission control. In general, any material with a constant cross section can be formed by extrusion. *See* EXTRUSION.

Jiggering is a mechanization of the hand-throwing process used by potters. It consists of molding one side of a piece by placing a slab of plastic material (usually cut from an extruded log) on a porous plaster of paris mold, placing the mold and plastic slab on a rotating head, and forming the other side of the object by forcing a template of the desired contour against the plastic slab. Dinner plates are usually formed by this process, and the powder used for this product is a mixture of clays, potter's flint, and feldspar. *See* CLAY; CLAY, COMMERCIAL; FELDSPAR.

Powder pressing is a process in which a powder containing 0–5% water is green-formed by compaction under pressure. This process is used for a wide variety of traditional and advanced ceramic products, including floor and wall tile, some refractories, spark plug insulators, and many electronic ceramics. In general, if the shape permits, powder pressing is used for green forming. There are two basic types of powder pressing, die pressing and isostatic pressing. In die pressing, which is limited to relatively simple shapes, a steel or tungsten carbide die consisting of a die cavity and internal punches is used. Powder is placed in the die cavity, and force is applied through the punches to compact the powder into the desired shape. Isostatic pressing is used to extend green forming by powder compaction into more complex shapes. For example, spark plug insulators are pressed isostatically by placing the powder around a central mandrel pin in a flexible mold which is compressed by using a pressure vessel to apply fluid pressure to the outside of the mold. The pressed blank is then ground on an automatic grinder to form the green part to the desired dimensions and contours. Most powders used for powder pressing are wet-blended to the desired composition, which includes organic binders and lubricants, and spray-dried so that they flow. *See* ELECTRICAL INSULATION.

In tape casting or the doctor-blade process, a powder slurry is drawn under a dam (doctor blade) to form a thin layer on a moving plastic belt (**Fig. 2**). This is the primary process for forming ceramic substrates for integrated electronic circuits. An organic liquid is used as the medium for the slurry to facilitate rapid removal by subsequent evaporation to form the green tape. *See* INTEGRATED CIRCUITS.

Injection molding is a process in which a plastic blend of ceramic powder and organic materials is extruded into a steel mold to form a green shape. The process is similar to injection molding of filled plastics. However, for ceramics the organic substance must be removed so that the powder shape can be densified. Injection molding is used for forming complex shapes. Thread guides and turbocharger rotors are two ceramic products that are formed by this process.

Removal of water and organics. After green forming, a drying or organic removal step is usually required before proceeding to the densification step. The process required depends on the green-forming process and the ceramic material being fabricated. For injection-molded parts, the organic (binder) removal step is especially critical, while drying is critical for slip-cast or extruded parts.

Densification. In the densification step the porous powder shape is converted into a dense part. The three primary processes used for final densification are sintering, hot pressing, and hot isostatic pressing. Sintering is often referred to as firing or vitrification, especially for traditional ceramics. Sintering involves heating a porous powder shape to a temperature sufficient to activate various thermal processes that lead to densification of the part. The two general mechanisms of densification during sintering are liquid-phase sintering and solid-state sintering. The driving force for sintering is reduction of the free surface energy. Most traditional ceramics are densified by liquid-phase sintering, as are alumina spark plug insulators. Materials such as dinnerware, sanitary ware, and electrical porcelain contain finely ground feldspar as one of the starting materials. When the part is heated, the feldspar melts and forms a viscous liquid which promotes densification by viscous flow. In many other ceramics, liquid phases are formed by chemical reaction between the individual starting materials. In many advanced ceramics, solid-state sintering is the predominant sintering mechanism. Solid-state sintering occurs by solid-state diffusion processes, and high-surface-area powders, generally below 1 micrometer in diameter, are especially critical to sintering by this process. *See* SINTERING.

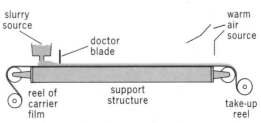

Fig. 2. Schematic diagram of doctor-blade tape casting process. (After D. W. Richerson, Modern Ceramic Engineering, Marcel Dekker, 1982)

Hot pressing is a process in which pressure is applied to a powder or powder compact in a die at elevated temperature (**Fig. 3**). The pressure enhances the thermal processes involved in sintering and often activates new processes. Dies are generally made of graphite. Materials that cannot be densified by sintering without pressure can be densified by using hot pressing. Hot pressing can also be used to produce materials with special properties, such as cutting-tool inserts. The principal disadvantages of hot pressing are cost and a limitation on the shapes that can be fabricated.

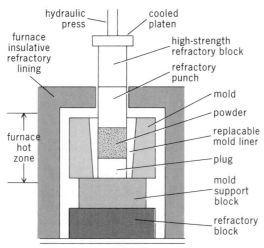

Fig. 3. Schematic diagram showing the essential elements of a hot press. (*After D. W. Richerson, Modern Ceramic Engineering, Marcel Dekker, 1982*)

Hot isostatic pressing (HIP) is similar to isostatic compaction of powders, except that the compaction process is carried out at elevated temperatures. The equipment consists of a cold-wall autoclave with an internal furnace. Gas, typically argon, is used as the pressurizing fluid in place of the water or oil used for cold isostatic compaction of powders. Hermetically sealed metal or glass enclosures (known as cans) are used to encase the powder compact and act as the barrier to transfer the gas pressure to an isostatic compaction force on the powder compact. Hot isostatic pressing is also used to further densify materials that have been sintered to eliminate continuous or interconnected porosity. This process is referred to as post-HIP, and a can is not required since the part acts as its own can. The primary advantages of hot isostatic pressing over hot pressing are the ability to densify more complex shapes and the ability to apply higher pressures to densify a wide range of materials. *See* POWDER METALLURGY.

Finishing. After densification, many ceramic products require some finishing to achieve the required dimensional tolerance or surface finish. Since ceramics generally have high hardness, the conventional machining used for finishing metals cannot be used. Diamond cutting, grinding, and core drilling are the most common finishing techniques, but ultrasonic cutting and laser drilling and cutting are frequently used. Electric discharge machining is used if the electrical conductivity of the material is high enough.

Vapor processes. The primary vapor processes used to fabricate ceramics are chemical vapor deposition and sputtering. Vapor processes have been finding an increasing number of applications. Chemical vapor deposition involves bringing gases containing the atoms to make up the ceramic into contact with a heated surface, where the gases react to form a coating. This process is used to apply ceramic coatings to metal and tungsten carbide cutting tools as well as to apply a wide variety of other coatings for wear, electronic, and corrosion applications. Chemical vapor deposition can also be used to form monolithic ceramics by building up thick coatings. A form of chemical vapor deposition known as chemical vapor infiltration has been developed to infiltrate and coat the surfaces of fibers in woven preforms. The coating on individual fibers leads to densification of the preform to produce ceramic-ceramic composites such as silicon carbide-fiber–reinforced silicon carbide that are being developed for applications in high-temperature aerospace engines. *See* HIGH-TEMPERATURE MATERIALS; VAPOR DEPOSITION.

Several variations of sputtering and other vacuum coating processes can be used to form coatings of ceramic materials. The most common process is reactive sputtering, used to form coatings such as titanium nitride on tool steel. This process involves vaporizing titanium from a titanium target by use of a magnetron that accelerates ions such as argon against the target in order to vaporize titanium atoms, which deposit on a substrate maintained at a fixed temperature in a low-pressure plasma containing nitrogen. The titanium and nitrogen react on the substrate (such as a cutting tool) to form a titanium nitride coating. *See* MAGNETRON; SPUTTERING.

Chemical processes. A number of different chemical processes are used to fabricate advanced ceramics. The chemical vapor deposition process described above as a vapor process is also a chemical process. Two other chemical processes finding increasing application in advanced ceramics are polymer pyrolysis and sol-gel technology.

Polymer pyrolysis. This involves the controlled heating of organometallic compounds to break down the organic molecules and remove the organic radicals. The residue is a ceramic material, and the starting organometallics are known as precursors. With appropriate selection of the precursor, a wide variety of oxide and nonoxide ceramics can be formed. The process is similar to the fabrication of carbon fibers or of the matrix in carbon-carbon composites by controlled pyrolysis of pitch. Silicon carbide fibers can be manufactured by using organometallic precursors such as polycarbosilane. Similar precursors can be used to incorporate a ceramic matrix in a woven preform of silicon carbide fibers to produce silicon carbide-fiber–reinforced silicon carbide composites. *See* CERMET.

Sol-gel technology. In addition to its use as a process for manufacturing advanced ceramic powders, sol-gel technology is used to fabricate advanced ceramics. This process involves the formation of a suspension of colloidal particles (sol) which is converted to a gel by chemical treatment. The gel is then dried and sintered to form a ceramic product. The overall process in which dense materials are fabricated directly from the preformed gel without going through a powder stage is known as the sol-gel monolith process. As a result of the fine pore size of the dried gel, the sintering temperatures are lower than those required for similar materials formed from powders. Many ceramic fibers are manufactured by the sol-gel monolith process, and the process is beginning to find many other applications in advanced ceramics in biomedical, electronic, and other fields. *See* COLLOID; GEL.

Melt processes. These are used to manufacture glass, to fuse-cast refractories for use in furnace linings, and to grow single crystals. *See* REFRACTORY.

Thermal spraying can also be classified as a melt process. In this process a plasma-spray gun is used to apply ceramic (or metal) coatings by melting and spraying powders onto a substrate. Powder particles are entrained in a gas stream in which a plasma is formed to melt (or soften) the particles as they are accelerated onto the substrate surface. For materials with lower melting points, a flame-spray gun can be used. In this process an oxygen-acetylene flame is used in place of a plasma, and the feed material can be a powder or a rod of the material to be deposited. Ceramic coatings applied by plasma spraying are used for corrosion protection in applications such as aircraft engine parts and for wear resistance in applications such as on rotating shafts in seals and slide bearings.

Applications

The selection of materials for engineering applications is based on performance requirements and cost, as well as other factors.

The general advantages of advanced structural ceramics over metals and polymers are high-temperature strength, wear resistance, and chemical stability, in addition to the enabling functions the ceramics can perform. Typical properties for some engineering ceramics are shown in the **table**.

High-temperature strength. This property of advanced ceramics is important in many potential applications, especially in components for the hot sections of engines and heat exchangers. The maximum use temperature for superalloys is 1800°F (1000°C). The only metals usable above this temperature are refractory metals that lack the oxidation resistance required for high-temperature applications in an oxidizing environment. Silicon nitride and silicon carbide have adequate oxidation resistance to be used in air up to 2600 and 2700°F (1400 and 1500°C), respectively. They also have adequate strength for many applications at these temperatures, although many silicon nitride materials are limited to use at lower temperatures because of additives that are used to aid in their fabrication. Many ceramic materials have higher melting points than silicon carbide and silicon nitride but lack adequate oxidation resistance for use at high temperatures. The other factor which is usually critical for advanced ceramics in high-temperature applications is thermal-shock fracture resistance. The thermal-shock fracture resistance under steady-state heat transfer is proportional to

$$\frac{\text{Strength}}{\text{Elastic modulus}} \times \frac{\text{thermal conductivity}}{\text{thermal expansion}}$$

Under highly transient conditions, the thermal conductivity is not a factor. Most engineering applications fall between the two extremes of steady-state and highly transient conditions. Comparison of the data in the table shows why silicon nitride and silicon carbide are far superior to alumina and zirconia for high-temperature applications where temperature gradients are expected. Two lower-temperature examples of an application involving thermal stress are ceramic stovetops and cookware. These materials have a thermal expansion near zero; therefore, stresses from thermal gradients are very low.

Wear resistance. Another important requirement for applications of materials is resistance to failure under impact loading. While metals generally exhibit ductible behavior, ceramic materials generally exhibit brittle failure; they are much more susceptible to failure due to high local stresses from impact loading. The toughness values in the table indicate the high toughness of partially stabilized zirconia relative to the other materials shown. In the same units, glass has a toughness of less than 1. The utilitarian fracture resistance of partially stabilized zirco-

Typical properties for some ceramic materials				
Property	Aluminum oxide	Silicon nitride	Silicon carbide	Partially stabilized zirconia
Density, g/cm^3	3.9	3.2	3.1	5.7
Flexure strength, MPa	350	850	450	790
Modulus of elasticity, GPa	407	310	400	205
Fracture toughness (K_{IC}), MPa·m$^{1/2}$	5	5	4	12
Thermal conductivity, W/mK	34	33	110	3
Mean coefficient of thermal expansion ($\times 10^{-6}$/°C)	7.7	2.6	4.4	10.2

nia under impact loading is quite different from that of glass and even of silicon nitride. For example, a hammer made from partially stabilized zirconia can be used to drive nails without chipping, and a partially stabilized zirconia shovel was dropped onto concrete from a height of three stories without breaking. In addition to partially stabilized zirconia, other materials such as alumina can be toughened by adding zirconia particles of the correct size and composition. Ceramic whisker- and fiber-reinforced ceramics possessing high toughness have also been developed. These advances have opened additional engineering applications for advanced ceramics.

In general, ceramic materials have a much higher hardness than metals, a property that leads to high wear resistance. Valve guides and cam followers for advanced engines, sandblast nozzles, grinding media, thread guides, cutting tools, pump parts, and extrusion dies are all applications for ceramics that result from their wear resistance. *See* WEAR.

Chemical stability. Ceramic materials also have better corrosion resistance than metals or polymers, particularly in erosive wear applications. This leads to applications in valves, pumps, and pipe linings for chemical, petrochemical, and other industries. *See* CORROSION.

For electronics, advanced ceramic materials have been developed which have piezoelectric, electrooptic, pyroelectric, and many other first- and second-order effects, and thus many special electronic, optical, or magnetic properties; this allows the ceramics to be tailored for specific advanced systems, a distinct advantage. *See* MAGNETIC MATERIALS; PIEZOELECTRICITY.

Enabling functions. Many of the applications of advanced ceramics are based on the enabling functions they can perform in advanced systems such as automotive engines, aerospace hardware, and electronics. For example, in advanced automotive engines, silicon nitride rotors enable the design of a turbocharger with a more rapid response to the accelerator, because the density of silicon nitride is lower than that of competitive metals, and its high-temperature strength, oxidation resistance, and resistance to thermal stress are good. The incentive to develop and apply advanced ceramics often lies with the manufacturer of a system, if the value added is sufficient to justify the required investment.

The enabling function of advanced ceramics is most apparent in high-temperature superconductors. In January 1986, J. G. Bednorz and K. A. Müller discovered superconductivity in lanthanum barium copper oxide and, in April 1986, announced their finding that it occurred at temperatures as high as 35 K ($-405°$F). Also, in February 1986, a group including C.-W. Chu and M. K. Wu discovered superconductivity in yttrium barium copper oxide up to 92 K ($-294°$F). Subsequent developments have resulted in higher-temperature ceramic superconductors. These events have generated a massive research and development effort around the world. The reason for the interest in this class of super-

conductors is its strong potential enabling functions, many of which may not yet be conceived. *See* SUPERCONDUCTIVITY.

The primary disadvantages of most advanced ceramics are in the areas of reliability, reproducibility, and cost. Major advances in reliability are being made through development of tougher materials such as partially stabilized zirconia and ceramic whiskers; and reinforced ceramics such as silicon-carbide-whisker–reinforced alumina used for cutting tools, and silicon-carbide-fiber–reinforced silicon carbide for high-temperature engine applications. Reproducibility is being improved by developments in manufacturing technology. Cost is expected to be reduced as materials science, manufacturing technology, and engineering design with ceramics are further developed.

The major applications for advanced ceramics are in electronics and include substrates for electronic circuits, electronic packages, capacitors, magnetic components, piezoelectric components, electronic sensors, and integrated optic components. Advanced ceramics are also finding many applications where wear resistance and corrosion resistance are critical, such as extrusion dies and pump components. Advanced ceramic components have been introduced into automotive and other engines, and these applications are expected to grow. Automotive engine applications include turbocharger rotors, valves, valve guides, valve seats and other valve-train components, fuel-injector nozzles, exhaust-port inserts, and advanced diesel engine components. Automotive gas turbines whose hot section consists wholly of advanced ceramic components are under development, and advanced ceramic composites are expected to play a major role in the engine for the aerospace plane as well as other aerospace systems. In the machine tool industry, advanced ceramic cutting tools have increased productivity up to tenfold over metal and carbide tools, and advanced ceramic bearings are being applied where high loads and high rigidity are needed. In communications, glass fiber-optic cable has revolutionized the electronic transmission of voice and data. *See* AUTOMOTIVE ENGINE.

In the future, advanced ceramics will play key enabling functions in a wide variety of advanced systems, and traditional ceramics will continue to fill important needs in consumer, building, and industrial products.   Dale E. Niesz

Bibliography. W. D. Kingery, H. K. Bowen, and D. R. Uhlmann, *Introduction to Ceramics*, 2d ed., 1976; L. Ponte, Dawn of the New Stone Age, *Reader's Digest*, July 1987; D. W. Richerson, *Modern Ceramic Engineering*, 1982; S. Saito, *Fine Ceramics*, 1987.

Cerargyrite

A mineral with composition AgCl (see **illus.**). Its structure is that of the isometric NaCl type, but well-formed cubic crystals are rare. The hardness

Cerargyrite crystals from Leadville, Colorado. (*Specimen from Department of Geology, Bryn Mawr College*)

is 2.5 on Mohs scale and specific gravity 5.5. Cerargyrite is colorless to pearl-gray but darkens to violet-brown on exposure to light. It is perfectly sectile and can be cut with a knife like horn; hence the name horn silver. Bromyrite, AgBr, is physically indistinguishable from cerargyrite and the two minerals form a complete series. Both minerals are secondary ores of silver and occur in the oxidized zone of silver deposits. *See* HALITE; SILVER.

Cornelius S. Hurlbut, Jr.

Cercaria

The larval generation which terminates the development of a digenetic trematode in the intermediate host, a mollusk or rarely an annelid. It becomes the adult fluke after entering the definitive host, a vertebrate. Access to the vertebrate may be either direct or indirect by entering a second intermediate, or vector, host which is ingested by the vertebrate. The intermediate host is usually aquatic and the cercaria has a tail used in swimming when it escapes from that host but the tail may be inactive, reduced, or absent and the larva unable to swim. When the tail is absent, the organism is called a cercariaeum. Larvae with unknown life cycles are commonly described and named as species such as *Cercaria micrura* or *Cercariaeum helicis*.

Cercariae vary from less than 0.006 to over 0.8 in. (0.15 to 20.0 mm) in length. Usually they can be obtained by crushing and examining freshly collected snails or by placing them in water to permit the larvae to escape. A hand lens or microscope is needed to detect small species.

Cercariae are classified into several types, based on the structure of the body and tail and also on the pattern of the excretory system. The body may have or lack such larval characters as eyespots (ocelli), a stylet in the oral sucker, and glands used for penetration and encystment. The tail may be forked or not and bear fins, setae, or other appendages; sometimes it is enlarged and may enclose the body (see **illus.**). The tail is always lost when the larva reaches the next host in the life cycle.

The cercaria is important in taxonomy because that stage of closely related trematodes usually is less variable than the adult, and thus indicates

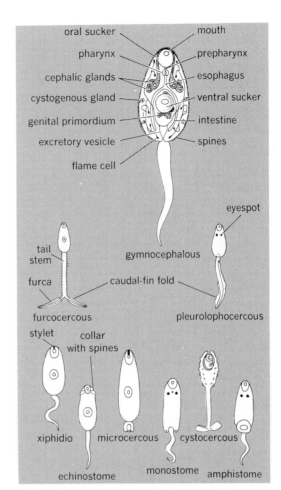

Various types of cercariae. (*After R. M. Cable, An Illustrated Laboratory Manual of Parasitology, Burgess, 1958*)

kinships that may be masked in the adult by adaptations to parasitism of the vertebrate host. *See* DIGENEA.

Raymond M. Cable

Cereal

Any member of the grass family (Gramineae) which produces edible grains usable as food by humans and livestock. Common cereals are rice, wheat, barley, oats, maize (corn), sorghum, rye, and certain millets. Triticale is cereal derived from crossing wheat and rye and then doubling the number of chromosomes in the hybrid. Occasionally, grains from other grasses (for example, teff) are used for food. Cereals are summer or winter annuals. Corn, rice, and wheat are the most important cereals. Today, as in ancient times, cereals provide more food for human consumption than any other crops. *See* BARLEY; CORN; CYPERALES; OATS; SORGHUM; RICE; RYE; WHEAT.

Cereal grains have many natural advantages as foods. They are nutritious. One kind or another can be grown almost anywhere on Earth. The grains are not bulky and therefore can be shipped inexpensively for long distances and stored for long periods of time. They are readily processed to give highly refined raw foods.

Preference for a cereal depends on the form and flavor of the food made from it, the amount of nourishment and contribution to health, its cost, its availability, and the food habits of a people.

Food products. Four general groups of foods are prepared from the cereal grains. (1) Baked products, made from flour or meal, include pan breads, loaf breads, pastries, pancakes, flatbreads, cookies, and cakes. (2) Milled grain products, made by removing the bran and usually the germ (or embryo of the seed), include polished rice, farina, wheat flour, cornmeal, hominy, corn grits, pearled barley, bulgur (from wheat), semolina (for macaroni products), prepared breakfast cereals, and soup, gravy, and other thickenings. (3) Beverages are made from fermented grain products (distilled or undistilled) and from boiled, roasted grains. Beverages, such as beer and whiskey, made from cereals are as old as recorded history. (4) Whole-grain products include rolled oats, brown rice, popcorn, shredded and puffed grains, breakfast foods, and home-ground meals made from wheat, corn, sorghum, or one of the other cereals. *See* DISTILLED SPIRITS.

Breeding. The long evolutionary development of the cereals has resulted in a wide array of genetic types. These and new mutants have been used to breed varieties that differ in adaptation, productivity, resistance to disease and insect pests, physical properties, composition, and nutrients.

Nutritional value. All cereal grains have high energy value, mainly from the starch fraction but also from the fat and protein. In general, the cereals are low in protein content, although oats and certain millets are exceptions. High-protein genetic types have been found, and, from their use in breeding, new varieties have been developed that possess a higher percentage of protein. Likewise, a better balance has been found among the amino acids in the protein in some lines of corn, barley, and sorghum, and research with wheat is promising. Also, the nature of the starchy fraction can be altered to give products with different physical properties. *See* GRAIN CROPS; GRASS CROPS; NUTRITION.   Louis P. Reitz

Cerebral palsy

A collection of syndromes (not a disease) of nonprogressive motor dysfunction arising from abnormal development of or damage to the brain, either prenatally, at birth, or postnatally. Most cases of cerebral palsy develop in utero. Premature birth is associated with an increased risk of cerebral palsy, with the lowest birth weights carrying the highest risk. A maximum of 15% of cases are related to birth injury or perinatal oxygen deprivation. *See* PREGNANCY DISORDERS.

Although the brain damage in cerebral palsy is nonprogressive and thus deterioration does not occur, the neurological manifestations of cerebral palsy may change with neurological maturation. The precise form of cerebral palsy rarely can be characterized prior to 6 months of age; often it cannot be characterized until the individual is 2 years old. Cerebral palsy is only rarely familial. Its incidence is stable at 0.1–0.3% of live births.

Forms of handicap. Cerebral palsy is classified by the form and distribution of the motor handicap as spasticity, dyskinesia, ataxia, and hypotonia. These four forms have considerable overlap. Spasticity, seen in 75% of cases, presents a clinical picture of muscle stiffness, weakness, and imbalance of muscle tone. Common findings are contractures of joints, resulting in shortened heel cords and thus in toe walking. Tightness of the adductor muscles in the thigh may result in a scissors gait. Painful dislocation of the hip is a common problem associated with severe spasticity. Severe involvement of the brainstem may result in difficulty speaking clearly or impair feeding. Dyskinetic syndromes (athetosis or dystonia) occur in 20% of cases. Both are characterized by a severe lack of voluntary muscle control. Athetosis is characterized by slow, writhing, involuntary movements occasionally combined with quick, distal, involuntary movements (chorea). Dystonia is characterized by more or less constant muscle stiffness. Dyskinetic syndromes show no symptoms during sleep and are aggravated by emotional tension. Unclear speech (dysarthria) can be quite severe. Ataxic syndromes, characterized by impaired coordination without altered motor tone, are uncommon. A fourth syndrome, characterized by severely decreased motor tone, is called atonic cerebral palsy.

Distribution of the altered motor tone is of great importance in predicting the degree of handicap, especially in the spastic forms. (1) Hemiplegia refers to involvement of one side of the body only. (2) Paraplegia refers to involvement of both legs with no involvement of the arms and hands. These two forms constitute about 50% of the spastic cases. Individuals with them can usually walk, and 80% have normal intelligence. Most of these individuals can become independent in society. (3) Spastic quadriplegia implies equal involvement of all four extremities; individuals frequently are severely retarded and have a small head (microcephalic). (4) Diplegia refers to involvement of the legs and lesser involvement of the arms and hands. It should probably be regarded as living a transitional form between paraplegia and quadriplegia and as having an intermediate prognosis.

A specific cerebral palsy syndrome due to severe neonatal jaundice is manifested by athetosis, deafness, and deficient upward gaze. Advances in obstetric and pediatric care have made this form uncommon. Other problems associated with cerebral palsy include mental retardation, seen in about 50% of cases. Epilepsy occurs in 25% of cases; it is treated with anticonvulsant drugs. *See* SEIZURE DISORDERS.

Treatment. Treatment of cerebral palsy is aimed at maximizing lifetime independence within the limitations of the individual's handicap. Appropriate education, in a normal class when feasible, is critical. Even the most severely affected individual can profit from training in self-care and communication skills. Common treatment modalities include physical and occupational therapy to prevent contractures and facilitate optimal motor control. Speech therapy is used to improve feeding technique and communication skills. Although these therapies are used, their long-term value has not been proven. Surgical procedures to correct contractures and improve muscle balance are valuable in the spastic syndromes. Surgical and pharmacological approaches to reducing spasticity and dyskinesia remain largely experimental.　Hart de Coudres Peterson

Bibliography. E. Blair and F. J. Stanley, Intrapartum asphyxia: A rare cause of cerebral palsy, *J. Pediat.*, 112:515–519, 1988; H. Galjaard et al. (eds.), *Early Detection and Management of Cerebral Palsy*, 1987; K. B. Nelson and J. H. Ellenberg, The asymptomatic newborn and risk of cerebral palsy, *Amer. J. Dis. Child.*, 141:1333–1335, 1987; K. B. Nelson and J. Ellenberg, Obstetric complications as risk factors for cerebral palsy or seizure disorders, *J. Amer. Med. Ass.*, 251:1983–1984, 1985; F. Stanley and E. Alberman, *The Epidemiology of the Cerebral Palsies*, 1984.

Cerenkov radiation

Light emitted by a high-speed charged particle when the particle passes through a transparent, nonconducting, solid material at a speed greater than the speed of light in the material. The blue glow observed in the water of a nuclear reactor, close to the active fuel elements, is radiation of this kind. The emission of Cerenkov radiation is analogous to the emission of a shock wave by a projectile moving faster than sound, since in both cases the velocity of the object passing through the medium exceeds the velocity of the resulting wave disturbance in the medium. This radiation, first predicted by P. A. Cerenkov in 1934 and later substantiated theoretically by I. Frank and I. Tamm, is used as a signal for the indication of high-speed particles and as a means for measuring their energy in devices known as Cerenkov counters. *See* SHOCK WAVE.

Direction of emission. Cerenkov radiation is emitted at a fixed angle θ to the direction of motion of the particle, such that $\cos \theta = c/nv$, where v is the speed of the particle, c is the speed of light in vacuum, and n is the index of refraction of the medium. The light forms a cone of angle θ around the direction of motion. If this angle can be measured, and n is known for the medium, the speed of the particle can be determined. The light consists of all frequencies for which n is large enough to give a real value of $\cos \theta$ in the preceding equation.

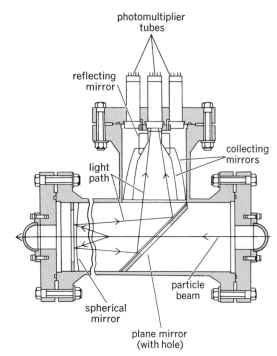

Fig. 1. Differential gas Cerenkov counter.

Cerenkov counters. Particle detectors which utilize Cerenkov radiation are called Cerenkov counters. They are important in the detection of particles with speeds approaching that of light, such as those produced in large accelerators and in cosmic rays, and are used with photomultiplier tubes to amplify the Cerenkov radiation. These counters can emit pulses with widths of about 10^{-10} s, and are therefore useful in time-of-flight measurements when very short times must be measured. They can also give direct information on the velocity of the passing particle. *See* PARTICLE DETECTOR; PHOTOMULTIPLIER.

Dielectrics such as glass, water, or clear plastic may be used in Cerenkov counters. Choice of the material depends on the velocity of the particles to be measured, since the values of n are different for the materials cited. By using two Cerenkov counters in coincidence, one after the other, with proper choice of dielectric, the combination will be sensitive to a given velocity range of particles. *See* DIELECTRIC MATERIALS.

The counters may be classified as nonfocusing or focusing. In the former type, the dielectric is surrounded by a light-reflecting substance except at the point where the photomultiplier is attached, and no use is made of the directional properties of the light emitted. In a focusing counter, lenses and mirrors may be used to select light emitted at a given angle and thus to give information on the velocity of the particle.

Cerenkov counters may be used as proportional counters, since the number of photons emitted in the light beam can be calculated as a function of the properties of the material, the frequency interval of the light measured, and the angle θ. Thus the number of photons which make up a certain size of pulse gives information on the velocity of the particle.

Gas, notably carbon dioxide (CO_2; **Fig. 1**), may also be used as the dielectric in Cerenkov counters. In such counters the intensity of light emitted is much smaller than in solid or liquid dielectric counters, but the velocity required to produce a count is much higher because of the low index of refraction of gas. William B. Fretter

Cerenkov astronomy. Faint flashes of Cerenkov light are emitted when energetic cosmic-ray particles penetrate the Earth's atmosphere. Observatories that are especially designed to record such radiation give information on the origin of cosmic rays and on some of the highest-energy phenomena to occur in nature.

The initiating radiation for the cosmic-ray air shower can be a very high energy gamma ray (**Fig. 2**). For such radiation the atmosphere is practically opaque; the probability of its reaching the ground without interacting is approximately 1 in 10^{12}. A cascade of electrons and positrons is generated from the interplay of two processes: electron-positron pair production from gamma rays and gamma-ray emission as the electrons and positrons are accelerated by the electric fields of nuclei in the atmosphere (bremsstrahlung). For a primary gamma ray having an energy of 10^{12} eV (1 teraelectronvolt), as many as a thousand or more electrons and positrons will contribute to the cascade. The combined Cerenkov light of the cascade is beamed to the ground over an area of a few hundred meters in diameter and marks the arrival direction of the initiating gamma ray

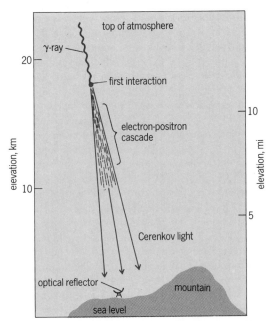

Fig. 2. Schematic view of air shower initiated by a very high energy gamma ray.

to about 1°. On a clear, dark night this radiation may be detected as a very short pulse of light lasting a few nanoseconds, by using an optical reflector (**Fig. 3**). *See* BREMSSTRAHLUNG; ELECTRON-POSITRON PAIR PRODUCTION.

Most cosmic-ray air showers are initiated by electrically charged particles. The magnetic fields of the Milky Way Galaxy prevent such particles from traveling in a straight line. For example, a 1-TeV proton travels along a twisted path with a radius

Fig. 3. The 34-ft (10-m) optical reflector at the Harvard-Smithsonian's Whipple Observatory near Tucson, Arizona.

of curvature of approximately 10^{-3} of a light-year. Therefore, the directional information regarding the source of the energetic cosmic ray is hopelessly scrambled. If the apparent arrival directions of such cosmic rays are plotted on a map of the sky, a uniform distribution is seen. However, high-energy gamma rays preserve their source direction; thus possible cosmic sources of high-energy gamma rays are seen as positional enhancements in the shower rate. One of the first clear source detections using this technique was the observations of Cygnus X-3 at teraelectronvolt energies in 1972. *See* MILKY WAY GALAXY.

Since this discovery, more than 20 sources of very high energy radiation have been observed by ground-based Cerenkov gamma-ray telescopes. The sources are predominantly identified with neutron stars or white dwarf stars in the Milky Way Galaxy. Many of the sources have been detected by observing a modulation in the shower rate at a period corresponding to the rotation period of the star. In the vicinity of the star, a beam of high-energy radiation is presumed to exist. The observed modulation is due, then, to that beam swinging into and out of the line of sight to Earth, just as the light from a rotating beacon to a distant observer appears to flash on and off with the rotation period of the beacon. The detailed shape of the intensity of radiation during a cycle is dependent on the shape of the beam. The presence of the periodic modulation in the shower rate allows a more sensitive search for such sources than would otherwise be possible. *See* NEUTRON STAR; PULSAR.

An alternative technique for improving the sensitivity of Cerenkov gamma-ray telescopes, (Fig. 3) exploits differences between the Cerenkov light images of gamma-ray showers and cosmic-ray showers. In this technique, the image of the each individual air shower is captured with an array of fast photomultipliers operating in the focal plane of the gamma-ray telescope. Comparison of the observed image parameters for each shower with an expected gamma-ray template results in rejection of more than 99% of the background cosmic-ray showers, while more than 50% of gamma-ray showers are retained. One advantage of the imaging technique for background suppression is that it does not depend on the presence of an assumed periodic signal at the source.

With this technique, radiation has been detected from the Crab Nebula. These detections, and detections at lower gamma-ray energies, generally support a theoretical model of the high-energy emission process in which the highest-energy radiation is due to Compton scattering between extremely relativistic electrons (with energies up to $\sim 10^{16}$ eV) and lower-energy photons in the nebula. In this picture, the lower-energy photons have been created by the relativistic electrons themselves as they spiral in the magnetic field of the nebula. The underlying power for all of this high-energy activity is the rotation of a rapidly spinning neutron star (spin period 33 milliseconds) which itself is the remnant of a relatively recent (1054) supernova explosion. *See* CRAB NEBULA.

The imaging technique was used to discover very high energy radiation from a distant galaxy, Markarian 421. This galaxy possesses an active nucleus at its center which powers radiation over a wide range of the electromagnetic spectrum. The fact that gamma rays to energies of 10^{12} eV are observed suggests that this source and others similar to it are copious producers of high-energy cosmic rays. *See* ASTROPHYSICS; HIGH-ENERGY; COSMIC RAYS; GALAXY; EXTERNAL; GAMMA-RAY ASTRONOMY   Richard C. Lamb

Bibliography. M. Punch et al., Detection of TeV photons from the active galaxy Markarian 421, *Nature*, 358:477–478, 1992; T. C. Weekes, Very high energy gamma-ray astronomy, *Phys. Rep.*, 160:1–121, 1988.

Ceres

The first asteroid discovered. It was found serendipitously by G. Piazzi on January 1, 1801. Although it is located at the heliocentric distance predicted by the Titius-Bode law for the "missing" planet between Mars and Jupiter, additional asteroids were not located thus, and so the significance, if any, of this "law" is unknown..

With an effective diameter of 580 mi (933 km), Ceres is the largest asteroid but not the brightest since it reflects only 10% of the visual light it receives. (Vesta, though only about half as large as Ceres, is the brightest asteroid since it is closer to the Sun, 2.4 versus 2.8 astronomical units, or 2.2 versus 2.6×10^8 mi, or 3.6 versus 4.2×10^8 km, and reflects 38% of its incident light.) Ceres' mass of 2.19×10^{21} lbm (9.95×10^{20} kg, that is, 1.7×10^{-4} that of the Earth) contains approximately 40% of the asteroid belt's total mass. Its relatively low density, approximately 2.3 that of water (144 lbm/ft^3 or 2.3 g/cm^3), may, at least in part, be due to the fact that its surface material, and hence possibly its interior, contains water of hydration.

Ceres is a spheroidal object with an equatorial diameter of 596 mi (959 km) and a polar diameter of 564 mi (907 km), displays no large-scale color or brightness variations over its surface, and has a rotation period of 9^h03^{min}. *See* ASTEROID; ASTRONOMICAL UNIT; PLANET.   Edward F. Tedesco

Bibliography. M. Standish and H. Hoffmann, Mass determinations of asteroids, in R. Binzel, T. Gehrels, and M. Matthes (eds.), *Asteroids II*, 1989.

Cerianthia

An order of the Zoantharia, typified by *Cerianthus*, which lives in sandy marine substrata (**illus.** *a* and *b*). The animal is enclosed in a sheath formed by mucus secreted from gland cells of the column

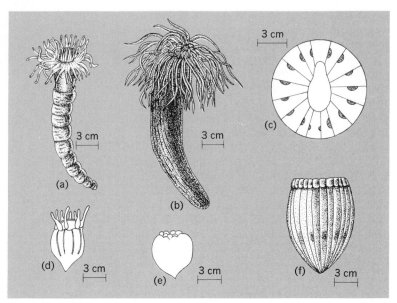

Ceriantharia. (a) *Cerianthus solitarius.* (b) *Pachycerianthus multiplicatus.* (c) *Mesenteric arrangement.* (d) *Cerianthula spinifer* larva. (e) *Ovactis aequatorialis* larva. (f) *Anactinia pelagica* larva.

ectoderm, in which discharged nematocysts, sand grains, and other foreign objects are embedded.

The polyp is a muscular, skeletonless, elongated, cylindrical body with a smooth wall. Long, slender, unbranching, freely retractile tentacles are arranged in two cycles and consist of smaller labial and larger marginal ones. A siphonoglyph termed the hyposulculus is present and a pedal disk is lacking.

The mesenteric arrangement is most characteristic (illus. c). Mesenteries are arranged bilaterally in couples, not in pairs, forming a single cycle. All are complete. The three most dorsal couples or directives appear first, and then the other two appear at both sides of the directives. Additional metacnemic couples are added to the ventral intermesenteric space and are arranged in quartets with regard to length. The longitudinal muscles are weakly developed in the ventral faces of the mesenteries, whose free edges bear filaments and acontialike threads or acontioids that seem to have an adhesive function.

Pelagic larvae (illus. d–f) known as *Arachnactis, Cerianthula, Ovactis, Anactinia,* and others always pass through the cerinula stage with three couples of the protocnemes. Life cycles have not been fully investigated. *See* ZOANTHARIA.   Kenji Atoda

Cerium

A chemical element, symbol Ce, atomic number 58, atomic weight 140.12. It is the most abundant metallic element of the rare-earth group in the periodic table. The naturally occurring element is made up of the isotopes ^{136}Ce 0.193%, ^{138}Ce 0.250%, ^{140}Ce 88.58%, and ^{142}Ce 11.07%. A radioactive alpha emitter, ^{142}Ce has a half-life of 5×10^{15} years. The oxide of the element was discovered in 1803 by M. H. Klaproth, and independently by J. J. Berzelius and W. Hisinger. Cerium occurs mixed with other

rare earths in many minerals, particularly monazite and blastnasite, and is found among the products of the fission of uranium, thorium, and plutonium.

Although the common valence of cerium is 3, it also forms a series of quadrivalent compounds and is the only rare earth which occurs as a quadrivalent ion in aqueous solution. Although it can be separated from the other rare earths in high purity by ion-exchange methods, it is usually separated chemically by taking advantage of its quadrivalent state. Ceric oxide, CeO_2, is the oxide usually obtained when cerium salts of volatile acids are heated. Ceric oxide is an almost white powder which is insoluble in most acids, although it can be dissolved in sulfuric acid or other acids when a reducing agent is present. The trivalent salts are white and the quadrivalent salts are usually yellow. The metal is an iron-gray color and it oxidizes readily in air, forming a gray crust of oxide. In the pure state it is not very pyrophoric, but when slightly oxidized or alloyed with iron, it becomes extremely pyrophoric. Misch metal, an alloy of cerium, is used in the manufacture of lighter flints. Cerium has the interesting property that, at very low temperatures or when subjected to high pressures, it exhibits a fourth allotropic form, face-centered cubic, which is diamagnetic and 18% denser than the common form. For other properties of cerium metal *see* RARE-EARTH ELEMENTS.

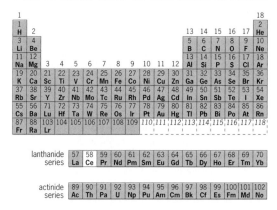

Crude mixtures of cerium with other rare earths have found extensive use in industry. It is used as a "getter" in the metal industry and as an opacifier and polisher in the glass industry. It is one of the main ingredients in Welsbach gas mantles and cored carbon arcs. Cerium metal, in common with the other rare earths, is almost immiscible in molten uranium, and can, therefore, be used as a liquid-liquid extraction agent to remove fission products from spent uranium fuel. The ceric salts are used in analytical chemistry as oxidation agents.

Frank H. Spedding

Cermet

A group of composite materials consisting of an intimate mixture of ceramic and metallic components.

Fabrication. Cermets can be fabricated by mixing the finely divided components in the form of powders or fibers, compacting the components under pressure, and sintering the compact to produce physical properties not found solely in either of the components. Cermets can also be fabricated by internal oxidation of dilute solutions of a base metal and a more noble metal. When heated under oxidizing conditions, the oxygen diffuses into the alloy to form a base metal oxide in a matrix of the more noble metal. *See* CORROSION; POWDER METALLURGY.

Components. Ceramic components may be metallic oxides, carbides, borides, silicides, nitrides, or mixtures of these compounds; the metallic components include a wide variety of metals whose selection depends on the application of the respective cermet. Some of the component materials are shown in the **table**.

Interactions. The reactions taking place between the metallic and ceramic components during fabrication of cermets may be briefly classified and described as follows:

1. Heterogeneous mixtures with no chemical reaction between the components, characterized by a mechanical interlocking of the components without formation of a new phase, no penetration of the metallic component into the ceramic component, and vice versa, and no alteration of either component (example, MgO–Ni). *See* PHASE EQUILIBRIUM.

2. Surface reaction resulting in the formation of a new phase as an interfacial layer that is not soluble in the component materials. The thickness of this layer depends on the diffusion rate, temperature, and time of the reaction (example, Al_2O_3–Be). *See* DIFFUSION.

3. Complete reaction between the components, resulting in the formation of a solid solution characterized by a polyatomic structure of the ceramic and the metallic component (example, TiC–Ni).

4. Penetration along grain boundaries without the formation of interfacial layers (example, Al_2O_3–Mo).

Bonding behavior. One important factor in the selection of metallic and ceramic components in cermets is their bonding behavior. Bonding may be by surface interaction or by bulk interaction. In cermets of the oxide-metal type, for example, investigators differentiate among three forms of surface interaction: macrowetting, solid wetting, and wetting assisted by direct lattice fit.

Combinations. One distinguishes basically between four different combinations of metal and ceramic components: (1) the formation of continuous interlocking phases of the metallic and ceramic components, (2) the dispersion of the metallic component in the ceramic matrix, (3) the dispersion of the ceramic component in the metallic matrix, and (4) the interaction between the metallic and ceramic components.

Characteristics. The combination of metallic and ceramic components can result in cermets characterized by increased strength and hardness, higher temperature resistance, improved wear resistance, and better resistance to corrosion, each characteristic depending on the variables involved in composition and processing. In general, these materials should be corrosion resistant, have high-temperature strength, temperature (thermal) shock resistance, and a certain ductility.

The yield strength σ of a cermet depends on the component materials, the volume fraction f of the dispersed phase, the particle diameter d of the dispersed material, and the mean spacing λ between particles. These variables are related by Eqs. (1) and (2), where A and B are material constants.

$$\lambda = \frac{2d}{3f}(1-f) \qquad (1)$$

$$\sigma = -A \log \lambda + B \qquad (2)$$

Applications. Friction parts as well as cutting and drilling tools have been successfully made from cermets for many years. Certain nuclear reactor fuel elements, such as dispersion-type elements, are also made as cermets.

Fiber reinforcement. Fiber-reinforced cermets consist either of a metallic matrix reinforced by ceramic fibers (for high-temperature strength) or a ceramic matrix with metallic fibers inserted (for better heat conductivity). The term fiber refers to a multicrystalline material approximately 0.5–2.5 micrometers (0.02–0.1 mil) in diameter. Whiskers which can be used instead of fibers are short single crystals approximately 1–10 μm in diameter. Combinations of powders and fibers can be made with short or continuous fibers, randomly dispersed or aligned (oriented). Special materials with directional properties can be made by insertion of aligned fibers.

Bulk interactions. Two different forms of bulk interaction between metals and ceramics can be distinguished; solid solution and formation of chemical compounds. Usually solid-solution

Representative components of cermets

Class	Ceramic	Metal addition
Oxides	Al_2O_3	Al, Be, Co, Co-Cr, Fe, stainless steel
	Cr_2O_3	Cr
	MgO	Al, Be, Co, Fe, Mg
	SiO_2	Cr, Si
	ZrO_2	Zr
	UO_2	Zr, Al, stainless steel
Carbides	SiC	Ag, Si, Co, Cr
	TiC	Mo, W, Fe, Ni, Co, Inconel, Hastelloy, stainless steel, Vitallium
	WC	Co
	Cr_3C_2	Ni, Si
Borides	Cr_3B_2	Ni
	TiB_2	Fe, Ni, Co
	ZrB_2	Ni
Silicides	$MoSi_2$	Ni, Co, Pt, Fe, Cr
Nitrides	TiN	Ni

bonding involves the addition, or formation, within the cermet of a small amount of the appropriate ceramic form of the metal constituent; examples of the type of phase involved are provided by the systems Al_2O_3–Cr_2O_3 and NiO–MgO for oxides, and TaC–Tic and NbC–ZrC for carbides. The systems form continuous series of solid solutions, but there are also many suitable systems in which solid solution occurs over a limited range only.

Formation of a compound in a bonding phase can best be shown by the examples of spinels, having the generalized formula $RO \cdot R'_2O_3$, where R could, for example, stand for Ni^{2+}, Mg^{2+}, Fe^{2+}, or Co^{2+}, and R' for Al^{3+}, Cr^{3+}, or Fe^{3+}. Much study has been made of the system Al_2O_3–Fe, without achieving the combination of properties required for the high-temperature engineering applications in view. *See* COMPOSITE MATERIAL; METAL MATRIX COMPOSITE.

Henry H. Hausner

Bibliography. P. Naylor, *Introduction to Metal Ceramic Technology*, 1992; J. Pask and A. Evans (eds.), *Surfaces and Interfaces in Ceramic and Ceramic-Metal Systems*, 1981; G. S. Upadhyaya (ed.), *Sintered Metal-Ceramic Composites*, 1985.

Cerussite

The mineral form of lead carbonate, $PbCO_2$. Cerussite is common as a secondary mineral associated with lead ores. In the United States it occurs mostly in the central and far western regions. Cerussite is white when pure but is

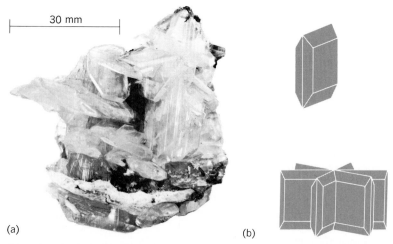

(a)   (b)

Cerussite crystals. (a) Specimen from Ems, Nassau (American Museum of Natural History specimen). (b) Common crystal habits (after C. S. Hurlbut, Jr., Dana's Manual of Mineralogy, 17th ed., John Wiley and Sons, 1959)

sometimes darkened by impurities. Hardness is 33/4 on Mohs scale and specific gravity is 6.5. Cerussite has orthorhombic symmetry and the same crystal structure as aragonite. Crystals may be tabular, enlongated, or arranged in clusters (see **illus.**). *See* CARBONATE MINERALS.

Robert I. Harker

Cesium

A chemical element, symbol Cs, with an atomic number of 55 and an atomic weight of 132.905, the heaviest of the alkali metals in group I of the periodic table (except for francium, the radioactive member of the alkali metal family). Cesium was discovered by R. Bunsen in 1860 by spectroanalysis, and was first isolated by electrolysis in 1881. It is a soft, light, very low melting temperature metal. It is the most reactive of the alkali metals and indeed is the most electropositive and the most reactive of all the elements. Little was known of its properties because of the relative unavailability and high cost of cesium compounds in the chemical market. In 1958, however, cesium salts became available much more readily and at lower prices as by-products of lithium chemicals manufacture. Knowledge of the properties and the reactions of cesium metal have developed accordingly. What is known of the chemical behavior of this most-reactive metal is intriguing, and it seems to offer unusual research possibilities.

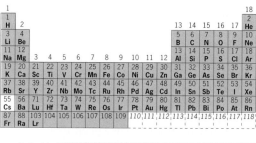

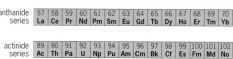

Chemical properties. Cesium reacts vigorously with oxygen to form a mixture of oxides in the same manner as do rubidium and potassium. In moist air, the heat of oxidation may be sufficient to melt and ignite the metal.

Cesium does not appear to react with nitrogen to form a nitride, but does react with hydrogen at high temperatures to form a fairly stable hydride.

Cesium reacts violently with water and even with ice at temperatures as low as $-116°C$ ($177°F$). Little is known about the reaction of cesium with carbon, but acetylides can be formed from cesium and acetylene.

The reaction with halogens is vigorous, and cesium is distinguished among the alkali metals for its ability, presumably due to its large ionic radius, to form stable polyhalides, such as CsI_3.

Cesium reacts with ammonia to form cesium amide and with carbon monoxide in the cold at low pressures to give a crystalline compound of indeterminate composition.

Cesium, in general, undergoes some of the same types of reactions with organic compounds as do the other alkali metals, but it is much more reactive. Thus, it adds directly to ethylene to form a brown solid, $C_2H_4Cs_2$, whereas the other alkali metals will add only to dienes or to olefins activated by aromatic groups. For a discussion of handling techniques *see* SODIUM.

Physical properties. The physical properties of cesium metal are summarized in the **table**.

Physical properties of cesium metal		
Property	Temp., °C	Value
Density	20	1.9 g/cm³
Melting point	28.5	
Boiling point	705	
Heat of fusion	28.5	3.8 cal/g
Heat of vaporization	705	146 cal/g
Viscosity	100	4.75 millipoises
Vapor pressure	278	1 mm
	635	400 mm
Thermal conductivity	28.5	0.044 cal/(s)(cm²)(°C)
Heat capacity	28.5	0.06 cal/(g)(°C)
Electrical resistivity	30	36.6 microhm-cm

Principal compounds. Cesium chloride is the most important cesium compound. The metal is made from the chloride, and the chloride is used as a constituent of getter mixtures for vacuum tubes. The fluoride, carbonate, and sulfate are also available and used in small commercial quantities.

Analytical methods. Cesium can be identified qualitatively by its blue flame. The fact that cesium forms an extremely insoluble alum may be used in the quantitative determination of cesium.

Occurrence. Cesium is not very abundant in the Earth's crust, at only 7 parts per million (ppm). However, this concentration still places cesium above beryllium, arsenic, uranium, and boron in abundance. There is only about 0.002 ppm of cesium in solution in seawater. Detectable amounts are found in plant and animal organisms, mineral waters, and soils.

Like lithium and rubidium, cesium is found as a constituent of complex minerals and not in relatively pure halide form as are sodium and potassium. Indeed, lithium, rubidium, and cesium frequently occur together in lepidolite ores, such as those from Rhodesia. Cesium is unlike lithium and rubidium, however, in that a cesium-rich mineral, pollucite, essentially $2Cs_2O \cdot 2Al_2O_3 \cdot 9SiO_2 \cdot H_2O$, does occur. It is found on the island of Elba, in South-West Africa, and in Manitoba. In the United States there are deposits in Maine and South Dakota.

Metallurgical extraction. Cesium metal is not produced on a commercial scale. In the limestone process for the conversion of lepidolite ore to lithium chemicals, however, a mixed alkali carbonate liquor is obtained by carbonation in a submerged combustion evaporator after the separation of the bulk of the lithium values as the hydroxide. Filtration after carbonation removes lithium carbonate and gives a filtrate containing the carbonates of potassium, rubidium, and cesium. For a description of the separation of the mixed alkali salts *see* RUBIDIUM.

Cesium metal is generally made by thermochemical processes. The carbonate can be reduced by metallic magnesium, or the chloride can be reduced by calcium carbide. Metallic cesium volatilizes from the reaction mixture and is collected by cooling the vapor.

Uses. Cesium metal is used in photoelectric cells, spectrographic instruments, scintillation counters, radio tubes, military infrared signaling lamps, and various optical and detecting devices. Cesium compounds are used in glass and ceramic production, as absorbents in carbon dioxide purification plants, as components of getters in radio tubes, and in microchemistry. Cesium salts have been used medicinally as antishock agents after administration of arsenic drugs. The isotope cesium-137 is supplanting cobalt-60 in the treatment of cancer. *See* ALKALI METALS.   Marshall Sittig

Bibliography. W. A. Hart et al., *The Chemistry of Lithium, Sodium, Potassium, Rubidium, Cesium, and Francium*, 1975.

Cestida

An order of the phylum Ctenophora (comb jellies) containing two monospecific genera, *Cestum* and *Velamen*, which have an unusual morphology. The transparent bodies of cestids are flattened in the tentacular plane and greatly elongated in the stomodeal plane so that they have the shape of a belt or ribbon (hence the specific name *Cestum veneris*, "Venus' girdle"; see **illus.**). The mouth is at the midpoint of the length. Individuals of *Cestum* may be more than 39 in. (1 m) long, and of *Velamen* about 8 in. (20 cm). Brown or yellow pigment spots sometimes occur on the tips of the body. If disturbed, Cestids, like other ctenophores, produce brilliant bioluminescence along their meridional canals.

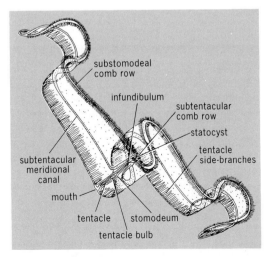

Cestum veneris.

They occur worldwide in tropical and subtropical waters; *C. veneris* is one of the most common species in the oceanic Atlantic. The extreme fragility of their bodies makes cestids difficult to collect and maintain, and living specimens have been seen by few biologists.

Because of the great lateral elongation of the body, the subtentacular comb rows are reduced to a few ctenes, but the substomodeal rows run along the entire aboral edge of the body. The beating of the comb rows propels the cestid slowly forward like a wing, with the oral edge leading. Two main tentacles arise on either side of the central stomodeum and lie in a groove along the oral edge; numerous fine side branches (tentilla) from these tentacles trail back over the flat sides of the body. The prey, mainly small crustaceans, are captured when they contact the body surface and stick to the tentilla. Contraction of the tentilla moves the prey into the oral groove, which transports it by ciliary action to the mouth. This feeding mechanism allows cestids to catch prey ranging from about 100 micrometers to several millimeters in size. It is energetically efficient, and fishing is continuous, without interruptions to transfer or handle prey. Cestids are also capable of rapid undulatory swimming along their long axis, mainly as an escape response to disturbance. They are frequently parasitized by hyperiid amphipods; predators on cestids include medusae, the ctenophore *Beroë*, and various fishes.

Like other ctenophores, cestids are simultaneous hermaphrodites, with ovaries and testes located along the meridional canals. Very little is known about the timing of their reproduction. Fertilized eggs develop first into typical cydippid larvae but soon begin to elongate and take on the typical cestid form. See CTENOPHORA.   Laurence P. Madin

Bibliography. G. R. Harbison, L. P. Madin, and N. R. Swanberg, On the natural history and distribution of oceanic ctenophores, *Deep-sea Res.*, 25:233–256, 1978; F. W. Harrison and J. A. Westfall (eds.), *Microscopic Anatomy of Invertebrates*, vol. 2, 1991; S. P. Parker (ed.), *Synopsis and Classification of Living Organisms*, 1982.

Cestoda

A subclass of tapeworms including most of the members of the class Cestoidea. All species are endoparasites of vertebrates, living in the intestine or related ducts.

Morphology. Like other members of the class, the cestodes have no digestive tract or mouth. Nutrition presumably occurs by absorption of food through the body surface. The body, or strobila, is usually very elongated and tapelike and frequently divided into segments, or proglottids, with replication of the hermaphroditic reproductive systems. In a few species there is duplication of both male and female organs within a single segment. The anterior end is usually modified into a holdfast organ, the scolex. Since a digestive tract is completely absent, the scolex is of solid construction, typically highly muscular with sucking depressions and hooks (**Fig. 1**). Behind the scolex there is usually a region of undifferentiated tissue, termed the neck, from which proliferation of new segments occurs. In some species a neck is not apparent, and segments begin immediately behind the scolex. The strobila, or chain of segments, typically arises by growth and differentiation, the smallest and least-differentiated segments being nearest to the neck. Young segments are always broader than long, but, as the segments grow in volume, they may become square or longer than broad. The body is clothed with what has been called a cuticle, but it has been shown that this noncellular layer is relatively complex (**Fig. 2**). This might be expected since these animals actively absorb such nutrients as carbohydrates and amino acids.

Nervous system. The nervous system consists basically of a pair of longitudinal lateral nerves running through the length of the strobila. Additional nerve trunks are frequently present. The trunks are connected by a ring-shaped commissure in each segment and by thickened commissures, a "brain," in the scolex. Although the tapeworms lack special sensory structures, the body surface has many sensory nerve endings.

Excretory system. The excretory or osmoregulatory system consists of protonephridia, or flame bulbs, which connect ultimately through a system of fine ducts to a pair of longitudinal lateral canals on either side. These canals traverse the length of the body.

Reproductive system. The reproductive systems develop progressively along the strobila, the male system usually becoming mature before the female. In some forms there are two complete hermaphroditic

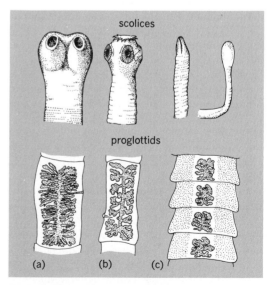

Fig. 1. Scolices and mature proglottids of (a) *Taenia saginata*, (b) *T. solium*, and (c) *Dibothriocephalus latus*. (After T. I. Storer and R. L. Usinger, *General Zoology*, 3d ed., McGraw-Hill, 1957)

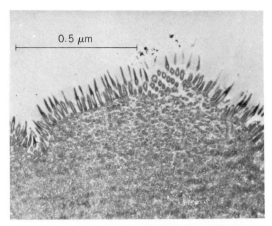

0.5 μm

Fig. 2. The "cuticle" of *Hymenolepis diminuta*. **(***Electron photomicrograph by A. H. Rothman***)**

systems. The male and female genital ducts commonly open into a common antrum, usually situated on the lateral margin of the segment. The testes are usually small rounded bodies, ranging in number from 1 to 1000 but most often about 100. Sperm are carried in a system of ducts to an eversible copulatory organ, the cirrus, which is frequently armed with spines or hooks. The ovary is single, commonly having two lobes. In the orders other than Cyclophyllidea, yolk glands occur as numerous follicles. Yolk cells from these glands are gathered in a duct system which enters the oviduct from the ovary. The oviduct also receives the vagina and eventually enlarges to form the uterus. The uterus begins developing after the gonads and their associated ducts have matured and varies in shape from a simple sac to a ramified network.

With growth, the reproductive systems differentiate, and fertilization occurs in a modified region of the oviduct where the ovum is enclosed with yolk cells in a shell. These eggs develop into embryos, or oncospheres, within the uterus. Fertilization may occur within a single proglottid, between segments in the same strobila, or between proglottids of separate worms. Hypodermic impregnation occurs in a few cases. The posterior proglottids become distended with embryos. In some orders, such as Tetraphyllidae, the sexually mature proglottids are shed from the body before significant development of embryos, and the free proglottids undergo "ripening" in the host intestine. In most other orders the gravid, embryo-filled proglottids are shed from the strobila and pass out of the host, with or without degeneration of the segment tissue. In the Pseudophyllidea, gravid proglottids are retained and the shelled embryos are shed through a uterine pore. The growth rates of cestodes show great variation. Different species of the same genus may show marked differences in growth rate and in the time during which a high growth rate, without senility, is maintained. The life of the sexually reproducing tapeworm varies from 4 or 5 days in some pseudophyllideans to 20 or more years in some cyclophyllideans. *See* CESTOIDEA; TETRAPHYLLIDEA.

Larval development. The details of larval development are known for only a few tapeworms. Cleavage leads to the formation of a six-hooked embryo, the oncosphere, which is enclosed in a ciliated embryophore in the Pseudophyllidea. Further embryonic development occurs in some other host species. Except for Cyclophyllidea, two intermediate hosts are usually required for embryonic development. Except for some taeniaoid tapeworms, the first intermediate host is always an arthropod, while the second is often a fish, but may be an invertebrate. Invariably, the embryo attains entrance to the intermediate host by being eaten, and the vertebrate host is infected by eating the intermediate host.

The postoncosphere development of all cestodes includes a procercoidlike stage. In most orders this is followed by the development of a plerocercoid larva in a second intermediate host. However, considerable modification of this developmental pattern occurs in the Cyclophyllidea, in which the postproceroid development continues in a single intermediate host and the plerocercoid is modified in one of several different ways. Other modifications of development in Cyclophyllidea include asexual reproduction of new individuals by budding. After differentiation and maturation of the scolex in the larval form, growth ceases until such time as the intermediate host is eaten by a vertebrate in which development of the strobila can occur. In general, the sexual strobilate phase of tapeworms shows considerable specificity with regard to the kind of vertebrate in which development occurs. It is rarely known whether this is due, in a given case, to a failure of contact of worm and host or to a physiological incompatibility. In many instances, such as the cestodes of birds, tapeworms occur in only a single vertebrate host species. *See* PSEUDOPHYLLIDEA.

Nutrition. The nutritional relationships of adult tapeworms have been extensively studied. The worms require carbohydrate for growth and reproduction and this requirement is satisfied only from the host ingesta. On the other hand, nitrogenous nutrients and many micronutrients may be obtained from the body stores of the host; deleting such materials from the host's diet has no appreciable effect on the worms. In at least one case, *Dibothriocephalus*, it has been shown that the anemia appearing in some humans harboring the worm is attributable to the absorption of vitamin B_{12} by the cestode. The energy metabolism of tapeworms is primarily fermentative. In air the rate of oxygen uptake is low and accounts for the oxidation of a small fraction of the carbohydrate metabolized.

Phylogeny. Most authorities agree that the tapeworms are ancient parasites, probably evolving as parasites of the earliest fishes. It seems probable that the tapeworms did not evolve from trematodes or other present-day groups of parasitic flatworms. The ancestry of the tapeworm may be directly derived from the acoele or rhabdocoele turbellarians and represents a line of evolution which is completely independent of other parasitic flatworms. These relationships remain obscure in the absence of any fossil records. *See* TURBELLARIA.   Clark P. Read

Cestodaria

A subclass of worms belonging to the class Cestoidea. Only a few species are known. All are endoparasites of primitive fishes. The subclass is usually divided into two orders, Amphilinidea and Gyrocotylidea. These worms differ from the other Cestoidea in being unsegmented, in not having the anterior end modified as a holdfast organ, and infrequently occurring as parasites of the coelomic cavity rather than the digestive tract. Some species have the posterior end modified into a holdfast organ. The animals are hermaphroditic and sexual reproduction occurs in the vertebrate host. The embryo or oncosphere bears 10 hooks, instead of the 6 found in other Cestoidea. *See* AMPHILINIDEA; GYROCOTYLIDEA.

In the only complete life history known, the worm undergoes a period of larval development in an invertebrate. When this invetebrate is eaten by the fish host, the worm develops to sexual maturity. *See* CESTOIDEA.   Clark P. Read

Cestoidea

A class of the phylum Platyhelminthes commonly referred to as tapeworms. All members are endoparasites, usually in the digestive tract of vertebrates. The class has been subdivided as follows:

Class Cestoidea
   Subclass Cestodaria
      Order: Amphilinidea
            Gyrocotylidea
   Subclass Cestoda
      Order: Proteocephaloidea
            Tetraphyllidea
            Lecanicephaloidea
            Trypanorhyncha
            Diphyllidea
            Pseudophyllidea
            Cyclophyllidea
            Nippotaeniidea

See separate articles on each group listed.

Morphology and life history. In size the tapeworms range from less than 0.04 in. (1 mm) to several feet in length. The class is differentially characterized by the presence of a cuticle rather than a cellular epidermis and by the total absence of a mouth and digestive tract. External cilia are never present, although the cuticle usually bears minute projections ranging from 0.1 to 1.0 micrometer

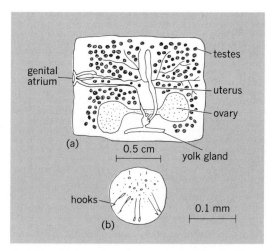

Cestoidea. (*a*) Sexually mature segment of *Taenia*. (*b*) Oncosphere of a cyclophyllidean tapeworm.

in diameter. In most species of the class the body is divided into proglottids, each proglottid containing one or two hermaphroditic reproductive systems (**illus.** *a*). The anterior end is usually modified into a holdfast organ, bearing suckers or sucking grooves, and frequently armed with hooks. Early embryonic development occurs in the parental body, usually in a uterus, to a hook-bearing stage, the oncosphere (illus. *b*). The oncosphere leaves the parental body through a uterine pore or by liberation of the terminal segment from the main body of the worm. Further development of the worm always occurs within the body of a host, most often an invertebrate, which commonly ingests the larval form. Growth of the larval worm, frequently with differentiation of the holdfast organ, occurs in this host; in some species asexual reproduction by budding occurs. Further larval growth and development of the holdfast may require a second host. Development of the sexual phase from the larva occurs in another host. Growth with strobilation and development of reproductive systems follow, the worm usually staying in the digestive tract. *See* PSEUDOPHYLLIDEA.

Nutrition. Food materials are presumed to be absorbed through the external surface. It has been shown that tapeworms have catalytic mechanisms for the active transport into the body of simple sugars and amino acids. Elaboration of digestive enzymes has not been demonstrated. The chemical composition of these worms is unique in that polysaccharide and fat represent a much larger proportion of the dry weight than does protein. *See* PLATYHELMINTHES.   Clark P. Read

Bibliography. A. C. Chandler and C. P. Read, *Introduction to Parasitology*, 10th ed., 1961; L. H. Hyman, *The Invertebrates*, vol. 2, 1951; E. R. Noble and G. A. Noble, *Parasitology: The Biology of Animal Parasites*, 5th ed., 1982; S. P. Parker (ed.), *Synopsis and Classification of Living Organisms*, 2 vols., 1982; R. A. Wardle and J. A. McLeod, *The Zoology of Tapeworms*, 1952.

Cetacea

An order of aquatic mammals including about 80 living species, of which the larger ones are called whales and the smaller ones dolphins or porpoises. Cetaceans live in all oceans and in several freshwater systems. They are remarkably adapted to aquatic life and die within a few hours or days on land. All have a smooth, streamlined body (**Fig. 1**); the forelimbs are flattened and rigid from shoulder to tip, without external fingers; the hindlimbs are absent, though represented by vestiges in the embryo or adult; the tail is flattened horizontally. The external ears are minute pits. The skin is hairless, though some fetal cetaceans have hairs on the snout and some adults have sensory bristles along the body. All cetaceans have a thick layer of blubber (subcutaneous fat) serving as heat insulation and as food reserve. *See* ADIPOSE TISSUE.

Structural and ecological adaptations. Cetaceans range in weight from 200 lb or 90 kg (harbor porpoise) to 176 tons or 160 metric tons (blue whale). Sex disparity in size is impressive in the sperm whale, a polygamous species; the full-grown male may weigh 61 tons (55 metric tons) and the female 16 (14.4 metric tons). Some whales make long annual migrations from warmer waters in which they breed to colder waters in which they feed. The California gray whale travels about 5000 mi (800 km) and returns each year. Maximum swimming speed is recorded for the killer whale

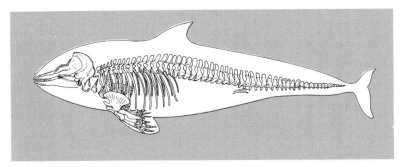

Fig. 1. Skeleton of a porpoise, highly specialized for an aquatic life. (*After Guide to the Hall of Biology of Mammals, Amer. Mus. Natur. Hist. Guide Leafl. ser. 76, 1933*)

sprinting at 30 knots (34.5 land miles per hour).

The sperm whale is one of the deepest divers, to a known depth of 3720 ft (1133 m) and may remain underwater for 75 min. Specialization of cetaceans for sensing their environment has led to extinction of smell, reduction of vision (one species is totally blind and another is nearly so), and extreme development of hearing. Some whales can perceive vibrations up to 200 kHz, as compared with the upper limit for humans of about 20 kHz. Vibrations serve for communication and echolocation (sonar). While the intelligence of cetaceans is debatable, by most standards (gross weight of brain, weight of brain in relation to cord, ready response to training, social interaction, and playfulness), the species which have been studied in captivity rate nearer the primates than do the dog, cat, rat, and

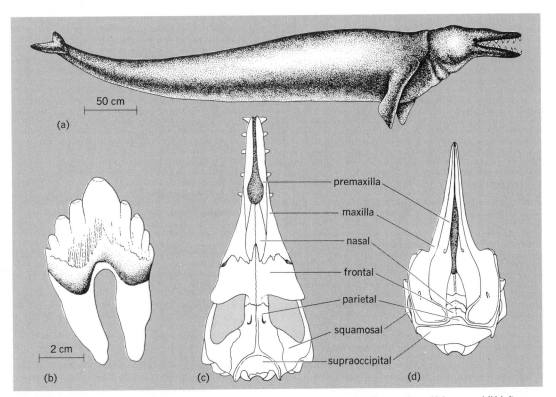

Fig. 2. Cetacea fossils. (*a*) *Zygorhiza kochii* (an archaeocete), restoration of the late Eocene from Alabama and (*b*) left upper premolar. (*c*) Skull of *Prozeuglodon stromeri* from early Oligocene of Egypt. (*d*) Skull of *Dephinodon dividum* from the middle Miocene of Maryland.

horse. The food of cetaceans is exclusively flesh. The toothed whales feed mainly on fishes and squids; the killer whale is a predator on other cetaceans and on seals, sea birds, fishes, and squids, but has never been known to attack a human. The whalebone whales feed mainly on macroplankton, especially euphausians.

Life cycle. So far as known, all cetaceans copulate belly to belly and quickly, near the surface of the sea. The gestation period is 9–16 months. A single, large precocious calf is born tail first, and it rises immediately to the surface for air. The nursing period may extend for 2 years (sperm whale). Cetacean milk is rich, being up to 50% fat, and low in sugars. It is forcibly squirted from two teats, normally buried in crypts but protruded during lactation. The blue whale calf gains an average of 10 lb (4.5 kg) an hour during the nursing months. Cetaceans are generally long-lived; as indicated by growth layers in the roots of the teeth, some sperm whales live to 75 years.

Taxonomy and fossil record. The ancestors of the cetaceans are completely unknown; they may have passed from land to sea via lakes, rivers, and estuaries in Cretaceous time. The earliest fossils are from middle Eocene beds and are clearly whales (**Fig. 2**). Separate lines of evolution have given rise to three suborders: Archaeoceti, Mysticeti, and Odontoceti. The bones of the braincase have progressively telescoped; the nostrils have moved to the top of the head; the teeth have in general been reduced in number and, in one line, remain now only in fetal life. No fossils are known which demonstrate the stages in loss of functional hindlimbs.

The zeuglodonts (Archaeoceti) were large, toothed forms with skull hardly or not at all telescoped. Their remains are known from middle Eocene beds of Africa and North America, and represent the oldest known cetaceans.

The whalebone whales (Mysticeti) are known from the middle Oligocene whales of Europe to the Recent whalebone whales of all oceans. They include the largest cetaceans. Their name is derived from horny, fringed filter plates of baleen, or whale "bone," suspended from the upper jaws. The external nares (blowholes) are double. Mysticetes and archaeocetes may have descended from a common stock. A remarkable archaeocete (Aetiocetus) from the late Oligocene of Oregon, described in 1966, was perhaps a close antecedent of the mysticetes. Its skull is moderately telescoped and has perhaps 44 teeth.

The toothed whales (Odontoceti) are known from the late Eocene whales of North America to Recent toothed whales, dolphins, and porpoises. The blowhole is single. Some odontocetes, but no mysticetes, live in fresh water. Evidence from blood chemistry suggests that the odontocetes are related to carnivores, and the mysticetes to ungulates. *See* MAMMALIA.   Victor B. Scheffer

Bibliography. S. Anderson and J. K. Jones, Jr. (eds.), *Recent Mammals of the World: A Synopsis*

of Families, 1967; R. Ellis, *Dolphins and Porpoises*, 1982; R. J. Harrison and J. E. King, *Marine Mammals*, 1968; R. Kellogg, The history of whales: Their adaptation to life in the water, *Quart. Rev. Biol.*, 3(1):29–76, and 3(2):174–208, 1928; S. Leatherwood and R. Reeves, *The Sierra Club Handbook of Whales and Dolphins*, 1983; S. P. Parker (ed.), *Synopsis and Classification of Living Organisms*, 2 vols., 1982; E. J. Slijper, *Whales and Dolphins*, 1976.

Cetane number

A number, usually between 30 and 60, that indicates the ability of a diesel engine fuel to ignite quickly after being injected into the cylinder. The higher the cetane number, the more easily the fuel can be ignited. In high-speed diesel engines, a fuel with a long ignition delay tends to produce rough operation. *See* COMBUSTION CHAMBER.

Automotive diesel engines use grades 1-D and 2-D of diesel fuel. Both grades have a minimum cetane number of 40. Low- and medium-speed diesel engines use grade 4-D, which has a minimum cetane number of 30.

To determine cetane number of a fuel sample, a specially designed diesel engine is operated under specified conditions with the given fuel. The fuel is injected into the engine cylinder each cycle at 13° before top center. The compression ratio is adjusted until ignition takes place at top center (13° delay). Without changing the compression ratio, the engine is next operated on blends of cetane (*n*-hexadecane), a short-delay fuel, and heptamethylnonane, which has a long delay. When a blend is found that also has a 13° delay under these conditions, the cetane number of the fuel sample may be calculated from the quantity of cetane required in the blend. *See* DIESEL ENGINE; DIESEL FUEL.   Donald Anglin

Bibliography. American Society for Testing and Materials, *Test Methods for Rating Motor, Diesel, and Aviation Fuels*, vol. 05.04, annually.

Cetomimiformes

An order of oceanic, mostly deep-water fishes that are structurally diverse and rare; most of the 41 species are known from one or a few specimens. Thus, their scientific study has been hindered, the anatomy is imperfectly known, and the relationships are in dispute. Five of the 10 families and 11 of the 21 genera currently placed in the order have been described since World War II. There is no fossil record.

Morphology and phylogeny. Cetomimiforms are all soft-rayed fishes. In most the mouth is large. Many are naked but a few have scales that are thin and deciduous or form an irregular mosaic; a few have the skin spinulose. Pelvic fins may be abdominal, thoracic, or jugular in position or, commonly, absent. In most forms the single dorsal and anal fins are placed rather well back and are opposed; an adipose fin is present in only one species. Studies now under way suggest that some kinds represent early developmental stages of other fishes, whereas some are the product of degenerative evolution in the deep seas. Cetomimiformes are probably polyphyletic and, when better known, the order may be dismembered and abandoned. The relationships of the constituent groups should be sought in the orders Beryciformes, Lampridiformes, and Salmoniformes.

Taxonomy. Because of the diversity, the five currently recognized suborders may be mentioned separately. Best known are the Cetomimoidei or whalefishes, also known as Cetunculi, a group of 3 families and 15 rare species of small, red or black deep-sea fishes with whale-shaped bodies and enormous mouths; they are bioluminescent. The Ateleopoidei (or Chondrobrachii) consist of 1 family, 3 genera, and 11 species of elongate fishes, the largest over half a meter, in which the long anal fin is continuous with the caudal and there is no dorsal fin. The Mirapinnatoidei (or Miripinnati) are tiny, perhaps larval fishes, all recently described. Three families, 4 genera, and 5 species are included. The Giganturoidei, with 2 families, 3 genera, and 6 species, are small mesopelagic fishes with large mouths and strong teeth; some have telescopic eyes. The Megalomycteroidei, or mosaic-scaled fishes, consist of 1 family, 4 genera, and 4 rare species of small, elongate deep-sea fishes with degenerate eyes and irregularly disposed scales. *See* ACTINOPTERYGII; OSTEICHTHYES; TELEOSTEI.

Reeve M. Bailey

Chabazite

A mineral belonging to the zeolite family of silicates. It commonly occurs in well-crystallized groupings of crystals with external rhombohedral symmetry (point group $\bar{3}2/m$) with nearly cubic angles. This well-developed external form suggests an internal structure compatible with space group $R\,\bar{3}m$; however, one structure refinement suggests lower symmetry (triclinic) with space group $P\,\bar{1}$. In addition to recognizing the distinct rhombohedral habit of chabazite crystals, the following physical properties are significant: hardness (on the Mohs hardness scale) in the range 4–5; light colors ranging from white to yellow, pink, and red; vitreous luster; and transparent to translucent in transmitted light. It is distinguished from calcite by a poorer rhombohedral cleavage and lack of effervescent reaction with dilute hydrochloric acid (HCl). *See* CRYSTAL STRUCTURE.

The ideal composition is $Ca_2Al_2Si_4O_{12}\cdot 6H_2O$ (where Ca = calcium, Al = aluminum, Si = silicon, O = oxygen, H_2O = water), but there is considerable chemical substitution of Ca by sodium (Na) and potassium (K), as well as (Na,K)Si for CaAl. The internal structure of chabazite consists of a framework linkage of (AlO_4) and (SiO_4) tetrahedra, with large cagelike openings bounded by rings of tetrahedra. The cages are connected to each other by open structural channels that allow for the diffusion of molecules through the structure of a size comparable to that of the diameter of the channels (about 0.39 nanometer in diameter). For example, argon (0.384 nm in diameter) is quickly absorbed by the chabazite structure, but *iso*-butane (0.56 nm in diameter) cannot enter the structure. In this manner, chabazite can be used as a sieve on a molecular level. *See* MOLECULAR SIEVE.

Chabazite is found, commonly with other zeolites, lining cavities in basalts as a result of low-temperature hydrothermal activity. Most of the fine chabazite crystal specimens that are exhibited in museums were found in large crystal-lined vugs in basalts. Notable localities are the Faroe Islands; the Giant's Causeway, Ireland; Seiser Alpe, Trentino, Italy; Aussig, Bohemia, former Czechoslovakia; Oberstein, Germany; and India. In the United States chabazite has been found at West Paterson, New Jersey, and Goble Station, Oregon. *See* ZEOLITE.

Cornelius Klein

Bibliography. G. Gottardi and E. Galli, *Natural Zeolites*, 1985; C. Klein and C. S. Hurlbut, Jr., *Manual of Mineralogy*, 21st ed., 1993.

Chaetodermomorpha

A subclass of burrowing, vermiform mollusks in the class Aplacophora. They are covered by a spicular integument and recognizable by the presence of a sensory cuticular oral shield, lack of a foot, and presence of paired gills in a posterior mantle cavity. Chaetoderms range in size from less than 0.08 in. (2 mm) to more than 2.8 in. (70 mm) and are found from shelf depths to hadal depths over 22,400 ft (7000 m). There are three families with 10 genera and 84 species worldwide. Chaetoderm species are numerically dominant in certain deep-sea localities. *See* DEEP-SEA FAUNA.

Spicules are aragonitic and sculptured by lengthwise ridges and grooves. They are overlapping, either held flat or slightly-to-perpendicularly raised in relation to the body. The underlying epidermis secretes both cuticle and spicules, as well as functioning for excretion through specialized papillae. Beneath the epidermis lie circular muscles, two sets of diagonal muscles, and four sets of heavy longitudinal muscle bands, the placement of which defines body shape.

Burrowing is slow, brought about by pushing the anterior end through the sediment by means of hydrostatic pressure; the longitudinal muscles then contract to bring the rest of the body forward.

The radula is nonrasping with two mirror-image teeth per row on a divided radular membrane, or it is specialized either as a rasping organ with distichous teeth on a unipartite membrane or as grasping pincers with two small distal denticles on a large cone. Food is entirely organic, either detritus or prey organisms, such as foraminiferans. The digestive system consists of a pharynx supplied with salivary glands, sometimes an esophagus, a stomach from which opens a blind digestive gland, and an intestine that runs from the stomach to the mantle cavity. Some families have a gastric shield at the posterior end of the stomach against which turns a mucoid rod.

The paired mantle cavity gills are typical for mollusks, of aspidobranch pattern with afferent and efferent vessels. A ventricle and paired auricles lie in the pericardium. The only blood vessel is the dorsal aorta, which runs anteriorly to the head; otherwise blood moves through open sinuses of the hemocoel. Paired ventral and lateral nerve cords arise from a bilobed cerebral ganglion and run posteriorly, connected by cross-commissures; the lateral cords join above the rectum as a large ganglion, which gives off a nerve to a chemoreceptory dorsal sensory organ.

The gonads are paired or fused and lie in the posterior part of the body; they empty into the pericardium, which in turn empties into paired U-shaped gametoducts. The latter are without elaboration and open separately into the cloaca. Sexes are separate. Embryology is unknown. *See* APLACOPHORA; MOLLUSCA.   Amelie H. Scheltema

Bibliography. L. v. Salvini-Plawen, Mollusca Caudofoveata, *Marine Invertebrates of Scandinavia,* vol. 4, 1975; A. H. Scheltema, Comparative morphology of the radulae and alimentary tracts in the Aplacophora, *Malacologia,* 20:361–383, 1981; A. H. Scheltema, Reproduction and rapid growth in a deep-sea aplacophoran mollusc, *Prochaetoderma yongei, Mar. Ecol., Prog. Ser.,* 37:171–180, 1987; E. R. Trueman and M. R. Clarke (eds.), *The Mollusca,* vol. 10: *Evolution,* 1985.

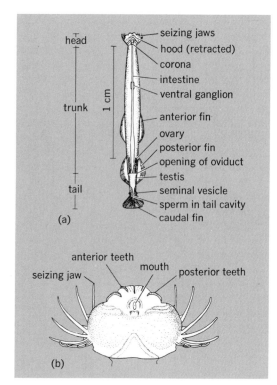

Sagitta enflata. (*a*) Dorsal view. (*b*) Head, ventral.

Chaetognatha

A phylum of abundant planktonic arrowworms. As adults they range in size from 0.2 to 4 in. (5 to 100 mm). Their bodies are tubular and transparent, and divided into three portions: head, trunk, and tail (**illus.** *a*). The head possesses one or two rows of minute teeth anterior to the mouth and usually 7–10 larger chaetae, or seizing jaws, on each side of the head. One or two pairs of lateral fins and a caudal fin are present. In mature individuals a pair of seminal vesicles protrudes from the sides of the tail segment just forward of the caudal fin.

Nine genera and about 42 species are recognized by some specialists. Most species belong to the genus *Sagitta*, which can be recognized by the presence of two pairs of teeth (illus. *b*) and two pairs of lateral fins. Important diagnostic features for species include the shape and position of the seminal vesicles and the number and arrangement of the anterior teeth.

Morphology. The body is covered by a thin hood of epidermis. When drawn forward, the hood covers the teeth and jaws and streamlines the anterior end of the body. Two small, dark eyes are found on the dorsal side of the head. Behind the eyes, and forming an irregular loop on the epidermis, is a structure called a corona ciliata, which is visible only when stained.

The nervous system consists of a dorsal ganglion, or brain, from which nerves lead to various portions of the head and body. A pair of nerves extends posteriorly from the brain and joins the prominent ventral ganglion which lies just beneath the epidermis.

The head musculature is quite complex, but the trunk has only six longitudinal bands of muscle, which restrict the body to simple lateral movements. Arrowworms are unable to constrict their bodies. Swimming is accomplished by rapid but brief movements of the caudal fin, followed by a quiet period. They do not appear to swim much, but drift passively most of the time.

The digestive system is simple. A mouth opens ventrally in the center of the head. A short esophagus leads to a straight intestine, which begins just behind the head and terminates in an anus opening ventrally at the septum separating the trunk and tail segments. The intestine is supported by dorsal and ventral mesenteries. A large coelom surrounds the intestine.

All chaetognaths are hermaphroditic. The ovaries are tubular and lie in the trunk segment just ahead of the septum dividing the trunk from the tail. The eggs in the ovaries increase in size at maturity, only a small fraction of the eggs maturing and being spawned at one time. Alongside the ovary is an oviduct, and contained within the oviduct is a narrow sperm duct. Fertilization is internal. The fertilized eggs are spawned free in the ocean, and the young chaetognaths hatch in some instances within 48 h. There is no larval stage.

The testes are situated in either side of the tail segment. As the sperm mature, they break away and often circulate in the tail cavity. From time to time some pass through short ducts leading from inside the tail cavity to the seminal vesicles. Small quantities of sperm are stored in the ducts prior to discharge.

Natural history. Chaetognaths are cosmopolitan forms which live not only at the surface but also at great depths; however, no one species is found in all latitudes and at all depths. One of the Arctic species, *Eukrohnia hamata*, may extend to the Antarctic by way of deep water across the tropics. A few species are neritic and are not found normally beyond the continental shelf.

Their food consists principally of copepods and other small planktonic crustaceans; however, they are very predacious and will even eat small fish larvae and other chaetognaths on rare occasions. The suggestion has been made that they feed on plants as well as animals, but this needs more supporting evidence. They seize their food with their pointed jaws and, aided by the teeth, push it into their mouths. Small crustacean larvae eaten one day appear to be digested by the next.

Along the Atlantic Coast of the United States they are most abundant over the continental shelf. Numbers of five or more per cubic meter of water are common along the coast; farther offshore only a fraction of this number is normally encountered. When very abundant, they may exceed $2.8/\text{ft}^3$ ($100/\text{m}^3$); however, this is unusual and often includes many young specimens.

Studies have shown them to be useful as indicator organisms. Certain species appear to be associated with characteristic types or masses of water, and when this water is displaced into an adjacent water mass, the chaetognaths may be used as temporary evidence for such displacement.

Their abundance and cosmopolitan distribution in marine waters, their little-known life history, their importance in the food chain both as predators and prey, and their value as indicator organisms invite further study. *See* SEAWATER FERTILITY.

E. Lowe Pierce

Bibliography. E. L. Pierce, The Chaetognatha over the continental shelf of North Carolina with attention to their relation to the hydrography of the area, *J. Mar. Res.*, 12(1):75–92, 1953; S. P. Parker (ed.), *Synopsis and Classification of Living Organisms*, 2 vols., 1982; R. von Ritter-Zahony, *Revision der Chaetognathen*, Deutsche Südpolar-Expedition 1901–1903, Bd. 13, Zool. 5, Heft 1, 1911; T. Tokioka, Chaetognaths of the Indo-Pacific, *Anat. Zool. Jap.*, 25(1,2):307–316, 1952.

Chaetonotida

An order of the phylum Gastrotricha. Members have Y-shaped pharyngeal lumina. *Neodasys* is a marine and macrodasyid-like form that reaches 0.8 mm (0.03 in.) in length and has front, side, and rear adhesive tubes. Others seldom exceed 0.3 mm (0.01 in.); they have only two rear adhesive tubes borne on a posterior furca, or none at all. Members of the family Xenotrichulidae have locomotor cilia grouped into cirri; all three genera are marine (**illus.** *a*). The family Chaetonotidae comprises half of

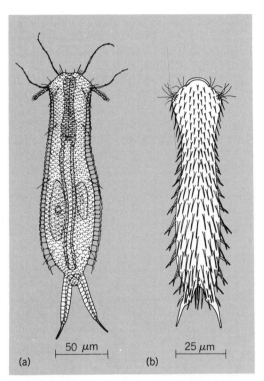

Marine gastrotrichs of the order Chaetonotida; dorsal views. (a) *Xenotrichula* (courtesy of W. D. Hummon). (b) *Chaetonotus* (after W. D. Hummon, Intertidal marine Gastrotricha from Colombia, Bull. Mar. Sci., 24:396–408, 1974).

all gastrotrichs: *Musellifer* and *Halichaetonotus* are marine; *Polymerurus* is fresh-water; *Aspidiophorus*, *Chaetonotus* (illus. *b*), *Heterolepidoderma*, *Ichthydium*, and *Lepidodermella* have species in each habitat. *Musellifer* lives in mud; all others inhabit sands of streams, beaches, or offshore banks, or live in the surface detritus of ponds or lake bottoms. The other seven genera, in four families, are all fresh-water and either are rare or tend toward a semiplanktonic life, especially *Neogossea* and *Stylochaeta*. Several chaetonotids are easily kept in aquatic microcosms, and a few, such as *L. squamata*, are readily cultured in pond water on wheat grains. *See* GASTROTRICHA.　　William D. Hummon

Chain drive

A flexible device of connected links used to transmit power. A drive consists of an endless chain which meshes with sprockets located on the shaft of a driving source, such as an electric motor/reducer, and a driven source, such as the head shaft of a belt conveyor.

Chains have been used for more than 2000 years. However, the modern contribution of the chain to industrialization began in 1873 with the development of a cast detachable chain. It was a simple cast-metal chain composed of identical links which could be coupled together by hand. This chain so greatly improved the performance of power takeoff drives for farm implements that mechanization became a practical reality. The first development after the success of the cast detachable chain was the cast pintle chain with a closed barrel design and steel pins. Other cast chain designs and variations evolved until an all-steel chain was developed.

Chain types. The new development, now called the roller chain (**Fig. 1**), found uses in the early 1900s on bicycles and other forms of conveyances. Constantly refined and improved, today's roller chain meets the demands of heavy-duty oil well drilling equipment, high-production agricultural machinery (**Fig. 2**), construction machinery, and similar equipment. It also meets the precise timing requirements of lighter-duty equipment such as printing, packaging, and vending equipment.

Another type of chain also evolved, called the

Fig. 2. Roller chain drive. (*FMC Corp.*)

engineering steel chain (**Fig. 3**). In a broad sense, the early designs of the engineering steel chain were a blend of the other two, the cast and the roller chain. The drive chains in the engineering steel chain category are usually identified by their offset/crank-link sidebar design. Generally, larger pitch sizes as compared to the roller chain and higher-strength chains characterize this group. A third group used for chain drives is the inverted-tooth (silent) chains (**Fig. 4**). A familiar application is their use as automotive timing chains in automobile engines.

Advantage. The use of chains for power transmission rather than another device, such as V-belts or a direct coupling to the power source, is usually based on the cost effectiveness and economy of chains and sprockets. Chains and sprockets offer the following advantages: large speed ratios; sufficient elasticity to absorb reasonable shocks; a constant speed ratio between the driving and driven shaft; long life without excessive maintenance; mechanical understandability regarding installation and functionality; coupling and uncoupling with simple tools; and a simple means to get power from its source to the location where needed. *See* BELT DRIVE.

Drive design. The design of a chain drive consists primarily of the selection of the chain and sprocket sizes. It also includes the determination of chain length, center distance, method of lubrication, and in some cases the arrangement of chain casings and idlers. Chain and sprocket selection is based on the horsepower and type of drive; the speeds and sizes of the shafting; and the surrounding conditions. A properly selected chain,

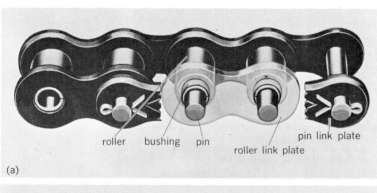

roller   bushing   pin   pin link plate   roller link plate

(a)

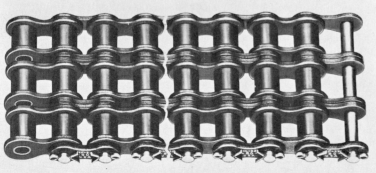

(b)

Fig. 1. Roller chains. (*a*) Single-strand. (*b*) Triple-strand.

Fig. 3. Engineering steel chain drive. (*Rexnord Inc.*)

following prescribed chain manufacturers' and the American Chain Association's techniques, is usually based on 15,000 hours of operation without breakage of components, considering chain wear not to exceed that which can be accommodated by the sprockets. Generally, chains are considered worn out when the roller chain exceeds approximately 3% elongation, the engineered steel chain exceeds approximately 5% elongation, and the inverted-tooth (silent) chain exhibits malfunction characteristics. To achieve the rated 15,000-h life, the environment must be clean and the chain lubricated as recommended by the manufacturer for the speed, the horsepower capacity, and the number of teeth on the smaller sprocket.

Chain and sprocket design. The particular design of the sideplate/sidebar/crank-link, pin, bushing, and roller of chains used in chain drives has been standardized to a substantial degree. The dimensional parameters regarding pitch, pin, bushing, roller, and side-plate sizes have been standardized. Interference between parts is usually controlled by the manufacturer, as is hardness of the chain parts, which determine the life of the chain. The selection of materials and heat treatments to obtain desired hardnesses are selected by manufacturers, but generally certain minimum hardnesses are required to meet minimum ultimate strength or breaking load criteria.

A sprocket is a wheel with teeth shaped to mesh with the chain. The sprocket tooth form, when properly selected, assures the success of the chain drive. Space limitations often determine the chain length and the number of teeth on the sprocket. Usually more than one combination of chain type, chain size, and number of sprocket teeth will satisfy a requirement. The final determination is based on economics and availability.

Lubrication. Lubrication of chains reduces joint wear as the links flex onto and off the sprockets. Lubricated bearing surfaces, that is, the chain joints, can carry high loads without galling. Chain capacity or horsepower ratings are determined for operation in a clean environment with proper lubrication. Lubrication extends the wear life of chains and sprockets operating in any environment, no matter how dirty or abrasive. Chains should not be greased. A nondetergent petroleum-base oil is recommended. For operation at high speeds, oil stream–force feed lubrication is required for cooling. An oil bath is effective at intermediate speeds, and manual lubrication is acceptable at slow speeds. *See* LUBRICANT; WEAR.

ANSI and ISO standards. The American National Standards Institute has established a committee for the standardization of transmission chains

Fig. 4. Inverted tooth/silent chain drive.

Chain description	ANSI standard number	ISO standard number	Title
Roller chain	B29.1	R606	(ANSI) Transmission roller chains and sprocket teeth (ISO) Short-pitch transmission roller chain
Inverted-tooth (silent) chain	B29.2	—	(ANSI) Inverted-tooth (silent) chains and sprocket teeth (ISO) No standard available
Engineering steel chain	B29.10	ISO3512	(ANSI) Heavy-duty offset sidebar power transmission roller chains and sprocket teeth (ISO) Heavy-duty crank-link transmission chains

ANSI and ISO standards for drive chains

and sprockets. Also, the International Standards Organization has established a committee to promulgate international standards for chains and chain wheels for power transmission and conveyors. The **table** identifies those standards which apply to drive chains. Typically, the standards identify those characteristics of a chain which ensure that one manufacturer's chain will couple with another and that the minimum ultimate strength or breaking load characteristics have been established for each chain (see table). The ANSI standard includes a supplemental section with horsepower rating tables and selection information. *See* CONVEYOR.   Victor D. Petershack

Bibliography. American Chain Association, *Chains for Power Transmission and Material Handling*, 1982.

Chain reaction (chemistry)

A chemical reaction in which many molecules undergo chemical reaction after one molecule becomes activated. In ordinary chemical reactions, every molecule that reacts must first become activated by collision with other rapidly moving molecules. The number of these violent collisions per second is so small that the reaction is slow. Once a chain reaction is started, it is not necessary to wait for more collisions with activated molecules to accelerate the reaction, which now proceeds spontaneously.

Photochemical reactions. A typical chain reaction is the photochemical reaction between hydrogen and chlorine as described by reactions (1).

$$Cl_2 + \text{light} \rightarrow Cl + Cl$$
$$Cl + H_2 \rightarrow HCl + H$$
$$H + Cl_2 \rightarrow HCl + Cl \tag{1}$$
$$Cl + H_2 \rightarrow HCl + H$$

The light absorbed by a chlorine molecule dissociates the molecule into chlorine atoms; these in turn react rapidly with hydrogen molecules to give hydrogen chloride and hydrogen atoms. The hydrogen atoms react with chlorine molecules to give hydrogen chloride and chlorine atoms. The chlorine atoms react further with hydrogen and continue the chain until some other reaction uses up the free atoms of chlorine or hydrogen. The chain-stopping reaction may be the reaction between two chlorine atoms to give chlorine molecules, or between two hydrogen atoms to give hydrogen molecules. Again the atoms may collide with the walls of the containing vessel, or they may react with some impurity which is present in the vessel only as a trace.

The length of the chain, that is, the number of molecules reacting per molecule activated, is determined by the relative rates of the competing reactions, namely, the chain-propagating reaction and the chain-stopping reactions. In the chain reaction just described, 10^6 molecules of hydrogen chloride may be formed by the photodissociation of 1 chlorine molecule.

In photochemical chain reactions, the length of the chain can be determined by measuring the number of photons of light absorbed, that is, the number of molecules activated, and dividing by the number of molecules which react chemically. *See* PHOTOCHEMISTRY.

Thermal reactions. In thermal reactions, the length of the chain may sometimes be estimated from a knowledge of the intermediate steps and the kinetics involved. The presence of a chain reaction can often be proved by adding a trace of an inhibitor, such as nitric oxide. If the reaction is slowed down greatly by a very small amount of a substance which reacts with the chain-propagating units, the reaction involves a chain. While the inhibitor is being consumed in this way, the reaction is slow. After an induction period, the inhibitor is consumed and the rapid chain reaction then takes place.

Chain reactions are erratic and are reproduced with difficulty in different laboratories because they depend so much on the presence and concentration of accidental impurities which act as inhibitors.

In many chemical reactions, particularly organic reactions at elevated temperatures, the chains are carried by free radicals which are very reactive fragments of molecules that have unshared electrons, such as $\cdot CH_3$, $\cdot C_2H_5$, $\cdot H$, and $\cdot OH$. The thermal decomposition of propane is a typical free-radical chain which follows reactions (2). One

$$C_3H_8 \rightarrow \cdot CH_3 + \cdot C_2H_5$$
$$\cdot CH_3 + C_3H_8 \rightarrow CH_4 + C_3H_7$$
$$\cdot C_3H_7 \rightarrow \cdot CH_3 + C_2H_4 \tag{2}$$
$$\cdot CH_3 + C_3H_8 \rightarrow CH_4 + \cdot C_3H_7$$

molecule of propane is decomposed into free radicals, $\cdot CH_3$ and $\cdot C_2H_5$, which then react with more propane to give the product methane and a free radical, $\cdot C_3H_7$, which decomposes into $\cdot CH_3$ and the product ethylene. The $\cdot CH_3$ reacts with more propane and continues the chain. The chain is terminated by collision of the free radicals with the wall or with each other, in reactions such as (3). Thus it is possible to obtain products of higher

$$\cdot CH_3 + \cdot C_3H_7 \rightarrow C_4H_{10} \tag{3}$$

molecular weight as well as products of lower molecular weight. The finding of these higher-molecular-weight products supports the theory of free-radical formation and chain reactions.

Certain oxidations in the gas phase are known to be chain reactions. The carbon knock which occurs at times in internal combustion engines is caused by a too-rapid combustion rate caused by chain reactions. This chain reaction is reduced by adding tetraethyllead which acts as an inhibitor.

The polymerization of styrene to give polystyrene and the polymerization of other organic materials to give industrial plastics involve chain reactions. The spoilage of foods, the precipitation of insoluble gums in gasoline, and the deterioration of certain plastics in sunlight involve chain reactions, which can be minimized with inhibitors. *See* ANTIOXIDANT; CATALYSIS; CHAIN REACTION (PHYSICS); CHEMICAL DYNAMICS; INHIBITOR (CHEMISTRY).

Farrington Daniels

Bibliography. J. H. Espenson, *Chemical Kinetics and Reaction Mechanisms*, 1981; H. Eyring et al., *Basic Chemical Kinetics*, 1980; K. J. Laidler, *Reaction Kinetics*, 2 vols., 1963; J. I. Steinfeld, J. Francisco, and W. Hase, *Chemical Kinetics and Dynamics*, 1989.

Chain reaction (physics)

A succession of generation after generation of acts of division (called fission) of certain heavy nuclei. The fission process releases about 200 MeV (3.2 × 10^{-4} erg = 3.2 × 10^{-11} joule) in the form of energetic particles including two or three neutrons. Some of the neutrons from one generation are captured by fissile species (^{233}U, ^{235}U, ^{239}Pu) to cause the fissions of the next generations. The process is employed in nuclear reactors and nuclear explosive devices. *See* NUCLEAR FISSION.

The ratio of the number of fissions in one generation to the number in the previous generation is the multiplication factor k. The value of k can range from less than 1 to less than 2, and depends upon the type and amount of fissile material, the rate of neutron absorption in nonfissile material, the rate at which neutrons leak out of the system, and the average energy of the neutrons in the system. When $k = 1$, the fission rate remains constant and the system is said to be critical. When $k > 1$, the system is supercritical and the fission rate increases. *See* REACTOR PHYSICS.

A typical water-cooled power reactor contains an array of uranium rods (about 3% ^{235}U) surrounded by water. The uranium in the form of UO$_2$ is sealed into zirconium alloy tubes. The water removes the heat and also slows down (moderates) the neutrons by elastic collision with hydrogen nuclei. The slow neutrons have a much higher probability of causing fission in ^{235}U than faster (more energetic) neutrons do. In a fast reactor, no light nuclei are present in the system and the average neutron velocity is much higher. In such systems it is possible to use the excess neutrons to convert ^{238}U to ^{239}U. Then ^{239}U undergoes radioactive decay into ^{239}Pu, which is a fissile material capable of sustaining the chain reaction. If more than one ^{239}Pu atom is provided for each ^{235}U consumed, the system is said to breed (that is, make more fissile fuel than it consumes). In the breeder reactor, the isotope ^{238}U (which makes up 99.3% of natural uranium) becomes the fuel. This increases the energy yield from uranium deposits by more than a factor of 60 over a typical water-moderated reactor, which

mostly employs the isotope ^{235}U as fuel.

A majority of power reactors use water as both the moderator and the coolant. However, a limited number of reactors use heavy water instead of light water. The advantage of this system is that it is possible to use natural uranium as a fuel so that no uranium enrichment is needed. Some other power reactors are gas-cooled by either helium or carbon dioxide and are moderated with graphite. *See* NUCLEAR REACTOR.   Norman C. Rasmussen

Bibliography. H. A. Enge and R. P. Redwine, *Introduction to Nuclear Physics*, 2d ed., 1995; S. Glasstone and A. Sesonske, *Nuclear Reactor Engineering*, 2 vols., 4th ed., 1993; K. S. Ram, *Basic Nuclear Engineering*, 1990.

Chalcanthite

A mineral with the chemical composition CuSO$_4$·5H$_2$O. Chalcanthite commonly occurs in blue to greenish-blue triclinic crystals or in massive fibrous veins or stalactites (see **illus.**). Fracture is conchoidal and luster is vitreous. Hardness is 2.5 on Mohs scale and specific gravity is 2.28. It has a nauseating taste and is readily soluble in water. It dehydrates in dry air to a greenish-white powder.

Chalcanthite is a secondary mineral associated with gypsum, melanterite, brochantite, and other sulfate minerals found in copper or iron sulfide deposits. It is also found in mine workings.

Although deposits of commercial size occur in arid areas, chalcanthite is generally not an important

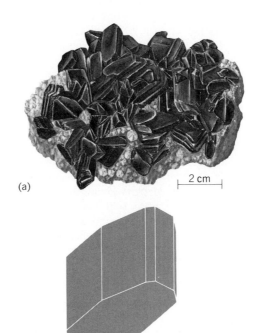

(a) |— 2 cm —|

(b)

Chalcanthite. (*a*) Crystals associated with quartz, Clifton, Arizona (*specimen from Department of Geology, Bryn Mawr College*). (*b*) Crystal habit (*after L. G. Berry and B. Mason, Mineralogy, W. H. Freeman, 1959*).

source of copper ore. Its occurrence is widespread in the western United States. *See* COPPER.

Edward C. T. Chao

Chalcedony

A fine-grained fibrous variety of quartz, silicon dioxide. The individual fibers that compose the mineral aggregate usually are visible only under the microscope. Subvarieties of chalcedony recognized on the basis of color differences (induced by impurities), some valued since ancient times as semiprecious gem materials, include carnelian (translucent, deep flesh red to clear red in color), sard (orange-brown to reddish brown), and chrysoprase (apple green). Chalcedony sometimes contains dendritic enclosures resembling plants or trees. Major kinds of impurities that give color to chalcedony are iron oxides (carnelian and sard), nickel (chrysoprase), and manganese. *See* GEM; QUARTZ.

Chalcedony occurs as crusts with a rounded, mammillary, or botryoidal surface and as a major constituent of nodular and bedded cherts. The hardness is 6.5–7 on Mohs scale. The specific gravity is 2.57–2.64. The ultrafine structure of chalcedony has been deduced from x-ray diffraction and electron microscopy to consist of a network of microcrystalline quartz with many micropores. The amount of amorphous silica, if any, is less than 10%. The yellowish color and anomalously low indices of refraction commonly observed under a transmitted light microscope result from scattering of light from the micropores. Paleozoic and older chalcedony is usually more coarsely crystallized than younger examples, grain growth of microcrystalline quartz being a result of time.

Crusts of chalcedony generally are composed of fairly distinct layers concentric to the surface. Agate is a common and important type of chalcedony in which successive layers differ markedly in color and degree of translucency. In the most common kind of agate the layers are curved and concentric to the shape of the cavity in which the material formed. The successive layers of chalcedony and agate usually differ in permeability to solutions, and much colored agate sold commercially is artificially pigmented by dyes or inorganic chemical compounds. *See* AGATE.

Raymond Siever

Bibliography. C. Frondel, *Dana's System of Mineralogy*, vol. 3: *Silica Minerals*, 1962.

Chalcocite

A mineral having composition Cu_2S, crystallizing in the orthorhombic system (below 217°F or 103°C), and having 96 formula units per unit cell. Cu atoms are tetrahedrally coordinated by S atoms, which form a face-centered cubic framework. Crystals are rare and small, usually with hexagonal

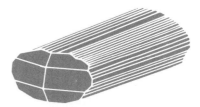

Chalcocite crystal habit. (*After C. S. Hurlbut, Jr., Dana's Manual of Mineralogy, 17th ed., John Wiley and Sons, 1959*)

outline because of twinning (see **illus.**). Most commonly, the mineral is fine-grained and massive with a metallic cluster and a lead-gray color which tarnishes to dull black on exposure. The Mohs hardness is 2.5–3, and the density 5.5–5.8. Chalcocite is an important copper ore found with cuprite, malachite, and azurite in zones of secondary enrichment of sulfide deposits at Miami, Morenci, and Bisbee, Arizona, and with bornite in sulfide veins at Butte, Montana, Kennecott, Alaska, and Tsumeb, South-West Africa. *See* BORNITE; COPPER.

Lawrence Grossman

Chalcopyrite

A mineral having composition $CuFeS_2$, crystallizing in the tetragonal system and having four formula units per unit cell. S atoms form a face-centered cubic network in which half the tetrahedral sites are filled with Cu and Fe atoms. Crystals are usually small and resemble tetrahedra (see **illus.**). Chalcopyrite is usually massive with a

Chalcopyrite, crystal habit. (*After C. S. Hurlbut, Jr., Dana's Manual of Mineralogy, 17th ed., John Wiley and Sons, 1959*)

metallic luster, brass-yellow color, and sometimes an iridescent tarnish. The Mohs hardness is 3.5–4.0, and the density 4.1–4.3. Chalcopyrite is a so-called fool's gold, but is brittle while gold is sectile. Pyrite, the most widespread fool's gold, is harder than chalcopyrite.

Chalcopyrite is the most widespread primary copper ore mineral, and many secondary copper minerals are its alteration products. It is an important source of Cu in massive, Ni-bearing sulfide deposits (Sudbury, Ontario; Noril'sk, Russia) that crystallized from sulfide melts which were immiscible with the silicate melts from which the basic igneous rocks associated with these deposits formed. It is commonly found in veins, some emplaced at high temperature (Braden mine, Chile; Cornwall, England) and others at lower temperature (Butte, Montana; Freiberg, Saxony; Tasmania; Rio Tinto, Spain). Chalcopyrite is also found in contact metamorphic deposits in limestone (Bisbee, Arizona) and as sedimentary deposits (Mansfeld, Germany). *See* COPPER; PYRITE.

Lawrence Grossman

Chalk

A fine-grained limestone primarily composed of the remains of minute marine pelagic organisms (see **illus.**), including coccoliths and rhabdoliths (algae) and planktic foraminifera (Protozoa). Larger fossil constituents (bivalves, echinoderms, ammonites) are present in lesser amounts. Coccoliths and planktic foraminifera consist of low-magnesium calcite, one of the most stable carbonate minerals at the Earth's surface. Because of this mineralogic stability, chalks remain porous and friable until buried to depths of more than half a mile. The small size of coccoliths means that chalks show typically an average grain size of less than 10 micrometers. Neither coccoliths nor planktic foraminifera evolved until the Jurassic—therefore true chalks are no older than about 195 million years before present.

Chalk accumulates slowly, commonly at rates of 80 ft (25 m) per million years or less, in areas protected from the influx of terrigenous clastic sediment (clay, silt, or sand) or shallow-water carbonate deposits. Thus, most chalks are deposited either in deep oceans or on shallower platforms (water depths ≥ 150 ft or 50 m) in broad seaways, far removed from land areas which act as sediment sources. Many of the best-known chalks—such as the chalk from the cliffs of Dover, the Austin and Selma Groups in the United States, Gulf Coast, and the Niobrara Limestone from the Western Interior— were formed during a worldwide high stand of sea level in the Late Cretaceous.

Typical chalk coccoliths. Note small grain size and porous fabric. Sample from late Oligocene chalk from the east side of Halton-Rockall Basin, North Atlantic Ocean.

Chalks are typically pure, light-colored carbonate deposits that are widely used in the manufacture of portland cement, as lime for fertilizers, and as powders and abrasives. Chalks are proved also to be major reservoirs for oil and gas production, especially in the Norwegian portion of the North Sea and in the United States Gulf Coast. *See* CALCITE; CARBONATE MINERALS; FERTILIZER; LIMESTONE.

P. A. Scholle

Bibliography. H. G. Reading (ed.), *Sedimentary Environments and Facies*, 3d ed., 1994; J. P. Riley and R. Chester (eds.), *Treatise on Chemical Oceanography*, vol. 5, pp. 265–388, 1976; P. A. Scholle, Chalk diagenesis and its relation to petroleum exploration: Oil from chalks, a modern miracle?, *Amer. Ass. Petrol. Geol. Bull.*, 61(7):982–1009, 1977; P. A. Scholle, D. G. Bebout, and C. H. Moore (eds.), *Carbonate Depositional Environments*, Amer. Ass. Petrol. Geo. Mem. 33, 1983; P. A. Scholle, N. P. James, and J. F. Read (eds.), *Carbonate Sedimentation and Petrology*, vol. 86, 1989.

Chameleon

The name for about 80 species of small-to-medium-sized lizards that comprise the family Chamaeleontidae and occur mainly in Africa and Madagascar. The American chameleons (*Anolis*) belong to a different family of lizards, the Iguanidae. This reptile is insectivorous and beneficial to humans. It commonly is found on vegetation, especially the green parts.

Chamaeleo chamaeleon is the most common species and is a typical example of the group. Its body is flattened from side to side; it has a long, prehensile tail; and both the forelimbs and hindlimbs have two digits that oppose the other three (see **illus.**). These feet and the tail make the chameleon well adapted for its arboreal habitat. The eyes are large and can move independently of each other in all directions. The tongue is also prehensile, being extensible for a great distance, about the length of the animal itself, and is a highly efficient organ for capturing insects. The head of the chameleon is triangular in profile and has a pointed crest.

Chameleons are noted for their ability to change color. Color changes appear to be related to environmental temperatures as well as other external stimuli. When the temperature is high or the animal excited, the chameleon is green in color. When the temperature is cool or the animal unmolested, it is gray in color. There are cells in the skin that contain chromatophores, pigment granules of various colors. These black, red, or yellow pigments are contained in stellate, or star-shaped, color cells. Under nervous stimulation the cell branches expand and the pigments diffuse into these areas and become visible, creating a change in skin color. Contraction of the cells causes the pigment to concentrate and appear as indefinite

Representative chameleon species.

spots of color. The ability to change color is protective, so that the animal can blend into its surroundings.

The chameleon is oviparous. The female digs out a hollow in the ground for a nest where several dozen eggs are laid and then covered with soil. The period of incubation varies inversely with the temperature and may be as short as 4 months or as long as 10 months. Parental care of the young has not been observed.

The armored chameleon (*Leandria perarmata*), known from one specimen in Madagascar, is a highly developed representative of a group of chameleons having one or more horns on the snout instead of a crest on the head. The body has a row of spines along either side as well as a crest of spines along the back. There is a bony hood on the nape of the neck and a serrated crest down to the eye level. One species, *C. bitaeniatus*, found in the mountainous areas of eastern Africa, is ovoviviparous, and the female produces eggs that are incubated and hatched within her body. After a period of development about six young are born. *See* CHROMATOPHORE; PROTECTIVE COLORATION; REPTILIA; SQUAMATA.   Charles B. Curtin

Chamois

One of several species of mammals included in the tribe Rupicaprini of the family Bovidae. The group is heterogeneous in form, but all are intermediate in characteristics between the goats and antelopes. The chamois is the only European species of the group and is indigenous to the mountainous areas, especially the Alps. About nine races are recognized, based on their geographical range. The chamois is, however, becoming rare.

The chamois (*Rupicapra rupicapra*) lives in small herds of both sexes in numbers from 10 to 50. The female leaves the herd after the rutting season for a sheltered area, and after a gestation period of about 20 weeks gives birth to a single young in the spring. The offspring are active almost immediately and

begin to forage when 10 days old. They are sexually mature at 3 years of age and the average life-span is about 10 years. The adult is almost 3 ft high and weighs about 90 lb (40 kg) maximum. Both sexes bear horns which are set close together on the forehead, project almost at right angles, and are straight except for the sharp curve backward at the top (see **illus.**). These animals have 32 teeth and the dental formula is I 0/3 C 0/1 Pm 3/3 M 3/3. A soft, pliable leather, known as chamois cloth, is obtained from the skin of this animal. *See* DENTITION.

The chamois (*Rupicapra rupicapra*).

The goral, serow, and Rocky Mountain goat are included in the same tribe of bovids as the chamois. Both the goral (genus *Naemorhedus*) and serow (genus *Capricornis*) are found in Asia. The goral lives in small herds in the Himalayas, existing on the sparse vegetation found on the rocky slopes. It is about 2 ft (0.6 m) high and has short horns. A single young is born in the early summer after a gestation period of 6 months. The male of the Rocky Mountain goat (*Oreamnos americanus*) is larger than the female, weighing between 200 and 300 lb (90 and 135 kg) and standing over 3 ft (1 m) high. Both sexes are covered with thick, long white hair and have horns and beards. These animals are vegetarians, feeding on moss, lichens, and other vegetation of the area. In the early spring the female bears one or two young, which are quite active soon after birth. *See* ANTELOPE; MAMMALIA.
                    Charles B. Curtin

Channel electron multiplier

A single-particle detector which in its basic form (**Fig. 1**) consists of a hollow tube (channel) of either glass or ceramic material with a semiconducting inner surface. The detector responds to one or

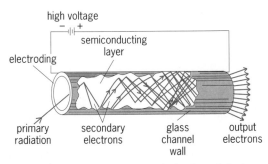

Fig. 1. Cutaway view of a straight, single-channel electron multiplier, showing the cascade of secondary electrons resulting from the initial, primary radiation event, which produces an output charge pulse. (After J. L. Wiza, Microchannel plate detectors, Nucl. Instrum. Meth., 162:587–601, 1979)

more primary electron impact events at its entrance (input) by producing, in a cascade multiplication process, a charge pulse of typically 10^4–10^8 electrons at its exit (output). Because particles other than electrons can impact at the entrance of the channel electron multiplier to produce a secondary electron, which is then subsequently multiplied in a cascade, the channel electron multiplier can be used to detect charged particles other than electrons (such as ions or positrons), neutral particles with internal energy (such as metastable excited atoms), and photons as well. As a result, this relatively simple, reliable, and easily applied device is employed in a wide variety of charged-particle and photon spectrometers and related analytical instruments, such as residual gas analyzers, mass spectrometers, and spectrometers used in secondary ion mass spectrometry (SIMS), electron spectroscopy for chemical analysis (ESCA), and Auger electron spectroscopy. *See* AUGER EFFECT; ELECTRON SPECTROSCOPY; MASS SPECTROMETRY; SECONDARY ION MASS SPECTROMETRY (SIMS); SPECTROSCOPY.

Photon detection. To directly detect photons, the photon energy must exceed the work function of the multiplier surface. Most channel electron multipliers require energies exceeding 5–10 eV for moderately efficient single-photon detection, limiting direct use to vacuum-ultraviolet wavelengths and shorter. Detection of longer-wavelength, lower-energy photons can be accomplished by the addition of a suitable photoelectron-emitting surface (photocathode) near the channel electron multiplier input, with an electric field to sweep liberated photoelectrons into the channel electron multiplier. *See* OPTICAL DETECTORS; PHOTOEMISSION; PHOTOMULTIPLIER; PHOTOTUBE.

Cascade multiplication. The cascade multiplication process at the heart of the channel electron multiplier's operation results from the secondary emission properties and high resistance (typically $10^9\ \Omega$) of the inner channel surface. For multiplication to occur, there must be a high probability (expressed as a high secondary emission coefficient) that an electron impacting the surface will liberate more than one secondary electron, each of which

is then accelerated toward the output to impact the surface and produce even more secondaries. In operation, it is necessary to apply a high voltage of the order of 1–4 kV between the input and output of the channel, thereby producing an electric field within the channel that accelerates secondary electrons to an energy sufficient to guarantee a high secondary emission coefficient. An electron impact energy of the order of 300 eV is generally required. High surface resistivity limits the current required from the high-voltage power supply to a few microamperes. *See* SECONDARY EMISSION.

Ion feedback. The large flux of electrons produced near the exit of a channel electron multiplier leads to a relatively high probability of electron impact ionization of residual gas molecules in the channel. The resulting ions are accelerated by the internal field toward the input, where they can impact the surface to liberate electrons that are then multiplied in the usual fashion. This is a potentially unstable condition called ion feedback and can lead to spurious outputs almost completely unrelated to real inputs. Several techniques are employed to reduce or eliminate ion feedback. Operating the channel electron multiplier in high vacuum (pressure less than 10^{-3} pascal or 10^{-5} torr) controls ion feedback by reducing residual gas density in the channel. Lowering the channel voltage limits the channel gain and hence the electron flux, thereby lowering the ionization rate. Finally, by introducing curvature in the channel, the distance that an ion can travel toward the input can be limited; since most ions are produced near the exit, limiting this distance also limits the multiplication gain and thus the amplitude of spurious ion feedback signals. Virtually all commercially available channel electron multiplier devices employ channel curvature to control ion feedback.

Configuration. A typical single channel electron multiplier will have a channel radius of 0.04 in. (1 mm) and a length of 4 in. (10 cm). The channel is often formed into a spiral or helix to conserve space and to control ion feedback. It is common to find the entrance flared into a funnel shape to

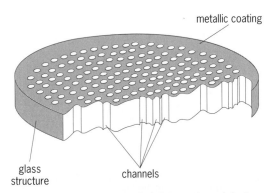

Fig. 2. Cutaway of a microchannel plate, or channel electron multiplier array, not to scale. Metallic coatings on both sides of the plate serve as input and output electrodes. (After J. L. Wiza, Microchannel plate detectors, Nucl. Instrum. Meth., 162:587–601, 1979)

increase the surface area sensitive to the primary event.

Microchannel plate. A related device is the channel electron multiplier array, often called a microchannel plate (**Fig. 2**). The channel electron multiplier array is usually a disk-shaped device with a diameter between 1 and 4 in. (2.5 and 10 cm) and a thickness of a fraction of a millimeter, and consists of millions of miniature channel electron multiplier devices arranged with channel axes perpendicular to the face of the disk. In one widely used version, the individual channels have a diameter of about 12 micrometers and are spaced at 15-μm intervals. Channel electron multiplier arrays find application as image intensifiers in night vision devices and are employed to add either large detection area or imaging capabilities, or both, to charged-particle detectors and spectrometers. Ion feedback in channel electron multiplier arrays is often controlled by using two arrays in tandem and arranging the channel axes at an angle to the axes of the disks, so that the channels in the second-stage array form a chevron or herringbone pattern with those in the input stage. *See* IMAGE TUBE (ASTRONOMY); LIGHT AMPLIFIER; PARTICLE DETECTOR.   Stuart B. Elston

Bibliography. M. Lampton, The microchannel image intensifier, *Sci. Amer.*, 245(5):62–71, November 1981; J. H. Moore, C. C. Davis, and M. A. Coplan, *Building Scientific Apparatus: A Practical Guide to Design and Construction,* 2d ed., 1989.

Channeling in solids

The steering of positively charged energetic particles between atomic rows or planes of a crystalline solid. The particles can be positive ions, protons, positrons, or muons. If the angle between the direction of the particle and a particular axis or plane in the crystal is within a small predictable limit (typically a few degrees or less), then the gradually changing electrostatic repulsion between the particle and each successive atomic nucleus of the crystal produces a smooth steering through the crystal lattice (**Fig. 1**). Thus, the trajectory of the channeled particle is restricted to the open spaces between atomic rows and planes of a crystal (**Fig. 2**). *See* CRYSTAL STRUCTURE.

An obvious consequence of this steered motion

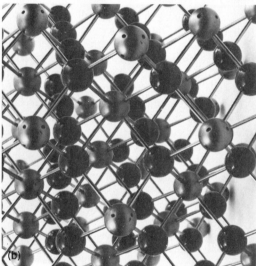

Fig. 2. Model of a cubic crystal lattice. (*a*) Model viewed along a ⟨100⟩ axis. The open (square) spaces are the ⟨100⟩ axial channels. (*b*) The same model viewed along a randomly chosen direction roughly 20° away from a ⟨100⟩ axis.

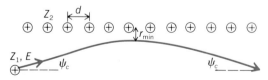

Fig. 1. Typical trajectory of a channeled ion (nuclear charge Z_1, energy E), illustrating the gentle steering caused by electrostatic repulsion from the regularly spaced nuclei of a crystal (nuclear charge Z_2, spacing d), so that the ion approaches no closer to the nuclei than r_{min}. The transverse angle ψ_c with respect to the channel axis remains almost constant as the ion penetrates through the crystal lattice.

is that it prevents violent collisions of the particles with atoms on the lattice sites. Hence, as compared with a randomly directed beam of particles, the channeled beam loses energy more slowly, penetrates more deeply, creates much less damage to the crystal along its track, and is prevented from participating in all close-encounter processes (nuclear reactions, Rutherford scattering, and so forth) with lattice atoms. *See* NUCLEAR REACTION; SCATTERING EXPERIMENTS (NUCLEI).

A related channeling phenomenon is the channeling of energetic electrons or other negative particles. In this case, the particles are attracted to the positively charged atomic nuclei, so that the probability of violent collisions with atoms on lattice sites is enhanced rather than being prevented, and the particles are steered along the rows or planes of nuclei rather than between them.

Blocking. A closely related phenomenon is called blocking. In this case, the energetic positive parti-

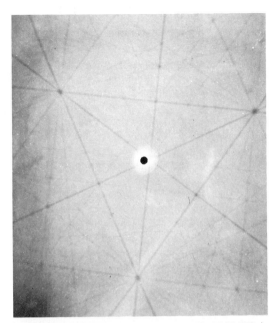

Fig. 3. Blocking pattern produced by a beam of 1-MeV He⁺ ions after backscattering from a germanium crystal onto a cellulose nitrate film 6 in. (15 cm) away. The large central spot is the hole in the film through which the incident beam reached the crystal. The intricate pattern of thin dark lines (that is, unbombarded regions of film) corresponds to the network of atomic planes along which backscattered particles are absent due to blocking. The wider spots at the intersection of several planes correspond to blocking along the major crystal axes.

cles originate from atomic sites within the crystal lattice by means of fission, alpha-particle decay, or by wide-angle scattering of a nonchanneled external beam in a very close encounter with a lattice atom. Those particles emitted almost parallel to an atomic row or plane will be deflected away from the row by a steering process similar to that shown in Fig. 1. Consequently, no particles emerge from the crystal within a certain critical blocking angle of each major crystallographic direction. A piece of film placed some distance from the crystal provides a simple technique for recording blocking patterns (**Fig. 3**). Theoretical considerations show that the same principle is involved in blocking as in channeling; hence, both phenomena exhibit an identical dependence on particle energy, nuclear charge, lattice spacing, and so forth. *See* NUCLEAR FISSION; RADIOACTIVITY.

Development. Channeling effects were predicted by J. Stark in 1912. However, despite the evident simplicity of the channeling phenomenon, firm experimental evidence for its existence was not recognized until the early 1960s, when it was observed that energetic heavy ions sometimes penetrated to unexpectedly large depths in polycrystalline aluminum and tungsten. In 1962, it was shown by computer simulation that these deep penetrations were probably due to particles being channeled along the open directions in some correctly oriented microcrystals. Single-crystal experiments in several laboratories subsequently confirmed that such channel-

ing was indeed an extremely general phenomenon, occurring for all charged nuclear particles (atomic nuclei, positrons, muons, and so forth) over an energy range from a few electronvolts up to hundreds of gigaelectronvolts. At about the same time, a comprehensive theoretical framework for predicting the behavior of channeled trajectories was developed, which led not only to an understanding of the channeling phenomenon but also to its widespread application in many other fields.

Applications. Applications of channeling include the location of foreign atoms in a crystal, the study of crystal surface structure, and the measurement of nuclear lifetimes.

Location of foreign atoms. The location of foreign (solute) atoms in a crystal is one of the simplest channeling applications. It is accomplished by measuring the yields of Rutherford back-scattered particles, characteristic x-rays, or nuclear reaction products produced by the interaction of channeled particles with the solute atoms. Such yields are enhanced for solute atoms that are displaced into channels of the crystal. Thus the solute atom sites can be identified by a triangulation technique, illustrated in **Fig. 4** for a two-dimensional model of a cubic lattice. Numbers in angle brackets ⟨ ⟩ identify the different kinds of crystal axes, whereas numbers in square brackets identify specific directions within a given kind. The shaded areas are shadowed by rows of host atoms (○) in the [10] and [11] channels. As shown by the table in Fig. 4, three possible sites for a foreign atom (●, ×, and □) are readily distinguished by comparing the channeling behavior along the ⟨10⟩- and ⟨11⟩-type directions. Channeled ions do

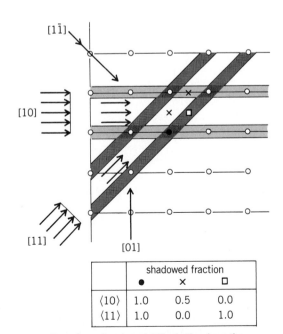

	shadowed fraction		
	●	×	□
⟨10⟩	1.0	0.5	0.0
⟨11⟩	1.0	0.0	1.0

Fig. 4. Two-dimensional model illustrating how the channeling effect may be used to locate foreign atoms in a crystal. (*After J. N. Mundy et al., eds., Methods of Experimental Physics, vol. 21, Solid State: Nuclear Methods, Academic Press, 1983*)

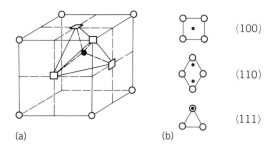

Key: ● solute atom □ vacancies ○ host atoms

Fig. 5. Tetravacancy–lute-atom complex. (a) Perspective view. (b) Projection of the solute atom into ⟨100⟩-, ⟨110⟩-, and ⟨111⟩-type axial channels. (After J. N. Mundy et al., eds., Methods of Experimental Physics, vol. 21, Solid State: Nuclear Methods, Academic Press, 1983)

not have close-encounter interactions with solute atoms in substitutional positions (●), since these are completely shadowed by atomic rows in both ⟨10⟩- and ⟨11⟩-type channels. The **x** interstitial positions (halfway along the sides of the until cells) are 50% shadowed in both the [10] and [01] channels, but lie in the center of the [11] and [1$\bar{1}$] channels. The □ interstitial positions (in the center of the square unit cell) are completely shadowed in both ⟨11⟩-type channels, but lie in the center of ⟨10⟩-type channels. *See* CRYSTAL DEFECTS.

This method has been used to determine the lattice positions of solute atoms that have been introduced into crystals by a variety of means (for example, by melting, diffusion, or ion implantation). For example, channeling measurements show that furnace or laser heating of silicon that has been implanted with energetic boron, arsenic, or other electrically active atoms causes these atoms to move onto normal (substitutional) lattice sites, sometimes to concentrations far in excess of solubility limits. These measurements also are used to determine the amount of lattice damage (created by the ion implantation) which remains after the heating. These and similar applications have proved extremely useful in the development of semiconductor devices. *See* ION IMPLANTATION; LASER-SOLID INTERACTIONS.

When energetic particles strike a crystal, atoms can be ejected from normal lattice sites, leaving vacant lattice sites (vacancies). Solute atoms can trap these vacancies, creating unique geometric configurations, such as the tetravacancy–solute-atom complex (**Fig. 5**). In this complex, the solute atom (for example, a tin atom in aluminum) becomes displaced from a normal lattice site into the tetrahedral interstitial site, surrounded by four lattice vacancies at equal distance. Such a solute atom lies in the center of ⟨100⟩ channels, is halfway to the center of ⟨110⟩ channels, and is completely shadowed in ⟨111⟩ channels. Thus, its position is easily identified by channeling measurements along these three axial channels. These vacancy–solute-atom complexes are very stable thermally, and probably form nucleation centers for the creation

of even larger vacancy clusters (voids) in irradiated materials. *See* RADIATION DAMAGE TO MATERIALS.

Study of surface structure. In a similar way, channeling techniques are used to study the structure of crystal surfaces. Because of the asymmetric forces between atoms on the surface of a crystal, the surface plane of atoms is often reconstructed (that is, it has a different atomic structure from that of the bulk); also, it may be relaxed inward or outward. In **Fig. 6**, a method for measuring an outward relaxation of the surface plane of atoms by the channeling technique is shown. A beam of ions directed perpendicular to the (111) surface (⟨111⟩ incidence) "sees" only one atom per row of atoms. However, because of the outward displacement of the surface atoms, a beam of ions incident along a nonperpendicular (for example, ⟨110⟩) axis "sees" two atoms per row at high ion energies (at which each surface atom casts a small shadow cone), and one atom per row at low ion energies (giving a large shadow cone). Information on surface relaxations (Δd) as small as 2×10^{-12} m and also on the vibrational amplitudes of the surface plane of atoms can be obtained by such studies. *See* LATTICE VIBRATIONS; SURFACE PHYSICS.

In addition, premelting at surfaces can be investigated. Channeling studies of the surface of lead near the melting point have shown that a thin surface layer becomes molten at a lower temperature than that of the bulk material. Such studies will contribute to an understanding of melting, which remains one of the more poorly understood physical phenomena.

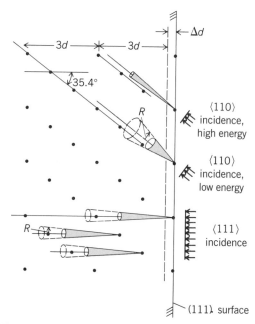

Fig. 6. Atomic configuration near the surface of a Pt(111) crystal, illustrating the use of channeling to investigate Δd, the surface relaxation. R = radius of shadow cone cast by surface atom; d = bulk (111) planar spacing. (After J. A. Davies et al., Measurement of surface relaxation by MeV ion backscattering and channeling, Phys. Lett., 54A:239–240, North Holland, 1975)

Measurement of nuclear lifetimes. A different type of application is the measurement of extremely short nuclear lifetimes. Nevertheless, the same basic principles of atom location are involved; namely, the ability, by means of channeling or blocking, to pinpoint accurately the location of a nucleus (relative to the crystal lattice) at the instant that it is struck by or emits an energetic positive particle. Suppose that a lattice nucleus under external beam bombardment captures a beam particle to form a compound nucleus, recoiling with known velocity from its lattice site, and that this nucleus subsequently decays by emitting an energetic positive particle (proton, alpha particle, fission fragment, and so forth). From the resulting blocking pattern of these emitted particles, the recoil distance before emission and hence the nuclear lifetime can be accurately determined. In this way, lifetimes as short as 10^{-18}s are directly observable.   John A. Davies; M. L. Swanson

Bibliography. L. C. Feldman, J. W. Mayer, and S. Thomas Picraux, *Materials Analysis by Ion Channeling*, 1982; J. N. Mundy et al. (eds.), *Methods of Experimental Physics*, vol. 21, *Solid State: Nuclear Methods*, 1983; E. Uggerhoj and A. Zucker (eds.), *Channeling and Other Penetration Phenomena*, 1989.

Chaos

System behavior that depends so sensitively on the system's precise initial conditions that it is, in effect, unpredictable and cannot be distinguished from a random process, even though it is deterministic in a mathematical sense. This article begins with a discussion of the notions of order, chaos, and noise as they occur in deterministic dynamical systems, the relation of chaos and periodicity, and the concept of an attractor. Applications of chaos to climate, electronic circuits, astronomy, acoustics, and atoms will then be discussed.

Throughout history, sequentially using magic, religion, and science, people have sought to perceive order and meaning in a seemingly chaotic and meaningless world. This quest for order reached its ultimate goal in the seventeenth century when newtonian dynamics provided an ordered, deterministic view of the entire universe epitomized in P. S. de Laplace's statement, "We ought then to regard the present state of the universe as the effect of its preceding state and as the cause of its succeeding state." In everday life, the predictable swing of a long, massive pendulum or the regular motion of the Sun, Moon, and planets provides reassurance of a mechanistic newtonian order in the world.

But if the determinism of Laplace and Newton is totally accepted, it is difficult to explain the unpredictability of a gambling game or, more generally, the unpredictably random behavior observed in many newtonian systems. Commonplace exam-ples of such behavior include smoke that first rises in a smooth, streamlined column from a cigarette, only to abruptly burst into wildly erratic turbulent flow (**Fig. 1**); and the unpredictable phenomena of the weather. *See* FLUID FLOW; TURBULENT FLOW.

At a more technical level, flaws in the newtonian view had become apparent by about 1900, leading J. H. Poincaré to remark, "Determinism is a fantasy due to Laplace," and J. C. Maxwell to assert, "The true logic of this world is the calculus of probabilities." The problem is that many newtonian systems exhibit behavior which is so exquisitely sensitive to the precise initial state or to even the slightest outside perturbation that, humanly speaking, determinism becomes a physically meaningless though mathematically valid concept. But even more is true. Many deterministic newtonian-system orbits are so erratic that they cannot be distinguished from a random process even though they are strictly determinate, mathematically speaking. Indeed, in the totality of newtonian-system orbits, erratic unpredictable randomness is overwhelmingly the most common behavior. *See* CELESTIAL MECHANICS; CLASSICAL MECHANICS; DETERMINISM; STOCHASTIC PROCESS.

Examples. These notions will be illustrated through three simple mapping systems which retain many features of general dynamical systems but are not encumbered by extraneous detail.

Highly ordered motion. An example of highly ordered motion is the discrete mapping of points around a circle of unit circumference in which each point

Fig. 1. Transition from order to chaos (turbulence) in a rising column of cigarette smoke. The initial smooth streamline flow represents order, while the erratic flow represents chaos.

is carried one-fifth way around the circle upon each iteration. After n iterations, a point initially at angular position θ_0 has been carried to position θ_n given by Eq. (1), where the angle θ has

$$\theta_n = (0.2)n + \theta_0 \qquad (1)$$

been normalized so that $\theta + 1 = \theta$. This mapping is obviously determinate since each θ_0 uniquely determines an "orbit" of θ_n iterates. The "motion" here is also highly ordered because, from Eq. (1), all orbits are periodic with $\theta_{n+5} = \theta_n$, because the entire circle of points is mapped as a rigid body upon each iteration, and because the angle of rotation is the precisely computable, terminating rational number, $\frac{1}{5} = 0.2$. Moreover, except for a displacement around the circle, all orbits are identical. This mapping system is thus fully ordered, strictly deterministic, and totally dull. In more general terms, the monotony of the streamline flow in Fig. 1 may be contrasted with the greater variety of behavior of the turbulent flow. Ordered motion while comfortingly simple is also rigidly constrained motion in which all or almost all capricious options have been discarded.

Ordered motion. A less constrained but still ordered motion is generated by the mapping which rigidly rotates the whole circle of points through the larger angle $\alpha = \sqrt{2}$ upon each iteration. Here the result of n iterations is given by Eq. (2), where

$$\theta_n = (\sqrt{2})n + \theta_0 \qquad (2)$$

again $\theta + 1 = \theta$. Like the mapping of Eq. (1), except for a displacement around the circle, all orbits are identical. However, here there is one exciting difference. Because the angle of rotation α is now irrational, the θ_n iterates of each θ_0 in Eq. (2) spread out uniformly around the circle, almost as if their positions were selected from a uniform random distribution. In fact, it is possible to rigorously prove for Eq. (2) that Eq. (3) is

$$\lim_{N \to \infty} \left(\frac{1}{N} \right) \sum_{n=0}^{N} f(\theta_n) = \int_0^1 f(\theta)\, d\theta \qquad (3)$$

satisfied, where f is any reasonable well-behaved function. Equation (3), a version of the ergodic theorem, is merely a sophisticated way to assert that all θ values occur with equal frequency and that the mapping of Eq. (2) therefore passes one test for randomness. However, this slight randomness in the mathematically deterministic Eq. (2) has appeared only because a sacrifice has been tacitly made for it. Indeed, the introduction of an irrational angle of rotation into Eq. (2) which yields a uniform θ distribution simultaneously also renders Eq. (2) not fully determinate from the physical viewpoint. Specifically, humans can never compute the precise decimal representation for $\sqrt{2}$. Thus, if ϵ is the error in the determination of $\sqrt{2}$, then the error $\Delta(n)$ in θ_n will be at least $\Delta(n) = n\epsilon$. Since this error clearly grows without bound with iteration

number n, physical determinism in Eq. (2) is completely lost when the error $\Delta(n)$ is about unity. Nonetheless, physical determinism over human time scales can be maintained, provided the error ϵ in the determination of $\sqrt{2}$ is sufficiently small.

It is now possible to proceed through a sequence of maps which become more "random" and less "physically determinate." For them, the error $\Delta(n)$ in each θ_n would grow as some polynomial in n, but the notions of order and physical determinism could still be maintained, at least over human time scales, by using humanly available accuracy. The great divide occurs when the error growth becomes exponential, yielding mathematically determinate systems which pass every test for randomness. Here the mapping equations require such massive input of data strings in order to maintain accuracy that, informationally speaking, they are not computing or determining the solution but rather merely copying out the solution being given to them. This case will be illustrated with a final example.

Chaotic motion. If the points on the circle of unit circumference move according to the "multiplicative" mapping equation (4), where $\theta + 1 = \theta$ as

$$\theta_n = 2^n \theta_0 \qquad (4)$$

before, then orbits starting with slightly differing θ_0 values clearly separate exponentially with iteration number n. In consequence, Eq. (4) exhibits that extreme sensitivity of final state to precise initial state characteristic of all chaotic systems; indeed, Eq. (4) is perhaps the simplest system which can serve as a paradigm for chaos.

However, Eq. (4) is no less mathematically deterministic than are Eqs. (1) and (2), since a θ_n set exists and is unique for each given θ_0. The θ_n iterates of Eq. (4) can nevertheless be unpredictably random and nondeterministic, as can be seen by considering the consequences for determinism of the exponentially separating orbits in Eq. (4). For example, if the spatial angle θ_0 is known to an accuracy of 10^{-31}, far beyond the accuracy available to contemporary science, even then, after only 100 iterations, the error in θ_{100} is of order unity, and the last vestige of determinism in Eq. (4) has been lost.

This issue may be further clarified by computing a lull set of θ_n iterates of Eq. (4), each having an accuracy of at least 2^{-1}, that is, at least one-binary-digit accuracy. If 2^{-m} is the accuracy of θ_0 required to compute a given θ_n, then Eq. (5) must be satisfied. Thus $m = n + 1$ or, for large n, $m \cong n$.

$$2^{-1} = 2^n 2^{-m} \qquad (5)$$

Now the situation becomes clear. In order to assure n informational bits of solution output, one per θ_n iterate, it is necessary to include a total of $m = n$ informational bits into the binary representation of θ_0. Equation (4) is thus seen to be merely a "copy" algorithm rather than a "deterministic" one. Alternatively stated, Eq. (4) is merely a fixed "language translation" algorithm which translates a "German" θ_0 into an "English" θ_n sequence.

Even greater insight into these matters can be obtained by writing the θ_0 of Eq. (4) in binary notation as a digit string of zeros and ones; typically it might be given by Eq. (6). Then, each

$$\theta_0 = 0.11101100000100\ldots \qquad (6)$$

iterate θ_n specified by Eq. (4) may be obtained by merely moving the "decimal" in Eq. (6) n places to the right and dropping the integer part. Now, the string of zeros and ones in Eq. (6) may be regarded as specifying a coin-toss sequence. Moreover, the set of all binary θ_0 sequences is in a one-to-one correspondence (essentially) with the set of all possible random coin-toss sequences. Consequently, almost all binary θ_0 sequences pass every humanly computable test for randomness. In short, they are random. A straightforward derivation then proves that almost all θ_0 yield random θ_n sequences despite that fact that Eq. (4) is mathematically deterministic.

Equation (4) is mathematically deterministic provided that θ_0 is given or somehow determined mathematically; however, in Eq. (4), randomness arises precisely because the infinite digit string for θ_0 is, in general, as random as a coin toss and therefore not computable by any finite algorithm. Moreover, and equally important, the exponentially sensitive dependence of final state upon initial state in Eq. (4) transforms randomness of the θ_0 digit string into randomness of the θ_n sequence. Indeed, the θ_n sequences of Eqs. (1) and (2) lack full randomness only because they lack this sensitive dependence upon initial state.

Equation (4), as mentioned above, is the epitome of chaos just as Eq. (1) is the epitome of order. In addition, Eq. (4) exhibits that richness of behavior inherent to all chaotic systems: everything that can happen does happen. In Eq. (4), for example, the full orbit is known once the θ_0 digit string of Eq. (6) is known. But here all digit strings are possible and, in fact, each digit string actually occurs for some θ_0. Thus, chaos results in richness of opportunity rather than meaninglessness.

Systems in the real world. The use of deterministic, ordered mathematical models to describe behavior of systems in the real world is so familiar that only chaos need be discussed. One example of chaos is the evolution of life on Earth. Were this evolution deterministic, the governing laws of evolution would have had built into them anticipation of every natural crisis which has occurred over the centuries plus anticipation of every possible ecological niche throughout all time. Nature, however, economizes and uses the richness of opportunity available through chaos. Random mutations provide choices sufficient to meet almost any crisis, and natural selection chooses the proper one. *See* ORGANIC EVOLUTION.

Another example concerns the problem that the human body faces in defending against all possible invaders. Again, nature appears to choose chaos as the most economical solution. Loosely speaking, when a hostile bacterium or virus enters the body, defense strategies are generated at random until a feedback loop indicates that the correct strategy has been found. A great challenge is to mimic nature and to find new and useful ways to harness chaos. *See* IMMUNITY.

Another matter for consideration is the problem of predicting the weather or the world economy. Both these systems have much in common with Eq. (4), although their governing equations are certainly more complicated. Nonetheless, like a θ_n sequence of Eq. (4), the weather and the economy are chaotic and can be predicted more or less precisely only on a very short time scale. Nonetheless, by recognizing the chaotic nature of the weather and the economy, it may eventually be possible to accurately determine the probability distribution of allowed events in the future given the present. At that point it may be asserted with mathematical precision that, for example, there is a 90% chance of rain 2 months from today. Much work in chaos theory seeks to determine the relevant probability distributions for chaotic systems. *See* WEATHER FORECASTING AND PREDICTION.

Finally, many physical systems exhibit a transition from order to chaos, as exhibited in Fig. 1, and much work studies the various routes to chaos. Examples include fibrillation of the heart and attacks of epilepsy, manic-depression, and schizophrenia. Physiologists are striving to understand chaos in these systems sufficiently well that these human maladies can be eliminated. *See* PERIOD DOUBLING.

Noise. Reduced to basics, chaos and noise are essentially the same thing. Chaos is randomness in an isolated system; noise is randomness entering this previously isolated system from the outside. If the noise source is included to form a composite isolated system, there is again only chaos. *See* ACOUSTIC NOISE; ELECTRICAL NOISE.   Joseph Ford

Chaos and periodicity. In systems where the number of possible states, none of which closely resembles any other one, is limited, approximate repetitions of earlier states must eventually occur. If such a system is not chaotic, the history following a near repetition of a state will nearly repeat the history following the original occurrence, so that near repetitions will continue to occur at regular intervals, and the system will vary periodically. If, then, a system of this sort is observed not to vary periodically, it must be chaotic. Absence of periodicity often affords the means by which chaos is most easily recognized, and it has sometimes served in place of sensitive dependence as a definition of chaos. For examples, a pendulum in a well-behaved clock does not swing chaotically; a flag in a moderate steady breeze may flap chaotically.

Many real systems exhibit nonperiodic variations superposed on periodic oscillations. The periodic components of these variations are entirely predictable and, like the diurnal and seasonal variations of the Earth's weather, are often externally forced. In such systems, which are also considered chaotic, two rather similar states will eventually evolve into states differing as much as states chosen from a long sequence, at similar phases of the periodic oscillations but otherwise randomly.

Attractors. Real-world systems generally entail some dissipative processes, and some external forcing that prevents them from coming to a standstill, like the clockwork that keeps a pendulum swinging or the wind that keeps a flag flapping. For such systems the set of states that can occur or be approximated again and again, after transient effects have subsided, is far more restricted than it would be if neither dissipation nor forcing were present; it is most drastically restricted when the system is not chaotic. This set of states is called the attractor of the system. Especially for simple systems, attractors are commonly represented by plane or multidimensional graphs in which each point represents a distinct state, the coordinates of the point equaling the values of some or all of the variables. For a chaotic system the graph is an infinite complex of curves or other manifolds, with finite gaps between any pair of manifolds, and the attractor is called a strange attractor.

Climate. Climate is sometimes identified with the set of all states of the climate system—the system consisting of the atmosphere and the upper portions of the underlying ocean and land surfaces—that may reasonably be expected to occur. It is thus identifiable with the attractor of the climate system. This system is dissipative and is forced by solar heating, and it is almost certainly chaotic; although it is not feasible to examine the actual climate system directly for sensitive dependence, mathematical models of the system, including some used in operational weather forecasting, invariably indicate sensitive dependence, while such features as migratory storms that cross the oceans and continents are not observed to occur in any periodic sequence.

Chaos can enrich the variety of weather patterns that make up the climate. Even though the weather has been observed for centuries, it is reasonable to expect something that is not known to have happened before—a record high or low temperature at some location, or a record rainfall that produces a record flood. Without chaos the weather would vary periodically, and records would simply be tied rather than broken.

Changes in external forcing will change the behavior of the climate system, thereby producing a new attractor, and hence a climatic change. Furthermore, if the state of the system normally fluctuates within one portion of the attractor for a long time and then enters into another portion, the transition will be perceived as an additional climatic change, perhaps indistinguishable from one externally produced. It is therefore sometimes preferable to identify the present climate with the portion of the attractor within which the state is presently fluctuating, thereby allowing for internally produced climatic changes.

Regardless of any chaotic weather variations occurring within the tenure of one climate, it is possible that the variations of the climate itself are chaotic. If this is so, only the periodic components of distant climatic changes can be predicted. Mathematical models of climate have not reached the degree of perfection needed to confirm or reject such a hypothesis, and recourse to observations is indicated. Where weather observations are absent or insufficient, proxy data, such as records of tree rings or oxygen isotope ratios, which are supposed to vary with climatic elements such as temperature, can be useful. There are indications of periodic variations with superposed nonperiodic variations; it is the latter that may be unpredictable. Some of the periodic variations appear to be associated with predictable changes in the Earth's orbital parameters. Some nonperiodic variations may result from irregular external forcing—perhaps nonperiodic volcanic activity. Others may be internally produced, and chaotic. *See* CLIMATIC PREDICTION; CLIMATOLOGY; DENDROCHRONOLOGY.　　　　　Edward N. Lorenz

Electronic circuits. Chaos is a ubiquitous phenomenon which is a subset of the dynamical behavior of nonlinear systems. In an electronic context, a nonlinear system is one where the output is not simply proportional to the input, and the response to a collection of excitations is not simply the sum of the individual responses to each excitation taken separately. This criterion embraces a large subset of electronic systems, including those in which there is multiple-valued behavior. Many chaotic systems observed in other disciplines are modeled well by electronic circuits. The dynamics are then susceptible to experimental analysis in a way that would be difficult in the source discipline. *See* NONLINEAR PHYSICS.

It is also possible to use electronic chaotic circuits for the direct experimental study of some arcane phenomena suggested by the rigorous mathematical analysis of nonlinear dynamical systems. Many such investigations have been reported. Intermittencies can be observed, trapping and long-lived chaotic transients are easily demonstrated, extensive catalogs of coexisting attractors can be found empirically, and synchronization and entrainment of chaotic systems can be explored, with applications to secure communications.

In analog electronic circuits, chaos can be found in overload situations, where a linear circuit is driven beyond the capacity of its power supply; in switchmode power supplies, where energy-efficient control is achieved by using dependent switches in association with a linear circuit; and in resonant circuits which are nonlinear. These resonant circuits divide into a group wherein the natural frequency is amplitude dependent (modeled by Duffing-like equations) and also a group which contain amplitude-dependent damping, modeled by Van der Pol-like equations. *See* DIFFERENTIAL EQUATION; ELECTRONIC POWER SUPPLY.

Categories of electrical chaotic system include purely electronic; electromechanical, in which the mechanical element is nonlinear whereas the coupled electronic circuit is linear (for example, ultrasonic cleaners); and control systems generally, in which either or both the control circuit and the system being controlled are nonlinear. There is an important class of chaotic system comprising coupled oscillators; a stable oscillator necessarily has a limit cycle and is therefore nonlinear. Two such oscillators (when coupled) may pull in and out of lock in a chaotic manner.

Analyses of chaos in continuous systems using a digital computer are sometimes grossly in error owing to the extreme sensitivity to initial conditions. However, all real electronic systems are described by continuous variables plus unavoidable added noise. Real digital systems are modeled as accurately as their analog equivalents when the number of distinguishable states is greater than the number of distinguishable levels in an analog version containing unavoidable noise. Digital filters containing registers which overflow exhibit chaos. Chaos is also found in systems containing phase detectors, owing to the ambiguity in phase angle modulo 360°, for similar reasons. *See* DIGITAL FILTER; PHASE-LOCKED LOOPS.

Chaos is found also in digital systems having more than one autonomous timing element or clock; it is therefore endemic in asynchronous parallel computation. Chaos is suspected to occur in computer networks, at the physical data level. *See* CONCURRENT PROCESSING.

Chaos in circuits is modeled reasonably well by circuit simulation packages that deal with nonlinearities in the device models by solving the dynamical equations by using numerical integration. However, the class of originally linear circuit analysis software packages that handle nonlinear circuits by methods such as harmonic balance fail completely to model chaotic dynamics.

David J. Jefferies

Astronomy. The methods of nonlinear dynamics have been applied to a large number of problems in astronomy. In particular, it is clear that chaos has played an important role in determining the dynamical structure and evolution of the solar system.

The Kirkwood gaps in the asteroid belt are now thought to be chaotic regions of space from which asteroids have been removed by the nonlinear gravitational perturbations of Jupiter. An asteroid in such a region can undergo large changes in its orbital elements which can cause it to become planet-crossing; the asteroid will eventually be removed from the region by a close approach to the planet. The existence of prominent gaps at the 1/3, 1/2, and 2/5 Jovian orbit-orbit resonances is consistent with the large chaotic regions which have been discovered at these locations by full numerical integrations and the use of algebraic mappings. The 2/3 resonance is associated with the stable Hilda group of asteroids and a much smaller chaotic zone. *See* ASTEROID.

Chaos has also been used to explain the delivery of one chondrite class of meteorites from the asteroid belt to the Earth. The 1/3 Kirkwood gap at 2.5 astronomical units has been identified as the source region for these meteorites, and studies of the dynamical behavior of asteroid collision fragments at the resonance show that perturbations by the outer planets can cause the orbits to become chaotic and achieve the high eccentricities necessary to become Earth-crossing. The time scales for this process are consistent with the ages of these chondrites determined by the length of time they have been exposed to the cosmic-ray environment of the solar system. *See* METEORITE.

The Saturnian satellite Hyperion exhibits chaotic behavior in its spin motion. Most natural satellites are locked in a 1/1 spin-orbit resonance where, as a result of tidal evolution, the orbital period of the satellite is equal to its spin period. However, Hyperion is distinctly nonspherical, and it has a large orbital eccentricity which is fixed by its 4/3 orbit-orbit resonance with the satellite Titan. As a result, Hyperion is in a chaotic spin state, with its rotational period changing constantly. Additional instabilities imply that its pole position may also have a chaotic behavior and that Hyperion is, in fact, tumbling. *See* SATURN.

The semimajor axis of a natural satellite can change significantly over the age of the solar system because of the tide that it raises on the parent planet. Consequently Kepler's third law implies that pairs of satellites can evolve into and out of resonance. This is an example of a dissipative dynamical system, since energy is lost in the form of tidal friction. Nonlinear dynamical studies have proved useful in determining the orbital histories of the satellite systems of the outer planets.

An 850-million-year numerical integration of the orbit of Pluto has shown some evidence of chaotic motion, although the chaos is unlikely to disrupt Pluto's stable 3/2 resonance with Neptune over the lifetime of the solar system. Long-term numerical integrations have been used to investigate the stability of the solar system over time scales comparable with a significant fraction of its age. Results show that the planets' orbits are chaotic, although there are no dramatic changes over several billion years. In this case the existence of chaos implies that a small error in the measurement of a planet's position will propagate exponentially such that its orbital location cannot be calculated for arbitrary times in the future. The evolution of a planetary orbit is connected with the evolution of the orientation of its spin axis (obliquity). In the case of Mars the obliquity varies chaotically from 0° to 60°, and this has important implications for climate change on the planet. *See* MARS; PLUTO; SOLAR SYSTEM.

Chaos has also helped solve problems in other branches of astronomy, including galactic dynamics and studies of stellar oscillations, and the number of applications of chaos to astronomy is expected to increase.   Carl D. Murray

Acoustics. Chaos physics has shed new light on the old problem of noise, a term which has its origin in acoustics. Noise had been thought to be the outcome of interacting processes for which a deterministic formulation and description is no longer feasible because the number of such processes is extremely large. However, chaos physics has shown that noise can be present in systems with only a few interacting processes, for which a deterministic formulation can easily be written down explicitly. An example of such a system is a driven nonlinear oscillator, for example, an electric circuit consisting of only a resistor, an inductance, and a varactor diode (as the necessary nonlinear element) in series, driven by a sinusoidally varying voltage.

A chaotic (irregular, never repeating) sound wave can be produced when the chaotic voltage across this diode is fed to a loudspeaker. But systems of this kind are not considered to be genuine acoustically chaotic systems. Genuine acoustic chaos is found in ultrasonics, thermoacoustics, musical acoustics, speech, and hearing. In ultrasonics it arises in the breakdown of liquids exposed to high-intensity sound, a phenomenon called acoustic cavitation. At too high an acoustic intensity the liquid ruptures to form bubbles or cavities (almost empty bubbles). They vibrate in the sound field that originally generated them, and emit sound. The total sound output of the cavities at high sound input (of a pure tone) leads to noise with a broadband spectrum. *See* CAVITATION.

A single sound frequency is thus transformed into an almost infinite number of neighboring sound frequencies. To study this transformation, an experiment has been conceived in which the sound output is monitored as the sound intensity is raised by digitizing the output of a hydrophone and storing the samples in a memory. Power spectra calculated from the stored data give the frequency content of the sound output. A period-doubling route to chaos is observed (**Fig. 2**). When the excitation level is raised, spectral lines appear exactly between the old lines by period doubling (frequency halving) until a broadband spectrum (chaos) is reached. Thus, acoustic cavitation has been identified as a chaotic system.

Because the cavities set into oscillation are the source of sound generation, their motion should become chaotic along with the sound output. Holographic observations of acoustically driven bubbles showed that they undergo period doubling to chaos in step with the acoustic output from the liquid.

Sound can be generated by heat—a fact known to glass blowers. When a gas-filled tube, closed at one end and open at the other, is heated at the closed end, the gas column starts to vibrate.

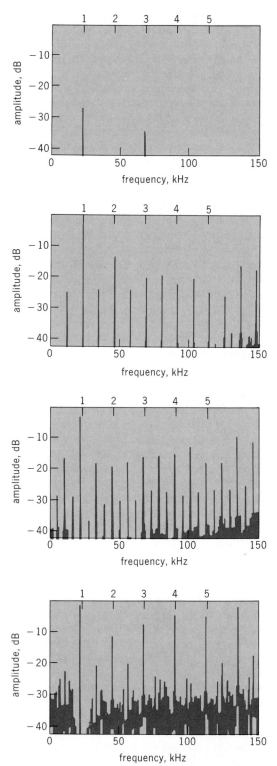

Fig. 2. Power spectra of acoustic cavitation noise at four different excitation levels, showing the successive filling of the spectrum by period doubling (frequency halving) when the sound input intensity is raised. Numbers at tops of the graphs indicate multiples of input frequency (harmonics).

Alternatively the open end may be cooled. When this self-excited oscillation is disturbed by another sound wave, the interaction may lead to chaotic sound waves.

In musical acoustics, signs of chaos are observed in string instruments, woodwind instruments (recorder, clarinet), the trumpet, and gongs (vibrated shells). Musicians, however, try to avoid the occurrence of bifurcations when playing their instruments. An example is the so-called wolf note that tends to appear in playing the cello. It is a quasiperiodic oscillation with two incommensurate frequencies that stem from the string and the bridge resonance. Oscillations of this type are also observed in woodwind instruments, there called multiphonics. Subharmonic sounds and chaos have also been found, for example, in the clarinet. *See* MUSICAL ACOUSTICS.

The human speech-production process is intrinsically nonlinear. To produce voice sounds the vocal cords are set into nonlinear vibration through the air flow between them. The fundamental frequency, the pitch, is determined by the length, mass, and tension of the vocal cords. There is no doubt from present knowledge of nonlinear oscilatory systems that the vocal cord system, and thus the human speech-production system, is susceptible to chaotic sound production. *See* SPEECH.

The ear is a very complex sound receiver with remarkable properties, for instance in frequency selectivity. They stem from nonlinearities and active filtering with feedback, that is, filtering with amplification of sound. Such systems may become unstable and start to oscillate themselves. The ear thus also acts as a sound emitter rather than a pure receiver. This may happen in reponse to a sound wave or spontaneously, a phenomenon called objective tinnitus. Many people suffer from this property of the ear, as they hear the emitted sound. *See* HEARING (HUMAN); HEARING IMPAIRMENT.

Werner Lauterborn

Atoms. A challenging problem is the behavior of quantal systems whose nonlinear, nonintegrable classical counterparts involve irregular (chaotic) trajectories, a subject commonly called quantum chaos. Because basic atomic structure is determined by the Coulomb electrostatic force, accurate quantal, semiclassical, or classical numerical calculations are possible. High-resolution atomic spectra, and how they are influenced by externally applied fields that rival the intraatomic Coulomb force binding a weakly bound atomic electron, can be recorded by using lasers or other sources and compared with theory.

In atomic three-body systems such as the helium atom, understanding and classifying the classical orbits, most of which are chaotic, is challenging enough. Quantizing them is a problem that has defied many researchers since the beginning of quantum theory early in the twentieth century. Thus, it is notable that the semiclassical quantization of the helium atom (in states with zero total angular momentum) has been accomplished.

Most atomic studies of quantum chaos have involved a weakly bound electron in the hydrogen atom (principal quantum number $n_0 \gg 1$) exposed to a strong, externally applied force F_{ext} that may be static or time varying. For $F_{ext} = 0$, the nonrelativistic, classical trajectories are regular, keplerian ellipses with angular frequency w_{at} for bounded motion and hyperbolas for unbounded motion; the corresponding quantal spectrum consists of the discrete (Bohr) levels with total energy E proportional to n_0^{-2} for $E < 0$ and a continuum of levels for $E > 0$. (Rydberg atoms, which have one of their electrons highly excited and approximate hydrogen, are also used.) *See* MATTER IN STRONG FIELDS; RYDBERG ATOM.

Static external fields. Hydrogen in a static magnetic field (B) is the most studied example. The linear (in B) paramagnetic interaction leads to regular classical dynamics and to the Zeeman effect of textbook quantum mechanics. As B increases, however, the nonlinear (quadratic in B) diamagnetic interaction becomes dominant, and irregular (chaotic) electron trajectories begin to appear in classical numerical computations. Experimental studies of the photoabsorption spectrum of hydrogen atoms and of helium, lithium, or other Rydberg atoms (via laser-driven transitions from low-lying quantal states to strongly perturbed states near $E = 0$) revealed a complicated quantal spectrum whose changing statistical properties reflect the onset of classically chaotic trajectories. Series of sharp spectral features observed with lithium Rydberg atoms for magnetic field strengths and energies where the classical (hydrogenic) orbits are all chaotic were well reproduced by quantal numerical calculations for hydrogen. Use of scaled energy spectroscopy, which exploits scaling relations derived for the classical dynamics of the hydrogen atom in the magnetic field and applies whether or not the electron's motion is chaotic, simplifies comparisons with semiclassical theory if the photoabsorption spectrum is recorded with both the laser photon energy and B being varied such that the scaled energy remains constant. Unstable classical periodic orbits (or even just orbits that close on themselves near the nucleus) of ever longer period, which proliferate at bifurcations specified by the theory of hamiltonian dynamics, were shown to correspond in a direct way with important spectral features observed with finite resolution. *See* DIAMAGNETISM; PARAMAGNETISM; ZEEMAN EFFECT.

Examples of even more complicated situations for which classical scaling relationships have also been exploited are highly excited hydrogen or hydrogenlike Rydberg atoms in the presence of either crossed or parallel electric and magnetic fields. Photoabsorption spectra up to and beyond $E = 0$ (well into the domain of classical chaos) have been recorded experimentally and compared with results of classical, semiclassical, and quantal theory.

Time-varying external fields. For an $F_{ext}(t)$ produced by a microwave electric field with angular frequency ω and amplitude F, exchange of energy between it and the atom can lead to deexcitation to lower bound states or excitation to higher bound states or the $E > 0$ continuum (that is, ionization). (Ionization can require net absorption of many tens

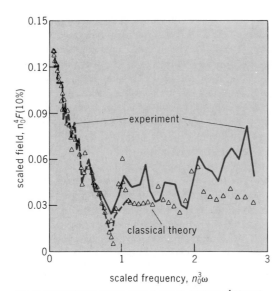

Fig. 3. Dependence of the scaled threshold field $n_0^4F(10\%)$ that produces an ionization probability of 10% after weakly bound hydrogen atoms are exposed to about 300 microwave field oscillations, on the scaled frequency $n_0^3\omega$.

G. Casati and B. Chirikov (eds.), *Quantum Chaos: Between Order and Disorder*, 1994; L. O. Chua and M. Hasler (eds.), Special issues on chaos in nonlinear electronic circuits, *IEEE Trans. Circ. Sys.*, vol. CAS-40, nos. 10 and 11 in CAS-I and no. 10 in CAS-II, 1993; M. C. Gutzwiller, *Chaos in Classical and Quantum Mechanics*, 1993; R. C. Hilborn, *Chaos and Nonlinear Dynamics: An Introduction for Scientists and Engineers*, 1993; W. Lauterborn and J. Holzfuss, Acoustic chaos, *Int. J. Bifurcations Chaos*, 1:13–26, 1991; E. N. Lorenz, *The Essence of Chaos*, 1993; T. Mullin (ed.), *The Nature of Chaos*, 1993; E. Ott, *Chaos in Dynamical Systems*, 1993; I. Peterson, *Newton's Clock: Chaos in the Solar System*, 1993; D. Ruelle, *Chance and Chaos*, 1993; M. Schroeder, *Fractals, Chaos, and Power Laws*, 1992.

Chaparral

A vegetation formation characterized by woody plants of low stature (3–9 ft or 1–3 m tall), impenetrable because of tough, rigid, interlacing branches, with small, simple, waxy, evergreen, thick leaves. The term refers to evergreen oak, Spanish *chaparro*, and therefore is uniquely southwestern North American. This type of vegetation has its center in California and occurs continuously over wide areas of mountainous to sloping topography. The Old World Mediterranean equivalent is called maquis or macchie, with nomenclatural and ecological variants in the countries ranging from Spain to the Balkans. Physiognomically similar vegetation occurs also in South Africa, Chile, and southwestern Australia in areas of Mediterranean climates, that is, with very warm, dry summers and maximum precipitation during the cool season.

The floras of these five areas with Mediterranean climates are altogether different, however, so only the assumption of close correlation between form and function in plants allows extrapolation of vegetation studies from one area to another.

California types. In western North America a number of kinds of so-called chaparral must be distinguished. In southern California the coastal sage formation consists of shrubs which are gray in color and low in stature, with soft, brittle wood; the formation contains *Artemisia californica*, shrubby species of *Salvia*, *Eriogonum fasciculatum* (typical form), and others. In the humid mountains of California, logged and burned coniferous forests have been replaced by a montane chaparral of the widespread western *Arctostaphylos patula* and *Ceanothus velutinus* plus the West Coast *Prunus emarginata*, the New Mexico–Californian–Cascade *Ceanothus integerrimus*, and the Californian endemics *Chamaebatia foliolosa*, *Castanopsis sempervirens*, *Quercus vacciniifolia*, and *Ceanothus cordulatus* (the last three at higher altitudes). North from Mexico along the Rocky Mountains to Denver and north to Cache Valley

or even hundreds of microwave photons, which signals a very high-order quantal multiphoton process.) The nature of the dynamics depends strongly on two ratios, the scaled frequency, $\omega/\omega_{at} = n_0^3\omega$, and the scaled amplitude, $F_{at} = n_0^4F$, where F_{at} is the Coulomb electric field at the Bohr (circular) orbit for initial state n_0. If the (scaled) threshold fields $n_0^4F(10\%)$ that produced an ionization probability of 10% after the atoms were exposed to about 300 microwave field oscillations are measured and their dependence on $n_0^3\omega$ is graphed (**Fig. 3**), locally higher thresholds show up as bumps near some rational-fraction values (for example, $^1/_2$, $^1/_1$, and $^2/_1$). These peaks were successfully explained via the stabilizing influence of classical, nonlinear trapping resonances. At one extreme, as $n_0^3\omega \to 0$, the measured threshold fields approach, as expected, the value $n_0^4F_0 \simeq 0.13$ for a static field. As $n_0^3\omega$ rises to near 1, classical, numerical Monte Carlo calculations (Fig. 3) that simulated the experiment reproduce the experimental curve (as do quantal calculations), but there are important, local exceptions. For example, a bump near $n_0^3\omega = 1.3$ is a quantal effect caused by the stabilizing influence of a (scarred) so called separatrix state. (Broadband noise added to the driving field to decrease its coherence was shown to be a new spectroscopic technique for finding such states experimentally.) When $n_0^3\omega \gtrsim 2$, however, the systematic rise of experimental thresholds above those of classical calculations confirmed a prediction of quantum theory and numerical calculations that quantal interference effects would tend to suppress the effects of classical chaos for high-scaled frequencies. *See* ATOMIC STRUCTURE AND SPECTRA; MONTE CARLO METHOD; NONRELATIVISTIC QUANTUM THEORY   Peter M. Koch.

Bibliography. J. R. Buchler and H. E. Kandrup (eds.), *Stochastic Processes in Astrophysics*, 1993;

in the Wasatch Mountains is a deciduous chaparral characterized by *Q. gambelii*. In northern California and southwestern Oregon and in the Tehachapi and adjacent mountains of southern California is an analogous vegetation type characterized by *Q. garryana* ssp. *breweri*.

The true chaparral of California, however, is different from the above. Its characteristic species include *Adenostema fasciculatum, Ceanothus cuneatus, Q. dumosa, Heteromeles arbutifolia, Rhamnus californica, R. crocea*, and *Cercocarpus betuloides*, plus a host of endemic species of *Arctostaphylos* and *Ceanothus* and other Californian endemics, both shrubby and herbaceous. These plants determine the formation's physiognomy. It is a dense, uniform-appearing, evergreen, shrubby cover with sclerophyllous leaves and deep-penetrating roots.

Plant life forms. Although the shrub life form is dominant, a variety of life forms is represented in chaparral. A floristic spectrum of Raunkiaer's life forms from an area of serpentine chaparral in Napa County, California, containing 67 species of vascular plants had 4% phanerophytes, 18% nanophanerophytes, 12% chamaephytes, 27% hemicryptophytes, 18% geophytes, and 21% therophytes. Comparable data from other chaparral regions show lower nanophanerophyte and geophyte percentages and a higher therophyte percentage. *See* PLANTS, LIFE FORMS OF.

Geographic variations. The Californian type of chaparral formation runs south from the Rogue River valley of southern Oregon through the lower California mountains, west of the crest of the Sierra Nevada, below the *Pinus ponderosa* belt, to northern lower California. In Oregon *Ceanothus cuneatus* and *Arctostaphylos viscida* are characteristic; *Adenostema fasciculatum*, for example, drops out north of Shasta County, California. In this northern area summer thunderstorms occur. Another variation is evident in Arizona. Again, such Californian plants as *Adenostema fasciculatum* and *Heteromeles arbutifolia* drop out as the climate changes from winter precipitation to a bimodal occurrence of rain with a maximum in summer. The Arizona chaparral is characterized by *Q. turbinella, Arctostaphylos pungens, Rhus trilobata*, and *Ceanothus greggii*, all more or less desert species in California.

Ecology. There is extreme floristic diversity, and therefore presumably also ecological diversity, within the vegetation commonly called chaparral. Since the basic floristic study of the formation has not yet been done, it is extremely difficult to extrapolate ecological or experimental physiological data from one area of chaparral to another.

Climate. Ecologically, chaparral occurs in a climate which is hot and dry in summer, cool but not much below freezing in winter, with little or no snow, and with winter precipitation which is excessive and leaches the soil of nutrients. The need for water and its supply are exactly out of phase. Figures describing chaparral climates are variable. Temperatures may be maritime as at coastal San Diego or continental as at Ash Mountain at 1750 ft (530 m) elevation on the west slope of the Sierra Nevada. Amplitudes of mean monthly temperatures at these stations are 46.2 and 69.4°F (7.9 and 20.8°C). Means are 60.6 and 63.5°F (15.9 and 17.5°C). Need for water potential evapotranspiration is 31.4 and 39.0 in. (785 and 974 mm) per year. Annual precipitations are 10 and 28 in. (250 and 700 mm) at these stations, with Redding, located at the northern end of the Sacramento Valley, having 38 in. (950 mm). Actual water use varies much less, being 10 in. (250 mm) at San Diego, 15.2 in. (380 mm) at Ash Mountain, and 16 in. (400 mm) at Redding. The differences between these figures and annual precipitation are runoff. In Oregon chaparral areas, need for water is less, about 28 in. (700 mm) per year, corresponding to the lower temperatures. However, actual water use is higher than in California, being 18.8–20.0 in. (470–500 mm) per year. In Arizona chaparral, runoffs are nil, and figures for actual water use are somewhat higher than in California, 14–20 in. (350–500 mm) per year.

A fair conclusion is that chaparral grows under no unique climate. It may, of course, still be differentiated from surrounding vegetation by climatic parameters. Its prevalence on south slopes, whereas some kind of woodland or forest occupies adjacent north slopes, is clear evidence of control by local climates.

Water relations. So far as water relations are concerned, the shrubs of the chaparral presumably transpire continuously during the dry summer since they are evergreen. They photosynthesize below the wilting point, and their roots penetrate very deeply (recorded to 28 ft or 8.5 m) as well as widely (ratio of root to crown spread 2 to 4). At great depths in the fractured rock, water may be perennially available although the soil itself is reduced to the permanent wilting point each summer. Some of the xeromorphic features of the plants may be related to low nitrogen supply, as has been found for ericaceous plants of acid bogs. *See* PLANT-WATER RELATIONS.

Soils. Chaparral soils are generally rocky, often shallow, or of extreme chemistry such as those derived from serpentine, and always low in fertility. In the very precipitous southern Californian mountains, soil erosion rates may be 0.04 in. (1 mm) per year over large watershed areas. The runoff figures mentioned above also contribute to low soil fertility through their leaching effects. The result is low available nitrogen. Quantitative data which would allow a nitrogen balance to be drawn up are lacking, although data do show that a single crop of *Ceanothus leucodermis* can double soil nitrogen contents. *See* SOIL.

Succession. Successionally chaparral is various. *Quercus durata* on serpentine, to which it is limited, may be a continuing type. On deep soils at higher foothill elevations, chaparral is often replaced by *Q. kelloggii*; on the still deeper soils at lower elevations, it may have replaced *Q. douglasii. Pinus sabiniana* comes up through dense chaparral stands, but it seems to affect the shrubs little. *Pinus halepensis* occupies a similar ecological position in the Mediterranean maquis. Fire often thickens a stand of chaparral since many of its species are crown sprouters; in other species seed germination is stimulated by fire. Careful management of deer or sheep grazing can keep burned chaparral areas open. Under natural conditions *Eriodictyon californicum* is successional to chaparral after fires, if replacement of the original shrubs does not follow directly by sprouting or seedings. *See* ECOLOGICAL SUCCESSION.   Jack Major

Character recognition

The process of converting scanned images of machine-printed or handwritten text (numerals, letters, and symbols) into a computer-processable format; also known as optical character recognition (OCR).

Systems. A typical OCR system (**Fig. 1**) contains three logical components: an image scanner, OCR software and hardware, and an output interface. The image scanner optically captures text images to be recognized. Text images are processed with OCR software and hardware. The process involves three operations: document analysis (extracting individual character images), recognizing these images (based on shape), and contextual processing (either to correct misclassifications made by the recognition algorithm or to limit recognition choices). The output interface is responsible for communication of OCR system results to the outside world.

Image scanner. Four basic building blocks form functional image scanners: a detector (and associated electronics), an illumination source, a scan lens, and a document transport. The document transport places the document in the scanning field, the light source floods the object with illumination, and the lens forms the object's image on the detector. The detector consists of an array of elements, each of which converts incident light into a charge or analog signal. These analog signals are then converted into an image. Scanning is performed by the detector and the motion of the text object with respect to the detector. After an image is captured, the document transport removes the document from the scanning field.

Over the years, advances in scanner technology made available higher resolution, often in the range of 300–400 pixels per inch (ppi). Recognition methods that use features (as opposed to template matching) use resolutions of at least 200 ppi and careful consideration of the gray scale. Lower resolutions and simple thresholding (that is, discrimination based only on whether the darkness of a pixel exceeds a certain threshold) tend to break thin lines or fill gaps, thus invalidating features.

Software and hardware. The software-hardware system that recognizes characters from a registered image can be divided into three operational steps: document analysis, character recognition, and contextual processing.

1. *Document analysis.* In this process, text is extracted from the document image. Reliable character segmentation and recognition depend upon both original document quality and registered image quality. Processes that attempt to compensate for poor-quality originals or poor-quality scanning include image enhancement, underline removal, and noise removal. Image enhancement methods emphasize discrimination between characters and objects that are not characters. Underline removal erases printed guidelines and other lines which may touch characters and interfere with character recognition. Noise removal erases portions of the image that are not part of characters. *See* IMAGE PROCESSING.

Prior to character recognition, it is necessary to isolate individual characters from the text image. Many OCR systems use connected components for this process. For those connected components that represent multiple or partial characters, more sophisticated algorithms are used. In low-quality or nonuniform text images, these sophisticated algorithms may not correctly extract characters, and thus recognition errors may occur. Recognition of

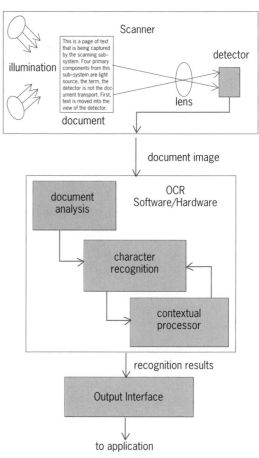

Fig. 1. General structure of an optical character recognition (OCR) system.

unconstrained handwritten text can be very difficult because characters cannot be reliably isolated, especially when the text is cursive handwriting.

2. *Character-recognition algorithms.* Two essential components in a character-recognition algorithm are the feature extractor and the classifier. Feature analysis determines the descriptors, or feature set, used to describe all characters. Given a character image, the feature extractor derives the features that the character possesses. The derived features are then used as input to the character classifier.

Template matching, or matrix matching, is one of the most common classification methods. In template matching, individual image pixels are used as features. Classification is performed by comparing an input character image with a set of templates (or prototypes) from each character class. Each comparison results in a similarity measure between the input character and the template. One measure increases the amount of similarity when a pixel in the observed character is identical to the same pixel in the template image. If the pixels differ, the measure of similarity may be decreased. After all templates have been compared with the observed character image, the character's identity is assigned as the identity of the most similar template.

Template matching is a trainable process because template characters may be changed. In many commercial systems, programmable read-only memories (PROMs) store templates containing single fonts. To retrain the algorithm, the current PROMs are replaced with PROMs that contain images of a new font. Thus, if a suitable PROM exists for a font, template matching can be trained to recognize that font. The similarity measure of template matching may also be modified, but commercial OCR systems typically do not allow this modification. *See* COMPUTER STORAGE TECHNOLOGY; SEMICONDUCTOR MEMORIES.

Structural classification methods utilize structural features and decision rules to classify characters. Structural features may be defined in terms of character strokes, character holes, or other character attributes such as concavities. For instance, the letter P may be described as a vertical stroke with a hole attached on the upper right side. For a character image input, the structural features are extracted and a rule-based system is applied to classify the character. Structural methods are also trainable, but construction of a good feature set and a good rule base can be time consuming.

Many character recognizers are based on mathematical formalisms that minimize a measure of misclassification. These recognizers may use pixel-based features or structural features. Some examples are discriminant-function classifiers, bayesian classifiers, artificial neural networks, and template matchers. Discriminant-function classifiers use hypersurfaces to separate the featural descriptions of characters from different semantic classes and, in the process, reduce the mean-squared error.

Bayesian methods seek to minimize the loss function associated with misclassification through the use of probability theory. Artificial neural networks, which are closer to theories of human perception, employ mathematical minimization techniques. Both discriminant functions and artificial neural networks are used in commercial OCR systems. *See* BAYESIAN STATISTICS; NEURAL NETWORK.

Character misclassifications stem from two main sources: poor-quality character images and poor discriminatory ability. Poor document quality, image scanning, and preprocessing can all degrade performance by yielding poor-quality characters. However, the character recognition method may not have been trained for a proper response on the character causing the error. This type of error source is difficult to overcome because the recognition method may have limitations and all possible character images cannot possibly be considered in training the classifier. Recognition rates for machine-printed characters can reach over 99%, but handwritten character recognition rates are typically lower because every person writes differently. This random nature often results in misclassifications.

3. *Contextual processing.* Contextual information can be used in recognition. The number of word choices for a given field can be limited by knowing the content of another field. For example, in recognizing the street name in an address, the street name choices can be limited to a lexicon by first correctly recognizing the postal code. Alternatively, the result of recognition can be postprocessed to correct the recognition errors. One method used to postprocess character recognition results is to apply a spelling checker to verify word spelling. Similarly, other postprocessing methods use lexicons to verify word results, or recognition results may be verified interactively with the user.

4. *Nonroman character recognition.* There are 26 different scripts in use that are other than roman. Some have had little work done on their recognition, for example, Kannada, while a significant amount of work has been done on others, for example, Japanese. In addition to alphanumerals, Japanese text uses Kanji characters (Chinese ideographs) and Kana (Japanese syllables). Therefore, it is considerably more difficult to recognize Japanese text because of the size of the character set (usually more than 3300 characters) and the complexity and similarity of the Kanji character structures. Low data quality is an additional problem in all OCRs. A Japanese OCR is usually composed of two individual classifiers (preclassifier and secondary classifier) in a cascade structure. The preclassifier first performs a fast coarse classification to reduce the character set to a short candidate list (usually containing no more than 100 candidates). The secondary classifier then uses more complex features to determine which candidate in the list has the closest match to the test pattern.

Output interface. The output interface allows character recognition results to be electronically transferred into the domain that uses the results. For example, many commercial systems allow recognition results to be placed directly into spread sheets, databases, and word processors. Other commercial systems use recognition results directly in further automated processing and, when the processing is complete, the recognition results are discarded. The output interface, while simple, is vital to the success of OCR systems because it communicates results to the outside world. *See* DATABASE MANAGEMENT SYSTEMS; WORD PROCESSING.

Applications. Commercial OCR systems can largely be grouped into two categories: task-specific readers and general-purpose page readers. A task-specific reader handles only specific document types. Some of the most common task-specific readers read bank checks, letter mail, or credit-card slips. These readers usually utilize custom-made image-lift hardware that captures only a few predefined document regions. For example, a bank-check reader may scan just the courtesy-amount field (where the amount of the check is written numerically) and a postal OCR system may scan just the address block on a mail piece. Such systems emphasize high throughput rates and low error rates. Applications such as letter-mail reading have throughput rates of 12 letters per second with error rates less than 2%. The character recognizer in many task-specific readers is able to recognize both handwritten and machine-printed text.

General-purpose page readers are designed to handle a broader range of documents such as business letters, technical writings, and newspapers. These systems capture an image of a document page and separate the page into text regions and nontext regions. Nontext regions such as graphics and line drawings are often saved separately from the text and associated recognition results. Text regions are segmented into lines, words, and characters, and the characters are passed to the recognizer. Recognition results are output in a format that can be postprocessed by application software. Most of these page readers can read machine-written text, but only

a few can read hand-printed alphanumerics.

Task-specific readers. Task-specific readers are used primarily for high-volume applications that require high system throughput. Since high throughput rates are desired, handling only the fields of interest helps reduce time constraints. Since similar documents possess similar size and layout structure, it is straightforward for the image scanner to focus on those fields where the desired information lies. This approach can considerably reduce the image-processing and text-recognition time. Application areas to which task-specific readers have been applied include assigning postal codes to letter mail, reading data entered in forms such as tax forms, automatic accounting procedures used in processing utility bills, verification of account numbers and courtesy amounts on bank checks, automatic accounting of airline passenger tickets, and automatic validation of passports.

1. *Address readers.* The address reader in a postal mail sorter locates the destination address block on a mail piece and reads the postal code in this block. In the United States, additional fields in the address block are read with high confidence, the system may generate a 9-digit ZIP code for the piece. This ZIP code is then used to generate a bar code which is sprayed on the envelope (**Fig. 2**).

The multiline optical character reader (MLOCR) used by the U.S. Postal Service locates the address block on a mail piece, reads the whole address, identifies the 9-digit ZIP code, generates a 9-digit bar code, and sorts the mail to the correct stacker. The character classifier recognizes up to 400 fonts, and the system can process up to 45,000 mail pieces per hour.

2. *Form readers.* A form-reading system needs to discriminate between preprinted form instructions and filled-in data. The system is first trained with a blank form. The system registers those areas on the form where the data should be printed. During the form-recognition phase, the system uses the spatial information obtained from training to scan the regions that should be filled with data. Some readers read hand-printed data as well as various

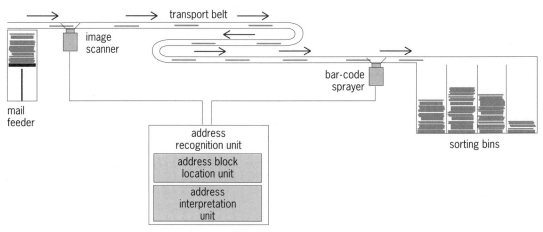

Fig. 2. Architecture of a postal address reading and sorting system.

machine-written text. They can read data on a form without being confused with the form instructions. Some systems can process forms at a rate of 5800 per hour.

3. *Bill-processing systems.* In general, a bill-processing system is used to read payment slips, utility bills, and inventory documents. The system focuses on certain regions on a document where the expected information is located, such as the account number and payment value.

4. *Check readers.* A check reader captures check images and recognizes courtesy amounts and account information on the checks. Some readers also recognize the legal amounts (written alphabetically) on checks and use the information in both fields to cross-check the recognition results. An operator can correct misclassified characters by cross-validating the recognition results with the check image that appears on a system console.

5. *Airline ticket readers.* In order to claim revenue from an airline passenger ticket, an airline needs to have three records matched: the reservation record, the travel-agent record, and the passenger ticket. However, it is impossible to match all three records for every ticket sold. Current methods, which use manual random sampling of tickets, are far from accurate in claiming the maximal amount of revenue. Several airlines use a passenger-revenue accounting system to account accurately for passenger revenues. The system reads the ticket number on a passenger ticket and matches it with the one in the airline reservation database. It scans up to 260,000 tickets per day and achieves a sorting rate of 17 tickets per second.

6. *Passport readers.* An automated passport reader is used to speed passengers returning to the United States through custom inspections. The reader reads a traveler's name, date of birth, and passport number on the passport and checks these against the database records that contain information on fugitive felons and smugglers.

General-purpose page readers. The two general categories are high-end page readers and low-end page readers. High-end page readers are more advanced in recognition capability and have higher data throughput. A low-end page reader usually does not come with a scanner, and it is compatible with many flat-bed scanners. Low-end page readers are used mostly in office environments with desktop workstations, which are less demanding in system throughput. Since they are designed to handle a broader range of documents, a sacrifice of recognition accuracy is necessary. Some commercial OCR software allows users to adapt the recognition engine to customer data for improving recognition accuracy. Some high-performance readers can detect type faces (such as boldface and italic) and output the formatted ASCII text in the corresponding style. *See* COMPUTER; COMPUTER VISION.

Sargur N. Srihari; Stephen W. Lam

Bibliography. J. Cohen, *Automatic Identification and Data Collection Systems*, 1995; M. Ogg and H. Ogg, *Optical Character Recognition: A Librarian's Guide*, 1992; J. C. Reimel, *Image Processing and Optical Character Recognition: How They Work and How to Implement Them*, 1993; G. Searfoss, *Jis-Kanji Character Recognition Method*, 1994; S. N. Srihari, High-performance reading machines, *Proc. IEEE*, 80:1120–1132, 1992; P. S. Wang (ed.), *Character and Handwriting Recognition: Expanding Frontiers*, 1990.

Characteristic curve

A curve that shows the relationship between two changing values. A typical characteristic curve is that which shows how the changes in the control-grid voltage of an electron tube affect the anode current. When three variables are involved, a family of characteristic curves is frequently drawn, with each curve representing one value of the third variable. Other common examples of curves include speed-torque characteristics of motors, frequency-gain characteristics of amplifiers, and voltage-temperature characteristics of thermocouples. The curves are produced by making a series of measurements and plotting the results.

With appropriate electronic circuits the measurements can now be made automatically and fast enough so that the entire characteristic curve is visible on the screen of a cathode-ray oscilloscope. *See* GRAPHIC RECORDING INSTRUMENTS; OSCILLOSCOPE.

John Markus

Charadriiformes

A large, diverse, worldwide order of shore and aquatic birds. It may be closely related to the pigeons (Columbiformes) on the one side and to the cranes, rails, and their allies (Gruiformes) on the other. The sandgrouse, here included in the Columbiformes, are sometimes placed in the Charadriiformes. Some workers place the flamingos (Phoenicopteriformes) and the ibises (Threskiornithidae; Ciconiiformes) in this order, but this is highly controversial. *See* CICONIIFORMES; COLUMBIFORMES; GRUIFORMES; PHOENICOPTERIFORMES.

Classification. The order Charadriiformes is arranged into three suborders and 17 families as follows: (1) Charadrii, with superfamily Jacanoidea containing the families Jacanidae (jacanas; 8 species) and Rostratulidae (painted snipe; 2 speices); superfamily Charadrioidea containing the families Graculavidae (Cretaceous of New Jersey), Presbyornithidae (Eocene of North and South America), Haematopodidae (oyster catchers; 7 species), Charadriidae (plovers and lapwings; 64 species), Scolopacidae (sandpipers, curlews, phalaropes, and snipe; 86 species), Recurvirostridae (stilts and avocets; 10 species), Dromadidae (crab plovers; 1 species), Burhinidae (thick-knees; 9 species), and Glareolidae (pratincoles; 16 species);

and superfamily Chionidoidea with the families Thinocoridae (seed snipe; 4 species) and Chionidae (sheathbills; 2 species). (2) Lari, with the families Stercorariidae (skuas; 5 species), Laridae (gulls and terns; 88 species), and Rynchopidae (skimmers; 3 species). (3) Alcae, with the single family Alcidae (auks, murres, and puffins; 23 species). Several of these families, such as the Charadriidae (plovers), Scolopacidae (sandpipers), and Laridae (gulls and terns), are divided into two or more subfamilies.

Fossil record. Being shore and water birds, the charadriiforms have a long and generally good fossil record, including some of the earliest fossils that are definitely assigned to a living order. The Graculavidae are Cretaceous birds from New Jersey whose affinities to Recent families have not been established. A number of other presumably charadriiform fossils are known from the Cretaceous, but their relationships are still uncertain. The Paleocene–early Eocene Presbyornithidae is known from abundant material from the western United States, Argentina, and Mongolia and may be the primitive group from which the other charadriiforms and perhaps several other orders have evolved. *Presbyornis* has a typical shorebirdlike postcranial skeleton and a ducklike skull, although there is some debate on the association of these elements. The larid and alcids have good fossil records, but most of the other families are represented by scattered remains and several are unrepresented as fossils. This lack arises presumably because of the fragile nature of the skeleton of most members of the order.

Suborders. The three suborders of charadiiforms are quite different groups, and each is best discussed separately.

Charadrii. The Charadrii are the typical shorebirds, usually found in marshy areas and along shores, but some are in dry areas, and a few, the phalaropes, are mainly aquatic. They can run and fly well. Most live in flocks, although most breed solitarily in nests placed on the ground. Males of the ruffs of Europe are much larger than females and court communally, in leks, with females coming to the leks and choosing particular males. The crab plovers nest colonially in tunnels dug into sand banks. The young are downy and leave the nest on hatching. The phalaropes (Scolopacidae: Phalaropodinae), painted snipes, and jacanas show sex reversal, with the females being larger than the males and usually more brightly colored, and assuming the lead in courtship; the males incubate and assume most of the care of the young. Most feed on insects and other small animals; the seed snipes are mainly vegetarian. The bills of many species are highly specialized for food capture, with the most bizarre being that of the wry-billed plover of New Zealand, in which the bill tip bends sharply to the right for probing under stones for insects. Many species breed in the Arctic or cool temperate regions and migrate long distances in large flocks. Some species have long transoceanic

migrations, for example, the bristle-thighed curlew, which flies from Alaska to Hawaii and then to Tahiti and surrounding islands. Many shorebirds were or still are of economic importance as game birds. The numbers of many species have been greatly reduced because of overhunting or loss of habitat, mainly migration and wintering grounds. A few species, for example, the Eskimo curlew, are severely threatened or extinct. *See* SEXUAL DIMORPHISM.

Lari. The Lari include the skuas, gulls, terns, and skimmers, predominantly aquatic birds that find their food by flying over the water. They are long-winged, excellent fliers with short legs, but they can walk well. The feet are webbed. Most species breed in large colonies, laying up to four eggs, and the downy young remain in or near the nest until they can fly. Most species can swim on the water surface, although terns do so less often. A few oceanic terns lack waterproof plumage and never alight on the water, sleeping on the wing. Although many species are marine, most are found near the coast and are not truly oceanic. Skimmers have a compressed, elongated lower jaw with which they skim the surface of the water for fish. Many species breed in the Arctic and cold temperate regions and migrate. The Arctic tern has the longest known migratory flight—22,000 mi (36,000 km) per year. Skuas have been seen closer to the poles than any other birds.

Alcae. Alcae include only the alcids, which are true marine, swimming and diving birds found only in the Northern Hemisphere. They are mainly black and white, and have webbed feet and reduced wings. Alcids are excellent divers, and swim underwater by using their wings, which are reduced to rather stiff, paddlelike structures. They have a quick, buzzy flight used mainly to reach their nesting sites. Alcids feed on fish and other aquatic animals. They breed in large colonies, on rocky ledges or in burrows. The young are downy, and in some species leave the nest before they are fully grown. The great auk of the North Atlantic, the penguin of a number of writers, is the largest known species and was flightless; it is now extinct. *See* AVES.
Walter J. Bock

Bibliography. P. A. Johnsgard, *The Plovers, Sandpipers and Snipes of the World*, 1981.

Charcoal

A porous solid product containing 85–98% carbon produced by heating carbonaceous materials such as cellulose, wood, peat, and coals of bituminous or lower rank at 930–1110°F (500–600°C) in the absence of air. Chars or charcoals are rendered more porous and more efficient for sorption by heating in air, carbon dioxide, or steam at 1650°F (900°C) for a brief period. The surface area of activated char produced by this technique is about 800,000 ft²/oz (1000 m²/g). Chars from cellulose or wood are soft and friable. They are used chiefly for decolorizing solutions of sugar and other foodstuffs and for removing objectionable tastes and odors from water. Chars from nutshells and coal are dense, hard carbons. They are used in gas masks and in chemical manufacturing for many mixture separations. Another use is for the tertiary treatment of wastewater. Residual organic matter is adsorbed effectively to improve the water quality.

The sorptive properties of chars are the result of their very large internal surface. The selectivity of the sorption can be modified by mixing additives to the char, and by controlling the partial pressure or concentration of components, the temperature of the mixture, and (in liquids) the acidity or polar environment. *See* ACTIVATED CARBON; ADSORPTION; CARBON; COKE; DESTRUCTIVE DISTILLATION; PYROLYSIS; WOOD CHEMICALS.   Joseph H. Field

Charge-coupled devices

Semiconductor devices wherein minority charge is stored in a spatially defined depletion region (potential well) at the surface of a semiconductor, and is moved about the surface by transferring this charge to similar adjacent wells. The formation of the potential well is controlled by the manipulation of voltage applied to surface electrodes. Since a potential well represents a nonequilibrium state, it will fill with minority charge from normal thermal generation. Thus a charge-coupled device (CCD) must be continuously clocked or refreshed to maintain its usefulness. In general, the potential wells are strung together as shift registers. Charge is injected or generated at various input ports and then transferred to an output detector. By appropriate design to minimize the dispersive effects that are associated with the charge-transfer process, well-defined charge packets can be moved over relatively long distances through thousands of transfers.

Control of charge motion. There are several methods of controlling the charge motion, all of which rely upon providing a lower potential for the charge in the desired direction. When an electrode is placed in close proximity to a semiconductor surface, the electrode's potential can control the near-surface potential within the semiconductor. The basis for this control is the same as for metal-oxide-semiconductor (MOS) transistor action. If closely spaced electrodes are at different voltages, they will form potential wells of different depths. Free charge will move from the region of higher potential to the one of lower potential. **Figure 1** shows a case where by alternating the voltage on three electrodes in proper phase, a charge packet can be moved to the right. **Figure 2** illustrates another scheme whereby an asymmetry built into a well can direct the charge in a given direction. Asymmetries of this type are easily created by using implanted ion layers or varying dielectric thickness. The three-

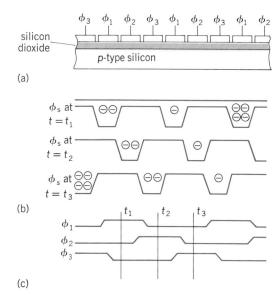

Fig. 1. Operation of three-phase charge-coupled shift register. (*a*) Cross section of register through channel. (*b*) Profile of surface potential ϕ_s for three different clock time intervals t_1, t_2, and t_3. (*c*) Voltage waveforms ϕ_1, ϕ_2, and ϕ_3 for the three-phase clocks.

phase structure shown in Fig. 1 has the ability to reverse the charge direction by a change in electrical phase.

Transfer efficiency. An important property of a charge-coupled device is its ability to transfer almost all of the charge from one well to the next. Without this feature, charge packets would be quickly distorted and lose their identity. This ability to transfer charge is measured as transfer efficiency, which must be very good for the structure to be

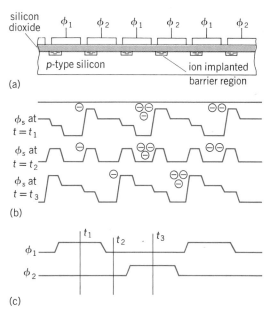

Fig. 2. Operation of two-phase charge-coupled shift register. (*a*) Cross section of register through channel. (*b*) Profile of surface potential ϕ_s for three different clock time intervals t_1, t_2, and t_3. (*c*) Voltage waveforms ϕ_1 and ϕ_2 for the two-phase clocks.

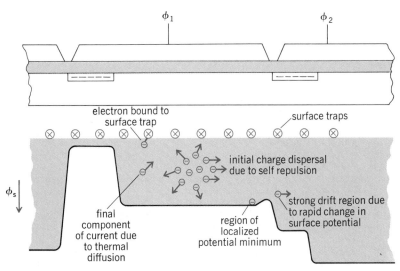

Fig. 3. Mechanisms determining charge-transfer rate. The three terms contributing to charge transfer include self-induced drift, channel drift fields, and thermal diffusion. Charge is left behind due to electron traps and localized potential minima.

useful in long registers. Values greater than 99.9% per transfer are not uncommon. This means that only 10% of the original charge is lost after 100 transfers.

Figure 3 shows a close-up of a stage of a charge-coupled device. Several mechanisms influence the transfer of charge from one well to the next. Initial self-induced drift acts to separate the charge. This repulsion of like charge is the dominant transfer mechanism for large signals, and is effective for the first 99% or so of the charge. Near the edge of the transfer electrode the potential gradient creates a field which sweeps the charge onward. Thermal diffusion accounts for the transfer of the remaining charge.

Electron traps. It would appear that, given sufficient time, almost all of the charge could be transferred. Two other mechanisms are at work to counter this. Within the silicon and at its surface are sites that can act as electron traps. This is especially true at the surface, where numerous surface states exist. These traps collect charge when exposed to a large charge packet and then slowly release it during later cycles of small charge packets. By stringing a large number of empty charge packets together, the traps can be emptied completely. When the first packet containing charge arrives, it could be completely consumed, recharging the traps.

Other than process steps that minimize the trap density, there are two methods to alleviate the severity of this problem. The first is never to allow a series of completely empty charge packets to occur. Instead of an empty charge packet, a minimum charge quantity is always present. This charge, called a fat zero, can be 10–20% of the well capacity. Under some conditions, this can reduce the trapping effects to tolerable levels. The second approach is to use a channel for the charge whose potential minimum does not occur at the surface. This is called a buried channel device, as opposed to a surface channel device. Since the charge is located within the bulk silicon below the surface, it is not exposed to the surface-state traps. Bulk traps remain, but because of their low density they are almost insignificant.

The process to shift the channel potential minimum below the surface can be either an ion-implant layer or an epitaxy layer combined with an implant layer. Because the charge is further removed from the surface control electrode, the maximum charge density has been reduced by a factor of 2 to 3. For the same reason, the fringing fields are greater and charge transfer can be much faster. The charge also moves with bulk mobility rather than the lower surface mobility, further enhancing performance. Fractional charge losses of as low as 5×10^{-5} at clock frequencies greater than 100 MHz have been reported for buried-channel charge-coupled-device structures. This means that such a structure could transfer 10^6 electrons from one well to another in less than 10 ns, leaving fewer than 50 electrons behind. *See* ION IMPLANTATION.

Localized potential minima. In addition to electron-trapping sites, there is another reason that charge can be left behind. Where the two adjacent surface electrodes come together, there is necessarily a gap. This gap is usually quite small, and sometimes may even be covered by one of the electrodes. However, the gap represents a region of poorly controlled surface potential. It is possible, under some conditions, for the transition from one potential well to the next to have perturbations in it. These perturbations, or glitches, can trap charge. They represent a localized minipotential well within the larger one. Charge trapped by the glitch will be left behind after a transfer. If the glitch remained filled, continued clocking of the structure would not represent a problem. However, the size of the glitch may change, depending upon electrode clock amplitude. Also, charge is released over the glitch as thermionic emission over a barrier potential. Thus a glitch can be emptied by a series of empty charge packets to trap the next packet-containing charge. Many times, glitches occur at input or output ports without detriment to the structure's operation, since their effect may be small. However, if a glitch occurs within the repetitive register, the

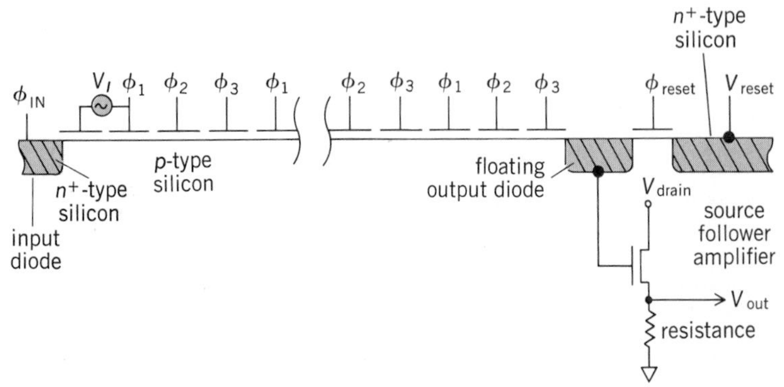

Fig. 4. Charge-coupled register showing analog input and output ports.

multiplication effect can have a serious impact on overall performance.

Lifetime. A second important property of a charge-coupled-device register is its lifetime. When the surface electrode is clocked high, the potential within the semiconductor also increases. Majority charge is swept away, leaving behind a depletion layer. If the potential is taken sufficiently high, the surface goes into deep depletion until an inversion layer is formed and adequate minority charge collected to satisfy the field requirements. The time it takes for minority charge to fill the well is the measure of well lifetime. The major sources of unwanted charge are the following: thermal diffusion of substrate minority charge to the edge of the depletion region, where it is collected in the well; electron-hole pair generation within the depletion region; and the emission of minority charge by traps. Surface-channel charge-coupled devices usually have a better lifetime, since surface-state trap emission is suppressed and the depletion regions are usually smaller.

Input and output ports. Once adequate transfer efficiency and sufficient lifetime have been achieved, input and output ports must be established. The port structure of a charge-coupled device depends upon its application. Analog registers require linear inputs and outputs with good dynamic range. Digital registers require precisely metered and detected ones and zeros. Imaging devices use photoemission at the register sites as input with analog-output amplifiers.

The most common input is shown in **Fig. 4**. This input structure relies upon a diode as a source of minority charge. Whenever the diode potential drops below the threshold potential of the adjacent gate, an inversion layer is formed beneath the gate. By pulsing the diode potential low or the adjacent gate potential high, charge can be injected into the register. To prevent the charge from returning to the diode, the next gate in the register immediately collects it. The amount of charge injected can be controlled by adjusting the channel potential difference between the first two gates.

Figure 4 also shows a common output circuit. The output diode is reset at the start of each cycle to the reset level. During the second part of the cycle, charge from the charge-coupled device register is dumped on the floating diode, causing its voltage to change. The diode is connected to a gate which can be used in an amplifier configuration. The example in Fig. 4 shows a source follower output. For digital applications, the output goes to a regenerative circuit with sufficient gain to produce full-level signals at the output.   Mark R. Guidry

Applications. Because of their unique properties, charge-coupled devices have found widespread use in a growing number of applications. Many solid-state imaging devices and analog-signal-processing devices have been successfully manufactured by using the principles of charge-coupling. Devices have been fabricated in both silicon and gallium arsenide, but silicon is the more prevalent.

Imagers. The most common use of charge-coupled devices is in solid-state imagers. In a charge-coupled-device imager, the photosites are used to convert an optical image into an electrical signal. Photons striking the surface of a semiconductor device will generate free electrons in an amount linearly proportional to their radiant energy. For a silicon device, electrons will be generated for incident photons with wavelengths of approximately 400–1100 nanometers, with the peak response occurring at 700–800 nanometers. This corresponds to the entire visible range of light, from blue to near-infrared. These photogenerated electrons can be collected in a regularly spaced array of photosites, each of which will then contain a charge packet of electrons. The amount of charge collected at each photosite will be directly proportional to the incident radiation of that photosite. If an image is focused on the surface of the device, the amounts of charge collected in the photosites will then be a faithful representation of the intensity of the image at each location. These charge packets correspond to picture elements, or pixels, each of which is a small part of the complete image. The number of photosites on the device determines the resolution of the final image. These charge packets are then transferred in parallel into a charge-coupled-device shift register, where they are then transferred serially to the output port. The output of the imager will be a series of electric signals whose amplitudes will represent the intensity of the image at each pixel.

Solid-state imagers offer many advantages over other imaging methods, including high reliability, high sensitivity, low power dissipation, and good spectral response over the entire visible spectrum. Charge-coupled-device imagers are produced in two formats, as linear arrays and as area arrays. Linear imaging devices (LIDs) consist of a single row of photosites, and scan images one line at a time. Area imaging devices (AIDs) consist of a matrix of photosites, and sense an entire field at one time. Linear imaging devices are used in applications where either the device or the image is moving at some constant speed, such as for inspection of objects on a conveyor belt. Other applications for linear imaging devices include use in facsimile equipment, photocopiers, mail sorters, and bar code readers, and for aerial mapping and reconnaissance.

Area imaging devices have been used in applications where neither the device nor the image is being moved in a regular manner, such as for closed-circuit television cameras, video cameras, and vision systems for robotics applications. Area imaging devices are also being used to replace conventional film for many kinds of astronomical observations. Charge-coupled-device imagers offer the astronomer many advantages over other detectors, such as good stability, linearity of output, and sensitivity of up to 50 times that of conventional film. When cooled to very low temperatures, on the order of $-150°F$ ($-100°C$), charge-coupled-device imagers can allow exposure times of several hours. This allows astronomers to detect fainter objects than ever before possible. The output signals from these devices can be fed into a computer to enhance the images and to extract other important data. *See* ASTRONOMICAL PHOTOGRAPHY; TELEVISION CAMERA; TELEVISION CAMERA TUBE.

Signal processing. Many applications for charge-coupled devices have been found in the processing of analog signal information. Since a charge-coupled device is an excellent analog shift register, it can be used as an analog delay line, where the delay is determined by the number of elements in the array and by the frequency at which it is clocked. The delay can be controlled externally by simply varying the clock frequency. It can also be used to scramble and descramble audio and video signals by varying the delay times of different sections of the signal. This could be used as a cable television descrambler, for example. By tapping a charge-coupled delay line, sampled analog filters can be produced that can be externally programmed to change their filter characteristics. Other uses for charge-coupled-device signal processors include applications as multiplexers and demultiplexers, correlators, and analog-to-digital converters. *See* COMPUTER STORAGE TECHNOLOGY; INTEGRATED CIRCUITS; SEMICONDUCTOR.   David E. Weisner

Bibliography. G. F. Amelio, Charge-coupled devices, *Sci. Amer.*, 230(2):22–31, February 1974; M. M. Blouke, *Charge-Coupled Devices and Other Solid State Optical Sensors*, 2 vols., 1990, 1991; S. Howell, *Astronomical CCD Observing and Reduction Techniques*, Astronomical Society of the Pacific Conference Series, vol. 23, 1992; G. Jacoby (ed.), *CCDs in Astronomy*, Astronomical Society of the Pacific Conference Series, vol. 8, 1990; J. Kristian and M. Blouke, Charge-coupled devices in astronomy, *Sci. Amer.*, 247(4):66–74, October 1982.

Charge-density wave

A possible ground state of a metal in which the conduction-electron charge density is sinusoidally modulated in space. The periodicity of this extra modulation is unrelated to the lattice periodicity. Instead, it is determined by the dimension of the conduction-electron Fermi surface in momentum space.

Description. The conduction-electron charge density $\rho_0(\vec{r})$ would ordinarily exhibit a dependence on position $\vec{r}$ having the same spatial periodicity as that of the positive-ion lattice. A metal with a charge-density wave (CDW) has an additional charge modulation described by Eq. (1). The fractional ampli-

$$\rho(\vec{r}) = \rho_0(\vec{r})[1 + f \cos{(\vec{Q} \cdot \vec{r} + \phi)}] \qquad (1)$$

tude of the charge-density wave is f and typically has a value of approximately 0.1. The wave vec-

tor $\vec{Q}$ of the charge-density wave is determined by the conduction-electron Fermi surface. In a simple metal, having a spherical surface of radius p_F in momentum space, the magnitude of $\vec{Q}$ is approximately the value in Eq. (2), where h is Planck's con-

$$Q \approx \frac{4\pi p_F}{h} \qquad (2)$$

stant. Although the wavelength of a charge-density wave is comparable to the spacing between lattice planes, their ratio is not a rational number. The charge-density wave is then said to be incommensurate. In such a case, the total energy of the metal is independent of the phase ϕ in Eq. (1). *See* FERMI SURFACE.

Origin. In a quasi-one-dimensional metal, for which conduction electrons are mobile in one direction only, a charge-density wave can be caused by a Peierls instability. This mechanism involves interaction between the electrons and a periodic lattice distortion having a wave vector Q parallel to the conduction axis. The linear-chain metal niobium triselenide ($NbSe_3$) is prototypical, and exhibits nonlinear conduction phenomena arising from electrically induced dynamic variations of the phase ϕ in Eq. (1).

For isotropic metals, and quasi-two-dimensional metals, Coulomb interactions between electrons are the cause of a charge-density wave instability. The exchange energy, an effect of the Pauli exclusion principle, and the correlation energy, an effect of electron-electron scattering, both act to stabilize a charge-density wave. However, the electrostatic energy attributable to the charge modulation in Eq. (1) would suppress a charge-density wave were it not for a compensating charge response of the positive-ion lattice. *See* EXCHANGE INTERACTION; EXCLUSION PRINCIPLE.

Lattice distortion. Suppose that $\vec{u}(\vec{r})$ is the displacement of a positive ion from its lattice site at $\vec{r}$. Then a wavelike displacement given by Eq. (3) will

$$\vec{u}(\vec{r}) = \vec{A} \sin{(\vec{Q} \cdot \vec{r} + \phi)} \qquad (3)$$

generate a positive-ion charge density that almost cancels the electronic charge modulation of Eq. (1). A typical value of the displacement amplitude A is about 1% of the lattice constant. Ion-ion repulsive interactions must be small in order to permit such a distortion. Consequently, charge-density waves are more likely to occur in metals having small elastic moduli.

Detection. The unambiguous signature of a charge-density wave is the observation of two satellites, on opposite sides of each Bragg reflection, in a single-crystal diffraction experiment, employing either x-rays, neutrons, or electrons. The satellites are caused by the periodic lattice displacement, Eq. (3). Charge-density waves were first seen by electron diffraction in layered metals like tantalum disulfide (TaS_2) and tantalum diselenide ($TaSe_2$), which have three charge-density waves. At reduced temperature, transitions from incommensurate to commensurate $\vec{Q}$'s are observed. The length of a charge-density wave in the latter case is then an integral multiple of some lattice periodicity. The charge-density wave in the elemental metal potassium has been observed by neutron diffraction. The wavelength of the charge-density wave in this case is 1.5% larger than the spacing between close-packed atomic planes. *See* ELECTRON DIFFRACTION; NEUTRON DIFFRACTION; X-RAY DIFFRACTION.

Fermi surface effects. If simple metals like sodium and potassium did not have a charge-density-wave structure, their conduction-electron Fermi surface would be almost a perfect sphere. Many electronic conduction phenomena would then be isotropic, and the low-temperature magnetoresistance would be essentially zero. The presence of a charge-density wave leads to a dramatic contradiction of such expectations. Conduction-electron dynamics will be modified by the presence of a new potential having the periodicity of Eq. (1). The Fermi surface will distort and become multiply connected. In high magnetic fields some electrons will travel in open orbits rather than in closed, cyclotron orbits. The low-temperature magnetoresistance will then exhibit sharp resonances as the magnetic field is rotated relative to the crystal axes. Such phenomena have been observed in sodium and potassium and have been explained with charge-density-wave theory. *See* MAGNETORESISTANCE.

$\vec{Q}$-domains. Generally, the $\vec{Q}$ direction will not be the same throughout an entire sample of, for example, a cubic crystal having a single charge-density wave. There will be a domain structure analogous to magnetic domains in a ferromagnet. The $\vec{Q}$ direction will (of course) prefer some specific axis described by direction cosines α, β, γ. In a cubic crystal there would be 24 equivalent axes and, therefore, 24 $\vec{Q}$-domain types. As a consequence, some physical properties of a sample will depend markedly on the orientation distribution of its $\vec{Q}$-domains. For example, the low-temperature resistivity of a potassium wire might be several times larger if its $\vec{Q}$-domains are oriented parallel to the wire, than the value obtained if the domains were oriented perpendicular. Since $\vec{Q}$-domain distribution can be altered by stress-induced domain regrowth, some physical properties will vary significantly from experiment to experiment, even on the same sample. Such behavior is observed in alkali metals. Techniques for the control of $\vec{Q}$-domain orientation have not yet been developed. *See* DOMAIN (ELECTRICITY AND MAGNETISM); ELECTRICAL RESISTIVITY.

Phasons. The energy decrease caused by the existence of an incommensurate charge-density wave is independent of the phase ϕ, Eq. (1). It follows that there are new low-frequency excitations which can be described by a slowly varying phase modulation of the charge-density wave, as represented approximately in Eq. (4).

$$\phi \to \phi(\vec{r}, t) = a(\vec{q}) \sin [\vec{q} \cdot \vec{r} - \omega(\vec{q})t] \qquad (4)$$

Quantized excitations of this type are called phasons. They exist only for small $\vec{q}$, $\vec{q} \parallel \vec{Q}$; and their frequency $\omega(\vec{q})$ approaches zero linearly with q.

A number of physical phenomena caused by phasons have been observed. Phasons give rise to a low-temperature anomaly in the heat capacity. The charge-density waves in lanthanum digerminide (LaGe$_2$) were first suspected from its anomalous heat capacity. The phason spectral density of potassium has been directly observed in point-contact spectroscopy. Phasons reduce the intensity of charge-density-wave diffraction satellites with increasing temperature and contribute a diffuse-scattering cloud which surrounds each satellite. The phason velocity in tantalum disulfide has been determined from measurements of the phason diffuse scattering. Conduction electrons are strongly scattered by phasons, and such processes modify the temperature dependence of the resistivity at low temperature. *See* BAND THEORY OF SOLIDS; CRYSTAL STRUCTURE; SPIN-DENSITY WAVE.

Albert W. Overhauser

Bibliography. F. Bassani et al. (eds.), *Highlights of Condensed-Matter Theory*, Proceedings of the International School of Physics "Enrico Fermi", Course 89, Varenna on Lake Como, 1983; T. Butz (ed.), *Nuclear Spectroscopy on Charge Density Wave Systems*, 1992; L. P. Gor'kov and G. Grüner (eds.), *Charge Density Waves in Solids*, 1990; G. Grüner, The dynamics of charge density waves, *Rev. Mod. Phys.*, 60:1129–1181, 1988.

Charged particle beams

Unidirectional streams of charged particles traveling at high velocities. Charged particles can be accelerated to high velocities by electromagnetic fields. They are then able to travel through matter (termed an absorber), interacting with it, losing energy, and causing various effects important in many applications. The velocities under consideration in this article exceed 100,000 m/s (about 60 mi/s or 200,000 mi/h), equivalent to an energy of 100 eV for a proton, and can approach the speed of light c (about 3×10^8 m/s or 6.7×10^8 mi/h). Examples of charged particles are electrons, positrons, protons, antiprotons, alpha particles, and any ions (atoms with one or several electrons removed or added). In addition, some particles are produced artificially and may be short-lived (pions, muons).

Excluded from consideration are particles of, for example, cosmic dust (micrometeorites), which are clumps of thousands or millions of atoms. *See* COSMIC RAYS; ELECTRONVOLT; ELEMENTARY PARTICLE; PARTICLE ACCELERATOR.

Particle properties. Fast charged particles are described in terms of the following properties (values for some particles are given in **Table 1**):

Charge, z, in multiples of the electron charge $e = 1.6022 \times 10^{-19}$ coulomb. At small velocities the charge may be less than the charge of the

TABLE 1. Properties of charged particles*

Ion	z	Lifetime, ns	Mass 10^{-24} g	u	MeV
Electron[†]	−1	Stable	0.910956	0.548593	511.004
Muon	1	2198.3	0.188357	0.113432	105.6598
Pion	1	26.04	0.248823	0.149846	139.578
Kaon	1	12.35	0.880322	0.530147	493.82
Sigma$^+$	1	0.081	2.120318	1.276895	1189.40
Sigma$^-$	−1	0.164	2.134436	1.285398	1197.32

Ion	z	Mass excess,[‡] MeV	Mass 10^{-24} g	u	MeV
1N	0	8.0714	1.674920	1.0086652	939.553
1H	1	7.2890	1.672614	1.0072766	938.259
2H	1	13.1359	3.343569	2.0135536	1875.587
3H	1	14.9500	5.007334	3.0155011	2808.883
3He	2	14.9313	5.006390	3.0149325	2808.353
4He	2	2.4248	6.644626	4.0015059	3727.328
6Li	3	14.0884	9.985570	6.0134789	5601.443
7Li	3	14.9073	11.647561	7.0143581	6533.743
7Be	4	15.7689	11.648186	7.0147345	6534.093
9Be	4	11.3505	14.961372	9.0099911	8392.637
10B	5	12.0552	16.622243	10.0101958	9324.309
11B	5	8.6677	18.276741	11.0065623	10252.406
12C	6	0	19.920910	11.9967084	11174.708
13C	6	3.1246	21.587011	13.0000629	12109.314
14C	6	3.0198	23.247356	13.9999504	13040.691
14N	7	2.8637	23.246166	13.9992342	13040.024
15N	7	.1004	24.901771	14.9962676	13968.741
16O	8	−4.7365	26.552769	15.9905263	14894.875
17O	8	−.8077	28.220304	16.9947441	15830.285
18O	8	−.7824	29.880881	17.9947713	16761.791
19F	9	−1.4860	31.539247	18.9934674	17692.058
20Ne	10	−7.0415	33.188963	19.9869546	18617.472
21Ne	10	−5.7299	34.851833	20.9883627	19550.265
22Ne	10	−8.0249	36.508273	21.9858989	20479.451

*From *American Institute of Physics Handbook*, 3d ed., McGraw-Hill, 1972.
[†]Electron masses to be divided by 1000.
[‡]Mass excess given for neutral atoms; it is used to calculate nuclear reaction Q values.

nucleus because electrons may be present in some of the atomic shells.

Rest mass, M; usually the energy equivalent Mc^2 (in MeV) is given.

Rest mass, m, of electron; $mc^2 = 0.51104$ MeV.

Mass in atomic mass units, u; $A_m = Mc^2/931.481$ MeV.

Kinetic energy, T, in MeV.

Velocity, v, in cm/s or m/s.

$\beta = v/c$; $c = 299{,}792{,}458$ m/s = speed of light.

For absorbers, the information needed is:

Atomic number, Z (number of protons in nucleus).

Average atomic weight, A (usually in g/mole, but numerically equal to mass in u).

Absorber thickness, x, in cm or g/cm^2.

Physical state (solid, liquid, gas, plasma).

See ATOMIC MASS UNIT; ENERGY; FUNDAMENTAL CONSTANTS; MASS.

Relation of velocity and energy. For small velocities ($\beta < 0.2$), the approximation $T = \frac{1}{2}Mc^2\beta^2$ is accurate to 3%. The expressions $\beta^2 = \zeta(\zeta + 2)/(\zeta + 1)^2$, and $T = Mc^2[(1/\sqrt{1 - \beta^2}) - 1]$, with $\zeta = T/Mc^2$), are correct for all velocities. For $\zeta > 100$, the expression $\beta^2 = 1 - (1/\kappa^2)$, with $\kappa = \zeta + 1$, is more suitable to provide accurate values. *See* RELATIVISTIC MECHANICS.

Range. If a parallel beam of monoenergetic particles (that is, a beam in which all particles have exactly the same kinetic energy T) enters an absorber with a flat and smooth surface, it is found that all the particles (with the exception of electrons) travel along almost straight lines, slow

TABLE 2. Calculated reduced average energy at various depths in copper of protons with $T = 144$ MeV*

x/mm	T_1/MeV
1	141
5	127
10	107
15	85
20	57

*From *American Institute of Physics Handbook*, 3d ed., McGraw-Hill, 1972.

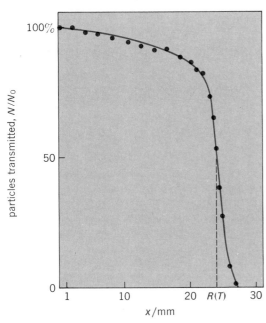

Fig. 1. Transmission curve for protons with kinetic energy $T = 144$ MeV through copper. (After L. Koschmieder, Zur Energiebestimmung von Protonen aus Reichweite-messungen, Z. Naturforsch., 19a:1414–1416, 1964)

down at approximately the same rate, and stop at approximately the same distance x from the surface (**Fig. 1**). The average distance traveled by the particles is called the mean range $R(T)$.

Energy loss and straggling. If the same beam travels through a thin absorber, it will emerge from it with a reduced average energy $\langle T_1 \rangle$ (**Table 2**). The difference between T and $\langle T_1 \rangle$ is called the average energy loss $\Delta = T - \langle T_1 \rangle$. Owing to the randomness of the number of collisions experienced by each particle, the range and the reduced energy fluctuate around the average values. This fluctuation is called straggling of energy loss or of range. (The shape of the curve in Fig. 1 for $x > 22$ mm is determined by range straggling.)

Charge state. At high velocities, an ion usually has the full charge ze of the nucleus. As soon as v drops below the velocity $u_K \cong zc/137$ of the K shell electrons, electrons in the absorber will be

attracted into K-shell orbits, thus reducing the total charge of the ion to a value $z^* = z - 1$ or $z - 2$. As the velocity drops further, more and more electrons will be attached to the ion; but since some of these electrons will be lost or gained as successive collisions take place, z^* must be considered as an average value which changes with v (**Fig. 2**). *See* ELECTRON CONFIGURATION.

Interactions. In traveling through matter, charged particles interact with nuclei, producing nuclear reactions and elastic and inelastic collisions with the electrons (electronic collisions) and with entire atoms of the absorber (atomic collisions). Usually, in its travel through matter a charged particle makes few or no nuclear reactions or inelastic nuclear collisions, but many electronic and atomic collisions. The average distance between successive collisions is called the mean free path, λ. In solids, it is of the order of 10 cm (4 in.) for nuclear reactions. It ranges from the diameter of the atoms (about 10^{-10} m) to about 10^{-7} m for electronic collisions. The mean free path, λ, depends on the properties of the particle and, most importantly, on its velocity.

Nuclear interactions. In nuclear reactions [for example, $Be(d,n)B$] the incident particle is removed from the beam. Therefore, a reduction in the fluence (number of particles in the beam per cm^2) will be observed. [The decrease in the number of particles in Fig. 1 for x less than about 22 mm (0.88 in.) is due to nuclear interactions.] Such an attenuation can be described by Eq. (1), where $e =$

$$\frac{N}{N_0} = e^{-x\Sigma} = e^{-x/\lambda} \qquad (1)$$

$2.71828 \dots$, $N_0 =$ initial particle fluence at $x = 0$, $N =$ particle fluence at x, and $\Sigma =$ probability for an interaction to take place per centimeter of absorber. The mean free path is $\lambda = 1/\sigma$; Σ is equal to $n\sigma$, where $\sigma =$ cross section per atom for nuclear reactions in square centimeters, and $n =$ number of atoms per cubic centimeter of absorber material. *See* ATTENUATION; E (MATHEMATICS); NUCLEAR CHEMISTRY; NUCLEAR REACTION; SCATTERING EXPERIMENTS (NUCLEI).

A rough estimate of the cross section for particles with $T/A_m > 10$ MeV can be obtained from Eq. (2).

$$\sigma = 5 \times 10^{-26} \text{ cm}^2 \, (A_m^{1/3} + A^{1/3})^2 \qquad (2)$$

For thin absorbers, $N/N_0 \cong 1 - x/\lambda + \cdots$.

An important nuclear interaction is Coulomb (or Rutherford) scattering: because both the incident particles and the nuclei of the absorber atoms have electric charge with values ze and Ze, respectively, a change in the direction of motion of the particles will take place during the passage of the particles near the nuclei. The total cross section for this process is only slightly less than the cross-sectional area of the total atom. Usually, though, the angular deflection is much less than $0.01°$, and only multiple scattering, the compounding of collisions with many atoms, will cause noticeable

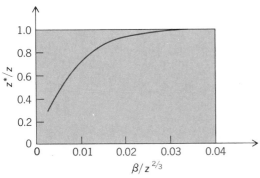

Fig. 2. Average charge z^* of a particle of velocity $v = \beta c$. (After American Institute of Physics Handbook, 2d ed., McGraw-Hill, 1963)

total deflections. If an observation of a very fine beam of particles were made along the direction of motion, the scattering events would be seen as small lateral displacements in random directions, and the final lateral displacement would be their vector sum. Although very few particles experience no deflection, the most probable location of the particles is still on the original line of the beam.

Bremsstrahlung. If a charged particle is accelerated, it can emit photons called bremsstrahlung. This process is of great importance for electrons as well as for heavy ions with $T \gg Mc^2$. It is used extensively for the production of x-rays in radiology. Electrons circulating in storage rings emit large numbers of photons with energies (100–1000 eV) not readily available from other sources. *See* ACCELERATION; BREMSSTRAHLUNG; SYNCHROTRON RADIATION.

Atomic collisions. At low velocities it may be convenient to consider separately collisions in which most of the energy loss is given as kinetic energy to a target atom. Usually, electronic excitation, electron rearrangements, and possibly ionization accompany this process. The term nuclear collision is used by some scientists. No simple quantitative description of atomic collisions is available. *See* SCATTERING EXPERIMENTS (ATOMS AND MOLECULES).

Electronic collisions. The interaction and energy transfer (**Fig. 3**) between the charged particle and the electrons are caused by the Coulomb force. In general, except in tenuous plasmas, electrons are bound. In gases, all electrons are bound to individual atoms or molecules in well-defined orbits. For these isolated molecules (henceforth, atoms will be included with molecules), electrons can be moved into other bound orbits (excitation) requiring a well-defined energy ϵ_2. Another possibility is the complete removal of the electron from the atom (ionization), requiring an energy $\epsilon \geq I$, where I is the ionization energy for the particular electron. The secondary electron, which is called a delta electron, will have kinetic energy $K = \epsilon - I$. In both processes, the charged particle will lose energy; the energy loss is ϵ_e or ϵ, respectively. Also, it will be deflected very slightly. However, the change in direction is so small that it does not show in Fig. 3; the larger deflection caused by Rutherford scattering at point *a* is visible. *See* ATOMIC STRUCTURE AND SPECTRA; DELTA ELECTRONS; EXCITED STATE.

In liquids and solids, only the inner electrons are associated with a specific nucleus (in aluminum metal the K- and L-shell electrons). Excitation and ionization processes for these electrons are very similar to those in free molecules. The outer electrons are either associated with several neighboring nuclei (nonconducting materials) or, in metals (in Al, the three M-shell electrons), form a plasmalike cloud. Collective or plasma excitations ($\epsilon \cong 20$ eV) take place with high probability, but direct ionization ($\epsilon \gg 20$ eV) also occurs. Because of the requirements of momentum conservation, the

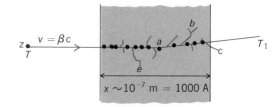

key:

⊤   ionization event

•─•   excitation event

Fig. 3. Energy loss by heavy charged particle. No details shown for energy losses of secondary electrons (delta electrons). Rutherford scattering at point *a*. At point *b*, delta electron experiences collision that results in tertiary delta electron. At *c*, delta electron escapes from absorber.

maximum energy loss which can occur is given by $\epsilon_M \simeq 2mv^2 = 2mc^2\beta^2$ for particles heavier than electrons. *See* SOLID-STATE CHEMISTRY.

The probability for energy losses ϵ by the incident particle is described by the energy loss spectrum $w(\epsilon)$. Theoretical values have been calculated by H. Bethe. An energy loss spectrum for heavy charged particles in adenine ($C_5N_5H_5$) is shown in **Fig. 4**. The structure between 3 and 30 eV relates to the outer electrons. Similar structures have been observed for many solids (including metals). Excitation and ionization of the K-shell of C (above 280 eV) and N (above 400 eV) cause further structure. The average energy loss per collision is defined by Eq. (3).

$$\langle \epsilon \rangle = \int \epsilon w(\epsilon)\, d\epsilon \left/ \int w(\epsilon)\, d\epsilon \right. \qquad (3)$$

Statistics of energy loss. The total energy loss δ of a particle traveling through matter is the sum of the energy losses ϵ_i in each collision: $\delta = \Sigma \epsilon_i = \epsilon_1 + \epsilon_2 + \epsilon_3 + \epsilon_4 + \cdots + \epsilon_v$, where v collisions have occurred, each with a probability given by $w(\epsilon)$ [Fig. 4]. If a large number of particles are observed, they will experience on the average $q = \langle v \rangle$ collisions (q is not an integer), and an average energy loss $\Delta = \langle \delta \rangle = q\langle \epsilon \rangle$, as long as collisions

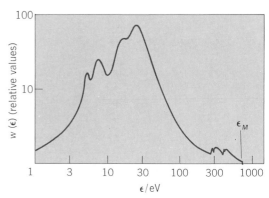

Fig. 4. Schematic single-collision spectrum $w(\epsilon)$ for heavy charged particles in adenine ($C_5N_5H_5$).

are uncorrelated with another. The number of collisions is distributed according to a Poisson distribution; the fraction $P(v)$ of particles having experienced exactly v collisions is given by Eq. (4). The distribution function for energy losses is

$$P(v) = \frac{q^v}{v!} e^{-q} \qquad (4)$$

called a straggling function $f(\Delta,x)$. Examples are given in **Figs. 5** and **6**. For fairly thick absorbers, $f(\Delta,x)$ is approximately a gaussian distribution of width proportional to $\sqrt{x}$. See DISTRIBUTION (PROBABILITY).

In many applications, the details of energy loss are not important, and a knowledge of the mean or average energy loss Δ is sufficient. If the total collision cross section per atom $w_t = \int w(\epsilon)d\epsilon$ is known (w_t in cm^2), the mean number of collisions is given by $q = xnw_t$, and the mean energy loss by Eq. (5). The quantity

$$\Delta = xn\langle\epsilon\rangle w_t \equiv xS \qquad (5)$$

stopping power S thus is defined by Eq. (6),

$$S \equiv n\langle\epsilon\rangle w_t \qquad (6)$$

in MeV/cm. Since knowledge of w_t and $\langle\epsilon\rangle$ is not extensive, S is frequently determined in experimental measurements in which a beam passes through an absorber, and S is calculated from Eq. (7).

$$S = \lim_{x \to 0} \frac{\Delta}{x} = \lim_{x \to 0} \frac{T - \langle T_1 \rangle}{x} \qquad (7)$$

Equation (5) is valid only if x is much smaller than the mean range, $R(T)$; otherwise, S varies significantly as the particle loses energy in the absorber. If x is not small, the following procedure can be used to obtain $\langle T_1 \rangle$, provided that $R(T)$ has been tabulated: Find $R(T)$ in the range table, calculate $y = R(T) - x$, and then find the energy T_1 corresponding to y in the range table.

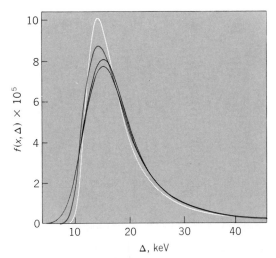

Fig. 6. Calculated straggling curve $f(x, \Delta)$ for 20-MeV protons incident on Al absorber of thickness 3.71×10^{-6} m. Various theoretical calculations are presented. (*After H. Bichsel and R. Saxon, Comparison of calculational methods for straggling in thin absorbers, Phys. Rev., A11:1286–1296, 1975*)

Stopping power. The stopping power is a function of the velocity v of the incident particle, its effective charge z^*, and the absorber material. **Figure 7** shows $S(T)$ for heavy ions of various elements in aluminum. S is expressed in MeV cm^2/g. This can be converted to MeV/cm by the formula $S(\text{MeV/cm}) = \rho S(\text{MeV cm}^2/\text{g})$, where ρ is the density of absorber material in g/cm^3. Atomic collisions dominate in region I. For region III, S can be calculated by using the theoretical Bethe expression, Eq. (8), where I_A = average excitation

$$S = \frac{0.30708}{\beta^2}\frac{Z}{A}\left[\ln\frac{2mc^2\beta^2}{I_A(1-\beta^2)} - \beta^2 - \frac{C}{\beta^2} - d(\beta)\right]$$
$$\cdot (z^*)^2[1 + G(z^*, \beta)]\ \text{MeV cm}^2/\text{g} \qquad (8)$$

energy of absorber (approximately $Z \times 10^{-5}$ MeV); C = shell correction constant; $d(\beta)$ = density correction, important for $T > Mc^2$; and $G(z^*,\beta)$ = correction due to the second Born approximation, important only for $\beta^2 < 0.01$. See PERTURBATION (QUANTUM MECHANICS).

A simpler approximate expression valid to about 10% for $z \leq 10$ in the same region is given by Eq. (9).

$$S = \frac{2.6z^2}{\beta^{1.66}Z^{.25}}\ \text{MeV cm}^2/\text{g} \qquad (9)$$
$$0.1 < \beta < 0.88$$

Range. A good approximation to the mean range $R(T)$ can be calculated from S using Eq. (10).

$$R(T) = \int_0^T \frac{d\tau}{S(\tau)} \qquad (10)$$

Usually, a numerical integration is performed to obtain R from a table of S or the Bethe formula.

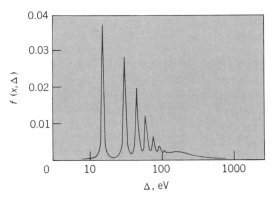

Fig. 5. Calculated straggling curve $f(x, \Delta)$ for 20-MeV protons incident on Al absorber of thickness 5.8×10^{-8} m. Spikes represent multiples of the "plasma loss" at 15 eV. (*After H. Bichsel and R. Saxon, Comparison of calculational methods for straggling in thin absorbers, Phys. Rev., A11:1286–1296, 1975*)

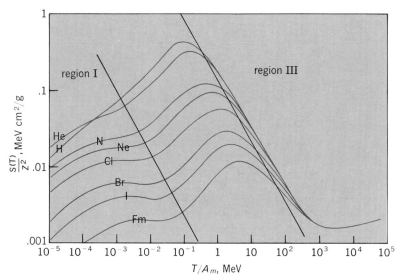

Fig. 7. *S(T)* for heavy ions in Al. (*After L. C. Northcliffe and R. F. Schilling, Range and stopping power tables for heavy ions, Nucl. Data Tables, A7:233, 1970*)

An approximation formula is Eq. (11). The range of

$$R = r \cdot \beta^s \cdot \frac{Z^{.25}}{z^2} \qquad (11)$$

$$z \leq 10$$

validity for this range formula is given in **Table 3**.

Channeling. In absorbers consisting of a single crystal, it has been found that the energy loss will be reduced if the direction of the particle beam coincides with certain preferred alignments of the crystal. It is believed that the particles travel through "open spaces" in the crystal, thus suffering a succession of collisions with relatively small energy losses and angular deflections, and tending to stay in the preferred direction (channel). Thus, even if the total number of collisions q were unchanged, the average energy loss per collision (ϵ) would be reduced, and the total energy loss Δ would be less. *See* CHANNELING IN SOLIDS.

Ionization. The secondary electrons of energies K produced in ionizing electronic collisions will travel through the absorber and will also suffer various collisions, producing further energetic electrons, and so on. This process continues until the electrons have energy $K < I$. It has been found experimentally that the total average number j of ions produced in this way (in the distance x) is proportional to the energy Δ lost by the particle: $j = \Delta/\omega$.

The constant of proportionality ω introduced in this definition has values between 20 and 45 eV for gases, about 3.6 eV for silicon, and 2.96 eV for germanium. It is almost, but not exactly, independent of particle energy and type. If particles lose all their energy in the material, the total ionization J is related to the kinetic energy T: $J = T/W$. The relation between W and ω is $T/W = \int dT/\omega$. $W = \omega$ only if ω is exactly independent of energy.

The ionization j along the path of a single particle increases with the distance traveled, approximately at the same rate as S. For a beam of particles, straggling also influences the total ionization at a given location. The function obtained from the combination (actually the convolution) of both effects is the Bragg curve.

Electrons. Although the interactions discussed earlier all occur for electrons, there are some major differences between electron beams and beams of heavier particles. In general, the path of an electron will be a zigzag. Angular deflections in the collisions will frequently be large. Electron beams therefore tend to spread out laterally, and the number of primary electrons in the beam at a depth x in the absorber decreases rapidly.

Since it is not possible to distinguish individual electrons, it is customary in a collision between two electrons to consider the one emerging with the higher energy as the primary electron. The maximum energy loss in a collision therefore is $mv^2/4$ (for $T \ll mc^2$). The stopping power expression therefore is somewhat different for electrons. *See* BETA PARTICLES.

Biological effects. In general, for the same dose (the energy deposited per gram along the beam line) heavy charged particles will produce, because of their higher local ionization, larger biological effects than electrons (which frequently are produced by x-rays). *See* NUCLEAR RADIATION (BIOLOGY); RADIATION BIOLOGY; RADIATION INJURY (BIOLOGY).

Observation. The most direct method of observing a beam of charged particles is to observe the electric current that they form (any flow of electric charges is an electric current). In all accelerators (such as cyclotrons, Van de Graaff generators, linear accelerators, and x-ray tubes) the beam current is measured as a primary monitor of the proper operation of the machine. It is not possible to identify the type of particles with current measurements (except for their electric charge). *See* PARTICLE DETECTOR.

Devices using ionization. If an electric field E is applied to an absorber irradiated with charged particles, the ions and electrons produced will travel in the direction **E,** and the resulting ionization current can be measured (electronic amplification usually is needed). If an oscilloscope is available, the ionization J associated with a single particle can be observed, and the energy (or energy loss) of the particle can be calculated from $T =$

TABLE 3. Range of validity of range formula			
Range of kinetic energy T, MeV	Range of β	r, g/cm²	s
$10 \leq T < 90$	$0.145 < \beta < 0.4$	0.116	1.84
$90 < T < 400$	$0.4 < \beta < 0.7$	0.275	2.33
$400 < T < 1000$	$0.7 < \beta < 0.88$	0.532	3.34

JW. Semiconductor detectors (chiefly silicon and germanium) are used extensively for this purpose, but gas-filled ionization chambers have also been used. Cloud chambers and bubble chambers use this principle, but individual ions or clumps of ionization are observed visually. Proportional counters, spark chambers, and Geiger-Müller tubes also operate on the same principle; but in the latter two only the presence of a particle is indicated, and *J* is not related to *T*. *See* ELECTRIC FIELD; GEIGER-MÜLLER COUNTER; IONIZATION CHAMBER.

Devices using excitation. The excited state of energy ϵ_e produced in excitation can decay with the emission of light (luminescence or scintillation). Early observations of radioactivity were made with this method (using ZnS screens and visual observation, usually with microscopes), and the method is used extensively with luminescent dials (for example, on wristwatches). The light emitted usually is detected and amplified with photomultipliers. Again, the energy *T* can be measured. Scintillators used are NaI(Tl), CsI, anthracene, stilbene, and various solids and liquids. *See* LUMINESCENCE; LUMINOUS PAINT; PHOTOMULTIPLIER; SCINTILLATION COUNTER.

A more indirect use of excitations and ionizations is in "chemical" devices (such as photographic emulsions, $FeSO_4$ solutions, and thermoluminescence). *See* PHOTOGRAPHIC MATERIALS; THERMOLUMINESCENCE.

Applications. Electron beams are used in the preservation of food. In medicine, electron beams are used extensively to produce x-rays for both diagnostic and therapeutic (cancer irradiation) purposes. Also, in radiation therapy, deuteron beams incident on Be and ^{3}H targets are used to produce beams of fast neutrons, which in turn produce fast protons, alpha particles, and carbon, nitrogen, and oxygen ions in the irradiated tissue. Energetic pion (about 100 MeV), proton (about 200 MeV), alpha (about 1000 MeV), and heavier ion beams can possibly be used for cancer therapy. The existence of a Bragg peak for these particles promises improvements in the dose distribution within the human body. *See* RADIOLOGY.

The well-defined range of heavy ions permits their implantation at given depths in solids (this is useful in the production of integrated circuits). Radiation damage studies are performed with charged particles in relation to development work for nuclear fission and fusion reactors. *See* ION IMPLANTATION; RADIATION DAMAGE TO MATERIALS.

Charged particle beams are used in many methods of chemical and solid-state analysis. Nuclear activation analysis can be performed with heavy ions. *See* ACTIVATION ANALYSIS; ELECTRON DIFFRACTION; ELECTRON SPECTROSCOPY; SECONDARY ION MASS SPECTROMETRY (SIMS).

Isotopes can be produced with fast charged ions. *See* ELEMENT 104; ELEMENT 105; ELEMENT 106; ELEMENT 107; ELEMENT 108; ELEMENT 109; LAWREN-CIUM; MENDELEVIUM; NOBELIUM; NUCLEAR CHEMISTRY; RADIOISOTOPE; TRANSURANIUM ELEMENTS.

Hans Bichsel

Radioactive secondary beams. Beams of nuclei with lifetimes as short as 10^{-6} s are used for studies in nuclear physics, astrophysics, biology, and materials science. Nuclear beams (or heavy-ion beams) are usually produced by accelerating naturally available stable isotopes. However, radioactive nuclei, most of which do not occur naturally on Earth, must be produced as required in nuclear reactions by using various accelerated beams. Because these radioactive nuclei are produced by the nuclear reactions of primary beams, they are called secondary particles and beams of such nuclei are called radioactive secondary beams. *See* RADIOACTIVITY.

Two methods can be used to produce radioactive beams; the methods differ in the way in which the ions of radioactive nuclei are extracted. The so-called isotope separator on line (ISOL) is used to select product nuclei. In this method, nuclei are extracted from a production target by thermal diffusion and then ionized and accelerated to a low energy (approximately 50 keV). The extracted ions are then selected in an isotope separator that consists of magnetic and electrostatic elements; the selected beam is then accelerated to the desired energy. The second method does not use an ion source but rather collects directly the recoil products from the production of nuclear reaction. A recoil mass separator is used to select the desired product. In many cases, these recoil products can be used directly in experiments. *See* ION SOURCES; MASS SPECTROSCOPE.

The recoil separator method has several advantages in separation of nuclei produced in heavy ion–induced reactions. In such reactions, the velocity of the center-of-mass system is large and product nuclei are emitted in a small-angle forward cone. In particular, nuclei that are produced by projectile fragmentation are emitted in the direction of the primary beam with almost the beam velocity.

For production and separation of radioactive nuclei, a heavy projectile of energy higher than a few hundred megaelectronvolts per nucleon results in high collection efficiency. For an experiment that requires good momentum resolution, the separated, secondary beam may be injected into a storage-cooler ring in which the radioactive nuclei are cooled to have a relative momentum broadening less than 10^{-3}. Such a cooler ring can also be used to decelerate or to accelerate the radioactive beam for experiments at various energies.

Radioactive secondary beams have made possible the study of the structure of nuclei far from stability. As an example, the sizes of neutron dripline nuclei such as lithium-11 (^{11}Li) and beryllium-14 (^{14}Be) were determined only after beams of these nuclei become available. Furthermore, the internal motion of nucleons inside a radioactive nucleus can be studied in reactions involving the radioactive nucleus as a projectile. Another important application occurs in the study of nuclear reactions of importance in hot stars and in supernovae. Such reactions, involving radioactive nuclei, are crucial for understanding nucleosynthesis in the universe. *See* EXOTIC NUCLEI; NUCLEAR STRUCTURE; NUCLEOSYNTHESIS.　　　　　　　　　　　Isao Tanihata

Bibliography. *American Institute of Physics Handbook*, 3d ed., 1972; F. H. Attix, *Introduction to Radiological Physics and Radiation Dosimetry*, 1986; R. D. Evans, *The Atomic Nucleus*, 1955, reprint 1982; K. R. Kase et al. (eds.), *The Dosimetry of Ionizing Radiation*, 3 vols., 1985, 1987, 1990; G. F. Knoll, *Radiation Detection and Measurement*, 2d ed., 1989.

Charged particle optics

The branch of physics concerned with the motion of charged particles under the influence of electric and magnetic fields.

Acceleration of charged particles. A positively charged particle that moves in an electric field experiences a force in the direction of this field. If the particle falls in the field from a potential of U volts to a potential of zero, its energy gain, measured in electronvolts, is equal to the product of U and the particle's charge. For example, if a singly and a doubly charged particle are accelerated by a potential drop of 100 V, the two particles will gain energies of 100 eV and 200 eV, respectively. If both particles were initially at rest, they would have final velocities proportional to the square root of K/m, where K is the energy increase and m is the mass of the particle. This relation describes the velocities of energetic particles accurately as long as these velocities are small compared to the velocity of light $c \approx 300,000$ km/s (186,000 mi/s), a speed that cannot be exceeded by any particle. *See* ELECTRIC FIELD; ELECTROSTATICS.

If an ensemble of ions of equal energies but of different masses is accelerated simultaneously, the ion masses can be determined from their arrival times after a certain flight distance. Such time-of-flight mass spectrometers have successfully been used, for instance, to investigate the masses of large molecular ions, up to and beyond 350,000 atomic mass units. *See* TIME-OF-FLIGHT SPECTROMETERS.

Deflection of charged particles. If a homogeneous electric field is established between two parallel-plate electrodes at different potentials, a charged particle in the space between the electrodes will experience a force in the direction perpendicular to them. If initially the particle moved parallel to the electrodes, it will be deflected by the electric force and move along a parabolic trajectory. Magnetic fields also deflect charged particles. In contrast to electrostatic fields, however, magnetic fields change only the direction of a particle trajectory and not the magnitude of the particle velocity. A charged particle that moves perpendicular to the field lines of a homogeneous magnetic field moves through a circular path (**Fig. 1**) whose radius is determined from the balance between the centrifugal force along this circle and the magnetic force. *See* MAGNETIC FIELD.

Charged particles that enter a magnetic field thus move along circles whose radii increase with the products of their velocities and their mass-to-charge ratios, m/q. If initially all particles start at the same potential U and are accelerated to the potential zero, they will move along radii that are proportional to the square root of $U(m/q)$. Thus, particles of different mass-to-charge ratios can be separated in a magnetic sector field (Fig. 1).

In the plane of deflection, charged particles that diverge from a point in some source are focused back to a point of the image (Fig. 1). In the perpendicular direction, however, the particles remain divergent. A straight line that connects the source and the image also passes through the center of curvature of the trajectory of the reference particle. The images of particles of different mass-to-charge ratios all lie in a plane that is usually inclined with respect to the particle beam.

A sector-field mass analyzer can be used to determine the masses of atomic or molecular ions in a cloud of such ions. Such systems can also be used to purify a beam of ions that are to be implanted in semiconductors in order to fabricate high-performance transistors and diodes. Finally, such magnetic sector fields are found in large numbers in all types of particle accelerators. *See* ION IMPLANTATION; MASS SPECTROSCOPE.

Axially symmetric lenses. An Einzel lens consists of three cylindrical tubes, the middle one of which is at a higher potential than the outer two. Positively charged particles entering such a device are first decelerated and then accelerated back to their initial energies. Since the decelerations and accelerations are perpendicular to the eqipotential surfaces, the particles experience forces that drive them toward the optic axis in some regions and away from it in others. However, the focusing actions are always stronger than the defocusing actions since they occur in regions in which the particles are moving more slowly, that is, in the center regions. Defocusing lenses cannot be built in this fashion unless potential-defining metal grids distort the

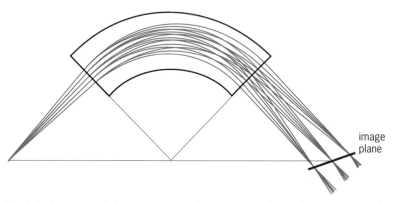

Fig. 1. Sector magnet that separates charged particles according to the products of their velocities and their mass-to-charge ratios. The straight line that connects the particle source and the image of the middle ion bundle also passes through the center of curvature of the corresponding central trajectory.

image plane

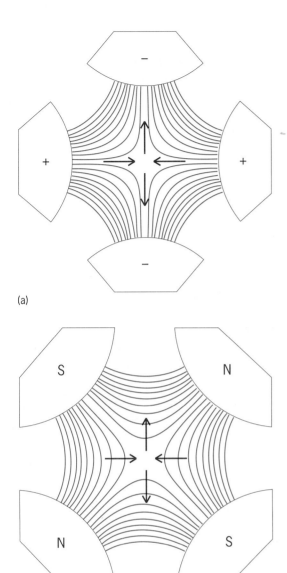

(a)

(b)

Fig. 2. Cross sections of *(a)* electric and *(b)* magnetic quadrupole lenses. Charged particles move through these lenses perpendicular to plane of drawing. Electric and magnetic field lines are shown. Arrows indicate directions of forces that drive charged particles toward or away from the optic axis. In both lenses, focusing occurs in the horizontal direction, while there is defocusing in the vertical direction.

equipotential surfaces. This statement also holds for axially symmetric lenses in which the potential on the center electrode has been chosen such that the charged particles are not decelerated but accelerated while passing through the lens. *See* ELECTROSTATIC LENS.

Axially symmetric magnetic lenses have also been constructed. Such lenses, also called solenoids, consist mainly of a coil of wire through which an electric current is passed. The charged particles are then constrained to move more or less parallel to the axis of such a coil. Steel tubes with rotationally symmetric geometries can be used to surround the coil to increase the magnetic field strength. *See* MAGNETIC LENS; SOLENOID (ELECTRICITY).

Axially symmetric electric and magnetic lenses are used extensively to focus low-energy particle beams. Particularly important applications are in television tubes and in electron microscopes. *See* CATHODE-RAY TUBE; ELECTRON MICROSCOPE; PICTURE TUBE.

Quadrupole lenses. By passing charged particles through electrode or pole-face arrangements (**Fig. 2**), a particle beam can also be focused toward the optic axis. In such quadrupole lenses the electric or the magnetic field strengths, and therefore the forces that drive the charged particles toward or away from the optic axis, increase linearly with the distance from the axis. This is the main property of the lens. In quadrupoles the focusing occurs in one direction only, while there is a defocusing action in the perpendicular direction. Focusing in both directions thus requires a combination of at least two quadrupole lenses. In quadrupole lenses the particle trajectories are bent toward the optic axis by the main field, while in axially symmetric lenses such a focusing action is achieved by the much weaker fringing fields. Quadrupole lens systems thus have much stronger focusing abilities than other types of lenses, and smaller field strengths can be used to focus more rigid particle beams.

While quadrupole lenses are found in systems in which low-energy particle beams must be focused, for instance, in mass spectrometers, such lenses have become indispensable for high-energy beams. Consquently, quadrupole lenses, especially magnetic ones, are found in many types of particle accelerators used in research in, for example, nuclear and solid-state physics, as well as in cancer irradiation treatment facilities. *See* CHARGED PARTICLE BEAMS; ELECTRON LENS; ELECTRON MOTION IN VACUUM; PARTICLE ACCELERATOR.   Hermann Wollnik

Bibliography. D. A. Dewolf, *Basics of Electron Optics*, 1990; P. W. Hawkes and E. Kasper, *Principles of Electron Optics*, vols. 1 and 2, 1989, vol. 3, 1994; H. Wollnik, *Optics of Charged Particles*, 1987.

Charles' law

A thermodynamic law, also known as Gay-Lussac's law, which states that at constant pressure the volume of a fixed mass or quantity of gas varies directly with the absolute temperature. Conversely, at constant volume the gas pressure varies directly with the absolute temperature. J. A. Charles and J. L. Gay-Lussac independently discovered the relation for an ideal gas. The relation is a useful and close approximation. *See* GAS; KINETIC THEORY OF MATTER.   Frank H. Rockett

Charm

A term used in elementary particle physics to describe a class of elementary particles.

Theory. Ordinary atoms of matter consist of a nucleus composed of neutrons and protons and surrounded by electrons. Over the years, however, a host of other particles with unexpected properties have been found, associated with both electrons (leptons) and protons (hadrons).

Leptons. The electron has as companions the mu meson (μ) and the tau meson (τ), approximately 200 times and 3700 times as heavy as the electron, respectively. These particles are similar to the electron in all respects except mass. In addition, there exist at least two distinctive neutrinos, one associated with the electron, v_e, and another with the mu meson, v_μ. In all, there are five or six fundamental, distinct, structureless leptons. *See* LEPTON.

Hadrons. A similar but more complex situation exists with respect to the hadrons. These particles number in the hundreds, and unlike the leptons they cannot be thought of as fundamental. In fact, they can all be explained as composites of more fundamental constitutents, called quarks. It is the quarks which now seem as fundamental as the leptons, and the number of quark types has also increased as new and unexpected particles have been experimentally uncovered. The originally simple situation of having an up quark (*u;* charge $+^2/_3$) and a down quark (*d;* charge $-^1/_3$) has evolved as several more varieties or flavors have had to be added. These are the strange quark (*s;* charge $-^1/_3$), with the additional property or quantum number of strangeness ($S = -1$), to account for the unexpected characteristics of a family of strange particles; the charm quark (*c;* charge $+^2/_3$), possessing charm ($C = +1$) and no strangeness, to explain the discovery of the J/ψ particles, massive states three times heavier than the proton; and a fifth quark (*b;* charge $-^1/_3$) to explain the existence of the even more massive upsilon (Υ) particles. *See* HADRON; J/PSI PARTICLE; QUARKS.

The quarks and leptons discovered so far appear to form a symmetric array (see **table**). Both the leptons and quarks come in pairs, although the anticipated partner (*t*) of the *b* quark has not yet been found.

Observations. The members of the family of particles associated with charm fall into two classes: those with hidden charm, where the states are a combination of charm and anticharm quarks ($c\bar{c}$), charmonium; and those where the charm property is clearly evident, such as the D^+ ($c\bar{d}$) meson and Λ_c^+ (*cud*) baryon.

Charmonium. In the charmonium family, six or seven states with various masses and decay modes have been identified. Although a detailed understanding of all these experimentally measured properties has not yet been achieved, everything seems to be in qualitative agreement with theoretical expectations.

Bare charm states. There are several identified bare charm states, including the D ($c\bar{d}$) mesons in both the $J^P = 0^-$ and $J^P = 1^+$ categories (where J is spin, and P is parity), and the Σ_c^{2+} (*cuu*) and Λ_c^+ (*cud*) charmed baryons. Information about the lifetimes of these states has been derived from experiments utilizing the high resolution of emulsions to measure the finite distance traveled by charmed particles. The lifetimes of the Λ_c^+ and D^0 have been determined to be on the order of 10^{-13} s with that of the D^+ about a factor of 7 longer. These values are in good agreement with theoretical expectations.

The Λ_c^+ charmed baryon has been observed to be produced in a variety of interactions, including neutrino-proton, proton-proton, electron-positron, and neutrino-neon reactions. A large number of decay modes have been observed, including *Kp, Kpπ, $\Lambda\pi$, $\Lambda\pi\pi\pi$,* and *Kp$\pi\pi$.*

Prospects. Although reasonable progress has been made in the study of charmed states, only a handful of states has been observed. Just as the basic SU(3) symmetry arose from a study of the numerous hadron strange and nonstrange resonances, the complete understanding of charm awaits the uncovering of additional states. *See* ELEMENTARY PARTICLE.   Nicholas P. Samios

Bibliography. I. S. Hughes, *Elementary Particles*, 3d ed., 1991; G. Kane, *Modern Elementary Particle Physics*, 2d ed., 1993; R. F. Schwitters, Fundamental particles with charm, *Sci. Amer.*, 237(4):56–70, 1977; M. Ye and T. Huang, *Charm Physics*, 1988.

Charophyceae

A group of branched, filamentous green algae, commonly known as the stoneworts, brittleworts, or muskgrasses, that occur mostly in fresh- or brackish-water habitats. They are important as significant components of the aquatic flora in some locales, providing food for waterfowl and protection for fish and other aquatic fauna; as excellent model systems for cell biological research; and as a unique group of green algae thought to be more closely related to the land plants.

Morphology. Charophytes are multicellular, branched, macroscopic filaments from a few inches to several feet in length. Colorless rhizoidal filaments anchor the plants to lake bottoms and other substrates. The main filaments are organized into short nodes forming whorls of branches, and much longer (up to 6 in. or 15 cm) internodal cells. The general morphology varies with environmental conditions such as depth of the water, light levels, and amount of wave action. Reproductive

Fundamental constituents of matter		
Family of particles	Charge	Particles
Leptons	0	v_e, v_μ, (v_τ)*
	-1	e, μ, τ
Quarks	$+^2/_3$	u, c, (t)*
	$-^1/_3$	d, s, b

*Existence uncertain.

structures occur at the nodes and consist of egg cell–containing structures, the nucules, and sperm cell–containing structures called globules. The biflagellated sperm cells are produced in antheridial filaments within the globules. In many charophytes, calicium carbonate (lime) is secreted on the cell walls, hence the name stoneworts or brittleworts. In some charophytes, the simple structure of nodal and intermodal cells is complicated by corticating elements that cover the cells of the main axis.

Taxonomy and phylogeny. Based on the morphology of the vegetative filaments and the reproductive structures, six extant genera are recognized: *Chara, Nitella, Tolypella, Nitellopsis, Lamprothamnium,* and *Lychnothamnus.* At the species level there is significant disagreement with regard to the importance and interpretation of morphological features, life cycles, and biogeography, especially for *Chara.* Hence, there is no agreement on how many valid species exist, but the maximum number of living species is probably fewer than 100. Among the special features that support the suggestion that the charophytes are closely related to the land plants are the morphologically complicated reproductive structures, the ultrastructure of the sperm cells, and the type of cell division. Some of these features have led some scientists to include other genera of green algae in this group known as the Charophyceae. Deoxyribonucleic acid (DNA) sequencing indicates that the charophytes are a distinct natural group that should be recognized at some taxonomic level (for example, as an order, Charales, or as a class, Charophyceae).

Life history. The charophytes are haploid organisms. The fusion of the sperm and egg cell produces a diploid resistant zygote which, after dormancy, undergoes meiosis to produce a new haploid generation. Thus, there is no alternation of generations. Asexual zoospores are not produced, but plants can reproduce vegetatively as the rhizoidal filaments spread and develop new plants. *See* REPRODUCTION (PLANT).

Fossils. Because the fertilized egg cells produce resistant, calcified zygotes, fossils (known as gyrogonites) provide a record of these organisms extending back to the Devonian Period (approximately 360–408 millions years ago). Many genera that once existed are now extinct. *See* ALGAE; CHLOROPHYCOTA; PALEOBOTANY.

Russell L. Chapman

Bibliography. H. C. Bold and M. J. Wynne, *Introduction to the Algae: Structure and Reproduction,* 2d ed., 1985; A. Sze, *A Biology of the Algae,* 2d ed., 1993.

Cheese

A food product selectively concentrated from major milk components. It is generally rich in flavor and contains high-quality nutrients. There are many varieties of cheese, all produced in the following general manner: Raw or pasteurized milk is clotted by acid, rennet, or both. The curd is cut and shaped into the special form of the cheese with or without pressing. Salt is added, or the cheese is brined after pressing.

Acid is produced during manufacture of cheese by fermentation of the milk sugar, lactose. This fermentation is initiated by the addition of a culture of specially selected acid bacteria (starter culture) to the milk. Acid production in cheese curd retards growth of bacteria that cause undesirable fermentations in cheese. Moreover, it favors the expulsion of the whey and the fusion of the curd particles. Fresh cheese (cottage or cream cheese) does not require any ripening, and it is sold soon after it is made. Other varieties of cheese are cured or ripened to obtain the desirable consistency, flavor, and aroma. The flavor and aroma of cheese are obtained by a partial breakdown of milk proteins and fat by the action of microbial, milk, and rennet enzymes. In hard varieties (Cheddar, Gouda, Edam, Emmentaler or Swiss, and provolone) this is done by the microorganisms in the interior of cheese; in semisoft or soft types (Limburger, Camembert, and Roquefort) by the organisms on, or in contact with, the surface of cheese. *See* MILK.

Cheese Microbiology

Microorganisms are essential to the manufacture of cheese, imparting distinctive flavor, aroma, consistency, and appearance.

Starter cultures. Lactic acid starter cultures are important in making cheese. Different types of lactic acid bacteria (*Lactococcus lactis, L. lactis cremoris, Streptoccus thermophilus,* and homofermentative lactobacilli) are used, depending upon the kind of cheese desired. The starter (both single and mixed strains of bacteria are used) must convert all

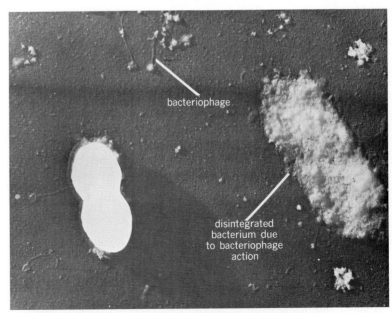

Fig. 1. Electron photomicrograph of *Lactococcus lactis* attacked by phages.

milk sugar left in the curd into lactic acid within a reasonable time. Several factors may prevent this: the occurrence of natural inhibitors in milk, antibiotics, and bacteriophages.

Some antibiotics (such as nisin) which affect the activity of the starter may be produced by microbes in the milk. Others may be excreted into the milk by cows treated for a particular disease; this happens if penicillin is used to treat mastitis. *See* ANTIBIOTIC.

Bacteriophages, or phages, are viruses which lyse sensitive bacterial cells (**Fig. 1**) and produce new phage particles. Phage particles may get into the milk with infected starter cultures or through contamination with phage-carrying dust particles. Phage particles slow down or totally inhibit the activity of the starter culture, causing insufficient souring and spoilage of cheese. Phage multiplication is influenced by temperature, pH, and calcium content of the medium. Phage outbreaks cause serious economic losses. They can be controlled by rigorous hygienic handling of starters, by culture rotation, or by culturing starters in calcium-free media. Attempts to isolate phage-resistant strains have not met with success. *See* BACTERIOPHAGE; STREPTOCOCCUS.

Flora of cheese. Cheeses of the hard type contain lactic acid lactococci and other bacteria present in the starter. Moreover, they contain all the microorganisms originally present in the raw milk or pasteurized milk. The types of bacteria most important for ripening are the lactococci, lactobacilli, micrococci, and propionic acid bacteria. They, together with the enzymes of rennet and milk, break down the proteins to peptides and amino acids, hydrolyze the milk fat to fatty acids, and frequently produce carbon dioxide gas which causes the holes in cheese (**Fig. 2**). The structure of cheese is greatly changed during ripening.

In semisoft and soft cheeses the lactic acid orig-

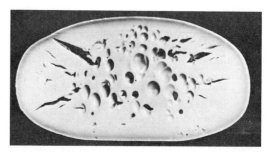

Fig. 3. Late blowing in Gouda cheese.

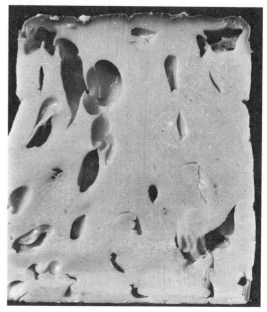

Fig. 4. Evidence of late gas production during the cheese ripening process.

inally produced by the starter is broken down afterward by molds, yeasts, and bacteria on the surface. The same flora decomposes the protein and the fat to a much greater extent than in hard cheeses. As a result, strong flavors are produced and the structure of the cheese becomes much softer. For the production of blue-veined cheese, needles are pushed into the interior to bring *Penicillium roqueforti* or the other molds, added during the manufacturing of the cheese, into contact with air they need for growth. The blue color is the color of the mold spores. The red color on the surface of some soft cheeses is caused by *Brevibacterium* (*Bacterium*) *linens* and micrococci. For good surface growth, soft cheeses must be cured in high-humidity air (caves or air-conditioned rooms).

Defects of cheese. In hard cheeses an abnormal gas formation is a problem. It can occur at almost any stage of manufacture or ripening. Early gas production can be caused by coliform bacteria or heterofermentative lactic bacteria. Gas production during cheese ripening (late gas, as in **Figs. 3** and **4**) may be caused by certain sporeforming bacteria, propionic acid bacteria, *Leuconostoc* species, and *Lactococcus lactis lactis* (biovar *diacetylactis*). The

Fig. 2. Swiss cheese with normal eye formation.

use of *L. lactis lactis* (biovar *diacetylactis*) and *L. lactis* as lactic starter cultures can cause fruity flavors, as well as gas formation, in Cheddar cheese. Other defects of hard cheese include insufficient or excessive acidity, various off flavors, and discoloration. Soft cheeses may be spoiled by gas production, excessive acidity, improper development of surface flora, and contamination with atypical molds.

Cheese blending. Cheeses of different ages are blended. The mixture, melted with the aid of emulsifying salts (citrates and phosphates), is packed in sealed containers (tins, paperboard, foil, or plastic). Few bacteria other than sporeformers survive the heat treatment. No substantial growth of the flora takes place in well-preserved processed cheese, but spoilage by anaerobic sporeformers may occur. *Clostridium sporogenes* causes putrefaction and slit openness and *C. tyrobutyricum* causes blowing of tins and packages. Acidity, salt content, and temperature of storage are important in controlling spoilage. *See* INDUSTRIAL MICROBIOLOGY.

Norman Olson

Cheese Manufacture

More than 150 countries make cheese, but 34 countries produce the major commercial quantities. Primitive cheesemaking exists in much of Africa, Latin America, and southwestern Asia, but advanced techniques are also found in these regions. Cheese manufacturing in developed world areas may be simple too, including that for the sheep-milk Broccio of Corsica, the mountain cheese of the Alps, the queso blanco of Venezuela, and the Pennsylvania pot cheese of the United States, but generally it is highly mechanized. Whether the method is primitive or sophisticated, the quality of the resulting cheese is usually excellent.

The primary objective of cheesemaking is to form a smooth acid curd, to reduce the size of the curd block and remove the whey, with or without prior cooking, and to salt and shape the curds. A different type of cheese emerges when the intensity of approximately eight steps is stressed or minimized as required; when special applications, usually microbial, are introduced; and when the environment is transformed to fit the optimum needs of a specific cheese type.

Materials. Key materials for cheesemaking include fresh or precultured milk, cultures, milk-coagulating enzyme preparations, special microorganisms, salt, and beta carotene or annatto color. The amounts used and the manner in which these materials are applied strongly influence the cheese character. Cheese may be made from the milk of the cow, sheep, goat, water buffalo, and other mammals, but the milk of the cow is most widely used despite some limitations. Sheep milk and water buffalo milk generally give more flavor to the cheeses, and the color is uniformly white because of a lack of carotene in such mammalian milks, but they are more expensive to make into cheese.

Major classes of cheeses. Two major classes of cheeses exist, fresh and ripened. Fresh cheeses are simpler to make than ripened, are more perishable, and do not develop as intense flavors, but give a mild acid, slightly aromatic flavor and soft, smooth texture.

Fresh cheeses. Three basic groups characterize fresh cheese types: group I—ricotta and Broccio; group II—cottage, Neufchâtel, and cream; and group III—mozzarella. Curd formation for these fresh cheese groups results from a combination of acid (pH 6.0) and heat (176°F or 80°C), as in group I; from acid alone to give a pH 4.6, as in group II; or from rennet (an enzyme preparation) at pH 6.3, as in group III. Essentially a dehydration of protein occurs, along with a partial or complete reduction of the negative electrical charges which surround the surfaces of the milk proteins. At a critical point, precipitation occurs, leading to a smooth gelatinous curd of varying strength. The curd may be scooped directly into cloth bags or perforated containers for immediate draining and eventual packaging, or the curd is cut and cooked, followed by drainage of whey, salting, and creaming.

Ricotta. Ricotta, or recooked cheese, in its most acceptable form is made from acidified whole milk heated to 176°F (80°C). By introducing large amounts of lactic starter culture, acid whey powder, food-grade acetic or citric acids, and small amounts of salt to cold milk and heating to the above temperatures in a kettle, smooth white particles appear which rise to the top and collect as a curd bed, which is left undisturbed. In about 30 min the hot curd is scooped into perforated containers for drainage and cooled. Later it is removed and consumer-packaged. The product is utilized directly or in a variety of Italian dishes.

Cottage. Cottage cheese is made from pasteurized skim milk, and in uniform discrete particles classified as small or large curd. A curd forms when the increasing lactic acid of milk during fermentation attains the isoelectric point of casein at pH 4.6. This soft curd additionally contains lactose, salt, and water. Later the curd matrix is cut and cooked to about 126°F (52°C). Separation of whey from the curd is rapid, and is followed by two or three water washings at warm to chill temperatures. Washing removes whey residues and acts as a cooling medium. After drainage of the last wash water, the chilled curd is blended with a viscous, salted creaming dressing to give 4.2% fat and 1% salt, and is packaged. One unsalted, uncreamed, nonfat form of cottage cheese has less flavor, calories, and sodium than standard cottage cheese. Another form is creamed to 9–11% fat and pressed as farmer's pressed cheese. *See* ISOELECTRIC POINT.

Cream and Neufchâtel. Cream and Neufchâtel cheeses resemble cottage cheese in manufacture, but they are made from high-fat mixes instead of skim milk, and no effort is undertaken to attain discrete particles. The minimum fat content of Neufchâtel cheese is 20%, and of cream cheese 33%. The cloth bags traditionally used to separate the whey from the curd have been replaced by centrifugal curd concentrators, which separate the stirred curds and whey at 165°F (74°C). The curd thereafter is pasteurized, treated with stabilizer or gums to prevent water leakage, and salted and homogenized hot. This hot mass is packaged and sealed directly, and tempered at room temperature for a number of hours. The products are used as spreads, in salads, and in cheesecake.

Cottage cheese keeps well at refrigerated temperatures for at least several weeks, but hot-pack cream and Neufchâtel cheeses, because of earlier exposure to high temperature and sealing hot in packages, maintain freshness for up to 2 months or more. Common microbial spoilage agents are molds and yeasts and frequently *Pseudomonas* bacteria which grow at low temperatures.

Mozzarella. Natural mozzarella cheese is normally made from pasteurized whole milk, but milks of 1 or 2% fat may be used if the cheeses are properly labeled. The warm cheese milk is incubated with lactic acid bacteria (*Lactococcus lactis, Streptococcus thermophilus,* or *Lactobacillus delbreuckii bulgaricus*), or may be directly acidified by the addition of food-grade acids such as acetic or citric. Added rennet coagulates the milk to a smooth curd, which is cut with wire knives. The curds, without cooking, may be drained of whey shortly after cutting or, depending upon the type of bacteria, may be cooked to 117°F (47°C) before whey removal. The blocks or patties of curd which result from this action are retained until a pH 5.2–5.5 is achieved, and then are milled into small cubes, placed in hot water, and stretched and molded until smooth. The resulting rectangular blocks are cooled and brined for 2–8 h, depending upon size, and dried and vacuum-packaged.

Acceptable natural mozzarella cheese has a bland, slightly acid flavor. It melts uniformly and smoothly when exposed to hot oven temperatures of 428°F (220°C) for a few minutes and, depending upon type, maintains its quality from several weeks to several months. Natural mozzarella cheese is used in a wide assortment of Italian dishes. Imitations containing vegetable fats, artificial flavors, and a variety of additives are made mainly for institutional and food supplementation use.

Ripened cheese. Ripened cheese is exposed to an optimum environment of temperature and moisture for a period of time to attain characteristic flavor, texture, and appearance. It may be made from raw, heat-treated, or pasteurized milk that is coagulated with a rennet preparation to form a smooth curd. After cutting and cooking to 95–131°F (35–55°C), the curds are salted, before or after pressing, and shaped. The pressed curds, usually salted, may be given a special microbial application, and then are usually held at 41–59°F (5–15°C) in rooms under controlled humidity (85–95%) to develop the desired traits. All standard ripened cheeses are salted, and the milks from which they are made are always coagulated with rennet, usually in the presence of small amounts of lactic acid and sometimes added calcium chloride.

Rennet milk coagulation occurs when rennin, a protease from rennet, hydrolyzes or splits kappa casein from casein into a whey-soluble component, glycomacropeptide. The cleavage of kappa casein by rennin destabilizes the casein molecule, permitting its dominant alpha and beta casein components in micelle form to precipitate. Such coagulated proteins are filamentous and, through strand overlapping under quiescent conditions, appear as a smooth, homogeneous, sweet (pH 6.3) gel or curd. This curd is cut and cooked, leading to a contraction which expresses whey. The dry curds thereafter are salted, pressed, and ripened. *See* MICELLE; RENNIN.

During ripening, many flavor compounds arise in the cheese. They include free fatty acids, amino acids, ketones, diacetyl, and alcohols. Their amounts in a balanced ratio, along with major components of the cheese, largely determine the characteristic flavor. Agents involved through proteolytic, lipolytic, decarboxylation, and deamination reactions include rennin, natural bacteria of milk, added microorganisms, natural milk enzymes, microbial enzymes, and added food-grade enzyme preparations. The microbial enzymes evolve from millions of microbial cells present in cheese; the sources of the added food-grade enzyme preparations usually are fungal.

Most ripened cheeses are contained in one of six basic groups. The characteristic cheeses in each group include: group I—Cheddar and Monterey; group II—Swiss (Emmentaler) and Gruyère; group III—Edam and Gouda; group IV—Muenster, brick, and Limburger; group V—provolone; and group VI—Camembert, Brie, and blue.

Cheddar and Monterey. For these cheeses the curds are formed at 88°F (31°C) by 0.2 qt (200 ml) of rennet in 2200 lb (1000 kg) of underheated whole milk previously inoculated with 1–2% lactic-type starter for 15–30 min. The curds are cut with wire knives, and cooked to 99°F (37°C) for 30–60 min. Then the whey is run off, and the curd bed is cut into rectangular blocks weighing approximately 11 lb (5 kg). These blocks usually are turned over every 15 min for 2 h in a step known as cheddaring, and the stringy nature of the curd evolves as sufficient lactic acid develops to give a pH of 5.3. The blocks, now flatter than at the start, are milled to small cubes, and dry-salted at the rate of 5 lb (2.3 kg) of salt per 220 lb (100 kg) of curd. These salted curds are pressed in single-service paper or cloth-lined stainless steel boxes. The standard 44- to 66-lb (20- to 30-kg) forms which result are removed, and repressed in plastic films of low oxygen permeability. The film-wrapped Cheddar cheese is ripened up to 1 year at 41–50°F (5–10°C). It is generally manufactured into various-size forms prior to reduction into consumer packages.

In modern industrial cheesemaking, another form

of Cheddar cheese, known as barrel, is made by the stirred-curd step in contrast to the cheddaring. This avoids the more lengthy period required for the latter. In the stirred-curd step, individual small cut curd particles, after cooking and whey separation, are stirred for about 30 min, salted, and packed into large film-lined metal or fiber barrels of 640-lb (290-kg) capacity. Here, after excess whey is removed, the curds are pressed and the containers sealed and placed in ripening rooms. Later, the cheese is removed and used largely for making processed cheese. Ripening cheese in large blocks appears to improve typical flavor quality, so that some cheese that is cheddared and destined for long ripening, too, may be held in 640-lb (290-kg) capacity film-lined, sealed boxes.

Monterey cheese resembles Cheddar, but has a higher moisture level and ripens more rapidly. Its curds are washed with water in the vat and not cheddared, but are stirred prior to salting and then added to lined standard stainless steel forms for pressing and eventual ripening.

Swiss (Emmentaler) and Gruyère. Swiss and Emmentaler cheeses are the same, but in the United States the term Swiss is widely used, whereas in Europe and elsewhere the name is Emmentaler. The cheeses are made in block or round forms, but in the United States the former shape dominates because it is easier to slice for sandwiches. Also, economics of production are enhanced.

Underheated milk (158°F or 70°C for 16 s), standardized or partly skimmed, is set with rennet to form a curd, accompanied by three special bacterial cultures, *Streptococcus thermophilus, Lactobacillus delbrueckii bulgaricus,* and *Propionibacterium shermanii.* These cultures influence the acid, eye, flavor, and texture development of the cheese. *Propionibacterium shermanii* is mainly responsible for eye and typical flavor formation.

Renneting requires about 30 min by using 0.2 qt (180 ml) of rennet per 2200 lb (1000 kg) of warm (88°F or 31°C) milk. The size of the curds after cutting is very small, about like peas. These are cooked to about 126°F (52°C) in 60 min, and stirred until the pH decreases to 6.3.

To make block Swiss cheese, these stirred, cooked curds and considerable whey are pumped into cloth-lined, perforated stainless steel chambers. Here a large block is formed under the warm whey, the whey is removed, and the bed of curd remaining is cut into about 100-lb (45-kg) sections. These are immersed in cool brine for up to several days. After removal and drying, the blocks are sealed with plastic or rubberized film, placed in wooden boxes, with room for expansion, and covered by lids. Exposure to warm temperature, about 73°F (23°C) for 2–3 weeks, produces the typical eyes and sweet, hazelnut flavor. Further ripening continues at 41°F (5°C) for 4–12 months before the cheese is ready for market.

Gruyère cheese shows eyes like Swiss or Emmental, but they are usually smaller. This 125-lb (57-kg) round wheel cheese is made mostly in France, Switzerland, and Finland. The surfaces of Gruyère cheese, unlike the larger 224-lb (102-kg) round wheel Emmentals, are not washed daily or wiped with cloths. This leads to a special microbial growth on the surface which imparts to the cheese more flavor of a unique nature best typified by the Comté Gruyère of the French Jura area.

Edam and Gouda. Both of these cheese types may contain eyes, but these are small and lack uniform distribution. Edam cheese is produced in its normal size as 5-lb (2.3-kg) round balls waxed in red. Gouda cheese, softer in body because whole milk is invariably used, appears as orange- or yellow-waxed, medium-sized flat wheels of about 11–22 lb (5–11 kg). Manufacturing is essentially similar for both.

Pasteurized milk is set with lactic culture and rennet, but acid development is constrained usually by removing some of the whey and replacing it with water. Before the cheese is pressed, the pH is usually 5.4. This higher pH gives a sweeter flavor to the cheese and permits other species of bacteria to function. In Europe, where most of this cheese is made, sodium nitrate may be added to the cheese milk to suppress spoilage bacteria, but the practice is diminishing, and instead a continuous bacterial spore centrifugal removal process is substituted. Where nitrates are used, only small amounts are introduced, most of which disappear during ripening.

Unique metal forms shape the cheese after light pressing. The cheeses are brined and waxed. Ripening occurs at 50°F (10°C) for 2–3 months.

Muenster, brick, and Limburger. Good-quality pasteurized milk is required for these cheeses. At times, as for brick cheese, the renneted curd may be washed with water to reduce the acidity and to increase moisture. A reddish bacterium, *Bacterium linens,* along with yeasts, grows on the cheese surfaces at 59°F (15°C) in a highly moist room for 11 days. The surfaces take on the brick-reddish color of the bacterium. The three cheeses are differentiated by the intensity of their flavor, softness of body, and sizes and shapes. Muenster has least intensity of flavor, followed by brick cheese.

Provolone. Originating in Italy, provolone cheese also is manufactured in large quantities in Argentina and the United States. It is a pasta filàta, or pulled-curd ripened cheese, and is generally smoked. The texture is smooth and flaky and the flavor highly aromatic or piquante. Initially, the cheese is made almost exactly like that of a fresh, low-moisture mozzarella using *Lactobacillus delbrueckii bulgaricus* as the starter. Following proper acid development in the vat, the curd is stretched and formed into various shapes: cylindrical, pear, or ball. Thereafter, it is bound with ropes or twine and hung in hickory smoke–filled rooms for 3 weeks or exposed to smoke compounds. Ripening occurs at about 44°F (7°C) for up to 12 months, and cheese sizes range from 3 to 500 lb (1.4 to 227 kg). A related

Italian type is caciocovàllo, literally meaning horse cheese.

Camembert, Brie, and blue. These are all rennet cheeses, and Camembert and Brie are made with pasteurized milk cultured to about 0.2% titratable acidity. The curds are not cooked and, following whey drainage and hooping in round forms, they are modified by the special application of white or blue-green mold spores. Introduction of the spores to the cheese may result from inoculating the milk, brine, or curds, or inoculating all three media.

Camembert and Brie are white mold cheeses about 1 in. (2.5 cm) thick whose manufacture is similar except that the diameter of the latter is larger. The characteristic feature of these cheeses is the appearance of a snow-white mat of *Penicillium caseicolum* or *P. camemberti* mold on the surfaces. These molds grow well only in an excessive air environment, and hence their appearance on the surface. They ripen the cheese from outside into the center through release of their many active enzymes, which transform the curds to a smooth, soft state. The cheeses are ready for consumption in 12–14 days at 50°F (10°C) and 95% relative humidity. Held thereafter in a refrigerated state for 40 days in supermarkets, the cheeses eventually become overripe. Ammoniacal flavor with the white surfaces becoming brown and the inner sections becoming light tan confirm an overripe state.

Blue cheese requires spores of *Penicillium roqueforti* or *P. glaucum.* These spores, appearing as a black powder, are present throughout the wheel of pressed, highly salted curd, and grow as filamentous blue-green mycelia when minimum air is supplied. In practice, the mold-inoculated wheels of cheese, from 5 to 12 lb (2.3 to 5.4 kg), are penetrated by a mechanical head containing 50 needles which create the long air channels. The mold grows along these air channels, and moves farther into the cheese if natural openings exist. Here the many lipolytic and proteolytic enzymes originating from the mold mycelia attack the cheese to give characteristic flavor. Molding occurs in 30 days after air channel formation at 50°F (10°C) and 95% relative humidity. Then the cheese is held at 41°F (5°C) during 2–6 months for more complete ripening.

The most famous blue cheese is Roquefort, made in southern France from sheep milk. Other widely known related cheeses are Stilton, Gorgonzola, Danish blue, and American blue.

Processed cheese. Processed cheese is made from natural types. Nearly any natural cheese can be processed, except that for blue cheese technical difficulties cause blackening of the blue mold due to the high heat.

Processed cheese is produced by grinding selected lots of natural cheese and adding cream, color, salt, and emulsifying agents. The mixture is blended and sent to cookers which heat the mass to 165–185°F (74–85°C). During the cooking, fat normally separates from the protein and water,

but this is corrected by adding anhydrous citrate and phosphate salts, usually at 3% levels. The salts raise the cheese pH to about 5.6–5.8, making the protein more soluble. Under these circumstances a stable emulsion of protein, fat, and water occurs to give a smooth homogeneous mass. The hot mass is packaged directly. Processed cheese foods and spreads are made similarly, but include more water and less protein, fat, and other solids.

Sliced processed cheese is attained by spreading the hot process cheese mass emerging from the cookers over moving cold steel rolls. The chilled cheese in thin, wide sheets passes over rotary knives and cutting bars to give squares lying on top of each other, which are packaged in film wrappers.

Production developments. The cheese industries of the world have become rapid-growth industries with high consumer acceptance of their product. Cheese-manufacturing plants may be very large, utilizing more than 2.2×10^6 lb (10^6 kg) of cheese milk daily. In the operational areas, cheese vats of 5500-lb (2500-kg) capacity are common, as are giant presses.

Mechanization of cheesemaking too has advanced through the introduction of ingenious cheddaring towers, block formers, and moving web belts. This has led to significantly higher rates of production, with less manual labor, while maintaining quality. True continuous making methods of natural cheese have yet to be realized. However, a unique process incorporating ultrafiltration membrane technology has potential for continuous manufacture of certain cheeses.

Membrane separation is an application of biotechnology to cheesemaking. In this process, skim or whole milk is pumped at low pressure, 48 lb/in.^{2} (3.4 kg/cm^2), through tubes or plates containing many small pores, with a molecular-weight cutoff of 20,000. The milk passes across the membranes, usually at 126–129°F (52–54°C). Much of its water, lactose, soluble salts, and nonprotein nitrogen pass through the pores as permeate. Retained are all the fat, protein, insoluble salts, and some serum, which contains water, lactose, soluble salts, and nonprotein nitrogen. This retentate increases in concentration with time, so that its fat and protein may be five times greater than that of the starting milk. Emerging from the ultrafiltration unit in its final concentrated form as a plastic fluid, this retentate has the same composition as some cheeses. Cheesemaking is completed without vats, as there is no whey to separate. Simple mechanical injection of culture, rennet, salt, color, and fungal spores into the plastic fluid concentrate may follow. A curd develops within 5–10 min, and is placed directly in a ripening room. This is a French process, known as MMV after the names of the inventors, Maubois, Mocquot, and Vassal. Its major advantages are much greater cheese yields due to complete retention of whey protein in the cheese, lower requirements for rennet, a high potential for continuous-process application, and production of a neutral-pH permeate with a reduced biochemical oxygen demand (BOD) value. Much cheese in Europe is made in this manner, particularly fresh, soft acid cheeses—Feta, Camembert, and St. Paulin.

Other variations of ultrafiltration retentate application to cheesemaking include milk retentate supplementation and direct ultrafiltration of cheese milks, but only up to 2:1 protein concentration. The advantages of this alternative ultrafiltration process include improved cheesemaking efficiency, energy savings, and higher quality of marginal cheeses. Use of milk retentates in cheesemaking in this manner has led to the production of natural Cheddar cheese of good quality with significantly reduced sodium levels, 0.015 oz/3.5 oz cheese (420 mg/100 g) or less, compared with approximately 0.02 oz (700 mg) for commercial Cheddar cheeses.

Ultrafiltration has led to whey protein concentrates of 90–95% protein. This nonfat product can be modified to give a texture similar to cheese and is used as a food ingredient to replace butterfat by up to 50% for the making of commercial low-fat cheese. Another technology for the fluid milk and cheese industries is microfiltration. This system follows the same principles as those for ultrafiltration except for membrane pore size. Ultrafiltration retains fat, casein, bacteria, and insoluble salts. Passage through a micromembrane retains fat, bacteria, and insoluble solids, but no protein, making the resulting permeate an almost sterile skim milk. The creamlike retentate obtained is heated to 302°F (150°C) for 2 s, and then it is blended with the almost-sterile skim milk, pasteurized, and cooled to proper temperatures for use in milk and cheese processing. Results from Europe, where much research has been conducted on this subject, indicate an almost 99.5% reduction in total bacteria. Also, quality cheese without gas defects or loss of flavor was produced. *See* ULTRAFILTRATION.   Frank V. Kosikowski

Bibliography. J. G. Davis, *Cheese*, vol. 3: *Manufacturing Methods*, 1976; F. V. Kosikowski, *Cheese and Fermented Milk Foods*, 2d ed., 1982; G. P. Sanders, H. E. Walter, and R. T. Tittsler, *General Procedure for Manufacturing Swiss Cheese*, USDA Circ. 851, 1955; A. L. Simon, *Cheese of the World*, 1956; U.S. Department of Agriculture, *Cheeses of the World*, 1972; L. L. Van Slyke and W. V. Price, *Cheese*, 1980.

Cheilostomata

An order of ectoproct bryozoans in the class Gymnolaemata. Cheilostomes possess delicate colonies composed of loosely grouped, highly complex, short, uncurved, box- or vase-shaped zooecia, with solid, porous, chitinous, or calcareous walls, and with apertures closed by lidlike opercula. *See* GYMNOLAEMATA.

Morphology. Cheilostome colonies may be encrusting threadlike networks; thin encrusting sheets; tabular, nodular, or globular masses; or erect tuft-like, twiglike, frondlike, or trellislike growths. These colonies are not divisible into distinct endozone and exozone regions. Although all lack stolons and monticules or maculae, and some have rhizoids or small coelomic chambers, most cheilostome colonies bear ovicells (brood chambers) developed at the distal ends of the normal autozooecia (feeding zooids). Many cheilostome colonies possess either one or both of two types of heterozooids: avicularia, which are bird-head-like heterozooids with a movable mandible that can be snapped at small animals attempting to settle on the colony; and vibracula, heterozooids with a bristlelike seta that sweeps animals and debris from the colony surface.

The walls of adjacent zooecia within a cheilostome colony are distinctly separate rather than fused together, and may be perforated by small openings filled with soft tissue. The zooecial walls may be thin chitinous membranes, moderately thick and firm chitinous walls, or thin to thick calcareous walls displaying a great variety of pores, pits, granules, spines, and lacy fretwork (especially the frontal walls, which form the external surface of the colony). Zooecia lack internal transverse partitions such as diaphragms. Round to highly complicated in outline, and noticeably smaller in transverse diameter than the zooecium itself, the aperture is closed by a membranous or chitinous lidlike operculum hinged to the edge of, and fitting snugly over, the aperture. The aperture may be flush with the colony surface or surrounded by spines or an elevated rim (peristome).

Life cycle. Each cheilostome zygote develops, usually sheltered in various ways by the parent zooid, into one larva. The larva usually swims freely for less than a day, and then attaches to a substrate and metamorphoses (with complete degeneration of its larval organs) into an ancestrular zooid. In a few species, the zygote is shed directly into the water and develops there into a larva (cyphonautes) which swims freely for up to several weeks before settling. Afterward, repeated asexual budding from the ancestrula produces the rest of the cheilostome colony (but no resistant resting bodies).

History and classification. Cheilostomes may well have evolved from ctenostomes. First appearing in the latest Jurassic, the cheilostomes rapidly expanded during Cretaceous time to become the dominant bryozoan group throughout the Cenozoic, a position which they still maintain today. Although ceilostomes are predominantly marine, some range into brackish waters; in addition to being abundant in level-bottom communities, cheilostomes extensively but inconspicuously encrust the framework of many Cenozoic and modern coral reefs. The cheilostomes have diversified into three major groups which appeared consecutively in geologic time. Anascan cheilostomes, the earliest, have a flexible, membranous, chitinous frontal wall which is completely open to the surrounding water. Cribrimorph cheilostomes possess similar flexible frontal walls but are partially protected externally by overarching, partly fused, calcareous spines. Ascophoran cheilostomes, the most highly evolved, display solid, shieldlike, calcareous frontal walls, below which is a special saclike hydrostatic-pressure device (ascus) used to protrude and retract the tentacular crown, or lophophore. *See* BRYOZOA; CTENOSTOMATA.   Roger J. Cuffey

Chelation

A chemical reaction or process involving chelate ring formation and characterized by multiple coordinate bonding between two or more of the electron-pair-donor groups of a multidentate ligand and an electron-pair-acceptor metal ion. The multidentate ligand is usually called a chelating agent, and the product is known as a metal chelate compound or metal chelate complex. Metal chelate chemistry is a subdivision of coordination chemistry and is characterized by the special properties resulting from the utilization of ligands possessing bridged donor groups, two or more of which coordinate simultaneously to a metal ion. *See* COORDINATION CHEMISTRY.

Ethylenediamine, $H_2NCH_2CH_2NH_2$, is a good example of a bidentate chelating agent consisting of two amino donor groups joined to each other by a two-carbon bridge. The coordination of both nitrogen atoms to the same metal ion would result in the formation of a five-membered chelate ring.

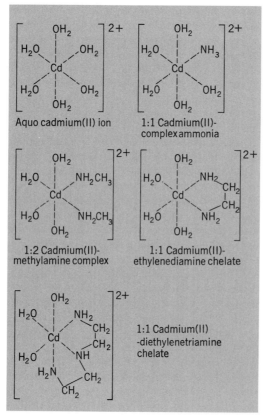

Fig. 1. Formulas of hydrated cadmium(II) ion, two cadmium(II) complexes, and two cadmium(II) chelates.

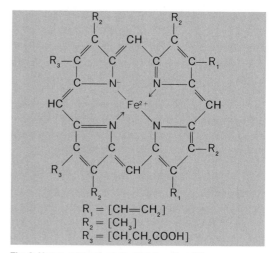

$R_1 = [CH{=}CH_2]$
$R_2 = [CH_3]$
$R_3 = [CH_2CH_2COOH]$

Fig. 2. Heme, a tetradentate chelate of iron(II).

If a chelating agent has three groups capable of attaching to a metal ion, as in diethylenetriamine, $NH_2CH_2CH_2NHCH_2CH_2NH_2$, it is tridentate (terdentate); if four, tetradentate (quadridentate); five, pentadentate (quinquidentate); six, hexadentate (sexadentate); and so on. In general, these chelating agents may be designated as multidentate or polydentate ligands. All chelating agents must be at least bidentate; tridentate agents give fused rings. An example of a nonchelated complex and two chelated complexes of the Cd(II) ion are illustrated in **Fig. 1**. In aqueous solution, metal ions are completely solvated, or hydrated, to give an aquo complex, as indicated for the Cd(II) ion in Fig. 1. Thus formation of a complex of a unidentate ligand involves the replacement of a water molecule by the unidentate donor group. Two water molecules are replaced by a single molecule of a bidentate ligand; three water molecules are replaced by a molecule of a terdentate ligand, and so on.

Many of the functional groups of both synthetic and naturally occurring organic compounds can form coordinate bonds to metal ions, producing metal-organic complexes or chelates, many of which are biologically active. Thus chelate compounds are frequently found in an interdisciplinary field of science called bioinorganic chemistry. The biological significance of chelates can be readily recognized if one notes that a large number of biologically important compounds are either metal chelates or chelating agents. This list includes the alpha amino acids, peptides, proteins, enzymes, porphyrins (such as hemoglobin), corrins (such as vitamin B_{12}), catechols, hydroxypolycarboxylic acids (such as citric acid), ascorbic acid (vitamin C), polyphosphates, nucleosides and other genetic compounds, pyridoxal phosphate (vitamin B_6), and sugars. The ubiquitous green plant pigment, chlorophyll, is a magnesium chelate of a tetradentate ligand formed from a modified porphin compound, and similarly the oxygen transport heme of red blood cells contains an Fe(II) chelate of the type illustrated in **Fig. 2**. *See* BIOINORGANIC CHEMISTRY;

ORGANOMETALLIC COMPOUND.

A rapidly growing body of experimental evidence indicates that chelation may be important in the pharmacological action of many drugs. The use of chelating agents to remove certain toxic cations such as lead and plutonium from the body is now widely recognized in medical practice. Intensive research has been undertaken to either develop or discover an effective synthetic or natural chelating agent for the removal of iron deposits in the body that result from certain hereditary metabolic disorders.

Applications. The ability of chelating agents to reduce the chemical activity of metal ions has found extensive application in many areas of science and industry. Ethylenediaminetetraacetic acid (EDTA), a hexadentate chelating agent (**Fig. 3**), has been employed commercially for water softening, boiler scale removal, industrial cleaning, soil metal micronutrient transport, and food preservation. Nitrilotriacetic acid (NTA) is a tetradentate chelating agent (**Fig. 4**) which, because of lower cost, has taken over some of the commercial applications of EDTA. Chelating agents of related type have been used in biological systems to produce metal-ion buffers. By selection of the appropriate chelating agent, the free metal-ion concentration can be maintained at a very low and constant concentration level, just as a relatively constant pH can be maintained through the use of a conventional hydrogen-ion buffer system. Furthermore, the colors of certain chelating agents are sensitive to metal-ion concentration in a manner completely analogous to the pH-dependent color changes observed with acid-base indicators; such chelating agents serve as metal-ion indicators in analytical chemistry. The solubility of many chelating agents and metal chelates in organic solvents permits their use in solvent extraction of aqueous solutions for the separation or analysis of metal ions.

Many commercially important dyes and pigments, such as copper phthalocyanines, are chelate compounds. Humic and fulvic acids are plant degradation products in lake and seawater sediments that have been suggested as important chelating agents which regulate metal-ion balance in natural waters. By virtue of its abundance, low toxicity, low cost, and good chelating tendencies for metal ions that produce water hardness, the tripolyphosphate ion (as its sodium salt) is used in large quan-

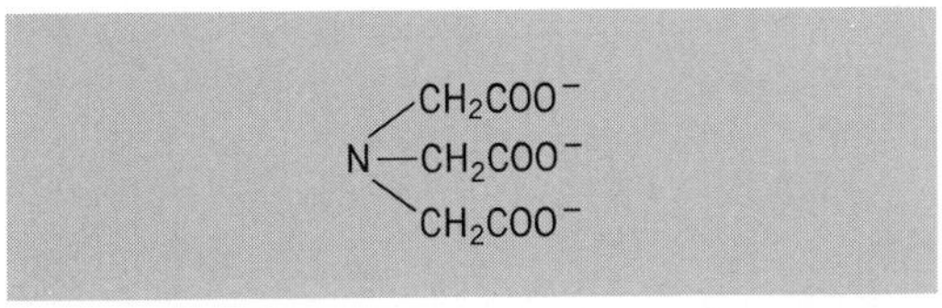

Fig. 4. Structural formula of NTA anion, a quadridentate ligand.

tities as a builder in synthetic detergents. Both synthetic ion exchangers and the mineral zeolites are chelating ion-exchange resins which are used in analytical and water-softening applications. As final examples, less conventional chelating agents are the multidentate, cyclic ligands, termed collectively crown ethers, which are particularly suited for the complexation of the alkali and alkaline-earth metals.

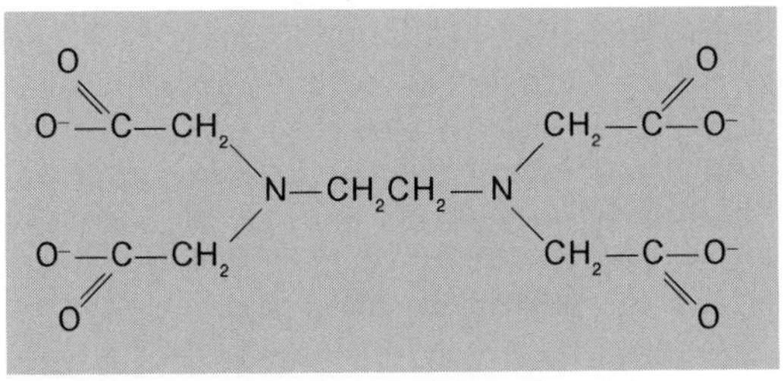

Stabilities of metal chelates in solution. One of the most striking properties of chelate ring compounds is their unusual thermodynamic and thermal stability. In this respect, they resemble the aromatic rings of organic chemistry. For example, in reaction (1), β-diketones in the enol form can lose a

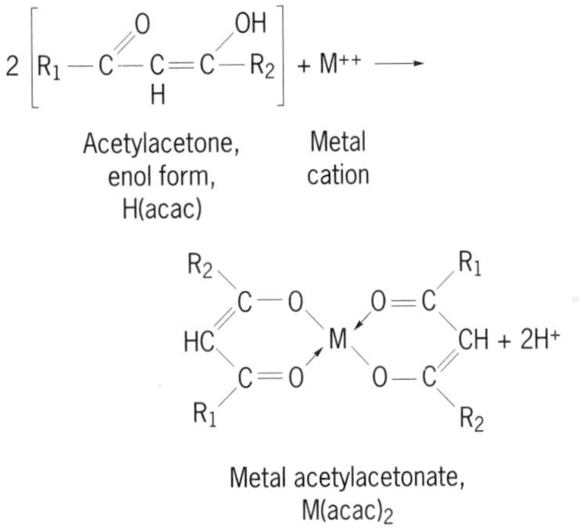

hydrogen ion and coordinate with a metal cation to give a six-membered ring of unusual thermal stability.

Beryllium acetylacetonate boils without decomposition at 270°C (518°F), and G. T. Morgan reported that scandium acetylacetonate, $Sc(acac)_3$, shows very little decomposition at 370°C (698°F). This remarkable stability contrasts sharply with the very low stability of coordination compounds containing simpler monodentate ketones, such as acetone.

Because of enhanced thermodynamic stability in solution, chelating agents may greatly alter the behavior of metal ions. The very insoluble compound, ferric hydroxide, will dissolve in a strongly alkaline solution of triethanol amine, $N(CH_2CH_2OH)_3$. Alternatively, the concentration of the ferric ion can be made vanishingly small at pH 2 by the addition of an equimolar amount of bis(orthohydroxybenzyl)ethylenediamine-*N,N'*-diacetic acid (HBED; **Fig. 5**).

Since about 1940, both theoretical and practical

Fig. 3. Structural formula of anion of EDTA, a sexadentate ligand.

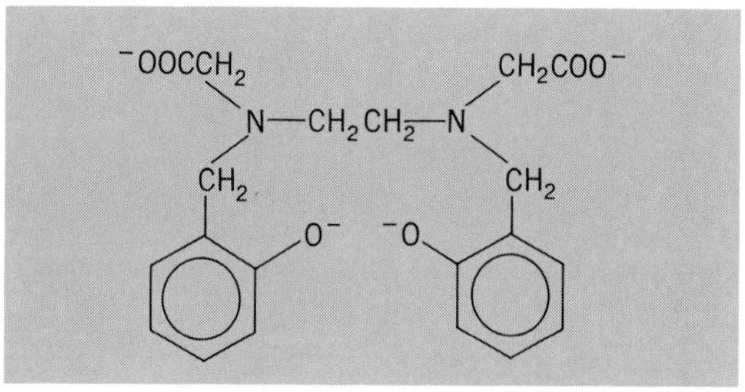

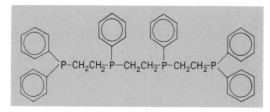

Fig. 5. Structural formula of anion of HBED, a sexadentate ligand.

considerations have focused attention on the factors which contribute to chelate stability. It is convenient to list such factors under three headings: (1) the nature of the metal cation, (2) the nature of the ligand, and (3) the formation of the chelate ring. It should be emphasized that these factors operate together, and their separation is somewhat artificial, but helpful for discussion purposes.

Role of metal in chelate stability. Since nitrogen, oxygen, and sulfur serve as the electron donor atoms in a majority of chelating agents, it is of interest to seek a relationship between the donor atom and the type of metal acceptor atom with which it combines. A large majority of the chelates of Li^+, Na^+, K^+, Rb^+, Cs^+, Mg^{2+}, Ca^{2+}, Sr^{2+}, Ba^{2+}, Al^{3+}, Ga^{3+}, In^{3+}, Tl^{3+}, Ti^{4+}, Zr^{4+}, Th^{4+}, Si^{4+}, Ge^{4+}, and Sn^{4+} contain oxygen as at least one of the donor atoms. It may be furnished as an acid, alcohol, ether, ketone, or other group. These ions coordinate less frequently through two nitrogen or sulfur atoms. Cations of other metals such as vanadium, niobium, tantalum, molybdenum, and uranium, and the cations Be^{2+}, Al^{3+}, and Fe^{3+} show a preference for oxygen as the donor atom, but they may coordinate through nitrogen, sulfur, or phosphorus under special conditions. Cr^{3+}, Fe^{2+}, and the platinum metals show increasing preference for coordination through nitrogen as opposed to oxygen, while Cu^+, Zn^{2+}, Ag^+, Au^+, Cu^{2+}, Cd^{2+}, Hg^{2+}, V^{3+}, Co^{3+}, and Ni^{2+} show a marked preference for nitrogen and sulfur as the donor atoms. The ions of the last group retain the ability to coordinate with oxygen in even greater degree than do the ions of the first group, but their tendency to form bonds through nitrogen is so great that it exceeds their oxygen-binding tendency.

It must be recognized that broad generalizations such as these have many exceptions, particularly in intermediate regions. On the other hand, such generalizations indicate clearly that attempts to arrange elements in the order of their chelating ability can be of significance only when cations of comparable type are selected. Thus, the stabilities of the alkali-metal, the alkaline-earth, and the rare-earth chelates decrease as the charge on the cation decreases or as the size of the cation increases. For example, the chelates of the alkaline-earth metal ions become less stable as the metal ion becomes larger (if the number of chelate rings remains the same), in the order Mg^{2+}, Ca^{2+}, Sr^{2+}, Ba^{2+}, Ra^{2+}. The relationship between ion size and chelate stability is of major importance in the separation of the rare-earth and transuranium elements by ion-exchange processes. The selectivity of the ion-exchange column is increased by the use of appropriate chelating agents in the eluting solution.

Stability sequences established for other metal ions are somewhat less satisfactory. Metal chelates of several substituted β-diketones decrease in stability in the order: $Hg^{2+} > (Cu^{2+}, Be^{2+}) > Ni^{2+} > Co^{2+} > Zn^{2+} > Pb^{2+} > Mn^{2+} > Cd^{2+} > Mg^{2+} > Ca^{2+} > Sr^{2+} > Ba^{2+}$. If one restricts stability comparisons to bivalent metals of the first transition series, the following order is obtained: $Zn^{2+} < Cu^{2+} > Ni^{2+} > Co^{2+} > Fe^{2+} > Mn^{2+}$. This latter listing of stabilities appears to be valid for a large variety of chelating ligands.

Lower valence states such as Ir(I) and Rh(I) are effectively coordinated by chelating ligands containing trivalent phosphorus or trivalent arsenic donor groups. For example, recently synthetic coordination chemists have synthesized a series of unusual chelating agents containing trivalent phosphorus, analogous to polyamines, an example of which is illustrated in **Fig. 6**.

General principles of selective coordination of metal ions by various types of donor atoms have now been worked out, and are described through concepts such as the principles of hard and soft acids and bases, and type A and B character of metal ions. These qualitative principles are based on well-known laws of ionic attraction and polarizabilities of atoms, ions, or molecular groups, as well as on general principles of molecular orbital theory.

Role of ligand in chelate stability. Two general types of groups give rise to coordinate bonds between ligands and metal. These are (1) primary acid groups in which the metal ion can replace hydrogen ions and (2) neutral groups which contain an atom with a free electron pair suitable for bond formation. If two groups from either class 1 or 2, or from both classes, are present in the same molecule in such positions that both groups can form bonds with the same metal ion, a chelate ring may be formed. For example, as shown in **Fig. 7**, in oxalic acid two groups of type 1 are present; in ethylenediamine two groups of type 2 are present; glycine possesses one of each type; and pyridoxylidine-glycine (the Schiff base

Fig. 6. "Tetraphos," a quadridentate ligand.

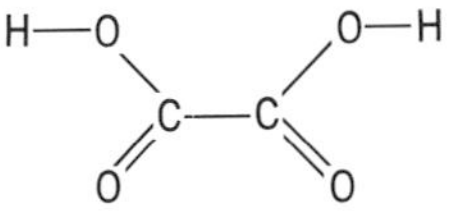

Oxalic acid; two type 1
(negative carboxylate)
donor groups

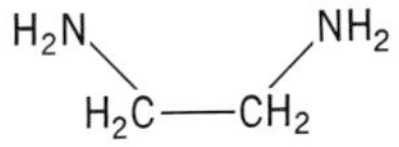

Ethylenediamine;
two type 2 (neutral amino)
donor groups

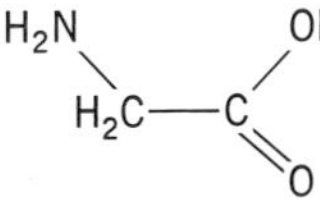

Glycine; one type 1
and one type 2
donor group

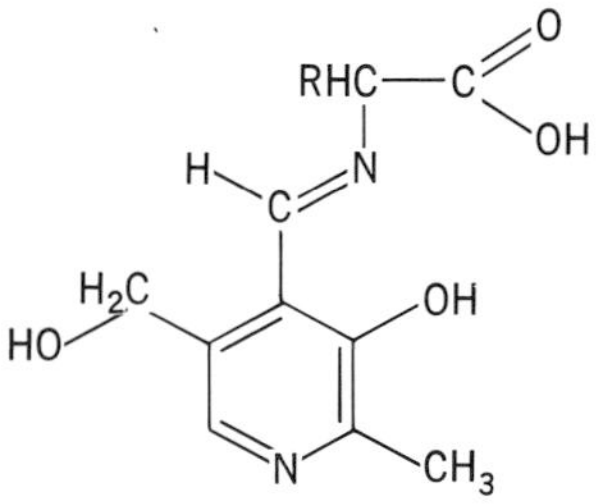

Amino acid Schiff base of
pyridoxal (vitamin B₆);
two type 1 (carboxylate and
phenolate) and one type 2
(azomethine nitrogen) donor
group

Fig. 7. Chelating ligands indicating the types of donor groups available for coordination.

of glycine and vitamin B₆) possesses a carboxylate (type 1), an aromatic phenolate (type 1), and an imino group (type 2) available for chelate formation around a metal ion.

In general, anything which increases the localization of negative charge on the donor atom increases its ability to coordinate to a metal atom. Since a hydrogen ion is bound to a ligand by an electron pair in groups of type 1, an increase in electron density on the donor atom will increase the ability

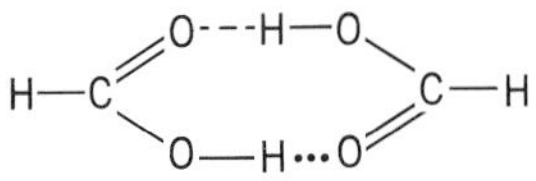

Dimer of formic acid;
intermolecular hydrogen bonds

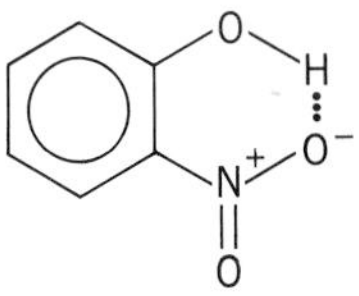

o-Nitrophenol; strong
intramolecular hydrogen
bond, relatively volatile

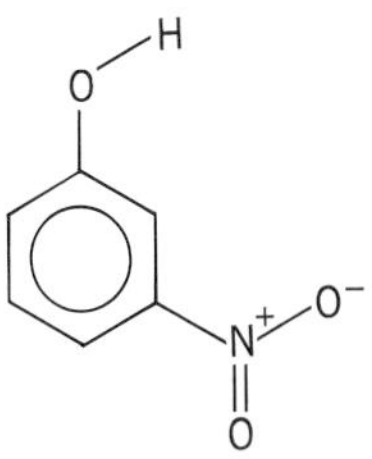

m-Nitrophenol;
low volatility

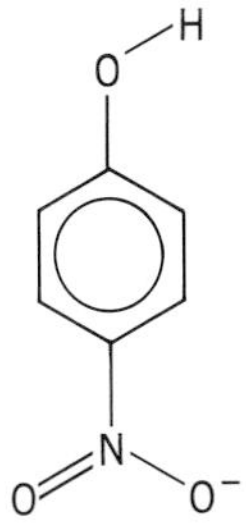

p-Nitrophenol;
low volatility

Fig. 8. Compounds forming intramolecular and intermolecular hydrogen bonds.

of the donor to bind either hydrogen ion or metal cation. The ability of a ligand to bind hydrogen ion is frequently referred to as its basic strength. It is surprising then that, for ligands of rather similar type, an increase in ligand basic strength implies an increase in its metal-chelating ability. A number of researchers have indicated this relationship by plotting the log of the equilibrium constant for the process represented by Eq. (2) against the log of

$$H^+ + L^- \rightleftharpoons HL \qquad K_1 = \frac{[HL]}{[H^+][L^-]} \qquad (2)$$

the equilibrium constant for the process of chelate dissociation shown by Eq. (3). L^- is the chelating

$$M^{n+} + L^- \rightleftharpoons M^{(n-1)+} \qquad K_2 = \frac{[ML^{(n-1)+}]}{[M^{n+}][L^-]} \qquad (3)$$

anion, such as the acetylacetonate anion,

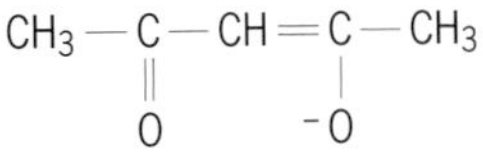

$$CH_3 - C - CH = C - CH_3$$
$$\quad\quad\quad || \quad\quad\quad\quad |$$
$$\quad\quad\quad O \quad\quad\quad\quad ^-O$$

The constant K_1 is the protonation constant (its reciprocal is the acid dissociation constant), and K_2 is designated the stability constant of the metal chelate.

For the organic chemist, the analogy between the hydrogen cation and the metal cation is even more clearly drawn. Rings formed by hydrogen bonding are referred to as chelates; thus, formic acid dimerizes through hydrogen-bond chelation as shown in **Fig. 8**. The high volatility of o-nitrophenol compared with the much lower volatility of its meta or para isomers (Fig. 8) can only be explained in terms of intramolecular versus intermolecular hydrogen bonding. The properties of salicylaldehyde, enhanced enolization in acetoacetic ester, and many other organic compounds are altered by internal chelate-ring formation involving hydrogen bonds. *See* HYDROGEN BOND.

The role of ligand structure on chelate stability is illustrated by studies which have been conducted on compounds of the type shown by **Fig. 9**, where A represents an electron-attracting group. In general, it was found that with an increase in the electron-attracting power of group A, electrons were pulled away from the nitrogen atom, resulting in both lower base strength and lower chelating ability for the ligand. As A is changed successively through the groups listed below, chelate stability increases in the order:

$$- NO_2 < - SO_3Na < \langle\bigcirc\rangle < - H < - CH_3$$

$$< - OH < - OCH_3$$

Least stable   Most stable

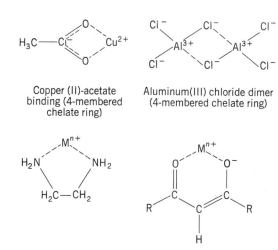

Fig. 9. Structure of a chelated copper compound.

Fig. 10. Metal chelates containing four-, five-, and six-membered rings.

Similar studies on substitute β-diketone chelates of the type

showed that, if R_1 were changed from a methyl group to an electron-withdrawing trifluoromethyl group, the stability of the resulting chelate is greatly decreased. In general, all molecular charge effects which can be invoked to shift charge in an organic molecule, such as inductive and resonance effects, will influence chelate stability. Thus the principles governing charge distribution and bond hybridization in organic chemistry are useful in working out the relationships between ligand structure and chelate stability.

Role of ring closure in chelate stability. The stability factors discussed above are applicable to coordination compounds generally, not to chelates alone. On the other hand, a number of stability factors may be considered to apply uniquely to chelates because of their ring structure. The most obvious variable in this category is ring size, a factor which is uniquely determined by the position of the donor atoms in the chelating ligand. When the groups are present in such a position as to form a five or six-membered ring, the resulting complex is the most stable although four-, seven-, eight-membered, and even larger rings are known. Examples of these would be found among biological ligands as well as in ion exchange resins. The existence of three-membered rings has not been established. Hydrazine, H_2NNH_2, which might in theory form a three-membered chelate ring, appears to be monodentate. There is some evidence for intermediate structures of metal-oxygen complexes

which may be considered three-membered chelate rings. Such compounds may be important reaction intermediates but are generally unstable and present in relatively low concentrations. The four-

membered chelate rings are frequently strained. Examples of four-membered chelate rings are copper(II)-carboxylate complexes, and the aluminum chloride dimer (**Fig. 10**). While five-membered rings are very common and are formed preferentially by saturated organic ligands, ligands with two double bonds tend to form six-membered structures. If only one double bond is present, five- or six-membered rings may form; five-membered saturated rings are shown in Fig. 10 by ethylenediamine-metal chelates, and the conjugated six-membered rings by the metal acetylacetonates.

Rings of seven or more members are comparatively uncommon, but their existence is well established. As the length of the chain between the two donor atoms increases, so does the tendency of the ligand to form polymetallic complexes. Under such circumstances, the two donor atoms on the same chelate molecule coordinate with different metal atoms rather than with one; thus, a polymeric chain, $M^+-NH_2CH_2CH_2CH_2CH_2NH_2-M^+$, may result instead of a ring structure.

The fact that chelate complexes are usually more stable than comparable nonchelate structures has been called the chelate effect. This effect is partly attributable to the fact that simultaneous rupture of both bonds holding the ligand to the metal is highly improbable, and if only one bond breaks there is a high probability that the broken bond will reform before the second bond is ruptured.

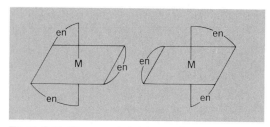

Fig. 11. Optical isomers of chelate complexes.

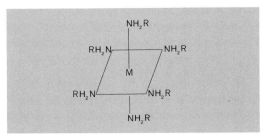

Fig. 12. Formula for an optically inactive nonchelate.

As the chain length between the two donor atoms increases, the chance for reformation of the broken bond declines; thus, large rings usually show a decrease in stability. On the other hand, in fused ring systems, formed by polydentate ligands such as ethylenediaminetetraacetic acid, the probability that at least one bond will reform before all bonds are ruptured results in increased complex stability. When the bonding atoms are rigidly positioned around the metal by the organic framework, as in the porphins, the resulting increase in stability is extremely high. It has been reported that the copper phthalocyanine complex, with a completely interlocked ring system, is stable in the vapor phase near $500°C$ ($930°F$).

Chelate compounds are differentiated from their nonchelate analogs by several properties besides high stability. Although not all chelates are volatile, the existence of low-boiling metal acetylacetonates and related structures is noteworthy. If the coordination number of the metal cation for the oxygen atoms of the acetylacetone (that is, the number of nearest oxygens around the cation) is equal to twice the ionic charge of the cation, the resulting acetylacetonate is volatile; thus, beryllium with a charge of 2 and a coordination number of 4 forms an acetylacetonate which boils at $270°C$ ($518°F$); aluminum with a charge of 3 and a coordination number of 6 forms an acetylacetonate which boils at $314°C$ ($597°F$). If the coordination number of the central cation is less than twice the ionic charge, less volatile saltlike complexes are formed.

Isomerism of all types, so important in organic chemistry, is of major concern in chelation, particularly to the biochemist, since desired biological properties are frequently restricted to a particular chelate isomer. Ring formation may result in optical activity where analogous nonchelate structures are inactive. Thus, the ethylenediamine chelate structures shown in **Fig. 11** are optical isomers, whereas the analogous methylamine complexes represented in **Fig. 12** are optically inactive. *See* CHEMICAL BONDING; CHEMICAL EQUILIBRIUM; COORDINATION COMPLEXES; STEREOCHEMISTRY; STERIC EFFECT (CHEMISTRY).

A. E. Martell; R. J. Motekaitis

Bibliography. N. W. Alcock, *Bonding and Structure: Structural Principles in Inorganic and Organic Chemistry*, 1991; I. Bertini, H. Gray, and J. Valentine, *Bioinorganic Chemistry*, 1993; R. Haydock (ed.), *Bonding and Structure of Solids*, 1991; A. E. Martell, The chelate effect, *Advances in Chemistry Series*, no. 62, American Chemical Society, pp. 272–294, 1967; A. E. Martell, *Inorganic Chemistry in Biology and Medicine*, 1980.

Chelicerata

A subphylum of the phylum Arthropoda. The Chelicerata can be defined as those arthropods with the anteriormost appendages as a pair of small pincers (chelicerae) followed usually by pedipalps and four pairs of walking legs, and with the body divided into two parts: the prosoma (corresponding approximately to the cephalothorax of many crustaceans) and the opisthosoma (or abdomen). There are never antennae or mandibles (lateral jaws). The Chelicerata comprise three classes: the enormous group Arachnida (spiders, ticks, mites, scorpions, and related forms); the Pycnogonida (sea spiders or nobody-crabs); and the Merostomata (including the extant Xiphosurida or horseshoe crabs). *See* ARACHNIDA; MEROSTOMATA; PYCNOGONIDA; XIPHOSURIDA.

With a few exceptions, the distinctive body and limb pattern of chelicerates is diagnostic. The Acarina (mites) have the prosoma and opisthosoma fused in a single armored globe. The segments of the prosoma are always fused (except in the minor order Solfugae or sun spiders), and the opisthosoma never bears locomotor appendages (although in the xiphosurids there are paired gills on six segments of the opisthosoma). Chelicerae are always present, but the form of the pedipalps varies greatly from tiny sensory appendages to enormous crablike chelae (in scorpions and certain minor orders). Four pairs of locomotor appendages follow the chelicerae and pedipalp on the prosoma; only in a few species of pycnogonids are there five or six pairs of walking legs. *See* ACARI.

Both Merostomata and Pycnogonida are marine, but the enormous numbers and varied forms of the Arachnida are almost entirely terrestrial. The respiratory structures of chelicerates include gills, booklungs, and tracheae. Sexes are normally separate, with genital openings at the anterior end of the opisthosoma. Some mites and other small chelicerates are omnivorous scavengers, but the majority of species of larger chelicerates are predaceous carnivores at relatively high trophic levels in their particular ecotopes. *See* ARTHROPODA.

W. D. Russell-Hunter

Chelonia

An order of the Reptilia, subclass Anapsida, including the turtles, terrapins, and tortoises. This order is also known as the Testudines. The group first appeared in the Triassic, and its representatives are among the commonest fossils from that time on. Members of the order are most frequently found in fresh-water streams, lakes, and ponds or in marshy areas. However, a number of strictly terrestrial species are known, and several are marine. Turtles occur on all the major continents and continental islands in tropic and temperature regions. The marine forms are basically tropic in distribution, but some individuals stray into temperate waters. *See* ANAPSIDA.

The largest carapace length attained by living forms is around 8 ft (2.4 m) in the marine leatherback turtle (*Dermochelys*), which weighs 1500 lb (675 kg). Members of the large land tortoise group (*Geochelone*) reach lengths of 4 ft (1.2 m) and weights of about 560 lb (250 kg). The smallest living species is probably the stinkpot (*Kinosternon odoratus*) of eastern North America, which attains a maximum length of about $4^{1}/_{2}$ in. (11 cm). The longevity of turtles is well known, with many captive tortoises having lived 50–60 years and others estimated to be as old as 150 years.

Taxonomy. The living turtles are usually divided into two major groups, the suborders Pleurodira and Cryptodira, based upon the structures of the head and neck. Both lines are thought to be evolved from primitive forms placed in the suborder Amphichelydia (Triassic to Eocene). This latter group differs most markedly from recent species in having elongate neural spines on the neck vertebrae so that the neck is not retractible into the shell (**Fig. 1**). Correlated with the lack of retractibility, the skull is not emarginated to make room for attachment of muscle from the cervical region. The pleurodires, on the other hand, have spines on only the most posterior cervicals and the head is retractile laterally. The skull is emarginate. In the cryptodires the cervical spines are uniformly reduced, the skull is usually emarginate, and the head is folded directly back to within the shell. In several cryptodires, notably in the marine turtles, the neck is secondarily nonretractible because of a reduction in the shell, and the skull is nonmarginate. The **table** shows the principal groups and distribution of the approximately 225 living species of the order.

Morphology. The Chelonia differ from most other vertebrates in possessing a hard bony shell which encompasses and protects the body (**Fig. 2**). The shell is made up of a dorsal portion, the carapace, and a ventral segment, the plastron, connected by soft ligamentous tissue or a bony bridge. The carapace is composed of the greatly expanded ribs and dorsal vertebrae overlain by a series of enlarged dermal ossifications and an outer covering of tough skin or horny scales. The plastron is similarly arranged with remnants of the interclavicle, clavicles, and gastralia fused with dermal ossifications and covered by skin or scales. Other peculiarities associated with the shell include the fusion of the ribs to the vertebrae and the reduction of trunk muscles, the presence of the pectoral girdle completely inside the ribs (found in no other animal), the highly modified short, thick humerus and femur, and the lungs attached dorsally to the shell. In addition, living turtles differ from the tuatara, snakes, lizards, and crocodilians in having an anapsid skull, no true teeth but horny beaks on the jaws, an immovable quadrate, and a single median penis in males. Teeth are present in ancient primitive turtles.

The rigid bony shell of turtles imposes a basic body plan subject to relatively little variation. Turtles are always recognizable as such, and the principal obvious differences between them are in the shell shape, limbs, head, and neck. The general outline of the shell is variable, but in most forms the shell is moderately high-arched and covered with epidermal scales. In some of the tortoises, such as *Geochelone*, the shell is very high, equaling the breadth. In the soft-shelled turtles, Trionychidae, and the saxicolous African tortoise (*Malacochersus*), the shell is greatly depressed to a thin, almost platelike form. No scales are present on the shells of the families Dermochelyidae, Carrettochelyidae, and Trionychidae, which are covered by thick skin.

The majority of turtles have limbs more or less adapted to aquatic or semiaquatic life with moderate to well-developed palmate webbed feet. However, in strictly terrestrial forms such as the tortoises, the limbs are elephantine with the weight of the body being borne on the flattened sole of the feet. The marine turtles and the river turtle (*Carrettochelys*) of southern New Guinea have the anterior limbs modified into paddlelike flippers, used to propel them through the water rapidly.

Physiology. Associated with the tendency of most turtles toward a life in or near water is the auditory apparatus. Even though an eardrum is present, hearing is adapted to picking up sounds transmitted through the water or substratum. However, there is

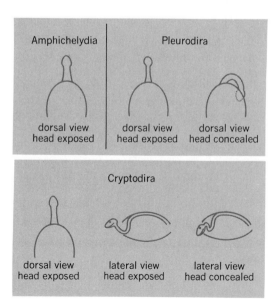

Fig. 1. Characteristics of turtle suborders, showing head in exposed and concealed positions.

Fig. 2. Common United States turtles. (*a*) Spotted turtle, *Clemmys guttata*. (*b*) Stinkpot, *Kinosternon odoratus*, (*c*) Box turtle, *Terrapene carolina*. (*d*) Painted turtle, *Chrysemys picta*. (*e*) Diamondback terrapin, *Malaclemys terrapin*. (*f*) Common snapping turtle, *Chelydra serpentina*. (*g*) Mud turtle, *Kinosternon subrubrum*. (*h*) Wood turtle, *Clemmys insculpta*. (*i*) Map turtle, *Graptemys geographica*. (*j*) Spiny soft-shelled turtle, *Trionyx spiniferus*. (*k*) River terrapin, *Chrysemys floridana*. (*After J. J. Shomon, ed., Virginia Wildlife, 15(6):27, 1954*)

evidence that airborne sound can be heard. Vision is also important, and turtles have color vision. Sounds are produced by many species through expulsion of air through the glottis. Respiration is by means of the rather rigid lungs, which are inflated and deflated by a series of special muscles. Several species with aquatic habits have special vacularized areas in the mouth or cloaca which act as auxiliary respiratory devices and make possible gaseous exchanges when the turtle is submerged in water. Most forms emit highly pungent oily substances from specialized cloacal glands, and these secretions probably are useful as recognition cues in the water. Most of the species are gregarious and diurnal, and territoriality is unknown in the order.

Families of the Chelonia

Group	Common name	Number of species	Distribution
Suborder Pleurodira			
Family Pelomedusidae	Side-necked turtles	14	Southern Africa, Madagascar, South America
Family Chelidae	Side-necked turtles	32	Australia, New Guinea, South America
Suborder Cryptodira			
Family Kinosternidae	Mud and musk turtles	22	North, Middle, and South America
Family Chelydridae	Snapping turtles	3	Middle and northern South America
Family Emydidae	Pond turtles and allies	102	All continents except Australia; only one or two South American species
Family Testudinidae	Tortoises	30	All continents except Australia; two South American species
Family Cheloniidae	Hawksbill, loggerhead, and green sea turtles	6	Tropical and subtropical seas
Family Dermocheylidae	Leatherback turtle	1	Tropical and subtropical seas
Family Trionychidae	Soft-shelled turtles	14	North America, Asia, central and southern Africa
Family Carretochelyidae	Fly River turtle	1	New Guinea

Reproduction. The courtship patterns of various turtles are distinctive. In general, aquatic forms mate in the water, but tortoises breed on land. The male mounts the female from above, and fertilization is internal. Sperm may be stored in the cloacal region of the female for extended periods before fertilization. Because of the presence of the large median penis in males, the sexes of many species can be distinguished by the longer and broader tail of the male. In addition, in many forms the plastron of the male is concave while in the female it is moderately to strongly convex. No doubt this characteristic of the female is associated with the spatial requirements for egg production and storage. All turtles lay shelled eggs which are buried in sand or soil in areas where females congregate. The shell is calcareous in most forms, but the marine turtles have leathery shells. Eggs are rather numerous, as many as 200 being laid by a single individual in some species, and are highly valued as human food. Incubation takes 60–90 days, and the little turtle cuts its way out of the shell with a small horny egg caruncle at the end of the snout.

Nutrition. Turtles feed on all types of organisms. Aquatic species may eat algae, higher plants, mollusks, crustaceans, insects, or fishes; terrestrial forms are similarly catholic in tastes. Most species are omnivores, but some have very specialized diets. The edges and internal surfaces of the horny beaks of these reptiles are frequently denticulate and modified to form specialized mechanisms adapted to handle particular food items.

Jay M. Savage

Phylogeny. Turtles have long been considered a "primitive" or relict reptile group that has maintained a consistent morphologic structure since its origin. Phylogenetic and functional work on the skulls of fossil and modern turtles suggest that this approach is incorrect. The Cryptodira and the Pleurodira probably represent a very early dichotomy which took place soon after the origin of the turtles. These two groups passed through similar stages during their phylogeny and repeatedly evolved parallel adaptations.

The basicranium of turtles has rarely been used in a comparative sense, and the morphology of this region is still poorly known in many families of turtles. Nonetheless, the basicranium is one of the most useful regions for phylogenetic work because of its extreme complexity and relative conservativism compared with other areas. The main arterial and venous circulation of the head, the cranial nerves, the brain, and the neck and jaw musculature are all related to features in the basicranium. Changes in any of these systems can usually be seen in the basicranium. Although turtle skulls are rare compared to shells, the fossil record contains a good series with basicrania dating from the Upper Triassic to the Recent.

Previous phylogenies, however, have been based primarily on shell criteria and vertebral characters. Two major living groups are usually distinguished: the Cryptodira, with vertical neck retraction, and the Pleurodira, with horizontal neck retraction. A few of the shell characters also distinguish the living forms: pelvis sutured to carapace and plastron in pleurodires, pelvis free in cryptodires. These

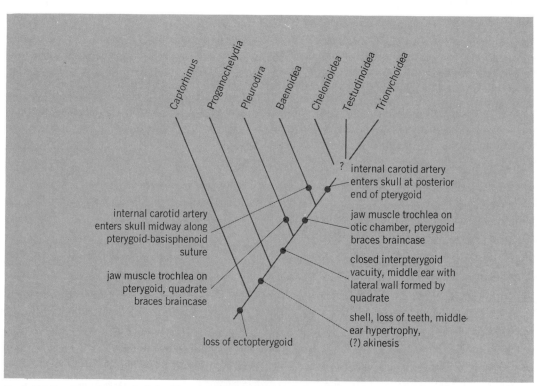

Fig. 3. Relationships of Chelonia derived from analysis of cranial features.

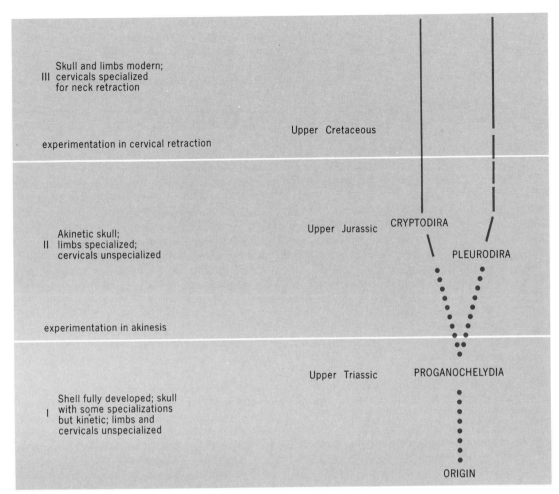

Fig. 4. Levels of organization in the order Chelonia.

features rather clearly separate living turtles into two groups, but when fossils are examined it becomes difficult to distinguish pleurodires and cryptodires. The neck retractile mechanisms had not evolved until the end of the Mesozoic; thus the earlier phylogeny of the two groups is difficult to determine by neck characters.

Work on the skulls of fossil and recent turtles, however, has resulted in the development of a new hypothesis of chelonian relationships. The use of cranial features in a shared-derived character analysis is expressed in **Fig. 3**. Arterial characters provide the basis for relating the major groups of cryptodires, whereas jaw mechanics and middle ear morphology are used in comparing Proganochelydia, Pleurodira, and Cryptodira. By using these characters, pleurodires and cryptodires can be recognized well into the Mesozoic as distinct lineages, and the divergence of the two groups from a common ancestor probably took place before the Jurassic.

The new phylogenetic information has enabled functional interpretations to be made concerning the biologic significance of the differences between cryptodires and pleurodires. These interpretations show that the two lineages have developed similar structures in parallel during their evolution (**Fig. 4**). A similar but nonhomologous jaw mechanism involving a trochlea to compensate for the expanded otic chamber (**Fig. 5**) and a method of bracing the palatoquadrate against the braincase are complex features evolved independently in both groups. Later in their evolution the neck retractile mechanisms evolved, but by this time the two groups had been separate for many millions of years.

Origin. The origin of turtles is more in doubt than ever. Previous workers have emphasized the peculiar adaptations of a Permian reptile from South Africa, *Eunotosaurus*. This animal, represented by postcranial remains but very little skull material, was suggested as an ancestor for turtles on the basis of its expanded ribs, which form a rudimentary shell. However, T. S. Parsons and E. E. Williams in 1961 and, in particular, C. B. Cox in 1969 showed that *Eunotosaurus* is not related to turtles. Cox stated that *Eunotosaurus* is a captorhinomorph and that its Chelonia-like features are due to structural convergence with turtles. *Eunotosaurus* lacks separate ribs on its last dorsal vertebra, and Cox held that this feature prevents *Eunotosaurus* from being a chelonian ancestor.

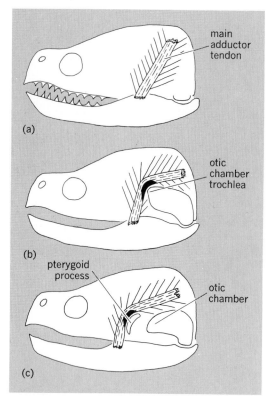

Fig. 5. Position of main jaw muscle tendon in (a) early reptiles, (b) cryptodires, and (c) pleurodires. The trochlea or pulley formed in turtles to get around the expanded otic chamber is independently derived in pleurodires and cryptodires.

No reptile known to science definitely possesses specialized characters in common with turtles that would allow it to be a close relative or ancestor of that order. Presumably the stem reptile group Captorhinomorpha includes the eventual forebears of turtles since captorhinomorphs probably were ancestral to all reptiles, but the intermediate forms are unknown. *See* REPTILIA.   Eugene S. Gaffney

Bibliography. P. W. Albrecht, *Tulane Stud. Zool.*, 14:81–99, 1967; R. L. Carroll, *Vertebrate Paleontology and Evolution*, 1988; C. B. Cox, *Bull. Brit. Mus. (Nat. Hist.)*, 18(5):167–196, 1969; E. S. Gaffney, *Bull. Amer. Mus. Nat. Hist.*, 155(5):387–436, 1975; M. Harless and H. Morlock, *Turtles: Perspectives and Research*, 1979; S. B. McDowell, *Bull. Mus. Comp. Zool.*, 125(2):23–39 1961; S. P. Parker (ed.), *Synopsis and Classification of Living Organisms*, 2 vols., 1982.

Chemical bonding

The force that holds atoms together in molecules and solids. Chemical bonds are very strong. To break one bond in each molecule in a mole of material typically requires an energy of many tens of kilocalories.

It is convenient to classify chemical bonding into several types, although all real cases are mixtures of these idealized cases. The theory of the various bond types has been well developed and

tested by theoretical chemists. *See* COMPUTATIONAL CHEMISTRY; MOLECULAR ORBITAL THEORY; QUANTUM CHEMISTRY.

The simplest chemical bonds to describe are those resulting from direct coulombic attractions between ions of opposite charge, as in most crystalline salts. These are termed ionic bonds. *See* COULOMB'S LAW; IONIC CRYSTALS; STRUCTURAL CHEMISTRY.

Other chemical bonds include a wide variety of types, ranging from the very weak van der Waals attractions, which bind neon atoms together in solid neon, to metallic bonds or metallike bonds, in which very many electrons are spread over a lattice of positively charged atom cores and give rise to a stable configuration for those cores. *See* CRYSTAL STRUCTURE; INTERMOLECULAR FORCES.

Covalent bond. But it is the normal covalent bond, in which two electrons bind two atoms together, as in

$$H-H, \quad H-Cl, \quad F-F, \quad \overset{H}{\underset{H}{\diagdown}}O, \quad \text{or} \quad \overset{H}{\underset{H}{\diagup}}\overset{H}{\underset{H}{C}}\overset{H}{\diagdown}$$

that is the most characteristic link in chemistry. The theory that accounts for it is a cornerstone that of chemical science. The physical and chemical properties of any molecule are direct consequences of its particular detailed electronic structure. Yet the theory of any one covalent chemical bond, for example, the H—H bond in the hydrogen molecule, has much in common with the theory of any other covalent bond, for example, the O—H bond in the water molecule. The current theory of covalent bonds current both treats their qualitative features and quantitatively accounts for the molecular properties which are a consequence of those features. The theory is a branch of quantum theory. *See* NONRELATIVISTIC QUANTUM THEORY; QUANTUM CHEMISTRY.

Hydrogen molecule. A brief outline of the application of quantum theory to the bond in the hydrogen molecule H—H follows. Here two electrons, each of charge $-e$, bind together two protons, each of charge $+e$, with the electrons much lighter than the protons. What must be explained, above all else, is that these particles form an entity with the protons 0.074 nanometer apart, more stable by $D = 109$ kcal (456 kilojoules) per mole than two separate hydrogen atoms, where D is the binding energy. In more detail, a molecular energy is involved (ignoring nuclear kinetic energy) that depends on internuclear distance, as shown in the **illustration**. This curve can be determined experimentally, and it can be used to interpret the characteristic spectroscopic properties of hydrogen gas. *See* MOLECULAR STRUCTURE AND SPECTRA.

The quantum theory accounts for the properties of isolated atoms by assigning atomic orbitals for individual electrons to move in, not more than two electrons at a time. For the hydrogen atom, the orbitals are labeled $1s$, $2s$, $2p_x$, $2p_y$, $2p_z$, and

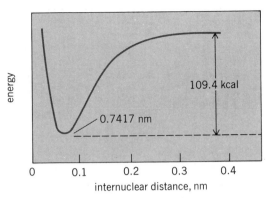

energy

109.4 kcal

0.7417 nm

| 0 | 0.1 | 0.2 | 0.3 | 0.4 |

internuclear distance, nm

Potential energy of the hydrogen molecule.

so on, with $1s$ the one having the lowest energy. For the molecule H_2 one electron, say electron 1, might be assigned to a $1s$ orbital on proton A, with $1s_A(1)$ written to signify this; similarly electron 2 might be assigned to the same kind of orbital on proton B, written as $1s_B(2)$. Since independent probabilities multiply and orbitals represent probability amplitudes, the description for the combined system shown in Eq. (1) is arrived

$$\phi(1, 2) = 1s_A(1)1s_B(2) \qquad (1)$$

at. Unfortunately, this fails to account for the bond properties; it gives a binding energy of only 10 kcal (41.9 kJ) per mole. *See* ATOMIC STRUCTURE AND SPECTRA; EXCLUSION PRINCIPLE.

An essential defect of Eq. (1) is the numbering of the electrons; it puts electron 1 on proton A, electron 2 on proton B. Electrons cannot be distinguished experimentally, so they should not be given unique numbers; the function $1s_A(2)1s_B(1)$ would be just as good as the foregoing. It is necessary to use a description that is not affected by interchange of electron labels, as in the additive combination of Eq. (2). (The difference

$$\phi(1, 2) = 1s_A(1)1s_B(2) + 1s_A(2)1s_B(1) \qquad (2)$$

combination also is an acceptable description, but it represents an excited state of the molecule.)

Any complete molecular electronic wave function should include electron spin. Symmetric space wave functions like Eq. (2) must be multiplied by antisymmetric spin wave functions to give total wave functions that are antisymmetrical with respect to interchange of electrons. For the ground state of hydrogen, and for the normal covalent bond elsewhere, this requirement means that the electron spins must be paired to give a total electron spin of zero.

The simple relationship described by Eq. (2) qualitatively accounts for the existence of the covalent bond; the predicted binding energy is $D = 74$ kcal (310 kJ) per mole; and the shape of the curve, with the minimum appearing at 0.080 nm, is right.

The description of Eq. (2) can be systematically improved. The charge acting on the electron may be changed from $+1e$ to the larger value, $+Ze$, which is more realistic for the actual molecule. With

$Z = 1.17$ this gives $D = 87$ kcal (364 kJ) per mole. Polarization effects may be introduced by taking Eq. (3), where $1\sigma_A = 1s_A + \lambda 2pz_A$ and $1\sigma_B =$

$$\phi(1, 2) = 1\sigma_A(1)1\sigma_B(2) + 1\sigma_A(2)1\sigma_B(1) \qquad (3)$$

$1s_B + \lambda 2pz_B$. This gives $D = 93$ kcal (389 kJ). Ionic terms may be introduced, acknowledging the possibility that both electrons may be on one atom, by taking Eq. (4) where C represents a constant.

$$\phi(1, 2) = C_1[1s_A(1)1s_B(2) + 1s_A(2)1s_B(1)]$$
$$+ C_2[1s_A(1)1s_A(2) + 1s_B(1)1s_B(2)] \qquad (4)$$

This also gives (with $Z = 1.19$) $D = 93$ kcal (389 kJ). Another possible approach is to include both ionic terms and polarization effects, and other terms involving $2s$, $3d$, $4f$, and other orbitals. If this is done, eventually one obtains the observed D value and a potential curve that is in complete agreement with experiment.

The linear mixing of terms such as $1s_A(1)1s_B(2)$ is called resonance; the method of mixing covalent and ionic structures is called the valence bond (VB) method. The particular mixing coefficients can be found by the variational principle: The best values for such parameters are those that make the total energy of the molecule, properly computed from quantum mechanics, a minimum. The energy expression contains only terms that have a direct classical interpretation: the kinetic energy of the electrons, their energy of repulsion for one another, their energy of attraction for the nuclei, and the nuclear-nuclear repulsion energy. *See* RESONANCE (MOLECULAR STRUCTURE).

Alternative descriptions of H_2 are possible, of which the most important is provided by the molecular orbital (MO) method. Here electrons are put one at a time into orbitals which are spread over the whole molecule, usually approximating these orbitals by linear combinations of atomic orbitals (LCAO). For H_2 the lowest molecular orbital is $\phi_1 \approx 1s_A + 1s_B$, the next $\phi_2 \approx 1s_A - 1s_B$. The simplest molecular orbital description is displayed in Eq. (5),

$$\phi(1, 2) = \phi_1(1)\phi_2(2) \qquad (5)$$

which represents an equal weighting of covalent and ionic structures; it gives $D = 61$ kcal (255 kJ) for $Z = 1.00$ and $D = 80$ kcal (335 kJ) for $Z = 1.20$. More suitable is a mixture of this function with the function obtained by promoting both electrons from ϕ_1 to ϕ_2. The result of this configuration interaction process has the form of Eq. (6), and

$$\phi(1, 2) = D_1\phi_1(2) + D_2\phi_2(1)\phi_2(2) \qquad (6)$$

it is identical with the valence bond function of Eq. (4). In this manner more terms can be added, using more orbitals, until, again, the accurate potential energy curve is obtained.

The most accurate description known for the chemical bond in H_2 is a very complicated electronic wave function. The calculated and observed values of D and other properties agree absolutely.

Complex molecules. The problem of the proper description of chemical bonds in molecules that are more complicated than H_2 has many inherent difficulties. The qualitative theory of chemical bonding in complex molecules preserves the use of many chemical concepts that predate quantum chemistry itself; among these are electrostatic and steric factors, tautomerism, and electronegativity. The quantitative theory is highly computational in nature and involves extensive use of computers and supercomputers.

The number of covalent bonds which an atom can form is called the covalence and is determined by the detailed electron configuration of the atom. An extremely important case is that of carbon. In most of its compounds, carbon forms four bonds. When these connect it to four other atoms, the directions of the bonds to these other atoms normally make angles of about 109° to one another, unless the attached atoms are crowded or constrained by other bonds. That is, covalent bonds have preferred directions. However, in accord with the idea that carbon forms four bonds, it is necessary to introduce the notion of double and triple bonds. Thus in the structural formula of ethylene, C_2H_4 (**1**), all lines denote covalent

bonds, the double line connecting the carbon atoms being a double bond. Such double bonds are distinctly shorter, almost twice as stiff, and require considerably more energy to break completely than do single bonds. However, they do not require twice as much energy to break as a single bond. Similarly, acetylene (**2**) is written with a triple bond, which is still shorter than a double bond. A carbon-carbon single bond has a length close to 1.54×10^{-8} cm, whereas the triple bond is about 1.21×10^{-8} cm long. *See* BOND ANGLE AND DISTANCE; VALENCE.

In many compounds the rules for writing bond formulas are not unique. For example, benzene, C_6H_6 (**3**), can be written in two forms. Evidence

proves that all six C-C bonds are equivalent, so neither formula can be correct. The correct picture is a blend of the two, in which the bonds have many properties intermediate between those of double and single bonds but in which the whole molecule

Spectroscopic properties of H_2O*		
Property	Observed value	Calculated value
r_{OH} (Å†)	0.957	0.962
∠(HOH) (deg)	104.5	104.6
Harmonic vibrational frequencies (cm^{-1})	3832	3912
	1649	1683
	3943	4041

*After B. H. Besler et al., *J. Chem. Phys.*, 89:360, 1988.
†1 Å = 10^{-10} m.

displays an additional stability. This resonance occurs whenever the structure is such that two or more different bond formulas can legitimately be drawn for the same geometry. *See* BENZENE; ELECTRON CONFIGURATION.

Many substances have some bonds which are covalent and others which are ionic. Thus in crystalline ammonium chloride, NH_4Cl, the hydrogens are bound to nitrogen by electron pairs, but the NH_4 group is a positive ion and the chlorine is a negative ion.

Both electrons of a covalent bond may come from one of the atoms. Such a bond is called a coordinate or dative covalent bond or semipolar double bond, and is one example of the combination of ionic and covalent bonding.

The hydrogen bond is a special bond in which a hydrogen atom links a pair of other atoms. The linked atoms are normally oxygen, fluorine, chlorine, or nitrogen. These four elements are all quite electronegative, a fact which favors a partially ionic interpretation of this kind of bonding. *See* ELECTRONEGATIVITY; HYDROGEN BOND.

To illustrate the level of accuracy of contemporary quantum-chemical calculations, the **table** gives observed and calculated values for certain spectroscopic properties of the molecule.   Robert G. Parr

Bibliography. J. Murell, J. M. Tedder, and S. F. Kettle, *The Chemical Bond*, 2d ed., 1985; L. Pauling, *The Nature of the Chemical Bond and the Structure of Molecules and Crystals*, 3d ed., 1960; L. Pauling and E. B. Wilson, Jr., *Introduction to Quantum Mechanics*, 1935, reprint 1985; M. J. Winter, *Chemical Bonding*, 1994.

Chemical conversion

A chemical manufacturing process in which chemical transformation takes place, that is, the product differs chemically from the starting materials. Most chemical manufacturing processes consist of a sequence of steps, each of which involves making some sort of change in either chemical makeup, concentration, phase state, energy level, or a combination of these, in the materials passing through the particular step. If the changes are of a strictly physical nature (for example, mixing, distillation, drying, filtration, adsorption, condensation), the step is referred to as a unit operation. If the changes are of a chemical nature, where conversion from one chemical species to another takes place (for example, combustion, polymerization, chlorination, fermentation, reduction, hydrolysis), the step is called a unit process. Some steps involve both, for example, gas absorption with an accompanying chemical reaction in the liquid phase. The term chemical conversion is used not only in describing overall processes involving chemical transformation, but in certain contexts as a synonym for the term unit process. The chemical process industry as a whole has tended to favor the former usage, while the petroleum industry has favored the latter. *See* CHEMICAL PROCESS INDUSTRY; UNIT PROCESSES.

Another usage of the term chemical conversion is to define the percentage of reactants converted to products inside a chemical reactor or unit process. This quantitative usage is expressed as percent conversion per pass, in the case of reactors where unconverted reactants are recovered from the product stream and recycled to the reactor inlet. *See* CHEMICAL ENGINEERING.   William F. Furter

Bibliography. N. Basta, *Shreve's Chemical Process Industries Handbook*, 6th ed., 1994.

Chemical dynamics

That branch of physical chemistry which seeks to explain time-dependent phenomena, such as energy transfer and chemical reaction, in terms of the detailed motion of the nuclei and electrons which constitute the system.

Reaction Kinetics

Although the ultimate state of a chemical system is specified by thermodynamics, the time required to reach that equilibrium state is highly dependent upon the reaction. For example, diamonds are thermodynamically unstable with respect to graphite, but the rate of transformation of diamonds to graphite is negligible. As a consequence, determining the rate of chemical reactions has proved to be important for practical reasons. Rate studies have also yielded fundamental information about the details of the nuclear rearrangements which constitute the chemical reaction.

Traditional chemical kinetic investigations of the reaction between species X and Y to form Z and W, reaction (1), sought a rate of the form given in Eq. (2), where $d[Z]/dt$ is the rate of appearance of

$$X + Y \rightarrow Z + W \qquad (1)$$

$$d[Z]/dt = kf([X], [Y], [Z], [W]) \qquad (2)$$

product Z, f is some function of concentrations of X, Y, Z, and W which are themselves functions of time, and k is the rate constant. Chemical reactions are incredibly diverse, and often the function f is quite complicated, even for seemingly simple reactions such as that in which hydrogen (H) and bromine (Br) combine directly to form hydrogen bromide (HBr). This is an example of a complex

reaction which proceeds through a sequence of simpler reactions, called elementary reactions. For reaction (3d), the sequence of elementary reactions

$$Br_2 \rightarrow 2Br \qquad (3a)$$

$$Br + H_2 \rightarrow HBr + Br \qquad (3b)$$

$$H + Br_2 \rightarrow HBr + Br \qquad (3c)$$

$$H_2 + Br_2 \rightarrow 2HBr \qquad (3d)$$

is a chain mechanism known to involve a series of steps, reactions (3a)–(3c). This sequence of elementary reactions was formerly known as the reaction mechanism, but in the chemical dynamical sense the word mechanism is reserved to mean the detailed motion of the nuclei during a collision.

Bimolecular processes. An elementary reaction is considered to occur exactly as written. Reaction (3b) is assumed to occur when a bromine atom hits a hydrogen molecule. The products of the collision are a hydrogen bromide molecule and a hydrogen atom. On the other hand, the overall reaction is a sequence of these elementary steps and on a molecular basis does not occur as reaction (3d) is written. With few exceptions, the rate law for an elementary reaction $A + B \rightarrow C + D$ is given by $d[C]/dt = k[A][B]$. The order (sum of the exponents of the concentrations) is two, which is expected if the reaction is bimolecular (requires only species A to collide with species B). The rate constant k for such a reaction depends very strongly on temperature, and is usually expressed as $k = Z_{AB}\rho \exp(-E_a/RT)$. Z_{AB} is the frequency of collision between A and B calculated from molecular diameters and temperature; ρ is an empirically determined steric factor which arises because only collisions with the proper orientation of reagents will be effective; and E_a, the experimentally determined activation energy, apparently reflects the need to overcome repulsive forces before the reagents can get close enough to react.

Unimolecular processes. In some instances, especially for decompositions, $AB \rightarrow A + B$, the elementary reaction step is first-order, Eq. (4), which

$$d[A]/dt = d[B]/dt = k[AB] \qquad (4)$$

means that the reaction is unimolecular. The species AB does not spontaneously dissociate; it must first be given some critical amount of energy, usually through collisions, to form an excited species AB*. It is the species AB* which decomposes unimolecularly.

Molecular Dynamics

In principle, it is possible to prepare two reagents in specific quantum states and to determine the quantum-state distribution of the products. In practice, this is very difficult, and experiments have mostly been limited to preparing one reagent or to determining some aspect of the product distribution. This approach yields data concerning the detailed aspects of the dynamics.

Bimolecular reactions. Molecular-beam and luminescence techniques have played a major role in the development of chemical dynamics. Since these techniques largely complement each other, they are illustrated by discussing the results of a single reaction, the formation of deuterium chloride (DCl) from atomic deuterium (D) and molecular chlorine (Cl_2), reaction (5).

$$D + Cl_2 \rightarrow DCl + Cl \qquad (5)$$

Chemiluminescence. Reaction (5) is 46 kilocalories per mole (192 kilojoules per mole) exoergic. If all of the exoergicity were to go into vibration of the newly formed DCl molecule, enough energy would be available to populate the $v' = 9$ vibrational level. In a gas-phase reaction at high pressure, much of this energy would be dissipated as heat at the walls of the container; but at very low pressures, where the frequency of collisions is small, DCl molecules in excited vibrational states, DCl*, will emit infrared emission prior to undergoing a collision.

An apparatus to study this infrared chemiluminescence is shown in **Fig. 1**. Deuterium atoms are made by dissociating D_2 gas in an electrical discharge, and together with Cl_2 are injected into the observation cell at the top. The reagents mix and react inside a vessel with walls maintained at 77 K ($-320°$F), which freeze out species hitting the wall. The pressure is kept low to minimize vibrationally deactivating collisions. Infrared emission from the products is gathered by mirrors at the end, taken out through the sapphire window, and analyzed with an infrared spectrometer. By analyzing the spectrum, it is possible to determine which vibration-rotation states are emitting and, as a consequence, which vibration-rotation states are formed in the reaction. **Figure 2** shows the relative distribution of vibrational states from the reaction, and also shows, for comparison, the relative distribution of vibrational states calculated from the Boltzmann equation for hot DCl (6000 K or 10,800°F). Thermal distributions at any other temperatures would still show a monotonic decline. (The

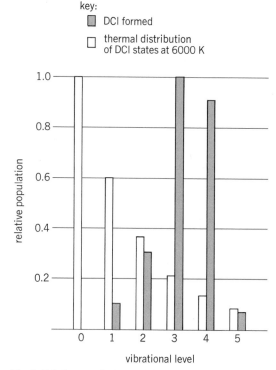

key:
- DCl formed
- thermal distribution of DCl states at 6000 K

Fig. 2. Relative populations of DCl molecules in different vibrational states formed in the reaction D + $Cl_2 \rightarrow$ DCl + Cl. 6000 K = 10,800°F.

population for $v' = 0$ is not determined by the chemiluminescence experiments, because that state does not emit.) The DCl formed in the reaction clearly has different properties than hot DCl: the vibrational population displays an inversion, and this system (the hydrogen isotope) was the active medium for the first chemically pumped laser. *See* CHEMILUMINESCENCE.

Molecular-beam experiments. Molecules can be isolated in molecular beams, and collisions between these isolated molecules can be observed by crossing two tenuous molecular beams in a region of otherwise high vacuum. **Figure 3** shows such an experiment. Gaseous atoms or molecules emerge from the ovens, and collimating slits select the particles which are all going in the same direction. The molecular beams cross at the center of rotation of a large platform which can be rotated under vacuum relative to the two beams. Large vacuum pumps maintain a high vacuum, which ensures that collisions take place only at the intersection of the two beams. Product molecules are ionized by electron bombardment, and detected with a quadrupole mass spectrometer housed within a region of ultrahigh vacuum.

Measurements are made of the scattered product intensity and speed at various scattering angles. For ease of interpretation, these data are transformed into the center-of-mass system in which the two reagents approach each other with equal and opposite momenta. **Figure 4** shows a contour map of the DCl intensity in the center-of-mass coordinate system in which the D atom is incident from the left and the Cl_2 molecule is incident from the right.

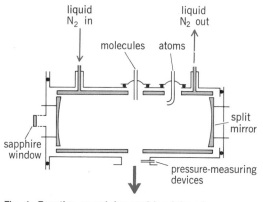

Fig. 1. Reaction vessel for studying infrared chemiluminescence between atoms and molecules at low pressure. (After D. H. Maylotte, J. C. Polanyi, and K. B. Woodall, J. Chem. Phys., 57:1547–1561, 1972)

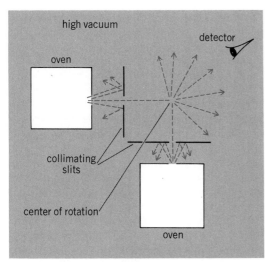

Fig. 3. Schematic of a molecular beam experiment; entire apparatus is under high vacuum.

The product DCl recoils backward (in the direction from which the D came) in a broad but nonetheless anisotropic distribution. The speed of the product is high, and corresponds to about half of the reaction exoergicity appearing in translation recoil of the products, with the balance appearing in vibration and rotation of the DCl; this is consistent with the chemiluminescence results. *See* MOLECULAR BEAMS.

The anisotropic product distribution shows that reaction occurs in the time less than a molecular rotation, about 1 picosecond. The partitioning of energy roughly equally between vibration and translation suggests that the major amount of energy is released in repulsion between the DCl and Cl. This repulsion is similar to that experienced by a Cl_2 molecule in photodissociation, also shown in Fig. 4. Because the deuterium atom is so light, the direction in which the product is expelled is a measure of the orientation of the Cl_2 molecule during reaction. For this reaction the collinear arrangement D-Cl-Cl is preferred, whereas bent arrangements are preferred for $D + I_2$.

Other investigations. Molecular-beam machines (and to some extent chemiluminescence machines) have been modified in various ways to explore even finer details of specific reactions. For example, electric and magnetic fields have been used to prepare reagents in various orientations or to determine the magnitude and polarization of the product rotational angular momentum; lasers have been used to prepare reagents in initial vibrational states and to determine the final vibration-rotation state of products by inducing fluorescence from the products; and reactions may be conducted at hyperthermal energies to produce dissociation or even ionization.

Advances in subnanosecond laser technology have made it possible to study a few bulk phase reactions under nearly collision-free circumstances. For example, H atoms can be formed by dissociating a hydrogen halide (HX) with a fast laser pulse, and reaction of the H can be monitored by a second pulse delayed enough to probe reaction products after only a few collisions. *See* ULTRAFAST MOLECULAR PROCESSES.

Information about chemical reactions has so far come from observations made on the disappearance of reagents or appearance of products. However, several experiments on systems such as $H + H_2$, K + NaCl, and ICN (iodine cyanide) have shown that it is possible to use lasers to probe the chemical system during the very short time in which the chemical bonds are rearranging. This forms the basis of a new spectroscopy of the transition region. *See* LASER PHOTOCHEMISTRY.

Unimolecular reactions. Unimolecular reactions are possible when the energy of an isolated molecule lies above the energy of the asymptotically separated products. Molecules were traditionally energized by collisions, and unimolecular reactions have been studied by using collisional excitation in both cross-beam and chemiluminescence experiments. Several laser methods—multiphoton excitation, stimulated emission pumping, and overtone excitation—can also be used to populate a very narrow range of energy levels in isolated molecules to study unimolecular reactions as well as the related process of photodissociation.

Considerable insight into unimolecular processes has been obtained. Energy initially deposited lo-

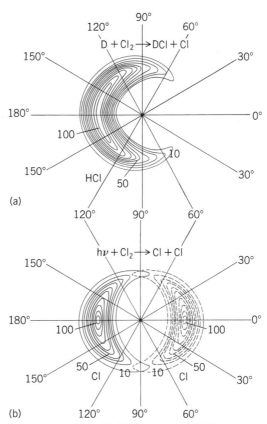

Fig. 4. Contour map of the DCl intensity. (*a*) Center-of-mass angular distribution of DCl from the reaction $D + Cl_2$. (*b*) Angular distribution of Cl atoms from photodissociation of Cl_2 molecules. Broken lines correspond to the second Cl atom. (*After D. R. Herschbach, Molecular dynamics of chemical reactions, Pure Appl. Chem. 47:61–73, 1976*)

cally is distributed on a picosecond time scale, and most processes seem to be described by a statistical model. Furthermore, bond-selective photochemistry (in which different reactions would occur for excitation of different molecular vibrations) seems unlikely, because reaction is usually slow compared to the energy redistribution process. *See* PHOTOCHEMISTRY.   Philip R. Brooks

Theoretical Methods

The goal of chemical dynamics is to understand kinetic phenomena from the basic laws of molecular mechanics, and it is thus a field which sees close interplay between experimental and theoretical research.

Energy distribution. An important question regarding the dynamics of chemical reactions has to do with the product energy distribution in exothermic reactions. For example, because the hydrogen fluoride (HF) molecule is more strongly bound than the H_2 molecule, reaction (6) releases a consider-

$$F + H_2 \rightarrow HF + H \qquad (6)$$

able amount of energy (more than 30 kcal/mol or 126 kJ/mol). The two possible paths for this energy release to follow are into translations, that is, with HF and H speeding away from each other, or into vibrational motion of HF.

In this case it is vibration, and this has rather dramatic consequences; the reaction creates a population inversion among the vibrational energy levels of HF—that is, the higher vibrational levels have more population than the lower levels—and the emission of infrared light from these excited vibrational levels can be made to form a chemical laser. A number of other reactions such as reaction (5) also give a population inversion among the vibrational energy levels, and can thus be used to make lasers.

Most effective energy. The rates of most chemical reactions are increased if they are given more energy. In macroscopic kinetics this corresponds to increasing the temperature, and most reactions are faster at higher temperatures. It seems reasonable, though, that some types of energy will be more effective in accelerating the reaction than others. For example, in reaction (7), where potassium

$$K + HCl \rightarrow KCl + H \qquad (7)$$

(K) reacts with hydrogen chloride (HCl) to form potassium chloride (KCl), studies in a molecular beam have shown that if HCl is vibrationally excited (by using a laser), this reaction is found to proceed approximately 100 times faster, while the same amount of energy in translational kinetic energy has a smaller effect. Here, therefore, vibrational energy is much more effective than translational energy in accelerating the reaction.

For reaction (6), however, translational energy is more effective than vibrational energy in accelerating the reaction. The general rule of thumb is that vibrational energy is more effective for endothermic reactions (those for which the new

molecule is less stable than the original molecule), while translational energy is most effective for exothermic reactions.

Lasers. As seen from above, lasers are also an important supplement to molecular-beam techniques for probing the dynamics of chemical reactions. Because they are light sources with a very narrow wavelength, they are able to excite molecules to specific quantum states (and also to detect what states molecules are in), an example of which is reaction (7). For polyatomic molecules—that is, those with more than two atoms—there is the even more interesting question of how the rate of reaction depends on which vibration is excited.

For example, when the molecule allyl isocyanide, $CH_2=CH-CH_2-NC$, is given sufficient vibrational energy, the isocyanide part ($-NC$) will rearrange to the cyanide ($-CN$) configuration. A laser can be used to excite a C-H bond vibrationally. An interesting question is whether the rate of the rearrangement process depends on which C-H bond is excited. Only with a laser is it possible to excite different C-H bonds and begin to answer such questions. This question of mode-specific chemistry, that is, the question of whether excitation of specific modes of a molecule causes specific chemistry to result, has been a subject of great interest. (For the example above, the reaction is fastest if the C-H bond closest to the NC group is excited.) Mode-specific chemistry would allow much greater control over the course of chemical reactions, and it would be possible to accelerate the rate of some reactions (or reactions at one part of a molecule) and not others. *See* LASER.

Models and methods. Many different theoretical models and methods have been useful in understanding and analyzing all of the phenomena described above. Probably the single most useful approach has been the calculation of classical trajectories. Assuming that the potential energy function or a reasonable approximation is known for the three atoms in reaction (6), for example, it is possible by use of electronic computers to calculate the classical

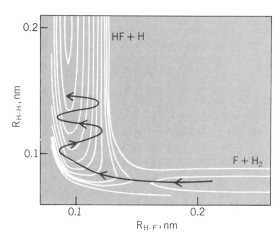

Fig. 5. Contour plot of the potential energy surface for the reaction F + H₂ = HF + H, with a typical reactive trajectory indicated.

motion of the three atoms. It is thus an easy matter to give the initial molecule more or less vibrational or translational energy, and then compute the probability of reaction. Similarly, the final molecule and atom can be studied to see where the energy appears, that is, as translation or as vibration.

It is thus a relatively straightforward matter theoretically to answer the questions and to see whether or not mode-specific excitation leads to significantly different chemistry than simply increasing the temperature under bulk conditions.

The most crucial step in carrying out these calculations is obtaining the potential energy surface—that is, the potential energy as a function of the positions of the atoms—for the system. **Figure 5** shows a plot of the contours of the potential energy surface for reaction (6). Even without carrying out classical trajectory calculations, it is possible to deduce some of the dynamical features of this reaction; for example, the motion of the system first surmounts a small potential barrier, and then it slides down a steep hill, turning the corner at the bottom of the hill. It is evident that such motion will cause much of the energy released in going down the hill to appear in vibrational motion of HF.

This and other theoretical methods have interacted strongly with experimental research in helping to understand the dynamics of chemical reactions. *See* INORGANIC PHOTOCHEMISTRY.

William H. Miller

Relaxation Methods

Considerable use has been made of perturbation techniques to measure rates and determine mechanisms of rapid chemical reactions. These methods provide measurements of chemical reaction rates by displacing equilibria. In situations where the reaction of interest occurs in a system at equilibrium, perturbation techniques called relaxation methods have been found most effective for determining reaction rate constants.

A chemical system at equilibrium is one in which the rate of a forward reaction is exactly balanced by the rate of the corresponding back reaction. Examples are chemical reactions occurring in liquid solutions, such as the familiar equilibrium in pure water, shown in reaction (8). The molar equilibrium

$$H_2O \underset{k_b}{\rightleftharpoons} H^+(aq) + OH^-(aq) \qquad (8)$$

constant at 25°C (77°F) is given by Eq. (9), where

$$K_{eq} = \frac{[H^+][OH^-]}{[H_2O]} = \frac{10^{-14}}{55.5} = 1.8 \times 10^{-16} \quad (9)$$

bracketed quantities indicate molar concentrations. It arises naturally from the equality of forward and backward reaction rates, Eq. (10). Here k_f and k_b

$$k_f[H_2O] = k_b[H^+][OH^-] \qquad (10)$$

are the respective rate constants that depend on temperature but not concentrations. Furthermore, the combination of Eqs. (9) and (10) gives rise

to Eq. (11). Thus a reasonable question might

$$K_{eq} = k_f/k_b = 1.8 \times 10^{-16} \qquad (11)$$

be what the numerical values of k_f in units of s^{-1} and k_b in units of dm^3 mol^{-1} s^{-1} must be to satisfy Eqs. (9) through (11) in water at room temperature. Stated another way, when a liter of 1 M hydrochloric acid is poured into a liter of 1 M sodium hydroxide (with considerable hazardous sputtering), how rapidly do the hydronium ions, $H^+(aq)$, react with hydroxide ions, $OH^-(aq)$, to produce a warm 0.5 M aqueous solution of sodium chloride? In the early 1950s it was asserted that such a reaction is instantaneous. Turbulent mixing techniques were (and still are) insufficiently fast (mixing time of the order of 1 ms) for this particular reaction to occur outside the mixing chamber. The relaxation techniques were conceived by M. Eigen, who accepted the implied challenge of measuring the rates of seemingly immeasurably fast reactions.

The essence of any of the relaxation methods is the perturbation of a chemical equilibrium (by a small change in temperature, pressure, electric-field intensity, or solvent composition) in so sudden a fashion that the chemical system, in seeking to reachieve equilibrium, is forced by the comparative slowness of the chemical reactions to lag behind the perturbation (**Fig. 6**).

Temperature jump. Reaction (8) has a nonzero standard enthalpy change, $\Delta H°$, associated with it, so that a small increase in the temperature of the water (H_2O) requires the concentrations of hydrogen ions [H$^+$] and hydroxide ions [OH$^-$] to increase slightly, and [H$_2$O] to decrease correspondingly, for chemical equilibrium to be restored at the new higher temperature. Thus a small sample cell containing a very pure sample of water may be made one arm of a Wheatstone conductance bridge, and further configured so that a pulse of energy from a microwave source (or infrared laser of appropriate wavelength) is dissipated in the sample liquid. The resulting rise in temperature of about 2°C (3.6°F) will produce a small increase in conductance that

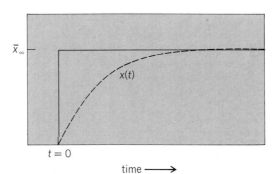

Fig. 6. Relaxational response to a rectangular step function in an external parameter such as temperature or pressure. The broken line represents the time course of the adjustment (relaxation) of the chemical equilibrium to the new temperature or pressure. (*After C. Bernasconi, Relaxation Kinetics, Academic Press, 1976*)

will have an exponential shape and a time constant or relaxation time $\tau \simeq 27$ microseconds; τ is the time required for the signal amplitude to drop to $1/e = 1/2.718$ of its initial value, where e is the base of natural logarithms.

In pure water at 25°C (77°F), $[H^+] = [OH^-] = 10^{-7} M$, and for small perturbations, the value for τ is given by Eq. (12), from which it follows

$$\begin{aligned} \tau^{-1} &= k_b([H^+] + [OH^-]) + k_f \\ &= k_b([H^+] + [OH^-] + K_{eq}) \end{aligned} \tag{12}$$

that $k_b \simeq 1.8 \times 10^{11}$ dm^3 mol^{-1} s^{-1}. This is an exceptionally large rate constant for a bimolecular reaction between oppositely charged ions in aqueous solution and is, in fact, larger than that for any other diffusive encounter between ions in water. Eigen and L. DeMaeyer, who first determined this rate constant (using another relaxation method called the electric-field jump method), attributed the great speed of the back reaction of the equilibrium, reaction (8), to the exceptionally rapid motion of a proton through water, accomplished by the successive rotations of a long string of neighboring water molecules (Grotthuss mechanism). Since sample solutions can be heated by a mode-locked laser on a picosecond time scale or by a bunsen burner on a time scale of minutes, the temperature jump (T-jump) relaxation method just described is very versatile. The choice of the particular means of effecting the temperature perturbation is dictated only by the requirement that the temperature rise somewhat more rapidly than the time constant of the chemical reaction to be explored, so that a tedious deconvolution can be avoided. The discharge of a high-voltage (15–30-kV) capacitor through the sample liquid containing sufficient inert electrolyte to make it a good electrical conductor is the now classic Joule heating T-jump method used by Eigen and coworkers in their pioneering studies. A schematic of such an apparatus is shown in **Fig. 7**. The 30-kV voltage generator charges the 0.1-microfarad condenser to the voltage at which the spark gap breaks down. The condenser then discharges across the spark gap

and through the sample cell, containing an aqueous 0.1 M ionic strength solution, to ground. The sample cell is an approximately 50 ml (3.05 in.^{3}) Plexiglas cell containing two platinum electrodes spaced 1 cm (0.4 in.) apart and immersed in an aqueous 0.1 M ionic strength solution. The surge of current raises the temperature of the 1-ml (0.061-in.^{3}) volume of solution between the electrodes by 10°C (18°F) in a few microseconds.

Electric-field jump. In a situation, such as reaction (8), in which electrically neutral reactant species dissociate into oppositely charged ions, an especially sensitive tool for measuring rate constants of forward and backward reactions is the electric-field jump (E-jump) technique with conductometric detection. In a strong electric field (of the order of 4 $\times 10^6$ V m^{-1}), a weak acid in solution is caused to dissociate to a greater degree than it would in the absence of the electric field. For weak electrolytes, such as aqueous acetic acid or ammonia, the effect is the order of 10% or less of the total normal dissociation, even at very high electric-field strengths. However, with a sensitive, high-voltage Wheatstone bridge, the exponential increase with time in the concentration of ions following a precipitous increase in electric-field strength is readily detected. The measured relaxation time (τ) is clearly that corresponding to the high-electric-field environment, but since the rate constants for these reactions differ little in and out of the electric field, no serious problem is posed.

A more serious concern is that the sample solution may have a very high electrical resistance, so that the supposedly square step function in the electric-field strength is not distorted by a significant voltage drop with concomitant heating of the sample liquid. Problems of working with high voltages, balancing capacitive and inductive effects in a very sensitive conductance bridge (now often circumvented by spectrophotometric detection), and the comparative difficulty of evaluating amplitudes of relaxations (as opposed to their readily determined time constants) are all factors that have worked against the wide use of the E-jump technique. There are many more ways of achieving a T-jump than an E-jump, and $\Delta H°$ values for chemical equilibria are readily available in the thermodynamic literature, whereas the extent to which a chemical equilibrium is displaced by an electric-field increment is rarely already known and is difficult to determine. Thus the commercialization of the T-jump method and the comparative neglect of the E-jump relaxation technique are readily understood.

Notwithstanding these difficulties, the E-jump technique is without peer for the investigation of the kinetics of solvent autoionization or for the exploration of the properties of weak electrolyte solutes in exotic solvents such as acetonitrile or xenon (the latter liquefied under a pressure of abou 50 atm or 5 megapascals), so long as the relaxation time to be measured lies in the range 30 nanoseconds $< \tau < 100$ μs.

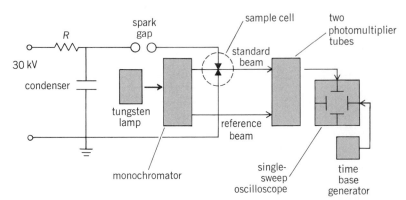

Fig. 7. Schematic of a Joule heating temperature-jump apparatus. (*After H. Eyring and E. M. Eyring, Modern Chemical Kinetics, Reinhold, 1963*)

Ultrasonic absorption. Two other relaxation methods more widely used than the E-jump technique are pressure jump (P-jump) and ultrasonic absorption. Each relies for its effectiveness on a volume change, $\Delta V°$, occurring in an aqueous sample equilibrium undergoing kinetic investigation. (In a nonaqueous solvent it will frequently be more important that $\Delta H°$ be large than that $\Delta V°$ be so for the equilibrium to be susceptible to study by these two relaxation techniques.) As electrically neutral, weak electrolyte solute species dissociate into ions in aqueous solution, there is an increase in the number of solvent molecules drawn into a highly ordered solvation sheath. The higher the charge density of the ion, the more water molecule dipoles are bound and the greater the change in $V°$ as reactants become products. Thus the dissociation of an aqueous neodymium(III) sulfate complex is particularly susceptible to study by one or more of the four or five ultrasonic absorption methods that cover the $f \simeq 100$ kHz–1 GHz sound frequency range. Unlike the T-jump and E-jump relaxation methods, which usually employ step function perturbations, the ultrasonic absorption techniques are continuous-wave experiments in which the sample chemical equilibrium absorbs a measurable amount of the sound wave's energy when the frequency of the sound wave (f) and the relaxation time of the chemical equilibrium bear the relation to one another given by Eq. (13).

$$\tau^{-1} = 2\pi f \qquad (13)$$

A particularly easy ultrasonic absorption experiment to understand and perform is the laser Debye-Sears technique. A continuously variable frequency sound wave is introduced by a quartz piezoelectric transducer into a 30-ml (1.83-in.^{3}) sample cell that has entrance and exit windows for a visible laser light beam that passes through the cell at about 90° to the direction of travel of the planar sound wave. The regions of compression and rarefaction in the sound wave act as a diffraction grating for the laser light beam. If a chemical equilibrium in the sample strongly absorbs a particular frequency of sound (f), the definition of the "diffraction grating" will deteriorate and the measured intensity of the first-order diffracted laser light will diminish. The frequency of minimum diffracted light intensity will be that of Eq. (12). **Figure 8** shows a diagram of the apparatus. The piezoelectric (quartz) tranducer cemented to the bottom of a plastic rod that is driven up and down by a stepping motor is controlled by a mini computer. The angle of diffraction of the laser beam by the alternating regions of compression and rarefaction in the liquid (suggested by the horizontal lines) is exaggerated in the diagram.

Ultrasonic absorption techniques have been used in kinetic investigations of complicated biophysical systems such as the order-disorder transitions that occur in liquid crystalline phospholipid membranes. While the ultrasonic techniques look through a conveniently broad time window at kinetic processes in solutions, this picture window is

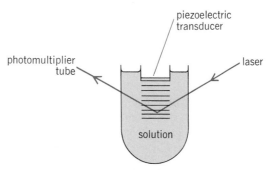

Fig. 8. Schematic of laser Debye-Sears apparatus for measuring ultrasonic absorption (about 15–300 MHz) in a sample liquid. (*After W. J. Gettins and E. Wyn-Jones, Techniques and Applications of Fast Reactions in Solution, D. Reidel, 1979*)

difficult to "see through" in that many equilibrium processes in solution can absorb sound energy and the responsible process is not instantly identified by a characteristic absorption of electromagnetic radiation as in a spectrophotometric T-jump or E-jump experiment. A further disadvantage arises from the great breadth of the ultrasonic absorption "peaks" in a plot of normalized sound absorption versus sound frequency. Unless multiple relaxation times in a chemical system are quite widely separated in time, they are difficult to resolve in an ultrasonic absorption spectrum. *See* ULTRASONICS.

Pressure jump. The typical pressure-jump (P-jump) experiment is one in which a liquid sample under about 200 atm (20 MPa) pressure is suddenly brought to atmospheric pressure by the bursting of a metal membrane in the sample cell autoclave. Relaxation times measured spectrophotometrically or conductometrically are thus accessible if $\tau > 100$ μs. This technique has proven particularly useful in the elucidation of micellar systems of great interest for catalysis and for petroleum recovery from apparently depleted oil fields.

The continuous- and stopped-flow techniques antedate somewhat the relaxation techniques described above, and have the sometimes important advantage of permitting kinetic measurements in chemical systems far from equilibrium. The stopped-flow experiment is one in which two different liquids in separate syringes are mixed rapidly in a tangential jet mixing chamber and then the rapid flow of mixed reactants is almost immediately brought to a halt in a spectrophotometric, conductometric, or calorimetric observation chamber. Reaction half-lives exceeding 2 ms are easily accessible. *See* SHOCK TUBE.

Other relaxation methods. Stopped-flow equipment has been used in concentration-jump and solvent-jump relaxation kinetic studies. An example of an application of the solvent-jump technique to a system insensitive to concentration-jump is a kinetic study of reaction (14) in mixed CCl_4–acetic

$$NOCl + n\text{BuOH} \rightarrow n\text{BuONO} + HCl \qquad (14)$$

acid solvents of varying composition (Bu = butyl). The thermodynamic treatment of the solvent jump is just about the only aspect of the presently known relaxation techniques that was not described in exhaustive detail by the earliest publications of Eigen and DeMaeyer. *See* CHEMICAL THERMODYNAMICS.

Edward M. Eyring

Bibliography. M. Baer (ed.), *Theory of Chemical Reaction Dynamics*, vol. 1, 1985; P. R. Brooks and E. F. Hayes, *State-to-State Chemistry*, ACS Symp. Ser. 56, 1977; F. A. Gianturco (ed.), *Collision Theory for Atoms and Molecules*, 1989; D. R. Herschbach, Molecular dynamics of elementary chemical reactions, *Angew. Chem. Int. Ed. Engl.*, 26:1221–1243, 1987; K. Kuchitsu (ed.), *Dynamics of Excited Molecules*, 1994; Y. T. Lee, Molecular beam studies of elementary chemical processes, *Angew. Chem. Int. Ed. Engl.*, 26:939–951, 1987; W. H. Miller (ed.), *Dynamics of Molecular Collisions*, 1976; P. Sykes, *A Guidebook to Mechanism in Organic Chemistry*, 6th ed., 1986; A. H. Zewail, *Femtochemistry: Ultrafast Dynamics of the Chemical Bond*, vols. 1 and 2, 1994.

Chemical ecology

The study of ecological interactions mediated by the chemicals that organisms produce. These substances, known as allelochemicals, serve a variety of functions, the growing list of which reflects the rapid discoveries made in this discipline. These compounds influence or regulate interspecific and intraspecific interactions of microorganisms, plants, and animals, and operate within and between all trophic levels—producers, consumers, and decomposers—and in terrestrial, fresh-water, and marine ecosystems.

Function is an important criterion for the classification of allelochemicals. Allelochemicals beneficial to the emitter are called allomones; those beneficial to the recipient are called kairomones. An allomone to one organism can be a kairomone to another. For example, floral scents benefit the plant (allomones) by encouraging pollinators, but also benefit the insect (kairomones) by providing a cue for the location of nectar.

The chemicals involved are diverse in structure and are often of low molecular weight (<10,000). They may be volatile (for example, monoterpene essential oils from peppermint, cyanide from trefoil, musks of mammals, mustard oils from cabbage, aldehyde pheromones in insects) or nonvolatile (such as nicotine alkaloids in tobacco, flavonoids in most plants), and water-soluble (phenols in many insect defenses) or fat-soluble (leaf waxes). Proteins, polypeptides, and amino acids are also found to play an important role.

Plant allelochemicals are often called secondary compounds or metabolites to distinguish them from those chemicals involved in primary metabolism, although this distinction is not always clear. The functions of secondary chemicals were a mystery until 1959, when G. Fraenkel emphasized their potential importance in the interactions of plants and animals. The role of chemicals in the ecology of microorganisms and of animals was recognized earlier: since the discovery of penicillin, scientists have known that fungi can produce substances that destroy bacteria, and the odors of such animals as stink bugs and skunks serve an obvious function.

Chemical defense in plants. Perhaps to compensate for their immobility, plants have made wide use of chemicals for protection against competitors, pathogens, herbivores, and abiotic stresses.

Production of defenses by plants is not cost-free; it requires energy that could be used for other purposes. Although the actual cost is usually not known, many plants do concentrate defensive compounds in those tissues that contain the highest energy reserves or growth potential, such as new leaves or seeds. Some plants may also change the amount of resources used for defense, in response to changes in their environment, and the availability of the raw materials for making defenses, for example, carbon from photosynthesis and nitrogen from soil.

Allelopathy. A chemically mediated competitive interaction between higher plants is referred to as allelopathy. This is one of the few examples in plants where the effects of chemicals can be obvious: observations that areas around the bases of walnut trees are free of plant growth led to the first description of allelopathy. In walnuts, the mechanism involves leaching of the chemical juglone (5-hydroxy napthoquinone) from the leaves to the ground, and this inhibits growth and germination of a variety of plants. Allelopathy appears to occur in many plants, may involve phenolics or terpenoids that are modified in the soil by microorganisms, and is at least partly responsible for the organization of some plant communities. *See* ALLELOPATHY.

Active and passive defenses. Chemicals that are mobilized in response to stress or attack are referred to as active or inducible chemicals, while those that are always present in the plant are referred to as passive or constitutive. In many plants, fungus attack induces the production of defensive compounds called phytoalexins, a diverse chemical group that includes isoflavonoids, terpenoids, polyacetylenes, and furanocoumarins. The phytoalexin is produced in the area immediately surrounding the fungus and probably acts by interfering with the nutrition or membrane permeability of the fungal cells. Plant susceptibility to fungus attack is partly related to the speed of production of phytoalexins. *See* PHYTOALEXINS.

Defensive chemicals can be induced by herbivore attack. For example, when snowshoe hares feed on paper birch there is an increase in the levels of phenolic resins in new growth. These levels decrease with time, and the activity of these induced chemicals is thought to cause population cycles of hares. There has been increasing evidence that inducible defenses, such as phenolics, are important in plant–insect interactions.

Constitutive defenses include the chemical hydrogen cyanide. Trefoil, clover, and ferns have been found to exist in two genetically different forms, one containing cyanide (cyanogenic) and one lacking it (acyanogenic); acyanogenic forms are often preferred by several herbivores. Acacia trees also have these two forms; the acyanogenic forms are protected from herbivores by ants that live in the tree and feed on special food bodies on the leaves. Other constitutive chemicals include some phenolic acids, flavonoids, pyrethrins, and alkaloids. *See* ALKALOID; FLAVONOID; PHENOL.

Diversity of activities. Chemical defenses frequently occur together with certain structures which act as physical defenses, such as spines and hairs. In tomatoes, glandular trichomes (hairlike structures) on the leaf surface contain the toxic chemical 2-tridecanone that is active against many insects, while other glands contain phenolics that polymerize like fast-setting glue.

While many chemicals protect plants by deterring herbivore feeding or by direct toxic effects, other defenses may act more indirectly. Chemicals that mimic juvenile hormones, the antijuvenile hormone substances found in some plants, either arrest development or cause premature development in certain susceptible insect species.

Plant chemicals potentially affect not only the herbivores that feed directly on the plant, but also the microorganisms, predators, or parasites of the herbivore. For example, the tomato plant contains an alkaloid, tomatine, that is effective against certain insect herbivores. The tomato hornworm, however, is capable of detoxifying this alkaloid and can thus use the plant successfully—but a wasp parasite of the hornworm cannot detoxify tomatine, and its effectiveness in parasitizing the hornworm is reduced. Therefore, one indirect effect of the chemical in the plant may be to reduce the effectiveness of natural enemies of the plant pest, thereby actually working to the disadvantage of the plant.

Types of plant defenses. Most plant chemicals can affect a wide variety of herbivores and microorganisms, because the modes of action of the chemicals they manufacture are based on a similarity of biochemical reaction in most target organisms (for example, cyanide is toxic to most organisms). In addition, many plant chemicals may serve multiple roles: resins in the creosote bush serve to defend against herbivores and pathogens, conserve water, and protect against ultraviolet radiation.

It is argued that there are two different types of defensive chemicals in plants. The first type occurs in relatively small amounts, is often toxic in small doses, and poisons the herbivore. These compounds, for example, some phenolic acids, alkaloids, and monoterpenes, may also change in concentration in response to plant damage; that is, they are inducible. These kinds of qualitative defensive compounds are the most common in short-lived or weedy species that are often referred to as unapparent. They are also characteristic of fast-growing species with short-lived leaves. In contrast, the second type of defensive chemicals often occurs in high concentrations, is not very toxic, but may inhibit digestion by herbivores and is not very inducible. These quantitative defenses, such as tannins, are most common in long-lived, so-called apparent plants such as trees that have slow growth rates and long-lived leaves. Some plants may use both types of defenses.

Aquatic habitats. There is accumulating evidence that marine plants may be protected against grazing by similar classes of chemicals to those found in terrestrial plants. In algae, for example, phenols appear to be an important defense against limpets. One interesting difference in the marine environment is the large number of halogenated organic compounds that are rare in terrestrial and fresh-water systems.

Evolution of defenses and adaptation. Through evolution, as plants accumulate defenses, herbivores that are able to bypass the defense in some way are selected for and leave more offspring than others. This in turn selects for new defenses on the part of the plant in a continuing process called coevolution.

Animals that can exploit many plant taxa are called generalists, while those that are restricted to one or a few taxa are called specialists. Specialists often have particular detoxification mechanisms to deal with specific defenses. For example, certain bruchid beetles that feed on seeds containing the toxic nonprotein amino acid canavanine possess enzyme systems that recognize this "false" amino acid and avoid incorporating it into proteins. In addition, they are able to convert the amino acid to ammonia via urea and generate energy in the process. Some generalists possess powerful, inducible detoxification enzymes, while others exhibit morphological adaptations of the gut which prevent absorption of compounds such as tannins, or provide reservoirs for microorganisms that accomplish the detoxification. Animals may avoid eating plants, or parts of plants, with toxins. For instance, monkeys choose low-toxin, high-nutrient plant tissues and are capable of learning which plants to avoid.

Some herbivores that have completely surmounted the plant toxin barrier use the toxin itself as a cue to aid in locating plants. The common white butterfly, *Pieris rapae*, for example, uses mustard oil glycosides, which are a deterrent and toxic to many organisms, to find its mustard family hosts. The monarch butterfly and other insects have gone so far as to store plant defensive chemicals in their bodies as protection against predators.

Chemical defense in animals. Many animals make their own defensive chemicals—such as all of the venoms produced by social insects (bees, wasps, ants), as well as snakes and mites. These venoms are usually proteins, acids or bases, alkaloids, or combinations of chemicals. They are generally injected by biting or stinging, while other defenses are produced as sprays, froths, or droplets from glands. For instance, the bombardier beetle expels hot quinones as a spray from its posterior. A response of one predatory mouse to this action is to bury the beetle's dangerous posterior into the sand before biting the head. There are also darkling beetles that mimic the bombardier's actions but do not have a defensive spray. While insects provide the best examples of chemical defense in animals, such defenses are also found in other groups, such as in stinging cells of jellyfish and in poisonous spurs on the duckbill platypus.

Animals frequently make the same types of toxins as plants, presumably because their function as protective agents is similar. Examples include the production of cyanide by millipedes and bracken fern, phenols in the secretions of grasshoppers and in most plant leaves, alkaloids in ant venoms and pepper plants, and cardiac glycosides in milkweed plants and beetles.

Other organisms, particularly insects, use plant chemicals to defend themselves. For example, the monarch butterfly sequesters or stores cardenolides from the milkweed plant, and the lubber grasshopper can sequester a variety of plant chemicals into its defensive secretion by feeding exclusively on certain plants. Sequestration may be a low-cost defense mechanism and probably arises when insects specialize on particular plants.

Microbial defenses. Competitive microbial interactions are regulated by many chemical exchanges involving toxins. They include compounds such as aflatoxin, botulinus toxin, odors of rotting food, hallucinogens, and a variety of antibiotics. *See* ANTIBIOTIC; TOXIN.

Microorganisms also play a role in chemical interaction with plants and animals that range from the production of toxins that kill insects, such as those produced by the common biological pest control agent *Bacillus thuringiensis*, to cooperative biochemical detoxification of plant toxins by animal symbionts.

Information exchange. A large area of chemical ecology concerns the isolation and identification of chemicals used for communication.

Insects. Pheromones, substances produced by an organism that induce a behavioral or physiological response in an individual of the same species, have been studied particularly well in insects. These signals are compounds that are mutually beneficial to the emitter and sender, such as sex attractants, trail markers, and alarm and aggregation signals.

Sex pheromones are volatile substances, usually produced by the female to attract males. Each species has a characteristic compound that may differ from that of other species by as little as a few atoms. For example, the pheromone of the cabbage looper moth is *cis*-7-dodecenyl acetate; the oriental fruit fly's is *cis*-8-dodecenyl acetate. The activity of these compounds can be destroyed by minor changes in their structure. In addition, sex pheromones generally are active at extremely low concentrations—a few molecules impinging on a moth's antenna may be sufficient to stimulate a response. The pheromone blend released by a female moth may be dominated by one or two components but also contains many trace components. The dominant compounds may attract males, but the full repertoire of male behavior that results in successful mating also involves the trace components.

Pheromones are typically synthesized directly by the animal and are usually derived from fatty acids. In a few cases the pheromone or its immediate precursors may be derived from plants, as in danaid butterflies. Male danaids visit certain nonhost plants solely to obtain pyrrolizidine alkaloids, which are used to make pheromones used in courtship.

Trail pheromones are used by social insects and some lepidopterans to recruit others of its species to a food source. These are synthesized by the animal as well as acquired from hosts, and are diverse in structure. The honeybee uses geraniol, which it acquires from nectar. Methyl 4-methylpyrrole 2-carboxylate, the trail pheromone of the leaf-cutting ant, may be synthesized in the gut by bacteria. The ideal trail pheromone loses its potency over time unless reinforced, and is therefore relatively unstable and difficult to analyze chemically. *See* PHEROMONE.

Vertebrates. Very little work has been done in identifying specific pheromones in vertebrates, particularly mammals. It is known, however, that they are important in marking territory, in individual recognition, and in mating and warning signals. Frequently these signals involve sebaceous oils from the skin, urine, or feces. Some mammals have a very complex series of glands; it is possible that microorganisms on these glands convert urine compounds to components of the signal chemical. The complexity of this chemical mix, and the complexity of the animal, means that the strong positive or negative response to single compounds that is found in some insects is not found as often in mammalian systems. In female primates of several species, mixtures of short-chain organic acids, such as acetic and butanoic, lead to sexual excitation in the male. These same chemicals have been found in human females, but in different concentrations. *See* REPRODUCTIVE BEHAVIOR; SCENT GLAND; TERRITORIALITY.

Plants and microorganisms. Chemical communication may also occur among plants and microorganisms, although it is rarer and less obvious than in animals. The release of ethylene by ripening fruit stimulates the ripening of nearby fruit, thus ensuring simultaneous presentation of an attractive mass for potential dispersers. Certain plants produce high concentrations of volatile isoprenes. The concentrations and composition of these compounds change under stress, but it is not known whether this signal, if it is one, is recognized by other plants.

Bacterial contact and recognition is accomplished by cell wall proteins and by secretions. This type of communication is important in strain recognition, and also takes place in fungi such as *Mucor* prior to mating. Here chemical communication is at the cellular level.

Value. The chemicals involved in chemical interactions between organisms are important in the pharmaceutical, perfume, and many other chemical industries. These substances, together with many antibiotics and pesticides, are based on compounds found in plants. However, information about chemical ecology is only just beginning to be exploited, particularly in the field of plant protection. For example, pheromones which are highly specific and nontoxic are used to trap insect pests for a variety of purposes, including monitoring and population reduction. As the mechanisms of pathogen resistance are understood, the proper chemical attributes may be bred or genetically engineered into plants. For example, the genes for production of a legume seed protein toxin have been transferred to tobacco leaves. The genes were expressed and the leaves became protected from insect attack. The potential for exploiting naturally occurring defenses may thus reduce reliance on costly, potentially hazardous synthetic chemicals. *See* ECOLOGY; GENETIC ENGINEERING; INSECT CONTROL, BIOLOGICAL; INSECTICIDE. Clive G. Jones; Alcinda C. Lewis

Bibliography. W. G. Abrahamson (ed.), *Plant-Animal Interactions*, 1989; W. J. Bell and R. T. Curde (eds.), *Chemical Ecology of Insects,* 1984; M. S. Blum, *Chemical Defenses of Arthropods,* 1981; R. F. Denno and M. S. McClure (eds.), *Variable Plants and Herbivores in Natural and Managed Systems*, 1983; J. B. Harborne, *Introduction to Ecological Biochemistry*, 1982; D. H. Nordlund, R. L. Jones, and W. J. Lewis (eds.), *Semiochemicals: Their Role in Pest Control*, 1981; G. A. Rosenthal and D. H. Janzen (eds.), *Herbivores: Their Interaction with Secondary Plant Metabolites* 1979.

Chemical energy

In most chemical reactions, heat is either taken in or given out. By the law of conservation of energy, the increase or decrease in heat energy must be accompanied by a corresponding decrease or increase in some other form of energy. This other form is the chemical energy of the compounds involved in the reaction. The rearrangement of the atoms in the reacting compounds to produce new compounds causes a change in chemical energy. This change in chemical energy is equal numerically and of opposite sign to the heat change accompanying the reaction.

Most of the world's available power comes from the combustion of coal or of petroleum hydrocarbons. The chemical energy released as heat when a specified weight, often 1 g, of a fuel is burned is called the calorific value of the fuel.

Depending on whether the pressure or volume of the system is kept constant, differing quantities of heat are liberated in a chemical reaction. The heat of reaction at constant pressure q_p is equal to minus the change in the chemical energy at constant pressure ΔH, called the change in the enthalpy; the heat of reaction at constant volume q_v is equal to minus the change in the chemical energy at constant volume ΔE, called the change in the internal energy. *See* ENTHALPY; INTERNAL ENERGY; THERMOCHEMISTRY.

It is not possible to measure an absolute value for the chemical energy of a compound; only changes in chemical energy can be measured. It is therefore necessary to make some arbitrary assumption as a starting point. One such assumption would be to take the chemical energies of the free atoms as zero and measure the chemical energies of all elements and compounds relative to this standard. If this were done, all chemical energies would then be negative quantities. Heat is given out when all elements and compounds are formed from their atoms. Since chemical energy can be regarded as a form of potential energy, it is interesting that the formation of chemical bonds is always accompanied by a decrease of potential energy. The reason, in qualitative terms at least, lies in the quantum theory. When chemical bonds are formed between atoms, for example, in the formation of a chlorine molecule from two chlorine atoms, electrons are shared between the two atoms, and this electron-sharing produces a lowering of the potential energies of the shared electrons, and thus, lowering of the potential energy of the molecule relative to the free atoms.

Although it would be more fundamental to take the chemical energies of the separated atoms as zero, in practice it is more convenient to take a more arbitrary starting point and to assume that the chemical energies of the elements are zero. For precision, the standard states of the elements at 77°F (25°C) and 1 atm (100 kilopascals) pressure are chosen. Thus, in the case of carbon the chemical energy of graphite, not diamond, is said to be zero at these states. Diamond then has a definite enthalpy value. *See* CHEMICAL EQUILIBRIUM; CHEMICAL THERMODYNAMICS; ENERGY SOURCES.

Thomas C. Waddington

Chemical engineering

A branch of engineering which involves the design and operation of large-scale chemical plants, petroleum refineries, and the like. In such industries, chemical engineers work in production, research, design, process and product development, marketing studies, data processing, sales, and, almost invariably, throughout top management. Chemical engineering ranks as the fourth most popular form of engineering, following electrical, civil, and mechanical (the latter three not necessarily in order).

The American Institute of Chemical Engineers (AIChE) has identified the 10 most outstanding achievements of chemical engineering as being production of fissionable isotopes, synthetic ammonia, petrochemicals, and chemical fertilizers, commercial-scale production of antibiotics, establishment of the plastics industry, establishment of the synthetic fibers industry and the synthetic rubber industry, development of high-octane gasoline, and electrolytic production of aluminum. Chemical engineering is also involved in a major way in nuclear energy, medicine, materials science, food production, space, undersea exploration, and, above all, in energy production and the development of new sources of energy. *See* CHEMICAL CONVERSION; CHEMICAL PROCESS INDUSTRY.

Associations and education. Chemical engineers are represented in the United States by the AIChE, which has over 70,000 members. It was founded in 1908. In other countries, chemical engineers are represented by national organizations such as the Canadian Society for Chemical Engineering, and the Institution of Chemical Engineers in Britain. About three-quarters of all chemical engineers work in private industry, with most of the others in government, education, and so on, or self-employed. There are probably 200,000 to 300,000 chemical engineers worldwide; they affect or control at some stage the materials or production of almost every article manufactured on an industrial scale.

The university education of a chemical engineer takes 4 years to the bachelor's degree, in common with most other forms of engineering. The proportion of chemical engineers who go on to master's and doctorate degrees, however, has been much higher over the years than for electrical, civil, or mechanical engineers.

Scope. Chemical engineering is broader in scope than electrical, civil, or mechanical engineering, for it draws more or less equally on the three main engineering cornerstones of mathematics, physics, and chemistry, while the other professions are based primarily on only the first two. The AIChE describes chemical engineering as "that branch of engineering concerned with the development and application of manufacturing processes in which chemical or certain physical changes of materials are involved … Chemistry, physics, and mathematics are the underlying sciences of chemical engineering, and economics its guide in practice." The chemical engineer is considered an engineering generalist because of a unique ability (among engineers) to understand and exploit chemical change. Familiar with all forms of matter and energy and their manipulation, the chemical engineer leaves detailed specialization in one area of technology, such as construction, machine design, or electronics to others.

Evolution of the discipline. Chemical engineering is the newest of the four big engineering professions

to develop, with its first attempts to emerge as a profession separate from chemistry occurring barely a century ago. Chemical engineering evolved from two main roots. The earlier one was industrial chemistry, in which the work of the chemical engineer emerged from that previously done by a team consisting of a chemist and a mechanical engineer. This emergence took place in England beginning in the 1880s, later in France, and not until fairly recently in Germany. The other main root, while also first described in England, was primarily an American innovation of the early twentieth century, and consisted of a unified approach to the unit operations. These were the physical separations such as distillation, absorption, and extraction, in which the principles of mass transfer, fluid dynamics, and heat transfer were combined in equipment design. The chemical and physical aspects of chemical engineering are known as unit processes and unit operations, respectively.

Although chemical engineering was conceived primarily in England, it underwent its main development in America, propelled at first by the petroleum and heavy-chemical industries, and later by the petrochemical industry with its production of plastics, synthetic rubber, and synthetic fibers from petroleum and natural-gas starting materials. As the supplies of petroleum and natural gas inexorably diminish in the world, chemical engineering research becomes increasingly important in the development of new energy sources and their large-scale implementation. *See* BIOCHEMICAL ENGINEERING; BIOMEDICAL CHEMICAL ENGINEERING; CHEMICAL PROCESS INDUSTRY; ELECTROCHEMICAL PROCESS; FOOD ENGINEERING; INDUSTRIAL FACILITIES; METAL AND MINERAL PROCESSING; NUCLEAR POWER; PILOT PRODUCTION; UNIT OPERATIONS; UNIT PROCESSES.   William F. Furter

Bibliography. W. F. Furter (ed.), *A Century of Chemical Engineering*, 1982; W. F. Furter (ed.), *History of Chemical Engineering*, ACS Advances in Chemistry Series, no. 190, 1980; S. Furusaki and J. Garside (eds.), *The Expanding World of Chemical Engineering*, 1994; D. Green (ed.), *Perry's Chemical Engineers' Handbook*, 6th ed., 1984; A. Heaton (ed.), *The Chemical Industry*, 2d ed., 1994.

Chemical equilibrium

In a dynamic or kinetic sense, chemical equilibrium is a condition in which a chemical reaction is occurring at equal rates in its forward and reverse directions, so that the concentrations of the reacting substances do not change with time. In a thermodynamic sense, it is the condition in which there is no tendency for the composition of the system to change; no change can occur in the system without the expenditure of some form of work upon it. From the viewpoint of statistical mechanics, the equilibrium state places the system in a condition of maximum freedom (or minimum restraint) compatible with the energy, volume, and composition of the system. The statistical approach has been merged with thermodynamics into a field called statistical thermodynamics; this merger has been of immense value for its intellectual stimulus, as well as for its practical contributions to the study of equilibria. *See* CHEMICAL THERMODYNAMICS; STATISTICAL MECHANICS.

Of the three viewpoints, the thermodynamic approach is by far the most powerful and fruitful in treating the quantitative relationships between the position of equilibrium and the factors which govern it. Since thermodynamics is concerned with relationships among observable properties, such as temperature, pressure, concentration, heat, and work, the relationships possess general validity, independent of theories of molecular behavior. Because of the simplicity of the concepts involved, this article will utilize that approach.

Chemical potential. Thermodynamics attributes to each chemical substance a property called the chemical potential, which may be thought of as the tendency of the substance to enter into chemical (or physical) change. Although the chemical potential of a substance cannot be directly measured (except on a relative basis), differences in chemical potential are measurable. (The units are those of energy per mole.)

The importance of the chemical potential lies in its relation to the affinity or driving force of a chemical reaction. Consider general reaction (1). Let

$$aA + bB \rightleftharpoons gG + hH \qquad (1)$$

μ_A be the chemical potential per mole of substance A, μ_B be the chemical potential per mole of B, and so on. Then, according to one of the fundamental principles of thermodynamics (the second law), the reaction will be spontaneous when the total chemical potential of the reactants is greater than that of the products. Thus, for spontaneous change (naturally occurring processes), notation (2) applies. When equilibrium is reached, the

$$[g\mu_G + h\mu_H] - [a\mu_A + b\mu_B] < 0 \qquad (2)$$

total chemical potentials of products and reactants become equal; thus Eq. (3) holds at equilibrium.

$$[g\mu_G + h\mu_H] - [a\mu_A + b\mu_B] = 0 \qquad (3)$$

The difference in chemical potentials in Eqs. (2) and (3) is called the driving force or affinity of the process or reaction; naturally, it is zero when the chemical system is in chemical equilibrium.

For reactions at constant temperature and pressure (the usual restraints in a chemical laboratory), the difference in chemical potentials becomes equal to the free energy change ΔG for the process in Eq. (4). The decrease in free energy

$$\Delta G = [g\mu_G + h\mu_H] - [a\mu_A + b\mu_B] \qquad (4)$$

represents the maximum net work obtainable from the process. When no more work is obtainable, the

system is at equilibrium. Conversely, if the value of ΔG for a process is positive, some useful work will have to be expended upon the process, or reaction, in order to make it proceed; the process cannot proceed naturally or spontaneously. (The term spontaneously as used here implies only that a process can occur. It does not imply that the reaction will be rapid or instantaneous. Thus, the reaction between hydrogen and oxygen is a spontaneous process in the sense of the term as used here, even though a mixture of hydrogen and oxygen can remain unchanged for years unless ignited or exposed to a catalyst.)

Since by definition a catalyst remains unchanged chemically throughout a reaction, its chemical potential does not appear in Eqs. (2), (3), and (4). A catalyst, therefore, can contribute nothing to the driving force of a reaction, nor can it, in consequence, alter the position of the chemical equilibrium in a system. *See* CATALYSIS.

In addition to furnishing a criterion for the equilibrium state of a chemical system, the thermodynamic method goes much further. In many cases, it yields a relation between the change in chemical potentials (or change in free energy) and the equilibrium concentrations of the substances involved in the reaction. To do this, the chemical potential must be expressed as a function of concentration (and other properties of the substance).

The chemical potential μ is usually represented by Eq. (5), where R is the ideal gas constant, T is

$$\mu = \mu^0 + RT \ln x + RT \ln f \qquad (5)$$

the absolute temperature, $\ln x = \log_e x = 2.3026 \log_{10} x$, x is the concentration of the substance, f is the activity coefficient of the substance, and μ^0 is the chemical potential of the substance in its standard state. *See* CONCENTRATION SCALES.

For substances obeying the laws of ideal solutions (or ideal gases), the last term, $RT \ln f$, is zero, since it is a measure of the deviation from ideal behavior caused by intermolecular or interionic forces. An ideal solution would then be a solution for which $RT \ln f$ is zero over the whole concentration range. For real solutions, the ideal or reference state where f is unity is generally chosen as a state of ideal purity (mole fraction = 1) for solids and solvents, and as a state of infinite dispersion (concentration = 0) for gases and solutes. Although the activity coefficient f is regarded as dimensionless, its numerical values will depend upon the particular concentration scale x with which it must be associated.

Although the choice of concentration scales is somewhat a matter of convenience, the following are conventionally used: $x = p =$ partial pressure, for gases; $x = c$ or $m =$ molar or molal concentrations, for solutes in electrolytic solutions; $x =$ mole fraction, for solids and solvents. When the choice is not established by convention, the mole fraction scale is to be preferred.

Activity and standard states. It is often convenient to utilize the product, fx, called the activity of the substance and defined by $a = fx$. The activity may be looked upon as an effective concentration of the substance, measured in the same units as the concentration x with which it is associated. The standard state of the substance is then defined as the state of unit activity (where $a = 1$) and is characterized by the standard chemical potential μ^0. Clearly, the terms μ^0, f, and x are not independent; the choice of the activity scale serves to fix the standard state. For example, for an aqueous solution of hydrochloric acid, the standard state for the solute (HCl) would be an (hypothetical) ideal 1 molar (or molal) solution, and for the solvent (H$_2$O) the standard state would be pure water (mole fraction = 1). The reference state would be an infinitely dilute solution; here the activity coefficients would be unity for both solute and solvent. For the vapor of HCl above the solution, the standard state would be the ideal gaseous state at 1 atm (100 kilopascals) partial pressure; the reference state would be a state of zero pressure. (For gases, the term fugacity is used instead of activity.) It should be noted that the reference state is a limiting state which in many cases can be reached only through an extrapolation from observed behavior. *See* FUGACITY.

Equilibrium constant. If the general reaction in Eq. (1) occurs at constant temperature T and pressure P when all of the substances involved are in their standard states of unit activity, Eq. (4) would become Eq. (6). The quantity ΔG° is

$$\Delta G^\circ = [g\mu_G^0 + h\mu_H^0] - [a\mu_A^0 + b\mu_B^0] \qquad (6)$$

known as the standard free energy change for the reaction at that temperature and pressure for the chosen standard states. (Standard state properties are commonly designated by a superscript, ΔG°, μ^0.) Since each of the standard chemical potentials (μ^0) is a unique property determined by the temperature, pressure, standard state, and chemical identity of the substance concerned, the standard free energy change ΔG° is a constant (parameter) characteristic of the particular reaction for the chosen temperature, pressure, and standard states.

If, in a reaction, Eq. (1), at constant temperature and pressure, the chemical potential of each substance is expressed in terms of Eq. (5), the free energy change for the reaction, from Eq. (4), becomes Eq. (7) in terms of the activities and the

$$\Delta G = \Delta G^\circ + RT \ln \frac{a_G^g a_H^h}{a_A^a a_B^b} \qquad (7)$$

standard free energy change, Eq. (6). Equation (7) is often written in the form of Eq. (8), where Q^0 is the

$$\Delta G = \Delta G^\circ + RT \ln Q^0 \qquad (8)$$

ratio of the activities of products to the activities of reactants, each activity bearing as an exponent the corresponding coefficient in the balanced equation for the reaction. The standard free energy change

ΔG° serves as a reference point from which the actual free energy change ΔG can be calculated in terms of the activities of the reacting substances.

When the system has come to chemical equilibrium at constant temperature and pressure, $\Delta G = 0$, from Eq. (3). Equation (7) then leads to the very important relation shown in Eq. (9), where the value of K^0 is shown as Eq. (10), and the activities are

$$\Delta G^\circ = -RT \ln K^0 \qquad (9)$$

$$K^0 = \left[\frac{a_G^g a_H^h}{a_A^a a_B^b} \right] \qquad (10)$$

the equilibrium values. The ratio of the activities at equilibrium, K^0, is called the equilibrium constant or, more precisely, the thermodynamic equilibrium constant. (The terms K^0 and Q^0 are written with superscripts to emphasize that they represent ratios of activities.) The equilibrium constant is a characteristic property of the reaction system, since it is determined uniquely in terms of the standard free energy change. The term $-\Delta G^\circ 0$ represents the maximum net work which the reaction could make available when carried out at constant temperature and pressure with the substances in their standard states. It should be clear from Eq. (6) that the magnitude of ΔG° is directly proportional to the amount of material represented in the reaction in Eq. (1). Likewise, Eqs. (7) to 10 denote this same proportionality through the exponents a, b, g, and h in the terms K^0 and Q^0. Naturally, the value of ΔG°, as well as K^0 and Q^0, will depend upon the particular concentration scales and standard states selected for the system, so it is essential that sufficient information be stated about a system to prevent any ambiguity.

Equations (8) and (10) can be combined in the form of Eq. (11). When Q^0 for a specified

$$\Delta G = RT \ln \frac{Q^0}{K^0} \qquad (11)$$

set of conditions is larger than K^0 (so that ΔG is positive), the proposed reaction cannot occur. On the other hand, when Q^0 is less than K^0, the proposed process or reaction can occur. The equilibrium constant thus serves as a measure of the position of chemical equilibrium for a system. For the proposed process for which Q^0 is greater than K^0, the reaction system would be moving away from its equilibrium state (impossible of its own accord!), and for a proposed process for which Q^0 is less than K^0, the process would bring the system closer to its equilibrium state (as in all naturally occurring processes).

Instead of activities, values of concentrations and activity coefficients at equilibrium may be used to express the form of the equilibrium constant K^0 in Eq. (12). This gives the equilibrium constant as a

$$K^0 = \left[\frac{x_G^g x_H^h}{x_A^a x_B^b} \right] \cdot \left[\frac{f_G^g f_H^h}{f_A^a f_B^b} \right] \qquad (12)$$

product of two terms, each of the same form as

K^0 itself. The first term, involving concentrations, is directly measurable if the system can be analyzed at equilibrium. On the other hand, the activity coefficient term, as seen in Eq. (13), is frequently difficult to evaluate.

$$\Gamma = \frac{f_G^g f_H^h}{f_A^a f_B^b} \tag{13}$$

Intensive studies of activity coefficients made upon a wide variety of chemical systems led to a number of simplifying principles and some useful theoretical treatments of the subject. For gases, the activity coefficients differ only slightly from unity for pressures up to 10 atm (1 megapascal) and can be evaluated from equation-of-state data. For mixtures of nonelectrolytes, the values also appear to be close to unity in many cases. For solutions of electrolytes, the activity coefficients vary greatly with concentration, and in many cases approach unity only below a useful or even meaningful concentration. The theoretical treatments of P. Debye, E. Hückel, and others have systematized the patterns of electrolyte behavior, making possible a reasonable estimate of the activity coefficients in many cases. *See* ACTIVITY (THERMODYNAMICS); SOLUTION.

In general, the function Γ, Eq. (13), approaches unity as the composition of the system approaches that of the reference state, so in practice most equilibrium constants K^0 are evaluated through some suitable extrapolation procedure involving Eq. (12). See the discussion following Eq. (5).

For many approximate calculations or when data for Γ are scarce, it is common to express the equilibrium constant as the concentration term only; that is, Eq. (14) holds. Unless Γ is a rather

$$K = \frac{x_G^g x_H^h}{x_A^a x_B^b} \tag{14}$$

insensitive function of concentration, the so-called constants obtained in this manner will not be constant at all as the composition is varied, and even though approximately constant, may vary considerably from the true value of K^0. Although the practice of assigning Γ a value of unity will often give adequate results and is frequently the only expedient available, the results should be used with caution.

It is appropriate to point out here that the kinetic concept of chemical equilibrium introduced by C. M. Guldberg and P. Waage (1864) led to the formulation of the equilibrium constant in terms of concentrations. Although the concept is correct in terms of the dynamic picture of opposing reactions occurring at equal speeds, it has not been successful in coping with the problems of activity coefficients and cannot lead to the useful relations, Eqs. (4) and (11), in terms of an energetic criterion for the position of equilibrium. Conversely, the thermodynamic approach yields no relationship between the driving force at the reaction and the

rate of approach to equilibrium. *See* CHEMICAL DYNAMICS.

The influence of temperature upon the chemical potentials, and hence upon the equilibrium constant, is given by the Gibbs-Helmholtz equation, Eq. (15). The derivative on the left represents the

$$\left[\frac{d \ln K^0}{dT} \right]_P = \frac{\Delta H^\circ}{RT^2} \tag{15}$$

slope of the curve obtained when values of $\ln K^0$ for a reaction, obtained at different temperatures but always at the same pressure P, are plotted against temperature. The standard heat of reaction ΔH° for the temperature T at which the slope is measured, is the heat effect which could also be observed by carrying out the reaction involving the standard states in a calorimeter at the corresponding temperature and pressure.

For endothermic reactions, which absorb heat (ΔH° positive), K^0 increases with increasing temperature. For exothermic reactions, which evolve heat (ΔH° negative), K^0 decreases with increasing temperature and the yield of products is reduced. A more useful arrangement of Eq. (15) is shown in Eq. (16). In practice, plots of $\ln K^0$ against

$$\left[\frac{d \ln K^0}{d(1/T)} \right]_P = \frac{-\Delta H^\circ}{R} \tag{16}$$

$1/T$ are nearly linear for many reactions where the value of ΔH° changes slowly with temperature. Hence, over small temperature ranges, Eq. (16) becomes, in integrated form, Eq. (17). This relation

$$\ln \frac{K_2^0}{K_1^0} = \frac{\Delta H^\circ}{R} \left[\frac{T_2 - T_1}{T_1 T_2} \right] \tag{17}$$

is much used for calculating heats of reaction from two equilibrium measurements or for determining a new equilibrium constant K_2^0 from values of K_1^0 and ΔH°.

For accurate work, or for extending the calculations over a wide range of temperature, ΔH° must be known as a function of temperature before Eq. (15) or (16) can be integrated. When sufficient heat capacity data are available, Kirchhoff's equation, involving the difference in heat capacities between the products and reactants, Eq. (18), may be combined with Eq. (15) to yield Eq. (19). In these equa-

$$\Delta H^\circ = \Delta H_0^\circ + \alpha T + \frac{\beta T^2}{2} + \frac{\gamma T^3}{3} \tag{18}$$

$$R \ln K^0 = -\frac{\Delta H_0^\circ}{T} + \alpha \ln T$$
$$+ \frac{\beta T}{2} + \frac{\gamma T^2}{6} + I \tag{19}$$

tions, α, β, and γ are determined from heat capacity data; the constants ΔH_0° and I require knowledge of one value of ΔH° and one value of K^0, or values of K^0 at two temperatures. *See* HEAT CAPACITY; THERMOCHEMISTRY.

When equilibria are studied under conditions of constant temperature and constant volume, and with use of volume concentrations to fix standard states, the preceding treatment will yield $\Delta E°$, the internal energy change, which is the calorimetric heat of reaction at constant volume.

Homogeneous equilibria. These involve single-phase systems: gaseous, liquid, and solid solutions. In most cases, solid solutions are so far from ideal that equilibrium constants cannot be evaluated, and such systems are treated in terms of the phase rule. *See* PHASE EQUILIBRIUM.

A typical gas-phase equilibrium is the ammonia synthesis shown in Eq. (20). The most natural

$$N_2 + 3H_2 \rightleftharpoons 2NH_3 \qquad (20)$$

concentration measures are mole fraction or partial pressure; molar concentrations might be used. The partial pressures p_i are defined in terms of mole fraction N_i and the total pressure P by $p_i = N_i P$; note that partial pressures in general are not directly observable. For low pressures, where activity coefficients are practically unity, Eq. (21) holds. In turn Eq. (21) may be shown as Eq. (22),

$$K_p^0 = \frac{p_{NH_3}^2}{p_{N_2} p_{H_2}^3} = \frac{N_{NH_3}^2}{N_{N_2} N_{H_2}^3} P^{-2} \qquad (21)$$

$$K_p^0 = K_N^0 P^{\Delta n} \qquad (22)$$

where Δn is the increase in the number of moles of gases (here $\Delta n = 2$). The mole fraction equilibrium constant K_N^0 is pressure dependent, but K_p^0 is independent of pressure because of the difference in standard states. Consequently, an increase in total pressure P must lead to an increase in K_N^0 in this case. If the increase in total pressure is due to a decrease in volume of the system, the result will be an increased yield of products (NH_3). An increase in pressure brought about by injection of an inert gas into a constant volume system would not affect the partial pressures of the reacting gases nor the ultimate yield of products. The value of K_N^0, and thus that of $\Delta G_N°$, will be affected by change in total pressure due to a change in the net work of mixing and unmixing the gases. This reaction, Eq. (20), is exothermic, so best yields will be obtained at lower temperatures. See Eq. (15).

A typical liquid-phase equilibrium is the dissociation of acetic acid in water, reaction (23) and Eq. (24). In this particular case, the activity coefficient

$$HC_2H_3O_2 + H_2O \rightleftharpoons H_3O^+ + C_2H_3O_2^- \qquad (23)$$

$$\frac{K^0}{\Gamma} = \frac{m_{H_3O^+} m_{C_2H_3O_2^-}}{m_{HC_2H_3O_2} N_{H_2O}} \qquad (24)$$

ratio Γ is slightly less than unity in dilute solutions; the reference state will be the infinitely dilute solution. The mole fraction of water in the applicable concentration range is close to unity, and so numerically plays little part in evaluation of K^0. For this reason, it is commonly omitted in the formulation of the equilibrium constant, and many erroneous explanations exist in the literature. Letting α be the fraction of acetic acid dissociated and m be the total concentration, $K^0/\Gamma = m\alpha^2/(1 - \alpha)$; inspection shows that α increases with dilution.

The solvent appears to be inert, since its chemical potential remains practically unchanged over the useful concentration range. As a result of this apparent inertness of the solvent, it is not possible to determine the extent of hydration of any dissolved species from equilibrium studies. Thus, where the actual ion is H^+, H_3O^+, or $H_9O_4^+$, it is the total stoichiometric concentration that is measured and used in Eq. (24). *See* IONIC EQUILIBRIUM.

Heterogeneous equilibria. These are usually studied at constant pressure, since at least one of the phases will be a solid or liquid. The imposed pressure may be that of an equilibrium gaseous phase, or it may be an externally controlled pressure.

In describing such systems, the nature of each phase must be specified. In the examples to follow, s, l, and g identify solid, liquid, and gaseous phases, respectively. For solutions or mixtures, the composition is needed, in addition to the temperature and pressure, to complete the specification of the system. If not obvious, the identity of the solvent must be given.

In the equilibrium shown as (25), the relationship of Eq. (26) holds. Here $K^0 = p/N$, the ratio of the

$$H_2O(l) \rightleftharpoons H_2O(g) \qquad (25)$$

$$\Delta G° = \mu_g^0 - \mu_l^0 = -RT \ln \frac{p}{N} \qquad (26)$$

vapor pressure p to the liquid mole fraction N. For pure water, the equilibrium constant is simply the standard vapor pressure p^0, and the Clausius-Clapeyron equation is just a special case of the Gibbs-Helmholtz equation, Eq. (15). Now when a small amount of solute is added, decreasing the mole fraction of solvent, the vapor pressure p must be lowered to maintain equilibrium (Raoult's law). The effect of the total applied pressure P upon the vapor pressure p of the liquid is given by the Gibbs-Poynting equation, Eq. (27). Here V_l and V_g

$$\left[\frac{dp}{dP}\right]_T = \frac{V_l}{V_g} \qquad (27)$$

are the molar volumes of liquid and vapor. The vapor pressure will increase as external pressure is applied (activity increases with pressure). If the external pressure is applied to a solution by a semipermeable membrane, an applied pressure can be found which will restore the vapor pressure (or activity) of the solvent to its standard state value. *See* OSMOSIS.

Solubility equilibria are of wide variety. For a solid, such as barium sulfate, $BaSO_4$, which dissociates as shown in Eq. (28), the equilibrium relationship is shown in Eq. (29). When the solid

$$BaSO_4(s) \rightleftharpoons Ba^{2+} + SO_4^{2-} \qquad (28)$$

$$K^0 = \frac{a_{Ba^2} + a_{SO_4}}{a_{BaSO_4}} \qquad (29)$$

state is pure, its mole fraction will be unity. If it is extremely finely divided, its activity coefficient will become greater than unity; with this increase in the activity of the solid state, the solubility must increase to maintain equilibrium. On the other hand, inclusion of foreign ions in the crystal lattice (solid solution formation) may lower the activity of the solid state.

When a gas, such as CO_2, is dissolved in a liquid, its equilibrium with the gas phase is shown in (30). Equation (31), Henry's law, represents the

$$CO_2(soln) \rightleftharpoons CO_2(g) \qquad (30)$$

$$K^0 = \frac{p}{N} \qquad (31)$$

equilibrium constant for this situation. When the gas dissociates in the liquid, reaction (32), then Eq. (33)

$$(H^+ + Cl^-)(aq) \rightleftharpoons HCl(aq) \rightleftharpoons HCl(g) \qquad (32)$$

$$K^0 = \frac{p}{m^2} \cdot \Gamma \qquad (33)$$

may be utilized. Here m is the molal concentration. The equilibrium constant must reflect this behavior through the proper exponents. Equation (33) might correctly imply that the molecules were dimerized in the gaseous phase, if it were not known from a study of vapor densities that in this case they are not.

Similarly, when a solute distributes itself between two immiscible phases, the equilibrium constant takes the form of Eq. (34). Here n is the ratio

$$K^0 = \frac{c_1}{c_2^n} \cdot \Gamma \qquad (34)$$

of the molecular weight in phase 1 to that in phase 2. The equilibrium concentrations c in Eq. (34) reflect the relative solubilities of the solute in the two phases; since solubilities may vary widely, distribution operations may provide an effective means for concentrating a widely dispersed solute. See EXTRACTION.

When two components form two immiscible phases at equilibrium, each condensed phase will be a saturated solution; complete immiscibility is impossible in principle, since the chemical potential of any component must be the same in both phases. The separation of a liquid system into two liquid phases is a manifestation of the nonideality of the solutions. For practical purposes, however, many solids may be regarded as immiscible because of the stringent requirements associated with formation of the crystal lattice.

In reactions involving condensed and immiscible phases, for example, reaction (35), there can be

$$Pb(s) + 2AgCl(s) \rightleftharpoons PbCl_2(s) + 2Ag(s) \qquad (35)$$

no change in concentration of any phase during the reaction. Then the Q^0 term in Eq. (10) will be constant, and ΔG can never become zero. Although a reaction is possible, there can be no equilibrium until one of the reactants is completely used up. There might, of course, be one condition of temperature and pressure for which ΔG could be zero. Such is the case in transition phenomena, or melting-freezing phenomena. From the phase-rule viewpoint, the system in reaction (35) lacks one degree of freedom if reaction is possible, so one phase must disappear in order to attain equilibrium.

Cecil E. Vanderzee

Bibliography. G. M. Barrow, *Physical Chemistry*, 5th ed., 1988; I. M. Klotz and R. M. Rosenberg, *Chemical Thermodynamics: Basic Theory Methods*, 5th ed., 1994; I. N. Levine, *Physical Chemistry*, 4th ed., 1994; G. N. Lewis and M. Randall, *Thermodynamics*, 2d ed., rev. by K. S. Pitzer and L. Brewer, 1961.

Chemical fuel

The principal fuels used in internal combustion engines (automobiles, diesel, and turbojet) and in the furnaces of stationary power plants are organic fossil fuels. These fuels, and others derived from them by various refining and separation processes, are found in the earth in the solid (coal), liquid (petroleum), and gas (natural gas) phases.

Special fuels to improve the performance of combustion engines are obtained by synthetic chemical procedures. These special fuels serve to increase the fuel specific impulse of the engine (specific impulse is the force produced by the engine multiplied by the time over which it is produced, divided by the mass of the fuel) or to increase the heat of combustion available to the engine per unit mass or per unit volume of the fuel. A special fuel which possesses a very high heat of combustion per unit mass is liquid hydrogen. It has been used along with liquid oxygen in rocket engines. Because of its low liquid density, liquid hydrogen is not too useful in systems requiring high heats of combustion per unit volume of fuel ("volume-limited" systems). In combination with liquid fluorine, liquid hydrogen produces extremely large specific impulses. See AIRCRAFT FUEL.

A special fuel which produces high flame temperatures of the order of 9000°F (5000°C) is gaseous cyanogen, C_2N_2. This is used with gaseous oxygen as the oxidizer. The liquid fuel hydrazine, N_2H_4, and other hydrazine-based fuels, with the liquid oxidizer nitrogen tetroxide, N_2O_4, are used in many space-oriented rocket engines. The boron hydrides, such as diborane, B_2H_6, and pentaborane,

B_5H_9, are high-energy fuels which are being used in advanced rocket engines. *See* BORANE.

For air-breathing propulsion engines (turbojets and ramjets), hydrocarbon fuels are most often used. For some applications, metal alkyl fuels which are pyrophoric (that is, ignite spontaneously in the presence of air), and even liquid hydrogen, are being used.

A partial list of additional liquid fuels and their associated oxidizers is shown in the **table**.

Liquid fuels and their associated oxidizers	
Fuel	Oxidizer
Ammonia	Liquid oxygen
95% Ethyl alcohol	Liquid oxygen
Methyl alcohol	87% Hydrogen peroxide
Aniline	Red fuming nitric acid
Furfural alcohol	Red fuming nitric acid

Fuels which liberate heat in the absence of an oxidizer while decomposing either spontaneously or because of the presence of a catalyst are called monopropellants and have been used in rocket engines. Examples of these monopropellants are hydrogen peroxide, H_2O_2, and nitromethane, CH_3NO_2.

Liquid fuels and oxidizers are used in most large-thrust (large propulsive force) rocket engines. When thrust is not a consideration, solid-propellant fuels and oxidizers are frequently employed because of the lack of moving parts such as valves and pumps, and the consequent simplicity of this type of rocket engine. Solid fuels fall into two broad classes, double-base and composites. Double-base fuels are compounded of nitroglycerin (glycerol trinitrate) and nitrocellulose, with no separate oxidizer required. The nitroglycerin plasticizes and swells the nitrocellulose, leading to a propellant of relatively high strength and low elongation. The double-base propellant is generally formed in a mold into the desired shape (called a grain) required for the rocket case. Composite propellants are made of a fuel and an oxidizer. The latter could be an inorganic perchlorate such as ammonium perchlorate, NH_4ClO_4, or potassium perchlorate, $KClO_4$, or a nitrate such as ammonium nitrate, NH_4NO_3, potassium nitrate, KNO_3, or sodium nitrate, $NaNO_3$. Fuels for composite propellants are generally the asphalt-oil-type, thermosetting plastics (phenol formaldehyde and phenolfurfural resins have been used) or several types of synthetic rubber and gumlike substances. Recently, metal particles such as boron, aluminum, and beryllium have been added to solid propellants to increase their heats of combustion and to eliminate certain types of combustion instability. *See* HYDROGEN PEROXIDE; ROCKET PROPULSION.

Wallace Chinitz

Bibliography. S. S. Penner, *Chemical Rocket Propulsion and Combustion Research*, 1962; G. A. Sutton, *Rocket Propulsion Elements: An Introduction to the Engineering of Rockets*, 5th ed., 1986.

Chemical microscopy

A scientific discipline in which microscopes are used to solve chemical problems. The unique ability to form a visual image of a specimen, to select a small volume of the specimen, and to perform a chemical or structural analysis on the material in the selected volume makes chemical microscopy indispensable to modern chemical analysis. *See* MICROSCOPE.

Microscopes are instruments which form images of objects too small to be seen with the unaided eye. Microscopes can also be combined with most analytical instruments. For example, a light microscope can be combined with a spectroscope, making it possible to determine the molecular composition of microscopic objects or structures. Similarly, an x-ray spectrometer can be combined with an electron microscope to determine the elemental composition of small objects. *See* ELECTRON MICROSCOPE; SPECTROSCOPY; X-RAY SPECTROMETRY.

Phase analyses can also be made microscopically. The boundaries of amorphous phases can usually be distinguished in the microscope, and an elemental or physical analysis can be used to identify the phase. An example of a physical analysis is the measurement of refractive index. Crystalline phases are even more amenable to microscopical analysis. For example, a polarizing microscope can be used to measure the optical properties of a crystalline phase and thus identify it. Or a transmission electron microscope can be used to select a tiny area of a crystalline phase and identify the crystal structure by means of electron diffraction. *See* ELECTRON DIFFRACTION.

While the idea of selecting a small volume for analysis is straightforward, the minimum volume that can be analyzed varies widely with the instrument used. Light microscopes can be used to identify particles as small as 1 micrometer in diameter and weighing about 1 picogram. A field ion microscope has been combined with a mass spectrometer and used to identify single atoms extracted from the surface of a specimen. *See* FIELD EMISSION MICROSCOPY; MASS SPECTROMETRY; OPTICAL MICROSCOPE.

After a portion of a specimen has been selected microscopically, it can be analyzed in many ways. An experienced microscopist may learn to recognize various structures by studying known materials, using published atlases, or an atlas that the individual microscopist has constructed. Analyses done in this fashion can be fast and simple. If the object or structure cannot be recognized, many means of analysis are available. For example, a polarizing microscope may be employed to identify the object by using optical crystallographic methods. Other light microscopes useful for chemical analy-

Micrograph of a portland cement formulation cured at 390–450°F (200°–230°C) for 72 h; gypsum and xonotlite crystals are growing into a cavity.

sis include phase-contrast and interference-contrast microscopes, microspectrophotometers, the confocal scanning laser microscope, and the laser Raman microscope. Physicochemical methods may be used to measure melting points, or mixed-melt phenomena and dispersion staining may also be used. *See* INTERFERENCE MICROSCOPE; LASER SPECTROSCOPY; PHASE-CONTRAST MICROSCOPE; RAMAN EFFECT.

Microscopes using other types of image-forming beams serve for chemical analysis. Scanning or transmission electron microscopes are powerful tools for chemical microscopy. Scanning electron microscopes are often fitted with x-ray spectrometers which are capable of both qualitative and quantitative analysis for most of the elements. Other electron microscopes capable of chemical analysis are the Auger electron microscope, field electron microscope, scanning tunneling microscope, and cathodoluminescence microscope. Microscopes which use ion beams, neutron beams, and x-ray beams also have analytical capabilities. *See* AUGER EFFECT; NEUTRON SPECTROMETRY; SCANNING ELECTRON MICROSCOPE; X-RAY MICROSCOPE.

A specific example of a chemical microscopical analysis involves portland cement which is formulated for use in geothermal-energy extraction wells (see **illus.**). In this micrograph, two types of crystals can be recognized by their morphology. If the microscopist does not recognize the crystals from their morphology, the crystals must be analyzed. This can be done in a number of ways. With a light microscope, it is possible to identify the crystals by scraping them from the sample and determining their optical properties through a variety of standard techniques. Another method is to examine each of the crystals by using x-ray or electron diffraction techniques. A third option is to perform an elemental analysis with an electron microscope fitted with an x-ray spectrometer. From the elemental analysis, it should be possible to identify the chemical compound that makes up the crystal. There should be no confusion resulting from the fact that the sample consists of more than one crystalline compound, because with the electron microscope a single crystal or a small portion of a crystal can be analyzed. Each crystal that appears different from the other can be analyzed quantitatively for its elemental composition. Knowledge of the combination of elemental composition and diffraction data nearly always leads to the identification of the crystals in the sample. This does require that the diffraction pattern for the crystals has been published and is accessible to the microscopist. If this information is not available, the microscopist can usually construct a list of data for the materials under consideration, so that in future work the individual crystals or amorphous materials can be recognized when they are encountered again.

In the example illustrated, only the commonly available microscopes, that is, the polarizing microscope, the scanning electron microscope, and the transmission electron microscope, were considered. Less commonly available microscopes, such as the Auger microscope, the laser Raman microscope, and the microspectrophotometer, can be used to identify crystalline and amorphous phases. *See* ANALYTICAL CHEMISTRY.   George Cocks

Bibliography. R. Barer and V. E. Cosslett, *Advances in Optical and Electron Microscopy*, vol. 10, 1987; E. M. Chamot, *Elementary Chemical Microscopy*, 1915; E. G. Ehlers, *Optical Mineralogy: Theory and Technique*, 1987; P. J. Elving (ed.), *Treatise on Analytical Chemistry*, pt. I, vol. 8, Ch. 16, 1986; H. J. Guntherod et al., *Scanning Tunneling Miucroscopy*, I: *General Principles and Applications to Clean and Adsorbate-Covered Surfaces*, 1992; R. E. Lee, *Scanning Electron Microscopy and X-Ray Microanalysis*, 1992; B. W. Rossiter and R. C. Baetzold, *Physical Methods of Chemistry: Investigations of Surfaces and Interfaces*, vol. 9, pt. B, 2d ed., 1993.

Chemical process industry

An industry, abbreviated CPI, in which the raw materials undergo chemical conversion during their processing into finished products, as well as (or instead of) the physical conversions common to industry in general. In the chemical process industry the products differ chemically from the raw materials as a result of undergoing one or more chemical reactions during the manufacturing process. The chemical process industries broadly include the traditional chemical industries, both organic and inorganic; the petroleum industry; the petrochemical industry, which produces the majority of plastics, synthetic fibers, and synthetic rubber from petroleum and natural-gas raw materials; and a series of allied industries in which chemical processing plays a substantial part. While the chemical process industries are primarily the realm of the chemical engineer and the chemist, they also involve a wide range of other scientific, engineering, and economic specialists.

For a discussion of the more prominent chemical process industries *see* ADHESIVE; BIOCHEMICAL ENGINEERING; BIOMEDICAL CHEMICAL ENGINEERING; CEMENT; CERAMICS; COAL CHEMICALS; COAL GASIFICATION; COAL LIQUEFACTION; DISTILLED SPIRITS; DYEING; ELECTROCHEMICAL PROCESS; EXPLOSIVE;

FAT AND OIL; FERMENTATION; FERTILIZER; FOOD MANUFACTURING; FUEL GAS; GLASS; GRAPHITE; HYDROCRACKING; INSECTICIDE; LIME (INDUSTRY); MANUFACTURED FIBER; NUCLEAR CHEMICAL ENGINEERING; NUCLEAR FUELS; PAPER; PETROCHEMICAL; PETROLEUM PROCESSING AND REFINING; PETROLEUM PRODUCTS; PLASTICS PROCESSING; POLYMER; RADIOACTIVE WASTE MANAGEMENT; RUBBER; WATER SOFTENING.   William F. Furter

Bibliography. G. Agam, *Industrial Chemicals, Their Characteristics and Development: Chemicals in the Real World*, 1994; N. Basta, *Shreve's Chemical Process Industries Handbook*, 6th ed., 1994; J. A. Kent (ed.), *Reigel's Handbook of Industrial Chemistry*, 8th ed., 1983.

Chemical reactor

A vessel in which chemical reactions take place. A combination of vessels is known as a chemical reactor network. Chemical reactors have diverse sizes, shapes, and modes and conditions of operation based on the nature of the reaction system and its behavior as a function of temperature, pressure, catalyst properties, and other factors.

Laboratory chemical reactors are used to obtain reaction characteristics. Therefore, the shape and mode of operation of a reactor on this scale differ markedly from that of the large-scale industrial reactor, which is designed for efficient production rather than for gathering information. Laboratory reactors are best designed to achieve well-defined conditions of concentrations and temperature so that a reaction model can be developed which will prove useful in the design of a large-scale reactor model.

Chemical reactions may occur in the presence of a single phase (liquid or gas), in which case they are called homogeneous, or they may occur in the presence of more than one phase and are referred to as heterogeneous. In addition, chemical reactions may be catalyzed. Examples of homogeneous reactions are gaseous fuel combustion (gas phase) and acid-base neutralization (liquid phase). Examples of heterogeneous systems are carbon dioxide absorption into alkali (gas-liquid); coal combustion and automobile exhaust purification (gas-solid); water softening (liquid-solid); coal liquefaction and oil hydrogenation (gas-liquid-solid); and coke reduction of iron ore (solid-solid). *See* CATALYSIS.

Modes of operation. Chemical reactors may be operated in batch, semibatch, or continuous modes.

Batch. When a reactor is operated in a batch mode, the reactants are charged, and the vessel is closed and brought to the desired temperature and pressure. These conditions are maintained for the time needed to achieve the desired conversion and selectivity, that is, the required quantity and quality of product. Batch operation is labor-intensive and therefore is commonly used only in industries involved in limited production of fine chemicals, such as pharmaceuticals.

Semibatch. In this type of reactor operation, one or more reactants are in the batch mode, while the coreactant is fed and withdrawn continuously. For example, a batch of liquid is exposed to a continuously fed and withdrawn gas phase.

Continuous. In a chemical reactor designed for continuous operation, there is continuous addition to, and withdrawal of, reactants and products from, the reactor system. The reaction time is the actual residence time of the molecules within the reactor. There are two extremes of residence or exposure time. If all molecules have the same reaction exposure time, the reactor is a plug- or piston-flow reactor; that is, reactant-product species move through the reactor as would a piston or plug, with no (zero) mixing in the direction of flow. If, however, the mixing is perfect (infinite) in the direction of flow, the reactor is a continuously fed stirred-tank reactor. For this type of reactor, concentrations and temperature are uniform throughout the vessel due to vigor of agitation, and the residence times are distributed around the mean value. In contrast, in the piston-flow reactor, concentrations and temperature are distributed nonuniformly between reactor inlet and outlet, and residence time is unique.

Selection of reactor. The choice between a continuously fed stirred-tank reactor and a piston-flow reactor for continuous operation is determined by reaction characteristics. The reactor environment with respect to temperature is likewise determined, and may be isothermal (heat removal or addition matching heat generation or extraction), adiabatic (no heat removal or addition in the reaction zone), or the intermediate case (partial heat removal or addition).

An example is the sequence of reactions shown below, where k_1 and k_2 represent rate coefficients.

$$\text{Ethylene} \xrightarrow{k_1} \text{ethylene oxide} \xrightarrow{k_2}$$

$$\text{carbon dioxide + water}$$

This reaction is exothermic (heat is released), and the rate coefficient k_1 increases with increase in temperature more slowly than does k_2. A decision must be made as to what reactor type, mode of operation, and environment should be employed. If large quantities of ethylene are to be treated annually, the continuous mode is economically justified. The desired product will determine the choice between a continuously stirred tank reactor and a piston-flow reactor.

The adiabatic environment is readily achieved in large-scale industrial reactors by the denial of heat exchange. Such an adiabatic reactor consists of a large-diameter tube packed with catalyst. The adiabatic temperature rise (in exothermic reactions) may require limitation due to safety and equilibrium factors in addition to integrity of the catalyst and reactor materials. These considerations led to the development of the staged adiabatic fixed-bed reactor system for sulfur dioxide oxidation and hydrocracking. In each case, interstage cooling is effected either by means of indirect heat exchange to generate steam or preheat reactants or by means of direct cooling by the addition of "cold" coreactant (cold-shot addition). The adiabatic reactor is the least expensive, since it does not require a costly heat-transfer surface area.

Gas-solid reactors. There are a number of different types of reactors designed for gas-solid heterogeneous reactions. These include fixed beds, tubular catalytic wall reactors, and fluid beds.

The design of these components involves consideration of the properties of solid catalysts. Catalytic agents (for example, platinum, palladium, vanadium pentoxide among other zeolites, metal oxides, sulfides) are usually supported upon porous solids, such as aluminum oxide and silicon dioxide. Thus the components are, typically, support, catalyst, and promoter. Characterization of these components is imperative, since deactivation over time periods of minutes (catalytic cracking), months (reforming), and years (ammonia synthesis) plagues all catalysts. The actual catalytic sites exposed to reactants may be partially inaccessible because of the diffusional limitations of the reactants and the nature of the sites dictated by the fluid-phase environment (oxidizing, reducing). Furthermore, the reactivity and yield selectivity per exposed catalyst site may change with catalyst crystallite size (dispersion), a phenomenon known as fractal behavior. Since the reactions and associated enthalpy changes are forcing functions that affect reactor performance, consideration of the complexities of heterogeneous catalytic phenomena is necessary both in reaction modeling and in reactor modeling. *See* HETEROGENEOUS CATALYSIS.

Fixed bed. A common catalytic reactor that consists of a tube or parallel array of tubes filled with solid catalyst particles is the fixed-bed reactor. It is commonly employed in processes such as partial oxidation, ammonia synthesis, and reforming. Minimization of tube surface area (large tube diameter) invites adiabaticity. In the general case (nonisothermal or nonadiabatic), temperature varies in axial and radial directions and radial heat-transfer limitations can cause "hot" or "quench" spots with consequent threats to safety and product quality. Radial temperature gradients can be minimized by use of small tube diameter; however, there will be consequent increase in heat-transfer surface and reactor cost. Usually a piston-flow reactor is used. When catalyst decay is rapid (as in catalytic cracking), fresh catalyst is added and spent solid removed continuously. This arrangement is known as a moving bed. *See* CRACKING.

Tubular catalytic wall reactor. Resistance to radial heat transfer can be vastly reduced by using this type of reactor, in which all the catalyst is impregnated upon the alumina wash-coated wall. This is the monolith tubular reactor used in auto-exhaust fume abatement. Catalyst replacement is obviously more difficult in this instance than in the conventional fixed bed; the tubular catalytic wall reactor cannot host catalysts of short life.

Fluid bed. When a fluid is passed upward through an unretained bed of fine solid particles, a velocity can be induced so that the bed moves, with bubbles of gas passing through the agitated solids. The bed behaves as a boiling fluid. Intensity of gas dispersion in the usually baffled bed induces rapid motion and circulation of the solid. Reaction heat is thus nearly uniformly dispersed and, unlike the fixed bed, the fluid bed approaches isothermality. Fine particles can be used with increase in surface area and reaction efficiency. Since the fluid bed is a multiphase system (gas-and-solids emulsion phases), bypassing or short-circuiting of unreacted species can occur, which reduces reactor efficiency. Staging or horizontal baffling can minimize bypassing and deleterious bubble growth.

The fluid bed can be operated in batch or continuous fashion with respect to the solids phase, while the fluiding (gas or liquid) phase is continuous. If catalyst life is short (seconds or minutes) or noncatalytic solid coreactant is converted, the continuous fluid bed must be employed. Residence time is complex.

A variation of the fluidized bed is the spouted-bed reactor, in which a jet of gas is injected at one or more points to disperse even rather large-sized particles with which the gas interacts (for example, drying of wheat, gas-solid reaction, or solid-catalyzed reaction). Solids may be batch or continuous.

At sufficiently high fluid velocities, the fluidized bed becomes entrained; that is, solids are carried out of the bed when fluid velocity exceeds particle terminal velocity. In a transport line or riser reactor, fresh solids are continuously fed at the reactor bottom with the entraining fluid. This is an ideal unit for rapidly decaying catalyst or solid noncatalytic coreactants. Modern catalytic cracking of oils to produce gasoline is largely done in the transport line reactor. Residence time approaches the piston-flow reactor limit as opposed to more complex residence time behavior of the continuous fluidized bed. Reactant exposure times are of the order of seconds, during which deactivating coke is laid down upon the catalyst. Coked catalyst is separated from the product vapors at the top of the reactor and is then sent to a regenerator, where oxygen-bearing gas is contacted with the coked catalyst to burn off the coke. The product of this gas-solid reaction, the regenerated cracking catalyst, is returned to the inlet of the transport line cracker. *See* FLUIDIZATION; FLUIDIZED-BED COMBUSTION.

Gas-liquid-solid reactors. Many different types have been developed for specific reaction conditions. The trickle-bed reactor employs a fixed bed of solid catalyst over which a liquid phase trickles downward in the presence of a cocurrent gas phase. This three-phase reactor, commonly employed for the removal of sulfur or nitrogen from high-boiling oil feedstocks, can pose problems of catalyst wetting, gas-liquid-solid heat/mass transfer, and liquid-phase bypassing. Reasonable catalyst life is required in trickle-bed operation.

An alternative is the slurry reactor, a vessel within which coreactant gas is dispersed into a liquid phase bearing suspended catalyst or coreactant solid particles. Unlike the trickle bed, liquid-solid wetting is complete. With short catalyst life or solid consumption, continuous feed and withdrawal of the liquid-solid phase is feasible, but with attendant problems of solid-liquid separation. Slurry reactors are usually of the continuously stirred tank type.

At high ratios of reactor length to diameter, the gas-liquid-solid reactor is often termed an ebullating-bed (high solids concentration) or bubble column reactor (low solids concentration). A trickle bed operating at high liquid holdup and countercurrent (upward) flow of gas becomes an ebullating bed.

Gas-liquid reactors assume a form virtually identical to the absorbers utilized in physical absorption processes. *See* ABSORPTION OPERATIONS.

Solid-solid reactions are often conducted in rotary kilns which provide the necessary intimacy of contact between the solid coreactants. *See* KILN.

James J. Carberry

Bibliography. J. J. Carberry, *Chemical and Catalytic Reaction Engineering*, 1976; J. J. Carberry, Remarks on the modeling of heterogeneous fluid-solid reactors, *Chem. Eng. Technol.*, 11:420–425, 1988; H. S. Fogler, *Elements of Chemical Reaction Engineering*, 1992.

Chemical senses

In vertebrates, the senses of smell (olfaction) and taste (gustation) plus the so-called common chemical sense constitute the external chemical senses, as contrasted with such internal chemoreceptors as the carotid sinus detectors of carbon dioxide in blood, glucose receptors of brain and certain visceral organs, and so on. The olfactory cells of vertebrates, usually located in the olfactory mucosa of the upper nasal passages, are specialized neural elements that are responsive to chemicals in the vapor phase. The floral fragrance of roses and the putrid smell of hydrogen sulfide are two examples of human olfactory sensations. Taste buds of the oral cavity, especially the tongue, are composed of modified epithelial cells responsive to chemicals in solution. Sweet, salty, sour, and bitter are the basic taste qualities experienced by humans. In certain fish (for example, catfish), taste buds occur over the body surface and barbels. The common chemical senses are composed of free nerve endings in the mucous membrane of the eye, nose, mouth, and digestive tract and are responsive to irritants or other chemicals in either the vapor or liquid phase. *See* CAROTID BODY; CHEMORECEPTION.

Chemical sensitivity occurs in single-cell and other lower organisms. Among invertebrates, sense organs occur as specialized hairs and sensilla, or minute cones supplied with sensory nerves and nerve cells. Characteristic of male moths, for example, are their distinctive bushy antennae, by which they detect and locate females by sex pheromones. Rodents, ungulates, carnivores, and other mammals also show sexual attraction to female odors produced by specialized glands. Whether humans in general are susceptible to pheromonal influences from other humans is highly debatable. *See* CHEMICAL ECOLOGY; PHEROMONE.

Taste plays an important role in selection and acceptance of food. Although the "sweet tooth" is widespread throughout the animal kingdom as well as humans, there are great species differences in sweet sensitivity, especially for artificial sweeteners. Besides the protective, inborn aversion to bitter (many poisons, but not all, are bitter), a single experience with the particular taste of a toxic substance which caused illness may establish a strong and persistent learned taste aversion. By contrast, a compensatory salt hunger may occur in persons or animals suffering salt deficiency. The intake of salt in civilized people, however, may be determined not only by physiological need but by social custom and habit, and excess intake with high incidences of hypertension has been reported in some groups. *See* HYPERTENSION; SALT (FOOD).

The limbic system of the brain, which modulates appetitive and emotional behavior and hedonic (pleasant vs. unpleasant) experiences, has both taste and olfactory neural pathways to it, providing the neural substrate for the pleasure or displeasure of sensations. *See* NEUROBIOLOGY; OLFACTION; SENSATION; TASTE.

Carl Pfaffmann

Bibliography. C. Pfaffmann, The pleasures of sensation, *Psychol. Rev.*, 67:253–268, 1960; G. M. Shepherd, *Neurobiology*, 1983.

Chemical separation techniques

A method used in chemistry to purify substances or to isolate them from other substances, for either preparative or analytical purposes. In industrial applications the ultimate goal is the isolation of a product of given purity, whereas in analysis the primary goal is the determination of the amount or concentration of that substance in a sample. In principle it is always more convenient to carry out quantitative determinations directly on portions of the original sample. In cases where the analytical methods available are not sufficiently selective to permit this direct approach, it is necessary to employ preliminary separations to reduce the concentration of, or to remove completely, those substances which interfere in the final estimation.

Although special considerations arise in a comparison of separation methods for engineering or laboratory analytical purposes because of differences in the scales of operations, the various separation processes are based on the same principles.

There are three factors of importance to be considered in all separations: (1) the completeness of recovery of the substance being isolated, (2) the extent of separation from associated substances, and (3) the efficiency of the separation. The recovery factor or yield R_A of a separation of substance A is defined as Eq. (1) where Q_A and $(Q_A)_0$ are the

$$R_A = \frac{Q_A}{(Q_A)_0} \qquad (1)$$

amount of A after and before the separation.

The degree of separation $S_{B/A}$ of two substances A and B is given by the separation factor R_B for B with respect to A, and is defined as Eq. (2). Although complete separations are

$$S_{B/A} = \frac{(Q_A)_0 Q_B}{(Q_B)_0 Q_A} \cong \frac{Q_B}{(Q_B)_0} \cong R_B \qquad (2)$$

usually preferred, they are not always necessary in analytical applications. The degree of purity will depend upon the choice of the method of final estimation. Sometimes merely a reduction in the quantity of foreign substance present is enough to simplify the subsequent analytical task.

The third factor, efficiency, is a measure of the amount of work required to obtain a given amount of product with a prescribed purity. This consideration is of much greater consequence in industrial separations in which both the scale and the cost of the operation are important.

There are many types of separations based on a variety of properties of materials. Among the most commonly used properties are those involving solubility, volatility, adsorption, and electrical and magnetic effects, although others have been used to advantage. The most efficient separation will obviously be obtained under conditions for which the differences in properties between two substances undergoing separation are at a maximum.

The common aspect of all separation methods is the need for two phases. The desired substance will partition or distribute between the two phases in a definite manner, and the separation is completed by physically separating the two phases. The ratio of the concentrations of a substance in the two phases is called its partition or distribution coefficient.

In analytical work the original phase is usually a liquid, that is, a solution of the sample, and the separation is brought about through the addition or formation of a solid, a liquid, or a gaseous second phase. Although the actual separation of the phases may be physical in nature, chemical reactions are usually required to convert or modify the substance to a form which permits the formation of the new phase or the partition of the substance to the second phase. In some separation methods this step may also be accomplished by physical means.

If two substances have very similar distribution coefficients, many successive steps may be required for a separation. The resulting process is called a fractionation.

Based on the nature of the second phase, the more commonly used methods of separation are classified as follows:

1. Methods involving a solid second phase include precipitation, electrodeposition, chromatography (adsorption), ion exchange, and crystallization. These methods involve a solid second phase either through the formation of a slightly soluble product, deposition as a metal on the surface of an electrode, or by physical or chemical adsorption on a suitable solid material.

2. The outstanding method involving a liquid second phase is solvent extraction, in which the original solution is placed in contact with another liquid phase immiscible with the first. Separations are achieved as a result of differences in the distribution of solutes between the two phases. Solid materials may also be separated by extraction with organic solvents.

3. Methods involving a gaseous second phase include gas evolution, distillation, sublimation, and gas chromatography. Mixtures of volatile substances can often be separated by fractional distillation. *See* CHROMATOGRAPHY; EXTRACTION.

George H. Morrison

Bibliography. J. C. King, *Separation Processes*, 2d ed., 1980; J. C. King and J. D. Navratil (eds.), *Chemical Separations*, vols. 1 and 2, 1986; E. S. Perry (ed.), *Techniques of Chemistry Separation and Purification*, 1978; R. H. Perry and D. Green, (eds.), *Perry's Chemical Engineers' Handbook*, 6th ed., 1984.

Chemical symbols and formulas

A system of symbols and notation for the chemical elements and the combinations of these elements which form numerous chemical compounds. This system of symbols, devised since about 1800 by chemists, consists of letters, numerals, and marks that are designed to denote the chemical element, formula, or structure of the molecule or compound. These symbols give a concise and instantly recognizable description of the element or compound. In many cases, through the efforts of international conferences, the symbols are recognized throughout the scientific world, and they greatly simplify the universal languge of chemistry.

Elements. Of the 109 presently known chemical elements 105 have been given symbols, usually derived from the name of the element. Examples of names and symbols are chlorine, Cl; fluorine, F; beryllium, Be; aluminum, Al; oxygen, O; and carbon, C. However, symbols for some elements are derived from Latin or other names for the element. Examples are Au, gold (from *aurum*); Fe, iron (from *ferrum*); Pb, lead (from *plumbum*); Na, sodium (from *natrium*); and K, potassium (from *kalium*). The symbols consist of one or, more commonly, two letters. The first letter is always a capital letter and is followed by a lowercase second letter.

Inorganic molecules and compounds. Simple diatomic molecules of a single element are designated by the symbol for the element with a subscript 2, indicating that it contains two atoms. Thus the hydrogen molecule is H_2; the nitrogen molecule, N_2; and the oxygen molecule, O_2. Polyatomic molecules of a single element are designated by the symbol for the element with a numerical subscript corresponding to the number of atoms in the molecule. Examples are the phosphorus molecule, P_4; the sulfur molecule, S_8; and the arsenic molecule, As_4.

Diatomic covalent molecules containing unlike elements are given a similar designation. The formula for hydrogen chloride is HCl; for iodine monochloride, ICl; and for hydrogen iodide, HI. The more electropositive element is always designated first in the formula.

For polyatomic covalent molecules containing unlike elements, numerical subscripts are used to designate the number of atoms of each element that are present in the molecule. Examples are phosphorus(III) chloride, PCl_3; arsine, AsH_3; ammonia, NH_3; and water, H_2O. Again, as in diatomic molecules, the more electropositive element is placed first in the formula.

Ionic inorganic compounds are designated by a similar notation. The positive ion is given first in the formula, followed by the negative ion; subscripts are again used to denote the number of ions of each element present in the compound. The formulas for several common compounds are sodium chloride, NaCl; ammonium nitrate, NH_4NO_3; aluminum sulfate, $Al_2(SO_4)_3$; and iron(III) oxide, Fe_2O_3.

More complex inorganic compounds are designated in a manner similar to that above. The positive ion is given first, but may contain attached or coordinated groups, and this is followed by the negative ion. Examples are hexammine-cobalt(III) chloride, $[Co(NH_3)_6]Cl_3$; dichlorobis(ethylenediamine)chromium(III) nitrate, $[Cr(en)_2Cl_2](NO_3)_3$, where en is the abbreviation for ethylenediamine; and potassium trioxalatoferrate(III), $K_3[Fe(C_2O_4)_3]$. Hydrates of inorganic compounds, such as copper(II) sulfate pentahydrate, are designated by the formula of the compound followed by the formula for water, the number of water molecules being designated by a numerical prefix. Thus the symbol for the above compound is $CuSO_4 \cdot 5H_2O$.

Organic compounds. Because there are many more organic than inorganic compounds, the designation or notation for the first group becomes exceedingly complex. Many different types of organic compounds are known; in the case of hydrocarbons, there are aromatic and aliphatic, saturated and unsaturated, cyclic and polycyclic, and so on. The system of notation used must distinguish between the various hydrocarbons themselves as well as setting this group of compounds apart from others such as alcohols, ethers, amines, esters, and phenols. *See* CHEMISTRY; COORDINATION COMPLEXES; INORGANIC CHEMISTRY; ORGANIC CHEMISTRY.   Wesley Wendlandt

Bibliography. B. P. Brock, W. H. Powell, and W. C. Fernelius (eds.), *Inorganic Chemical Nomenclature: Principles and Practice*, 1990; J. C. Richer, R. Panico, and W. H. Powell (eds.), *A Guide to IUPAC Nomenclature of Organic Compounds*, 1993.

Chemical thermodynamics

The application of thermodynamic principles to systems involving physical and chemical transformations in order to (1) develop quantitative relationships among the identifiable forms of energy and their conjugate variables, (2) establish the criteria for spontaneous change, for equilibrium, and for thermodynamic stability, and (3) provide the macroscopic base for the statistical-mechanical bridge to atomic and molecular properties. The thermodynamic principles applied are the conservation of energy as embodied in the first law of thermodynamics, the principle of internal entropy production as embodied in the second law of thermodynamics, and the principle of absolute entropy and its statistical thermodynamic formulation as embodied in the third law of thermodynamics.

Basic concepts. The basic goal of thermodynamics is to provide a description of a system of interest in order to investigate the nature and extent of changes in the state of that system as it undergoes spontaneous change toward equilibrium and interacts with its surroundings. This goal implicitly carries with it the concept that there are measurable properties of the system which can be used to adequately describe the state of the system and that the system is enclosed by a boundary or wall which separates the system and its surroundings. Properties that define the state of the system can be classified as extensive and intensive properties. Extensive properties are dependent upon the mass of the system, whereas intensive properties are not. Typical extensive properties are the energy, volume, and numbers of moles of each component in the system, while typical intensive properties are temperature, pressure, density, and the mole fractions or concentrations of the components.

Extensive properties can be expressed as functions of other extensive properties, for instance as in Eq. (1), where the volume V of the system is

$$V = V(U, S, \{n_i\}) \qquad (1)$$

expressed in terms of the internal energy U, the entropy S, and $\{n_i\}$, the set of numbers of moles of the various components labeled by the index i. A suitable transformation procedure can be used to replace extensive variables by conjugate intensive variables. For example, the volume can be expressed as in Eq. (2a) or (2b). Since temperature

$$V = V'(P, S, \{n_i\}) \qquad (2a)$$

$$v = V''(P, T, \{n_i\}) \qquad (2b)$$

T and pressure P are particularly convenient variables to control and measure in chemical systems, the last form is of great utility. All extensive thermodynamic properties X can be rewritten in this form, namely as Eq. (3), and since all such properties are

$$X = X(T, P, \{n_i\}) \qquad (3)$$

linear homogeneous functions of the mass, it can be shown that at a given temperature and pressure Eq. (4) holds, where $\overline{X}_i$ is the partial molar value of

$$X = \sum_i n_i \overline{X}_i \qquad (4)$$

the extensive property for the ith component, and is given by Eq. (5), where the notation $\{n_i\}'$, means

$$\overline{X}_i = (\partial X / \partial n_i)_{T, P, \{n_i\}'} \qquad (5)$$

that all of the mole numbers are constant except the ith one involved in the derivative. $\overline{X}_i$ is itself intensive.

Specification of boundaries. The concept of a boundary enclosing the system and separating it from the surroundings requires specification of the nature of the boundary and of any constraints the boundary places upon the interaction of the system and its surroundings. Boundaries that restrain a system to a particular value of an extensive property are said to be restrictive with respect to that property. A boundary which restrains the system to a given volume V is a fixed wall. A boundary which is restrictive to one component of a system but not to the other components is a semipermeable wall or membrane. A system whose boundaries are restrictive to energy and to mass or moles of components is said to be an isolated system. A system whose boundaries are restrictive only to mass or moles of components is a closed system, whereas an open system has nonrestrictive walls and hence can exchange energy, volume, and mass with its surroundings. Boundaries can be restrictive with respect to specific forms of energy, and two important types are those restrictive to thermal energy but not work (adiabatic walls) and those restrictive to work but not thermal energy (diathermal walls).

Reversible and irreversible processes. Changes in the state of the system can result from processes taking place within the system and from processes involving exchange of mass or energy with the surroundings. After a process is carried out, if it is possible to restore both the system and the surroundings to their original states, the process is said to be reversible; otherwise the process is irreversible. All naturally occurring spontaneous processes are irreversible. The first law defines the internal energy as a state function or property of the state of a system, and restricts the system and its surroundings to those processes which conserve energy. The second law established which of the permissible processes can occur spontaneously.

First law of thermodynamics. The total energy E of a system is the sum of its kinetic energy T, its potential energy V, and its internal energy U, Eq. (6). If a system has constant mass and its

$$E = T + V + U \qquad (6)$$

center of mass is moving with uniform velocity in a uniform potential, then changes in the total energy of the system δE are equal to changes in its internal energy δU. Chemical thermodynamics concentrates on the internal energy of the system, but kinetic and potential energy changes of the system as a whole can be important for chemical systems. The principle of conservation of energy requires that the change in the internal energy of a system be the result of energy transfer between the system and its surroundings. The internal energy U is a function of the set of extensive variables associated with the various forms of internal energy. Each form of internal energy is manifest by the product of an extensive variable and its conjugate intensive variable. **Table 1** lists several forms of internal energy, their conjugate pair of variables, and their corresponding work terms.

The internal energy of the system is given by the fundamental equation of state, Eq. (7). Processes

$$U = U(S, V, \{n_i\}, \{X_i\}) \qquad (7)$$

which give rise to a change in U are then limited to those for which Eq. (8) holds. Since all the

$$dU = (\partial U / \partial S)_{V, \{n_i\}, \{X_j\}} dS + (\partial U / \partial V)_{S, \{n_i\}, \{X_j\}} dV$$
$$+ \sum_i (\partial U / \partial n_i)_{S, V, \{n_i\}', \{X_j\}} dn_i$$
$$+ \sum_y (\partial U / \partial X_j)_{X, V, \{n_i\}, \{X_j\}'} dX_j \qquad (8)$$

extensive state properties are linear homogeneous functions, the coefficients of the differential terms are themselves intensive and correspond to the conjugate variable of the respective extensive variable. Their product is thus the differential work associated with the appropriate form of external energy. Equation (8) then becomes Eq. (9), where

$$dU = T dS - p dV + \sum_i \mu_i dn_i + \sum_j I_j dX_j \quad (9)$$

μ_i is the chemical potential of the ith component and I_j is the conjugate potential for X_j. The internal energy change given by this expression is dependent only upon the state properties of the system, and hence is independent of the process causing the change. *See* CONSERVATION OF ENERGY; ENERGY; INTERNAL ENERGY; WORK.

Heat. Thermal energy exchange or heat (that form of energy transferred as a result of temperature differences between a system and its surroundings) plays a central role in thermodynamics, and is singled out from the other forms of energy or work. This is expressed by Eq. (10), where δq

$$dU = \delta q + \delta w \qquad (10)$$

TABLE 1. Internal energy and generalized work			
Type of energy	Intensive factor	Extensive factor	Element of work
Mechanical			
Expansion	Pressure (P)	Volume (V)	$-PdV$
Stretching	Surface tension (γ)	Area (A)	γdA
Extension	Tensile stretch (F)	Length (l)	Fdl
Thermal	Temperature (T)	Entropy (S)	TdS
Chemical	Chemical potential (gm)	Moles (n)	μdn
Electrical	Electric potential (E)	Charge (Q)	EdQ
Gravitational	Gravitational field strength (mg)	Height (h)	$mgdh$
Polarization			
Electrostatic	Electric field strength (E)	Total electric polarization (P)	EdP
Magnetic	Magnetic field strength (H)	Total magnetic polarization (M)	HdM

is the differential thermal energy (heat) absorbed by the system from the surroundings and δw is the differential work performed on the system by the surroundings. Equating Eqs. (9) and (10) yields Eq. (11). Since δw is the work performed

$$\delta q = TdS - PdV + \sum_i \mu_i dn_i$$
$$+ \sum_j I_j dX_j - \delta w \quad (11)$$

by the surroundings on the system, Eq. (11) can be rewritten as Eq. (12), where conservation

$$\delta q = TdS - (P - P_s)dV + \sum_i (\mu_i - \mu_{i_s})dn_i$$
$$+ \sum_j (I_j - I_{j_s})dX_j \quad (12)$$

laws for the nonthermal extensive properties have been utilized and where the subscript s on the intensive variable identifies it as the value for the surroundings. It is convenient to write this equation as Eqs. (13), where $(-\delta a)$ is the sum of

$$\delta q = TdS - \delta a \quad (13a)$$

$$dU = TdS + \delta w - \delta a \quad (13b)$$

the nonthermal differential work terms in Eq. (12). The term δa can be either zero or nonzero. If it is zero, the heat absorbed by the system is equal to TdS. In an adiabatic process δq is zero and $TdS = \delta a$, and hence if δa is nonzero, it must correspond to an internally generated thermal energy. This is frequently referred to as the uncompensated heat of a process, since it does not result from the transfer of heat from the surroundings. The first law or energy conservation principle can provide no further insight concerning either the sign or magnitude of δa. This will remain for the statement of the second law to consider. Of course, given the initial and final states of a system, the first law permits thermochemical calculations pertaining to such changes. *See* HEAT.

Heat capacity. The heat capacity of a system is of particular importance in such thermochemical calculations. The heat capacity is the amount of thermal energy that can be absorbed by a system for a unit rise in temperature. This is defined by Eq. (14), where C_{process} is the heat capacity

$$\delta q = C_{\mathrm{process}}\, dT \quad (14)$$

of a system for a given type of process. Three commonly considered processes for closed systems and their respective heat capacities are the constant-volume process C_v, the constant-pressure process C_p, and the saturated-vapor process C_s. Further understanding is gained by examination of Eqs. (9) and (10). For a closed system in which only mechanical (PV) work is possible, the internal energy change for a constant volume process is given by Eq. (15), and therefore Eqs. (16) hold.

$$dU = \delta q = C_v dT = TdS \quad (15)$$

$$C_v = (\partial U/\partial T)_V \quad (16a)$$

$$\Delta S = \int_{T_1}^{T_2} (C_v/T)dT \quad (16b)$$

In the same closed system, the internal energy change for a constant pressure process is given by Eq. (17). For convenience, a new state function

$$dU + PdV = \delta q = C_p dT = TdS \quad (17)$$

called the enthalpy is defined by Eqs. (18), which

$$H \equiv U + PV \quad (18a)$$

$$dH = dU + PdV + VdP \quad (18b)$$

for a constant-pressure process yield $dH = dU + PdV$; therefore Eqs. (19) hold. The heat capacity

$$C_p = (\partial H/\partial T)_p \quad (19a)$$

$$\Delta S = \int_{T_1}^{T_2} (C_p/T)dT \quad (19b)$$

is an extensive property of a system, but it is not a state function since its value is path- or process-dependent. *See* ENTHALPY; HEAT CAPACITY.

Second law of thermodynamics. There are many possible and essentially equivalent statements of the second law. It will suffice to state the empirical result that in all spontaneous processes the uncompensated heat δa in Eqs. (13) is always positive. Equation (13a) can be rewritten as Eq. (20), where the term $\delta q/T$ is the contribution

$$dS = \delta q/T + \delta a/T \quad (20)$$

to the entropy due to heat exchange with the

surrounding ($d_e S$), while $\delta a / T$ is the contribution to the entropy produced internally as a result of the interconversion of work terms ($d_i S$). The second law can then be summarized as Eqs. (21), where $d_i S$ greater than zero applies to

$$dS = d_e S + d_i S \qquad (21a)$$

$$d_i S \geq 0 \qquad (21b)$$

irreversible processes. When $d_i S = 0$, that is, for a reversible process, Eq. (22) holds. This is the

$$dS = \delta q_{\text{rev}} / T \qquad (22)$$

basic equation for establishing the thermodynamic temperature scale based upon the theoretical limits of reversible cycles. The requirement that $d_i S > 0$ for spontaneous processes provides the criteria for examining the specific conditions for spontaneous paths, and the criteria for establishing the equilibrium states of a system. *See* CARNOT CYCLE; TEMPERATURE.

In an isolated system, $dU = 0$, for any process that takes place whether spontaneous or not, whereas $dS = d_i S$ since $d_e S = 0$. Any spontaneous process must therefore increase S until S reaches a maximum value at which point only reversible processes can take place. If a random fluctuation perturbs the equilibrium state, the system will spontaneously return to the equilibrium state. Thus states in the vicinity of the equilibrium state are said to be unstable with respect to such perturbations. *See* ENTROPY.

Helmholtz free energy. While isolated systems are of theoretical value, they do not play an important role in practical chemical systems, and consequently criteria for systems undergoing changes at constant temperature and either constant volume or constant pressure are required. Examination of Eq. (11) indicates that if a state function defined by Eqs. (23)

$$A \equiv U - TS \qquad (23a)$$

$$dA = dU - TdS - SdT \qquad (23b)$$

is combined with Eq. (13b), then Eq. (24) holds,

$$dA = -\delta a + \delta w - SdT \qquad (24)$$

which for constant-temperature processes is Eqs. (25), and where $-\delta w_{\text{max}}$ is the maximum work that

$$dA = -\delta a + \delta w \quad \text{Spontaneous process} \qquad (25a)$$

$$dA = \delta w_{\text{max}} \quad \text{Reversible process} \qquad (25b)$$

can be performed by the system under constant temperature conditions. If processes take place at constant temperature and constant extensive variables ($V, \{n_i\}, \{X_i\}$), then $dA = -\delta a$, and all spontaneous processes are accompanied by a decrease in A and equilibrium is achieved when A is a minimum. The state function A is the Helmholtz free energy, and its characteristic variables are $A(T, V, \{n_i\}, \{X_i\})$. *See* FREE ENERGY.

Gibbs free energy. If a state function is defined by Eqs. (26), combining this with Eq. (13b) yields

$$G \equiv U + PV - TS = H - TS \qquad (26a)$$

$$dG = dU + PdV + VdP - TdS - SdT \qquad (26b)$$

Eq. (27), which for a constant temperature and pressure process is Eqs. (28). Here $-\delta w_{\text{net}}$ is the

$$dG = -\delta a + \delta w + PdV + VdP - SdT \qquad (27)$$

$$dG = -\delta a + \delta w + PdV \quad \text{Spontaneous process} \qquad (28a)$$

$$dG = \delta w_{\text{max}} + PdV = \delta w_{\text{net}} \quad \text{Reversible process} \qquad (28b)$$

next maximum work a system can perform in excess of expansion work under conditions of constant temperature and pressure. If processes take place at constant temperature and pressure and constant extensive variables ($\{n_i\}, \{X_j\}$), then $dG = -\delta a$, and all spontaneous processes are accompanied by a decrease in G and equilibrium is achieved when G is a minimum. The state function G is the Gibbs free energy or free enthalpy, and its characteristic variables are $G(T, P, \{n_i\}, \{X_j\})$.

Equations of state. **Table 2** summarizes the fundamental equation of state for the internal energy and entropy, as well as the derived equations of state for practical conditions. A more complete understanding of the relationship of equations involving intensive variables as independent variables is based on the mathematical recognition that intensive variables are Legendre transformations of the corresponding conjugate extensive variables. The properties of these transformations are such that derived equations involving intensive variables only incompletely define the state of the system, though they do completely define changes in state. *See* PARTIAL DIFFERENTIATION.

Affinity and chemical equilibrium. Many chemical systems can be considered closed systems in which a single parameter ξ can be defined as a measure of the extent of the reaction or the degree of advancement of a process. If the reaction proceeds or the process advances spontaneously, entropy must be produced according to the second law and δa must be positive. In terms of the advancement parameter ξ, this uncompensated heat δa can be given by Eq. (29), where $\underline{A}$ is the affinity of the

$$\delta a = \underline{A} d\xi = T d_i S \qquad (29)$$

process or reaction. The affinity is related to internal entropy production by Eq. (30). The condition

$$\underline{A} = T d_i S / d\xi \geq 0 \qquad (30)$$

that the entropy production is zero represents equilibrium, and hence $\underline{A} = 0$ is an equivalent condition for equilibrium in a closed system. For spontaneous processes, since the signs of $\underline{A}$ and $d\xi$ must be the same, for positive $\underline{A}$ the process must

TABLE 2. Equations of state and characteristic variables

Basic function	Equation of state	Differential form
Internal energy (U)	$v(S, V, \{n_i\}, \{X_i\})$	$dU = TdS - PdV + \sum_i \mu_i dn_i + \sum_j l_j dX_j$
Entropy (S)	$S(U, V, \{n_i\}, \{X_i\})$	$dS = (1/T)dU - (P/T)dV + \sum_i (\mu_i/T)dn_i + \sum_j (l_j/T)dX_j$
Enthalpy (H) $[H = U + PV]$	$H(S, P, \{n_i\}, \{X_i\})$	$dH = TdS + VdP + \sum_i \mu_i dn_i + \sum_j l_j dX_j$
Helmholtz free energy (A) $[A = U - TS]$	$A(V, T, \{n_i\}, \{X_i\})$	$dA = -SdT - PdV + \sum_i \mu_i dn_i + \sum_j l_j dX_j$
Gibbs free energy (G) $[G = U + PV - TS]$	$G(P, T, \{n_i\}, \{X_j\})$	$dG = -SdT + VdP + \sum_i \mu_i dn_i + \sum_j l_j dX_j$

advance or go in a forward direction in the usual sense of chemical reactions or physical processes, while for negative $\underline{A}$ the process must proceed in the reverse direction.

Equations (13b) and (26b) can be combined to give Eqs. (31) which indicates that the affinity is itself a state function, Eq. (32).

$$dG = -SdT + VdP - \delta a \qquad (31a)$$

$$= -SdT + VdP - \underline{A}d\xi \qquad (31b)$$

$$\underline{A} = -(\partial G/\partial \xi)_{P,T} = \underline{A}(T, P, \xi) \qquad (32)$$

Consider a closed system in which a chemical reaction can be characterized by the stoichiometry of reaction (33). The stoichiometry requires that at

$$\alpha A + \beta B \rightarrow \gamma C + \delta D \qquad (33)$$

each time element t in the reaction the number of moles of the ith component n_i be given by Eq. (34), where n_i^0 is the number of moles of i

$$n_i = n_i^0 + v_i \xi \qquad (34)$$

in the initial or original state ($t = 0$), v_i is the stoichiometric coefficient for the ith component as given in the balanced equation (the convention is that v_i is positive for products and negative for reactants), and ξ is the degree-of-advancement parameter whose range is normally taken to be zero to unity. In terms of differential changes in advancement Eq. (35) holds. For closed systems

$$dn_i = v_i d\xi \qquad (35)$$

(constant temperature and pressure) in which only thermal, expansion, and chemical work terms are included, Eqs. (36) and (37) hold. The condition

$$dG = +\sum_i \mu_i dn_i = -\delta a \qquad (36a)$$

$$= \left(\sum_i v_i \mu_i\right) d\xi = -\underline{A}d\xi \qquad (36b)$$

$$\underline{A}(T, P, \xi) = -\sum_i v_i \mu_i \qquad (37)$$

for equilibrium is $\underline{A} = 0$, and thus for a chemical reaction, equilibrium is achieved when Eq. (38)

$$\sum_i v_i \mu_i = 0 \qquad (38)$$

holds. If electrical work is included in Eq. (36), Eqs.

(39) and (40) hold. Since $\underline{A} = 0$ is the equilibrium

$$dG = \sum_i \mu_i dn_i + EdQ = -\delta a \qquad (39a)$$

$$= \left(\sum_i v_i \mu_i + zFE\right) d\xi = -\underline{A}d\xi \qquad (39b)$$

$$\underline{A}(T, P, E, \xi) = -\sum_i v_i \mu_i - zFE \qquad (40)$$

condition, equilibrium in an electrochemical system is given by Eq. (41), where z is the number of

$$\sum_i v_i \mu_i = -zFE \qquad (41)$$

equivalents of charge and F is the Faraday constant (the number of coulombs of charge per equivalent).

More than one reaction can take place in a chemical system, each characterized by a degree-of-advancement parameter, and thus for r independent reactions, Eqs. (42) hold, where the

$$dG = \sum_i \mu_i dn_i = -\delta a \qquad (42a)$$

$$= \sum_r \underline{A}_r \delta \xi_r \qquad (42b)$$

$$= \sum_r \left(\sum_i v_{ir} \mu_{ir} \delta \xi_r\right) \qquad (42c)$$

equilibrium condition is Eq. (43). At equilibrium

$$\sum_r \underline{A}d\xi_r = 0 \qquad (43)$$

each of the $\underline{A}_r$ must be zero, but for the spontaneous condition, inequality (44) holds. In

$$\sum_r \underline{A}_r d\xi_r > 0 \qquad (44)$$

a two-reaction system inequality (45) holds, but

$$\underline{A}_1 d\xi_1 + \underline{A}_2 d\xi_2 > 0 \qquad (45)$$

now $\underline{A}_1$ and $d\xi_1$ do not necessarily have the same sign. If their signs are different, the first reaction can be driven in the nonspontaneous direction by the second reaction. The reactions are then said to be coupled, and this is a common situation in biological systems. *See* CHEMICAL EQUILIBRIUM.

Chemical potential. The affinity of a chemical reaction establishes the spontaneous direction of the reaction, and consequently methods for determining the affinity are important in thermochemical studies. As shown above, the affinity is simply related to the stoichiometric coefficients of the reaction and the chemical potentials of the reactants and products in the reaction. It is necessary therefore to investigate some of the properties of the chemical potential and to develop convenient methods of using it to calculate the affinity.

The chemical potential of a single-phase pure substance can be expressed as $\mu_i = \mu_i(T,P)$, whereas for a component in single-phase solution $\mu_i = \mu_i(T,P,\{x_i\})$, where $\{x_i\}$ is the set of independent mole fractions ($x_i = n_i/\Sigma\, n_i$). All intensive thermodynamic variables are homogeneous functions of zero degree in mass, and hence Eq. (46) holds, where $\overline{I}i$ is given by Eq. (47). Equation (46) is

$$\sum_i n_i \overline{I}_i = 0 \qquad (46)$$

$$\overline{I}_i = (\partial I_i/\partial n_i)_{T,P,\{n_i\}'} \qquad (47)$$

a form of the Gibbs-Duhem relationship. Since the chemical potential is intensive, the Gibbs-Duhem equation for a given solution phase can be written as Eq. (48). This is an important result in phase

$$\sum_i x_i \overline{\mu_i} = 0 \qquad (48)$$

equilibria in heterogeneous systems, and places restraints on the number of independent variables in such systems. *See* PHASE EQUILIBRIUM.

The chemical potential can be represented in several forms, but for chemical studies the form which expresses that it is a partial molar quantity, Eq. (49), is most useful. Since the order of

$$\mu_i = (\partial G/\partial n_i)_{T,P,\{n_i\}'} \qquad (49)$$

differentation of exact functions is immaterial, temperature, and pressure derivatives of μ_i are given by Eqs. (50) and (51), where $\overline{S}_i$ and $\overline{V}_i$

$$(\partial\mu_i/\partial T)_{P,\{n_i\}} = \partial^2 G/\partial T\,\partial n_i$$
$$= -(\partial S/\partial n_i)_{T,P,\{n_i\}} = -\overline{S}_i \quad (50)$$

$$(\partial\mu_i/\partial P)_{T,\{n_i\}} = \partial^2 G/\partial P\,\partial n_i$$
$$= -(\partial V/\partial n_i)_{T,P} = \overline{V}_i \qquad (51)$$

are the partial molar entropy and volume of the ith component. Two additional useful differential coefficients are given by Eqs. (52) and (53), where

$$[\partial(\mu_i/T)/\partial(1/T)]_{P,\{n_i\}} = \overline{H}_i \qquad (52)$$

$$(\partial\overline{H}_i/\partial T)_{P,\{n_i\}} = \overline{C}_{P,i} \qquad (53)$$

$\overline{H}_i$ and $\overline{C}_{P,i}$ are the partial molar enthalpy and constant-pressure heat capacity.

It is quite apparent that a knowledge of the chemical potentials of pure substances and of substances in solution provides the basis of the thermal properties of the substance, as well as the

basis for reaction spontaneity. Usually the chemical potential of a substance is expressed in terms of a standard state and a convenient measure of the deviation from that state. Various functional forms could be used, but it is customary to use Eq. (54), where $\mu_i^{\ominus}$ is the chemical potential in a

$$\mu_i(T, P, \{x_i\}) = \mu_i^{\ominus}(T, P, \{x_i\})$$
$$+ RT \ln a_i^*(^*T, P, \{x_i\}) \quad (54)$$

designated standard state, R is the gas constant, and a_i^* is the relative activity of the ith substance. The activity is frequently written as Eq. (55), where

$$a_i^* = f_i^* x_i \qquad (55)$$

$f_i^*\ (T,P,\{x_i\})$ is the activity coefficient on the mole fraction basis. Two basic situations arise as the mole fraction approaches its limits of 0 to 1, and it is these limits that determine the functional form of f_i^*. Combining Eq. (54) with (55) gives Eq. (56).

$$\mu_i = \mu_i^* + RT\ \ln f_i^* + RT\ \ln x_i \qquad (56)$$

If the

$$\lim_{x_i \to 1} f_1^* = 1$$

then Eq. (57), the Raoult law convention, holds

$$\lim_{x_i \to 1} \mu_i = \mu_i^* = \mu_i^*(T, P) \qquad (57)$$

where μ_i^* is the chemical potential of pure i. The other limit,

$$\lim_{x_i \to 0} f_i = 1$$

implies that

$$\lim_{x_i \to 1} f_i$$

equals some finite value, say f_i^∞, and therefore Eq. (58), the Henry law convention, holds, where

$$\lim_{x_i \to 1} \mu_i = \mu_i^{\ominus} + RT\ \ln f_i^\infty = \mu_i^\infty \qquad (58)$$

f_i^∞ is the activity coefficient at mole fraction unity determined by the limiting behavior of the chemical potential in an infinitely dilute solution of i, and μ_i^∞ is the chemical potential i would have if its dilute solution behavior persisted up to mole fraction one. The two situations can be summarized by Eqs. (59),

$$\mu_i = \mu_i^*(T, P) + RT\ \ln f_i^* x_i \quad \text{Raoult's law} \quad (59a)$$

$$\mu_i = \mu_i^\infty(T, P, x_i) + RT\ \ln f_i^\infty x_i \quad \text{Henry law}$$
$$(59b)$$

where f_i^* and f_i^∞ are the activity coefficients on the Raoult or Henry law basis, respectively. *See* ACTIVITY (THERMODYNAMICS).

The activities discussed above are based upon mole fractions. It is frequently more convenient to use other measures of relative amounts, for example, the molality m, defined as the moles of solute per kilogram of solvent, and the molarity c, defined as the moles of solute per liter of solution. If this is done, the chemical potentials are given by Eq. (60) or (61), where $\mu_i^{\infty,m}$ and $\mu_i^{\infty,c}$ are infinite dilution

$$\mu_i = \mu_i^{\infty,m} + RT \ln f_i^m \, m_i \qquad (60)$$

$$\mu_i = \mu_i^{\infty,c} + RT \ln f_i^c c_i \qquad (61)$$

based standard state chemical potentials on the molality and molarity convention, and f_i^m and f_i^c are activity coefficients on the same bases. In each case

$$\lim_{m_i, c_i \to 0} f_i = 1$$

The chemical potential of gases is frequently discussed in terms of its fugacity or pressure, and Eq. (54) is then written as Eq. (62) or (63), where

$$\mu_i = \mu_i^0(T) + RT \ln P_i^* \qquad (62)$$

$$\mu_i = \mu_i^0(T) + RT \ln f_i P_i \qquad (63)$$

P_i^* is the fugacity of substance i and is equal to $f_i P_i$, where f_i is the fugacity coefficient and P_i is the partial pressure of i. The fugacity coefficient is defined such that the

$$\lim_{P \to 0} f_i = 1$$

The standard chemical potential $\mu_i^0(T)$ is the value of the chemical potential of a perfect gas, and is a function of temperature only. *See* FUGACITY.

The chemical potential of pure liquids or solids is given by Eq. (64), where $P^\ominus$ is the pressure in a designated standard state. The last term of Eq. (64)

$$\mu_i(T, P) = \mu_i^*(T, P)$$
$$= \mu_i^\ominus(T, P^\ominus) + \int_{P^\ominus}^P \overline{V}_i dP \qquad (64)$$

is negligible if $(P - P^\ominus)$ is not very large, since $\overline{V}_i$ for condensed phases is relatively small. Generally the standard chemical potential is taken from tables of Gibbs free energies of formation $\Delta G^\ominus$ of pure gases, liquids, or solids or of substances at infinite dilution in particular solvents.

Thermodynamical relationships. The criteria for equilibrium in a chemical system at constant temperature and pressure are given by Eq. (65).

$$\underline{A} = -\sum v_i \mu_i = 0 \qquad (65)$$

If a reaction takes place in a gaseous mixture, substitution of Eq. (62) for the μ_i gives Eq. (66a) or (66b), and Eq. (67) holds, where $\Delta G_{\text{react}}^\circ$ is the

$$\sum v_i(\mu_i^0(T) + RT \ln P_i^*) = 0 \qquad (66a)$$

$$\sum v_i \mu_i^0(T) = -RT \ln \prod_i (P_i^*)^{v_i} \qquad (66b)$$

$$\Delta G_{\text{react}}^\circ(T) = -RT \ln K_{p*} \qquad (67)$$

Gibbs free energy change for a reaction going from a standard state of reactants to a standard state of products in accordance with the stoichiometry of

the reaction, and K_{p*} is the equilibrium constant for the reaction in terms of fugacities. At low pressures $P_i^* = P_i$ and the equilibrium constant for reaction (33) is given by Eq. (68). For a reaction

$$K_p = P_c^\gamma P_d^\delta / P_a^\alpha P_b^\beta \qquad (68)$$

in solution for which the chemical potential is given on a molarity basis, Eqs. (69)–(71) hold,

$$\sum v_i(\mu_i^{\infty,c} + RT \ln a_i^c) = 0 \qquad (69)$$

$$\sum v_i \mu_i^{\infty,c} = -RT \ln \prod_i (a_i^c)^{v_i} \qquad (70)$$

$$\Delta G_{\text{react}}^{\infty,c} = -RT \ln K_a^c \qquad (71)$$

where K_a^c is the equilibrium constant for the reaction in terms of molarity-based activities. For dilute solutions, $a_i = c_i$, and for reaction (33), Eq. (72) holds. Similar results can be obtained for

$$K_c = c_c^\gamma c_d^\delta / c_a^\alpha c_b^\beta \qquad (72)$$

other concentration-gased activities. The activities can be based on whatever measures of activity are most convenient. Clearly the more general expression of the equilibrium is given by Eq. (73).

$$\Delta G_{\text{react}}^\ominus = -RT \ln K_a \qquad (73)$$

The standard enthalpy, entropy, heat capacity, and volume changes for a chemical reaction can be obtained directly from the appropriate temperature derivatives of the standard free energy of the reaction or its equivalent, the equilibrium constant.

The condition for a reaction to take place spontaneously in the direction from reactants to products requires that $\underline{A}$ be positive, and hence Eqs. (74) hold, where Q_a is an expression of the form

$$\underline{A} = -\sum_i v_i \mu_i > 0 \qquad (74a)$$

$$\underline{A} = -\left(\sum_i v_i \mu_i + RT \ln \prod_i a_i^{v_i}\right) > 0 \quad (74b)$$

$$\underline{A} = RT \ln K_a - RT \ln Q_a > 0 \qquad (74c)$$

$$\underline{A} = RT \ln K_a/Q_a > 0 \quad \text{or} \quad K_a/Q_a > 1 \quad (74d)$$

of the equilibrium constant, but involving activities of reactants in their initial state and the activities of the products in their final states. Again, the bases of the activities in Q_a, as in K_a, are arbitrary and selected for convenience.

Third law of thermodynamics. Most understanding of the classical thermodynamics of chemical systems is based upon the first and second laws. As these systems are studied on a molecular rather than on a macroscopic basis, it is apparent that the first and second laws cannot be addressed to this endeavor in a direct manner. Although implicit in the concept of the existence of the fundamental equations of state for U or S is an absolute value of these functions, and therefore an extensive quantity which could be calculated on the basis of molecular properties from quantum mechanics and statistical mechanics, neither the first nor second law considers anything but differences in these state functions. The second law does indeed indicate the existence of an absolute zero for an intensive variable, the temperature, but this is not sufficient to bridge the areas of classical and statistical thermodynamics. *See* ABSOLUTE ZERO.

It is found experimentally that for many isothermal processes involving pure phases, Eq. (75)

$$\lim_{T \to 0} \Delta S = 0 \qquad (75)$$

holds. This includes phase transitions between different crystalline modifications, solid-state chemical reactions, and even the solid-liquid transition in helium. This, along with Eq. (76), implies that

$$S(T, P) - S(0 \text{ K}) = \int_0^T (C_p/T) dT \qquad (76)$$

at zero absolute temperature the entropy of pure crystalline phases are equal. If the entropy of pure phases are equal at $T = 0$, it is reasonable to take the value $S(0 \text{ K})$ to be zero. The statement of the third law then is that the entropy of all pure crystalline phases at 0 K is zero. This makes it possible, by using Eq. (76), to calculate the absolute or third-law entropy of a substance from experimental measurements of their heat capacities. Comparison of such experimental values with those calculated by statistical thermodynamic methods has provided evidence for the validity of the third law. In some cases thorough investigation of apparent discrepancies from the third law have led to new conclusions concerning the molecular structure of the substances or new information on the energy level system for the molecules. Calculations of the thermodynamic properties for a gas from the spectroscopic properties of molecules is an important result stemming from the third law. *See* STATISTICAL MECHANICS.

Thermodynamics of irreversible processes. Classical equilibrium thermodynamics is primarily concerned with calculations for reversible processes, and deals with irreversibility in terms of inequalities. In the case of irreversible processes in systems slightly removed from equilibrium, the rate of internal entropy production d_iS/dt is related to the fluxes J_i associated with thermal, concentration, or other differences in intensive parameters or potentials X_i. This entropy production is then given by Eq. (77). The fluxes include heat conduction, diffusion,

$$d_iS/dt = \sum_i J_i X_i \geq 0 \qquad (77)$$

electric conduction, and other direct effects.

In addition, a flux of one type may be coupled to a potential difference of another type. For example, a thermal gradient can result in a mass flux (thermal diffusion), or a concentration gradient in any energy flux. Thermal conductivity, thermoosmosis, and thermoelectric effects are all coupled effects. The fluxes are thus found to be given by Eq. (78),

$$J_i = \sum_i L_{ij} X_j \qquad (78)$$

where the L_{ij} are called the phenomenological coefficients. If $L_{ij} \neq 0$, there is a coupling between the flux J_i and the gradient X_j. Microscopic reversibility implies that not far from equilibrium, $L_{ij} = L_{ji}$, and this is known as the Onsager reciprocity relationship. These results, together with the theorem of minimum entropy production, are the basis of investigations of irreversible processes near equilibrium. *See* THERMOELECTRICITY.

Far removed from equilibrium, thermodynamics must be formulated somewhat differently and more cautiously. The interplay of thermodynamic stability and kinetics can give rise to macroscopic structures with both temporal and spatial coherence called dissipative structures. Much theoretical effort has been directed to these studies because of their apparent relevance to biological structures. *See* THERMODYNAMIC PRINCIPLES; THERMODYNAMIC PROCESSES.   Robert A. Pierotti

Chemiluminescence

The type of luminescence wherein a chemical reaction supplies the energy responsible for the emission of light (ultraviolet, visible, or infrared) in excess of that of a blackbody (thermal radiation) at the same temperature and within the same spectral range. Below 900°F (500°C), the emission of any light during a chemical reaction is a chemiluminescence. The blue inner cone of a bunsen burner or the Coleman gas lamp are examples. *See* BLACKBODY.

Reactions. Many chemical reactions generate energy. Usually this exothermicity appears as heat, that is, translational, rotational, and vibrational energy of the product molecules; whereas, for a visible chemiluminescence to occur, one of the reaction products must be generated in an excited electronic state (designated by an asterisk) from which it can undergo deactivation by emission of a photon. Hence a chemiluminescent reaction, as shown in reactions (1) and (2), can be regarded as

$$A + B \rightarrow C^* + D \qquad (1)$$

$$C^* \rightarrow C + h\nu \qquad (2)$$

the reverse of a photochemical reaction.

Energy. The energy of the light quantum $h\nu$ (where h is Planck's constant, and ν is the light frequency) depends on the separation between the ground and the first excited electronic state of C; and the spectrum of the chemiluminescence usually matches the fluorescence spectrum of the emitter. Occasionally, the reaction involves an additional step, the transfer of electronic energy from C^* to another molecule, not necessarily otherwise involved in the reaction. Sometimes no discrete excited state can be specified, in which case the chemiluminescence spectrum is a structureless continuum associated with the formation of a molecule, as in the so-called air afterglow: $NO + O \rightarrow NO_2 + h\nu$ (green light). *See* HEAT RADIATION; LUMINESCENCE; PHOTOCHEMISTRY.

Efficiency. The efficiency of a chemiluminescence is expressed as its quantum yield ϕ, that is, the number of photons emitted per reacted molecule. Many reactions have quantum yields much lower (10^{-8} $h\nu$ per molecule) than the maximum of unity. Einsteins of visible light (1 einstein $= Nh\nu$, where N is Avogadro's number), with wavelengths from 400 to 700 nanometers, correspond to energies of about 70 to 40 kcal per mole (300 to 170 kilojoules per mole). Thus only very exothermic, or "exergonic," chemical processes can be expected to be chemiluminescent. Partly for this reason, most familiar examples of chemiluminescence involve oxygen and oxidation processes; the most efficient examples of these are the enzyme-mediated bioluminescences. The glow of phosphorus in air is a historically important case, although the mechanism of this complex reaction is not fully understood. The oxidation of many organic substances, such as aldehydes or alcohols, by oxygen, hydrogen peroxide, ozone, and so on, is chemiluminescent. The reaction of heated ether vapor with air results in a bluish "cold" flame, for example. The efficiency of some chemiluminescences in solution, such as the oxidation of luminol (**1**) and, especially, the reaction of some oxalate esters (**2**) with hydrogen

(**1**)   (**2**)

peroxide, can be very high (ϕ = 30%). *See* BIOLUMINESCENCE.

Other aspects. It is believed that the requirements for chemiluminescence are not only that there be sufficient exothermicity and the presence of a suitable emitter, but also that the chemical process be very fast and involve few geometrical changes, in order to minimize energy dissipation through vibrations. For example, the transfer of one electron from a powerful oxidant to a reductant (often two radical ions of opposite charge generated electrochemically) is a type of process which can result, in some cases, in very effective generation of electronic excitation. An example, with 9,10-diphenylanthracene (DPA), is shown in reaction (3). The same is true of the decomposition of

$$DPA^{\overline{\cdot}} + DPA^{\overset{+}{\cdot}} \rightarrow DPA^* + DPA \qquad (3)$$

four-membered cyclic peroxides (**3**) into carbonyl products, as shown in reaction (**4**), which may be

(**3**)

the prototype of many chemiluminescences.

Therese Wilson

Electrogenerated chemiluminescence. Also known as electrochemiluminescence, electrogenerated chemiluminescence is a luminescent chemical reaction in which the reactants are formed electrochemically. Electrochemical reactions are electron-transfer reactions occurring in an electrochemical cell. In such a reaction, light emission may occur as with chemiluminescence; however, the excitation is from the application of a voltage to an electrode. In chemiluminescence, the luminophore is excited to a higher energetic state by means of a chemical reaction initiated by mixing of the reagents. In electrogenerated chemiluminescence, the emitting luminophore is excited to a higher energy state by reactions of species that are generated at an electrode surface by the passage of current through the working electrode. Upon decay to the electronic ground state, light emitted by the luminophore (fluorescent or phosphorescent) can be detected. The luminophore is typically a polycyclic hydrocarbon, an aromatic heterocycle, or certain transition-metal chelates. *See* ELECTRON-TRANSFER REACTION.

Reaction mechanism. There are many reactions which give rise to electrogenerated chemiluminescence. However, they all share some common features. A typical reaction scheme involves the oxidation of a luminophore (Z), as in reaction (5), and

$$Z \longrightarrow Z^+ + e^- \qquad (5)$$

reduction of a second molecule of the luminophore, as in reaction (6), where e^- is an electron. The ex-

$$Z + e^- \longrightarrow Z^- \qquad (6)$$

cited state of the luminophore (Z^*) is formed by a homogeneous charge-transfer reaction (7), between

$$Z^+ + Z^- \longrightarrow Z^* + Z \qquad (7)$$

the oxidized and reduced luminophore. The excited luminophore decays to the ground state and emits a photon at a wavelength characteristic of the luminophore, which is measured by means of a photomultiplier detector [reaction (8)].

$$Z^* \overset{h\nu}{\longrightarrow} Z \qquad (8)$$

An example is the oxidative-reduction reaction using ruthenium tris(2,2'-bipyridine) [$Ru(bpy)_3{}^{2+}$], and oxalate $C_2O_4{}^{2-}$. The luminophore $Ru(bpy)_3{}^{2+}$ and oxalate are oxidized by application of a positive voltage to the electrode [reactions (9) and (10)]. In

$$Ru(bpy)_3{}^{2+} \longrightarrow Ru(bpy)_3{}^{3+} + e^- \qquad (9)$$

$$C_2O_4{}^{2-} \longrightarrow C_2O_4{}^- \cdot + e^- \qquad (10)$$

both reactions, one electron is removed for each molecule of starting material. The oxidized oxalate rapidly disassociates [reaction (11)]. The products

$$C_2O_4{}^- \cdot \longrightarrow CO_2 + CO_2{}^- \cdot \qquad (11)$$

formed are carbon dioxide and, importantly, a strong reducing agent, $CO_2{}^- \cdot$ radical anion. The term oxidative-reduction is descriptive of the process of forming a strong reducing agent through an electrochemical oxidation reaction. An exothermic and energetic reaction between the reducing agent and the oxidized luminophore occurs. Provided the enthalpy of the reaction is greater than the excitation energy, the excited state of the luminophore results from reaction (12). After the

$$Ru(bpy)_3{}^{3+} + CO_2{}^- \cdot \longrightarrow Ru(bpy)_3{}^{2+*} + CO_2 \qquad (12)$$

emission reaction [reaction (8)], the luminophore is returned to the initial state and is able to again participate in the reaction sequence, and thus it is able to emit many photons during each measurement cycle.

Applications. Chief among the developments since the early research and discovery of electrogenerated chemiluminescence was the construction of instrumentation for detection of electrogenerated chemiluminescence. These instruments made it possible for the methodology to be used by practitioners other than electrochemists.

Measurement of the light intensity of electrogenerated chemiluminescence is very sensitive and is proportional to the luminophore concentration. Trace amounts of luminophore as low as 10^{-13} mol/liter can be detected, making electrogenerated chemiluminescence very useful in analytical and diagnostic applications.

A commercial application of the phenomenon forms the basis of a highly sensitive technique for detection of biological analytes such as deoxyribonucleic acid (DNA), ribonucleic acid (RNA), proteins, antibodies, haptens, and therapeutic drugs in the clinical laboratory. The technique combines a binding assay method and a system for detecting electrogenerated chemiluminescence. The reaction is an oxidative-reduction type of mechanism using tripropyl amine and $Ru(bpy)_3{}^{2+}$. The concentration of analyte from a blood or serum sample is proportional to the intensity of the light from the electrogenerated chemiluminescence reaction. The reaction is carried out with a luminophore that is specially bound to the analyte of interest. The process of specifically binding a label (that is, a luminophore) to an analyte and measuring the extent of binding to determine concentration is referred to as a binding assay. An immunoassay uses as the binding reaction an antibody-antigen reaction. By covalently bonding the luminophore to the antibody, an electrogenerated chemiluminescence–active label is produced. The binding reaction may be of many types; antibody-antigen, ligand-receptor, DNA hybridization, and others.

Relating the intensity of the electrogenerated chemiluminescence to concentration requires the integration of several types of systems: a biological binding reaction that is selective for the analyte and attaches the luminophore; an electrochemiluminescent reaction causing the luminophore to emit light; and an instrument which integrates the electrochemical cell, light measurement system, and means for sample handling and preparation.

Separation scientists requiring more sensitive detection system capabilities for chromatography have used electrogenerated chemiluminescence as a substitute for more traditional methods of detection, such as fluorescence and spectrophotometry.

Jonathan K. Leland; Laurette Nacamulli; Hongjun Yang

Bibliography. A. J. Bard (ed.), *Electroanalytical Chemistry*, vol. 1, 1966, vol. 10, 1977; A. J. Bard and L. R. Faulkner, *Electrochemical Methods*, 1980; A. K. Campbell, *Chemiluminescence: Principles and Applications in Biology and Medicine*, 1988; P. E. Stanley and L. J. Kricka (eds.), *Bioluminescence and Chemiluminescence*, 1991.

Chemiosmosis

The coupling of metabolic and light energy to the performance of transmembrane work through the intermediary of electroosmotic gradients. Processes include synthesis of adenosinetriphosphate (ATP) by oxidative phosphorylation or by photosynthesis, production of heat, accumulation of small molecules by active transport, movement of bacterial flagella, uptake of deoxyribonucleic acid (DNA) during bacterial conjugation, genetic transformation and bacteriophage infection, and insertion or secretion of proteins into or through membranes.

Oxidative phosphorylation. During the 1940s and 1950s, mitochondria were shown to be the powerhouses of the eukaryotic cell and the site of synthesis of ATP by oxidative phosphorylation. In the oxidation portion of ATP synthesis, reductants, such as reduced nicotinamide adenine dinucleotide (NADH) and succinate, are generated during metabolism of carbohydrates, lipids, and protein. These compounds are oxidized through the series of redox reactions performed by membrane-bound complexes, called electron transport or respiratory chains. The respiratory chains have common features. All are found associated with the inner mitochondrial membrane, and each chain pumps protons from inside the mitochondrion to the cytosol. Each begins with a membrane-bound dehydrogenase enzyme which oxidizes the soluble reductant. The dehydrogenase complex transfers electrons to a lipid-soluble quinone coenzyme, such as ubiquinone, which in turn passes electrons to a series of cytochromes. Cytochromes are proteins which have a heme moiety. Unlike the oxygen-carrier protein hemoglobin, which maintains its heme iron in the reduced state, the irons of cytochromes undergo a cycle of oxidation-reduction, alternating between the ferrous and ferric states. During reduction a cytochrome accepts an electron from the reduced side of the chain and passes it to the cytochrome on the oxidized side of the chain. The terminal cytochrome interacts with molecular oxygen, forming water. The overall reaction for the mitochondrial NADH oxidase is expressed in (1). The reaction is exergonic, with

$$NADH + H^+ + {}^1/_2O_2 \longrightarrow NAD^+ + H_2O \qquad (1)$$

a standard free-energy change ($\Delta G^{\circ\prime}$) at pH 7 of -52.6 kcal/mol. *See* CYTOCHROME; HEMOGLOBIN; MITOCHONDRIA.

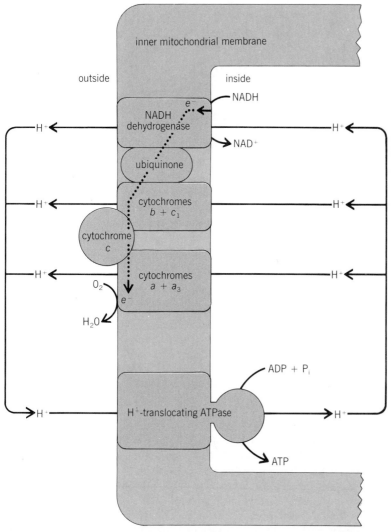

Mitochondrial oxidative phosphorylation. The chemiosmotic proton circuit of the inner mitochondrial membrane is depicted. NADH oxidase is composed of three proton-translocating units connected in series to form an electron transport chain. Electrons flow down a redox potential gradient from NADH to oxygen (broken line). Protons are pumped up an electrochemical gradient from inside to outside the mitochondrion, generating a proton motive force. Uptake of protons by the proton-translocating ATPase couples the phosphorylation of ADP to ATP.

The phosphorylation half of oxidative phosphorylation is catalyzed by a specific H^+-translocating adenosinetriphosphatase (ATPase) enzyme. The ATPase is also a membrane-bound enzyme located in the inner mitochrondrial membrane, catalyzing reaction (2), where ADP is adenosinediphosphate

$$ADP + P_i + H^+ \longrightarrow ATP + H_2O \qquad (2)$$

and P_i is inorganic phosphate. The reaction occurs with a standard free-energy change, $\Delta G^{\circ\prime}$, of $+7.3$ kcal/mol. The two processes, oxidation and phosphorylation, are metabolically coupled, so that mitochondria continually synthesize ATP by using energy derived from the respiratory chain. In the case of NADH oxidase, the net reaction is shown as (3).

$$NADH + {}^1/_2O_2 + 3ADP + 3P_i + 4H^+ \longrightarrow$$
$$NAD^+ + 3ATP + 4H_2O \quad (3)$$

In the overall biological reaction, three ATP's are synthesized for each NADH reduced, even though enough energy was available for six or seven ATP's. This assumes that the actual free-energy change, ΔG, is approximately the same as the standard free-energy change at pH 7, $\Delta G^{\circ\prime}$. Calculations suggest that the free energy of formation of ATP is probably greater than -7.3 kcal/ mol, perhaps as much as -10 to -15 kcal/mol, but it is difficult to determine this parameter in a living system. The stoichiometry is a function of the molecular mechanism of coupling.

Most early postulates about the mechanism by which the redox energy of NADH is converted into the energy-rich phosphoric anhydride bond of ATP involved the formation of a high-energy chemical intermediate during the flow of electrons down the respiratory chain. This chemical intermediate could then interact with ADP, forming a high-energy nucleotide which could finally interact with P_i, producing ATP. For two decades this chemical intermediate proved elusive. The search culminated in the formulation of the chemiosmotic hypothesis by Peter Mitchell in 1961. For this contribution Mitchell was awarded the Nobel prize in medicine in 1978.

Mitchell postulated that chemical energy, that is, the energy of a chemical bond, can be reversibly converted into electroosmotic energy. The reactions are catalyzed by enzyme complexes which function as primary ion pumps. From the work of Mitchell and of others, the respiratory chain and the ATPase have both been shown to be proton pumps. The respiratory chain transports protons out of the mitochondrion into the cell cytosol, creating an electrochemical gradient of protons. When the ATPase hydrolyzes ATP, it also pumps protons out of the mitochondrion, hence the name H^+-translocating ATPase. Since the free energy produced by respiration is so much greater than that derived from ATP hydrolysis, proton translocation by the respiratory chain creates a force which drives the uptake of protons by the ATPase and consequently the synthesis of ATP. A diagram of the coupling of oxidation and phosphorylation is shown in the **illustration**.

Mitchell termed the force derived from proton translocation the proton motive force (pmf), by analogy with the electromotive force (emf) of electrochemical cells. Since the pmf is produced by pumping of H^+ ions across the mitochondrial membrane, it has both electrical and chemical components. The electrical or membrane potential ($\Delta\psi$) is due to the separation of positive and negative charges across the mitochondrial membrane. The chemical component results from the separation of H^+ and OH^-. Since pH = $-\log$ [H^+], [H^+] being the concentration of H^+ ions, the chemical proton gradient is measured as a pH difference, ΔpH. Thus, pmf = $\Delta\psi - (2.3RT/F) \cdot \Delta$pH and pmf = $\Delta G/F$, where R is the gas constant, T is the temperature, and F is the Faraday constant.

The concept of chemiosmosis is now well accepted, although some still question whether the pmf is the primary source of energy for phosphorylation. Most effort is concentrated on the molecular mechanisms of chemiosmotic coupling. It is clear that respiratory chains pump out protons, but questions such as which components directly transport protons, how many protons are translocated per pair of electrons, and what is the catalytic mechanism of proton translocation are still not adequately answered. It is clear that the ATPase transports protons outward during ATP hydrolysis and inward during synthesis, but the number of protons per ATP is controversial. The protons may directly interact with substrate within an active site, participating directly in catalysis. Conversely, binding of protons may change the shape or conformation of the ATPase enzyme in such a way as to alter its affinity for ATP. These are not trivial distinctions. How these macromolecular complexes work, how chemical energy is transformed into electrochemical and back into chemical energy, cannot be understood without the answers to the more basic questions. *See* ADENOSINETRIPHOSPHATE (ATP); BIOLOGICAL OXIDATION.

Bacterial oxidative phosphorylation. Bacteria do not contain mitochondria, but many of the functions of the mitochondrial membrane are carried out by the bacterial cytoplasmic membrane. All bacteria contain a H^+-translocating ATPase in their cytoplasmic membrane. This enzyme is nearly identical to that of mitochondria. In fact, the genes for the bacterial and mitochondrial versions are clearly derived from a single evolutionary precursor. Many bacteria also use respiratory chains. Oxygen is not always the terminal electron acceptor of those chains. In some, nitrate or other oxidants can serve this role. But all of the chains are proton pumps. Thus, oxidative phosphorylation in bacteria is also chemiosmotic in nature. This resemblance to mitochondria is more than chance. The evidence, although mostly circumstantial, suggests that mitochondria, chloroplasts, and perhaps other eukaryotic organelles were originally free-living bacteria. These bacteria and larger proto-eukaryotic cells became mutually symbiotic, so that neither was complete or viable without the other. The animal and plant kingdoms arose from these endosymbiotic events. *See* BACTERIAL PHYSIOLOGY AND METABOLISM.

Photosynthesis. Photosynthesis is the conversion of light energy into chemical energy. Overall photosynthetic bacteria and the chloroplasts of eukaryotic plants capture sunlight or other light and use that energy to generate both ATP and a reductant for use in biosynthesis. The mechanism of photophosphorylation, that is, the use of light energy to drive the phosphorylation of ADP to ATP, resembles that of oxidative phosphorylation. Chloroplasts use a H^+-translocating ATPase for phosphorylation. Again, the genes for the chloroplast ATPase are derived from the same evolutionary precursor as the mitochondrial and bacterial genes. Electron transport chains are also components of membranes found within chloroplasts. These chains have components similar to those of mitochondria, but the direction of electron flow is reversed. Water is oxidized to produce oxygen. Nicotinamide adenine dinucleotide phosphate ($NADP^+$) is reduced to NADPH, which is used for CO_2 fixation and the synthesis of carbohydrates. The energy to drive these endergonic reactions is derived from light through the absorption of photons by chlorophyll-containing photosystems. The chloroplast electron transport chain comprises a proton pump, generating a pmf which drives the phosphorylation of ADP to ATP by the ATPase. *See* PHOTOSYNTHESIS.

Thermogenesis. Not all of the energy of the proton motive force is coupled productively. It was noted above that enough chemiosmotic energy is generated by respiration to allow for phosphorylation of six or seven ATP. Yet, at best only three are produced. If not coupled to the performance of work, the excess energy may be lost as heat. In some cases, heat production or thermogenesis through the dissipation of the pmf is regulated. Some mammals, for example, cold-adapted animals, hibernating animals, and infants of hairless species (including humans), have a specialized form of adipose tissue called brown fat. The inner membrane of brown-fat mitochondria has unique proton channels which open or close depending on the need for heat. When open, the channels allow for the return of protons extruded by respiration. This cycling of protons uncouples the pmf from ATP synthesis. The energy from proton cycling becomes heat energy. By controlling the rate of the cycle, animals can regulate body temperature. *See* ADIPOSE TISSUE; THERMOREGULATION.

Other chemiosmotic systems. Oxidative phosphorylation and photophosphorylation are but specialized examples of chemiosmotic energy coupling. In the broader sense, the pmf is an ion current analogous to an electric current. Electric generators are machines which convert stored energy into a current of electrons. Among the forms of useful energy are chemical energy, such as that derived from fossil fuels, and light energy in the case of solar cells. Electricity is transmitted to motors, which couple electrical energy to the performance of work. Bacterial cells, mitochondria, and chloroplasts have protonic generators and protonic motors. Respiratory and photosynthetic electron transport chains are generators of proton currents pmf's, which then drive the various motors of the cell or organelle. When the H^+-translocating ATPase is "plugged in," the proton current drives phosphorylation. There are other motors present in the cell. Most membranes contain specific transport systems for small molecules, such as ions, sugars, and amino acids. Many of these transport systems are protonic; that is, they use the energy of the pmf to drive the accumulation or extrusion of their substrate. To give one example, in many bacteria the transport system for the sugar lactose consists of a single membrane protein which catalyzes the simultaneous cotransport of both lactose and a proton. Entry of protons through this carrier protein is driven by the pmf. Since a molecule of lactose enters the cell with each proton, entry and accumulation of lactose is thus coupled to the pmf. *See* BIOPOTENTIALS AND IONIC CURRENTS.

Other metabolic events have been found to use the pmf. Flagellar rotation in bacteria is coupled to the pmf. The flagellum is a motor which uses a flow of protons to do mechanical work, just as a paddle wheel uses a flow of water to turn it. Another example of a membrane event which uses the pmf is the uptake of DNA by bacterial cells. Foreign DNA can enter cells by sexual conjugation, by direct uptake (transformation), or by injection of viral DNA by bacteriophage. Similarly, some proteins destined to be secreted by cells require a pmf to be inserted into, or translocated through, the cytoplasmic membrane. Exactly how the pmf functions in the transport of DNA or protein is not clear. In conclusion, chemiosmosis is a universal phenomenon involved in many membrane and transmembrane events. *See* BACTERIAL GENETICS; BACTERIOPHAGE; CELL MEMBRANES.   **Barry Rosen**

Bibliography. P. Mitchell, Keilin's respiratory chain concept and its chemiosmotic consequences (Nobel Prize lecture), *Science*, 260:1148–1159, 1979; D. G. Nicholls, *Bioenergetics: An Introduction to the Chemiosmotic Theory*, 1982; B. P. Rosen (ed.), *Bacterial Transport*, 1978.

Chemistry

The science that embraces the properties, composition, and structure of matter, the changes in structure and composition that matter undergoes, and the accompanying energy changes. It is important to distinguish chemical change, implicit in this definition, and changes in physical form. An example of the latter is the conversion of liquid water to solid or gas by cooling or heating; the water substance is unchanged. In chemical change, such as the rusting of iron, the metal is consumed as it reacts with air in the presence of water to form the new substance, iron oxide.

Modern chemistry grew out of the alchemy of the Middle Ages, and the attempts to transmute base metals into gold. Seminal observations were made in the early eighteenth century on the changes in volume of air during combustion in a closed vessel, and the French chemist Antoine Lavoisier in the 1770s interpreted these phenomena in essentially modern terms.

Atoms and elements. Underlying all of chemistry is the concept of elementary units of matter which cannot be subdivided. This idea was adumbrated in classical Greek writings, and was clearly expressed by the Englishman John Dalton in 1803, who called these units atoms. Different kinds of atoms were recognized, each corresponding to one of the chemical elements such as oxygen, sulfur, tin, iron, and a few other metals. By the mid-nineteenth century, about 80 elements had been characterized, and these were organized on the basis of regularities in behavior and properties, into a periodic table. *See* ELEMENT (CHEMISTRY); PERIODIC TABLE.

In the early twentieth century, observations of radiation from various sources and its impact on solid targets led to the recognition of three fundamental particles that are common to all elements; the electron, with negative charge; the proton, with positive charge; and the neutron, with zero charge. An atom consists of a nucleus containing protons and neutrons, and a diffuse cloud of electrons, equal in number to the number of protons and arranged in orbitals of progressively higher energy levels as the distance from the nucleus increases. The atomic number of an element (Z) is defined as the number of protons in the nucleus; this is the sequence of ordering in the periodic table. The mass number corresponds to the total number of protons and neutrons. *See* ATOMIC NUMBER; ELECTRON; NEUTRON; PROTON.

Isotopes. Most elements exist as isotopes, which have differing numbers of neutrons. All isotopes of an element exhibit the same chemical behavior, although isotopes can be separated on the basis of differences in atomic mass. The known elements total 106; of these, 88 have been detected in one or more isotopic forms in the Earth's crust. The other elements, including all but one of those with atomic number above 92, are synthetic isotopes produced in nuclear reactions that take place in nuclear piles or particle accelerators. Most of the isotopes of these heavier elements and also some lighter ones are radioactive; that is, the nuclei are unstable and decay, resulting in the emission of radiation. *See* ISOTOPE; PARTICLE ACCELERATOR; RADIOACTIVITY.

Molecules and chemical reactions. Molecules are combinations of two or more atoms, bonded together in definite proportions and specific geometric arrangements. These entities are chemical compounds; a molecule is the smallest unit. The bonding of atoms in compounds involves the distribution of electrons, and is the central concern of chemistry.

Compounds result from chemical reactions of atoms or molecules. The process involves formation and breaking of bonds, and may be either exothermic, in which the net bond charges lead to a more stable (lower-energy) system and heat is evolved, or endothermic, in which energy must be added to overcome a net loss of bonding energy.

A simple case is the reaction of hydrogen and oxygen to give water, which can be expressed as reaction (1).

$$2H_2 + O_2 \rightarrow 2H_2O \qquad (1)$$
$$\Delta H = 572 \text{ kilojoules}$$

The equation is balanced; no atoms are gained or lost in a chemical reaction. The symbols represent the nature of the initial and final materials and also the relative amounts. Thus H_2O represents a molecule of water or a mole, which is the quantity in grams (or other mass units) equivalent to the molecular weight. The symbol ΔH indicates the energy (enthalpy) change for the process. The reaction of hydrogen and oxygen is highly exothermic, and the sign of the energy charge is therefore negative since the system has lost heat to the surroundings. *See* ENTHALPY; MOLE (CHEMISTRY); STOICHIOMETRY.

Bonds. Bonds can be broadly classified as ionic or covalent. An ion is an atom or molecule which has an electric charge. Ionic compounds can be illustrated by salts such as sodium chloride, NaCl, in which a positive sodium ion, Na^+, and negative chloride ion, Cl^-, are associated by electrostatic attractions in regular locations of a crystal lattice. In solution the ions are solvated by water molecules and can conduct an electric current.

In covalent molecules, bonds are formed by the presence of pairs of electrons in overlapping orbitals between two atoms. Thus when two hydrogen atoms ($H\cdot$) come within bonding distance, a molecule of hydrogen is formed in an exothermic reaction, by formation of a covalent bond. In this case the heat of reaction represents the energy of the H-H bond [reaction (2)].

$$2H\cdot \rightarrow H{-}H \qquad (2)$$
$$\Delta H = -435 \text{ kilojoules}$$

See CHEMICAL BONDING.

Chemical compounds. A compound is specified by the elements it contains, the number of atoms of each element, the bonding arrangement, and the characteristic properties. The number of unique compounds that have been isolated from natural sources or prepared by synthesis is enormous; as of 1990, over 10 million substances were registered in the file maintained by Chemical Abstracts (American Chemical Society). Most of these are organic compounds, containing from a few to many hundred carbon atoms. The element carbon, unlike any others, can form long chains of covalently bonded atoms. Moreover, there can be many compounds, called isomers, with the same atomic composition. Thus a molecular formula such as $C_8H_{16}O$ can represent many thousand different compounds. *See* CARBON; MOLECULAR ISOMERISM.

Branches. Traditionally, five main subdivisions are designated for the activities, professional organizations, and literature of chemistry and chemists.

Analytical chemistry. This subdivision is an overarching discipline dealing with determination of the composition of matter and the amount of each component in mixtures of any kind. Analytical measurements are an integral and indispensable part of all chemical endeavor. Originally, analytical chemistry involved detection, separation, and weighing of the substances present in a mixture. Determination of the atomic ratio and thence the molecular formula of a compound is a prerequisite for any other investigation; the development of balances and techniques for doing this on milligram quantities of material had an enormous impact on organic chemistry. Advances since the 1950s have involved increasingly sophisticated instrumentation; mass spectrometers are a notable example. Other important methods include high-resolution chromatography and various applications of electrochemistry. A constant goal in analytical chemistry is the development of methods and instruments of greater sensitivity. It is now possible to detect trace compounds such as environmental pollutants at the picogram level. *See* ANALYTICAL CHEMISTRY.

Biochemistry. Biochemistry is the study of living systems from a chemical viewpoint; thus it is concerned with the compounds and reactions that occur in plant and animal cells. Most of the substances in living tissues, including carbohydrates, lipids, proteins, nucleic acids, and hormones, are well-defined organic substances. However, the metabolic and regulatory processes of these compounds and their biological function are the special province of biochemistry. One of the major areas is the characterization of enzymes and their cofactors, and the mechanism of enzyme catalysis. Other topics of interest include the transport of ions and molecules across cell membranes, and the target sites of neurotransmitters and other regulatory molecules. Biochemical methods and thinking have contributed extensively to the fields of endocrinology, genetics, immunology, and virology. *See* BIOCHEMISTRY.

Inorganic chemistry. This discipline is concerned with any material in which metals and metalloid elements are of primary interest. Inorganic chemistry is therefore concerned with the structure, synthesis, and bonding of a very diverse range of compounds. One of the early interests was the composition of minerals and the discovery of new elements; from this has grown the specialized area of geochemistry. Early synthetic work emphasized compounds of the main group elements, and particularly in this century, complex compounds of the transition metals. These studies have led to soluble transition-metal catalysts, and a greatly increased understanding of catalytic processes and the pivotal role of metal atoms in major biochemical processes, such as oxygen transport in blood, photosynthesis, and biological nitrogen fixation. Other contributions of inorganic chemistry are seen in advanced ceramics, high-performance composite materials, and the growing number of high-temperature superconductors. *See* CATALYSIS; CERAMICS; COMPOSITE MATERIAL; INORGANIC CHEMISTRY; PHOTOSYNTHESIS.

Organic chemistry. This subdivision is centered on compounds of carbon. Originally these were the compounds isolated from plant and animal sources, but the term was early broadened to include all compounds in which a linear or cyclic carbon chain is the main feature. Two of the major thrusts have been the elucidation of new structures and their preparation by synthesis; another long-standing interest has been study of the reaction mechanisms and rearrangments of organic compounds. Structure work on naturally occurring compounds progressed over a 150-year period from simple straight-chain compounds with 2–10 carbon atoms, hydrogen, and 1 or 2 oxygen atoms to antibiotics and toxins with many rings and as many as 100 carbon atoms. In modern work, nuclear magnetic resonance spectroscopy and x-ray diffraction have become indispensable tools. Paralleling structural studies has been the synthesis of increasingly complex target molecules. Synthetic work is directed also to the preparation of large numbers of compounds for screening as potential drugs and agricultural chemicals. Plastics, synthetic fibers, and other high polymers are other products of organic chemistry. *See* NUCLEAR MAGNETIC RESONANCE (NMR); ORGANIC CHEMISTRY; X-RAY DIFFRACTION.

Physical chemistry. This discipline deals with the interpretation of chemical phenomena and the underlying physical processes. One of the classical topics of physical chemistry involves the thermodynamic and kinetic principles that govern chemical reactions. Another is a description of the physical states of matter in molecular terms. Experimentation and theoretical analysis have been directed to the understanding of equilibria, solution behavior, electrolysis, and surface phenomena. One of the major contributions has been quantum chemistry, and the applications and insights that it has provided. The methods and instruments of physical chemistry, including such hardware as spectrometers and magnetic resonance and diffraction instruments, are an integral part of every other area. *See* CHEMICAL THERMODYNAMICS; PHYSICAL CHEMISTRY; QUANTUM CHEMISTRY.

Others. Each broad area of chemistry embraces many specialized topics. There are also a number of hybrid areas, such as bioorganic and bioinorganic chemistry, analytical biochemistry, and physical organic chemistry. Each of these areas has borrowed extensively from and contributed to every other one. It is better to view chemistry as a seamless web, rather than a series of compartments. *See* BIOINORGANIC CHEMISTRY.   James A. Moore

Chemometrics

A chemical discipline that uses mathematical and statistical methods to design or select optimal measurement procedures and experiments and to provide maximum chemical information by analyzing chemical data. Chemometrics is actually a collection of procedures, mathematics, and statistics that can help chemists perform well-designed experiments and proceed rapidly from data, to information, to knowledge of chemical systems and processes.

Medicinal chemists use chemometrics to relate measured or calculated properties of candidate drug molecules to their biological function; this subdiscipline is known as quantitative structure activity relations (QSAR). Environmental chemists use chemometrics to find pollution sources or understand the effect of point pollution sources on regional or global ecosystems by analyzing masses of environmental data. Forensic chemists analyze chemical measurements made on evidence (for example, gasoline in an arson case) or contraband to determine its source. Experimental physical chemists use chemometrics to unravel and identify physical or chemical states from spectral data acquired during the course of an experiment. *See* FORENSIC CHEMISTRY; MEDICINAL CHEMISTRY; PHYSICAL CHEMISTRY.

In analytical chemistry, chemometrics has seen rapid growth and widespread application, primarily due to the computerization of analytical instrumentation. Automation provides an opportunity to acquire enormous amounts of data on chemical systems. Virtually every branch of analytical chemistry has been impacted significantly by chemometrics; commercial software implementing chemometrics methods has become commonplace in analytical instruments. *See* ANALYTICAL CHEMISTRY.

Whether the analyst is concerned with a single sample or, as in process analytical chemistry, an entire chemical process (for example, the human body, a manufacturing process, or an ecosystem), chemometrics can assist in the experimental design, instrument response, optimization, standardization, and calibration as well as in the various steps involved in going from measurements (data), to chemical information, to knowledge of the chemical system under study.

Tensorial calibration. Chemical processes are usually controlled by acquiring information on physical properties (such as temperature, pressure, and flow rate) and chemical properties (composition) at one or more locations in a chemical reactor. These data are then fed to process control computers that open or close valves and provide heating or cooling of the process to optimize yield and quality of the product. Sensors that measure product in terms of intermediate or starting material composition are calibrated by using pure standards. One problem often encountered is that the sensor may be sensitive to an unsuspected interferent in the process, causing the reported composition data to be erroneous. Simple sensors generating only one measurement or datum can be classified as zero-order sensors and cannot separate the signal generated by the analyte from the interferent. This is a serious problem in process control.

First order. To solve the problem of separating the signals, chemists have turned to multivariate calibration using first-order instruments. These are instruments capable of producing a vector of measurements, a first-order tensor, per sample and include spectrometers and arrays of nonselective zero-order sensors. For the calibration of such instruments, methods such as classical multilinear regression (MLR), principal components regression (PCR), and partial least-squares regression (PLS) have become popular, especially in infrared and near-infrared spectrophotometry. Besides being able to analyze for multiple analytes in one sample while correcting for interferences, the methods have also been used to predict physical properties from spectral data. While these methods correct for interferences, the interferents must be included in the calibration step according to a good statistical experimental design. If an uncalibrated interferent is present in a sample to be analyzed, these methods can detect its presence but cannot, in general, correct for its effect, and therefore the results are biased.

First-order calibration is used in many areas of process control. The physical properties of polymers, such as tensile strength and the ability to incorporate dyes for color, can be predicted from on-line spectral data acquired during a polymerization process before the process is complete. Another important application involves the use of on-line fiber-optic-based near-infrared spectrometers to predict the octane number of gasoline at various stages of refining and blending. Accurate knowledge of fuel properties during production can save millions of dollars per year at a large refinery. A multivariate calibration method is used to relate the spectral data from calibration samples to one or more known performance properties. If the calibration model passes various statistical tests, it can be used in the refinery. *See* PROCESS CONTROL.

Second order. Quite often the relationship between the analytical measurements and the analyte concentration, or physical property, is nonlinear. Methods are available for calibration and analysis in these cases, for example locally weighted regression, nonlinear partial least squares, and neural networks. *See* LEAST-SQUARES METHOD; NEURAL NETWORK.

A common problem in environmental science is determining the concentrations of pollutants in very complex samples containing completely unknown components. For example, in order to determine the migration of toxic chemicals in the ground near a known or suspected dump site, environmental analytical chemists sample ground and subsurface water from monitoring wells located around the site. Environmental analyzers have been developed that can be lowered down the wells for in-place analysis in order to avoid the time, expense, and other problems associated with taking hundreds of samples to the laboratory. The in-place analyzers must be calibrated, and the calibration models must be capable of accurate determination of the toxic chemicals, even though what may be present in the wells is not fully known. When an unknown interferent is present, it must be physically separated from the analyte by chromatography; or the analyst can move up to second-order calibration using an instrument capable of acquiring a matrix of data, second-order tensor, per sample. These instruments involve all so-called hyphenated methods, for example, gas chromatography–mass spectrometry (GC/MS) and liquid chromatography–ultraviolet, and include as well tandem mass spectrometers (MS/MS), two-dimensional nuclear magnetic resonance spectrometers (2D-NMR), and emission-excitation fluorescence spectrometers. Methods to analyze these data include the generalized rank annihilation method (GRAM) and residual bilinearization; they come in a variety of algorithms according to the mathematical characteristics (for example, bilinearity) of the data. The most important benefit associated with second-order calibration (the second-order advantage) is the possibility to analyze for analytes in the presence of unknown interferents. Also, under certain conditions these methods yield qualitative information about sample components as well as quantitative information. This characteristic is particularly important for environmental or medical applications and assures the analyst that the analyzer is operational. *See* CALIBRATION; CHROMATOGRAPHY; GAS AND ATMOSPHERIC ANALYSIS.

Standardization. The composition of many agricultural and food products is determined by spectrometers. For example, near-infrared reflectance (NIR) is commonly used to determine the moisture, protein, and fat concentration in wheat or other grains in farm fields. These data are useful for determining harvest time, irrigation, and fertilizer requirements and for setting the value of the product. Either the spectrometers must be calibrated individually or, more desirably, a reference instrument can be calibrated and the calibration model then used with several other similar instruments. Unfortunately, the latter is problematic since no two analytical instruments are exactly alike, even if they come from the same company and have the same model numbers. Also, a single instrument's response to a standard reference sample will change over time because of subtle changes in its components. To circumvent these and similar problems, chemometricians have developed the topic of instrument standardization. This is fundamentally different than calibration, which is used to relate instrument response to the property of interest. The goal of standardization is to correct the response of an instrument to be in accord with another instrument or with itself over the time it is in service.

Standardization can be as simple as using a stable wavelength reference such as a laser line to correct for shifts in wavelength that can invalidate calibration and produce incorrect analyses. There are multivariate instrument standardization methods that use multiple standardization or transfer samples to calculate the parameters of a model that can, for example, correct the response obtained from one instrument so that the response is like that obtained from another instrument. This approach can facilitate the use of a calibration model among several instruments. In process analytical chemistry, this is a major advantage, since a calibration model developed on one instrument, perhaps a high-quality laboratory spectrometer, can be transferred to several process analyzers; thus the need to calibrate each one is avoided, often a very costly process. Also, as the process analyzers change over time (for example, drift), they can be restandardized to generate the same response as when they were first put into service. *See* INSTRUMENT SCIENCE.

Curve resolution. Chromatography is widely used in product testing and quality control, especially in the pharmaceutical industry. As the components of a sample are separated in a chromatogram, it is imperative that the purity of each component be assured in order to avoid having a contaminant in the final product. To help solve this problem, chromatographers employ rapid scanning or diode array spectrometers as detectors so that the spectrum of each component eluting can be checked for purity.

When two analytes coelute near each other during a chromatographic separation of a mixture sample, a single peak in the chromatogram may result. If the analyst has previous knowledge of the shape of a pure analyte elution profile, it may be possible to resolve the mixture peak into the two pure analyte peaks by using, for example, Fourier deconvolution. Fourier deconvolution uses the fast Fourier transform algorithm to mathematically extract a curve with a known shape from a more complex mixture curve, itself composed of a number of curves.

If a spectrometer is used as the detector, multivariate curve resolution methods based on principal components analysis, factor analysis, or singular value decomposition can be used to resolve the mixtures into their component parts, thereby detecting the presence of a product contaminant. *See* CURVE FITTING; FACTOR ANALYSIS.

Pattern recognition. Perhaps the oldest activity in modern chemometrics is the application of data analysis methods developed in computer science and electrical engineering under the heading of pattern recognition to chemical data. As with most of the multivariate methods mentioned above, a pattern recognition application begins when a series of measurements is made on a collection of samples called the training set. For example, the concentrations of a number of trace elements may be measured on several quartzite samples acquired from three known quarries involved in an archeological study. One goal would be to determine if the pattern of trace-element concentrations can be used to distinguish the samples from a given quarry from all of the others. If this training step is successful, the rule or model can be used to classify samples taken from statues or monuments in order to determine their origin. Several studies of this type have been carried out in archeology, where trace-element patterns in antiquities (such as statues or arrowheads) have been traced back to their origins in order to study trade routes or cultural diversity.

Many similar studies have been conducted in forensic chemistry, drug design, screening, taxonomy, and product quality determination. In drug design, structural, chemical, or physical properties are used to classify previously untested drugs as active or inactive in a particular drug screening test. The chemometric methods used are called multivariate classification or supervised learning methods, and they are the same as those used in archeological studies. If the methods are successful, they can be used to predict the activity of untested candidate drug compounds and even to indicate which of the structural, chemical, or physical properties are the most related to biological activity, giving the medicinal chemist information useful for finding more potent drugs.

A medicinal chemist may want to subject a subset of a large set of chemical compounds to a biological screening test. The subset would be selected to represent the structural diversity of the full set as much as possible. Based on structural properties available for each compound, cluster analysis (a type of pattern recognition) might determine that the many compounds can be arranged in, say, 20 groups or clusters, with the compounds belonging to any one group being similar to its class members. The chemist need only test one compound per group, thereby saving considerable expense but getting a good coverage of available compounds.

Other areas. There are several other areas of chemometrics research. Experimental design is a well-developed topic in statistics that chemists use to get the maximum amount of pertinent information from the smallest investment of time, money, or effort. Using one of several multivariate optimization methods, computers can optimally tune complex instruments to get the best possible results. Wherever experiments generating data, particularly large quantities of data, are being conducted, modern chemometrics methods can be applied to make the best measurements possible and move quickly from data to information to knowledge. *See* STATISTICS.   Bruce Kowalski

Bibliography. S. D. Brown, R. S. Bear, Jr., and T. B. Blank, Chemometrics, *Fundamental Rev.: Anal. Chem.*, 64:22R–49R, 1992; S. J. Haswell (ed.), *Practical Guide to Chemometrics*, 1992; H. Martens and T. Naes, *Multivariate Calibration*, 1989; D. L. Massart et al., *Chemometrics: A Textbook*, 1988; M. A. Sharaf, D. L. Illman, and B. R. Kowalski, *Chemometrics*, 1986.

Chemoreception

The ability of organisms to detect changes in the chemical composition of their exterior or interior environment. It is a characteristic of every living cell, from the single-celled bacteria and protozoa to the most complex multicellular organisms. Chemoreception allows organisms to maintain homeostasis, react to stimuli, and communicate with one another. *See* HOMEOSTASIS.

At the single-cell level, bacteria orient toward or avoid certain chemical stimuli (chemotaxis); algal gametes release attractants which allow sperm to find oocytes in a dilute aqueous environment; and unicellular slime molds are drawn together to form colonial fruiting bodies by use of aggregation pheromones. *See* CELLULAR ADHESION; TAXIS.

In multicellular organisms, both single cells and complex multicellular sense organs are used to homeostatically maintain body fluids (interoreceptors) as well as to monitor the external environment (exteroreceptors). The best-studied interoreceptors are perhaps the carotid body chemoreceptors of higher vertebrates, which monitor the levels of oxygen, carbon dioxide, and hydrogen ions in arterial blood. The best-studied exteroreceptors are those associated with taste (gustation) and smell (olfaction). Such receptors may occur anywhere on the bodies of different organisms, from antennae and tongues to legs and fins, and range from single hair cells in some invertebrates to the complex nasal epithelia of higher vertebrates. Internal communication is also effected by chemical means in multicellular organisms. Thus both hormonal and neural control involve the perception, by cells, of control chemicals (hormones and neurotransmitters, respectively). *See* CAROTID BODY; CHEMICAL SENSES; OLFACTION; SENSE ORGAN; TASTE; TONGUE.

Basic mechanism of action. Although tremendous diversity can be seen in the evolution of complex chemosensory structures, chemoreception is ultimately a property of single cells. The basic mechanism underlying chemoreception is the interaction of a chemical stimulus with receptor molecules in the outer membrane of a cell. These molecules are believed to be proteins which, because of their three-dimensional shapes and chemical properties, will have the right spatial and binding "fit" for interaction with only a select group of chemicals (the same basic mechanism by which enzymes are specific for various substrates). The interaction between a chemical stimulus and a receptor molecule ultimately leads to structural changes in membrane channels by mechanisms that are not totally clear. In some instances, the chemical stimulus–receptor complex activates an enzyme (adenylate cyclase) that synthesizes cyclic adenosinemonophosphate (cAMP), which acts as a second messenger interacting with membrane channels and changing their conductance. In other instances, the chemical stimulus interacts with the channel protein directly, altering its conductance. In either case, the net result is usually a change in membrane conductance (permeability) to specific ions which changes both the internal chemical composition of the cell and the charge distribution across the cell membrane. In single-celled organisms, this may be sufficient to establish a membrane current which may elicit responses such as an increase or decrease in ciliary movement. In multicellular organisms, it usually results in changes in the rate of release of hormones or the stimulation of neurons. *See* CELL MEMBRANES.

Characteristics of chemoreceptors. The basic characteristics of all chemoreceptors are specificity (the chemicals that they will respond to); sensitivity (the magnitude of the response for a given chemical stimulus); and range of perception (the smallest or largest level of stimulus that the receptor can discriminate). Specificity is a consequence of the types of proteins found in the membrane of a receptor cell. Each cell will have a mosaic of different receptor molecules, and each receptor molecule will show different combinations of excitatory or inhibitory responses to different molecules. In an excitatory response, there is a net flux of positive ions into the cell (depolarization); for an inhibitory response, there is a net flux of negative ions into the cell (hyperpolarization). In single cells, or in primary sensory neurons, the receptor current will spread along the membrane by passive electrotonic means. The stronger the stimulus—that is, the more of the chemical present—the more receptors affected, the greater the change in conductance, and the larger the membrane current.

In animals with nervous systems, these changes in conductance of primary sensory cells can lead to one of two events. In some receptors, if the current is excitatory and sufficient in magnitude (threshold), an action potential will be generated at a spike-initiating zone on the neuron. Other receptors are not able to generate action potentials but respond by releasing a neurotransmitter (the depolarizing current causes a change in membrane conductance of the transmitter substance) that acts on a second-order neuron which is excitable and therefore can generate action potentials. *See* BIOPOTENTIALS AND IONIC CURRENTS.

The sensitivity of a chemoreceptor reflects both the amount of chemical substance required to initiate a change in membrane potential or discharge of the receptor cell, and the change in potential or discharge for any given change in the level of the chemical stimulus. There are real limits as to the extent of change in membrane conductance or firing frequency. Thus, for more sensitive cells, there is a smaller range over which they can provide information about the change in concentration of any given chemical before it has reached its maximum conductance or discharge rate and has saturated.

In most chemoreceptors, this problem is reduced by a variety of mechanisms. To begin with, the relationship between stimulus intensity and neuronal discharge frequency is usually logarithmic. This means that the high-intensity end of the scale is compressed, greatly extending the range of discrimination of the receptor. Although this may seem to decrease the sensitivity of the receptor at higher stimulus intensities in absolute terms, the increment in discharge remains the same for any given percentage change in stimulus intensity. In other words, a doubling of the stimulus intensity will produce the same increase in receptor potential anywhere over the full range of sensitivity of the cell. Receptor adaptation, a decrease in receptor discharge despite a constant chemical stimulus, also extends the dynamic range over which receptors operate. Finally, in chemoreceptive organs of multicellular organisms, the interaction of chemoreceptors with different threshold levels (range fractionation) can also extend the dynamic range of sensory perception.

Chemosensory systems can be extremely sensitive. Humans can detect 1 molecule of mercaptan in 5×10^{10} molecules of air, while marine crabs have been shown to respond to as little as 10^{-17} lb (10^{-15} g) of prey tissue in 0.264 gal (1 liter) of seawater. Perhaps most impressive, however, is the ability of the antennal chemoreceptor cells of the male silkworm (*Bombyx mori*) to detect a single molecule of female pheromone. Only about 90 molecules per second impinging on a single receptor are required to alter the firing rate of a cell, and stimulation of only 40 chemoreceptors out of roughly 20,000 per antenna is sufficient to evoke a behavioral response (excited wing flapping). *See* PHEROMONE.

Chemoreceptor tuning. In animals, the responsiveness of some chemoreceptors can be either enhanced or attenuated by other neural input. These influences come in the form of efferent inputs from the central nervous system, from neighboring receptors, or even from recurrent branches of the chemoreceptor's own sensory axons. The net effect is either (1) to increase the acuity of the receptors (excitatory input brings the membrane potential of the receptor cell closer to threshold, requiring less chemical stimulus to elicit a response); or (2) to extend the range of responsiveness of the receptors (inhibitory input lowers the membrane potential of the receptor cell, requiring more chemical stimulus to bring the cell to threshold). For example, chemi-

cal sensitivity is greatly heightened in most animals when they are hungry.

Central integration of input. Any given chemoreceptor cell can have any combination of receptor proteins, each of which may respond to different chemical molecules with either an increase or a decrease in the membrane potential. Thus, chemoreceptor cells do not exhibit a unitary specificity to a single chemical substance, but rather an action spectrum to various groups of chemicals. The ability of animals to distinguish such a large number of different, complex, natural chemical stimuli resides in the ability of higher centers in the nervous system to "recognize" the pattern of discharge of large groups of cells. Sensory quality does not depend on the activation of a particular cell or group of cells but on the interaction of cells with overlapping response spectra.

Structural adaptations. Despite the common, basic mechanism underlying chemoreception in all organisms, there is a great diversity in the design of multicellular chemoreceptive organs, particularly in animals. The complex structures of most of these organs reflect adaptations that serve to filter and amplify chemical signals. Thus, the antennae in many insects, and the irrigated protective chambers, such as the olfactory bulb of fishes and nasal passages of mammals, increase the exposure of chemoreceptor cells to the environment. At the same time, they allow the diffusion distances between chemoreceptive cells and the environment to be reduced, thereby increasing acuity. In terms of filtering, they may serve to convert turbulent or dispersed stimuli into temporal patterns that can be more easily interpreted. The extent to which such structural adaptations are seen in various organisms tends to reflect the relative importance of chemoreception to the organism, which, to a large extent, reflects the habitat in which the organism lives. *See* CHEMICAL ECOLOGY.   William Milsom

Bibliography. H. Acker and R. G. O'Regan (eds.), *Physiology of the Peripheral Arterial Chemoreceptors,* 1983; V. G. Dethier, *The Hungry Fly,* 1976; R. Eckert and D. Randall, *Animal Physiology,* 1983; T. V. Getchell and G. M. Shepherd, Responses of olfactory receptor cells to step impulses of odour at different concentrations in the salamander, *J. Physiol. (London),* 282:521–540, 1978; G. M. Shepherd, *Neurobiology,* 1988.

Chemostat

An apparatus (see **illus.**) for the continuous cultivation of microorganisms, such as bacteria, yeasts, molds, and algae, or for the cultivation of plant cells. The nutrients required for cell growth are supplied continuously to the culture vessel by a pump connected to a medium reservoir. The cells in the vessel grow continuously on these nutrients. Residual nutrients and cells are removed from the vessel (fermenter) at the same rate by an overflow,

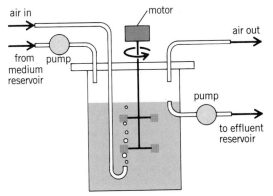

Schematic representation of chemostat apparatus.

thus maintaining the culture in the fermenter at a constant volume.

Parameters. An important feature of chemostat cultivation is the dilution rate, defined as the volume of nutrient medium supplied per hour divided by the volume of the culture. During chemostat cultivation, an equilibrium is established (steady state) at which the growth rate of the cells equals the dilution rate. The higher the dilution rate, the faster the organisms are allowed to grow. Above a given dilution rate the cells will not be able to grow any faster, and the culture will be washed out of the fermenter. The chemostat thus offers the opportunity to study the properties of organisms at selected growth rates. This is particularly important because in their natural environment microorganisms seldom grow at their maximum rate. Under nutrient limitation, cells may display properties which also are of great importance in a number of applications, such as industrial fermentation and wastewater treatment. *See* FERMENTATION; WATER TREATMENT.

The nutrient medium which is fed to the fermenter contains an excess of all growth factors except one, the growth-limiting nutrient. The concentration of the cells (biomass) in the fermenter is dependent on the concentration of the growth-limiting nutrient in the medium feed. Upon entering the fermenter, the growth-limiting nutrient is consumed almost to completion, and only minute amounts of it may be found in the culture and the effluent. Initially, when few cells have been inoculated in the growth vessel, even the growth-limiting nutrient is in excess. Therefore, the microorganisms can grow at a rate exceeding their rate of removal. This growth of cells causes a fall in the level of the growth-limiting nutrient, gradually leading to a lower specific growth rate of the microorganisms. Once the specific rate of growth balances the removal of cells by dilution, a steady state is established in which both the cell density and the concentration of the growth-limiting nutrient remain constant. Thus the chemostat is a tool for the cultivation of microorganisms almost indefinitely in a constant physiological state.

To achieve a steady state, parameters other than the dilution rate and culture volume must be kept constant (for example, temperature and pH). The fermenter is stirred to provide a homogeneous suspension in which all individual cells in the culture come into contact with the growth-limiting nutrient immediately. Furthermore, stirring is also required to achieve optimal distribution of air (oxygen) in the fermenter when aerobic cultures are in use.

Laboratory chemostats usually contain 0.5 to 10.5 quarts (0.5 to 10 liters) of culture, but industrial chemostat cultivation can involve volumes up to 343,000 gal (1300 m^3) for the continuous production of microbial biomass.

Advantages. The chemostat offers a number of advantages for the cultivation of cells as compared with growth in a batch culture. In the latter, a closed system, organisms grow in excess nutrients at their maximum rate, and the nutrient concentration, products, and biomass change continuously. When a nutrient becomes depleted, a rapid fall in the growth rate takes place. This often leads to the death of cells. In the chemostat, however, the constancy of all parameters allows accurate and reproducible experiments. By varying the dilution rate, within limits, the rate of growth of the organisms can be changed at will. The density of cells in the cultures can be chosen by the appropriate concentration of the growth-limiting nutrient in the medium reservoir. Depending on the question to be answered, the type of growth-limiting nutrient can be selected. Of course, possible choices are limited by the nature and capabilities of the organisms studied.

The chemostat can be used to grow microorganisms on very toxic nutrients since, when kept growth-limiting, the nutrient concentration in the culture is very low. The chemostat can be used to select mutants with a higher affinity to the growth-limiting nutrient or, in the case of a mixed population, to select the species that are optimally adapted to the growth limitation and culture conditions. The chemostat is of great use in such fields of study as physiology, ecology, and genetics of microorganisms. *See* BACTERIAL GENETICS; BACTERIAL PHYSIOLOGY AND METABOLISM; MICROBIOLOGY.

Mathematical description. The operation of a chemostat can also be described in mathematical terms. Growth of a microorganism can be described by the empirical formula of J. Monod (1942) as a function of the growth-limiting substrate, Eq. (1), in which μ is the specific growth rate

$$\mu = \mu_{max} \frac{C_s}{K_s + C_s} \qquad (1)$$

(h^{-1}), μ_{max} is the maximum specific growth rate, C_s is the concentration of the growth-limiting substrate, and K_s is a Monod saturation constant, numerically equal to the substrate concentration at which $\mu = \frac{1}{2}\mu_{max}$. The relationship between C_s and μ is a typical saturation curve. When an organism is grown in a closed system (batch culture) with, initially, excess substrate, it will grow at $\mu_{\max}$. During growth its environment will constantly change, but if the conditions remain favorable, growth will continue until the growth-limiting compound is depleted. Near the end of growth, μ will fall because of the factors described by Eq. (1), and will finally become zero.

The chemostat can be considered as an open culture system in which fresh (sterilized) medium is introduced at a constant flow rate ϕ, and from which the culture fluid emerges at the same flow rate. At a constant volume v and an in-flow rate ϕ, the dilution rate D is defined by Eq. (2), in which

$$D = \frac{\phi}{V} \tag{2}$$

the dilution rate is expressed in h^{-1}.

Monod demonstrated that over a large range of growth rates a fixed relationship exists between the amount of (growth-limiting) substrate consumed and the amount of biomass produced, Eq. (3),

$$\frac{dC_x}{dt} = -Y''_{sx}\frac{dC_s}{dt} \tag{3}$$

in which C_x is the biomass concentration and t is time. Y''_{sx} is the yield factor and is defined as the amount (weight) of cell material produced per amount (weight, or mole) of substrate consumed. Y''_{sx} is not always a constant.

If the medium in the fermenter is inoculated (for example, with bacteria), the culture will grow at a given rate. At the same time, a quantity of bacteria will be washed out because the culture is continuously fed and diluted with fresh medium. It thus follows that accumulation of biomass in the culture is equal to growth minus washout.

The balance equation is Eq. (4). Hence if μ is

$$\frac{dC_x}{dt} = \mu C_x - DC_x = (\mu - D)C_x \tag{4}$$

greater than D, C_x will increase, while if μ is less than D, C_x will decrease. If μ equals D, Eq. (4) will be zero and an equilibrium will exist.

It can be shown mathematically that, irrespective of the starting conditions, a steady state, with μ equal to D, must inevitably be reached, provided that D does not exceed a critical value.

In order to calculate the steady-state concentrations of biomass and the growth-limiting nutrient in the culture, mass balance equations similar to Eq. (4) for the nutrients entering, being consumed, and leaving the culture must also be made. In Eq. (5), C_s is the substrate concentration in the culture,

$$\frac{dC_s}{dt} = D(C_{si} - C_s) - \frac{\mu C_x}{Y''_{sx}} \tag{5}$$

and C_{si} the concentration of the substrate entering the vessel. The net change in C_{si} per unit of time is equal to the dilution rate multiplied by the difference in substrate concentration entering and leaving the culture, minus the substrate consumed. The substrate consumed is expressed as the growth

divided by the yield, Eq. (3). At steady state, both Eqs. (4) and (5) are zero. This, when combined with Eq. (1), will lead to the equilibrium concentrations $\overline{C}_x$ for biomass [Eq. (7)] and $\overline{C}_s$ for the substrate [Eq. (6)]. Here K_s, $\mu_{\max}$, and Y''_{sx} are constants for

$$\overline{C}_s = K_s(D/\mu_{\max} - D) \tag{6}$$

$$\overline{C}_x = Y''_{sx}(C_{si} - \overline{C}_s)$$
$$= Y''_{sx}\left(C_{si} - \frac{K_s \cdot D}{\mu_{\max} - D}\right) \tag{7}$$

a microorganism under the specified conditions of temperature, medium composition, and the nature of the growth-limiting substrate. For C_{si} and D, any realistic constant value can be chosen. From Eq. (6) it appears that $\overline{C}_s$ solely depends on D. Equation (7) shows that $\overline{C}_x$ depends on D and C_{si} and is proportional to C_{si} if $\overline{C}_s \ll C_{si}$, which is usually the case. If K_s, $\mu_{\max}$, and Y''_{sx} are known for a given microorganism, the relationship between C_x or C_s, and D can be predicted at a chosen C_{si}.   J. Gijskuenen

Bibliography. R. G. Burns and J. H. Slater (eds.), *Experimental Microbial Ecology*, 1982; D. Herbert, R. Elsworth, and R. C. Telling, The continuous culture of bacteria: A theoretical and experimental study, *J. Gen. Microbiol.*, 14:601–622, 1956; J. R. Norris and D. W. Ribbonds (eds.), *Methods in Microbiology*, vol. 2, 1970; S. J. Pirt, *Principles of Microbe and Cell Cultivation*, 1975; H. Veldkamp, *Continuous Culture in Microbial Physiology and Ecology*, 1976.

Chemostratigraphy

A subdiscipline of stratigraphy and geochemistry that involves correlation and dating of marine sediments and sedimentary rocks through the use of trace-element concentrations, molecular fossils, and certain isotopic ratios that can be measured on components of the rocks. The isotopes used in chemostratigraphy can be divided into three classes: radiogenic (strontium, neodymium, osmium), radioactive (radiocarbon, uranium, thorium, lead), and stable (oxygen, carbon, sulfur). Trace-element concentrations (that is, metals such as nickel, copper, molybdenum, and vanadium) and certain organic molecules (called biological markers or biomarkers) are also employed in chemostratigraphy. *See* DATING METHODS; ROCK AGE DETERMINATION.

Radiogenic isotope stratigraphy. Radiogenic isotopes are formed by the radioactive decay of a parent isotope to a stable daughter isotope. The application of these isotopes in stratigraphy is based on natural cycles of the isotopic composition of elements dissolved in ocean water, cycles which are recorded in the sedimentary rocks. The element commonly used is strontium, but osmium and neodymium isotopes are used as well. *See* ISOTOPE; RADIOISOTOPE.

Strontium (Sr) has four naturally occurring, stable

isotopes, with mass numbers (sum of protons and neutrons) 88, 87, 86, and 84. Strontium-87 is radiogenic, formed by the radioactive decay of rubidium-87. Strontium replaces calcium in calcium carbonate and other calcium-bearing minerals (such as aragonite, apatite, and plagioclase). Calcite typically contains 500–2000 parts per million strontium, and aragonite (another form of calcium carbonate) contains 2000–9000 ppm. Strontium is the major cation in strontianite ($SrCO_3$) and celestite ($SrSO_4$), but its principal occurrence in minerals is as a trace element.

The ocean is a large reservoir of dissolved strontium. The isotopic composition of strontium in the oceans reflects the isotopic composition and relative proportions of strontium entering the ocean. Strontium is delivered to the oceans by dissolution in river water [with an average ratio of strontium-87 to strontium-86 ($^{87}Sr/^{86}Sr$) of 0.710] and by dissolution and recrystallization of submarine carbonates. Strontium is removed from the oceans by incorporation into precipitate minerals such as calcium carbonate as well as by inorganic precipitation of evaporites, phosphorites, and ferromanganese oxides. Seawater also exchanges strontium with ocean-floor rocks at mid-ocean ridges. Ocean-floor rocks (basalt) have a relatively low average $^{87}Sr/^{86}Sr$ ratio of 0.703. The variations in the $^{87}Sr/^{86}Sr$ ratio in seawater over millions of years are largely due to the changing inputs of continent-derived strontium delivered by rivers versus strontium derived from exchange of seawater with sea-floor basalt. Comparison of the strontium isotope curve and the geologic record indicate that the $^{87}Sr/^{86}Sr$ ratio in seawater is highest during periods of mountain building and continental collision, when there is a large flux of material from the continents due to increased erosion rates. Conversely, the $^{87}Sr/^{86}Sr$ ratio is lowest in seawater during times when the continents are splitting apart and when sea-floor spreading rates are greatest. *See* SEAWATER.

Measurements of the $^{87}Sr/^{86}Sr$ ratio of calcium-bearing marine precipitates (calcium carbonate, anhydrite, gypsum, and phosphate minerals) show that the $^{87}Sr/^{86}Sr$ ratio of strontium dissolved in seawater has fluctuated over the past 600 million years between the limits of 0.7068 and 0.7092. Because the average strontium atom remains in seawater 3–4 million years before it is removed, which is much longer than the mixing time of the oceans (1000 years), the $^{87}Sr/^{86}Sr$ ratio in seawater is the same throughout the oceans at any given time. Consequently, calcite that forms in the ocean in different places at the same time has the same $^{87}Sr/^{86}Sr$ ratio. When the $^{87}Sr/^{86}Sr$ ratio is changing rapidly with time in seawater, such as between the late Eocene and the present (the past 40 million years), excellent age resolution can be obtained for stratigraphic studies. *See* EOCENE.

An assumption in using strontium isotopes (or any geochemical method) in stratigraphic studies is that the $^{87}Sr/^{86}Sr$ ratio remains unaltered during diagenesis (all the chemical and physical changes that occur in the sediment following its deposition), and hence retains the original strontium isotopic signature. Careful inspection and sample selection prior to analysis are necessary to assess the degree of diagenetic alteration. *See* DIAGENESIS; STRONTIUM.

Stable isotope stratigraphy. The elements hydrogen (H), carbon (C), nitrogen (N), oxygen (O), and sulfur (S) owe their isotopic distributions to physical and biological processes that discriminate between the isotopes because of their different atomic mass. The use of these isotopes in stratigraphy is also facilitated by cycles of the isotopic composition of seawater, but the isotopic ratios in marine minerals are also dependent on water temperature and the mineral-forming processes.

Oxygen isotope stratigraphy. Oxygen isotope stratigraphy has developed since the mid-1950s following the pioneering work of Harold Urey; it has become the most widely used method for dating and correlating marine sediments deposited during the Quaternary (Pleistocene and Holocene). Oxygen isotope stratigraphy is based on the ratio of two isotopes of oxygen (oxygen-18 and oxygen-16) in the calcium carbonate ($CaCO_3$) shells of marine fossils. *See* QUATERNARY.

Detailed measurements of the ratio of oxygen-18 relative to oxygen-16 ($^{18}O/^{16}O$) in planktonic foraminifera from sediments cored in the deep ocean show that the ocean changed periodically over the past 3 million years because of alternating glacial (or ice age) and interglacial conditions. During glacial periods, water depleted in oxygen-18 is transferred to and stored on the continents as glaciers, leaving the oceans enriched in oxygen-18 (higher $^{18}O/^{16}O$ ratio). Although both the water temperature and the $^{18}O/^{16}O$ ratio in the water determine the $^{18}O/^{16}O$ ratio in the carbonate shells, the fluctuations of the $^{18}O/^{16}O$ ratio between interglacial and glacial periods are mainly caused by fluctuating continental ice volume. Each isotopic fluctuation representing a glacial-interglacial cycle has been assigned a stage number, with odd numbers corresponding to interglacial periods and even numbers corresponding to glacial periods (numbered 1 through 23). These stages are globally synchronous and can be intercalibrated with other stratigraphic scales, such as magnetostratigraphy and biostratigraphy. There is much evidence that these climatic fluctuations (called Milankovitch cycles) are a result of changes in the incoming solar radiation reaching the surface of the Earth. The dominant periodicities of these cycles are 100,000, 40,000, and 23,000 years. *See* GLACIAL EPOCH; INSOLATION.

Carbon isotope stratigraphy. Stable carbon (C) isotope stratigraphy involves measurements of the ratio of carbon-13 to carbon-12 ($^{13}C/^{12}C$) in carbonate ($CaCO_3$) fossil shells and organic matter. Organic matter and calcium carbonate are converted to carbon dioxide (CO_2) prior to simultaneous measurement of the ratios $^{13}C/^{12}C$ and $^{18}O/^{16}O$ on a gas-source mass spectrometer.

The carbon isotopic composition in marine organisms (calcite shells or organic tissue) reflects the local and global changes in the cycling of nutrients and CO_2 in the ocean, as well as ocean circulation and ocean-atmosphere interactions. The $^{13}C/^{12}C$ ratio of both organic material and carbonate material can be used as a stratigraphic tool. The $^{13}C/^{12}C$ ratio of a sample depends on the $^{13}C/^{12}C$ ratio of the source [atmospheric CO_2 for land plants, both dissolved CO_2 and bicarbonate (HCO_3^-) for aquatic environments] and the isotopic fractionation produced by equilibrium and kinetic effects (the fractionation of isotopes of the same element in physical or chemical processes occurs because of their slight mass differences). In general, organic carbon is depleted in carbon-13 relative to carbonate carbon in the marine environment. A major focus of carbon isotope studies in stratigraphy is the assessment of detailed variations and excursions of the $^{13}C/^{12}C$ ratio on a stratigraphic level. For example, during periods of increased productivity in the surface layer of the ocean, the carbon-12 is preferentially removed by phytoplankton during photosynthesis, enriching the surface water in carbon-13. Calcium carbonate and organic tissue that form during these periods have an increased $^{13}C/^{12}C$ ratio. Many organic carbon-rich, laminated black shales of Jurassic and Cretaceous age contain organic carbon that is enriched in carbon-13.

Sulfur isotope stratigraphy. The isotopic composition [the ratio of sulfur-34 to sulfur-32 ($^{34}S/^{32}S$)] of sulfur in the sulfate molecules (SO_4^{2-}) dissolved in seawater has varied systematically through Phanerozoic time (the past 600 million years). Sulfate is a major constituent of the marine evaporite minerals gypsum and anhydrite, which are the materials commonly used as recorders of the ocean isotopic ratios. The $^{34}S/^{32}S$ ratio in seawater reflects a complex balance of the sulfate delivered to the oceans by rivers; it also reflects the relative importance of sulfur removal as reduced sulfur in pyrite, as opposed to oxidized sulfur in gypsum and anhydrite. *See* ANHYDRITE; GYPSUM; PYRITE.

Radioactive isotope stratigraphy. Radiocarbon [the radioactive isotope of carbon (^{14}C)] and the isotopes uranium-234 (^{234}U) and thorium-230 (^{230}Th) are used in radioactive isotope stratigraphy.

Radiocarbon stratigraphy. Carbon-14 is used in dating and stratigraphy of both marine and terrestrial sediments younger than 50,000 years. Radiocarbon is continually produced in the upper atmosphere by the capture of neutrons by nitrogen (^{14}N), forming carbon-14, which is radioactive with a half-life of about 5730 years. The carbon-14 enters the hydrosphere and biosphere as CO_2, and it is incorporated into plant and animal organic tissues and hard parts (such as calcium carbonate). When the plant or animal dies, exchange with the atmosphere ceases; the carbon-14 begins to decay, starting the radioactive clock.

Uranium-thorium stratigraphy. Marine minerals such as calcite incorporate minor amounts of the radioactive isotope uranium-234 (^{234}U), which has a half-life of 2.4 million years and decays to thorium-230, which is also radioactive with a half-life of 70,000 years. Because marine calcite forms almost free of thorium-230, the accumulation of radiogenic thorium-230 can be used to measure the age of marine calcites up to about 300,000 years old. This technique is valuable for measuring the age of coral reefs. *See* THORIUM; URANIUM.

Molecular stratigraphy. Certain organic molecules that can be linked with a particular source (called biomarkers) have become useful in stratigraphy. The sedimentary distributions of biomarkers reflect the biological sources and inputs of organic matter (such as that from algae, bacteria, and vascular higher plants), and the depositional environment. *See* DEPOSITIONAL SYSTEMS AND ENVIRONMENTS.

One method of molecular stratigraphy uses the composition of long-chain alkenones (lipids whose molecules comprise chains of 37–39 carbon atoms). These compounds are produced by certain photosynthetic algae (coccolithophorids) that regulate the fluidity of their membranes in waters of different temperatures by biosynthetically controlling the extent of unsaturation in their alkenones. The degree of unsaturation of alkenones (expressed as the alkenone unsaturation index, U_{37}^K) in marine sediments varies as a function of water temperature, which varies from glacial to interglacial times. A molecular stratigraphic record of sea surface temperatures in Quaternary sequences has been developed and intercalibrated with the oxygen isotope record for the past half million years. Alkenones are found in marine sediments throughout the Quaternary and Tertiary.

Trace elements. Certain trace metals, such as nickel, copper, vanadium, magnesium, iron, uranium, and molybdenum, are concentrated in organic-rich sediments in proportion to the amount of organic carbon. Although the processes controlling their enrichment are complex, they generally form in an oxygen-poor environment (such as the Black Sea) or at the time of global oceanic anoxic events, during which entire ocean basins become oxygen poor, resulting in the death of many organisms; hence large amounts of organic carbon are preserved in marine sediments. The trace-metal composition of individual stratigraphic units may be used as a stratigraphic marker (or "fingerprint"), making it possible to correlate, for example, black shales from location to location within a basin. *See* GEOCHEMISTRY; MARINE SEDIMENTS; STRATIGRAPHY.   B. Lynn Ingram; Donald J. DePaolo

Bibliography. S. C. Brassell et al., Molecular stratigraphy: A new tool for climate assessment, *Nature*, 320:129–133, 1986; G. Faure, *Principles of Isotope Geology,* 2d ed., 1986; J. Hoefs, *Stable Isotope Geochemistry,* 2d ed., 1980; H. D. Holland, *The Chemical Evolution of the Atmosphere and Oceans,*

1984; J. Kennett, *Marine Geology*, 1982; R. E. Taylor, A. Long, and R. S. Kra (eds.), *Radiocarbon after Four Decades: An Interdisciplinary Perspective*, 1992.

Chemotaxonomy

The use of biochemistry in taxonomic studies. Living organisms produce many types of natural products in varying amounts, and quite often the biosynthetic pathways responsible for these compounds also differ from one taxonomic group to another. The distribution of these compounds and their biosynthetic pathways correspond well with existing taxonomic arrangements based on more traditional criteria such as morphology. In some cases, chemical data have contradicted existing hypotheses, which necessitates a reexamination of the problem or, more positively, chemical data have provided decisive information in situations where other forms of data are insufficiently discriminatory.

Historical perspective. Chemotaxonomy in its crudest form was practiced by primitive cultures as they began to label and classify edible plants by taste, smell, color, and whether or not they were poisonous. In the case of poisonous plants, for example, the Greek philosopher Socrates was forced (for political reasons) to take his own life by drinking a broth of poison hemlock, *Conium maculatum*, which contains the toxic alkaloid coniine. The extensive world explorations by post-Renaissance European adventurers and merchants were fueled by the desire of European societies for exotic spices and condiments. The post-Linnaean taxonomists of the 1800s utilized descriptive chemical characters in their work. Thus, A. P. de Candolle, a Swiss taxonomist, recognized the antifever properties of *Cinchona* species, although not until 1904 was the antimalarial substance, quinine, completely identified. Today, as P. M. Smith has shown, routine chemotaxonomic surveys often uncover many such compounds of practical as well as taxonomic value.

Natural product classification. Modern chemotaxonomists often divide these natural products into two major classes: (1) micromolecules, that is, those compounds with a molecular weight of 1000 or less, such as alkaloids, terpenoids, amino acids, fatty acids, flavonoid pigments and other phenolic compounds, mustard oils, and simple carbohydrates; and (2) macromolecules, that is, those compounds (often polymers) with a molecular weight over 1000, including complex polysaccharides, proteins, and the basis of life itself, deoxyribonucleic acid (DNA).

Analysis techniques. A crude extract of a plant can be separated into its individual components, especially in the case of micromolecules, by using one or more techniques of chromatography, including paper, thin-layer, gas, or high-pressure liquid chromatography. The resulting chromatogram provides a visual display or "fingerprint" characteristic of a plant species for the particular class of compounds under study. **Figure 1** shows the paper chromatographic pattern (or fingerprint) of flavonoid pigment spots of *Parinari parilis*. The flavonoid spots are normally visible only when observed under long-wave ultraviolet light (360 nanometers) and have been outlined for clarity. *See* CHROMATOGRAPHY.

Spectroscopy. The individual, separated spots can be further purified and then subjected to one or more types of spectroscopy, such as ultraviolet, infrared, or nuclear magnetic resonance or mass spectroscopy (or both), which may provide information about the structure of the compound. Thus, for taxonomic purposes, both visual patterns and structural knowledge of the compounds can be compared from species to species. *See* SPECTROSCOPY.

X-ray crystallography. Because of their large, polymeric, and often crystalline nature, macromolecules (for example, proteins, carbohydrates, DNA) can be subjected to x-ray crystallography, which gives some idea of their three-dimensional structure. These large molecules can then be broken down into smaller individual components and analyzed by using techniques employed for micromolecules. In fact, the specific amino acid sequence of portions or all of a cellular respiratory enzyme, cytochrome *c*, has been elucidated and used successfully for chemotaxonomic comparisons in plants and especially animals. *See* X-RAY CRYSTALLOGRAPHY.

Amino acid sequences. Cyctochrome *c* is a small protein or polypeptide chain consisting of approximately 103–112 amino acids, depending on the animal or plant under study. About 35 of the amino acids do not vary in type or position within the

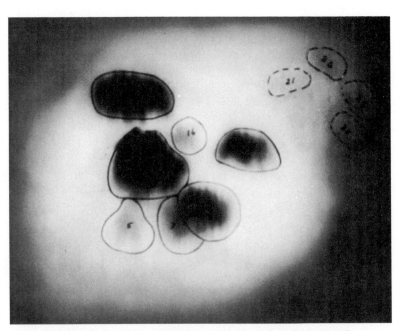

Fig. 1. Two-dimensional paper chromatogram ("fingerprint") of *Parinari parilis* (Chrysobalanaceae), a Brazilian plant. A portion of the extract was spotted on the paper in the lower right-hand corner and separated into the pattern in solvents flowing from right to left and bottom to top. The pattern was photographed under long-wave ultraviolet light. (*Courtesy of Ralph Rocklin*)

chain, and are probably necessary to maintain the structure and function of the enzyme. Several other amino acid positions vary occasionally, and always with the same amino acid substitution at a particular position. Among the remaining 50 positions scattered throughout the chain, considerable substitution occurs, the number of such differences between organisms indicating how closely they are related to one another. Thus, the horse and bakers' yeast, not unexpectedly, differ from each other in 41 of these variable sites, and the yeast cytochrome is also slightly longer by several amino acids. The horse, however, differs by only two amino acid substitutions from its relatives—the pig, cow, and sheep—all of which have identical cytochrome *c* sequences.

When such substitutional patterns were subjected to computer analysis, an evolutionary tree was obtained showing the degree of relatedness among the 36 plants and animals examined. This evolutionary tree is remarkably similar to evolutionary trees or phylogenies constructed on the basis of the actual fossil record for these organisms. Thus, the internal biochemistry of living organisms reflects a measure of the evolutionary changes which have occurred over time in these plants and animals. Since each amino acid in a protein is the ultimate product of a specific portion of the DNA code, the substitutional differences in this and other proteins in various organisms also reflect a change in the nucleotide sequences of DNA itself. *See* GENETIC CODE; PHYLOGENY.

Electrophoresis. In the case of proteins, however, it is often not necessary to know the specific amino acid sequence of a protein (ascertainable by a most laborious process), but, rather, to observe how many different proteins, or forms of a single protein, are present in different plant or animal species. The technique of electrophoresis is used to obtain a pattern of protein bands of spots much like the chemical fingerprint of micromolecules. Because each amino acid in a protein carries a positive, negative, or neutral ionic charge, the total sum of

charges of the amino acids constituting the protein will give the whole protein a net positive, negative, or neutral charge. A protein extract of seeds, for example, is placed into a slab of a semisolid gel of starch, agar, or polyacrylamide. The gel is placed in contact with electrically conductive salt solutions, and an electric current is passed through the system. Because of their differing charges, the various proteins in the extract migrate at various rates toward the positive (or negative) pole, spreading out into a series of separate bands. A colored marker dye which moves at a specific rate indicates when the electrophoretogram is done. The slab of gel containing the proteins, which are colorless, is then soaked in an appropriate stain or dye which complexes (directly or through a substrate-enzyme reaction) with and visualizes the proteins, giving the desired protein band pattern or fingerprint. Such a gel is shown in **Fig. 2**. The several columns of band patterns in Fig. 2 represent the variation in forms of a single protein enzyme within individual seeds from a single tree of the red maple, *Acer rubrum*. Thus electrophoresis is sensitive enough to pick out protein (and hence genetic) differences between individual offspring of a single tree. *See* ELECTROPHORESIS; PROTEIN.

By using such electrophoretic techniques in animal studies, protein differences between species of the fruit fly, *Drosophila*, have been examined. Electrophoretic patterns like those shown in Fig. 2 were obtained for five enzyme systems sampled in 27 species of *Drosophila* which were arranged in nine groups of 3 species each. Each group of 3 species, called a triad, consisted of two closely related sibling species and a third related but morphologically distinct species. For each enzyme among the 27 species, the number of different electrophoretic forms (bands) ranged from 13 for acid phosphatase to 27 different forms (bands) for leucine amino peptidase. Statistical analysis of these electrophoretic data confirmed that in most cases the sibling species of each triad were more closely related to each other than either was to the related

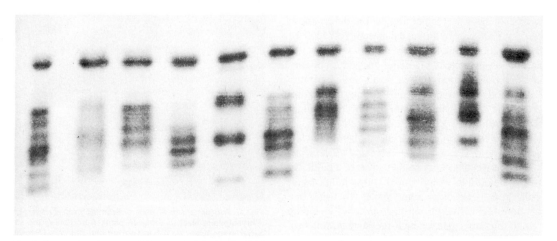

Fig. 2. Electrophoretograms of the protein enzyme phosphoglucoisomerase (PGI). Each column represents the protein band pattern for a single seed from the same tree of red maple, *Acer rubrum*. Note the variation in band patterns between the 11 individual seeds (columns). (*Courtesy of G. M. Iglich*)

but distinct third species. In some cases, however, and despite morphological similarity, the protein data suggested a closer relationship between a sibling species and its triad relative species than between the former and its own sibling. It has been suggested that in these cases the morphology of the organism might not evolve as rapidly as its biochemistry, and thus the biochemical differences may be more accurate indicators of actual genetic and taxonomic relationships. In other animals and plants such morphological similarity may represent parallel but unrelated developments, rather than actual taxonomic affinities. Often biochemistry can clarify such systematic difficulties.

Electrophoretic techniques have also been applied to the direct sequencing of the DNA nucleotides which make up the specific genes in plants and animals. Rather than using the very complex nuclear DNA, these studies have concentrated on the smaller, more manageable DNA sequences which occur independently in subcellular organelles such as chloroplasts and mitochondria. Each of these organelles contains its own DNA complement which codes for many of the structural and enzymatic proteins required for organellar function. Such organellar DNA can be cleaved into smaller portions consisting of one or a few genes by special enzymes. These enzymes, called restriction endonucleases, cleave the DNA nucleotide chain at specific points. The resulting fragments are separated by electrophoresis (similar to that used in protein studies) into diagnostic patterns. Fragments which differ in their pattern or mobility indicate portions of the DNA molecule where the nucleotide sequence has changed over time. These differences among species allow taxonomic comparisons between groups of organisms, and most importantly, the DNA itself is examined rather than its terminal product, the protein. *See* RESTRICTION ENZYME.

By using other techniques of molecular biology, such as DNA hybridization and genetic cloning, the specific gene function of these individual fragments may be identified. Their nucleotide sequences can be determined and then compared for different taxa. Such data may prove useful at several different taxonomic levels. *See* GENETIC ENGINEERING.

While the organellar DNA does not contain the number of genetic messages of the organism that nuclear DNA does, and its transmission from parent to offspring may vary somewhat depending on the organism, the convenient size of organellar DNA and its potential for direct examination of the genetic code suggest that it is a potent macromolecular approach to chemosystematics. *See* GENETIC CODE.

Specific chemotaxonomic applications. In terms of taxonomic studies, the chemistry of plants has been used extensively, and in some cases it provides the primary method of distinguishing between plant groups. Fungi, for example, are distinguished from plants because they lack the chlorophyll pigments typical of photosynthetic plants. Within the fungi, it has been found that some of them synthesize the

amino acid lysine via the precursor aminoadipic acid, whereas others synthesize lysine via the precursor diaminopimelic acid. The presence of one or the other of these biosynthetic pathways (and cell wall composition) correlates with current taxonomic arrangements within the fungi and provides information as to which groups of fungi are closely related to each other. *See* FUNGI.

In contrast, the major divisions of algae are recognized on the basis of the different types of chlorophyll and their starch reserves. *See* ALGAE.

Lichens, which are organisms consisting of an alga and a fungus living together in a symbiotic (and often complex) relationship, are regularly identified by the unusual chemical components (for example, depsides, depsidones) produced by the fungal symbiont. In fact, many of the compounds are unique to lichens, and lichen identification often depends greatly on these diagnostic components when few reliable morphological characters are available. *See* LICHENES.

In bacteria, beyond a certain point, the external appearance of a cell is no longer sufficiently diagnostic, and bacteria are then classified on the basis of the types of substrates on which they will grow or digest, what type of respiratory by-products they produce, whether they will grow in air (aerobic) or without it (anaerobic) or equally well in both cases (facultative), and most recently, by differences in cell wall chemistry. These distinctions in bacteria are based on differences in amino acids or amino acid chains (peptides) which in combination with different kinds of sugar polymers make up the peptidoglycans that form the bacterial cell wall. For example, it has been shown that in the coryneform bacteria some genera (*Mycobacterium*, *Corynebacterium*, *Nocardia*) are identical in their cell wall composition, while in other genera (*Microbacterium*) individual species may be recognized by their cell wall chemistry. *See* BACTERIAL TAXONOMY.

In green plants, and particularly in the flowering plants (angiosperms), micromolecular data have been most useful. One such group of compounds, the flavonoid pigments, have been effectively employed at many taxonomic levels. One group of these pigments, the anthocyanins, are responsible for the red-to-orange and the blue range of colors typical of most flowers. The second group, the anthoxanthins, are pale yellow or colorless to the naked eye, but occur in the largest number and variety and are easily separated into distinct chromatographic patterns or fingerprints. These patterns are clearly observable under long-wave ultraviolet light (Fig. 1). *See* FLAVONOID.

Documentation of hybrids. One of the earliest uses of flavonoid patterns was in a classic study of chemical documentation of hybridization between species in the legume genus *Baptisia*. Occasionally, when two species of *Baptisia* occur together, hybridization occurs. The hybrids resulting from this fortuitous type of cross often look different from both parents. Some early taxonomists even

Comparative distribution of flavonoids in fossil and extant species of oak (*Quercus*) and related taxa*

Taxon	A						B						C		D	E			
	1	3	5	9	10	11	2	4	12	13	16	17	14	15	7	6	8	18	19
Quercus consimilis	+	+	.	.	.	.	+	+	.	.	.	.			+	+	+	.	+
Q. acutissima	+	+	+	.	.	.	+	+	.	.	.	.			+	+	+	.	+
Q. chenii	+	+	.	+	+	+	+	+	.	.	.	.			+	+	+	.	.
Q. myrsinaefolia	.	.					.	.	+	+	+	.	+	+	+				
Q. stenophylla							.	.	+	+	+	.	+	+	+				
Q. variabilis							.	+	.	+	+	+	+	+	tr				
Castanea dentata							.	.	.	.	+	+	+	+	tr	.	.	+	.

*From K. J. Niklas and D. E. Giannasi, Angiosperm paleobiochemistry of the Succor Creek flora (Miocene), Oregon, U.S.A., *Amer. J. Bot.*, 65:943–952, 1978.
†A = glycoflavones; B = flavonols; C = flavanonols; D = ellagic acid; E = unknown; + = presence of compound; tr = trace amounts.

described them as new species of *Baptisia* rather than recognizing them as transient hybrids. It was suspected that these "new" species were hybrids. Researchers first examined the flavonoid profiles of the two parents and found them to be different from one another. The profile of the suspected hybrid proved to be a summation of the two contributing parents, a phenomenon termed complementation. If the hybrid had instead been a legitimate species, its flavonoid profile would have been expected to be different from either of the two species present in the area owing to its own morphological and chemical evolution as an individual species. Indeed, so distinct are the flavonoid profiles of each *Baptisia* species that at least one hybrid was shown to possess a complementary profile involving up to four different species.

The same approach has been used employing other classes of compounds such as terpenes to study cases of suspected hybridization in other taxa such as the junipers (*Juniperus*). In one case, suspected hybridization between *J. ashei* and *J. virginiana*, based on earlier morphological work, was shown by terpene chemistry to be unfounded. In contrast, terpene chemistry indicated that hybridization had occurred between *J. virginiana* and *J. scopulorum* when no such definite conclusions could be drawn from morphological and ecological information alone.

Phytoalexin studies. In another approach, advantage has been taken of the distribution of phenolic "antibodies," or phytoalexins, produced by plants in response to invasion by bacteria (both pathogenic or nonpathogenic). It has been shown that inoculation of droplets of water on leaves of species of the legume genus *Trigonella* with the bacterium *Helminthosporium carbonum* (a nonpathogenic bacterium) elicits the secretion of phytoalexins by the host plant into the waterdroplets. Analysis of the waterdroplets shows the presence of several classes of phenolic compounds (pterocarpans, flavonoids, coumarins). Remarkably, the distribution of host plant phytoalexin types induced by the bacterium is closely correlated with the subgeneric groupings of *Trigonella* species based on morphological and other nonchemical features. In this case,

chemotaxonomic correlations are based on a biological relationship between host and pathogen rather than internal host chemistry alone. *See* PHYTOALEXINS.

Fossil chemotaxonomy. Flavonoids have been found to be preserved in fossil angiosperm leaves from the western United States that are about 22,000,000 years old. The flavonoid profiles of the fossils, which could be compared with profiles of extant (living), related species, included elm (*Ulmus*), hackberry (*Celtis*), maple (*Acer*), oak (*Quercus*), and *Zelkova*. The flavonoid chemistry of the fossil oak *Quercus consimilis* proved especially interesting since paleobotanists considered the fossil oak species to be most closely related, morphologically, to two extant Asian species, *Q. myrsinaefolia* and *W. stenophylla*. Using combined gas chromatography and mass spectroscopy, researchers obtained steroid, fatty acid, and alkane profiles of the fossil leaf, demonstrating that it was an oak. The flavonoid profile of the fossil oak leaf, however, was not like that of the previously proposed living relatives, but was in fact nearly identical to that of two other extant Asian oaks, *Q. acutissima* and *Q. chenii*, which, incidentally, also have a leaf morphology similar to that of the fossil. Thus, in the **table**, the occurrence of flavonoids of group A in the fossil oak (taxon 1) shows it to be chemically most similar to *Q. acutissima* and *Q. chenii* (taxa 2 and 3, respectively) rather than to the putative relatives (see taxon 4) that were chosen on the basis of morphology alone and that lack pigment group A. Other randomly chosen, superficially similar taxa (taxa 5 and 6) also do not match the fossil species. *See* PALEOBIOCHEMISTRY.

Although the chemical data confirmed that the fossil was an oak and pointed out its close relationship to two living oak species not previously suspected on the basis of morphology alone, perhaps more important was the fact that (1) a definite taxonomic and evolutionary link exists between extant Asian oaks and the extinct oaks of western North America, and (2) the chemistry of fossils can be compared with that of living relatives to determine how much evolutionary change, if any, has occurred over millions of years.

Potential. Obviously, in studies of existing taxonomic systems, a knowledge of biochemistry can be a powerful adjunct tool, and in many cases can indicate possible evolutionary relationships between organisms more precisely than other evidence alone can. Indeed, the potential of chemistry in taxonomy has finally been recognized, resulting in a close synergism between chemist and taxonomist, and in the establishment of the chemotaxonomist, a person trained in both fields. *See* ANIMAL SYSTEMATICS; NUMERICAL TAXONOMY; PLANT TAXONOMY.

David E. Giannasi

Bibliography. R. Adams and B. L. Turner, *Taxon*, 19:728–751, 1970; R. E. Alston and B. L. Turner, *Biochemical Systematics*, 1963; M. O. Dayhoff (ed.), *Atlas of Protein Sequence and Structure*, Nat. Biomed. Res. Foun., 1972; J. L. Hubby and L. H. Throckmorton, Protein differences in *Drosophila*, IV, *Amer. Natural.*, 102:193–205, 1968; J. L. Ingham, Phytoalexin induction and its chemosystematic significance in the genus *Trigonella, Biochem. Sys. Ecol.*, 9:275–281, 1981; K. J. Niklas and D. E. Giannasi, *Amer. J. Bot.*, 65:943–952, 1978; P. M. Smith, *The Chemotaxonomy of Plants*, 1976.

Chemotherapy

The use of chemical agents (drugs) to treat disease. In theory, the term can mean pharmacologic (chemical) therapy of any disease. In practice, it has been used almost exclusively for the drug treatment of parasitic and neoplastic diseases. When the term chemotherapy is used without a qualifying adjective, it has been understood to mean cancer chemotherapy, and it is in this context that it is discussed here.

History. The father of chemotherapy was Paul Ehrlich. Ehrlich and his successors searched for drugs that would selectively kill invading parasites (such as bacteria, fungi, protozoa, and worms) without harming the host—in other words, that would exhibit selective toxicity. Although the earliest success (Ehrlich's salvarsan, 1910) and the greatest success (Alexander Fleming's penicillin, 1926) of chemotherapy were antibacterial agents, cancer chemotherapy was recognized before long as an area of great importance. However, relatively little progress was made until 1941, when Charles Brenton Huggins and C. V. Hodges published their work on sex hormone therapy for advanced metastatic cancers of the prostate and breast. In 1945, nitrogen mustard (mechlorethamine), a derivative of a World War I poison gas, was introduced for the treatment of lymphomas and some solid tumors. Since 1945, the rapid expansion of basic science research and empirical testing of drugs for anticancer effects have resulted in the introduction of approximately 30 useful drugs. *See* ANTIBIOTIC.

Status. From its halting beginnings as palliative therapy for advanced breast and prostate cancer, chemotherapy has progressed to a point at which it can cure several types of cancer (paradoxically, those that are most rapidly fatal without chemotherapy), produce remissions of several years in others, and yield palliation in many others.

Depending on the cancer, chemotherapy may be the primary means of therapy or an adjunct to primary surgical or radiation therapy, in which case chemotherapy is termed the adjuvant therapy. Chemotherapy is almost always the primary therapy in tumors that are widely disseminated from the start, for example, bone marrow or lymphatic neoplasms. Surgery or radiotherapy is usually the primary therapy of choice in solid tumors and other neoplasms that are initially well localized. However, even a small, well-circumscribed tumor may invade blood vessels and seed distant sites with micrometastases. Such metastases will grow after the primary tumor is removed, and may eventually kill the patient. Therefore, adjuvant chemotherapy to eliminate micrometastatic disease is now considered necessary to effect a cure in tumors that are prone to early metastasis.

Types of cancers for which a cure is relatively common by using chemotherapy include acute lymphocytic leukemia, acute myelocytic leukemia, choriocarcinoma, Hodgkin's disease, non-Hodgkin's lymphoma (Burkitt's), rhabdomyosarcoma, and testicular carcinoma.

Good-to-excellent results (remission in 20 to 80% of patients and disease-free survival for 2 to 8 years) using chemotherapy are obtained for breast carcinoma (adjuvant), Ewing's sarcoma (adjuvant), hairy cell leukemia, ovarian carcinoma, prostatic carcinoma, and Wilm's tumor (adjuvant).

The use of chemotherapy yields moderate results (remission or prolonged survival in some patients) for adrenocortical carcinoma, bladder carcinoma, brain glioblastoma, cervical carcinoma, and chronic leukemias (lymphocytic or myelocytic). Moderate results are also obtained for endometrial carcinoma, follicular lymphoma, gastric carcinoma, lung carcinoma (small cell), and mycosis fungoids.

Poor results (improvement in survival not demonstrated) are obtained with chemotherapy for colorectal carcinoma, hepatocellular carcinoma, lung carcinoma (non-small-cell), malignant melanoma, and pancreatic carcinoma.

Principles. A successful chemotherapeutic agent is toxic to invading (or abnormal) cells but has little or no effect on host (or normal) cells. A high degree of selective toxicity is relatively easy to achieve in antimicrobial drugs: the disease-inducing organism usually has biochemical and physiological processes not shared by the host. Furthermore, because the organism is foreign, it evokes host-defense mechanisms that aid the drug in eradicating the disease. Parasite-specific biochemical processes are obvious targets for selectively toxic chemotherapy. For example, bacteria have a cell wall but animal cells do not.

Synthesis of this cell wall requires enzymes unique to bacteria, and blockade of cell wall synthesis results in death or severe growth impairment of bacteria. Penicillin selectively blocks one or more enzymes responsible for the synthesis and maintenance of the cell wall.

Cancer cells stem from the same genome as the normal cells of the host and therefore have few, if any, processes that are unique. It would appear that a key difference is the absence of a normal growth control process in cancer cells, and other processes differ only quantitatively, not qualitatively. Thus, discovery of useful targets for selectively toxic drugs has been very slow, and the best drugs discovered to date are only partially selective in their toxicity. As a result, the therapeutic index (ratio of median toxic dose to median therapeutic dose) for the cancer chemotherapeutic agents is much lower than that for any antimicrobial drug. Cancer cells also demonstrate rapid turnover and genetic instability; therefore cancer cells may develop resistance to drugs rapidly. For example, an enzyme that is essential for cell division (and susceptible to drug inhibition) in the parent cancer cell line may be bypassed in a mutant descendant cell. Therefore, special multidrug treatment protocols that minimize the opportunity for the neoplastic cells to become resistant have been developed. *See* ONCOLOGY.

Nevertheless, some differences between cancer cells and normal cells exist, permitting selective toxicity. The most important is the fact that most cancer cells divide more rapidly than normal cells. In fact, except in specialized tissues that must replenish themselves continuously (intestinal epithelium, gonadal germ cells, and lymph and blood cells), the cells of most tissues divide slowly or not at all. Dividing cells are more susceptible to drugs that interfere with replication of the genetic material—deoxyribonucleic acid (DNA) and ribonucleic acid (RNA)—and with the synthesis of proteins (for example, enzymes) necessary to support rapid cell division. Antitumor drugs are conventionally divided into two major subgroups: drugs that are most effective in one phase of the cell division cycle of the cancer cell (cell-cycle-specific) and those that are effective at any time during the cycle (cell-cycle-nonspecific). *See* CELL CYCLE; CELL DIVISION.

The first major subgroup—cell-cycle-specific drugs—includes three classes of antitumor drugs: antimetabolites, peptide antibiotics, and alkaloids. Azacytadine, cytarabine, fluorouracil, mercaptopurine, methotrexate, and thioguanine are all antimetabolites. Bleomycin is an example of a peptide antibiotic. Alkaloid drugs include podophyllin (etoposide, teniposide), vincristine, and vinblastine.

Cell-cycle-nonspecific drugs (the second major subgroup) are divided into four drug classes: alkylating agents, antibiotics, hormones and endocrine inhibitors, and miscellaneous drugs.

The alkylating agents include busulfan, cyclophosphamide, mechlorethamine, melphelan, and thiotepa. Doxorubicin, daunorubicin, dactinomycin, plicamycin, and mitomycin are antibiotics. Examples of hormones and endocrine inhibitors are diethylstilbestrol, tamoxifen, megestrol, leuprolide, bromocriptine, aminoglutethimide, prednisone, and mitotane. Finally, miscellaneous drugs include cisplatin, nitrosureas, and interferons.

The logarithmic growth curve that characterizes neoplasms predicts that a tumor cell must undergo 27 doublings before it is detectable by the most sensitive x-ray techniques, and 30 before it is palpable, but only 5 to 10 additional doublings before it is fatal to the host. The log-kill principle of chemotherapy (see **illus.**) describes the probable effect of a given dose of an anticancer drug as reducing the total body tumor burden by a fixed number of log units. Thus, an effective dose of a drug given to a patient with 10^{12} leukemia cells might be expected to reduce the total tumor burden by 3 log units or 99.9% of the total. However, 10^9 tumor cells would still remain in the host. To achieve a cure, this dose would have to be repeated several times. In the case of a solid tumor, cure could be expedited by surgical removal of most of the tumor mass. Unfortunately, the viable cancer cells remaining after any chemotherapeutic treatment might be expected to include one or more that were resistant to the drug.

In the illustration, which is a graphic representation of the log-kill hypothesis, the broken curve indicates the progression of the neoplasm with no treatment; clinical manifestations (earliest possi-

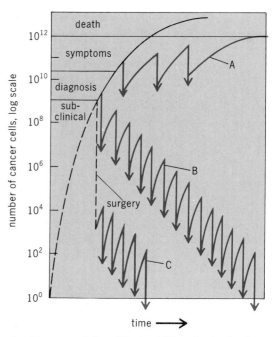

Graphic representation of the log-kill hypothesis, showing natural history of a hypothetical neoplasm with and without various treatments. (*After S. E. Salmon and A. C. Sartorelli, Cancer chemotherapy, in B. G. Katzung, ed., Basic and Clinical Pharmacology, 4th ed., Appleton and Lange, 1989*)

ble diagnosis, symptoms, death) are indicated. The solid curves indicate the results of application of a treatment capable of achieving a 99.9% eradication of tumor cells. If chemotherapy is not initiated until late in the growth of the tumor, and is not repeated frequently (curve A), only brief and incomplete remissions of the disease will be achieved, and the patient will die after a short delay. If therapy is repeated frequently enough to maintain and increase each partial response (curve B), all tumor cells may eventually be eradicated and the patient will be cured. If the total mass of tumor is rapidly reduced at the onset of therapy, for example, by surgery (curve C) and residual tumor is then attacked repeatedly with chemotherapy, a complete cure can be achieved much sooner. To achieve cure by any means, chemotherapy must be repeated long after all clinical evidence of the tumor has been eliminated.

To maximize cell kill and to reduce the emergence of resistant cell clones, the use of combinations of drugs has become commonplace in cancer treatment. The drugs in the most effective combinations (1) attack different biochemical targets, thus minimizing the chance that a cancer cell will be resistant to all the drugs; (2) have different toxicities, so that relatively high doses can be given without appreciably increased risk to the host; and (3) can be repeated at intervals, thus permitting the host to recover from toxic effects while multiplying the number of log-kills of tumor cells.

Drug selection. The selection of drugs for a given type of cancer, and for a given patient, is usually based almost entirely on experience. However, selection of drugs for hormone-dependent cancers can be guided by application of the pharmacologic principle that drugs must combine with receptors to produce their effects. Because endocrine receptors have been well characterized, it is possible to take a specimen of tumor from a surgical biopsy of the breast and determine the numbers of estrogen and progestin receptors present. The presence of many of these receptors is prognostic of a good response to antiestrogen therapy. Another means of predicting drug response entails culturing cells from a tumor and measuring the effect of candidate drugs on them. This clonogenic assay has not yet proven to be of great value in selecting drugs, but may provide valuable models for testing new cancer agents.

Measuring clinical response. Responses to chemotherapy are usually described as complete (total disappearance of all signs of disease), or partial (at least 50% decrease in size of measurable lesions or total tumor burden). A response of less than 50% is considered disease progression or no response. Because drug-resistant clones of cells may be present even in a patient who has had a complete remission, the duration of these remissions must then be followed over time to measure the total benefit.

Toxicity of chemotherapy. Because most cancer chemotherapeutic agents have a low therapeutic index, some drug toxicity is almost universal in patients treated with these chemicals. The prevention or management of this toxicity has became an important part of cancer chemotherapy, since the toxicity may be lethal (bone marrow suppression) or may be so unpleasant (nausea and vomiting) that patients refuse to continue therapy. Antibiotics are widely used to prevent infection, blood or blood products are used to treat anemia and prevent bleeding, and antinauseants are used to reduce nausea and vomiting. Toxicities that have not been well controlled to date, and can be avoided only by limiting the total dose, include cardiac failure, pulmonary fibrosis, and sterility, especially in males.

A second major type of toxicity associated with the use of cancer chemotherapeutic agents is the induction of new cancers. It has been recognized that many anticancer agents are carcinogenic in the laboratory. In humans, secondary neoplasms most often take the form of acute myelogenous leukemia. There is clinical evidence that up to 10% of leukemias being diagnosed today are secondary neoplasms, that is, leukemias induced by the treatment of other cancers. The drugs that appear most likely to cause cancer include melphelan, azathioprine, carmustine, chlorambucil, lomustine, cyclophosphamide, and procarbazine. *See* CANCER (MEDICINE); LEUKEMIA.   Bertram Katzung

Bibliography. B. Chabner, *Pharmacologic Principles of Cancer Treatment*, 1982; A. DeVita, K. Hellman, and S. A. Rosenberg. *Cancer: Principles and Practice of Oncology*, 1982; C. M. Haskell, *Cancer Treatment*, 1980; K. Hellman and S. K. Carter, *Fundamentals of Cancer Chemotherapy*, 1987; B. G. Katzung (ed.), *Basic and Clinical Pharmacology*, 4th ed., 1989.

Cherry

Sweet or sour fruit of the *Prunus* genus, having cultivated and wild varieties.

Cultivated varieties. The two principal cherries of commerce are the sweet cherry (*Prunus avium*) and the sour cherry (*P. cerasus*). Both are of ancient origin and seem to have come from the region between the Black and Caspian seas. They were probably carried into Europe by birds before humans were there. The cherry was mentioned in 300 B.C. by the Greek botanist Theophrastus. It was taken to America from Europe.

Cherries of minor importance are the dwarf or western sand cherries (*P. besseyi*) of the plains region of North America; the Duke cherries, which are supposedly natural hybrids between the sweet and sour cherry; and the Padus cherries, which bear their small fruits in long clusters or racemes rather than in short fascicles.

Sweet cherries may be divided into two groups, firm-fleshed types known as Bigarreaus, represented by the Napoleon (also called the Royal

Anne), and soft-fleshed types known as Hearts, represented by the Black Tartarian. Sour cherries may also be divided into two groups, clear-juice or Amarelle types, represented by the Montmorency, and colored-juice or Morello types, represented by the English Morello.

In North America the principal sweet commercial varieties are the Napoleon (white), Bing, Lambert, Van, Schmidt, and Windsor (dark). The principal commercial variety of sour cherry is the Montmorency.

Trees are propagated by budding into seedlings of the wild sweet (mazzard) cherry or of *P. mahaleb,* commonly called the perfumed cherry of southern Europe. The former is best suited to the sweet cherry, and the latter to the sour cherry. *See* PLANT PROPAGATION; REPRODUCTION (PLANT).

The sweet cherry is somewhat hardier than the peach, and the sour cherry is hardier than the sweet cherry. Cultivated varieties are usually planted 25–30 ft (7.5–9 m) apart and allowed to grow to heights of only about 15–20 ft (4.5–6 m) for ease of culture and harvest. Sour cherry trees may reach 30–40 ft (9–12 m) but are kept at 15–20 ft (4.5–6 m) and planted 18–22 ft (5.4–6.6 m) apart. Cherry trees do best in well-drained sandy loam soils. They will not tolerate wet soil. Sweet varieties require cross-pollination; common sour varieties are self-fruitful (self-pollinated). *See* FRUIT; FRUIT, TREE; ROSALES.

R. Paul Larsen

Wild varieties. The wild cherry tree, *P. serotina,* grows to a height of 100 ft (30 m) and may reach an age of 200 years. It belongs to the rose family, and is an important timber species of cherry in the United States. Native in the eastern half of the United States and adjacent Canada, it reaches its largest size in the southern Appalachian Mountains. The deciduous leaves are long-pointed, thickish, and shining above (**Fig. 1**). The edible fruit is a shiny black drupe found in long clusters. The hard, strong wood is a red-brown and is used for furniture,

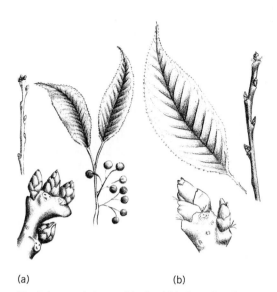

(a)   (b)

Fig. 2. Leaves, twigs, and buds of (a) pin or fire cherry (*Prunus pensylvanica*) and (b) wild cherry (*P. serotina*).

often as an imitation mahogany.

The sweet cherry or mazzard (*P. avium*), which grows to 70 ft (21 m), is naturalized over a large part of the United States. It has fruits borne in umbel-like clusters. It also differs from the wild cherry in having more ovate leaves with rounded teeth (**Fig. 2**).

The Japanese flowering cherries are varieties of *P. serrulata,* which attract much attention at blossoming time in early May.

Arthur H. Graves/Kenneth P. Davis

Diseases. A destructive disease of cherry in the orchard and after harvest is brown rot, caused by the fungus *Monilinia fructicola.* Infections occur first in blossoms, and later in the maturing fruit, causing rot (**Fig. 3**). Cherry leaf spot, caused by the fungus *Coccomyces hiemalis,* results in leaf spotting, yellowing, and premature defoliation. Without well-functioning leaves, trees lose vigor and decline in productivity. Powdery mildew, caused by the fungus *Podosphaera oxyacanthae,* impairs the ability of leaves to supply sugars and other products needed by the tree for normal development. These three diseases can be effectively controlled with timely sprays of recommended fungicides.

The major bacterial diseases of cherry are bacterial canker caused by *Pseudomonas syringae* (affecting leaves, branches, and fruit) and crown gall, due to *Agrobacterium tumefaciens,* which causes a tumorlike growth on the crown and roots.

Important virus (or viruslike) diseases are Prunus ring spot, prune dwarf, little cherry, and X disease ("buckskin"). Virus diseases affect certain tissues (wood, bark, leaves, seeds, pollen) of certain branches or even the entire tree. The symptoms vary with each disease, but usually involve small, mottled, yellow, or missing leaves, and small and poorly colored fruit. Tree growth and yield suffer. Preventive control measures include planting

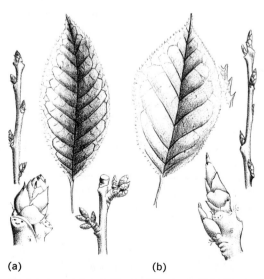

(a)   (b)

Fig. 1. Leaves, twigs, and buds of (a) sweet cherry (*Prunus avium*) and (b) choke cherry (*P. virginiana*).

Fig. 3. Brown rot disease of sweet cherry.

resistant varieties and certified virus-free stock and, where applicable, spraying for the control of insect vectors that transmit the pathogens. *See* PLANT PATHOLOGY; PLANT VIRUSES AND VIROIDS.

Michael Szkolnik

Bibliography. J. M. Ogawa and H. English, *Diseases of the Temperate Zone Tree Fruit and Nut Crops*, 1991; *Virus Diseases of Small Fruits*, USDA Agr. Handb. 631, 1987; C. Wilson and M. E. Wisniewski (eds.), *Biological Control of Postharvest Diseases: Theory and Practice*, 1994.

Chert

A hard, dense sedimentary rock composed of fine-grained silica (SiO_2). Chert is characterized by a semivitreous to dull luster and a splintery to conchoidal fracture, and is most commonly gray, black, reddish brown, or green. Chert is also used as a field term to describe silica-rich rocks which may be impure; common impurities include carbonates, iron and manganese oxides, and clay minerals. When impurities change the texture of the rock to the extent that it is less dense and hard than chert, and has the appearance of unglazed porcelain, the rock is then called porcellanite or siliceous shale. The term flint is synonymous with chert, but its use has become restricted to archeological artifacts and to nodular chert that occurs in chalk. The term chert, however, is preferred for the nodular deposits. Jasper refers to red or yellow quartz chert associated with iron ore or containing iron oxide. Novaculite is a white chert of great purity and uniform grain size, and is composed chiefly of quartz; the term is mostly restricted to descriptions of Paleozoic cherts in Oklahoma and Arkansas. Chert synonyms that have become obsolete include silexite, petrosilex, phthanite, and hornstone. *See* JASPER.

Composition. The silica that composes chert occurs in four forms: quartz, chalcedony, opal-CT, and opal-A. Chalcedony is a microscopically fibrous form of the mineral quartz with water trapped in void spaces parallel to the fibers.

The poorly understood opal-CT phase is probably an interstratified mixture of the silica minerals cristobalite and tridymite, although it has been suggested to be solely disordered tridymite. In chert, the chalcedony, quartz, and opal-CT are secondary forms of silica derived from the dissolution and later precipitation of a primary silica phase, which for most chert is biogenic silica (opal-A). The main rock-forming types of biogenic silica are the tests and frustules of the siliceous plankton diatoms, radiolarians, silicoflagellates, and ebriidians, and the siliceous spicules of sponges. The composition of chert changes with time and temperature, beginning with opal-A, which transforms to opal-CT and finally to quartz or chalcedony. Under special conditions, opal-A can transform directly to quartz. *See* CHALCEDONY; OPAL; QUARTZ.

Diagenesis. Opal-A and opal-CT are metastable phases within the Earth's crust. The diagenetic transformation of opal-A to opal-CT and then to quartz is primarily controlled by temperature and time, but also by surface area, pore-water chemistry, sediment permeability, and host-sediment composition. The mineralogical transformations are commonly, but not invariably, accompanied by textural transformations. For example, diatom or radiolarian ooze (unconsolidated marine sediment composed mostly of diatom frustules or radiolarian tests) or diatomaceous or radiolarian earth (weakly consolidated oozes that have been incorporated into on-land deposits), which are composed of opal-A, transform into porcellanite (most commonly composed of opal-CT), which in turn transforms into chert (most commonly composed of quartz). *See* DIAGENESIS; MARINE SEDIMENTS; RADIOLARIAN EARTH.

Occurrence. Chert occurs mainly in three forms: bedded sequences (see **illus**.), nodular, and massive. Bedded chert consists of rhythmically interlayered beds of chert and shale, or in pre-Phanerozoic formations with alternations of chert and siderite or hematite. Bedded sequences can be hundreds of feet thick stratigraphically and cover areas of hundreds of square miles. Individual beds are commonly $1/2$–8 in. (1–20 cm) thick.

Rhythmically bedded radiolarian chert from the Franciscan Complex Diablo Range, California; of Late Jurassic age.

Intercalated shale layers are commonly, but not invariably, thinner than the associated chert layers. In many places individual chert beds are laminated. Chert nodules and lenses occur primarily in chalk, limestone, and dolomite, and are the only types of chert recovered by the Deep Sea Drilling Project from open-ocean sediment. Chert nodules are well known from many places in western Europe, where their dark color contrasts strikingly with the white host chalk. Nodules vary in size from $1/2$ in. to 3 ft (1 cm to 1 m). Fossils and sedimentary structures characteristic of the host rock are preserved within the nodules. Massive cherts occur in the interstices between basalt pillows, and as the basal member of bedded chert that overlies pillow basalts in ophiolites. *See* BASALT; CHALK; DOLOMITE ROCK; LIMESTONE.

Origin. When a supply of silica is available, chert forms in three ways: by replacement of mainly carbonate rock, by deposition from turbidity currents composed primarily of biogenic silica, and by precipitation of silica from water under either hydrothermal or low-temperature hypersaline conditions. The replacement of chalk and limestone by silica has been well documented in Deep Sea Drilling Project cores and in some deposits on land. The silica is derived from the dissolution of biogenic silica deposited with the biogenic carbonate. The resultant chert most commonly forms nodules, but the silica may also replace beds of limestone completely, thereby forming bedded chert. Most bedded chert, however, is probably turbidite sequences, although additional work is necessary to confirm this hypothesis. Transient, sediment-laden density currents (turbidity currents) that flowed down the sides of submarine basins carried mostly biogenic silica which settled in layers. The layers later transformed into cherts through diagenetic processes. Pelagic or hemipelagic clays were deposited in the basin between times of turbidite deposition, thus creating the rhythmically bedded chert-shale sequences found in many mountain belts. In some places, the shales may be the turbidites and the cherts the pelagic deposits. Of relatively minor volumetric importance is the primary precipitation of silica. Inorganic precipitation of silica takes place in hypersaline lakes and lagoons. Chert also forms by deposition of silica from hydrothermal solutions into the interstices between basalt pillows, and in other localized areas within ophiolite sequences. *See* TURBIDITE; TURBIDITY CURRENT.

Distribution. The distribution of chert is tied to the distribution of siliceous plankton, which in turn depends on oceanographic conditions. After the plankton die, their shells accumulate in great quantities on the sea floor, especially around the polar regions (diatoms) and the equatorial belt of high biological productivity (radiolarians and diatoms). Shells also accumulate in other areas where cold, nutrient-rich subsurface water upwells, such as off the west coasts of continents and in marginal seas such as the Philippine and Japan seas. Marine siliceous deposits, along with the underlying oceanic crust, are incorporated into mountain belts by uplift of oceanic crust or by obduction and thrust faulting at subduction plate margins. Such on-land cherts of every age are found at many locations around the world. *See* BACILLARIOPHYCEAE.

Radiolarians and sponge spicules occur in Phanerozoic chert. Diatoms first evolved during the Mesozoic Era and came into prominence in the Tertiary, when they became the dominant precursor of chert. The source of silica for pre-Phanerozoic cherts, which are commonly associated with banded iron formations, is equivocal. Direct evidence of a biological source is lacking, and inorganic precipitation of silica is generally postulated; however, future studies may yield information that would indicate an additional source. *See* SEDIMENTARY ROCKS.   James R. Hein

Bibliography. S. R. Aston (ed.), *Silicon Geochemistry and Biogeochemistry*, 1983; J. R. Hein, *Bibliography of Fine-Grained Siliceous Deposits*, USGS Open-File Rep. 80–391, 1980; A. Iijima, J. R. Hein, and R. Siever (eds.), *Siliceous Deposits in the Pacific Region*, 1983.

Chestnut

Any of seven species of deciduous, nut-bearing trees of the genus *Castanea* (order Fagales) native to the Northern Hemisphere and introduced throughout the world. The nuts are actually fruits, with the shells enclosing cotyledons. Trees bear both male and female flowers in late spring but must be cross-pollinated for nut production. Nuts are borne in a spiny involucre or bur that opens to release the nuts in late fall. *See* FAGALES.

Varieties. Japanese chestnuts (*C. crenata*) and Chinese chestnuts (*C. mollissima*) are grown in Asia and the United States for their nuts, and many cultivars have been selected. European chestnuts (*C. sativa*) are an important food source, both cooked whole and ground into flour. They are

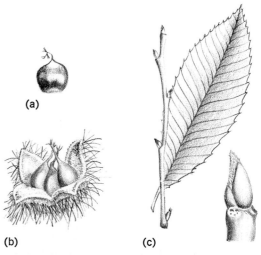

(a)

(b)   (c)

American chestnut (*Castanea dentata*). (*a*) Nut. (*b*) Bur. (*c*) Leaf, twig, and bud.

native to the Caucasus mountains, and distributed throughout southern Europe. American chestnuts (*C. dentata*; see **illus.**) have smaller nuts than Asian or European species and are usually sweeter. Only American trees served as an important source of lumber, because of the length of their unbranched trunks; all chestnut species have been used as a source of tannin for the leather-tanning industry. American and Chinese chinquapins (*C. pumila* and *C. henryi*) have very small nuts that are an important source of food for wildlife. All of the species can be crossed, and hybrids have been selected primarily as orchard cultivars.

Diseases. In 1838 a root disease was reported on European chestnut in Portugal, and soon after this "ink disease" was found in several other parts of southern Europe. The pathogen, *Phytophthora cinnamomi*, causes brownish-black lesions on the roots that exude an inky-blue stain. The lesions expand, coalesce, and girdle the root, resulting in tree death. Breeding with ink disease–resistant Asian species has produced new cultivars, and careful sanitation and site selection allow European chestnuts to still be grown. In the United States, ink disease probably accounted for the recession of chestnut species from large areas in the Gulf and Atlantic states and inland to the foothills and mountains of Mississippi, Alabama, Georgia, Tennessee, Maryland, Virginia, and the Carolinas. The fungus is assumed to have entered the United States in the mid-1800s.

The second disaster for American and European chestnuts was also a fungus disease. *Cryphonectria* (formerly *Endothia*) *parasitica* was first reported in New York City in 1904 and was found to be widespread throughout the northeast region of the United States. This fungus, causing chestnut blight, had probably entered the United States on imported Japanese chestnuts in the late 1800s. The initial spread was on nursery stock (most major mail-order nurseries sold Japanese chestnuts at the turn of the century), but spores were also carried on the fur, feet, and feathers of the birds, animals, and insects that walked up and down the trees. Wounds in the bark allow access and initial fungal growth, and the resulting canker expands to kill the cambium and eventually the twigs, branches, and trunk. The fungus does not kill the root collar, and the dormant embryos there sprout and grow until wounded, infected, and killed, and the cycle is repeated. In the northern part of the natural range of American chestnut (northern Georgia to southern Maine, and west through Ohio, Kentucky, and Tennessee), sprout clumps have survived well, but farther south repeated chestnut blight cycles kill the sprout clumps. American chinquapins are also very susceptible to chestnut blight, and their sprouting system (relying on the old root system, instead of forming new roots as chestnut does) may make them more liable to be killed by blight.

Chestnut blight was first reported in Europe on chestnuts in Italy in 1938. The epidemic there proceeded as in the United States, but natural virus infection of the fungus now provides a biological control. The fungal strains with viruses are less virulent (hypovirulent), and can be inoculated into natural cankers to transmit the viruses and establish biological control in orchards. Hypovirulent strains have been used in the United States for control of blight fungus populations in orchards and forest stands of American chestnut sprouts. Improved control may result from new genetically engineered strains. In addition, trees are bred for resistance by crossing susceptible trees with resistant Chinese and Japanese chestnuts.

The next potential disaster for chestnut trees in the United States and Europe is infestation with a small wasp native to Asia called the Oriental chestnut gall wasp (*Dryocosmus kuriphilus*). Eggs laid in leaf and flower buds develop into galls and heavy infestations can kill the trees. The insect has been in the United States since 1974 (on Chinese chestnut trees in orchards in Georgia), and is now infesting American chestnut trees at the southern part of the range. Japanese chestnut breeders released cultivars with some resistance to the insect, and American chinquapins also seem to have good resistance. *See* FOREST AND FORESTRY; PLANT PATHOLOGY; TREE.   Sandra L. Anagnostakis

Chevrel phases

A series of ternary molybdenum chalcogenide compounds. They were reported by R. Chevrel, M. Sergent, and J. Prigent in 1971. The compounds have the general formula $M_xMo_6X_8$, where M represents any one of a large number (nearly 40) of metallic elements throughout the periodic table; x has values between 1 and 4, depending on the M element; and X is a chalcogen (sulfur, selenium or tellurium). The Chevrel phases are of great interest, largely because of their striking superconducting properties.

Crystal structure. Most of the ternary molybdenum chalcogenides crystallize in a structure in which the unit cell, that is, the repeating unit of the crystal structure, has the overall shape of a rhombohedron with a rhombohedral angle close to 90°. Some of the ternary molybdenum chalcogenides display a slight distortion of the rhombohedral crystal structure at, or below, room temperature to a triclinic structure in which the three axes of the unit cell, and the three angles between them, are unequal.

The building blocks of the Chevrel-phase crystal structure are the M elements and Mo_6X_8 molecular units or clusters. Each Mo_6X_8 unit is a slightly deformed cube with X atoms at the corners, and Mo atoms at the face centers. One of these structures, that of $PbMo_6S_8$, is shown in the **illustration**. *See* CRYSTAL STRUCTURE; CRYSTALLOGRAPHY.

Superconductivity. Many of the Chevrel-phase compounds exhibit superconductivity, a phenomenon in which a metal, when cooled below its superconducting transition temperature T_c, loses

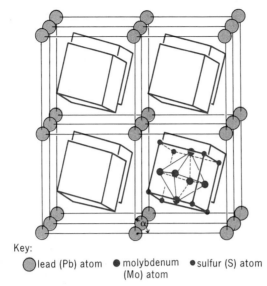

Key:

◗ lead (Pb) atom ● molybdenum • sulfur (S) atom
(Mo) atom

Crystal structure of PbMo₆S₈. Each lead atom is surrounded by eight Mo₆S₈ units, the structure of which is shown in the lower right part of the figure. The rhombohedral angle α is indicated also.

all resistance to flow of an electric current. Several of the Chevrel-phase compounds have relatively high values of T_c, the maximum being about 15 K ($-433°$F) for $PbMo_6S_8$. Prior to 1986, the highest T_c of any known material was 23 K ($-418°$F) for the A15 compound Nb_3Ge. *See* A15 PHASES.

Since 1987, superconductivity at temperatures above the boiling point of liquid nitrogen (77 K or $-321°$F) has been discovered in several families of copper oxide compounds. A value of T_c of approximately 122 K ($-240°$F) has been observed in a compound comprising the elements thallium, barium, calcium, copper, and oxygen. As in conventional superconductors, the superconductivity is associated with electron pairs, called Cooper pairs; but the attractive mechanism responsible for the formation of the Cooper pairs may be different in the high-T_c superconducting oxides than in conventional superconductors, like the Chevrel phases and the A15 phases, where it involves the interaction between the negatively charged electrons and the positively charged ions of the crystal lattice.

The superconductivity of any superconducting compound can be destroyed with a sufficiently high magnetic field, called the upper critical magnetic field $H_{c2}(T)$, which depends on the temperature T and varies from material to material. As the temperature is lowered, $H_{c2}(T)$ generally increases from zero at T_c to a maximum value, $H_{c2}(0)$, as the temperature approaches absolute zero. The Chevrel-phase $PbMo_6S_8$ has a value of $H_{c2}(0)$ of about 60 teslas (600 kilogauss), the largest value observed for any material prior to 1986. The highest $H_{c2}(0)$ that had been previously reported for a non-Chevrel-phase material was 40 teslas (400 kilogauss) for the A15 compound Nb_3Ge. In comparison, the values of $H_{c2}(0)$ for the highest T_c copper oxide superconductors may reach several hundred teslas, values so large that they cannot readily be measured by using the magnetic fields and techniques that are presently available in the laboratory.

A number of Chevrel-phase compounds of the form RMo_6X_8, where R is a rare-earth element with a partially filled $4f$ electron shell and X is S or Se, display magnetic order at low temperatures in addition to superconductivity. The superconductivity is primarily associated with the mobile $4d$ electrons of Mo, while the magnetic order involves the localized $4f$ electrons of the R atoms which occupy regular positions throughout the lattice. Superconductivity has been found to coexist with antiferromagnetic order, but to be destroyed by the onset of ferromagnetic order. *See* ANTIFERROMAGNETISM; FERROMAGNETISM; SUPERCONDUCTIVITY.   M. Brian Maple

Bibliography. G. Burns, *High-Temperature Superconductivity: An Introduction*, 1991; O. Fischer and M. B. Maple (eds.), *Topics in Current Physics*, vol. 32, 1982; T. H. Geballe and J. K. Hulm, Superconductivity: The state that came in from the cold, *Science*, 239:367–374, 1988; H. S. Kwok and D. T. Shaw (eds.), *Superconductivity and Its Applications*, 1988; M. B. Maple and O. Fischer (eds.), *Topics in Current Physics*, vol. 34, 1982.

Chevrotain

The name for four species of mammals which constitute the family Tragulidae in the order Artiodactyla. These animals, also known as mouse deer, are the smallest ruminants, growing to a maximum height of 12 in. (30 cm) at the shoulder. The water chevrotain (*Hyemoschus aquaticus*) is found in west-central Africa along the banks of rivers in Sierra Leone through the Cameroons to the Congo. It feeds principally on aquatic vegetation. The other species are all members of the genus *Tragulus*, and range through the forested areas of Sumatra into Borneo and Java. These are the Indian chevrotain (*T. meminna;* see **illus.**), the larger Malay chevrotain (*T. napu*), and the lesser Malay

Indian chevrotain (*Tragulus meminna*).

chevrotain (*T. javanicus*). They are differentiated by the pattern of markings (stripes or spots) on their coats. *Tragulus javanicus* has a coat of uniform color. The chevrotain lacks horns or antlers. There are two well-developed toes on the feet, and the upper canines of the male are elongate and protrude from the mouth as small tusks. The chevrotain is a shy animal which leads a solitary life except during the breeding season. After a gestation period of 120 days, one or two young are born. There is a total of 34 teeth with the dental formula I 0/3 C 1/1 Pm 3/3 M 3/3. The Eocene fossil traguloid, *Archaeomeryx*, which was unearthed in Mongolia, shows many general similarities to the modern chevrotains. The main line of evolutionary development of the traguloids occurred in Eurasia. *See* ARTIODACTYLA; DENTITION.   Charles B. Curtin

Chickenpox and shingles

Chickenpox (varicella) and shingles (herpes zoster) are two different forms of disease caused by the varicella-zoster virus, which is a deoxyribonucleic acid (DNA) virus closely related to herpes simplex and Epstein-Barr viruses. Initial infection causes varicella, a common childhood infection characterized by fever, malaise, and a rash consisting of dozens to hundreds of small fluid-filled lesions (vesicles) that are individually surrounded by reddened skin. Successive crops of lesions appear that eventually ulcerate and crust over during the two-week course of the disease. The virus is spread from person to person by the highly infectious respiratory secretions and lesion drainage. Varicella is rarely a serious disease in normal children but can be severe in immunocompromised individuals or in the rare adult who escaped childhood infection. Primary infection results in immunity to a new varicella-zoster virus, but the original virus lies dormant in nerve ganglia cells. *See* EPSTEIN-BARR VIRUS; HERPES.

At some time in their life, approximately 10% of the population suffers subsequent reactivation of latent virus, which spreads to the skin overlying the affected nerve and causes a localized eruption of vesicles called herpes zoster. The vesicles are similar in appearance and in infectiousness to varicella lesions. This syndrome is usually well tolerated, although elderly persons may develop chronic pain at the site of reactivation. Herpes zoster in immunocompromised individuals may be prolonged or may disseminate to vital organs.

Varicella or herpes zoster in a normal host is self-limited and does not typically require antiviral therapy. In individuals with underlying immune disorders, treatment with the antiviral drug acyclovir decreases the duration and severity of disease. Previously uninfected immunocompromised individuals or pregnant women recently exposed to varicella-zoster virus can be partially protected from subsequent disease through the administration of varicella-zoster immune globulin. However, antibody tests often indicate preexisting immunity from asymptomatic or forgotten childhood varicella. *See* ANIMAL VIRUS; VIRUS INFECTION, LATENT, PERSISTENT, SLOW.   Frederick P. Heinzel

Chicle

A gummy exudate used in the manufacture of chewing gum. It is contained in the bark of a tall evergreen tree, *Manilkara zapota* (see **illus.**), belonging to the sapodilla family (Sapotaceae). The species is a native of Mexico and Central America. The latex (secretion) is collected and carefully boiled to remove excess moisture. When the wa-

Fruit of *Manilkara zapota*. (*After L. H. Bailey, The Standard Cyclopedia of Horticulture, vol. 3, Macmillan, 1937*)

ter content is reduced to 33%, the chicle is poured off and molded into blocks. Crude chicle contains resin, arabin, gutta, sugar, calcium, and different soluble salts. For refining, it is broken up, washed in strong alkali, neutralized with sodium acid phosphate, rewashed, dried, and powdered. The resulting product is an amorphous, pale-pink powder, insoluble in water, and forming a sticky paste when heated. In the manufacture of chewing gum, the chicle is cleaned, filtered, and sterilized, and various flavoring materials and sugar are added. *See* EBENALES; RUBBER.   Perry D. Strausbaugh/Earl L. Core

Chicory

A perennial herb, *Cichorium intybus* (Asteraceae), with a long taproot, a coarse branching stem, and a basal rosette of numerous leaves. Although the plant is a native of Europe, it has become a common weed in the United States. It is used as a salad plant or for greens. The roasted root is also used as an adulterant of coffee. *See* CAMPANULALES; SPICE AND FLAVORING.   Perry D. Strausbaugh/Earl L. Core

Child-Langmuir law

A law governing space-charge-limited flow of electron current between two plane parallel electrodes in vacuum when the emission velocities of the electrons can be neglected. It is often called the three-halves power law, and is expressed by the formula below.

$$j\,(\text{A/cm}^2) = \frac{\epsilon}{9\pi}\left(\frac{2e}{m}\right)^{1/2}\frac{V^{3/2}}{d^2}$$
$$= 2.33 \times 10^{-6}\frac{V\,(\text{volts})^{3/2}}{d\,(\text{cm})^2}$$

Here ϵ is the dielectric constant of vacuum, $-e$ the charge of the electron, m its mass, V the potential difference between the two electrodes, d their separation, and j the current density at the collector electrode, or anode. The potential difference V is the applied voltage reduced by the difference in work function of the collector and emitter. The Langmuir-Child law applies, to a close approximation, to other electrode geometries as well. Thus for coaxial cylinders with the inner cylinder the cathode, it leads to a deviation from the true value of the current density of 13% at most. *See* SPACE CHARGE.   Edward G. Ramberg

Chilopoda

A class of the Myriapoda commonly known as the centipedes. Like all myriapods, centipedes are ground dwellers whose spatial movements are restricted largely by a dependence upon high environmental moisture. Unlike the others, centipedes are evidently exclusively carnivorous and predatory, a way of life reflected in their great agility or fleetness and especially in the extraordinary modification of the first trunk appendages into a pair of usually massive raptorial pincers, the prehensors (**Fig. 1**). Each prehensor contains a poison gland from which venom is conducted through a terminal claw into the victim's body. The poison immobilizes or kills arthropods and even some small vertebrates, but so far as is known it seems only harmlessly painful to human beings.

Excluding the last two or three trunk segments, each segment bears a single pair of functional legs. The genital ducts open at the posterior end of the body. Spiracles open laterally or dorsally; tracheal and circulatory systems are present and often elaborate. The antennae are unbranched; the eyes, when present, are either of the compound type or appear as simple ocelli. The mandibles have a partially free and movable gnathal portion. There are two pairs of maxillae, as in symphylans and insects. Some centipedes are anamor-

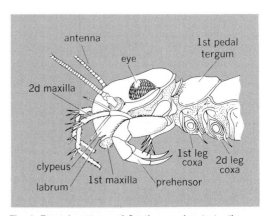

Fig. 1. Frontal anatomy of *Scutigera coleoptrata*, the common house centipede. (*After R. E. Snodgrass, A Textbook of Arthropod Anatomy, Cornell University Press, 1952*)

phic, some are epimorphic.

Distribution. In terms of families, genera, and individuals, the Diplopoda, or millipedes, are most abundant in the tropics, but this is not true of centipedes as a group, for whereas certain orders are basically tropical (Scutigeromorpha, Scolopendromorpha), one order, the Lithobiomorpha, is essentially temperate, and the Geophilomorpha is abundant in both zones. Indeed, there are some Lithobiomorpha and Geophilomorpha that occur as far north as the Arctic Circle. In general, centipedes seem less affected by temperature and more sensitive to environmental moisture than are millipedes.

Taxonomy. The class is divisible into two subclasses, the Notostigmophora and the Pleurostigmophora. The notostigmophorous centipedes comprise a single order, Scutigeromorpha. Its members, which are peculiar in embodying primitive as well as highly advanced characters, are signalized by possession of dorsal respiratory openings (stomata), of compound-type eyes, of long flagellate, multisegmental antennae, and of long thin legs with multisegmental tarsi. The trunk has 15 leg-bearing segments but only seven terga. All are anamorphic. The order is probably known to most persons through acquaintance with the common house centipedes, *Scutigera coleoptrata*, one of which is shown in **Fig. 2**.

Pleurostigmophora. The Pleurostigmophora, in contrast, have lateral respiratory openings, or spira-

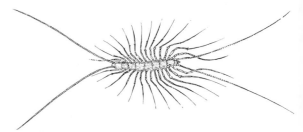

Fig. 2. Chilopoda. *Scutigera coleoptrata*, the house centipede; body length about 1 in. (25 mm). (*After R. E. Snodgrass, A Textbook of Arthropod Anatomy, Cornell University Press, 1952*)

cles. They are reducible into four orders. Of these, the Lithobiomorpha seem most like the Scutigeromorpha, with which some classifications ally them: both are anamorphic and have 15 leg-bearing trunk segments. In the Lithobiomorpha, however, when eyes are present, they are ocellar. The majority of these centipedes are rather small in size, few exceeding $1\frac{1}{2}$ in. (3.7 cm). Like the scutigeromorphs, they are rapid runners. Although the order is typically temperate in distribution, there are a few mainly tropical or subtropical groups, but apparently few species are exclusively tropical. The order Craterostigmomorpha, represented by a single known species inhabiting Tasmania and New Zealand, resembles the Lithobiomorpha in having 15 leg-bearing segments with associated sternites; they differ notably in possessing 21 tergites and large, peculiar prehensors. In fact, many of their characteristics seem annectant, linking them both with the Lithobiomorpha and the Scolopendromorpha.

Scolopendromorpha. The Scolopendromorpha (**Fig. 3***a*) are the dominant tropical chilopods, being the most abundant centipedes in the tropics, where the order exhibits its greatest elaboration into species and genera. They include also the largest of centipedes, some achieving lengths in excess of a foot. The order in addition includes a sizable temperate zone representation whose members can be quite small. The order is divisible into two families, the Scolopendridae, which possess eyes, and the Cryptopidae, which are blind. Depending upon the group, there are either 21 or 23 pairs of legs. All are epimorphic.

Geophilomorpha. The Geophilomorpha (Fig. 3*b*) represent the most specialized of all centipedes. Unlike most other chilopods, which are voracious hunters emerging at night to seek their prey in the open, the geophilomorphs are adapted to the special requirements of life in the soil, in the close confines of leaf litter, in general in the crevice-cranny type of habitat. All are dorsoventrally flattened, and their bodies are long and pliable, permitting them to squeeze through tight openings. All are blind and epimorphic. In all species the spiracles occur as an unbroken series from the second through the last or next-to-last leg-bearing segment. Depending upon the family, genus, or even the species, mouthparts display a very wide range of variations, in contrast to the uniformity encountered in most other centipedes. Unique to them is the intraspecific variability in number of trunk segments in all but one family. For the whole order the number of trunk segments bearing legs ranges approximately from 33 to more than 183.

As has been mentioned already, the Scutigeromorpha, Lithobiomorpha, and Craterostigmomorpha are anamorphic, the young hatching with less than the adult number of pairs of legs, thereafter undergoing molts until the adult complement is achieved. The Scolopendromorpha and Geophilomorpha are epimorphic; that is, upon hatching, the young already possess the adult complement of

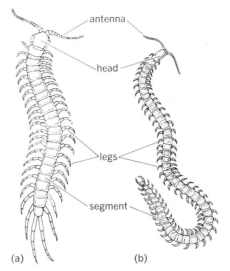

Fig. 3. Epimorphic chilopods. (*a***) Scolopendromorpha, *Scolopocryptops sexspinosus*; body length about 2.5 in. (65 mm). (***b***) Geophilomorpha, unidentified species, 1.6 in. (40 mm) long. (***After R. E. Snodgrass, A Textbook of Arthropod Anatomy, Cornell University Press, 1952***)**

leg-bearing segments, and successive molts merely permit an increase in size. There is evidence to suggest that all centipedes continue to molt even after reproduction capacity is gained and perhaps throughout life; in some species this may entail many years. Finally, it is interesting to note that in the epimorphic orders, and also the Craterostigmomorpha, the female broods her eggs and, after they have hatched, even guards the young for a time. Theoretically, the young Epimorpha emerge from the egg in a semiembryonic condition, so that without the attention of the female they would succumb to the fungi and bacteria of the forest floor. None of the anamorphic Chilopoda is known to practice brooding.

R. E. Crabill

Chimaeriformes

The only order of the chondrichthyan subclass Holocephali. The chimaeriforms (ratfishes) are a distinctive group of marine bottom-feeding fishes that chiefly inhabit the deeper layers of the Atlantic and Pacific oceans. During the winter months some species move into coastal waters, and a few species may be restricted to this environment.

Like the elasmobranchs (sharks, skates, and rays), the ratfishes have a cartilaginous skeleton (partly calcified), a urea retention mechanism, and clasper organs in the male for internal fertilization. Unlike the elasmobranchs, however, they have the upper jaw fused to the braincase (holostylic condition), a complete hyoid arch that is not involved in jaw suspension, four gill slits opening into a common outer chamber covered by an opercular skin fold, a single branchial opening on each side of the head, no spiracle in the adult, dental plates rather than teeth, a persistent notochord surrounded by calcified centra, and a narrow, tapering tail. *See* ELASMOBRANCHII.

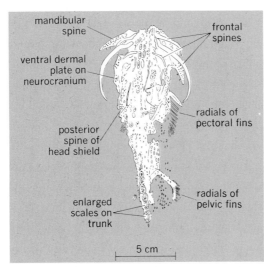

Fig. 1. Permian chimaeriform *Menaspis*; dorsal view. (*After C. Patterson, The phylogeny of the chimaeroids, Phil. Trans. Roy. Soc. London, 249:101–219, 1965*)

Fossil record. The fossil record for the chimaeriforms is generally poor and fragmentary. All the available evidence leaves the question of ancestry unanswered, but it may have involved some

group of placoderms. The ratfishes first appeared in the Devonian, and their earliest radiation occurred during the late Paleozoic. This radiation involved groups known mostly from tooth plates, such as the copodontiforms, psammodontiforms, chondrenchelyiforms, petalodontiforms, and helodontiforms. *See* PLACODERMI.

Evolution. The main line of chimaeriform evolution apparently began with Mississippian to Permian forms called menaspoids. These fishes had flattened heads, dermal plates on the neurocranium, tooth plates without tritors, a persistent notochord without centra, and a dorsal fin without an anterior bordering spine (**Fig. 1**). By the beginning of the Jurassic the menaspoids had been replaced by their presumed descendants, the myracanthoids. Fishes belonging to this group had a somewhat deeper skull and the dermal armor on the skull was more reduced or absent. Tritors appeared on some of the tooth plates, and there was a large clasper on the front of the head. Centra were present around the notochord and these were fused anteriorly to form a synarcuum. The dorsal fin was bordered by a spine, as in modern ratfishes. The myracanthoid radiation was apparently more modest than the menaspoid.

The large Lower Jurassic *Squaloraja* probably arose from some primitive myracanthoid stock. This genus had a long rostrum with frontal claspers (**Fig. 2**). It also had a synarcuum followed by ring centra around the notochord. The branchial arches were situated under the neurocranium and the pectoral fins were dibasal, as in the modern representatives. However, the absence of an ethmoid canal, tritors on the tooth plate and a dorsal spine, as well as the extensive squamation, indicate that *Squaloraja* was not ancestral to the modern ratfishes.

Modern ratfishes (**Figs. 3** and **4**) appeared during the Middle Jurassic. They are characterized by a laterally compressed head with a variably developed rostrum, which is frequently exotically shaped, and an ethmoidal canal. Dermal plates have disappeared in the head region, and the dorsal fin spine, which primitively was composed of osteodentine, is made up almost entirely of lamellar bone. The pectoral fins are dibasal and fairly large, and the caudal fin is tapered to almost whiplike proportions. Placoid scales cover the body, in contrast to the more complicated compound scales

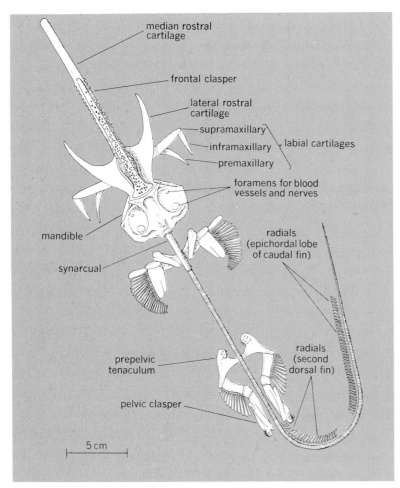

Fig. 2. Lower Jurassic chimaeriform *Squaloraja*. Restoration of the skeleton in dorsal view. (*After C. Patterson, The phylogeny of the chimaeroids, Phil. Trans. Roy. Soc. London, 249:101–219, 1965*)

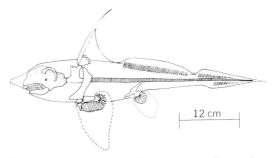

Fig. 3. Upper Jurassic chimaeriform *Ischyodus*. Restoration of the female; shown in lateral view. (*After C. Patterson, The phylogeny of the chimaeroids, Phil. Trans. Roy. Soc. London, 249:101–219, 1965*)

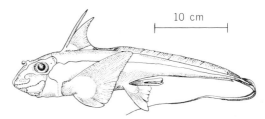

Fig. 4. Modern chimaeriform *Chimaera*. (*After H. B. Bigelow and W. C. Schroeder, Fishes of the Western North Atlantic, pt. 2, Sears Foundation for Marine Research, 1953*)

of the primitive chiameriforms.

Extant forms. The living ratfishes are divided into three families: the Chimaeridae, the Rhinochimaeridae, and the Callorhinchidae, which can be readily distinguished by the shape of the rostrum. Some 28 species are recognized. Most of them feed on mollusks and crustaceans and occasionally on smaller fishes. *See* CHONDRICHTHYES.   Bobb Schaeffer

Bibliography. H. B. Bigelow and W. C. Schroeder, *Fishes of the Western North Atlantic*, pt. 2, Sears Foundation for Marine Research, 1953; E. S. Herald *Living Fishes of the World*, 1961; C. Patterson, The phylogeny of the chimaeroids, *Phil. Trans. Roy. Soc. London*, 249:101–219, 1965.

Chimera

An individual animal or plant made up of cells derived from more than one zygote or otherwise genetically distinct.

Animals

Although some chimeras do arise naturally, most are produced experimentally, either by mixing cells of very early embryos or by tissue grafting in late embryos or adults. Experimental chimeras have been used to study a number of biological questions, including the origin and fate of cell lineages during embryonic development, immunological self-tolerance, tumor susceptibility, and the nature of malignancy. *See* CELL LINEAGE.

Mixing embryo cells. Two techniques used to form chimeras by mixing embryo cells are aggregation and injection.

Aggregation chimeras. The first experimental mammalian chimeras were produced from mouse embryos in the early 1960s, first by Andrei Tarkowski and later by Beatrice Mintz. The technique involves removing the zonae pellucidae from around 8–16 cell embryos of different strains of mice and pushing the morulae together so that the cells can aggregate. After a short period of laboratory culture, during which the aggregate develops into a single large blastocyst, the embryo is returned to a hormone-primed foster mother (**Fig. 1**). Chimeric offspring are recognized in several ways. If derived from embryos of pigmented and albino strains, they may have strips of pigmented skin and patches of pigment in the eye. Internal chimerism can be detected by use of chromosomal markers or genetically de-

termined enzyme variants. Chimeras accept skin grafts from the two component strains, but reject grafts from third-party strains. Aggregation chimeras formed from embryos of strains A and B are denoted A ↔ B, and chimeras developing from two embryos are often known as tetraparental animals. Up to 15 mouse embryos have been aggregated to form a single giant blastocyst. However, the offspring from such experiments are always normal, so that size regulation must occur after implantation. On average, 50% of aggregation chimeras will be XX ↔ XY. Sex determination seems to depend on the relative number of XX and XY cells in the fetal gonads, and in mice most of these animals develop into phenotypic males.

Injection chimeras. This technique was first described for mouse embryos by Richard Gardner in 1968. A blastocyst of the host mouse strain is removed from its zona pellucida and held on a suction pipette. Cells of the donor strain are injected through a fine glass needle, either into the blastocoele cavity or into the center of the inner cell mass (the group of cells from which the fetus is derived). After a short period of culture, the blastocyst is returned to a foster mother. By analogy with aggregation chimeras, injection chimeras are denoted A ↔ B and are recognized by similar, genetically determined markers (pigment formation, and enzyme, serum, and urinary protein variants). A variety of cells have been injected into blastocysts in this way. Cells from adults fail to either grow or become incorporated into the fetus. Early-cleavage-stage embryos injected into the cavity of giant blastocysts (formed by aggregating several embryos in culture as described above) develop inside their zonae into "blastocysts within blastocysts." In contrast, individual cells or groups of cells isolated from embryos of about the same age as the host become incorporated into the host embryo and grow and differentiate along with it. By taking appropriately

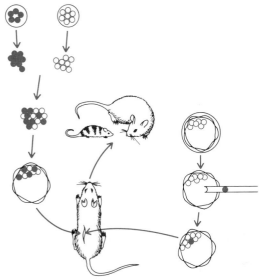

Fig. 1. Techniques for making aggregation chimeras (left) and injection chimeras (right) from early mouse embryos.

marked cells from different positions in the donor embryo, placing them in different positions in the host blastocyst, and following their contribution to the late-gestation embryo or adult, important information was obtained about cell interactions and lineages in mouse development.

Another kind of cell—the pluripotent stem cell of mouse teratocarcinomas—was found to give rise to normal tissues in adult chimeras after injection into the mouse blastocyst. Teratocarcinomas are tumors consisting of a disorganized mixture of adult and embryonic tissues. They develop spontaneously from germ cells in the gonads of certain mouse strains, or from cells in early embryos transplanted to ectopic sites. All the differentiated tissues in the tumor arise from pluripotent stem cells known as embryonal carcinoma (EC) cells. When embryonal carcinoma cells are injected into a genetically marked host blastocyst, they continue to divide and participate in normal development, and give rise to fully differentiated cells in all tissues of the adult, including skin, muscle, nerve, kidney, and blood.

Embryonal carcinoma cells from several sources, including spontaneous and embryo-derived tumors and cultured lines selected to carry specific mutations or even human chromosomes, have contributed to normal chimeras. However, embryonal carcinoma cells from some other sources fail to integrate, but produce teratocarcinomas in the newborn animal or adult. The factors controlling successful integration are not yet fully understood, but must include such things as the relative division rate of the embryonal carcinoma cells, their biochemical similarity to cells of the inner cell mass, and their chromosomal constitution. On general grounds, embryonal carcinoma cells should be expected to give rise also to fully functional germ cells, so that EC → blastocyst chimeras might be used to generate nonchimeric mice carrying specific mutations. The fact that certain embryonal carcinoma cells give rise to tumors when injected under the skin or into the body cavity, but behave normally in the blastocyst, has been used to support the idea that cancers can develop not only as a result of gene mutations but also as a result of disturbances in environmental factors controlling normal cell differentiation (epigenetic theory of cancer). *See* ONCOLOGY.

Interspecies chimeras. A number of interspecies chimeras have been produced by aggregating sheep and goat embryos and reimplanting them in sheep. The offspring have tissues containing a mixture of both sheep and goat cells. The goat, for example, may have patches of both wool and hair. Interspecies chimeras have also been made between rat and mouse, but these do not develop in the uterus, presumably because of immunological rejection by the foster mother. This rejection does not occur in sheep for unknown reasons.

Tissue grafting. Animals that have accepted skin or organ grafts are technically chimeras. Radiation chimeras are produced when an animal is exposed to x-rays, so that blood-forming stem cells in the bone marrow are killed and then replaced by a bone marrow transplant from a genetically different animal. Lymphoid cells in the process of differentiating from stem cells in the donor marrow recognize the recipient as "self" and do not initiate an immune response against the host cells. By removing the thymus from the irradiated host and replacing it with a thymus from another animal prior to the bone marrow transplant, it has been shown that this organ plays an important role in the generation of immunological self-tolerance. *See* TRANSPLANTATION BIOLOGY.

Natural occurrence. Naturally occurring chimeras in humans are rare and are most easily recognized when some cells are XX and others XY. Such individuals are usually hermaphrodite and probably result from fertilization of the egg by one sperm and the second polar body by another, with both diploid cells then contributing to the embryo (the small polar bodies normally degenerate). Blood chimeras are somewhat more common in animals such as cattle where the blood vessels in placentas of twins fuse, so that blood cells can pass from one developing fetus to the other. The female sibling of male and female cattle twins is sterile (a freemartin), because sex hormones from the male fetus interfere with sexual differentiation in the female. Blood chimerism always occurs in marmosets, which produce twins at most pregnancies, but no abnormalities in sexual function are found.   Brigid Hogan

Plants

In modern botanical usage a chimera is a plant consisting of two or more genetically distinct kinds of cells. Chimeras can arise either by a mutation in a cell in some part of the plant where cells divide or by bringing together two different plants so that their cells multiply side by side to produce a single individual. They are studied not only because they are interesting freaks or ornamental, but also because they help in the understanding of many of the developmental features of plants that would otherwise be difficult to investigate.

Grafting. The first type of chimera to be used in this way resulted from grafting. Occasionally a bud forms at the junction of the scion and stock incorporating cells from both, and it sometimes happens that the cells arrange themselves so that shoots derived from the bud will contain cells from both plants forever. A plant of this kind is *Laburnocytisus adami,* formed in 1825 by grafting *Cytisus purpureus* onto *Laburnum anagyroides.* The flowers are brown instead of the purple or yellow of the scion and stock. It has the treelike habit of *Laburnum,* its leaves resemble those of *Laburnum* except for the surfaces, which are like those of *Cytisus,* and its seeds always grow into *Laburnum* trees. Occasionally a branch grows out wholly like *Laburnum* or, more rarely, wholly like *Cytisus. See* PLANT PROPAGATION.

At first people thought that *Laburnocytisus* and other similar plants derived from grafting must have been nonsexual hybrids, the result of fusing two somatic cells, but there was no evidence that this

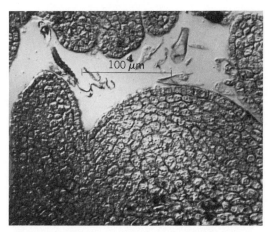

Fig. 2. Section through growing point of *Laburnocytisus adami*.

could occur and result in viable hybrid cells. The occasional reversion to pure *Laburnum* or *Cytisus* branches and the fate of its seeds militated against this theory.

Further investigation showed that the plant consists of a skin of *Cytisus* cells overlying a core of *Laburnum* cells (**Fig. 2**). The skin is only one cell deep, and the flowers appear brown because a purple epidermis covers yellow cells inside the petals. The germ cells which go to form the embryos in the seeds are always formed from the second layer of the shoot, and so always produce *Laburnum* plants. Reversions are due to some buds being formed wholly from the *Cytisus* skin or by the *Laburnum* tissue bursting through the skin in bud formation.

Apical meristem. *Laburnocytisus adami* has been synthesized only once, and all the specimens in existence have been propagated vegetatively from the original. This implies great stability in the constitution of the chimera, and for a long while after the plant's origin, nobody knew any mechanism whereby a shoot could maintain such a stable arrangement of genetically diverse cells. It was in attempts to solve this problem that it was discovered that flowering plants have growing points (apical meristems) where the outer cells are arranged in layers parallel to the surface, and that this periclinal layering is due to the fact that the outer cells divide only anticlinally, that is, by walls perpendicular to the surface of the growing point (Fig. 2). In many plants there are two such tunica layers and, because cell divisions are confined to the anticlinal planes, each layer remains discrete from the other and from the underlying nonlayered tissue called the corpus. The epidermis of leaves, stems, and petals is derived from the outer layer of the growing point, and the discreteness of this layer accounts for the stability of the *Laburnocytisus* chimera. *See* APICAL MERISTEM.

An elegant proof of the existence of these self-perpetuating layers in apical meristems came with the synthesis of polyploid chimeras in *Datura* and *Vaccinium*. This was done by treating the embryos or buds with colchicine, a drug which causes nuclei which divide in its presence to double their chromosome number. These tetraploid cells and their progeny are bigger than ordinary diploid cells, and so they can be identified in sections cut through the growing point. After the treated meristems had been allowed to grow and produce lateral buds, the buds were sectioned and each tunica layer was seen to contain only cells with the same ploidy, but one layer often consisted of cells of a different ploidy from the other tunica layers and from the corpus. The exclusively anticlinal divisions of the tunica layers clearly prevent the mixing of cells of different ploidy, and prevent the chimera from becoming unstable from competition between the cells of different ploidy.

Periclinal chimera. With this type of chimera, where the different cells can be identified under the microscope by their relative sizes, it is possible to trace into stems, leaves, and flowers which tissues are derived from each layer in the growing point. For leaves, this can also be done with variegated chimeras where the genetic difference between the cells rests in the plastids due to a mutation whose effect is to prevent the synthesis of chlorophyll. Tracts of cells whose plastids lack this pigment appear white or yellow instead of green.

A common form of variegated chimera has leaves with white margins and a green center (**Fig. 3**). The white margin is derived from the second layer of the tunica, and the green center is derived from inner cells of the growing point. (The outer tunica

Fig. 3. Variegated *Pelargonium*, a periclinal chimera whose second tunica layer is genetically white and whose corpus is genetically green.

Fig. 4. Variegated *Chlorophytum*, a periclinal chimera whose outer cell layer is genetically green and proliferates at the leaf margins to give green tissue in an otherwise genetically white plant.

layer contributes no color to the leaves of most plants, because it gives rise only to the epidermis, whose cells usually do not develop chloroplasts.) The white leaf tissue overlies the green in the center of the leaf, but does not mask the green color. Chimeras with green leaf margins and white centers are usually due to a genetically green tunica proliferating abnormally at the leaf margin in an otherwise white leaf (**Fig. 4**).

Periclinal chimeras can be used to study the destiny of different regions of the growing point, and how the leaves and so forth are constructed; but chimerical plants sometimes do not behave exactly like nonchimerical plants. Nevertheless, they have supplied valuable evidence, sometimes the only evidence, on which to base a view on some developmental problems. Chimeras show, for example, that there is considerable diversity in the number of layers that go to make each kind of organ, and this affects ideas about the homology of different organs.

Sectorial chimera. Since the somatic mutation that initiates most variegated and polyploid chimeras would normally occur in a single cell of a growing point or embryo, it often happens that it is propagated into a tract of mutant cells to form a sector of the plant. If the mutation resulted in a failure to form green pigment, the tract would be seen as a white stripe. Such chimeras are called sectorial, but they are normally unstable because there is no mechanism to isolate the mutant sector and, in the flux that occurs in a meristem of growing

and dividing cells, one or other of the two sorts of cells takes over its self-perpetuating layer in the growing point. The sectorial chimera therefore becomes nonchimerical or else a periclinal chimera.

Mericlinal chimera. However, in one class of chimera an isolating mechanism can stabilize the sectorial arrangement. This propagates stripes of mutant tissue into the shoot, but because the tunica and corpus are discrete from each other, the plant is not fully sectored and is called a mericlinal chimera.

Many chimeras of this type have a single tunica layer; those with green and white stripes in the leaves have the mutant cells in sectors of the corpus. It was not until C. Thielke tried to find the reason why these chimeras are stable that attention was directed to the fact that they are always plants with leaves in two ranks, and consequently the lateral growth of the growing point occurs by cell expansion only in the plane connecting alternate leaves. This results in the longitudinal divisions of the corpus cells being confined to planes at right angles to the plane containing the leaves. A mutation in one cell therefore can result in a vertical sheet of mutant cells which, in the case of a plastid defect, manifests itself as a white stripe in every future leaf. Transverse sections through the bud confirm that the cells behave as predicted.

Roots. The growing points of roots may also become chimerical, but in roots there is no mechanism to isolate genetically different tissues as there is in shoots, and so chimeras are unstable. However, there can be sufficient stability to do experiments with induced root chimeras on the destiny of cells.

Cultivated plants. Since the general acceptance of the existence of organisms with genetically diverse cells, many cultivated plants have been found to be chimeras. This knowledge has explained several phenomena hitherto puzzling. In carnations, for example, white flowers have arisen from red varieties due to the red variety being a periclinal white-red chimera whose normal stability was upset. Flecks of color often indicate the chimerical nature of such plants. Color changes in potato tubers occur similarly because the plants are periclinal chimeras. *See* SOMATIC CELL GENETICS.   F. A. L. Clowes

Bibliography. F. A. L. Clowes, Chimeras and the origin of lateral root primordia in *Zea mays, Ann. Bot.,* 42:801–807, 1978; F. A. L. Clowes, *Morphogenesis of the Shoot Apex,* 1972; K. Esau, *Anatomy of Seed Plants,* 1977; J. T. O. Kirk and R. A. E. Tilney-Bassett, *The Plastids,* 1978.

Chimney

A vertical hollow structure of masonry, steel, or reinforced concrete, built to convey gaseous products of combustion from a building or process facility. A chimney should be high enough to furnish adequate draft and to discharge the products of combustion without causing local air pollution. The height and diameter of a chimney determine the draft.

Construction specifications. For adequate draft, small industrial boilers and home heating systems depend entirely upon the enclosed column of hot gas. A draft is produced because the density of the hot gas inside is lower than that of the air outside. In contrast, stacks, which are chimneys for large power plants and process facilities, usually depend upon force-draft fans and induced-draft fans to produce the draft necessary for operation, and the chimney is used only for removal of the flue gas. Some stacks burn off the gases at the top and are known as flarestacks. *See* FAN.

For fire safety, chimneys for residential construction and for small buildings must extend at least 3 ft (0.9 m) above the level where they pass through the roof and at least 2 ft (0.6 m) higher than any ridge within 10 ft (3 m) of them. Some stacks extend as high as 500 ft (150 m) above ground level, thus providing supplementary natural draft.

A chimney or stack must be designed to withstand lateral loads from wind pressure or seismic forces (earthquakes), as well as vertical loads from its own weight. Wind pressure on a cylindrical surface is about two-thirds that on a plane surface. Thus with a wind pressure of 30 lb/ft^2 (1440 newtons/m^2), the pressure per foot of chimney height is 20 times the diameter, in feet, of the chimney (the pressure in newtons per meter of height is 960 times the diameter in meters). Depending upon geographical location, horizontal inertia loads due to an earthquake can be as high as 35% of the weight of the chimney and can result in greater overturning moments and bending stresses than wind loading. *See* LOADS, DYNAMIC.

Construction materials. Small chimneys used in residential construction are commonly made of brick or unreinforced masonry, while stacks are usually made of steel. In the early 1900s it was generally more economical to construct tall chimneys from masonry or reinforced concrete. However, modern construction costs for tall chimneys favor the use of steel since it allows for more rapid fabrication and erection compared with masonry or reinforced concrete. Where flue gases are particularly corrosive to steel, castable or masonry linings or corrosion-resistant steels (stainless) are often used; or the stack is designed with a corrosion allowance. Sometimes a steel stack has a double steel shell, consisting of concentric cylinders with an air space between the two. The inner shell serves mainly to convect the gases, while the outer shell withstands the wind or seismic loads. *See* REINFORCED CONCRETE; STAINLESS STEEL; STEEL.

Tall steel chimneys of small diameter cannot economically be made self-supporting and must be guyed. Where land costs are at a premium or where land is not available for guying, such as at congested process facilities, it is often more economical to support slender steel stacks with a derrick-type structure of steel latticed or trussed construction as opposed to constructing a self-supported stack. Modern steel stacks are usually shop welded into sections, which are then assembled in the field by flange bolting or welding. *See* JOINT (STRUCTURES); TRUSS.

Concrete chimneys may be plain or reinforced. If the bending moment due to wind or seismic forces on concrete chimneys does not produce excessive tension on the leeward side, reinforcing is unnecessary. To prevent temperature cracking, some plain concrete stacks have a fire-clay lining with an air space between the lining and the outer shell. Masonry or concrete linings are often used in construction of concrete chimneys, resulting in a chimney within a concrete chimney. The outer chimney withstands the lateral loads from wind or earthquake, and the inner one withstands the thermal loads and the acid attacks.

Except for rectangular flues and chimneys commonly used in residential construction, masonry chimneys are usually constructed of perforated radial brick molded to suit the diameter of the chimney. Because the compressive strength of the brick is much greater than that of the mortar, the design strength is determined by the tensile strength of the mortar. Unlike its steel or reinforced counterpart, a brick chimney cannot resist high tensile stresses. *See* BRICK; MASONRY; MORTAR.

Accessory structures. Tall chimneys and stacks, particularly flarestacks, are usually provided with a ladder and rest platforms to allow for inspection and maintenance. Safety regulations require either a cage around the ladder, which increases wind loading, or a safety climb device attached to the ladder to prevent a fall.

Tall stacks are usually fitted with some form of lightning protection and are always grounded at the base. Depending upon the lightning activity in a particular area, a tall stack may be fitted with a lightning dissipator at the top with a special copper line to ground to prevent static buildup and lightning strikes. *See* LIGHTNING AND SURGE PROTECTION.

Cylindrical stacks are subject to a phenomenon known as Kármán vortex oscillations due to the alternating vortices that are shed from opposite sides of the cylinder during gentle winds. Masonry (or gunite-lined stacks) and guyed stacks are generally not susceptible to this phenomenon, because the stack damping ratio is raised in the presence of an internal lining or guying, which tends to abate the buildup of oscillations from the Kármán vortex street. For unlined, self-supported, steel stacks, vortex oscillations are usually controlled by adding strakes or fins to the top third of the stack to spoil the airflow. *See* KÁRMÁN VORTEX STREET.

Foundations. Foundations for tall stacks and chimneys are made from reinforced concrete and are usually octagonal. For very soft soils, the foundation strength is augmented by piles. The design of the foundation is controlled almost entirely by the overturning moment from wind or seismic forces. *See* FOUNDATIONS; PILE FOUNDATION.

Joseph Vellozzi

Chinchilla

The name given to two species of rodents which, together with four species of viscachas, make up the family Chinchillidae. These animals are native to several areas of South America and are widely bred on farms in North America and Europe for their fur, which is long, fine, and expensive. The wild population is protected in Chile since the killing of wild stocks in the early 1900s almost led to extinction.

Species. The two species of chinchilla are *Chinchilla brevicaudata* and *C. lanigar*. These animals resemble the squirrel in size and shape and are characterized by long, muscular hindlimbs, with elongate feet bearing four toes, and short forelimbs (see **illus.**). Blunt claws occur on the flexible fingers. These animals have 20 teeth with a dental formula of I 1/1 C 0/0 Pm 1/1 M 3/3. *See* DENTITION.

The chinchilla, with more hair per square inch than any other animal, is valued for its fur.

Chinchillas are gregarious, nocturnally active animals and are found in arid, mountainous regions where they feed principally on vegetation. They often seek shelter in burrows or rock crevices, so that their capture is difficult. The female, which is larger than the male, bears one to six offspring twice each year after a gestation period of 105–111 days.

Viscacha. There are four species of viscacha belonging to two genera, *Lagidium* (three species) and *Lagostomus*. The mountain viscacha (*Lagidium viscaccia*) lives in burrows near rocks in the foothills of the Andes. It is larger than the chinchilla and has a poor-quality fur, which is woven with wool into cloth. The plains viscacha (*Lagostomus maximus*) inhabits burrows in the pampas region of Argentina. It has coarse fur and is exclusively herbivorous. *See* RODENTIA.   Charles B. Curtin

Chinook

A mild, dry, extremely turbulent westerly wind on the eastern slopes of the Rocky Mountains and closely adjoining plains. The term is an Indian word which means "snow-eater," appropriately applied because of the great effectiveness with which this wind reduces a snow cover by melting or by sublimation. The chinook is a particular instance of a type of wind known as a foehn wind. Foehn winds, initially studied in the Alps, refer to relatively warm, rather dry currents descending the lee slope of any substantial mountain barrier. The dryness is an indirect result of the condensation and precipitation of water from the air during its previous ascent of the windward slope of the mountain range. The warmth is attributable to adiabatic compression, turbulent mixing with potentially warmer air, and the previous release of latent heat of condensation in the air mass and to the turbulent mixing of the surface air with the air of greater heat content aloft.

In winter the chinook wind sometimes impinges upon much colder stagnant polar air along a sharp front located in the foothills of the Rocky Mountains or on the adjacent plain. Small horizontal oscillations of this front have been known to produce several abrupt temperature rises and falls of as much as 45–54°F (25–30°C) at a given location over a period of a few hours. Damaging winds sometimes occur as gravity waves, which are triggered along the interface between the two air masses.

In the Alpine regions adverse psychological and physiological effects have been noted in humans during prolonged periods of foehn wind. These phenomena have been referred to as foehn sickness. *See* FRONT; ISENTROPIC SURFACES; PRECIPITATION (METEOROLOGY); WIND; WIND STRESS.

Frederick Sanders; Howard B. Bluestein

Chipmunk

A member of the tribe Marmotini in the rodent family Sciuridae (see **illus.**). There are 18 species. The eastern chipmunk (*Tamias striatus*) is found in wooded areas of eastern Canada and the United States. The western species, although quite similar to the eastern form, are included in the separate genus *Eutamias*.

These rodents are intermediate between the squirrels and marmots, having lost the typical bushy tail, tufted ears, and silky fur of the squirrel. They are diurnal animals, active in collecting food such as nuts, grains, and seeds. They fill their large cheek pouches with gathered food to carry it to storage places for the winter.

The animals construct extensive burrows of several chambers at the bottom of a downward sloping entry tunnel, which is about 3 ft (1 m) long. The chambers, used for hoarding food and for nesting, are below the frost line. While chipmunks are not true hibernators, they tend to remain in their underground chambers during the winter months. In the early spring they emerge from the burrows and mating occurs. After a gestation period of 5 weeks six or more young are born, blind and helpless. The eyes open after 1 month, and at

Representative species of chipmunk.

3 months the chipmunks are independent. These animals can be tamed and make good pets. *See* RODENTIA.   Charles B. Curtin

Chiroptera

An order of mammals (bats) in which the front limbs are modified as wings, thus making the chiropterans the only truly flying mammals. Bats form the second largest order of living mammals (16 families, 171 genera, some 840 species). They range from the limit of trees in the Northern Hemisphere to the southern tips of Africa, New Zealand, and South America, but most species are confined to the tropics. On many oceanic islands they are the only native land mammals.

The wing is formed by webs of skin running from the neck to the wrist (propatagium, or antebrachial membrane), between the greatly elongated second, third, fourth, and fifth fingers (chiropatagium), and from the arm and hand to the body (usually the side) and hindlegs (plagiopatagium). There is also usually a web between the hindlegs (uropatagium, or interfemoral membrane) in which the tail, if present, is usually embedded for at least part of its length (**Figs. 1** and **2**). The 16 living families may be briefly characterized as follows.

Pteropodidae. These are in general the most primitive of living bats and are placed in the suborder Megachiroptera, characterized by more primitive ears and shoulder joints. Most still retain a claw on the second digit (absent in all other bats, suborder Microchiroptera), and few have developed an echolocation (sonar) mechanism, found in all Microchiroptera. The teeth, however, are highly modified for eating fruit or nectar. The family, with 38 genera and 149 species, is widely distributed in the tropics and subtropics of the Eastern Hemisphere. While some species are quite small, the family includes the largest of all bats, with wingspreads of up to 5½ ft (1.5 m).

Rhinopomatidae. This insect-eating family, with one genus and two species, is found chiefly in arid regions of northern Africa and southern Asia, and is characterized by long wirelike tails and rudimentary nose leaves; these are dermal outgrowths of unknown function above the nostrils.

Emballonuridae. This insectivorous family includes 12 genera with 45 species and is found in the tropics of both Eastern and Western hemispheres. Like the Pteropodidae, but unlike other families of bats, these bats have well-developed bony processes behind the eye sockets. The tail extends only partly across the uropatagium.

Noctilionidae. This tropical American family, represented by two species in one genus, includes a highly specialized fish-eating species. Fish are detected by echolocation and gaffed by the long clawed feet. The tail is as in the Emballonuridae.

Nycteridae. This family of insect eaters, with 1 genus and 12 species, is found in Africa and southern Asia. These bats have an extensive basin behind the nose, which is partly bridged over by flaps of skin, leaving a mere slit between them.

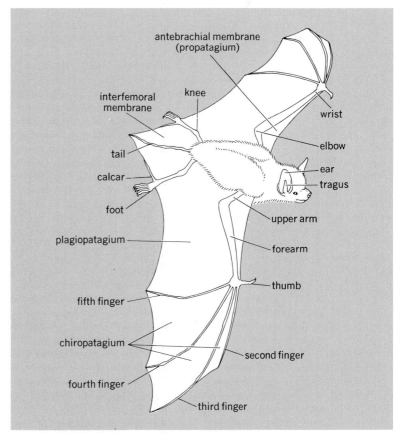

Fig. 1. Anatomical features of bat. (*After R. Peterson, Silently by Night, McGraw-Hill, 1964*)

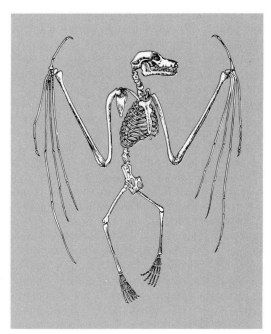

Fig. 2. Skeleton of *Pteropus*, giant fruit bat (lacking tail). (*After R. Peterson, Silently by Night, McGraw-Hill, 1964*)

Megadermatidae. The four genera (with five species) of this family occur in tropical Africa, southeastern Asia and adjoining islands, and northern Australia. The nose leaf is well developed and simple; the ears are very large and are jointed together across the forehead. Some species are insect-eating; others feed on small vertebrates, including other bats.

Rhinolophidae. These insect-eating bats are widely distributed in the Eastern Hemisphere. They are remarkable for their extremely complex nose leaves. There are 11 genera represented by 129 species.

Phyllostomatidae. While most of the 120 species (in 50 genera) of this tropical and subtropical American family possess simple nose leaves, there is tremendous variety in structure, reflecting an equal diversity in food habits. Primitively insect-eating, many have become fruit or nectar feeders, and a few are predators on small vertebrates, including other bats.

Desmodontidae. These are the true vampires, essentially confined to the mainland of tropical America. The teeth and tongue are highly modified for taking of blood. This family includes three genera with three species.

Natalidae. These bats (one genus and four species) are tropical American insect-eating species with large funnellike ears.

Furipteridae. This insect-eating family, confined to tropical South America, is represented by two species in two genera. The thumb is reduced in size and largely enclosed in the wing membrane.

Thyropteridae. The two species (in one genus) of this family are confined to the tropical American mainland. The large suction disks on the thumbs and hindfeet enable them to roost on the smooth inner surfaces of large rolled-up leaves.

Myzopodidae. The single species of this family is confined to Madagascar, eats insects, and has suckers on the thumbs and feet rather like those of the Thyropteridae.

Vespertilionidae. This nearly cosmopolitan family, with 279 species in 34 genera, occurs almost everywhere that bats occur. Almost all are insect-eating and a few catch fish. In all, the tail is long, extending to the edge of the uropatagium. Most have no special facial modifications. A few have very large ears or small simple nose leaves. In spite of its many species, the family shows little structural diversity. Echolocation, present in all families of bats except the Pteropodidae, is perhaps most highly developed here and is used for catching insects as well as avoiding obstacles.

Mystacinidae. The single insect-eating species of this family is confined to New Zealand. It has a short tail, not reaching the edge of the uropatagium, and stout hindlegs and body.

Molossidae. These are widely distributed in the tropics and subtropics. Feeding on insects, they have long tails which extend beyond their uropatagia. The body and hindlegs are stoutly built. The family includes 81 species in 10 genera.

Fossil record. Bats have a poor fossil record, but have been distinct at least since the Eocene, some 50,000,000 years ago. One unusually well-preserved early form, *Icaronycteris*, combined a primitive insect-eating dentition and a retained claw on the second digit with the advanced type of shoulder joint seen in the Vespertilionidae. *See* ECHOLOCATION; MAMMALIA..   Karl F. Koopman

Bibliography. G. M. Allen, *Bats*, 1939; R. Peterson, *Silently by Night*, 1964.

Chitin

A polysaccharide found abundantly in nature. Chitin forms the basis of the hard shells of crustaceans, such as the crab, lobster, and shrimp. The exoskeleton of insects is also chitinous, and the cell walls of certain fungi contain this substance. Chitin can be obtained as an amorphous powder after dissolution of the calcium carbonate with mineral acids and removal of the proteins. It is insoluble in water, dilute mineral acids, and alkalies, and in these respects resembles cellulose; it is, however, insoluble in Schweizer's reagent.

Dissolution takes place in concentrated mineral acids, and chitin, apparently unchanged, is precipitated on dilution. Hydrolysis, however, takes place on standing in concentrated acid with change in specific rotation, $[\alpha]_D^{20} - 15° \rightarrow +56°$; and D-glucosamine can be isolated by cautious hydrolysis with acid or with chitinase, an enzyme preparation from snails. Chitin is a long, unbranched molecule consisting entirely of N-acetyl-D-glucosamine units, with the structure shown, linked by β-1,4 bonds. It may be contemplated as cellulose in which the hydroxyl groups on the second carbon are replaced with $NHCOCH_3$ groups.

$$\text{(chemical structure of chitin — repeating N-acetyl-D-glucosamine units)}$$

Chitin is considered to be synthesized in nature by an enzyme which is capable of effecting a glycosyl transfer to the N-acetyl-D-glucosamine from uridinediphosphate-N-acetyl-D-glucosamine to a preformed chitodextrin acceptor, forming the polysaccharide. This stepwise enzymic transfer results in the production of the long chain of β-N-acetyl-D-glucosamine units, which is the insoluble chitin. *See* OPTICAL ACTIVITY; POLYSACCHARIDE.   William Z. Hassid

Chiton

A number of the class Polyplocophora in the phylum Mollusca. Chitons are also called loricates or coat-of-mail shells, and the Polyplacophora were formerly placed with the solenogastres (now class Aplacophora) in the class Amphineura. Of the five minor molluscan classes, only the Polyplacophora have any numerical or ecological significance. There are nearly 600 living species placed in 43 genera and possibly about 300 identified fossil species. All chitons are marine and, except for a few deep-sea forms, all live in the low intertidal and upper sublittoral, typically on wave-swept rocks. The flattened elliptical body bears eight articulated shell plates dorsally on the mantle and a ventral suctorial foot, features which are clearly adapted for life adhering to hard and uneven surfaces in the lower littoral zone (**Fig. 1**). Normally, chitons can resist the strongest surf action but, in the unlikely natural event of a chiton being washed off its rock (or if removed by a human collector), the articulated shell allows it to curl up to protect the soft foot

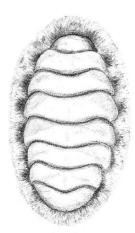

Fig. 1. Dorsal view of a mossy chiton (*Mopalia muscosa*) showing the eight articulated plates of the shell and the pallial girdle with calcareous spicules.

and gills of its underside, like a pill bug or a fossil trilobite.

Distribution. Chiton species living on both sides of the Atlantic are relatively small (0.4–1.2 in. or 1–3 cm long) and unobtrusive. They include the common green chiton, *Chaetopleura apiculata*, along the Atlantic coast of North America, and *Lepidochitona cinerus* and *Tonicella marmorea*, both common on rocky shores of Scandinavia and the British Isles. A much greater variety, including much larger forms, is found around the Indo-Pacific. The Pacific coast of North America has about 130 species, many startlingly colored and over 2 in. (5 cm) long, including the massive species of *Cryptochiton* which may be up to 12 in. (30 cm) in length with the shell plates overgrown by a tough leathery mantle. A similarly varied and numerous fauna of chitons is found on the rocky shores of Tasmania and southern Australia. Only four genera (all placed in the order Lepidopleurida) have living species offshore and in deeper waters (to 20,000 ft or 6000 m), but they may be related to the earliest fossil chitons (*Helminthochiton* from Lower Ordovician).

Gills (ctenidia). The compound gills of chitons (**Fig. 2**) appear to be structurally and functionally homologous with the ctenidia found in the three major molluscan groups (gastropods, bivalves, and cephalopods) and are similarly housed in a semi-internal space enclosed by the mantle (pallium). The chiton body is elongate (unlike other mollusks), and thus the mantle cavity has been drawn out into two narrow pallial grooves running between the foot and the broad mantle edge or "girdle" on each side. The molluscan functional pattern is again exemplified with each of these pallial grooves being divided into an inhalant and exhalant mantle cavity, with the kidney and genital openings, along with the central anus, discharging in the exhalant stream. In chitons, the functional division is a ctenidial curtain forming a perforated screen by means of ciliary junctions between the tips of leaflets on adjacent ctenidia (Fig. 2). Each ctenidium closely resembles the most primitive gastropod type (the aspidobranch gill with alternating ctenidial leaflets on either side of the ctenidial axis in which run the afferent and efferent blood vessels). The respiratory water current is caused by the lateral cilia on the faces of the leaflets, and blood and water move in opposite directions with the usual molluscan physiological efficiency of a countercurrent system. However, the original ctenidia are multiplied to form lateral series numbering from 4 to 80 on each side and functionally linked in the ctenidial curtain which divides the pallial grooves (Fig. 2) into an anterior-outer inhalant mantle cavity and a posterior-inner exhalant cavity. As growth continues in adult chitons, ctenidia are added anteriorly, irregularly and independently on either side but so that there is a broad correlation between gill number and adult size. Asymmetry in ctenidial numbers between the left and right sides of single specimens occurs in

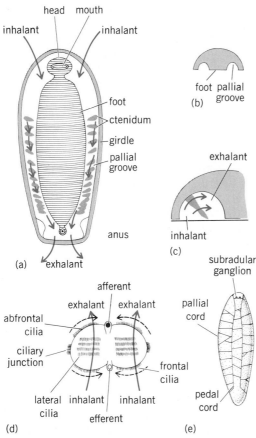

Fig. 2. Plans of functional anatomy in chitons. (a) Ventral view. (b, c) Cross sections of chitons to show the arrangement of the pallial grooves and their functional division into inhalant and exhalant parts by the ctenidia. (d) Ctenidial plates from a gill. (e) Plan of the nervous system. (After W. D. Russell-Hunter, A Life of Invertebrates, Macmillan, 1979)

most chiton species which have been studied and, in some populations, involves more than half the individuals. Thus the ctenidia of chitons cannot be considered as paired structures. Temporary lifting of the mantle edge or girdle can result in a temporary inhalant current to the mantle grooves anywhere in the front of the animal. The exhalant current is always posterior, and the feces, along with the excretory and reproductive products, are discharged into this posterior current.

Digestive system. The alimentary canal and associated organs are clearly adapted for continuous grazing of attached algae and diatoms from rock surfaces. There is a long radula, and prominent salivary and sugar glands secrete into the posterior esophagus. Amylase is prominent among their secretions, and digestion is largely extracellular, the digestive diverticula being also mainly secretory. There is a long posterior gut that is concerned with consolidation of feces.

Nervous system. The nervous system consists of a double ladder of pallial and pedal cords, and the only ganglia are subradular. Connected with this very primitive nervous system are a surprising number of sense organs. There are osphradia on either side of the anus, tactile organs in the mantle

girdle and on the snout, taste receptors in the buccal region, and otocysts near the pedal cords. Also, to a varying extent in different species, there are peculiar sense organs embedded in pits through the shell plates; these are termed megalaesthetes and microaesthetes. Little or nothing is known about their functioning, although the microanatomy of some suggests the structures of a simple eye. *See* EYE (INVERTEBRATE).

Reproduction. The sexes are separate, and external fertilization occurs after spawning, which usually shows some lunar periodicity. The zygote develops into a trochophore larva which becomes elongate and develops a mantle rudiment. About the time that it settles to the bottom, it secretes six shell plates. After an interval a larger plate is added anterior to the series, and still later a small last plate is added at the posterior end. At no stage in the development is there a "budding zone" for shell plates. In the young postlarva there are initially no ctenidia; after the first of these appear in the posterior parts of the pallial grooves, they are added to with growth of the chitons throughout life. The replicated structures in chitons (ctenidia, shell plates, renal lobes, auriculoventricular openings) are not metamerically arranged in segmental series of unit subdivisions. *See* GASTROPODA; MOLLUSCA; MONOPLACOPHORA; POLYPLACOPHORA.

W. D. Russell-Hunter

Bibliography. S. P. Parker (ed.), *Synopsis and Classification of Living Organisms*, 2 vols., 1982; W. D. Russell-Hunter, *A Life of Invertebrates*, 1979; W. D. Russell-Hunter and S. C. Brown, Ctenidial number in relation to size in certain chitons, with a discussion of its phyletic significance, *Biol. Bull.*, 128:508–521, 1965; C. M. Yonge, On the mantle-cavity and its contained organs in the Loricata, *Quart. J. Micros. Sci.*, 81:367–390, 1939.

Chlamydia

A unique genus of bacteria with a growth cycle differing from those of all other microorganisms: *Chlamydia* grow only in living cells and cannot be cultured on artificial media. Although capable of synthesizing macromolecules, they have no system for generating energy; the host cell's energy system fuels the chlamydial metabolic processes.

Infectious particle. The chlamydial infectious particle, called the elementary body, is round and small (about 350–450 nanometers in diameter). It enters a susceptible host cell and changes to a metabolically active and larger (approximately 800–1000 nm in diameter) reticulate body that divides by binary fission. The entire growth cycle occurs within a vacuole that segregates the *Chlamydia* from the cytoplasm of the host cell. The reticulate bodies change back to elementary bodies, and then the cell lyses and the infectious particles are released. The growth cycle takes about 48 h.

Chlamydial diseases. Diseases are caused by three species of *Chlamydia*. *Chlamydia trachomatis*, occurring in humans, is susceptible to sulfonamides and produces inclusions that stain with iodine because they contain glycogen. *Chlamydia psittaci*, occurring in birds, lower animals, and humans, is sulfa resistant and the inclusions do not stain with iodine. The TWAR strains have been given their own species category, *C. pneumoniae*. The TWAR elementary body is pear shaped rather than round, and there is little deoxyribonucleic acid (DNA) relatedness.

Chlamydia trachomatis. *Chlamydia trachomatis* is almost exclusively a human pathogen, and one of the most common. Those strains infecting humans have no known animal reservoir. Infections occur in two distinct epidemiologic patterns. In many developing countries, *C. trachomatis* causes trachoma, a chronic follicular keratoconjunctivitis. It is the world's leading cause of preventable blindness, affecting approximately 500 million people, with millions losing their sight. In areas where this condition is highly endemic, virtually the entire population is infected within the first few years of life. Most active infections are found in childhood. *See* EYE DISORDERS.

Scarring can develop as a result of severe inflammation of the conjunctiva. Over a period of years, the scars shrink and distort the upper eyelid, causing an in-turning of the eyelashes which damages the cornea and causes blindness. By age 60, more than 20% of a population can be blinded as a result of trachoma.

Chlamydia trachomatis can be spread sexually. In the United States, it is the most common sexually transmitted bacterial pathogen; an estimated 4.5 million cases occur each year. The most common manifestation of this infection is nongonococcal urethritis in males. The cervix is the most commonly infected site in women. Ascending infections can occur in either sex, resulting in epididymitis in males or endometritis and salpingitis in females. Chlamydial infection of the fallopian tube can cause late consequences such as infertility and ectopic pregnancy, even though the earlier infection is asymptomatic. For some women, their first knowledge of having had a chlamydial infection occurs when they are being evaluated for infertility or are hospitalized with an ectopic pregnancy. Thus chlamydial infection in the female can be particularly insidious and dangerous. *See* SEXUALLY TRANSMITTED DISEASES.

The infant passing through the infected birth canal can acquire the infection and may develop either conjunctivitis (called inclusion conjunctivitis of the newborn, or inclusion blennorrhea) or pneumonia. In the United States, *C. trachomatis* is the leading cause of conjunctivitis in the first month of life, and of pneumonia in the first 6 months.

All of the diseases mentioned above involve mucous membranes. There is a more invasive form of *C. trachomatis* that causes a systemic sexually transmitted disease called lymphogranuloma venereum. Lymphogranuloma venereum has a worldwide distribution, although it is more common in some trop-

ical countries. This disease has a predilection for lymphoid tissue involvement. It occurs in stages: the primary stage involves small, superficial, usually painless genital lesions; in the secondary stage, inguinal buboes (infected lymph nodes) are the common finding. If untreated, the disease may progress to stages involving widespread tissue destruction of genital and intestinal tracts.

Chlamydia psittaci. *Chlamydia psittaci* is virtually ubiquitous among avian species and is a common pathogen among lower mammals. It is economically important in many countries as a cause of abortion in sheep, cattle, and goats. It causes considerable morbidity and mortality in poultry, particularly turkeys and ducks. *Chlamydia psittaci* can infect humans, causing the disease psittacosis. Psittacosis can occur as pneumonia or a febrile toxic disease without respiratory symptoms. Apparently, the chlamydiae that infect turkeys, ducks, and psittacine birds are most infectious for humans. Psittacosis is a potential threat to the health of pet-bird owners and is an occupational hazard in the poultry industry. *Chlamydia psittaci* derived from mammals can also infect humans.

Chlamydia pneumoniae (TWAR). *Chlamydia pneumoniae* appears to be a human pathogen with no animal reservoir. It is of worldwide distribution and may be the most common human chlamydial infection. It appears to be an important cause of respiratory disease, being found in association with sporadic cases of community-acquired pneumonia and epidemics of mild pneumonia. In addition, *C. pneumoniae* infection has been linked to coronary artery disease.

Treatment. Tetracycline is considered to be the drug of choice in the treatment of chlamydial diseases. Erythromycin is used for those who are tetracycline intolerant, as well as for pregnant women or young children. *See* MEDICAL BACTERIOLOGY.

Julius Schachter

Bibliography. J. T. Grayston et al., A new respiratory tract pathogen: *Chlamydia pneumoniae* strain TWAR, *J. Infect. Dis.*, 161:618–625, 1990; K. K. Holmes et al. (eds.), *Sexually Transmitted Diseases*, 1984; J. Schachter and C. R. Dawson, *Human Chlamydial Infections*, 1978.

Chlorine

A chemical element, symbol Cl, of atomic number 17 and atomic weight 35.453. Chlorine exists as a greenish-yellow gas at ordinary temperatures and pressures. It is second in reactivity only to fluorine among the halogen elements, and hence is never found free in nature, except at the elevated temperatures of volcanic gases. It is estimated that 0.045% of the Earth's crust is chlorine. It combines with metals, nonmetals, and organic materials to form hundreds of chlorine compounds, the most important of which are discussed here.

Chlorine and its common acid derivative, hydrochloric (or muriatic) acid, were probably noted

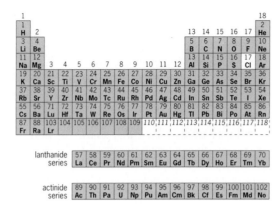

by experimental investigators as early as the thirteenth century. C. W. Scheele identified chlorine as "dephlogisticated muriatic acid" in 1774, and H. Davy proved that a new element had been found in 1810. Extensive production started 100 years later. During the twentieth century, the amount of chlorine used has been considered a measure of industrial growth.

Physical properties. The atomic weight of naturally occurring chlorine is 35.453 (based on carbon at 12). It is formed of stable isotopes of mass 35 and 37; radioactive isotopes have been made artificially. The diatomic gas has a molecular weight of 70.906. The boiling point of liquid chlorine (golden-yellow in color) is $-33.97°C$ ($-29.15°F$) at 760 mm Hg (10^2 kilopascals) and the melting point of solid chlorine (tetragonal crystals) is $-100.98°C$ ($-149.76°F$). The critical temperature is $144°C$ ($292°F$); the critical pressure is 78.7 atm; the critical volume is 1.745 ml/g; and density at the critical point is 0.573 g/ml.

Thermodynamic properties include heat of sublimation at 7370 ± 10 cal/mole at 0 K, heat of evaporation at 4882 cal/mole at $-33.97°C$, heat of fusion at 1531 cal/mole, vapor heat capacity at a constant pressure of 1 atm of 8.32 cal/(mole °C) at 0°C (32°F) and 8.46 cal/(mole °C) at 100°C (212°F). Other properties are shown in **Figs. 1–5**. Chlorine forms solid hydrates, $Cl_2·6H_2O$ (pale-green crystals) and $Cl_2·8H_2O$. It hydrolyzes in water as shown in reaction (1).

$$Cl_2 + H_2O \rightarrow HClO + HCl \qquad (1)$$

Chemical properties. Chlorine is one of four closely related chemical elements which have been called the halogen elements. Fluorine is more active chemically, and bromine and iodine are less active. Chlorine replaces iodine and bromine from their salts. It enters into substitution and addition reactions with both organic and inorganic materials. Dry chlorine is somewhat inert, but moist chlorine unites directly with most of the elements. *See* HALOGEN ELEMENTS.

Natural compounds. Sodium chloride, NaCl, is used directly as mined (rock salt), or as found on the surface, or as brine. It may also be dissolved, purified, and reprecipitated for use in foods or when chemical purity is required. Its main uses are in the production of soda ash and chlorine products. Farm use, refrigeration, dust and ice control, water treatment, food processing, and food preservation are other uses. Calcium chloride, $CaCl_2$, is usually obtained from brines or as a by-product of chemical processing. Its main uses are in road treatment, coal treatment, concrete conditioning, and refrigeration. *See* HALITE.

Inorganic compounds. Wet chlorine reacts with metals to form chlorides, most of which are soluble in water. It also reacts with sulfur and phosphorus and with other halogens as in reactions (2).

$$
\begin{aligned}
H_2 + Cl_2 &\rightarrow 2HCl \\
2Fe + 3Cl_2 &\rightarrow 2FeCl_3 \\
2S + Cl_2 &\rightarrow S_2Cl_2 \\
S + Cl_2 &\rightarrow SCl_2 \\
S + 2Cl_2 &\rightarrow SCl_4 \qquad\qquad (2)\\
P_4 + 6Cl_2 &\rightarrow 4PCl_3 \\
P_4 + 10Cl_2 &\rightarrow 4PCl_5 \\
Br_2 + Cl_2 &\rightarrow 2BrCl \\
2F_2 + Cl_2 &\rightarrow ClF + ClF_3
\end{aligned}
$$

Oxygen-containing compounds. The oxides of chlorine, dichlorine monoxide, Cl_2O, chlorine monoxide, ClO, chlorine dioxide, ClO_2, chlorine hexoxide, Cl_2O_6, and chlorine heptoxide, Cl_2O_7, are all made indirectly. Cl_2O is commonly called chlorine monoxide also. Chlorine dioxide, a green gas, has become increasingly important in commercial bleaching of cellulose, water treatment, and waste treatment. It is usually liberated at the plant site by the action of a reducing agent on a chlorate, as shown in reaction (3).

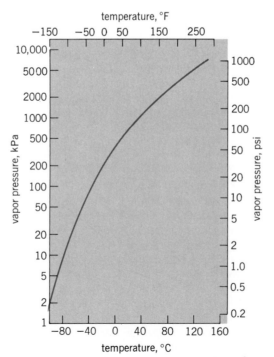

Fig. 1. Vapor pressure of liquid chlorine. (*After Diamond Shamrock Corp., Chlorine Handbook, 1976*)

$$2NaClO_3 + H_2SO_4 + SO_2 \rightarrow 2ClO_2 + 2NaHSO_4 \quad (3)$$

Sodium and calcium hypochlorite solutions, made by passing chlorine gas into alkaline solutions, are in general use for their oxidizing power or bleaching power. Various solid hydrates and basic compounds may be prepared and sold, but the most common, called bleaching powder, has been assigned various formulas. The stability of these compounds varies with the water and metallic impurity present. One formula, $Ca(OCl)_2 \cdot CaCl_2 \cdot Ca(OH)_2 \cdot 2H_2O$, would correspond to 35% bleach. $CaOCl_2$ is the simplest formula to use. Hypochlorite production began in earnest in 1823.

Many special processes are used, and mixtures are prepared to stablize high-available chlorine for bleaching purposes without obtaining detrimental insoluble materials. High-test hypochlorite (HTH) is calcium hypochlorite, $Ca(OCl)_2$, containing 70% available chlorine. Production started in 1923 and increased rapidly. Bleaching and sanitation uses have been increased by swimming pool requirements and account for approximately 90% of the production, the rest being exported. Calcium hypochlorite used in place of chlorine for water treatment is required in some heavily populated areas. *See* ANTIMICROBIAL AGENTS.

The corresponding acid for hypochlorites is

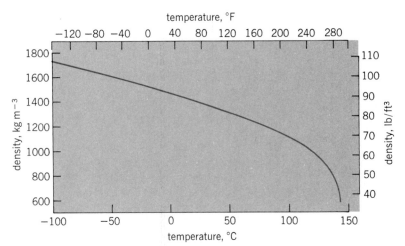

Fig. 2. Density of saturated liquid chlorine. (*After Diamond Shamrock Corp., Chlorine Handbook, 1976*)

hypochlorous acid, HClO, which may be prepared, as shown in reaction (4), by action of carbonic acid on a hypochlorite.

$$NaClO + H_2CO_3 \rightarrow NaHCO_3 + HClO \quad (4)$$

Chlorites such as $NaClO_2$ are produced by reduction of calcium chlorate by hydrochloric acid to chlorine dioxide, followed by absorption and

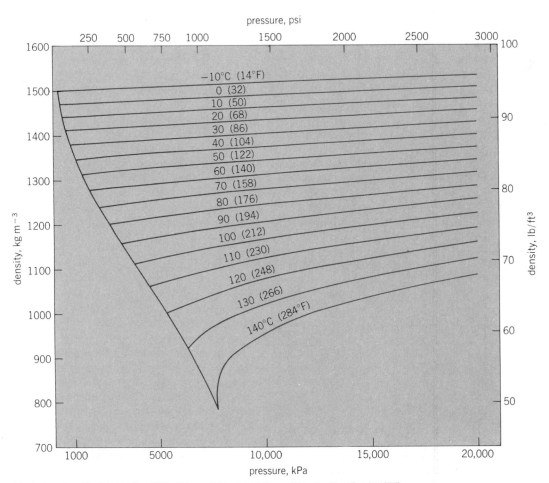

Fig. 3. Density of liquid chlorine. (*After Diamond Shamrock Corp., Chlorine Handbook, 1976*)

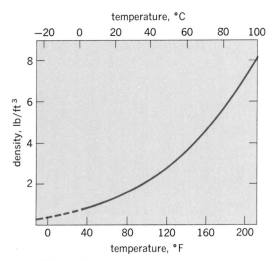

Fig. 4. Relationship between temperature and density of saturated chlorine gas. (*Hooker Chemical Corp.*)

reduction with caustic and peroxide, as shown in reactions (5) and (6). The use of sodium chlorite

$$Ca(ClO_3)_2 + 4HCl \rightarrow 2ClO_2 + Cl_2 + CaCl_2 + 2H_2O \quad (5)$$

$$2ClO_2 + 2NaOH + H_2O_2 \rightarrow 2NaClO_2 + O_2 + 2H_2O \quad (6)$$

permits controlled bleaching, and it is stable unless heated. With organic matter present, explosions can result, however. The corresponding acid for chlorites is chlorous acid, $HClO_2$.

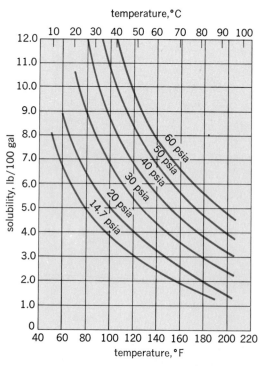

Fig. 5. Equilibrium solubility of chlorine in water. The data were calculated from partial pressure values. (*After Chlorine Institute, Inc., Chlorine Manual, 4th ed., 1969*)

Acidified sodium chlorite bleaches are very popular for cellulose and textile processing. *See* BLEACHING.

Chlorates may be prepared, reaction (7), by

$$NaCl + 3H_2O \rightarrow NaClO_3 + 3H_2 \quad (7)$$

direct electrolysis of a chloride in cells in which the products of electrolysis are allowed to mix. Graphite anodes are used, and cooling coils or jackets are provided to remove heat. The effluent may be cooled to precipitate the sodium chlorate. Calcium chlorate may be prepared by chlorination of lime with heating of the acidified solution to 50–70°C (120–160°F), followed by filtration and removal of insolubles. Sodium chlorate is used as an intermediate in perchlorate production. It is a weed killer, and is also used in dye preparation, textile and fur processing, and metallurgical operations. Potassium chlorate is used in match manufacture and for fireworks. The corresponding acid for chlorates is chloric acid, $HClO_3$, which can exist in water solution up to 30% concentration.

Potassium chlorate, $KClO_3$, is a white powder or colorless monoclinic crystals. It is poisonous and may explode on contact with combustible substances.

Sodium chlorate, $NaClO_3$, is a colorless, odorless, cubic or trigonal crystal material.

Perchlorates may be produced by electrolysis of sodium chlorate, reaction (8), using platinum anodes, followed by conversion to any desired salt, reaction (9). The corresponding acid is perchloric

$$4NaClO_3 \rightarrow 3NaClO_4 + NaCl \quad (8)$$

$$NaClO_4 + KCl \rightarrow KClO_4 + NaCl \quad (9)$$

acid, $HClO_4$, a colorless, fuming liquid that can be used as an oxidizing agent.

Potassium perchlorate, $KClO_4$, and ammonium perchlorate, NH_4ClO_4, are important as fuels for rockets and jet propulsion and as explosives. *See* OXIDIZING AGENT.

Chlorides. Hydrogen chloride, HCl, is a colorless, pungent, poisonous gas which liquefies at 82 atm at 51°C (124°F). It boils at −85°C (−121°F) at 1 atm (10^2 kPa). This acid is frequently produced by the LeBlanc process. The reactions are illustrated in reactions (10) and (11). Its major production is

$$NaCl + H_2SO_4 \rightarrow NaHSO_4 + HCl \quad (10)$$

$$NaHSO_4 + NaCl \rightarrow Na_2SO_4 + HCl \quad (11)$$

as the by-product of many organic chlorinations. It can be made by direct reaction of chlorine and hydrogen in an open combustion chamber submerged in cooled, aqueous hydrochloric acid solution. Constant-boiling solutions at 760 mm (10^2 kPa) pressure contain 20.24% HCl, but a saturated solution at 15°C contains 43.4% HCl and has a specific gravity of 1.231. It is used as a strong acid and as a reducing agent.

Aluminum chloride, $AlCl_3$, is an anhydrous,

white, deliquescent, hexagonal crystalline substance. Either scrap aluminum or the oxide (bauxite) may be chlorinated. Scrap or pig aluminum is melted at 660°C (1220°F) and chlorinated, and aluminum chloride vapor is condensed. Bauxite is calcined at 980°C (1800°F), mixed with coal or coke, pulverized, briquetted with asphalt, recalcined to 18% carbon, heated to 870°C (1600°F) in a bauxite-lined vertical kiln, and chlorinated, reaction (12).

$$Al_2O_3 + 3C + 3Cl_2 \rightarrow 2AlCl_3 + 3CO \qquad (12)$$

Aluminum chloride is a catalyst for production of cumene, styrene, and isomerized butane. Of the aluminum chloride uses in anhydrous form, ethylbenzene production uses 25%, dyes 30%, detergents 15%, ethyl chloride 10%, drugs 8%, and miscellaneous production 12%. Hydrated and liquid forms are also available, 50% of which are used in drug and cosmetic production.

Titanium tetrachloride, $TiCl_4$, is a clear, colorless liquid. Production of titanium metal became of considerable interest in the 1950s for military uses. This required production of titanium tetrachloride from chlorination of rutile, TiO_2, as in reaction (13),

$$TiO_2 + 2Cl_2 \rightarrow TiCl_4 + O_2 \qquad (13)$$

or ilmenite, $FeO \cdot TiO_2$. Usually mixtures of carbon and rutile are chlorinated. $TiCl_4$ is also used as a polymerization catalyst and as a smoke screen agent and for sky writing. *See* SCREENING SMOKE.

Zirconium tetrachloride, $ZrCl_4$, is a colorless solid. Titanium technology is applicable to other metals, among which zirconium became of interest in the late 1950s. Zirconium tetrachloride is manufactured by chlorination of zirconium carbide or zirconium cyanonitride. It is also made by action of chlorine and carbon on the ores zircon, $ZrSiO_4$, and zirconia, ZrO_2, or by treating ores with carbon tetrachloride or phosgene.

Phosphorus trichloride, PCl_3, and phosphorus oxychloride, $POCl_3$, are important reagents in organic chemical synthesis. The oxychloride is a clear, colorless, fuming liquid. Chlorine is bubbled through phosphorus pentoxide in phosphorus trichloride, and the oxychloride is removed by distillation. Reaction (14) illustrates this process.

$$P_2O_5 + 3PCl_3 + 3Cl_2 \rightarrow 5POCl_3 \qquad (14)$$

Ferric chloride, $FeCl_3$, is a solid composed of dark, hexagonal crystals. Much chlorine from chemical processes is converted to ferric chloride, which is then used for the manufacture of salts, pigments, pharmaceuticals, and dyes and for photoengraving, preparation of catalysts, and waste and sewage treatment.

Evidence for the formation of coordination complexes is observed when an insoluble chloride such as silver chloride dissolves in the presence of excess chloride ion to give the complex ion $AgCl_3{}^{2-}$.

Other common chloro complexes are those of copper, cobalt, tin, and platinum, $CuCl_2{}^+$, $CoCl_4{}^{2-}$, $SnCl_6{}^{2-}$, and $PtCl_6{}^{2-}$, respectively. *See*

COORDINATION COMPLEXES.

Chloroplatinates. These are compounds containing the anion $PtCl_6{}^{2-}$, which is derived from chloroplatinic acid. This acid is produced when platinum is dissolved in aqua regia. Of the many salts known, the ammonium and potassium chloroplatinates are the most useful because of their low solubility. The formation of precipitate is used as a qualitative test for the ammonium and potassium ions. *See* AQUA REGIA; PLATINUM.

Other compounds. Phosgene, $COCL_2$, is a very poisonous gas. The pure product is a colorless liquid that boils at 7.48°C (45.5°F). It is produced by the reaction of dry carbon monoxide and chlorine gases, conducted over activated charcoal, reaction (15). Phosgene is used primarily in the manufacture

$$CO + Cl_2 \rightarrow COCl_2 \qquad (15)$$

of toluene diisocyanate, which is important in making urethane foams and special rubbers. Other isocyanates are being used in making adhesives.

Monochloracetic acid, $CH_2ClCOOH$, white deliquescent crystals, is made by chlorination of acetic acid with a catalyst in acid-resistant equipment. It is used as a chemical intermediate for making dyes, coumarin, pharmaceuticals, cosmetics, weed killers, and insecticides. Dichloroacetic acid, $CHCl_2COOH$, results from further chlorination of acetic acid. Trichloroacetic acid, CCl_3COOH, is a white crystalline material which results from still further chlorination of acetic acid. It is used medicinally, and the sodium salt is used as a weed killer. *See* INSECTICIDE.

Other chlorinated organic compounds are produced in large quantities for a wide variety of uses.

Safety precautions. Chlorine attacks the tissues of the nose, throat, and lungs. Its pungent odor allows easy detection, which should not be ignored. Concentrations of 15–30 ppm in air for even a short time will irritate the mucous membranes, the respiratory system, and the skin and coughing will usually result. The threshold limit value (TLV) for an 8-h day is 1 ppm. Higher concentrations are dangerous. In extreme cases the difficulty of breathing may increase to the point where death can occur from suffocation. Chlorine reacts violently with many materials. Explosive mixtures are formed with hydrogen, and metals such as iron will begin to burn in it with only a slight amount of heating. For example, use of chlorine should be avoided in service with titanium metal, as an explosion will result if titanium comes into contact with dry chlorine. Many organic reactions with chlorine are highly exothermic. Entire industries based on chlorine reactions have excellent safety records, but each use must be carefully considered, and each operation checked for safety hazards. Gas masks should be available. *See* INDUSTRIAL HEALTH AND SAFETY; RESPIRATOR.

Natural occurrence. Because many inorganic chlorides are quite soluble in water, they are leached out of land areas by rain and ground water to accumulate in the sea or in lakes that have no outlets.

Seawater contains 18.97 g of chloride ion per kilogram (3% sodium chloride). Solar evaporation produces large deposits of salts in landlocked areas. Similar evaporation in the past is responsible for vast underground deposits of rock salt and brines in Michigan, central New York, the Gulf Coast of Texas, Stassfurt in Germany, and elsewhere. These deposits are mainly of sodium chloride, the supply of which is unlimited for practical purposes. Other rocks and minerals in the Earth's surface average slightly over 0.03% chloride. *See* HALOGEN MINERALS; SALINE EVAPORITE.

Manufacture. The first electrolytic process was patented in 1851 by Charles Watt in Great Britain. In 1868 Henry Deacon produced chlorine from hydrochloric acid and oxygen, reaction (16), at

$$4HCl + O_2 \rightarrow 2Cl_2 + 2H_2O \tag{16}$$

400°C (750°F) with copper chloride absorbed in pumice stone as a catalyst. The electrolytic cells now used may be classified for the most part as diaphragm and mercury types. Both make caustic (NaOH or KOH), chlorine, and hydrogen. The economics of the chlor-alkali industry mainly involve the balanced marketing or internal use of caustic and chlorine in the same proportions as obtained from the electrolytic cell process.

Diaphragm cells. The Hooker diaphragm cell illustrates the principles of operation with porous asbestos pulp diaphragms. Diaphragms separate the anode compartment, containing the brine feed to the cell and chlorine produced, from the cathode compartment. The cathode compartment contains the sodium hydroxide (caustic) produced as a solution in undecomposed brine (which has percolated through the diaphragm) and hydrogen gas.

To minimize back diffusion and migration of caustic, the flow rate of brine through the diaphragm is faster than salt can be electrolyzed, so that only part of the salt is converted. Diaphragms must be renewed if brine is not sufficiently purified or if oils from graphite and calcium or iron from cell bodies cut down the flow rate. These impurities are all collected by the diaphragms. Diaphragm cells produce solutions containing about 10% sodium hydroxide and 15% sodium chloride. This is used directly in some chemical processes. Usually commercial caustic is evaporated to 50 or 73% solutions or to dry sodium hydroxide, NaOH. Most of the salt then crystallizes out and is returned to the process.

In general, very little unused chlorine capacity exists in the industry. Dow diaphragm cells represent the largest installed capacity, followed by Hooker, Diamond Alkali, and other types of diaphragm cells. Dow diaphragm cells are erected in blocks (traditionally about 50 per unit) which operate as a group in contrast to single-cell units in all other diaphragm installations. In Dow cells the electric current passes through a multiple unit series without electrical cables or bus bars between cells. Abutting frames are pressed together to form a tight block, with each unit connected electrically to the next cell within the frames of the series. Chlorine and hydrogen gases are each collected in inverted trough concrete headers on top of the cells, and caustic at the side through a trap.

Modern diaphragm cell installations operate at currents of 60–900 kA/m² (5.6–84 kA/ft²), and in the range of 3.5 V per cell. The voltage is determined by the sum of anode and cathode potentials (dependent on surface characteristics of each electrode, temperature, and current density, which affect the chlorine and hydrogen overvoltages), the resistance through the electrolyte, the resistance through the diaphragm, the resistance through anode and cathode leads and across contacts, and the diffusion potential.

Traditionally, anodes are made of graphite. In the mid-1960s and 1970s, researchers developed anodes made of the platinum group metals and having high, near-metallic conductivities. The best results have been obtained with ruthenium dioxide and titanium oxide solid solutions. These anodes, known as dimensionally stable anodes, have become the world standard anode material—possessing long life, low operating voltages, and good efficiency and cost. Dow Chemical Company, in its conversion plans for metal anodes, includes the use of its own coating system as well as that of Diamond Shamrock Technologies. Some plantinized titanium is also being used in anode production.

Graphite anodes must be replaced periodically, and are therefore an additional item of expense in cell operation. Graphite is oxidized to carbon dioxide gas and trace-chlorinated organics, which leave the cell with the chlorine gas. Iron screen

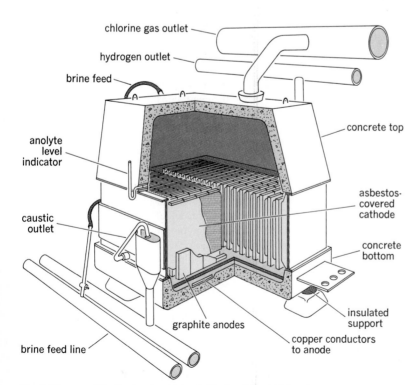

Fig. 6. Diagram of the Hooker type S-4 cell. (*Hooker Chemical Corp.*)

chlorine gas outlet

hydrogen outlet

brine feed

anolyte level indicator

caustic outlet

brine feed line

concrete top

asbestos-covered cathode

concrete bottom

insulated support

graphite anodes

copper conductors to anode

cathodes and concrete cell bodies are smaller items of expense, and need not be replaced as often as the graphite. Some diaphragm cells are cylindrical, such as the historic Vorce, Wheeler, and Gibbs cells. Cylindrical cells usually have less concrete, since the vessels are made of iron, and replacement of these parts is even less frequent. Nelson and Allen-Moore cells are historic rectangular diaphragm cells.

Figure 6 shows a Hooker diaphragm cell, which illustrates the principles of the diaphragm type. Chlorine is produced on the graphite anodes, which are covered with incoming salt brine. Chlorine gas bubbles rise to the top of the anodes and on through a reservoir of incoming brine in the lower portion of the concrete top; they are then collected from the chlorine gas outlet by pipelines connected to each cell. The chlorine contains water vapor, which makes it a very corrosive material. Wet chlorine must be handled in rubber-lined steel, glass, plastic, or similar corrosion-resistant material. However, when cool and dry, chlorine may be handled in equipment made of black iron, steel, copper, nickel, or lead. Processing of chlorine consists of cooling, drying (with sulfuric acid), pumping, and perhaps liquefying for storage or shipment. Liquefaction occurs at increased pressure (usually about 100 psi or 700 kPa), perhaps with some cooling or by decreasing temperature to about −40°C (−40°F) at low pressure. Shipments have been common in 100-lb (45-kg), 150-lb (68-kg), and 1-ton (0.9-metric ton) cylinders; in 16-, 30-, 55-, and 85-ton (14-, 27-, 50-, and 77-metric ton) railroad tank cars; and in tank barges of 550 and 1110 tons (495 and 999 metric tons) capacity. Usually barges contain four or six tanks containing 85 to 185 tons (77 to 167 metric tons) each.

Hydrogen gas and caustic are produced inside the asbestos-covered iron screen cathode pockets shown in Fig. 6. The caustic solution drops from the outlet into a funnel (to break the electric current path) and is collected and pumped to the evaporators. Hydrogen is collected as shown behind the cell, scrubbed with caustic to remove chlorine, and often converted into ammonia or hydrochloric acid or used for hydrogenation of oils.

Mercury cells. This type of cell has been operated during the entire period of commercial production of chlorine, starting with the Castner cell and continuing in the United States with the Mathieson cell. They achieved increased importance in Germany during World War II, and other countries later renewed their interest. New mercury cell plants have been erected by many companies in the United States.

In the mercury cell the cathode is metallic mercury to which current is led by the steel body of the cell or other metallic contacts. Sodium amalgam is produced in the cell. It is led away from the cell to a decomposer also containing graphite which, in this case, serves as a cathode. The amalgam serves as an anode in a short-circuited cell.

Pure water is added in the decomposer to produce concentrated sodium hydroxide solutions and

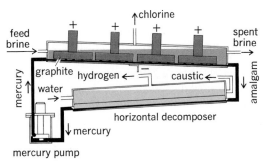

Fig. 7. A mercury cell for producing chlorine.

hydrogen from the sodium amalgam. Such caustic is usually considered quite pure (depending on the purity of the water and some other factors). It is often sold without further treatment as 50%-strength caustic, or may be evaporated to 73% or solid products. The direct 50% product constitutes the main economy of mercury cell installations compared with diaphragm cell caustic evaporator installations. However, mercury cells operate basically at 0.8 V higher than diaphragm cells, representing higher power costs. Furthermore, the cost of mercury (of which there are losses in operation) is considerable.

Mercury cells overflow some brine continuously to maintain salt concentration in the electrolyzer. This brine is usually resaturated, purified, and recycled. Sodium amalgam forms in the electrolyzer, rather than caustic and hydrogen. This occurs because the discharge potential of hydrogen is higher than that of sodium because of the high overvoltage of hydrogen on mercury. Cells are usually constructed of steel, and are rubber-lined where necessary for protection against wet chlorine. Graphite anodes or the new metal anodes are parallel to the mercury surface, as shown in **Fig. 7**, and are suspended from the cover by graphite or other conducting pins. Whereas the decomposition voltage in diaphragm cells is about 2.3 V, in mercury cells it is about 3.1 V.

The tremendous interest in mercury cells arises from the large units which have been developed. In Europe mercury cells previously were operated at currents of up to 40,000 A, but since 1950 designs developed by all manufacturers of cells increased the operating range to 100–300 kA. Besides the higher amperage, multilevel layouts and extremely close spacing of cells cut down floor space requirements tremendously. Other innovations include improvements in cell cover sealing arrangements, automatic anode adjustments, decomposer arrangements, and cleaning devices.

Other methods. Electrolysis of potassium chloride brine in either diaphragm or mercury cells produces potassium hydroxide, KOH, in place of sodium hydroxide. Molten sodium chloride is electrolyzed in cells, such as the Downs cell, operating at 600°C (1100°F) to produce sodium metal rather than sodium hydroxide. Caustic cell liquor can also be converted to the carbonates as alternate products instead of the hydroxides originally produced, resulting in soda ash, Na_2CO_3, and potassium carbonate, K_2CO_3. An interesting new idea related to both the mercury cell and the molten salt cell is the Szechtman cell. Mercury is replaced by molten lead flowing in a closed circuit. Either molten sodium chloride or other molten alkali chlorides could be electrolyzed to produce a variety of co-products with the chlorine.

Hydrochloric acid is often in oversupply because of its production as a by-product of organic syntheses. The chlorine may be recovered by any one of four available processes: catalytic oxidation of gaseous HCl (Deacon process), direct oxidation of HCl by an inorganic oxidizing agent such as sulfur trioxide, SO_3, electrolysis of HCl, or formation of metal chlorides and oxidation to metal oxide and chlorine.

Small amounts of chlorine are also made as by-products of the electrolysis of fused magnesium chloride, $MgCl_2$, in the production of magnesium metal,and of the electrolysis of fused lithium chloride in lithium metal production. A nonelectrolytic process, the nitrosyl chloride process, has been operating in the United States for many years, and oxidation of HCl with HNO_3 is practiced in some other countries.

Germany, Great Britain, France, Italy, and Spain have been the major chlorine producers in Europe; the United States and Canada are the leading Western Hemisphere producers. Latin America, Japan, and India also have a number of plants. *See* ELECTROCHEMICAL PROCESS.

Uses. Chlorine is an excellent oxidizing agent. Historically, the use of chlorine as a bleaching agent in the paper, pulp, and textile industries and as a germicide for drinking water preparation, swimming pool purification, and hospital sanitation has made community living possible.

Chlorine is used to produce bromine from bromides found in brines and seawater. The automotive age increased the production of bromine tremendously for the manufacture of ethylene dibromide for use in gasoline. Of the total bromine produced, such use for ethylene dibromide reached 95% some years ago. Later the use of other bromides increased at a faster rate than ethylene dibromide. Use of bromine has rapidly grown in manufacturing fire retardants for plastics and polymers, as has the use of bromide in high-density fluids for oil recovery. Considering the bromide ions involved as being represented by NaBr in seawater and $CaBr_2$ in brines, the reactions for production of bromine are (17) and (18). Both processes are followed by

$$2NaBr + Cl_2 \rightarrow 2NaCl + Br_2 \qquad (17)$$

$$CaBr_2 + Cl_2 \rightarrow CaCl_2 + Br_2 \qquad (18)$$

concentration and purification steps. *See* BROMINE.

Compounds of chlorine are used as bleaching agents, oxidizing agents, solvents, and intermediates in the manufacture of other substances. *See* HERBICIDE.

Joe Downey; Frederick W. Koerker; Robert W. Belfit, Jr.
Bibliography. J. Bowser, *Inorganic Chemistry*,

1993; Chlorine Institute, Inc., *Chlorine Inst. Bull.*, various dates; Chlorine Institute, Inc., *Chlorine Manual*, 5th ed., 1986; F. A. Cotton and G. Wilkinson, *Advanced Inorganic Chemistry*, 5th ed., 1988; Electrochemical Society, Inc., *Annu. Rep. Chlor-Alkali Comm. Ind. Electrolytic Div.*, annually; *Kirk-Othmer Encyclopedia of Chemical Technology*, vol. 4, 4th ed., 1993.

Chlorite

One of a group of layer silicate minerals, usually green in color, characterized by a perfect cleavage parallel to (001). The cleavage flakes are flexible but inelastic, with a luster varying from pearly or vitreous to dull and earthy. The hardness on the cleavage is about 2.5. The specific gravity varies between 2.6 and 3.3 as a function of composition.

Chlorite is a common accessary mineral in low- to medium-grade regional metamorphic rocks and is the dominant mineral in chlorite schist. It can form by alteration of ferromagnesian minerals in igneous rocks and is found occasionally in pegmatites and vein deposits. It is a common constituent of altered basic rocks and of alteration zones around metallic ore bodies. Chlorite also can form by diagenetic processes in sedimentary rocks. *See* DIAGENESIS.

The crystal structure of chlorite consists of a 2:1 layer, similar to that in mica, with octahedrally coordinated cations sandwiched between two tetrahedral sheets that are inverted relative to one another. Substitution of Al or Fe^{3+} for Si in the tetrahedral sheets gives a net negative charge to the 2:1 layers, which must be balanced by a positively charged octahedral sheet in the interlayer space.

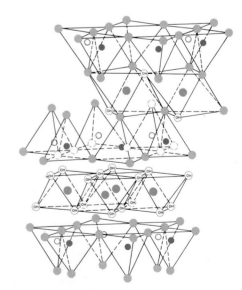

● } silicon (partially replaced
○ } by aluminum)
● magnesium, aluminum, and/or iron
⊕ hydroxyls
● oxygens

Diagram of the structure of chlorite. (*After R. E. Grim, Clay Mineralogy, McGraw-Hill, 1953*)

The composition of the 2:1 layer can be expressed as

$$\left(R_{3-a-b-c}^{2+}R_a^{1+}R_b^{3+}\square_c\right)\left(Si_{4-x}R_x^{3+}\right)O_{10}(OH)_2$$

and that of the interlayer as

$$\left(R_{3-d-e-f}^{2+}R_d^{1+}R_e^{3+}\square_f\right)(OH)_6$$

with $\square$ = vacancy. Enough R^{3+} cations must be present in the interlayer to create a net positive charge on that sheet. Long hydrogen bonds link basal oxygens of each tetrahedral sheet with surface hydroxyl groups of the interlayer sheet (see **illus.**). Different stacking arrangements of the layers and interlayers are possible. *See* MICA.

Most chlorites are trioctahedral with close to 3.0 octahedral cations present in both the 2:1 layer and the interlayer. The main octahedral cations present in these sheets are Mg, Fe^{2+}, Fe^{3+}, and Al, but with important substitutions of Cr, Mn, Ni, V, Cu, or Li in certain species. Species names are given according to the dominant divalent octahedral cation present: clinochlore for Mg dominant, chamosite for Fe^{2+} dominant, nimite for Ni dominant, and pennatite for Mn^{2+} dominant. A few dioctahedral chlorites are known also. *See* AUTHIGENIC MINERALS; CLAY MINERALS.

S. W. Bailey

Chloritoid

A hydrous iron aluminum silicate mineral with an ideal formula of $Fe_2^{2+}Al_4O_2(SiO_4)_2(OH)_4$. Chloritoid occurs as platy, black or dark green crystals, rarely more than a few millimeters in size. Its density ranges from 3.46 to 3.80 g/cm³, and its hardness on the Mohs scale is 6.5.

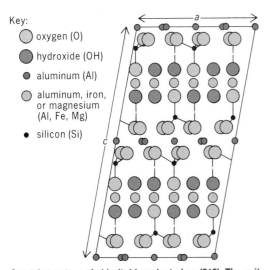

Key:
- ○ oxygen (O)
- ◓ hydroxide (OH)
- • aluminum (Al)
- ◐ aluminum, iron, or magnesium (Al, Fe, Mg)
- • silicon (Si)

Crystal structure of chloritoid, projected on (010). The unit cell for one structural type of chloritoid, $2M_2$, is shown. The unit cell parameters are a = 0.9482 nanometers, b = 0.5485 nm, c = 1.8180 nm, β = 101.8°. (*After P. H. Ribbe, ed., Orthosilicates, Reviews in Mineralogy, vol. 5, Mineralogical Society of America, 1980*)

Crystal form. Chloritoid most commonly forms monoclinic crystals, having a single twofold rotation axis perpendicular to a mirror plane. This is the symmetry of the prismatic crystal class, symbolized as $2/m$. The atomic structure of chloritoid is characterized by silicon atoms surrounded by four oxygen atoms in a tetrahedral arrangement. These tetrahedral clusters form layers that alternate with layers of ferrous iron (Fe^{+2}) and aluminum (Al; see **illus.**) The iron and aluminum are surrounded by six oxygen (O) and hydroxide (OH) ions in an octahedral arrangement in the ratio $[Fe_2^{2+}AlO_2(OH)_4]^-$ and are sandwiched between layers of $(SiO_4)^{4-}$ tetrahedra. The sandwiches of silica tetrahedra–iron and aluminum octahedra–silica tetrahedra are stacked alternately with layers of aluminum. Other structural forms of chloritoid, called polytypes, are created by variations in the stacking of the tetrahedral-octahedral-tetrahedral sandwiches. *See* CRYSTAL STRUCTURE; CRYSTALLOGRAPHY.

In thin section under the polarizing microscope, chloritoid can appear to be rectangular, with a length two or three times the width. It is observed to be pleochroic, having a color of bluish or greenish gray if the long dimension of the crystal is parallel to the polarizing direction, and pale gray to colorless if the long dimension of the crystal is perpendicular to the polarizing direction. Crystals are commonly twinned across planes parallel to the long dimension. The indices of refraction range from 1.713 to 1.740, with a birefringence (δ) of about 0.010. The mineral has a higher-than-average index of refraction and tends, therefore, to stand out from the other minerals in thin section. Chloritoid exhibits anomalous interference colors in cross-polarized light. *See* BIREFRINGENCE; PLEOCHROISM.

Composition. The composition of chloritoid typically deviates from the ideal formula. Magnesium (Mg) substitutes for as much as 40% of the iron, although the ratio Mg/(Mg + Fe) is generally 0.15 to 0.20. Manganese has been found to substitute for 17% of the iron, but manganese contents are generally less than 1% of the iron. A variety of chloritoid, called ottrelite, contains manganese in substitution for iron in amounts of about 60%. Ferric iron (Fe^{3+}) substitutes for less than 14% of the aluminum, and titanium occurs in trace amounts.

Occurrence. Chloritoid is typically found in low-grade, metamorphosed shales, which are commonly called pelitic schists. It occurs as a comparatively large mineral set in a matrix composed of quartz and fine-grained muscovite. It first appears in most metamorphic terrains near the biotite isograd, that is, near the first appearance of biotite; however, the first appearance of chloritoid depends on many factors, including pressure, oxidation state, and availability of proper rock compositions in the metamorphic terrain. In low-grade rocks, chloritoid is found in association with chlorite, muscovite, and, in some rocks, paragonite. At medium grades of metamorphism, chloritoid can be found with garnet or staurolite in a muscovite and quartz matrix.

The reaction responsible for the synthesis of chloritoid in pelitic schists is not well documented but may occur as in reaction (1), where H_2O may

$$12\,\text{pyrophyllite} + 4\,\text{chlorite} \longrightarrow$$
$$9\,\text{chloritoid} + 49\,\text{quartz} + 10\,H_2O \quad (1)$$

be water or a supercritical fluid phase.

Chloritoid breaks down during metamorphism by either reaction (2) or (3).

$$\text{Chloritoid} + \text{quartz} \longrightarrow$$
$$\text{garnet} + \text{staurolite} + \text{chlorite} + H_2O \quad (2)$$

$$\text{Chloritoid} + \text{muscovite} + \text{quartz} \longrightarrow$$
$$\text{garnet} + \text{staurolite} + \text{biolite} + H_2O \quad (3)$$

The stoichiometric coefficients in these two reactions depend on the Fe/Mg ratios in the minerals, which in turn depend on the pressure and temperature of the reaction. Reaction (2) is found to occur in medium- to high-pressure terrains, whereas reaction (3) occurs in low-pressure terrains.

Experimental studies of the stability of chloritoid have been conducted over a limited range in temperature and pressure and in the possible compositions of chloritoid. The low-temperature stability limit of chloritoid has not been well determined. Calculations indicate that reaction (1) proceeds at a temperature near 400°C (750°F) at 500 megapascals (5 kilobars). The high-temperature stability limit of chloritoid has been studied experimentally under conditions appropriate for reaction (2). The results indicate that chloritoid is stable up to temperatures near 550°C (1020°F) at 500 MPa (5 kbar) and 575°C (1070°F) at 1000 MPa (10 kbar), although the precise temperature and pressure conditions of reaction (2) have not been determined. Reactions at low pressures, including reaction (3), have not been investigated.

Chloritoid is increasingly being recognized as a constituent in rocks that formed under high-pressure conditions. It is found in association with glaucophane in blueschist-facies metamorphic rocks, and with amphibole and pyroxene in eclogite-facies metamorphic rocks. These are rocks that formed under conditions thought to prevail at the base of the Earth's crust or in the mantle. Experimental studies of metamorphism of basalt under these conditions indicate the formation of chloritoid at pressures exceeding 2300 MPa (23 kbar) and at a temperature of 650°C (1200°F). In these high-pressure occurrences of chloritoid, the chloritoid is rich in magnesium, having a value of Mg/(Mg + Fe) ranging from 0.38 to 0.40. *See* METAMORPHIC ROCKS. **Theodore C. Labotka**

Bibliography. W. A. Deer, R. A. Howie, and J. Zussman, *An introduction to the Rock-Forming Minerals*, 1992; C. Klein and C. S. Hurlbut, Jr., *Manual of Mineralogy*, 21st ed., 1993.

Chloromonadida

An order of the class Phytamastigophorea, also known as the Chloromonadina. These poorly known flagellates are grass-green or colorless, somewhat flattened, and have two equal flagella, one anterior, the other trailing. All known genera are free-swimming, although *Reckertia* and *Thaumatomastix* form pseudopodia. They vary in size from 30 to 100 micrometers. Chromatophores are small disks, stigmas are lacking, and fat is the storage product. Trichocysts are found in three genera. The nucleus is large, with nucleoli and chromosomes visible during interphase. One or two anterior vacuoles are present and a reservoir seems to be present in *Trentonia* and *Gonyostomum* (see **illus.**). Life cycles are unknown, but longitudinal di-

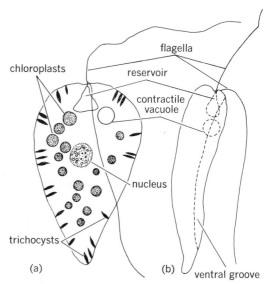

Gonyostomum semen. (*a*) Dorsal view. (*b*) Side view.

vision occurs. *Gonyostomum* sometimes occurs as bloom in cedar swamps, and *Vacuolaria* is sometimes common there. The taxonomic position of the class is poorly defined. *See* CILIA AND FLAGELLA; PHYTAMASTIGOPHOREA; PROTOZOA.

James B. Lackey

Chlorophyceae

A large and diverse class of plants, commonly called green algae, in the chlorophyll *a-b* phyletic line (Chlorophycota). Estimated number of taxa varies widely; 560 genera and 8600 species are conservative estimates. *See* CHLOROPHYCOTA.

Characteristics. The green algae exhibit great morphological diversity while sharing fundamental biochemical and ultrastructural features. Their photosynthetic pigments are similar to those in higher plants and include chlorophyll *a* and *b*, α-, β-, and γ-carotene, and various xanthophylls, especially lutein, violaxanthin, zeaxanthin, antheraxanthin, and neoxanthin. Chloroplasts vary in number and shape, but always have two membranes, two to five thylakoids per lamella, and usually one or more pyrenoids. A cell wall, which may be calcified, is usually present, and often contains cellulose, hydroxyproline glycosides, xylan, and mannan. The chief food reserve is starch, stored in the chloroplast as granules which often sheathe a pyrenoid. Motile cells usually have two or four apically inserted smooth flagella of approximately equal length. In a few genera, motile cells have more than four apical flagella, one or two pairs of subapical flagella, or a subapical crown of numerous flagella. Flagellar scales and hairs are rare. There is sometimes an eyespot, which lies within the chloroplast. *See* CELL PLASTIDS; CHLOROPHYLL.

Phylogeny. Almost all somatic cell types known for algae occur among the Chlorophyceae, the exceptions being rhizopodial unicells and complex multicellular thalli differentiated into macroscopic organs. In the traditional view of phylogeny within the green algae, the progenitor is a motile unicell (monad) with a wall and a pair of equal, smooth, apical flagella, similar to present-day *Chlamydomonas*. In one line of evolution (volvocine), monads joined to form motile colonies. In a different evolutionary line, monads lost their flagella, forming nonmotile solitary cells and colonies (tetrasporine line), which then underwent specialization and elaboration (chlorococcine line). Multicellular thalli (ulotrichine line) were made possibly by the evolution of desmoschisis, a type of cell division in which the wall of the progeny and that of the parent become an integral structure. Traditionally, the ulotrichine line has been considered to lead from unbranched filaments (Ulotrichales) through forms with both prostrate and erect branched systems (Chaetophorales) to the higher plants, with two very distinctive groups (Zygnematales and Oedogoniales) as early offshoots and a third equally distinctive group (charophytes) diverging from a more advanced position. Siphonous and vesicular green algae (siphonine line) were believed to have evolved prior to the origin of desmoschisis.

Ultrastructural studies, however, have revealed differences in details of nuclear and cell division, cell coverings, plasmodesmata, pyrenoids, and flagellar structure that are correlated among themselves and with certain traditional characters to a degree that strongly suggests that the ulotrichine line is polyphyletic, with desmoschisis having evolved at least four times. Moreover, these studies suggest that the ultimate ancestral green flagellate was prasinophycean (asymmetrical and covered with scales) rather than *Chlamydomonas*-like. Integration of these studies and inferences suggests four phyletic lines: chlorophycean, ulvophycean, charophycean, and pleurastrophycean.

Chlorophycean phyletic line. This phyletic group has motile cells that are usually walled and with two or more apically arising flagella, their basal bodies associated with four or more relatively narrow bands of microtubules in a cruciate arrangement.

The group includes the volvocine, tetrasporine, and chlorococcine lines, as well as the Chlorosarcinales, Microsporales, Sphaeropleales, Oedogoniales, and Chaetophorales. It is believed to be the most derived of the four phyletic lines and the only one with a chlamydomonad ancestor.

Volvocales and Chlorococcales. The order Volvocales includes all Chlorophyceae that normally are flagellate and motile. The cells are solitary or united into colonies of definite structure, called coenobia. Some taxonomists place the unicellular forms in a separate order, Chlamydomonadales, and interpret the coenobial forms as being multicellular. *Chlamydomonas*, presumably similar to the volvocalean archetype, has two smooth

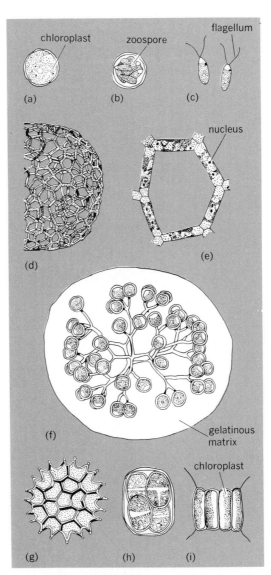

Fig. 1. Chlorococcales. (*a*) *Chlorococcum* (Chlorococcaceae), vegetative cell; (*b*) cell with zoospores; (*c*) zoospores; (*d*) *Hydrodictyon* (Hydrodictyaceae), portion of coenobium; (*e*) portion enlarged; (*f*) *Dictyosphaerium* (Dictyosphaeriaceae), colony in gelatinous matrix; (*g*) *Pediastrum* (Scenedesmaceae), coenobium; (*h*) *Oocystis* (Oocystaceae), colony (*from G. M. Smith, Fresh-water Algae of the United States, 2d ed., McGraw-Hill, 1950*); (*i*) *Scenedesmus* (Scenedesmaceae), coenobium (*from G. M. Smith, Cryptogamic Botany, vol. 1, 2d ed., McGraw-Hill, 1955*).

flagella, a chloroplast that commonly is cup-shaped or H-shaped, a pyrenoid, a nucleus, an eyespot, and contractile vacuoles. The protoplast is enclosed in a wall (theca). Within the Volvocales there are notable evolutionary trends: isogamy through anisogamy to oogamy; increase in number of cells; and increase in polarity, resulting in morphological and functional differentiation of component cells. *Volvox*, terminating these trends, has a spherical coenobium composed of as many as 50,000 cells. The Tetrasporales, regarded by some taxonomists as a suborder of the Volvocales, are essentially unicellular Volvocales that have lost their flagella and become nonmotile in their vegetative phase.

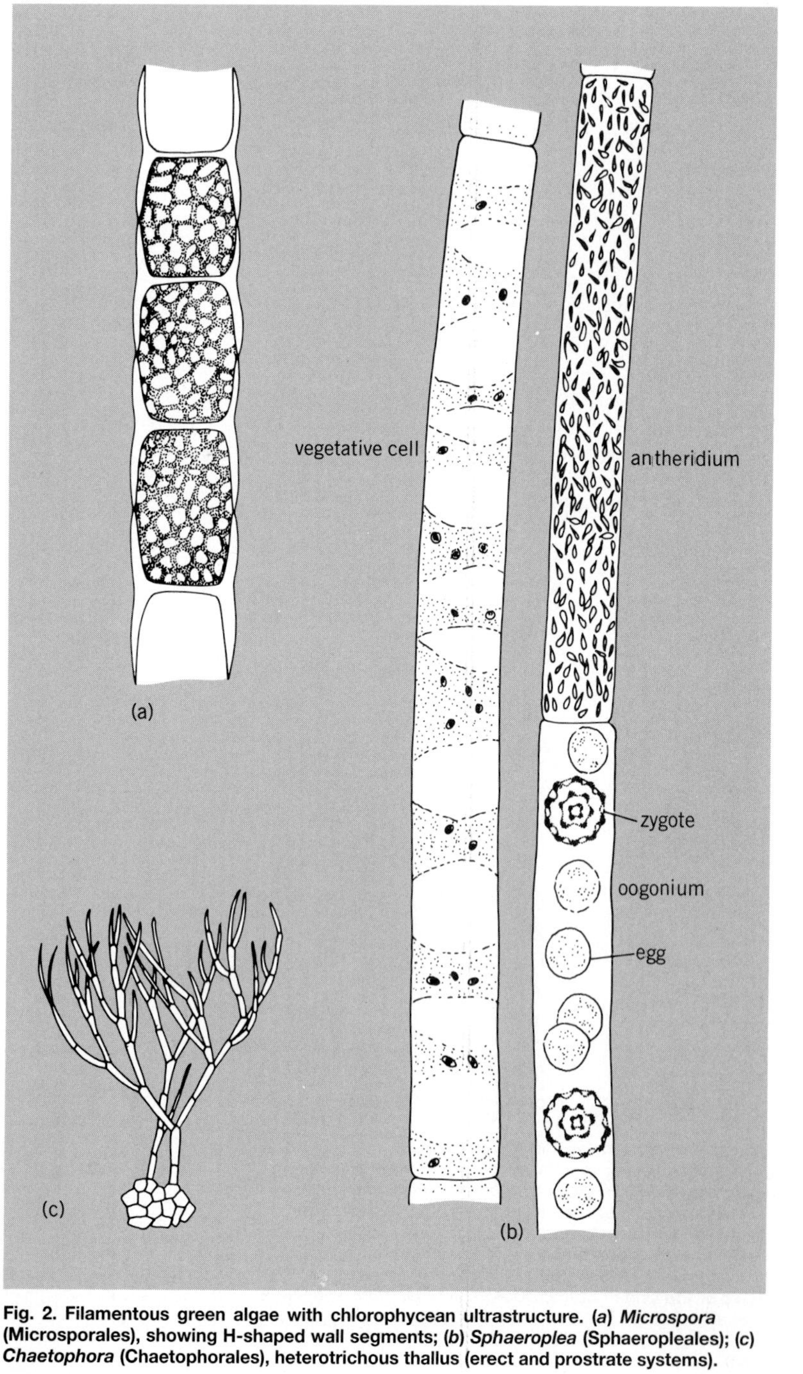

The cells generally have an internal organization similar to that of *Chlamydomonas*. They are usually massed in gelatinous colonies of indefinite shape, but in some genera the thallus is saccate, dendroid, or reticulate. *See* VOLVOCALES.

The order Chlorococcales comprises a large and diverse assemblage of nonmotile algae that appear to follow the Tetrasporales phylogenetically, sharing their inability to form multicellular thalli, but differing cytologically in that vegetative cells lack eyespots and contractile vacuoles and tend to be nonpolar. Most Chlorococcales are solitary cells of various shapes (spherical, ellipsoid, reniform, lunate, acicular, polygonal) and sizes (to 200 micrometers maximum dimension). Cells are free or attached by a gelatinous stalk. The wall is plain or ornamented (spines, bristles, knobs, horns) and uniformly or asymmetrically thickened. In many genera, however, the cells are joined into colonies of indefinite or definite structure. Colonies of indefinite structure result from coalescence of gelatinous envelopes (Coccomyxaceae) or joining of successive progenies by persistent remnants of parental walls (Dictyosphaeriaceae, **Fig. 1***f*). Colonies of definite structure (coenobia) result from coherence of the cells of a progeny, whether the cells are nonmotile (Scenedesmaceae, Fig. 1*i*) or initially motile (Hydrodictyaceae, Fig. 1*d, e, g*). Asexual reproduction is by cleavage of a protoplast to form autospores or autocolonies (cells or colonies having the same shape as the parent) or zoospores. After being released from the parental wall, autospores and autocolonies enlarge to adult size. Zoospores either metamorphose individually into nonmotile cells or settle collectively to form an autocolony. Sexual reproduction is usually isogamous.

The Chlorococcales constitute an important component of fresh-water plankton and soil microflora, but occupy other aquatic and subaerial habitats, including snow and ice. Some are the algal component (phycobiont) of lichens, while others occur in the tissues of aquatic and terrestrial plants and aquatic animals. *Oophila*, for example, lives in the mucilage of salamander eggs. *Prototheca* is an intestinal pathogen of various domestic animals and humans. *Chlorella*, commonly found in a wide variety of aquatic habitats, is used extensively in physiological research and is grown in mass cultures as a protein source for poultry, livestock, and humans. Nearly 200 genera of Chlorococcales are recognized, distributed among 15 or 16 families. They are almost exclusively fresh-water.

In the orders Volvocales, Tetrasporales, and Chlorococcales, cell division is of the type termed eleutheroschisis, in which the daughter protoplasts either remain naked or secrete new walls separate from the parental wall, which ruptures or gelatinizes to release the progeny (zoospores, autospores, or gametes). In theory, multicellularity was made possible by the evolution of desmoschisis, a process by which daughter cells make permanent contributions to the parental wall. In multicellular algae with uninucleate cells, there is a regular sequence of

Fig. 2. Filamentous green algae with chlorophycean ultrastructure. (*a*) *Microspora* (Microsporales), showing H-shaped wall segments; (*b*) *Sphaeroplea* (Sphaeropleales); (*c*) *Chaetophora* (Chaetophorales), heterotrichous thallus (erect and prostrate systems).

karyokinesis, cytokinesis, and cell-wall deposition. The relationship between daughter and parental walls is not always clear, however; numerous intermediate situations have been demonstrated. A relatively small group of green algae (mainly in soil) exhibit desmoschisis but lack intercellular connections (plasmodesmata) and thus form only cuboidal (sarcinoid) or irregular packets. Both chlorophycean and charophycean phyletic lines are represented, with members of the former assigned to the order Chlorosarcinales and those of the latter to the order Chlorokybales. In a few genera, rudimentary filaments result from end-to-end coherence of daughter cells that do not contribute to the parental wall and thus are equivalent to autospores. Such genera can be assigned to the Chlorococcales. Long but unbranched filaments can also be produced in the absence of desmoschisis of which there are two well-known fresh-water examples. In *Microspora* (**Fig. 2***a*), each daughter cell forms a partial wall, so that the filament wall is composed of segments that are H-shaped in optical section, each segment covering the lower half of one cell and the upper half of the subtending cell. The cells are quadrate, each with a reticulate chloroplast lacking pyrenoids. The nucleus lies in a bridge of cytoplasm that crosses the middle of the central vacuole. In *Sphaeroplea* (Fig. 2*b*), daughter cells secrete an entire wall, but the parental wall soon breaks apart. Mature cells are 15–16 times longer than wide and have a curious coenocytic organization, in which a linear series of vacuoles is separated by transverse cytoplasmic bands, each containing several nuclei and a parietal girdle-shaped chloroplast with several pyrenoids or numerous discoid chloroplasts, certain of which contain pyrenoids. Sexual reproduction involves oogamy or an advanced form of anisogamy. *Microspora* and *Sphaeroplea* are traditionally assigned to their own families and, in the present classification, to their own orders.

Oedogoniales. The order Oedogoniales and the coextensive family Oedogoniaceae comprise three genera of filamentous fresh-water algae with several unique features, including (1) an elaborate method of cell division that results in the accumulation of apical caps; (2) zoospores and antherozoids with a subapical crown of numerous flagella; and (3) a highly specialized type of oogamy. *Oedogonium*, with simple filaments, comprises several hundred species that grow attached to various substrates, including stones, wood, and aquatic angiosperms. In *Bulbochaete* and *Oedocladium*, which have fewer species, the filaments are branched. *See* OEDOGONIALES.

Chaetophorales. Traditionally, the ulotrichine line was considered to begin with the unbranched filaments of *Ulothrix* and continue through various genera with branched filaments composed of uninucleate cells, each containing a parietal laminate chloroplast. If more than one order (Ulotrichales) was recognized, the branched forms were separated as the Chaetophorales. Modern studies have shown, however, that this morphological spectrum encompasses four phyletic lines as defined by ultrastructural features. *Ulothrix* is ulvophycean, as are *Trentepohlia* and probably all marine genera previously assigned to the Chaetophorales. *Microthamnion* is pleurastrophycean, while *Coleochaete* is charophycean. Residual chlorophycean forms, which include *Uronema* (unbranched) and *Chaetophora* (branched), constitute the order Chaetophorales *sensu stricto* with about 28 genera distributed among three families. Except for *Uronema*, members of the family Chaetophoraceae typically have a thallus differentiated into a prostrate portion composed of loose or pseudoparenchymatous filaments and an erect, freely branched portion (heterotrichous thallus, Fig. 2*c*). Ultimate branches are usually attenuate, often terminating in a long multicellular hyaline hair. In the Aphanochaetaceae, many cells bear unsheathed unicellular hairs, often with a bulbous base. In *Schizomeris*, the only member of the family Schizomeridaceae, the juvenile is similar to *Ulothrix*, but during maturation all cells in the upper portion of a filament undergo repeated division in various planes, resulting in a parenchymatous cylinder indistinctly marked into bands by the persistent transverse walls of the uniseriate cells.

Ulvophycean phyletic line. Ulvophyceae have motile cells that are scaly or naked, are radially symmetrical, and have two or more flagella arising apically from a cruciate root system, but the distal ends of the basal bodies lie in counterclockwise rotation rather than the clockwise rotation seen in Chlorophyceae. Cytokinesis is effected by a precocious cleavage furrow that impinges on microtubules of the persistent spindle. This phyletic line, which is predominantly marine, includes the Ulotrichales, Ctenocladales, Ulvales, Trentepohliales, Acrosiphoniales, Cladophorales, Siphonocladales, Bryopsidales, Dasycladales, and possibly Cylindrocapsales and Prasiolales.

Ulotrichales. The simplest thallus in the ulvophycean phyletic line is the unbranched filament of *Ulothrix* (**Fig. 3**), the only certain member of the family Ulotrichaceae and the order Ulotrichales. Other genera previously aligned with *Ulothrix* have been shown to be chlorophycean (such as *Uronema*, now in the Chaetophorales) or charophycean (such as *Klebsormidium*, *Stichococcus*, and *Raphidonema*, now in the Klebsormidiales) or to be reinterpreted as filamentous Chlorococcales (such as *Binuclearia*). Each cell of the *Ulothrix* filament has a nucleus and a parietal laminate or cylindrical chloroplast with one or more pyrenoids. Filaments attach (at least initially) by a modified basal cell to stones or wood, forming extensive stands in various aquatic habitats, such as the shores of lakes and harbors. The life history of fresh-water species involves only one somatic phase, a haploid gametophyte, with meiosis occurring in the production of zoospores during germination of the zygospore. Alternation of a filamentous gametophyte with a filamentous sporophyte has been reported for a marine species.

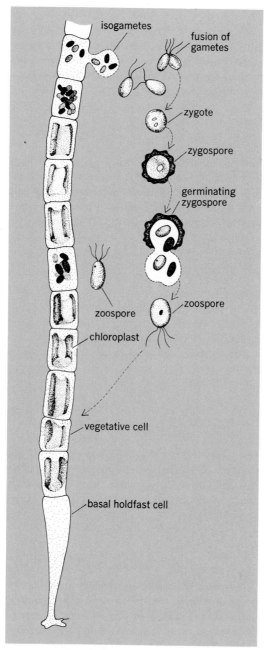

Fig. 3. *Ulothrix* (Ulotrichales).

Ctenocladales. Small green algae with branched filaments are widespread in marine habitats, and have traditionally been assigned to the Chaetophorales, but all prove to have ulvophycean rather than chlorophycean ultrastructure. The order Ctenocladales has been proposed to receive them, but some workers refer them to the Ulvales, an order usually restricted to algae with parenchymatous thalli. In these marine forms, which constitute the family Ulvellaceae, the thallus usually consists solely of prostrate filaments that are free or coherent and pseudoparenchymatous. It is affixed to, or immersed in, a solid substrate, usually an aquatic organism. Free erect filaments, if produced, are short, the cells moniliform or irregularly swollen. Colorless anucleate setalike

projections of the cell wall are produced in many genera. Sporangia and gametangia are often conspicuously larger than vegetative cells and undergo sequential cleavage. Swarmers are released by the abrupt rupture of an elongate exit papilla. Various ulvophycean genera that previously were assigned to the Chaetophorales but that lack the special features of the Ulvelaceae are tentatively placed in the Ctenocladaceae.

Ulvales. The order Ulvales comprises green algae with thalli in the form of biseriate filaments, monostromatic blades, tubes, or sacs, and distromatic blades. Cytologically, they are similar to *Ulothrix*, and some workers do not segregate them from the Ulotrichales. Various life histories have been demonstrated. *Ulva* (sea lettuce) and its close relative *Enteromorpha* occur abundantly in the intertidal zone, especially in harbors and estuaries. As treated here, the order comprises five families (Capsosiphonaceae, Percursariaceae, Ulvaceae, Monostromataceae, and Gomontiaceae) with about 12 genera.

Trentepohliales. The order Trentepohliales, with the single family Trentepohliaceae, comprises a small, specialized group of subaerial algae. The thallus is composed of branched uniseriate filaments loosely arranged in an erect tuft or cohering laterally to form a prostrate disk. Sporangia and gametangia are clearly differentiated from vegetative cells. Starch is lacking. Carotenoid pigments are abundant, coloring the thallus yellow-green, yellow, orange, or red, and often imparting the odor of violets. *Trentepohlia*, which has both prostrate and erect systems, grows on rocks, tree trunks, leaves, and wooden structures. *Cephaleuros* grows within the leaves and twigs of various plants in tropical and subtropical regions, including those of commercial plantings of tea and coffee. It is parasitic, inducing a massive wound response in many hosts.

Acrosiphoniales. Thalli in the order Acrosiphoniales are composed of unbranched or branched filaments, each cell usually containing many nuclei and a perforate cylindrical chloroplast with numerous pyrenoids. The life history often includes a vesicular sporophyte derived from the zygote. The vesicle produces haploid quadriflagellate zoospores that give rise to filamentous gametophytes. Gametes and zoospores are liberated through a distinct pore, which is operculate in one family. The order includes two families, Codiolaceae with unbranched filaments and Acrosiphoniaceae with profusely branched filaments, comprising three or four genera restricted to cold marine and brackish waters.

Cladophorales. In the order Cladophorales, the simple or branched filaments have multinucleate cells, as in most Acrosiphoniales, but the characteristic life history is an alternation of isomorphic somatic phases. The cell wall is thick and lamellate. The chloroplast is a parietal network with numerous pyrenoids. *Cladophora* is one of the most common algae in all parts of the world and in all aquatic habitats. Certain species form spherical masses (*Cladophora* balls) that roll to and fro on the bottom of shallow lakes.

Siphonocladales. In the Siphonocladales, an order of tropical marine algae closely related to the Cladophorales, the multinucleate cells are often vesicular rather than cylindrical, and when cylindrical may anastomose in one or more planes. The chief feature of the order supposedly is the occurrence of a unique process of cell division, called segregative division. The protoplast cleaves into multinucleate portions of varying size, which round up, secrete a wall, and expand until they are in complete mutual contact. In some genera the daughter vesicles expand outward and upward, forming branches. The enormous size of the primary vesicle of certain species of *Valonia* has made this genus a favorite subject of biophysical studies, especially in the fields of permeability and solute absorption. In the few species of Siphonocladales in which sexual reproduction has been observed, the thalli are diploid gametophytes, with meiosis occurring during the production of biflagellate isogametes. The failure to observe segregative division in more than a few members of the Siphonocladales and the paucity of information on life histories obscure the border between this order and the Cladophorales. Some authors combine the two orders.

Bryopsidales. Many green algae (almost entirely marine) have thalli composed of nonseptate multinucleate filaments or tubes. These forms, which constitute the order Bryopsidales, are abundant and diverse in most tropical waters. *Halimeda*, which has a calcified thallus, is a major contributor to the buildup of coral reefs and infilling of atoll lagoons. *See* BRYOPSIDALES; HALIMEDA.

Dasycladales. In another group of tropical, essentially marine green algae, the thalli are noncellular, but unlike those in the Bryopsidales, they exhibit radial symmetry, with whorls of loosely arranged or densely aggregated branches arising from the primary axis. These forms constitute the order Dasycladales. Most members have calcified thalli, and there is a rich fossil record extending at least to the Cambrian and including more than a hundred extinct genera. Some genera have a unique life history, involving the fragmentation of an enormous primary nucleus to form numerous small secondary nuclei, which migrate into gametangia. The gametangia cleave into uninucleate units, which develop into operculate cysts containing biflagellate isogametes. Meiosis is believed to occur prior to or during fragmentation of the primary nucleus. *Acetabularia* (mermaid's wine glass) is frequently used in morphogenetic experimentation, since its large and readily accessible nucleus is quite amenable to manipulation. *See* DASYCLADALES.

Charophycean phyletic line. This phyletic group has motile cells that are scaly or naked, asymmetrical, devoid of eyespots, and with two laterally or subapically arising flagella, their basal bodies associated with a broad band of microtubules (multilayered structure) and usually an additional, smaller microtubular root. The distal ends of the basal bodies show counterclockwise rotation. Cytokinesis is effected either by centripetal growth of a furrow that impinges on microtubules of the persistent spindle or by means of a cell plate in the presence of a phragmoplast, the microtubules of which proliferate from the persistent spindle. This group includes the Chlorokybales, Klebsormidiales, Zygnematales, and Coleochaetales, as well as the charophytes (treated here as the class Charophyceae).

Chlorokybales. Packet-forming algae with charophycean ultrastructure have been segregated from the Chlorosarcinales as the order Chlorokybales. So far only one genus, *Chlorokybus*, is known.

Klebsormidiales. Rudimentary filaments that dissociate easily and lack holdfast cells are formed by members of the order Klebsormidiales. Plasmodesmata are absent. Each cell contains a nucleus and a parietal laminate chloroplast. Zoospores, which lack eyespots, are formed singly in unspecialized cells. Two families (Klebsormidiaceae and Elakatotrichaceae) with at least seven genera are tentatively recognized.

Zygnematales. The order Zygnematales is a large and well-known group of fresh-water and subaerial green algae exhibiting two somatic types, unicells (desmids) and unbranched uniseriate filaments. The cell wall is composed of inner fibrillar cellulose layers and an outer slippery pectic layer. Plasmodesmata are absent. Each cell has a nucleus and one or more distinctly shaped chloroplasts. The most distinctive feature of the order is sexual reproduction by conjugation of ameboid or passive gametes (hence the alternate name, Conjugales). Flagellate cells are unknown. The zygote secretes a thick wall and undergoes a period of dormancy. Meiosis occurs at some point (variable, depending upon the species) between conjugation and germination.

Members of the Zygnemataceae (especially *Spirogyra* and *Zygnema*) form the slippery skeins common in stagnant water. Mesotaeniaceae, often called saccoderm desmids, are essentially unicellular Zygnemataceae. The Desmidiaceae and Peniaceae together constitute the placoderm desmids. The cells vary in shape, but are always composed of mirror-image semicells often demarcated by a median constriction. The cell wall has pores and is frequently ornamented. Placoderm desmids are abundant in slightly acidic fresh water. *See* ZYGNEMATALES.

Coleochaetales. Members of the order Coleochaetales are aquatic epiphytes or endophytes. The thallus consists of cells that are clustered or united into filaments. In *Coleochaete*, the only genus in the family Coleochaetaceae, the thallus may be filamentous, pseudoparenchymatous, or rudimentarily parenchymatous. Most or all cells bear one or more cytoplasmic setae, each with a basal gelatinous sheath. Each cell contains a nucleus and usually a parietal laminate chloroplast with a pyrenoid traversed by one or more thylakoids. Asexual reproduction is by scaly biflagellate zoospores, lacking eyespots and formed within ordinary cells. Sexual reproduction is oogamous, with minute colorless antherozoids being formed singly in conical antheridia, and eggs singly in spherical or flask-shaped oogonia. Fertilization occurs in place. The zygote enlarges greatly and secretes a thick wall. Neighboring branches produce a pseudoparenchymatous or parenchymatous sheath around the zygote, suggesting the possibility of the transfer of substances. After a period of dormancy (winter), the zygote germinates meiotically to form 8–32 biflagellate zoospores. Although exhibiting features conducive to the development of a terrestrial life, *Coleochaete* probably is not in the direct line of evolution of any extant embryophyte.

Pleurastrophycean phyletic line. Pleurastrophyceae have motile cells that are thecate or naked and more or less flattened. The flagella have a cruciate microtubular root system showing counterclockwise rotation of the basal bodies. The ancestral flagellate is believed to resemble *Tetraselmis*, a marine genus usually aligned with Prasinophyceae. The Pleurastrophyceae, while apparently a distinct group, is small. The few genera that have been assigned to it have been taken from several orders, including Chlorococcales, Chlorosarcinales, and Chaetophorales.

Micromonadophyceae. In addition to the four phyletic lines described here, each of which includes monads as well as multicellular algae, there is a residual group of primitive green flagellates for which the name Micromonadophyceae has been proposed. These monads are scaly or secondarily naked and have one to four flagella arising from an apical pit or lateral depression. The interzonal mitotic spindle persists during cytokinesis. This group corresponds to the class Prasinophyceae in the present classification.

The ultrastructural classification described in this article could be incorporated in the traditional scheme with minimal difficulty by according the rank of subclass to each major group, a treatment in keeping with the presumed monophyletic origin of green algae. For the sake of consistency, however, Prasinophyceae and Charophyceae are treated elsewhere in this work as separate classes. *See* ALGAE; CHAROPHYCEAE; PRASINOPHYCEAE.

Paul C. Silva; Richard L. Moe

Bibliography. H. C. Bold and M. J. Wynne, *Introduction to the Algae: Structure and Reproduction*, 1985; P. Bourrelly, *Les Algues d'Eau Douce . . .*, tome 1: *Les Algues Vertes*, 1972; K. R. Mattox and K. D. Stewart, Classification of the green algae: A concept based on comparative cytology, in D. E. G. Irvine and D. M. John (eds.), *Systematics of the Green Algae*, 1984; S. P. Parker (ed.), *Synopsis and Classification of Living Organisms*, 2 vols., 1982.

Chlorophycota

A division of the plant kingdom (also known as Chlorophyta or Chlorophycophyta) comprising all algae that have chlorophyll *a* and *b* except the Euglenophyceae, and that in all other respects are so different as to suggest a separate origin of their photosynthetic pigments. Three classes, Charophyceae (charophytes), Chlorophyceae (green algae), and Prasinophyceae, are recognized. *See* ALGAE; CHAROPHYCEAE; CHLOROPHYCEAE; PRASINOPHYCEAE.

Paul C. Silva; Richard L. Moe

Chlorophyll

The generic name for the intensely colored green pigments which are the photoreceptors of light energy in photosynthesis. These pigments belong to the tetrapyrrole family of organic compounds, which includes the open-chain bile pigments and the large ring compounds. The large-ring compounds are composed of porphyrins, dihydro- and tetrahydroporphyrins, as well as their derivatives chelated with metals such as iron (Fe) or magnesium (Mg). *See* PHOTOSYNTHESIS.

Occurrence. Five closely related chlorophyll groups, designated *a* through *e*, occur in higher plants and algae. The principal chlorophyll (Chl) group is the Chl *a*, found in all oxygen-evolving organisms; photosynthetic bacteria, which do not evolve O_2, contain instead bacteriochlorophyll (Bchl). Higher plants and green algae contain Chl *b*, the ratio of Chl *b* to Chl *a* being 1:3. Chlorophyll *c* (of two or more types) is present in diatoms and brown algae. Chlorophyll *d*, isolated from marine red algae, has not been shown to be present in the living cell in large enough quantities to be observed in the absorption spectrum of these algae. Chlorophyll *e* has been isolated from cultures of two algae, *Tribonema bombycinum* and *Vaucheria hamata*. Small amounts of biochemical precursors of chlorophyll, that is, protochlorophyll and magnesium protoporphyrin, are also found in all green plants. In certain algae, open-chain metal-free tetrapyrrole pigments called phycobilins are found attached to proteins. Purple photosynthetic bacteria contain bacteriochlorophylls *a* or *b*, and the green bacteria contain, in addition to Bchl *a*, chlorobium chlorophyll. *See* ALGAE; BACTERIA; BACTERIAL PHYSIOLOGY AND METABOLISM; PHYCOBILIN.

In higher plants the chlorophylls and the above-mentioned pigments are contained in lipoprotein bodies, the plastids. At the highest magnification of the light microscope one may just see tiny grana in the plastids of higher plants. A granum is made up of 10–100 disks and resembles a stack of pennies. The disk, or thylakoid, is the basic photosynthetic apparatus and may be thought of as a flattened balloon; its continuous membrane is 5–8 nanometers thick and it encloses a space about 8 nm wide. The outer portion of the membrane differs in structure and function from the inner portion, but the exact molecular organization is not known. Within the membrane are the chlorophylls, which constitute 10% of the dry weight of the membrane, and two kinds of photosynthetic units, photosystem I and II. A photosynthetic unit is made up of a packet of enzymes together with several hundred chlorophyll molecules and carotenoid molecules. *See* CAROTENOID; CELL PLASTIDS.

Photosystem II absorbs shorter wavelengths of light than I and is thought to contain a high ratio of chlorophyll *b* to *a*. Photosystem I absorbs longer wavelengths and contains a high ratio of *a* to *b*. The major difference lies in the presence of certain long-wavelength-absorbing forms of Chl *a* in photosystem I.

Functions. Chlorophyll molecules have three functions. (1) They serve as antennae to absorb light quanta. (2) They transmit this energy from one chlorophyll to another over distances usually of 1.5–2 nm by a process of resonance transfer, so that the energy finally comes to reside in special chlorophyll molecules, P700 or P680, in the receptor site of photosystem I or II. (3) This chlorophyll molecule, in close association with enzymes, undergoes a chemical oxidation; that is, an electron of high potential is ejected from the molecule; this electron can then be made to do chemical work, that is, reduction of another compound. In this way the energy of light quanta is converted into chemical energy.

Light-induced oxidation of reaction-center chlorophyll molecules leads to photobleaching, which is detected spectroscopically by an absorbance decrease. In addition, loss of an electron transforms the reaction-center molecule, for example, from P700 to P700$^+$; the latter species is detected by the electron spin resonance technique, as this species has an unpaired electron. A similar species, P890$^+$, is produced in photosynthetic bacteria.

Chemistry. The chlorophylls are cyclic tetrapyrroles in which four 5-membered pyrrole rings join to form a giant macrocycle. Chlorophylls are members of the porphyrin family, which plays important roles in respiratory pigments, electron transport carriers, and oxidative enzymes. *See* PORPHYRIN.

It now appears that the chlorophyll *a* group may be made up of several chemically distinct Chl *a* species. The structure of monovinyl chlorophyll *a*, the most abundant of the Chl *a* species, is shown in **Fig. 1**. This molecule has now been synthesized in the laboratory. The characteristic features of chlorophyll *a* are that it is a magnesium chelate of a dihydroporphyrin with a cyclopentanone ring (V) and is esterified with phytol. Chlorophyll *a* consists of four 5-membered rings (I–IV) which form part of the large macro ring. Rings I–III are pyrrolic nuclei, whereas ring IV is a dihydropyrrolic nucleus, that is, containing two extra hydrogen atoms. In the 6 position is an oxidized propionic acid group esterified with methanol which forms the cyclopentanone ring V. This ring contains the carbonyl oxygen at position 9 and the enolizable hydrogen atom at 10. The small rings are linked together through methine bridges

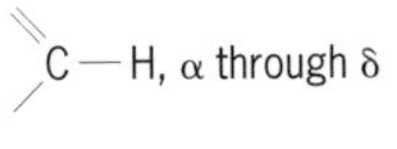

$$\text{C} - \text{H}, \ \alpha \text{ through } \delta$$

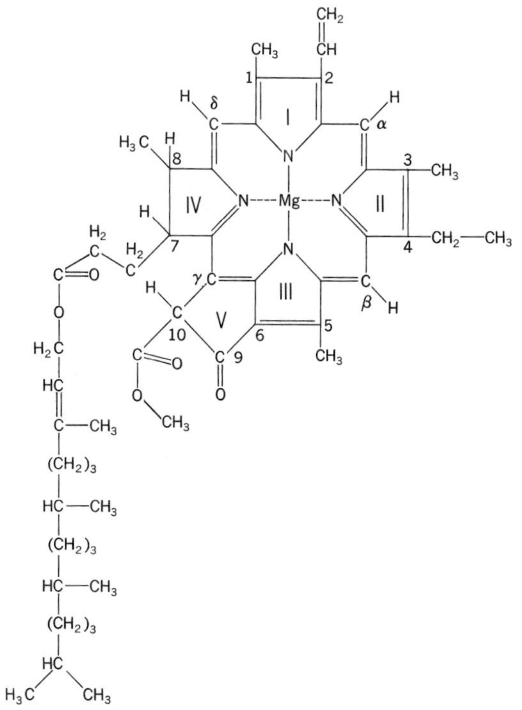

Fig. 1. Structure of chlorophyll *a* ($C_{55}H_{72}O_5N_4Mg$).

to form the large inner 16-membered ring of carbon and nitrogen atoms attached to each other through alternating single and double bonds. The alicyclic 5-membered ring V, which contains a keto C=O group at position 9, is unique to chlorophylls.

The other chemical species of Chl *a* may differ from the monovinyl Chl *a*, shown in Fig. 1, by the replacement of the ethyl group (at position 4), by a vinyl group, or by having alcohols other than phytol at position 7.

The parent compound, porphyrin or porphin, consists of four pyrrole nuclei and is red, as in protoporphyrin. When a dihydropyrrole replaces one pyrrolic nucleus, the resulting compound is a dihydroporphyrin or chlorin and is green, as in chlorophyll. When two dihydropyrroles replace two pyrrolic nuclei, as in bacteriochlorophyll, the main absorption is in the far-red.

To get the structure of the following compounds, substitute in the chlorophyll *a* the atoms or groups in the position noted.

Chlorophyll *b*: in position 3, substitute —CHO for —CH$_3$.

Chlorophyll *c*: in position 7, substitute acrylic acid

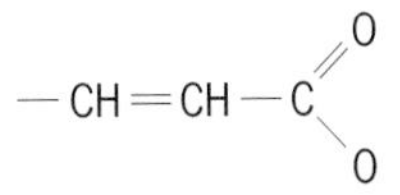

$$-\text{CH}=\text{CH}-\text{C}\overset{\displaystyle \text{O}}{\underset{\displaystyle \text{O}}{\Big\backslash}}$$

and replace H atoms at position 7 and 8 by a double bond.

Chlorophyll *d*: in position 2, substitute —CHO.

Bacteriochlorophyll *a*: this is a tetrahydropor-

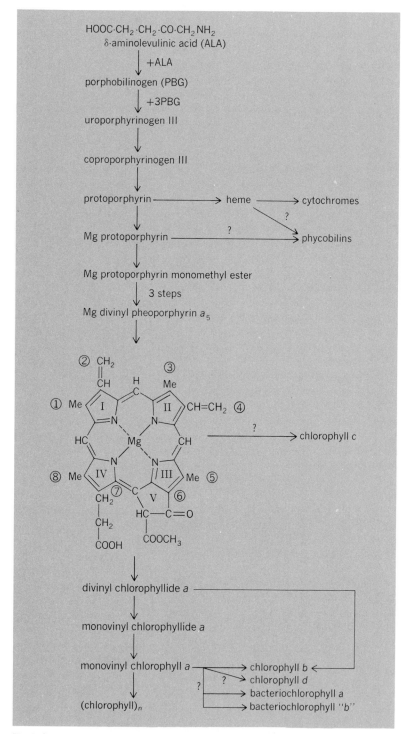

Fig. 2. One of the major biosynthetic routes for monovinyl *a* and some related compounds.

phyrin (extra hydrogen atoms on both rings II and IV); remove double bond between 3 and 4 and add an H atom at 3 and 4; at 2, substitute —CO·CH$_3$. In Bchl *a* from *Rhodospirillum rubrum*: substitute in position 7 geranyl-geraniol, C$_{20}$H$_{33}$OH, a relatively unsaturated alcohol, in place of phytol.

Chlorobium chlorophyll 660: 2 is —CHOHCH$_3$; at 10, remove COOCH$_3$ and replace by H; at 7, farnesol (C$_{15}$) replaces phytol (C$_{20}$); at β or γ, a CH$_3$ or C$_2$H$_5$ replaces H.

Pheophytin: remove Mg and add two H

atoms on two of the N atoms.

Pheophorbide: remove Mg and phytol.

Protochlorophyll: in positions 7 and 8, remove H atoms and add a double bond.

Vinyl pheoporphyrin a_5: in positions 7 and 8, remove H atoms and add a double bond; also remove Mg and phytol.

Coordination number of Mg. Spectroscopic investigations suggest that the coordination properties of the central Mg atom are very important in understanding the association of one Chl molecule with other molecules (another Chl molecule, solvent molecules, proteins, and so forth). The coordination number of Mg in Chl or Bchl is larger than 4. One or both of the axial positions are occupied by an electron donor (nucleophile) group. In solutions of Chl, this could be a molecule of a polar solvent (Lewis base), for example, diethyl ether or pyridine. In a nonpolar solvent, another Chl molecule can act as electron donor through the keto C=O group of ring V. In bifunctional solvents like dioxane or pyrazine (pyr), aggregates may be formed (for example, Chl-pyr-Chl-pyr-Chl-pyr-Chl...). Thus, due to the greater-than-4 coordination number of Mg, Chl can exist as a monomer, dimer, trimer, tetramer, and as an aggregate of *n* number of Chl molecules. The monomers absorb red light maximally in the 660–670-nm region, whereas the aggregates absorb red light in the 680–700-nm region. On the other hand, the Chl·H$_2$O·Chl adduct is suggested to absorb at as far as 740 nm; the (Chl·H$_2$O)$_2$ adduct may absorb around 700 nm.

The relationship of the above-mentioned forms of Chl in solutions to different spectral forms of Chl in living cells remains speculative. It is indeed possible that different spectral forms in living cells represent the different aggregation states of Chl. However, care must be exercised in extrapolating solution data to a living-cell situation. There could be several reasons—not mutually exclusive—for shifts in absorption bands; these include complexing with different proteins, different microenvironment (solvents), exciton splitting of absorption bands, chemical modification of the macrocycle as in the aforementioned Chl *a* chemical species, and, possibly, different binding and orientation of the chromophore on the membrane. Much more research is needed to understand the exact physicochemical nature of the different spectral forms of Chl (Bchl) in living cells.

Reaction-center chlorophylls. Green plants have two types of reaction-center chlorophylls (the number after P represents their long-wavelength absorption bands): P680 for pigment system II and P700 for pigment system I. Photosynthetic bacteria may have only one reaction center. However, its far-red absorption maximum is different in different bacteria: P840 in green bacteria, P870 in *Rhodospirillum rubrum*, P890 in *Chromatium*, and P985 in *Rhodopseudomonas viridis*. As noted, upon illumination with strong light, these reaction-center molecules undergo oxidation, and an electron spin resonance signal is observed due to the production of P$^+$ (unpaired electron on the reaction-center molecule). This signal has a half-bandwidth of 7 gauss for P700 and about 9 gauss for P870. (These signals are tremendously narrowed when deuterated samples are used.) Moreover, these signals are much narrower than for Chl (or Bchl) monomers in solution, and have been interpreted as arising from dimers. The possibility exists that these signals are either from (B)Chl·H$_2$O·(B)Chl or (B)Chl·(H$_2$O)$_2$·(B)Chl. The dimer nature of P890 is well established, but P700, in its oxidized form, is most likely a chemically modified form of Chl, for example, an enol. It is not yet clear why P680 and P700 are different. Perhaps association with other pigments and proteins, or chemical differences, may explain the difference.

Biosynthesis. The two major pigments of protoplasm, green chlorophyll and red heme, are synthesized from ALA (δ-aminolevulinic acid) along the same biosynthetic pathway to protoporphyrin, as shown by tracer and enzyme studies. ALA is converted in a series of enzymic steps, identical in plants and animals, to protoporphyrin. Here the pathway branches to form a series of porphyrins chelated with iron, as heme and related cytochrome pigments; and a series of porphyrins chelated with magnesium which are precursors of chlorophyll (**Fig. 2**). See HEMOGLOBIN.

In plants, ALA is probably not formed from succinyl CoA and glycine by plastids. However, ALA has been shown to be converted by isolated plastids to Chl a. Therefore, all of the enzymes from ALA to chlorophyll are contained in the chloroplasts. In higher plants, light and a special protein (holochrome) are required to convert protochlorophyllide to chlorophyllide; in this photoreaction two H atoms are added to the 7 and 8 positions of ring IV. In a few plants, such as *Chlorella*, this reduction can occur enzymically and chloroplasts can be formed in the dark if glucose is supplied as a source of energy. Among additional factors required for chlorophyll formation are Fe, Mg, adenosinetriphosphate (ATP), nicotinamide adenine dinucleotide (NAD), and O$_2$. Concomitant with chlorophyll synthesis, the disk, or thylakoid, membranes are also synthesized. The possible origins of the phycobilin pigments, chlorophylls b, c, and d, and the bacteriochlorophylls are shown in Fig. 2.

Isolation and separation. Isolation of chlorophylls a and b consists in extracting leaves, such as nettles or spinach, which have little chlorophyllase, with 80% acetone containing some Na$_2$CO$_3$ or dilute NH$_3$ (to neutralize plant acids). Petroleum ether is added and the acetone is washed out with water; then methanol is used to remove carotenoids. Finally, the petroleum ether is washed free of acetone and methanol with water, which causes the chlorophyll to precipitate. It is filtered into a layer of talc, and the talc is washed with petroleum ether to remove carotenes. The chlorophyll is then extracted with ether. The ether is dried with anhydrous Na$_2$SO$_4$, and chlorophyll is then precipitated. Separation of the chlorophylls, dissolved in a small volume of pyridine and diluted with petroleum ether, is achieved by chromatography on powdered sucrose or polyethylene columns. The column is developed with 0.5% isopropanol in pentane. "Crystalline" chlorophyll a is obtained by addition of water to an ether solution of chlorophyll which is slowly evaporated in vacuum. See CHROMATOGRAPHY.

S. Granick; Govindjee

Fluorescence. Chlorophylls, the important protagonists of plant and bacterial photosynthesis, reemit a fraction of the light energy they absorb as fluorescence. Irrespective of the wavelength of the absorbed light, the emitted fluorescence is always on the long-wavelength side of the lowest energy absorption band, in the red or infrared region of the spectrum.

The fluorescent properties of a particular chlorophyll are functions of the structure of the molecule and its immediate environment. Thus, the fluorescence spectrum of chlorophyll in the living plant is always shifted to longer wavelengths (peak at 685 nm) relative to the fluorescence spectrum of a solution of the same pigment (peak at approximately 660 nm). This redshift is characteristic of chlorophyll–protein complexes.

Even in dilute solutions the capacity of chlorophyll to fluoresce depends on the nature of the solvent. In solvents which can combine with the central Mg atom of chlorophyll by donating a pair of electrons to it, chlorophyll is fluorescent. In solvents which lack this property, chlorophyll is dimeric or polymeric and nonfluorescent at room temperature. The aggregates are formed by combining the carbonyl group of one molecule with the Mg atom of the other.

The most widespread chlorophylls in nature, chlorophylls (Chl) a and b, fluoresce with a quantum efficiency of 0.33 and 0.16, respectively, in dilute solution in ethyl ether. In the living cell the quantum efficiency drops to 0.03 for Chl a and to zero for Chl b. This is due to the property of Chl b which transfers all its excitation energy to Chl a, which in turn channels most of its excitation to photosynthesis, allowing only a small fraction to escape as fluorescence.

An excited Chl a molecule in ethyl ether has a mean lifetime of five-billionths of a second, whereas in the living plant this is reduced to one- to two-billionths of a second. A long-lived excited state of Chl a (the triplet state) has been observed under special conditions, such as illumination of concentrated solutions in dry hydrocarbon solvents at low temperatures. Under these conditions Chl a emits phosphorescence at a spectral maximum of 750 nm. Weak phosphorescence of Chl a has been recently observed in living cells. However, when a chemical reductant (such as dithionite) is added to chromatophores prepared from photosynthetic bacteria, triplets of Bchl can be observed by electron spin resonance techniques.

Govindjee; George Papageorgiou

Bibliography. M. B. Bazzaz and R. G. Brereton, *Fed. Europ. Biochem. Soc. Lett.*, 138:104, 1982;

M. B. Bazzaz, C. V. Bradley, and R. G. Brereton, *Tetrahedron Lett.*, 23:1211, 1982; Govindjee (ed.), *Bioenergetics of Photosynthesis*, 1975; Govindjee (ed.), *Photosynthesis*, vol. 1, 1982; Govindjee and R. Govindjee, Primary events in photosynthesis, *Sci. Amer.*, 231:68, 1974; E. Rabinowitch, *Photosynthesis and Related Processes*, 1956; E. Rabinowitch and Govindjee, *Photosynthesis*, 1969; C. A. Rebeiz, H. Daniell, and J. R. Mattheis, *4th Symposium on Biotechnology in Energy Production and Conservation*, 1982; D. R. Sanadi and L. Packer (eds.), *Current Topics in Bioenergetics*, 1973; L. P. Vernon and G. R. Sealy (eds.), *The Chlorophylls*, 1966.

Choanoflagellida

An order of the class Zoomastigophorea, superclass Mastigophora, subphylum Sarcomastigophora, in the phylum Protozoa. They are principally small, single-celled or colonial, structurally simple, colorless flagellates distinguished by having the anterior end surrounded by a thin protoplasmic collar, within which is an ingestive area for particulate matter, for example, bacteria. A single flagellum arises from the center of this collar. The genus *Monosiga* is single, sometimes with a stalk, sometimes free in the plankton. *Desmarella* is a linear colony (see **illus.**), and *Astrosiga* and *Sphaerosiga* are colonies radiating from a center. *Proterospongia* cells arise in a common jelly, the zooids being organically connected. *Diploeca* lives in an attached lorica. *Stelexomonas* and *Aulomonas* inhabit tubular loricae. *Diplosiga* has a double colony. *Sportelloeca* and *Pleurasiga* live in complex loricae. *See* PROTOZOA; SARCOMASTIGOPHORA; ZOOMASTIGOPHOREA.

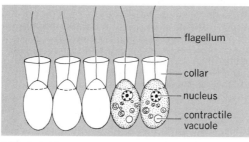

A linear colony of the choanoflagellate, *Desmarella moniliformis*.

The botanist P. Bourrelly puts these organisms in the order Monosigales. It is generally agreed, however, that the group shows relationships to the sponges. They are widespread in fresh and salt water and are common in inshore waters.

James B. Lackey

Bibliography. B. M. Honigberg et al., A revised classification of the phylum Protozoa, *J. Protozool.*, 11(1):7–20, 1964; R. E. Norris, Neustonic marine Craspedomonadales (choanoflagellates) from Washington and California, *J. Protozool.*, 12(4):589–602, 1965; S. P. Parker (ed.), *Synopsis and Classification of Living Organisms*, 2 vols., 1982.

Choke (electricity)

An inductor that is used to prevent electric signals and energy from being transmitted along undesired paths or into inappropriate parts of an electric circuit or system. Power-supply chokes prevent alternating-current components, inherent to a power supply, from entering the electronic equipment. Radio-frequency chokes (RFCs) prevent radio-frequency signals from entering audio-frequency circuits. The printed circuit boards used in virtually all electronic equipment such as computers, television sets, and high-fidelity audio systems typically have one or more chokes. The purposes of these chokes are the (1) attenuation of spurious signals generated in the equipment itself so that these signals will not be transmitted to other parts of the circuit or beyond the overall system to other electronic devices; (2) prevention of undesired signals or electrical noise generated in other parts of the system from adversely affecting circuit performance; and (3) prevention of ripple from the power supply from degrading system behavior. Waveguide chokes keep microwave energy from being transmitted to the wrong part of a waveguide system. *See* ELECTRICAL NOISE; ELECTRONIC POWER SUPPLY; PRINTED CIRCUIT; RIPPLE VOLTAGE; WAVEGUIDE.

In its simplest form, a choke or an inductor is a coil of wire (usually copper) wound around and insulated from a core, which may or may not be ferromagnetic. Ferromagnetic cores tend to increase inductance, reduce physical size, and reduce electromagnetic coupling between circuit elements, and they may increase power loss and resultant heating. Such cores often lead to nonlinear or swinging chokes, commonly found in power supplies, where the nonlinearity may be an advantage. The basic principle of operation derives from the fact that it is impossible to change instantaneously the energy stored in a magnetic field. The various configurations are designed to control the magnetic field in an appropriate manner. The graphic symbols used to represent the various types of chokes or inductors in electric circuits are shown in the **illustration**. *See* MAGNETIC FIELD; MAGNETIC MATERIALS.

Chokes come in a wide variety of inductance ranges, power-handling capabilities, fabrication

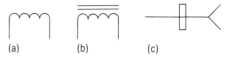

Graphic symbols for chokes or inductors in electric circuits. (*a*) Choke or inductor with air core. (*b*) Choke or inductor with magnetic core. (*c*) Waveguide choke.

technologies, and intended applications. In many cases they are specially designed for a particular situation. Chokes are available in inductance sizes ranging from a fraction of a microhenry to tens of henrys or higher. The frequency range of intended use is a major consideration. *See* INDUCTANCE; INDUCTOR.

Edwin C. Jones, Jr.

Bibliography. D. G. Fink and D. Christiansen (eds.), *Electronics Engineers Handbook*, 3d ed., 1989; Institute of Electrical and Electronics Engineers, *Graphic Symbols for Electrical and Electronics Diagrams*, IEEE 315–1975, 1975; W. T. McLyman, *Transformer and Inductor Design Handbook*, 2d ed., 1988.

Choked flow

Fluid flow through a restricted area whose rate reaches a maximum when the fluid velocity reaches the sonic velocity at some point along the flow path. The phenomenon of choking exists only in compressible flow and can occur in several flow situations. *See* COMPRESSIBLE FLOW.

Flow through varying-area duct. Choked flow can occur through a convergent flow area or nozzle attached to a huge reservoir (**illus.** *a*). Flow exits the reservoir through the nozzle if the back pressure is less than the reservoir pressure. In all cases considered here, the reservoir pressure is assumed to be a constant. When the back pressure is decreased slightly below the reservoir pressure, a signal from beyond the nozzle exit is transmitted at sonic speed to the reservoir. The reservoir responds by sending fluid through the nozzle. Further, the maximum velocity of the fluid exists at the nozzle throat where the area is smallest.

When the back pressure is further decreased, fluid exits the reservoir more rapidly. Eventually, however, the velocity at the throat reaches the sonic velocity. Then the fluid velocity at the throat is sonic, and the velocity of the signal is also sonic. Therefore, further decreases in back pressure are not sensed by the reservoir, and correspondingly will not induce any greater flow to exit the reservoir. The nozzle is thus said to be choked, and the mass flow of fluid is a maximum. Thus, choking in a converging nozzle occurs when the Mach number (defined as the ratio of fluid velocity to the sonic velocity) at the throat equals 1. *See* MACH NUMBER; NOZZLE; SOUND; SUPERSONIC DIFFUSER.

Flow with friction. Choked flow can also occur through a long constant-area duct attached to a reservoir (illus. *b*). As before, flow from the reservoir through this duct is induced when the back pressure is decreased below the reservoir pressure, and a signal is transmitted through the duct to the reservoir.

As fluid flows through the duct, friction between the fluid and the duct wall reduces the pressure acting on the fluid. As pressure is reduced, other

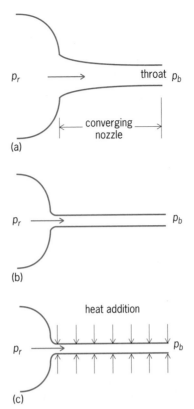

Examples of choked flow. (*a*) Flow through a varying-area duct or nozzle. (*b*) Flow through a constant-area duct. (*c*) Frictionless flow through a constant-area duct with heat addition. P_b = back pressure; P_r = reservoir pressure.

fluid properties are affected, such as sonic velocity, density, and temperature. The maximum Mach number occurs at the nozzle exit. As the back pressure is decreased, flow exits more rapidly through the duct, but eventually the Mach number at the exit reaches 1. Any further decrease in back pressure is not sensed by the reservoir and so causes no increase in flow rate. Thus, when the Mach number is 1 at the duct exit, the flow is said to be choked, and the mass flow rate through the duct is a maximum.

Frictionless flow with heat addition. A reservoir with a constant-area duct attached may also be considered in the case that the flow through the duct is assumed to be frictionless, but heat is added to the system along the duct wall (illus. *c*). As fluid receives energy in the form of heat, fluid properties again change. The maximum Mach number occurs at the duct exit. As the total amount of heat increases, the Mach number at the duct exit increases, and eventually reaches 1. At this point, the mass flow through the duct is a maximum and the flow is said to be choked. Any further heat addition results in a decrease in mass flow through the duct. *See* FLUID FLOW; GAS DYNAMICS.

William S. Janna

Bibliography. J. D. Anderson, Jr., *Modern Compressible Flow: With Historical Perspective*, 2d ed., 1990; W. S. Janna, *Introduction to Fluid Mechanics,*

3d ed., 1993; J. E. A. John, *Gas Dynamics*, 2d ed., 1984.

Cholera

A disease caused by infection and colonization of the small intestine by the bacterium *Vibrio cholerae*. The primary symptom is severe diarrhea. It has been estimated that severe diarrhea accounts for 5 million deaths each year, primarily among children, in developing countries, and cholera is responsible for a significant portion. With proper treatment, however, cholera is fatal to fewer than 1% of the infected individuals. The high death rate in developing countries is primarily due to lack of proper facilities to care for the diseased. *See* DIARRHEA.

Vibrio cholerae is a facultatively anaerobic, gram-negative, curved rod-shaped bacterium. It has a simple flagellum and is rapidly motile. Most epidemics are the result of waterborne organisms. Attack rates of *V. cholerae* are 10 times as high for children as for adults in endemic areas, but in areas of fresh cholera outbreaks as many adults as children are affected. This may be due to a buildup of natural immunity to the bacteria in those exposed since childhood.

The diarrhea that is symptomatic of cholera is related to production of a bacterial toxin that attaches to epithelial cells of the small intestine of infected individuals. This toxin is made of two parts; one part is responsible for binding to cells, while the other is responsible for the toxic action. The toxic portion causes cellular levels of adenate cyclase to rise. As a result, the concentration of cyclic adenine monophosphate (cyclic AMP) increases in intestinal cells which excrete fluid. The fluid is isotonic; that is, it contains the same concentration of electrolytes as the cells, so that the body loses both water and electrolytes.

There is a 12–48-h incubation period between the ingestion of *V. cholerae* and manifestation of symptoms. The disease runs its course in 2–7 days. With prompt fluid and electrolyte replacement, either by intravenous injection or oral preparations, recovery is quite rapid and death is very rare. Untreated attacks, however, can result in death from electrolyte loss and dehydration.

Immunization provides minimal protection, and lasts for a maximum of about 60 days. Though there is active research in this field, which is based on the detailed knowledge of the molecular action of the toxin, no long-term protection is yet available. The best way to prevent cholera is to avoid infection. With proper hygiene this can be easily accomplished by a traveler. For inhabitants of developing countries, however, prevention requires permanently clean water supplies and sanitary disposal of sewage.   Daniel Kaizer

Bibliography. E. Braunwald et al. (eds.), *Harrison's Principles of Internal Medicine*, 11th ed., 1987; J. Holmgren, Actions of cholera toxin and the prevention and treatment of cholera, *Nature*, 292:413–417, 1981; M. M. Levine et al., Present status of cholera vaccines, *Biochem. Soc. Transact.*, 12(2):200–202, 1984.

Cholesterol

A cyclic hydrocarbon alcohol commonly classified as a lipid because it is insoluble in water but soluble in a number of organic solvents. It is the major sterol in all vertebrate cells and the most common sterol of eukaryotes, but it is absent from most prokaryotes. In vertebrates, the highest concentration of cholesterol is in the myelin sheath that surrounds nerves and in the plasma membrane that surrounds all cells. In these membranes, the cholesterol-to-phospholipid ratio is generally between 0.5 and 1. Insects and most invertebrates cannot synthesize cholesterol; therefore they must rely on dietary cholesterol for use in their membranes and as a precursor of ecdysone, a molting hormone required during growth and development. *See* ECDYSONE; LIPID.

Free and esterified forms. Cholesterol can exist either in the free (unesterified) form, in which the hydroxyl group (OH) is free (see structure below),

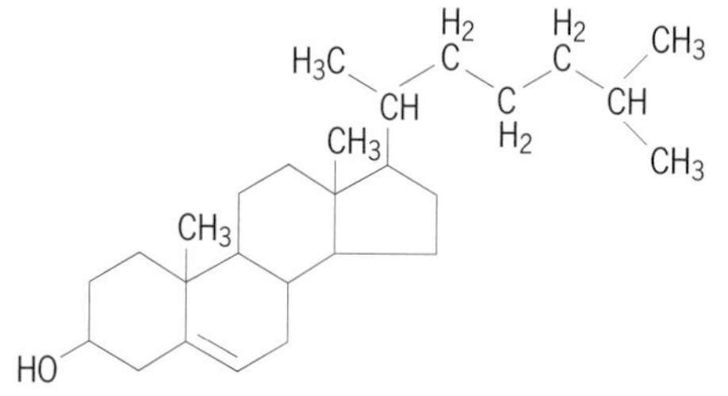

or in the esterified form, in which a fatty acid is bound to the hydroxyl group of cholesterol by an ester bond. The free form is found in membranes with the hydroxyl group at the membrane-aqueous environment interphase and the hydrocarbon tail buried in the membrane. Cholesteryl esters are normally found in lipid droplets either within the cells of steroidogenic tissues, where it can be converted to free cholesterol and then to steroid hormones, or in the middle of spherical lipid-protein complexes, called lipoproteins, that are found in blood. *See* CELL MEMBRANES.

In human blood plasma, free cholesterol and ester cholesterol are present in a ratio of approximately 1:3, and the total content ranges 150–250 mg per 100 ml of plasma in normal persons. The principal acid esterified is linoleic; oleic acid is the next in abundance, followed by some saturated fatty acids, chiefly palmitic, and some esters of arachidonic acid. The total amount of cholesterol in the plasma can vary with age, diet, exercise, or following the use of hypolipidemic drugs. The human red blood cell, in contrast, contains about 100 mg of cholesterol per 100 ml of packed cells, and this is virtually all free cholesterol. The cholesterol of nervous tissue is chiefly free cholesterol, which in adults does not exchange with other cholesterol stores of the body. The adrenal cortex and the gonads are rich in ester cholesterol; this is in dynamic exchange with plasma cholesterol.

Function. Cholesterol, together with phospholipids and proteins, is important in the maintenance of normal cellular membrane fluidity. At physiological temperatures, the cholesterol molecule interacts with the fatty acids of the membrane phospholipids and causes increased packing of the lipid molecules and hence a reduction of membrane fluidity. Thus, all vertebrate cells require cholesterol in their membranes in order for the cell to function normally. Cholesterol is also important as a precursor for a number of other essential compounds, including steroid hormones, bile acids, and vitamin D.

Synthesis and metabolism. Cellular cholesterol is obtained both from the diet, following its absorption in the intestine, and from synthesis within all cells of the body. Foods that are particularly high in cholesterol include eggs, red meat, and organs such as liver and brain. About 40–50% of the dietary cholesterol is absorbed from the intestine per day. In contrast, plant sterols are very poorly absorbed.

Cholesterol synthesis occurs in all vertebrate cells but is highest in the liver, intestine, and skin, and in the brain at the time of myelination. Two carbon precursors are converted to lanosterol, a 30-carbon intermediate, which is then rapidly degraded to the 27-carbon cholesterol. This whole process requires over 40 enzymes and is highly regulated by the cholesterol status of the cell. The regulatory enzyme in the biosynthetic process is 3-hydroxy-3-methylglutaryl coenzyme A reductase (HMG-CoA reductase). This is the target enzyme for a number of drugs that are used clinically to reduce blood cholesterol levels. These drugs work in part by binding to and inactivating HMG-CoA reductase, the rate-limiting enzyme in the biosynthetic pathway, with a resulting decrease in the rate of cholesterol synthesis. *See* COENZYME; ENZYME.

Steroid hormones are derived from cholesterol and are required for the control of many different cell functions. The conversion of cholesterol to the steroid hormones cortisol and aldosterone occurs in the adrenal glands, and conversion of cholesterol to estrogen, testosterone, or progesterone occurs in the testes, ovary, or placenta. *See* HORMONE; STEROID.

Cholesterol is also a precursor of the bile acids that are synthesized in the liver. Bile acids, together with unesterified cholesterol, phospholipids, and other minor constituents, are stored in the gallbladder. In response to the presence of food in the intestine, the gallbladder contracts and the liver is stimulated to produce more bile that is eventually secreted into the small intestine, where the bile acids emulsify (solubilize) dietary fats. This emulsification process allows the intestine to subsequently absorb fat from the diet. Most of the bile acids and cholesterol that were originally produced in the gallbladder are reabsorbed from the intestine and are returned to the liver. This process is called enterohepatic circulation. However, about 5% of this cholesterol and bile acid is retained and is excreted in the feces. This pathway represents the major route by which vertebrates excrete cholesterol from the body. *See* GALLBLADDER.

Cholesterol is also the precursor of vitamin D, a hormone that is required for control of normal calcium metabolism. One of the initial steps occurs in the skin in response to ultraviolet light; however, further modifications are required in the liver and kidney in order to form the biologically active vitamin D. *See* CALCIUM METABOLISM; LIPID METABOLISM; VITAMIN D.

Plasma lipoproteins and atherosclerosis. Cholesterol and cholesteryl esters are essentially insoluble in water. In order to transport these compounds around the body in the blood, the liver and intestine produce various lipid-protein complexes, called lipoproteins, which serve to solubilize the otherwise insoluble lipids. Lipoproteins are large, complex mixtures of cholesterol, cholesteryl esters, phospholipids, triglycerides (fats), and various proteins. The major lipoproteins include chylomicrons, very low density lipoprotein (VLDL), low-density lipoprotein (LDL), and high-density lipoprotein (HDL).

People are usually required to fast for approximately 14 h before they give blood for cholesterol analysis. The plasma (blood from which all the cells have been removed) contains VLDL, LDL, and HDL. Chylomicrons are normally absent from the plasma of fasted individuals because the chylomicrons are rapidly metabolized and removed from the blood during the fast. All the cholesterol in the plasma is contained in lipoproteins.

Total plasma cholesterol levels of less than 200 mg/100 ml are considered desirable. Values of 200–239 or greater than 239 mg per 100 ml are considered, respectively, borderline high or high risk values, indicating the potential for a heart attack. High levels of low-density lipoprotein in the plasma are associated with increased risk of atherosclerosis, heart attack, and death. Atherosclerosis, "hardening of the arteries," involves deposition of cholesterol and other lipids in the artery wall. These deposits, together with the increased division of cells already present in the artery wall, can result in narrowing of the artery. The final blockage often results from a blood clot. When this occurs in one of the arteries of the heart, the muscle cells may die, perhaps resulting in a heart attack. *See* ARTERIOSCLEROSIS.

Low-density lipoprotein is normally removed from the blood after binding to its receptor, a protein found on the surface of cells. This receptor mediates the internalization of the LDL, and its cholesteryl ester core, into cells, especially liver cells. Certain individuals have a mutation in the LDL receptor gene and protein which results in a defect in the normal removal of LDL from the blood. As a consequence, the blood LDL levels increase, putting these individuals at increased risk for atherosclerosis and heart attacks. This genetic disorder, called familial hypercholesterolemia, is found in about 0.2% of the United States population.

Diets low in cholesterol and saturated fats often result in a reduction in total plasma and LDL cholesterol levels. Such changes in blood cholesterol levels are thought to be beneficial and to reduce the incidence of heart attacks.

High-density lipoproteins also transport cholesterol in the plasma. However, in contrast to LDL, HDL levels are inversely correlated with the risk of heart attacks. High-density lipoprotein levels greater than 40 mg/100 ml, between 35 and 40 mg/100 ml or less than 35 mg/100 ml are considered desirable, borderline high risk, or high risk respectively. Interestingly, premenopausal women generally have higher HDL cholesterol levels than men and a decreased incidence of heart attacks.

Gallstones. Gallstones are found in the gallbladder or in the bile duct. The stones can be as large as the egg of a small bird. Many of these stones contain significant amounts of cholesterol that initially came out of solution and formed crystals in the gallbladder. *See* GALLBLADDER DISORDERS.   Peter A. Edwards

Bibliography. N. B. Myant, *Cholesterol Metabolism, LDL, and the LDL Receptor*, 1990; M. Sugano and A. C. Beynen (eds.), *Dietary Proteins, Cholesterol Metabolism and Atherosclerosis*, 1990; P. L. Yeagle (ed.), *The Biology of Cholesterol*, 1988.

Choline

A compound used by the animal organism as a precursor of acetylcholine and as a source of methyl groups. It is a strongly basic hygroscopic substance with the formula below. It is questionable whether

$$(CH_3)_3 \equiv N^+ - CH_2 - CH_2OH$$

this very necessary metabolite should be considered a vitamin. Choline is determined microbiologically by using a mutant of the mold *Neurospora crassa*.

A choline deficiency has been produced in a number of animal species. The degree of deficiency achieved depends on the amount of choline precursors, particularly methyl donors such as methionine, present in the diet. Choline deficiency is associated with fatty livers, poor growth, and renal lesions. It is a lipotropic agent. There is no direct evidence of disease in humans due to choline deficiency, although there have been suggestions that some of the liver, kidney, or pancreas pathology seen in various nutritional deficiency states may be related to choline insufficiency. Choline is found in acetylcholine, which is necessary for nerve impulse propagation, and in phospholipids.

There is no evidence that choline acts as a coenzyme. Choline functions as a donor of methyl groups to quaternary nitrogen and sulfonium compounds.

Human beings eat 50–600 mg of choline per day, but only excrete 2–4 mg. Consequently, conventional load tests are of no value in studying choline requirements, and no knowledge of human requirements exists. *See* ACETYLCHOLINE; VITAMIN.

Stanley N. Gershoff

Choline, trimethyl-β-hydroxyethylammonium hydroxide, is a quaternary compound which is made by the reaction of trimethylamine and ethylene oxide in either an aqueous or an alcoholic solvent. If choline salts are desired, the reaction can be carried out with the corresponding trimethylamine salt, or the base can be neutralized with the corresponding acid. The salts in common use are choline chloride, choline bitartrate, choline dihydrogen citrate, and tricholine citrate.

Choline salts are sold as liquids and solids. The liquids, such as a 65% solution of tricholine citrate, are prepared by the aqueous quaternization procedure, decolorized with charcoal, and then evaporated to the desired strength. The solid types are prepared in either aqueous or alcoholic media and are crystallized by cooling concentrated solutions.   Richard J. Turner

Chondrichthyes

A class of vertebrates comprising the cartilaginous, jawed fishes. The Chondrichythyes have traditionally included the subclasses Elasmobranchii (sharks, skates, and rays) and Holocephali (ratfishes).

A classification scheme for the Chondrichthyes follows; for detailed information see separate articles on each group listed.

Class Chondrichthyes
 Subclass Elasmobranchii
  Order: Cladoselachii
   Pleurocanthodii
   Selachii
   Batoidea
 Subclass Holocephali
  Order Chimaeriformes

A group of Devonian armored fishes, the Placodermi, has usually been regarded as ancestral to the Chondrichthyes, but this derivation is not certain. Another group of primitive jawed fishes called acanthodians, which are considered by many as ancestral to the higher bony fishes, exhibit certain primitive elasmobranch-like features. In any case it is probable that the elasmobranchs and ratfishes arose independently of each other sometime during the Silurian or Early Devonian. *See* ACANTHODII; PLACODERMI.

Characteristics. The most distinctive feature shared by the elasmobranchs and ratfishes is the absence of true bone. In both groups the endoskeleton is cartilaginous; in some cases it may be extensively calcified. This cartilaginous endoskeleton probably represents a retained ancestral condition rather than a derived one. Because even calcified cartilage is rarely preserved, the fossil record of the Chondrichthyes is represented mainly by teeth and spines, with only occasional associated skeletons. *See* SKELETAL SYSTEM.

Other characteristics of the Chondrichthyes include placoid scales, clasper organs on the pelvic fins of males for internal fertilization, a urea-retention mechanism, and the absence of an air (swim) bladder. Both groups have primarily always been marine predators, although they have repeatedly invaded fresh water throughout their long history. The elasmobranchs have probably always fed as they do today, on other fishes as well as on soft- and hard-bodied invertebrates. The ratfishes have most likely concentrated on invertebrates, although modern forms occasionally also feed on smaller fishes. *See* COPULATORY ORGAN; SCALE (ZOOLOGY); SWIM BLADDER.

Elasmobranchs. Sharks are typically fusiform fishes, with well-developed dentitions, one or two dorsal fins, and a heterocercal tail (**illus.** *a*). They inhabit all the oceans, ranging from tropical to arctic zones. A few genera occur in deep water, and a few others have become acclimated to fresh water. There are about 250 living genera.

The other elasmobranchs, skates and rays, have a depressed body, greatly enlarged pectoral fins, and a much reduced tail (illus. *b*). Most of them are bottom feeders that inhabit coastal regions. The devil rays, which are pelagic plankton feeders, are an exception. The skates and rays include about 340 genera and are found throughout the world.

Chimaeroids. The chimaeroids are distinguished from the elasmobranchs by the presence of a skin flap covering the gill openings (in elasmobranchs the gill openings reach the surface separately), a rounded head profile, a small mouth, a nearly diphycercal tail, and sharp-edged tooth plates (illus. *c*). Most species live at considerable depths, although some occur regularly in coastal waters, others only during the winter months. The chimaeroids are a small group of three families containing only 28 genera, but they are widely distributed in the Atlantic and Pacific oceans.

Bobb Schaeffer

Bibliography. H. C. Bigelow and W. C. Schroeder, *Fishes of the Western North Atlantic*, 2 pts., 1948, 1953; E. S. Herald, *Living Fishes of the World*, 1961; S. P. Parker (ed.), *Synopsis and Classification of Living Organisms*, 2 vols., 1982; A. S. Romer, *Vertebrate Paleontology*, 3d ed., 1966; B. Schaeffer, Comments on elasmobranch evolution, in P. W. Gilbert et al. (eds.), *Sharks, Skates, and Rays*, 1967.

Chondrostei

The most archaic of three organizational levels (infraclasses) of the subclass Actinopterygii (rayfin fishes). Classification of this group follows; all are fossil orders except Polypteriformes and Acipenseriformes.

Order: Palaeonisciformes
Haplolepiformes
Dorypteriformes
Tarrasiiformes
Ptycholepiformes
Luganoiiformes
Redfieldiformes
Perlediformes
Peltopleuriformes
Phanerorhynchiformes
Saurichthyiformes
Polypteriformes
Acipenseriformes

Phylogeny and systematics. Chondrosteans of the order Palaeonisciformes appeared first in the Lower Devonian, and by Middle Devonian were abundant contemporaries of the early crossopterygians and lungfishes, representative of the other two subclasses of bony fishes. Palaeonisciformes were diversified and abundant in fresh and inshore marine waters of the late Paleozoic and the Triassic. In the Jurassic they gave rise to the forebears of the sturgeons (order Acipenseriformes), which persist in the modern fauna as highly specialized and in some ways degenerate chondrosteans. Some authors have confusingly applied the name Chondrostei exclusively to this order. Even more like the palaeonisciforms than the sturgeons are the surviving African fishes of the older Polypteriformes, which are known only since the Eocene but are probably much older. *See* ACIPENSERIFORMES; CROSSOPTERYGII; DIPNOI; PALAEONISCI-

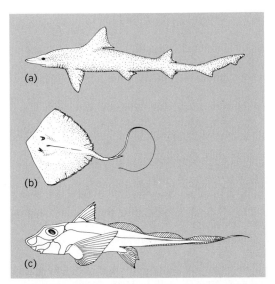

Modern representative chondrichthyans. (*a*) Shark. (*b*) Skate. (*c*) Chimaeroid. (*After A. S. Romer, Vertebrate Paleontology, University of Chicago Press, 1962*)

FORMES; POLYPTERIFORMES.

By the Upper Permian the oldest holosteans had evolved, a notable structural advance over the Chondrostei. Perhaps several parallel modifications from the palaeonisciforms contributed to the Holostei, which dominated the bony fish fauna for most of the Mesozoic, before itself giving way in the Cretaceous to the superiority of the Teleostei, which still prevail.

Structure. Primitive chondrosteans were mostly small- or moderate-sized fishes with a heavy armor of rhomboidal, enameled scales. The heterocercal tail was preceded on the midline, above and below, by series of enlarged fulcral scales. There was usually a spiracle behind the eye. The head was heavily plated and relatively inflexible, with the maxilla firmly bound to the cheek bones. The hyomandibular suspension from the skull was very oblique; the angle of the jaw was far back; and the coronoid process of the mandible was little developed. Thus, the space available for jaw muscles was restricted. Feeding was accomplished largely by biting and gulping, aided by simple conical teeth. As a result of the above structural features, movements of the orobranchial chamber were restrained, and respiratory and feeding movements were limited. In higher actinopterygians these restrictions are overcome by progressive evolutionary improvements. *See* ACTINOPTERYGII; HOLOSTEI; SCALE (ZOOLOGY); TELEOSTEI.   Reeve M. Bailey

Bibliography. E. Jarvik, *Basic Structure and Evolution of Vertebrates*, 2 vols., 1981; A. S. Romer, *Vertebrate Paleontology*, 3d ed., 1966.

Chonotrichida

An order of the Holotrichia. This is a small group of curious, vase-shaped ciliates, commonly found as ecotocommensals on marine crustaceans. They attach to their hosts by a short, secreted stalk,

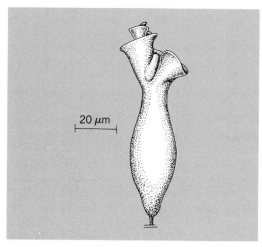

Spirochona, an example of a chonotrichid.

and their bodies are practically devoid of ciliature. *Spirochona* (see **illus.**) is a common example of this order. *See* CILIOPHORA; HOLOTRICHIA; PROTOZOA.   John O. Corliss

Chopping

The act of interrupting an electric current, beam of light, or beam of infrared radiation at regular intervals. This can be accomplished mechanically by rotating a vibrating mirror in the path of the beam to deflect it away from its intended source at regular intervals. A current can be chopped with an electromagnetic vibrator having contacts on its moving armature. A current can also be chopped electronically by passing it through a multivibrator or other switching circuit. Chopping is generally used to change a direct-current signal into an alternating-current signal that can more readily be amplified. Control systems for guided missiles make extensive use of chopping. *See* MULTIVIBRATOR; VIBRATOR.

Chopping has been increasingly used inside analog integrated circuits. Solid-state switches and capacitors are used to chop operational amplifiers, greatly improving their offset voltages. Chopping is also used in analog large-scale-integrated switched-capacitor filters as a means for reducing their undesirable $1/f$ (inverse-frequency) noise. *See* AMPLIFIER; INTEGRATED CIRCUITS; OPERATIONAL AMPLIFIER; SWITCHED CAPACITOR.   Eric J. Swanson

Bibliography. R. L. Geiger, P. E. Allen, and N. R. Strader, *VLSI Design Techniques for Analog and Digital Circuits*, 1990.

Chordata

The highest phylum in the animal kingdom, which includes the lancelets or amphioxi (Cephalochordata), the tunicates (Urochordata), the acorn worms and pterobranchs (Hemichordata), and the vertebrates (Craniata) comprising the lampreys, sharks and rays, bony fish, amphibians, reptiles, birds, and mammals. Members of the first three groups, the lower chordates, are small and strictly marine. The vertebrates are free-living; the aquatic ones are primitively fresh-water types with marine groups being advanced; and the members include animals of small and medium size, as well as the largest of all animals. *See* CEPHALOCHORDATA; HEMICHORDATA; TUNICATA; VERTEBRATA.

Characteristics. The typical chordate characteristics are the notochord, the dorsal hollow nerve cord, the pharyngeal slits, and a postanal tail.

Notochord. The notochord appears in the embryo as a slender, flexible rod filled with gelatinous cells and surrounded by a tough fibrous sheath, and contains, at least in some forms, transverse striated muscle fibers; it lies above the primitive gut. In lower chordates and the early groups of vertebrates, the notochord persists as the axial support (antitelescoping device) for the body throughout life, but it is surrounded and gradually replaced by segmental vertebrae in the higher fish.

Nerve cord. The dorsal hollow nerve cord grows from a specialized band of ectoderm along the middorsal surface of the embryo by a folding together of two parallel ridges. The anterior end enlarges slightly in larval tunicates and somewhat more in lancelets, but enlarges greatly in the vertebrates to form the brain. Vertebral evolution is characterized by continual enlargement of the brain. In the crainates or vertebrates, the brain is enclosed in the braincase or cranium, and the spinal cord is enclosed by the neural arches. *See* NERVOUS SYSTEM (VERTEBRATE).

Pharyngeal slits. Paired slits develop as outpocketings of the posterior end of the mouth on the sides of the embryonic pharynx, a part of the digestive system, and are retained in all aquatic chordates. Pharyngeal slits originated as adaptations for filter feeding but soon became the primary respiratory organ, as blood vessels line the fine filaments on the margins of each slit. Water passing over the gills serves for gas exchange in addition to the original filter-feeding function, which was soon lost in the vertebrates. Internal gills were lost with the origin of tetrapods; larval and some adult amphibians possess external gills which are different structures. The pharyngeal slits in embryonic tetrapods close early in life, with the pharyngeal pouches becoming the site for development of glands, for example, the thyroid and the tonsils. *See* RESPIRATORY SYSTEM.

Postanal tail. The chordate tail is part of the skeletal support, muscles, and nervous system which continues posteriad to the anus or posterior opening of the digestive system. It is a feature not found in any other animal group and serves to increase the force available to the animal for locomotion.

Affinities. Much controversy still exists about the limits, origin, and affinities of the chordates. For example, opinions differ considerably as to whether the Hemichordata and the Pogonophora are related to the Chordata, although there is no question that the Hemichordata are closely related and part of the pharyngeal-slit filter-feeding radiation; the Hemichordata are here considered as members of the phylum Chordata, not as a separate phylum. Almost all workers agree that the Echinodermata are the closest relatives of the Chordata because of evidence ranging from embryonic development to biochemical resemblances, but there is dispute over which group is the more primitive. A peculiar, possibly echinoderm, fossil group, the Calcichordata, has been suggested as a close relative and possibly an intermediate group between the chordates and the echinoderms. *See* ECHINODERMATA; POGONOPHORA.

Evolutionary origins. The Chordata apparently arose from a group of elongated, segmented worms with three sets of body musculature (longitudinal, circular, and transverse) and transverse septa. The first change was the evolution of a segmented coelom, associated with improved locomotion; these animals possessed a hydrostatic skeleton and moved with a sinusoidal or peristaltic locomotion. The first chordate feature to appear was the notochord, which provided a stronger skeleton and permitted the reduction of the transverse and circular muscles. A notochord resulted in a fixed body length and the loss of peristaltic locomotion. The dorsal longitudinal muscles enlarged, and with this modification came the evolution of the dorsal hollow nerve cord, dorsal because of closer proximity with the major mass of musculature. Having a notochord for support rather than a hydrostatic skeleton permitted the appearance of pharyngeal slits through the lateral walls of the anterior parts of the body, which served for increased filter feeding and subsequently for respiration. The presence of the notochord also permitted the appearance of a postanal tail and increased force for locomotion.

The earliest chordate with all of the typical features of the phylum probably looked much like the present-day lancelet or amphioxus (Cephalochordata), which burrows in shifting sands and needs considerable force to move through the heavy sand. Presumably all other chordates developed from this ancestral type, with their differing characteristics evolving because of conditions of their differing habitats. Tunicates (Urochordata) are sessile organisms that live on hard substrate, and have lost most chordate features in the metamorphosed adult and have evolved a tough tunic. Their larvae retained the ancestral chordate features which are necessary for a mobile larval stage. The features were retained in several tunicate groups in which the adult stage was lost and the organisms were permanent free-swimming pelagic forms. Although zoologists have argued in the past that vertebrates may have evolved from such permanent tunicate larval forms, it is far more likely that the vertebrates descended directly from an amphioxuslike form. Another group, the acorn worms, burrowed in muddy bottoms and lived in tubes with two openings. They lost most of the notochord, the dorsal nerve cord, and segmentation of the coelom, but still possess pharyngeal slits. They evolved an anterior bulblike proboscis as a locomotory organ, and a collar around the body behind the mouth to prevent forward flow of water expelled from the pharyngeal slits. A new larval form similar to that found in echinoderms also evolved. The pterobranchs evolved from the acorn worms. They are sessile and live on hard substrate; therefore, a protective tube with only one opening evolved. Filter feeding via pharyngeal slits no longer worked, and the collar evolved into a pair of feeding tentacles. It is argued that the Echinodermata evolved from a pterobranchlike ancestor, acquiring a five-part symmetry. Thus, chordates would be primitive relative to the echinoderms. The final group to evolve was the Vertebrata, which left the oceans to invade fresh waters. They retained the full set of chordate features but had to evolve several additional ones. Size and swimming ability increased in order to swim upstream against the currents. Many features, including an upturned (heterocercal) tail and flattened ventral surface, modified in connection with this change. The problem of water balance, because of an increased inward flow of water across the body surface, was solved when the kidneys, with the nephron as the basic unit, evolved to rid the body of excess water. Finally, dermal bone evolved as armored protection against predators. Embryological development of the nerve cord also changed with the appearance of the neural crest, a unique vertebrate feature which is involved in the development of bony scales, teeth, gill bars, pigment cells, and several parts of the nervous system.

Fossil record. There are no chordate remains known from Cambrian rock strata, in which animal fossils first became common; fossil tunicates, hemichordates, and lancelets are also unknown, as these earliest chordates were soft-bodied and highly unlikely to fossilize. The earliest known vertebrates were the fish of the Ordovician Period, when bone first appeared; thereafter, vertebrates are common in the fossil records. Agnathan fish appeared in the Ordovician, and the earliest gnathostomes in the Silurian. The Devonian was a time of vast vertebrate radiation, with the sharks and all major subgroups of bony fish and of amphibians (slightly later) appearing. Reptiles originated in the Carboniferous and radiated broadly throughout the Mesozoic Era. The first bird, *Archaeopteryx,* comes from the Jurassic, as do the archaic animals. *See* AVES; CARBONIFEROUS; MESOZOIC; ORDOVICIAN; REPTILIA; SILURIAN.

Environmental adaptations. The chordates are a radiation of filter-feeding animals based on the pharyngeal slits; the diversity of body types from sand-dwelling lancelets, mud-burrowing acorn worms, and sessile tunicates to eellike larvae of the lamprey depends largely upon the nature of the substrate. As vertebrates became larger, filter feeding was abandoned for active feeding on macrofood. The earliest vertebrates evolved in fresh water and were bottom dwellers with poor swimming abilities. A hard, dermal, bony armor evolved as protection in slow-swimming early fish against larger, active arthropod predators. Better-swimming groups evolved, with gradual reduction of the heavy dermal scales and the origin of paired fins and girdles. Jaws and teeth evolved for feeding on larger food particles. Although fish respire via their gills, lungs appeared early in vertebrate history as an accessory respiratory organ using air in stagnant waters. Kidneys serve as a water balance organ. The major line of fish evolution remained in fresh waters, with side branches becoming marine secondarily a number of

times. Tetrapods left the waters because of feeding and other advantages on the land, not because they were forced out of the water by drought conditions. Gills were lost and lungs took over respiration completely, fins became limbs, and kidneys took over nitrogenous waste elimination. Reproduction was still aquatic, with eggs and larval life in the waters. Reptiles were the first true terrestrial tetrapods with water-impervious skin, specialized extraembryonic membranes, and a dry-shelled egg. Mammals and birds acquired a high, constant body temperature and also an insulated body covering of hair or feathers, respectively.

The lower chordates are minor elements in the seas, whereas the vertebrates are dominant members of the fauna in the fresh and marine waters and on land because of their larger size, diversity, and activity. Chordate species number only about 40,000 (17,000 fishes, 2200 amphibians, 6000 reptiles, 9000 birds, and 4400 mammals) of the estimated more than 1,000,000 species of living animals. *See* ANIMAL KINGDOM.   Walter J. Bock

Bibliography. M. J. Benton, *Vertebrate Paleontology,* 1990; R. L. Carroll, *Vertebrate Paleontology and Evolution,* 1988.

Chorion

The outermost of the several extraembryonic membranes in amniotes (reptiles, birds, and mammals) enclosing the embryo and all of its other membranes. The chorion, or serosa, is composed of an outer layer of ectodermal cells and an inner layer of mesodermal cells, collectively the somatopleure. Both layers are continuous with the corresponding tissue of the embryo. The chorion arises in conjunction with the amnion, another membrane that forms the outer limb of the somatopleure which folds up over the embryo in reptiles, birds, and some mammals. The chorion is separated from the amnion and yolk sac by a fluid-filled space, the extraembryonic coelom, or body cavity. In those mammals in which the amnion forms by a process of cavitation in a mass of cells, instead of by folding, the chorion forms directly from the trophoblastic capsule, the extraembryonic ectoderm, which becomes gradually underlain by extraembryonic mesoderm.

In reptiles and birds the chorion fuses with another extraembryonic membrane, the allantois, to form the chorioallantois, which lies directly below the shell membranes. An extensive system of blood vessels develops in the mesoderm of this compound membrane which serves as the primary respiratory and excretory organ for gaseous interchanges. In all mammals above the marsupials, the chorion develops special fingerlike processes (chorionic villi) extending outward from its surface. To a varying degree in different species of mammals, the villous regions of the chorion come into more or less intimate contact with the uterine mucosa, or uterine lining, of the mother, thereby forming the various placental types. *See* ALLANTOIS; AMNIOTA; FETAL MEMBRANE; GERM LAYERS.

Nelson T. Spratt, Jr.

Choristida

An order of sponges of the class Demospongiae, subclass Tetractinomorpha, in which at least some of the megascleres are tetraxons, usually triaenes. Monaxonid spicules may occur as well. Triaenes characteristically lie in tracts which radiate from the center of the sponge to the periphery, with the three shorter rays lying just below or in the cortex. In some cases the shorter rays extend beyond the dermis to form a spicule flush with the protuding monaxonis spicules (**Fig. 1**). Microsclere types are chiefly aster, streptasters, or sigmas. A well-developed cortex comprising an outer gelatinous layer and an inner fibrous layer is often present. *Geodia* has a stony cortex formed of numerous, closely packed, spiny, spherical microscleres.

Many choristidan sponges are radially symmetrical; spherical or ellipsoidal shapes are common. Others are encrusting or massive; very few form branching colonies. Some species have basal tufts or mats of long, thin spicules which anchor them in mud or sand on the sea bottom (**Fig. 2**).

Choristidans are common in tidal regions and shallow waters of all seas, and some species

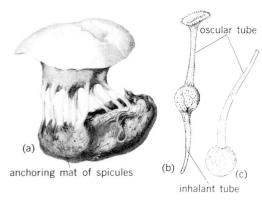

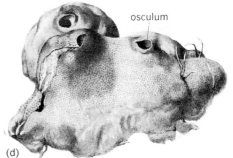

Fig. 2. Choristidans. (*a*) *Thenea wyvilli*, with basal mat of spicules. (*b*) *Disyringa dissimilis*, with separate oscular and inhalant tubes. (*c*) *Tribrachion schmidti*, with oscular tube. (*d*) *Geodia gibberosa*.

extend down to depths of at least 11,550 ft (3500 m). Sponges with spicules similar to those of existing choristidans are scattered through the fossil record from Carboniferous times onward. *See* DEMOSPONGIAE.

Willard D. Hartman

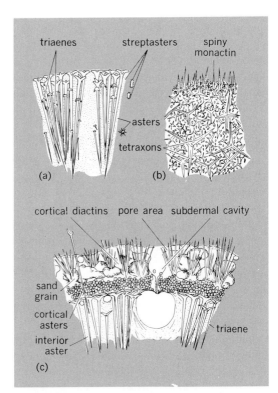

Fig. 1. Choristidans. (*a*) *Ancorina* section, showing spicule arrangement. (*b*) *Pachastrella* section, showing spicule arrangement. (*c*) *Geodia* section, showing skeletal arrangement.

Chromadorida

An order of nematodes in which the amphid manifestation is variable but within superfamilies some constancy is apparent. The various amphids are reniform, transverse elongate loops, simple spirals, or multiple spirals not seen in any other orders or subclasses. The cephalic sensilla are in one or two whorls at the extreme anterior. In all taxa the cuticle shows some form of ornamentation, usually punctations that are apparent whether the cuticle is smooth or annulated. When developed, the stoma is primarily esophastome and is usually armed with a dorsal tooth, jaws, or protrusible rugae. The corpus of the esophagus is cylindrical; the isthmus is not seen; and the postcorpus, in which the heavily cuticularized lumen forms the cresentic valve, is distinctly expanded. The esophagointestinal valve is triradiate or flattened. The females usually have paired reflexed ovaries.

There are four chromadorid superfamilies: Choanolaimoidea, Chromadoroidea, Comesomatoidea, and Cyatholaimoidea. Choanolaimoidea is distinguished by a complex stoma in two parts. The group occupies marine habitats; some species are predaceous, but for many the feeding habits are unknown. Chromadoroidea comprises small to moderate-sized free-living forms that are mainly marine but are also found in fresh water and soil. Known species either are associated with algal substrates or are nonselective deposit feeders in soft-bottom sediments. Comesomatoidea, containing only one family, the Comesomatidae, is found in marine habitats, but the feeding habits are unknown. Cyatholaimoidea is found in marine, terrestrial, and fresh-water environments. *See* NEMATA.

Armand R. Maggenti

Chromatic aberration

The type of error in an optical system in which the formation of a series of colored images occurs, even though only white light enters the system. Chromatic aberrations are caused by the fact that the refraction law determining the path of light through an optical system contains the refractive index n, which is a function of wavelength λ. Thus the image position and the magnification of an optical system are not necessarily the same for all wavelengths, nor are the aberrations the same for all wavelengths.

In this article the chromatic aberrations of a lens system are discussed. For information on other types of aberration *see* ABERRATION (OPTICS); REFRACTION OF WAVES.

Dispersion formula. When the refractive index of glass or other transparent material is plotted as a function of the square of the wavelength, the result is a set of dispersion curves which appear to have an asymptote in the near-ultraviolet region and a straight portion in the near-infrared (up to 1 micrometer). In the glass catalogs the indices are given for selected wavelengths between 0.365 and 1.01 μm, which are the absorption (emission) bands of certain chemical elements. For an extended discussion of dispersion *see* ABSORPTION OF ELECTROMAGNETIC RADIATION; OPTICAL MATERIALS.

For the visible region, the Hartmann formula, Eq. (1), where a and b are constants for a given glass,

$$n = a/(\lambda - b) \qquad (1)$$

has been much used. However, if an attempt is made to apply Eq. (1) to the near-ultraviolet or the near-infrared, it proves to be insufficient. Over this more extended range, n can be given as a function of the wavelength by Eq. (2).

$$n = a + b\lambda^2 + \frac{c}{\lambda^2 - 0.028} + \frac{d}{(\lambda^2 - 0.028)^2} \qquad (2)$$

This formula, in which c and d are additional constants, enables one to compute n for any wavelength if it is given for four. An equivalent formula is shown by Eq. (3), where $a_1(\lambda)$, $a_2(\lambda)$,...

$$n = n_1 a_1(\lambda) + n_2 a_2(\lambda) + n_3 a_3(\lambda) + n_4 a_4(\lambda) \qquad (3)$$

are functions of the form of Eq. (2), which assume

Values of the four universal functions $a(\lambda)$ for various wave lengths				
λ	a_1	a_2	a_3	a_4
1.0140	0.000000	0.000000	0.000000	+1.000000
0.7682	+0.031555	−0.276197	+1.051955	+0.192687
0.6563	0.000000	0.000000	+1.000000	0.000000
0.6438	−0.004774	+0.051075	+0.966511	−0.012813
0.5893	−0.024952	+0.326272	+0.744598	−0.045919
0.5876	−0.025492	+0.336338	+0.735480	−0.046326
0.5461	−0.033080	+0.597795	+0.479049	−0.043764
0.4861	0.000000	+1.000000	0.000000	0.000000
0.4800	+0.009340	+1.036699	−0.052699	+0.006659
0.4358	+0.143980	+1.193553	−0.394569	+0.057036
0.4047	+0.366779	+1.045064	−0.487634	+0.075791
0.3650	+1.000000	0.000000	0.000000	0.000000

for λ_1, λ_2,... the values 1, 0, 0, 0; 0, 1, 0, 0; 0, 0, 1, 0; and 0, 0, 0, 1, respectively. Choosing $\lambda_1 = 0.365 = \lambda^{**}$, $\lambda_2 = 0.4861 = \lambda_F$, $\lambda_3 = 0.6563 = \lambda_C$, $\lambda_4 = 1.014 = \lambda^*$, one finds in the **table** the four universal functions $a(\lambda)$ tabulated for different values of λ. Note that for any wavelength Eq. (4) holds.

$$a_1 + a_2 + a_3 + a_4 = 1 \qquad (4)$$

Instead of giving the indices of a glass for the wavelengths specified, one can specify the glass by the refractive index n_F at one wavelength F, the dispersion $\delta = n_F - n_C$, and the partial dispersions in the ultraviolet and infrared, defined respectively by Eqs. (5). The partial dispersion for an arbitrary

$$P^{**} = \frac{n^{**} - n_F}{n_F - n_C} \qquad P^* = \frac{n_F - n^*}{n_F - n_C} \qquad (5)$$

wavelength λ is then given by Eq. (6).

$$P = P^{**} a_1(\lambda) + a_2(\lambda) + P^* a_4(\lambda) \qquad (6)$$

In the literature the Abbe number, defined by Eq. (7), where n_D is the mean index for the D lines

$$\nu = (n_D - 1)/(n_F - n_C) \qquad (7)$$

of sodium, is frequently used to designate optical glass.

In **Fig. 1**, $(n_F - 1)$ is shown plotted against $(n_F - n_C)$ for various optical materials. One sees that in

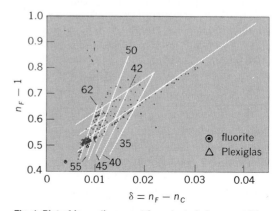

Fig. 1. Plot of $(n_F - 1)$ versus δ for selected glasses and for fluorite and Plexiglas. The numbers on the lines dividing the glasses into groups represent ν values.

this kind of plot glasses of the same type lie on a straight line, while on the ordinary plot of n_D versus ν they lie on hyperbolas.

Color correction. A system of thin lenses in contact is corrected for two wavelengths λ_A and λ_B if the power of the combination is the same for both wavelengths as in Eq. (8), where the K_k's are the

$$\phi_A = \phi_B = \Sigma(n_A - 1)K_k = \Sigma(n_B - 1)K_k \quad (8)$$

difference s between the first and last curvatures of the lenses, and the summation is over all the lenses, each with its particular value of n_A, n_B, and K_k. Two cemented lenses are corrected for wavelengths C and F, for instance, if Eqs. (9) hold.

$$\begin{aligned} \phi_1 + \phi_2 &= \phi \\ \phi_1/\nu_1 + \phi_2/\nu_2 &= \phi_C - \phi_F = 0 \end{aligned} \quad (9)$$

See LENS (OPTICS).

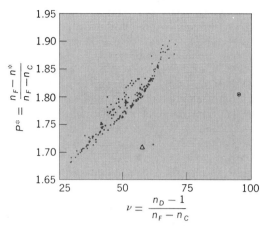

Fig. 3. Plot of P^* versus ν for materials of Fig. 1.

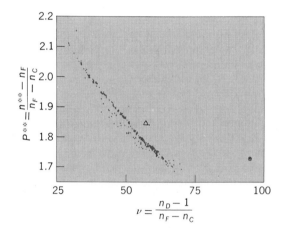

Fig. 2. Plot of P^{**} versus ν for materials of Fig. 1.

The two lenses are also corrected for a third wavelength if and only if, in addition, one has $P_1 = P_2$, where P_1 and P_2 are given by Eq. (6).

A system corrected for three colors is called an apochromat (in microscopy this term traditionally demands freedom from asymmetry in addition). An apochromat for the ultraviolet portion of the spectrum is possible only if the two glasses in **Fig. 2** have the same P^{**} value. For the infrared, the glasses must have the same P^* value (**Fig. 3**). The $\nu - 1$ values for the two glasses should lie as far apart as possible to give low values for the powers.

Three lenses can be corrected for four wavelengths and therefore practically for the whole spectrum if the glasses lie on the straight line on the plot of P^{**} against P^* (**Fig. 4**). Such a system may be called a superachromat.

In lenses with finite thicknesses and distances, there are in gaussian optics two errors to be corrected. One is a longitudinal aberration, which means that the gaussian images do not lie in the same plane, and the other is a lateral aberration, which means that the images in different colors have different magnifications.

In the presence of longitudinal aberration, it is best to balance the lateral aberration so that the apparent sizes of the images as seen from the exit pupil coincide.

A system of two uncorrected lenses, such as a simple ocular, with one finite distance, cannot be corrected for both color errors. Two finite distances are needed to balance both color errors at the same time.

In a general system, all image errors are functions of the wavelength of light. However, in a lens system corrected for color, it is easily possible, with a small adjustment, to balance the correction of the aperture rays (spherical aberration) with respect to color by introducing a small amount of lateral color aberration.

If only two colors can be corrected, the choice of the colors depends on the wavelength sensitivity of the receiving instrument. For visual correction, the values for C and F are frequently brought together. Some optical systems contain filters to permit only a narrow spectral band to pass the instrument. This makes correction for color errors easier.

If light of a large band of wavelengths traverses the instrument, it is frequently desirable to use catadioptric systems, such as the Schmidt camera.

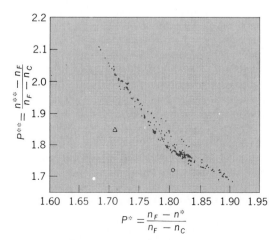

Fig. 4. Plot of P^{**} versus P^* for materials of Fig. 1.

The mirror or mirrors of these systems are used to obtain the necessary power without introducing color errors, and an afocal lens system can be added to correct monochromatic aberrations. *See* SCHMIDT CAMERA.   Max Herzberger

Bibliography. E. U. Condon and H. Odishaw, *Handbook of Physics*, 2d ed., 1967; M. Herzberger, *Modern Geometrical Optics*, 1958, reprint 1978 F. A. Jenkins and H. E. White, *Fundamentals of Optics*, 4th ed., 1976; J. Mayer-Arendt, *Introduction to Classical and Modern Optics*, 2d ed., 1984; Optical Society of America, *Handbook of Optics*, 1978.

Chromatography

A physical method of separation in which the components of a mixture of substances are separated from each other by differences in their distribution between two phases, one of which is stationary (stationary phase) while the other (mobile phase) moves through it in a definite direction. The substances must interact with the stationary phase to be retained and separated by it.

Retention and separation. Retention results from a combination of reversible physical interactions that can be characterized as adsorption at a surface, absorption in an immobilized solvent layer, and electrostatic interactions between ions. When the stationary phase is a porous medium, accessibility to its regions may be restricted and a separation can result from size differences between the sample components. More than one interaction may contribute simultaneously to a separation mechanism. The general requirements are that all interactions must be reversible, and that the two phases can be separated (two immiscible liquids, a gas and a solid, and so forth) in such a way that a distribution of sample components between phases and mass transport by one phase can be established. *See* ABSORPTION; ADSORPTION.

Reversibility of the interactions can be achieved by purely physical means, such as by a change in temperature or by competition; the latter condition is achieved by introducing substances into the mobile phase that have suitable properties to ensure reversibility for the interactions responsible for retention of the sample components. Since this competition with the sample components is itself selective, it provides a general approach to adjusting the outcome of a chromatographic experiment to obtain a desired separation. It is an absolute requirement that a difference in the distribution constants for the sample components in the chromatographic system exist for a separation to be possible.

Methods. A distinction between the principal chromatographic methods can be made in terms of the properties of the mobile phase and configuration of the stationary phase. In gas chromatography the mobile phase is an inert gas, in supercritical fluid chromatography the mobile phase is a fluid (dense gas above its critical pressure and temperature), and in liquid chromatography the mobile phase is a liquid of low viscosity. The stationary phase can be a porous, granular powder with a narrow particle-size distribution packed into a tube (called a column) as a dense homogeneous bed. This configuration is referred to as a packed column and is nearly always used in liquid chromatography and is commonly used in supercritical fluid and gas chromatography. Alternatively, the stationary phase can be distributed as a thin film or layer on the wall of an open tube of capillary dimensions, leaving an open space through the center of the column. This configuration is referred to as an open tubular column (or incorrectly as a capillary column); and it is commonly used in gas chromatography, frequently used in supercritical fluid chromatography, but rarely used in liquid chromatography.

Thin-layer chromatography is a form of liquid chromatography in which the stationary phase is spread as a thin layer over the surface of a glass or plastic supporting structure. The stationary phase must be immobilized on the support by using a binder to impart the desired mechanical strength and stability to the layer. The samples are applied to the layer as spots or bands near the bottom edge of the plate. The separation is achieved by contacting the bottom edge of the plate below the line of samples with the mobile phase, which proceeds to ascend the layer by capillary action. This process is called development and is performed in a chamber, with the lower edge of the layer in contact with the mobile phase and the remaining portion of the layer in contact with solvent vapors from the mobile phase. The chamber may be a simple device such as a covered jar or beaker or a more elaborate device providing control of the mobile-phase velocity and elimination or control of the vapor phase. Thin-layer chromatography is the most popular form of planar chromatography having virtually replaced paper chromatography in laboratory practice. *See* GAS CHROMATOGRAPHY; GEL PERMEATION CHROMATOGRAPHY; LIQUID CHROMATOGRAPHY; SUPERCRITICAL-FLUID CHROMATOGRAPHY.

Uses. Chromatographic methods provide a means of analyzing samples (to determine component identity and relative amount), of isolating significant quantities of purified material for further experimentation or commerce, and for determining fundamental physical properties of either the samples or the mobile or stationary phases (for example, diffusion coefficients, solubilities, or thermodynamic properties). There are virtually no boundaries to the sample types that can be separated. Examples include organic and inorganic compounds in the form of fixed gases, ions, polymers, as well as other species. Applications are found in all areas of technological development, making chromatography one of the most widely used laboratory procedures in chemistry. Depending on intent, chromatography can be applied to trace quantities at the limit of detector response (for example, 10^{-15} g) or to kilogram amounts in preparative separations.

Instrumentation. Modern chromatographic methods are instrumental techniques in which the optimal conditions for the separation are set and varied by electromechanical devices external to the column or layer. Separations are largely automated, with important features of the instrumentation being control of the flow and composition of the mobile phase, introduction of the sample onto the stationary phase, and on-line detection of the separated components. In column chromatography the sample components are detected in the presence of the mobile phase after they have exited the stationary phase. In thin-layer chromatography the sample components are detected in the presence of the stationary phase, resulting in different detection strategies.

Instrument requirements differ by the needs of the method employed. Gas chromatography, for example, employs a mobile phase of constant composition at a few atmospheres of column inlet pressure and variation in the temperature of the column to effect a separation. Liquid chromatography uses a pump to select or vary the composition of the mobile phase with a high column inlet pressure (typically a few hundred atmospheres) and a constant temperature for the separation. These differences in optimized separation conditions result in different equipment configurations for each chromatographic method.

Interpretation. The results of a chromatographic experiment are summarized in a chromatogram (**Fig. 1**), a two-dimensional record of the detector response to the sample components (y axis) plotted against the residence time of the components in column chromatography or migration distance in planar chromatography (x axis). Individual compounds or mixtures of unseparated compounds appear as peaks in the chromatogram. These peaks are ideally symmetrical and occur at positions in the chromatogram that are characteristic of their identity, with a distribution around the mean position (apex of the peak) that is characteristic of the kinetic properties of the chromatographic system. The area inscribed by the peak is proportional to the amount of substance separated in the chromatographic system.

Information readily extracted from the chromatogram includes an indication of sample complexity (the number of observed peaks), qualitative substance identification (determined by peak position), relative composition of the sample (peak dimensions; area or height), and a summary of the kinetic characteristics of the chromatographic system (peak shapes).

There is a synergistic relationship between the peak profiles and the properties of the detector. The detector may have an approximately equal response to all substances, in which case the peak sizes are roughly equal to their relative concentration in the sample; or the detector may have a selective response to some property of the sample components, such as a particular chromophore or the presence of a particular element, in which case the peak sizes have to be interpreted with respect to prior knowledge of the way a particular compound responds to the detector. This is also a useful feature, because the information in the chromatogram can be edited to suit an individual application. For example, the determination of organophosphorus pesticides in environmental samples by gas chromatography can be made with a detector that responds selectively to phosphorus, so that the information contained in the chromatogram is limited to the number of phosphorus-containing compounds in the sample and is easier to interpret than a chromatogram in which all compounds present in the sample are revealed by the detector.

Quality of separation. The object of a chromatographic separation is to obtain a minimum acceptable separation (resolution) between all components of interest in a sample within the shortest possible time. The resolution between two peaks in a chromatogram depends on how well the peak maxima are separated and how wide the two peaks are. This can be expressed numerically, at least for peaks of approximately equal height, by the ratio of the separation of the two peak maxima divided by the average peak widths at their base. When two peaks are separated such that they are just touching at their base, the value calculated for their resolution is 1.5; for difficult-to-separate samples a lower resolution value of 1.0, representing 94% peak separation (6% of the peak areas overlap), is

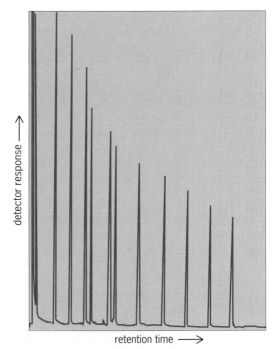

Fig. 1. Typical chromatogram obtained by gas chromatography.

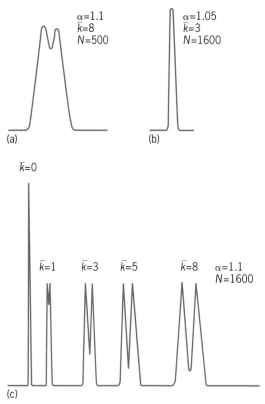

Fig. 2. Observed changes in resolution in a two-component separation for different values of the separation factor, average capacity factor, or number of theoretical plates. (*a*) Viewed vertically, this chromatogram indicates the change in resolution at the same average capacity factor and separation factor values when the number of theoretical plates is varied. (*b*) Viewed vertically, this chromatogram indicates the relationship between resolution and changes in the separation factor with the same number of theoretical plates and average capacity factor value. (*c*) Viewed horizontally, this chromatogram illustrates the change in resolution as the average capacity factor is varied with the same value for the separation factor and number of theoretical plates. (*After P. J. Schoenmakers, Optimization of Chromatographic Selectivity, Elsevier, 1986*)

an adequate goal for identification and quantification based on the characteristic shape of the individual peaks. Resolution is also simply related to the properties of the chromatographic system by the equation below, where R_S is the observed res-

$$R_S = \frac{N^{1/2}}{4}\frac{\alpha - 1}{\alpha}\frac{k_2}{1 + k_2}$$

olution, N is the column efficiency measured as the number of theoretical plates, α is the separation factor (a measure of the relative peak maxima positions; $\alpha = k_2/k_1$), k is the capacity factor (the ratio of the time a substance spends in the stationary and mobile phases), and the subscripts 1 and 2 refer to the peak order (peak 2 emerges from the column after peak 1). To a first approximation, the three terms in the equation can be treated as independent variables and optimized separately to obtain a desired separation in the chromatogram.

Efficiency. The efficiency of a chromatographic system is expressed as a number of theoretical plates. This terminology was adopted from the

application of the theory of fractional distillation columns to gas chromatography when this technique was introduced. The term has remained in use, although any analogies between chromatography and fractional distillation are inappropriate and the concept of a theoretical plate has no physical meaning as presently used in chromatography. From a mathematical perspective, efficiency is a characteristic property of the extent of peak dispersion that occurs during the time a compound is resident in the chromatographic system.

Systems with large numerical values for their efficiency are preferred to optimize resolution. Since the resolution is proportional to $N^{1/2}$, unless N can be increased by large increments only small changes in resolution will be obtained. The numerical value for N is governed by kinetic factors that control peak broadening (N affects only peak widths and not peak positions). The chromatographic system should be optimized to minimize peak broadening, leading to better separations. All things being equal, N could never be too large, and chromatographic systems with intrinsically large values of N are desirable; the corollary is also true—systems that have intrinsically small values of N are undesirable and diminish the prospects of achieving a desired separation unless other factors in the chromatographic system can be adjusted to compensate for poor kinetic performance of the column (**Fig. 2***a*).

The rate theory of peak broadening recognizes three processes that contribute to peak widths beyond purely instrumental contributions: (1) resistance to mass transfer between phases prevents instantaneous equilibrium within the chromatographic system; (2) flow anisotropy in packed beds results from variations in the flow characteristics of the bed in regions of unequal packing density; (3) longitudinal diffusion is the natural consequence of molecular diffusion along the axis of migration of the mobile phase. The purpose of column design is to minimize these contributions to peak broadening so as to achieve the most favorable value of N. The optimum column design is different for each chromatographic method, although it can be easily predicted from the characteristic properties of the chromatographic system and the desired operating conditions (see **table**).

Resistance to mass transfer is often the major cause of peak dispersion in chromatography, and it is related to the absolute magnitude and the relative magnitude of the solute diffusion coefficients in the mobile and stationary phases, and the fact that the relative velocity of the mobile phase is significant on the time scale for these other processes. Resistance to mass transfer, therefore, prevents true equilibrium from being established in the chromatographic system, resulting in additional peak dispersion from that predicted from an equilibrium model.

In gas chromatography the rate of radial diffusion

Approximate values of characteristic parameters in predicting peak broadening			
Parameter	Gas	Supercritical fluid	Liquid
Diffusion coefficient (m^2/s)	10^{-1}	10^{-4} to 10^{-3}	10^{-5}
Density (g/cm^3)	10^{-3}	0.3–0.8	1
Viscosity (poise)	10^{-4}	10^{-4} to 10^{-3}	10^{-2}
Column length (m): packed	1–5	0.1–1.0	0.05–1.0
open tubular	10–100	5–25	
Column diameter (mm), open tubular	0.1–0.7	0.02–0.1	
Average particle diameter (μm)	100–200	3–10	3–10
Column inlet pressure (atm)	<10	<600	<400
Efficiency (N): packed	10^3 to 10^4	10^4 to 8×10^4	5×10^3 to 5×10^4
open tubular	10^4–10^6	10^4–10^5	

defines the useful range of column radii for open tubular columns, and the difference in diffusion processes between the mobile and stationary phases dictates that the liquid stationary-phase film should be thin compared to the dimensions of the column radius. High efficiency in gas chromatography can be obtained with open tubular columns of 0.1–0.5-mm diameter, liquid films of 0.1–2.0-micrometer thickness, and column lengths of 5–100 m or more. Open tubular columns of these dimensions offer little flow resistance, and since gases have low viscosities, long columns are practically feasible and compatible with the low operating pressures favored in modern instrument design. Packed columns provide lower efficiencies, since long columns have undesirably high column inlet pressure requirements and the column packing structure results in peak broadening from flow anisotropy, which is unimportant for open tubular columns.

The mobile-phase diffusion coefficients are less favorable in supercritical fluids and liquids than they are for gases. To minimize the contribution of radial mass transfer to peak broadening, the dimensions of an open tube must be reduced proportionately, resulting in columns with internal diameters of about 0.05–0.10 mm being required for supercritical fluids, and <0.01 mm for liquids. Small column diameters present significant problems in column preparation and instrument design. These are difficult but possible to achieve by using supercritical fluids, but cause exceptional problems in liquid chromatography. Packed columns are invariably used in the practice of liquid chromatography. To minimize flow anisotropy and stationary-phase mass transfer contributions to peak broadening, the columns must have homogeneously packed beds of small particles with a narrow average particle diameter (3–10 μm); the total column length, and therefore the maximum number of theoretical plates, is limited by the viscosity of the mobile phase and the available column operating pressure (see table). These same restrictions apply to supercritical fluids; however, since their characteristic physical properties are more favorable than those for liquids, supercritical fluids are capable of more efficient separations (larger value for N) than can be obtained in liquid chromatography. Thus, it is generally fea-

sible to optimize resolution through varying N only in gas chromatography and in a more limited way in supercritical fluid chromatography. For liquid chromatography the largest practical value for N is used for the separation, and the other parameters in the equation are varied to improve resolution.

Selectivity. The separation factor, α, in the equation is determined by the difference in the distribution coefficients for the two peaks, which is responsible for their relative positions in the chromatogram. Thus, it is the thermodynamic properties of the system that are responsible for the mechanism by which the two components are selectively recognized and therefore retained to different extents. Numerical analysis of the term selectivity reveals its critical importance to obtaining a desired separation. First of all, a separation can result only when α has a value greater than 1.0 ($\alpha=1$ corresponds to the observed resolution $R_s=0$), but only a relatively small increase in the value of α close to its minimum value considerably increases the possibility of obtaining a separation (Fig. 2b).

In gas chromatography the mobile phase behaves essentially as an ideal gas and does not contribute to the selectivity of the system. To vary α, a new stationary phase (column) must be selected or the temperature of the system varied. In liquid chromatography there is a high level of flexibility gained by being able to easily modify the properties of the mobile phase, as well as the possibility of exploiting retention mechanisms that are not available in gas chromatography. These factors account for its widespread use. The properties of the mobile phase are easily varied by changing either the identity or composition of the mobile phase from the wide range of solvents available, or by using additives in the mobile phase to change the properties of individual sample components (for example, buffers, complexing agents, and micelles), as well as by changing the type of stationary phase (column) used for the separation.

In practice, gas chromatography and liquid chromatography should be considered as complementary techniques. Separations by gas chromatography are restricted to thermally stable compounds with significant vapor pressure at the temperatures required for their separation. The upper temperature limit for common stationary phases is in the range 200–400°C (390–750°F). Few compounds with a molecular weight above 1000 have sufficient vapor pressure to be separated in this temperature range, and many low-molecular-weight compounds are known to be labile at temperatures required for their vaporization. The only requirement for separation by liquid chromatography is that the sample have sufficient solubility in an available solvent whose properties are suitable for the separation. This criterion is much easier to meet in general and results in many of the applications for liquid chromatography as being those for which gas chromatography is unsuitable. Included are applications to high-molecular-weight synthetic polymers, biopolymers, ionic compounds, and many thermally labile polar compounds of chemical interest.

Supercritical fluids have solvating properties that are intermediate between those of gases and liquids. Liquids are virtually incompressible under the conditions used in liquid chromatography, so their capacity for intermolecular interactions is fixed. By contrast, fluids are highly compressible, and their density, which is proportional to their solvating capacity, can be varied over a wide range by simply changing the operating pressure or temperature of the column. This feature is unique to supercritical fluid chromatography, and it is the principal method of varying the separation factor α. The most common mobile phase is carbon dioxide, a relatively nonpolar fluid. More polar fluids, such as water, ammonia, or methanol, tend to have unfavorable critical constants or are highly corrosive to columns and instrument components, limiting their use. Mixed mobile phases can be used to vary selectivity, such as carbon dioxide–methanol mixtures, but miscibility problems and high critical constants for the mixed mobile phases may restrict the range of properties available for experimentation. Supercritical fluid chromatography can provide faster and more efficient separations then liquid chromatography, but it is more restricted than liquid chromatography in the choice of mobile phases and retention mechanisms to vary selectivity. However, it finds applications in many areas where the results from gas and liquid chromatography are unsatisfactory. Examples are the separations of middle-molecular-weight compounds, low-molecular-weight organic polymers, fats and oils, and organometallic compounds. *See* CHEMICAL SEPARATION TECHNIQUES.

Separation time. The capacity factor k in the equation represents the compromise between the need for retention to achieve resolution and the overall separation time. Numerical evaluation of this term indicates that a minimum value of k is required to obtain close-to-maximum resolution in the chromatographic system, but larger values of k do not increase this resolution significantly and lead to unfavorable separation times (Fig. 2c). The most difficult components to separate in a mixture will ideally have k values between 1 and 3, while k values greater than 10–20 have little further

influence on resolution. Increasing the residence time of substances in a chromatographic system beyond a certain point does not contribute to their further separation. In practice, larger values than the optimum values may be required to provide sufficient space to fit all the components of a complex mixture into the chromatogram.

Planar chromatography. The separation mechanisms for thin-layer and column liquid chromatography are essentially the same. However, the two processes differ in that in column liquid chromatography all substances migrate the same distance and become separated in time, while in thin-layer chromatography all substances have the same separation time and are separated in space. In column liquid chromatography the mobile phase moves through the column at a constant velocity, while in thin-layer chromatography its velocity is usually controlled by capillary forces and declines with distance from the solvent entry position. These forces are generally too weak to achieve the optimum velocity required to minimize zone broadening. Compared to a constant mobile-phase velocity, longer separation times and a reduced separation potential results. The useful development distance for a separation is restricted, since eventually the mobile-phase velocity becomes so low that zones begin to broaden faster than their centers are moving apart. The optimum development length depends on properties of the mobile and stationary phases, particularly the average particle size of the layer; and it is typically between 5 and 15 cm for commercially available materials.

A general discussion of zone broadening in thin-layer chromatography is inherently more complex than in column liquid chromatography for reasons which relate to both the practice of the technique and the limitations of subsequent theoretical treatments. Because substances are separated in space, individual zones experience only those theoretical plates through which they travel; and therefore the

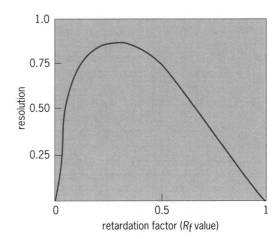

Fig. 3. Variation of resolution of two closely migrating zones as a function of the R_f value of the faster moving zone. (After C. F. Poole and S. K. Poole, Chromatography Today, Elsevier, 1991)

efficiency N is a function of the migration distance of the substance in the chromatogram. The migration of individual zones occurs across several regions of different local velocity and can be represented only by some average value that is difficult to determine. In practice, when the mobile-phase velocity is controlled by capillary forces, the major contribution to zone broadening is longitudinal diffusion supplemented by a smaller contribution from flow anisotropy. Separations in thin-layer chromatography occur with 0–5000 theoretical plates, depending on migration distance, and with a capacity for baseline resolved peaks of about 10–14 in the chromatogram.

The general variation of resolution with migration distance is more complex than is the case for column liquid chromatography and is approximately represented by a special curve (**Fig. 3**). The fundamental parameter used to characterize the position of a sample zone in a thin-layer chromatogram is the retardation factor, or R_f value. It represents the ratio of the distance migrated by the sample to the distance traveled by the solvent front in the same time. The boundary conditions for R_f values are $1 \geq R_f \geq 0$ (Fig. 3). There is no separation possible for substances that do not migrate from their origin ($R_f = 0$) or do not interact with the stationary phase and move with the solvent front ($R_f = 1$). A maximum in the resolution of two closely spaced peaks is observed at an R_f of about 0.3, but the resolution does not vary much in the range $R_f = 0.2$–0.5, which is the optimum region in which to obtain a separation. When the difference in R_f values for two substances exceeds 0.1, separations are easy to achieve; for R_f values less than 0.05, a separation is very difficult or impossible to achieve because of an inadequate range of efficiency values. Therefore, selective separation systems are required.

A common method of improving the separation potential of thin-layer chromatography is to increase the number of development steps used for the separation. This process is known as multiple development. A reduction in zone dimensions is achieved by a refocusing mechanism that is well understood from a phenomenological perspective but is difficult to characterize quantitatively. At the start of each development the solvent front contacts the bottom portion of the zone first, and this region of the zone starts moving forward before the more distant regions of the zone still ahead of the solvent front. The result is a compression of the sample zone such that its width is reduced in size compared to zones migrated the same distance in a single development. This process can be automated so that a large number of developments can be used in an individual separation, resulting in a peak capacity for baseline resolved peaks of about 25–40, a considerable increase over the separation capacity obtained by using a single development.

The ultimate separation capacity of column liquid chromatography is greater than that of thin-layer chromatography (at least as normally prac-

ticed). However, for simple separations where a high sample throughput is required, where crude samples are to be analyzed with minimum sample preparation, and where chemical reactions are to be used for detection, thin-layer chromatography is often preferred to column liquid chromatography. The reasons are that the stationary phase is not reused and multiple samples can be separated in parallel lanes in contrast to the single-sample sequential separations characteristic of column chromatography. After the separation the components are immobilized on the stationary phase and can be treated with chemical reagents to change their detection properties without time constraints. The types of samples that are suitable for analysis by thin-layer chromatography are the same as those normally separated by column liquid chromatography, and a choice between the two approaches is made on the basis of practical considerations such as those outlined above. *See* ANALYTICAL CHEMISTRY.
Colin F. Poole

Bibliography. F. Geiss, *Fundamentals of Thin-Layer Chromatography*, 1987; E. Heftmann, *Chromatography*, pt. A and B, 1991; M. L. Lee and K. E. Markides, *Analytical Supercritical Fluid Chromatography and Extraction*, 1990; C. F. Poole and S. K. Poole, *Chromatography Today*, 1991; C. F. Poole and S. K. Poole, Instrumental thin-layer chromatography, *Anal. Chem.*, 66:27A–37A, 1994.

Chromatophore

A pigmented structure found in many animals, generally in the integument. The term is usually restricted to those structures that bring about changes in color or brightness. A majority of chromatophores are single cells that are highly branched and contain pigment granules that can disperse or aggregate within the cell. However, in coleoid cephalopod mollusks (all mollusks except *Nautilus*), the chromatophores function as miniature organs, and changes in the dispersion of pigment are brought about by muscles. Although the mode of action of the two types of chromatophore is completely different, the effect is the same: pigment either is spread out over a large area of the body or is retracted into a small area.

The movement of pigment takes place in many chromatophores simultaneously, so that the effect is a change in the quality of light reflected from the surface of the animal. The color change functions as a camouflage from predator or prey, but it may also serve for regulating temperature, protecting against harmful radiation, and in some animals, signaling. Light stimulates the responses of chromatophores, and although in some species light may affect the chromatophores directly, light generally acts indirectly via the eyes and central nervous system.

Occurrence. Single-cell chromatophores are found in some annelids, in insects (migratory locusts, some grasshoppers, and stick insects), and in echinoderms (some sea urchins). They are much more conspicuous in crustaceans (shrimps and prawns), in fishes (especially in bony fish and teleosts), in anuran amphibians (frogs and toads), and in a few reptiles.

The chromatophores may be uniformly distributed in the skin (chameleons), or they may occur in patches (flounders) or lines (around the abdomen in shrimps). Chromatophores of various colors may be distributed unevenly across the body, and occur at different depths in the skin. This characteristic can be important for enhancing or suppressing colors produced in the skin by reflecting structures.

Colors produced. Chromatophores produce their colors by reflection after absorption of light. Generally, the light comes from above, but it may come from below after reflection from an underlying structure. The most common type of chromatophore contains melanin (and is, therefore, often called a melanophore), which absorbs all wavelengths so that the chromatophore appears black; other types have red (erythrophores) or yellow (xanthophores) pigments. These pigments generally derive from carotenoids in vertebrates and from ommochromes in invertebrates. It should be noted that although a chromatophore may appear red in the laboratory or in a shallow tidal pool, it will appear black at depths of 165 ft (50 m) or more, and many of the red chromatophores of marine animals may act (like the black ones) as neutral-density filters for matching background brightness rather than for providing color.

Chromatophores do not usually contain green or blue pigments. These colors are often produced structurally, by reflecting or refracting structures (iridophores, also called iridocytes). The skin of many animals contains structures known as leucophores which, being broadband reflectors, can also produce greens and blues. Chromatophores in cephalopods and amphibians often function in conjunction with iridophores and leucophores to produce beautiful and complex color patterns over the whole body.

Crustaceans and vertebrates. Chromatophores contain pigment granules that move within them, giving them an appearance that ranges from spotted to fibrous on the five-stage scale that is widely used to measure the degree of chromatophore expansion. If the pigment within the particular cell is black or brown, the integument takes on a dark appearance when most of the chromatophores are in the last stage of dispersion (stage 5). If the pigment color is yellow or cream, the animal tends to look paler if all the chromatophores are at that stage.

Shrimp or frog chromatophores respond actively to the background illumination (**Fig. 1**). After only an hour or two, changes in the state of the chromatophores become evident with the aid of a microscope. These changes are usually brought about by hormones that are released from a particular site and circulated throughout

Fig. 1. Light- and dark-adapted frogs. (*After J. Pierce, J. Exp. Zool., 89:293–295, 1942*)

the body. In shrimp, the hormones acting on the chromatophores originate in organs located in the eyestalk and also in the central nervous system. In the frog, the hormone responsible for color change comes from the pars intermedia of the pituitary organ; it is a peptide, called melanocyte-stimulating hormone, that disperses the pigment granules, thus making the skin darker. In teleosts, the control system is more complicated because there is a second hormone, melanin-concentrating hormone from the hypothalamus, that suppresses melanocyte-stimulating hormone, causing pigment aggregation in all color classes of chromatophores, and hence paling.

In crustaceans, elasmobranch fishes, anurans, and lizards, control of the chromatophores is thought to be exclusively hormonal. Such hormonal control is true also of some teleosts; in others the control is part hormonal and part neural; while in still others control is purely neural, as in the chameleon. Where nerves are involved, the speed of the response is faster, the chromatophores responding in minutes rather than hours. *See* NEUROSECRETION.

The chromatophores of crustaceans often have pigments of different colors, and they enable the integument to take on the background hue for concealment. When they form patterns, such as lines and bands, they may also serve to conceal the animal disruptively by breaking up the outline of the body. In fish, anurans, and reptiles, camouflage is again a major function, but in terrestrial vertebrates with chromatophores, changes in color may also serve for temperature regulation, at least

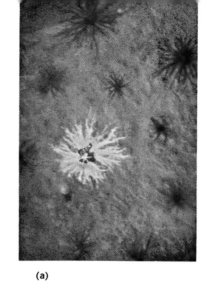

(a)

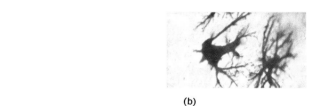

(b)

(a-c) Skin of a prawn (*Leander serratus*), with red and white chromatophores showing (*a*) pigment mostly dispersed in the branches of one white and several red cells; (*b*) successive stages in dispersal of pigment in two red cells; (*c*) twofold effect of injecting prawn with sinus-gland extract — red pigment becoming less dispersed and some converted into a blue diffused outside the chromatophore. (*F. G. W. Knowles, Endeavour, 14:99, 1955*)

(d) Skin of a squirrelfish (*Holocentrus ascensionis*) with chromatophores as seen by transmitted light: a few large finely branched melanophores and many small erythrophores (seen as balls of concentrated red) over a screen of larger oval iridophores (looking grayish and granular) and a deeper and more evenly spaced layer of nearly parallel elongate reflecting bodies (appearing straw-colored). (*H. B. Goodrich, Lerner Marine Laboratory, Bimini, B.W.I.*)

(e) Young flounders (*Parophrys velulus*), originally indistinguishable in color, showing adaptive coloration attained during prolonged periods of time (43 days) over a given bottom color such as black, red, blue, or white. (*E. F. B. Fries, Hopkins Marine Station, Pacific Grove, Calif.*)

(f) Parrotfish skin with chromatophores as seen by reflected light: melanophores, with black pigment widely dispersed in their branches and smaller, less sharply defined, yellow-to-orange xanthophores over meshed chains of brightly whitish iridophores. (*H. B. Goodrich, Lerner Marine Laboratory, Bimini, B.W.I.*)

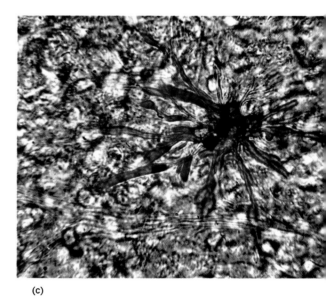

(c)

(d)

(e)

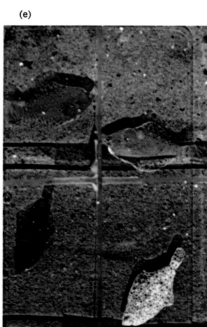

(f)

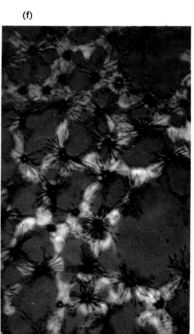

when the temperature is excessively high or low. In some teleosts, neurally controlled chromatophores permit the rapid color changes that are used for social signaling, for example during sexual or territorial encounters.

Cephalopods. Each cephalopod chromatophore organ comprises an elastic sac containing pigment granules. Attached to the sac is a set of 15–25 radial muscles that are striated and contract rapidly. Associated with the radial muscles are axons from nerve cell bodies that lie within the brain. Active nerve cells cause the radial muscles to contract and the chromatophore sac expands; when the nerves are inactive, energy stored in the elastic sac causes the chromatophore to retract as the muscles relax. The chromatophores receive only nerve impulses, and there is no evidence that they are influenced by hormones.

The chromatophores are ultimately controlled by the optic lobe of the brain under the influence of the eyes. Two consequences follow from the fact that cephalopod chromatophores are under the direct control of the brain. First, color change is instantaneous (an octopus can change from almost white to jet black in less than a second). Such a rapid change may cause a predator to hesitate, permitting escape; also, when the animal reaches the sea floor, it can vanish almost at once. Second, patterns can be generated in the skin in a way impossible in other animals. Thus, cephalopods can use the chromatophores not just to match the background in general color but to break up the body visually (disruptive coloration) so that the predator does not see the whole animal.

Concealment is obviously a major function. It is possible that cephalopod chromatophores evolved for purposes of camouflage after the ancestral cephalopods had abandoned the molluscan shell in the interest of speed and agility. However, because the chromatophores are neurally controlled and patterns can be produced in the skin, they can also be used for signaling. A characteristic of cephalopods is that some species make displays as conspicuous as those of fish or birds. Included are sexual signals destined for members of the same species, and warning signals, such as the large black eyespots used against predators. Signaling is especially well developed in some shallow-water forms, such as the Caribbean reef squid.

Finally, cephalopod chromatophores can be used for countershading and for maintaining countershading after disorientation. Animals that are generally illuminated from above tend to have a dark upper surface and a light lower surface, concealing them from a viewer from the side. This characteristic is true of fish and cephalopods. However, when a fish becomes momentarily disorientated and rolls over on its side, it becomes conspicuous because its countershading is fixed. When a squid rolls over, the chromatophores on the ventral surface of the body expand to maintain the countershading (**Fig. 2**). Such versatility is possible only because the chromatophores are neurally controlled. *See* PIGMENTATION; PROTECTIVE COLORATION.

J. B. Messenger

Chromite

The only ore mineral of chromium. Chromite is jet black to brownish black, has a submetallic luster, and gives a brown streak. It belongs to the spinel group of minerals and has cubic symmetry. The unit cell of chromite contains 32 oxygens and 24 cations, of which 8 are in 4-fold coordination and 16 in 6-fold coordination. Naturally occurring chromite has the general formula $(Mg,Fe^{2+})(Cr,Al,Fe^{3+})_2O_4$ and ranges from 15 to 64 wt % Cr_2O_3, with minor amounts of nickel, titanium, zinc, cobalt, and manganese. The specific gravity of chromite ranges from 4 to 5, depending on its composition. Pure chromite, $Fe^{2+}Cr_2O_4$, is extremely rare in nature and has been found only in meteorites.

Most chromite mined worldwide comes from two kinds of deposits, stratiform and podiform. Stratiform deposits, which occur as tabular bodies, are found in large, layered igneous intrusions, $1.9–3.2 \times 10^9$ years old. Examples are found in South Africa, Zimbabwe, Finland, Brazil, Greenland, and the United States. About 99% of the total chromite resources, more than 3.0×10^{10} tons (2.7×10^{10} metric tons), is contained in stratiform deposits in southern Africa. Podiform deposits having irregular shape are found in a group of rocks called ophiolites, which occur primarily in

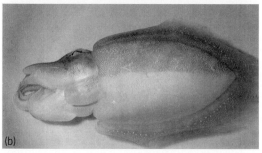

Fig. 2. Orientation of a cuttlefish. (*a*) The animal has a pale underside because all the chromatophores on the ventral mantle are retracted. (*b*) When the cuttlefish is rolled over onto its right side, the chromatophores of the upper (left) half of the ventral mantle expand to maintain the countershading.

folded mountain belts and island arcs. Turkey, the Philippines, Russia, Albania, New Caledonia, Iran, Cyprus, Greece, and the United States contain podiform deposits totaling about 3.0×10^8 tons (2.7×10^8 metric tons). World consumption is about 1×10^7 tons (9×10^6 metric tons) per year; therefore, resources are adequate for centuries.

Minor amounts of chromite have also been mined from the erosion products of podiform deposits and their host rocks, mostly from heavy-mineral concentrations in beach sands.

Chromite has a variety of uses. Chromium is extracted from it to make stainless steel and other alloys for which resistance to oxidation and corrosion is important. Chromium is also used as a plating and tanning agent. The mineral chromite is made into refractory lining for steel-making furnaces. *See* CHROMIUM; SPINEL; STAINLESS STEEL.

Bruce R. Lipin

Chromium

A chemical element, symbol Cr, atomic number 24, and atomic weight 51.996, which is the weighted average for several isotopes weighing 50 (4.31%), 52 (83.76%), 53 (9.55%), and 54 (2.38%). The orbital arrangement of the electrons is $1s^2$, $2s^2$, $2p^6$, $3s^2$, $3p^6$, $3d^5$, $4s^1$. The stability of the half-filled d shell doubtless accounts for this rather unusual arrangement. In the crust of the Earth, chromium is the twenty-first element in abundance, which ranks it along with vanadium, zinc, nickel, and copper. Traces of chromium are present in the human body; in fact, it is essential to life.

The element was discovered in 1797 and isolated the following year by the French chemist L. N. Vauquelin. It was named chromium because of the many colors of its compounds. It occurs in nature largely as the mineral chromite ($FeO \cdot Cr_2O_3$), which is a spinel, but the ore is usually contaminated with Al^{3+}, Fe^{3+}, Mn^{2+}, and Mg^{2+}. Smaller quantities are found as the beautiful yellow mineral crocoite ($PbCrO_4$). Chromite is found in many parts of the world, but the main source is South Africa. The American ores are less pure and are seldom used, though at one time they were the main source of chromium and chromium compounds in the United States. *See* CHROMITE; CROCOITE; SPINEL.

Chemistry. As a transition metal, chromium exists in all oxidation states from 2− to 6+ (**Table 1**). The chemistry of its aqueous solutions, at least in the 3+ (chromic) state, is complicated by the fact that the compounds exist in many isomeric forms, which have quite different chemical properties.

At high temperature, metallic chromium reacts with many nonmetallic elements to give compounds in which the valences seem quite anomalous. These compounds are quite analogous to intermetallic compounds. Some examples are CrH, CrH_2, Cr_4B, Cr_3B_4, Cr_7C_3, Cr_3C_2, Cr_3Si, Cr_3Si_2, CrN, Cr_3P, CrP, CrP_2, CrS, Cr_7S_8, CrSe, and Cr_7Se_8. Many of these are interstitial compounds—that is, the nonmetal atoms fit into interstices between the chromium atoms. The compounds resemble metals in physical properties. *See* INTERMETALLIC COMPOUNDS; TRANSITION ELEMENTS.

Coordination compounds. The compounds which chromium forms with π-acceptor ligands usually contain chromium in a low oxidation state. This implies a high electron density on the metal atoms, which can be delocalized into the ligands. Some π-acceptor ligands are CO, NO, RNCO, PR_3, AsR_3, and dithioketones and other sulfur-containing ligands. Compounds such as $Cr(CO)_6$ and $Na_2[Cr(CO)_5]$ are often considered to be Werner coordination compounds, but they differ greatly from the classical ammines which A. Werner studied and in which electrons furnished by the ligands are shared with the metal ion. There is no sharp line between the two classes of compounds; $K_3[Cr(CN)_6]$ is a typical Werner complex in which the metal shows the normal oxidation state of 3+, but $K_3[Cr(CN)_4]$ is a π-acceptor complex in which the oxidation state of chromium is 1+. *See* COORDINATION CHEMISTRY; COORDINATION COMPLEXES.

Organochromium compounds. The first organochromium compound was made by F. Hein in 1919 by the reaction of $CrCl_3$ with phenylmagnesium bromide in ether. He did not understand the nature of the product, and it was not until 1954 that it was shown to be a sandwich compound. Many similar compounds containing a variety of unsaturated compounds—particularly aromatic hydrocarbons and cyclopentadiene—have become known. In general, all of these compounds follow the effective atomic number rule: The total number of electrons around the metal is equal to the number in the next rare gas—krypton. *See* METALLOCENES; ORGANOMETALLIC COMPOUND.

Chromium carbonyl. This compound, $[Cr(CO)_6]$, like other metal carbonyls, is an extremely toxic, volatile liquid. One or more of the carbon monoxide molecules can be replaced by other groups, as in $[Cr(CO)_5X]$ (X = I, CN, NCS), $[Cr(CO)_x(CNR)_y]$, $[Cr(CO)_x(CH_3CN)_y]$, $[Cr(CO)_x$-(pyridine)$_y$], $[Cr(CO)_x (NH_3)_y]$, $[Cr(CO)_x(PCl_3)_y]$

TABLE 1. Compounds of chromium

Oxidation state	Typical compound	Remarks
2−	$NA_2[Cr(CO)_5]$	
1−	$NA_2[Cr_2(CO)_{10}]$	
0	$Cr(CO)_6$	Chromium hexacarbonyl; π-bonded complexes; the only colorless compound of chromium
	$Cr(C_6H_6)_2$	Bis-benzene chromium
1+	$(C_6H_5C_6H_4)_2CrI$	Bis-biphenyl chromium(I) iodide
2+	$CrCl_2$ (white), $(NH_4)_2SO_4 \cdot 6H_2O$ (blue), $Cr_2(OOCCH_3)_4 \cdot 2H_2O$ (red)	Chromous salts; sensitive to air; strong reducing agents; the acetate is almost insoluble in water
3+	$CrCl_3$ (bright purple), $CrCl_3 \cdot 6H_2O$ (violet or green), $KCr(SO_4)_2 \cdot 12H_2O$ (deep purple)	The third compound is an alum

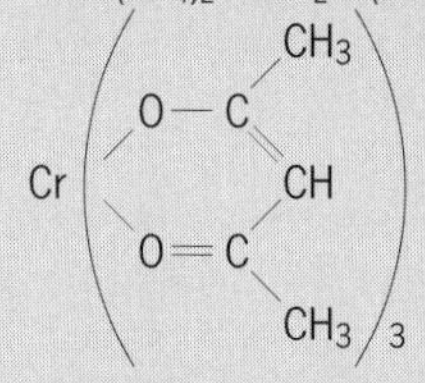

(red violet)

Acetylacetonate; insoluble in water; soluble in nonpolar solvents; somewhat volatile

Oxidation state	Typical compound	Remarks
4+	CrO_2, $CrCl_4$	CrO_2 is paramagnetic and is used in magnetic tapes
5+	$Ba_3(CrO_4)_2$ (black-green)	Converted by acids to Cr(III) and Cr(VI)
6+	CrO_3 (ruby red)	Commonly called chromic acid, although it is actually the anhydride
	Cr_2Cl_2 (cherry-red liquid)	Chromyl chloride; reacts violently with water to give $H_2Cr_2O_7$ and HCl
	Na_2CrO_4 (yellow)	Also many other soluble chromates
	$PbCrO_4$ (yellow)	An important paint pigment
	$Na_2Cr_2O_7$ (orange)	Dichromate—used as a source of nearly all other chromium compounds
	$Na_2Cr_3O_{10}$ (orange)	Trichromate; of little importance
	$Na_2Cr_4O_{13}$ (orange-red)	Tetrachromate; of little importance
	$KCrO_3Cl$ (orange)	Chlorochromate; hydrolyzes in water to $K_2Cr_2O_7$ and HCl

(in all of these $x = 3$, 4, or 5 and $y = 1$, 2, or 3). Even polydentate ligands can enter the complex, as in $[Cr(CO)_4(AA)]$ (AA = dipyridyl, 1,10-phenanthroline, ethylenediamine, 8-aminoquinoline, and so on) and in $[Cr(CO)_3$-(diethylenetriamine)]. The dipyridyl compound $[Cr(dipy)_3]^0$ can be reduced to $[Cr(dipy)_3]^-$ or oxidized to $[Cr(dipy)_3]^{+\ or\ 2+}$. All of these are air-sensitive and must be handled in an inert atmosphere. *See* METAL CARBONYL.

Bivalent state. The 2+ oxidation state of chromium is better known than the lower oxidation states, and compounds such as the white $CrCl_2$ and the blue $CrSO_4 \cdot (NH_4)_2SO_4 \cdot 6H_2O$ are easily prepared by reduction of compounds in the 3+ state by zinc in acid solution [reaction (1)]. These substances absorb

$$2CrCl_3 + Zn \longrightarrow 2CrCl_2 + ZnCl_2 \qquad (1)$$

oxygen from the air rapidly; $CrCl_2$ is sometimes used to absorb the last traces of oxygen from gas streams. The red acetate, $[Cr_2(OOCCH_3)_4] \cdot 2H_2O$ [structure (**1**)], is insoluble in water, so it can be handled briefly in the air. Like several other acetates of bivalent metals, it is dimeric and contains a metal-metal bond. The acetate groups bridge the two chromium atoms, and the water molecules complete the octahedral structure about each chromium atom.

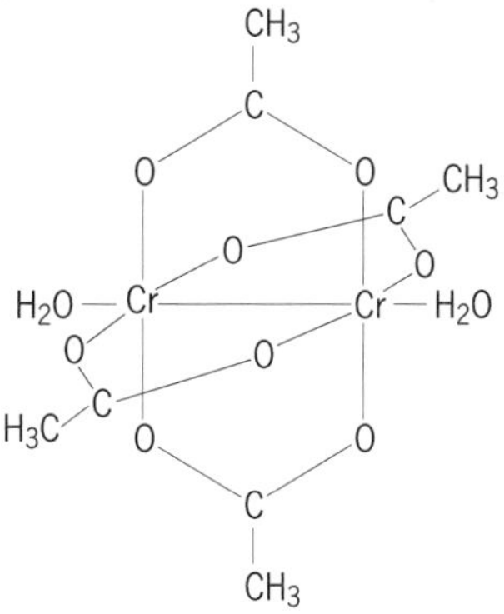

(**1**)

Trivalent state. The 3+ stage is a normal one for chromium, and compounds in that state are stable in air. They can be reduced only by strong reducing agents, and oxidized to the 6+ state only by strong oxidizing agents. Anhydrous chromium(III) chloride forms beautiful bright purple crystals. It cannot be formed by dehydration of the hydrated form, as hydrolysis takes place with the formation of oxychlorides. Instead, it is prepared by the action of chlorine on chromium metal at elevated temperature, or by the reaction of chromium(III) oxide and carbon tetrachloride in the presence of carbon at red heat [reaction (2)]. It is insoluble in

$$Cr_2O_3 + 3CCl_4 \xrightarrow{\Delta} 2CrCl_3 + 3COCl_2 \qquad (2)$$

water (due to its polymeric nature), but dissolves readily if a little Cr^{2+} is present. Supposedly, the Cr^{2+} compound dissolves and reduces an equivalent amount of $CrCl_3$, which thus becomes $CrCl_2$. This, in turn, is oxidized as it reduces more $CrCl_3$, and the reaction continues until all of the $CrCl_3$ has gone into solution; thus, chromium(II) may be considered to be catalytic in its action.

Chromium 3+ forms a great many complex ions, and its chemistry is largely that of the complexes. The red-violet acetylacetone complex (**2**) is note-

(**2**)

worthy in that it is somewhat volatile; this volatility is markedly increased if the methyl hydrogen atoms are replaced by fluorine atoms. The tris-hexafluoroacetonylacetate (**3**) vaporizes when

(**3**)

heated to a few degrees above room temperature. The oxygen atoms of the acetylacetone rings occupy adjacent corners of an octahedron, so the three chelate rings lie (approximately) in three mutually perpendicular planes. On this account, the molecule exists in two isomeric forms; when the substance is in solution, one of these turns the plane of polarization to the right (dextro isomer) and the other to the left (levo isomer). The isomers have been at least partially separated by passing the vapor through a column of powdered dextro quartz at 55°C (131°F). *See* OPTICAL ACTIVITY.

Like many trivalent metal ions, Cr^{3+} forms alums, of which the deep purple $KCr(SO_4)_2 \cdot 12H_2O$ is typical. This forms octahedral crystals which can be grown to very large size (8 in. or 20 cm or more on each edge). In this alum, as in others, six molecules of water are coordinated to the chromium ion; the other water molecules are hydrogen-bonded to the sulfate ions. The formation and crystallization of potassium or ammonium alum is often used in the purification of chromium compounds. *See* ALUM.

The hydrated chromium(III) salts show an interesting isomerism; this is best illustrated by the chloride $CrCl_3 \cdot 6H_2O$, which exists in three distinct forms, having the fomulas $[Cr(H_2O)_6]Cl_3$, $[Cr(H_2O)_5Cl]Cl_2 \cdot H_2O$, and $[Cr(H_2O)_4Cl_2]Cl \cdot 2H_2O$. The first of these is violet; the other two are different shades of green. In the violet compound,

the coordination sphere of the metal ion is filled by six molecules of water. It exists in dilute solutions of the salt, and can be obtained in crystalline form by saturating a concentrated solution of a chromium(III) salt with hydrogen chloride gas at 0°C (32°F). In the two green forms, the coordination sphere contains both water molecules and chloro groups. The remaining water molecules are interstitial; that is, they fill holes in the crystal lattice and are held by hydrogen bonding. In each case, the chloro groups in the coordination sphere are precipitated only slowly upon the addition of silver nitrate solution, while the ionic chloride is precipitated at once.

The chromium(III) complexes, like those of cobalt(III), are inert, while those of the metals in the divalent stage are labile. H. Taube and his students utilized these properties in a very ingenious way to study the mechanism of oxidation-reduction reactions. They reduced $[Co(NH_3)_5Cl]^{2+}$ with $[Cr(H_2O)_6]^{2+}$, as shown in reaction (3). The

$$[Co(NH_3)_5Cl]^{2+} + [Cr(H_2O)_6]^{2+} + 5H_3O^+ \longrightarrow$$
$$[Co(H_2O)_6]^{2+} + [Cr(H_2O)_5Cl]^{2+} + 5NH_4^+ \quad (3)$$

interesting point in this experiment is that the chloride which was originally attached to the cobalt is found, at the end of the experiment, attached to the chromium. That it is the same chlorine was shown by using isotopic chlorine in the cobalt complex. Even in a solution containing another chloride, the labeled chlorine is found in the chromium complex. There must be an intermediate in which the chloride is attached to both metals: $[(NH_3)_5Co—Cl—Cr(H_2O)_5]^{4+}$. If additional chloride ion is present in the solution, it will appear, at least in part, in the chromium complex, which is then $[Cr(H_2O)_4Cl_2]^+$. This added chloride probably enters the complex as a nonbridging ligand. Other groups which can attach themselves to two metal ions (to form a bridge) give similar results. When $[Co(NH_3)_6]^{3+}$ is substituted for $[Co(NH_3)_5Cl]^{2+}$, the reduction is very slow because the ammonia molecules cannot form a bridge. In this case, the reaction takes place by a so-called outer-sphere mechanism—that is, an electron is transferred from the chromium complex to the cobalt complex, without the transfer of an atom. *See* OXIDATION-REDUCTION.

The chloro-erythro chromium(III) ion undergoes an unusual reaction in the presence of a Cr^{2+} ion [reaction (4)]. Apparently, the Cr^{2+} ion forms a

$$\overset{\overset{\text{H}}{|}}{[(NH_3)_5CrOCr(NH_3)_4Cl]^{4+}} + 5H_3O^+ \overset{Cr^{2+}}{\longrightarrow}$$
$$[Cr(NH_3)_5H_2O]^{3+} + [Cr(H_2O)_5Cl]^{2+} + 4NH_4^+ \quad (4)$$

bridge through the coordinated chloro group, thus reducing the adjacent chromium atom to the 2+ state and weakening the bond between it and the —OH bridge. The reduced chromium atom loses the attached ammonia molecules and is ready to attack another chloro-erythro ion. Thus, the Cr^{2+} serves as a catalyst, being regenerated in each step.

There are many chromium(III) ammines; if $[Cr(NH_3)_6]^{3+}$ is considered as the parent of the series, it is possible to replace one or more ammonia molecules by univalent negative groups such as F^-, Cl^-, Br^-, I^-, or CH_3COO^- or divalent groups such as SO_4^{2-} or $C_2O_4^{2-}$. The ammonia molecules can also be replaced by amines—methyl amine, pyridine, ethylenediamine, dipyridyl, 1,10-phenanthroline, and so on. Molecules and ions containing both neutral and negative groups are common, as illustrated by such substances as $[Cr(NH_3)_5Cl]^{2+}$, $[Co(en)_2(NH_3)Cl]^{2+}$ (en = ethylenediamine), and $[Cr(en)_2Cl_2]^+$. The neutral and negative groups can be part of the same coordinating molecule; the amino acid anions (**4**) and ethylenediaminetetraacetate ion (**5**) form very stable complexes.

$$R\!-\!CH\!-\!C\!=\!O$$
$$\mid \qquad \mid$$
$$NH_2 \quad O^-$$

(**4**)

$$
\begin{array}{ccc}
COO^- & & COO^- \\
\mid & & \mid \\
CH_2 & & CH_2 \\
\mid & & \mid \\
N\!-\!CH_2\!-\!CH_2\!-\!N \\
\mid & & \mid \\
CH_2 & & CH_2 \\
\mid & & \mid \\
COO^- & & COO^-
\end{array}
$$

(**5**)

It is interesting that analogous chromium(III) and cobalt(III) complexes are usually similar in physical characteristics—they have very similar colors, crystallize in the same form, and often have similar solubilities. However, they frequently differ markedly in their chemical behavior. The chromium(III) ammines are classified as inert, but they are more reactive than the corresponding cobalt(III) compounds. On standing in water solution, they slowly hydrolyze; the solutions become dark red, and yield only intractable syrups upon evaporation or addition of a nonsolvent.

Many chromium(III) ammines exist in isomeric forms. For example, the ion $[Cr(en)_2Cl_2]^+$ exists in cis and trans forms, and the cis form exists in dextro and levo modifications (**Fig. 1**).

Three coordinated bidentate groups, whether alike or different, always give complexes in dextro and levo forms, and if the bidentate group is unsymmetrical, there will also be cis and trans forms (often called facial and meridonal; **Fig. 2**). Two tridentate groups, attached to the Cr^{3+} ion, also yield cis (facial) and trans (meridonal) isomers. **Figure 3** shows the structures of the isomers of the diethylenetriamine complex ($NH_2CH_2CH_2NHCH_2CH_2NH_2$). These last coordi-

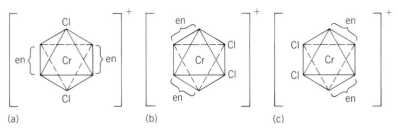

Fig. 1. Isomeric forms of the dichloro-bis-ethylenediamine chromium(III) ion [Cr(en)$_2$Cl$_2^+$] (en = ethylenediamine). (a) Trans isomer. (b) Dextro-cis isomer. (c) Levo-cis isomer.

nate ions are not optically active, for each has at least one plane of symmetry. An unsymmetrical tridentate chelating agent, however, would give a complex which would exist in dextro and levo forms. It can be seen that the possibilities for isomerism are almost unlimited.

Chromium complexes containing coordinated water molecules tend to hydrolyze in water, that is, to lose protons [reaction (5)]. The OH group,

$$[Cr(H_2O)_6]^{3+} + H_2O \longrightarrow [Cr(H_2O)_5OH]^{2+} + H_3O^+ \quad (5)$$

having three unshared pairs of electrons, can simultaneously coordinate with more than one atom of metal, so that dimers, trimers, and polymers form readily [reactions (6)]. However, the reaction

$$[Cr(H_2O)_5OH]^{2+} + [Cr(H_2O)_6]^{3+} \longrightarrow$$

$$\begin{array}{c} H \\ | \\ [(H_2O)_5CrOCr(H_2O)_5]^{5+} \end{array} + H_2O$$

$$\begin{array}{c} H \\ | \\ O \\ \diagup \ \diagdown \\ [(H_2O)_4Cr \qquad Cr(H_2O)_4]^{4+} + 2H_2O \quad (6) \\ \diagdown \ \diagup \\ O \\ | \\ H \end{array}$$

need not stop at this point, for water molecules remaining in the coordination sphere can lose protons, resulting in continuation of the process

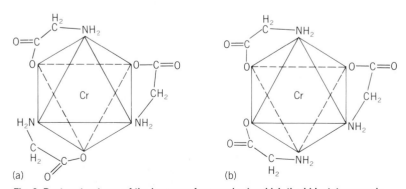

Fig. 2. Dextro structures of the isomers of a complex in which the bidentate group is unsymmetrical. (a) Dextro-facial: all N atoms are cis to each other. (b) Dextro-meridonal: two N atoms are trans to each other.

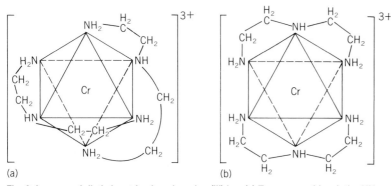

Fig. 3. Isomers of diethylenetriamine chromium(III) ion. (*a*) Trans or meridonal; the NH₂ groups of each triamine are trans to each other. (*b*) Cis or facial; the NH₂ groups of each triamine molecule are cis to each other.

until the particle becomes so large that it is no longer soluble and forms a colloid or a precipitate. This process is called olation; it is, of course, aided by the addition of a base. If an olated polymer is heated, the ol group (OH) can lose a proton [reaction (7)]. This is called oxolation. It is greatly

$$[(H_2O)_4Cr \underset{\underset{H}{O}}{\overset{\overset{H}{O}}{\diamond}} Cr(H_2O)_4]^{4+} + H_2O \longrightarrow$$

$$[(H_2O)_4Cr \underset{\underset{H}{O}}{\overset{O}{\diamond}} Cr(H_2O)_4]^{3+} + H_3O^+ \quad (7)$$

aided by an increase in temperature. When the oxolated solution is cooled, the process is reversed, but very slowly.

These reactions are important in the tanning of leather. In chrome tanning, dichromate is reduced by sulfur dioxide, sugar, or other reducing agents in the presence of sulfuric acid. This gives one-third-basic chromium(III) sulfate, $Cr(OH)SO_4$, which is polymeric. It is important that the pH and temperature be controlled carefully, for changes in either produce changes in the composition of the chromium complex. When the hide to be tanned is soaked in $Cr(OH)SO_4$ solution, the protein forms chromium complexes which are resistant to weather and bacterial action. The exact mechanism of the tanning process is not well understood, although much work has been done on it.

Higher oxidation states. Chromium(IV) exists in the form CrO_2, which is paramagnetic and is used in magnetic tapes. It is formed by heating other oxides of high-valent chromium (for example, CrO_3 and Cr_3O_8) in water vapor to 300–400°C (570–750°F) under pressures up to 3000 atm (30 megapascals). Materials such as iron oxides and antimony oxide are often added to modify the magnetic properties of the product. *See* MAGNETIC MATERIALS.

The oxidation state of 4 in CrF_4 and in $CrCl_4$ is

also known. The former is prepared by the action of fluorine on chromium metal or on CrF_3 or $CrCl_3$. (Some CrF_5 is formed simultaneously.) The chloride $CrCl_4$ is made by heating $CrCl_3$ in chlorine gas to 600°C (1110°F). If an alkali metal chloride is ground with $CrCl_3$ and the mixture is fluorinated, the complex M_2CrF_6 is formed (M = alkali metal). Chromium(IV) chromates are also known, but they have not been well characterized—the best known are Ba_2CrO_4 and Sr_2CrO_4. The barium salt is made by heating a mixture of chromium(III) oxide, barium chromate(VI), and barium hydroxide in an atmosphere of nitrogen [reaction (8)].

$$Cr_2O_3 + BaCrO_4 + 5Ba(OH)_2 \longrightarrow$$
$$3Ba_2CrO_4 + 5H_2O \quad (8)$$

Compounds containing chromium in the 5+ state are known, but are of little importance. Such compounds as CrF_5 and $CrOF_3$ are known, as well as chromates(V) of which the alkali and alkaline-earth salts are the best known—$M_3^ICrO_4$ and $M_3^{II}(CrO_4)_2$.

Chromium(VI) is best known in the form of chromate(VI), CrO_4^{2-}, and dichromate(VI), $Cr_2O_7^{2-}$. Chromium does not form polyacids to the same extent as its congeners molybdenum and tungsten, but trichromates $Cr_3O_{10}^{2-}$ and tetrachromates $Cr_4O_{13}^{2-}$ are known. They exist only in very strongly acid solution and are of little importance. Both chromates and dichromates are well known and are widely used. In water solution, they exist in equilibrium with each other [reaction (9)]. Thus, the orange dichromate

$$Cr_2O_7^{2-} + H_2O \rightleftharpoons 2CrO_4^{2-} + 2H^+ \quad (9)$$

is predominant in acid solution and the yellow chromate in basic solution. The equilibrium is shifted toward chromate upon dilution with water, but the effect is much less pronounced than that produced by addition of base. In either event, the equilibrium is displaced very rapidly. Since heavy-metal chromates are much less soluble than the corresponding dichromates, the addition of Pb^{2+}, for example, causes the precipitation of $PbCrO_4$, thus shifting the equilibrium toward the formation of chromate. This trend continues until the acidity of the solution becomes great enough to prevent further precipitation.

The first step in the extraction of chromium from its ores consists of oxidizing the element to chromate, so that all of the chromium compounds of commerce have come through that intermediate. For most uses, the chromate is converted to dichromate.

Chromic acid is a softer acid than sulfuric; that is, the chromate ion is more easily deformed than is the sulfate ion. Chromates of hard bases resemble the corresponding sulfates in crystal form and solubility, but those of soft bases tend to be less soluble and deeper in color than might be expected.

Thus, silver chromate is only about one-fiftieth as soluble as silver sulfate, and it is deep maroon in color. Chromic acid is a much weaker acid than sulfuric; also, it readily forms dichromate ion, whereas the corresponding disulfate (commonly called pyrosulfate) is formed only under very acid conditions, as by strong heating of a solid acid sulfate [reaction (10)]. Another striking difference is

$$2NaHSO_4 \longrightarrow Na_2S_2O_7 + H_2O \qquad (10)$$

found in the strong oxidizing property of chromic and dichromic acids.

Other chromium(VI) compounds which are of interest are the halochromates $KCrO_3X$ (X = F, Cl, Br, I) and the chromyl halides, CrO_2X_2 (X = F, Cl, Br). Chromyl chloride is a dark red, volatile liquid (bp 117°C or 243°F) which reacts vigorously with water.

Chromic acid, H_2CrO_4, was formerly used for many industrial oxidations—such as the conversion of toluene to benzoic acid and the oxidation of naphthalene to phthalic anhydride—but has been replaced largely by catalytic oxidation.

Analytical methods. For the quantitative analysis for chromium, the usual procedure is to oxidize the chromium to the 6+ state with sodium peroxide in basic solution [reaction (11)]. The excess sodium

$$2Cr(OH)_3 + 3Na_2O_2 \longrightarrow$$
$$2Na_2CrO_4 + 2NaOH + 2H_2O \quad (11)$$

peroxide is destroyed by boiling. The solution is then acidified and titrated with iron(II) sulfate, as shown in reaction (12a)—this may also be represented by reaction (12b), where only the

$$Na_2Cr_2O_7 + 6FeSO_4 + 7H_2SO_4 \longrightarrow$$
$$Cr_2(SO_4)_3 + 3Fe_2(SO_4)_3 + Na_2SO_4 + 7H_2O \quad (12a)$$

$$Cr_2O_7{}^{2-} + 6Fe^{2+} + 14H^+ \longrightarrow$$
$$2Cr^{3+} + 6Fe^{3+} + 7H_2O \quad (12b)$$

ions taking part in the reaction are noted. The excess Fe^{2+} is back-titrated with permanganate. *See* QUANTITATIVE CHEMICAL ANALYSIS.

In the qualitative analysis scheme, chromium falls into the sodium sulfide group, the ions of which are not precipitated by chloride ion or by sulfide ion in acid solution. After these ions are removed and the solution is boiled to drive out any sulfide which remains, the solution is made basic. If chromium is the only element of the group which can be present, sodium peroxide is added to convert it to chromate. (If other metals of this group are present, they must be removed before the test for chromium is made.) The addition of a solution of barium acetate precipitates the bright yellow barium chromate. The test may be confirmed by dissolving the precipitate in a minimum amount of nitric acid and adding 3% hydrogen peroxide and amyl alcohol. The peroxide gives a blue peroxide $[CrO(O)_2)_2]$, which is extracted into the amyl alcohol layer. The color

TABLE 2. Oxidation-reduction potential for some chemical reactions of chromium	
Reaction	Oxidation potential, ($E°$), V
$Cr^{2+} + 2e^- \rightleftharpoons Cr$	−0.91
$Cr^{3+} + 3e^- \rightleftharpoons Cr$	−0.74
$Cr^{3+} + e^- \rightleftharpoons Cr^{2+}$	−0.41
$CrO_4{}^{2-} + 4H_2O + 3e^- \rightleftharpoons$ $Cr(OH)_3 + 5OH^-$	−0.13
$Cr(OH)_3 + 3e^- \rightleftharpoons Cr + 3OH^-$	−1.3
$[Cr(OH)_4(H_2O)_2]^- + 3e^- \rightleftharpoons$ $Cr + 4OH^- + 2H_2O$	−1.2
$CrO_4{}^{2-} + 4H_2O + 3e^- \rightleftharpoons$ $Cr(OH)_3 + 5OH^-$	−0.12 ($E°B$)*
$Cr_2O_7{}^{2-} + 14H^+ + 5H_2O$ $+ 6e^- \rightleftharpoons 2[Cr(H_2O)_6]^{3+}$	+1.33
*In basic solution.	

is not persistent, so it must be observed at once.

A very delicate test for chromium involves the addition of diphenylcarbazide, $CO(NHNHC_6H_5)_2$, to a slightly acid chromium(VI) solution. This gives an intense red-violet color, which is said to be sensitive to 0.003 part per million of chromium. The test can be made quantitative by comparing the color with that of standard solutions. Modern methods depending upon atomic absorption and activation analysis are increasingly used in the analysis of substances containing very small amounts of chromium. *See* QUALITATIVE CHEMICAL ANALYSIS.

Metal. For the preparation of pure chromium, the chromite ore is heated in the air with sodium carbonate and lime, the latter being added to combine with the aluminum and other impurities and to give a frit with the proper physical properties [reaction (13)]. Any aluminum which has gone into

$$4Fe(CrO_2)_2 + 8Na_2CO_3 + 7O_2 \longrightarrow$$
$$2Fe_2O_3 + 8Na_2CrO_4 + 8CO_2 \quad (13)$$

solution is precipitated as aluminum hydroxide by addition of carbon dioxide or sulfuric acid. In the laboratory, this change is easily effected by fusing the powdered ore with NaOH and $NaClO_3$ [reaction (14)]. In these reactions, both the iron and

$$6Fe(CrO_2)_2 + 24NaOH + 7NaClO_3 \longrightarrow$$
$$3Fe_2O_3 + 12Na_2CrO_4 + 7NaCl + 12H_2O \quad (14)$$

the chromium are oxidized; the iron stays in an insoluble form, but the chromate formed is readily soluble in water. Of course, if the material is to be used to make ferrochrome or some other iron-chromium alloy, it is not necessary to separate the two metals in the ore.

Properties. Pure chromium metal has a bluish-white color, reflects light well, and takes a high polish. When pure, it is ductile, but even small amounts of impurities render it brittle. The metal melts at about 1900°C (3452°F) and boils at 2642°C (4788°F). Chromium shows a wide range of oxidation states; the compounds in which the metal is in a low oxidation state are powerful reducing agents, whereas those showing a high oxidation state are strong oxidizing agents. Some oxidation-reduction potentials are shown in **Table 2**.

In spite of the negative value of the oxidation potential ($E°$) for the first reactions shown in Table 2, the metal is resistant to atmospheric corrosion and to attack by most acids (except HF, HCl, and H_2SO_4). It reacts with fluorine at red heat to give CrF_4 and CrF_5, with chlorine to give $CrCl_3$, and (at 750–800°C or 1380–1470°F) with iodine to give CrI_2 and CrI_3. After passivation by nitric acid, the metal is resistant to HF.

Uses. The bright color and resistance to corrosion make chromium highly desirable for plating plumbing fixtures, automobile radiators and bumpers, and other decorative pieces. Unfortunately, chrome plating is difficult and expensive. It must be done by electrolytic reduction of dichromate in sulfuric acid solution. This requires the addition of six electrons per chromium ion. This reduction does not take place in one step, but through a series of steps, most of which are not clearly understood. The current efficiency is low (maybe 12%), and the chromium plate contains microscopic cracks and other flaws, and so it does not adequately protect the metal under it from corrosion. It is customary, therefore, to first plate the object with copper, then with nickel, and finally, with chromium.

Alloys. In alloys with iron, nickel, and other metals, chromium has many desirable properties. Chrome steel is hard and strong and resists corrosion to a marked degree. Stainless steel contains roughly 18% chromium and 8% nickel. Some chrome steels can be hardened by heat treatment and find use in cutlery; still others are used in jet engines. Nichrome and chromel consist largely of nickel and chromium; they have low electrical conductivity and resist corrosion, even at red heat, so they are used for heating coils in space heaters, toasters, and similar devices. Other important alloys are Hastelloy C (Cr, Mo, W, Fe, Ni), used in chemical equipment which is in contact with HCl, oxidizing acids, and hypochlorite. Stellite [Co, Cr, Ni, C, W (or Mo)], noted for its hardness and abrasion resistance at high temperatures, is used for lathes and engine valves, and Inconel (Cr, Fe, Ni) is used in heat treating and in corrosion-resistant equipment in the chemical industry. *See* ALLOY; HEAT TREATMENT (METALLURGY); STAINLESS STEEL.

Compounds. Chromium compounds are widely used in the tanning of leather and as mordants in the dye industry. The chief tanning compound is the basic sulfate [approximate formula $Cr(OH)SO_4$]. The hide must first be dehaired and defatted, and then soaked in the chrome solution. The chemistry of the process is not fully understood, but essentially the chromium reacts with the protein matter of the hide, forming coordinate bonds with the nitrogen and oxygen atoms, thus binding the entire skin into a wear- and weather-resistant unit. In the use of chromium compounds as mordants, chromium(III) hydroxide is precipitated within the fibers of the fabric to be dyed. It is permanently anchored there, and the dye adheres to it, either through chemical adsorption or reaction. For example, azo dyes with functional groups in positions ortho to the azo group form stable complexes such as structure (**6**). *See* DYE; LEATHER AND FUR PROCESSING.

Several chromium compounds are used as paint pigments—chrome oxide green (Cr_2O_3), chrome yellow ($PbCrO_4$), chrome orange ($PbCrO_4 \cdot PbO$), molybdate orange (a solution of $PbSO_4$, $PbCrO_4$, and $PbMoO_4$), chrome green (a mixture of $PbCrO_4$ and Prussian blue), and zinc yellow (potassium zinc chromate). Several of these, particularly zinc yellow, are used to inhibit corrosion. The gems ruby, emerald, and alexandrite owe their colors to traces of chromium compounds. *See* CORROSION; EMERALD; PAINT; RUBY.

Dichromates are widely used as oxidizing agents, as rust inhibitors on steel, and as wood preservatives. In the last application, they kill fungi, termites, and boring insects. The wood can still be painted and glued, and retains its strength. Other chromium compounds find use as catalysts, as drilling muds, and in photochemical reactions. The last are important in the printing industry. A metal plate is coated with a colloidal material (for example, glue, shellac, or casein) containing a dichromate. On exposure to strong light under a negative image, the dichromate is reduced to Cr^{3+}, which reacts with the colloid, hardening it and making it resistant to removal by washing. The unexposed material is washed off, and the metal plate is etched with acid to give a printing plate. *See* PRINTING.

Biological aspects. Chromium is essential to life. A deficiency (in rats and monkeys) has been shown to impair glucose tolerance, decrease glycogen reserve, and inhibit the utilization of amino acids. It has also been found that inclusion of chromium in the diet of humans sometimes, but not always, improves glucose tolerance. Certain chromium(III) compounds enhance the action of insulin.

On the other hand, chromates and dichromates are severe irritants to the skin and mucous membranes, so workers who handle large amounts of these materials must be protected against dusts and mists. Continued breathing of the dusts finally leads to ulceration and perforation of the nasal septum. Contact of cuts or abrasions with chromate may lead to serious ulceration. Even on normal skin, dermatitis frequently

(6)

results. Cases of lung cancer have been observed in plants where chromates are manufactured.

John C. Bailar, Jr.

Bibliography. J. Bowser, *Inorganic Chemistry*, 1993; F. A. Cotton and G. Wilkinson, *Advanced Inorganic Chemistry*, 5th ed., 1988; D. Katakis and G. Gordon, *Mechanisms of Inorganic Reactions*, 1987; *Kirk-Othmer Encyclopedia of Chemical Technology*, vol. 4, 4th ed., 1993; S. Langard, *Biological and Environmental Aspects of Chromium*, 1983; M. E. Weeks, The discovery of the elements, 7th ed., *J. Chem. Educ.*, pp. 271–281, 1968; A. F. Wells, *Structural Inorganic Chemistry*, 5th ed., 1983.

Chromophycota

A division of the plant kingdom (also known as Chromophyta) comprising nine classes of algae: Bacillariophyceae (diatoms), Chrysophyceae (golden or golden-brown algae), Cryptophyceae, Dinophyceae (dinoflagellates), Eustigmatophyceae, Phaeophyceae (brown algae), Prymnesiophyceae, Raphidophyceae, and Xanthophyceae (yellow-green algae). Some of these classes are closely related, while others stand so far apart that they are sometimes assigned to their own divisions. The chief unifying character is the presence of chlorophyll *c* rather than chlorophyll *b* as a complement to chlorophyll *a* (although only chlorophyll *a* is present in Eustigmatophyceae). The chloroplasts are usually brown or yellowish because of large amounts of β-carotene and various xanthophylls, many of which are restricted to one or more classes. Storage products include lipids, starch, and glucans (glucose polymers with β-1,3 linkages). In all classes except Dinophyceae, the chloroplast is surrounded by chloroplast endoplasmic reticulum that is continuous with the nuclear envelope, and the deoxyribonucleic acid of the chloroplast forms an annular genophore. Except in Cryptophyceae, thylakoids are in groups of three. In most classes, motile cells bear two unequal flagella, one of which may be almost completely reduced and at least one of which bears two rows of hairlike appendages. Algae in this division range in size and complexity from unicellular flagellates to gigantic kelps. *See* ALGAE; BACILLARIOPHYCEAE; CHRYSOPHYCEAE; CRYPTOPHYCEAE; DINOPHYCEAE; EUSTIGMATOPHYCEAE; PHAEOPHYCEAE; PRYMNESIOPHYCEAE; RAPHIDOPHYCEAE; XANTHOPHYCEAE.

Paul C. Silva; Richard L. Moe

Chromosome

Any of the organized components of each cell which carry the individual's hereditary material, deoxyribonucleic acid (DNA). Chromosomes are found in all organisms with a cell nucleus (eukaryotes) and are located within the nucleus.

The simplest organisms (prokaryotes) do not have a cell nucleus or true chromosomes. Each chromosome contains a single extremely long DNA molecule that is packaged by various proteins into a compact domain within the tiny nucleus. A full set, or complement, of chromosomes is carried by each sperm or ovum in animals and each pollen or ovule in plants. This constitutes the haploid (*n*) genome of that organism and contains a complete set of the genes characteristic of that organism. Sexually reproducing organisms in both the plant and animal kingdoms begin their development by the fusion of two haploid germ cells and are thus diploid (2*n*), with two sets of chromosomes in each body cell. These two sets of chromosomes carry virtually all the thousands of genes of each cell, with the exception of the tiny number in the mitochrondria, which are essential for generation of energy-rich adenosinetriphosphate (ATP). *See* DEOXYRIBONUCLEIC ACID (DNA); GENE.

Chromosomes can change their conformation and degree of compaction throughout the cell cycle. During interphase, the major portion of the cycle, the DNA of active genes is available to the enzymes that are essential for ribonucleic acid (RNA) synthesis, and for a fraction of interphase (the DNA synthetic or S phase) all the DNA is available for DNA synthesis. During interphase, chromosomes are not visible under the light microscope because, although they are very long, they are extremely thin. However, during cell division (mitosis or meiosis), the chromosomes become compacted into shorter and thicker structures that can be seen under the microscope. At this time they appear as paired rods with defined ends, called telomeres, and they remain joined at a constricted region, the centromere, until the beginning of anaphase of cell division. *See* CELL CYCLE; CELL DIVISION.

Chromosomes are distinguished from one another by length and position of the centromere. In this way, chromosomes can be divided into metacentric groups (the centromere is in the middle of the chromosome), acrocentric groups (the centromere is closer to one end), or telocentric groups (the centromere is at the end, or telomere). The centromere thus usually lies between two chromosome arms, one often being longer than the other, which contain the genes and their regulatory regions, as well as other DNA sequences that have no known function. In many species, regional differences in base composition and in the time at which the DNA is replicated serve as the basis for special staining techniques that make visible a series of distinctive bands on each arm, and these can be used to identify the chromosome.

Composition. Chromosomes are made up essentially of DNA and proteins. The DNA is in the form of an extremely long, threadlike double-stranded helix. Each strand has a continuous backbone of millions of alternating phosphate and deoxyribose sugar units. A nucleotide base is attached to each sugar molecule and can be either adenine (A), cytosine (C), guanine (G), or thymine (T). The two

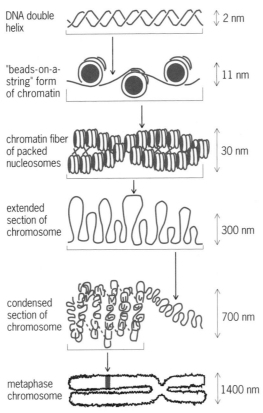

DNA double helix — 2 nm

"beads-on-a-string" form of chromatin — 11 nm

chromatin fiber of packed nucleosomes — 30 nm

extended section of chromosome — 300 nm

condensed section of chromosome — 700 nm

metaphase chromosome — 1400 nm

Fig. 1. Organization of DNA into chromosomes. (*From B. Alberts et al., Molecular Biology of the Cell, 2d ed., Garland Publishing, 1989*)

complementary strands of the double helix are held together by hydrogen bonds between specific nucleotide base pairs: two hydrogen bonds between each AT base pair and three hydrogen bonds between each GC base pair. Since A can pair only with T, and G can pair only with C, each strand carries the information needed to make a new DNA strand complementary to itself (and identical to the other strand) in the process of DNA synthesis (replication), or to make a strand of RNA complementary to itself in the process of RNA synthesis (transcription). *See* NUCLEOPROTEIN.

A linear sequence of bases in a messenger RNA molecule is translated into a linear series of amino acids in a polypeptide chain or protein on the basis of a nonoverlapping triplet code; that is, each successive amino acid in a growing polypeptide chain is specified by the next set of three nucleotide bases in an RNA message synthesized on a DNA template. Most of the estimated 5000–100,000 genes present in eukaryotes act by encoding proteins in this way. For an important minority of the genes, the RNA transcript itself is the functional gene product. Examples are the small nuclear and nucleolar RNAs involved in preparing mature ribosomal and messenger RNAs, and the ribosomal and transfer RNAs involved in protein synthesis. *See* RIBONUCLEIC ACID (RNA).

Each nucleus in the cell of a human or other mammal contains some 6 billion base pairs of DNA which, if stretched out, would form a very thin thread about 6 ft (2 m) long. This DNA has to be packaged into the chromosome within a nucleus that is much smaller than a printed dot (**Fig. 1**). Each chromosome contains a single length of DNA comprising a specific portion of the genetic material of the organism. Tiny stretches of DNA, about 140 base pairs long and containing acidic phosphate groups, are individually wrapped around an octamer consisting of two molecules of each of the four basic histone proteins H2a, H2b, H3, and H4. This arrangement produces small structures called nucleosomes and results in a sevenfold compaction of the DNA strand. Further compaction is achieved by binding the histone protein H1 and several nonhistone proteins, resulting in a supercoiled structure in which the chromosome is shortened by about 1600-fold in the interphase nucleus and by about 8000-fold during metaphase and anaphase, where the genetic material must be fully compacted for transport to the two daughter cells. At the point of maximum compaction, human chromosomes range in size from about 2 to 10 micrometers in length, that is, less than 0.0004 in. *See* NUCLEOSOME.

Number. Each diploid (*2n*) organism has a characteristic number of chromosomes in each body (somatic) cell, which can vary from two in a nematode worm and one species of ant, to hundreds in some butterflies, crustaceans, and plants which have undergone polyploidization in their evolution (see **table**). The diploid number of chromosomes includes a haploid (*n*) set from each parent. Many one-celled organisms are haploid throughout most of their life cycle. The fission yeast (*Schizosaccharomyces pombe*) has $n = 3$ chromosomes, while the budding yeast (*Saccharomyces cerevisiae*), the common bread

Diploid numbers of chromosomes for selected species	
Species	Chromosome number
Gray kangaroo	16
Domestic horse	64
Zebra	32
Indian muntjac	6,7
Chinese muntjac	46
Cats	38
Domestic dog	78
Fox	34
Gorilla	48
Human	46
Chicken	78
Budding yeast	32
Fission yeast	6
Nematode	2
Scorpion	12
Fruit fly	8
Hermit crab	254
Corn (maize)	20
Wheat	42
Goldfish	104
Salamander	24
Rattlesnake	36

mold, has $n = 16$ chromosomes. *See* POLYPLOIDY.

The human diploid number is 46. Gorilla and chimpanzee chromosomes are very similar to those of the human, but both of these great apes have 48 chromosomes because only in the human was chromosome number 2 formed by fusion of two different acrocentric chromosomes characteristic of their common primate ancestor. Members of some groups of animals, such as the horses, show marked differences in chromosome number from one species to another. For example, the zebra has only half as many chromosomes as does the domestic horse. In other groups, such as the cats, all the member species share the same number of chromosomes.

There is some relationship between the number of chromosomes and their size. Marsupials, which are metatherians, usually have a diploid number of 14–16 chromosomes as well as larger and fewer chromosomes than do most eutherian mammals. However, there are some interesting exceptions. For example, like other deer, the Chinese muntjak has 46 chromosomes, but the closely related Indian muntjak has only 6 much larger chromosomes in the XX female and 7 in the XY_1Y_2 male. Each of these large chromosomes is composed of several of the smaller Chinese muntjak chromosomes as a result of a massive reshuffling of the genome. Some of the chromosomes in certain classes of organisms with large numbers of chromosomes are very tiny, and have been called microchromosomes. In birds and some reptiles, there are about 30–40 pairs of microchromosomes in addition to 5–7 or so pairs of regular-sized macrochromosomes. The number of microchromosomes is constant in any species carrying them, and only their size distinguishes them from the widespread macrochromosomes. At least three microchromosomes in birds have been shown to contain genes, and all are thought to.

In some species of insects, plants, flatworms, snails, and rarely vertebrates (such as the fox), the number of chromosomes can vary because of the presence of a variable number of accessory chromosomes, called B chromosomes. It is not clear what role, if any, B chromosomes play, but they appear to be made primarily of DNA that does not contain functional genes and does not have much effect on the animal or plant even when present in multiple copies.

Telomeres. Telomeres are essential for chromosome stability. A telomere caps each end of every chromosome and protects it from being digested by enzymes (exonucleases) present in the same cell, possibly by having a short single-stranded DNA segment that folds back on itself with unusual G-G pairing, leaving no free end to be degraded. Most important, the telomere permits DNA replication to continue to the very end of the chromosome, thus assuring its stability. The telomere is also involved in attachment of the chromosome ends to the nuclear membrane and in pairing of homologous chromosomes during meiosis.

The structure of telomeric DNA is very similar in virtually all eukaryotic organisms except the fruit fly (*Drosophila*). One strand of the DNA is rich in guanine and is oriented 5' to 3' toward the end of the chromosome, and the other strand is rich in cytosine and is oriented 5' to 3' toward the centromere. Replication of DNA always occurs in the 5' to 3' direction, starting from an RNA primer complementary to the opposite strand of the DNA. Thus, in the absence of some provision for a special template structure, the end of the chromosome arm would be shortened by the length of the RNA primer each time the DNA is replicated. In order to avoid such shortening, in each replication cycle, at least in the germ line, an enzyme called a telomerase adds additional telomere repeats on the G-rich strand at the end of each telomere. There is some evidence that the telomere region becomes shorter in somatic cells with repeated cell divisions, and hence with age, because fewer copies of the telomere repeat are present in human adult somatic cells than in human embryonic cells or sperm.

In most organisms, the telomere consists of multiple copies of a very short DNA repeat. For example, each human telomere contains about 2 million copies (10,000–15,000 kilobases) of a tandemly repeating TTAGGG sequence. Although the specific number and composition of the repeat units differ among various organisms, widely diverse organisms may share the same repeat unit, as do humans and slime molds. In fact, the telomere of one organism may function in a different organism; for example, a human telomere can function in a yeast cell. However, the sequences added to that telomere by yeast telomerase will be those specific for the yeast cell.

The fruit fly is an exception. Its telomere is composed of several types of very long DNA repeats, one called HeT and another called a TART sequence. These can act as transposable elements and are not synthesized by a telomerase. Instead, the infrequent addition for a single copy several thousand bases pairs long to each telomere counteracts the gradual shortening of the chromosome end at each cycle of DNA replication.

Centromeres. The centromere is the chromosome structure which is responsible for proper segregation of each chromosome pair during cell division. The chromatids in mitosis and each pair of homologous chromosomes in meiosis are held together at the centromere until anaphase, when they separate and move to the spindle pole, thus being distributed to the two daughter cells. The kinetochore, which is the attachment site for the microtubules that guide the movement of the chromosomes to the poles, is organized around the centromere.

The molecular composition of the centromere is known in detail in only two species, the budding yeast and the fission yeast. In the budding yeast, the entire sequence necessary for centromeric function is no more than 120 base pairs long and consists of two short protein-binding regions flanking a longer AT-rich sequence. The DNA sequence of the centromere of each of the 16 chromosomes in this budding yeast differs, but the centromere of one chromosome can substitute for that of a different chromosome in this species. In the fission yeast, the centromeric DNA is much more complex, consisting of long, direct and inverted repeats flanking a core element of approximately 5,000 base pairs. Each of the three centromeres in the fission yeast is a different length, ranging from 40,000 to 120,000 base pairs. A centromere from a chromosome of one organism cannot function in the other.

The molecular structures of centromeres in other species, including mammals, are still unclear, although most appear to be even larger and more complex than those of fission yeast. All centromeres seem to contain sequences that bind proteins, and these are contained in a series of short, highly repetitive DNA sequences. In a wide variety of species, some of the proteins bound to the centromere are sufficiently similar that they can be detected by antibodies present in the serum of humans with an autoimmune disease, the CREST type of scleroderma. As a general rule, only closely related species share similar centromeric sequences. In humans and great apes, one of these repetitive families is called alpha satellite DNA. The precise sequence of its repeats of 170-base-pair length differs slightly even on different human chromosomes, so that the type of alpha satellite present can be used to identify specific human chromosomes by in situ hybridization.

The repetitive DNA making up and surrounding the centromere is called heterochromatin because it remains condensed throughout the cell cycle and hence stains intensely. In humans, this region includes multiple copies of the alpha satellite DNA as well as several other types of satellite DNA. Satellites I, II, and III consist of many copies of short repeat units, some only five to eight base pairs long, and they can be partially purified by density-gradient centrifugation because their average base composition, and thus their density, differs from that of the rest of the DNA. Such repetitive-sequence DNAs can undergo changes in composition and in number, with the result that the size of the centromeric heterochromatin region can vary between chromosomes, and even between members of the same pair of homologous chromosomes, usually without any apparent effect on centromeric function.

Nucleolus organizer regions. One or more pairs of chromosomes in each species have a region called a secondary constriction which does not stain well. This region contains multiple copies of the genes that transcribe, within the nucleolus, the ribosomal RNA (rRNA), which is an essential component of the ribosomes on which proteins are synthesized. In humans, all five pairs of acrocentric chromosomes usually have a cluster of rRNA genes, each containing up to 40 or more gene copies.

These genes are clustered in other species as well, often on a single pair of chromosomes. The rRNA genes take part in forming a nucleolus, and as a result the nucleolus organizer regions can often be found still associated during metaphase, although rRNA synthesis, like that of all other genes, ceases during cell division. The presence of such associations has been used as an indication that the rRNA genes on chromosomes in association were active. A silver-staining technique is used to identify only active rRNA gene clusters. The number of active rRNA genes may be regulated, and an organism that has too few copies of the rRNA genes may develop abnormally or not survive. *See* RIBOSOMES.

Chromosome bands and staining methods. The classical chromosome stains, such as orcein or Giemsa, produce intense, uniform staining of every chromosome, except for the centromere which is less intense, and are particularly effective for demonstrating the ends of each arm and the position of the centromere. This type of stain can be used to identify specific chromosomes only in species in which the chromosomes in the complement differ quite a bit in length or in the position of the centromere.

Staining with quinacrine mustard produces consistent, bright and less bright fluorescence bands (Q bands) along the chromosome arms because of differences in the relative amounts of CG or AT base pairs. The distinctive Q-band pattern of each chromosome makes it possible to identify every chromosome in the human genome. Quinacrine fluorescence can also reveal a difference in the amount or type of heterochromatin on the two members of a homologous pair of chromosomes, called heteromorphism or polymorphism. Such differences can be used to identify the parental origin of a specific chromosome, such as the extra chromosome in individuals who have trisomy 21.

Many methods have been devised to enhance the banding patterns inherent in chromosome structure in mammals, birds, reptiles, and other organisms. Two methods involve treating chromosomes in various ways before staining with Giemsa. Giemsa or G-band patterns are essentially identical to Q-band patterns; reverse Giemsa or R-band patterns are the reverse, or reciprocal, of those seen with Q or G banding.

In humans, most other mammals, and birds (macrochromosomes only), the Q-, G-, and R-banding patterns are so distinctive that each chromosome pair can be individually identified, making it possible to construct a karyotype, or organized array of the chromosome pairs from a single cell (**Fig. 2**). The chromosomes are identified on the basis of the banding patterns, and the pairs are arranged and numbered in some order, often based on length. In the human karyotype, the autosomes are numbered 1 through 22, and the sex chromosomes are called X and Y. The short

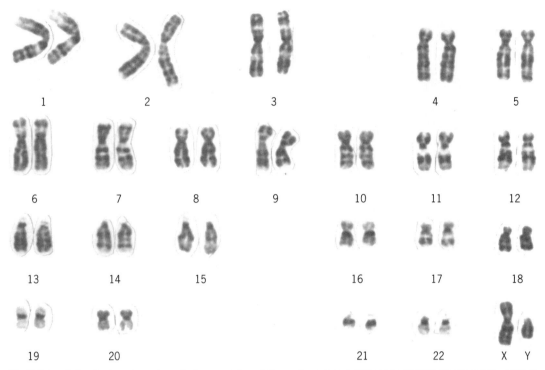

Fig. 2. G-banded metaphase karyotype of a human male cell. Every chromosome pair can be identified by its banding pattern. Chromosome 1 is about 12 μm long.

arm of a chromosome is called the p arm, and the long arm is called the q arm; a number is assigned to each band on the arm. Thus, band 1q23 refers to band 23 on the long arm of human chromosome 1.

G and R bands. G bands and R bands differ in a variety of ways. In humans, each R band may contain up to 100 or more genes. The majority of genes appear to be in the R bands, including all the housekeeping genes, which are active in all cells, and some of the tissue-specific genes, which are active in only certain cell types. R bands are rich in many short interspersed repeat DNA sequences. In contrast, only tissue-specific genes (those that are active in only certain types of cells) are located in the G bands. G bands are replicated later than R bands, although not as late as heterochromatin. G bands are rich in long interspersed repeat DNA sequences.

The polytene chromosomes present in *Drosophila* or other dipteran fly salivary glands (**Fig. 3***b*) are also banded, but these bands have a different origin than G and R bands. Polytene chromosomes are produced by multiple (up to 10 or 13) rounds of DNA replication, or endoreduplication, of the genes in somatically paired dipteran chromosomes, without any separation of the duplicated strands. Thus, each of the approximately 5000 bands may contain a single gene, or very few genes at most. The activity of a gene may result in the formation of a puff in the polytene chromosome. Polytene chromosomes are present not only in dipteran insects but also

in specialized tissues of plant embryos. Endoreduplication also occurs in certain specialized cells in mammals, notably in trophoblast cells of the placenta, but the endoreduplicated chromosomes do not remain attached to each other, so the cells are polyploid, with increased numbers of chromosome sets rather than polytene chromosomes.

Other staining methods. There are methods which make it possible to stain only selected regions of chromosomes. For example, C-banding techniques produce dark staining of heterochromatin (especially in the centromeric regions) and light staining of the euchromatin. Heterochromatin does not contain genes and is replicated very late. Restriction-enzyme banding is useful for distinguishing different types of repeated-sequence DNAs in heterochromatin. Replication banding is used to determine when DNA in a particular band is replicated during the cell cycle. It is based on the incorporation of radioactive molecules (for example, tritium) which can later be detected by autoradiography or, for better resolution, bromodeoxyuridine, detectable by specific antibodies or by selective destruction of DNA that has incorporated bromodeoxyuridine. Replication banding is particularly useful because it occurs even in many species in which standard G- or R-banding techniques do not produce banding. This diverse group includes fish, amphibia, and some plants. In many of these organisms, replication banding is the best method to identify individual chromosomes in the complement. Replication banding has also been used to

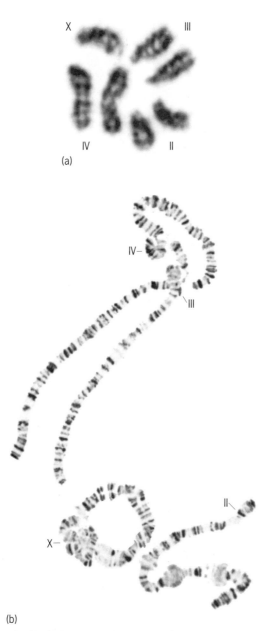

Fig. 3. Chromosomes of the fungus gnat (*Sciara coprophila*). (*a*) Mitotic metaphase spread from an XO male fly, showing somatic pairings of homologous chromosomes. Chromosome IV is about 5 μm long. (*b*) Polytene chromosome (containing identical chromosomes) spread from a female fly.

carries a particular gene or set of linked genes, other methods are necessary. Some of these can be used to identify both the chromosome carrying a specific gene and the chromosome band in which a gene or isolated piece of DNA is located. *See* LINKAGE (GENETICS).

One method involves the use of somatic cell hybrids. Cells from two species, for example, mouse and human, are fused together to form a hybrid cell containing chromosomes from both parents. Such hybrid cells tend to lose chromosomes from one parent, usually the human chromosomes from a rodent-human hybrid cell, with the result that any human gene still present in the hybrid cell after it has lost most of the human chromosomes must be located on a remaining chromosome. In mapping studies, a panel of hybrids, each containing a different partial set of human chromosomes, is analyzed to identify the single human chromosome present in all the hybrids that have a specific gene, and only in those hybrids. This approach can be extended to the regional localization of the gene by using a second panel composed of hybrids that contain different segments of the chromosome to which the gene has been mapped. *See* SOMATIC CELL GENETICS.

A second widely used method for mapping is in situ hybridization. It is based on annealing (hybridizing) single-stranded, labeled copies of the gene or DNA segment directly to denatured (single-stranded) DNA in chromosomes on a microscope slide. The gene is labeled by radioactivity or fluorescence so that its location on a chromosome band can be determined microscopically. Fluorescence in situ hybridization (FISH) is the most widely used technique for mapping genes. About 3000 human genes have been mapped to specific chromosome locations, but this is only a small fraction of the estimated 50,000–100,000 genes in the human genome.

The banding patterns of portions of chromosomes have been maintained over long evolutionary distances. Correspondences are very close between human and chimpanzee or gorilla chromosomes, but quite a number of correspondences have been retained between more distantly related species, for example, human and cat. Once a gene is mapped to a specific chromosome band in one organism, comparative banding analysis provides a clue to where it may be located in the second species. *See* GENETIC MAPPING.

Imprinting. A chromosome carries the same complement of genes, whether it is transmitted from the father or the mother, and most of these genes appear to be functionally the same. However, a small number of mammalian genes are functionally different, depending on whether they were transmitted by the egg or by the sperm. This phenomenon is known as imprinting. It appears to be caused by the inactivation of certain genes in sperm, probably by methylation of cytosine residues within the regulatory (promotor) region

identify the inactive X chromosome in mammalian female cells, because the inactive X replicates later than the active X.

Genetic mapping. Genes that are close to one another on a chromosome are usually inherited together, rather than becoming separated by crossing over between the paired homologous chromosomes during meiosis; that is, they show genetic linkage. Genes that are farther apart on a chromosome are more frequently separated from each other by crossing over. However, in order to identify the chromosome in the complement which of the imprinted gene. As a result of imprinting, normal development of the mammalian embryo requires the presence of both a maternal and a paternal set of chromosomes. Parthenogenesis, the formation of a normal individual from two sets of maternal chromosomes, is therefore not possible in mammals. In contrast, some lizards reproduce parthenogenetically and have only maternal chromosomes.

Sex chromosomes. In most mammals, including humans, the sex of an individual is determined by whether or not a Y chromosome is present. Thus XX and the rare XO individuals are female, while XY and the uncommon XXY individuals are male. In contrast, sex in the fruit fly depends on the balance of autosomes and X chromosomes. Thus, in diploids, XX and the rare XXY flies are female, while XY and the rare XO flies are male. In both mammals and fruit flies, males are the heterogametic sex, producing gametes that contain either an X or a Y chromosome; and females are the homogametic sex, producing only gametes containing an X. In birds and butterflies, however, females are the heterogametic sex and males the homogametic sex; fertilized eggs with two Z chromosomes develop as males and those with a Z and a W chromosome develop as females. Other sex-determining systems are used by some classes of organisms, while sex in some species is determined by a single gene or even by environmental factors such as temperature (some turtles and alligators) or the presence of a nearby female (*Bonellia*, a marine worm) rather than by a chromosome-mediated mechanism.

The X chromosome in eutherian mammals has been conserved for more than 60–80 million years, as shown by the fact that the X chromosomes of primates, carnivores, pigs, and camels all show identical gene content and similar banding patterns. The X chromosome usually makes up about 5% of the length of the haploid complement in most mammals, although in some species the X chromosome is larger because it contains increased amounts of heterochromatin or, less commonly, it has undergone a translocation, exchanging unequal segments of a chromosome arm with another chromosome.

The X chromosome contains a relatively large proportion of the genes that have been mapped in the human. This is true in part because the inheritance of a gene located on the X chromosome is easy to follow. A single copy of a mutated X-linked gene will be expressed in a male, whereas a single copy of a mutated gene on an autosome may have no effect if the normal gene copy on the homologous chromosome produces sufficient gene product for normal function.

If the genes on both X chromosomes were fully expressed in female cells, then male cells, which have only one X, would exhibit only half as much gene product as female cells. In the mammalian female, genes on only one X chromosome are expressed, and genes on any additional X chromosomes are inactivated. This X inactivation (a type of chromosome differentiation) randomly occurs during an early stage in embryonic development, and is transmitted unchanged to each of the daughter cells. Females are therefore mosaics of two types of cells, those with an active maternally derived X and those with an active paternally derived X. This finding made it possible to demonstrate that some tumors are monoclonal in origin, that is, they are derived from a single cell, because the same X chromosome is inactivated in every cell in the tumor.

Species other than mammals do not show this type of dosage compensation mechanism for sex-linked genes, and some show none at all. Included are birds, with their ZW/ZZ sex-determining mechanism, and amphibia, with either an XX/XY or a ZW/ZZ sex-determining mechanism. *Drosophila* uses a different mechanism for dosage compensation: the activity of genes on the single X chromosome in the males is increased, so that the level of gene product is equivalent to that in females.

The Y chromosome is one of the smallest chromosomes in the genome in most mammalian species, and sometimes, as in the gibbon, it appears as only a dot in metaphase. Usually the mammalian Y chromosome has a very high proportion of heterochromatin, as does the large Y chromosome in *Drosophila*. It is thus not surprising that only a few genes are located on the Y chromosome in mammals, as in *Drosophila*, or that most of these genes are concerned with either sex determination or the production of sperm. The W chromosome in birds is correspondingly small and is largely heterochromatic, but its genic content is virtually unknown. In some species of insects and other invertebrates, no Y chromosome is present, and sex in these species is determined by the X:autosome balance (XX female, XO male). *See* CELL NUCLEUS; GENETICS; HUMAN GENETICS; SEX DETERMINATION; SEX-LINKED INHERITANCE.

Orlando J. Mille; Dorothy A. Mille

Bibliography. N. Cooper, *The Human Genome Project*, 1994; A. T. Sumner, *Chromosome Banding*, 1990; R. P. Wagner, M. P. Maguire, and R. L. Stallings, *Chromosomes: A Synthesis*, 1993.

Chromosome aberration

Any numerical or structural change in the usual chromosome complement of a cell or organism.

Heteroploidy. Numerical changes (heteroploidy) are of two types, polyploidy and aneuploidy. Polyploidy is a change in the number of chromosome sets. The polyploid condition has both advantages and disadvantages. For example, tetraploid (4n) plants can be fertile because each chromosome can pair in meiosis with a homologous chromosome and segregate properly to form euploid $2n$ gametes or germ cells. These plants are larger than diploid varieties and produce larger fruit making them valuable commercially. Triploid ($3n$) plants, however, are usually sterile because of the inability of every chromosome to find a homologous chromosome to pair with in meiosis. The result is improper segregation (nondisjunction) of chromosomes and aneuploidy in the progeny. Triploidy rarely occurs in animals. Triploid reptiles and frogs are seen only in populations that reproduce parthenogenetically from unfertilized eggs that have not undergone the meiotic divisions that could produce aneuploid ova. Triploidy occurs in about 1% of human pregnancies, but it is almost always an embryonic lethal condition. *See* MEIOSIS; MITOSIS; POLYPLOIDY.

Aneuploidy is a change in the number of chromosomes from the diploid ($2n$) number (usually found in the somatic cells of sexually reproducing organisms, including animals and plants) or the haploid (n) number (usually found in germ cells and the haplophase of some unicellular organisms.) Aneuploidy involves either an increase or a decrease in the number of chromosomes. It usually involves a single chromosome, and any chromosome in the complement can be involved. Aneuploidy is the result of aberrant segregation of one or more chromosomes during meiosis or mitosis. If malsegregation or nondisjunction occurs during meiosis, one daughter cell receives two copies of the chromosome and the other daughter cell receives none. Fertilization of such an aneuploid germ cell by a euploid gamete will produce a zygote that has either three copies (trisomy) or one copy (monosomy) of the chromosome. Malsegregation of a chromosome can also take place during a mitotic division in a somatic cell, producing trisomic or monosomic cells in an otherwise euploid individual. This outcome is important primarily in the origin and progression of some forms of cancer. In humans, nearly 20% of ova and 7% of sperm may be aneuploid, and at least 3% of recognized pregnancies are trisomic and 1% are XO, that is, having a single sex chromosome per cell. Also, nearly half of all miscarriages and 3% of stillbirths are the result of aneuploidy.

Autosomal trisomy. The most common trisomy in human liveborns is trisomy 21, or Down syndrome, which is a major cause of mental retardation and congenital heart disease. Individuals with trisomy 18 and trisomy 13 also occur but are much less common. Most autosomal trisomies are lethal to embryos, leading to spontaneous abortion. The incidence of trisomy for any autosome increases exponentially with maternal age. For trisomy 21, the risk is about 1 in 100 for women over 35 years of age, and much greater for women over age 40. In about 80% of cases, the extra chromosome 21 is inherited from the mother and in 20% from the father, the latter case showing no paternal age effect on incidence. *See* DOWN SYNDROME.

Sex chromosome aneuploidy. In humans, there are more types of aneuploidy involving the sex chromosomes than the autosomes. The most common is XO, occurring in about 1% of pregnancies, with the risk being slightly higher in very young mothers. Although 99% of XO fetuses die early in pregnancy, the other 1% (about 1 in 10,000 liveborn females) survive. The high frequency of deaths of most XO fetuses is somewhat puzzling because the somatic cells in XX females have only a single active X chromosome. It is believed that the cause of death may be the presence of one or more genes on the tiny shared (homologous) segment of X and Y that remain active on both the Y and the otherwise inactive X chromosome. Adults who are XO tend to be short, with some webbing of the neck. They rarely develop secondary sexual characteristics or have children because the germ cells essential for ovarian development are usually absent. These features are characteristic of Turner syndrome. *See* HUMAN GENETICS.

Trisomy for the human X chromosome, commonly called XXX, is not associated with embryonic death or congenital malformations. The reason is that in all mammals, including humans, only a single X chromosome is active in each somatic cell; additional X chromosomes are inactivated, so almost all of their genes fail to be expressed. These are adult individuals with as many as five X chromosomes, and while they are physically normal they do show some degree of mental retardation.

In contrast to autosomal trisomy, sex chromosome aneuploidy increases only slightly with maternal age, and the extra X chromosome comes from the mother in only about 60% of the cases. About 1 of every 1000 liveborn females is XXX, while 1 of every 1000 liveborn males is XXY and 1 is XYY. An additional X chromosome can be present in either egg or sperm; additional Y chromosomes can be present only in sperm. The XXX and XXY individuals display minimal phenotypic manifestations of their increased number of chromosomes, although XXY males are usually sterile and have an increased risk of mild mental retardation. Individuals who are XYY generally are indistinguishable from XY individuals, although they are questionably at a slightly increased risk of antisocial behavior. The presence of a Y chromosome leads to male sex differentiation no matter how many X chromosomes are present, because of the presence of a single, critical gene, called *SRY*, on the Y chromosome. A mutation of this gene has been found in some XY individuals who developed as females.

Structural abnormalities. Structural abnormalities (chromosome mutations) involve the gain, loss, or rearrangement of chromosome segments after the continuity of the deoxyribonucleic acid (DNA) strand in one or more chromosomes is disrupted (**Fig. 1**).

Deletion. A deletion involves the loss of a chromosome segment and the genes it carries. A

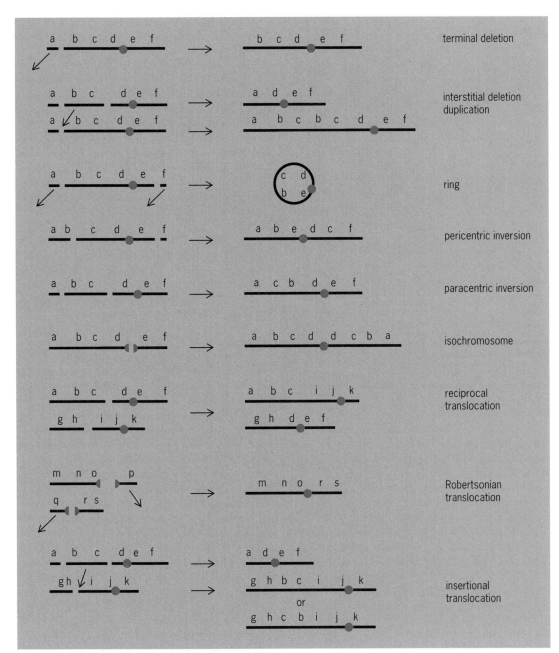

Fig. 1. Diagram of various types of structural abnormalities.

terminal deletion involves the loss of a segment extending from the point of disruption (breakpoint) to the end of the same arm of a chromosome. It is relatively uncommon because the broken end of the chromosome is usually repaired during DNA replication, resulting in a dicentric chromosome that is unstable because its two centromeres tend to be pulled toward opposite spindle poles at anaphase of cell division. The result is the breakage and eventual loss of the chromosome. An interstitial deletion involves the loss of the segment between two breakpoints in one arm of a chromosome (**Fig. 2**). The effect of such a loss depends on the genes that are included in the missing segment. If a deletion is associated with a genetic disease, the chromosome breakpoint provides a clue to the location of the gene responsible for the disease. For example, deletions were useful in mapping and isolating the human gene for retinoblastoma.

Fragments and duplication. When one break occurs in each arm of a chromosome, the broken ends of the internal centromeric fragment may join, resulting in the formation of a stable ring chromosome (Fig. 2). Each of the two end segments lacks a centromere, and such acentric fragments are lost during cell division, resulting in deletion of both end segments. Ring chromosomes are subject to reduction in size, as well as doubling. An individual who has a ring chromosome may thus show phenotypic effects not only of deletion but of duplication of part of the chromosome. A duplication more commonly occurs in other ways. For example,

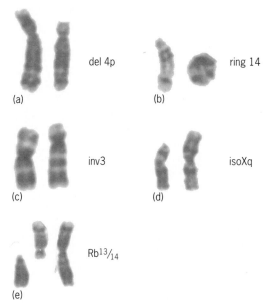

Fig. 2. G-banded human chromosomes illustrating structural chromosome abnormalities present in different individuals. The normal chromosome(s) is on the left in each case. (a) Terminal deletion of the short arm of chromosome 4 (4p). (b) Ring chromosome 14. (c) Pericentric inversion of chromosome 3. (d) Isochromosome of the long arm of the X. (e) Robertsonian translocation of chromosomes 13 and 14.

a chromosome segment can undergo tandem or inverted duplication at the usual chromosome site, or the second copy of the segment may be carried on another chromosome.

Inversion. An inversion is generated by disrupting the DNA strand in a chromosome at two breakpoints and rejoining the broken ends with the interstitial segment in the opposite orientation. This process will invert the order of the genes on the segment (Fig. 2). The centromere is included in the inverted segment in pericentric inversions but not in paracentric inversions. Thus, pericentric inversions can often be identified by an altered position of the centromere, while paracentric inversions can be identified only by an altered banding pattern or altered gene order.

Translocation. A translocation involves the interchange of one or more chromosome segments between two or more chromosomes. A reciprocal translocation involves the reciprocal exchange of the segment produced by a single break in one chromosome for the segment produced by a single break in another chromosome. A Robertsonian translocation (Fig. 2) is produced by the rejoining of the long arms and centromere of two acrocentric or telocentric chromosomes after disruptions in the short arm or at the centromere. It results in the reduction of chromosome number by one, except in the rare case in which the two short arms rejoin and the tiny fragment retains a functional centromere. An insertional translocation is produced when the interstitial segment between two breakpoints in one chromosome is inserted into a breakpoint in another chromosome. A complex transloca-

tion involves rearrangement of segments from three or more chromosomes. *See* GENE AMPLIFICATION; MUTATION.

Consequences of translocations and inversions. If a translocation breakpoint disrupts a gene, the gene's function will be blocked or abnormal, and such can have deleterious effects on development or function. Sometimes a normally silent gene is activated by a chromosome rearrangement that places it next to a strong promoter of gene expression, and this change is important as a cause of cancer. If a translocation does not block the function of an essential gene or activate a normally silent gene, the individual carrying the rearrangement will be normal.

In an individual carrying an inversion on one of a pair of homologous chromosomes, pairing leads to the formation of a loop containing the inverted segment. Crossing over within the loop leads either to the formation of gametes with a duplication of one segment of the inversion and a deficiency of the other segment, or to two abnormal chromosomes, one with two centromeres and the other lacking a centromere. *See* CROSSING-OVER (GENETICS).

Causes. Structural aberrations can occur spontaneously or be induced by agents that break chromosomes, such as x-rays, radioactive substances, ultraviolet rays, and certain chemicals. The most frequent cause may be the presence of enormous numbers of a few types of short interspersed elements (SINES), that is, DNA sequences that occur once every few thousand base pairs throughout the genome of most metazoans, including humans. These elements predispose to the occurrence of errors during DNA replication or genetic recombination at meiosis that can lead to the deletion or duplication of the region between two nearby interspersed repeats on one chromosome. They may also play a role in the formation of inversions and, possibly, translocations. *See* MUTAGENS AND CARCINOGENS.

Another cause of structural aberrations is also inherent in the genome: the great abundance of short repeats of a 2-, 3-, or 4-base-pair unit. Some trinucleotide repeats, such as $(CGG)_n$ or $(CAG)_n$, can undergo expansion during meiotic and mitotic cell divisions. This expansion sometimes affects gene function and leads to disease. The most common type of X-linked mental retardation in humans is the result of heritable expansions, in the *FMR-1* gene, of a specific trinucleotide repeat, $(CGG)_n$, where the number of expansions (n) is increased from the normal 8–20 or so to 50–200 or more. For unknown reasons, this expanded region tends to undergo breakage under some conditions, and this particular form of mental retardation is called the fragile X syndrome. There are dozens, if not hundreds, of similar fragile sites in the human and other genomes.

Imprinting. The function of a gene that is inherited from the father may differ from that of the same gene inherited from the mother, a phenomenon known as imprinting. The mechanism for imprinting is not fully understood, but differences in DNA methylation of genes in sperm compared to ova appear to be involved. Imprinting is important in some human diseases, such as Prader-Willi and Angelman syndromes. Although deletions of the same region on chromosome 15 have been observed in some individuals with either of these syndromes, individuals who received the deleted chromosome 15 from the father developed the Prader-Willi syndrome, whereas those who received the deleted chromosome 15 from the mother developed Angelman syndrome. Thus, although each syndrome is associated with the presence of a single undeleted chromosome 15, the outcome depended on the parental origin.

Abnormal chromosomes in tumor cells. Specific chromosome aberrations play an important role in the development of many, if not all, cancers. For example, most patients with chronic myelogenous leukemia have a translocation between chromosome 9 and 22 which fuses the normally silent *c-abl* oncogene with the expressed *bcr* gene. The result is the production of an abundant *bcr-abl* fusion gene product and tumor development (**Fig. 3***a* and *b*). Tumor cells tend to be chromosomally unstable, and further chromosome aberrations may enhance tumor malignancy. Translocations and tri-

somies may lead to additional oncogene products, whereas deletions may remove genes that suppress tumor growth.

Some tumor cells have an elongated region on a chromosome arm that contains an increased number of copies (amplification) of an oncogene. Such regions stain uniformly, rather than being banded, and are called homogeneously staining regions (HSRs). The amplified oncogenes are sometimes extrachromosomal, that is, are present on very tiny collections of chromatin resembling small chromosomes that lack centromeres; these are called double minutes (DMs). *See* ONCOGENES; ONCOLOGY.

Evolution. Chromosome complements are remarkably diverse throughout both plant and animal kingdoms, and chromosome aberrations may have played an important role in the reproductive isolation that fosters speciation. For example, polyploidization creates a reproductive barrier that favors the formation of a new, polyploid species. Some species contain very large chromosome numbers, such as a fern with about 1000 chromosomes, a crayfish with over 350 chromosomes, and a butterfly with over 400 chromosomes.

Structural chromosome changes have also been a common occurrence in evolution. As described above, when a translocation or inversion involves

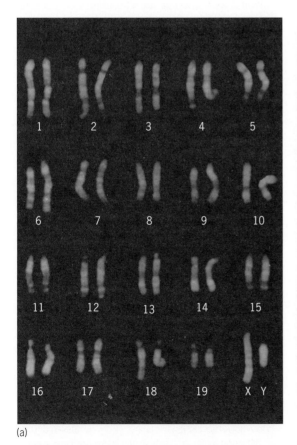

(a)

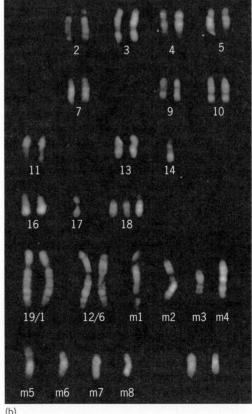

(b)

Fig. 3. Q-banded chromosomes of (*a*) normal mouse metaphase cell, arranged according to the standard karyotype, (*b*) and metaphase karyotype of a mouse cancer cell showing numerical and structural changes. Chromosomes 2–18 are structurally normal, but noteworthy are the monosomy 17 and 14 and trisomy 18.

one of a pair of homologous chromosomes, abnormal gametes are produced and fertility is reduced. However, in a small, inbreeding population, both male and female parents could receive a copy of the rearranged chromosome or chromosomes, and each parent could pass them on to an offspring, who would thus have a matched set of rearranged chromosomes. The latter would pair normally at meiosis, leading to the production of normal gametes. In this way, the altered chromosome could spread through a small, inbreeding population and might replace the initial chromosome arrangement, becoming fixed in the population. *See* POPULATION GENETICS.

Chromosome rearrangements do not change the banding patterns of the chromosome segments. Therefore, it is possible to compare the karyotypes of species to determine what changes have been fixed in their evolution. For example, there is a preponderance of Robertsonian translocations in lemurs compared to other primates, and a preponderance of pericentric inversions in the chromosomes of the great apes and humans. The telocentric chromosomes of the European mouse, *Mus musculus domesticus*, undergo frequent Robertsonian translocations and, indeed, one mouse was found in which 18 of the 19 autosomes had undergone such translocations. At this time there is no evidence that chromosome changes alone have led to the creation of a new species, but it is clear that they can lead to sterility in certain outcrosses and to the reproductive isolation that is critical for speciation. *See* CHROMOSOME; RECOMBINATION (GENETICS); SPECIATION.

Orlando J. Miller; Dorothy A. Miller

Bibliography. C. J. Epstein, *The Consequences of Chromosome Imbalance*, 1986; G. J. Stine, *The New Human Genetics*, 1989; E. Thesman and M. Susman, *Human Chromosomes: Structure, Behavior, Effects*, 3d ed., 1993; B. K. Vig, *Chromosome Segregation and Aneuploidy*, 1993.

Chromosphere

A transparent, tenuous layer of gas occurring in the atmosphere of the Sun and resting on the opaque photosphere. It is a thermal buffer zone between the low temperature at the top of the photosphere (4400 K or 7500°F) and the high temperature at the bottom of the corona ($0.5–1 \times 10^6$ K or $1–2 \times 10^{6°}$F). Its temperature of about 8000 to 20,000 K (14,000 to 36,000°F) is due to the input of mechanical energy. The chromosphere consists of a homogeneous atmosphere between 1500 and 2000 km (900 and 1200 mi) thick, and an embedded fur of hairy spikes known as spicules, some 2000 to 10,000 km (1200 to 6000 mi) high. The interface between the chromosphere and the corona is a thin layer, the transition zone, in which the temperature rises and the density of the gas falls very abruptly to coronal levels. *See* SUN. John W. Evans

Chronograph

A device for recording the epoch of an event. In its older form the astronomical chronograph includes a drum rotated at constant speed and a pen actuated by an electromagnet. A spiral line is traced on paper on the drum. Signals from a clock produce a set of time marks and signals made by an observer produce other marks, so that the epoch of the events observed can be determined.

Modern chronographs are of the digital printing type. In one form rotating type wheels carry numbers. In another form the time is accumulated electronically, and when a signal is given the output is printed by keys. A totalizing chronograph prints the mean of several signals. *See* TIME-INTERVAL MEASUREMENT. William Markowitz

Chronometer

A large, strongly built watch especially designed for precise timekeeping on ships at sea. The name is sometimes loosely applied to any fine watch. *See* WATCH.

The features that distinguish a chronometer from a watch are (1) a heavy balance wheel, the axis of which is kept always vertical by mounting the entire instrument within two concentric rings, so pivoted as to permit the chronometer to remain undisturbed despite considerable tilting of the box containing it, as the ship rolls and pitches; (2) a balance spring wound in cylindrical shape, instead of a nearly flat helix; (3) a special escapement; and (4) a fusee, by means of which the power of the mainspring is made to work through a lever arm of continuously changing length, being shortest when the spring is tightly wound and longest when it has run down, thus regulating the transmitted power so that it is approximately constant at all times. *See* ESCAPEMENT; SPRING (MACHINES).

These mechanical chronometers are being replaced by quartz digital chronometers, which operate on the same principle as a quartz watch. *See* QUARTZ CLOCK.

Oceangoing ships formerly relied completely on chronometers keeping Greenwich mean time to determine longitude. The broadcast of radio time signals that became widespread in the 1920s, and subsequently the loran, Omega, and satellite navigation systems, have made Greenwich mean time available to mariners at almost any instant, and chronometers are no longer indispensable for determining longitude at sea. However, they are still a necessary backup, and naval vessels will not leave port without one or more chronometers aboard. *See* CLOCK; HOROLOGY; LORAN; OMEGA; SATELLITE NAVIGATION SYSTEMS; TIME. Steven J. Dick

Bibliography. R. T. Gould, *The Marine Chronometer*, 1990; M. E. Whitney, *The Ship's Chronometer*, 1985.

Chrysoberyl

A mineral having composition $BeAl_2O_4$ and crystallizing in the orthorhombic system. Chrysoberyl crystals are usually tabular parallel to the front pinacoid and frequently in pseudohexagonal twins (see **illus.**). There is good prismatic cleavage. The hardness is 8.5 (Mohs scale) and the specific gravity is 3.7–3.8. The luster is vitreous and the color various shades of green, yellow, and brown. There are two gem varieties of chrysoberyl. Alexandrite, one of the most prized of gemstones, is an emerald green but in transmitted or in artificial light is red. Cat's eye, or cymophane, is a green chatoyant variety with an opalescent luster. When cut en cabochon, it is crossed by a narrow beam of light. This property results from minute tabular cavities that are arranged in parallel position.

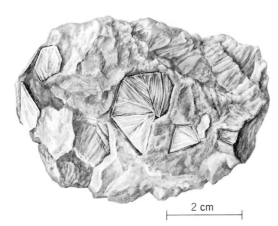

2 cm

Chrysoberyl crystals in pegmatite, Greenwood, Maine. (*Specimen from Department of Geology, Bryn Mawr College*)

Chrysoberyl is a rare mineral found most commonly in pegmatite dikes and occasionally in granitic rocks and mica schists. Gem material is found in stream gravels in Ceylon and Brazil. The alexandrite variety is found in the Ural Mountains. In the United States chrysoberyl is found in pegmatites in Maine, Connecticut, and Colorado. *See* BERYLLIUM; GEM.   Cornelius S. Hurlbut, Jr.

Chrysocolla

A silicate mineral with composition essentially $(Cu,Al)_2H_2Si_2O_5(OH)_4 \cdot nH_2O$; iron, and more rarely manganese, may substitute for copper. Although acicular monoclinic crystals have been reported, the wide variation in the composition of analyzed specimens suggests that chrysocolla is a hydrogel or gelatinous precipitate rather than a well-crystallized mineral. This suggestion is reinforced by the fact that x-ray diffractions are weak and ill defined. The mineral characteristically occurs in impure amorphous-to-cryptocrystalline crusts and masses with conchoidal fracture.

There is a wide variation in physical properties commensurate with the variation in chemical composition. The hardness varies from 2 to 4 on Mohs scale, the specific gravity varies from 2.0 to 4.0, and the refractive index is given variously from 1.40± to 1.60. The luster is vitreous to greasy; and the color is normally green to greenish blue but may be brown or, with manganese present, black.

Chrysocolla is a secondary mineral occurring in the oxidized zones of copper deposits, where it is associated with malachite, azurite, native copper, and cuprite. It is also found in alluvial gravels, indicating that copper is carried in solution far from its primary source. Chrysocolla is a minor ore of copper and a minor gem. Most gem material is essentially chalcedony colored by incorporated chrysocolla. *See* GEM; SILICATE MINERALS.

Cornelius S. Hurlbut, Jr.

Bibliography. C. Klein and C. S. Hurlbut, Jr., *Manual of Mineralogy*, 21st ed., 1993.

Chrysomonadida

An order of the class Phytamastigophorea. Many botanists consider this group a part of the class Chrysophyceae, the golden-brown algae. Chrysomonads, also known as Chrysomonadina, are usually small flagellates, *Mallomonas* being about the largest. They are yellow to brown because of phycocrysin in the usual one or two

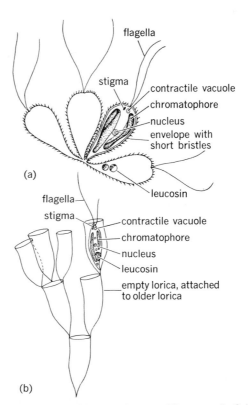

Chrysomonads. (*a*) Portion of colony of *Synura uvella*. Cell size is 20–40 μm, and colonies 100–400 μm. (*b*) *Dinobryon sertularia* colony. Cells measure 30–44 μm.

chromatophores, but some lack chromatophores. *Uroglena* colonies may be quite large. Many species form diagnostic siliceous cysts. Palmelloid colonies (*Hydrurus*) consist of a tough, gelatinous matrix holding many nonflagellate cells. Starch is not formed, but fats are, and the refractive carbohydrate leucosin is common. The flagella are usually two, rarely three, and are subequal. Nuclei are small. *See* CILIA AND FLAGELLA.

Synura and *Dinobryon* are colonial types which produce enough oil to be a source of tastes and odors in drinking water (see **illus.**). *Dinobryon* often shows large numbers of cysts in the open ends of empty tests of old colonies. Chrysomonads may ingest food through the area near the flagellar base. Chrysomonadida are common in cooler fresh water, and certain types (Coccolithophora and Silicoflagellata) abound in the ocean. *See* CHRYSOPHYCEAE; COCCOLITHOPHORIDA; PHYTAMASTIGOPHOREA; PROTOZOA; SILICOFLAGELLATA.

James B. Lackey

Chrysophyceae

A relatively large and diverse class of algae in the chlorophyll *a–c* phyletic line (Chromophycota). In protozoological classification, these organisms constitute an order, Chrysomonadida, of the class Phytomastigophora. Some workers align Chrysophyceae (golden or golden-brown algae) with Bacillariophyceae (diatoms) and Xanthophyceae (yellow-green algae) in the division Chrysophyta.

Chrysophytes typically are flagellate unicells, either free-living or attached, and solitary or colonial. There are, however, ameboid and plasmodial forms, solitary or colonial nonflagellate cells, filaments, and blades. Fresh-water forms, which are usually found in cold clear water, are more common than marine forms.

Although many unicellular chrysophytes have naked protoplasts, others are covered with organic or siliceous scales, or surrounded by a siliceous, cellulosic-pectic, or (rarely) calcareous lorica. Cells that compose blades and filaments have a polysaccharide wall. The statospore, an internally formed resting stage or cyst, occurs in the life history of most chrysophytes. It is urn-shaped, with a siliceous spiny body and a pectic plug. Similar cysts, assigned to the families Archaeomonadaceae and Chrysostomaceae, are found in the fossil record as far back as the Late Cretaceous.

Motile cells bear two subapically inserted, unequal flagella—a hairy (mastigoneme-bearing) flagellum directed forward, and a shorter, smooth flagellum directed backward. In some genera, the smooth flagellum is greatly reduced and may be represented only by its basal region, which may be transformed into a photoreceptive system, often in combination with an eyespot. Contractile vacuoles may be present in fresh-water forms.

Most chrysophytes are photosynthetic, but some are osmotrophic or phagotrophic. Each cell contains one or two chloroplasts (rarely more), which conform to the biochemical and ultrastructural patterns typical of Chromophycota. The chlorophylls are masked by carotenoids (especially β-carotene and fucoxanthin), producing the characteristic golden-brown color. Chloroplast endoplasmic reticulum is present, thylakoids are in groups of three, and chloroplast deoxyribonucleic acid is distributed in a ring. The chief storage product is chrysolaminaran, which is a glucose polymer with β-1,3 linkages, but lipids are also stored.

Asexual reproduction in unicellular forms is by longitudinal binary fission, autospores (nonflagellate cells that are miniatures of the parent), or zoospores, and in multicellular forms by fragmentation or zoospores. Sexual reproduction, observed rarely and in only a few species, is isogamous.

A satisfactory classification of the approximately 1000 species of chrysophytes has not yet been elaborated. One scheme emphasizes somatic organization, by analogy with green algae (Chlorophyceae), while another scheme emphasizes details of flagellation. Studies using electron microscopy and laboratory culture have led to the removal of certain groups to other classes. The choanoflagellates—collared, colorless flagellate unicells—were formerly aligned with chrysophytes or placed in their own class (Craspedophyceae), but similarity to sponge choanocytes supports their placement among animals, as the order Choanoflagellida of the class Zoomastigophora. Members of the order Isochrysidales, characterized by having two equal flagella, have been transferred to the class Prymnesiophyceae. The bicosoecids, a small group of colorless unicells with a lorica formed of spiral or annular elements and with one of the two flagella serving as a contractile stalk, are sometimes appended to the Chrysophyceae or, alternatively, assigned to the Zoomastigophora. Finally, silicoflagellates, which are characterized by an elaborate siliceous endoskeleton and a unique protoplast, are placed in the subclass Dictyochophycidae or referred to their own class. They are a relictual group common in the fossil record as far back as the Early Cretaceous but represented in modern seas by only a few taxa. *See* ALGAE; BACILLARIOPHYCEAE; BICOSOECIDA; CHOANOFLAGELLIDA; CHRYSOMONADIDA; XANTHOPHYCEAE.   Paul C. Silva; Richard L. Moe

Bibliography. S. P. Parker (ed.), *Synopsis and Classification of Living Organisms*, 2 vols., 1982.

Chytridiomycetes

A monophyletic group of true fungi in the subdivision Mastigomycotina, characterized by the presence of a zoosporic state in the life cycle. The zoospore has a single, posteriorly directed, whiplash-type of flagellum; a few species are polyflagellated. The Chytridiomycetes are generally regarded as primitive and are probably representative of the ancestral group for the true fungi.

The thallus may be unicellular, colonial, or filamentous and consists of a single reproductive body (monocentric) or many reproductive bodies (polycentric). The asexual reproductive body comprises a zoosporangium that releases zoospores. Most species are haploid and have no known sexual reproduction. Where sexual reproduction is known, it is highly varied in form. In the least complex species, the thallus consists merely of a naked (having no cell wall) zoosporangium within a host cell. In the most complex species (for example, *Allomyces*), the thallus is polycentric and filamentous with both asexual and sexual reproduction, and with haploid and diploid states. *See* REPRODUCTION (PLANT).

The five orders are classified primarily on differences in zoospore ultrastructure and include the Chytridiales, Spizellomycetales, Blastocladiales, Monoblepharidales, and Neocallimastigales.

Chytrids are cosmopolitan in distribution and are found in environments from the tundra to the equatorial rainforests, in alkaline or acid soil, in peat bogs, and in fresh or brackish water. Many are saprobes, but some are parasites of microflora and fauna such as algae and rotifers. Some (for example, *Coelomomyces*) are of interest because they destroy mosquitoes and others are parasites of vascular plants and are of economic concern as vectors of plant viruses. The Neocallimastigales are obligate anaerobes in the rumen and digestive tract of herbivores, where they are important in the breakdown of cellulose and hemicellulose fiber. Many chytrids have been isolated and grown in pure culture, but others are obligate parasites. *See* EUMYCOTA; FUNGI; MASTIGOMYCOTINA.

Donald J. S. Barr

Bibliography. L. Margulis et al. (eds.), *Handbook of Protoctista*, 1990.

Ciconiiformes

An order of predominantly long-legged, long-necked wading birds including herons, ibises, spoonbills, storks, and their allies, and also the hawklike New World vultures which were previously placed in the Falconiformes. The flamingos have traditionally been placed in this order, but they show a number of unique features and differences; they will be placed in a separate order, Phoenicopteriformes. Some workers have suggested that the ibises are members of the Charadriiformes and that the herons should be placed in a separate order. *See* CHARADRIIFORMES; FALCONIFORMES; PHOENICOPTERIFORMES.

Classification. The order Ciconiiformes is divided into four suborders and seven families: Ardeae, with the family Ardeidae (herons; 62 species); Balaenicipites, with the family Balaenicipitidae (shoe-billed stork; 1 species); Ciconiae, with the families Scopidae (hammerhead; 1 species), Threskiornithi-

dae (ibises and spoonbills; 33 species), and Ciconiidae (storks; 17 species); and Cathartae, containing the families Teratornithidae (Miocene to Pleistocene of South and North America) and Cathartidae (New World vultures; 7 species). Several of these families are divided into subgroups, the most distinct of which are the ibises (Threskiornithinae) and the spoonbills (Plataleinae). The affinities of the New World vultures to the ciconiiforms, and especially to the storks (Ciconiidae), have been demonstrated rather convincingly. For many decades ornithologists have queried the inclusion of these birds in the Falconiformes, but their true affinities had been obscure.

Fossil record. Except for the Cathartae, the fossil record of the Circoniiformes is scattered, considering that these are large wading birds, and does not illustrate anything special about the relationships and distribution of these birds.

Characteristics. The herons (Ardeidae), shoe-billed stork (Balaenicipitidae), hammerhead (Scopidae), ibises and spoonbills (Threskiornithidae), and storks (Ciconiidae) are mainly wading birds with strong legs, living in marshes and other wet areas. They feed on fish, amphibians, and other animals, which are caught in various ways depending on the structure of the bill. Most are diurnal, but a few are nocturnal. Some of the storks are scavengers. Most species are colonial and nest in mixed, often huge, colonies in trees or on the ground, as well as a few on cliff ledges; the hammerhead builds a huge, domed nest. All are strong fliers, usually having to cover a long distance between the nesting site and feeding areas; some are excellent soarers. Most species have elaborate courtship displays and form tight pair bonds; many species of herons possess specialized courtship plumes. The young remain in the nest and are cared for by both adults until they are able to fly. These species are tropical to cool temperate, with those breeding in colder areas migrating to warmer areas for the winter. Many species of herons and egrets had been intensively hunted for their courtship plumes; some were almost extinct before fashions of apparel changed and the birds received protection. The numbers of many species have been drastically reduced, and several are threatened mainly because of lack of the needed wetland habitat. Numbers of the white stork of Europe, which nests readily on human structures and is a symbol of fertility, have been reduced greatly in much of its range because of accidents with wires and loss of wetlands.

Cathartidae. The New World vultures appear to be typical hawks and had been placed in the Falconiformes since the beginnings of avian classification but with ever-increasing doubt. It has been shown rather convincingly that they should be placed in the Ciconiiformes and are closest to the storks. They are placed in a separate suborder to emphasize their specialization as scavengers. These vultures are large soaring birds; the Andean condor has the largest wing span of any living land bird.

Vultures locate their food from the air either by sight or by smell; these abilities differ in the several species. Vultures may be solitary or hunt in loose flocks; larger concentrations may exist during the winter. They nest solitarily, with the nest placed on the ground or on a cliff ledge. The one to three young remain in the nest until they can fly. Most species are common, but the California condor has decreased steadily in numbers and is now extinct in the wild. Survival of this species will depend on captive breeding and reintroduction of birds to the wild.

The fossil history of the New World vultures is excellent. It demonstrates that the Cathartidae had their early evolution in the Old World and invaded the New World only late in the Neogene. More interesting are the related Teratornithidae known from North and South America, which include the birds with the largest wing spans. The relatively small *Teratornis merriami* had a wing spread of up to 3.8 m (12 ft), and the larger *T. incredibilis* had an estimated wing span of up to 5.9 m (19 ft). However, *Argentavis magnificens* from the late Miocene of Argentina had an estimated wing span of 7–7.6 m (22.5–24 ft) and a weight of about 120 kg (264 lb), making it the largest known flying bird by far. *See* AVES.

Walter J. Bock

Bibliography. J. Hancock and H. Elliot, *The Herons of the World*, 1978.

Cidaroida

An order of the subclass Cidaroidea in which the narrow ambulacra comprise two columns of simple plates, and each broad ambulacral plate carries only one primary tubercle. They are unique among echinoids as the only Paleozoic order surviving to the present day. The earliest representatives were the Carboniferous Archaeocidaridae with a flexible test and more than two columns of plates in the interambulacra. Neoteny in the Permian and Triassic families led to forms with only two columns in the interambulacra, and in the Jurassic the test assumed the rigid, globular shape it has in modern forms. After the Mesozoic, cidaroids waned in northern faunas, but they have remained prominent and beautiful elements in Indonesian and Australasian faunas. *See* ECHINODERMATA; ECHINOIDEA; NEOTENY.

Howard B. Fell

Cilia and flagella

Centriole-based, motile cell extensions. These organelles are usually indistinguishable in fine structure as seen with the electron microscope, but quantitatively there are many (several hundred) cilia and few or fewer (usually one or two) flagella, on one cell. Bacterial or prokaryotic flagella are entirely different organelles that are not considered in this article, which concerns only eukaryotic (higher-cell) flagella. *See* BACTERIA.

Characteristics and occurrence. Flagella move with undulatory motion in which successive bending waves progress along the length of the organelle (**Fig. 1**), whereas cilia move with flexural motion consisting of a planar effective stroke, with the organelle extended perpendicular to the cell body, followed by a nonplanar curving recovery stroke, with the organelle pulled parallel to the cell body. Cilia and flagella are low-Reynolds-number systems, which implies that viscous forces are more important to the motion of the organelles than inertial forces are. On a macroscopic scale, this is equivalent to swimming in molasses, and the fluid can be thought of as being clawed forward by the effective stroke of the cilium or as being pushed away by the propagating undulatory wave of the flagellum. Beat frequencies of cilia and flagella in different organisms range from about 2 to more than 50 per second. During a beat, bends usually originate and grow in restricted regions at the base of the organelle in the form of circular arcs. They then propagate toward the tip at rates of several hundred micrometers per second without changing amplitude or form. On sperm tails, bends of equal magnitude but of opposite direction are separated by straight regions of uniform length to give a symmetrical waveform that is superficially sinusoidal. A similar but asymmetrical waveform on a shorter cilium produces one typical form of flexural motion. Both organelles function to move water past the cell. Their action may bring food and oxygen into an animal, or it may propel the cell to a new environment. Cilia often move sheets of mucus at velocities of about 0.008 in. (0.2 mm) per second, either in water or over surfaces exposed to humid air, as in the human respiratory tract. Particles trapped in such sheets are effectively cleared from the epithelial surface. *See* CELL MOTILITY.

Distribution. Cilia were first described by A. van Leeuwenhoek in 1676. The words cilium (eyelash) and flagellum (whip) are accurate descriptions of the appearance of these cell organelles when they are seen under the light microscope. Cilia are present on protozoa, such as *Paramecium*, and on metazoan cells of many different tissue types. For example, in humans, many cells lining the respiratory and reproductive tracts, the ear and the olfactory epithelium, as well as ependymal cells in the brain, have functioning cilia. A flagellum is present on human sperm; in fact, the sperm of most animals, and the male gametes of many lower plants are flagellated. Even the *Ginkgo* spermatozoon is ciliated. Derivatives that are similar to cilia but nonmotile are found on many sensory structures in a variety of animals and include insect pressure receptors and vertebrate photoreceptors. In addition, many ordinary types of cells of vertebrates, for example, from the thyroid, the kidney, or the pituitary gland, also possess modified nonmotile derivatives that resemble cilia, and other cell lines can be induced to grow them in tissue

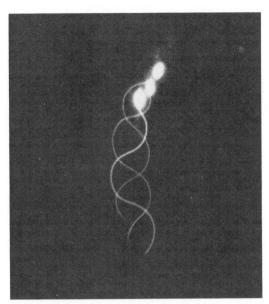

Fig. 1. Sea urchin sperm shown in three positions by dark-field microscopy. Note undulatory waveform as it swims. (*From C. J. Brokaw, Nonsinusoidal bending waves of sperm, J. Exp. Biol., 43:155–169, 1965*)

culture. *See* CILIOPHORA; EPITHELIUM; SPERM CELL; TISSUE CULTURE.

Size. Relative to cell size, both cilia and flagella are very long organelles. Flagella may be more than 50 micrometers long and, in sperm, may be four or more times the cell length. Certain compound cilia, such as the comb plates of ctenophores, are truly macroscopic structures, visible to the naked eye. In these structures, many thousands of individual cilia are joined together laterally, and the length of each cilium runs to a few millimeters. Usually, however, cilia range from 5 to 15 μm in length.

Metachronism. Fields of cilia or flagella such as those in invertebrate flame cells can beat synchronously. Often, however, even on a single cell, cilia beat so that coordinated waves of bending appear to cross the field. Originally, these waves were described as the sort that are seen rippling across a wheat field when the wind is blowing. The phenomenon of beating slightly out of phase is known as metachronism. Several types of metachronism are recognized, since the plane of ciliary beat may be either perpendicular (diaplectic) or parallel (orthoplectic) to the direction of the metachronal wave. Metachronal coordination is usually effected by purely mechanical means; that is, viscoelastic coupling establishes a phase difference between individual cilia so that there is minimal mechanical interference between one beating cilium and its neighbors. In a ciliated epithelium the cells can be functionally linked together so that metachronal waves pass smoothly from cell to cell.

Behavior. Under normal conditions, most cilia and flagella beat continuously, although some cilia (for example, mammalian respiratory cilia and mammalian sperm) require special activation for beating. Many organisms are able to alter properties of ciliary beat, including form, frequency, the direction of the effective stroke, or the direction of bend propagation; sometimes, the ciliary stroke can be arrested. Cells usually alter beat properties by common mechanisms leading to increases in second messengers, including internal calcium ion (Ca^{2+}) or cyclic nucleotide concentrations. For example, in *Paramecium*, depolarization of the cell membrane opens voltage-sensitive calcium channels in the ciliary membrane, which leads to an increase in calcium ion concentration in the cilium above 10^{-7} M. This in turn leads to slowed and then to backward swimming at concentrations above 10^{-6} M. When calcium ion is pumped out of the cilium, the normal beat resumes. Different second messengers may have different effects. Cyclic adenosinemonophosphate (cAMP) increases normal beat frequency in *Paramecium* cilia, leading to faster forward swimming. Such processes allow the cell to respond to various stimuli and form the basis of behavioral responses of free-swimming ciliated cells. The same messenger may have different modes of action in different cilia; for example, calcium ion activates and increases beat frequency in mammalian respiratory cilia.

Ultrastructure. The electron microscope reveals that the cilium or flagellum is really an internal organelle since it is bounded by the cell membrane and enclosed at the tip. The main internal structure of the cilium is the axoneme. Under the electron microscope a single axoneme contains a fixed pattern of microtubules. The microtubules are not simple single units; rather, nine doublet microtubules are found on the periphery of the axoneme surrounding two central elements. This is the so-called 9 + 2 pattern (**Fig. 2**).

Microtubule arrangement. Each peripheral doublet is composed of one complete and one partial

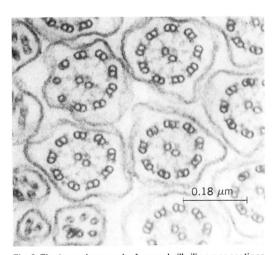

Fig. 2. Electron micrograph of mussel gill cilia cross sections showing 9 + 2 pattern of axoneme. At the left are cross sections through tips at various levels. (*From P. Satir, Studies on cilia, II: Examination of the distal region of the ciliary shaft and the role of the filaments in motility, J. Cell Biol., 26:805–834, 1965*)

0.18 μm

microtubule. The microtubules are themselves composed of subunits arranged into microfibers or protofilaments. The complete microtubule, labeled subfiber A, consists of a ring of 13 protofilaments. The incomplete microtubule, subfiber B, is a C-shaped structure of 10 or 11 protofilaments. In a transverse section the doublets appear as figure eights, with two short arms and several linkages extending from one end. The doublets form a ring around the central pair. The diameter of this ring is very constant, about 0.2 μm, even in different types of cilia or in cilia of different species.

Microtubule pattern variation. The 9 + 2 pattern is present in all known motile cilia. Motile flagella, especially sperm tails, sometimes possess altered patterns, although these are usually simple variations upon the basic array. Flatworm sperm, for example, show a 9 + 1 pattern (one central element instead of two), although somatic cilia of the same animal are 9 + 2. Insect sperm show even greater divergences. Mammalian sperm have the 9 + 2 pattern, but in addition have a set of thick fibers alongside the axoneme. The most simply organized motile flagella in eukaryotes are the 6 + 0 and 3 + 0 forms present in male gametes of certain gregarine protozoa. In these flagella, the doublet tubules appear to possess normal arms, but the spokes and central pair are lacking. Nonmotile flagellar derivatives usually have 9 + 0 patterns and lack both the arms and the central pair. All these patterns are constant within any one species of animal or plant, with the exception of certain very rare variants that are probably mistakes in assembly.

Symmetry. If the arms are disregarded, there is a plane of bilateral symmetry in the normal cilium which passes between two peripheral doublets, through the central pair, and through one doublet on the side opposite. This doublet is numbered 1, and the plane of bilateral symmetry is also the plane of the effective stroke. By looking from the cell surface and outward along the axoneme, looking clockwise from subfiber B of doublet number 1, the sequence is subfiber B, subfiber A, arms of doublet number 1, subfiber B, subfiber A, arms of doublet number 2, and so on. The arms always extend from subfiber A of any doublet N toward subfiber B of the adjacent doublet. In this manner the doublets can be numbered unequivocally. The two peripheral doublets between which the plane of bilateral symmetry passes are the numbers 5 and 6, and these may be specially distinguished in some cases by being connected by a distinctive bridge.

Axonemal linkages. The axonemal microtubules are interconnected into a functional whole by groups of projections extending in different directions from each subfiber A (**Fig. 3**). These include the two circumferentially oriented rows of dynein arms. The outer arms repeat at spacings of about 24 nanometers. The outer arms are uniform, but the inner arms are sometimes of two or three types with a more complicated spacing. There are also several types of circumferentially oriented links, some of which form elastic connections, some inelastic connections, between doublets. The periodicity of these links is about 96 nm. Radially oriented spoke groups project toward the central sheath with a major period of 96 nm; the spoke groups often comprise three individual spokes, each of which ends in an expanded spoke head. The spokes are spaced at intervals of 32, 24, and 40 nm, with the first spoke of each group in alignment with a set of dynein arms. There are six central sheath projections per spoke group. Such vernier alignments may prove to be important in the regulation of beat form.

Morphogenesis. At the base of the cilium or flagellum there is a basal body, or kinetosome, that is similar to, and sometimes derived from, a centriole. The basal body may have extensions of various sorts attached to it, notably a basal foot that indicates effective stroke direction and prominent striated rootlet fibers in many cilia. Ordinarily, the ciliary axoneme originates and grows in a membrane protrusion which forms just above the basal body, either at the cell surface or deeper inside the cytoplasm. The basal body remains attached to the cell membrane throughout morphogenesis by a structure that extends from the microtubules to the membrane, where it is seen as a ciliary necklace. The necklace forms a barrier that segregates the ciliary membrane from the general cell membrane. As morphogenesis proceeds, from a pool of subunits, axonemal microtubules polymerize above the basal body. Continuity of the microtubules between axoneme and basal body may be traced through a complex transition zone. Evidently, polymerization of the

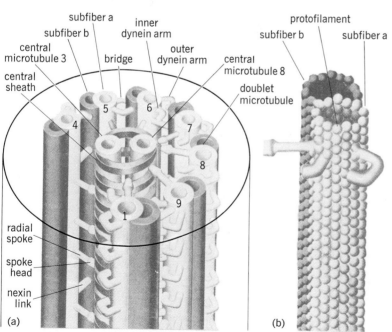

Fig. 3. Ultrastructure of a cilium. (*a*) Three-dimensional reconstruction with doublets 2 and 3 removed to show spoke periodicities more clearly, (*b*) Three-dimensional wall structure of a doublet showing tubulin subunits. (*After P. Satir, How cilia move, Sci. Amer., 231(4):44–52, 1974*)

axonemal microtubules takes place at the growing tip of the cilium. Certain cells such as the ameboflagellate *Naegleria* can grow or resorb the cilia in response to internal programming during the cell cycle, or upon physiological stimulation. *See* CENTRIOLE.

Genetic control. Morphogenesis is under genetic controls, in part by nuclear genes. For example, certain nuclear mutants in *Chlamydomonas* fail to polymerize the central microtubules. Other mutants lack radial spokes or either the outer or the inner row of dynein arms. In these cases, the mutant flagella are partially or completely paralyzed, or the beat form or frequency is altered. Paralyzed and behavioral mutants have also been found in other species, ranging from *Paramecium* to humans. Approximately 1 in 40,000 people suffer from an inherited genetic defect originally known as Kartagener's syndrome, in which the cilia of the bronchial tract and the sperm flagella (in males) are paralyzed, in some instances because dynein arms are completely lacking on the doublet microtubules. People with this syndrome have considerable respiratory difficulty, and males are infertile. These people also have a 50% chance of their heart and other internal organs being on the opposite side of the body compared with normal anatomy, possibly as a result of ciliary immotility during embryonic development.

Growth parameters. The extent of each axonemal component is strictly determined. In mussel gill lateral cilia, all subfiber B's of the peripheral doublets end at the same level. Simultaneously the arms and the spokes also terminate. However, both the central pair and the subfiber A's of the doublets continue, the central pair to the exact end of the ciliary tip, where the elements are topped by a distinctive finial, the central pair cap. Every continuation of subfiber A is unique in length so that subfiber A's of doublets 3 and 8 are overall about 1 μm, or 10%, longer than subfiber A's of doublets 1, 4, and 5. A general reduction in axonemal diameter accompanies microtubule termination and gives the cilium a distinctive conical tip. These growth parameters and the shape of the tip are different for different kinds of cilia and flagella. In certain mammalian cilia the tip is blunt, and the membrane is decorated externally by a cell coat, the ciliary crown.

Chemical composition. Cilia may be isolated en masse from ciliated protozoa, such as *Tetrahymena*, and flagella may be isolated as sperm tails. Such preparations are suitable for chemical analysis, and reasonably pure preparations of axonemes and of membranes can be obtained in quantities adequate for study. The major protein component (70–80%) of the axoneme is tubulin, the structural protein of the microtubules. The second largest component (10–15%) is dynein, the axonemal adenosinetriphosphatase protein (ATPase). The remaining 10–15% of the axonemal protein is distributed among approximately 250 distinct polypeptides that can

be visualized by two-dimensional electrophoresis. Some of these polypeptides can be assigned to specific axonemal structures, but most have not yet been otherwise characterized. The molecular unit of tubulin is a heterodimer of α and β subunits, each a globular protein about 4 nm long and 5 nm wide. One $\alpha\beta$ tubulin heterodimer (molecular weight 100,000) contains one molecule of bound guanosine triphosphate and one more loosely bound guanosine diphosphate. Axonemal and cytoplasmic microtubules are similar in most properties, but they differ in their stability to depolymerization. In *Chlamydomonas*, axonemal tubulin is acetylated locally after synthesis, while tubulin in most other parts of the cell is not. Another difference is that the midwall of the doublet microtubules is not tubulin, but proteins related to intermediate filament proteins, termed tektins. This may account for the differential stability or other unique properties of the axonemal microtubules.

The axonemal adenosinetriphosphatase (ATPase), dynein, consists of a group of related globular proteins of slightly different solubilities with high molecular weights in the range of $1–2 \times 10^6$. Isolated dynein (**Fig. 4**) resembles a bouquet of two or three globular masses attached to a common base by slender stalks. Analysis after

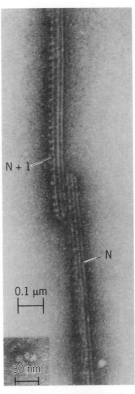

Fig. 4. Sliding of doublet microtubules from an axoneme after destruction of the control system. The dynein arms of the lower doublet (N) have interacted with subfiber B of the upper doublet (N + 1), displacing it toward the ciliary tip. Inset shows an isolated dynein molecule. (*After P. Satir, Structural analysis of the dynein cross bridge cycle, in F. D. Warner et al., eds., Cell Movement, vol. 1, Alan Liss, 1989; inset courtesy of K. Barkalow*)

brief protease digestion of the molecule shows that each head contains at least one distinctive heavy polypeptide chain (molecular weight 4–5×10^5) that has ATPase activity, and each chain can be cleaved into two distinctive fragments by ultraviolet light in the presence of vanadate ions. In addition, purified dynein contains two or three intermediate-size chains (approximately 1×10^5) and several types of light chains (approximately 1–3×10^4). Outer and inner arm dyneins of the same axoneme may be different biochemically and structurally. Inner arm dyneins may be closely associated with other axonemal proteins, including small amounts of actin and centrin, in a so-called regulatory complex. The dynein genes of sea urchin and several other organisms have been cloned, and amino acid sequences of the heavy chains have been derived from the deoxyribonucleic acid (DNA) sequences. Each axonemal heavy chain is probably the product of a different gene. The sequences of the ATPase sites of the various dyneins seem highly conserved. Transcription of the axonemal dyneins of tubulins and other ciliary proteins is increased after experimental deciliation of cells.

The membranes of flagella and cilia appear similar in structure, but they differ in composition from the adjacent cell membranes. Like other membranes, the ciliary membrane is a phospholipid bilayer into which proteins are inserted. Some major membrane components of the cilia and flagella are glycoproteins, including immobilization antigens and other molecules involved in mating or cell recognition. Some ciliary membranes contain specific ion channels, including the voltage-sensitive calcium ion channel responsible for backward swimming in *Paramecium*.

Axonemes sometimes contain target proteins for the second messengers that control their behavior, including calmodulin which binds calcium and loosely or tightly bound protein kinases that may phosphorylate other axonemal proteins in the presence of cyclic nucleotides. A small polypeptide that copurifies with the outer arm dynein is phosphorylated in a cAMP-dependent manner and might act as a regulatory light chain of this dynein.

Mechanism of movement. Cilia and flagella are active structures, and the energy for their motion is provided by the dephosphorylation of adenosine-triphosphate (ATP) at the dynein arms distributed along most of the length of the organelle. The membranes of cilia and flagella can be removed selectively by treatment with a nonionic detergent, such as Triton X-100. The motile mechanism in the resulting demembranated cilia and flagella is undamaged, so that when placed in an appropriate saline medium containing added ATP, the organelles regain motility and their pattern of beating closely resembles that of the same organelles in the living organism. An abrupt decrease in ATP concentration causes beating axonemes to set into a rigor state in which the

stationary axonemes maintain the bent waveforms that they had at the moment the ATP concentration was lowered. The preservation of these rigor bends results from the dynein arms forming fixed cross-bridges between adjacent doublets in the absence of ATP. Movements between doublets can be regenerated by local addition of ATP; they are the result of a cyclic process in which the binding and hydrolysis of a molecule of ATP at a dynein arm from subfiber A of one doublet (N) causes it to release its cross-bridge attachment to the B subfiber of the adjacent doublet (N + 1), change its angle, reattach to a new site closer to the basal end of the B subfiber, and then pull. This paradigm is known as the sliding microtubule model of ciliary motility. Both inner and outer dynein arms cooperate to produce sliding with the same polarity. Microtubule sliding can be seen in a beating axoneme by attaching gold beads to different parts of the structure and observing their periodic motion in the light microscope.

The outer dynein arms can be quantitatively extracted from certain axonemes. This causes the beat frequency to fall. The beat frequency also decreases in mutants of *Chlamydomonas* where the outer dynein arms or specific portions of them are missing. When corresponding mutants lack a specific type of inner arm, the beat frequency is largely unchanged but the bending pattern of the beat is altered. The suggestion is that sliding produced by the outer dynein arms is a primary determinant of beat frequency, while the inner arms primarily regulate beat form.

Active sliding of the doublet tubules can be demonstrated directly by brief treatment of demembranated axonemes with the protease trypsin. Trypsin rapidly destroys most of the spokes and circumferential links while leaving the arms and doublet tubules relatively intact. When ATP is then added, the treated axonemes no longer generate bending waves, but elongate and grow thinner as the doublets slide apart (Fig. 4). Isolated dynein arms will rebind to axonemal or other microtubules and slide them across glass surfaces in the presence of ATP. Dynein and tubulin are the only proteins necessary to produce sliding. This sliding microtubule mechanism is applicable to other microtubule-based forms of cell motility.

Since all dynein arms operate in the same way, the normal development and propagation of bends in the axoneme requires the presence of a suitable control system to generate appropriately phased localized sliding movements between the axonemal doublets. Trypsin damages this control system that normally limits sliding, leading to an uncoupling of sliding from bending.

The control system permits sliding to be asynchronous; one possibility is that sliding switches back and forth between the two bilaterally symmetrical halves of the axoneme and the other, during each stroke cycle. Inhibitors that act on the switches cause beating to cease abruptly at one particular stroke position. Such arrested cilia can be moved from one position to another by replacing one inhibitor with another, and microtubules from about half of each axoneme prepared from the arrested cilia will slide normally after trypsin treatment. This indicates that arrest is an active state in which the dynein arms producing bending to one side remain potentiated, while those producing bending to the reverse side are inhibited.

The main elements thought to convert the fundamental ATP-powered sliding interaction into local bending are the spokes. The spoke heads appear to be attached to the central sheath at points where bends develop, so as to provide the needed resistance to sliding, while the central tubules and sheath act as a fulcrum around which bending occurs. The presence of spokes affects the behavior of the inner dynein arms. Flagellar mutants of motile *Chlamydomonas* that possess axonemes lacking spokes appear capable of tubule sliding but not of bending. The 3 + 0 flagella in sperm of certain gregarines mentioned above lack both spokes and central tubules, yet generate helical bending waves of low frequency, which indicates that spokes and central tubules are not absolutely required for bending. However, their interactions may play a critical role in generating the asymmetric bending waves characteristic of normal ciliary motion and in the control of beat parameters. *See* ADENOSINETRIPHOSPHATE (ATP).   Peter Satir

Bibliography. R. A. Bloodgood (ed.), *Ciliary and Flagellar Membranes*, 1990; F. D. Warner, E. R. Gibbons, and P. Satir, *Cell Movement*, vol.1, 1989.

Ciliatea

The single class of the subphylum Ciliophora. This group has the characteristics of those defined for the subphylum. This protozoan class is divided into the subclasses Holotrichia, Peritrichia, Suctoria, and Spirotrichia. *See* CILIOPHORA; HOLOTRICHIA; PERITRICHIA; SPIROTRICHIA; SUCTORIA.   John O. Corliss

Ciliophora

A subphylum of the Protozoa. The ciliates are a fairly homogeneous group of highly differentiated, unicellular organisms. Over 5000 species have been described, and many more surely exist but remain to be discovered. Typically, ciliates are larger than most other protozoa, ranging from 10 to 3000 micrometers or about 0.004 to 0.12 in. Some larger species are easily visible to the naked eye. The majority of them are free-living forms, found abundantly in a variety of fresh- and salt-water habitats, although a few entire groups live in association with other organisms, generally as harmless ecto- or endocommensals. Their principal value to humans is as experimental animals in a host of investigations concerned with

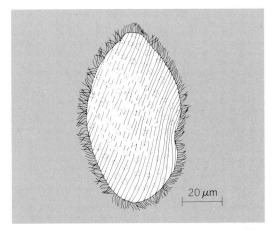

Fig. 1. *Opaline ranarum*, an opalinid; not considered a ciliate by many protozoologists.

fundamental problems of biology.

Systematics. Classification of ciliates followed here is that published in the "Honigberg Report," which appeared in 1964. That classification scheme, of the entire phylum Protozoa, was determined by an international committee of distinguished protozoologists. It is a reasonable and useful classification. Separate articles appear on each group included in the classification listed below. Subordinal divisions of some orders are commonly recognized by protozoologists, but such taxa are not considered here.

Subphylum Ciliophora
  Class Ciliatea
    Subclass Holotrichia
      Order: Gymnostomatida
           Trichostomatida
           Chonotrichida
           Apostomatida
           Astomatida
           Hymenostomatida
           Thigmotrichida
    Subclass Peritrichia
      Order Peritrichida
    Subclass Suctoria
      Order Suctorida
    Subclass Spirotrichia

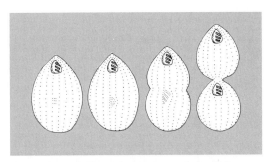

Fig. 2. Binary fission and stomatogenesis in ciliate *Tetrahymena*. Argentophilic basal bodies form part of silverline system and infraciliature.

Order: Heterotrichida
Oligotrichida
Tintinnida
Entodiniomorphida
Odontostomatida
Hypotrichida

Protociliata or opalinids (**Fig. 1**) are entirely excluded. They are considered members of the subphylum Sarcomastigophora, because they possess only one type of nucleus, a symmetrogenic rather than a homothetogenic type of binary fission, and true syngamy, or sexual reproduction with anisogamous gametes, rather than conjugation. There are four genera of opalinids which are large, mouthless, multiflagellated forms found almost exclusively as saprozoic commensals in the posterior end of the alimentary tract of frogs and toads. *See* SARCO-MASTIGOPHORA.

Major subdivisions of the ciliates are reduced to the four subclasses named above. Within the Holotrichia are included the Chonotrichida, a group formerly accorded a high-level, independent taxonomic status. *See* HOLOTRICHIA.

Characteristics. The usual ciliate life cycle is fairly simple. An individual feeds and undergoes binary fission, and the filial products repeat the process. Some commensal or parasitic forms have a more complicated life history, but it is never as involved as the malarial species of the subphylum Sporozoa. Some ciliates, including free-living species, have a cystic stage in their cycle. As in other kinds of Protozoa this stage often serves as a protective phase during adverse environmental conditions, such as desiccation or lack of food. It also may be important in distribution, and thus possibly in preservation, of the species. *See* EUCOCCIDA.

Six major characteristics aid in distinguishing the Ciliophora from other protozoan groups. Not all of these are entirely unique, but when taken together they are definitely distinctive of ciliates.

Mouth. Most Ciliophora possess a true mouth or cytostome often associated with a buccal cavity containing compound ciliary organelles. However, some ciliates are completely astomatous, that is, mouthless. Nutrition is heterotrophic in ciliates. Some species are solely or primarily herbivorous since they eat bacteria or algae; some are carnivorous, eating other Protozoa or occasionally small aquatic invertebrate Metazoa; some are omnivorous; and still others live a saprozoic, or saprobic, existence, obtaining all their nutritive needs from materials dissolved in the medium. The process of stomatogenesis, or new mouth formation, which must take place before the completion of binary fission, is a morphogenetic phenomenon of great interest to students of Protozoa. Various modes of stomatogenesis exist in different ciliate groups. Their study helps in postulation of phylogenetic and evolutionary interrelationships within this subphylum of highly differentiated unicellular animals, as well as in throwing light on the important and not yet solved biological process of cell division and its control.

Ciliation. The Ciliophora possess simple cilia or compound ciliary organelles, often in abundance, in at least one stage of their life cycle. Morphologically, cilia are relatively short and slender hairlike structures, whose ultrastructure is known, from electron microscope studies, to be composed of nine peripheral and two central fibrils. Compound ciliary organelles include the undulating membrane, which is essentially a single sheet of fused cilia; the membranelle, a more or less fused block of cilia, typically two to four rows wide and of greater length; and the cirrus, a tuft of closely opposed cilia which is approximately circular in cross section near its base or proximal end but tapered or

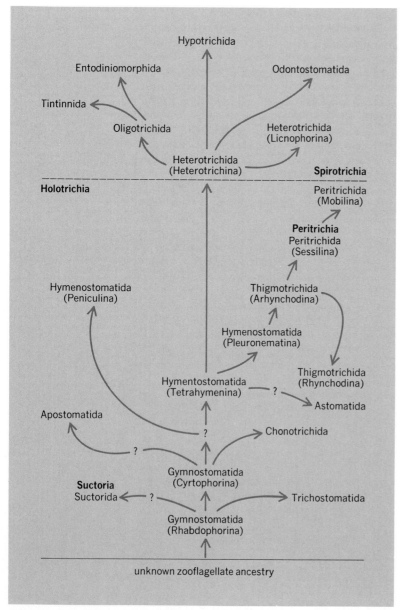

Fig. 3. Phylogenetic tree showing orders of the Ciliophora (names in boldface are of subclasses, and in parentheses of suborders).

even fimbriate at its distal end. Functionally, cilia and cirri serve principally as locomotor organelles. Membranes and membranelles are characteristically associated with the mouth or buccal areas and serve to bring food into the oral opening, although they sometimes aid in locomotion as well. Membranelles are typically arranged as an adoral zone. *See* CILIA AND FLAGELLA.

Infraciliature. The presence, without exception, of some sort of infraciliature located at a subpellicular level in the cortex is another characteristic of Ciliophora. The infraciliature consists essentially of basal bodies, or kinetosomes, associated with cilia and ciliary organelles at their bases, plus certain more or less interconnecting fibrils. The basal bodies are argentophilic, that is, they readily stain with silver stains, and are the most important components of the so-called silverline system present in all ciliates (**Fig. 2**). Various argentophilic fibrils, the contractile vacuole pores, and the cell anus (cytoproct or cytopyge) are included in this system. The controversial neuromotor apparatus of ciliates, best known in hypotrichs, is not well understood. Anatomically, it appears to embrace certain parts of the silverline system, although parts of it are definitely not argentophilic. Much remains to be learned of its function.

Nuclear apparatus. Ciliophora possess two kinds of nuclei, and at least one of each is usually present. The smaller, or micronucleus, contains recognizable chromosomes and behaves much as the single nucleus in cells of metazoan organisms. Its mitotic divisions, however, appear to be acentric (without centrioles). The larger, or macronucleus, does not show mitosis but is considered indispensable in controlling metabolic functions, and is recognized as having genic control over all phenotypic characteristics of ciliates. Micronuclei are typically spherical or ovoid and show little variety in shape. Macronuclei vary in different species from compact bodies to C- or E-shaped forms, or from nodulated chains, which look like a string of tiny linked sausages, to bizarre dendritic configurations. Both nuclei divide in fission, but in sexual phenomena new macronuclei arise from what may be considered micronuclear origin. *See* GENETICS.

Fission. Ciliophora exhibit a type of binary fission commonly known as transverse division. In ciliates the splitting results in two filial organisms, the anterior or proter and the posterior or opisthe which, geometrically speaking, show homothety with respect to identical structures possessed by each (Fig. 2). Thus, homothetogenic is both a broader and more exact descriptive term. Indeed, in a number of groups the fission is more nearly longitudinal than transverse. Some ciliates show a budding type of asexual reproduction; some regularly reproduce within a cystic membrane.

Reproduction. Ciliophora lack true sexual reproduction. Ciliates do not show syngamy, with fusion of free gametes. Processes such as conjugation are considered to be sexual phenomena, since meiosis

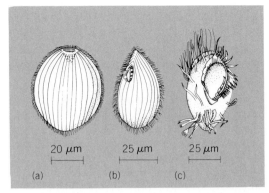

Fig. 4. Ciliates (not drawn to same scale). (*a*) Primitive form. *Holophrya*. (*b*) Intermediate form, *Tetrahymena*. (*c*) Highly complex form, *Diophrys*.

and chromosome recombination are involved, but not sexual reproduction. In addition to conjugation, certain ciliates exhibit forms of sexual phenomena known as autogamy and cytogamy. *See* REPRODUCTION (ANIMAL).

Evolution of ciliates. Ciliated protozoa, by virtue of their universal possession of an infraciliature and relatable patterns of somatic and buccal ciliature, appear to be the most taxonomically compact group in the phylum Protozoa. They also seem to lend themselves most readily to interpretation of their own phylogenetic interrelationships, that is, their own evolutionary history from the conjectured time of the first recognizable ciliate on the phylogenetic tree of the animal kingdom. Handicaps to study include lack of a usable fossil record, the usually microscopic size, and the very unicellularity which places all complexities of organization of necessity at a subcellular level. However, the student of the ciliated protozoa may still recognize, with a certain amount of reasonable, if indirect, supporting evidence, certain evolutionary lines or trends among the several orders. Most fruitful lines of such investigation have involved comparative study of life cycles, infraciliature, mouthparts, and the morphogenetic phenomenon of stomatogenesis. A possible genealogical tree of Ciliophora is given in **Fig. 3**. The change in somatic and buccal ciliature in the evolution of ciliates is emphasized in three present-day forms which, allegedly, are representative of the most primitive, intermediate, and most highly evolved orders (**Fig. 4**). *See* PROTOZOA.

John O. Corliss

Bibliography. T.-T. Chen (ed.), *Research in Protozoology*, 2 vols., 1967; J. O. Corliss, *The Ciliated Protozoa: Characterization, Classification, and Guide to the Literature*, 1961; J. O. Corliss, The value of ontogenetic data in reconstructing protozoan phylogenies, *Trans. Amer. Microsc. Soc.*, 87:1–20, 1968; B. M. Honigberg et al., A revised classification of the phylum Protozoa, *J. Protozool.*, 11:7–20, 1964; R. R. Kudo, *Protozoology*, 5th ed., 1966; D. L. Mackinnon and R. S. J. Hawes, *An Introduction to the Study of Protozoa*, 1961; S. P. Parker (ed.), *Synopsis and Classification of Living Organisms*, 2 vols.,

1982; D. R. Pitelka, *Electron-Microscopic Structure of Protozoa*, 1963.

Cinchona

A genus of trees belonging to the madder family (Rubiaceae), occurring indigenously in the cool, cloud forests of the Andes from Colombia to Peru. Many species have been described, most of which may be variants of *Cinchona pubescens* or *C. officinalis*. The bark contains several alkaloids, the most important of which is quinine. This bitter substance is the most specific drug used in the treatment of malaria. The great demand for quinine and the wasteful methods used in collecting the materials threatened extinction of the plants; therefore cultivation was begun. Now there are extensive cinchona plantations in India, Java, Ceylon, Australia, and Jamaica. *See* QUININE; RUBIALES.   Perry D. Strausbaugh/Earl L. Core

Cinematography

The process of producing the illusion of a moving picture. Cinematography includes two phases: the taking of the picture with a camera and the showing of the picture with a projector. The camera captures the action by taking a series of still pictures at regular intervals; the projector flashes these pictures on a screen at the same frequency, thus producing an image on the screen that appears to move. This illusion is possible only because of the persistence of vision of the human eye. The still pictures appear on the screen many times a second, and although the screen is dark equally as long as it is lighted by the projected image, they do not seem to be a series of pictures but appear to the viewer to be one continuous picture.

This article discusses motion picture cameras, motion picture projectors, and wide-screen processes. For related information *see* CAMERA; MAGNETIC RECORDING; OPTICAL PROJECTION SYSTEMS; OPTICAL RECORDING; PHOTOGRAPHIC MATERIALS; PHOTOGRAPHY; STEREOPHONIC SOUND.

Cameras

Still photographs are taken by motion picture cameras (movie cameras) at the rate of 24 per second, even faster at times. The photographs are sharp and clear, and if they were superimposed on one another would be found to be extremely uniform with respect to position. This last feature is essential in order to have the image appear steady on the screen.

A motion picture camera consists of five basic parts: the lens, the shutter, the gate, the film chamber, and the pull-down mechanism.

Lens. The lens on a motion picture camera collects the light from the scene being photographed and focuses it on the photographic emulsion in the camera aperture. Lenses vary in focal length. The focal lengths most often used on 35-mm cameras are between 30 and 50 mm. Other lenses in common use vary from wide-angle (14.5 to 25 mm), through long-focal-length (60 to 250 mm), to telephoto (300 to 1000 mm). Lenses of shorter focal length have a wider angle of view; those of longer focal length give a larger image size on the film. Lenses for the 16-mm camera which give the same angle of view and the same relative image size are approximately one-half the focal length of those used on a 35-mm camera. Variable-focal-length lenses (zoom lenses) are useful to cinematographers and directors and are used extensively not only for filming sport events but also in making feature films, documentaries, and television films. *See* FOCAL LENGTH; TELEPHOTO LENS; ZOOM LENS.

To protect the lens from extraneous light and prevent lens flare, a lens shade must be used. On a motion picture camera this shade is called a matte box. It completely surrounds the lens and acts as a lens shade, but it also has slots to hold various types of filters (such as diffusion, fog, color correcting, and polarizing), and optically flat glass for use when needed. These items are used by cinematographers for the many effects required in making a professional motion picture.

Lenses for motion picture cameras have focusing mounts and can be focused on objects as close as 2 or 3 ft (0.6 to 0.9 m). They are fastened to the camera with threaded or bayonet mounts and can be changed when a lens of a different focal length is needed. Although some older cameras have turrets on the front of them which hold three or four lenses at one time, making it a simple matter to change from one lens to another, all modern professional cameras have solid fronts because of the size and weight of the zoom lens, and because the faster lenses now used require closer tolerances in the positional accuracy of the lens mount relative to the film plane.

The lens has an iris diaphragm which can be opened and closed to control the amount of light reaching the film, thus controlling the exposure. The f-number is a ratio of the focal length of the lens to the diameter of the lens opening, and a lens with a given f-number will always allow the same amount of light per unit area to strike the film regardless of the focal length of the lens. The T-system used in cinematography takes into account all of the light losses encountered in a lens, such as the number of reflecting surfaces inside the lens and the various types of coating on the surfaces. T-stops are determined by the amount of light transmitted through the lens, while f-stops are determined by a mathematical formula of the focal length of the lens divided by the diameter of the iris diaphragm opening. Since the T-stops system is more accurate as far as light transmission is concerned, this is usually used for exposure, while the f-number is used to determine the depth of field, that is, a range of subject distances between which all objects will

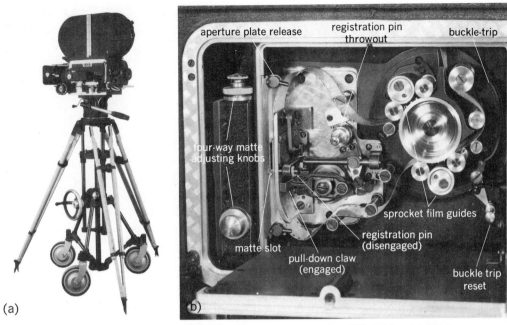

Fig. 1. Mitchell studio camera (BNC). (*a*) Overall view. (*b*) Film-moving mechanism. (*Mitchell Camera Corp.*)

be in sharp focus on the film. *See* LENS (OPTICS).

Shutter. The shutter in a motion picture camera rotates and exposes the film according to its angle of opening. When the shutter is open to its widest angle, the film receives its maximum exposure. Many cameras have variable shutters; that is, the angle of opening can be changed while the camera is running. Such shutter openings usually vary from 180° when the shutter is wide open to 0° when it is closed. Some cameras have a variable shutter which opens to 235° at its widest opening. The shutter in a motion picture camera is almost always located between the lens and the film.

Gate. The aperture called the gate is the passageway through which the film is channeled while it is being exposed. It consists of the aperture plate, which is in front of the film and masks the frame, or picture; the pressure plate, which is in back of the film and holds it firmly against the aperture plate; and the edge guides, which keep the film stable laterally.

Film chamber. This holds the unexposed film at one end and collects the exposed film at the other. Although some motion picture cameras have an interior film chamber, it is usually a separate piece of equipment called the film magazine. Magazines come in 400-ft (120-m) and 1000-ft (300-m) capacities. One thousand feet of 35-mm film, exposed at the normal speed of 24 frames per second, and with a four-perforation pull-down, lasts slightly more than 11 min. The magazines are loaded with film in a darkroom or in a lightproof changing bag and are fitted on the camera as needed, making camera loading easy and rapid.

Pull-down mechanism. The part of the pull-down mechanism called the intermittent movement pulls

the film down through the gate of the camera one frame at a time; in a conventional 35-mm camera, each frame is four perforations high. Some wide-screen cameras have frames five or six perforations high. The pull-down claw engages the perforations and pulls the film down into place to be exposed. At the bottom of its stroke, the claw remains stationary for a moment to position the film and then disengages itself and returns to the upper portion of the stroke to pull another frame into place. During the time the claw is returning to the top of its stroke, the film is stationary and the shutter opens and exposes the film. Some of the more expensive cameras have registration pins which engage the film while the picture is being taken. This ensures that the film is perfectly still and is in exactly the same position as each frame is being exposed. This feature is especially important in special effects photography where independently photographed images are superimposed.

Mobile cameras. When sound is being recorded, cameras must be absolutely quiet. In the early days of sound, cameras were put in enclosures called blimps. Almost all modern cameras are self-blimped, which enhances their portability. The Mitchell BNC (Blimped News Camera), introduced in 1935, was the first such camera (**Fig. 1**), and remained the worldwide industry standard for 35 years. Although this camera was portable, at approximately 125 lb (55 kg), fully loaded, it was not hand-holdable. In 1968 the Arriflex BL camera (**Fig. 2***a*) was introduced. The current model of this camera is the 35BL-4S. In 1972 Panavision introduced the lightweight, very silent Panaflex camera (Fig. 2*b*), and in 1979 the extremely silent Moviecam camera (Fig. 2*c*) was introduced. These

Fig. 2. Hand-holdable cameras with 1000-ft (300-m) magazines. (*a*) Arriflex 35BL-4S camera system with 135-mm T2.1 Zeiss lens (*Arnold and Richter, Gmbh*). (*b*) Panaflex Platinum camera system with Primo T2.4, 18- to 74-mm zoom lens (*Panavision*). (*c*) Super America camera system with video monitor and Mini-Worrall head (*Moviecam*).

later cameras range in weight from 30 to 40 lb (14 to 18 kg), including the lens and a 400-ft (120-m) load of film.

These smaller and lighter cameras have enabled production companies to achieve more mobility and to shoot many pictures on actual locations away from studios, using hotels, cafes, and even private homes in small towns as sets to give the pictures more authenticity. Most feature films, as well as those made for television, are made by independent producers who take advantage of these realistic backgrounds and at the same time save money on stage rentals.

When they go on location, most companies use mobile units which are complete with all the equipment necessary to make a professional motion picture. These vehicles can carry two or three complete camera packages, two or more sound outfits which have been reduced in size even more than the cameras, grip equipment which is used for construction where necessary, camera supports and dollies, and lightweight lamps and cables which feed from a gasoline-powered generator built into the vehicle. Some of these conveyances include space for makeup and wardrobe, although these two departments are usually housed in a separate unit.

Motors. Up until 1970 most sound cameras were driven by 220-VAC (volts alternating current) three-phase synchronous motors, while the sound film, 35-mm perforated iron oxide-coated film running over a sprocket, was driven by a similar synchronous motor. After 1970, however, almost all professional 35-mm productions in the United States, and many 16-mm sound films as well, changed to a new type of motor for driving the camera and a new method of recording synchronous sound, both of which have many advantages over the older system. The motor used on the camera is a direct-current motor, which runs off batteries (12 to 36 V) at a synchronous speed. The speed of the motor is controlled by a crystal oscillator which is so precise that the speed of the

motor varies less than one-half a frame of picture in 1000 ft (300 m) of film. Most productions (16 mm as well as 35 mm) use these "crystal motors."

Sound. All sound is recorded on sprocketless 14-in. (6-mm) tape. Since tape is an elastic medium, some sort of "sync" pulse must be put on the tape in order to synchronize the recorded sound with the picture when they are put together in a "married" print. The sync pulse is usually an inaudible 1-V, 60-Hz (in Europe, 50 Hz) pulse put on the tape at the time of recording. This pulse can be one generated at the camera and sent to the sound recorder, which is exactly 60-Hz when the camera is running precisely 24 frames/s; or a similar pulse from a crystal oscillator either built into or attached to the tape recorder on which the sound is being recorded. The latter method is the one most commonly used on professional motion picture productions. It is the only system in which there is no physical or electrical connection between sound and camera. Without this connection the camera is completely free; it can be in a separate vehicle, car, boat, or aircraft, while the sound-recording equipment is in another. The only thing required to make a synchronous sound picture with this system is that a sync stick, or clap stick, be used so that sound can have an audible point of reference and the camera can have a visible point of reference.

After the sound is recorded on the 14-in. (6-mm) tape, it is put through a resolver, which transfers the sound from the tape to 16-mm or 35-mm perforated iron oxide–coated film. The resolver corrects for the aforementioned variations in sound-track recording by using the sync pulse as a reference. With the sound on the perforated film it can be precisely synchronized with the picture, using sync-stick marks when the picture is printed for release.

There are two types of sound tracks, optical and magnetic, on release prints, the prints seen by the audience. All 35-mm and practically all 16-mm release prints have optical sound tracks. A 16-mm film may have a magnetic sound track if only one or two prints are to be made, but this is

Fig. 3. Slate with data.

seldom the case. An optical sound track is printed photographically on the film; a magnetic sound track is printed in the same manner as on a tape recorder, after the film is coated with an iron oxide stripe in the area reserved for the sound track. All Super 8 films have magnetic sound tracks.

All 65-mm–70-mm films, those shot on 65-mm film in the camera and printed on 70-mm film for release, have magnetic sound tracks. The 70-mm prints have six-track sound, one track on each side inside the perforations and two tracks on each side outside the perforations. The space for the tracks outside the perforations is made possible by the additional width of 2.5 mm on each side.

Slate. In any motion picture a slate with all pertinent information is of utmost importance (**Fig. 3**). The slate is fastened to the sync stick, and the information is photographed at the beginning of each take. The slate has places for all information relating to the production, such as the name of the picture and its production number for identification at the laboratory, where the film is processed, and the name of the director and the camera operator. In addition, there are spaces for the scene number and the take number, and places to indicate whether the shot is an interior or exterior, a day or night shot, or sound or MOS (silent); MOS comes from the early European director's pronunciation of "mit-out sound." The term "MOS" is still used extensively throughout the motion picture industry instead of the expression "silent."

Time code. Current practice makes increasing use of some method of coding the film and sound track to facilitate post production, especially by permitting transfer to videotape for highly automated editing. Methods have been developed for optically printing time code along the edge of the film beside every frame. The code is machine-readable, and is also human-readable in some systems. A method has also been introduced for printing the human-readable key number, which

normally appears as a latent image along the edge of the film, as a machine-readable latent-image bar code. All these schemes facilitate the task of conforming the edit decisions, made in the video domain, back to film for final cutting and assembly.

Camera support equipment. A number of devices have been developed to take advantage of the increased mobility of cameras. Their purpose is to give the camera a smooth fluid motion to follow the cinematic action in ever more difficult and ingenious ways. All of these devices are designed to move in such a manner that the film viewer is drawn into the illusion of the scene. A bumpy or jerky camera motion would make the viewer aware of the camera's presence and destroy the illusion.

Crab dolly. One of the first devices developed to permit camera movement was the crab dolly (**Fig. 4**). This dolly can be steered in the usual manner by turning the wheels for curves, and it can be put in a mode where all four wheels turn in the same direction so that it can go forward and backward and also crab across the stage sideways. The camera can be raised or lowered while the dolly is in motion, making it possible to get interesting and creative camera movements.

Cranes and boom arms. A crane is a larger and more versatile version of the crab dolly. Available in a wide range of sizes, some cranes are slightly larger than a dolly, similar in configuration to a dolly equipped with a boom arm; others extend to 30 ft (9 m) in the air. Cranes are used extensively to achieve large sweeping moves for dramatic effects.

Camera cars. Trucks specially fitted to provide a smooth-moving platform for motion picture cameras (**Fig. 5**) are extremely useful in photographing

Fig. 4. Fisher crab dolly.

fast-moving action such as a car chase. These vehicles have become extremely sophisticated. They can support a camera smoothly at highway speeds, in conventional or crab mode, on a boom arm with battery or generator power to satisfy lighting needs.

Steadicam. This is a unique device to support cameras in a mobile situation (**Fig. 6**). It provides a stable platform for a hand-held camera supported by the camera operator by means of a vest and supporting spring arm. The mass of the camera and its supporting structure is balanced about a gimbal. The operator guides the camera by gently grasping the system at the gimbal, and is able to walk, run, or go up or down stairs, and still provide totally smooth camera motion.

Film. The film used in the standard motion-picture camera is 35 mm (wide) and is perforated along both edges. There are 64 perforations (or sprocket holes) to each foot of film.

Motion-picture film consists of a cellulose acetate base approximately 0.006 in. (0.15 mm) thick and coated with a light-sensitive emulsion. In color film, several layers of emulsion are applied; each of three of the layers is sensitive to one of the three primary colors of light: blue, green, and red. The film is made in large rolls about 54 in. (1.37 m) wide and as long as several thousand feet. It is slit into 35-mm strips, perforated, and packed in lightproof bags and cans in rolls 100, 200, 400, and 1000 ft (30, 60, 120, and 300 m) in length.

Smaller widths such as 16 and 8 mm are also made from these wide rolls if they are of the same emulsion type. These sizes are seldom used for feature films but are used extensively by professionals in the audiovisual field and for news and low-budget films for television. The kinds of

Fig. 6. Steadicam, operated by inventor, Garrett Brown.

motion picture film are numerous and varied to meet the needs of a many-faceted industry: black and white, color, high and low speed, fine and coarse grain, high and low contrast, and wide and narrow exposure latitude. These film characteristics describe a particular type of film emulsion.

There are two different types of film: negative film, from which a print is made in order to see the original subject in its true likeness (for example, Kodacolor, used in amateur photography), and reversal film, in which a negative is first formed in the original film and from this a positive is formed in the same piece of film (for example, Kodachrome, a film familiar to amateurs). In the negative film two pieces of film are necessary to get a picture that can be projected; in the reversal film only one piece of film is required, making it a much less expensive process. In Super 8, as well as regular 8, the reversal film is generally used because of the cost factor. In 16-mm and 35-mm professional work, the original, that is, the film used in the camera, is never used for projection. A work print is made in order to edit the film and the original is made to conform to the edited work print. The release prints are made from the conformed work print and then the sound is added. The original film is all-important and is kept in a vault at the laboratory; it is used only for making prints.

Aspect ratio. The picture taken in standard 35-mm motion picture cameras is masked by the aperture plate, which varies according to the camera. The silent aperture, that is, the aperture used on cameras

Fig. 5. Camera car. (*Shotmaker Co.*)

that do not leave room on the film for a sound track, is almost the entire width of the film between perforations, slightly less than 1 in. (25 mm) and approximately 34 in. (19 mm) high. This gives an aspect ratio (the ratio of its width to its height) of 1.33:1 (4/3). Sound apertures are masked down to a width of 0.868 in. (22 mm), to allow room for the sound track, and a height of 0.631 in. (16 mm), which gives an aspect ratio of 1.37:1.

Projectors

The projector system in a modern motion picture theater has five main assemblies: the optical sound head, which reproduces optical (photographically recorded) sound; the projector head, which projects the image onto the screen; the lamphouse, which furnishes the illumination for the picture; the shutter; and the platter system, which feeds the film through the projector head. On some projectors, there is a second sound head for the reproduction of magnetic (magnetically recorded) sound.

Optical sound head. This consists of an exciter lamp and a photoelectric cell. The optical sound track is 20 frames ahead of the picture on 35-mm film (26 frames ahead on 16-mm film). If the film has a magnetic sound track in addition to the optical one, it is first threaded over the magnetic sound head, which is above the projector head (**Fig. 7**). The magnetic sound track is 28 frames behind the picture on 35-mm film and 23 frames behind on 70-mm film (26 frames ahead on 16-mm film, the same as optical sound).

Fig. 7. Motion picture projector. The white ribbon shows the path of film from the feed magazine over the magnetic sound head, down through the projector head, and bypassing the optical sound head on its way to the take-up magazine. (*Twentieth Century Fox*)

Fig. 8. Nonrewind platter system. (*Kinotone*)

Projector head. This consists of the projection lens and the projector intermittent. The projection lens is located in the front of the projector head between the aperture and the screen. The film is put in the projector aperture upside down and with the sound track on the right. The image is inverted by the lens and appears right side up on the screen. The sound track, if it were visible, would appear on the left side of the screen. The focal length of the lens is determined by the size of the image desired on the screen and the distance between projector and screen. The lens usually has a fixed speed of $f/2$ and has no iris diaphragm.

The projector intermittent uses a Geneva movement to pull the film through the gate. This movement drives a 16-toothed sprocket one-quarter of a revolution at a time. With each movement a new frame is pulled into place. The film is wrapped around this sprocket wheel and its perforations on both sides engage four or five teeth on the wheel at all times. This distributes the stress caused by the acceleration and deceleration over many perforations and results in less wear and tear on the film, substantially increasing its life. A framing device is incorporated in the projector head so that the frame can be moved up or down to position the picture correctly and put the frame lines at the top and bottom of the screen.

Lamphouse. All modern projectors employ xenon arc lamps in place of the previously used carbon arc lamps. The xenon arc lamps form a small plasma arc in a sealed glass bulb. A concave reflector behind the lamp collects the light and concentrates it on the film in the projector aperture. Depending on the size of the screen, the lamps generally range from 1 to 7 kW in power input. *See* ARC LAMP.

Platter system. Most modern theaters use a platter system (**Fig. 8**) rather than the convential 2000-ft (600-m) reels used in older theaters. Conventional reels are labor-intensive and require two projectors to achieve a smooth transition (changeover) between subsequent reels of a motion picture. In the platter system, only one projector is needed. All reels of a motion picture are spliced together and loaded onto one of the platters with the start of the picture at the center of the reel. The film is then threaded from the center of the reel, through the projector, and onto a second platter. When the show is over, it is only necessary to rethread the projector, but starting from the second platter.

Shutter. A projector has a two-bladed shutter located between the lamphouse and the gate in the projector head. The shutter cuts off the light to the screen while the film is being moved down from one frame to the next and opens when the new frame has been moved into place. It then closes and opens a second time before another frame has been brought into position. This makes two exposures per frame, or 48 light impulses hitting the screen in 1 s, even though the picture was shot at 24 frames per second. This reduces the flickering effect that would be noticeable if only 24 light impulses per second were flashed on the screen.

Universal types. Universal projectors can show 35-mm prints, both normal and anamorphic, with optical sound, four-track magnetic sound, or both. They can also show 70-mm normal and anamorphic with six-track magnetic sound. The 35-mm sprockets are between and below the 70-mm sprockets, and either film can be run by selecting the correct lens and threading the film through the gate and through the appropriate sound head.

Wide-Screen Processes

Until 1952 the motion picture industry as a whole used film and equipment that was well standardized. Film was 35 mm wide, the aspect ratio was 1.33:1, and the camera had a four-perforation pull-down mechanism. These standards had been in effect since early in the twentieth century. With the advent of sound in 1926, standard camera speed became established at 24 frames per second, and most sound tracks were reproduced optically. Beginning in 1952, however, many new processes were introduced which departed from these standards and utilized a multiplicity of film sizes, aspect ratios, and types of sound tracks. Some processes which employ 35-mm film use a means of getting more picture on the film. The 1.85:1 ratio has practically become a standard when referring to wide screen. Four-track, six-track, and seven-track magnetic sound has become fairly common.

Cinerama. The first commercially successful wide-screen process was Cinerama, developed by F. Waller. First shown in 1952, the system employed three separate, matched film strips projected by three separate projectors. The projected image height was equivalent to six perforations, and the width the equivalent of three full 35-mm apertures. The deeply curved screen consisted of 1200 overlapping strips, arranged in such a manner as to minimize lateral reflections. A fourth 35-mm film strip carried seven sound tracks for full stereophonic reproduction. The complexities of running these projectors in exact synchronism, in addition to jitter problems between the three panels, caused the system to be simplified some years later to a single 70-mm-wide film with multiple sound tracks and a 1.25:1 anamorphic "squeeze." The first picture made in this manner was *Mad Mad Mad Mad World* (1964).

Cinemascope. The single-film approach was anticipated by Cinemascope, developed by 20th Century-Fox, based on earlier work of the physicist H. Chrétien. Special lens adapters were designed that produced a linear 2:1 anamorphic squeeze when attached to conventional lenses. Integral anamorphic lenses were subsequently developed which were simpler to use. A special projector lens was used to unsqueeze the picture (**Fig. 9**). The first feature filmed in Cinemascope was *The Robe* (1953). The format continues to be used.

VistaVision. This process, developed by Paramount, utilized an eight-perforation–pull-down, 35-mm movement, operating from left to right rather than top to bottom. Conventional spherical lenses were used, and the resulting format was 37.7 mm wide by 25 mm high. *White Christmas* (1954) was the first picture produced by this process. The need for special projection equipment eventually caused VistaVision to be discontinued. It is still

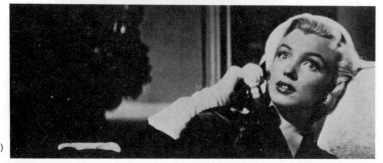

Fig. 9. Action of Cinemascope anamorphic lens. (*a*) The image "squeezed" onto the film by an anamorphic lens. (*b*) The "unsqueezed" image as it appears on the screen. (*Twentieth Century Fox*)

used, however, for shooting background plates for process photography since it provides a large format that will not degrade as much as a 35-mm format during the duplicating process.

Todd-AO. In the mid-1950's B. O'Brien in cooperation with promoter M. Todd developed the Todd-AO wide-screen process. This process used a 70-mm print derived directly from a 65-mm negative, five perforations high, with six magnetic sound tracks arrayed as previously noted. A series of special lenses was developed to provide from 37 to 128° of angular coverage. The first picture produced in Todd-AO was *Oklahoma* (1955). As originally presented, Todd-AO used a deeply curved screen, but it was subsequently converted to flat-screen projection. Super Panavision, similar to Todd-AO in format, has been widely used. Mitchell 35- and 65-mm cameras have been used for these processes, as well as cameras specially designed and built for the process.

Current screen formats. Films for theatrical release have now been standardized in two basic formats in the United States, as contrasted with the plethora of wide-screen and multiscreen formats that appeared and disappeared during the 1950s and 1960s. With rare exceptions all films for theatrical presentation are now shot either (1) in the 2.35:1 aspect ratio, using the 35-mm anamorphic system that was originated by Cinemascope but that now exists largely through the use of Panavision anamorphic lenses and those developed by Todd-AO, or (2) in the 1.85:1 aspect ratio, which is achieved by cropping the standard 35-mm frame top and bottom. In Europe, the popular aspect ratio is 1.66:1.

The 1.85:1 format is extremely wasteful of film, and there have been several attempts to introduce a system involving three-perforation pull-down in the camera as well as in the projector to eliminate this waste.

Techniscope. This was a promising format that has now virtually disappeared in the United States. It was developed in the Technicolor Laboratories in Rome, Italy. The process involves shooting the original camera negative with the camera modified to pull down two perforations, rather than four, in a standard 35-mm camera. The taking lenses are the normal complement of spherical lenses. In the laboratory the negative is optically printed through an anamorphic lens which stretches the image vertically by a factor of 2:1 so that the print is identical to one which would have resulted from a negative shot in the Cinemascope anamorphic process. A number of films were shot in this process, but it fell into disfavor in the United States because the increase in granularity and the decrease in resolution due to using a negative area one-half that of the standard 35-mm size resulted in a film that was not of acceptable quality when compared with the 1.85:1 format or the anamorphic format. However, in Europe and elsewhere Techniscope is still an acceptable and frequently used process.

Super 16. An alternative means of arriving at current theatrical formats, called Super 16, was pioneered by R. Ericson in Sweden. This process involves photographing with a 16-mm camera that is modified so that the full width of the negative is photographed, including that area reserved for sound track in the final release print. The negative is then enlarged, usually through liquid-gate optical printing, to a 35-mm format with a 1.65:1 aspect ratio.

70-mm presentation. There has been a major move back to theatrical presentation in the 70-mm format originated by Todd-AO in the mid-1950s. More than 1000 theaters in the United States are equipped for this format. The 70-mm print permits the use of high-quality multitrack audio provided by several sound systems. The six magnetic tracks on a 70-mm print are ideal for high-fidelity audio reproduction. The 70-mm prints are usually enlarged from 35-mm negatives shot anamorphically or in the 1.85:1 aspect ratio. Motivated by competition with television and in particular the coming of high-definition television, there is growing interest in film origination in 65-mm, since it would provide much greater resolution than a 35-mm negative. To meet this anticipated need, new 65-mm cameras have been developed (**Fig. 10**).

Imax. Epitomizing this trend to larger formats, the Imax process films on a 65-mm negative moving horizontally through the camera, 15 perforations per frame. The resulting aspect ratio is 1.33:1. The 70-mm prints are projected on a large flat screen.

Fig. 10. CP-65 65-mm camera system. (*Cinema Products Corp.*)

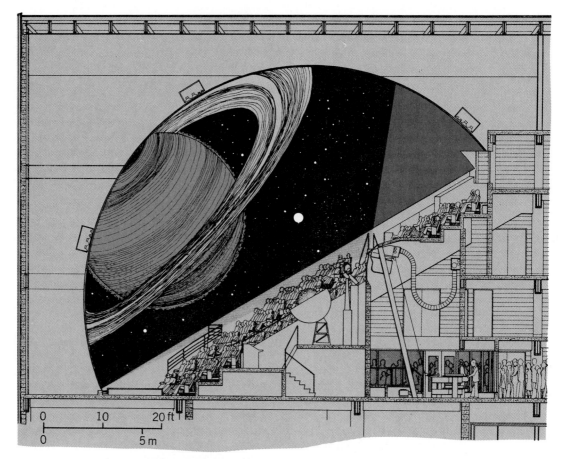

Fig. 11. Cross-sectional view of typical Omnimax theater.

They can also be photographed and projected with a fisheye lens on a hemispheric dome in a process called Omnimax (**Fig. 11**). The projector is of a unique design that utilizes a rolling loop to rapidly advance the film with no damage and absolute flatness in the film gate. *See* PLANETARIUM.

Showscan. This process uses the conventional 70-mm, five-perforation format, but is filmed and projected at 60 frames per second. This frame rate virtually eliminates all filmic artifacts, such as strobe and flicker, to provide a heightened sense of reality.

Edmund M. DiGiulio

Bibliography. S. Carlson and V. Carlson, *Professional Cameraman's Handbook*, 4th ed., 1994; F. P. Clark, *Special Effects in Motion Pictures*, 1982; F. Detmers, *American Cinematographer's Manual*, 6th ed., 1986; J. Mercer, *An Introduction to Cinematography*, 1979; D. W. Samuelson, *Hands-on Manual for Cinematographers*, 1994; D. W. Samuelson, *Motion Picture Camera and Lighting Equipment*, 2d ed., 1987; D. W. Samuelson, *Motion Picture Camera Techniques*, 1984; D. Viera, *Lighting for Film and Electronic Cinematography*, 1993.

Cinnabar

A mineral of composition HgS, crystallizing in the hexagonal system, and having three formula units per unit cell. Each Hg atom is octahedrally coordinated by three pairs of S atoms, each pair at a different distance from the Hg atoms. Crystals are rare, usually of rhombohedral habit and often in penetration twins (see **illus.**). Cinnabar most commonly occurs in fine, granular, massive form. It has perfect prismatic cleavage, a Mohs hardness of 2.0–2.5, and a density of 8.09. It has either an adamantine luster and vermilion red color or a dull luster and brownish-red color.

Metacinnabar is an isometric polymorph in which the Hg atoms occupy tetrahedral sites in a face-centered cubic framework of S atoms. It is grayish-black and has a hardness of 3 and a density of 7.65. It is found with cinnabar and inverts to it when heated to 750–930°F (400–500°C).

Cinnabar is deposited from hydrothermal solu-

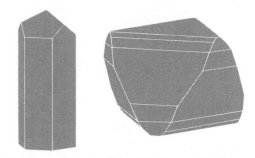

Cinnabar crystal habits. (*After L. G. Berry and B. Mason, Mineralogy, W. H. Freeman, 1959*)

tions in veins and as impregnations near recent volcanic rocks and hot springs. It is the principal ore of mercury. Notable occurrences are Almadén, Spain; Idria, Italy; near Belgrade, in former east Yugoslavia; Kweichow and Hunan provinces, China; Turkistan; New Almaden and New Idria, California; Terlingua, Texas; and several localities in Utah, Nevada, New Mexico, Oregon, and Idaho. *See* MERCURY (ELEMENT).   Lawrence Grossman

Cinnamon

An evergreen shrub or small tree, *Cinnamomum zeylanicum*, of the laurel family (Lauraceae). A native of Sri Lanka, the plant (see **illus.**) is now

Cinnamon (*Cinnamomum zeylanicum*). (*USDA*)

in cultivation in southern India, Burma, parts of Malaya, West Indies, and South America. In cultivation the trees are cut back and long, slender suckers grow up from the roots. The bark is removed from these suckers, dried and packaged for shipping. Cinnamon is a very important spice for flavoring foods. It is used in confectionery, gums, incense, dentifrices, and perfumes. Cinnamon oil is used in medicine and as a source of cinnamon extract. *See* MAGNOLIALES; SPICE AND FLAVORING.
    Perry D. Strausbaugh/Earl L. Core

Circle

The curve that is the locus of points in a plane with equal distance (radius) from a fixed point (center) (**Fig. 1**). In elementary mathematics, circle often refers to the finite portion of the plane bounded by a curve (circumference) all points of which are equidistant from a fixed point of the plane,

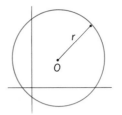

Fig. 1. Circle of radius *r* and center *O*.

that is, a circular disk. Circles are conic sections and are defined analytically by certain second-degree equations in cartesian coordinates. They were extensively studied by the ancient Greeks, who formulated the famous problem of "squaring the circle," that is, to construct, with compasses and unmarked straightedge only, a square whose area is equal to that of a given circle. It was not until 1882 that this was shown to be impossible, when F. Lindemann proved that the ratio of the length of a circle to its diameter (denoted by π) is not the root of any algebraic equation with integer coefficients. That π is irrational (that is, not the quotient of two integers) was shown by A. M. Legendre in 1794. Numerous approximations of π appeared quite early; for example, 3 (*Book of Kings*); $3\frac{1}{7} > \pi > 3\frac{10}{71}$ (Archimedes); $\sqrt{10}$ (*Ch'ang Höng*, A.D. 78–139); and 3.1416 (Aryabhata, A.D. 476–550). Electronic computers have calculated π to over 10,000 decimal places. Interesting expressions are

$$\pi = 4(1 - \tfrac{1}{3} + \tfrac{1}{5} - \tfrac{1}{7} + \cdots)$$
$$\pi = 2 \cdot 2(2 \cdot 4/3 \cdot 3)(4 \cdot 6/5 \cdot 5)(6 \cdot 8/7 \cdot 7) \cdots$$

The area of a circle (circular disk) with radius r is πr^2; the length (circumference) is $2\pi r$. The area enclosed by a circle is greater than that bounded by any other curve of the same length. If a circular disk can cover each three points of an arbitrary plane set, then the disk can cover the whole set. It is, moreover, the only disk that has this property. *See* ANALYTIC GEOMETRY; CONIC SECTION.
    Leonard M. Blumenthal

A great many properties of the circle are in relation to a given triangle. Such, for example, is the nine-point circle theorem. Let the altitudes of any triangle *ABC* intersect each other in the orthocenter *H*, and intersect the opposite sides in *D*, *E*, and *F*, respectively. Then the circle *DEF* passes through the midpoints of each of the six segments *AB*, *BC*,

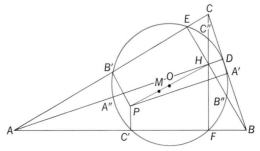

Fig. 2. Nine-point circle and Euler line *PMH*.

CA, *AH*, *BH*, *CH*. It is called the nine-point circle of the triangle *ABC*, and also of each of the triangles *HBC*, *HCA*, *HAB*, whose orthocenters are *A*, *B*, *C*, respectively. Feuerbach's theorem states that this nine-point circle is tangent both to the inscribed circle and to the three escribed circles of each of these triangles.

The center *O* of the nine-point circle (**Fig. 2**) of any triangle lies midway between the orthocenter *H* and the circumcenter *P* on the so-called Euler line that passes through these points and the centroid *M*.

J. Sutherland Frame

Bibliography. P. Beckmann, *A History of Pi*, 4th ed., 1977, reprint 1990; J. L. Coolidge, *Treatise on the Circle and the Sphere*, 1971; D. Pedoe, *Circles: A Mathematical View*, 1979.

Circuit (electricity)

A general term referring to a system or part of a system of conducting parts and their interconnections through which an electric current is intended to flow. A circuit is made up of active and passive elements or parts and their interconnecting conducting paths. The active elements are the sources of electric energy for the circuit; they may be batteries, direct-current generators, or alternating-current generators. The passive elements are resistors, inductors, and capacitors. The electric circuit is described by a circuit diagram or map showing the active and passive elements and their connecting conducting paths.

Devices with an individual physical identity such as amplifiers, transistors, loudspeakers, and generators, are often represented by equivalent circuits for purposes of analysis. These equivalent circuits are made up of the basic passive and active elements listed above.

Electric circuits are used to transmit power as in high-voltage power lines and transformers or in low-voltage distribution circuits in factories and homes; to convert energy from or to its electrical form as in motors, generators, microphones, loudspeakers, and lamps; to communicate information as in telephone, telegraph, radio, and television systems; to process and store data and make logical decisions as in computers; and to form systems for automatic control of equipment.

Electric circuit theory. This includes the study of all aspects of electric circuits, including analysis, design, and application. In electric circuit theory the fundamental quantities are the potential differences (voltages) in volts between various points, the electric currents in amperes flowing in the several paths, and the parameters in ohms or mhos which describe the passive elements. Other important circuit quantities such as power, energy, and time constants may be calculated from the fundamental variables. For a discussion of these parameters *see* AD-

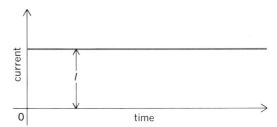

Fig. 1. Direct current, which is constant in magnitude and does not vary with time.

MITTANCE; CONDUCTANCE; ELECTRICAL IMPEDANCE; ELECTRICAL RESISTANCE; REACTANCE; SUSCEPTANCE; TIME CONSTANT.

Electric circuit theory is an extensive subject and is often divided into special topics. Division into topics may be made on the basis of how the voltages and currents in the circuit vary with time; examples are direct-current, alternating-current, nonsinusoidal, digital, and transient circuit thoery. Another method of classifying circuits is by the arrangement or configuration of the electric current paths; examples are series circuits, parallel circuits, series-parallel circuits, networks, coupled circuits, open circuits, and short circuits. Circuit theory can also be divided into special topics according to the physical devices forming the circuit, or the application and use of the circuit. Examples are power, communication, electronic, solid-state, integrated, computer, and control circuits. *See* CIRCUIT (ELECTRONICS); NEGATIVE-RESISTANCE CIRCUITS.

Direct-current circuits. In dc circuits the voltages and currents are constant in magnitude and do not vary with time (**Fig. 1**). Sources of direct current are batteries, dc generators, and rectifiers. Resistors are the principal passive element. For a discussion of direct-current circuits *see* DIRECT-CURRENT CIRCUIT THEORY.

Magnetic circuits. Magnetic circuits are similar to electric circuits in their analysis and are often included in the general topic of circuit theory. Magnetic circuits are used in electromagnets, relays, magnetic brakes and clutches, computer memory devices, and many other devices. For a detailed

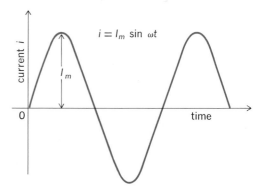

Fig. 2. Alternating current, which periodically reverses direction with time. In this example, the current varies sinusoidally with time.

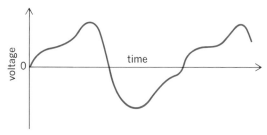

Fig. 3. Nonsinusoidal voltage wave.

treatment *see* MAGNETIC CIRCUITS.

Alternating-current circuits. In ac circuits the voltage and current periodically reverse direction with time. The time for one complete variation is known as the period. The number of periods in 1 s is the frequency in cycles per second. A cycle per second was named a hertz (in honor of Heinrich Rudolf Hertz's work on electromagnetic waves).

Most often the term ac circuit refers to sinusoidal variations. For example, the alternating current in **Fig. 2** may be expressed by $i = I_m \sin \omega t$. Sinusoidal sources are ac generators and various types of electronic and solid-state oscillators; passive circuit elements include inductors and capacitors as well as resistors. The analysis of ac circuits requires a study of the phase relations between voltages and currents as well as their magnitudes. Complex numbers are often used for this purpose. For a detailed discussion *see* ALTERNATING-CURRENT CIRCUIT THEORY.

Nonsinoidal waveforms. These voltage and current variations vary with time but not sinusoidally (**Fig. 3**). Such nonsinusoidal variations are usually caused by nonlinear devices, such as saturated magnetic circuits, electron tubes, and transistors. Circuits with nonsinusoidal waveforms are analyzed by breaking the waveform into a series of sinusoidal waves of

Fig. 4. Transient electric current.

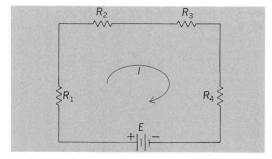

Fig. 5. Series circuit.

different frequencies known as a Fourier series. Each frequency component is analyzed by ac circuit techniques. Results are combined by the principle of superposition to give the total response. *See* NONSINUSOIDAL WAVEFORM.

Electric transients. Transient voltage and current variations last for a short length of time and do not repeat continuously (**Fig. 4**). Transients occur when a change is made in the circuit, such as opening or closing a switch, or when a change is made in one of the sources or elements. For a discussion of dc and ac transients *see* ELECTRIC TRANSIENT.

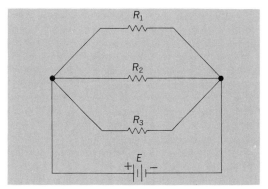

Fig. 6. Parallel circuit.

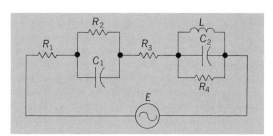

Fig. 7. Series-parallel circuit.

Series circuits. In a series circuit all the components or elements are connected end to end and carry the same current, as shown in **Fig. 5**. *See* SERIES CIRCUIT.

Parallel circuits. Parallel circuits are connected so that each component of the circuit has the same potential difference (voltage) across its terminals, as shown in **Fig. 6**. *See* PARALLEL CIRCUIT.

Series-parallel circuits. In a series-parallel circuit some of the components or elements are connected in parallel, and one or more of these parallel combinations are in series with other components of the circuit, as shown in **Fig. 7**.

Electric network. This is another term for electric circuit, but it is often reserved for the electric circuit that is more complicated than a simple series or parallel combination. A three-mesh electric network is shown in **Fig. 8**. *See* NETWORK THEORY.

Coupled circuits. A circuit is said to be coupled if two or more parts are related to each other through some common element. The coupling may

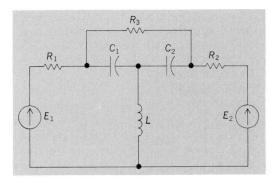

Fig. 8. A three-mesh electric network.

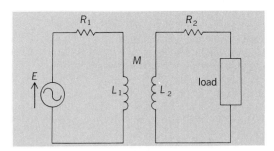

Fig. 9. Inductively coupled circuit.

be by means of a conducting path of resistors or capacitors or by a common magnetic linkage (inductive coupling), as shown in **Fig. 9**. *See* COUPLED CIRCUITS.

Open circuit. An open circuit is a condition in an electric circuit in which there is no path for current flow between two points that are normally connected. *See* OPEN CIRCUIT.

Short circuit. This term applies to the existence of a zero-impedance path between two points of an electric circuit. *See* SHORT CIRCUIT.

Integrated circuit. In the integrated circuit the entire circuit is contained in a single piece of semiconductor material. Sometimes the term is also applied to circuits made up of deposited thin films on an insulating substrate. *See* INTEGRATED CIRCUITS; SEMICONDUCTOR.

Clarence F. Goodheart

Bibliography. N. Balabanian, *Electric Circuits*, 1994; W. Hayt, Jr., and J. E. Kemmerly, *Engineering Circuit Analysis*, 5th ed., 1993; L. P. Huelsman, *Basic Circuit Theory*, 3d ed., 1990; D. E. Johnson, J. L. Milburn, and J. R. Johnson, *Electric Circuit Analysis*, 2d ed., 1991; T. J. Maloney, *Electric Circuits*, 2d ed., 1988; R. J. Smith, *Circuits, Devices, and Systems*, 5th ed., 1991.

Circuit (electronics)

An interconnection of electronic devices, an electronic device being an entity having terminals which is described at its terminals by electromagnetic laws. Most commonly these are voltage–current laws, but others, such as photovoltaic relationships, may occur.

Basic Concepts

Some typical electronic devices are represented as shown in **Fig. 1**, where a resistor, a capacitor, a diode, transistors, an operational amplifier, an inductor, a transformer, voltage and current sources, and a ground are indicated. Other devices (such as vacuum tubes, switches, and logic gates) exist, in some cases as combinations of the ones mentioned. The interconnection laws are (1) the Kirchhoff voltage law, which states that the sum of voltages around a closed loop is zero, and (2) the Kirchhoff current law, which states that the sum of the currents into a closed surface is zero (where often the surface is shrunk to a point, the node, where device terminals join). **Figure 2** represents an electronic circuit which is the interconnection of resistors (R, R_{B1}, R_{B2}, R_E, R_L), capacitors (C), a battery voltage source (V_{CC}), a current source (i_s), a bipolar transistor (T), and a switch (S). Functionally Fig. 2 represents a high-pass filter when S is open, and an oscillator when S is closed and the current source is removed. *See* AMPLIFIER; BATTERY; CAPACITOR; CURRENT SOURCES AND MIRRORS; DIODE; ELECTRIC FILTER; ELECTRONIC SWITCH; INDUCTOR; KIRCHHOFF'S LAWS OF ELECTRIC CIRCUITS; LOGIC CIRCUITS; OPERATIONAL AMPLIFIER; OSCILLATOR; RESISTOR; TRANSFORMER; TRANSISTOR; VACUUM TUBE.

Active and passive devices. The devices in an electronic circuit are classified as being either passive or active. The passive devices change signal energy, as is done dynamically by capacitors and statically by transformers, or absorb signal energy, as occurs in resistors, which also act to convert voltages to currents and vice versa. The active devices, such as batteries, transistors, operational amplifiers, and vacuum tubes, can supply signal energy to the circuit and in many cases amplify signal energy by transforming power supply energy into signal energy. Often, though, they are used for other purposes, such as to route signals in logic circuits. Transistors can be considered the workhorses of modern electronic circuits, and consequently many types of transistors have been developed, among which the most widely used are the bipolar junction transistor (BJT), the junction field-effect transistor (JFET), and the metal-oxide-silicon field-effect transistor (MOSFET). *See* ELECTRONIC POWER SUPPLY.

Fortunately, most of these transistors occur in pairs, such as the *npn* and the *pnp* bipolar junction transistors, or the *n*-channel and the *p*-channel MOSFETs, allowing designers to work symmetrically with positive and negative signals and sources. This statement may be clarified by noting that transistors can be characterized by graphs of output current i versus output voltage v that are parametrized by an input current (in the case of the bipolar junction transistor) or input

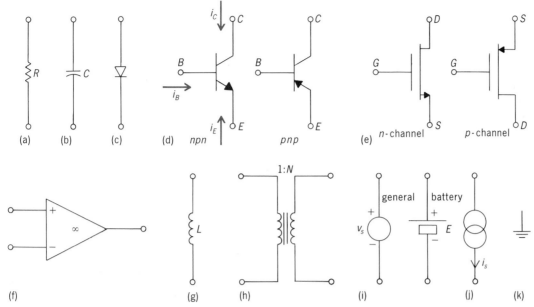

Fig. 1. Representation of some typical electronic devices. (*a*) Resistor. (*b*) Capacitor. (*c*) Diode. (*d*) Bipolar junction transistors (BJTs). (*e*) Metal-oxide-semiconductor field-effect transistors (MOSFETs). (*f*) Operational amplifier. (*g*) Inductor. (*h*) Transformer. (*i*) Voltage sources. (*j*) Current source. (*k*) Ground.

voltage (in the MOSFET and JFET cases). Typically, the curves for an *npn* bipolar junction transistor or an *n*-channel field-effect transistor are used in the first quadrant of the output *i-v* plane, while for a *pnp* bipolar junction transistor or a *p*-channel field-effect transistor the same curves show up in the third quadrant. Mathematically, if $i = f(v)$ for an *npn* bipolar junction transistor or *n*-channel field-effect device, then $i = -f(-v)$ for a *pnp* bipolar junction transistor or *p*-channel field-effect device when the controlling parameters are also changed in sign.

Transistor properties. Because the transistors are so basic to the operation of electronic circuits, their performance will be briefly discussed.

Bipolar transistors. These have three terminals, designated as the base *B*, the collector *C*, and the emitter *E*. These terminals connect to two diode junctions, *B-C* and *B-E*, these forming back-to-back diodes. The *B-E* junction is often forward-biased, in which case its voltage is about 0.7 V, while the *B-C*

junction is reverse-biased for linear operation. In the case of linear operation, the bipolar junction transistor is much more than two back-to-back diodes because it has a very thin base which allows almost all of the current i_E entering the emitter to be collected by the collector. Thus, the collector current is nearly equal to the emitter current. This is expressed in Eq. (1), where the transistor parameter

$$i_C = -\alpha i_E \tag{1}$$

α is very close to 1. (The negative sign arises because the positive direction of current is assumed into the terminals, while one current must come out when the other goes in.) By Kirchhoff's current law for a sphere around the transistor ($i_B + i_C + i_E = 0$), the collector current can be expressed in terms of the base current to obtain Eq. (2), where the parameter β, given by Eq. (3), is very large. From

$$i_C = \beta i_B \tag{2}$$

$$\beta = \frac{\alpha}{1 - \alpha} \tag{3}$$

this it follows that in linear operation the (bipolar junction) transistor acts like a current-controlled current source which, when used with base current as input and collector current as output, can have a high current gain β (typically 20 to 600). Because a current can be changed into a voltage via resistors, the transistor in its linear mode of operation also can be used to obtain a high voltage gain. For example, if the current source, the three capacitors, the two resistors labeled *R*, and the switch are replaced with a capacitor-coupled voltage source v_s between the point *B* and ground in Fig. 2 the voltage gain is given by Eq. (4), and can be chosen large in

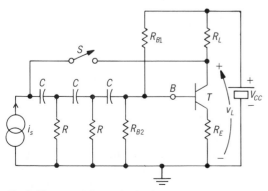

Fig. 2. Diagram of electronic circuit.

$$\frac{v_L}{v_s} = -\alpha \frac{R_L}{R_E} \tag{4}$$

magnitude by appropriately choosing the ratio of the load resistance R_L to the emitter resistance R_E to be large.

Besides biasing of the junctions for linear operation, any state of the two junctions can occur. For example, both junctions might be forward-biased, in which case the transistor is said to be in saturation and acts nearly as a short circuit between E-C, while if the junctions are simultaneously back-biased the transistor is said to be cut off and acts as an open circuit between all terminals. The transistor can be controlled between saturation and cutoff to make it act as an electronically controlled switch. This mode of operation is especially useful for binary arithmetic, as used by almost all digital computers, where 0 and 1 logic levels are represented by the saturation and cutoff transistor states.

MOSFET. These also have three regions of operation: cutoff, saturated, and resistive. The MOSFET also has three terminals, the gate G, the drain D, and the source S. A key parameter characterizing the MOSFET is a threshold voltage V_{th}. When the G-S voltage is below the threshold voltage, no drain current flows and the transistor is cut off. When the G-S voltage is above threshold, then for D-S voltages large in magnitude the MOSFET acts as a voltage-controlled current source, with the drain current given by Eq. (5), where K can conveniently

$$i_D = \frac{K(v_{GS} - V_{th})^2}{2} \tag{5}$$

be controlled by process parameters. Finally, for D-S voltages of small magnitude, the drain current law is given by Eq. (6), in which case the MOSFET

$$i_D = K\left[(v_{GS} - V_{th})v_{DS} - \frac{v_{DS}^2}{2}\right] \tag{6}$$

acts as a resistor between drain and source which can be varied by the G-S voltage v_{GS}. This resistor is nonlinear, because of the square term, but for very small values of v_{DS} can be considered linear [of conductance $K(v_{GS} - V_{th})$].

The MOSFET is a versatile device, acting as a voltage-controlled current source in the saturation region and approximately as a voltage-controlled resistor in the resistive region. It can also be electronically controlled between cutoff and the resistive region to make it act as a switch, while for small signals around an operating point in the saturation region it acts as a linear amplifier. Another feature of the MOSFET is that, besides the categories of *n*-channel and *p*-channel devices, there are also enhancement- and depletion-mode devices of each category. In practice, for electronic circuit considerations, an *n*-channel device has $V_{th} > 0$ for enhancement-mode devices and $V_{th} < 0$ for depletion-mode devices, while the signs are reversed for *p*-channel devices.

Biasing of circuits. Since active devices usually supply signal energy to an electronic circuit, and since energy can only be transformed and not created, a source of energy is needed when active devices are present. This energy is usually obtained from batteries or through rectification of sinusoidal voltages supplied by power companies. When inserted into an electronic circuit, such a source of energy fixes the quiescent operation of the circuit; that is, it allows the circuit to be biased to a given operating point with no signal applied, so that when a signal is present it will be processed properly. To be useful, an electronic circuit produces one or more outputs; often inputs are applied to produce the outputs. These inputs and outputs are called the signals and, consequently, generally differ from the bias quantities, though often it is hard to separate signal and bias variables. For example, i_s in Fig. 2 would be an input signal, while V_{CC} would be a bias supply voltage. The voltage v_L would contain an output signal but would also include a bias component. The resistors R_{B1}, R_{B2}, R_E, and R_L are used to set the bias point of the transistor, but since they also affect the signal-handling capabilities, their choice is important in the design of the circuit. Biasing of electronic circuits is an important, nontrivial, and often overlooked aspect of their operation. *See* BIAS OF TRANSISTORS.

Analog versus digital circuits. Electronic circuits are also classified as analog or digital. Analog circuits work with signals that span a full range of values of voltages and currents, while digital circuits work with signals that are at prescribed levels to represent numerical digits. Analog signals generally are used for continuous-time processes, while digital ones most frequently occur where transitions are synchronized via a clock. However, there are situations where it is desirable to transfer between these two classes of signals, that is, where analog signals are needed to excite a digital circuit or where a digital signal is needed to excite an analog circuit. For example, it may be desired to feed a biomedically recorded signal, such as an electrocardiogram into a digital computer, or it may be desired to feed a digital computer output into an analog circuit, such as a temperature controller. For such cases, there are special electronic circuits, called analog-to-digital and digital-to-analog converters. *See* ANALOG-TO-DIGITAL CONVERTER; DIGITAL-TO-ANALOG CONVERTER.

Feedback. An important concept in electronic circuits is that of feedback. Feedback occurs when an output signal is fed around a device to contribute to the input of the device. For example, in Fig. 2, when the switch S is closed, the voltage v_L is fed around the transistor T back to the input point; removal of i_s then allows v_L to contribute to its own generation, resulting in oscillations if the proper conditions are met. Consequently, when positive feedback occurs, that is, when the output signal returns to reinforce itself upon being fed back, it can lead to the generation of signals which may or may not be wanted. Circuit designers need to be conscious of all possible feedback paths that are present in their circuits so that they can ensure that unwanted oscillations do not occur. In the case of negative feedback, that is, when the output signal returns to weaken itself, then a number of improvements in circuit performance often ensue; for example, the circuit can be made less sensitive to changes in the environment or element variations, and deleterious nonlinear effects can be minimized. *See* CONTROL SYSTEMS; FEEDBACK CIRCUIT.

Specific Circuits

In designing integrated electronic circuits, one of the most useful tools is the current mirror. Two basic current mirrors are that shown in **Fig. 3***a* for taking current out of a terminal attached to point A, and that shown in Fig. 3*b* for sending current into a terminal attached to point B. In Fig. 3*a*, the base-to-emitter voltages of both transistors are identical and given by V_{BE}, with typically $V_{BE} = 0.7$ V (since the base-to-emitter junction of T_1 is a forward-biased diode). The current in the resistor i_R is then given by Ohm's law as Eq. (7) since the short circuit

$$i_R = \frac{E - V_{BE}}{R} \qquad (7)$$

between collector and base makes T_1 a diode-connected transistor that forces the voltage $E - V_{BE}$ to be across R. From Kirchhoff's current law applied to a sphere encircling T_1, it follows that this current is about equal to the emitter current i_{E1} of T_1 (since the current into the base of transistor T_2 is very small). If the two transistors are identical, then $i_{E2} = i_{E1}$ (because the base-to-emitter voltages are the same). Finally, the collector current i_s of T_2 is about equal to its emitter current (by the construction and characteristics of transistors so that this current is given by Eq. (8), mirroring the current i_R.

$$i_s = i_R \qquad (8)$$

One of the most versatile circuits is the differential pair, since it finds increasing use in both analog and digital circuits. A bipolar-junction-transistor differential pair is shown in **Fig. 4**, where the dc bias current source I_E can be constructed from the output of a current mirror of the type of Fig. 3*a*. If the differential input voltage v_{id} is defined by Eq. (9), then it can be shown that the differential output voltage v_{od} is given by Eq. (10),

$$v_{id} = v_{i1} - v_{i2} \qquad (9)$$

$$v_{od} = \alpha R I_E \tanh \frac{v_{id}}{2V_T} \qquad (10)$$

where V_T is the thermal voltage ($V_T = 25$ mV at room temperature), α is the parameter alpha (defined above) for the two transistors (which are assumed identical), and tanh[·] is the hyperbolic tangent function. As Eq. (10) shows, the differential pair performs as a differential voltage-controlled voltage source. An MOS differential pair is obtained simply by replacing the bipolar junction transistors

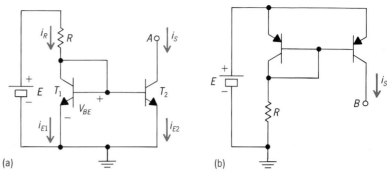

(a)   (b)

Fig. 3. Basic current mirrors. (*a*) Sink. (*b*) Source.

in Fig. 4 by MOSFETs, although a somewhat more complicated input-output law results. *See* DIFFERENTIAL AMPLIFIER.

Analog circuits. By replacing the resistive loads of the differential amplifier of Fig. 4 with the current mirror of Fig. 3*b*, a differential voltage-controlled current source (DVCCS) is generated, as shown in **Fig. 5**, where from the above Eq. (11) follows. Since

$$i_o = i_{c2} - i_{c1} = a I_E \tanh \frac{v_{id}}{2V_T} \qquad (11)$$

$\tanh (x) \simeq x$ when x is very small in magnitude, for small differential inputs the linear law (12) holds.

$$i_0 = \frac{\alpha I_E v_{id}}{2V_T} \qquad (12)$$

An application of the differential voltage-controlled current source is seen by connecting its output to a capacitor, in which case an integrator results. Connecting the output of a differential voltage-controlled current source to its input can result in a resistor.

Operational amplifiers. The differential pair forms the input stage to the operational amplifier (op amp), an extremely important electronic circuit device. The operational amplifier is typically realized by taking v_{od} of Fig. 4, greatly amplifying it, terminating with an output stage that allows for loading, and improving the input terminals so that miniscule input current is drawn. From this

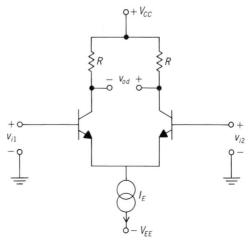

Fig. 4. Differential pair based on bipolar junction transistors.

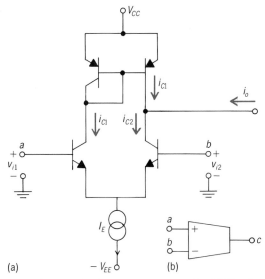

Fig. 5. Differential voltage-to-current converter. (a) Circuit. (b) Symbol.

description, it follows that an operational amplifier in the linear region is characterized by the input-output voltage relationship given by Eq. (13), with

$$v_o = K v_{id} \qquad (13)$$

K tending to infinity. Since v_o is finite, this means that either $v_{id} \simeq 0$ or the output is saturated at a bias voltage of the operational amplifier. In either case, for most practical purposes the input current can be assumed to be zero. Therefore, in the linear region the operational amplifier has the very interesting description given by Eq. (14), in which case its input

$$v_{id} = 0, \quad i_{\text{input}} = 0 \qquad (14)$$

looks like a simultaneous short and open circuit (while its output can be "anything").

By applying feedback through a direct connection of the output to the negative input, the unity-gain buffer amplifier satisfying Eq. (15) results. The

$$v_o = v_i \qquad (15)$$

buffer amplifier is shown in **Fig. 6a**. If the positive input is grounded and negative feedback is applied, then the negative input must be also at ground potential and, since the operational amplifier draws no current, the negative input terminal is said to be a virtual ground. Using the concept of the virtual ground, it is readily seen that the circuit of Fig. 6b functions as an integrator, given by Eq. (16), where

$$v_o = \frac{-v_i}{RCs} \qquad (16)$$

s is the derivative operator (and hence its inverse, $1/s$, is the integral operator). The circuit of Fig. 6c functions as a summer, given by Eq. (17). Using the

$$v_o = -R_F \left(\frac{v_{i1}}{R_1} + \frac{v_{i2}}{R_2} \right) \qquad (17)$$

three circuits of Fig. 6, any set of linear differential equations with constant coefficients can be simulated, and arbitrary transfer functions realized. The

operational amplifier is one of the most useful of the electronic circuit devices. *See* ANALOG COMPUTER.

Applying positive feedback in operational amplifier circuits, some interesting results can also be obtained. For example, the circuit of **Fig. 7a** is a practical way to obtain a negative resistance; its operation depends on Eq. (18). When the operational

$$i = \frac{v - v_o}{R} \qquad (18)$$

amplifier is in its linear region, that is, when notation (19) is valid, Eq. (20) holds, giving the negative

$$-V_{EE} < v_o < V_{CC} \qquad (19)$$

$$v_o = \left(1 + \frac{R_F}{R_1} \right) v \qquad (20)$$

resistor equation (21). When the operational ampli-

$$i = -\left(\frac{R_F}{R_1 R} \right) v \qquad (21)$$

fier is forced into saturation the behavior of the circuit is given by Eqs. (22) and (23) [Fig. 5]. The

$$i = \frac{v - V_{CC}}{R} \qquad (22)$$

$$\text{when } v < V_+ = \frac{V_{CC}}{1 + (R_F/R_1)}$$

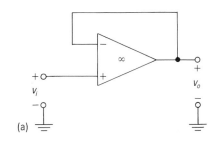

(a)

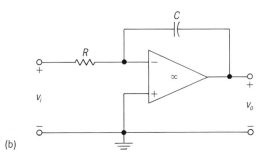

(b)

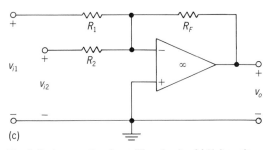

(c)

Fig. 6. Basic operational amplifier circuits. (a) Unity-gain (isolation) amplifier. (b) Integrator. (c) Summer.

$$i = \frac{v + V_{EE}}{R} \qquad (23)$$

$$\text{when } v > -V_- = -\frac{V_{EE}}{1 + (R_F/R_1)}$$

resulting transfer characteristic is shown in Fig. 7*b*. This negative resistor is multiple-valued when the input voltage v is used as the independent (that is, control) variable. Hence, an attempt to use it as a voltage-controlled device will result in its exhibiting hysteresis, since a switch onto the upper curve occurs at $v = V_+$ whereas a switch off the upper curve occurs at $-V_-$. *See* HYSTERESIS; NEGATIVE-RESISTANCE CIRCUITS; OPERATIONAL AMPLIFIER.

Schmitt triggers. Other circuits exhibiting hysteresis are Schmitt trigger circuits (**Fig. 8**), where positive feedback is again used. In these circuits the output is taken as the operational amplifier output voltage, which saturates at the bias voltages. As shown in the input-output curves of Fig. 8, the Schmitt triggers give binary-valued hysteresis, which makes them useful for storage of binary information or for maintaining a constant output in the presence of noise.

Role of nonlinearity. Since the characteristics of the circuits of Figs. 7 and 8 are very nonlinear, they serve as examples to illustrate that nonlinear theory plays an important role in the area of electronic circuits. There are many other instances where nonlinearities are important, for example, in the construction of analog multipliers where the output is the product of two inputs. (Such a multiplier can be obtained via the differential pair of Fig. 5 if I_E is made to vary with an input. This is achievable by using the current sink of Fig. 3*a* to generate I_E. With this circuit the voltage E becomes the second input.) Likewise, nonlinearities are required in the modern theories of neural networks, where so-called sigmoid-type nonlinearities are used to obtain convergence toward set patterns. (The hyperbolic tangent function realized by the differential pair is a sigmoid-type of nonlinearity.) *See* NEURAL NETWORK.

Filters. One of the most common uses of analog active circuits is in the construction of electrical filters. Electrical filters are circuits whose input-output characteristics allow signals at certain frequencies (called the passband) to pass through unattenuated while signals at unwanted frequencies (called the stopband) are eliminated. By appropriately positioning the passband and the stopband, various filter types such as low-pass, band-pass, and high-pass can be attained. Filter design often concentrates on low-pass filters, since through relatively elementary transformations the band-pass and high-pass responses can be obtained from the low-pass transfer function. The transfer function, $H(s)$, is the ratio of the output v_o to the input v_i as a function of the complex frequency variable s.

Maximally flat filters are common with these resulting from using the Butterworth polynomials, $B_n(s)$, to obtain the low-pass transfer function given

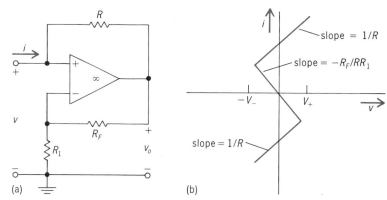

Fig. 7. Negative resistor circuit. (*a*) Diagram. (*b*) Voltage-current characteristic.

by Eq. (24). Here, $B_n(s)$ is given by Eq. (25),

$$H(s) = 1/B_n(s) \qquad (24)$$

$$B_n(s) = (s - s_1) \cdot \ldots \cdot (s - s_n) \qquad (25)$$

where $s_1, \ldots, s_n$ are the $2n$th roots of $(-1)^{n+1}$ with negative real parts. As a function of frequency, f, the magnitude of the transfer function satisfies Eq. (26), so that it is equal to 1 at dc and to $1/\sqrt{2}$ at

$$|H(j2\pi f)| = \frac{1}{[1 + (2\pi f)^{2n}]^{1/2}} \qquad (26)$$

$f = 1/2\pi$ [termed the 3-decibel attenuation point]. The substitution of Eq. (27) shifts the 3-dB point to the frequency $\Omega/(2\pi)$; the substitution of Eq. (28)

$$s = \frac{S}{\Omega} \qquad (27)$$

$$s = \frac{\Omega}{S} \qquad (28)$$

changes the low-pass characteristic to high-pass.

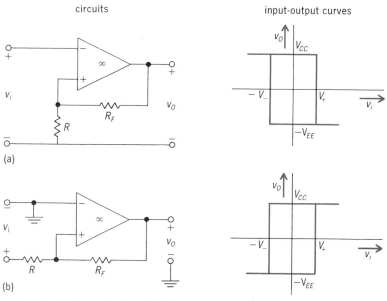

Fig. 8. Schmitt trigger circuits and their input-output curves. (*a*) Circuit with isolated input (negative gain). $V_+ = V_{CC}/[1 + (R_F/R)]$; $V_- = V_{EE}/[1 + (R_F/R)]$. (*b*) Circuit with coupled input (positive gain). $V_+ = RV_{CC}/R_F$; $V_- = RV_{EE}/R_F$.

The substitution of Eq. (29) leads to a band-pass

$$s = \Omega_o \left(\frac{S}{\Omega} + \frac{\Omega}{S} \right) \qquad (29)$$

characteristic (with Ω_o adjusting the bandwidth and Ω adjusting the center frequency).

Since the complex frequency variable s also serves as the derivative operator, a description of the filter in terms of differential equations can be obtained from the transfer function. One way these differential equations can be realized is with the electronic circuits of Fig. 6. Alternatively, the transfer function can be realized by specialized circuits created for the purpose of filtering. Indeed, because of the importance of filters to technology, their theory is extensive, and vast tables of filter transfer functions and circuits to realize them have been compiled. *See* ELECTRIC FILTER.

Digital circuits. The digital computer is based on digital electronic circuits. Although some of the circuits are quite sophisticated, such as the microprocessors integrated on a single chip, the concepts behind most of the circuits involved in digital computers are quite simple compared to the circuits used for analog signal processing. The most basic circuit is the inverter; a simple realization based upon the MOS transistor is shown in **Fig. 9a**. The upper (depletion-mode) transistor acts as a load "resistor" for the lower (enhancement-mode) transistor, which acts as a switch, turning on (into its resistive region) when the voltage at point A is above threshold to lower the voltage at point B. Adding the output currents of several of these together into the same load resistor gives a NOR gate, a two-input version of which is shown in Fig. 9b; that is, the output is high, with voltage at V_{DD}, if and only if the two inputs are low. Placing the drains of several of the enhancement-mode switches in series yields the NAND gate, a two-input version of which is shown in Fig. 9c; that is, the output is low if and only if both inputs are high. From the circuits of Fig. 9, the most commonly used digital logic circuits can be constructed. Because these circuits are so simple, digital circuits and digital computers are usually designed on the basis of negation logic, that is, with NOR and NAND rather than OR and AND circuits. *See* DIGITAL COMPUTER; INTEGRATED CIRCUITS; MICROPROCESSOR.

Conversion. Because most signals in the real world are analog but digital computers work on discretizations, it is necessary to convert between digital and analog signals. As mentioned above, this is done through digital-to-analog and analog-to-digital converters. Most approaches to digital-to-analog conversion use summers of the type shown in Fig. 6c, where the voltages representing the digital bits are applied to input resistors, either directly or indirectly through switches gated on by the digital bits which change the input resistance fed by a dc source (as is the case in the R-to-2R type of analog-to-digital converters).

One means of doing analog-to-digital conversion is to use a clocked counter that feeds a digital-

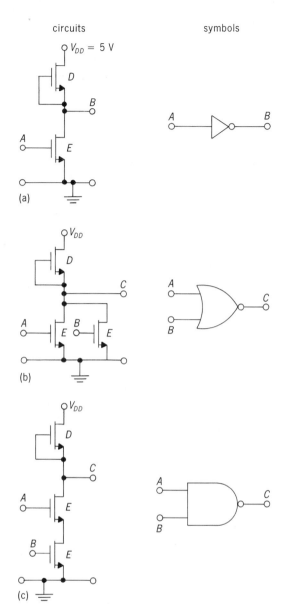

circuits   symbols

(a)

(b)

(c)

Fig. 9. Digital logic gates and their symbols. D = depletion-mode transistor; E = enhancement-mode transistor. (a) Inverter. (b) NOR gate. (c) NAND gate.

to-analog converter, whose output is compared with the analog signal to stop the count when the digital-to-analog output exceeds the analog signal. The counter output is then the analog-to-digital output. The comparator for such an analog-to-digital converter is similar to an open-loop operational amplifier (which changes saturation level when one of the differential input levels crosses the other). Other types of analog-to-digital converters, called flash converters, can do the conversion in a shorter time by use of parallel operations, but they are more expensive.

Other circuits. The field of electronic circuits is very broad and there are a very large number of other circuits besides those discussed above. For example, the differential is a key element in operational amplifier design and in biomedical data acquisition devices which must also be interfaced with specialized electronic sensors. Light-emitting and -detecting diodes allow for signals to be transmitted and received at optical frequencies. Liquid crystals are controlled by electronic circuits and are useful in digital watches, flat-panel color television displays, and electronic shutters. *See* BIOMEDICAL ENGINEERING; ELECTRONIC DISPLAY; LIGHT-EMITTING DIODE; LIQUID CRYSTALS; OPTICAL DETECTORS; TRANSDUCER.

Design

Because some circuits can be very complicated, and since even the simplest circuits may have complicated behavior, the area of computer-aided design (CAD) of electronic circuits has been extensively developed. A number of circuit simulation programs are available, some of which can be run on personal computers with good results. These programs rely heavily upon good mathematical models of the electronic devices. Fortunately, the area of modeling of electronic devices is well developed, and for many devices there are models that are adequate for most purposes. But new devices are constantly being conceived and fabricated, and in some cases no adequate models for them exist. Thus, many of the commercial programs allow the designer to read in experimentally obtained data for a device from which curve fitting techniques are used to allow an engineer to proceed with the design of circuits incorporating the device. Reproducibility and acceptability of parts with tolerances are required for the commercial use of electronic circuits. Consequently, theories of the reliability of electronic circuits have been developed, and most of the computer-aided design programs allow the designer to specify component tolerances to check out designs over wide ranges of values of the elements. Finally, when electronic circuits are manufactured they can be automatically tested with computer-controlled test equipment. Indeed, an area that will be of increasing importance is design for testability, in which decisions on what to test are made by a computer using knowledge-based routines, including expert systems. Such tests can be carried out automatically with computer-controlled data-acquisition and display systems. *See* CIRCUIT (ELECTRICITY); COMPUTER-AIDED DESIGN AND MANUFACTURING; EXPERT SYSTEMS; RELIABILITY (ENGINEERING); ROBOTICS.   Robert W. Newcomb

Bibliography. P. R. Gray and R. G. Meyer, *Analysis and Design of Analog Integrated Circuits*, 2d ed., 1984; D. A. Hodges and H. G. Jackson, *Analysis and Design of Digital Integrated Circuits*, 2d ed., 1988; J. Millman and A. Grabel, *Microelectronics*, 2d ed., 1987; A. S. Sedra and K. C. Smith, *Microelectronic Circuits*, 1982; G. C. Temes and J. W. LaPatra, *Introduction to Circuit Synthesis and Design*, 1977.

Circuit breaker

A device to open or close an electric power circuit either during normal power system operation or during abnormal conditions. A circuit breaker

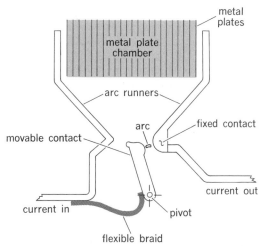

Fig. 1. Cross section of interrupter for a typical medium-voltage circuit breaker.

serves in the course of normal system operation to energize or deenergize loads. During abnormal conditions, when excessive current develops, a circuit breaker opens to protect equipment and surroundings from possible damage due to excess current. These currents are usually the result of short circuits created by lightning, accidents, deterioration of equipment, or sustained overloads. *See* CIRCUIT (ELECTRICITY); LIGHTNING AND SURGE PROTECTION.

Formerly, all circuit breakers were electromechanical devices. In these breakers a mechanism operates one or more pairs of contacts to make

Fig. 2. Bulk oil circuit breaker for 133-kV application.

or break the circuit. The mechanism is powered either electromagnetically, pneumatically, or hydraulically. The contacts are located in a part termed the interrupter. When the contacts are parted, opening the metallic conductive circuit, an electric arc is created between the contacts. This arc is a high-temperature ionized gas with an electrical conductivity comparable to graphite. Thus the current continues to flow through the arc. The function of the interrupter is to extinguish the arc, completing circuit-breaking action.

Current interruption. In alternating-current circuits, arcs are usually extinguished at a natural current zero, when the ac voltage applied across the arcing contacts reverses polarity. Within a short period around a natural current zero, the power input to the arc, equal to the product of the instantaneous current and voltage, is quite low. There is an opportunity to remove more energy from the arc than is applied to it, thus allowing the gas to cool and change from a conductor into an insulator. *See* AL-TERNATING CURRENT.

In direct-current circuits, absence of natural current zero necessitates the interrupter to convert the initial arc into one that could only be maintained by an arc voltage higher than the system voltage, thus forcing the current to zero. To accomplish this,

the interrupter must also be able to remove energy from the arc at a rapid rate. *See* DIRECT CURRENT.

Different interrupting mediums are used for the purpose of extinguishing an arc. In low- and medium-voltage circuits (1110–15,000 V) the arc is driven by the magnetic field produced by the arc current into an arc chute (**Fig. 1**). In the arc chute the arc is either split into several small arcs between metal plates or driven tightly against a solid insulating material. In the former case the splitting of the arc increases the total arc voltage, thus increasing the rate of energy dissipation. In the latter case the insulating material is heated to boiling temperatures, and the evaporated material flows through the arc, carrying a great deal of energy with it.

Oil and gas-blast circuits. For outdoor applications at distribution and subtransmission voltage (10 kV and above), oil breakers are widely used. In the United States, bulk oil breakers are used (**Fig. 2**), and in European and many other countries, "low-oil-content" breakers are quite popular. The principles of operation of both kinds of oil breakers are basically the same. Only the amount of oil used and the detailed engineering design differ. In oil breakers, the arc is drawn in oil. The intense heat of the arc decomposes the oil, generating high

Fig. 3. Air blast circuit breaker rated for 500 kV.

Fig. 4. Sulfur hexafluoride circuit breakers, 500-kV 3-kA.

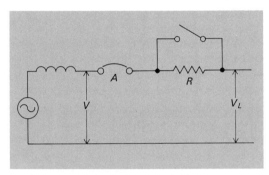

Fig. 5. Resistor insertion to reduce switching surge.

pressure that produces a fluid flow through the arc to carry energy away. At transmission voltages below 345 kV, oil breakers used to be popular. They were, however, increasingly replaced by gas-blast circuit breakers such as air-blast (**Fig. 3**) and sulfur hexafluoride (SF$_6$) circuit breakers (**Fig. 4**).

In air-blast circuit breakers, air is compressed to high pressures (approximately 50 atm = 5 × 10^6 pascals). When the contacts part, a blast valve is opened to discharge the high-pressure air to ambient, thus creating a very high-velocity flow near the arc to dissipate the energy. In SF$_6$ circuit breakers, the same principle is employed, with SF$_6$ as the medium instead of air. In the "puffer" SF$_6$ breaker, the motion of the contacts compresses the gas and forces it to flow through an orifice into the neighborhood of the arc. Both types of SF$_6$ breakers have been developed for EHV (extra-high-voltage) transmission systems.

For EHV systems, it was discovered that closing of a circuit breaker may cause a switching surge which may be excessive for the insulation of the system. The basic principle is easy to understand. If a breaker is closed at the peak of the voltage wave to energize a single-phase transmission line

which is open-circuited at the far end, reflection can cause the transient voltage on the line to reach twice the peak of the system voltage. If there are trapped charges on the line, and if it happens that at the moment of breaker-closing the system voltage is at its peak, equal in magnitude to but opposite to the polarity of the voltage due to the trapped charges left on the line, the switching surge on the line can reach a theoretical maximum of three times the system voltage peak.

One way to reduce the switching surge is to insert a resistor in series with the line (**Fig. 5**) for a short time. When switch A in Fig. 5 is closed, the voltage is divided between the resistance and the surge impedance Z of the line by the simple relationship $V_L = V[Z/(R + Z)]$, where V is voltage impressed, V_L is voltage across the transmission line, R is resistance of the resistor, and Z is surge impedance of the line. Only V_L will travel down the line and be reflected at the other end. The magnitude of the switching surge is thus considerably reduced.

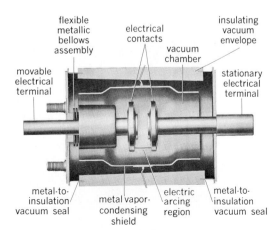

Fig. 6. Cutaway view of vacuum interrupter.

Vacuum breakers. The vacuum breaker, another electromechanical device, uses the rapid dielectric recovery and high dielectric strength of vacuum. A pair of contacts is hermetically sealed in a vacuum envelope (**Fig. 6**). Actuating motion is transmitted through bellows to the movable contact. When the contacts are parted, an arc is produced and supported by metallic vapor boiled from the electrodes. Vapor particles expand into the vacuum and condense on solid surfaces. At a natural current zero the vapor particles disappear, and the arc is extinguished. Vacuum breakers of up to 242 kV have been built (**Fig. 7**).

Solid-state breakers. The other type of breaker uses a thyristor, a semiconductor device which in the off state prevents current from flowing but which can be turned on with a small electric current through a third electrode, the gate. At the natural current zero, conduction ceases, as it does in arc interrupters. This type of breaker does not require a mechanism. Semiconductor breakers have been built to carry continuous currents up to 10,000 A.

Semiconductor circuit breakers can be made to operate in microseconds if the commutation principle is applied. **Figure 8** illustrates the commutation principle for an hvdc (high-voltage direct-current) circuit, but it can easily be extended to ac circuits. During normal operation, the circuit breaker (CB in the diagram) would be closed from the hvdc source. In this diagram, inductances L_1 and L_2 represent the circuit inductance on either side of the breaker. Suppose that a fault occurs which applies a short circuit between points A and B. The current will commence to increase, its rate being determined by L_1 and L_2. When the increased current is detected, the contacts of the circuit breakers are opened, drawing an arc, and the switch (S in the diagram) is closed, causing

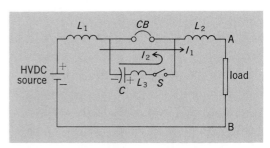

Fig. 8. Commutation principles of circuit interruption.

the precharged capacitors C to discharge through the circuit breaker. The current I_2 so produced is traveling in such a direction as to oppose I_1 and drive it to zero, thereby giving the circuit breaker an opportunity to interrupt.

Thyristors can be used for both circuit breakers and switches. The closing and opening operations are, of course, not mechanical but are controlled by the gates. Such a circuit breaker was built for very special switching applications, such as thermonuclear fusion research.   Thomas H. Lee

Bibliography. D. G. Fink and H. W. Beaty (eds.), *Standard Handbook for Electrical Engineers*, 13th ed., 1993; K. Nakanishi (ed.), *Switching Phenomena in High-Voltage Circuit Breakers*, 1991; M. H. Rashid, *Power Electronics*, 2d ed., 1992.

Circuit testing (electricity)

The testing of electric circuits to determine and locate any of the following circuit conditions: (1) an open circuit, (2) a short circuit with another conductor in the same circuit, (3) a ground, which is a short circuit between a conductor and ground, (4) leakage (a high-resistance path across a portion of the circuit, to another circuit, or to ground), and (5) a cross (a short circuit or leakage between conductors of different circuits). Circuit testing for complex systems often requires extensive automatic checkout gear to determine the faults defined above as well as many quantities other than resistance. *See* OPEN CIRCUIT; SHORT CIRCUIT.

In cable testing, the first step in fault location is to identify the faulty conductor and type of fault. This is done with a continuity tester, such as a battery and flashlight bulb or buzzer (**Fig. 1**), or an ohmmeter.

Murray loop test. Useful for locating faults in relatively low-resistance circuits, the Murray loop

Fig. 7. Vacuum circuit breaker, 242-kV 40-kA.

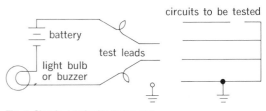

Fig. 1. Simple continuity test setup.

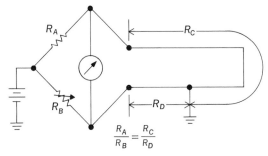

Fig. 2. Murray loop for location of ground fault.

is shown in **Fig. 2** with a ground fault in the circuit under test. A known "good" conductor is joined to the faulty conductor at a convenient point beyond the fault but at a known distance from the test connection. One terminal of the test battery is grounded. The resulting Wheatstone bridge is then balanced by adjusting R_B until a null is obtained, as indicated by the detector in Fig. 2. Ratio R_A/R_B is then known. For a circuit having a uniform ratio of resistance with length, circuit resistance is directly proportional to circuit length. Therefore, the distance to the fault is determined from the procedure given by Eqs. (1)–(3). From Eq. (3)

$$R_C \propto l + (l - x) \qquad R_D \propto x \qquad (1)$$

$$\frac{R_A}{R_B} = r = \frac{R_C}{R_D} = \frac{2l - x}{x} \qquad (2)$$

$$x = \frac{2l}{r - 1} \qquad (3)$$

and a knowledge of total length l of the circuit, once ratio r has been measured, the location of the fault x is determined. If circuit resistances are not uniform with distances, as when the known faultless conductor is different in size from the faulty conductor, additional calculation taking into consideration the resistance per unit length of the conductors is necessary.

If the fault is a short circuit or a cross instead of a ground, the battery is connected to the conductor to which the short or cross has taken place (**Fig. 3**). The test circuit is then equivalent to the one used to locate a ground (Fig. 2). The bridge is balanced and

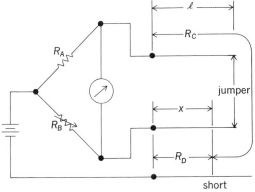

Fig. 3. Murray loop for location of short or cross fault.

the calculations carried out as before. *See* BRIDGE CIRCUIT.

Varley loop test. This is similar to the Murray loop test except for the inclusion of the adjustable resistance R. The Varley loop (**Fig. 4**) is used for fault location in high-resistance circuits.

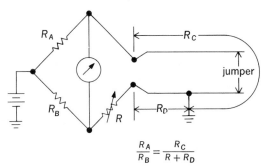

$$\frac{R_A}{R_B} = \frac{R_C}{R + R_D}$$

Fig. 4. Varley loop for location of leakage to ground.

Open circuit. An alternating-current capacitance bridge can be used for locating an open circuit as shown in **Fig. 5**. One test terminal is connected to the open conductor and the other terminal to a conductor of known continuity in the cable. All conductors associated with the test are opened at a convenient point beyond the fault but at a known distance from the test connection. An audio oscillator supplies the voltage to the bridge, which

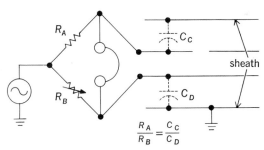

$$\frac{R_A}{R_B} = \frac{C_C}{C_D}$$

Fig. 5. Alternating-current capacitance bridge used in location of an open circuit in one conductor.

is balanced by adjusting R_B for a null as detected by the earphones. Measured ratio R_A/R_B equals the ratio of capacitances between the lines and the grounded sheath. Because each capacitance is proportional to the length of line connected to the bridge, the location of the open circuit can be determined from Eq. (4).

$$\frac{R_A}{R_B} = \frac{C_C}{C_D} \qquad (4)$$

For convenience in carrying out the tests for fault location, the fault location bridge has switches for setting up the various loop test circuits. Basically it is a bridge like other bridges used in circuit testing. *See* CIRCUIT (ELECTRICITY); OHMMETER; RESISTANCE MEASUREMENT; WHEATSTONE BRIDGE.

Charles E. Applegate

Bibliography. A. D. Helfrick and W. D. Cooper, *Electronic Instrumentation and Measurement Techniques*, 4th ed., 1990; L. Schnell (ed.), *Technology of Electrical Measurements*, 1993; L. M. Thompson, *Electrical Measurements and Calibration*, 2d ed., 1994.

Circulation

Those processes by which metabolic materials are transported from one region of an organism to another. Ultimately, the essential gases, nutrients, and waste products of metabolism are exchanged across cell membranes by diffusion. Diffusion is the movement of material, by random motion of molecules, from a region of high concentration to one of low concentration. The amount of material moved from one place to another depends on the difference in concentrations and on the distance between the two points. The greater the distance, the less movement of material per unit time for a given difference in concentration. Consequently, in all but the smallest animals, convection (or bulk circulation) of materials to the cell must be employed to supplement diffusion.

Protoplasmic movement aids diffusion at the intracellular level. In multicellular animals, however, either the external medium or extracellular body fluids, or both, are circulated. In sponges and coelenterates (**Fig. 1**a and b), water is pumped through definite body channels by muscular activity or, more often, by cilia or flagella on the cells lining the channels. Even external water currents can be tapped for this purpose. It is generally assumed that flows driven by these mechanisms will be slow. However, this may not be the case.

In sponges, flow driven by flagella in flagellated chambers enters through pores in the body wall and exits through the large central osculum. The cross-sectional area of all the flagellated chambers is approximately 6000 times that of the osculum. Hence, the exceptionally low flow velocity in the flagellated chambers increases markedly as the total volume of water is forced out through the osculum. In fact, water may flow through the osculum at velocities of 5 cm · s^{-1}, approaching those attained in major arterial vessels in vertebrates. This is an example of the principle of continuity, which states that the total volume of fluid moving past any point in a circulation (providing it has no major leaks) must be the same as that flowing past any other point. In regions of large cross-sectional area, the velocity of flow is low, whereas when cross-sectional area is small the flow velocity will be high.

Coelenterates have a body wall derived from two cell layers; an outer ectoderm is separated from an inner endoderm by a noncellular gelatinous material (mesoglea). All higher animals have bodies consisting of three cell layers, with the ectoderm being separated from the endoderm by a cellular layer of mesoderm. The mesoderm

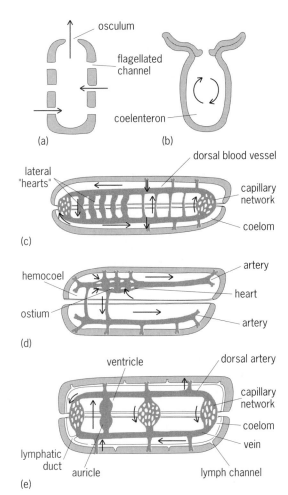

Fig. 1. Systems of internal transport. (*a*) Sponge type, with flagellated channels. (*b*) Coelenterate type. (*c*) Oligochaete type, with coelom and closed blood system. (*d*) Crustacean-molluscan type, with blood system open to hemocoel which is derived from primary cavity or blastocoel. (*e*) Vertebrate type, with coelom, closed vascular system, and lymphatic channels. (*After C. L. Prosser, Comparative Animal Physiology, 3d ed., W. B. Saunders, 1973*)

proliferates and separates to develop a fluid-filled body cavity or coelom. The coelom separates the ectoderm (together with an outer layer of mesoderm) from the endoderm (which has an inner layer of mesoderm). Coelomic fluid is moved around by body movements or ciliary activity, but in larger animals this movement is usually inadequate to supply the metabolic requirements of the organs contained within the coelom. These needs are provided for by pumping a fluid, blood, to them through vessels, the blood vascular system (Fig. 1c–e).

Open and Closed Circulatory Systems

When the blood is in a separate compartment from the rest of the extracellular fluid, the vascular system is described as closed. In such a system, the blood is circulated by a pump, the heart, through special channels, blood vessels; it comes into close association with the tissues only in the capillaries, fine vessels with walls only one cell thick. In some tissues or regions, larger blood spaces may exist, called sinuses. A closed vascular system is found in most annelids (segmented worms and leeches), cephalopod mollusks (squids and octopods), holothurian echinoderms (sea cucumbers), and vertebrates (Fig. 1*c* and *e*).

In most vertebrates, a functional but anatomically closed connection exists between the extracellular spaces (between the cells) and the blood vascular system in the form of lymph channels. Lymph is derived from the noncellular component of blood (plasma), modified in its passage through the tissues, and is picked up by blind-ending lymphatic vessels, which conduct the lymph to the veins (Fig. 1*e*). The presence of a lymphatic system in fish is controversial. In many fishes, a secondary circulation exists which parallels the primary circulation in extent and connects to it by narrow channels, which are small enough to exclude most red blood cells from the secondary circulation. It is unlikely that the secondary circulation is the evolutionary forerunner of a true lymphatic system, which is first observed in lungfishes, or that the secondary circulation subserves the same function as a true lymphatic system.

In most arthropods (crustaceans, insects), most mollusks (shellfish), and many ascidians (sea squirts), the extracellular spaces are confluent with the blood system. In these animals, blood is pumped through a limited network of vessels into a body cavity called a hemocoel (Fig. 1*d*). After bathing the tissues, blood (called hemolymph in these organisms) collects in sinuses and returns to the heart. This is the open vascular system. In animals with open circulatory systems, the coelom is much reduced.

Dynamics

A pump is required to circulate the blood in animals. The pump (usually called a heart) imparts propulsive energy to the blood, which flows from regions of high fluid energy to regions of low fluid energy (or down an energy gradient). The total energy of flowing blood consists of pressure energy, imparted by the pump, and energy contained in blood due to its motion (kinetic energy). Even in mammals, where blood flows very rapidly, the kinetic energy component is small compared with pressure energy and is usually ignored. Consequently, it is usual to refer to blood flow as taking place down a pressure gradient rather than energy gradient.

As the blood courses around the circulatory system, pressure energy is lost as heat. This loss of energy is described as resistance to flow. In closed circulations, flow resistance is concentrated in short narrow regions of blood vessels, known as resistance vessels. These are fine vessels (diameter of 0.02 mm), and since they have a muscular coat they are able to change their diameter to regulate flow. However, it is not the friction between the wall and blood that causes energy dissipation but rather friction between the various layers of the

flowing blood (internal friction or viscosity). Blood flow in tubes is streamlined; the layer of blood at the wall is stationary while that in the middle flows fastest. Hence, slower-moving layers close to the wall tend to slow down and stop faster-moving layers, while they, in turn, will try to speed up slower-flowing layers. It is this internal friction which must be overcome by flowing blood, and the higher the viscosity of the fluid, the more energy will be dissipated in doing this. For instance, it takes much more effort to force treacle (a high-viscosity fluid) than water, at the same flow rate, through the same-diameter pipe. Blood is also much thicker (or more viscous) than water.

In a closed circulation, the total peripheral resistance (R) can be expressed by the equation below, in which P_1 = pressure in the outflow

$$R = \frac{P_1 - P_2}{Q}$$

vessels of the heart, P_2 = pressure in the inflow vessels, and Q = the output of a single propulsive chamber (ventricle). This equation is a simplified form of a formula used to describe flow in tubes (Poiseuille's law) and is a direct analog of Ohm's law for the relationship between electrical potential difference (pressure gradient), current (flow), and resistance. The resistance of the vascular system will depend on its geometry, as well as the viscosity of the fluid. Of the geometric factors, the radius of the tubes is far more important than length because only the radius is a variable in the circulation. In fact, flow per unit time changes in proportion to the fourth power of the radius for a given fall in pressure along the vessel. Hence, in the resistance vessels, halving the radius by muscular contraction will reduce flow to one-sixteenth of what it was before for the same pressure gradient.

In open circulations, the concept of total peripheral resistance cannot apply. Certainly, the pump imparts propulsive energy to the blood which is dissipated, due to viscous losses, as the blood courses through the hemocoel. But a pressure difference between the outflow and inflow vessels of the heart can, at best, indicate only the resistance of the major shunts in the circulation. A shunt is a short circuit between the outflow and inflow vessels. In the simplest possible case, when the pump sits in the hemocoel and there are no blood vessels, the heart activity only stirs the blood, and pressure differences across the heart are mostly a reflection of its filling and emptying mechanisms.

Physiology of Open and Closed Systems

In open blood systems, there is no separation between extracellular fluid and blood, so the total volume of hemolymph in these animals is large (up to 40% of the body weight). In closed circulations, blood is separated from fluid around the cells, and blood volume is much smaller, about 5–10% of the body weight. In both open and closed systems, blood is conveyed directly to the organs, but only in closed systems can its distribution be regulated with any precision. The best that can be done to facilitate the normal functioning of open circulations is to regulate hemolymph flow to a particular region by opening or closing valves of the junction of the major arteries and the heart.

On the outflow side of the pump (arterial side), closed vascular systems are effectively overfilled with blood, and the elastic blood vessel walls bear down on their contained volume and maintain a high pressure, even when the pump is in the filling phase (diastole). The arterial system is "topped up" again with each ejection of the pump (systole). Obviously, blood pressure can be maintained only if rapid escape of blood from the arteries is prevented by having a high resistance to flow in the periphery of the circulation. As a consequence, almost continuous blood flow is provided to the tissues by the elastic recoil of the stretched arterial walls during diastole. In open systems, peripheral flow resistance is low, as are the pressures generated in these systems. Futhermore, pressures in the outflow vessels of the pump will be highly pulsatile, reaching a peak in systole (the pump-ejection phase) and perhaps falling to zero in diastole (the pump-filling phase). Likewise, flow will be extremely pulsatile, often stopping between heartbeats.

In both open and closed circulatory systems, the volume of blood pumped by the heart must be the same volume as returns to the heart in any given time period. However, only in closed circulations does this have important consequences with regard to the rate at which blood flows through the vessels in the various regions of the vascular system. The velocity of blood flow at any part of a closed system depends on the cross-sectional area of the vessels in that part. Since the vessels that arise from or join to the heart must necessarily be about the same size, flow velocity in the veins is almost as rapid as in the arteries. Furthermore, since the cross-sectional area of the vessels within all the tissues is many times greater than vessels leaving the heart, the flow in the tissue vessels is very slow (usually less than 1 mm · s^{-1}), allowing plenty of time for exchange across cell walls.

Components of Circulatory Systems

The two principal components of all circulatory systems are hearts and blood vessels.

Hearts. The circulatory pumps are the hearts, all of which operate by causing a wave of muscular contraction followed by a wave of relaxation (peristaltic wave) to travel over the walls of a tube. When the muscle contracts, the volume is reduced and fluid contents are expelled.

Tubular heart. If the heart persists in adult animals as a tube, such as the dorsal vessel of annelids or the dorsal heart of insects (**Fig. 2**b), it is called a tubular heart. The peristaltic wave passes along the tube in an anterior direction, pushing the blood before it in the same way the air in a balloon is squeezed

down to one end by pulling the balloon through a cupped hand. Therfore, valves are unnecessary to ensure unidirectional flow of blood. In earthworms, the peristaltic waves travel up the dorsal vessel at rates of 2–4 cm · s^{-1} about 10 times each minute. Vessels in the gills of hagfishes and octopods also contract rhythmically and propel the blood.

Multiple and chambered hearts. In the majority of animals, the zone of propulsive activity is restricted to a localized region. Some animals have many hearts: earthworms have five pairs of lateral hearts connecting the dorsal and ventral vessels (Fig. 2e); octopods and squids have hearts which boost blood flow through the gas exchanger (gills) in addition to a main or central heart (Fig. 2f); sea cucumbers may have over 150 hearts between dorsal and ventral vessels (Fig. 2i). However, many animals have only one heart, and in order to pump a volume equivalent to that pumped by a long contractile vessel, the lumen is greatly enlarged and usually divided into a number of chambers (chambered heart). To ensure undirectional flow of blood, chambered hearts require one-way valves. Valves are flaps of tissue situated around the edges of orifices between heart chambers or in vessels.

Contractile chambers. The more powerful the heart muscle becomes, the faster the blood can be driven into the outflow vessels, but filling the heart then requires a greater force. In vertebrates, there is often enough energy in the fast-flowing venous blood to do this, but other chambers may be necessary to fill the main propulsive chamber (or ventricle) in stages. These chambers are auricles and must have sufficiently thin walls to be expanded by the energy of the inflowing blood, yet must be powerful enough to fill the ventricle when they contract.

Most animals with chambered hearts have a single auricle, but in mollusks there is one for each pair of gills, so there may be from one to four (Fig. 2f and h). Fishes have a single auricle, but in amphibians the auricle is divided into two atria. In birds and mammals, the ventricle is divided, giving two separate circulations: one to the body and the other to the lungs. Fishes and amphibians have an extra contractile chamber, the sinus venosus, which fills the auricle when it contracts. Elasmobranchs and amphibians also have an extra contractile chamber on the ventricular outflow pathway, the conus arteriosus. Its role has not been established, but it could be in actively closing the outflow valves of the heart.

All vertebrate hearts, and many in invertebrates (such as mollusks and arthropods; Fig. 2f and g), are enclosed in a small portion of the coelom called the pericardial cavity. This cavity is fluid-filled and serves to prevent the heart from being buffeted by other body organs, but it can also aid in returning blood to the heart. If the pericardial wall is rigid, as in elasmobranchs and most mollusks and crustaceans, one chamber of the heart cannot contract unless another is expanding. If the ventricle starts to contract, the reduction in volume will tend

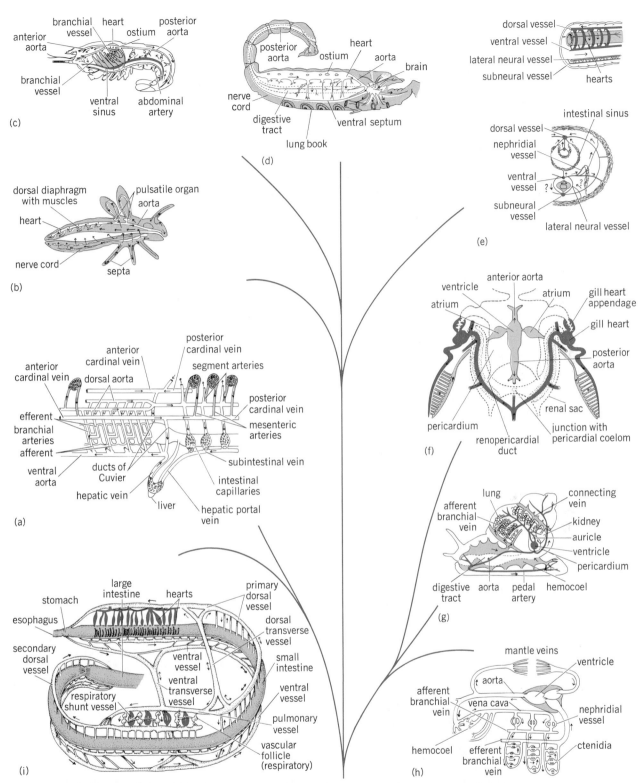

**Fig. 2. Representative invertebrate and ancestral vertebrate circulatory systems on a schematic evolutionary tree. In all diagrams the arrows indicate the direction of blood flow. (*a*) Ancestral vertebrate, represented by *Amphioxus*. (*b*) Insect: a main dorsal vessel carries blood from the heart. (*c*) Crustacean: circulation in the lobster. (*d*) Arachnid, represented by the scorpion *Bathus*. (*e*) Annelid: cross section and longitudinal section. (*f*) Cephalopod mollusk, represented by the closed circulation in the octopus. (*g*) Gastropod mollusk: an open circulation represented by the snail *Helix*. (*h*) Bivalve mollusk: an open circulation represented by the fresh-water mussel *Anodonta*. (*i*) Echinoderm represented by the sea cucumber, *Stichopus*. (*Part a after A. J. Waterman et al., Chordate Structure and Function, Macmillan, 1971; b, c, e after K. Schmidt-Nielsen, Animal Physiology, 2d ed., Cambridge University Press, 1979; d, g, h after W. F. Hamilton and P. Dow, eds., Handbook of Physiology, Sec. 2, Circulation, vol. 3, American Physiological Society, 1965; f after E. Florey, An Introduction to General and Comparative Animal Physiology, W. B. Saunders, 1966; i after C. F. Herreid et al., Blood vascular system of the sea cucumber, Stichopus moebi, J. Morphol., 150:423, 1976)*

to increase the volume of the pericardial cavity, and since it has rigid walls, the pressure inside it will be reduced. This suction pressure is transmitted through the thin auricular wall and draws blood in from outside the pericardium. This mechanism ensures successful filling of the heart even in open blood systems.

In tubular hearts, blood will tend to be sucked into the lumen when the muscle relaxes behind the wave of contraction. It has even been suggested that the major function of the dorsal contractile vessel in annelids is to prime the lateral hearts with blood. In insects, the tubular heart is suspended by alary or aliform muscles attached to the external skeleton, and when these contract the expansion of the lumen sucks blood through valved openings (ostia) into the heart (Fig. 2b).

Electrophysiology. The wave of contraction which passes across the heart is driven by an electrical impulse (action potential) which arises spontaneously, either in modified heart muscle cells, or in special nerve cells located on or near the heart. These cells form the pacemaker, which sets the heart rhythm. When nerve cells initiate the heartbeat, the pacemaker is called neurogenic. A pacemaker of muscle cells is called myogenic. Myogenic pacemakers are found in vertebrates, mollusks, echinoderms, and perhaps in some annelids. Neurogenic pacemakers are found in most arthropods. Many hearts have more than one pacemaker. In tunicates, the tubular heart pumps into the open circulation in two directions. After several hundred beats the rhythm slows and stops, and the direction of the wave of contraction reverses when the heart starts up again. Consequently, the tunicate heart must have at least two pacemakers. In frogs, heart contraction can be driven by electrical impulses arising in the sinus venosus, atria, or ventricle. Usually the sinus pacemaker beats fastest and drives all the others.

In birds and mammals, the heart is large and generates high pressures. To prevent the pressure set up by the contraction of one part of the heart from stretching, and perhaps rupturing, the relaxed part, all of the ventricular muscle must be activated simultaneously. This is achieved by conveying the electrical impulse to all parts of the ventricle through specialized conduction pathways composed of modified muscle cells. *See* CARDIAC ELECTROPHYSIOLOGY.

Chemical and mechanical excitation. Many hearts are innervated by nerves which regulate the beat. When these nerves are active, they liberate chemicals such as noradrenalin or acetylcholine from their terminals, and these neurotransmitters affect the cardiac muscles directly. In general, the pacemaker of myogenic hearts is inhibited by acetylcholine; excitation is produced by noradrenaline (vertebrates) or serotonin (mollusks). In neurogenic hearts, gamma aminobutyric acid (GABA) is inhibitory, whereas glutamic acid is excitatory. Neurotransmitters affect not only the rate but also the strength of cardiac contraction. For example, noradrenaline increases the amount of blood pumped by a single ventricle (stroke volume) while acetylcholine decreases stroke volume. *See* ACETYLCHOLINE; ENDOCRINE MECHANISMS.

Mechanical factors may also affect rate and strength of heart contraction. In earthworms, mollusks, and some fishes, stretching the pacemaker region of the myocardium increases its rhythm. Moreover, in all vertebrates, and probably in all mollusks as well, the length of the muscle fibers in the heart at the end of diastole is directly proportional to the strength of the next muscle contraction (Starling's law of the heart).

Many animals, both vertebrate and invertebrate, take advantage of muscular activity in the body, such as during exercise, as an aid to circulation of the blood. In vertebrates, valved thin-walled veins run through blocks of skeletal muscle and are compressed when the muscle contracts, squeezing blood toward the heart (muscle pump). In other animals, the blood functions directly in locomotion. Spiders have no leg extensor muscles, so leg extension is brought about by forcing hemolymph into the leg at high pressure (50 kilopascals), which is generated by the contraction of lateral cephalothoracic muscles depressing the carapace. Backflow into the abdominal heart (which can generate pressures of only 13 kPa) is prevented by valves on the outflow vessels at the junction of the cephalothorax and abdomen. But there are no valves in the veins, and blood returns rapidly to the abdomen.

Caudal heart. Hagfishes have a unique caudal heart. A longitudinal rod of cartilage separates two chambers, and when body muscles on one side contract, the rod is bent to that side. The bend in the rod causes the volume of the chamber on the actively contracting side to expand so that it fills with blood, while the volume of the chamber on the other side is decreased, expelling blood. Valves at the inflow and outflow ends of the chambers ensure unidirectional flow of blood. *See* HEART (INVERTEBRATE); HEART (VERTEBRATE).

Blood vessels. Blood ejected from the heart is conveyed by vessels which are usually called arteries or aortas. In some animals, structural differences between outflow and inflow vessels are not obvious, and they are usually referred to simply as blood vessels. In closed systems, the arteries (outflow vessels) divide and subdivide so that ultimately tubes only a few micrometers thick (capillaries) run between the cells of each organ.

Capillaries. In vertebrates, each capillary consists of a single layer of endothelial cells surrounded by a basement membrane. In some echinoderms with well-developed circulatory systems (such as holothurians; Fig. 2i) capillary structure is similar to that in vertebrates, while in cephalopods (such as the octopus) capillaries are extremely small (1 micrometer in diameter) but are usually more than one cell thick. The total number of capillaries in a vertebrate is large, and in humans it is enormous: over 50 billion in the whole body. Therefore, although each capillary is small the total cross-sectional area of all capillaries is perhaps a thousand times greater than that of the main arterial vessels. Consequently, blood flows very slowly in the capillaries, about one-thousandth of the velocity in the aorta, allowing lots of time for exchange of materials with the cells.

In open circulations, after a greater or lesser number of branchings blood vessels ultimately open to the spaces between the cells. Even so, networks of fine blood pathways may occur, especially in gas-exchange organs, nephridia, and masses of nervous tissue (such as brains or ganglia). In animals with closed circulatory systems, a plexus of fine capillaries brings blood close to the external environment in skin (annelids, frogs), respiratory trees (holothurians), gills (fishes), and lungs. Similar close associations between blood and external media are seen in animals with open circulatory systems (Fig. 2c and d). For instance, gills of shrimp look similar to those of fish in all but the finest morphological details. Book lungs of spiders are unique structures in which blood is moved across rows of fine air tubes, stacked one on the other, in channels only a few micrometers in width. In insects, air is distributed directly to the body cells by way of the trachea, a system of tubes independent of the circulation. Fine blood channels are lacking in these animals. Nevertheless, the circulation in insects reduces the diffusion distances for metabolites, nutrients, and hormones. Furthermore, in large flying insects it plays an important role in controlling body temperature, particularly in the thoracic region where the large flight muscles are located.

Veins and portal systems. After traversing the capillaries, blood is collected into large vessels which return it to the heart. In cephalopods and vertebrates, these collecting vessels are called veins. In open circulations, channels returning blood to the heart exist, but the pattern of blood flow is less precise than in closed systems. In insects and arachnids, longitudinal membranes impose some direction on blood movement (Fig. 2b and d).

In many vertebrates, venous blood is transported to another organ (such as the liver or kidney) on its way back to the heart. In these organs the veins divide into a capillary network supplying blood to the tissues at low pressure. This is a portal blood supply, and there are a large number of these in vertebrates. The hepatic portal system occurs in all vertebrates and serves to transport materials from the intestine, where they are absorbed, to the liver, where they are stored (Fig. 2a). Another prominent portal system is the renal portal system. It occurs in all vertebrates except mammals, and transports blood from the caudal parts of the body to the kidneys. The function of the renal portal system is not known. *See* KIDNEY; LIVER.

Contraction. Many blood vessels have muscular coats, the muscle cells being rhythmically contractile (myogenic rhythm). Contraction of blood vessels is found in the dorsal and ventral vessels and some capillaries of annelids, in the gill vessels of cephalopods and cyclostomes, and also in the fine vessels leading to the capillary beds in higher vertebrates. In these small vertebrate vessels (called arterioles, with a diameter of 50–200 μm), the muscles are in a continual state of activity, modulating the radius of the vessel and therefore the blood flow. This activity can be altered by nerves, by blood-borne agents such as adrenaline, and also at the local level by changes in the level of tissue metabolites (a fall in oxygen tension in the body tissues causes the muscles to relax).

Aortic elasticity. The aortas (or arteries leaving the heart) are fairly elastic in nearly all animals. In closed circulations, the stroke volume is stored by the elastic distension of the arteries and is fed to the periphery between cardiac ejections. This elastic reservoir (or Windkessel effect) is exemplified by the arterial vessels of vertebrates. In humans, the whole arterial tree participates in producing a Windkessel effect. In contrast, fishes have a very short ventral aorta, and only a very elastic bulb (bulbus cordis) just outside the ventricle provides a pressure reservoir, which smooths blood flow through the gills. Many mollusks with open circulatory systems have a similar elastic expansion of the aortic wall just beyond the ventricle. *See* BLOOD VESSELS.

Evolution of Vertebrate Circulation

The evolution of an organ system which is not preserved in fossils can only be inferred from investigations of extant species. Thus, understanding must always be clouded by uncertainty. For example, a major pattern of increasing complexity, which emerges from comparative studies of circulatory systems, is related in vertebrates to life on land. More promising are investigations of the early stages of development of the heart and circulation. These show that all types of vertebrate circulations can be related to a common ancestral pattern (Fig. 2a). The ancestral pattern of circulation in vertebrates is for a ventral heart to pump blood anteriorly in a ventral vessel, connecting to the dorsal vessel through the gas exchanger (gills; Fig. 1e). The gills are situated on the high-pressure side of the circulation, and blood flows posteriorly in the dorsal vessel.

Annelid worms exhibit a superficial resemblance to the circulation in the ancestral vertebrate in the pattern of dorsal and ventral vessels (Fig. 1c), except that the heart is dorsal, flow in the dorsal vessels is anteriorly directed, and flow in the ventral vessel is posteriorly directed. More important, in most invertebrates the gas exchanger, when it exists as a discrete entity, is on the low-pressure side of the circulation. This arrangement limits metabolic scope, a problem which is solved in large, active invertebrates (such as cephalopods) by the development of high-pressure, prebranchial hearts.

Apparently, the chordate stock arose from ancestors in common with primitive echinoderms, a group with a very poorly developed circulation. Hence, the apparent similarities between the circulations in vertebrates and invertebrates are superficial and presumably arose as an evolutionary response to similar physiological demands. This is an example of convergent evolution due to common selection pressures, the circulatory systems in vertebrate and invertebrate groups being analogous rather than homologous. *See* CARDIOVASCULAR SYSTEM.   David R. Jones

Circulation disorders

Circulation disorders include both localized disturbances of circulation and diseases of the circulatory system.

Circulatory system. The function of the circulatory system is to transport and distribute substances either used or produced by cells or both. Excluded are those materials that are discharged directly from sweat glands, digestive glands, and renal tubule cells. Included, however, are nutritive and metabolic substances, hormones, waste products, water, and heat.

The circulating fluids are distributed between the heart, blood vessels, capillaries, intercellular spaces and lymphatics and within the cells. The blood and body fluids are in a constant state of dynamic equilibrium (see **illus.**). Blood flows through the vessels to the capillaries where some fluid passes through the endothelium to the intercellular spaces to bathe the cells. Fluid with contained electrolytes and metabolic substances can then pass into and out of the cells. At the distal end of the capillaries most of this fluid passes back into the vascular compartment. A portion of this fluid is returned to the circulation by way of the lymphatics. *See* CARDIOVASCULAR SYSTEM; LYMPHATIC SYSTEM.

Vascular disturbances. Disturbances in this pattern can either result in or from disease conditions. An example is edema, which is an abnormal accumulation of fluid in the cells, tissue spaces, or cavities of the body. There are three main factors in the formation of generalized edema and a fourth which plays a role in the formation of local edema. They are the permeability of the capillary wall, the colloid osmotic pressure of the plasma proteins, and the hydrostatic pressure in the capillaries. The fourth factor, which is of importance in local edema formation, is lymphatic obstruction.

An example of edema formation secondary to a decrease in the colloid osmotic pressure of the

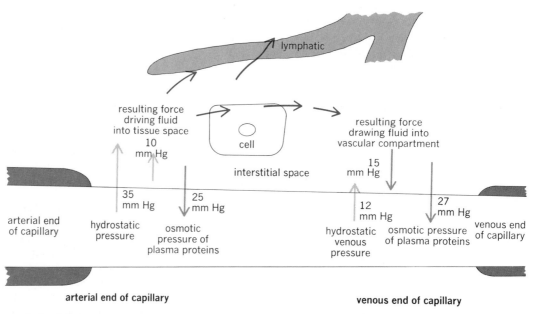

Fluid movements and resulting pressures at the capillary level of circulating blood.

plasma proteins is nephrotic edema. In chronic Bright's disease there is a marked loss of urine albumin and the plasma protein level drops as a result.

Cardiac edema follows the generalized venous congestion of cardiac failure and is an example of edema formation resulting from increased hydrostatic pressure in the capillaries.

Increased permeability of the capillary walls plays an important role in the formation of inflammatory edema, the edema of severe infections, metabolic intoxications, asphyxia, anaphylactic reactions, secondary shock, and acute nephritis. *See* EDEMA; HYPERTENSION.

Deficiencies. A deficiency of circulating blood volume, both cellular elements and fluid, is called oligemia. This may be the result of an acute blood loss or it may be of a chronic nature, such as an anemia combined with dehydration. Anemia, or oligochromemia, is a deficiency of circulating red cell volume or, more specifically, hemoglobin content. This is the oxygen-carrying component of the circulating red blood cell. The normal value for the adult human is 14–16 g/100 ml of blood. The norm for most domestic animals is 10–12 g/100 ml of blood, except for the dog with a norm of 13 g. *See* ANEMIA; HEMOGLOBIN.

Anemia can result from a variety of causes. It may be secondary to a chronic nutritional deficiency with an inadequate intake of iron. Iron is a necessary substance used by the blood-forming tissue to make hemoglobin. Anemia can also result from a defect in the blood-forming tissue (the bone marrow) so that it is unable to use the materials available to make red blood cells. It can also be the result of a displacement of blood-forming tissue, as from a tumor. It may also follow periods of acute blood loss. These are just a few examples of the causes of anemia. *See* BLOOD; HEMATOPOIESIS.

Pancytopenia, or oligocythemia, is a deficiency of all circulating blood cellular elements. This is usually the result of a deficiency of the blood-forming tissue, the bone marrow.

Ischemia. The decrease of blood flow to an organ or tissue is known as ischemia. This can be sudden as when a vessel is ligated, when a thrombus or blood clot forms, or when an embolus comes to lodge in the vessel. A gradual occlusion can follow arteriosclerotic changes in the vessel wall with resulting diminution of the lumen and blood-carrying capacity of the vessel. The effect of a sudden occlusion depends to a great extent on the collateral circulation to the organ or tissue involved. If an adequate collateral circulation comes to be established, the tissue survives; it not, it dies and an infarct results.

An infarct is a region of necrosis resulting from a vascular obstruction. The usual cause is occlusion of an artery or vein by a thrombus or embolus. If the vessel is the sole source of blood supply, the tissue dies. *See* ARTERIOSCLEROSIS; EMBOLISM; INFARCTION; THROMBOSIS.

Plethora. An excess of blood is referred to as plethora. This increase may be the result of an increase in the size or the number of red blood cells. The increase in red cell volume may be a polycythemia vera, or true polycythemia, which is a primary increase in the number of red blood cells with no regard to the needs of the organism. Polycythemia, or erythrocytosis, is usually a secondary increase in red cells following conditions of chronic hypoxia, such as congenital heart disease, emphysema, or residence at high altitudes. Serous plethora is an increase in the watery part of the blood.

Hyperemia. Hyperemia, or congestion, refers to an excess of blood within an organ or tissue. This condition may be localized or generalized. Active hyperemia is congestion which is caused by an active dilatation of arterioles and capillaries. This occurs under certain physiological conditions, such as in the muscle when there is an increased need for blood during exercise. It also occurs in pathological states such as inflammation. *See* INFLAMMATION.

Passive hyperemia is a condition which results in an accumulation of blood in the venous system. It may be generalized or localized and can result from any obstruction or hindrance to the outflow of blood from the venous circuit. The generalized form can result from valvular diseases of the heart, such as mitral or aortic stenosis or insufficiency, or myocardial failure from any cause. Tricuspid valvular disease is slightly more frequent in animals. *See* HEART DISORDERS.

Diseases of the lungs such as emphysema, fibrosis, or pulmonary hypertension of any origin can result in right ventricular failure and generalized venous congestion. The late stages of these conditions can result in cor pulmonale, which is a hypertrophy and dilatation of the right ventricle secondary to an obstruction to the pulmonary blood flow associated with a generalized venous congestion.

Localized venous congestion results when a main vein from a region is occluded either by a thrombus or some extrinsic pressure such as a tumor or enlarged lymph nodes.

In congestion the organ is usually wet and bloody. Microscopically there is an enlargement of the veins and capillaries associated with edema formation.

Hemorrhage. The escape of blood from within the vascular system is hemorrhage. This process can be the result of trauma to, or disease of, the vessel wall. Diapedesis is the passage of the corpuscular elements of the blood through an intact vessel wall.

The trauma which results in hemorrhage may be direct, such as a cut from a knife, or it may be indirect, such as a blow to the head, resulting in a tearing of cerebral or meningeal vessels.

The causes of hemorrhage other than trauma can be divided into three main groups. In the first group are those conditions in which there is a disease process affecting the vessel wall, such as arteriosclerosis or aneurysm formation. An infarct, or tissue death from any case, can result in hemorrhage.

In the second group are conditions in which there is an acute process affecting the vessel wall, as in septicemia, poisoning by heavy metals, or even anoxia.

The third and last group consists of those conditions in which there is a defect in the blood itself, which results in hemorrhage. Under this heading are included the blood-clotting disorders, thrombocytopenia, leukemia, and pernicious anemia.

Apoplexy, or stroke, is an acute vascular lesion of the brain. This can be the result of hemorrhage of, thrombosis in, or embolism to a cerebral vessel. *See* HEMORRHAGE.

Thrombosis. Thrombosis is the formation of a thrombus, which is a solid body formed during life and composed of the elements of the blood: platelets, fibrin, red cells, and leukocytes.

Thrombosis is essentially platelet deposition and may occur on a vessel wall anywhere that the endothelium is damaged. However, because the platelets release thromboplastinogen, which activates the clotting mechanism, thrombosis and blood coagulation may occur together. Platelets normally exhibit a tendency to stick together. This tendency is increased if the number of platelets is increased, as in thrombocytosis, if the velocity of the stream is decreased below a certain speed, or if the endothelium is roughened. These are the same factors which promote thrombus formation.

Thrombi may form in the veins, arteries, capillaries, or within the heart. The most common sites for the formation of thrombi are in the veins.

The venous thromboses can be divided into two groups: venous thrombosis (phlebothrombosis) and thrombophlebitis. Phlebothrombosis is the more important and is often a sequela of generalized circulatory failure, trauma, or prolonged bed rest from any cause.

Thrombophlebitis is the formation of a thrombus secondary to inflammation in the wall of the vein. Arterial thrombosis is usually the result of local causes, for example, arteriosclerosis of the vessel wall.

Embolism. The sudden blocking of an artery or vein by a clot or other substance which has been brought to its place by the blood current is an embolism. The material that is carried in the circulation in this process is an embolus. Emboli may be composed of thrombi, fat, air, tumor cells, masses of bacteria or parasites, bone marrow, amniotic fluid, or atheromatous material from the vessel wall.

Emboli originating in the right side of the heart or the great venous system of the body come to lodge in the lungs, those from the portal system in the liver, and those from the pulmonary veins or left side of the heart in some segment of the peripheral arterial tree.

One of the dire consequences of an embolus

is infarction or death of the tissue supplied by the occluded vessel. This occurs if the collateral circulation is inadequate to supply the tissue with blood. *See* DEATH; VASCULAR DISORDERS.

Romeo A. Vidone

Bibliography. E. Chung, *Quick Reference to Cardiovascular Disease*, 3d ed., 1987; W. R. Felix, Jr., *Noninvasive Diagnosis of Peripheral Vascular Disease*, 1987; S. B. McKenzie, *Textbook of Hematology*, 1988; N. C. Staub and A. E. Taylor (eds.), *Edema*, 1984; J. H. Wood, *Cerebral Blood Flow: Physiologic and Clinical Aspects*, 1987.

Cirque

A cliffed rock basin, shaped like half a bowl, at the head of a mountain valley. Cirques may be shallow if glacier erosion is slight, but may be 1650–2650 ft (500–800 m) from the top of the headwall to the cirque floor if erosion is deep. Some cirques used repeatedly by glaciers over long periods of years are excavated profoundly. Many cirques contain small glaciers today that were inherited from a huge cirque cut by glaciers long ago. Well-formed cirques have steep rock walls and floors that slope down-valley or back toward the base of the headwall. Some cirques are cup-shaped rock basins holding rainwater; a lake formed in them is a tarn. If glacial deposits, such as till or a small moraine on the cirque floor, form a depression for a lake, the lake is known as a moraine-dammed lake.

If the glacier occupying a cirque is moving, it pulls away from the headwall, leaving an opening between the glacier head and the headwall. This opening is the bergschrund (see **illus.**). Rocks fall and rubble slides into the bergschrund, along with avalanching snow and ice, and water from melting snow above. Rock debris thus gets into the ice and is carried away to be used as an abrasive tool, scouring and rasping the cirque floor. Due to earlier rock removal by the glacier plucking at the headwall, and hence a release of confining pressure, adjacent rock deeper within the cliff may break away or split off from the once-solid headwall. This produces cracks which become filled with water. The water freezes into ice when the bergschrund is open, and cold air sinks or blows down into it at night. This is ice wedging, which further loosens and separates blocks of rock from the headwall. As the glacier moves away, it pulls these rocks with it, thus gradually extending the glacier headward and enlarging the cirque.

It is not known for certain how a cirque forms. Presumably, it starts as a small hollow or niche in the mountainside at the head of a stream valley. Excavation of such a hollow is by removal of fine material (sand, silt, clay) around the melting edge of a shrinking snowbank or firn field (an accumulation of old snow changed into ice granules). This form

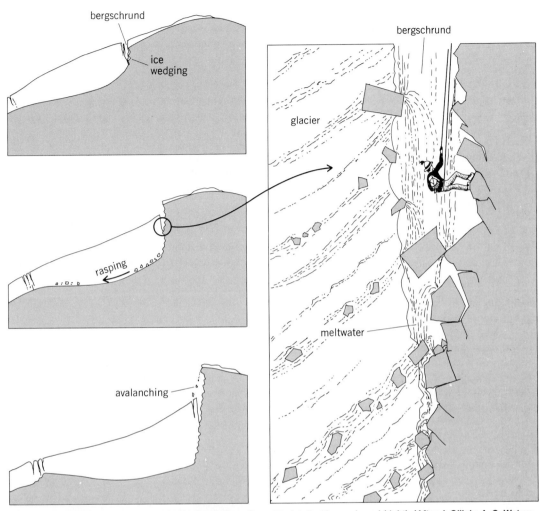

Progressive stages of cirque erosion in the head of a valley, with detail of bergschrund (right). (*After J. Gilluly, A. C. Waters, and A. O. Woodford, Principles of Geology, 4th ed., W. H. Freeman, 1975*)

of erosion is known as nivation, and takes place solely by sheetwash and rivulet flow as the snow or firn edge melts. Chemical decomposition of rock fragments is intensified two to four times by the influence of snow meltwater, and solutes are readily washed away. Quantitative tests have supported this process. Since the effect of repeated freezing and thawing of water is recognized as restricted to the uppermost 4 in. (10 cm) of the ground in alpine regions, it is insignificant in nivation. Freeze-thaw action may occur only around the edges and not underneath snow or firn. This happens only in spring and summer and is not possible in winter. Thus, if a snowbank or firn field melts each summer, a hollow might be deepened after many years into a cirque, but this has never been proved. If a snowbank or firn field does not melt each summer but increases in size and volume each year, as would be expected during the onset of glaciation, excavation of the hollow will cease. However, cirques occur in glaciated mountains all over the world. *See* GLACIATED TERRAIN.

Sidney E. White

Cirrhosis

A liver disease characterized by a marked increase in fibrous connective tissue, resulting in a firm, nodular, distorted liver.

Etiology. There are numerous causes of cirrhosis. In the United States the majority of cases are caused by excessive alcohol consumption, and the condition is referred to as alcoholic cirrhosis. In the past, alcoholic cirrhosis was thought to be secondary to poor nutrition associated with excessive drinking, but studies have conclusively demonstrated that alcohol is a liver toxin. How alcohol leads to fibrosis in the liver is still not entirely understood, but some cases are preceded by alcoholic hepatitis. *See* ALCOHOLISM; HEPATITIS.

Cirrhosis may occur as a result of the healing of severe fulminant hepatitis or chronic active hepatitis. Some cases are caused by obstruction of the bile duct by calculi (stones) and are referred to as secondary biliary cirrhosis. Primary biliary cirrhosis is primarily a disease of middle-aged women and is caused by an autoimmune destruction of bile ducts. This disease is slowly progressive and initially begins as inflammation in and around larger intrahepatic bile ducts; it may take several years before the liver becomes cirrhotic. Autoimmune hepatitis, sometimes referred to as lupoid hepatitis and characteristically seen in young women and associated with serum autoantibodies, may progress to cirrhosis. *See* ANTIBODY.

Relatively few cases of cirrhosis are caused by genetically determined deficiencies in certain substances. These include Wilson's disease (caused by a decrease or absence of ceruloplasmin which binds to copper in the blood), alpha 1 antitrypsin deficiency (caused by a decrease in alpha 1 antitrypsin which is produced in the liver), and hemosiderosis (caused by an inborn error of iron metabolism).

Symptoms. The signs and symptoms of cirrhosis are nonspecific and frequently related to the complications. As the liver becomes fibrotic, there is obstruction of the blood flow through the liver. This results in portal hypertension, an increase in blood pressure within the portal vein and its tributaries. This obstruction of blood flow through the liver results in the formation of new collateral venous channels which bypass the liver. The most important collateral channels are those in the region of the lower esophagus. These channels, called esophageal varices, are characteristically underneath the epithelial lining of the esophagus and frequently become dilated. These can erode through the lining of the esophagus and cause severe bleeding. The obstructed hepatic blood flow also causes congestion of the spleen, leading to a markedly enlarged spleen (splenomegaly). Also, most people with cirrhosis eventually develop fluid in their abdomen (ascites) and are at an increased risk of developing a spontaneous intraabdominal infection. Some individuals will develop hemorrhoids due to portal hypertension.

In addition to obstruction of blood flow, the bile ducts within the liver are distorted and frequently partially obstructed by the increased connective tissue. This results in jaundice, a yellow discoloration of all tissues and organs, including the skin. Some individuals with advanced cirrhosis develop renal failure, a condition referred to as hepatorenal syndrome. Also, there is a definite increase in liver cell cancer in cirrhotic persons. *See* JAUNDICE.

Morphological changes. The liver may be slightly enlarged, but as the disease progresses it usually becomes smaller due to progressive loss of liver cells. In the final stage the liver may weigh as little as 14–18 oz (400–500 g; normal is 50–60 oz or 1400–1700 g). When examined microscopically, liver cells of varying size and shape can be observed that are surrounded by dense fibrous connective tissue which contains inflammatory cells and distorted bile ducts.

Treatment. The therapy of cirrhosis is aimed primarily at preventing or reducing the complications.

Some experimental animal studies and early human trials used (unsuccessfully) the drug colchicine to prevent the development of fibrosis. Bleeding esophageal varices (collateral venous channels) are a frequent serious complication of cirrhosis. Various techniques are used to control the bleeding. In some individuals with severe portal hypertension, vascular shunts are made to reduce the pressure in the portal vein by bypassing the liver. Most frequently the portal vein is surgically connected to the inferior vena cava so that some of the blood in the portal vein does not pass through the liver. *See* CARDIOVASCULAR SYSTEM; LIVER DISORDERS.

Samuel P. Hammar

Bibliography. S. Grisolia (ed.), *Cirrhosis, Hepatic Encephalopathy, and Ammonium Toxicity*, 1990; A. G. Johnson and D. R. Triger, *Liver Diseases and Gallstones: The Facts*, 1992; R. W. Watson (ed.), *Liver Pathology and Alcohol*, 1991; D. G. Wight, *Atlas of Liver Pathology*, 1993.

Cirripedia

A subclass of the Crustacea, permanently attached when adult, and called barnacles. The carapace forms a complete covering or mantle over the rest of the body and is usually strengthened by calcareous plates. The body within the mantle consists of a mouth region and thorax. The

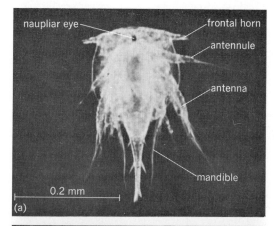

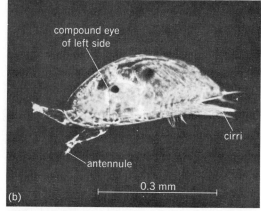

Fig. 1. Larval stages of *Balanus*. (*a*) Nauplius. (*b*) Cypris. (*Photographs by D. P. Wilson*)

Characteristics and some genera of Cirripedia

Order	Characteristics	Some genera
Thoracica	Permanently attached, stalked or sessile, independent or commensal barnacles, typically with calcareous plates in mantle; hermaphroditic	Lepas, Scalpellum, Conchoderma, Alepas, Balanus, Coronula, Verruca
Acrothoracica	Burrowing barnacles living in shells, coral, or limestone; bisexual with dwarf males; cirri poorly developed, often reduced in number	Trypetesa, Lithoglyptes, Kochlorine
Ascothoracica	Parasites, attached only by prehensile antennules, in body cavity of coelenterates and echinoderms; abdomen developed; cirri reduced	Synagoga, Laura, Baccalaureus, Ulophysema,
Rhizocephala	Internal parasites of decapod crustacea; body a formless ramifying mass among the host tissues; no gut; eggs and larvae produced in an external sac on host's body	Sacculina, Loxothylacus, Thompsonia

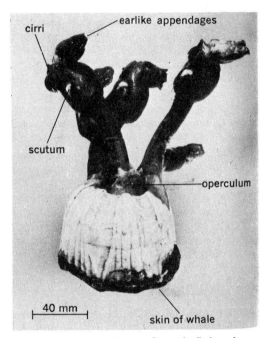

Fig. 2. *Conchoderma auritum* on *Coronula diadema* from a humpback whale. (*Photograph by V. B. Scheffer*)

Thereafter cement is secreted from glands in the antennules, and the animal is permanently attached.

The Cirripedia are divided into four orders (see **table**). A fifth order, Apoda, has been suppressed, the only representative having been shown to be a transitory larval stage of a parasitic isopod crustacean. Only the Thoracica, the goose barnacles and acorn barnacles (**Figs. 2** and **3**), are at all conspicuous, and only the latter of any economic significance.

Most acorn barnacles live in shallow waters or between tide marks, where they may be present in immense numbers. These intertidal forms have economic importance. They settle on any suitable immersed surface, including the hulls of ships and submerged equipment. Their presence interferes

abdomen is usually vestigial. Typically the mouth appendages are paired mandibles with palps, maxillulae, and maxillae. The thorax bears six pairs of biramous appendages (cirri) composed of numerous segments, each with a considerable armament of setae. Compound eyes occur only in the larvae, there is no heart, and typically adults are hermaphroditic. The female genital pore is on the base of cirrus I, the male genital pore on an elongated penis lying medianly, posterior to cirrus VI. Cross-fertilization is normal, and the eggs are incubated in the mantle cavity and hatch into free-swimming nauplius larvae (**Fig. 1**a). By successive molts a further five nauplius larvae follow. The sixth nauplius (or metanauplius) molts into an entirely different larval form, the cypris (Fig. 1b), with a bivalved shell and resembling the ostracod genus *Cypris*. The cypris is characteristic of all Cirripedia. It has prominent antennules and well-developed though short cirri. The cypris seeks a suitable substrate or host and attaches by the antennules.

Fig. 3. Glass ball, formerly a Japanese fishing float, heavily fouled with **Lepas anatifera.** (*Photograph by R. Shomura, Pacific Oceanic Fishery Investigations, U.S. Fish and Wildlife Service, Honolulu*)

with efficient operation and increases running costs. Large sums have been spent devising antifouling paints and techniques to discourage settlement of barnacles. Equal attention has been paid to the detailed life history and biology of barnacles and their larvae.

Remains of Cirripedia are known from the Ordovician, but it is doubtful if they occurred earlier. Disarticulated shell plates, but few near-complete shells, are found. *See* ACROTHORACICA; ASCOTHORACICA; BARNACLE; RHIZOCEPHALA; THORACICA.

H. G. Stubbings

Bibliography. H. G. Bronn (ed.), *Klassen und Ordnungen des Tierreichs*, vol. 5, bk. 3, pt. 1, 1940; D. P. Henry, The Cirripedia of Puget Sound with a key to the species, *Univ. Wash. Publ. Oceanogr.*, 4(1):1–48, 1940; D. P. Henry, Studies on the sessile Cirripedia of the Pacific Coast of North America, *Univ. Wash. Publ. Oceanogr.*, 4(3):99–131, 1942; S. P. Parker (ed.), *Synopsis and Classification of Living Organisms*, 2 vols., 1982; H. G. Stubbings, *Balanus balanoides*, L.M.B.C. Mem. Typical Brit. Mar. Plants Animals 37, 1975..

Citric acid

A hydroxytricarboxylic acid, general formula $C_6H_8O_7$, with the structure shown below. It is

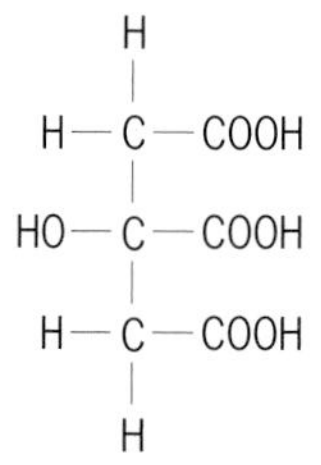

$$
\begin{array}{c}
\text{H} \\
| \\
\text{H}-\text{C}-\text{COOH} \\
| \\
\text{HO}-\text{C}-\text{COOH} \\
| \\
\text{H}-\text{C}-\text{COOH} \\
| \\
\text{H}
\end{array}
$$

available primarily as anhydrous material but also as the monohydrate. The major commercial salts are sodium and potassium, with calcium, diammonium, and ferric ammonium (complex) also available. *See* ACID AND BASE.

Citric acid and its salts are widely used because they are nontoxic, safe to handle, and easily biodegraded. They are universally accepted, without restriction on level, as food ingredients, including acceptance by the Joint FAO/WHO Expert Committee on Food Additives and the U.S. Food and Drug Administration. Because of their food use, specifications for purity are included in the *Food Chemicals Codex* (except diammonium citrate). In addition, specifications for citric acid, sodium citrate, and potassium citrate are included in the *U.S Pharmacopeia* and many pharmacopeia throughout the world.

Occurrence. Citric acid occurs in relatively large quantities in citrus fruits. It also occurs in other fruits, in vegetables, and in animal tissues and fluids either as the free acid or as citrate ion (**Table 1**). It is an integral part of the Krebs (citric acid) cycle involving the metabolic conversion of carbohydrates, fats, and proteins in most living organisms. *See* CITRIC ACID CYCLE.

Manufacture. Prior to World War I, all of the world's citric acid was produced by extraction from cull citrus fruit. Today, essentially all of the commercial citric acid is produced by fermentation. Processes employed are surface or submerged fermentation by mold (*Aspergillus niger*) and submerged fermentation by yeast (*Candida guilliermondii, C. lipolytica*), using a variety of substrates including sucrose, molasses, corn syrup, enzyme-treated starch, and normal paraffins. Citric acid is recovered from the fermentation broth by solvent extraction or more commonly by precipitation as calcium citrate, followed by treatment with sulfuric acid to convert the calcium citrate to calcium sulfate and citric acid. The calcium sulfate is removed by filtration, and the citric acid solution is further purified. Crystallization of citric acid from a hot aqueous solution (above the transition temperature of 36.6°C or 97.9°F) yields anhydrous citric acid; crystallization from a cold solution yields the monohydrate. Although total chemical syntheses for citric acid have been published, they have never achieved commercial success. *See* FERMENTATION; INDUSTRIAL MICROBIOLOGY.

Properties. Key properties of anhydrous citric acid are summarized in **Table 2**. Citric acid is a relatively strong organic acid (see dissociation constants), and is very soluble in water.

Uses. Citric acid is widely used in the food and pharmaceutical industries. In foods it is used primarily to produce a tart taste and to complement fruit flavors in carbonated beverages, beverage powders, fruit-flavored drinks, jams and jellies, candy, sherbets, water ices, and wine. It is also used to reduce pH in certain canned foods to make

TABLE 1. Citrate content of natural products			
Product	Percent citric acid	Product	Percent citric acid
Lemon juice	4.0–8.0	Tomato	0.25
Orange juice	0.6–1.0	Cabbage	0.05–0.07
Tangerine juice	0.9–1.2	Corn	0.02
Grapefruit juice	1.2–2.1	Eggplant	0.01
Strawberry	0.65–0.82	Peas	0.05
Raspberry	1.1–1.3	Cow milk	0.08–0.23
Black currant	1.5–3.0	Human milk	0.35–1.25
Red currant	0.7–1.4	Chicken organs	0.01–0.07
Gooseberry	0.98–0.99		

TABLE 2. Properties of anhydrous citric acid

Property	Value
Formula	$H_3C_6H_5O_7$
Molecular weight	192.13
Dissociation constants	K_1 8.2×10^{-4}
	K_2 1.8×10^{-5}
	K_3 3.9×10^{-7}
Melting point	153°C (307°F)
Solubility, g/100 ml at 25°C (77°F)	
Water	181
Ethanol	59
Ether	0.75

heat treatment more effective, and in conjunction with antioxidants to chelate trace metals and retard enzymatic activity. *See* FOOD MANUFACTURING.

In pharmaceuticals, citric acid provides the acid source in effervescent tablets in addition to being used to adjust pH, impart a tart taste, and chelate trace metals. It is also used as a blood anticoagulant. *See* PHARMACEUTICAL CHEMISTRY.

Citric acid, because of its low toxicity, relative noncorrosiveness, and biodegradability, is also being used for applications normally reserved for the strong mineral acids. These include preoperational and operational cleaning of iron and copper oxides from boilers, nuclear reactors, and heat exchangers; passivation of stainless steel tanks and equipment; and etching of concrete floors prior to coating. It is also used as a dispersant to retard settling of titanium dioxide slurries and as a sequestering and pH control agent in the textile industry. *See* TEXTILE CHEMISTRY.

Salts. Since citric acid is a tribasic acid, it can form acid and neutral salts, and will buffer over a broad pH range. The salts which are readily available commercially are trisodium citrate (dihydrate and anhydrous), tripotassium citrate (monohydrate), calcium citrate (tetrahydrate), diammonium citrate (anhydrous), and ferric ammonium citrate. *See* BUFFERS (CHEMISTRY); PH.

Trisodium citrate dihydrate, the salt which is most widely used, is a stable white crystal or granule. It is used as an emulsifier in processed cheese products where it prevents fat separation, imparts good meltdown properties, and produces slices with proper flexibility. In other dairy products, such as ice cream, whipping cream, and evaporated milk, it acts as a stabilizer and viscosity control agent. The sharpness of high-acid beverages is mellowed with sodium citrate, and it is used as a buffer to control pH in jams and jellies, gelatin desserts, and many pharmaceutical preparations. It is also used as a blood anticoagulant. Its largest single industrial use is as a detergent builder since it is rapidly biodegradable, environmentally acceptable, and can chelate calcium, magnesium, and other metal ions. Sodium citrate is also used as a water conditioner, set-retardant for cement, buffer, and scrubbing agent to remove sulfur dioxide from stack gases or process tail gases. In most applications the dihydrate is used since it is less expensive. Occasionally, certain dry formulations require the use of the anhydrous salt. *See* CHEESE; DETERGENT.

Potassium citrate is a white crystalline granule or powder which readily absorbs moisture from the air. It is often used as a substitute for sodium citrate in special food products where sodium ion is undesirable. Calcium citrate is a stable, white, free-flowing powder used as a source of calcium either for nutritional purposes or for functional purposes (that is, as a firming agent). Ferric ammonium citrate is a complex salt, of undetermined structure, composed of iron, ammonia, and citric acid. Product containing 14.5–16% iron is green in color, and product containing 14.5–18.5% iron is brown. Both absorb moisture readily and are affected by light. They are used as a nutrient source of iron in food and in pharmaceutical syrups and elixirs. Diammonium citrate is a white granule or powder which is stable in air and used in dry formulations for metal cleaning.   Fred Sauer

Bibliography. National Research Council, *Food Chemicals Codex*, 3d ed., 1981; Pfizer Chemical Division, Technical Literature: *Citrate Salts in Foods*, 1983, *Citric Acid and Citrates*, 1978, *Food Acidulants*, 1981, *Organic Chelating Agents*, 1984; *Scientific Literature Review on GRAS Food Ingredients: Citrates*, PB 223 850, National Technical Information Service, Springfield, Virginia, April 1973; *Scientific Literature Review on GRAS Food Ingredients: Citric Acid*, PB 241 967, National Technical Information Service, Springfield, Virginia, October 1974.

Citric acid cycle

In aerobic cells from animal and certain other species, the major pathway for the complete oxidation of acetyl coenzyme A (the thioester of acetic acid with coenzyme A); also known as the Krebs cycle or tricarboxylic acid cycle. Reduced electron carriers generated in the cycle are reoxidized by oxygen via the electron transport system; water is formed, and the energy liberated is conserved by the phosphorylation of adenosinediphosphate (ADP) to adenosinetriphosphate (ATP). Reactions of the cycle also function in metabolic processes other than energy generation. The role of the cycle in mammalian tissues will be emphasized in this article. *See* ADENOSINEDIPHOSPHATE (ADP); ADENOSINETRIPHOSPHATE (ATP); COENZYME; ENZYME.

Reactions. The first step in the cycle involves the condensation of the acetyl portion of acetyl coenzyme A (CoA) with the four-carbon compound oxaloacetate to form citrate, a tricarboxylate containing six carbons (see **illus.**). A shift of the hydroxyl group of citrate to an adjacent carbon results in the formation of D-threo-isocitrate, which in turn is oxidized to the five-carbon compound α-ketoglutarate and carbon dioxide (CO_2). In a second oxidative decarboxylation reaction, α-ketoglutarate, in the presence of CoA, is converted to succinyl CoA and another molecule of CO_2.

Citric acid cycle.

In the subsequent formation of the four-carbon compound succinate and CoA, the energy in the thioester bond of succinyl CoA is conserved by the formation of guanosine triphosphate (GTP) from guanosine diphosphate (GDP) and inorganic phosphate. Fumarate is formed from succinate by the removal of two atoms of hydrogen, and the unsaturated compound is then hydrated to L-malate. The dehydrogenation of malate forms oxaloacetate, the starting four-carbon compound of the metabolic cycle. Thus, beginning with the two-carbon acetyl group, one completion of the cycle results in the formation of two molecules of carbon dioxide. The obligatory role of the intact cycle for the complete oxidation of acetyl CoA has been demonstrated by inhibiting enzymes required for specific reactions (for example, inhibition of succinate dehydrogenase by the substrate analog malonate) or by altering the regeneration or depletion of an intermediate of the cycle.

Electron transport and oxidative phosphorylation. The oxidation of acetyl CoA to CO_2 in the cycle occurs without direct reaction with molecular oxygen. The oxidations occur at dehydrogenation reactions in which hydrogen atoms and electrons are transferred from intermediates of the cycle to the electron carriers nicotinamide adenine dinucleotide (NAD^+) and flavin adenine dinucleotide (FAD). The NAD-specific dehydrogenase reactions are isocitrate dehydrogenase [reaction (1)], α-ketoglutarate dehydrogenase (2), and malate dehydrogenase (3). FAD is the coenzyme for succinate dehydrogenase, (4). The electrons from NADH and $FADH_2$ are trans-

Isocitrate + NAD^+ $\longrightarrow$

$$\alpha\text{-ketoglutarate} + CO_2 + NADH + H^+ \quad (1)$$

α-Ketoglutarate + CoA + NAD^+ $\longrightarrow$

$$\text{succinyl CoA} + CO_2 + NADH + H^+ \quad (2)$$

$$\text{Malate} + NAD^+ \longleftrightarrow \text{oxaloacetate} + NADH + H^+ \quad (3)$$

$$\text{Succinate} + FAD \longleftrightarrow \text{fumarate} + FADH_2 \quad (4)$$

ferred to molecular oxygen via a series of electron transport carriers, with regeneration of NAD^+ and FAD. The energy liberated in the electron transport chain is partially conserved by the formation of ATP from ADP and inorganic phosphate, by a process called oxidative phosphorylation. The energy generated as oxygen accepts electrons from the reduced coenzymes generated in one turn of the cycle results in the maximal formation of 11 molecules of ATP. Because GTP obtained by phosphorylation of GDP at the succinyl CoA to succinate step of the cycle is readily converted to ATP by nucleotide diphosphokinase, as in reaction (5), the

$$\text{GTP} + \text{ADP} \longleftrightarrow \text{GDP} + \text{ATP} \quad (5)$$

yield is 12 molecules of ATP per molecule of acetyl CoA metabolized. *See* NICOTINAMIDE ADENINE DINUCLEOTIDE (NAD).

The electron transport and oxidative phosphorylation systems and the enzymes required for the citric acid cycle are located in the mitochondria of cells. These mitochondrial systems are the major source of ATP for energy-consuming reactions in most tissues. The citric acid cycle does not occur in all cells. For example, mature human red blood cells do not contain mitochondria and the cycle is absent. In these cells, ATP is formed by the anaerobic conversion of glucose to lactate (anaerobic glycolysis).

See MITOCHONDRIA; PHOSPHATE METABOLISM.

Regulation. A major rate-limiting step of the citric acid cycle in aerobic mammalian tissues (for example, heart) is at NAD-specific isocitrate dehydrogenase [reaction (1)]. The activity of the enzyme is dependent on the concentration of the substrate (magnesium isocitrate): it is activated by ADP, calcium (Ca^{2+}), and citrate, and it is inhibited by NADH and reduced nicotinamide adenine dinucleotide phosphate (NADPH). Differences in energy demand affect the rate of citric acid flux and concentrations of modulators of NAD-dependent isocitrate dehydrogenase. At rest, the flux through the cycle is slowed, the cellular concentration of the isocitrate dehydrogenase inhibitor NADH is raised; and the activator ADP is lowered; the opposite occurs during high energy demand. The rate of cycle oxidation in liver mitochondria increases with decreased NADPH concentration; increased mitochondrial free Ca^{2+} enhances cycle flux. *See* NICOTINAMIDE ADENINE DINUCLEOTIDE PHOSPHATE (NADPH).

Formation of acetyl CoA and intermediates. Acetyl CoA is formed from carbohydrates, fats, and the carbon skeleton of amino acids. The origin of a precursor and the extent of its utilization depend on the metabolic capability of a specific tissue and on the physiological state of the organism. For example, most mammalian tissues have the capacity to convert glucose to pyruvate in a reaction called glycolysis. Pyruvate is then taken up from cellular cytosol by mitochondria and oxidatively decarboxylated to acetyl CoA and carbon dioxide by pyruvate dehydrogenase, as in reaction (6).

Pyruvate + NAD^+ + CoA $\longrightarrow$

$$\text{acetyl CoA} + CO_2 + NADH + H^+ \quad (6)$$

Acetyl CoA is also the end product of fatty acid oxidation in mitochondria. However, the fatty acid oxidation pathway occurs in fewer tissues than does glycolysis or the citric acid cycle. For example, nervous tissue utilizes the complete oxidation of glucose but not of fatty acids to maintain energy needs. In prolonged starvation, the level of blood glucose declines to a concentration inadequate to support the optimal energy needs of brain, whereas the level of blood ketone bodies (formed from fatty acids in liver) rises. In this case, the oxidation of ketone bodies (acetoacetate and 3-hydroxybutyrate) via acetyl CoA supplements the diminished oxidation of glucose to fulfill the energy requirements of the brain.

The amino acids follow varied pathways for forming compounds that can enter the citric acid cycle. For example, the paths of degradation of leucine and lysine lead directly to formation of acetyl CoA; only part of the carbons of aromatic amino acids and of isoleucine are converted to acetyl CoA. Pyruvate, formed by transamination of alanine with the citric acid cycle intermediate α-ketoglutarate [reaction (7)],

Alanine + α-ketoglutarate $\longleftrightarrow$ pyruvate + glutamate   (7)

can be oxidatively decarboxylated to acetyl CoA by pyruvate dehydrogenase [reaction (6)] or carboxylated to the cycle intermediate oxaloacetate by pyruvate carboxylase [reaction (8)]. Oxaloacetate

Pyruvate + CO_2 + ATP $\longrightarrow$

oxaloacetate + ADP + P_1 (8)

can also be formed by aspartate aminotransferase [reaction (9)]. Portions of the carbon skeletons of

Aspartate + α-ketoglutarate $\longleftrightarrow$

oxaloacetate + glutamate   (9)

valine, isoleucine, methionine, and threonine are converted to methylmalonyl CoA, which rearranges to the citric acid cycle intermediate succinyl CoA. *See* AMINO ACIDS.

Role in lipogenesis and gluconeogenesis. In addition to the cycle's role in yielding catabolic energy, portions of it can supply intermediates for synthetic processes, such as the synthesis of the fatty acid moiety of triglycerides from glucose (lipogenesis), and formation of glucose from the carbon skeletons of certain amino acids, lactate, or glycerol (gluconeogenesis).

Lipogenesis. When dietary intake exceeds the energy needs of the body, the excess calories are deposited as body fat. Under these conditions in humans, the synthesis of fatty acids from glucose occurs mainly in the liver. It is favored by metabolic changes resulting principally from a rise in blood insulin: (1) The rate of pyruvate formation increases because of the rise in tissue glucose and enhancement of glycolysis. (2) Increases in enzyme activities catalyzing the conversion of pyruvate to acetyl CoA at pyruvate dehydrogenase [reaction (6)] and to oxaloacetate at pyruvate carboxylase [reaction (8)] raise the concentrations of both of these substrates for citrate synthesis. When this occurs at a rate exceeding that of the citric acid cycle, the citrate concentration rises and citrate exits from the mitochondria to the cytosol. (3) In the cytosol, citrate is cleaved to oxaloacetate and acetyl CoA in a reaction requiring CoA and ATP. The acetyl CoA is converted to palmitate and other long-chain fatty acids in a series of condensation steps requiring CO_2, ATP as energy source, and NADPH as reductant. *See* LIPID METABOLISM.

Gluconeogenesis. Dietary deprivation of an adult human for more than 2–3 days results in the depletion of liver glycogen stores supporting blood glucose, and the oxidation of fatty acids derived from body triglyceride depots becomes the principal body energy source. However, certain tissues, such as brain and red and white blood cells, remain partially or wholly dependent on glucose as the energy source. In the starved state, where blood insulin decreases and glucagon increases, increased mobilization of amino acids from skeletal muscle proteins occurs, and carbons from some of these amino acids become available for glucose synthesis. The interactions of degradation pathways of individual amino acids in various tissues result in markedly increased blood alanine, an important substrate for gluconeogenesis.

Some of the steps in the conversion of alanine to glucose are as follows: (1) Alanine is taken up from the bloodstream by the liver and converted to pyruvate by transamination [reaction (7)]. (2) The further metabolism of pyruvate in liver mitochondria is affected by the increase in the rate of fatty acid oxidation in the starved state, which raises the levels of acetyl CoA and NADH. Since NADH inhibits pyruvate dehydrogenase [reaction (6)], and acetyl CoA activates pyruvate carboxylase [reaction (8)], the conversion of pyruvate to oxaloacetate rather than acetyl CoA is favored. The increased NADH displaces the malate dehydrogenase reaction [reaction (3)] from oxaloacetate toward malate. Malate is transported from the mitochondria to the cytosol, where it is reoxidized by NAD^+ to oxaloacetate by cytosolic malate dehydrogenase. (3) Oxaloacetate is converted to phosphoenolpyruvate (PEP) by the PEP-carboxykinase reaction [reaction (10)].

Oxaloacetate + GTP $\longrightarrow$ PEP + CO_2 + GDP   (10)

Phosphoenolpyruvate is an intermediate of both gluconeogenesis and glycolysis. In the starved state, the levels of modulators, metabolites, and so forth activate certain rate-limiting steps favoring the formation of glucose from PEP, and also inhibit key enzyme activities facilitating glycolysis. The net effect of these opposing trends is to funnel the flux of carbons from amino acids toward glucose synthesis. *See* BIOLOGICAL OXIDATION; CARBOHYDRATE METABOLISM; CELL (BIOLOGY); GLUCOSE; GLYCOGEN; METABOLISM.

Gerhard W. E. Plaut

Citron

Citrus medica, a species of true citrus. The plant has a long and interesting history, being the first contact between citrus, which came from the Far East, and western Judaeo-Christian civilization. A citron, the Etrog, was the "hadar" or "goodly fruit" offering at the ancient Jewish Feast of the Tabernacles. At the time of the first Jewish revolt against Rome in A.D. 66–70, the rebels minted their own coins with the Etrog substituting for Nero's imperial visage.

Commercially, citrons are still grown almost exclusively in the Mediterranean area, principally in Italy, Sicily, Corsica, Greece, and Israel. The tree is evergreen, as are all citrus, and frost-tender. It is thorny, straggly, shrubby, and tends to be short-lived.

The fruit is scarcely edible fresh, having a very

Commercial citron (*Citrus medica*), approximately one-half natural size. (*a*) Foliage and fruit. (*b*) Cross section of fruit. (*From J. Horace McFarland Co.*)

thick skin with little flesh and that lacking in juice (see **illus.**). However, it is very fragrant and was valued in for its aroma and its fragrant peel oil, used in perfumes and as a moth repellent. Later, when the citron was the only known citrus fruit, it was very highly valued. Today, it is grown commercially only as a source of candied peel for use in cakes and confections. The actual candying is usually done in the importing country, the citron peel being exported in brine. Traditionally the fruit was halved and held in large unsealed casks in seawater, a mild fermentation taking place for a week or more, after which additional coarse salt was added and the casks sealed. Today brining is more typically done in a 15% salt solution to which about 2000 parts per million of SO_2 has been added as a preservative and 1% $CaCl_2$ to firm the tissues. The candying process involves first leaching out the brine with boiling water and then transfers through successive syrups of increasing strength up to about 75%.

Confusion sometimes arises due to the name "citron" also being used for a small, wild, inedible melon in the United States and for lemons (*C. limon*) in France. *See* FRUIT; FRUIT, TREE.

William Grierson

Citronella

A tropical grass, *Cymbopogon nardus*, from the leaves of which oil of citronella is distilled. This essential oil is pale yellow, inexpensive, and much used in cheap perfumes and soaps. It is perhaps best known as an insect repellent. A large acreage is devoted to the cultivation of this grass in Java and Sri Lanka. *See* CYPERALES; ESSENTIAL OILS.

Perry D. Strausbaugh/Earl L. Core

Civet

Any of 18 species of carnivores which are assigned to the family Viverridae. Also included in this family are genets, linsangs, and mongooses. *See* MONGOOSE.

Civets are small to medium size with a pointed muzzle, long head, slender body, and long, bushy tail. They have short limbs and nonretractile claws; they are digitigrade, that is, they walk on their toes. The Indian civet (*Viverra zibetha*) and the smaller African civet are two better-known species.

Civets are nocturnal and remain hidden in brush areas during the day. They have well-developed perianal glands, from which a scented substance used in perfumery is secreted. The elongate muzzle is a consequence of the long jaw required to hold 36–40 teeth (dental formula I 3/3 C 1/1 Pm 4/4 M 2/2). *See* DENTITION.

Genets are smaller, arboreal members of the family. There are nine species, all indigenous to Africa, and the small spotted genet (*Genetta genetta*) has a range extending to France and Spain. They are solitary, nocturnal carnivores found in forested areas, preying on small mammals and birds. Scent glands are not well developed, and retractile claws make them good climbers. *See* CARNIVORA; SCENT GLAND.

Charles B. Curtin

Civil engineering

A branch of engineering that encompasses the conception, design, construction, and management of residential and commercial buildings and structures, water supply facilities, transportation systems for goods and people, as well as control of the environment for the maintenance and improvement of the quality of life. Civil engineering is a people-serving profession; it includes planning and design professionals in both the public and private sectors, contractors, builders, educators, and researchers who strive to meet the needs and desires of the community.

The civil engineer holds the safety, health, and welfare of the public paramount. Civil engineering projects and systems should conform to governmental regulations and statutes; should be built economically to function properly for a reasonable period of time with a minimum of maintenance and repair while withstanding anticipated usage and weather; and should conserve energy and allow hazard-free construction while providing healthful, safe, and environmentally sound utilization by society.

Because the desired objectives are so broad and encompass an orderly progression of interrelated components and information to arrive at the visually pleasing, environmentally satisfactory, and energy-frugal end point, civil engineering projects are actually systems requiring the skills and inputs of many diverse technical specialties, all of which are subsets of the overall civil engineering profession.

The infrastructure is the foundation of the modern industrialized urban society. The infrastructure includes roads; mass transit; railroads; bridges; airports; storage buildings; terminals; communication and control towers; water supply and treatment systems; storm water control systems; wastewater collection, treatment and disposal systems; as well as living and working areas, recreational buildings, and ancillary structures for civil and civic needs. Without a well-maintained and functioning infrastructure, the urban area, and society, cannot stay healthy, grow, and prosper. Civil engineers, with their various technical specialties, play a major role in developing workable solutions to construct, renovate, repair, maintain, and upgrade this infrastructure. The civil engineer works with other professionals in developing functional projects, arriving at realistic cost estimates, and advocating reasonable investment strategies.

Civil engineers who move into management combine their technical training and skills with the ability to organize and properly employ the four basics of any project—personnel, time, materials, and money. Civil engineers in management may work for private engineering firms, for industries, for the military, for governmental agencies, or for regional authorities. The civil engineer may also choose a career in education. The teaching civil engineer educates students in technical specialties, inculcates engineering ethics and standards of safety, and engages in research and scholarly endeavors. Civil engineering faculty members are frequently involved as consultants or specialists on boards or commissions for standards, planning, or educational certification.

Photogrammetry, surveying, and mapping. The civil engineer in this specialty precisely measures the Earth's surface to obtain reliable information for locating, planning, and designing engineering projects. This specialty involves everything from traditional land surveying to high-technology methods using aerial surveying, satellites, and computer-processing of photographic imagery. The information obtained by optical sighting, radio signal, laser scan, or sonic beam is converted to maps to provide accurate locations for designing planned developments, boring tunnels, building highways or pipelines, plotting flood control, irrigation or hydroelectric projects with dams and other structures, delimiting subsurface geologic formations that may affect construction projects, and aiding many other building uses. *See* AERIAL PHOTOGRAPH; PHOTOGRAMMETRY; REMOTE SENSING; SURVEYING; TOPOGRAPHIC SURVEYING AND MAPPING.

Community and urban planning. Those engaged in this segment of civil engineering evaluate environmental, social, and economic factors in affecting the use and development of land and natural resources as they plan to establish planned developments, recreational park areas, or industrial complexes for regions, cities, or portions of a community. They work with other professionals to coordinate required infrastructure to ensure social, economic, and environmental well-being. *See* LAND-USE PLANNING.

Geotechnical engineering. Civil engineers in this specialty analyze and evaluate the behavior of earth materials and the ability of these materials to support structures on or below the ground. They design and establish procedures to prevent the pressure or weight of structures from compressing the supporting earth and causing settlement. They are also concerned with methods to stabilize slopes and fills, to protect structures and infrastructure from earthquakes, and to mitigate the unwanted effects of ground water. *See* ENGINEERING GEOLOGY; FOUNDATION; PERMAFROST; PILE FOUNDATION; ROCK MECHANICS; SOIL MECHANICS.

Construction engineering. Civil engineers in this area manage and direct the physical construction of a project from start to finish; this field is also known as construction management. Construction engineers apply the knowledge of construction methods and equipment along with principles of financing, scheduling, planning, organization, and coordination to convert the paper designs into completed usable facilities. They maintain a continuous record of the personnel, time, materials, and costs expended and prepare periodic reports depicting the project's progress to completion. *See* CONSTRUCTION ENGINEERING; CONSTRUCTION METHODS; CRITICAL PATH METHOD (CPM); ENGINEERING AND ARCHITECTURAL CONTRACTS.

Structural engineering. In this specialty, civil engineers plan, design, and evaluate a wide variety of structures, including buildings, bridges, offshore platforms, space platforms, amusement park rides, towers, and any other construction that must support its own weight and the loads it must carry. These structures must be designed for, and capable of withstanding, the loads due to rain, snow, or ice; the forces due to wind, hurricanes, and earthquakes; the effects of temperature changes and the like. The structural engineer must determine which construction materials or combinations of them such as steel, concrete, stone, brick, aluminum, plastics, and glass are most economical, safe, and appropriate for the project under the site-specific conditions. *See* BRIDGE; BUILDINGS; STRUCTURAL ANALYSIS; STRUCTURAL DESIGN; STRUCTURAL MATERIALS; STRUCTURES (ENGINEERING).

Environmental engineering. In this branch of the profession, civil engineers plan, design, construct, operate, and supervise systems to protect human health and the ecological balances necessary for environmental quality in both natural and human-made environments. These systems include development and treatment of drinking water; collection and treatment of sanitary and industrial wastes to prevent contamination of the land and water; containment of hazardous and toxic materials; safe disposal of garbage, refuse, and other solid wastes; minimization or elimination of air pollution caused by industrial manufacturing or combustion processes; and design for containment of radioactive discharges. The environmental engineer is involved, either personally or through a team effort, to reduce, mitigate, or eliminate the hazards and risks associated with air, food, and water contaminants, radiation, toxic chemicals, solid wastes, disease vectors, safety hazards, and habitat alterations to preserve or conserve ecological biomes. *See* AIR POLLUTION, ENVIRONMENTAL ENGINEERING; HAZARDOUS WASTE; INDUSTRIAL WASTE WATER; LAND RECLAMATION; SEWAGE TREATMENT; WATER POLLUTION; WETLANDS.

Water resources engineering. Civil engineers who specialize in this area deal with all aspects of the physical control of water. They plan, evaluate, design, construct, supervise, and operate systems to control floods; to supply water for cities; to develop irrigation; to manage and control river navigation, locks, and banks; to prevent beach erosion; and to maintain waterfront facilities. They are also involved in the planning and design of harbors, docks, wharfs, port facilities, canals, and offshore platforms and systems. They are involved with other civil engineers in planning and designing flood control dikes, dams, and hydroelectric power impoundments. *See* CANAL; COASTAL ENGINEERING; DAM; HARBORS AND PORTS; RESERVOIR; REVETMENT; RIVER ENGINEERING; WATER SUPPLY.

Waste management and risk assessment. Civil engineers involved in this area must function as a part of a team. The improper disposal of hazardous or toxic wastes, as well as the indiscriminate dumping of wastes in landfills, has created a situation that impacts on the land and subsurface water supplies. A subset of environmental engineering has evolved that is specifically concerned with the management of these sites. At the same time it is imperative that the available time, money, and personnel be utilized to treat these existing sites in a systematic and cost-effective manner. One method of establishing the hierarchy for treating the existing sites is to perform a risk assessment and establish which areas pose the greatest threat to people and natural resources. The civil engineers in this area of work must develop treatability procedures and estimate costs needed to reduce the risk. The data must then be presented to the public to explain the trade-offs of potential risk and the costs necessary to reduce them, since the locally affected community must be willing to expend time, effort, and money to clean up and manage the site. *See* RISK ANALYSIS.

Transportation engineering. Civil engineers working in this specialty plan, design, construct, and maintain facilities to safely and efficiently move people and goods. Accomplishing this task involves modal system planning for pedestrians, bikeways, streets, roads, highways, mass transit, railroads, airports, ports, and harbors. The ancillary structures to the vehicles and the travel way, which includes parking areas and terminals as the transfer facilities between the various modes of traffic, must be considered. Transportation engineers must apply technological acumen and consider the economic, social, and political factors that impact on each system. It is essential that transportation planning be done in conjunction with community and urban planners. The goal is an acceptable means of enhancing the movement of goods and people from residence to place of employment or entertainment, to shopping areas, and to health care facilities while always permitting quick response of emergency vehicles. The prosperity and quality of life of a community are intimately tied up with the transportation system. *See* AIRPORT; HIGHWAY ENGINEERING; RAILROAD ENGINEERING; TRANSPORTATION ENGINEERING.

Pipeline engineering. Civil engineers in this highly specialized task of transporting liquids, gases, or slurries plan, design, maintain, and operate the pipelines in which these various types of noncombustible to highly combustible materials are moved from one location to another. The engineers determine pipeline design, location, and the environmental and economic impacts on the region that the line traverses. They select the material for constructing the line based on the qualities of durability and safety. Further, they specify installation techniques, methods of testing, and controls for maintaining proper pressure and rate of flow of the material within the line. When a hazardous or toxic material is to be carried, safety is a major concern. *See* ENGINEERING; PIPELINE.

Kenneth Lazuruk; Gerald Palevsky

Bibliography. American Society of Civil Engineers, *The Civil Engineering Technologist*, 1993; American Society of Civil Engineers, *Our Past, The Present, Your Future . . . in Civil Engineering*, 1993; N. S. Grigg, Infrastructure and economic development: Civil engineering perspective, *J. Prof. Iss. Eng. Educ. Prac.*, 119:51–61, January 1993; W. J. Hall et al., *Civil Engineering in the 21st Century: A Collection of Papers*, 1987; W. J. Hall et al., *Civil Engineering in the 21st Century: A Vision and a Challenge for the Profession*, 1988; F. S. Merritt, J. T. Ricketts, and M. K. Loftin, *Merritt's Civil Engineering Handbook*, 4th ed., 1995.

Cladding

An old jewelry art, now employed on an industrial scale to add the desirable surface properties of an expensive metal to a low-cost or strong base metal. In the process a clad metal sheet is made by bonding or welding a thick facing to a slab

Fig. 1. Rolls of copper clad with copper-nickel facing for minting composite coins.

of base metal; the composite plate is then rolled to the desired thickness. The relative thickness of the layers does not change during rolling. Cladding thickness is usually specified as a percentage of the total thickness, commonly 10%.

Uses. Gold-filled jewelry has long been made by this process; the surface is gold, the base metal bronze or brass with the cladding thickness usually 5%. The process is used to add corrosion resistance to steel and to add electrical or thermal conductivity, or good bearing properties, to strong metals. One of the first industrial applications, about 1930, was the use of a nickel-clad steel plate for

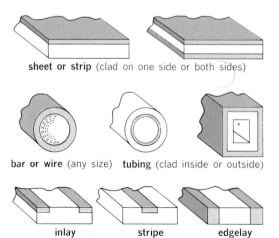

sheet or strip (clad on one side or both sides)

bar or wire (any size)   **tubing** (clad inside or outside)

inlay   stripe   edgelay

Fig. 2. Types of cladding.

a railroad tank car to transport caustic soda; by 1947 stainless-clad steels were being used for food and pharmaceutical equipment. Corrosion-resistant pure aluminum is clad to a strong duralumin base, and many other combinations of metals are widely used in cladding; a development includes a technique for cladding titanium to steel for jet-engine parts.

Today's coinage uses clad metals as a replacement for rare silver. Since 1965 dimes and quarters have been minted from composite sheet consisting of a copper core with copper-nickel facing. The proportion of core and facing used duplicates the weight and electrical conductivity of silver so the composite coins are acceptable in vending machines (**Fig. 1**).

A three-metal composite sole plate for domestic steam irons provides a thin layer of stainless steel on the outside to resist wear and corrosion. A thick core of aluminum contributes thermal conductivity and reduces weight, and a thin zinc layer on the inside aids in bonding the sole plate to the body of the iron during casting.

Cladding supplies a combination of desired properties not found in any one metal. A base metal can be selected for cost or structural properties, and another metal added for surface protection or some special property such as electrical conductivity. Thickness of the cladding can be made much heavier and more durable than obtainable by electroplating.

Combinations. The following clad materials are in common use.

Stainless steel on steel. Provides corrosion resistance and attractive surface at low cost for food display cases, chemical processing equipment, sterilizers, and decorative trim.

Stainless steel on copper. Combines surface protection and high thermal conductivity for pots and pans, and for heat exchangers for chemical processes.

Copper on aluminum. Reduces cost of electrical conductors and saves copper on appliance wiring.

Copper on steel. Adds electrical conductivity and corrosion resistance needed in immersion heaters and electrical switch parts; facilitates soldering.

Nickel or monel on steel. Provides resistance to corrosion and erosion for furnace parts, blowers, chemical equipment, toys, brush ferrules, and many mechanical parts in industrial and business machines; more durable than electroplating.

Titanium on steel. Supplies high-temperature corrosion resistance. Bonding requires a thin sheet of vanadium between titanium and steel.

Bronze on copper. Usually clad on both sides, for current-carrying springs and switch blades; combines good electrical conductivity and good spring properties.

Silver on copper. Provides oxidation resistance to surface of conductors, for high-frequency electrical coils, conductors, and braiding.

Silver on bronze or nickel. Adds current-carrying capacity to low-conductivity spring material; cladding sometimes is in form of stripes or inlays with silver areas serving as built-in electrical contacts.

Gold on copper. Supplies chemical resistance to a low-cost base metal for chemical processing equipment.

Gold on nickel or brass. Adds chemical resistance to a stronger base metal than copper; also used for jewelry, wristbands, and watchcases.

Types. Cladding can be added to both sides of a sheet or strip of base metal. Tubing can be supplied with a clad surface on inside or outside; round and rectangular wire can be clad similarly (**Fig. 2**).

For some forms of electrical contact, the composite materials are bonded side by side, or silver is inset as a stripe on one side or along the edges. This construction can place solid silver just where it is needed to form an electrical contact with no waste of costly metal.

Another related form of cladding is found in thermostatic bimetals in which equal thicknesses of low- and high-expansion metals are bonded together. With a change in temperature, differing expansion rates of the two metals cause the composite material to bend and thus operate valves in automobile cooling systems, or electrical contacts in room thermostats.

Clad wires with properly chosen proportions of materials of different thermal-expansion rates can match the thermal expansion of types of glass used for vacuum-tight seals for conductors in lamp bulbs and hermetically sealed enclosures.

In making parts from clad metal, the composite material can be bent, drawn, spun, or otherwise formed just the same as the base metal without breaking the bond. The maximum service temperature is limited by the melting point of the material at the juncture of the two metals; annealing temperatures during manufacturing are similarly limited.

Cut edges of clad sheets expose the base metal and thus may require special protection. Welding of thick clad sheets sometimes offers special problems in maintaining the integrity of the protective surface, but joining methods are generally the same as for the base metal. *See* ELECTROPLATING OF METALS; METAL COATINGS.   Robert W. Carson

Cladoselachii

An order of extinct elasmobranch fishes including the oldest and most primitive of sharks. Best known is *Cladoselache* (see **illus**.) of the Late Devonian, of which complete specimens, including even muscle and other soft tissues, have been obtained from shales in the region of Cleveland, Ohio. Primitive features are broad-based paired fins, amphistylic jaw support, and absence of claspers. The teeth, termed *Cladodus* when found separately, and the *Ctenacanthus* spines borne by

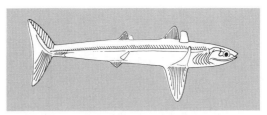

Cladoselache, a Late Devonian sharklike fish. The original specimens range from about 1 1/2 to 4 ft (0.4 to 1.2 m) in length.

some cladoselachians are found in Carboniferous and Permian as well as Devonian deposits, but whether they pertain to true cladoselachians or to hybodont sharks descended from them is generally doubtful. *See* ELASMOBRANCHII.   Alfred S. Romer

Clamping circuit

An electronic circuit that effectively functions as a switch to connect a signal point to a fixed-reference voltage or current level, either at a specific time interval or at some prescribed amplitude level of the signal itself. The circuit is also called simply a clamp. Clamps have many applications, serving as clippers, limiters, transmission gates, and so on. They are frequently used to reset the starting level of periodic waveforms, such as sweep generators, and to establish a direct-current (dc) level in a signal which may have lost its dc component because of capacitance coupling. They are also used in many frequency and voltage comparison circuits and in control circuits. *See* CLIPPING CIRCUIT; GATE CIRCUIT; LIMITER CIRCUIT.

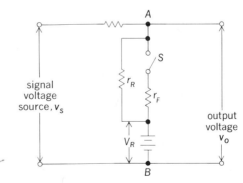

Fig. 1. Elements of a clamping circuit.

The basic elements of a clamping circuit are shown in **Fig. 1**. The clamp between terminals A and B is shown as a switch S in series with reference voltage V_R, having a large resistance r_R when the switch is open and a small resistance r_F when the switch is closed.

Voltage-amplitude-controlled clamp. In **Fig. 2**a the diode functions as a clamp whenever the potential at point A starts to rise above $V_R + V_D$, where V_D is the small forward voltage of the diode

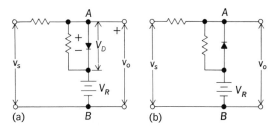

Fig. 2. Single diode clamp circuits. (*a*) Positive-polarity clamp. (*b*) Negative-polarity clamp.

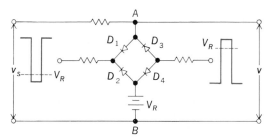

Fig. 3. Four-diode bidirectional keyed clamp. *D* = diode.

(approximately 0.7 V for silicon); then the diode is in its forward-biased condition and acts as a very low resistance. Such a clamp is referred to as a voltage-amplitude-controlled, or continuous, clamp. The circuit of Fig. 2*b* is similar, except that the polarity is reversed. These clamps function only when a fixed polarity of signal with respect to V_R appears at point A, and are therefore referred to as unidirectional clamps.

Keyed, or synchronous, clamp. If a clamp functions at specific time intervals controllable from separate voltage or current sources rather than from the

signal itself, it is a keyed, or synchronous, clamp, and the sources, usually pulses, used to actuate the clamping action are called keying, or clamping, pulses. Such a keyed clamp may be unidirectional but more often it is a bidirectional clamp, defined as a clamp that functions at the prescribed time irrespective of the polarity of the signal source at the time the keying pulses are applied.

A bidirectional clamp using four diodes with two opposite-polarity keying pulses is shown in **Fig. 3**. The peak of the negative pulse is established at a level negative with respect to V_R, causing D_2 to conduct heavily when the pulse is applied, while that of the positive-going pulse is above V_R, causing D_4 to be forward-biased and to conduct heavily. If, at the same time, point A is above V_R, D_1 conducts and point A is clamped to V_R, while if it is below V_R, D_3 conducts and point A is clamped to V_R. When point A is exactly at V_R, all diodes are forward-biased and conducting. Between clamping pulse intervals, all diodes are reverse-biased, and the clamp is open. Because of the balanced nature of the circuit, the effect of the offset voltage of the diodes v_o is eliminated. A unidirectional keyed clamp results if the left or right pair of diodes, together with its keying pulses, is eliminated.

In form, the bidirectional keyed clamp is the essential element of the diode transmission gate and the sample-and-hold circuit, and the voltage-controlled diode clamp is the main element of the diode limiter.

DC restorer. A dc restorer is a clamp circuit used to establish a dc reference level in a signal without modifying to any important degree the waveform of the signal itself. For this function to be performed, the signal must have a self-contained reference

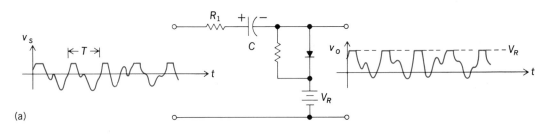

(a)

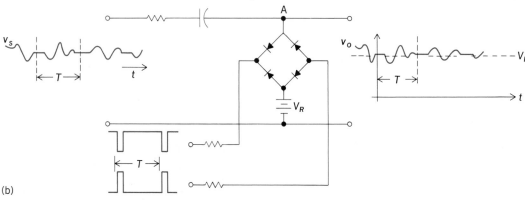

(b)

Fig. 4. DC restorers. (*a*) Diode clamp. (*b*) Keyed clamp.

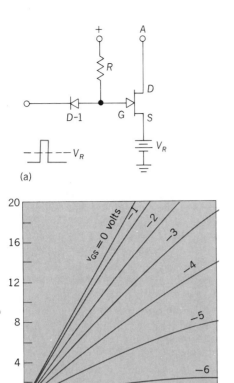

(a)

(b)

Fig. 5. Example of bidirectional clamp which uses complementary field-effect transistors. (a) Circuit. (b) The low-voltage characteristics of a low-resistance field-effect transistor of the n-channel type.

level which repeats at periodic intervals. A typical example of such a waveform is that constituting the video signal of the television system. *See* TELEVISION.

An example of a simple waveform, assumed to be periodic at intervals of T, applied to a single-diode voltage-controlled clamp is shown in **Fig. 4***a*. Restoration of the peak of the waveform to the level of V_R depends upon current flowing through the capacitance when the input level is above V_R and the diode is forward-biased. The capacitance charges in the direction shown during such successive peaks, and the peak level is finally established at V_R. The circuit does not operate if the peak of the waveform at point A is not above the level of V_R initially. The reverse time constant $\{R_1 + [R_2 r_R/(R_2 + r_R)]\}C$ be long compared to the period T, while the forward time constant $(R_1 + r_F)C$ must be very short, with $(R_1 + r_F)$ as small as possible. A bidirectional keyed clamp is required to function as a dc restorer on the waveform shown in Fig. 4*b*. A bidirectional keyed clamp thus establishes the recurrent reference level regardless of the signal polarity between pulses.

Triode clamp. A three-terminal, high-impedance device such as a field-effect transistor (FET) may be used as a keyed clamp to eliminate the need for balanced keying pulses. One common form of such a clamp is shown in **Fig. 5***a* using an *n*-channel

junction FET having the low-voltage characteristics shown in Fig. 5*b*.

When no keying pulse is applied, diode *D*-1 conducts and the gate of the FET is held sufficiently negative with respect to the source that its drain current is cut off; hence, the drain-source terminals represent essentially an open circuit. When the keying pulse is applied, *D*-1 cuts off and sufficient gate current flows through R to cause the drain-source path through the FET to be a very low resistance, thus essentially short-circuiting point A to V_R. The junction FET is a symmetrical device with the source and drain interchangeable; therefore the clamp will function whether A is positive or negative with respect to V_R before the clamp pulse is applied. *See* TRANSISTOR.   Glenn M. Glasford

Bibliography. C. H. Chen (ed.), *Digital Waveform Processing and Recognition*, 2d ed., 1995; G. Glasford, *Analog Electronic Circuits*, 1986; G. Glasford, *Digital Electronic Circuits*, 1988; A. S. Sedra and K. C. Smith, *Microelectronic Circuits*, 3d ed., 1992.

Clarification

The removal of small amounts of fine, particulate solids from liquids. The purpose is almost invariably to improve the quality of the liquid, and the removed solids often are discarded. The particles removed by a clarifier may be as large as 100 micrometers or as small as 2 micrometers. Clarification is used in the manufacture of pharmaceuticals, beverages, rayon, nylon, and other fiber and film polymers; in the reconditioning of electroplating solu-

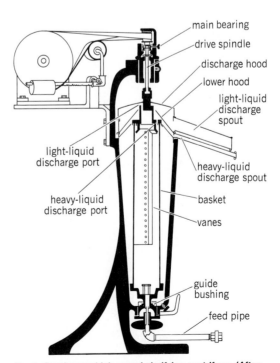

Fig. 1. Continuous high-speed clarifying centrifuge. (*After W. L. Bader and J. T. Banchero, Introduction to Chemical Engineering, McGraw-Hill, 1955*)

tions; in the recovery of dry-cleaning solvent; and for the purification of drinking water and waste-water. The filters in the feed line and lubricating oil system of an internal combustion engine are clarifiers.

The methods of clarification include gravity sedimentation, centrifugal sedimentation, filtration, and magnetic separation. Clarification differs from other applications of these mechanical separation techniques by the low solid content of the suspension to be clarified (usually less than 0.2%) and the substantial completion of the particle removal.

Gravity sedimentation is employed, usually in continuous settling tanks of simple construction, to concentrate the solid fraction and to clarify the liquid fraction of suspensions amenable to separation by this method. Gravity clarifiers differ from thickeners only in the concentration of solids in the feed and in the demand that the overflow be practically particle free. *See* SEDIMENTATION (INDUSTRY); THICKENING.

When the settling rate is too slow for gravity sedimentation to be feasible, centrifugal force up to approximately 100,000 times the force of gravity may be employed to clarify a suspension. In a separator called a centrifuge the suspension is passed through a rapidly rotating tube or basket (**Fig. 1**). The relatively dense solids are forced to the walls of the rotor, and the clarified liquid overflows a dam in the end of the centrifuge. *See* CENTRIFUGATION; ULTRACENTRIFUGE.

Clarifying filters comprise a versatile class of mechanical separators that are effective over the entire range of particle sizes encountered in clarification (from 0.1 mm down to molecules with a molecular weight on the order of 1000), regardless of relative densities and in spite of high viscosities. Sand or coal filters are used extensively for potable and industrial water clarification. Precoat filters are used for water and suspensions carrying slimy, amorphous impurities. Disk and plate filters (**Fig. 2**) service a wide variety of clarifying demands, removing particles over a range of 0.1 to 5 μm. Cartridge filters are in-line units with cleanable or replaceable elements that can remove particles in the range of 0.5 to 50 μm. Ultrafilters (also called microfilters and hyperfilters) contain fibrous sheets or porous membranes with carefully sized pores. These can remove particles as small as 0.002 μm. *See* FILTRATION; STERILIZATION; ULTRAFILTRATION.

Magnetic separators are effective for the removal of ferrous particles. *See* MAGNETIC SEPARATION METHODS.

Clarification processes often depend on flocculating agents for their success. These are additives that cause the suspended solids to agglomerate into flocs that settle more rapidly or are more readily filtered than their smaller components. **Shelby A. Miller**

Bibliography. C. O. Bennett and J. E. Myers, *Momentum, Heat and Mass Transfer*, 3d ed., 1993; R. H. Perry and D. Green (eds.), *Perry's Chemical Engineer's Handbook*, 6th ed., 1984; W. L. McCabe, J. C. Smith, and P. Harriot, *Unit Operations of Chemical Engineering*, 5th ed., 1993.

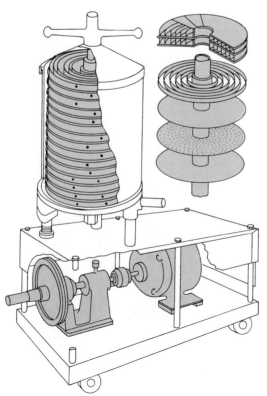

Fig. 2. Disk-and-plate clarifying filter. (*After R. H. Perry and D. Green, eds., Perry's Chemical Engineers' Handbook, 6th ed., McGraw-Hill, 1984*)

Classical field theory

The mathematical discipline that studies the behavior of distributions of matter and energy when their discrete nature can be ignored; also known as continuum physics or continuum mechanics. The discrete nature of matter refers to its molecular nature, and that of energy to the quantum nature of force fields and of the mechanical vibrations that exist in any sample of matter. The theory is normally valid when the sample is of laboratory size or larger, and when the number of quanta present is also very large. *See* PHONON; PHOTON; QUANTUM MECHANICS.

Classical field theories can be formulated by the molecular approach, which seeks to derive the macroscopic (bulk) properties by taking local averages of microscopic quantities, or by the phenomenological approach, which ignores the microscopic nature of the sample and uses properties directly measurable with laboratory equipment. This article follows the phenomenological course, although the microscopic treatment sometimes yields profounder insights. The problems considered below illustrate a selection of classical field theories without long mathematical discussions. Partial differential equations are used because the neglect of microscopic structure allows quantities like density and pressure to be expressed by continuously varying numbers.

Bending of a beam. A first example, leading to an ordinary differential equation, is the bending of a solid beam. To calculate the bending, isolate a segment of length dx (see **illus.**), and take account of the conditions that produce a mechanical equilibrium. The forces exerted up and down on the beam must balance, as well as the moments or torques tending to turn it. These conditions, combined with some geometry, lead to an equation from which the curvature of the beam can be calculated.

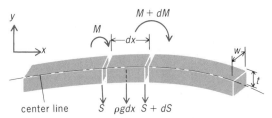

Portion of a rectangular solid beam, showing quantities used in calculating the bending of the beam.

The quantity $M(x)$ is defined to be the moment or torque exerted by the part of the beam to the right of point x on the part to the left, and similarly $S(x)$ is the shear force exerted from right to left. If $\rho(x)$ is the beam's linear density, it follows from definitions that S and M change as in Eqs. (1) and (2), where g is the acceleration of gravity. To find

$$dS = -\rho g dx \qquad \frac{dS}{dx} = -\rho g \qquad (1)$$

$$dM = S dx \qquad \frac{dM}{dx} = S \qquad (2)$$

the bending, the beam is assumed to consist of parallel fibers; those above the center line are in tension and those below in compression. It is easy to see that at any point x, M is as given in Eq. (3), where R is the beam's radius of curvature, E is

$$M = \frac{E}{R} I \qquad I = \int y^2 dA \qquad (3)$$

Young's modulus of elasticity for the material, dA is an element of area, and I is the moment of inertia of the cross section. If the beam is nearly horizontal, Eq. (4) relates R to the second derivative of y. For

$$\frac{d^2 y}{dx^2} = \frac{1}{R} \qquad (4)$$

the rectangular cross section shown, I is evaluated around the center line and is given by Eq. (5).

$$I = {}^{1}/_{12} \omega t^3 \qquad (5)$$

See MOMENT OF INERTIA; SHEAR; STATICS.

Combining Eqs. (1)–(4) gives Eq. (6) for the

$$\frac{d^4 y}{dx^4} = -\frac{\rho g}{E I} \qquad (6)$$

shape of the beam. It can be integrated, requiring four boundary conditions, to find the curve under

different conditions of loading; for example, if the beam is of length l and is supported horizontally at one end, the sag Y at the other end, given in Eq. (7), varies as l^4/t^3. Historically, the analysis in

$$Y = -\frac{\rho g}{E I} \frac{l^4}{8 t^3} \qquad (7)$$

terms of the moment of inertia I was begun by G. W. Leibniz in 1694, and results equivalent to the foregoing were obtained by C. Coulomb in 1773. The representation of the beam as a sheaf of fibers of infinitesimal thickness leads to the field equation (6), which is extremely simple in form and involves only the bulk properties of the material. *See* LOADS, TRANSVERSE.

Diffusion. In a vessel of fluid (liquid or gas) a small quantity of a different fluid is released and spreads slowly (in the absence of convection) through the vessel. To calculate the rate at which it spreads, let $n(x)$ be the number of molecules of the new fluid per unit volume, and $\mathbf{j}(x)$ be the flow (molecules per unit area per unit time) produced by any nonuniform distribution of n. This current has the direction in which n changes most rapidly, and the simplest assumption is that it is given approximately by Eq. (8), proposed by A. Fick in

$$\mathbf{j}(x) = -D \nabla n(x) \qquad (8)$$

1855, where D is the diffusivity, a coefficient which for simplicity is here assumed independent of x. If the molecules of the new fluid are neither created nor destroyed, $\mathbf{j}$ satisfies the conservation equation (9), and Fick's law becomes the field equation (10)

$$\nabla \cdot \mathbf{j} + \frac{\partial n}{\partial t} = 0 \qquad (9)$$

$$\frac{\partial n}{\partial t} = D \nabla^2 n \qquad (10)$$

giving the variation of n with position and time. *See* CALCULUS OF VECTORS.

If the initial distribution of n is $n_0(x)$ and the region is so large that its boundaries are far away, this equation is easy to solve. Let $\tilde{n}(k)$ be the Fourier transform of $n_0(x)$, so that Eq. (9) is solved by Eq. (11) where the integration is over all values of k; this

$$n(x, t) = \int \tilde{n}(k) \exp(i\mathbf{k} \cdot \mathbf{x} - k^2 D t) d^3 k \quad (11)$$

expression satisfies Eq. (9) whatever the function $\tilde{n}$ may be. If $t = 0$, the value of the integral is n_0, and if $t > 0$, Eq. (11) shows what happens as time goes on. For any $\tilde{n}$, as t becomes large, the distribution spreads and becomes uniform. (If $t < 0$, the integral shows correctly only in exceptional cases what happened earlier.)

The diffusion equation contains a single parameter, the diffusivity D. It can be determined from experiment and also in other ways, for diffusion can be analyzed as a random molecular process. The drag β that a diffusing particle experiences as it moves through the fluid is defined by Eq. (12),

$$F = -\beta v \tag{12}$$

where v is the particle velocity. Then the diffusivity can be calculated as in Eq. (13), where k is Boltz-

$$D = \frac{kT}{\beta} \tag{13}$$

mann's constant and T is the absolute temperature. Evidently the warmer the environment and the less the resistance, the faster the diffusion. Equation (13) was first given by A. Einstein in 1905. *See* DIFFUSION.

Temperature, T, is another field quantity in classical physics, and the argument used for diffusion makes it plausible that heat diffusing through a solid follows the same law. Equation (14) duplicates the diffusion equation and has

$$\frac{\partial T}{\partial t} = \alpha^2 \nabla^2 T \tag{14}$$

the same solutions. The coefficient α is calculated in the theory of solids by methods that differ according to the physical properties of the solid. *See* CONDUCTION (HEAT).

Hydrodynamics. The calculation of the flow of a fluid presents great mathematical difficulties; in fact, the essentially chaotic nature of turbulence often makes it impossible to represent flow in terms of a continuously varying field. The following discussion is therefore restricted to nonturbulent motion. *See* TURBULENT FLOW.

The basic equation of fluid flow was given by L. Euler in 1755. In modern notation, it can be derived as follows: A small volume of the fluid moves with velocity **v**. The force exerted on it by the pressure p of the surrounding fluid is

$$-\oint p d\mathbf{A}$$

where dA is an outward-directed element of area, and this is transformed by a vector identity into

$$-\int \nabla p \, dV$$

That is to say, the force on the element of fluid is $-\nabla p$ per unit volume. If p is the density of the fluid, Newton's law gives the equation of motion, Eq. (15), where the gravitational force on the element

$$\frac{\rho d\mathbf{v}}{dt} = -\nabla p + p\mathbf{g} \tag{15}$$

is included. It is more convenient mathematically to study changes in velocity at a given point in space than to follow an element of fluid as it moves. It is easy to show that Eq. (16) is valid, which gives Euler's equation (17).

$$\frac{d\mathbf{v}}{dt} = \frac{\partial \mathbf{v}}{\partial t} + (\mathbf{v} \cdot \nabla)\mathbf{v} \tag{16}$$

$$\frac{\partial \mathbf{v}}{\partial t} = -(\mathbf{v} \cdot \nabla)\mathbf{v} - \frac{1}{\rho \nabla} p + \mathbf{g} \tag{17}$$

Solutions of Euler's equation are as varied as the conditions under which fluids flow; to see what it does and does not contain let us look at a very simple case, the propagation of sound through a fluid. Let $p = p_0 + p'$ and $\rho = \rho_0 + \rho'$, where p_0 and ρ_0 are the ambient values, and assume that the amplitude is so small that second-order terms in p, ρ, and **v** can be neglected, as well as **g**. In addition, **v** can be represented as $\nabla \phi$, where ϕ is called the velocity potential. Then Euler's equation gives Eqs. (18). Equations (19)

$$\nabla \left(\frac{\partial \phi}{\partial t} + \frac{p'}{\rho_0} \right) = 0 \tag{18}$$
$$\rho_0 \frac{\partial \phi}{\partial t} + p' = 0$$

$$\rho_0 \frac{\partial^2 \phi}{\partial t^2} + \frac{\partial p'}{\partial t} = 0 \tag{19}$$
$$\rho_0 \nabla^2 \phi + \frac{\partial \rho'}{\partial t} = 0$$

compare the time derivative of Eqs. (18) with the conservation equation (9) expressed in terms of ϕ. An equation for ϕ is possible if p' can be expressed in terms of ρ'. To do this requires a hypothesis that is not included in either Euler's equation or the conservation law, namely, an equation of state for the fluid. If $(\partial p/\partial \rho)_0$ is denoted by c^2, comparison of Eqs. (18) and (19) gives Eq. (20), which is

$$\nabla^2 \phi - \frac{1}{c^2} \frac{\partial^2 \phi}{\partial t^2} = 0 \tag{20}$$

d'Alembert's equation for a wave traveling with velocity c.

The foregoing example shows how the equation of motion for the acoustical field arises from three hypotheses: Newton's second law, the conservation of the fluid, and its equation of state. Whereas the previous examples of field equations could have been derived by reasoning from the microscopic properties of matter, Eq. (20) would have been very difficult to derive in this way. *See* FLUID-FLOW PRINCIPLES; HYDRODYNAMICS; SOUND; WAVE EQUATION; WAVE MOTION.

Electromagnetic field. The theory of the electromagnetic field, which J. C. Maxwell developed during the 1860s, was intended as a phenomenological theory of the ether analogous to the theories outlined above. There is of course no ether, and therefore no phenomenological properties, but this was not known at the time, and to discover the properties of ether was generally considered the most important task of physics. Maxwell based his work on a microscopic model of the ether involving tiny whirling vortices, but when it was finished the model's phenomenological constants had almost entirely disappeared from the equations; only one remained. The electric current could be calculated from the theory in two ways, and the constant, now called c, is determined by the ratio of the two resulting numbers. During the succeeding 40 years

Maxwell's equations were regarded as a clever device that gave correct answers while avoiding the important questions.

In terms of the electrodynamic potentials, using the modern International System of Units (SI), Maxwell's equations can be written in the form of Eqs. (21); here $\mathbf{A}(x)$ and $\phi(x)$ are vector and

$$\nabla^2 \mathbf{A} - \epsilon\mu \frac{\partial^2 \mathbf{A}}{\partial t^2} = -\mu \mathbf{j}$$
$$\nabla^2 \varphi - \epsilon\mu \frac{\partial^2 \varphi}{\partial t^2} = -\frac{1}{\epsilon}\rho \qquad (21)$$

scalar potentials, respectively, and $\mathbf{j}(x)$ and $\rho(x)$ are the current and charge densities, respectively, that produce them. They occur on the right sides multiplied by μ and $1/\epsilon$, respectively, and since $\mathbf{j}$ is simply the result of moving ρ, the units are effectively different in the two equations. Their ratio is $c^2 = 1/(\epsilon\mu)$; in Maxwell's day its value was approximately known. In empty space, $\mathbf{j} = \rho = 0$, and the equations are d'Alembert's for waves traveling at a speed c. The correspondence between this c and the measured speed of light was convincing evidence that light is an electromagnetic phenomenon.

Maxwell's equations are still phenomenological in content, but they are now considered to describe the electromagnetic fields and potentials and not properties of the ether. They are fully relativistic and survive in form, though not exactly in content, in the modern theory of quantum electrodynamics. *See* ELECTROMAGNETIC RADIATION; MAXWELL'S EQUATIONS; QUANTUM ELECTRODYNAMICS; RELATIVISTIC ELECTRODYNAMICS.

Gravitational field. During the nineteenth century, tentative efforts were made to create a theory of gravity along the same lines as Maxwell's theory of electromagnetism. The results, however, were trivial, and the development of special relativity showed that they could not possibly be correct. Only with a reformulation of the entire problem in terms of curved space-time was Einstein able in 1915 to create a classical theory of the gravitational field. Like the classical theories mentioned above, it gives its results in terms of phenomenological constants: the speed of light and the force of attraction between two unit masses one unit distance apart. It is very successful in explaining not only the phenomena of gravitation known in 1915 but also various new facts that have been learned since. Unlike Maxwell's equations, however, Einstein's do not give reasonable results in the context of a quantum theory of gravity. They must represent some sort of approximation, but so far no successful quantum version has been developed with which they can be compared. *See* GRAVITATION; QUANTUM GRAVITATION; RELATIVITY.

Mathematical development. The foregoing examples illustrate some of the most important classical field theories. Solving the equations has produced a vast body of mathematics. Computers have aided in special calculations, but many mathematicians are working on the analytical theory of partial differential equations, and new results continue to be produced. *See* DIFFERENTIAL EQUATION.   **David Park**

  Bibliography. G. Carrier, *Partial Differential Equations*, 1988; G. Joos and I. M. Freeman, *Theoretical Physics*, reprint 1987; L. Landau, *Course of Theoretical Physics: The Classical Theory of Fields*, 4th ed., 1980.

Classical mechanics

The science dealing with the description of the positions of objects in space under the action of forces as a function of time. Some of the laws of mechanics were recognized at least as early as the time of Archimedes (287?–212 B.C.). In 1638, Galileo stated some of the fundamental concepts of mechanics, and in 1687, Isaac Newton published his *Principia*, which presents the basic laws of motion, the law of gravitation, the theory of tides, and the theory of the solar system. This monumental work and the writings of J. d'Alembert, J. L. Lagrange, P. S. Laplace, and others in the eighteenth century are recognized as classic works in the field of mechanics. Jointly they serve as the base of the broad field of study known as classical mechanics, or Newtonian mechanics. This field does not encompass the more recent developments in mechanics, such as statistical, relativistic, or quantum mechanics.

The general principles of classical mechanics are stated in mathematical form. With mathematical logic, one can deduce countless possible motions of bodies and then compare the predictions with experimental observations. Classical mechanics illustrates the essential nature of a physical theory, and it is usually an important ingredient in or a starting point for the various branches of modern physics. Its study offers one the opportunity to become acquainted with mathematical techniques and procedures which are useful in other fields.

In the broad sense, classical mechanics includes the study of motions of gases, liquids, and solids, but more commonly it is taken to refer only to solids. In the restricted reference to solids, classical mechanics is subdivided into statics, kinematics, and dynamics. Statics considers the action of forces that produce equilibrium or rest; kinematics deals with the description of motion without concern for the causes of motion; and dynamics involves the study of the motions of bodies under the actions of forces upon them. An important example of a force whose effect on bodies is often studied is the Earth's gravitational force. For some of the more important areas of classical mechanics *see* BALLISTICS; CELESTIAL MECHANICS; COLLISION (PHYSICS); DYNAMICS; ENERGY; FORCE; GRAVITATION; KINEMATICS; LAGRANGE'S EQUATIONS; MASS; MOTION; PRECESSION; RIGID-BODY DYNAMICS; STATICS; WORK.

  Newell S. Gingrich

Classification, biological

A human construct for grouping organisms into hierarchical categories. The most inclusive categories of any classification scheme are called kingdoms, which are delimited so that organisms within a single kingdom are more related to each other than to organisms grouped in the other kingdoms. Classification (grouping) is a part of biological systematics or taxonomy, science that involves naming and sorting a organisms into groups. Historically, organisms have been arranged into kingdoms based on practical characteristics, such as motility, medicinal properties, and economic value for food or fiber. From the time of Aristotle until the nineteenth century, simple plant-animal classification systems grouped organisms in two kingdoms based more on superficial resemblance than on evolutionary relationships. If an organism was colored green or grew from roots, it was classified as a plant; if it moved, it was an animal. Fungi had roots and so were placed with plants even though fungi were not green. Single-celled organisms that were motile and ingested food were placed with animals. However, since C. Darwin presented powerful evidence for evolution by natural selection, the most natural classification is held to be that which reflects evolutionary relationships.

Beyond two kingdoms. Beginning in the seventeenth century, the light microscope revealed an array of minute organisms (microbes) for which the plant-animal grouping was inadequate. Some microbes had both plant- and animallike characteristics; euglena are green but also motile, for example. In 1861, John Hogg introduced a third kingdom to accommodate those organisms which do not fit neatly into either the plant or animal kingdom. This was called Kingdom Protoctista.

Later in the nineteenth century the German biologist Ernst Haeckel proposed a three-kingdom system that evolved through several versions. Haeckel's third kingdom, Protista, set more primitive organisms apart from plants and animals. Organisms in the plant kingdom obtained nutrients by photosynthesis and had walls of cellulose around their cells but lacked motility. Organisms placed in the animal kingdom were motile, ingested nutrients, and lacked walls around their cells. Organisms that did not fit in either the plant or animal kingdom were placed in Kingdom Protista. A major group within this kingdom was the Monera, which comprised the bacteria and blue-green algae, and was distinguished by lack of a cell nucleus. In the three-kingdom scheme, poison ivy, maple trees, rice, pines and mosses are members of the plant kingdom because they are green, are rooted, and have cell walls. Llamas, eagles, honeybees, and lobsters are members of the animal kingdom because they move, ingest food, and lack cell walls. Bacteria, yeasts, and other microbes are placed in Kingdom Protista. *See* PROTISTA.

Scientific advances. In the nineteenth and twenti-

eth centuries, advances such as electron and light microscopy, biochemistry, genetics, ethology, and greater knowledge of the fossil record provided new evidence upon which to construct more sophisticated classification schemes. Proposals were made to assign organisms into four, five, and even thirteen kingdoms. Earlier two-kingdom and three-kingdom systems were devised without awareness of the profound distinction between prokaryotes and eukaryotes, which Edouard Chatton (1937) recognized as a fundamental evolutionary discontinuity. Prokaryotic cells do not have either a nucleus or any other internal membrane-bounded structures, the so-called organelles. By contrast, eukaryotic cells have both a nucleus and organelles (**Fig. 1**). The deoxyribonucleic acid (DNA) of eukaryotes is combined with protein to form chromosomes. All bacteria are prokaryotes. Plants, fungi, animals, and protoctists are eukaryotes. *See* EUKARYOTAE; PROKARYOTAE.

Four kingdoms. The four-kingdom system of Herbert F. Copeland (1956) divided Haeckel's protistas into the two kingdoms Monera and Protoctista based on prokaryotic and eukaryotic cell structure, respectively. Thus, Copeland's kingdoms were

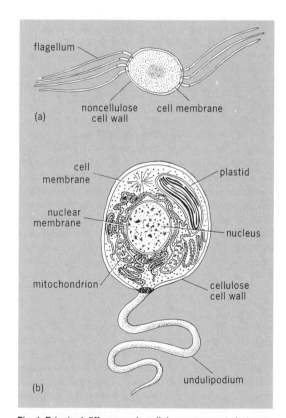

Fig. 1. Principal differences in cellular components between prokaryotes and eukaryotes. (*a*) Prokaryotic (bacterial) cells bear flagella but lack a nucleus and organelles. (*b*) Eukaryotic (protozoan, animal, fungal, plant) cells usually have undulipodia, a membrane-bounded nucleus, and organelles such as plastids and mitochondria. Mitochondria, plastids, and probably even undulipodia are descended from prokaryotes engulfed in another cell which set up an endosymbiotic partnership. (*After L. Margulis and D. Sagan, The Microcosmos Coloring Book, Harcourt Brace Jovanovich, 1988*)

(1) Monera (prokaryotes, including bacteria and blue-green algae); (2) Protoctista (all multicellular and unicellular eukaryotes except plants and animals, including red, brown, and green algae, protozoa, slime molds, and all fungi); (3) Plantae (multicellular, green eukaryotes with walled cells); and (4) Animalia (multicellular nongreen eukaryotes that lack walled cells).

Five kingdoms. Robert H. Whittaker (1959) proposed the first five-kingdom classification. He removed the fungi from both the Plantae and Protoctista and established fungi as a separate kingdom. Fungi differ fundamentally in morphology and reproduction from plants and also absorb nutrients rather than photosynthesize. Whittaker's five kingdoms were Monera (prokaryotic nutrient absorbers and producers—cyanobacteria and other phototrophs); Protista (all unicellular eukaryotes, except yeast and other fungi); Plantae (multicellular eukaryotic photosynthetic nutrient producers); Fungi (multicellular eukaryotic nutrient absorbers); and Animalia (multicellular eukaryotes that ingest nutrients). In the modification of Whittaker's scheme, L. Margulis and K. Schwartz (1988) include genetic and developmental features as well as nutritional modes and structure.

Beyond five kingdoms. One criticism of Whittaker's five-kingdom scheme is that the kingdom Protista encompassed a much greater diversity of organisms than did the other four kingdoms. G. F. Leedale responded to this problem (1974), suggesting an expanded classification system of thirteen kingdoms that did not force diverse organisms into a particular kingdom for the sake of classificational tidiness. In fact, some of Leedale's kingdoms contain just a single phylum. Multikingdom classification systems aim at a more natural classification, that is, one that reflects evolutionary relationships and focuses on the unique characteristics of phyla that may be the sole surviving representatives of much more extensive taxonomic groups that are now largely extinct.

Current perspectives. By the late 1980s, biologists widely accepted a classification system that classifies all organisms composed of membrane-bound cells into five kingdoms based on key characteristics of function and structure (**Fig. 2**). These are Prokaryotae (Monera; with two subkingdoms), Protoctista (or Protozoa in some classification schemes), Fungi, Animalia, and Plantae.

Important characteristics for classification. One characteristic used in classifying organisms into kingdoms is the mode by which the organism obtains nutrients, that is, by heterotrophy (absorption or ingestion) or autotrophy (chemotrophy or phototrophy). All autotrophs synthesize their nutrients by using carbon dioxide as the source of carbon. Chemoautotrophs obtain energy from hydrogen sulfide, ammonia, methane, or other inorganic compounds. Chemoautotrophy is used only by prokaryotes. Photoautotrophic organisms gain energy from light. They use solar energy captured

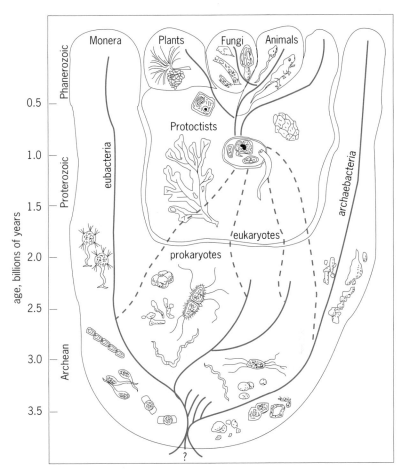

Fig. 2. Five-kingdom classification scheme, showing evolutionary relationships between the kingdoms. Approximate dates of the appearance of organisms are based on direct fossil evidence. (*After L. Margulis, R. Guerrero, and P. Bunyard, Gaian: The thesis, the mechanisms, and the implications, Florin Publishers, London, 1995*)

via a complex of pigment and protein molecules including chlorophyll. All green plants, and those protoctists and monerans capable of photosynthesis, are the photoautotrophs. Ingesters (which take in particulate food) and decomposers (which absorb their food) include animals, fungi, and all the colorless protoctists. All organisms not capable of photosynthesis obtain their nutrients directly (by eating them) or indirectly (by eating the organisms that eat them) from photosynthetic organisms. The only exception is chemoautotrophs and their symbiotic partners such as the giant red tube worms found in deep ocean trenches. Hot water spewing forth from submarine vents is rich in sulfides, methane, and other compounds from which, using oxygen, chemautotrophic bacteria obtain energy. The tube worms harbor the bacteria in special organs called trophosomes. *See* HYDROTHERMAL VENT.

Another key characteristic used in classification is the presence or absence of an embryo, an early developmental stage of multicellular organisms that is produced by sexual union of sperm with an egg. Prokaryotes, fungi, and protoctists lack embryos. Animals and plants have embryos. *See* EMBRYOLOGY.

Two organs of motility, flagella and undulipodia,

also help delineate kingdoms. Prokaryotes move by means of a flagellum that rotates at its point of attachment to the cell and lacks microtubules. On the other hand, a eukaryote's motile organ is an undulipodium, which does not rotate but "waves" or undulates. The undulipodium shaft is made up of a (9 + 2) array of microtubules, which mainly consist of tubulin protein. Although single microtubules are in all eukaryotes, their (9 + 2) array is found only in the animals, plants, and protoctists, and not in monerans and fungi. *See* CILIA AND FLAGELLA.

Multicellularity itself is not a key characteristic used to distinguish kingdoms, because each of the five kingdoms includes many organisms that are multicellular. Many bacteria are multicellular; their unit of behavior and growth consists of a group of many prokaryotic cells. However, multicellular bacteria lack the complex junctions between cells that characterize multicellular animals. Kingdom Protoctista includes certain multicellular organisms (kelp is an example) as well as tiny one-celled organisms. Most fungi, plants, and animals are multicellular.

Kingdom Prokaryotae (Monera). This kingdom is composed of small prokaryotic organisms that may be a single cell, a colony of cells, or long mycelial filaments of cells, or have stalklike appendages. The genes are borne on a circular thread of DNA rather than chromosomes as in eukaryotes. Those monerans that move either are propelled by flagella as described above or glide by some currently unknown mechanism.

Moneran cell walls are composed of peptidoglycans, that is, nitrogenous sugar bound to short chains of amino acids, but never of cellulose or chitin. Their metabolism includes a range of responses to oxygen, from aerobic to anaerobic modes. Bacteria are virtuosos of biochemical diversity. Blue-green bacteria photosynthesize in sunlit ponds; spirochete bacteria live inside termite intestines and obtain nutrients by fermenting sugars derived from wood eaten by the host insect; and purple-sulfur bacteria, which deposit sulfur rather than emit oxygen, live in salt marshes, and use hydrogen sulfide rather than water as the source of hydrogen atoms for their photosynthesis. *See* BACTERIA.

Monerans are always capable of reproducing asexually, that is, forming offspring with only a single parent. Moneran cells may divide by fission (division into equal cells) or by budding (division into unequal cells). Bacterial sex is not a reproductive act but the donation of genes from one bacterium to another.

Archaebacteria. Bacteria that produce methane from hydrogen and carbon dioxide, that is, methanogenic bacteria, differ strikingly from all other living organisms. The ribonucleic acid (RNA) molecules of the protein synthesis apparatus of methanogens differs so much from that of other living organisms that these bacteria appear only distantly related to typical bacteria (eubacteria) and to eukaryotic cells. Because protein synthesis is fundamental to the existence or growth of all life-forms, and the sequences of components in the molecules (small RNA) making up the protein synthetic machinery are highly conserved, it is assumed that the evolutionary history of organisms can be inferred from these molecular sequences. The five-kingdom classification has been revised so that archaebacteria, meaning "old bacteria," are set apart from typical bacteria (eubacteria) as two separate subkingdoms of Prokaryotae. *See* ARCHAEBACTERIA.

Kingdom Protoctista. This kingdom consists of both single-celled and multicellular eukaryotes, including nucleated algae, seaweeds, protozoa, water molds (undulipodiated fungi), and slime molds. (In some classifications, slime molds are placed in the kingdom Fungi.) Giant kelp (brown algae) measure up to 330 ft (100 m) long and are the largest of the 250,000 protocitist species. Protocists lack embryos, an exclusive feature of animals and plants. They all have eukaryotic chromosomes, but some lack protein associated with the chromosomes. Mitotic cell division may be absent, standard, or idiosyncratic. An immense variety of sexual reproduction strategies have evolved in protoctists.

Nutritional modes vary: heterotrophs absorb or ingest. The nutritional mode of protoctists often depends on presence of light and food; the same organism may photosynthesize in light when food is scarce but feed in the dark when food is present. Autotrophs are always photoautotrophs, that is, they harness light energy via photosynthesis, and are not chemoautotrophs. Amebas, radiolarians, ciliates, and foraminiferans are heterotrophic microbes that ingest or absorb their food. Red, brown, and green algae are photoautotrophs. Slime molds and chytrids are mycelial and multicellular heterotrophic protoctists that form undulipodiated cells. *See* ALGAE; PHOTOSYNTHESIS; PROTOZOA.

Kingdom Fungi. All fungi are eukaryotes that form spores; they all lack embryos and undulipodia in all life cycle stages. Bread mold, puffballs, yeasts, and truffles are examples. Mushrooms and shelf fungi are the largest, but some fungi (mostly yeasts) are single celled. A multicellular fungal body often branches into filaments (hyphae) composed of cells that are incompletely separated from each other. Chitin makes up fungal cell walls, rather than the cellulose that composes plant cell walls. Fungi are heterotrophs: These absorptive decomposers excrete digestive enzymes which break down food outside the body, then absorb through their walls the small molecules that result from the breakdown. Fungi always lack chlorophyll and never make their own food by photosynthesis. Of the 250,000 known species of fungi, most are aerobic and terrestrial, although a few inhabit fresh or salt water. Some fungi live on other fungi, others live on plants or on animals. Athlete's foot and moniliasis are animal diseases caused by fungi.

Fungi differ from plants and animals not only in nutritional mode but also in pattern of development. Fungi reproduce by spores, which are tiny propagules that resist heat and drying. Some fungi are sexual, but all fungi lack embryos.

A lichen is a symbiotic partnership between a fungus and an oxygen-producing chlorophyll-containing autotrophic partner, usually a blue-green bacterium (moneran) or a green alga (protoctist). The fungus generally receives photosynthate—carbohydrate and nitrogenous compounds produced by photosynthesis—from the photosynthetic symbiont. The fungus protects its partner from ultraviolet and visible light damage and from moisture loss. Lichens are classified with fungi rather than with monerans or protoctists, by analogy with the concept that photosynthetic protoctists ought to be classified according to their life cycles and the structure of the nonplastid part of their cells. *See* FUNGI; LICHENES.

Kingdom Plantae. Organisms in this kingdom are eukaryotes with cellulosic cell walls. Plants develop from an embryo stage and are multicellular. Mosses, liverworts, club mosses, horsetails, ferns, and the seed plants (cycads, ginkgos, conifers, and flowering plants) are typical of the 400,000 plant species.

Plant embryos are the products of sexual reproduction, the fertilization of a larger female cell by a smaller male cell. However, many plants can bypass a sexual stage and reproduce asexually. Propagation of strawberry plants by sending out runners or of apple trees by cuttings are examples of asexual reproduction.

Nearly all plants photosynthesize by using chlorophyll and other pigments contained in plastids, organelles within most plant cells. Most plants benefit from symbiotic fungi that transport soil nutrients into their roots. Some plants are parasitic; dodder, for example, lacks photosynthetic pigments and depends on fusions with green plants for growth. Plant are aerobes and also convert solar energy into food. *See* PLANT KINGDOM.

Kingdom Animalia. Size alone is not an adequate criterion for placing an organism in the animal or any other kingdom. The smallest animals are smaller than many multicellular monerans and protoctists. Members of Kingdom Animalia are eukaryotes that usually develop from a blastula embryo, which is a liquid-filled hollow sphere of cells. (Plants also develop from an embryo but never form blastulas.) Ecologically, animals are consumers whereas plants are producers. Animals are heterotrophic, although tiny ones may be absorptive; most have mouths and ingest food. Behavior such as response to light, gravity, and certain chemicals occurs in members of all five kingdoms, but animals, particularly mammals and birds, have complex behaviors.

Vertebrates (animals with backbones) and invertebrates (animals supported by means other than backbones) are members of the animal kingdom.

Most animals (excluding sponges) have tissues and have a special sort of multicellularity; animal cells interconnect via complex cell junctions (gap junctions, desmosomes). Many employ undulipodia as organs of sensory perception, motility, and feeding. Cells lining the human nose have sensory undulipodia. Unlike plant and fungal cells, animal cells do not have a wall; rather, the cell is bounded only by a membrane.

Future perspectives. Modern classification is based on evidence derived from biochemistry and molecular biology, genetics (including chromosomal cytology), and detailed morphology of extant organisms and their fossils. Because information is drawn from such diverse sources, and because more than 30 million—possibly 100 million—species are probably alive today, informed judgments must be made to integrate the information into classification schemes. Estimates of the number of species on Earth range from 10 to 30 million, of which only about 1.7 million have been formally classified in the taxonomic literature of biology to date. Thus, it must be anticipated that biological classification schemes will continue to be revised as new evidence is weighed. For example, archaebacteria differ fundamentally from all more complex cells. It is possible that eukaryotes evolved from an ancient common ancestor. This ancestor, called the urkaryote, engulfed and then became host for bacterial symbionts. From such cells, eukaryotic cells containing mitochondria and plastids descended. *See* ANIMAL SYSTEMATICS; BACTERIAL TAXONOMY; PLANT TAXONOMY; VIRUS CLASSIFICATION.

Karlene V. Schwartz

Bibliography. H. F. Copeland, *The Classification of Lower Organisms*, 1956; H. F. Copeland, The kingdom of organisms, *Quart. Rev. Biol.*, 13:383–420, 1938; G. F. Leedale, How many are the kingdoms of organisms?, *Taxon*, 23:261–270, 1974; L. Margulis, Biodiversity: Molecular biological domains, symbiosis and kingdom origins, *BioSystems*, 27:39–51, 1992; L. Margulis and K. V. Schwartz, *Five Kingdoms: An Illustrated Guide to the Phyla of Life on Earth*, 2d ed., 1988; R. H. Whittaker, New concepts of kingdoms of organisms, *Science*, 163:150–160, 1969; R. H. Whittaker, On the broad classification of organisms, *Quart. Rev. Biol.*, 34:210–226, 1959; R. H. Whittaker and L. Margulis, Protist classification and the kingdoms of organisms, *BioSystems*, 10:3–18, 1978.

Clathrate compounds

Well-defined addition compounds formed by inclusion of molecules in cavities existing in crystal lattices or present in large molecules. The constituents are bound in definite ratios, but these are not necessarily integral. The components are not held together by primary valence forces, but are the consequence of a tight fit preventing the smaller partner, the guest, from escaping from the cavity of the host.

Inclusion compounds

Host substance	Shape of cavity	Guest substance examples
Lattice inclusion compounds		
Urea	Channel	Derivatives of straight-chain hydrocarbons
Thiourea	Channel	Branched-chain hydrocarbons
Deoxycholic acid	Channel	Paraffins, fatty acids, aromatic hydrocarbons
Dinitrodiphenyl	Channel	Diphenyl derivatives
Hydroquinone, phenol	Cage	Hydrogen chloride, sulfur dioxide, acetylene
Gas hydrates	Cage	Halogens, inert gases, hydrocarbons
Trithymotide	Cage	Benzene, chloroform
Nickel dicyanobenzene	Cage	Benzene, chloroform
Cyclodextrins	Channel or cage	Hydrocarbons, iodine, aromats
Molecular inclusion compounds		
Cyclodextrins	Cage	Hydrocarbons, iodine, aromats
Bis (N,N'-alkyl benzidines)	Cage	Benzene, dioxane
Crown ether compounds	Cage	Inorganic cations
Ionophore antibiotics	Cage	Inorganic cations
Inclusion compounds of macromolecular substances		
Clay minerals	Channel or sheet	Hydrophilic substances
Graphite	Sheet	Oxygen, bisulfate ion, alkali metals
Cellulose, starch	Channel	Hydrocarbons, dyes, iodine

Thus, the geometry of the molecules is the decisive factor.

Clathrate compounds are of theoretical interest because they represent a special type of bonding. In practice they can be used for separation of hydrocarbons, for stablization of drugs or pesticides, and as enzyme models.

Inclusion compounds can be subdivided into (1) lattice inclusion compounds (inclusion within a lattice which, as such, is built up from smaller single molecules); (2) molecular inclusion compounds (inclusion into larger ring molecules with holes); and (3) inclusion compounds of macromolecules (see **table**).

The best-known lattice inclusion compounds are the urea and thiourea channel inclusion compounds, which are formed by mixing hydrocarbons, carboxylic acids, or long-chain fatty alcohols with solutions of urea. Urea, in this case the host lattice, crystallizes in the presence of the other molecules in a particular crystal structure which contains long channels or tubes 0.4–0.5 nanometer

in diameter. The hydrocarbons are accommodated in these channels, but only unbranched molecules find enough space to fit into the urea channel. The molar ratio of urea to hydrocarbon is simply determined by the lengths of the hydrocarbon molecule, not by any functional group. The longer the paraffin chain, the more urea is necessary in order to envelop the paraffin (**Fig. 1**). Thiourea has a similar lattice structure, but a larger diameter of the channel. Therefore, only branched paraffins are included; the unbranched ones are too small, and cannot be held tightly (principle of closest packing), as shown in **Fig. 2**.

Other representatives of lattice inclusion compounds are the choleic acids, which are adducts of deoxycholic acid with fatty acids, and other lipoic substances. Most likely, these compounds play a role in the digestion process by emulsifying or dissolving fat and fat-soluble substances. Hydroquinone and phenol, cyclic anhydrides of phenol carboxylic acids, such as *o*-trithymotide and tetrasalicylide, as well as some other aromatic compounds, form an open crystal lattice which can accommodate smaller gas and solvent molecules (clathrates in the stricter sense of the word). The gas hydrates, which have been known since about 1810 (for example, $Cl_2 \cdot 6H_2O$), are inclusion compounds of gases in a somewhat expanded ice lattice. The gas or solvent molecules are inserted into definite places within the ice lattice and are surrounded by water molecules on all sides.

The cyclodextrins (cycloamyloses) are cyclic degradation products of starch which contain six, seven, or eight glucose residues (α, β, γ-cyclodextrin) and have the shape of large-ring molecules, the cavity diameters being 0.6–1.0 nm. Here, a great number of inclusion compounds in solution or in the crystalline state can be prepared with various kinds of molecules, the only requirement being the fit of the guest within the cyclodextrin cavity. α-Cyclodextrin forms

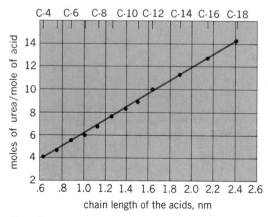

Fig. 1. Dependence of the urea/fatty acid composition of the inclusion compound on the chain length of the fatty acid. (After W. Schlenk, Jr., Organic occlusion compounds, Fortschr. Chem. Forschg., 2:92–145, 1951)

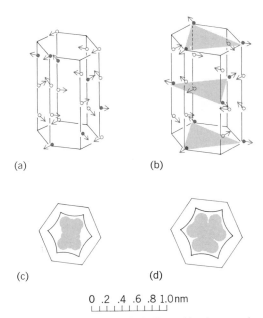

(a)   (b)

(c)   (d)

0 .2 .4 .6 .8 1.0 nm

Fig. 2. Schematic drawing of the lattices of (*a*, *c*) urea and (*b*, *d*) thiourea; *c* and *d* show accommodation of unbranched and branched paraffin chains, respectively.

blue iodine inclusion compounds in which the host molecules are stacked to form a cylinder reminiscent of the starch helix (**Fig. 3**). Polyiodide, located within the thus formed channellike cavity, consists of I_2, I_3^-, or I_5^- units in α-cyclodextrin, as well as in starch. A similar structure is likely for the blue iodine polyvinyl alcohol inclusion compound which exhibits a strong dichroism when stretched. This is used technically to prepare (light) polarizing sheets and spectacles.

Crown ether compounds are cyclic or polycyclic polyether compounds (for example, with the repeating unit ...O—CH_2—CH_2...) capable of including another atom in the center of the ring.

In this way, sodium or potassium compounds can be solubilized in organic solvents. Similarly, a series of ionophore antibiotics can complex inorganic cations. *See* MACROCYCLIC COMPOUND.

Some clay minerals are made up of distinct silicate layers. Between these layers some free space may exist in the shape of channels. Smaller hydrocarbon molecules can be accommodated reversibly within these channels. This phenomenon is used in some technical separation processes for separating hydrocarbons (molecular sieves). Furthermore, ion-exchange processes used for water deionization are based on similar minerals. *See* CLAY MINERALS; MOLECULAR SIEVE; ZEOLITE.

Enzymes are believed to accommodate their substrates in active sites, pockets, or clefts prior to the chemical reaction which then changes the chemical structures of the substrates. These binding processes are identical to those of low-molecular-weight inclusion compounds. On the other hand, some low-molecular-weight inclusion compounds can mimic enzyme action, such as ester hydrolysis, but only with modest efficiency.

Friedrich Cramer; Wolfram Saenger; D. Gauss

Bibliography. J. L. Atwood, *Inclusion Phenomena and Molecular Recognition*, 1990; P. Bernier (ed.), *Chemical Physics of Intercalation II*, 1993; D. J. Cram and J. M. Cram, Design of complexes between synthetic hosts and organic guests, *Accounts Chem. Res.*, 11:8–14, 1978; S. A. Jenekhe (ed.), *Macromolecular Host-Guest Complexes*, 1992.

Clathrinida

An order of sponges in the subclass Calcinea of the class Calcarea. These sponges have an asconoid structure and lack a true dermal membrane or cortex. The spongocoel is lined with choanocytes. This order contains the family Clathrinidae; *Clathrina*, *Ascute*, and *Dendya* are examples. *See* CALCAREA; CALCINEA.   Willard D. Hartman

Clavaxinellida

An order of sponges of the class Demospongiae, subclass Tetractinomorpha, with monaxonid megascleres arranged in a radial pattern. Microscleres include asters, sigmas, and small monactinal or diactinal spicules often provided with spines. Spongin is rare.

In the suborder Hadromerina, the megascleres are always monactinal and usually have a terminal knob at one end (**Fig. 1**). Microscleres in the form of streptasters, asters, sigmas, or small spined diactinals may occur. The megascleres tend to be arranged in tracts radiating from the center of the sponge; spongin is usually rare. In the suborder Axinellina, monactinal or diactinal megascleres or both occur in plumose tracts (**Fig. 2**). An abundance of spongin is usually present in the form of fibers in

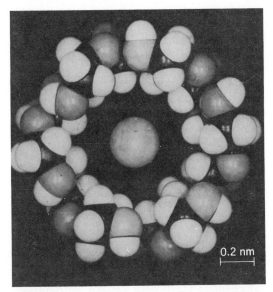

Fig. 3. Molecular model of α-dextrin–iodine compound seen in the direction of the *c* axis, that is, in the direction of the iodine chains, which lie in channels.

0.2 nm

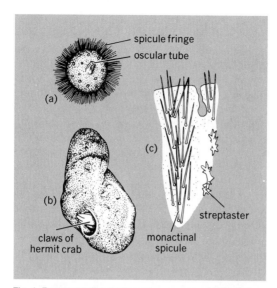

Fig. 1. Representative hadromerine sponges. (*a*) *Radiella sol,* deep-sea species with a peripheral fringe of spicules. (*b*) *Suberites ficus* living on shell occupied by hermit crab. (*c*) Spicule arrangement of *Spirastrella.*

which the megascleres are embedded. Microscleres include raphides, sigmas, and asters. A specialized dense axial skeleton is usually present.

The union of these groups to form the order Clavaxinellida is supported by the similarity of spicule types and their arrangement in radiating or plumose patterns and by the occurrence of oviparity in most of the species in which sexual processes are known. However, biochemical evidence suggests that the Axinellina and Hadromerina should be recognized as independent orders and that the Epipolasina are polyphyletic and should be distributed among several existing orders.

Clavaxinellidan sponges vary greatly in shape, from radially symmetrical species which are spherical to encrusting or massive species and upright branching types. They occur in tidal and shallow waters of all seas and extend to depths

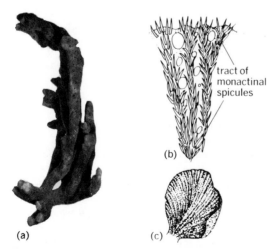

Fig. 2. Representative axinelline sponges. (*a*) *Axinella polycapella.* (*b*) Section through *Axinella* species showing plumose arrangement of spicule tracts. (*c*) Enlarged portion of *b* showing spicule arrangement.

of at least 18,150 ft (5500 m). Sponges comparable to existing clavaxinellidans occur scattered through the fossil record from Cambrian strate upward. *See* DEMOSPONGIAE.   Willard D. Hartman

Clay

A term used to refer to the finest-grain particles in a sediment, soil, or rock. According to the Wentworth scale (see **table**), clay is finer than silt, characterized by a grain size of less than approximately 4 micrometers. However, the term clay can also refer to a rock or a deposit containing a large component of clay-size material. Thus clay can be composed of any inorganic materials, such as clay minerals, allophane, quartz, feldspar, zeolites, and iron hydroxides, that possess a sufficiently fine grain size. Most clays, however, are composed primarily of clay minerals. *See* CLAY MINERALS; FELDSPAR; QUARTZ; ZEOLITE.

Wentworth scale for size classification of sediment particles

Particle	Grain size, mm
Boulder	>256
Cobble	64–256
Pebble	4–64
Granule	2–4
Sand	1/16–2
Silt	1/256–1/16
Clay	<1/256

Although the composition of clays can vary, clays can share several properties that result from their fine particle size. These properties include plasticity when wet, the ability to form colloidal suspensions when dispersed in water, and the tendency to flocculate (clump together) and settle out in saline water. *See* COLLOID.

Origin and occurrence. Clays occur most abundantly in nature in soils, sediments, sedimentary rocks, and hydrothermal deposits.

Clays, together with organic matter, water, and air, are one of the four main components of soil. Clays can form directly in a soil by precipitation from solution (neoformed clays); they can form from the partial alteration of clays already present in the soil (transformed clays); or they can be inherited from the underlying bedrock or from sediments transported into the soil by wind, water, or ice (inherited clays). *See* SOIL.

The type of clays neoformed in a soil depends on the composition of the soil solution, which in turn is a function of climate, drainage, original rock type, vegetation, and time. Generally, neoformed clays that have undergone intense leaching, such as soils formed under wet, tropical climates, are composed of the least soluble elements, such as ferric iron, aluminum, and silicon. These soils contain clays

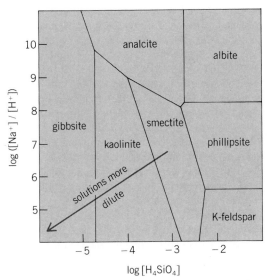

Example of a stability diagram for the system Na₂O-K₂O-Al₂O₃-SiO₂-H₂O drawn for log ([K⁺]/[H⁺]) = 4. The soluble species in brackets are in activity units. (*After J. I. Drever, The Geochemistry of Natural Waters, Prentice-Hall, 1982*)

such as gibbsite, kaolinite, goethite, and amorphous oxides and hydroxides of aluminum and iron. Clays formed in soils that are found in dry climates or in soils that are poorly drained can contain more soluble elements, such as sodium, potassium, calcium, and magnesium, in addition to the least soluble elements. These soils contain clays such as smectite, chlorite, and illite, and generally are more fertile than those formed under intense leaching conditions. The importance of the composition of soil solution to the type of clay neoformed at equilibrium can be shown quantitatively in mineral stability diagrams, such as in the **illustration**. *See* CHLORITE; GOETHITE; ILLITE; KAOLINITE.

Examples of clays formed by the transformation of other clays in a soil include soil chlorite and soil vermiculite, the first formed by the precipitation of aluminum hydroxide in smectite interlayers, and the second formed by the leaching of interlayer potassium from illite. Examples of inherited clays in a soil are illite and chlorite-containing soils formed on shales composed of these minerals. *See* SHALE.

Clays also occur abundantly in sediments and sedimentary rocks. For example, clays are a major component of many marine sediments. These clays generally are inherited from adjacent continents, and are carried to the ocean by rivers and wind, although some clays (such as smectite and glauconite) are neoformed abundantly in the ocean. Clays also are a chief constituent of shale, are found in pore spaces in sandstones, and are found dispersed in limestones, dolomites, and coals. The ashes that remain after coal is burned, for example, are the residue of clays and silts washed into coal swamps and later incorporated into the coal. Hydrothermal clays can form abundantly where rock has been in contact with hot water or steam. Illite and chlorite, for

example, form during the deep burial of sediments, and smectite and chlorite form by the reaction of hot, circulating waters at ocean ridges. Kaolinite can form hydrothermally where hot springs invade volcanic ash, given proper solution chemistries. *See* COAL; DOLOMITE; GLAUCONITE; LIMESTONE; MARINE SEDIMENTS; SANDSTONE; SEDIMENTARY ROCKS.

Properties and uses. Various clays possess special properties which make them important industrially. Bentonite, a smectite formed primarily from the alteration of volcanic ash, swells; is readily dispersible in water; and possesses strong absorptive powers, including a high cation exchange capacity. These properties lead to uses in drilling muds, as catalysts and ion exchangers, as fillers and absorbents in food and cosmetics, and as binders for taxonite and fertilizers. Swelling clays also must be taken into account in building design. In agriculture, swelling clays in a soil may lead to undesirable tilth and water runoff characteristics, and to unexpected reactions with soil additives, such as the catalytic conversion of pesticides into other compounds, or the fixation of ammonia fertilizer. *See* BENTONITE; CATALYSIS; ION EXCHANGE; SOIL CHEMISTRY.

Kaolinite-rich clays are used as paper-coating materials because they are white and show desirable rheological properties; as additives to rubber because they can bind with organic compounds; and as refractory materials due to their high melting point. Other important uses for clays include the manufacture of brick, ceramics, molding sands, decolorizers, detergents and soaps, medicines, adhesives, liners for ponds and landfills, lightweight aggregate, desiccants, molecular sieves, pigments, greases, paints, plasticizing agents, emulsifying, suspending, and stabilizing agents, and many other products. Ore deposits sometimes are composed of clays (for example, lateritic nickel and bauxites), and clay in shale may play an important role in the generation of petroleum. *See* CLAY, COMMERCIAL; REFRACTORY.

Dennis D. Eberl

Bibliography. R. Bennett and M. H. Hulbert, *Clay Microstructure*, 1986; J. I. Drever, *The Geochemistry of Natural Waters*, 1982; R. E. Grim, *Applied Clay Mineralogy*, 1962; R. E. Grim, *Clay Mineralogy*, 2d ed., 1968.

Clay, commercial

Commercial clays, or clays utilized as raw material in manufacturing, are among the most important nonmetallic mineral resources. The value of clays is related to their mineralogical and chemical composition, particularly the clay mineral constituents kaolinite, montmorillonite, illite, chlorite, and attapulgite. The presence of minor amounts of mineral or soluble salt impurities in clays can restrict their use. The more common mineral impurities are quartz, mica, carbonates, iron oxides and sulfides, and feldspar. In addition, many clays contain some organic material. *See* CLAY MINERALS.

Clay is an abundant raw material; however, certain high-grade types of clay deposits are limited in geographic occurrence and extent. Examples are the white kaolin clays found in abundance only in Georgia and South Carolina; the high-quality bentonites found in Wyoming, South Dakota, California, Texas, and Mississippi; and the attapulgite clays found in Georgia and Florida.

Kaolinitic clays. Clays containing a preponderance of the clay mineral kaolinite are known as kaolinitic clays. Several commercial clays are composed predominantly of kaolinite. These are china clays, kaolines, ball clays, fireclays, and flint clays. The terms china clay and kaolin are used interchangeably in industry. *See* KAOLINITE.

China clay. China clays are high-grade white kaolins found in the southeastern United States, England, and many other countries. In Georgia and South Carolina, the largest producing states, the deposits are composed almost wholly of the mineral kaolinite and occur as lenticular-shaped bodies generally 6–25 ft (1.8–7.5 m) in thickness. Many grades of kaolin are used in the manufacture of ceramics (whitewares, refractories, and porcelain), paper, rubber, paint, plastics, insecticides, adhesives, catalysts, and ink. They are also used for many other industrial purposes.

Kaolin has the desirable properties of being white in color, very fine in particle size, nonabrasive (hardness 2–2.5 on Mohs scale), and chemically inert in most uses. The individual kaolin particle is a thin, flat, pseudohexagonal platelet, so tiny that approximately 10,000,000 spread on a postage stamp would form a layer thinner than the thickness of a human hair. This thin, flat particle shape is a distinct advantage in many uses. The grades of kaolin that are commercially available generally are based on particle size and on color, or brightness.

By far the largest consumer of white kaolins is the paper industry, which uses them to make paper products smoother, whiter, and more printable. The kaolin is used both as a filler in the sheet to enhance opacity and receptivity to ink and as a thin coating (about 0.005 in. or 0.013 cm) on the surface of the sheet to make it smoother and whiter for printing. The clay coating makes possible sharp photographic illustrations and brilliant color printing. Other important properties of kaolin for paper manufacture are softness of texture, ease of dispersion in the coating formulation, and ability to produce a high-gloss finish.

Because of the trend toward whiter coatings and lighter-weight paper (to minimize postal charges), the kaolin producers have developed new products. The colorant in kaolin is iron and titanium minerals; through flotation procedures or selective flocculation, a portion of the iron and titanium can be removed, making a significantly whiter product. To aid in the development of lighter-weight coatings, a delaminated kaolin is being produced. The thicker kaolin particles are separated by force to produce thin, white particles which give excellent coated-sheet properties with lighter coat weights.

In ceramics the kaolin clays are used in white-wares, sanitary ware, special refractories, and porcelain insulators. In whitewares and sanitary ware the kaolin provides a white body, gives easy molding properties, and adds strength, dimensional stability, and smooth surfaces to the finished product. Refractoriness, dimensional stability, and chemical inertness make the kaolins uniquely suitable for special refractories. In addition, the excellent dielectric properties of kaolin are very suitable for porcelain electric insulators. *See* CERAMICS; PORCELAIN.

In the manufacture of both natural and synthetic rubber, kaolin clays are used as a functional filler. The kaolin adds strength, abrasion resistance, rigidity, and whiteness. It costs less than most other fillers used in rubber.

In paint and ink kaolins are used as extenders because of their chemical inertness, smooth flow properties, ease of dispersion, nonabrasiveness, relatively low cost, and the high pigment volume concentrations that can be attained.

In plastics kaolin is used to provide smooth surfaces, dimensional stability, and better resistance to chemical attack, and to improve physical and electrical properties, to minimize water absorption, to reduce brittleness, and to lower costs.

In insecticides the inertness, low abrasiveness, and good adsorption and flow properties of kaolin make it an effective carrying agent in dust and spray forms.

A relatively new field is the chemical modification of kaolinite to make it an effective catalyst for use in petroleum refining. The kaolin is treated with sulfuric acid and calcined to produce the catalyst. Also, kaolin, calcined to drive off the structural water, is used as a source of alumina and silica to produce zeolites, which are used as molecular sieves. Molecular sieves are becoming widely used in petroleum refining.

Because the United States has very small reserves of bauxite, kaolin, which contains 38% Al_2O_3, has been studied as a source of alumina. Many patents utilizing either bases or acids to extract the alumina have been issued. Some companies which are basic producers of aluminum metal have acquired large reserves of kaolin, but to date no processing plants have been constructed.

Calcined clay is another commercial product of the kaolins. It is used in paint, ceramics, plastics, paper, and other materials. The calcined kaolins have the advantage of increased whiteness. The kaolinite is changed during the calcination to the minerals mullite and cristobalite. The hardness after calcination is about 6.5 to 7 on Mohs scale, and therefore the calcined kaolin makes an exceptional, very fine polishing agent. This product is used in toothpaste, automobile polishes, and silver and brass polishes. High-temperature calcined kaolins (1803–2703°F or 984–1484°C) are used as grog by the refractory industry.

Ball clay. Ball clays are composed mainly of the mineral kaolinite but usually are much darker in color than kaolin. The term ball clay is used for a fine-grained, very plastic, refractory bond clay. Most ball clays contain minor amounts of organic material and the clay mineral montmorillonite. Usually ball clays are finer grained than china clays. This fineness, together with the montmorillonite and organic material, gives ball clays excellent plasticity and strength. For these reasons and because they fire to a light-cream color, ball clays are commonly used in whitewares and sanitary ware. Commercial deposits of ball clay are located in western Kentucky, western Tennessee, northern Mississippi, and northeastern Texas.

Fireclay. This term is used for clays that will withstand temperatures of 2730°F (1500°C) or higher. Such clays are composed primarily of the mineral kaolinite. The most common fireclays are the underclays, which occur directly under coal seams. Not all under-clays are fireclays because many contain materials that lower the fusion point to below 2730°F (1500°C). Fireclays are generally light to dark gray in color, contain minor amounts of mineral impurities such as illite and quartz, and fire to a cream or buff color. Most fireclays are plastic, but some are nonplastic and very hard; the latter are known as flint clays.

Fireclays are used primarily by the refractories industry. The refractoriness of fireclays is proportional to the amount of alumina present in the clay and is reduced by impurities such as calcium carbonate and iron compounds. The foundry industry uses fireclay to bind sands into shapes in which metals can be cast. From 10 to 15% fireclay is necessary to bind the sand grains together. Fireclay-bonded sands give the metal a smoother surface than when other clays, such as bentonite, are used, but equivalent or higher mold strengths can be attained with approximately one-third as much bentonite. In many cases even though the strength properties of bentonite-bonded sands are higher, fireclays are used if the cost of clay and transportation is lower. Large quantities of fireclay are mined in Pennsylvania, West Virginia, Kentucky, Ohio, and Missouri.

Flint clay. This term is used for a special type of fireclay. Flint clays are composed essentially of kaolinite and are also refractory but are nonplastic and very hard.

Diaspore clay. This clay is composed of the minerals diaspore and kaolinite. Diaspore is a hydrated aluminum oxide with an Al_2O_3 content of 85% and a water content of 15%. This mineral is quite hard (6.5–7 on Mohs scale) and very refractory. Diaspore clay is used almost exclusively by the refractories industry in making refractory brick. However, after calcination, it is sometimes used as an abrasive material. Diaspore clay is produced commercially in Missouri and Pennsylvania. It is found in nature mixed with flint and plastic fireclays. High-grade diaspore clay contains 65–70% Al_2O_3. When its Al_2O_3 content is 50–65%, this material is called burley clay. Because of extensive reserves of diaspore clay, the U.S. Bureau of Mines has worked out a process for the production of metallic aluminum from diaspore clay. Under present economic conditions, however, it can not compete with bauxite in the production of aluminum. *See* BAUXITE.

Mullite. Mullite is a high-temperature conversion product of many aluminum silicate minerals, including kaolinite, pinite, topaz, dumortierite, pyrophyllite, sericite, andalusite, kyanite, and sillimanite. Mullite is used in refractories to produce materials of high strength and great refractoriness. Mullite does not spall, withstands the shock of heating and cooling exceptionally well, and is resistant to slag erosion. It is used in making spark plugs, laboratory crucibles, kiln furniture, saggars, and other special refractories. Mullite crystals occur as long needlelike or lathlike forms. The intermeshing of these crystals produces high-strength bodies. The only natural occurrence of mullite is on the island of Mull in the Western Isles of Scotland, and here it is found in such small quantities that it has no commercial significance.

Bentonites. Those clays that are composed mainly of the clay mineral montmorillonite and are formed by the alteration of volcanic ash are known as bentonites. They are used in many industries; the most important uses are as drilling muds and catalysts in the petroleum industry, as bonding clays in foundries, as bonding agents for taconite pellets, and as adsorbents in many industries. *See* MONTMORILLONITE.

The largest producing areas of bentonite are northeastern Wyoming, western South Dakota, central and eastern Texas, and northeastern Mississippi. The Wyoming and South Dakota bentonites are known as sodium bentonites, because the montmorillonite has a relatively high sodium content. The Texas and Mississippi bentonites are known as calcium bentonites, because the montmorillonite has a relatively high calcium content. Sodium montmorillonite and calcium montmorillonite have significantly different physical properties which regulate their use and acceptance by many industries.

The term bentonite is a rock term, but in industrial usage it has become almost synonymous with swelling clay. Bentonite contains minor amounts of other clay minerals, particularly illite, chlorite, and kaolinite, and up to approximately 30% cristoballite, the high-temperature form of silicon dioxide. The properties of the bentonites are largely dependent on the type and amount of montmorillonite present.

Drilling mud. Drilling mud consists of bentonite, water, a weighting material such as barite, and various electrolytes. This mud is circulated in the hole at all times while the drilling is progressing. The functions of the drilling mud are to remove the drill cuttings from the drill hole, to form a filter cake on the wall of the drill hole to keep the drilling fluid in the hole and prevent water in the rock formations from entering, to cool and lubricate the bit, and to prevent blowouts. Bentonite, especially the sodium variety, imparts high viscosity and shear strength to the mud and also imparts a property called thixotropy. A thixotropic body acts as a fluid when agitated and as a thick gel when standing. Because the properties imparted by the bentonites to the drilling fluid are so important to the success of the oil industry, these clays are an extremely important mineral commodity.

Bonding clay. Bentonites are used in the foundry industry to bind sands into desired shapes in which metals can be cast. Only 3–5% bentonite is needed to bond the sand grains together. Because of their fine particle size and their nature of water adsorption, bentonites give the mold a higher green, dry, and hot strength than does any other type of clay.

Another use of bentonite as a bonding agent is in the taconite industry. Taconite, low-grade iron ore, is crushed into a fine powder and the iron particles are separated from silica and other rock particles magnetically. The fine iron particles are pelletized with the aid of bentonite, of which 12–18 lb (54–72 kg) is used to pelletize a ton of ore.

Other uses. Bentonites are also used as bleaching clays to remove coloring matter from oils, and as clarifying agents for products such as wines and beers. Bentonite is used as an adsorbent for oils, insecticides, alkaloids, vitamins, proteins, and many other materials. Calcium montmorillonites generally have better decolorizing and adsorbent properties than the sodium variety. Bentonite suspensions in water are widely used in industry, in addition to that suspension used as a drilling mud by the petroleum industry. Some applications are as fire retardants, as media for suspending materials for medicinal purposes, and as media for suspending lumps of coal to separate them from heavier impurities. Sodium bentonites are the better suspending agents because of their higher viscosities. Large quantities of sodium bentonite are used to line irrigation ditches and to seal leaks in dams, because it forms an impermeable cake or film by swelling and filling the pores. Sodium montmorillonite swells in water to many times its original size. Other uses are as catalysts, emulsion stabilizers, deinking agents, suspending agents in enamels, plasticizers in ceramics and pastes, and ingredients in cosmetics. *See* BENTONITE.

Attapulgite clays. Attapulgite is a hydrated magnesium aluminum silicate with a needlelike shape. It is commercially produced from a small area in southwestern Georgia and northwestern Florida. The needlelike shape gives attapulgite its unusual properties; each individual needle is exceedingly small, about 1 micrometer in length and approximately 0.01 micrometer across. Attapulgite is used as a suspending agent, and gives high viscosity because of the interaction of the needles. Some com-

mercial uses are as an oil well drilling fluid, in adhesives as a viscosity control, in oil base foundry sand binders, as thickeners in latex paints, in liquid suspension fertilizers, and as a suspending agent and thickener in pharmaceuticals. Other uses are as adsorbent beds for pets, floor adsorbents, carriers for agricultural chemicals, catalyst, flatting agent in paint, and anticaking agent. An unusual use is as a coating on paper used in NCR (no carbon required) multicopy business forms. The attapulgite acts as a catalyst to convert the dye intermediates to the colored dyes when the encapsulated intermediates are released by pressure.

Miscellaneous clays. Most of these clays and shales contain mixtures of differing proportions of illite, chlorite, kaolinite, and montmorillonite, plus a variety of nonclay minerals. By far the largest user of these miscellaneous clays is the structural clay products industry. This industry manufactures brick, drain tile, sewer pipe, conduit tile, glazed tile, terra cotta, and other items.

The clays that can be used for the different structural clay products necessarily have wide variations in properties. For example, a clay that can be used for conduit tile must be very plastic and have high green and dry strength and uniform shrinkage; for drain tile or common brick, these properties do not have to be controlled so closely. In general, however, the properties of clays that are important in the manufacture of structural clay products are plasticity, green strength, dry strength, drying and firing shrinkage, vitrification range, and fired color. These properties are largely dependent on the composition of the clay and the particle size of the constituents.

Mining and processing. Almost all the commercial clays are mined by open-pit methods, with overburden-to-clay ratios ranging as high as 10 to 1. The overburden is removed by motorized scrapers, bulldozers, shovels, or draglines. The clay is won with draglines, shovels, or bucket loaders, and transported to the processing plants by truck, rail, aerial tramways, or belt conveyors, or as slurry in pipelines.

The clay is processed dry or in some cases, wet. The dry process usually consists of crushing, drying, and pulverizing. The clay is crushed to egg or fist size or smaller and dried usually in rotary driers. After drying, it is pulverized to a specified mesh size, such as 90% retained on a 200-mesh screen with the largest particle passing a 30-mesh screen. In other cases, the material may have to be pulverized to 99.9% finer than 325 mesh. The material is shipped in bulk or in bags. All clays are produced by this method.

Where more exacting products must be produced, as in the case of kaolins for the paper industry and bentonites for certain pharmaceutical uses, wet processing is used. In the case of kaolins, the material is slurried in water at the mine face at about 35–40% solids with the aid of a dispersant. The slurry is pumped to a degritting station, where the very coarse impurities are removed, and then through pipelines to the processing plant. The general processing steps are particle size fractionation; that is, separation into coarse and fine particles, leaching out iron impurities, dewatering by filtration, and drying and pulverization. Fractionation is done by centrifuging or by gravity settling; dewatering by centrifuges, filter presses, or rotary vacuum drum filters; and drying by rotary, apron, drum, or spray driers. Most of the kaolin is shipped dry bulk by rail, but about 20% is bagged and shipped by rail or truck. Some kaolin is shipped in slurry form in tank cars at 70% solids.

Properties. Most clays become plastic when mixed with varying proportions of water. Plasticity of a materal can be defined as the ability of the material to undergo permanent deformation in any direction without rupture under a stress beyond that of elastic yielding. Clays range from those which are very plastic, called fat clay, to those which are barely plastic, called lean clay. The type of clay mineral, particle size and shape, organic matter, soluble salts, adsorbed ions, and the amount and type of nonclay minerals all affect the plastic properties of a clay.

Strength. Green strength and dry strength properties are very important because most structural clay products are handled at least once and must be strong enough to maintain shape. Green strength is the strength of the clay material in the wet, plastic state. Dry strength is the strength of the clay after it has been dried. Plasticity and green strength are closely related and are affected largely by the same variables. Dry strength is dependent on the proportion of fine particles present, the degree of hydration of the colloidal fraction, the method of forming the ware, and the extent of drying. The presence of a small amount of montmorillonite, which is of very fine particle size and highly hydrated, generally increases the dry strength.

Shrinkage. Both drying and firing shrinkages are important properties of clay used for structural clay products. Shrinkage is the loss in volume of a clay when it dries or when it is fired. Drying shrinkage is dependent on the water content, the character of the clay minerals, and the particle size of the constituents. Drying shrinkage is high in most very plastic clays and tends to produce cracking and warping. It is low in sandy clays or clays of low plasticity and tends to produce a weak, porous body. Montmorillonite in relatively large amounts (10–25%) causes excessive shrinkage, cracking, and slow drying. Firing shrinkage depends on the volatile materials present, the types of crystalline phase changes that take place during firing, and the dehydration characteristics of the clay minerals.

Vitrification range. The temperature range of vitrification, or glass formation, is a very important property in structural products. Vitrification is due to a process of gradual fusion in which some of the more easily melted constituents begin to produce an increasing amount of liquid which makes up the glassy bonding material in the final fired product. Some clays have a short vitrification range so that the temperature of the kiln must be very closely regulated. Illites, montmorillonites, and chlorites all have lower vitrification temperatures than kaolinite. Some nonclay minerals such as calcite and feldspar lower the vitrification temperature of the body by acting as fluxes. The degree of vitrification developed depends on the duration of firing as well as on the temperature attained. Usually the degree of vitrification is regulated by the amount of shrinkage and porosity that is needed in the final product. There is, however, a practical limit as to the amount of shrinkage and reduction in porosity than can be attained at a given temperature.

Color. Color is important in most structural clay products, particularly the maintenance of uniform color. The color of a product is influenced by the state of oxidation of iron, the state of division of the iron minerals, the firing temperature and degree of vitrification, the proportion of alumina, lime, and magnesia in the clay material, and the composition of the fire gases during the burning operation. The best white-burning clays contain less than 1% Fe_2O_3. Buff-burning clays contain 1–5% Fe_2O_3 and red-burning clays contain 5% or more Fe_2O_3. Other constituents also affect the color, but finely divided iron-bearing minerals are considered to be the principal colorants.

Uses. All types of clay and shale are used in the structural products industry but, in general, the clays that are used are considered to be relatively low grade. Clays that are used for conduit tile, glazed tile, and sewer pipe are underclays and shales that contain large proportions of kaolinite and illite. The semirefractory plastic clays found directly beneath the coal seams make the best raw material for the above mentioned uses. Brick and drain tile can be made from a wide variety of clays depending on their location and the quality of product desired. Clays used for brick and drain tile must be plastic enough to be shaped. In addition, color and vitrification range are very important. For common brick, drain tile, and terra-cotta, shales and surface clays are usually suitable, but for high-quality face bricks, shales and underclays are used. Geographic location is a prime factor in the type of clay used for structural clay products because, in general, these products cannot be shipped great distances without excessive transportation costs. Many raw materials of questionable quality are utilized in certain areas because no better raw material is available nearby. *See* BRICK; TILE.

Lightweight aggregate is produced from many types of clays and shales. The raw material is heated very rapidly in rotary kilns or sintering machines to the temperature range between incipient and complete fusion. After fusion has developed a molten jacket around the particle, certain constituents, if present, release gas to produce bloating and vesiculation. The molten jacket must be viscous enough to retain the expanding gas. Shales containing illites, montmorillonites, or chlorites, plus nonclay materials such as carbonates, sulfates, and organic matter, are the best raw material for lightweight aggregate. Adequate testing of a clay or shale is the only way to determine whether or not it will make a suitable lightweight aggregate. Mineral and chemical composition, particle size distribution, fusion temperature, and final strength of the aggregate particles are all important factors which control the production of lightweight aggregate from a clay or shale. The presence of a high percentage of kaolinite causes the material to be too refractory and the presence of excess fluxing agents causes the material to melt much too rapidly to control the vesiculation necessary to make the material lightweight.

The cement industry uses large quantities of impure clays and shales. Clays are used to provide alumina and silica to the charge for the cement kiln. Generally, a suitable clay can be found in the area in which the cement is being manufactured. *See* CEMENT; POTTERY; REFRACTORY.   Haydn H. Murray

Bibliography. W. E. Brownell, *Structural Clay Products*, 1976; H. Van Olphen, *An Introduction to Clay Colloid Chemistry*, 2d ed., 1977, reprint 1991; B. Velde, *Introduction to Clay Minerals: Chemistry, Origins, Uses, and Environmental Significance*, 1992; W. E. Worrall, *Clays and Ceramic Raw Materials*, 1986.

Clay minerals

Fine-grained, hydrous, layer silicates that belong to the larger class of sheet silicates known as phyllosilicates. Their structure is composed of two basic units. (1) The tetrahedral sheet is composed of silicon-oxygen tetrahedra linked to neighboring tetrahedra by sharing three corners to form a hexagonal network (**Fig. 1**). The fourth corner of each tetrahedron (the apical oxygen) points into and forms a part of the adjacent octahedral sheet. (2) The octahedral sheet is usually composed of aluminum or magnesium in sixfold coordination with oxygen from the tetrahedral sheet and with hydroxyl. Individual octahedra are linked laterally by sharing edges (**Fig. 2**). Tetrahedral and octahedral sheets taken together form a layer, and individual layers may be joined to each other in a clay crystallite by interlayer cations, by van der Waals and electrostatic forces, or by hydrogen bonding.

Because clay minerals are nearly ubiquitous in the Earth's upper crust, they offer a unique record of earth processes and earth history. Thus, the study of clay minerals forms an important branch of the science of geology. It has been suggested also that clay minerals may have been a necessary precursor for the origin of life by providing protection for primitive organic molecules, and by catalyzing their transformation into more complex substances. *See* PREBIOTIC ORGANIC SYNTHESIS.

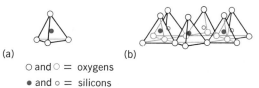

○ and ○ = oxygens

● and ○ = silicons

Fig. 1. Diagrammatic sketch showing (a) single silica tetrahedron and (b) sheet structure of silica tetrahedrons arranged in a hexagonal network. (*After R. E. Grim, Clay Mineralogy, McGraw-Hill, 1953*)

Classification. Clay minerals are classified by their arrangement of tetrahedral and octahedral sheets. Thus, 1:1 clay minerals contain one tetrahedral and one octahedral sheet per clay layer; 2:1 clay minerals contain two tetrahedral sheets with an octahedral sheet between them; and 2:1:1 clay minerals contain an octahedral sheet that is adjacent to a 2:1 layer (see **table**).

Ionic substitutions may occur in any of these sheets, giving rise to a complex chemistry for many clay minerals. For example, cations small enough to enter into tetrahedral coordination with oxygen, such as Fe^{3+} and Al^{3+}, can substitute for Si^{4+} in the tetrahedral sheet. Cations such as Mg^{2+}, Fe^{2+}, Fe^{3+}, Li^+, Ni^{2+}, Cu^{2+}, and other medium-sized cations can substitute for Al^{3+} in the octahedral sheet. Still larger cations such as K^+, Na^+, and Cs^+ can be located between layers and are called interlayer cations. F^- may substitute for $(OH)^-$ in some clay minerals. *See* COORDINATION CHEMISTRY.

Clay minerals and related phyllosilicates are classified further according to whether the octahedral sheet is dioctahedral or trioctahedral. In dioctahedral clays, two out of three cation positions in the octahedral sheet are filled, every third position being vacant. This type of octahedral sheet is sometimes known as the gibbsite sheet, with the ideal composition $Al_2(OH)_6$. In trioctahedral clay minerals, all three octahedral positions are occupied, and this sheet is called a brucite sheet, composed ideally of $Mg_3(OH)_6$. Some dioctahedral and trioctahedral clay minerals and related phyllosilicates are listed in the table.

Clay minerals can be classified further according to their polytype, that is, by the way in which adjacent 1:1, 2:1, or 2:1:1 layers are stacked on top of each other in a clay crystallite. For example, kaolinite shows at least four polytypes: *b*-axis ordered kaolinite, *b*-axis disordered kaolinite, nacrite, and dickite. Serpentine shows many

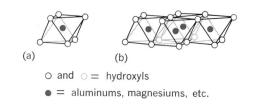

○ and ○ = hydroxyls

● = aluminums, magnesiums, etc.

Fig. 2. Diagrammatic sketch showing (a) single octahedral unit and (b) sheet structure of octahedral units. (*After R. E. Grim, Clay Mineralogy, McGraw-Hill, 1953*)

Some dioctahedral and trioctahedral clay minerals and related phyllosilicates

Type	Layer structure*	Mineral	Idealized formula
		Dioctahedral	
1:1		Kaolinite	$Al_2Si_2O_5(OH)_4$
2:1		Pyrophyllite	$Al_2Si_4O_{10}(OH)_2$

	O + nH$_2$O	Dioctahedral smectite
		  Beidellite
		  Montmorillonite
		Dioctahedral vermiculite
			$Al_2(Si_{3.7}Al_{.3})O_{10}(OH)_2Na_{.3} \cdot nH_2O$
			$(Al_{1.7}Mg_{.3})Si_4O_{10}(OH)_2Na_{.3} \cdot nH_2O$
			$Al_2(Si_{3.2}Al_{.8})O_{10}(OH)_2Mg_{.4} \cdot nH_2O$

		Illite Muscovite Celadonite Leucophyllite	$Al_2(Si_{3.2}Al_{.8})O_{10}(OH)_2K_{.8}$ $Al_2(Si_3Al)O_{10}(OH)_2K$ $(Fe,Al,Mg)_2Si_4O_{10}(OH)_2K$
	O + nH$_2$O	Mixed-layer illite/smectite illite + smectite (see above)	
2:1:1		Dioctahedral chlorite	$Al_4Si_4O_{10}(OH)_8$
		Trioctahedral	
1:1		Serpentine	$Mg_3Si_2O_5(OH)_4$
2:1		Talc	$Mg_3Si_4O_{10}(OH)_2$

	O + nH$_2$O	Trioctahedral smectite
		  Saponite
		  Hectorite
		Trioctahedral vermiculite
			$Mg_3(Si_{3.7}Al_{.3})O_{10}(OH)_2Na_{.3} \cdot nH_2O$
			$(Mg_{2.7}Li_{.3})Si_4O_{10}(OH)_2Na_{.3} \cdot nH_2O$
			$Mg_3(Si_3Al)O_{10}(OH)_2Mg_{.5} \cdot nH_2O$

		Phlogopite	$Mg_3(Si_3Al)O_{10}(OH)_2K$
2:1:1		Trioctahedral chlorite	$Mg_6Si_4O_{10}(OH)_8$
Chain	nH$_2$O	Sepiolite Palygorskite (attapulgite)	$Mg_8Si_{12}O_{30}(OH)_4(OHH)_4 \cdot 8H_2O$ $Mg_5Si_8O_{20}(OH)_2(OHH)_4 \cdot 4H_2O$

*Tetrahedral sheets are drawn as trapezoids, octahedral sheets as rectangles, and interlayer cations as circles. The c-axis is approximately parallel to the table's columns.

polytypes, the best-known of which is chrysotile, a mineral that is used to manufacture asbestos products. *See* KAOLINITE; SERPENTINE.

Finally, clays are named on the basis of chemical composition. For example, two types of swelling clay minerals are the 2:1, dioctahedral smectites termed beidellite and montmorillonite. The important difference between them is in the location of ionic substitutions. In beidellite, charge-building substitutions are located in the tetrahedral sheet; in montmorillonite, the majority of these substitutions are located in the octahedral sheet. Other examples of chemistry used in classification are nontronite, an iron-rich beidellite, and sauconite, a zinc-containing beidellite.

Another family of clay minerals is the chain clays, which have a structural resemblance to the chainlike arrangement of silica tetrahedra in pyroxene. In sepiolite and palygorskite, 2:1 layers are joined at their corners to form long channels that can contain water, a few exchangeable cations, and other substances.

Because clay minerals are composed of only two types of structural units (octahedral and tetrahedral sheets), different types of clay minerals can articulate with each other, thereby giving rise to mixed-layer clays. The most common type of mixed-layer clay is mixed-layer illite/smectite, which is composed of an interstratification of various proportions of illite and smectite layers. The interstratification may be random or ordered. The ordered mixed-layer clays may be given separate names. For example, a dioctahedral mixed-layer clay containing equal proportions of illite and smectite layers that are regularly interstratified is termed potassium rectorite. A regularly interstratified trioctahedral mixed-layer clay mineral containing approximately equal proportions of chlorite and smectite layers is termed corrensite.

Properties. Many of the properties of clay minerals are related to their crystal structure. Some of these properties are discussed below.

Kaolinite-serpentine group. These 1:1 layer silicates possess a c dimension of approximately 0.7 nanometer. The dioctahedral clays include the polytypes of kaolinite mentioned previously. The trioctahedral minerals include varieties of serpentine such as chrysotile, antigorite, lizardite, and amesite. These clays are nonswelling in water, with the exception of halloysite, a variety of kaolinite which can swell to about 1.0 nm. Kaolinites, however, can be made to swell by using intercalation compounds. Kaolinites can be distinguished from serpentines in x-ray diffraction analysis by their smaller b dimension, and by heat treatment: the kaolinite structure will decompose at 550°C (1020°F), whereas the serpentine structure will not. Also, serpentines are more susceptible to acid attack and will not intercalate. The 1:1 clay minerals possess a cation exchange capacity of 3–15 milliequivalents per 100 g, this arising mainly from broken bonds on crystal edges. Kaolinites are used in the manufacture of

ceramics, paper, rubber, and medicine. A variety of serpentine (chrysotile) is used to manufacture asbestos products such as fireproof cloth and brake linings. *See* HALLOYSITE.

Pyrophyllite-talc group. These 2:1 layer silicates possess a c-dimension of slightly more than 0.9 nm and exist in several polytypes and chemical varieties. Talc generally shows a triclinic structure (1Tc), but a disordered variety is called kerolite. Minnesotaite is an iron-rich variety of talc, and willemseite is a nickel-rich variety. Polytypes of pyrophyllite are monoclinic, triclinic, and disordered pyrophyllite. Generally, these 2:1 minerals possess a high thermal stability, have a low cation-exchange capacity, and do not swell in water or in intercalation agents. *See* PYROPHYLLITE; TALC.

Smectite group. These 2:1 clays possess a variable c dimension because of their ability to swell. It ranges generally from 1.2 to 1.5 nm in air, depending on the type of interlayer cation, on the layer charge, and on the relative humidity. When saturated with ethylene glycol, however, smectites will swell to approximately 1.7 nm regardless of these factors, and therefore this treatment is a commonly used test for smectite. The ability to swell and other unusual properties associated with this group arise from isomorphous substitutions in the tetrahedral and octahedral sheets which give rise to a negative charge on the 2:1 layers. This charge is balanced by interlayer cations which usually are hydrated.

The association of water with interlayer cations gives rise to crystalline (or first-stage) swelling for smectites. Smectites may undergo further osmotic (second-stage) swelling in wet environments if the interlayer cation is Na^+ or Li^+. In third-stage swelling, 2:1 layers are dispersed completely in water. An osmotically swelling smectite may be transformed into a smectite that undergoes only the more limited form of crystalline swelling by exchanging interlayer Na^+ for a divalent cation such as Ca^{2+}. Other properties related to the expanded interlayer region are a large cation-exchange capacity, a large surface area, and a Brönsted acidity related to a greater degree of dissociation for interlayer water. Many of these properties may be lost, either reversibly or irreversibly, by heating smectite in air to drive off interlayer water, thereby causing the 2:1 layers to collapse around interlayer cations. Water also can be driven out of the interlayer by increasing negative charge on 2:1 layers. This process happens spontaneously in nature during burial metamorphism, wherein layer charge is increased, leading to water expulsion and layer collapse around interlayer K^+, thereby transforming smectite into illite. The many industrial uses for smectite include drilling muds, binders, cation exchangers, and catalysts.

Vermiculite group. Clays in this group are similar to smectite, except that a larger layer charge leads to a decreased ability to swell, although some can swell osmotically under certain conditions. Their c dimension is about 1.4 nm, and generally, unlike smectite, they will not swell further in ethylene glycol. Many vermiculites will collapse to 1.0 nm on potassium exchange and on heating in air. Like smectite, these clays also possess special properties related to the expanding interlayer region, including a large cation-exchange capacity and surface area. Macroscopic vermiculite is exploded by heating in air for use in potting soil and insulation. Some micas and illites can be transformed into vermiculite by replacing interlayer K$^+$ with cations of greater hydration energy. *See* VERMICULITE.

Illite group. These clays possess a *c* dimension of about 1.0 nm. They are nonswelling and possess a small cation-exchange capacity, unless they are interlayered with smectite to form mixed-layer illite/smectite. Illite/smectites show properties intermediate between pure illite and smectite. Illite's layer charge and potassium content are less than those of a true mica. *See* ILLITE.

Chlorite group. Chlorites, like vermiculites, show a *c* dimension of about 1.4 nm, but unlike vermiculite, they will not collapse on heating or potassium saturation. Chlorites share many polytypes and chemical varieties. *See* CHLORITE.

Sepiolite and palygorskite. The structure of these minerals are similar, except that sepiolite shows a *b* dimension of about 1.21 nm, whereas that for palygorskite is about 1.04 nm. This difference arises from the fact that palygorskite incorporates only two linked pyroxenelike chains in each 2:1 layer rather than three. Both clays possess a fibrous morphology and channels which can accommodate water and a few cations. The ability of these channels to absorb organic substances gives rise to their use in clarification. Sepiolite also is used to manufacture meerschaum tobacco pipes. *See* SEPIOLITE; ZEOLITE.

Origin. A primary requirement for the formation of clay minerals is the presence of water, because clay minerals are hydrous silicates. Hence clay minerals are not expected to form on the Moon because there is no water on the Moon. Evidence for the presence of water on Mars, and the unusual catalytic properties of Martian soil, suggest that clay minerals may be present on this planet. Likewise, the presence of clay minerals in some meteorites suggests that these materials have been exposed to water during some part of their long and complex history.

Clay minerals form on Earth in many different environments, including the weathering environment, the sedimentary environment, and the diagenetic-hydrothermal environment. Clay minerals composed of the more soluble elements (for example, smectite and sepiolite) are formed in environments in which these ions can accumulate (for example, in a dry climate, in a poorly drained soil, in the ocean, or in saline lakes), whereas clay minerals composed of less soluble elements (for example, kaolinite and halloysite) form in more dilute water such as that found in environments that undergo severe leaching (for example, a hilltop in

the wet tropics), where only sparingly soluble elements such as aluminum and silicon can remain. Illite and chlorite are known to form abundantly in the diagenetic-hydrothermal environment by reaction from smectite. *See* CLAY; CLAY, COMMERCIAL; LITHOSPHERE; SILICATE MINERALS.   Dennis D. Eberl

Bibliography. A. G. Cairns-Smith and H. Hartman (eds.), *Clay Minerals and the Origin of Life*, 1987; R. E. Grim, *Clay Mineralogy*, 2d ed., 1968; A. C. Newman, *Chemistry of Clays and Clay Minerals*, 1986; B. Velde, *Introduction to Clay Minerals: Chemistry, Origins, Uses, and Environmental Significances*, 1992.

Clear-air turbulence

Turbulence above the boundary layer but not associated with cumulus convection. The atmosphere is a fluid in turbulent motion. That turbulence of a scale sensed by humans in aircraft is primarily associated with the boundary layer within a kilometer or so of the Earth, where it is induced by the surface roughness, or in regions of deep convection such as cumulus cloud development or thunderstorms. However, aircraft occasionally encounter turbulence when flying at altitudes well above the surface and far from convective clouds. This phenomenon has been given the rather unsatisfactory name of clear-air turbulence (CAT).

What is a primarily sensed in clear-air turbulence by the human is vertical acceleration. This acceleration will depend on the person's location in the plane, the speed of flight relative to the air, and the response characteristics of the airframe. A plane with a wing that generates aerodynamic lift more efficiently or an airframe with less weight per unit wing area will respond more strongly to a given gust magnitude. When allowances are made for different tolerance thresholds in different humans, a rough scale for subsonic aircraft has become accepted, with one-tenth the acceleration of gravity (*g*) as the threshold for light clear-air turbulence, 0.5 *g* for moderate, and 1 *g* for severe. *See* AEROELASTICITY.

Occurrence. Clear-air turbulence is encountered in the atmosphere with probability depending on flight altitude, geographical location, season of the year, and meteorological conditions. Given this variability and the small scale of the phenomenon, it is difficult to establish reliable statistics on the frequency of its occurrence. A number of extensive investigations have been carried out with this aim. One of these was a series of 90 flights by the National Aeronautics and Space Administration (NASA) supersonic aircraft YF-12A. At commercial-jet cruising levels (around 7.5 mi or 12 km), clear-air turbulence was encountered during approximately 12% of flight time in winter and 4% in summer. Above 11 mi (18 km) altitude (in the stratosphere) the frequency falls off rapidly. Other NASA studies have estimated clear-air turbulence frequency below 7.5 mi (12 km) to be somewhat increased, especially over mountainous terrain. The turbulent patches varied from 0.5 or 1.5 mi (1 or 2 km) in length to as large as 30 mi (50 km), although such large patches were very infrequent. The depth of the turbulent air was found to be almost always less than 0.6 mi (1 km).

Although clear-air turbulence may be encountered in unexpected meteorological contexts, there are highly favored locations for its occurrence. One is in the vicinity of the jet stream, particularly in ridges and troughs where the wind direction is turning sharply. A second and even more common location of occurrence is in the lee of a mountain range when a strong air flow is distorted by being forced over the range. In this situation a gravity lee wave is generated, which propagates to stratospheric heights. At various altitudes and distances from the mountain, this wave may break, and as many as a dozen or more patches of clear-air turbulence, light to severe, may be formed. *See* JET STREAM.

Forecasting and detection. Despite knowledge of these favored meteorological areas, it is not possible to forecast with confidence the precise location of a patch of clear-air turbulence. Warning forecasts for substantial portions of routes are typically given to pilots when conditions of clear-air turbulence prevail.

In view of this situation, effort has been expended to develop remote-sensing systems to give warning of a patch of clear-air turbulence with sufficient lead time to be avoided by minor diversions of flight path or at least to assure that all passengers are seated with safety belts fastened. Some ground-based techniques have the capability to produce a unique clear-air turbulence signature; of these, ultrasensitive radar probably has had the most demonstrable success. However, it is clearly impracticable to attempt to monitor any significant portion of commercial flight paths with costly ground-based instrumentation. Airborne infrared and microwave sensors, some using multiple frequencies, detect sharp temperature gradients or water-vapor concentration irregularities. The usefulness of these as clear-air turbulence warning systems is a subject of vigorous debate and investigation. *See* AERONAUTICAL METEOROLOGY; METEOROLOGY.

Flight safety. Despite sophisticated design techniques applied to airframe response and despite pilot avoidance procedures, clear-air turbulence is still a factor in 10% of air transport accidents and safety incidents in the United States. Of all weather-related accidents, at least 20% may be associated with turbulence in flight.

Origin and explanation. The early observational documentations of clear-air turbulence excited much theoretical interest and speculation as to the fluid-dynamic explanation of this phenomenon. The consensus of researchers is that clear-air turbulence is the result of Kelvin-Helmholtz instability, a breakdown of smooth flow that occurs when the

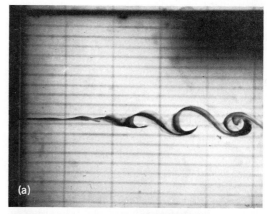

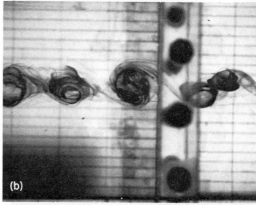

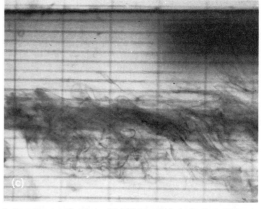

Laboratory realization of (*a*) Kelvin-Helmholtz instability, (*b*) the subsequent generation of turbulent eddies, and (*c*) mixing and dissipation. Fluid flow is left to right. (*Courtesy of Drs. G. G. Koop and F. K. Browand*)

destabilizing velocity gradient of the fluid becomes large relative to the stabilizing density gradient.

It was initially obvious that this hypothesis was consistent with the occurrence of clear-air turbulence in the jet stream and in distorted flow downwind of mountain ranges where velocity gradients are large. Further quantitative experiments in the field identified a number of clear-air turbulence events precisely under the theoretically predicted conditions. In the laboratory it has been possible to reproduce the instability mechanism and follow its breakdown into turbulence (see **illus.**). This is the dynamic mechanism widely thought to be the fundamental one in clear-air turbulence.

One way of viewing clear-air turbulence is as an

increase in energy of the smaller scales (30 ft to 0.6 mi, or 10 m to 1 km) of atmospheric motion. This is best presented in a spectral diagram, that is, a graph of energy versus wavelength.

Aside from the practical implications of clear-air turbulence for air transport, this phenomenon plays a role of undetermined magnitude in the dissipation of the kinetic energy of the atmosphere. *See* UPPER-ATMOSPHERE DYNAMICS.

M. G. Wurtele; L. J. Ehernberger

Bibliography. F. K. Lutgens and E. J. Tarbuck, *The Atmosphere: An Introduction to Meteorology*, 5th ed., 1991.

Cleavage (embryology)

The subdivision of eggs into cells called blastomeres. It occurs in eggs activated by fertilization or parthenogenetic agents. Cleavages follow one another so rapidly that there is little opportunity for daughter cells to grow before they divide again. Consequently the size of blastomeres diminishes progressively, although many times unequally, during cleavage. By contrast, the nucleus of each daughter cell enlarges following each cleavage with the result that the ratio of the volume of the nucleus to the volume of cytoplasm (the nucleoplasmic ratio) progressively increases. The cleavage period is said by some authorities to terminate when the nucleoplasmic ratios of various blastomeres attain values characteristic of adult tissues. Cells continue to divide thereafter, but each daughter cell then undergoes a period of growth prior to its division with the result that the nucleoplasmic ratio tends to remain approximately constant for each cell type following termination of cleavage. According to others, cleavage terminates with formation of the definitive blastula. Cleavage appears to be an essential step in development. Although some differentiation occurs in eggs of certain animals when cleavage is blocked experimentally, it is limited and infrequent. *See* BLASTULATION.

Chromosomal behavior. During cleavage the hereditary material located on the chromosomes behaves as it does during any mitotic division. Each chromosome present in the activated egg duplicates itself lengthwise, and the original or duplicate of each chromosome enters each daughter cell. Appropriate distribution of chromosomes depends upon formation of a mitotic spindle. The cleavage plane which divides each parent cell forms at right angles to the spindle and usually passes through the equator of the latter. Location of the spindle, in turn, is controlled largely by the cytoplasmic organization of the egg (which changes with time) and to some extent by its yolk content. Consequently these cleavage patterns are controlled indirectly by the same factors. The rate of cleavage is likewise controlled by the cytoplasm and its yolk content. Because of their large size and the fact that cleavages occur on a predictable schedule under constant conditions,

dividing blastomeres have been studied extensively by those investigators interested in all aspects of mitotic division. Cleavage is peculiar among mitotic divisions because daughter cells remain together and develop as an integrated system. *See* MITOSIS.

Blastomere differentiation. Because mitosis virtually guarantees nuclear identity in all blastomeres, nuclei of blastomeres can be exchanged with no deleterious effects. Moreover, the nucleus can be removed from an amphibian blastomere and transplanted into an enucleated egg which can then be activated to develop parthenogenetically. Eggs so treated develop normally. Thus differentiation of blastomeres in different directions cannot be the result of differential distribution of genetic material during cleavage. Instead, it is believed that cleavage is frequently instrumental in segregating special cytoplasmic areas or materials into different blastomeres. Identical genetic material would then encounter different substrates in different blastomeres, and its action on these substrates could cause different blastomeres and their progeny to differentiate in different directions. *See* CELL DIFFERENTIATION.

Cleavage types. In the eggs of some animals, for example, in those of the tunicate *Styela*, this sorting out of localized cytoplasmic areas is strikingly evident even during the first cleavage. Consequently when the first two blastomeres are isolated experimentally, they develop into partial rather than whole larvae. Eggs in which the developmental fates of individual blastomeres are controlled so rigidly by their ooplasmic content are called mosaic eggs. Their cleavage planes always bear a fixed relation to such localized cytoplasmic areas; therefore these eggs are said to undergo determinate cleavage. In the eggs of other animals, for example, in those of frogs and rabbits this sorting-out of localized cytoplasmic areas does not become differential until the second cleavage. Eggs of this type in which a part can regulate to form the whole organism are called regulative eggs, and they are said to undergo indeterminate cleavage. The chief difference between eggs of these two types is the fact that the pattern of localization of special cytoplasmic areas is more complex in precleavage stages of mosaic eggs (in which it is bilateral) than of regulative eggs (in which it is radial).

Thus cleavage does more than merely subdivide the substance of the egg quantitatively into smaller units, the blastomeres, which are then of such a size that they can readily undergo the subsequent events of blastulation, gastrulation, and interaction that are involved in formation of tissues and organs. Sooner or later, cleavage segregates different cytoplasmic areas into different blastomeres, thus subdividing the substance of the egg qualitatively. These qualitative cytoplasmic differences among blastomeres are then sufficient to account for the initial establishment of different lines of differentiation in the progeny of different blastomeres, even though the genetic content of all blastomeres is identical. Various types of cleavage encountered in the animal kingdom are shown

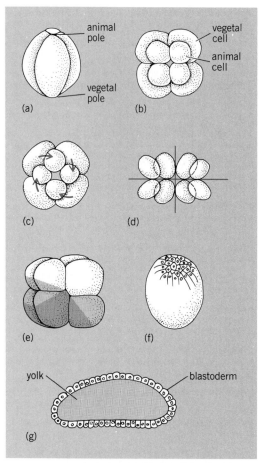

Various types of cleavage of invertebrate eggs. (*a*) Four-cell stage. (*b–d*) Eight-cell stages viewed from the animal pole: (*b*) radial; (*c*) spiral; (*d*) disymmetrical. (*e*) Bilateral (shading shows bilateral distribution of presumptive germ layers). (*f*) Discoidal. (*g*) Superficial. (*Parts b, c, d, f after A. Richards, Outline of Comparative Embryology, John Wiley and Sons; part e from R. L. Watterson, Analysis of Development, 1955*)

in the **illustration**. Most striking of these are the cleavage cells either from a disk sitting on the massive yolk (discoidal cleavage; illus. *f*) or completely enclosing the central massive yolk (superficial cleavage; illus. *g*). *See* CELL LINEAGE; OVUM.

                                        Ray L. Watterson

Bibliography. I. Balinsky, *Introduction to Embryology*, 4th ed., 1975; T. W. Torrey and A. Fiduccia, *Morphogenesis of the Vertebrates*, 4th ed., 1979.

Cleft lip and cleft palate

Two of the most common congenital anomalies in humans, resulting from incomplete closure of the lip and palate during early embryonic life. During the first trimester of pregnancy, the face and mouth are formed by the fusion of several different parts. The lip is fully fused 6 or 7 weeks after fertilization. The palate, which forms the roof of the mouth and separates the oral cavity from the nasal cavity, is fully fused 10 weeks after fertilization. If fusion fails to occur or breaks down, an opening, or cleft, occurs in the lip, the palate, or both. Although cleft

lip and cleft palate are associated with separate embryologic events, that is, are separated by a long time on the embryonic time scale, both often occur in an affected individual. Clefts vary in frequency among racial subgroups, with incidence ranging from 1 per 250 live births to 1 per 750 live births. *See* MOUTH.

Clefts of the lip may occur on one side (unilateral, **Fig. 1**) or both sides (bilateral). When they occur in the exact midline of the lip, they are often associated with severe anomalies of the brain. The cleft usually extends through the lip and nostril floor. The underlying dental arch is also typically involved.

The palate consists of an anterior bony portion (hard palate) and a posterior muscular portion (soft palate). The soft palate alone may be cleft, or both the soft and hard palate may be cleft (**Fig. 2**), but rarely is the hard palate cleft with the soft palate intact. A variant of cleft palate is the submucous cleft palate, in which the muscles of the palate are cleft but the overlying mucous membrane is intact.

Causes. Clefts are the only major abnormality in approximately half of newborns who have them. In the other half, they occur as a part of a pattern of multiple anomalies (a syndrome). It has been determined that most clefts are associated with genetic factors; the genetic patterns range from autosomal dominant inheritance (50% risk of inheritance) in many syndromes to a genetic predisposition for clefting (about 4% risk of inheritance). Clefting is often associated with chromosome abnormalities, intrauterine disturbances (such as tears in the am-

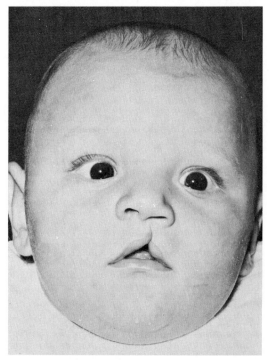

Fig. 1. Unilateral, incomplete cleft lip in which the notch does not extend to the nose.

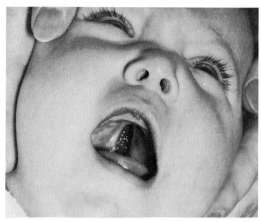

Fig. 2. Cleft palate, resulting in a fissure in the palate connecting the nasal and oral cavities.

nion), and teratogenic (malformation-causing) substances, such as alcohol, anticonvulsant drugs, and excessive levels of retinoic acid (vitamin A). *See* HUMAN GENETICS.

Secondary complications. Cleft lip is both an esthetic and a functional problem because of the disruption of the lip musculature. The defect in the floor of the nose causes asymmetry of the nose. The cleft of the dental arch causes orthodontic and occlusal (bite) problems, including congenitally missing teeth. The palatal cleft may result in some minor difficulties with feeding in early life, but a more significant problem is abnormal speech, including excessive nasal resonance (hypernasality) and articulation disorders. Clefting is also associated with chronic middle-ear disease (ear infections) and mild hearing loss. Additional structural or functional disorders can be associated with other features of a syndrome that includes cleft lip or cleft palate. *See* HEARING (HUMAN); SPEECH.

Management. Because of the combination of esthetic, structural, and functional requirements for total repair of clefts, that is, surgical, dental, ear, hearing, and speech, the care of children with clefts has usually been managed by comprehensive teams of specialists, including plastic surgeons, speech pathologists, audiologists, geneticists, otolaryngologists, oral surgeons, orthodontists, and pediatricians.

Cleft lip is typically repaired within the first few months of life, and the palate is most often surgically closed before speech development.

Extensive dental work is normally deferred until some of the permanent teeth have erupted. Middle-ear disease is usually treated aggressively through surgery in order to prevent long-term hearing loss. In general, the outlook for children with these problems is very favorable, and in many cases the problems associated with clefts are completely remediable. Genetic counseling is extremely important. *See* CONGENITAL ANOMALIES.

Robert Shprintzen

Bibliography. J. Hobbs (ed.), *Cleft Lip and Cleft Palate*, Cleft Palate Foundation, 1989; D. R. Millard, *Cleft Craft: The Evolution of Its Surgery*, 1980; R. J. Shprintzen et al., Anomalies associated with cleft lip, cleft palate, or both, *Amer. J. Med. Genet.*, 20:585–596, 1985 ; R. J. Shprintzen and C. B. Croft, Abnormalities of the eustachian tube orifice in individuals with cleft palate, *Int. J. Pediatr. Otorhinolaryngol.*, 3:15–23, 1981; J. E. Trost, Articulatory additions to the classical description of the speech of persons with cleft palate, *Cleft Palate J.*, 18:193–203, 1981; K. Vargervik, Growth characteristics of the premaxilla and orthodontic treatment principles in bilateral cleft lip and palate, *Cleft Palate J.*, 20:289–302, 1983.

Clevis pin

A fastener with a head at one end and a hole at the other used to join a clevis to a rod. A clevis is a yoke with a hole formed or attached at one end of a rod (see **illus.**). When an eye or hole of a second

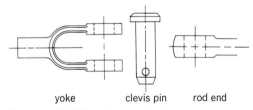

yoke   clevis pin   rod end

Clevis pin which joins yoke to rod end.

rod is aligned with the hole in the yoke, a clevis pin can be inserted to join the two. A cotter pin can then be inserted in the hole of the clevis pin to hold it in, yet the fastening is readily detachable. This joint is used for rods in tension where some flexibility is required.   Paul H. Black